South Asian Civilizations

A Bibliographic Synthesis

The research for and preparation of SOUTH ASIAN CIVILIZATIONS: A BIBLIOGRAPHIC SYNTHESIS was made possible in large part through grants from the Research Materials Program of the National Endowment for the Humanities, an independent federal agency.

South Asian Civilizations

A Bibliographic Synthesis

Maureen L. P. Patterson

in collaboration with

William J. Alspaugh

The University of Chicago Press · Chicago and London

Maureen L. P. Patterson is an associate professorial lecturer in the Department of South Asian Languages and Civilizations at The University of Chicago, and Bibliographer and Head of the South Asia Collection in The University of Chicago Library.

The University of Chicago Press, Chicago 60637
The University of Chicago Press, Ltd., London

Printed in the United States of America

88 87 86 85 84 83 82 81 1 2 3 4 5

On the cover:
Early twentieth century embossed brass plate from Jaipur, diameter 24 inches. Sūrya, the Sun God, is in the center, surrounded by the twelve signs of the solar zodiac. On the rim are the twenty-eight lunar zodiac emblems.
-- From the collection of Maureen L.P. Patterson, photographed by Nancy Campbell Hays.

On the spine:
Photograph of baked clay seal from Mohenjo Daro, depicting elephant and Indus Valley script, third millenium B.C.

Library of Congress Cataloging in Publication Data

Patterson, Maureen L. P.
South Asian civilizations: a bibliographic synthesis.

Includes index.
1. South Asia--Civilization--Bibliography.
I. Alspaugh, William J. II. Title.
Z3185.P37 [DS339] 016.954 81-52518
ISBN 0-226-64910-5 AACR2

Dedicated

to

George V. Bobrinskoy

and

Milton B. Singer

who brought

Social Sciences to the Humanities

and

Humanities to the Social Sciences

and

South Asia to Chicago

Contents

Preface ix

Introduction xiii

Scope and Purpose xiv

Selection: Limits, Inclusions and Exclusions xv

A Note on Administrative Documents xvi

Structure and Organization xix

On the Use of the Bibliography xxiii

Note on Transliteration xxx

List of Abbreviations xxxi

Maps xxxviii

THE OUTLINE OF HEADINGS 1

THE BIBLIOGRAPHIC ENTRIES 85

PART ONE
Overview of the Great Tradition

Chapter One — Traditional South Asia: Enduring Structures and Concepts through Space and Time — 87

PART TWO
Four Ages of Historical Evolution:
Subcontinental and Regional

Chapter Two — Prehistory and Protohistory of South Asia to 600 BC: The Paleolithic through the Vedic Age — 161

Chapter Three — Ancient India: c. 6th Cent. BC to 6th Cent. AD, from the Time of the Buddha through the Imperial Guptas — 173

Chapter Four — Early "Medieval" South Asia, 600-1526 AD: Emergence of Regional Traditions and Penetration of Islam — 209

Chapter Five — The Mughals, Marathas, and the Rise of British Power: South Asia in an Era of World Integration and Interaction, 1526-1818 — 249

PART THREE
Transformations in the Modern Age: National Level

Chapter Six	The Raj: Princely and British India, from Company to Empire to Independence (1818-1947)	287
Chapter Seven	The Present-Day South Asian Subcontinent in its Global Context, 1947-	351
Chapter Eight	India as Nation-State: The Challenge of Development in the World's Largest Democracy, 1947-	357
Chapter Nine	The Islamic State of Pakistan: Genesis, Division, and Development, 1947-71, 1971-	459

PART FOUR
Transformations in the Modern Age: The Eight Geo-Cultural Areas

Chapter Ten	Ceylon to Sri Lanka: Cosmopolitan Island, Colony to Nation-State, 1796-1948, 1948- ; The Maldives	483
Chapter Eleven	The Dravidian South of India: Cultural Distinctness Versus National Integration, 1800-	503
Chapter Twelve	Middle India: Contrasts of Tradition and Modernity in an Area of Transition between North and South; Persistence of Tribal Cultures, Princely Conservatism and Urban Progress, 1818-	535
Chapter Thirteen	The Northwest: The Indus Valley and Mountain Frontier, 1799-	577
Chapter Fourteen	North India: The Populous Hindi-Speaking Ganga Plains, India's Political and Cultural Heartland, 1801-	597
Chapter Fifteen	The Northeast: The Bengal-Bangladesh and Assam Area of the Ganga Delta and Brahmaputra Valley, 1813-	619
Chapter Sixteen	The Himalayas and Eastern Mountain Rim of India, Nepal and Bhutan: Fringes of Tibetan, Buddhist, and Southeast Asian Cultures, 1816-	653
Chapter Seventeen	The Indic Diaspora: South Asian Communities Throughout the World	673

PART FIVE
Reference Resources

Chapter Eighteen	Introductions and General Research Guides for Travellers and Scholars	681
	AUTHOR INDEX	707
	SUBJECT INDEX	809

Preface

Serious western study of all aspects of South Asia is a phenomenon of the period following World War II and the consequent achievement of independence in the subcontinent. During the nineteenth and the first half of the twentieth centuries academic interest in the Indic cultural realm was focussed primarily on classical languages and literatures, the religious and philosophical traditions of the elite, and their artistic expressions. Scholarly writing in German, French, and English concentrated on comparative philology and religion, as well as on art measured against the accepted western standards of Greece and Rome. With the gradual British domination of most of India, administrators were forced to learn about the land and peoples they were sent out to govern, and Christian missionaries, once they had established a footing on the subcontinent, began to investigate local beliefs and practices, the better to convert the subjects of the new raj.

The scholars, armchair Indologists most of whom had never travelled to the land of their concern, and the practitioners of administration and evangelism produced innumerable books, essays, and documents in many western languages, but predominantly in English. The newly introduced printing presses, increasing educational opportunities, and an enhanced communication system soon encouraged Indians to express themselves both for and against the new ideas from the West. Writing and publication on all subjects and in new literary forms soon proliferated in all South Asian languages. Gradually, published materials from all over the subcontinent were collected and deposited in libraries in Calcutta, Madras, Bombay, and other administrative centers of British India as well as in Britain, the ultimate seat of government for much of the Indian land mass until the mid-twentieth century. Next came the production of lists and catalogs, necessary tools for the control of what by the end of the nineteenth century was regularly coming off the presses and flowing toward the official receptacles of the India Office and British Museum in London as well as to several depositories within India itself. We are blessed with the results of the work of J. Blumhardt and many others in language by language catalogs published by the India Office Library and the British Museum. Alphabetical lists of the holdings of the Imperial Library in Calcutta, the Connemara Library in Madras, and several other collections help to show us the scope and direction of publishing during the British raj. Later analytic tools, descriptive and classificatory in nature, such as the Indian National Bibliography (begun in 1957) continue the tradition of listing acquisitions, organized by language and broad subject.

The development of research in the United States on South Asia as a world area -- within the general context of post-World War II area studies -- demonstrated the need for an overall bibliography on all aspects of subcontinental life. In the first plan to coordinate South Asian studies in North America, prepared by W. Norman Brown at the University of Pennsylvania in 1949, the library development section was written by Horace I. Poleman, the Sanskritist who developed the South Asia section at the Library of Congress. It included the statement that a comprehensive bibliography on the area was urgently needed. This was the first time that scholars had seen the need for a work that pulled together materials on the many faces of Indic civilization -- in the humanities and in the social sciences -- and that transcended the specialized subjects that had previously been given bibliographic attention. The need was expressed again at the 1957 Washington conference on South Asia library resources, but nothing came of it. In fact, the notion of a general bibliography usually obtained lower priority than collection and placement of materials on South Asia in American libraries. When Patrick Wilson demonstrated in his Government and Politics in India and Pakistan, 1885 to 1955 (bibliographic entry 12293) what could be done on just the nationalist period, a mere 70-year span, by listing over 5000 items, mostly in English and mostly accessible in the United States, the idea of adequately covering the whole civilization in a single bibliography became a challenge to be met.

At the University of Chicago in the mid-fifties, Robert Redfield and Milton Singer laid the groundwork for a civilizational approach to South Asian studies through their joint interdisciplinary project on comparative cultures and civilizations. By 1956 the College faculty had approved the launching of a year-long course, Introduction to Indian Civilization (one of three non-Western civilizations offered at the undergraduate level). The interdisciplinary staff of the Indian Civilization course prepared reading materials, and in due course decided to gather their reading lists into a formal bibliography. By 1961 this emerged into Patterson and Inden's South Asia: An Introductory Bibliography (27656).

The present work evolved out of this original effort. While its goal is the same -- to introduce the reader to selected western-language publications organized in a detailed classification structure -- and while about half of the original 4,369 entries are included here, the framework is radically different in conception. It balances dimensions of time, space, and event relegating disciplinary distinctions to a secondary level.

After several years of sorting and classifying cards by conventional disciplines, we realized that to do justice to the complexity and "foreignness" of Indic civilization we had to depart from standard western academic categories. We had labored with separate chapters on religion and philosophy (defined in primarily western terms), and chapters on art, literature, and social structure, all of them carrying entries from the beginning to the present. Many entries demanded inclusion in several chapters. We failed to show that certain religious, art, and literary forms developed at the same time. After much discussion and experimentation, we decided to change the basic classification scheme radically so that we could show interrelationships and juxtapositions of ideas and events within chronological and geographic blocs that better reflected South Asian reality than did the Eurocentric categories we had started with. While we lost a lot of time and had to jettison many already typed sheets, we gained a lot of experience and insight into treatment of South Asian materials.

We had rejected the Bibliography of Asian Studies classification in which materials on standard disciplines are presented, country by country, in long alphabetical lists -- and the disciplines themselves are arranged from "anthropology" to "technology" in mechanical order of the alphabet. For lack of the requisite funding level of the large-scale operation that William Skinner established for his bibliography on modern Chinese society, we were unable to contemplate computerization and the development of multiple subject codes for each bibliographic item.

We had to be satisfied with a three-dimension classification: fundamentally chronological, secondarily geographic and topical. We have entered most items only once, but a few titles defied our attempts to limit their appearance and have been repeated. Actually duplications are more than anticipated; intentional and unintentional, they total about one percent of the entries, or 280 items.

Other works designed to assist beginning students of South Asia include South Asia: A Bibliography for Undergraduate Libraries (27658), where entries have been rated according to levels as defined by the editors, and J. M. Mahar's India (27653), which provides useful annotations to some books within a standard disciplinary structure. Mahar's book is limited to India as a current political entity, although many of the histories he includes necessarily deal with parts of the subcontinent now in other nation-states. A French contribution to this genre is J.-L. Chambard's Bibliographie de civilsation de l'Inde contemporaine (27648), which is restricted to the modern period and also to India. Broader in scope, larger in size, and more complex than its predecessors, our book will serve the same purpose of introducing the vast literature on all aspects of South Asia to a variety of users.

The publication in 1962 of South Asia: An Introductory Bibliography coincided with the establishment of the Library of Congress' book-procurement program in South Asia under the terms of an amendment to Public Law 480 of the 83d Congress. Under this scheme, the Library of Congress authorized newly established field offices in New Delhi and Karachi to collect all local publications deemed to be of research value and to send copies of them to United States libraries participating in this acquisitions program. The University of Chicago Library was one of the original dozen participants and as such soon began to receive large shipments of books and periodicals. The Library of Congress soon followed the dispatch of books with Accessions Lists and eventually with preliminary cataloging cards. Within a few years it became clear that we had at our disposal the making of a supplement to our 1962 bibliography. Not only could we consult the increasingly sophisticated Accessions Lists and actually use extra sets of cards available upon request, but we also had the books, documents, and periodicals themselves to examine so that we could discover the exact coverage of a book or article and could place it correctly in a projected new bibliography. It is safe to say that we could never have contemplated a bibliography on the scale of the present one without the "PL 480" program and the fact that Chicago participated in it at a comprehensive level and that we were able to control and make accessible the materials we received. We must record our gratitude to the Library of Congress for establishing this imaginative program and to its field staff for carrying it out with such success and thoroughness. The extent to which we have been able to give prominence to the scholarship from South Asia is testimony to the coverage and currency of the Library of Congress program.

Successful completion of this project has benefitted from support from several institutions and very many persons. I thank the University of Chicago Library for providing space, equipment, supplies, and administrative support, as well as forbearance as I encountered snags and delays. I am pleased that the Library recognizes the value of this project for the development and interpretation of our extensive South Asia collection. The Committee on Southern Asian Studies initially made several small grants which effectively established the project. The Association for Asian Studies' generous and crucial grant in 1974 came with the enthusiastic support of the late Richard L. Park. This provided me with time and confidence to look for further funding for what had turned into an enterprise of considerable dimensions. In 1975 I applied to the National Endowment for the Humanities (NEH) and was successful in receiving a reference tool grant. Since then the Endowment has awarded supplementary grants and extensions of time up to December 1980. I wish to record my gratitude to NEH and especially to Dr. George F. Farr for his patient support these last several years. Other persons have helped in funding this book. Albert Mayer, the New York architect who recently presented his personal papers and books on India to the University of Chicago Library, came through with a monetary contribution at a moment of great need. I am beholden to him for his confidence in this project. And to the Misses Lillian and Elizabeth Barbour, University of Chicago alumnae of yesteryear (1915 and 1920), I am grateful for funds which tided us over a critical juncture.

Many people have worked with me on this book in many capacities and for varying periods of time. While I cannot mention everyone associated with the project, I must pay special tribute to the contributions of Sara Lindholm, Philip Oldenburg, Paul Greenough, Mary Carmen Lynn, Joan Erdman, Robert Emmett, Kris Kasselman, Carol Sakala, Cynthia Livermore, Ruta Pempe, Katherine Ewing, and Stephen Kontos. Fruitful and often lively discussions among Joan Erdman, Bob Emmett, and myself led to the development of a format of outline, entries, and index. With Carol Sakala joining the project, we were able to establish principles for an outline content which departed drastically and successfully from the conventional discipline orientation of the early days of the project. The principles of this outline are recognizable in Sakala's Women of South Asia: A Guide to Resources (00950). But without any doubt it is the collaboration of William J. Alspaugh which has made it possible to turn this project into a finished book. Since September 1978 we have deliberated over each heading, each entry, and the order and structure of the book as a whole, until we arrived at the wording and meaning that felt right and achieved the logical sequences we desired. To this task he has brought persistent energy and enthusiasm, unfailing intellectual integrity, as well as wit and good humor through thick and thin. His contribution of time to the project has been far beyond what our funds could recompense him for.

I have frequently consulted South Asia colleagues at Chicago and visitors to Chicago on outline details and selection of entries. I am particularly indebted to Clinton Seely, Edward Dimock, C. M. Naim, A. K. Ramanujan, Richard Taub, Donald Nelson, Pramod Chandra, Sara Schastok, Brian Silver, Dan Ehnbom, Joan Erdman, Karine Schomer, Franklin Presler, and Leo Rose for advice on the content and form of sections dealing with their academic specialties. Joan Erdman, especially, has been a constant source of welcome and constructive criticism on matters of form as well as substance. The late J. A. B. van Buitenen was an early supporter of the project; I have not taken lightly his friendly admonition to supply Indic words with diacritical marks.

I must acknowledge a very special debt of gratitude to a very special person, Chauncy D. Harris. His understanding of bibliographic production, his enthusiastic support, and the provision of funds at several critical junctures enabled us to finish this book.

I must thank Karen O'Connor for cheerfully and competently typing drafts of the outline as we produced them. Our three manuscript typists have performed miracles in successfully transforming over 28,000 entries and all the index material from unordered information on often barely legible cards into beautiful sheets ready for the camera. Our typists did much more than press the keys -- they served as critics in matters of style and consistency, and often on questions of substance, as befitted their own status as advanced graduate students. We are grateful to Allan Johnson and Deborah Malamud who have shared the typing from beginning to end, and to Ann Reichenbach who joined them for a crucial middle period. We thank Nita Kumar for able assistance in preparation of the massive author index, the alphabetization of which, in double-quick time, was achieved by Richard Peiser and two assistants. Dan Greenway has prepared the maps crucial to the location of designated geo-cultural areas and linguistic regions. Needless to say, none of the persons I have mentioned should be held accountable for errors; that responsibility is entirely mine.

It gives me special pleasure to thank the University of Chicago Press for accepting this book for publication and providing additional funding as well as special attention.

Introduction

A bibliography is the charting or mapping of an intellectual field or area, both by defining its limits and by placement of references to pertinent books and other written materials within these limits. For those who would venture into the vast, almost limitless, area of Indic civilization, this book presents charts -- some detailed, some sketchy -- of material showing highways, broad avenues, lanes, and paths that the scholar may take on his travels in this domain. Many ways are well worn and highly developed, while others are rough and ill-marked. Taken together, the charts drawn here comprise an overall guide to the civilizations of the subcontinent. Broad directional indicators guide the traveller, but to the extent that he uses his own source of direction as well as other instruments of navigation, he can explore side roads and bypaths of this complex of cultures.

Few bibliographies produced in the subcontinent, or elsewhere for that matter, have presented selected materials on any basis other than alphabetical, using the broad categories of recognized academic disciplines. Rather than list entries uncritically, with equal weight given to each bibliographic entry, as in a card catalog, we have made critical judgments in terms of intrinsic research value. We have selected those titles deemed to be important on the basis of inspection or use and quotation in respectable published scholarly works.

The philosophical and practical basis for this approach is laid out in an eloquent and detailed fashion by George Sarton, the famous historian of science, in his stimulating article "Synthetic Bibliography" (Isis 3,2 (1920) 159-70). He makes a careful distinction between analytic bibliography, in which each citation is placed on the same level, and synthetic bibliography, which by critical and selective means seeks to exclude items judged to be of lesser importance. A library cataloger's job is analytical, therefore, in making cards for each bibliographic item presented regardless of judgment of quality. The job of a "synthetic" bibliographer, as defined by Sarton, is "to include everything which is important, to place it in its proper perspective and to exclude everything which is not important, with plenty of exceptions however." The pitfalls in this approach should be obvious; avoidance of these pitfalls inheres in the capacity of the bibliographer to make informed judgments. It is this approach that we set out to follow, and we hope that for the most part we have been successful. And it is, following Sarton, the reason for subtitling this book "A Bibliographic Synthesis."

This bibliography reveals certain features of the study of South Asia as a field. Categories we had expected to be represented by a substantial number of publications turned out to be underpopulated; many categories which we had expected to be crowded turned out in fact to be almost the exclusive preserve of one writer.

Research tends not to be planned in terms of schemes for overall coverage. One's teachers, the emphases at one's university, the accessibility of materials and even of locale for field work often determine a young scholar's choice of topic or field. Scholarly fads, fancies, and cycles also enter the picture. A rush to Vedic studies is followed by work on the Mahabharata, as soon as the critical edition is available; historians take a new look at the Puranas, and suddenly a wide range of scholars is doing the same; geographers and anthropologists have recently turned their attention to pilgrimage, its extent and meaning; Kashmir Śaivism has been rescued from obscurity in a spurt of research and publication; the village studies of the 1950s and 60s tended to cluster in the North Indian heartland, while places such as Bihar, the Andhra delta, and peninsular Gujarat were ignored. Now whole tracts of India are "out of bounds" for research, especially by non-Indians. "Untouchables" have been the subject of more studies than Brahmans; analyses of kingship and authority have supplanted dynastic histories; and the interfacing of disciplines, whether anthropology and medicine, sociology and linguistics, or psychoanalysis and religion, is increasingly in vogue either in works by individuals or by groups in workshop style research.

In many ways the plethora and paucity of entries in the various sections of this book reflect the intensity and direction of research to date. Thus the bibliography may function to alert younger scholars to areas relatively unsaturated. By and large, researches have not been conducted according to some carefully coordinated master plan, but have been much more haphazard, verging on the serendipitous.

Yet there are some systematic, planned approaches to social science and historical research in modern India. The Census organization has throughout its hundred-year history asked a series of questions and presented the resultant descriptions and analyses of social, economic, linguistic, and religious data in its thousands of published volumes. In other attempts to look at broad areas of research, note trends, and pinpoint lacunae, Indian government bodies are producing multivolume surveys of research by academic disciplines (Indian Council of Social Science Research), drawing up plans for historical research in fields deemed neglected, and producing "nationalist" histories to counter so-called imperialist interpretations of the past century (Indian Council of Historical Research). As a result of work on the histories of literatures in India's various languages and preparation of the multivolume Encyclopedia of Indian Literatures, the Sahitya Akademi is indicating subjects that need study and interpretation.

The following sections of this Introduction discuss the scope and purpose of the volume, its limits and selection principles, its structure and organization into parts and chapters, and finally, access and format of the bibliographic entries. We have tried to anticipate users' questions and provide a guide into the book's nooks and crannies.

Scope and Purpose

The focus of this book is South Asia, defined geographically as the subcontinental mainland between the Himalayas and the Indian Ocean, plus the adjacent islands. In present political terms this comprises India, Pakistan, Bangladesh, Nepal, Bhutan, and the island states of Sri Lanka and the Maldives. In civilizational terms the scope is the Indic civilization of the subcontinent plus its extensions and overlappings into Afghanistan, Tibet, and Burma and outliers in South East Asia and beyond (particularly in modern times).

South Asia, site of one of the four centers of earliest civilization (the others being China, the Fertile Crescent, and the Mediterranean), developed over several millenia into the distinct culture realm it is today through the invasion, interaction, and melding of various civilizational layers -- Harappan, Dravidian, Aryan, Islamic, and Western. By titling this book South Asian Civilizations, we highlight the separate existence of historical layers within, and contribution of these layers to, the distinctive culture complex of this world region today -- Indic civilization. The major goal of this book is to identify the principal units and components of Indic civilization within a three-fold structuring of time, space, and topic. This structure provides an organizational framework for presenting the major western-language citations.

The tendency within each South Asian nation today is to study itself as a restricted unit defined by latter-day nationalism. The tendency is exacerbated by existing obstacles to scholarly interaction among the nations and by the lack of free exchange of publications. While this situation is understandable in studies of current economic or political development, it is dangerous in social, religious, and artistic studies to ignore or play down historical bonds and commonalities that transcend political boundaries. We hope to provide a corrective to conceptual fragmentation and perhaps stimulate South Asian scholars to take a larger view by emphasizing the civilizational context, on-going complex interrelationships, and unifying factors in the bibliographic framework and in the relative positioning of the bibliographic entires. Within the overall civilizational context we identify a number of geo-cultural areas, macroregions, middle-level cultural-linguistic regions, and smaller units which are used as classificatory devices for organizing the literature within broad chronological periods. Topical divisions within each time-space unit include political, economic, social, religio-philosophical, literature, and art sections as and when the corpus of materials dictates.

Our goal is to guide the student through the mass of recent western-language publications on South Asia toward some of the best and most stimulating. Beyond this goal we have developed an approach and a model that we hope will be adopted or adapted in future bibliographies. This book may be the last attempt at a detailed bibliography of South Asian civilization. The literature threatens to become too vast even for a highly selective work limited to western-language sources. Future bibliographies might best be regional or topical. If regional, they should include the rich materials in appropriate South Asian languages. We shall have fulfilled one of our goals if future compilations proceed from the conceptual framework and classificatory refinement we have developed.

While this book is limited to western-language works, there is a great difference between the amount and subject matter of writing in English and in the regional languages. From our observation of publications received in the "PL 480" program over the last two decades, it is clear that the very large categories of such social sciences as economics, politics, and international relations are dominated by English materials. Relatively little solid analytical work is published in South Asian languages. On the other hand, in the regional chapters where we looked for materials on local politics, caste, religious movements, and modern literature, research and experience indicate that much of the significant writing is in regional languages. The message here is that western-language materials represent only the tip of the iceberg; the vast bulk of sources for the study of regional, subregional, and local history and society lies in the mass below the surface. For western scholars this means acquiring new language skills, but for a South Asian generation of researchers trained to use western methods and materials, and often confined to western languages, it means that invaluable resources await them in their own backyard, resources that they are naturally qualified to use.

Although we tapped western-language references for this book, we were unable to handle Russian and other Slavic materials. We have, however, included translations from the Russian. This exclusion, we recognize, is a serious deficiency and one that other bibliographers must remedy. We are not alone in "disregarding" Russian scholarship, as Wendy O'Flaherty points out in "Disregarded Scholars" in a recent issue of South Asian Review (27422). Generally, South Asians themselves are unable to tackle the large number of important Russian studies of South Asian archaeology, art, linguistics, literature, and certain historical periods. There is also a rapidly growing corpus of South Asian studies in the Japanese language, which we have had to omit. Here again the serious scholar of economic history, archaeology, art, and linguistics ignores at his peril the publications by Japanese scholars of the subcontinent.

South Asians have, of course, used their own languages for writing epics, poetry and stories, religious treatises and tracts, local history and genealogy, biographies and hagiographies. Linguistic partisanship is now bringing about the production of a wide variety of studies in regional languages, studies of substance and quality that must be recognized. In sum, we can no longer be satisfied that we have covered all significant works if we restrict our coverage to the "traditional" languages of serious western research, i.e., English, French, and German. There is, therefore, a real limitation in this book, but one we have had to confront and admit.

In constructing this bibliography, we have kept in mind the needs and concerns of several audiences. For the person unfamiliar with the history and cultural diversity of this strategic part of the world, the indexes and outline will point to the most important, up-to-date, and generally accessible western-language books and articles. For the college and secondary school teacher, the book will offer a course outline for teaching on any aspect of the Indic civilization, and will facilitate the preparation of lectures on unfamiliar parts of South Asia's complex of cultures. For students -- both undergraduate and graduate -- the book can provide an innovative and highly refined organization of some 28,000 carefully selected titles. For researchers -- both in and out of academe -- the book may be used to deepen their knowledge on areas beyond their specialties.

Selection: Limits, Inclusions, and Exclusions

Bibliographies must have limits, and one of the limits of this one is its restriction by and large to the holdings of the University of Chicago libraries. Given our substantial South Asia collection this is simply a limit rather than a limitation. The most important reason for imposing this limit was our need to examine books and articles for placement in the highly refined categories of the conceptual structure. We estimate that Chicago has more than 90 percent of the titles listed. We have not indicated in the text those titles which Chicago does not own. However, since the project was also seen as a collection-development tool, we expect to acquire those books which we discovered missing. Those publications we deemed significant enough to include, on the basis of evidence from various sources, even though we could not examine them, are believed to be generally accessible to researchers in North America through interlibrary loan or photocopying. If it seemed that the only place a particularly striking title was available was in a British or South Asian library, we sadly omitted that work. While this approach may appear parochial, we decided it was practical since we expect the majority of users of this book to be in North America. It will be a source of satisfaction if this does not prove to be the case.

Our principles of selection have been based on language, accessibility, uptodateness, and length. That is to say, we have restricted ourselves to western-language (other than Slavic), generally available, recent books as well as reasonably long periodical articles. We define as accessible those publications known to be in major American research libraries, available by interlibrary loan in North America or, in the case of dissertations, through commercial photocopying. We have emphasized the most recent books and articles on the premise that they would not have been included in earlier bibliographies. Since bibliographies by nature build upon one another, we reasoned that many of the nineteenth-century classics would have been listed in one or another of our predecessors. However, this work is self-contained because most books we list on a subject refer to those older works which have survived the test of time. In general, we preferred to include books rather than articles. We were satisfied to list articles in the case of subjects that have only recently become foci of research, and where we could not find book length titles. We have limited our selection of articles to those from substantial scholarly journals, except in some cases where we could locate only an article from a popular magazine (such as the Illustrated Weekly of India, Social Welfare, or Yojana) to represent a category. Since dissertations from the subcontinent are hard if not impossible to obtain, we have not listed any, in accord with our principle of accessibility.

In general, we include scholarly, popular, and polemic works representing varying viewpoints. By no means do we include all significant articles from every important western or South Asian journal. To have done so would have required more space and more time than we had at our disposal. Our aim was rather to select representative articles from major journals. Readers will become aware of these journals by close attention to bibliographic entries or to the list of abbreviations, or by going to indexes or specialized reference tools identified in various sections. We have been selective in citing chapters from collections or edited volumes of essays by many authors. By citing a few contributions to such works we hope to encourage the reader to inspect the volume itself.

When we faced the question of dealing with modern writers and literature, we chose to present materials about the writers, together with anthologies and collections of their works, rather than titles of individual novels, dramas, and the like. Library catalogs and specialized reference works will enable the reader to identify individual works of a prominent writer. Wherever possible we have listed translations of works by classical and medieval writers as well as studies of them.

In general we have concentrated on selecting nontechnical works of the greatest interest to a broad range of South Asianists as well as to general readers. In certain fields such as numismatics, epigraphy, linguistics, archaeology, and art history we have excluded technical studies and site reports. The same is true for technical studies in physical anthropology, geography, and economics.

We have referred to but have not included many important articles in mammoth productions such as Hastings' Encyclopaedia of Religion and Ethics, the New Encyclopedia Britannica, and L'Encyclopédie de la Pléiade. Readers are urged to note the treasures of South Asian scholarship imbedded in these multivolume works.

Constraints of time for preparation of this work and of space in the finished volume have no doubt contributed to weakness of selection or inadequacy of representation in some sections. We preferred to set up a category with relatively weak or few entries in order to show a topic apparently underresearched or materials unavailable to us. There is, therefore, much room for development and improvement within many subdivisions of the conceptual framework.

The section on administrative documents which follows deals with, and in some sense compensates for, a major exclusion of this bibliography. The bibliography does not include references to individual volumes in many series of official publications of the British and independent governments in South Asia.

A Note on Administrative Documents

In this special section we will introduce the main categories of administrative documents and suggest means of access to titles in these lengthy series. By and large, we do not give citations to individual gazetteers, settlement reports, or census volumes. Only a few volumes in the many series of the Archaeological Survey of India are included. We have provided, whenever they were available, references to the series as a whole and to reference works which provide access to the volumes of a series. Historians of modern South Asia, as well as anthropologists and other social scientists, should be familiar with the documents described here, as well as with the hundreds of reports on all subjects by official committees and royal commissions, many of which are included in the British parliamentary papers but only some of which are cited in this book.

In the British period, we have identified four categories of descriptive and administrative documents which form a crucial component of the source literature for studying the past two centuries of Indian history. They continue to be basic material for research on modern nations of the subcontinent. These four categories of publications are interrelated and have been built one upon the other; taken together they form a local administrator's view of the basic units of centralized administration: districts, provinces, and states, and the country as a whole. The four categories of documents can be characterized, from earliest to latest and by increasing administrative utility, as follows:

1. general descriptions and early surveys
2. revenue surveys and settlement reports at subdistrict (taluka) and district levels
3. historical, geographic, and statistical accounts primarily at the district level, later developed into gazetteers
4. demographic surveys, later developed into decennial census reports, in the British period by British province and princely state, and later by national and subnational units

We may identify a fifth category, not necessarily restricted to or aimed at the district or state level, which includes linguistic, ethnographic, archaeological, geological, botanical, and other such surveys.

Examples of the first category of publications are Alexander Hamilton, A New Account of the East-Indies . . . , 1727 (07944), Francis Buchanan-Hamilton, Journey from Madras . . . , 1807 (19135), and Thomas Williamson, East India Vade-Mecum, 1810 (11964). To these may be added a large number of parliamentary and administrative reports prepared by the East India Company as it gained de facto political power in India. One important investigation was the Fifth Report of the Select Subcommittee of the House of Commons which was presented to Parliament in 1812 (07981). The Fifth Report covered details of economic, social, and cultural life of a kind that were later incorporated into the settlement report and gazetteer literature.

Secondly, in the late eighteenth century, land revenue and settlement reports at taluka and district levels were compiled and written, and gradually extended to all territories administered by the East India Company. These surveys and reports set forth the boundaries of villages, talukas, and districts, estimate and describe the population, evaluate the land holdings and crop production, and form the basis for establishing the amount of revenue to be paid to the government. Village records and field investigations by the new administrators were the basic building blocks for these reports, which in turn eventually led to the compilation of district accounts and memoirs, later called gazetteers. A good guide to the settlement reports up to 1899 is Campbell's Index-Catalogue of Indian Official Publications in the Library, British Museum (27523). The Gokhale Institute's Bibliography of the Economic History of India (10853) lists its substantial holdings of settlement reports. N. G. Barrier describes these documents in an article in Indian Archives 23,1-2 (1974) in which he describes how to find and use them.

The third category, gazetteers, are much more than geographical indexes or dictionaries arranged in alphabetical order. Beginning with works such as Robert Montgomery Martin's History, Antiquities, Topography and Statistics of Eastern India . . . (00524), published in 1838, many historical, geographical, and statistical accounts of administrative units were published in the nineteenth century. Sometimes these works have been called memoirs, and sometimes manuals or district handbooks. Until 1869 district accounts were haphazardly produced and were not uniform in format or coverage. Then William Wilson Hunter was commissioned by the government to draw up an all-India plan for compilation and publication of gazetteers at the district, provincial, and imperial (All India) levels. These were primarily intended to be guides for administrators, and secondarily served as reference works for scholars. At the district and princely state levels nearly 1400 descriptive and statistical volumes were published. At the provincial level only one edition (1908-9) of the Provincial Gazetteer was published, with volumes for each province and major princely state. The 1909 edition of the Imperial Gazetteer of India was the largest, with twenty-six volumes, listing alphabetically all administrative units (27781). Since Independence in 1947, India has published new editions of district gazetteers as well as a gazetteer of India in four volumes (27779). Three books on the gazetteer literature may be consulted for details: Campbell's Index-Catalogue (27523), S. B. Chaudhuri's History of the Gazetteers of India (27778) and in 1970 Henry Scholberg's The District Gazetteers of British India: A Bibliography (27783).

The fourth category, census reports from South Asia, is a major source of data for economic, anthropological, sociological, linguistic, and historical research. Beginning in 1824, city censuses were taken sporadically (Allahabad, 1824; Benares, 1827-28; Dacca, 1830). Estimates for larger territorial units were made from time to time. In 1849 the Governor-General directed presidency and provincial governments to report population counts on a quinquennial basis. These reports, largely unpublished, were founded on revenue and statistical surveys, and did not involve any uniform collecting method or standard publication format. In the 1850s other censuses were planned and some were completed. A scheme for an all-India census in 1861 was postponed because preparations were interrupted by the "Mutiny" of 1857 and its aftermath. By 1869 the Governor-General had appointed W. W. Hunter to organize and direct the Statistical Survey and coordinate efforts to count, classify, and describe the population, as part of the All-India plan. In 1872 the first general census was published, based on counts made with uniform schedules and taken between 1867 and 1872 in most parts of British-controlled territory. While the 1872 Census -- as it has come to be known -- was neither synchronous nor comprehensive in coverage, it proved to be the beginning of modern census operations, which would provide invaluable demographic, socio-cultural, and economic data for the subcontinent.

Subsequent decennial censuses for 1881 through 1941 have offered administrators and scholars all-India facts and statistics that comprise the most complete and continuous record for any comparable population. Sociocultural data, in particular on caste and community, are especially rich in the 1921 and 1931 census reports. Linguistic questions (mother tongue, bilingualism, literacy, etc.) were also investigated and eventually inspired the compilation of the eleven-volume Linguistic Survey of India (02321). The 1941 Census -- the last before partition -- was greatly abbreviated because of wartime strictures. Post-1947 census operations have been continued in India, Pakistan, and Bangladesh.

The 1951 Census of India remained modest in scope, but the 1961 Census was the most far-reaching and voluminous to date. Approximately 1,400 volumes were planned, not all of which have yet been published. In contrast to the 1931 Census, the 1961 reports limit data on castes to information on Scheduled Castes and Tribes. However, the 1961 Census goes further than any other census in the publication of individual monographs on crafts, fairs, and festivals, and on villages selected to represent a wide variety of socioeconomic and geographic features. Atlases to illustrate census findings have been produced on a national as well as a state level. From 1951, District Census Handbooks were prepared, complementing the gazetteers by providing detailed socioeconomic data culled from or expanding upon the state census volumes. Special volumes on large cities, regionalization, and other topics have been published, and in some states attention has been given to distinctive features, such as the volumes on temples of Madras State.

The 1971 Census of India was similarly ambitious in design, though it will probably not be as voluminous. Special emphases in this census were on fertility, migration patterns, and urban data. Publication is slow, with only about 778 volumes out as of late 1980. Because 1971 was the hundredth anniversary of the Indian census in its modern and comprehensive form, a special series of Census Centenary Monographs was published to show its historical development and trace changes in categories of enumeration and definitions. The first two Centenary Monographs, Indian Census in Perspective, by S. C. Srivastava (27759), and Indian Census through a Hundred Years, by D. Natarajan (27760), provide the historical context and development of this monumental research resource. N. G. Barrier has edited an important new book, The Census in British India: New Perspectives (New Delhi: Manohar, 1981), in which a panel of scholars explores the uses and pitfalls of the vast and varied data in the census reports. While these discussions focus on the accuracy and value of the data produced during the British raj, many of the questions and comments are applicable to the volumes that compose independent India's demographic data base.

Pakistan has published three censuses in the period since its creation. The 1951 Pakistan Census is contained in eight volumes, with sixty-three District Census Reports covering both East and West Pakistan in considerable detail. The 1961 Census consists of ten volumes, all of which are primarily statistical. Pakistan's most recent census is 1972 (17788). The first census of Bangladesh was taken in 1974 (25275).

After an early one-volume Census of Ceylon in 1827, decennial censuses of the island's population were taken regularly from 1871 to 1931, and again in 1946 and 1953. While some of the early reports contain much historical and descriptive material, the Ceylon censuses primarily provide statistical data. No census appears to have been made at all in the 1960s, but the decennial census was resumed in 1971 and the report for that year is now published (1978) in Sri Lanka's three official languages (Sinhala, Tamil, and English) (27765).

For Nepal, population counts were made in 1911 and approximately every ten years since. However, the Census of Population, Nepal, 1952-54, appears to be the first count to be published, in 1958 in a slim volume of statistics. The 1962 Census came out in 1966 in four volumes, entirely in the Nepali language. The 1971 Nepal census was produced in English, bringing it into line with the Indian and Pakistani census publications, which up to this point have all been in English.

References to administrative documents in the bibliography will be found under outline headings such as "Bibliography and Reference" and "Demography and Population Policy," in appropriate historical sections, and for topics which were the subject of committees and commissions of inquiry. In the Author Index, entries for particular states and nations offer listings of official reports.

Structure and Organization

The Outline of Headings

The framework of this volume is an Outline of Headings, which appears on pages 1 through 83. The over 28,000 bibliographic entries are organized in terms of this outline of headings into five parts which are divided into eighteen chapters. These parts and chapters are described below following some general statements about classification and the outline headings.

This Outline of Headings synthesizes resources for the study of South Asian civilizations in five parts. Parts One and Five -- Chapters One and Eighteen respectively -- are not chronological, but rather provide an overview of the Great Tradition and a summary of reference resources. Parts Two, Three, and Four include Chapters Two through Seventeen, which start from prehistory and protohistory and move chronologically and by geo-cultural areas to the present. Part Two treats of events and people up to about 1800 AD. Such a large literature exists on South Asia after that date that we felt the need to separate national-level issues and persons from those belonging to a particular region or locality. Parts Three and Four present national and area-by-area materials respectively.

The individual headings of the Outline are used within the Bibliographic Entries (pages 85 to 708) to designate each chapter and its subdivisions. Each chapter is divided into from four to eleven subdivisions at the large roman-numeral level. Each chapter's large roman-numeral division (I, II, . . .) differs: sometimes it represents a further chronological differentiation, sometimes it designates disciplinary distinctions, and sometimes geo-cultural specifics. Within these large roman-numeral sections are capital-letter level headings (A, B, . . .) subdivided by fields of study. These fields of study are large topics under which appear (at arabic-numeral level headings, 1, 2, . . .), specifications of the field. A further subdivision by type, event, or individual authors brings us to the level of most of the bibliographic entries, at small letter headings (a, b, . . .), although entries are often made at the arabic-numeral and small roman-numeral levels as well. Sometimes a further subdivision into small roman numerals (i, ii, . . .) is necessary to provide specific distinctions within a topic. Because of the fineness of the subdivisions, this Outline of Headings substitutes for annotations to each entry.

Our principles of classification are from the earliest to the latest; from subcontinental or pan-Indian to regional and local; from the general to the specific. We have devised a system which gathers material from several disciplines within a single period, sorts it by spatial unit, and presents it in a consistent sequence -- political context, economic conditions, social development, religio-philosophical traditions, and literary and artistic expression. This sequence is replicated throughout the Outline of Headings.

So that the reader may better grasp the whole, we have presented the complete Outline of Headings following this Introduction. Subordination of sections is indicated by indentation and typographical convention. At appropriate places we include in both the Outline of Headings and the Bibliographic Entries cross-references to related sections, which appear in square brackets. Parentheses are used to indicate additional or definitional information for a heading, dates of individuals or events, or statistics such as a city's population or literacy rate. Key words from the Outline of Headings appear also in the Subject Index. The Outline gives five-digit serial numbers at the headings where the entries begin. Taken in the aggregate, the headings constitute a detailed outline of the units of South Asian civilizations. As such, the Outline is in itself a convenient reference tool.

The Bibliographic Entries

The Bibliographic Entries, in five parts divided into eighteen chapters, are the main text of the volume. The following paragraphs further characterize each part and present notes on each chapter and on particular meanings and usage of terms.

<u>Part One</u>, which we call "Overview of the Great Tradition," is a single chapter, Chapter One, "Traditional South Asia: Enduring Structures and Concepts through Time and Space." In Part One we set the civilizational tone of the whole book. If Indic civilization exhibits any unity or perennial character, it resides in that cultural core we call Hinduism. This umbrella term, which defies definition except in negative ways, refers to a congeries of beliefs and practices carried on by persons in India who are neither Muslim nor Christian nor Buddhist nor many other things, but these people often participate in or adapt Hindu practices. While the practices may vary dramatically from place to place, or from person to

person according to social position, there is an identifiable Hindu world view at a high level of abstraction in terms of which external civilizational entities may be comprehended. If Sanskrit is its linguistic vehicle, then its social expression is a hierarchical structure with the Brahman at the top.

In Chapter One we note two basic approaches to the study of Indic civilization. One is centered on the northern heartland, Āryavarṭa, and the other emanates from the Tamil southern part of the Hindu central core. We hope to dispel the notion that some sort of dynamic northern Hinduism gradually engulfed the peninsula. Throughout our outline we emphasize the variety of Indic cultural forms. We differentiate Part One from all the other parts because it contains fundamental statements about Indic civilization. Here the reader finds reference to "dawn-to-dusk" histories of various regions and topics (political, economic, cultural, scientific, and so forth); and to introductions and overall treatments of social systems, religio-philosophical traditions, literature, art, and architecture. For example, this chapter contains a history of Tamil literature through the ages, whereas a book on medieval or modern Tamil literature is placed in the appropriate later chapter defined by its time period. We put materials here on such "timeless" performing arts as classical music and dance as well as regional and folk performances. However, contemporary folksongs and folk literature of various regions appear in the area chapters in a separate division within "literature."

Part Two, which begins the chronological parts of the book, is entitled "Four Ages of Historical Evolution: Subcontinental and Regional." It consists of Chapter Two through Chapter Five, which cover the period from prehistory to approximately 1800 AD. In this part and in Part Four, when we have introduced regions and areas, the dates for opening or closing each section emerge from events in that place. For example, in Chapter Five, on the Mughal-Maratha period, the important opening date in Ceylon is 1505, when the Portuguese arrived, and the closing date is 1795, when the Dutch lost control to the British. Chapter Two presents materials on rapidly expanding studies of pre- and protohistory in the subcontinent. Modern techniques have opened up whole new vistas in the short time since the discovery of Harappan civilization in 1921 and the gradual realization of its possibly extensive spread. This chapter also contains entries on the Vedic period, which is almost exclusively the extraordinary corpus of literary compositions of the incoming Aryan tribes -- the four Vedas themselves and their associated works. There is as yet no documentation of these tribal invasions; their origin is inferred from comparative Indo-European philological studies. The civilizational levels represented in Chapter Two set the stage for the next chapter.

Chapter Three, which we have called "Ancient India: c. 6th Cent. BC to 6th Cent. AD . . . ," sets forth the formative period of Indic civilization and presents materials on subcontinent-wide developments in religion, literature, and art. We include the Sanskrit epics; although they may have begun to take shape in an earlier period, it was in this period that they attained their present form. Whereas in Chapter One we present perennial concepts and practices of indigenous Indian religions, in Chapter Three we organize materials illustrating their development during this period. For example, we include bibliographic entries on the emergence of theistic Hinduism, the life of Buddha, and the early history of the Sangha, early Jainism, classical Sanskrit writers, and major sites and styles of Gandharan and Gupta art.

Chapter Four is entitled "Early 'Medieval' South Asia . . . ." We use quotes for the word "medieval" to show that we do not mean the quality of "Dark Ages" in Western history. This chapter includes substantial material on the rise of bhakti, full-blown devotional Hinduism addressed to a personal god and increasingly expressed through regional languages rather than Sanskrit. Studies of earlier theistic Hinduism, however, are presented in Chapter Three (section V.B.), and materials on the earliest theistic developments in Hindu mythology and iconography in Chapter One (section IV.B.). In Chapter Four we begin to emphasize regional traditions and demonstrate our practice of starting with Sri Lanka, moving to South India, and then proceeding north and west, then east, ending with what we term the Himalayan Rim (see Map 2, page xxxix). By this sequence, we intend to give greater prominence to Ceylon and the South than is usually given in works which cover the subcontinent, and to underscore the importance of the bhakti movement and Śaṅkara's Vedānta, both of which originated in South India and spread north.

Chapter Five, "The Mughals, Marathas, and the Rise of British Power . . . ," focusses on Mughal and Maratha efforts to develop a unitary state in India. The inclusive dates for this chapter are 1526 and 1818, from Babar's defeat of the Afghans and control of Delhi to the British defeat of the Marathas, the last Indian power which attempted to gain all-India hegemony. Works on Muslim rule in India which concentrate on the Mughal period but have sizable sections on pre-Mughal history are placed in this chapter. We include materials on the growth of Sikhism here, but writings on the Sikh kingdom of the Punjab and modern Sikhism are in Chapter Thirteen (IV.A.3.).

Part Three is entitled "Transformations in the Modern Age: National Level" and includes Chapters Six through Nine, which cover the period from 1818 to the present. We have not included Sri Lanka, the Maldive Islands, Nepal and Bhutan in

Part Three despite the fact that they are nation-states. Entries concerning these political entities are found in Chapters Ten and Sixteen. We do not intend to diminish their stature as independent nation states today but rather continue their treatment in this book as integral parts of the subcontinental civilizational whole. Furthermore, the amount of literature on each was not enough to warrant separate chapters.

Chapter Six, on "The Raj . . . ," covers both Princely and British India, and presents literature pertaining to the period 1818-1947 for mainland South Asia. The division of chapters at 1947 is a concession to historical events; we recognize that many books deal with the political history of modern India, with 1947 as the midpoint. We chose 1818 because it is the date when the British eliminated the last remaining Indian military obstacle to their de facto political control of the subcontinent. Materials on India in growing confrontation and encounter with British political power and sociocultural influence, and books and articles which treat national-level issues, events, and personalities as well as transregional literatures and movements are listed here. While the term "raj" ("rule") can properly apply to a regime or jurisdiction of a princely state or other sovereign entity, its current use is overwhelmingly as a code for British rule in India after 1857, which is our usage in the Outline of Headings. In contrast to usage in Chapter Five, the term "European" is used in Chapter Six as a synonym for "British" (as in 11930).

Chapters Seven, Eight, and Nine cover the subcontinent from 1947 to the present. Chapter Seven, "The Present-Day South Asian Subcontinent in its Global Context," deals with modern developments in the Indian ocean area and relations among the South Asian nation-states, and places the South Asian nations in world politics. Literature on the creation of Bangladesh in 1971 is in Chapter Seven under the rubric of relations among South Asian nations and the Indo-Pakistani war of 1971 (section IV.B.) Materials on the People's Republic of Bangladesh since 1971 are in Chapter Fifteen, since Bangladesh is treated as part of the northeast geo-cultural area of the Ganga delta.

Chapter Eight, "India as Nation-State . . . ," covers the voluminous literature on modern India after 1947. It includes over 5,000 entries, culled from the mass of writing currently being produced. We have been very selective, particularly with respect to periodical articles on politics and economics, some of which appear to be instant analysis rather than thoughtful commentary.

Chapter Nine, "The Islamic State of Pakistan . . . ," organizes the literature on Pakistan from its foundation as a state in 1947 through its division in 1971, and from 1971 to the present. It outlines the development of Pakistan insofar as we could locate books, articles, and government documents. There is no adequate bibliographic apparatus within the country, few indexes, and no guide to periodical literature.

Part Four consists of Chapters Ten through Seventeen, which cover "Transformations in the Modern Age: The Eight Geo-Cultural Areas." We have developed the concept of geo-cultural areas as groupings of cultural-linguistic units. Seven geo-cultural areas refer to the parts of the subcontinent which are included in the South Asian nation-states. These seven geo-cultural areas are: the Island of Ceylon, the Dravidian South of India, Middle India, the Northwest, North India, the Northeast, and the Himalayan Rim. The eighth geo-cultural area encompasses South Asian communities in all other parts of the world. The bibliographic entries in Part Four number nearly 8,700. For a view of the seven geo-cultural areas of the subcontinent readers should refer to the map on page xxxix. A second map shows present political boundaries at national, provincial, and state levels.

The first geo-cultural area, Sri Lanka (Ceylon) and the Maldive Islands, is considered in Chapter Ten, "Ceylon to Sri Lanka . . ." This chapter comprises materials on Sri Lanka from the time of its establishment as a British colony to the present. While Ceylon has nearly always been a separate political entity, we treat it throughout as a distinctive area within Indic civilization. We include the now independent republic of the Maldive Islands in this chapter for two reasons. Their closest cultural affinity is with Ceylon, and during the British period they were administered from Colombo, the capital of Ceylon.

Chapter Eleven covers a geo-cultural area and is called "The Dravidian South of India. . . ." This area includes the four southernmost cultural-linguistic regions of India from 1800 to the present. Since Madras Presidency included parts of each linguistic region, many publications deal with this British administrative unit and are placed in a separate section of the chapter (section II.). With territorial reorganization following independence, four language-based states were set up. We treat the Tamil-speaking state of Tamilnadu as a continuation of Madras Presidency in the same section. Three major sections (III., IV., V.) complete the chapter and reflect the fact that each linguistic region included major Princely States. We include here under Andhra Pradesh (III.) materials on the Nizam's Dominions (later Hyderabad State) even though not all of Hyderabad was Telugu-speaking. Similarly, for Kerala we include works on Travancore and Cochin

States, and for Karnataka works on Mysore as a princely state. The Outline of Headings clearly shows these political adjustments through time.

With Chapter Twelve, "Middle India . . . ," we deal with the large area that is transitional between North and South. By our definition, this area of hill, plateau, and desert has two main components: a band of princely states stretching from coast to coast (most of the 562 principalities recognized by the British are found here), and large concentrations of adivasis, indigenous preliterate tribal peoples. The chapter covers an area which is now five different states and two union territories. It begins with materials (section I.) on two major administrative categories: the groupings of principalities in Princely India under the British Raj, proceeding from west to east, and the units of British rule. The next section (II.) deals with adivasis, again moving from west to east. We chose to retain Chota Nagpur (much of it in Bihar State) as a whole and place it here because it is undeniably part of the band of tribal peoples in Middle India, but its industrial development is dealt with in Chapter Fourteen. Later sections contain works on Goa, Maharashtra, Gujarat, Rajasthan, Madhya Pradesh, and Orissa.

Chapter Thirteen, "The Northwest . . . ," includes materials on the huge area watered by the Indus River and its tributaries. It is marked on the west and north by the mountain frontier which divides Indic civilization from the civilizations of the Middle East and Central Asia. The entries follow a sequence that starts with Sind and proceeds up the Indus River to the Kashmir region toward the river's source in Tibet. We treat the Punjab ("panch āb," or "five waters," which are tributaries of the Indus) as a cultural-linguistic whole. The literature on Ranjit Singh's Sikh State as well as on the subsequent British province, Punjab, is in this section (IV.). To accommodate the post-1947 divisions, publications on partitioned Punjab are placed under Pakistani and Indian sections as appropriate. However, with respect to Punjabi literature, we retain an undivided category. The Kashmir region is similarly treated primarily in geo-cultural terms.

"North India . . ." is the geo-cultural area named in Chapter Fourteen's title. This encompasses the present Hindi-speaking states of Haryana, Uttar Pradesh, and Bihar, and the union territory of Delhi. With 200 million persons (1981 Census) -- twenty-nine percent of India's total of about 684,000,000 -- North India is the political and cultural heartland, the perennial site of India's capitals, and the conservative core of the Indic cultural realm. Even though it is the Hindi and Urdu region par excellence, we have chosen to treat these languages and literatures as pan-South Asian (in Chapters Six, Eight, and Nine) because of their spread beyond North India's limits. Kumaon and Garhwal, the northern mountain region of Uttar Pradesh, are included in Chapter Sixteen (section III.) with other regions of the Himalayan Rim.

In Chapter Fifteen, "The Northeast . . . ," we include bibliographic entries on the cultural regions of the Gangetic delta and the Brahmaputra Valley. Since the Bengal Presidency was the overall administrative unit for most of this area during the British period, we treat it first under Political History (section I.A.). Then we present materials on West Bengal State, which we see as the Indian portion of the Presidency after the 1947 partition of the subcontinent. After parallel treatment of economic, social, and cultural materials in India, we turn to a separate section (II.) on Bangladesh (from 1971) and East Pakistan (1947-71). Together, however, these sections add up to a bibliography on a modern Bengali cultural-linguistic region that crosses recent political boundaries. The section on Assam (III.) which follows presents materials on the Brahmaputra Valley region and adjacent foothills of the Himalayas, including materials on tea plantations, as well as on those tribals who have settled in the valley and foothills.

Chapter Sixteen covers materials on the extensive geo-cultural area denoted in its title, "The Himalayas and Eastern Mountain Rim of India, Nepal, and Bhutan: Fringes of Tibetan, Buddhist, and Southeast Asian Cultures." The common element in the discrete cultural segments dealt with here is the fact of mountain or island ecology and what that implies in terms of differentiation of peoples in scores of isolated cultural-linguistic pockets. It is the environment and general way of life -- the highland-lowland dichotomy and island separation -- that set off these cultures from the rest of the subcontinent. Although the area is not entirely Indic, Tibetan, or Burmese in orientation, it is treated as an extension of the main Indian tradition. Since we presented the Kashmir region in Chapter Thirteen, we start this chapter with a section on the Western Pahari-speaking region of Himachal Pradesh, including the erstwhile Punjab Hill States. Readers will also find materials on Kumaon and Garhwal, Nepal, Sikkim and the Darjeeling district of West Bengal, Bhutan, and the small Indian states bordering Assam. We include the Andaman and Nicobar Islands at the end of Chapter Sixteen, since we saw them as southernmost extensions of the Himalayan Rim, outcrops if you will, in the Bay of Bengal. This represents a geographical extension rather than a cultural statement.

Chapter Seventeen, "The Indic Diaspora . . . ," treats South Asian communities widely scattered throughout the world. Nineteenth- and twentieth-century emigration from the subcontinent, for whatever reasons, has created far-flung outposts of Indic civilization. Large enough groups of South Asians have settled around the world to assure continuation in new lands of a consciousness of origin and, for the most part, of on-going social and economic ties to the homeland. Research on the dispersed South Asian communities has only recently begun, however, and scholarly coverage is uneven. For example, we need scholarly analyses of the sizable groups of South Asians who have been lured by the recent explosion of employment opportunities to Saudi Arabia, the Yemens, and the Persian Gulf States. So far only newspapers and popular magazines have explored this phenomenon. Population pressures in the subcontinent are leading to the transplanting of more and more South Asians, along with their whole paraphernalia of culture. We expect to see great expansion of the Indic diaspora, and a concomitant development of research and writing on the subject.

Part Five is called "Reference Resources" and contains Chapter Eighteen, "Introductions and General Research Guides for Travellers and Scholars." It gathers together useful practical introductions and guides to places, libraries, and languages of the subcontinent and includes scholarly works such as those under the "geography" headings in section II. Popular introductions to various places, journalistic travellers' accounts, and "how-to-do-it" travel and hotel guides are also in section II. Materials for teaching about South Asia are in section III, and materials in section IV will assist in the location of scholarly publications. Section V, on language tools, presents the most accessible and current dictionaries, readers, and grammars for the major literary languages of the subcontinent. We do not include in this book references to the hundreds of works on South Asia's many nonliterary languages, although we include references which will lead the reader to them. While Chapter One plays a special and fundamental role in overviewing and previewing the chapters which follow it, Chapter Eighteen provides reference materials which give the reader tools of a technical and practical nature.

On the Use of the Bibliography

This section describes the various ways in which readers can use this volume. The multilevel and multipurpose nature of this book means that it will be used by both introductory and advanced students and scholars. Those beginning their study of South Asia can focus on the general sections of each chapter or on the popular introductions in Chapter Eighteen. Persons at an advanced level, who probably have specialized in one field of study or one part of the subcontinent, can become acquainted with other parts of Indic civilization through perusal of the Outline of Headings. Librarians can locate specific subjects or identify particular subjects and authors through the indexes or place particular works in their geographic and chronological contexts through use of the Outline of Headings and its serial numbers.

A user will come to this volume to look for a particular author and his work, or a title where the author is unknown, or a general or specific topic. In each case, the user will adopt a strategy depending upon what is known and unknown. For example, Milton B. Singer's When a Great Tradition Modernizes can be located in the bibliography as follows: (1) use the Author Index to find the listing under "Singer, Milton B.," which will give fifteen separate five-digit clusters. You may, if you choose, look up each serial number in the Bibliographic Entries, or (2) look in the Subject Index under "Great Tradition" or "modernization" where you will find not only a five-digit number referring to Singer's volume (00651) but also five-digit serial numbers referring to other volumes dealing with its topic. You may compare the serial numbers in the Subject and Author Indexes, narrowing the search for this particular book in the Bibliographic Entries, or (3) turn to the one- or two-digit Arabic numeral pages listed before the serial numbers in the Subject Index. On these pages (1-8, 48) of the Outline of Headings you will find sections which deal with the subject matter of the Singer book, and its larger chronological and geographic contexts which are in this case "timeless" and "South Asia." Then you can use the outline to find further sections of Bibliographic Entries in the same field of study as the Singer volume, as well as the volume itself.

A user interested in ancient Indian social history could proceed as follows. (1) Check the Subject Index under "history, ancient," and find page numbers 10-13, referring to the Outline of Headings, and serial numbers 04009-586 referring to the Bibliographic Entries. (2) Check the Outline of Headings, pages 10-13 which contains Chapter Three, sections I through V, and in section III, "History by Topic: Political, Economic, Social, and International," find sections A through E, wherein section C (on page 12) is called "Dharma: the Person and the Social Order; Law and the Family . . . " and the first section is "General Studies of Social Life in the Ancient Period . . . " The serial numbers for this section will lead the user to those Bibliographic Entries specifically concerned with the topic of interest, ancient Indian social history. (3) In the Bibliographic Entries, numbers 04009 to 04586 appear on twelve pages, and by scanning the section headings and book titles you will find several sections related to the chosen topic, such as in section I.D. "General Surveys of Ancient History" (04086 - 04107) and III.C. "Dharma: the Person and the Social Order . . . " You may find other titles of interest within these pages. If you find that a single author, for instance Romila Thapar, has written several books or articles on this subject you may wish to consult the Author Index under her name, "Thapar, Romila," to find her other works.

Before turning to a description of the indexes, the Bibliographic Entries, the maps, and a note on transliteration, we should caution the reader about the use of names in this bibliography. We have not been able to be consistent in the spelling, transliteration, and order of elements in names that originate in South Asian languages. Wherever possible we have followed the usage in the book or article for listing places, groups, and persons in the Bibliographic Entries and the Indexes. In the Outline of Headings we have attempted to be consistent and have provided alternative spellings and glosses where the difference is significant. In the Outline of Headings, chapters One through Five, we use standardized transliteration of classical languages, but in the later chapters we follow contemporary and popular usage. In the Bibliographic Entries we use the original transliterations.

We recommend to users three means of access to the Bibliographic Entries: (1) the Author Index, (2) the Subject Index, and (3) the Outline of Headings.

The Author Index

The Author Index (pages 707 through 808) lists alphabetically authors, joint authors, editors, compilers, and translators of texts (but not translators of studies) for all Bibliographic Entries. If more than four authors exist for a book, the Bibliographic Entries contains only the first author followed by et al., but in the Author Index each of the several authors is listed independently. Most original authors and translators of classical texts appear in the Author Index, but if a real or supposed author of a classical text cannot be located in the Author Index, check the Subject Index for a listing.

The Author Index includes corporate and title entries where no person is identifiable as author. For Indian government documents we follow Library of Congress procedure and order the entries chronologically. That is, under "India" for the pre-1947 period, under "India (Dominion)" for 1947-50, and under "India (Republic)" since 1950. Chairmen of Committees and Commissions have been listed, insofar as possible, in the Author Index.

Personal names are given in full, to the extent possible, in the Author Index, whereas forenames are usually reduced to initials within the Bibliographic Entries. You may find out an author's full name by noting the Bibliographic Entry serial number and consulting the Author Index to find where that serial number appears. There is no standard method of alphabetizing Indic or Perso-Arabic names. We have attempted to provide consistency in this volume but if you do not find an individual's name on the first try you should look under the other separate elements of the name. In general, when we found discrepant spellings of names in several references, we adopted a single form. Many South Asian names have multiple elements and it is difficult to determine which element should be used for alphabetizing. Names ending with elements which occur frequently such as Ayyar, Chand, Khan, Lal, Rao, Sastri, and Singh may be alphabetized under the penultimate element. Muslim names vary widely by time and region, and are especially difficult to alphabetize. For these names, we use final, penultimate, or first elements to alphabetize, depending on two main authorities, the Library of Congress National Union Catalog and title pages of the works themselves. Cross-references are usually given for names where the final element is questionable. For example, "Singh" is a final element in many South Asian names. While there are many listings under "Singh" in the Author Index, some well-known names such as Karni Singh and Khushwant Singh are alphabetized by the penultimate element, that is, by "K." For Khushwant Singh, there is also a listing in the Subject Index under "Khushwant Singh" which gives several serial numbers for articles about Khushwant Singh and his writing, but not for works by him. In general, authors' names appear in the Subject Index only when we have listed works about them, or autobiographies or their collected speeches.

The Subject Index

The Subject Index lists key words from the headings and important terms taken from the titles of books and articles and our notes -- concepts, authors, scholarly fields, persons, places, historical events and movements, sects, communities, castes, and tribes. We have not attempted to index every book by every significant word in its title, or concept in its contents, but we have tried to provide the user with access to numerous subjects. Glosses are given for Indic words to aid non-specialists. For translations and definitions, we suggest the reader refer to standard reference works such as 00144 (Philips), 01121 (Stutley), 01597 (Liebert), 02318 (Dictionary of Oriental Literatures), and 27797 (Monier-Williams).

Listings in the Subject Index include three types of numbers: small roman numerals, and one- or two-digit arabic numbers, both of which refer to pages of the volume, and five-digit serial numbers which refer to Bibliographic Entries. For example, the listing for "gazetteers,"

page *page* *serial numbers*
gazetteers, xvii, 83, 27778-83

means that in the Introduction on page xvii there is information about gazetteers; on page 83 in the Outline of Headings there is reference to gazetteers, and finally, in the Bibliographic Entries, numbers 27778 to 27783 are gazetteers or references to them.

The guiding principle in preparing the Subject Index was "what would people look under?" but since not all interests can be anticipated users may have to do a little searching to find what they want. Some general statements about the construction of this index may help. If one looks under a particular political unit each of the large sections of the Outline of Headings on that political unit will be listed and blocks of serial numbers will be given for the Bibliographic Entries. For instance, for Maharashtra the listing begins:

Maharashtra, xxi
- art, 8, 03405, 05483-93, 05572-607, 06808-29
- bibliography, 27716
- British period, 62, 20584-611, 20685-773
- drama and dance, 8, 03029-30, 03032
- general history, 2, 00449-51

The subheadings for this listing refer to time periods, types of works, and specific topics such as art or drama, in alphabetical order.

However, if your subject of interest is a topic, then consult the listing for that particular topic. For instance, if you are interested in famines, famine control, and famine relief, you will find a listing as follows:

famines. For regions not listed below, *see* agriculture
- ancient, 04369
- Assam, 25740
- Bangladesh, 75, 25344-50
- Bengal, 73, 24450-9
- Bihar, 72, 24079-84
- British India, 36, 10992, 11012-23, 19273
- India (Rep.), 46, 14826-30
- Kerala, 19994
- Maharashtra, 64, 21283-90
- Orissa, 22318
- South Asia, general, 12231

This list will lead you to the specific places in the Outline and in the Entries where famine is mentioned. The cross-reference following "famines" indicates that a more general level for "famine" in this volume is "agriculture" and further works on famine will be found under this more general heading. The listing for agriculture gives the next higher level of heading, "economic conditions," which is the most general heading in the Subject Index for this topic.

In a similar way, the Subject Index will lead you from the topic "planning, urban" to "urbanization" to "social conditions." "Social conditions," the most general heading in the Subject Index for this topic, will lead mainly to sections of the Outline of Headings under "Society and Social Change" and Bibliographic Entries for this heading. For some listings, you will be referred directly to the next higher level. For instance, in the listing,

universities. *See* education; *see also* names of
universities and colleges

all the page and serial numbers appear under "education." We have endeavored to avoid duplicating large sections with many subheads for general categories such as government, economics, and education. If you are looking for references to a specific topic and place, such as post-1947 education in Tamil Nadu, you should look not only under "education, Tamil Nadu," but also see listings for "education, India (Rep.)" where you will find all-India works which include material on Tamil Nadu education. The sections on British India, India (Rep.), Pakistan, are general; i.e., they are nation-wide, All-India, or at least transregional.

Subheadings in the Subject Index use code words to identify chapters. In the chart Guide to Chapters and Serial Numbers, which follows on page xxix, for the convenience of the user we give serial numbers, code words, and page numbers for each chapter. This chart summarizes the structure of the Bibliographic Entries.

The Bibliographic Entries

For each type of bibliographic entry we have designed a standard format, which incorporates a main entry (personal or corporate author, editor, compiler, translator or title), title (where title is not the main entry), place of publication, publisher, date of publication, and pagination. In addition, where appropriate, we have provided the editors and title of a book in which an article or essay appears, series information in parentheses, and additional information in square brackets. Wherever possible we have changed roman numerals to arabic numbers, for example, in citing journal volumes and volumes of British parliamentary papers. Names of publishers are reduced to the minimal entry needed for clarity such as "Munshiram" for Munshiram Manoharlal. A list of abbreviations used in the Bibliographic Entries appears at the end of this Introduction. In addition we have abbreviated names of journals, names of series, and frequently used words. The latter appear in a list of "General Abbreviations" which also follows this Introduction.

In the case of reprints, we have entered the best new editions which are currently available for purchase. We note in square brackets the date of the original publication. In the entries, spellings follow the usage of the author where we could consult the original. Certain spellings alternate between English and American usage.

Dissertations are identified as "Diss.," "Ph.D. Diss.," and "Unpub. Ph.D. Diss.," and the University and year awarded are given. In most cases, American dissertations are listed in Dissertation Abstracts International and are identified by a serial number (e.g. "UM 77-29,597") by which photocopies or microfilm copies may be ordered from University Microfilms International, P.O. Box 1764, Ann Arbor, Michigan 48106. Copies of University of Chicago dissertations may be ordered from Photoduplication Department, Joseph Regenstein Library, 1100 E. 57th Street, Chicago, Illinois 60637. Harvard University dissertations are available from the Photographic Department in Harvard's Widener Library, Cambridge, Massachusetts 02138. For further information on obtaining dissertations, see 27696 (Shulman).

The types of Bibliographic Entries and descriptions of their components are illustrated in the following examples.

1. Standard format for a book:

   06281 NILAKANTA SASTRI, K.A. Development of religion in South India. Bombay: Orient Longmans, 1963. 148p.

06281	serial number
NILAKANTA SASTRI, K.A.	main entry (author)
Development of religion . . .	title of book
Bombay:	place of publication
Orient Longmans,	publisher
1963.	date of publication
148p.	pagination

2. Corporate author format:

   10254 INDIA. INDIAN CENTRAL CMTEE. Report, 1928-29. London: HMSO, 1929. 428p. (Cmd 3451; Parl. Pap. 1929/30: 10) [appointed by Lord Irwin to work with Simon Cmsn.]

10254	serial number
INDIA. INDIAN CENTRAL CMTEE.	main entry (corporate author)
Report, 1928-29.	title
London:	place of publication
HMSO,	publisher (see abbreviations list)
1929.	date of publication
428p.	pagination
(Cmd 3451; Parl. . . .)	series information (see abbreviations list)
[appointed by Lord Irwin . . .]	additional information

3. Translator format:

06293 FILLIOZAT, J., tr. Un texte tamoul de dévotion vishnouite: le Tiruppāvai d'Āṇṭāl. Pondicherry: IFI, 1972. 120p. (Its pub., 45)

06293	serial number
FILLIOZAT, J., tr.	translator. Full name appears in author index.
Un texte tamoul . . .	title. We do not translate titles.
Pondicherry:	place of publication, given in standard English
IFI,	publisher (see abbreviations list)
1972.	date of publication
120p.	pagination
(Its pub., 45)	publication number 45 of series from Institut français d'Indologie (IFI)

4. Article formats:

06287 YOCUM, G.E. Sign and paradigm: myth in Tamil Śaiva and Vaiṣṇava Bhakti poetry. In H.M. Buck & G.E. Yocum, eds. Structural approaches to South Indian studies. Chambersburg, PA: Wilson Books, 1974, 227-234.

06283 VIPULANANDA, Swami. The development of Tamilian religious thought. In TC 5 (1956) 251-66.

In	indicates the book or journal in which the article appears
TC	name of journal (see abbreviations list)
5	volume number of journal
(1956)	year of publication of volume
251-66	pagination of article

5. Title formats:

25286 Islam and family planning. Dacca: Dir. of Population Control & Family Planning, 1977. 43p.

01927 Pilgrim centres of India. In Vivekananda Kendra Patrika 3,1 (1974). 408p.

408p.	indicates that title is entire issue of the journal

6. Dissertation format:

06288 ATE, L.M. Periyāḻvār's Tirumoḻi: a Bāla Kṛṣṇa text from the devotional period in Tamil literature. Ph.D. diss., U. of Wisconsin, 1978. [UM 78-15,034]

[UM 78-15,034]	University Microfilms order number for this dissertation

Entries appear under headings from the Outline of Headings at an appropriate level. For example, Chapter Four, VI. C. looks like this:

C. "Greater India": Colonization and Indianization of South-East Asia

06273 COEDÈS, G. The Indianized states of Southeast Asia. Tr. by S.B. Cowing. Ed. by W.F. Vella. Honolulu: EWCP, 1968. 403p. [1st French ed., 1944]

06274 MAJUMDAR, R.C. Hindu colonies in the Far East 2nd rev. & enl. ed. Calcutta: KLM, 1963. 280p.

06275 ______. India and South East Asia. Ed. by K.S. Ramachandran & S.P. Gupta. Delhi: B.R., 1979. 218p.

06276 SIRISENA, W.M. Sri Lanka and South-East Asia: Political, religious and cultural relations from A.D. c. 1000 to c. 1500. Leiden: Brill, 1978. 186p.

If there are several subheadings under a higher level heading, an entry begins like this

D. Religio-Philosophical Traditions in Early Medieval Dravidian India: Blending of Popular Bhakti, the Pan-Indian Brahmanic Orthodoxy of Vedānta, and the Āgamic Traditions

1. General Studies of the South Indian Religious Milieu

06277 ARUMUGA MUDALIAR, S. Concepts of religion in Sangam literature and in devotional literature. In TC 11 (1964) 252-71.

06278 HANUMANTHA RAO, B.S.L. Religion in Āndhra: a survey of religious developments in Āndhra from early times up to AD 1325. Guntur: the author, 1973. 346p.

06279 HART, G.L., III. The nature of Tamil devotion. In M.M. Deshpande and P.E. Hook, eds. Aryan and Non-Aryan in India. Ann Arbor: UMCSSAS, 1979, 11-35.

Some headings give additional information, such as the cross-reference in Chapter Fourteen, I.,

I. HARYANA: HINDI-SPEAKING STATE CREATED FROM PUNJAB IN 1966 [see also Chap. THIRTEEN, IV.A.]

or the literacy rate for a state as in Chapter Twelve, IV. C. 7.,

7. Education in Maharashtra since 1818 (47.4% literacy in 1981)

or the population of a city as in Chapter Fifteen, I. D. 5.,

5. Calcutta (1981 pop. 9,165,650)

The running heads in the Bibliographic Entries indicate, on the left page, the Chapter number and short title, and on the right page, the roman numeral section of the Outline of Headings.

Maps

The volume includes two maps to guide users of this bibliography. One map shows the seven geo-cultural areas of the subcontinent which we have designed for this volume and the linguistic regions within each area. The second map indicates the political boundaries of nations, states and provinces within the subcontinent. For a detailed set of maps of the subcontinent, both contemporary and historical, we recommend use of The Historical Atlas of South Asia edited by Joseph Schwartzberg (00156).

GUIDE TO CHAPTERS AND SERIAL NUMBERS

PART	CHAPTER	SERIAL NUMBERS	CHAPTER CODE	PAGES
ONE Overview of the Great Tradition	One	00001 - 03482	General	87-157
TWO Four Ages of Historical Evolution: Subcontinental and Regional	Two	03483 - 04008	Prehistory; or Harappan; or Vedic	161-172
	Three	04009 - 05625	Ancient	173-208
	Four	05626 - 07385	"Medieval"	209-247
	Five	07386 - 08986	Mughal	249-284
THREE Transformations in the Modern Age: National Level	Six	08987 - 11981	British India	287-349
	Seven	11982 - 12269	South Asia	351-356
	Eight	12270 - 17282	Republic of India	357-458
	Nine	17283 - 18288	Pakistan	459-480
FOUR Transformations in the Modern Age: The Eight Geo-Cultural Areas	Ten	18289 - 19115	Sri Lanka	483-501
	Eleven	19116 - 20578	South India	503-534
	Twelve	20579 - 22425	Middle India	535-575
	Thirteen	22426 - 23262	Northwest	577-595
	Fourteen	23263 - 24240	North India	597-618
	Fifteen	24241 - 25833	Northeast	619-652
	Sixteen	25834 - 26736	Himalayan Rim	653-671
	Seventeen	26737 - 26951	Diaspora; Overseas	673-678
FIVE Reference Resources	Eighteen	26952 - 28017	Introductions; Reference	681-703

Note on Transliteration

Diacritical marks have been added to words in the headings after typing the camera-ready copy; probably some are missing. For the first five chapters of the Outline of Headings we have presented names and concepts in transliteration from non-Roman scripts. Readers will thus find, particularly in the first five chapters, Sanskrit, Tamil, Arabic and other non-Western terms with diacritical marks. We have used the transliteration scheme generally accepted by western scholarly journals. The reader may find inconsistencies, however, in the rendering of the palatal c, ch, chh and the various sibilants ś, ṣ, s, and in the representation of nasals before k, g and some other consonants. For certain letters pure and popular transliterations coexist, such as svāmī/swami, vrata/brata, and satī/suttee. Beginning with Chapter Six we have tended to use popular, anglicized spellings for names of persons, places, and concepts.

Non-English words in the Bibliographical Entries are given as we found them on the title page, or in the National Union Catalog, or wherever we obtained the citation. Thus there is no consistency of spelling among the entries. The Subject Index shows both "pure" and "popular" transliterations for a number of terms.

Perhaps the best way to state our philosophy regarding transliteration and consistency is to borrow the following statement from Sir Henry Yule and his Hobson-Jobson (09011):

> My intention has been to give the headings of the articles under the most usual of the popular, or, if you will, vulgar quasi-English spellings, whilst the Oriental words, from which the headings are derived or corrupted, are set forth under precise transliteration, the system of which is given in a following "Nota Bene." When using the words and names in the course of discursive elucidation, I fear I have not been consistent in sticking either always to the popular or always to the scientific spelling, and I can the better understand why a German critic of a book of mine, once upon a time, remarked upon the *etwas schwankende yulische Orthographie*. Indeed it is difficult, it never will for me be possible, in a book for popular use, to adhere to one system in this matter without the assumption of an ill-fitting and repulsive pedantry.

List of Abbreviations

General Abbreviations

admin.	administration, -tive	econ.	economy, -ic	p.	pages
agri.	agriculture, -al	ed.	edited, -tor, -tion	pop.	population
anthro.	anthropology, -ical	educ.	education, -al	Proc.	Proceedings
archaeol.	archaeology, -ical	eval.	evaluation	pub.	published, -ers, -ication
assn.	association	genl.	general	Q.	Quarterly
assoc.	association	Govt.	Government	R.	Review, Revue
bibl.	bibliography	hist.	history, -ical	Rep.	Republic
Bull.	Bulletin	incl.	including	res.	research
c.	circa	info.	information	rev.	revised
Cmsn.	Commission	Inst.	Institute	rpt.	reprint
Cmttee.	Committee	Intl.	International	S.A.	South Asian
comp.	comparative	J.	Journal	ser.	series
comp.	compiled, -er	mgmt.	management	Soc.	Society
conf.	conference	Min.	Ministry	st.	studies
coop.	cooperation, -tive	natl.	national	stat.	statistics, -al
corp.	corporation	ND	New Delhi	suppl.	supplement
Dept.	Department	ns	new series	tr.	translated, -or, -tion
dev.	development	NY	New York	Trans.	Transactions
Dir.	Director, -ate	or.	oriental	U.	University
diss.	dissertation	org.	organization	U.T.	Union Territory

Abbreviations of Journals, Series, and Publishers

AA	American Anthropologist (Washington)
AAR	American Academy of Religion
AAS	Association for Asian Studies
AAS(J)	Asian and African Studies (Jerusalem)
AAWG	Abhandlungen der Akademie der Wissenschaften in Göttingen
AC	Ancient Ceylon (Colombo)
ABORI	Annals of the Bhandarkar Oriental Research Institute (Poona)
ActaOr(B)	Acta Orientalia (Budapest)
ActaOr(C)	Acta Orientalia (Copenhagen)
Adm	Administrator (Mussorie)
AF	Altorientalische Forschungen (Leipzig)
AFS	Asian Folklore Studies (Nagoya)
AGSW	Abhandlungen der Geistes- und Sozialwissenschaften Klasse, Akademie der Wissenschaften und der Literatur
AI	Ancient India (Delhi)
AICC	All-India Congress Committee
AID	Agency for International Development
AIILSG	All-India Institute of Local Self-Government (Bombay)
AIIS	American Institute of Indian Studies
AIOC	All-India Oriental Conference, Proceedings
AITM	Ancient Indian tradition and mythology
AJES	Aligarh Journal of English Studies
AJS	American Journal of Sociology (Chicago)
AKM	Abhandlungen für die Kunde des Morgenlandes, Deutsche Morgenländische Gesellschaft
ALB	Brahmavidyā: Adyar Library Bulletin (Madras)
AnthSI	Anthropological Survey of India
ANUP	Australian National University Press
AO	Archiv Orientální (Prague)
AOS	American oriental series
AOS	American Oriental Society
AP	Ancient Pakistan (Karachi)
APSR	American Political Science Review (Washington)
AR	Asiatic Review

ArtAs Artibus Asiae (Ascona)

ArtsAs Arts Asiatiques (Paris)

AS Asian Survey (Berkeley)

AS/EA Asiatische Studien / Études asiatiques (Bern)

ASB Asiatic Society of Bengal

ASBangla Asiatic Society of Bangladesh

ASH Asian studies at Hawaii

ASI Archaeological Survey of India

ASP Asiatic Society of Pakistan

AsProf Asian Profile (Hong Kong)

AsSt Asian Studies (Quezon City)

ATS Asian Thought and Society (Oneonta, NY)

AUJR(L) Agra University Journal of Research (Letters)

AV Artha Vijñāna (Poona)

AVARD Association of Voluntary Agencies for Rural Development

AVik Artha Vikas (Vallabh Vidyanagar)

BAnthSI Bulletin, Anthropological Survey of India (Calcutta)

BARD Bangladesh Academy for Rural Development

BBTRI Bulletin of the Bihar Tribal Research Institute (Ranchi)

BDA Bulletin of the Department of Anthropology (Delhi)

BDCRI Bulletin of the Deccan College Research Institute (Poona)

BDS Bangladesh Development Studies (Dacca)

BEFEO Bulletin de l'École française de l'Extrême-Orient (Paris)

BER Bangladesh Economic Review (Dacca)

BHS Bangladesh Historical Studies (Dacca)

BHU Banaras Hindu University

BI Bibliotheca Indica

BIDE Bangladesh Institute of Development Economics

BIDS Bangladesh Institute of Development Studies

BIHM Bulletin of the Institute for the History of Medicine (Hyderabad)

BITCM Bulletin of the Institute of Traditional Cultures (Madras)

BMDSS Bulletin of the Madras Development Seminar Series (Madras)

BORI Bhandarkar Oriental Research Institute

BOS Bhandarkar oriental series

BPP Bengal Past and Present (Calcutta)

BPS Buddhist Publication Society

BRMIC Bulletin of the Ramakrishna Mission Institute of Culture (Calcutta)

BSAF Beiträge zur Südasienforschung, Südasien-Institut, Universität Heidelberg

BSOAS Bulletin of the School of Oriental and African Studies (London)

BT Bulletin of Tibetology (Gangtok, Sikkim)

BTRI Bulletin of the Tribal Research Institute (Chhindwara)

BV Bharatiya Vidya (Bombay)

BVB Bharatiya Vidya Bhavan

CA Current Anthropology (Chicago)

CAJ Central Asiatic Journal (Wiesbaden)

CamUP Cambridge University Press

CAP Carolina Academic Press

CAS Contributions to Asian Studies (Leiden)

CASS Centre of Advanced Studies in Sanskrit, publications

CDPRD Community Development and Panchayati Raj Digest (Hyderabad)

CEDA Centre for Economic Development and Administration

CHJ Ceylon Historical Journal (Colombo)

CHJSS Ceylon Journal of Historical and Social Studies (Peradeniya)

CHM Cahiers d'histoire mondiale / Journal of World History (Paris)

CI Census of India

CIIL Central Institute of Indian Languages

CIL Contemporary Indian Literature (New Delhi)

CIS Contributions to Indian Sociology (Delhi)

CISRS Christian Institute for the Study of Religion and Society

CJH Ceylon Journal of Humanities (Peradeniya)

CLS Christian Literature Society

CNRS Centre National de Recherche Scientifique

CNS Contributions to Nepali Studies (Kirtipur)

Cont. of Pub. Controller of Publications, Government of India

CornellUP Cornell University Press

CORS Chaukhambha Oriental Research Studies

CPI Communist Party of India

CR Calcutta Review

CRSA Canadian Review of Sociology and Anthropology (Calgary)

CSS Chowkhambha Sanskrit studies

CSSH Comparative Studies in Society and History (Ann Arbor)

CSSO Chowkhambha Sanskrit Series Office

CTL	Current trends in linguistics
CUDL	Calcutta University, Dept. of Letters, Journal
DCBC	Deccan College building centenary silver jubilee series
DCPRI	Deccan College Postgraduate and Research Institute
DG	Deccan Geographer (Hyderabad)
DI	Demography India (Delhi)
DPMIB	Directorate of Publications, Ministry of Information and Broadcasting
DRT	Disputationes Rheno-Trajectinae
DSI	Dissertationsreihe des Südasien-Instituts der Universität Heidelberg
DUP	Duke University Press
DUPCSSA	Duke University Program in Comparative Studies on Southern Asia
DUS	Dacca University Studies
EA	Eastern Anthropologist (Lucknow)
E&W	East and West (Rome)
EDCC	Economic Development and Cultural Change (Chicago)
EE	Eastern Economist (New Delhi)
EFEO	École française d'Extrême-Orient
EHR	Economic History Review (Cambridge, Eng.)
EJ(L)	Economic Journal (Lahore)
EPW	Economic and Political Weekly (Bombay)
ES	Economic Studies (Calcutta)
EW	Economic Weekly (Bombay)
EWCP	East-West Center Press
FAO	Food and Agriculture Organization, United Nations
FBI	Freiburger Beiträge zur Indologie
FEQ	Far Eastern Quarterly
FN	Fortnightly (London)
Folklore(C)	Folklore (Calcutta)
Folklore(L)	Folklore (London)
GIAPA	Grundriss der Indo-Arischen Philologie und Altertumskunde
GIPE	Gokhale Institute of Politics and Economics
GJ	Geographical Journal (London)
GJRI	Ganganatha Jha Research Institute
GM	Gandhi Marg (New Delhi)
GOS	Gaekwad's oriental series
GRI	Geographical Review of India (Calcutta)
HCIP	History and culture of the Indian people
HIIHC	Heras Institute of Indian History and Culture
HIL	A history of Indian literature
HimR	Himalayan Review (Kathmandu)
HJ	Historical Journal (London)
HMSO	Her/His Majesty's Stationery Office
HO	Handbuch der Orientalistik (as series)
HO	Human Organization (Ithaca, NY)
HR	History of Religions (Chicago)
HRAF	Human Relations Area Files
HUP	Harvard University Press
IA	Indian Antiquary (Bombay)
IAC	Indo-Asian Culture (New Delhi)
IAD	Idarah-i Adabiyat-i Delli
IAF	Internationales Asienforum (Munich)
IAIC	International Academy of Indian Culture
IAnth	Indian Anthropologist (Delhi)
IAS	Indian Anthropological Society
IATR	International Association of Tamil Research
IC	Indian Culture (Calcutta)
ICAR	Indian Council of Agricultural Research
ICCR	Indian Council for Cultural Relations
IChHR	Indian Church History Review
ICHR	Indian Council of Historical Research
ICPS	Institute of Constitutional and Parliamentary Studies
ICQ	Indian Cultures Quarterly (Jabalpur)
ICSSR	Indian Council of Social Science Research
ICWA	Indian Council of World Affairs
IDS	Indian Documentation Service
IEJ	Indian Economic Journal (Bombay)
IER	Indian Economic Review (Delhi)
IESHR	Indian Economic and Social History Review (Delhi)
IFI	Institut français d'indologie
IGJ	Indian Geographical Journal (Madras)
IHQ	Indian Historical Quarterly (Calcutta)
IHR	Indian Historical Review (New Delhi)
IHS	Institute of Historical Studies
IHRI	Indian Historical Research Institute
IIC	Indian International Center
IIJ	Indo-Iranian Journal (Dordrecht)
IIMEO	Istituto Italiano per il Medio ed Extremo Oriente
IIPA	Indian Institute of Public Administration

IIPO	Indian Institute of Public Opinion
IJE	Indian Journal of Economics (Allahabad)
IJEA	Indian Journal of Agricultural Economics (Bombay)
IJHM	Indian Journal of the History of Medicine (Madras)
IJHS	Indian Journal of the History of Science
IJIR	Indian Journal of Industrial Relations (New Delhi)
IJLE	Indian Journal of Labour Economics (Lucknow)
IJPA	Indian Journal of Public Administration (New Delhi)
IJPH	Indian Journal of Public Health (Calcutta)
IJPS	Indian Journal of Political Science (Calcutta)
IJS	Indian Journal of Sociology (New Delhi)
IJSR	Indian Journal of Social Research (Meerut)
IJSW	Indian Journal of Social Work (Bombay)
IL	Indian Literature (New Delhi)
ILJ	Indian Labour Journal (New Delhi)
ILO	International Labour Organization
ILP	India - the land and people
INC	Indian National Congress
IndBH	Indological Book House
Indica	Indica (Bombay)
IPSR	Indian Political Science Review (Delhi)
IQ	India Quarterly (New Delhi)
IS	International Studies (Delhi)
ISAE	Indian Society of Agricultural Economics
ISB	Indian Sociological Bulletin (Ghaziabad)
IsC	Islamic Culture (Hyderabad)
ISHI	Institute for the Study of Human Issues
ISPCK	Indian Society for Promoting Christian Knowledge
ISPP	Indian Studies Past and Present (Calcutta)
ISPQS-H&A	Indian Society for Prehistoric and Quaternary Studies - History and archaeology series
IT	Indologica Taurinensia; Official Organ of the International Association of Sanskrit Studies (Turin)
ITL	Indian theological library
IWI	Illustrated Weekly of India (Bombay)
IWT	Indian Writing Today (Bombay)
IYIA	Indian Yearbook of International Affairs (Madras)
JAAR	Journal of the American Academy of Religion (Missoula, MT)
JAAS(L)	Journal of Asian and African Studies (Leiden)
JAAS(T)	Journal of Asian and African Studies (Tokyo)
JAH	Journal of Asian History (Wiesbaden)
JAHRS	Journal of the Andhra Historical Research Society (Rajahmundry)
JAIH	Journal of Ancient Indian History (Calcutta)
JAnthSB	Journal of the Anthropological Society of Bombay
JAOS	Journal of the American Oriental Society (New Haven, CT)
JAS	Journal of Asian Studies (Ann Arbor, MI)
JASBangla	Journal of the Asiatic Society, Bangladesh (Dacca)
JASBengal	Journal of the Asiatic Society of Bengal (Calcutta)
JASBombay	Journal of the Asiatic Society, Bombay
JASCalcutta	Journal of the Asiatic Society, Calcutta
JASP	Journal of the Asiatic Society, Pakistan
JAU	Journal of Annamalai University (Annamalainagar)
JBBRAS	Journal of the Bombay Branch, Royal Asiatic Society
JBORS	Journal of the Bihar and Orissa Research Society (Patna)
JBPP	Journal of the Bihar Puravid Parishad (Patna)
JBRS	Journal of the Bihar Research Society (Patna)
JCCP	Journal of Commonwealth and Comparative Politics (London)
JCL	Journal of Commonwealth Literature (Leeds)
JComPolSt	Journal of Commonwealth Political Studies (London)
JCPS	Journal of Constitutional and Parliamentary Studies (New Delhi)
JD	Journal of Dharma (Bangalore)
JDS	Journal of Development Studies (London)
JEH	Journal of Economic History (New York)
JESHO	Journal of the Economic and Social History of the Orient (Leiden)
JGJKSV	Journal of the Ganganatha Jha Kendriya Sanskrit Vidyapeetha (Allahabad)
JGJRI	Journal of the Ganganatha Jha Research Institute (Patna)
JGRS	Journal of the Gujarat Research Society (Bombay)
JHS	Journal of Haryana Studies (Kurukshetra)
JIAI	Journal of Indian Art and Industry (London)
JIAP	Journal of the Indian Academy of Philosophy (Calcutta)

JIAS	Journal of the Indian Anthropological Society (Calcutta)
JICH	Journal of Imperial and Commonwealth History (London)
JIDSA	Journal of the Institute of Defense Studies and Analysis (New Delhi)
JIER	Journal of the Institute of Economic Research (Dharwar)
JIF	Journal of Indian Folkloristics (Mysore)
JIH	Journal of Indian History (Trivandrum)
JILI	Journal of the Indian Law Institute (New Delhi)
JIMS	Journal of the Indian Musicological Society (Baroda)
JIP	Journal of Indian Philosophy (Dordrecht)
JISOA	Journal of the Indian Society of Oriental Art (Calcutta)
JITP	Journal of the Institute of Town Planners (New Delhi)
JIWE	Journal of Indian Writing in English (Annamalainagar)
JKS	Journal of Kerala Studies (Trivandrum)
JKU(H)	Journal of Karnataka University (Humanities)
JKU(SS)	Journal of Karnataka University (Social Sciences)
JMA	Journal of the Music Academy (Madras)
JMSUB	Journal of the Maharaja Sayajirao University of Baroda
JMU	Journal of Madras University
JNAA	Journal of the National Academy of Administration (Mussoorie)
JOIB	Journal of the Oriental Institute (Baroda)
JORM	Journal of Oriental Research (Madras)
JOSA	Journal of the Oriental Society of Australia (Sydney)
JPHS	Journal of the Pakistan Historical Society (Karachi)
JPS	Journal of Peasant Studies (London)
JPTS	Journal of the Pali Text Society (London)
JPUHS	Journal of the Punjab University Historical Society (Lahore)
JRAI	Journal of the Royal Anthropological Institute (London)
JRAS	Journal of the Royal Asiatic Society (London)
JRASCB	Journal of the Royal Asiatic Society, Ceylon Branch (Colombo)
JRIHR	Journal of the Rajasthan Institute of Historical Research (Jaipur)
JRLB	John Rylands Library Bulletin (Manchester)
JRSP	Journal of the Research Society of Pakistan (Lahore)
JSAL	Journal of South Asian Literature (East Lansing, MI)
JSAMES	Journal of South Asian and Middle Eastern Studies (Villanova, PA)
JSR	Journal of Social Research (Ranchi)
JSS	Journal of Sikh Studies (Amritsar)
JSSR	Journal for the Scientific Study of Religion
JTS	Journal of Tamil Studies (Madras)
JUB	Journal of the University of Bombay
JUG	Journal of the University of Gauhati
JUP	Journal of the University of Poona
JUPHS	Journal of the Uttar Pradesh Historical Society (Lucknow)
JUSI	Journal of the United Service Institution of India (New Delhi)
KG	Khadi Gramodyog (Bombay)
LEW	Literature East and West (College Park, MD)
LGQ	Local Government Quarterly (Dacca)
LHI	Lake House Investments (Colombo)
LK	Lalit Kalā (New Delhi)
LKC	Lalit Kālā Contemporary (New Delhi)
MAS	Modern Asian Studies (Cambridge)
MASB	Memoirs of the Asiatic Society of Bengal (Calcutta)
MCS	Modern Ceylon Studies (Peradeniya)
MED	Monographs on the economics of development
MEDC	Maharashtra Economic Development Council
MI	Man in India (Ranchi)
MIB	Ministry of Information and Broadcasting
MIDS	Madras Institute of Development Studies
MIQ	Medieval India Quarterly (Aligarh)
MIS	Münchener indologische Studien
MO	Mysore Orientalist
Motilal	Motilal Banarsidass
MPGOI	Manager of Publications, Government of India
MPGOP	Manager of Publications, Government of Pakistan
MPSSA	Michigan papers on South and Southeast Asia
MR	Modern Review (Calcutta)
MSUASC	Michigan State University, Asian Studies Center
MSUB	Maharaja Sayajirao University of Baroda
Mushiram	Munshiram Manoharlal
MW	Muslim World (Hartford)
NAI	National Archives of India

NCERT	National Council of Educational Research and Training
NGJI	National Geographical Journal of India (Varanasi)
NGSI	National Geographical Society of India
NIA	New Indian Antiquary (Bombay)
NICD	National Institute of Community Development
NIFP	National Institute of Family Planning
NIPA	National Institute of Public Administration
NIRD	National Institute of Rural Development
NUJ	Nagpur University Journal
OA	Oriental Art (London)
OAW	Österreichische Akademie der Wissenschaften
OBRC	Oriental Books Reprint Corporation
OECD	Organization for Economic Cooperation and Development
O&M	Objets et mondes (Paris)
OH	Our Heritage (Calcutta)
OHRJ	Orissa Historical Research Journal (Bhubaneswar)
OLZ	Orientalische Literaturzeitung (Berlin)
Orbis	Orbis: a Journal of World Affairs (Philadelphia)
ORT	Orientalia Rheno-Traiectina
OSGP	Office of the Superintendent of Government Printing
OTJ	Oriental translation fund
OUP	Oxford University Press
PA	Pacific Affairs (Vancouver)
P&P	Past and Present (Oxford)
PAPS	Proceedings of the American Philosophical Society (Philadelphia)
PARD	Pakistan Academy for Rural Development
Parl.Pap.	Parliamentary Papers (Great Britain)
PDMIB	Publications Division, Ministry of Information and Broadcasting
PDR	Pakistan Development Review (Islamabad)
PEJ	Pakistan Economic Journal (Lahore)
PIDE	Pakistan Institute of Development Economics
PIHC	Proceedings of the Indian History Congress
PO	Poona Orientalist
POS	Poona oriental series
PPH	People's Publishing House
PPP	Punjab Past and Present (Patiala)
PSR	Political Science Review (Jaipur)
PUF	Presses Universitaires de France
PUP	Princeton University Press
PWM	Prince of Wales Museum of Western India
PWMB	Prince of Wales Museum of Western India, Bulletin
QER	Quarterly Economic Report, Indian Institute of Public Opinion (New Delhi)
QJLSGI	Quarterly Journal of the Local Self-Government Institute (Hyderabad)
QJMS	Quarterly Journal of the Mythic Society (Bangalore)
QR	Quarterly Review
QRHS	Quarterly Review of Historical Studies (Calcutta)
RAI	Royal Anthropological Institute
R&C	Race and Class (London)
R&S	Religion and Society (Bangalore)
RARD	Regional Academy of Rural Development
RAS	Royal Asiatic Society, London
RASB	Royal Asiatic Society of Bengal
RASCB	Royal Asiatic Society, Ceylon Branch
RBI	Reserve Bank of India
RL	Roopa Lekha (New Delhi)
RMIC	Ramakrishna Mission Institute of Culture
RT	Round Table (London)
SA	South Asia (Nedlands, Australia)
SAR	South Asian Review (London)
SAS	South Asian Studies (Jaipur)
SB	Sociological Bulletin (New Delhi)
SBB	Sacred books of the Buddhists
SBE	Sacred books of the East
SBH	Sacred books of the Hindus
SE	Southern Economist (Bangalore)
Sem	Seminar (New Delhi)
SER	Southern Economic Review (Madras)
SGKAO	Schriften zur Geschichte und Kultur des alten Orients
SHR	Studies in the history of religions
SI	Studia Islamica (Paris)
SIAK	Schriften des Institut für Asienkunde
SIAS	Studies in Indian and Asian civilisations
SIE	Studies in Indian Epigraphy (Mysore)
SIET Studies	Small Industry Extension Training Studies (Hyderabad)
SISSWPS	South India Saiva Siddhanta Works Publication Society
SLJAS	Sri Lanka Journal of South Asian Studies

SN	Sangeet Natak (New Delhi)
SocAct	Social Action (New Delhi)
SocSci	Social Scientist (Trivandrum)
SOU	States of our Union
SP	Sessional Papers, Ceylon Parliament
SPB	Sanskrit Pustak Bhandar
SPP	Sarada Pitha Pradipa (Dwarka)
SPS	Satapitaka series
SR	Sikh Review (Calcutta)
SSAC	Studies in South Asian cultures
SSI	Schriftenreihe des Südasien-Instituts der Universität Heidelberg
StM	Studia Missionalia
SVUOJ	Sri Venkatesvara University Oriental Journal (Tirupati)
SWJA	Southwestern Journal of Anthropology (Albuquerque, NM)
TAPS	Transactions of the American Philosophical Society (Philadelphia)
TASSI	Transactions of the Archaeological Society of South India (Madras)
TC	Tamil Culture (Madras)
TISS	Tata Institute of Social Sciences
TPH	Theosophical Publishing House
TSB	Tibet Society Bulletin (Bloomington, IN)
UA	United Asia (Bombay)
UCalP	University of California Press
UChiP	University of Chicago Press
UCR	University of Ceylon Review (Peradeniya)
UMCSSAS	University of Michigan Center for South and Southeast Asian Studies
UMichP	University of Michigan Press
UNESCO	United Nations Educational, Social and Cultural Organization
UNESCO series	UNESCO collection of representative works
UPaP	University of Pennsylvania Press
UPH	University Press of Hawaii
URPT	Urban and Rural Planning Thought (New Delhi)
USAID	United States Agency for International Development
UWashP	University of Washington Press
UWiscP	University of Wisconsin Press
VBA	Visvabharati Annals (Santiniketan)
VFPA	Viking Fund publications in anthropology
VGS	Veröffentlichungen der Glassenapp Stiftung
VIJ	Vishveshvaranand Indological Journal (Hoshiarpur)
VIS	Visveshvaranand indological series
VKFKS	Veröffentlichungen der Kommission für Sprachen und Kulturen Südasiens, Österreichische Akademie der Wissenschaften
VKNAW,AL	Verhandelingen der Koninklijke Nederlandse Akademie van Wettenschappen, Afdeling Letterkunde
VQ	Visvabharati Quarterly (Santiniketan)
VVRI	Vishveshvaranand Vedic Research Institute
WA	World anthropology
WHO	World Health Organization
WIS	Woolner indological series
WLWE	World Literature Written in English
YUP	Yale University Press
ZDMG	Zeitschrift der Deutschen Morgenländischen Gesellschaft (Wiesbaden)
ZMR	Zeitschrift für Missionswissenschaft und Religionswissenschaft
ZRGG	Zeitschrift für Religions- und Geistesgeschichte (Cologne)

Maps

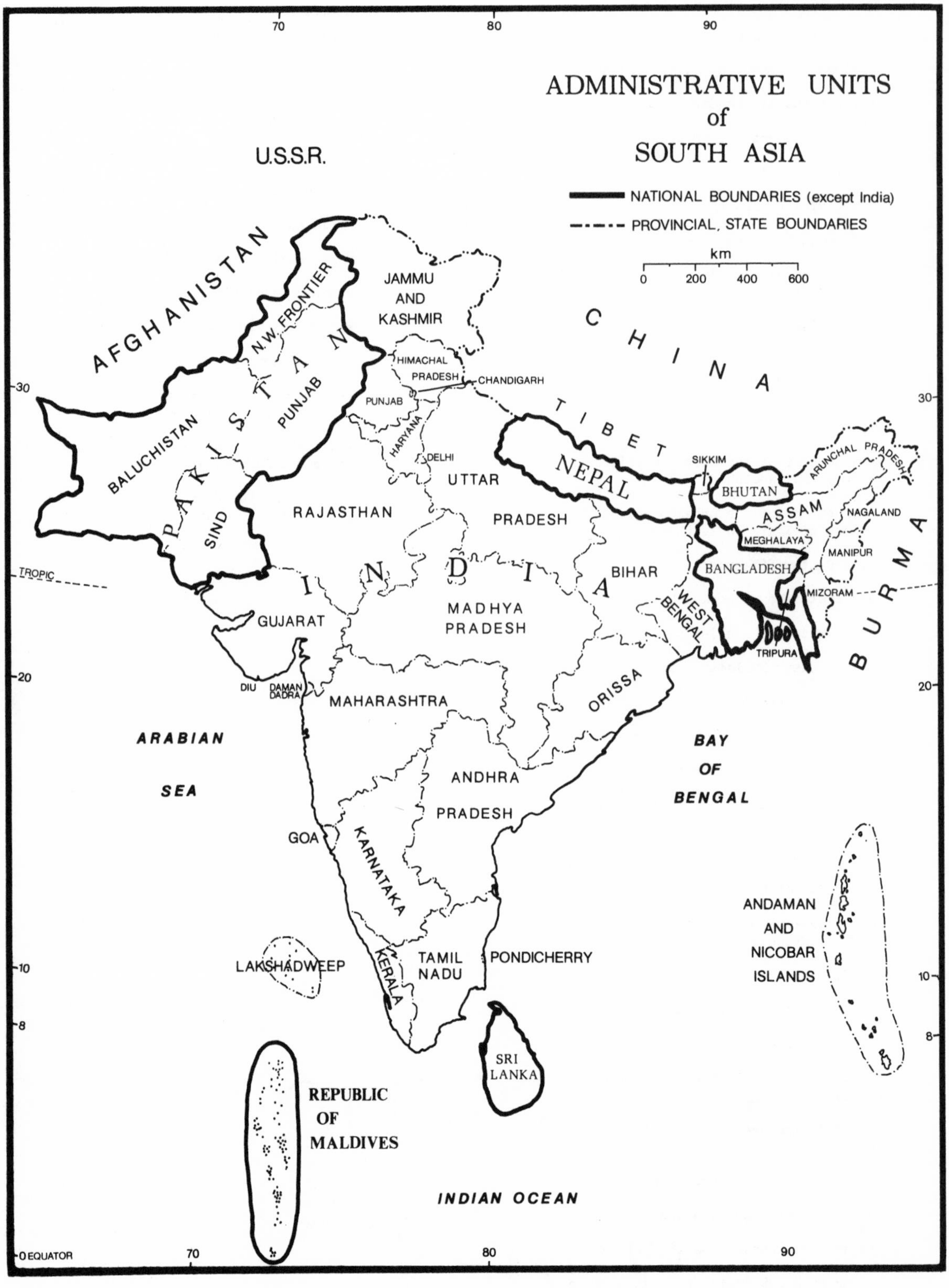
ADMINISTRATIVE UNITS of SOUTH ASIA
NATIONAL BOUNDARIES (except India)
PROVINCIAL, STATE BOUNDARIES
km
0 200 400 600
70
80
90
U.S.S.R.
AFGHANISTAN
PAKISTAN
N.W. FRONTIER
PUNJAB
BALUCHISTAN
SIND
JAMMU AND KASHMIR
HIMACHAL PRADESH
CHANDIGARH
PUNJAB
HARYANA
DELHI
CHINA
TIBET
NEPAL
SIKKIM
BHUTAN
ARUNCHAL PRADESH
ASSAM
NAGALAND
MEGHALAYA
MANIPUR
BANGLADESH
MIZORAM
TRIPURA
BURMA
INDIA
RAJASTHAN
UTTAR PRADESH
BIHAR
WEST BENGAL
GUJARAT
MADHYA PRADESH
ORISSA
TROPIC
DIU
DAMAN
DADRA
MAHARASHTRA
ARABIAN SEA
BAY OF BENGAL
ANDHRA PRADESH
GOA
KARNATAKA
LAKSHADWEEP
KERALA
TAMIL NADU
PONDICHERRY
SRI LANKA
ANDAMAN AND NICOBAR ISLANDS
REPUBLIC OF MALDIVES
INDIAN OCEAN
30
20
10
8
0 EQUATOR

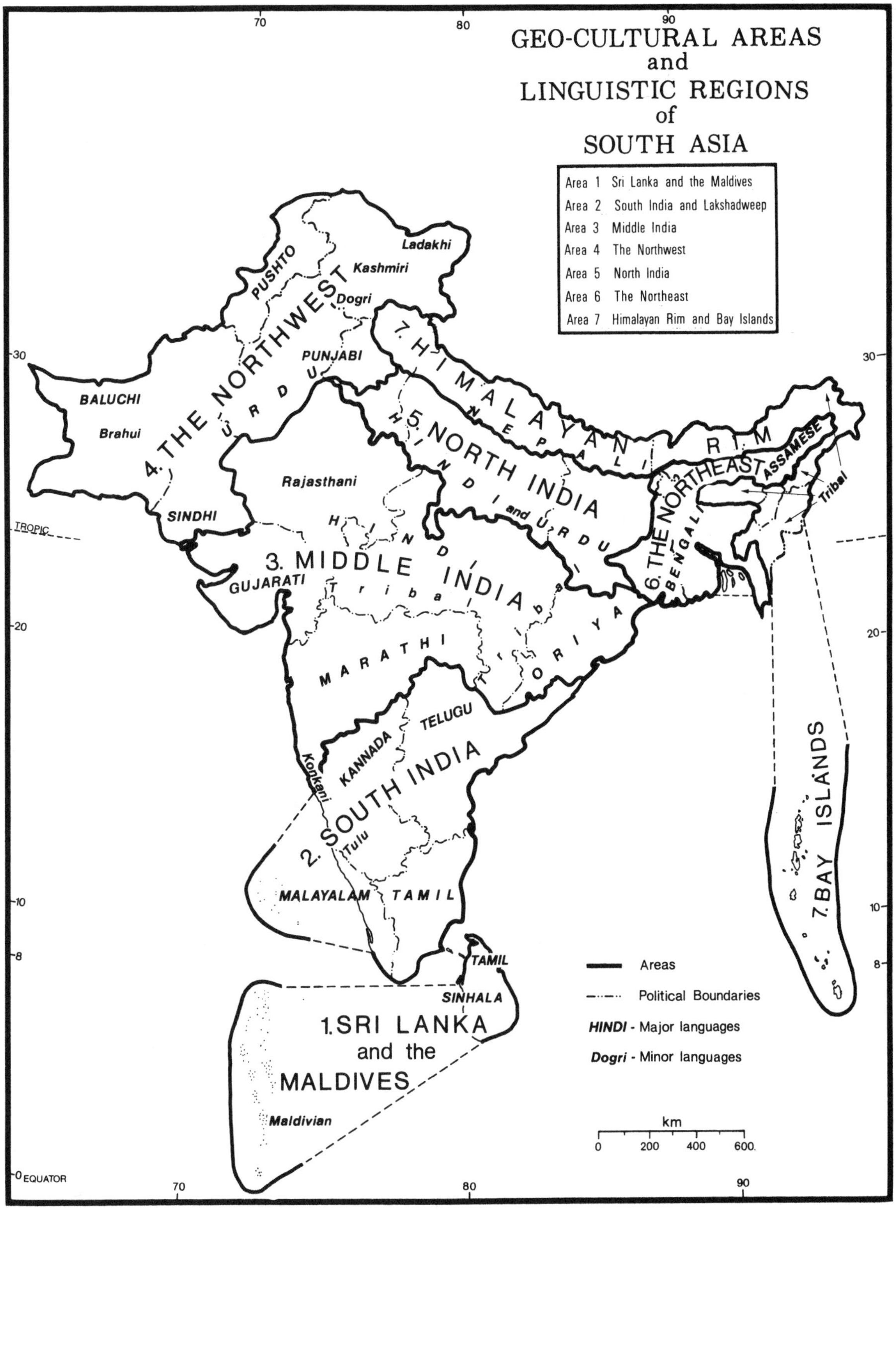
GEO-CULTURAL AREAS
and
LINGUISTIC REGIONS
of
SOUTH ASIA
Area 1 Sri Lanka and the Maldives
Area 2 South India and Lakshadweep
Area 3 Middle India
Area 4 The Northwest
Area 5 North India
Area 6 The Northeast
Area 7 Himalayan Rim and Bay Islands
1. SRI LANKA and the MALDIVES
2. SOUTH INDIA
3. MIDDLE INDIA
4. THE NORTHWEST
5. NORTH INDIA
6. THE NORTHEAST
7. HIMALAYAN RIM
7. BAY ISLANDS
PUSHTO
Kashmiri
Ladakhi
Dogri
PUNJABI
URDU
BALUCHI
Brahui
SINDHI
Rajasthani
HINDI
HINDI and URDU
NEPALI
ASSAMESE
Tribal
BENGALI
GUJARATI
Tribal
ORIYA
MARATHI
TELUGU
KANNADA
Konkani
Tulu
MALAYALAM
TAMIL
TAMIL
SINHALA
Maldivian
TROPIC
EQUATOR
70
80
90
30
20
10
8
0
Areas
Political Boundaries
HINDI - Major languages
Dogri - Minor languages
km
0 200 400 600

The Outline of Headings

PART ONE: OVERVIEW OF THE GREAT TRADITION

CHAPTER ONE: TRADITIONAL SOUTH ASIA: ENDURING STRUCTURES AND CONCEPTS THROUGH TIME AND SPACE

I. HISTORY AND CURRENT STATE OF CLASSICAL INDIC STUDIES

A. Indology

1. Bibliography and Methodology - incl. Catalogs of Sanskrit Manuscripts 00001
2. Festschriften 00015
3. Collected Essays 00029
4. History of Indology 00042
5. Studies of Individual Indologists and Their Work 00059

B. Tamil Studies and Dravidology

1. Bibliography and Reference 00067
2. Studies 00073

II. HISTORY OF SOUTH ASIA

A. Historiography, Sources, and Research Aids

1. Bibliographies 00092
2. Studies of Sources and Methodology 00097
3. Historiography
   a. surveys and general studies 00105
   b. biographies and studies of historians 00121
   c. issues and debates 00128
4. Chronologies, Handbooks, Dictionaries 00138
5. Historical Geography - Atlases and Reference Works 00150
6. Biographical Dictionaries and Essays 00157

B. General Histories

1. Thematic Interpretations of South Asian History 00163
2. Introductory Surveys 00174
3. General Histories for Reference or Advanced Study 00190
4. Collected Essays 00198

C. Topical Histories

1. Cultural Histories (Literature, Arts, Religion) 00203
2. Historical Geography - Studies 00216
3. Political History: Institutions and Ideas 00221
4. Economic History 00236
5. History of Science and Technology
   a. bibliography 00247
   b. general surveys 00252
   c. cosmology and cosmography 00269
   d. astronomy and astrology (jyotiṣa), calendrical science 00274
   e. mathematics 00290
   f. medicine
      i. bibliography and reference 00295
      ii. traditional Hindu medicine: Āyurveda and Siddha systems 00303
      iii. Indian pharmacology 00330
   g. chemistry and alchemy (rasaśāstra) 00336
   h. technology 00340
6. History of External Contacts and Foreign Relations
   a. general 00350
   b. China, Japan, and Southeast Asia 00361
   c. Iran and Central Asia 00368
   d. the Indian Ocean 00370
   e. the Gypsies: a western Indian migratory group 00375

II. D. Regional Histories

1. Sri Lanka: the Island of Ceylon 00379
2. South India: the Dravidian regions of the Peninsula
   a. general 00395
   b. Tamil Nadu 00406
   c. Andhra 00418
   d. Kerala 00420
   e. Karnataka 00430
3. Middle India: Area of Transition between North and South
   a. the Deccan 00441
   b. Goa 00446
   c. Maharashtra 00449
   d. Gujarat 00452
   e. Rajasthan 00463
   f. Madhya Pradesh 00472
   g. Orissa 00475
4. The Northwest: the Indus Valley and Mountain Frontier
   a. Sind 00484
   b. Baluchistan 00487
   c. Punjab 00491
   d. the Pathan borderland 00498
   e. Kashmir, Jammu, and Ladakh 00500
5. North India: the Ganga Plains and Āryavarta Cultural Heartland (Haryana, U.P., and Bihar) 00510
6. The Northeast: the Ganges Delta and Brahmaputra Valley
   a. Bengal 00521
   b. Assam 00525
7. The Himalayan Rim of India, Nepal, and Bhutan 00537

E. Auxiliary Techniques for the Study of the Past

1. Numismatics
   a. bibliographies and catalogs 00546
   b. surveys and studies 00551
2. Epigraphy and Paleography
   a. bibliography and reference 00559
   b. compilations of texts 00564
   c. studies 00569
3. Archaeology
   a. bibliography and reference 00575
   b. history of South Asian archaeology 00577
   c. methodology 00586
   d. collections of studies 00593
   e. museums and museology of South Asia 00600

III. INDIC SOCIAL SYSTEMS

A. Bibliography and Reference 00612

B. History and Methodology of Social Anthropological Studies of South Asia 00621

C. Anthropological Approaches to Indic Society

1. Overviews 00639
2. Festschriften 00655
3. Other Essay Collections 00664

D. Unity and Diversity of Indic Civilization

1. Is South Asia a Cultural Unit? 00678
2. Cultural Regions 00682
3. Ethnic Diversity
   a. early Western views of the "races of India" 00690
   b. recent studies of ethnic diversity: race and caste 00700
4. Physical Anthropology 00710

E. Social Structure and Caste Systems

1. Bibliography 00715
2. Definition of Caste; Distinguishing Jāti from Other Social Classifications 00719
3. General Studies 00731
4. Essay Collections 00737
5. Varṇāśramadharma: the Traditional Rationalization of Caste 00741
6. Caste among Muslims and other Non-Hindus 00752
7. Early Modern Views of Caste by Indians and Europeans (to c. 1945) 00757
8. Conceptual and Theoretical Analyses of Caste 00770
9. Homo Hierarchicus and the Sociology of Louis Dumont 00783
10. Caste Ranking and Its Determinants
   a. general studies of caste ranking 00793
   b. the concept of dominant caste 00812
   c. ideas of purity and pollution 00818

III. E. 10. d. social mobility of castes and individuals
- i. general studies 00825
- ii. Sanskritization: upward mobility by adoption of classical behavior patterns; desanskritization 00827

11. Food Habits and the Role of the Betel-nut 00837

F. Transmission of Culture: Traditional Systems of Communication and Education

1. Networks and Centers of Cultural Transmission 00846
2. Sanskrit Learning 00852
3. Histories of Education 00859

G. The Village, Home of 80% of South Asians

1. Bibliography 00864
2. Methodology and Overviews 00867
3. Collections of Village Studies [for individual village studies see Chaps. Ten-Sixteen] 00884

H. Urban Centers and Urbanization 00888

J. The Traditional Economy

1. the Jajmani System 00893
2. Land Tenure, Revenue, and Taxation 00905
3. Craftsmen, Guilds, and other Occupational Groups 00910

K. Traditional Legal Systems: Hindu Dharmaśāstra and Muslim Sharīʿat

1. Bibliography 00916
2. General Surveys and Essay Collections 00918
3. Classical Hindu Law [see also Chap. Three, III. C.] 00925
4. Hindu Law in Modern India 00934
5. Islamic Law 00940

L. Women: Status and Role

1. Bibliography 00947
2. General Studies 00951

M. Kinship, Family, and the Person

1. Bibliography and Methodology 00960
2. Kinship and the Family
   - a. general studies 00967
   - b. kinship terminology 00979
   - c. family types 00990
   - d. intra-family roles and relationships 01000
   - e. gotra and pravara: exogamous lineage groups within endogamous castes 01002
3. Marriage 01006
4. Women: Dowry, Property Rights, Status of Widows 01016
5. Life and Death Saṃskāras
   - a. general 01023
   - b. upanayana and dīkṣa: rites of initiation 01028
   - c. the Hindu sacrament of marriage 01040
   - d. death and ancestor rites 01043
6. The Person and the Group 01052
7. Personal Names and Naming Patterns 01062

N. The Adivasis: Tribal Peoples

1. Bibliography and Reference 01073
2. General Studies of Ādivāsīs [For studies of specific tribes see regional chapters Ten through Sixteen] 01077
3. From Tribe to Caste: Acculturation through Sanskritization and Other Processes 01091
4. Tribal Religion, incl. Totemism and Shamanism 01097

IV. RELIGIO-PHILOSOPHICAL TRADITIONS OF SOUTH ASIA - THE INDIGENOUS INDIC RELIGIONS: HINDUISM, BUDDHISM, JAINISM

A. Philosophy and Religious Thought

1. Reference
   - a. bibliography 01101
   - b. other reference works 01107
   - c. history and methodology of the study of Indic thought and religion 01113
   - d. Hinduism - bibliography and reference 01116
   - e. Buddhism - bibliography and reference
     - i. bibliography 01123
     - ii. dictionaries and other reference works on Buddhism 01135

IV. A. 1. e. iii. histories of Buddhist studies 00141
f. Jainism - bibliography and reference 01144
2. Surveys of Indic Thought and Religion - General
a. overall thematic interpretations 01154
b. introductory surveys 01159
c. general surveys for reference and advanced study 01167
d. essay collections 01173
e. texts in translation -- anthologies and collections 01184
3. Surveys of Hinduism
a. general introductions and surveys 01188
b. essay collections 01210
c. texts in translation 01218
4. Surveys of Buddhism
a. general introductions to Buddhism 01224
b. surveys of Buddhism in South Asia 01235
c. essay collections 01249
d. texts in translation - anthologies and collections 01265
5. Surveys of Jainism
a. introductions 01273
b. essay collections 01289
c. texts in translation 01295
6. Philosophy and Doctrine of the Indic Religions - General and Comparative Studies
a. general 01296
b. surveys of Hindu philosophy 01312
c. surveys of Buddhist philosophy 01319
d. surveys of Jaina philosophy 01328
e. comparisons among the Indic philosophies and religions 01335
f. East and West: general comparative studies 01342
g. comparisons with specific Western philosophies or schools 01352
7. Key Concepts and Problems Shared by the Indic Religions
a. general studies of key concepts 01360
b. metaphysics and theory of knowledge
i. general studies 01368
ii. idealism, materialism, and scepticism in Indic philosophy 01379
iii. concepts of the absolute; Hindu brahman and Buddhist śūnyatā 01391
iv. māyā: the world as illusion 01401
v. epistemology 01411
vi. logic and theories of meaning 01426
vii. kāla: concept of time 01437
c. samsāra: the cycle of death and rebirth
i. general studies 01434
ii. Indic psychology - concepts of self (ātman) and non-self (anātman) 01436
iii. karma and transmigration 01480
iv. mokṣa and nirvāṇa: liberation from rebirth 01498
d. ethics and values
i. general studies 01509
ii. the nature of man and the meaning of human life 01525
iii. dharma/dhamma: Hindu and Buddhist concepts of duty and moral order 01535
iv. the problem of evil 01548
v. ahiṁsā: the philosophy of non-violence 01555
vi. sanctity of the cow 01563

B. Mythology, Symbolism, and Iconography of the Indic Religions: Hinduism, Buddhism, and Jainism

1. Comparative Studies and Common Themes
a. general studies of Indic myths and symbols 01576
b. general studies of Indic iconography 01588
c. sexual metaphors and symbolism 01607
d. specific symbols
i. serpents (nāgas), elephants, and other animals and birds 01611
ii. trees and other plants 01628
iii. the cakra (wheel) 01642
iv. other symbols 01647
2. Buddhist Mythology and Iconography
a. general studies 01655
b. the Buddha image 01664
c. the stūpa 01679
3. Jaina Mythology and Iconography
a. general studies 01687
b. images of Mahāvīra and other Tīrthaṅkaras 01693
4. Hindu Theism: Images of God and the Gods in Myth and Art
a. general studies of the Hindu mythology and pantheon 01696
b. Devī and the Mātṛikās: the female principle and the Mother Goddess
i. general studies 01711
ii. studies of specific goddesses 01725
c. Śiva Mahādeva, "the great god": mythology and iconography
i. general 01739

IV. B. 4. c. ii. Śiva Naṭarāja, "Lord of the Dance" 01748
iii. histories of the cult of Śiva 01754
d. Viṣṇu, "pervading" preserver of the Universe
i. general mythology and iconography 01759
ii. avatāra, "descent" of God: the theory of divine incarnation 01767
iii. Kṛṣṇa, the last and most prominent avatāra of Viṣṇu 01774
iv. other avataras of Viṣṇu 01792
v. Hanumān, monkey-chief and ally of Rāma 01802
e. Brahmā, the Creator, and Dattātreya; the "Trinity" of Brahma, Viṣṇu, and Śiva 01804
f. Gaṇeśa, Vināyaka, or Gaṇapati ("Lord of the minor spirits"), elephant-headed son of Śiva and Pārvatī 01807
g. Kārttikeya, six-headed son of Śiva and Pārvati; also called Skanda, Subrahmanya, Murugan in S. India 01817
h. Sūrya (the sun), moon, and astral deities 01826
j. Gaṅgā and Yamunā, deified rivers 01837
k. yakṣas and other genii and demons 01845
l. folk deities of South India: Aiyaṉṉār, Śāstā, Ayyappan and others 01851

C. Religious Practice in the Indic Religions: Hinduism, Buddhism, and Jainism

1. Religion and Society; Sociology and Anthropology of Religion; Legitimation of Power 01860
2. Temples and Other Religious Institutions - General Studies
a. temples: their role in economy, society, and culture 01877
b. religious orders and institutions: monasteries, maṭhas, and āśramas 01889
3. Pilgrimage and Sacred Centers
a. pilgrimage as ritual and communication 01905
b. general guides and studies of sacred centers throughout the subcontinent 01920
c. Sri Lanka: Kandy and Kataragama 01934
d. South Indian sacred centers
i. general 01947
ii. Tirupati in Andhra and the Śrī Veṅkaṭeśwara temple 01956
iii. Chidambaram in Tamilnadu and the Naṭarāja temple 01962
iv. Madurai and the temple of Mīṇākṣī 01966
v. Kāñchīpuram and the temple of Varadārāja 01969
vi. other South Indian sacred centers 01972
e. Middle India
i. Paṇḍharpur and the cult of Viṭhobā in Mahārāṣhṭra; Nāsik on the Godāvarī 01993
ii. Dwārkā and Somnāth in Gujarāt 02003
iii. Rājāsthān's sacred centers 02009
iv. Purī in Orissa, and the cult of Jagannāth 02015
f. North India: the Ganga Plains and the Āryāvarta heartland
i. Kurukṣhetra, and its sacred region 02031
ii. Braj and the Kṛṣṇa centers of Mathurā and Vṛindāvan 02036
iii. Prayāga and the Saṅgam - confluence of the Gaṅgā and Yamunā at Allahabad 02040
iv. Kāśī, capital of Hindudom; the modern Benares/Banāras/Varānasi 02043
v. Bihar and its sacred centers: Gayā, Buddha Gayā, and Rājgīr 02057
g. the Northeast: Ganges Delta and Brahmaputra Valley 02066
h. the Himalayan Rim and the Kashmir area
i. the Indian Himalayas and the Kashmir area 02068
ii. Nepal 02074
4. Festivals and the Sacred Calendar
a. general studies 02078
b. specific festivals 02098
5. Rites and Ritual; Mantra (Ritual Formulae); Pūjā 02024
6. Popular Religious Practice; Omens, Sorcery and Shamanism 02135

D. The Religious Life of the Individual in the Indic Religions

1. Mysticism 02142
2. Yoga: Methods of Spiritual Advancement
a. reference 02153
b. general studies 02156
c. dhyāna ("meditation"): the central practice of yoga 02173
d. psychological and scientific evaluations 02181
3. Sannyāsa: Renunciation of Worldly Goals in order to Attain Mokṣa (Liberation)
a. origin and history of Indian asceticism 02186
b. the role of asceticism for society and the individual 02194
c. warrior ascetics 02200
d. religious suicide 02204
4. Lives of Ascetics
a. general studies of sannyāsis, monks, and saints 02209

IV. D. 4. b. biographies and autobiographies of Indian and Western sādhus, saints, and mystics 02220

V. RELIGIO-PHILOSOPHICAL TRADITIONS FROM OUTSIDE THE SUBCONTINENT: CHRISTIANITY, ISLAM, ZOROASTRIANISM, JUDAISM

A. Christianity in South Asia

1. Bibliography and Reference 02234
2. Surveys and Studies
a. general surveys 02237
b. the Syrian Church of Kerala and the St. Thomas Christians 02249

B. Islam in South Asia

1. Bibliography and Reference 02257
2. Surveys and Studies
a. introductions to Islam as a world religion 02262
b. Islam in South Asia: histories and surveys 02268
3. Muslim Society in South Asia 02275
4. Interactions of Islam and Hinduism 02282

C. Indian Zoroastrianism and the Parsi Community
1. General Introductions to Zoroastrianism by Indians and Others 02288
2. The Avesta: the Zoroastrian Scripture in Zend (Ancient Persian) 02297
3. Histories and Studies of the Parsis Since Their Immigration to India in the 7th Century AD 02301

D. Judaism 02311

VI. LANGUAGES AND LITERATURES

A. Bibliography and Reference 02315

B. South Asian Languages and Scripts: Historical and Comparative Linguistic Studies

1. South Asia as a Linguistic Area 02329
2. General Studies of South Asian Linguistics 02335
3. Comparative Indo-Aryan Philology 02347
4. Comparative Dravidian Linguistics
a. bibliography 02353
b. general studies 02357
5. Scripts

C. Surveys and Studies of South Asian Literature

1. General History of Indian Literature 02387
2. Literary Criticism and Aesthetics 02398
3. Comparative Studies among South Asian Literatures 02411
4. Anthologies 02418

D. Folk Literature and Oral Tradition [For folklore of specific regions, see chaps. Ten through Sixteen]

1. Bibliography and Reference 02424
2. Folklorists and Folklore Research 02432
3. Studies of Folklore and Folk Literature 02440
4. Collections of Folk Tales and Folksongs 02449

E. Pan-South Asian Languages and Literatures

1. Sanskrit Literature
a. histories and surveys of Sanskrit literature 02463
b. regional contributions to Sanskrit literature 02486
c. Sanskrit aesthetics and poetic theory 02496
2. Persian and Arabic Literatures of South Asia 02519
3. Urdu Language and Literature
a. bibliography and reference 02528
b. general histories and surveys 02531
c. anthologies of Urdu literature 02538
4. Hindi Language and Literature [see VI. F. 5. below]
5. English Language and Literature in South Asia [see Chap. Eight, X. C. 5.]

F. Regional Languages and Literatures

1. Sinhala of Sri Lanka and its Literature 02541
2. South Indian Regional Languages and Literatures
a. Tamil of Tamil Nadu and Sri Lanka
i. language 02548
ii. literature 02559
b. Kannada of Karnataka 02577

VI. F. 2. c. Telugu of Andhra 02581
d. Malayalam of Kerala 02586
3. Middle Indian Regional Languages and Literatures
a. Konkani of Goa and the West Coast 02593
b. Marathi of Maharashtra 02598
c. Gujarati 02603
d. Oriya of Utkal/Orissa 02609
4. The Northwest: the Indus Valley and Mountain Frontier
a. Sindhi 02612
b. Baluchi 02617
c. Punjabi 02621
d. Dogri, an Indo-Aryan language of Jammu 02630
e. Kashmiri, a Dardic language 02631
f. Pashto, language of the Pathans 02636
5. North India: Hindi, its Dialects and Related Languages [for Urdu, see VI. E. 3. above] 02640
6. The Northeast: Languages and Literatures of Bengal and Assam
a. Bengali language and literature
i. bibliography 02654
ii. surveys, studies, and anthologies 02656
b. Assamese language and literature 02669
7. Nepali Language and Literature 02677

VII. PERFORMING ARTS: MUSIC, DANCE, AND DRAMA OF SOUTH ASIA

A. Classical Texts of Music and Dance [for Sāmaveda, see Chapter Two, V. B. 2.; see also Chapter Three, VIII. C. 3. b.] 02680

B. Music of India

1. Inter-regional Studies
a. bibliography, discography, and reference works 02686
b. surveys and studies of Indian music
i. introductions and descriptive surveys 02696
ii. historical studies and early Western views of Indian music 02722
iii. comparative studies 02734
c. musical theory
i. traditional aesthetics, and music theory 02743
ii. rāga: melodic structures 02753
iii. tāla: rhythm 02759
iv. śruti and svara: scale and note 02764
d. the problem of developing notation for traditional music and dance 02775
e. Indian musical instruments
i. general 02779
ii. wind instruments 02790
iii. string instruments 02793
iv. percussion: tablā, mṛdaṅgam, and other drums 02800
f. the musician in Indian society 02810
2. North Indian or Hindustani Music
a. general introductions 02816
b. theory of Hindustani music
i. aesthetics 02826
ii. rāga system of North India 02829
iii. tāla: rhythm in Hindustani music 02834
c. vocal music of Northern India 02838
d. musicians of Hindustani music 02843
3. South Indian or Karnatak/Carnatic Music
a. general introductions 02852
b. theory of Karnatak music 02867
c. musicians and composers 02873
4. Devotional Music of Various Religious Traditions 02881
5. Traditions of Nepal, Sri Lanka, and Other Regions 02891
6. Ethnomusicology and Folk Music [for regional folksongs, see Chaps. Ten-Sixteen] 02897

C. Classical Dance, Dance-Drama, and Theatre of South Asia

1. Bibliography and Reference 02904
2. Introductions and Descriptive Studies
a. general 02910
b. dance 02918
c. drama and the theatre 02932
e. Classical Dance and Dance-Drama
a. general introductions and studies 02946
b. Bharata Nāṭyam and related dance styles of Tamilnadu 02957
c. Kathākalī and other dance-drama traditions of Kerala 02969
d. Kathak, rhythmic dance of the North Indian princely courts 02985
e. Manipuri, Vaiṣṇava ritual dance of the hill-state of Manipur 02938
f. mudrās: poses and gestures of classical dance-drama 02990

VII. D. Mediating Traditions: Regional and Folk Performances

1. General Studies 02995
2. Puppetry and Shadow Plays 03005
3. Regional Performances
    a. Kandyan and other dances of Sri Lanka 03014
    b. Karnataka's Yakṣagāna: dance-drama of South Kanara district 03026
    c. Middle India
        i. folk dance and village theatre of Maharashtra, Gujarat and Rajasthan 03029
        ii. Chhau and Odissi dances, folk plays of Orissa 03036
    d. folk dance and popular theatre of North India, Bengal, and Nepal 03051

VIII. ARCHITECTURE, ART, AND CRAFTS

A. Introductions, Surveys and Research Tools

1. Bibliography and Reference 03056
2. Catalogs and Guides to Collections and Exhibits 03065
3. Histories and Surveys of South Asian Art 03078
4. Festschriften and Commemorative Volumes 03109
5. Aesthetics 03113
6. Erotic Art 03130
7. Hindu Art of South Asia (see IV. B. 4. above]
8. Buddhist and Jain Art of South Asia [see also IV. B. 2. & 3. above] 03140

B. Architecture

1. Bibliography and Reference Works 03149
2. Surveys and Studies 03155
3. Temples and Temple Sculpture: Hindu, Buddhist, and Jain 03174
4. "Indo-Islamic" Architecture 03188

C. Sculpture [see also Iconography, IV.B., above]

1. Histories and Surveys of Indian Sculpture 03197
2. Catalogs and Guides to Collections and Exhibits 03208
3. Techniques 03228
4. Bronze and Other Metal Sculpture 03232
5. Terra Cotta and Ivory Sculpture 02343

D. Painting

1. Bibliography 03262
2. Introductory Surveys 03265
3. Miniatures 03279
4. Techniques 03286

E. Industrial and Decorative Arts and Handicrafts

1. General Studies 03294
2. Design Motifs 03308
3. Personal Adornment: Costume, Coiffure, Jewelry, and Armor 03310
4. Textiles and Textile History 03324
5. Embroidery 03339
6. Carpets 03347

F. Folk Art - General Studies 03350

G. Introductions to Regional Art Traditions: Architecture, Sculpture, and Painting

1. Sri Lanka 03361
2. South India: Tamilnadu, Andhra, Karnataka, and Kerala
    a. general 03379
    b. temples and other architecture 03386
    c. sculpture and painting 03395
3. Middle India 03401
4. The Northwest: Indus Valley and Mountain Frontier 03419
5. North India: the Ganga Plains from Delhi to Bihar 03432
6. The Northeast Area of Bengal and Assam 03439
7. Nepal and the Indian Himalayan Rim
    a. general surveys 03447
    b. catalogs of collections and exhibits of Nepali art 03459
    c. temples, sculpture, and painting 03469

PART TWO: FOUR AGES OF HISTORICAL EVOLUTION: SUBCONTINENTAL AND REGIONAL

CHAPTER TWO: PREHISTORY AND PROTOHISTORY OF SOUTH ASIA TO 600 BC: THE PALAEOLITHIC THROUGH THE VEDIC AGE

I. GENERAL SURVEYS AND STUDIES OF PREHISTORY AND PROTOHISTORY

A. Reference

1. Bibliography 03483
2. Chronology and Methodology 03488

B. General Surveys and Studies

1. General Studies 03493
2. Surveys of Prehistory by Region 03509
3. Studies of Early Technology 03525
4. Prehistoric Art and Rock Paintings 03532
5. Burial Practices 03543

II. THE EARLY, MIDDLE, AND LATE STONE AGES: HUNTING AND GATHERING BANDS

A. The Early Stone Age (Palaeolithic), up to 10,000 BC: Handaxe and Flake Industries 03546

B. the Late Stone Age (Mesolithic): Microliths 03559

III. THE NEOLITHIC AND CHALCOLITHIC ("COPPER-STONE") AGE: BEGINNINGS OF FOOD PRODUCTION, USE OF COPPER AND BRONZE, AND FIXED SETTLEMENTS

A. General 03568

B. Pre-Harappan Sites in Afghanistan, Baluchistan, and the Indus Valley 03578

C. The Harappan Civilization of the Indus Valley (c. 2500-1500? BC)

1. Bibliography and Reference 03589
2. General Studies 03595
3. Harappa and Mohenjo Daro: Urban Centers of Indus Valley Civilization 03612
4. Other Harappan Sites 03621
5. External Contacts and Trade 03628
6. The Indus Script: Attempts at Decipherment 03637
7. Decline of Harappan Civilization: Floods, Invasion, or...? 03651

D. Neolithic-Chalcolithic Sites in non-Indus South Asia

1. The Ganga Plains: Ochre-Colored Pottery and the Copper Hoards Culture 03662
2. Peninsular India and Sri Lanka 03670

IV. THE IRON AGE AND THE ARYAN INVASIONS

A. General Histories and Studies

1. General 03686
2. Beginnings of Iron Technology 03689

B. South India and Ceylon in the Iron Age

1. The Megaliths and the Iron Age 03691
2. The Dravidians: Hypotheses on their Origin and Linguistic Affiliations 03715

C. Northern India in the Vedic and Epic Ages (c. 1500-600 BC)

1. Sources
   a. historical and geographical evidence from the Vedas 03730
   b. archaeology 03734
2. General History of the Vedic and Epic Ages in Northern India (c. 1500-600 BC)
   a. the Vedic Age 03745
   b. the Epic Age 03759
3. The Invasion of the Aryans, Indo-European-Speaking Tribes from Central Asia; the Debate on Their Origins 03771
4. Kingship, Political Organization and Warfare in Northern India 03781
5. Economic and Social Life 03787
6. The Beginnings of Science in Vedic India 03793

V. THE FOUNDATIONS OF INDIC RELIGIOUS TRADITION: ŚRUTI, THE VEDIC LITERATURE, FROM THE ṚGVEDA SAṀHITĀ THROUGH THE UPANISADS

A. General Studies of the Veda (Supreme Sacred "Knowledge") as a Whole

1. Bibliography and Reference 03798
2. Histories of Vedic Literature 03806
3. General Studies of Vedic Religion and Philosophy 03812
4. Vedic Myths, Symbols, and Deities 03830
5. Vedic Ritual: Yajña, or Sacrifice 03858
6. Selections from Vedic Literature in Translation 03873
7. Vedic Recitation 03876

B. The Vedic Saṁhitās: the Basic "Collection" of Each of the Four Vedas

1. Ṛgveda Samhitā: Laudatory Stanzas (ṛc/ṛg) in 1028 Hymns
   a. translations and selections 03881
   b. studies in the Ṛgveda Saṁhitā 03891
2. Sāmaveda Saṁhita: Collection of Chants (sāman) for the Soma Sacrifice
   a. translations 03909
   b. studies in the Sāmaveda Saṁhitā 03912
3. Yajurveda Saṁhitā: Sacrificial (yajus) Formulas
   a. translations 03917
   b. studies in the Yajurveda Saṁhitā 03922
4. Atharvaveda Saṁhitā: Priestly (atharvan) Formulas for Domestic Ritual, Healing, and Defense Against Evil and Enemies
   a. translations 03926
   b. studies in the Atharvaveda Saṁhitā 03929

C. The Brāhmaṇas: Prose Interpretations of the Rituals and Mantras of Each Veda

1. General Studies 03933
2. Brāhmaṇas of the Ṛg Veda 03941
3. Brāhmaṇas of the Sama Veda 03945
4. Brāhmaṇas of the Yajur Veda 03957
5. Brāhmaṇas of the Atharva Veda 03960

D. The Āraṇyakas, Esoteric "Forest Texts" 03962

E. The Vedic Upaniṣads: Philosophical Discussions Presaging the Vedānta ("End of the Veda")

1. Reference 03967
2. The Principal Upaniṣads in Translation 03968
3. Studies of the Upaniṣads 03981

VI. THE VEDĀṄGAS ("LIMBS OF THE VEDA"): EXEGESIS OF VEDIC TEACHINGS FOR PRACTICAL APPLICATION IN RITUAL, LAW AND DOMESTIC LIFE [For Vedāṅgas other than the Kalpasūtra, see Chap. Three]

A. General 03995

B. The Kalpasūtras: Rules Relating to Sacrifices and Rituals [For Gṛhyasūtras, see Chap. Three, III. C. 3. a.]

1. Śrautasūtras: Rules for Vedic Sacrifice 03998
2. Śulvasūtras: Rules for Construction of Sacrificial Altars 04006

CHAPTER THREE: ANCIENT INDIA: c. 6th CENT. BC TO 6th CENT. AD, FROM THE TIME OF THE BUDDHA THROUGH THE IMPERIAL GUPTAS

I. GENERAL HISTORIES OF THE ANCIENT PERIOD, c. 600 BC TO c. 600 AD

A. Historiography and Chronology 04009

B. Sources: Auxiliary Techniques for Study of the Past

1. Literary sources
   a. classical Greek accounts 04018
   b. early Indian texts as sources 04029
   c. the Epics and Purāṇas as historical sources 04038
   d. Chinese accounts 04052
2. Epigraphy 04056
3. Numismatics 04063

C. Historical Geography 04078

D. General Surveys of Ancient History 04086

II. HISTORY BY AREA AND DYNASTY, c. 600 BC TO c. 600 AD

A. North India: Kingdoms and Empires of the Ganga Plains and Nepal

1. General Studies of Ancient North India 04108
2. The Earliest Kingdoms & Dynasties: Kośala, Magadha, and the Nandas 04115
3. The Mauryan Empire
   a. general studies of the Mauryas 04117
   b. Chandragupta Maurya: founder of the first Indian Empire 04121
   c. Aśoka: Buddhist convert and Emperor
      i. biographies and studies 04124
      ii. the Edicts, on rock and pillar 04132
4. Post-Mauryan Dynasties: Śungas and Kānvas 04142
5. The Imperial Guptas: 320-550 AD 04144

B. The Northwest: Invasion and Assimilation of Foreign Peoples in the Panjab-Malwa Area

1. General Histories 04158
2. The Indo-Greek Dynasties: Successors of Alexander the Great 04165
3. The Indo-Parthians and other Iranians 04171
4. The Śakas, Indo-Scythians from Central Asia 04175
5. The Kuṣāṇas: Pretenders to Empire, Patrons of Buddhism and Transmitters of Buddhism to Central Asia and China 04178
6. The Hūṇas 04193

C. Middle India and the Deccan: the Andhra Sātavāhanas, and their Successors the Vakāṭakas and Kalacuris 04195

D. Dravidian Kingdoms of South India before, during, and after the Sangam/Caṅkam Age

1. General Studies of Ancient South India 04202
2. The Legend of Agastya, and the Meeting of Aryan and Dravidian Cultures in the South 04214
3. Early Kingdoms of the Tamils: Cōḷas, Ceras and Pāṇḍyas 04219
4. The Ikṣvākus and Other Dynasties of Andhra 04222
5. The Pallavas of Kāñchīpuram, Capital of Toṇḍaimaṇḍalam, 250-900 AD 04227

E. Lanka: Prince Vijaya and the Aryanization of Ceylon

1. The Pālī Chronicles: the Dīpavaṃśa, Mahāvaṃśa and its Continuation, the Cūlavaṃśa 04229
2. General Studies of Ancient Sri Lanka 04242

III. HISTORY BY TOPIC: POLITICAL, ECONOMIC, SOCIAL, AND INTERNATIONAL

A. Political Forms and Ideas, the Military and the Art of War

1. Reference 04250
2. General Studies of the Political System 04253
3. Political Theory
   a. general 04265
   b. ideas of authority and kingship 04277
   c. the Arthaśāstra: the first treatise on statecraft, attrib. to Kauṭilya (Cānakya), Prime Minister of Chandragupta Maurya (c. 324-300 BC)
      i. bibliography 04293
      ii. translations 04295
      iii. studies 04299
   d. later statecraft texts: the Nītisāra and Śukranīti 04317
4. Aryan and non-Aryan Tribal States, Kṣatriya and Others 04320
5. Evidences of Democracy: Village Assemblies, and Tribal "Republics" 04328
6. Diplomacy and International Law 04336
7. The Art of War and the Military System 04341

B. Economic Life: Agriculture, Public Finance, Commerce and Industry

1. General Studies 04346
2. Economic Thought 04360
3. The Agrarian System: Agriculture, the Cultivator and his Overlords; Irrigation 04362
4. The State and the Economy: Taxation, Public Finance and Enterprise 04372
5. Commerce and Industry; Trade Routes 04377
6. The Role of Slavery 04386

III. C. Dharma: the Person and the Social Order; Law and the Family according to the Brahmanical and Buddhist Literature

1. General Studies of Social Life in the Ancient Period, 600 BC to 600 AD
   a. the time of the Buddha 04392
   b. from the Mauryas through the Guptas 04395
2. Dharma as Expressed in Early Legal Traditions
   a. general studies of ancient law 04405
   b. the Dharmasūtras: prose compilations of "canonical" and "secular" law in the Vedic tradition 04414
   c. Manusmṛti: the foundation of Hindu law, and the chief Dharmaśāstra (metrical and codified expansions on the Dharmasūtras)
      i. translations 04419
      ii. studies 04422
   d. other dharmaśāstras, incl. general studies of dharmasāstra literature 04428
   e. Varnāśramadharma: social stratification and the "origins" of the caste system 04440
3. Domestic Life: Kinship, Marriage, Sexual Life, and the Status of Women
   a. Gṛhyasūtras: fundamental texts of household rites and sacraments (saṃskāras)
      i. translations 04457
      ii. studies 04463
   b. kinship and marriage 04467
   c. the roles and status of women 04474
   d. the Kāmasūtra: manual of erotics and social life, c. 300 AD
      i. translations of Vātsyāyana's Kāmasūtra 04482
      ii. studies 04486
4. The Tirukkuṟaḷ of Tiruvaḷḷuvar (5th cent. AD?): Classic South Indian Text on Ethics, Polity and Love, "the Tamil Veda"
   a. bibliography 04488
   b. translations 04489
   c. studies 04497
5. Education and Learning 04508
6. Urbanization and Town Planning 04519

D. History of Science in Ancient India

1. General Studies of Ancient Indian Science 04525
2. Astronomy and Astrology, Developed from the Jyotiṣa Vedāṅga, and Mathematics
   a. general studies, incl. calendrical science 04530
   b. early astronomer-mathematicians: Āryabhaṭa I (b. 476 AD), and Varāhamihira (c. 505 AD) 04533
   c. ancient Indian geometry, developed from the Śulvasūtras [see also Chap. Two, VI. B. 2] 04540
3. Beginnings of Indic Medicine: Āyurveda and Other Systems
   a. general studies 04545
   b. classical texts in translation: the Caraka and Suśruta Saṁhitās (comp. 200 BC to 200 AD) 04552

E. Foreign Contacts

1. General Studies 04561
2. The Greco-Roman World 04569
3. Southeast and East Asia 04584

IV. GENERAL STUDIES OF ANCIENT INDIC RELIGION AND PHILOSOPHY, AND OF SOME MINOR TRADITIONS

A. General Studies: Śramanas (Buddhist, Jaina and Other Unorthodox Sects) in Conflict with Vedic Brahmanism 04587

B. Materialists: The Cārvāka or Lokāyata 04594

C. Ājīvikas: An Ascetic Śramana Order Similar to Jainism 04599

D. The Apostle Thomas and the Beginnings of Indian Christianity 04601

V. RELIGIO-PHILOSOPHICAL TRADITIONS: FROM BRAHMANISM TO HINDUISM

A. The Epics: the Mahābhārata and the Rāmāyaṇa

1. General Studies Covering Both the Mahābhārata and the Rāmāyaṇa 04607
2. The Mahābhārata of Vyāsa (including the Bhagavad-gītā): India's Great Epic Recounting the Wars of the Pāṇḍavas and Kauravas
   a. bibliography and reference 04614
   b. complete translations 04620

V. A. 2. c. abridged translations, selections, and retellings from the Mbh (other than the Bhagavadgītā) 04625
d. selected studies 04635
e. translations and studies of the Harivaṃśa, an appendix to the Mbh giving the genealogy of Kṛṣṇa 04656
3. The Bhagavad Gītā: the Quintessence of Hinduism and the Central Scripture of the Viṣṇu-Kṛṣṇa Cult
a. translations 04659
b. selected studies 04675
4. The Rāmayaṇa of Vālmīki: the Story of Rāma, King and Avatāra
a. bibliography and reference 04695
b. complete translations 04698
c. abridged translations, selections, and re-tellings 04702
d. studies 04709

B. The Emergence of Theistic Hinduism: from Communal Ritual to Personal Devotion, from Yajña to Pūjā

1. General Studies 04731
2. Early Worship of Śiva
a. general studies of early Śaivism 04739
b. the Śaiva āgamas: basic Sanskrit texts held to be the word of Śiva and equal in authority to the Vedas 04744
c. the Pāśupatas: a Śaiva ascetic order 04754
3. Early Worship of Viṣṇu
a. general studies of early Vaiṣṇavism 04764
b. the Bhāgavata Dharma: the rise of bhakti ("devotion") 04772
c. the Pāñcarātra saṁhitās/āgamas 04775
d. the Vaikhānasas: insistence on ritual 04789

C. The Ṣaḍḍarśana: the "Six (Orthodox) Systems" of Hindu Philosophy

1. General Studies of and Comparisons among the Six Āstika Systems 04793
2. Sāṁkhya, attrib. to Kapila (pre-6th Cent. BC): Duality of Matter and Spirit, Prakṛti-Puruṣa
a. translations of Sāṁkhya-kārikā ("verses on Sāṁkhya") of Īśvarakṛṣṇa (3rd cent. AD?) and other texts 04798
b. studies of Sāṁkhya 04805
3. Yoga: the Aṣṭānga ("Eightfold") Yoga of Patañjali (2nd cent. BC): Liberation through Personal Discipline
a. translations of Patañjali's Yogasūtra 04818
b. studies of Pātañjala Rāja Yoga 04822
4. Nyāya, the Methods of Logical Thinking; and Vaiśeṣika, Theory of the Atomic Nature of Reality
a. translations of the Nyāyasūtra of Gautama (2nd cent. BC?) 04832
b. translation of the Vaiśeṣikasūtra of Kaṇāda 04835
c. studies of Nyāya-Vaiśeṣika (incl. trans. of classical commentaries) 04837
5. Pūrva-mimāṃsā, or Karma-mimāṃsā: Proof of the Vedic Texts
a. translations of the Purva-mimāṃsā-sūtra of Jaimini (4th cent. BC?) 04862
b. studies of the Pūrva-mimāṃsā (incl. trans. of classical commentaries) 04864
6. The Vedānta, or Uttara-Mimāṃsā: the Culmination of Upaniṣadic Thought, and the Philosophical Foundation of Later Hinduism: Translations of the Brahmasūtra, or Vedāntasūtra, of Bādarāyana (200-250 AD?) 04870

VI. RELIGIO-PHILOSOPHICAL TRADITIONS: BUDDHISM

A. Gautama the Buddha, ("the Enlightened One"), and the Beginnings of the Dharma/Dhamma

1. Siddhārtha, Prince of the Śākyas (c. 560-480 BC)
a. biographies: the person and the sacred legend 04875
b. translations and studies of sources 04889
c. the iconography of the Buddha image [see Chap. One, IV. B. 2. b.]
d. disciples and other associates 04907
2. Early Buddhism and Contiguous Traditions 04911
3. General Studies of the Origin and Early Development of Buddhism 04923

B. Early History of the Saṅgha: the Monastic Community Founded by the Buddha and Supported by the Laity

1. General Studies of the Monastic Order 04935
2. Early Buddhist Councils, Saṅgītis: Definition of the Canon and Tradition 04942
3. Emergence of Sectarianism: the Sthaviras and Mahāsaṅghikas, Precursors of Hīnayāna and Mahāyāna 04951
4. Aśoka Maurya: Buddhist Cakravartin, World Emperor and Patron of the Dharma/dhamma (see also II. A. 3. c., above] 04955
5. Missionary Activities and the Expansion of Buddhism 04961

VI. C. The Tripiṭaka, the "Three Baskets" of Sacred Literature: the Pāli Canon and its translations; Non-Canonical Works

1. General Guides and Studies 04966
2. Translations from the Canon
   a. collections 04972
   b. selected translations 04975
3. Vinaya-piṭaka: Rules of the Monastic Order 04979
4. Sutta (sūtra)-piṭaka: Collections of Teachings Attributed to the Buddha
   a. the four major nikāyas ("collections") 04984
   b. the Khuddaka-nikāya, or minor anthology, incl. the Dhammapada, the Therā- and Therī-Gāthā, and the Jātaka 04989
5. Abhidhamma-piṭaka: Seven Collections of Philosophical and Psychological Treatises 04996
6. Semi- and Non-Canonical Works in Pāli
   a. the Milindapañha: the "Questions of King Menander" to the Buddhist monk Nāgasena (c. 150 BC) 05003
   b. the Jātaka Tales, stories of the Buddha's former lives
      i. translations 05007
      ii. studies of the Jātakas in religion, literature, and art 05009
   c. other non-canonical Pāli literature 05015

D. Hīnayāna, "the Lesser Vehicle," Salvation through Personal Discipline and Meditation: the Theravāda/Sthaviravāda and Other Schools

1. Early History of Theravāda Buddhism 05017
2. Surveys and Studies of Theravāda Doctrine 05019
3. Meditation: Central to Theravāda 05029
4. Buddhaghoṣa (5th cent. AD), Greatest Exponent of Theravāda, and his Viśuddhimagga, "Path of Purity" 05036
5. Establishment and Early History of Buddhism in Sri Lanka (from c. 240 BC) 05041

E. Mahāyāna, the "Great Vehicle": Salvation through Faith in the Bodhisattvas (c. 100 BC to 100 AD)

1. Surveys and Histories 05045
2. Origins of Mahāyāna 05052
3. Mahāyāna Canon: Sanskrit Sūtras and Commentaries Added to the Tripiṭaka
   a. general: selections and anthologies of Mahāyāna texts 05060
   b. the Prājñāparamitā sūtra literature, "Perfection in Wisdom"
      i. translated texts 05062
      ii. studies 05068
   c. the Saddharmapuṇḍarīka sūtra, "Lotus of the True Law" 05076
   d. other sūtra texts 05079
4. Major Mahāyāna Doctrines and Schools
   a. the Bodhisattvas, "ones whose essence is Perfect Knowledge" 05084
   b. the Mādhyamika ("middle way") school founded by Nāgarjuna (c. 159-250 AD), and the concept of Śūnyatā ("Emptiness"
      i. translations and studies of major texts 05090
      ii. general studies of the Mādhyamika philosophy 05095
   c. the Yogācara or Vijñānavāda school of Asaṅga and Vasubandhu (c. 300 AD)
      i. translations and studies of major texts 05109
      ii. general studies of the Yogācara school 05115
      iii. doctrine of Trikāya, "three bodies" of the Buddha 05124

VII. RELIGIO-PHILOSOPHICAL TRADITIONS: JAINISM

A. The Tīrthaṅkaras: the 24 "Ford-finders" or Prophets of the Jaina Tradition

1. the First 23 Tīrthaṅkaras: Ṛsabha to Pārśvanātha 05130
2. Vardhamāna Mahāvīra, the 24th Tīrthaṅkara (c. 5th cent. BC, Contemporary of Gautama Buddha) 05133

B. Early History of Jainism, and the Division into Śvetāmbara and Digambara Sects 05141

C. The Jaina Canon, in Ardhamāgadhī (a Prakrit of Magadha) and Sacred Texts in Sanskrit and Other Prakrits 05150

VIII. LANGUAGE, LITERATURE, AND THE PERFORMING ARTS (c. 6th CENT. BC TO 6th CENT. AD)

A. Early Indic Linguistic Science, Developed from the Vedāngas Concerned with Vedic Exegesis

1. General Studies in Early Indian Linguistics; Belief in the Power of Speech (Vāc) and Ritual Formulas (Mantra) 05162

VIII. A. 2. The Śīkṣa Vedāṅga: Phonetics 05175
3. The Nirukta Vedāṅga: Etymology-Lexicography and the Nirukta of Yaska 05178
4. The Vyākaraṇa Vedāṅga: Grammar
a. general studies of the Sanskrit grammarians 05183
b. Pāṇini (4th cent. BC?) and the systematization of classical Sanskrit
i. reference 05190
ii. the Aṣṭhādhyāyi of Pāṇini: translations 05195
iii. studies 05197
c. Patañjali and his Mahābhāṣya, "Great Commentary" on Pāṇini (c. 150 BC) 05219
d. Bhartṛhari (c. 450-510 AD), author of Vākyapadīya, a treatise on grammar and its philosophy, and of Mahābhāṣya-dīpikā, a commentary on Patañjali
i. texts in translation 05221
ii. studies 05224
5. Tolkāppiyam: the Earliest Extant Tamil Grammar (c. 2nd cent. BC) 05230

B. Middle Indo-Aryan Language and Literature: Pali, the Prakrits, and Apabhraṃśa

1. General and Reference 05237
2. Pāli 05240
3. Prākrits and Apabhraṃśa: Transitional Stages in the Emergence of the Modern Indo-Aryan Languages 05246

C. The Beginnings of Classical Sanskrit Literature: Kāvya, including Drama (Nāṭya), Narrative Verse (Sargabandha), and Stories (Kathā)

1. Kāvya - General Studies 05261
2. Classical Sanskrit Drama - General Studies
a. bibliography 05264
b. general histories and surveys 05266
c. special topics 05277
3. Early Dramatic Theory and Criticism
a. general 05284
b. the Nāṭyaśāstra of "Bharata-Muni" (compiled 5th cent. BC - 2nd cent. AD): classic text of drama, dance and music
i. translations 05289
ii. studies 05294
c. the Abhinayadarpaṇa of Nandikeśvara; the "Mirror of Gesture" 05300
4. Early Sanskrit Drama and Poetry in Translation, with Studies of Major Authors
a. Aśvaghoṣa (1st cent. AD) - his Buddhacarita and Saundarānanda, both based on the Buddha's life, are the earliest extant Sanskrit mahākāvyas 05302
b. Śūdraka, king and playwright (c. 3rd cent. AD?), reputed author of Mṛcchakaṭikā, "the Little Clay Cart" 05308
c. Bhāsa (c. 4th cent. AD), reputed author of Svapnavāsavadatta - "Vāsavadatta seen in a dream" - and other recently discovered plays 05312
d. Kālidāsa (c. 400 AD): India's greatest poet and dramatist
i. bibliography and reference 05323
ii. general studies of Kālidāsa: his life and work 05326
iii. studies of special topics 05336
iv. translations of Kālidāsa's plays and poems: complete or selected 05347
v. Śakuntalā: the first Indian nāṭaka (heroic drama) to inspire the admiration of the West 05349
vi. Vikramorvaśīya, drama of the nymph Urvaśī 05353
vii. Mālavikāgnimitra, drama of the king and the princess 05355
viii. Meghadūta, "The Cloud Messenger": Kālidāsa's most famous poem, in extended lyric form 05358
ix. Raghuvaṃśa: a mahākāvya relating the "Dynasty of Raghu", of Rāma's lineage 05363
x. Kumārasambhava: a mahākāvya on the birth of the war-god Skanda, son of Śiva and Pārvati 05368
xi. Ṛtusaṁhāra: a lyric poem on the six seasons, attributed to Kālidāsa 05374
e. Visākhadatta (5th cent. AD), Gupta courtier and author of Mudrārākṣasa, "Minister Rākṣasa and his Signet Ring," a semi-historical play 05376
f. other kāvya (poems and plays) and anthologies 05380
5. Kathā, "Story Literature": Collections of Fables and Tales
a. general studies 05387
b. Bṛhatkathā, "The Great Story" of Guṇāḍhya (c. 4th cent. AD?): prototype of Sanskrit story literature; Prakrit original is lost 05389
c. Pañcatantra, "The Five Treatises", attrib. to Viṣṇuśarma (date unknown), didactic fables aiming at goals of secular and material success

VIII. C. 5. c. i. translations 05394
ii. studies of the Pañcatantra and its worldwide diffusion 05400
d. collections of tales from classical literature 05406

D. Classical Tamil Literature in the Kingdoms of the Pāṇḍyas, Cōḻas and Cēras

1. General Studies of Ancient Tamil Literature 05412
2. The Poems of the Sangam/Caṅkam Age (c. 1st-4th cents. AD): Works of the Three Legendary "Academies"
a. general
i. translations 05415
ii. studies 05418
b. Akam "love" poetry: the "interior landscape"
i. translations 05428
ii. studies 05430
c. Puṟam "heroic" or war poetry" the "exterior," collections of the bards 05434
3. The Early Tamil Epics (Comparable to Sanskrit Mahākāvyas) of the Post-Sangam Period
a. the Cilappatikāram/Shilappadikāram "The lay of the anklet" by Prince Ilaṅkōvaṭikal/Ilango Adigal (c. 450 AD): leading epic of the Jaina cycle
i. translations 05437
ii. studies 05440
b. the Maṇimēkalai, "The Jewel Belt," by Cāttanār (c. 550 AD): a sequel to Cilappatikāram but partisan to Buddhism 05446

IX. ART AND ARCHITECTURE OF THE ANCIENT PERIOD (600 BC TO 600 AD)

A. General Surveys of Ancient Indian Art (c. 600 BC - 600 AD) 05449

B. Mauryan and Early "Buddhist" Art [for Iconography of the Buddha, see Chap. One, IV. B. 2. b., above; for Mauryan pillar and Sarnath railing, see E. 2., below] 05461

C. Post-Mauryan Art During the Period of Competing Dynasties

1. Śunga, Kanva and "Mitra" Dynasties in Madhyadeśa (Northern and Middle India)
a. Bodhgayā and the Mahābodhi temple 05468
b. Sānchī 05472
c. Bhārhut 05479
2. Western India and the Buddhist "Cave-Temples" 05483
3. Southern India: the Veṅgī Region (Krishna-Godavari Deltas) under the Āndhra-Sātavāhanas (200 BC - 225 AD) and the Īkṣvākus (c. 230-275)
a. general studies 05494
b. Jaggayapeṭa stūpa; Amarāvatī: center of Buddhism in Āndhradeśa 05499
c. Nāgārjunakoṇḍa 05509

D. The Period of the Śakas and Kuṣāṇas in the North and Northwest (Present Day India, Pakistan and Afghanistan): 1st cent. BC to 4th cent. AD

1. General Studies 05516
2. Gandhāra: "Indo-Greek" Buddhist Art under the Patronage of the Kuṣāṇas
a. general studies of Gandharan art 05522
b. Begrām (ancient Kapīśī): cosmopolitan emporium and ivory-carving center 05538
c. Bāmiyān Valley: Buddhist monastic center with rock-cut colossal Buddhas, stupas and frescoes 05544
d. Taksaśīlā (Taxila): center of education, religion, trade and art 05549
3. Mathurā: on the Yamunā (Jumna) River: Preeminent School of Buddhist-Jain-Hindu Sculpture and Architecture (1st-4th cents. AD) [see also E. 2., below] 05552

E. The Gupta-Vākāṭaka Period: The Golden Age of Ancient Indian Civilization (320-600 AD)

1. General Studies of Gupta Art 05554
2. Mathurā and Sārnāth: Buddha Images and Other Sculptures [see also D. 3., above] 05562
3. Deogarh and Central India: Beginnings of Hindu Temple Construction (c. 5th cent. AD) 05572
4. Western India (Gujarat-Sind-SW Rajasthan) in the Gupta Period 05582
5. Ajaṇṭā and Bāgh: Sculptures and Frescoes of the Buddhist Cave Temples 05591
6. Eastern India (Bihar and Orissa) During the Gupta Period 05608

IX. F. Siṁhāla/Ceylon in the Anurādhapura Period (4th cent. BC - 8th cent. AD): Importation and Naturalization of Indian Buddhist Styles

1. General Studies 05613
2. Anurādhapura, the Capital City 05617
3. Sīgiriya/Sīgiri: the "Lion-Mountain" Rock Fortress, 473-491 AD 05622

CHAPTER FOUR: EARLY "MEDIEVAL" SOUTH ASIA, 600-1526 AD: EMERGENCE OF REGIONAL TRADITIONS AND PENETRATION OF ISLAM

I. GENERAL HISTORIES OF THE PERIOD, 600-1526 AD

A. Historiography and Historians of Medieval India 05626

B. Sources

1. Accounts of Travellers
   a. al-Bīrūnī, Ibn Batutā, and other Arab accounts 05636
   b. Buddhist pilgrims and other Chinese and Tibetan sources 05647
   c. European travellers 05660
2. Indian Texts as Sources 05669
3. Numismatic and Epigraphic Evidence 05675

C. General Histories of the Period, 600-1526 AD 05687

D. Hindu Law: Emergence of the Mītākṣara and Dayābhāga Traditions 05699

E. Economic Life and the Question of Feudalism

1. General Studies, incl. Trade and Commerce 05704
2. The Debate over the Nature and Dating of Indian Feudalism 05711

F. Aspects of Society and Culture 05722

G. History of Science in Early Medieval South Asia

1. General Studies 05731
2. Astronomy and Mathematics: Brahmagupta (b. 598 AD); Bhāskara I (c. 600); Mahāvīrācārya (c. 850); Bhāskara II (b. 1114) 05732
3. Medicine: the Introducation and Development of Ūnānī Tibb, Greco-Arab Medicine 05739

II. RELIGIO-PHILOSOPHICAL TRADITIONS: THE RISE OF BHAKTI (DEVOTIONAL HINDUISM), ECLIPSE AND ABSORPTION OF BUDDHISM, PENETRATION OF ISLAM

A. The Purāṇas, "Ancient Stories": Encyclopedic Storehouses of Hindu Myth and Basic Texts of the Bhakti Sects (compiled 4th-16th cents. AD)

1. Reference and Methodology 05744
2. General Studies in the Purāṇas 05751
3. The Bhāgavata Purāṇa/Śrīmad Bhāgavatam: the Principal Vaiṣṇava Mahāpurāna, Compiled in Tamil-speaking South India Narrating Lord Kṛṣṇa's Life
   a. translations 05761
   b. studies 05770
4. The Viṣṇu Purāṇa (c. 450): a Vaiṣṇava Mahāpurāṇa 05779
5. The Brahmavaivarta Purāṇa (compiled 750-1550): a Mahāpurāṇa Basic to Rādhā-Kṛṣṇa Bhakti 05783
6. Śiva, Liṅga and Skanda Purāṇas: Basic Mahāpurāṇas of Śaivism 05788
7. Agni, Garuḍa and Nārada Purāṇas: The "Encyclopedic" Mahāpurāṇas 05792
8. The Matsya Purāṇa: a Mahāpurāṇa 05801
9. The Mārkaṇḍeya Purāṇa: a Mahāpurāṇa Containing the Devī-Māhātmya, "Glorification of the Goddess" 05807
10. Other Mahāpurāṇas 05812
11. The Upapurāṇas [For Viṣṇudharmottara-purāṇa see Chap. Four, IX. B] 05823

B. Bhaktimārga: the Path of Devotion to a Personal God, Expressed Through Sanskrit and the Regional Languages

1. General Studies of the Development of Bhakti on an All-India Level 05828
2. Sanskrit Hymns of Praise: Stotra/Stuti/Stava 05839
3. The Development of Śāktism: Worship of Śakti, the Female "Energy" of the Divine, as Devī, the Great Goddess 05848

C. Tantrism in the Buddhist and Hindu Traditions: Esoteric Yoga Emphasizing the Union of Male and Female Principles

1. General Studies of Tantraśāstra 05857
2. Tantric Iconography and Symbolism, Hindu and Buddhist 05869
3. Hindu Tantrism: Texts and Studies 05886

II. C. 4. Vajrayāna, the "Thunderbolt-vehicle": Buddhist Tantrism in India and Tibet
- a. general studies of the origins and development of Vajrayāna 05894
- b. the cult of Tārās, savioress-consorts of Buddhas and Bodhisattvas 05913
- c. selected Tantric texts in translation 05917

D. The Submergence of Buddhism in Medieval India 05923

E. Jainism in Medieval India 05930

F. The Entry of Islam: Brought by Arabs to Sindh (710 AD), and by Turks and Afghans to the Northwest (after 1000 AD)

1. General Studies of Early Islam in India 05932
2. Sufism: Islamic Mysticism
   - a. general introductions to Sufism 05937
   - b. studies of early Sufism in India (beginning c. 1015 AD) 05943
3. Islam and the Indic Religions: Mutual Perceptions and Interactions 05957

III. MEDIEVAL SANSKRIT LITERATURE

A. Medieval Poetic Theory and Criticism

1. the Alaṁkāra-śāstra: Aesthetics of Stanzaic Poetry
   - a. general studies 05965
   - b. Bhāmaha (c. 725 AD), author of the Kāvyālaṁkāra, first treatise on poetics after the Nāṭyaśāstra 05971
   - c. later alaṁkāra writers; Daṇḍin (c. 750 AD), author of the Kāvyadarśa 05973
2. The Rasa ("Flavor" of Aesthetic Experience) and Dhvani ("Resonance") Theories
   - a. general studies 05977
   - b. the Dhvanyāloka of Ānandavardhana of Kashmir (c. 850): interaction of rasa and bhakti 05980
   - c. Abhivanagupta (c. 1000 AD): Kashmir Śaiva theorist of theology and poetics; concept of Śāntarasa (rasa of "repose") [For his philosophical works, see VII. B. 2. b., below] 05988
   - d. the Kāvyaprakāśa of Mammaṭa (c. 1100 AD) of Kashmir 05994
   - e. other major writers on Sanskrit poetics 05998

B. Medieval Sanskrit Drama, Poetry and Prose in Translation, with Studies of Major Authors

1. Harṣavardhana, King of Kanauj (606-648 AD) and Dramatist 06005
2. Bāṇabhaṭṭa (c. 625 AD): Novelist and Biographer of King Harṣa
   - a. translations 06011
   - b. studies 06017
3. Bhavabhūti (c. 700 AD), Author of Nāṭakas ("Heroic Dramas") Based on Rāmāyaṇa, and of the Prakaraṇa ("Romantic Play") Mālatīmādhava
   - a. translations 06023
   - b. studies 06031
4. Bhartṛhari the Poet (c. 7th cent.?), Sometimes Identified with Bhartṛhari the Grammarian 06037
5. Bilhaṇa (11th cent. AD), Love-poet of Kashmir 06047
6. Other Medieval Sanskrit Poets and Dramatists, and Their Works 06054

C. Medieval Sanskrit Narrative Literature: Kathā, Ākhyāyikā, and Campū; Popular Tales and Fables

1. Medieval Sanskrit Versions of the Lost Prakrit Bṛhatkathā: by Somadeva and Kṣemendra of Kashmir, and Budhasvāmin of Nepal 06071
2. Hitopadeśa, "Book of Good Counsel": Bengali Sanskrit Version of the Pañcatantra 06079
3. The Vetālapañcaviṁśatī, "Twenty-five Tales of a Vampire" 06086
4. The Śukasaptati, "Seventy Tales of a Parrot" 06089

IV. ART AND ARCHITECTURE OF EARLY MEDIEVAL INDIA (WORKS ON A TRANSREGIONAL LEVEL)

A. General Studies 06096

B. Selected Sanskrit Texts for Art and Architecture: Translations and Studies 06103

V. SRI LANKA: THE ISLAND OF CEYLON FROM THE 7TH CENT. AD TO THE EARLY PORTUGUESE PERIOD (1550 AD)

A. Histories of Medieval Simhala

1. The Decline of Anurādhapura; Invasions, Conquest (1029 AD) and Rule by the Cōḻa Kings of South India 06116
2. The Period of Rule from Polonnāru (1070-1230 AD), incl. Conquest by the Kaliṅga King Magha (1215-1235 AD) 06121
3. Dambadeniya,Gampola, Kotte and other Kingdoms up to 1550 AD; Contacts with China and the Arabs 06130

B. Economic and Social Life 06135

C. Literature of Ceylon in Sanskrit, Pali, Sinhala 06144

D. Religio-Philosophical Traditions: the Formation of a Characteristic Sinhalese Buddhism 06149

E. Art and Architecture in Medieval Ceylon

1. General Studies 06164
2. The Efflorescence of Art in the Capital City of Polonnāruwa 06171

VI. THE DRAVIDIAN SOUTH AND ADJACENT AREAS OF THE DECCAN IN THE MEDIEVAL PERIOD (c. 600-1565 AD)

A. General and Political Histories

1. Conflict of Rival Kingdoms 06176
2. The "Great" Pallavas of Kāñchī and Mahābalipuram/Mamallāpuram (575-903 AD) 06185
3. The Cōḻas/Chȯlas of Tanjore (846-1177 AD): Imperial Consolidation and Overseas Expansion 06196
4. The Western Cālukyas of Vātāpi/Bādāmi (550-753 AD): the Rāstrakūṭa Interregnum (753-973 AD), and the Eastern Cālukyas of Vengī (617-1190 AD) 06205
5. The Hoysalas of Dvārasamudra (1190-1340 AD), successors to the Cālukyas 06215
6. The Early Penetration of Muslim Power into South India 06239

B. Economic and Social Life in Early Medieval South India

1. General Studies of Economic History 06243
2. The Agrarian System and Feudalism 06255
3. Economic and Social Role of South Indian Temples 06263

C. "Greater India": Colonization and Indianization of Southeast Asia 06273

D. Religio-Philosophical Traditions in Early Medieval Dravidian India: Blending of Popular Bhakti, the Pan-Indian Brahmanic Orthodoxy of Vedānta and the Āgamic Traditions

1. General Studies of the South Indian Religious Milieu 06277
2. Vaiṣṇava and Śaiva Saint-singers in Popular Tamil: the Āḻvārs and the Nāyaṉārs (6th-10th cent. AD)
   a. general and comparative studies and translations 06285
   b. the Āḻvārs, 12 Vaiṣṇava saints, and their collected songs, the Nālāyira Divyaprabandham, "the 4,000 hymns" 06288
   c. the Nāyaṉārs, 63 Śaiva saints and their collected songs, the Tirumuṟai
      i. general studies and translations 06303
      ii. Māṇikkavācakar (9th cent.), author of the Tiruvācakam, "sacred utterances" 06308
      iii. the Periya Purāṇam by Cēkkiḻār (12th cent.): epic hagiography of the 63 Nāyaṉārs 06320
3. The Advaita ("Non-Dual") Vedānta of Śaṅkarācārya (788-820 AD): the Philosophic Basis of Pan-Indian Hindu Orthodoxy
   a. general surveys and studies of Vedānta 06324
   b. pre-Śaṅkara Vedānta; Gauḍapāda (c. 700 AD), traditional founder of Advaita Vedānta and paramaguru (teacher's teacher) of Śaṅkarācārya 06336
   c. Śaṅkara (788-820 AD), Nāmbūdiri Brāhmaṇ from Kerala, leads Hindu resurgence against Buddhism and establishes India-wide network of ascetic orders
      i. Śaṅkara's works translated from the Sanskrit, and studies of particular works 06345
      ii. biographical studies 06361
      iii. general studies of Śaṅkarācārya's thought 06368
      iv. Śaṅkara and contemporary religious trends: his relation to bhakti and his confrontation with the Buddhists 06379
      v. Śaṅkara and his successors in the Advaita Vedānta tradition 06387

VI. D. 4. Rāmānuja (1017?-1137? AD), Ācārya of Śrīraṅgam Temple, and his Viśiṣṭādvaita ("Qualified Non-Dualism")
- a. Yāmunācārya (10th cent. AD), Rāmānuja's guru and reconciler of Pāñcarātra theism and Vedānta 06408
- b. Rāmānuja's works translated from Sanskrit, and studies of individual works 06415
- c. general studies of Rāmānuja's life and philosophy 06426
- d. special topics in Rāmānuja's philosophy 06443
- e. Śrī-Vaiṣṇavism after Rāmānuja: the split into Tengalai (southern school at Śrīrangam) and Vadagalai (northern school at Tirupati, 13th cent.)
  - i. general studies 06453
  - ii. the Tengalai school at Śrīraṅgam and its leader Piḷḷai Lokācārya (1264-1327 AD) 06460
  - iii. the Vadagalai school at the Śrī Venkaṭeśvara temple at Tirupati and its leader, Vedānta Deśika 06463

5. Madhva (1197-1276 AD?) of Udipi, Karṇāṭaka: Vaiṣṇava Founder of the School of Dvaita ("Dualistic") Vedānta
   - a. works of Madhvācārya, translated from Sanskrit 06469
   - b. general studies of Madhva and his Dvaita Vedānta 06475
   - c. the Haridāsas of Karṇāṭaka: Kannaḍa bhakta-poets inspired by Madhva's teachings 06488
6. The Bhedābheda ("Different/Non-Different") Schools: Bhāskara (9th cent. AD), and Nimbārka (11th cent. AD), the Telugu Brāhman Devotee of Gopālakṛṣṇa and Rādhā 06495
7. The Śuddhādvaita ("Pure Non-Dual") Vedānta of Vallabhācārya (1479-1531 AD?): Telugu Brahman Propagator of Rādhā-Kṛṣṇa Bhakti and Puṣṭimārga Throughout India 06500
8. Śaivism in Early Medieval South India (c. 600-1565 AD): General Studies (incl. Śāktism) 06508
9. The Śaiva Siddhānta: a Blending of the Bhakti of the Tamil Saints with the Philosophy of the Śaivāgamas
   - a. Śaiva Siddhānta texts, translated from the Tamil 06519
   - b. studies of Śaiva Siddhānta 06525
10. The Tamil Siddhas: Śaiva Tantric Adepts, Possessors of the Siddhis, "Supernormal Powers" 06534
11. The Vīraśaiva Movement of the Lingāyat Caste-Sect of Karnātaka (from c. 12th cent. AD)
    - a. bibliography 06537
    - b. Basava (12th cent. AD) and other Śaraṇas, founding saint-poets and their Kannaḍa vacanas ("sayings") 06538
    - c. religious and sociocultural studies of Vīraśaivism and the Lingāyats) 06557
12. Jainism and Remnants of Buddhism in the South 06569
13. Islam in Early Medieval South India 06572

E. Regional Languages and Literatures of South India in the Early Medieval Period (600-1565 AD)

1. Tamil
   - a. the Tamil Rāmāyaṇa of Kamban/Kampar (c. 10th to 12th cent. AD): Cōḻa period retelling of the Vālmīki epic 06575
   - b. other Tamil writers and texts 06585
2. Malayālam of Kerala 06593
3. Kannaḍa of Karnataka [see also VI. D. 5. c. & VI. D. 11., above] 06596
4. Telugu of Andhra 06599

F. Art and Architecture of Medieval South India (600-1565 AD)

1. General; Architectural Texts 06607
2. Art under the Pāṇḍya Dynasty (586-1323 AD) 06611
3. Art under the Pallava Dynasty (575-903 AD): Mahābalipuram and other Sites 06613
4. Art under the Cōḷas (850-1177 AD) 06632
5. Art under the Western Cālukya Dynasty of Bādāmi (550-753 AD) 06648
6. Art under the Eastern Cālukyas of Veṅgī (617-1190 AD) and the Kākatīyas of Warangal (1000-1425 AD) 06660
7. Art under the Hoysaḷas of Karṇāṭaka (1110-1317 AD) 06670
8. Art of the Vijayanagara Dynasties (1336-1565 AD) 06678

VII. MIDDLE INDIA IN THE EARLY MEDIEVAL PERIOD (c. 600-1526 AD)

A. General Histories by Area and Dynasty

1. Major Powers in the Maharashtra Area (the Cāḷukyas of Vāṭāpi and Veṅgī Ruled this Area c. 550-753 and 973-1190 AD)
   - a. the Rāṣṭrakūṭas (753-973 AD), interregnum between the two Cāḷukya dynasties 06680
   - b. the Yādavas of Devagiri (1150-1313 AD), a successor state of the later Cāḷukyas; annexed by the Delhi Sultanate in 1313 06683
   - c. the Bāhmanī Sultanate in the northern Deccan (independent of Delhi 1345; split into five sultanates c. 1530 AD) 06687

VII. A. 2. Early Medieval Dynasties in the Orissa Area (600-1526 AD): Bhaumakāras, Eastern Gaṅgas, and Gajapatis 06694
3. The Gondwāna, Bāghelkhaṇḍ and Bundelkhaṇḍ Areas of Central India: Tribal States and the Candella Dynasty 06702
4. The Pivotal Malwa Plateau: the Rajput Paramāras/Pawārs of Dhār and Later Muslim Rulers 06708
5. Hindu and Muslim Kingdoms of the Gujarat Area 06712
6. The Rajasthan Area: Emergence of the Rajput Military Aristocracy, the Hindu Bulwark Against Islam
a. bardic poetry and other sources of medieval Rajput history 06724
b. general studies of Rajput history (600-1526 AD) 06731

B. Religio-Philosophical Traditions, incl. the Rise and Dominance of Bhakti and Sufi Movements in Middle India (600-1526 AD)

1. General Studies 06742
2. The Early Maharashtrian Santas: the Vārkarī Panth (Cult of Viṭhobā at Paṇḍharpur) and the Beginnings of Marathi Literature
a. general studies and selected translations 06744
b. Jñāneśvara/Dnyāndev (1275-1296 AD): protegé of the Yādava king of Devagiri, and first religious poet in Marathi; the Jñāneśvarī, his verse commentary on the Gītā 06757
c. Nāmdeva (1270-1350 AD), a tailor by caste and travelling Bhakta; propagandist of nāmakīrtan, "repetition of the names" of God 06769
3. The Mahānubhāva/Mānbhāo Sect Founded by Cakradhara under the Yādavas (13th cent. AD): Esoteric Kṛṣṇa Devotees and Rivals of the Vārkarīs 06772
4. Gujarat and Rajasthan: Trends in Religion and Religious Literature - Hindu, Jain, Muslim
a. general 06777
b. Narsiṁha Mahetā/Mehtā (1414-1481 AD) and Gujarati bhakti 06781
c. Mīrābāī (1515-1546 AD): Rajput princess and Kṛṣṇa devotee, from Mewāṛ to Dwārkā 06783
d. Jaina religion and religious literature 06790
3. Islam and Muslim life in Gujarat and Rajasthan 06797
5. Orissa: Religion and Literature [for Caitanya, see also X. C. 3. e., below] 06802

C. Art and Architecture in Early Medieval Middle India (600-1526 AD)

1. General Studies 06806
2. Maharashtra
a. general studies 06808
b. Buddhist cave sculptures at Aurangabad (7th cent. AD) 06813
c. Ellora: cave-temples and sculptures - Buddhist (c. 359-700 AD), Brahmanical (7th-8th cents. AD), and Jain (8th-13th cents. AD) 06816
d. Brahmanical cave-temples of Elephanta (Ghārapurī) Island in Bombay Harbor (450-750 AD) 06825
3. Art and Architecture of the Gujarat-Rajasthan-Malwa Area (600-1526 AD)
a. general studies 06830
b. Western Indian painting 06831
c. sculpture 06846
d. architecture
i. texts on Hindu and Jain temple architecture 06853
ii. temples of Gujarat, Rajasthan, and Malwa 06855
iii. Muslim architecture 06876
4. Hindu and Jain architecture of Bundelkhaṇḍ and Baghelkhaṇḍ Area
a. Khajuraho: capital of the Candellas and site of 30 temples constructed 950-1050 AD 06880
b. other sites in Bundelkhaṇḍ-Baghelkhaṇḍ 06896
5. Art and Architecture of Early Medieval Orissa
a. general studies 06900
b. Sanskrit texts on temple construction in the Orissan tradition 06910
c. Bhuvaneśvara/Bhubaneshwar: "temple city" built 8th-13th cent. AD) 06913
d. Konārak: temple of Sūrya in the form of the Sun God's chariot 06916
e. Mukhaliṅgam: temples of the eastern Gaṅga dynasty, 13th cent. 06923

VIII. THE INDUS VALLEY IN THE EARLY MEDIEVAL PERIOD (600-1526 AD): SINDH, PANJAB, KASHMIR AND THE NORTHWEST MOUNTAIN FRONTIER

A. General Histories by Major Sub-areas

1. Sindh and Baluchistan; the Early Arab Incursions 06925

VIII. A. 2. Panjāb, "Land of the Five Rivers": Avenue for Invasion, Trade and Cultural Interchange 06929

3. Kashmir: Mountain Refuge of Hindu and Buddhist Culture During the Early Muslim Invasions; Beginning of Muslim Rule in 1339 AD

a. the Rājataraṅginī of Kalhaṇa (fl. 1148 AD): chronicle of the Hindu kings of Kashmir; other sources 06937

b. general studies of early medieval Kashmir 06944

B. Religio-Philosophical Traditions: Buddhism, Hinduism, and Islam in the Early Medieval Indus Valley

1. Buddhism: Displacement by Śaivism and Islam, Except for Lamaistic Remnants in Ladākh 06955

2. Kashmir Śaivism: Regional School Combining Monistic, Realistic, and Tantric Elements Based on the Śaivāgamas and the Śivasūtras

a. general studies of Kashmir Śaivism, called Trika ("Triad") school; the Śiva-sūtra 06956

b. Abhinavagupta (c. 1000): leading exponent and systematizer of Kashmir Śaivism [for his works on poetics, see III. A. 2. c., above]; his teacher Utpaladeva, and his disciple, Kṣemarāja 06966

c. Śaiva bhakti in Kashmir: the poetry of Lalla Ded (14th cent.) and Bhaṭṭa Nārāyana 06976

3. Earliest Development of Islam in the Indus Valley Area; Lives and Poetry of the Ṣūfī Mystics (Beginning 11th cent. AD) 06993

C. Art and Architecture of the Indus Valley 06996

IX. NORTH INDIA: THE UPPER AND MIDDLE GANGA PLAINS IN THE EARLY MEDIEVAL PERIOD (600-1526 AD)

A. General Histories

1. Harṣavardhana (ruled 606-647 AD) of Kānyakubja/Kanauj: the Last Great Hindu Empire-Builder of North India [see also III. B. 1.,2., above] 07002

2. Later Hindu Dynasties of North India, incl. General History of Kanauj 07006

3. The Delhi and Jaunpur Sultanates (1206-1526 AD): Muslim Dominance of North India

a. general studies 07014

b. the early Sultāns: the Māmluks or "slave" dynasty (1206-1290 AD), the Khaljīs (1290-1320 AD) 07023

c. the later Sultāns: the Tughluqs (1320-1411 AD), the Sayyīds (1414-1451 AD), and the Lodīs (1451-1526 AD) 07037

B. Political, Economic and Social Life in Early Medieval North India (600-1526 AD)

1. Political and Military Organization

a. pre-Sultanate (600-1206 AD) 07056

b. the Delhi Sultanate (1206-1526) 07058

2. Economic and Social Conditions

a. pre-Sultanate period (600-1206 AD) 07070

b. period of the Delhi Sultanate (1206-1526 AD) 07077

C. Religio-Philosophical Traditions: the Meeting of Hinduism and Islam [for Buddhism in Medieval Bihar see X. C., below]

1. Studies of the General Religious Milieu 07084

2. Early Bhakti in North India: Egalitarian, Centered on Rama Worship, and Expressed Exclusively in Hindi Vernacular

a. general studies 07089

b. Rāmānanda (1400-1470 AD) of Banāras: organizer and inspirer of North Indian Rāma-bhakti; his Camār disciple Ravidāsa/Raidās 07093

c. Kabīr (1440-1518 AD), Muslim weaver of Banāras, and supposed disciple of Rāmānanda: Hindu-Muslim eclectic and reformer

i. Kabīr's poems in translation 07096

ii. studies of Kabīr and his followers, the Kabīr Panth 07102

3. Sufism and Muslim Literature in North India: Shaikh Nizām-ud Dīn Awliya (d. 1325 AD), and the Chishtī Order in Delhi

a. general studies 07111

b. Amīr Khusrau (1253-1325 AD) of Delhi: follower of Nizām-ud-Dīn Awliya, and religious-secular literary genius in Persian and early Hindi 07121

D. Language: Emergence of the Earliest Forms of Hindi-Urdu 07131

IX. E. Art and Architecture of North India in the Early Medieval Period (600-1526 AD)

1. Schools of Early North Indian Painting [see also Western Indian Painting, VII. C. 3. b., above] 07136
2. Islamic Architecture of the Sultanate Period 07159

X. THE BENGAL AREA, INCL. BIHAR AND ASSAM, IN THE EARLY MEDIEVAL PERIOD (600-1538 AD): THE LOWER GANGA AND THE BRAHMAPUTRA VALLEYS

A. General and Political Histories

1. Buddhist and Hindu Dynasties: the Pālas (730-1197 AD), the Senas (1095-1204 AD), and other Kingdoms 07174
2. Muslim Rule in Bengal up to the Mughal Period (1204-1538 AD) 07182
3. Early Medieval Assam (Kāmarūpa): Entry of Ahom People from Burma and Beginning of their Rule (13th cent. AD) 07192

B. Economic and Social Life in Early Medieval Eastern India (600-1538 AD) 07197

C. Religio-Philosophical Traditions and Their Literature in the Early Medieval Bengal Area (600-1538 AD): Developments in Buddhism, Hinduism and Islam

1. The General Religious Milieu 07204
2. Buddhism Under Pāla Patronage: the Dominance of Mahāyāna and Vajrayāna (Tantrism); the Buddhist Sahajiya Cult
   a. general studies 07211
   b. Buddhist literature in Sanskrit and Old Bengali; dohās and caryā songs 07219
3. Vaiṣṇavism in the Bengal Area: the Culmination of the Bhakti-Vedānta Tradition in Caitanya (1486-1533 AD)
   a. Bengal Vaiṣṇavism and its literature - general studies and translations 07228
   b. the Bengali Rāmāyaṇas of Kṛttibās (15th cent. AD) and others 07242
   c. the Gīta-Govinda of Jayadeva (12th cent. AD): erotic-devotional poem on Rādhā and Kṛṣṇa
      i. translations from the Sanskrit 07244
      ii. studies 07250
   d. Rādhā-Kṛṣṇa bhakti; the poems of Vidyāpati in Maithilī, and of Caṇḍidāsa in Bengali 07258
   e. Caitanya (1486-1533 AD), called Śrī Gaurāṅga, central figure of Gauḍiya (Gauḍ=Bengal) Vaiṣṇava bhakti, and founder of the Acintya-Bhedābheda school of Vedānta
      i. general studies of the Caitanya movement 07264
      ii. the Śrī Caitanya-caritāmṛta and later biographies of Caitanya 07270
      iii. studies and expositions of Caitanya's teachings 07278
      iv. lives and works of Caitanya's disciples, the Six Gosvāmins 07284
   f. Śankaradeva (1486?-1568 AD) and the Vaiṣṇava movement in Assam 07292
4. Śaiva and Other Hindu Sects in the Bengal Area
   a. general studies 07299
   b. the Nāthas: esoteric cult of Haṭhayoga (psycho-physiological practices) and its Ādi-Siddha Gorakṣa/Gorakh Nātha (13th cent. AD?) 07303
   c. Manasā, goddess of snakes, adopted into Hinduism from tribal religion 07309
5. The Navya-Nyāya School of Hindu Logic in Mithilā and Bengal; Gaṅgeśa (13th cent.) and his Tattva-cintāmaṇi 07316
6. Early Development of Islam in the Bengal Area 07328

D. Language: Old and Early Middle Bengali (c. 950-1500 AD) and Related Languages 07335

E. Art and Architecture of the Bengal Area in the Early Medieval Period (600-1538 AD) under the Pāla, Sena and other Dynasties

1. General Studies 07340
2. Manuscript Illustration and other Painting 07342
3. Sculpture in Stone, Bronze and Terracotta 07350
4. Architecture: Buddhist, Hindu, and Muslim 07361

XI. THE HIMALAYAN RIM: THE NEPAL AREA AND BHUTAN IN THE EARLY MEDIEVAL PERIOD (600-1530 AD)

A. General Histories 07369

B. Religio-Philosophical Traditions 07379

C. Art and Architecture of Nepal 07380

CHAPTER FIVE: THE MUGHALS, MARATHAS, AND THE RISE OF BRITISH POWER: SOUTH ASIA IN AN ERA OF WORLD INTEGRATION AND INTERACTION, 1526-1818

I. REFERENCE WORKS, SOURCES, AND GENERAL HISTORIES OF SOUTH ASIA IN THE MUGHAL-MARATHA PERIOD (1526-1818)

A. Bibliography and Reference 07386

B. Historiography and Sources; Numismatics 07393

C. General Histories of the Mughal-Marāṭhā Period

1. General Histories and Studies of "Muslim Rule in India," incl. the Pre-Mughal Period 07404
2. General Studies of South Asia During the Period of Mughal Rule (1526-1707) 07424
3. General Studies of South Asia During the Period of Maratha Supremacy (1674-1818) 07437

II. THE MUGHAL EMPIRE: POLITICAL AND ADMINISTRATIVE UNIFICATION OF THE SUBCONTINENT UNDER MUSLIM RULE

A. The Rise and Consolidation of Mughal Rule: Bābar to Shāh Jahān

1. Bābar (1483-1539): Descendant of Chingīz Khān and Timur, and Founder of the Mughal Empire 07448
2. Humāyūn (1508-1556), and the Interregnum (1538-1545) of the Afghan, Sher Shāh 07457
3. Akbar (1542-1615): Indianization of Mughal Rule, Bureaucracy, and Cultural Rapprochement of Hindus and Muslims
   a. original sources: Indian and European 07468
   b. biographies and political studies 07473
4. Jahāngīr (1569-1627): Patron of the Arts; His Empress Nūr Jahān 07480
5. Shāh Jahān (1592-1666): Imperial Expansion, and Patronage of Architecture and Scholarship; Builder of the Tāj Mahal 07490

B. Aurangzīb and His Successors: Decline of the Mughals

1. Aurangzīb (1619-1707): Rejection of Akbar's Religious Toleration, Promotion of Sunnī Orthodoxy; Wars with Sikhs, Rajputs and the Marathas
   a. original sources, incl. European travellers' accounts 07494
   b. biographies and studies of Aurangzīb; Dārā Shukoh, Sufi elder brother and rival for the throne 07505
2. Later Mughal Emperors - General Accounts 07513
3. The Fall of the Mughals; Analyses from Aligarh Muslim U. and Elsewhere 07524

C. Political Structure and Administrative System of the Mughal Empire

1. Political Thought and Concepts of Authority 07529
2. General Studies of Politics and Administration 07533
3. Provincial and Local Government [see also regional sections in this chapter, below] 07544
4. The Mughal Military Elite: the Mansabdārī System
   a. general studies of the Mughal aristocracy 07548
   b. biographies of Mughal nobles, ministers, and generals 07557
   c. the Mughal military system and warfare 07565
5. Law and Judicial Administration Under the Mughals 07572
6. Foreign Relations of the Mughals 07579

D. Economic Activity and Institutions Under the Mughals

1. General Economic Histories 07585
2. The Agrarian System Under the Mughals: Land Tenure and Revenue 07597
3. Public Finance; Money and Banking 07605
4. Transport and Communication Under the Mughals 07611
5. Trade and Commerce Under the Mughals 07616
6. Industries and Urbanization Under the Mughals 07623

E. Social and Cultural Life Under the Mughal Empire

1. General Studies 07629
2. Caste and Social Stratification 07641
3. Social and Cultural Role of Women 07644
4. Education and Learning 07646

F. Religions Under the Mughals: Hinduism, Islam and the State [see also regional sections below for Christianity, Sikhism, etc]

1. General Studies of the Religious Policy of the Mughals 07653

II. F. 2. Akbar's Syncretic "Divine Faith," the Dīn-i-Ilāhī, and his policy of Religious Tolerance 07664
3. Aurangzīb's Persecution of Hindus, Sikhs, and Shiᶜas in the Name of Sunnī Orthodoxy 07671
4. Developments Within Indian Islam Under the Mughals
a. general studies 07674
b. Shaikh Ahmad Sirhindī (1564-1625), Naqshbandīya Sufi, reconciler of Sufism and Sunnī orthodoxy 07677
c. Shāh Walīullāh of Delhi (1703-1763), pre-modern reformer and revitalizer of Indian Islam 07680
5. Christianity and the Mughal Empire 07685

G. Literature of Court and Camp: Persian and Early Urdu Under the Mughal Empire

1. Indo-Persian Literature: Blossoming of Verse, Letter-Writing and History 07688
2. Development of Literary Urdu out of the Dakhnī of the Provincial Sultanates 07703

H. Art and Architecture under the Mughals

1. Indian Miniature Painting - Collections from Mughal and Other Periods 07711
2. Painting Under the Mughals [for regional traditions see below]
a. general surveys and studies 07728
b. painters and painting from the courts of Humāyūn and Akbar 07750
c. the school of Jahāngīr, and later Mughal court painting 07763
d. "popular" schools of Mughal painting 07772
3. Mughal Architecture: Forts, Palaces, Gardens; Mosques and Tombs
a. general studies 07775
b. the imperial capitals: Delhi, Āgrā, and Fatehpur Sikrī 07784
c. the Tāj Mahal in Āgrā: Shāh Jahān's memorial to his Empress, Mumtāz 07792
4. Other Arts Under the Mughals 07798

III. THE EUROPEAN RE-DISCOVERY OF INDIA: TRAVELLERS, TRADERS AND MISSIONARIES (FROM 1498)

A. General

1. Historical Interpretations of European Expansion and its Impact on South Asia 07803
2. General Histories of Political, Economic, and Cultural Contacts 07811
3. Travel Accounts by Europeans
a. general studies of early European travellers in South Asia 07821
b. major collections of travel accounts 07826
c. accounts and studies by Italians, Spaniards, and other Europeans (not included in the sections below) 07834

B. The Portuguese Settlement of South Asia after Vasco da Gama's Arrival in 1498

1. Bibliography and Reference 07841
2. Document Collections (in Portuguese) 07852
3. Biographies and Accounts of Portuguese Travellers And Administrators 07858
4. Early Portuguese Histories of the Estado da India, in Original or Translation 07866
5. Recent Histories of the Portuguese Enterprise in India 07874
6. The Establishment of the Roman Catholic Church in India Under the Portuguese
a. documents 07883
b. studies 07888

C. The Verenigde Oostindische Compagnie (V.O.C.) - "United East Indies Company" of the Netherlands (Founded 1602): Dutch Traders in South Asia

1. Bibliography and Reference 07891
2. Documents and Travellers' Accounts 07893
3. Studies of Dutch Activities in South Asia 07899

D. The French in India: From Trade to Imperial Ambition

1. Bibliography and Reference 07902
2. Document Collections 07905
3. French Travellers' Accounts 07909
4. Histories of French Activities in India: Commercial and Military Policies Dictated by World-wide Anglo-French Rivalry
a. general studies 07915

III. D. 4. b. La Compagnie Royale des Indes Orientales (founded 1664) and its successors; François Martin and the establishment of Pondicherry as the center of French India 07918
c. Joseph François Dupleix (1697-1764), and his challenge to British hegemony through alliance with native states; the diary of Ānanda Ranga Pillai, dubāsh of Dupleix 07926
d. after the defeat of French imperial aspirations: the War of the American Revolution, the French Revolution and the Napoleonic era (1763-1815)

E. The British in India: from Trade to Administration (1600-1818)

1. Early British Travellers 07941
2. The East India Company, Founded 1600 by Royal Charter Under Elizabeth I to Gain Access to the Eastern Spice Trade
a. general histories of the Company 07951
b. sources: official documents and correspondence 07963
c. politics and administration of the Company 07973
d. trade activities of the Company 07998
3. Lord Robert Clive (1725-74) and the Establishment of the British Indian State: Final Victory Over the Mughals and French [see also Bengal and Assam, IX., below]
a. biographies and studies of Lord Robert Clive, Governor of Bengal (1758-60, and 1765-67) and Mansabdār of the Mughal Empire 08005
b. the Battle of Plassey (1757) and other engagements 08017
4. The Rule of the Early Governors-General from Calcutta (1774-1813), under the Regulating Act of 1773
a. Warren Hastings, 1774-85 08026
b. Charles Cornwallis, First Marquess Cornwallis, 1786-93 and 1805 08038
c. Sir John Shore, Lord Teignmouth, 1793-98 08040
d. Richard Wellesley,Earl of Mornington, Marquess Wellesley, 1798-1805 08042
e. Gilbert Elliot, Earl of Minto I, 1807-13 08046

IV. CEYLON: INDIGENOUS KINGDOMS AND EUROPEAN INVADERS (1505-1795)

A. Political, Economic, and Social History of Sri Lanka

1. Bibliography and Sources 08048
2. Accounts of Ceylon by Early European Travellers 08049
3. The Kingdom of Kandy in the Central Ceylon Highlands (1593-1815) 08055
4. The Tamil Kingdom of Jaffna in the Northern Coastal Region 08065
5. The Coming of the Portuguese (1505) and Their Rule in Coastal Ceylon (1594-1658) 08069
6. Dutch-Portuguese Rivalry and Dutch Rule in Ceylon (1658-1795) 08082

B. Religions of Ceylon During the Period 1505-1795: Buddhism, Hinduism, Islam, Roman Catholic and Protestant Christianity 08098

C. Literature 08104

D. Art and Architecture 08109

V. SOUTH INDIA IN THE MUGHAL-MARATHA PERIOD (1565-1818)

A. General and Political Histories of South India in the Mughal-Maratha Period

1. Bījāpur and Golkoṇḍā: the Adil Shāhī and Qutb Shāhī Sultanates of the Southern Deccan 08112
2. Hyderabad Under the Early Nizāms: Asaf Jāh I (1671-1768) Asserts Independence of the Declining Mughals 08126
3. The Malabar Coast: Portuguese, Dutch, and British Settlements; the Rise of Travancore; the Muslim Sea-power of the Zamorin at Calicut 08130
4. The Coromandel/Cōḻamaṇḍalam Coast: the Nayaks of Madurai and Tanjore, Maratha Rule, and European Coastal Settlements 08148
5. Mysore/Karnātaka: the Wadiyār Dynasty and the Interregnum Under Haidar Alī (c. 1722-1782) and his son Tipū Sultān (1753-1799) 08162
6. The Beginnings of British Administration in South India: Fort St. George (built 1640) and the Presidency of Madras
a. selected records and correspondence 08179
b. general studies of early British policy and administration, early resistance to British rule 08187

B. Economic and Social History of South India in the Mughal-Maratha Period (1565-1818)

1. The Coromandel Coast and the Northern Circars: Tamil Nadu and Andhra
a. general studies 08191
b. colonial life in early Fort St. George, Madras 08199

V. B. 2. The Malabar Coast 08203
3. Mysore and its Kanara Coast 08206

C. Religion and Society in South India in the Mughal-Maratha Period (1565-1818)

1. Hinduism 08207
2. Islam: Sufis and the Māppilla Shahīds (Martyrs) 08212
3. Christian Churches: Syrian, Roman Catholic, and Protestant 08216

D. Languages and Literatures of South India: Late Medieval Developments in Sanskrit and the Dravidian Regional Languages (1565-1818) 08228

E. Art and Architecture of Late Medieval South India (1565-1818) 08232

VI. MIDDLE INDIA DURING THE MUGHAL-MARATHA PERIOD (1565-1818)

A. General and Political History

1. The Ahmadnagar and Berar Sultanates of the Northern Deccan
a. Ahmadnagar: Muslim resistance to Mughal imperialism under Sultān Chānd Bībī (d. 1600) and Malik Ambar (1549-1626), the Abyssinian "slave" Prime Minister 08239
b. Berar/Vidarbha: the ʿImād-Shāhī dynasty 08246
2. The Marathas: from Anti-Mughal Guerrilla Warfare to India-wide Supremacy
a. sources 08247
b. general histories of the Maratha power, 17th-19th cents. 08253
c. studies of Maratha institutions: administrative, fiscal, judicial and military 08263
d. Shivājī Chhatrapati (1627-1680): the Maratha revolt against the Mughals
i. contemporary records and biographies 08271
ii. later biographies and studies of Shivājī 08278
iii. Shivājī's descendants: Sambhājī I, Rājārām I and his queen Tārā Bāī; rival Chhatrapatis at Satara and Kolhapur 08292
e. the Peshwās at Poona: Chitpāvan Brāhmaṇ prime-ministers of the Chhatrapatis, and de facto rulers, 1713-1818
i. the peak of Maratha expansion: the first four Peshwās (1713-72); defeat by the Afghans at Pānipat, 1761 08296
ii. Maratha provincial feudatories, origins of later Princely States: the Bhonsles of Nāgpur, Āngres of Kolābā, Scindias/Shiṇḍes of Gwalior, Hoḷkars of Indore, and Gaikwāḍs of Baroda 08305
iii. the Maratha Confederacy under the later Peshwās and the Regent Nānā Phadnīs (1741-1800): confrontations with growing British power, to 1818 08316
3. Goa: Portuguese Presence on the Konkan Coast, 1510-1961 08334
4. Gujarat: from Muslim Kingdom to Mughal Province (1572); Maratha Raids and Occupation; Dutch Settlements [for Surat and the British see 7. b. below] 08340
5. Rajput Princes of Rajasthan: Hindu Martial Aristocracy, in Mughal Service Until Revolt Against Aurangzīb; Relations with Marathas and British
a. general studies 08350
b. Mewār/Udaipur: home of the Sisodiā clan 08358
c. Mārwār/Jodhpur: desert stronghold of the Rāṭhod clan 08364
d. Amber and Jaipur: the Kacchwāhs 08371
e. Ajmer 08376
6. Central India and Orissa 08377
7. Growth of British Power in Middle India, 1608-1818
a. general studies 08379
b. East India Company headquarters at Surat in Gujarat (1613-1687), and Bombay in Maharashtra (from 1687) 08385

B. Economic and Social History of Middle India During the Mughal-Maratha Period (1526-1818)

1. General Economic and Social History 08391
2. The Agrarian System and Village Life 08402
3. Trade and Commerce; the Ports of Surat and Bombay 08413

C. Religion and Society in Middle India During the Mughal-Maratha Period (1526-1818)

1. Later Maharashtrian Santas (Poet-saints) [see also Chap. Four, VII. B. 2. for Early Santas]
a. general studies; minor poet-saints 08424
b. Ekanātha (c. 1548-c. 1609), Brāhmaṇ bhakta in the Dnyāneśvara tradition 08427
c. Tukārāma (1608-1649), most popular of the santas 08432

VI. C. 1. d. Rāmadāsa (1608-1681), supposed preceptor of Shivājī 08443
2. Dādū (1544-1603) and the Dādū Pantha: Bhakta Followers of Kabīr in Rajasthan 08450
3. Islamic Religious Developments 08457

D. Languages and Literatures of Middle India in the Mughal-Maratha Period (1526-1818) 08458a

E. Art and Architecture of Middle India in the Mughal-Maratha Period (1526-1818)

1. Painting
a. Deccani painting of the Five Sultanates; Malwa and Bundelkhaṇḍ 08463
b. Gujarati painting 08475
c. Rajasthani painting
i. general 08476
ii. Bundī and Koṭā school 08492
iii. Mewāṛ/Udaipur school 08501
iv. other Rajasthani schools 08507
v. the "Mālwā school," an extension of Rajasthani painting 08516
2. Architecture 08520
3. Decorative and Industrial Arts 08526

VII. THE INDUS VALLEY AND NORTHWEST MOUNTAIN FRONTIER IN THE MUGHAL-MARATHA PERIOD (1526-1799)

A. General and Political History

1. Sind and Baluchistan 08530
2. Panjab and the Sikhs, from Guru Nānak (1469-1538) to the Rise of Ranjīt Singh
a. sources 08531
b. general histories of the Panjab and the Sikhs: from religious sect to military power, between Mughals and Afghans 08535
c. Hindu states of the Panjab Hills 08555
3. Jammu and Kashmir 08557

B. Economic and Social History of the Indus Valley Area in the Mughal-Maratha Period (1526-1799) 08561

C. Religious Traditions of the Sikhs: Syncretism of Hinduism and Islam in the Panjab (1469-1799)

1. General Studies of Sikhism
a. bibliography 08565
b. histories and surveys 08567
c. philosophy, ethics, and doctrine 08580
d. Sikh shrines and ceremonies 08585
2. General Studies of the Ten Gurus, from Nānak to Gobind Singh 08594
3. Guru Nānak (1469-1539): Follower of Kabīr and the North Indian Santas, and Founder of Sikhism
a. bibliography and sources on Guru Nanak 08598
b. works of Guru Nānak: translations and commentaries 08601
c. biographies of Guru Nānak 08609
d. general studies of Guru Nānak's teachings 08616
e. Guru Nānak and Islam, and other comparative studies 08630
4. The Later Gurus: Transformation from Panth (Sect) to Militant Khālsā (Brotherhood of the "Pure")
a. Guru Rām Dās (1534-1581), the fourth Guru 08636
b. Guru Har Gobind (1595-1644), sixth guru and the beginnings of militarization 08637
c. Guru Tegh Bahādur (1621-1675), ninth guru and martyr to Aurangzīb's persecution 08639
d. Guru Gobind Singh (1666-1708): the tenth and last human Guru, founder of the Khālsā 08647
5. The Guru Granth Sahib or Ādi Granth, the Sikh Scriptures: Installed in Gurdwārās as Guru After 1708 08661

D. Religious Traditions: Hinduism, Islam, and Buddhism in the Indus Valley Area (1526-1799)

1. Hinduism: Survival in the Face of Islam and Sikhism 08667
2. Islam: Sufi Mysticism and Poetry
a. Sindh: Shāh Abdul Karīm (1536-1624), Shāh Abdul Latīf (1698-1752), and other Sufi poets 08671
b. Panjabi Sufi poets 08686
3. Buddhism in Ladakh 08689

E. Language and Literature of the Indus Valley Area in the Mughal-Maratha Period (1526-1799): Baluchi, Pashto, Panjabi 08690

VII. F. Art and Architecture of the Indus Valley Area

1. Pahārī Painting of the HIndu Principalities of the Panjab Hills
   - a. general studies 08695
   - b. the Basohli school (c. 1650-1750) 08712
   - c. the Kāngrā school (c. 1750-1850) 08719
   - d. Pahārī art of particular hill-states: Jammū, Chāmbā, Guler, Kulu, Maṇḍī, Gaṛhwāl 08732
2. Art Under Sikh Rulers; Pahārī Painters on the Panjab Plains 08750
3. Islamic Art and Architecture of Lahore 08753

VIII. NORTH INDIA: THE UPPER AND MIDDLE GANGA PLAINS IN THE MUGHAL-MARATHA PERIOD (1526-1801)

A. General and Political History [for Mughal Central Government, see II. above]

1. The Upper Ganga Plains (Haryana, Delhi, and Western U.P.), incl. Rohilkhaṇḍ 08755
2. The Avadh/Oudh Area of Eastern U.P. 08762
3. The Bihar Area: Mithilā, Magadha, Tirhut 08778

B. Economic and Social History of North India in the Mughal-Maratha Period (1526-1801) 08784

C. Religious Traditions and Their Literatures in North India during the Mughal-Maratha Period (1526-1801); Emergence of Avadhī and Brajbhāṣā, Early Forms of Hindī [See also Chap. Four, II. F., above]

1. Rāma-bhakti in Avadh: Tulsidās (1532-1623) and his Rāmāyana in Avadhi, Rāmcaritmānas ("Holy Lake of the Acts of Rāma")
   - a. translations of the Rāmcaritmānas, and other works of Tulsīdās 08790
   - b. studies 08800
2. The Rādhā-Kṛṣṇa Bhakti Sampradāyas (Sects) of Braj, Centered on Mathurā and Vrindāban
   - a. the Vallabha Sampradāya: Sūrdās (1483-1563) and the Aṣṭachāp ("eight-signatures") group of poets 08813
   - b. the Rādhāvallabha Sampradāya: Goswāmi Hit Harivaṃś and his Caurāsī Pad 08825
   - c. the Nimbārka Sampradāya: Ghanānand (1719-1739) 08826
3. Islam in North India 08827

D. Language and Literature in North India During the Mughal-Maratha Period (1526-1801) 08832

IX. BENGAL AND ASSAM: THE GANGA DELTA AND THE BRAHMAPUTRA VALLEY IN THE MUGHAL-MARATHA PERIOD (1538-1813)

A. General and Political Histories

1. General Studies of the Bengal Sūbah Under the Mughals 08840
2. Early Mughal Rule to 1707: Conquest of Afghan Successors of Sher Shāh 08843
3. Northeast Kingdoms of Koch Bihār, Kāmrūp, and the Ahom State of Assam 08848
4. European Settlements in Bengal - Portuguese, Dutch, Danish, Belgian and French 08853
5. The Mughal Sūbah of Bengal, 1707-1757, and its Administrators 08861
6. British Assumption of Political Power: Dyarchy of the East India Company and Mughal Provincial Government [see also III. E. 3. above] 08872

B. Economic and Social History of the Bengal-Assam Area in the Mughal-Maratha Period (1538-1813)

1. General Economic History 08889
2. The Agrarian Order: Peasants, Zamīndārs, and the Revenue System
   - a. land system and revenue under Mughal and early British rule (to 1793) 08894
   - b. the 1793 Permanent Settlement of Lord Cornwallis, Governor-General 08903
3. Commerce and Industry; the Indigenous Economy and the East India Company 08910
4. Urban Centers
   - a. traditional urban centers 08920
   - b. Fort William (est. 1669) and the developing colonial city of Calcutta 08924

C. Religion and Religious Literature in the Bengal-Assam Area in the Mughal-Maratha Period (1538-1813)

1. General Developments in Religion and Philosophy 08932

IX. C. 2. Spread of Śakti Worship and Tantric Rituals; Rāmprasād Sen (1718-1775) 08935
3. Vaiṣṇavism After Caitanya; the Sahajiya Cult; the Philosophy of Madhusūdana Sarasvatī (1540-1648) 08940
4. The Bāuls, "Mad" Singers of Bengal: Hindu-Muslim Mysticism and Social Egalitarianism 08946
5. Islam in Bengal 08953
6. Early Protestant Missions in Bengal: William Carey in the Danish Enclave at Serampore/Śrīrāmpur 08954

D. Language and Literature of the Bengal-Assam Area in the Mughal-Maratha Period (1538-1813) 08962

E. Art and Architecture of the Bengal-Assam Area in the Mughal-Maratha Period (1538-1813) 08968

X. NEPAL AND THE HIMALAYAN RIM IN THE MUGHAL-MARATHA PERIOD (1526-1816)

A. General and Political History 08973

B. Art and Architecture 08985

PART THREE: TRANSFORMATIONS IN THE MODERN AGE: NATIONAL LEVEL

CHAPTER SIX: THE RAJ: PRINCELY AND BRITISH INDIA, FROM COMPANY TO EMPIRE TO INDEPENDENCE (1818-1947)

I. RESEARCH TOOLS AND GENERAL HISTORY OF THE BRITISH PERIOD

A. Bibliography, Historiography and Reference

1. Bibliography 08987
2. Historiography 08997
3. Chronologies, Handbooks, and Dictionaries 09007
4. Biographical Sources 09012

B. General History of the British Period

1. Overall Assessments and Thematic Interpretations 09026
2. Introductory Surveys 09045
3. General Histories for Reference or Advanced Study 09053
4. Essay Collections 09062
5. Documentary Histories 09067

II. POLITICAL AND ADMINISTRATIVE HISTORY OF BRITISH INDIA AND RELATIONS WITH THE PRINCELY STATES

A. The Central Policy-Making and Executive Organs in England and India

1. Constitutional History and Documents 09073
2. General History of Politics and Policies at the Center 09084
3. The Home Government in London 09093
4. The Supreme Government of India: the Governors-General (and, after 1858, Viceroys) and their Administrations (to 1899)
a. general 09100
b. Earl of Moira, Marquess of Hastings, 1814-1823 (Francis Rawdon) 09107
c. Earl Amherst, 1823-28 (William Pitt Amherst) 09110
d. Lord William Bentinck, 1828-35 (William Cavendish-Bentinck 09111
e. Earl of Auckland,1835-42 (George Eden) 09116
f. Earl of Ellenborough, 1842-44 (Edward Law) 09117
g. Viscount Hardinge, 1844-48 (Henry Hardinge) 09120
h. Marquess of Dalhousie, 1848-56 (James Andrew Broun-Ramsay) 09121
j. Earl Canning, 1856-62 - first Viceroy, from 1858 (Charles John Canning) 09129
k. Earl of Elgin, 1862-63 (James Bruce) 09131
l. Lord Lawrence, 1863-69 (John Laird Mair Lawrence) 09134
m. Earl of Mayo, 1869-72 (Richard Southwell Bourke) 09139
n. Earl of Northbrook, 1872-76 (Thomas George Baring) 09141
o. Earl of Lytton, 1876-80 (Edward Robert Bulwer Lytton) 09143
p. Marquess of Ripon, 1880-84 (George Frederick Samuel Robinson) 09144
q. Marquess of Dufferin, 1884-88 (Frederick Temple Blackwood) 09147

II. A. 4. r. Marquess of Lansdowne, 1888-94 (Henry Charles Keith Petty-Fitzmaurice) 09149
s. Earl of Elgin II, 1894-99 (Victor Alexander Bruce) 09151
5. Legislative Councils 09152

B. Administrative Organization of British India

1. General Histories and Studies of Administration 09159
2. Biographies and Studies of Leading Administrators 09170
3. The Indian Civil Service (ICS) and Other Public Services of British India
a. general studies of the public services, and official reports 09179
b. recruitment and training for the ICS; Haileybury College, and the competitive system 09194
c. accounts and memoirs by officials 09200
4. Provincial, District and Local Government 09214
5. Police Administration and Crime in British India
a. history, organization and personal accounts 09222
b. thugs/ṭhags, dacoits and other underworld types 09231
6. Law and Judicial Administration
a. history of the judicial system in British India 09244
b. Hindu and Muslim personal and family law under British administration 09260
c. adaptation and effects of British law in India; law and caste 09272
7. Military Organization and History
a. general history of the armed forces, British and Indian 09283
b. selected unit histories 09298
c. biographies, memoirs and studies of British military men in India 09314

C. Princely India: From Mughal Allegiance to British Paramountcy [for Individual States, See Index]

1. Biographical Guides and Other Reference Works 09335
2. General History and Studies of the Native States 09343
3. Political Relations Between the Paramount Power and Princes; the Indian Political Service 09356
4. Moves Toward Federation and Integration: the Chamber of Princes (Est. 1921), and the Government of India Act, 1935 09376

D. Foreign Relations of the Government of India

1. General Diplomatic History: Relations with Western Nations 09384
2. India as Part of the British Empire and Commonwealth; Relations with the Middle East 09395
3. Relations with Burma: British Conquest and Annexation, 1824-1886; a Province of India, 1886-1935 09405
4. "The Great Game" of British-Russian Rivalry in Central Asia
a. general studies 09408
b. Afghanistan and the North-West frontier 09421
c. Tibet and the Himalayan frontier 09439

III. GROWTH OF INDIAN NATIONALISM IN RESPONSE TO EXPANDING BRITISH POWER (TO 1919)

A. Background to Nationalism: Early Civil and Military Discontent

1. Early Opposition to British Rule (to 1857) 09454
2. 1857: "Sepoy Mutiny" or "War of Independence"?
a. bibliography and historiography 09458
b. document collections 09469
c. selected personal accounts and biographies [for more of this huge literature see bibliographies in a. above] 09473
d. history of the Revolt of 1857-59
i. nineteenth century British accounts 09486
ii. re-interpretations by Marxists, nationalists, and twentieth century scholars 09491
iii. some recent popular narratives 09513
e. aftermath and effects 09521

B. Indian Nationalism and the "Freedom Movement" - General Histories and Studies

1. Bibliography and Reference 09524
2. Histories of Modern Indian Political Thought 09530
3. History of Indian Nationalism and the Independence Movement
a. interpretations by contemporaries, Indian and British 09546
b. post-independence assessments of the nationalist movement 09554
c. role of women in the Freedom Movement 09583
4. Collective and Comparative Biographies of National Leaders 09587
5. Social Background of Nationalists 09598
6. The Indian National Movement and the World: International Context and Relations 09605

III. C. The Indian National Congress (est. 1885): the First All-India Organization for Political and Social Reform

1. General History of the INC 09630
2. The Founding (1885) and Early Years of Congress (to 1905): Emphasis on Moderation and Petition of Grievances
    a. general studies 09645
    b. early Congress leaders: A.O. Hume, W.C. Bonnerjee, Dadabhai Naoroji, Pherozeshah Mehta, Surendranath Banerjea 09651
    c. Gopal Krishna Gokhale (1866-1915), Congress Moderate leader, and member of Imperial Legislative Council: disciple of M.G. Ranade and "political guru" of M.K. Gandhi 09668

D. The Politicization of Nationalism, 1905-1919: From Lord Curzon's Raj to Gandhian Non-Cooperation; Rise of the Muslim League; the Great War, 1914-18

1. The Extremists and Revolutionaries: Religious Nationalism and Approval of Violence; Boycotts and the Swadeshi Movement
    a. general studies 09679
    b. Bal Gangadhar Tilak (1856-1920): Maharashtrian editor of Kesari and Mahratta, and pioneer in mass mobilization [see also Chapter Twelve, I. C. 2. b.] 09697
    c. Bipin Chandra Pal (1858-1932): Bengali editor of New India 09713
    d. Aurobindo Ghose (1872-1950): Bengali editor of Bande Mātaram [see also VII. C. 7., below] 09718
    e. Lajpat Rai (1865-1928): Panjabi lawyer and Arya Samajist 09727
    f. the Revolutionaries: terrorism and armed conspiracy; the Lahore conspiracy, the Anusilan Samiti of Bengal, the Hindustan Ghadar Party among Punjabis overseas 09738
    g. the Home Rule Leagues , founded 1916 by B.G. Tilak and Annie Besant: demand for self-rule at War's end 09758
2. The Indian Muslims Between Nationalism and Communalism (1880's-1919) [for Muslim Religion and Thought see VII. C. 2. c., below]
    a. general studies of Muslims under the Raj: relations to British and Hindus after the end of the Mughal Empire and the "Mutiny" 09762
    b. early Muslim leaders - biographies and studies
        i. Sir Sayyid Ahmad Khan (1817-1898): advocate of Western education to restore Muslim political fortunes, opponent of Indian National Congress [for his religious and educational views see VII. D. 2., below] 09789
        ii. other early Muslim political leaders 09797
    c. Muslim political organization (to 1919): loyalty to the British and protection of Muslim rights; rapprochement with Congress in the 1916 Lucknow Pact 09810
3. British Reactions to Nationalist Petitions and Bombs: Repression and Constitutional Change
    a. Lord Curzon, Marquess of Kedleston (Viceroy, 1899-1904, 1904-1905), and his administration [for Partition of Bengal, see Chap. Fifteen, II. A. 5. c.] 09816
    b. Earl of Minto II (Viceroy, 1905-1910; Gilbert John Elliot-Murray-Kynynmound)
        i. general studies of Lord Minto and his administration 09823
        ii. the "Morley-Minto Reforms," or Indian Councils Act of 1909: increased Indian council membership and the beginning of communal representation 09829
    c. Lord Hardinge of Penshurst (Viceroy, 1910-16) (Charles Hardinge)
        i. general studies of Lord Hardinge and his administration 09838
        ii. visit of King-Emperor George V, the Delhi Durbar of 1911, and the moving of the capital from Calcutta to Delhi, 1912 09839
    d. repressive measures in response to nationalist agitation and German support of conspirators
        i. the Rowlatt Acts (March 1919) and nationwide hartals (general strikes) called by M.K. Gandhi 09841
        ii. the massacre of civilians at Jallianwala Bagh, Amritsar (April 1919) 09843

IV. NON-COOPERATION AND CONSTITUTIONAL PROGRESS TOWARDS INDEPENDENCE AND PARTITION, 1919-47

A. Mohandas Karamchand Gandhi (1869-1948), called the Mahātmā ("Great Soul")

1. Bibliography and Reference 09854
2. Gandhi's Writings 09861
3. General Biographical Studies of M.K. Gandhi
    a. selected biographies and biographical studies 09873

IV. A. 3. b. personal accounts by Gandhi's associates 09890
c. assessments of Gandhi's life and historic role 09909
4. The Transformation of Indian Politics Under Gandhi's Leadership
a. general studies of Gandhi's political career 09928
b. Gandhi's political and social thought - beginnings of "Gandhism" 09934
c. Gandhi's new strategy of satyāgraha ("truth force"): reliance on moral force and ahiṃsā ("non-violence") 09955

B. The Nationalist Movement: Proliferation of Strategies in Response to Devolution of Power by British, 1919-47

1. General Studies of the Nationalist Movement and its Context, 1919-47 09970
2. The Khilafat and Non-cooperation Movements (1919-1924): High Tide of Hindu-Muslim Unity 09986
3. Responsive Cooperation: Political Parties Formed from Congress for Elections and Council Entry
a. National Liberal Federation (est. 1918); Tej Bahadur Sapru; V.S. Srinivasa Sastri; C.Y. Chintamani; H.N. Kunzru 10008
b. the Swaraj Party (est. 1922): C.R. Das, Motilal Nehru, Vithalbhai Patel 10021
4. The Rise of the Left: Communists and Socialists
a. general studies of leftist movements in India, 1919-1947 10033
b. the Communist Party of India (est. 1925)
i. CPI documents and British official reports 10039
ii. general history of the CPI 10048
iii. memoirs and biographies of Indian Communists and foreign agents 10056
c. M.N. Roy: from Communism to Radical Humanism
i. bibliography 10065
ii. writings of M.N. Roy and of Ellen Roy 10066
d. the Congress Socialist Party (est. 1934): socialists within the Indian National Congress 10087
e. the Hindustan Socialist Republican Army and other terrorist groups 10105
5. Communalism and the Growth of Hindu-Muslim Tensions (1917-47): Religious Communities as the Basis of Politics
a. general studies 10115
b. Muslims and the Congress, from the Lucknow Pact (1916) to the Nehru Report (1928): demand for separate electorates 10125
c. Hindu Communalism: the politicization of orthodox Hindus; the Hindu Mahasabha; Pandit M.M. Malaviya, Swami Shraddhananda 10130
6. Gandhi's Resumption of Congress Leadership: the Civil Disobedience Movement - Salt Satyagraha - of 1930 10142
7. Other Major Congress Leaders
a. Jawaharlal Nehru (1889-1964) [see also Chap. Eight, III. D. 2.] 10147
b. Subhas Chandra Bose, 1897-1945 [see also IV. D. 4. 3, below] 10153
c. Vallabhbhai Patel, 1875-1950 10176
d. Abul Kalam Azad, 1888-1958 10192
e. Chakravarti Rajagopalachari, 1879-1972 10197
f. Rajendra Prasad, 1884-1963 [see Chap. Eight, II. E. 2. b. i.]

C. Constitutional Developments, the Government of India Acts of 1919 and 1935: from Dyarchy to Federation

1. General History of Constitutional Changes, 1919-1947 10210
2. The Montagu-Chelmsford ("Montford") Reforms, 1919
a. Edwin S. Montagu, Secretary of State for India, and Lord Chelmsford, Viscount (Frederick John Napier Thesiger), Viceroy 1916-21: biographical studies 10223
b. Government of India Act, 1919: provincial dyarchy with increased Indian representation 10228
c. Lord Reading, 1st Marquess (Rufus Daniel Isaacs), Viceroy 1921-26: the Reforms Enquiry Committee, 1924 (Sir A.P. Muddiman, chm.) 10244
3. The Simon Commission, 1927, to Evaluate the 1919 Reforms, and Plan New Constitution; Widespread Boycotts 10250
4. Lord Irwin, Earl of Halifax (Edward Wood), Viceroy 1926-31: British Offer of Dominion Status, Congress Demand for Pūrṇa Swarāj ("Complete Independence") 10255
5. The Round Table Conference, 1930-32, in London: Federation, Position of Princes, and Communal Questions 10260
6. Lord Willingdon, Marquess of Willingdon (Freeman Freeman-Thomas), Viceroy 1931-36 10269
7. The Government of India Act of 1935: Elections Under the Communal Award, Popular Provincial Ministries, Refusal of Princes to Accede to Federation 10272

IV. D. The End of the Raj: World War II: Partition, Independence and the Integration of the Princely States (1939-1948)

1. General Histories, Studies and Documents 10288
2. Indian Muslims between Nationalism and Separatism
   a. general studies of the period, 1928-1947 10308
   b. origin of the idea of Pakistan, and its realization
      i. Sir Muhammad Iqbal and Rahmat Ali [see also VII. D. 3. and VIII. C. 2. c. below for Iqbal as philosopher and poet] 10320
      ii. documents and sources 10332
      iii. the birth of Pakistan 10339
3. Mahomed Ali Jinnah (1876-1948): Qā᾿id-i-Aᶜẓam ("Great Leader") of the Muslims and Creator of Pakistan
   a. bibliography and reference 10358
   b. Jinnah's writings 10363
   c. biographies and studies 10371
4. Other Muslim Organizations
   a. the Khaksar Movement (1926-46): a militaristic Islamic nationalist group led by Inayat Allah Khan Mashriqi (1888-1963) 10389
   b. Jamᶜīat al-ᶜulamā-i-Hind, a pro-Congress group of Muslim scholars 10392
5. Indian Nationalism During World War II
   a. Lord Linlithgow, Marquess of Linlithgow (Victor Alexander John Hope), Viceroy 1936-43: declared India at war, without consultation; Indian responses 10394
   b. India and the Indian Army in WWII 10398
   c. the Cripps Mission (March-April 1942) to gain Indian support for war effort, backed by U.S. emissary Louis Johnson 10404
   d. Gandhi's "Quit India" ultimatum, arrest of Congress leaders, "Revolt of 1942" and government repression 10413
   e. Azad Hind ("Free India"), est. 1943 under Japanese auspices by Subhas Chandra Bose, and its Indian National Army (INA) 10432
   f. the Sapru Committee (1943-45): attempt to mediate communal and minority conflict 10446
   g. Archibald Percival Wavell, 1st Earl Wavell (Viceroy, Oct. 1943-Mar. 1947) 10448
6. Post-War Constitutional Negotiations: Congress, League and Attlee's Labour Government (elected July 1945)
   a. the Simla Conference (June-July 1945): Jinnah's intransigence prevents agreement on communal representation 10451
   b. the INA trials (1945-46) and the Royal Indian Navy mutiny (Feb. 1946) 10456
   c. the Cabinet Mission (March 1946) to help Indians frame their constitutional future; Jinnah's rejection of the Mission's proposals and his call for Muslim "Direct Action" 10461
   d. the Interim Government headed by J. Nehru (took office Sept. 1946), and the Constituent Assembly (met 29 Jan. 1947) 10467
7. Divide and Quit: Mountbatten's Mission to Transfer Power
   a. Louis Mountbatten, 1st Earl Mountbatten of Burma: last Viceroy and first Governor-General of the Dominion of India, 1947-48 10468
   b. transfer of power and partition: the Independence of India Act, and the Dominions of Pakistan and India, August 14 and 15, 1947 10474
8. Aftermath of Partition
   a. transfer of populations and intercommunal violence among Muslims, Sikhs, and Hindus; resettlement of refugees 10490
   b. economic and political consequences of partition 10511
   c. Mahatma Gandhi's final efforts in behalf of Hindu-Muslim peace 10517
   d. Gandhi's assassination by Chitpavan Brahman, unreconciled to partition and to Gandhi's alleged favoritism to Muslims; the murder trial 10521
   e. the integration of the Princely States into the Dominions of India and Pakistan 10534

V. CHANGING PATTERNS OF SOCIAL AND CULTURAL ORGANIZATION AND COMMUNICATION, 1813-1947

A. Initial British Views of Indian Society and the Question of Interference vs. Cultural Laissez-faire

1. Rationales for Social and Educational Policy: Utilitarian and Evangelical 10537
2. Early Western Accounts of Indian Society 10546

V. B. Education under the Raj: Agency for Westernization and National Identity

1. Bibliography 10547
2. General Histories, Studies and Document Collections 10551
3. Education under the East India Company (1813-1853): Search for an Educational Policy 10568
4. From Wood's Despatch on Education (1854) to the Hunter Commission Report (1882): Beginnings of University Education 10576
5. Expansion and Indianization of Education (1884-1947): Prelude to Independence
    a. general studies and documents 10582
    b. higher education 10590
    c. primary and secondary education 10600
    d. vocational and technical education 10607
    e. adult education and literacy 10612
6. Indian Nationalist Educational Thought and Experiments
    a. the National Education movement (1905-1922) 10615
    b. Rabindranath Tagore and Vishva-Bharati: his experimental institutions of Santiniketan and Sriniketan 10621
    c. Gandhian educational ideas and the Wardha scheme of Basic Education 10630
    d. Muslim educational leaders 10641

C. Science and Technology under the Raj

1. The Introduction and Development of Modern Science in India 10649
2. The Indian Scientific Community
    a. institutions and associations for scientific research, from the founding of the Asiatic Society, Calcutta, 1784 10656
    b. Indian and Western scientists 10661

D. Public Health and Medical Services under the Raj 10673

E. Cities and Urbanization under the Raj 10686

F. Social Welfare and Reform under the Raj

1. General Studies 10693
2. Early British Social Intervention: Collision of Traditional Customs with Christian Morality (up to 1857)
    a. satī/suttee, "a woman who is true," used for the practice of widow-burning (outlawed in 1829) 10708
    b. female infanticide 10716
    c. slavery 10720
3. Efforts to Raise the Status of Women in Indian Society (after 1857)
    a. general 10722
    b. child-marriage, the "age of consent" controversy, and the problem of widow-remarriage 10725
    c. courtesans and temple prostitutes: dancing ("nautch") girls and devadāsīs 10732
    d. pardā/purdah ("curtain"): seclusion of women in the zenānā ("female quarters") 10734
    e. legal status of women - ownership and inheritance of property 10737
    f. women's leaders and organizations: progress towards enfranchisement and equality 10741
4. Stratification and Untouchability: Social and Economic Discrimination on the Basis of Caste
    a. studies of social stratification 10746
    b. general studies of the problems of Untouchables, about one-fifth of all Hindus 10749
    c. early efforts at "elevation of the depressed classes" by missionaries and Indian reformers 10758
    d. Gandhi's work for the "Harijans" ("children of God"): the first All-India movement for abolition of untouchability 10760
    e. Bhimrao Ramji Ambedkar (1892-1956): Mahar economist, lawyer, Constitution framer and Untouchable political leader; his confrontation with Gandhi 10771
5. Later Western Censure of Indian Society in the Name of Reform: "Mother India" (1927) and its Critics 10788

G. Journalism and the Press under the Raj

1. General Histories of the Indian Press, in Western and Regional Languages 10796
2. Biographies and Memoirs of Leading Journalists in India 10822
3. Government and the Press: Freedom of the Press Versus Censorship 10838

VI. ECONOMIC HISTORY OF INDIA IN THE BRITISH PERIOD, 1818-1947

A. Bibliography and Reference 10853

B. Economic History of the Raj

1. General Studies 10857
2. Demography and Population 10879
3. Secular Trends and Structural Changes; National Income 10884

C. Economic Thought: Indian and British Views

1. Surveys of Modern Indian Economic Thought 10900
2. The "Drain Theory," "Aborted Growth," and other Economic Critiques of British Rule 10908
3. British Economic Thought and India Policy 10922

D. The Agrarian Base

1. General Studies of Agricultural Development 10930
2. Land Tenure and Revenue Systems; Beginnings of Land Reform 10943
3. The Indian Village and the Peasantry Under the Raj [See also Chap. One, III. G., and regional chaps. Ten- Sixteen]
   a. general studies of rural conditions 10962
   b. early British views of the "Indian village community" 10966
   c. rural reconstruction: Gandhian and other programs 10977
   d. peasant indebtedness, moneylenders, and the cooperative movement 10983
   e. agricultural laborers 10992
   f. peasant movements and unrest 10996
4. Famine and Famine Policy 11012
5. Water-supply: Irrigation and Flood Control 11025
6. Crops: Field and Plantation; Forestry 11029

E. Transportation and Commerce under the Raj

1. General Studies 11034
2. Indian Railways and Shipping 11040
3. Foreign Economic Relations and Tariffs; Balance of Payments 11056

F. Indian Industry under the Raj

1. Decline of Traditional Handicrafts 11077
2. Origins and Growth of India's Modern Industry 11084
3. The Indian Business Community
   a. indigenous business groups: transformation to industrial entrepreneurship 11092
   b. businessmen, firms and the managing agency system 11094
4. Studies of Specific Industries 11106
5. The Industrial Worker in India
   a. general studies 11111
   b. the trade union movement and its leaders 11127
   c. labor policy and legislation 11141

G. Government Economic Policy, Investment, and Currency

1. Public Finance and Taxation 11148
2. Banking and Monetary Policy; the Reserve Bank of India 11163
3. Public and Private Investment 11183
4. The Beginnings of National Economic Planning 11192

VII. SOCIO-RELIGIOUS REVIVAL AND REFORM, 1818-1947: NATIONAL AND TRANSREGIONAL LEADERS AND MOVEMENTS

A. General Studies of Social and Religious Change 11199

B. Hindu Response to British Culture and Reforms

1. General Studies of the "Hindu Renaissance" 11219
2. Ram Mohan Roy and the Brāhmo Samāj: an Ethical Hinduism Purified of Idolatry and Other "Abuses"
   a. Rājā Rām Mohan Roy (1772?-1833):
      i. works 11228
      ii. biographies and studies 11233
   b. the Brāhmo Samaj (est. 1828 as Brāhma Sabhā): Ram Mohan's religious organization 11248
   c. the later Brāhmo Samāj: leaders and factions, the turn to social and political activity 11251
3. The Dev Samāj of Satyānand Agnihotri, 1850-1929: Offshoot of the Brāhmo Samāj in North India 11263
4. Swami Dayānand and the Āryā Samāj: Revival of the Vedas in the Service of Social and Religious Reform
   a. Swami Dayānand Saraswatī (1824-1883): Gujarati Brahman, from sannyāsi to social reformer

VII. B. 4. a. i. works 11269
ii. biographies and studies 11276
b. the Āryā Samāj (est. 1875): movement for change in Panjab and North India, stimulated by the Brāhmos and in reaction to Christian missionaries 11286
5. Śrī Rāmakrishna and his Disciples: Vedānta for the Modern World
a. Rāmakrishna Paramahaṁsa (1834-1886): from Bengali Kālī Bhakta to Advaita Vedāntin 11294
b. Swami Vivekānanda (1863-1902): Bengali apostle to India and the West, founder of Rāmakrishna Mission and Vedānta Societies
i. works and sources 11313
ii. biographies and studies 11318
c. Sister Niveditā (Margaret Noble, 1867-1911): British disciple of Swami Vivekānanda 11338
d. the Rāmakrishna movement: modern missionaries of Indic culture and social service 11344
6. The Theosophical Society (est. 1875): Amalgam of Westernized Sanskritic Hinduism and Occultism
a. general histories and studies of the Theosophical Movement in India 11353
b. Annie Besant (1847-1933) and Theosophical involvement in politics and social problems 11360
7. Sri Aurobindo (Aravinda Ghose, 1872-1950): from England-Returned Intellectual to Bengali Extremist to Mystic-Philosopher and Super-Man
a. bibliography and reference 11367
b. writings of Sri Aurobindo 11374
c. studies of Sri Aurobindo and his philosophy of Integral Yoga 11376
d. The Mother/La Mère: Aurobindo's French Śakti and successor at the Pondicherry Ashram 11400
8. Ramana Mahārṣi (1879-1950): Jīvanmukta, Living Exemplar of Advaitic Self-Realization in Modern Tamilnadu 11405
9. Swāmī Śivānanda Sarasvatī (1887-1963): Vedāntin and Ayurvedic physician, Founder of the Divine Life Society 11419
10. Academic Philosophers: Blending of Hindu Tradition and Western Scholarship
a. general studies 11425
b. Sir Sarvepalli Rādhākrishnan (1888-1975): Interpreter of Hindu Philosophy to the World 11432

C. Islam and the Muslims under the Raj: Crisis of Belief and Identity (1818-1947)

1. Pre-Mutiny Muslim Revivalist Movements: Attempts to Restore Islamic Orthodoxy and Muslim Rule
a. Sayyid Ahmad of Rae Bareli (1786-1831): adaptation of Arabian Wahhabism to the tradition of Shāh Walī Allāh 11443
b. the Farā᾽idī Movement [see Chap. Fifteen, I. E. 3.]
2. Post-Mutiny Islamic Modernists: Accommodation to Secular British Rule and Western Science and Culture
a. general studies 11447
b. Sir Sayyid Ahmad Khan (1817-98): modernizing theologian and educator in opposition to the orthodox ʿulamā 11466
c. the Muhammadan Anglo-Oriental College (after 1920, Aligarh Muslim Univ.), founded 1875 by Sayyid Ahmad Khan, and the Aligarh Movement 11475
3. ʿAllāma Dr. Muḥammad Iqbāl (1877-1938): Foremost Philosophical Thinker of Modern Islam in South Asia, between Fundamentalism and Westernism
a. bibliography 11482
b. religious and philosophical writings of Iqbal 11487
c. studies of Iqbal's religio-philosophical ideas 11495
4. Islamic Conservatism in Modern India: the Network of Madrasas (religious schools) centred on Deoband, U.P. 11516
5. Mirzā Ghulām Aḥmad of Qādiyan, Punjab (1835-1908) and the Aḥmadīyah Movement: Progressive, Heterodox Interpretation of Islam 11518

D. Christianity under the Raj (1813-1947): from Foreign Missionary Dominance to Indianization

1. General Histories and Studies of Churches and Missions 11528
2. Major Church Leaders: Biographies and Studies 11540
3. Christianity and Hinduism: Mutual Views and Interactions 11555
4. Christians in Social Welfare and Reform 11564

VIII. MODERN LITERATURES UNDER THE RAJ: GENERAL STUDIES AND LITERATURES IN TRANSREGIONAL LANGUAGES (HINDI, URDU, AND ENGLISH), 1800-1947

A. General Surveys and Studies

1. Studies of Modern Indian Literatures 11567

VIII. A. 2. Collections and Anthologies 11581

B. Hindi Literature under the Raj

1. Bibliography and General Studies of the Development of Modern Hindi and its Literature 11584
2. The Making of Modern Hindi, Based on North Indian Dialects: Developed as Administrative Language by Fort William College and Serampore Mission 11593
3. Hariścandra (1850-85), Called Bhāratendu ("Moon of India"): Journalist, Dramatist and Poet from Benares 11598
4. Premchand, pseud. of Dhanpat Rai Srivastava (1880-1936): Pioneer Urdu and Hindi Novelist and Short Story Writer
   a. biographies and studies 11600
   b. translations of Premchand's works 11609
5. Twentieth Century Hindi Poetry: Mystic-Romanticism (Chayavad), Nationalism and Progressivism 11615
6. Other Major Hindi Writers of Fiction, Drama, and Poetry - Studies and Translations 11625

C. Urdu Literature under the Raj

1. General Studies of Modern Urdu Literature 11631
2. Urdu Poetry: the Ghazal and Other Forms
   a. general studies 11634
   b. Mirzā Asadullāh Khān Ghālib (1797-1869): poet and letter-writer in Persian and Urdu
      i. bibliography 11642
      ii. works in translation 11643
      iii. biographies and studies 11649
   c. Sir Muḥammad Iqbāl (1877-1938): Urdu and Persian poet [for his role in politics and philosophy see above IV. D. 2. b. i. and VII. D. 3.]
      i. works in translation 11672
      ii. critical studies 11678
   d. modernist and nationalist poets 11692
3. Modern Urdu Prose: Development of the Novel and Short Story
   a. Urdu fiction in translation 11695
   b. studies of Urdu fiction 11697

D. English Literature by South Asian Writers (to 1947) [See also Chap. Eight, X. C. 5.]

1. Bibliography 11703
2. General Studies of Indo-Anglian Literature 11710
3. Indo-English Fiction: Novels and Short Stories 11726
4. Indo-Anglian Poetry and Drama
   a. general studies and anthologies 11743
   b. early imitative Indo-English poetry from the Bengal Renaissance 11762
   c. poetry of Hindu and nationalist inspiration 11770

IX. ART AND ARCHITECTURE UNDER THE RAJ

A. General Studies 11781

B. Painting

1. General 11788
2. "Company Painting," by Indian Artists for British Patrons 11792
3. "Bazaar" Painting of Calcutta 11794
4. Modern Painting of India (1808-1930)
   a. the Bengal school 11800
   b. Amrita Sher-Gil (1913-1941): confluence of Western and Indian styles 11821
   c. leading painters of other schools 11825

C. Architecture: Uniformity of Style through Hybridization of European and Indian Elements 11830

X. INDIA AND THE WEST: MUTUAL ENCOUNTERS DURING THE PERIOD OF BRITISH RULE

A. Orientalism: The Western Discovery of India's Great Tradition

1. General Studies 11836
2. Sir William Jones (1746-1794), Founder of the Asiatic Society of Bengal in 1786 11847
3. Friedrich Max Müller (1823-1900), Editor of Sacred Books of the East 11852
4. Ananda Kentish Coomaraswamy (1877-1947): Anglo-Ceylonese Apostle of Indian Art and Culture 11854

X. B. Indian Inspiration in Western Philosophy and Literature 11858

C. The Indian Discovery of the West: Travellers to Europe and America 11870

D. Images of India in Western Fiction [individual works of fiction not included]

1. General Studies and Reference Works 11875
2. Flora Annie Steel (1847-1929) 11891
3. Rudyard Kipling (1865-1936): "Voice of Anglo-India"
   a. bibliographies and collections 11893
   b. biographies and studies 11898
4. E.M. Forster (1879-1970): Symbolic Interpretations of India and Anglo-India 11909
5. Other Significant Writers 11923

E. The European Experience in India under the Raj

1. Journals and Reminiscences of Residents and Travellers 11930
2. Sahibs and Memsahibs: British Life in India
   a. general studies 11949
   b. the hill-station: retreat from the tropics, and islands of British social life 11960
   c. British artists of the Indian scene 11974

CHAPTER SEVEN: THE PRESENT-DAY SOUTH ASIAN SUBCONTINENT IN ITS GLOBAL CONTEXT, 1947-

I. BIBLIOGRAPHY AND REFERENCE 11982

II. THE INDIAN OCEAN AREA: ITS GEOPOLITICAL AND ECONOMIC SIGNIFICANCE 11986

III. THE SOUTH ASIAN NATIONS IN WORLD POLITICS

A. General 12012

B. China and the Subcontinent 12031

C. USSR and the Subcontinent 12043

D. USA and the Subcontinent 12051

IV. RELATIONS AMONG THE SOUTH ASIAN NATIONS

A. General Studies 12059

B. India-Pakistan Relations

1. General Studies 12066
2. The Kashmir Conflict over Accession to India (October 1947)
   a. documents of India, Pakistan and the United Nations 12077
   b. studies of the Kashmir conflict 12084
3. The 1965 Indo-Pakistan War, UN Ceasefire Resolution, and the Tashkent Accord (January 1966) 12100
4. The Breakup of Pakistan, the Birth of Bangladesh, and the Indo-Pak War of 1971
   a. reference works and document collections 12113
   b. general studies of the Bangladesh liberation movement and its international context 12120
   c. Pakistan Army repression and genocide in East Bengal, and the exodus of 6,000,000 refugees to India 12138
   d. Indian intervention and the 1971 war 12158
   e. the Simla Agreement of 1972, and its aftermath 12184
5. India-Pakistan-Bangladesh Relations after 1972: Normalization? 12191

C. Sri Lankan Relations with other South Asian States 12199

V. POLITICS AND GOVERNMENT: SUBCONTINENTAL AND COMPARATIVE STUDIES 12203

VI. ECONOMIC INSTITUTIONS AND DEVELOPMENT - SUBCONTINENTAL AND COMPARATIVE STUDIES

A. General Studies 12231

B. Economic Resources

1. General Studies 12238

2. Water Resources: Dispute over Use of Indus and Ganga Rivers 12239

VI. C. Economic Development and International Economic Cooperation 12247

VII. SOCIAL CHANGE AND DEVELOPMENT 12265

CHAPTER EIGHT: INDIA AS NATION-STATE: THE CHALLENGE OF DEVELOPMENT IN THE WORLD'S LARGEST DEMOCRACY, 1947-

I. THE DOMINION OF INDIA, 1947-1950: TRANSITION FROM EMPIRE TO REPUBLIC WITHIN THE COMMONWEALTH [See also Chap. Six. IV. D. 7]

A. General Studies and Document Collections 12270

B. The Constituent Assembly, 1946-1950 12274

II. THE REPUBLIC OF INDIA, 1950-: POLITICAL SYSTEM AND INSTITUTIONS

A. Bibliography and Reference

1. Bibliography 12286
2. The Study of Indian Politics, and Political Science in India - Trends and Methodology 12294

B. General Studies of India's Political System 12300

C. The Constitution of India, Adopted 26 January 1950

1. Texts of the Constitution 12319
2. Commentaries on the Constitution 12320
3. Studies of the Constitution, Constitutional Law, and Constitutional History 12326
4. Central Provisions of the Constitution
   a. fundamental rights 12350
   b. directive principles of state policy 12368
   c. emergency provisions, incl.President's Rule in the States 12373
   d. amendment procedures 12380

D. Indian Democracy and the Problems of National Integration

1. General Studies 12386
2. Secularism as the Answer to Religious Conflict
   a. general studies of India as a secular state; freedom of religion 12411
   b. survivals of communalism in Indian political life 12435
   c. the Indian Muslim community - political expectations 12445
   d. bans on cow-slaughter: collision of Hindu and Muslim values 12460
3. Regionalism and Language Problems
   a. general studies of India's language problems 12469
   b. the official language: continued use of English, or Hindi only? 12485
   c. linguism: cultural-linguistic regionalism as the basis of political units 12504
4. Indian Federalism: Division of Powers between the Union and the States
   a. general studies 12516
   b. the process of states reorganization: consolidation and rationalization on cultural-linguistic lines 12532
   c. the Princes as pensioners of the Republic; the privy purses and their final abolition in 1971 12538

E. The Union Executive

1. General Studies - the Central Policy-making Offices 12546
2. The President and Vice-President
   a. the offices: their powers and functions 12552
   b. India's Rashtrapatis: documents, biographies, and studies of the Presidents
      i. Rajendra Prasad (1884-1963), Pres. 1950-62 12565
      ii. Sarvepalli Radhakrishnan (1888-1975), Pres. 1962-67 12575
      iii. Zakir Husain (1897-1969), Pres. 1967-69 12580
      iv. V.V. Giri (1894-1980), Pres. 1969-74 12587
      v. Fakhruddin Ali Ahmed (1905-1977), Pres. 1974-77 12591
      vi. N. Sanjeeva Reddy (1913-), Pres. 1977-
3. The Prime Minister and the Council of Ministers (the Cabinet and Ministers of State) [for indiv. PM's see III. D., below] 12593
4. The Attorney-General for India: a Separate Office Co-equal with the Council of Ministers 12601
5. Public Administration and the Bureaucracy
   a. bibliography and reference 12602
   b. general studies of Indian administration 12606

II. E. 5. c. the All-India Services (Administrative, Police, Forest, Medical and Health) and other public services
- i. general studies 12627
- ii. the Public Service Commissions, recruitment and training 12640
- iii. the Indian bureaucrat - sociological studies of background and behavior 12648
- iv. personal accounts and biographies of public servants 12657

d. administrative problems, corruption, reform
- i. general studies of corruption; the Santhanam Committee Report, 1964 12670
- ii. commissions of inquiry and advisory committees 12682
- iii. the Administrative Reforms Commission (1966-69) and other efforts at reform 12682
- iv. the citizen vs. the bureaucracy; proposals for a Lokpal and Lokayukta ("people's protector, advocate") or ombudsman 12691

e. police administration and operations; paramilitary forces 12700

6. The Armed Forces of Independent India: Generals and Jawans
   - a. general studies in military history and administration 12717
   - b. the military and society 12730
   - c. memoirs and biographies of "old soldiers" 12735
7. The Indian Foreign Service
   - a. studies of Foreign Service administration 12744
   - b. memoirs and biographies of India's diplomats 12749

F. Parliament

1. General Studies of India's Parliament 12762
2. The Rajya Sabha (Council of States) 12774
3. The Lok Sabha (House of the People) 12778
4. Parliamentary Procedure 12783
5. MP's and Parliamentary Privileges; Who's Whos and Biographies 12787
6. Committees and Parliamentary Control of Finance and Administration 12799

G. The Union Judiciary and the Legal System

1. Bibliography 12814
2. General Studies of the Indian Judiciary 12816
3. The Supreme Court
   - a. general studies and reference 12821
   - b. Justices of the Supreme Court - studies and biographies 12835
4. Judicial Review, and Relations of the Judiciary with Other Branches 12845
5. The Indian Legal System 12851
6. The Indian Legal Profession - Studies and Biographies of Lawyers and Judges 12865

H. The 22 States and the 9 Union Territories [for individual States and Territories, see Chapters Ten-Sixteen]

1. General Studies of State Government and Administration 12876
2. The Office of the State Governor 12883
3. The State Legislature and the Chief Minister 12892
4. The High Courts and State Judiciaries 12898
5. The Union Territories, under Presidentially-Appointed Administrators 12904
6. Inter-governmental Relations in India
   - a. bibliography and general studies 12907
   - b. centre-state relations 12912
   - c. inter-state relations, incl. boundary and water disputes 12925

J. Local Government: District, Municipal, Village

1. General Studies 12938
2. District Administration 12947
3. Municipal Administration 12961
4. Panchayati Raj: Democratic Decentralization for Self-Government and Community Development
   - a. bibliography and reference 12980
   - b. reports from the Government and the Indian National Congress 12982
   - c. general studies of gram panchayats (village councils) and Panchayati Raj 12989
   - d. nyaya panchayats ("judicial councils"): village-level courts 13005

III. THE INDIAN POLITICAL PROCESS, 1947-: PARTIES, ELECTIONS, LEADERS

A. Bibliography and Reference 13007

III. B. General Studies

1. General History of Indian Politics since Independence 13009
2. Politics and Society
    a. general studies of political culture and participation 13037
    b. political elites and leadership 13060
    c. caste and Indian politics 13072
    d. political protest and violence
        i. general 13083
        ii. student political unrest 13093
3. Journalistic Accounts of Indian Politics 13105
4. Political Cartoons and Satire 13114

C. Political Parties, Movements, and Ideologies

1. Bibliography and Reference 13124
2. General Studies of the Party System - at the All-India Level
    a. the working of the party system 13126
    b. party ideologies - general and comparative studies 13141
3. The Indian National Congress (est. 1885) after Independence
    a. general studies of the Congress Party 13151
    b. INC organization 13159
    c. Congress programme and ideology: "a socialistic pattern of society" 13164
4. Socialism and the Socialist Parties: Successors to the Congress Socialist Party after 1948
    a. general studies of socialism in India 13171
    b. the Socialist parties 13179
    c. Socialist leaders: biographies, studies and writings
        i. Rammanohar Lohia (1910-1967) 13186
        ii. other socialist leaders 13192
5. The Communist Parties of India after Independence
    a. general studies of Indian Communism 13198
    b. the Communist Party of India (CPI, est. 1925): Soviet-oriented, ally of Congress after 1970 13218
    c. The Communist Party of India (Marxist): Peking-oriented up to 1964 split, later independent 13223
    d. the Naxalbari (W. Bengal) peasant uprising, 1967: Maoist revolutionary violence 13235
    e. the Communist Party of India (Marxist-Leninist): Naxalite split from CPI (M) in 1969 13246
6. Communal (Religio-centric) Parties and Supporting Groups
    a. general studies of Hindu communal political groups 13253
    b. Akhil Bharat ("All-India") Hindu Mahasabha (est. 1915) and its ideologue, Veer Savarkar (1883-1966) [see also Chap. Six IV. B. 5. c.] 13258
    c. Bharatiya Jana Sangh ("Indian Peoples Party," est. 1951) 13265
    d. the Rashtriya Swayamsevak Sangh ("National Volunteer Organization," est. 1925): not a party, but a self-styled "cultural organization" with great political influence 13279
    e. the Indian Union Muslim League and other Muslim political groups 13290
    f. the Shiromani Akali Dal (est. 1920): Sikh Communal party 13295
7. The Swatantra Party (est. 1959): Voice of Economic Conservatism and the Private Sector 13298
8. The Republican Party of India (est. 1957): Heir to Dr. B.R. Ambedkar's Movement of Former Untouchables 13301
9. The Heritage of Gandhism 13304

D. Politics at the Centre: Elections, Prime Ministers and their Administrations

1. The Indian Electoral System
    a. bibliography and reference 13316
    b. election law and procedures 13323
    c. general studies of India's national elections 13332
2. Pandit Jawaharlal Nehru (1889-1964): India's First Prime Minister, 1947-64
    a. bibliography 13348
    b. Nehru's writings and speeches 13349
    c. biographical studies 13353
    d. political studies of Nehru's thought and administration 13362
    e. Panditji's legacy and the problem of succession 13375
3. India's Elections During the Nehru Years
    a. 1952: the first election under universal franchise 13380
    b. 1957 election: Communist victory in Kerala challenges Congress monopoly 13385
    c. 1962: India's third Lok Sabha election 13388
4. Lal Bahadur Shastri (1904-1966): Prime-Minister, 1964-66
    a. writings and speeches 13399
    b. biographies and studies 13402
5. Indira Nehru Gandhi (1917-): Prime Minister, 1966-77, 1980-
    a. bibliography 13409
    b. writings and speeches 13410
    c. biographies and studies 13413

III. D. 6. Indira vs. the Congress Organization, 1966-75
a. the 1967 Lok Sabha elections: post-Nehru surfacing of ideological differences 13430
b. the 1969 Presidential election of V.V. Giri over N. Sanjeeva Reddy: conflict of P.M. and Congress "Syndicate" 13446
c. the Congress split, Nov. 1969, into Cong (R), the "ruling" Congress headed by Smt. Gandhi, and Cong (O), the "organisation" Congress headed by Morarji Desai 13449
d. the fifth Lok Sabha elections 1971: Indira's populist appeal for socio-economic reform, Garibi Hatao! ("Abolish Poverty") 13455
e. the "Indira Wave" (1971-73): triumph in elections and in Bangladesh 13466
f. Jayaprakash Narayan's call for "total revolution" (the J.P. Movement): focus of growing socioeconomic unrest and opposition to Indira
i. J.P.'s writings and speeches 13470
ii. biographies and political studies 13478
g. the High Court's conviction of the P.M. for 1971 election law violations 13492
7. The Emergency (25 June 1975 to 20 March 1977)
a. why emergency? rationales for and against 13495
b. the 20-Point Economic Programme 13510
c. Fundamental Rights and the debate over constitutional amendment
i. general studies of Emergency and the Constitution 13517
ii. 42nd Amendment: attempt to institutionalize and perpetuate emergency rule - passed 18 December 1976, repealed 28 March 1977 13522
iii. detention under Emergency provision, and accounts by detenus 13527
d. Indira vs. the press; censorship and the underground journals 13538
e. the National Population Policy (April 1976) and charges of "Forced sterlilization" [see also V. B. 5. a., below] 13544
f. Sanjay Gandhi (1946-1980), the P.M.'s son, and his Youth Congress 13546
g. the Sixth Lok Sabha elections, 1977, one year later than scheduled
i. general studies and election results 13550
ii. manifestoes of the contesting parties 13560
h. the Shah Commission of Inquiry, and other investigations into abuses during the Emergency 13565
j. overall assessments of the Emergency and "Indira Raj" 13576
8. The Janata Party in Power (March 1977 to August 1979): Coalition of Indira's Opposition Led by Jayaprakash Narayan
a. general studies of Janata and its administration 13605
b. Morarji Ranchodji Desai (1896-   ): Prime Minister, 1977-1979 13621
9. Charan Singh (1899-   ) P.M. Aug. 1979-Jan. 1980, the Defeat of Janata, and the 1980 Mid-Term Election of the Seventh Lok Sabha 13626
10. The Return to Power of Indira Gandhi (Jan. 1980-   ) 13636
11. Other Recent Contenders for the Prime Ministership 13640

E. State and Local Politics, 1947- [see also Regional Chaps. Ten-Sixteen]

1. General Studies of State Politics 13651
2. Politics at the Local Level: District, Municipal, Village
a. urban politics 13667
b. politics of panchayati raj and rural leadership 13673

IV. INDIA'S INTERNATIONAL RELATIONS, 1947- [for relations within the subcontinent see Chap. Seven]

A. General

1. Bibliography, Reference and Document Collections 13683
2. General Studies of India's Foreign Policy 13691
3. Political Parties and India's Foreign Policy 13716
4. Epochs of India's Foreign Policy
a. the Nehru Years, 1947-64
i. general studies 13726
ii. the Asian Relations Conference (1947) and the Bandung Asian-African Conference (1955) and its Five Principles (Panchasheel) 13737
b. Lal Bahadur Shastri's foreign policy, 1964-66 13741
c. Indira Gandhi's foreign policy, 1966-77 13742
d. the Janata Party's foreign policy, 1977-79 13744
5. Neutralism and Nonalignment: Continuation of Nehru's Major Foreign Policy Principles 13748

IV. B. India's Security and Defense

1. General Studies 13759
2. Nuclear Weapons Policy, before and after India's First Nuclear Explosion (18 May 1974) at Pokharan, Rajasthan 13772
3. Indian Attitudes towards the Non-Proliferation Treaty and Arms Control 13787

C. India in the World Economy

1. Foreign Exchange and Balance of Payments
   a. general 13794
   b. the rupee: devaluation in 1949 and 1966, and delinking from sterling in 1975 13804
2. India's Foreign Trade
   a. bibliography, reference, and statistics 13813
   b. general studies of India's foreign trade 13819
   c. imports and tariff policy 13831
   d. India's exports and export markets 13840
3. Foreign Aid and Investment
   a. bibliography, reference, and statistics 13855
   b. general studies of foreign investment (public and private) 13858
   c. foreign aid 13865
   d. private foreign investment
      i. general 13879
      ii. the role of multinational corporations 13893

D. India's Relations with Specific Countries and Areas

1. General Studies (multilateral) 13901
2. China-India Relations
   a. general studies 13908
   b. Sino-Indian border disputes and the 1962 War
      i. documents 13916
      ii. general studies of the Sino-Indian border dispute 13923
      iii. India, China and the problem of Tibet 13938
      iv. the 1962 War in Ladakh and NEFA: Indian military debacle 13942
3. USSR-India Relations
   a. bibliography 13960
   b. general studies of Indo-Soviet relations 13962
   c. Soviet policy towards India - perceptions and strategies 13978
   d. the 1971 Indo-Soviet Treaty of Peace, Friendship, and Cooperation: alliance without alignment? 13987
   e. Indo-Soviet economic relations 13994
4. United States-India Relations
   a. general studies 14003
   b. memoirs of U.S. and Indian diplomats 14017
   c. major issues of U.S. - India relations 14025
   d. U.S. - India economic relations - trade and general studies 14033
   e. U.S. economic assistance to India
      i. general studies: Point Four (1950), Technical Cooperation Mission (1952) and other development programs 14036
      ii. PL 480: sale of U.S. surplus agricultural commodities for rupees 14046
      iii. private foreign assistance through foundations and voluntary agencies 14054
5. United Kingdom-India Relations since Independence 14056
6. India in the British Commonwealth and Relations with Commonwealth Nations 14063
7. India and Europe
   a. the European Economic Community (Common Market) 14070
   b. the Comecon Nations of Eastern Europe 14080
8. India and the Middle East 14085
9. India and Southeast Asia 14093
10. Japan-India Relations 14102
11. India's Relations with Latin America and Africa 14105
12. India in the United Nations 14109

V. PLANNING FOR INDIA'S DEVELOPMENT: STRUCTURE AND INSTITUTIONS OF THE ECONOMY

A. Bibliography and Reference

1. Bibliographies and Reference Works 14122
2. The State of Economic Research on India: Trends and Methodology 14128

B. Demography and Population Policy (1981 pop. 683,810,051)

1. Bibliography, Statistics; Status of Population Studies 14132
2. General Studies of India's Population; Population and Economic Development 14141

V. B. 3. Distribution and Composition of the Population: Sex Ratio, Regional Differences, and Migration 14161
4. Studies of Fertility and Mortality in India 14173
5. Population Policy and Control [see also VIII. G. 4., below] 14183

C. Economic Geography and Natural Resources 14194

D. Output, Income, and Standards of Living

1. National Product and National Income: Estimates and Studies 14203
2. Income Distribution and Standard of Living 14212
3. Regional and State Differences in Income and Living Levels 14221

E. Economic Development and the Planning Process

1. Economic History of India since Independence 14228
2. Economic Growth and Development
a. general studies 14241
b. essay collections 14255
c. models and projections of economic growth 14264
d. comparisons with other developing nations 14272
e. poverty and the social context of development 14277
3. Economic Philosophies and Ideologies of India after 1947
a. general studies 14286
b. Gandhian economic thought - Sarvodaya ("uplift of all"): utopian vision or viable alternative? [for Bhoodan and Gramdan see VI. D. 3. c., below]
i. general studies 14292
ii. Acharya Vinoba Bhave, leading exponent and practitioner of Gandhian economics 14312
c. "socialistic pattern of society" advocated by the Indian National Congress, and other socialists 14323
d. economic ideas of Indian Marxists 14335
e. economic conservatism: advocates of free enterprise and the private sector 14340
4. Traditional Values in Economic Modernization: the Weber Thesis and other Interpretations 14347
5. Indian Planning: Process and Experience
a. general studies 14368
b. essay collections on planning 14389
c. the machinery of planning: the Planning Commission and the bureaucracy 14400
d. the Five-Year Plans - documents and studies
i. general studies of the Plans, their implementation and results 14416
ii. the First Five-Year Plan, 1951-55 14423
iii. the Second Five-Year Plan, 1956-60 14431
iv. the Third Five-Year Plan, 1961-65 14436
v. the "Plan Holiday," 1966-8: three annual plans during reconstitution of the Planning Commission 14448
vi. the Fourth Five-Year Plan, 1969-74 14452
vii. the Fifth Five-year Plan, 1974-78 14461
viii. the Draft Five-Year Plan, 1978-83: the Sixth Plan in the making 14466
e. subnational aspects of planning in India: zones, regions, states, and districts
i. regional development and planning 14471
ii. planning at the state and district levels 14483

F. India's Financial and Monetary System Since 1947

1. General Studies 14489
2. Public Finance
a. general studies 14497
b. finances of the Central Government 14509
c. Centre-state financial relations
i. general studies 14521
ii. the Finance Commissions, established by the Constitution to allocate certain taxes between Centre and states 14531
d. state finance 14551
e. local and municipal finance 14557
3. Taxation and Tax Reform in India Since 1947
a. documents 14563
b. general studies of Indian taxation 14571
c. agricultural taxation 14589
d. state and local taxation in India 14597
e. tax avoidance and evasion 14602
4. Banking and Monetary Policy, and other Financial Institutions
a. general studies 14610
b. the Reserve Bank of India (est. 1935), India's central bank, and its monetary management 14623
c. prices and inflation 14642
d. development banking and industrial finance 14656

V. F. 4. e. commercial banking
i. general studies 14662
ii. nationalization of banks, 1969 14670
f. indigenous financial agencies 14681
g. savings and capital formation
i. general studies 14683
ii. India's capital markets 14691

G. The Cooperative Movement in India Since Independence [for rural cooperatives see VI. E. 5., below]

1. Bibliography and Reference 14700
2. General Studies 14702
3. Cooperative Banks, and Credit in the Non-Agricultural Sector 14717

VI. RECONSTRUCTING RURAL INDIA: AGRICULTURAL DEVELOPMENT AND SOCIAL CHANGE SINCE 1947

A. Bibliography and Reference

1. Bibliographies and Atlases 14723
2. Statistical Collections and Guides to Statistics 14734
3. Research in Indian Agriculture - Surveys and Reviews 14737

B. Agricultural Development through Planning

1. Indian Agriculture and its Problems - Descriptive Studies 14743
2. Agricultural Development
a. general studies 14757
b. the "Green Revolution," beginning 1965 with the use of high-yielding varieties (HYV's) 14771
3. Agricultural Planning
a. strategies and administration 14782
b. the Intensive Agricultural Districts Programme (IADP) 14797
c. food policy and supply
i. general studies 14806
ii. the Food Corporation of India and government marketing 14819
iii. famines and famine policy 14826
d. agricultural price policy 14831
4. Agricultural Technology and Innovation
a. modernization and its effects - general studies 14842
b. innovation and the peasant 14845
c. high-yielding varieties and other seed programs 14858
d. fertilizers 14866
e. mechanization of agriculture 14871
f. irrigation and water management
i. general studies 14874
ii. irrigation policies and projects 14888
iii. land reclamation and colonization 14895

C. The Land and its Agricultural Products

1. Land Use and Crops - general studies 14897
2. Food and Commercial Crops 14904
3. Forestry 14917
4. Animal Husbandry, Fishing, and Wildlife 14924

D. Land Tenure and Reform Since Independence

1. Bibliographies and Reviews of Research 14946
2. General Studies of Land Tenure and Agrarian Relations 14950
3. Land Reform by Legislation, Persuasion and Direct Action
a. documents 14963
b. studies of land reform and land reform legislation, enacted by the states under Central guidance 14971
c. Bhoodan ("land-gift"), and Gramdan ("village-gift"): Gandhian reform from below through moral persuasion, led by Vinoba Bhave 14986

E. Peasant Society and Rural Social Change

1. Bibliography 14998
2. The Indian Village in an Era of Planned Social Change - General Studies 15001
3. Planning for Rural India: from Community Development to Integrated Rural Development
a. The Community Development Programme (est. 1952)
i. bibliography 15017
ii. studies 15018
iii. collections of essays and case studies 15034
b. Community Development and local government: dual control by bureaucracy and elected panchayats
i. panchayati raj - agency for integrated development? 15044

VI. E. 3. b. ii. district, block, and village level development administration 15050
c. communication and education in rural development 15058
d. rural electrification 15071
4. Rural Labor in India
a. the Agricultural Labour Enquiry, and other government reports 15075
b. general studies of rural labor 15083
c. bonded labor 15100
5. Rural Financial Institutions, Credit, and Cooperatives
a. rural credit - general studies 15103
b. banking in the rural economy 15118
c. rural credit cooperatives 15129
d. other cooperative institutions and general studies of rural cooperation 15138
e. small and marginal farmers - special problems 15147
6. Rural Industrialization; Khadi (Handloom) and other Cottage Industries 15151
7. Rural Settlements and Housing 15165

VII. INDIAN INDUSTRY, COMMERCE, AND LABOR SINCE 1947

A. Industry and Industrialization

1. Bibliography and Reference 15171
2. General Studies of Indian Industry and its Development 15175
3. Industrial Geography and Interstate Differences 15192
4. Industrial Policy and Planning
a. documents 15198
b. studies 15201
5. The Public Sector: Government Ownership of Key Industries and Services
a. bibliography and reference 15207
b. documents 15212
c. general studies of the public sector 15217
d. management and control of public enterprises 15230
e. financing of public sector undertakings 15245
6. The Joint Sector: Mixed Participation of Public and Private Firms 15251
7. The Private Sector
a. general studies of private business and its management 15255
b. private economic power and its social control
i. problems of economic concentration and monopolies 15266
ii. the Managing Agency system and its abolition in 1970 15277
iii. government regulation and licensing of business 15283
c. business communities of independent India
i. Indian entrepreneurs and managers - social and economic studies 15289
ii. studies of individuals or groups important in transregional business 15302
iii. business organizations 15310
iv. Indian politics and business 15314
8. Small Industries and Industrial Cooperatives
a. general studies of modern small-scale industry (non-cottage) 15319
b. industrial estates: government-supported areas for facilitating industrial enterprises 15335
c. industrial cooperatives 15341
9. Studies of Specific Industries
a. mining and mineral resources - general studies 15346
b. energy resources and production
i. surveys of energy resources and demand 15351
ii. energy policy 15357
iii. coal resources and production 15363
iv. petroleum resources and production 15365
v. atomic energy development 15369
vi. new energy alternatives: bio-gas (gobar), solar, and geothermal power 15375
c. iron and steel industry 15382
d. the textile industry 15391
e. tourism 15397
f. other Indian industries 15405

B. India's Transport and Communication System

1. General Studies 15415
2. Railways 15423
3. Road Transport 15431
4. Urban Mass Transit 15438
5. Water Transport: Inland and Maritime Shipping 15444
6. Air Transport 15448
7. Posts and Telecommunications 15455

VII. C. India's Internal Commerce

1. Commercial Policy and General Studies 15460
2. Marketing and Distribution; the State Trading Corporation 15464
3. Interstate Trade 15473
4. The Indian Consumer 15474

D. Labor in the Indian Economy since 1947

1. Bibliography and Reference 15483
2. The Labor Market
   a. general studies of employment and unemployment 15492
   b. educted manpower and unemployment 15512
   c. the "brain drain" 15525
   d. women in the labor force 15531
3. Labor and Manpower Policy 15548
4. Labor Legislation 15569
5. Wages, Wage Policy, and Productivity
   a. wage determination and productivity 15576
   b. wage policy 15586
6. The Indian Industrial Worker
   a. general studies 15593
   b. problems of recruitment, commitment, and absenteeism 15604
7. Industrial Relations
   a. general studies 15613
   b. personnel management and policies 15624
   c. workers' participation in management: towards industrial democracy 15631
   d. the trade union movement: All-India Trade Union Congress, Indian National Trade Union Congress, and other unions
      i. general studies of the labor movement 15640
      ii. the Indian labor leadership 15652
      iii. the Gandhian approach to labor relations 15655
   e. labor disputes and collective bargaining; strikes, lockouts and gheraos ("surrounding" an employer to enforce demands) 15658
   f. trade unions and politics 15667

VIII. CONTEMPORARY INDIAN SOCIETY: STRUCTURE AND CHANGE SINCE 1947

A. The Study of Indian Society: Sources and Trends in the Behavioral Sciences

1. Bibliography 15677
2. Trends and Methodology in Anthropology, Sociology, and Psychology 15685
3. Applied Social Science and Problems of Indian Society 15703

B. Social Change and Social Policy since Independence

1. General Studies of Social Change 15713
2. Social Policy and Planning 15733
3. Law and Social Change 15744

C. Social Categories in Contemporary India

1. Changing Patterns of Social Stratification - General Studies 15750
2. Caste (jati): Hierarchical Structure in the Context of Change
   a. general studies 15761
   b. "Untouchables" in post-Independence India
      i. general studies 15766
      ii. untouchability and the law; constitutional abolition under Article 17 15778
3. The Adivasis ("aboriginals"), Tribal Peoples in Independent India [see also Chap. One, III. M. & regional chaps. below] 15785
4. The "Backward Classes," Including Scheduled Castes and Scheduled Tribes, in Public Policy and Law
   a. general studies 15806
   b. "protective discrimination" in legislatures, jobs, and education 15821
5. Elites and other Socio-economic Classes
   a. general studies of India's elites 15830
   b. the Indian intellectual 15834
6. India's Minority Communities [for minorities in regions see Chaps. Ten- Sixteen]
   a. general studies 15843
   b. India's 80 million Muslims: a conspicuous and diverse minority 15848
   c. India's Christian communities: c. 15,000,000 souls 15850
   d. Anglo-Indians (Eurasians): culturally ambivalent All-India minority of 100,000-300,000 15861
7. Women in Changing India 15868

VIII. D. Kinship and the Family: Changing Structures and Relationships since 1947

1. General Studies 15887
2. Family Structure: the Trend from Joint to Nuclear Family 15895
3. Marriage: Changing Patterns and Attitudes [see also Chap. One III. L. 3 & 4]
    a. general studies 15904
    b. age at marriage 15907
    c. reform of dowry and brideprice customs; the Dowry Prohibition Act, no. 28 of 1961 15915
    d. marriage arrangements: love marriage, arranged marriage, matrimonial advertisement 15918
    e. intercaste and other intergroup marriages 15926
    f. divorce 15930
4. Childhood and Youth: Growing Up in Indian Society
    a. child-rearing and socialization 15936
    b. Indian youth and the generation gap: attitudes and values 15951
5. Aging and the Aged: Growing Old in India Today 15968
6. Family and Personal Law: Towards a Uniform Civil Code?
    a. general studies across community lines 15973
    b. Hindu law in secular India
        i. general studies of Hindu law since Independence 15980
        ii. the Hindu Code Bill (passed 1955), and other attempts at codification and reform 15985
        iii. Hindu law relating to kinship and succession 15996
        iv. Hindu law of marriage 16001
    c. Muslim law in secular India 16009

E. Urbanization: Cities and Towns in Independent India

1. Bibliography 16021
2. General Studies of Urbanization 16027
3. Morphology and Functions of Indian Urban Centers; Land Use 16044
4. Urban Society and its Problems
    a. general studies 16056
    b. housing 16065
    c. slums 16076
5. Urban Planning and Development 16082
6. Rural-Urban Relationships 16102

F. Social Problems and Social Service in Independent India

1. Bibliography and Reference 16113
2. General Studies of Social Welfare [see also E. above] 16116
3. The Central Social Welfare Board and other Organizations, Public and Private 16126
4. Public Assistance and Social Insurance Schemes 16135
5. Professional Social Work and Education 16141
6. Social Problems and Services
    a. child welfare 16150
    b. prostitution and "immoral traffic in women" 16164
    c. the physically handicapped - the blind, deaf, crippled 16174
    d. beggars and beggary 16180
    e. juvenile delinquency, crime, and corrections 16184
    f. alcohol and drug abuse: prohibition and control 16201

G. Health Services and Medical Systems in Independent India

1. Bibliography and Reference 16207
2. General Studies of Health Services and Administration 16217
3. Major Public Health Problems
    a. sanitation and pollution control 16236
    b. nutrition and malnutrition 16249
    c. studies of major diseases 16260
    d. mental health and hygiene 16269
4. Family Planning: Knowledge, Attitudes, and Practice (KAP) [see also V. B. 5., above]
    a. bibliographies and surveys of research 16275
    b. general studies of family planning 16283
    c. attitudes and acceptance: family planning education and communication 16300
    d. selected studies of birth control methods in India; abortion, sterilization, IUCD 16311
5. Indigenous and Cosmopolitan Systems of Medicine: Competition and Collaboration
    a. general studies 16328
    b. indigenous medical systems in contemporary India 16333
6. Health Professionals and Institutions
    a. physicians, vaidyas, hakims and other practitioners 16346
    b. medical education 16357
    c. hospitals and other institutions 16372

VIII. H. Education in India since 1947

1. Bibliography and Reference 16377
2. General Studies of Indian Education since Independence 16385
3. Educational Policy and Planning
   a. general studies 16400
   b. the Education Commission of 1964-66: report and critiques 16415
   c. education and national goals of development and national integration 16421
   d. educational finance, economics, and administration 16430
   e. manpower policy and education 16438
4. Sociology of Education; Education and Social Change 16442
5. Indian Educators and Educational Thought 16455
6. Higher Education
   a. bibliography and reference 16474
   b. government reports on higher education 16480
   c. general studies of higher education in India 16485
   d. administration of higher education; the University Grants Commission 16508
   e. university teachers and teaching 16517
   f. examination system and educational standards 16526
   g. postgraduate and professional education
      i. teacher education 16539
      ii. commerce, management, and public administration education 16549
      iii. legal education 16557
      iv. engineering education 16563
      v. agricultural education: universities and rural institutes 16566
      vi. medical education [see VIII. G. 6. b., above]
7. Students in Indian Higher Education [for students in politics see III. B. 2. d. ii., above] 16575
8. Elementary and Secondary Education
   a. elementary education (ages 6-14), mandated under Directive Principles of the Constitution
      i. general studies; primary and middle schools 16588
      ii. Basic Education and Work-Experience: the Gandhian heritage 16595
   b. secondary education
      i. general studies 16607
      ii. vocational and technical education 16617
   c. "Public Schools" and other private institutions 16625
9. Curriculum and Textbook Questions [see also, VIII. H. 6. e., above] 16631
10. Language Problems in Multilingual India
   a. general studies 16639
   b. the problems of medium of instruction at various levels: Hindi, English, regional language, mother tongue? 16648
   c. English in independent India: function and status 16653
11. Illiteracy (70%, as of 1980) and its eradication 16660
12. Social, i.e. Adult, Education 16670
13. Special Problems of Women and Girls in Indian Education 16686

IX. RELIGIO-PHILOSOPHICAL TRADITIONS IN SECULAR INDIA

A. Contemporary Indian Philosophy 16692

B. Hinduism: Transregional Trends and Movements 16706

C. Sects and Cults deriving from Hinduism, in India and the West, using English and Modern Media

1. The Export of "Hinduism" to the West - General Studies 16722
2. Sathya Sai Baba: Popular "Miracle-Man" (1926-) 16737
3. Meher Baba (1894-1969): Parsi Spiritual Leader in the Yogic Tradition 16745
4. Acharya Rajneesh (1931-): Poona Magnet for Foreign Spiritual seekers 16753
5. The Hare Kṛṣṇa Movement: Modern Followers of Caitanya Vaiṣṇavism 16756

D. The Buddhist Revival in Contemporary India 16761

E. Jainism in Contemporary India 16768

F. Islam in Secular India 16774

G. Judaism in India Today 16780

H. Christianity: Continuing Indigenization in Theology and Personnel

1. Bibliography and Reference 16781
2. General Studies 16784
3. Indian Christian Theology and the Dialogue with Hinduism 16787
4. Christian Evangelization and the Resistance to it: the Niyogi Committee and Legislation on Conversion 16806

VIII. H. 5. The Roman Catholic Church in India 16811
6. Protestant and Other Denominations 16820

X. CULTURE AND COMMUNICATION IN INDEPENDENT INDIA

A. Mass Media and Communication

1. Bibliography and Reference 16829
2. General Studies 16831
3. Government and the Media: Law, Censorship, and Press Freedom 16847
4. Journalism and the Indian Press since Independence
a. general studies 16861
b. memoirs and biographies of Indian journalists 16882
c. news agencies and news management 16891
5. The Indian Publishing Industry: Books and Periodicals 16897
6. Libraries and Information Services 16909
7. Public Relations and Advertising 16931
8. Radio and Television Broadcasting
a. general studies 16935
b. radio (ākāshvānī): All-India Radio government monopoly 16941
c. television: Doordarshan government network 16944
d. Satellite Instructional Television Experiment (SITE) for rural development 16949
9. Indian Cinema: World's Largest Film Industry
a. bibliography and reference 16959
b. general studies of Indian cinema 16964
c. film censorship 16988

B. The Arts in India; The New Role of Government as Patron since 1947 16991

C. Literatures of Independent India - the Pan-Indian Languages and General Literary Scene

1. General Studies of Indian Literatures in Various Languages
a. surveys and studies 16993
b. anthologies - prose and poetry 17012
c. fiction: studies of novels and short stories 17025
d. poetry - studies 17028
e. studies of contemporary Indian theatre 17034
2. Hindi Literature of Independent India
a. general studies 17038
b. fiction 17040
c. poetry 17049
3. Urdu Literature in India since 1947 17054
4. Sanskrit and its Literature in Modern India 17062
5. Indo-English Literature since Independence
a. general studies 17070
b. linguistic studies of Indian English 17087
c. Indo-English poetry - anthologies and general studies 17093
d. Indian writers in English - studies of individuals
i. Mulk Raj Anand (1905-) 17105
ii. R.K. Narayan (1906-) 17118
iii. Raja Rao (1909-) 17131
iv. Nissim Ezekiel (1924-) 17136
v. Dom Moraes (1938-) 17142
vi. A.K. Ramanujan (1929-) 17145
vii. Manohar Malgonkar (1913-) 17147
viii. Anita Desai (1937-) 17152
ix. Kamala Markandaya (1924-) 17155
x. Khushwant Singh (1915-) 17161
xi. Ruth Prawer Jhabvala (1927-) 17166
xii. other prominent Indo-Anglian writers, including overseas Indians 17173

D. Contemporary Art in India

1. General Studies 17184
2. Studies of Individual Artists 17205

E. Music, Dance, and Other Performing Arts in Independent India [see Chap. One, VII.]

XI. SCIENCE AND TECHNOLOGY IN INDIA SINCE 1947

A. General Studies 17231

B. Science Policy and Development 17244

C. Science and Indian Society 17256

XI. D. The Indian Scientist

1. Science as a Profession in India 17263
2. Scientific Societies and Research Organizations 17267
3. Biographies and Studies of Indian Scientists 17272

CHAPTER NINE: THE ISLAMIC STATE OF PAKISTAN: GENESIS, DIVISION, AND DEVELOPMENT, 1947-71, 1971-

I. REFERENCE AND GENERAL

A. Bibliography and Reference 17283

B. General Histories of Pakistan since 1947 17293

II. PAKISTAN GOVERNMENT AND POLITICS, 1947- : ALTERNATION OF CIVIL AND MILITARY RULE, AND THE SEARCH FOR A VIABLE CONSTITUTION

A. Government Structure: Administration, Legislatures, and Judiciary

1. General Studies of Pakistan's Political System 17306
2. Constitutional History and Law - General Studies 17316
3. Executive Offices; President (Governor-General before 1956), Prime Minister and Council of Ministers 17324
4. Administration and Bureaucracy
    a. general studies 17326
    b. the Civil Service 17338
    c. corruption and administrative reform 17352
5. Pakistan's Armed Forces and their Political Role 17364
6. The Police Service of Pakistan (PSP) and other Security Forces 17375
7. Parliament 17377
8. The Judiciary and the Legal System: Interaction of Parliamentary Legislation and Islamic Law 17379
9. Islam and the Political System 17392
10. Federalism and National Integration 17411

B. The Political Process

1. General Histories and Studies of Pakistan Politics 17421
2. Politics and Society 17441
3. Pakistan's Political Parties
    a. general studies of political parties 17448
    b. the Pakistan Muslim League 17453
    c. the Awami League, founded 1949 by Sheikh Mujibur Rahman 17456
    d. the National Awami Party, founded 1957 by Maulana Abdul Hamid Bhashani, in split from Awami League 17460
    e. the Pakistan People's Party, founded 1967 by Zulfiqar Ali Bhutto 17462
    f. the Jamāʿāt-i-Islāmī, founded 1941 by Maulana Syed Abulʿ Alā Maudoodi 17467
4. Elections and Election Law - General Studies 17473

C. Phases of Pakistan's Political Development, 1947-

1. 1947-58: Founding, Consolidation, and Constitution-making
    a. general studies 17478
    b. Quaid-i-Azam Mahomed Ali Jinnah (1876-1948), founder and first Governor-General [see Chap. Six, IV. D. 3]
    c. Liaquat Ali Khan (1895-1951), first Prime Minister of Pakistan 17485
    d. the Constituent Assemblies and the Constitution of 1956 17489
2. 1958-62: Martial Law under Army-Bureaucratic Rule
    a. general studies 17500
    b. Field Marshal Mohammad Ayub Khan, leader of the 1958 "Revolution" 17508
3. 1962-69: Presidency of Ayub Khan under the New Constitution
    a. the Constitution of 1962: from parliamentary to presidential government 17516
    b. the general elections of 1965 17529
    c. the Presidency of Ayub Khan, 1965-69, and his "Basic Democracies" program 17538
    d. 1969: political crisis and resignation of Ayub Khan 17544
4. 1969-71: Martial Law under General Agha Muhammad Yahya Khan
    a. general studies 17551
    b. the general election of 1970: victories of Zulfiqar Ali Bhutto and Mujibur Rahman in West and East wings 17555
    c. the culmination of tensions between East and West Pakistan [for 1971 war and creation of Bangladesh, see Chapter Seven, IV. B. 4]
5. 1972-77: Rule of Zulfiqar Ali Bhutto and his Pakistan People's Party, and its Program of "Islamic Socialism"

II. C. 5. a. general studies 17568
b. Zulfiqar Ali Bhutto (1928-1979): sources and studies 17579
c. the Constitution of 1973: return to parliamentary government 17592
6. 1977- : Reimposition of Martial Law under Gen. Mohammad Zia-ul Haq
a. general studies 17601
b. the trial and execution of former Prime Minister Bhutto on the charge of murder 17610

D. Provincial and Local Government and Politics in Pakistan

1. Provincial Government and Politics 17620
2. Local Government
a. general studies 17621
b. the "Basic Democracies" program 1959-69 under Ayub Khan - general studies 17629
c. Divisional and District government 17645
d. municipal government 17649
e. sub-district government: village and tehsil/thana 17651

E. Pakistan's Foreign Relations [for Relations within South Asia, see Chapter Seven]

1. Bibliography and Reference 17656
2. Documents and Sources 17657
3. General Studies of Pakistan's Foreign Relations 17661
4. Islam as a Factor in Foreign Policy 17682
5. Defense and Security
a. general studies 17685
b. Pakistan's nuclear policy 17690
6. International Economic Relations of Pakistan
a. foreign exchange and balance of payments 17697
b. foreign trade 17703
c. foreign aid and investment 17712
7. Pakistan's Relations with Specific Countries and Areas
a. United States-Pakistan relations
i. general studies 17724
ii. American economic and military assistance 17731
b. China-Pakistan relations 17737
c. USSR-Pakistan relations 17743
d. Pakistan's relations with the United Kingdom and the Commonwealth (withdrew from Commonwealth 1971) 17749
e. Pakistan and the Middle East 17753
f. Pakistan's relations with other nations 17762
g. Pakistan and the United Nations 17765

III. THE PAKISTAN ECONOMY: PROBLEMS OF DEVELOPMENT

A. Bibliography and Reference 17770

B. Demography and Population Policy

1. Bibliography 17781
2. General Studies of Pakistan's Population 17783
3. Population Structure and Distribution; Fertility and Mortality 17792
4. Population Policy and Control 17800

C. Output, Income, and Standards of Living 17805

D. Economic Development and Planning

1. General Studies of Pakistan's Economy since 1947 17810
2. Economic Growth and Development 17823
3. Economic Thought; Islam and Modernization 17836
4. Pakistan's Economic Planning
a. general studies 17846
b. the Plans
i. the Two-Year Development Plan (1949-50) and the Six-Year Development Programme (1951-57) 17858
ii. the First Five-Year Plan, 1955-60 17860
iii. the Second Five-Year Plan, 1960-65 17863
iv. the Third Five-Year Plan, 1965-70 17871
v. the Fourth Five-Year Plan, 1970-75 17877
vi. the Fifth Five-Year Plan, 1978-83 17883
c. economic disparities of East and West Pakistan [see Chap. Fifteen, II. C. 3. b.]

E. Pakistan's Financial and Monetary System

1. Public Finance 17884
2. Taxation 17889
3. Banking and Monetary Policy
a. the State Bank of Pakistan (est. 1948) and commercial banks 17894

III. E. 3. b. prices and inflation 17903
c. savings and capital formation 17908
4. The Cooperative Movement in Pakistan 17913

F. Agriculture and Rural Development

1. Bibliography, Reference, and Statistics 17915
2. General Studies of Pakistan's Agriculture 17923
3. Agricultural Development and the "Green Revolution" 17931
4. Agricultural Planning 17942
5. Agricultural Technology and Innovation [see also F. 3., above] 17950
6. Irrigation and Water Management 17958
7. Land Use and Agricultural Products 17974
8. Land Tenure and Reforms; Agricultural Credit 17978
9. Peasant Society and Rural Social Change 17992

G. Pakistan's Industry

1. Bibliography and Reference 17998
2. General Studies of Industrialization 18002
3. The Public Sector 18015
4. The Private Sector and the Pakistani Business Communities 18020
5. Industrial Management and Finance 18026
6. Energy Resources and Production 18030
7. Studies of Specific Industries 18033

H. Labor in Pakistan's Economy

1. Labor Force, Wages, and Unemployment 18042
2. Labor and Manpower Policy and Legislation 18051
3. Industrial Relations and Trade Unions 18059

J. Transportation and Internal Commerce 18067

IV. SOCIETY AND SOCIAL CHANGE IN PAKISTAN

A. General Studies of Pakistan Society 18073

B. Social Categories in Pakistan: Class, Caste and Tribe

1. Social Stratification and Minorities 18086
2. Women in Pakistan Society 18091

C. Kinship and the Family: Changing Structures and Relationships

1. General Studies 18094
2. Marriage: Changing Patterns and Attitudes 18097
3. Family and Personal Law 18102

D. Urbanization in Pakistan

1. General Studies 18111
2. Urban Society and its Problems 18120

E. Social Problems and Social Service in Pakistan 18124

F. Health Services and Medical Systems

1. General Studies 18131
2. Family Planning 18137

G. Education in Pakistan

1. Bibliography and Statistics 18146
2. General Studies of Education 18150
3. Educational Policy and Planning
a. general studies 18159
b. education and manpower planning 18176
4. Higher Education 18182
5. Elementary and Secondary Education 18194
6. Literacy and Adult Education (1972 literacy 21.7%) 18198
7. Special Problems of Female Education 18200
8. Pakistani Students: Problems, Attitudes, and Unrest 18201

V. RELIGIO-PHILOSOPHICAL TRADITIONS IN THE ISLAMIC STATE OF PAKISTAN

A. Islam in Pakistan: Conflict of Orthodoxy and Modernism (In 1980, 98.2% of Pakistanis were Muslim)

1. General Studies 18206
2. Maulana Sayyid Abulʿalā Maudūdi (1903-79): Foremost Exponent of Islamic Fundamentalism 18218

V. B. The Ahmadiyyas: Are they Muslim? 18224

C. Religious Minorities: Christian, Zoroastrian, Hindu 18235

D. Contemporary Philosophy in Pakistan 18238

VI. CULTURE AND COMMUNICATION IN PAKISTAN

A. Mass Media and Communication

1. Government and the Media: Law, Censorship, and Press Freedom 18241
2. Journalism and the Press 18247
3. Book Publishing and Libraries 18250
4. Radio and Television, and Cinema 18255

B. Literatures of Pakistan in Urdu and English [for Bengali Literature of E. Pakistan see Chap. Fifteen, II. F. 1., below] 18261

C. Contemporary Art and Music of Pakistan 18276

VII. SCIENCE AND TECHNOLOGY IN PAKISTAN 18284

PART FOUR: TRANSFORMATIONS IN THE MODERN AGE: THE EIGHT GEO-CULTURAL AREAS

CHAPTER TEN: CEYLON TO SRI LANKA: COSMOPOLITAN ISLAND, COLONY TO NATION-STATE, 1796-1948, 1948- ; THE MALDIVES

I. GENERAL HISTORIES AND STUDIES OF SRI LANKA SINCE 1796 18289

II. GOVERNMENT AND POLITICS OF SRI LANKA SINCE 1796

A. British Rule in Ceylon, 1796-1948

1. General Histories 18295
2. Foundation of British Rule, 1796-1833
   a. capture of the maritime Provinces from the Dutch, and conquest of the Kandyan Kingdom 18300
   b. colonial government, to the Colebrooke-Cameron Reforms, 1833 18311
3. Consolidation of British Rule, 1834-1910 18319
4. Constitutional Reform and the National Movement, 1911-48
   a. communal riots of 1915 between Buddhists and Muslims 18334
   b. the Ceylon nationalist movement
      i. general studies 18342
      ii. the Ceylon National Congress, founded 1919 18350
      iii. other nationalist parties 18355
   c. the Donoughmore Commission (1928) and the 1931 Constitution 18356
   d. Ceylon government and politics, 1931-48 18360
   e. the Soulbury Constitutional Commission, 1944-45 18362

B. Independent Ceylon/Sri Lanka - Government and Politics, 1948-

1. Constitutional Law and History - General Studies 18365
2. The Constitution of 1948 18369
3. Political Process in Ceylon/Sri Lanka, 1948-
   a. general studies 18371
   b. political parties
      i. general studies 18389
      ii. Marxist parties 18392
      iii. communal parties 18402
   c. the electoral system and elections 18403
   d. political leaders of Sri Lanka 18411
4. The Insurrection of April 1971 by the Janatha Vimukthi Peramuna (People's Liberation Front), Ceylon's "Guevarists"
   a. bibliography 18430
   b. studies 18432
5. The 1972 Constitution: Ceylon Becomes the Republic of Sri Lanka 18445
6. The 1978 Constitution: from Parliamentary to Presidential System 18451

C. Political System and Institutions - British and Independent Ceylon

1. Religion, Nationalism, and the State
   a. general studies 18455
   b. Buddhism under Christian-secular British rule 18461

II. C. 1. c. Buddhism in Independent Sri Lanka and the constitutional directive to "protect and foster the Buddhist Sāsana" 18466
2. Language, Communalism and National Integration
a. general studies 18473
b. the Tamils of Ceylon (22% of tot. pop.): problems of citizenship and official language 18489
3. Public Administration and Bureaucracy
a. general studies 18504
b. the Ceylon Civil Service, and other government services 18510
4. The Legislature in Ceylon 18519
5. The Multiple Legal Systems of Ceylon 18524

D. Local Government in Ceylon 18541

E. Sri Lanka's Foreign Relations

1. General Studies; the Policy of Non-Alignment 18553
2. Relations with Specific Nations and Areas [for Indo-Ceylon relations see Chap. Seven, IV. C.] 18565
3. Sri Lanka in the World Economy since 1948
a. foreign trade; balance of payments 18569
b. foreign investment and aid 18576

III. THE CEYLON ECONOMY: FROM PLANTATION COLONY TO SOCIALIST WELFARE STATE

A. Bibliography and Reference 18581

B. Economic History of Ceylon since 1796 18584

C. Demography and Population Policy

1. General Studies of Ceylon's Population; Population and Economic Development 18598
2. Fertility and Mortality; Distribution of Population 18605
3. Population Policy and Control 18610

D. Output, Income, and Standards of Living 18614

E. Natural Resources 18620

F. Economic Development and Planning in Sri Lanka

1. General Studies of Development 18622
2. Buddhist Values in Economic Modernization; the Weber Thesis 18636
3. Economic Policy and Planning
a. general studies 18641
b. development plans 18648

G. Ceylon's Financial and Monetary System

1. Public Finance and Taxation 18654
2. Banking and Monetary Policy; Other Financial Institutions 18663
3. The Cooperative Movement 18676

H. Restructuring Agriculture and Rural Society in Sri Lanka

1. General Studies of Ceylon Agriculture 18682
2. Agricultural Planning and Development
a. general studies 18687
b. agricultural technology and innovation 18697
c. irrigation and water management 18699
d. integrated river basin schemes 18705
3. The Plantation Sector
a. history of plantation agriculture and export economy 18712
b. major plantation crops: tea, rubber, coconut 18718
4. The Peasant Sector
a. general studies 18728
b. pioneer peasant colonization: a continuing development from the 19th century 18735
5. Land Tenure and Reform
a. land policy under British rule: the Land Commission of 1927 18751
b. land tenure in independent Ceylon; the Land Reform Law of 1972 18762

J. Industry in Sri Lanka

1. General Studies 18776
2. Public Corporations 18782

K. Transport and Communication 18787

III. L. Labor in Ceylon's Economy

1. General Studies; Labor Force and Employment 18791
2. Labor Policy and Legislation 18797
3. Industrial Relations and Trade Unions 18802

IV. SOCIETY AND SOCIAL CHANGE IN CEYLON

A. Social Categories in Ceylon

1. Social Stratification: Caste and Class 18815
2. Ethnic, Religious and Linguistic Groups [incl. Kinship and Marriage Patterns]
   a. general studies 18819
   b. the Veddas: Ceylon's disappearing aborigines 18829
   c. the Kandyan and Low-Country Sinhalese: the "paradox" of a Buddhist caste society 18835
   d. the Hindu Tamils, native and Indian immigrant [see also II. C. 2. b., above] 18850
   e. Ceylon's Muslims ("Moors"): Arabs, Indians, and Malays 18859
   f. the Burghers and Euro-Ceylonese 18867
   g. women 18869

B. Rural Society and Social Change

1. General Studies 18872
2. Village Studies 18877
3. Rural and Community Development 18882
4. Agricultural Credit 18889

C. Cities and Urbanization

1. General Studies 18893
2. Colombo: Ceylon's Cosmopolitan Capital and Cultural Center (1977 est. pop. 800,000) 18898
3. Other Cities and Towns 18907

D. Social Problems and Social Welfare in Sri Lanka 18909

E. Health Services and Medical Systems 18920

F. Education in Ceylon (78% literacy in 1971)

1. Bibliography 18930
2. History of Education since 1796 18931
3. Educational Policy and Development 18943
4. Higher Education 18953
5. Elementary and Secondary Education 18968

V. RELIGIO-PHILOSOPHICAL TRADITIONS IN BUDDHIST CEYLON, 1796-

A. The Resurgence and Dominance of Theravada Buddhism

1. Bibliography 18973
2. General Studies of Buddhism in Modern Ceylon since 1796 18974
3. The Buddhist Revival in the Mid-19th Century; Olcott and the Theosophists; Anagarika Dharmapala (1874-1933) 18983
4. Traditional Buddhist Monasticism in Modern Ceylon 18989
5. Resurgence of Monastic and Lay Buddhism after 1956 18996
6. Buddhism and Folk-Religion: Interactions and Syncretism
   a. Buddha and the Sinhalese pantheon 19004
   b. Sinhalese rituals of exorcism and healing 19013

B. Hinduism in Modern Ceylon; the Śaiva Murugan Cult among the Tamils 19028

C. Christianity in Modern Ceylon: Missionary Dominance and "Ceylonization"

1. General Studies 19033
2. The Roman Catholic Church 19041
3. The Anglicans and other Protestants 19048

D. Islam in Modern Ceylon since 1796 [see also IV. A. 2. e., above] 19055

VI. MEDIA AND THE ARTS

A. The Mass Media: Press, Broadcasting, Cinema 19056

B. Literatures of Modern Ceylon

1. Sinhala, Tamil and English 19072
2. Folk Literature 19082

VI. C. Art and Architecture of Modern Sri Lanka 19089

D. Science in Modern Sri Lanka 19099

VII. THE MALDIVE ISLANDS: ISLAMIC REPUBLIC IN THE INDIAN OCEAN; FORMER BRITISH PROTECTORATE ADMINISTERED FROM CEYLON TO 1965 19102

CHAPTER ELEVEN: THE DRAVIDIAN SOUTH OF INDIA: CULTURAL DISTINCTNESS VERSUS NATIONAL INTEGRATION, 1800-

I. OVERALL STUDIES OF SOUTH INDIA

A. Political Studies 19116

B. Economic Studies 19122

C. Social and Cultural Studies 19127

II. MADRAS PRESIDENCY TO MADRAS STATE TO TAMILNADU

A. Government and Politics since 1800

1. The British Raj in the South, 1800-1947
   a. accounts by officials and travellers 19134
   b. government and politics of the Madras Presidency 19142
   c. local government and politics 19156
2. The Nationalist Movement in the Madras Presidency 19163
3. The Justice Party, Anti-Brahmanism, and the Dravidian Movement
   a. general studies 19178
   b. E.V. Ramaswami Naicker (1878-1973): founder of the Self-Respect Movement (1925) and the Dravida Kazhagam (DK, 1944) 19188
4. Pondicherry: French Enclave Ceded to India 1954, Now a Union Territory 19195

B. Post-Independence Government and Politics in Madras State and Tamilnadu

1. General Studies; Political System and Administration 19196
2. The Period of Congress Rule, 1946-1956; K. Kamaraj, Congress Leader 19199
3. DMK Rule, 1967-
   a. the Dravida Munnetra Kazhagam (DMK), the party of Tamil regionalism
      i. general studies 19206
      ii. C.N. Annadurai (1908-1969): founder of DMK and Chief Minister of Tamil Nadu, 1967-69 19214
   b. Tamilnadu politics under DMK rule, 1967- 19223
4. Language and Politics; Anti-Hindi Agitation 19233
5. Local Government and Panchayati Raj 19238

C. The Economy of Madras Presidency and Tamilnadu

1. Bibliography and Reference 19243
2. General Economic History 19247
3. Demography (1981 pop. 48,297,456) 19257
4. Economic Development and Planning 19259
5. Agriculture in Madras/Tamilnadu since 1818
   a. general studies of agricultural development 19270
   b. agricultural technology and innovation 19286
   c. land tenure and reform
      i. the ryotwari and other tenure systems of Madras Presidency 19295
      ii. land reform 19305
   d. rural credit and cooperatives 19311
6. Industry and Transportation 19316
7. Labor and Trade Unions 19326

D. Society and Social Change in Madras Presidency and Tamil Nadu since 1818

1. General Studies 19333
2. Castes and the Caste System in Madras
   a. general studies 19340
   b. Brahman castes 19353
   c. Non-Brahman castes 19358
   d. Adi-Dravida, or "untouchable", castes 19363
3. Adivasis (Tribals) of Tamilnad
   a. general studies 19371
   b. the Todas of the Nilgiri Hills 19386
   c. the Kotas of the Nilgiri Hills 19398

II. D. 4. Religious Minorities [see also E. 3., below]
a. Christians 19405
b. Muslims 19410
5. Villages and Rural Society 19417
6. Cities and Urbanization in Madras
a. general studies 19426
b. Madras, metropolis of the South (1981 pop. 4,276,635)
i. history and general studies 19431
ii. slums, urban problems, and development 19444
7. Social Problems and Social Welfare 19454
8. Health Services and Medicine 19458
9. Education (literacy 45.78% in 1981)
a. general studies 19469
b. higher education; universities of Madras (1857), Annamalai (1929), Madurai (1966) 19476

E. Religio-Philosophical Traditions of Tamil Nadu since 1818

1. General Studies; Interactions of Hinduism and Christianity 19486
2. Hinduism
a. general studies 19492
b. temples and endowments -- their political and economic role 19514
3. Christianity; from Missionary to Indian Direction 19523

F. Media and the Arts in Tamilnadu

1. Journalism and the Press 19545
2. Cinema of Tamilnadu and its Political Role [see also II. B. 3. b., above] 19549
3. Modern Tamil Literature; the "Pure Tamil" Movement
a. general studies 19552
b. modern Tamil prose 19564
c. modern Tamil poetry
i. general studies 19580
ii. C. Subrahmanya Bharati (1882-1921) 19583
4. Folk Literature of Tamil Nadu 19597

III. ANDHRA PRADESH: THE TELUGU-SPEAKING AREA OF MADRAS PRESIDENCY AND HYDERABAD STATE

A. General and Political History of Andhra since 1818

1. General Studies 19604
2. The Nizam's Dominions to 1949, and Hyderabad State to 1956
a. general studies 19611
b. Communist-led peasant uprising against Nizam and landlords, 1946-51 19633
3. The Nationalist Movement in Andhra and Provincial Politics [see also II. A. 2., above] 19641
4. Andhra Politics after Independence: the Demand for Vishala ("Greater") Andhra versus Subregionalisms
a. the formation of Andhra State, 1953, from the Madras Telugu districts 19649
b. general studies of politics: Andhra State 1953-56, Andhra Pradesh (Hyderabad + Andhra State) 1956- 19653
c. election studies 19670
d. subregionalism of Telangana (Telugu districts of former Hyderabad State), 1968- 19681
e. Maoist armed uprisings by Naxalite peasants in Srikakulam District and elewhere, and their suppression 19694
5. Administration, State and Local
a. state and district administration 19700
b. Panchayati Raj introduced in 1959 19708

B. The Andhra Economy since 1818

1. General Economic History 19722
2. Economic Development and Planning 19725
3. Agriculture
a. general studies 19738
b. land tenure and reform 19756
4. Industry in Andhra 19767
5. Labor in the Andhra Economy 19776
6. Commerce and Transportation 19782

C. Society and Social Change in Andhra

1. General Studies 19784
2. Social Categories
a. castes in Andhra 19792
b. tribes of Andhra 19803
3. Villages and Rural Society 19817
4. Cities and Urbanization 19834

III. C. 5. Health and Social Welfare 19848
6. Education (literacy 29.94% in 1981) 19857

D. Religions of Modern Andhra: Hinduism, Islam and Christianity 19870

E. Media and the Arts in Andhra

1. Journalism and the Press 19883
2. Telugu and Urdu Literatures of Modern Andhra
a. general studies 19885
b. Swami Tyagaraja (1767-1847): Vaisnava dramatist and composer 19896
c. Kandakuri Viresalingam (1848-1919) 19903
d. Guruzada Venkata Apparao (1861-1915): innovative poet in the colloquial language 19906
3. Folk Literature 19910

IV. KERALA AND LAKSHADWEEP/LACCADIVES: THE MALAYALAM-SPEAKING REGION OF SOUTHWEST SOUTH INDIA

A. Government and Politics since 1800

1. Malabar District under the Madras Presidency 19912
2. The Princely States of Travancore and Cochin up to 1949 19917
3. The Nationalist Movement in Kerala 19937
4. Politics of Post-Independence Kerala: Multi-partism based on Castes/Communities
a. the Travancore-Cochin Union, 1949-56, and the establishment of Kerala 19945
b. general studies of Kerala politics 19946
c. election studies 19958
d. Kerala Communists and experiments in coalition 19969
5. Local Government and Politics 19986
6. Lakshadweep/Laccadives: Indian Ocean Union Territory since 1956 19990

B. The Kerala Economy since 1800

1. General Economic History 19993
2. Demography (1981 pop. 25,403,217) 19995
3. Economic Development and Planning 20002
4. Agriculture in Kerala
a. general studies 20012
b. land tenure and reform 20020
c. agrarian unrest and peasant movements 20033
5. Industry and Transportation in Kerala 20042
6. Labor in the Kerala Economy 20051

C. Society and Social Change in Kerala since 1800

1. General Studies of Kerala's Elaborate Social Structure 20055
2. Social Categories in Kerala
a. general studies, incl. kinship and marriage 20067
b. the Nambudiri Brahmans (1% of Kerala's pop.) 20081
c. the Nayars (16% of Kerala's pop.)
i. general studies 20086
ii. kinship and marriage 20094
d. the Ezhava/Ilavas: an "untouchable" caste group (22% of Kerala's pop.) 20105
e. Kerala Christians: the Syrian, Roman Catholic and other communities (21% of Kerala's pop.) 20114
f. the Mappillas of Malabar, and other Muslims (19% of Kerala's pop.); the Moplah rebellions 20122
g. Muslim islanders of Lakshadweep 20135
h. the Cochin Jews 20140
j. Adivasis (Tribals) of Kerala (1.25% of Kerala's pop.) 20144
3. Villages and Rural Society 20153
4. Cities and Urbanization 20157
5. Education in Kerala (69.17% literacy in 1981) 20160

D. Religio-Philosophical Traditions of Modern Kerala

1. Hinduism (60% of Kerala's pop.)
a. general studies 20167
b. Narayana Guru Swami (1840-1928): Ezhava Vedantin and social reformer [see also C. 2. d. above] 20172
2. Christianity (21% of Kerala's pop.): Indigenous and Missionary Churches [see also C. 2. e., above] 20177
3. Islam (18% of Kerala's pop.) [see also C. 2. f. above] 20187

E. Media and the Arts in Modern Kerala

1. Journalism and the Press 20188
2. Modern Malayalam Literature
a. general studies 20191

IV. E. 2. b. modern Malayalam fiction 20199
c. modern Malayalam poetry
i. Vallathol Narayana Menon (1878-1958): nationalist and poetic innovator 20206
ii. Kumaran Asan (1873-1924): Ezhava poet and social reformer 20210
iii. Ulloor S. Paramesvara Iyer (1877-1949) 20213
iv. G. Sankara Kurup (1901-) 20216
3. Folk Literature 20219

V. KARNATAKA: THE KANNADA-SPEAKING NORTHWEST REGION OF SOUTH INDIA

A. General and Political Histories, 1799-

1. Mysore State under the Wadiyar Maharajas (1799-1831, 1881-1947) and under Direct British Rule (1831-1881)
a. general studies 20223
b. administrators: Princes, Diwans, and British Chief Commissioners 20232
2. Coorg: A British Chief Commissioner's Province, 1834-1947; District of Karnataka, 1956- 20244
3. The Nationalist Movement in Karnataka 20247
4. Government and Politics after Independence: from Mysore State to United Karnataka 20251
5. Local Government and Politics 20259

B. The Karnataka Economy since 1799

1. General Economic History 20267
2. Demography (1981 pop. 37,043,451) 20269
3. Economic Development and Planning 20280
4. Finance, Taxation, and Banking 20295
5. Agriculture in Karnataka
a. general studies of agricultural development 20305
b. agricultural technology and innovation; irrigation 20327
c. land tenure and reform 20333
6. Industry in Karnataka 20341
7. Labor and Trade Unions 20351
8. Transport and Communication 20355

C. Society and Social Change

1. Social Categories, incl. Kinship and Marriage
a. general studies 20361
b. kinship and marriage (not specific to one group) 20380
c. Gauda Saraswat Brahmans of N. & S. Kanara districts 20393
d. Vokkaligas (20%) and Lingayats/Virasaivas (13%): rival dominant groups of Karnataka 20400
e. Coorgs/Kodagus: the ruling warrior caste of Coorg 20408
f. scheduled castes of Karnataka, the Adi Karnatakas 20415
g. Adivasis (tribals) of Karnataka 20423
2. Villages and Rural Society
a. village studies 20425
b. community development and rural social change 20449
3. Cities and Urbanization in Karnataka
a. general studies 20457
b. Bangalore; capital of Karnataka (1981 pop. 2,913,537) 20465
c. Mysore City, princely capital of Mysore (1971 pop. 355,685) 20481
d. Hubli and Dharwar, twin cities of NW Karnataka (1971 pop. 379,166) 20486
3. Mangalore, port city of South Kanara District (1971 pop. 215,122) 20489
4. Social Problems and Social Welfare 20497
5. Health Services and Family Planning 20504
6. Education in Karnataka (38.41% literacy in 1981) 20517

D. Religions of Modern Karnataka

1. Hinduism, incl. Virasaivism and Folk Religions 20533
2. Christianity 20555

E. Kannada Literature of Modern Karnataka

1. General Studies 20557
2. Modern Kannada Fiction and Drama 20565
3. Modern Kannada Poetry 20571
4. Folk Literature 20576

CHAPTER TWELVE: MIDDLE INDIA: CONTRASTS OF TRADITION AND MODERNITY IN AN AREA OF TRANSITION BETWEEN NORTH AND SOUTH; PERSISTENCE OF TRIBAL CULTURES, PRINCELY CONSERVATISM AND URBAN PROGRESS, 1818-

I. MIDDLE INDIA IN THE BRITISH PERIOD, 1818-1947: ADMINISTRATIVE DIVERSITY

A. General Studies and Accounts 20579

B. Princely States of Middle India

1. Princely States of Maharashtra (Integrated in 1948)
a. general studies 20584
b. Kolhapur and its feudatories; the Non-Brahman movement [see also I. C. 2. d., below] 20591
c. Satara, lapsed to British administration, 1849 20603
d. Nagpur, lapsed to British administration, 1853 20609
2. Princely States of Present-day Gujarat (Merged 1948-49, Unified in 1956)
a. general studies of Kathiawad and other states 20612
b. Baroda under the Gaikwads 20624
3. Rajputana: Princely States of Present-day Rajasthan (Unified in 1949)
a. general studies 20634
b. Mewar/Udaipur: the premier Rajput state 20645
c. Marwar/Jodhpur 20647
d. Jaipur 20651
e. Bikaner 20657
f. the Jat State of Bharatpur 20659
4. Princely States of Present-day Madhya Pradesh (Integrated in 1948, Unified in 1956)
a. general studies 20662
b. Gwalior under the Scindia/Shinde family 20671
c. the Muslim State of Bhopal and its Nawabs 20676
5. Princely States of Present-day Orissa (Integrated in 1949) 20680

C. The British Raj in Middle India

1. Bombay Presidency (Parts of Karnataka, Maharashtra, Gujarat, and Sind): Government and Administration
a. reference and sources 20685
b. general studies of administration 20691
c. British administrators 20701
d. law and the judiciary 20708
e. local government 20714
2. Nationalism in Bombay Presidency [see also Chap. Six, III. C]
a. the rise of regionalism and nationalism; Congress in Bombay (after 1885) 20710
b. Bal Gangadhar Tilak (1856-1920): the Shivaji and Ganapati festivals and mass nationalism 20739
c. post-Tilak nationalism: Gandhian non-cooperation and participation in constitutional reform 20745
d. socio-political protest movements by Non-Brahmans and "untouchable" Mahars [see also I. B. 1. b., above] 20752
3. Central Provinces and Berar/Vidarbha (British Districts of Madhya Pradesh and Parts of Maharashtra)
a. history and administration under the Raj 20764
b. nationalism and politics in C.P. and Berar 20769
4. The British Raj in Orissa, 1803-1947
a. general histories 20774
b. formation of Orissa Province from Oriya-speaking districts of Bihar, Central Provinces, and Madras Presidency 20779
c. nationalism and constitutional change 20788

II. ADIVASIS OF MIDDLE INDIA: TRIBAL PEOPLES OF THE HILLS AND FORESTS, SINCE 1818

A. Tribes of Western MIddle India

1. The Bhils of the Malwa Plateau 20798
2. Tribes of Maharashtra 20819
3. Tribes of Gujarat 20829
4. Tribes of Rajasthan 20838

B. Tribes of Central Middle India

1. General Studies 20843
2. The Gond Group of Dravidian-speaking Tribes (1971 pop. 4,000,000+) 20862
3. Other Major Tribes of Gondwana 20881

C. Tribes of the Chota Nagpur Plateau (Bihar, Orissa, and M.P.)

1. General Studies 20892

II. C. 2. The Santals: the Largest Mundari-speaking Tribal Group (1971 pop. 3,786,899)
a. bibliography and reference 20911
b. general studies 20913
c. social and psychological studies 20921
d. cultural change and social unrest; the 1855 Santal Insurrection and the Kharwar Movement of 1871 20928
e. Santal religion and folklore 20940
3. The Mundas: a Mundari-speaking Tribal Group (1971 pop. 1,080,546)
a. reference 20948
b. general studies 20949
c. Munda political and social movements: from Birsa Munda to Jaipal Singh 20955
d. Munda religion and folklore 20964
4. The Bhumij: a Hinduized Munda Tribe, Claiming Rajput Descent 20969
5. The Hos and Kols: Munda Tribes 20977
6. The Oraons/Kurukhs: A Dravidian-speaking Tribal Group 20983
7. Other Tribes of Chota Nagpur 20994

D. Tribes of the Orissa Highlands
1. General Studies 21007
2. The Saoras/Savaras 21011
3. The Juangs 21018
4. Other Tribes of Highland Orissa 21023

III. GOA: FROM PORTUGUESE COLONY TO UNION TERRITORIES

A. General and Political History
1. Portuguese Rule, 1818-1961 [see also Chap. Five], and the Liberation Movement 21036
2. The Union Territory of Goa, Daman and Diu (1962-); the U.T. of Dadra and Nagar Haveli (Liberated 1959)
a. the India-Portugal struggle over Goa 21043
b. Indian Army's Liberation of Goa, 1961 21051
c. politics and elections of G. D. and D., 1962- 21059
d. the question of merger: rival claims of Karnataka and Maharashtra 21067

B. The Goan Economy
1. General Studies; Development and Planning 21071
2. Goan Agriculture
a. general studies 21084
b. land tenure and reform 21089

C. Society and Religion in Modern Goa 21092

D. Literatures of Modern Goa
1. Modern Literature in Konkani and Portuguese 21099
2. Folk Literature 21107

IV. MAHARASHTRA: THE MARATHI-SPEAKING REGION OF WESTERN AND CENTRAL INDIA, 1818-

A. General and Political History
1. Bombay State,1947-60 21110
2. The Samyukta ("United") Maharashtra Movement, and the Establishment of Maharashtra State, 1960 21115
3. General Studies of Maharashtra Politics, 1960- 21126
4. Election Studies, 1960- 21132
5. The Shiv Sena ("Army of Shivaji"): Urban Middle-class Party of Maharashtrian Nativism 21139
6. Administration and Reorganization 21148
7. Local Government and Politics
a. general studies 21152
b. district administration and the zilla parishad 21161
c. village panchayats and local officials 21167
d. urban administration and politics - general studies 21172
e. Bombay City - government and politics
i. historical studies, 1818-1947 21178
ii. Bombay municipal administration and politics - general studies 21185
iii. election studies 21189

B. The Economy of Maharashtra since 1818
1. General Economic History, 1818-1947 21196
2. Demography (1981 pop. 62,693,898) 21205
3. Surveys of Economic Conditions since 1947 21209
4. Economic Development and Planning 21219

IV. B. 5. Finance and Banking 21227
6. Agriculture
a. agriculture in the Bombay Presidency, 1818-1947 21234
b. agricultural development since 1947 21240
c. agricultural technology and innovation; irrigation 21247
d. land tenure and reform 21257
e. rural credit and cooperatives 21268
f. agrarian unrest; the Deccan Riots of 1875 21273
g. famines and famine relief 21283
7. Industry in Maharashtra since 1818
a. general studies 21291
b. studies of specific industries and industrialists 21296
c. small-scale and cottage industries 21306
8. Labor in Maharashtra since 1854
a. general studies 21309
b. wages and employment 21320
c. labor policy and legislation 21324
d. labor movement and trade unions 21327
9. Commerce and Transportation 21331

C. Society and Social Change in Maharashtra since 1818

1. Social Reform and Reformers in Maharashtra and Bombay Presidency
a. general studies 21342
b. Mahadev Govind Ranade (1842-1901): High Court Justice and founder of the National Social Conference, 1887- 21347
c. women's reform movements 21256
d. other social reformers 21370
2. Social Categories in Maharashtra incl. Kinship and Marriage [see also II. A. above]
a. general studies 21377
b. Brahman castes: Chitpavan and Deshastha [for Saraswats, see Chap. Eleven, V. C. 1. b.] 21389
c. Non-Brahman castes: Marathas and others 21393
d. Mahars and other "Untouchables"
i. general studies 21403
ii. conversion of Mahars to Buddhism under Dr. Ambedkar (1956) and its political consequences 21413
e. religious minorities
i. the Parsis: Zoroastrians of Bombay and other cities 21431
ii. Muslim groups of Maharashtra 21443
iii. the Christians of Maharashtra 21450
iv. the Bene Israel: an indigenous Jewish community 21456
v. the "Neo-Buddhists" (Nava Bauddhas): [see C. 2. d. ii., above]
3. Villages and Rural Development
a. villages of the Konkan coast 21459
b. villages of the Deccan Plateau (Desh, Marathwada, and Nag-Vidarbha) 21464
4. Cities and Urbanization
a. general studies 21485
b. Bombay City, capital of Maharashtra (1981 pop. 8,292,759) [for govt. and politics, see IV. A. 7. e., above]
i. historical studies since 1818 21497
ii. the Bombay metropolitan area and problems of migration 21507
iii. urban planning and economic development 21516
iv. urban mass transportation 21527
v. housing and slums 21531
vi. urban social problems and welfare 21537
c. Poona/Pune, Maharashtra's cultural center (1981 pop. 1,685,266) 21543
5. Social Problems and Social Welfare 21559
6. Health Services and Family Planning 21562
7. Education in Maharashtra since 1818 (47.37% literacy in 1981)
a. general history of education, 1818-1947 21569
b. educational policy and development since 1947 21577
c. elementary and secondary schools and teachers 21585
d. higher education
i. general studies 21593
ii. university students 21601

D. Religio-Philosophical Traditions of Maharashtra since 1818

1. Hinduism
a. general studies 21606
b. Ramchandra Dattatraya Ranade (1886-1956): a modern mystic 21615
c. the cult of Sai Baba (d. 1918), Muslim-Hindu saint 21619
2. Christianity in Maharashtra 21625

IV. E. Literature and Media in Maharashtra since 1818

1. Modern Marathi Literature
   a. general studies 21633
   b. modern Marathi fiction 21637
   c. modern Marathi poetry 21646
   d. modern Marathi drama and theatre 21650
2. Folk Literature 21652
3. Publishing and the Press in Maharashtra 21659
4. The Film Industry in Maharashtra: Center of Hindi and Marathi Cinema 21662

V. GUJARAT: THE GUJARATI-SPEAKING REGION OF WESTERN MIDDLE INDIA

A. Political History [for Bombay Pres. and Princely States, see I. above]

1. From Independence to the Formation of Gujarat State (1947-1960) 21663
2. General Studies of Gujarat Politics since 1960 21665
3. Election Studies 21681
4. Local Government and Politics
   a. general studies 21690
   b. district administration 21695
   c. village government and panchayats 21699

B. The Gujarat Economy since 1818

1. General Economic History to 1947 21706
2. Demography (1981 pop. 33,960,905) 21709
3. Surveys of Economic Conditions after 1947 21711
4. Economic Development and Planning 21715
5. Finance and Taxation 21720
6. Agriculture in Gujarat
   a. surveys and descriptive studies 21722
   b. agricultural development and planning 21735
   c. agricultural technology and innovation 21746
   d. agricultural cooperatives in Gujarat 21753
   e. land tenure and reform 21762
7. Industry in Gujarat 21773
8. Labor and Trade Unions in Gujarat 21786
9. Commerce and Transportation in Gujarat 21797

C. Society and Social Change in Gujarat since 1818

1. Social Reform in the 19th Century 21803
2. Social Categories in Gujarat
   a. general studies 21811
   b. kinship and marriage (not specific to one group) 21821
   c. Brahman castes 21831
   d. Patidars and other intermediate castes 21835
   e. "untouchable" castes of Gujarat 21841
   f. Muslims of Gujarat [see also, IV. C. 2. e. ii., above] 21847
   g. tribals of Gujarat [see II. A. above]
3. Villages and Rural Society
   a. village studies 21854
   b. community development and modernization 21864
4. Cities and Urbanization
   a. general studies 21869
   b. Ahmedabad: industrial city and center of Gandhism (1981 pop. 2,515,195) 21875
   c. Baroda/Vadodara: former Maratha princely capital (1971 pop. 1,980,065) 21884
5. Social Welfare and Health Services 21889
6. Education in Gujarat since 1818 (43.75% literacy in 1981)
   a. general studies 21895
   b. higher education 21904

D. Religion of Modern Gujarat

1. General Studies of Gujarati Hinduism 21913
2. The Svaminarayana Sect: reformist Vaishnavism founded by Swami Sahajananda, 1781-1830 21921

E. Literature and Media in Modern Gujarat

1. Modern Gujarati Literature 21932
2. Folk Literature of Gujarat 21947
3. Journalism and the Press in Modern Gujarat 21950

VI. RAJASTHAN: THE FORMER PRINCELY STATES OF NORTHWEST MIDDLE INDIA

A. Political History since 1949 [for Princely States, see I. B. above]

1. General Studies 21951

VI. A. 2. Election Studies 21963
3. Administration 21975
4. Local Government and Politics
a. general studies of democratic decentralization/panchayati raj 21979
b. district administration and zila parishads 21991
c. village panchayats and politics 21996
d. municipal politics and administration 22003

B. The Economy of Rajasthan

1. Demography (1981 pop. 34,102,912) 22010
2. Economic Development and Planning 22015
3. Finance and Banking 22023
4. Agriculture: Problems of a Desert Region
a. general studies 22025
b. agricultural development and innovation; irrigation, and the Rajasthan Canal 22037
c. land tenure and reform 22043
5. Industrial Development of Rajasthan
a. general studies 22054
b. small scale industry 22062
6. Labor in Rajasthan 22066
7. Commerce and Transportation 22071

C. Society and Social Change in Modern Rajasthan

1. Social Categories
a. general studies incl. kinship and marriage 22074
b. the Rajputs 22084
c. Jats and other Hindu castes 22090
d. "Untouchables": Bhangis and other Scheduled Castes 22094
e. the Meos: a Muslim caste of Mewat, in NE Rajasthan 22095
f. tribals of Rajasthan [see also II. A. above] 22101
2. Villages and Rural Social Development 22105
3. Cities and Urbanization 22117
4. Social Welfare and Health Services 22128
5. Education in Modern Rajasthan (24.05% literacy in 1981) 22135

D. Religions of Modern Rajasthan 22142

E. Literatures of Modern Rajasthan

1. Rajasthani and its Emergence as a Literary Language 22145
2. Folk Literature 22150

VII. MADHYA PRADESH: INDIA'S LARGEST STATE, IN THE UPLANDS OF CENTRAL MIDDLE INDIA

A. Political History [for British Period, see I. B. 4. and I. C. 3., above]

1. Politics of Madhya Pradesh (est. 1956) 22155
2. Election Studies 22160
3. Local Government and Politics 22167

B. The Madhya Pradesh Economy

1. Demography (1981 pop. 52,131,717) 22177
2. Surveys of Economic Conditions 22180
3. Economic Development and Planning 22188
4. Agriculture
a. general studies 22198
b. agricultural cooperatives 22213
c. land tenure and reform 22216
5. Industry, Labor, and Transportation in Madhya Pradesh 22221

C. Society and Social Change (27.82% literacy in 1981)

1. Social Categories [for Tribals, see II. B. above] 22229
2. Villages and Rural Society 22243
3. Cities and Urbanization 22254
4. Social Problems and Social Welfare, incl. Dacoity in the Chambal Valley 22263

D. Religions of Madhya Pradesh

1. Hinduism 22273
2. Christianity and its Missionary Activities 22280
3. Tribal Religions [see II. B., above]

E. Literatures of Madhya Pradesh

1. Hindi Literature [see Chap. Six, VIII. B., and Chap. Eight, X. C. 2.]
2. Folk Literature 22285

VIII. ORISSA (UTKAL): THE ORIYA-SPEAKING REGION OF EASTERN MIDDLE INDIA

A. Political History [for British Period, see I. B. 5. and I. C. 4., above]

1. General Studies of Orissa Politics 22287
2. Election Studies 22299
3. Administration and the Judiciary 22306
4. Local Government and Politics 22309

B. The Orissa Economy

1. General Economic History, 1818-1947 22315
2. Demography (1981 pop. 26,272,054) 22319
3. Surveys of Economic Conditions since 1947 22322
4. Economic Development and Planning 22327
5. Agriculture
   a. general studies 22329
   b. land tenure and reform 22340
6. Industry in Orissa 22348

C. Society and Social Change

1. Social Categories [for Tribals see II. D., above] 22357
2. Villages and Rural Society 22366
3. Cities and Urbanization 22375
4. Social Welfare and Health Services 22379
5. Education (34.12% literacy in 1981) 22382

D. Religious Traditions of Modern Orissa

1. Puri and the Vaishnava Cult of Jagannath [see also Chap. One, IV. C. 3. e. iv.]; Religious Endowments 22386
2. Mahimā Dharma (Ālekha): a Reformist Hindu Sect, est. mid-19th century 22394
3. Śākta and Śaiva Cults 22401
4. Christian Missionary Activities 22403

E. Literatures of Modern Orissa

1. Oriya Literature 22404
2. Folk Literature 22420

CHAPTER THIRTEEN: THE NORTHWEST: THE INDUS VALLEY AND MOUNTAIN FRONTIER, 1799-

I. GENERAL STUDIES OF THE NORTHWEST

A. The British Period: Accounts by Officials and Travellers 22426

B. Post-1947 Studies and Accounts 22439

II. SIND: THE SINDHI-SPEAKING LOWER INDUS VALLEY, A PROVINCE OF PAKISTAN SINCE 1947

A. General and Political History

1. The British Period in Sind (Annexed 1843, Part of Bombay Presidency until 1936)
   a. general studies and accounts 22440
   b. politics and nationalism, 1937-1947 22461
2. Sind Politics since 1947: A Province of Pakistan 22463

B. The Sind Economy

1. General Studies 22466
2. Agriculture 22474

C. Society and Social Change

1. General Studies 22486
2. Karachi: Pakistan's Largest City and Major Port, Capital of Sind Province (1978 pop. 3,500,000) 22493

D. Modern Sindhi Literature in Pakistan and India 22508

III. BALUCHISTAN: THE ARID BASINS AND HILLS OF SOUTHWESTERN PAKISTAN

A. General and Political History

1. The British Period (1839-1947): the Khanate of Kalat, Other Chiefdoms, and British Baluchistan 22515
2. Government and Politics after 1947 22523

III. B. The Baluchistan Economy 22527

C. Society and Social Change 22532

D. Languages and Literatures of Modern Baluchistan: Baluchi and Brahui 22550

IV. THE PUNJAB: THE PLAINS AND FOOTHILLS OF THE MIDDLE INDUS VALLEY

A. General and Political History since 1799

1. Bibliography and Sources 22554
2. General Histories of Modern Punjab since 1799 22559
3. The Sikh Kingdom of the Punjab, 1799-1849
   a. general studies 22564
   b. Maharaja Ranjit Singh (1780-1839) and the consolidation of the Sikh Khālsā 22570
   c. the Anglo-Sikh wars, and annexation of the Punjab in 1849 22581
4. The Princely States of the Punjab, 1799-1947 22602
5. The British Province of the Punjab, 1849-1947
   a. general studies of British rule 22611
   b. administrative studies 22622
   c. district and local government 22628
   d. nationalist politics in the Punjab
      i. general studies 22632
      ii. parties and leaders: the Unionist Party, Congress, Muslim League, and the Sikh Akali Dal 22644
      iii. communalism and partition: conflict of Sikhs, Muslims, and Hindus 22659
6. The Indian Punjab - Government and Politics since 1947
   a. general studies 22667
   b. the Sikh demand for a Punjabi-speaking state, and the partition into Punjab and Haryana states 22674
   c. election studies, 1947- 22689
   d. administrative studies 22699
   e. local government and politics 22703
7. The Pakistani Punjab - Government and Politics since 1947 22715

B. The Economy of the Punjab Region

1. The Economy of British Punjab, 1849-1947
   a. bibliography 22722
   b. general studies, incl. industry 22724
   c. agriculture
      i. general studies 22731
      ii. land tenure, revenue and reform; agrarian unrest 22737
2. The Economy of the Indian Punjab since 1947
   a. demography (1981 pop. 16,669,755) 22747
   b. economic development and planning 22751
   c. agriculture in the Punjab, "the granary of India"
      i. agricultural development and planning 22756
      ii. agricultural technology and innovation 22774
      iii. irrigation 22783
      iv. land tenure and reform 22783
   d. industry 22792
   e. labor 22795
   f. commerce and transportation 22799
3. The Economy of the Pakistani Punjab since 1947 22805

C. Society and Social Change in the Punjab Region since 1800

1. General Studies of Punjabi Society 22815
2. Social Categories of the Punjab 22822
3. Kinship and Marriage Patterns 22841
4. Villages and Rural Society
   a. villages of pre-partition British Punjab 22849
   b. villages of the Indian Punjab 22855
   c. villages of the Pakistani Punjab 22871
5. Cities and Urbanization
   a. general studies 22887
   b. Lahore: Mughal city and capital of Pakistani Punjab (1972 pop. 2,200,000) 22893
   c. Islamabad City and Capital Territory and its twin-city Rawalpindi (Pakistan) - 1972 pop., 235,000 & 615,392 22896
   d. Chandigarh: a union territory and capital of both India's Punjab and Haryana states (1971 pop. 257,251) 22899
   e. Amritsar: sacred city of the Sikhs (1971 pop. 8,835,500) 22910
6. Social Welfare and Health Services 22914
7. Education
   a. education in the British Punjab 22919
   b. education in the Indian Punjab (40.74% literacy in 1981) 22931
   c. education in the Pakistani Punjab 22936

IV. D. Religious Traditions of the Modern Punjab

1. General Studies 22941
2. Sikhism
    a. general studies 22944
    b. the Akali movement for reformation of Gurdwaras, 1920-25 22950
    c. the Namdhari (Kuka) sect 22955
    d. the Nirankari sect and the conflict with the Akali orthodoxy 22960
3. The Hindu Tradition
    a. the Arya Samaj in Punjab 22966
    b. Swami Ram Tirth (1873-1906): modern Punjabi yogi 22970
4. Islam in Modern Punjab 22975
5. Christianity and Missionary Activity in Modern Punjab 22980

E. Literature and Media in Modern Punjab

1. Languages of Modern Punjab: Punjabi, Urdu, Siraiki 22991
2. Modern Punjabi Literature in India and Pakistan
    a. general studies 22996
    b. Bhai Vir Singh (1872-1957): Sikh nationalist writer 23011
    c. Amrita Pritam (1919-): poetess and novelist 23018
3. Hindi and Urdu Literature of the Punjab [see Chap. Six, VIII. B. & C., Chap. Eight, X. C. 2. & 3., and Chap. Nine, VI. B.]
4. Folk Literature 23021
5. Journalism and the Press in Modern Punjab 23030

V. THE NORTHWEST FRONTIER PROVINCE (NWFP) AND TRIBAL AREAS SINCE THE MID-1800's

A. General and Political History

1. General Histories of the Period 23033
2. The British Raj after 1849: NWFP (est. 1901), Tribal Agencies, and Princely States
    a. accounts by officials, soldiers, and travellers 23035
    b. political studies of British rule 23048
    c. Indian nationalism; Abdul Ghaffar Khan (1891-), "the Frontier Gandhi" 23060
3. NWFP and Centrally Administered Tribal Areas of Pakistan since 1947
    a. general studies 23071
    b. agitation for "Pakhtunistan/Pushtunistan," Pathan separatism supported by Afghanistan 23074

B. The Economy of the Northwest Frontier 23081

C. Society and Social Change on the Northwest Frontier

1. Social Categories
    a. general studies 23096
    b. the Pathans: Pushtu-speaking tribal group 23103
    c. Kafirs and other peoples of Chitral 23116
2. Peshawar, capital of NWFP (1972 pop. 268,368) 23124
3. Education on the Northwest Frontier 23128

VI. THE KASHMIR REGION: THE UPPER INDUS VALLEY AND THE KARAKORAM MOUNTAINS

A. General and Political History since 1819

1. Ranjit Singh's Conquest of the Sultanate (1819), and Sikh Rule of Kashmir until 1846 23131
2. The Princely State of Jammu and Kashmir under the British Raj (1846-1957)
    a. Gulab Singh (1792-1857): Dogra Maharaja of Jammu, and his conquest of Kashmir with British backing; his successors 23133
    b. accounts by officials and travellers 23142
    c. J & K relations with the Government of India, 1847-1948 23157
    d. nationalism and communalism; a Hindu Maharaja in a Muslim-majority state 23164
3. Post-Independence Kashmir
    a. the question of Maharaja Hari Singh's accession to India or Pakistan and the resulting conflict [see also Chap. Seven, IV. B. 2] 23174
    b. the Indian state of Jammu and Kashmir
        i. special constitutional status and integration 23175
        ii. Sheikh Mohammad Abdullah (1905-): charismatic leader of Kashmir since 1930 23183
        iii. general studies of Kashmir government and politics since 1947 23190
    c. "Azad Kashmir": Pakistan-administered area of J & K 23203

B. The Economy of the Kashmir Region 23208

VI. C. Society and Social Change (18.6% literacy in 1971) 23225

D. Religions of the Kashmir Region: Islam, Hinduism, Buddhism 23242

E. Literatures of the Kashmir Area

1. Modern Kashmiri Literature 23247
2. Modern Dogri Literature of Jammu 23252
3. Hindi 23256
4. Folk Literatures of Jammu, Kashmir and Ladakh 23257

CHAPTER FOURTEEN: NORTH INDIA: THE POPULOUS HINDI-SPEAKING GANGA PLAINS, INDIA'S POLITICAL AND CULTURAL HEARTLAND, 1801-

I. HARYANA: HINDI-SPEAKING STATE CREATED FROM PUNJAB IN 1966 [see also Chap. Thirteen, IV. A.]

A. Government and Politics since 1966

1. General Studies 23263
2. Election Studies 23269
3. Local Government and Politics 23272

B. The Haryana Economy

1. Demography 23274a
2. Economic Development and Planning 23276
3. Agriculture in Haryana
   a. general studies 23282
   b. land tenure and reform 23292
4. Industry, Labor, and Commerce 23294

C. Society and Social Change

1. Social Categories; Kinship and Marriage 23300
2. Villages and Rural Society; Urbanization 23303
3. Health and Family Planning 23308
4. Education (35.84% literacy in 1981) 23313

D. Literatures of Haryana: Hindi [see Chap. Six VIII. B., & Chap. Eight X. C. 2.] and Folk 23318

II. DELHI, PERENNIAL SITE OF INDIA'S CAPITALS: FROM BRITISH DISTRICT TO UNION TERRITORY

A. General and Political History

1. The British Period, 1803-1947 23320
2. Delhi Politics since 1947 23325
3. Administrative Studies 23333
4. Local Government and Politics
   a. Delhi and New Delhi 23335
   b. panchayati raj and village government in Delhi U.T. 23341

B. The Delhi Economy

1. Demography 23343
2. Economic Development and Planning 23346
3. Agriculture 23351
4. Industry and Labor 23356

C. Society and Social Change

1. Social Categories; Kinship and Marriage 23362
2. Villages and Rural Society 23369
3. Urbanization and Urban Problems: Delhi Urban Area (1981 pop. 5,227,730)
   a. historical studies 23379
   b. urbanization and social change 23386
   c. urban problems 23398
   d. urban planning and development 23412
4. Health Services and Family Planning 23424
5. Education (61.06% literacy in 1981) 23434

III. UTTAR PRADESH: THE GANGA-YAMUNA DOAB AND THE PLAINS OF ROHILKHAND AND AWADH/OUDH

A. General and Political History since 1801
[for 1857 "Mutiny," see Chap. Six, III. A. 2.]

1. The Nawabs of Oudh from 1801 to Company Annexation in 1856 23441
2. Rohilkhand: Ceded to the Company by Oudh in 1801 23448
3. British Rule: The United Provinces of Agra and Oudh (formerly North-Western Provinces and Oudh)
   a. accounts by officials and travellers 23450
   b. British administration 23456
   c. Indian nationalism and U.P. provincial politics, to 1947 23467
   d. the growth of Muslim separatism in the U.P. [see also Chap. Six, III. D. 2.] 23486
4. Uttar Pradesh Government and Politics since 1947
   a. general studies of politics 23491
   b. election studies 23508
   c. mob violence and police firings 23515
   d. administration and judiciary 23520
   e. local government and politics
      i. general studies 23523
      ii. district administration and politics; zila parishads 23530
      iii. municipal government 23533
      iv. village panchayats and administration 23545
      v. nyaya panchayats (village courts) 23555

B. The Economy of Uttar Pradesh since 1801

1. General Economic History to 1947 23558
2. Demography of India's Most Populous State (1981 pop. 110,858,091) 23561
3. Surveys of Economic Conditions since 1947 23568
4. Economic Development and Planning 23571
5. Finance and Banking 23584
6. Agriculture in the U.P. since 1801
   a. surveys and descriptive studies 23590
   b. agricultural development and planning 23598
   c. agricultural technology and innovation; irrigation 23610
   d. agricultural labor 23618
   e. agricultural credit and cooperatives 23623
   f. land tenure, revenue, and reform in British India
      i. general studies of the land system 23629
      ii. the Taluqdari system of Oudh: predominance of great landlords 23637
      iii. the NW Provinces and the land settlement of 1833 23642
   g. land tenure and reform since Independence 23649
   h. peasant movements and agrarian unrest in the U.P. since 1801 23656
7. Industry of the U.P. since 1801
   a. general studies 23664
   b. small-scale industry 23674
8. Labor and Trade Unions 23678
9. Commerce and Transportation 23686

C. Society and Social Change in the U.P. since 1801

1. Social Categories
   a. general studies 23688
   b. kinship and marriage (not specific to one group) 23707
   c. Brahman castes of U.P. 23718
   d. the Kayasthas: a high-caste scribal group 23725
   e. Rajputs of U.P. 23732
   f. merchant castes of U.P. 23735
   g. Jats and other agricultural castes 23738
   h. Scheduled castes: Chamars, Bhangis and others 23743
   j. Muslims of the U.P. (15.5% of the 1971 pop.) 23759
   k. Adivasis (tribals) of the U.P. [for tribals of the Tarai, see Chap. Sixteen, III. C.] 23773
2. Villages and Rural Society
   a. village studies of "Senapur," "Karimpur," etc. 23780
   b. rural change and community development
      i. general studies 23799
      ii. the Pilot Project at Etawah, 1948-54 23813
   c. language, communication, and rural development 23819
3. Cities and Urbanization
   a. general studies 23824
   b. the "KAVAL towns": Kanpur, Agra, Varanasi, Allahabad, Lucknow 23836
   c. other urban centers of U.P. 23855
4. Social Problems and Social Welfare 23864
5. Health Services and Family Planning 23871
6. Education in the U.P. since 1801 (27.38% literacy in 1981)
   a. general studies 23887

III. C. 6. b. higher education
i. Banaras Hindu University (est. 1915) 23893
ii. Aligarh Muslim University [see also Chap. Six, VII. C. 2. c.] 23902
iii. Allahabad University 23905

D. Religious Traditions of the U.P. since 1801 [see also Sacred Centers, Chap. One, IV. C. 3. f.] 23910

E. Literatures of U.P.

1. Hindi and Urdu Literature [for Hindi and Urdu Literature, see Chap. Six, VIII. B. & C., and Chap. Eight, X. C. 2. & 3.]
2. Folk Literature 23933

IV. BIHAR: THE MIDDLE GANGA PLAINS AND THE CHOTA NAGPUR PLATEAU

A. General and Political History since 1801

1. Bihar under the Raj: Part of Bengal Pres. to 1912; 1912-36 Bihar & Orissa Prov.; 1936-47 Bihar Prov. - General Studies and Sources 23944
2. Nationalism and Provincial Politics in British Bihar
a. general studies 23954
b. Gandhi at Champaran 1917: the first test of satyagraha 23964
3. Bihar Government and Politics since 1947
a. general studies 23974
b. election studies 23999
c. riots and communal violence 24008
d. administrative studies 24011
e. local government and politics 24014

B. The Bihar Economy since 1801

1. Demography (1981 pop. 69,823,154) 24030
2. Economic Development and Planning
a. general studies 24033
b. the Damodar Valley Corporation (est. 1948) 24051
3. Agriculture in Bihar since 1801
a. agricultural development and planning 24056
b. agricultural technology and innovation; irrigation and water control 24073
c. famines and famine relief 24079
d. land tenure, land reform, and agrarian relations 24085
e. peasant movements and organizations 24101
4. Industry in Bihar 24106
5. Labor and Trade Unions in Bihar 24123

C. Society and Social Change in Bihar since 1801

1. Social Categories; Kinship and Marriage
a. general studies 24133
b. Brahman castes: Maithil, Gayawal, Bhumihar, and others 24139
c. intermediate castes [for Kayasthas see III. C. 1. d., above]
d. Muslims of Bihar 24149
e. Adivasis (tribals) [for tribes of Chota Nagpur area, see Chap. Twelve, II. C.]
2. Villages and Rural Development 24158
3. Cities and Urbanization
a. general studies 24171
b. Patna, site of ancient Pataliputra, and capital of Bihar (1971 pop. 490,265) 24180
c. Jamshedpur: Tata Iron and Steel Co. (TISCO) center in Singhbhum Dist. (1971 pop. 465,200) 24187
d. Ranchi: political center of Chota Nagpur tribal region (1971 pop. 256,011) 24193
4. Social Welfare and Health Services 24198
5. Education in Bihar since 1801 (26.01% literacy in 1981) 24204

D. Religious Traditions of Modern Bihar [for tribal religions see Chap. Twelve, II. C.] 24221

E. Literatures and Media in Modern Bihar

1. Maithili Literature of North Bihar [see also Chap. One, VI. F. 5.; for Hindi and Urdu Literature, see Chap. Six, VIII. B. & C. and Chap. Eight, X. C. 2. & 3.] 24226
2. Folk Literature 24228
3. Journalism and the Press 24236

CHAPTER FIFTEEN: THE NORTHEAST: THE BENGAL-BANGLADESH AND ASSAM AREA OF THE GANGA DELTA AND BRAHMAPUTRA VALLEY, 1813-

I. BENGAL: THE BENGALI-SPEAKING GANGA DELTA

A. Bengal Presidency: General and Political History, 1813-1947

1. Sources and Reference Works 24241
2. General Histories of Bengal, incl. Local Histories 24250
3. Administration and Judiciary; the Rule of the Lieutenant Governors 24261a
4. Local Government in Bengal, 1813-1947 [for Calcutta, see I. D. 5., below] 24277
5. Nationalism and Bengal Provincial Politics
   a. general studies 24283
   b. early nationalist organizations 24286
   c. Partition of Bengal 1905, India-wide nationalist protest, and re-unification, 1912 24289
   d. later Bengal nationalism: extremism, Gandhism, constitutionalism 24305
   e. Bengal provincial politics - general studies 24326
   f. Muslims in Bengal politics, 1813-1947 24332
   g. A.K. Fazlul Huq (1873-1962), leader of the Krishak Praja Party and the first Premier of Bengal, 1937-42 24341

B. The Indian State of West Bengal - General and Political History since 1947 24349

1. West Bengal Politics - Surveys and General Studies 24349
2. Chief Ministers and other Politicians 24363
3. West Bengal Communist Parties: CPI, CPM, CPML (Naxalites) [see also: Chap. Eight, III. C. 5] 24369
4. Election Studies 24377
5. Administrative Studies 24387
6. Local Government and Politics [for Calcutta, see I. D. 5., below] 24390

C. The Economy of Bengal Presidency and West Bengal State since 1813

1. General Economic History 24397
2. Demography (West Bengal 1981 pop. 54,485,560) 24417
3. Surveys of Economic Conditions since 1947 24422
4. Economic Development and Planning 24429
5. Agriculture since 1813
   a. agriculture in Bengal under the Raj
      i. general studies 24436
      ii. plantation and commercial crops: tea, jute, indigo, opium, forests 24443
      iii. famines and famine control - incl. 1943 Famine 24450
   b. agricultural development in West Bengal since 1947
      i. general studies 24460
      ii. agricultural technology and innovation 24468
   c. rural credit and cooperatives 24474
   d. land tenure, land revenue, and reform
      i. land tenure and revenue under the British 24478
      ii. land reform since 1947 24495
6. Industry in Bengal since 1813
   a. general and historical studies 24510
   b. studies of specific industries - incl. small-scale 24521
7. Labor and Trade Unionism in Bengal
   a. general studies 24533
   b. industrial relations 24536
   c. trade unions and the labor movement 24540
8. Commerce and Transportation in Bengal 24545

D. Society and Social Change since 1813

1. Social Reform and Intellectual Awakening in 19th Century Bengal
   a. general studies 24551
   b. the "Bengal Renaissance" [see also Chap. Six, VII. B] 24561
2. Social Categories in Bengal; Kinship and Marriage
   a. general studies 24578
   b. kinship and marriage (not specific to one group) 24598
   c. the bhadralok ("respectable people") and other elites 24612
   d. Brahman castes of Bengal 24621
   e. intermediate groups: professional, commercial, agricultural, and artisan castes 24626
   f. scheduled castes and tribes of Bengal [for Santals, see Chap. Twelve, II. C. 2] 24633
   g. Muslims of Bengal 24647
   h. Europeans, Jews, and Armenians 24655
   j. women in Bengal 24660
3. Villages and Rural Society in Bengal since 1813
   a. rural society and change under the Raj 24665
   b. general studies of rural society and village studies in West Bengal since 1947 24671

I. D. 3. c. rural community development in W. Bengal since 1947 24688
4. Cities and Urbanization - General Studies 24695
5. Calcutta (1981 pop. 9,165,650)
a. historical studies and descriptions 24708
b. municipal government and politics 24731
c. the Calcutta conurbation (1971 pop. 7,040,345)
i. Howrah and other contiguous cities 24747
ii. relations of city and hinterland 24752
d. socio-economic studies 24759
e. urban planning and development; the Calcutta Metropolitan Planning Organization 24772
f. urban problems and services
i. general studies 24784
ii. slums (bustees/bastis) and housing 24786
iii. transportation and water supply 24791
6. Social Problems and Social Welfare in West Bengal
a. general studies 24804
b. refugees from East Bengal - problems of resettlement 24810
7. Health Services and Family Planning 24815
8. Education in Bengal since 1813 [see also: Rabindranath Tagore, Visvabharati, Chap. Six, V. B. 6. b; Vidyasagar (Ishwar Chandra Sarma) I. F. 2. b., below]
a. general histories and studies (literacy 40.88% in 1981) 24824
b. higher education
i. general studies 24836
ii. the University of Calcutta (est. 1857); Sir Asutosh Mukherjee (1864-1924), High Court judge and educator 24839
iii. other universities and colleges 24847
iv. student attitudes and unrest 24853
c. elementary and secondary education 24855
d. education of Muslims in Bengal, 1813-1947 24860
e. education of women in Bengal 24866

E. Religious Traditions of Modern Bengal [see also: Brahmo Samaj, Chap. Six, VII. B. 2; Ramakrishna, Vivekananda, Chap. Six, VII. B. 5; Sacred Centers, Chap. One, IV. C. 3. g.]

1. General Studies; Folk Religion 24873
2. Hinduism
a. Vaiṣṇava, Śākta, and other sects 24881
b. Lord Dharma and his cult: admixture of Hindu, Buddhist, and tribal elements, appealing to lower castes 24897
c. Śrī Ānandamāyī Mā and her ashram 24902
3. Islam in Modern Bengal; the Farāʿidī/Ferazi Movement 24910
4. Christianity in Modern Bengal 24915

F. Literature and Media in Modern Bengal

1. Bengali Literature - General Studies and Anthologies
a. surveys 24919
b. fiction 24927
c. poetry 24936
d. drama and theatre 24947
2. Modern Bengali Literature - the Formative Period
a. general studies 24952
b. Vidyasagar (Ishwar Chandra Sarma, 1820-91): social and educational reformer, and artificer of modern literary Bengali 24968
c. Bankim Chandra Chatterji/Chattopadhyay (1838-94): government official and leading nationalist novelist 24976
3. Gurudev Rabindranath Tagore (1861-1941): Multifaceted Creative Genius, Patriot-Internationalist, and Nobel Laureate
a. bibliography 24992
b. anthologies and collected works 24998
c. poems and plays in translation 25004
d. philosophical works and letters 25012
e. biography and autobiography 25026
f. commemorative volumes 25043
g. critical studies of Tagore's works 25049
4. Saratchandra Chatterji (1876-1938): Novelist of Social Realism 25068
5. Kazi Nazrul Islam (1899-1976): Nationalist Muslim Poet of Undivided Bengal 25079
6. Post-Tagore Bengali Writers 25086
7. Folk Literature of Bengal
a. folklorists and folklore studies 25109
b. collections of folktales and folksongs 25121
8. Journalism and the Press in Modern Bengal 25127
9. The Bengali Cinema 25138

II. THE PEOPLE'S REPUBLIC OF BANGLADESH (THE FORMER EAST PAKISTAN, 1947-71), 1971-

A. Bibliography and Reference 25141

B. Government and Politics, 1947-

1. General Surveys 25150
2. East Pakistan, 1947-71: An Unequal and Uneasy Partnership with West Pakistan [for Pakistan National Politics, see Chap. Nine]
   a. general studies of provincial politics 25159
   b. the demand for provincial autonomy, the 1971 War, and Independence [see also Chap. Seven, IV. B. 4.] 25165
   c. Sheikh Mujibur Rahman (1922-1975): Awami League leader and first President of Bangladesh 25176
3. The Constitution and Formation of the Nation of Bangladesh 25183
4. Bangladesh Politics since 1971
   a. general political studies, incl. elections 25194
   b. the 1975 coups, assassination of President Mujib, and the martial law regime of Gen. Ziaur Rahman (1936-81) 25208
   c. dilemmas of secularism in a Muslim nation 25218
5. Administrative Studies, 1947- 25221
6. Local Government and Politics since 1947 25229
7. Bangladesh Foreign Relations, 1971- [See also Chap. Seven]
   a. general studies 25251
   b. foreign economic relations: dependence on foreign aid and rebuilding of the export economy 25256

C. The Bangladesh Economy since 1947

1. Bibliography and Reference 25267
2. Demography
   a. bibliography 25272
   b. general studies of the Bangladesh population 25273
   c. population policy and control 25283
3. Surveys of Economic Conditions since 1947
   a. general studies 25287
   b. economic inequality of East Pakistan, 1947-71 25303
4. Economic Development and Planning since 1947 25314
5. Agriculture in Bangladesh since 1947
   a. bibliography 25331
   b. agricultural conditions
      i. general studies 25335
      ii. floods, cyclones and famines 25344
   c. rice and other food crops; the promotion of wheat 25351
   d. jute, tea, and other commercial crops 25359
   e. agricultural planning and development
      i. general studies 25372
      ii. agricultural research, technology, and innovation 25383
      iii. irrigation and water control 25399
      iv. the Comilla project: Bangladesh Academy of Rural Development (est. 1957) 25411
   f. rural credit and cooperatives 25431
   g. rural labor and unemployment 25440
   h. land tenure and reform 25444
6. Industry in Bangladesh since 1947
   a. general studies 25455
   b. small-scale and cottage industries 25466
7. Labor and Trade Unions in Bangladesh since 1947 25469
8. Commerce and Transportation in Bangladesh 25475

D. Society and Social Change in Bangladesh since 1947

1. General Studies 25487
2. Social Categories, incl. Kinship and Marriage
   a. general studies 25493
   b. Muslims of Bangladesh (85.4% in 1974) incl. the Bihari Muslim minority 25497
   c. Hindus (6.9% caste Hindu, 6.6% scheduled castes, in 1974) 25503
   d. tribals (Buddhist, Hindu, Muslim and other): meeting with Burmese culture 25506
   e. women of Bangladesh 25516
3. Villages and Rural Society
   a. village studies 25528
   b. stratification and exploitation 25540
   c. community development; the svanirvār ("self-reliance") program 25547
4. Cities and Urbanization
   a. general studies 25561
   b. Dacca: Mughal provincial capital; capital and cultural center of Bangladesh (1974 pop. 1,679,572) 25566
5. Social Problems and Social Welfare 25572

II. D. 6. Health Services and Family Planning
a. health and medical services 25584
b. family planning 25590
7. Education in Bangladesh since 1947
a. general studies 25606
b. higher education; University of Dacca (est. 1921) 25616
c. elementary and secondary education 25627
d. rural education and literacy (1974 literacy 22.2%) 25631

E. Religions of Bangladesh: Islam, Hinduism, Buddhism 25636

F. Literature and Media in Bangladesh

1. Bengali Literature since 1947 25645
2. Folk Literature 25654
3. Journalism and the Press 25662

G. Art of Bangladesh 25665

III. ASSAM: THE PLAINS AND FOOTHILLS OF THE BRAHMAPUTRA VALLEY

A. General and Political History since 1826

1. Assam under the British (annexed 1826)
a. general studies 25677
b. accounts by travellers and officials 25687
c. administrative studies and local government, 1826-1947 25691
d. nationalist movement and provincial politics 25695
2. Government and Politics of Assam since 1947
a. states reorganization: separation of the tribal hill areas from Assam [see also Chap. Sixteen, VII] 25700
b. general studies of Assam politics 25706
c. election studies 25712
d. local government and panchayati raj 25716

B. The Assam Economy since 1826

1. Economic History; Dominance of the Tea Plantations 25722
2. Demography (1981 est. pop. 19,903,000) 25734
3. Surveys of Economic Conditions since 1947; Flood Control 25737
4. Economic Development and Planning 25742
5. Agriculture in Assam since 1826
a. general studies of agricultural development 25748
b. land tenure and reform 25763
6. Industry and Labor 25765

C. Society and Social Change in Assam since 1826

1. Social Categories of Assam
a. general studies 25775
b. Bengalis in Assam (19.7% of pop. in 1971): unwelcome immigrants, Hindu and Muslim 25779
c. Assamese Hindus and Muslims 25783
d. tribals of Assam [see also Chap. Sixteen, VII] 25785
2. Villages and Rural Society 25794
3. Social Services, Health, and Education 25803

D. Religions of Assam: Hinduism, Islam, Folk Religions 25806

E. Modern Assamese Literature

1. General Studies 25814
2. Lakshminath Bezbarua (1868-1938): Nationalist Poet, Dramatist and Fiction Writer 25823
3. Folk Literature 25826

CHAPTER SIXTEEN: THE HIMALAYAS AND EASTERN MOUNTAIN RIM OF INDIA, NEPAL AND BHUTAN: FRINGES OF TIBETAN, BUDDHIST, AND SOUTHEAST ASIAN CULTURES, 1816-

I. GENERAL STUDIES OF THE NORTHERN AND EASTERN BORDERLAND SINCE 1800

A. Historical Accounts and Studies 25834

B. Political Studies 25840

C. Economic, Social, and Cultural Studies 25848

II. HIMACHAL PRADESH: THE WESTERN PAHARI-SPEAKING REGION

A. General and Political History since 1800

1. The Himachal Area under the Raj: Rajput Hill States and British Districts of Punjab 25856
2. Government and Politics since 1948 (from Union Territory to State, 1971) 25859

B. The Economy of Himachal Pradesh

1. Demography 25869
2. Economic Development and Planning 25870
3. Agriculture 25877

C. Society and Social Change in Himachal Pradesh 25880

D. Religion and Folklore 25892

III. KUMAON AND GARHWAL: THE U.P. HIMALAYAS, SACRED SOURCE OF THE GANGA AND YAMUNA

A. General History and Accounts of the Central Himalayas since 1815 25899

B. The Economy of the U.P. Himalayas 25905

C. Society and Social Change in the Central and Eastern Pahari-Speaking Areas 25912

D. Religions and Folklore of the Garhwal and Kumaon Himalayas [For Sacred Centers, see Chap. One, IV. C. 3. h.] 25928

IV. NEPAL: INDEPENDENT HIMALAYAN KINGDOM BETWEEN INDIA AND TIBET

A. General and Political History since 1816

1. General Histories of Modern Nepal 25944
2. Accounts by Travellers and Officials 25951
3. The Hindu Monarchy of Nepal: A Rajput Dynasty
   a. general studies 25957
   b. hereditary rule by Rana prime ministers ("maharajas"), 1846-1951 25962
   c. King Tribhuvana Bir Bikram Shaha Deva (1906-1955) and the restoration of royal authority in 1951 25969
   d. King Mahendra Bir Bikrama Shaha Deva (1920-72): continued autocracy under 1962 "Panchayat" Constitution
      i. general studies 25970
      ii. the 1959 and 1962 Constitutions 25975
   e. King Birendra Bir Bikram Shaha Deva (1945-): rejection of parliamentary democracy in favor of partyless Panchayat System 25989
4. Nepali Politics
   a. general studies 25993
   b. pre-1951 politics: demand for a constitution and opposition to the Ranas 26007
   c. 1951-61: experiment with party politics 26009
   d. the Panchayat System: a "partyless democracy"? 26014
5. Administrative Studies 26022
6. Law and Judiciary 26036
7. Local Government and Politics 26039
8. Foreign Relations of Nepal: from Isolationism to Non-Alignment
   a. documents 26041
   b. general studies 26044
   c. relations with British India: protectorate and buffer state 26053
   d. Nepal and its neighbors
      i. relations with India and other South Asian nations 26064
      ii. relations with Tibet and China 26075
      iii. Sino-Indian rivalries over Nepal 26079
   e. foreign economic relations of Nepal: trade and aid 26085

B. The Nepal Economy

1. General Economic History of Modern Nepal 26100
2. Demography and Population Policy 26102
3. Surveys of Economic Conditions 26110
4. Economic Development and Planning 26122
5. Finance and Banking 26140
6. Agriculture
   a. general studies of agricultural development 26148
   b. agricultural technology and innovation; irrigation 26161
   c. agrarian relations, land tenure and reform 26166
7. Industry in Nepal 26174
8. Labor in Nepal 26180
9. Commerce and Transportation 26184

IV. C. Society and Social Change in Nepal since 1816

1. Social Categories, incl. Kinship and Marriage
   a. general studies 26190
   b. Tibeto-Nepalese peoples of the northern border: Sherpas and other Bhotiyas 26205
   c. peoples of the middle hills and valleys
      i. the Magar, Gurung, and Rai, sources of the Gurkha regiments [see also Chap. Six, II. B. 7. b.] 26223
      ii. the Newars: dominant group of the Kathmandu Valley 26243
      iii. other groups of the middle region 26250
   d. Brahmans and Chetris: Nepali Hindu castes 26260
   e. peoples of the Tarai, marshy plain and forests of the Indian border
      i. the Tharus, immigrants from the Indian Tarai 26264
      ii. Nepali Muslims (2% of pop.), mostly merchants of the Tarai 26269
   f. women of Nepal 26272
2. Villages and Rural Development 26280
3. Urbanization, Migration, and Settlement Patterns 26286
4. Social Welfare and Health Services, incl. Family Planning 26294
5. Education in Nepal (16% literacy) 26303

D. Religions of Nepal: Buddhism, Hinduism, Islam and Folk Cults 26318

E. Literatures of Modern Nepal

1. Modern Literature in Nepali 26340
2. Newari Literature 26351
3. Folk Literature 26353

V. SIKKIM STATE AND DARJEELING DISTRICT OF WEST BENGAL (SINCE 1817)

A. General and Political History

1. General Histories of Modern Sikkim 26358
2. The Sikkim Raj as a British Protectorate, 1817-1947 26360
3. Sikkim as an Indian Protectorate, 1947-1975: from Buddhist Theocracy towards Constitutional Democracy 26369
4. Integration of Sikkim as an Indian State, 1975- (1981 pop. 315,682) 26380
5. The Darjeeling Area, Ceded by Sikkim in 1835 26385

B. The Economy of Sikkim and Darjeeling 26389

C. Society and Religion: Buddhist Lepchas and Bhotes, and Hindu Nepalese (33.83% literacy in 1981) 26396

VI. BHUTAN/DRUKYUL: INDEPENDENT BUDDHIST MONARCHY OF THE EASTERN HIMALAYAS

A. General and Political History since 1772

1. General Histories and Accounts of Modern Bhutan 26412
2. Government and Politics 26416
3. Foreign Relations of Bhutan
   a. general studies 26423
   b. relations with British India, 1772-1947 26425
   c. relations with Independent India, 1947- 26431

B. Society and Religion in Bhutan (1977 pop. 1,100,000) 26436

VII. THE NORTHEAST INDIAN MOUNTAIN RIM: TRIBAL INTERFACE WITH BURMA AND CHINA

A. General Studies of the Arunachal, Purvanchal and Meghalaya Areas Bordering Assam

1. Historical Accounts and Studies 26441
2. Political Studies 26451
3. Economic, Social, and Cultural Studies 26460
4. Religions and Folklore of the NE Tribal Areas 26467

B. Arunachal Pradesh: the Former North-East Frontier Agency (NEFA) of the Eastern Himalaya (1981 pop. 628,050)

1. Historical and Political Studies
   a. the British period, 1827-1947 26475
   b. post-1947: from NEFA (1954) to Arunachal Pradesh U.T. (1972) 26478
2. Economic and Social Development (29.09% literacy in 1981) 26482
3. Tribal Peoples of Arunachal
   a. general studies 26486

VII. B. 3. b. tribals of Kameng District 26493
c. tribals of Subansiri District 26496
d. tribals of Siang District 26503
e. tribals of Lohit District 26509
f. tribals of Tirap District 26512

C. Nagaland: Fiercely Independent Naga Tribes of the Indo-Burmese Border

1. Historical and Political Studies
a. general studies 26515
b. accounts by travellers and officials 26519
c. Nagaland State (est. 1963) - government and politics (1981 pop. 773,281) 26521
d. continuing independence demands and guerrilla insurgency 26531
2. Economic and Social Development (41.99% literacy in 1981) 26540
3. The Naga Tribes - Ethnographic Studies 26556
4. Folklore 26574

D. Manipur: Former Princely State, Founded by a Hinduized Naga in 1714 (1981 pop. 1,433,691)

1. Historical and Political Studies (Statehood Granted 1972) 26575
2. Economic and Social Development (41.99% literacy in 1981) 26579
3. Social Categories of Manipur
a. the Meitei Hindu community: Brahmans, Kshatriyas and outcastes 26582
b. Purums and other tribal groups of Manipur 26584
4. Chaitanya Vaisnavism of Manipur, State Religion 1714-1949 26596
5. Manipuri Language and Literature (Tibeto-Burman Language in Bengali Script) 26599
6. Manipuri Dancing [See Chap. One, VII. C. 3. e.]

E. Mizoram: Land of the Christianized Mizo Tribes of the Lushai Hills (1981 pop. 487,774)

1. Historical and Political Studies (from Assam District to U.T., 1972)
a. general studies 26604
b. the Mizo National Front under Laldenga (1919-), and the armed struggle for secession 26606
2. Economic and Social Development (59.59% literacy in 1981) 26610
3. Tribals of Mizoram - Ethnography and Religion (86% Christian) 26613

F. Tripura: Former Princely State, Bengali-Speaking Hindu Salient into Bangladesh (1981 pop. 2,060,189)

1. Historical and Political Studies (Statehood Granted 1972) 26627
2. Economic and Social Development (41.58% literacy in 1981) 26636
3. Social Categories in Tripura
a. Bengali residents and refugees from Bangladesh 26644
b. tribals of Tripura (30% of pop.), incl. Bodo-speaking Tripuris, Riangs, Chakmas, and Kukis 26645

G. Meghalaya ("Abode of Clouds"): The Garo, Khasi, and Jaintia Hills of the Shillong Plateau (1981 pop. 1,327,874)

1. Historical and Political Studies (Autonomous Status within Assam, 1970; Statehood, 1972) 26649
2. Economic and Social Development (33.22% literacy in 1981) 26656
3. Matrilineal Tribes of Meghalaya
a. general studies 26669
b. the Garos, a Bodo (Tibeto-Burman) speaking people 26671
c. the Khasis, a Mon-Khmer speaking people 26684
d. other tribes of Meghalaya 26697
4. Religions in Meghalaya: Preference for Christianity over Hinduization (1971, 47% Christian, 18% Hindu, 3% Muslim, 31% Tribal) 26699
5. Languages and Literatures of Meghalaya 26701

VIII. THE ANDAMAN AND NICOBAR ISLANDS: INDIA'S OCEAN FRONTIER IN THE BAY OF BENGAL

A. General and Historical Studies (British Chief Commissioner's Province, a U.T. since 1956) (1981 pop. 188,254; Literacy 51.27%) 26707

B. The Economy of the Bay Islanders 26714

C. Tribals of the Andamans and Nicobars (1971 pop. 18,102) 26720

CHAPTER SEVENTEEN: THE INDIC DIASPORA: SOUTH ASIAN COMMUNITIES THROUGHOUT THE WORLD

I. SOUTH ASIAN COMMUNITIES OVERSEAS AFTER 1800 - GENERAL STUDIES

- A. Histories and Surveys 26737
- B. Sociological Studies of Overseas Indians 26753
- C. Export of Indian Coolies to British Tropical Colonies 26758

II. THE SUGAR PLANTATION COLONIES AND THEIR SUCCESSOR INDEPENDENT NATIONS

- A. Mauritius: Anglo-French Island in the Indian Ocean (South Asian pop. 66%) 26761
- B. The Caribbean and South America: British, French, and Dutch Colonies
  1. General Studies 26773
  2. The Guianas: Guyana, Surinam, and French Guiana 26775
  3. Trinidad and Tobago 26791
- C. Fiji: British Islands in the South Pacific, Independent since 1970 (South Asian pop. 51%) 26803

III. SOUTH ASIANS IN AFRICA SINCE 1800

- A. General Studies 26816
- B. South Africa: the Smallest and Most Vulnerable Minority of the Apartheid System (South Asian pop. 3%)
  1. Histories and General Studies 26819
  2. Early Indian Emigration to the Crown Colony of Natal, 1860-1893 26825
  3. Gandhi and the Birth of Satyagraha, 1893-1914 [See also Chap. Six, IV. A.] 26827
  4. Continuing Discrimination against South Asians, 1914- 26832
- C. East and Central Africa: British and German Colonies
  1. General Studies 26842
  2. British Colonial Rule: Indians as Laborers, Traders, and Minor Bureaucrats 26853
  3. South Asians under the Independent African States
     - a. general studies 26857
     - b. the 1972 expulsion of Asians from Uganda by Idi Amin 26865

IV. SOUTH ASIANS IN THE MIDDLE EAST 26871

V. SOUTH ASIANS IN SOUTHEAST ASIA AND HONG KONG

- A. General Studies 26874
- B. Burma: Part of the Indian Empire until 1937; Expulsion of Indians from Independent Burma, in 1962 26877
- C. Malaysia and Singapore: South Asians as a Third Minority between Malays and Chinese (South Asian pop. 11%) 26881
- D. The Hong Kong Indian Community 26891

VI. SOUTH ASIAN COMMUNITIES IN THE UNITED KINGDOM

- A. General Studies 26892
- B. Indian Immigrants to Britain
  1. General Studies 26903
  2. The Sikhs: a Distinctive and Visible Punjabi-speaking Minority 26911
  3. The Ugandan Indian Refugees 26917
- C. Pakistani and Bangladeshi Muslims in the U.K. 26919
- D. South Asian Women: Varying Adaptations to British Society 26925

VII. SOUTH ASIANS IN NORTH AMERICA

A. General Studies 26928

B. Canada, a Commonwealth Partner

1. Early Immigration: South Asian Laborers on the West Coast before Exclusion 1913-1947 26932
2. Post-Independence Immigration; Encouragement of Professional and Technical Immigrants after 1967 26936

C. The United States

1. Early Immigration: Swamis, Sikhs, and Students, 1893-1945 26941
2. The Post-War Influx of Students and Elite Immigrants, 1945- 26942

PART FIVE: REFERENCE RESOURCES

CHAPTER EIGHTEEN: INTRODUCTIONS AND GENERAL RESEARCH GUIDES FOR TRAVELLERS AND SCHOLARS

I. GENERAL REFERENCE 26952

II. PHYSICAL AND HUMAN ECOLOGY: A SCHOLAR'S AND TRAVELLER'S INTRODUCTION

A. Overall Works on India and South Asia

1. Reference Works 26957
2. Selected Introductions 26967
3. Geography and Climate; Atlases
   a. bibliography and reference 26984
   b. atlases 26994
   c. surveys and studies 27007
4. Natural History 27024
5. Travellers' Accounts 27047
6. Travel, City, and Hotel Guides 27066
7. Images and Stereotypes of South Asia and South Asians 27080

B. Overall Introductions to Pakistan

1. Reference 27087
2. Introductions 27091
3. Geography and Natural History 27110
4. Travellers' Accounts 27118
5. Travel, City, and Hotel Guides 27127

C. Sri Lanka

1. Reference 27130
2. Introductions 27133
3. Geography and Natural History 27142
4. Travellers' Accounts 27151
5. Travel Guides 27155

D. South India: Tamil Nadu, Kerala, Karnataka, Andhra Pradesh

1. Introductions 27158
2. Geography 27171
3. Travellers' Accounts 27176
4. Travel, City, and Hotel Guides 27179

E. Middle India: Maharashtra, Gujarat, Rajasthan, Madhya Pradesh, Orissa

1. Introductions 27184
2. Geography and Natural History 27197
3. Travel, City, and Hotel Guides 27204

F. Indus Valley Region and Mountain Frontier: Sind, Baluchistan, Punjab, NWFP, Kashmir

1. Introductions 27212
2. Geography 27227
3. Travellers' Accounts 27234
4. Travel, City, and Hotel Guides 27248

II. G. The Ganga Plains of North India: Haryana, Delhi, Uttar Pradesh, Bihar

1. Introductions 27256
2. Geography and Natural History 27266
3. Travellers' Accounts 27271
4. Travel, City, and Hotel Guides 27276

H. The Northeast: The Bengal-Bangladesh and Assam Area of the Ganga Delta

1. Bengal and Assam
   a. introductions 27283
   b. geography 27289
   c. travel, city, and hotel guides 27293
2. Bangladesh
   a. introductions 27300
   b. geography and natural history 27307

J. The Himalayas and Eastern Mountain Rim of India, Nepal, and Bhutan

1. India and Bhutan
   a. introductions 27312
   b. geography and natural history 27342
   c. travellers' accounts 27346
   d. travel, city, and hotel guides 27356
2. Nepal
   a. introductions 27361
   b. geography and natural history 27373
   c. travellers' accounts 27381
   d. travel, city, and hotel guides 27399

III. TEACHING AND STUDY OF SOUTH ASIA

A. The State of Academic Study of South Asia (Outside the Subcontinent)

1. The United States and Canada 27408
2. Europe and the United Kingdom 27420

B. Guides to Study in South Asia: Teaching and Research Centers 27424

C. Teaching and Research Aids

1. Syllabi 27448
2. Indic Names and Their Transliteration 27453
3. Almanacs and Calendars 27463
4. Who's Whos and Biographical Dictionaries
   a. general 27465
   b. professional 27486
5. Dictionaries of Anglo-Indian Terms 27496

IV. SOUTH ASIAN RESEARCH MATERIALS: LOCATION AND ACCESS

A. Location and Acquisition of Research Materials

1. Library Collections
   a. United States 27503
   b. United Kingdom
      i. general 27511
      ii. British Library (formerly British Museum) 27520
      iii. India Office Library and Records 27524
      iv. The School of Oriental and African Studies, London University 27531
   c. South Asia 27533
2. Archival and Manuscript Collections
   a. America and Europe 27544
   b. South Asia 27554
3. Publishers and Bookdealers in South Asia
   a. "Books in Print" for Indian books in English 27566
   b. book industry of South Asia: directories and journals 27571
4. Access to Periodical Literature on and from South Asia
   a. lists and bibliographies of periodicals 27583
   b. guides to contents of periodicals 27597
5. Access to Books: Reviews of Current Publications 27623
6. Access to Festschriften 27628

B. General Bibliographies Containing South Asia Materials

1. Bibliographies of Bibliographies 27631
2. Bibliographies of Reference Works 27637
3. General Bibliographies for South Asia
   a. South Asia and India 27645
   b. Pakistan 27660
4. Special Subject Bibliographies 27676
5. Bibliographies of Theses and Dissertations 27687

IV. B. 6. Regional Bibliographies
a. Sri Lanka 27700
b. South India 27707
c. Middle India 27713
d. Indus Valley and Mountain Frontier 27718
e. the Ganga Plains of North India 27729
f. the Northeast: Assam and the Bengals 27730
g. the Himalayan Rim 27736

C. Statistical and Codified Information on South Asia

1. Guides to the Statistics of South Asia 27748
2. Major Statistical Compendia
a. South Asian censuses: guides and descriptions 27756
b. national statistical yearbooks and abstracts [volumes also pub. at state and district level] 27766
3. Gazetteers: Historical and Geographical Compendia 27778

V. TOOLS FOR THE STUDY OF THE LITERARY LANGUAGES OF SOUTH ASIA

A. Bibliographies and Reference Works on South Asian Languages 27784

B. Pan-South Asian Languages

1. Sanskrit: Vedic and Classical
a. dictionaries 27791
b. learning aids: grammars and readers 27798
2. Pali and Prakrits
a. dictionaries 27807
b. learning aids 27811
3. Persian 27816
4. Hindi, Urdu, and Hindustani
a. dictionaries 27819
b. grammars 27827
c. introductory texts 27832
d. readers 27842

C. Regional Literary Languages

1. Sinhala: the Indo-Aryan Language of Sri Lanka 27849
2. South Indian Dravidian Languages
a. Tamil
i. dictionaries 27860
ii. learning aids 27867
b. Malayalam of Kerala
i. dictionaries 27877
ii. learning aids 27882
c. Kannada of Karnataka
i. dictionaries
ii. learning aids 27890
d. Telugu of Andhra Pradesh
i. dictionaries 27896
ii. learning aids 27900
3. Middle India
a. Marathi of Maharashtra
i. dictionaries 27908
ii. learning aids 27915
b. Konkani of Goa and the West Coast 27922
c. Gujarati
i. dictionaries 27925
ii. learning aids 27930
d. Oriya of Orissa
i. dictionaries 27934
ii. learning aids 27938
4. Indus Valley and Mountain Frontier
a. Sindhi
i. dictionaries 27942
ii. learning aids 27947
b. Baluchi 27949
c. Panjabi
i. dictionaries 27953
ii. learning aids 27957
d. Kashmiri: the Dardic language of Kashmir 27967
e. Pashto of the Frontier 27972
5. The Ganga Plains of North India [for Hindi, see V. B. 4. above]
6. The Northeast: Bengal-Bangladesh and Assam
a. Bengali of West Bengal and Bangladesh
i. dictionaries 27984
ii. learning aids 27992
b. Assamese 28001
7. Nepal
a. Nepali: an Indo-Aryan language 28008
b. Newari: a Tibeto-Burman language 28016

The Bibliographic Entries

Part One
Overview of the Great Tradition

1

Traditional South Asia: Enduring Structures and Concepts through Space and Time

I. HISTORY AND CURRENT STATE OF CLASSICAL INDIC STUDIES

A. Indology

1. Bibliography and Methodology - including Catalogs of Sanskrit Manuscripts

00001 AUFRECHT, T. Catalogus catalogorum: an alphabetical register of Sanskrit works and authors. Wiesbaden: Steiner, 1962. 3 v. in 2. [Rpt. of 1891-1903 ed. Continued by New catalogus catalogorum]

00002 CHAUDHURI, S. Bibliography of indological studies in 1953: a survey of periodical publications. Calcutta: ASB, 1958. 54p. [1st pub in JASBengal (Letters) 3d ser. 22,1 (1956) suppl. 1-43]

00003 ______. Bibliography of indological studies in 1954: a survey of periodical publications. In JASBengal (Letters) 3d ser. 23 (1957) 1-64.

00004 ______. Bibliography of indological studies in 1956: a survey of periodical publications. Calcutta: ASB, 1978. 303p.

00005 DANDEKAR, R.N. Vedic bibliography; an up-to-date, comprehensive, and analytically arranged register of all important work done since 1930 in the field of the Veda and allied antiquities including Indus Valley civilisation. v. 1 Bombay: Karnatak Pub. House, 1946. 398p.; v. 2 Poona: U. of Poona, 1961. 760p.; v. 3 Poona: BORI, 1973. 1082p. [Continues L. Renou's Bibliographie védique]

00006 JANERT, K.L., et al. Indische Handschriften. Wiesbaden: Steiner, 1962-. 3 v. (Verzeichnis der orientalischen Handschriften in Deutschland, 2:1-3)

00007 KOSAMBI, D.D. Combined methods in Indology. In IIJ 6 (1962) 177-202.

00008 MUKHERJEE, A.K. Guide to selected reference tools and Indological source materials: classified and annotated. Calcutta: World Press, 1979. 267p.

00009 New catalogus catalogorum; an alphabetical register of Sanskrit and allied works and authors. Madras: U. of Madras, 1949-. [10 v. issued as of 1978. Continues T. Aufrecht, Catalogus catalogorum]

00010 PANDURANGI, D.T. The wealth of Sanskrit manuscripts in India and abroad. Bangalore: Pandurangi, 1978. 42p.

00011 POLEMAN, H.I. A census of Indic manuscripts in the United States and Canada. NY: Kraus Reprint Corp., 1967. 542p. [Rpt. of 1938 ed.]

00012 RAGHAVAN, V. Bibliography of books, papers and other contributions of Dr. V. Raghavan. Ahmedabad: New Order Book Co., 1968. 370p.

00013 ______. Manuscripts, catalogues, editions; steps taken for the collection, preservation, and utilisation of manuscripts. Madras: Bharati Vijayam Press, 1963. 111p.

00014 RENOU, L. Bibliographie védique. Paris: Adrien-Maisonneuve, 1931. 339p. [Cont. by R.N. Dandekar's Vedic bibliography]

2. Festschriften

00015 BENDER, E., ed. Indological studies in honor of W. Norman Brown. New Haven: AOS, 1962. 253p.

00016 CHATTERJI, S.K., et al., eds. Some aspects of Indo-Iranian literary and cultural traditions: commemoration volume of Dr. V.G. Paranjpe. Delhi: Ajanta, 1977. 159p.

00017 CHATTOPADHYAYA, D., ed. History and society: essays in honour of Professor Niharranjan Ray. Calcutta: K.P. Bagchi, 1978. 642p.

00018 DAVE, J.H., et al., eds. Munshi indological felicitation volume...to Dr. K.M. Munshi on his completion of seventy-five years.... Bombay: BVB, 1963. 412p. [1st pub. as BV, 20-21 (1960-61)]

00019 Dr. V. Raghavan shashtyabdapurti felicitation volume; a souvenir of the 61st birthday celebrations and a collection of essays contributed in his honour by his friends, colleagues, and students on that occasion. Madras: Dr. V. Raghavan Shashtyabdapurti Felicitation Cmtee., Kuppuswami Sastri Res. Inst., 1971. 419p.

00020 GANESAN, S., ed. Prof K.A. Nilakanta Sastri felicitation volume. Madras: Prof. K.A. Nilakanta Sastri Felicitation Cmtee., 1971. 497p.

00021 GOPAL, L., et al., eds. D.D Kosambi commemoration volume. Varanasi: D.D. Kosambi Cmtee., Banaras Hindu University, 1977. 320p.

00022 HEESTERMANN, J.C. & G.H. SCHOKKER & V.I. SUBRAMANIAM, eds., Pratidānam: Indian, Iranian, and Indo-European studies presented to Franciscus Bernardus Jacobus Kuiper on his sixtieth birthday. The Hague: Mouton, 1968. 627p. (Janua Linguarum. Series Major, 34)

00023 JAYAWICKRAMA, N.A., ed. Paranavitana felicitation volume on art and architecture and oriental studies.... Colombo: M.D. Gunasena, 1965. 353p.

00024 K.C. Chaṭṭopādhyaya memorial volume. Allahabad: Dept. of Ancient Hist., Culture and Archaeol., Allahabad U., 1975. 175p.

00025 KRÜGER, H. Neue Indienkunde; new indology: Festschrift Walter Ruben zum 70 Geburtstag. Berlin: Akademie Verlag, 1970. 552p.

00026 Languages and areas: studies presented to George V. Bobrinskoy. Chicago: UChiP, 1967. 189p.

00027 SAKSENA, B.R., et al., eds. Umesha Mishra commemoration volume. Allahabad: GJRI, 1970. 793p.

00028 SUBRAMANYAM, R. & N. RAMESAN, eds. Sri Mallampalli Somasekhara Sarma commemoration volume. Hyderabad: Govt. of Andhra Pradesh, 1976. 578p. [Pub. as JAHRS 35 (1975-76)]

3. Collected Essays

00029 ALSDORF, L. Kleine Schriften. Ed. by A. Wezler. Wiesbaden: Steiner, 1974. 762p.

00030 BROWN, W.N. India and Indology: selected articles. Ed. by R. Rocher. Delhi: Motilal, 1978. 367p.+28pl.

00031 FRANKE, R.O. Kleine Schriften. Ed. by O. von Hinüber. Wiesbaden: Steiner, 1978. 2 v. 1547p. (Glasenapp-Stiftung, 17)

00032 FILLIOZAT, J. Laghu-Prabandhāḥ. Choix d'articles d'Indologie. Leiden: Brill, 1974. 508p.

00033 GOETZ, H. Studies in the history, religion and art of classical and mediaeval India. Ed. by H. Kulke. Wiesbaden: Steiner, 1974. 208p.

00034 KIRFEL, W. Kleine Schriften. Ed. by R. Birwe. Wiesbaden: Steiner, 1976. 464p.

00035 PRINSEP, J. Essays on Indian antiquities, historic, numismatic, and palaeographic.... Ed. by E. Thomas. Varanasi: Indological Book House, 1971. 2 v. [1st pub. 1858]

00036 SASTRI, S. Essays on Indology. Delhi: Meharchand Lachmandass, 1963. 236p.

00037 SHASTRI, D.N. & D.R. PAL & P. KUMAR, eds. Studies in indology. Delhi: Inst. of Indology, 1973? 212p.

00038 SIRCAR, D.C., ed. Pracyavidya-Tarangini: golden jubilee volume of the Department of Ancient History and Culture. Calcutta: U. of Calcutta, 1969. 540p.

00039 STCHERBATSKY, Th. Papers of Th. Stcherbatsky. Tr. from Russian by H.C. Gupta. Ed. by D. Chattopadhyaya. Calcutta: ISPP, 1969. 136p.

00040 TUCCI, G. Opera minora. Roma: G. Bardi, 1971. 2 v.

00041 ZACHARIAE, T. Opera minora zur indischen Wortforschung, zur Geschichte der indischen Literatur und Kultur, zur Geschichte der Sanskritphilologie. Ed. by C. Vogel. Wiesbaden: Steiner, 1977. 2 v. (Glasenapp-Stiftung, 12)

4. History of Indology

00042 CHATTERJEE, A.K. A brief history of Indological studies. In JAIH 9, 1/2 (1975-6) 23-56.

00043 CHINMULGUND, P.J. & V.V. MIRASHI, eds. Review of Indological research in last 75 years. Poona: Bharatiya Charitrakosha Mandal, 1967. 849p. (M.M. Chitraoshastri Felicitation Volume)

00044 DANDEKAR, R.N. Decade of Vedic studies in India and abroad. In ABORI 56 (1975) 1-25.

00045 ______. Progress of Indic studies, 1917-1942. Poona: BORI, 1942. 406p.

00046 ______. Recent trends in Indology. Poona: BORI, 1978. 131p. (BOS 11)

00047 ______. Some trends in Indological studies. In ABORI 58/59 (1977/78) 525-41.

00048 DANDEKAR, R.N. & V. RAGHAVAN, eds. Oriental studies in India. ND: Organising Cttee., 26th Internatl. Congress of Orientalists, 1964. 268p.

00049 GULIK, R. VAN Siddham: an essay on the history of Sanskrit studies in China and Japan. Nagpur: Internatl. Academy of Indian Culture, 1956. 240p. (Sarasvati vihara series, 36)

00050 O'FLAHERTY, W.D. Disregarded scholars: a survey of Russian Indology. In SAR 6 (1972) 332-5.

00051 PARPOLA, A. Indological studies in Scandinavia. In JAIH 4,1/2 (1970-71) 218-25.

00052 RAGHAVAN, V. Indological studies in India. Delhi: Motilal, 1964. 46p.

00053 ______. Sanskrit and allied Indian studies in U.S. Gauhati: Gauhati U., 1975. 167p.

00054 ______. Sanskrit and allied Indological studies in Europe. Madras: U. of Madras, 1956. 117p.

00055 ______. Some aspects of recent research in Sanskrit and Indology; some trends and desiderata. In ALB 40 (1976) 115-41.

00056 ROCHER, R. The beginning of Indological studies. In JAIH 3, 1/2 (1969-70) 1-16.

00057 RUBEN, W. Indological studies in the German Democratic Republic. In VQ 27, 3/4 (1961-62) 197-211.

00058 TISCHLER, J. Statistische Methoden in der Indologie. In ZDMG 123 (1973) 316-27.

5. Studies of Individual Indologists and Their Work

00059 CORREIA-AFONSO, J., ed. Henry Heras, the scholar and his work. Bombay: HIIHC, 1976. 36p.

00060 DANDEKAR, R.N., ed. Ramakrishna Gopal Bhandarkar as an indologist: a symposium. Poona: BORI, 1976. 200p.

00061 GEROW, E. Renou's place in Vedic exegetical tradition. In JAOS 88 (1968) 310-333.

00062 PHADKE, H.A. R.G. Bhandarkar. ND: NBT, 1968. 89p.

00063 RICHARDS, J.F., ed. Symposium: the achievement of Georges Dumézil. In JAS 34,1 (1974) 117-67. [essays by A. Hiltebeitel, J. Gonda, C.S. Littleton, D.M. Knipe]

00064 ROCHER, R. Alexander Hamilton (1762-1824), a chapter in the early history of Sanskrit philology. New Haven: AOS, 1968. 128p. (AOS, 51)

00065 Suniti Kumar Chatterji: the scholar and the man. Calcutta: Jijnasa, 1970. 149p. [31-149 bibl. of his works]

00066 TOPE, T.K. Modern sage: brief sketch of the life and learning of M.M. Dr. P.V. Kane, National Research Professor of Indology. Poona: Brahman Sabha, 1960. 139p.

B. Tamil Studies and Dravidology

1. Bibliography and Reference

00067 MANAVALAN, A.A. Tamil research through journals: an annotated bibliography. Madras: Internatl. Inst. of Tamil St., 1975. 228p.

00068 NÖLLE, W. Dravidian studies: a review. Delhi: Jain Bros., 1965. 60p.

00069 THANI NAYAGAM, X.S. A bibliographical guide to Tamil studies. In TC 9 (1961) 333-334.

00070 ______. The bibliography of Tamil studies. In TC 10 (1963) 98-108.

00071 ______. A reference guide to Tamil studies: books. Kuala Lumpur: Malaya U. Press, 1966. 122p.

00072 THOMAS, A. M. Dissertations in Tamilology. Madras: Internatl. Inst. of Tamil St., 1977. 289p.

2. Studies

00073 ARAVAANAN, K.P., ed. Dravidians and Africans. Madras: Tamil Koottam, 1977. 188p.

00074 ARUNACHALAM, K.P.P. Research papers on Tamilology. Madras: Thamizhkkoottam, 1972. 80p.

00075 BUCH, H.M. & G.E. YOCUM, eds. Structural approaches to South India studies. Chambersburg, PA: Wilson Books, 1974. 224p.

00076 DAVID, H.S. Suggestions to research schools and lexicographers in Tamil and Dravidology. In TC 12,4 (1966) 269-85.

00077 FILLIOZAT, J. Les Dravidiens dans la civilisation indienne. In J. des savants (1969) 74-91.

00078 ______. La place des études tamoules dans l'Indologie. In his Laghu-prabandhāḥ. Leiden: Brill, 1974, 401-414. [1st pub. in Indologica Tauriniensia 1 (1973) 21-26]

00079 INTL. CONF. SEM. OF TAMIL STUDIES, 1ST, U. OF MALAYA, 1966. I.A.T.R. who's who.... n.p., 1966. 96p.

00080 INTL. CONF. SEM. OF TAMIL STUDIES, 1ST, KUALA LUMPUR. Proceedings. Kuala Lumpur: IATR, 1968. 764p.

00081 INTL.CONF. SEM. OF TAMIL STUDIES, 2ND, 1968, MADRAS. Plenary sessions papers. Madras: IATR, 1968.

00082 INTL. CONF. SEM. OF TAMIL STUDIES, 3RD, COLLEGE DE FRANCE, PARIS. Proceedings. Ed. by X.S. Thani Nayagam & F. Gros. Pondicherry: IFI, 1973. 279p.

00083 MANICKAM, V.S. A glimpse of Tamilology. Ed. by V. Sp. Manickam. Thiruchirappalli: Academy of Tamil scholars of Tamil Nadu, 1968, 213-67.

00084 MEENAKSHISUNDARAM, K. The contribution of European scholars to Tamil. Madras: U. of Madras, 1974. 370p.

00085 NAGASWAMY, R., ed. South Indian studies. Madras: Soc. for Archaeol., Hist., & Epigraphical Res., 1978. 190p.

00086 NAVARATNAM, K. Tamil element in Ceylon culture. Kurumpasiddy: Eelakesari Ponniah Mem. Pub. Soc., 1959. 111p.

00087 SJOBERG, A.F., ed. Symposium on Dravidian civilisation. Austin: Jenkins, 1971. 173p.

00088 SLATER, G. The Dravidian element in Indian culture. ND: Ess Ess Publications, 1976. 165p.

00089 SRINIVASA AIYANGAR, M. Tamil studies; or, Essays on the history of the Tamil people, language, religion and literature. Madras: Guardian Press, 1914. 427p.

00090 STEIN, B., ed. Essays on South India. Honolulu: UPH, 1975. 213p.

00091 THANI NAYAGAM, X.S. Tamil studies abroad: a symposium. Kuala Lumpur: IATR, 1968. 269p.

II. HISTORY OF SOUTH ASIA

A. Historiography, Sources, and Research Aids

1. Bibliographies

00092 ABIDI, S.A. & S.K. SHARMA, eds. Fifty years of Indian historical writings. ND: Gitanjali, 1974. 248p. [Index to articles in JIH, vols. 1-50 (1921/22-1972).]

00093 KERN INSTITUTE, LEIDEN. Annual bibliography of Indian archaeology for the year 1926-. Leiden: Brill. [Includes books and articles on ancient history, archaeology, epigraphy, iconography, numismatics, art, "medieval" history. v. 21, 1964-66, pub. 1972]

00094 SADHU RAM. Index to the Indian Historical Quarterly, 1925-1963. ND: Vijay Mohan, 1970. 187p.

00095 SEN, S.P., ed. Indian History Congress; Silver jubilee souvenir volume. Calcutta: The Congress, 1963. 267p.

00096 SIDDIQUE, A.F.M. Subject index to articles published in the journal Bengal, Past and Present. Dacca: Centre for Social Studies, 1978. 48p. (Its bibliography ser., 1) [index to v. 1-81 of BPP]

2. Studies of Sources and Methodology

00097 GOSWAMY, B.N. The records kept by priests at centres of pilgrimage as a source of social and economic history. In IESHR 3 (1966) 174-184.

00098 MENDIS, G.C. Problems of Ceylon history. Colombo: Colombo Apothecaries, 1966? 87p.

00099 NILAKANTA SASTRI, K.A. & H.S. RAMANA. Historical method in relation to Indian history. Madras: Central Art Press, 1956. 184p.

00100 ______. Historical method in relation to problems of South Indian history. Madras: U. of Madras, 1941. 56p. (Bul. of the Dept. of Indian Hist. & Archaeol., 7)

00101 ______. Sources of Indian history with special reference to South India. Bombay: Asia, 1964. 113p.

00102 PROBLEMS OF HISTORICAL WRITING IN INDIA: proceedings of the seminar held at the India International Centre, New Delhi, 21-25 January, 1963. ND: India Intl. Centre, 1963. 146p.

00103 THAPAR, R. The scope and significance of regional history. In her Ancient Indian social history. ND: Orient Longman, 1978, 361-376.

00104 TRAUTMANN, T.R. Length of generation and reign in ancient India. In JAOS 89 (1969) 564-577.

3. Historiography
a. Surveys and general studies

00105 DE SOUZA, J.P. & G.M. KULKARNI, eds. Historiography in Indian languages: Dr. G.M. Moraes felicitation volume. Delhi: Oriental Publishers, 1972. 275p.

00106 FAUJA SINGH, ed. Historians and historiography of the Sikhs. ND: Oriental, 1978. 296p.

00107 GOKHALE, B.G. The Theravada view of history. In JAOS 85,3 (1965) 354-60.

00108 GHOSAL, U.N. The beginnings of Indian historiography and other essays. Calcutta: Ramesh Ghosal, 1944. 320p.

00109 GOONERATNE, Y. Nineteenth century histories of Ceylon. In CJHSS 8 (1965) 106-118.

00110 MAJUMDAR, R.C. Historiography in Modern India. Bombay: Asia, 1970. 61p.

00111 Past and present: symposium on attitudes and approaches to a study of our history. In Seminar, 39 (1962) 9-52.

00112 PATHAK, V.S. Ancient historians of India: a study in historical biographies. Bombay: Asia, 1966. 184p.

00113 PHILIPS, C.H., ed. Historians of India, Pakistan, and Ceylon. London: OUP, 1961. 504p.

00114 PRASAD, S.N. A survey of work done on the military history of India. Calcutta: K.P. Bagchi, 1976. 98p. (Indian Council of Hist. Research; Survey ser., 3)

00115 SEN, S.P., ed. Historians and historiography in modern India. Calcutta: Inst. of Hist. Studies, 1973. 464 p.

00116 ______. History in modern Indian literature. Calcutta: Inst. of Hist. Studies, 1975. 226p.

00117 SUBRAHMANIAN, N. Historiography. Madurai: Koodal, 1973. 506p.

00118 THAPAR, R. The tradition of historical writing in early India. In IChHR 4,1 (1972) 1-22.

00119 VOIGT, J.H. British policy towards Indian historical research and writing 1870-1930. In IESHR 3,2 (1966) 137-49.

00120 WARDER, A.K. An introduction to Indian historiography. Bombay: Popular, 1972. 196p.

b. biographies and studies of historians

00121 BANERJEE, T.S. Sardar K.M. Panikkar: the profile of a historian (a study in modern Indian historiography). Calcutta: Ratna Prakashan, 1977. 157p.

00122 CAIRNS, G.E. Social progress and holism in T.M.P. Mahadevan's philosophy of history. In PEW 20,1 (1970) 73-82.

00123 MAHADEVAN, T.M.P. & G.E. CAIRNS, eds. Contemporary Indian philosophers of history. Calcutta: World Press, 1977. 311p.

00124 PANIKKAR, K.M. An autobiography. Tr. from Malayalam by K. Krishnamurthy. Madras: OUP, 1977. 372p.

00125 RULE, P. The pursuit of progress: a study of the intellectual development of Romesh Chunder Dutt, 1848-1888. Calcutta: Editions Indian, 1977. 170p. (U. of Melbourne Indian studies, 2)

00126 SARKAR, J.N. Making of a princely historian: letters of Sir J.N. Sarkar to Dr. Raghubir Sinh of Sitamau. Ed. by S.R. Tikekar. Maharashtra State Board for Archives and Archaeol., 1975. 284p.

00127 TIKEKAR, S.R. On historiography: a study of methods of historical research and narration of J.N. Sarkar, G.S. Sardesai and P.K. Gode. Bombay: Popular, 1964. 71p.

c. issues and debates

00128 CHAUDHARY, V.C.P. Secularism versus communalism: an anatomy of the national debate on five controversial history books. Patna: Navdhara Samiti, 1977. 137p.

00129 DEVAHUTI, ed. Problems of Indian historiography. Delhi: D.K., 1979. 190p.

00130 MALIK, S.C. Indian civilization: new images of the past for a developing nation. In Kenneth David, ed. The new wind: changing identities in South Asia. The Hague: Mouton, 1977. 85-94.

00131 STEIN, B. Early Indian historiography: a conspiracy hypothesis. In IESHR 6 (1969) 41-59.

00132 SUBRAHMANIAN, N. Historiography: India and the West. In BITCM (1962), pt. 2 254-80.

00133 THAPAR, R. & H. MUKHIA & BIPAN CHANDRA. Communalism and the writing of Indian history. Delhi: PPH, 1969. 57p.

00134 THAPAR, R. The past and prejudice. ND: PDMIB, 1973. 53p.

00135 WARDER, A.K. Desiderata in Indian historiography: an essay. In JESHO 2 (1959) 206-18.

00136 WEBSTER, J.C.B., ed. History and contemporary India. Bombay: Asia, 1971. 123p.

00137 WIELENGA, B. Marxist views on India in historical perspective. Madras: CLS, 1976. 155p.

4. Chronologies, Handbooks, Dictionaries

00138 BHATTACHARYA, S. A dictionary of Indian history. Calcutta: U. of Calcutta, 1967. 888p.

00139 BURGESS, J. The chronology of Indian history: medieval and modern. Delhi: Cosmo, 1972. 483p. (St. in Indian hist., 1) [Rpt. of The chronology of modern India .... Edinburgh: J. Grant, 1913.]

00140 CUNNINGHAM, A. Book of Indian eras, with tables for calculating Indian dates. Varanasi: Indological Book House, 1970. 227p. [1st pub. 1883]

00141 GAHLOT, P. Ready reckoner for Indian eras. Jodhpur: Rajasthan Sahitya Mandir, 1979. 82p.

00142 GAHLOT, S.V. Historians' calendar: giving equivalent dates of Christian, Vikram, Shaka, Hijari, Bengali, and Kollam eras. Jodhpur: Hindi Sahitya Mandir, 1979-. [v. 1, 1544-1643 AD]

00143 KETKAR, V.B. Indian and foreign chronology. In JASBombay Extra no. (1905) 214p.

00144 PHILIPS, C.H., ed. Handbook of oriental history. London: Royal Histl. Soc., 1951. 265p.

00145 RICKMERS, C.M.D. The chronology of Indian history, from the earliest times to the beginning of the sixteenth century. Delhi: Cosmo, 1972. 409p. (Studies in Indian Hist., 2) [Orig.: The chronology of India.... Westminster: A. Constable, 1899.]

00146 SEWELL, R. Indian calendar, with tables for the conversion of Hindu and Muhammadan dates into A.D. dates and vice versa... London: Swan Sonnenschein, 1896. 106p.

00147 SHARMA, J.S. India since the advent of the British: a descriptive chronology from 1600 to Oct. 2, 1969. Delhi: S. Chand, 1970. 817p. (Natl. Bibl., 7)

00148 VAN WIJK, W.E. Decimal tables for the reduction of Hindu dates from the data of the Sūrya-Siddhānta. The Hague: Nijhoff, 1938. 33p.

00149 VENKATACHELAM, K. Chronology of ancient Hindu history. Gandhinagar: K. Venkatachela, 1957. 2 v. in 1.

5. Historical Geography - Atlases and Reference Works

00150 BAJPAI, K.D., et al., eds. Geographical encyclopaedia of ancient and medieval India, based on Vedic, Puranic, tantric, Jain, Buddhistic literature and historical records. Varanasi: Indic Academy, 1967-. [pt. 1, A-D, 120p., no more pub.]

00151 DEY, N.L. The geographical dictionary of ancient and medieval India. 3rd ed. ND: Oriental Books Reprint Corp., 1971. 262p. [1st ed. 1899]

00152 DAVIES, C.C. An historical atlas of the Indian peninsula. 2nd ed. Bombay: OUP, 1959. 94p. [1st ed. 1949]

00153 GUPTA, P. Geographical names in ancient Indian inscriptions. Delhi: Concept, 1977. 176p.

00154 LEHMANN, E. & H. WEISSE. Historisch-geographisches Kartenwerk; v. 1, Indien, Entwicklung seiner Wirtschaft und Kultur. Leipzig: Verlag Enzyklopädie, 1958. 90 maps in 60p.

00155 SRINIVAS KINI, K. & U.B. SHANKAR RAO. Oxford pictorial atlas of Indian history. 8th ed. London: OUP, 1963. 72p.

00156 SCHWARTZBERG, J.E., ed. A historical atlas of South Asia. Chicago: UChiP, 1978. 382p., incl. 650 maps.

6. Biographical Dictionaries and Essays

00157 BEALE, T.W. An oriental biographical dictionary. Ed. by H.G. Keene. Lahore: Sind Sagar Academy, 1975. 431p. [Rpt. of 1894 ed.]

00158 KULKARNI, V.B. Heroes who made history. 2nd ed. Bombay: BVB, 1965. 211p. [1st ed. 1951]

00159 MADHAVANANDA, Swami & R.C. MAJUMDAR, eds. Great women of India. Almora: Advaita Ashrama, 1953. 551p.

00160 POOL, J.J. Famous women of India. 2nd rev. & abridged ed. Calcutta: S. Gupta, 1954. 150p. [1st ed. 1892: Women's influence in the East....]

00161 SAXENA, T.P. Women in Indian history: a biographical dictionary. ND: Kalyana, 1979. 114p.

00162 WILLIAMS, L.F.R., ed. Great men of India. n.p., 19--. 640p.

B. General Histories

1. Thematic Interpretations of South Asian History

00163 ANTONOVA, K., & G. BONGARD-LEVIN & G. KOTOVSKY. A history of India. Moscow: Progress, 1979. 2 v., 264, 342p.

00164 CHAND, T. Material and ideological factors in Indian history. Allahabad: U. of Allahabad, 1966. 97p.

00165 GOETZ, H. The crisis of the migration period and other key problems of Indian history. In his Studies in the history, religion, and art of classical and medieval India. Ed. by H. Kulke. Wiesbaden: Steiner, 1974. 64-86.

00166 KOSAMBI, D.D. An introduction to the study of Indian history. Bombay: Popular, 1975. 69 + 415p.

00167 MALIK, S.C., ed. Dissent, protest, and reform in Indian civilization. Simla: IIAS, 1977. 391p. [Its Transactions]

00168 NEHRU, J.L. The discovery of India. Ed. by R.I. Crane. Garden City: Anchor Books, 1960. 426p. [1st pub. NY: J. Day, 1946, 595p.]

00169 PANIKKAR, K.M. Survey of Indian history. Bombay: Asia, 1957. 272p. [1st ed. 1947]

00170 RAIKAR, Y.A. Indian history, a study in dynamics. Baroda: Faculty of Arts, MSUB, 1960. 52p.

00171 SAVARKAR, V.D. Six glorious epochs of Indian history. Tr. by S.T. Godbole, ND: Bal Savarkar, 1971. 568p.

00172 SEN, S.P., ed. The North and the South in Indian history: contact and adjustment. Calcutta: Inst. Hist. St., 1976. 226p.

00173 SUBRAHMANIAN, N. Hindu responses to medieval and modern western challenges. In IYIA 17 (1974) 487-509.

2. Introductory Surveys

00174 ALI, K. A new history of Indo-Pakistan: from Dravidians to Sultanates. 4th rev. ed. Lahore: Aziz, 1978. 174p.

00175 DANIÉLOU, ALAIN. Histoire de l'Inde. Paris: Fayard, 1971. 379p.

00176 GOETZ, H. Geschichte Indiens. Stuttgart: W. Kohlhammer, 1962. 221p.

00177 KOPF, D., & C.J. Bishop. The Indian world. St. Louis: Forum Press, 1977. 86p.

00178 MORELAND, W.H., & A.C.CHATTERJEE. A short history of India. 4th ed. NY: McKay, 1965. 694p. [1st pub. 1936]

00179 NILAKANTA SASTRI, K.A., & G. SRINIVASACHARI. Life and culture of the Indian people: a historical survey. 2nd rev. ed. Bombay: Allied, 1974. 284p. [1st ed. 1966]

00180 PURI, B.N. A study of Indian history. Bombay: BVB, 1971. 285p.

00181 QURESHI, I.H., ed. A short history of Pakistan. Karachi: U. of Karachi, 1967. 4 v.

00182 RUBEN, W. Einführung in die Indienkunde; ein Überblick über die historische Entwicklung Indiens. Berlin: Deutscher Verlag der Wissenschaften, 1954. 390p.

00183 SPEAR, T.G.P. A history of India, v. 2. Baltimore: Penguin, 1965. 284p. [Mughal and after; for v. 1, see Thapar, R.]

00184 ______. India, a modern history. Ann Arbor: UMichP, 1961. 491p.

00185 THAPAR, R. A history of India, v. 1. Baltimore: Penguin, 1966. 381p. [pre-Mughal, for v. 2 see Spear, T.G.P.]

00186 TINKER, H. South Asia; a short history. NY: Praeger, 1966. 287p.

00187 WATSON, F. A concise history of India. NY: Scribners, 1975. 192p.

00188 WHEELER, R.E.M. Five thousand years of Pakistan. London: C. Johnson, 1950. 149p.

00189 WOLPERT, S.A. A new history of India. NY: OUP, 1977. 471p.

3. General Histories for Reference or Advanced Study

00190 CHOPRA, P.N. & B.N. PURI & M.N. DAS. A social, cultural, and economic history of India. Delhi: Macmillan, 1974. 3 v. in 1.

00191 DE BARY, W.T. et al., eds. Sources of Indian tradition. NY: ColUP, 1958. 961p. [trans. sources]

00192 DODWELL, H.H., ed. Cambridge history of India. Cambridge: CamUP, 1922-53. 6 v. + suppl.

00193 MAJUMDAR, R.C. & H.C. RAYCHAUDHURI & K.K. DATTA, eds. An advanced history of India. 3rd ed. Delhi: Macmillan, 1973. 1126p.

00194 ______. The history and culture of the Indian people. Bombay: Bharatiya Vidya Bhavan, 1951-77. 11 v.

00195 MUKERJEE, R.K. A history of Indian civilization, v. 1: ancient and classical traditions; v. 2: medieval and modern synthesis. 2nd ed. Bombay: Hind Kitabs, 1958-1966. 2 v.

00196 NILAKANTA SASTRI, K.A. & G. SRINIVASACHARI. Advanced history of India. Bombay: Allied, 1971. 874p.

00197 SMITH, V.A. The Oxford history of India. 3rd ed. Ed. by T.G.P. Spear. Oxford: OUP, 1958. 898p. [1st ed. 1920]

4. Collected Essays

00198 GHOSHAL, U.N. Studies in Indian history and culture. 2nd rev. ed. Bombay: Orient Longmans, 1965. 385p. [1st ed. 1944]

00199 PRAKASH, BUDDHA. Aspects of Indian history and civilization. Agra: Shiva Lal Agarwala, 1965. 389p.

00200 RAVINDRAN, T.K., ed. Journal of Indian history: golden jubilee volume. Trivandrum: Dept. of History, U. of Kerala, 1973. 933p.

00201 SATCHIDANANDA MURTY, K. Readings in Indian history, politics and philosophy. London: Allen & Unwin, 1967. 392p.

00202 [Special issue on Indian history] In CHM 6,2 (1960) 209-430. [13 essays]

C. Topical Histories

1. Cultural Histories (Literature, Arts, Religion)

00203 BARNETT, L.D. Antiquities of India: an account of the history and culture of ancient Hindustan. NY: Putnam's, 1914. 306p.

00204 BASHAM, A.L., ed. A cultural history of India. Oxford: OUP, 1975. 585p. [Reincarnation of G.T. Garratt's Legacy of India, 1937]

00205 ______. Studies in Indian history and culture. Calcutta: Sambodhi, 1964. 248p.

00206 ______. The wonder that was India; a survey of the culture of the Indian subcontinent before the coming of the Muslims. London: Sidgwick & Jackson, 1963. 568p. [1st ed. 1957]

00207 The cultural heritage of India. Calcutta: RMIC, 1953-78. 5 v., 3699 p. [1st ed. 1937]

00208 FILLIOZAT, J. India, the country and its traditions. Tr. by M. Ledesert. London: Harrap, 1962. 276p.

00209 GARRATT, G.T. The legacy of India. Oxford: OUP, 1937. 428p.

00210 Handbuch der Orientalistik, Zweite Abteilung: Indien. Genl. ed. Jan Gonda. Leiden: Brill, 1966-.

00211 MACDONELL, A. A. India's past; a survey of her literature, religions, languages and antiquities. Oxford: OUP, 1927. 293p.

00212 MÉTRAUX, G.S. & F. CROUZET, eds. Studies in the cultural history of India. Agra: Shiva Lal Agarwala, 1965. 512p.

00213 MUKERJEE, R.K. The culture and art of India. London: Allen & Unwin, 1959. 447p. + 54 plates.

00214 RAWLINSON, H.G. India; a short cultural history. NY: Praeger, 1952. 454p. [1st ed. 1938]

00215 SIVARAMAMURTI, C. Some aspects of Indian culture. ND: Natl. Museum, 1969. 177p.

2. Historical Geography - Studies

00216 JANAKI, V.A. Some aspects of the political geography of India. Baroda: MSUB, 1977. 265p.

00217 LAW, B.C. Historical geography of ancient India. Delhi: Ess Ess, 1976. 354p.

00218 PANIKKAR, K.M. Geographical factors in Indian history. Bombay: BVB, 1969. 128p.

00219 RAZA, M. & A. AHMAD. Historical geography; a trend report. In A survey of research in geography. Bombay: Popular, 1972, 147-69. [sponsored by ICSSR]

00220 SIRCAR, D.C. Studies in the geography of ancient and medieval India. 2nd ed., rev. Delhi: Motilal, 1971. 400p.

3. Political History: Institutions and Ideas

00221 BHATIA, H.S., ed. Origin & development of legal & political system in India. ND: Deep & Deep, 1976. 2 v., 206, 220p.

00222 BROWN, D.M. The white umbrella - Indian political thought from Manu to Gandhi. Berkeley: UCalP, 1953. 205p.

00223 FOX, R.G., ed. Realm and region in traditional India. Durham: Duke U., Program in comp. st. on Southern Asia, 1977. 307p. (Its monograph 14)

00224 INDEN, R. Ritual, authority and cyclic time in Hindu kingship. In J.F. Richards, ed. Kingship and authority in South Asia. Madison: South Asian Studies, U. of Wisconsin, 1978. 28-73. (Its Publication Series, 3)

00225 JAYASWAL, K.P. Hindu polity; a constitutional history of India in Hindu times. 4th ed. Bangalore: Bangalore Print. & Pub. Co., 1967. 414p.

00226 KENNEDY, R.S. The king in early South India, as chieftain and emperor. In IHR, 3,1 (1976) 1-15.

00227 MAJUMDAR, R.C., ed. Readings in political history of India, ancient, mediaeval, and modern. Delhi: B.R., 1976. 279p.

00228 MOORE, R.J., ed. Tradition and politics in South Asia. ND: Vikas, 1979. 266p.

00229 PANIKKAR, K.M. The ideas of sovereignty and state in Indian political thought. Bombay: BVB, 1963. 114p.

00230 RICHARDS, J.F., ed. Kingship and authority in South Asia. Madison: South Asian Studies, U. of Wisconsin, 1978. 303p. (Its Publication Series, 3)

00231 SARKAR, B.K. The political institutions and theories of the Hindus; a study in comparative politics. Leipzig: Markert & Petters, 1922. 242p.

00232 SCHWARTZBERG, J.E. The evolution of regional power configurations in the Indian subcontinent. In R.G. Fox, ed., Realm and region in traditional India. Durham: Duke U., Program in Comparative Studies on Southern Asia, 197-233.

00233 SINGH, N. The theory of force and organisation of defence in Indian constitutional history; from earliest times to 1947. Bombay: Asia, 1969. 290p.

00234 SINHA, H.N. The development of Indian polity. Bombay: Asia, 1963. 589p.

00235 UPADHYAY, G. Political thought in Sanskrit kāvya. Varanasi: Chaukhambha Orientalia, 1979. 432p. (CORS 15)

4. Economic History

00236 Annotated bibliography on the economic history of India (1500 AD to 1947 AD). Poona: GIPE, 1977. 3 v., 1865p. [to be 4 v.]

00237 BENJAMIN, N. Economic history of India (1526-1900): a bibliographic essay. In AV, 12,4 (1970) 594-626.

00238 CHATTOPADHYAYA, A.K. Slavery in India; an exhaustive study from the ancient times to the present. Calcutta: Nagarjun Press, 1962. 138p.

00239 CHAUDHURI, K.N. & C.J. DEWEY, eds. Economy and society: essays in Indian economic and social history. Delhi: OUP, 1979. 358p.

00240 DATTA, B. The evolution of economic thinking in India. Calcutta: Federation Hall Soc., 1962. 16 + 52p.

00241 MALIK, S.C. India c. 1000 B.C. - A.D. 1000: interpreting economic patterns in a civilizational framework. In EA 29,3 (1976) 249-58.

00242 MOOKERJI, RADHA KUMUD. Indian shipping; a history of the sea-borne trade and maritime activity of the Indians from earliest times. Allahabad: Kitab Mahal, 1962. 206p. [1st pub. 1912]

00243 MORRIS, M.D. & B. STEIN. The economic history of India: a bibliographic essay. In JEH 21,2 (1961) 179-207.

00244 RUBEN, W., ed. Die ökonomische und soziale Entwicklung indiens: Sowietische Beiträge zur indischen Geschichte. Berlin: Akademie Verlag, 1961. 2 v., 308, 239p.

00245 SPENGLER, J.J. Indian economic thought; a preface to its history. Durham: DUP, 1971. 192p.

00246 VOLLMER, F.J. Eigentumsbeschränkungen in Indien. Wiesbaden: Steiner, 1975. 147p. (BSAF, 21)

5. History of Science and Technology
a. bibliography

00247 PINGREE, D.E. Census of the exact sciences in Sanskrit; series A. vol 1. Philadelphia: American Philosophical Society, 1970-. 3 v. (Its memoirs, 81,86)

00248 SEN, S.N., ed. A bibliography of Sanskrit works on astronomy and mathematics. ND: Natl. Inst. of Sci. of India, 1966. v. 1, 258p. [No more pub.]

00249 ______. A survey of source materials. In D.M. Bose & S.N. Sen & B.V. Subharayappa, eds., A concise history of science in India. ND: Indian Natl. Sci. Academy, 1971, 1-57.

00249 SWAMY, B.G.L. Sources for a history of plant sciences in India. I. Epigraphy. In IJHS 8,1/2 (1973) 61-98.

00251 WILSON, P. Science in South Asia, past and present; a preliminary bibliography of writings on science in India, Pakistan and Ceylon. NY: State Education Dept., 1966. 100p.

b. general surveys

00252 BOSE, D.M., ed. A concise history of science in India. ND: Indian Natl. Sci. Academy, 1971. 689p.

00253 CHATTOPADHYAYA, D.P. Science and society in ancient India. Calcutta: Research India, 1977. 441p.

00254 FILLIOZAT, J. Ancient Indian science. In R. Taton, ed. History of science; ancient and medieval science from the beginnings to 1450. NY: Basic Books, 1963, 133-160.

00255 ______. Science in medieval India. In R. Taton, ed. History of science; ancient and medieval science from the beginnings to 1450. NY: Basic Books, 1963, 442-426.

00256 JAGGI, O.P. History of science and technology in India. Delhi: Atma Ram, 1969. 5 v.

00257 ______. Scientists of ancient India and their achievements. Delhi: Atma Ram, 1966. 258p.

00258 MAJUMDAR, G.P. The history of botany and allied sciences (agriculture, medicine, arbori-horticulture) in ancient India. (c. 2000 BC to 100 AD) In Archives internationales d'histoire des sciences 4,14 (1951) 100-35.

00259 PRAKASH, SATYA. Founders of sciences in ancient India. ND: Res. Inst. of Ancient Sci. Studies, 1965. 675p.

00260 SARKAR, B.K. Hindu achievements in the exact sciences; a study in the history of scientific development. London: Longmans, Green, 1918. 82p.

00261 SARTON, G. Introduction to the history of science. Washington: Carnegie Inst., 1927-48. 5 v. [material on India, passim]

00262 Scientists: Dhanvantari, Caraka, Suśhruta, Varāhamihira, Āryabhaṭa, Bhāskarācārya. ND: PDMIB, 1976. 108p.

00263 SEAL, B.N. The positive sciences of the ancient Hindus. London: Longmans, Green, 1915. 295p.

00264 SEN, S.N. Scientific works in Sanskrit, translated into foreign languages and vice-versa in the 18th and 19th century A.D. In IJHS 7,1 (1972) 44-70.

00265 SINHA, S. Science, technology, and culture; a study of the cultural traditions and institutions of India and Ceylon in relation to science and technology. ND: ICC, dist. Manoharlal, 1970. 283p.

00266 SYMPOSIUM ON THE HISTORY OF SCIENCES IN INDIA, CALCUTTA, 1961. Proceedings. ND: Natl. Inst. of Sciences, 1963. 343p.

c. cosmology and cosmography

00267 BHATTACHARYYA, N.N. Brahmanical, Buddhist and Jain cosmography. In JIH 47 (1969) 43-64.

00268 DANDEKAR, R.N. Universe in Hindu thought. Bangalore: Bangalore U., 1972. 41p.

00269 ______. Universe in Vedic thought. In J. Ensink & P. Gaeffke, eds. India Maior. Leiden: Brill, 1972, 91-114.

00270 KIRFEL, W. Die Kosmographie der Inder nach den Quellen dargestellt. Bonn: K. Schroeder, 1920. 401p.

00271 MCGOVERN, W.M. Manual of Buddhist philosophy. v. 1 Cosmology. London: K. Paul, Trench, Trubner, 1923. 205p. [no more pub.]

00272 SIRCAR, D.C. Cosmography and geography in early Indian literature. Calcutta: ISPP, 1967. 250p.

00273 SIVARAMA MENON, C.P. Early astronomy and cosmology; a reconstruction of the earliest cosmic system. London: Allen & Unwin, 1932. 192p.

d. astronomy and astrology (jyotiṣa), calendrical science

00274 BENTLEY, J. A historical view of the Hindu astronomy..... Osnabrück: Biblio Verlag, 1970. 282p. [Rpt. 1825 ed.]

00275 BILLARD, R. L'Astronomie indienne; investigation des textes sanskrits et des données numériques. Paris: EFEO, 1971. 181p. (Its pub., 83)

00276 Calendar in Hindu tradition. In BITCM (1968) pt. 1, 41-144. [seminar report]

00277 CHAKRAVARTY, A.K. Origin and development of Indian calendrical science. In ISPP 15,3 (1974) 219-80.

00278 DIKSHIT, S.B. English translations of Bharatiya. jyotish sastra. (History of Indian astronomy). Tr. from Marathi by R.V. Vaidya. Delhi: MPGOI, 1969-. v. 1-.

00279 FILLIOZAT, J. Notes d'astronomie ancienne de l'Iran et de l'Inde. In JA 250 (1962) 325-350.

00280 GIBSON, G.E. The Vedic nakṣatras and the zodiac. In W.J. Fischel, ed. Semitic and oriental studies.... Berkeley: UCalP, 1951. 149-65.

00281 KAYE, G.R. Hindu astronomy. Calcutta: ASI, 1926. 134p. (Its memoirs, 18)

00282 MUKHERJI, K.N. Popular Hindu astronomy: taramaṇḍalas and nakshatras. Calcutta: Nirmal Mukherjea, 1969. 218p.

00283 NEUGEBAUER, O. Tamil astronomy. In Osiris 10 (1952) 252-76.

00284 PINGREE, D.E. Astronomy and astrology in India and Iran. In Isis 54 (1963) 229-246.

00285 ______. Sanskrit astronomical tables in the United States. Philadelphia: APS, 1968. 77p. [pub. as TAPS ns 58,3]

00286 SARMA, K.V. A bibliography of Kerala and Kerala-based astronomy and astrology. Hoshiarpur: VVRI, 1972. 116p. (VIS, 324) [1st pub. in VIJ 11-12 (1972-73)]

00287 SENGUPTA, P.C. Ancient Indian chronology, illustrating some of the most important astronomical methods. Calcutta: U. of Calcutta, 1947. 287p.

00288 SOMAYAJI, D.A. A critical study of the ancient Hindu astronomy in the light and language of the modern. Dharwar: Karnatak U., 1971. 186p.

00289 WAERDEN, B.L. VAN DER. Tamil astronomy. In Centaurus, 4 (1956) 221-34.

e. mathematics

00290 BAG, A.K. Mathematics in ancient and medieval India. Varanasi: Chaukhambha Orientalia, 1979. 344p. (CORS, 16)

00291 CLARK, W.E. Hindu-Arabic numerals. In Indian studies in honor of Charles Rockwell Lanman. Cambridge: HUP, 1929, 217-36.

00292 DATTA, B.B. & A.N. SINGH. History of Hindu mathematics, a source book. Bombay: Asia, 1963. 2 v., 260, 314p. [1st pub. 1955-58]

00293 KAYE, G.R. Indian mathematics. Calcutta: Thacker, Spink, 1915. 73p. [also pub. in Isis 2,6 (1919) 326-56]

00294 SRINIVASIENGAR, C.N. The history of ancient Indian mathematics. Calcutta: World Press, 1967. 157p.

f. medicine
i. bibliography and reference

00295 BAGCHI, A.K. Sanskrit and modern medical vocabulary: a comparative study. Calcutta: Ṛddhi, 1978. 119p.

00296 CHAUDHURI, S. Select bibliography on Indian system of medicine. In QJMS 53 (1962) 64-74.

00297 GOVINDA REDDY, C. Recent Indian medical historiography. In BIHM 5,1 (1975) 43-54 [bibl. for 1971]; 5,3 (1975) 179-190 [bibl. for 1972]; 5,4 (1975) 253-267 [bibl. for 1973]; 6,3 (1976) 200-218 [bibl. for 1974]. [to be continued periodically]

00298 150 year old bibliography of Siddha medical literature. In BIHM 2,3 (1972) 150-55.

00299 RADHAKRISHNA, P. Current work in history of medicine in India for 1964. In IJHM 13,2 (1968) 48-55.

00300 RAMA RAO, B. A check-list of Sanskrit medical manuscripts in India. ND: Central Council for Res. in Indian Medicine and Homoeopathy, 1972. 101p.

00301 SRIKANTA MURTHY, K.R. Luminaries of Indian medicine, from the earliest times to the present day. Mysore: 1968. 152p. [Pub. serially in the National Medical Journal, Mysore]

00302 SUBRAHMANYA SASTRY, V.V. A brief account of the writers and books on Indian herbs, drugs and bazaar medicines in English and other European languages. In BIHM 4,2 (1974) 61-75.

ii. traditional Hindu medicine: Āyurveda and Siddha systems

00303 BASHAM, A.L. The practice of medicine in ancient and medieval India. In C. Leslie, ed. Asian medical systems: a comparative study. Berkeley: UCalP, 1976, 18-43.

00304 BHAGVAT SINH JEE, Maharaja of Gondal. A short history of Aryan medical science. Delhi: New Asian, 1978. 206p. [Rpt. of 1896 ed.]

00305 BHATIA, S.L. A history of medicine: with special reference to the Orient. ND: Mgmt. Cttee., Dr. B.C. Roy Natl. Award Fund, Office of the Medical Cncl. of India, 1977. 263p.

00306 ______. Medical science in ancient India. Bangalore: Bangalore U., 1972. 50p.

00307 DASH, B. Concept of agni in āyurveda; with special reference to agnibala parīkṣa. Varanasi: CSSO, 1971. 212p. (CSS,81)

00308 ______. Fundamentals of ayurvedic medicine. Delhi: Bansal, 1978. 246p.

00309 FILLIOZAT, J. The classical doctrine of Indian medicine, its origins and its Greek parallels. Tr. from French by D.R. Chanana. Delhi: Munshiram, 1964. 298p. [1st French ed. 1949]

00310 GUPTA, S.P. Psychopathology in Indian medicine (āyurveda): with special reference to its philosophical bases. Aligarh: Ajaya, 1977. 568p.

00311 HOERNLE, A.F.R. Studies in the medicine of ancient India. Oxford: OUP, 1907. 252p.

00312 JOLLY, J. Indian medicine. Tr. from German by C.G. Kashikar. 2d rev. ed. ND: Munshiram, 1977. 197p. [1st German ed., 1910]

00313 KESWANI, N.H. Medical education in India since ancient times. In C.D. O'Malley, ed. The history of medical education.... Berkeley: UCalP, 1970.

00314 ______. The science of medicine & physiological concepts in ancient & medieval India. ND: S.K. Manchanda, 1974. 185p.

00315 KUTUMBIAH, P. The siddha and rasa siddha schools of Indian medicine. In IJHM, 18,1 (1973) 21-33.

00316 MUKHOPADHYAYA, G.N. History of Indian medicine, containing notices, biographical and bibliographical, of the ayurvedic physicians and their works on medicine, from the earliest ages to the present time. 2d ed. ND: OBRC, 1974. 3 v. [Rpt. of 1923-29 ed.]

00317 ______. The surgical instruments of the Hindus: with a comparative study of the surgical instruments of the Greek, Roman, Arab, and the modern European surgeons. ND: R.K. Naahar, 1977. 283 + 32p. + 41 pls. [Rpt. of 1913-14 ed.]

00318 MÜLLER, R.F.G. Kritische Skizze zur Entwicklung der Medizin der Indoarier. In WZKS 4 (1960) 14-35.

00319 OJHA, D. & A. KUMAR. Panchakarma-therapy in ayurveda. Varanasi: Chaukhamba Amarabharati Prakashan, 1978. 219p.

00320 RAMACHANDRA RAO, V., ed. Regional seminar-cum-workshop on history of medicine in India. s.l., s.n., 1976? [held Oct. 9, 10, 11, 1970 at S.V. Medical College, Tirupati]

00321 SAMBOO, G. La médecine de l'Inde, autrefois et aujourd'hui. Paris: Éditions du Scorpion, 1963. 288p.

00322 SHARMA, S., ed. Realms of ayurveda: scientific excursions by nineteen scholars. ND: Arnold-Heinemann, 1979. 336p.

00323 SHUKLA, H.C. The Indian medical concept of human variation; two monographs. Hamburg: Arbeitsgemeinschaft Ethnomedizin, 1973. 124p.

00324 SINGHAL, G.P. & D.S. GAUR. Surgical ethics in ayurveda. Varanasi: CSSO, 1963. 99p.

00325 SUBBA REDDY, D.V., ed. Western epitomes of Indian medicine. Hyderabad: Osmania medical college, 1966. 115p.

00326 Theories and philosophies of medicine: with particular reference to Greco-Arab medicine, Ayurveda, and traditional Chinese medicine. 2nd ed. ND: Inst. of Hist. of Medicine and Medical Res., 1973. 523p.

00327 THYAGARAJAN, R. A hand book of common remedies in siddha system of medicine. ND: Central Cncl. for Res. in Indian Medicine and Homoeopathy, Min. of Health and Family Planning, 1975. 83p.

00328 VAKIL, R.J. Our glorious heritage. Bombay: Times of India Press, 1966. 106p.

00329 ZIMMER, H.R. Hindu medicine. Baltimore: Johns Hopkins Press, 1947. 203p.

00330 ZIMMERMAN, F. Ṛtu-sātmya. Le cycle des saisons et le principe d'appropriation. In Puruṣārtha 2 (1975) 87-105.

iii. Indian pharmacology

00331 MEHTA, P.M. The concept of the wholesome and unwholesome (diet) in Ayurveda. In JGRS 27 (1965) 232-240.

00332 NADKARNI, K.M. Dr. D.M. Nadkarni's Indian materia medica: with ayurvedic, unani-tibbi, siddha, allopathic, homeopathic, naturopathic, and home remedies. Bombay: 3rd ed. Popular, 1976. 2 v.

00333 ORTA, G. DA. Colloquies on the simples and drugs of India. Tr. from Portuguese by Clements Markham. London: H. Sotheran, 1913. 508p. [1st pub. Goa 1563]

00334 SHARMA, P.V. Introduction to dravyaguna (Indian pharmacology). Varanasi: Chaukhambha Orientalia, 1976. 226p. (Jaikrishnadas ayurveda series, 5)

00335 SRIVASTAVA, G.P. History of Indian pharmacy. Calcutta: Pindars, 1954. 276p. [1st ed. 1953]

g. chemistry and alchemy (rasaśāstra)

00336 MUKHERJI, B. Rasa-jala-niti; or ocean of Indian chemistry and alchemy. Calcutta: K.C. Neogi, 1926-38. 5 v.

00337 RAY, P.R. History of chemistry in ancient and medieval India. Calcutta: Indian Chemical Soc., 1956. 494p. [Includes abridged version of P.C. Ray's History of Hindu chemistry]

00338 ______. Origin and tradition of alchemy. In IJHS 2,1 (1967) 1-21.

00339 RAY, P.C. A history of Hindu chemistry. London: Oxford, Williams and Norgate, 1902-09. 2 v.

h. technology

00340 ALLCHIN, F.R. Upon the antiquity and methods of gold mining in ancient India. In JESHO 5 (1962) 195-211.

00341 BHARDWAJ, H.C. Aspects of ancient Indian technology: a research based on scientific methods. Delhi: Motilal, 1979. 212p.

00342 CHAKRABARTI, D.K. Research on early Indian iron. In IHR 4,1 (1977) 96-105.

00343 DELOCHE, J. Les ponts anciens de l'Inde. Paris: EFEO, 1973. 90p. (Its Pub. 93)

00344 DIKSHIT, M.G. History of Indian glass. Bombay: U. of Bombay, 1969. 212p.

00345 GHORI, S.A.K. & A. RAHMAN. Paper technology in medieval India. In IJHS 1,2 (1966) 133-150.

00346 MACGEORGE, G.W. Ways and works in India; being an account of the public works in that country from the earliest times to the present day. Westminster: A. Constable, 1894. 565p.

00347 NEOGI, P. Copper in ancient India. Patna: Janaki, 1979. 77p. [Rpt. 1918 ed.]

00348 RAGHAVAN, V. Yantras or mechanical contrivances in ancient India. 2nd ed. Bangalore: Indian Inst. of Culture, 1956. 33p. (Its Trans., 10)

00349 TRIER, J. Ancient paper of Nepal.... Copenhagen: Gyldendal, 1972. 274p. (Jutland Archaeological Society publications, 10)

6. History of External Contacts and Foreign Relations

a. general

00350 KAUL, H.K., ed. Travellers' India: an anthology. Delhi: OUP, 1979. 535p.

00351 LAL, C. Hindu America; depicting the imprints of Hindu culture on the two Americas. Hoshiarpur: VVRI, 1956. 360p. (VIS, 133)

00352 LEIFER, W. India and the Germans; 500 years of Indo-German contacts. Bombay: Shakuntala, 1971. 350p.

00353 RAGHUVIRA. India and Asia: a cultural symphony: a collection of some notes, articles, poems, and letters of the late Prof. Dr. Raghuvira. ND: IAIC, 1978. 499p.

00354 JOSHI, P.M., ed. Studies in the foreign relations of India, from the earliest times to 1947: Prof. H.K. Sherwani felicitation volume. Hyderabad: State Archives, Govt. of Andhra Pradesh, 1975. 601p.

00355 CHANDRA, L., et al., eds. India's contribution to world thought and culture. Madras: Vivekananda Rock Mem. Cttee., 1970. 705p.

00356 JAIRAZBHOY, R.A. Foreign influence in ancient India. Bombay: Asia, 1964. 195p.

00357 NILAKANTA SASTRI, K.A. Cultural expansion of India. Gauhati: U. of Gauhati, 1959. 94p.

00358 PRAKASH, BUDDHA. India and the world: researches in India's policies, contacts and relationships with other countries and peoples of the world. Hoshiarpur: VVRI, 1964. 292p.

00359 SALETORE, B.A. Karnāṭaka's trans-oceanic contacts. Dharwar: Karnatak U., 1956. 100p.

00360 SINGHAL, D.P. India and world civilization. East Lansing: Michigan State U. Press, 1969. 2 v., 435, 384p.

b. China, Japan and Southeast Asia

00361 BAGCHI, P.C. India and China: a thousand years of cultural relations. 2d ed., rev. & enl. Westport, CT: Greenwood Press, 1971. 234p. [1st ed. 1944]

00362 LAL, CHAMAN India and Japan - friends of fourteen centuries. Hoshiarpur: VVRI, 1959. 230p.

00363 NAKAMURA, H. Japan and Indian Asia; their cultural relations in the past and present. Calcutta: KLM, 1961. 93p.

00364 NILAKANTA SASTRI, K.A. South India and South-East Asia: studies in their history and culture. Mysore: Geetha Book House, 1978. 280p.

00365 PANIKKAR, K.M. India and China: a study of cultural relations. Bombay: Asia, 1957. 107p.

00366 PARANAVITANA, S. Ceylon and Malaysia. Colombo: Lake House Investments Ltd., 1966. 234p.

00367 WALES, H.G.Q. The indianization of China and of South-east Asia. London: Quaritch, 1967. 25 + 158p.

c. Iran and Central Asia

00368 BAGCHI, P.C. India and central Asia. Calcutta: Natl. Cncl. of Educ., 1955. 184p.

00369 DAVAR, F.C. Iran and India through the ages. Bombay: Asia, 1962. 312p.

d. the Indian Ocean

00370 NAIR, B.N. Time and tide in Indo-Madagascan cultural exchanges. In JKS 2,3 (1975) 293-344.

00371 NAMBIAR, O.K. Our seafaring in the Indian Ocean. Bangalore: Jeevan, c1975. 192p.

00372 NTSOHA, D. Religion and social conflict in the South-Western Indian Ocean: studies in Indo-Malagascan culture. Tr. from French by B.N. Nair. In JKS 2,4 (1975) 531-603 and 3,1 (1976) 1-95.

00373 PANIKKAR, K.M. India and the Indian Ocean; an essay on the influence of sea power on Indian history. NY: Macmillan, 1945. 109p.

00374 TOUSSAINT, A. History of the Indian Ocean. Tr. from French by F. Guicharnaud. Chicago: UChiP, 1966. 292p. [1st pub. 1961]

e. the gypsies: a western Indian migratory group

00375 LAL, CHAMAN. Gipsies: forgotten children of India. London: A. Probsthain, 1963. 214p.

00376 MCDOWELL, B. Gypsies, wanderers of the world. Washington: Natl. Geog. Soc., 1970. 215p.

00377 RISHI, W.R. Roma; the Panjabi emigrants in Europe, Central and Middle Asia, the USSR and the Americas. Patiala: Pubjabi U., 1976. 119p.

00378 Roma; half-yearly journal of the life, language and culture of Roma (the Gypsies of Europe, the Americas, the USSR, etc.) Chandigarh: Roma Pub., 1975-.

D. Regional Histories

1. Sri Lanka: the Island of Ceylon

00379 ARASARATNAM, S. Ceylon. Englewood Cliffs, NJ: Prentice-Hall, 1964. 182p.

00380 CODRINGTON, H.W. A short history of Ceylon. Rev. ed. London: Macmillan 1952. 246p.

00381 COELHO, V. Across the Palk Straits: India-Sri Lanka relations. ND: Abhinav, 1976. 188p.

00382 History of Ceylon. Colombo: U. of Ceylon. 1959-. v. 1, pt. 1, up to the end of the Anuradhapura period, 410p.; v. 1, pt. 2., 1017-1505 AD, 500p.; v. 2 not yet pub.; v. 3, 1800-1046, 578p.

00383 LUDOWYK, E.F.C. The story of Ceylon. London: Faber & Faber, 1962. 328p.

00384 NICHOLAS, C.W. & S. PARANAVITANA. A concise history of Ceylon, from the earliest times to the arrival of the Portuguese in 1505. Colombo: Ceylon U. Press, 1961. 368p.

00385 PAKEMAN, S.A. Ceylon. London: E. Benn, 1964. 256p.

00386 PEIRIS, E. Studies, historical and cultural. Colombo: Colombo Catholic Press, 1978. 272p.

00387 PERERA, L.H.H. & M. RATNASABAPATHY. Ceylon and Indian history (from early times to 1505 AD) 2d ed. Colombo: W.M.A. Wahid, 1954. 400p. (1st ed. 1951)

00388 PILLAY, K.K. South India and Ceylon. Madras: U. of Madras, 1963. 200p.

00389 PREMATILLEKE, L. & K. INDRAPALA. Senarat Paranavitana commemoration volume. Leiden: Brill, 1978. 300p. (Studies in South Asian culture, 7)

00390 RAGHAVAN, M.D. India in Ceylonese history, society and culture. Bombay: Asia, 1964. 190p.

00391 WEERASOORIA, N.E. Ceylon and her people. Colombo: LHI, 1970-71. 4 v., 1217p.

00392 WICKRAMASINGHE, M. Aspects of Sinhalese culture. 3rd rev. ed. Dehiwala: Tisara Prakasakayo, 1973. 174p.

00393 _____. Sinhala language and culture. Dehiwala: Tisara Prakasakayo, 1975. 155p.

00394 ZEYLANICUS. Ceylon; between Orient & Occident. London: Elek Books, 1970. 288p.

2. South India: the Dravidian Regions of the Peninsula

a. general

00395 CHOPRA, P.N. & T.K. RAVINDRAN & N. SUBRAHMANIAN. History of South India. New Delhi: S. Chand, 1979. 3 v., 805p.

00396 KRISHNASWAMI AIYANGAR, S. Ancient India and South Indian history and culture. Poona: Oriental Book Agency, 1941. 2 v., 1755p. [1st pub. 1911]

00397 _____. Some contributions of South India to Indian culture. 2nd ed. Calcutta: U. of Calcutta, 1942. 428p. [1st ed. 1923]

00398 MAHALINGAM, T.V. Readings in South Indian history. Delhi: B.R., 1977. 229p.

00399 _____. South Indian polity. 2nd ed. rev. Madras: U. of Madras, 1967. 531p. [1st ed. 1955]

00400 NAGASWAMY, R., ed. South Indian studies. Madras: Soc. for Archaeological, Historical & Epigraphical Res., 1978. 195p.

00401 NARAYANAN, M.G.S. Re-interpretations in South Indian history. Trivandrum: College Book House, 1977. 119p.

00402 NILAKANTA SASTRI, K.A. A history of South India from prehistoric times to the fall of Vijayanagar. 4th ed. Madras: OUP, 1976. 521p.

00403 _____., ed. Foreign notices of South India: from Megasthenes to Ma Huan. Madras: U. of Madras, 1972. 341p. [1st pub. 1939]

00404 SREENIVASA MURTHY, H.V. History and culture of South India, to 1336 A.D. Mangalore: Vivek, 1975. 263p.

00405 SUBRAHMANYA AIYER, K.V. Historical sketches of ancient Dekhan. v. 1 Madras: Modern Printing Works, 1917, 429p.; v. 2,3 Coimbatore: K.S. Vaidyanathan, 1967, 288, 177p.

b. Tamil Nadu

00406 AROKIASWAMI, M. The Kongu country, being the history of the modern districts of Coimbatore and Salem from the earliest times to the coming of the British. Madras: U. of Madras, 1956. 420p.

00407 HUSAINI, A.Q. The history of the Pāṇḍya country. Karaikudi: Selvi Pathippakam, 1962. 192p.

00408 KALIDOS, R. History and culture of the Tamils: from prehistoric times to the president's rule. Dindigul: Vijay, 1976. 382p.

00409 LUDDEN, D.E. Agrarian organization in Tinnevelly District, 800 to 1900 A.D. Ph.D diss, U. of Pennsylvania, 1978. 441p. [UM 78-24,744]

00410 NAGARAJAN, K.S. Jain contribution to Tamil culture. Madras: Dhanraj Baid Jain College, 1977. 58p.

00411 NILAKANTA SASTRI, K.A. The culture and history of the Tamils. Calcutta: KLM, 1964. 184p.

00412 _____. The Pandyan Kingdom: from the earliest times to the 16th century. Madras: Swathi, 1972. 252p. [1st pub. 1929]

00413 PILLAY, K.P.K. A social history of the Tamils. Madras: U. of Madras, 1969. pt. 1, 601p. [no more pub.]

00414 RAJAYYAN, K. Selections from history of Tamilnadu, 1565-1965. Madurai: Madurai Pub. House, 1978. 312p.

00416 RAMASWAMI SASTRI, K.S. The Tamils and their culture. Annamalainagar: Annamalai U., 1967. 196p.

00416 SRINIVASAN, C.R. Kanchipuram through the ages. Delhi: Agam Kala, 1979. 326p.

00417 SUBRAHMANIAN, N. History of Tamilnad. Madurai: Koodal, 1972-. 2 v.

c. Andhra

00418 BALENDU SEKARAM, K. The Andhras through the ages. Hyderabad: Sri Saraswati Book Depot, 1973. 2 v. in 1.

00419 SATYANARAYANA, K. A study of the history and culture of the Andhras. ND: PPH, 1975. v. 1, 408p.

d. Kerala

00420 KODER, S.S. Cochin Synagogue 400th anniversary celebrations: exhibits. Cochin: The Synagogue, 1968? 300p.

00421 KRISHNA AYYAR, K.V. A short history of Kerala. Ernakulam: Pai, 1966. 218p.

00422 KRISHNA IYER, L.A. Social history of Kerala. Madras: Book Centre Pub., 1968-70. 2 v., 184, 179p.

00423 KUNJAN PILLAI, E.P.N. Studies in Kerala history. Trivandrum: the author, 1970. 423p.

00424 NARAYANAN, M.G.S. The ancient and medieval history of Kerala: recent developments and the rationale for inter-disciplinary approach. In JKS 3,3/4 (1976) 441-56.

00425 RAVINDRAN, T.K. Institutions and movements in Kerala history. Trivandrum: Charithram, 1978. 176p.

00426 SHUNGOONNY MENON, P. A history of Travancore from the earliest times. Madras: Higginbotham, 1878. 523p.

00427 SREEDHARA MENON, A. Cultural heritage of Kerala: an introduction. Cochin: East-West, 1978. 296p.

00428 ______. A survey of Kerala history. Kottayam: Sahitya Pravarthaka Co-operative Soc., 1967. 446p.

00429 VELUTHAT, K. Brahman settlements in Kerala: historical studies. Calicut: Sandhya Pub., Calicut U., 1978. 115p.

e. Karnataka

00430 DESAI, P.B. A history of Karnataka; from prehistory to unification. Dharwar: Kannada Res. Inst., Karnatak U., 1970. 483p.

00431 DIWAKAR, R.R. Karnataka through the ages; from prehistoric times to the day of the independence of India. Bangalore: Lit. and Cult. Dev. Dept., Govt. of Mysore, 1968. 1084p.

00432 GURURAJA BHATT, P. Studies in Tuluva history and culture; from the pre-historic times up to the modern. Kallianpur: the author, 1975. 452p.

00433 Karnatak Historical Research Society...: golden jubilee souvenir. Dharwar: The Society, 1970. 127p.

00434 Karnataka darshana; volume presented to Shri R.R. Diwakar on his sixtieth birthday. Bombay: R.S. Hukkerikar, 1955. 564p.

00435 KALGHATGI, T.G., ed. Jainism and Karnatak culture. Karnatak U., 1977. 152p.

00436 MUTHANNA, I.M. Karnataka: history, administration, and culture. Bangalore: the author, 1977. 541p.

00437 RAMESH, K.V. A history of South Kanara: from the earliest times to the fall of Vijayanagara. Dharwar: Karnatak U., 1970. 340p.

00438 SREENIVASA MURTHY, H.V. & R. RAMAKRISHNAN. A history of Karnataka, from the earliest times to the present day. ND: S. Chand, 1977. 364p.

00439 SRIKANTHA SASTRI, S. Sources of Karnataka history. Mysore: U. of Mysore, 1940. 238p.

00440 Śrīkanthikā: Dr. S. Srikantha Sastri felicitation volume. Mysore: Geetha Book House, 1973. 395p.

3. Middle India: Area of Transition between North and South

a. the Deccan

00441 ALAVI, R.A. Studies in the history of medieval Deccan. Delhi: IAD, 1977. 100p. [Its Or. series, 42]

00442 BAWA, V.K., ed. Aspects of Deccan history: Hyderabad: Inst. of Asian Studies, 1963. 229p.

00443 BHANDARKAR, R.G. Early history of the Dekkan down to the Mahomedan conquest. 3d ed. Calcutta: Chuckervertty, Chatterjee, 1928. 260p.

00444 SHERWANI, H.K., ed. History of medieval Deccan, 1295-1724. Hyderabad: Govt. of Andhra Pradesh, 1973-74. 2 v.

00445 YAZDANI, G., ed. The early history of the Deccan. London: OUP, 1960. 2 v., 857p. + 65 pl.

b. Goa

00446 KOSAMBI, D.D. The village community in the 'old conquests' of Goa. In his Myth and reality. Bombay: Popular, 1962, 152-71. [1st pub. in JUB 15,4 (1947) 63-78]

00447 MENEZES, A. DE. Goa, historical notes. Panjim, Goa: Casa J.D. Fernandes, 1978-.

00448 PEREIRA, R.G. Goa. Tr. from Portuguese by A.V. Couto. Panaji: Pereira, 1978-.

c. Maharashtra

00449 Dawn of civilization in Maharashtra: an exhibition of archaeological finds in Maharashtra, of the prehistoric period to the third century A.D. Bombay: Prince of Wales Museum of Western India, 1975. 134p.

00450 BHAGWAT, A.K., ed. Maharashtra, a profile: Vishnu Sakharam Khandekar felicitation volume. Kolhapur: V.S. Khandekar Amrit Mahotsava Satkar Samiti, 1977. 593p.

00451 KANE, P.V. Ancient civilization and geography of Maharashtra. In JASBombay 24 (1917) 613-57.

d. Gujarat

00452 FORBES, A.K. Rās-mālā: Hindu annals of western India, with particular reference to Gujarat. ND: Heritage, 1973. 715p. [Rpt. of 1878 ed.]

00453 MAJMUDAR, M.R. Cultural history of Gujarat, from early times to pre-British period. Bombay: Popular, 1965. 364p.

00454 ______. Historical and cultural chronology of Gujarat from earliest times to 942 AD. Baroda: MSUB, 1960. 342p.

00455 MALABARI, B.M. Gujarat and the Gujaratis. 3d ed. Bombay: Fort Printing, 1889. 358p.

00456 MEHTA, R.N. Khambhat (Cambay): topographical, archaeological and toponymical perspective. In JMSUB 24,1 (1975) 17-29.

00457 MUNSHI, K.M., ed. The Glory that was Gurjaradesa. Bombay: BVB, 1943-. 3 v.

00458 SALETORE, B.A. Main currents in the ancient history of Gujarat. Baroda: MSUB, 1960. 73p.

00459 SANKALIA, H.D. Studies in the historical and cultural geography and ethnogeography of Gujarat. Poona: DCPRI, 1949. 245p.

00460 SUBBARAO, B. Baroda through the ages. Baroda: U. of Baroda, 1953. 130p.

00461 WILBERFORCE-BELL, H. The history of Kathiawad from the earliest times. ND: Ajay Book Service, 1980. 312p. [Rpt. 1916 ed.]

00462 WILLIAMS, L.F.R. The black hills. Kutch in history and legend. London: Weidenfeld & Nicolson, 1955. 276p.

e. Rajasthan

00463 AGARAWALA, R.A. History, art & architecture of Jaisalmer. Delhi: Agam Kala, 1979. 98p.

00464 BANERJI, A.C. Lectures on Rajput history. Calcutta: KLM, 1962. 192p.

00465 DEVRA, G.L. Some aspects of socio-economic history of Rajasthan: Jagdish Singh Gahlot commemoration volume. Jodhpur: Sri Jagdish Singh Gahlot Res. Inst., 1980. 252p.

00466 PRABHAKARA, M. Cultural heritage of Rajasthan. Jaipur: Panchsheel Prakashan, 1972. 138p.

00467 QANUNGO, K.R. Studies in Rajput history. Delhi: S. Chand, 1960. 111p.

00468 SARDA, H.B. Ajmer, historical and descriptive. Ajmer: Fine Art Printing Press, 1941. 458p.

00469 SHARMA, D., ed. Rajasthan through the ages. Bikaner: Rajasthan State Archives, 1966-. 2 v.

00470 SHARMA, G.N. Rajasthan studies. Agra: Lakshmi Narain Agarwal, 1970. 247p.

00471 TOD, J. Annals and antiquities of Rajast'han or, the central and western Rajpoot states of India. ND: K.M.N. Pub., 1971. 2 v. 631, 637p. [Rpt. 1829-32 ed.]

f. Madhya Pradesh

00472 BHATTACHARYYA, P.K. Historical geography of Madhya Pradesh from early records. Delhi: Motilal, 1977. 318p.

00473 HUGHES, A. Gwalior. Gwalior: Vidya Mandir Prakashan, 1979. 51p.

00474 JAIN, K.C. Malwa through the ages, from the earliest times to 1305 A.D. Delhi: Motilal, 1972. 555p.

g. Orissa

00475 BANERJI, R.D. History of Orissa: from the earliest times to the British period. Delhi: Bharatiya, 1980. 2 v. [Rpt. 1930-31 ed.]

00476 CHATTERJI, S.K. The people, language, and culture of Orissa. Bhubaneswar: Orissa Sahitya Akademi, 1966. 79p.

00477 GANGULY, D.K. Historical geography and dynastic history of Orissa, up to the rise of the imperial Gangas. Calcutta: Punthi Pustak, 1975. 311p.

00478 MAHTAB, H.K. The history of Orissa. Cuttack: Prajatantra Prachar Samity, 1959-60. 2 v., 538p.

00479 MITTAL, A.C. Early history of Orissa from earliest times up to the 1st century AD. Barnaras: BHU, 1962. 468p. (Jain Cultural Res. Soc., Sanmati pub., 16)

00480 ORISSA CULTURAL FORUM, comp. Culture. Cuttack: Rashtrabhasha Samabaya Prakashan, 1978. 156p.

00481 SAHU, N.K., ed. A history of Orissa. Delhi: Bharatiya, 1980. 2 v., 401p. [Rpt. of the 1950-56 ed.; sel. from W.W. Hunter, A. Stirling, J. Beames, etc.]

00482 ______., ed. New aspects of history of Orissa. Sambalpur: Sambalpur U., 1971-78. 2 v.

00483 Utkal Univ. history of Orissa. Cuttack: Utkal U., 1964. v. 1 (to 500 AD), 568p. + 21 pl.; v. 6 (19th cent.), 545p. [no more pub.]

4. The Northwest: the Indus Valley and Mountain Frontier

a. Sind

00484 HAIG, M.R. The Indus delta country: a memoir, chiefly on its ancient geography and history. Karachi: Indus, 1972. [Rpt. 1894 ed.]

00485 LAMBRICK, H.T. Sind: a general introduction. Hyderabad: Sindhi Adabi Board, 1964. 274p. (History of Sind series, 1)

00486 Sind through the centuries: an introduction to Sind, a progressive province of Pakistan. Karachi: Sind Through the Centuries Seminar, 1975. 88p.

b. Baluchistan

00487 BALOCH, M.K.B.M. Searchlights on Baloches and Balochistan. Ed. by M. J. Hussain. Karachi: Royal Book Co., 1974. 387p.

00488 Balochistan through the ages: selection from government record. Quetta: Nisa Traders, 1979. 2 v. [comp. from district gazetteers]

00489 BALUCH, M.S.K. History of Baluch race and Baluchistan. 2d ed. Quetta: Gosha-e-Adab, 1977. 298p. [1st pub. 1958]

00490 BROHI, N. Studies in Brahui history. Karachi: Pakistan Herald Press, 1977. 114p.

c. Punjab

00491 FAUJA SINGH, ed. History of the Punjab. Patiala: Punjabi U., 1972-. v. 1 (to Aśoka), 354p.; v. 3 (1000-1526 AD), 420p. [to be 8 v.]

00492 ______., ed. Sirhind through the ages. Patiala: Punjabi U., 1972. 154p.

00493 GREWAL, J.S., ed. Studies in local and regional history. Amritsar: Guru Nanak U., 1974. 207p.

00494 HARBANS SINGH & N.G. BARRIER, eds. Punjab past and present: essays in honour of Dr. Ganda Singh. Patiala: Pubjabi U., 1976. 511p.

00495 SURI, V.S. Panjab through the ages.... Chandigarh: Panjab Itihas Prakashan, 1971. 92p.

00496 THAPAR, R. The scope and significance of regional history. In her Ancient Indian social history. ND: Orient Longmans, 1978, 361-76.

00497 TREVASKIS, H.K. The land of the five rivers: an economic history of the Punjab from the earliest times to the year 1890. London: OUP, 1928. 372p.

d. the Pathan borderland

00498 CAROE, O. The Pathans 550 B.C.-A.D. 1957. NY: St. Martins, 1958. 521p.

00499 SPAIN, J.W. The Pathan borderland. The Hague: Mouton, 1963. 293p.

e. Kashmir, Jammu, and Ladakh

00500 BAMZAI, P.N.K. A history of Kashmir: political, social, cultural, from the earliest times to the present day. 2d rev. ed. ND: Metropolitan Book Co., 1973. 866p.

00501 FERGUSON, J.P. Kashmir; an historical introduction. London: Centaur Press, 1961. 214p.

00502 IQBAL, S.M. & K.L. NIRASH, eds. The culture of Kashmir. ND: Marwah, 1978. 244p.

00503 KAUL, G.L. A six millennium review of Kashmir; describing physical, political, social, cultural, economic & religious upheavals. Srinagar: Chronicle Pub. House, 1969. 304p.

00504 PATHIK, J. Cultural heritage of the Dogras. ND: Light & Life, 1980 177p.

00505 PETECH, L. The kingdom of Ladakh: c. 950-1842 A.D. Rome: Instituto italiano per il Medio ed Estremo Oriente, 1977. 191p. (Serie orientale Roma, 51)

00506 SAXENA, K.S. Political history of Kashmir (B.C. 300-A.D. 1200). Lucknow: Upper India Pub. House, 1974. 364p.

00507 SNELLGROVE, D.L. & T. SKORUPSKI. The cultural heritage of Ladakh. Warminster, Eng.: Aris & Phillips, 1977-. v. 1, 144p.

00508 SUFI, G.M.D. Kashīr, being a history of Kashmir from the earliest times to our own. ND: Light & Life, 1974. 2 v. [Rpt. of 1949 ed.]

00509 WAKEFIELD, W. History of Kashmir & the Kashmiris: the happy valley. Delhi: Seema, 1975. 300p. [Rpt. 1879 ed.]

5. North India: the Ganga Plains and Āryavarta Cultural Heartland (Haryana, U.P., and Bihar)

00510 AQUIQUE, M. Economic history of Mithila, c. 600 B.C.-1907 A.D. ND: Abhinav, 1974. 224p.

00511 CHAUDHARI, R.K. History of Bihar. Patna: Motilal, 1958. 421p.

00512 CROOKE, W. The North-western provinces of India: their history, ethnology, and administration. 2d ed. Karachi: OUP, 1972. [1st ed. 1897]

00513 DIWAKAR, R.R. Bihar through the ages. Bombay: Orient Longmans, 1959. 891p.

00514 MISHRA, V. Cultural heritage of Mithila. Allahabad: Mithila Prakasana, 1979. 416p.

00515 MUZTAR, B.K. Kurukshetra: political and cultural history. Delhi: B.R., 1978. 174p.

00516 PANDEY, M.S. Historical geography and topography of Bihar. Delhi: Motilal, 1963. 226p.

00517 PRAKASH, BUDDHA. Hariyana through the ages. Kurukshetra: Kurukshetra U., 1970. 95p.

00518 PRASAD, B., ed. Comprehensive history of Bihar. Patna: Kashi Prasad Jayaswal Res. Inst. v. 1 pt. 1, 1044 + 55p.; v. 1 pt. 2, 758 + 79p.

00519 THAKUR, U. History of Mithila (c. 3000 BC-1556 AD). Darbhanga: Mithila Res. Inst., 1956. 462p.

00520 YADAV, K.C., ed. Haryana: studies in history and culture. Kurukshetra: Kurukshetra U., 1968. 150p.

6. The Northeast: the Ganges Delta and Brahmaputra Valley

a. Bengal

00521 BHATTACHARYYA, A. Historical geography of ancient and early medieval Bengal. Calcutta: Sanskrit Pustak Bhandar, 1977. 158p.

00522 The history of Bengal. Dacca: Dacca U., 1943-48. v. 1 (Hindu period), ed. by R.C. Majumdar, 729p. + 80 pl.; v. 2 (Muslim period 1200-1757), ed. by J.N. Sarkar, 530p.

00523 MAJUMDAR, R.C. History of ancient Bengal. Calcutta: G. Bharadwaj, 1971. 699p.

00524 MARTIN, R.M. The history, antiquities, topography and statistics of eastern India...surveyed under the orders of the supreme government.... London: W.H. Allen, 1838. 3 v. [Rpt. by: Delhi: Cosmo Publications, 1976. 5 v. (Studies in Indian History, 11-15)]

b. Assam

00525 BARUA, B.K. A cultural history of Assam. 2d ed. Gauhati, Lawyer's Book Stall, 1969-. v. 1, 244p.

00526 ______. Early geography of Assam. Nowgong, Assam: Shri K.K. Barooah, 1952. 72p.

00527 BARUA, K.L. Early history of Kāmarūpa, from the earliest times to the end of the sixteenth century. 2d ed. Gauhati: Lawyers Book Stall, 1966. 238p.

00528 ______. Studies in the early history of Assam.... Ed. by M. Neog. Jorhat: Asam Sahitya Sabha, 1973. 342p.

00529 BASU, N.K. Assam in the Ahom age, 1228-1826; being politico-economic and soci-cultural studies. 1st ed. Calcutta: SPB, 1970. 365p.

00530 BHUYAN, S.K. Studies in the history of Assam. Gauhati: Srimati Laksheswari Bhuyan, 1965. 270p.

00531 CHATTERJI, S.K. The place of Assam in the history and civilization of India. Gauhati: U. of Gauhati, 1955. 84p.

00532 CHAUDHURI, P.C. The history of civilisation of the peoples of Assam to the twelfth century A.D. Gauhati: Dept. of Hist. and Antiquarian Studies in Assam, 1959. 538p.

00533 GAIT, E.A. A history of Assam. 3d rev. ed. Rev. by B.K. Barua and H.V.S Murthy. Calcutta: Thacker Spink, 1963. 349p. [1st ed. 1906]

00534 LAKSHMI DEVI. Ahom-tribal relations: a political study. Gauhati: Assam Book Depot, 1968. 275p.

00535 NATH, R.M. The back-ground of Assamese culture. 2d ed. Gauhati: Dutta Baruah, 1978. 158p.

00536 PURI, B.N. Studies in early history and administration in Assam. Gauhati: Gauhati U., 1968. 84p.

7. The Himalayan Rim of India, Nepal, and Bhutan

00537 CHAKRAVARTI, B. A cultural history of Bhutan. Chittaranjan: Hilltop, 1979-. v. 1-. [to be 2 v.]

00538 CHARAK, S.D.S. Himachal Pradesh. ND: Light & Life, 1978-.

00539 DAS, N. The dragon country: the general history of Bhutan. Bombay: Orient Longmans, 1974. 99p.

00540 GOPAL, L. & T.P. VERMA. Studies in the history and culture of Nepal. Varanasi: Bharati Prakashan, 1977. 72p.

00541 KAUSHAL, R.K. Himachal Pradesh; a survey of the history of the land and its people. Bombay: Minerva Book Shop, 1965. 152p.

00542 LÉVI, S. Le Nepal. Étude historique d'un royaume hindou. Paris: E. Leroux, 1905-08. 3 v.

00543 SAYMI, D. The lotus & the flame; an account on Nepalese culture. Kathmandu: Dept. of Info., Min. of Communication, 1972. 158p.

00544 VAIDYA, K.L. The cultural heritage of the Himalayas. ND: National, 1977. 183p.

00545 Vaṁśāvalī. History of Nepal. Tr. from Parbatiya by S.S. Singh and P. Gunanand. Ed. by D. Wright. Kathmandu: Nepal Antiquated Book Pub., 1972. 320p. [1st pub. 1877]

E. Auxiliary Techniques for the Study of the Past

1. Numismatics

a. bibliographies and catalogs

00546 BAL KRISHNAN. Ancient Indian coinage; a select bibliography. ND: Res. Inst. of Ancient Scientific Studies, 1968. 55p.

00547 GOONETILEKE, H.A.I. A bibliography of Ceylon coins and currency, ancient, mediaeval and modern. In CJHSS 6 (1963) 187-239.

00548 GUPTA, P.L. Bibliography of Indian numismatics. Varanasi: Numismatic Soc. of India, 1977-1979. 2 v.

00549 ______. A bibliography of the hoards of punch-marked coins of ancient India. Bombay: Numismatic Soc. of India, 1955. 23p.

00550 SINGHAL, CHANAN RAM. Bibliography of Indian coins. Ed. by A.S. Altekar. Bombay: Numismatic Soc. of India, 1950-52. 2 v., 163, 220p.

b. surveys and studies

00551 BAJPAI, K.D. Indian numismatic studies. ND: Abhinav, 1976. 188p.

00552 BROWN, C.J. The coins of India. Bologna: Forni, 1967. 120p. (Heritage of India series) [1st ed. 1922]

00553 ELLIOT, W. Coins of Southern India. Varanasi: Prithivi Prakashan, 1970. 159p. [Rpt. 1886 ed.]

00554 GUPTA, P.L. Coins. ND: Natl. Book Trust, 1969. 241p.

00555 NUMISMATIC SOC. OF INDIA. Golden jubilee volume. Varanasi: 1961. 510p. [Its Journal 23 (1961)]

00556 ______. Sixty years of the Numismatic Society of India, 1910-1971: history and presidential addresses. Varanasi: 1973. 581p.

00557 SIRCAR, D.C. Studies in Indian coins. Delhi: Motilal, 1968. 405p.

00558 THAKUR, U. Mints and minting in India. Varanasi: CSSO, 1972. 192p. (CSS, 88)

2. Epigraphy and Paleography

a. bibliography and reference

00559 CHAUDHURI, S. Bibliography of studies in Indian epigraphy, 1926-50. Baroda: Oriental Inst., 1966. 113p. (M.S.U. oriental series, 6)

00560 GOONETILEKE, H.A.I. Writings on Ceylon epigraphy. In CHJ 10, 1/4 (1960-61) 171-205.

00561 SCHARPÉ, A., et al., eds. Corpus topographicum Indiae antiquae: a sodalibus Universitatis Gandavensis et Universitatis Lovaniensis editum. Gent: U. of Gent, 1974-.

00562 SIRCAR, D.C. Epigraphical studies in India: some observations. In SIE 3 (1976) 9-25.

00563 ______. Indian epigraphical glossary. Delhi: Motilal Banarsidass, 1966. 560p.

00564 Corpus Inscriptionum Indicarum. Calcutta: Govt. of India, 1877-. [v. 6, 1977, pub. by ASI. Individual volumes entered in appropriate historical sections]

00565 Epigraphia Indica. Delhi, etc: ASI, 1888/91-. v. 1-. [irregular]

00566 Inscriptions of Ceylon. Colombo: Dept. of Archaeol., 1970-. v. 1-.

00567 SEWELL, R. The historical inscriptions of Southern India (collected till 1923) and outlines of political history. Ed. by S. Krishnaswami Aiyangar. Madras: U. of Madras, 1932. 451p.

00568 South Indian inscriptions. Delhi: ASI, 1890-.

c. studies

00569 BÜHLER, G. Indian paleography. Appendix to: IA 33 (1904), 102p. [Reprinted: Calcutta: ISSP, 1959. 138p.]

00570 BURNELL, A.C. Elements of south-Indian palaeography, from the fourth to the seventeenth century A.D.; being an introduction to the study of south-Indian inscriptions and mss. 2d. enl. and impr. ed. London: Trubner [Mangalore, Basel mission press],1878. 147p. + 34 pl.

00571 DANI, A.H. Indian palaeography. Oxford: OUP, 1963. 297p.

00572 MAHALINGAM, T.V. Early South Indian palaeography. Madras: U. of Madras, 1967. 341p.

00573 SIRCAR, D.C. Indian epigraphy. Delhi: Motilal, 1965. 475p.

00574 ______. Introduction to Indian epigraphy and palaeography. In JAIH 4, 1/2 (1970-71) 72-139.

3. Archaeology
a. bibliography and reference

00575 COUNCIL FOR OLD WORLD ARCHAEOLOGY. COWA bibliography: Southern Asia; area 16, no. 1-. Cambridge, MA: 1958-. no. 1-. [title varies]

00576 HINGORANI, R.P. Site index to A.S.I. circle reports: a cumulative site index to annual progress reports (1881 to 1921) of various circles of the Archaeological Survey of India. ND: AIIS, 1978. 262p.

b. history of South Asian archaeology

00577 ABU IMAM. Sir Alexander Cunningham and the beginnings of Indian archaeology. Dacca: ASP, 1966. 276p. (Its pub., 19)

00578 DEVENDRA, D.T. Seventy years of Ceylon archaeology. In ArtAs 22, 1/2 (1959) 23-40.

00579 GHOSH, A. Fifty years of the Archaeological Survey of India. In AI 9 (1953) 29-52.

00580 LAL, B.B. Indian archaeology since independence. Delhi: Motilal, 1964. 107p.

00581 MALONEY, C. Archaeology in South India: accomplishments and prospects. In B. Stein, ed. Essays on South India. Honolulu: UPH, 1975. 1-40. (ASH, 15)

00582 MARKHAM, C.R. Archaeological survey. In his A memoir of the Indian surveys. London: W.H. Allen, 1871, 170-203.

00583 RAY, S. Story of Indian Archaeology (1784-1947). ND: ASI, 1961. 131 p. + 47 pl.

00584 SANKALIA, H.D. Born for archaeology: an autobiography. Delhi: B.R., 1978. 183p.

00585 ______. Indian archaeology today. Rev. and enl. ed. Delhi: Ajanta, 1979. 204p. [1st ed. 1962]

c. methodology

00586 AGRAWAL, D.P. & B.M. PANDE, eds. Ecology and archaeology of western India: proceedings of a workshop held at the Physical Research Laboratory, Ahmedabad, February 23-26, 1976. Delhi: Concept, 1977. 255p.

00587 LESHNIK, L.S. Sociological interpretation in archaeology. In MI 47 (1967) 8-14.

00588 MALIK, S.C. Archaeology as a source in writing socio-cultural and socio-economic history. In EA 21 (1968) 291-304.

00589 ______. Indian civilization: the formative period; a study of archaeology as anthropology. Simla: IIAS, 1968. 204p.

00590 ______. The future of archaeological research in India--some thoughts. In JMSUB 15,1 (1966) 79-89.

00591 SANKALIA, H.D. Archaeology and tradition. In Indica 1,1 (1964) 3-17.

00592 ______. New archaeology, its scope and application to India. Lucknow: Ethnographic and Folk Culture Soc., 1977. 122p.

d. collections of studies

00593 DEO, S.B. Archaeological congress and seminar papers. Nagpur: Nagpur U., 1972. 296p.

00595 HAMMOND, N., ed. South Asian archaeology: papers from the first international conference of South Asian archaeologists held in the University of Cambridge. London: Duckworth, 1973. 308p.

00595 LOHUIZEN-DE LEEUW, J.E. VAN, ed. Papers from the third international conference of the Association of South Asian Archaeologists in Western Europe held in Paris. Leiden: Brill, 1979. 189p. + 94 pl.

00596 LOHUIZEN-DE LEEUW, J.E. VAN & J.M.M. UBAGHS, eds. South Asian archaeology 1973: papers from the second international conference of the Association for the Promotion of South Asian Archaeology in Western Europe held in the University of Amsterdam. Leiden: Brill, 1974. 187p. + 48pl.

00597 MISRA, V.D. Some aspects of Indian archaeology. Allahabad: Prabhat, 1977. 128p.

00598 SANKALIA, H.D. Aspects of Indian history and archaeology. Delhi: B.R., 1977. 330p.

00599 TADDEI, M., ed. Papers from the fourth international conference of the Association of South Asian Archaeologists in Western Europe held in Naples. Naples: Istituto Universitario Orientale, 1979. 938p. + many illus., plans, maps. (Seminario dei Studi Asiatici, Series Maior, 6)

e. museums and museology of South Asia

00600 AGRAWAL, U. Brief directory of museums in India. ND: Museums Assoc. of India, 1977. 94p.

00601 ______. Index to the Journal of Indian museums, vol. I-XXVIII, 1945-1972. ND: Museums Assoc. of India, 1973. 66p.

00602 ANAND, M.R., ed. Museum - house of the muses. [special issue] In Marg 19,1 (1965). 57p. + pls. [illus. survey of Indian museums]

00603 DE SILVA, P.H. Les musées de Céylan. In Museum 19 (1966) 219-299.

00604 DAR, S.R. Archaeology and museums in Pakistan. Lahore: Lahore Museum, 1975. 54p.

00605 ______. Repositories of our cultural heritage: a handbook of museums in Pakistan (1851-1979). Lahore: Lahore Museum, 1979. 126p.

00606 Directory of museums in U. P. In Saṅgrahālaya-purātatva patrikā (Bull. of mus. & archaeol. in U. P.) 13 (1974) 3-48.

00607 DWIVEDI, V.P., ed. Museums and museology: new horizons: essays in honour of Dr. Grace Morley on her 80th birthday. Delhi: Agam, 1980. 339p.

00608 GHOSH, D.P. Studies in museum and museology in India. Calcutta: Indian Pub., 1968. 155p.

00609 INDIA (REP.) ARCHAEOLOGICAL SURVEY. Archaeological remains, monuments, and museums. Delhi: 1964, 2 v., 379p.

00610 ROY, S., ed. [special issue on museums] In EA 29,1 (1976) 1-146.

00611 SIVARAMAMURTI, C. Directory of museums in India. ND: Min. of Scientific Res. & Cultural Affairs, 1959. 141p. + 30 pl.

III. INDIC SOCIAL SYSTEMS

A. Bibliography and Reference

00612 Anthropological bibliography of South Asia, together with a directory of anthropological field research. The Hague: Mouton, 1958-. v. 1 & 2 comp. by E. von Fürer-Haimendorf. v. 3 & n.s. v. 1 comp. by H. Kanitkar & E. von Fürer-Haimendorf. 748, 459, 562, 346p. [last v. 1976]

00613 Asian social science bibliography, 1966-. Ed. by Nand Kishore Goil. Delhi: Hindustan, 1970-. (Inst. of Economic Growth; Documentation series, 1-.) [continues: Southern Asia Social Science Bibliography. v. 1-14. 1952-65. Calcutta: UNESCO Res. Centre. Annual. Title varies.]

00614 KANITKAR, J.M., ed. A bibliography of Indology. v. 1, Indian anthropology. Ed., rev. & enl. by D.L. Banerjee & A.K. Ohdedar. Calcutta: Natl. Library, 1960. 290p.

00615 RAHMAN, M.H. & N. AHMED. Select annotated bibliography on social science research work in Bangladesh, 1972-1978. Dacca: Social Science Res. Cncl., Min. of Planning, 1979. 323p.

00616 RAY, S.K. Bibliographies of eminent Indian anthropologists, with life-sketches. Calcutta: AnthSI, 1974. 184p.

00617 ______. Bibliography of anthropology of India; including index to current literature, 1960-1964. Calcutta: AnthSI, 1976. 323p.

00618 ROY, S. Anthropologists in India: short-biography, bibliography, and current projects. New Delhi: Indian Anthropological Assoc., 1970. 218p.

00619 A survey of research in sociology and social anthropology. Bombay: Popular, 1972-4. 3 v. [Sponsored by ICSSR.]

00620 VIDYARTHI, L.P. Rise of anthropology in India: a social science orientation. Delhi: Concept, 1978. 2 v., 384, 476p. [bibl. essays]

B. History and Methodology of Social Anthropological Studies of South Asia

00621 AMES, M.M. Detribalized anthropology and the study of Asian civilizations. In PA 49,2 (1976) 313-24. [on Milton Singer's approach]

00622 BÉTEILLE, A. & T.N. MADAN, eds. Encounter and experience: personal accounts of fieldwork. ND: Vikas, 1975. 225p.

00623 BOSE, N.K. Fifty years of science in India: progress of anthropology and archaeology. Calcutta: Indian Science Congress Assoc., 1963. 50p.

00624 CHOUDHURY, N.C. Plea for anthropology museums in India. In EA 29,1 (1976) 37-56.

00625 DUMONT, L. & D.F. POCOCK. For a sociology of India. In CIS 1 (1957) 7-22.

00626 ELWIN, V. The tribal world of Verrier Elwin, an autobiography. Bombay: OUP, 1964. 356p.

00627 FOX, R. Avatars of Indian research. In CSSH 12 (1970) 59-72.

00628 GARDNER, P.M. Phenomenal levels in the structure of Indian civilization. In S. Vatuk, ed., American studies in the anthropology of India. ND: Manohar, 1978, 14-34.

00629 GHURYE, G.S. I and other explorations. Bombay: Popular, 1973. 352p.

00630 MADAN, T.N. For a sociology of India. In CIS 9 (1966) 9-16.

00631 ______. For a sociology of India. Some clarifications. In CIS ns 1 (1967) 90-93.

00632 MALIK, S.C. Understanding Indian civilization: a framework of enquiry. Simla: IIAS, 1975. 138p. (SIAS,1)

00633 MUKHERJEE, R. The value-base of social anthropology: the context of India in particular. In CA 17,1 (1976) 71-95.

00634 OPLER, M.E. The themal approach in cultural anthropology and its application to North Indian data. In SWJA 24,3 (1968) 215-27.

00635 SINHA, S. Anthropology of Nirmal Kumar Bose. In his (ed.) Aspects of Indian culture & society.... Calcutta: IAS, 1972, 1-22.

00636 ______., ed. Field studies on the people of India: methods and perspectives: in memory of Professor Tarak Chandra Das. Calcutta: IAS, 1978. 307p.

00637 SRINIVAS, M.N. & A.M. SHAH & E.A. RAMASWAMY, eds. The Fieldworker and the field: problems and challenges in sociological investigation. Delhi: OUP, 1979. 288p.

00638 VIDYARTHI, L.P. The rise of social anthropology in India, 1774-1972. In K. David, ed. The new wind: changing identities in South Asia. The Hague: Mouton, 1977. 61-84. (WA)

C. Anthropological Approaches to Indic Society

1. Overviews

00639 BHARATI, A. Great tradition and little traditions: Indological investigations in cultural anthropology. Varanasi: CSSO, 1978. 384p.

00640 BOSE, N.K. An anthropological view of Indian civilization. In MI 52,2 (1972) 97-112.

00641 COHN, B.S. India: the social anthropology of a civilization. Englewood Cliffs, N.J.: Prentice-Hall, 1971. 164p.

00642 DELEURY, G.A. Le modèle indou: essai sur les structures de la civilisation de l'Inde d'hier et d'aujourd'hui. Paris: Hachette, 1978. 365p.

00643 DUMONT, L. La civilisation indienne et nous. Paris: A. Colin, 1975. 142p.

00644 KARVE, I. The cultural process in India. In A. Aiyappan, ed., Society in India. Madras: Social Sciences Assoc., 1956, 29-48.

00645 LANNOY, R. The speaking tree: a study of Indian culture and society. London: OUP, 1971. 466p.

00646 LEHMAN, F.K. Some anthropological parameters of a civilisation; the ecology and evolution of India's high culture. Ph.D. diss., Columbia U., 1959. 754p. [UM 60-1146]

00647 MANDELBAUM, D.G. Society in India, v. 1: Continuity and change; v. 2: Change and continuity. Berkeley: UCalP., 1972. 2 v., 665 + 51p.

00648 PANIKKAR, K.M. Essential features of Indian culture. Bombay: BVB, 1964. 60p.

00649 RAGHAVAN, V. Variety and integration in the pattern of Indian culture. In FEQ 15 (1956) 497-506.

00650 SINGER, M.B. The cultural pattern of Indian civilization: a preliminary report of a methodological field study. In FEQ 15,1 (1955) 23-36.

00651 ______. When a great tradition modernizes: an anthropological approach to Indian civilization. NY: Praeger, 1972. 430p.

00652 SINGER, M.B. & B.S. COHN, eds. Structure and change in Indian society. Chicago: Aldine, 1968. 507p. (VFPA, 47)

00653 TYLER, S.A. India: an anthropological perspective. Pacific Palisades, CA.: Goodyear, 1973. 224p.

00654 VIDYARTHI, L.P. South Asian culture: an anthropological perspective. Delhi: Oriental, 1976. 140p.

2. Festschriften

00655 The Anthropologist; special volume. Delhi: U. of Delhi, 1969. 2 v. in 1. [papers in honor of Prophilla Chander Biswas]

00656 BALA RATNAM, L.K., ed. Anthropology on the march; recent studies of Indian beliefs, attitudes, and social institutions. A commemorative volume in honour of L.K. Ananta Krishna Iyer. Madras: Book Centre, 1963. 390p.

00657 DEVADAS PILLAI, S., ed. Aspects of changing India; studies in honour of Prof. G.S. Ghurye. Bombay: Popular, 1976. 414p.

00658 KAPADIA, K.M., ed. Professor Ghurye felicitation volume. Bombay: Popular, 1954. 283p.

00659 KRISHNASWAMY, K.S. et al., eds. Society and change: essays in honour of Sachin Chaudhuri. Bombay: OUP, 1977. 327p.

00660 MADAN, T.N. & S. GOPALA. Indian anthropology; essays in memory of D.N. Majumdar. Bombay: Asia, 1962. 420p.

00661 PRADHAN, M.C., ed. Anthropology and archaeology; essays in commemoration of Verrier Elwin, 1902-64. Bombay: OUP, 1969. 328p.

00662 SINHA, S., ed. Aspects of Indian culture and society; essays in felicitation of Professor Nirmal Kumar Bose. Calcutta: IAS, 1972. 248p.

00663 UNNITHAN, T.K. & INDRA DEVA & Y. SINGH, eds. Towards a sociology of culture in India; essays in honour of Professor D.P. Mukerji. ND: Prentice Hall, 1965. 441p.

3. Other Essay Collections

00664 AIYAPPAN, A. & L.K. BALA RATNAM, ed. Society in India. Madras: Social Sciences Assoc., 1956. 252p.

00665 BOSE, N.K. Cultural anthropology. Bombay: Asia, 1961. 140p.

00666 ______. Cultural anthropology and other essays. Calcutta: Indian Associated Pub., 1953. 289p.

00667 ______. Culture and society in India. Bombay: Asia, 1967. 440p.

00668 DUMONT, L. Religion, politics & history in India, collected papers in Indian sociology. The Hague: Mouton, 1970. 166p.

00669 GABORIEAU, M. & A. THORNER, eds. Asie du Sud, tradition et changements. Paris: CNRS, 1979. 676p. [Colloques internationaux, 582]

00670 GHURYE, G.S. Anthropo-sociological papers. Bombay: Popular, 1963. 381p.

00671 ______., et al., ed. Papers in sociology. Silver jubilee memorial volume. Bombay: U. of Bombay, 1947. 130p.

00672 KOSAMBI, D.D. Myth and reality; studies in the formation of Indian culture. Bombay: Popular, 1962. 187p.

00673 LESHNIK, L.S. & G.-D. SONTHEIMER, eds. Pastoralists and nomads in South Asia. Wiesbaden: Harrassowitz, 1975. 276p. (SSI)

00674 PIERIS, R., ed. Some aspects of traditional Sinhalese culture; a symposium. Peradeniya: U. of Ceylon, 1956. 113p.

00675 SINGER, M.B., ed. Traditional India: structure and change. Philadelphia: American Folklore Soc., 1959. 312p. [pub. as J. of American folklore 71, 281 (1958)]

00676 SRIVASTAVA, R., ed. Social anthropology in India: contemporary perspectives: selections from the Journal of Social Research, 1958-1977. ND: Books Today, 1979. 257p.

00677 VATUK, S., ed. American studies in the anthropology of India. ND: Manohar, 1978. 517p.

D. Unity and Diversity of Indic Civilization

1. Is South Asia a Cultural Unit?

00678 MASON, P., ed. India and Ceylon: unity and diversity: a symposium. London: OUP, 1967. 311p.

00679 MOOKERJI, RADHA KUMUD. The fundamental unity of India (from Hindu sources). London: Longmans, Green, 1914. 140p.

00680 PANDIT, P.B. India as a sociolinguistic area. Poona: U. of Poona, 1972. 92p.

00681 RAGHAVAN, V. Variety and integration in the pattern of Indian culture. In FEQ 15,4 (1956) 497-505.

2. Cultural Regions

00682 BECK, B.E.F. Centers and boundaries of regional caste systems: toward a general model. In C.A. Smith, ed. Regional Analysis. NY: Academic Press, 1976, v. 2, 255-288.

00683 BHATT, B.L. India and Indian regions: a critical overview. In D.E. Sopher, ed. An exploration of India. Ithaca: Cornell U. Press, 1980, 35-64.

00684 BOSE, N.K. Cultural zones of India. In GRI 18,4 (1956) 1-12.

00685 CRANE, R.I., ed. Regions and regionalism in South Asian studies: an exploratory study. Durham: DUPCSSA, 1967. 281p. [Monograph & occ. paper series 5]

00686 RICHARDS, F.J. Cultural regions of India. In Geography 15 (1929) 20-29.

00687 SABERWAL, S. Regions and their social structures. In CIS ns 5 (1971) 82-98.

00688 SOPHER, D.E. The geographic patterning of culture in India. In his An exploration of India; geographic perspectives on society and culture. Ithaca: Cornell U. Press, 1980, 289-326.

00689 SUBBARAO, B. Regions and regionalism in India. In EW 10 (1958) 1215-20.

3. Ethnic Diversity
a. early views of the "races of India"

00690 BAINES, J.A. Ethnography (castes and tribes). Strassburg: K.J. Trübner, 1912. 211p. (GIAPA,2,5)

00691 CHAKRABERTY, C. The racial history of India. Calcutta: Vijaya Krishna, 1947. 359p.

00692 CHANDA, R. Races of India. In CUDL 8 (1922) 295-312.

00693 CROOKE, W. Races of Northern India. Delhi: Cosmo, 1973. 270p. [1st ed. 1907]

00694 GUHA, B.S. An outline of the racial ethnology of India. Calcutta: Indian Science Congress Assoc., 1937. 139p.

00695 HODSON, T. C. India, census ethnography, 1901-1931. Delhi: MP, 1937. 118p.

00696 KITTS, E.J. A compendium of the castes and tribes found in India. Comp. from the (1881) census reports. Bombay: Educ. Soc. Press, 1885. 90p.

00697 MAJUMDAR, D.N. Races and cultures of India. 4th rev. and enl. ed. Bombay: Asia, 1973. 457p.

00698 RISLEY, H.H. India. Ethnographic appendices. Calcutta: Supt. of Govt. Printing, 1903. 251p. (CI 1901,1,3)

00699 ______. The people of India. 2d ed., ed. by W. Crooke. Delhi: OBRC, 1969. 472p.

b. recent studies of ethnic diversity: race and caste

00700 BÉTEILLE, A. Race and descent as social categories in India. In Daedalus 96 (1967) 444-63.

00701 CHATTERJI, S.K. The Indian synthesis, and racial and cultural intermixture in India. Presidential address, All India Oriental Conf., 17th session, 1953. Ahmedabad: R.C. Parikh, 1953. 50p.

00702 ______. Kirāta-jana-kṛti = The Indo-Mongoloids, their contribution to the history and culture of India. Rev. 2nd ed. Calcutta: ASB, 1974. 187p.

00703 CHAUDHURI, N.C. The continent of Circe; being an essay on the peoples of India. London: Chatto & Windus, 1965. 320p.

00704 DESHPANDE, M.M. & P.E. HOOK. Aryan and non-Aryan in India. Ann Arbor: UMCSSAS, 1979. 315p.

00705 GANKOVSKY, YU. V. The people of Pakistan: an ethnic history. Tr. from Russian by I. Gavrilov. Moscow: Nauka, 1971. 246p. [Rpt. Lahore: PPH, n.d.]

00706 MALONEY, C. Peoples of South Asia. NY: Holt, Rinehart & Winston, 1974. 584p.

00707 MASICA, C.P. Aryan and Non-Aryan elements in North Indian agriculture. In M.M. Deshpande and P.E. Hook, eds., Aryan and Non-Aryan in India. Ann Arbor: UMCSSAS, 1979, 55-152.

00708 RÉGAMEY, C. Bibliographie analytique des travaux relatifs aux éléments anaryens dans la civilization et les langues de l'Inde. In BEFEO 34 (1934) 429-566.

00709 SCHERMERHORN, R.A. Ethnic plurality in India. Tucson: U. of Arizona Press, 1978. 369p.

4. Physical Anthropology

00710 RAKSHIT, HIRENDRA K., ed. Anthropology in India; v. 2 physical anthropology. Calcutta: AnthSI, 1976. 167p.

00711 ______. Bio-anthropological research in India: proceedings of the Seminar in Physical Anthropology and Allied Disciplines. Calcutta: AnthSI, 1975. 293p.

00712 SEN, D.K. Racial studies in India: recent trends. In JIAS 2,1 (1967) 1-18.

00713 SINGH, I.P. Twenty-five years of physical anthropology in India - an appraisal. In EA 27,3 (1974) 183-94.

00714 STOUDT, H.W. The physical anthropology of Ceylon. Colombo: Colombo Museum, 1961. 180p. (Ceylon Natl. Museums' Ethnog. series, 2)

E. Social Structure and Caste Systems

1. Bibliography

00715 SINHA, S. Caste in India; a trend report. In A survey of research in sociology and social anthropology. Bombay: Popular, 1974, v. 1, 233-75. [sponsored by ICSSR]

00716 ______. Trends of research on caste in India. In his Anthropology in India. Calcutta: AnthSI, 1976, 169-197.

00717 SRINIVAS, M.N., et al. Caste: a trend report and a bibliography. In Current Sociology 8,2 (1959) 135-85.

00718 VIDYARTHI, LALITA PRASAD. Caste studies. In his Rise of anthropology in India. Delhi: Concept, 1978, 136-153. [bibl. essay]

2. Definition of Caste: Distinguishing Jāti from Other Social Classifications

00719 BERREMAN, G.D. Caste as social process. In SWJA 23 (1967) 351-70.

00720 ______. Caste in cross-cultural perspective. In G. DeVos and H. Wagatsuma, eds. Japan's invisible race: caste in culture and personality. Berkeley: UCalP, 1966, 275-324.

00721 ______. Caste in India and the United States. In AJS 66 (1960) 120-127.

00722 ______. Caste, racism, and stratification. In CIS 6 (1962) 122-25.

00723 BÉTEILLE, A. Class and caste: a rejoinder. In MI 46,2 (1966) 172-76.

00724 BOSE, N.K. Class and caste. In MI 45,4 (1965) 265-74. [also in EW 17 (1965) 1337-40.]

00725 DUMONT, L. Caste, racism and stratification. In CIS 5 (1961) 20-43.

00726 HSU, F.L.K. Clan, caste, and club. Princeton: Van Nostrand, 1963. 353p.

00727 KARVE, I. What is caste? (1) Caste as extended kin: (2) Caste as status group. In EW 10 (1958) 125-38, 881-88.

00728 KLASS, M. Caste: the emergence of the South Asian social system. Philadelphia: ISHI, 1980. 212p.

00729 LEACH, E.R. Caste, class, and slavery: the taxonomic problem. In A.V.S. de Reuck & J. Knight, eds. Caste and race.... London: Churchill, 1967, 5-16.

00730 ______. Introduction: what should we mean by caste. In his (ed.) Aspects of caste in South India, Ceylon, and North-West Pakistan. Cambridge: CamUP, 1969. 147p.

3. General Studies

00731 BERREMAN, G.D. Caste and other inequities: essays on inequality. Meerut: Folklore Inst., 1979. 325p. (Kirpa Dai series in folklore and anthro., 2)

00732 BOSE, D. The problems of Indian society. Bombay: Popular, 1968. 206p.

00733 BOSE, N.K. The structure of Indian society. Tr. from Bengali by A. Béteille. ND: Orient Longmans, 1975. 171p.

00734 KARVE, I. Hindu society; an interpretation. 2nd ed. Poona: Deshmukh Prakashan, 1968. 18p.

00735 MENCHER, J.P. The caste system upside down, or the not-so-mysterious East. In CA 15,4 (1974) 469-478.

00736 PRABHU, P.N. Hindu social organization - a study in social, psychological and ideological foundations. 5th rev. & enl. ed. Bombay: Popular, 1971. 390p. [1st ed. 1954]

4. Essay Collections

00737 AHRENS, H. & K.G. SCHWERIN, eds. Aspekte sozialer Ungleichheit in Südasien. Wiesbaden: Steiner, 1975. 215p. (BSAF, 17)

00738 BÉTEILLE, A. Castes: old and new; essays in social structure and social stratification. Bombay: Asia, 1969. 254p.

00739 Class and Caste in India. [Annual number.] In EPW 14,7-8 (1979) 221-484.

00740 LEACH, E.R., ed. Aspects of caste in South India, Ceylon, and north-west Pakistan. Cambridge: CamUP, 1969. 147p.

5. Varṇāśramadharma: the Traditional Rationalization of Caste

00741 DAS, V. A sociological approach to the Caste Purāṇas: a case study. In SB 17 (1968) 141-164.

00742 FOX, R.G. Varṇa schemes and ideological integration in Indian society. In CSSH 11 (1969) 27-45.

00743 GAJENDRAGADKAR, S.N. Caste system in the Mahābhārata. In JUB ns 30 (1961) 23-38.

00744 JHA, V.N. Varṇasaṃkara in the Dharma Sūtras: theory and practice. In JESHO 23,3 (1970) 273-288.

00745 MEES, G.H. Dharma and society: a comparative study of the theory and the ideal of varṇa ('natural class') and the phenomena of caste and class. Delhi: Seema, 1980. 206p. [Rpt. 1935 ed.]

00746 PRASAD, N. The myth of the caste system. Patna: Samjna Prakashan, 1957. 319p.

00747 ROCHER, L. Caste & occupation in classical India: the normative texts. In CIS ns 9,1 (1975) 139-51.

00748 SHARMA, K.N. On the word 'varṇa'. In CIS ns 9,2 (1975) 293-297.

00749 SRINIVAS, M.N. Varṇa and caste. In his Caste in modern India and other essays. NY: Asia, 1962, 63-69.

00750 TAGORE, S.M. The caste system of the Hindus. Varanasi: IndBH, 1963. 33p.

00751 TAMBIAH, S.J. From varṇa to caste through mixed unions. In J. Goody, ed. The character of kinship. Cambridge: CamUP, 1973, 191-230.

6. Caste among Muslims and Other Non-Hindus

00752 AHMAD, IMTIAZ. Ashraf-ajlaf dichotomy in Muslim social structure in India. In IESHR 3,3 (1966) 268-278.

00753 AHMAD, IMTIAZ, ed. Caste and social stratification among Muslims in India. 2nd ed. rev. and enl. ND: Manohar, 1978. 314p. [1st ed. 1973]

00754 HARJINDER SINGH, ed. Caste among non-Hindus in India. ND: National, 1977. 172p.

00755 KHAN, Z.R. Caste and Muslim peasantries of North India and East and West Pakistan. In CRSA 5 (1968) 192-203. [also in MI, 48 (1968) 133-48]

00756 NEWMAN, R.S. Caste and the Indian Jews. In EA 28,3 (1975) 175-214.

7. Early Modern Views of Caste by Indians and Europeans (to c. 1945)

00757 BHATTACHARYA, J.N. Hindu castes and sects; an exposition of the origin of the Hindu caste system and the bearing of the sects towards each other and towards other religious systems. Calcutta: Editions Indian, 1968. 496p. [1st ed. 1896]

00758 BOUGLÉ, C.C.A. Essays on the caste system. Trans. by D.F. Pocock. Cambridge: CamUP, 1971. 228p. [1st French ed. 1908]

00759 DUMONT, L. & D.F. POCOCK. A.M. Hocart on caste - religion and power. In CIS 2 (1958) 45-63.

00760 DUTT, N.K. Origin and growth of caste in India. 2nd ed. Calcutta: KLM. v. 1, 1931, 2nd ed. 1968, 278p.; v. 2, 1965, 169p.

00761 GHURYE, G.S. Caste and race in India. 5th ed. Bombay: Popular, 1969. 504p. [1st ed. 1932; titles vary]

00762 HOCART, A.M. Caste: a comparative study. NY: Russell & Russell, 1968. 157p. [Rpt. of 1st ed. 1950]

00763 HUTTON, J.H. Caste in India, its nature, function and origins. 4th ed. Bombay: OUP, 1963. 324p.

00764 JACKSON, A.M.T. Note on the history of the caste system. In JASBengal 3 (1907) 509-15.

00765 O'MALLEY, L.S.S. Indian caste customs. Cambridge: CamUP, 1932. 190p.

00766 ROBERTS, J., ed. Caste, in its religious and civil character, opposed to Christianity. London: Longman, Brown, Green & Longmans, 1847. 148p.

00767 PILLAI, G.K. Origin and development of caste. Allahabad: Kitab Mahal, 1959. 271p. (His India without misrepresentation, 3)

00768 SENART, E.C.M. Caste in India, the facts and the system. London: Methuen, 1930. 220p.

00769 WILSON, J. Indian caste. ND: Deep, 1976. 2 v., 450, 228p. [Rpt. 1877 ed.]

8. Conceptual and Theoretical Analyses of Caste

00770 ATAL, Y. A conceptual framework for the analysis of caste. In SB 16,2 (1967) 20-38.

00771 BAILEY, F.G. Closed social stratification in India. In European J. of Sociology 4 (1963) 107-124.

00772 BÉTEILLE, A. Ideas and interests: some conceptual problems in the study of social stratification in rural India. In Social Sciences J. 21,2 (1969) 219-234.

00773 CHAUHAN, B.R. The nature of caste and sub-caste in India. In SB 15,1 (1966) 40-51.

00774 D'SOUZA, V.S. Caste and endogamy: a reappraisal of the concept of caste. In JAnthSB n.s. 11,1 (1959) 11-42.

00775 ______. Caste structure in India in the light of set theory. In CA 13,1 (1972) 5-22.

00776 GARDNER, P.M. Toward a componential model of Indian caste. In JSR 11,1 (1968) 37-48.

00777 HARPER, E.B. A comparative analysis of caste: the United States and India. In B.S. Cohn and M.B. Singer, eds. Structure and change in Indian society. Chicago: Aldine, 1968, 51-80.

00778 KHARE, R.S. The one and the many: varṇa and jāti as a symbolic classification. In S. Vatuk, ed. American studies in the anthropology of India. ND: Manohar, 1978, 35-64.

00779 KOLENDA, P. Caste in contemporary India: beyond organic solidarity. Menlo Park: Benjamin/Cummins, 1978. 181p.

00780 MARRIOTT, M. Hindu transactions: diversity without dualism. In B. Kapferer, ed. Transaction and meaning.... Philadelphia: ISHI, 1976, 109-142.

00781 MARRIOTT, M. & R.B. INDEN. Caste systems. In New Encyclopedia Britannica (1974) v. 14, 982-91.

00782 ______. Toward an ethnosociology of South Asian caste systems. In Kenneth David, ed. The new wind: changing identities in South Asia. The Hague: Mouton, 1977. 227-38. (WA)

9. Homo Hierarchicus and the Sociology of Louis Dumont

00783 DUMONT, L. Homo hierarchicus; an essay on the caste system. Translated by Mark Sainsbury. Chicago: UChiP, 1970. 386p. [1st French ed. 1967]

00784 BÉTEILLE, A. Homo hierarchicus, homo equalis. In MAS 13,4 (1979) 529-48.

00785 DOUGLAS, M. Louis Dumont's structural analysis. In her Implicit meaning; essays in anthropology. London: Routledge & Kegan Paul, 1975, 181-192.

00786 LEVY, P. Le problème des castes dans Homo Hierarchicus de Louis Dumont. In JESHO 13 (1970) 91-9.

00787 LYNCH, O.M. Method and theory in the sociology of Louis Dumont: a reply. In Kenneth David, ed. The new wind: changing identities in South Asia. The Hague: Mouton, 1977. 239-62. (WA)

00788 MADAN, J.N., et al. On the nature of caste in India: a review symposium on Louis Dumont's Homo Hierarchicus. In CIS ns 5 (1971) 1-81.

00789 MARRIOTT, M. Homo Hierarchicus [book rev.] In AA 71,6 (1969) 1166-1175.

00790 ______. Interpreting Indian society: a monistic alternative to Dumont's dualism. In JAS 36,1 (1976) 189-95.

00791 PARRY, J. Egalitarian values in an hierarchical society. In SAR 7,2 (1974) 95-122.

00792 Symposium: the contributions of Louis Dumont. In JAS 35,4 (1976) 579-650. [articles by P. Kolenda, J.D.M. Derrett, J.M. Masson & S. Barnett, L. Fruzzetti, & A. Ostor]

10. Caste Ranking and Its Determinants
a. general studies of caste ranking

00793 APPADURAI, A. Right and left hand castes in South India. In IESHR 11 (1974) 216-59.

00794 BERREMAN, G.D. The study of caste ranking in India. In SWJA 21 (1965) 115-29.

00795 COVE, J.J. A multi-dimensional model of caste ranking. In EA 26,2 (1973) 129-144.

00796 ______. A multi-dimensional model of caste ranking. In MI 53,1 (1973) 29-45.

00797 DAVID, K. And never the twain shall meet? mediating the structural approaches to caste ranking. In H.M. Buck & Glenn E. Yocum, eds., Structural approaches to South India studies. Chambersburg, Pa.: Wilson Books, 1974, 43-80.

00798 D'SOUZA, V.S. Caste status and its correlates. In JSR 7 (1964) 119-25.

00799 FREED, S.A. An objective method for determining the collective caste hierarchy of an Indian village. In AA 65 (1963) 879-891.

00800 GOUGH, E.K. Criteria of caste ranking in South India. In MI 39 (1959) 115-26.

00801 HALE, S.M. Stratification and local organization: the case of rural development in India. In CAS 10 (1977) 116-129.

00802 HIEBERT, P.G. Caste and personal rank in an Indian village: an extension in techniques. In AA 71 (1969) 434-53.

00803 MAHAR, P.M. Multiple scaling technique for caste ranking. In MI 39,2 (1959) 127-147.

00804 MARRIOTT, M. Caste ranking and community structure in five regions of India and Pakistan. Poona: DCPRI, 1965. 111p. (DCBC, 30)

00805 ______. Caste ranking and food transactions: a matrix analysis. In B.S. Cohn & M.B. Singer, eds. Structure and change in Indian society. Chicago: Aldine, 1968, 133-72.

00806 ______. Interactional and attributional theories of caste ranking. In MI 39 (1959) 92-107.

00807 MAYER, A.C. Some hierarchical aspects of caste. In SWJA 12 (1956) 117-44.

00808 ORANS, M. Caste ranking: sacred-secular, tails & dogs. In E. Gerow & M.D. Lang, eds. Studies in the language and culture of South Asia. Seattle: UWashP, 1974, 135-50.

00809 SHARDA, B.D. Status attainment in rural India. Delhi: Ajanta, 1977. 186p.

00810 SILVERBERG, J. Caste-ascribed 'status' vs. caste-irrelevant roles. In MI 39 (1959) 148-62.

00811 STEVENSON, H.N.C. Status evaluation in the Hindu caste system. In JRAI 84 (1954) 45-65.

b. the concept of dominant caste

00812 BHATT, A. Dominant caste and political process. In M.N. Srinivas & S. Seshaiah & V.S. Parthasarathy, eds. Dimensions of social change in India. Bombay: Allied, 1977, 297-319.

00813 DUBE, S.C. Caste dominance and factionalism. In CIS ns 2 (1968) 58-81.

00814 GARDNER, P.M. Dominance in India; a reappraisal. In CIS ns 2 (1968) 82-97.

00815 OOMMEN, T.K. The concept of dominant caste: some queries. In CIS ns 4 (1970) 73-83.

00816 SRINIVAS, M.N. The dominant caste in Rampura. In AA 61,1 (1959) 1-16.

00817 ______. The social system of a Mysore village. In M. Marriott, ed., Village India. Chicago: UChiP, 1955, 1-36.

c. ideas of purity and pollution

00818 DUMONT, L. & D. POCOCK, eds. Pure and impure. In CIS 3 (1959) 9-39.

00819 HARPER, E.B. Ritual pollution as an integrator of caste and religion. In his (ed.) Religion in South Asia. Seattle: UWashP, 1964, 150-97. [also in JAS 23 (1964) 150-97.]

00820 KHARE, R.S. Ritual purity and pollution in relation to domestic sanitation. In EA (1962) 125-34.

00821 ORENSTEIN, H. The structure of Hindu caste values: a preliminary study of hierarchy and ritual defilement. In Ethnology 4 (1965) 1-15.

00822 ______. Toward a grammar of defilement in Hindu sacred law. In B.S. Cohn & M.B. Singer, eds. Structure and change in Indian society. Chicago: Aldine, 1968, 115-32.

00823 SARAF, S. The Hindu ritual purity-pollution complex. In EA 22 (1969) 161-76.

00824 SINGH, T.R. Some aspects of ritual purity and pollution. In EA 19 (1966) 131-42.

d. social mobility of castes and individuals
i. general studies

00825 SILVERBERG, J., ed. Social mobility in the caste system in India: an interdisciplinary symposium. The Hague: Mouton, 1968. 155p. (Comp. Studies in Society and History, suppl. 3)

00826 SRINIVAS, M.N. Mobility in the caste system. In M.B. Singer & B.S. Cohn, eds. Structure and change in Indian society. Chicago: Aldine, 1968, 189-200.

ii. Sanskritization: upward mobility by adoption of classical behavior patterns; desanskritization

[Tribal acculturation through Sanskritization see III. M. 3. below]

00827 BARNABAS, A.P. Sanskritisation. In EW 13,15 (1961) 613-18.

00828 BOEL, J. Sanskritization and westernization - an analysis of social change in India. In SocAct 17 (1967) 411-19.

00829 DUBE, L. On the applicability of the concept of Sanskritization: comment on Hetukar Jha. In IESHR 15,4 (1978) 521-22. [Dr. Jha's reply, 522-24]

00830 GOULD, H.A. Sanskritisation and westernisation: further comments. In EW 14 (1962) 48-51.

00831 RASTOGI, P.N. Functional analysis of Sanskritization. In EA 16,1 (1963) 10-19.

00832 SRINIVAS, M.N. The cohesive role of Sanskritization. In P. Mason, ed. India & Ceylon: unity & diversity. London: OUP, 1976, 67-82.

00833 ______. A note on Sanskritization and westernization. In FEQ 15 (1956) 481-96.

00834 SRIVASTAVA, S.K. The process of desanskritization in village India. In L.K. Bala Ratnam, ed. Anthropology on the march. Madras: Book Centre, 1963, 263-267.

00835 STAAL, J.F. Sanskrit and Sanskritization. In JAS 22 (1963) 261-75.

00836 VIDYARTHI, L.P. The changing life of an Indian priestly caste: a case of desanskritisation. In ISB 2 (1965) 183-95.

11. Food Habits and the Role of the Betel-nut

00837 CHAKRAVARTY, I. Saga of Indian food; a historical & cultural survey. ND: Sterling, 1972. 183p.

00838 CHARPENTIER, C.-J. The use of Betel in Ceylon. In Anthropos 72, 1/2 (1977) 108-18.

00839 FERRO-LUZZI, G.E. Food avoidances of Indian tribes. In Anthropos 70, 3/4 (1975) 385-427.

00840 KHARE, R.S. Culture and reality: essays on the Hindu system of managing food. Simla: IIAS, 1976. 210p.

00841 ______. The Hindu hearth and home. Durham: CAP, 1976. 315p.

00842 MILLOT, J. Inde et bétel. In O&M 5 (1965) 73-122.

00843 PRAKASH, OM. Food and drinks in ancient India, from earliest times to c. 1200 A.D. Delhi: Munshiram, 1961. 341p.

00844 SHARMA, K.N. Hindu sects and food patterns in north India. In L.P. Vidyarthi, ed. Aspects of religion in Indian society. Meerut: Kedar Nath Ram Nath, 1961, 45-58. [also in JSR 4 (1961) 45-58]

00845 THIERRY, S. Le bétel, l'Inde et Asie du S.-E. Paris: Museum natl. d'histoire naturelle, 1969. 304p. (Catalogues du Musée de l'Homme)

F. Transmission of Culture: Traditional Systems of Communication and Education

1. Networks and Centers of Cultural Transmission

00846 COHN, B.S. & M. MARRIOTT. Networks and centers in the integration of Indian civilization. In JSR 1 (1958) 1-9.

00847 DAMLE, Y.B. Communication of modern ideas and knowledge in Indian villages. In Public Opinion Q. 20 (1956) 257-70.

00848 HOCKINGS, P. Communication networks. In M.N. Srinivas & S. Seshaiah & V.S. Parthasarathy, eds. Dimensions of social change in India. Bombay: Allied, 1977, 475-86.

00849 MARRIOTT, M. Changing channels of cultural transmission in Indian civilization. In L.P. Vidyarthi, ed. Aspects of religion in Indian society. Meerut: Kedar Nath Ram Nath, 1961, 13-25.

00850 SINGER, M.B. Text and context in the study of contemporary Hinduism. In his When a great tradition modernizes. NY: Praeger, 1972, 39-54. [1st pub ALB 25,1-4 (1961) 274-303]

00851 SRINIVAS, M.N. & A. BÉTEILLE. Networks in Indian social structure. In Man 64 (1964) 165-168.

2. Sanskrit Learning

00852 BROWN, W.N. Class and cultural traditions in India. In M.B. Singer, ed. Traditional India: structure and change. Philadelphia: American Folklore Soc., 1959, 241-45.

00853 GHURYE, K.G. Preservation of learned tradition in India. Bombay: Popular, 1950. 70p.

00854 INGALLS, D.H.H. The Brahman tradition. In M.B. Singer, ed. Traditional India: structure and change. Philadelphia: American Folklore Soc., 1959, 209-15.

00855 PANT, M.R. On Sanskrit education. Kathmandu: Pant, 1979. 202p.

00856 SARASWATI, B. Study of specialists in traditional learning: the Pandits of Kashi. In JIAS 10,2 (1975) 103-116.

00857 ______. Traditional modes of learning in Indian civilization. In S. Sinha, ed. Aspects of Indian culture and society.... Calcutta: IAS, 1972, 153-69.

00858 Seminar on Sanskrit learning through the ages. In MO 3 (1970) 1-300.

3. Histories of Education

00859 Education in Ceylon: from the sixth century B.C. to the present day; a centenary volume. Colombo: Min. of Educ. & Cultural Affairs, 1969. 3 v.

00860 GURUMURTHY, S. Education in South India: ancient and medieval periods. Madras: New Era, 1979. 183p.

00861 HAMIUDDIN KHAN, M. History of Muslim education. Karachi: Academy of Educ. Res., All Pakistan Educ. Conf., 1967-. v. 1, 712-1750 AD, 260p.; v. 2, 1751-1854 AD, 217p.

00862 JAYASEKERA, U.D. Early history of education in Ceylon (from earliest times up to Mahāsena). Colombo: Dept. of Cultural Affairs, 1969. 220p.

00863 KEAY, F.E. A history of education in India and Pakistan. 4th rev. ed., with add. chapter by D.D. Karve. London: OUP, 1964. 238p. (Teaching in India series, 26) [1st ed. 1918. Titles vary]

G. The Village, Home of 80% of South Asians

1. Bibliography

00864 ADAMS, J. & U.J.WOLTEMADE. Studies of Indian village economics. In IESHR 7,1 (1970) 109-137.

00865 CHAUHAN, B.R. Rural studies; a trend report. In A survey of research in sociology and social anthropology. Bombay: Popular, 1974, 82-114. [sponsored by ICSSR]

00866 Village studies; analysis and bibliography. v. 1: India 1950-1975. Brighton: Bowker, for Inst. of Dev. Studies, U. of Sussex, 1976. 329p.

2. Methodology and Overviews

00867 ADAMS, J. The analysis of rural Indian economy: economics and anthropology. In MI 52,1 (1972) 1-20.

00868 ADAMS, J. & U.J. WOLTEMADE. Village economy in traditional India: a simplified model. In HO 29,1 (1970) 49-56.

00869 ATAL, Y. Studies of the village in India. In his Social sciences: the Indian scene. ND: Abhinav, 1976, 142-65.

00870 BÉTEILLE, A. The study of agrarian systems: an anthropological approach. In MI 52,2 (1972) 150-73.

00871 BOSE, N.D., ed. Peasant life in India; a study in Indian unity & diversity. 2d ed. Calcutta: AnthSI, 1967. 60p. (Its Memoir, 8)

00872 DASGUPTA, B. A typology of village socio-economic systems from Indian village studies. In EPW 10,33/35 (1975) 1395-1414.

00873 DUMONT, L. & D.F. POCOCK. Village studies. In CIS 1 (1957) 23-41.

00874 GANGULI, B.N. The Indian peasant as an analytical category. In SB 23,2 (1974) 153-68.

00875 HOBSBAWM, E.J., et al., ed. Peasants in history; essays in honour of Daniel Thorner. Calcutta: OUP, 1980. 319p.

00876 KESSINGER, T.G. Anthropology and history: the study of social and economic change in rural India. In J. of Interdisc. Hist. 3,2 (1972) 313-322.

00877 MANDELBAUM, D.G. Village, region, civilization. In his Society in India. Berkeley: UCalP, 1972, v. 2, 325-424.

00878 MARRIOTT, M. Little communities in an indigenous civilization. In his (ed.) Village India. Chicago: UChiP, 1955, 171-222.

00879 NATH, V. The village and the community. In R. Turner, ed., India's urban future. Berkeley: UCalP, 1962, 141-56.

00880 PANDE, V.P. Village community in India: origin, development and problems. London: Asia, 1967, 258p.

00881 SRINIVAS, M.N. The Indian village: myth and reality. In J.G.M. Beattie & R.G. Lienhardt, eds., Studies in social anthropology.... London: OUP, 1975, 41-85.

00882 ______. Village studies and their significance. In A.R. Desai, ed., Rural sociology in India. Bombay: Popular, 1969, 785-95. [1st pub. in EA 8 (1955) 215-28]

00883 ______. Village studies, participant observation and social science research in India. In EPW 10,33-35 (1975) 1387-94.

3. Collections of Village Studies [for individual village studies see Chaps. Ten-Sixteen]

00884 FUKUTAKE, T. & T. OUCHI & C. NAKANE. The socio-economic structure of the Indian village: surveys of villages in Gujarat and West Bengal. Tr. from Japanese by J.R. McEwan. Tokyo: Inst. of Asian Econ. Affairs, 1964. 174p.

00885 MALONEY, C., ed. South Asia; seven community profiles. NY: Holt, Rinehart & Winston, 1974. 304p.

00886 SRINIVAS, M.N., ed. India's villages. 2nd rev. ed. NY: Asia, 1960. 222p. [1st ed. 1954]

00887 MARRIOTT, M., ed. Village India. Chicago: UChiP, 1955. 269p.

H. Urban Centers and Urbanization

00883 BARNOW, F. & M. SHODHAN. Notes on the urban history of India. Copenhagen: School of Architecture, 1977. 100p.

00884 BHATTACHARYA, B. Urban development in India, since pre-historic times. Delhi: Shree Pub. House, 1979. 360p.

00890 FOX, R.G., ed. Urban India: society, space, and image. Durham: DUPCSSA, 1970. 244p. (Its Monograph 10)

00891 GHURYE, G.S. Cities and civilization. Bombay: Popular, 1962. 306p.

00892 REDFIELD, R. & M.B. SINGER. The cultural role of cities. In EDCC 4 (1954) 53-73. [also in MI 36 (1956) 161-94]

J. The Traditional Economy

1. The Jajmānī System

00893 BEIDELMAN, T.O. A comparative analysis of the jajmani system. Locust Valley, NY: J.J. Augustin, 1959. 86p. (AAS monograph, 8)

00894 BENSON, J. South Indian Jajmani system. In Ethnology 15,3 (1976) 239-50.

00895 BRONGER, D. Jajmani system in southern India? In P. Meyer-Dohm, ed. Economic and social aspects of Indian development. Tübingen: Horst Erdmann, 1975, 207-45.

00896 HARPER, E.B. Two systems of economic exchange in village India. In AA 16,5, pt. 1 (1959) 760-78.

00897 KOLENDA, P.M. Toward a model of the Hindu jajmani system. In HO 22 (1963) 11-31.

00898 KUSHNER, G. A synthetic model of the Hindu jajmani system. In MI 47 (1967) 35-60.

00899 NEALE, W.C. Reciprocity and redistribution in the Indian village. In K. Polanyi, ed. Trade and markets in the early Empires. Glencoe: Free Press, 1957, 218-36.

00900 ORANS, M. Maximizing in jajmaniland: a model of caste relations. In AA 70 (1968) 875-97.

00901 ORENSTEIN, H. Exploitation or function in the interpretation of jajmani. In SWJA 18 (1962) 302-16.

00902 POCOCK, D.F. Notes on jajmāni relationships. In CIS 6 (1962) 78-95.

00903 REINICHE, M.-L. La notion de Jajmani. Qualification abusive ou principe d'intégration? In Puruṣārtha 3 (1977) 71-108.

00904 WISER, W.H. The Hindu jajmani system. Lucknow: Lucknow Pub. House, 1958. 160p. [1st pub. 1936]

2. Land Tenure, Revenue, and Taxation

00905 ABEYSINGHE, A. Ancient land tenure to modern land reform in Sri Lanka. Colombo: Centre for Society & Religion, 1978-. v. 1-.

00906 GHOSAL, U.N. Contributions to the history of the Hindu revenue system. 2d ed. Calcutta: Saraswat Library, 1972. 447p. [1st pub. 1929]

00907 MOOKERJI, RADHA KUMUD. Indian land system, ancient, mediaeval and modern (with special reference to Bengal). Alipore: W. Bengal Govt. Press, 1958. 84p. [1st pub. 1941]

00908 SHARMA, R.S., ed. Land revenue in India: historical studies. Delhi: Motilal, 1971. 129p.

00909 STEIN, B. Integration of the agrarian system of South India. In R. Frykenberg, ed. Land control & social structure in Indian history. Madison: UWiscP, 1969, 175-216.

3. Craftsmen, Guilds, and other Occupational Groups

00910 COOMARASWAMY, A.K. The Indian Craftsman. London: Probsthain, 1909. 130p.

00911 HOPKINS, E.W. Ancient and modern Hindu guilds. In his India, old and new. NY: Scribner's, 1902.

00912 KRAMRISCH, S. Traditions of the Indian craftsman. IN M.R. Singer, ed. Traditional India: structure and change. Philadelphia: American Folklore Soc., 1959, 224-30.

00913 LAMB, H.B. The Indian merchant. In Singer, M.B., ed. Traditional India: structure and change. Philadelphia: American Folklore Soc., 1959, 231-40.

00914 MASANI, R.P. Banking castes and guilds in India. In JAnthSB 14 (1931) 605-36.

00915 PAL, M.K. Crafts and craftsmen in traditional India. ND: Kanak, 1978. 348p.

K. Traditional Legal Systems: Hindu Dharmaśāstra and Muslim Sharīʿat

1. Bibliography

00916 ALEXANDROWICZ, C.H., ed. A bibliography of Indian law. London: OUP, 1958. 69p.

00917 ROCHER, L. Droit Hindou ancien. In J. Gilissen, ed. Bibliographical introduction to legal history and ethnology. Brussels: U. Libre de Bruxelles, l'Inst. de Sociologie, 1965. sect. E/6. 48p.

2. General Surveys and Essay Collections

00918 DERRETT, J.D.M. Essays in classical and modern Hindu law. Leiden: Brill, 1976-78. 4 v., 1764p.

00919 ______. Religion, law and the state in India. London: Faber & Faber, 1958. 572p.

00920 DEVADASON, E.D. Christian law in India: law applicable to Christians in India. Madras: Dev. Services (India), 1974. 414p.

00921 GALANTER, M. The uses of law in Indian studies. In Languages and areas; studies presented to George V. Bobrinskoy. Chicago: UChiP, 1967, 37-44.

00922 ISHWARAN, K. Customary law in village India. In D.C. Buxbaum, ed. Family law and customary law in Asia. The Hague: Nijhoff, 1968, 234-251.

00923 SETHNA, M.J. Parsi law and a uniform civil code in India. In Indian advocate, 10 (1970) 131-142.

00924 SMITH, G. & J.D.M. DERRETT. Hindu judicial administration in pre-British times and its lesson for today. In JAOS 95,3 (1975) 417-423.

3. Classical Hindu Law [see also Chap. Three, III. C]

00925 DATTA, B.N. Hindu law of inheritance (an anthropological study). Calcutta: Nababharat, 1957. 246p.

00926 DERRETT, J.D.M. Dharmaśāstra and juridical literature. Wiesbaden: Harrassowitz, 1973. 75p. (HIL, 4,2)

00927 ______. History of Indian law (dharmaśāstra). Leiden: Brill, 1973. 39p. (HO, 2,3,1)

00928 JHA, G.N. Hindu law in its sources. Allahabad: Indian Press, 1930. 577p.

00929 JOLLY, J. Hindu law and custom. Tr. by B. Ghosh. Varanasi: Bharatiya, 1975. 341p. [Rpt. 1928 ed.; 1st German ed. 1896]

00930 LINGAT, R. The classical law of India. Tr. by J.D.M. Derrett. Berkeley: UCalP, 1973. 303p. [1st French ed. 1967]

00931 ROCHER, L. "Lawyers" in Classical Hindu law. In Law and Society R. 3,2 (1969) 383-403.

00932 SARKAR, U.C. Epochs in Hindu legal history. Hoshiarpur: VVRI, 1958. 440p.

00933 SASTRY, K.R.R. Hindu jurisprudence: a study in historical jurisprudence. Calcutta: Eastern Law House, 1961. 294p.

4. Hindu Law in Modern India

00934 DERRETT, J.D.M. A strange rule of smṛti and a suggested solution. In JRAS (1958) pt. 1/2, 17-25.

00935 KANE, P.V. Hindu customs and modern law. Bombay: U. of Bombay, 1950. 122p.

00936 RAGHAVACHARIAR, N.R. Hindu law: principles and precedents. Madras: Madras Law Journal Office, 1970. 1234p.

00937 ROUTH, S.K. Elements of Hindu law. Comilla: N. Routh, 1974. 292p.

00938 SARKAR, U.C. Hindu law: its character and evolution. In JILI 6 (1965) 213-35.

00939 VARADACHARIAR, S. The Hindu judicial system. Lucknow: Lucknow U., 1946. 267p.

5. Islamic Law

00940 FYZEE, A.A.A. Compendium of Fatimid law. Simla: IIAS, 1969. 160p.

00941 ______. Outlines of Muhammadan Law. 2d ed. London: OUP, 1955. 443p. [1st pub. 1949]

00942 HASSAN, S.R. The reconstruction of legal thought in Islam: a comparative study of the Islamic and the Western systems of law in the latter's terminology, with particular reference to the Islamic laws suspended by the British rule in the sub-continent. Lahore: Law Pub. Co., 1974. 220p.

00943 MULLA, D.F. Principles of Mahomedan law. 16th ed. by M. Hidayatullah. Bombay: N.M. Tripathi, 1968. 62 + 392p.

00944 MUSLEHUDDIN, M. Philosophy of Islam law and the orientalists: a comparative study of Islamic legal system. Lahore: Islamic Pub., 1977. 302p.

00945 SAKSENA, K.P. Muslim law as administrated in India and Pakistan. 4th ed. Lucknow: Eastern Book Co., 1963. 1232p.

00946 VERMA, B.R. B.R. Verma's Mohammedan law in India and Pakistan. 5th ed., rev. by B. Malik, R.B. Sethi. Allahabad: Delhi Law House, 1978. 886p.

K. Women: Status and Role

1. Bibliography

00947 AGNEW, V. A review of the literature on women. In JIH 55, 1/2 (1977) 307-24.

00948 DASGUPTA, K. Women on the Indian scene; an annotated bibliography. ND: Abhinav, 1976. 391p.

00949 RESEARCH UNIT ON WOMEN'S STUDIES, S.N.D.T. WOMEN'S U., BOMBAY. A select bibliography on women in India. Bombay: Allied, 1976. 131p.

00950 SAKALA, C. Women of South Asia; a guide to resources. Millwood, NY: Kraus Intl., 1980. 517p.

2. General Studies

00951 ALTEKAR, A.S. The position of women in Hindu civilization: from prehistoric times to the present day. 2nd ed. Delhi: Motilal, 1959. 380p. [1st ed. 1938]

00952 BAIG, T.A. India's woman power. ND: S. Chand, 1976. 301p.

00953 Indian Womanhood thru the Ages. In Vivekananda Kendra Patrika 4,2 (1975) 380p.

00954 MAUDOODI, SYED ABŪL ᶜALĀ. Purdah & the status of women in Islam. Tr. & ed. by al-Ash ari. Lahore: Islamic Pub., 1972. 231p.

00955 MAYO, K. Slaves of the gods. London: J. Cape, 1933. 256p. [1st pub. 1929]

00956 MUKHERJI, P. Hindu women: normative models. Calcutta: Orient Longmans, c1978. 118p.

00957 ROY, S. Status of Muslim women in north India. Delhi: B.R., 1979. 241p.

00958 SEN GUPTA, S., ed. Women in Indian folklore; a short survey of their social status and position: linguistic and religious study. Calcutta: Indian Pub., 1969. 62 + 327p. (Indian Pub. folklore series, 15)

00959 UPADHYAYA, H.S. On the position of women in Indian folk culture. In AFS 27,6 (1968) 81-106.

L. Kinship, Family and the Person

1. Bibliography and Methodology

00960 DUBE, L. Sociology of kinship; a trend report. In A survey of sociology and social anthropology. Bombay: Popular, 1974, v. 2, 233-366. [sponsored by ICSSR]

00961 ______. Sociology of kinship: an analytical survey of literature. Bombay: Popular, 1974. 154p. [Rpt. of above]

00962 MADAN, T.N. The joint family: a terminological clarification. In Intl. J. of Comp. Sociology, 3 (1962) 1-16.

00963 RAMU, G.N. Researches on the family in India. In MI 52,3 (1972) 212-227.

00964 SHAH, A.M. Annotated bibliography. In his The household dimension of the family in India. Berkeley: UCalP 1974, 175-269.

00965 ______. Basic terms and concepts in the study of the family in India. In IESHR 1 (1964) 1-36.

2. Kinship and the Family
a. general studies

00967 DAVIS, M. Rank and rivalry in the Bengali Hindu family. In EA 30,1 (1977) 67-87.

00965 AHMAD, IMTIAZ, ed. Family, kinship and marriage among Muslims in India. ND: Manohar, 1976. 367p.

00968 DUMONT, L. & D.F. POCOCK. Kinship. In CIS 1 (1957) 43-64. [review of I. Karve, Kinship organization in India]

00969 FERREIRA, J.V. Totemism in India. Bombay: OUP, 1965. 304p.

00970 GHURYE, G.S. Family and kin in Indo-European culture. 2d ed. Bombay: Popular Book Depot, 1962. 333p.

00971 GORE, M.S. The traditional Indian family. In M.F. Nimkoff, ed. Comparative family systems. Boston: Houghton Mifflin, 1965, 209-31.

00972 JACOBSON, D. Flexibility in Indian kinship and residence. In K. David, ed. The new wind: changing identities in South Asia. The Hague: Mouton, 1977. 263-86. (WA)

00973 KAPADIA, K.M. Hindu kinship: an important chapter in Hindu social history. Bombay: Popular Book Depot, 1947. 320p.

00974 ______. Marriage and family in India. 3rd ed. Bombay, OUP, 1966. 395p.

00975 KARVE, I. Kinship organization in India. 3rd ed. NY: Asia, 1968. 431p. [1st ed., 1953]

00976 KURIAN, G., ed. The family in India; a regional view. The Hague: Mouton, 1974. 391p.

00977 MANDELBAUM, D.G. Family and kinship relations. In his Society in India. Berkeley: UCalP, 1972, v. 1, 31-158.

00979 TRAUTMANN, T.R., ed. Kinship and history in South Asia: four lectures. Ann Arbor: UMCSSAS, 1974. 157p.

b. kinship terminology

00979 AZIZ AHMAD. Muslim kinship terminology in Urdu. In JESHO 20,3 (1977) 344-50.

00980 BHARATI, A. Kinship term avoidance and substitution in North Indian middle class milieux. In Sociologus ns 13 (1963) 112-120.

00981 CHATTOPADHYAY, K.P. On terms of kinship and social relationship. In T.N. Madan & Gopala Saran, eds. Indian anthropology; essays in memory of D.N. Majumdar. Bombay: Asia, 1962, 339-51.

00982 DUMONT, L. The Dravidian kinship terminology as an expression of marriage. In Man 54 (1953) 34-39.

00983 ______. Le vocabulaire de parenté dans l'Inde du Nord. In L'Homme 2,2 (1962) 5-48.

00984 FRUZZETTI, L. & A. OSTOR. Is there a structure to North Indian kinship terminology? In CIS ns 10,1 (1976) 63-95.

00985 STIRRAT, R.L. Dravidian and non-Dravidian kinship terminologies in Sri Lanka. In CIS 11,2 (1977) 271-93.

00986 TURNER, J. A formal semantic analysis of a Hindi kinship terminology. In CIS ns 9,2 (1975) 263-292.

00987 VATUK, S. A structural analysis of the Hindi kinship terminology. In CIS ns 3 (1969) 94-115.

00988 VREEDE-DE STUERS, C. Terminologie de parenté chez les Musulmans Ashrāf de l'Inde du Nord. In Bijdragen tot de Taal-, Land- en Volkenkunde (The Hague) 119 (1963) 254-266.

00989 YALMAN, N. The semantics of kinship in South India and Ceylon. In M.B. Emeneau & C.A. Ferguson, ed. Linguistics in South Asia. The Hague: Mouton, 1969, 607-26. (CTL, 5)

c. family types

00990 DERRETT, J.D.C. The history of the juridical framework of the joint Hindu family. In CIS 6 (1962) 17-47.

00991 EHRENFELS, U.R. VON. Matrilineal joint family patterns in India. In G. Kurian, ed. The family in India.... The Hague: Mouton, 1974, 91-106.

00992 ______. Mother-right in India. London: OUP, 1941. 229p.

00993 ISHWARAN, K. The interdependence of elementary and extended family. In G. Kurian, ed. The family in India.... The Hague: Mouton, 1974. 163-77. [1st pub. in CAS 1 (1971) 16-27]

00994 KOLENDA, P.M. Region, caste and family structure: a comparative study of the Indian "joint" family. In M.B. Singer & B.S. Cohn, eds. Structure and change in Indian society. Chicago: Aldine, 1968, 339-396.

00995 ______. Regional differences in Indian family structure. In R.E. Crane, ed. Regions and regionalism in South Asian studies. Durham: DUPCSSA, 1967, 147-226.

00996 KUMAR, J. Family structure in the Hindu society of rural India. In G. Kurian, ed. The family in India.... The Hague: Mouton, 1974, 43-74.

00997 MUKHERJEE, B. The structural features of the tribal families in India. In G. Kurian, ed. The family in India: a regional view. The Hague: Mouton, 1974, 75-90.

00998 NAIK, R.D. Some structural aspects of urban family. Bombay: Somaiya, 1979. 120p. (TISS series, 45)

00999 SONTHEIMER, G.-D. The joint Hindu family; its evolution as a legal institution. ND: Munshiram, 1977. 250p.

d. intra-family roles and relationships

01000 GORE, M.S. The husband-wife and mother-son relationships. In SBII (1962) 91-102.

01001 WIESINGER, R. The parent-daughter relationship among the Hindus. In Sociologus 15 (1965) 143-161.

e. gotra and pravara: exogamous lineage groups within endogamous castes

01002 CHEKKI, D.A. Inter-kin marriage: a theoretical framework. In MI 48 (1968) 337-44.

01003 GHURYE, G.S. Two Brahmanical institutions: gotra and charana. Bombay: Popular, 1972. 324p.

01004 KARANDIKAR, S.V. Hindu exogamy. Bombay: Taraporevala, 1929. 308p.

01005 MADAN, T.N. Is the Brahmanic gotra a grouping of kin? In SWJA 18 (1962) 59-77.

3. Marriage

01006 DUMONT, L. Dravidien et Kariera: l'alliance de mariage dans l'Inde du Sud, et en Australie. The Hague: Mouton, 1975. 148p.

01007 ______. Hierarchy and marriage alliance in South Indian kinship. London: RAI, 1957. 45p.

01008 ______. Marriage in India: the present state of the question. In CIS 5 (1961) 75-95; 7 (1964) 77-98; 9 (1966) 90-114.

01009 HARA, M. A note on the rākṣasa form of marriage. In JAOS 94,3 (1974) 296-306.

01010 KEMPER, S.E.G. Sinhalese astrology, South Asian caste systems, and the notion of individuality. In JAS 38,3 (1979) 477-497.

01011 PETROS, Prince of Greece. A study of polyandry. The Hague: Mouton, 1963. 601p.

01012 RIVERS, W.H.R. The marriage of cousins in India. In JRAS (1907) 611-40.

01013 ______. The origin of hypergamy. In JBORS 7 (1921) 9-24.

01014 SUR, A.K. Sex and marriage in India; an ethnohistorical survey. Bombay: Allied, 1973. 194p.

01015 THANKAPPAN NAIR, P. Marriage and dowry in India. Calcutta: Minerva, 1978. 205p.

4. Women: Dowry, Property Rights, Status of Widows

01016 AGARWALA, S.N. Widow remarriages in some rural areas of northern India. In Demography 4,1 (1967) 126-34.

01017 CHAUDHURI, R.L. Hindu woman's right to property, past and present. Calcutta: KLM, 1961. 156p.

01018 Dowry custom. In Vivekananda Kendra Patrika 2,2 (1973) 256p.

01019 HINCHCLIFFE, D. Widows dower-debt in India. In Islam & the modern age 4 (Aug. 1973) 5-22.

01020 HOOJA, S.L. Dowry system in India; a case study. Delhi: Asia Press, 1969. 236p.

01021 SIVARAMAYYA, BHAMIDIPATI. Women's rights of inheritance in India; a comparative study of equality & protection. Madras: Madras Law Journal Office, 1974. 215p.

01022 TAMBIAH, S.J. Dowry and bridewealth and the property rights of women in South Asia. In J. Goody & S.J. Tambiah. Bridewealth & dowry. Cambridge: CamUP, 1973, 59-169.

5. Life and Death Saṃskāras
a. general

01023 DAYANANDA SARASVATI, Swami. The Sanskār vidhi = the procedure of sacraments of Swami Dayanand Saraswati. Tr. by V.N. Shastri. ND: Sarvadeshik Arya Pratinidhi Sabha, 1976. 369p.

01024 PANDEY, R.B. The Hindu sacraments (saṃskāras). In Cultural Heritage of India. Calcutta: RMIC, 1962, v. 2, 390-413.

01025 ______. Hindu saṃskāras; socio-religious study of the Hindu sacraments. 2d rev. ed. Delhi: Motilal, 1969. 327p. [1st pub. 1949]

01026 SARASWATI, B. Brahmanic ritual traditions in the crucible of time. Simla: IIAS, 1977. 299p.

01027 STEVENSON, M. The rites of the twice born. ND: OBRC, 1971. 474p. [1st pub. 1920]

b. upanayana and dīkṣā: rites of initiation

01023 AGRAWAL, B.C. Dīkshā ceremony in Jainism: an analysis of its socio-political ramifications. In EA 25,1 (1972) 13-20.

01029 ALTEKAR, A.S. Yajnopavīta or "the sacred thread". In JBDRS 20 (1934) 135-139.

01030 BASU, A. Dīkṣā. In C.J. Bleeker, ed. Initiation. Leiden: Brill, 1965. 81-86.

01031 BHATTACHARYYA, N.N. Indian puberty rites. In ISPP 9 (1968) 271-302, 303-42.

01032 DANGE, S.A. Death and rebirth in initiation ceremonies. In IA, 3rd ser., 1 (1964) 104-09.

01033 GONDA, J. Dīkṣā. In his Change and continuity in Indian religion. The Hague: Mouton, 1965, 315-462.

00134 GOUGH, E.K. Female initiation rites on the Malabar coast. In JRAI 85 (1955) 45-80.

01035 GUPTE, B.A. Janeu, or the Hindu thread ceremony. In MI 5 (1925) 237-244.

01036 JOSHI, R.V. Notes on Guru, Dīkṣā, and Mantra. In Ethnos 37 (1972) 103-112.

01037 OLSON, C. The existential, social and cosmic significance of the Upanayana rite. In Numen 24,2 (1977) 152-60.

01038 PRAMANIK, P. A sacred thread giving ceremony at a Bengalee Hindu Brahmin family of Dhanbad, Bihar. In Folklore (c) 19 (1978) 34-44.

01039 TOOMEY, P.M. The upanayana and samavartana rites: a paradox of 'two dharmas'. In IAnth 6,1 (1976) 40-45.

c. the Hindu sacrament of marriage

01040 APTE, U.M. The sacrament of marriage in Hindu society, from Vedic period to dharmaśāstras. Delhi: Ajanta, 1978. 254p.

01041 CHATTERJEE, K.N. Hindu marriage - past and present. Varanasi: Tara, 1972. 397p.

01042 CHATTERJI, C.K. Studies in the rites and rituals of Hindu marriage in ancient India. Calcutta: SPB, 1978. 372p.

d. death and ancestor rites

01043 DUMONT, L. La dettes vis-à-vis des ancêtres et la catégorie de sapiṇḍa. In Puruṣārtha 4 (1980) 15-38.

01044 HABENSTEIN, R.W. & W.M. LAMEIS. Hindu India. In Funeral customs the world over. Milwaukee: Bulfin Press, 1960, 114-27.

01045 KAUSHIK, M. The symbolic representation of death. In CIS ns 10 (1976) 265-92.

01046 KNIPE, D.M. Sapiṇḍīkaraṇa: the Hindu rite of entry into heaven. In F.E. Reynolds & E.H. Waugh, eds. Religious encounters with death.... University Park, PA: Penn State U. Press, 1977.

01047 ORENSTEIN, H. Death and kinship in Hinduism: structural and functional interpretations. In AA 72,6 (1970) 1357-77.

01048 PEREIRA, T. Symbolism and its role in the death rites of Hinduism. In Laurentianum 15 (1979) 434-54.

01049 PUTHNANGADY, PAUL. Le rite funéraire en Inde. In Maison-Dieu 101 (1970) 51-56.

01050 SHASTRI, D.R. Origin and development of the rituals of ancestor worship in India. Calcutta: Bookland, 1963. 399p.

01051 SOUNDARA RAJAN, K.V. Rites (Saṃskāras) connected with death (Preta) and after (Pitṛ). In BITCM Pt. 2 (1966) 259-75.

6. The Person and the Group

01052 BHATTACHARYYA, K. The status of the individual in Indian philosophy. In PEW 14,2 (1964) 131-44.

01053 DE SMET, R. Towards an Indian view of the person. In M. Chatterjee, ed. Contemporary Indian philosophy. London: Allen & Unwin, 1974, 51-75.

01054 DUMONT, L. The functional equivalents of the individual in caste society. In CIS 8 (1965) 85-99.

01055 FRUZZETT, L. & A. OSTOR & S. BARNETT. The cultural construction of the person in Bengal and Tamil Nadu. In CIS ns 10,1 (1976) 157-82.

01056 JOSHI, K.S. Yoga and personality. Allahabad: Udayana, 1967. 163p.

01057 KAKAR, S., ed. Identity and adulthood. Delhi: OUP, 1979. 134p.

01058 MALLIK, B.K. The individual and the group, an Indian study in conflict. London: Allen & Unwin, 1939. 181p.

01059 NARAIN, D. Hindu character, a few glimpses. Bombay: U. of Bombay, 1957. 238p.

01060 SPRATT, P. Hindu culture and personality: a psycho-analytic study. Bombay: Manaktalas, 1966. 400p.

01061 THAKUR, U. The history of suicide in India, an introduction. Delhi: Munshiram, 1963. 229p.

7. Personal Names and Naming Patterns

01062 DIL, A. A comparative study of the personal names and nicknames of the Bengali-speaking Hindus and Muslims. In W.M. Gunderson, ed. Studies on Bengal. East Lansing: MSUASC, 1975, 51-70. (Its occ. papers, 26)

01063 EMENEAU, M.B. Towards an onomastics of South Asia. In JAOS 98,2 (1978) 113-30.

01064 FULLER, M. "The naming of names" in Indian folk belief. In AFS 24,1 (1965) 63-79.

01065 JUNGHARE, I.Y. Socio-psychological aspects and linguistic analysis of Marathi names. In Names 23 (1975) 31-43.

01066 KANE, P.V. Naming a child or a person. In IHQ 14,2 (1938) 224-44.

01067 KARVE, I. Personal names in India. In G.S. Ghurye et al., eds. Papers in sociology; silver jubilee memorial volume. Bombay: Bombay U., 1947, 37-48.

01068 MASANI, R.P. Folk culture reflected in names. Bombay: Popular, 1966. 120p.

01069 SEN, P.K. Proper names: some theories and considerations. In JIAP 16,1 (1977) 1-20.

01070 SHANTA. Handbook of Hindu names. Calcutta: ARNICA International, 1969. 201p.

01071 SJOBERG, A.F. Telugu personal names: a structural analysis. In Bh. Krishnamurti, ed. Studies in Indian linguistics. Poona & Annamalainagar: Centre of Advanced Studies in Linguistics, 1968, 313-21.

01072 TEMPLE, R.C. Dissertation on the proper names of Panjābīs, with special reference to the proper names of villagers in the Eastern Panjab. Bombay: Education Society's Press, 1883. 115p.

M. The Adivasis: Tribal Peoples

1. Bibliographies and Reference

01073 BOSE, S. Scheduled tribes: a select bibliography. Surat: Centre for Social Studies, 1979. 121p.

01074 PATHY, J., et al. Tribal studies in India: an appraisal. In EA 29,4 (1976) 399-417.

01075 VIDYARTHI, L.P., ed. Rise of anthropology in India: a social science orientation. v. 1 The tribal dimensions. Delhi: Concept, 1978. 384p. [bibl. essays]

01076 ______. Tribal ethnography in India: a trend report. In A survey of research in sociology and social anthropology. Bombay: Popular, 1972, v. 3, 31-133. [sponsored by ICSSR]

2. General Studies of Adivasis [For studies of specific tribes see regional chapters Ten through Sixteen]

01077 BHOWMIK, K.L. Tribal India; a profile in Indian ethnology. Calcutta: World Press, 1971. 224p.

01078 BOSE, N.K. Tribal life in India. ND: NBT, 1971. 84p.

01079 CHATTOPADHYAYA, K. Tribalism in India. ND: Vikas, 1978. 302p.

01080 DUBE, S.C., ed. Tribal heritage of India. ND: Vikas, for IIAS, 1977. v. 1, 212p. [to be 4 v.]

01081 GHURYE, G.S. The scheduled tribes of India. New Brunswick, NJ: Transaction Books, 1980. 404p. [1st pub. 1943]

01082 FOX, R.G. Professional primitives: hunters and gatherers of nuclear South Asia. In MI 49 (1969) 139-60.

01083 FUCHS, S. The aboriginal tribes of India. Delhi: Macmillan, 1974. 307p.

01084 Hill India. In Vivekananda Kendra Patrika 1,2 (1972) 364p.

01085 MUKHOPADHYAY, S. The Austrics of India: their religion and tradition. Calcutta: K.P. Bagchi, 1975. 148p.

01086 RAGHAVIAH, V. Nomads. ND: Bharateeya Adimajati Sevak Sangh, 1968. 413p.

01087 ______, ed. Tribes of India. ND: Bharatiya Adimjati Sevak Sangh, 1969-70. 2 v.

01088 SARKAR, S.S. The aboriginal races of India. Calcutta: Bookland, 1954. 151p.

01089 The tribal people of India. Rev. ed. ND: PDMIB, 1973. 192p.

01090 VIDYARTHI, L.P. & B.K. RAI. The tribal culture of India. Delhi: Concept, 1977. 487p.

3. From Tribe to Caste: Acculturation through Sanskritization, and Other Processes.

01091 BAILEY, F.G. "Tribe" and "caste" in India. In CIS 5 (1961) 7-19.

01092 BOSE, N.K. The Hindu method of tribal absorption. In his Cultural anthropology and other essays. Calcutta: Indian Associated Pub. Co., 1953, 45-64.

01093 DUMONT, L. Tribe and caste in India. In CIS 6 (1962) 120-22.

01094 RATHA, S.N. Caste as a form of acculturation. Gauhati: Gauhati U., 1977. 119p.

01095 SINHA, S. Tribal cultures in peninsular India as a dimension of little tradition in the study of Indian civilization: a preliminary statement. In M.B. Singer, ed. Traditional India: structure and change. Philadelphia: American Folklore Soc., 1959, 504-18. [also in MI 37,2 (1957) 93-118]

01096 WATSON, J.B. Caste as a form of acculturation. In SWJA 19 (1963) 356-79.

4. Tribal Religion, including Totemism and Shamanism

01097 HERMANNS, M. Die Religiös-magische Weltanschauung der Primitivstamme Indiens. Wiesbaden: Steiner, 1964-73. 3 v.

01098 DAS, T.C. Religious beliefs of the Indian tribes. In Cultural Heritage of India. Calcutta: RMIC, 1956, v. 4, 421-32.

01099 VIDYARTHI, L.P. & B.K. RAI. Religious life of the tribals. In their The tribal culture of India. Delhi: Concept, 1977, 236-71.

01100 PRESLER, H.H. Primitive religions in India. Madras: CLS, 1971. 349p. (ITL, 6)

IV. RELIGIO-PHILOSOPHICAL TRADITIONS OF SOUTH ASIA - THE INDIGENOUS INDIC RELIGIONS: HINDUISM, BUDDHISM, JAINISM

A. Philosophy and Religious Thought

1. Reference
a. bibliography

01101 ADAMS, C.J., ed. A reader's guide to the great religions. 2nd ed. NY: Free Press, 1977. 521p. [1st ed. 1965]

01102 A bibliography of Indian philosophy. Madras: Dr. C.P. Ramaswami Aiyar Res. Endowment Cttee.,1963-68. 2v.

01103 International bibliography of the history of religions. Leiden: Brill, 1952-. [annual]

01104 NAKAMURA, H. Religions and philosophies of India: a survey with bibliographical notes. Tokyo: Hokuseido Press, 1973-. 3 v.

01105 POTTER, K.H. Bibliography of Indian philosophies. Delhi: Motilal, 1970. 811p. (Encyclopedia of Indian philosophies, 1) [suppl. in JIP 2 (1972-74) 65-112, 175-209, 397-413; 4 (1976-77) 295-99; 6 (1978) 87-127, 195-231, 299-324.]

01106 Religion: a select bibliography. Amritsar: Guru Nanak U. Library, 1972. 256p. [English, Hindi, Panjabi, Urdu]

b. other reference works

01107 AL-FARUQI, I.R., ed. & D.E. SOPHER, map ed. Historical atlas of the religions of the world. NY: Macmillan, 1974. 346p. [Chapters on Hinduism, Jainism, Sikhism, Zoroastrianism, Buddhism.]

01108 Encyclopedia of religion and ethics. Ed. by James Hastings, et al. NY: Scribner's, 1955. 13 v. [Rpt. 1908-26 ed.]

01109 MORRISON, D. A glossary of Sanskrit from the spiritual tradition of India. Petaluma, CA: Nilgiri Press, 1977. 38p.

01110 TYBERG, J.M. The language of the gods: Sanskrit keys to India's wisdom. 2nd ed. Los Angeles: East-West Cultural Centre, 1976. 297p. [1st ed. 1943 as Sanskrit keys to the wisdom religion....]

01111 WALKER, G.B. The Hindu world: an encyclopedic survey of Hinduism. NY: Praeger, 1968. 2 v., 608, 695p.

01112 ZAEHNER, R.C., ed. The concise encyclopedia of living faiths. Boston: Beacon Press, 1967. 431p. [1st pub. 1959]

c. history and methodology of the study of Indic thought and religion

01113 FANGER, A.C. Anthropological approaches to the study of religion. In EA 20 (1967) 197-214.

01114 HALBFASS, W. The study of Indian philosophy in Germany and Austria: a survey of recent contributions, 1965-1972. In JOIB 25,3/4 (1976) 364-75.

01115 NOELLE, W. Helmuth von Glasenapp, interpreter of Indian thought. ND: Max Mueller Bhavan German Cultural Inst., 1964. 108p.

d. Hinduism - bibliography and reference

01116 DOWSON, J. A classical dictionary of Hindu mythology and religion. 11th ed. London: Routledge & Kegan Paul, 1968. 411p. (Trubner's Oriental series, no. 6) [1st ed. 1891]

01117 GARRETT, J. A classical dictionary of India; illustrative of the mythology, philosophy, literature, antiquities, arts, manners, customs &c. of the Hindus. Delhi: Oriental Pub., 1971. 793p. [1st pub. 1871]

01118 HEIN, N.J. Hinduism. In C.J. Adams, ed. A reader's guide to the great religions. 2nd ed. NY: Free Press, 1977, 106-55. [1st ed. 1966]

01119 HOLLAND, B. Popular Hinduism and Hindu mythology: an annotated bibliography. Westport, CT: Greenwood Press, 1979. 394p.

01120 MANI, V. Puranic Encyclopaedia; a comprehensive dictionary with special reference to the epic and puranic literature. 1st English ed. Delhi: Motilal, 1975. 922p. [1st Malayalam ed. 1964]

01121 STUTLEY, M. & J. STUTLEY. Harper's dictionary of Hinduism: its mythology, folklore, philosophy, literature and history. NY: Harper & Row, 1977. 372p.

01122 WOOD, E. Vedanta dictionary. NY: Philosophical Library, 1963. 225p.

e. Buddhism - bibliography and reference
i. bibliography

01123 BEAUTRIX, P. Bibliographie du Bouddhisme. Brussells: Inst. Belge des Hautes Études Bouddhiques, 1970-. v. 1 Editions de textes. 206p.

01124 BECHERT, H., ed. Systematische Übersicht über die buddhistische Sanskrit-Literatur = A systematic survey of Buddhist Sanskrit literature. Wiesbaden: Steiner, 1979-. v. 1, Vinaya-texte. 78p.

01125 GARD, R., ed. Buddhist text information. NY: Inst. for Adv. Study of World Religion. Nov., 1974-.

01126 HANAYAMA, S. Bibliography on Buddhism. Tokyo: Hokuseido Press, 1961. 869p.

01127 NAKAMURA, H. A survey of Conservative Buddhism in South Asia with bibliographical notes. In J. of Intercultural Studies 2 (2955) 85-122. ["Conservative" = Hinayana]

01128 ______. A survey of Mahayana Buddhism with bibliographical notes. In J. of Intercultural Studies 3 (1976) 60-145; 4 (1977) 77-135.

01129 MARCH, A.C. A Buddhist bibliography. London: Buddhist Lodge, 1935. 257p.

01130 PRZYLUSKI, J. & M. LALOU, eds. Bibliographie bouddhique. Paris: Libraire Orientaliste, P. Geunthner, 1930-67. v. 1-31.

01131 REGAMEY, C. Buddhistische Philosophie. Bern: A. Francke, 1950. 86p. (Bibl. Einführungen in das Studium der Philosophie 20/21)

01132 REYNOLDS, F.E. From philology to anthropology: a bibliographic essay on works related to early Theravada and Sinhalese Buddhism. In B.L. Smith, ed. The two wheels of dhamma.... Chambersburg, PA: AAR, 1972, 107-21. (Amer. Academy of Religion monograph series, 3)

01133 ______. Buddhism. In C.J. Adams, ed. A reader's guide to the great religions. 2nd ed. NY: Free Press, 1977, 156-222. [1st ed. 1966]

01134 SATYAPRAKASH, ed. Buddhism: a select bibliography. Gurgaon: IDS, 1976. 172p. (Subject bibliography series, 1)

ii. dictionaries and other reference works on Buddhism

01135 Hobogirin. Dictionnaire encyclopédique du Bouddhisme d'après les sources chinoises et japonaises. Tokyo: Maison française-japonaise. 1929-37 and 1967-. [5 fasc. to 1931]

01136 HUMPHREYS, C., ed. A popular dictionary of Buddhism. NY: Citadel Press, 1963. 223p.

01137 KERN, H. Manual of Indian Buddhism. Varanasi: Indological Book House, 1968. 149p. [Rpt. 1896 ed.]

01138 LING, T.O., ed. A dictionary of Buddhism. NY: Scribner's, 1972. 277p.

01139 MALALASEKERA, G.P., ed. Encyclopedia of Buddhism. Colombo: Govt. of Ceylon Press, 1961-.

01140 NYANATILOKA, Mahathera . Buddhist dictionary. Rev. ed. Colombo: Frewin, 1956. 198p.

iii. history of Buddhist studies

01141 CONZE, E. Recent progress in Buddhist studies. In his Thirty years of Buddhist studies. Columbia, SC: U. of S. Carolina Press, 1968, 1-32. [1st pub. in The Middle Way 34-35 (1959 & 1960) 6-14, 144-50; 93 ff.]

01142 DE JONG, J.W. Brief history of Buddhist studies in Europe and America. Varanasi: Bharat-Bharati, 1976. 94p. [1st pub. in Eastern Buddhist ns 7,1/2 (1974) 55-106; 49-82.]

01143 DELUBAC, H. La rencontre du bouddhisme et de l'occident. Paris: Aubier, 1952. 258p.

f. Jainism - bibliography and reference

01144 ALSDORF, L. Les Études jaina, état présent et tâches futures. Paris: Collège de France, 1975. 83p.

01145 CAILLAT, C. Notes de bibliographie jaina et moyen-indienne. In JA 260 (1972) 409-32.

01146 CHAKRAVARTI, A. Jaina literature in Tamil. Rev. ed. ND: Bharatiya Jnanapitha, 1974. 232p. (Its Murti-Devi Jaina granthamala: English ser., 3)

01147 FOLKERT, K.W. Jaina studies: Japan, Europe, India. In Sambodhi 5,2-3 (1976) 138-47.

01148 ______. The Jainas. In C.J. Adams, ed. A reader's guide to the great religions. 2nd ed. NY: Free Press, 1977, 231-246.

01149 GUÉRINOT, A.A. Essai de bibliographie Jaina. Paris: Leroux, 1906. 568p.

01150 JAIN, C.L. Jain bibliography. Calcutta: Satis Chandra Sed, 1945. 2 v.

01151 JAINI, P.S. The Jainas and the Western scholar. In Sambodhi 5,2-3 (1976) 121-31.

01152 KASLIWAL, K.C. Jaina grantha bhandārs in Rajasthan. Jaipur: Shri Digamber Jain Atishaya Kshetra Shri Mahavirji, 1967. 370p. (Shri Mahavir granthmala grantha, 13)

01153 NAKAMURA, H. Bibliographical survey of Jainism. In J. of Intercultural Studies 1 (1974) 51-75.

2. Surveys of Indic Thought and Religion - General

a. overall thematic interpretations

01154 BANERJI, N.V. The spirit of Indian philosophy. ND: Arnold-Heinemann, 1974. 380p.

01155 DAMODARAN, K. Indian thought; a critical survey. Bombay: Asia, 1967. 520p.

01156 GONDA, J. Change and continuity in Indian religion. The Hague: Mouton, 1965. 484p. (DRT, 9)

01157 RADHAKRISHNAN, S. Eastern religions and Western thought. 2nd ed. London: OUP, 1940. 396p.

01158 SCHWEITZER, A. Indian thought and its development. Tr. by Mrs. C.E.B. Russell. NY: Henry Holt, 1936. 272p.

b. introductory surveys

01159 HERMAN, A.L. An introduction to Indian thought. Englewood Cliffs, NJ: Prentice-Hall, 1976. 301p.

01160 HOPKINS, E.W. The religions of India. 2nd ed. ND: Munshiram, 1970. 612p. [1st pub. 1885]

01161 MACNICOL, N. Indian theism, from the Vedic to the Muhammadan period. 2nd ed. Delhi: Munshiram, 1968. 292p. [1st pub. 1915]

01162 ______. The living religions of the Indian people. London: Student Christian Movement, 1934. 323p.

01163 REGINER, R. Religions du Monde - l'Inde. Paris: Bloud & Gay, 1963. 135p.

01164 RENOU, L. Religions of ancient India. 2nd ed. ND: Munshiram, 1972. 139p.

01165 YOUNGER, P. The Indian religious tradition. Varanasi: Bharatiya Vidya Prakashan, 1970. 138p.

01166 ______. Introduction to Indian religious thought. Philadelphia: Westminster Press, 1972. 142p.

c. general surveys for reference and advanced study

01167 BHANDARKAR, R.G. Vaiṣṇavism, Śaivism and minor religious systems. Varanasi: IndBH, 1965. 167p. [Rpt. 1913 ed.]

01168 DASGUPTA, S.N. A history of Indian philosophy. Cambridge: CamUP, 1922-25. 5 v. [Also abridged ed. by R.R. Agarwal & S.K. Jain. Allahabad: Kitab Mahal, 1969. 230p.]

01169 ELIOT, C.N.E. Hinduism and Buddhism. NY: Barnes & Noble, 1954. 3 v. [Rpt. 1921 ed.]

01170 FARQUHAR, J.N. Outline of the religious literature of India. Delhi: Motilal, 1967. 451p. [Rpt. 1920 ed.]

01171 GONDA, J., et al. Die religionen Indiens. Stuttgart: Kohlhammer, 1960-64. 3 v. [French ed., Paris: Payot, 1962-66. 3 v.]

01172 RADHAKRISHNAN, S. Indian philosophy. London: Allen & Unwin, 1923-27. 2 v.

01173 TUCCI, G. Storia della filosofia Indiana. Bari: Editori Laterza, 1957. 604p.

01174 ZIMMER, H. Philosophies of India. Ed. by J. Campbell. Princeton: PUP, 1969. 687p. [1st pub. 1951]

d. essay collections

01175 BISHOP, D.H., ed. Indian thought: an introduction. ND: Wiley Eastern, 1975. 427p.

01176 HEIMANN, B. Facets of Indian thought. London: Allen & Unwin, 1964. 177p.

01177 HIRIYANNA, M. Indian philosophical studies. Mysore: Kavyalaya, 1957-72. 2 v. in 1.

01178 MAHADEVAN, T.M.P., ed. Spiritual perspectives: essays in mysticism and metaphysics. ND: Arnold-Heinemann, 1975. 303p.

01179 MAZUMDER, A.K. & (Swami) PRAJNANANANDA. The bases of Indian culture: commemoration volume of Swami Abhedananda. Calcutta: Ramakrishna Vedanta Math, 1971. 689p.

01180 MOORE, C.A., ed. The Indian mind; essentials of Indian philosophy and culture. Proceedings of the East-West Philosophers' Conference. Honolulu: East-West Center Press, 1967. 480p.

01181 SAKSENA, S.K. Essays on Indian philosophy. Honolulu: UPH, 1970. 127p.

01182 SHARMA, A. Thresholds in Hindu-Buddhist studies. Calcutta: Minerva, 1979. 231p.

01183 SIRCAR, D.C. Studies in the religious life of ancient and medieval India. Delhi: Motilal, 1971.

e. texts in translation: anthologies & collections

01184 GERBER, W., ed. The mind of India. NY: Macmillan, 1967. 256p.

01185 PANIKKAR, R., tr. The Vedic experience: mantramañjarī. An anthology of the Vedas for modern man and contemporary celebration. Berkeley: UCalP, 1977. 937p.

01186 MÜLLER, F. MAX, ed. The sacred books of the East. Delhi: Motilal, 1962-66. 50 v. [Rpt. 1879-1910 ed.]

01187 RADHAKRISHNAN, S. & C.A. MOORE, eds. A source book in Indian philosophy. Princeton: PUP, 1957. 683p.

3. Surveys of Hinduism
a. general introductions and surveys

01188 BANERJI, M. Invitation to Hinduism. ND: Arnold-Heinemann, 1978. 160p.

01189 BIARDEAU, M. Clefs pour la pensée Hindoue. Paris: Éditions Seghers, 1972. 246p.

01190 BOUQUET, A.C. Hinduism. London: Hutchinson U. Library, 1966. 160p.

01191 CHAUDHURI, N.C. Hinduism, a religion to live by. NY: OUP, 1979. 340p.

01192 CHENNAKESAVAN, S. A critical study of Hinduism. NY: Asia, 1974. 159p.

01193 DANDEKAR, R.N. Hinduism. In C. Bleeker & G. Widengren, eds. Historia Religionum. Leiden: Brill, 1971, v. 2, 237-345.

01194 DAY, C.B. Peasant cults in India. San Francisco: Chinese Materials Center, 1974. 126p.

01195 FARQUHAR, J.N. The crown of Hinduism. ND: OBRC, 1971. 468p. [1st pub. 1913]

01196 GLASENAPP, H. VON. Der Hinduismus; Religion und Gesellschaft im heutigen Indien. Munich: K. Wolff, 1922. 503p.

01197 HOPKINS, T.J. The Hindu religious tradition. Encino, CA: Dickenson, 1971. 156p.

01198 KLOSTERMAIER, K. Hinduismus. Koln: Bachem, 1965. 467p.

01199 MAHADEVAN, T.M.P. Outlines of Hinduism. 2nd rev. ed. Bombay: Chetana, 1960. 312p. [1st ed. 1956]

01200 MONIER-WILLIAMS, M. Religious thought and life in India: Vedism, Brāhmanism, and Hindūism.... ND: OBRC, 1974. 520p. [Rpt. 1883 ed.]

01201 ORGAN, T.W. The Hindu quest for the perfection of man. Columbus: Ohio State U. Press, 1970. 439p.

01202 ______. Hinduism; its historical development. Woodbury, NY: Barron's Educ. Series, 1974. 425p.

01203 RENOU, L. The nature of Hinduism. Tr. from French by P. Evans. NY: Walker, 1963. 155p.

01204 SARMA, D.S. Hinduism through the ages. 4th ed. Bombay: BVB, 1973. 300p. [1st ed. 1956]

01205 SEN, K.M. Hinduism. Baltimore: Penguin, 1961. 160p.

01206 SHOURIE, A. Hinduism, essence and consequence: a study of the Upanishads, the Gita, and the Brahmasutras. ND: Vikas, 1979. 414p.

01207 STROUP, H.H. Like a great river; an introduction to Hinduism. NY: Harper & Row, 1972. 200p.

01208 WILSON, H.H. Religious sects of the Hindus. Ed. by E.R. Rost. 2nd ed. Calcutta: Susil Gupta, 1958. 221p. [1st pub. 1861]

01209 ZAEHNER, R.C. Hinduism. London: OUP, 1962. 272p.

b. essay collections

01210 GUÉNON, R. Études sur l'hindouisme. Paris: Éditions traditionnelles, 1968. 286p.

01211 HINNELLS, J.R. & E.J. SHARPE, eds. Hinduism. Newcastle on Tyne: Oriel, 1972. 224p.

01212 MORGAN, K.W., ed. The religion of the Hindus. NY: Ronald Press, 1953. 434p.

01213 NARANG, G.C. Glorious Hinduism. ND: New Book Soc. of India, 1966. 160p.

01214 NAVARATNAM, K. Studies in Hinduism. Jaffna: M.D. Navaratnam, 1963. 263p.

01215 Religious Hinduism; a presentation and appraisal. By Jesuit scholars. Allahabad: St. Paul Pub., 1964. 330p.

01216 SMITH, B.L., ed. Hinduism: new essays in the history of religions. Leiden: Brill, 1976. 231p. (SHR, 33)

01217 SUNDARARAJAN, K.R., et al. Hinduism. Patiala: Punjabi U., 1969. 128p.

c. texts in translation

01218 EMBREE, A.T., ed. The Hindu tradition. NY: Modern Library, 1966. 363p.

01219 JOHNSON, C., ed. Vedanta: an anthology of Hindu scripture, commentary and poetry. NY: Harper & Row, 1971. 243p.

01220 MACNICOL, N., ed. Hindu scriptures; hymns from the Rigveda, five Upanishads, the Bhagavadgita. London: J.M. Dent, 1938. 293p.

01221 RAGHAVAN, V., tr. The Indian heritage; an anthology of Sanskrit literature. 3rd ed. Bangalore: Indian Inst. of World Culture, 1963. [1st ed. 1956]

01222 RENOU, L., ed. Hinduism. NY: G. Braziller, 1961. 255p.

01223 Sacred books of the Hindus. Allahabad: Panini Office, 1919-26. 31 v. [Rpt. NY: AMS Press, 1974]

4. Surveys of Buddhism
a. general introductions to Buddhism

01224 CONZE, E. Buddhism; its essence and development. NY: Philosophical Library, 1951. 212p.

01225 GARD, R.A., ed. Buddhism. NY: Braziller, 1961. 256p.

01226 JACOBSON, N.P. Buddhism: the religion of analysis. Carbondale, IL: S. Illinois U. Pr., 1970. 202p.

01227 JAYATILLEKE, K.N. The message of the Buddha. Ed. by N. Smart. NY: Free Press, 1974. 262p.

01228 PRATT, J.B. The pilgrimage of Buddhism & a Buddhist pilgrimage. NY: Macmillan, 1928. 758p.

01229 RAHULA, W. What the Buddha taught. Rev. ed. NY: Grove Press, 1974. 151p. [1st ed. 1959]

01230 ROBINSON, R. The Buddhist religion; a historical introduction. Belmont, CA: Dickenson, 1970. 136p.

01231 SANGHARAKSHITA, Bhikshu. A survey of Buddhism. Bangalore: Indian Inst. of World Culture, 1957. 500p.

01232 ______. The Three Jewels: an introduction to Buddhism. London: Rider, 1967. 276p.

01233 WAYMAN, A. Buddhism. In C.J. Bleeker & G. Widengren, ed. Historia Religionum. Leiden: Brill, 1971. v. 2, 372-464.

01234 ZÜRCHER, E. Buddhism; its origin and spread.... London: Routledge & K. Paul, 1962.

b. surveys of Buddhism in South Asia

01235 AHIR, D.C. Buddhism in the Punjab, Haryana, and Himachal Pradesh. ND: Delhi: Maha Bodhi Soc., 1971. 113p.

01236 ______. India's debt to Buddhism. ND: Maha Bodhi Soc., 1964. 112p.

01237 BARTHÉLEMY SAINT-HILAIRE, J. Buddhism in India and Sri Lanka. ND: Chetana, 1975. 172p. [extracts from his Buddha and his religion, 1882]

01238 BECHERT, H. Ceylon. In his Buddhismus, Staat und Gesellschaft in den Ländern Theravada-Buddhismus. Frankfurt: A. Metzner, 1966, v. 1, 199-369. (SIAK, 17½)

01239 ______. Buddhism in Ceylon and studies on religious syncretism in Buddhist countries. Göttingen: Vandenhoeck & Ruprecht, 1978. 341p. (AAWG, ser. 3,108)

01240 COPLESTON, R.S. Buddhism; primitive and present, in Magadha and in Ceylon. NY: Longmans, Green, 1892. 501p.

01241 DE SILVA, W.A. History of Buddhism in Ceylon. In B.C. Law, ed. Buddhistic studies. Calcutta: Thacker, Spink, 1931, 453-528.

01242 GOKHALE, B.G. Buddhism in Maharashtra: a history. Bombay: Popular, 1976. 191p.

01243 KHOSLA, S. History of Buddhism in Kashmir. ND: Sagar, 1972. 188p.

01244 LING, T.O. The Buddha: Buddhist civilization in India and Ceylon. London: Temple Smith, 1974. 287p.

01245 ______. Sinhalese Buddhism in recent anthropological writing: some implications. In Religion 1,1 (1971) 49-59.

01246 RAHULA, W. History of Buddhism in Ceylon; the Anuradhapura period, 3d century BC-10th century AD. 2d ed. Colombo, M.D. Gunasena, 1966. 351p. [1st ed. 1956]

01247 TARANATHA, JO-NAN-PA. Taranatha's history of Buddhism in India. Tr. from Tibetan by Lama Chimpa & A. Chattopadhyaya. Ed. by D. Chattopadhyaya. Simla: IIAS, 1970. 472p.

01248 WARDER, A.K. Indian Buddhism. 2d rev. ed. Delhi: Motilal, 1980. 627p. [1st ed. 1970]

c. essay collections

01249 BAPAT, P.V., ed. 2500 years of Buddhism. Delhi: PDMIB, 1956. 499p.

01250 BARUA, B.M. Studies in Buddhism. Ed. by B.N. Chaudhury. Calcutta: Saraswat Library, 1974. 427p.

01251 Buddha jayanti special issue. In JBRS (1956) 1-332.

01252 CONZE, E. Thirty years of Buddhist studies; selected essays. Columbia, SC: U. of S. Carolina Press, 1968. 274p.

01253 COUSINS, L. & A. KUNST & K.R. NORMAN, eds. Buddhist studies in honour of I.B. Horner. Boston: D. Reidel, 1974. 239p.

01254 Gautama Buddha 25th centenary volume. [special issue] In IHQ 32,2/3 (1956) 109-356.

01255 LAMOTTE, É., et al. Towards the meeting with Buddhism. Rome: Ancora, 1970. 2 v., 144, 140p.

01256 LAW, B.C. Historical gleanings. Delhi: Nag, 1976. 101p. [Rpt. 1922 ed.]

01257 NARAIN, A.K., ed. Studies in history of Buddhism: papers presented at the International Conference on the History of Buddhism at the University of Wisconsin, Madison...August 19-21, 1976. Delhi: B.R., 1980. 421p.

01258 ______. Studies in Pali and Buddhism; a memorial volume in honor of Bhikkhu Jagdish Kashyap. Delhi: B.R., 1979. 422p.

01259 PIYADASSI, ed. A felicitation volume presented to the Ven. Narada Mahathera. Kandy: BPS, 1979. 193p.

01260 OBEYESEKERE, G. & F. REYNOLDS & B.L. SMITH. The two wheels of Dhamma: essays on the Theravada tradition in India & Ceylon. Chambersburg, PA: AAR, 1972. 121p. (Amer. Academy of Religion Studies in Religion, 3)

01261 PREBISH, C.S., ed. Buddhism, a modern perspective. University Park: Pennsylvania State U. Press, 1975. 330p.

01262 SANKRITYAYAN, et al. Buddhism: the Marxist approach. Delhi: PPH, 1970. 86p.

01263 STORY, F. Collected writings. Kandy: BPS, 1973-. v. 1, 382p.; v. 2, 286p.

01264 WIJESEKERA, O.H. DE A., ed. Malalasekera commemoration volume. Colombo: Malalasekera Comm. Vol. Ed. Cmtee., 1976. 362p.

d. texts in translation - anthologies and collections

01265 BEYER, S., ed. Buddhist experience: sources and interpretations. Belmont, CA: Dickenson, 1974. 274p.

01266 BURTT, E.A., ed. Teachings of the compassionate Buddha. NY: Mentor, 1955. 247p.

01267 CONZE, E., tr. Buddhist scriptures. Baltimore: Penguin, 1968. 249p. [1st pub. 1959]

01268 CONZE, E., et al., tr. Buddhist texts through the ages. Oxford: B. Cassirer, 1954. 322p.

01269 DE BARY, W., ed. The Buddhist tradition in India, China, & Japan. NY: Modern Library, 1969. 417p.

01270 HAMILTON, C., ed. Buddhism: a religion of compassion. NY: Liberal Arts, 1952. 248p.

01271 Sacred books of the Buddhists. London: 1895-. [32 v. as of 1976; various editors and publishers]

01272 STREIK, L, ed. World of Buddha: a reader. Garden City, NY: Doubleday, 1969. 286p.

5. Surveys of Jainism
a. introductions

01273 BHATTACHARYA, H.S. The Jaina prayer. Calcutta: U. of Calcutta, 1964. 117p.

01274 CAILLAT, C. & A.N. UPADHYE & B. PATIL. Jainism. Delhi: Macmillan, 1974. 92p.

01275 DELLA CASA, C. Jainism. In C. Bleeker & G. Widengren, eds. Historia Religionum. Leiden: Brill, 1971, 346-371.

01276 DURBIN, M.A. A transformational model of linguistics and its implications for an ethnology of religion: a case study of Jainism. In AA 72,2 (1970) 334-42.

01277 GLASENAPP, H. VON. Der Jainismus, eine indische Erlösungsreligion. Berlin: A. Hager, 1925. 505p.

01278 GUÉRINOT, A.A. La religion djaina; histoire, doctrine, culte, coutumes, institutions. Paris: P. Geuthner, 1926. 351p.

01279 GUSEVA, N.R. Jainism. Tr. by Y.S. Redkar. Bombay: Sindhu, 1971. 108p. [1st Russian ed. 1968]

01280 JAIN, J.P. Religion and culture of the Jains. ND: Bharatiya Jnanpith, 1975. 196p. (its Murtidevi granthamala: English series, 6)

01281 JAIN, K.C. Jainism in Rajasthan. Sholapur: Jaina Samskṛti Samrakshaka Sangha, 1963. 284p. (Jīvarāja Jaina granthamālā, no. 15)

01282 JAIN, U.K. Jaina sects and schools. Delhi: Concept, 1975. 162p.

01283 JAINI, J.L. Outlines of Jainism. Cambridge: CamUP, 1940. 156p. [1st pub. 1916]

01284 JAINI, P.S. The Jaina path of purification. Berkeley: UCalP, 1979. 374p.

01285 LATTHE, A.B. An introduction to Jainism. Delhi: Jain Mittra Mandal, 1964. 78p. 1st pub. 1905

01286 MEHTA, M.L. Jaina culture. Varanasi: P.V. Res. Inst., 1969. 152p. (Parshvanath Vidyashram series, 13)

01287 SCHUBRING, W. The religion of the Jainas. Tr. from German by Amulyachandra Sen & T.C. Burke. Calcutta: Sanskrit College, 1966. 43p. (Calcutta Sanskrit College Res. series, 52)

01288 STEVENSON, M.S. The heart of Jainism. ND: Munshiram, 1970. 336p. [1st pub. 1915]

b. essay collections

01289 BHANAWAT, N. & P.S. JAIN, eds. Bhagwan Mahavira and his relevance in modern times. Bikaner: Akhil Bharatavarshiya Sadhumargi Jain Sangha, 1976. 222p.

01920 DWIVEDI, R.C., ed. Contribution of Jainism to Indian culture. Delhi: Motilal, 1975. 306p.

01291 KALGHATGI, T.G., ed. Jainism and Karnatak culture. Dharwar: Karnatiak U., 1977. 242p.

01292 SCHUBRING, W. Kleine Schriften. Ed. by K. Bruhn. Wiesbaden: Steiner, 1977. 496p. (VGS, 13)

01293 TALIB, G.S., ed. Jainism. Patiala: Pubjabi U., 1975. 115p.

01294 UPADHYE, A.N., et al., eds. Mahāvīra and his teachings. Bombay: Bhagavan Mahavira 2500th Nirvana Mahotsava Samiti, 1977. 462p.

c. texts in translation

01295 Sacred books of the Jainas. Ed. by S.C. Ghoshal, et al. Arrah: K.D. Prasada, Central Jaina Pub. House, 1917-40. 11 v. [Rpt. NY: AMS Press, 1973]

6. Philosophy and Doctrine of the Indic Religions - General and Comparative Studies

a. general

01296 BELVALKAR, S.K. & R.D. RANADE. History of Indian philosophy. 2d ed. ND: OBRC, 1974-. v. 2, 514p. [to be 8 v.? Rpt. 1927 ed.]

01297 BERARD, Father. Indian mind. Mangalore: Codialbail Press, 1962. 287p.

01298 CHATTOPADHYAYA, D., ed. Studies in the history of Indian philosophy: an anthology of articles by scholars, eastern and western. Calcutta: K.P. Bagchi, 1978-79. 3 v.

01299 DAMODARAN, K. Man and society in Indian philosophy. ND: PPH, 1970. 94p.

01300 FILLIOZAT, J. Les philosophies de l'Inde. Paris: PUF, 1970. 127p.

01301 FRAUWALLNER, E. History of Indian philosophy. Tr. by V.M. Bedekar. NY: Humanities Press, 1974. 2 v. [1st German ed. 1953-56]

01302 GANDHI, V.R. The systems of Indian philosophy. Ed. by K.K Dixit. Bombay: Shri Mahavira Jain Vidyalaya, 1970. 148p.

01303 GROUSSET, R. Les philosophies indiennes; les systèmes. Paris: Desclée de Brouwer, 1931. 2 v.

01304 HIRIYANNA, M. The essentials of Indian philosophy. London: Allen & Unwin, 1949. 216p.

01305 MAHADEVAN, T.M.P. Invitation to Indian philosophy. ND: Arnold-Heinemann, 1974. 435p.

01306 PULIGANDLA, R. Fundamentals of Indian philosophy. Nashville: Abingdon, 1975. 363p.

01307 RAJU, P.T. The philosophical traditions of India. London: Allen & Unwin, 1971. 256p.

01308 REYNA, R. Introduction to Indian philosophy; a simplified text. Bombay: Tata McGraw Hill, 1971. 257p.

01309 SHARMA, C. Indian philosophy; a critical survey. NY: Barnes & Noble, 1962. 405p.

01310 SINHA, J.N. Outlines of Indian philosophy. Calcutta: Sinha Pub. House, 1963. 435p.

01311 WARDER, A.K. Outline of Indian philosophy. Delhi: Motilal, 1971. 262p.

b. surveys of Hindu philosophy

01312 BHATTACHARJEE, S.S. The Hindu theory of cosmology: an introduction to the Hindu view of man and his universe. Calcutta: Bani Prakashani, 1978. 164p.

01313 BOWES, P. The Hindu religious tradition: a philosophical approach. Bombay: Allied, 1976. 322p.

01314 CHANDRA, PRATAP. The Hindu mind. Simla: IIAS, 1977. 152p.

01315 CHATTERJEE, S.C. The fundamentals of Hinduism: a philosophical study. Calcutta: Das Gupta, 1950. 186p.

01316 GUÉNON, R. Introduction to the study of Hindu doctrines. Tr. by M. Pallis. London: Luzac, 1045. 351p.

01317 PEREIRA, J., ed. Hindu theology: a reader. Garden City, NY: Image Books, 1976. 558p.

01318 RADHAKRISHNAN, S. The Hindu view of life. NY: Macmillan, 1928. 133p.

c. surveys of Buddhist philosophy

01319 GUENTHER, H.V. Buddhist philosophy in theory & practice. Baltimore: Penguin, 1972. 240p.

01320 INADA, K. Some basic misconceptions of Buddhism. In Intl. Philosophical Q. 9,1 (1969) 101-119.

01321 KALUPAHANA, D.J. Buddhist philosophy; a historical analysis. Honolulu: UPH, 1977. 189p.

01322 KEITH, A.B. Buddhist philosophy in India and Ceylon. Oxford: OUP, 1923. 339p.

01323 LA VALLÉE POUSSIN, L. DE. Le Bouddhisme: opinions sur l'histoire de la dogmatique. Paris: G. Beauchesne, 1909. 420p.

01324 ______. Le Dogme et la Philosophie de Bouddhisme. Paris: G. Beauchesne, 1930. 213p.

01325 TAKAKUSU, J. & W.-T. CHAN & C.A. MOORE. The essentials of Buddhist philosophy. 3rd ed. Bombay: Asia, 223p. [1st ed. 1947]

01326 THOMAS, E.J. History of Buddhist thought. 2nd ed. London: Routledge & K. Paul, 1951. 316p. [1st ed. 1933]

01327 WAYMAN, A. Who understands the four alternatives of the Buddhist texts? In PEW 27,1 (1977) 3-21.

d. surveys of Jaina philosophy

01328 BHATTACHARYA, N.N. Jain philosophy: historical outline. ND: Munshiram, 1976. 220p.

01329 GOPALAN, S. Outlines of Jainism. ND: Wiley Eastern, 1973. 205p.

01330 JAIN, C.R. Fundamentals of Jainism. Meerut: Veer Nirvan Bharti, 1974. 121p.

01331 KALGHATGI, T.G. Jaina view of life. Sholapur: Jaina Samskṛti Samraksaka Sangha, 1969. (Jīvarāja Jaina granthamālā, 20)

01332 MEHTA, M.L. Jaina philosophy. Varanasi: P.V. Res. Inst., 1971. 234p. (Parshvanath Vidyashram series, 16)

01333 SCHUBRING, W. The doctrine of the Jainas. Tr. by W. Beurlen. Delhi: Motilal, 1962. 335p. [1st German ed. 1935]

01334 TATIA, NATHMAL. Studies in Jaina philosophy. Banaras: Jain Cultural Res. Soc., 1951. 327p.

e. comparisons among the Indic philosophies and religions

01335 COOMARASWAMY, A.K. Hinduism and Buddhism. Westport, CN: Greenwood Press, 1971. 86p. [Rpt. 1943 ed.]

01336 FRENZ, A., ed. Grace in Saiva siddhanta, Vedanta, Islam, and Christianity: papers presented at the seminar held at Tamil Nadu Theological Seminary, Arasaradi, Madurai, on Saturday, October 11th, 1975. Madurai: Tamil Nadu Theological Seminary, 1975. 128p.

01337 MEHTA, J.L., ed. Vedānta and Buddhism: proceedings of the third all-India seminar held at the Centre of Advanced Study in Philosophy, BHU.... Varanasi: Centre of Advanced Study in Philosophy, BHU, 1968. 186p.

01338 MONIER-WILLIAMS, M. Buddhism: in its connection with Brahmanism and Hinduism and its contrast with Christianity. 2nd ed. Varanasi: CSSO, 1964. 563p. [1st ed. 1889]

01339 RAJU, P.T. Buddhism & Vedanta. In IAC 6,1 (1957) 24-48.

01340 RAMAKRISHNAN, V. Perspectives in Śaivism. Madras: Dr. S. Radhakrishnan Inst. for Advanced Study in Philosophy, U. of Madras, 1978. 134p.

01341 RUEGG, D. The study of Indian and Tibetan thought. Leiden: Brill, 1967. 48p.

f. East and West: general comparative studies

01342 BURTT, E.A. What can western philosophy learn from India? In PEW 5,3 (1955) 195-210.

01343 DEVARAJA, N.K. Hinduism and Christianity. Bombay: Asia, 1969. 126p.

01344 GISPERT-SAUCH, G., ed. God's word among men: papers in honour of Fr. Joseph Putz, Frs. J. Bayart, J. Volckaert, and P. De Letter. Delhi: Vidyajyoti Inst. of Religious Studies, 1973. 384p.

01345 HEIMANN, B. Indian and Western philosophies; a study in contrasts. London: Allen & Unwin, 1937. 156p.

01346 MOORE, C.A., ed. Essays in East-West philosophy: an attempt at world philosophical synthesis. Honolulu: UPH, 1951. 467p.

01347 RADHAKRISHNAN, S. East and West; some reflections. NY: Harper, 1956. 140p.

01348 ______. History of philosophy, eastern and western. London: Allen & Unwin, 1952-53. 2 v.

01349 SARKAR, A.K. Changing phases of Buddhist thought; a study in the background of east-west philosophy. Patna: Bharati Bhawan, 1968. 147p.

01350 SMART, N. The yogi and the devotee: the interplay between the Upanishads and Catholic theology. London: Allen & Unwin, 1968. 174p.

01351 SRINIVASAN, G. Studies in East-West philosophy. ND: Arnold-Heinemann, 1974. 111p.

g. comparisons with specific Western philosophers or schools

01352 BETTY, L.S. The Buddhist-Humean parallel: postmortem. In PEW 21,3 (1971) 237-254.

01353 DE SILVA, M.W.P. Buddhist and Freudian psychology. Colombo: LHI, 1973. 193p.

01354 GOCHHWAL, B.S. The concept of perfection in the teachings of Kant and the Gita. 1st ed. Delhi: Motilal, 1967. 184p.

01355 MEHTA, J.L. Heidegger and the comparison of Indian and Western philosophy. In PEW 20,3 (1970) 287-96.

01356 POTTER, K.H. Realism, speech-acts & truth-gaps in Indian & Western philosophy. In JIP 1,1 (1970) 13-21.

01357 RAJU, P.T. Thought and reality - Hegelianism and advaita. London: Allen & Unwin, 1937. 285p.

01358 SINGH, JAIDEVA. Philosophy of evolution: Western and Indian. Prasārānga: U. of Mysore, 1970. 127p.

01359 SINGH, RAM LAL. An inquiry concerning reason in Kant and Samkara. Allahabad: Chugh, 1978. 263p.

7. Key Concepts and Problems Shared by the Indic Religions

a. general studies of key concepts

01360 BALBIR SINGH. The conceptual framework of Indian philosophy. Delhi: Macmillan, 1976. 354p.

01361 BROWN, W.N. The content of cultural continuity in India. JAS 20 (1961) 427-434.

01362 ______. Man in the universe: some cultural continuities in Indian thought. Berkeley: UCalP, 1970. 128p.

01363 GOKHALE, B.G. Indian thought through the ages, a study of some dominant concepts. Bombay: Asia, 1963. 236p.

01364 INGALLS, D.H.H. Dharma and mokṣa. In PEW 7 (1957) 41-48.

01365 POTTER, K.H. Presuppositions of India's philosophies. Englewood Cliffs, NJ: Prentice-Hall, 1963. 276p.

01366 RAO, K.L.S. The concept of śraddhā in the Brāhmaṇas, Upanisads and Gita. Patiala: Roy Pub., 1971. 197p.

01367 VAN BUITENEN, J.A.B. Dharma and Mokṣa. In PEW 7 (1957) 33-40.

b. metaphysics and theory of knowledge
i. general studies

01368 BHATTACHARYA, H.S. Reals in the Jaina metaphysics. Bombay: Seth Santi Das Khetsy Charitable Trust, 1966. 412p.

01369 CHATHIMATTAM, J.B. Consciousness and reality; an Indian approach to metaphysics. Bangalore: Dharmaram College, 1967. 259p.

01370 DIXIT, K.K. Jaina ontology. Ahmedabad: L.D. Inst. of Indology, 1971. 203p.

01371 DRAVID, R.R. The problem of universals in Indian philosophy. Delhi: Motilal, 1972. 473p.

01372 JHA, R.C. The Vedāntic and the Buddhist concept of reality as interpreted by Śaṁkara and Nāgārjuna. Calcutta: KLM, 1973. 156p.

01373 PADMARAJIAH, Y.J. A comparative study of the Jaina theories of reality and knowledge. Bombay: Jain Sahitya Vikas Mandal, 1963. 423p.

01374 RAMAIAH, C. The problem of change and identity in Indian philosophy. Tirupati: Sri Venkateswara U., 1978. 107p.

01375 SEN, S. A study of universals, with special reference to Indian philosophy. Santiniketan: Visva-Bharati, 1978. 168p.

01376 SILBURN, L. Instant et cause; le discontinu dans la pensée philosophique de l'Inde. Paris: J. Vrin, 1955. 439p.

01377 STCHERBATSKY, Th. The central conception of Buddhism & the meaning of the word 'dharma'. Calcutta: Susil Gupta, 1956. 96p. [Rpt. 1923 ed.]

01378 ZAVERI, J.S. Theory of atom in the Jaina philosophy: a critical study of the Jaina theory of paramanu pudgala in light of modern scientific theory. Ladnun, Rajasthan: Agama & Sahitya Prakashan, Jaina Vishva Bharati, 1975. 149p.

ii. idealism, materialism, and scepticism in Indic philosophy

01379 CHATTERJEE, D. Skepticism and Indian philosophy. In PEW 27,2 (1977) 195-209.

01380 CHATTOPADHAYA, D. Sources of Indian idealism. In AF 5 (1977) 205-31.

01381 DASGUPTA, S.N. Indian idealism. Cambridge: CamUP, 1962. 206p. [Rpt. 1933 ed.]

01382 MAY, J. La philosophie bouddhique idéaliste. In AS/EA 25 (1971) 265-323.

01383 MITTAL, K.K. Materialism in Indian thought. ND: Munshiram, 1974. 336p.

01384 POTTER, K.H. The background of skepticism, East and West. In JIP 3,3/4 (1975) 299-313.

01385 RAJU, P.T. Idealistic thought of India. London: Allen & Unwin, 1953. 454p.

01386 RIEPE, D.M. The naturalistic tradition in Indian thought. Seattle: UWashP, 1961. 308p.

01387 SASTRI, P.S. Indian idealism: epistemology & ontology. Delhi: Bharatiya Vidya Prakashan, 1975. 2 v.

01388 SHASTRI, D.N. Critique of Indian realism; a study of the conflict between the Nyāya-Vaiśeṣika & the Buddhist Dignāga school. Agra: Agra U., 1964. 562p.

01389 SINHA, J.N. Indian realism. London: K. Paul, Trench, Trubner, 1938. 287p.

01390 TUCCI, G. Linee di una storia del materialsmo indiano. Rome: R.A.N. dei Lincei, 1924-29. 2 v.

iii. concepts of the absolute; Hindu brahman and Buddhist śūnyatā

01391 ARANJANIYIL, A.G. The absolute of the Upanishads: personal or impersonal? Bangalore: Dharmaram, 1975. 131p.

01392 BAREAU, A. L'Absolu en philosophie bouddhique: évolution de la notion d'asaṃskṛta. Paris: Centre de documentation universitaire, 1951. 307p.

01393 BHATTACHARYA, A.R. Brahman of Śaṅkara and Śūnyatā of Mādhyamikas. In IHQ 32 (1956) 270-85.

01394 BHATTACHARYYA, K.C. Search for the absolute in Neo-Vedanta. Ed. by G.B. Burch. Honolulu: UPH, 1976. 203p.

01395 CHAUDHURI, H. The concept of Brahman in Hindu philosophy. In PEW 4,1 (1954) 47-66.

01396 DE JONG, J.W. The problem of the absolute in the Madhyamaka school. [and] Emptiness. In JIP 2 (1972) 1-6, 7-15.

01397 LACOMBE, O. L'Absolu selon le Védânta, les notions de Brahman et d'Atman dans les systèmes de Cankara et Râmânoudja. Nouvelle edition. Paris: Geunther, 1966. 416p. (Annales du Musée Guimet. Bibliothèque d'études, 49)

01398 MUKHERJI, S. The Jaina philosophy of non-absolutism: a critical study of Anekāntavāda. 2nd ed. Delhi: Motilal, 1978. 289p. [1st pub. 1944]

01399 STRENG, F.J. Emptiness, a study in religious meaning. Nashville: Abingdon Press, 1967. 252p.

01400 SUNDARA, R.G. Brahman: a comparative study of the philosophies of Sankara and Ramanuja. Waltair: Andhra U., 1974. 196p.

iv. māyā: the world as illusion

01401 BURCH, G.B. The Hindu concept of existence. In Monist 50 (1966) 44-54.

01402 DEVANANDAN, P.D. The concept of māyā; an essay in historical survey of the Hindu theory of the world, with special reference to the Vedanta. London: Lutterworth Press, 1950. 234p.

01403 GOUDRIAAN, T. Māyā divine and human: a study of magic and its religious foundations in Sanskrit texts, with particular attention to a fragment on Viṣṇu's Māyā preserved in Bali. Delhi: Motilal, 1978. 516p.

01404 HACKER, P. Vivarta. Studien zur Geschichte der illusionistischen Kosmologie und Erkenntnistheorie der Inder. Wiesbaden: Steiner, 1953. 58p.

01405 JOSHI, R.B. The origin of maya in Sankara's philosophy. In JIH 37 (1959) 179-99, 289-311.

01406 PRAJNANANANDA, Swami. Indefinable māyā in Advaita Vedānta. In A.K. Mazumder & Swami Prajnanananda, eds. The bases of Indian culture. Calcutta: Ramakrishna Vedanta Math, 1971, 139-60.

01407 RAMACHANDRAN, T.P. The concept of the vyāvahārika in Advaita Vedānta. Madras: Centre of Advanced Study in Philosophy, U. of Madras, 1969. 192p. (Madras U. philosophical series, 12)

01408 REYNA, R. The concept of Māyā, from the Vedas to the 20th century. Bombay: Asia, 1962. 120p.

01409 SARATHCHANDRA, E.R. From Vasubandhu to Śāntarakṣita; a critical examination of some Buddhist theories of the external world. In JIP 4,1-2 (1976) 69-107.

01410 SHASTRI, P.D. The doctrine of māyā in the philosophy of the Vedānta. London: Luzac, 1911. 138p.

v. epistemology

01411 BOTHRA, P. The Jaina theory of perception. Delhi: Motilal, 1976. 133p.

01412 COWARD, H. & K. SIVARAMAN. Revelation in Indian thought: a Festschrift in honour of Professor T.R.V. Murti. Emeryville, CA: Dharma Pub., 1977. 193p.

01413 JAYATILLEKE, K.N. Early Buddhist theory of knowledge. London: Allen & Unwin, 1963. 520p.

01414 MATILAL, B.K. Epistemology, logic, and grammar in Indian philosophical analysis. The Hague: Mouton, 1971. 183p. (Janua Linguarum. Series minor, 111)

01415 MISHRA, C. The problem of nescience in Indian philosophy. Darbhanga: Mithila Inst. of Post-Graduate Studies and Res. in Sanskrit Learning, 1977. 79 + 418p.

01416 OBERHAMMER, G., ed. Offenbarung, geistige Realität des Menschen. Vienna: Indological Inst., U. of Vienna, 1974. 237p. [seminar papers]

01417 PONNIAH, V. The Śaiva Siddhānta theory of knowledge. Annamalainagar: Annamalai U., 1952. 351p.

01418 PRASAD, JWALA. History of Indian epistemology. 2nd ed. rev. & enl. Delhi: Munshiram, 1958. 406p. [1st pub. 1939]

01419 RAGHUNATHAN, N. Reason and intuition in Indian culture. Madras: U. of Madras, 1969. 86p.

01420 SATPRAKASHANANDA, Swami. Methods of knowledge, perceptual, non-perceptual, and transcendental, according to Advaita Vedānta. London: Allen & Unwin, 1965. 366p.

01421 SEN, N.L. A critique of the theories of viparyaya. Calcutta: Rabindra Bharati, 1965. 259p.

01422 SINHA, J.N. Indian epistemology of perception. Calcutta: Sinha Pub. House, 1969. 224p.

01423 SPRUNG, M., ed. The problem of two truths in Buddhism and Vedānta. Dordrecht: D. Reidel, 1973. 126p.

01424 SUZUKI, D.T. Reason and intuition in Buddhist philosophy. In C.A. Moore, ed. Essays in East-West philosophy. Honolulu: UPH, 1951, 17-48.

01425 THRASHER, A.W. Maṇḍana Miśra on the indescribability of Avidyā. In WZKS 21 (1977) 219-37.

vi. logic and theories of meaning

01426 BARLINGAY, S.S. A modern introduction to Indian logic. Delhi: Natl. Pub. House, 1965. 238p.

01427 CHAKRAVARTI, N.B. The Advaita concept of falsity; a critical study. Calcutta: Sanskrit College, 1967. 90p.

01428 DIXIT, K.K. Indian logic: its problems as treated by its schools. Vaishali (Muzaffarpur): Res. Inst. of Prakrit, Jainology, and Ahimsa, 1975. 246p. (Prakrit Jaina Inst. res. pub. series, 10)

01429 KUNJUNNI RAJA, K. Indian theories of meaning. Madras: Adyar Library, 1963. 360p.

01430 MATILAL, B.K. Reference and existence in Nyaya and Buddhist logic. In JIP 1,1 (1970) 83-110.

01431 SHARMA, C. Dialectics in Buddhism and Vedanta. Benares: Nand Kishore, 1952. 272p.

01432 SHARMA, D. The differentiation theory of meaning in Indian logic. The Hague: Mouton, 1969. 129p.

01433 SMART, N. Doctrine and argument in Indian philosophy. London: Allen & Unwin, 1964. 255p.

01434 STCHERBATSKY, TH. Buddhist logic. NY: Dover, 1962, 2 v. [1st pub. 1930-32]

01435 VIDYABHUSANA, S.C. History of Indian logic: ancient, medieval, and modern schools. Delhi: Motilal, 1971. 648p.

01436 WARDER, A.K. The concept of a concept. In JIP 1,2 (1971) 181-96.

vii. kāla: concept of time

01437 BASHAM, A.L. Ancient Indian ideas of time and history. In D.C. Sircar, ed. Prācyavidyā-Taraṅginī.... Calcutta: U. of Calcutta, 1969, 49-63.

01438 BHARTRHARI. The Kālasamuddeśa of Bhartṛhari's Vākyapadīya, together with Helārāja's commentary. Tr. by P.S. Sharma. ND: Motilal, 1972. 153p.

01439 COOMARASWAMY, A.K. Time and eternity. Ascona: Artibus Asiae, 1947. 140p. (Art. As. suppl. 8)

01440 ELIADE, M. Time and eternity in Indian thought. In J. Kitagawa, ed. Man and time. London: Routledge & K. Paul, 1957, 173-200. [Bollingen series, 30]

01441 KHARE, R.S. The concept of time and time-reckoning among the Hindus: an anthropological view point. In EA 20 (1967) 47-53.

01442 LINGAT, R. Time and the Dharma (on Manu I, 85-86). In CIS 6 (1962) 7-16. [1st pub. in French in JA 249 (1961) 487-95]

01443 MANDAL, K.K. A comparative study of the concepts of space and time in Indian thought. Varanasi: CSSO, 1968. 223p. (CSS, 65)

01444 MITCHINER, J.E. The saptarsi yuga: elucidation of a cyclical era. In JAIH 10 (1976-77) 52-95.

01445 MOOKERJEE, S. The Jaina conception of time. In VQ 27,2 (1961) 122-39.

01446 NAKAMURA, H. Time in Indian and Japanese thought. In J.T. Fraser, ed. The voices of time. NY: G. Braziller, 1966, 77-91.

01447 POCOCK, D.F. The anthropology of time reckoning. In CIS 7 (1964) 18-30.

01448 ŚASTRI, S. Conception of time in post-Vedic Sanskrit literature. In his Essays on Indology. Delhi: Meharchand Lachhmandass, 1963, 149-204.

01449 SCHAYER, S. Contribution to the problem of time in Indian philosophy. Krakow: Nakladem Polskiej Akademii Umiejetnosci, 1938. 76p. (Mém. de la Commission Orientaliste, 31)

01450 SEN, S.K. Time in Sāṁkhya-yoga. In Indian Philosophical Q. * (1968) 407-426.

01451 SHAMASASTRY, R. The Vedic calendar. ND: Ganga Pub., 1979. 79p.

01452 SINHA, B.M. Time and temporality in Sāṁkhya and Abhidharma Buddhism. ND: Munshiram, 1980.

01453 Time and temporality [special issue]. In PEW 24,2 (1974) 119-214.

c. saṃsāra: the cycle of death and rebirth
i. general studies

01454 JOSHI, G.N. The evolution of the concepts of atman and moksa in the different systems of Indian philosophy. Ahmedabad: Gujarat U., 1965. 868p.

01455 PARAMESWARA, P. Soul, karma, and re-birth. Bangalore: 1973. 212p.

ii. Indic psychology - concepts of self (ātman) and non-self (anātman)

01456 ABHEDANANDA, Swami. The Upanishadic doctrine of the self: an analytical study of the nature of the self as revealed in the Upanishads. ND: Oriental, 1978. 139p.

01457 BAGCHI, A. Indian definition of mind. Calcutta: Sanskrit College, 1975. 117p.

01458 BEIDLER, W. The vision of self in early Vedanta. Delhi: Motilal, 1975. 266p.

01459 BHATTACHARYA, K. L'Ātman-Brahman dans le Bouddhisme ancien. Paris: EFEO, 1973. 186p.

01460 BIARDEAU, M. Ahaṃkāra, the ego principle of the Upanishads. In CIS 9 (1966) 62-84.

01461 BON, B.K., ed. Jīva-ātma or finite self: the concept of the individual finite self in twelve different systems of philosophy. Vrindaban: Inst. of Oriental Philosophy, 1963. 123p.

01462 CATALINA, F.V. A study of the self concept of Sankhya Yoga philosophy. Delhi: Munshiram, 1968. 163p.

01463 CHANDRA, P. Metaphysics of perpetual change: the concept of self in early Buddhism. Bombay: Somaiya, 1978. 275p.

01464 CHENNAKESAVAN, S. The concept of mind in Indian philosophy. New York: Asia, 1960. 164p.

01465 DEUTSCH, E.S. The self in advaita Vedanta. In Int. Philosophical Q. 6 (1966) 5-21.

01466 HACKER, P. Die Idee der Person im Denken von Vedānta-Philosophen. In his Kleine Schriften. Wiesbaden: Steiner, 1978, 270-93. [1st pub. in StM 13 (1963) 30-52.]

01467 HULIN, M. Le principe de l'ego dans la pensée indienne classique: la notion d'ahaṃkāra. Paris: Inst. de civilisation indienne, 1978. 375p.

01468 INADA, K.K. Whitehead's "actual entity" and the Buddha's anātman. In PEW 21,3 (1971) 303-16.

01469 JAIN, S.C. Structure and functions of soul in Jainism. ND: Bharatiya Jnanpith, 1978. 239p.

01470 JOHANNSON, R.E.A. The dynamic psychology of early Buddhism. London: Curzon Press, 1979. 236p.

01471 LUYSTER, R.W. The concept of the self in the Upanisads: its origin and symbols. In PEW 20,1 (1970) 51-62.

01472 MURPHY, G. & L.B. MURPHY, eds. Asian psychology. NY: Basic Books, 1968. 238p. [texts and commentary; pp. 1-108 on India]

01473 ORGAN, T.W. The self in Indian philosophy. The Hague: Mouton, 1964. 184p.

01474 PARRINDER, G. The indestructible soul; the nature of man and life after death in Indian thought. London: Allen & Unwin, 1973. 116p.

01475 ROBINSON, R. Some Buddhist and Hindu concepts of intellect - will. In PEW 22,3 (1972) 299-307.

01476 ROȘU, ARION. Les conceptions psychologiques dans les textes médicaux indiens. Paris: Collège de France, l'Inst. de Civilisation, 1978. 287p. [its Publications, IN-8, 43]

01477 RHYS DAVIDS, C.A.F. The birth of Indian psychology and its development in Buddhism. ND: OBRC, 1978. 444p. [Rpt. 1936 ed.]

01478 SAKSENA, S.K. Nature of consciousness in Hindu philosophy. 2nd ed. Delhi: Motilal, 1971. 223p. [1st pub. 1944]

01479 SHUKLA, P.C. Concept of soul in Indian philosophy. ND: Newman, 1976. 187p.

iii. karma and transmigration

01480 ARYA, U. Hindu contradictions of the doctrine of Karma. In E&W 22,1-2 (1972) 93-100.

01481 DE SILVA, L.A. Reincarnation in Buddhist and Christian thought. Colombo: Study Centre for Religion and Society, 1968. 176p.

01482 DE SMET, R. Copernican reversal: the Gītakāra's reformulation of Karma. In PEW 27,1 (1977) 53-63.

01483 GHOSE, A. The problem of rebirth. Pondicherry: Sri Aurobindo Ashram, 1969. 189p. [Rpt.]

01484 GLASENAPP, H. VON. The doctrine of karman in Jain philosophy. Trans. by G.B. Gifford & rev. by the author, ed. by H.R. Kapadia. Bombay: Bai Vijibai Jivanlal Panalal Charity Fund, 1942. 186p. [1st German ed. 1915]

01485 KALGHATGI, T.G. Karma and rebirth. Ahmedabad: L.D. Inst. of Indology, 1972. 75p.

01486 KOLENDA, P.M. Religious anxiety and Hindu fate. In E.B. Harper, ed. Religion in South Asia. Seattle: U. of Washington Press, 1964, 71-81. [also in JAS 23 (1964) 71-81.]

01487 MCDERMOTT, J.P. Is there group Karma in Theravāda Buddhism? In Numen 23,1 (1976) 67-80.

01488 ______. The Kathavatthu Kamma debates. In JAOS 95,3 (1975) 424-33.

01489 MEHTA, MOHAN LAL. Jaina psychology: a psychological analysis of the Jaina doctrine of Karma. Amritsar: Sohanlal Jaindharma Pracharak Samiti, 1957. 220p.

01490 NĀRADA, Thera. Kamma, or the Buddhist law of causation. In D.R. Bhandarkar, ed. B.C. Law Volume, Part 2. Poona: 1946, 158-75.

01491 O'FLAHERTY, W.D., ed. Karma and rebirth in classical Indian traditions. Berkeley: UCalP, 1980. 342p.

01492 PANIKKAR, R. The law of karman and the historical dimension of man. In PEW 22,1 (1972) 25-43.

01493 RAMASUBRAMANIAM, V. Metempsychosis: a study of Tamilian traditions, folklore and philosophy. In BITCM (1970) pt. 1, 1-38.

01494 REAT, N.R. Karma and rebirth in the Upanishads and Buddhism. In Numen 24,3 (1977) 163-85.

01495 TILAK MAHARAJ, Swami. Rebirth. Wadakancheri: Jnana Asram, 1968. 114p.

01496 VEEZHINATHAN, N. The concept of Karma in Jainism and Buddhism. In BITCM (1974) pt. 1, 95-105.

01497 WALLI, K. Theory of karman in Indian thought. Varanasi: Bharata Manisha, 1977. 363p. (Bharata Manisha res. series, 10)

iv. mokṣa and nirvāṇa: liberation from rebirth

01498 CAVE, S. Redemption, Hindu and Christian. London: OUP, 1919. 263p.

01499 ELAYATH, K.N.N. The concept of jīvanmukti. Trivandrum: Academic Pub., 1975. 56p.

01500 GLASENAPP, H. VON. Immortality and salvation in Indian religions. Trans. by E.F.J. Payne. Calcutta: Susil Gupta, [1963]. 112p. [1st German ed. 1938]

01501 LAD, A.K. A comparative study of the concept of liberation in Indian philosophy. Burhanpur: Girdharlal Keshavdas, 1967. 208p.

01502 LA VALLÉE-POUSSIN, LOUIS DE. Nirvāṇa. Paris: G. Beauchesne, 1925. 194p.

01503 MIYAMOTO, S. Freedom, independence, and peace in Buddhism. In PEW 1,4 (1952) 30-40; 2,3 (1952) 208-25.

01504 Moksha and liberation [special issue]. In J. of Dharma 2,1 (1977) 3-98.

01505 RUPP, G. The relationship between nirvāṇa and saṃsāra: an essay on the evolution of Buddhist ethics. In PEW 21,1 (1971) 55-68.

01506 SMART, N. Living liberation: jīvanmukti and nirvāṇa. In E.J. Sharpe & J.R. Hinnels, eds. Man and his salvation.... Manchester: Manchester U. Press, 1973, 281-90.

01507 STCHERBATSKY, TH. The conception of Buddhist nirvana. Rev. & enl. ed. Varanasi: Bharatiya Vidya Prakashan, 1968. 1 v. [1st ed. 1927]

01508 WELBON, G.R. The Buddhist nirvāṇa and its Western interpreters. Chicago: UChiP, 1968. 320p.

d. ethics and values
i. general studies

01509 BHARGAVA, D. Jaina ethics. Delhi: Motilal, 1968. 296p.

01510 BHATTACHARYA, H.S. Jain moral doctrine. Bombay: Jain Sāhitya Vikās Maṇḍala, 1976. 83p.

01511 CHANDAVARKAR, G.A. A manual of Hindu ethics. 3rd rev. ed. Poona: Oriental Book Agency, 1925.

01512 CRAWFORD, S.C. The evolution of Hindu ethical ideals. Calcutta: KLM, 1974. 241p.

01513 DASGUPTA, S. Development of moral philosophy in India. Bombay: Orient Longmans, 1961. 226p.

01514 GUPTA, S.N. The Indian concept of values. ND: Manohar, 1978. 197p.

01515 HIRIYANNA, M. Indian conception of values. Mysore: Kavyalaya, 1975. 372p.

01516 HINDERY, R. Comparative ethics in Hindu and Buddhist traditions. Delhi: Motilal, 1978. 307p.

01517 HOPKINS, E.W. Ethics of India. Port Washington, NY: Kennikat Press, 1968. 265p. [1st pub. 1924]

01518 KING, W.L. In the hope of nibbana; an essay in Theravada Buddhist ethics. La Salle, IL: Open Court, 1964. 298p.

01519 LAW, B.C. The concept of morality in Buddhism and Jainism. In JASBombay 34/35 (1959/60) 1-21.

01520 MAITRA, S.K. The ethics of Hindus. ND: Asian Pub. Services, 1978. 344p. [Rpt. 1925 ed.]

01521 SADDHATISSA, H. Buddhist ethics; essence of Buddhism. London: Allen & Unwin, 1970. 202p.

01522 SHARMA, I.C. Ethical philosophies of India. Ed. & rev. by S.M. Daugert. London: Allen & Unwin, 1965. 374p.

01523 SOGANI, K.C. Ethical doctrines in Jainism. Sholapur: Lalchand Hirachand Doshi, 1967. 302p. (Jīvarāja Jaina granthamālā, 19)

01524 TACHIBANA, S. The ethics of Buddhism. London: Curzon Press, 1975. 288p. [rpt. 1926 ed.]

ii. the nature of man and the meaning of human life

01525 DANDEKAR, R.N. Man in Hindu thought: a broad outline. In ABORI 43 (1962) 1-57.

01526 DE SMET, R.V. Early trends in the Indian understanding of man. In PEW 22,3 (1972) 259-68.

01527 HORNER, I.B. The early Buddhist theory of man perfected. London: Williams & Norgate, 1936. 162p.

01528 LEVY, J. The nature of man according to the Vedanta. London: Routledge & K. Paul, 1956. 101p.

01529 RADHAKRISHNAN, S., ed. The concept of man: a study in comparative philosophy. 2nd ed. London: Allen & Unwin, 1966. 546p.

01530 RAJU, P.T. The concept of man in Indian thought. In S. Radhakrishnan & P.T. Raju, eds. The concept of man; a study in comparative philosophy. London: Allen & Unwin, 1960, 206-305.

01531 REGAMEY, C. Menschseins-ideale in der orientalischen Kulturen: Indien. As. St. 13 (1960) 55-81.

01532 ROSS, F.H. The meaning of life in Hinduism and Buddhism. London: Routledge & K. Paul, 1952. 162p.

01533 SMITH, B.L. Toward a Buddhist anthropology: the problems of the secular. In JAAR 36,3 (1968) 203-16.

01534 WHITE, D. Human perfection in the Bhagavadgītā. In PEW 21,1 (1971) 43-54.

iii. the concept of dharma/dhamma: Hindu and Buddhist concepts of duty and moral order

01535 BROWN, W.N. Duty as truth in ancient India. In PAPS 116,3 (1972) 252-268. [rpt. in his India and Indology. Delhi: Motilal, 1978, 102-19.]

01536 CARTER, J.R. Dhamma as a religious concept: a brief investigation of its history in the Western academic tradition and its centrality within the Sinhalese Theravāda tradition. In JAAR 44,4 (1976) 661-674.

01537 CONZE, E. Dharma as a spiritual, social and cosmic force. In P. Kunz, ed. The concept of order. Seattle: UWashP, 1967. 239-252.

01538 CREEL, A.B. Dharma in Hindu ethics. Calcutta: KLM, 1977. 178p.

01539 GOKHALE, B.G. Dharma as a political concept in early Buddhism. In JIH 46 (1968) 249-61.

01540 HACKER, P. Dharma im Hinduismus. In his Kleine Schriften. Wiesbaden: Franz Steiner, 1978, 496-509. [1st pub. ZMR 49 (1965) 93-106]

01541 ______. Der Dharmabegriff des Neuhinduismus. In his Kleine Schriften. Wiesbaden: Franz Steiner, 1978, 510-25. [1st pub. in ZMR 42 (1958) 1-15]

01542 HAZRA, R.C. Dharma according to Kautilya. In OH 11,2 (1963) 59-100.

01543 KOLLER, J.M. Dharma: an expression of universal order. In PEW 22,2 (1972) 131-44.

01544 KUPPUSWAMY, B. Dharma and society: a study in social values. Delhi: Macmillan, 1977. 211p.

01545 LARSON, G.J. The trimurti of dharma in Indian thought: paradox or contradiction. In PEW 22,2 (1972) 145-53.

01546 O'FLAHERTY, W.D. & J.D.M. DERRETT, eds. The concept of duty in South Asia. ND: Vikas, 1977. 240p.

01547 STERNBACH, L. Bibliography on dharma and artha in ancient and mediaeval India. Wiesbaden: Harrassowitz, 1973. 152p.

iv. the problem of evil

01548 BOYD, J.W. Satan and Māra: Christian and Buddhist symbols of evil. Leiden: Brill, 1975. 188p. (SHR, 27)

01549 HERMAN, A.L. The problem of evil and Indian thought. Delhi: Motilal, 1976. 329p.

01550 LING, T.O. Buddhism and the mythology of evil: a study in Theravāda Buddhism. London: Allen & Unwin, 1962. 179p.

01551 MUDGAL, S.G. Evil in the systems of Indian philosophy. In Indian philosophy and culture 15 (1970) 39-47.

01552 NAYAK, G.C. Evil, karma, and reincarnation. Santiniketan: Centre of Advanced Study in Philosophy, Visva-Bharati, 1973. 176p.

01553 O'FLAHERTY, W.D. The origins of evil in Hindu mythology. Berkeley: UCalP, 1976. 411p.

01554 Suffering and evil. [special issue] In J. of Dharma 2,3 (1977) 245-338.

v. ahiṃsā: the philosophy of nonviolence

01555 DWIVEDI, R.C., ed. Contribution of Jainism to Indian culture. ND: Motilal, 1975. 306p. [with special reference to non-violence; 1973 seminar papers.]

01556 KOTHARI, V.P. The law of non-violence (ahiṃsā) and its relevance for all times. Ed. by D.H. Bishop. Sholapur: Jaina Samskrti Samrakshaka Sangha, 1975. 73p. (Jīvarāja Jaina granthamala, 26)

01557 KOTTURAN, G. Ahimsa: Gautama to Gandhi. ND: Sterling, 1973. 228p.

01558 SANDHU, S.S. Nonviolence in Indian religious thought and political action. Philadelphia: Dorrance, 1977. 130p.

01559 SCHMIDT, H.-P. The origin of ahiṃsā. In Mélanges d'Indianisme à la mémoire de Louis Renou. Paris: E. de Boccard, 1968, 625-656.

01560 SUTANTAR SINGH. Nonviolence and the Sikhs. Delhi: Rachna, 1975. 78p.

01561 TAHTINEN, U. Ahiṃsā: non-violence in the Indian tradition. London: Rider, 1976. 148p.

01562 WALLI, K. The conception of ahiṃsā in Indian thought, according to Sanskrit sources. Varanasi: Bharata Manisha, 1974. 48 + 219p. (Bharata Manisha res. series, 3)

vi. sanctity of the cow

01563 ALSDORF, L. Beiträge zur Geschichte von Vegetarismus und Rinderverehrung in Indien. Wiesbaden: Steiner, 1962. 69p. (AGSW, 6)

01564 BENNETT, J.W. On the cultural ecology of Indian cattle. CA 8,2 (1967) 251-52.

01565 BROWN, W.N. The sanctity of the cow in Hinduism. In JMU 28 (1957) 29-41. [also in EW 16 (1964) 245-55; also in his India and Indology.... Delhi: Motilal, 1978, 90-101]

01566 CROOKE, W. The veneration of the cow in India. In Folklore (L) 23 (1912) 275-306.

01567 DANDEKAR, V.M. India's sacred cattle and cultural ecology. EPW 4 (1969) 1559-67.

01568 FREED, S.A. & R.S. FREED. Cattle in a north Indian village. In Ethnology 11 (Oct. 1972) 349-408.

01569 GUBERNATIS, A. DE. The worship of the bull and the cow in India, and the Brāhmanic legends relating to it. In his Zoological mythology, or the legends of animals. Detroit: Singing Tree Press, 1968, 41-90.

01570 HARRIS, M. The cultural ecology of India's sacred cattle. In CA 7,1 (1966) 51-60.

01571 HESTON, A.W. An approach to the sacred cow of India. In CA 12,2 (1971) 191-209.

01572 MARGUL, T. Present-day worship of the cow in India. In Numen 15,1 (1968) 63-80.

01573 RAJ, K.N. India's sacred cattle: theories and empirical findings. In EPW 6,13 (1971) 717-22.

01574 ROY, P. The sacred cow in India. In Rural Sociology 20 (Mar. 1955) 8-15.

01575 SHARMA, M.L. The myth of the sacred cow. In J. of Popular Culture 2 (1968) 457-467.

B. Mythology, Symbolism, and Iconography of the Indic Religions: Hinduism, Buddhism, and Jainism

1. Comparative Studies and Common Themes
a. general studies of Indic myths and symbols

01576 BHATTACHARYA, A. The sun and the serpent lore of Bengal. Calcutta: KLM, 1977. 288p.

01577 BOSCH, F.D.K. The golden germ; an introduction to Indian symbolism. The Hague: Mouton, 1960. 264p. (Indo-Iranian monographs, 2)

01578 BOSCH, F.D.K. Rémarques sur les influences reciproques de l'iconographie et de la mythologie indiennes. In ArtsAs 3 (1956) 22-47.

01579 BROWN, W.N. Mythology of India. In S.N. Kramer, ed. Mythologies of the ancient world. Garden City, NY: Doubleday, 1961, 277-330.

01580 IONS, V. Indian mythology. London: Hamlyn, 1967. 141p.

01581 KIRFEL, W. Symbolik des Buddhismus. Stuttgart: Hiersemann, 1959. 128p. (Symbolik der Religionen, 5)

01582 ______. Symbolik des Hinduismus und des Jinismus. Stuttgart: Hiersemann, 1959. 167p. (Symbolik der Religionen, 4)

01583 NOBLE, M.E. & A.K. COOMARASWAMY. Myths of the Hindus and Buddhists. NY: Henry Holt, 1914. 399p.

01584 THOMAS, P. Epics, myths and legends of India: a comprehensive survey of the sacred lore of the Hindus, Buddhists and Jains. 12th ed. Bombay: Taraporevala, 1961. 134p.

01585 VITSAXIS, B. Hindu epics, myths, and legends in popular illustrations. Delhi: OUP, 1977. 98p.

01586 WAYMAN, A. Climactic times in Indian mythology and religion. In HR 4 (1965) 295-318.

01587 ZIMMER, H.R. Myths and symbols in Indian art and civilization. Ed. by J. Campbell. Princeton: PUP, 1972. 248p. (Bollingen series, 6)

b. general studies of Indic iconography

01588 AUBOYER, J. Moudra et hāsta ou la langage par signes. In OA 3 (1950-51) 153-61.

01589 BANERJEA, J.N. The development of Hindu iconography. 2d ed. Calcutta: U. of Calcutta, 1956. 653p. + 48pl.

01590 BHATTASALI, N.K. Iconography of Buddhist and Brahmanical sculptures in the Dacca Museum. Dacca: Rai S.N. Bhadra Bahadur, 1929. 274p.

01591 COOMARASWAMY, A.K. Indian images with many arms. In his The dance of Śiva, fourteen Indian essays. NY: Sunwise Turn, 1924, 67-71.

01592 DETMOLD, G. & M. RUBEL. The gods and goddesses in Nepal: a traveller's guide to the Hindu and Buddhist deities in the Kathmandu valley of Nepal, with a comrehensive glossary to aid in their identification. Kathmandu: Ratna Pustak Bhandar, 1979. 129p.

01593 GOPINATHA RAO, T.A. Elements of Hindu iconography. 2nd ed. NY: Paragon Book Reprint Corp., 1968. 2 v. in 4. [Rpt. 1914-16 ed.]

01594 ______. Talamana: or, Iconometry, being a concise account of the measurements of Hindu images as given in the Agamas and other authoritative works: with illustrative drawings. ND: IndBK, 1977. 115p. [Rpt. 1920 ed.] (ASI memoir, 3)

01595 JOUVEAU-DUBREUIL, G. Iconography of southern India. Tr. by A.C. Martin. Varanasi: Bharatiya, 1978. 135p. [Rpt. 1937 ed.]

01596 KOOIJ, K.R. VAN. Religion in Nepal. Leiden: Brill, 1978. 33p. + 24 l. of pl. (Iconography of religions, 13, 15)

01597 LIEBERT, G. Iconographic dictionary of the Indian religions: Hinduism-Buddhism-Jainism. Leiden: Brill, 1976. 377p.

01598 PARANAVITANA, S. The god of Adam's Peak. In ArtAs, suppl. 18 (1958). 77p. [on Saman=Yama]

01600 RAU, H. Multiple arms in Indian God-images. In ALB 39 (1975) 275-93.

01601 RUBEL, M. The gods of Nepal; an introduction to the deities of Hinduism and Buddhism, with a glossary to aid in their identification. 2d ed. Kathmandu: Bhimratna Harsharatna, 1968. 52p.

01602 SAHAI, B. Iconography of minor Hindu and Buddhist deities. ND: Abhinav, 1975. 295p.

01603 SINGH, S.B. Brahmanical icons in northern India: a study of images of five principal deities from earliest times to circa 1200 A.D. ND: Sagar, 1977. 226p.

01604 SIVARAMAMURTI, C. Geographical and chronological factors in Indian iconography. In AI 6 (1950) 21-63 + 28pl.

01605 SMITH, H.D. Hindu 'deśika' figures; some notes on a minor iconographic tradition. In Religion 8,1 (1978) 40-67.

01606 TAIMNI, I.K. An introduction to Hindu symbolism. Madras: Theosophical Pub. House, 1965. 118p.

c. sexual metaphors and symbolism

01607 KIRK, J.A. Sport of the gods: religion and sexuality in India. In Iliff Review, 35 (1978) 41-53.

01608 MACY, J. The dialectics of desire. In Numen 22,2 (1975) 145-60.

01609 MASSON, J.L. Sex & yoga: psychoanalysis & the Indian religious experience. In JIP 2, 3/4 (1974) 307-20.

01610 O'FLAHERTY, W.D. Women, androgynes, and other mythical beasts. Chicago: UChiP, 1980. 382p.

d. specific symbols
i. serpents (nāgas), elephants, and other animals and birds

01611 BANERJEE, P. Naga cult in ancient India. In IAC 15,4 (1966) 297-314.

10612 BHATTACHARYA, A.K. The Indian national bird in art & literature. In Cultural Forum 6,2 (1964) 111-19.

01613 CHHABRA, B.C. Elephant in Indian art. In JIH 60,3 (1963) 485-9.

01614 GORAKSHKAR, S., ed. Animal in Indian art: catalogue of the exhibition held at the Prince of Wales Museum of Western India, Bombay from 30 September to 21 October, 1977. Bombay: Prince of Wales Museum of Western India, 1979. 75p. + 22pl.

01615 IYER, K.B. Animals in Indian sculpture. Bombay: Taraporevala, 1977. 91p. + 28pl.

01616 KRISHAN, Y. The Naga cult in Indian art and literature. In OA 13 (1967) 180-92.

01617 MAJUPURIA, T.C. Sacred and symbolic animals of Nepal: animals in the art, culture, myths, and legends of the Hindus and Buddhists. Kathmandu: Sahayogi Prakashan, 1977. 214p. + 9pl.

01618 MUKHERJEE, A.K. Peacock, our national bird. ND: PDMIB, 1979. 48p.

01619 NAIR, P.T. Peacock worship in India. In AFS 33,2 (1974) 93-170.

01620 NILAKANTA. The elephant lore of the Hindus; the elephant-sport (maṭanga līlā) of Nīlakaṇṭha. Tr. by F. Edgerton. New Haven: YUP, 1931. 129p.

01621 SEMEKA-PANKRATOV, E. A semiotic approach to the polysemy of the symbol nāga in Indian mythology. In Semiotica 26,1-3 (1979) 237-90.

01622 SEN, A. Animal motifs in ancient Indian art. Calcutta: KLM, 1972. 138p.

01623 SINHA, B.C. Serpent worship in ancient India. ND: Books Today, 1979. 103p. + 26pl.

01624 SUKUMARA BARAKATHA. Hastividyārṇava. Ed. by P.C. Choudhury. Gauhati: Pub. Board, Assam, 1976. 266p. [English & Assamese]

01625 THANKAPPAN NAIR, P. The peacock, the national bird of India. Calcutta: KLM, 1977. 340p.

01626 VOGEL, F.P. The goose in Indian literature and art. Leiden: Brill, 1962. 74p.

01627 ______. Indian serpent-lore: or, The nagas in Hindu legend and art. Varanasi: Prithivi Prakashan, 1972. 318p. + 30pl. [Rpt. 1926 ed.]

ii. trees and other plants

01628 BÉNISTI, M. Le Médaillon lotiforme dans la sculpture indienne du IIIe siècle avant J.-C. au VIIe siècle après J.-C. Paris: Klincksieck, 1952. 43p. + 26pl.

01629 BISWAS, T.K. & P.K. DEBNATH. Aśoka (saraca indica Linn) - a cultural and scientific evaluation. In IJHS 7,2 (1972) 99-114.

01630 COOMARASWAMY, A.K. The inverted tree. In QJMS 29 (1938) 111-49.

01631 GUPTA, S.L. Sacred plants in Hindu religion. In ICQ 21,3 (1964) 2-10; 22 (1965) 6-19.

01632 ______. Sacred trees in Hinduism: mango. In ICQ 22,3 (1965) 81-88.

01633 GUPTA, S.M. Plant myths and traditions in India. Leiden: Brill, 1970. 117p.

01634 KRISHAN, Y. Symbolism of the lotus-seat in Indian art. In AO 12 (1966) 36-48 + pl.

01635 MAJUPURIA, T.C. & I. MAJUPURIA. Sacred and useful plants & trees of Nepal: in religion, myths, mythologies & medicines of Hindus & Buddhists. Kathmandu: Sahayogi Prakashan, 1978. 199p. + 13pl.

01636 MITRA, R. & L.D. KAPOOR. Kamala - the national flower of India - its ancient history and uses in Indian medicine. In IJHS 11,2 (1976) 125-32.

01637 RANDHAWA, M.S. The cult of trees and tree-worship in Buddhist-Hindu sculpture. ND: All India Fine Arts & Crafts Soc., 1964. 66p.

01638 SAHAY, K.N. Tree-cult in tribal culture. In Folklore (C) 5 (1964) 241-57.

01639 SEN GUPTA, S., ed. Tree symbol worship in India; a new survey of a pattern of folk-religion. Calcutta: Indian Pub., 1965. 170p. (Indian folklore series, 5)

01640 SINHA, B.C. Tree worship in ancient India. ND: Books Today, 1979. 103p. + 23pl. (Worship in India series, 1)

01641 VIENNOT, O. Le culte de l'arbre dans l'Inde ancienne, textes et monuments brahmaniques et bouddhiques. Paris: PUF, 1954. 289p.

iii. the cakra (wheel)

01642 AGRAWALA, V.S. Wheel flag of India; chakradhvaja. Varanasi: Prithivi Prakashan, 1964. 104p.

01643 AUBOYER, J. Quelques réflexions à propos du cakra, arme offensive. In ArtsAs 11,1 (1965) 119-30.

01644 KARUNARATNE, T.B. Buddhist wheel symbolism. Kandy: BPS, 1969. 34p.

01645 ______. Le symbole bouddhique de la roue. In Samadhi 6,1 (1972) 31-45; 6,3 (1972) 120-34.

01646 PRZLYUSKI, J. The solar wheel of Sārnāth and in Buddhist monuments. In JISOA 4,1 (1936) 45-51.

iv. other symbols

01647 BHARATI, A. Symbolik der Berührung in der hinduistisch-buddhistischen Vorstellungswelt. In Studium Generale 17 (1964) 609-620.

01648 DEB, H.K. The Svastika and the Oṃkāra. In JASBengal ns 17 (1921) 31-247.

01649 FREED, S.A. & R.S. FREED. Origin of the swastika: ceremonies in India have shed new light on an ancient symbol. In Natural History 89,1 (1980) 68-75.

01650 GAIROLA, C.K. Évolution du pūrṇa ghaṭa (vase d'abondance) dans l'Inde et l'Inde extérieure. In ArtsAs 1 (1954) 209-26.

01651 HAVELL, E.B. The Himalayas in Indian art. London: J. Murray, 1924. 94p. + 24pl.

01652 MOTI CHANDRA. Nidhiśringa (Cornucopia): a study in symbolism. In PWMB 9 (1964-65) 1-33.

01653 NAUDOU, J. Symbolisme du miroir dans l'Inde. In ArtsAs 13 (1966) 59-82.

01654 ROSU, A. Pūrṇaghaṭa et le symbolisme du lotus dans l'Inde. In ArtsAs 8,3 (1961) 163-94.

2. Buddhist Mythology and Iconography
a. general studies

01655 BANERJI, A. Origins of early Buddhist church art. Calcutta: Sanskrit College, 1967. 58p.

01656 BHATTACHARYYA, D.C. Studies in Buddhist iconography. ND: Manohar, 1978. 115p. + 12pl.

01657 COOMARASWAMY, A.K. Elements of Buddhist iconography. Cambridge: HUP, 1935. 95p. + 15pl.

01658 FOUCHER, A.C.A. Étude sur l'iconographie bouddhique de l'Inde. Paris: E. Leroux, 1900-05. 2 v.

01659 GETTY, A. The gods of northern Buddhism: their history, iconography and progressive evolution through the northern Buddhist countries.... Tokyo: Tuttle, 1962. 220p. [1st ed. 1914]

01660 GOMBRICH, R. Feminine elements in Sinhalese Buddhism. In WZKS 16 (1972) 67-93.

01661 HALDAR, J.R. Early Buddhist mythology. ND: Manohar, 1977. 221p.

01662 ______. Links between early and later Buddhist mythology. Calcutta: Centre of Advanced Study, Dept. of Ancient Indian Hist. & Cult., U. of Calcutta, 1972. 45p.

01663 SAUNDERS, E.D. Symbolic gestures in Buddhism. In ArtAs 21 (1958) 47-68.

b. the Buddha image

01664 AGRAWALA, V.S. Origin of the Buddha image. In Śatabda-Kaumudī; centenary volume. Nagpur: Central Museum, 1964, v. 1, 29-35.

01665 COOMARASWAMY, A.K. The Buddha's cūḍā, hair, uṣṇīṣa and crown. In JRAS (1928) 815-41 + 5pl.

01666 ______. The origins of the Buddha image. ND: Munshiram, 1972. 42p. + 73figs. [1st pub. in Art Bull. 9,4 (1927) 287-317]

01667 ______. Uṣṇīṣa and chatra: turban and umbrella. In PO 3 (1938) 1-19.

01668 DEVENDRA, D.T. The Buddha image and Ceylon. Kandy: K.G.V. DeSilva, 1957. 92p. + 29pl.

01669 FOUCHER, A.C.A. On the iconography of the Buddha's nativity. Tr. by H. Hargreaves. Delhi: MP, 1934. 27p. (ASI memoir, 46)

01670 ______. L'origine grecque de l'image du Bouddha. In Annales du Musée Guimet 38 (1912) 231-72.

01671 GANGOLY, O.C. The antiquity of the Buddha-image; the cult of the Buddha. Calcutta: Bani, 1965. 21p.

01672 KRISHAN, Y. The hair on the Buddha's head and Usnisa. In E&W 16 (1966) 275-89.

01673 ______. The origin of the crowned Buddha image. In E&W 21,2/3 (1971) 91-96.

01674 PANDEY, D.B. The Dharmachakrapravartana in literature and art. ND: Oriental, 1978. 78p. + 39pl.

01675 ROWLAND, B. The evolution of the Buddha image. NY: Asia Soc., 1963. 146p.

01676 SINHA, D.K. The absence of the Buddha image in the pre-Kushan period. In IHQ 39,1/2 (1963) 69-79. [also in JGJRI 20/21 (1963-65) 97-110]

01667 SNELLGROVE, D.L. The image of the Buddha. NY: Kodansha, 1978. 482p.

01678 SUNASINGHE, S. A contribution to the development of the Buddha image. In CJHSS 3 (1960) 59-71.

c. the stūpa

01679 BAREAU, A. & M. BÉNISTI. La construction et le culte du stūpa d'après les Vinayapiṭaka. In BEFEO 50,2 (1960) 229-74.

01680 ______. Étude sur le stūpa dans l'Inde ancienne. In BEFEO 50,1 (1960) 37-116.

01681 COMBAZ, G. L'évolution du stūpa en Asie. In Mélanges Chinois et Bouddhiques, 2-3-4 (1933-5) 165-305, 93-114, 1-125.

01682 GOVINDA, A. Quelques aspects du symbolisme des stūpa. In Samadhi 8,3/4 (1974) 154-72.

01683 ______. Some aspects of stūpa symbolism. London: Kitabistan, 1940. 126p.

01684 MUS, P. Barabudur; esquisse d'une histoire du bouddhisme fondée sur la critique archéologique des textes. NY: Arno Press, 1978. 802p. [Rpt. 1935 ed.]

01685 ______. Barabudur; les origines du stūpa et la transmigration, essai d'archéologie religieuse comparée. In BEFEO 32 (1932) 269-439; 33 (1933) 578-980; 34 (1934) 175-400.

01686 PARANAVITANA, SENARAT. The stupa in Ceylon. Colombo: Archaeol. Dept., 1946. 152p.

3. Jaina Mythology and Iconography
a. general studies

01687 BHATTACHARYYA, A.K. Jaina iconography. In Arts and Letters 34 (1960) 9-16.

01688 BHATTACHARYA, B.C. The Jaina iconography. 2nd rev. ed. Delhi: Motilal, 1974. 171p. [1st pub. 1939]

01689 BURGESS, J. Digambara Jaina iconography. Ed. by R.P. Hingorani. Varanasi: Ashutosh Prakashan Sansthan, 1979. 61p. [1st pub. in IA 32 (1903)]

01690 JHA, S. Aspects of Brahmanical influence on the Jaina mythology. Delhi: Bharat-Bharati, 1978. 296p.

01691 JAIN, J. & E. FISCHER. Jaina iconography. Leiden: Brill, 1978. 2 v., 79p. + 94pl. (Iconography of religions, 13:12,13)

01692 SŪTRADHĀRAMAṆḌANA. Jaina iconography in Rupamandana of Sūtradhāra Srī Maṇḍana, son of Kṣetra of Medapaṭa: text of sixth chapter.... Tr. by R.P. Hingorani. Varanasi: Kishor Vidya Niketan, 1978. 46p.

b. images of Mahāvīra and other Tīrthaṅkaras

01693 COOMARASWAMY, A.K. "The Conqueror's Life" in Jaina painting. In JISOA 3 (1935) 129-44.

01694 NAWAB, S.M., ed. The life of Lord Shri Mahavira as represented in the Kalpasutra paintings. 168 paintings.... Ahmedabad: Nawab, 1978. 96p. + 34pl.

01695 TIWARI, M.N.P. A note on some Bahubali images from North India. In E&W 23,3/4 (1973) 347-53.

4. Hindu Theism: Images of God and the Gods in Myth and Art
a. general studies of the Hindu pantheon

01696 BARNETT, L.D. Hindu gods and heroes: studies in the history of the religion of India. Delhi: Ess Ess, 1977. 120p. [Rpt. 1922 ed.]

01697 BHATTACHARJI, S. The Indian theogony; a comparative study of Indian mythology from the Vedas to the Puranas. London: CamUP, 1970. 396p.

01698 DANDEKAR, R.N. God in Hindu thought. In ABORI 48/49 (1968) 433-65.

01699 DANIÉLOU, A. Hindu polytheism. NY: Pantheon, 1964. 537p. (Bollingen series, 73) [French version pub. 1960]

01700 DEFOURNY, M. Le mythe de Yayāti dans la littérature épique et purānique: étude de mythologie hindoue. Paris: Les Belles Lettres, 1978. 189p.

01701 GONDA, J. The Hindu trinity. In Anthropos, 63/64 (1968-69) 212-26.

01702 GUPTA, S.M. From daityas to devatā in Hindu mythology. Bombay: Somaiya, 1973. 115p. + 56pl.

01703 KINSLEY, D.R. The sword and the flute: Kālī and Kṛṣṇa, dark visions of the terrible and the sublime in Hindu mythology. Berkeley: UCalP, 1975. 167p.

01704 NARAYAN, R.K. Gods, demons, and others. NY: Viking Press, 1967. 241p.

01705 O'FLAHERTY, W.D., tr. & ed. Hindu myths: a sourcebook. Baltimore: Penguin, 1975. 358p.

01706 ROBERTS, J.M. & CHIEN CHIAO & TRILOKI N. PANDEY. Meaningful god sets from a Chinese personal pantheon and a Hindu personal pantheon. In Ethnology 14,2 (1975) 121-49.

01707 SAMPURNANAND. Evolution of the Hindu pantheon. Bombay: BVB, 1963. 102p.

01708 SHARMA, B.N. Iconography of Revanta. ND: Abhinav, 1975. 86p. + 18pl.

01709 SOMPURA, P.O. Album of Hindu iconography. Ahmedabad: The Late Sri Balwantrai Prabhashankar Sompura, 1976. 127p. [Hindi & English]

01710 VAN BUITENEN, J.A.B. & C. DIMMITT, tr. & eds. Classical Hindu mythology: a reader in the Sanskrit Purāṇas. Philadelphia: Temple U. Press, 1978. 373p.

b. Devī and the Mātṛkās: the female principle and the Mother Goddess

i. general studies

01711 BHATTACHARYA, N.N. The Indian Mother Goddess. 2nd rev. & enl. ed. ND: Manohar, 1977. 319p. [1st pub. in ISPP 11,4 (1970) 327-98; 12,1 (1970) 65-124.]

01712 BRUBAKER, R.L. The ambivalent mistress: a study of South Indian village goddesses and their religious meaning. Unpub. Ph.D. diss., U. of Chicago, 1978. 403p.

01713 CROOKE, W. The cults of the mother goddesses in India. In Folklore (L) 30 (1919) 282-308.

01714 DAS, S.K. Śakti, or divine power. Calcutta: U. of Calcutta, 1924. 298p.

01715 DIKSHIT, S.K. The mother goddess: a study regarding the origin of Hinduism. ND: S.K. Dikshit, n.d. 280p.

01716 DURDIN-ROBERTSON, L. The goddesses of India, Tibet, China and Japan. Clonegal, Ireland: Cesara, 1976. 532p. [p. 1-221 on India]

01717 FANE, H. The female element in Indian culture. In AFS 34 (1975) 51-112.

01718 GROSS, R.M. Hindu female deities as a resource for the contemporary rediscovery of the goddess. In JAAR 46 (1978) 269-92.

01719 HARPER, K. An iconological study on the origins and development of the Sāptamātṛkās. Unpub. Ph.D. diss., UCLA, 1977. 293p. [UM 77-30,914]

01720 KOOIJ, K.R. VAN. Worship of the goddess according to the Kālikāpurāṇa. Leiden: Brill, 1972-. v. 1-. (ORT, 14)

01721 KOSAMBI, D.D. At the crossroads: a study of mother-goddess cult sites. In his Myth and reality. Bombay: Popular, 1962, 82-109. [1st pub. in JRAS (1960) 17-31, 135-44.]

01722 KRAMRISCH, S. The Indian great goddess. In HR 14,4 (1975) 235-65.

01723 MOTI CHANDRA. Studies in the cult of the Mother Goddess in ancient India. In PWMB 12 (1973) 1-47.

01724 SRIVASTAVA, M.C.P. Mother goddess in Indian art, archaeology & literature. Delhi: Agam, 1979. 231p. + 12 pl.

ii. studies of specific goddesses

01725 AGRAWALA, R.C. Mātṛkā reliefs in early Indian art. In E&W 21,1-2 (1971) 79-90.

01726 CHANDRA, P. The cult of Śrī Lakshmī & four carved discs. In Anand Krishna, ed. Chhavi.... Banaras: BHU, 1971, 139-148.

01727 COOMARASWAMY, A.K. Early Indian iconography, II, Sri-Laksmi. In Eastern Art 1,3 (1929) 174-89.

01728 DASH, M.P. Worship of Sāpta Mātṛkās and their representation in Orissan temples. In OHRJ 11,2 (1962) 114-23.

01729 DHAL, U.N. Goddess Laksmi: origin and development. ND: Oriental, 1978. 229p.

01730 FREED, R.S. & S.A. FREED. Two mother goddess ceremonies of Delhi State in the great and little traditions. In SWJA 18 (1962) 246-77.

01731 KINSLEY, D. Freedom from death in the worship of Kālī. In Numen 22,3 (1975) 183-207.

01732 MISRA, B. Śītalā: the small-pox goddess of India. In AFS 28,2 (1969) 133-42.

01733 NOBLE, M.E. [Sister NIVEDITA]. Kali the mother. Almora: Advaita Ashrama, 1950. 114p. [1st pub. 1900]

01734 SARKAR, D.C. Foreigners in ancient India and Lakṣmī and Sarasvatī in art and literature. Calcutta: U. of Calcutta, 1970. 192p.

01735 SHULMAN, D. The murderous bride: Tamil versions of the myth of Devī and the buffalo-demon. In HR 16,2 (1976) 120-46.

01736 SOUNDARA RAJAN, K.V. & R.T. PARIKH. A magnificent Sāptamātrikā group and Pārvatī from Vadaval, North Gujarat. In PWMB 7 (1959-62) 46-54.

01737 SPINK, W. Jogeśvarī: a brief analysis. In JISOA, Moti Chandra Comm. Issue (1978), 1-35.

01738 SRIVASTAVA, B. Iconography of Śakti: a study based on Śrītattvanidhi. 1st ed. Varanasi: Chaukhambha Orientalia, 1978. 173p. + 8pl. (CORS, 9)

c. Śiva Mahādeva, "the great god": mythology and iconography

i. general

01739 ADICEAM, M.E. Les images de Śiva dans l'Inde du Sud. In ArtsAs 11 (1964) 23-44; 12 (1965) 83-112; 13 (1966) 83-99; 17 (1968) 143-72; 19 (1969) 85-106. [series begun by J. Filliozat, 01743]

01740 AGRAWALA, V.S. Śiva Mahadeva, the great God: an exposition of the symbolism of Śiva. Benares: Veda Academy, 1966. 66p.

01741 DESSIGANE, R. & P.Z. PATTABIRAMIN & J. FILLIOZAT. Les légendes çivaïtes de Kāñcīpuram; analyse de textes et iconographie. Pondichéry: IFI, 1964. 152p. & 99pl. (Its Pub., 27)

01742 ______. La légende des jeux de Çiva a Madurai, d'après les textes et les peintures. Pondichéry: IFI, 1960. 127p. (Its Pub., 19)

01743 FILLIOZAT, J. Les images de Śiva dans l'Inde du Sud. In ArtsAs 8 (1961) 43-56. [series cont. by M.E. Adiceam, 01739]

01744 GOSWAMI, N. A study of the ūgra-mūrtis of Śiva. Ph.D. diss., U. of Pennsylvania, 1972. 403p. [UM 73-13,406]

01745 O'FLAHERTY, W.D. Asceticism & eroticism in the mythology of Śiva. London: OUP, 1973. 386p.

01746 ______. The symbolism of the third eye of Śiva in the Purāṇas. In Purana 11 (1969) 273-84.

01747 SHARMA, B.N. Iconography of Sadasiva. ND: Abhinav, 1976. 82p.

ii. Śiva Naṭarāja, "Lord of the Dance"

01748 BONER, A. Zur Komposition des Śiva Naṭarāja im Museum Rietberg. In ArtAs 27,4 (1965) 301-10.

01749 COOMARASWAMY, A.K. The dance of Siva. NY: Farrar Straus, 1957. 119p. [Rpt. 1918 ed.; essays]

01750 GOSWAMI, O. The birth of Shiva: the dancing God. In Sangeet Kala Vihar, English supp. 1,4 (1970) 21-36.

01751 SIVARAMAMURTI, C. Nataraja in art, thought, and literature. ND: Natl. Museum, dist. by PDMIB, 1974. 417p.

01752 SOMASUNDARAM PILLAI, J.M. Siva-Nataraja, the cosmic dancer in Chidambaram. J.M. Annamalainagar: J.M. Somasundaram Pillai, 1970. 99p.

01753 SRIVIVASAN, P.R. The Nataraja concept in Tamilnad art. In RL 27, (1956) 24-35; 27,2 (1956) 4-11.

iii. histories of the cult of Śiva

01754 BHATTACARYA, B. Saivism and the phallic world. ND: Oxford & IBH, 1975. 2 v., 1048p.

01755 JASH, P. History of Śaivism. Calcutta: Roy and Chaudhury, 1974. 205p.

01756 MILES, A. The land of the lingam. London: Hurst & Blackett, 1933. 288p.

01757 SIDDHANTASHASTREE, R.K. Śaivism through the ages. ND: Munshiram, 1975. 188p.

01758 ZIESENISS, A. Studien zur Geschichte des Śivaismus. ND: IAIC, 1958-. (Śatapiṭaka, 7) [v.2, Śaiva-Systematik des Vṛhaspatitattva, 192p.]

d. Viṣṇu, "pervading" preserver of the universe
i. general mythology and iconography

01759 BEGLEY, W.E. Vishnu's flaming wheel: the iconography of the sudarśana-cakra. NY: NYU Press, 1973. 103p. + 80pl.

01760 BIDYABINOD, B.B. Varieties of the Vishnu image. ND: Indological Book Corp., 1977. (ASI memoirs, 2) [Rpt. 1920 ed.]

01761 CHANDA, R. Archaeology and Vaishnava tradition. ND: Indological Book Corp., 1977. 173p. (ASI memoirs, 5) [Rpt. 1920 ed.]

01762 DESAI, K.S. Iconography of Viṣṇu (in northern India, up to the mediaeval period). ND: Abhinav, 1973. 159p.

01763 KAKATI, B.K. Vishnuite myths and legends in folklore setting. Gauhati: Sri Tarini Das, 1952. 140p.

01764 MACHEK, V. Origin of the god Viṣṇu. In Archiv Orientalni 28 (1960) 103-26.

01765 PAL, P. Vaisnava iconology in Nepal: a study in art and religion with 110 illustrations. Calcutta: Asiatic Soc., 1970. 186p.

01766 SMITH, H.D., ed. Vaiṣṇava iconography. Madras: Pāñcarātrā Pariśodhana Pariṣad, 1969. 306p. [Sanskrit text with intro. and notes in English.]

ii. avatāra, "descent" of God: the theory of divine incarnation

01767 AGARWAL, U. Worship of Viṣṇu: his incarnations in India in the medieval period. In OA 16,3 (1970) 252-58.

01768 DAS, B. Kṛṣhṇa: a study in the theory of Avatāras. Adyar, Madras: TPH, 1924. 112p.

01769 GUPTA, S.M. Vishnu and his incarnations. Bombay: Somaiya, 1974. 68p. + 26pl.

01770 HACKER, P. Zur Entwicklung der Avatāralehre. In his Kleine Schriften. Wiesbaden: Steiner, 1978. 404-28. [1st pub. in WZKS 4 (1960) 47-70.]

01771 PANDEY, R.K. The concept of avatārs: with special reference to Gita. Delhi: B.R., 1979. 92p.

01772 PARRINDER, E.G. Avatār and incarnation: the Wilde lectures in natural and comparative religion in the University of Oxford. London: Faber, 1970. 296p. [NY: Barnes & Noble]

01773 SOIFER, D. Toward an understanding of Vishnu's avatāras. In Purāṇa 18,2 (1976) 128-48.

iii. Kṛṣṇa, the last and most prominent avatāra of Viṣṇu

01774 AGRAWALA, R.C. Kṛṣṇa and Balarāma in Rajasthana sculptures and epigraphs. In IHQ 30 (1954) 339-53.

01775 ARCHER, W.G. The loves of Krishna in Indian painting & poetry. London: Allen & Unwin, 1957. 127p.

01776 BANERJEE, P. The life of Krishna in Indian art. ND: Natl. Museum, dist. PDMIB, 1978. 348p.

01777 BHATTACHARYA, S.K. Kṛṣṇa-cult. ND: Associated, 1978. 231p.

01778 CHAKRAVARTI, A.C. The story of Kṛṣṇa in Indian literature. Calcutta: Indian Associated Pub. Co, 1976. 146p.

01779 FRITH, N. The legend of Krishna. London: Sheldon Press, 1975. 238p.

01780 JOSHI, N.P. Iconography of Balarāma. ND: Abhinav, 1979. 125p. + 19pl.

01781 JOSHI, R.V. Le rituel de la dévotion Kṛṣṇaite. Pondichéry: IFI, 1959. 142p.

01782 KINSLEY, D.R. "Through the looking glass:" divine madness in the Hindu religious tradition. In HR 13,4 (1974) 270-305.

01783 ______. The divine player; a study of Kṛṣṇa-līlā. Ph.D. diss., U. of Chicago, 1970. 423p.

01784 LAL, K. The religion of love. Delhi: Arts & Letters, 1971. 102p.

01785 MAJUMDAR, B. Kṛṣṇa in history and legend. Calcutta: U. of Calcutta, 1969. 307p.

01786 MASSON, J.L. The childhood of Kṛṣṇa: some psychoanalytic observations. In JAOS 94,4 (1974) 454-459.

01787 MUNSHI, K.M. Krishnavatara. Bombay: Bharatiya Vidya Bhavan, 1962-71. 6 v.

01788 SHARMA, U.M. The immortal cowherd and the saintly carrier: an essay in the study of cults. In SB 19 (1970) 137-51.

01789 SINGER, M.B., ed. Krishna; myths, rites and attitudes. Honolulu: East-West Center Press, 1966. 277p.

01790 SPINK, W.M. Krishnamandala, a devotional theme in Indian art. Ann Arbor: UMCSSAS, 1971. 133p.

01791 VARMA, M. Lord Krishna: love incarnate. ND: Delhi, Vikas, 1978. 226p.

iv. other avatāras of Viṣṇu

01792 BIARDEAU, M. Narasiṃha, mythe et culte [and] Narasiṃha et ses sanctuaires. In Puruṣārtha 1 (1975) 31-48, 49-66.

01793 DEVI, V.Y. Vāmana Trivikrama. In JIH 43,3 (1965) 833-53.

01794 GAIL, A.J. Parasurāma, Brahmane und Krieger; Untersuchen über Ursprung und Entwicklung eines Avatāra Viṣṇu und Bhakta Śivas in der indischen Literatur. Wiesbaden: Harrasowitz, 1977. 252p.

01795 ______. Viṣṇu als Eber in Mythos und Bild. In Beiträge zur Indienforschung.... Berlin: Museum für indische Kunst, 1977, 127-68. (Its Veröffentlichungen, 4)

01796 GUPTA, S. Viśvakṣena, the divine protector. In WZKS 20 (1976) 75-89.

01797 MUNSHI, K.M. Bhagawan Parashurama. 2nd rev. ed. Bombay: BVB, 1965. 509p.

01798 SHARMA, B.N. Viṣṇu-Trivikrama in literature, art, and epigrams. In E&W 18 (1968) 323-34.

01799 SINGH, T. The origin of the concept of Matsyavatāra. In JBRS 51 (1965) 19-28.

01800 SWAIN, A.C. A study of the man-lion myth. In IA, 3rd ser. 5,1 (1971) 38-54.

01801 TRIPATHI, G.C. Der Ursprung und die Entwicklung der Vāmana-Legende in der indischen Literatur. Wiesbaden: Harrasowitz, 1968. 253p.

v. Hanumān, monkey-chief and ally of Rāma

01802 ARYAN, K.C. & S. ARYAN. Hanuman in art and mythology. Delhi: Rekha, 1975. 187p.

01803 WOLCOTT, L.T. Hanuman: the power-dispensing monkey in North Indian folk religion. In JAS 37,4 (1978) 653-62.

e. Brahmā, the creator; and Dattātreya, the "trinity" of Brahmā, Viṣṇu, and Śiva

01804 BHATTACHARYYA, T. The cult of Brahmā. 2d ed., rev. and enl. Varanasi, CSSO, 1969. 318p. (CSS, 70)

01805 DAVE, S.K. The cult of Brahmā - a brief review. In Purana 19 (1977) 342-346.

01806 JOSHI, H.S. Origin and development of Dattātreya worship in India. Baroda: MSUB, 1965. 225p.

f. Gaṇeśa, Vināyaka, or Gaṇapati ("lord of the minor spirits"), elephant-headed son of Śiva and Pārvatī

01807 AGRAWALA, P.K. Some Varanasi images of Ganapati and their iconographic problem. In ArtAs 39,2 (1977) 139-155.

01808 ARAVAMUTHAN, T.G. Gaṇesa: Clue to a cult and a culture. In JORM 18 (1949) 221-45.

01809 DHAVALIKAR, M.K. A note on two Gaṇesa statues from Afghanistan. In E&W 21,3/4 (1971) 331-336.

01810 GETTY, A. Gaṇesa; a monograph on the elephant-faced God. Oxford: OUP, 1936. 103p. + 40pl.

01811 NAVARATNAM, R. Aum Gaṇesa: the peace of god. Jaffna: Vidya Bhavan, 1978. 270p.

01812 RIVIERE, J.R. The problem of Gaṇesa in the Purāṇas. In Purāṇa 4 (1962) 96-102.

01813 SHARMA, B.N. Iconography of Vaināyakī. ND: Abhinav, 1979. 92p. + 17pl.

01814 SHARMA, B.R. Gaṇapati and his most sacred places for pilgrimage in India. In Bhavan's J. 22,3 (1975) 17-27.

01815 SRIVASTAVA, V.C. Historiography of Gaṇesa-cult in ancient India. In K.C. Chattopadhyaya Memorial Volume. Allahabad: Dept. of Ancient Hist, Culture & Archaeol., Allahabad U., 1975, 137-57.

01816 VERNEUIL DE MARVAL, A. Gaṇesha ou Gaṇapati: son histoire d'après les sculptures des temples hindous. Neuchatel: Ides et Calendes, 1975. 43p.

g. Kārttikeya, six-headed son of Śiva and Pārvatī; also called Skanda, Subrahmanya, Murugan in S. India

01817 AGRAWALA, P.K. Skanda in the purāṇas and classical literature. In Purāṇa 8,1 (1966) 135-58.

01818 BECHERT, H. Eine alte Gottheit in Ceylon und Südindien. In WZKS 12/13 (1968-69) 33-42.

01819 CHATTERJEE, A.K. The cult of Skanda-Kārttikeya in ancient India. Calcutta: Punthi Pustak, 1970. 167p.

01820 DESSIGANE, R. & P.S. PATTABIRAMIN. La légende de Skanda; selon le Kandapurāṇam tamoul et l'iconographie. Pondicherry: Inst. Francais d'Indologie, 1967. 288p. (Publications de IFI, 31)

01821 L'HERNAULT, F. L'iconographie de Subrahmaṇya au Tamilnad. Pondichery: IFI, 1978. 272p. + 61pl.

01822 NAVARATNA, R. Kārttikeya, the divine child: the Hindu testament of wisdom. Bombay: BVB, 1973. 271p.

01823 SHULMAN, D.D. Murukaṉ, the mango and Ekāmbareśvara-Śiva: fragments of a Tamil creation myth? In IIJ 21,1 (1979) 27-40.

01824 SINHA, K. Kārttikeya in Indian art and literature. Delhi: Sundeep, 1979. 175p. + 14pl.

01825 SIVANANDA, Swami. Lord Shanmukha and his worship. Rev. and enl. Sivanandanagar: Divine Life Soc., 1970. 32 + 140p.

h. Sūrya (the sun), moon, and astral deities

01826 GUPTA, S.M. Surya; the sun god. Bombay: Somaiya, 1977. 71p. + 36pl.

01827 KAYE, G.R. Hindu astronomical deities. In JASBengal ns 16,1 (1920) 57-75.

01828 MITRA, DEBALA. A study of some graha-images of India and their possible bearing on the Nava-Devas of Cambodia. In JASBengal, 4th ser. 7,1/2 (1965) 13-37.

01829 PAL, P. & D.C. BHATTACHARYYA. The astral divinities of Nepal. Varanasi: Prithivi Prakashan, 1969. 82p.

01830 PANDEY, L.P. Sun-worship in ancient India. Delhi: Motilal, 1971. 368p.

01831 RAGHAVAN, V. Worship of the sun. In Purana 12 (1970) 205-30.

01832 SHAH, U.P. Some Surya images from Saurashtra, Gujerat and Rajasthan. In Baroda Museum and Picture Gallery, Bulletin, 19 (1966) 37-53.

01833 SRIVASTAVA, V.C. The Puranic records on the sun-worship. In Purana 11 (1969) 229-72.

01834 ______. Sun-worship in ancient India. Allahabad: Indological Pub., 1972. 463p. + 30pl.

01835 STIETENCRON, H.VON. Indische Sonnenpriester. Sāmba und die Śākadvīpīya-Brāhmaṇa: eine textkritische und religionsgeschichtliche Studie zum indischen Sonnenkult. Wiebaden: Harrassowitz, 1966. 287p. (SSI, 3)

01836 VARENNE, J. La lune, mythe et rites dans l'Inde. In La lune, mythes et rites. Paris: Éditions du seuil, 1962, 233-260.

j. Gaṅgā and Yamunā, deified rivers

01837 DARIAN, S. Gaṅgā and Sarasvatī; an incidence of mythological projection. In E&W ns 26,1/2 (1976) 153-66.

01838 ______. The Ganges in myth and history. Honolulu: UPH, 1978. 219p.

01839 GLYNN, C. Some reflections on the origins of the type of Gaṅgā image. In JISOA ns 5 (1972-73) 16-27.

01840 SIVANANDA, Swami. Mother Ganges. Sivanandanagar: Divine Life Society, 1962. 89p.

01841 SIVARAMAMURTI, C. Gaṅgā. ND: Orient Longmans, 1976. 99p.

01842 STIETENCRON, H. VON. Gangā und Yamunā; zur symbolischen Bedeutung der Flussgöttinnen an indischen Tempeln. Wiesbaden: Harrassowitz, 1972. 162p. (FBI, 5)

01843 VIENNOT, O. Les divinités fluviales Gangā et Yamunā aux portes des sanctuaires de l'Inde; essai d'évolution d'un thème decoratif. Paris: PUF, 1964. 212p.

01844 VOGEL, J.P. Gangā et Yamunā dans l'iconographie Brahmanique. In Études asiatiques.... Paris: G. Van Oest, 1925, v. 2, 385-402.

k. yakṣas and other genii and demons

01845 AGARWALA, V.S. Yakshas and Nagas in Indian folk-art tradition. In Folklore (C) 7,1 (1966) 1-9.

01846 BARUA, P.R. The Yakṣa belief in early Buddhism. In JASPak 10,1 (1965) 1-13.

01847 COOMARASWAMY, A.K. Yakṣas. ND: Munshiram, 1971. 127p. + 73 p. of ill. [1st pub. 1928-31]

01848 FILLIOZAT, J. Étude de démonologie indienne. Le Kumāratantra de Rāvaṇa et les textes parallèles indiens, tibétains, chinois, cambodgien, et arabe. Paris: Imprimerie nationale, 1937. 192p. (Cahiers de Soc. Asiatique 1st ser., 4)

01849 MOTI CHANDRA. Some aspects of Yaksha cult in ancient India. In PWMB 3 (1952-53) 43-62.

01850 VARENNE, J. Anges, démons et génies dans l'Inde. In Génies, anges et démons. Paris: Éditions du Seuil, 1971, 259-293. (Sources orientales, 8)

1. folk deities of South India: Aiyannār, Śāstā, Ayyappan, and others

01851 ADICEAM, M.E. Contribution à l'étude d'Aiyanār-śāstā. Pondicherry: IFI, 1967. 128p. + 25pl.

01852 DUMONT, L. A structural definition of a folk deity of Tamil Nad: Aiyanār the Lord. In CIS 3 (1959) 75-87.

01853 ELMORE, W.T. Dravidian gods in modern Hinduism; a study of the local and village deities of southern India. Lincoln: U. of Nebraska, 1915. 149p.

01854 HORNELL, J. The ancient village gods of south India. In Antiquity 18 (1944) 78-87.

01855 PYYAPPAN. Lord Ayyappan: the dharma sasta. 2nd ed. Bombay: BVB, 1966. 53p.

01856 SRINIVAS, M.N. A brief note on Ayyappa, the south Indian deity. In K.M. Kapadia, ed. Professor Ghurye felicitation volume. Bombay: Popular, 1955, 238-43.

01857 THOMAS, P.T. Sabarimalai and its Sastha: an essay on the Ayyappa movement. Madras: CLS, for CISRS, 1973. 62p.

01858 WHITEHEAD, H. The village gods of South India. NY: Garland, 1980. 175p. [Rpt. 2nd ed., 1921]

01859 ZIEGENBALG, B. Genealogy of the South Indian gods. Tr. from German by G.F. Metzger. Madras: Higginbotham, 1869. 208p.

C. Religious Practice in the Indic Religions: Hinduism, Buddhism, and Jainism

1. Religion and Society; Sociology and Anthropology of Religion; Legitimation of Power

01860 BECHERT, H. Einige fragen der religionssoziologie und struktur des Südasiatischen Buddhismus. In Intl. Yearbook for the Sociology of Religion 4 (1968) 251-95.

01861 BHARATI, A. A functional analysis of Indian thought and its social margins. Varanasi: CSSO, 1964. 175p. (CSS, 37)

01862 DUMONT, L. & D.F. POCOCK. On the different aspects or levels in Hinduism. In CIS 3 (1959) 40-54.

01863 GHURYE, G.S. Gods and men. Bombay: Popular, 1962. 300p.

01864 GUPTA, K.P. Sociology of Indian tradition and tradition of Indian sociology. In SB 23,1 (1974) 14-43.

01865 HARPER, E.B., ed. Religion in South Asia. Seattle: UWashP, 1964. 199 p. [also in JAS 23 (1964)]

01866 HERTEL, B.R. Church, sect, and congregation in Hinduism: an examination of social structure and religious authority. In JSSR 16,1 (1977) 15-26.

01867 MANDELBAUM, D.G. Religion in India and Ceylon: some new formulations of structure and theme. In EW 16, 5/6/7 (1964) 219-28.

01868 NASH, M., et al. Anthropological studies in Theravada Buddhism. New Haven: Yale U., 1966. 223p.

01869 PFEIFFER, M. Hinduismus des Gegenwart; ein Literaturbericht. In Verkundigung und Forschung 1 (1974) 24-56.

01870 PRESLER, H.H. Patronage for public religious institutions in India. In Numen 20,2 (1973) 116-24.

01871 Religion and politics in medieval south India: papers of a seminar held by the Inst. of Asian Studies and Andhra University. Hyderabad: Inst. of Asian Studies, 1972. 170p.

01872 SINHA, S. Sociology of religion; a trend report. In A survey of research in sociology and social anthropology. Bombay: Popular, 1974, v. 2, 508-30. [Sponsored by ICSSR]

01873 SMITH, B.L., ed. Religion and legitimation of power in Sri Lanka. Chambersburg, PA: ANIMA Books, Conococheague Assoc., 1978. 244p.

01874 ______, ed. Religion and the legitimation of power in South Asia. Leiden: Brill, 1978. 186p.

01875 VIDYARTHI, L.P., ed. Aspects of religion in Indian society. Meerut: Kedar Nath Ram Nath, 1961. 410p.

01876 WEBER, M. The religion of India; the sociology of Hinduism and Buddhism. Tr. & ed. by H.H. Gerth & D. Martindale. Glencoe, IL: Free Press, 1958. 392p. [1st German ed. 1921]

2. Temples and Other Religious Institutions - General Studies

a. temples: their role in economy, society, and culture

01877 APPADURAI, A. & C.A. BRECKENRIDGE. The South Indian temple: authority, honour and retribution. In CIS 10,2 (1976) 189-211.

01878 FÜRER-HAIMENDORF, C. VON. The role of the monastery in Sherpa society. In Ethnologica 2 (1960) 12-28.

01879 HARDY, F. Ideology and cultural contexts of the Srivaisnava temple. In IESHR 14,1 (1977) 119-51.

01880 HIRT, H.F. The Dravidian temple complex: a South Indian cultural dominant. In Bombay Geog. Magazine, 8/9 (1961) 95-103.

01881 INDIA (REP). HINDU RELIGIOUS ENDOWMENTS CMSN. Report; 1960-62. Delhi: Govt. of India Press, 1962. 524p.

01882 MECUNE, E.B. The role of the temple in the social and economic life of India. In BITCM (1960) pt. 1, 5-19.

01883 MAHALINGAM, T.V. Studies in the South Indian temple complex. Dharwar: Kannada Res. Inst., Karnatak U., 1970. 89p.

01884 PILLAY, K.K. The temple as a cultural centre. In JORM 29 (1959-60) 83-94.

01885 RAMACHANDRA RAO, S.K. The Indian temple, its meaning. Bangalore: IBH, 1979. 151p.

01886 The sacred complex in India [special issue]. In JSR 17,1 (1974) 1-137.

01887 VARADACHARI, V.K. V.K. Varadachari's The law of Hindu religious and charitable endowments. 2nd ed., rev. by V.P. Sarathi. Lucknow: Eastern Book Co., 1977. 827p.

01888 VIRASWAMI PATHAR, S. Temple and its significance. Tiruchirapalli: Viraswami Pathar, 1974. 383p.

b. religious orders and institutions: monasteries, maṭhas, āśramas

01889 BARUA, R.B. The Theravāda Sangha. Dacca: ASBangla, 1978. 358p.

01890 DESJARDINS, A. Ashrams. Les yogis et les sages. New ed. Geneve: La Palatine, 1969. 223p.

01891 DEO, S.B. History of Jaina monachism from inscriptions and literature. Poona: Deccan College, 1956. 655p. (Its Diss. series, 6)

01892 DESIKĀCHĀRYA, N. The origin and growth of Śrī Brahmatantra Parakāla Mutt. Bangalore: Bangalore Press, 1949. 407p.

01893 DUTT, S. Buddhist monks and monasteries of India: their history and their contribution to Indian culture. London: Allen & Unwin, 1962. 397p.

01894 FARQUHAR, J.N. The organization of the sannyāsis of the Vedānta. In JRAS (1925) 479-86.

01895 FERGUSON, F.N. Bodily symbolism in Hindu ashrams and the replication of social experience. In W.C. McCormack & S.A. Wurm, eds. Language and thought.... The Hague: Mouton, 1977, 283-95.

01896 GNANAMBAL, K. Religious institutions and caste panchayats in South India. Calcutta: AnthSI, 1976. (Its memoir, 18)

01897 HATTIANGDI, G.S., ed. Fifty years of bliss. Bombay: for Shri Chitrapur Math, Shirali, N.K., 1965. 351p.

01898 MAQUET, J. Expressive space & Theravada values. In Ethnos 6,1 (1975) 1-23.

01899 MARGUL, T. L'āśram hindou contemporain. In Studia Religionznawcze 1 (1969) 173-206.

01900 MILLER, D.M. & D.C. WERTZ. Hindu monastic life: the monks and monasteries of Bhubaneswar. Montreal: McGill-Queen's U. Press, 1976. 228p.

01901 MOFFITT, J. Varieties of contemporary Hindu monasticism. In VK 57 (1970), 91-99, 128-36.

01902 SADANANDA GIRI, Swami. Society and sannysin: a history of the Dasnami sannyasins. Rishikesh: Giri, 1976. 109p.

01903 SADLER, A.W. Three types of monastic temple in Hindu India. In Horizons 2 (1975) 1-23.

01904 SARKAR, J.N. A history of Dāsnāmi Nāgā Sanyāsis. Allahabad: Sri Panchayata Akhara Mahanirvani, 1958. 286p.

3. Pilgrimage and Sacred Centers
a. pilgrimage as ritual and communication

01905 ADAMO, P. Le bain dans le Gange; sa signification. In BEFEO 58 (1971) 197-212.

01906 BHARATI, A. Pilgrimage in the Indian tradition. In HR 3 (1963) 135-67.

01907 ______. Pilgrimage sites and Indian civilization. In J.W. Elder, ed. Chapters in Indian civilization. Rev. ed. Dubuque: Kendall, Hunt, 1970, v. 1, 83-126.

01908 BHARDWAJ, S.M. Hindu places of pilgrimage in India; a study in cultural geography. Berkeley: UCalP, 1973. 258p.

01909 GOSWAMY, B.N. The records kept by priests at centres of pilgrimage as a source of social and economic history. In IESHR 3,2 (1966) 174-84.

01910 JACQUES, C. Les pèlerinages en Inde. In Les Pèlerinages. Paris: Éd. du Seuil, 1960, 157-97. (Sources Orientales, 3)

01911 JHA, M. The Hindu pilgrimage and pilgrims. In his Dimensions of Indian civilization. ND: Classical, 1979, 154-72.

01912 NĀRĀYAṆA BHAṬṬA. The sāmānya-praghaṭṭaka of Nārāyaṇa Bhaṭṭa's Tristhalīsetu. Ed. & tr. by R.G. Salomon. Ph.D. diss., U. of Pennsylvania, 1976. 2 v., 901p. [UM 76-12,334]

01913 PRESLER, H.H. What it costs to make a pilgrimage. In ICQ 23,3 (1966) 74-80.

01914 RAMACHANDRIAH, N.S. Pilgrims and pilgrimages in the Kannada land and literature. In JKU (H) 20 (1976) 15-29.

01915 SALOMON, R. Tīrtha-pratyāmnāyāḥ: ranking of Hindu pilgrimage sites in classical Sanskrit texts. In ZDMG 129,1 (1979) 102-28.

01916 STODDARD, R.H. An analysis of the distribution of major Hindu holy sites. In NGJI, 14 (1968) 148-55.

01917 TURNER, V.W. Process, performance, and pilgrimage: a study in comparative symbology. ND: Concept, 1979. 164p. (Ranchi anth. series, 1)

01918 VIDYARTHI, L.P. & M. JHA. Symposium on the sacred complex in India. Ranchi: Council of Social and Cultural Res. & Dept. of Anthropology, Ranchi U., 1974. 137p. [Rpt. of JSR 17,1 (1974)]

01919 WIJAYATILAKE, S.R. Buddhist India: the pilgrim path. Colombo: Colombo Apothecaries, 1969. 75p.

b. general guides and studies of sacred centers throughout the subcontinent

01920 BHATT, B.L. The religious geography of South Asia: some reflections. In NGJI 23, 1/2 (1977) 26-39.

01921 DAVE, F.H. Immortal India. Bombay: BVB, 1959-61. 4 v.

01922 GLASENAPP, H. VON. Heilige Stätten Indiens. Munich: G. Miller, 1928. 183p.

01923 GOSWAMI, B.B. & S.G. MORAB. Comparative study of sacred complexes in India - a working paper. In JSR 13,2 (1970) 95-106.

01924 India's sacred shrines & cities. Madras: Natesan, 1940. 245p.

01925 KANE, P.V. Tīrthayātrā (pilgrimages to holy places). In his History of Dharmaśāstra.... 2d ed. Poona: BORI, 1973, v. 4, 552-827. [Includes descriptive list of tīrthas, p. 723-827]

01926 LAL, K. Holy cities of India. Delhi: Asia Press, 1961. 335p.

01927 Pilgrim centres of India. In Vivekananda Kendra Patrika 3,1 (1974). 408p.

01928 SARASWATI, B. Sacred complexes in Indian cultural traditions. In EA 31,1 (1978) 81-92.

01929 SIRCAR, D.C. The Śākta pīṭhas. Delhi: Motilal, 1973. 132p.

01930 STODDARD, R.H. Hindu holy sites in India. Ph.D. diss., U. of Iowa, 1966. 200p. [UM 67-2684]

01931 THAKUR, U. The holy places of North India as mentioned in the Skanda Purāṇa. In Purāṇa 15,1 (1973) 93-120.

01932 ______. The holy places of South India as depicted in the Skanda Purāṇa. In Purāṇa 19 (1977) 305-320; 20 (1978) 103-120, 246-267.

01933 ______. The holy places of West India as mentioned in the Skanda-Purāṇa. In Purāṇa 18,2 (1976) 162-96.

c. Sri Lanka: Kandy and Kataragama

01934 ALUWIHARE, R. The Kandy Esala Perahera. Colombo: M.D. Gunasena, 1964. 27p.

01935 DASSANAYAKE, M.B. The Kandy Esala perahera; spectacular pageant. Colombo: Lake House Bookshop, 1970. 32p.

01936 GOLOUBEW, V. Le temple de la Dent à Kandy. In BEFEO, 32 (1932) 441-74.

01937 HASSAN, M.C.A. The story of the Kataragama mosque and shrine. Colombo: S.A.M. Thauoos, 1968. 36p. + 3pl.

01938 HAUSHERR, K. Kataragama: Das Heiligtum im Dschungel Südost Ceylons - aus geographischer Sicht. In H. Bechert, ed. Buddhism in Ceylon and studies on religious syncretism in Buddhist countries. Göttingen: Vandenhoeck & Ruprecht, 1978, 234-80.

01939 HOCART, A.M. The temple of the tooth in Kandy. London: Luzac, 1931. 42p. [with plates & plans of this important Buddhist temple]

01940 OBEYESEKERE, G. Social change and the deities: rise of the Kataragama cult in modern Sri Lanka. In Man ns 12 (1975) 377-96.

01941 PFAFFENBERGER, B. The Kataragama pilgrimage: Hindu-Buddhist interaction and its significance in Sri Lanka's polyethnic social system. In JAS 38,2 (1979) 253-270.

01942 SENARATNE, K.M.L.B. Kandy esala maha perahera and its connected ceremonies. Kandy: Bravi, 1974. 38p.

01943 SENEVIRATNE, H.L. Aristocrats and rituals in contemporary Ceylon. In JAAS (L) 11,1/2 (1976) 97-101.

01944 ______. Āsala Perahära in Kandy. In CJHSS 6 (1963) 169-80.

01945 ______. The natural history of a Buddhist liturgy; being a study in the nature and transformation of Kandyan Sinhalese metropolitan ritual. Ph.D. diss., U. of Rochester, 1972. 412p. [UM 73-25,851]

01946 WIRZ, P. Kataragama, the holiest place in Ceylon. With illus. and photos. by the author. Tr. from German by D.B. Pralle. Colombo: LHI, 1966. 57p.

d. South Indian sacred centers
i. general

01947 BALARAM IYER, T.G.S. & T.R. RAJAGOPALAN. South temples: pilgrims' guide: a sketch of the various important temples of South India with a map in addition. 3d ed. Madurai: Sri Karthikeiya Pub., 1979. 104p. [1st pub. 1977]

01948 CLOTHEY, F.W. Pilgrimage centers in the Tamil cultus of Murukan. In JAAR 40,1 (1972) 79-95.

01949 JAGADEESAN, N. Sri Vaishnava sacred centers. In his Homage to a historian. Madurai: Koodal, 1976, 105-40.

01950 MEENA, V. Temples of South India. Kanyakumari: Hari Kumari Arts, 1976. 130p.

01951 PADMANABHAN, S.P. Temples of South India. Nagercoil: Kumaran Pathippagam, 1977. 137p.

01952 RAMA RAO, M. The temples of Kalinga. Tirupati: Sri Venkatesvara U., 1965. 54p. (Its Hist. series, 1)

01953 RAMESAN, N. Temples and legends of Andhra Pradesh. Bombay: BVB, 1962. 179p.

01954 SHULMAN, D.D. Tamil temple myths: sacrifice and divine marriage in the South Indian Saiva tradition. Princeton: PUP, 1980. 471p.

01955 STEIN, B., ed. South Indian temples: an analytical reconsideration. ND: Vikas, 1978. 155p.

ii. Tirupati in Andhra and the Śrī Venkaṭeśwara temple

01956 KRISHNASVAMI AIYANGAR, S. A history of Tirupati. Madras: C. Sambaiya Pantulu, 1940-41. 2 v.

01957 RAMACHANDRAN, S.P. Sree Venkatesa puraana. Madras: Lotus, 1978. 124p.

01958 SITAPATI, P. Sri Venkateswara, the lord of the seven hills, Tirupati. Bombay: BVB, 1968. 209p.

01959 Sreevenkateswara mahatmyam. Ṛajahmundry: Gollapudi Veeraswamy, 1975. 92p.

01960 SRINIVASA RAO, V.N. Tirupati, Sri Venkatesvara-Balaji; origin, significance & history of the shrine. Madras: Umadevan, 1949. 252p.

01961 VIRARAGHAVACHARYA, T.K.T. History of Tirupati: the Thiruvengadam temple. 2d ed. Tirupati: Tirumala-Tirupati Devasthanams, 1976. 3 v. [1st ed. 1962]

iii. Chidambaram in Tamilnadu and the Naṭarāja temple

01962 KULKE, H. Cidambaramāhātmya: eine Untersuchung der religionsgeschichtlichen und historischen Hintergrunde für die Entstenhung der Tradition einer südindischen Tempelstadt. Wiesbaden: Harrassowitz, 1970. 243p. (FBI, 3)

01963 NATARAJAN, B. The city of the cosmic dance: Chidambaram. ND: Orient Longmans, 1974. 164p. + 8pl. (Southern art series, 2)

01964 RAMAKRISHNA AIYER, V.G. The economy of a South Indian temple. Annamalainagar: Annamalai U., 1946. 168p.

01965 SATYAMURTI, T. The Nataraja Temple: history, art, and architecture. ND: Classical, 1978. 64p. + 7pl.

iv. Madurai and the temple of Mīnākṣī

01966 PALANIAPPAN, K. The great temple of Madurai = English version of the book Koilmanagar. Madurai: Sri Meenakshisundareswarar Temple Renovation Cmtee., 1963. 141p. + 18pl. [Rpt. 1970]

01967 SHENOY, J.P.L. Madura, the temple city. 2d ed. Madras: P.L. Shenoy, 1955. 95p.

01968 THIAGARAJAN, K. Meenakshi Temple, Madurai. Madurai: Meenakshi Sundareswarar Temple Renovation Cmtee., 1965. 119p.

v. Kāñchīpuram, and the temple of Varadārāja

01969 RAMAN, K. VENKATA. Śrī Varadārājaswāmi temple; a study of its history, art and architecture. ND: Abhinav, 1975. 206p. + 12pl.

01970 SRINIVASAN, C.R. Kanchipuram through the ages. Delhi: Agam, 1979. 326p.

01971 VARADA TATACHARYA, R. The Temple of Lord Varadaraja, Kanchi: a critical survey of Dr. K.V. Raman's Sri Varadarajaswami Temple, Kanchi. Kanchi: Sri Tatadesika Tiruvamsastar Sabha, 1978. 206p. + 11pl.

vi. other South Indian sacred centers

01972 BURGESS, J. The ritual of the temple of Rameshvaram. In IA 12 (1883) 315-26.

01973 HARI RAO, V.N. History of the Srirangam Temple. Tirupati: Sri Venkateswara U., 1976. 261p.

01974 ______., tr. Kōil Oḻugu, the chronicle of the Śrī Raṅgam Temple. Madras: Rouchouse, 1961. 168p.

01975 INDIA (REP.) CENSUS OF INDIA, 1961. Temples of Madras State. Madras: 1965-69. [v. 9, pt. 11-D., 7 v.]

01976 INDUCHUDAN, V.T. The golden tower: a historical study of the Tirukkulasekharapuram and other temples. Trichur: Cochin Devaswom Board, 1971. 296p.

01977 ______. The secret chamber; a historical, anthropological & philosophical study of the Kodungallur Temple. Trichur: Cochin Devaswom Board, 1969. 323p.

01978 KALIYANAM, G. Guide and history of Sri Andal Temple, Srivilliputtur. Srivilliputtur: Sri Nachiar Devasthanam, 1971. 72p. + 13pl.

01979 NĀRĀYAṆABHAṬṬAPĀDA. Narayaneeyam. Tr. from Sanskrit by R. Varmha. Cochin: Rama Varmha Thampuran, 1978. 150p. [Kṛṣṇa at Guruvāyur]

01980 PADMANABHAN, S. The forgotten history of the Land's End. Nagercoil: Kumaran Pattippagam, 1971. 92p. [On Kaṇyakumari - Cape Comorin]

01981 PILLAI, K.K. The Sucīndram temple. Adyar: Kalakshetra Pub., 1953. 519p.

01982 RAMALINGESWARA RAO, T. A profile of Kalady (Sankara's birth place in picturesque Kerala). Madras: V. Ramaswamy Sastrulu, 1969. 51p.

01983 ______. Sringeri revisited. Madras: the author, 1968. 76p.

01984 SOMALAY. Palani, the hill temple of Muruga. Palani: Arulmigu Dhandayuthapani Swamy Temple, 1975. 80p.

01985 SUNDARAM, K. The Simhachalam Temple. Simhachalam: Simhachalam Devasthanam, 1969. 295p.

01986 UDAYALINGA RAO, S. Holy Srisailam: all about Srisailam. Kurnool: Balasaraswathi Book Depot, 1973. 63p. + 10pl.

01987 VAIDYANATHAN, K.R. Pilgrimage to Sabari. Bombay: BVB, 1978. 148p. + 10pl.

01988 ______. Sri Krishna, the Lord of Guruvayur. 2nd ed. Bombay: BVR, 1977. 175p. [1st ed. 1974]

01989 VANAMAMALAI PILLAI, N. The Setu and Rameswaram. Rameswaram: V. Narayanan, 1929. 197p.

01990 VENKATARAMAN, K.R., ed. Kālady: birth place of Śrī Śaṅkara. Parli: P.S. Narayanan, for Sri Sankara Seva Samiti, 1966. 232p.

01991 ______. Śaṁkara and his Śāradā Pīṭha in Śriṅgeri; a study in growth and integration. Calcutta: Kalpa Printers and Publ., 1969. 64p.

01992 ______. The throne of transcendental wisdom: Sri Śaṁkarācārya's Śāradā Pīṭha in Sringeri. Tiruchirapalli: Trichinopoly United Printers, 1959. 175p.

e. Middle Indian sacred centers
i. Paṇḍharpur and the cult of Viṭhobā in Maharashtra; Nāśik on the Godāvarī

01993 ACHARYA, HEMLATA. Changing role of religious specialists in Nasik - a pilgrim city. In M.S.A. Rao, Urban sociology in India. ND: Orient Longmans, 1974, 401-417.

01994 ______. Nasik: a socio-cultural study. In JAnthSB ns 14,1 (1969) 51-65.

01995 DELEURY, G.A. The cult of Viṭhobā. Poona: DCPRI, 1960. 224p.

01996 ______. Renaître en Inde. Paris: Stock, 1976. 333p.

01997 KARVE, I. On the road: a Maharashtrian pilgrimage. In JAS 22 (1962) 13-29.

01998 KESHAVADAS, Swami. Lord Pāṇḍuranga and his minstrels. Bombay: BVB, 1977. 188p.

01999 MATE, M.S. Temples and legends of Maharashtra. Bombay: BVB, 1962.

02000 UPADHYAYA, BALDEV. Vārakarī: the foremost Vaiṣṇava sect of Mahārāṣṭra. In IHQ 15 (1939) 265-77.

02001 VAUDEVILLE, C. Paṇḍharpur, the city of saints. In H.M. Buck & G.E. Yocum, eds. Structural approaches to South Indian studies. Chambersburg, PA: Wilson Books, 1974, 137-161.

ii. Dwārkā and Somnāth in Gujarat

02002 DESAI, S.H. Dwarka. 2nd ed. Junagadh: Sorath Res. Soc., 1977. 60p.

02003 ______. Prabhas and Somnath. 2nd ed. Junagadh: Sorath Res. Soc., 1975. 108p.

02004 DHAKY, M.A. & H.P. SHASTRI. The riddle of the temple of Somanātha. Varanasi: Bharata Manisha, 1974. 49p.

02005 MUNSHI, K.M. Somanatha, the shrine eternal. 4th ed. Bombay: BVB, 1976. 186p. [1st ed. 1951]

02006 SANKALIA, H.D. Antiquity of modern Dwarka, or Dwarka in literature and archaeology. In JASBombay ns 38 (1963) 74-84.

02007 ______. Dwarka in literature and archaeology. In SPP 11,2 (1971) 14-30.

02008 UPADHYAY, V.S. The sacred geography of Dwarka. In JSR 17,1 (1974) 52-74.

iii. Rajasthan's sacred centers

02009 BINFORD, M.R. Mixing in the color of Rām of Rānujā: a folk pilgrimage to the grave of a Rajput hero-saint. In B.L. Smith, ed. Hinduism.... Leiden: Brill, 1976, 120-142.

02010 GUPTA, D.P. Mount Abu - the Olympus of Rajasthan. 4th ed. Ajmer: Sasta Sahitya Press, 1960. 108p. + 3pl.

02011 JAIN, K.C. Holy places: Brahmanical places. In his Ancient cities and towns of Rajasthan. Delhi: Motilal, 1972, 394-415.

02012 JINDEL, R. Culture of a sacred town: a sociological study of Nathdwara. Bombay: Popular, 1976. 233p.

02013 LAL, K. Abu; Ajmer [and Pushkar]. In his Holy cities of India. Delhi: Asia Press, 1961, 66-86, 87-104.

02014 MEHTA, J.S. Abu to Udaipur: celestial Simla to City of Sunrise. Delhi: Motilal, 1970. 197p. + 32pl.

iv. Puri in Orissa, and the cult of Jagannāth

02015 CHAKRABORTI, HARIPADA. The cult of Jagannatha in Indian culture. In U. Thakur & Y.K. Mishra, eds. The heritage of India. Bodh Gaya: L.N. Mishra Comm. Vol. Pub. Cmtee., 1978, 451-58.

02016 DAS, P. A story of the Puri temple. In IAC 10 (1961) 231-40.

02017 DAS, R.K. Legends of Jagannath, Puri. Bhadrak: Pragati Udyog, 1978. 190p.

02018 ESCHMANN, A. & H. KULKE & G.C. TRIPATHI, eds. The cult of Jagannath and the regional tradition of Orissa. ND: Manohar, 1978. 537p.

02019 GEIB, R. Indradyumna-Legende: ein Beitrag zur Geschichte des Jagannātha-Kultes. Wiesbaden: Harrassowitz, 1975. 195p. (FBI, 7)

02020 JHA, M. The beggars of a pilgrim's city: anthropological, sociological, historical and religious aspects of beggars and lepers of Puri. Varanasi: Kishor Vidya Niketan, 1979. 129p.

02021 MAHAPATRA, K. The Jagannatha temples in eastern India. Bhubaneswar: Mahapatra, 1977. 127p.

02122 MISHRA, K.C. The cult of Jagannātha. Calcutta: KLM, 1971. 251p.

02023 MOHAPATRA, G. The land of Viṣṇu: a study on Jagannātha cult. Delhi: B.R., 1979. 508p.

02024 PATNAIK, N. Cultural tradition in Puri: structure and organization of a pilgrim centre. Simla: IIAS, 1977. 97p.

02025 RÖSEL, J. Pilger und Tempelpriester; indische Wallfahrtsorganization, dargestellt am Beispiel der südostindischen Tempelstadt Puri. In IAF 7 (1976) 322-54.

02026 ______. Über die Bedeutung von Tempelstadten für Entstehen und Bestand indischer Regionalreiche - Der Jagannāth-Tempel und das Regionalreich von Orissa. IN IAF 9 (1978) 41-59.

02027 Shree Jagannath Smarika. ND: Sri Neelachala Seva Sangha, 1969. 2 v., 82, 44p. [Articles in English or other languages, commemorating founding of New Delhi Shree Jagannath Temple]

02028 TRIPATHI, G.C. The evolution of the concept of Jagannātha as a deity. In JOIB 25,3/4 (1976) 272-85.

02029 ______. The influence of some philosophical systems on the mode of worship of Kṛṣṇa-Jagannātha. In ZRGG 27,3 (1975) 206-21.

02030 TRIPATHY, P., comp. Shree Jagannath Temple manual. Puri: Shree Jagannath Temple, 1971. 203p.

f. North India: the Ganga Plains and the Āryavarta heartland

i. Kurukshetra, and its sacred region

02031 AGRAWALA, R.C. Kurukshetra in early Sanskrit literature. In JIH 33 (1955) 85-90.

02032 ______. Kurukshetra in later Sanskrit literature. In K.C. Yadav, ed. Haryana: studies in history and culture. Kurukshetra: Kurukshetra U., 1968, 6-41.

02033 MAJUMDAR, R.C. The antiquity and importance of Kurukshetra. In JHS 4 (1972) 1-10.

02034 PHOGAT, S.R. Tirthas of Kurukshetra. In JHS 8 (1976) 14-32.

02035 SHARMA, I. Kurukshetra in medieval times. In JHS 6 (1974) 30-36.

ii. Braj and the Kṛṣṇa centers of Mathurā and Vrindāvan; Naimiṣa/Nimsār in U. P.

02036 GROWSE, F.S. Mathurā: a district memoir. 3rd ed. rev. Ahmedabad: New Order Book Co., 1978. 434p. + 30 pl. [Rpt. 1883 ed.]

02037 ______. The tīrthas of Vrindā-vana and Gokula. In JASBengal 41 (1872) 313-331.

02038 KLOSTERMAIER, K. In the paradise of Krishna: Hindu and Christian seekers. Tr. from German by A. Fonseca. Philadelphia: Westminster, 1971. 118p.

02039 SARASWATI, B. The holy circuit of Nimsar. In JSR 8,2 (1965) 35-49.

iii. Prayāga and the Saṅgam - the confluence of the Gaṅgā and Yamunā at Allahabad

02040 CHATTOPADHYAYA, K. Religious suicide at Prayag. In JUPHS 10 (1937) 65-79.

02041 GODE, P.K. Some evidence from datable sources about the practice of committing religious suicide at the confluence of the Ganges and the Jamna. In N.G. Kalelkar, ed. S.K. De Felicitation Volume. Poona, 1960. 353-356.

02042 KANTAWALA, S.G. Prayāga māhātmya - a study. In Purāṇa 9,1 (1967) 103-120.

iv. Kāśī: capital of Hindudom; the modern Benares / Banāras / Vārāṇasī

02043 CAPE, C.P. Benares, the stronghold of Hinduism. London: C.H. Kelly, 1910. 262p.

02044 DUBE, K.K. Tourism and pilgrimage in Varanasi. In NGJI 14 (1968) 176-85.

02045 ECK, D.L. Kāśī, city and symbol. In Purāṇa 20,2 (1978) 169-92.

02046 HAVELL, E.B. Benares, the sacred city. London: Blackie, 1905. 226p.

02047 MECKING, L. Benares: ein kulturgeographisches Charakterbild. In Geographische Zeitschrift 19 (1913) 20-35, 77-96.

02048 PANDEY, R.B. Varanasi, the heart of Hinduism. Varanasi: Orient Pub., 1969. 150p.

02049 PANDEY, R. Kasi through the ages. Delhi: Sundeep, 1979. 167p.

02050 SARASWATI, B.N. Kashi: myth and reality of a classical cultural tradition. Simla: IIAS, 1975. 81p.

02051 SEN, R. The holy city, Benares. Chittagong: M.R. Sen, 1912. 280p.

02052 SHERRING, M.A. Benares, the sacred city of the Hindus, in ancient and modern times. Delhi: B.R., 1975. 388p.

02053 SINGH, A.N. The economics of a religious city: a case study of Varanasi. In JSR 15,1 (1972) 58-70.

02054 SINHA, S. & B.N. SARASWATI. Ascetics of Kashi: an anthropological exploration. Varanasi: N.K. Bose Mem. Foundation, 1978. 286p.

02055 SUKUL, K.N. Varanasi down the ages. Patna: K.N. Sukul, 1974. 328p.

02056 VIDYARTHI, L.P. & M. JHA & B.N. SARASWATI. The sacred complex of Kashi: a microcosm of Indian civilization. Delhi: Concept, 1979. 319p.

v. Bihar and its sacred centers: Gayā, Buddha Gayā and Rājgīr

02057 BARUA, B.M. Gaya and Buddha-Gaya. Calcutta: Chuckervertty Chatterjee, 1931-34. 2 v., 41 pl.

02058 BARUA, D.K. Buddha Gaya temple: its history. Buddha Gaya: Buddha Gaya Temple Mgmt. Cmtee., 1975. 64p. + 8 pl.

02059 JACQUES, C., tr. Gayā Māhātmya. Pondicherry: IFI, 1962. 432p. [Its pub., 20]

02060 KURAISHI, M.H. A guide to Rajgir. 9th ed. Delhi: MP, 1956. 37p.

02061 ROY CHOUDHURY, P.C. Temples and legends of Bihar. Bombay: BVB, 1965. 189p.

02062 SIRCAR, D.C. Gaya-tirtha. In JIH 32 (1954) 283-289.

02063 STABLEIN, M. Textual and contextual patterns of Tibetan Buddhist pilgrimage in India. In TSB 12 (1978) 7-38.

02064 VIDYARTHI, L.P. The sacred complex in Hindu Gaya. 2nd ed. Delhi: Concept, 1978. 232p. [1st ed. 1961]

02065 ______. Thinking about a sacred city. In EA 13 (1960) 203-215. [Gaya]

g. the Northeast: Ganges Delta and Brahmaputra Valley

02066 BARUA, B.K. & H.V. SREENIVASA MURTHY. Temples and legends of Assam. Bombay: BVB, 1965. 136p.

02067 ROY CHOUDHURY, P.C. Temples and legends of Bengal. Bombay: BVB, 1967. 167p.

h. the Himalayan Rim and the Kashmir area
i. the Indian Himalayas and the Kashmir area

02068 GANHAR, J.N. Jammu, shrines and pilgrimages. ND: Ganhar, 1975. 180p. + 12 pl.

02069 GOSWAMY, K. The Bāthū shrine and the Rajas of Guler: a brief study of a Vaishnava establishment. In JIH 43 (1965) 577-585.

02070 MUHAMMAD, G. Festivals and folklore of Gilgit. In Memoirs, ASBengal 1 (1905) 93-127.

02071 NAUTIYAL, G.P. Call of Badrinath; contains description of Badrinath, Kedarnath, Yamnotri, Gangotri, Kailas-Mansarovar, etc. 4th ed. Badrinath: Shri Badrinath-Kedarnath Temples Cmtee., 1962. 127p.

02072 RAGAM, V.R. Pilgrim's travel guide, the Himalayan region. Guntur: Sri Sita Rama Nama Sankirtana Sangham, 1963. 76p.

02073 SEN, D. In the mountains: inner Himalayan shrines - Badrinath. In IAC 2 (1952) 182-187.

ii. Nepal

02074 JHA, M. Aspects of a great traditional city in Nepal: an anthropological appraisal. Varanasi: Kishor Vidya Niketan, 1978. 188p. [1st pub. 1971 as The sacred complex in Janakpur.]

02075 ROY CHOUDHURY, P.C. Temples and legends of Nepal. 1st ed. Bombay: BVB, 1972. 93p.

02076 UEBACH, H. Das Nepālamāhātmyam des Skandapurāṇam. Legenden um die hinduistischen Heiligtumer Nepals. Munich: W. Fink, 1970. 255p.

02077 WYLIE, T. A Tibetan religious geography of Nepal. Rome: IIMEO, 1970. 66p. (Serie Orientale Roma, 42)

4. Festivals and the Sacred Calendar
a. general studies

02078 AGRAWALA, V.S. Ancient Indian folk cults. Varanasi: Prithivi Prakashan, 1970. 216p.

02079 ANDERSON, M.M. The festivals of Nepal. London: Allen & Unwin, 1971. 288p.

02080 ANDERSON, R.L. & E.M. SOUTHWICK. Festivals and holidays of Nepal. Kathmandu: American Women's Org., 1968. 60p.

02081 BALARATNAM, L.K. South Indian fasts and festivities. In QJMS 34 (1943) 63-73.

02082 BUCK, C.H. Faiths, fairs and festivals of India. ND: Asian Pub. Services, 1977. 262p. [Rpt. 1917 ed.]

02083 Festivals of India. In Vivekananda Kendra Patrika 6,1 (1977) 380p.

02084 FREED, R.S. & S.A. FREED. Calendars, ceremonies and festivals in a north Indian village: necessary calendric information for fieldwork. In SWJA 20,1 (1964) 67-90.

02085 GNANAMBAL, K. Festivals of India. Calcutta: AnthSI, 1969. [Its memoir, 19]

02086 GUPTE, B.A. Hindu holidays and ceremonials. Calcutta: Thacker, Spink, 1919. 285p.

02087 HUART, A. Hindu calendar and festivals. In R. de Smet & J. Neuner, eds. Religious Hinduism. Allahabad: St. Paul Pubs., 1968. 136-144.

02088 INDIA. IMPERIAL RECORD DEPT. An alphabetical list of the feasts and holidays of the Hindus and Muhammadans. Calcutta: 1914. 123p.

02089 INDIA (REP.) CENSUS OF INDIA, 1961. Fairs and festivals....[Pt. 7-B in each state census vol.]

02090 JAGADISA AYYAR, P.V. South-Indian festivities. Madras: Higginbothams, 1921. 202p.

02091 MALURKAR, S.L. Determination of seasons, religious festivals and temples in ancient India. In QJMS 54, 1/2 (1963) 18-29.

02092 MUKERJI, A.C. Hindu fasts and feasts. Allahabad: Indian Press, 1916.

02093 SHARMA, B.N. Festivals of India. ND: Abhinav, 1978. 156p. + 45 pl.

02094 THOMAS, P. Festivals and holidays of India. Bombay: Taraporevala, 1971. 115p.

02095 UNDERHILL, M.M. The Hindu religious year. London: OUP, 1921. 194p.

02096 WELBON, G.R. & G.E. YOCUM, eds. Religious festivals in South India and Sri Lanka. ND: Manohar, 1980. 332p. (Studies in Religion in S. India and Sri Lanka, 1)

b. specific festivals

02097 BHATTACHARYA, T. Gangasagar mela: a pilgrim's guide. Tr. from Bengali by B. Mukhopadhyay. Calcutta: KLM, 1976. 115p.

02098 BISTA, K.B. Tīj ou la fête des femmes. In O&M 9 (1969) 7-18.

02099 BONAZZOLI, G. Prayāga and its Kumbha Melā. In Purāna 19,1 (1977) 81-179.

02100 BOSE, N.K. The spring festival of India. In MI 7 (1927) 111-173. [Also in his Cultural anthropology and other essays. Calcutta: Indian Associated Pub. Co., 1953. 76-135.]

02101 CLOTHEY, F.W. Skanda-Ṣāṣṭi: a festival in Tamil India. In HR 8 (1969) 236-259.

02102 CROOKE, W.J. The Divali, the lamp festival of the Hindus. In Folk-lore (L) 34 (1923) 267-92.

02103 DEEP, D.K. The Nepal festivals: with some articles enquiring into Nepalese arts, religion, and culture. Kathmandu: Ratna Pustak Bhandar, 1978-. v. 1-.

02104 DUMONT, L. La double fête de Madura. In Marco Polo 22 (1956) 35-48.

02105 GARGI, B. Ramlila in Ramnagar. In SN 13 (1967) 27-34.

02106 GODAKUMBURA, C.E. Sinhalese festivals, their symbolism, origins and proceedings. In JRASCB ns 14 (1970) 91-130.

02107 GOVER, C.E. The Pongal festival in Southern India. In JRAS (1871) 91-118.

02108 GULATI, R.K. Pongal: a deeply tradition-oriented festival of the south. In JSR 11,2 (1968) 150-54.

02109 HEIN, N. The Ram Lila. In M.B. Singer, ed. Traditional India: structure and change. Philadelphia: American Folklore Soc., 1959, 279-304. (J. of American Folklore 71, 281)

02110 HELFER, M. Fanfares villageoises au Népal. In O&M 9 (1969) 51-58.

02111 JEST, C. La fête du Janaipurnima à Patan. In O&M 6 (1966) 143-52.

02112 KRASA, M. Kumbha Mela, the greatest pilgrimage in the world. In New Orient 4 (1965) 180-184.

02113 [Kumbha Mela special issue] In ICQ 24,3 (1967) 25-60.

02114 LONG, J.B. Festival of repentance: a study of Mahāśivarātri. In JOIB 12 (1972) 15-38.

02115 MARRIOTT, M. The feast of love. In M. Singer, ed. Krishna: myths, rites, and attitudes. Honolulu: EWCP, 1966, 200-12.

02116 MILLER, D.B. Holi-Dulhendi: licensed rebellion in a North Indian village. In SA 3 (1973) 15-22.

02117 NAIR, P.T. Onam - the national festival of Kerala. In Folklore (C) 9 (1968) 46-55.

02118 ______. Para festival of the Nairs of Kerala. In Folklore (C) 11 (1970) 177-187.

02119 ROY, D.K. & I. DEVI. Kumbha, India's ageless festival. Bombay: BVB, 1955. 204p.

02120 SANGAR, S.P. Hindu festivals as reflected in the literature of Sūr Dās. In JIH 40 (1962) 223-32.

02121 SEN, A.C. The Car festival of India. In IAC 14 (1965) 84-95.

02122 SHASTRI, A.N. Dūrgā-pūjā. In BV 10 (1949) 241-62.

02123 VERMA, S.N., ed. Kulu dussehra: international folk dance festival, 1976, Oct. 2 - Oct. 9. Kulu: Dussehra Festival Cmtee., 1976. 63p.

5. Rites and Ritual; Mantra (Ritual Formulae); Pūjā

02124 ABBOTT, J. The keys of power: a study of Indian ritual and belief. Secaucus, NJ: University Books, 1974. 560p. [Rpt. 1932 ed.]

02125 BHATTACHARYA, N.N. Ancient Indian rituals and their social contents. Delhi: Manohar, 1975. 184p.

02126 CHARPENTIER, J. The meaning and etymology of pūjā. In IA 56 (1927) 93-99, 130-136.

02127 DIEHL, C.G. Instrument and purpose; studies on rites and rituals in South India. Lund: C.W.K. Gleerup, 1956. 394p.

02128 DAS, V. Structure and cognition: aspects of Hindu caste and ritual. Delhi: OUP, 1977. 147p.

02129 GONDA, J. The Indian mantra. In Oriens 16 (1963) 244-97.

02130 MCDERMOTT, A.C.S. Towards a pragmatics of mantra recitation. In JIP 3,3/4 (1975) 283-98.

02131 OSTOR, A. Puja in society: a methodological and analytical essay on an ethnographic category. In EA 31,2 (1978) 119-76.

02132 PADOUX, A. Contributions a l'étude du mantraśāstra. In BEFEO 65,1 (1978) 65-86.

02133 SARAF, S. Hindu ritual idiom: cosmic perspective and basic orientations. In A. Bharati, ed. The realm of the extra-human. The Hague: Mouton, 1976, 151-64.

02134 WAYMAN, A. The significance of mantras, from the Veda down to Buddhist Tantric practice. In ALB 39 (1975) 65-89.

6. Popular Religious Practice; Omens, Sorcery, and Shamanism

02135 AIYAPPAN, A. Deified men and humanized gods: some folk bases of Hindu theology. In K. David, ed. The new wind: changing identities in South Asia. The Hague: Mouton, 1977, 95-104. (WA)

02136 BIJALWAN, C.D. Hindu omens. ND: Sanskriti & Arnold-Heinemann, 1977. 176p.

02137 CROOKE, W. The popular religion and folk-lore of northern India. 2nd ed., rev. Delhi: Munshiram, 1968. 2 v., 294, 358p. [1st ed. 1894]

02138 JACQUES, C. Le monde du sorcier en Inde. In Le monde du sorcier. Paris: Seuil, 1966, 234-280. (Sources orientales, 7)

02139 JONES, R.L. Shamanism in South Asia: a preliminary survey. In HR 7 (1968) 330-47.

02140 O'MALLEY, L.S.S. Popular Hinduism, the religion of the masses. NY: Johnson Rpt. Co., 1970. 246p. [Rpt. 1934 ed.]

02141 OMAN, J.C. Cults, customs, and superstitions of India. Delhi: Vishal, 1972. 336p. [Rpt. 1908 ed.]

D. The Religious Life of the Individual in the Indic Religions

1. Mysticism

02142 DASGUPTA, S.N. Hindu mysticism: six lectures. Chicago: Open Court, 1927. 168p.

02143 MASSON, J.M. The oceanic feeling: the origins of religious sentiment in ancient India. Dordrecht: Reidel, 1980. (Studies of classical India, 3)

02144 MATILAL, B.K. The logical illumination of Indian mysticism: an inaugural lecture delivered before the University of Oxford on 5 May, 1977. Delhi: OUP, 1978. 36p.

02145 MATILAL, B.K. Mysticism and reality: ineffability. In JIP 3,3/4 (1975) 217-52. [With comments by J.H. Hattiangadi: Why is Indian Philosophy Mystical? 253-58.]

02146 OBERHAMMER, G., ed. Tranzendenzerfahrung, Vollzugshorizont des Heils. Das Problem in indischer und christlicher Tradition. Leiden: Brill, 1978. 253p. (Pub. of the De Nobili Res. Library, 5)

02147 OTTO, R. Mysticism East and West: a comparative analysis of the nature of mysticism. Tr. by B.L. Bracey and R.C. Payne. NY: Macmillan, 1932. 262p.

02148 SHASTRI, H.P., tr. Indian mystic verse. 2nd enl. ed. London: Shanti Sadan, 1963. 203p.

02149 SOGANI, K.C. Fundamentals of Jaina mysticism. In VIJ 3,2 (1965) 255-72.

02150 STAAL, J.F. Exploring mysticism: a methodological essay. Berkeley: UCalP, 1975. 230p.

02151 WINSLOW, J.C. The Indian mystic. London: Student Christian Movement, 1926.

02152 ZAEHNER, R.C. Hindu and Muslim mysticism. NY: Schocken, 1969. 234p. [1st pub. 1960]

2. Yoga: Methods of Spiritual Advancement
a. reference

02153 DIGAMBARAJI, Swami & M. SAHAI. Yoga kosa: yoga terms explained with reference to context. Lonavla, Dist. Poona: Kaivalyadhama S.M.Y.M. Samiti, 1972-. v. 1, pt. 1 & 2, 156p. + 37 pl.

02154 RAY, R.K. Encyclopedia of yoga. Varanasi: Prachya Prakashan, 1975. 421p.

02155 WOOD, E. Yoga dictionary. NY: Philosophical Library, 1956. 178p.

b. general studies

02156 CHAUDHURI, H. Drug mysticism and yoga. In Darshana Intl. 9,3 (1969) 22-32.

02157 DANIÉLOU, A. Yoga, the method of re-integration. London: Johnson, 1949. 164p.

02158 DATE, V.H. The yoga of the saints: analysis of spiritual life. 2nd rev. ed. ND: Munshiram, 1974. 252p. [1st ed. 1944]

02159 ELIADE, M. Shamanism and Indian yoga techniques. In P.A. Sorokin, ed. Forms and techniques of altruistic and spiritual growth. Boston: Beacon, 1954, 70-84.

02160 ______. Techniques du Yoga. Paris: Gallimard, 1948. 266p.

02161 ______. Yoga: essai sur les origines de la mystique indienne. Paris: P. Guethner, 1936. 346p.

02162 ______. Yoga: immortality and freedom. Tr. by W. Trask. Princeton: PUP, 1969. 536p.

02163 FEUERSTEIN, G.A. The essence of yoga: a contribution to the psychohistory of Indian civilization. NY: Grove Press, 1974. 224p.

02164 FEUERSTEIN, G. & J. MILLER. A reappraisal of yoga: essays in Indian philosophy. London: Rider & Co., 1971. 176p.

02165 GHOSH, J. A study of yoga. 2nd rev. ed. Delhi: Motilal, 1977. 274p.

02166 JOSHI, K.S. Prāṇāyāma: the science of yogic breathing. Varanasi: Chaukhambha Orientalia, 1977. 160p. (CORS, 7)

02167 VARENNE, J., tr. Upanishads du Yoga. Paris: Gallimard, 1971. 171p.

02168 ______. Yoga and the Hindu tradition. Tr. by D. Coltman. Chicago: UChiP, 1976. 253p.

02169 WERNER, K. Yoga and Indian philosophy. Motilal, 1977. 192p.

02170 WOOD, E. Great systems of Yoga. NY: Citadel Press, 1966. 168p. [1st ed. 1954]

02171 ______. Yoga: an explanation of the practices and philosophy of Indian Yoga.... Baltimore: Penguin, 1968. 271p. [1st pub. 1959]

02172 YOGENDRA, J. & J.C. VAZ, eds. Yoga today. Madras: Macmillan, 1971. 236p.

c. dhyāna ("meditation"): the central practice of yoga

02173 ANTES, P. & B. UHDE. Aufbruch zur Ruhe: Texte und Gedanken über Meditation in Hinduismus, Buddhismus, Islam. Mainz: M. Grünewald, 1974. 155p.

02174 CONZE, E., tr. Buddhist meditation. London: Allen & Unwin, 1956. 183p.

02175 KIYOTA, MINORU, ed. Mahāyāna Buddhist meditation: theory and practice. Honolulu: UPH, 1978. 312p.

02176 Meditation [special issue]. In JD 2,2 (1977) 125-88.

02177 OBERHAMMER, G. Strukturen yogischer Meditation. Untersuchungen zur Spiritualität des Yoga. Wien: OAW, 1977. 244p. (VKSKS, 13)

02178 RAMAKRISHNA VEDANTA CENTRE. Meditation. By monks of the Ramakrishna Vedanta Centre. London: 1972. 161p.

02179 SATPRAKASHANANDA, Swami. Meditation: its process, practice, and culmination. St. Louis: Vedanta Soc., 1976. 264p.

02180 SIDDHESWARANANDA, Swami. La méditation selon le yoga-vedanta. Paris: Adrien-Maisonneuve, 1945. 153p.

d. psychological and scientific evaluations

02181 BEHANAN, K.T. Yoga: A scientific evaluation. NY: Dover, 1960. 270p. [1st ed. 1937]

02182 BROSSE, T. Études instrumentales des techniques du Yoga. (Expérimentation psychosomatique). Paris: ÉFEO, 1963. 130p. (Its Pub., 52)

02183 COSTER, G. Yoga and western psychology; a comparison. London: OUP, 1934. 248p.

02184 INDIA (REP.) CMTEE. ON EVALUATION OF THERAPEUTICAL CLAIMS OF YOGIC PRACTICES. Report. ND: Min. of Educ., 1962. 72p.

02185 JACOBS, H. Western psychotherapy and Hindu-Sadhana. A contribution to comparative studies in psychology and metaphysics. NY: Intl. U. Press, 1961. 231p.

3. Saṅnyāsa: Renunciation of Worldly Goals in order to Attain Mokṣa (Liberation)
a. origin and history of Indian asceticism

02186 BHAGAT, M.G. Ancient Indian asceticism. ND: Munshiram, 1976. 367p.

02187 CAILLAT, C. L'ascetisme chez les Jaina. In Archives de sociologie des religions 9,18 (1964) 45-53.

02188 GHURYE, G.S. Ascetic origins. In SB 1 (1952) 162-84.

02189 OLIVELLE, P. A definition of world renunciation. In WZKS 19 (1975) 75-83.

02190 SKORPEN, E. The philosophy of renunciation East & West. In PEW 21,3 (1971) 283-302.

02191 SKURZAK, L. Indian asceticism in its historical development. In ALB 31-32 (1967-68) 202-210.

02192 SPROCKHOFF, J.F. Saṃnyāsa; Quellenstudien zur Askese in Hinduismus. I. Untersuchen über die Saṃnyāsa-Upaniṣads. Wiesbaden: Steiner, 1976. 384p. (AKM, 42:1)

02193 TIWARI, K.N. Dimensions of renunciation in Advaita Vedanta. Delhi: Motilal, 1977. 156p.

b. the role of asceticism for society and the individual

02194 CANTLIE, A. Aspects of Hindu asceticism. In I. Lewis, ed. Symbols and sentiments. London: Academic Press, 1976, 247-68.

02195 DUMONT, L. World renunciation in Indian religions. In CIS 4 (1960) 33-62.

02196 HOLCK, H.F. Some observations on the motives and purposes of asceticism in ancient India. In AS/EA 23, 1/2 (1969) 45-57.

02197 MASSON, J.M. The psychology of the ascetic. In JAS 35,4 (1976) 611-25.

02198 SINGER, P. Hindu holy men: a study in charisma. Ph.D. diss., Syracuse U., 1961. 469p. [UM 62-3055]

02199 THAPAR, R. Renunciation: the making of a counter-culture? In N. Jagadeesan & S. Jeyapragasam, ed. Homage to a historian. Madurai: Koodal, 1976, sect. 2, 1-50. [Rpt. in her Ancient Indian social history. ND: Orient Longmans, 1978, 63-104]

c. warrior ascetics

02200 FARQUHAR, J. The fighting ascetics of India. In JRLB 9 (1925) 431-52.

02201 GHOSH, J.M. The sannyāsis in Mymensingh. Dacca: Pran Ballav Chakrabarty, 1923. 156p.

02202 LORENZEN, D.N. Warrior ascetics in Indian history. In JAOS 98,1 (1978) 61-75.

02203 ORR, W.G. Armed religious ascetics in Northern India. In JRLB 24 (1940) 81-100.

d. religious suicide

02204 CAILLAT, C. Fasting unto death according to the Jaina tradition. In ActaOr (C) 38 (1977) 43-66.

02205 GANDHI, R.S. Sati as altruistic suicide. In CAS 10 (1977) 141-57.

02206 OLIVELLE, P. Ritual suicide and the rite of renunciation. In WZKS 22 (1978) 19-44.

02207 STIETENCRON, H. VON. Suicide as a religious institution. In HV 27 (1967) 7-24.

02208 TUKOR, T.K. Sallekhanā is not suicide. Ahmedabad: L.D. Inst. of Indology, 1976. 112p.

4. Lives of Ascetics
a. general studies of sannyasis, monks, saints

02209 BALSE, M. Mystics and men of miracles in India. ND: Heritage, 1976. 185p.

02210 BANKEY BEHARI. Sufis, mystics and yogis of India. Bombay: BVB, 1962. 384p.

02211 BRENT, P. Godmen of India. NY: Quadrangle, 1972. 346p.

02212 GHURYE, G.S. Indian sādhus. Bombay: Popular, 1964. 300p. [1st ed. 1953]

02213 KRISHNA MURTHY, R. The saints of the Cauvery delta. ND: Concept, 1979. 136p.

02214 MAHADEVAN, T.M.P., ed. A seminar on saints. Madras: Ganesh, 1960. 455p.

02215 ______. Ten saints of India. 3rd ed. Bombay: BVB, 1971. 147p.

02216 MENEN, A. The mystics. NY: Dial Press, 1974. 239p.

02217 OMAN, J.C. The mystics, ascetics, and saints of India; a study of sadhuism.... Delhi: Vishal, 1972. [1st pub. 1903]

02218 Ramanand to Ram Tirath; lives of the saints of northern India, including the Sikh Gurus. 2nd ed. Madras: Natesan, 1947. 239p.

02219 SINGH, P. Saints and sages of India. ND: New Book Soc., 1948. 152p.

b. biographies and autobiographies of Indian and Western sādhus, saints and mystics

02220 BHARATI, A. The ochre robe. Seattle: UWashP, 1962. 294p. [Autobiog. of a European swami]

02221 ISHERWOOD, C. My guru and his disciple. NY: Farrar, Straus, Giroux, 1980. 338p. [on Swami Prabhavananda]

02222 KRISHNASWAMI AIYAR, R. The saint of Sringeri. Madurai: Sri Ramakrishna Press, 1963. 263p.

02223 LE SAUX, H. [ABHISHIKTANANDA]. Guru and disciple. Tr. from French by H. Sandeman. London: SPCK, 1974. 176p.

02224 MAHADEVAN, T.M.P., ed. The sage of Kanchi. ND: Arnold-Heinemann, 1975. 93p. [on Srī Chandrasekharendra Sarasvatī, Sankarāchārya of Kānchī]

02225 NANAMOLI, Bhikkhu. A thinker's notebook; posthumous papers of a Buddhist monk. Ed. by (Bhikkhu) Nyānaponika. Kandy: The Forest Hermitage, 1972. 254p. [orig. name Osbert Moore]

02226 PUROHIT SWAMI. An Indian monk: his life & adventures. London: MacMillan, 1932. 204p.

02227 RAMA, Swami (1903-72). A bunch of reminiscences. Tr. by R.S. Kelkar. ND: Om Rama-Yoga Sangam, 1972. 214p.

02228 RAMA, Swami (1925-). Living with the Himalayan masters: spiritual experiences of Swami Rama. Ed. by Swami Ajaya. Honesdale, PA: Himalayan Intl. Inst. of Yoga Sciences & Philosophy, 1978. 490p.

02229 SANGHARAKSHITA, Bhikshu. The thousand-petalled lotus: an English Buddhist in India. London: Heinemann, 1976. 318p. [orig. name D.P.E. Lingwood]

02230 SIVAGANACHARYA, Swami. Life and work of an Indian saint; being the autobiography of.... Ed. by G. Krishna Sastri. Mylapore: Vedic Mission, 1912. 129p.

02231 SRI KRISHNA PREM. Initiation into Yoga: an introduction to the spiritual life. Wheaton, IL: Theosophical Pub. House, 1976. 128p. [orig. name Ronald Nixon]

02232 TALEYARKHAN, FEROZA. Sages, saints, and Arunachala Ramana. Madras: Orient Longmans, 1970. 275p.

02233 YOGANANDA, Paramahansa. Autobiography of a yogi. 7th ed. Los Angeles: Self-Realization Fellowship, 1956. 514p. [1st ed. 1946]

V. RELIGIO-PHILOSOPHICAL TRADITIONS FROM OUTSIDE THE SUBCONTINENT: CHRISTIANITY, ISLAM, ZOROASTRIANISM, JUDAISM

A. Christianity in South Asia

1. Bibliography and Reference

02234 BAAGØ, K. Library of Indian Christian theology: a bibliography. Madras: CLS, 1969. 102p.

02235 HAMBYE, E.R. A bibliography on Christianity in India. Serampore?: Church History Assoc. of India, 1976. 183p.

02236 MENACHERY, G., ed. The St. Thomas Christian encyclopaedia of India. Trichur: St. Thomas Christian Encyclopaedia of India, 1973. v. 2, 218p.

2. Surveys and Studies
a. general surveys

02237 BOYD, R.H.S. India and the Latin captivity of the Church; the cultural context of the Gospel. London: CamUP, 1975. 165p.

02238 FIRTH, C.B. An introduction to Indian church history. Madras: CLS, 1961. 278p. (Christian students' library, 23)

02239 GIBBS, M.E. The Anglican Church in India, 1600-1970. Delhi: ISPCK, 1972. 437p.

02240 HOUPERT, J.C. Christianity in India and Ceylon, AD 52-1964. Madras: Good Pastor Depot, 1965. 132p.

02241 KAYE, J.W. Christianity in India: An historical narrative. London: Smith, Elder, 1859. 522p.

00242 MORAES, G.M. A history of Christianity in India. Bombay: Manaktalas, 1964. 320p.

02243 NEILL, S. The story of the Christian church in India and Pakistan. Grand Rapids: W.B. Eerdmans, 1970. 183p.

02244 PERUMALIL, H.C. & E.R. HAMBYE, eds. Christianity in India; a history in ecumenical perspective. Alleppey: Prakasam, 1973. 355p.

02245 SUBRAMANYAM, K.N. The Catholic community in India. Madras: Macmillan, 1970. 146p.

02246 TAYLOR, R.W. Jesus in Indian paintings. Madras: CLS, for CISRS, 1975. 184p. (Confessing the faith in India series, 11)

02247 THOMAS, P. Christians and Christianity in India and Pakistan; a general survey of the progress of Christianity in India from apostolic times to the present day. London: Allen & Unwin, 1954. 260p.

00248 THOMAS, P. Churches in India. Delhi: PDMIB, 1964. 56p.

b. the Syrian Church of Kerala and the St. Thomas Christians

02249 BROWN, L.W. The Indian Christians of St. Thomas. Cambridge: CamUP, 1956. 315p.

02250 DANIEL, D. The Orthodox Church of India. v. 1, history. ND: the author, n.d. 184p.

02251 DELHI ORTHODOX SYRIAN CHURCH SOCIETY. The orthodox Syrian Church, Delhi; souvenir, 1964. 112p.

02252 KEAY, F.E. A history of the Syrian Church in India. 2nd ed. Madras: SPCK in India, 1951. 111p.

02253 MATHEW, C.P. & M.M. THOMAS. The Indian churches of St. Thomas. Delhi: ISPCK, 1967. 168p.

02254 PODIPARA, P.J. The hierarchy of Syro-Malabar Church. Alleppey: Prakasam, 1976. 214p.

02255 VELLIAN, J., ed. The Malabar Church. Rome: Pont. Inst. Orientalium St., 1970. 312p. (Orientalia Christiana Analecta, 186)

02256 VERGHESE, P. Die Syrischen Kirchen in Indien. Stuttgart: Evangelisches Verlagswerk, 1974. 222p.

B. Islam in South Asia

1. Bibliography and Reference

02257 Encyclopaedia of Islam. New ed. Leiden: Brill, 1960-79. 4 v. + Index. [1st ed. 1913-34]

02258 GIBB, H.A.R. & J.H. KRAMERS, eds. Shorter encyclopaedia of Islam. Ithaca: CornellUP, 1953. 671p.

02259 HUGHES, T.P. A dictionary of Islam; being a cyclopaedia of the doctrines, rites, ceremonies and customs, together with the technical and theological terms of the Muhammadan religion. Lahore: Premier, 1965. 750p.

02260 ROTHERMUND, D., ed. Islam in Southern Asia: a survey of current research. Wiesbaden: Steiner, 1975. 126p. (BSAF, 16)

02261 SIDDIQI, I.H. Modern writings on Islam and Muslims in India. Aligarh: Intl. Book Traders, 1974. 112p.

2. Surveys and Studies
a. introductions to Islam as a world religion

02262 ARBERRY, A.J. Revelation and reason in Islam. London: Allen & Unwin, 1957. 122p.

02263 GIBB, H.A.R. Mohammedanism; an historical survey. 2nd ed. London: OUP, 1953. 206p. [1st ed. 1949]

02264 GUILLAUME, A. Islam. 2nd ed., rev. Baltimore: Penguin, 1961. 209p. [1st ed. 1954]

02265 HODGSON, M.G.S. The venture of Islam: conscience and history in a world civilization. Chicago: UChiP, 1974. 3 v.

02266 MAHMUD, S.F. A short history of Islam. Karachi: OUP, 1960. 724p.

02267 RAHMAN, FAZLUR. Islam. 2nd ed. Chicago: UChiP, 1979. 285p. [1st ed. 1966]

b. Islam in South Asia: histories and surveys

02268 AZIZ AHMAD. An intellectual history of Islam in India. Edinburgh: Edinburgh U. Press, 1969. 226p. (Islamic surveys, 7)

02269 ______. Studies in Islamic culture in the Indian environment. Oxford: OUP, 1964. 311p.

02270 HOLLISTER, J.N. The Shi'a of India. 2nd ed. ND: OBRC, 1979. [Rpt. 1953 ed.]

02271 ISHAQ, M. India's contribution to the study of Hadith literature; a survey of the growth and development of Hadith literature in the subcontinent of Pakistan and India from the earliest time down to the nineteenth century; together with the lives and the works of the leading Muhaddithun of the time. Dacca: U. of Dacca, 1955. 270p.

02272 LAWRENCE, B.B. The rose and the rock: mystical and rational elements in the intellectual history of South Asian Islam. Durham: DUPCSSA, 1978. 200p. (Its monograph, 15)

02273 QURESHI, I.H. & S.A.A. RIZVI & J. BURTON-PAGE. The Indian sub-continent. In P.M. Holt & A.K.S. Lampton & B. Lewis, eds. The Cambridge history of Islam. Cambridge: CamUP, 1970. v. 2, 1-120.

02274 TITUS, M.T. Islam in India and Pakistan; a religious history of Islam in India and Pakistan. Calcutta: Y.M.C.A. Pub. House, 1959. 328p. (Heritage of India series)

3. Muslim society in South Asia

02275 IMAM, ZAFAR, ed. Muslims in India. ND: Orient Longmans, 1975. 307p.

02276 JAᶜFAR SHARIF. Islam in India; or, the Qānūn-i-Islām; the customs of the Musalmans of India; comprising a full and exact account of their various rites and ceremonies from the moment of birth to the hour of death. Tr. from Urdu by G.A. Herklots. New ed., rev. by W. Crooke. ND: OBRC, 1972. [1st pub. 1832]

02277 LAL, K.S. Growth of Muslim population in medieval India, A.D. 1000-1800. Delhi: Research, 1973. 272p.

02278 MADAN, T.N., ed. The Muslim communities of South Asia. Delhi: Vikas, 1976. 183p. [1st pub. in CIS, ns 6 (1972)]

02279 MARIKAR, A.I.L. & A.L.M. LAFIR & A.H. MACAN MARKAR. Glimpses from the past of the Moors of Sri Lanka. Colombo: Moors' Islamic Cultural Home, 1976. 224p.

02280 MUJEEB, M. The Indian Muslims. London: Allen & Unwin, 1967. 590p.

02281 QURESHI, I.H. The Muslim community of the Indo-Pakistan subcontinent., 610-1947: a brief historical analysis. 2nd ed. Karachi: Maᶜaref, 1977. 385p.

4. Interactions of Islam and Hinduism

02282 ATTAR SINGH, ed. Socio-cultural impact of Islam on India. Chandigarh: Panjab U., 1976. 200p.

02283 CHAND, TARA. Influence of Islam on Indian culture. Allahabad: Indian Press, 1963. 322p. + 61pl. [Rpt. of 1954 ed.]

02284 MUJEEB, M. Islamic influence on Indian society. Meerut: Meenakshi, 1972. 204p.

02285 MUJTABAI, F. Aspects of Hindu-Moslem cultural relations. ND: Natl. Book Bureau, 1978. 144p.

02286 NADVI, S.S. The education of Hindus under Muslim rule. Karachi: Academy of Educ. Conf., 1963. 138p.

02287 SULAIMAN, S.M. & M.M. ISMAIL. Islam, Indian religions, and Tamil culture. Madras: Dr. S. Radhakrishnan Inst. for Advanced Study in Philosophy, U. of Madras, 1977. 81p.

C. Indian Zoroastrianism and the Parsi Community

1. General Introduction to Zoroastrianism by Indians and Others

02288 BHARUCHA, E.S.D. Zoroastrian religion and customs. 3rd rev. and enl. ed. Bombay: Taraporevala, 1979. 210p. [Rpt. 1928 ed.]

02289 BOYCE, M. Zoroastrianism. In C.J. Bleeker & G. Widengren, eds. Historia religionum. Leiden: Brill, 1971, v. 2, 211-236.

02290 DABU, K.S. Message of Zarathushtra: a manual of Zoroastrianism, the religion of the Parsis. 2nd ed., rev. & enl. Bombay: New Book Co., 1959. 187p.

02291 DHALLA, M.N. History of Zorastrianism. NY: OUP, 1938. 525p.

02292 ______. Zoroastrian theology: from the earliest times to the present day. NY: 1914. 384p.

02293 HAUG, M. The Parsis: essays on their sacred language, writings, and religion. ND: Cosmo, 1978. 427p. [Rpt. 1884 ed.]

02294 MASANI, R.P. The religion of the good life: Zoroastrianism. 2nd ed. London: Allen & Unwin, 1954. 189p. [1st ed. 1938]

02295 Sir J.J. Zarthoshti Madressa centenary volume. Bombay: Parsi Punchayet Funds and Properties, 1967. 196p.

02296 ZAEHNER, R.C. The dawn and twilight of Zoroastrianism. NY: Putnam, 1961. 371p.

2. The Avesta: the Zoroastrian Scripture in Zend (Ancient Persian)

02297 DARMESTETER, J., tr. The Zend-Avesta. Delhi: Motilal, 1965. 3 v. (SBE, 4,23,31) [Rpt. 1880-87 ed.]

02298 DHABHAR, E.B.N., tr. (Translation of) Zand-i khurtak Avistāk. Bombay: K.R. Cama Oriental Inst., 1963. 476p.

02299 DUCHESNE-GUILLEMIN, J., tr. The hymns of Zarathustra. London: Murray, 1952. 162p.

02300 TARAPOREWALA, I.J.S., tr. The divine songs of Zarathustra. Bombay: Taraporewala, 1951. 1166p.

3. Histories and Studies of the Parsis since their Immigration to India in the 7th century A.D.

02301 BALSARA, P.P. Highlights of Parsi history. Bombay, 1963. 73p.

02302 HAHN, E. The Parsis. In New Yorker 34 (18 Oct. 1958) 110-40.

02303 KARAKA, D.F. History of the Parsis, including their manners, customs, religion & present position. London: Macmillan, 1884. 2 v.

02304 KATRAK, S.K.H. Who are the Parsees? Karachi: 1965. 310p.

02305 KULKE, E. Die Parsen: Bibliographie über eine indische Minorität. Freiburg: Bertelsmann Universitatsverlag, 1968. 52p. [text in German and English]

02306 MENANT, D. The Parsis in India. Rev. by M.M. Murzban. Bombay: M.M. Murzban, 1917. 2v. [1st French ed. 1898]

02307 MIRZA, K. Outlines of Parsi history. Bombay: Mirza, 1974. 516p.

02308 MODI, J.J. The religious ceremonies and customs of the Parsees. 2nd ed. Bombay: J.B. Karani's, 1937. 455p.

02309 NANAVUTTY, P. The Parsis. ND: NBT, 1977. 191p.

02310 VIMADALAL, J.R. What a Parsee should know. 2nd ed. Bombay: Vimadalal, 1970. 66p.

D. Judaism

02311 ELIYA, E. The synagogues in India. Kiryat Motzkin, Israel: Eliahu, 1978. 127p.

02312 FISCHEL, W.J. Ha-Yehudim b'Hoddu; helkom b'hayim hakalkaliim w'hamediniim. Jerusalem: Ben-Zvi Inst., Hebrew U., 1960. 215p. [English title: The Jews in India....]

02313 JAPHETH, M.D. The Jews of India; a brief survey. Bombay: 1969. 33p.

02314 LORD, J.H. The Jews in India and the Far East: being a reprint of articles contributed to "Church and synagogue" with appendices. Westport, CN: Greenwood Press, 1976. 120p. [Rpt. 1907 ed.]

VI. LANGUAGES AND LITERATURES

A. Bibliography and Reference

02315 ACHARYA, K.P., ed. Classified bibliography of articles in Indian linguistics. Mysore: CIIL, 1978. 106p.

02316 BRETON, R.J.L. Atlas géographique des langues et des ethnies de l'Inde et du subcontinent: Bangladesh, Pakistan, Sri Lanka, Népal, Bhoutan, Sikkim. Québec: Presses de l'U. Laval, 1976. 648p.

02317 ______. Les langues de l'Inde depuis l'indépendance; étude de géographie culturelle du monde indien: Inde, Pakistan, Népal, Céylan. 2nd ed., rev. Aix-en-Provence: La Pensée universitaire, 1968. 285p.

02318 Dictionary of Oriental Literatures. Ed. by Jaroslav Průšek; vol. 2, South and South-East Asia. Ed. by Dušan Zvavitel. NY: Basic Books, 1974. 191p.

02319 EMENEAU, M.B. A union list of printed Indic texts and translations in American libraries. NY: Kraus, 1967. 540p. [Rpt. 1935 ed.; 4491 entries, mainly pre-1800 works in Sanskrit, Pali, Prakrit, Apabhramsa]

02320 FUSSMAN, G. Atlas linguistique des parlers dardes et kafirs. Paris: EFEO, 1972. 451p. (Its Pub., 86)

02321 GRIERSON, G.A. Linguistic survey of India. Delhi: Motilal, 1967-68. 11 v. [1st ed. Calcutta: OSGP, 1903-22]

02322 HUGONIOT, R.D., ed. A bibliographical index of the lesser known languages and dialects of India and Nepal. Kathmandu: Summer Inst. of Linguistics, 1970. 312p.

02323 INDIA (REP.) CENSUS OF INDIA, 1961. Language tables, v. 1 India, Part II-c(ii). ND: 1964. 244+534p.

02324 The National bibliography of Indian literature, 1901-1953. General editors: B.S. Kesavan & Y.M. Mulay & V.Y. Kulkarni. ND: Sahitya Akademi, 1962-74. 4 v., 2875p.

02325 NIGAM, R.C. Language handbook on mother tongues in census. ND: Office of the Registrar General, 1972. 61+339p. (Census centenary monograph, 10) [Census of India, 1971]

02326 PATIL, H.S. & S. MASIHUL HASSAN. Indian literature (select bibliographies). ND: ICCR, 1972. 262p. (Aspects of Indian culture, 3)

02327 SARKAR, A., ed. Handbook of languages and dialects of India. Calcutta: KLM, 1964. 109p.

02328 VARMA, S. G.A. Grierson's linguistic survey of India: a summary. Hoshiarpur: VVRI, 1972-76. 3 v. (VIS, 58,59,59a)

B. South Asian Languages and Scripts: Historical and Comparative Linguistic Studies

1. South Asia as a Linguistic Area

02329 EMENEAU, M.B. India and historical grammar; lecture on diffusion and evolution in comparative linguistics, and lecture on India and the linguistic areas.... Annamalainagar: Annamalai U., 1965. 74p. (Its Pub. in linguistics, 5)

02330 ______. India as a linguistic area. In Language 32 (1956) 3-16.

02331 ______. Onomatopoetics in the Indian linguistic area. In Language 45 (1969) 274-299.

02332 MASICA, C.P. Defining a linguistic area: South Asia. Chicago: UChiP, 1976. 234p.

02333 PANDIT, P.B. India as a sociolinguistic area. Poona: U. of Poona, 1972. 92p.

02334 RAMANUJAN, A.K. & C.P. MASICA. Toward a phonological typology of the Indian linguistic area. In M.B. Emeneau & C.A. Ferguson, ed. Linguistics in South Asia. The Hague: Mouton, 1969, 543-77. (CTL, 5)

2. General Studies of South Asian Linguistics

02335 ALL INDIA CONFERENCE OF LINGUISTS, 1st, Poona, 1970. Proceedings. Poona: Linguistic Soc. of India, 1971. 270p.

02336 ALL INDIA CONFERENCE OF LINGUISTS, 2nd, Delhi, 1972. Proceedings. Poona: Linguistic Soc. of India, 1974. 178p.

02337 DIL, A.S., ed. Studies in Pakistani linguistics. Lahore: Linguistic Res. Group of Pakistan, 1965. 231p. (Pakistani linguistics series, 5)

02338 ______. Pakistani linguistics, 1963. Selected papers presented at the Second Pakistan Conference of Linguistics. Lahore: Linguistic Res. Group of Pakistan, 1964. 316p.

02339 ______. Pakistani linguistics. Lahore: Linguistic Research Group of Pakistan, 1963. 210p. [papers of 1st Pakistan Conf. of Linguists, 1962]

02340 EMENEAU, M.B., et al., ed. Linguistics in South Asia. The Hague: Mouton, 1969. 814p. (CTL, 5)

02341 FERGUSON, C.A. & J.J. GUMPERZ, ed. Linguistic diversity in South Asia: studies in regional, social, and functional variation [special issue]. In Intl.

J. of American Linguistics 26,3 (1960). 188p.

02342 GUMPERZ, J.J. Language in social groups: essays by John Gumperz. Stanford: Stanford U. Press, 1971. 350p.

02343 KACHRU, B.B. & S.N. SRIDHAR, eds. Aspects of sociolinguistics in South Asia. [special issue]. In Intl. J. of the Sociology of Language, 16 (1978) 5-121.

02344 KRISHNAMURTI, BH. Studies in Indian linguistics (Prof. M.B. Emeneau ṣaṣṭipūrti volume). Poona & Annamalainagar: Centres of Advanced Study in Linguistics, 1968. 377p.

02345 PATTANAYAK, D.P. Aspects of applied linguistics. NY: Asia, 1970. 105p.

02346 RAGHU VIRA. India's national language. ND: TAIC, 1965. 351p. (Śatapiṭaka series, 36)

3. Comparative Indo-Aryan Philology

02347 BEAMES, J. A comparative grammar of the modern Aryan languages of India: to wit, Hindi, Panjabi, Sindhi, Gujarati, Marathi, Oriya and Bangali. Delhi: Munshiram, 1966. 3 v. in 1. [1st pub. 1872-79]

02348 BLOCH, J. Application de la cartographie à l'histoire de l'Indo-Aryen. Paris: Impr. nationale, 1963. 78p. (Cahiers de la Société asiatique, 13)

02349 ______. Indo-Aryan, from the Vedas to modern times. Rev. ed. Tr. from French by A. Master. Paris: Adrien-Maisonneuve, 1965. 337p.

02350 TURNER, R.L. Collected papers, 1912-1973. London: OUP, 1975. 435p.

02351 ______. A comparative dictionary of the Indo-Aryan languages. London: OUP, 1962-68. 2 v., 842p. [Indexes comp. by D.R. Turner. London: OUP, 1969. 357p.]

02352 TURNER, R.L. & D.R. TURNER. A comparative dictionary of the Indo-Aryan languages, phonetic analysis. London: OUP, 1971. 231p.

4. Comparative Dravidian Linguistics
a. bibliography

02353 AGESTHIALINGOM, S. & S. SAKTHIVEL. A bibliography of Dravidian linguistics. Annamalainagar: Annamalai U., 1973. 362p.

02354 ANDRONOV, M.S. Materials for a bibliography of Dravidian linguistics. Kuala Lumpur: Dept. of Indian Studies, U. of Malaya, 1966. 44p.

02355 MONTGOMERY, S.E. Supplemental material for a bibliography of Dravidian linguistics. In B. Krishnamurti, ed. Studies in Indian linguistics. Annamalainagar: Poona U. & Annamalai U., 1968, 234-46.

02356 RAJANNAN, B. Dravidian languages and literatures: a contribution toward a bibliography of books in English and in a few other European languages, on, about, and translated from the Dravidian languages. Madurai: Madurai U., 1973. 279p.

b. general studies

02357 ANDRONOV, M.S. Dravidian languages. Tr. from Russian by D.M. Segal. Moscow: Nauka, 1970. 199p.

02358 ______. Two lectures on the historicity of language families. Annamalainagar: Annamalai U., 1968. 35p.

02359 AGESTHIALINGOM, S. & N. KUMARASWAMI RAJA, eds. Dravidian linguistics: seminar papers. Annamalainagar: Annamalai U., 1969. 279p.

02360 AGESTHIALINGOM, S. & S.V. SHANMUGAN, eds. Third seminar on Dravidian linguistics. Annamalainagar: Annamalai U., 1972. 415p.

02361 BLOCH, J. The grammatical structure of Dravidian languages. Poona: S.M. Katre, 1954.

02362 BURROW, T. Collected papers on Dravidian linguistics. Annamalainagar: Annamalai U., 1968. 340p.

02363 BURROW, T. & M.B. EMENEAU. Dravidian etymological dictionary. Oxford: OUP, 1961. 609p. [with supplement: 1968. 185p.]

02364 CALDWELL, R. A comparative grammar of the Dravidian or South-Indian family of languages. Rev. and ed. by J.L. Wyatt and T. Ramakrishna Pillai. 3rd ed. ND: OBRC, 1974. 640p. [Rpt. 1913 ed.]

02365 EMENEAU, M.B. Brahui and Dravidian comparative grammar. Berkeley: UCalP, 1962. 91p.

02366 ______. Dravidian comparative phonology; a sketch. Annamalainagar: Annamalai U., 1970. 128p. [1st pub. 1959]

02367 ______. The non-literary Dravidian languages. In his (ed.) Linguistics in South Asia. The Hague: Mouton, 1969, 334-42. (CTL, 5)

02368 ______. The South Dravidian languages. In JAOS 87 (1967) 365-413.

02369 EMENEAU, M.B. & T. BURROW. Dravidian borrowings from Indo-Aryan. Berkeley: UCalP, 1962. 121p.

02370 HIREMATH, R.C. & J.S. KULLI, eds. Proceedings of the Third All India Conference of Dravidian Linguists. Dharwar: Karnatak U., 1976. 304p.

02371 KRISHNAMURTI, BH. Comparative Dravidian studies. In M.B. Emeneau & C.A. Ferguson, eds. Linguistics in South Asia. The Hague: Mouton, 1969, 309-33. (CTL, 5)

02372 RAMESH, K.V. The Tuḷu language: a historical survey. In QJMS 48 (1957-58) 90-101.

02373 SUBRAHMANYAM, P.S. The central Dravidian languages. In JAOS 89 (1969) 739-50.

02374 ______. The position of Tulu in Dravidian. In Indian linguistics 29 (1968) 47-65.

02375 ZVELEBIL, K. Comparative Dravidian phonology. The Hague: Mouton, 1970. 202p. (Janua linguarum. Series practica, 80)

02376 ______. An introduction to the comparative study of Dravidian. In AO 33 (1965) 367-96.

02377 ______. One hundred years of Dravidian comparative philology. In TC 9 (1961) 181-201.

5. Scripts

02378 BANERJI, R.D. The origin of the Bengali script. Calcutta: Nababharat, 1973. 112p. [Rpt. 1919 ed.]

02379 BÜHLER, G. On the origin of the Indian Brahma alphabet. 3rd ed. Varanasi: CSSO, 1963. 124p. (CSS, 33)

02380 CONTRACTOR, M.K. The International Education Year and common script for India: an appeal. Nanpur, Surat: Contractor, 1973. 127p.

02381 GUPTA, S.P. & K.S. RAMACHANDRAN, eds. The origin of Brahmi script. Delhi: D.K., for Indian History and Culture Soc., 1979. 128p. (History and historians of India series, 2)

02382 INDIA (REP.) CENTRAL HINDI DIRECTORATE. Devanagari through the ages. ND: 1967. 72p.

02383 KABIR, HUMAYUN, et al. A common script for Indian languages; a symposium. ND: Min. of Sci. Res. & Cultural Affairs, 1963. 62p.

02384 KANNAIYAN, V. Scripts in and around India. Madras: Govt. Museum, 1960. 44p.

02385 NAIM, C.M. Arabic orthography and some non-Semitic languages. In G.L. Tikku, ed. Islam and its cultural divergence.... Urbana: U. of Illinois Press, 1971, 113-144.

02386 Romanization; a symposium on the possibilities of a single script through romanization. In Seminar 40 (1962) 10-36.

02387 SARAN, S. India's national writing. Delhi: Munshiram, 1969. 160p.

C. Surveys and Studies of South Asian Literature

1. General History of Indian Literature

02387a BAUSANI, A. Storia delle letterature del Pakistan: urdu, pangiābi, sindhī, pasc'tô, bengalī pakistana. Milan: Nuova Accademia editrice, 1958. 370p.

02388 BHATTACHARYYA, N.N. History of Indian erotic literature. ND: Munshiram, 1975. 135p.

02389 DIMOCK, E.C. et al. The literatures of India, an introduction. Chicago: UChiP, 1974. 292p.

02390 A history of Indian literature. Ed. by J. Gonda. Wiesbaden: Harrassowitz, 1973-.

02391 MUKHERJEE, S. Towards a literary history of India. Simla: IIAS, 1975. 103p.

02392 NAGENDRA, ed. Indian literature.... Agra: Lakshmi Narain Agarwal, 1959. 671p.

02393 PODDAR, A., ed. Indian literature (proceedings of a seminar). Simla: IIAS, 1972. 530p.

02394 RENOU, L. Indian literature. Tr. from French by P. Evans. NY: Walker, 1964. 152p.

02395 SEN, S.P., ed. Historical biography in Indian literature. Calcutta: IHS, 1979. 348p.

02396 WEBER, A.F. The history of Indian literature. Tr. from German by J. Mann and T. Zachariae. 6th ed. Varanasi: CSSO, 1961. 360p. (CSS, 8)

02397 WINTERNITZ, M. A history of Indian literature, v. 1 & 2. Tr. by S. Ketkar and H. Kohn. Calcutta: U. of Calcutta, 1933. 634, 673p. [v. 3, pts. 1 & 2, tr. by S. Jhā. Delhi: Motilal, 1963-67. 720p. 1st German ed. 1908-22]

2. Literary Criticism and Aesthetics

02398 CHAITANYA, K., et al. Aspects of Indian poetics. ND: PDMIB, 1969. 46p.

02399 DESHPANDE, M. On the notion of similarity in Indian poetics. In JIP 2,1 (1972) 21-52.

02400 GEROW, E. Indian poetics. Wiesbaden: Harrassowitz, 1977. p. 218-301. (HIL, 5:3)

02401 GHOSHAL, S.N. Elements of Indian aesthetics. Varanasi: Chaukhambha Orientalia, 1978-. v. 1, 242p.

02402 GOKAK, V.K. The concept of Indian literature. ND: Munshiram, 1979. 275p.

02403 LAL, P. The concept of an Indian literature; six essays. Calcutta: Writers Workshop, 1968. 49p.

02404 KRISHNAMOORTHY, K. Some thoughts on Indian aesthetics and literary criticism. Mysore: U. of Mysore, 1968. 90p.

02405 _____. Studies in Indian aesthetics and criticism. Mysore: D.V.K. Murthy, 1979. 271p.

02406 MCCUTCHION, D. Western and Indian approaches to literature. In Mahfil 4,1 (1967) 21-33.

02407 MUKHERJI, R.R. Imagery in poetry: an Indian approach. Calcutta: SPB, 1972. 168p.

02408 NAGENDRA, ed. Literary criticism in India. Meerut: Sarita Prakashan, 1976. 320p.

02409 RAGHAVAN, V. & NAGENDRA, ed. An introduction to Indian poetics. Bombay: Macmillan, 1970. 144p.

02410 SUKLA, A.C. The concept of imitation in Greek and Indian aesthetics. Calcutta: Rupa, 1977. 308p.

3. Comparative Studies among South Asian Literatures

02411 HART, G.L., III. The relation between Tamil and classical Sanskrit literature. Wiesbaden: Harrassowitz, 1976, 317-51. (HIL, 10:2)

02412 _____. Some related literary conventions in Tamil and Indo-Aryan and their significance. In JAOS 94,2 (1974) 157-67.

02413 RAGHAVAN, V., ed. Ramayana, Mahabharata, and Bhagavata writers: Kamban, Pampa, Nannaya-Tikkana, Madhava Kandali, Ekanath, Krittivasa, Sarala Dasa, Potana, Tunchattu Eluttacchan, Tulasi Das, Premananda, Bopadeva. ND: PDMIB, 1978. 134p.

02414 SUBRAHMANYA SASTRI, P.S. An enquiry into the relationship of Sanskrit and Tamil. Trivandrum: U. of Travancore, 1946. 112p.

02415 SUBRAMANYAM, K.N. The South in the Indian literary tradition. In IAC 18 (1969) 44-57.

02416 VAUDEVILLE, C., tr. Bārahmāsā: les chansons des douze mois dans les littératures Indo-Aryennes. Pondicherry: IFI, 1965. 97p.

4. Anthologies

02417 ALPHONSO-KARKALA, J.B. An anthology of Indian literature. Harmondsworth: Penguin, 1971. 630p.

02418 DUTT, TORU. Ancient ballads and legends of Hindustan. London: Kegan Paul, Trench & Co., 1882. 139p.

02419 GHOSH, O., ed. The dance of Shiva and other tales from India. NY: New American Library, 1965. 341p.

02420 PANCHAPAKESA AYYAR, A.S. Famous tales of India. Madras: Ramaswamy Sastrulu, 1954. 394p.

02421 PURAN SINGH. The spirit of oriental poetry. 2nd ed. Patiala: Panjabi U., 1969. 279p. [1st ed. 1926]

02422 SANTHANAM, K.I., ed. An anthology of Indian literatures. Bombay: BVB, 1969. 724p.

02423 SHAH, I.A. The golden treasury of Indian literature. London: Low, Marston, 1938. 294p.

D. Folk Literature and Oral Tradition [For folklore of specific regions, see Chapters Ten through Sixteen.]

1. Bibliography and Reference

02424 DEVA, I. Folklore studies; a trend report. In A survey of research in sociology and social anthropology. Bombay: Popular, 1972, v. 3, 197-239. [sponsored by ICSSR]

02425 HANDOO, J. A bibliography of Indian folk literature. Mysore: CIIL, 1977. 419p.

02426 KIRKLAND, E.C. A bibliography of South Asian folklore. Bloomington: Indiana U. Res. Center in Anthropology, Folklore, and Linguistics, 1966. 291p. (Asian folklore studies, 4)

02427 SAKTHIVEL, S. Folklore literature in India: a review. Kothaloothu, Madurai Dist.: Meena Pathippakam, 1976. 110p.

02428 SEN GUPTA, S. A bibliography of Indian folklore and related subjects. Calcutta: Indian Pub., 1967. 196p. (Indian folklore series, 11)

02429 THOMPSON, S. & J. BALYS, eds. The oral tales of India. Bloomington: Indiana U. Press, 1958. 448p. [Motif index to folktales in 259 sources] (Folklore series, 10)

02430 VIDYARTHI, L.P. Folklore research in India. In A. Dundes, ed. Varia Folklorica. The Hague: Mouton, 1978, 201-62. (WA)

02431 _____. Folklore researches in India. In his Rise of anthropology in India. Delhi: Concept, 1978, v. 1, 331-433. [bibl. essay]

2. Folklorists and Folklore Research

02432 HANCHETT, S. Recent trends in the study of folk Hinduism and India's folklore. In JIF 1,1 (1978) 40-54.

02433 HANDOO, J. Current trends in folklore. Mysore: Inst. of Kannada Studies, U. of Mysore, 1978. 157p.

02434 ISLAM, M. A history of folktale collections in India and Pakistan. Dacca: Bengali Academy, 1970. 336p.

02435 MISRA, B. Verrier Elwin's field methods and fieldwork in India: an appraisal. In AFS 30,1 (1971) 97-132.

02436 OSMAN, M.T. William Crooke: an appraisal of his contributions to folklore studies and ethnography of India. In Folklore (C) 12 (1971) 200-17.

02437 SEN GUPTA, S., ed. Folklore research in India; official proceedings and speeches at the All-India Folklore Conference, Calcutta. Calcutta: Indian Pub., 1964. 122p. (Folklore series, 4)

02438 UPADHYAYA, H.S. Reminiscences of an octogenarian folklorist (Stith Thompson). In AFS 27,2 (1968) 107-45.

02439 VIDYARTHI, L.P. Essays in Indian folklore; papers presented to the centenary festival of Rai Bahadur S.C.

Roy. Calcutta: Indian Pub., 1973. 199p. (Folklore series, 22)

3. Studies of Folklore and Folk Literature

02440 BARUA, H. Nature-songs of the folk-people of India. In IAC 11 (1962) 133-51.

02441 PANDE, T. Themes of Indian folksongs. In Folklore (C) 12,11 (1971) 424-34.

02442 SARKAR, B.K. The folk-element in Hindu culture; a contribution to socio-religious studies in Hindu folk-institutions. ND: OBRC, 1972. 312p. [1st pub. 1917]

02443 SEN GUPTA, S. An objective view of folklore study in India. Jammu: Dogri Res. Inst., 1971. 48p.

02444 SEN GUPTA, S. & K.D. UPADHYAYA, ed. Studies in Indian folk culture; folk-songs, folk-arts, and folk-literature. Calcutta: Indian Pub., 1964. 187p.

02445 SRIVASTAVA, S.L. Folk culture and oral tradition; a comparative study of regions in Rajasthan and eastern U.P. ND: Abhinav, 1974. 404p.

02446 THOMPSON, S. & W.E. ROBERTS. Types of Indic oral tales: India, Pakistan, Ceylon. Helsinki: Suomalainen Tiedeakatemia, 1960. 181p. (Folklore Fellows communication, 180)

02447 VATUK, V.P. Thieves in my house: four studies in Indian folklore of protest and change. Varanasi: Vishwavidyalaya Prakashan, 1969. 107p.

02448 WADLEY, S.S., ed. Folk literature of South Asia. [special issue] In JSAL 11,1/2 (1975) 176p.

4. Collections of Folk Tales and Folksongs

02449 BARUA, H. Folksongs of India. ND: Indian Council for Cultural Relations, 1963. 88p.

02450 CROOKE, W., comp. The talking thrush and other tales from India. Retold by W.H. Robinson. NY: Dutton, 1938. 217p. [1st pub. 1899]

02451 EDWARDES, S.M. Folk tales from northern India from the collection made by the late Dr. William Crooke. In IA 53 (1924) 1-24; 54 (1925) 25-40; 55 (1926) 41-56.

02452 GOVER, C.E. The folk-songs of Southern India. 2nd ed. Tirunelveli, Madras: South India Saiva Siddhanta Works Pub. Soc., 1959. 300p.

02453 GRAY, J.E.B. Indian tales and legends. London: OUP, 1961. 230p.

02454 HERTEL, J., ed. Indische Märchen. Düsseldorf: Diederichs, 1967. 421p.

02455 JACOBS, J., ed. Indian fairy tales. NY: Dover, 1969. 255p. [Rpt. 1892 ed.]

02456 JETHABHAI, G. Indian folklore (being a collection of tales illustrating the customs and manners of the Indian people.) Tr. by N.M. Dhruva. Limbdi: H.S. Dubal, 1903. 236p. [1st Gujarati ed. 1885]

02457 KINCAID, C.A. Folk tales of Sind and Guzarat. Ahmedabad: New Order Book Co., 1976. 121p. [1st pub. 1925]

02458 KUNHAPPA, M. Three bags of gold, and other Indian folk tales. NY: Asia, 1963. 134p.

02459 MACFARLANE, I. Tales and legends from India. London: Chatto & Windus, 1965. 136p.

02460 MASUD-UL-HASAN. Famous folk tales of Pakistan. Lahore: Ferozsons, 1976-.

02461 NATESA SASTRI, S.M. Indian folktales. 2nd ed. Madras: Guardian Press, 1908. 533p.

02462 STEEL, F.A. & JASIMUDDIN & C. PAINTER, comps. Folk tales of Pakistan; adapted from stories collected by.... Lahore: OUP, 1966. 109p.

E. Pan-South Asian Languages and Literatures

1. Sanskrit Literature
a. histories and surveys of Sanskrit literature

02463 AGARWAL, H.R. A short history of Sanskrit literature. 2nd rev. and enl. ed. Delhi: Munshiram, 1963. 323p.

02464 ARTOLA, G.T. The banner of Kāmadeva and other topics of Sanskrit literature and Indian culture. Bombay: Popular, 1977. 101p. (Monographs of the Dept. of Sanskrit and Indian Studies, U. of Toronto, 3)

02465 BANERJI, S.C. A companion to Sanskrit literature; ... containing brief accounts of authors, works, characters, technical terms, geographical names, myths, legends .... Delhi: Motilal, 1971. 729p.

02466 ______. Flora and fauna in Sanskrit literature. Calcutta: Naya Prokash, 1980. 192p.

02467 BURROW, T. The Sanskrit language. 2nd rev. ed. London: Faber & Faber, 1973. 438p. [1st ed. 1961]

02468 CHAITANYA, K. A new history of Sanskrit literature. 2nd ed. Bombay: Asia, 1977. 490p. [1st ed. 1962]

02469 DE, S.K. History of Sanskrit literature. Calcutta: U. of Calcutta, 1947. 511p.

02470 GHOSH, J. Epic sources of Sanskrit literature. Calcutta: Sanskrit College, 1963. 223p.

02471 GOWEN, H.H. A history of Indian literature from Vedic times to the present day. NY: Greenwood Press, 1968. 593p. [1st pub. 1931]

02472 KEITH, A.B. Classical Sanskrit literature. ND: YMCA Pub. House, 1966. 135p.

02473 ______. A history of Sanskrit literature. London: OUP, 1966. 575p.

02474 KRISHNAMACHARIAR, M. History of classical Sanskrit literature.... Delhi: Motilal, 1970. 1246p. [1st pub. 1937]

02475 KUNHAN RAJA, C. Survey of Sanskrit literature. Bombay: BVB, 1962. 363p.

02476 MACDONELL, A.A. A history of Sanskrit literature. NY: Haskell House, 1968. 472p. [Rpt. 1900 ed.]

02477 MILLER, B.S., ed. Sanskrit issue. In Mahfil 7,3/4 (1971) 257p.

02478 RAGHAVAN, V. Sanskrit: essays on the value of the language and the literature. Madras: Sanskrit Educ. Soc., 1972. 180p.

02479 RENOU, L., ed. & tr. Anthologie sanskrite; textes de l'Inde ancienne. Paris: Rayot, 1947. 406p.

02480 ______. Littérature sanskrite. Paris: Adrien Maisonneuve, 1945. 160p.

02481 SEREBRYAKOV, I.D. Sketches of ancient Indian literature. Tr. from Russian by H.C. Gupta. In ISPP 15,1&2 (1973) 1-117, 119-217.

02482 SHASTRI, G.B. A concise history of classical Sanskrit literature. 2nd ed. Delhi: Motilal, 1974. 220p. [1st ed. 1943. An introduction to classical Sanskrit]

02483 SIVARAMAMURTI, C. Sanskrit literature and art, mirrors of Indian culture. ND: Lakshmi Book Store, 1970. 125p. (ASI memoir, 73) [1st pub. 1955]

02484 VENKATAKRISHNA RAO, U. A handbook of classical Sanskrit literature. Bombay: Orient Longmans, 1967. 251p.

02485 WARDER, A.K. Indian Kāvya literature. Delhi: Motilal, 1972-. v. 1-3, 281, 393, 305p.

b. regional contributions to Sanskrit literature

02486 BANERJI, S.C. Cultural heritage of Kashmir; a survey of Kashmir's contribution to Sanskrit literature. Calcutta: SPB, 1965. 180p.

02487 ______. Sanskrit beyond India: a survey of the diffusion of Sanskrit language and literature and their influence on world literature and culture. Calcutta: Saraswat Library, 1978. 244p.

02488 DANDEKAR, R.N., ed. Sanskrit and Maharashtra: a symposium. Poona: U. of Poona, 1972. 139p.

02489 DATTA, K.K. Bengal's contributions to Sanskrit literature. Calcutta: Sanskrit College, 1974. 102p. (Its Res. series, 103)

02490 DE, S.K. Bengal's contribution to Sanskrit literature, and studies in Bengal Vaisnavism. Calcutta: KLM, 1960. 153p. [Rpt. from ISPP]

02491 EASWARAN NAMPOOTHIRY, E. Sanskrit literature of Kerala; an index of authors and their works. Trivandrum: College Book House, 1972. 162p.

02492 KUNJUNNI RAJA, K. The contribution of Kerala to Sanskrit literature. Madras: U. of Madras, 1958. 310p. (Its Sanskrit series, 23)

02493 MITRA, R.L. The Sanskrit Buddhist literature of Nepal. Calcutta: SPB, 1971. 341p. [1st pub. 1882]

02494 NAGARAJAN, K.S. Contribution of Kashmir to Sanskrit literature. Bangalore: 1970. 729p.

02495 VENKITASUBRAMONIA IYER, S. Kerala Sanskrit literature; a bibliography. Trivandrum: Dept. of Sanskrit, U. of Kerala, 1976. 512p.

c. Sanskrit aesthetics and poetic theory

02496 AKLUJKAR, A. Stylistics in the Sanskrit tradition. In B.B. Kachru & H.F.W. Stahlke, eds. Current trends in stylistics. Champaign, IL: Linguistic Res., Inc., 1972, 1-14.

02497 BHAT, G.K. Sanskrit drama: a perspective on theory and practice. Dharwar: Karnatak U., 1975. 122p.

02498 CHAKRABARTI, T. Indian aesthetics and science of language. Calcutta: SPB, 1971. 191p.

02499 CHAITANYA, K. Sanskrit poetics; a critical and comparative study. London: Asia, 1966. 466p.

02500 DE, S.K. History of Sanskrit poetics. 2nd rev. ed. Calcutta: KLM, 1976. 2 v. in 1, 361 + 341p. [Rpt. of 1960 ed. 1st pub. 1923-25]

02501 ______. Sanskrit poetics as a study of aesthetics. Berkeley: UCalP, 1963. 118p.

02502 ______. Some problems of Sanskrit poetics. Calcutta: KLM, 1959. 267p.

02503 DWIVEDI, R.C., ed. Principles of literary criticism in Sanskrit. Delhi: Motilal, 1969. 309p.

02504 GEROW, E.M. A glossary of Indian figures of speech. The Hague: Mouton, 1971. 348p.

02505 GIRI, K. Concept of poetry, an Indian approach: studies in Sanskrit poetry and poetics. Calcutta: SPB, 1975. 216p.

02506 HIRIYANNA, M. Art experience. Mysore: Kavyalaya, 1954. 86p.

02507 INGALLS, D.H.H. General introduction. In his An anthology of Sanskrit court poetry. Cambridge: HUP, 1965, 611p. (HOS, 44)

02508 JHA, K. Figurative poetry in Sanskrit literature. Delhi: Motilal, 1975. 212p.

02509 KANE, P.V. History of Sanskrit poetics. 4th ed. Delhi: Motilal, 1971. 446p.

02510 KATRE, S.M. Introduction to Indian textual criticism. Poona: S.M. Katre, 1954. 148p.

02511 KRISHNAMOORTHY, K. Essays in Sanskrit criticism. Dharwar: Karnatak U., 1974. 325p.

02512 MASSON, J.M. Obscenity in Sanskrit literature. In Mahfil 7,3-4 (1971) 197-207.

02513 MUKHERJI, A.D. Sanskrit prosody: its evolution. Calcutta: Saraswat Library, 1976. 261p.

02514 MURTI, M.S. Sanskrit compounds: a philosophical study. Varanasi: CSSO, 1974. 360p. (CSS, 93)

02515 PANDEY, K.C. Comparative aesthetics. 2nd ed. Varanasi: CSSO, 1959-72. 2 v.

02516 RAGHAVAN, V. The number of rasas. Adyar: Adyar Library, 1940. 192p.

02517 VIJAYAWARDHANA, G.H. Outlines of Sanskrit poetics. Varanasi: CSSO, 1970. 170p. (CSS, 76)

02518 VOGEL, C. Die Jahreszeiten in Spiegel der altindischen Literatur. In ZDMG 121 (1971) 284-326.

2. Persian and Arabic Literatures of South Asia

02519 ʿABD AL-GHANI, M. Pre-Mughal Persian in Hindustan; a critical survey of the growth of Persian language and literature from the earliest time to the advent of Mughal rule. Allahabad: Allahabad Law Journal, 1941. 505p.

02520 AHMAD, M.G. ZUBAID. The contribution of Indo-Pakistan to Arabic literature: from ancient times to 1857. Lahore: Sh. Muhammad Ashraf, 1968. 539p. [Rpt. 1946 ed.]

02521 GOREKAR, N.S. Indo-Iran relations: cultural aspects. Bombay: Sindhu, 1970. 211p.

02522 HEINZ, W. Der indische Stil in der persischen Literatur. Wiesbaden: Steiner, 1973. 132p.

02523 MAREK, J. Persian literature in India. In Jan Rypka ed. History of Iranian literature. Dordrecht, Holland: D. Reidel, 1968, 713-734. [biblio., 832-838]

02524 SADARANGANI, H.I. Persian poets of Sind. Karachi, Sindhi Adabi Board, 1956. 319p.

02525 SCHIMMEL, A. Islamic literatures of India. Wiesbaden: Harrassowitz, 1973. 60p. (HIL, 7:5) [Persian, Arabic, Turkish]

02526 STOREY, C.A. Persian literature; a bio-bibliographical survey. London: Luzac, 1927-71. [History of India, v. 1, sect. 2, fasc. 3, 433-779]

02527 TIKKU, G.L. Persian poetry in Kashmir 1339-1846. Berkeley: UCalP, 1971. 321p.

3. Urdu Language and Literature
a. bibliography and reference

02528 FLEMMING, L.A. & G.C. NARANG. An additional bibliography of English sources for the Urdu language and literature. In LEW 15,1 (1972) 17-37.

02529 NAIM, C.M. A bibliography of English sources for the Urdu language and literature. In LEW 7 (1963) 11-18.

02530 PRITCHETT, F.W. Urdu literature: a bibliography of English language sources. ND: Manohar, 1979. 162p.

b. general histories and surveys

02531 ASIRI, F.M. Studies in Urdu literature. Santiniketan: Visvabharati, 1952. 146p. (Its Studies, 19)

02532 BAILEY, T.G. A history of Urdu literature. Calcutta: Assoc. Press, 1932. 119p. [Rpt. Lahore: al Biruni, 1977]

02533 NAZ. An outline of Urdu literature. Lahore: Ferozsons, 1971. 98p.

02534 SADIQ, M. A history of Urdu literature. London: OUP, 1964. 429p.

02535 SAKSENA, R.B. A history of Urdu literature. Lahore: Sind Sagar Academy, 1975. 379p.

02536 SCHIMMEL, A. Classical Urdu literature from the beginning to Iqbāl. Wiesbaden: Harrassowitz, 1975. 262p. (HIL, 7:3)

02537 SINGH, M. Handbook of Urdu literature. Lahore: Careers, n.d. 166p.

c. anthologies of Urdu literature

02538 ALI, AHMAD. The falcon and the hunted bird. Karachi: Kitab, 1950. 98p.

02539 ALI, AHMED, ed. The golden tradition, an anthology of Urdu poetry. NY: ColUP, 1973. 286p.

02540 MATTHEWS, D.J. & C. SHACKLE, tr. An anthology of classical Urdu love lyrics: text and translations. London: OUP, 1972. 283p.

4. Hindi Language and Literature
[see VI. F. 5. below]

5. English Language and Literature of South Asia
[see Chap. Eight, X. C. 5.]

F. Regional Languages and Literatures

1. Sinhala of Sri Lanka and its Literature

02541 DE SILVA, M.W.S. Sinhalese. In M.B. Emeneau & C.S. Ferguson, ed. Linguistics in South Asia. The Hague: Mouton, 1969, 245-48. (CTL, 5)

02542 ______. Sinhalese and other island languages in South Asia. Tübingen: Narr, 1979. 75p.

02543 GEIGER, W. Literatur und Sprache der Singhalesen. Strassburg: Trübner, 1900. 93p.

02544 GODAKUMBURA, C.E. Sinhalese literature. Colombo: Colombo Apothecaries, 1955. 376p.

02545 PINTO, M.N. A short history of Sinhalese literature: from the earliest times to the present day. Colombo: Gunasena, 1954. 78p.

02546 REYNOLDS, C.H.B., et al. An anthology of Sinhalese literature up to 1815. Tr. by W.G. Archer, et al. London: Allen & Unwin, 1970. 377p.

02547 WICKRAMASINGHE, M. Landmarks of Sinhalese literature. Tr. by E.R. Sarathchandra. 2nd rev. ed. Colombo: M.D. Gunasena, 1963. 211p. [1st ed. 1948]

2. South Indian Regional Languages and Literatures
a. Tamil of Tamil Nadu and Sri Lanka
i. language

02548 AGESTHIALINGOM, S. & S.V. SHANMUGAM. The language of Tamil inscriptions, 1250-1350 A.D. Annamalainagar: Annamalai U., Dept. of Linguistics, 1970. 288p.

02549 ANDRONOV, M.S. The Tamil language. Tr. by V. Korotky. Moscow: Nauka, 1965. 53p. (Languages of Asia and Africa) [1st Russian ed. 1960]

02550 KAMATCHINATHAN, A. The Tirunelvēli Tamil dialect. Annamalainagar: Annamalai U., 1969. 188p.

02551 MEENAKSHISUNDARAM, T.P. A history of the Tamil language. Poona: DCPRI, 1965. 246p. (DCBC, 22)

02552 ______. Prof. T.P. Meenakshisundaran sixty-first birthday commemoration volume.... Annamalainagar: Annamalai U., 1961. 251p. [his collected papers]

02553 POPE, G.U. A handbook of the Tamil language. ND: Asian Educ. Services, 1979. 205p. [Rpt. 1904 ed.]

02554 SATHASIVAM, A. Linguistics in Ceylon: Tamil. In M.B. Emeneau & C.A. Ferguson, eds. Linguistics in South Asia. The Hague: Mouton, 1969, 752-759. (CTL, 5)

02555 VELUPPILLAI, A. Pandya inscriptions; a language study. Jaffna: Jaffna Archaeol. Soc., 1972. 325p.

02556 ZVELEBIL, K. Paḻḻar speech: a contribution to Tamil dialectology. In Linguistics, 21 (1966) 87-97.

02557 ______. Tamil in 550 A.D.; an interpretation of early inscriptional Tamil. Prague: Ucelovynakl Orientalniho Ustavu, 1964. 74p.

02558 ZVELEBIL, K. & J. VACEK. Introduction to the historical grammar of the Tamil language. Prague: Oriental Inst. in Academia, 1970. 222p.

ii. literature

02559 ARUNACHALAM, M. An introduction to the history of Tamil literature. Tiruchitrambalam, Tanjavur Dist.: Gandhi Vidyalayam, 1974. 365p.

02560 ASHER, R.E. Aspects de la littérature en prose dans le Sud de l'Inde. In BEFEO 59 (1972) 123-188.

02561 JESUDASAN, C. & H. JESUDASAN. A history of Tamil literature. Calcutta: YMCA Pub. House, 1961. 305p.

02562 JOHN SAMUEL, G. Collected papers on Tamil literature. Madras: Mani Pathippakam, 1979. 136p.

02563 MEENAKSHISUNDARAM, T.P. A history of Tamil literature. Annamalainagar: Annamalai U., 1965. 211p.

02564 ______. The pageant of Tamil literature. Madras: Sekar Pathippagam, 1966. 126p.

02565 PERCIVAL, P. Tamil proverbs with their English translations. 3rd ed. London: H.S. King, 1875. 573p. [1st pub. 1834]

02566 RAGHAVA AIYANGAR, M. Some aspects of Kerala and Tamil literature. Tr. by J. Parthasarathi. Trivandrum: U. of Kerala, 1973. 178p. [Rpt. 1948-50 ed.]

02567 SEMINAR ON THE LITERARY HERITAGE OF THE TAMILS, MADRAS, 1978. Literary heritage of the Tamils...: seminar papers. Madras: Intl. Inst. of Tamil Studies, 1979. 728p.

02568 SOMASUNDARAM PILLAI, J.M. Two thousand years of Tamil literature; an anthology with studies and translations. Madras: South India Saiva Siddhanta Works Pub. Soc., 1959. 376p.

02569 UWISE, M.M. Muslim contribution to Tamil literature. Kandy: Tamil Manram, 1953. 131p.

02570 VAIYAPURI PILLAI, S. History of Tamil language & literature. Madras: New Century Book House, 1956. 206p.

02571 VEDACHALAM PILLAI, N.R.S. Ancient and modern Tamil poets. Madras: SISSWPS, 1971. 84p.

02572 WHITE, E.E. The wisdom of the Tamil people. ND: Munshiram, 1975. 130p.

02573 ZVELEBIL, K. The smile of Murugan on Tamil literature of South India. Leiden: Brill, 1973. 378p.

02574 ______. Tamil literature. Wiesbaden: Harrassowitz, 1974. 316p. (HIL, 10:1)

02575 ______. Tamil literature. Leiden: Brill, 1975. 307p. (HO, 2:2:1)

02576 ZVELEBIL, K.V. & D. NELSON, eds. Tamil issue. In Mahfil 5,3/4 (1968) 1-121.

b. Kannada of Karnataka

02577 MUGALI, R.S. History of Kannada literature. ND: Sahitya Akademi, 1975. 143p.

02578 NAYAK, H.M. Kannada, literary and colloquial; a study of two styles. Mysore: Rao and Raghavan, 1967. 156p.

02579 RICE, E.P. A history of Kanarese literature. Calcutta: Assoc. Press, 1921. 128p.

02580 UMARJI, V.R. Kannada language: its origin & development. Dharwar: Karnatak Historical Res. Soc, 1969. 98p.

c. Telugu of Andhra

02581 CHENCHIAH, P. & M. BHUJANGA RAO. A history of Telugu literature. Calcutta: Assn. Press, 1928. 132p.

02582 RADHAKRISHNA SARMA, C. Landmarks in Telugu literature: a short survey of Telugu literature. Madras: Lakshminarayana Granthamala, 1975. 80p.

02583 ______. Ramblings in Telugu literature. Madras: Lakshminarayana Granthamala, 1978. 98p.

02584 RAJU, P.T. Telugu literature (Andhra literature). Bombay: Intl. Book House, 1944. 154p.

02585 VENKATA SITAPATI, G. History of Telugu literature. ND: Sahitya Akademi, 1968. 314p.

d. Malayalam of Kerala

02586 AYYAPPAPANICKER, K. A short history of Malayalam literature. Trivandrum: Dept. of Public Relations, Govt. of Kerala, 1977. 69p.

02587 CHAITANYA, K. A history of Malayalam literature. ND: Orient Longmans, 1971. 596p.

02588 CHANDRASEKHAR, A. The history of linguistic studies in Malayalam. In VIJ 12,1/2 (1974) 48-67.

02589 GEORGE, K.M. A survey of Malayalam literature. Bombay: Asia, 1968. 354p.

02590 KUNJUNNI RAJA, K., et al., eds. Pratibhanam; a collection of research papers presented to Dr. P.K. Narayana Pillai.... Trivandrum: Dr. P.K. Shashtipoorthi Cmtee., 1970. 282p.

02591 LEELADEVI, R. History of Malayalam literature. Trivandrum: Educ. Supplies Depot, 1977. 196p.

02592 PARAMESWARAN NAIR, P.K. History of Malayalam literature. Tr. from Malayalam by E.M.J. Venniyoor. ND: Sahitya Akademi, 1967. 296p.

3. Middle Indian Regional Languages and Literatures

a. Konkani of Goa and the West Coast

02593 DA CUNHA RIVARA, J.H. An historical essay of the Konkani language. In A.K. Priolkar. The printing press in India.... Bombay: Marathi Samshodhana Mandala, 1958, 149-236.

02594 KATRE, S.M. The formation of Konkani. Poona: DCPRI, 1966. 183p. (DCBC, 23)

02595 KELEKAR, R. A bibliography of Konkani literature in Devanagari, Roman and Kannada characters. Goa: Gomant Bharati Pub., 1963. 87p.

02596 PEREIRA, J. A brief history of literary Konkani. In Mahfil 8,2/3 (1972) 59-83.

02597 SHANBHAG, D.N., ed. Essays on Konkani language and literature; Professor Armando Menezes felicitation volume. Dharwar: Konkani Sahitya Prakashan, 1970. 118p.

b. Marathi of Maharashtra

02598 BERNTSEN, R.M. The speech of Phaltan; a study in linguistic variation. Ph.D. diss., U. of Pennsylvania, 1973. 291p. [UM 73-24,116]

02599 BLOCH, J. The formation of the Marathi language. Tr. from French by D.R. Chanana. Delhi: Motilal, 1970. 416p.

02600 DESHPANDE, K. Marathi sahitya; review of the Marathi literature up to 1960. ND: Maharashtra Info. Centre, 1966. 105p.

02601 MANWARING, A. Marathi proverbs. Oxford: OUP, 1899. 271p.

02602 SOUTHWORTH, F.C. Marathi. In M.B. Emeneau & C.A. Ferguson, eds. Linguistics in South Asia. The Hague: Mouton, 1969, 99-104. (CTL, 5)

c. Gujarati

02603 JHAVERI, K.M. Further milestones in Gujarati literature. Bombay: N.M. Tripathi, 1924. 279p.

02604 ______. Milestones in Gujarati literature. Bombay: K.M. Jhaveri, 1914. 295p.

02605 JHAVERI, M.M. History of Gujarati literature. ND: Sahitya Akademi, 1978. 260p.

02606 MUNSHI, K.M. Gujarāt and its literature, from early times to 1852. 3rd ed. Bombay: BVB, 1967. 292p.

02607 PANDIT, P.B. Gujarati. In M.B. Emeneau & C.A. Ferguson, eds. Linguistics in South Asia. The Hague: Mouton, 1969, 105-21. (CTL, 5)

02608 SHASTRI, P.N. & P. LAL. The Writers Workshop handbook of Gujarātī literature. Calcutta: Writers Workshop, 1974-. v. 1, A-F, 94p.

d. Oriya of Utkal/Orissa

02609 MANSINHA, M. History of Oriya literature. Delhi: Sahitya Akademi, 1962. 282p.

02610 TRIPATHI, K. A brief history of Oriya literature. Berhampur: Bijoy Book Store, 1972. 106p.

02611 ______. The evolution of Oriya language and script. Cuttack: Utkal U., 1963. 392p.

4. The Northwest: the Indus Valley and Mountain Frontier

a. Sindhi

02612 AJWANI, L.H. History of Sindhi literature. ND: Sahitya Akademi, 1970. 225p.

02613 DASWANI, C.J. & S. PARCHANI. Sociolinguistic survey of Indian Sindhi. Mysore: CIIL, 1978. 128p.

02614 JOTWANI, M.W. Sindhi literature and society. ND: Rajesh, 1979. 124p.

02615 KHUBCHANDANI, L.M. Sindhi. In M.B. Emeneau & C.A. Ferguson, eds. Linguistics in South Asia. The Hague: Mouton, 1969, 201-34. (CTL, 5)

02616 SCHIMMEL, A. Sindhi literature. Wiesbaden: Harrassowitz, 1974. 41p. (HIL, 8:4)

b. Baluchi

02617 BAUSANI, A. Baluchi language and literature. Tr. from Italian by B. Blair. In Mahfil 7,1/2 (1971) 43-54.

02618 KAMIL AL-QADRI, S.M. Baluchi language and literature. In Pakistan Q. 17,1 (1969) 60-65.

02619 ______. Bibliography of Baluchi and Brahui language and literature. In Pakistan Q. 17,1 (1969) 76-84.

02620 ROOMAN, M.A. A brief survey of Baluchi literature and language. Karachi: Pakistan Historical Soc., 1967. 41p. (PHS pub., 51)

c. Punjabi

02621 BAHL, K.C. Panjabi. In M.B. Emeneau & C.A. Ferguson, eds. Linguistics in South Asia. The Hague: Mouton, 1969, 153-200. (CTL, 5)

02622 GRIERSON, G.A. Bibliography of the Panjabi language. In IA 35 (1906) 65-72.

02623 GUPTA, B.R. Annotated bibliography of Panjabi language. In Parkh 1 (1971) 1-22.

02624 HARBANS SINGH. Aspects of Punjabi literature. Ferozepore Cantt.: Bawa Publishing House, 1961. 96p.

02625 Linguistic atlas of the Punjab. Patiala: Dept. of Anthropological Linguistics, Punjabi U., 1973. 242p.

02626 MOHAN SINGH. A history of Panjabi literature (1100-1932).... 3rd ed. Jullundur: Sadasiva, 1971. 226p. [1st ed. 1951]

02627 NAJM HUSAIN SAYYID. Recurrent patterns in Punjabi poetry. Lahore: Majlis Shah Hussain, 1968. 112p.

02628 QURAISHI, W. A survey of Panjabi language and literature. In JPHS 15,2 (1967) 101-29.

02629 SEREBRYAKOV, I.D. Punjabi literature: a brief outline. Tr. from Russian by T.A. Zalite. Lahore: Progressive Books, 1975. 117p. [1st English ed. 1968]

d. Dogri, an Indo-Aryan language of Jammu

02630 SHIVANATH. History of Dogri literature. ND: Sahitya Akademi, 1976. 194p.

e. Kashmiri, a Dardic language

02631 COOK, N.C. The way of the swan; poems of Kashmir. Bombay: Asia, 1958. 148p.

02632 KACHRU, B.B. Kashmiri and other Dardic languages. In M.B. Emeneau & C.A. Ferguson, eds. Linguistics in South Asia. The Hague: Mouton, 1969, 284-306. (CTL, 5)

02633 KAUL, J.L. Kashmiri literature. Mysore: U. of Mysore, 1970. 73p.

02634 ______. Studies in Kashmiri. Srinagar: Kapoor, 1968. 339p.

02635 KOUL, O.N. Linguistic studies in Kashmiri. Chandigarh: Bahri, 1977. 103p. (Series in Indian languages and linguistics, 9)

f. Pashto, language of the Pathans

02636 AHMED, A.S., tr. Mataloona: Pukhto proverbs. 2nd rev. ed. Karachi: OUP, 1975. 59p.

02637 BAUSANI, A. Pashto language & literature. Tr. from Italian by B. Blair. In Mahfil 7,1/2 (1971) 55-69.

02638 ENEVOLDSEN, J., ed. Sound the bells, O moon, arise and shine. Peshawar: University Book Agency, 1970. 92p.

02639 RAVERTY, H.G., tr. Selections from Pushto poetry. Lahore: al-Biruni, 1978. 348p. [Rpt. 1880 ed.]

5. North India: Hindi, its Dialects and Related Languages [for Urdu, see VI. E. 3. above]

02640 AGGARWAL, N.K., ed. A bibliography of studies on Hindi language and linguistics. Gurgaon: Indian Documentation Service, 1978. 184p.

02641 CHOUDHARY, R.K. A survey of Maithili literature. Deoghar: Shanti Devi, 1976. 273p.

02642 DWIVEDI, R.A. A critical survey of Hindi literature. Delhi: Motilal, 1966. 304p.

02643 GARCIN DE TASSY, J.H. Histoire de la littérature hindoui et hindoustani; biographie, bibliographie et estraits. 2nd ed., rev. NY: B. Franklin, 1968. 3 v. [1st ed. 1839]

02644 HANDA, R.L. History of Hindi language and literature. Bombay: BVB, 1978. 504p.

02645 JHA, S. The formation of the Maithili language. London: Luzac, 1958. 638p.

02646 JINDAL, K.B. A history of Hindi literature. Allahabad: Kitab Mahal, 1955. 384p.

02647 KEAY, F.E. A history of Hindi literature. 3rd ed. Calcutta: YMCA Pub. House, 1960. 110p.

02648 MISHRA, J. A history of Maithili literature. Allahabad: Tirabhukti, 1949-50. 2 v.

02649 ______. History of Maithili literature. ND: Sahitya Akademi, 1976. 308p.

02650 NARULA, S.S. Hindi language: a scientific history. 2nd ed. Delhi: Oriental, 1976. 136p.

02651 PANDEY, I.P. Hindi literature: trends & traits. Calcutta: KLM, 1975. 248p.

02652 SAKSENA, B. Evolution of Awadhi (a branch of Hindi). Delhi: Motilal, 1971. 562p. [1st pub. 1937]

02653 VAJPEYI, A.P. Persian influence on Hindi. Calcutta: U. of Calcutta, 1935. 212p.

6. The Northeast: Languages and Literatures of Bengal and Assam
a. Bengali language and literature
i. bibliography

02654 ČIŽIKOVA, K.L. & C.A. FERGUSON. Bibliographical review of Bengali studies. In M.B. Emeneau & C.A. Ferguson, eds. Linguistics in South Asia. The Hague: Mouton, 85-98. (CTL, 5)

02655 MUKHERJI, J.M. Bengali literature in English; a bibliography. Calcutta: M.C. Sarkar, 1970. 108p.

ii. surveys, studies, and anthologies

02656 ASHRAF, S.A. Muslim traditions in Bengali literature. Karachi: Bengal Lit. Soc., U. of Karachi, 1960. 83p.

02657 CHATTERJI, S.K. The origin and development of the Bengali language. London: Allen & Unwin, 1970-72. 3 v. [Rpt. 1926 ed.]

02658 DIMOCK, E.C., ed. & tr. The thief of love; Bengali tales from court and village. Chicago: UChiP, 1963. 305p.

02659 FUCHAS, Mother. Bengali language and dialects. In Folklore (C) 16,7 (1975) 232-55.

02660 GHOSH, J.C. Bengali literature. NY: AMS Press, 1978. 198p. [Rpt. 1948 ed.]

02661 HAQ, M.E. Muslim Bengali literature. Karachi: Pakistan Pub., 1957. 231p.

02662 RAY, A. & L. RAY. Bengali literature. Bombay: Intl. Book House, 1942. 126p.

02663 SEN, D.O. History of Bengali language and literature. 2nd ed. Calcutta: U. of Calcutta, 1954. 865p. [1st pub. 1911]

02664 SEN, S. History of Bengali literature. Rev. ed. ND: Sahitya Akademi, 1971. 394p. [1st ed. 1960]

02665 SENGUPTA, N.G. A book of Bengali verse from 10th to 20th century. Calcutta: Indian Pub., 1969. 114p.

02666 YUSUF JAMAL, Begam, tr. Poems from East Bengal. Selections from East Bengal poetry of the last five hundred years: 1389-1954. Karachi: Pakistan PEN, 1954. 144p.

02667 ZBAVITEL, D. Bengali literature. Wiesbaden: Harrassowitz, 1976. 307p. (HIL, 9:3)

02668 ______. The development of the baromasi in the Bengali literature. In AO 29,4 (1961) 582-619.

b. Assamese language and literature

02669 BARUA, B.K. Assamese literature. Bombay: Intl. Book House, 1941. 102p.

02670 ______. History of Assamese literature. ND: Sahitya Akademi, 1964. 203p.

02671 BARUA, H. Assamese literature. ND: NBT, 1965. 282p.

02672 BHUYAN, S.K. Studies in the literature of Assam. 2nd ed. Gauhati: Lawyer's Book Stall, 1962. 254p. [1st ed. 1956]

02673 KAKATI, B.K. Assamese, its formation and development; a scientific treatise on the history and philology of Assamese language. 2nd ed., rev. & ed. by G.C. Goswami. Gauhati: Lawyer's Book Stall, 1962. 432p.

02674 NEOG, D. New light on history of Asamiya literature from the earliest until recent times, including an account of its antecedents. Dispur: Suwani Prakas, 1962. 464p.

02675 SARMA, S.N. Assamese literature. Wiesbaden: Harrassowitz, 1976. 118p. (HIL, 9:2)

02676 SHASTRI, P.N., & P. LAL. The Writers Workshop handbook of Assamese literature. Calcutta: Writers Workshop, 1972-. v. 1, 114p.

7. Nepali Language and Literature

02677 CLARK, T.W. Nepali and Pahari. In M.B. Emeneau & C.A. Ferguson, eds. Linguistics in South Asia. The Hague: Mouton, 1969, 249-76. (CTL, 5)

02678 SRIVASTAVA, D. Nepali language, its history and development. Calcutta: Calcutta U., 1962. 145p.

02679 TANASARMA. An introduction to Nepali literature. Nepal R. 1,9 (1969) 396-410.

VII. PERFORMING ARTS: MUSIC, DANCE AND DRAMA OF SOUTH ASIA

A. Classical Texts of Music and Dance [for Sāmaveda, see Chap. Two, V. B. 2.; see also Chap. Three, VIII. C. 3. b.]

02680 DHANAÑJAYA. The Dāsarūpa; a treatise on Hindu dramaturgy. Tr. by G.C.O. Haas. NY: ColUP, 1912. 169p. (Indo-Iranian series, 7)

02681 JĀYASENĀPATI. Nṛttaratnāvalī. Ed. by V. Raghavan. Madras: Govt. Oriental Manuscripts Library, 1965. 677p.

02682 KUMBHĀ, Mahārāṇā of Udaipur. Saṅgītarāja. Vol. 1. Ed. by Premlata Sharma. Varanasi: BHU, 1963. [English intro. 1-153]

02683 LATH, M. A study of Dattilam: a treatise on the sacred music of ancient India. ND: Impex India, 1978. 472p.

02684 NATH, R. A study of the Sanskrit texts on the inter-relationship of the performing and the plastic arts. In J. of the Natl. Centre for the Performing Arts 8,2 (1979) 1-22.

02685 ŚARṄGADEVA. The Saṁgītaratnākara. v. 4, chapter on dancing. Tr. from Sanskrit by K. Kunjunni Raja & R. Burnier. In ALB 23,3/4 (1959) 1-262.

B. Music of India

1. Inter-regional studies
a. bibliography, discography, and reference works

02686 BARNETT, E.B. A discography of the art music of India. Ann Arbor: Soc. for Ethnomusicology, 1975. 54p.

02687 ______. Special bibliography: the art music of India. In Ethnomusicology 14,2 (1970) 278-312.

02688 BRUNET, J. Oriental music: a selected discography. NY: Foreign Area Materials Center, U. of the State of NY, 1971. 100p.

02689 DANIÉLOU, A. A catalogue of recorded classical and traditional Indian music. Paris: UNESCO, 1952. 200p.

02690 Index to the Journal of the Music Academy, Vols. 21-30. In JMA 30,1 (1959) i-xlix.

02691 India in sound and rhythm; a catalog of recorded Indian music. ND: Educ. Resources Center, 1978. 103p.

02692 MUSIC ACADEMY, MADRAS. Index to the articles published in the annual conference - souvenirs from the earliest period up to the 49th Conference, 1975-76. Madras, 1977. 16p.

02693 POWERS, H.S. Indian music and the English language. In Ethnomusicology 9 (1965) 1-12.

02694 RAJAN, T.N. A classification scheme for Indian music literature. In SN 16 (1970) 73-88.

02695 RAMASWAMI AIYAR, M.S. Bibliography of Indian music. In JRAS (1941) 233-46. [Discusses Sanskrit texts]

b. surveys and studies of Indian music
i. introductions and descriptive surveys

02696 AGARWALA, V.K. Traditions and trends in Indian music. Meerut: Rastogi, 1966. 88p.

02697 Aspects of Indian music [AIR Symposium]. ND: PDMIB, 1970. 103p.

02698 BAKE, A.A. The music of India. In The New Oxford History of Music. London: OUP, 1957, v. 1, 195-227.

02699 BROWN, R.E. India's music. In J. Elder, ed. Chapters in Indian civilization.... Dubuque: Kendall, Hunt, 1970, 137-78.

02700 ______. India's music. In D.P. McAllester, ed. Readings in ethnomusicology. NY: Johnson Reprint, 1971, 293-329.

02701 DEVA, B.C. Indian music. ND: ICCR, 1974. 172p.

02702 ______. An introduction to Indian music. ND: PDMIB, 1973. 130p.

02703 FYZEE RAHAMIN, A.B. The music of India. ND: OBRC, 1979. 95p. + 16pl. [Rpt. 1925 ed.]

02704 GOSWAMI, O. The story of Indian music; its growth and synthesis. Bombay: Asia, 1961. 332p.

02705 HOLROYDE, P. Indian music: a vast ocean of promise. London: Allen & Unwin, 1972. 291p. [also pub. NY: Praeger, 1972: Music of India]

02706 JAIRAZBHOY, N.A. Music. In A.L. Basham, ed. A cultural history of India. Oxford: OUP, 1975, 212-42.

02707 JOSHI, B. Understanding Indian music. Bombay: Asia, 1963. 102p.

02708 KUPPUSWAMY, G. & M. HARIHARAN. Indian music: a perspective. Delhi: Sundeep, 1980. 262p.

02709 ______, eds. Readings on Indian music. Trivandrum: College Book House, 1979. 239p.

02710 MASSEY, R. & J. MASSEY. The music of India. London: Kahn & Averill, 1976. 189p.

02711 MENON, R.R. The sound of Indian music: a journey into raga. ND: Indian Book Co., 1976. 85p.

02712 NIJENHUIS, E. TE, tr. Dattilam: a compendium of ancient Indian music. Leiden: Brill, 1970. 477p.

02713 ______. Musicological literature. Wiesbaden: Harrassowitz, 1977. 51p. (HIL, 6:1)

02714 POPLEY, H.A. The music of India. 3rd ed. ND: YMCA Pub. House, 1966. 184p.

02715 PRAJNANANANDA, Swami. Music, its form, function, and value. ND: Munshiram, 1979. 181p.

02716 RAM, V. Glimpses of Indian music. Allahabad: Kitab Mahal, 1962. 192p.

02717 SHARMAN, G. Filigree in sound: form and content in Indian music. ND: Vikas, 1970. 176p.

02718 SHIRALI, V.D. Sargam: an introduction to Indian music. ND: Abhinav/Marg, 1977. 125p. + 14pl.

02719 SORRELL, N. Indian music in performance: a practical introduction. NY: NYU Press, 1980.

02720 SUBBA RAO, T.V. Studies in Indian music. Bombay: Asia, 1962. 248p.

02721 WADE, B.C. Music in India: the classical traditions. Englewood Cliffs, NJ: Prentice Hall, 1979. 252p.

ii. historical studies and early Western views of Indian music

02722 BHATTACHARYA, A. A treatise on ancient Hindu music. Calcutta: K.P. Bagchi, 1978. 176p.

02723 FOX-STRANGWAYS, A.H. The music of Hindostan. ND: OBRC, 1975. 364p. + 17pl. [Rpt. 1914 ed.]

02724 JONES, W. & N.A. WILLARD. Music of India. 2nd rev. ed. Calcutta: Sushil Gupta, 1962. 122p. [1st pub. 1793]

02725 NIJENHUIS, E.TE. Indian music: history and structure. Leiden: Brill, 1974. 142p. + 14pl. (HO, 2:6)

02726 PINGLE, B.A. History of Indian music, with particular reference to theory and practice. 3rd ed. Calcutta: A. Gupta, 1962. 124p.

02727 PRAJNANANANDA, Swami. Historical development of Indian music; a critical study. 2nd new ed. Calcutta: KLM, 1973. 495p.

02728 ______. A historical study of Indian music. Calcutta: Anandadhara Prakashan, 1965. 503p.

02729 ______. A history of Indian music. Calcutta: Ramakrishna Vedanta Math, 1963-. v. 1, ancient period, 210p.

02730 ______. Music of the South-Asian peoples: a historical study of music of India, Kashmere, Ceylon and Bangladesh, and Pakistan. Calcutta: Ramakrishna Vedanta Math, 1979-. v. 1, 382p. [to be 3 v.]

02731 ROSENTHAL, E. The study of Indian music and its instruments; a study of the present & a record of the past; together with Sir William Jones celebrated treatise in full.... ND: OBRC, 1970. 220p. + 19pl. [1st pub. 1928]

02732 TAGORE, S.M., comp. Hindu music from various authors. 3rd ed. Varanasi: CSSO, 1965. 423p. (CSS, 49) [1st pub. 1882]

02733 ______., comp. Universal history of music. Varanasi: CSSO, 1963. 354p. (CSS, 31) [Rpt. 1896 ed.]

iii. comparative studies

02734 ASHTON, R., ed. Music east and west. ND: ICCR, 1966. 217p.

02735 BALOCH, A. Spanish Cante Jondo and its origin in Sindhi music. Hyderabad (Sind): Mehran Arts Council, 1968. 62p.

02736 BHATKHANDE, V.N. A comparative study of some of the leading music systems of the 15th, 16th, 17th and 18th centuries. Baroda: Indian Musicological Soc., 1972. 113p.

02737 HALL, F. Influence of Indian dance on the West. In SN 28 (1973) 30-49.

02738 JUNIUS, M. Indian and Western music: structural differences and similarities. In Indian Horizons 21,2-3 (1972) 93-101.

02739 MENUHIN, Y. The possible influences of Indian classical music on future Western music. In Orbis Musicae (Tel Aviv) 1,2 (1972) 105-11.

02740 Music of India; studies in cultural exchange. In CAS 12 (1978) 3-82. [5 articles by D. Reck, R.E. Brown, B.C. Wade, D.M. Neuman, B. Silver]

02741 PRAJNANANANDA, Swami. Music of the nations: a comparative study. ND: Munshiram, 1973. 223p.

02742 PRASAD, O. Contemporary Indian music: a classification with special reference to the field of Banaras. In MI 58,3 (1978) 208-31.

c. musical theory
i. traditional aesthetics and music theory

02743 CLEMENTS, E. Introduction to the study of Indian music; an attempt to reconcile modern Hindustani music with ancient musical theory and to propound an accurate and comprehensive method of treatment of the subject of Indian musical intonation. Allahabad: Kitab Mahal, 196-. 104p. [1st pub. 1903]

02744 DEVA, B.C. Psychoacoustics of music and speech. Madras: Music Academy, 1967. 306p.

02745 GHOSH, N. Fundamentals of rāga and tāla, with a new system of notation. Bombay: Popular, 1968. 121p.

02746 ISAAC, L. Theory of Indian music. Madras: Shyam Printers, 1967. 256p.

02747 JAIRAZBHOY, N.A. A possible basis of Bharata's melodic system. In JIMS 4,4 (1973) 5-18.

02748 RAMASWAMI SASTRI, K.S. Indian aesthetics; music and dance. Tirupati: Sri Venkateswara U., 1966. 74p.

02749 SINHA, P. An approach to the study of Indian music. Calcutta: Indian Pub., 1970. 119p.

02750 ______. The structure of Indian music: the basic concepts. In Folklore (C) 9,12 (1968) 468-479.

02751 SWARUP, B. Theory of Indian music. 2nd ed., rev. Allahabad: Swarup, 1950. 238p.

02752 VERMA, K.K. Ananda in the aesthetics of Indian music. In SN 9 (1968) 25-40.

ii. rāga: melodic structures

02753 BANDYOPADHYAYA, S. The origin of rāga: a concise history of the evolution, growth, and the treatment of raga from the age of Bharatamuni to Bhatkhande. 2nd ed. ND: Munshiram, 1977. 82p.

02754 DEVA, B.C. Rāga rūpa; introduction to the methodology of rāga classification. In JMA 33 (1962) 142-76.

02755 NIJENHUIS, E.TE. Continuity in Indian rāga tradition. In JMA 43 (1972) 146-69.

02756 POWERS, H.S. Mode and raga. In Musical Q. 49,4 (1958) 448-60.

02757 VERMA, K.K. Musicometry of Indian melody. In SN 17 (1970) 5-37.

02758 SUBBA RAO, B. Bharatiya sangeet: raga nidhi; encyclopedia of Indian ragas, a comparative study of Hindustani and Karnatak ragas. Poona: Vishnu Digambar Smarak Samiti, 1956-66. 4 v., 907p.

iii. tāla: rhythm

02759 CHANDOLA, A.C. Metalinguistic structure of Indian drumming: a study of musicolinguistics. In Language and Style 2 (1969) 288-95.

02760 NEOG, M. & K. CHANGKAKATI. Rhythm in the Vaishnava music of Assam. Gauhati: Bargit Res. Cmtee., Asam Sangeet Natak Akademi, 1962. 146p.

02761 RATANJANKAR, S.N. Comparative study of tāla systems of Hindustani and Karnatak music. In JMA 38 (1967) 113-29.

02762 STEWART, R.M. The modes of rhythmic expression in contemporary Indian and western music. In JMA 35 (1964) 68-76.

02763 VENKATARAMA IYER, V.T. & R. VENKATARATHNAM. The theory of musicometrics. In JMA 44 (1973) 217-26.

iv. śruti and svara: scale and note

02764 CHANDOLA, A.C. Some systems of musical scales and linguistic principles. In Semiotica 2,2 (1970) 135-50.

02765 JAIRAZBHOY, N.A. Factors underlying important notes in North Indian music. In Ethnomusicology 16,1 (1972) 63-81.

02766 KHAN, A.K. & B.K. KAPILESHWARI. Indian musical scales. In SN 8 (1968) 73-124.

02767 LEELA, S.V. Notes and their places in Indian music, made simple. Madras: Leipzig Printers, n.d. 22p.

02768 LENTZ, D.A. Tones and intervals of Hindu classical music.... Lincoln: U. of Nebraska, 1961. 25p.

02769 LOBO, A. Indian musical "ma-grama" of bharata: world's only perfect scale. In JIMS 2,3 (1971) 37-60.

02770 Musical scale. In SN 17 (1970) 5-74. [3 articles by K.K. Verma, A. Lobo, R. Sathyanarayana]

02771 Musical scales: report of symposium, February, 1973. ND: Sangeet Natak Akademi, 1975. 176p.

02772 SATHYANARAYANA, R. Śruti: the scale foundation. In SN 17 (1970) 58-74.

02773 SHRINGY, R.K. The concept of śruti as related to svara - a textual and critical study. In JMA 44 (1973) 111-28.

02774 TAGORE, S.M. The twenty-two musical srutis of the Hindus. Calcutta: Bengal Academy of Music, 1886. 51p.

d. the problem of developing notation for traditional music and dance

02775 BENESH, R. & J. BENESH & M. BALCHIN. Notating Indian dance. In SN 9 (1968) 5-24.

02776 BOATWRIGHT, H. A handbook on staff notation for Indian music. Bombay: BVB, 1960. 56p.

02777 KAUFMANN, W. Musical notations of the Orient. Bloomington: Indiana U. Press, 1967. 498p. [183-263 on India]

02778 ______. Some reflections of the notations of Vedic chant. In H. Tischler, ed. Essays in musicology. Bloomington: Indiana U. School of Music, 1968, 1-18.

e. Indian musical instruments
i. general

02779 BALLINGER, T.O. & P.H. BAJRACHARYA. Nepalese musical instruments. In SWJA 16 (1960) 398-416.

02780 BALOCH, N.A. Musical instruments of the Lower Indus Valley of Sind. Hyderabad (Sind): Mehran Arts Council, 1966. 75p.

02781 DEVA, B.C. Musical instruments. ND: NBT, 1977. 106p.

02782 ______. Musical instruments of India: their history and development. Calcutta: KLM, 1978. 306p.

02783 KOTHARI, K.S. Indian folk musical instruments. ND: Sangeet Natak Akademi, 1968. 99p.

02784 ______. The Langas. A folk-musician caste of Rajasthan. In SN 27 (1973) 5-26.

02785 KRISHNASWAMI, S. Musical instruments of India. Boston: Crescendo, 1971. 102p. [1st pub. 1965]

02786 MULLER, M. Classical Indian musical instruments. Copenhagen: Musikhistorisk Museum, 1969. 20p.

02787 SACHS, C. Die Musikinstrumente Indiens und Indonesiens. Berlin: W. de Gruyter, 1923. 192p.

02788 SAMBAMOORTHY, P. Catalogue of musical instruments exhibited in the Government Museum, Madras. Rev. ed. Madras: Govt. of Madras, 1962. 32p. + 14 pl. [1st pub. 1931]

02789 TARLEKAR, G.H. & N. TARLEKAR. Musical instruments in Indian sculpture. Pune: Pune Vidyarthi Griha Prakashan, 1972. 104p.

ii. wind instruments

02790 DESHPANDE, V.H. & S.N. RATANJANKAR. Harmonium and Hindustani classical music. In Sangeet Kala Vihar 1,4 (1970) 51-59.

02791 JAIRAZBHOY, N.A. A preliminary survey of the oboe in India. In BITCM (1971) pt. 1, 213-28.

02792 SAMBAMOORTHY, P. The flute. 3rd ed., rev. and enl. Madras: Indian Music Pub. House, 1967. 143p. [1st ed. 1927]

iii. string instruments

02793 HANSEN, J. [Swami PREM VEDANT]. A simple introduction to Indian classical music: a small collection of notes made to introduce non-Indian students of classical music to the sitar, its heritage and tradition, with lessons for beginners. 2nd ed. Baroda: H. Jan, 1973-.

02794 LEELA, S.V. Veena, self-taught: an introduction to Carnatic music. Madras: V.P.S. Printers, 1976. 34p.

02795 RAGHAVAN, V. The Indian origin of the violin. JMA 19,1 (1948) 65-70.

02796 RAM AVTAR. Learn to play on sitar. ND: Pankaj Pub., 1978. 56p.

02797 SAMBAMOORTHY, P. Śruti vādyas (drones). ND: All India Handicrafts Board, 1957. 48p. + 23 pl. (Sangita Vadyalaya Series, 1)

02798 SCHRAMM, H. Traditional Indian melodies for sitar. NY: Southern Music Pub., 1969. 49p.

02799 SHANKAR, L.N. The art of violin accompaniment in South Indian classical music. Ph.D. diss., Wesleyan U., 1974. 206p. [UM 74-23,027]

iv. percussion: tablā, mṛdangam, and other drums

02800 BROWN, R.E. The mṛdanga: a study of drumming in South India. Ph.D. diss., UCLA, 1965. 2 v., 363, 388p. [UM 65-6947]

02801 HARI HARA SARMA, T.R. The art of mridhangam (a practical guide). Madras: Sri Jaya Ganesh Tala Vadya Vidyalaya, 1969. 93p.

02802 HARTENBERGER, J.R. Mṛdangam manual: a guidebook to South Indian rhythm for Western musicians. Ph.D. diss., Wesleyan U., 1974. 626p. [UM 74-23,024]

02803 KRISHNASWAMI, S. Drums of India through the ages. In JMA 38 (1967) 72-82.

02804 MURPHY, D. The structure, repair and acoustical properties of the classical drums of India, with special reference to mṛdanga and tablā. In JMA 36 (1965) 223-247.

02805 RAM AVTAR. Learn to play on tabla. ND: Pankaj Pub., 1977. 32p.

02806 RAMAMURTY, D. The theory and practice of mridanga (Mridanga tatwam). Tr. from Telugu by V. Veerabhadram. Rajahmundry: Ramamurty, 1973. 336p.

02807 SAMBAMOORTHY, P. Laya vadyas (time-keeping instruments). ND: All India Handicrafts Board, 1959. 56p. + 32 pl. (Sangita Vadyalaya Series, 2)

02808 STEWART, R.M. The tablā in perspective. Ph.D. diss., UCLA, 1974. 444p. [UM 74-12,474]

02809 VENKATARAMA IYER, T. The art of playing mridangam: a percussion instrument in Karnataka music. Madras: Bharati Vijayam Press, 1969. 95p.

f. the musician in Indian society

02810 BRAHASPATI, K.C.D. Mussalmans and Indian music. In JIMS 6,2 (1975) 27-49.

02811 DANIÉLOU, A. The situation of music and musicians in countries of the Orient. Florence: Leo S. Olschki, 1971. 124p.

02812 GERSON-KIWI, E. The musician in society: East and West. In Cultures 1,1 (1973) 175-204.

02813 KESKAR, B.V. Indian music; problems and prospects. Bombay: Popular, 1967. 93p.

02814 LAMSWEERDE, F. VAN. Musicians in Indian society: an attempt at a classification. In Tropical Man 2 (1969) 7-30.

02815 RIZVI, D. Great musicians of India. Bombay: I.B.H., 1968. 85p.

2. North Indian or Hindustani Music
a. general introductions

02816 BALOCH, N.A. Development of music in Sind. Hyderabad (Sind): Sind U. Press, 1973. 32p.

02817 BANDYOPADHYAYA, S. The music of India: a popular handbook of Hindustani music. 2nd rev. ed. Bombay: Taraporevala, 1958. 84p.

02818 BHATKHANDE, V.N. A short historical survey of the music of upper India. Baroda: Indian Musicological Soc., 1974. 43p. [Rpt. of 1916 speech]

02819 DESHPANDE, V.H. Indian musical traditions; an aesthetic study of the gharanas in Hindustani music. Tr. by S.H. Deshpande. Bombay: Popular, 1973. 116p.

02820 ______. Maharashtra's contribution to music. ND: Maharashtra Info. Centre, 1972. 83p.

02821 GUPTA, B.L. The Gwalior School of Music. In JIMS 4,1 (1973) 5-15.

02822 JOSHI, G.N. Music in Maharashtra. In Sangeet Kala Vihar 1,3 (1970) 5-12.

02823 KARNANI, C. Listening to Hindustani music. Bombay: Orient Longman, 1976. 167p.

02824 NEUMAN , D.M. Gharāṇās: the rise of musical "houses" in Delhi and neighboring cities. In B. Nettl, ed. Eight urban musical cultures. Urbana: U. of Illinois Press, 1978, 186-222.

02825 RANADE, G.H. Music in Maharashtra. ND: Maharashtra Info. Center, 1967. 58p.

b. theory of Hindustani music
i. aesthetics

02826 RANADE, G.H. Hindustani music: its physics and aesthetics. 3rd ed., rpt. Bombay: Popular, 1971. 204p. [1st pub. 1939]

02827 SAXENA, S.K. Aesthetics of Hindustani music. In SN 28 (1973) 5-23.

02828 SINGH, T.J. Aesthetics of Hindustani musical forms. In SN 16 (1970) 23-32.

ii. rāga system of Northern India

02829 BOSE, N.K. Melodic types of Hindusthan; a scientific interpretation of the rāga system of Northern India. Bombay: Jaico, 1960. 748p.

02830 DANIÉLOU, A. The rāgas of northern Indian music. London: Cresset, 1968. 403p. [1st pub. 1949]

02831 JAIRAZBHOY, N.A. The rāgs of North Indian music: their structure and evolution. Middletown, CT: Wesleyan U. Press, 1971. 222p.

02832 KAUFMANN, W. The rāgas of North India. Bloomington: Indiana U. Press, 1968. 625p. (Asian Studies Res. Inst., Oriental studies, 1)

02833 POWERS, H. Review of Kaufmann's Rāgas of North India. In Ethnomusicology 13,2 (1969) 350-64.

iii. tāla: rhythm in Hindustani music

02834 BHOWMICK, K.N. Banaras school of tablā-playing. In JMA 44 (1973) 129-41.

02835 ROACH, D. The Banaras bāj - the tablā tradition of a northern Indian city. In Asian Music 2,2 (1972) 29-41.

02836 ROBERTSON, D. Tablā; a rhythmic introduction to Indian music. NY: Peer Intl., 1968. 54p.

02837 SAXENA, S.K. Form and content in Hindustani rhythm. In SN 18 (1970) 5-19.

c. vocal music of Northern India

02838 BOSE, S. Thumri in Hindustani music. In Sangeet Kala Vihar 1,2 (1970) 29-32.

02839 DESAI, C. The origin and development of khyāl. In JMA 40 (1969) 147-82.

02840 SINHA, P. Vocal music of North India: classical forms and styles. In Folklore (C) 10,2 (1969) 63-73.

02841 WADE, B. Chīz in khyāl: the traditional composition in the improvised performance. In Ethnomusicology 17,3 (1973) 443-59.

02842 ______. Khyāl: a study in Hindustani classical vocal music. Ph.D. diss., UCLA, 1971. 2 v., 526, 124p. [UM 72-3195]

d. musicians of Hindustani music

02843 ATHAVALE, V.R. Pandit Vishnu Digambar. ND: NBT, 1967. 55p.

02844 ERDMAN, J.L. The Maharaja's musicians: the organization of cultural performances at Jaipur in the nineteenth century. In S. Vatuk, ed. American studies in the anthropology of India. ND: Manohar, 1978, 342-70.

02845 MENON, R.R. K.L. Saigal, the pilgrim of the swara. Delhi: Clarion Books, 1978. 111p.

02846 NEUMAN, D.M. The life of music in north India; the organization of an artistic tradition. Detroit: Wayne State U. Press, 1980. 296p.

02847 RAM AVTAR. The torch bearer of Indian music: Maharshi Vishnu Digambar Paluskar. ND: Pankaj Pub., 1978. 40p.

02848 RATANJANKAR, S.N. Pandit Bhatkhande. ND: NBT, 1967. 61p.

02849 RAYCHAUDHURI, M. Studies in artistic creativity: personality structure of the musician. Calcutta: Rabindra Bharati, 1966. 256p.

02850 SHANKAR, R. My music, my life. NY: Simon & Schuster, 1968. 160p.

02851 SILVER, B. On becoming an ustād: six life sketches in the evolution of a gharāṇā. In Asian Music 7,2 (1976) 27-58.

3. South Indian or Karnatak/Carnatic Music

a. general introduction

02852 BENARY, B.L. Within the Karnatik tradition. Ph.D. diss., Wesleyan U., 1973. 313p. [UM 73-27,621]

02853 BRAHASPATI, K.C.D. Muslim influence on Venkatamakhi and his school. In SN 13 (1969) 5-26.

02854 DAY, C.R. The music and musical instruments of southern India and the Deccan. Delhi: B.R., 1974. 181p. [Rpt. 1891 ed.]

02855 DURGA, S.A.K. Voice-culture with special reference to South Indian music. In BITCM (1970) 71-100.

02856 JAYALAKSHMI, S.S. Musical systems of ancient Tamils. In JIMS 6,1 (1975) 19-44.

02857 L'ARMAND, K. & A. L'ARMAND. Music in Madras: the urbanization of a cultural tradition. In Bruno Nettl, ed. Eight urban musical cultures. Urbana: U. of Illinois Press, 1978, 115-45.

02858 PODUVAL, R.V. The music of Kerala and other essays. Trivandrum: St. Joseph's Press, 195-. 90p.

02859 RAMAKRISHNAN, E.M. Fundamentals of South Indian or Karnatak music in a nutshell. Madras: 1967. 48p.

02860 RANGARAMANUJA AYYANGAR, R. History of South Indian (Carnatic) music, from Vedic times to the present. Madras: the author, 1972. 368 + 170p.

02861 RIES, R.E. The cultural setting of south Indian music. In BITCM (1967) pt. 1, 7-21.

02862 SAMBAMOORTHY, P. A dictionary of South Indian music and musicians. Madras: Indian Music Pub. House, 1952-. v. 1-3 [covers A-N], 535p.

02863 ______. History of Indian music. Madras: Indian Music Pub. House, 1960. 264p.

02864 ______. South Indian music. Madras: Indian Music Pub. House, 1960-1969. 6 v.

02865 SUBRAHMANYA AYYAR, C. The grammar of South Indian (Karnatic) music. 2nd ed., rev. Madras: Ananda Press, 1951. 149p.

02866 WHITE, E.E. Appreciating India's music: an introduction, with an emphasis on the music of South India. Boston: Crescendo, 1971. 96p. [1st pub. 1957]

b. theory of Karnatak music

02867 ADYANTHAYA, N.M. Melody music of India; how to learn it. Mangalore, 1965. 292p.

02868 KAUFMANN, W. The ragas of South India: a catalogue of scalar material. Bloomington: Indiana U. Press, 1976. 723p.

02869 KUCKERTZ, J. Form und Melodiebildung der karnatischen Musik Südindiens in Umkreis der vorderorientalischen und der nordindischer Kunstmusik. Wiesbaden: Harrassowitz, 1970. 254p.

02870 MUKUND, S. The unique system of 72 scales of Karnatak music. In JMA 43 (1973) 88-95.

02871 POWERS, H.S. The background of the South Indian raga-system. Ph.D. diss., Princeton U., 1958. 3 v., 222, 84, 10p.

02872 RAMACHANDRAN, K. Mathematical basis of the thala system, Carnatic music. 1st ed. Madras, 1962. 48p.

c. musicians and composers

02873 BENARY, B. Composers and tradition in Karnatik music. In Asian Music 3,2 (1972) 42-51.

02874 HIGGINS, J.B. From prince to populace; patronage as a determinant of change in South Indian (Karnatak) music. In Asian Music 7,2 (1976) 20-26.

02875 RANGARAMANUJA AYYANGAR, R. Musings of a musician: recent trends in Carnatic music. Bombay: Wilco Pub. House, 1977. 128p.

02876 SAMBAMOORTHY, P. Great composers. Madras: Indian Music Pub. House, 1962. 164p. [1st ed. 1959]

02877 SITA, S. Some less known composers of Karnatik music. In BITCM 2 (1969) 1-34.

02878 VENKITASUBRAMONIA IYER, S. Some less known composers of Kerala. In JMA 40 (1969) 89-106.

02879 ______. Swati Tirunal and his music. Trivandrum: College Book House, 1975. 296p.

02880 VIDYA SHANKAR. Shyama Sastry. ND: NBT, 1970. 83p.

4. Devotional Music of Various Religious Traditions

02881 Bhajans: a collection of songs of praise in various languages used at the NBCLC. 3rd ed. Bangalore: National Biblical Catechetical and Liturgical Centre, 1977. 64p.

02882 BHATTACHARYYA, S.P. Indian hymnology. In Cultural heritage of India. Calcutta: RMIC, 1956, v. 4, 464-78.

02883 DANIÉLOU, A. Musique religieuse dans l'Inde. In Encyclopédie des musiques sacrées. Paris: Labergerie, 1968, 162-69.

02884 Music in prayers in the Hindu, Christian, Zoroastrian and Islamic religions. In BITCM (1963) pt. 1, 29-78.

02885 QURESHI, REGULA. Indo-Muslim religious music, an overview. In Asian Music 3,2 (1972) 15-22.

02886 ______. Mysticism and devotion in the music of the Qawwali. NY: Asia Soc., 1977.

02887 ______. Tarannum: the chanting of Urdu poetry. In Ethnomusicology 13 (1969) 425-68.

02888 Sikh sacred music. ND: Sikh Sacred Music Soc., 1967. 90p.

02889 SIMON, R.L. Bhakti ritual music in South India: a study of the bhajana in its cultural matrix. Ph.D. diss., UCLA, 413p. [UM 75-25,189]

02890 SINGER, M.B. Search for a great tradition in cultural performances. In his When a great tradition modernizes. NY: Praeger, 1972, 67-80.

5. Traditions of Nepal, Sri Lanka and Other Regions

02891 HRIDAYA, C.D. Nepalese music. Tr. by T. Manandhar. Kathmandu: Nepal Bhasha Parishad, 1957. 18p.

02892 KULATILLAKE, C. DE S. A background to Sinhala traditional music of Sri Lanka. Colombo: Dept. of Cultural Affairs, 1976. 25p.

02893 ______. Metre, melody, and rhythm in Sinhala music. Colombo: Sinhala Music Res. Unit, Sri Lanka Broadcasting Corp., 1976. 52p.

02894 RAY, S. Music of eastern India; vocal music in Bengali, Oriya, Assamese, and Manipuri, with special emphasis on Bengali. Calcutta: KLM, 1973. 264p.

02895 SHARMA, B.L. Contribution of Rajasthan to Indian music. In JIMS 2,2 (1971) 32-47.

02896 SURYA SENA, D. Of Sri Lanka I sing: the life and times of Devar Surya Sena, OBE, MA, LLB, ARCM. Colombo: Surya Sena, 1978. 306p.

6. Ethnomusicology and Folk Music [for regional folksongs, see Chaps. Ten - Sixteen]

02897 BHATTACHARYA, S.B. Ethno-musicology and India. Calcutta: Indian Pub., 1968. 100p.

02898 CHAUHAN, I.E.N. Ethnomusicology and Kinnaur: a suggested methodology. In SN 27 (1973) 27-48.

02899 HENRY, E.O. The variety of music in a North Indian village: reassessing cantometrics. In Ethnomusicology 20,1 (1976) 49-66.

02900 PARMAR, S. Folk music and mass media. ND: Communication Pub., 1977. 112p.

02901 SEN GUPTA, S. On ethnomusicology and India. In Folklore (C) 9,7 (1968) 229-242.

02902 SEN GUPTA, S. & S. PARMAR. Bibliography of India and Pakistan: C., folk music, ballad, song, dance and drama. In Folklore (C) 7,5 (1966) 193-202; 7,6 (1966) 212-28.

02903 SINHA, P. Folk-classical continuum in Indian music. In Folklore (C) 10 (1969) 355-73, 439-63; 11 (1970) 9-19.

C. Traditional Dance, Dance-Drama, and Theatre of South Asia

1. Bibliography and Reference

02904 BOSE, M. Classical Indian dancing: a glossary. Calcutta: General Printers and Pub., 1970. 216p.

02905 MEHTA, C.C., ed. Bibliography of stageable plays in Indian languages. ND: MSUB & Bharatiya Natya Sangha, 1963-65. 2 v.

02906 NAQVI, G.A. The Indian stage: select bibliography. In Cultural News from India 3,4 (1962) 31-40.

02907 RAMASUBRAMANIAN, V. An inter-regional vocabulary of Indian theatrical terms. In BITCM (1962) pt. 2, 361-76; (1963) pt. 1, 169-83.

02908 RICHMOND, F. Asian theatre materials: a selected bibliography. In The Drama Review 15,3 (1971) 312-23.

02909 VAN ZILE, J. Dance in India: an annotated guide to source materials. Providence: Asian Music Pub., 1973. 129p.

2. Introductions and Descriptive Studies
a. general

02910 BOWERS, F. Theatre in the East: a survey of Asian dance & drama. NY: Grove Press, 1969. 374p. [1st pub. 1956]

02911 BRANDON, J.R., ed. The performing arts in Asia. Paris: UNESCO, 1971. 168p.

02912 GARGI, B. Theater und Tanz in Indien. Darmstadt: Fladung, 1960. 152p.

02913 KUPPUSWAMY, G. & M. HARIHARAN, eds. Readings on music and dance. Delhi: B.R., 1979. 211p.

02914 NAWAB, V.S. 419 illustrations of Indian music & dance in Western Indian style. Ahmedabad: Sarabhai Manilal Nawab, 1964. 85p.

02915 SCHRAMM, H. Musical theatre in India. In Asian Music 1,1 (1968-69) 31-40.

02916 VARMA, K.M. Nāṭya, nṛtta & nṛtya - their meaning & relationship. Bombay: Orient Longmans, 1957. 86p.

02917 VASUDEV, U. Notes on the relationship of music and dance in India. In Ethnomusicology 7,1 (1963) 33-38.

b. dance

02918 ANAND, M.R., ed. Invitation to the dance: Bhagavata Mela, Yakshagana, Kuchipudi, Krishnattam. [special issue] In Mārg, 19,2 (1966). 48p.

02919 BANERJI, P. Dance of India. Allahabad: Kitabistan, 1956. 239p. [5th ed. rev. & enl.]

02920 BHAVNANI, E. The dance in India: the origin and history, foundation, the art, and science of the dance in India, classical, folk, and tribal. Bombay: Taraporevala Sons, 1965. 261p.

02921 BOWERS, F. The dance in India. NY: ColUP, 1953. 175p.

02922 NARASIMHACHARYA, V.V. Contribution of the Telugu region to the dance art. In JMA 45 (1974) 192-210.

02923 RAGINI DEVI. Dance dialects of India. Delhi: Vikas, 1972. 227p.

02924 ______. Dances of India, with an appendix on Indian music. 3rd ed. Calcutta: S. Gupta, 1962. 87p.

02925 RAM GOPAL & S. DADACHANJI. Indian dancing. London: Phoenix House, 1951. 119p.

02926 SARABHAI, M. Indian dancing for the young. Bombay: BVB, 1967. 44p.

02927 ______. The sacred dance of India. Bombay: BVB, 1979. 43p.

02928 SHASTRI, K.V. Dance in Sanskrit literature. In JIMS 4,4 (1973) 19-53.

02929 SINGHA, R. & R. MASSEY. Indian dances: their history and growth. London: Faber, 1967. 264p.

02930 SRINIVASA IYENGAR, C.R. Indian dance. Madras: Blaze Pub., 1948. 226p.

02931 VENKATACHALAM, G.R. Dance in India. Bombay: Nalanda Pub., n.d., 131p.

c. drama and the theatre

02932 ANAND, M.R. The Indian theatre. NY: Roy Pub., 1951. 60p.

02933 BENEGAL, S. A panorama of theatre in India. Bombay: Popular, for ICCR, 1968. 132p.

02934 BHALLA, M.M. A handful of dreams: essays and reviews in search of Indian theatre. Ed. by A. Bhalla. Delhi: Kailash Book Co., 1970. 109p.

02935 GARGI, B. Theatre in India. NY: Theatre Arts Books, 1962. 245p.

02936 GUPTA, C.B. The Indian theatre, its origin & development up to the present day. Banaras: Motilal, 1954. 215p.

02937 PAPPACENA, E. Teatro indiano. Bari: Andriola, 1962. 270p.

02938 RANGACHARYA, A. The Indian theatre. ND: NBT, 1971. 163p.

02939 RANGANATH, H.K. The Karnatak theater. Dharwar: Karnatak U., 1960. 242p.

02940 RICHMOND, F. Some religious aspects of Indian traditional theatre. In Drama Review 15,3 (1971) 123-131.

02941 ______, ed. Theatre in India. [special issue]. In JSAL 10,2/3/4 (1975) 378p.

02942 SRIRAMA SASTRY, P. Surabhi theatres. Hyderabad: Andhra Pradesh Sangeeta Nataka Akademi, 1975. 47p.

02943 Theatre in India. [special issue]. In World Theatre 5,2 (1956) 91-177.

02944 Theatres, Indian and western: their mutual impacts: a seminar. In BITCM (1962) pt. 1, 41-105.

02945 VARADPANDE, M.L. Traditions of Indian theatre. ND: D.K., 1978. 104p.

3. Classical Dance and Dance-Drama
a. general introductions and studies

02946 AMBROSE, K. & RAM GOPAL. Classical dances & costumes of India. NY: Macmillan, 1951. 95p. + 14pl.

02947 BALAKRISHNA MENON, K.C. Indian classical dances. Calcutta: Rabindra Bharati, 1967. 126p.

02948 DE ZOETE, B. The other mind; a study of dance in south India. NY: Theatre Arts Books, 1960. 171p. [1st pub. 1953]

02949 DURGA, S.A.K. The opera in South India. Delhi: B.R., 1979. 152p.

02950 JAGANATHAN, M. Indian ballet: a round-up. In Indian Horizons 24,1 (1975) 23-44.

02951 KHOKAR, M. Traditions of Indian classical dance. Delhi: Clarion Books, 1979. 168p. + 8pl.

02952 RAM GOPAL. Rhythm in the heavens: an autobiography. London: Secker & Warburg, 1957. 212p.

02953 RAMASWAMI SASTRI, K.S. Indian dance as a spiritual art; along with the history of Indian dance. Madras: The author, 1961. 63p.

02954 SARABHAI, M. The eight nayikas: heroines of the classical dance of India. NY: Dance Perspectives, 1965. 49p. (Dance perspectives, 24)

02955 VATSYAYAN, K.M. Classical Indian dance in literature and the arts. ND: Sangeet Natak Akademi, 1968. 431p. + 96p. of ill.

02956 ______. Indian classical dance. ND: PDMIB, 1974. 61p. + 87pl.

b. Bharata Nāṭyam and related dance styles of Tamilnadu

02957 HIGGINS, J.B. The music of Bharata Natyam. Ph.D. diss., Wesleyan U., 1973. 553p. [UM 73-27,623]

02958 JONES, C.R. Bhāgavata Mēḷa Nāṭakam, a traditional dance-drama form. In JAS 22 (1963) 193-200.

02959 KHOKAR, M. Bhāgavata Mēḷa and Kuchipudi. In Mārg 10,4 (1957) 27-36.

02960 ______. Dancing Bharata Natyam: a manual on adavus, the basic 'dance-units' of the art. Bombay: BVB, 1979. 67p.

02961 KRISHNA IYER, E. Bhagavata Mela; dance-drama of Bharata Natya. In SN 13 (1969) 46-56.

02962 ______. Bharata natya and other dances of Tamil Nad. Baroda: College of Indian Music, Dance & Dramatics, MSUB, 1957. 88p.

02963 ______. The renaissance in Bharata Natya & its future. In JIMS 2,1 (1971) 41-55.

02964 NILAKANTA SASTRI, K.A. & K.R. VENKATARAMAN. The Tamils & the art of dance. In BITCM (1971) pt. 2, 10-33.

02965 Problems facing Bharata Natyam today. In BITCM (1967) pt. 2, 253-308.

02966 RANGANATHAN, E. Kuravanji Nattiya Nadagam; a dance-drama from Madras state. In Comp. Drama 4,2 (1970) 110-19.

02967 SARABHAI, M. Understanding Bharata natyam; lectures at Baroda University. Baroda: MSUB, 1965. 166p.

02968 SATHYANARAYANA, R. Bharatanatya; a critical study. Mysore: Sri Varalakshmi Academies of Fine Arts, 1969. 400p.

c. Kathākalī and other dance-drama traditions of Kerala

02969 DANIÉLOU, A. & K.M. VATSYAYAN. Kathākalī, le théâtre dansé de l'Inde. Berlin: Intl. Inst. for Comp. Studies, 1964. 44p.

02970 DEVASSEY, M.K. Costumes & accessories in Kathakali. ND: MPGOI, 1964. p. 26-74. (Census of India, 1961, v.2, pt. 7-A)

02971 HALL, F. Noh, Kabuki, Kathakali. In SN 7 (1968) 33-75.

02972 IYER, K.B. Kathakali: the sacred dance drama of Malabar. London: Luzac, 1955. 136p.

02973 JONES, B.T. Mōhiniyāṭṭam: a dance tradition of Kerala, South India. In P.A. Rowe & E. Stodelle, eds. Dance Research Monograph One, 1971-72. NY: Cmtee. on Res. in Dance, 1973, 7-48.

02974 JONES, C.R. The temple theatre of Kerala: its history & description. Ph.D. diss., U. of Pennsylvania, 1967. 209p. [UM 68-4586]

02975 JONES, C.R. & B.T. JONES. Kathakali: an introduction to the dance-drama of Kerala. NY: Theatre Arts Books, 1970. 115p.

02976 Kathakali, its history, present position and future. In BITCM (1961) pt. 1, 17-53.

02977 KUNJUNNI RAJA, K. Kutiyattam - an introduction. ND: Sangeet Natak Akademi, 1964. 38p.

01978 KURUP, K.K.N. The cult of teyyam and hero worship in Kerala. Calcutta: Indian Pub., 1973. 87p.

02979 PANCHAL, G. Koothampalam Sanskrit stage of Kerala. In SN 8 (1968) 17-30.

02980 PANDEYA, A.C. The art of Kathakali. 2nd ed. Allahabad: Kitabistan, 1961. 224p.

02981 RAGHAVAN, M.D. Folk plays and dances of Kerala. Trichur: Rama Varma Archaeol. Soc., 1947. 58p.

02982 RAPHY, S. Charittu-natakam; dramatic opera of Kerala. In SN 12 (1969) 56-73.

02983 VASUDEV, U. Kathakali - dance theatre of India. In The World of Music 10,1 (1968) 22-35.

02984 ZARRILLI, P.B. Kālarippayatt and the performing artist East and West: Past, Present, Future. Ph.D. diss., U. of Minnesota, 1978. 645p. [UM 78-13,472]

d. Kathak, rhythmic dance of the North Indian princely courts

02985 In praise of Kathak. In Mārg 12,4 (1959) 66-73.

02986 ISHAQ, S. Evolution of classical dancing in Pakistan; a study. Karachi: Printers Combine, 1969. 24p.

02987 KHOKAR, M. Kathak. In his Traditions of Indian classical dance. Delhi: Clarion Books, 1979, 94-103.

e. Manipuri, Vaiṣṇava ritual dance of the hill-state of Manipur

02988 KHOKAR, M. Dance and ritual in Manipur. In SN 10 (1968) 35-47.

02989 LIGHTFOOT, L. Dance rituals of Manipur, India; an introduction to Meitei Jagoi. Hong Kong: Standard Press, 1958. 79p.

f. mudrās: poses and gestures of classical dance-drama

02990 Dictionary of mudrās. In Marg 11,1 (1957) 18-25.

02991 GOPINATH, C. & S.V. RAMANA RAO. The classical dance poses of India. 2nd ed. Madras: Natana Niketan, 1955. 53p.

02992 HUGHES, R.M. [LA MÉRI]. The gesture language of the Hindu dance. NY: Benjamin Blom, 1964. 100p. [Rpt. 1941 ed.]

02993 IKEGAMI, Y. A stratification analysis of the hand gestures in Indian classical dancing. In Semiotica 4,4 (1971) 365-391.

02994 PREMAKUMAR. The language of Kathākalī. A guide to mudrās. Allahabad: Kitabistan, 1948. 102p.

D. Mediating Traditions: Regional and Folk Performances

1. General Studies

02995 ANAND, M.R. The dancing foot. Delhi: PDMIB, 1967. 35p. [Rpt. 1957 ed.]

02996 BANERJI, P. The folk-dance of India. 2nd rev. & enl. ed. Allahabad: Kitabistan, 1959. 206p.

02997 DAS GUPTA, S.P. A short introduction to the variety of folk dances in India. In Folklore (C) 4 (1963) 163-91.

02998 GANDHI, S. Experiments in folk drama. In SN 11 (1969) 52-68.

02999 GARGI, B. Folk theater of India. Seattle, UWashP, 1966. 217p.

03000 KLIMKEIT, H.-J. Die "Teufelstanze" von Südindien. In Anthropos 71,3/4 (1976) 555-78.

03001 MATHUR, J.C. Drama in rural India. Bombay: ICCR, 1964. 121p.

03002 MUKHOPADHYAY, D.D., ed. Lesser known forms of performing arts in India. ND: Sterling, 1978. 132p.

03003 SPREEN, H.L. & R. RAMANI. Folk dances of south India. 2nd ed. London: OUP, 1948. 134p.

03004 VATSYAYAN, K.M. Traditions of Indian folk dance. ND: Indian Book Co., 1976. 280p.

2. Puppetry and Shadow-Plays

03005 Asian puppets - wall of the world. Intro. by M. Helstein. Los Angeles: UCLA Museum of Cultural History, 1979. 152p. [1st pub. 1976]

03006 CONTRACTOR, M. Various types of traditional puppets of India. In Marg 21,3 (1968) 2-21, 27-43.

03007 JACOB, G. & H. JENSEN & H. LOSCH. Das indische Schattentheater. Stuttgart: W. Kohlhammer, 1931. 156p. (Das orientalische Schattentheater, 2)

03008 PANI, J. Ravana chhaya. ND: Sangeet Natak Akademi, 1978. 35p.

03009 SELTMANN, F. Schattenspiel in Kerala. In Bijdragen Tot de Taal-land-en Volkenkunde 128,4 (1972) 458-490.

03010 SORENSEN, N.R. Shadow theatre in Andhra Pradesh. In SN 33 (1974) 14-39.

03011 STACHE-ROSEN, V. Schattenspiele und Bildervorführungen, zwei formen der religiösen Volksunterhaltung in Indien. In ZDMG 126,1 (1976) 136-48.

03012 TILAKASIRI, J. Puppetry in Sri Lanka. Colombo: Dept. of Cultural Affairs, 1976. 29p. + 14pl. [Rpt. 1961 ed.]

03013 UPADHYAYA, K.S. & K. SANJIVA PRABHU. Yaksagana puppets. In J. of the National Centre for the Performing Arts 5,3 (1976) 1-14.

3. Regional Performances
a. Kandyan and other dances of Sri Lanka

03014 DE ZOETE, B. Dance and magic drama in Ceylon. London: Faber & Faber, 1957. 237p.

03015 GOONATILLEKA, M.H. Masks and mask systems of Sri Lanka. Colombo: Tamarind Books, 1978. 93p.

03016 ______. Mime, mask and satire in Kolam of Ceylon. In Folklore (L) 81 (1970) 161-73.

03017 KANDIAH, T. Tamil drama in Ceylon: a tradition usurped. In SAR 5,1 (1971) 29-40.

03018 MAKULOLUWA, W.B. Dances of Sri Lanka. Colombo: Dept. of Cultural Affairs, 1976. 49p.

03019 PERTOLD, O. The ceremonial dances of the Sinhalese. In AO 2 (1930) 108-38, 201-54, 385-426 [incl. 35pl., index 423-26].

03020 RAGHAVAN, M.D. Kandyan dancing. In BITCM (1961) pt. 1, 1-8.

03021 ______. Sinhala nātum; dances of the Sinhalese. Colombo: M.D. Gunasena, 1967. 303p.

03022 SARATHCHANDRA, E.R. Folk drama of Ceylon. Colombo: Dept. of Cultural Affairs, 1966. 180p.

03023 ______. The Sinhalese folk play and the modern stage. Colombo: Ceylon U., Press, 1953. 139p.

03024 SENEVIRATNA, A. Kandyan dance; a traditional dance form in Sri Lanka. In SN 32 (1974) 5-25.

03025 VITHIANANTHAN, S. Tamil folk drama in Ceylon. In TC 11 (1964) 165-72.

b. Karnataka's Yakṣhagāna: dance-drama of South Kanara district

03026 ASHTON, M.B. Yakṣhagāna Badagatittu Bayalata: a South Indian dance drama. Ph.D. diss., Michigan State U., 1972. 346p. [UM 73-5319]

03027 ASHTON, M.B. & B. CHRISTIE. Yakṣagāna, a dance drama of India. ND: Abhinav, 1977. 108 + 46p.

03028 KARANTH, K.S. Yaksagana. Mysore: Inst. of Kannada Studies, U. of Mysore, 1975. 196p.

c. Middle India
i. folk dance and village theatre of Maharashtra, Gujarat, and Rajasthan

03029 ABRAMS, T. Tamāshā: people's theatre of Maharashtra State, India. Ph.D. diss., Michigan State U., 1974. 431p. [UM 74-27,381]

03030 AGARKAR, A.J. Folk-dance of Maharashtra. Bombay: Rajabhau Joshi, 1950. 170p.

03031 DESAI, S.R. Bhavāī: a medieval form of ancient Indian dramatic art (nāṭya) as prevalent in Gujarat. Ahmedabad: Gujarat U., 1972. 654p.

03032 KHANAPURKAR, D.P. Tamasha. In EA 7 (1953) 19-36.

03033 NADKARNI, D.G. Marathi Tamasha yesterday and today. In SN, 12 (1969) 19-28.

03034 RICHMOND, F.P. Bhavai: village theatre of West India. In Papers in International & World Affairs, Michigan State U., 1969 series, 2, 13-28.

03035 SHUKLA, H. Folk dances of Gujarat. Ahmedabad: Dir. of Info. & Tourism, 1966. 28p.

ii. Chhau and Odissi dances, folk plays of Orissa

03036 ARDEN, J. The Chhau dancers of Purulia. In Tulane Drama Review 15,2 (1971) 65-75.

03037 BHATTACHARYYA, A. Chhau dance of Purulia. Calcutta: Rabindra Bharati U., 1972. 112p.

03038 ______. Substrat anthropologique des danses cchau de Purulia. In O&M 13,2 (1973) 67-80.

03039 BLANK, J. The story of the Chou dance of the former Mayurbanj State, Orissa. Ph.D. diss., U. of Chicago, 1973. 160p., film, & tape.

03040 CHAUDHURI, D., ed. Chho dance: a socio-cultural profile. Calcutta: Akademi of Folklore, 1977. 27p.

03041 Chhau dances of India. [special issue]. In Mārg 22,1 (1968) 45p. [articles by S. Kothari, J. Pani]

03042 KOTHARI, S. The Chhau Dance. In Sangeet Kala Vihar 1,2 (1970) 25-28.

03043 ______. The Chhau dances. In World of Music 11,4 (1969) 38-55.

03044 ______. Gotipua dancers of Orissa. In SN 8 (1968) 18-43.

03045 PATNAIK, D.N. Folk plays of Orissa. In SN 32 (1974) 26-33.

03046 ______. Odissi dance. Bhubaneswar: Orissa Sangeet Natak Akademi, 1971. 110p.

03047 PATTANAIK, K.K. et al., eds. Dance & music of Orissa. Cuttack: Kala Vikash Kendra, 1958. 53p.

03048 RECK, D. The music of Matha Chhau. In Asian Music 3,2 (1972) 8-14.

03049 SINGH DEO, J.B. Chhau, mask dance of Seraikela. Cuttack: Jayashree Devi, 1973. 98p.

03050 VATSYAYAN, K.M. A study of Mayurbhanj Chhau in relation to other dance forms of Orissa. In JMA 45, 1-4 (1974) 118-130 + 7pl.

d. folk dance and popular theatre of North India, Bengal and Nepal

03051 BHATTACHARYYA, A. Yatra of Bengal. In SN 12 (1969) 29-39.

03052 FARBER, C. Problems of studying urban specialists: 'jatra' in Calcutta. In JIAS 10,2 (1975) 117-32.

03053 HEIN, N.J. The miracle plays of Mathura. New Haven: Yale U. Press, 1972. 313p.

03054 JERSTAD, L.G. Mani-rimdu; Sherpa dance-drama. Seattle: UWashP, 1969. 192p.

03055 SARKAR, P. Jatra: the popular traditional theatre of Bengal. In JSAL 10,2/3/4 (1974) 87-107.

VIII. ARCHITECTURE, ART, AND CRAFTS

A. Introductions, Surveys and Research Tools

1. Bibliography and Reference

03056 CIRLOT, J.E. A dictionary of symbols. Tr. from Spanish by J. Sage. NY: Philosophical Library, 1962. 400p.

03057 Encyclopedia of world art. NY: McGraw Hill, 1959-1968. 15v.

03058 HINGORANI, R.P., ed. Journal of Indian museums; an index to its first twenty volumes. Varanasi: American Academy of Benares, 1969. 51p. (Index to journals, 6)

03059 JAGDISH CHANDRA, comp. Bibliography of Indian art, history and archaeology, v. 1: Indian art. Delhi: Delhi Printers Prakashan, 1978. 316p.

03060 KERN INSTITUTE, LEIDEN. Annual bibliography of Indian archaeology. Leyden: Brill, 1928-. [v. 1, for 1926; v. 21, for 1964-66, pub. 1972]

03061 MITRA, H. Contributions to a bibliography of Indian art and aesthetics. Santiniketan: Visva-Bharati, 1951. 240p. [guide to Sanskrit texts]

03062 PATIL, H.S. & R.N. SAR. The arts. Bombay: ICCR, 1966. 225p. (Aspects of Indian culture: select bibl., 1)

03063 SHUKLA, L.K. A study of Hindu art & architecture, with especial reference to terminology. Varanasi: CSSO, 1972. 297p. (CSS, 82)

03064 WESTHEIM, P. Indische Baukunst. Berlin: E. Wasmuth, 1920. 16p. + 48pl.

2. Catalogs and Guides to Collections and Exhibits

03065 The arts of India and Nepal: the Nasli and Alice Heeramaneck Collection. NY: October House, 1966. 185p.

03066 ASHTON, L., ed. The art of India and Pakistan; a commemorative catalogue of the exhibition held at the Royal Academy of Arts, London, 1947-48. London: Faber & Faber, 1950. 291p. + 160pl.

03067 COMBAZ, G. L'Inde et l'Orient classique. Paris: P. Geuthner, 1937. 2 v., 165pl. (Pub. du Musée Guimet; Documents d'art et d'archeologie, 1)

03068 COOMARASWAMY, A.K. Catalogue of the Indian collections in the Museum of Fine Arts, Boston. Boston: Museum of Fine Arts, 1923-30. 5 v.

03069 DAVIDSON, J.L. Art of the Indian subcontinent from Los Angeles collections. Los Angeles: W. Ritchie Press, 1968. 128p.

03070 GOETZ, H. Handbook of the collections: Baroda Museum and Picture Gallery. Baroda: 1952. 76p.

03071 HACKIN, J. Guide-catalogue du Musée Guimet. Les collections bouddhiques de l'Inde centrale et Gandhara, Turkestan, Chine septestrienale, Tibet. Paris: G. Van Oest, 1923. 175p. + 24pl.

03072 IRWIN, J., ed. Indian art at the Victoria and Albert Museum. In Marg 29,4 (1976) 70p.

03073 KHANDALAVALA, K. & MOTI CHANDRA. Miniatures and sculptures from the collections of the late Sir Cowasji Jehangir, Bart. Bombay: Prince of Wales Museum, 1965. 44p. + 72pl.

03074 LOMMEL, A. Indische Kunst. Ausstellung des staatlichen Museums für Völkerkunde. Munich: the Museum, 1958. 114p.

03075 MONOD, O. Le Musée Guimet: Inde, Khmer, Tchampa, Thailande, Java, Népal, Tibet, Afghanistan, Pakistan, Asie Centrale. Paris: Ed. des Musées Nationaux, 1966. 433p.

03076 MUSEUM FÜR INDISCHE KUNST. BERLIN. Katalog 1971. Ausgestellte Werke. Berlin: Staatliche Museen Preussischer Kulturbesitz, 1971. 154p. + 64pl.

03077 SRIVASTAVA, V.N. & S. MISRA. Inventory of Mathura Museum since 1949 up to date. In Saṅgrahālaya Pūratatva Patrikā. Bulletin of Museums & Archaeology in U.P. 11-12 (1973) 42-120.

3. Histories and Surveys of South Asian Art

03078 AGRAWALA, V.S. The heritage of Indian art. Delhi: PDMIB, 1976. 186p. [Rpt. of 1964 ed.]

03079 ANDREWS, F.H., ed. The influence of Indian art. Delhi: Delhi Printers Prakashan, 1978. 206p. [Rpt. 1924 ed.]

03080 AUBOYER, J. Les arts de l'Inde et des pays indianisés. Paris: PUF, 1968. 186p.

03081 ______. Introduction a l'étude de l'art de l'Inde. Rome: IIMEO, 1965. 138p.

03082 BUSSAGLI, M. & C. SIVARAMAMURTI. 5000 years of the art of India. NY: H.N. Abrams, 1971. 335p. + 397 col. ill.

03083 COOMARASWAMY, A.K. The arts & crafts of India & Ceylon. ND: Today & Tomorrow's, 1971. 255p. [1st pub. 1913]

03084 ______. History of Indian and Indonesian art. NY: Dover, 1965. 295 + 128p. [1st pub. 1927]

03085 ______. Introduction to Indian art. 2nd ed. Delhi: Munshiram, 1969. 104p. + 32 p. of ill. [1st ed. 1923]

03086 CRAVEN, R.C. A concise history of Indian art. London: Thames & Hudson, 1976. 252p.

03087 DEHEJIA, V. Looking again at Indian art. ND: PDMIB, 1978. 156p.

03088 FISCHER, K. Schöpfungen indischer Kunst: von den frühesten Bauten und Bildern zum Mittelalterlichen Tempel. 2nd ed. Cologne: M. DuMont Schauberg, 1961. 412p.

03089 FRANZ, H.G. Hinduistische und islamische Kunst Indiens. Leipzig: E.A. Seemann, 1967. 437p.

03090 Glimpses of wonder and beauty, Indian heritage. Bombay: Marg Pub., 1980. 125p.

03091 GOETZ, H. The art of India: five thousand years of Indian art. 2nd ed. NY: Greystone Press, 1964. 281p. [1st ed. 1959]

03092 HAVELL, E.B. Handbook of Indian art. London: Murray, 1920. 222p. + 79 pl.

03093 ______. Indian sculpture and painting. London: Murray, 1908. 278p. + 78 pl.

03094 KHAN, F.A. Architecture and art treasures in Pakistan; prehistoric, protohistoric, Buddhist, and Hindu periods. Karachi: Elite, 1969. 200p.

03095 KRAMRISCH, S. The art of India; traditions of Indian sculpture, painting and architecture. 3rd ed. Greenwich, CT: Phaidon Pub., 1965. 231p.

03096 MISRA, R.N. Ancient artists and art-activity. Simla: IIAS, 1975. 88p.

03097 MODE, H. The woman in Indian art. Tr. from German by Marianne Herzfeld. NY: McGraw-Hill, 1970. 51p.

03098 MOOKERJEE, A.C. The arts of India from prehistoric to modern times. Rev. ed. Calcutta: Oxford & IBH, 1966. 33 + 141p.

03099 PAL, P., ed. Aspects of Indian art. Leiden: Brill, 1972. 171p.

03100 RAU, H. Die Kunst Indiens bis zum Islam. Stuttgart: H.E. Günther, 1958. 63p.

03101 RAWSON, P.S. Indian art. NY: Dutton, 1972. 159p.

03102 ROWLAND, B. The art and architecture of India, Buddhist, Hindu, Jain. Baltimore: Penguin, 1970. 512p. [1st pub. 1933]

03103 SINHA, B.P. Archaeology and art of India. Delhi: Sundeep, 1979. 188p. + 14 pl.

03104 SMITH, V.A. A history of fine art in India and Ceylon, from the earliest times to the present day. Rev. & enl. by K. Khandalavala. London: OUP, 1962. 219p. + 200 pl. [1st pub. 1911]

03105 SOLOMON, W.E.G. The charm of Indian art. ND: Asian Educ. Services, 1978. 142p. + 11 pl. [Rpt. 1926 ed.]

03106 SWARUP, S. 5000 years of arts and crafts in India and Pakistan; a survey of sculpture, architecture, painting, dance, music, handicrafts, and ritual decorations from the earliest times to the present day. Bombay, 1968. 272p.

03107 TAKATA, O. & T. UENO. The art of India. Tokyo: Nihon Keizai Shimbun, 1966. 2 v. [English and Japanese text]

03108 ZIMMER, H.R. The art of Indian Asia, its mythology and transformations. Ed. by J. Campbell. NY: Pantheon, 1955. 2 v., 509, 18p. + 662 pl. (Bollingen series, 39)

4. Festschriften and Commemorative Volumes

03109 Chhavi: golden jubilee volume, Bhārat Kalā Bhavan, 1920-70. Banaras: BHU, 1971. 410p. + 26 pl. + 594 fig.

03110 Dr. Moti Chandra commemoration volume. [Special issue] In JISOA ns 7 (1976-77) 93p. + 25 pl.

03111 Dr. Vasudev Saran Agrawala Commemoration Volume. [Special issues] In JISOA ns 4 (1971-72) 98p. + 24 pl.; 5 (1972-73) 133p. + 35 pl.

03112 IYER, K.B., ed. Art and thought, issued in honour of Dr. Anand K. Coomaraswamy on the occasion of his 70th birthday. London: Luzac, 1947. 259p.

5. Aesthetics

03113 AGRAWALA, V.S. Studies in Indian art; 45 papers. Varanasi: Vishwavidyalaya Prakashan, 1965. 288p.

03114 ANAND, M.R. Hindu view of art. London: Allen & Unwin, 1933. 245p. + 16 pl.

03115 COOMARASWAMY, A.K. The intellectual operation in Indian art. In JISOA 3 (1935) 1-12.

03116 ______. The transformation of nature in art. 2nd ed. Cambridge: HUP, 1935. 245p.

03117 DATTA, B.N. Indian art in relation to culture. Calcutta: Nababharat, 1978. 110p. + 10 pl. [Rpt. 1956 ed.]

03118 GUPTA, S. The beautiful in Indian arts. ND: Munshiram, 1979. 118p.

03119 HANUMANTHA RAO, G. Comparative aesthetics, Eastern and Western. Mysore: D.V.K. Murthy, 1974. 261p.

03120 HAVELL, E.B. The art heritage of India, comprising Indian sculpture and painting; and Ideals of Indian art. Rev. ed. Bombay: Taraporevala, 1964. 199p. [1st pub. 1928 & 1920]

03121 NANDI, S.K. Studies in modern Indian aesthetics. Simla: IIAS, 1975-. v. 1, 306p.

03122 PANDEY, K.C. A bird's eye view of Indian aesthetics. In J. of Aesthetics and Art Criticism 24 (1965) 59-73.

03123 PANDIT, S. An approach to the Indian theory of art and aesthetics. ND: Sterling, 1977. 148p.

03124 RAPHAEL, R. The metaphysical basis of Coomaraswamy's aesthetics. In Indian Horizons 25,3/4 (1976) 9-21.

03125 RAU, H. Reflections on Indian art. Bombay: Shakuntala, 1976. 179p. + 26 pl.

03126 RAY, N.R. An approach to Indian art. Chandigarh: Panjab U., 1974. 299p.

03127 SEMINAR ON INDIAN AESTHETICS AND ART ACTIVITY, SIMLA, 1966. Indian aesthetics and art activity.... Simla: IIAS, 1968. 327p. (IIAS Trans., 2)

03128 SUBRAMANYAN, K.G. Moving focus: essays on Indian art. ND: Lalit Kala Akademi, 1978. 122p. + 14 pl.

03129 TAGORE, R.N. Angel of surplus: some essays and addresses on aesthetics. Ed. by S.K. Ghose. Calcutta: Visva-Bharati, 1978. 155p.

6. Erotic Art

03130 ANAND, M.R. Kama Kala: some notes on the philosophical basis of Hindu erotic sculpture. NY: Nagel, 1958. 45p. + 58 pl.

03131 DANIÉLOU, A. La sculpture érotique hindoue. Paris: Buchet-Chastel, 1973. 240p.

03132 DESAI, D. Erotic sculpture of India: a socio-cultural study. ND: Tata McGraw-Hill, 1975. 269p. + 47 pl.

03133 FOUCHET, M.P. The erotic sculpture of India.... NY: Criterion Books, 1959. 95p.

03134 LAL, K. The cult of desire: an interpretation of the erotic sculpture of India. 2nd ed. NY: University Books, 1967. 104p.

03135 LEESON, F. Kāma shilpa; a study of Indian sculptures depicting love in action. Bombay: Taraporevala, 1962. 132p.

03136 MAJUPURIA, T.C. & I. MAJUPURIA. Erotic themes of Nepal: an analytical study and interpretations of religion-based sex expressions misconstrued as pornography. Kathmandu: Shakuntala Devi, 1978. 268p. + 21 pl.

03137 RAWSON, P. Erotic art of the East; the sexual theme in oriental painting and sculpture. NY: Putnam, 1968. 380p. + 32 pl.

03138 THOMAS, P. Kama Kalpa: the Hindu ritual of love... 4th ed. Bombay: Taraporevala, 1957. 151p. + 99 pl.

03139 TUCCI, G. Rati-Līlā: Studie über die erotischen Darstellungen in der nepalesischen Kunst. Tr. from Italian by G. Glaesser. Munich: Nagel, 1969. 174p.

7. Hindu Art of South Asia [see IV. B. above]

8. Buddhist and Jain Art of South Asia

03140 FISCHER, E. & J. JAIN. Kunst und Religion in Indien: 2500 Jahren Jainismus. Zurich: Rietberg Museum, 1975.

03141 FRANZ, H.G. Buddhistische Kunst Indiens. Leipzig: E.A. Seemann, 1965. 381p.

03142 GHOSH, A., ed. Jaina art and architecture. ND: Bharatiya Jnanpith, 1974-1975. 3 v.

03143 GRUNWEDEL, A. Buddhist art in India. Tr. from German by A.C. Gibson. Rev. & enl. by J. Burgess. 2nd ed. Santiago de Compostela: S. Gupta, 1965. 228p.

03144 HALLADE, M. Inde: un millénaire d'art bouddhique. Rencontre de l'Orient et de l'Occident. Fribourg: Office du Livre, 1968. 284p.

03145 MITRA, DEBALA. Buddhist monuments. Calcutta: Sahitya Samsad, 1971. 307p. + 112p. of ill.

03146 SHAH, U.P. Studies in Jaina art. Banaras: Jaina Cultural Res. Soc., 1955. 166p.

03147 SHAH, U.P. & M.A. DHAKY, eds. Aspects of Jaina art and architecture. Ahmedabad: Gujarat State Committee for the Celebration of 2500th Anniversary of Bhagavān Mahāvīra Nirvāṇa, 1975. 480p. + 129 pl.

03148 VOGEL, J.-P. Buddhist art in India, Ceylon, and Java. ND: OBRC, 1977. 115p. + 39 pl. [Rpt. of 1935 ed.]

B. Architecture

1. Bibliography and Reference Works

03149 ACHARYA, P.K. A dictionary of Hindu architecture: treating of Sanskrit architectural terms, with illustrative quotations from śilpaśāstras, general literature, and archaeological records. Varanasi: Bharatiya Pub. House, 1979. 861p. [Rpt. 1927 ed.]

03150 ______. An encyclopedia of Hindu architecture. London: OUP, 1946. 684p. (Mānasara series, 7)

03151 AIYAR, S.A. Historical index to the study of Indian temple architecture. Bombay: Chandra Print. Press, 1972. 23p.

03152 COOMARASWAMY, A.K. Indian architectural terms. In JAOS 48,3 (1928) 250-75.

03153 CRESWELL, K.A.C. A bibliography of the architecture, arts and crafts of Islam to 1st Jan., 1960. Cairo: American U. of Cairo Press, 1961. 1330 p. [Architecture, India, p. 97-194]

03154 ______. A provisional bibliography of the Muhammadan architecture of India. Bombay: British India Press, 1922. [Rpt. from IA 51 (1922) 81-108, 165-79]

2. Surveys and Studies

03155 ACHARYA, P.K. Hindu architecture in India and abroad. Bhopal: J.K. Pub. House, 1979. 508p. + 36 pl. (Mānasara series, 6) [Rpt. 1946 ed.]

03156 ANANTHALWAR, M.A. & A. REA. Indian architecture. Madras: A.V.I. Iyer, 1921. 3 v.

03157 BATLEY, C. The design development of Indian architecture. 2nd ed. Bombay: Taraporevala, 1965. 12p. + 52 pl.

03158 BROWN, P. Indian architecture. 5th ed. Bombay: Taraporevala, 1965-68. 2 v. [1st pub. 1942-43; v. 1, Hindu and Buddhist period; v. 2, Islamic period]

03159 COOMARASWAMY, A.K. The symbolism of the dome. In IHQ 14 (1938) 1-56.

03160 CUNNINGHAM, A. An essay on the Arian order of architecture, as exhibited in the temples of Kashmir. In JASBengal 195 (1848) 241-326 + 18 pl.

03161 FABRI, C.L. An introduction to Indian architecture. Bombay: Asia, 1963. 104p.

03162 FERGUSSON, J. History of Indian and eastern architecture. Rev. & ed. by J. Burgess. Delhi: Munshiram, 1967. [Rpt. 1910 ed.; 1st ed. 1876]

03163 FISCHER, K. Dächer, Decken und Gewölbe indischer Kultstätten und Nutzbauten. Wiesbaden: Steiner, 1974. 190p. + 32 pl.

03164 GANGOLY, O.C. Indian architecture. Bombay: Kutub, 1946. 67p. + 106 pl.

03165 GOETZ, H. Building and sculpture techniques in India. In Archaeology 15,4 (1962) 252-61; 16,1 (1963) 47-53.

03166 GROVER, S. The architecture of India: Buddhist and Hindu. ND: Vikas, 1980. 231p.

03167 GUTSCHOW, N. & J. PIEPER. Indien: von den Klöstern im Himalaya zu den Tempelstädten Südindiens: Bauformen und Stadtgestalt einen bestandigen Tradition. Cologne: DuMont, 1978. 424p.

03168 HAVELL, E.B. The ancient and medieval architecture of India: a study of Indo-Aryan civilization. London: Murray, 1915. 230p. + 83 pl.

03169 ______. Indian architecture, its psychology, structure and history from the first Muhammadan invasion to the present day. ND: S. Chand, 1971. 260p. + 129 pl. [Rpt. 1913 ed.]

03170 LAROCHE, E. Indische Baukunst. Munich: F. Beruckmann, 1921-22. 6 v.

03171 ROGERS, M.B. A study of the makara and kirttimukha with some parallels in Romanesque architectural ornament of France and Spain. Ph.D. diss., U. of Chicago, 1965. 287p.

03172 SOMPURA, P.O. Album of Indian architectural designs. Ahmedabad: The Late Shri Balwantrai Prabhashankar Sompura, 1977. 223p.

03173 VOLWAHSEN, A. Living architecture: Indian. Tr. by A.E. Keep. London: MacDonald, 1969. 192p.

3. Temples and Temple Sculpture: Hindu, Buddhist, and Jain

03174 AGRAWALA, V.S. Evolution of the Hindu temple, and other essays. Varanasi: Prithivi Prakashan, 1965. 73p.

03175 BURGESS, J. Report on the Buddhist cave temples and their inscriptions. Varanasi: IndBH, 1964. 140p. (Archaeol. Survey of W. India, 4) [Rpt. 1883 ed.]

03176 CHANDRA, PRAMOD. The study of Indian temple architecture. In his (ed.) Studies in Indian temple architecture. ND: AIIS, 1975, 1-39.

03177 ______., ed. Studies in Indian temple architecture: papers presented at a seminar held in Varanasi, 1967. ND: AIIS, 1975. 317p. + 68 pl.

03178 FERGUSSON, J. & J. BURGESS. The cave temples of India. Delhi: OBRC, 1969. 536p. [1st pub. 1880]

03179 GOSWAMI, A. Indian temple sculpture. Calcutta: Rupa, 1959. 48p. + 107p. of ill.

03180 KAIL, O.C. Buddhist cave temples of India. Bombay: Taraporevala, 1975. 138p.

03181 KRAMRISCH, S. The Hindu temple. Delhi: Motilal, 1976. 2 v. 466p. + 80 pl. [Rpt. of the 1946 ed. pub. by U. of Calcutta.]

03182 KRISHNA DEVA. Temples of north India. ND: NBT, 1968. 87p.

03183 LOUIS-FRÉDERIC [pseud.] The art of India: temples and sculpture.... NY: H.N. Abrams, 1960. 464p.

03184 MEHTA, R.J. Masterpieces of Indian temples. Bombay: Taraporevala, 1974. 67 + 100p.

03185 MICHELL, G. The Hindu temple: an introduction to its meaning and forms. London: Elek, 1977. 192p.

03186 SOUNDARA RAJAN, K.V. Indian temple styles; the personality of Hindu architecture. ND: Munshiram, 1972. 184p.

03187 The temples of India. ND: Dept. of Tourism, 1964. 123p.

4. "Indo-Islamic" Architecture

03188 BROWN, P. Indian architecture, v. 2 Islamic period. Bombay: Taraporevala, 1968. 146p., 250 ill.

03189 DESAI, Z.A. Indo-Islamic architecture. ND: PDMIB, 1970. 61p.

03190 ______. Mosques of India. ND: PDMIB, 1966. 52p.

03191 FISCHER, K. & C.-M.F. FISCHER. Indische Baukunst islamischer Zeit. Baden-Baden: Holle, 1976. 108p.

03192 HUSAIN, A.B.M. The manara in Indo-Muslim architecture. Dacca: ASP, 1970. 258p. + 98 pl.

03193 MEHTA, R.J. Masterpieces of Indo-Islamic architecture. Bombay: Taraporevala, 1976. 70 + 100p.

03194 TARAFDAR, M.R. Notes on Indo-Muslim architecture. In JASPak 11,2 (1966) 127-41.

03195 TERRY, J. The charm of Indo-Islamic architecture. An introduction to the Northern phase. Bombay: Taraporevala, 1955. 40p. + 61 pl.

03196 VOLWAHSEN, A. Islamisches Indien. Munich: Hirmer, 1969. 192p. (Weltkulturen und Baukunst)

C. Sculpture
[see also Iconography, IV. B., above]

1. Histories and Surveys of Indian Sculpture

03197 COHN, W. Indische plastik. Berlin: B. Cassirer, 1922. 90p.

03198 COOMARASWAMY, A.K. Viśvakarma.... 1st series, 100 examples of Indian sculpture. London: the author, 1912. 59p. + 104 pl. [series discontinued]

03199 FABRI, C.L. Discovering Indian sculpture; a brief history. ND: Affiliated East-West Press, 1970. 84p.

03200 FORMAN, W. Indian sculpture: masterpieces of Indian, Khmer and Cham art. Tr. from French by I. Urwin. Rev. ed. Feltham: Hamlyn, 1970. 35p. + 238 pl. [1st ed. 1970]

03201 HALLADE, M. La composition plastique dans les reliefs de l'Inde; art ancien, art bouddhique, gupta et post-gupta. Paris: Adrien-Maisonneuve, 1942. 107p. (Études d'art indien)

03202 KRAMRISCH, S. Indian sculpture. Calcutta: YMCA Pub. House, 1933. 240p. + 50 pl.

03202 MATHUR, N.L. Sculpture in India; its history and art. 2nd rev. & enl. ed. ND: the author, 1976. 114p., incl. 56 pl.

03204 MEHTA, R.J. Masterpieces of Indian sculpture. Bombay: Taraporevala, 1968. 50p. + 100 pl.

03205 RAWSON, P.S. Indian sculpture. NY: Dutton, 1966. 160p.

03206 SARASVATI, S.K. A survey of Indian sculpture. Calcutta: KLM, 1957. 207p. + 40 pl.

03207 SIVARAMAMURTI, C. Indian sculpture. ND: Allied, 1961. 164p.

2. Catalogs and Guides to Collections and Exhibits

03208 AGRAWALA, V.S. A handbook of the sculptures in the Curzon Museum of Archaeology, Muttra. Allahabad: Supt. of Govt. Press, 1966. 60p. + 22 pl. [1st ed. 1939, 47p.]

03209 Bronzes of India and greater India. Providence, RI: Rhode Island School of Design Museum of Art, 1955. 20p.

03210 CHANDRA, P. The stone sculptures in the Allahabad Museum. Poona: AIIS, 1971. 211p. + 174 pl. [AIIS Pub., 2]

03211 CRAVEN, R.C. Indian sculpture in the John and Mable Ringling Museum of Art. Gainesville: U. of Florida Press, 1961. 28p.

03212 GRAVELY, F.H. & C. SIVARAMAMURTI. Guide to the archaeological galleries; an introduction to South Indian temple architecture and sculpture. 3rd ed. Madras: Govt. Museum, 1954. 50p. [1st pub. 1939]

03213 ______. Illustrations of Indian sculpture, mostly southern, for use with the Guide to the archaeological galleries. Madras: Govt. Museum, 1939. 2p. + 23 pl.

03214 GUPTA, P.L., ed. Patna Museum catalogue of antiquities; stone sculptures, metal images, terracottas and minor antiquities. Patna: Patna Museum, 1965. 367 + 58p.

03215 HACKIN, J. La sculpture indienne et tibétaine au Musée Guimet. E. Leroux, 1931. 24p. + 51 pl.

03216 HEERAMANECK, A.N. Masterpieces of Indian sculpture, from the former collections of Nasli M. Heeramaneck. NY: Paragon Book Gallery, 1979. 149 pl.

03217 KALA, S.C. Sculptures in the Allahabad Municipal Museum. Allahabad: Kitabistan, 1946. 75p.

03218 KHAN, M.A.W. Stone sculptures in the Alampur Museum. Ed. by N. Ramesan. Hyderabad: Govt. of Andhra Pradesh, 1973. 131p. (Its Archaeol. series, 39)

03219 KRAMRISCH, S. Indian sculpture in the Philadelphia Museum of Art. Philadelphia: UPaP, 1961. 183p.

03220 LEFEBVRE D'ARGENCÉ, R.-Y. & T. TSE. Indian and South-east Asian stone sculptures from the Avery Brundage collection. Pasadena: Pasadena Art Museum, 1969. 116p.

03221 LIPPE, A. The art of India: stone sculpture. NY: Asia Soc., 1962. 64p.

03222 ______. The Freer Indian sculptures. Washington: Smithsonian Inst., 1970. 15 + 54p.

03223 LOHUIZEN-DE LEEUW, J.E. VAN. Descriptive catalog; Indian sculpture in the von der Heydt collection. Zurich: Atlantis, 1964. 250p.

03224 MAJUMDAR, N.G. A guide to the sculptures in the Indian Museum [Calcutta]. Delhi: Manager of Pub., 1937. 2 v. [v. 1, Early Indian schools; v. 2, the Graeco-Buddhist school of Gandhara.]

03225 MOTI CHANDRA. Stone sculpture in the Prince of Wales Museum. Bombay: PWM, 1974. 26 + 61p. + 43 pl.

03226 PAL, P. The sensuous immortals; a selection of sculptures from the Pan-Asian collection. Los Angeles: Los Angeles County Museum of Art, 1977. 264p.

03227 SIVARAMAMURTI, C. Masterpieces of Indian sculpture in the National Museum. ND: PDMIB, 1971. 42p.

3. Techniques

03228 BONER, A. Principles of composition in Hindu sculpture, cave temple period. Leiden: Brill, 1962. 260p.

03229 KRISHNAN, M.V. Wax modeling and lost-wax process of metal casting (a comparative study of South Indian and Banaras methods). In Prajna 10,2 (1965) 237-48.

03230 RAWSON, P. The methods of Indian sculpture. In Asian Review ns 1 (1964) 115-27.

03231 REEVES, R. Cire perdue casting in India. ND: Crafts museum, 1962. 124p.

4. Bronze and Other Metal Sculpture

03232 AGRAWALA, P.K. Early Indian bronzes. Varanasi: Prithvi Prakashan, 1977. 158 + 72p.

03233 BALKRISHNAN. Indian bronzes: select bibliography. In Cultural News from India 3,6 (1962) 33-58.

03234 BRIJ BHUSHAN, J. Indian metalware. Bombay: All India Handicrafts Board, Min. of Commerce and Industry, Govt. of India, 1961. 88p.

03235 CHANDRA, P. Master bronzes of India; exhibition at the Art Institute of Chicago.... Chicago: Art Inst., 1965. 6p. + 61 pl.

03236 KAR, C. Indian metal sculpture. Bombay: Taraporevala, 1952. 46p. + 61 pl.

03237 KHANDALAVALA, K. Masterpieces in South India and Nepalese bronzes in the collection of Mr. S.K. Bhadwar of Bombay. In Marg 4,4 (1950) 8-27.

03238 MEHTA, R.J. Masterpieces of Indian bronzes and metal sculpture. Bombay: Taraporevala, 1971. 46p. + 100 pl.

03239 MITRA, D. Bronzes from Achutrajpur, Orissa. Delhi: Agam Kala Prakashan, 1978. 185p. + 29 pl.

03240 MUKHERJEE, M. Folk metal craft of eastern India. ND: All India Handicrafts Board, Min. of Commerce, Govt. of India, 1977. 15p. + 12 pl.

03241 SIVARAMAMURTI, C. Indian bronzes. Bombay: Marg Pub., 1962. 72p.

03242 THAPAR, D.R. Icons in bronze; an introduction to Indian metal images. Bombay: Asia, 1961. 171p.

5. Terra Cotta and Ivory Sculpture

03243 COOMARASWAMY, A.K. Archaic Indian terracottas. In Marg 6,2 (1952) 22-35.

03244 ______. Archaic Indian terracottas. In IPEK, Jahrbuch für prähistorische und ethnographische Kunst 3 (1928) 64-76 + 7 pl.

03245 DASGUPTA, C.C. Bibliography of ancient Indian terracotta figurines. In JASBengal 3rd ser. 4 (1938) 67-120; 10 (1944) 61-79.

03246 ______. Origin and evolution of Indian clay sculpture. Calcutta: Calcutta U., 1961. 323p. + 195 pl.

03247 ______. Some unpublished ancient Indian terracottas preserved in the British Museum. In ArtAs 13,4 (1950) 254-69.

03248 ______. Unpublished ancient Indian terracottas preserved in the Musée Guimet. In ArtAs 14,4 (1951) 283-305.

03249 DHAVALIKAR, M.K. Masterpieces of Indian terracottas. Bombay: Taraporevala, 1977. 64p. + 50 pl.

03250 DWIVEDI, V.P. Indian ivories: a survey of Indian ivory and bone carvings from the earliest to the modern times. Delhi: Agam Prakashan, 1976. 152p. + 26 pl.

03251 FISCHER, K. Old Indian terracottas and contemporary art. In RL 25,1 (1954) 26-42.

03252 GANGOLY, O.C. Indian terracotta art. London: Mayflower, 1959. 17p.

03253 KRAMRISCH, S. Indian terracottas. In JISOA 7 (1939) 89-110.

03254 MOTI CHANDRA. Ancient Indian ivories. In PWMB 6 (1957-59) 4-63.

03255 ______. Indian ivories. ND: Arnold-Heinemann, 1977. 70p.

03256 ______. Terracottas in Bharat Kala Bhavan. In Chhavi.... Banaras: BHU, Bharat Kala Bhavan, 1971, 1-15.

03257 Portfolio on Indian terracottas. In Marg 23,1 (1969) 13-32.

03258 SANKALIA, H.D. & M.K. DHAVALIKAR. The terracotta art of India. In Marg 23,1 (1969) 33-54.

03259 SARASWATI, B.N. & N.K. BEHURA. Pottery techniques in peasant India. Calcutta: AnthSI, 1966. 208p. (Its memoirs, 13)

03260 SHAH, U.P. Terracottas from former Bikaner State. In LK 8 (1960) 55-62.

03261 VERMA, K.M. The Indian technique of clay modelling. Shantiniketan: Proddu, 1970. 310p.

D. Painting

1. Bibliography

03262 COOMARASWAMY, A.K. One hundred references to Indian painting. In ArtAs 4,1 (1930-32) 41-57.

03263 CRESWELL, K.A.C. A bibliography of painting in Islam. Cairo: Impr. de l'Institut Français d'Archéologie Orientale, 1953. 100p.

03264 HINGORANI, R.P. Painting in South Asia: a bibliography. Delhi: Bharatiya, 1976. 253p.

2. Introductory Surveys

03265 ARCHER, W.G. Indian painting. NY: OUP, 1957. 22p. + 15 pl.

03266 ______. Paintings of India - the correct perspective. In RL 34,1/2 (1965) 63-75.

03267 BARRETT, D.E. & B. GREY. Painting of India. Geneva: A. Skira, 1963. 216p.

03268 BROWN, P. Indian painting. Calcutta: Assn. Press, 1918. 115p. + 17 pl.

03269 CHAITANYA, K. A history of Indian painting. ND: Abhinav, 1976-79. 2 v., 180p. + 150 pl.

03270 KHANDALAVALA, K.J. The development of style in Indian painting. Delhi: Macmillan, 1974. 99p. + 8 pl.

03271 KRAMRISCH, S. A survey of painting in the Deccan. Hyderabad: Archaeol. Dept. of the Nizam's Govt., 1937. 234p. + 26 pl.

03272 MEHTA, N.C. Studies in Indian painting.... Bombay: Taraporevala, 1926. 127p. + 61 pl. [600-1870 AD]

03273 MOTI CHANDRA. Studies in early Indian painting. Bombay: Asia, 1974. 160p. + 62 pl.

03274 PAL, P. & C. GLYNN. The sensuous line: Indian drawings from the Paul F. Walter Collection. Los Angeles: L.A. Co., Museum of Art, 1976. 72p. [cat. of an exhibit]

03275 RANDHAWA, M.S. & J.K. GALBRAITH. Indian painting; the scenes, themes and legends. Boston: Houghton Mifflin, 1968. 142p.

03276 RAWSON, P.S. Indian painting. NY: Universe Books, 1961. 169p.

03277 ROWLAND, B. & A.K. COOMARASWAMY. The wall-paintings of India, Central Asia, and Ceylon. Boston: Merrymount Press, 1938. 94p. + 36 pl.

03278 SIVARAMAMURTI, C. Indian painting. ND: NBT, 1970. 130p.

3. Miniatures

03279 ARCHER, W.G. Indian miniatures. Greenwich, CT: New York Graphic Soc., 1960. 16p., 100 ill.

03280 BUSSAGLI, M. Indian miniatures. Tr. by Raymond Rudorff. London: P. Hamlyn, 1969. 158p. + 73 pl. [1st Italian ed. 1966]

03281 DAHMEN-DALLAPICCOLA, A.L. Indischen Miniaturen: Malerei der Rajput-Staaten. Baden-Baden: Holle, 1976. 107p.

03282 ______. Rāgamālā Miniaturen von 1475 bis 1700. Wiesbaden: Harrassowitz, 1975. 439p.

03283 DIMAND, M.S. Indian miniature paintings. NY: Crown Pub., 1967. 28p., 10 col. ill.

03284 GOETZ, H. Geschichte der indischen Miniaturmalerei. Berlin: W. de Gruyter, 1934. 57p.

03285 HAJEK, L. Miniatures from the East. Photographs by Werner Forman. Tr. by A. Jappel. London: Spring Books, 1960. 108p. + 53 pl.

4. Techniques

03286 AGRAWAL, O.P. A study on the techniques of Indian wall paintings. In J. of Indian Museums 25/26 (1969-70) 90-116.

03287 BHATTACHARYA, A.K. Technique of Indian painting: a study chiefly made on the basis of the śilpa texts. Calcutta: Saraswat Library, 1976. 174p.

03288 COOMARASWAMY, A.K. The technique and theory of Indian painting. In JUPHS 23,1/2 (1950) 5-34.

03289 DE SILVA, R.H. The evolution of the technique of Sinhalese wall painting and comparison with Indian painting methods. In AC 1 (1971) 90-104.

03290 GUNASINGHE, S. La technique de la peinture indienne d'après les textes du Śilpa. Paris: PHF, 1957. 96p. (Musée Guimet, Annales: Bibliothèque d'études, 62)

03291 JOHNSON, B.B. A preliminary study of the technique of Indian miniature painting. In P. Pal, ed. Aspects of Indian Art. Leiden: Brill, 1972, 139-46.

03292 SIVARAMAMURTI, C. Conventions in the art of painting. In JORM 9 (1935) 255-69.

03293 ______. The painter in ancient India. ND: Abhinav, 1978. 93p. + 31 pl.

E. Industrial and Decorative Arts and Handicrafts

1. General Studies

03294 ABRAHAM, J.M. Handicrafts in India. ND: Graphics Columbia, 1964. 188p.

03295 Bihar handicrafts [special issue]. In Marg 20 (1966) 2-60. [Articles by Mulk Raj Anand, J.C. Mathur, P.L. Gupta, Jasleen Dhamija, M. Archer and Sachchidananda.]

03296 BIRDWOOD, G.C.M. Industrial arts of India. London: Chapman & Hall, 1880. 344p. + 93pl.

03297 BUSSABARGER, R.F. & B.D. ROBINS. The everyday art of India. NY: Dover, 1968. 205p.

03298 CHATTOPADHYAYA, K. Indian handicrafts. ND: Allied, 1963. 95p.

03299 Crafts Museum. ND: Crafts Museum, All India Handicrafts Board, Min. of Foreign Trade, Govt. of India, 1971. 154p.

03300 INDIA (REP.). CENSUS OF INDIA, 1961. [Handicraft reports appear as pt. VII-A of state Census reports.]

03301 Indian handicrafts. Rev. ed. ND: PDMIB, 1968. 72p.

03302 KELKAR, D.G. Lamps of India. Delhi: PDMIB, 1961. unpaged.

03303 MEHTA, R.J. The handicrafts and industrial arts of India. A pictorial and descriptive survey of Indian craftsmanship as seen in masterpieces... Bombay: Taraporevala, 1969. 157p.

03304 MIRZA, A. Handicrafts of West Pakistan. Karachi: West Pakistan Ind. Dev. Corp., 1964. 109p.

03305 MUKHARJI, T.N. Art-manufactures of India: specially compiled for the Glasgow International Exhibition, 1888. ND: Navrang, 1974. 451p. [1st pub. 1888]

03306 SHUKLA, M.S. A history of gem industry in ancient & medieval India. Varanasi: Bharat-Bharati, 1972-.

03307 UPADHYAY, M.N. Handicrafts of India (especially Andhra Pradesh). Secunderabad: Andhra Pradesh Book Dist., 1966. 88p. + 20 p. of ill.

2. Design Motifs

03308 BHAVNANI, E. Decorative designs and craftsmanship in India; with over 10,001 designs and motifs from the crafts of India. Bombay: Taraporevala, 1969. 109p. + 175pl.

03309 INDIAN INSTITUTE OF ART IN INDUSTRY, CALCUTTA. 5000 Indian designs and motifs. Ed. by A.C. Mookerjee. Calcutta: Sahitya Samsad, 1965. 13p. + 200p. of ill. [1st pub. 1958]

3. Personal Adornment: Costume, Coiffure, Jewelry, and Armor

03310 BIRDWOOD, G.C.M. Catalogue of the collection of Indian arms and objects of India.... London: Griggs, 1898. 20p. + 30pl.

03311 BRIJ BHUSHAN, J. The costumes and textiles of India. Bombay: Taraporevala, 1958. 92p. + 87 p. of ill. + 150pl.

03312 ______. Indian jewelry, ornaments and decorative designs. 2nd ed. Bombay: Taraporevala, 1964. 189p.

03313 BRUNEL, F. Jewellery of India: five thousand years of tradition. ND: NBT, 1972. 82p.

03314 CHAUDHURI, N.C. Culture in the vanity bag, being an essay on clothing and adornment in passing and abiding India. Bombay: Jaico, 1976. 146p.

03315 DAR, S.N. Costumes of India and Pakistan; a historical and cultural study. Bombay: Taraporevala, 1969. 244p. + 44pl.

03316 DONGERKERY, K. The Indian sari. ND: All India Handicrafts Board, 1959. 99p.

03317 ______. Jewelry and personal adornment in India. ND: ICCR, 1970. 77p.

03318 EGERTON, W.E. Indian and Oriental armour. Harrisburg, PA: Stackpole Books, 1968. 178p. [1st pub. 1880]

03319 FABRI, C.L. Indian dress: a brief history. Orient Longmans, 1977. 92p. [1st pub. 1960]

03320 GHURYE, G.S. Indian costume... Bombay: Popular, 1951. 319p.

03321 PALCHOUDHURI, I. Ancient hair styles of India. Calcutta: Rupa, 1974. 44p.

03322 PANT, G.N. Indian arms and armour. ND: Army Educ. Stores, 1978-. [to be 4 v.]

03323 RAWSON, P.S. The Indian sword. London: Jenkins, 1968. 108p.

4. Textiles and Textile History

03324 CHAKRABORTI, M.K. & L. CHATTERJEE. Batik-o-tex print. Calcutta: KLM, 1970. 50p.

03325 Homage to kalamkari. Bombay: Marg Pub., 1980. 134p.

03326 Indian batik paintings. ND: Dhoomi Mal's Gallery, 1971. 5p. + 18pl.

03327 IRWIN, J. The Kashmir shawl. London: HMSO, 1974. 62p. + 50p. of pl. (Victoria and Albert Museum, monograph 29)

03328 ______. A select bibliography of Indian textiles. In Journal of Indian Textile History 1 (1955) 66-76.

03329 IRWIN, J. & M. HALL. Indian painted and printed fabrics. Ahmedabad: Calico Museum of Textiles, 1971. 203p.

03330 IRWIN, J. &. P.R. SCHWARTZ. Studies in Indo-European textile history. Ahmedabad: Calico Museum of Textiles, 1966. 124p.

03331 JAYAKAR, P. & J. IRWIN, eds. Textiles & ornaments of India; a selection of designs. NY: Arno, 1972. 93p. [Rpt. of 1956 ed.]

03332 MANCHANDA, J. Traditional fabrics of India. ND: Samkaleen Prakashan, 1978. 36p.

03333 MEHTA, R.J. Masterpieces of Indian textiles: hand spun--hand woven--traditional. Bombay: Taraporevala, 1970. 56p. + 88pl.

03334 MEHTA, R.N. Bāndhas of Orissa. Journal of Indian Textile History 6 (1961) 62-74.

03335 MOTI CHANDRA. Kashmir shawls. In PWMB 2 (1952-53) 1-24.

03336 SARASVATI, S.K. Indian textiles. Delhi: PDMIB, 1961. 48p.

03337 TALWAR, K. & K. KRISHNA. Indian pigment paintings on cloth. Ahmedabad: Calico Museum of Textiles, 1979. 166p. + 58pl.

03338 Textiles and embroideries of India. Bombay: Marg Pub., 1965. 80 + 72p.

5. Embroidery

03339 ARYAN, S. Himachal embroidery. ND: Rekha, 1976. 82p. + 24pl.

03340 CHATTOPADHYAYA, K. Indian embroidery. ND: Wiley Eastern, 1977. 76p.

03341 COUSIN, F. Blouses brodées du Kutch; coupe et décor. O&M 12,3 (1972) 287-312.

03342 DONGERKERY, K. Romance of Indian embroidery. Bombay: Thacker, 1951. 62p.

03343 IRWIN, J. Indian embroidery. London: HMSO, 1951. 9p. + 28pl.

03344 IRWIN, J. & M. HALL. Indian embroideries. Ahmedabad: Calico Museum of Textiles, 1973. 222p. + 62pl. (Historic textiles of India at the Calico Museum, 2)

03345 NANAVATI, J.M. & M.P. VORA & M.A. DHAKY. The embroidery and bead work of Kutch and Saurashtra. Baroda: Dept. of Archaeol., Gujarat State, 1966. 125p. + 104p. of ill.

03346 Painting with the needle: a survey of Indian embroidery. [special issue] In Marg 17 (1964) 2-72.

6. Carpets

03347 Carpets of India. In Marg 18 (1965) 2-45. [Articles by K. Chattopadhyaya, C.G. Ellis, J. Irwin, J. Dhamija, H.K. Wattal and P.N. Kaul]

03348 CHATTOPADHYAYA, K. Carpets and floor coverings of India. Bombay: Taraporevala, 1969. 68p.

03349 Indian carpets. Bombay: Marg Pub., 1966. 45p.

F. Folk Art - General Studies

03350 ARCHER, W.G. Vertical man, a study in primitive Indian sculpture. London: Allen & Unwin, 1947. 122p.

03351 ARYAN, K.C. Folk bronzes of north western India. Delhi: Rekha, 1973. 123p.

03352 COOMARASWAMY, A.K. The nature of 'folklore' and 'popular' art. In QJMS 27,1/2 (1936) 1-12.

03353 DAS, A.K. Tribal art and craft. Delhi: Agam, 1979. 190p.

03354 DHAMIJA, J. Indian folk arts and crafts. ND: NBT, 1970. 115p.

03355 Folk paintings of India. ND: Inter-Natl. Cultural Centre, 1961. 49p.

03356 KRAMRISCH, S. Unknown India: ritual art in tribe and village. Philadelphia: Philadelphia Museum of Art, 1968. 127p.

03357 MOOKERJEE, A.C. Indian primitive art. Calcutta: Oxford Book & Stationery, 1959. 79p.

03358 PATEL, A. Folk terracottas of Gujarat. In MSUB 12 (1963) 63-70.

03359 RAY, S.K. The folk art of India. Calcutta: Yogalayam, 1967. 23p. + 16pl.

03360 REEVES, R. Folk arts of India: metal, ceramics, jewelry, textiles and wood; an exhibition of the Ruth Reeves Memorial Collection, Syracuse University. Ed. by A.K. Schmeckebier. Syracuse: School of Art, Syracuse U., 1967. 93p.

G. Introductions to Regional Art Traditions: Architecture, Sculpture, and Painting

1. Sri Lanka

03361 CEYLON. MIN. OF CULTURAL AFFAIRS. Register of ancient monuments. Colombo: 1972. 814p.

03362 COOMARASWAMY, A.K. Bronzes from Ceylon.... Colombo: Colombo Museum, 1914. 31p. (Its Memoirs, ser. A, 1)

03363 DE SILVA, P.H.D.H. A catalogue of antiquities and other cultural objects from Sri Lanka (Ceylon) abroad. Colombo: Natl. Museums of Sri Lanka, 1975. 506p., incl. 103pl.

03364 DHANAPALA, D.B. Buddhist paintings from shrines and temples in Ceylon. NY: New American Library, 1964. 24p. + 4p. of ill.

03365 ______. Peintures de temples et de sanctuaires a Ceylan. Paris: Flammarion, 1964. 96p.

03366 ______. The story of Sinhalese painting. Maharagama: Saman Press, 1957. 58p.

03367 DOHANIAN, D.K. The Mahayana Buddhist sculpture of Ceylon. NY: Garland, 1977. 167p. + 75pl.

03368 GODAKUMBURA, C.E. Architecture of Sri Lanka. Colombo: Dept. of Cultural Affairs, Sri Lanka, 1976. 43p. + 14pl. (The Culture of Sri Lanka, 5) [1st ed. 1963]

03369 LUDOWYK, E.F.C. The footprint of the Buddha. London: Allen & Unwin, 1958. 182p.

03370 MODE, H. Die buddhistische Plastik auf Ceylon. Leipzig: Seemann, 1963. 145p.

03371 MUDIYANSE, N. Mahayana monuments in Ceylon. Colombo: M.D. Gunasena, 1967. 135p.

03372 PARANAVITANA, S. Glimpses of Ceylon's past. Colombo: LHI, 1972. 199p.

03373 PARANAVITANA, S. & W.G. ARCHER. Ceylon: paintings from temple, shrine and rock. NY: New York Graphic Society, 1957. 29p. + 32pl. (UNESCO world art ser., 8)

03374 RAGHAVAN, M.D. Art and architecture of Ceylon. In BITCM (1966) pt. 2, 243-50.

03375 SENAVERATNE, J.M. Guide to Mihintale. Colombo: Archaeol. Dept., 1952. 26p.

03376 WIJESEKERA, N.D. A comparative study of early Sinhalese paintings with contemporary Indian paintings. In CHJ 1,2 (1951) 97-108.

03377 ______. Early Sinhalese sculpture. Colombo: M.D. Gunasena, 1962. 256p. + 82pl.

03378 WILLEY, A. Ancient bronzes in the Colombo museum. In Spolia Zeylanica 6,22 (1909) 57-74.

2. South India: Tamilnadu, Andhra, Karnataka, and Kerala

a. general

03379 JOUVEAU-DUBREUIL, G. Archéologie du sud de l'Inde. Paris: P. Geuthner, 1914. v. 1, architecture, 192p.; v. 2, iconography, 152p.

03380 ______. Dravidian architecture. Ed. with pref. and notes by S. Krishnaswami Aiyangar. Varanasi: Bharat-Bharati, 1972. 47p.

03381 KRAMRISCH, S. Dravida and Kerala in the art of Travancore. Ascona: Artibus Asiae, 1953. 50p. + 24pl.

03382 NAGASWAMI, R. The art of Tamilnadu. Madras: Dept. of Archaeol., Govt. of Tamilnadu, 1972. 16p. + 125 p. of ill.

03383 RAJENDRA PRASAD, B. Art of South India, Andhra Pradesh. Delhi: Sundeep, 1980. 230p. + 20pl. (Art of South India series, 2)

03384 SOUNDARA RAJAN, K.V. The art of south India: Tamil Nadu & Kerala. Delhi: Sundeep, 1978. 218p. + 25pl.

03385 YAZDANI, G. Bidar, its history and monuments. London: OUP, 1947. 240p. + 130pl.

b. temples and other architecture

03386 DAS, R.K. Temples of Tamilnad. Bombay: BVB, 1964. 275p.

03387 INDIA (REP.) CENSUS OF INDIA, 1961. Temples of Madras State. Madras: 1965-69. [v. 9, pt. 11-D, 7 v.]

03388 JAUHARI, M. South India and its architecture. Varanasi: Bharatiya Vidya Prakashan, 1969. 136p.

03389 MAHALINGAM, T.V. Studies in the South Indian temple complex. Dharwar: Kannada Res. Inst., Karnatak U., 1970. 89p.

03390 NARASIMHACHAR, R. Architecture and sculpture in Mysore. Bangalore: Govt. Press, 1917. (Mysore Archaeol. series, 1)

03391 SARKAR, H. Monuments of Kerala. ND: ASI, 1973. 75p. + 6pl.

03392 SOUNDARA RAJAN, K.V. The matrix of South Indian architecture. In JIH 43,3 (1965) 783-825.

03393 SRINIVASAN, K.R. Temples of South India. ND: NBT, 1972. 223p.

03394 Temples of South India. Rev. ed. ND: PDMIB, 1973. 50p. + 20pl.

c. sculpture & painting

03395 ARAVAMUTHAN, T.G. Portrait sculpture in South India. London: India Soc., 1931. 100p. + 32pl.

03396 GANGOLY, O.C. South Indian bronzes: a historical survey of south Indian sculpture with iconographical notes based on original sources. Rev. and enl. 2nd ed. Calcutta: Nababharat, 1978. 142p. + 50 pl.

03397 GRAVELEY, F.H. Catalogue of South Indian Hindu metal images in the Madras Government Museum. Madras: Govt. Press, 1932. 144p. + 23pl.

03398 NIGAM, M.L. Sculptural heritage of Andhradesa. Hyderabad: Booklinks Corp., 1975. 60 + 20p.

03399 SIVARAMAMURTI, C. South Indian bronzes. ND: Lalit Kalā Akademi, 1963. 86p.

03400 ______. South Indian paintings. ND: Nath Museum, 1968. 174p.

3. Middle India

03401 AGARAWALA, R.A. History, art & architecture of Jaisalmer. Delhi: Agam Kala, 1979. 98p. + 26pl.

03402 AZEVEDO, C. DE. A arte de Goa, Damao e Diu. Lisbon: Commissao Executiva do V Centenario de nascimento de Vasco da Gama, 1469-1969, 1970. 60p. + 50pl.

03403 BURGESS, J. & H. COUSENS. The architectural antiquities of northern Gujarat, more especially of...Baroda State. Varanasi: Bharatiya, 1975. 118p. + 57pl.

03404 COUSENS, H. The architectural antiquities of western India. London: India Soc., 1926. 86p. + 57pl.

03405 DEGLURKAR, G.B. Temple architecture and sculpture of Maharashtra. Nagpur: Nagpur U., 1974. 184p. + 47pl. (Temples of the Vidarbha region, 4)

03406 ELSON, V.C. Dowries from Kutch: a women's folk art in India. Los Angeles: Museum of Cultural History, U. of California, 1979. 127p.

03407 ELWIN, V. The tribal art of middle India. Bombay: OUP, 1951. 213p.

03408 FABRI, C.L. History of the art of Orissa. Bombay: Orient Longmans, 1974. 220p. + 61pl.

03409 FISCHER, E. & H. SHAH. Rural craftsmen and their work; equipment and techniques in the Mer village of Ratadi in Saurashtra, India. Ahmedabad: Natl. Inst. of Design, 1970. 227p.

03410 GOETZ, H. The art and architecture of Bikaner State. Oxford: B. Cassirer, 1950. 180p.

03411 GUNE, V.T., ed. Ancient shrines of Goa; a pictorial survey. Panjim: Dept. of Info., Goa, Daman & Diu, 1965. 25p. + 72pl.

03412 JOSHI, O.P. Painted folklore and folklore painters of India: a study with reference to Rajasthan. Delhi: Concept, 1976. 119p. + 11pl.

03413 MAJMUDAR, M.R. Gujarat, its art-heritage. Bombay: U. of Bombay, 1968. 168p. + 70p. of ill.

03414 MITRA, R.L. The antiquities of Orissa. Calcutta: Baptist Mission Press, 1875-80. 2 v. [Rpt. in ISPP 2-4 (1960-63), passim]

03415 MITTERWALLNER, G. VON. Chaul, eine unerforschte Stadt an der Westküste Indiens. (Wehr-, Sakral-, und Profanarchitektur.) Berlin: W. de Gruyter, 1964. 238p. (Neue Münchner Beiträge zur Kunstgeschichte, 6)

03416 RAVAL, R.M. Silavat painting: folk painting of Gujerat & Saurashtra. In Folklore (C) 3 (1962) 249-53.

03417 SAKSENA, J. Art of Rajasthan: henna and floor decorations. Delhi: Sundeep, 1979. 241p. + 24pl.

03418 SHAH, U.P. & K.K. GANGULI, eds. Western Indian art. Calcutta: Indian Soc. of Oriental Art, 1966. 94 + 51p. [Pub. as JISOA, special no., 1965-68]

4. The Northwest: Indus Valley and Mountain Frontier

03419 ANAND, M.R., ed. The art of living in the Punjab village. In Marg 28,1 (1974) 9-40.

03420 ARYAN, K.C. Punjab murals. ND: Rekha, 1977. 122p.

03421 BARGER, E. & P. WRIGHT. Excavations in Swat and explorations in the Oxus Territories of Afghanistan. Delhi: MPGOI, 1941. 67p. (ASI Memoirs, 64)

03422 COUSENS, H. The antiquities of Sind, with historical outline. Varanasi: Bharatiya, 1975. 184p. [Rpt. 1929 ed.]

03423 GANGULY, M.M. Orissa and her remains, ancient and medieval. Calcutta: Thacker, Spink, 1912. 540p. & 27pl.

03424 GOETZ, H. Studies in the history and art of Kashmir and the Indian Himalaya. Wiesbaden: Harrassowitz, 1969. viii, 197p. & 47p. of ill. (SSI, 4)

03425 KAK, R.C. Ancient monuments of Kashmir. London: India Soc., 1933. 172p. + 77pl.

03426 KANG, K. & N. SANDHU. Punjab murals. Chandigarh: Public Relations Dept., Punjab, 1978. 16p. + 21pl.

03427 PAL, P. Bronzes of Kashmir. ND: Munshiram, 1975. 255p. + 120pl.

03428 SNELLGROVE, D.L. & T. SKORUPSKI. The cultural heritage of Ladakh. Boulder, CO: Prajna Press, 1977. 144p. + 20pl.

03429 STEIN, M.A. An archaeological tour of Upper Swāt and adjacent hill tracts. Calcutta: Govt. of India Pub. Branch, 1930. 115p. (ASI Memoirs, 42)

03430 TUCCI, G. Explorations récentes dans le Swāt. In Museon 79 (1966) 42-58.

03431 WALIULLAH KHAN, M. Lahore and its important monuments. 2nd rev. ed. Karachi: Dept. of Archaeol. and Museums, 1964. 91p. [1st pub. 1959]

5. North India: the Ganga Plains from Delhi to Bihar

03432 CHATTERJI, S.C. Magadha architecture and culture. Calcutta: U. of Calcutta, 1942. 112p. + 30pl.

03433 FÜHRER, A.A. The monumental antiquities and inscriptions in the North-Western Provinces and Oudh. Varanasi: IndBH, 1969. 425p. [1st pub. 1891]

03434 MISHRA, V.K. Mithila art and architecture. Allahabad: Mithila Prakasana, 1978. 45p. + 24pl.

03435 PATIL, D.R. The antiquarian remains in Bihar. Patna: Kashi Prasad Jayaswal Res. Inst., 1963. 665p. (Hist. res. ser., 4)

03436 SHARMA, Y.D. Delhi and its neighbourhood. ND: ASI, 1964. 128p.

03437 STEPHEN, C. Archaeology and monumental remains of Delhi. Allahabad: Kitab Mahal, 1967. 284p. [1st pub. 1876]

03438 VEQUAUD, Y. The women painters of Mithila. London: Thames & Hudson, 1977. 112p. [1st French ed. 1976]

6. The Northeast Area of Bengal and Assam

03439 CHAUDHURI, P.D. Archaeology in Assam. Gauhati: State Dept. of Archaeol., 1964. 59p.

03440 DAS GUPTA, R. Eastern Indian manuscript painting. Bombay: Taraporevala, 1972. 112p.

03441 DATTA, B.K. Bengal temples. ND: Munshiram, 1975. 88p. + 14pl.

03442 HASAN, S.M. A guide to ancient monuments of East Pakistan. Dacca: Soc. for Pakistan St., 1970. 180p.

03443 MCCUTCHION, D. Hindu Muslim artistic continuities in Bengal. In JASP 13,3 (1968) 233-52.

03444 ______. The temples of Bankura District. Calcutta: Writers Workship, 1967. 16p.

03445 ______. Temples of Birbhum. In VQ 31,4 (1965-66) 315-43.

03446 SARASVATI, S.K. Muslim architecture in Bengal. In JISOA 9 (1941) 12-36.

7. Nepal and the Indian Himalayan Rim
a. general surveys

03447 ARAN, L. The art of Nepal: a guide of the masterpieces of sculpture, painting, and woodcarving. Kathmandu: Sahayogi, 1978. 237p. + 32pl.

03448 BANERJEE, N.R. Some thoughts on the development of Buddhist art in Nepal. In E&W 22,1/2 (1972) 63-78.

03449 ELWIN, V. The art of the north-east frontier of India. Shillong: North-East Frontier Agency, 1969. 211p. [1st pub. 1959]

03450 LÉVI, S. The art of Nepal. In Indian Arts & Letters 1,2 (1925) 49-67.

03451 MADANJEET SINGH. Himalayan art; wall-painting and sculpture in Ladakh, Lahaul, and Spiti, the Siwalik Ranges, Nepal, Sikkim, and Bhutan. Greenwich, CT: New York Graphic Soc., 1968. 295p. [Rev., small-format ed. London: Macmillan, 1971, 287p.]

03452 OHRI, V.C. Arts of Himachal. Simla: State Museum, Himachal Pradesh, 1975. 230p. (Studies in arts of Himachal series, 1)

03453 PAL, P. The arts of Nepal. Leiden: Brill, 1974-78. pt. 1, sculpture, 87p. + 300pl.; pt. 2, painting, 184p. + 219pl. (HO, 7:3:2)

03454 RAY, A. Art of Nepal. ND: ICCR, 1973. 78p. + 80p. of ill.

03455 SHARMA, P.R. Étude préliminaire sur l'art & l'architecture du bassin de la Karnali, Népal de l'ouest. Paris: CNRS, 1972. 116p.

03456 VAIDYA, K.L. The cultural heritage of the Himalayas. ND: National, 1977. 183p.

03457 VOGEL, J.P. Antiquities of Chamba State. Calcutta: Supt. Govt. Print., 1911-57. 2 v.

03458 WALDSCHMIDT, E. & R.L. WALDSCHMIDT. Nepal: art treasures from the Himalayas. Tr. from German by D. Wilson. London: Elek, 1969. 160p. [1st pub. 1967]

b. catalogs of collections and exhibits of Nepali art

03459 FOUCHER, A. Catalogue des peintures népalaises et tibétaines de la collection B.H. Hodgson a la bibliothéque de l'Institut de France. In Mémoires. Academie des inscriptions et belles-lettres (Paris), 1st ser., 11 (1897) 1-30.

03460 KRAMRISCH, S. The art of Nepal. NY: Asia Soc., 1964. 159p.

03461 ______. Art of Nepal and Tibet. In Philadelphia Museum of Art Bull. 55 (1960) 23-38.

03462 LEE, S.E. Manuscript and bronze from Nepal. In Bull. of the Detroit Inst. of Arts 21 (1942) 60-70.

03463 MALLMANN, M.-T. DE. Les bronzes népalais de la collection Sylvain Lévi. In ArtAs 27,1/2 (1964) 134-50.

03464 MONOD, O. Népal; sculptures et peintures des collections royales, Musée Guimet. Paris: Musée Guimet, 1966. 8p.

03465 PAL, P. Nepal: where the gods are young. NY: Asia Soc., 1975. 135p.

03466 ______. Paintings from Nepal in the Prince of Wales Museum. In PWMB 10 (1967) 1-26.

03467 THAPA, R.J. & N.R. BANERJEE. Nepalese art. Kathmandu: Dept. of Archaeol., 1966. 85p.

03468 TOTH, E. The art of Nepal in the "Francis Hopp" Museum of Eastern Asiatic Arts. Budapest: Revai Nyomda, 1963. 44p., 14 figs.

c. temples, sculpture, and painting

03469 BANERJEE, N.R. Nepalese architecture. Delhi: Agam, 1980. 272p. + 35pl.

03470 BERNIER, R.M. The Nepalese pagoda: origins and style. ND: S. Chand, 1979. 219p. + 47pl.

03471 ______. The temples of Nepal; an introductory survey. Kathmandu: Voice of Nepal, 1970. 239p.

03472 CHETWODE, P. Temple architecture in Kulu. In Royal Society of Arts, London. Journal 116 (Oct. 1968) 924-946.

03473 COOMARASWAMY, A.K. Bronzes from Nepal. In Museum of Fine Arts, Boston. Bulletin 16,95 (June 1918) 33-39.

03474 DAS GUPTA, R. Nepalese miniatures. Varanasi: Bharatiya Vidya Prakashan, 1968. 55p.

03475 JAMSPAL, L., ed. Himalayan Buddhist art: thangka prints. Delhi: Shiva Pub., 1973-. 3 v.

03476 JETTMAR, G. Die Holztempel des oberen Kulutales; in ihren historischen, religiösen und kunstgeschichtlichen Zusammenhängen. Wiesbaden: Steiner, 1974. 133p. + 48pl.

03477 JOSEPH, M. Viharas of Kathmandu Valley; reliquaries of Buddhist culture. In OA ns 17,2 (1971) 121-42.

03478 KHANDALAVALA, K. Some Nepalese and Tibetan bronzes in the collection of Mr. R.S. Sethna of Bombay. In Mārg 4,1 (1950) 21-40.

03479 KRAMRISCH, S. Nepalese paintings. In JISOA 1 (1933) 129-47.

03480 SESTINI, V. & E. SOMIGLI. Sherpa architecture. Tr. from Italian by T. Paterson. Geneva: UNESCO, 1978. 77p.

03481 SNELLGROVE, D.L. Shrines and temples of Nepal. In ArtsAs 8 (1961) 3-10, 93-120.

03482 WIESNER, U. Nepalese temple architecture; its characteristics and its relations to Indian development. Leiden: Brill, 1978. 117p. + 16pl. (Studies in South Asian culture, 8)

Part Two

Four Ages of Historical Evolution: Subcontinental and Regional

2

Prehistory and Protohistory of South Asia to 600 B.C.: The Paleolithic through the Vedic Age

I. GENERAL SURVEYS AND STUDIES OF PREHISTORY AND PROTOHISTORY

A. Reference

1. Bibliography

03483 DALES, G.F. Recent trends in the pre- and protohistoric archaeology of South Asia. In PAPS 110 (1966) 130-39.

03484 KING, D.E., ed. Comprehensive bibliography of Pakistan archeology: paleolithic to historic times. East Lansing: Asian Studies Center, Michigan State U., 1975. 95p. (S. Asia Ser. Occ. Paper, 24)

03485 MISRA, V.N. & M. NAGAR. Twenty-five years of Indian prehistory (1947-1972) - a review of research. In K.S. Mathur & S.C. Varma, eds. Man and society. Lucknow: Ethnog. and Folk Culture Soc., 1972, 1-54. [bibl. 34-54]

03486 SEN, D.D. Research trends in prehistory in India. In H.K. Rakshit, ed. Anthropology in India. Calcutta: AnthSI, 1976, v. 2, 10-24.

2. Chronology and Methodology

03487 AGRAWAL, D.P. & S. KUSUMGAR. Prehistoric chronology and radiocarbon dating in India. ND: Munshiram, 1974. 170p.

03488 ALLCHIN, B. The Indian stone-age sequence. In JRAI 93,2 (1963) 210-234.

03489 DALES, G.F. Archaeological and radiocarbon chronologies for protohistoric S. Asia. In N. Hammond, ed. South Asian archaeology. Park Ridge, NJ: Noyes Press, 1973, 157-70.

03490 MALIK, S.C. Peninsular India: problems of Pleistocene chronology and a tentative scheme of climatic phases and stone industries. In Anthropos 60 (1965) 198-203.

03491 MISRA, V.N. Problems of terminology in Indian prehistory. In EA 15,2 (1962) 113-24.

03492 ROY, S.B. Ancient India: a chronological study, 1500-400 B.C. ND: Inst. of Chronology, 1975. 162p. [a traditional Hindu approach]

B. General Surveys and Studies

1. General Studies

03493 AGRAWAL, D.P. & D.K. CHAKRABARTI, eds. Essays in Indian protohistory. Delhi: B.R., 1979. 392p.

03494 AGRAWAL, D.P. & A. GHOSH, eds. Radiocarbon and Indian archaeology. Bombay: Tata Inst. of Fundamental Res., 1973. 526p.

03495 ALLCHIN, B. & R. ALLCHIN. The birth of Indian civilization; India and Pakistan before 500 B.C. Baltimore: Penguin, 1968. 365p.

03496 FAIRSERVIS, W.A. The roots of ancient India; the archaeology of early Indian civilization. NY: Macmillan, 1971. 482p.

03497 FOOTE, R.B. Prehistoric and protohistoric antiquities of India. Delhi: Leeladevi, 1979. 246p. [1st pub. 1916]

03498 GHOSH, A.K., ed. Perspectives in palaeoanthropology: Professor D. Sen festschrift. Calcutta: KLM, 1974. 380p.

03499 GORDON, D.H. The pre-historic background of Indian culture. Westport, CT: Greenwood Press, 1975. 199p. [Rpt. of 1960 ed.]

03500 JAIN, K.C. Prehistory and protohistory of India. ND: Agam, 1979. 367p.

03501 MALIK, S.C. Indian civilisation; the formative period; a study of archaeology as anthropology. Simla: IIAS, 1968. 204p.

03502 MISRA, V.N. & M.S. MATE, eds. Indian prehistory: 1964. Poona: DCPRI, 1965. 266p. (DCBC, 32)

03503 PIGGOTT, S. Prehistoric India to 1000 B.C. 2nd ed. London: Cassell, 1962. 295p.

03504 SANKALIA, H.D. Prehistory of India. ND: Munshiram, 1977. 16 + 211p.

03505 ______. The prehistory and protohistory of India and Pakistan. Poona: DCPRI, 1974. 592p.

03506 SEN, D.D. & A.K. GHOSH, eds. Studies in prehistory; Robert Bruce Foote memorial volume. Calcutta: KLM, 1966. 194p.

03507 SUBBARAO, B. The personality of India: a study in the development of material culture in India and Pakistan. Baroda: Faculty of Arts, MSUB, 1956. 135p. (MSUB series, 3)

03508 WHEELER, R.E.M. Early India and Pakistan: to Ashoka. Rev. ed. NY: Praeger, 1968. 241p.

2. Surveys of Prehistory by Region

03509 AGRAWAL, D.P. & B.M. PANDE. Ecology and archaeology of western India. Delhi: Concept, 1977. 255p. [Gujarat-Rajasthan]

03510 CHAKLADAR, H.C. The prehistoric culture of Bengal. In MI 31,4 (1952) 129-64.

03511 DANI, A.H. Prehistory and protohistory of eastern India. Calcutta: KLM, 1960. 248p. [covers Assam, East and West Bengal, Bihar, Orissa]

03512 DERANIYAGALA, S. Prehistoric Ceylon - a summary in 1968. In AC 1 (1971) 3-46.

03513 GRAZIOSI, P. Prehistoric research in northwestern Punjab; anthropological research in Chitral. Leiden: Brill, 1964. 61p. + 95 pl.

03514 JOSHI, R.V. Stone age cultures of central India. Poona: DCPRI, 1978. 96p.

03515 KOSAMBI, D.D. Pilgrim's progress: a contribution to the prehistory of the Western Deccan plateau. In his Myth and reality. Bombay: Popular, 1962, 110-51.

03516 MISRA, V.N. Pre- and proto-history of the Berach Basin, South Rajasthan. Poona: DCPRI, 1967. 216p. (DCBC, 41)

03517 MOHAPATRA, G.C. The stone age cultures of Orissa. Poona: DCPRI, 1962. 242p.

03518 NARAYAN, B. Archaeology in Bihar. In JBPP 1 (1977) 1-74.

03519 OHRI, V.C., ed. Prehistory of Himachal Pradesh: some latest findings. Simla: State Museum, Dept. of Languages & Culture, Himachal Pradesh, 1979. 67p.

03520 RAMACHANDRA DIKSHITAR, V.R. Pre-historic South India. Madras: U. of Madras, 1951. 264p.

03521 SANKALIA, H.D., et al. From history to prehistory at Nevasa. Poona: DCPRI, 1960. 549p. [in Maharashtra]

03522 SHARMA, R.K. & RAHMAN ALI. Archaeology of Bhopal region. Delhi: Agam Kala, 1980. 136p. + 12 pl.

03523 SOLHEIM, W.G. & S. DERANIYAGALA. Archaeological survey to investigate Southeast Asian prehistoric presence in Ceylon. Colombo: Ceylon Dept. of Archaeology, 1972. 40p. [AC, occ. paper, 3]

03524 SUDERSEN, V. Geomorphology and pre-history of South India. Delhi: B.R., 1979. 156p.

3. Studies of Early Technology

03525 POSSEHL, G.L. The chronology of gabarbands and palas in western South Asia. In Expedition 17,2 (1975) 33-37.

03526 RAIKES, R.L. The ancient gabarbands of Baluchistan. In E&W 15 (1964-65) 26-35.

03527 RAY, A. & D.K. CHAKRABARTI. Studies in ancient Indian technology and production: a review. In JESHO 18,2 (1975) 219-32.

03528 SINHA, B.P., ed. Potteries in ancient India. Patna: Dept. of Ancient Indian Hist. & Archaeol., Patna U., 1969. 315p.

03529 SANKALIA, H.D. Functional significance of the O.C.P. and P.G.W. shapes and associated objects. In Purātattva 7 (1974) 47-52.

03530 ______. Some aspects of prehistoric technology in India. ND: Indian Natl. Sci. Acad., 1970. 69p.

03531 ______. Stone age tools: their techniques, names and probable functions. Poona: DCPRI, 1964. 215p.

4. Prehistoric Art and Rock Paintings

03532 Bhimbhetka. In Marg 28,4 (1975) 46p. [Madhya Pradesh]

03533 BROOKS, R.R.R. Reconstructing stone age paintings. In Archaeology 28 (1975) 92-97.

03534 BROOKS, R.R.R. & V.S. WAKANKAR. Stone age painting in India. New Haven: YUP, 1976. 128p. + 67 pl.

03535 GAJJAR, I.N. Ancient Indian art and the West: a study of parallels, continuity, and symbolism from proto-historic to early Buddhist times. Bombay: Taraporevala, 1971. 179p.

03536 KHATRI, A.P. Rock paintings of Adamgarh (Central India) and their age. In Anthropos 59,5/6 (1964) 759-69.

03537 MATHPAL, Y. Prehistoric art of Bhimbetka, Central India: a preliminary study. In JUP 41 (1974) 95-107.

03538 ______. Rock art of India. In JIH 56,1 (1976) 27-53.

03539 SANKALIA, H.D. Pre-historic art in India. ND: Vikas, 1978. 109p.

03540 [Special issue on rock painting] In Prachya Pratibha 3,2 (1975) 1-96.

03541 WAKANKAR, V.S. Painted rock shelters of India. In Rivista di Scienze Preistoriche 17,1/4 (1962) 237-253.

03542 ______. Peintures rupestres indiennes. In O&M 3,2 (1963) 129-50.

5. Burial Practices

03543 GUPTA, S.P. Disposal of the dead and physical types in ancient India. Delhi: Oriental, 1972. 346p.

03544 LESHNIK, L.S. Archaeological interpretation of burial in the light of central Indian ethnography. In Zeitschrift für Ethnologie 92,1 (1967) 23-32.

03545 SINGH, P. Burial practices in ancient India; a study in the eschatological beliefs of early man as revealed by archaeological sources. Varanasi: Prithivi Prakashan, 1970. 204p.

II. THE EARLY, MIDDLE, AND LATE STONE AGES: HUNTING AND GATHERING BANDS

A. The Early Stone Age (Paleolithic), up to 10,000 B.C.: Handaxe and Flake Industries

03546 DETERRA, H. & T.T. PATERSON. Studies on the Ice Age in India and associated human culture. Washington: Carnegie Inst., 1939. 354p. (Its pub., 493)

03547 GHOSH, A.K. Concept of chopper/chopping tool complex in India. In A.K. Ghosh, ed. Perspectives in palaeoanthropology. Calcutta: KLM, 1974, 221-34.

03548 ______. The palaeolithic cultures of Singhbhum. In TAPS 40,1 (1970) 1-68.

03549 JAYASWAL, V. Palaeohistory of India: a study of the prepared core technique. Delhi: Agam Kala Prakashan, 1978. 243p.

03550 ______. Some aspects of techniques in palaeolithic cultures of India: a comparative review. In EA 27,3 (1974) 235-50.

03551 ______. A techno-typological review of the middle palaeolithic cultures of India. In Purātattva 7 (1974) 13-16.

03552 KENNEDY, K.A.R. The search for fossil man in India. In A. Basu, et al., eds. Physical anthropology and its expanding horizons.... Bombay: Orient Longmans, 1978, 93-112.

03553 MOVIUS, H.L. Pebble-tool terminology in India and Pakistan. In MI 37,2 (1957) 149-56.

03554 PATERSON, T.T. & H.J.H. DRUMMOND. Soan, the palaeolithic of Pakistan. Karachi: Pakistan Dept. of Archaeol., 1962. 171p. (Its Memoir, 2)

03555 SANKALIA, H.D. New evidence for early man in Kashmir. In CA 12,4/5 (1971) 558-62.

03556 ______. A revised study of Soan culture. In Anthropologist 14,1 (1967) 1-40.

03557 SEN, D.D. Lower palaeolithic culture complex and chronology in India. In MI 34,2 (1954) 121-50.

03558 ______. The Nalagarh palaeolithic culture. In MI 35,3 (1955) 177-84.

B. The Late Stone Age (Mesolithic): Microliths

03559 ALLCHIN, B. The late stone age of Ceylon. In JRAI 88,2 (1958) 179-201.

03560 ______. The stone-tipped arrow: late stone age hunters of the tropical old world. London: Phoenix, 1966. 224p.

03561 LAL, B.B. Birbhanpur, a microlithic site in the Damodar Valley, West Bengal. In AI 14 (1958) 4-48.

03562 LESHNIK, L.S. More microliths from Gujarat and some thoughts on Langhnaj. In A.K. Ghosh, ed. Perspectives in palaeoanthropology. Calcutta: KLM, 1974, 249-58.

03563 MALIK, S.C. The late stone age industries from excavated sites in Gujarat, India. In ArtAs 28 (1966) 162-74.

03564 PADDAYA, K. Mesolithic culture of the Shorapur doab, peninsular India. In Anthropos 69,3-4 (1974) 590-607.

03565 SANKALIA, H.D., et al. Excavations at Langhnaj, 1944-63. Poona: DCPRI, 1965. 1 v.

03566 SHARMA, G.R. Seasonal migrations and mesolithic lake cultures of the Ganga Valley. In K.C. Chattopadhyaya Memorial volume. Allahabad: Dept. of Ancient Hist., Culture and Archaeol., Allahabad U., 1975, 1-20.

03567 ZEUNER, F. & B. ALLCHIN. The microlithic sites of Tinnevelly District, Madras State. In AI 12 (1956) 4-20.

III. THE NEOLITHIC AND CHALCOLITHIC ("COPPER-STONE") AGE: BEGINNINGS OF FOOD PRODUCTION, USE OF COPPER AND BRONZE, AND FIXED SETTLEMENTS

A. General

03568 AGRAWAL, D.P. The copper bronze age in India: an integrated archaeological study of the copper bronze age in India in the light of chronological, technological, and ecological factors, ca. 3000-500 B.C. Delhi: Munshiram, 1971. 270p.

03569 ALLCHIN, F.R. Early domestic animals in India and Pakistan. In P.J. Ucko & G.W. Dimbleby, eds. The domestication and exploitation of plants and animals. Chicago: Aldine, 1969, 317-22.

03570 CLASON, A.T. Wild and domestic animals in prehistoric and early historic India. In EA 30,3 (1977) 241-289.

03571 DECARDI, B. Excavations and reconnaisance in Kalat, West Pakistan; the prehistoric sequence in the Surab region. In AP 2 (1965) 86-182 + 9 pl.

03572 KRISHNASWAMI, V.D. The neolithic pattern of India. In AI 16 (1960) 25-64.

03573 LAMBERG-KARLOVSKY, C.C. Archeology and metallurgical technology in prehistoric Afghanistan, India, and Pakistan. In AA 69,2 (1967) 145-62.

03574 SANKALIA, H.D. The chalcolithic cultures of India. In S.B. Deo, ed. Archaeological congress and seminar papers. Nagpur: Nagpur U., 1972, 157-87 (inc. comments).

03575 ______. Iranian influence on early Indo-Pakistani cultures. In Indica 6,2 (1969) 59-80.

03576 SOUNDARA RAJAN, K.V. Chronological and cultural aspects of the Indian neolithic, based on recent data. In JIH 42,1 (1964) 107-17.

03577 VISHNU-MITTRE. Protohistoric records of agriculture in India. In Bose Res. Inst., Trans. 31,3 (1968) 87-106 + 43 p.

B. Pre-Harappan Sites in Afghanistan, Baluchistan, and the Indus Valley

03578 CASAL, J.-M. Nindowari, a Chalcolithic site in South Baluchistan. In Pakistan Archaeol. 3 (1966) 10-21.

03579 DALES, G.F. A review of the chronology of Afghanistan, Baluchistan and the Indus valley. In Amer. J. of Archaeol. 72 (1968) 305-7.

03580 DANI, A.H. Origins of Bronze Age cultures in the Indus Valleys - a geographic perspective. In Expedition 17,2 (1975) 12-18.

03581 FAIRSERVIS, W.A. Archaeological surveys in the Zhob and Loralai districts, West Pakistan. In APAMNH 47,2 (1959) 277-448.

03582 ______. Excavations in the Quetta valley, West Pakistan. In APAMNH 45,2 (1956) 169-402.

03583 KHAN, F.A. Excavations at Kot Diji. In AP 2 (1965) 13-85 + 34 pl.

03584 KHAN, G.M. Pre- and early Harappan controversy in the context of Indus valley civilization. In JPHS 23,4 (1975) 233-45.

03585 LAMBERG-KARLOVSKY, C.C. Archeology and metallurgical technology in pre-historic Afghanistan, India, and Pakistan. In AA 69,2 (1967) 145-62.

03586 RAIKES, R.L. New prehistoric bichrome ware from the plains of Baluchistan, West Pakistan. In E&W 14 (1963) 56-68.

03587 ______. The prehistoric climate of Baluchistan and the Indus Valley. In AA 63 (1961) 265-81.

03588 SHAFFER, J.G. Prehistoric Baluchistan: with excavation report on Said Qala Tepe. Delhi: B.R., 1978. 195p. (ISPQS - H&A, 3)

C. The Harappan Civilization of the Indus Valley (c. 2500-1500? BC)

1. Bibliography and Reference

03589 ANDERSON, B. Indus Valley civilization; a bibliography 1954-66. In Indica 4 (1967) 107-24.

03590 BRUNSWIG, R.H., JR. Comprehensive bibliography of the Indus civilization and related subjects and areas. In Asian Perspectives 16 (1974) 75-111.

03591 MUGHAL, M.R. Present state of research on the Indus Valley civilization. Karachi: Dept. of Archaeol. & Museums, Min. of Educ. & Culture, Govt. of Pak., 1973. 28p.

03592 PANDE, B.M. & K.S. RAMACHANDRAN. Bibliography of the Harappan culture. Ed. by H. Field. Miami: Field Res. Projects, 1971. 46p.

03593 PARPOLA, A. Bibliographic aids for the study of the Indus civilization: a critical survey. In Purātattva 8 (1975-76) 150-56.

03594 POSSEHL, G.L. Bibliography. In his Ancient cities of the Indus. ND: Vikas, 1979, 361-422.

2. General Studies

03595 CASAL, J.-M. La civilisation de l'Indus et ses énigmes. Paris: Fayard, 1969. 225p.

03596 CHAKRABARTI, D.K. Concept of urban revolution and the Indian context. In Purātattva 6 (1972-73) 27-31. [followed by comments, with related articles by D.P. Agrawal & S.P. Gupta, 32-42]

03597 CHANDRA, R.G. Studies of Indus Valley terracottas. Varanasi: Bharatiya Pub. House, 1973. 56p.

03598 DIKSHIT, K.N. Prehistoric civilization of the Indus Valley. 2nd ed. Madras: U. of Madras, 1967. 53p.

03599 FAIRSERVIS, W.A. The origin, character, and decline of an early civilization. In American Museum Novitates 2302 (1967) 1-48.

03600 HERAS, H. Studies in proto-Indo-Mediterranean culture. Bombay: Indian Hist. Res. Inst., 1953. 216p.

03601 INDIAN ARCHAEOLOGICAL SOCIETY. Archaeological Congress and Seminar, 1972...Late Harappan and other chalcolithic cultures of India: a study in inter-relationship. Ed. by Udai Vir Singh. Kurukshetra: B.N. Chakravarty U., 1976. 177p.

03602 MACKAY, E.J.H. Early Indus civilizations. 2nd ed. rev. by D. Mackay. London: Luzac, 1948. 169p. [1st ed. 1935]

03603 MANCHANDA, O. A study of the Harappan pottery, in comparison with the pre-Harappan and the post-Harappan ceramic industries of the Indian subcontinent. Delhi: Oriental, 1972. 406p.

03604 MODE, H. Das frühe Indien. Stuttgart: G. Kilpper, 1959. 267p. + 96 pl.

03605 POSSEHL, G.L., ed. Ancient cities of the Indus. ND: Vikas, 1979. 422p.

03606 PRAKASH, BUDDHA. Ṛgveda and the Indus Valley civilization. Hoshiarpur: VVRI, 1966. 179p. + 17 pl.

03607 RAY, S.B. Harappan chronology: an integrated study. In Purātattva 7 (1974) 65-9.

03608 SHENDGE, M.J. The civilized demons: the Harappans in Rgveda. ND: Abhinav, 1977. 441p.

03609 SULLIVAN, H.P. A re-examination of the religion of the Indus valley civilization. In HR 4 (1964) 115-25.

03610 WHEELER, R.E.M. Civilizations of the Indus Valley and beyond. NY: McGraw-Hill, 1966. 144p.

03611 ______. The Indus civilization: supplementary volume to the Cambridge History of India. 3rd ed. Cambridge: CamUP, 1968. 143p. + 34 pl. (Cambridge Hist. of India suppl., 1) [1st ed. 1953]

3. Harappa and Mohenjo Daro: Urban Centers of Indus Valley Civilization

03612 DALES, G.F. New investigations at Mohenjo-daro. In Archaeology 18 (1965) 145-50.

03613 KHAN, A.N., ed. Proceedings of International Symposium on Moenjodaro, 1973. Karachi: Natl. Book Foundation, 1975. 187p.

03614 LAMBRICK, H.T. Stratigraphy at Mohenjo Daro. In JOIB 20,4 (1971) 363-69.

03615 MACKAY, E.J.H. Further excavation at Mohenjo-daro, being an official account of archaeological excavations at Mohenjo-daro carried out by the government of India between the years 1927 and 1931. Delhi: MP, 1938. 2 v.

03616 MARSHALL, J.H. Mohenjo-daro and the Indus civilization, being an official account of archaeological excavations at Mohenjo-daro carried out by the Government of India between 1922 and 1927. London: A. Probsthain, 1931. 3 v.

03617 MATE, M.S. Harappan fortifications: a study. In IA 4 (1970) 75-83.

03618 MUGHAL, M.R. The early Harappan period in the greater Indus Valley and Northern Baluchistan. Ph.D. diss., U. of Pennsylvania, 1970. [UM 71-19263]

03619 VAN LOHUIZEN-DE LEEUW, J.E. Moenjo Daro: a cause of common concern. In J.E. van Lohuizen-de Leeuw & J.M.M. Ubaghs, eds. South Asian Archaeology 1973. Leiden: Brill, 1974, 1-11.

03620 VATS, M.S. Excavations at Harappa, being an account of archaeological excavations at Harappa carried out between the years 1920-21 and 1933-34. Varanasi: Bharatiya, 1974-75. 2 v. [Rpt. 1940 ed.]

4. Other Harappan Sites

03621 ALLCHIN, F.R. & J.P. JOSHI. Mālvan: further light on the southern extension of the Indus civilization. In JRAS (1970) pt. 1, 20-28.

03622 DALES, G.F. Harappan outposts on the Makran coast. In Antiquity 36 (1962) 86-92.

03623 DUTTA, BIMAL CHANDRA. Rupar: the ancient town of Harappan settlers in East Punjab. In Ethnos 35,1/4 (1970) 123-41.

03624 LESHNIK, L.S. The Harappan "port" at Lothal: another view. In AA 70,5 (1968) 911-22.

03625 MACKAY, E.J.H. Chanhu Daro excavations, 1935-36. Boston: AOS, 1943. 338p.

03626 RAO, S.R. Lothal and the Indus civilization. NY: Asia, 1973. 215p.

03627 THAPAR, B.K. Kalibangan: a Harappan metropolis beyond the Indus valley. In Expedition 17,2 (1975) 19-32.

5. External Contacts and Trade

03628 CHAKRABARTI, D.K. Gujarat Harappan connection with West Asia: a reconstruction of the evidence. In JESHO 18,3 (1975) 337-42.

03629 DURING CASPERS, E.C.L. Sumer, coastal Arabia and the Indus Valley in protoliterate and early dynastic eras. Supporting evidence for a cultural linkage. In JESHO 22,2 (1979) 121-35.

03630 DURING CASPERS, E.C.L. & A. GOVINDANKUTTY. R. Thapar's Dravidian hypothesis for the locations of Meluḫḫa, Dilmun and Makan; a critical reappraisal. In JESHO 21,2 (1978) 113-45.

03631 KHAN, F.A. The Indus Valley and early Iran. Karachi: Dept. of Archaeol. and Museums, 1964. 104p.

03632 KRAMER, S.N. The Indus civilization and Dilmun: the Sumerian paradise land. In Expedition 6,3 (1964) 44-52.

03633 LAMBERG-KARLOVSKY, C.C. Trade mechanisms in Indus-Mesopotamia interrelations. In JAOS 92,1 (1972) 222-29. [also in Purātattva 6 (1972-73) 103-17.]

03634 PARPOLA, S. & A. PARPOLA & R.H. BRUNSWIG, JR. The Meluḫḫa village: evidence of acculturation of Harappan traders in late 3rd millenium Mesopotamia? In JESHO 20,2 (1977) 129-65.

03635 RAO, S.R. Shipping and maritime trade of the Indus people. In Expedition 7,3 (1965) 30-37.

03636 THAPAR, R. Possible identification of Meluḫḫa, Dilmun and Makan. In JESHO 18,1 (1975) 1-42. [With comments by Dilip Chakrabarti In 18,3 337-42.]

6. The Indus Script: Attempts at Decipherment

03637 AALTO, P. Indus script and Dravidian. In SIE 2 (1976) 16-30. [survey of translation attempts]

03638 ALEKSEEV, G.V., et al. Soviet studies on Harappan script. Ed. by H. Field & E.M. Laird. Tr. from Russian by H.C. Pande. Coconut Grove, FL: Field Res. Projects, 1969. 35p. (Its Occ. paper, 6)

03639 CHAKRAVORTI, B.B. The message of the Indus script. Nabapalli: Bani Chakraborty, 1976. 122p. [also in Folklore (C) 17,1 through 17,7 (1976) passim.]

03640 KINNIER WILSON, J.V. Indo-Sumerian: a new approach to the problems of the Indus script. Oxford: Clarendon Press, 1974. 55p.

03641 KOSKENNIEMI, K. & A. PARPOLA. Corpus of texts in the Indus script. Helsinki: Dept. of Asian and African Studies, U. of Helsinki, 1979. 197p.

03642 KOSKENNIEMI, S. & A. PARPOLA & S. PARPOLA. Materials for the study of the Indus script. 1. A concordance to the Indus inscriptions. Helsinki: Suomalainen Tiedeakatemia, 1973. 528p.

03643 MAHADEVAN, I. The Indus script: texts, concordance, and tables. ND: ASI, 1977. (ASI Memoirs, 77) 829p.

03644 MITCHINER, J.E. Studies in the Indus Valley inscriptions. ND: Oxford & IBH, 1978. 86p.

03645 PARPOLA, A. Tasks, methods and results in the study of the Indus script. In JRAS (1975) 2, 178-209.

03646 PARPOLA, A., et al. Decipherment of the proto-Dravidian inscriptions of the Indus civilization: a first announcement. Copenhagen: Scandinavian Inst. of Asian St., 1969. 72p. (Its Special Pub., 1)

03647 ______. Further progress in the decipherment of the Indus Valley script. Copenhagen: Scandinavian Inst. of Asian St., 1969. 47p. (Its Special Pub., 2)

03648 Special number on the decipherment of the Mohenjo-daro script. In JTS 2,1 (1970) 1-276.

03649 VACEK, J. The problem of the Indus script. In AO 38,2 (1970) 198-212.

03650 ZIDE, A.R.K. & K.V. ZVELEBIL, eds. The Soviet decipherment of the Indus Valley script: translation and critique. The Hague: Mouton, 1976. 142p. (Janua linguarum, series practica, 156)

7. Decline of Harappan Civilization: Floods, Invasion, or ... ?

03651 DALES, G.F. Civilization and floods in the Indus valley. In Expedition 7,4 (1965) 10-19.

03652 ______. The decline of the Harappans. In Scientific American 214,5 (1966) 92-100.

03653 ______. The mythical massacre of Mohenjo-daro. In Expedition 6,3 (1964) 36-43.

03654 DALES, G.F. & R.L. RAIKES. The Mohenjo-daro floods: a rejoinder. In AA (1968) 957-61.

03655 LAMBRICK, H.T. The Indus flood-plain and the "Indus" civilization. In GJ 133 (1967) 483-95.

03656 POSSEHL, G.L. The Mohenjo-daro floods: a reply. In AA 69 (1967) 32-40.

03657 RAIKES, R.L. The end of the ancient cities of the Indus. In AA 66 (1964) 284-99.

03658 ______. Kalibangan: death from natural causes. In Antiquity 42 (1968) 286-91.

03659 ______. The Mohenjo-daro floods. In Antiquity 39 (1965) 196-203.

03660 ______. The Mohenjo-daro floods - riposte. In Antiquity 41 (1967) 309-10.

03661 SAXENA, K.K. End of Harappan civilization: an appraisal of the data. In IAC 17,3 (1968) 20-36.

D. Neolithic-Chalcolithic Sites in non-Indus South Asia

1. The Ganga Plains: Ochre-colored Pottery and the Copper Hoards Culture

03662 GAUR, R.C. The ochre coloured pottery: a reassessment of the evidence. In J.E. van Lohuizen-de Leeuw & J.M.M. Ubaghs, eds. South Asian archaeology 1973. Leiden: E.J. Brill, 1974, 53-62.

03663 GUPTA, S.P. Further copper hoards: a reassessment in the light of new evidence. In JBRS 51,1/4 (1965) 1-7.

03664 ______. Indian copper hoards: the problem of homogeneity, stages of development, origin, authorship and dating. In JBRS 49,1/4 (1963) 147-66.

03665 LAL, B.B. Further copper hoards in the Gangetic Basin and a review of the problem. In AI 7 (1951) 20-39.

03666 MISRA, V.D. The Chalcolithic cultures of Uttar Pradesh. In K.C. Chattopadhyaya memorial volume. Allahabad: Dept. of Ancient Hist., Culture & Archaeol., Allahabad U., 1975, 57-68.

03667 NATH, S. The copper-hoards of the Ganga valley: a new appraisal of the problem. In JOIB, 19 (1970) 254-264.

03668 PIGGOTT, S. Prehistoric copper hoards of the Gangetic basin. In Antiquity 18 (1944) 173-82.

03669 Seminar on OCP & NBP. Proceedings. In Purātattva 5 (1971-72) 1-104. [held May 11, 1971, ND; bibl. on ochre coloured pottery and northern black polished ware, 65-79]

2. Peninsular India and Sri Lanka

03670 ALLCHIN, F.R. Neolithic cattle-keepers of South India; a study of the Deccan ashmounds. NY: CamUP, 1963. 189p.

03671 ______. Utnur excavations. Hyderabad: Govt. of Andhra Pradesh, 1961. 75p. (Its Archaeol. series, 5)

03672 DEO, S.B. & Z.D. ANSARI. Chalcolithic Chandoli. Poona: DCPRI, 1965. 206p.

03673 DERANIYAGALA, S. Stone implements from a Balangoda culture site in Ceylon: Bellan Bandi Palassa. In AC 1 (1971) 47-89.

03674 KARTHIKEYA SARMA, I. Patapadu revisited; a new painted pottery culture of south-east India. In Puratattva 1 (1967-68) 68-84.

03675 KENNEDY, K.A.R. & K.C. MALHOTRA. Human skeletal remains from Chalcolithic and Indo-Roman levels from Nevasa: an anthropometric and comparative analysis. Poona: DCPRI, 1966. 135p.

03676 LESHNIK. L.S. Early settled farmers in Central India and the Deccan. In Heidelberg U., Sudasien-Inst., Jahrbuch, 1966. Wiesbaden: 1967, 43-55.

03677 MUJUMDAR, G.G. & S.N. RAJAGURU. Ashmound excavations at Kupgal. Poona: DCPRI, 1966. 60p.

03678 NAGARAJA RAO, M.S. New evidence for Neolithic life in India: excavations in the southern Deccan. In Archaeology 20 (1967) 28-35.

03679 ______. Protohistoric cultures of the Tungabhadra Valley: a report on Hallur excavations. Dharwar: the author, 1971. 144p.

03680 NAGARAJA RAO, M.S. & K.C. MALHOTRA. The stone age hill dwellers of Tekkalakota: preliminary report of the excavations at Tekkalakota. Poona: DCPRI, 1965. 164p.

03681 PADDAYYA, K. Investigations into the neolithic culture of the Shorapur Doab, South India. Leiden: Brill, 1973. 137p.

03682 RAMI REDDY, V. The bone-tool technology of the South Indian neolithic culture with special reference to Palavoy. In EA 29,3 (1976) 231-48.

03683 SANKALIA, H.D. Earliest farmers in the Narmada Valley. In IAC 11 (1962) 31-38.

03684 SARKAR, S.S. Ancient races of the Deccan. ND: Munshiram, 1972. 212p.

03685 THAPAR, B.K. Prakash 1955: a chalcolithic site in the Tapti valley. In AI 20/21 (1964-65) 5-167.

IV. THE IRON AGE AND THE ARYAN INVASIONS

A. General Histories and Studies

1. General

03686 BANERJEE, N.R. The iron age in India. ND: Munshiram, 1965. 264p.

03687 SOUNDARA RAJAN, K.V. The Iron Age culture provinces of India. In BV 23 (1963) 1-4.

03688 SUBRAHMANYAM, B.R. Iron Age in India - its beginnings. In JMSUB 15,1 (1966) 69-78.

2. Beginnings of Iron Technology

03689 CHAKRABARTI, D.K. The beginning of iron in India. In Antiquity 50,198 (1976) 114-124.

03690 ______. Distribution of iron ores and the archaeological evidence of early iron in India. In JESHO 20,2 (1977) 166-84.

B. South India and Ceylon in the Iron Age

1. The Megaliths and the Iron Age

03691 BANERJI, A. Problem of Black and Red ware. In MI 44,4 (1964) 341-53.

03692 DEO, S.B. Mahurjhari excavation, 1970-72. Nagpur: Nagpur U., 1973. 110p.

03693 ______. Problem of South Indian megaliths. Dharwar: Kannada Res. Inst., Karnatak U., 1973. 85p.

03694 GUPTA, P. & A. BASU & P.C. DUTTA. Ancient human remains. Calcutta: Anthropological Survey of India, 297p. 74p. (ASI memoir, 20)

03695 GUPTA, S.P. Gulf of Oman: the original home of Indian megaliths. In Purātattva 4 (1970-71) 4-18.

03696 GURURAJA RAO, B.K. Megalithic culture in South India. Mysore: U. of Mysore, 1972. 390p.

03697 JOUVEAU-DUBREUIL, G. Vedic antiquities. 2nd ed. Hyderabad: Akshara, 1976. 55p. [1st pub. 1922; on the rock-cut tombs discovered at Mennapuram, Kerala]

03698 KENNEDY, K.A.R. The physical anthropology of the megalith-builders of South India and Sri Lanka. Canberra: ANUP, 1975. 93p. (Oriental mono. ser., 17)

03699 KRISHNA IYER, L.A. Kerala megaliths and their builders. Madras: U. of Madras, 1967. 74p.

03700 KRISHNASWAMI, V.D. Megalithic types of South India. In AI 5 (1949) 35-45 + 9pl.

03701 LAL, B.B. From the Megalithic to the Harappan: tracing back the graffiti on the pottery. In AI 16 (1962) 4-24.

03702 LESHNIK, L.S. Pastoral nomadism in the archaeology of India and Pakistan. In World Archaeol. 4 (1972) 150-66.

03703 ______. South Indian megalith burials: the Pandukal complex. Wiesbaden: Steiner, 1974. 309p.

03704 NARASIMHAIAH, B. Neolithic and megalithic cultures in Tamil Nadu. Delhi: Sundeep, 1980. 257p.

03705 NOBLE, W.A. Nilgiri Dolmens, South India. In Anthropos 71,1/2 (1976) 90-128.

03706 PARPOLA, A. Arguments for an Aryan origin of the South Indian megaliths. Madras: Tamilnadu Dept. of Archaeol, 1973. 74p. (TNDA pub., 32)

03707 RAMACHANDRAN, K.S. A bibliography on Indian megaliths. Madras: Tamilnadu Dept. of Archaeology, Govt. of Tamilnadu, 1971. 184p. (TNDA pub., 15)

03708 ______. Gulf of Oman: original home of the Indian megaliths, a reappraisal. In Purātattva 6 (1972-73) 20-26.

03709 RAMI REDDY, V. The problem of ashmounds in South India: a fresh look. In EA 30,2 (1977) 193-211.

03710 SAHNEY, V. The Iron Age of South India. Ph.D. diss., U. of Pennsylvania, 1965. [UM 66-295] 232p.

03711 SRIVASTAV, K.M. The problem of the black-and-red ware in proto-historic India. In JOIB 20 (1971) 372-417.

03712 SUBBARAO, B. Megalithic problem of South India and the Dravidian languages. In TASSI (1960-62) 132-151.

03713 SUBBAYYA, K.K. Archaeology of Coorg with special reference to Megaliths. Mysore: Geetha, 1978. 269p.

03714 SUNDARA, A. The early chamber tombs of South India: a study of the iron age megalithic monuments of north Karnataka. Delhi: University Pub., 1975. 315p.

2. The Dravidians: Hypotheses on their Origin and Linguistic Affiliations

03715 BALAKRISHNAN NAYAR, T. The problem of Dravidian origins: a linguistic, anthropological, and archaeological approach. Madras: U. of Madras, 1977. 238p.

03716 ______. Where did the Dravidians come from? In TC 10,4 (1963) 121-133.

03717 BOUDA, K. Dravidisch und Uralaltaisch. In Lingua 5 (1956) 129-44.

03718 FUCHS, S. The Dravidian problem. In JASBombay 41/42 (1966-67) 153-63.

03719 FÜRER-HAIMENDORF, C. VON. New aspects of the Dravidian problem. In TC 2,2 (1953) 127-35.

03720 ______. When, how, and from where did the Dravidians come to India? In IAC 2,3 (1954) 238-47.

03721 JOSEPH, P. The Dravidian problem in the South Indian culture complex. Madras: Orient Longmans, 1972. 100p.

03722 LAHOVARY, N. Dravidian origins and the West (newly discovered ties with the ancient culture and languages, including Basque, of the pre-Indo-European Mediterranean World). Bombay: Orient Longmans, 1963. 419p.

03723 MCALPIN, D.W. Elamite and Dravidian: further evidence of relationship. In CA 16,1 (1975) 105-9. [comments & reply: 109-16]

03724 ______. Linguistic prehistory: the Dravidian situation. In M.M. Deshpande & P.E. Hook, eds. Aryan and non-Aryan in India.... Ann Arbor: UMCSSAS, 1979, 175-90.

03725 MENGES, K.H. Dravidian and Altaic. In Anthropos 72,1/2 (1977) 129-79.

03726 RAMACHANDRA DIKSHITAR, V.R. Origin and spread of the Tamils. Madras: SISSWPS, 1971. 129p. [1st pub. 1947]

03727 SIRCAR, D.C. The Dravidian problem. In MI 35 (1955) 31-38.

03728 SJOBERG, A. Who are the Dravidians? In her (ed.) Symposium on Dravidian civilization. NY: Jenkins, 1971, 1-32.

03729 ZVELEBIL, K. Harappa and the Dravidians: an old mystery in a new light. In New Orient 4,3 (1965) 65-69.

C. Northern India in the Vedic and Epic Ages (c. 1500-600 BC)

1. Sources

a. historical and geographical evidence from the Vedas

03730 BHARGAVA, M.L. The geography of Rgvedic India: a physical geography of Sapta Saindhava. Lucknow: Upper India Pub. House, 1964. 157p.

03731 DWIVEDI, R.K. The Sarasvatī River Complex in the Mahabharata. In K.C. Chattopadhyaya memorial volume. Allahabad: Dept. of Ancient Hist., Culture & Archaeol., Allahabad U., 1975, 158-76.

03732 GODBOLE, N.N. Rig-Vedic (Prachin) Sarasvati; its origin, its flow and its disappearance in the sands of Rajasthan. Jaipur: Cabinet Secretariat, 1963. 37p.

03733 SAXENA, D.P. Regional geography of Vedic India. Kanpur: Grantham, 1976. 173p.

b. archaeology

03734 CHAKRABARTI, D.K. The Aryan hypothesis in Indian archaeology. In ISPP 9,4 (1968) 343-58.

03735 DANI, A.H. Excavations in the Gomal Valley. In AP 5 (1970-71) 1-177 + 88pl.

03736 ______. Timargarha and Gandhara grave culture. In AP 3 (1967) 1-386 + 57pl.

03737 FACCENNA, D. Results of the 1963 excavation campaign at Barama I (Swat-Pakistan). In E&W 15 (1964-65) 7-32.

03738 FAIRSERVIS, W.A. Problems in post-Harappan archaeology in the lower Indus valley and Baluchistan. In JMSUB 15,1 (1966) 21-24.

03739 LAL, B.B. Excavations at Hastināpura and other explorations in the Upper Ganga and Sutlej Basins 1950-52: new light on the dark age between the end of the Harappā Culture and the early historical period. In AI 10/11 (1954-55) 5-151.

03740 ROY, S.R. The pre-N.B.P. ware ceramic industry of Bihar. In JBRS 53 (1967) 53-57.

03741 SOUNDARA RAJAN, K.V. Community-movements in protohistoric India: an archaeological perspective. In JOIB 12,1 (1962) 69-82.

03742 STACUL, G. Excavations in a rock shelter near Ghaligai (Swat, W. Pakistan). Preliminary report. In E&W 17 (1967) 185-219.

03743 ______. The gray pottery in the Swat Valley and the Indo-Iranian connections, ca. 1500-300 B.C. In E&W 20 (1970) 92-102.

03744 TRIPATHI, V. The painted grey ware: an iron age culture of northern India. Delhi: Concept, 1976. 150p.

2. General History of the Vedic and Epic Ages in Northern India (c. 1500-600 BC)

a. the Vedic Age

03745 BASU, J. India of the age of the Brāhmaṇas.... Calcutta: Sanskrit Pustak Bhandar, 1969. 61 + 295p.

03746 BHARGAVA, P.L. India in the Vedic age; a history of Aryan expansion in India. 2nd rev. and enl. ed. Lucknow: Upper India Pub. House, 1971. 396p. [1st ed. 1956]

03747 CHATTOPADHYAYA, K.P. Ancient Indian culture and migrations. Calcutta: Sanskrit College, 1965. 114p. [Its res. ser., 43]

03748 DANDEKAR, R.N. Indian pattern of life and thought - a glimpse of its early phases. In IAC 8,1 (1959) 47-59.

03749 DANGE, S.A. Cultural sources from the Veda. Bombay: BVB, 1977. 116p.

03750 DAS, A.C. Rgvedic culture. Varanasi: Bharatiya, 1979. 565p. [Rpt. of 1925 ed.]

03751 GHURYE, G.S. Vedic India. Bombay: Popular, 1979. 471p.

03752 KARAMBELKAR, V.W. The Atharvavedic civilization, its place in the Indo-Aryan culture: a cultural history of the Indo-Aryans from the Atharva Veda. Nagpur: the author, 1959. 315p.

03753 LA VALLÉE POUSSIN, L. DE. Indo-européens et Indo-iraniens; l'Inde jusque vers 300 av.J.-C. Paris: Boccard, 1924. 345p.

03754 LAW, N.N. Age of the Rgveda. Calcutta: KLM, 1965. 166p.

03755 MITRA, P. Life and society in the Vedic Age.

Calcutta: Sanskrit Pustak Bhankar, 1966. 106p.

03756 PRAKASH, BUDDHA. Political and social movements in ancient Punjab (from the Vedic age up to the Maurya period.) Delhi: Motilal, 1964. 276p.

03757 RENOU, L. Vedic India. Tr. from French by P. Spratt. Delhi: IndBH, 1971. 160p. (His Classical India, 3)

03758 THAPAR, R. Ancient Indian social history. ND: Orient Longmans, 1978. 296p. [collected essays]

b. the Epic Age

03759 AGARWALA, G.C., ed. Age of Bharata War. Delhi: Motilal, 1979. 343p.

03760 CHANDRA, A.N. The date of Kurukshetra War. Calcutta: Ratna Prakashan, 1978. 188p.

03761 DE, S.C. Historicity of Ramayana and the Indo-Aryan society in India and Ceylon. Delhi: Ajanta, 1976. 334p.

03762 GOLDMAN, R.P. Gods, priests, and warriors: the Bhṛgus of the Mahābhārata. NY: ColUP, 1977. 195p.

03763 GUPTA, S.P. & RAMACHANDRAN, K.S., eds. Mahabharata: myth and reality, differing views. Delhi: Agam, 1976. 263p.

03764 JAGANNANDHA RAO, N. The age of the Mahabharata war. Varanasi: Bharat-Bharati, 1978. 68p.

03765 MAJUMDAR, A.K. Economic background of the epic society. Calcutta: Progressive, 1977. 256p.

03766 MIRASHI, V.V. The date of the Bhārata War. In JOIB 25,3/4 (1976) 286-98.

03767 ROY, S.B. Date of Mahabharata battle. Gurgaon: Academic Press, 1976. 223p.

03768 SIDHANTA, N.K. The heroic age of India. A comparative study. ND: OBRC, 1975. 232p. [Rpt. 1929 ed.]

03769 SIRCAR, D.C., ed. The Bhārata war and purāṇic genealogies. Calcutta: U. of Calcutta, 1969. 196p.

03770 VYAS, S.N. India in the Ramayana age; a study of the social and cultural conditions in ancient India as described in Valmiki's Ramayana. Delhi: Atma Ram, 1967, 358p.

3. The Invasion of the Aryans, Indo-European-Speaking Tribes from Central Asia: the Debate on their Origins

03771 BHARGAVA, P.L. The original home of the Aryans and Indo-Iranian migrations. In ABORI 48/49 (1968) 219-226.

03772 CHAKLADAR, H.C. The Aryan occupation of eastern India. Calcutta: KLM, 1962. 114p.

03773 CHILDE, V.G. The Aryans: a study of Indo-European origins. NY: Knopf, 1926. 221p.

03774 DUTT, N.K. The Aryanisation of India. 2nd ed. Calcutta: KLM, 1970. 159p. [1st ed., 1925]

03775 GHOSE, N.N. The Aryan trail in Iran and India; a naturalistic study of the Vedic hymns and the Avesta. Calcutta: U. of Calcutta, 1937. 333p.

03776 SETHNA, K.D. The Aryans, the domesticated horse and the spoked chariot-wheel. In JASBombay ns 38 (1963) 44-68.

03777 ______. The problem of Aryan origins: from an Indian point of view. Calcutta: S. & S., 1980. 150p.

03778 SOUTHWORTH, F.C. Lexical evidence for early contacts between Indo-Aryan and Dravidian. In M.M. Deshpande & P.E. Hook, eds. Aryan and non-Aryan in India. Ann Arbor: UMCSSAS, 1979, 191-234.

03779 TALUKDAR, J.N. The Aryan question. In JASBengal 16, 1/4 (1974) 15-34.

03780 TILAK, B.G. The Arctic home in the Vedas, being also a new key to the interpretation of many Vedic texts and legends. Poona: Kesari, 1903. 500p.

4. Kingship, Political Organization, and Warfare in Northern India

03781 BASU, P.C. Indo-Aryan polity: Rigvedic period. Delhi: Nag, 1977. [1st pub. 1919]

03782 GHOSHAL, U.N. A history of Hindu public life, v. 1: period of the Vedic Samhitas, the Brahmanas, and the older Upanishads. Calcutta: R. Ghoshal, 1945? 175p.

03783 HEESTERMAN, J.C. The ancient Indian royal consecration; the rājasūya described according to the Yajus texts and annotated. The Hague: Mouton, 1957. 235p.

03784 ______. Conundrum of the King's authority. In J.F. Richards, ed. Kingship and authority in South Asia. Madison: South Asian Studies, U. of Wisconsin, 1978, 1-27. (Its Pub. series, 3)

03785 PRADHAN, S.N. Chronology of Ancient India: from the times of the rigvedic king Divodasa to Chandragupta Maurya, with glimpses of the political history of the period. Varanasi: Bharatiya, 1979. 291p. [1st pub. 1927]

03786 SINGH, S.D. Ancient Indian warfare, with special reference to the Vedic peiod. Leiden: Brill, 1965. 203p.

5. Economic and Social Life

03787 BANERJI, S.C. Aspects of ancient Indian life, from Sanskrit sources. Calcutta: Punthi Pustak, 1972. 179p.

03788 CHAKRABORTY, C. Common life in the Rgveda and Atharvaveda: an account of the folklore in the Vedic period. Calcutta: Punthi Pustak, 1977. 278p.

03789 ICAR. Agriculture in ancient India. ND: 1964. 167p.

03790 KOSAMBI, D.D. The Vedic "Five Tribes". In JAOS 87,1 (1967) 33-39.

03791 PRAKASH, BUDDHA. Political and social movements in ancient Panjab: from the Vedic age up to the Maurya period. Delhi: Motilal, 1964. 276p.

03792 SARMAH, J. Philosophy of education in the Upanishads. ND: Oriental, 1978. 303p.

6. The Beginnings of Science in Vedic India

03793 DIKSHIT, S.B. English translation of Bharatiya jyotish sastra (History of Indian astronomy), v. 1: history of astronomy during the Vedic and Vedanga periods. Tr. from Sanskrit by R.V. Vaidya. Delhi: Manager of Publications, GOI, 1969. 3 v.

03794 MEHTA, D.D. Positive sciences in the Vedas. ND: Arnold Heinemann, 1974. 269p.

03795 SARMA, K.V. Astronomy in India: Vedic period. In VIJ 14,1 (1976) 133-52.

03796 SHASTRI, V. Sciences in the Vedas. ND: Sarvadeshik Arya Pratinidhi Sabha, 1970. 231p.

03797 VAIDYA, R.V. Astronomical light on Vedic culture. Bombay: Makarand Sahitya, 1965. 114p.

V. THE FOUNDATIONS OF INDIC RELIGIOUS TRADITION: ŚRUTI, THE VEDIC LITERATURE, FROM THE ṚGVEDA SAṀHITĀ THROUGH THE UPANIṢADS

A. General Studies of the Veda (Supreme Sacred "Knowledge") as a Whole

1. Bibliography and Reference

03798 BLOOMFIELD, M. A Vedic Concordance. Delhi: Motilal, 1964. 1078p. [Rpt. of 1st ed. 1906]

03799 DANDEKAR, R.N. A decade of Vedic studies in India and abroad. In ABORI 56,1-4 (1975) 1-25.

03800 ______. Vedic bibliography: an up-to-date, comprehensive, and analytically arranged register of all important work done since 1930 in the field of the Veda and allied antiquities including the Indus Valley civilisation. v. 1. Bombay: Karnatak Pub. House, 1946. 398p.; v. 2. Poona: U. of Poona, 1961. 760p.; v. 3. Poona:

BORI, 1973. 1082p. [continues L. Renou, Bibliographie védique, 03803]

03801 DANDEKAR, R.N. Vedic religion and mythology: a survey of the work of some Western scholars. In JUP 21 (1965) 1-53.

03802 MACDONELL, A.A. & A.B. KEITH. Vedic index of names and subjects. Delhi: Motilal, 1967. 2 v. [1st ed. 1912]

03803 RENOU. L. Bibliographie védique. Paris: Adrien-Maisonneuve, 1931. 339p. [contd. by Dandekar, 03800]

03804 SANTUCCI, J.A. An outline of Vedic literature. Missoula, MT: Scholars Press, for American Academy of Religion, 1976. 69p. (AAR aids for the study of religion, 3)

03805 WERNER, K. On interpreting the Vedas: survey article. In Religion 7 (1977) 189-200.

2. Histories of Vedic Literature

03806 GHOSE, N.N. Indo-Aryan literature and culture (origins). 2nd ed. Varanasi: CSSO, 1965. 287p. (CSS, 51)

03807 GONDA, J. Old Indian. Leiden: Brill, 1971. 230p. (HO, 2:1:1)

03808 ______. Vedic literature (saṁhitās and brāhmaṇas). Wiesbaden: Harrassowitz, 1975. 463p. (HIL, 1:1)

03809 RAMMOHUN ROY, Raja. The Vedas: the scripture of the Hindus. Rev. & enl. ed. by J.L. Shastri. Delhi: Nag Publishers, 1977. 69p. [1st pub. 1832]

03810 SHARMA, S.N. A history of Vedic literature. Varanasi: CSSO, 1973. 142p. (CSS, 92)

03811 TILAK, B.G. The Orion, or researches into the antiquity of the Vedas. Bombay: Radhabhai Atmaram Sagoon, 1893. 227p.

3. General Studies of Vedic Religion and Philosophy

03812 BARUA, B.M. A history of pre-Buddhistic Indian philosophy. Delhi: Motilal, 1970. 444p. [1st pub. 1921]

03813 BHAT, G.K. Vedic themes: articles on Vedic topics. Delhi: Ajanta, 1978. 119p.

03814 BLOOMFIELD, M. The religion of the Veda, the ancient religion of India, from Rigveda to Upanisads. NY: Putnam's, 1908. 300p.

03815 CHAKRABARTI, S.C. On the transition of Vedic sacrificial lore. In IIJ 21,3 (1979) 181-88.

03816 DAYANANDA SARASVATI, Swami. Introduction to the commentary on the Vedas. Tr. from Sanskrit by G. Ram. 2nd ed. Delhi: Sarvadeshik Arya Pratinidhi Sabha, 1958. 312p.

03817 HAUER, J.W. Die Anfänge der Yogapraxis im alten Indien; eine Untersuchung über die Wurzeln der indischen Mystik nach Ṛgveda und Atharvaveda. Berlin: W. Kohlhammer, 1922. 210p.

03818 KAELBER, W.O. Tapas, birth, and spiritual rebirth in the Veda. In HR 15,4 (1976) 343-86.

03819 KAMBLE, B.R. Caste and philosophy in pre-Buddhist India. Aurangabad: Parimal, 1979. 288p.

03820 KEITH, A.B. Religion and philosophy of the Vedas and Upanishads. Cambridge: HUP, 1925. 2 v. (HOS, 31,32)

03821 KUIPER, R.B.J. The basic concept of Vedic religion. In HR 15,2 (1975) 107-20.

03822 LA VALLÉE-POUSSIN, L. DE. Notions sur les religions de l'Inde: Le Védisme. Paris: Bloud, 1909. 126p.

03823 MERKREBS, A.H. Vedic Ṛta: its origin and early development. In JOIB 25,1 (1975) 1-16.

03824 OLDENBERG, H. Die Religion des Veda. Berlin: W. Hertz, 1894. 620p.

03825 PRABHAVANANDA, Swami. Vedic religion and philosophy. Madras: Sri Ramakrishna Math, 1968. 172p.

03826 RODHE, S.O. Deliver us from evil: studies in the Vedic ideas of salvation. Lund: C.W.K. Gleerup, 1946. 207p.

03827 SMITH, R.M. From ritual to philosophy in India. In JIP 4,1/2 (1976) 181-97.

03828 WATSON, I. Sruti and philosophy. In Numen 19,2/3 (1972) 204-15.

03829 WERNER, K. Religious practice and yoga in the time of the Vedas, Upanishads and early Buddhism. In ABORI 56,1/4 (1975) 179-94.

4. Vedic Myths, Symbols, and Deities

03830 AGRAWALA, V.S. Sparks from the Vedic fire: a new approach to Vedic symbolism. Varanasi: School of Vedic Studies, Banaras Hindu U., 1962. 132p.

03831 ATKINS, S.D. Pūṣan in the Ṛgveda. Princeton: the author, 1941. 102p.

03832 BALI, S. Bṛhaspati in the Vedas and the Purāṇas. Delhi: Nag, 1978. 206p.

03833 BROUGH, J. Soma and amanita muscaria. In BSOAS 34 (1971) 331-62.

03834 COOMARASWAMY, ANANDA KENTISH. Early Indian iconography, I, Indra. In Eastern Art 1,1 (1928) 33-41.

03835 DANDEKAR, R.N. Vedic mythological tracts. Delhi: Ajanta, 1979. 383p. (His Select writings, 1)

03836 ______. Yama in the Veda. In D.R. Bhandarkar, et al., eds. B.C. Law Volume, Part I. Calcutta: Indian Res. Inst., 1945, 194-210.

03837 GANGULI, K.K. Agni - a primal deity of the Ṛgveda. In JAIH 9,1-2 (1975-76) 1-22.

03838 GONDA, J. Triads in the Veda. Amsterdam: North Holland, 1976. 246p.

03839 ______. The Vedic god Mitra. Leiden: Brill, 1972. 147p.

03840 HILLEBRANDT, A. Vedische Mythologie. 2nd rev. ed. Breslau: M.&H. Marcus, 1927-29. 2 v., 1045p.

03841 JOSHI, J.R. Minor Vedic deities. Poona: U. of Poona, 1978. 220p.

03842 ______. Prajāpati in Vedic mythology and ritual. In ABORI 53 (1972) 101-25.

03843 ______. Some minor divinities in Vedic mythology and ritual. Poona: DCPRI, 1977. 156p.

03844 KNIPE, D.M. In the image of fire: Vedic experiences of heat. Delhi: Motilal, 1975. 187p.

03845 ______. One fire, three fires, five fires: Vedic symbols in transition. In HR 12,1 (1972) 28-41.

03846 KRAMRISCH, S. Pūṣan. In JAOS 81,2 (1961) 104-22.

03847 MACDONELL, A.A., ed. The Bṛhad-devatā, attributed to Śaunaka. Delhi: Motilal, 1965. 2 v. [Rpt. of 1904 ed. by HUP (HOS 5,6)]

03848 ______. Vedic mythology. NY: Gordon Press, 1974. 174p. [Rpt. of 1897 ed.]

03849 RENOU, L. Études védiques et pāṇinéenes. Paris: E. de Boccard, 1956-67. 16 v., 2223p. (Pub. de l'Inst. de Civilisation Indienne, fasc. 1, 2, 4, 6, 9, 10, 12, 14, 16, 17, 18, 20, 22, 23, 26, 27)

03850 SAHAI, B. Agni in North Indian art. In J. of the Bihar Res. Soc. 53 (1967) 143-57.

03851 SCHMIDT, H.-P. Bṛhaspati und Indra: Untersuchungen zur vedischen Mythologie und Kulturgeschichte. Wiesbaden: Harrassowitz, 1968. 260p.

03852 SRINIVASAN, D. The myth of the Paṇis in the Rig Veda. In JAOS 93,1 (1973) 44-57.

03853 ______. The religious significance of multiple bodily parts to denote the divine: findings from the Ṛg Veda. In AS 29,2 (1975) 137-79.

03854 SWAMY, B.G.L. Sources for a history of plant sciences in India. II the Ṛg Vedic soma plant. In IJHS 11,1 (1976) 11-48.

03855 WASSON, R.G. SOMA brought up-to-date. In JAOS 99,1 (1979) 100-105.

03856 WASSON, R.G. & W.D. O'FLAHERTY. Soma, divine mushroom of immortality. NY: Harcourt, Brace, & World, 1971. 380p. [Rpt. of 1968 ed.]

03857 WERNER, K. Symbolism in the Vedas and its conceptualisation. In Numen 24,3 (1977) 223-40.

5. Vedic Ritual: Yajña, or Sacrifice

03858 AGUILAR, H. The sacrifice in the Ṛgveda: doctrinal aspects. Delhi: Bharatiya Vidya Prakashan, 1976. 222p.

03859 CALAND, W. & V. HENRY. L'agnistoma: description complète de la forme normale du sacrifice de soma dans le culte védique. Paris: E. Leroux, 1906-07. 2 v.

03860 CONVERSE, H.S. The agnicayana rite: indigenous origin. In HR 14,2 (1974) 81-95.

03861 DANGE, S.A. Sexual symbolism from the Vedic ritual. Delhi: Ajanta, 1979. 251p.

03862 GONDA, J. The significance of the right hand and the right side in Vedic ritual. In Religion 2,1 (1972) 1-23.

03863 INDUCHUDAN, V.T. Kerala Yajna with foreign participation. In IWI 96,21 (1975) 12-15. [a modern reenactment]

03864 KASHIKAR, C.G. Vedic sacrificial rituals through the ages. In IA 1 (1964) 77-89.

03865 MYLIUS, K. Das Schlussbad im altindischen Somakult, der Avabhṛta. In Ethnographische-Archäologische Zeitschrift 17,4 (1976) 589-630.

03866 POTDAR, K.R. Sacrifice in the Rig Veda. Bombay: BVB, 1953. 299p.

03867 RENOU, L. Vocabulaire du rituel védique. Paris: C. Klincksieck, 1954. 176p.

03868 SCHNEIDER, U. Der Somaraub des Manu: Mythus und Ritual. Wiesbaden: O. Harrassowitz, 1971. 89p. (Freiburger Beiträge zur Indologie, 4)

03869 SEN, C. A dictionary of the Vedic rituals, based on the śrauta and gṛhya sūtras. Delhi: Concept, 1978. 168p.

03870 THITE, GANESH. Vijñāna; a kind of divination-rites in the Vedic literature. In WZKS 22 (1978) 5-17.

03871 VAN BUITENEN, J.A.B. The Pravargya, an ancient Indian iconic ritual described and annotated. Poona: DCPRI, 1968. 159p.

03872 ______The Samaveda in the Pravargya ritual. In Mélanges d'indianisme à la mémoire de Louis Renou.... Paris: Boccard, 1968, 179-86. (Pub. d'Inst. de civilisation indienne serie in - 8, 28)

6. Selections from Vedic Literature in Translation

03873 DWIVEDI, R. Selections from Brāhmaṇas and Upaniṣads. Delhi: Motilal, 1965. 215p.

03874 EDGERTON, F., tr. The beginnings of Indian philosophy: selections from the Rig Veda, Atharva Veda, Upanisads, and Mahabharata. Cambridge: HUP, 1965. 362p.

03875 VARENNE, J., tr. Le Véda. Paris: Éditions Planète, 1967. 455p.

7. Vedic Recitation

03876 BAKE, A.A. The music of India. In E. Wellesz, ed. Ancient and oriental music. London: OUP, 1957, 195-227.

03877 ______. The practice of Sāmaveda. In AIOC (Baroda) 7 (1935) 143-55.

03878 BON, Swami B.H. The uniqueness of Vedic reading. In SPP 7,1 (1967) 1-13.

03879 RAGHAVAN, V. The present position of Vedic recitation and Vedic śākhās. Kumbhakonam: Vedic Dharma Paripalana Sabha, 1962. 24p.

03880 STAAL, J.F. Nambudiri veda recitation. The Hague: Mouton, 1961. 101p.

B. The Vedic Saṁhitās: the Basic "Collection" of Each of the Four Vedas

1. Ṛgveda Saṁhitā: Laudatory Stanzas (rc/rg) in 1,028 Hymns

a. translations and selections

03881 BOSE, A.C., tr. Hymns from the Vedas. Bombay: Asia, 1966. 387p.

03882 DHARMA DEVA, Vidya Martanda, tr. The Rigveda with Dayananda Saraswati's commentary. ND: Sarvadeshik Arya Pratinidhi Sabha, 1974-. [to be 12 v.]

03883 GELDNER, K.F., tr. Der Ṛig-veda aus dem Sanskrit ins Deutsche übersetzt. Cambridge: HUP, 1951. 4 v. (HOS 33-36) [1st pub. 1923]

03884 GOPALACHARYA, M.R. The heart of the Rigveda. Bombay: Somaiya, 1971. 464p.

03885 GRIFFITH, R.T.H., tr. Hymns of the Ṛgveda. 6th ed. Delhi: Motilal, 1973. 707p. [1st ed. 1892]

03886 MÜLLER, F.M. & H. OLDENBERG, tr. Vedic hymns. Delhi: Motilal, 1967. 2 v. [Rpt. of 1891-97 ed., SBE 32, 46]

03887 RAU, W. [Index to Ṛgveda translations in L. Renou's Études védiques et pāṇinéennes.] In OLZ 64 (1969) 1/2, 74-83.

03888 THOMAS, E.J. Vedic hymns. London: Murray, 1923. 128p.

03889 VELANKAR, H.D., tr. Ṛgveda maṇḍala VII. Bombay: BVB, 1963. 119 + 285p.

03890 ______., tr. Ṛksūktaśatī; selected hymns from the Rgveda.... Bombay: BVB, 1972. 367p.

b. studies in the Ṛgveda Saṁhitā

03891 BERGAIGNE, A.H.J. Abel Bergaigne's Vedic religion. Tr. from French by V.G. Paranjpe. Delhi: Motilal, 1978. 4 v. in 1. [1st pub. 1878-97]

03892 CHAKRAVARTHY, G.N. The concept of cosmic harmony in the Rg Veda. Mysore: Prasaranga, U. of Mysore, 1966. 16 + 138 + 39p.

03893 DANGE, S.A. Vedic concept of 'field' and the divine fructification: a study in fertility and sex-symbolism, with special reference to the Ṛgveda. Bombay: U. of Bombay, 1971. 236p.

03894 ESTELLER, A. Around the Ṛgveda-saṁhita - text as palimpsest. In MO 1 (1968) 59-77.

03895 ______. The quest for the original ṚgVeda. In ABORI 50 (1969) 1-40.

03896 GONDA, J. Hymns of the Ṛgveda not employed in the solemn ritual. Amsterdam: North Holland, 1978. 138p.

03897 ______. The vision of the Vedic poets. The Hague: Mouton, 1963. 372p.

03898 GRISWOLD, H. DE W. Religion of the Rigveda. Delhi: Motilal, 1971. 392p. [1st pub. 1923]

03899 KESHAVA IYENGAR, B.R. The Rigvedic Purushasukta: hymns 1-16, sukta 90, mandala 10: a non-traditional approach. Bangalore: Vedanta Book Agencies, 1977. 46p.

03900 KRAMRISCH, S. The triple structure of creation in the Ṛg Veda. In HR 2 (1963) 256-85.

03901 ______. Two: its significance in the Ṛgveda. In E. Bender, ed. Indological studies in honor of W. Norman Brown. New Haven: AOS, 1962, 109-36. (AOS, 47)

03902 MACDONELL, A.A., tr. Hymns from the Rigveda. ND: YMCA Pub. House, 1966. 98p. (Heritage of India series) [1st ed. 1923]

03903 OGIBENIN, P.L. Structure d'un mythe védique: le mythe cosmogonique dans le Ṛgveda. Tr. from Russian. The Hague: Mouton, 1973. 170p.

03904 ROCHER, L. The meaning of purāṇa in the Ṛgveda. In WZKS 21 (1977) 5-24.

03905 SRINIVASAN, D.M. Concept of cow in the Rigveda. Delhi: Motilal, 1979. 161p.

03906 UPADHYAYA, B.S. Women in Ṛgveda. 3rd rev. ed. ND: S. Chand, 1974. 243p.

03907 VENKATASUBBIAH, A. Contributions to the interpretation of the Ṛgveda. Mysore: U. of Mysore, 1967. 298p.

03908 VENKATASUBBIAH, A. Satyaloka in Ṛgveda: a study. Hoshiarpur: Vishveshvaranand Inst., 1974. 500p. (VIS 48)

2. Sāmaveda Saṁhitā: Collection of Chants (Sāman) for the Soma Sacrifice
a. translations

03909 DEVI CHAND, tr. Sama Veda. Hoshiarpur: the author, 1963. 370p.

03910 DHARMA DEVA, Vidya Martanda, tr. Hymns of the Samaveda Sanhita. Jwalapur: the author, 1967. 909p.

03911 GRIFFITH, R.T.H., tr. Hymns of the Samaveda. 4th ed. Varanasi: CSSO, 1963. 338p. (CSS, 28) [1st ed.: Benares: E.J. Lazarus, 1893.]

b. studies in the Sāmaveda Saṁhitā

03912 FADDEGON, BAREND. Studies in the Sāmaveda. Amsterdam: North Holland, 1951. 83p. (VKNAW, AL, ns 57,1)

03913 HOOGT, J.V. VAN DER. The Vedic chant studied in its textual and melodic form. Wageningen: H. Veenman, 1930. 123p.

03914 IYER, S. The Sāmans. In JUB 31,2 (1962) 35-61; 31,2 (1963) 89-126.

03915 RAGHAVAN, V. Sāma Veda and music. In JMA 33 (1962) 127-33.

03916 RENOU, L. Les versets du Sāmaveda d'origine non-Ṛgvédique. In JA 240 (1952) 133-41.

3. Yajurveda Saṁhitā: Sacrificial (Yajus) Formulas
a. translations

03917 DEVI CHAND, tr. Yajur Veda. 2nd ed. ND: S. Paul, 1965. 519p.

03918 GRIFFITH, R.T.H., tr. The texts of the White Yajur Veda. 3rd ed. Banaras: B.N. Yadav, 1957. 216p. [1st pub. 1899]

03919 KEITH, A.B., tr. the Veda of the Black Yajus school, entitled Taittirīya Saṁhitā. Cambridge: HUP, 1914. 2 v. (HOS 18, 19)

03920 RAO, M.C.R., tr. Rudra-adhyaaya: also known as Namaka-chamaka. Meerut: Anu Prakashan, 1975. 127p.

03921 ROLLAND, P., tr. Le Vārāhagṛhyapuruṣa; et autres extraits des Vārāhaparisiṣṭa à caractère domestique. Aix-en-Provence: U. de Provence; dist. Paris: Ophys, 1975. 218p. (Études indiennes, 3)

b. studies in the Yajurveda Saṁhitā

03922 BHAWE, S.S. Die Yajus' des Aśvamedha, Versuch einer Rekonstruktion dieses Abschnittes des Yajurveda auf Grund der Überlieferung seiner fünf Schulen. Stuttgart: W. Kohlhammer, 1939. 135p. (Bonner or. st., 25)

03923 PANDEY, U.K. Political concepts and institutions in the Śukla Yajurveda. Patna: Janaki Prakashan, 1979. 180p.

03924 SMITH, R.M. On the White Yajurveda Vaṃśa. E&W 16,1 (1966) 112-25.

03925 THITE, G.U. Magico-religious application of the White Yajurveda. In CASS Studies, no. 1. Poona: U. of Poona, 1972, 65-81.

4. Atharvaveda Saṁhitā: Priestly (Atharvan) Formulas for Domestic Ritual, Healing, Defense against Evil and Enemies
a. translations

03926 BLOOMFIELD, M., tr. Hymns of the Atharvaveda.... Delhi: Motilal, 1964. 716p. [Rpt. of 1897 ed., SBE 42]

03927 GRIFFITH, R.T.H., tr. Hymns of the Atharvaveda. Varanasi: CSSO, 1968. 2 v. (CSS, 66) [1st pub. 1895-96]

03928 WHITNEY, W.D., tr. Atharva-veda saṁhitā. Cambridge: HUP, 1905. 2 v. (HOS 7,8) [Rpt. Delhi: Motilal, 1962]

b. studies in the Atharvaveda Saṁhitā

03929 BLOOMFIELD, M. The Atharvaveda and the Gopatha Brāhmaṇa. ND: Asian Pub. Services, 1978. 126p. [Rpt. of 1898 ed.]

03930 KARAMBELKAR, V.W. The Atharva-veda and the Ayurveda. Nagpur: U. of Nagpur, 1961. 312p.

03931 SHENDE, N.J. Kavi and kāvya in the Atharvaveda. Poona: U. of Poona, 1967. 186p.

03932 ______. The religion and philosophy of the Atharvaveda. Poona: BORI, 1952. 251p. (BOS, 8)

C. The Brāhmaṇas: Prose Interpretations of the Rituals and Mantras of Each Veda

1. General Studies

03933 BANERJI, A.C. Studies in the Brāhmanas. Delhi: Motilal, 1963. 185p.

03934 BODEWITZ, H.W. The daily evening and morning offering (Agnihotra) according to the Brāhmanas. Leiden: Brill, 1976. 211p.

03935 GONDA, J. The etymologies in the ancient Indian Brāhmaṇas. In Lingua 5,1 (1955-56) 61-85.

03936 LEVI, S. La doctrine du sacrifice dans les "Brāhmaṇas". 2nd ed. Paris: Presses universitaires de France, 1966. 16 + 196p.

03937 MACDONALD, K.S. The Brāhmaṇas of the Vedas. Delhi: Bharatiya Book Corp., 1979. 211p. [Rpt. 1896 ed.]

03938 MALAMOUD, C. Théologie de la dette dans les Brāhmaṇa.... In Puruṣārtha 4 (1980) 39-62.

03939 THITE, G.U. Sacrifice in the Brāhmaṇa-texts. Poona: U. of Poona, 1975. 350p.

03940 VARENNE, J., tr. Mythes et legendes extraits des Brāhmaṇas. Paris: Gallimard, 1967. 207p.

2. Brāhmaṇas of the Ṛg Veda

03941 HAUG, M., tr. The Aitareya Brāhmaṇam of the Rigveda: containing the earliest speculations of the Brahmans on the meaning of the sacrificial prayers and on the origin, performance, and sense of the rites of the Vedic religion. Delhi: Bharatiya Pub. House, 1976-77. 2 v. [1st pub. 1863]

03942 KEITH, A.B., tr. Rigveda Brāhmaṇas: the Aitareya and Kauṣītaki Brāhmaṇas. Cambridge: HUP, 1920. 555p. (HOS 25) [Rpt. Delhi: Motilal, 1971]

03943 SHARMA, A. Analysis of three epithets applied to the Śūdras in Aitareya Brāhmaṇa VII. 29. 4. In JESHO 18,3 (1975) 300-17.

03944 SHENDE, N.J. The hotṛ and other priests in the Brāhmaṇas of the Ṛgveda. In JUB ns 32,2 (1963) 48-88.

3. Brāhmaṇas of the Sāma Veda

03945 BODEWITZ, H.W., tr. Jaiminīya Brāhmaṇa, I. 1-65, translation and commentary with a study: agnihotra and prāṇāgnihotra. Leiden: Brill, 1973. 357p.

03946 BOLLEE, W.B., tr. Ṣaḍviṁśa Brāhmaṇa. Utrecht: A. Storm, 1956. 118p.

03947 CALAND, W. Das Jaiminīya-Brāhmaṇa in Auswahl. Amsterdam: J. Muller, 1919. 326p.

03948 ______., tr. Pancaviṁśa-Brāhmaṇa: the Brāhmaṇa of twenty-five chapters. Calcutta: ASB, 1931. 660p. [BI 255]

03949 HOFFMAN, K. Die Weltentstehung nach dem Jaiminīya-Brāhmaṇa. In Münchener Studien zur Sprachwissenschaft 27 (1970) 59-67.

03950 HOPKINS, E.W. Gods and saints of the Great Brāhmaṇa. In Trans. of the Conn. Academy of Arts and Sciences 15 (1909) 23-69.

03951 JORGENSEN, H. Das Mantrabrāhmaṇa: 2. prapāṭhaka. Darmstadt: 1911. [Chāndogyabrāhmaṇa]

03952 OERTEL, H. Contributions from the Jaiminīya to the history of Brāhmaṇa literature. In JAOS 18 (1897) thru 28 (1907) passim.; 7th series In Trans. of Conn. Academy of Arts and Sciences 15 (1909) 155-216.

03953 ______. Extracts from the Jaiminīya Brāhmaṇa and Upaniṣad Brāhmaṇa. In JAOS 15 (1893) 233-51.

03954 SHUKLA, K.S. Ṣaḍviṁśa Brāhmaṇa: a study. In SPP 11,1 (1971) 31-37.

03955 STONNER, H. Das Mantrabrāhmaṇa; 1. prapāṭhaka. Halle: 1901. 53p. [Chāndogyabrāhmaṇa]

03956 TSUJI, N. On the frontier of the Adbhūta-Brāhmana. In ABORI 48-49 (1968) 173-78.

4. Brāhmaṇas of the Yajur Veda

03957 DEVASTHALI, G.V. Religion and mythology of the Brāhmaṇas, with particular reference to the Śatapatha-Brāhmaṇa. Poona: U. of Poona, 1965. 177p. (The Bhau Vishnu Ashtekar Vedic res. ser., 1)

03958 DUMONT, P.E. [Translations from the Taittirīya-Brāhmaṇa.] In PAPS, from 92 (1948) through 113 (1969) passim. [13 sections]

03959 EGGELING, J., tr. Śatapatha-brāhmaṇa, according to the text of the Mādhyandina school. Delhi: Motilal, 1966. 5 v. [1st pub. 1882-1900. SBE 12, 26, 41, 43, 44]

5. Brāhmaṇas of the Atharvaveda

03960 BLOOMFIELD, M. Position of the Gopatha-Brāhmaṇa in Vedic literature. In JAOS 19,2 (1898) 1-11.

03961 PATYAL, H.C. Gopatha Brāhmaṇa: English translation with notes and introduction. Ph.D. diss., U. of Poona, 1969. 646p.

D. The Āraṇyakas "Forest Texts"

03962 DESHPANDE, I.C. Philosophical thoughts in the Āraṇyakas. In IA ser. 3,3,1/4 (1969) 169-76.

03963 KEITH, A.B., tr. Aitareya āraṇyaka. Oxford: OUP, 1909. 390p.

03964 ______. The Śāṅkhāyana āraṇyaka. In JRAS (1908) 363-88.

03965 ______., tr. The Śāṅkhāyana Āraṇyaka with an appendix on the Mahāvṛata. London: RAS, 1908. 361p. (OTF 18)

03966 OERTEL, H., tr. The Jaiminīya or Talavakāra Upaniṣad Brāhmaṇa. JAOS 16 (1896) 79-260.

E. The Vedic Upaniṣads: Philosophical Discussions Presaging the Vedānta ("End of the Veda")

1. Reference

03967 JACOB, G.A. A concordance to the principal Upanishads and Bhagavadgītā. Delhi: Motilal, 1963. 1083p. [1st pub. 1891]

2. The Principal Upaniṣads in Translation

03968 GHOSE, A. Kena Upanishad. Pondicherry: Sri Aurobindo Ashram, 1970. 124p.

03969 HIRIYANNA, M., tr. Īśavāsyopaniṣad....with the commentary of Śaṁkarācarya. Mysore: Kavyalaya Pub., 1972. 40p.

03970 HUME, R.E. The thirteen principal Upaniṣads. NY: OUP, 1971. 587p. [1st pub. 1921]

03971 MAHADEVAN, T.M.P., ed. Upaniṣads: the selections from 108 Upaniṣads. ND: Arnold-Heinemann, 1975. 240p.

03972 MASCARO, J., tr. The Upanishads. Harmondsworth: Penguin Books, 1965. 142p.

03973 MITRA, R. & E.B. COWELL, tr. The twelve principal Upaniṣads. Delhi: Nag, 1978-. 3 v. [Rpt. of 1931-32 ed.]

03974 MÜLLER, F.M., tr. Upanishads. Delhi: Motilal, 1965. 2 v. [Rpt. of 1879-84 ed. SBE 1,15]

03975 NIKHILANANDA, Swami, tr. The Māṇḍukyopaniṣad; with Gauḍapāda's Kārikā and Śaṅkara's commentary. 6th ed. Mysore: Sri Ramakrishna Ashrama, 1974. 315p.

03976 ______., tr. The Upanishads. NY: Harper, 1949-59. 4 v., 1497p.

03977 PRABHAVANANDA, Swami & F. MANCHESTER, tr. The Upanishads; breath of the eternal. Hollywood: Vedanta Press, 1947. 210p.

03978 PUROHIT, Swami, & W.B. YEATS, trs. The ten principal Upanishads. London: Faber, 1970. 150p. [1st pub. 1937]

03979 RADHAKRISHNAN, S., tr. The principal Upanishads. London: Allen & Unwin, 1969. 958p. [1st pub. 1953]

03980 VAN BUITENEN, J.A.B., tr. The Maitrayanīya Upaniṣad. The Hague: Mouton, 1962. 157p.

2. Studies of the Upaniṣads

03981 BEHM, A.J. The theodicy of the Upanishads. In JOSA 7,1/2 (1970) 5-14.

03982 CHAKRAVARTI, S.C. The philosophy of the Upanishads. Delhi: Nag, 1979. 272p. [Rpt. of 1935 ed.]

03983 DAVE, T.N. Taittirīya Upaniṣad - a mine of cultural and philosophical information. In SPP 5,2 (1965) 51-66; 6,1 (1966) 3-18.

03984 DEUSSEN, P. The philosophy of the Upanishads. Tr. from German by A.S. Geden. NY: Dover, 1966. 429p. [1st English translation 1906]

03985 EDGERTON, F. The Upanishads; what do they seek and why. In JAOS 49 (1929) 97-121.

03986 GOMAN, T.G. & R.S. LAURA. A logical treatment of some Upaniṣadic puzzles and changing conceptions of sacrifice. In Numen 19,1 (1972) 52-67.

03987 HANEFELD, E. Philosophische Haupttexte der alteren Upaniṣaden. Wiesbaden: Harrassowitz, 1976. 199p. (Freiburger Beiträge zur Indologie, 9)

03988 KADANKAVIL, K.T. The quest of the real: a study of the philosophical methodology of Muṇḍakopaniṣhad. Bangalore: Dharmaram, 1975. 292p.

03989 MODAK, M.S. Spinoza and the Upanishads; a comparative study. Nagpur: Nagpur U., 1970. 120p.

03990 RADHAKRISHNAN, S. The philosophy of the Upaniṣads. Rev. ed. London: Allen & Unwin, 1924. 143p.

03991 RANADE, R.D. A constructive survey of Upanishadic philosophy, being an introduction to the thought of the Upanishads. 2nd ed. Bombay: BVB, 1968. 340p. [1st ed. Poona: Oriental Book Agency, 1926. 438p.]

03992 RUBEN, W. Die Philosophen der Upanishaden. Bern: A. Francke, 1947. 338p.

03993 SEN GUPTA, A. Kaṭha Upaniṣad: Sāṁkhya point of view. Kanpur: M. Sen, 1967. 68p.

03994 VITSAXIS, B. Plato and the Upaniṣads. ND: Arnold-Heinemann, 1977. 93p.

VI. THE VEDĀṄGAS ("LIMBS OF THE VEDA"): EXEGESIS OF VEDIC TEACHINGS FOR PRACTICAL APPLICATION IN RITUAL, LAW AND DOMESTIC LIFE

[For Vedāṅgas other than the Kalpasūtra, see Chapter Three]

A. General

03995 APTE, V.M. The Vedāngas. In Cultural Heritage of India. Calcutta: RMIC, 1958, v. 1, 264-292.

03996 RENOU, L. Sur le genre du sūtra dans la littérature sanskrite. In JA 251 (1963) 165-216.

03997 SITARAMIAH, G. The vedāngas and their value. QJMS 32 (1941-42)

B. The Kalpasūtras: Rules Relating to Sacrifices and Rituals

[For Gṛhyasūtras, see Chapter Three, III. C. 3. a.]

1. Śrautasūtras: Rules for Vedic Sacrifice

03998 CALAND, W., tr. Das Śrautasūtra von Āpastamba; aus dem Sanskrit übersetzt. Wiesbaden: M. Sandig, 1969. 2 v., 468, 459p. [Rpt. of 1924-28 ed.]

03999 ______. Über das rituelle Sūtra des Baudhāyana. In AKM 12,1 (1903) 1-65.

04000 GHOSHAL, S.N., tr. The Vaitānasūtra: annotated English translation. In IHQ 34 (1958) supp. 10 + 53p.; 35 (1959) supp., 1-113; 36,1 (1960) 115-132.

04001 KASHIKAR, C.G. A survey of the Śrautasūtras. In JUB ns 35,2, Arts number 41 (1966) 188p.

04002 PARPOLA, A., tr. The Śrautasūtras of Lāṭyāyana and Drahyāyana and their commentaries; an English translation and study. Helsinki: Soc. Scientiarum Fennica, 1968-69. v. 1, pts. 1 & 2, 141, 273p. (Commentationes humanorum litterarum, 42(2), 43(2))

04003 SINGH, K.P. A critical study of the Katyāyana-śrauta-sūtra. Varanasi: BHU, 1969. 217p. (BHUSS, 3)

04004 VAN GELDER, J.M., tr. The Mānava Śrauta Sūtra. ND: IAIC, 1963. 332p. (SPS, 27)

04005 VISHVA BANDHU & BHIM DEVA & PITAMBAR DATT. Vaitāna-śrauta-sūtra with the commentary called Ākṣepūvidhi by Somāditya. Hoshiarpur: VVRI, 1967. 34 + 263p. (WIS, 13)

2. Śulvasūtras: Rules for Construction of Sacrificial Altars

04006 BAG, A.K. The knowledge of geometrical figures, instruments and units in the śulbasūtras. In E&W 21,1/2 (1971) 111-19.

04007 SATYAPRAKASH &. R.S. SHARMA, trs. Āpastamba-Śulba-sūtram. ND: Mahalakshmi Pub. House, 1968. 841p. (Ratna Kumari pub. series, 5)

04008 ______. Baudhāyana-Śulbasūtram. ND: Res. Inst. of Ancient Scientific St., 1968. 34 + 215p. (Ratna Kumari pub. series, 4)

3

Ancient India: c. Sixth Century B.C. to Sixth Century A.D., from the Time of the Buddha through the Imperial Guptas

I. GENERAL HISTORIES OF THE ANCIENT PERIOD, c. 600 BC-c. 600 AD

A. Historiography and Chronology

04009 CHOUDHARY, R.K. Problems and methods of socio-economic history of ancient India in a new perspective. In JBRS 54 (1968) 76-126.

04010 GHOSHAL, U.N. History and historians of ancient India. In QRHS 3,1/2 (1963-64) 10-19.

04011 ______. History and historians of ancient India in the modern age. In IAC 9 (1961) 353-84.

04012 MALIK, S.C. Indian civilization: the first phase, problems of a sourcebook. Simla: IIAS, 1971. 305p. (Its Trans., 17) [Proc. of Seminar on a Sourcebook of Ancient Indian and Asian Civilization, Simla, 1970]

04013 MORRISON, B.M. Sources, methods and concepts in early Indian history. In PA 41 (1968) 71-85.

04014 MUKHERJEE, B.N. Central and South Asian documents on the old Śaka era. Varanasi: Bharat-Bharati, 1973. 135p.

04015 THAKUR, V.K. Archaeology and the writing of ancient Indian history. In JBPP 1 (1977) 94-103.

04016 THAPAR, R. Ideology and the interpretation of early Indian history. In K.S. Krishnaswamy, et al, eds. Society and change.... Bombay: OUP, 1977, 1-19.

04017 ______. Interpretations of ancient Indian history. In History & Theory 7 (1968) 318-35.

B. Sources: Auxiliary Techniques for Study of the Past

1. Literary Sources
a. classical Greek accounts

04018 KALOTA, N.S. India as described by Megasthenes. Delhi: Concept, 1978. 128p.

04019 MAJUMDAR, R.C. The classical accounts of India. Calcutta: KLM, 1960. 504p.

04020 MCCRINDLE, J.W., tr. Ancient India, as described by Ktesias the Knidian. Delhi: Manohar, 1973. 104p. [1st pub. in IA, 1881; rpt. of 1882 ed.]

04021 ______. Ancient India as described by Ptolemy. Ed. by R.C. Jain. Rev. ed. ND: Today & Tomorrow's, 1974. 468p. [1st pub. in IA, 1884]

04022 ______. The Christian topography of Cosmas, an Egyptian monk. London: Hakluyt Soc., 1897. 398p.

04023 ______. McCrindle's Ancient India, as described by Megasthenes and Arrian. Ed. by R.C. Jain. ND: Today & Tomorrow's, 1972. 263p. [1st pub. in IA, 1876-77; rpt. 1877 ed.]

04024 PIRENNE, J. Un problème-clef pour la chronologie de l'Orient: la date du "Périple de la mer Érythrée". In JA 249 (1961) 441-59.

04025 PURI, B.N. India in classical Greek writings. Ahmedabad: New Order Book Co., 1963. 259p.

04026 SALETORE, B.A. Ptolemy and western India. In JIH 40 (1962) 41-84.

04027 SCHOFF, W.H., tr. The Periplus of the Erythraean sea; travel and trade in the Indian Ocean by a merchant of the first century. 2nd ed. ND: OBRC, 1974. 323p. [Rpt. 1912 ed.]

04028 SINNATAMBY, J.R. Ceylon in Ptolemy's geography. Colombo: the author, 1968. 73p.

b. early Indian texts as sources

04029 AGRAWALA, V.S. India as described by Manu. Varanasi: Prithvi Prakashan, 1970. 55p.

04030 ______. India as known to Pāṇini; a study of the cultural material in the Aṣhṭādhyayi. 2nd ed., rev. and enl. Varanasi: Prithvi Prakashan, 1963. 612p. [1st pub. 1953]

04031 BANERJI, S.C. Aspects of ancient Indian life, from Sanskrit sources. Calcutta: Punthi Pustak, 1972. 179p.

04032 JAIN, J.C. Life in ancient India as depicted in the Jain canons. Bombay: New Book Co., 1947. 420p.

04033 JAIN, J.P. The Jaina sources of the history of ancient India, 100 B.C. - A.D. 900. Delhi: Munshiram, 1964. 321p.

04034 LAW, B.C. India as described in early texts of Buddhism and Jainism. Delhi: Bharatiya, 1980. 315p. [Rpt. 1941 ed.]

04035 PURI, B.N. India in the time of Patañjali. 2nd ed. Bombay: BVB, 1968. 272p.

04036 SHASTRI, A.M. India as seen in the Bṛihatsaṁhitā of Varāhamihira. Delhi: Motilal, 1969. 556p.

04037 UPADHYAYA, B.S. India in Kālidāsa. Allahabad: Kitabistan, 1947. 385p.

c. the Epics and Purāṇas as historical sources

04038 AWASTHI, A.B.L. History from the Puranas. Lucknow: Kailash Prakashan, 1975. 176p.

04039 CHAUDHURI, S.B. Ethnic settlements in ancient India, a study on the Puranic lists of the peoples of Bharatavarsa. Calcutta: General Printers & Publishers, 1955. 212p.

04040 DESHPANDE, V.V. Nature and significance of Itihāsa and Purāṇa in Vedic Puruṣārtha Vidyās. In Purāṇa 16,1/2 (1974) 47-66, 245-60; 18/2 (1976) 197-211.

04041 KANTAWALA, S.G. Cultural history from the Matsyapurāṇa. Baroda: MSUB, 1964. 477p.

04042 ______. The purāṇas and epics as sources of religious, social, and cultural history of India. In JMSUB 19,1 (1970) 45-58.

04043 LEWIS, C.A. The connection between the geographical texts of the Purāṇas and those of Mahābhārata. In Purāṇa 18,1 (1976) 56-74.

04044 PAI, G.K. Cultural history from the Kūrma Purāna. Cochin: Sukrtindra Oriental Res. Inst., 1975. 544p.

04045 PARGITER, F.E. Ancient Indian historical tradition. Delhi: Motilal, 1971. 370p. [Rpt. 1922 ed.]

04046 PARUI, S.S. Kurukṣetra in the Vāmana Purāṇa. Calcutta: Punthi Pustak, 1976. 225p.

04047 PATIL, D.R. Cultural history from the Vāyu Purāṇa. Delhi: Motilal, 1973. 348p.

04048 SETHNA, K.D. Megasthenes and the problem of Indian chronology as based on the Purāṇas. In Purāṇa 8 (1966) 267-294.

04049 SINGH, R.B. Jaina Puranas as a source of social history. In U. Thakur & U.K. Mishra, eds. The heritage of India. Bodh Gaya: L.N. Mishra Commem. Vol. Pub. Cmtee., 1978, 292-95.

04050 SMITH, R.M. Dates and dynasties in earliest India; translation and justification of a critical text of the Purāṇa dynasties. Ed. by J.L. Shastri. Delhi: Motilal, 1970. 517p.

04051 THAPAR, R. Genealogy as a source of social history. In her Ancient Indian social history. ND: Orient Longmans, 1978, 326-60. [1st pub. IHR 2,2 (1976) 259-81]

d. Chinese accounts

04052 BEAL, S., tr. Travels of Fa-hian and Sung-yun, Buddhist pilgrims, from China to India (400 A.D. & 518 A.D.). NY: Kelly, 1970. 73 + 208p. [1st pub. 1869]

04053 GILES, H.A., tr. The travels of Fa Hsien (399-414 AD), or Record of the Buddhistic kingdoms. Cambridge: CamUP, 1923. 96p.

04054 LEGGE, J., tr. A record of the Buddhistic kingdoms, being an account by the Chinese monk Fa-hien of his travels in India and Ceylon (399-414).... NY: Paragon, 1965. 123 + 45p. [Rpt. 1886 ed.]

04055 LI, YUNG-HSI, tr. A record of the Buddhist countries. Peking: Chinese Buddhist Assn., 1957. 93p.

2. Epigraphy

04056 BANERJEE, M. A study of important Gupta inscriptions: historical, social, religious & literary. Calcutta: SPB, 1976. 65p.

04057 CHAKRAVARTI, H.P. Early Brahmi records in India (c. 300 B.C. - c. 300 A.D.); an analytical study: social, economic, religious, and administrative. Calcutta: SPB, 1974. 235p.

04058 FLEET, J.F. Inscriptions of the early Gupta kings and their successors. 3rd rev. ed. Varanasi: IndBH, 1970. 605p. (Corpus inscriptionum indicarum, 3) [1st pub. 1963]

04059 MAHALINGAM, T.V. Early South Indian palaeography. Madras: U. of Madras, 1967. 341p.

04060 SHARMA, T.R. Personal and geographical names in the Gupta inscriptions. Delhi: Concept, 1978. 377p.

04061 SHASHI KANT. The Hāthīgumphā inscription of Khāravela and the Bhabru Edict of Aśoka. Delhi: Prints India, 1971. 111p.

04062 SIRCAR, D.C., ed. Select inscriptions bearing on Indian history and civilization. Vol. 1: From the 6th century BC to the 6th century AD. Calcutta: U. of Calcutta, 1942. 41+530p. [Rev. enl. ed. 1965. 552p.+62pl.]

3. Numismatics

04063 CUNNINGHAM, A. Coins of ancient India, from the earliest times down to the seventh century A.D. Varanasi: IndBH, 1963. 118p. [Rpt. 1891 ed.]

04064 DAS GUPTA, K.K. A tribal history of ancient India: a numismatic approach. Calcutta: Nababharat, 1974. 336p. + 12 pl.

04065 LAHIRI, A.N. Corpus of Indo-Greek coins. Calcutta: Poddar Pub., 1965. 287p.

04066 MAITY, S.K. Early Indian coins and currency system. ND: Munshiram, 1970. 136p.

04067 MITCHINER, M. Indo-Greek and Indo-Scythian coinage. Sanderstead: Hawkins Pub., 1975-76. 9 v. in 3.

04068 MUKHERJEE, B.N. Nanā on lion; a study in Kushāṇa numismatic art. Calcutta: Asiatic Soc., 1969. 159p. + 15 pl.

04069 PRAKASH, S. & R. SINGH. Coinage in ancient India; a numismatic archaeochemical and metallurgical study of ancient Indian coins. ND: Res. Inst. of Ancient Scientific Studies, 1968. 546p.

04070 RHYS DAVIDS, T.W. On the ancient coins and measures of Ceylon. Chicago: Obol Intl., 1975. 60p. [Rpt. 1877 ed.]

04071 SHARAN, M.K. Tribal coins; a study (the Yaudheyas, the Mālavas, the Audumbaras, and the Kuṇindas). ND: Abhinav, 1972. 358p.

04072 SHASTRI, A.M., ed. Coinage of the Śātavāhanas and coins from excavations; papers presented at the numismatic seminars held under the auspices of the Nagpur University on 11th and 12th November 1970. Nagpur: Nagpur U., 1972. 142p.

04073 ______., ed. Coins and early Indian economy: papers presented at a Seminar on Coins as a Source of Economic History of Ancient India, held at Patna University on 2nd October 1969. Varanasi: Numismatic Soc. of India, 1976. 179p. (Its Memoirs ser., 6)

04074 SINGH, O.P. Religion and iconography on early Indian coins. Varanasi: Bharati Prakashan, 1978. 112p. + 7 pl.

04075 SIRCAR, D.C., ed. Early Indian indigenous coins. Calcutta: U. of Calcutta, 1970. 175p.

04076 ______. Early Indian numismatic and epigraphical studies. Calcutta: Indian Museum, 1977. 170p.

04077 THOMAS, E. Ancient Indian weights. Varanasi: Prithvi Prakashan, 1970. 74p.

C. Historical Geography

04078 CHAUDHURY, B.N. Buddhist centres in ancient India. Calcutta: Sanskrit College, 1969. 292p.

04079 CUNNINGHAM, A. The ancient geography of India. New enl. ed. Varanasi: Bharatiya, 1975. 491 + 78p. [1st pub. 1871]

04080 DUBE, B. Geographical concepts in ancient India. Varanasi: NGSI, 1967. 183p.

04081 GUPTA, P. Geographical names in ancient Indian inscriptions. Delhi: Concept, 1977. 176p.

04082 ______. Geography in ancient Indian inscriptions, up to 650 A.D. Delhi: D.K., 1973. 315p.

04083 LAW, B.C. Geographical essays relating to ancient geography of India. Delhi: Bharatiya, 1976. 225p. [Rpt. 1938 ed.]

04084 ______. Geography of early Buddhism. Varanasi: Bharatiya, 1973. 88p. [Rpt. 1932 ed.]

04085 ______. Historical geography of ancient India. Delhi: Ess Ess, 1976. [Rpt. 1954 ed.]

D. General Surveys of Ancient History

04086 BHAGI, M.L. Ancient India; culture and thought. Ambala Cantt: Indian Pub., 1963. 200p.

04087 BHATTACHARJEE, A. History of ancient India. ND: Sterling, 1979. 422p.

04088 GOKHALE, B.G. Ancient India: history and culture. Bombay: Asia, 1959. 224p.

04089 JHA, D.N. Ancient India: an introductory outline. ND: PPH, 1977. 134p.

04090 KOSAMBI, D.D. The culture and civilization of ancient India. ND: Vikas, 1970. 243p. [1st pub. 1965]

04091 KRISHNASWAMI AIYANGAR, S. History of ancient India. Delhi: Seema, 1980. 451p. [Rpt. 1911 ed.]

04092 LA VALLÉE POUSSIN, L. DE. Dynasties et histoire de l'Inde depuis Kanishka jusqu'aux invasions musulmanes. Paris: Boccard, 1935. 396p.

04093 ______. L'Inde aux temps des Mauryas et des barbares, Grecs, Scythes, Parthes et Yue-tchi. Paris: Boccard, 1930. 376p.

04094 MAJUMDAR, A.K. Concise history of ancient India. ND: Munshiram, 1977, 1973-. v. 1, 560p.

04095 MAJUMDAR, R.C. Ancient India. Rev. ed. Delhi: Motilal, 1960. 538p. [1st pub. 1927]

04096 ______., ed. The age of imperial unity. Bombay: BVB, 1960. 735p. (HCIP, 2)

04097 ______., ed. The classical age. Bombay: BVB, 1954. 745p. (HCIP, 3)

04098 MAJUMDAR, R.C. & A.S. ALTEKAR, eds. The Vakataka-Gupta age (circa 200 - 550 A.D.) Delhi: Motilal, 1967. 515p.

04099 MASSON-OURSEL, P. & H. DE WILLMAN-GRABOWSKA & P. STERN. Ancient India and Indian civilization. Tr. from French by M.R. Dobie. NY: Barnes & Noble, 1967. 24 + 435p. [1st English ed. 1933]

04100 MCNEILL, W.H. & J.W. SEDLAR, eds. Classical India. NY: OUP, 1969. 291p. (Readings in world history, 4)

04101 NILAKANTA SASTRI, K.A., comp. Age of the Nandas and Mauryas. 2nd ed. Delhi: Motilal, 1967. 449p. [1st ed. 1952]

04102 RAPSON, E.J. Ancient India: from the earliest times to the first century AD. 3rd ed. Cambridge: CamUP, 1916. 199p. [1st ed. 1914]

04103 RAYCHAUDHURI, H.C. Political history of ancient India, from the accession of Parikshit to the extinction of the Gupta dynasty. 6th ed., rev. & enl. Calcutta: U. of Calcutta, 1953. 680p.

04104 RENOU, L. La civilisation de l'Inde ancienne, d'après les textes sanskrits. Paris: Flammarion, 1950. 264p.

04105 RHYS DAVIDS, T.W. Buddhist India. Delhi: Motilal, 1971. 332p. [Rpt. 1903 ed.]

04106 RUBEN, W. Die gesellschaftliche Entwicklung im alten Indien. Berlin: Akademie-Verlag, 1973. 6 v., 1851p.

04107 THAKUR, U. Some aspects of ancient Indian history and culture. ND: Abhinav, 1974. 322p.

II. HISTORY BY AREA AND DYNASTY, c. 600 BC TO c. 600 AD

A. North India: Kingdoms and Empires of the Ganga Plains and Nepal

1. General Studies of Ancient North India

04108 CHATTOPADHYAY, S. Bimbisāra to Aśoka: with an appendix on the later Mauryas. Calcutta: Roy & Chowdhury, 1977. 225p.

04109 ______. Early history of North India, from the fall of the Mauryas to the death of Harsa, c. 200 BC - AD 650. 2nd ed. Calcutta: Academic Pub., 1968. 375p.

04110 JAYASWAL, K.P. Chronology and history of Nepal, 600 B.C. to 880 A.D. In JBORS 22 (1936) 157-264.

04111 JOSHI, N.P. Life in ancient Uttarapātha: material civilisation of northern India from c. 200 B.C. to c. 300 A.D. as revealed by the sculptures, terracottas, and coins. Varanasi: BHU, 1967. 306p.

04112 MISHRA, Y.K. Socio-economic and political history of Eastern India. Delhi: D.K., 1978. 152p.

04113 PRASAD, HARI KISHORE. The political and socio-religious condition of Bihar, 185 BC to 319 AD. Varanasi: CSSO, 1970. 262p. (CSS, 78)

04114 REGMI, D.R. Ancient Nepal. 3rd ed. Calcutta: KLM, 1969. 364p. [1st ed. 1960]

2. The Earliest Kingdoms and Dynasties: Kośala, Magadha, and the Nandas

04115 LAW, B.C. The Magadhas in ancient India. Delhi: Nag, 1976. 50p. [Rpt. 1946 ed.]

04116 PATHAK, V. History of Kośala up to the rise of the Mauryas. Delhi: Motilal, [1963]. 479p.

3. The Mauryan Empire
a. general studies of the Mauryas

04117 MONAHAN, F.J. The early history of Bengal. Varanasi: Bharatiya, 1974. 248p. [Rpt. 1925 ed.]

04118 NARAYANAN, M.G.S. The Mauryan problem in Sangam works in historical perspective. In JIH 53,2 (1975) 243-54.

04119 RAMACHANDRA DIKSHITAR, V.R. The Mauryan polity. 2nd ed. Madras: Madras U., 1953. 243p.

04120 WADDELL, L.A. Report on the excavations at Pataliputra (Patna), the Palibothra of the Greeks. Delhi: Sanskaran Prakashak, 1975. 83p. + 10 pl. [Rpt. 1903 ed.]

b. Chandragupta Maurya: founder of the first Indian Empire

04121 BHARGAVA, P.L. Chandragupta Maurya. Lucknow: Upper India Pub. House, 1935. 138p.

04122 GOPAL, L. Chandragupta Maurya. ND: NBT, 1969. 77p.

04123 MOOKERJI, R.K. Chandragupta Maurya and his times. 4th ed. Delhi: Motilal, 1966. 263p. [1st ed. 1952]

c. Aśoka: Buddhist convert and Emperor
i. biographies and studies

04124 AROKIASWAMY, M. Aśoka and his Ujjain line of descendants. In JIH 53,3 (1975) 371-91.

04125 BHANDARKAR, D.R. Aśoka. Calcutta: U. of Calcutta, 1969. 366p.

04126 EGGERMONT, P.H.L. The chronology of the reign of Aśoka Moriya: a comparison of the data of the Aśoka inscriptions and the data of the tradition. Leiden: Brill, 1956. 222p.

04127 FUSSMAN, G. Quelques problèmes Aśokéens. In JA 262,3/4 (1974) 369-89.

04128 GOKHALE, B.G. Aśoka Maurya. NY: Twayne, 1966. 194p.

04129 MOOKERJI, R.K. Aśoka. 3rd ed., rev. and enl. Delhi: Motilal, 1962. 289p. [1st ed. 1928]

04130 SMITH, V.A. Aśoka, the Buddhist emperor of India. 2nd ed., rev. and enl. Delhi: S. Chand, 1964. 252p. (Rulers of India) [Rpt. 1901 ed.]

04131 THAPAR, R. Aśoka and the decline of the Mauryas. London: OUP, 1961. 283p.

ii. the Edicts, on rock and pillar

04132 BARUA, B.M. Aśoka and his inscriptions. 3rd ed. Calcutta: New Age, 1968-69. v. 1, pt. 1 & 2, 388, 104p.; v. 2, 102p.

04133 BLOCH, J., tr. Les inscriptions d'Aśoka. Paris: Les Belles Lettres, 1950. 216p.

04134 BONGARD-LEVIN, G. Megasthenes' "Indica" and the inscriptions of Aśoka. In ISPP 2 (1961) 203-11.

04135 CUNNINGHAM, A. Inscriptions of Aśoka. Varanasi: IndBH, 1961. 141p. (Corpus inscriptionum indicarum, 1) [1st pub. 1877]

04136 HULTZSCH, E. Inscriptions of Aśoka. Delhi: IndBH, 1969. 260p. + 55 pl. (Corpus inscriptionum indicarum, 1) [1st pub. 1925 as new ed. of Cunningham, 04135]

04137 LAW, B.C. Historical and geographical aspects of the Aśokan inscriptions. In JIH 41 (1963) 345-62.

04138 NIKAM, N.A. & R. MCKEON, tr. & eds. The edicts of Aśoka. Chicago: UChiP, 1958. 69p.

04139 SCHNEIDER, U. Die grossen Felsen-Edikte Aśokas. Wiesbaden: Harrassowitz, 1978. 197p. (FBI, 10)

04140 SIRCAR, D.C. Aśokan studies. Calcutta: Indian Museum, 1979. 150p. + 11 pl.

04141 ______., tr. Inscriptions of Aśoka. 3rd ed., rev. ND: PDMIB, 1975. 80p.

4. Post-Mauryan Dynasties: Śungas and Kānvas

04142 LAHIRI, B. Indigenous states of northern India, circa 200 B.C. to 320 A.D. Calcutta: U. of Calcutta, 1974. 398p.

04143 SINHA, B.C. History of the Śunga dynasty. Varanasi: Bharatiya, 1977. 200p.

5. The Imperial Guptas: 320 - 550 A.D.

04144 BANERJI, R.D. The age of the imperial Guptas. Benares: BHU, 1933. 250p. + 41 pl.

04145 BHATIA, O.P.S. The imperial Guptas. Delhi: Surjeet Book Depot, 1962. 386p.

04146 CHAKRABORTI, H.P. India as reflected in the inscriptions of the Gupta period. ND: Munshiram, 1978. 248p.

04147 GOKHALE, B.G. Samudra Gupta: life and times. Bombay: Asia, 1962. 120p.

04148 GOYAL, S.R. A history of the Imperial Guptas. Allahabad: Central Book Depot, 1967. 432p.

04149 GUPTA, P.L. The imperial Guptas. Varanasi: Vishwavidyalaya Prakashan, 1974-. v. 1, 402p.

04150 JOSHI, N.P. New light on the Gupta era and the chronology of early Gupta kings. In VIJ 14,2 (1976) 245-60.

04151 MAITY, S.K. Gupta civilization: a study. Calcutta: SPB, 1974. 104p.

04152 ______. The Imperial Guptas and their times, cir. AD 300-550. ND: Munshiram, 1975. 286p.

04153 MOOKERJI, R.K. The Gupta Empire. 4th ed. Delhi: Motilal, 1969. 174p.

04154 PATHAK, H. Cultural history of the Gupta period: based on epigraphic and numismatic records. Delhi: Bharatiya, 1978. 316p. + 12 pl.

04155 RAMACHANDRA DIKSHITAR, V.R. The Gupta polity. Madras: U. of Madras, 1952. 427p.

04156 SINGH, J.P. History and coinage of Skandagupta Kramāditya. Varanasi: Dept. of Ancient Indian History, Culture & Archaeology, BHU, 1976. 140p. (Its monographs, 9)

04157 THOMAS, E. Records of the Gupta dynasty; illustrated by inscriptions, written history, local tradition, and coins, to which is added a chapter on the Arabs in Sind. Varanasi: IndBH, 1973. 64p. [Rpt. 1876 ed.]

B. The Northwest: Invasion and Assimilation of Foreign Peoples in the Panjab-Malwa Area

1. General Histories

04158 ᶜALI IBN HAMID, AL-KUFI. The Chachnamah: an ancient history of Sind, giving the Hindu period down to the Arab conquest. Tr. from Persian by M.K. Fredunbeg. Delhi: IAD, 1979. 207p. (Its Oriental rpt. ser., 45) [Rpt. 1900 ed.]

04159 GOSWAMI, J. Cultural history of ancient India: a socio-economic and religio-cultural survey of Kapiśa and Gandhāra. Delhi: Agam Kala, 1979. 120p. + 16 pl.

04160 MARSHALL, J. Guide to Taxila. 4th ed. Cambridge: CamUP, 1960. 196p. [1st pub. 1918]

04161 MOHAN, M.V.D. The north-west India of the second century B.C. Ludhiana: Indological Res. Inst., 1974. 315p.

04162 PRAKASH, BUDDHA. Glimpses of the ancient Panjab. Patiala: Punjabi U., Dept. of Punjab Hist. Studies, 1966. 101p.

04163 SHUKLA, D.C. Early history of Rajasthan. Delhi: Bharatiya Vidya Prakashan, 1978. 252p.

04164 WHEELER, R.E.M. Chārsada, a metropolis of the North-west Frontier, being a report on the excavations of 1958. London: OUP, 1962. 130p.

2. The Indo-Greek Dynasties: Successors of Alexander the Great

04165 EGGERMONT, P.H.L. Alexander's campaigns in Sind and Baluchistan and the siege of the Brahmin town of Harmatelia. Leuven: Leuven U. Press, 1975. 233p.

04166 NARAIN, A.K. The Indo-Greeks. Oxford: OUP, 1962. 201p.

04167 PARANAVITANA, S. The Greeks and the Mauryas. Colombo: LHI, 1971. 188p.

04168 RAWLINSON, H.G. Bactria, from the earliest times to the extinction of Bactrio-Greek rule in the Punjab. Delhi: Bharatiya, 1978. 150p.

04169 TARN, W.W. The Greeks in Bactria and India. 2nd ed. Cambridge: CamUP, 1951. 507p. [1st ed. 1938]

04170 WOODCOCK, G. The Greeks in India. London: Faber, 1966. 199p.

3. The Indo-Parthians and Other Iranians

04171 MACDOWALL, D.W. The dynasty of the later Indo-Parthians. In Numismatic Chronicle 7th ser. 5 (1965) 137-48.

04172 MUKHERJEE, B.N. An Agrippan source; a study in Indo-Parthian history. Calcutta: Pilgrim Pub., 1969. 341p.

04173 ______. The Pāradas; a study in their coinage and history. Calcutta: Pilgrim Pub., 1972. 149p.

04174 PRAKASH, BUDDHA. The Parthians - a reappraisal. In VIJ 2 (1964) 307-18.

4. The Śakas: Indo-Scythians from Central Asia

04175 CHATTOPADHYAYA, S. The Śakas in India. 2nd ed. Santiniketan: Visva-Bharati, 1967. 115p.

04176 MOHAN, V.M. The Śakas in India and their impact on Indian life and culture. Varanasi: Chaukhambha Orientalia, 1976. 196p. (CORS, 4)

04177 SALOMON, R. The Kṣatrapas and Mahākṣatrapas of India. In WZKS 17 (1973) 5-25.

5. The Kuṣāṇas: Pretenders to Empire, Patrons of Buddhism, and Transmitters of Buddhism to Central Asia and China

04178 AYUBI, F., ed. Kushan culture and history, no. 2. Kabul: Historical and Literary Society of Afghanistan Academy, 1971. 118p.

04179 BASHAM, A.L., ed. Papers on the date of Kanishka. Leiden: Brill, 1968. 478p. (ANU Oriental monograph ser., 4) [from London conference, 1960]

04180 CHATTERJI, B. Kushāṇa State and Indian society: a study in post-Mauryan polity and society. Calcutta: Punthi Pustak, 1975. 288p.

04181 DANI, A.H. Kushāna civilization in Pakistan. In JASP 14 (1969) 1-20.

04182 KONOW, S. Kharoshti inscriptions, with the exception of those of Aśoka. Calcutta: Govt. of India Pub. Branch, 1929. 127 + 192p. (Corpus inscriptionum indicarum, 2:1)

04183 KUMAR, B. The early Kuṣāṇas; a history of the rise and progress of the Kuṣāṇa power under the early Kuṣāṇa rulers - from Kujula Kadphises to Vāsudeva. ND: Sterling, 1973. 329p.

04184 MUKHERJEE, B.N. Disintegration of the Kushāṇa Empire. Varanasi: Dept. of Ancient Indian History, Culture and Archaeol., BHU, 1976. 108p. (Its monographs, 8)

04185 ______. The Kushāṇa genealogy. Calcutta: Sanskrit College, 1967. 212p. (Studies in Kushāṇa Genealogy and Chronology, 1)

04186 ______. The Kushanas and the Deccan; Part 1, Kanishka I and the Deccan (a study in the problem of relationship). Calcutta: Pilgrim Pub., 1968. 166p.

04187 PURI, B.N. India under the Kushāṇas. Bombay: BVB, 1965. 268p.

04188 ______. Kuṣāṇa bibliography. Calcutta: Naya Prokash, 1977. 196p.

04189 SHARMA, G.R., ed. Kuṣāṇa studies. Allahabad: U. of Allahabad, 1968. 97p. + 28 pl.

04190 SIRCAR, D.C. Some problems concerning the Kuṣāṇas. Dharwar: Kannada Res. Inst., Karnatak U., 1971. 44p.

04191 UNESCO CONFERENCE ON HISTORY, ARCHAEOLOGY, AND CULTURE OF CENTRAL ASIA IN THE KUSHAN PERIOD, DUSHANBE, 1968. Kushan studies in U.S.S.R.; papers presented by the Soviet scholars. Calcutta: ISPP, 1970. 186p. (Soviet indology series, 3)

04192 ZEIMAL, E.V. Kushanskiia khronologiia. Moscow: Nauka, 1968. 186p. [25p. English summary]

6. The Hūṇas

04193 BISWAS, A. The political history of the Hūṇas in India. ND: Munshiram, 1973. 243p.

04194 THAKUR, U. The Hūṇas in India. Varanasi: CSSO, 1967. 344p. (CSS, 58)

C. Middle India and the Deccan: The Āndhra-Sātavāhanas and Their Successors, the Vākāṭakas and the Kalacuris

04195 CHATTOPADHYAY, S. Some early dynasties of South India. Delhi: Motilal, 1974. 216p.

04196 MIRASHI, V.V. Inscriptions of the Vakatakas. ND: ASI, 1963. 76 + 141p. + 41 pl. (Corpus inscriptionum indicarum, 5)

04197 NAIDU, D.S. Andhra Satavahanas; origins, chronology, and history of the early rulers of the dynasty. Vijayawada: Bharath Pub., 1970. 153p.

04198 PANDEY, R.B. Vikramāditya of Ujjayini (the founder of the Vikrama era). Banaras: Shatadala Prakashana, 1951. 268p.

04199 SIRCAR, D.C. Ancient Malwa and the Vikramāditya tradition. Delhi: Munshiram, 1969. 202p.

04200 ______. The successors of the Sātavāhanas in lower Deccan. Calcutta: U. of Calcutta, 1939. 417p.

04201 SURYAVANSHI, B.S. The Abhiras, their history and culture. Baroda: MSUB, 1962. 119p.

D. Dravidian Kingdoms of South India Before, During, and After the Sangam/Caṁkam Age

1. General Studies of Ancient South India

04202 AROKIASWAMI, M. The classical age of the Tamils. Madras: U. of Madras, 1967. 119p.

04203 KANAKASABHAI, K.V. The Tamils 1800 years ago. Tirunelveli: SISSWPS, 1956. 264p. [1st pub. 1904]

04204 MISHRA, P.K. The Kadambas. Allahabad: Mithila Prakasana, 1979. 178p. + 10 pl.

04205 NAGASWAMI, R. Studies in ancient Tamil law and society. Madras: Inst. of Epigraphy, Tamilnadu State Dept. of Archaeol., 1978. 140p. (TNSDA pub., 47)

04206 RATNASWAMI, S. A short history of the ancient Tamils and their literature. Annamalainagar: Thaiyalnayaki Veliyeedu, dist. ND: Munshiram, 1979. 151p.

04207 SIVARAJA PILLAI, K.N. Chronology of the early Tamils.... Madras: U. of Madras, 1932. 284p.

04208 SOUNDARA RAJAN, K.V. Determinant factors in the early history of Tamilnad. In JIH 45 (1967) 647-71; 46 (1968) 39-64.

04209 SRINIVASA AIYANGAR, P.T. History of the Tamils from the earliest times to 600 AD. Madras: C. Naidu, 1929. 635p.

04210 SUBRAHMANIAN, N. Pre-Pallavan Tamil index: index of historical material in pre-Pallavan Tamil literature. Madras: U. of Madras, 1966. 823p.

04211 ______. Sangam polity: the administration and social life of the Sangam Tamils. Bombay: Asia, 1967. 416p.

04212 ______. The territorial limits of Tamilaham of the Sangam age. In JMU 33,1 (1961) 33-45.

04213 THANI NAYAGAM, X.S., comp. Tamil culture and civilization; readings: the classical period. Bombay: Asia, 1971. 233p.

2. The Legend of Agastya, and the Meeting of Aryan and Dravidian Cultures in the South

04214 FILLIOZAT, J. Agastya et la propagation du brahmanisme au sud-est asiatique. In ALB 31/32 (1967-68) 442-49.

04215 GHURYE, G.S. Indian acculturation: Agastya and Skanda. Bombay: Popular, 1977. 232p.

04216 NARAYANAN, M.G.S. Aspects of Aryanisation in Kerala. Trivandrum: Kerala Hist. Soc., 1973. 53p.

04217 NILAKANTA SASTRI, K.A. Agastya. In Tijdschrift voor Indische Taal-, Land-, en Volkenkunde 76,4 (1936) 471-545.

04218 ______. Cultural contacts between Aryans and Dravidians. Bombay: Manaktalas, 1967. 88p.

3. Early Kingdoms of the Tamils: Cōḻas, Cēras, Pāṇḍyas

04219 MALONEY, C. The beginnings of civilization in South India. In JAS 29,3 (1970) 603-16.

04220 MANICKAVASAGOM PILLAI, M.E. Culture of the ancient Cheras; a study in cultural reconstruction. Kovilpatti: Manjula, 1970. 300p.

04221 AIYAR, K.G. Cēra kings of the Sangam period. London: Luzac & Co., 1937. 183p.

4. The Īkṣvakus and Other Dynasties of Andhra

04222 GOPALACHARI, K. Early history of the Andhra country. Madras: U. of Madras, 1941. 226p.

04223 KRISHNA MURTHY, K. Nāgārjunakoṇḍa; a cultural study. Delhi: Concept, 1977. 289p. + 46 pl.

04224 KRISHNARAO, B.V. A history of the early dynasties of Andhradesa, c. 200-625 A.D. Madras: V. Ramaswami Sastrulu, 1942. 716p.

04225 RAMA RAO, M. Īkṣvakus of Vijayapurī. Tirupati: Sri Venkateswara U., 1967. 97p.

04226 SANKARANARAYANAN, S. The Viṣṇukuṇḍis and their times: an epigraphical study. Delhi: Agam Prakashan, 1977. 278p.

5. The Pallavas of Kāñchīpuram, Capital of Toṇḍaimaṇḍalam. 250 - 900 A.D.

04227 MAHALINGAM, T.V. The early Pallavas of Kāñcī. In his Kāñchīpuram in early South Indian history. Bombay: Asia, 1969, 25-52.

04228 SIRCAR, D.C. The early Pallavas. In JIH 14 (1935) 149-64.

E. Lanka: Prince Vijaya and the Aryanization of Ceylon

1. The Pāli Chronicles: the Dīpavaṃśa, Mahāvaṃśa, and its Continuation, the Cūlavaṃśa

04229 BECHERT, H. Zum Ursprung der Geschichtsschreibung im indischen Kulturbereich. Göttingen: Vandenhoeck & Ruprecht, 1969. p. 35-58. (NAWG, 1969:2)

04230 GEIGER, W., tr. Cūlavaṃśa, being the more recent part of the Mahāvaṃśa. Tr. from German by Mrs. C.M. Rickmers. London: Pali Text Soc., 1929-30. 2 v., 362, 365p. (Its Translation ser., 18, 20)

04231 ______. The Dīpavaṃśa and Mahāvaṃśa and their historical development in Ceylon. Tr. from German by E.M. Coomaraswamy. Colombo: Govt. Printer, 1908. 129p.

04232 ______. The Mahāvaṃśa, or the great chronicle of Ceylon. London: Luzac, 1964. 300p. [1st pub. 1912]

04233 LAW, B.C. On the chronicles of Ceylon. Calcutta: RASB, 1947. 76p.

04234 ______., ed. The chronicle of the island of Ceylon or the Dīpavaṃśa: a historical poem of the 4th century A.D. In CHJ 7 (1957-58) 1-266.

04235 MALALASEKARA, G.P., tr. Vamsatthappakāsinī: commentary on the Mahavamsa. London: OUP, 1935. 2 v., 711p.

04236 MENDIS, G.C. The Pali Chronicles of Ceylon: an examination of the opinions expressed about them since 1879. In UCR 4 (1946) 1-24.

04237 OLDENBERG, H., tr. Dipavamsa: an ancient Buddhist historical record. London: Williams & Norgate, 1879. 227p.

04238 PERERA, L.S. The Pali chronicles of Ceylon. In C.H. Philips, ed. Historians of India, Pakistan and Ceylon. London: OUP, 1961, 29-43.

04239 STILL, J. Index to the Mahavansa, together with chronological table of wars and genealogical trees. Colombo: H. Ross Cottle, Govt. printer, 1907. 83p.

04240 SENEVIRATNE, M. Some Mahavamsa places: or, History happened here. Colombo: LHI, 1979. 152p.

04241 SMITH, B. The ideal social order as portrayed in the chronicles of Ceylon. In his (ed.) The two wheels of Dhamma.... Chambersburg, PA: American Academy of Religion, 1972, 31-57. (Its monograph ser., 3)

2. General Studies of Ancient Sri Lanka

04242 BASHAM, A.L. Prince Vijaya and the Aryanisation of Ceylon. In CHJ 1,3 (1952) 163-71.

04243 DE LANEROLLE, S.D. Origins of Sinhala culture. Colombo: LHI, 1976. 76p.

04244 JAYASEKERA, U.D. The early people of Ceylon. In IAC 17,2 (1968) 12-28.

04245 LAW, B.C. Some early Buddhist kings of Ceylon. In JIH 46,1 (1968) 1-18.

04246 MENDIS, G.C. The Vijaya legend. In Paranavitana felicitation volume.... Colombo: M.D. Gunasena, 1965, 263-79.

04247 MURPHEY, R. The ruins of ancient Ceylon. In JAS 16,2 (1957) 181-200.

04248 PARKER, H. Ancient Ceylon; an account of the aborigines and of part of the early civilization. London: Luzac, 1909. 695p.

04249 SIVARATNAM, C. The Tamils in early Ceylon. Colombo, 1968. 187p.

III. HISTORY BY TOPIC: POLITICAL, ECONOMIC, SOCIAL AND INTERNATIONAL

A. Political Forms and Ideas, the Military and the Art of War

1. Reference

04250 CHAUDHURI, P.K. Political concepts in ancient India: a glossary of political terms. ND: S. Chand, 1977. 190p.

04251 DISKALKAR, D.B. Designations of public officials in ancient India. In JUP 19 (1964) 107-33.

04252 GARDE, D.K. & P.P. APTE. Bibliography of political thought and institutions in ancient and medieval India. In JUP 25 (1967) 99-133; 35 (1971) 131-66; 39 (1974) 83-112.

2. General Studies of the Political System

04253 ALTEKAR, A.S. State and government in ancient India. 4th ed. Delhi: Motilal, 1962. 407p. [1st ed. 1949]

04254 DANDEKAR, R.N. The system of government under the Guptas. In J.H. Dave, ed. Munshi indological felicitation volume. Bombay: BVB, 1963, 340-354.

04255 GANGULY, D.K. Aspects of ancient Indian administration. ND: Abhinav, 1979. 352p.

04256 GHOSHAL, U.N. A history of Indian public life. v. 2: The pre-Maurya and the Maurya periods. Bombay: OUP, 1967. 324p.

04257 KUNTE, M.M. The vicissitudes of Aryan civilization in India: the history of the Vedic and Buddhistic polities, their origin, prosperity, and decline. Delhi: Heritage, 1974. 599p. [Rpt. 1880 ed.]

04258 LAW, N.N. Aspects of ancient Indian polity. Bombay: Orient Longmans, 1960. 238p.

04259 MOOKERJI, RADHA KUMUD. Local government in ancient India. Oxford: OUP, 1920. 229p.

04260 NATH, B. Judicial administration in ancient India. Patna: Janaki Prakashan, 1979. 164p.

04261 SALETORE, B.A. Ancient Indian political thought & institutions. Bombay: Asia, 1963. 695p.

04262 SHARMA, R.S. Aspects of political ideas and institutions in ancient India. 2nd ed., rev. & enl. Delhi: Motilal, 1968. 336p. [1st ed., 1959]

04263 SIRCAR, D.C. Studies in the political and administrative systems in ancient and medieval India. Delhi: Motilal, 1974. 300p.

04264 THAKUR, U. Corruption in ancient India. ND: Abhinav, 1979. 200p.

3. Political Theory
a. general

04265 BASHAM, A.L. Some fundamental political ideas of ancient India. In C.H. Philips, ed. Politics and society in India. London: Allen & Unwin, 1963, 11-23.

04266 GHOSHAL, U.N. A history of Indian political ideas: the ancient period and the period of transition to the middle ages. London: OUP, 1968. 589p. [Rpt., with corrections, of 1959 ed.]

04267 GOKHALE, B.G. The early Buddhist view of the state. In JAOS 89,4 (1969) 731-38.

04268 GUPTA, R.K. Political thought in the smṛti literature. Allahabad: Political Science Dept., U. of Allahabad, 196-. 354p.

04269 JAUHARI, M. Politics and ethics in ancient India; a study based on the Mahābhārata. Varanasi: Bharatiya, 1968. 393p.

04270 MABBETT, I.W. Truth, myth, and politics in ancient India. ND: Thomson Press, 1971. 158p.

04271 PILLAI, P.V. Perspectives on power: India and China: an analysis of attitudes towards political power in the two countries between c. seventh and second centuries B.C. ND: Manohar, 1977. 230p.

04272 PRASAD, BENI. Theory of government in ancient India. 2nd rev. ed. Allahabad: Central Book Depot, 1968. 399p.

04273 PURI, B.N. History of Indian administration. v. 1, ancient period. Bombay: BVB, 1968. 186p.

04274 ROY, B.P. Political ideas and institutions in the Mahabharata, based on Poona critical edition. Calcutta: Punthi Pustak, 1975. 423p.

04275 VARMA, V.P. Studies in Hindu political thought and its metaphysical foundations. 3rd rev. & enl. ed. Delhi: Motilal, 1974. 509p. [1st ed. 1954]

b. ideas of authority and kingship

04276 ARMELIN, I. Le Roi détenteur de la roue solaire en révolution, "cakravartin": selon le brahmanisme et selon le bouddhisme. Paris: P. Geuthner, 1975. 70p. (Cahiers de notices philologiques, grammaticales et bibliographiques; Serie Indologie)

04277 AUBOYER, J. Le trône et son symbolisme dans l'Inde ancienne. Paris: PUF, 1949. 228p.

04278 BASHAM, A.L. Ancient Indian kingship. In Indica 1,2 (1964) 119-27.

04279 BHARATIYA, R.K. The Hindu king and public welfare. In Prajna 9,1 (1963) 212-223.

04280 DREKMEIER, C. Kingship and community in early India. Stanford: Stanford U. Press, 1962. 369p.

04281 DUMONT, L. The conception of kingship in ancient India. In CIS 6 (1962) 48-77.

04282 GOKHALE, B.G. Early Buddhist kingship. In JAS 26,1 (1966) 15-22.

04283 GONDA, J. Ancient Indian kingship from the religious point of view. Leiden: E.J. Brill, 1966. 147p.

04284 HARA, M. The king as a husband of the earth (mahīpati). In AS/EA 27,2 (1973) 97-114.

04285 HEESTERMAN, J.C. The ancient Indian royal consecration; the rājasūya described according to the Yajus texts and annotated. The Hague: Mouton, 1957. 235p.

04286 HETTIARACHCHY, T. History of kingship in Ceylon up to the fourth century A.D. Colombo: LHI, 1972. 208p.

04287 JHA, D.D. Theory and practice of Dvairājya (double kingship) in ancient India. In JBRS 61,1/4 (1975) 37-54.

04288 LOSCH, H. Rājadharma. Einsetzung und Aufgabenkreis des Königs im Lichte des Purāṇas. Bonn: Selbstverlag der orientalischen Seminars der U. Bonn, 1959. 397p. (Bonner orientalische Studien, ns 8)

04289 PRAKASH, OM. King and Brāhmaṇas vis-à-vis Prayaścitta and Daṇḍa. In K.C. Chattopadhyaya memorial volume. Allahabad: Dept. of Hist., Culture and Archaeol., Allahabad U., 1975, 96-107.

04290 ROCHER, L. A few considerations on monocracy in ancient India. In Recueils de la Société Jean Bodin pour l'Histoire Comparative des Institutions 20 (1970) 639-75.

04291 SINHA, H.N. Sovereignty in ancient Indian polity; a study in the evolution of the early Indian state. London: Luzac, 1938. 344p.

04292 SPELLMAN, J.W. Political theory of ancient India; a study of kingship from the earliest times to ca. A.D. 300. Oxford: OUP, 1964. 288p.

c. the Arthaśāstra, the first treatise on statecraft, attrib. to Kauṭilya (Cāṇakya), Prime Minister of Chandragupta Maurya (c. 324-300 BC)

i. bibliography

04293 GHOSHAL, U.N. & R.G. BASAK. A general survey of the literature of Artha-śāstra and Nīti-śāstra. In The cultural heritage of India. Calcutta: RMIC, 1962, v. 2, 451-64.

04294 STERNBACH, L. Bibliography of Kauṭilīya Arthaśāstra. Hoshiarpur: VVRI, 1973. 39p. (VIS, 63)

ii. translations

04295 KANGLE, R.P., tr. The Kauṭilīya Arthaśāstra. 2nd ed. Bombay: U. of Bombay, 1969-72. v. 1, text, 283p; v. 2, translation, 516p. [1st ed. 1960-65]

04296 MEYER, J.J., tr. Das altindische Buch vom Welt- und Staatsleben. Das Arthaçāstra des Kauṭilya. Graz: Akademische Druck- und Verlagsanstalt, 1977. 80 + 983p. [1st pub. 1925-26]

04297 RAMASWAMY, T.N., tr. Essentials of Indian statecraft; Kauṭilya's Arthaśāstra for contemporary readers. Bombay: Asia, 1963. 152p.

04298 SHAMASASTRY, R., tr. Kauṭilya's Arthaśāstra. 7th ed. Mysore: Mysore Print. and Pub. House, 1961. 484p. [1st ed. 1909]

iii. studies

04299 BASAK, R.G. Some aspects of Kauṭilya's political thinking. Burdwan: U. of Burdwan, 1967. 51p.

04300 BRELOER, B. Kauṭaliya-studien I-III. Bonn: Schroeder, 1927-28. 2 v.

04301 ______. Staatsverwaltung im alten Indien. Leipzig: Harrassowitz, 1934. 560p. (His Kauṭaliya-studien, 3)

04302 BRUCKER, E. Wirtschaft und Finanzen im Staate Kauṭilyas unter besonderer Berücksichtigung der historischen und sozialen Verhältnisse. Wurzburg: Julius-Maximilians-U., 1966. 158p.

04303 CHOUDHARY, R.K. Kauṭilya's political ideas and institutions. Varanasi: CSSO, 1971. 444p. (CSS, 73)

04304 CHUNDER, P.C. Kauṭilya on love and morals. Calcutta: Jayanti, 1970. 208p.

04305 HEESTERMAN, J.C. Kauṭalya and the ancient Indian state. In WZKS 15 (1971) 5-22.

04306 KANGLE, R.P. Some recent work on the Kauṭilya Arthaśāstra. In JASBombay 43/44 (1968-69) 227-38.

04307 KONOW, S. Kauṭalya studies. Delhi: Oriental, 1975. 71p. [1st pub. 1945]

04308 KRISHNA RAO, M.V. Studies in Kauṭilya. 3rd rev. ed. ND: Munshiram, 1979. 171p.

04309 RITSCHL, E. & M. SCHETELICH. Studien zum Kauṭiliya Arthaśāstra. Berlin: Akademie-Verlag, 1973. 392p. (SGKAO, 9)

04310 SCHARFE, H. Untersuchungen zur Staatsrechtslehre des Kauṭalya. Wiesbaden: Harrassowitz, 1968. 349p.

04311 SCHLINGLOFF, D. Arthaśāstra-Studien. In WZKS 9 (1965) 1-38.

04312 SINHA, B.P. Readings in Kauṭilya's Arthaśāstra. Delhi: Agam Prakashan, 1976. 184p.

04313 STERNBACH, L. The subhāṣita-saṁgraha-s as treasuries of Cāṇakya's sayings. Hoshiarpur: VVRI, 1966. 187p. (VIS, 36)

04314 TRAUTMANN, T. Kauṭilya and the Arthaśāstra: a statistical investigation. Leiden: Brill, 1971. 227p.

04315 VOIGT, J.H. Nationalist interpretations of Arthaśāstra in Indian historical writing. In S.N. Mukherjee, ed. South Asian affairs; no. 2; The movement for national freedom in India. London: OUP, 1966, 46-66.

04316 WILHELM, F. Politische Polemiken im Staatslehrbuch des Kauṭalya. Wiesbaden: Harrassowitz, 1960. 158p. (Münchener Indologische Studien, Bd. 2)

d. later statecraft texts: the Nītisāra and Śukranīti

04317 DUTT, M.N., tr. Kamandakīya nītisāra: or, The elements of polity. 2nd ed. Varanasi: CSSO, 1979. 254p. (CSS, 97)

04318 GOPAL, L. The Śukranīti: a nineteenth century text. Varanasi: Bharati Prakashan, 1978. 112p.

04319 SARKAR, B.K., tr. The Śukranīti. Allahabad: Panini Office, 1914. 270p. (SBH, 13:1-4)

4. Aryan and Non-Aryan Tribal States, Kṣatriya and Others

04320 CHAUBEY, B.B. Historical account of the Tṛtsus. In VIJ 13,1/2 (1975) 50-71.

04321 CHOUDHARY, R.K. The Vrātyas in ancient India. Varanasi: CSSO, 1964. 204p. (CSS, 38)

04222 CHOUDHURY, M. Tribes of ancient India. Calcutta: Indian Museum, 1977. 161p.

04323 DASGUPTA, K.K. A tribal history of ancient India: a numismatic approach. Calcutta: Nababharat, 1974. 336p. + 12pl.

04324 JHA, H.N. The Licchavis (of Vaiśāli). Varanasi: CSSO, 1970. 247p. (CSS, 75)

04325 LAW, B.C. Ancient mid-Indian Ksatriya tribes. Varanasi: Bharatiya, 1975. v. 1, 166p.

04326 ______. Some Ksatriya tribes of ancient India. Varanasi: Bharatiya, 1975. 303p. + 13pl. [Rpt. 1924 ed.]

04327 ______. Tribes in ancient India. 2nd ed. Poona: BORI, 1973. 428p. (BOS, 4)

5. Evidences of Democracy: Village Assemblies and Tribal "Republics"

04328 GHOSHAL, U.N. On the working of village assemblies, economic guilds, religious congregations and other assemblies during the Gupta period. In JASBengal, 4th ser. 1,2 (1959) 177-82.

04329 MAJUMDAR, R.C. Corporate life in ancient India. 3rd ed. Calcutta: KLM, 1969. 391p. [1st pub. 1919]

04330 MISHRA, S. Janapada state in ancient India. Varanasi: Bharatiya, 1973. 336p.

04331 MISRA, S. Ancient Indian republics: from the earliest times to the 6th century A.D. Lucknow: Upper Indian Pub. House, 1976. 327p.

04332 MOHAN, M.V.D. Republican polity of the ancient Uttarapātha. In VIJ 13,1/2 (1975) 216-24.

04333 MUKHERJI, S. The republican trends in ancient India. Delhi: Munshiram, 1969. 220p.

04334 RUBEN, W. Some problems of the ancient Indian republics. In H. Krüger, ed., Kunwar Mohammed Ashraf, an Indian scholar and revolutionary, 1903-1962. Delhi: PPH, 1969. p. 5-29.

04335 SHARMA, J. Republic in ancient India, 1500 B.C. - 500 B.C. Leiden: Brill, 1968. 278p.

6. Diplomacy and International Law

04336 BHATIA, H.S., ed. International law and practice in ancient India. ND: Deep & Deep, 1977. 224p.

04337 LAW, N.N. Inter-state relations in ancient India. London: Luzac, 1920.

04338 MUKHERJEE, T.B. Inter-state relations in ancient India. Meerut: Meenakshi, 1967. 212p.

04339 MUKHERJI, B. Kautilya's concept of diplomacy: a new interpretation. Calcutta: Minerva, 1976. 110p.

04340 ROY, S.L. Diplomacy in ancient India, from the early Vedic period to the end of the sixth century AD. Calcutta: A. Roy, 1978. 226p.

7. The Art of War and the Military System

04341 CHAKRAVARTI, P.C. The art of war in ancient India. Delhi: Oriental, 1972. 212p.

04342 DATE, G.T. The art of war in ancient India. London: OUP, 1929. 105p.

04343 MAJUMDAR, B.K. The military system in ancient India. 2nd ed. Calcutta: KLM, 1960. 167p.

04344 RAMACHANDRA DIKSHITAR, V.R. War in ancient India. Madras: Macmillan, 1944. 416p. [1st pub. 1929]

04345 SINHA, S.P. Art of war in ancient India; 600 BC - 300 AD. In CHM 4,1 (1957) 123-60.

B. Economic Life: Agriculture, Public Finance, Commerce and Industry

1. General Studies

04346 ADHYA, G.L. Early Indian economics; studies in the economic life of northern and western India, c. 200 B.C. - 300 A.D. Bombay: Asia, 1966. 219p.

04347 BANERJEE, N.C. Economic life and progress in ancient India. 2nd ed. Calcutta: U. of Calcutta, 1945-. v. 1, Hindu period, 341p.

04348 BOSE, A.N. Social and rural economy of northern India, c. 600 BC- 200 AD. 2nd ed. Calcutta: KLM, 1961-67. 2 v. [1st ed. 1942-45]

04349 DARIAN, S.G. The economic history of the Ganges to the end of Gupta times. In JESHO 13,1 (1970) 62-87.

04350 DAS, D.R. Economic history of the Deccan, from the first to the sixth century A.D. Delhi: Munshiram, 1967. 324p.

04351 DAS, S. Socio-economic life of northern India, c. A.D. 550 to A.D. 650. ND: Abhinav, 1980. 413p.

04352 JHA, D.N. Studies in early Indian economic history. Delhi: Anupama, 1980. 102p.

04353 MAITY, S.K. Economic life in northern India in the Gupta period, cir. A.D. 330-550. Rev. 2nd ed. Delhi: Motilal, 1970. 314p. [1st ed. 1957]

04354 MUKHERJEE, B.N. The economic factors in Kushana history. Calcutta: Pilgrim Pub., 1970. 114p.

04355 NIGAM, S.S. Economic organisation in ancient India, 200 B.C. - 200 A.D. ND: Munshiram, 1975. 329p.

04356 PRANANATHA, Vidyalankara. A study of the economic conditions of ancient India. London: RAS, 1929. 172p.

04357 SALETORE, R.N. Early Indian economic history. Bombay: N.M. Tripathi, 1973. 856p.

04358 SHARMA, R.S. Stages in ancient Indian economy. In his Light on early Indian society and economy. Bombay: Manaktalas, 1966, 52-89.

04359 SIRCAR, D.C., ed. Early Indian trade and industry. Calcutta: U. of Calcutta, 1972. 142p.

2. Economic Thought

04360 RANGASWAMI AIYANGAR, K.V. Aspects of ancient economic thought. Varanasi: BHU, 1943. 211p.

04361 SHAH, K.T. Ancient foundations of economics in India. Bombay: Vora, 1954. 175p.

3. The Agrarian System: Agriculture, the Cultivator and his Overlords; Irrigation

04362 CODRINGTON, H.W. Ancient land tenure and revenue in Ceylon. Colombo: Ceylon Govt. Press, 1950. 77p. [Rpt. 1938 ed.]

04363 GANGULI, R. Some materials for the study of agriculture and agriculturists in ancient India. Serampore: N.C. Mukherjee, 1932. 147p.

04364 GHOSHAL, U.N. The agrarian system in ancient India. 2nd ed. Calcutta: Saraswat Library, 1973. 143p. [1st ed. 1929]

04365 GOPAL, L. Aspects of history of agriculture in ancient India. Varanasi: Bharati Prakashan, 1980. 185p.

04366 ______. Ownership of agricultural land in ancient India. In JBRS 46,1/4 (1960) 27-44.

04367 KRISHNASWAMY, S.Y. Major irrigation systems of ancient Tamilnad. In Intl. Conference Seminar of Tamil Studies, 1st, 1966, Proceedings. Kuala Lumpur: 1968, 451-461.

04368 NICHOLAS, C.W. A short account of the history of irrigation works up to the 11th century. In JRASCB ns 7,1 (1960) 43-69.

04369 PANDEY, L.P. Famines in ancient India. In JIH 53,1 (1975) 25-32.

04370 PERERA, L.S. Proprietary and tenurial rights in ancient Ceylon. In CJHSS 2,1 (1959) 1-36.

04371 PURI, B.N. Irrigation and agricultural economy in ancient India. In ABORI 48/49 (1968) 383-390.

4. The State and the Economy: Taxation, Public Finance and Enterprise

04372 GOPAL, L. Irrigation-tax in ancient India. In IHQ 38,1 (1962) 65-70.

04373 JHA, D.N. Revenue system in post-Maurya and Gupta times. Calcutta: Punthi Pustak, 1967. 234p.

04374 KHER, N.N. Agrarian and fiscal economy in the Mauryan and post-Mauryan age (cir. 324 B.C. - 320 A.D.). Delhi: Motilal, 1973. 468p.

04375 SARKAR, K.R. Public finance in ancient India. ND: Abhinav, 1978. 271p.

04376 THAPAR, R. State weaving shops of the Mauryan period. In J. of Indian textile history 5 (1960) 51-59.

5. Commerce and Industry; Trade Routes

04377 BALKRISHNA. The beginnings of the silk industry in India. In JIH 4,1 (1925) 42-52.

04378 CHAKRABORTI, H.P. Trade and commerce of ancient India, c. 200 BC - c. 650 AD. Calcutta: Academic Pub., 1966. 354p.

04379 EGGERMONT, P.H.L. The Murundas and the ancient trade-route from Taxila to Ujjain. In JESHO 9 (1966) 257-96.

04380 GOPAL, L. Textiles in ancient India. In JESHO 4 (1961) 53-69.

04381 MOTI CHANDRA. Trade and trade routes in ancient India. ND: Abhinav, 1977. 259p. [Tr. from Hindi]

04382 SARKAR, H.B. Bengal and her overland routes in India and beyond. In JASBengal 16,1/4 (1974) 92-119.

04383 SINGARAVELU, S. The origin and development of barter trade in Tamilnad. In TC 11 (1964) 317-28.

04384 SRIVASTAVA, B.R. Trade and commerce in ancient India, from the earliest times to c. A.D. 300. Varanasi: CSSO, 1968. 346p. (CSS, 59)

04385 THAKUR, U. A study in barter and exchange in ancient India. In Indian Numismatic Chronicle 6,1 (1967) 3-17.

6. The Role of Slavery

04386 BONGERT, Y. Réflexions sur le problème de l'esclavage dans l'Inde ancienne, à propos de quelques ouvrages récents. In BEFEO 51 (1963) 143-94.

04387 CHANANA, D.R. Slavery in ancient India as depicted in Pali & Sanskrit texts. ND: PPH, 1960. 203p.

04388 CHOUDHARY, R.K. Visti (forced labour) in ancient India. In IHQ 38,1 (1962) 44-59.

04389 GUNASINGHE, P.A.T. Slavery in Ceylon during the period of the Anuradhapura kingdom. In CHJ 10,1-4 (1960-61) 47-59.

04390 RAI, G.K. Forced labor in ancient and early medieval India. In IHR 3,1 (1976) 16-42.

04391 RUBEN, W. Die Lage der Sklaven in der altindischen Gesellschaft. Berlin: Academie-Verlag, 1957. 111p.

C. Dharma: the Person and the Social Order; Law and the Family according to the Brahmanical and Buddhist Literature

1. General Studies of Social Life in the Ancient Period, c. 600 BC - 600 AD
a. the time of the Buddha

04392 FICK, R. The social organisation in North-East India in Buddha's time. Tr. from German by S.K. Maitra. Varanasi: IndBH, 1972. 365p. [1st English ed. 1920]

04393 SINGH, M.M. Life in north-eastern India in pre-Mauryan times, with special reference to c. 600 BC - 325 BC. Delhi: Motilal, 1967. 308p.

04394 WAGLE, N.K. Society at the time of the Buddha. Bombay: Popular, 1966. 314p.

b. from the Mauryas through the Guptas

04395 AUBOYER, J. Daily life in ancient India, from approximately 200 B.C. to 700 A.D. Tr. from French by S.W. Taylor. London: Weidenfeld & Nicholson, 1965. 344p.

04396 BHATTACHARYA, S.C. Some aspects of Indian society from c. 2nd century B.C. to c. 4th century A.D. Calcutta: KLM, 1978. 313p.

04397 ELLAWALA, H. Social history of early Ceylon. Colombo: Dept. of Cultural Affairs, 1969. 191p.

04398 RAJAMANIKKAM, M. Aspects of social life of the Tamils in the Sangam age (300 BC - AD 300). In Intl. Conference Seminar of Tamil Studies, 1st, 1966, Proceedings. Kuala Lumpur: 1968, 332-337.

04399 SALETORE, R.N. Life in the Gupta age. Bombay: Popular, 1943. 623p.

04400 SHARMA, R.S. Light on early Indian society and economy. Bombay: Manaktalas, 1966. 168p.

04401 SINGARAVELU, S. Social life of the Tamils; the classical period. Kuala Lumpur: Dept. of Indian Studies, U. of Malaya, 1966. 214p. (Its Monograph series)

04402 SIRCAR, D.C., ed. Social life in ancient India. Calcutta: U. of Calcutta, 1971. 169p.

04403 ______. Studies in the society and administration of ancient and medieval India. v. 1. Society. Calcutta: KLM, 1967. 321p.

04404 THAPAR, R. Ancient Indian social history: some interpretations. ND: Orient Longman, 1978. 396p.

2. Dharma as Expressed in Early Legal Traditions
a. general studies of ancient law

04405 CHAUDHURI, R.K. Studies in ancient Indian law and justice. Bankipore: Motilal, 1953. 68p.

04406 DERRETT, J.D.M. The right to earn in ancient India: conflict between expediency and authority. In JESHO 1 (1958) 66-97.

04407 INGALLS, D.H.H. Authority and law in ancient India. In Authority and law in the ancient orient. Suppl. to JAOS 17 (1954) 34-45.

04408 KANE, P.V. History of Dharmaśāstra. Poona: BORI, 1930-62. 5 v. in 7. (Govt. oriental ser., B:6)

04409 NATARAJA AYYAR, A.S. Mīmāṃsā jurisprudence; the sources of Hindu law. Allahabad: GJRI, 1952. 84p. (Its ser., 2)

04410 SENGUPTA, N.C. Evolution of ancient Indian law. London: Probsthain, 1953. 348p.

04411 ______. Sources of law and society in ancient India. Calcutta: Art Press, 1914. 102p.

04412 STERNBACH, L. Juridical studies in ancient Indian law. Delhi: Motilal, 1965. 2 v., 548, 469p.

04413 THAKUR, U. An introduction to homicide in India: ancient and early-medieval period. ND: Abhinav, 1978. 117p.

b. the Dharmasūtras: prose compilations of canonical and secular law in the Vedic tradition

04414 BANERJI, S.C. Dharma-sūtras: a study in their origin and development. Calcutta: Punthi Pustak, 1962. 551p.

04415 BÜHLER, G., tr. The sacred laws of the Āryas. Delhi: Motilal Banarsidass, 1969. 2 v., 312, 360p. (SBE, 2, 14) [1st pub. 1879-82; Āpastamba, Gautama, Vasiṣṭha, Baudhāyana Dharmasūtras in trans.]

04416 HAZRA, R.C. The judicial pramāṇas (means of proof) known or mentioned in the extant Dharmasūtras of Gautama and others. In OH 16,1 (1968) 1-56.

04417 MITRA, VEDA. India of Dharma Sūtras. ND: Arya Book Depot, 1965. 299p.

04418 PATKAR, M.M. Topics of law and litigation in the Dharmasūtras with glossary. In PO 26,3-4 (1961) 65-104.

c. Manusmṛti: the foundation of Hindu law, and the chief Dharmaśāstra (metrical and codified expansions on the Dharmasūtras)
i. translations

04419 BÜHLER, G., tr. The Laws of Manu. Delhi: Motilal, 1967. 620p. (SBE, 25) [1st pub. 1886]

04420 BURNELL, A.C. & E.W. HOPKINS, tr. The ordinances of Manu. London: K. Paul, Trench, Trübner, 1891. 399p.

04421 STREHLY, G., tr. Les lois de Manou. Paris: Leroux, 1893. 402p.

ii. studies

04422 BANERJEE, N.V. Studies in the Dharmaśāstra of Manu. ND: Munshiram, 1980. 117p.

04423 BHARUCI (6th Cent. AD?) Bharuci's commentary on the Manusmṛti: (the Manu-śāstra-vivaraṇa, books 6-12); text, translation, and notes. Ed. by J.D.M. Derrett. Wiesbaden: Steiner, 1975. 2 v., 316, 489p. [the earliest commentary]

04424 BROWN, D.M. Some modern views of the Manusaṁhitā. In ALB 31-32 (1967-68) 95-112.

04425 MANICKAM, T.M. Dharma according to Manu and Moses. Bangalore: Dharmaram, 1977. 358p.

04426 PATWARDHAN, M.V. Manusmṛti: the ideal democratic republic of Manu. Delhi: Motilal, 1968. 225p.

04427 VAIDYANATHA AYYAR, R.S. Manu's land and trade laws: their Sumerian origin and evolution up to the beginning of the Christian era. Delhi: Oriental, 1976. 164p. [Rpt. 1927 ed.]

d. other dharmaśāstras, incl. general studies of dharmaśāstra literature

04428 CHATTOPADHYAYA, S. Social life in ancient India (in the background of Yajñavalkya-smṛti). Calcutta: Academic Pub., 1965. 178p.

04429 DERRETT, J.D.M. Dharmaśāstra and juridical literature. Wiesbaden: Harrassowitz, 1973. 75p. (HIL, 4:2)

04430 DUTT, M.N., tr. The Dharma shāstra: or, the Hindu law codes. Varanasi: Chaukhamba Amarabharati Prakashan, 1977-. v. 1, 533p. (Chaukhamba Amarabharati studies, 5)

04431 JAYASWAL, K.P. Manu and Yajñavalkya - a comparison and a contrast; a treatise on the basic Hindu law. Calcutta: Butterworth, 1930. 331p.

04432 JOLLY, J., tr. The institutes of Vishnu. Delhi: Motilal, 1965. 316p. (SBE, 7) [Rpt. 1880 ed.]

04433 ______., tr. The minor law books. Delhi: Motilal, 1965. 396p. (SBE, 33) [Rpt. 1889 ed.; inc. Nārada's and Bṛihaspati's Dharmaśāstras]

04434 ______., tr. Nāradīya dharmaśāstra; or, The institutes of Nārada. Varanasi: Bharatiya, 1978. 143p. [Rpt. 1876 ed.]

04435 KANE, P.V. Kātyāyanasmṛti on vyavahāra (law and procedure). Bombay: the author, 1933. 372p.

04436 LOSCH, H. Die Yajñavalkyasmṛti; ein Beitrag zur Quellenkunde des indischen Rechts. Leipzig: Harrassowitz, 1927. 60 + 132p.

04437 PATKAR, M.M. Nārada, Bṛhaspati, and Kātyāyana: a comparative study in judicial procedure. ND: Munshiram, 1978. 185p.

04438 SHARAN, M.K. Court procedure in ancient India: on the basis of Dharmaśāstra literature. ND: Abhinav, 1978. 280p.

04439 SRISA CHANDRA VIDYARNAVA, tr. Yajñavalkya Smṛiti, with the commentary of Vijñāneśvara, called the Mitākṣara.... Allahabad: Panini Office, 1918. 440p. (SBH, 21)

e. varṇāśramadharma: social stratification and the "origins" of the caste system

04440 AMBEDKAR, B.R. Who were the Shudras? How they came to be the fourth Varna in the Indo-Aryan society. Bombay: Thackers, 1970. 268p. [Rpt. 1946 ed.]

04441 BASU, J. The role of Āśramas in the life of the ancient Hindus. In JIH 42,3 (1964) 847-76.

04442 BRINKHAUS, H. Die altindischen Mischkastensysteme. Wiesbaden: Steiner, 1978. 232p. (Alt- und neuindische Studien, 19)

04443 DANIÉLOU, A. Les quatre sens de la vie et la structure sociale de l'Inde traditionnelle. Paris: Librairie academique Perrin, 1963. 251p.

04444 DAS, V. A sociological approach to the caste Purāṇas: a case study. In SB 17 (1968) 141-64.

04445 GHOSHAL, U.N. Status of Brāhmaṇas in the Dharmasūtras. In IHQ 23,2 (1947) 83-92.

04446 ______. The status of Śūdras in the Dharmasūtras. In IC 14,1 (1947) 21-27.

04447 GOPAL, L. Economic groups and caste system in ancient India. In JIH 43,3 (1965) 771-81.

04448 HOPKINS, E.W. The social and military position of the ruling caste in ancient India, as represented by the Sanskrit epic; with an appendix on the status of woman. Varanasi: Bharat-Bharati, 1972. 320p. [1st pub. 1889]

04449 JHA, V.N. Varṇasaṁkara in the Dharmasūtras; theory and practice. In JESHO 13,3 (1970) 273-88.

04450 MAITY, A. Note on caste in ancient India. In MI 40,1 (1960) 65-67.

04451 OLIVELLE, P. The notion of āśrama in the Dharmasūtras. In WZKS 18 (1974) 27-35.

04452 PILLAI, K.K. The caste system in the Sangam age. In JIH 40,3 (1962) 513-36.

04453 RUBEN, W. Über die frühesten Stufen der Entwicklung der alt-indischen Śūdras. Berlin: Academie-Verlag, 1965. 59p.

04454 SHARMA, R.S. Śūdras in ancient India (a survey of the Lower Orders down to c. A.D. 500). Delhi: Motilal, 1958. 318p.

04455 THAPAR, R. Social mobility in ancient India with special reference to elite groups. In R.S. Sharma, ed. Indian society: historical probings.... ND: PPH, 1974, 95-123.

04456 UPADHYAY, G.P. Brāhmaṇas in ancient India: a study in the role of the Brāhmaṇa class from c. 200 BC to c. AD 500. ND: Munshiram, 1979. 272p.

3. Domestic Life: Kinship, Marriage, Sexual Life, and the Status of Women

a. Gṛhyasūtras: fundamental texts of household rites and sacraments (saṁskāras)

i. translations

04457 CALAND, W., tr. Altindisches Zauberritual; Probe einer Übersetzung der wichtigsten Theile des Kauśika sūtra. Wiesbaden: M. Säding, 1967. 195p. [Rpt. 1900 ed.]

04458 ______., tr. Jaiminigṛhyasūtra. Lahore: Punjab Sanskrit Book Depot, 1922. 80 + 62p.

04459 GONDA, J., tr. The Savayajñas (Kauśikasūtra 60-68). Amsterdam: North Holland, 1965. 461p. (VKNAW, AL ns 71:2)

04460 OLDENBERG, H., tr. The grihya-sūtras; rules of Vedic domestic ceremonies. Delhi: Motilal, 1967. 2 v., 444, 415. (SBE, 29, 30) [Rpt. 1886-92 ed.]

04461 ROLLAND, P., tr. Un rituel domestique védique: le Varāhagṛhyasūtra. Gap: Ophrys, 1971. 214p. (Pub. universitaires de lettres et sciences humaines d'Aix-en-Provence)

04462 SHARMA, N.N., tr. Aśvalāyana gṛhyasūtram, with Sanskrit commentary of Narāyaṇa. Delhi: Eastern Book Linkers, 1976. 225p.

ii. studies

04463 APTE, V.M. Social and religious life in the Grihya Sutras. Bombay: Popular, 1954. 280p.

04464 CHATTOPADHYAYA, A. Some social aspects in the Āpastambagṛhyasūtra. In IA ser. 3 2,3 (1967) 37-42.

04465 KRISHNA LAL. Mantras employed in the Gṛhyasūtras for placing the fuel sticks in the fire in the upanayana ritual. In JOIB 17,2 (1967) 129-36.

04466 TSUJI, N. The marriage-section of the Āgniveśya-Gṛhyasūtra. In Memoirs of the Res. Dept. of the Toyo Bunko (Tokyo) 19 (1960) 43-77.

b. kinship and marriage

04467 CHATTERJEE, C.K. Studies in the rites and rituals of Hindu marriage in ancient India. Calcutta: SPB, 1978. 372p.

04468 CHATTERJEE, H. Studies in the social background of the forms of marriage in ancient India. Calcutta: SPB, 1972-74. 2 v., 623p.

04469 SENGUPTA, N. Evolution of Hindu marriage, with special reference to rituals, c. 1000 B.C. - A.D. 500. Bombay: Popular, 1965. 191p.

04470 SINGH, S.D. Polyandry in ancient India. ND: Vikas, 1978. 212p.

04471 TRAUTMANN, T.R. Consanguineous marriage in Pali literature. In JAOS 93,2 (1973) 158-80.

04472 ______. Cross-cousin marriage in ancient North India? In his (ed.) Kinship and history in South Asia. Ann Arbor: UMCSSAS, 1974, 61-103. (MPSSA, 7)

04473 WAGLE, N.K. Kinship groups in the Jātakas. In T.R. Trautman, ed. Kinship and history in South Asia. Ann Arbor: UMCSSAS, 1974, 105-57. (MPSSA, 7)

c. the roles and status of women

04474 HART, G.L., III. Woman and the sacred in ancient Tamilnad. In JAS 32,2 (1973) 233-50.

04475 HORNER, I.B. Women under primitive Buddhism: laywomen and almswomen. Delhi: Motilal, 1975. 391p. [Rpt. 1930 ed.]

04476 JAYAL, S. The status of women in the epics. Delhi: Motilal, 1966. 335p.

04477 LAW, B.C. Women in Buddhist literature. Colombo: W.E. Bastian, 1930. 128p.

04478 MEYER, J.J. Sexual life in ancient India: a study in the comparative history of Indian culture. Delhi: Motilal, 1971. 591p. [1st German ed. 1915]

04479 MOTI CHANDRA. The world of courtesans. Delhi: Vikas, 1973. 245p.

04480 NADARAJAH, D. Women in Tamil society: the classical period. Kuala Lumpur: U. of Malaya, 1969. 189p.

04481 TALIM, M. Woman in early Buddhist literature. Bombay: U. of Bombay, 1972. 242p.

d. the Kāmasūtra: manual of erotics and social life, c. 500 A.D.
i. translations of Vātsyāyana's Kāmasūtra

04482 BASU, B.N., tr. Kama-sutra, the Hindu art of love. 12th ed. Calcutta: Medical Book Co., 1955. 197p.

04483 BERGMANN, J.N. Les Kama-Soutra des sages de l'Inde. Paris: Trèfle d'or, 1968. 201p.

04484 BURTON, R.F., tr. The Kama sutra of Vatsyayana. London: Allen & Unwin, 1963. 296p. [1st pub. 1883]

04485 UPADHYAYA, S.C., tr. Kama sutra. Bombay: Taraporevala, 1963. 272p.

ii. studies

04486 CHAKLADAR, H.C. Social life in ancient India: studies in Vatsyayana's Kamasutra. Delhi: Bharatiya, 1976. 212p. [Rpt. 1929 ed.]

04487 FIŠER, I. Indian erotics of the oldest period. Prague: U. Karlova, 1966. 139p.

4. The Tirukkuṟal of Tiruvaḷḷuvar (5th Cent. A.D.?): Classic South Indian Text on Ethics, Polity, and Love, "the Tamil Veda"
a. bibliography

04488 THIRUMALAI MUTHUSWAMY, A. A bibliography on Tirukkural. Madurai: Meenakshi Puththaka Nilayam, 1962. 50p.

b. translations

04489 BALASUBRAMANIAM, K.M., tr. Tirukkuṟal of Tiruvaḷḷuvar. Madras: Manali Lakshmana Mudaliar Specific Endowments, 1962. 69 + 527p.

04490 BHARATI, S., tr. Thirukkural couplets. Madras: SISSWPS, 1971. 270p.

04491 POPE, G.U., tr. The "sacred" Kural of Tiruvalluva-Nāyanār. 2nd ed. Calcutta: YMCA Pub. House, 1958. 424p. [Rpt. 1886 ed.]

04492 POPLEY, H.A., tr. The sacred Kural, or the Tamil Veda of Tiruvaḷḷuvar. 2nd rev. ed. Calcutta: YMCA, 1958. 157p. [1st ed. 1931]

04493 RAJAGOPALACHARI, C., tr. Kural, the great book of Tiruvalluvar. Bombay: BVB, 1965, 200p. [Selections from books 1 & 2]

04494 RAMACHANDRA DIKSHITAR, V.R., tr. Tirukkuṟal of Tiruvaḷḷuvar. Madras: Adyar Library, 1949. 271p.

04495 SREENIVASAN, K. Tirukkural, an ancient Tamil classic. Bombay: BVB, 1969. 139p.

04496 VANMIKANATHAN, G. The Tirukkural; a unique guide to moral, material, and spiritual prosperity. Tiruchirapalli: Tirukkural Prachar Sangh, 1969. 1 v.

c. studies

04497 ARULAPPA, R. Thirukkural, a Christian book? Madras: Meipporul Pub., 1974. 62p.

04498 DEVASENAPATHI, V.A. The ethics of the Tirukkural. In Annals of Oriental Research (Madras) 20,1/2 (1965) 1-46; 21,1 (1966) 47-72. [Srimati Sornamal Endowment lecture]

04499 DURAISWAMY PILLAI, A.S. An introduction to the study of Tiruvalluvar; a lecture. Madurai: Visalakshi Pathipagam, 1961. 115p.

04500 KAMALIAH, K.C. Preface in the Kuṟaḷ: a comparative study of the first forty couplets of the Kural. Madras: M. Seshachalam, 1973. 192p.

04501 MAHARAJAN, S. Tiruvalluvar. ND: Sahitya Akademi, 1979. 89p.

04502 MUTHURAMAN, M. Gita and Kural. Madras: Higginbothams, 1971. 63p.

04503 PURNALINGAM PILLAI, M.S. Critical studies in Kural. Tinnevelly: Bibliotheca, Munnirpallam, 1929. 95p.

04504 SANJEEVI, N., ed. First All-India Tirukkural Research Seminar papers, May 1972. Madras: U. of Madras, 1973. 37 + 154p.

04505 SANKARAN, K. Kamban's treatment of Tirukkural. Madras: Pooram Pub., 1978. 287p.

04506 SASTRY, K.R.R. [Swami RAMANANDA BHARATI] Manu and Thiruvalluvar; a comparative study. Madras: Sangam Pub., 1973. 63p.

04507 Thirumathi Sornamal Endowment lectures on Tirukkural, 1959-60 to 1968-69. Madras: U. of Madras, 1971. 2 v.

4. Education and Learning

04508 ACHYUTHAN, M. Educational practices in Manu, Pāṇini, and Kauṭilya. Trivandrum: College Book House, 1974. 122p.

04509 ALTEKAR, A.S. Education in ancient India. 6th ed., rev. & enl. Varanasi: Nand Kishore, 1965. 347p.

04510 DATTA, B.K. Libraries and librarianship of ancient and medieval India. Delhi: Atma Ram, 1970. 247p.

04511 KEAY, F.E. Ancient Indian education: an inquiry into its origin, development, and ideals. ND: Cosmo, 1980. 191p. [Rpt. 1918 ed.]

04512 MOOKERJI, RADHA KUMUD. Ancient Indian education; Brahmanical and Buddhist. 4th ed. Delhi: Motilal, 1969. 655p. [1st ed. 1947]

04513 NANAVATY, J.J. Educational thought: a critical study (in the perspective of history) of ideas and concepts which shaped the pattern and determined the content of education in ancient and medieval India. Poona: Joshi & Lokhande Prakashan, 1973-. v. 1, 263p.

04514 PARANAVITANA, S. The Mahāvihāra and other ancient seats of learning. In Education in Ceylon. Colombo: Min. of Educ. and Cultural Affairs, 1969. v. 1, 51-60.

04515 SARKAR, S.C. Educational ideas and institutions in ancient India. Patna: Janaki Prakashan, 1979. 195p.

04516 THANI NAYAGAM, X.S. Patterns of studenthood in ancient India. In Pedagogica Historica 9 (1969) 477-506.

04517 ______. The typology of ancient Indian education. In Paedagogica Historica 3,2 (1963) 353-77.

04518 TREHAN, G.L. Learning and libraries in ancient India: a study. Chandigarh: Library Literature House, 1975. 74p. (Library literature in India ser., 2)

5. Urbanization and Town Planning

04519 BEGDE, P.V. Ancient and mediaeval town-planning in India. ND: Sagar Pub., 1978. 245p.

04520 DUTT, B.B. Town planning in ancient India. Delhi: New Asian Pub., 1977. 379p. [Rpt. 1925 ed.]

04521 GHOSH, A. The city in early historical India. Simla: IIAS, 1973. 98p.

04522 PURI, B.N. Cities of ancient India. Meerut: Meenakshi, 1966. 139p.

04523 RAI, J. The rural-urban economy and social changes in ancient India, 300 B.C. to 600 A.D. Varanasi: Bharatiya, 1974. 419p.

04524 RAY, A. Villages, towns and secular buildings in ancient India c. 150 B.C. - c. 350 A.D. Calcutta: KLM, 1964. 159p.

D. History of Science in Ancient India

1. General Studies of Ancient Indian Science

04525 CLARK, W.E. Science. In G.T. Garratt ed. The Legacy of India. Oxford: Clarendon Press, 1937, 335-68.

04526 FILLIOZAT, J. India and scientific exchanges in antiquity. In CHM 1 (1954) 351-71.

04527 ______. La science indienne antique. In R. Taton ed. Histoire generale des sciences. Paris: Presses Universitaires de France, 1957-63, v. 1, 156-83.

04528 MAJUMDAR, RAMESH CHANDRA. Growth of scientific spirit in ancient India. In Science and Culture 18 (1953) 463-72.

04529 WINTER, H.J.J. Science. In A.L. Basham, ed. A cultural history of India. Oxford: Clarendon Press, 1975, 141-61.

2. Astronomy and Astrology, Developed from the Jyotiṣa vedāṅga, and Mathematics
a. general studies, incl. calendrical science

04530 CHAKRAVARTY, A.K. Origin and development of Indian calendrical science. Calcutta: ISPP, 1975. 62p. [1st pub. in ISPP 15,3 (1974) 219-80]

04531 PINGREE, D. Representation of the planets in Indian astrology. In IIJ 8 (1965) 249-67.

04532 SENGUPTA, P.C. Ancient Indian chronology, illustrating some of the most important astronomical methods. Calcutta: U. of Calcutta, 1947. 287p.

b. early astronomer-mathematicians: Āryabhaṭa I (b. 476 AD), and Varāhamihira (c. 505 AD)

04533 CHIDAMBARAM AIYAR, N., tr. The Brihat Jātaka [of Varaha Mihira]. 2nd ed. Madras: Thompson, 1905. 248p.

04534 CLARK, W.E., tr. Āryabhatīya of Āryabhata; an ancient Indian work on mathematics and astronomy. Chicago: UChiP, 1930. 90p.

04535 KERN, H., tr. The Bṛhat Saṁhitā [of Varāha Mihira]. Calcutta: Baptist Mission Press, 1865. [Text in Sanskrit; 64p. introduction in English]

04536 MENON, K.N. Āryabhaṭa, astronomer mathematician. ND: PDMIB, 1977. 64p.

04537 NEUGEBAUER, O. & D. PINGREE. The Pañchasiddhāntika of Varāhamihira. Copenhagen: Munksgaard, 1970-71. 2 pts. (Kongelige Danske Videnskabernes Selskab, Historisk-filologiske Skifter, 6:1)

04538 SHASTRI, AJAY MITRA. Varāhamihira and Bhadrabāhu. In VIJ 12,1/2 (1974) 361-83.

04539 THIBAUT, G. & S. DVIVEDI, tr. The Panchasiddhāntikā: the astronomical work of Varāha Mihira. Varanasi: CSSO, 1968. 336p. (CSS, 68) [1st pub. 1889]

c. ancient Indian geometry, developed from the Śulvasūtras
[see also Chap. Two, VI. B. 2]

04540 BAG, A.K. The knowledge of geometric figures, instruments and units in the Śulbasūtras. In E&W 21,1/2 (1971) 111-19.

04541 DATTA, B.B. The science of the śulba, a study in early Hindu geometry. Calcutta: U. of Calcutta, 1932. 239p.

04542 MILHAUD, G. La géometrie d'Āpastamba. In Revue générale des sciences pures et appliquées 21 (1910) 512-20.

04543 MUELLER, C. Die Mathematik der Śulvasūtra, eine Studie zur Geschichte indischer Mathematik. In Abhandlungen aus dem Mathematischen Seminar der Hamburgischer U. 7 (1929) 173-204.

04544 THIBAUT, G. On the Śulvasūtras. In JASBengal 44 (1875) 227-75.

3. Beginnings of Indic Medicine: Āyurveda and Other Systems
a. general studies

04545 EMMERICK, R.E. Contributions to the study of the Jīvaka-pustaka. In BSOAS 62,2 (1979) 235-43.

04546 HALDAR, J.R. Medical science in Pali literature. Calcutta: Indian Museum, 1977. 72p.

04547 KUTUMBIAH, P. Ancient Indian medicine. Bombay: Orient Longmans, 1962. 225p.

04548 MITRA, J. History of Indian medicine from pre-Mauryan to Kuṣāṇa period. Varanasi: Jyotiralok Prakashan, 1974. 165p.

04549 REHM, K.E. Die Rolle des Buddhismus in der indischen Medizin und das Spitalproblem. Zürich: Juris Druck Verlag, 1969. 57p.

04550 SHARMA, P.V. Indian medicine in the classical age. Varanasi: CSSO, 1972. 265p. (CSS, 85)

04551 SUBBA REDDY, D.V. Glimpses of health and medicine in Mauryan Empire. Hyderabad: Upgraded Dept. of History of Medicine, Osmania Medical College, 1966. 97p.

b. classical texts in translation: the Caraka and Suśruta Saṁhitās (comp. 200 BC-200 AD)

04552 BHISHAGRATNA, K.L., tr. An English translation of the Sushruta Samhita.... Calcutta: the author, 1907-16. 3 v.

04553 CARAKA. The Caraka saṁhitā expounded by the worshipful Ātreya Punarvasu, comp. by the great sage Āgniveśa and redacted by Caraka and Dridhabala. With tr. in Hindi, Gujarati & English by Shree Gulabkunverba Ayurvedic Soc. Jamnagar: 1949. 6 v. [v. 5 running English translation]

04554 ESSER, A.M., tr. Die Ophthalmologie des Suśruta. Leipzig: J.A. Barth, 1934. 83p.

04555 HOERNLE, A.F.R. The Bower Manuscript. Calcutta: Supt. of Govt. Printing, 1893. 240p. + 54pl. (ASI, New imperial ser., 22)

04556 ______. Studies in ancient Indian medicine. In JRAS (1906) 283-302, 915-941; (1907) 1-18; (1908) 997-1027; (1909) 857-93. [mainly on Suśruta & Caraka]

04557 KAVIRATNA, A.C., tr. Charaka-saṁhitā. Calcutta: the author, 1888-1912. 3 v.

04558 RAY, P.R. & H.N. GUPTA. Caraka saṁhitā; a scientific synopsis. ND: Natl. Inst. of Sciences of India, 1965. 120p.

04559 SANKARAN, P.S. Sushruta's contribution to surgery. Varanasi: IndBH, 1976. 154p.

04560 SHARMA, R.K. & B. DASH. Āgniveśa's Caraka saṁhitā. Varanasi: CSSO, 1976-77. 2 v., 619, 597p. (CSS, 94)

E. Foreign Contacts

1. General Studies

04561 ASTHANA, S. History and archaeology of India's contacts with other countries, from earliest times to 300 B.C. Delhi: B.R., 1976. 275p. + 32pl.

04562 CHATTOPADHYAYA, S. The Achaemenids and India. 2nd rev. ed. ND: Munshiram, 1974. 79p.

04563 HOURANI, G.F. Arab seafaring in the Indian Ocean in ancient & early medieval times. Princeton: PUP,

1951. 131p.

04564 PRASAD, P.C. Foreign trade and commerce in ancient India. ND: Abhinav, 1977. 255p.

04565 SIRCAR, D.C. Foreigners in ancient India and Lakṣmī and Sarasvatī in art and literature. Calcutta: U. of Calcutta, 1970. 192p.

04566 THAPAR, R. The image of the barbarians in early India. In CSSH 13,4 (1971) 408-36.

04567 ______. The impact of trade c. 100 BC-300 AD in India. In H. Kruger, ed. Kunwar Mohammed Ashraf.... Delhi: PPH, 1969, 30-38.

04568 THAPLIYAL, U.P. Foreign elements in ancient Indian society, 2nd century BC to 7th century AD. ND: Munshiram, 1979. 194p.

2. The Greco-Roman World

04569 BANERJEE, G.N. Hellenism in ancient India. Calcutta: Butterworth, 1919. 373p.

04570 CASAL, J.M. & G. CASAL. Fouilles de Virampatnam-Arikamedu; rapport de l'Inde et de l'Occident aux environs de l'ère chrétienne. Paris: Impr. nationale, 1949. 70p.

04571 CHAPEKAR, N.M. Ancient India and Greece: a study of their cultural contacts. Delhi: Ajanta, 1977. 92p.

04572 DE JONG, J.W. The discovery of India by the Greeks. In AS/EA 27,2 (1973) 115-142.

04573 DERRETT, J.D.M. Greece and India: the Milindapañha, the Alexander-romance and the Gospels. In ZRGG 19,1 (1967) 33-64.

04574 FILLIOZAT, J. Les relations extérieures de l'Inde. Pondicherry: IFI, 1956-. v. 1, 60p. (Its pub., 2)

04575 LAMOTTE, E. Alexandre et le Bouddhisme. In BEFEO 44 (1947-51) 147-62.

04576 ______. Du quelques influences Grecques et Scythes sur le Buddhisme. In Académie des inscriptions et belles lettres, Comptes-rendus des séances (1956) 458-504.

04577 MCCRINDLE, J.W., tr. The invasion of India by Alexander the Great, as described by Arrian, Q. Curtius, Diodoros, Plutarch, and Justin.... NY: Barnes & Noble, 1969. 432p. [New ed., 1st pub. 1896]

04578 MEILE, P. Les Yavanas dans l'Inde Tamoule. In JA 232,1 (1940-41) 85-123.

04579 PEIRIS, E. Greek and Roman contacts with Ceylon. In CHJ 10,1-4 (1960-61) 8-30.

04580 RAWLINSON, H.G. Intercourse between India and the western world, from the earliest times to the fall of Rome. Delhi: Rai Book Service, 1977. 196p.

04581 WARMINGTON, R.H. The commerce between the Roman Empire and India. 2nd ed., rev. and enl. Delhi: Vikas, 1974. 417p. [1st pub. 1928]

04582 WHEELER, R.E.M. Arikamedu: an Indo-Roman trading station. In AI 2 (1946) 17-124.

04583 ______. Flames over Persepolis: turning-point in history. NY: Reynal, 1968. 180p.

3. Southeast and East Asia

04584 CHHABRA, B.C. Expansion of Indo-Aryan culture during Pallava rule, as evidenced by inscriptions. Delhi: Munshiram, 1965. 137p.

04585 CHRISTIE, A. The provenance and chronology of the early Indian cultural influence in South-East Asia. In H.B. Sarkar, ed. R.C. Majumdar felicitation volume. Calcutta: KLM, 1970, 1-14.

04586 NILAKANTA SASTRI, K.A. The beginnings of intercourse between India and China. In IHQ 14,2 (1938) 380-87.

IV. GENERAL STUDIES OF ANCIENT INDIC RELIGION AND PHILOSOPHY, AND OF SOME MINOR TRADITIONS

A. General Studies: Śramanas (Buddhists, Jains, and other Unorthodox Sects) in Conflict with Vedic Brahmanism

04587 BANERJEE, P. Early Indian religions. Delhi: Vikas, 1973. 241p.

04588 DAHLQUIST, A. Megasthenes and Indian religion: a study in motives and types. Delhi: Motilal, 1977. 315p. [Rpt. 1962 ed.]

04589 GONDA, J. Selected studies, v. 4: History of ancient Indian religion. [presented to the author by the staff of the Oriental Institute, Utrecht Univ.] Leiden: Brill, 1975. 540p.

04590 JAINI, P. Śramanas: their conflict with Brahminical society. In J. Elder, ed. Chapters in Indian civilization. Dubuque, IA: Kendall/Hunt, 1970, v. 1, 39-81.

04591 PANDE, G.C. Śramana tradition; its history and contribution to Indian culture. Ahmedabad: L.D. Inst. of Indology, 1978. 76p.

04592 SCHRADER, F.O. VON. Über den Stand der indischen Philosophie zur Zeit Mahāviras und Buddhas. Leipzig: 1902. 68p.

04593 THAPAR, R. Ethics, religion, and social protest in the first millennium B.C. in northern India. In her Ancient Indian social history. ND: Orient Longmans, 1978, 40-62. [1st pub. in Daedalus 104,2 (1975) 119-33]

B. Materialists: The Cārvāka or Lokāyata

04594 CHATTOPADHYAYA, D.P. Lokayata, a study in ancient Indian materialism. ND: PPH, 1959. 696p.

04595 KOLLER, J.M. Skepticism in early Indian thought. In PEW 27,2 (1977) 155-64.

04596 SHASTRI, D.R. Charvaka philosophy. Calcutta: Purogami Prakashani, 1967. 52p.

04597 ______. Materialists, sceptics, and agnostics. In Cultural Heritage of India. Calcutta: RMIC, 1953, v. 3, 168-83.

04598 ______. A short history of Indian materialism, sensationalism and hedonism. Calcutta: Calcutta Book Co., 1930. 48p.

C. Ājīvikas: an Ascetic Śramana Order Similar to Jainism

04599 BASHAM, A.L. History and doctrines of the Ājīvikas, a vanished Indian religion. London: Luzac, 1951. 304p.

D. The Apostle Thomas and the Beginnings of Indian Christianity

04600 CHERIYAN, C.V. A history of Christianity in Kerala, from the Mission of St. Thomas to the arrival of Vasco Da Gama (A.D. 52-1498). Kottayam: Kerala Hist. Soc., 1973. 163p.

04601 FARQUHAR, J.N. The apostle Thomas in North India. In JRLB 10,1 (1926) 80-111.

04602 ______. The apostle Thomas in South India. In JRLB 11,1 (1927) 20-50.

04603 GEORGE, V.C. Apostolate and martyrdom of St. Thomas. Bombay: Society of St. Paul, 1969. 193p.

04604 HAMBYE, E.R. Some eastern testimonies concerning early and medieval Christianity in India. In Indian history congress, Proceedings (1958) 582-590.

04605 MEDLYCOTT, A.E. India and the Apostle Thomas; an inquiry with a critical analysis of the Actae Thomae. London: D. Nutt, 1905. 303p.

04606 PERUMALIL, A.C. The apostles in India. 2nd enl. ed. Patna: Xavier Teachers' Training Inst., 1971. 234p.

V. RELIGIO-PHILOSOPHICAL TRADITIONS: FROM BRAHMANISM TO HINDUISM

A. The Epics: The Mahābhārata and the Rāmāyaṇa

1. General Studies Covering Both the Mahābhārata and the Rāmāyaṇa

04607 DE JONG, J.W. Recent Russian publications on the Indian epic. In ALB 39 (1975) 1-42.

04608 HOPKINS, E.W. Epic mythology. Varanasi: IndBH, 1968. 277p. [Rpt. 1915 ed.]

04609 KANE, P.V. The two epics. In ABORI 47 (1967) 11-58.

04610 KARMARKAR, A.P. Religion and philosophy of the epics. In Cultural Heritage of India. Calcutta: RMIC, 1962, v. 2, 80-94.

04611 PUSALKER, A.D. Studies in the Epics and Purāṇas. Bombay: BVB, 1963. 234p. [112-230 reviews scholarship on Epics and Purāṇas to 1963]

04612 RUBEN, W. Die homerischen und die altindischen Epen. Berlin: Akademie-Verlag, 1975. 62p.

04613 SARMA, B. Ethico-literary values of the two great epics of India: an ethical evaluation of the Mahabharata and the Ramayana. ND: Oriental, 1978. 248p.

2. The Mahābhārata of Vyāsa (including the Bhagavadgītā): India's Great Epic Recounting the Wars of the Pāṇḍavas and Kauravas

a. bibliography and reference

04614 LAL, P. An annotated Mahabharata bibliography. Calcutta: Writers Workshop, 1967. 31p.

04615 LONG, J.B. The Mahābhārata: a select annotated bibliography. Ithaca, NY: South Asia Program, Cornell U., 1974. 93p. (South Asia occ. papers and theses, 3)

04616 O'FLAHERTY, W.D. [review of J.A.B. van Buitenen, tr., The Mahābhārata]: In Religious Studies Review 4,1 (1978), 19-27. [bibl. essay covering much recent scholarship]

04617 RICE, E.P. The Mahābhārata: analysis and index. London: OUP, 1934. 112p.

04618 SORENSEN, S. An index to the names in the Mahābhārata with short explanations and a concordance to the Bombay and Calcutta editions and P.G. Roy's translation. Delhi: Motilal, 1978. 807p. [1st ed. 1904]

04619 SUKTHANKAR, V.S. Prolegomena. In his The Mahābhārata, for the first time critically edited. Poona: BORI, 1933, v. 1, i-cx.

b. complete translations

04620 DUTT, M.N., tr. A prose English translation of the Mahabharata. Calcutta: H.C. Dass, 1895-1905. 5 v.

04621 FAUCHE, H., tr. Le Mahābhārata; poème épique de Krishna-Dwaipāyana, plus commément appelé Veda-Vyasa. Paris: B. Duprat, 1863-99. 12 v.

04622 LAL, P., tr. The Mahabharata. Calcutta: Writers Workshop, 1968-.

04623 ROY, P.C., tr. The Mahabharata of Krishna-Dwaipayana Vyasa. Calcutta: Oriental Pub., 1962. 12 v. [Rpt. of 1887-96 ed.]

04624 VAN BUITENEN, J.A.B., tr. The Mahābhārata. Chicago: UChiP, 1973-. [3 v. to 1978]

c. abridged translations, selections, and re-tellings from the MBh.(other than Bhagavadgītā)

04625 ARNOLD, E., tr. Indian idylls. Boston: Roberts Brothers, 1883. 318p.

04626 BALLIN, L., tr. Le Mahābhārata; IX Çalyaparva et Livres X, XI, XII. Paris: E. Leroux, 1899. 2 v. [continuation of T. Fauche translation]

04627 BUCK, W. Mahabharata. Berkeley: UCalP, 1973. 417p.

04628 DUTT, R.C. The Mahābhārata condensed into English verse. London: M.M. Dent, 1898.

04629 HOPKINS, E.W. Legends of India. New Haven: YUP, 1928. 193p.

04630 MACFIE, J.M. The Mahābhārata, a summary. Madras: CLS, 1921. 265p. [based on M.N. Dutt translation]

04631 NARASIMHAN, C.V., tr. Mahabharata; an English version based on selected verses. NY: ColUP, 1965. 254p.

04632 RAJAGOPALACHARI, C. Mahabharata. Bombay: BVB, 1977. 332p.

04633 SRINIVASA RAO, C.V. Mahabharata (abridged). Bangalore: Bangalore Press, 1956-61. 3 v., 240, 301, 416p.

04634 SUBRAMANIAM, K., tr. Mahabharata. 2nd ed. Bombay: BVB, 1971. 766p. [1st pub. 1965]

d. selected studies

04635 AUTRAN, C. L'épopée Indoue; étude de l'arrière-fonds ethnographique et religieux. Paris: Éditions Denoël, 1946. 408p.

04636 DUMEZIL, G. The destiny of a king. Tr. by A. Hiltebeitel. Chicago: UChiP, 1973. 170p.

04637 ______. Mythe et Épopée. Paris: Gallimard, 1968-73. 3 v., 653, 406, 366p.

04638 GEHRTS, H. Mahābhārata: das Geschehen und seine Bedeutung. Bonn: Bouvier, 1975. 295p.

04639 GOLDMAN, R.P. Gods, priests, and warriors: the Bhṛgus of the Mahābhārata. NY: ColUP, 1977. 195p.

04640 HELD, G.J. The Mahābhārata; an ethnological study. London: K. Paul, Trench, Trubner, 1935. 348p.

04641 HILTEBEITEL, A. The burning of the forest myth. In B.L. Smith, ed. Hinduism.... Leiden: Brill, 1976, 208-24. (SHR, 33)

04642 ______. The Mahābhārata and Hindu eschatology. In HR 12,2 (1972) 95-135.

04643 ______. The ritual of battle: Kṛishṇa in the Mahābhārata. Ithaca: CornellUP, 1976. 368p.

04644 HOLTZMANN, A., JR. Das Mahābhārata und seine Theile. Kiel: C.F. Haesler, 1892-95. 4 v.

04645 HOPKINS, E.W. The great epic of India; its character and origin. Calcutta: Punthi Pustak, 1969. 485p. [Rpt. 1901 ed.]

04646 JAIN, R.C. Jaya: the original nucleus of Mahabharat. Delhi: Agam, 1979. 375p.

04647 KLAES, N. Conscience and consciousness: ethical problems of Mahabharata. Bangalore: Dharmaram College, 1975. 144p.

04648 MEHTA, M.M. The Mahābhārata - a study of the critical edition [with special reference to the Suparṇākhyāna of the Ādiparvan]. In BV 31 (1971) 67-118.

04649 SCHEUER, J. Śiva dans le Mahābhārata: l'histoire d'Ambā/Śikhaṇḍin. In Puruṣārtha 2 (1975) 67-86.

04650 SHARMA, R.K. Elements of poetry in the Mahabharata. Berkeley: UCalP, 1964. 175p.

04651 SINHA, J.P. The Mahabharata: a literary study. ND: Meharchand Lachhmandas, 1977. 127p.

04652 SMITH, M.C. The Mahabharata's core. In JOAS 95 (1975) 479-82.

04653 SUKTHANKAR, V.S. The Bhṛgus and the Bhārata: a text-historical study. In ABORI 18 (1944) 1-76.

04654 ______. On the meaning of the Mahābhārata. Bombay: Asiatic Soc. of Bombay, 1957. 146p. (Its Monograph, 4)

04655 VAN NOOTEN, B.A.A.J. The Mahābhārata; attributed to Kṛṣṇa Dvaipāyana Vyāsa. NY: Twayne, 1971. 153p.

c. translations and studies of the Harivaṁśa, an appendix to the MBh., giving the genealogy of Kṛṣṇa

04656 DUTT, M.N., tr. A prose English translation of Harivamsha. Calcutta: H.C. Dass, Elysium Press, 1897. 951p.

04657 LANGLOIS, S.A., tr. Harivansa, ou, Histoire de la famille de Hari.... Paris: Oriental Translation Fund, 1823-35. 2 v. (Oriental Translation Fund, 36)

04658 THOREAU, H.D., tr. The transmigration of the seven Brahmans; a translation of the Harivansa of Langlois. Ed. by A. Christy. NY: W.E. Rudge, 1932. 66p.

3. The Bhagavadgītā: the Quintessence of Hinduism and Central Scripture of the Viṣṇu-Kṛṣṇa Cult

a. translations

04659 ARNOLD, E., tr. The song celestial; or, Bhagavad-gita. Boston: Roberts Bros., 1885. 185p.

04660 BESANT, A., tr. The Bhagavad-gita; the Lord's song. 11th Adyar ed. Madras: TPH, 1967. 260p.

04661 BHAKTIVEDANTA SWAMI, A.C., tr. Bhagavad-gītā, as it is. NY: Bhaktivedanta Book Trust, 1975. 330p.+28pl.

04662 BOLLE, K.W., tr. The Bhagavadgītā: a new translation. Berkeley: UCalP, 1979. 318p.

04663 DEUTSCH, E., tr. The Bhagavad Gītā. NY: Holt, Rinehart & Winston, 1968. 192p.

04664 EDGERTON, F., tr. The Bhagavadgītā. Cambridge: HUP, 1944. 2 v. (HOS, 38, 39)

04665 MAHADEVA SASTRY, A., tr. The Bhagavad Gita: with the commentary of Sri Sankaracharya. 7th ed. Madras: Samata Books, 1977. 522p. [1st ed. 1918]

04666 MASCARO, J., tr. The Bhagavad gītā. Baltimore: Penguin Books, 1972. 121p.

04667 NIKHILANANDA, Swami, tr. The Bhagavad Gita. NY: Ramakrishna-Vivekananda Center, 1944. 386p.

04668 PRABHAVANANDA, Swami & C. ISHERWOOD, tr. The Song of God, Bhagavad-gita. London: Dent, 1975. 187p. [1st ed. 1944]

04669 RADHAKRISHNAN, S., tr. The Bhagavad Gita. NY: Harper, 1948. 388p.

04670 SARGEANT, W., tr. The Bhagavad Gita. NY: Doubleday, 1978. 751p.

04671 SIVANANDA, Swami, tr. The Bhagavad Gita. 7th ed. Sivanandanagar: Divine Life Soc., 1969. 630p.

04672 TILAK, B.G. Srimad-Bhagavadgita-Rahasya, or Karma-Yoga-Sastra. Tr. into English by B.S. Sukhtankar from Tilak's Marathi translation of the original Sanskrit. 2nd ed. Poona: Tilak Bros., 1965. 1220p. [1st ed. 1936]

04673 VAN BUITENEN, J.A.B. The Bhagavadgītā in the Mahābhārata. Chicago: UChiP, 1981.

04674 ZAEHNER, R.C., tr. Bhagavad-Gita, with commentary based on the original sources. London: OUP, 1969. 480p.

b. selected studies

04675 AGRAPURA, J.G. The upside-down tree of the Bhagavadgita, Ch. 15. In Numen 22,2 (1975) 131-44.

04676 BAZAZ, P.N. The role of Bhagavad Gita in Indian history. ND: Sterling, 1975. 747p.

04677 BHAVE, V. Talks on the Gita. 4th ed. Varanasi: Sarva Seva Sangh Prakashan, 1970. 254p.

04678 DATE, V.H. Brahma-yoga of the Gītā. ND: Munshiram, 1971. 647p.

04679 DESHPANDE, M.S. Śrī Gītā-sāra = Essence of the Gītā. 3rd ed. Bombay: BVB, 1977. 77p.

04680 DIVATIA, H.V. The art of life in the Bhagavad-gita. 5th ed. Bombay: BVB, 1970. 155p.

04681 FEUERSTEIN, G. Introduction to the Bhagavad-gītā: its philosophy and cultural setting. London: Rider, 1974. 191p.

04682 GANDHI, M.K. The gospel of selfless action, or the Gita according to Gandhi. Tr. by M.H. Desai. Ahmedabad: Navajivan, 1951. 390p.

04683 GHOSE, A. Essays on the Gītā. Pondicherry: Sri Aurobindo Birth Centenary Library, 1970. 575p. [1st pub. 1922]

04684 IMAM, SYED MEHDI. The drama of Prince Arjuna; being a revaluation of the central theme of the Bhagvad Gita. Delhi: Motilal, 1973. 118p.

04685 KAVEESHWAR, G.W. The ethics of the Gītā. Delhi: Motilal, 1971. 316p.

04686 KHAIR, G.S. Quest of the original Gita. Bombay: Somaiya, 1969. 248p.

04687 KOSAMBI, D.D. Social and economic aspects of the Bhagavad Gita. In JESHO 4 (1961) 198-224. [revised in his Myth and reality. Bombay: Popular, 1962, 12-41]

04688 LAJPAT RAI, Lala. The message of the Bhagawad Gita. Bombay: R.M. Kapadia, 1921. 68p.

04689 LARSON, G.J. The Bhagavad Gita as cross-cultural process: toward an analysis of the social locations of a religious text. In JAAR 43,4 (1975) 651-70.

04690 MAINKAR, T.G. A comparative study of the commentaries on the Bhagavadgītā. Delhi: Motilal, 1969. 65p.

04691 PARADKAR, M.D., ed. Studies in the Gita. Bombay: Popular, 1970. 444p.

04692 RANADE, R.D. The Bhagavadgita as a philosophy of God-realization; being a clue through the labyrinth of modern interpretations. Bombay: BVB, 1965. 287p.

04693 ROY, S.C. The Bhagavad Gītā and modern scholarship. London: Luzac, 1941. 263p.

04694 SHARAN, M.K. The Bhagavad-gita and Hindu sociology. Delhi: Bharat Bharati Bhandar, 1977. 144p.

4. The Rāmāyaṇa of Vālmīki: the Story of Rāma, King and Avatāra

a. bibliography and reference

04695 BHATT, G.H., ed. Introduction. In The Vālmīki-Rāmāyaṇa, critically edited for the first time. Baroda: Oriental Inst., 1960-72. v. 1, p. i-xlix. [incl. concordance to other eds.; each of 7 v. has English intro.]

04696 ______. Pada-index of the Vālmīki-Rāmāyaṇa. Baroda: Oriental Int., 1961-66. 2 v., 1354p. (GOS, 129, 153)

04697 GORE, N.A. Bibliography of the Ramayana. Poona: the author, 1943. 99p.

b. complete translations

04698 DUTT, M.N., tr. The Ramayana. Calcutta: Girish Chandra Chackravarti, 1890-94. 7 v.

04699 GRIFFITH, R.T.H., tr. The Ramayana of Valmiki. 3rd ed. Varanasi: CSSO, 1963. 576p. (CSS, 29) [1st pub. 1870-89]

04700 SEN, M.L., tr. The Ramayana. Calcutta: Oriental Pub. Co., 1927. 3 v.

04701 SHASTRI, H.P. The Ramayana. London: Shanti Sadan, 1957-59. 3 v.

c. abridged translations, selections, and retellings

04702 BUCK, W. Ramayana : [King Rama's way]. Berkeley: UCalP, 1976. 432p.

04703 CHANDRASEKHARA AIYER, N. Ramayana. Bombay: BVB, 1954. 234p.

04704 COLLIS, M. Quest for Sita.... NY: J. Day, 1947. 162p.

04705 MENEN, A. The Ramayana. NY: Scribner, 1954. 276p.

04706 NARAYAN, R.K. The Ramayana: a shortened modern prose version of the Indian epic. NY: Viking, 1972. 171p.

04707 RAJAGOPALACHARI, C. Ramayana. 7th ed. Bombay: BVB, 1971. 320p.

04708 SRINIVASA RAO, C.V., tr. The Ramayana. Bangalore: Bangalore Press, 1970. 412p.

d. studies

04709 ALL INDIA RAMAYANA CONFERENCE, TRIVANDRUM, 1973. Sree Rama Sahasranama Dasakoti Archana festival; All India Ramayana Conference special souvenir, 1972-1973. Trivandrum: Sree Seetha Ramabhaktha Sabha, 1973. 242p.

04710 ANTOINE, R. Rama and the bards: epic memory in the Ramayana. Calcutta: Writers Workshop, 1975. 114p.

04711 ATHAVALE, P.V. Valmiki Ramayana: a study. Bombay: Associated Advertisers & Printers, 1976. 209p.

04712 BROCKINGTON, J.L. Religious attitudes in Vālmīki's Rāmāyaṇa. In JRAS (1976) 108-29.

04713 BULCKE, C. The Rāmāyaṇa: its history and character. In PO 25 (1960) 36-60.

04714 CHATTERJI, S.K. The Rāmāyaṇa: its character, genesis, history, expansion, and exodus: a resume. Calcutta: Prajna, 1978. 27 + 46p.

04715 DESAI, S.N. Rāmāyaṇa - an instrument of historical contact and cultural transmission between India and Asia. In JAS 30,1 (1970) 5-20.

04716 GHURYE, G.S. The legacy of the Ramayana. Bombay: Popular, 1979. 280p.

04717 GUPTA, P.H. My studies in the Ramayana. Visakhapatnam, 1968. 240p.

04718 PANDURANGA RAO, I. Women in Valmiki. Hyderabad: Andhra Mahila Sabha, 1978. 143p.

04719 PATHAK, M.M. Similes in the Rāmāyaṇa. Baroda: MSUB, 1968. 314p.

04720 RAGHAVAN, V. The greater Ramayana. Varanasi: All-India Kashiraj Trust, 1973. 91p.

04721 ______. The Ramayana in Greater India. Surat: South Gujarat U., 1975. 274p. + 14 pl.

04722 ______. Ramayana - Triveni. Madras: Ramayana Pub. House, 1970. 69p.

04723 ______. The two brothers, Rama and Lakshmana. Madras: Raghavan, 1976. 44p.

04724 RAMASWAMI NAICKER, E.V. The Ramayana: a true reading. 2nd ed. Trichy: Periyar Self-Respect Propaganda Inst. Pub., 1972. 68p.

04725 SANKALIA, H.D. Ramayana: myth or reality? ND: PPH, 1973. 86p.

04726 SEN, N. Comparative studies in oral epic and the Vālmīki Rāmāyaṇa: a report on the Bālākaṇḍa. In JAOS 86 (1966) 397-409.

04727 SHARMA, R. A socio-political study of the Vālmīki Rāmāyaṇa. Delhi: Motilal, 1971. 473p.

04728 SUBRAMANIA AIYAR, N. The concept of tapas in Valmiki Ramayana. Madras: Samskrita Academy, 1977. 21p.

04729 THAPAR, R. Exile and the kingdom: some thoughts on the Rāmāyaṇa. Bangalore: Mythic Society, 1978. 43p.

04730 WAGLE, N.K. A study of kinship groups in the Rāmāyaṇa of Vālmīki. In G. Kurian, ed. The family in India: a regional view. The Hague: Mouton, 1974, 17-42.

B. The Emergence of Theistic Hinduism: From Communal Ritual to Personal Devotion: From Yajña to Pūjā

1. General Studies

04731 AGRAWALA, V.S. Ancient Indian folk cults. Varanasi: Prithvi Prakashan, 1970. 216p.

04732 BANERJEA, J.N. Religion in art and archaeology: Vaiṣhṇavism and Śaivism. Lucknow: U. of Lucknow, 1968. 134p.

04733 BHAGABAT KUMAR, Sastri. The bhakti cult in ancient India. Calcutta: B. Banerjee, 1922[?]. 411p.

04734 CHATTOPADYAYA, S. Evolution of Hindu sects up to the time of Śaṁkarācārya. ND: Munshiram, 1970. 216p.

04735 DANDEKAR, R.N. Vaiṣṇavism and Śaivism. In his (ed.) Ramakrishna Gopal Bhandarkar as an Indologist. Poona: BORI, 1976, 21-111.

04736 ESNOUL, A.-M. Le courant affectif a l'intérieur du brahmanisme ancien. In BEFEO 48,1 (1954) 141-207.

04737 GONDA, J. Visnuism and Sivaism: a comparison. London: Athlone, 1970. 228p.

04738 GOSWAMI, B.K. The Bhakti cult in ancient India. 2nd ed. Varanasi: CSSO, 1965. 411p. (CSS, 52)

2. Early Worship of Śiva
a. general studies of early Śaivism

04739 BANERJEE, P. Some aspects of the early history of Saivism. In IAC 14,3 (1965) 215-31.

04740 NANDIMATH, S.C. Saivism in the Vedic, epic and Pauranika periods. In JKU(H) 12 (1968) 1-21.

04741 RAJAMANIKKAM, M. Śaivism in the pre-Pallava period. In TC 5 (1956) 328-39.

04742 SADANANDA, Swami. Origin and early history of Śaivism in South India. Madras: U. of Madras, 1974. 484p. (Its Hist. ser., 6) [Rpt. 1939 ed.]

04743 SUBRAMANIAM, K.R. The origin of Śaivism and its history in the Tamil land. In JMU (1929) suppl., 1-82.

b. the Śaiva-āgamas: basic Sanskrit texts held to be the Word of Śiva and equal in authority to the Vedas

04744 ARUNACHALAM, M. The Śaiva Āgamas. In Śaiva Siddhānta 3,2 (1968) 90-112.

04745 ______. Worship in the Agamas. In Śaiva Siddhānta 5,3-4 (1970) 115-64.

04746 BHATT, N.R. Analyse du Pūrvakāmikāgama. In BEFEO 64 (1977) 1-38.

04747 BRUNNER, H. Analyse du Kiraṇāgama. In JA 253 (1965) 309-28.

04748 ______. Importance de la littérature āgamique pour l'étude des religions vivantes de l'Inde. In IT 3/4 (1975-76) 107-24.

04749 FILLIOZAT, J. Introduction; les Āgama Civaites. In N.R. Bhatt, ed. Rauravagama. Pondicherry: IFI, 1961, v. 1, i-xv.

04750 GNOLI, R. Gli Āgama Scivaiti nell'India settentrionale. In IT 1 (1973) 61-69.

04751 GONDA, J. The Śivaite Āgama literature [and] The individual Agamas. In his Medieval religious literature in Sanskrit. Wiesbaden: Harrassowitz, 1977, 163-79, 180-215. (HIL, 2:1)

04752 NANDIMATH, S.C. Śaivāgamas: their literature and theology. In JKU(H) 6 (1962) 1-34; 7 (1962) 1-48.

04753 Temples and Āgamas. In BITCM (1974) pt. 2, 185-229. [seminar report]

c. the Pāśupatas, a Śaiva ascetic order

04754 BANERJEA, J.N. Lakulīśa - the founder or the systematiser of the Pāśupata Order. In Indian History Congress, Proc. of the 14th session, Jaipur, 1951, 32-36.

04755 BHANDARKAR, D.R., ed. An Ekliṅgjī stone inscription and the origin and history of the Lakulīśa sect. In JBBRAS 22 (1904-7) 151-65.

04756 ______. Lakulīśa. In ASI annual report (1906-7) 179-92.

04757 CHAKRABORTI, H., tr. Pāśupata sūtram, with Panchārtha-Bhāṣya of Kaundinya...with an introduction on the history of Śaivism in India. Calcutta: Academic Pub., 1970. 223p.

04758 HARA, M. Nakulīśa-Paśupata-Darśanam. In IIJ 2 (1958) 8-32.

04759 INGALLS, D.H. Cynics and Pāśupatas: the seeking of dishonor. In Harvard Theological R. 55 (1962) 281-98.

04760 MAHALINGAM, T.V. The Pāśupatas in the South. In JIH 27 (1949) 43-53.

04761 PANIGRAHI, K.C. Sculptural representations of Lakulisa and other Pasupata teachers. In JIH 38 (1960) 635-43.

04762 SCHULTZ, F.A. Die philosophisch-theologischen Lehren des Pāśupata-Systems nach den Pañcārthabhāṣya und der Rātnaṭīka. Walldorf-Hessen: Verlag fur Orientkunde, 1958. 68p. (Beiträge zur Sprach- und Kulturgeschichte des Orients, 10)

04763 SRIVASTAVA, V.C. The antiquity of the Pasupata sect. In K.C. Chattopadhyaya memorial volume. Allahabad: Dept. of Ancient Hist., Culture and Archaeol., 1975, 109-25.

3. Early Worship of Viṣṇu
a. general studies of early Vaiṣṇavism

04764 DANDEKAR, R.N. The beginnings of Vaiṣṇavism. In IT 3/4 (1975-76) 169-86.

04765 GONDA, J. Aspects of early Vishṇuism. 2nd ed. Delhi: Motilal, 1969. 270p.

04766 ______. Vedic cosmology and Viṣṇuite bhakti. In IT 5 (1977) 85-112.

04767 JAISWAL, S. The origin and development of Vaiṣṇavism: Vaiṣṇavism from 200 BC to AD 500. Delhi: Munshiram, 1967. 266p.

04768 RAMANUJAM, B.V. History of Vaishnavism in South India up to Ramanuja. Annamalainagar: Annamalai U., 1973. 271p.

04769 RAYCHAUDHURI, H.C. Materials for the study of the early history of the Vaishnava sect. ND: OBRC, 1975. 146p.

04770 SIRCAR, D.C. Early history of Vaiṣṇavism. In Cultural Heritage of India. Calcutta: RMIC, 1956, v. 4, 108-45.

04771 SOLOMON, T.J. Early Vaiṣṇava Bhakti and its autochthonous heritage. In HR 10,1 (1970) 32-48.

b. the Bhāgavata Dharma: the rise of bhakti ("devotion")

04772 SINHA, J.N. Bhāgavata religion: the cult of Bhakti. In Cultural Heritage of India. Calcutta: RMIC, 1956, v. 4, 146-59.

04773 VAUDEVILLE, C. Evolution of love-symbolism in Bhāgavatism. In JAOS 82 (1962) 31-40.

04774 VYAS, R.N. The Bhāgavata bhakti cult and three Advaita ācāryas, Saṅkara, Rāmānuja, and Vallabha. Delhi: Nag, 1977. 240p.

c. the Pāñcarātra saṁhitās/āgamas

04775 APTE, P.P. Pāñcarātra: name and origin. In R.N. Dandekar, ed. CASS studies, no. 2. Poona: U. of Poona, 1974, 83-110. (CASSP, E:3)

04776 BHATT, S.R. The philosophy of Pancharatra: Advaitic approach. Madras: Ganesh, 1968. 136p.

04777 ______. Why Pāñcarātra was condemned as non-Brahmanic. In IHQ 39,1/2 (1963) 27-37.

04778 ESNOUL, A.-M. Padmatantra. In IT 3/4 (1975-76) 223-32.

04779 GONDA, J. Medieval religious literature in Sanskrit. Wiesbaden: Harrassowitz, 1977. 316p. (HIL 2:1) [chaps. 4-8, p. 39-139, cover Pāñcarātra Samhitās]

04780 GUPTA, S., tr. Lakṣmitantra. A Pāñcarātra text. Leiden: Brill, 1972. 398p.

04781 KRISHNASWAMI AIYANGAR, S., tr. Parama Saṁhitā, of the Pāñcharātra. Baroda: Oriental Inst., 1940. 483p. (GOS, 86)

04782 RAGHAVAN, V. The name Pāñcarātra: with an analysis of the Sanatkumāra-Saṁhita in manuscript. In JAOS 85 (1965) 73-79.

04783 SCHRADER, F.O. Introduction to the Pāñcarātra and the Ahirbudhnya saṁhitā. Madras: Adyar Library and Res. Centre, 1973. 199p. (Adyar Library series, 5) [1st pub. 1915]

04784 SMITH, H.D. A descriptive bibliography of the printed texts of the Pāñcarātrāgama. Baroda: Oriental Inst., 1975-. v. 1, 560p. (GOS, 158)

04785 ______. The Smith āgama collection: Sanskrit books and manuscripts relating to Pāñcarātra studies: a descriptive catalogue. Syracuse, NY: Maxwell School of Citizenship & Public Affairs, Syracuse U., 1978. (Foreign and Comparative Studies/South Asian special pub., 2)

04786 ______. The "Three Gems" of the Pāñcarātra Canon - a critical appraisal. In C.J. Bleeker, ed. Ex Orbe Religionum. Leiden: Brill, 1972, 42-51.

04787 ______. A typological survey of definitions: the name "Pāñcarātra." In JORM 34-35 (1973) 102-17.

04788 VAN BUITENEN, J.A.B. The name "Pāñcarātra." In HR 1 (1962) 291-99.

d. the Vaikhānasas: insistence on ritual

04789 GONDA, J. Vaikhānasa literature. In his Medieval religious literature in Sanskrit. Wiesbaden: Harrassowitz, 1977, 140-52. (HIL, 2:1)

04790 ______. Some notes on the use of Vedic mantras in the ritual texts of the Vaikhānasas. In IIJ 14 (1972) 1-31.

04791 GOUDRIAAN, T. Kāśyapa's Book of Wisdom, a ritual handbook of the Vaikhānasas. The Hague: Mouton, 1965.

04792 ______. Vaikhānasa daily worship according to the handbooks of Atri, Bhṛgu, Kāśyapa, and Marīci. In IIJ 12,3 (1970) 162-215. [Tamil & Telugu Vaiṣṇava Brāhmans]

C. The Ṣaḍdarśana: the "Six (Orthodox) Systems" of Hindu Philosophy

1. General Studies of and Comparisons Among the Six Āstika Systems

04793 BERNARD, T. Hindu philosophy. NY: Philosophical Library, 1947. 207p.

04794 COWELL, E.B. & A.E. GOUGH, tr. The Sarva-darśana-saṁgraha; or, review of the different systems of Hindu philosophy. London: K. Paul, Trench, Trubner, 1914. 281p.

04795 MÜLLER, F.M. The six systems of Indian philosophy. 4th ed. Varanasi: CSSO, 1971. 478p. (CSS, 16) [1st pub. 1894]

04796 RAGHAVAN, V., ed. Founders of philosophy; Kapila, Patañjali, Kaṇāda, Gautama, Jaimini, Bādarāyana. ND: PDMIB, 1975. 84p.

04797 SEN GUPTA, A. Essays on Sāṁkhya and other systems of Indian philosophy. Rev. & enl. ed. Allahabad: M.R. Sen, 1977. 351p.

2. Sāṁkhya, attrib. to Kapila (Pre-6th Cent. BC): Duality of Matter and Spirit, Prakṛti-Puruṣa
a. translations of the Sāṁkhya Kārikā ("verses on sāṁkhya") of Īśvara Kṛṣṇa (3rd cent. AD?) and other texts

04798 COLEBROOKE, H.T. & H.H. WILSON, tr. The Sāṅkhya Kārikā, with the Bhāṣhya or commentary of Gauṛapāda. Oxford: Oriental Translation Fund, 1837. 260p.

04799 ESNOUL, A.-M., tr. Les strophes du Sāṁkhya, avec le commentaire de Gauḍapāda. Paris: Les Belles-Lettres, 1964. (Collection Émile Senart, 9)

04800 JHA, G.N., tr. Tattva-kaumudi: Vacaspati Miśra's commentary on Sāṁkhya-kārikā. Rev. & re-ed. by M.M. Patkar. 3rd ed. Poona: Oriental Book Agency, 1965. 255p. (POS 10)

04801 KUNHAN RAJA, C. The Sāṅkhya Kārikā of Īśvarakṛṣṇa; a philosopher's exposition. Hoshiarpur: VVRI, 1963. 204p. (WIS, 4)

04802 MAINKAR, T.G., tr. The Sāṁkhyakārikā with commentary of Gauḍapāda. Poona: Oriental Book Agency, 1964. 174p. (POS 9)

04803 SURYANARAYANA SASTRI, S.S., tr. The Sāṅkhya-kārikā of Īśvara Kṛiṣhṇa. Madras: U. of Madras, 1935. 129p.

04804 TAKAKUSU, J. La Sāṁkhyakārikā étudiée à la lumière de sa version chinoise. In BEFEO 4 (1904) 1-65, 978-1064.

b. studies of Sāṁkhya

04805 BAHADUR, K.P. The wisdom of Saankhya. ND: Sterling, 1978. 222p.

04806 BHATTACHARYA, D.P. Sāṁkhya-yoga theory of causality:an advaitic study. In CR 3rd ser. 2,1 (1970) 45-60.

04807 CHAKRAVARTI, P.B. Origin and development of the Sāṁkhya system of thought. 2nd ed. ND: OBRC, 1975. 325p. [Rpt. 1951 ed.]

04808 GARBE, R. VON. Die Sāṁkhya-Philosophie; eine Darstellung des Indischen Rationalismus nach dem Quellen. Leipzig: H. Haessal, 1894. 347p.

04809 HULIN, M. Sāṁkhya literature. Wiesbaden: Harrassowitz, 1978. 162p. (HIL, 6:3:3)

04810 JOHNSTON, E.H. Early Sāṁkhya: an essay on its historical development according to the texts. Delhi: Motilal, 1974. 91p. [Rpt. 1937 ed.]

04811 KEITH, A.B. A history of the Sāṁkhya philosophy: the Sāṁkhya system. Delhi: Nag, 1975. 126p. [Rpt. 1918 ed.]

04812 LARSON, G.J. Classical sāṁkhya: an interpretation of its history and meaning. 2nd rev. ed. Delhi: Motilal, 1979. 315p.

04813 MAJUMDAR, A.K. The Sāṅkhya conception of personality; or, a new interpretation of the Sāṅkhya philosophy. Calcutta: Calcutta U., 1930. 158p.

04814 RAMAKRISHNA RAO, K.B. Theism of pre-classical Sāṁkhya. Mysore: U. of Mysore, 1966. 444p.

04815 SEN GUPTA, A. Classical Sāṁkhya; a critical study. Lucknow: Monoranjan Sen, 1969. 178p.

04816 SINHA, N., tr. Sāṁkhya philosophy. Allahabad: Panini Office, 1915. 575p. (SBH, 11) [various texts in translation]

04817 SOLOMON, E.A. The commentaries of the Sāṁkhya Kārikā - a study. Ahmedabad: Gujarat U., 1974. 215p.

3. Yoga: the Aṣṭānga ("Eightfold") Yoga of Patañjali (2nd Cent. BC?): Liberation through Personal Discipline
a. translations of Patañjali's Yogasūtra

04818 KRISHNAMACHARYA, E. The yoga of Patañjali. Visakhapatnam: Mithila Pub. House, 1976-. v. 1 -.

04819 MISHRA, R.S. Yoga sūtras: the textbook of Yoga psychology. Garden City: Anchor, 1973. 538p. [1st pub. 1963]

04820 PRAVHAVANANDA, Swami, & C. ISHERWOOD, tr. How to know God; the Yoga aphorisms of Patañjali. NY: Harper, 1953. 224p.

04821 WOODS, J.H., tr. Yoga system of Patañjali.... Delhi: Motilal, 1966. 381p. [1st pub. 1914; HOS, 17]

b. studies of Pātañjala Rāja Yoga

04822 BHATTACHARYA, H. Yoga psychology. In Cultural Heritage of India. Calcutta: RMIC, 1953, v. 3, 53-90.

04823 DASGUPTA, S.N. The study of Patañjali. Calcutta: U. of Calcutta, 1920. 207p.

04824 ______. Yoga as philosophy and religion. NY: Krishna Press, 1974. 200p. [Rpt. 1924 ed.]

04825 ______. Yoga philosophy in relation to other systems of Indian thought. Delhi: Motilal, 1974. 380p. [1st pub. 1930]

04826 ELIADE, M. Patañjali and yoga. Tr. by C.L. Markham. NY: Funk & Wagnalls, 1969. 216p. [1st French ed. 1962]

04827 FEUERSTEIN, G. The Yoga-sūtra of Patañjali: an exercise in the methodology of textual analysis. ND: Arnold-Heinemann, 1979. 116p.

04828 JANACEK, A. The methodological principle in Yoga according to Patañjali's Yogasūtra. In AO 19 (1951) 514-67.

04829 KOELMAN, G.M. Pātañjala yoga, from related ego to absolute self. Poona: Papal Athenaeum, 1970. 280p.

04830 SATYA PRAKASH SARASVATI, Swami. Pātañjala Raja yoga. ND: S. Chand, 1975. 347p.

04831 SATYANANDA SARASWATI. Four chapters on freedom: commentary on Yoga sūtras of Patañjali. Monghyr: Bihar School of Yoga, 1976. 288p.

4. Nyāya, the Methods of Logical Thinking; and Vaiśeṣika, Theory of the Atomic Nature of Reality
a. translations of the Nyāyasūtra of Gautama (2nd cent. BC?)

04832 CHATTOPADHYAYA, D.P. & M.K. GANGOPADHYAYA, tr. Nyāya philosophy; literal translation of Gautama's Nyāya-sūtra and Vātsyāyana's Bhāṣya... Calcutta: ISPP, 1967-. 3 v.

04833 JHA, G.N., tr. Gautama's Nyāyasūtras with Vātsyāyana-Bhāsya. Poona: Oriental Book Agency, 1939. 567p.

04834 RUBEN, W., tr. Die Nyāyasūtras.... Leipzig: F.A. Brockhaus, 1928. 269p. (AKM, 18:2)

b. translations of the Vaiśeṣikasūtra of Kaṇāda

04835 GOUGH, A.E., tr. The Vaiśeṣhika aphorisms of Kaṇāda with comments from the Upaskāra of Śankara-Miśra and the Vivṛitti of Jaya-Narāyaṇa-Tarkapañchānana. Benares: E.J. Lazarus, 1873. 310p.

04836 SINHA, N., tr. The Vaiśesika sūtras of Kanāda. Allahabad: Panini Office, 1923. 285p. (SBH, 6)

c. studies of Nyāya-Vaiśeṣika (incl. trans. of classical commentaries)

04837 BAHADUR, K.P. The wisdom of Nyaaya. ND: Sterling, 1978. 246p. (Wisdom of India series, 3)

04838 ______. The wisdom of Vaisheshika. ND: Sterling, 1979. 207p. (Wisdom of India series, 4)

04839 BHARTIYA, M.C. Causation in Indian philosophy (with special reference to Nyāya-Vaiśeṣika). Ghaziabad, U.P.: Vimal Prakashan, 1973. 297p.

04840 BHATTACHARYYA, J.V., tr. Jayanta Bhaṭṭa's Nyāyamañjarī: the compendium of Indian speculative logic. Delhi: Motilal, 1978-.

04841 BIJALWAN, C.D. Indian theory of knowledge based upon Jayanta's Nyāyamañjarī. ND: Heritage, 1977. 288p.

04842 BULCKE, C. The theism of Nyāya-vaiśeṣika, its origin and early development. Delhi: Motilal, 1968. 58p.

04843 CHAKRAVARTI, K.K. The logic of Gotama. Honolulu: UPH, 1977. 147p.

04844 ______. The Nyāya-Vaiśeṣika theory of universals. In JIP 3,3/4 (1975) 363-82.

04845 CHATTERJEE, S.C. The Nyāya theory of knowledge. 2nd ed. Calcutta: U. of Calcutta, 1950. 421p. [1st ed. 1939]

04846 CHATTERJI, J.C. The Hindu realism; being an introduction to the metaphysics of the Nyāya-Vaiśeṣhika system of philosophy. Allahabad: Indian Press, 1912. 181p.

04847 FADDEGON, B. The Vaiçeṣika system. Amsterdam: J. Muller, 1918. 614p.

04848 GANGOPADHYAY, M.K. The concept of upādhi in Nyāya logic. In JIP 1,2 (1971) 146-66.

04849 GROHMA, O. Theorien zur Bunten Farbe im älteren Nyāya und Vaiśeṣika bis Udayana. In WZKS 19 (1975) 147-82.

04850 GUPTA, B. Die Wahrnehmungslehre in der Nyāyamañjarī. Walldorf-Hessen: Verlag fur Orientkund H. Vodran, 1963. 141p. (Beiträge zur Sprach- und Kulturgeschichte des Orients, 16)

04851 HALBFASS, W. Conceptualizations of 'being' in classical Vaiśeṣika. In WZKS 19 (1975) 183-98.

04852 ______. Zum Begriff der Substanz (dravya) im Vaiśeṣika. In WZKS 20 (1976) 141-66.

04853 JHA, G.N., tr. Tarkabhāṣā; or exposition of reasoning. Poona: Oriental Book Agency, 1967. 104p.

04854 JUNANKAR, N.S. Gautama, the Nyāya philosophy. Delhi: Motilal, 1978. 664p.

04855 KAVIRAJ, G.N. Gleanings from the history and bibliography of Nyāya-Vaiśeṣika literature. In ISPP 2 (1961) 609-64; 3 (1961) 1-29.

04856 KEITH, A.B. Indian logic and atomism; an exposition of the Nyāya and Vaiçeṣika systems. ND: Greenwood Press, 1968. 291p. [Rpt. 1921 ed.]

04857 POTTER, K.H., ed. Encyclopedia of Indian philosophies; v. 2, Indian metaphysics and epistemology: the tradition of Nyāya-Vaiśeṣika up to Gaṅgeśa. Delhi: Motilal, 1977. 744p.

04858 RAMANUJAM, P.S. A study of vaiśeṣika philosophy: with special reference to Vyomaśivācārya. Mysore: U. of Mysore, 1979. 226p.

04859 RANDLE, H.N. Indian logic in the early schools: a study of the Nyāyadarśana in its relation to the early logic of other schools. ND: OBRC, 1976. 404p. [Rpt. 1930 ed.]

04860 SCHUSTER, N. Inference in the vaiśeṣikasūtras. In JIP 1,4 (1972) 341-95.

04861 VISVANĀTHA NYĀYAPANCĀNANA BHATTĀCĀRYA. Bhāṣāpariccheda with Siddhānta-muktāvalī. Tr. by Swami Madhavananda. 3rd ed. Calcutta: Advaita Ashrama, 1977. 282p.

5. Pūrva Mīmāṁsā or Karma Mīmāṁsā: Proof of the Vedic Texts
a. translations of the Pūrva-mīmāṁsāsūtra of Jaimini (4th cent. BC?)

04862 JHA, G., tr. the Pūrva-mīmāṁsā-sūtras of Jaimini. Allahabad: Panini Office, 1916. 506p. (SBH, 10)

04863 SANDAL, M.L., tr. The Mīmāṁsā Sūtras of Jaimini. Allahabad: Panini Office, 1923-25. 1022p. (SBH, 27)

b. studies of Pūrva-mīmāṁsā (incl. trans. of classical commentaries)

04864 EDGERTON, F., tr. The Mīmāṅsā nyāya prakāśa; or, Āpadevī: a treatise on the Mīmāṅsā system by Āpadeva. New Haven: YUP, 1929. 308p.

04865 JHA, G.N., tr. The Çlokavartika of Kumārīla Bhaṭṭa. Calcutta: Roy. As. Soc. of Bengal, 1909. 555p. (Bibliotheca Indica, v. 146)

04866 ______. Prabhākara school of pūrva mīmāṁsā. Delhi: Motilal, 1978. 317p. [1st pub. 1911]

04867 ______. Pūrva-mīmāṁsā, in its sources. With a critical bibliography by Umesha Mishra. 2nd ed. Varanasi: BHU, 1965. 449p.

04868 KEITH, A.B. Karma-Mīmāṁsā. ND: OBRC, 1978. 112p. [Rpt. 1921 ed.]

04869 SANDAL, M.L. Introduction to the Mīmāṁsā sūtras of Jaimini. Allahabad: Panini Office, 1925. 240p. (SBH, 28)

6. The Vedānta, or Uttara-Mīmāṁsā: the Culmination of Upaniṣadic Thought, and the Philosophical Foundation of Later Hinduism: translations of the Brahmasūtra, or Vedānta-sūtra, of Bādārayana (200-250 AD?)

04870 GAJENDRAGADKAR, S.N., tr. The Brahma-sūtras of Bādarāyana: with commentary of Śaṁkarācārya, II. 2. Bombay: U. of Bombay, 1965. 177p.

04871 RADHAKRISHNAN, S., tr. The Brahma Sūtra: philosophy of spiritual life. NY: Harper, 1960. 606p.

04872 RENOU, L. Sur la forme des Brahmasūtra. In E. Bender, ed. Indological studies in honor of W. Norman Brown. New Haven: AOS, 1962, 195-203. (AOS, 47)

04873 SIVANANDA, Swami, tr. Brahma sūtras. 2nd rev. ed. Delhi: Motilal, 1977. 686p.

04874 THIBAUT, G., tr. The Vedanta sūtras, with the commentary of Shankarāchārya. Delhi: Motilal, 1962. 3 v. (SBE, 34, 38, 48) [1st pub. 1890-1904]

VI. RELIGIO-PHILOSOPHICAL TRADITIONS: BUDDHISM

A. Gautama the Buddha ("the Enlightened One"), and the Beginnings of the Dharma/Dhamma

1. Siddhārtha, Prince of the Sakyas (c. 560-480 BC)
a. biographies: the person and the sacred legend

04875 AMBEDKAR, B.R. The Buddha and his Dhamma. Bombay: People's Education Soc., 1957. 599p.

04876 DIWAKAR, R.R. Bhagawan Buddha. Bombay: BVB, 1960. 199p.

04877 FOUCHER, A.C.A. The life of the Buddha; according to the ancient texts and monuments of India. Tr. by S.B. Boas. Westport, CT: Greenwood Press, 1972. 272p. [This version 1st pub. 1962]

04878 ______. La vie du Bouddha, d'après les textes et les monuments de l'Inde. Paris: Payot, 1949. 383p.

04879 JENNINGS, J.G., tr. The Vedantic Buddhism of the Buddha: a collection of historical texts. Delhi: Motilal, 1974. 117 + 679p. [Rpt. 1948 ed.]

04880 LAMOTTE, E. La legend du Bouddha. In Revue de l'histoire des religions 134 (1947) 37-71.

04881 MARSHALL, G.N. Buddha, the quest for serenity. Boston: Beacon Press, 1978. 239p.

04882 IKEDA, D. The living Buddha; an interpretive biography. Tr. by B. Watson. NY: Weatherhill, 1976. 148p. [1st Japanese ed. 1973]

04883 NĀṆAMOLI, Bhikku, tr. The life of the Buddha, as it appears in the Pali Canon.... Kandy: Buddhist Pub. Soc., 1972. 369p.

04884 ROCKHILL, W.W., tr. The life of the Buddha, and the early history of his order. Derived from Tibetan works in the Bkah-hgyur and Bstan-hgyur.... London: Trubner, 1884. 273p.

04885 SAUNDERS, K.J. Gotama Buddha: a biography, based on the canonical books of the Theravadin. ND: Light & Life, 1978. 111p. [Rpt. 1922 ed.]

04886 SENART, É.C.M. Essai sur la legende du Buddha, son caractère et ses origines. 2nd ed., rev. Paris: E. Leroux, 1882. [1st pub. in JA, 1873-75]

04887 THOMAS, E.J. The life of Buddha as legend and history. London: Routledge & K. Paul, 1975. 297p. [1st pub. 1927]

04888 WARREN, H.C. The life of the Buddha. Ed. & enl. by P. Kumar. Delhi: Eastern Book Linkers, 1978. 113p.

b. translations and studies of sources

04889 AŚVAGHOṢA. The Buddhacarita: or, acts of the Buddha. Tr. by E.H. Johnston. 2nd ed. ND: OBRC, 1972. 2 v. in 1. [1st pub. 1935-36]

04890 ______. The Buddha-karita: or, life of Buddha. Tr. by E.B. Cowell. ND: Cosmo, 1977. 207 + 175p. [1st pub. 1894]

04891 ______. The Fo-sho-hing-tsan-king, a life of Buddha. Tr. by S. Beal from the Chinese translation of Dharmaraksha (420 AD). Delhi: Motilal, 1966. 380p. (SBE, 19) [1st pub. 1883]

04892 BAREAU, A. La date du nirvana. In JA 241 (1953) 27-62.

04893 ______. La jeunesse du Bouddha dans les Sūtrapitaka et les Vinayapiṭaka anciens. In BEFEO 61 (1974) 199-274.

04894 ______. Recherches sur la biographie du Bouddha dans les Sūtrapiṭaka et les Vinayapiṭaka anciens. Paris: EFEO, 1963-71. 2 v., 405, 342p.

04895 BHATTACHARYYA, N.N. Note on the biography of the Buddha. In JIH 53,1 (1975) 1-12.

04896 FOUCAUX, P.E., tr. Le Lalita Vistāra. Paris: Leroux, 1884-92. 2 v.

04897 HIRSCH, P. Buddha's erste Meditation. AS/EA 17,3/4 (1964) 100-154.

04898 JOHNSTON, E.H., tr. The Buddha's mission and last journey: Buddhacarita XV-XVIII. In ActaOr(C) 15,1 (1936) 26-62.

04899 JONES, J.J., tr. The Mahāvastu. London: Luzac, 1949, 1952-56. 3 v. (SBB, 16, 18, 19)

04900 KROM, N.J., ed. The life of Buddha on the stūpa of Barabudur, according to the Lalitavistāra text. Varanasi: Bharatiya, 1974. 131p. + 30 pl. [Rpt. of 1926 ed.]

04901 LAW, B.C. A note on the Mahāvastu. Delhi: Bharatiya, 1978. 180 + 38 p. [Rpt. 1930 ed.]

04902 MITRA, R.L., tr. The Lalita-vistāra; or, Memoirs of the early life of Śākya Siṁha. Calcutta: ASB, 1881-86. 288p. (BI, ns 90) [Chaps. 1-15 only; no more pub.]

04903 MUS, P. Le Buddha paré. Son origine indienne. Çākyamuni dans le Mahāyānisme moyen. In BEFEO 28,1/2 (1928) 153-280.

04904 RAHULA, T. A critical study of the Mahāvastu. Delhi: Motilal, 1978. 435p.

04905 SENART, É.C.M., tr. Le Mahāvastu.... Paris: Imprimerie nationale, 1882-97. 3 v.

04906 SNELLGROVE, D.L. Śākyamuni's final nirvāna. In BSOAS 36,2 (1973) 399-411.

c. the iconography of the Buddha image [see Chap. One, IV. B. 2. b.]

d. disciples and other associates

04907 MIGOT, A. Un grand disciple du Bouddha: Sariputra. Son role dans l'histoire du bouddhisme et dans le dévelopement de l'Abhidharma. In BEFEO 46,2 (1954) 405-554.

04908 MUKHERJEE, B. Die Überlieferung von Devadatta, dem Widersacher des Buddha in den canonische Schriften. Munich: Kitzinger, 1966. 158p. [reviewed by David Ruegg in T'oung Pao (1968) 164-68]

04909 OMODEO SALÉ, M. La vita di Sariputra e le sette dell'hinayana. Milan: A. Martello, 1959. 194p.

04910 SASAKI, S. The story of the great disciples of Buddha: Ananda and Maha-kasyapa. NY: First Zen Buddhism Inst., 1931. 32p.

2. Early Buddhism and Contiguous Traditions

04911 BHATTACHARYA, V.S. The basic conception of Buddhism. Calcutta: U. of Calcutta, 1934. 103p.

04912 HORSCH, P. Buddhismus und Upaniṣaden. In J.C. Heesterman, et al., eds. Pratidānam. The Hague: Mouton, 1968, 462-78. (Janua linguarum, series major, 8)

04913 JOSHI, L.M. Brahmanism, Buddhism and Hinduism; an essay on their origins and interactions. Kandy: Buddhist Pub. Soc., 1970. 75p.

04914 LAMOTTE, É. & J. PRZYLUSKI. Bouddhisme et Upanishad. In BEFEO 32 (1932) 141-69.

04915 LEE, O. From acts to non-action to acts. In HR 6,4 (1967) 273-302.

04916 NAGRAJ, MUNI. The contemporaneity and the chronology of Mahāvīra and Buddha. Ed. & trans. by Muni Mahendra Kumarji 'Diviteeya'. ND: Today and Tomorrow's, 1970. 167p.

04917 OLDENBERG, H. Die Lehre der Upanishaden und die Anfänge des Buddhismus. Göttingen: Vandenhoeck & Ruprecht, 1915. 366p.

04918 RAMAKRISHNA RAO, K.B. The Buddhacarita and the Sāṁkhya of Arada Kalama. In ALB 58 (1964) 231-44.

04919 RHYS-DAVIDS, C.A.F. Relations between early Buddhism and Brahmanism. In IHQ 10,2 (1934) 274-87.

04920 UPADHYAYA, K.N. Early Buddhism and the Bhagavadgita. Delhi: Motilal, 1971. 567p.

04921 VARMA, V.P. The Vedic tradition and the origins of Buddhism. In JBRS 46 (1960) 276-308.

04922 WARDER, A.K. On the relationship between early Buddhism and other contemporary systems. In BSOAS 18 (1956) 43-63.

3. General Studies of the Origin and Early Development of Buddhism

04923 BAREAU, A. Le Parinirvāṇa du Bouddha et la naissance de la religion bouddhique. In BEFEO 61 (1974) 275-300.

04924 BARUA, B.M. Gayā and Buddha-Gayā: early history of the holy land. Varanasi: Bharatiya, 1975. 2 v. [Rpt. 1931-34 ed.]

04925 BASHAM, A.L. The rise of Buddhism in its historical context. In AsSt 4,3 (1966) 395-411.

04926 COOMARASWAMY, A.K. Buddha and the Gospel of Buddhism. Rev. by Doña Luisa Coomaraswamy. NY: Harper & Row, 1963. 369p. [1st ed. 1916]

04927 DUTT, S. The Buddha and five after-centuries. Calcutta: Sahitya Samsad, 1978. 259p. + 13 pl.

04928 LAMOTTE, E. Histoire du Bouddhisme des origines a l'ère Śaka. Louvain: Publications Universitaires, 1958. 862p.

04929 MIZUNO, K. Primitive Buddhism. Tr. from Japanese by K. Yamamoto. Ube: Karin Bunko, 1969. 295p. (The Karin Buddhological series, 2)

04930 OLDENBERG, H. Buddha: his life, his doctrine, his order. Tr. by W. Huey. Delhi: IndBH, 1971. 454p. [Rpt. 1921 ed.; 1st German ed. 1897]

04931 PANDE, G.C. Studies in the origins of Buddhism. 2nd ed. Delhi: Motilal Banarsidass, 1975. 208p. [1st ed. Allahabad: U. of Allahabad, 1957. 600p.]

04932 REYNOLDS, F. The two wheels of dhamma: a study of early Buddhism. In B.L. Smith, ed. The two wheels of dhamma.... Chambersburg, PA: American Academy of Religion, 1972, 6-30. (AAR monographs, 3)

04933 TĀRĀNĀTHA. Tārānātha's history of Buddhism in India. Tr. from Tibetan by Lama Chimpa, Alaka Chattopadhyaya. Ed. by D.P. Chattopadhyaya. Simla: IIAS, 1970. 472p.

04934 VARMA, V.P. Early Buddhism and its origins. Delhi: Munshiram, 1973. 505p.

B. Early History of the Saṅgha: the Monastic Community Founded by the Buddha and Supported by the Laity

1. General Studies of the Monastic Order

04935 BECHERT, H. The Theravāda Buddhist saṅgha. In JAS 29,4 (1970) 261-78.

04936 DE, G.D. Democracy in early Buddhist samgha. Calcutta: Calcutta U., 1955. 120p.

04937 DUTT, N. Early monastic Buddhism, rev. & enl. ed. Calcutta: Calcutta Oriental Book Agency, 1960. 311p.

04938 DUTT, S. Early Buddhist monasticism; 600 BC - 100 BC. NY: Asia, 1960. 196p. [Rpt. 1924 ed.]

04939 NJAMMASCH, M. Hierarchische Strukturen in den budhistischen Klöstern Indiens in der ersten Hälfte des ersten Jahrtausends unserer Zeitrechnung: Untersuchungen zur Genesis des indischen Feudalismus. In Ethnographische-Archäologische Zeitschrift 11,4 (1970) 515-39.

04940 PREBISH, C.S. The Pratimokṣa puzzle: fact versus fantasy. In JAOS 94,2 (1974) 168-76.

04941 SINGH, M.M. Life in the Buddhist monastery during the 6th century BC. In JBRS 40 (1954) 131-54.

2. Early Buddhist Councils, Saṅgītis: Definition of the Canon and Tradition

04942 BAREAU, A. Les premiers conciles bouddhiques. Paris: PUF, 1955, 150p.

04943 DEMIÉVILLE, P. À propos du concile de Vaiśalī. In T'oung Pao 50 (1951) 239-96.

04944 DUTT, N. The second Buddhist council. In IHQ 35,1 (1959) 45-56.

04945 FRANCKE, R.O. The Buddhist councils at Rājagṛiha and Veśalī as alleged in Cullavagga XI, XII. In JPTS (1908) 1-80.

04946 HOFINGER, M. Étude sur la concile de Vaiśalī. Louvain: Bureaux du Museon, 1946. 300p.

04947 LA VALLÉE POUSSIN, L. DE. The Buddhist councils. In IA 37 (1908) 1-18, 81-106.

04948 PREBISH, C. Review of scholarship on the Buddhist councils. In JAS 33,2 (1974) 239-254.

04949 PRZYLUSKI, J. Le concile de Rājagraha. Paris. Guenther, 1926-29. 3 v.

04950 PURI, B.N. The first Buddhist Council: a solemn synod, a quasi-judicial body or an assembly of the elders against the heretics? In JIH 52,1 (1974) 57-67.

3. Emergence of Sectarianism: the Sthaviras and Mahāsaṅghikas, Precursors of Hīnayāna and Mahāyāna

04951 BECHERT, H. Zur Geschichte der buddhistischen Sekten in Indien und Ceylon. In La Nouvelle Clio, 7/9 (1955-57) 311-360.

04952 CONZE, E. Buddhist thought in India; three phases of Buddhist philosophy. London: Allen & Unwin, 1962. 302p.

04953 DUTT, N. Buddhist sects in India. Calcutta: KLM, 1970. 317p.

04953 NATTIER, J.J. & C.S. PREBISH. Mahāsamghika origins: the beginnings of Buddhist sectarianism. In HR 16,3 (1977) 237-72.

4. Aśoka Maurya: Buddhist Cakravartin, World Emperor and Patron of the dharma/dhamma [see also II. A. 3. c., above]

04955 BECHERT, H. Aśoka's "Schismenedikt" und der Begriff Saṅghabheda. In WZKS 5 (1961) 18-52.

04956 FILLIOZAT, J. The festivities of the Dhamma as practised by Aśoka; the Devas of Aśoka: "Gods" or "Divine Majesties"? In ISPP 8 (1966) 3-35.

04957 GOKHALE, B.G. Buddhism and Aśoka. Baroda: Padmaja, 1948. 296p.

04958 KERN, F. Aśoka, Kaiser und Missionar. Ed. by W. Kirfel. Bern: Francke, 1956. 207p.

04959 LAMOTTE, É. Aśoka et les missionaires bouddhiques. In Studia Missionalia 12 (1962) 35-49.

04960 PRZYLUSKI, J. The legend of Emperor Aśoka in Indian and Chinese texts. Tr. from French by D.K. Biswas. Calcutta: KLM, 1967. 252p.

5. Missionary Activities and the Expansion of Buddhism

04961 Aśoka and the expansion of Buddhism. In P.V. Bapat, ed. 2500 years of Buddhism. ND: PDMIB, 56-96. [essays by P.V. Bagat, P.C. Bagchi, J.N. Takasaki, V.V. Gokhale, R.C. Majumdar]

04962 GLASENAPP, H. VON. Der Buddhismus in Indien und im fernen Osten; Schicksale und Lebensforme einer Erlösungsreligion. Berlin: Atlantis-Verlag, 1936. 402p.

04963 HOFINGER, M. L'action missionnaire du bouddhisme ancien: fondement doctrinal, formes et méthodes de la prédication. In Studia Missionalia 12 (1962) 10-34.

04964 SAHA, K. Buddhism and Buddhist literature in Central Asia. Calcutta: KLM, 1970. 162p.

04965 ZÜRCHER, E. The Buddhist conquest of China.... Leiden: Brill, 1972. 2 v., 470p. [Rev. rpt. of 1959 ed.]

C. The Tripiṭaka, the "Three Baskets" of Sacred Literature: The Pali Canon and its Translations; Non-Canonical Works

1. General Guides and Studies

04966 BANERJEE, A.C. Sarvāstivāda literature. Calcutta: World Press, 1979. 270p. [Rpt. 1957 ed.]

04967 HUMPHREYS, C., ed. A Buddhist students manual. London: Buddhist Soc., 1956. 279p.

04968 MALALASEKARA, G.P. Dictionary of Pali names. London: Murray, 1960. 2 v.

04969 MASSON, J. La religion populaire dans le canon Bouddhique Pali. Louvain: Bureaux du Museon, 1942. 154p.

04970 WARDER, A.K. The Pali canon and its commentaries as an historical record. In C.H. Philips, ed. Historians of India, Pakistan & Ceylon. London: OUP, 1961, 44-56.

04971 WOODWARD, F.L., et al., eds. Pāli Tipiṭakam concordance. London: Pali Text Soc., 1952-. (3 vol. pub. to 1979)

2. Translations from the Canon
a. collections

04972 PALI TEXT SOCIETY, LONDON. Translation series. London: OUP, 1909-. [41 v. to 1974]

04973 Sacred books of the Buddhists. London: 1895-. [32 v. as of 1976; editors and publishers vary]

b. selected translations

04974 ALLEN, G.F., tr. The Buddha's philosophy: selections from the Pali canon and an introductory essay. NY: Macmillan, 1959. 194p.

04975 BURLINGAME, E.W., tr. Buddhist parables. NY: YUP, 1922. 348p.

04976 MAURICE, D., comp. The lion's roar; an anthology of the Buddha's teachings, selected from the Pāli canon. London: Rider, 1962. 255p.

04977 THOMAS, E.J. Early Buddhist scriptures. Ed. and tr. from Pali. London: K. Paul, Trench, Trubner, 1935. 232p.

04978 WARREN, H.C. Buddhism in translation. NY: Atheneum, 1963. 496p. [1st pub. 1896; trans. from Pali]

3. Vinaya-piṭaka: Rules of the Monastic Order

04979 FRAUWALLNER, E. The earliest Vinaya and the beginnings of Buddhist literature. Rome: IIMEO, 1956. 218p. (Serie orientale Roma, 8)

04980 HORNER, I.B., tr. The Book of the Discipline (Vinaya-piṭaka). London: OUP, 1938-. 5 v. (SBB, 10, 11, 13, 14, 20)

04981 MISRA, G.S.P. The age of vinaya. ND: Munshiram, 1972. 298p.

04982 PREBISH, C.S. Recent progress in Vinaya studies. In A.K. Narain, ed. Studies in Pali and Buddhism. Delhi: B.R., 1979, 297-306.

04983 RHYS-DAVIDS, T.W. & H. OLDENBERG, tr. Vinaya texts. Delhi: Motilal, 1968. 3 v. (SBE, 13, 17, 20) [1st pub. 1881-85]

4. Sutta(Sūtra)-piṭaka: Collection of Teachings Attributed to the Buddha
a. the four major nikāyas ("collections")

04984 BARUA, D.K. An analytical study of four Nikayas. Calcutta: Rabindra Bharati U., 1971. 626p.

04985 HARE, E.M., tr. Woven cadences of early Buddhists. London: OUP, 1944. 229p. (SBB, 15)

04986 NYANATILOKA, tr. The Buddha's path to deliverance in its threefold division and seven stages of purity, being a systematic exposition in the words of the Sutta-piṭaka. 3rd ed. Colombo: Bauddha Sahitya Sabha, 1969. 199p.

04987 RHYS-DAVIDS, T.W., tr. Buddhist Suttas. Delhi: Motilal, 1968. 320p. (SBE, 11) [1st pub. 1900; from Pali Suttapitaka]

04988 SWEARER, D.K. Two types of saving knowledge in the Pāli sūtras. In PEW 22,4 (1972) 355-72.

b. the Khuddaka-nikāya, or minor anthology, incl. the Dhammapada, the Therā- and Therīgāthā, and the Jātaka

04989 BABBITT, I., tr. The Dhammapada. NY: New Directions, 1965. 123p. [Rpt. 1936 ed.]

04990 BURLINGAME, E.W., tr. Buddhist legends; from the original Pali text of the Dhammapada commentary. Cambridge: HUP, 1921. 3 v. (HOS, 28-30)

04991 LAL, P., tr. The Dhammapada. Tr. from Pali. NY: Farrar, Straus & Giroux, 1967. 184p.

04992 LIENHARD, S. Sur la structure poétique des Therātherīgāthā. In JA 263,3/4 (1975) 375-96.

04993 MÜLLER, F.M., tr. The Dhammapada.... Delhi: Motilal, 1968. 224p. (SBE, 10) [1st pub. 1881]

04994 RADHAKRISHNAN, S., tr. The Dhammapada. London: OUP, 1950. 194p.

04995 RHYS DAVIDS, C.A.F, tr. Psalms of the early Buddhists.... London: H. Frowde, 1909-13. 2 v. (Pali Text Soc., trans. ser., 1, 4) [from Therigatha and Theragata]

5. Abhidhamma-piṭaka: Seven Collections of Philosophical and Psychological Treatises

04996 GOVINDA, A. The psychological attitude of early Buddhist philosophy and its systematic representation according to Abhidhamma tradition. NY: S. Weiser, 1974. 191p.

04997 GUENTHER, H.V. Philosophy and psychology in the Abhidharma. 3rd ed. Berkeley: Shambala, 1976. 270p. [1st ed. 1957]

04998 KASHYAP, J. The Abhidhamma philosophy: the psycho-ethical philosophy of early Buddhism. Sarnath: The Mahabodhi Soc., 1942-43. 2 v.

04999 NĀRADA, Mahathera, tr. A manual of abhidhamma; being Abhidhammattha sangaha of Bhadanta Anuruddhacariya. 2nd rev. ed. Kandy: BPS, 1968. 451p.

05000 NYANATILOKA, Thera. Guide through the Abhidhamma Pitaka.... 3rd ed. Kandy: BPS, 1971. 177p. [1st pub. 1938]

05001 SILANANDA, Brahmachari. An introduction to abhidhamma: Buddhist philosophy and psychology. Calcutta: Jadab Barua Pub., 1979. 190p.

05002 TAKAKUSA, J. On the Abhidharma literature of the Sarvāstivādins. In JPTS (1904-5) 67-147.

6. Semi- and Non-Canonical Works in Pali
a. the Milindapañha: the "Questions of King Menander" to the Buddhist monk Nāgasena (c. 150 BC)

05003 BASU, R.N. A critical study of the Milindapañha: a critique of Buddhist philosophy. Calcutta: KLM, 1978. 128p.

05004 DEMIÉVILLE, P. Les versions Chinoises du Milindapañha. In BEFEO 24 (1924) 1-258.

05005 RHYS-DAVIDS, C.A.F. The Milinda Questions: an inquity into its place in the history of Buddhism with a theory as to its author. London: G. Routledge, 1930. 168p.

05006 RHYS-DAVIDS, T.W., tr. The questions of King Milinda. Delhi: Motilal, 1965. 2 v. (SBE, 35, 36) [1st pub. 1890-94]

b. the Jātaka Tales, stories of the Buddha's former lives
i. translations

05007 COWELL, E.B., ed. The Jātaka; or, stories of the Buddha's former births. London: Luzac, 1969. 7 v. in 3. [Rpt. 1895-1913 ed.]

05008 SPEYER, J.S., tr. The Jātakamālā; or, garland of birth-stories of Āryaśūra. Delhi: Motilal, 1971. 350p. [1st pub. 1895]

ii. studies of the Jātakas in religion, literature, and art

05009 BASHAM, A. The Pāli Jātakas. In LEW 12,2/4 (1968) 114-28.

05010 DE, G.D. Significance and importance of Jātakas. Calcutta: U. of Calcutta, 1951. 184p.

05011 FEER, H.L. A study of the Jātakas; analytical and critical. Tr. from French by G.M. Foulkes. Calcutta: Susil Gupta, 1963. 120p. [1st pub. in JA 7th ser. 5 (1875) 357-423; 6 (1875) 243-306]

05012 FOUCHER, A.C.A. Les représentations de Jātaka dans l'art bouddhique. Paris: E. Leroux, 1919. 220p.

05013 ______. Les vies antérieures du Bouddha d'après les textes et les monuments de l'Inde. Paris: PUF, 1955. 370p.

05014 SEN, B.C. Studies in the Buddhist Jātakas: tradition and polity. Calcutta: Saraswat Library, 1974. 271p.

c. other non-canonical Pali literature

05015 LAW, B.C. Non-canonical Pali literature. In ABORI 12 (1931) 97-143.

05016 WAYMAN, A. & H. WAYMAN, tr. The lion's roar of Queen Śrīmālā, a Buddhist scripture of the Tathāgatagarbha theory. NY: ColUP, 1974. 142p.

D. Hīnayāna, "The Lesser Vehicle", Salvation through Personal Discipline and Meditation: the Theravāda/Sthaviravāda and Other Schools

1. Early History of Theravāda Buddhism

05017 GOKHALE, B.G. Theravāda Buddhism in western India. In JAOS 92,1 (1972) 230-236.

05018 SWEARER, D.K. Knowledge as salvation: a study in early Buddhism. Ph.D. diss., Princeton U., 1967. 300p. [UM 68-2524]

2. Surveys and Studies of Theravāda Doctrine

05019 BAREAU, A. Les sectes bouddhiques du Petit Vehicule. Saigon: EFEO, 1955. 310p. (EFEO Pub. 38)

05020 HORNER, I.B. The early Buddhist theory of man perfected; a study of the arhat. London: Williams & Norgate, 1936. 328p.

05021 JAYATILLEKE, K.N. The message of the Buddha; a posthumous work edited by N. Smart. London: Allen & Unwin, 1975. 362p.

05022 NYANAPONIKA, Mahāthera, ed. Pathways of Buddhist thought: essays from "The Wheel." London: Allen & Unwin, 1971. 256p.

05023 PIYADASSI, W., Thera. The Buddha's ancient path. London: Rider, 1964. 240p.

05024 PRASAD, C.S. Theravāda and Vibhajjavāda: a critical study of the two appellations. In E&W 22,1-2 (1972) 101-113.

05025 REYNOLDS, F.E. The several bodies of Buddha: reflections on a neglected aspect of Theravāda tradition. In HR 16,4 (1977) 374-89.

05026 SADDHATISSA, H. The Buddha's way. London: Allen & Unwin, 1971. 139p.

05027 THITTILA, U, Mahāthera. The fundamental principles of Theravāda Buddhism. In K.W. Morgan, ed. The path of the Buddha.... NY: Ronald Press, 1956, 67-112.

05028 WILLIAMS, P.M. Buddhadeva and temporality. In JIP 4,3/4 (1977) 279-94.

3. Meditation: Central to Theravāda

05029 CONZE, E. Buddhist meditation. London: Allen & Unwin, 1956. 183p.

05030 KING, W.-L. Theravāda meditation: the Buddhist transformation of yoga. University Park, PA: Pennsylvania State U. Press, 1980.

05031 NYANAPONIKA, Thera. The heart of Buddhist meditation: Satipaṭṭhāna, a handbook of mental training based on the Buddha's way of mindfulness, with an anthology of relevant texts translated from the Pali and Sanskrit. NY: Citadel Press, 1969. 223p.

05032 PE MAUNG TIN. Buddhist devotion and meditation. London: S.P.C.K., 1964. 90p.

05033 RHYS DAVIDS, C.A.F. Dhyāna in early Buddhism. In IHQ 3 (1927) 689-715.

05034 SWEARER, D.K. Control and freedom: the structure of Buddhist meditation in the Pāli suttas. In PEW 23,4 (1973) 435-54.

05035 VAJIRAÑANA, P., Mahāthera. Buddhist meditation in theory and practice; a general exposition according to the Pāli Canon of the Theravāda School. Colombo: M.D. Gunasena, 1962. 498p.

4. Buddhaghoṣa (5th Cent. AD), Greatest Exponent of Theravāda, and His Viśuddhimagga, "Path of Purity"

05036 DHAMMARATANA, U. Guide through Visuddhimagga. Varanasi: Maha Bodhi Soc., 1964. 163p.

05037 JAYAWICKRAMA, N.A., tr. The inception of discipline, and the Vinaya nidāna....the Bāhiranidāna of Buddhaghoṣa's Samantapāsādika, the Vinaya commentary. London: Luzac, 1962. 222p. (SBB, 21)

05038 LAW, B.C. The life and work of Buddhaghoṣa. Calcutta: Thacker, Spink, 1923. 183p. (Calcutta oriental series, 9. E. 3.)

05039 NĀṆAMOLI, Bhikkhu, tr. The path of purification. Colombo: R. Semage, 1956. 886p. [Trans. of Viśuddhimagga by Buddhaghoṣa]

05040 PE MAUNG TIN, tr. The path of purity. London: Luzac, 1922-31. 3 v. (Pali Text Soc., trans. ser., 11, 17, 22)

5. Establishment and Early History of Buddhism in Sri Lanka (From c. 240 BC)

05041 ADIKARAM, E.W. Early history of Buddhism in Ceylon. Colombo: D.S. Puswella, 1953. 146p. [1st pub. 1946]

05042 PARANAVITANA, S. Pre-Buddhist religious beliefs in Ceylon. In JRASCB 31,82 (1929) 302-28.

05043 RAHULA, W. History of Buddhism in Ceylon: the Anuradhapura period; 3rd century BC - 10th century AD. 2nd ed. Colombo: M.D. Gunasena, 1966. 43 + 351p.

05044 REYNOLDS, F.E. Dhammadipa: a study of Indianization and Buddhism in Śri Lanka. In Ohio J. of Religion 2,1 (1974) 63-78.

E. Mahāyāna, "The Great Vehicle": Salvation through Faith in the Bodhisattvas (c. 100 BC to 100 AD)

1. Surveys and Histories

05045 DUTT, N. Mahayana Buddhism. Calcutta: KLM, 1973. 304p.

05046 FOX, D.A. The vagrant lotus: an introduction to Buddhist philosophy. Philadelphia: Westminster, 1973. 223p.

05047 NAKAMURA, H. Critical survey of Mahāyāna and esoteric Buddhism based upon Japanese studies. In Acta Asiatica 6 (1964) 57-88; 7 (1964) 36-94.

05048 NILAKANTA SASTRI, K.A. Mahayana Buddhism in South India - some aspects. In Bull. of Tibetology 3 (1965) 11-21.

05049 PARANAVITANA, S. Mahayanism in Ceylon. In Ceylon J. of Science, sect. G.2,1 (1928) 37-51.

05050 SUZUKI, B.L. Mahayana Buddhism: a brief outline. NY: Macmillan, 1969. 158p.

05051 SUZUKI, D.T. On Indian Mahayana Buddhism. Ed. by E. Conze. NY: Harper & Row, 1968. 284p.

2. Origins of Mahāyāna

05052 BARUA, B.M. Mahayana in the making. In Asutosh Mookerji Silver Jubilee Volume. Calcutta: Calcutta U., 1927, v. 3, 163-80.

05053 GOMEZ, L.O. Proto-Mādhyamika in the Pali canon. In PEW 26,2 (1976) 137-66.

05054 HIRAKAWA, A. The rise of Mahāyāna Buddhism and its relation to the worship of Stūpas. In Memoirs of the Res. Dept. of the Toyo Bunko 22 (1963) 57-106.

05055 JONES, E.T. Hinduism and the development of Mahāyāna Buddhism. In J. of the Society for Asian Studies (Provo, UT) 2 (1969) 57-68.

05056 KIMURA, R. A historical study of the terms Hīnayāna and Mahāyāna and the origins of Mahāyāna Buddhism. Patna: Indological Book Corp., 1978. 202p. [Rpt. 1927 ed.]

05057 LAMOTTE, É. Sur la formation du Mahāyāna. In Asiatica; Festschrift Friedrich Weller.... Leipzig: Harrassowitz, 1954, 377-96.

05058 NAKAMURA, H. Historical studies of the coming into being of Mahāyāna sūtras. In Proc. of the Okurayama Oriental Res. Inst., 2 (1956) 1-22.

05059 SANKRITYAYANA, R. Les origines du Mahāyāna. In JA 225 (1934) 195-208.

3. Mahāyāna Canon: Sanskrit Sūtras and Commentaries Added to the Tripiṭaka

a. general: selections and anthologies of Mahāyāna texts

05060 COWELL, E.B., tr. Buddhist Mahayana texts. Delhi: Motilal, 1968. 207 + 208p. (SBE, 49) [Rpt. 1894 ed.]

05061 THOMAS, E.J., tr. The quest of enlightenment. London: John Murray, 1950. 89p.

b. the Prajñāpāramitā sūtra literature, "Perfection in Wisdom"

i. translated texts

05062 CONZE, E., tr. Aṣṭasahārika prajñāpāramitā; the perfection of wisdom in eight thousand ślokas. Calcutta: Asiatic Soc., 1970. 225p. (BI, 284) [1st pub. 1958]

05063 ______., tr. Buddhist Wisdom books, containing the Diamond Sūtra and the Heart Sūtra. London: Allen & Unwin, 1958. 110p.

05064 ______., tr. The large sūtra on perfect wisdom, with the divisions of the Abhisamayālankāra. Berkeley: UCalP, 1975. 679p.

05065 ______., tr. The perfection of wisdom in eight thousand lines and its verse summary. Bolinas: Four Seasons Foundation, 1973. 325p.

05066 ______., tr. Selected sayings from the perfection of wisdom. London: Buddhist Soc., 1955. 215p.

05067 ______., tr. The short Prajñāpāramitā texts. London: Luzac, 1974. 217p.

ii. studies

05068 BEAUTRIX, P. Bibliographie de la littérature Prajñāpāramitā. Brussels: Inst. Belge des Hautes Études Bouddhiques, 1971. 58p. [Its Pub., serie "Bibliographies", 3]

05069 CONZE, E. The iconography of the Prajñāpāramitā. In OA 2,2 (1949) 47-52; 3,3 (1951) 104-9.

05070 ______. The ontology of the Prajñāpāramitā. In PEW 3,2 (1953) 117-29.

05071 ______. The Prajñāpāramitā literature. The Hague: Mouton, 1960. 124p.

05072 HANAYAMA, S. A summary of various research on the Prajñāpāramitā literature by Japanese scholars. In Acta Asiatica 10 (1966) 16-93.

05073 HIKATA, R. An introductory essay on the Prajñāpāramitā sūtra. In his Suvikrāntavikrāmiparipṛcchā Prajñāpāramita-sūtra. Fukuoka: Kyushu U., 1958, 1-72.

05074 MITCHELL, D.W. The paradox of Buddhist wisdom. In PEW 26,1 (1976) 55-68.

05075 SUZUKI, D.T. The philosophy and religion of the Prajñāpāramitā. In his Essays in Zen Buddhism, 3rd series. London: Luzac, 1927-34, v. 3, 207-88.

c. the Saddharmapuṇḍarīka sutra, "Lotus of the True Law"

05076 FUJITA, K. One vehicle or three? Tr. from Japanese by L. Hurvitz. In JIP 3,1/2 (1975) 79-166.

05077 HURVITZ, L., tr. Scripture of the Lotus Blossom of the Fine Dharma. NY: ColUP, 1976. 421p. (Records of civilization - sources and studies, 94) [Tr. from the Chinese of Kumārajīva]

05078 KERN, H., tr. The Saddharmapuṇḍarīka, or the lotus of the true law. Delhi: Motilal, 1968. 454p. (SBE, 21) [Rpt. 1884 ed.]

d. other sūtra texts

05079 BAREAU, A. The superhuman personality of the Buddha and its symbolism in the Mahāparinirvāna sūtra of the Dharmaguptaka. In J.M. Kitagawa & C.H. Long, eds. Myths and Symbols.... Chicago: UChiP, 1969, 9-21.

05080 EMMERICK, R.E., tr. The Sutra of golden light; being a translation of the Suvarnabhasottamasūtra. London: Luzac, 1970. 108p. (SBB, 27)

05081 STCHERBATSKY, T., tr. Madhyānta-vibhaṅga: discourse on discrimination between middle and extremes. Osnabrück: Biblio Verlag, 1970. 106 + 58p. (Bibliotheca Buddhica, 30) [Rpt. 1936 ed.]

05082 SUZUKI, D.T. Studies in the Lankāvatāra-sūtra.... London: Routledge, 1930. 464p.

05083 THURMAN, R.A.F., tr. The holy teaching of Vimalakīrti: a Mahāyāna scripture. University Park, PA: Pennsylvania State U. Press, 1976. 166p.

4. Major Mahāyāna Doctrines and Schools

a. the Bodhisattvas, "ones whose essence is Perfect Knowledge"

05084 DAYAL, H. The bodhisattva doctrine in Buddhist Sanskrit literature. Delhi: Motilal, 1970. 392p. [1st pub. 1932]

05085 LAMOTTE, É. Mañjuśrī. In T'oung Pao 48,1-3 (1960) 1-96.

05086 LÉVI, S. Maitreya le consolateur. In Études d'orientalisme publiées par le Musée Guimet à la mémoire de Raymonde Linossier. Paris: E. Leroux, 1932, v. 2, 355-402.

05087 MALLMAN, M.-T. DE. Étude iconographique sur Mañjuśri. Paris: EFEO, 1964. 284p. (Its pub., 55)

05088 ______. Introduction à l'étude d'Avalokiteçvara. Paris: PUF, 1967. 354p.

05089 RAHULA, W. L'idéal du Bodhisattva dans le Theravāda et le Mahāyāna. In JA 259 (1971) 63-70.

b. the Mādhyamika ("Middle Way") school, founded by Nāgārjuna (c. 150-250 AD), and the concept of Śūnyatā ("Emptiness")

i. translations and studies of major texts

05090 BHATTACHARYA, K., tr. The dialectical method of Nāgārjuna. (Trans. of the "Vigrahavyāvartanī") In JIP 1,3 (1971) 217-61.

05091 INADA, K.K., tr. Nāgārjuna: a translation of his Mūlamadhyamakakārikā. Tokyo: Hokuseido Press, 1970. 204p.

05092 LAMOTTE, É., tr. Le traité de la grand vertu de sagesse, de Nāgārjuna. Louvain: Bureaux du Muséon, 1944-49. 2 v. (Bibliothèque du Muséon, 18) [Mahāprajñāpāramitāśāstra]

05093 MATICS, M.L., tr. Entering the path of enlightenment: the Bodhicāryavatāra of the Buddhist poet Śāntideva. London: Allen & Unwin, 1971. 318p.

05094 STRENG, F. Emptiness: a study of religious meaning. NY: Abingdon, 1967. 252p. [trans. & study of Mūlamadhyamakakārikā]

ii. general studies of the Mādhyamika philosophy

05095 CASEY, D.F. Nāgārjuna and Chandrakīrti: a study of significant differences. In Trans. of the Intl. Congress of Orientalists in Japan 9 (1964) 34-45.

05096 CHATALIAN, G. A study of R.H. Robinson's Early Mādhyamika in India and China. In JIP 1,4 (1972) 311-40.

05097 HUA, JAN YUN. Nāgārjuna, one or more? In HR 10,2 (1970) 139-55.

05098 KATZ, N. Appraisal of the Svātantrika-Prasaṅgika debates. In PEW 26,3 (1976) 253-67.

05099 MURTI, T.R.V. The central philosophy of Buddhism: a study of the Mādhyamika system. London: Allen & Unwin, 1955. 372p.

05100 NARAIN, H. Śūnyavāda: a reinterpretation. In PEW 13,4 (1964) 311-38.

05101 PANDEYA, R.C. The Mādhyamika philosophy: a new approach. In PEW 14,1 (1964) 3-24.

05102 RINPOCHE, SAMDHONG, tr. Mādhyamika dialectic and the philosophy of Nāgārjuna. Sarnath: Central Inst. of Higher Tibetan Studies, 1977. 233p. (The Dalai Lama Tibetan Indology studies, 1)

05103 ROBINSON, R.H. Early Mādhyamika in India and China. Madison: UWiscP, 1976. 347p.

05104 SASTRI, P.S. Nāgārjuna & Āryadeva. In IHQ 31,3 (1955) 193-202.

05105 STRENG, F.J. The Buddhist doctrine of two truths as religious philosophy. In JIP 1,3 (1971) 262-271.

05106 VENKATA RAMANAN, K. Nāgārjuna's philosophy as presented in the Mahā-prajñāpāramitā-śāstra. Rutland, VT: Tuttle, 1966. 409p.

05107 WALLESER, M. The life of Nāgārjuna from Tibetan and Chinese sources. In B. Schindler, ed. Hirth anniversary volume.... London: Probsthain, 1923, 421-55.

05108 WAYMAN, A. Contributions to the Mādhyamika school of Buddhism. In JAOS 89 (1969) 141-52.

c. the Yogācāra-Vijñānavāda school of Asaṅga and Vasubandhu (c. 300 AD)

i. translations and studies of major texts

05109 ANACKER, S. Vasubandhu's Karmasiddhiprakaraṇa and the problem of the highest meditations. In PEW 22,3 (1972) 247-258.

05110 CHAUDHURI, S. Analytical study of the Abhidharmakośa. Calcutta: Sanskrit College, 1976. 249p.

05111 HAKEDA, Y.S., tr. The awakening of faith, attributed to Aśvaghosha. NY: ColUP, 1967. 128p.

05112 LAMOTTE, É. La somme du grand véhicule d'Asaṅga. Louvain: Bureaux du muséon, 1938. 99p. [Mahāyāna saṁgraha]

05113 RAHULA, W., tr. Le compendium de la super-doctrine (philosophie) (Abhidharmasamuccaya) d'Asaṅga. Paris: EFEO, 1971. 236p.

05114 STCHERBATSKY, T., tr. The soul theory of the Buddhists. Varanasi: Bharatiya, 1970. 122p. [from Vasubandu's Abhidharmakosa]

ii. general studies of the Yogācāra school

05115 FRAUWALLNER, E. On the date of the Buddhist master of the law, Vasubandhu. Rome: IIMEO, 1951. 69p. (Serie orientale Roma, 3)

05116 JAINI, P. On the theory of the two Vasubandhus. In BSOAS 21 (1958) 45-53.

05117 KAJIYAMA, Y. Bhāvaviveka, Sthiramati & Dharmapāla. In WZKS 12/13 (1968-69) 193-203.

05118 LÉVI, S., et al. Un système de philosophie bouddhique: matériaux pour l'étude du système Vijñāptimātra. Paris: Librairie H. Champion, 1932. 207p.

05119 RUEGG, D.S. The meanings of the term Gotra and the textual history of the Ratnagotravibhāga. In BSOAS 39,2 (1976) 341-63.

05120 TUCCI, G. On some aspects of the doctrines of Maitreya (nātha) and Asaṅga. Calcutta: U. of Calcutta, 1930. 81p.

05121 UEDA, YOSHIFUMU. Two streams of thought in Yogācāra philosophy. In PEW 17,1-4 (1967) 155-65.

05122 WAYMAN, A. The Yogācāra idealism. In PEW 15 (1965) 65-73.

05123 YAMADA, I. Vijnāptimātratā of Vasubandu. In JRAS (1977) 158-76.

iii. the doctrine of trikāya, "three bodies" of the Buddha

05124 CHINZEN, A. The triple body of the Buddha. In Eastern Buddhist 2 (1922) 1-29.

05125 GUENTHER, H.V. The psychology of the three kāyas. In Uttara Bharati 2 (1955) 27-50.

05126 KRISHAN, Y. La doctrine de kāya dans le Bouddhisme. In Samādhi 6,4 (1972) 189-96.

05127 LA VALLÉE-POUSSIN, L. DE. Buddhist dogma: the three bodies of the Buddha. In JRAS (1906) 943-77.

05128 MASSON-OURSEL, P. Les trois corps du Bouddha. In JA (1913) 581-618.

05129 NAGAO, G. On the theory of the Buddha-body. In Eastern Buddhist ns 6 (1973) 25-53.

VII. RELIGIO-PHILOSOPHICAL TRADITIONS: JAINISM

A. The Tīrthaṅkaras: the 24 "Ford-finders," or Prophets of the Jaina Tradition

1. The First 23 Tīrthaṅkaras: Ṛṣabha to Pārśvanātha

05130 BLOOMFIELD, M. The life and stories of the Jaina savior Pārçvanātha. NY: Arno Press, 1979. 254p. [Rpt. 1919 ed.]

05131 JAINI, P. Jina Ṛṣabha as an avatara of Viṣṇu. In BSOAS 40,2 (1977) 321-37.

05132 KALGHATGI, T.G., ed. Tīrthankara Pārśvanātha: a study. Mysore: Dept. of Jainology and Prakrits, U. of Mysore, 1977. 214p.

2. Vardhamāna Mahāvīra, the 24th Tīrthaṅkara (5th cent. B.C. - contemporary of Gautama Buddha)

05133 DULAHARAJ, Muni. Lord Mahavira: life and teachings. Churu: Adarsh Sahitya Sangh, 1970. 74p.

05134 JACOBI, H.G. On Mahāvīra and his predecessors. In IA 9 (1880) 158-63.

05135 JAIN, A.K., ed. Lord Mahavira in the eyes of foreigners. ND: Meena Bharati, 1975. 168p.

05136 JAIN, H.L. & A.N. UPADHYE. Mahāvīra, his times and his philosophy of life. ND: Bharatiya Jnanpith, 1974. 60p.

05137 JAIN, K.C. Lord Mahāvīra and his times. Delhi: Motilal, 1974. 406p.

05138 LALWANI, K.C. Śramana Bhagavān Mahāvīra: life and doctrine. Calcutta: Minerva, 1975. 206p.

05139 LAW, B.C. Mahāvīra: his life and teachings. London: Luzac, 1937. 113p.

05140 PRAGWAT, R.B. Lord Mahavira, omniscient teacher of truth: his life and teachings. Ed. by V.G. Nair. 2nd ed. Bangalore: Shri Adinath Jain Swetambar Temple, 1969. 48p.

B. Early History of Jainism and the Division into Śvetāmbara and Digambara Sects

05141 CAILLAT, C. Atonements in the ancient ritual of the Jaina monks. Ahmedabad: L.D. Inst. of Indology, 1975. 209p. [Tr. from French]

05142 CHATTERJEE, A.K. A comprehensive history of Jainism, up to 1000 AD. Calcutta: KLM, 1978. 400p.

05143 DESAI, P.B. Jainism in South India and some Jaina epigraphs. Sholapur: Jaina Samskrti Samrakshaka Sangha, 1957. 454p.

05144 DIXIT, K.K. Early Jainism. Ahmedabad: L.D. Inst. of Indology, 1978. 99p.

05145 ______. A new contribution to the discussion of Jaina monastic discipline. In Sambodhi 5,2/3 (1976) 13-48.

05146 JAIN, K.P. The Digambara and Śwetāmbara sects of Jainism. In S.M. Katre, ed. A volume of studies in Indology presented to Prof. P.V. Kane. Poona: Oriental Book Agency, 1941, 228-37.

05147 NAHAR, P.C. Antiquity of the Jain sects. In IA 61 (1932) 121-26.

05148 RAMAN, K.V. Jainism in Tondaimandalam. In BITCM (1974) pt. 1, 1-23.

05149 SINGH, F.P. Aspects of early Jainism, as known from the epigraphs. Varanasi: BHU, 1972. 139p.

C. The Jaina Canon, in Ardhamāgadhī (a Prakrit of Magadha), and Sacred Texts in Sanskrit and Other Prakrits

05150 HANAKI, T., tr. Anuogaddaraim. Vaishalī, Bihar: Res. Inst. of Prakrit, Jainology & Ahimsa, 1970. 62 + 246p.

05151 JACOBI, H.G., tr. Jaina sūtras. Delhi: Motilal, 1964. 2 v., 234, 456p. (SBE, 22, 45) [Rpt. 1884-95 ed.]

05152 JAIN, S.A., tr. Reality. Calcutta: Vira Sasana Sangha, 1960. 300p. [Tr. of Pūjyapāda's commentary Sarvārthasiddhi]

05153 KAPADIA, H.R. A history of the canonical literature of the Jainas. Bombay: Gujarati Printing Press, 1941. 272p.

05154 LALWANI, K.C., tr. Kalpa sūtra of Bhadrabāhu Svāmi. Delhi: Motilal, 1979. 207p. + 7pl.

05155 ______. Uttarādhyāyana sūtra: the last testament of Bhagavān Mahāvīra. Calcutta: Prajñānam, 1977. 488p.

05156 LAW, B.C. Some Jaina canonical sūtras. Bombay: Bombay Branch, Royal Asiatic Soc., 1949. 213p.

05157 MALVANIA, D. & A.P. SHAH, eds. Āgamic index. Ahmedabad: L.D. Inst. of Indology, 1970-. (Lalbhai Dalpatbhai series, 28)

05158 ROTH, G. What the Jaina sources can teach us. In JOIB 24,1/2 (1974) 175-86.

05159 Sacred books of the Jainas. Ed. by Sarat Chandra Ghoshal. Arrah: Central Jaina Pub., 1917-40. 11 v. [Rpt. NY: AMS Press, 1973]

05160 SEN, M. A cultural study of the Niśītha cūrṇi. Amritsar: Sohanlal Jaindharma Pracharak Samiti, 1975. 409p.

05161 STEVENSON, J., tr. The Kalpa sūtra and Nava tatva; two works illustrative of the Jaina religion and philosophy. Varanasi: Bharat-Bharati, 1972. 144p. [1st pub. 1848]

VIII. LANGUAGE, LITERATURE, AND THE PERFORMING ARTS (c. 6th CENT. BC TO 6th CENT. AD)

A. Early Indic Linguistic Science, Developed from the Vedāṅgas Concerned with Vedic Exegesis

1. General Studies of Early Indian Linguistics; Belief in Power of Speech (vac) and Ritual Formulas (mantra)

05162 BASU, P.L. A study of the Hindu concept of Vāk: the power of the word in an oral society. Ph.D. diss., Princeton U., 1978. 192p. [UM 78-19,237]

05163 BIARDEAU, M. Théorie de la connaissance et philosophie de la parole dans le brahmanisme classique. Paris: Mouton, 1964. 484p.

05164 BROWN, W.N. The creative role of the goddess Vāc in the Rig Veda. In J.C. Heesterman, et al., eds. Pratidānam.... The Hague: Mouton, 1968, 393-97. (Janua Linguarum, ser. major, 34) [also in Mahfil 7, 3/4 (1971) 19-27]

05165 CHAKRAVARTI, P.C. The linguistic speculations of the Hindus. Calcutta: U. of Calcutta, 1933. 496p.

05166 GONDA, J. Notes on names and the name of God in ancient India. Amsterdam: North Holland, 1970. 113p.

05167 LIEBICH, B. Zur Einführung in die indische einheimische Sprachwissenschaft. Heidelberg: C. Winter, 1919-20. 4 v. (Sitzungsberichte der Heidelberger Akademie der Wissenschaften, 10-11)

05168 MAZUMDAR, P.K. The philosophy of language: in the light of Pāṇinian and the Mīmāṁsāka schools of Indian philosophy. Calcutta: SPB, 1977. 146p.

05169 PADOUX, A. Recherches sur la symbolique et l'énergie de la parole dans certains textes tantriques. 2nd ed. Paris: Inst. de civilisation indienne, 1975. 391p.

05170 RENOU, L. Les pouvoirs de la parole dans le Ṛgveda. In his Études védiques et Pāṇiniennes. Paris: Boccard, 1955, v. 1, 1-27.

05171 RUEGG, D.S. Contributions à l'histoire de la philosophie linguistique indienne. Paris: Boccard, 1959. 132p.

05172 STAAL, J.F. The concept of metalanguage and its Indian background. In JIP 3,3/4 (1975) 315-54.

05173 ______. Sanskrit philosophy of language. In M.B. Emeneau & C.A. Ferguson, ed. Linguistics in South Asia. The Hague: Mouton, 1969, 499-531. (CTL, 5)

05174 TAMBIAH, S.J. The magical power of words. In Man 3,2 (1968) 175-208.

2. The Śikṣā Vedānga: Phonetics

05175 ALLEN, W.S. Phonetics in ancient India. London: Cumberlege, 1953. 96p.

05176 KIELHORN, F. Remarks on the Śikshās. In IA 5 (1876) 141-44, 193-200.

05177 VARMA, S. Critical studies in the phonetic observations of Indian grammarians. Delhi: Munshiram, 1961. 190p. [1st pub. 1929]

3. The Nirukta Vedāṅga: Etymology-Lexicography and the Nirukta of Yāska

05178 BHATTACHARYA, B. Yāska's Nirukta and the science of etymology. Calcutta: KLM, 1958. 118p.

05179 MEHENDALE, M.A. Nirukta notes. Poona: DCPRI, 1965-78. 2 v., 72, 80p.

05180 PRASAD, M. Language of the Nirukta. Delhi: D.K., 1975. 436p.

05181 SARUP, L., tr. The Nighaṇṭu and the Nirukta; the oldest Indian treatise on etymology, philology, and semantics. Delhi: Motilal, 1967. 670p. [1st pub. 1920]

05182 SKOLD, H. The Nirukta, its place in old Indian literature, its etymologies. Lund: C.W.K. Gleerup, 1926. 375p.

4. The Vyākaraṇa Vedāṅga: Grammar

a. general studies of the Sanskrit grammarians

05183 BURNELL, A.C. On the Aindra school of Sanskrit grammarians, their place in the Sanskrit and subordinate literatures. Varanasi: Bharat-Bharati, 1976. 120p. [Rpt. 1875 ed.]

05184 DESHPANDE, M. Critical studies in Indian grammarians. I: the theory of homogeneity [savarnya]. Ann Arbor: UMCSSAS, 1975. 221p.

05185 KIELHORN, F. Katyayana and Patañjali; their relation to each other and to Panini. 2nd ed. Varanasi: IndBH, 1963. 56p. [1st pub. 1876]

05186 SARMA, K.M.K. Paṇini, Katyāyana, and Patanjali. Delhi: Sri Lal Bahadur Shastri Rashtriya Sanskrit Vidyapeeth, 1968. 185p.

05187 SCHARFE, H. Grammatical literature. Wiesbaden: Harrassowitz, 1977. 216p. (HIL, 5:2)

05188 SHASTRI, K.C. Bengal's contribution to Sanskrit grammar in the Pāṇinian and Candra systems: pt. 1. Gen. introduction. Calcutta: Sanskrit College, 1972. 389p.

05189 STAAL, J.F., ed. A reader on the Sanskrit grammarians. Cambridge: MIT, 1972. 557p.

b. Pāṇini (4th cent. BC?) and the systematization of classical Sanskrit

i. reference

05190 CARDONA, G. A note on Pāṇini technical vocabulary. In JOIB 19 (1970) 195-212.

05191 ______. Pāṇini: a survey of research. The Hague: Mouton, 1976. 384p. (Trends in linguistics, 6)

05192 DVIVEDI, H.P. Studies in Pāṇini: technical terms of the Aṣṭādhyāyī. Delhi: Inter-India, 1978. 208p.

05193 KATRE, S.M. Pāṇinian studies, I-VII. Poona: DCPRI, 1967-74. 4 v., 1466p. [incl. index and list of roots in Dhātupāṭha, dictionaries of Pāṇini and of Gaṇapāṭha]

05194 LAHIRI, P.C. Concordance Pāṇini-Patañjali (Mahābhaṣya). Breslau: M.& H. Marcus, 1935. 114p.

ii. the Aṣṭādhyāyī of Pāṇini: translations

05195 RENOU, L., tr. La grammaire de Pāṇini. Paris: EFEO, 1966. 2 v. [1st ed. 1948-54]

05196 VASU, S.C. The Aṣḥṭādhyāyī of Pāṇini. Allahabad: Indian Press, 1891-98. 8 v. in 2.

iii. studies

05197 AL-GEORGE, S. Sign (Lakṣaṇa) and propositional logic in Pānini. In E&W 19,1/2 (1969) 176-93.

05198 BAHULIKAR, S. Concerning the structure of Pāṇini's Aṣṭādhyāyī. In Indian Linguistics 34,2 (1973) 75-99.

05199 CARDONA, G. Pāṇini's Kārakas: agency, animation and identity. In JIP 2,3/4 (1974) 231-306.

05200 ______. Some principles of Pāṇini's grammar. In JIP 1,1 (1970) 40-74.

05201 ______. Studies in Indian grammarians. 1: the method of description reflected in the Śiva-Sūtras. Philadelphia: American Philosophical Soc., 1969. 48p. (TAPS, 59)

05202 DESHPANDE, M. Pāṇinian procedure of Taparakaraṇa: a historical investigation. In Zeitschrift für Vergleichende Sprachforschung 86 (1972) 207-254.

05203 DEVASTHALI, G.V. Anubandhas of Pāṇini. Poona: U. of Poona, 1967. 224p. (CASS, 13:2)

05204 FADDEGON, B. Studies on Pāṇini's grammar. Amsterdam: North Holland, 1936. 72p. (VKNAW, AL, 38:1)

05205 GOLDSTUECKER, T. Pāṇini: his place in Sanskrit literature. An investigation of some literary and chronological questions which may be settled by a study of his work. Ed. by S.N. Shastri. Varanasi: CSSO, 1965. 300p. (CSS, 48) [1st pub. 1861]

05206 MAHAVIR. Pāṇini as grammarian: with special reference to compound formations. Delhi: Bharatiya Vidya Prakashan, 1978. 105p.

05207 MISRA, V.N. The descriptive technique of Pāṇini; an introduction. The Hague: Mouton, 1966. 175p. (Janua linguarum. Series practica, 18)

05208 NATH, N.C. Pāṇinian interpretation of the Sanskrit language. Varanasi: BHU, 1969. 239p. (Its Sanskrit ser., 2)

05209 RENOU, L. Études védiques et pāṇinéennes. Paris: E. de Boccard, 1956-67. 16 v., 2223p. (Pub. de l'Inst. de Civilisation Indienne, fasc. 1, 2, 4, 6, 9, 10, 12, 14, 16, 17, 18, 20, 22, 23, 26, 27)

05210 ______. Pāṇini. In M.B. Emeneau & C.A. Ferguson, eds. Linguistics in South Asia. The Hague: Mouton, 1969, 481-98. (CTL, 5)

05211 ROCHER, R. La théorie des voix du verbe dans l'école pāṇinéenne (le 14e āhnika). Brussels: Presses universitaires de Bruxelles, 1968. 348p.

05212 SCHARFE, H. Pāṇini's metalanguage. Philadelphia: American Philosophical Soc., 1971. 53p. (Its Memoirs, 89)

05213 SEN, S. Pāṇinica. Calcutta: Sanskrit College, 1970. 10 + 34p.

05214 STAAL, J.F. Euclid and Pāṇini. In PEW 15 (1965) 99-116.

05215 THIEME, P. Pāṇini and the Pāṇinīyas. In JAOS 76 (1956) 1-23.

05216 ______. Pāṇini and the Veda: studies in the early history of linguistic science in India. Allahabad: Globe Press, 1935. 132p.

05217 WEZLER, A. Bestimmung und Angabe der Funktion von Sekundar-Suffixen durch Pāṇini. Wiesbaden: Steiner, 1975. 155p.

05218 ______. Paribhāṣā IV, V und XV; Untersuchungen zur Geschichte der einheimischen indischen grammatischen Scholastik. Bad Homburg: Gehlen, 1969. 266p.

c. Patañjali and his Mahābhāṣya, "Great Commentary" on Paṇini (c. 150 BC)

05219 JOSHI, S.D., tr. Patañjali's Vyākaraṇa-mahābhāṣya. Poona: U. of Poona, 1968-74. 5 v. (CASS, C: 3, 5....)

05220 LIMAYE, V.P. Critical studies on the Mahābhāṣya. Hoshiarpur: VVRI, 1974. 972p. (VIS, 49)

d. Bhartṛhari (c. 450-510 AD), author of Vākyapadīya, a treatise on grammar and its philosophy, and of Mahābhāṣya-dīpikā, a commentary on Patañjali

i. texts in translation

05221 BIARDEAU, M., tr. Vākyapadīya Brahmakāṇḍa, avec la vṛtti de Harivṛṣabha. Paris: Boccard, 1964. 193p.

05222 SUBRAMANIA IYER, K.A., tr. The Vākyapadīya of Bhartṛhari, with the Vṛtti; chapter I. Poona: DCPRI, 1965. 40 + 136p. (DCBC, 26)

05223 ______. The Vākyapadīya of Bhartṛhari, kāṇḍa, II. Delhi: Motilal, 1977. 61 + 205p.

ii. studies

05224 COWARD, H.G. Bhartṛhari. Boston: Twayne, 1976. 150p.

05225 NAKAMURA, H. Bhartṛhari the scholar. In IIJ 4 (1960) 282-305.

05226 RAGHAVAN PILLAI, K. The Vākyapadīya: studies in the Vākyapadīya. Delhi: Motilal, 1971-. v. 1, cantos I & II., 239p.

05227 RAU, W. Die handschriftliche Überlieferung des Vākyapadīya und seiner Kommentare. Munich: Fink, 1971. 55p.

05228 SASTRI, GAURINATH. The philosophy of word and meaning; some Indian approaches with special reference to the philosophy of Bhartṛhari. Calcutta: Sanskrit College, 1959. 292p.

05229 SUBRAMANIA IYER, K.A. Bhartṛhari; a study of the Vākyapadīya in the light of the ancient commentaries. Poona: DCPRI, 1969. 597p. (DCBC, 68)

5. Tolkāppiyam: Earliest Extant Tamil Grammar (c. 2nd Cent. BC)

05230 AGESTHIALINGOM, S. & N. KUMARASWAMI RAJA, eds. Studies in early Dravidian grammars: proceedings of the Seminar on Early Dravidian Grammars. Annamalainagar: Annamalai U., 1978. 356p.

05231 ILAKKUVANAR, S. Tholkāppiyam in English; with critical studies. Madurai: "Kural Neri" Pub. House, 1963. 545p.

05232 NATARAJA SARMA, T. The simile in Tamil; a comparative study of Tolkāppiyam uvamai iyal and Thandiyalankaram uvamai ani. Nagercoil: Jayakumari Stores, 1971. 59p.

05233 NATARAJAN, T. The language of Sangam literature and Tolkāppiyam. Madurai: Madurai Pub. House, 1977. 329p.

05234 SUBRAHMANYAN, S. A critical study of Tolkāppiyam (eḻettu and col.) and Naṉṉūl. Nagercoil: Doss Book Centre, 1977-. pt. 1, v. 1, Phonology, 176p.

05235 VELLAIVARANAN, K. A history of Tamil literature: Tolkāppiam. Annamalainagar: Annamalai University, 1957. 320p.

05236 ZVELEBIL, K.V. Tolkāppiyam. In JTS 4 (1972) 43-60.

B. Middle Indo-Aryan Language and Literature: Pāli, the Prākṛits, and Apabhraṁśa

1. General and Reference

05237 BANERJI, S.C. A companion to Middle Indo-Aryan literature. Calcutta: KLM, 1977. 351p.

05238 MEHENDALE, M.A. Some aspects of Indo-Aryan linguistics. Bombay: U. of Bombay, 1968. 123p.

05239 SEN, S. A comparative grammar of Middle Indo-Aryan. Poona: Linguistic Soc. of India, 1960. 256p. (Its Special Pub., 1)

2. Pāli

05240 BANERJI, S.C. An introduction to Pāli literature. Calcutta: Punthi Pustak, 1964. 150p.

05241 ELIZARENKOVA, T.Y. & V.N. TOPOROV. The Pāli language. Moscow: Nauka, 1976. 263p.

05242 GEIGER, W. Pali language and literature. Tr. by B.K. Ghosh. 2nd ed. Delhi: OBRC, 1968. 250p. [Rpt. 1943 ed.; 1st German ed. 1916]

05243 LAW, B.C. A history of Pāli literature. Varanasi: Bharatiya, 1974. 2 v., 689p. [Rpt. 1933 ed.]

05244 MALALASEKERA, G.P. The Pāli literature of Ceylon. Colombo: M.D. Gunasena, 1958. 329p. [1st pub. 1928]

05245 WARDER, A.K. Pāli metre: a contribution to the history of Indian literature. London: Luzac, 1967. 252p.

3. Prākṛits and Apabhraṁśa: Transitional Stages in the Emergence of the Modern Indo-Aryan Languages

05246 ALSDORF, L. Apabhraṁśa-studien. Leipzig: Deutsche Morganlandische Gesellschaft, 1937. 113p. (AKM, 22:2)

05247 BANERJEE, S.R. A bibliography of Prakrit language. Calcutta: Sanskrit Book Depot, 1977. 31p.

05248 ______. The eastern school of Prakrit grammarians: a linguistic study. Calcutta: Vidyasagar Pustak Mandir, 1977. 133 + 30 p.

05249 CHANDRA, K.R., ed. Proceedings of the Seminar on Prakrit Studies, 1973. Ahmedabad: L.D. Inst. of Indology, 1978. 37 + 184p.

05250 DANDEKAR, R.N. & A.M. GHATAGE, eds. Proceedings of the Seminar in Prakrit Studies, June 23-27, 1969. Poona: U. of Poona, 1970. 246p.

05251 HANDIQUI, K.K., tr. Pravarasena's Setubandha. Ahmedabad: Prakrit Text Soc., 1976. 806p. (Its series, 20)

05252 JAIN, J.C. The importance of Vasudevahiṇḍi. In WZKS 19 (1975) 103-16.

05253 JHA, M. Magadhī and its formation. Calcutta: Sanskrit College, 1967. 262p. (Its Res. ser., 60)

05254 KATRE, S.M. Prakrit languages and their contribution to Indian culture. 2nd ed. Poona: DCPRI, 1964. 95p. (DCBC, 17)

05255 LANMAN, C.R., tr. Rāja-çekhara's Karpūra-mañjarī. Cambridge: HUP, 1901. 289p.

05256 NITTI-DOLCI, L. The Prākrita grammarians. Tr. from French by P. Jha. Delhi: Motilal, 1972. 240p.

05257 PISCHEL, R. Comparative grammar of the Prākrit languages. Tr. from German by S. Jha. 2nd ed. Delhi: Motilal, 1965. 437 + 204p.

05258 RISHABH CHANDRA, K. A critical study of Paumcariyam. Vaishali: Res. Inst. on Prakrit, Jainology and Ahimsa, 1972. 641p.

05259 UPADHYE, A.N., tr. Kamsavaho; a Prākrit poem in classical style by Rāma Pānivāda. Delhi: Motilal, 1966. 213p.

05260 VARARUCHI. The Prākrita-prakāśa, with the commentary of Bhāmaha. Tr. by E.B. Cowell. Hertford: S. Austin, 1854. 204p.

C. The Beginnings of Classical Sanskrit Literature: Kāvya, including Drama (Nāṭya), Narrative Verse (Sarga bandha), and Stories (Kathā)

1. Kāvya - General Studies

05261 ARYA, U. Man in kāvya. Delhi: Motilal, 1971. 38p. [In LEW 15,2 (1971) 183-208]

05262 RENOU, L. Sur la structure du kāvya. In JA 247 (1959) 1-114. [grammar, phraseology, vocabulary]

05263 WARDER, A.K. Indian Kāvya literature. Delhi: Motilal, 1972-. v. 1-3, 281, 393, 305p.

2. Classical Sanskrit Drama - General Studies
a. bibliographies

05264 RAGHAVAN, V. A bibliography of English translations of Sanskrit dramas. In IL 3 (1959) 141-53.

05265 SCHUYLER, M. A bibliography of the Sanskrit drama .... NY: ColUP, 1906. 105p.

b. general histories and surveys

05266 BHATT, S.C. Drama in ancient India. ND: Amrit Book Co., 1961. 100p.

05267 BYRSKI, M.C. Concept of ancient Indian theatre. ND: Munshiram, 1974. 207p.

05268 DANGE, S.A. & S.S. DANGE. Critiques on Sanskrit dramas. Moradabad: Darshana Printers, 1963. 123p.

05269 GHOSH, M. Contributions to the history of the Hindu drama: its origin, development and diffusion. Calcutta: KLM, 1958. 63p.

05270 KEITH, A.B. The Sanskrit drama in its origin, development, theory and practice. London: OUP, 1970. 405p. [Rpt. 1924 ed.]

05271 KONOW, S. The Indian drama (the Sanskrit drama). Tr. S.N. Ghosal. Calcutta: General Printers & Pub., 1969. 92 + 213p. [1st German ed. 1920]

05272 LEVI, S. Le théâtre indien. Paris: Collège de France, Librairie H. Champion, 1963. 2 v. in 1. [1st pub. 1890. English tr. by N. Mukherjee. Calcutta: Writers Workshop, 1978-.]

05273 RANGACHARYA, A. Drama in Sanskrit literature. 2nd rev. ed. Bombay: Popular, 1967. 229p.

05274 SHEKHAR, I. Sanskrit drama: its origin and decline. 2nd ed. ND: Munshiram, 1977. 214p. + 9 pl. [also includes regional dramas]

05275 WELLS, H.W. The classical drama of India: studies in its values for the literature and theatre of the world. Westport, CT: Greenwood Press, 1975. 196p. [Rpt. 1963 ed.]

05276 WILSON, H.H., et al. Theatre of the Hindus. Calcutta: Susil Gupta, 1955. 224p. [1st pub. 1871]

c. special topics

05277 BHAT, G.K. Tragedy and Sanskrit drama. Bombay: Popular, 1974. 166p. [Includes English tr. of Bhāsa's Ūrbhanga and Karnabhāra.]

05278 ______. The Vidūṣaka. Ahmedabad: New Order Book Co., 1959. 308p.

05279 CHANDRA, K.R. Proportion of Prakrit in our ancient classical dramas. In JOIB 24,1/2 (1974) 155-74.

05280 DALAL, M.L. Conflict in Sanskrit drama. ND: Somaiya, 1973. 342p.

05281 DIKSHIT, R. Women in Sanskrit dramas. ND: Mehar Chand Lachhman Das, 1964. 425p.

05282 PARIKH, J.T. Sanskrit comic characters. Surat: Popular Book Store, 1962. 72p.

05283 URSEKAR, H.S. Music in Sanskrit drama. In JASBombay 41/42 (1966-67) 124-44.

3. Early Dramatic Theory and Criticism
a. general

05284 BHAT, G.K. Sanskrit drama: a perspective on theory and practice. Dharwar: Karnatak U., 1975. 122p.

05285 MAINKAR, T.G. Studies in Sanskrit dramatic criticism. Delhi: Motilal, 1971. 136p.

05286 ______. The theory of the saṁdhis and the saṁdhyaṅgas. Delhi: Ajanta, 1978. 193p.

05287 RAGHAVAN, V. Sanskrit drama: theory and performance. In Comparative Drama 1,1 (1967) 36-48.

05288 SHASTRI, S.N. The laws and practice of Sanskrit drama. Varanasi: CSSO, 1961. v. 1, 556p. (CSS, 14)

b. the Nāṭyaśāstra of "Bharata-muni" (compiled 5th cent. BC - 2nd cent. AD): classic text of drama, dance, and music
i. translations

05289 BHAT, G.K. Bharata-nāṭya-mañjarī: Bharata on the theory and practice of drama: a selection from Bharata's Nāṭyaśāstra. Poona: BORI, 1975. 120 + 277p.

05290 DAUMAL, R. Bharata; l'origine du théâtre, la poésie et la musique en Inde. Traductions de textes sacrés et profanes. Paris: Gallimard, 1970. 210p.

05291 GHOSH, M.M., tr. The Nāṭyaśāstra; a treatise on ancient Indian dramaturgy and histrionics, ascribed to Bharata Muni. Rev. 2nd ed. Calcutta: Manisha Granthalaya, 1967-. v. 1, 537p. [1st ed. 1950]

05292 MASSON, J.L. & M.V. PATWARDHAN. Aesthetic rapture; the Rasādhyaya of the Nāṭyaśāstra. Poona: DCPRI, 1970. 2 v.

05293 NAIDU, B.V.N., et al., tr. Tāṇḍava Lakṣaṇam; or, the fundamentals of ancient Hindu dancing; being a translation into English of the fourth chapter of the Nāṭya śāstra of Bharata, with a glossary of the technical dance terms.... ND: Munshiram, 1971. 177p. [1st pub. 1936]

ii. studies

05294 APPA RAO, P.S.R. A monograph on Bharata's Naatya Saastra: Indian dramatology. Tr. from Telugu by P. Sri Rama Sastry. Hyderabad: Naatya Maalaa Pub., 1967. 186p.

05295 GHOSH, M.M. The date of Bharata Nāṭya Śāstra. In CUDL 25,4 (1934) 1-54.

05296 KALE, P. The theatric universe: a study of the Nāṭyaśāstra. Bombay: Popular, 1974. 196p.

05297 KUNHAN RAJA, C. Aristotle's katharsis and Bharata's Sthāyibhāvas. In ALB 12 (1948) 1-16.

05298 RANGACHARYA, A. Introduction to Bharata's Nāṭya-Śāstra. Bombay: Popular, 1966. 80p.

05299 SUBRAHMANYAM, P. Bharata's art, then and now. Bombay: Bhulabhai Memorial Inst., 1979. 93p.

c. the Abhinayadarpana of Nandikeśvara; "mirror of gesture"

05300 COOMARASWAMY, A.K. & G.K. DUGGIRALA, tr. The mirror of gesture, being the Abhinaya darpana of Nandikeśvara. 2nd ed. ND: Munshiram, 1970. 52p. + 15 pl. [1st pub. 1917]

05301 GHOSH, M.M., tr. Nandikesvara's Abhinayadarpanam: a manual of gesture and posture used in ancient Indian dance and drama. 3rd ed. rev. Calcutta: Manisha Granthalaya, 1975. 141p.

4. Early Sanskrit Drama and Poetry in Translation, with Studies of Major Authors
a. Aśvaghoṣa (1st cent. AD) - his Buddhacarita and Saundarānanda, both based on the Buddha's life, are the earliest extant Sanskrit mahākāvyas

05302 COWELL, E.B., tr. The Buddha-karita: or life of Buddha. ND: Cosmo, 1977. 382p. [1st pub. 1894 as SBE, 49]

05303 DATTA, S.K. Aśvaghoṣa as a poet and a dramatist: a critical study. Burdwan: U. of Burdwan, 1979. 159p.

05304 JOHNSTON, E.H., tr. The Buddhacarita: or, acts of the Buddha. ND: OBRC, 1972. 2 v. in 1. [1st pub. 1935-36]

05305 ______., tr. The Saundarānanda of Aśvaghoṣa. Delhi: Motilal, 1975. 171 + 123p. [Rpt. of 1928-32 ed.]

05306 LAW, B.C. Aśvaghoṣa. Calcutta: RASB, 1946. 92p.

05307 SEN, S. The language of Aśvaghoṣa's Saundarānanda. In JASBengal 26 (1930) 181-206.

b. Śūdraka, king and playwright (c. 3rd cent.?), reputed author of Mṛcchakaṭikā, "The little clay cart"

05308 DEVASTHALI, G.V. Introduction to the study of Mṛcchakaṭikā. Poona: Oriental Book House, 1951. 184p.

05309 OLIVER, R.P., tr. Mṛcchakaṭikā = The little clay cart: a drama in ten acts, attributed to King Sūdraka. Westport, CT: Greenwood Press, 1975. 250p. [Rpt. 1938 ed.]

05310 RYDER, A.W., tr. Mṛcchakaṭikā.... The little clay cart. Cambridge: HUP, 1905. 176p.

05311 VAN BUITENEN, J.A.B., tr. Two plays of ancient India. NY: ColUP, 1968. 278p. [Sudraka's Mṛcchakaṭikā and Visākhadatta's Mudrarākṣasa]

c. Bhāsa (c. 4th cent. AD), reputed author of Svapnavāsavadatta "Vāsavadattā seen in a dream", and other recently discovered plays

05312 BHAT, G.K. Bhāsa-studies. Kolhapur: Maharashtra Granth Bhandar, 1968. 147p. (His collected papers, 1)

05313 JANVIER, E.P., tr. Madhyama Vyāyoga. Mysore: Wesleyan Mission Press, 1921. 44p.

05314 KUNBAE, BAK. Avimāraka and Bālacarita: Bhāsa's two plays. ND: Meharchand Lachmandas, 1968. 324p.

05315 MASSON, J.L. & D.D. KOSAMBI, tr. Avimāraka, love's enchanted world. Delhi: Motilal, 1970. 151p.

05316 PUSALKER, A.D. Bhāsa: a study. 2nd rev. ed. ND: Munshiram, 1968. 613p. [Rpt. 1940 ed.]

05317 RANGACHAR, S. Pratijñāyaugandharāyaṇam, a play in four acts. Rev. 3rd ed. Mysore: Samskrita Sahitya Sadana, 1962. 178p.

05318 RAO, A. & B.G. RAO, tr. Three plays of Bhāsa. ND: Orient Longmans, 1971. 165p.

05319 SANKARA RAMA SASTRI, C. Svapnavāsavadattā, a Sanskrit play ascribed to Bhāsa. 2nd ed. Madras: Sri Balamanorama Press, 1966. 242p.

05320 SUKTHANKAR, V.S., tr. Vāsavadattā. London: OUP, 1923. 93p.

05321 UNNI, N.P. New problems in Bhāsa plays. Trivandrum: College Book House, 1978. 338p.

05322 WOOLNER, A.C. & L. SARUP, tr. Thirteen Trivandrum plays, attributed to Bhasa. London: OUP, 1930-31. 2 v.

d. Kālidāsa (c. 400 AD): India's Greatest Poet and Dramatist
i. bibliography and reference

05323 BANERJI, S.C. Kālidāsa-kośa; a classified register of the flora, fauna, geographical names, musical instruments, and legendary figures in Kālidāsa's works. Varanasi: CSSO, 1968. 83p. (CSS, 61)

05324 NARANG, S.P. Kālidāsa bibliography. ND: Heritage, 1976. 412p.

05325 SCHARPE, A. Kālidāsa-lexicon. Bruges: De Tempel, 1954-75. v. 1 (romanized texts), pts. 1 & 2, 134, 149p.; v. 2 (references & concordance of quotations), pts. 1 & 2, 276, 253p.

ii. general studies of Kālidāsa, his life and work

05326 BHAWE, S.S. Kālidāsa, the national poet of India. 2nd ed. Baroda: Good Companions, 1964. 88p.

05327 KARMARKAR, R.D. Kālidāsa. Dharwar: Karnatak U., 1960. 239p.

05328 KRISHNAMOORTHY, K. Kālidāsa. NY: Twayne, 1972. 155p.

05329 KUNHAN RAJA, C. Kālidāsa; a cultural study. Waltair: Andhra U., 1956. 210p.

05330 MAINKAR, T.G. Kālidāsa, his art & thought. Poona: Deshmukh Prakashan, 1962. 215p.

05331 MIRASHI, V.V. & N.R. NAVLEKAR. Kālidāsa; date, life, and works. Bombay: Popular, 1969. 473p.

05332 NAGAIAH, S. Kālidāsa. Madras: Super Power Press, 1978. 220p.

05333 RUBEN, W. Kālidāsa; die menschliche Bedeutung seiner Werke. Berlin: Akademie-Verlag, 1956. 111p.

05334 SABNIS, S.A. Kālidāsa, his style and his times. Bombay: N.M. Tripathi, 1966. 480p.

05335 SINGH, A.D. Kālidāsa: a critical study. Delhi: Bharatiya, 1977. 350p.

iii. studies of special topics

05336 BHANDARE, L.S. Imagery of Kālidāsa. Bombay: Popular, 1968. 122p.

05337 CHAKLADAR, H.C. The geography of Kālidāsa. In ISPP 4 (1963) 208-25, 375-78, 411-57.

05338 HARRIS, M.B. Kalidasa; poet of nature. Boston: Meador, 1936. 105p.

05339 INGALLS, D.H.H. Kālidāsa and the attitudes of the golden age. In JAOS 96 (1976) 15-26.

05340 Kālidāsa & south Indian literatures. Madras: Sanskrita Academy, 1977. 40p.

05341 LAW, B.C. Geographical aspect of Kālidāsa's works. Delhi: Bharatiya, 1976. 46p. [Rpt. 1953 ed.]

05342 MANSINHA, M. Kālidāsa & Shakespeare. ND: Motilal, 1969. 156p.

05343 SIVARAMAMURTI, C. Kālidāsa and painting. In JORM 7 (1933) 160-85.

05344 TRIVEDI, R.D. Viṣṇu & his incarnations in the works of Kālidāsa. In E&W 22,1/2 (1972) 51-62.

05345 VENKATARAMAYYA, M. Rāmagiri of Kālidāsa. In JIH 41 (1963) 69-72.

05346 YADAV, B.R. A critical study of the sources of Kālidāsa. Delhi: Bhavana Prakashan, 1974. 247p.

iv. translations of Kālidāsa's plays and poems, complete or selected

05347 FAUCHE, H., tr. Oeuvres completes de Kālidāsa. Paris: A. Durand, 1859-60. 2 v. in 1.

05348 RYDER, A.W., tr. Shākuntalā and other writings of Kālidāsa. NY: E.P. Dutton, 1959. 216p. [1st pub. 1912]

v. Śakuntalā: the first Indian nātaka (heroic drama) to inspire the admiration of the West

05349 BOSE, R.M. Kālidāsa: Abhijñāna-Śakuntalam; a synthetic study, with about 30,000 quotations & references. 5th ed., rev. Calcutta: Modern Book Agency, 1970. 885p.

05350 DEVADHAR, C.R., tr. Abhijñāna-Śakuntalā. Delhi: Motilal, 1966. 368p.

05351 EMENEAU, M.B., tr. Abhijñāna-Śakuntalā. Berkeley: UCalP, 1962. 115p. [tr. from the Bengali recension]

05352 JONES, W., tr. Śacontalā; or, The fatal ring: an Indian drama. London: Printed for Edwards, by J. Cooper, 1792. 152p.

vi. Vikramorvaśīya, drama of the nymph Urvaśī

05353 COWELL, E.B., tr. Vikramorvaśī. Hertford: S. Austin, 1851. 110p.

05354 KALE, M.R., tr. The Vikramorvaśīyam of Kālidāsa. 11th ed. Delhi: Motilal, 1967. 402p.

vii. Mālavikāgnimitra, drama of the king and the princess

05355 GEROW, E., tr. Mālavikā & Agnimitra: a tr. of Kālidāsa's play. In Mahfil 7,3/4 (1971) 67-128.

05356 KALE, M.R., tr. The Mālavikāgnimitra. 6th rev. & enl. ed. Bombay: A.R. Sheth, 1968. 384p.

05357 TAWNEY, C.H., tr. Mālavikāgnimitra: a Sanskrit play by Kālidāsa. 3rd ed. Varanasi: IndBH, 1964. 160p. [1st ed. 1875]

viii. Meghadūta, "the Cloud Messenger": Kālidāsa's most famous poem in extended lyric form

05358 EDGERTON, F. & E. EDGERTON, tr. The cloud messenger. Ann Arbor: UMichP, 1964. 87p.

05359 NATHAN, L., tr. The transport of Love = The Meghadūta of Kālidāsa. Berkeley: UCalP, 1976. 116p.

05360 ROOKE, G.H., tr. Meghadūta. London: OUP, 1935. 82p.

05361 ROYCHOWDHURY, K.C. Kālidāsa's imagery in "Meghadūta". In IL 19,2 (1976) 92-118.

05362 WILSON, H.H., tr. The Megha dūta: or, Cloud messenger: a poem in the Sanskrit language. 4th ed. Varanasi: CSSO, 1973. 151p. (CSS, 9) [Rpt. 1843 ed.]

ix. Raghuvaṁśa, a mahākāvya relating the history of Raghu, of Rāma's lineage

05363 ANANTAPADMANABHAN, K.N., tr. Raghuvaṁśam of Kālidāsa. Madras: Ramayana Pub. House, 1973. 296p.

05364 ANTOINE, R., tr. The dynasty of Raghu. Calcutta: Writers Workshop, 1972. 230p.

05365 JOHNSTONE, P.D.L., tr. Raghuvaṁśa. London: J.M. Dent, 1902. 200p.

05366 RANGANATHAN, P. Kālidāsa's Raghuvaṁśa; a study. ND: Ranganathan, 1964. 140p. [1st pub. in the Sunday Standard, 1962]

05367 RENOU, L, tr. Raghuvaṁśa, or Le raghuvaṁça. Paris: P. Guethner, 1928. 218p.

x. Kumārasaṁbhava, a mahākāvya on the birth of the war-god, Skanda, son of Śiva and Pārvatī

05368 GRIFFITH, R.T.H., tr. The birth of the war god [Kumārasaṁbhava]. London: W.H. Allen, 1853. 89p.

05369 KALE, M.R., tr. Kālidāsa's Kumārasaṁbhava, cantos I-VIII, complete. 6th ed. Delhi: Motilal, 1967. 175 + 168p.

05370 SARKAR, R. The poetical transmutation of some philosophical concepts in Kumārasaṁbhava. In IT 3/4 (1975-76) 413-24.

05371 SURYAKANTA. Kālidāsa's vision of Kumārasaṁbhava, a study of the Kumāra-problem; a key to the correct comprehension of Kālidāsa's poem and philosophy. Delhi: Mehar Chand Lachman Das, 1963. 150p.

05372 TUBINI, B. La naissance de Kumāra (Kumārasaṁbhava) .... Paris: Gallimard, 1958. 176p.

05373 WALTER, O., tr. The divine marriage. Tr. from German by G.B. Burch. Mystic, CT: L. Verry, 1970. 77p. [1st German ed. 1913]

xi. Ṛtusaṁhara, a lyric poem on the six seasons, attributed to Kālidāsa

05374 KALE, M.R., tr. The Ṛitusaṁhāra of Kālidāsa. 2nd ed. Delhi: Motilal, 1967. 175p.

05375 WILSON, H.H., tr. Ṛitu-saṁhāra: or, an account of seasons. Varanasi: IndBH, 1966. 32p.

e. Viśākhadatta (5th cent. AD): Gupta courtier and author of Mudrārākṣasa, "Minister Rākṣasa and his signet ring," a semi-historical play

05376 DEVASTHALI, G.V. Introduction to the study of Mudrā-rākṣasa. Bombay: K.B. Dhavale, 1948. 174p.

05377 RAY, S.R., tr. Mudrā-rākṣhasam. Calcutta: Prankrishna Chakravarty, 1918. 545p.

05378 RUBEN, W. Der Sinn des Dramas "Das Siegel und Rākshasa" (Mudrārākṣhasa). Berlin: Academie-Verlag, 1956. 211p.

05379 VAN BUITENEN, J.A.B., tr. Two plays of ancient India. NY: ColUP, 1968. 278p. [Sūdraka's Mṛcchakaṭikā and Viśākhadatta's Mudrārākṣasa]

f. other kāvya (poems & plays) and anthologies

05380 CAPPELLER, C., tr. Bhāravi's poem Kirātārjunīya, or, Arjuna's combat with the Kirāta. Cambridge: HUP, 1912. 206p. (HOS, 15) [in German]

05381 GHOSH, M.M., tr. Glimpses of sexual life in Nanda-Maurya India: translation of the Caturbhāṇī, together with a critical edition of text. Calcutta: Manisha Granthalaya, 1975. 389p.

05382 LAL, P. Great Sanskrit plays: in new English transcreations. Norfolk, CT: New Directions, 1964. 396p. [1st pub. 1957]

05383 NANDARGIKAR, B.R., tr. The Jānakīharaṇam, of Kumāradāsa. Bombay: Indu-Prakash Steam-press, 1907. 533p.

05384 SWAMINATHAN, R. Jānakīharaṇa of Kumāradāsa: a study, critical text, and English translation of cantos xvi-xx. Ed. by V. Raghavan. Delhi: Motilal, 1977. 275p.

05385 WELLS, H.W., tr. Classical triptych: Śakuntalā, The little clay cart, Nāgānanda; new rendering into English verse. Mysore: Literary half-yearly, U. of Mysore, 1970. 394p.

05386 ______. Sanskrit plays from epic sources. Baroda: MSUB, 1968. 258p.

5. Kathā (Story Literature): Collections of Fables and Tales

a. general studies

05387 STERNBACH, L. The Kathā literature and the Purāṇas. In Purana 7,1 (1965) 19-86.

05388 ______. The kāvya-portions in the kathā-literature (Pancatantra, Hitopadeśa, Vikramacarita, Vetālapañcaviṁśatikā, & Śukasaptati); an analysis. ND: Meharchand Lachhmandas, 1971-. 2 v., 411, 388p.

b. Bṛhatkathā, "The great story" of Guṇādhya (c. 4th cent. AD?): prototype of Sanskrit story literature; Prakrit original is lost

05389 JAIN, J.C., tr. The Vasudevahiṇḍi: an authentic Jain version of the Bṛhatkathā [Saṅghadāsagaṇi Vācaka]; with selected translations compared to the Bṛhatkathāślokasaṅgraha, Kathāsaritsāgara, Bṛhatkathāmañjarī, and some important Jaina works, including the unpublished Majjhimakhaṇḍa. Ahmedabad: L.D. Inst. of Indology, 1977. 740p.

05390 LACÔTE, F. Essai sur Guṇāḍhya et la Bṛhatkathā. Paris: E. Leroux, 1908. 335p.

05391 ______, tr. Bṛhat-Kathā çlokasaṁgraha, I-XXVIII. Paris: Imprimérie Nationale, 1908-29. 2 v. in 1.

05392 NELSON, D. Bṛhatkathā studies: the problem of an Ur-text. In JAS 37,4 (1978) 663-76.

05393 PRASAD, S.N. Studies in Guṇādhya. Varanasi: Chaukhambha Orientalia, 1977. 163p. (CORS, 6)

c. Pañcatantra, "the five treatises," attrib. to Viṣṇuśarma (date unknown): didactic fables aiming at secular and material success
i. translations

05394 EDGERTON, F. The Pañchatantra reconstructed; an attempt to establish the lost original... on the basis of the principal extant versions. New Haven: American Oriental Soc., 1924. 2 v.

05395 ______, tr. The Pañchatantra. London: Allen & Unwin, 1964. 151p.

05396 HERTEL, J., tr. Tantrākhyāyikā. Die älteste fassung des Pañcatantra. Leipzig: Teubner, 1909. 2 v.

05397 LANCEREAU, É., tr. Pañcatantra. Paris: Gallimard, 1965. 383p.

05398 RICE, S. Ancient Indian fables and stories; being a selection from the Pañchatantra. Folcroft, PA: Folcroft Library Editions, 1974. 126p. [Rpt. 1924 ed.]

05399 RYDER, A.W., tr. The Panchatantra. Chicago: UChiP, 1962. 470p. [1st pub. 1925]

ii. studies of the Pañcatantra and its world-wide diffusion

05400 BROWN, W.N. The Pañcatantra in modern Indian folklore. JAOS 39 (1919) 1-54.

05401 FALK, H. Quellen des Pañcatantra. Wiesbaden: Harrassowitz, 1978. 205p. (FBI, 12)

05402 GEIB, R. Zur Frage nach der Urfassung des Pañcatantra. Wiesbaden: Harrassowitz, 1969. 196p. (FBI, 2)

05403 HERTEL, J. Das Pañcatantra, seine geschichte und seine verbreitung. Leipzig: B.G. Teubner, 1914. 459p.

05404 ______. Über das Tāntrākhyāyikā, die Kaśmīrische rezension des Pañcatantra. Leipzig: B.G. Teubner, 1904. 28 + 154p.

05405 RUBEN, W. Das Pañchatantra und seine Morallehre. Berlin: Akademie-Verlag, 1959. 305p.

d. collections of tales from classical literature

05406 ADAVAL, N. The story of King Udayana as gleaned from Sanskrit, Pali & Prakrit sources. Varanasi: CSSO, 1970. 292p. (CSS, 74)

05407 GHOSE, O.K. Tales from the Indian classics. Bombay: Jaico, 1961.

05408 KRISHNASWAMI AIYAR, V. Stories from Indian classics. Tr. from Sanskrit by P. Sankaranarayanan. Bombay: BVB, 1966. 175p.

05409 NARAVANE, V.S. Stories from the Indian classics. Bombay: Asia, 1962. 303p.

05410 VAN BUITENEN, J.A.B. Tales of ancient India. Chicago: UChiP, 1959. 260p.

05411 ______, tr. The hermit and the harlot. In Mahfil 7,3/4 (1971) 149-166. [a tale by Baudhāyana]

D. Classical Tamil Literature in the Kingdoms of the Pāṇḍyas, Cōḻas, and Cēras

1. General Studies of Ancient Tamil Literature

05412 SOMASUNDARA BHARATHIAR, N.S. The papers of Dr. Navalar Somasundara Bharathiar. Ed. by S. Sambasivan. Madurai: Navalar Puthaka Nilayam, 1967. 143p.

05413 SOMASUNDARAM PILLAI, J.M. A history of Tamil literature with texts and translations from the earliest times to 600 A.D. Annamalainagar: 1968. 424p.

05414 THANI NAYAGAM, X.S. The period of ethical literature in Tamil: third century to the seventh century A.D. In J.C. Heesterman, et al., eds. Pratidānam.... The Hague: Mouton, 1968, 601-14.

2. The Poems of the Saṅgam/Caṅkam Age (c. 1st-4th Cent. AD): Works of Three Legendary "Academies"
a. general
i. translations

05415 GROS, F., tr. Le Paripāṭal, texte tamoul. Pondicherry: IFI, 1968. 63 + 319p. (Its pub., 35)

05416 HART, G.L., III. Poets of the Tamil anthologies; ancient poems of love and war. Princeton: PUP, 1979. 212p.

05417 THANGAPPA, M.L., tr. Hues and harmonies from an ancient land: a translation of Tamil poetry. Madras: Pandian Pub., 1970. 55p.

ii. studies

05418 HART, G.L., III. The poems of ancient Tamil: their milieu and their Sanskrit counterparts. Berkeley: UCalP, 1975. 308p.

05419 JESUDASAN, C. Peaks of Sangam poetry. Trivandrum: Ramalakshi Press, 1960. 91p.

05420 MARR, J.R. The translations of Cankam literature. In TC 12,2/3 (1966) 223-29.

05421 NILAKANTA SASTRI, K.A. Sangam literature: its cults & culture. Madras: Swathi, 1972. 98p.

05422 PERIAKARUPPAN, R. Tradition and talent in Cankam poetry. Madurai: Madurai Pub. House, 1976. 331p.

05423 RAMANUJAN, A.K. Form in classical Tamil poetry. In A.F. Sjoberg, ed. Symposium on Dravidian civilization. NY: Pemberton, 1971, 73-104.

05424 The Sangham age; being essays on early Tamil literature together with English renderings of selected poems of the Sangham age. Calcutta: Bharathi Tamil Sangham, 1968. 187p.

05425 THANI NAYAGAM, X.S. Landscape and poetry; a study of nature in classical Tamil poetry. 2nd ed. Bombay: Asia, 1966. 151p. [1st ed. 1963]

05426 ______. Nature in ancient Tamil poetry, concept and interpretation. Tuticorin: Tamil Literature Soc., 1953. 185p.

05427 VARADARAJAN, M. The treatment of nature in Sangam literature (ancient Tamil literature). Madras: SISSWPS, 1969. 436p.

b. akam, "love" poetry: the "interior landscape"
i. translations

05428 RAMANUJAN, A.K., tr. The interior landscape; love poems from a classical Tamil anthology. Bloomington: Indiana U. Press, 1967. 125p.

05429 SHANMUGAM PILLAI, M. & D.E. LUDDEN, tr. Kuṟontokai: an anthology of classical Tamil love poetry. Madurai: Koodal Pub., 1976. 463p.

ii. studies

05430 HART, G.L., III. Some aspects of kinship in ancient Tamil literature. In T.R. Trautman, ed. Kinship & history in South Asia. Ann Arbor: UMCSSAS, 1974, 29-60. (MPSSA, 7)

05431 LIENHARD, S. Tamil literary conventions and Sanskrit Muktaka poetry. In WZKS 20 (1976) 101-10.

05432 MANICKAM, V.S. The Tamil concept of love. Madras: SISSWPS, 1962. 339p.

05433 RAMACHANDRAN, C.E. Ahananuru in its historical setting. Madras: U. of Madras, 1974. 148p.

c. puṟam, "heroic" or war poetry: the "exterior," collections of the bards

05434 ANNAMALAI, E. A fraternity with diversity and individuality; Tamil heroic poetry. In Mahfil 6,2/3 (1970) 83-89.

05435 KAILASAPATHY, K. Tamil heroic poetry. London: OUP, 1968. 282p. [hist. & sociological background]

05436 VANAMAMALAI, N. A study of the historical ballads of Tamilnad. In Intl. Conference Seminar of Tamil Studies, 1st, 1966, Proceedings. Kuala Lumpur: 1968, 597-620.

3. The Early Tamil Epics (Comparable to Sanskrit Mahākāvyas) of the Post-Sangam Period

a. the Cilappatikāram/Shilappadikāram, "The lay of the anklet" by Prince Ilankōvaṭikaḷ/Ilango Adigal (c. 450 AD), leading epic of the Jaina cycle

i. translations

05437 DANIELOU, A., tr. The Shilappadikaram (The ankle bracelet). NY: New Directions, 1965. 211p.

05438 KARUNANITHI, M. Tale of the anklet = Silappathikāram. English rendering by T.G. Narayanaswamy. Madras: Tamizhkani Pathippagam, 1976. 83p. [Play based on the Tamil epic Cilappatikāram by Ilankōvatikal; rpt. 1968 ed.]

05439 RAMACHANDRA DIKSHITAR, V.R. The Cilappatikāram. 2nd ed. Madras: SISSWPS, 1978. 436p. [1st ed. 1939]

ii. studies

05440 ALPHONSO-KARKALA, J.B. Thematic and structural antithesis in Shilappadikaram. In IL 15,1 (1972) 56-62.

05441 BECK, B.E.F. The study of a Tamil epic: several versions of Sillapadikaram compared. In JTS 1 (1972) 23-38.

05442 MUDALIAR, V.S. Gleanings from Silappathikaram. Madras: 1968. 46p.

05443 RAMANATHAN, S. Music in Cilappatikaaram. Ph.D. diss., Wesleyan U., 1974. 325p. UM 74-23,026

05444 VANAMAMALAI, N. The folk motif in Silappadikaram. In Intl. Conference Seminar of Tamil Studies, 1st, 1966, Proceedings. Kuala Lumpur: 1968, 138-65.

05445 VARADARAJAN, M. Ilango Adigal. ND: Sahitya Akademi, 1967. 72p.

b. the Maṇimēkalai, "The jewel belt," by Cāttaṉār (c. 550 AD): a sequel to Cilappatikāram, but partisan to Buddhism

05446 GUNASEGARAM, S. Maṇimēkalai. In TC 10 (1963) 42-52.

05447 KANDASWAMY, S.N. Buddhism as expounded in Maṇimēkalai. Annamalainagar: Annamalai U., 1978. 410p.

05448 KRISHNASWAMI AIYANGAR, S. Maṇimēkhalai in its historical setting. London: Luzac, 1928. 35 + 235p.

IX. ART AND ARCHITECTURE OF THE ANCIENT PERIOD (C. 600 BC - 600 AD)

A. General Surveys of Ancient Indian Art (C. 600 BC - 600 AD)

05449 AGRAWALA, P.K. Early Indian bronzes. Varanasi: Prithvi Prakashan, 1977. 158 + 72p.

05450 BACHHOFER, L. Early Indian sculpture. NY: Hacker Art Books, 1972. 2 v. [Rpt. 1929 ed.]

05451 CHANDA, R.P. The beginnings of art in Eastern India with special reference to sculptures in the Indian Museum, Calcutta. Calcutta: Government of India Central Publications Branch, 1927. 54p. (ASI Memoir, 30)

05452 CODRINGTON, K. DE B. Ancient India. London: E. Benn, 1926. 65p. + 76 pl.

05453 COOMARASWAMY, A.K. Early Indian architecture. In Eastern Art 2 (1930) 209-35; 3 (1931) 181-217.

05454 GANGULY, A.B. Fine arts in ancient India. ND: Abhinav, 1979. 180p. + 8 pl.

05455 GOETZ, H. Imperial Rome and the genesis of classic Indian art. In his Studies in the history, religion and art of classical and medieval India. Ed. by H. Kulke. Wiesbaden: Steiner, 1974, 3-48. (SSI, 16) [1st pub. in E&W 10,3/4 (1959) 153-261.

05456 GOKHALE, B.G. The Mithuna motif in early Buddhist art. In Indica 13,1/2 (1976) 49-58.

05457 MOTI CHANDRA & P.L. GUPTA. Jewellery moulds in ancient India. In PWMB 8 (1962-64) 8-17.

05458 PIGGOTT, S. The earliest Buddhist shrines. In Antiquity 17,65 (1943) 1-10.

05459 RAY, N.R. Maurya and post-Maurya art: a study in social and formal contrasts. ND: ICHR, 1975. 143 + 75p.

05460 SARASVATI, S.K. Early sculpture of Bengal. 2nd ed. Calcutta: Sambodhi, 1962. 128p.

B. Mauryan and Early "Buddhist" Art [for Iconography of the Buddha, see Chap. One IV. B. 2. b.; for Mauryan pillars and Sarnath railing, see E.2. below]

05461 BANERJI, A. Mauryan sculptures in Banaras. In RL 24 (1953) 11-22.

05462 FOUCHER, A.C.A. The beginnings of Buddhist art, and other essays in Indian and Central Asian archaeology. Paris: P. Geuthner, 1917. 316p. + 50 pl.

05463 IRWIN, J. "Asokan" pillars: a reassessment of the evidence - II: capitals. In Burlington 117,4 (1975) 631-43.

05464 ______. "Asokan" pillars: a reassessment of the evidence - IV: symbolism. In Burlington 118,4 (1976) 734-52.

05465 MITRA, A.K. Mauryan art. In IHQ 3,3 (1927) 541-60.

05466 SINHA, B.P. & L.A. NARAIN. Pataliputra excavation, 1955-56. Patna: Bihar Dir. of ARchaeology and Museums, 1970. 56p.

05467 WADDELL, L.A. Report on the excavations at Pataliputra (Patna). Calcutta: Bengal Secretariat Press, 1903. 83p.

C. Post-Mauryan Art During the Period of Competing Dynasties

1. Śunga, Kānva, and "Mitra" Dynasties in Madhyadeśa (Northern and Middle India)

a. Bodhgayā and the Mahābodhi temple

05468 BHATTACHARYYA, T. The Bodhgayā temple. 2nd ed. Calcutta: KLM, 1966. 40p.

05469 COOMARASWAMY, A.K. La sculpture de Bodhgayā. Paris: Éditions d'art et d'histoire, 1935. 72p. + 50 pl. [Ars Asiatica suppl. 18]

05470 MITRA, R.L. Buddha Gayā, the great Buddhist temple, the hermitage of Śākya Muni. Delhi: IndBH, 1972. 257p. + 51 pl. [1st pub. 1878]

05471 MYER, P. Temple at Bodh-Gayā. In Art Bulletin 40,4 (1958) 277-98.

b. Sānchī

05472 CHANDRA, PRAMOD. Yakṣha and Yakṣhī images from Vidīśā. In Ars Orientalis 6 (1966) 157-65.

05473 CUNNINGHAM, A. The Bhilsa topes; or, Buddhist monuments of Central India.... Varanasi: IndBH, 1966. 236p. [1st pub. 1854]

05474 MAISEY, F.C. Sanchi and its remains. Delhi: IndBH, 1972. 142p.

05475 MARSHALL, J.H. A guide to Sanchi. 3rd ed. Delhi: MP, 1955. 168p. + 10 pl. [1st pub. in 1918]

05476 ______. Monuments of Sanchi. London: Probsthain, 1940. 3 v.

05477 SPINK, W.M. Sanchi; catalogue. NY: U. of the State of New York, Foreign Area Materials Center, 1968. 100p.

05478 SUGIMOTO, T. A study in Jātaka-scenes depicted in the gateways of Sānchī stūpa. In JBRS 54 (1968) 202-15.

c. Bhārhut

05479 BARUA, B.M. Barhut. Patna: Indological Book Corp., 1979. 375p. + 51 pl. [Rpt. 1934-37 ed.]

05480 COOMARASWAMY, A.K. La sculpture de Bhārhut. Paris: Éditions d'art et d'histoire, 1956. 97p.+51 pl.

05481 CUNNINGHAM, A. The stūpa of Bhārhut.... 2nd ed. Varanasi: IndBH, 1962. 143p. + 57 pl. [1st ed. 1879]

05482 SPAGNOLI, M.M. Relationship between the perspective and compositional structure of the Bhārhut sculptures and Gandhārān art. In E&W 20,3 (1970) 327-47.

2. Western India and the Buddhist "Cave Temples"

05483 BARRETT, D. A guide to the Kārla caves. Bombay: Bhulabhai Memorial Inst., 1957. 12p. + 20 pl.

05484 DEHEJIA, V. Early Buddhist caves at Junnar. In ArtAs 31,2/3 (1969) 147-66 + 17 figs.

05485 ______. Early Buddhist rock temples; a chronology. Ithaca: Cornell U. Press, 1972. 240p. + 90 figs. + 11 tables.

05486 DESHPANDE, M.N. The rock-cut caves of Pītalkhora in the Deccan. In AI 15 (1959) 66-93.

05487 DIKSHIT, M.G. Buddhist art of Western India. In Indica 8,1 (1971) 1-18.

05488 KHANDALAVALA, K.J. & MOTI CHANDRA. The date of the Kārla Chaitya. In LK 3/4 (1956) 11-26 + 12 pl.

05489 KRISHAN, Y. Udaigiri and Khandagiri caves and early Buddhist art. In OA 15,2 (1969) 116-18.

05490 LEYDEN, R.V. The Buddhist caves at Lonād. In JISOA 15 (1947) 84-88.

05491 SPINK, W. On the development of early Buddhist art in India. In Art Bulletin 40,2 (1958) 95-104.

05492 TRABOLD, J.L. A chronology of Indian sculpture: the Śātavāhana chronology at Nāsik. In ArtAs 32,1 (1970) 49-88.

05493 WAUCHOPE, R.S. Buddhist cave temples of India. Calcutta: General Printing Co., 1933. 21p. + 51 pl.

3. Southern India: The Vengī Region (Kṛiṣhṇā-Godāvarī Deltas) Under the Āndhra-Sātavāhanas (200 BC - 225 AD) and the Īkṣvākus (C. 230 - 275)

a. general studies

05494 AIYAPPAN, A. & P.R. SRINIVASAN. Guide to the Buddhist antiquities. Rev. ed. Madras: Govt. of Madras, 1960. 10p. + 54 pl. (Madras Govt. Museum, Guide series, 2)

05495 BAREAU, A. Le site bouddhique de Guntupalle. In ArtsAs 23 (1971) 69-92.

05496 GANGOLY, O.C. Andhra sculptures. Hyderabad: Govt. of Andhra Pradesh, 1973. 102p. + 27 pl. (Archaeol. series, 36)

05497 PANCAMUKHI, R.S. Buddhist art in Andhradesa: predecessor of Calukyan style. In J.H. Date, ed. Munshi indological felicitation volume. Bombay: BVB, 1963, 310-320. [Pub. as BV 20 (1960) and 21 (1961)]

05498 REA, A. South Indian Buddhist antiquities; including the stupas of Bhaṭṭiprōḷu, Guḍivāḍa and Ghaṇṭasālā, and other ancient sites in the Kṛiṣhṇā District, Madras Presidency.... Varanasi: IndBH, 1969. 51p. (ASI, new imperial ser., 15) [1st pub. 1894]

b. Jaggayapeṭa stūpa and Amarāvati, center of Buddhism in Āndhradeśa

05499 BARRETT, D. The later school of Amarvati. In Art and Letters 28,2 (1954) 41-53.

05500 ______. Sculptures from Amaravati in the British Museum. London: British Museum, 1954. 76p.

05501 BURGESS, J. The Buddhist stupas of Amaravati and Jaggayyapeta. Varanasi: IndBH, 1970. 131p. (Archaeol. survey of Southern India, ns 1) [1st pub. 1887]

05502 ______. Notes on the Amaravati stupa. Varanasi: Prithivi Prakashan, 1972. 57p. (Archaeol. survey of Southern India, ns 3) [1st pub. 1882]

05503 D'ANCONA, M.L. Amaravati, Ceylon, and three imported bronzes. In Art Bulletin 32,1 (1952) 1-17.

05504 DEHEJIA, V. Early activity at Amaravati. In Archives of Asian art 23 (1969-70) 41-54.

05505 GHOSH, A. & H. SARKAR. Beginnings of sculptural art in Southeast India: a stele from Amaravati. In AI 20/21 (1964-65) 168-77.

05506 GUPTA, R.N. Sculptures of Amaravati. In QJMS 52 (1961) 97-103.

05507 SIVARAMAMURTI, C. Amaravati sculptures in the Madras Government Museum. Madras: 1942. (Bulletin of the Madras Government Museum, ns, v. 4) 376p. + 65 pl.

05508 STERN, P. & M. BÉNISTI. Évolution de style indien d'Amaravati. Paris: PUF, 1961. 116p.

c. Nāgārjunakoṇḍa

05509 Nāgārjunakoṇḍa sculptures. In Mārg 18 (1965) 2-56. [Articles by M.R. Anand and A. Ray]

05510 KRISHNA MURTHY, K. Nāgārjunakoṇḍa: a cultural study. Delhi: Concept Pub. Co., 1977. 289p. + 46 pl.

05511 LONGHURST, A.H. The Buddhist antiquities of Nāgārjunakoṇḍa, Madras Presidency. Delhi: MP, 1938. 67p. (ASI Memoirs, 54)

05512 RAMACHANDRA RAO, P.R. The art of Nāgārjunakoṇḍa. Madras: Rachana, 1956. 150p. + 56 pl.

05513 RAMACHANDRAN, T.N. Nāgārjunakoṇḍa. ND: ASI, 1938. 46p. + 48 pl. (ASI Memoirs, 71)

05514 SARKAR, H. & B.N. MISRA. Nāgārjunakoṇḍa. 2nd ed. ND: ASI, 1972. 83p.

05515 SUBRAHMANYAM, R., et al. Nāgārjunakoṇḍa, 1954-60. ND: ASI, 1975-. v. 1, 215p. + 101 pl. (ASI Memoirs, 75)

D. The Period of the Śakas and Kuṣāṇas in the North and Northwest (Present-day India, Pakistan, and Afghanistan), 1st Cent. BC - 4th Cent. AD

1. General Studies

05516 CHANDRA, R.G. Indo-Greek jewellery. ND: Abhinav, 1979. 136p. + 12 pl.

05517 FOUCHER, A.C.A. La vielle route de l'Inde, de Bactres à Taxila. Paris: Éd. d'art et d'histoire, 1942-47. 2 v., 426p. (Mémoires de la Délégation archéologique française en Afghanistan, 1)

05518 LOHUIZEN-DE LEEUW, J.E. VAN. Gandhāra and Mathurā: their cultural relationship. In P. Pal, ed. Aspects of Indian art. Leiden: Brill, 1972, 27-43.

05519 ______. The "Scythian" period; an approach to the history, art, epigraphy and palaeography of North India from the 1st century BC to the 3rd century AD. Leiden: Brill, 1949. 435p.

05520 MARSHALL, J.H. A guide to Taxila. Cambridge: CamUP, 1960. 196p. [1st pub. 1918]

05521 ROSENFIELD, J.M. The dynastic arts of the Kushans. Berkeley: UCalP, 1967. 377p.

2. Gandhāra: "Indo-Greek" Buddhist Art Under the Patronage of the Kuṣāṇas
a. general studies of Gandhāran art

05522 AUBOYER, J. L'Afghanistan et son art. Paris: Editions Cercle d'Art, 1968. 176p.

05523 BURGESS, J. The Gandhāra sculptures. Delhi: Bharatiya, 1978. 38p. + 13pl. [1st pub. in JIAI 1891-96]

05524 BUSSAGLI, M. L'arte del Gandhara in Pakistan e i suoi incontri con l'arte dell' Asia centrale. Rome: C. Colombo, 1958. 128p. (Catalogue for IIMEO, Museo Civico di Torino)

05525 DANI, AHMAD HASAN. Gandhara art of Pakistan. Peshawar: Dept. of Archaeology, U. of Peshawar, 1968. 41p.

05526 DEYDIER, H. Contribution a l'étude de l'art du Gandhara. Paris: Adrien-Maisonneuve, 1950. 325p. [A critical and analytical bibliog. of Gandharan art between 1922 and 1949.]

05527 DYE, J.M. Two fragmentary Gandhāran narrative reliefs in the Peshawar Museum: a study of Gandhāran representations of the Four Encounters. In ArtAs 38,2/3 (1976) 219-45.

05528 FOUCHER, A.C.A. L'art greco-bouddhique du Gandhāra; étude sur les origines de l'influence classique dans l'art bouddhique de l'Inde et de l'Extrême-Orient. Paris: E. Leroux, 1905-51. 2 v. in 4.

05529 HALLADE, M. Gandharan art of North India and the Graeco-Buddhist tradition in India, Persia, and Central Asia. NY: Abrams, 1968. 266p. + 203 pl.

05530 MARSHALL, J.H. The Buddhist art of Gandhara: the story of the early school, its birth, growth and decline. Cambridge: CamUP, 1960. 117p. + 111 pl.

05531 LYONS, I. & H. INGHOLT. Gandharan art in Pakistan. NY: Pantheon Books, 1957. 203p.

05532 ROWLAND, B., JR. Ancient art from Afghanistan; treasures of the Kabul Museum. NY: Asia Soc., 1966. 144p.

05533 ______. A cycle of Gandhara. In Bulletin of the Boston Museum of Fine Arts 62 (1965) 114-129.

05534 ______. Gandhara sculpture from Pakistan museums. (Exhibition circulated by the Smithsonian Institution Traveling Exhibition Service) NY: Asia Soc., 1960. 64p.

05535 ______. The Hellenistic tradition in Northwestern India. In Art Bulletin 31 (1949) 1-10.

05536 SCHLUMBERGER, D. The excavations at Surkh Kotal and the problem of Hellenism in Bactria and India. London: OUP, 1961. 95p.

05537 SCHMITT, E. Ornamente in der Gandharakunst und rezenten Volkskunst im Hindukush und Karakorum. Wiesbaden: Harrassowitz, 1971. 334p. (DSI, 10)

b. Begrām (ancient Kāpiśī): cosmopolitan emporium and ivory-carving center

05538 AUBOYER, J. Ancient Indian ivories from Begram. In JISOA 16 (1948) 34-46.

05539 DAVIDSON, J.L. Begram ivories and early Indian sculpture. In P. Pal, ed. Aspects of Indian Art. Leiden: Brill, 1972, 1-14.

05540 GHIRSHMANN, R. Begrām, recherches archéologiques et historiques sur les Kouchāns. Cairo: Impr. de l'Inst. français d'archéologie orientale, 1946. 232p. + 54 pl.

05541 HACKIN, J. Nouvelles recherches archéologiques à Begrām (ancienne Kāpiçī) (1939-1940) Paris: Impr. nationale - Presses universitaires, 1954. 353p. + pl. (Mémoires de la délégation archéologique française en Afghanistan, XI)

05542 HACKIN, J. & J.R. HACKIN. Recherces archéologiques à Begram. Paris: Les éditions d'art et d'histoire, 1939. 2 v. (Mémoires de la délégation archéologique française en Afghanistan, IX)

05543 SIVARAMAMURTI, C. Begrām ivories: the traditions of the master craftsman. In Mārg 24,3 (1971) 9-14.

c. Bāmiyān Valley: Buddhist monastic center with rock-cut colossal Buddhas, stūpas, and frescoes

05544 Bāmiyān - a special issue. In Mārg 24,2 (1971) 2-44. [contribs. by Mulk Raj Anand, B.B. Lal, N.H. Dupree, B. Rowland, R. Sengupta]

05545 GODARD, A. & Y. GODARD & J. HACKIN. Les antiquités bouddhiques de Bāmiyān. Paris: G. Van Qest, 1928. 113p., 27 figs. & plans, 47 pl. Memoires de la delegation archéologique française en Afghanistan, 2)

05546 HACKIN, J. The colossal Buddhas at Bamiyan: their influence on Buddhist sculpture. In Eastern Art 1 (1929) 109-16.

05547 KLIMBURG-SALTER, D.E. Buddhist painting of the Hindu Kush: Bamiyan, Fondukistan, Foladi, Kakrak. Ph.D. diss., Harvard U., 1976. 312p.

05548 MIZUNO, SEIICHI, ed. Haibak and Kashmir-Smast; Buddhist cave-temples in Afghanistan and Pakistan surveyed in 1960. Kyoto: Kyoto U., 1962. 197p. [Japanese and English text]

d. Takṣaśīla (Taxila): center of education, religion, trade, and art

05549 ASHFAQ NAQUI, SYED. Taxila, centre universitaire de l'ancienne Asie. In Samadhi 8,2 (1974) 73-90.

05550 MARSHALL, J.H. Excavations at Taxila: the stūpas and monasteries at Jaulian. ND: Indological Book Corp., 1979. 75p. + 15 pl. [Rpt. 1921 ed.]

05551 ______. Taxila, an illustrated account of archaeological excavations carried out at Taxila under the orders of the Govt. of India between the years 1913 and 1934. Cambridge: CamUP, 1951. 3 v.

3. Mathurā: On the Yamunā (Jumna) River: Pre-eminent School of Buddhist-Jain-Hindu Sculpture and Architecture (1st - 4th Cents. AD)
[See also E. 2., below]

05552 HARLE, J.C. Late Kuṣāṇa, early Gupta: a reverse approach. In N. Hammond, ed. South Asian archaeology .... Park Ridge, NJ: Noyes Press, 1973, 231-41.

05553 SMITH, V.A. The Jain stūpa and other antiquities of Mathurā. 2nd ed. Varanasi: IndBH, 1969. 63p. [Rpt. 1901 ed.]

F. The Gupta-Vākāṭaka Period: The Golden Age of Ancient Indian Civilization (320 - 600 AD)

1. General Studies of Gupta Art

05554 AGRAWALA, P.K. Gupta temple architecture. Varanasi: Prithivi Prakashan, 1968. 107p.

05555 AGRAWALA, V.S. Gupta art: a history of Indian art in the Gupta period 300 - 600 AD. Ed. by P.K. Agrawala. Varanasi: Prithivi Prakashan, 1977. 128p. [based on collected essays and lectures]

05556 GOETZ, H. The last masterpiece of Gupta art: the great temple of Yaśovarman of Kanauj at Gwalior. In his Studies in the history, religion and art of classical and medieval India. Ed. by H. Kulke. Wiesbaden: Steiner, 1974, 49-63. (SSI, 16) [1st pub. in Art & Letters 29,2 (1974) 49-63]

05557 ______. School of Gupta. In Encyclopedia of World Art. NY: McGraw-Hill, 1959-68, v. 7, 248-263.

05558 HARLE, J.C. Gupta sculpture: Indian sculpture of the fourth to the sixth centuries AD. Oxford: OUP, 1974. 57p. + 40 pl.

05559 KRAMRISCH, S. Die figurale Plastik der Guptazeit. In Wiener Beiträge für Kunst und Kulturgeschichte Asiens 5 (1931) 15-39.

05560 PAL, P. The ideal image: the Gupta sculptural tradition and its influence. NY: Asia Soc., 1978. 144p.

05561 SOUNDARA RAJAN, K.V. Brahmanical early structural architectural - some aspects. In TASS 1 (1960-62) 158-65.

2. Mathurā and Sārnāth: Buddha Images and Other Sculptures [See also D. 3. above]

05562 AGRAWALA, V.S. Masterpieces of Mathurā sculpture. Varanasi: Prithivi Prakashan, 1965. 27p.

05563 ______. Sārnāth. Delhi: MP, 1956. 26p. + 10 pl.

05564 DASGUPTA, C.C. Some terracottas from Mathurā preserved in the Francis Hopp Museum of Asiatic Arts. In JASBengal 3rd ser. 9,1 (1943) 211-20.

05565 JOSHI, N.P. Mathurā sculptures: a handbook to appreciate sculptures in the Archaeological Museum. Mathura: Archaeological Museum, 1966. 118p. + 102p. of illustrations.

05566 MAJUMDAR, B. A guide to Sārnāth. Delhi: MPGOI, 1937. 122p.

05567 MARSHALL, J.H. & S. KONOW. Excavations at Sārnāth, 1908. In ASI Annual Report (1907-8) 43-80.

05568 Mathurā of the Gods. In Mārg 15 (1962) 2-60. [Kushāna and Gupta]

05569 ROSENFIELD, J.M. On the dated carvings of Sārnāth. In ArtAs 26 (1963) 10-26.

05570 SAHNI, D.R. Guide to the Buddhist ruins of Sārnāth. 5th ed. Delhi: MP, 1933. 49p.

05571 VOGEL, J.P. Archaeological museum at Mathurā. Delhi: IndBH, 1971. 209p. [Rpt. 1910 ed.]

3. Deogaṛh and Central India: Beginnings of Hindu Temple Construction (C. 5th Cent. AD)

05572 AGRAWALA, V.S. A survey of Gupta art and some sculptures from Nāchnā Kuṭhāra and Khoh. In LK 9 (1961) 16-26.

05573 BANERJEE, N.R. New light on the Gupta temples at Deogarh. In JASB 4th ser. 5,1/2 (1963) 37-49.

05574 BANERJI, R.D. Temple of Siva at Bhumara. Calcutta: Supt. Govt. Printing, 1924. 14p. (ASI Memoirs, 16)

05575 CHANDRA, PRAMOD. A Vāmana temple at Marhiā and some reflections on Gupta architecture. In ArtAs 32 (1970) 125-45.

05576 MITRA, R.L. On the temples of Deogarh. In JASBengal 52,1 (1883) 164-204.

05577 PATIL, D.R. The monuments of Udaygiri Hill. Gwalior: Archaeological Dept., 1948. 52p.

05578 SOUNDARA RAJAN, K.V. Beginnings of the temple plan. In PWMB 6 (1957-59) 74-81.

05579 SPINK, W.M. A temple with four Uchchakalpa doorways at Nāchnā Kuṭhāra. In Anand Krishna, ed. Chhavi .... Banaras: B.H.U., Bharat Kala Bhavan, 1971, 161-172.

05580 VATS, P.M.S. The Gupta temple at Deogarh. Delhi: MPGOI, 1952. 48p. (ASI Memoirs, 70)

05581 VIENNOT, O. Le problème des temples à toit plat dans l'Inde du Nord. In ArtsAs 18 (1968) 23-84.

4. Western India (Gujarat-Sind-SW Rajasthan) in the Gupta Period

05582 AGRAWALA, R.C. Some unpublished sculptures from southwestern Rajasthan. In LK 6 (1959) 63-71.

05583 MEHTA, R.N. & S.N. CHOWDHARY. Excavation at Devnimori; a report of the excavation conducted from 1960 to 1963. Baroda: MSUB, 1966. 197p. (MSU archaeol. ser., 8)

05584 MOTI CHANDRA. A study in the terracottas from Mirpurkhas. In PWMB 7 (1959-62) 1-22.

05585 PAL, P. Some Rajasthani sculptures of the Gupta period. In Bull., Allen Mem. Art Museum, Oberlin College 28 (1971) 10-26.

05586 RAO, S.R. Excavations at Amreli - a Kshatrapa-Gupta town. In Bull. of the Baroda Mus. & Picture Gallery, 18 (1966) 1-114.

05587 SCHASTOK, S.W. Sixth-century Indian sculptures from Sāmālajī: style and iconography. Ph.D. diss., U. of Michigan, 1980. 470p., incl. 210 pl.

05588 SHAH, U.P. Gupta sculptures from Idar state (Gujarat). In J. of India Museum 9 (1953) 90-103.

05589 ______. Sculptures from Sāmālajī and Roḍā (North Gujarat) in the Baroda Museum. Baroda: V.L. Devkar, 1960. 136p.

05590 ______. Some early sculptures from Abu and Bhinmal. In Bull. of the Baroda Mus. & Picture Gallery, 12 (1955-56) 43-56.

5. Ajaṇṭā and Bāgh: Sculptures and Frescoes of the Buddhist Cave-Temples

05591 BEGLEY, W.E. The chronology of Mahāyāna Buddhist architecture and painting at Ajaṇṭā. Ph.D. diss., U. of Pennsylvania, 1966. 291p. [UM 67-3050]

05592 BURGESS, J. Notes on the Banddha rock temples of Ajanta. Bombay: Govt. Central Press, 1879. 111p. (Archaeol. survey of Western India, 9)

05593 DHAVALIKAR, M.K. Ajanta: a cultural study. Poona: U. of Poona, 1974. 157p. + 43 pl.

05594 GHOSH, A. Ajanta murals; an album of eighty-five reproductions in colour. ND: ASI, 1967. 71p. + 95 pl.

05595 GOETZ, H. Ajanta; portfolio. ND: NBT, 1964. 5p. + 6 pl.

05596 GOLOUBEW, V. Documents pour servir à l'étude d'Ajanta: les peintures de la première grotte. Paris & Brussels: G. Van Oest, 1927. 48p. + 66 pl.

05597 INDIA SOCIETY, LONDON. Ajanta frescoes; being reproductions in colour and monochrome of frescoes in some of the caves at Ajanta, after copies taken in 1909-1911 by Lady Herringham and her assistants. London: OUP, 1915. 28p. + 42 pl.

05598 MARSHALL, J.H., et al. The Bagh caves in the Gwalior state. Delhi: Delhi Printers Prakashan, 1978. 78p. + 26 pl. [Rpt. of 1927 ed.]

05599 ROWLAND, B. The Ajanta caves; early Buddhist paintings from India. NY: New American Library, 1963. 24p. + 31 pl.

05600 SINGH, M. The cave paintings of Ajanta. London: Thames & Hudson, 1965. 189p.

05601 ______. India; paintings from Ajanta caves. NY: New York Graphic Soc., 1954. 10p. + 32 pl.

05602 SPINK, W.M. Ajanta: a brief history. In P. Pal, ed. Aspects of Indian art. Leiden: Brill, 1972, 49-58.

05603 ______. Ajanta and Ghaṭoṭkāchā: a preliminary analysis. In Ars Orientalis 6 (1966) 135-55.

05604 ______. Ajanta's chronology: the crucial cave. In Ars Orientalis (1975) 143-69 + 16 pl.

05605 ______. Bāgh: a study. In Archives of Asian Art 30 (1976-77) 53-65.

05606 WEINER, S.L. Ajaṇṭā: its place in Buddhist art. Berkeley: UCalP, 1977. 138p. + 28 pl.

05607 YAZDANI, G. Ajanta. London: OUP, 1930-55. 4 v.

6. Eastern India (Bihar and Orissa) during the Gupta Period

05608 ASHER, F.M. The art of eastern India, 300-800. Minneapolis: U. of Minnesota Press, 1980. 260p.+253 pl.

05609 BROADLEY, A.M. The Buddhistic remains of Bihar. In JASBengal 41,1 (1872) 209-312.

05610 CHANDRA, PRAMOD. Some remarks on Bihar sculpture from the fourth to the ninth century. In P. Pal, ed. Aspects of Indian art. Leiden: Brill, 1972, 59-64.

05611 DONALDSON, T. Doorframes on the earliest Orissan temples. In ArtAs 38,2/3 (1976) 189-218.

05612 SAHAI, S. Some Brahmanical rock-sculptures from Sultanganj. In JBRS 49 (1963) 137-46.

F. Siṁhāla/Ceylon: Anurādhapura Period (4th Cent. BC - 8th Cent. AD): Importation and Naturalization of Indian Buddhist Styles

1. general studies

05613 DEVENDRA, D.T. Classical Sinhalese sculpture: 300 B.C. to A.D. 1000. London: Alec Tiranti, 1958. 48p.

05614 GODAKUMBURA, C.E. A bronze Buddha image from Ceylon. In ArtAs 26 (1963) 230-36.

05615 PARANAVITANA, S. Art of the ancient Sinhalese. Colombo: LHI, 1971. 141p.

05616 ______. [sections on arts] in H.C. Ray, et al., eds. University of Ceylon History of Ceylon. Colombo: Ceylon U., 1959, v. 1,1, 256-68, 395-409 + pls.

2. Anurādhapura, the Capital City

05617 BANDARANAYAKE, S. Sinhalese Buddhist architecture: the vihāras of Anurādhapura. Leiden: Brill, 1974. 438p. (SSAC, 4)

05618 DERANIYAGALA, S. The citadel of Anurādhapura 1969: excavations in the Gedige area. In AC 2 (1972) 48-169.

05619 FERNANDO, W.B.M. Ancient city of Anurādhapura. 3rd ed. Colombo: Archaeological Dept., 1970. 66p. + 30pl. [1st ed. 1965 & 2nd ed. 1967 ed. by C.E. Godakumbara]

05620 LOHUIZEN-DE LEEUW, J.E. VAN. The rock-cut sculptures at "Isurumuni." In Ceylon Today 19,7/8 (1970) 35-47.

05621 PERERA, A.D.T.E. A possible identification of a significant sculpture at Isurumuniya temple, Anuradapura. A man and a horse's head. E&W 29,1/2 (1970) 122-43.

3. Sīgiriya/Sīgiri: the "Lion Mountain" Rock Fortress (473-491 AD)

05622 DE SILVA, R.H. Sīgiriya. Colombo: Dept. of Archaeology, 1971. 27p. + 29pl.

05623 PARANAVITANA, S. Sīgiri, the abode of a God-king. In JRASCB ns 1 (1950) 129-83.

05624 ______. The story of Sīgiri. Colombo: Lake House Investments, 1972. 281p.

05625 SWAAN, W. Sīgiriya: the rock fortress of the parricide king. In his Lost cities of Asia.... NY: G.P. Putnam, 1966, 66-76.

4

Early "Medieval" South Asia, 600–1526 A.D.: Emergence of Regional Traditions and Penetration of Islam

I. GENERAL HISTORIES OF THE PERIOD, 600-1526 AD

A. Historiography and Historians of Medieval India

05626 CHAUBE, R.K. India as told by the Muslims. Varanasi: Prithivi Prakashan, 1969. 258p.

05627 GREWAL, J.S. Medieval India: history and historians. Amritsar: Guru Nanak U., 1975. 150p.

05628 ______. Muslim rule in India: the assessments of British historians. Bombay: OUP, 1970. 218p.

05629 HAMEED-UD-DIN. Historians of Afghan rule in India. In JAOS 82 (1962) 44-51.

05630 HARDY, P. Historians of medieval India: studies in Indo-Muslim historical writing. London: Luzac, 1960. 146p.

05631 ______. The Muslim historians of the Delhi sultanate: is what they say really what they mean? In JASP, 9 (1964) 59-63.

05632 HASAN, M., ed. Historians of medieval India. Meerut: Meenakshi, 1968. 290p.

05633 LUNIYA, B.N. Some historians of medieval India. Agra: Lakshmi Narain Agarwal, 1969. 200p.

05634 SARKAR, J.N. History and historians of medieval India. In QRHS 3,1/2 (1963-64) 51-81.

05635 ______. Ideas of history in mediaeval India. In QRHS 4,1/2 (1964-65) 20-67.

B. Sources

1. Accounts of Travellers
a. al-Bīrūnī, Ibn Battūta, and other Arab accounts

05636 DANI, A.H., ed. Alberuni's Indica: a record of the cultural history of South Asia about A.D. 1030. Islamabad: U. of Islamabad Press, 1973. 244p. [based on Eduard Sachau translation]

05637 GIBB, H.A.R., tr. The travels of Ibn Battuta, A.D. 1325-1354. Cambridge: CamUP, 1971. [v. 3, 539-771 on South Asia]

05638 HASAN IBN YAZĪD, ABŪ ZAID (AL-SIRAF). Aḥbār as-Sīn wa l-Hind. Relation de la Chine et de l'Inde rédigée en 851. Tr. by J. Sauvaget. Paris: Belles Lettres, 1948. 41 + 162p.

05639 HUSAIN, M., tr. The Reḥla of Ibn Battūta: India, Maldive Islands, and Ceylon. Baroda: MSUB, 1976. 77 + 300p. + 7pl. (GOS, 122) [Rpt. 1953 ed.]

05640 JAHN, K. Rashīd al-Dīn's history of India; collected essays, with facsimiles and indices. The Hague: Mouton, 1965. 108p. (Central Asiatic studies, 10)

05641 KHAN, M.S. Al-Bīrūnī and the political history of India. In Oriens 25/26 (1976) 86-115.

05642 REINAUD, J.T., comp. & tr. Fragments arabes et persans inédits: relatifs a l'Inde, anterieurement au XIe siècle. Amsterdam: Oriental Press, 1974. 227p. [Rpt. 1845 ed.]

05643 SACHAU, E.C., tr. Alberuni's India. Ed. by A.T. Embree. NY: Norton, 1971. 246p.

05644 SAID, H.M., ed. Al-Bīrūnī: commemorative volume: proceedings of the International Congress held in Pakistan on the occasion of millenary of Abū Raihān Muhammad ibn Ahmad al-Bīrūnī 973-ca 1051 A.D., November 26, 1973 thru' December 12, 1973. Karachi: Hamdard National Foundation, Pakistan, 1979. 844p.

05645 SHASTRI, A.M. Sanskritic sources of Alberuni. In JIH 52,2/3 (1974) 327-60.

05646 SIDDIQI, I.H. & Q.M. AHMAD, tr. A fourteenth century Arab account of India under Sultan Muhammad Bin Tughluq; being English translation of the chapters on India, from Shihab al-Din al- Umari's Masalik al-absar fi-mamalik al-amsar. Aligarh: Siddiqi Pub. House, 1972. 86p.

b. Buddhist pilgrims and other Chinese and Tibetan sources

05647 BARTHÉLEMY-SAINT-HILAIRE, J. Hiouen-thsang in India. Tr. from French by L. Ensor. 2nd ed. Calcutta: Anil Gupta, 1965. 107p.

05648 BEAL, S., tr. Si-Yu-Ki: Buddhist records of the Western world. NY: Paragon, 1968. 2 v.

05649 GROUSSET, R. In the footsteps of the Buddha. NY: Grossman, 1971. 337p. [1st pub. 1932; tr. from French by J.A. Underwood]

05650 JOSHI, L.M. Studies in the Buddhistic culture of India during the 7th and 8th centuries AD. Delhi: Motilal, 1967. 538p.

05651 LÉVI, S. Les missions de Wang Hiuen-ts'e dans l'Inde. In JA 15 (1900) 297-341, 401-68.

05652 MEUWESE, C. L'Inde du Bouddha, vue par des pèlerins chinois sous la dynastie Tang. Paris: Calman-Levy, 1968. 320p.

05653 MINH-CHAU, Thich. Hsuan Tsang, the pilgrim & scholar. Nha-Trang, Vietnam: Vietnam Buddhist Inst., 1963. 139p.

05654 ROERICH, G., tr. Biography of Dharmasvamin (Chag lo tsa-ba Chos-rje-dpal): a Tibetan monk pilgrim. Patna: K.P. Jayaswal Res. Inst., 1959. 45 + 119p.

05655 SEN, N.C., tr. Accounts of India and Kashmir in the dynastic histories of the T'ang period. Santiniketan: Visva-Bharati, 1968. 84p.

05656 SEN, S.N. India through Chinese eyes. Madras: U. of Madras, 1956. 199p.

05657 SIRCAR, D.C. A Chinese account of India - 732 AD. In JIH 44,2 (1966) 351-57.

05658 TAKAKUSU, J., tr. A record of the Buddhist religion as practised in India and the Malay archipelago (AD 671-695). Delhi: Munshiram, 1966. 240p. [1st pub. 1896; acct. by I-Tsing]

05659 WATTERS, T. On Yuan Chwang's travels in India (A.D. 629-645). Ed. by T.W. Rhys Davids & S.W. Bushell. ND: Munshiram, 1973. 401-357p. [1st pub. 1904-05]

c. European travellers

05660 BARBOSA, D. The book of Duarte Barbosa.... Tr. from Portuguese by M.L. Dames. London: Hakluyt Soc., 1918-21. 2 v.

05661 ______. Description of the coasts of E. Africa and Malabar in the beginning of the 16th century. Tr. from Spanish by Lord H.E.J. Stanley. NY: B. Franklin, 1973. 236p. [Rpt. 1866 ed.; orig. in Portuguese]

05662 BENJAMIN BEN JONAH, of Tudela. The itinerary of Benjamin of Tudela. Tr. from Hebrew by M.N. Adler.

NY: P. Feldheim, 196-. 2 v. in 1. [Rpt of 1907 ed.]

05663 JORDANUS CATALANI. Mirabilia descripta; the wonders of the East, by Friar Jordanus...Bishop of Columbum in India the Greater (c. 1330). Tr. from Latin by H. Yule. London: Hakluyt Soc., 1863. 68p. (Its 1st ser., 31)

05664 MAJOR, R.H., tr. & ed. India in the fifteenth century, being a collection of narratives.... London: Hakluyt Soc., 1857. 220p. (Its 1st ser., 22) [Accts. by Abd-er-Razzak, Nicolo Conti, Athanasius Nikitin, Hieronimo di Santo Stefano]

05665 NIKITIN, A.N. Die Fahrt des Athanasius Nikitin über die drei Meere; Reise eines russischen Kaufmannes nach Ostindien, 1466-72. Tr. from Russian by K.H. Meyer. Leipzig: P. Schraepler, 1920. 47p.

05666 POLO, M. The book of Ser Marco Polo, the Venetian, concerning the Kingdoms and marvels of the East. Tr. from Italian by H. Yule; rev. by H. Cordier. London: Murray, 1903. 2 v.

05667 ______. The description of the world. Tr. from Italian by A.C. Moule & P. Pelliot, 1938. 2 v.

05668 ______. The travels of Marco Polo. Tr. from Italian by A. Ricci. London: G. Routledge, 1931. 439p.

2. Indian Texts as Sources

05669 ASKARI, SAYED HASAN. Historical value of the Sufi hagiographical works of the Sultanate period. In JBRS 52 (1966) 143-84.

05670 FURER-HAIMENDORF, C. VON. The historical value of Indian Bardic literature. In C.H. Philips, ed., Historians of India, Pakistan, and Ceylon. London: OUP, 1961, 87-93.

05671 GUPTA, D.K. Society and culture in the time of Dandin. Delhi: Meharchand Lachhmandas, 1972. 458p.

05672 HANDIQUI, K.K. Yaśastilaka and Indian culture: or, Somadeva's Yaśastilaka and aspects of Jainism and Indian thought and culture in the tenth century. Sholapur: Jaina Saṁskṛti Samrakshaka Saṅgha, 1968. 544p. (Jīvarāja Jaina granthamālā, 2)

05673 JAMKHEDKAR, A.P. Kuvalayamālā - a cultural study. In Nagpur U.J. 21,1/2 (1970-71) 1-146.

05674 SHASTRI, A.M. India, as seen in the Kuṭṭanīmata of Dāmodaragupta. Delhi: Motilal, 1975. 319p. + 111pl.

3. Numismatic and Epigraphic Evidence

05675 BENDREY, V.S. A study of Muslim inscriptions; with special reference to the inscriptions published in the Epigraphia Indo-Moslemica, 1907-38. Bombay: Karnatak Pub. House, 1944. 197p.

05676 CUNNINGHAM, A. Coins of mediaeval India, from the seventh century down to the Muhammedan conquests. Varanasi: IndBH, 1967. 108p. [1st pub. 1894]

05677 Epigraphia Indica. Arabic and Persian Supplement. Dehi: MPGOI, 1951-. [biennial; supercedes Epigraphia Indo-Moslemica of the Dept. of Archaeology]

05678 GOPAL, K.K. Administrative divisions in the inscriptions of early mediaeval India. In IHQ 39,1/2 (1963) 80-97.

05679 HENIGE, D.P. Some phantom dynasties of early and medieval India: epigraphic evidence and the abhorrence of a vacuum. In BSOAS 38,3 (1975) 525-49.

05680 KARASHIMA, N. & Y. SUBBARAYALU & T. MATSUI. A concordance of the names in Cōḻa inscriptions. Madurai: Sarvodaya Ilakkiya Pannai, 1978. 3 v.

05681 KARIM, ABDUL. A fresh study of the Muslim coins of Bengal of the Afghan period. In J. of the Numismatic Soc. of India 27 (1965) 65-80.

05682 RODGERS, C.J. Catalogue of the coins [in the Indian Museum, Calcutta]: Pt. 1. Sultans of Delhi and their contemporaries in Bengal, Gujarat, Jaunpur, Malwa, the Dekkhan, and Kashmir. Calcutta: the Museum, 1893. 172p.

05683 Seminar on Medieval Inscriptions, Aligarh Muslim U., 1970. Proceedings. Aligarh: Aligarh Muslim U., 1974. 169p.

05684 SINGHAL, C.R., comp. Catalogue of the coins in the Prince of Wales Museum of Western India, Bombay. The sultans of Gujarat. Bombay: PWM, 1935. 154p.

05685 SIRCAR, D.C. Some epigraphical records of the medieval period from eastern India. ND: Abhinav, 1979. 157p. + 10pl.

05686 WRIGHT, H.N., ed. Catalogue of the coins in the Indian museum, Calcutta: v. 2, The sultans of Delhi & contemporary dynasties of India. Delhi: IndBH, 1972. 280p. [Rpt. of 1907 ed.; suppl. by Shamsuddin Ahmad. Delhi: MPGOI, 1939. 152p.]

C. General Histories of the Period, 600-1526 AD

05687 MAJUMDAR, R.C., ed. The age of imperial Kanauj. Bombay: BVB, 1955. 585p. (HCIP, 4) [7th-10th centuries AD]

05688 ______. The struggle for Empire. Bombay: BVB, 1957. 940p. (HCIP, 5) [10th-13th centuries AD]

05689 MEHTA, J.L. Advanced study in the history of medieval India. ND: Sterling, 1979-. [to be 3 v.]

05690 NIZAMI, K.A. Studies in medieval Indian history and culture. Allahabad: Kitab Mahal, 1966. 171p.

05691 PANDEY, A.B. Early medieval India. 3rd ed. Allahabad: Central Book Depot, 1970. 366p.

05692 ______. Society and government in medieval India. Allahabad: Central Book Depot, 1965. 297p.

05693 PRASAD, I. History of mediaeval India; from 647 AD to the Mughal conquest. 3rd ed. Allahabad: Indian Press, 1966. 621p.

05694 RAY, H.C. The dynastic history of northern India (early mediaeval period). 2nd ed. ND: Munshiram, 1973. 2 v. [Rpt. 1931-36 ed.]

05695 SINGH, MEERA. Medieval history of India. ND: Vikas, 1978. 423p.

05696 AL-SIRHINDI, YAHYA IBN AHMAD. The Tarikh-i Mubarakshahi. Tr. by K.K. Basu. Karachi: Karimsons, 1977. 299p. [Rpt. 1932 ed.]

05697 SRIVASTAVA, A.L. The history of India, 1000 AD - 1707 AD. Agra: Shiva Lal Agarwala, 1964. 724p.

05698 VAIDYA, C.V. History of mediaeval Hindu India. ND: Cosmo, 1979. 3 v.

D. Hindu Laws: Emergence of the Mītākṣara and Dāyabhāga Traditions

05699 COLEBROOKE, H.T., tr. Jimutavahana. Mitacshara and Daya-Bhaga; two treatises on the Hindu law of inheritance. Calcutta: B. Banerjee, 1883. 120 + 205p.

05700 DERRETT, J.D.M. Law and the social order in India before the Muhammadan conquests. In JESHO 7 (1969) 73-120. [Rpt. in his Religion, law and the state in India. London: Faber & Faber, 1968, 171-224.]

05701 PAWATE, I.S. Dāya-vibhāga: or, the individualization of communal property and the communalization of individual property in the Mitakshara law. 2nd ed., rev. and enl. Dharwar: Karnatak U., 1975. 458p.

05702 VACASPATI MIŚRA. The vivādachintāmaṇi. Tr. by G.N. Jha. Baroda: Oriental Inst., 1942. 348p. (GOS, 99)

05703 ______. Vyavahāracintāmaṇi, a digest on Hindu legal procedure. Ed. by L. Rocher. Gent: 1956. 414p. (Gentse Orientalistische Bijdragen, 1)

E. Economic Life and the Question of Feudalism

1. General Studies, incl. Trade and Commerce

05704 CHITNIS, K.N. Socio-economic aspects of medieval India. Poona: R.K. Chitnis, 1979. 516p.

05705 JAIN, P.C. Socio-economic exploration of medieval India from 800 to 1300 AD. Delhi: B.R., 1976. 330p.

05706 KOSAMBI, D.D. Indian feudal trade charters. In JESHO 2 (1959) 281-93.

05707 MISHRA, S.M. India's foreign trade as known from the Samaraiccakaha and the Kuvalayamala. In JOIB 24,1/2 (1974) 187-200.

05708 SARKAR, B.K. Inland transport and communication in mediaeval India. Calcutta: U. of Calcutta, 1925. 87p.

05709 SHARMA, R.S. Usury in early mediaeval India (A.D. 400-1200). In CSSH 8 (1965) 56-77.

05710 VERMA, H.C. Medieval routes to India: Baghdad to Delhi: a study of trade and military routes. Calcutta: Naya Prokash, 1978. 345p.

2. The Debate over the Nature and Dating of Indian Feudalism

05711 CHOUDHARY, R.K. Some historical aspects of feudalism in ancient India (down to the 14th century A.D.); based mainly on the epigraphic sources. In JIH 37 (1959) 383-406; 38 (1960) 193-203.

05712 COULBORN, R. Feudalism, Brahminism and the intrusion of Islam upon Indian history. In CSSH 10,3 (1968) 356-74.

05713 GOPAL, K.K. The assembly of the Sāmantas in early mediaeval India. In JIH 42 (1964) 241-50.

05714 GOPAL, L. On feudal polity in ancient India. In JIH 41,2 (1963) 405-13.

05715 ______. On some problems of feudalism in ancient India. In ABORI 44 (1963) 1-32.

05716 ______. Sāmanta - its varying significance in ancient India. In JRAS (1963) 21-37.

05717 SHARMA, R.S. Indian feudalism: c. 300-1200. Calcutta: U. of Calcutta, 1965. 319p.

05718 ______. Land grants to vassals and officials in northern India, c. A.D. 1000-1200. In JESHO 4 (1961) 70-105.

05719 SINHA, G.P. Post-Gupta polity (A.D. 500-750): a study of feudal elements and rural administration. Calcutta: Punthi Pustak, 1972. 262p.

05720 SIRCAR, D.C. Controversy on certain problems of early Indian history. In JAIH 8,1/2 (1974-75) 203-32.

05721 ______. Land system and feudalism in ancient India. Calcutta: U. of Calcutta, 1966. 139p.

F. Aspects of Society and Culture

05722 CHOUDHARY, A.K. Early medieval village in north-eastern India, A.D. 600-1200: mainly a socio-economic study. Calcutta: Punthi Pustak, 1971. 411p.

05723 COMFORT, A., tr. The Koka Shastra, being the Ratirahasya of Kokkoka, and other medieval Indian writings on love. London: Allen & Unwin, 1964. 171p.

05724 LUNIYA, B.N. Life and culture in medieval India. Indore: Kamal Prakashan, 1978. 634p.

05725 OJHA, P.N. Aspects of medieval Indian society and culture. Delhi: B.R., 1978. 224p.

05726 RASHID, A. Society and culture in medieval India, 1206-1556 A.D. Calcutta: KLM, 1969. 288p.

05727 SAHU, K.P. Some aspects of north Indian social life, 1000-1526 A.D. (with a special reference to contemporary literatures). Calcutta: Punthi Pustak, 1973. 306p.

05728 SATISH CHANDRA. Sri Rebala Lakshminarasa Reddy Endowment lectures: 1976. Tirupati: Sri Venkateswara U., 1977. 48p. [Lectures on social change]

05729 UPADHYAYA, S.C., tr. The Hindu secrets of love: Rati rahasya of Pandit Kokkoka. Bombay: Taraporevala, 1965. 140p. + 79 pl.

05730 YADAVA, B.N.S. Problem of the interaction between socio-economic classes in the early medieval complex. In IHR 3,1 (1976) 43-58.

G. History of Science in Early Medieval South Asia

1. General Studies

05731 SYMPOSIUM ON AL-BĪRŪNĪ AND INDIAN SCIENCE. Proceedings. In IJHS 10,2 (1975) 1-278. [held at ND, Nov. 8-9, 1971]

2. Astronomy and Mathematics: Brahmagupta (b. 598), Bhāskara I (c. 600), Mahāvīrācārya (c. 850), Bhāskara II (b. 1114)

05732 BHĀSKARĀCĀRYA. Līlāvatī. Tr. by H.T. Colebrooke. Allahabad: Kitab Mahal, 1967. 173p. [1st pub. 1817]

05733 CHATTERJEE, BINA, ed. & tr. The Khaṇḍakhādyaka (an astronomical treatise) of Brahmagupta, with the commentary of Bhaṭṭotpāla. Calcutta: World, 1970. 2 v., 315, 238p.

05734 DATTA, B.B. The two Bhāskaras. In IHQ 6,4 (1930) 727-36.

05735 KAYE, G.R. The Bakhshālī Manuscript; a study in mediaeval mathematics. Calcutta: ASI, 1927-33. 3 pts. 237p. + 47 pl. (Its New imperial series, 43)

05736 PRAKASH, S. A critical study of Brahmagupta and his works, a most distinguished Indian astronomer and mathematician of the sixth century A.D. ND: Indian Inst. of Astronomical & Sanskrit Res., 1968. 344p.

05737 RANGACARYA, M., tr. The Gaṇitasārasaṅgraha of Mahāvīrācārya. Madras: Government Press, 1912. 158 + 325p.

05738 SHUKLA, K.S., tr. Bhaskara I and his works. Lucknow: Dept. of Math. and Astronomy, Lucknow U., 1963. 2 v.

3. Medicine: The Introduction and Development of Unānī Tibb, Greco-Arab Medicine

05739 KESHWANI, N.H. & R.L. VERMA. Unānī medicine in medieval India - its teachers and texts [and] The physiological concepts of Unānī medicine. In N.H. Keshwani, ed. The science of medicine and physiological concepts of ancient and medieval India. ND: All-India Inst. of Medical Sciences, 1974, 127-144, 145-166.

05740 SUBBA REDDY, D.V. The origins and growth of indigenous unānī medical literature in medieval India. In IJHM 14,1 (1969) 20-25; 15,1 (1970) 14-19.

05741 ULLMAN, M. Die Medizin im Islam. Leiden: Brill, 1970. 379p. (HO, suppl. 6:1)

05742 UMMUL FAZAL & M.A. RAZZACK, eds. A hand book of common remedies in unānī system of medicine. ND: Central Council for Res. in Indian Medicine and Homoeopathy, Min. of Health and Family Planning, 1976. 173p.

05743 VERMA, R.L. The growth of Greco-Arabian medicine in medieval India. In IJHS 5,2 (1970) 348-63.

II. RELIGIO-PHILOSOPHICAL TRADITIONS: THE RISE OF BHAKTI (DEVOTIONAL HINDUISM), ECLIPSE AND ABSORPTION OF BUDDHISM, PENETRATION OF ISLAM

A. The Purāṇas, "Ancient Stories": Encyclopedic Storehouses of Hindu Myth and Basic Texts of the Bhakti Sects (Compiled 4th - 16th Cents. AD)

1. Reference and Methodology

05744 DEVI, A.K. A biographical dictionary of Purāṇic personages. Calcutta: Vijaya Krishna Bros., 194-. 69p.

05745 GUPTA, A.S. Purāṇas and their references. In Purana 7,2 (1965) 321-51.

05746 MANI, V. Purāṇic encyclopedia: a comprehensive dictionary of the epic and Puranic literature. Delhi: Motilal, 1975. 922p.

05747 PUSALKER, A.D. Studies in the epics and Purāṇas. Bombay: BVB, 1963. 230p. [205-30 is review of scholarship on Purāṇas]

05748 RAMACHANDRA DIKSHITAR, V.R. The Purāṇa index. Madras: U. of Madras, 1951-55. 3 v. [to Bhāgavata, Brahmāṇḍa, Matsya, Vāyu, Vishṇu Puraṇas]

05749 RIVIÈRE, J.R. European translations of purāṇic texts. In Purāṇa 5 (1963) 243-50.

05750 TRIPATHI, G.C. The significance of contents-analysis for the reconstruction of a Purāṇic text. In Purāṇa 17,1 (1975) 38-51.

2. General Studies in the Purāṇas

05751 ALI, S.M. The geography of the Purāṇas. ND: PPH, 1966. 234p.

05752 AGRAWALA, V.S. The purāṇas and the Hindu religion. In Purāṇa 6,2 (1964) 333-46.

05753 ______. Purāṇa-vidyā. In Purāṇa 6,1 (1964) 187-99.

05754 BIARDEAU, M. Etudes de mythologie Hindoue; cosmogonies Purāṇiques. In BEFEO 54 (1968) 19-46; 55 (1969) 59-105; 58 (1971) 17-89.

05755 GUPTA, A.S. Purāṇa, itihāsa and ākhyāna. In Purāṇa 6,2 (1964) 451-61.

05756 HAZRA, RAJENDRA CHANDRA. Studies in the Purāṇic records on Hindu rites and customs. 2nd ed. Delhi: Motilal Banarsidass, 1975. 367p. [1st pub. in U. of Dacca Bulletin 10 (1940)]

05757 OM PRAKASH. Political ideas in the Purāṇas. Allahabad: Panchanada Pub., 1977. 27 + 157p.

05758 The Purāṇas. In Cultural heritage of India. Calcutta: RMIC, 1962, v. 2, 223-98. [essays by R.N. Dandekar, R.C. Hazra, C.S. Venkateswaran]

05759 ROY, S.N. Historical and cultural studies in the Purāṇas. Allahabad: Pauranic Pub., 1978. 346p.

05760 SINGH, M.R. Geographical data in the early Purāṇas; a critical study. Calcutta: Punthi Pustak, 1972. 405p.

3. The Bhāgavatapurāṇa/Śrīmad Bhāgavatam: The Principal Vaiṣṇava Mahāpurāna, Compiled in Tamil-speaking South India, Narrating Lord Kṛṣṇa's Life. C. 950

a. translations

05761 BHAKTIVEDANTA SWAMI, A.C., tr. Śrīmad-Bhāgavatam. NY: Bhaktivedanta Book Trust, 1972. 10 v.

05762 BURNOUF, E. & M. HAUVETTE-BESNAULT & A. ROUSSEL, tr. Le Bhāgavata Purāṇa. Paris: Imprimerie Royal, 1840-98. 5 v.

05763 DUTT, M.N., tr. A prose English translation of Śrīmadbhāgabatam. Calcutta: H.C. Dass, 1895-96. 3 v.

05764 MADHAVANANDA, Swami, tr. Uddhava gītā; or the last message of Shri Krishna. 3rd ed. Calcutta: Advaita Ashrama, 1971. 376p.

05765 PRABHAVANANDA, Swami, tr. Śrīmad Bhāgavatam; the wisdom of God. NY: Putnam's, 1943. 340p.

05766 RAGHUNATHAN, N., tr. Śrīmad Bhāgavatam. Madras: Vighneswara, 1976. 2 v., 692, 746p.

05767 ROUSSEL, A. Légendes morales de l'Inde, empruntées au Bhāgavata Purāṇa et au Mahābhārata. Paris: Gustave-Paul Maisonneuve et Larose, 1969. 2 v., 340, 370p. [Rpt. 1900-01]

05768 SANYAL, J.M., tr. Shrīmad-Bhāgbatam of Krishna-Dwaipāyana Vyāsa. Calcutta: Oriental Pub. Co., 1952. 5 v.

05769 TAGARE, G.V., tr. Bhāgavatapurāṇa. Delhi: Motilal, 1976-78. 5 v., 2241p. (AITM, 7-11)

b. studies

05770 BASU, A. Preface to the study of the Bhāgavata Purāṇa. Belgaum: Academy of Comp. Philosophy and Religion, 1973. 156p.

05771 BHATTACHARYA, S. The philosophy of the Srīmad-Bhāgavata. Santiniketan: Visva-Bharati, 1960-62. 2 v.

05772 BHAKTIVINODE, T. The Bhāgavat: its philosophy, its ethics and its theology. Calcutta: Gauḍiya Maṭh, 1936. 256p.

05773 GAIL, A. Bhakti im Bhāgavatapurāṇa. Religionsgeschichtliche Studien zur Idee der Gottesliebe in Kult und Mystik des Viṣṇuismus. Wiesbaden: Harrassowitz, 1969. 135p. (MIS, 6)

05774 HOPKINS, T.J. The social teaching of the Bhāgavata Purāṇa. In M.B. Singer, ed. Krishna: myths, rites, and attitudes. Honolulu: EWCP, 1966, 3-22.

05775 RUKMANI, T.S. A critical study of the Bhāgavata Purāṇa, with special reference to bhakti. Varanasi: CSSO, 1970. 370p.

05776 TRIPATHI, K.S. A cultural study of the Śrīmad-Bhāgavata. Varanasi: BHU, 1969. 493p.

05777 VAN BUITENEN, J.A.B. On the archaism of the Bhāgavata Purāṇa. In M.B. Singer, ed. Krishna: myths, rites, and attitudes. Honolulu: EWCP, 1966, 23-40.

05778 VYAS, R.N. The synthetic philosophy of the Bhāgavata. Delhi: Meharchand Lachhmandas, 1974. 183p.

4. The Viṣṇu Purāṇa (C. 450): A Vaiṣṇava Mahāpurāṇa

05779 DUTT, M.N., tr. Prose English translation of Vishṇupurāṇam. 2nd ed. Varanasi: CSSO, 1972. 464p. (CSS, 90) [1st pub. 1894]

05780 MACFIE, J.M. The Vishṇu Purāṇa; a summary with introduction and notes. Madras: CLS, 1926. 258p.

05781 PENNER, H.H. Cosmogony as myth in the Vishṇu Purāṇa. In HR 4 (1966) 283-99.

05782 WILSON, H.H., tr. The Vishṇu Purāṇa: a system of Hindu mythology and tradition. 3rd ed. Calcutta: Punthi Pustak, 1979. 72 + 562p. [Rpt. 1961 ed.; 1st pub. 1864-77]

5. The Brahmavaivarta Purāṇa (Compiled 750 - 1550): A Mahapurana Basic to Rādhā-Kṛṣṇa Bhakti

05783 BONAZZOLI, G. General introduction to the Brahmavaivarta Purāṇa: its Anukramaṇikās and their significance. In Purāṇa 17,2 (1975) 118-48.

05784 BROWN, C.M. God as mother: a feminine theology in India: an historical and theological study of the Brahmavaivarta Purāṇa. Hartford, VT: C. Stark, 1974. 264p.

05785 RAWAL, A.J. Geographical and ethnic data in the Brahmavaivarta Purāṇa. In Purāṇa 17,1 (1975) 24-37.

05786 ______. Society and socio-economic life in the Brahmavaivarta Purāṇa. In Purāṇa 15,1 (1973) 6-92.

05787 SEN, R.N., tr. Brahmavaivarta Purāṇam. NY: AMS Press, 1974. 2 v. [Rpt. of 1920 ed., SBH 24]

6. Śiva, Liṅga, and Skanda Purāṇas: Basic Mahāpurāṇas of Śaivism

05788 AWASHTHI, A.B.L. Studies in Skanda Purāṇa. Lucknow: Kailash Prakashan, 1965-. v. 1, 320p.

05789 Liṅga-purāṇa. Delhi: Motilal, 1973. 2 v., 808p. (AITM, 5, 6)

05790 Śiva-purāṇa. Delhi: Motilal, 1970. 4 v., 2120p. (AITM, 1-4)

05791 THAKUR, U. The holy places of Eastern India as depicted in the Skanda-Purāṇa. In Purāṇa 14,1 (1972) 40-57.

7. The Agni, Garuḍa, and Nārada Purāṇas: The "Encyclopedic" Mahāpurāṇas

05792 ABEGG, E., tr. Der Pretakalpa des Garuḍa-Purāṇa. Berlin: W. de Gruyter, 1921. 272p.

05793 BIRWÉ, R. The Amarakośa and the lexicographical chapters of the Agnipurāṇa. In JAOS 96 (1976) 383-403.

05794 DAMODARAN NAMBIAR, K. Nārada Purāṇa, a critical study. Varanasi: All-India Kashiraj Trust, 1979. 503p. [1st pub. in Purāṇa 15 (1973) - 18 (1976)]

05795 DUTT, M.N., tr. The Agni purāṇam. Varanasi: CSSO, 1967. 2 v. (CSS, 54) [1st pub. 1903-04]

05796 ______. The Garuḍapuraṇam. 2nd ed. Varanasi: CSSO, 1968. 784p. (CSS, 67) [1st pub. 1908]

05797 Garuḍa-purana. Delhi: Motilal, 1978-. v. 1 (chap. 1-146), 423p. (AITM, 12)

05798 GYANI, S.D. Agni Puraṇa: a study. Varanasi: CSSO, 1964. 339p. (CSS, 42)

05799 MISHRA, B. Polity in the Agni Puraṇa. Calcutta: Punthi Pustak, 1965. 206p.

05800 WOOD, E., tr. Garuḍa-puraṇa. Allahabad: Panini Office, 1911. 169p.

8. The Matsya Purāṇa: A Mahāpurāṇa

05801 AGRAWALA, V.S. Matsya Purāṇa, a study; Matsyapurāṇasilanam, an exposition of the ancient Purāṇa-Vidyā. Varanasi: All-India Kashiraj Trust, 1963. 427p.

05802 AKHTAR, J.D., ed. The Matsya Purāṇam. Delhi: Oriental Pub., 1972. 868p. (Sacred Books of the Aryans, 1)

05803 GOLDMAN, R.P. Myth as literature in ancient India: the saga of Śukrācārya and the demons (Matsyapurāṇa, 47). In Mahfil 7,3-4 (1971) 45-62.

05804 HOHENBERGER, A. Die indische Flutsage und das Matsyapurāṇa. Leipzig: Harrassowitz, 1930. 217p.

05805 The Matsya purāṇam. Tr. by a taluqdar of Oudh. Allahabad: Panini Office, 1916-17. 1 v. (SBH, 17)

05806 RAMACHANDRA DIKSHITAR, V.R. The Matsya Purāṇa, a study. Madras: U. of Madras, 1935. 140p.

9. The Mārkaṇḍeya Purāṇa, a Mahāpurāṇa, Containing the Devīmāhātmya, "Glorification of the Goddess"

05807 AGRAWALA, V.S., tr. Devī-Māhātmyam: the glorification of the great goddess. Varanasi: All-India Kashiraj Trust, 1963. 257p.

05808 DESAI, N.Y. Ancient Indian society, religion, and mythology as depicted in the Mārkaṇḍeya-Purāṇa; a critical study. Baroda: MSUB, 1968. 292p.

05809 PARGITER, F.E., tr. Mārkaṇḍeya purāṇa. Delhi: IndBH, 1969. 730p. [Rpt. 1888-1904 ed.]

05810 SHANKARANARAYANAN, S., tr. Glory of the Divine Mother; Devīmāhātmyam. Pondicherry: Dipti Pub., 1968. 322p.

05811 VARENNE, J., tr. Celebration de la grande Deesse: Devī-Māhātmya. Paris: Belles Lettres, 1975. 230p.

10. Other Mahāpurāṇas

05812 AGRAWALA, V.S. Vāmana-Purāṇa - a study. Varanasi: Prithvi Prakashan, 1964. 190p.

05813 ANANTHAKRISHNA SASTRY, R., tr. Lalita Sahasranāma, with Bhāskararāya's commentary. 3rd ed. Adyar: TPH, 1951. 432p. [from Brahmānda-purāna]

05814 BHATTACHARYA, A.B., et al., tr. The Kūrma Purāṇa. Varanasi: All-India Kashi Raj Trust, 1972.

05815 CHATTERJEE, A. Padma-purāṇa; a study. Calcutta: Sanskrit College, 1967. 268p.

05816 DUMONT, P.E., tr. L'Īśvaragītā; le chant de Śiva, texte extrait du Kūrma-Purāṇa. Baltimore: Johns Hopkins Press, 1933. 251p.

05817 GUPTA, A.S., ed. Vāmana Purāṇa. Tr. by M.N. Mukhopadhyaya, et al. Varanasi: All-India Kashiraj Trust, 1968. 710p.

05818 HOHENBERGER, A. Das Bhaviṣyapurāṇa. Wiesbaden: Harrassowitz, 1967. 143p. (MIS, 45)

05819 ______. Das Vāmanapurāṇa. In IJJ 7,1 (1963) 1-57.

05820 LASZLO, F. Die Parallelversion der Manusmṛti in Bhavisyapurāṇa. Wiesbaden: Steiner, 1971. 198p. (AKM, 40:2)

05821 RAMACHANDRA DIKSHITAR, V.R. Some aspects of Vāyu Purāṇa. Madras: U. of Madras, 1933. 52p.

05822 SHETH, S. Religion and society in the Brahma Purāṇa. ND: Sterling, 1979. 341p.

11. The Upapurāṇas
[For Viṣṇudharmottara-purāṇa see Chap. Four, IX. B.]

05823 HAZRA, R.C. Studies in the Upapurāṇas. Calcutta: Sanskrit College, 1958-. v. 1, 397p.; v. 2, 574p.

05824 JAHN, W., tr. Das Saurapurāṇam, ein Kompendium spätindischer Kulturgeschichte und des Sivaismus. Strassburg: Trübner, 1909. 207p.

05825 LALYE, P.G. Studies in Devī Bhāgavata. Bombay: Popular, 1973. 400p.

05826 SANYAL, N.C. The Devī-Bhāgavata as the real Bhāgavata. In Purāṇa 11,1 (1969) 127-58.

05827 VIJNANANANDA, Swami, tr. The Śrīmad Devī bhāgawatam. 2nd ed. ND: OBRC, 1977. 1192p. [Rpt. 1921-23 ed.; SBH, 26]

B. Bhakti Mārga: The Path of Devotion to a Personal God, Expressed through Sanskrit and the Regional Languages

1. General Studies of the Development of Bhakti on an All-India Level

05828 APPASAMY, A.J. The theology of Hindu Bhakti. Madras: CLS, 1970. 130p. (ITL, 5)

05829 BANKEY BEHARI. Minstrels of God. 2nd ed. Bombay: Bharatiya Vidya Bhavan, 1970. 344p.

05830 BHATTACHARYA, S.A. A study of the cult of devotion. In ALB 25 (1961) 587-602.

05831 CARPENTER, J.E. Theism in medieval India. ND: OBRC, 1977. 552p. [Rpt. 1921 ed.]

05832 GONDA, J. Medieval religious literature in Sanskrit. Wiesbaden: Harrassowitz, 1977. 316p. (HIL, 2:1)

05833 GOPALAKRISHNA NAIDU, G.T. The holy trinity, the three saintly ladies of ecstatic mysticism: comparative studies of Divine Mother Sri Sarada Devi, Sri Mira Bai and Sri Andal. Coimbatore: Mercury Book Co., 1974. 58p.

05834 HALIM, A. Religious movements in northern India, (1414-1526); Bhakti cult. In JASP 7 (1962) 47-87.

05835 KULENDRAN, S. Grace; a comparative study of the doctrine in Christianity and Hinduism. London: Lutterworth Press, 1964. 279p.

05836 RAGHAVAN, V. The great integrators: the saint-singers of India. Delhi: PDMIB, 1966. 184p.

05837 YADAVA, B.N.S. Social significance of the main religious trends and ideologies during the early medieval period. In K.C. Chattopadhyaya memorial volume. Allahabad: Dept. of Ancient Hist., Culture & Archaeol., Allahabad U., 1975, 39-49.

05838 ZELLIOT, E. The medieval Bhakti movement in history: an essay on the literature in English. In B.L. Smith, ed. Hinduism: new essays in the history of religions. Leiden: Brill, 1976, 143-68. (SHR, 33)

2. Sanskrit Hymns of Praise: Stotra/Stuti/Stava

05839 BAKE, A.A. The appropriation of Śiva's attributes by Devī. In BSOAS 27,3 (1955) 519-25. [based on Saundaryalaharī]

05840 BHATTACHARYYA, S.P. The stotra literature of old India. In IHQ 1,2 (1925) 340-60.

05841 BROWN, W.N., tr. The Mahīmnastava, or praise of Shiva's greatness, attrib. to Puṣpadanta. Poona: AIIS, 1965. 80p. (AIIS pub., 1)

05842 ______. The Saundaryalaharī, or Flood of Beauty. Cambridge: HUP, 1958. 247p. + 49 pl. [traditionally ascribed to Śaṅkarācārya]

05843 GONDA, J. Stotra literature. In his Medieval religious literature in Sanskrit. Wiesbaden: Harrassowitz, 1977, 232-70. (HIL, 2:1)

05844 SUBRAMANIAN, V.K., tr. Saudaryalaharī = the ocean of divine beauty of Śaṅkarācārya. Delhi: Motilal, 1977. 112p.

05845 KṚṢṆALĪLĀŚUKAMUNI. The Bilvamaṅgalastava. Tr. F. Wilson. Leiden: Brill, 1973. 173p.

05846 ______. The love of Krishna; the Kṛṣṇakarṇāmṛta of Līlāśuka Bilvamaṅgala. Tr. by F. Wilson. Philadelphia: UPaP, 1975. 463p. (Haney Foundation series, 14)

05847 WOODROFFE, J.G. Hymns to the goddess. Madras: Ganesh, 1973. 335p.

3. The Development of Śāktism: Worship of Śakti, the Female "Energy" of the Divine, Devī, the Great Goddess

05848 BEANE, W.C. Myth, cult, and symbols in Śākta Hinduism: a study of the Indian mother goddess. Leiden: Brill, 1977. 288p.

05849 BHATTACHARYA, N.N. History of the Śākta religion. ND: Munshiram, 1974. 188p.

05850 GIRI, R.N. Śakti (the Power) in the philosophy of the Purānas. In Purāṇa 12 (1970) 231-51.

05851 KRISHNA WARRIER, A.G., tr. Śākta Upaniṣads. Madras: Adyar Library, 1967. 95p.

05852 PAYNE, E.A. The Śāktas: an introductory and comparative study. NY: Garland Pub., 1979. 153p. [Rpt. 1933 ed.]

05853 PUSHPENDRA KUMAR. Śakti cult in ancient India, with special reference to the Purāṇic literature. Varanasi: Bharatiya, 1974. 317p.

05854 SINHA, J.N. The cult of divine power: Śaktisādhanā. 5th ed. Calcutta: Sinha Pub. House, 1977. 128p.

05855 ______. Shākta monism: the cult of Shakti. Calcutta: Sinha Pub. House, 1966. 52p.

05856 SIRCAR, D.C. Śakti cult. In his (ed.) The Śakti cult and Tārā. Calcutta: U. of Calcutta, 1967, 1-106.

C. Tantrism in the Hindu and Buddhist Traditions: Esoteric Yoga Emphasizing the Union of Male and Female Principles

1. General Studies of Tantraśāstra

05857 BHARATI, A. The Tantric tradition. Westport, CT: Greenwood Press, 1977. 349p. [Rpt. 1965 ed.]

05858 BOSE, D.N. Tantras, their philosophy and occult secrets. Calcutta: Oriental, 195-. 186p.

05859 CHAKRAVARTI, C. Tantras: studies in their religion and literature. Calcutta: Punthi Pustak, 1963. 129p.

05860 CHATTOPADHYAYA, S. Reflections on the Tantras. Delhi: Motilal, 1978. 105p.

05861 DOUGLAS, N. Tantra yoga. ND: Munshiram, 1971. 125p.

05862 ELIADE, M. Yoga and Tantrism. In his Yoga: immortality and freedom. 2nd ed. Tr. by W.R. Trask. Princeton: PUP, 1973, 200-273. (Bollingen series, 56) [1st French ed. 1954]

05863 RAMACHANDRA RAO, S.K. Tantra, mantra, yantra: the tantra psychology. ND: Arnold-Heinemann, 1979. 79p. + 4pl.

05864 RAWSON, P. Tantra; the Indian cult of ecstasy. London: Thames & Hudson, 1973. 128p.

05865 SARAF, S. The Tantric tradition. In EA 27,2 (1974) 99-156. [comparative evaluation of A. Bharati's Tantric Tradition]

05866 SINGH, L.P. Tantra, its mystic and scientific basis. Delhi: Concept, 1976. 203p.

05867 WOODROFFE, J. Shakti and Shākta: essays on the Shakta Tantrashāstra. 4th ed. Madras: Ganesh, 1951. 734p.

05868 ZIMMER, H. Zur Bedeutung des indischen Tantra-yoga. In Eranos Jahrbuch 1 (1933) 9-94.

2. Tantric Iconography and Symbolism, Hindu and Buddhist

05869 ARGUELLES, J. & M. ARGUELLES. Maṇḍala. Berkeley: Shambala, 1972. 140p.

05870 BHATTACHARYA, B. The Indian Buddhist iconography, mainly based on the Sādhanāmālā and other cognate Tantric texts. 2nd ed., rev. & enl. Calcutta: KLM, 1958. 478p. [1st ed. 1924, 220p.]

05871 LAUF, D.I. Das Bild als Symbol im Tantrismus; die indischen Tantras als praktische Führer zur seelischen Ganzheit des Menschen. München: H. Moos, 1973. 76p.

05872 MALLMANN, M.-T. DE. Un aspect de Sarasvatī dans le Tantrisme bouddhique. In BEFEO 63 (1976) 369-74.

05873 ______. Dieux polyvalents du tantrisme bouddhique. In JA 252 (1964) 365-77.

05874 ______. Divinités hindoues dans le tantrisme bouddhique. In ArtsAs 10 (1964) 67-86. [English tr. by S.W. Taylor in Zentralasiatische Studien 2 (1968) 41-54]

05875 ______. Notes d'iconographie tantrique. In ArtsAs 2 (1955) 35-46; 9 (1962-63) 73-79; 20 (1969) 21-40; 32 (1976) 173-88.

05876 MEISEZAL, R.O. Amogapāśa; some Nepalese representations and their Vajrayānic aspects. In Monumenta Serica 26 (1967) 455-97 + 10pl.

05877 ______. Die Göttin Vajravārāhī; eine ikonographische Studie nach einem Sādhanā text von Advayavajra. In Oriens, 18-19 (1965-66) 228-303.

05878 MOOKERJEE, A.C. Tantra art: its philosophy and physics. ND: R. Kumar, 1967. 152p. [1st pub. 1966]

05879 RAWSON, P. The art of Tantra. London: Thames & Hudson, 1973. 216p.

05880 SARASWATI, S.K. Tantrayāna art: an album with introduction and notes. Calcutta: Asiatic Soc., 1977. 100p. + 134pl.

05881 SHANKARANARAYANAN, S. Sri chakra. Pondicherry: Dipti Pub., 1970. 122p.

05882 SLUSSER, M.S. Vajrācārya (Gautamavajra) - some Nepalese stone sculptures: a reappraisal within their cultural and historical context. In ArtAs 35,1-3 (1973) 79-138, incl. 20pl.

05883 SRIVASTAVA, B. Iconography of Śakti: a study based on Śrītattvanidhi. Varanasi: Chaukhambha Orientalia, 1978. 173p. + 8pl.

05884 TUCCI, G. Theory and practice of mandala. Tr. by A.H. Brodrick. London: Rider, 1961. 146p. [1st Italian ed., 1949]

05885 VARENNE, J. Le tantrisme: la sexualité transcendée. Paris: CELT, 1977. 255p. (Bibliothèque de l'irrationel) (Le Domaine invisible)

3. Hindu Tantrism: Texts and Studies

05886 BHATTACHARYA, S.C.V. Principles of tantra = The Tantra-tattva of Śrīyukta Śiva Candra Vidyārṇava Bhaṭṭācārya Mahodaya. 5th ed. Madras: Ganesh, 1978. 2 v.

05887 GOUDRIAAN, T. Khaḍya-Rāvaṇa and his worship in Balinese and Indian Tantric sources. In WZKS 21 (1977) 143-69.

05888 GUPTA, S. & D.J. HOENS & T. GOUDRIAAN. Hindu tantrism. Leiden: Brill, 1974. 208p. (HO, 2:4:2)

05889 KUNDU, N.L. Non-dualism in Śaiva and Śākta philosophy. Calcutta: Śrī Śrī Bhairabī Jogeśwarī Maṭh, 1964. 199p.

05890 MUKHERJEE, A.C. Tantra āsana, a way to self-realization. Basel: Ravi Kumar, 1971. 161p.

05891 WOODROFFE, J.G. The world as power. 5th ed. Madras: Ganesh, 1974. 477p. [1st pub. 1921]

05892 ______, tr. Tantra of the great liberation (Mahānirvāṇa Tantra). NY: Dover, 1972. 506p. [1st pub. 1913]

05893 ______. Tantrarāja tantra and Kāma-kalā-vilāsa. Madras: Ganesh, 1971. 245p. [1st pub. 1921]

4. Vajrayāna, the "Thunderbolt-Vehicle": Buddhist Tantrism in India and Tibet
a. general studies of the origins and development of Vajrayāna

05894 BAGCHI, P.C. The cult of the Buddhist Siddhācāryas. In Cultural heritage of India. Calcutta: RMIC, 1956, v. 4, 273-79.

05895 ______. Studies in the Tantras. Part 1. [A collection of articles which were published in the IHQ and the Calcutta Oriental Journal between 1930 & 1934] Calcutta: U. of Calcutta, 1939. 114p.

05896 BHATTACHARYYA, B. An introduction to Buddhist esoterism. 2nd ed. Varanasi: CSSO, 1964. 184p. (CSS, 46) [1st ed. 1932]

05897 BLOFELD, J. The way of power: a practical guide to the Tantric mysticism of Tibet. London: Allen & Unwin, 1970. 255p.

05898 DARIAN, S.G. Antecedents of Tantrism in the Saddharma-Puṇḍarīka. In AS/EA 24 (1970) 105-125.

05899 DASGUPTA, S.B. An introduction to tāntric Buddhism. 3rd ed. Calcutta: U. of Calcutta, 1974. 211p. [1st ed. 1950]

05900 DUTT, N. Tantric Buddhism. In Bulletin of Tibetology 1,2 (1964) 5-16.

05901 ELDER, G.R. Problems of language in Buddhist tantra. In HR 15,3 (1976) 231-50.

05902 GLASENAPP, H. VON. Buddhistische Mysterien, die geheimen Lehren und Riten des Diamantfahrzeugs. Stuttgart: W. Spemann, 1940. 201p.

05903 ______. Die Entstehung des Vajrayāna. In ZDMG 90 (1936) 546-72.

05904 GUENTHER, H.V. Tantra and revelation. In HR 7 (1968) 279-301.

05905 ______. The Tantric view of life. Berkeley: Shambhala, 1973. 190p.

05906 ______. Treasures on the Tibetan middle way: a newly revised edition of Tibetan Buddhism without mystification. Berkeley: Shambhala, 1976. 156p.

05907 ______. Yuganaddha, the tantric view of life. 2nd ed., rev. Varanasi: CSSO, 1969. 218p. (CSS, 3)

05908 JHAVERY, M.B. Comparative and critical study of Mantrasāstra with treatment of Jain Mantravāda, being the introduction to Śrī Bhairava Padmāvatī Kalpa. [Skt. poem of Mallishena]. Ahmedabad: Sarabhai Manilal Nawab, 1944. 364 + 74 + 136p.

05909 JOSHI, L.M. Original homes of Tantrika Buddhism. In JOIB 16 (1967) 223-38.

05910 SANKRITYAYANA, R. L'origine du Vajrayāna. In JA 225 (1934) 209-30.

05911 Studies of esoteric Buddhism and Tantrism, in commemoration of the 1,150th anniversary of the founding of Koyasan. Koyasan, Japan: Koyasan U., 1965. 866p. (1-370 in English)

05912 WAYMAN, A. The Buddhist Tantras: light on Indo-Tibetan esoterism. London: Routledge & K. Paul, 1974. 247p.

b. the cult of Tārās, savioress-consorts of Buddhas and Bodhisattvas

05913 DHAVALIKAR, M.K. The origin of Tārā. In BDCRI 25 (1963-64) 15-20.

05914 SASTRI, H. The origin and cult of Tārā. ND: Indological Book Corp, 1977. 27p. + 2pl.

05915 SIRCAR, D.C. Tārā. In his The Śakti cult and Tārā. Calcutta: U. of Calcutta, 1967, 107-68.

05916 WAYMAN, A. Female energy and symbolism in the Buddhist tantras. In HR 2 (1952) 73-111.

c. selected Tantric texts in translation

05917 BHATTACHARYYA, B. Guhyasamāja Tantra, Tathāgataguhyaka. Baroda: Oriental Inst., 1931. 38 + 212p. [Sanskrit text; English intro.]

05918 ______. Sādhanāmālā. Baroda: Oriental Inst., 1928. 2 v. (GOS, 26, 41) [English intro., v. 2, 11-177; Sanskrit text]

05919 SNELLGROVE, D., tr. The Hevajra Tantra. London: OUP, 1959. 2 v.

05920 TAJIMA, R. Étude sur le Mahāvairocana-Sūtra. Paris: Maisonneuve, 1936. 186p.

05921 TUCCI, G. Some glosses on the Guhyasamāja. In Mélanges chinois et bouddhiques 3 (1934) 339-53.

05922 WAYMAN, A. Yoga of the Guhyasamājatantra: the arcane lore of forty verses: a Buddhist tantra commentary. Delhi: Motilal, 1977. 388p.

D. The Submergence of Buddhism in Medieval India

05923 BAGCHI, P.C. Decline of Buddhism in India and its causes. In Sir Asutosh Mookerjee Silver Jubilee Volume. Calcutta: Calcutta U., 1927, v. 3, 405-21.

05924 HOFFMAN, H. Das Kālacakra, die letzte Phase des Buddhismus in Indien. In Saeculum 15 (1964) 125-31.

05925 JOSHI, L.M. Reviews on some alleged causes of the decline of Buddhism in India. In JGJRI 22,1/2 (1965-66) 23-28.

05926 ______. Studies in the Buddhistic culture of India, during the 7th and 8th centuries A.D. Delhi: Motilal, 1967. 538p.

05927 MITRA, R.C. The decline of Buddhism in India. Santiniketan: Visva-Bharati, 1954. 164p. (Its Studies, 20) [Also pub. in VBA 6 (1954) 1-164]

05928 POMERANTZ, G.S. The decline of Buddhism in medieval India. In Diogenes 96 (1976) 38-66.

05929 RAMACHANDRA RAO, S.K. The Indian background of Tibetan religion. In Brahmavādin 11,1 (1976) 219-240.

E. Jainism in Medieval India

05930 CAILLAT, C. L'offrande de distiques (dohāpāhuḍa): traduction de l'apabhraṁśa. In JA 264,1/2 (1976) 63-95.

05931 WILLIAMS, R.H.B. Jaina Yoga; a survey of the mediaeval śravakācāras. London: OUP, 1963. 296p.

F. The Entry of Islam: Brought by Arabs to Sindh (710 AD) and by Turks and Afghans to the Northwest (After 1000 AD)

1. General Studies of Early Islam in India

05932 ARNOLD, T.W. The spread of Islam in India. In his The preaching of Islam; a history of the propagation of the Muslim faith. Lahore: Sh. Muhammad Ashraf, 1961, 257-96. [Rpt. of 1896 ed.]

05933 HARDY, P. Modern European and Muslim explanations of conversion to Islam in South Asia: a preliminary survey of the literature. In JRAS (1977) 177-206.

05934 NABI, M.N. Development of Muslim religious thought in India from 1200 A.D. to 1450 A.D. Aligarh: Aligarh Muslim U., 1962. 210p.

05935 RICHARDS, J.F. The Islamic frontier in the East: expansion into South Asia. In South Asia 4 (1974) 90-109. [review article]

05936 SRIVASTAVA, A.L. A survey of India's resistance to medieval invaders from the North-West; causes of eventual Hindu defeat. In JIH 43,2 (1965) 349-68.

2. Sufism: Islamic Mysticism
a. general introductions to Sufism

05937 ARBERRY, A.J. An introduction to the history of Sufism. London: Longmans, Green, 1943. 84p.

05938 ______. Sufism; an account of the mystics of Islam. NY: Harper and Row, 1970. 141p. [1st pub. 1950]

05939 NICHOLSON, R.A. Studies in Islamic mysticism. Cambridge: CamUP, 1921. 282p.

05940 SCHIMMEL, A. Mystical dimensions of Islam. Chapel Hill: U. of N. Carolina Press, 1975. 506p.

05941 SMITH, M. The Ṣūfī path of love; an anthology of Sufism. London: Luzac, 1954. 154p.

05942 TRIMINGHAM, J.S. The Sufi orders in Islam. Oxford: OUP, 1973. 344p.

b. studies of early Sufism in India (beginning c. 1015)

05943 AKHTER, M.S. A critical appraisal of the Sufi hagiographical corpus of medieval India. In IsC 52,3 (1978) 139-50.

05944 BEGG, W. The big five of India in Sufism. Ajmer: 1972. 214p.

05945 CHATTERJI, S.K. Islamic mysticism; Iran and India. In Indo-Iranica 1,2 (1946-47) 9-35.

05946 EATON, R.M. Sufi folk literature and the expansion of Indian Islam. In HR 14,2 (1974) 117-27.

05947 HAQ, M.E. Sufi movement in India. In Indo-Iranica 3,2 (1948) 1-12; 3,3 (1949) 11-43.

05948 KHAN, Y.H. Sufism in India. In IsC 30 (1956) 239-62.

05949 LAWRENCE, B.B. An overview of Sufi literature in the Sultanate period, 1206-1526 A.D. Patra: Khuda Bakhsh Oriental Public Library, 1979. 76p.

05950 MOINUL HAQ, S. Rise of the Naqshbandī and Qādirī Silsilahs in the subcontinent. In JPHS 25,1 (1977) 1-33.

05951 NIZAMI, KHALIQ AHMAD. Khānqah life in medieval India. In Studia Islamica 8 (1957) 51-70.

05952 RIZVI, S.A.A. A history of Sufism in India. ND: Munshiram Manoharlal, 1978-. v. 1, 432p. [Early Sufism and its history in India to 1600 AD]

05953 SCHIMMEL, A. The influence of Sufism on Indo-Muslim poetry. In J.P. Strelka, ed. Anagogic qualities of literature. U. Park: Penn. State U. Press, 1971, 181-210.

05954 SIDDIQUI, M.H. The memoirs of Sufis written in India: reference to Kashaf-ul-mahjub, Siyar-ul-auliya, and Siyar-ul-arifin. Baroda: Dept. of Persian, Urdu, and Arabic, MSUB, 1979. 105p.

05955 SIDDIQUI, M.S. Origin and development of the Chishtī order in the Deccan, 1300-1538 AD. In IsC 51 (1977) 209-19.

05956 SUBHAN, J.A. Sufism, its saints and shrines; an introduction to the study of Sufism with special reference to India. NY: S. Weiser, 1970. 412p. [1st pub. 1938]

3. Islam and the Indic Religions: Mutual Perceptions and Interactions

05957 BANKEY BEHARI. Sufis, mystics, and yogis of India. Bombay: Bharatiya Vidya Bhavan, 1962. 384p.

05958 FRIEDMANN, Y. Medieval Muslim views of Indian religions. In JAOS 95,2 (1975) 214-21.

05959 GIMARET, D. Bouddha et les bouddhistes dans la tradition musulmane. In JA 257 (1969) 273-316.

05960 KHAN, Y.H. L'Inde mystique au moyen age, Hindous et Musulmans. Paris: A. Maisonneuve, 1929. 211p.

05961 LAWRENCE, B.B. Shahrastānī on the Indian religions. The Hague: Mouton, 1976. 297p. (Religion and society, 4)

05962 RIZVI, S.A.A. Sufis and Natha yogis in mediaeval northern India (XII to XVI centuries). In JOSA 7,1/2 (1970) 119-33.

05963 SEN, K.M. Medieval mysticism of India. Tr. from Bengali by M.M. Ghosh. London: Luzac, 1936. 241p.

05964 YUSUF, S.M. The early contacts between Islam and Buddhism. In UCR 13,1 (1955) 1-28.

III. MEDIEVAL SANSKRIT LITERATURE

A. Medieval Poetic Theory and Criticism

1. The Alaṁkāra-śāstra: Aesthetics of Stanzaic Poetry

a. general studies

05965 BHATTACHARYA, S.P. Kashmīr Śaiva darśana's impress on alaṅkāras in alaṅkāraśāstra. In JOIB 1,3 (1952) 245-52.

05966 _____. Neo-Buddhist nucleus in Alaṁkārasāstra. JASBengal 22,1 (1956) 49-66.

05967 BHATTACHARYYA, S.M., tr. The alaṁkāra section of the Agni-purāṇa. Calcutta: KLM, 1976. 240p.

05968 CHATTERJI, H.N. Comparative studies in Pāli and Sanskrit alaṅkāras. Calcutta: SPB, 1960.

05969 LAHIRI, P.C. Concepts of rīti and guṇa in Sanskrit poetics. Columbia: South Asia Books, 1974. 215p. [Rpt. 1937 ed.]

05970 RAGHAVAN, V. Studies on some concepts of the Alaṁkāra shāstra. Madras: Adyar Library, 1973. 345p.

b. Bhāmaha (c. 725 AD), author of the Kāvyālaṁkāra, first treatise on poetics after the Nāṭyaśāstra

05971 GNOLI, R., tr. Commentary on the Kāvyālaṁkāra of Bhāmaha. Rome: IIMEO, 1962. 110p. [Comm. by Udbhaṭa]

05972 NAGANATHA SASTRY, P.V., tr. Kāvyālaṅkāra of Bhāmaha. 2nd ed. Delhi: Motilal, 1970. 134p.

c. later alaṁkāra writers; Daṇḍin (c. 750), author of the Kāvyadarśa

05973 BÖHTLINGK, O. VON, tr. Poetik (Kāvyadarça). Leipzig: A. Haessel, 1890. 138p.

05974 GUPTA, D.K. A critical study of Daṇḍin and his works. Delhi: Meharchand Lachhmandas, 1970. 466p.

05975 _____. Society and culture in the time of Daṇḍin. Delhi: Meharchand Lachhmandas, 1972. 458p.

05976 VAMANA. The Kāvyalaṅkāra sūtra of Vāmana; with his own gloss, the Kavipriya. In Indian Thought (Allahabad) 3 (1911) 267-96, 301-56; 4 (1912) 1-32, 101-34.

2. The Rasa ("Flavor" of Aesthetic Experience) and Dhvani ("Resonance") Theories

a. general studies

05977 NANDI, T.S. The origin and development of the theory of rasa and dhvani in Sanskrit poetics. Ahmedabad: Gujarat U., 1973. 466p.

05978 PRABHAKARA SASTRI, J. Lollaṭa's theory of rasa. In JOIB 15 (1965-66) 157-65.

05979 SANKARAN, A. Some theories of literary criticism in Sanskrit, or, the theories of rasa and dhvani. Madras: U. of Madras, 1929. 161p.

b. the Dhvanyāloka of Ānandavardhana of Kashmir (c. 850): interaction of rasa and bhakti

05980 CHARI, V.K. The Indian theory of suggestion (dhvani). In PEW 27,4 (1977) 391-408.

05981 JACOBI, H.G., tr. Dhvanyāloka; die Principien der Poetik. Leipzig: Brockhaus, 1903. 159p.

05982 KRISHNAMOORTHY, K. The Dhvanyāloka and its critics. Mysore: Kāvyālaya, 1968. 352p.

05983 _____. Germs of the theory of dhvani. In ABORI 28 (1947) 190-211.

05984 _____., tr. Dhvanyāloka of Ānandavardhana. Dharwar: Karnatak U., 1974. 406p.

05985 MASSON, J.L. Philosophy and literary criticism in ancient India. In JIP 1,2 (1971) 167-80.

05986 RENOU, L. Le dhvani dans la poétique Sanskrite. In ALB 18 (1954) 6-25.

05987 SHARMA, M.M. The dhvani theory in Sanskrit poetics. Varanasi: CSSO, 1968. 287p.

c. Abhinavagupta (c. 1000 AD): Kashmir Śaiva theorist of theology and poetics; concept of śāntarasa, rasa of "repose." [For his philosophical works, see Chap. Four, VIII. B. 2. b.]

05988 BHATTACHARYA, S.P. Śānta rasa and its scope in literature. Calcutta: Sanskrit College, 1976. 255p.

05989 GEROW, E. & A. AKLUJKAR. On Śānta Rasa in Sanskrit poetics. In JAOS 92 (1972) 80-88. [rev. of Masson and Patwardhan]

05990 GNOLI, R., tr. The aesthetic experience according to Abhinavagupta. Tr. of part of the Abhinavabharati.... 2nd rev. ed. Varanasi: CSSO, 1968. 125p. (CSS, 62) [1st ed. 1956]

05991 MASSON, J.L. Abhinavagupta as a poet. In JOIB 19 (1970) 247-53.

05992 MASSON, J.L. & M.V. PATWARDHAN. Śāntarasa and Abhinavagupta's philosophy of aesthetics. Poona: BORI, 1969. 206p. (BOS, 9)

05993 PANDEY, K.C. Abhinavagupta; an historical and philosophical study. 2nd ed., rev. & enl. Varanasi: CSSO, 1963. 1014p. (CSS, 1)

d. the Kāvyaprakāśa of Mammaṭa (c. 1100) of Kashmir

05994 DWIVEDI, R.C., tr. The poetic light: Kāvyaprakāśa of Mammaṭa. Delhi: Motilal, 1966-70. 2 v., 193, 591p.

05995 FILLIOZAT, P.-S. Une théorie indienne du langage poétique: les modes d'expression du sens selon Mammaṭa. In Poetique 11 (1972) 315-20.

05996 GAJENDRAGADKAR, A.B., tr. The Kāvyaprakāśa of Mammaṭa; first, second, third, and tenth ullāsas. 3rd ed. Bombay: Popular, 1970. 42 + 518p.

05997 JHA, G.N., tr. The Kāvya-prakāsha of Mammaṭa. Varanasi: Bharatiya Vidya Prakashan, 1967. 2 v., 563p. [1st ed. 1898]

e. other writers in Sanskrit poetics

05998 BALLANTYNE, J.R. & P. MITRA, tr. The Mirror of Composition, a treatise on poetical criticism, being an English translation of the Sāhitya-darpana of Viśwanātha Kavirāja. Banaras: Motilal, 1956. 444p. [Rpt. from BI ed. of 1865]

05999 CHATTOPADHYAYA, S. Nāṭaka-lakṣaṇa-ratna-kośa in the perspective of ancient Indian drama and dramaturgy. Calcutta: Punthi Pustak, 1974. 343p.

06000 GANGOPADHYAY, A. Contribution of Appaya Dīkṣita to Indian poetics. Calcutta: SPB, 1971, 134p.

06001 HAAS, G.C.O. The Daśarūpa [of Dhanañjaya]; a treatise on Hindu dramaturgy. NY: ColUP, 1912. 169p.

06002 KLOSTERMAIER, K. The Bhaktirasāmṛtasindhubindu of Viśvanātha Cakravartin. In JAOS 94,1 (1974) 96-107.

06003 RAGHAVAN, V. Bhoja's Śṛṅgāra prakāśa. 3rd rev. enl. ed. Madras: Raghavan, 1978. 981p.

06004 VENKATESWARAN, C.S. Rajaśekhara and his Kāvyamīmāṁsā. Madras: Kuppuswami Sastri Res. Inst., 1970. 12p. [1st pub. in JORM 37 (1967-68) 1-12]

B. Medieval Sanskrit Drama, Poetry, and Prose in Translation, With Studies of Major Authors

1. Harṣavardhana, King of Kanauj (606-648 AD) and Dramatist

06005 BHATTACHARYA, A.N. & M. DAS, tr. Ratnāvalī. Calcutta: Modern Book Agency, 1967. 410 + 72p.

06006 LEHOT, M., tr. Ratnāvalī. Paris: Les Belles Lettres, 1933. 81 + 104p. [In French]

06007 NARIMAN, G.K. & A.V.W. JACKSON & C.J. OGDEN, tr. Priyadarśikā, a Sanskrit drama. NY: ColUP, 1923. 131p.

06008 SANKARA RAMA SASTRI, C., tr. Nāgānanda of Harsha Deva. 6th ed. Madras: Sri Balamanorama Press, 1967. 252p.

06009 SCHUYLER, M. A bibliography of the plays attributed to Harṣadeva. In Verhandlungen des Internationalen Orientalisten-Kongresses....Leiden (1904) 33-37.

06010 WORTHAM, B.H. The Buddhist legend of Jimutavāhana from the Kathā-sarit-sāgara...dramatized in the Nāgānanda, a Buddhist drama by Sri Harsha Deva. London: Routledge, 1911. 105p.

2. Bāṇabhaṭṭa (C. 625), Novelist and Biographer of King Harṣa

a. translations

06011 COWELL, E.B. & F.W. THOMAS, tr. Harṣa-carita. London: RAS, 1897. 284p.

06012 KALE, M.R., tr. Bāṇa's Kādambarī. Bombay: Jaico, 1960. 265p.

06013 KUNHAN RAJA, C. Kādambarī. Bombay: BVB, 1963. 198p. [a retelling]

06014 QUACKENBOS, G.P., tr. The Sanskrit poems of Mayūra ...with...Bāna's Caṇḍīśataka. NY: ColUP, 1917. 362p.

06015 RIDDING, C.M., tr. Kādambarī. London: RAS, 1896. 231p.

06016 VISHVANATHAN, S., tr. Harshacharita, the first ucchhvāsa. 2nd ed. Madras: Sri Balamanorama Press, 1964. 168p.

b. studies

06017 AGRAWALA, V.S. The deeds of Harsha, being a cultural study of Bāṇa's Harshacharita. Ed. by P.K. Agrawala. Varanasi: Prithvi Prakashan, 1969. 269p.

06018 KANSARA, N.M. Bāṇa and Dhanapāla as Sanskrit novelists. In VIJ 14,2 (1976) 223-38.

06019 KARMARKAR, R.D. Bāṇa. Dharwar: Karnatak U., 1964. 118p.

06020 KRISHNAMOORTHY, K. Bāṇabhaṭṭa. ND: Sahitya Akademi, 1976. 83p.

06021 SHARMA, N. Bāṇabhaṭṭa; a literary study. Delhi: Munshiram, 1968. 255p.

06022 SIVARAMAMURTI, C. Painting and allied arts revealed in Bāṇa's works. In JORM 7 (1933) 59-81.

3. Bhavabhūti (C. 700), Author of Nāṭakas ("Heroic Drama") Based on Rāmāyaṇa, and of the Prakaraṇa ("Romantic Play") Mālatīmādhava

a. translations

06023 BELVALKAR, S.K., tr. Rāma's later history; or, Uttara-rāma-carita. Cambridge: HUP, 1915. 88 + 102p. (HOS, 21-23; v. 21, English translation)

06024 BHAT, G.K., tr. Uttara-rāma-carita. 2nd rev. ed. Surat: Popular Pub., 1965. 178 + 471p.

06025 KALE, M.R., tr. Mālatīmādhava, with the commentary of Jagadhara. 3rd ed. ND: Motilal, 1967. 1 v. [1st pub. 1913]

06026 ______., tr. Uttararamacharita. Bombay: G. Narayan, 1911. 352p.

06027 KARMARKAR, R.D., tr. Uttararāmacarita [Rāma's later history]. Poona: Aryabhushan Press, 1954. 312p.

06028 PICKFORD, J., tr. Mahāvīracharita; the adventures of the great hero Rāma. London: Trubner, 1871. 172p.

06029 STCHOUPAK, N., tr. Uttararāmacarita (la dernière aventure de Rāma). Paris: Les Belles Lettres, 1935. 304p.

06030 STREHLY, G., tr. Mādhava et Mālatī. The Mālatīmādhava. Paris: E. Leroux, 1885. 174p.

b. studies

06031 BETAI, R. Principal sentiment in the Uttara-Rāmacharita. In JGRS 32 (1970) 202-10.

06032 BHAT, G.K. Bhavabhūti. ND: Sahitya Akademi, 1979. 80p.

06033 GERA, V. Mind and art of Bhavabhūti. ND: Meharchand Lachhmandas, 1973. 292p.

06034 HARSHE, R.G. Observations on the life and works of Bhavabhūti. Tr. from French by J.B. Khanna. Delhi: Meharchand Lachhmandas, 1974. 103p. [1st French ed. 1938]

06035 KARMARKAR, R.D. Bhavabhūti. Dharwar: Karnatak U., 1963. 119p.

06036 MIRASHI, V.V. Bhavabhūti and his date, life and works. Delhi: Motilal, 1974. 411p.

4. Bhartṛhari the Poet (C. 7th Cent.?), Sometimes Identified with Bhartṛhari the Grammarian

06037 AKLUJKAR, A. Two textual studies of Bhartṛhari. In JAOS 89 (1969) 547-63.

06038 COWARD, H.G. Bhartṛhari. Boston: Twayne, 1976. 150p.

06039 KALE, M.R., tr. The Nīti and Vairagya śatakas of Bhartṛhari. 7th ed. Delhi: Motilal, 1971. 275p.

06040 KOSAMBI, D.D., tr. The epigrams attributed to Bhartṛhari. Bombay: BVB, 1948. [Sanskrit text; English intro. 56-81]

06041 MILLER, B.S., tr. Bhartrihari: Poems. NY: ColUP, 1967. 156p.

06042 ______. The hermit and the love-thief; Sanskrit poems of Bhartrihari and Bilhaṇa. NY: ColUP, 1978. 127p.

06043 RYDER, A.W., tr. Women's eyes. San Francisco: A.M. Robertson, 1910. 100p.

06044 MORE, P.E., tr. A century of Indian epigrams. NY: Harper, 1899. 124p.

06045 SCOTT, D., tr. Bhartrihari says. London: F. Muller, 1940. 93p.

06046 WORTHAM, B.H., tr. The Śatakas of Bhartrihari. London: Trübner, 1886. 71p.

5. Bilhaṇa (11th Cent. AD), Love Poet of Kashmir

06047 ARNOLD, E., tr. The Chaurapanchāsika, an Indian love lament. London: K. Paul, Trench, Trubner, 1896. 53p.

06048 BANERJI, S.C. & A.K. GUPTA. Bilhaṇa's Vikramāṅkadevacaritam; glimpses of the history of the Cāḷukyas of Kalyāṇa. Calcutta: Sambodhi Pub., 1965. 323p.

06049 GOMBRICH, R., tr. The fifty stanzas of a thief. In Mahfil 7,3-4 (1971) 175-86.

06050 MILLER, B.S., tr. The hermit and the love-thief; Sanskrit poems of Bhartrihari and Bilhaṇa. NY: ColUP, 1978. 127p.

06051 ______., tr. Phantasies of a love-thief: the Caurapañcāśika attributed to Bilhaṇa. NY: ColUP, 1971. 233p. (Studies in Oriental culture, 6)

06052 MISRA, B.N. Studies on Bilhaṇa and his Vikramāṅkadevacarita. ND: K.B. Pub., 1976. 135p.

06053 TADPATRIKAR, S.N., tr. Caurapañcāśika, an Indian love lament of Bilhaṇakavi. Poona: Oriental Book Agency, 1966. 43p.

6. Other Medieval Sanskrit Poets and Dramatists, and Their Works

06054 BANDYOPADHYAY, P. Observations on similes in the Naiṣadhacarita. Calcutta: SPB, 1966. 142p.

06055 BEDI, B.P.L., tr. The art of the temptress; translation of the 1200 year old Sanskrit classic the Kuṭṭnī māhātmyam of Dāmodar Gupta. Bombay: Pearl Pub., 1968. 218p.

06056 BHATT, B.N. Śrīkaṇṭhacaritam; a study. Baroda: MSUB, 1973. 180p. [by Maṅkha, fl. 1136-1150]

06057 CHANDRA PRABHA. Historical mahākāvyas in Sanskrit, eleventh to fifteenth century A.D. ND: Meharchand Lachhmandas, 1976. 435p.

06058 GUPTA, D.K. A critical study of Daṇḍin and his works. Delhi: Meharchand Lachhmandas, 1970. 466p.

06059 HANDIQUI, K.K., tr. The Naiṣadhacarita of Śrīharsha (cantos 1-22). 3rd ed. Poona: DCPRI, 1965. 647p. [1st pub. 1934]

06060 INGALLS, D.H.H., tr. An anthology of Sanskrit court poetry; Vidyākara's 'Subhāṣitaratnakośa'. Cambridge: HUP, 1965. 611p. (HOS, 44)

06061 ______., tr. Sanskrit poetry, from Vidyākara's treasury. Cambridge: HUP, 1968. 346p.

06062 KALE, M.R., tr. The Daśakumāracarita, with a commentary. 4th ed. ND: Motilal, 1966. 524p. [by Dandin; Rpt. 1917 ed.]

06063 LAL, P., tr. The farce of the drunk monk; a 1-act Sanskrit play of the 7th century. Calcutta: Writers Workshop, 1968. 30p. [by Mahendra Vikrama Varma Pallava, king of Kanchi, fl. 600-630]

06064 LOCKWOOD, M. & A.V. BHAT, tr. Bhagavadajjuka prahāsana: a philosophical farce. Madras: CLS, 1978. 126p. [by Mahendra Vikrama Varma Pallava, king of Kāñchī, fl. 600-630]

06065 MAAN SINGH. Subandhu and Daṇḍin. ND: Meharchand Lachhmandas, 1979. 577p.

06066 MERWIN, W.S. & J.M. MASSON, tr. Sanskrit love poetry. NY: ColUP, 1977. 204p.

06067 QUACKENBOS, G.P., tr. The Sanskrit poems of Mayūra. NY: ColUP, 1917. 362p.

06068 RYDER, A.W., tr. Daṇḍin's Dasha-kumāra-charita, the ten princes. Chicago: UChiP, 1927. 240p.

06069 STERNBACH, L. Unknown verses attributed to Kṣemendra. Lucknow: Akhila Bharatiya Sanskrit Parishad, 1979. 147p.

06070 UNNI, N.P. Kulaśekhara Varman: the royal dramatist of Kerala. In JKS 3 (1976) 239-316, 325-406.

C. Medieval Sanskrit Narrative Literature: Kathā, Ākhyāyikā, and Campū: Popular Tales and Fables

1. Medieval Sanskrit Versions of the Lost Prakrit Bṛhatkathā, by Somadeva and Kṣemendra of Kashmir, and Budhasvāmin of Nepal

06071 BOTTO, O. Il poeta Kṣemendra e il suo Daśavatāracarita. Torino: U. di Torino, 1951. 49p. (Its Facoltà di lettere e filosofia, pub., 3:1)

06072 DATTARAY, R. A critical survey of the life and works of Kṣemendra. Calcutta: SPB, 1974. 184p.

06073 LACÔTE, F., tr. Bṛhatkathāçlokasaṁgraha. Paris: Imprimerie Nationale, 1908-29. 2 v. [by Budhasvāmin; French tr.]

06074 MANKOWSKI, L. VON. Der Auszug aus dem Pañcatantra in Kshemendras Brihatkathāmañjarī. Leipzig: Harrassowitz, 1892. 80p.

06075 MATEN, E.P., tr. Budhasvāmin's Bṛhatkathāślokasaṁgraha: a literary study of an ancient Indian narrative. Leiden: Brill, 1973. 116p.

06076 TAWNEY, C.H., tr. The Kathākoça: or, treasury of stories. ND: OBRC, 1975. 260p. [Rpt. 1895 ed.]

06077 ______. The ocean of story...Somadeva's Kathā sarit sāgara, or ocean of streams of story. Delhi: Motilal, 1968. 10 v. [Rpt. of 1924-28 ed.]

06078 WORTHAM, B.H., tr. The Buddhist legend of Jīmūtavāhana from the Kathā-sarit sāgara, dramatized in the Nāgānanda, a Buddhist drama by Srī Harsha Deva. London: Routledge, 1911. 105p.

2. Hitopadeśa, "Book of Good Counsel": Bengali Sanskrit Version of the Pañcatantra

06079 ARNOLD, E., tr. The book of the good counsels. The Hitopadesa. Edinburgh: J. Grant, 1905. 162p.

06080 JOHNSON, F., tr. Hitopadeśa, the book of wholesome counsel. Rev. by L.D. Barnett. NY: F.A. Stokes, 1929. 201p.

06081 KALE, M.R., tr. The Hitopadeśa of Nārāyaṇa. 6th ed. Delhi: Motilal, 1967. 283p. [1st pub. 1906]

06082 LANCEREAU, E., tr. Hitopadeśa, ou L'instruction utile. Paris: Maisonneuve, 1882. 387p.

06083 MULLER, F.M., tr. Hitopadeśa; eine alte indische Fabelsammlung. Leipzig: F.A. Brockhaus, 1844. 185p.

06084 STERNBACH, L. The Hitopadeśa and its sources. New Haven: AOS, 1960. 109p. (AOS, 44)

06085 WILKINS, C., tr. Fables and proverbs from the Sanskrit, being the Hitopadeśa. London: G. Routledge, 1886. 277p. [Rpt. Gainesville, FL: Scholars' Facsimilies & Reprints, 1968]

3. The Vetālapañcaviṁśatī, "Twenty-five Tales of a Vampire"

06086 EMENEAU, M.B., tr. Jhambhaladatta's version of the Vetālapañcaviṁśatī. New Haven: AOS, 1934. 155p. (AOS, 4)

06087 RENOU, L., tr. Contes du vampire. Paris: Gallimard, 1963. 232p.

06088 RICCARDI, T., tr. A Nepali version of the Vetālapañcaviṁśatī. New Haven: AOS, 1971. 206p. (AOS, 54)

4. The Śukasaptati, "Seventy Stories of a Parrot"

06089 CHANDRA, PRAMOD, ed. Ṭuṭi-nāma = Tales of a parrot = Das Papageienbuch; complete colour facsimile of the manuscript in...Cleveland Museum of Art. Graz: Academische Druck-und Verlaganstalt, 1976. 2 v. [ms. of Persian version]

06090 MATHUR, G.L., tr. Erotic Indian tales from...the Sanskrit classic Śukasaptati. Delhi: Hind Pocket Books, 1971. 202p.

06091 SCHMIDT, R. Des textus ornatior der Çukasaptati; ein Beitrag zur Märchenkunde. Stuttgart: W. Kohlhammer, 1896. 70p.

06092 ______, tr. Die Marāṭhī-übersetzung der Śukasaptati. Leipzig: F.A. Brockhaus, 1897. 175p. (AKM, 10:4) [Marathi & German]

06093 ______,tr. Die Çukasaptati: textus simplicior. Kiel: C.F. Haeseler, 1894. 101p.

06094 ______,tr. Die Śukasaptati (textus ornatior). Stuttgart: W. Kohlhammer, 1899. 149p.

06095 WORTHAM, B.H., tr. The enchanted parrot, being a selection from the Śuka saptati or the Seventy tales of a parrot. London: Luzac, 1911. 127p.

IV. ART AND ARCHITECTURE OF EARLY MEDIEVAL INDIA (WORKS ON A TRANSREGIONAL LEVEL)

A. General Studies

06096 BURTON-PAGE, J. A study of fortification in the Indian subcontinent from the thirteenth to the eighteenth century A.D. In BSOAS 23 (1960) 508-22. [Review of S. Toy, Strongholds of India, 06102]

06097 CHANDRA, R.P. Medieval Indian sculpture in the British museum. London: K. Paul, Trench, Trubner, 1936. 77p. + 24pl.

06098 CODRINGTON, K.D.B. An introduction to the study of medieval Indian sculpture. London: E. Goldston, 1929. 31p. + 24pl.

06099 DHAKY, M.A. The Vyāla figures on the mediaeval temples of India. Varanasi: Prithivi Prakashan, 1965. 32p.

06100 DE LIPPE, A. Indian mediaeval sculpture. Amsterdam: North Holland, 1978. 411p., inc. 312pl.

06101 PLAESCHKE, H. & I. PLAESCHKE. Hinduistische Kunst: das indische Mittelalter. Leipzig: Koehler und Amelang, 1978. 177p.

06102 TOY, S. Strongholds of India. Melbourne: Wm. Heinemann, 1957. 136p.

B. Selected Sanskrit Texts for Art and Architecture; Translations and Studies

06103 ACHARYA, P.K. A summary of the Mānasāra; a treatise on architecture and cognate subjects... Leiden: N.V. boekhandel en drukkerij, 1918. 76p.

06104 ______,tr. Architecture of mānasāra. London: OUP, 1934. 268p. (Mānasāra, 4)

06105 BOSE, P.N. Principles of Indian śilpaśāstra with the text of Mayaśāstra. Delhi: Bharatiya, 1978. 114p. [Rpt. 1926 ed.]

06106 GOSWAMY, B.N. & A.L. DAHMEN-DALLAPICCOLA, tr. An early document of Indian art: the citralakshana of Nagnajit. ND: Manohar, 1976. 176p.

06107 GUNASINGHE, S. La technique de la peinture indienne d'après les textes du Śilpa. Paris: PUF, 1957. 96p.

06108 KRAMRISCH, S. The Vishnudharmottara (part III); a treatise on Indian painting and image-making. 2nd rev. & enl. ed. Calcutta: Calcutta U. Press, 1928. 117p. [an appendix to the Viṣṇupurāṇa; 1st pub. 1924]

06109 LAUFER, B., tr. Das Citralakshana nach dem tibetischen Tanjur... Leipzig: Harrassowitz, 1913. 193p.

06110 MALLMANN, M.-T. DE. Les enseignements iconographiques de l'Agnipurāṇa. Paris: PUF, 1963. 371p.

06111 MEISTER, M.W. Maṇḍala and practice in Nāgara architecture in North India. In JAOS 99,2 (1979) 204-219.

06112 PILLAI, G.K. Way of the shilpis, or Hindu approach to art and sciences. Allahabad: Indian Press, 1948; London: Luzac, 1949, 356p. [speculative interp. of Mānasāra]

06113 SHAH, P., tr. Viṣṇudharmottara-Purāṇa; 3rd khāṇḍa. Baroda: Oriental Inst., 1958-61. 2 v. (GOS, 130, 137)

06114 SIVARAMAMURTI, C. Chitrasūtra of the Vishnudharmottara. ND: Kanak, 1978. 232p. + 46pl.

06115 ______. Śrī Harṣa's observations on painting with special reference to Naiṣadhīya Carita. In JORM 7 (1933) 331-50.

V. SRI LANKA: THE ISLAND OF CEYLON FROM THE 7th CENT. AD TO THE EARLY PORTUGUESE PERIOD (1550 AD)

A. Histories of Medieval Siṁhala

1. The Decline of Anurādhapura; Invasions, Conquest (1029 AD), and Rule by the Cōḷa Kings of South India

06116 OBEYESEKERE, G. Gaja bahu and the Gaja bahu synchronism; an enquiry into the relationship between myth and history. In CJH 1,1 (1970) 25-56.

06117 PARANAVITANA, S. The capital of Ceylon during the 9th and 10th centuries. In Ceylon J. of Science 2 (1928-33) 141-47.

06118 PERERA, B.J. Some political trends during the late Anuradhapura and Polonnaruwa period. In CHJ 10, 1-4 (1960-61) 60-76.

06119 SPENCER, G.W. The politics of plunder: the Cholas in eleventh century Ceylon. In JAS 35,3 (1976) 405-19.

06120 WIJETUNGA, W.M.K. Some aspects of Cola administration of Ceylon in the eleventh century. In UCR 23 (1965) 67-82.

2. The Period of Rule from Poḷonnāru (1070-1235 AD), incl. the Conquest by the Kaliṅga King Māgha (1215-35 AD)

06121 CODRINGTON, H.W. The decline of the medieval Sinhalese kingdom. In JRASCB ns 7,1 (1960) 93-103.

06122 INDRAPALA, K., ed. The collapse of the Rajarata civilization in Ceylon and the drift to the south-west; a symposium. Peradeniya: Ceylon Studies Seminar, U. of Ceylon, 1971. 126p.

06123 KIRIBAMUNE, S. The royal consecration in medieval Sri Lanka: the problem of Vikramabāhu I and Gajabāhu II. In SLJSAS 1,1 (1976) 33-51.

06124 LIYANAGAMAGE, A. A forgotten aspect of the relations between the Sinhalese and the Tamils; the Upāsakajanālaṅkāra: a re-examination of its date and authorship and its significance in the history of South India and Ceylon. In CHR 25 (1978) 95-142.

06125 NILAKANTA SASTRI, K.A. Vijayabāhu I, the Liberator of Lanka. In JRASCB ns 5 (1954) 45-71.

06126 SAPARAMADU, S.D., ed. The Poḷonnāruva period. 3rd ed. Dehiwala: Tisara Prakasakayo, 1973. 206p. [1st pub. as CHJ 4 (1955)]

06127 SIRISENA, W.M. The Kalinga dynasty of Ceylon and the theory of its South-East Asian origin. In CJHSS ns 1,1 (1971) 11-47.

06128 SMITH, B.L. The Polonnaruva period (ca. 993-1293 AD): a thematic bibliographical essay. In his (ed.), Religion and legitimation of power in Srī Lanka. Chambersburg, PA: Conocochegue Assoc., 1978, 119-54.

06129 TAYLOR, K. The devolution of kingship in twelfth century Ceylon. In K.R. Hall & J.K. Whitmore, eds. Explorations of early Southeast Asian history. Ann Arbor: UMCSSAS, 1976, 257-302.

3. Dambadeniya, Gampola, Kotte and Other Kingdoms up to 1550; Contacts with China and the Arabs

06130 DE ALWIS, C.M. Antiquities of the kingdom of Kotte. Ratmalana: Deaf School Press, 1976. 46p. + 7pl.

06131 KULASURIYA, A.S. Regional independence and elite change in the politics of 14th century Sri Lanka. In JRAS (1976) 136-55.

06132 LIYANAGAMAGE, A. The decline of Polonnaruwa and the rise of Dambadeniya, circa 1180-1270 AD. Colombo: Dept. of Cultural Affairs, 1968. 213p.

06133 PATHMANATHAN, S. The Kingdom of Jaffna. Colombo: Arul M. Rajendran, 1978-. v. 1, 294p.

06134 SOMARATNE, G.P.V. The political history of the Kingdom of Kotte, 1400-1521. Nugegoda: Deepanee Printers, 1975. 362p.

B. Economic and Social Life

06135 ARIYAPALA, M.B. Society in mediaeval Ceylon: the state of society in Ceylon as depicted in the Saddharma-ratnavaliya and other literature of the thirteenth century. Colombo: Dept. of Cultural Affairs, 1968. 415p.

06136 BROHIER, R.L. Ancient irrigation works in Ceylon. Colombo: Govt. Press, 1934-35. 157p. [in 3 parts]

06137 GEIGER, W. Culture of Ceylon in mediaeval times. Ed. by H. Bechert. Wiesbaden: O. Harrassowitz, 1960. 286p.

06138 GUNAWARDANA, R.A.L.H. Irrigation and hydraulic society in medieval Ceylon. In P&P 53 (1971) 3-27.

06139 INDRAPALA, K. South Indian mercantile communities in Ceylon, c. 950-1250. In CJHSS ns 1,2 (1971) 101-13.

06140 LEACH, E.R. Hydraulic society in Ceylon. In P&P, no. 15 (1959) 2-26.

06141 PATHMANATHAN, S. Feudal polity in medieval Ceylon; an examination of the chieftancies of the Vaṇṇi. In CJHSS ns 2,1 (1972) 131-55.

06142 SIRIWEERA, W.I. Land tenure and revenue in mediaeval Ceylon (AD 1000-1500). In CJHSS ns 2,1 (1972) 1-49.

06143 ______. The theory of the king's ownership of land in ancient Ceylon: an essay in historical revision. In CJHSS ns 1,1 (1971) 48-61.

C. Literature of Ceylon in Sanskrit, Pali, Sinhala

06144 DE SILVA, S.M.W. Some linguistic peculiarities of Sinhalese poetry. In Linguistics 60 (1970) 5-26.

06145 JAYAWICKRAMA, N.A., tr. The chronicle of the Thūpa, and the Thūpavaṃsa, being a translation and edition of Vācissaratthera's Thūpavaṃsa. London: Luzac, 1971. 34 + 286p. (SBB, 28)

06146 PARANAVITANA, S. Sīgiri Graffiti, being Sinhalese verses of the eighth, ninth, and tenth centuries. London: OUP, 1956. 2 v., 277, 472.

06147 SAPARAMADU, S.D., ed. The Polonnaruva period. 3rd ed. Dehiwala: Tisara Prakasakayo, 1973. 206p. [1st pub. as CHJ 4 (1955); literature 91-112]

06148 WANIGATUNGA, S. An eminent scholar and poet. In Education in Ceylon. Colombo: Min. of Education and Cultural Affairs, 1969, v. 1, 265-279 [on Śrī Rāhula]

D. Religio-Philosophical Traditions: the Formation of a Characteristic Sinhalese Buddhism

06149 BAREAU, A. Le rayonnement des anciens monastères bouddhiques de Ceylan. In Studia missionalia 12 (1962) 50-67.

06150 GOMBRICH, R. The consecration of a Buddhist image. In JAS 26,1 (1966) 23-36.

06151 GUNAWARDANA, R.A.L.H. Buddhist Nikāyas in mediaeval Ceylon. In CJHSS 9,1 (1966) 55-66.

06152 ______. Monasticism and economic interest in early medieval Sri Lanka. Tucson: U. of Arizona Press, 1979. (AAS monograph, 35)

06153 ______. Some economic aspects of monastic life in the later Anurādhapura period: two new inscriptions from Madirigiriya. In CJHSS ns 2,1 (1972) 60-74.

06154 KALUPAHANA, D.J. Schools of Buddhism in early Ceylon. In CJH 1,2 (1970) 159-90.

06155 LAW, B.C., tr. A manual of Buddhist historical traditions (Saddhamma-Saṅgaha). Calcutta: U. of Calcutta, 1941. 140p.

06156 NARADA, Mahathera. A manual of Abhidhamma; being Abhidhammattha sangaha of Bhandantu Anuruddhacariya. 2nd rev. ed. Kandy: BPS, 1968. 451p.

06157 PANDITHA, V. Buddhism during the Polonnaruva period. In CHJ 4 (1955) 113-29.

06158 PARANAVITANA, S. Mahāyānism in Ceylon. In Ceylon J. of Science, sect. G, 2,1 (1928) 25-71 + 5pl.

06159 ______. The religious intercourse between Ceylon and Siam in the thirteenth and fifteenth centuries. In JRASCB 32,85 (1932) 190-212.

06160 RHYS DAVIDS, C.A., tr. Compendium of philosophy. London: Luzac, 1972. 298p. (PTS translation series, 8) [1st pub. 1916; tr. of Anuruddha's Abhidammattha-sangaha]

06161 SARVESVARA IYER, P. Puranic Saivism in Ceylon during the Polonnaruwa period. In Intl. Conference Seminar of Tamil Studies, 1st, 1966. Proceedings. Kuala Lumpur: 1968, 462-474.

06162 SMITH, B.L. Religious assimilation in early medieval Sinhalese society. In A.K. Narain, ed. Studies in Pali and Buddhism. Delhi: B.R., 1979, 347-368.

06163 WICKRAMASINGHE, M. Tantrism in Ceylon - Tisa Vera Lithic diagram. In CHJ 1,4 (1952) 55-66.

E. Art and Architecture in Medieval Ceylon

1. General Studies

06164 BANDARANAYAKE, S. Buddhist tree-temples in Sri Lanka. In J.E. van Lohuizen-de Leeuw & J.M.M. Ubaghs, eds. South Asian archeology 1973. Leiden: Brill, 1974, 136-60.

06165 DOHANIAN, D.K. The colossal Buddha at Aukana. In Archives of the Chinese Art Society of America 19 (1965) 16-25, plus 11 illus.

06166 LIYANARATNE, J., tr. Le Purāṇa Mayamataya. Manuel astrologique sinhalais de construction. Paris: EFEO, 1976. 16 + 138p. [Its Pub., 109]

06167 MUDIYANSE, N. The art and architecture of the Gampola period, 1341-1415 AD. Colombo: M.D. Gunasena, 1963. 194p.

06168 ______. Śilpaśāstra works in Sri Lanka. In JRAS (1978) 69-73.

06169 PREMATILLEKE, L. & R. SILVA. A Buddhist monastery type of ancient Ceylon showing Mahayana influences. In ArtAs 30,1 (1968) 61-84.

06170 WARD, W.E. Recently discovered Mahiyangana paintings. In ArtAs 15 (1952) 108-13.

2. The Efflorescence of Art in the Capital City of Polonnāruwa

06171 DOHANIAN, D.K. The Wata-da-ge in Ceylon: the circular relic-house of Polonnaruva and its antecedents. In Archives of Asian art 23 (1969-70) 31-40.

06172 FERNANDO, P.E.E. Sculptures at Gal Vihara, Polonnaruva. In UCR 18 (1960) 50-66.

06173 FERNANDO, W.B.M. Ancient city of Polonnaruva. Colombo: Archaeological Commissioner, 1967. 41p.

06174 GODAKUMBURA, C.E. Bronzes from Polonnaruva. In JRASCB ns 7,2 (1961) 239-50.

06175 PARANAVITANA, S. Art and architecture of Ceylon: Polonnaruva period. Colombo: Arts Council of Ceylon, 1954. 84p., inc. 73pl.

VI. THE DRAVIDIAN SOUTH AND ADJACENT AREAS OF THE DECCAN IN THE MEDIEVAL PERIOD (c. 600-1565 AD)

A. General and Political Histories

1. Conflict of Rival Kingdoms

06176 BALAMBAL, V. Feudatories of South India, 800-1070 A.D. Allahabad: Chugh Publications, 1978. 210p.

06177 IBRAHIM KUNJU, A.P. Studies in medieval Kerala history. Trivandrum: Kerala Hist. Soc., 1975. 156p.

06178 KRISHNA RAO, M.V. The Gangas of Talkad; a monograph on the history of Mysore from the fourth to the close of the eleventh century. Madras: B.G. Paul, 1936. 306p.

06179 KRISHNASWAMI AIYANGAR, S. Evolution of Hindu administrative institutions in South India. Madras: U. of Madras, 1931. 387p.

06180 MORAES, G.M. The Kadamba kula; a history of ancient and mediaeval Karnataka. Bombay: B.X. Furtado, 1931. 504p.

06181 RAMA RAO, M. Karnataka-Andhra relations, 220 A.D.-1323 A.D. Dharwar: Kannada Research Institute, Karnatak U., 1974. 94p.

06182 SALETORE, B.A. Ancient Karṇāṭaka; v. 1: History of Tuḷuva. Poona: Oriental Book Agency, 1936. 659p. (Poona Oriental Ser., 53)

06183 SETHURAMAN, N. The imperial Pandyas: mathematics reconstructs the chronology. Kumbakonam: Sethuraman, 1978. 251p.

06184 SHEIKH ALI, B. History of the western Gangas. Mysore: Prasaranga, U. of Mysore, 1976. 416p.

2. The "Great" Pallavas of Kāñchī and Mahābalipuram/Mamallāpuram (575-903 AD)

06185 GOPALAN, R. History of the Pallavas of Kanchi. Madras: U. of Madras, 1928. 245p.

06186 GOVINDASAMY, M.S. The role of feudatories in Pallava history. Annamalainagar: Annamalai U., 1965. 180p.

06187 HERAS, H. The Pallava genealogy; an attempt to unify the Pallava pedigree of the inscriptions. Bombay: IHRI, 1931. 27p.

06188 ______. Studies in Pallava history. Madras: B.G. Paul, 1933. 115p.

06189 MAHALINGAM, T.V. The Banas in South Indian history. In JIH, 29 (1951) 253-305.

06190 ______. Kāñcīpuram in early South Indian history. NY: Asia Pub. House, 1969. 243p.

06191 ______. Problems in later Pallava chronology and genealogy. In JIH 43,3 (1965) 917-28.

06192 MINAKSHI, C. Administration and social life under the Pallavas. Madras: U. of Madras, 1977. 421p. (Its Hist. ser., 13) [1st ed. 1938]

06193 SATHIANATHAIER, R. Studies in the ancient history of Toṇḍaimaṇḍalam. Madras: Rochouse & Sons, 1944. 54p.

06194 STEIN, B. All the kings' Mana: perspectives on kingship in medieval South India. In J.F. Richards, ed. Kingship and authority in South Asia. Madison: South Asian Studies, U. of Wisconsin, 1978, 115-67. (Its Pub. series, 3)

06195 VENKATASUBBA AYYAR, V. South Indian inscriptions: v. 12, the Pallavas. Madras: ASI, 1943. 204p.

3. The Cōḻas/Cholas of Tanjore (850-1177 AD): Imperial Consolidation and Overseas Expansion

06196 BIDDULPH, C.H. Coins of the Cholas. Varanasi: Numismatic Soc. of India, 1968. 65p. + 5pl.

06197 KRISHNAMURTHI, S.R. A study on the cultural developments in the Chola period. Annamalainagar: Annamalai U., 1966. 172p.

06198 NILAKANTA SASTRI, K.A. The Cōḻas: with over 100 illustrations. 2nd ed., rev. Madras: U. of Madras, 1975. 812p. + 37pl. [Rpt. 1955 ed.]

06199 ______. Studies in Cola history and administration. Madras: U. of Madras, 1932. 210p.

06200 SETHURAMAN, N. The Cholas: mathematics reconstructs the chronology. Kumbakonam: Sethuraman, 1977. 193p.

06201 SPENCER, G.W. & K.R. HALL. Toward an analysis of dynastic hinterlands: the Imperial Cholas in 11th century South India. In AsProf 2,1 (1974) 51-62.

06202 SRIVASTAVA, B. Rajendra Chola. ND: NBT, 1973. 103p.

06203 STEIN, B. The segmentary state in South Indian history. In R.G. Fox, ed. Realm and region in traditional India. Durham: DUPCSSA, 1977, 3-51. (Its monograph, 14)

06204 SUBBARAYALU, Y. Political geography of the Chola country. Madras: State Dept. of Archaeology, Govt. of Tamilnadu, 1973. 111 + 90p. (TNDA pub. 30)

4. The Western Cālukyas of Vāṭāpi/Badāmi (550-753 AD); the Rāstrakūṭa interregnum (753-973 AD), and the Eastern Cālukyas of Veṅgī (617-1190 AD)

06205 ALTEKAR, A.S. Rashtrakutas and their times. 2nd rev. ed. Poona: Oriental Book Agency, 1967. 441p. (POS, 36)

06206 GANGULY, D.C. The Eastern Chālukyas. Benares: the author, 1937. 228p. [1st pub. in IHQ 8 (1932) thru 13 (1937)]

06207 KATARE, S.L. The Cālukyas of Kalyāṇī. In IHQ 17,1 (1941) 11-34.

06208 KRISHNA MURARI. The Cāḷukyas of Kalyāṇī, from circa 973 A.D. to 1200 A.D.: based mainly on epigraphical sources. Delhi: Concept, 1977. 402p.

06209 NAGARAJA RAO, M.S., ed. The Chalukyas of Badami: seminar papers. Bangalore: Mythic Society, 1978. 318p. +81pl.

06210 RAMAMURTY. Social and cultural life of the eastern Chalukyas of Vengi. Hyderabad: Maulana Abul Kalam Azad Oriental Res. Inst., 196-. 95p.

06211 RAYCHAUDHURI, G.C. Aspects of Western Cālukya administration. In JAIH 8,1-2 (1974-75) 125-66.

06212 ______. History of the Western Cālukyas. In JAIH 8,1-2 (1974-75) 1-124.

06213 VENKATA RAMANAYYA, N. The eastern Cālukyas of Veṅgī. Madras: Vedam Venkataray Sastry, 1950. 359p.

06214 VENKATAKRISHNA RAO, B. History of the Eastern Chalukyas of Vengi, 610-1210 A.D. Hyderabad: Andhra Pradesh Sahitya Akademi, 1973. 596p.

5. The Hoysaḷas of Dvārasamudra (1190-1340 AD), Successors to the Cālukyas

06215 DERRETT, J.D.M. The Hoysalas, a medieval Indian royal family. Madras: OUP, 1957. 257p.

06216 SHEIK ALI, B., ed. The Hoysaḷa dynasty. Mysore: U. of Mysore, 1972. 376p.

06217 SUBRAHMANIAN, N. The Hoysalas. In JIH 42 (1964) 877-85.

6. The Vijayanagara Dynasties (1336-1565 AD): Reassertion of Brahmanic Orthodoxy in the Context of the Bhakti Movement and Challenge of Islam

06218 ABD-ER-RAZZAK. Narrative of the voyage of Abd-er-Razzak, Ambassador from Shah Rokh, AD 1442. Tr. by R.H. Major. In R.H. Major, ed. India in the 15th century... London: Hakluyt Soc., 1857. 49p. (Its 1st ser., 22)

06219 FILLIOZAT, V. L'épigraphie de Vijayanagar du debut à 1377. Paris: EFEO, 1973. 179p. (Its pub., 91)

06220 HERAS, H. The Aravidu dynasty of Vijayanagar. Madras: B.G. Paul, 1927. 130p.

06221 ______. Beginnings of Vijayanagara history. Bombay: IHRI, 1929. 144p.

06222 KRISHNASVAMI AIYANGAR, S. Sources of Vijayanagar history. Madras: U. of Madras, 1919. 394p.

06223 KRISHNASWAMI, A. The Tamil country under Vijayanagar. Annamalainagar: Annamalai U., 1964. 418p.

06224 MAHALINGAM, T.V. Administration and social life under Vijayanagar. Madras: U. of Madras, 1969-75. 2 v., 317, 456p.

06225 NILAKANTA SASTRI, K.A. & N. VENKATARAMANAYYA. Further sources of Vijayanagara history. Madras: U. of Madras, 1946. 3 v.

06226 PAES, D. & F. NUNIZ. The Vijayanagar Empire. Tr. from Portuguese by R. Sewell. Ed. by V. Filliozat. ND: NBT, 1977. 180p. [1st pub. 1900]

06227 RAMA RAO, M. Krishnadeva Raya. ND: NBT, 1971. 74p.

06228 RAMA SHARMA, M.H. The history of the Vijayanagar Empire. Bombay: Popular, 1978-.

06229 RAMALINGA REDDY, D. Vijayanagar & its lessons for modern India. Madras: U. of Madras, 1968. 59p.

06230 SALETORE, B.A. Social and political life in the Vijayanagara empire (1346-1646). Madras: B.G. Paul, 1934. 2 v., 470, 523p.

06231 SEWELL, R. A forgotten empire: Vijayanagar; a contribution to the history of India. ND: NBT, 1970. 407p. [1st pub. 1900; tr., with intro., of D. Paes & F. Nunes, Chronica dos reis de Bisnaga]

06232 SHASTRY, B.S. The first decade of Portuguese-Vijayanagara relations. In JIH 42,1 (1974) 147-55.

06233 SREE RAMA SARMA, P. Saluva dynasty of Vijayanagar. Hyderabad: Prabhakar Pub., 1979. 296p.

06234 VENKATARAMANAYYA, N. Prolegomena to the study of the history of Vijayanagara. Pt. 3. In Itihās 3 (1975) 53-88.

06235 ______. Studies in the history of the third dynasty of Vijayanagara. Madras: U. of Madras, 1935. 527p.

06236 ______. Vijayanagar; origin of the city and the empire. Madras: U. of Madras, 1933. 191p.

06237 VANKATA RATNAM, A.V. Local government in the Vijayanagara Empire. Mysore: U. of Mysore, 1972. 188p.

06238 Vijayanagara sexcentenary commemoration volume. Dharwar: Vijayanagara Empire Sexcentenary Assoc., 1936. 380p. + 45pl.

7. The Early Penetration of Muslim Power into South India

06239 ABDUL RAHIM, M. Islam in Negapatam. In Bull. of Inst. of Trad. Cultures (Jul 1974) 85-99.

06240 IBRAHIM KUNJU, A.P. Genesis and spread of Islam in Kerala. In JKS 3,3/4 (1976) 479-88.

06241 KRISHNASVAMI AIYANGAR, S. South India and her Muhammadan invaders. London: OUP, 1921. 257p.

06242 VENKATARAMANAYYA, N. The early Muslim expansion in South India. Madras: U. of Madras, 1942. 216p.

B. Economic and Social Life in Early Medieval South India

1. General Studies of Economic History

06243 APPADORAI, A. Economic conditions in Southern India, 1000-1500 A.D. Madras: U. of Madras, 1936. 2 v.

06244 CHATTOPADHYAYA, B. Coins and currency systems in South India, c. A.D. 225-1300. ND: Munshiram, 1977. 352p.

06245 GURURAJACHAR, S. Some aspects of economic and social life in Karṇāṭaka, A.D. 100-1300. Mysore: U. of Mysore, 1974. 200p.

06246 HALL, K.R. Price-making and market hierarchy in early medieval South India. In IESHR 14,2 (1977) 207-30.

06247 KAMAT, J.K. Social life in medieval Karṇāṭaka. ND: Abhinav, 1980. 142p.

06248 KRISHNAMOORTHY VAIDEHI, A. Social and economic conditions in the Eastern Deccan, from A.D. 1000 to A.D. 1250. Secunderabad, A.P.: the author, 1970. 315p.

06249 KUPPUSWAMY, G.R. Economic conditions in Karnataka, A.D. 973-A.D. 1336. Dharwar: Karnatak U., 1975. 231p.

06250 MAHALINGAM, T.V. Economic life in the Vijayanagar empire. Madras: U. of Madras, 1951. 224p.

06251 MATHEW, K.S. Society in medieval Malabar: a study based on Vadakkaṅ Pāṭṭukal. Kottayam: Jaffe Books, 1979. 110p.

06252 STEIN, B. Coromandel trade in medieval India. In J. Parker, ed. Merchants and scholars.... Minneapolis: U. of Minnesota Press, 1965, 49-62.

06253 ______. Peasant, state and society in medieval South India: a study of economic, social, religio-cultural, and political systems, from the 7th century to the arrival of the Europeans. ND: OUP, 1980. 450p.

06254 SUNDARAM, K. Studies in economic and social conditions of medieval Andhra, A.D. 100-1600. Machilipatnam: Triveni Publishers, 1968. 96p.

2. The Agrarian System and Feudalism

06255 BECK. B.E.F. The authority of the king: prerogatives and dilemmas of kingship as portrayed in a contemporary oral epic from South India. In J.F. Richards, ed. Kingship and authority in South Asia. Madison: South Asian Studies, U. of Wisconsin, 1978, 168-91. (Its Pub., 3)

06256 CHAUDHARY, R.K. Some aspects of feudalism in South India: from the earliest times to 15th century A.D., based mainly on inscriptions. In JIH 53,1 (1975) 63-104.

06257 GUPTA, K.M. The land system in South India between c. 800 A.D. and 1200 A.D. (in the light of the epigraphic and literary evidence). Lahore: Motilal, 1933. 239p.

06258 KARASHIMA, N. Allur and Isanamangalam: two South Indian villages of the Cola times. In IESHR 3,2 (1966) 150-62.

06259 LUDDEN, D. Ecological zones and the cultural economy of irrigation in southern Tamilnadu. In SA ns 1,1 (1978) 1-13.

06260 MURTON, B.J. Agrarian system dynamics in interior Tamil Nadu before 1800 A.D. In NGJI 21,3/4 (1975) 151-65.

06261 STEIN, B. Brahman and peasant in early South Indian history. In ALB 31-32 (1967-68) 229-69.

06262 ______. The state and the agrarian order in medieval South India: a bibliographical critique. In his Essays on South India. Honolulu: UPH, 1975, 64-91.

3. Economic and Social Role of South Indian Temples

06263 APPADURAI, A. King, sects and temples in South India, 1350-1700 AD. In IESHR 14,1 (1977) 47-73.

06264 KESAVAN, V. The role of temples in Kerala society, 1100-1500. In JKS 3,2 (1976) 181-94.

06265 NAGASWAMY, R. South Indian temple - as an employer. In IESHR 2,4 (1965) 367-72.

06266 NATARAJAN, D. Endowments in early Tamil Nadu. In BITCM (1974) pt. 2, 101-18.

06267 SPENCER, G.W. Religious networks and royal influence in eleventh-century South India. In JESHO 12,1 (1969) 42-56.

06268 ______. Royal initiative under Rajaraja I: the auditing of temple accounts. In IESHR 7,4 (1970) 431-42.

06269 ______. Temple money-lending and livestock redistribution n early Tanjore. In IESHR 5 (1968) 279-93.

06270 STEIN, B. The economic function of a medieval South Indian temple. In JAS 19 (1960) 163-76.

06271 ______. The state, the temple and agricultural development -- a study in medieval South India. In EW 13,4/6 (1961) 179-87.

06272 ______. Temples in Tamil country, 1300-1750 AD. In IESHR 14,1 (1977) 11-45.

C. "Greater India": Colonization and Indianization of South-East Asia

06273 COEDÈS, G. The Indianized states of Southeast Asia. Tr. by S.B. Cowing. Ed by W.F. Vella. Honolulu: EWCP, 1968. 403p. [1st French ed., 1944]

06274 MAJUMDAR, R.C. Hindu colonies in the Far East. 2nd rev. & enl. ed. Calcutta: KLM, 1963. 280p.

06275 ______. India and South East Asia. Ed. by K.S. Ramachandran & S.P. Gupta. Delhi: B.R., 1979. 218p.

06276 SIRISENA, W.M. Sri Lanka and South-East Asia: Political, religious and cultural relations from A.D. c. 1000 to c. 1500. Leiden: Brill, 1978. 186p.

D. Religio-Philosophical Traditions in Early Medieval Dravidian India: Blending of Popular Bhakti, the Pan-Indian Brahmanic Orthodoxy of Vedānta, and the Āgamic Traditions

1. General Studies of the South Indian Religious Milieu

06277 ARUMUGA MUDALAIR, S. Concepts of religion in Sangam literature and in devotional literature. In TC 11 (1964) 252-71.

06278 HANUMANTHA RAO, B.S.L. Religion in Āndhra: a survey of religious developments in Āndhra from early times up to AD 1325. Guntur: the author, 1973. 346p.

06279 HART, G.L., III. The nature of Tamil devotion. In M.M. Deshpande and P.E. Hook, eds. Aryan and Non-Aryan in India. Ann Arbor: UMCSSAS, 1979, 11-35.

06280 NANDI, R.N. Religious institutions and cults in the Deccan, c. A.D. 600- A.D. 1000. Delhi: Motilal, 1973. 203p.

06281 NILAKANTA SASTRI, K.A. Development of religion in South India. Bombay: Orient Longmans, 1963. 148p.

06282 PRASAD, D. Saints of Telangana. Hyderabad, A.P.: Abul Kalam Azad Res. Inst., 1969. 148p.

06283 VIPULANANDA, Swami. The development of Tamilian religious thought. In TC 5 (1956) 251-66.

06284 YOCUM, G.E. Shrines, shamanism, and love poetry: elements in the emergence of popular Tamil bhakti. In JAAR 41,1 (1973) 3-17.

2. Vaiṣṇava and Śaiva Saint-singers in popular Tamil: the Āḻvārs and Nāyaṉārs (6th-10th Cent. AD)

a. general and comparative studies, and translations

06285 ARUMUGA MUDALIAR, S. The period of religious revival in Tamil literature. In TC 6 (1957) 294-308.

06286 RAMACHANDRA DIKSHITAR, V.R. Early Tamil religious literature. In IHQ 18,1 (1942) 1-19.

06287 YOCUM, G.E. Sign and paradigm: myth in Tamil Śaiva and Vaiṣṇava Bhakti poetry. In H.M. Buck & G.E. Yocum, eds. Structural approaches to South Indian studies. Chambersburg, PA: Wilson Books, 1974, 227-234.

b. the Āḻvārs, 12 Vaiṣṇava saints, and their collected songs, the Nālāyira Divyaprabandham, "the 4000 hymns"

06288 ATE, L.M. Periyāḻvār's Tirumoḻi: a Bāla Krsna text from the devotional period in Tamil literature. Ph.D. diss., U. of Wisconsin, 1978. [UM 78-15,034]

06289 BALASUBRAMANIAN, R. The mysticism of Poygai Āḻvār. Madras: Vedanta, 1976. 71p.

06290 BHARATI, S. Alvar saints and acharyas; containing their lives, works, and teachings. 2nd enl. ed. Madras: Shuddhananda Library, 1968. 116p.

06291 DAMODARAN, G. The literary value of Tiruvāymoḻi. Tirupati: Sri Venkateswara U., 1978. 350p.

06292 DEVASENAPATHI, V.A. The mysticism of Nammāḻvār. In JORM 39 (1969-70) 23-36.

06293 FILLIOZAT, J., tr. Un texte tamoul de dévotion vishnouite: le Tiruppāvai d'Āṇṭāḷ. Pondicherry: IFI, 1972. 120p. (Its pub., 45)

06294 GAYATHRI, P.K. Alvars and their philosophy. In Brahmavadin 11,1 (1976) 53-75.

06295 HARDY, F. The Tamil Veda of a śūdra saint (the Śrivaisnava interpretation of Nammāḻvār). In Gopal Krishna, ed. Contributions to South Asian studies, 1. Delhi: OUP, 1979, 29-87.

06296 HOOPER, J.S.M. Hymns of the Alvars. Calcutta: Assn. Press, 1929. 94p.

06297 NILAKANTA SASTRI, K.A. Vaishnavism and the early Alvars. In TASSI (1960-62) 120-24.

06298 RAJAGOPALA CHARIAR, T. The Vaishnavite reformers of India. 2nd ed. Madras: G.A. Natesan, 1909. 128p.

06299 RAJAGOPALAN, V., tr. Godā's Garland of songs, Tiruppāvai. Madras: Rajalakshmi Pathippakam, 1974. 83p.

06300 SRINIVASA RAGHAVAN, A. Nammalvar. ND: Sahitya Akademi, 1975. 96p.

06301 VARADACHARI, K.C. Āḻvārs of South India. Bombay: BVB, 1966. 200p.

06302 VARADACHARI, V.K. The divine song of Godā; English translation of Āṇḍāḷ's Tiruppāvai. Madras: Visual Graphics, dist. Higginbotham's, 1967. 63p.

c. the Nāyaṉārs, 63 Śaiva saints and their collected songs, Tirumuṟai

i. general studies and translations

06303 ATHILAKSHMI. Tamil Nayanars in Telugu literature. In TC 6 (1957) 71-77.

06304 KARAVELANE, tr. Karaikkalammaiyar. Pondicherry: IFI, 1956. 14 + 50p. (Its pub., 1)

06305 KINGSBURY, F. & G.E. PHILLIPS, tr. Hymns of the Tamil Śaivite saints. Calcutta: Assn. Press, 1921. 132p.

06306 RAMACHANDRA DIKSHITAR, V.R. Tamil Śaiva mystic poets in mediaeval South India. In IHQ 19,2 (1943) 173-78.

06307 SPENCER, G.W. The sacred geography of the Tamil Shaivite hymns. In Numen 17 (1970) 232-244.

ii. Māṇikkavācakar (9th cent.), author of Tiruvācakam, "sacred utterances"

06308 BALASUBRAMANIAN, K.M., tr. The Tiruvembavai in Tamil by Saint Manikkavachagar. Madras: SISSWPS, 1954. 19p.

06309 KELLER, C.A. L'homme intérieur chez Māṇikkavāçagar, poète et mystique Tamoul. In AS/EA 24 (1971) 81-104.

06310 MOWRY, M.L. The structure of love in Māṇikkavācakar's Tiruvācakam. In H.M. Buck & G.E. Yocum, eds. Structural approaches to South India studies. Chambersburg, PA: Wilson Books, 1974, 207-224.

06311 NAVARATNAM, R. A new approach to Tiruvacagam. Annamalainagar: Annamalai U., 1971. 328p.

06312 ______. Tiruvāchakam; the Hindu testament of love. Bombay: BVB, 1963. 246p.

06313 POPE, G.U., tr. The Tiruvācagam or "sacred utterances" of the Tamil poet, saint & sage Māṇikka-vācagar. Oxford: OUP, 1900. 354 + 84p.

06314 SCHOMERUS, H.W., tr. Die Hymnen des Māṇikkavāsaga (Tiruvāsaga). Jena: E. Diederichs, 1923. 213p.

06315 VANMIKANATHAN, G. Maanichavaacagar, poet and mystic; an original interpretation of the Tiruvaacagam. Tiruchirapalli: Tirukkural Prachar Sangh, 1970. 104p.

06316 ______. Manikkavachakar. ND: Sahitya Akademi, 1976. 83p.

06317 ______. Pathway to God through Tamil literature. ND: A Delhi Tamil Sangam Pub., 1971-. v. 1, 528p. (Thiruvaachakam)

06318 YOCUM, G.E. Māṇikkavācakar's image of Śiva. In HR 16,1 (1976) 20-41.

06319 ______. A study of Māṇikkavācakar's Tiruvācakam: the setting and significance of a Tamil devotional text. Ph.D. diss., U. of Pennsylvania, 1976. 316p. [UM 77-10,240]

iii. the Periya Purāṇam of Cēkkilār (12th cent.): epic hagiography of the 63 Nāyaṉārs

06320 BHARATI, S. The grand epic of Śaivism. Madras: SISSWPS, 1970. 257p.

06321 MARR, J.T. The Periya Purāṇam frieze at Tārācuram: episodes in the lives of the Tamil Śaiva saints. In BSOAS 42,2 (1979) 268-89, inc. 12pl.

06322 NAMBI AROORAN, K. Glimpses of Tamil culture: based on Periyapuranam. Madurai: Koodal, 1977. 218p.

06323 SCHOMERUS, H.W., tr. Schivaistische Heiligenlegenden (Periya Purāṇa und Tiruvātavūrarpurāṇa). Jena: E. Diederichs, 1925. 306p.

3. The Advaita ("Non-Dual") Vedānta of Śaṅkarācārya (788-820 AD): the Philosophical Basis of Pan-Indian Hindu Orthodoxy

a. general surveys and studies of Vedānta

06324 DESHPANDE, B. The universe of Vedanta. Bombay: Indian Institute of Socialist Studies, 1974. 167p.

06325 DEUSSEN, P. The system of the Vedānta; according to Bādarāyana's Brahma-sūtras and Çaṅkara's commentary thereon.... Chicago: Open Court, 1912. 513p. [1st German ed. 1883]

06326 DEUTSCH, E. Advaita Vedānta: a philosophical reconstruction. Honolulu: EWCP, 1969. 119p.

06327 DEUTSCH, E. & J.A.B. VAN BUITENEN, eds. A source book of Advaita Vedānta. Honolulu: UPH, 1971. 335p.

06328 GHATE, V.S. Le Védānta: étude sur les Brahmasūtras et leur cinq commentaires. Paris: E. Leroux, 1918. 146p.

06329 KRISHNASWAMY IYER, K.A. Vedānta; or, the science of reality. Holenarsipur: Adhyatma Prakasha Karyalaya, 1965. 543p.

06330 MAHADEVAN, T.M.P. The insights of Advaita. Mysore: U. of Mysore, 1970. 117p.

06331 MOHATTA, R.G. Vedanta in practice. Tr. from Hindi by B. Bhattacharya. Bombay: BVB, 1966. 152p.

06332 NAGARAJA RAO, P. Introduction to Vedanta. 3rd ed. Bombay: BVB, 1966. 243p.

06333 PANDEY, R.R. Some philosophical problems of the Vedānta-Siddhāntamuktāvalī. In WZKS 20 (1976) 167-86.

06334 PRITHIPAL, D. Advaita Vedānta: action and contemplation. Varanasi: Bharatiya, 1969. 144p.

06335 RANADE, R.D. Vedānta: the culmination of Indian thought. Bombay: BVB, 1970. 234p.

b. pre-Śankara Vedānta; Gauḍapāda (c. 700 AD), traditional founder of Advaita Vedānta and paramaguru (teacher's teacher) of Śaṅkarācārya

06336 BHATTACHARYA, V.S., tr. The āgamaśāstra of Gauḍapāda. Calcutta: U. of Calcutta, 1943. 146 + 308p.

06337 CONIO, C. The philosophy of Māṇḍukya kārikā. Varanasi: Bharatiya, 1971. 238p.

06338 LESIMPLE, E. Māṇḍukya Upaniṣad et Kārikā de Gaudapāda. Paris: Adrien-Maisonneuve , 1944. 46 + 23p.

06339 MAHADEVAN, T.M.P. Gauḍapāda: a study in early Advaita. 4th ed. Madras: U. of Madras, 1975. 292p. [1st pub., 1952]

06340 NAKAMURA, H. Upaniṣadic tradition and the early school of Vedānta as noticed in Buddhist scripture. In Harvard J. of Asiatic Studies 18 (1955) 74-104.

06341 ______. The Vedānta as noticed in medieval Jain literature. In E. Bender, ed. Indological studies in honor of W. Norman Brown. New Haven: AOS, 1962, 186-194. (AOS, 47)

06342 POTTER, K.H. Was Gauḍapāda an idealist? In M. Nagatomi, et al., eds. Sanskrit and Indian studies; essays in honour of Daniel H.H. Ingalls. Dordrecht: R. Reidel, 1980, 183-200.

06343 SAHASRABUDHE, M.T. A survey of the pre-Śaṅkara Advaita Vedānta. Poona: U. of Poona, 1968. 274p.

06344 VETTER, T. Die Gauḍapādīya-kārikās; zur Entstehung und zur Bedeutung von (A)dvaita. In WZKS 22 (1978) 95-131.

c. Śaṅkara (788-820 AD); a Nāmbūdiri Brāhmaṇ from Kerala, leads Hindu resurgence against Buddhism and establishes India-wide network of ascetic orders

i. Śaṅkara's works translated from Sanskrit, and studies of particular works

06345 BOSE, P.S., tr. Sarva-siddhānta-saṁgraha. Calcutta: B.N. Mukherjee, 1929. 97p. [attrib. to Saṅkara]

06346 CHINMAYANANDA, Swami. Talks of Sankara's Vivekachoodamani. Bombay: Central Chinmaya Mission Trust, 1970. 2 v.

06347 COHEN, S.S. Advaitic sādhanā: or The yoga of direct liberation: containing English translation of Māṇḍukyopaniṣad and Ātmabodha. Delhi: Motilal, 1975. 92p.

06348 DAS, R.V. Introduction to Shankara; being parts of Shankara's commentary on the Brahma sutras rendered freely into English. Calcutta: KLM, 1968. 156p.

06349 DATE, V.H., ed. Vedānta explained; Śaṁkara's commentary on the Brahma-sūtras. 2nd ed. ND: Munshiram, 1973. 2 v. [Rpt. 1954-59 ed.]

06350 GUSSNER, R.E. Śaṅkara's Crest Jewel of Discrimination: a stylometric approach to the question of authorship. In JIP 4,3/4 (1977) 265-78.

06351 ______. Stylometric study of the authorship of seventeen Sanskrit hymns attributed to Śaṅkara. In JAOS 96 (1976) 259-67.

06352 JAGADANANDA, Swami, tr. Upadeśa sāhasrī; a thousand teachings of Sri Śaṅkarācārya. 4th ed. Madras: Sri Ramakrishna Math, 1970. 301p.

06353 ______, tr. Vākyāvritti and Ātmajñānopadeshavidhi of Śrī Śankarāchārya. Madras: Sri Ramakrishna Math, 1967. 113p.

06354 MADHAVANANDA, Swami, tr. Vivekachudamani of Shri Shankaracharya. 7th ed. Calcutta: Advaita Ashrama, 1966. 228p.

06355 MAHADEVAN, T.P.M., tr. The hymns of Śaṅkara. Madras: Ganesh, 1970. 256p. (Jayanti series, 12)

06356 ______, tr. Self-knowledge (Atma-bodha) of Śri Śaṅkaracarya. Madras: Akhila Bharata Sankara Seva Samiti, 1964. 100p. (Jayanti series, 9)

06357 MAYEDA, S. Śaṅkara's Upadeśasāhasrī. Tokyo: Hokuseido Press, 1973. 370p.

06358 NIKHILANANDA, Swami, tr. Self-knowledge: an English translation of Śaṅkaracharya's Atmabodha. NY: Ramakrishna-Vivekananda Center, 1946. 228p.

06359 PRABHAVANANDA, Swami & C. ISHERWOOD, tr. Shankara's Crest-jewel of discrimination (Viveka-chudamani). 2nd ed. Hollywood: Vedanta Press, 1971. 162p.

06360 VIMUKTANANDA, Swami, tr. Aparokshanubhuti or Self-Realization. Calcutta: Advaita Ashrama, 1955. 78p. [1st pub. 1938]

ii. biographical studies

06361 HACKER, P. Śaṅkara der Yogin und Śaṅkara der Advaitin. In WZKS 12/13 (1968-69) 127-35.

06362 KUPPUSWAMI, A. Śrī Bhāgavatpāda Śankarācārya. Varanasi: CSSO, 1972. 179p. (CSS, 89) [a traditional hagiography]

06363 MADHAVA, called VIDYARANYA. Sankara-dig-vijaya: the traditional life of Sri Sankaracharya. Tr. by Swami Tapasyananda. Madras: Sri Ramakrishna Math, 1978. 208p.

06364 MAHADEVAN, T.M.P. Sankaracharya. ND: NBT, 1968. 119p.

06365 NARAYANA SASTRI, T.S. The age of Śaṅkara. 2nd enl. ed. Madras: B.G. Paul, 1971. 288p.

06366 SIVARAMAMURTI, C. Bhagavatpāda. Śri Śaṅkarāchārya. ND: Śaṅkara Academy of Sanskrit Culture and Classical Arts, 1972. 42p. [iconography]

06367 VYAS, R.N. The Bhāgavata bhakti cult and three advaita ācāryas: Śaṅkara, Rāmānuja, and Vallabha. Delhi: Nag, 1977. 240p.

iii. general studies of Śaṅkarācārya's thought

06368 DATTA, C. The place of action and knowledge in the Bhagavadgītā according to Śaṅkara. In Prajñā 11,2 (1966) 106-24.

06369 DEVARAJA, N.K. An introduction to Śaṅkara's theory of knowledge. Delhi: Motilal, 1962. 225p.

06370 INGALLS, D.H.H. The study of Śaṁkarācārya. In ABORI 33 (1952) 1-14.

06371 JOSHI, S. The message of Śaṅkara. Allahabad: Lokbharti Pub., 1968. 196p.

06372 KARMARKAR, R.D. Śaṅkara's Advaita. Dharwar: Karnatak U., 1966. 111p.

06373 KRISHNA WARRIER, A.G. God in Advaita. Simla: IIAS, 1977. 234p.

06374 MAYEDA, S. On the cosmological view of Śaṁkara. In ALB 39 (1975) 186-204.

06375 MENON, Y.K. & R.F. ALLEN. The pure principle; an introduction to the philosophy of Shankara. East Lansing: Michigan State U. Press, 1960. 127p.

06376 MUKHARJI, N.M. A study of Śaṅkara. Calcutta: U. of Calcutta, 1942. 266p.

06377 SINARI, R. The phenomenological attitude in the Śaṅkara Vedānta. In PEW 22,3 (1972) 281-90.

06378 VENKATARAMA IYER, M.K. Advaita vedānta, according to Śaṁkara. NY: Asia, 1965. 213p.

iv. Śaṅkara and contemporary religious trends: his relation to bhakti and his confrontation with the Buddhists

06379 BHATT, B.N. Śaṁkaracarya's advaita and pratyabhijna system - a comparison. In JOIB 19 (1969) 53-59.

06380 BHATTACHARYA, A.R. Śaṅkara & the Buddhist speculations. In J. of the Assam Res. Soc., 14 (1960) 43-53.

06381 BHATTACHARYA, K. Śaṅkara's criticism of Buddhism. In J. of the Indian Academy of Philosophy 1 (1962) 53-64.

06382 CHAKRAVARTI, K.C. Vision of reality. Calcutta: KLM, 1969. 371p.

06383 INGALLS, D.H.H. Shankara's arguments against the Buddhists. In PEW 3,4 (1954) 291-306.

06384 MISHRA, A.P. The development and place of bhakti in Śāṅkara vedanta. Allahabad: Sanskrit Dept., U. of Allahabad, 1967. 254p.

06385 MUDGAL, S.G. Śaṅkara, a reappraisal: impact of Buddhism and Sāṁkhya on Śaṅkara's thought. Delhi: Motilal, 1965. 195p.

06386 PIANTELLI, M. Śaṅkara e la rinascita del brāhmaṇesimo. Fossano: Esperienze, 1974. 315p.

v. Śaṅkara and his successors in the Advaita Vedānta tradition

06387 The Age of Vidyaraṇya. Calcutta: Kalpa Printers and Publ., 1976. 3 v. in 1.

06388 BHATTACHARYA, A. Studies in post-Śaṁkara dialectics. Calcutta: U. of Calcutta, 1936. 322p.

06389 BHATTACHARYA, D.C. Post-Śaṅkara Advaita. In Cultural Heritage of India. Calcutta: RMIC, 1953,3, 255-80.

06390 BIARDEAU, M. La philosophie de Maṇḍana Miśra, vue à partir de la Brahmasiddhi. Paris: EFEO, 1969. 343p.

06391 BOETZELAER, J.M. VAN. Sureśvara's Taittirīyopaniṣadbhāṣyavārtikam. Leiden: Brill, 1971. 211p. (ORT, 12)

06392 FILLIOZAT, P.-S. L'Āryaśataka d'Appāyyadīkṣita, stances de dévotion à Śiva. In JA 253 (1965) 51-82.

06393 GRANOFF, P.E. Philosophy and argument in late Vedānta; Śrī Harṣa's Khāṇḍanakhaṇḍakhādya. Dordrecht: D. Reidel, 1978. 275p.

06394 GUPTA, S. Studies in the philosophy of Madhusūdana Saraswatī. Calcutta: SPB, 1966. 230p.

06395 HACKER, P. Relations of early Advaitins to Vaiṣṇavism. In WZKS 9 (1965) 147-54.

06396 HERMAN, A.L. Indian theodicy: Śaṁkara & Rāmānuja on Brahma Sūtra II. 1. 32-36. In PEW 21,3 (1971) 265-82.

06397 MĀDHAVA, called VIDYĀRAṆYA. Jīvanmuktiviveka. Tr. by S. Subramanya Sastri, rev. by A.G. Krishna Warrier. In ALB 41 (1977) 433p. 1st pub. 1935

06398 ______. Panchadashi; a treatise on Advaita metaphysics. Tr. by H.P. Shastri. 2nd ed. London: Shanti Sadan, 1966. 486p.

06399 MARTIN-DUBOST, P. Çaṅkara et le Vedānta. Paris: Editions du Seuil, 1973. 187p.

06400 MEENAKSHISUNDARAM, T.P. Advaita in Tamil. In MUJ 46,2 (1974) 1-67.

06401 RADHAKRISHNAN, S. The Vedanta according to Śaṁkara and Rāmānuja. London: Allen & Unwin, 1928. 287p.

06402 RÜPING, K. Studien zur Frühgeschichte der Vedānta-Philosophie. Wiesbaden: Steiner, 1977-.

06403 SARMA, V.A. Citsukha's contribution to Advaita: with special reference to the Tattva-pradīpika. Mysore: Kāvyālaya, 1974. 248p.

06404 SINHA, J.N. Problems of post-Śaṁkara Advaita Vedānta. Calcutta: Sinha Pub. House, 1971. 232p.

06405 SIVARAM, M. Ānanda and the three great acharyas. ND: Vikas, 1976. 165p.

06406 SRINIVASACHARI, P.N. Advaita and Viśiṣṭādvaita. NY: Asia, 1961. 226p.

06407 Three great āchāryas Śankara, Rāmānuja, Madhwa. Critical sketches of their life and times: an exposition of their philosophical systems. Madras: Natesan, 1923. 344p.

4. Rāmānuja (1017?-1137? AD), Ācārya of Śrīraṅgam Temple, and his Viśiṣṭādvaita ("Qualified Non-Dualism")

a. Yāmunācārya,(10th cent. AD), Rāmānuja's guru and reconciler of Pāñcarātra theism and Vedānta

06408 DHAVAMONY, M. Yāmuna's Catusśloki: an analysis and interpretation. In IT 3/4 (1975-76) 197-208.

06409 MESQUITA, R. Recent research on Yāmuna. In WZKS 18 (1974) 183-208.

06410 ______. Yāmunamuni: Leben, Datierung, und Werke. In WZKS 17 (1973) 177-93.

06411 NARASIMHACHARI, M. Contribution of Yāmuna to Viśistādvaita. Madras: Prof. M. Rangacharya Mem. Trust, 1971. 340p.

06412 NEEVEL, W. Yāmuna's Vedānta and Pāñcarātra: integrating the classical and the popular. Missoula, MT: Scholars Press, 1977. 300p.

06413 OBERHAMMER, G. Yāmunamunis Interpretation von Brahmasūtram 2, 2, 42-45. Eine Untersuchung zur Pāñcarātra Tradition der Rāmānuja-Schule. Vienna: H. Höhlaus, 1971. 135 p. (Österreichische Akademie der Wissenschaften Phil.-Hist. Klasse, Sitzungsberichte 274:4)

06414 VAN BUITENEN, J.A.B. Yāmuna's Āgama Prāmāṇyam, or Treatise on the validity of Pāñcarātra. Madras: Ramanuja Res. Soc., 1971. 276p.

b. Rāmānuja's works translated from Sanskrit, and studies of individual works

06415 HOHENBERGER, A., tr. Vedāntadīpa; seine Kurzauslegung der Brahmasūtren des Bādarāyana, Bonn: Selbstverlag des Orientalischen Seminars der Universität, 1964. 274 p. (Bonner orientalistische Studien, ns 14)

06416 LACOMBE, O., tr. La doctrine morale et métaphysique de Rāmānuja. Paris: Adrien-Maisonneuve, 1938. 255 + 132p.

06417 NARASIMHA AYYANGAR, M.B., tr. Rāmānuja's Vedāntasāra. Madras: Adyar Library, 1953 455p. (Its series,83)

06418 RAGHAVACHAR, S.S. Introduction to the Vedārthasaṅgraha of Śrī Rāmānujāchārya. 2nd ed. Mangalore: Sharada Press, 1973. 124p. [1st ed. 1956]

06419 ______. Śrī Rāmānuja on the Gītā. Mangalore: Sri Ramakrishna Ashrama, 1969. 213p.

06420 ______, tr. Vedārthasaṁgraha of Śrī Rāmānujācārya. 2nd ed. Mysore: Sri Ramakrishna Ashrama, 1968. 192p. [1st ed. 1956]

06421 RANGACHARYA, M. & M.B. VARADARAJA AIYANGAR, tr. The Vedānta-sūtras with the Śrī-bhāṣhya of Rāmānujācārya. 2nd rev. ed. Madras: Educational Pub. Co., 1961-65. 3 v. [v. 1 1st pub. 1899]

06422 SAMPATKUMARAN, M.R., tr. The Gītābhāṣya of Rāmānuja. Madras: Prof. M. Rangacharya Mem. Trust, 1969. 585p.

06423 VAN BUITENEN, J.A.B., tr. Rāmānuja on the Bhagavadgītā; a condensed rendering of his Gītābhāṣya. Delhi: Motilal, 1968. 187p. [1st pub. 1953]

06424 ______, tr. Vedārthasaṁgraha. Poona: DCPRI, 1956. 316p. (Its monograph, 16) [by Rāmānuja]

06425 YAMUNACHARYA, M. Rāmānuja's teaching in his own words. Bombay: BVB, 1963. 160p.

c. General studies of Rāmānuja's life and and philosophy.

06426 BHARADWAJ, K.D. The philosophy of Rāmānuja. ND: ND: Sir Shankar Lall Charitable Trust Soc., 1958. 259p.

06427 BHATT, S.R. Studies in Rāmānuja Vedānta. ND: Heritage, 1975. 200p.

06428 CARMAN, J.B. The theology of Rāmānuja: an essay in interreligious understanding. New Haven: YUP, 1974. 333p.

06429 ESNOUL, A.-M. Rāmānuja et la mystique vishnouite. Paris: Éditions du Seuil, 1964. 190p.

06430 HOHENBERGER, A. Rāmānuja, ein Philosoph indischer Gottesmystik; seine Lebensanschauung nach den wichtigen Quellen. Bonn: Selbstverlag des Orientalischen Seminars der Universitat, 1960. 159p. (Bonner orientalische Studien, ns 10)

06431 KUMARAPPA, B. The Hindu conception of the deity as culminating in Rāmānuja. London: Luzac, 1934. 356p.

06432 MAJUMDAR, A.K. Bhakti renaissance. Bombay, BVB, 1965. 86p.

06433 PARTHASARATHY, R. Ramanujacharya. ND: NBT, 1969. 72p.

06434 RAGHAVACHAR, S.S. Viśiṣṭādvaita. Madras: Dr. S. Radhakrishnan Inst. for Advanced Study in Philosophy, U. of Madras, 1977. 63p.

06435 RAMAKRISHNANANDA, Swami. Life of Sri Ramanuja. 3rd ed. Madras: Sri Ramakrishna Math, 1977. 273p. [serialized in Vedanta Kesari, 1949-54]

06436 SEN GUPTA, A. A critical study of the philosophy of Rāmānuja. Varanasi: CSSO, 1967. 263p. (CSS, 55)

06437 SHARMA, A. Viśiṣṭādvaita Vedānta: a study. ND: Heritage, 1978. 83p.

06438 SRINIVASACHARI, P.N. The philosophy of Viśiṣṭādvaita. Adyar: Adyar Library, 1946. 640p. (Its series, 39)

06439 SRISAILA CHAKRAVARTI, V.R. The philosophy of Śrī Rāmānuja (Viśiṣṭādvaita). Madras: V.S.R. Chakravarti, 1974. 356p.

06440 VARADACHARI, K.C. Viśiṣṭādvaita and its development. Tirupati: Chakravarthy Pub., 1969. 129p.

06441 VIDYARTHI, P.B. Early Indian religious thought: a study in the sources of Indian theism with special reference to Rāmānuja. ND: Oriental, 1976. 239p.

06442 ______. Śrī Rāmānuja's philosophy and religion: a critical exposition of Viśiṣṭādvaita. Madras: Prof. M. Rangacharya Mem. Trust, 1977. 591p.

d. special topics in Rāmānuja's philosophy

06443 ANANTHARANGACHAR, N.S. The philosophy of sādhanā in Viśiṣṭādvaita. Mysore: U. of Mysore, 1967. 304p.

06444 LAZARUS, F.K. Rāmānuja and Bowne; a study in comparative philosophy. Bombay: Chetana, 1962. 332p.

06445 LESTER, R.C. Rāmānuja and Śrī-Vaiṣṇavism: the concept of prapatti or śaraṇāgati. In HR (1966) 266-82.

06446 ______. Rāmānuja on the Yoga. Adyar, Madras: TPH, 1976. 181p.

06447 LOTT, E.J. God and the universe in the Vedāntic theology of Rāmānuja: a study in his use of the self-body analogy. Madras: Ramanuja Res. Soc., 1976. 247p.

06448 PLOTT, J.C. A philosophy of devotion: a comparative study of bhakti and prapatti in Viśiṣṭādvaita and St. Bonaventura and Gabriel Marcel. Delhi: Motilal, 1974. 657p.

06449 RAGHAVACHAR, S.S. Sri Ramanuja on the Upanishads. Madras: Prof. M. Rangacharya Mem. Trust, 1972. 150p.

06450 VIDYARTHI, P.B. Divine personality and human life in Rāmānuja. ND: Oriental, 1978. 367p.

06451 ______. Knowledge, self, and God in Rāmānuja. ND: Oriental, 1978. 327p.

06452 WILSON, J.G. Śaṅkara, Rāmānuja and the function of religious language. In Religious Studies 6 (1970) 57-68.

e. Śrī Vaiṣṇavism after Rāmānuja; the split into Tengalai (southern school at Śrīraṅgam) and Vadagalai (northern school at Tirupati, 13th cent.)

i. general studies

06453 AIYANGAR, A.N.K. The three sects (rahasyatraya) of Viśiṣṭādvaita. In ALB 19 (1955) 223-31.

06454 JAGADEESAN, N. History of Śrī Vaishṇavism in the Tamil country: post-Rāmānuja. Madurai: Koodal, 1977. 460p.

06455 RAGHAVAN, V.K.S.N. History of viśiṣṭādvaita literature. Delhi: Ajanta, 1979. 132p.

06456 RANGACHARYA, V. Historical evolution of Śrī-Vaiṣṇavism in South India. In Cultural heritage of India. Calcutta: RMIC, 1956, v. 4, 163-85.

06457 STEIN, B. Social mobility and medieval South Indian sects. In J. Silverberg, ed. Social mobility in the caste system in India. The Hague: Mouton, 1968, 78-94.

06458 SUBBU REDDIAR, N. The two sects of South Indian Vaiṣṇavism. In SVUOJ 17,1/2 (1974) 57-70.

06459 VENKATACHARI, K.K.A. The Maṇipravāḷa literature of the Śrīvaiṣṇava Ācāryas, 12th to 15th century A.D. Bombay: Ananthacharya Res. Inst., 1978. 192p.

ii. the Tengalai school at Śrīraṅgam and its leader, Piḷḷai Lokācārya (1264-1327 AD)

06460 LESTER, R.C. Aspects of the Vaiṣṇava experience: Rāmānuja and Piḷḷai Lokācārya on human effort and divine grace. In Indian Philosophical Annual 10 (1974-5) 10p.

06461 ______, tr. Śrīvacana bhūṣaṇa of Piḷḷai Lokācārya. Madras: Kuppuswamy Sastri Res. Inst., 1979. 124p.

06462 PAUL, M.N., tr. The Vedānta Tattva-Traya of Śrī Lokāchārya Swami. Allahabad: Allahabad Press, 1904. 83p. (Vedānta series, 5)

iii. the Vadagalai school at the Śrī Veṅkaṭeśvara temple in Tirupati and its leader, Vedānta Deśika

06463 DESIKA CHARIAR, N.V. & K. RANGA AYENGAR, tr. Haṁsasandeśa of Vedānta Deśika. Madras: Vedanta Desika Res. Soc., 1973. 280p. [Rpt. 1903 ed.]

06464 GNANAMBAL, K. Śrīvaishṇavas and their religious institutions. In BAnthSI 20,3/4 (1971) 97-187.

06465 RAJAGOPALA AYYANGAR, M.R., tr. Srī Vedānta Deśika's (Veṅkaṭanātha's) Saṅkalpa-sūryodaya, a drama in ten acts. Tirupati: Tirumala Tirupati Devasthanams, 1965. 250p.

06466 ______,tr. Śrīmad Rahasyatrayasāra. Kumbakonam: Agnihothram Ramanuja Thathachaniar, 1956. 256p.

06467 SINGH, S. Vedānta Deśika: his life, works & philosophy. Banaras: CSSO, 1958. 316p. (CSS, 5)

06468 SRINIVASA CHARI, S.M. Advaita & Viśiṣṭādvaita, a study based on Vedānta Deśika's Śatadūṣani. NY: Asia, 1961. 204p.

5. Madhva (1197-1296 AD?), of Udipi, Karnataka: Vaiṣṇava Founder of Dvaita ("Dualistic") Vedanta

a. works of Madhvācarya, translated from Sanskrit

06469 KRISHNAMURTI SHARMA, B.N. Sri Madhva's teachings in his own words. 3rd ed. Bombay: BVB, 1979. 204p.

06470 NAGARAJA SARMA, R. Reign of realism in Indian philosophy. Madras: National Press, 1937. 695p.

06471 RAGHAVENDRACHARYA, H.N., tr. Brahma-mīmāṁsā. Mysore: U. of Mysore, 1965-.

06472 SIAUVE, S., tr. Les hiérarchies spirituelles selon l'Anuvyākhyāna de Madhva. Pondicherry: IFI, 1971. 114p. (Its pub., 43)

06473 ______,tr. La voie vers la connaissance de Dieu (Brahma-Jijñāsa) selon l'Anuvyākhyāna de Madhva. Pondicherry: IFI, 1957. 109p. (Its pub., 6)

06474 SUBBA RAU, S., tr. The Vedanta-sutras with the commentary by Sri Madhwacharya. 2nd ed., rev. Tirupati: Sri Vyasa Press, 1936. 59 + 294p. [1st pub. 1904]

b. general studies of Madhva and his Dvaita Vedānta

06475 GLASENAPP, H. VON. Madhvas Philosophie des Vishnu Glaubens. Bonn: K. Schroeder, 1923. 119p. (Geistesströmungen des Ostens, 2)

06476 HANUMANTHA RAO, S. Hindu religious movements in medieval Deccan. In JIH 25 (1936) 103-13. [Madhva & his successors]

06477 KASHYAP, R.A. & R. PURNAIYA. An introduction to Madhva ontology. Bangalore: Tattva Viveka Pub., 1973. 132p.

06478 KRISHNAMURTI SHARMA, B.N. A history of the Dvaita school of Vedanta and its literature. Bombay: Booksellers' Pub. Co., 1960-61. 2 v.

06479 ______. Philosophy of Sri Madhvacarya. Bombay: BVB, 1962. 375p.

06480 NAGARAJA RAO, P. The epistemology of Dvaita Vedānta. Madras: Adyar Library, 1976. 120p. (Its series, 107)

06481 NARAIN, K. A critique of Madhva refutation of the Śaṁkara school of Vedānta. Allahabad: Udayana, 1964. 392p.

06482 ______. An outline of Madhva philosophy. Allahabad: Udayana, 1962. 231p.

06483 PADMANABHACHARYA, C.M. Life & teachings of Sri Madhvacharya. Udipi: Paryaya Sri Palimar Mutt, 1970. 185p.

06484 RAGHAVACHAR, S.S., tr. Śrīmad Viṣṇu Tattva Vinirṇaya. Mangalore: Sri Ramakrishna Ashrama, 1959. 98p.

06485 RAMACHANDRAN, T.P. Dvaita Vedānta. ND: Arnold-Heinemann, 1976. 132p.

06486 SIAUVE, S. La doctrine de Madhva, Dvaita-Vedānta. Pondicherry: IFI, 1968. 397p. (Its pub.,38)

06487 SUBBANNACHAR, N.V. Madhva methodology. In Indian philosophy and culture 15,3 (1970) 24-35.

c. the Haridāsas of Karṇāṭaka: Kannaḍa bhakta-poets, inspired by Madhva's teachings

06488 ACHARYA, B.T. Haridasa sahitya: the Karnatak mystics and their songs. Bangalore: Indian Inst. of Culture, 1953. 16p.

06489 KARMARKAR, A.P. & N.B. KALAMDANI. Mystic teachings of the Haridāsas of Karnātak. Dharwar: Karnatak Vidyavardhak Sangha, 1939. 129p.

06490 KRISHNA RAO, M.V. A brief survey of mystic tradition in religion and art in Karnataka. Madras: Wardha Pub. House, 1959. 217p.

06490a ______. Purandara and the Haridasa movement. Dharwar: Karnatak U., 1966. 242p.

06491 KRISHNAMURTI SARMA, B.N. The Vaiṣṇava saints of Karṇāṭaka. In Cultural history of India. Calcutta, RMIC, 1956, v. 4, 349-55.

06492 KUPPUSWAMY, G. & M. HARIHARAN. Compositions of Haridasas. Trivandrum: College Book House, 1979. 194p.

06493 RANADE, R.D. Pathway to God in Kannada literature. Bombay: BVB, 1960. 344p.

06494 SITARAMIAH, V. Purandaradāsa. ND: NBT, 1971. 145p.

6. The Bhedābheda ("Different-non-Different") Schools: Bhāskara (9th cent. AD), and Nimbārka (11th cent. AD), Telugu Brahman Devotee of Gopālakṛṣṇa and Rādhā

06495 BOSE, R. Vedānta-Parijāta-Saurabha of Nimbārka & Vedānta-Kaustubha of Srīnivāsa. Calcutta: ASB, 1940-43. 2 v.

06496 CHAUDHURI, R. The Nimbārka school of Vedānta. In Cultural heritage of India. Calcutta: RMIC, 1953, v. 3,

333-46.

06497 MISHRA, U. Nimbārka school of Vedānta. 2nd ed. Allahabad: Tirabhukti, 1966. 125p.

06498 SINHA, J.N. The philosophy of Nimbārka. Calcutta: Sinha Pub. House, 1973. 152p.

06499 SRINIVASACHARI, P.N. The philosophy of Bhedābheda. Madras: Adyar Library, 1972. 311p. (Its series, 74) [Rpt. 1934 ed.]

7. The Śuddhādvaita ("Pure Non-Dual") Vedānta of Vallabhācārya (1479-1531 AD?), Telugu Brahman Propagator of Rādhā-Kṛṣṇa Bhakti and Puṣṭimārga throughout India

06500 BARZ, R. The Bhakti sect of Vallabhācārya. Delhi: Thomson Press, 1976. 264p. (Australian National U., Oriental monograph ser., 18)

06501 BHATT, G.H. The school of Vallabha. In Cultural heritage of India. Calcutta: RMIC, 1953, v. 3, 347-59.

06502 GLASENAPP, H. VON. Doctrines of Vallabhāchārya. Tr. from German by L. Amin. Kapadvanj, Gujarat: Shuddhadvaita Samsada, 1959. 65p.

06503 MARFATIA, M.I. The philosophy of Vallabhācārya. Delhi: Munshiram, 1967. 343p.

06504 PAREKH, M.C. Shri Vallabhāchārya: life, teachings, and movement: a religion of grace. 2nd ed. Rajkot: Shrī Bhāgavata Dharma Mission, 1969. 299p. (Shrī Bhāgavata dharma series, 3) [1st pub. 1943]

06505 SHAH, J.G. A primer of Anu-Bhāshya. Rev. ed. Kapadvanji Shuddhadvaita Samsada, 1960. 156p. [Rpt. 1927 ed.]

06506 ______. Shri Vallabhāchārya: his philosophy and religion. Nadiad: Pushtimargiya Pustakalaya, 1969. 501p.

06507 ______,tr. Tattvārthadīpanibandha. Bombay: S. Narayandas & J. Asanmal Charity Trust, 1943. 253p.

8. Śaivism in Early Medieval South India (c. 600-1565 AD): General Studies (incl. Śāktism)

06508 Aruṇagirināthar [special section]. In BITCM (1975) pt. 2, 127-68.

06509 BRUNNER, H. Le Sādhaka, personage oublié du Śivaīsme du Sud. In JA 263,3/4 (1975) 411-43.

06510 BRUNNER-LACHAUX, H., tr. Somaśambhupaddhati: Pt. 1. Le rituel quotidien... Pt. 2. Rituels occasionels dans la tradition śivaīte de l'Inde du Sud. Pondicherry: IFI, 1963-68. 2 v., 372p. + 8pl.; 394p. + 7pl. (IFI series, 25:1,2)

06511 FILLIOZAT, J. Un text de la religion Kaumāra le Tirumurukāṟṟuppaṭai. Pondicherry: IFI, 1973. 132p.

06512 FLEET, J.F., tr. Inscriptions at Ablur. In Epigraphia Indica 5 (1898-99) 213-65. [evidence for Kālamukha Śakti-pariṣad in Karnataka]

06513 LORENTZEN, D. The Kāpālikas and Kālamukhs, two lost Śaivite sects. ND: Thomson, 1972. 214p.

06514 MAHALINGAM, T.V. The cult of Śakti in Tamilnad. In BITCM (1965) pt. 1, 17-29.

06515 RAJAMANICKKAM PILLAI, M.P. The development of Śaivism in South India (A.D. 300-1300). Dharmapuram: Gnanasambandam Press, 1964. 358p.

06516 SUBRAMANIA, N. Śakti worship in the south. In VK 53,1 (1966) 46-50.

06517 SWAMY, B.G.L. The Golaki school of Śaivism in the Tamil country. In JOH 53,2 (1975) 167-210.

06518 VENKATA SUBBIAH, A. A twelfth century university in Mysore. In QJMS 7 (1917) 157-96.

9. The Śaiva Siddhānta: a Blending of the Bhakti of the Tamil Saints with the Philosophy of the Śaivāgamas

a. Śaiva Siddhānta texts, translated from the Tamil

06519 DEVASENAPATHI, V.A. Śaiva Siddhānta as expounded in the Śivajñāna-siddhiyār and its six commentaries. Madras: U. of Madras, 1966. 322p. [1st pub. 1960]

06520 MATTHEWS, G., tr. Śiva-ñana-bōdham, a manual of Śaiva religious doctrine. Oxford: OUP, 1948. 82p. [by Meykanda Deva, 13th cent.]

06521 NALLASWAMI PILLAI, J.M., tr. Śivagñāna Botham of Meykand Deva. Dharmapuram: Gnanasambandam Press, 1945. 111p. [1st ed. 1895]

06522 ______,tr. Thiruvarutpayan of Umāpathi Śivāchārya. Dharmapuram: Gnanasambandam Press, 1945. 168p.

06523 NATARAJAN, B., tr. Tirumantiram = Holy hymns. Madras: ITES Pub., 1979-. [to be 10 v.]

06524 PIET, J.H., tr. A logical presentation of the Śaiva Siddhānta philosophy. Madras: CLS, 1952. 167p. (Indian Res. ser., 8) [Tr. with commentaries, of Śiva-Jñana-bodha]

b. studies of Śaiva Siddhānta

06525 Collected lectures on Śaiva Siddhānta, 1946-54. Annamalainagar: Annamalai U., 1965. 529p.

06526 Collected lectures on Śaiva Siddhānta, 1963-1973. Annamalainagar: Annamalai U., 1978. 397p.

06527 DEVASENAPATHI, V.A. Of human bondage and divine grace. Annamalainagar: Annamalai U., 1959. 114p.

06528 DHAVAMONY, M. Love of God according to Śaiva Siddhānta: a study in the mysticism and theology of Śaivism. Oxford: OUP, 1971. 402p.

06529 KELLER, C.A. Dieu, l'âme et le monde selon le Śaiva-Siddhānta (philosophie religieuse de l'Inde du Sud). In AS/EA 32,2 (1978) 97-111.

06530 NALLASWAMI PILLAI, J.M. Studies in Śaiva Siddhānta. Dharmapuram: Gnanasambandham Press, 1962. 274p. [1st pub. 1911]

06531 PARANJOTI, V. Śaiva Siddhānta. 2nd rev. ed. London: Luzac, 1954. 240p.

06532 SCHOMERUS, H.W. Der Çaiva-Siddhānta: eine Mysktik Indiens. Leipzig: J.C. Hinrichs, 1912. 444p.

06533 VAN TROY, J. The social structure of the Śaiva-Siddhāntika ascetics: 700-1300 AD. In Indica 11,2 (1974) 77-86.

10. The Tamil Siddhas: Śaiva Tantric Adepts, Possessors of the Siddhis, "Supernormal Powers"

06534 ARUNACHALAM, M. The siddha cult in Tamilnad. In BITCM (1977) pt. 1, 85-117.

06535 SUBRAMANIA AIYAR, A.V. The poetry & philosophy of the Tamil Siddārs; an essay in criticism. Tirunelveli: S. Mahadevan, 1957. 87p.

06536 ZVELEBIL, K.V. The poets of the powers. London: Rider, 1973. 144p.

11. The Vīraśaiva movement of the Lingāyat Caste-Sect of Karṇāṭaka (from c. 12th cent. AD)

a. bibliography

06537 ALLCHIN, R. Attaining to the void: a review of recent contributions in English to the study of Vīraśaivism. In Religious Studies 7 (1971) 339-59.

b. Basava (12th cent. AD) and other Śaraṇas, founding saints-poets and their Kannaḍa vacanas ("sayings")

06538 BHOOSNURMATH, S.S. Man the divine: a critical exposition of Shoonya sampadane. Condensed by C.H. Prahlada Rao. Adoni: Sri Swamiji of Mandagiri Kalmath, 1979. 292p.

06539 CHIDANANDA MURTHY, M. Basavanna. ND: NBT, 1972. 111p.

06540 DESAI, P.B. Basavesvara and his times. Dharwar: Kannada Res. Inst., Karnatak U., 1968. 406p.

06541 HIREMATH, R.C. Sri Channabasavesvara: life and philosophy. Dharwar: Karnatak U., 1978. 162p.

06542 KAMBI, V.S. Philosophy of the Śūnyasaṁpādane. Dharwar: Kumaresha Granthamale, 1973-.

06543 KUMARA SWAMIJI. Buddha and Basava. Dharwar: V.R. Koppal, 1957. 207p.

06544 MAHADEVI, M. Revolution in Kalyana. Dharwar: Suyidhana Sugrantha Maale, 1973. 146p.

06545 MANJAPPA, H. Basava: the dimension of universal man. Tr. by A. Mylar Rao. Dharwar: Hardekar Manjappa Smaraka Granthamale, 1966. 104p.

06546 MENEZES, L.M.A., tr. Songs from the śaraṇas and other poems. Dharwar: Karnatak U., 1971. 67p.

06547 MENEZES, L.M.A. & S.M. ANGADI, tr. Essence of Ṣaṭsthala: vacanas of Tōṇṭada Siddhaliṅgēśvara. Dharwar: Karnatak U., 1978. 481p.

06548 ______, tr. Vacanas of Basavanna, a selection. Sirigere, Karnataka: Annana Balaga, 1967. 498p. [1st pub. 1965, 160p.]

06549 NANDIMATH, S.C. & L.M.A. MENEZES & R.C. HIREMATH, tr. Śūnyasaṁpādane. Dharwar: Karnatak U., 1965-68. 3 v.

06550 RAMANUJAN, A.K., tr. Speaking of Śiva. Baltimore: Penguin, 1973. 199p.

06551 SAMARTHA, M.P. The compassionate Basava; an evaluative study of a medieval saint-reformer of Karnataka, India. Ph.D. diss, Hartford Seminary Foundation, 1972. 229p. [UM 73-15,937]

06552 Śri Basaveśvara: 8th centenary commemoration volume. Bangalore: Got. of Mysore, 1967. 540p.

06553 THEODORE, A.S. & D.K. HAKARI, tr. Thus spoke Basava; English renderings of Basava's vachanas. Bangalore: Bassava Samiti, 1965. 82p.

06554 THIPPERUDRA SWAMY, H. Basaveshwara. ND: Sahitya Akademi, 1975. 53p.

06555 ______. The Vīraśaiva saints, a study. Tr. by S.M. Angadi. Mysore: Rao and Raghavan, 1968. 374p.

06556 UMASHANKAR, P. A garland of pearls: or, Basavamālā: an interpretation of the vachanas of Lord Basaveshwar. Hubli: Shri Jagadguru Gangadhar Dharma Pracharak Mandal, 1978. 48p.

b. religious and sociocultural studies of Vīraśaivism and the Lingāyats

06557 BRUNNER, H. De la consommation du nirmālya de Śiva. In JA 257 (1969) 213-63.

06558 CHITNIS, K.N. Viraśaiva Maṭhas in the Keladi Kingdom. In JKU(SS) 3 (1967) 124-31.

06559 HUNASHAL, S.M. The Lingayat movement; a social revolution in Karnatak. Dharwar: Karnatak Sahitya Mandira, 1947. 268p.

06560 KAMBI, V.S. Forms of Indian philosophical literature and other papers. Dharwar: Shri Vidya Prakashan, 1979. 105p.

06561 ______. Philosophy of the Śunyasaṁpādane. Dharwar: Kumaresha Granthamale, 1973-.

06562 KUMARA SWAMIJI. The Vīrashaiva philosophy and mysticism. 2nd ed. Dharwar: V.R. Koppal, 1960. 288p. [1st ed. 1949]

06563 MCCORMACK, W.C. Lingāyats as a sect. In JRAI 93 (1963) 59-71.

06564 NANDI, R.N. Origin of the Vīraśaiva movement. In IHR 2,1 (1975) 32-46.

06565 NANDIMATH, S.C. A handbook of Vīraśaivism. 2nd rev. ed. Delhi: Motilal, 1979. 43 + 175p. [1st ed. 1942]

06566 SAKHARE, M.R. History and philosophy of Lingayat religion. Dharwar: Karnatak U., 1978. 444p. [1st pub. 1942]

06567 SHARMA, A. Vīraśaivism: a study in sectarian Hinduism. In Indica 12,2 (1975) 101-13.

06568 SHIVARUDRAPPA, A.D.G. Contributions of Veerashaiva Maṭhas to the development of education in Karnatak from the 12th to the 18th century AD. In JKU(H) 20 (1976) 126-42.

12. Jainism and Remnants of Buddhism in the South

06569 BANERJI, A. Traces of Buddhism in South India, c. 700-1600 A.D. Calcutta: Scientific Book Agency, 1970. 109p.

06570 SALETORE, B.A. Mediaeval Jainism, with special reference to the Vijayanagar Empire. Bombay: Karnatak Pub. House, 1938. 426p.

06571 SINGH, R.B.P. Jainism in early medieval Karnataka, c. A.D. 400-1200. Delhi: Motilal, 1975. 175p.

13. Islam in Early Medieval South India

06572 ABDUL RAHIM, M. Islam in Negapatam. In BITCM 1974 pt. 2, 85-100.

06573 CHERIAN, A. The genesis of Islam in Malabar. In Indica 6,1 (1969) 1-13.

06574 IBRAHIM KUNJU, A.P. Islam in Kerala. In JKS 4,4 (1977) 493-602.

E. Regional Languages and Literatures of South India in the Early Medieval Period (c. 600-1565 AD)

1. Tamil

a. the Tamil Rāmāyaṇa of Kamban/Kampar (c. 10th-12th cent. AD): Cōḻa period re-telling of the Vālmīki epic

06575 MAHARAJAN, S. Kamban. ND: Sahitya Akademi, 1972. 80p.

06576 PONNIAH, S.M., tr. Sri Paduka: the exile of the Prince of Ayodhya. Athens: Center for Intl. Studies, Ohio U., 1969. 86p. [canto 2 of Kamban Rāmāyaṇa]

06577 RAJAGOPALACHARI, C., tr. The Ayodhya canto of the Ramayana as told by Kamban. London: Allen & Unwin, 1961. 127p.

06578 SANKARAN, K. Kamban's treatment of Tirukkural: a treatise in English. Madras: Pooram Pub., 1978. 287p.

06579 SHANKAR RAJU NAIDU, S. A comparative study of Kamba Ramayanam and Tulasi Ramayan. Madras: U. of Madras, 1971. 591p.

06580 SHULMAN, D.D. Divine order and divine evil in the Tamil Tale of Rāma. In JAS 38,4 (1979) 651-69.

06581 SINGARAVELU, S.A. A comparative study of the story of Rama in South India and Southeast Asia. Kuala Lumpur: IATR, 1966. 55p.

06582 SUBRAMANYA AIYAR, V.V. Introduction to Kamba Ramayanam - a study. Delhi: Delhi Tamil Samgam, 1950. 378p.

06583 ______. Kamba Ramayana; a study. Bombay: BVB, 1965. 342p.

06584 VENKATARAMA AIYER, C.P. Kamban and his art. Madras: C. Coomaraswamy Naidu, 1913. 112p.

b. other Tamil writers and texts

06585 APPUSWAMI, P.N. Muttollayiram: a Tamil classic of over 1300 years ago: a fragment of 110 verses. Calcutta: Kurinji, 1977. 117p.

06586 GNANAMURTHY, T.E. A critical study of Cīvakacintāmaṇi. Coimbatore: Kalaikathir, 1966. 372p.

06587 GROS, F., tr. Le Paripāṭal. Pondicherry: IFI, 1968. 319p. (Its pub., 35)

06588 JAYARAMAN, N. Life and letters of Kapilar. Madurai: Madurai Pub. House, 1978. 248p.

06589 LANGTON, M., tr. The story of King Nala & Princess Damayanti, a narrative poem...from the Tamil of Puhalendi Pulavar. Madras: CLS, 1950. 215p. (Indian Res. Ser., 4)

06590 NANDAKUMAR, P. Classical Tamil poetry. In Indian Horizons 25,1/2 (1976) 61-74.

06591 POPE, G.U., tr. Nāladiyār, or, Four hundred quatrains in Tamil. Oxford: OUP, 1893. 440p.

06592 SUBRAMANIA AIYAR, A.V., tr. Kapilarahaval: a medieval Tamil poem on caste. Madras: Subramania Aiyar, 1975. 123p.

2. Malayālam of Kerala

06593 GEORGE, K.M. Rāmacaritam and the study of early Malayalam. Kottayam: National Book Stall, 1956. 218p.

06594 VELAYUDHAN PILLAI, P.V. Early Malayalam prose; a study. Trivandrum: Kwality Printers, 1973. 190p.

06595 ZVELEBIL, K. From proto-South Dravidian to Malayalam. In AO 38,1 (1970) 45-67.

3. Kannaḍa of Karnataka [see also VI. D. 5. c. & VI. D. 11., above]

06596 RAMANUJAN, A.K. & M.G. KRISHNAMURTHI. Some Kannada poems. Calcutta: Writers Workshop, 1967. 16p.

06597 SITARAMIAH, V.R. Mahākavi Pampa. Bombay: Popular, 1967. 245p.

06598 SURYANARAYANARAO, M.K. Kannaḍa versions of the Purāṇas. In Purāṇa 6,1 (1964) 147-73.

4. Telugu of Andhra

06599 BROWN, C.P., tr. Verses of Vemana. Hyderabad: Andhra Pradesh Sahitya Akademi, 1967. 289p. [1st pub. 1929]

06600 JANAKIRAM, A. Glimpses into Telugu classics. Hyderabad: Andhra Mahila Sabha, 1976. 78p.

06601 RADHAKRISHNA SARMA, C. Tales from Telugu: 18 tales retold in English from Manchana's poem, Keyurabaahu charitramu. Madras: Lakshminarayana Granthamala, 1975. 48p.

06602 ROGHAIR, G.H. The epic of Palnāḍu: a study and translation of Palnāti vitrula kathā, a Telugu oral tradition as sung by Aliśeṭṭi Gāleyya. Ph.D. diss., U. of Wisconsin, 1977. 2 v., 248, 363p. [UM 77-19,781]

06603 ______. The role of Brahmā Nāyuḍu in the Epic of Palnāḍu. In JIF 1,2 (1978) 15-26.

06604 VENKATAVADHANI, D. Pothana. ND: Sahitya Akademi, 1972. 98p.

06605 VENKATESWAR RAO, N. Vemana. ND: Sahitya Akademi, 1969. 93p.

06606 ______, ed. Vemana through Western eyes. Madras: Seshachalam, 1969. 96p.

F. Art and Architecture of Medieval South India

1. General; Architectural Texts

06607 DAGENS, B. Les enseignements architecturaux de l'Ajitāgama et du Rauravāgama. Pondicherry: IFI, 1977. 148p. (Its pub., 57)

06608 ______,tr. Mayamata, traité sanskrit d'architecture. Pondicherry: IFI, 1970. 2 v., 732, 580p. (IFI pub., 40:1,2)

06609 PROCTOR, R.C. Some rules and precepts among Tamils for construction of houses, villages, towns and cities during the mediaeval age. In JRASCB 30 (1927) 337-360. [Based on the Sarasothimālai, 1310 AD]

06610 SOUNDARA RAJAN, K.V. Early temple architecture in Karnataka and its ramifications. Dharwar: Kannada Res. Inst., 1969. 73p.

2. Art under the Pāṇḍya Dynasty (586-1323 AD)

06611 NAGASWAMY, R. Some contributions of the Pāṇḍyas to South Indian art. In ArtAs 27 (1965) 265-74.

06612 SIVARAMAMURTI, C. Kalugamalai and early Pandyan rock-cut shrines. Bombay: N.M. Tripathi, 1961. 46p. (Heritage of Indian art series, 3)

3. Art under the Pallava Dynasty (575-903 AD): Mahābalipuram and Other Sites

06613 DUMARCAY, J. & F. L'HERNAULT. Temples Pallava construits: étude architecturale, étude iconographique. Paris: EFEO, 1975. 124p. (Mémoires archéologiques, 9)

06614 GANGOLY, O.C. The art of the Pallavas. NY: G. Wittenborn, 1957. 29p.

06615 HARI RAO, V.N. The Vīrattāneśvara temple at Tiruttani. In JIH 42 (1964) 433-41.

06616 JOUVEAU-DUBREUIL, G. Pallava antiquities. London: Probsthain, 1916-18. 2 v., 76, 74p. [tr. from French]

06617 LOCKWOOD, M. & G. SIROMONEY & P. DAYANANDAN. Mahabalipuram studies. Madras: CLS, 1974. 111p.

06618 LONGHURST, A.H. Pallava architecture, Part I (Early period). Simla: Govt. of India Press, 1924. 41p. (ASI memoirs, 17)

06619 ______. Pallava architecture, Part II (intermediate or Māmalla Period). Calcutta: Govt. of India Central Pub. Branch, 1928. 50p. (ASI memoirs, 33)

06620 ______. Pallava architecture, Part III (the later or Rājasiṁha Period). Calcutta: Govt. of India Central Pub. Branch, 1930. 25p. (ASI Memoirs, 40)

06621 MATE, M.S. Origin of Pallava art: the Undavalli caves. In E&W 20,1/2 (1970) 108-16.

06622 MINAKSHI, C. The Historical Sculptures of the Vaikuṇṭha-perumāḷ Temple, Kāñchī. Delhi: MPGOI, 1941. 61p. (ASI memoirs, 41)

06623 NARASIMHAN, V.M. Some Pallava icons. In LK 7 (1960) 19-28.

06624 ______. Two more Pallava temples in Rājasiṁha style. In LK 3/4 (1956) 63-66.

06625 RAMACHANDRAN, T.N. Cave temple paintings of Sittannavasal. In LK 9 (1961) 30-34.

06626 RAMASWAMI, N.S. Māmallapuram: an annotated bibliography. Madras: New Era, 1980. 119p.

06627 REA, A. Pallava architecture. Madras: Govt. Press, 1909. 49p. + 124p. (ASI new imperial ser., 34)

06628 SIVARAMAMURTI, C. Mahābalipuram. 3rd ed. ND: 1972. 35p.

06629 SRINIVASAN, K.R. Cave temples of the Pallavas. ND: Director General of Archeology, 1964. 206p. (Architectural survey of temples, 1)

06630 ______. The Dharmarāja ratha & its sculptures, Mahābalipuram. ND: Abhinav, 1975. 112 + 32p.

06631 ______. The Pallava Architecture of South India. In AI 14 (1958) 114-38.

4. Art under the Cōḷas (850-1177 AD)

06632 BALASUBRAHMANYAM, S.R. Early Chola art. London: Asia, 1967-. pt.1, 265p. + 115pl.

06633 ______. Early Chola temples: Parantaka I to Rajaraja I, A.D. 907-985. Bombay: Orient Longman, 1971. 351p. + 156p. of ill.

06634 ______. Four Chola temples. Bombay: N.M. Tripathi, 1963. 72p. (Heritage of Indian art series, 4.)

06635 ______. Later Chola temples: Kulottunga I to Rajendra III (A.D. 1070-1280). Madras: Mudgala Trust, 1979. 470p.

06636 ______. Middle Chola temples: Rajaraja I to Kulottunga I, A.D. 985-1070. Faridabad: Thomson Press, 1975. 424p. + 102p.

06637 BANERJEE, N.R. The Valiśvara temple at Tiruvaliśvaram. In JAS Bengal 4th ser. 4,3/4 (1962) 169-77.

06638 BARRETT, D.E. Early Cola architecture and sculpture; 866-1014 A.D. London: Faber, 1974. 142p. + 50pl.

06639 ______. Early Cola bronzes. Bombay: Bhulabhai Mem. Inst., 1965. 46p. + 102pl.

06640 BHOOTHALINGAM, M. Movement in stone; a study of some Chola temples. ND: Soumani, 1969. 90p.

06641 DHAKY, M.A. Coḷa Sculpture. In Anand Krishna, ed. Chhavi.... Banaras: B.H.U., Bharat Kala Bhavan, 1971, 263-289.

06642 MAHALINGAM, T.V. The Nāgeśvarasvāmi temple. In JIH 47,1 (1967) 1-94.

06643 MARR, J.R. The Periya Purāṇam frieze at Tārācuram: episodes in the lives of the Tamil Śaiva saints. In BSOAS 62,2 (1979) 268-89 + 12pl.

06644 NAGASWAMY, R. Some Aḍavallān and other bronzes of the early Chola period. In LK 10 (1961) 34-40.

06645 RAMACHANDRAN, T.N. Bronze images from Tiruvenkadu-Śvetaraṇya (Tanjore district). In LK 3/4 (1956) 55-62.

06646 SRINIVASAN, P.R. Rare sculptures of the early Chola period. In LK 5 (1959) 59-67.

06647 VENKATARAMAN, B. Temple art under the Chola queens. Faridabad: Thomson Press, 1976. 154p. + 28pl.

5. Art under the Western Cālukya Dynasty of Bādāmi (550-753 AD)

06648 ANNIGERI, A.M. A guide to the Pattadakal temples. Dharwar: Kannada Res. Inst., 1961. 63p.

06649 BANERJI, R.D. Basreliefs of Badami. Calcutta: Govt. of India, 1928. 62p. (ASI memoirs, 25)

06650 GUPTA, R.S. The art and architecture of Aihole; a study of early Chalukyan art through temple architecture and sculpture. Bombay: Taraporevala, 1967. 126p. + 140pl.

06651 In praise of Aihole, Badami, Mahakuta, Pattadakal. Bombay: Marg Pub., 1980. 133p.

06652 LIPPE, A. Additions and replacements in early Chālukya Temples. In Archives of Asian art. 23 (1969/1970) 6-23. [Suppl. in 23 (1970/1971) 80-83.]

06653 ______. Some sculptural motifs on early Calukya temples. In ArtAs 29,1 (1967) 5-24.

06654 MICHELL, G.A. An architectural description and analysis of the early Western Calukyan temples. Ph.D. diss., London U., School of Oriental and African Studies, 1974. 332p.

06655 RAMA RAO, M. Early Calukyan architecture; a review. In JIH 41 (1963) 431-57.

06656 RAO, S.R. A note on the chronology of early Chalukyan Temples. In LK 15 (1970) 9-18.

06657 REA, A. Chalukyan architecture, including examples from the Ballari District, Madras Presidency. Delhi: IndBH, 1970. 40p. + 114pl. (ASI new imperial ser., 21) [1st pub. 1896]

06658 SIVARAMAMURTI, C. Western Chāḷukya paintings at Badami. In LK 5 (1959) 49-58.

06659 TARR, G. The architecture of the early Western Chalukyas. Ph.D. diss., UCLA, 1969. 548p. [UM 70-15,948]

6. Art under the Eastern Cālukyas of Veṅgī (617-1190 AD) and the Kākatīyas of Warangal (1000-1425 AD)

06660 DIVAKARAN, O. Les temples d'Alampur et de ses environs au temps des Calukya de Badami. In ArtsAs 24 (1971) 51-101.

06661 GOPALA REDDY, Y. Ganapur group of temples. In JAHRS 29(1963) 27-39.

06662 GOPALAKRISHNA MURTHY, S. The sculpture of the Kakatiyas. Hyderabad: Govt. of Andhra Pradesh, 1964. 44p. + 22pl. (Its Archaeol. ser., 34)

06663 RADHAKRISHNA SARMA, M. Temples of Telingāna: the architecture, iconography, & sculpture of the Cālukya and Kākatīya temples. Hyderabad: dist. Booklinks, 1972. 307p.

06664 RAMA RAO, M. Early Cālukyan temples of Āndhra Desa. Hyderabad: Govt. of Andhra Pradesh, 1965. 44p. (Its Archaeol. ser., 20)

06665 ______. Eastern Cālukyan temples of Āndhra Desa. Hyderabad: Govt. of Andhra Pradesh, 1964. 48p. (Its Archaeol. ser., 19)

06666 ______. The temples of Alampur. In JIH 39,3 (1961) 369-91.

06667 RAMESAN, N., ed. Alampur. Bombay: Marg Pub., 1978. 4p. + 10pl.

06668 SIVARAMAMURTI, C. Early Eastern Chalukya sculpture. Madras: Supt. Govt. Press, 1957. 71p. + 35pl.

06669 YAZDANI, G. The temples of Palampet. Calcutta: Supt. Govt. Printing, 1922, 174-85. (ASI memoirs, 6)

7. Art under the Hoysaḷas of Karṇāṭaka (1110-1317 AD)

06670 DEL BONTÀ, R.J. The Hoysalas: architectural development and artists, 12th and 13th centuries AD. Ph.D. diss., U. of Michigan, 1978. 488p. [UM 78-13,636]

06671 In praise of Hoysala art. Bombay: Marg Pub., 1980. 106p. [1st pub. in Marg 31 (1977) 1-106]

06672 KAMESVARA RAO, V. Vimanas of the Hoysala Temples. In JAHRS 30,1/4 (1964-65) 43-49.

06673 MAITY, S.K. Masterpieces of Hoysala art: Halebid, Belur, Somnathpur. Bombay: Taraporevala, 1978. 52p. + 50pl.

06674 NAGARAJ, N. Belur. Bangalore: Art Pub., 1979. 39p. + 10pl.

06675 NARASIMHACHAR, R. The Kesava temple at Somanathapur. Mysore: Dir. of Archaeology and Museums, 1977. 17p. + 23pl. (Karnataka archaeol. ser., 1)

06676 SAMA RAO, P. Hoysala architecture and sculpture. In Prabuddha Bharata 71,3 (1966) 118-22 + 8pl.

06677 SETTAR, S. Hoysaḷa sculptures in the National Museum, Copenhagen. Copenhagen: The Museum, 1975. 172p.

8. Art of the Vijayanagara Dynasties (1336-1565 AD)

06678 KAMESWARA RAO, V. Select Vijayanagara temples of Rāyalaseema. Hyderabad: Govt. of Andhra Pradesh, 1976. 230 + 67p. (Its Archaeol. ser., 49)

06679 LONGHURST, A.H. Hampi ruins. Madras: Govt. Press, 1917. 144p.

VII. MIDDLE INDIA IN THE EARLY MEDIEVAL PERIOD (c. 600-1526 AD)

A. General Histories by Area and Dynasty

1. Major Powers in the Mahārāshṭra Area (The Cālukyas of Vāṭāpi and Veṅgī Ruled in this Area c. 550-753 AD and 973-1190 AD)

a. the Rāṣṭrakūṭas (753-973 AD): interregnum between the two Cālukya dynasties

06680 ALTEKAR, A.S. Rāṣṭrakūṭas and their times. 2nd rev. ed. Poona: Oriental Book Agency, 1967. 441p. (POS, 36)

06681 NILAKANTA SASTRI, K.A. Amogavarsa I and Karka Suvarnavarsa of Lata. In JIH 26 (1948) 21-25.

06682 REU, B.N. The early Rashtrakutas of the Deccan and the present Mysore State. In JIH 16 (1937) 253-58.

b. the Yādavas of Devagiri (1150-1313 AD): a successor state of the later Cāḷukyas; annexed by the Delhi Sultanate in 1313

06683 AHLUWALIA, M.S. Khalji annexation of Devagiri - a study of the political relations between the North and the South. In S.P. Sen, ed. The North and the South in Indian history.... Calcutta: IHS, 1976, 134-46.

06684 NARASIMHA MURTHY, A.V. The Sēvuṇas of Devagiri. Mysore: Rao & Raghavan, 1971. 272p.

06685 RITTI, S. The Seunas: the Yadavas of Devagiri. Dharwar: Dept. of Ancient Indian History and Epigraphy, Karnatak U., 1973. 364p.

06686 VERMA, O.P. The Yādavas and their times. Nagpur: Vidarbha Samshodhan Mandal, 1970. 404p.

c. the Bāhmanī Sultanate in the northern Deccan (independent of Delhi 1345; split into five sultanates c. 1530 AD)

06687 HUSAIN, A.M. Khandesh in a new light, based on a study of Persian and Arabic sources. Bangalore: Mythic Society, 1963. 41p.

06688 ______. A short history of Khandesh 1382-1601. In QJMS 51 (1960-61) 120-28, 180-86; 52 (1961-62) 6-20; 53 (1962-63) 30-40.

06689 HUSAINI, A.Q. Bahman Shah, the founder of the Bahmani kingdom of the Deccan. London: Probsthain, 1960. 192p.

06690 KING, J.S., tr. The history of the Bāhmanī dynasty. Founded on the Burhān-i-ma'āsir [of ʿAlī ibn ʿAzīz Allāh]. London: 1900. 35+ 157p. [Rpt. from IA]

06691 SHERWANI, H.K. The Bahmanis of the Deccan. Hyderabad: Mgr. of Pub., 1953. 453p.

06692 ______. Mahmud Gawan, the great Bahmani wazir. Allahabad: Kitabistan, 1942. 267p.

06693 SINHA, S.K. Mediaeval history of the Deccan, v. 1. Bahmanids. Hyderabad: Govt. of Andhra Pradesh, 1964. 228p. (Its Archaeol. ser., 18)

2. Early Medieval Dynasties in the Orissa Area (600-1526): the Bhauma-kāras, Eastern Gaṅgas, and Gajapatis

06694 ACHARYA, P. Studies in Orissan history, archaeology, and archives. Cuttack: Cuttack Student's Store, 1969. 560p.

06695 DAS, B.R. The Bhauma-Karas: Buddhist kings of Orissa and their times. ND: Oriental, 1978. 246p. + 31pl.

06696 MISRA, B. Dynasties of mediaeval Orissa. Calcutta: K.N. Chatterji, 1933. 111p.

06697 MUKHOPADHYAY, P. History of the Gajapati kings of Orissa and their successors. Calcutta: General Trading, 1953. 179p.

06698 NEMA, S.R. Political history of the Soma-Vamsi kings of south Kosala and Orissa. ND: Oriental, 1978. 331p.

06699 RAJAGURU, S.N. History of the Gaṅgas. Bhubaneswar: State Museum, 1968-72. 2 v., 224, 293p.

06700 RAMACHANDRA RAO, C.V. Administration and society in medieval Andhra (AD 1038-1538) under the later Eastern Gaṅgas and the Sūrya-vaṁśa Gajapatis. Nellore: Manasa, 1976. 394p.

06701 SUBUDDHI, U. The Bhauma-karas of Orissa. Calcutta: Punthi Pustak, 1978. 187p. +7pl.

3. The Gondwānā, Bāghelkhaṇḍ, and Bundelkhaṇḍ Areas of Central India: Tribal States and the Candella Dynasty

06702 BOSE, N.S. History of the Chandellas of Jejakabhukti. Calcutta: KLM, 1956. 213p.

06703 MIRASHI, V.V. Inscriptions of the Kalachuri-Chedi era. Ootacamund: Govt. Epigraphist, 1955. 2 v.

06704 MITRA, S.K. The early rulers of Khajuraho. Calcutta: KLM, 1958. 253p.

06705 POGSON, W.R. A history of the Boondelas. Delhi: B.R., 1974. 174p. + 9pl. [Rpt. 1928 ed.]

06706 VIDYA PRAKASH. Khajuraho; a study in the cultural conditions of Chandella society. Bombay: Taraporevala, 1967. 217p.

06707 WILLS, C.U. The territorial system of the Rajput Kingdoms of mediaeval Chhattisgarh. In JASB ns 15 (1920) 197-262.

4. The Pivotal Mālwā Plateau: the Rajput Paramāras/Pawārs of Dhār and Later Muslim Rulers

06708 BHATIA, P. The Paramāras, c. 800-1305 A.D. ND: Munshiram, 1970. 443p.

06709 DAY, U.N. Medieval Malwa; a political and cultural history, 1401-1562. Delhi: Munshiram, 1965. 452p.

06710 GANGULY, D.C. The history of the Paramāra dynasty. Dacca: Dacca U., 1933. 387p. (Dacca U. bull., 17)

06711 SETH, K.N. The growth of the Paramara power in Malwa. Bhopal: Progress Publishers, 1978. 261p.

5. Hindu and Muslim Kingdoms of the Gujarāt Area

06712 BAYLEY, E.C. The local Muhammadan dynasties; Gujarat. London: W.H. Allen, 1886. 519p.

06713 CHAUBE, J. History of Gujarat Kingdom. ND: Munshiram, 1975. 320p.

06714 COMMISSARIAT, M.S. A history of Gujarat. Bombay: Orient Longmans, 1938. 2 v. [v. 1, Pre-Muslim to 1572]

06715 DESAI, Z.A. Mirʿat-i-Sikandarī as a source for the study of cultural and social conditions of Gujarat under the sultanate, 1403-1572. In JOIB 10 (1961) 235-78.

06716 ______. Muslims in the 13th century Gujarat, as known from Arabic inscriptions. In JOIB 10 (1961) 353-64.

06717 JANAKI, V.A. Gujarat as the Arabs knew it; a study in historical geography. Baroda: MSUB, 1969. 84p.

06718 LOKHANDWALA, M.F., tr. Zefar al wālih bi muzaffar wa ālihi; an Arabic history of Gujarat...by Abdullāh Muhammed al-Makki al-Āṣafi al-Ulughkhani Ḥajji ad-Dabir. Baroda: MSUB, 1970-74. 2 v., 1055p. (GOS, 152, 157)

06719 MAJUMDAR, A.K. Chaulukyas of Gujarat; a survey of the history and culture of Gujarat from the middle of the tenth to the end of the thirteenth century. Bombay: BVB, 1956. 545p.

06720 MISRA, S.C. Muslim communities in Gujarat, preliminary studies in their history and social organization. Bombay: Asia, 1964. 207p.

06721 ______. The rise of Muslim power in Gujarat; a history of Gujarat form 1209 to 1442. London: Asia, 1963. 252p.

06722 TIRMIZI, S.A.I. Some aspects of medieval Gujarat. Delhi: Munshiram, 1968. 150p.

06723 VIRJI, K.J. Ancient history of Saurashtra. Bombay: 1952. 354p.

6. The Rajasthan Area: Emergence of the Rajput Military Aristocracy, the Hindu Bulwark against Islam

a. Bardic poetry and other sources of medieval Rajput history

06724 HOERNLE, A.F.R., tr. The Prithvirāja rāsau [of Chand Bardāī]. Pt. 2, fasc. 1. Calcutta: Asiatic Society, 1881. (BI, 77)

06725 SARAN, P. Descriptive catalog of non-Persian sources of medieval Indian history, covering Rajasthan and adjacent regions. NY: Asia, 1965. 234p.

06726 SMITH, J.D. Introduction to the language of the historical documents from Rājasthān. In MAS 9,4 (1975) 433-64.

06727 SMITH, J.D., tr. The Vīsaladevarāsa. Cambridge: CamUP, 1976. 335p.

06728 TESSITORI, L.P. Bardic and historical survey of Rajputana. Scheme for the bardic and historical survey of Rajputana. In JASBengal 10 (1914) 373-410.

06729 VAUDEVILLE, C. Les duhās de Dhola-mārū; une ancienne ballade du Rajasthan. Pondicherry: IFI, 1962. 148p.

06730 WATERFIELD, W., tr. The lay of Alha, a saga of Rajput chivalry as sung by minstrels of northern India. London: OUP, 1923. 278p.

b. general studies of Rajput history (c. 600-1526 AD)

06731 AHLUWALIA, M.S. Muslim expansion in Rajasthan: the relations of Delhi Sultanate with Rajasthan, 1206-1526. Delhi: Yugantar, 1978. 247p.

06732 ASOPA, J.N. Origin of the Rajputs. Delhi: Bharatiya, 1976. 282p. (Studies in Rajput history & culture, 1)

06733 AWASTHI, A.B.L. Rajput politics. Lucknow: Kailash Prakashan, 1964. 95p.

06734 CHATTOPADHYAYA, B.D. Origin of the Rajputs: the political, economic, and social processes in early medieval Rajasthan. In IHR 3,1 (1976) 59-82.

06735 DAY, U.N. Mewar under Maharana Kumbha, 1433 A.D.-1468 A.D. ND: Rajesh, 1978. 194p.

06736 HAMEED-UD-DIN. The Lodi Sultans and the Rajput states. In JIH 39 (1961) 313-26.

06737 JAIN, K.C. Ancient cities and towns of Rajasthan; a study of culture and civilization. Delhi: Motilal, 1972. 645p.

06738 SHARMA, D. Early Chauhān dynasties: a study of Chauhān political history, Chauhān political institutions, and life in the Chauhān dominions, from 800 to 1316 A.D. 2nd rev. ed. Delhi: Motilal, 1975. 407p. [1st pub. 1959]

06739 _____. SHARMA, D. Lectures on Rajput history and culture. Delhi: Motilal, 1970. 165p.

06740 SINGH, R.B. History of the Cāhamānas. Varanasi: Nand Kishore, 1964. 486p.

06741 _____. Origin of the Rajputs. Gorakhpur: Sahitya Sansar Prakashan, 1975. 296p.

B. Religio-Philosophical Traditions, incl. the Rise and Dominance of Bhakti and Sufi Movements in Middle India (c. 600-1526 AD)

1. General Studies

06742 PAHADIYA, S.M. Buddhism in Malwa. ND: K.B. Pub., 1976. 182p.

06743 PANSE, M.G. Religion and politics in the early Medieval Deccan (AD 1000-1350). In JIH 45 (1967) 673-87.

2. The Early Mahārāshṭrian Santas: the Vārkarī Pantha (Cult of Viṭhobā at Paṇḍharpur) and the Beginnings of Marāṭhī Literature

a. general studies and selected translations

06744 ABBOTT, J.E., tr. Bhanudās. Poona: Scottish Mission Industries, 1926. 49 + 55p. (Poet-saints of Maharashtra, 1) [from Mahīpati's Bhaktavijaya, chapters 42,43]

06745 _____,tr. Stotramālā. A garland of Hindu prayers. Poona: Scottish Mission Industries, 1929. 331p. (Poet-saints of Maharashtra, 6)

06746 ABBOTT, J.E. & N.R. GODBOLE, tr. Nectar from Indian saints; an English translation of Mahīpati's Marathi Bhaktalīlāmrita, chapters 1-12, 41-51. Poona: Aryabhushan Press, 1935. 498p. (Poet-saints of Maharashtra, 11)

06747 _____,tr. Stories of Indian saints: an English translation of Mahīpati's Marathi Bhaktavijaya. Poona: Aryabhushan Press, 1933-34. 2 v. (Poet-saints of Maharashtra, 9-10)

06748 GAJENDRAGADKAR, K.V. The Mahārāshṭra saints and their teachings. In Cultural heritage of India. Calcutta: RMIC, 1956, v. 4, 356-76.

06749 KHANOLKAR, S. Saints of Maharashtra. Bombay: BVB, 1978. 179p.

06750 KINCAID, C.A., tr. Tales of the saints of Paṇḍharpur. Bombay: OUP, 1919. 120p. [from Mahīpati's Bhaktavijaya]

06751 MACNICOL, N. Psalms of Maratha saints, 108 hymns translated from the Marathi. Calcutta: Association Press, 1920. 94p.

06752 PATEL, B. The rosary and the lamp. Bombay: Girnar Publications, 1966. 247p.

06753 RANADE, R.D. Pathway to God in Marathi literature. Bombay: BVB, 1961. 337p.

06754 SARDAR, G.B. The saint-poets of Maharashtra: their impact on society. Tr. by K.A. Mehta. Bombay: Orient Longmans, 1969. 160p.

06755 UPADHYAYA, B. Vārakarī: the foremost Vaiṣṇava sect of Mahārāṣṭra. In IHQ 15 (1939) 265-77.

06756 UPADHYE, P.M. Saint literature in Marathi. In Ind Lit 19,5 (1976) 49-62.

b. Jñāneśvara/Dnyāndev (1275-1296 AD), protegé of the Yādava king of Devagiri, and first religious poet in Marathi; the Jñāneśvarī, his verse commentary on the Gītā

06757 BAHIRAT, B.P. The philosophy of Jñānadeva. Pandharpur: Pandharpur Res. Soc., 1956. 220p.

06758 _____,tr. Amritānubhava. Bombay: Popular, 1963. 93p.

06759 BHAGWAT, R.K., tr. Sri Jñānadeva's Bhāvārtha dīpika: otherwise known as Jnāneshwarī. Madras: Samata Books, 1979. 689p.

06760 DANDEKAR, S.V. Dnyānadeo. ND: Maharashtra Information Centre, 1967. 94p.

06761 EDWARDS, J.F. Dnyāneshwar, the out-caste brahmin. Poona: the author, 1941. 525p. (Poet-saints of Maharashtra, 12)

06762 PRADHAN, V.G., tr. Jñāneshvarī (Bhāvārthadīpika); a song-sermon on the Bhagavadgītā. Tr. from the Marathi. Ed., with an intro. by H.M. Lambert. London: Allen & Unwin, 1967-69. 2 v., 336, 352p. (UNESCO series)

06763 SARAF, R.N. Shri Jñāneshwar: comparative & critical study of his philosophy. Belgaum: Academy of Comparative Philosophy and Religion, 1975. 78p.

06764 SEN, G.C. Saint Jñānadeva of Maharashtra (1275-1314). In IL 25,3 (1971) 34-40.

06765 SHARMA, S.R. Teachings of Jñānadeva. Bombay: BVB, 1965. 47p.

06766 SUBEDAR, M., tr. Gītā explained. Bombay: the author, 1945. 318p. [English prose trans. of Jnāneshvarī]

06767 VAUDEVILLE, C. The cult of the divine name in the Haripāṭh of Dñāndev. In WZKS 12/13 (1968-69) 395-406.

06768 _____,tr. L'invocation. Le Haripāṭh de Dnyāndev. Paris: EFEO, 1969. 170p. (Its pub., 73)

c. Nāmadeva (1270-1350 AD), a tailor by caste and travelling Bhakta; propagandist of nāma-kīrtan, "repetition of the names" of God

06769 KARANDIKAR, M.A. Namdev. ND: Maharashtra Information Centre, 1970. 30p.

06770 MACHWE, P.B. Namdev: life & philosophy. Patiala: Punjabi U., 1968. 142p.

06771 NĀMADEVA. Saint Nāmdeva: selected poems. Beas: Radha Soami Satsang Beas, 1977. 132p.

3. The Mahānubhāva/Mānbhāo Sect Founded by Cakradhara under the Yādavas (13th cent. AD): Esoteric Kṛṣṇa Devotees and Rivals of the Vārkarīs

06772 FELDHAUS, A. The Devatācakra of the Mahānubhāvas. In BSOAS 43,1 (1980) 101-09.

06773 JOSHI, P.M. Glimpses of history in Mahānubhāva texts. In Indica 13,1/2 (1976) 67-74.

06774 RAESIDE, I.M.P. A bibliographical index of Mahānubhāva works in Marathi. In BSOAS 23,3 (1960) 464-507.

06775 ______. The Mahānubhāvas. In SOAS 39,3 (1976) 585-600.

06776 VERMA, O.P. The Mahānubhāva sect: a reassessment. In NUJ 19,1/2 (1968) 34-41.

4. Gujarat and Rajasthan: Trends in Religion and Religious Literature - Hindu, Jain, Muslim
a. general

06777 DAVE, S.K. The minor Purāṇas of Gujarat: a brief survey. In Purāṇa 17,2 (1975) 149-62.

06778 KALANI, K.L. Saint literature in Gujarati. In IL 19,5 (1976) 36-48.

06779 RAIKAR, Y.A. Śrī Cakradhar: a medieval saint from Gujarat. In JOIB 12 (1962) 113-118.

06780 SHARMA, G.N. Śaivism in medieval Rajasthan. In ALB 28 (1964) 221-30.

b. Narasiṁha Mahetā/Mehtā (1414-1481 AD) and Gujarātī bhakti

06781 MALLISON, F. Notes on the biography of Narasiṁha Mahetā. In ABORI 55,1-4 (1975) 189-201.

06782 NARASIṀHA MEHETĀ. English version of the selected poems of Mehtā Narsiṅha. Junagadh: Shantiprasad Parmanandas Vaishnav, 1979. 75p.

c. Mīrābāī (1515-1546 AD): Rajput princess and Kṛṣṇa devotee, from Mewār to Dwārkā

06783 BANKEY BEHARI. Bhakta Mira. 2nd ed. Bombay: BVB, 1971. 190p.

06784 GOETZ, H. Mira Bai; her life and times. Bombay: BVB, 1966. 45p.

06785 KURAL, S., tr. The devotional poems of Mirabai. Calcutta: Writers Workshop, 1973. 87p.

06786 MEHTA, S.S. Mirabai, the saint of Mewad. Bombay: S.S. Mehta Bhatwadi Girgaon, 133p.

06787 NILSSON, U.S. Mira Bai. ND: Sahitya Akademi, 1969. 70p.

06788 PANDEY, S.M. Mīrābāī and her contributions to the Bhakti movement. In HR 5 (1965) 54-73.

06789 TANDAN, R.C., tr. Songs of Mirabai. Allahabad: Hindi Mandir, 1934. 72p.

d. Jaina religion and religious literature

06790 ARAI, T. Jaina kingship as viewed in the Prabandhacintāmaṇi. In J.F. Richards, ed. Kingship and authority in South Asia. Madison: South Asian Studies, U. of Wisconsin, 1978, 74-114. (Its Pub. series, 3)

06791 BAUMANN, G., tr. Drei Jaina-Gedichte in Alt-Gujarātī. Wiesbaden: Steiner, 1975. 176p.

06792 MOOKERJEE, S., tr. Hemacandra's Pramāna-mīmāṁsā. Varanasi: Tara Pub., 1970. 29 + 82p. (Prachya Bharati series, 11)

06793 NARANG, S.P. Hemacandra's Dvyasrayakavya: a literary and cultural study. ND: Devvani Prakashan, 1972. 21 + 283p.

06794 SHARMA, J.P. The life and scholarship of a Jaina monk. In As. Prof. 3 (1975) 195-215. [Hemachandra]

06795 SHETH, C.B. Jainism in Gujarat (AD 1100 to 1600). Bombay: Shree Vijaydevsur Sangh Gnan Samity, 1953. 282p.

06796 VIDYABHUSANA, A.C., tr. Gujarat Jaina jātakas, or Lord Ṛshabha's Pūrvabhāvas; being an English trans. of Book 1, Canto 1 of Hemacandra's Trishashtiśalāka-purusha-carita. Lahore: Punjab Sanskrit Book Depot, 1925. 118p. (Its series, 8)

e. Islam and Muslim life in Gujarat and Rajasthan

06797 ANSARI, A.S. Sayyid Muhammad Jawnpuri and his movement: a historico-heresiological study of the Mahdiyyah in the Indo-Pakistan sub-continent. In Islamic studies 2 (1963) 41-74.

06798 NIZAMI, K.A. Shaikh Ahmad Maghribi as a great historical personality of medieval Gujarat. In Medieval India 3 (1975) 234-59.

06799 QURAISHI, M.A. Muslim education and learning in Gujarat, 1297-1758. Baroda: MSUB, 1972. 328p.

06800 SALMIN, M.A. The holy saint of Ajmer. Bombay: the author, 1949. 85p.

06801 SHARAB, A.H. The life and teachings of Khawaja Moinud-din Hasan Chishti. Ajmer: Khawaja Pub., 1959. 98p.

5. Orissa: Religion and Literature [For Caitanya, see also X. C. 3. e. below]

06802 DASH, M.P. Interrelation between Vaiṣṇavism and Śaktism in Orissa. In OHRJ 11 (1964) 273-281.

06803 MUKHERJEE, P. History of the Chaitanya faith in Orissa. ND: Manohar, 1979. 126p.

06804 MUKHOPADHYAY, P. The history of medieval Vaishnavism in Orissa. Calcutta: R. Chatterjee, 1940. 200p.

06805 SEN, P.R. Oriya literature in the early stages. In D.R. Bhandarkar, ed. B.C. Law Volume. Pt. 2. Poona: BORI, 1946, 197-207.

C. Art and Architecture in Early Medieval Middle India (600-1526 AD)

1. General Studies

06806 TRIVEDI, H.V. Cultural affinity of Gujarat and Malwa. In JOIB 6 (1955-56) 99-102.

06807 VIENNOT, O. Temples de l'Inde centrale et occidentale. Étude stylistique et essai de chronologie relative du VIe au milieu de Xe siècle. Paris: Maisonneuve, 1976. 2 v., 265p. + 71pl.

2. Maharashtra
a. general studies

06808 DEO, S.B. Mārkaṇḍi temples. Nagpur: Nagpur U., 1973. 58p.

06809 GANGOLY, O.C. The art of the Rashtrakutas. Bombay: Orient Longmans, 1958. 26p. + 40pl.

06810 GUPTE, R.S. & B.D. MAHAJAN. Ajanta, Ellora and Aurangabad caves. Bombay: Taraporevala, 1962. 288p.

06811 SPINK, W. Ajaṇṭā to Ellorā. Bombay: Mārg, for UMCSSAS, 1967. 67p. [Also in Mārg 29,2 (1967) 6-67]

06812 VERMA, O.P. A survey of Hemāḍpanti temples in Maharashtra. Nagpur: Nagpur U., 1973. 31p. + 36pl. (Temples of the Vidarbha Region, 2)

b. Buddhist cave sculptures at Aurangabad (7th cent. AD)

06813 ANAND, M.R. The Lesser Vehicle, The Greater Vehicle and the Worshippers of the Many Gods: (The background of the Aurangabad cave sculptures). In Mārg 16,3 (1963) 15-33.

06814 LEVINE, D.B. Aurangabad: a stylistic analysis. In ArtAs 28 (1966) 175-204.

06815 RAY, A. Aurangabad sculptures. Calcutta: KLM, 1966. 49p.

c. Ellora: cave temples and sculptures - Buddhist (c. 350-700 AD), Brahmanical (7th-8th cent. AD), and Jain (8th-13th cent. AD)

06816 BURGESS, J. Report on the Elura cave temples and the Brahmanical and Jaina caves in western India; completing the results of the fifth, sixth, and seventh seasons' operations of the Archaeological Survey, 1877-78, 1878-79, 1879-80. Varanasi: IndBH, 1970. 89p. (Archaeological survey of western India, 5) [1st pub. 1882]

06817 CHATHAM, D.C. Stylistic sources and relationships of the Kailāsa temple at Ellora. Ph.D. diss., U. of California at Berkeley, 1977. 398p. [UM 77-31,315]

06818 GOETZ, H. The Kailasa of Ellora and the chronology of Rashtrakuta art. In his Studies in the history, religion and art of classical and medieval India. Ed. by Hermann Kulke. Wiesbaden: Steiner, 1974, 91-107. [1st pub. in ArtAs 15,1/2 (1952) 84-107]

06819 GUPTE, R.S. The iconography of the Buddhist sculptures (caves) of Ellora. Aurangabad: Marathwada U., 1964. 164p.

06820 PEREIRA, J. Monolithic Jinas [the iconography of the Jain Temples of Ellora]. Delhi: Motilal, 1977. 185p. + 7pl.

06821 RANADE, P.V. Ellora paintings. Aurangabad: Parimal, 1980. 82p. + 21pl.

06822 SEELY, J.B. The wonders of Elora: or, The narrative of a journey to the temples and dwellings excavated out of a mountain of granite and extending upwards of a mile and a quarter at Elora, in the East Indies, by the route of Poona, Ahmed-Nuggur, and Toka, returning by Dowlutabad and Aurungabad, with some general observations on the people and country. 2nd ed. with considerable additions and improvements. Delhi: B.R., 1975. 597p. + 12pl. [Rpt. 1825 ed.]

06823 SPINK, W. Ellora's earliest phase. In Bulletin of the American Academy of Benares 1 (1967) 11-22.

06824 TIWARI, R.G. The Daśavatāra cave (no. XV) of Ellora: its time. In PO 26 (1961) 24-40.

d. Brahmanical cave-temples of Elephanta (Ghārapurī) Island in Bombay Harbor (450-750 AD)

06825 BURGESS, J. The rock-temples of Elephanta. Bombay: D.H. Sykes, 1871. 80p.

06826 CHANDRA, PRAMOD. Elephanta caves, Gharapuri; a pictorial guide. Rev. ed. Bombay: Bhulabhai Mem. Inst., 1970. 10p. + 30pl.

06827 GUPTE, R.S. The dating of the Elephanta caves. In JIH 43,2 (1965) 513-30.

06828 NEFF, M. Elephanta. In Mārg 8,4 (1960) 20-60.

06829 SASTRI, HIRANAND. A guide to Elephanta. ND: Kanak, 1978. 84p. + 32pl. [Rpt. of 1934 ed., with new essay by Ratan Parimoo, 54-78]

3. Art and Architecture of the Gujarat-Rajasthan-Malwa Area (600-1526 AD)

a. general studies

06830 SHAH, U.P. & K.K. GANGULI, eds. Western Indian art. In JISOA special no. (1965-66) 94p. + 51pl.

b. Western Indian painting

06831 BROWN, W.N. A descriptive and illustrated catalogue of miniature paintings of the Jaina Kalpasūtra as executed in the early western Indian style. Washington: Smithsonian Inst., 1934. 66p. + 45pl. (Freer Gallery, Oriental studies, 2)

06832 ______. Early Śvetāmbara Jaina miniatures. In Indian Art and Letters 3,1 (1929) 1-11.

06833 ______. Early Vaiṣṇava miniature paintings from Western India. In his India and Indology. Delhi: Motilal, 1978, 215-42. [1st pub. in Eastern Art 2(1930) 167-206]

06834 ______. A Jaina manuscript from Gujarat illustrated in early Western Indian and Persian styles. In Ars Islamica 4 (1937) 154-72.

06835 ______. Manuscript illustrations of the Uttarādhyayana sūtra. New Haven: AOS, 1941. 54p. (AOS, 21)

06836 ______. The story of Kālaka; texts, history, legends, and miniature paintings of the Śvetāmbara Jain hagiographical work, the Kālakācāryakathā. Washington: Smithsonian Inst., 1933. 149p. + 15pl. (Freer Gallery, Oriental studies, 1)

06837 ______. Stylistic varieties of early Western Indian miniature painting about 1400 A.D. In JISOA 5 (1937) 2-12.

06838 ______,tr. The Vasanta vilāsa; a poem of the spring festival in Old Gujarati accompanied by Sanskrit and Prakrit stanzas and illustrated with miniature paintings. New Haven: AOS, 1962. 251p. (AOS, 46)

06839 COOMARASWAMY, A.K. Catalogue of the Indian collections.... Part 4: Jaina paintings and manuscripts. Boston: Museum of Fine Arts, 1924. 74p. + 39pl.

06840 GOETZ, H. Decline and rebirth of medieval Indian art: Western Indian painting. In Marg 4,2 (1950) 36-48 + 8pl.

06841 KHANDALAVALA, K. & MOTI CHANDRA. An illustrated Kalpasūtra painted at Jaunpur in AD 1465. In LK 12 (1962) 9-15 & 9pl.

06842 MOTI CHANDRA. Jain miniature paintings from Western India. Ahmedabad: Sarabhai Manilal Nawab, 1949. 199p. + 100pl.

06843 MOTI CHANDRA & U.P. SHAH. New documents of Jaina painting. Bombay: Shri Mahavira Jaina Vidyalaya, 1975. 104p. + 41pl.

06844 NAWAB, SARABHAI MANILAL. Masterpieces of Kalpasūtra paintings. Ahmedabad: 1956. 23 + 82p. (Jain art pub. ser., 7)

06845 ______. The oldest Rajasthani paintings from Jain bhandars. Ahmedabad: 1959. 81p. + 140p. of ill. (Jain art pub. ser., 5)

c. sculpture

06846 DIKSHIT, M.G. Some Buddhist bronzes from Sirpur, Madhya Pradesh. In PWMB 5 (1955-57) 1-11.

06847 KUMAR, K. A Dhyāna-yoga Maheśamūrti, and some reflections on the iconography of the Maheśamūrti images. In ArtAs 37,1/2 (1975) 105-20.

06848 MAJMUDAR, H.A. Some medieval sculptures of North Gujarat. Ahmedabad: Gujarat U., 1968. 200p.

06849 NANAVATI, J.M. & M.A. DHAKY. The ceilings in the temples of Gujarat. Baroda: Gujarat Dept. of Archaeology, 1963. 117p. [Pub. as Bull. of the Museum & Picture Gallery, Baroda, 16/17 (1963-64)]

06850 SHAH, U.P. Bronze hoard from Vasantagadh. In LK 1/2 (1955-56) 55-65.

06851 ______. Western Indian sculpture and the so-called Gupta influence. In P. Pal, ed. Aspects of Indian art. Leiden: Brill, 1972, 44-48.

06852 SOUNDARA RAJAN, K.V. Some iconographic elements of pre-medieval Rajasthan temples. In LK 8 (1960) 15-24.

d. architecture
i. texts on Jain and Hindu temple architecture

06853 BHATTACHARYA, T. The canons of Indian art; or, a study of Vastuvidyā. 2nd ed. Calcutta: KLM, 1963. [1st pub. 1947]

06854 SOMPURA, P.O. The Vastuvidyā of Viśvakarma. In Pramod Chandra, ed. Studies in Indian temple architecture.... ND: AIIS, 1975, 47-56.

ii. temples of Gujarat, Rajasthan, and Malwa

06855 AGRAWALA, R.C. An early Pratihāra temple at Buchkala. In BV 27 (1967) 55-58 + 6p. of ill.

06856 ______. Khajurāho of Rajasthan: the Temple of Āmbikā at Jagat. In ArtsAs 10,1 (1964) 43-65.

06857 BANERJI, A. Monuments of Bijolya. In JAS Calcutta 7,1/2 (1965) 99-106 + 10pl.

06858 COUSENS, H. Somanatha and other medieval temples in Kathiawad. Calcutta: Govt. of India Central Pub. Branch, 1931. 92p. (ASI new imperial ser., 45)

06859 DHAKY, M.A. Brahmāṇasvāmi temple at Varman. In JOIB 14 (1965) 381-87.

06860 ______. The chronology of the Solaṅki temples of Gujarat. In J. of the Madhya Pradesh Itihasa Parishad 3 (1961) 1-83.

06861 ______. The genesis and development of Māru-Gurjara temple architecture. In Pramod Chandra, ed. Studies in Indian Temple Architecture.... ND: AIIS, 1974, 114-165.

06862 ______. Kiradu and the Māru-Gurjara style of temple architecture. In Bulletin of the American Academy of Benares 1 (1967) 35-46.

06863 ______. Some early Jaina temples in Western India. In Shri Mahavira Jaina Vidyalaya Golden Jubilee Volume. Bombay: Shri Mahavira Jaina Vidyalaya, 1968, 290-347.

06864 ______. The temple of Mahāvīra at Ahar and the Viṣṇu temple, Ekliṅgjī. In JAS Calcutta 14 (1972) 11-17.

06865 GAUDANI, H.R. & M.A. DHAKY. The Mūlanāthadeva temple in Maṇḍali. In JGRS 29 (1967) 253-57.

06866 ______. Some newly discovered and less known Māru-Gurjara temples in northern Gujarat. In JOIB 17 (1967) 149-56.

06867 GOETZ, H. Osiān, one of the first monuments of medieval Indian art. In his Studies in the history, religion and art of classical and medieval India. Ed. by H. Kulke. Wiesbaden: Steiner, 1974, 87-90. (SSI, 16) [1st pub. in Western Railway Magazine (1953)]

06868 KRISHNA DEVA. Bhūmija temples. In Pramod Chandra, ed. Studies in Indian Temple Architecture, ND: AIIS, 1974, 90-113.

06869 ______. Extensions of Gupta art: art and architecture of the Pratīhāra age. In Moti Chandra, ed. Seminar on Indian Art History 1962. ND: Lalit Kala Akademi, n.d., 85-106.

06870 MEISTER, M.W. A preliminary report on the Śiva temple at Kusumā. In Archives of Asian Art 27 (1973-4) 76-90.

06871 NANAVATI, J.M. & M.A. DHAKY. The Maitraka and the Saindhava monuments of Gujarat. In BV 22,1/4 (1962) 33-42.

06872 ______. The Maitraka and the Saindhava monuments of Gujarat. Ascona: Artibus Asiac, 1969. 83p. (ArtAs suppl., 26)

06873 SOMPURA, K.F. The structural temples of Gujarat, up to 1600 A.D. Ahmedabad: Gujarat U., 1968. 560p. + 61pl. + 165p. of ill.

06874 SOUNDARA RAJAN, K.V. Architectural affiliations of early Saurashtra temples. In IHQ 37 (1961) 1-7.

06875 VIENNOT, O. Un type rare de temple à trois chapelles au site d' Āmvān (Rajasthan). In ArtsAs 26 (1973) 125-156.

iii. Muslim architecture

06876 BURGESS, J. On the Muhammadan architecture of Bharoch, Cambay, Dholka, Champanir, and Mahmudabad in Gujarat. Delhi: IndBH, 1971. 47p. + 77pl. (Archaeol. survey of western India, 6) [1st pub. 1896]

06877 ______. The Muhammadan architecture of Ahmadabad. Calcutta: Thacker, Spink, 1900-1905. 2 v., 196p. + 197pl.

06878 DHAKY, M.A. The minarets of the Hilāl Khān Qāẓi Mosque, Dhoḷkā. In JASCalcutta 14,1 (1972) 18-24.

06879 YAZDANI, G. Mandu: The City of Joy. Dhār: [Oxford printed], 1929. 131p. + 4pl.

4. Hindu and Jain Architecture of the Bundelkhaṇḍ-Bāghelkhaṇḍ Area

a. Khajurāho: capital of the Candellas and site of 30 temples constructed 950-1050 AD

06880 AGARWAL, U. Khajuraho sculptures and their significance. Delhi: S. Chand, 1964. 220p.

06881 ANAND, M.R. & C. FABRI & S. KRAMRISCH. Homage to Khajuraho. 2nd ed. Bombay: Marg Pub., 1962. 68p.

06882 BALASUBRAHMANYAM, S.R. Khajuraho. In JORM 29 (1959-60) 67-78.

06883 CHANDRA, PRAMOD. The Kaula-Kāpālika cults at Khajurāho. In LK 1/2 (1955-56) 98-107.

06884 DHAMA, B.L. & S.C. CHANDRA. Khajuraho. ND: MPGOI, 1953. 36p. + 212pl.

06885 FLORY, M. Les temples de Khajuraho. Paris: Delpire, 1965. 162p.

06886 GOETZ, H. The historical background of the great temples of Khajuraho. In his Studies in the history, religion, and art of classical and medieval India. Ed. by H. Kulke. Wiesbaden: Steiner, 1974, 108-21. (SSI, 16) [1st pub. in ArtsAs 5 (1958)]

06887 KRISHNA DEVA. Krishṇa-Līlā scenes in the Lakshmaṇa temple, Khajurāho. In LK (1960) 82-90.

06888 ______. The temples of Khajuraho in Central India. In AI 15 (1959) 43-65.

06889 LAL, KANWAR. Apsaras of Khajuraho. Delhi: Asia Press, 1966. 34p.

06890 ______. Immortal Khajuraho. Delhi: Asia Press, 1965. 253p. + 234pl.

06891 MEISTER, M.W. Juncture and conjunction: punning and temple architecture. In ArtsAs 41 (1979) 226-235.

06892 NATH, R. The art of Khajuraho. ND: Abhinav, 1980. 181p. + 64pl.

06893 TRIPATHI, L.K. Dīkpāla images on the Khajurāho temples. In Bharati 9,2 (1965-66) 103-135.

06894 VIDYA PRAKASH. Khajuraho; a study in the cultural conditions of Chandella society. Bombay: Taraporevala, 1967. 217p.

06895 ZANNAS, E. Khajurāho; text and photos. With intro. by J. Auboyer. The Hague: Mouton, 1960. 227p. + 91pl.

b. other sites in Bundelkhaṇḍ-Bāghelkhaṇḍ

06896 BANERJI, R.D. The Haihayas of Tripuri and their monuments. Calcutta: Govt. of India Pub., 1931. 152p. + 57pl. (ASI memoirs, 23)

06897 BRUHN, K. The Jina-images of Deogarh. Leiden: Brill, 1969. 520p. (SSAC, 1)

06898 NATH, R. The art of Chanderi: a study of the 15th century monuments of Chanderi. ND: Ambika, 1979. 67p. + 14pl.

06899 SHARMA, R.K. The temple of Chaunsaṭha-yoginī at Bheraghat. Delhi: Agam Kala, 1978. 184p. + 75pl.

5. Art and Architecture of Early Medieval Orissa

a. general studies

06900 ACHARYA, P. Studies in the temple architecture in Orissa. In OHRJ 12,1 (1964) 9-21.

06901 DEHEJIA, V. Early stone temples of Orissa. ND: Vikas, 1979. 217p.

06902 DONALDSON, T. Propitious-apotropaic eroticism in the art of Orissa. In ArtAs 37,1/2 (1975) 75-100.

06903 GANGOLY, O.C. Orissan sculpture and architecture. Calcutta: Oxford Book and Stationery, 1956. 21p. + 41pl.

06904 MAHAPATRA, K.N. Note on the hypaethral temple of sixty-four yoginis at Hirapur. In OHRJ 2 (1953) 23-40.

06905 MITRA, D. Bronzes from Achutrajpur, Orissa. Delhi: Agam Kala, 1978. 185p. + 29pl.

06906 ______. Four little-known Khakhara temples of Orissa. In JASCalcutta 4th ser. 2,1 (1960) 1-23.

06907 PANIGRAHI, K.C. Bhauma art and architecture of Orissa. In ArtsAs 4 (1957) 275-92 + 23pl.

06908 SARASWATI, S.K. Temples of Orissa. In OHRJ 1 (1952) 233-253.

06909 WILLETTS, W. An 8th century Buddhist monastic foundation; excavation at Ratnāgiri in the Cuttack district of Orissa. In OA 9 (1963) 15-21. [Also in Asian R. ns 1 (1964) 19-33]

b. Sanskrit texts on temple construction in the Orissan tradition

06910 BONER, A. Extracts from the Śilpasārinī. In Pramod Chandra, ed. Studies in Indian temple architecture. ND: AIIS, 1975, 57-79.

06911 BONER, A. & S.R. SARMA, tr. Śilpa prakāśa; medieval Orissan Sanskrit text on temple architecture by Rāmacandra Kaulacāra . Leiden: Brill, 1966. 177p. + 72pl. + 102p. of Sanskrit text.

06912 BOSE, N.K. Canons of Orissan architecture. Calcutta: R. Chatterjee, 1932. 191p.

c. Bhuvaneśvara/Bhubaneshwar: "temple-city" built 8th-13th cent. AD

06913 DE, S.C. Svarṇa Jaleśwar, one of the early temples of Bhubaneswar. In OHRJ 10,4 (1962) 18-22.

06914 LAL, KANWAR. Temples and sculptures of Bhubaneswar. Delhi: Arts & Letters, 1970. 124p. + 63p. of ill.

06915 PANIGRAHI, K.C. Archaeological remains at Bhubaneshwar. Bombay: Orient Longmans, 1961. 274p.

d. Konārak: temple of Sūrya in the form of the Sun God's chariot

06916 BONER, A. & S.R. SARMA, tr. New light on the Sun Temple of Konārka; four unpublished manuscripts relating to construction, history, and ritual of this temple. Varanasi: CSSO, 1972. 283p.

06917 EBERSOLE, R. Black pagoda. Gainesville: U. of Florida Press, 1957. 105p.

06918 ELISOFON, E. Erotic spirituality; the vision of Konarak. NY: Macmillan, 1971. 125p.

06919 GANGOLY, D.C. Konarak. Calcutta: Jiten Bose, 1956. 36p.

06920 LAL, KANWAR. Miracle of Konark. Delhi: Asia Press, 1967. 85p.

06921 MEHTA, R.J. Konarak, the sun-temple of love. Bombay: Taraporevala, 1969. 46p.

06922 MITRA, D. Konarak. ND: ASI, 1968. 113p.

e. Mukhaliṅgam: temples of the Eastern Ganga dynasty, 13th cent.

06923 BARRETT, D.E. Mukhalingam temples. Bombay: N.M. Tripathi, 1960. 31p. + 83pl.

06924 SURYANARAYANA MURTY, A. Śrī Mukhaliṅgam temples, including the worship of Lord Śiva, his attributes. Bombay: BVB, 1978. 56p.

VIII. THE INDUS VALLEY IN THE EARLY MEDIEVAL PERIOD (600-1526 AD): SINDH, PANJAB, KASHMIR, AND THE NORTHWEST MOUNTAIN FRONTIER

A. General Histories by Major Sub-areas

1. Sindh and Baluchistan; the Early Arab Incursions

06925 BALUCH, M.S.K. The great Baluch; life and times of Ameer Chakar Rind, 1454-1551 A.D. Quetta: Baluchi Academy, 1965. 266p.

06926 MAJUMDAR, R.C. The Arab invasion of India. Lahore: Sheikh Mubarak Ali, 1974. 60p.

06927 PATHAN, M.H. Arab kingdom of al-Mansurah in Sind. Hyderabad: Institute of Sindhology, U. of Sind, 1974. 216p.

06928 TALUKDAR, M.H.R. The Arab invasions of Al-Sind and Al-Hind. In JPHS 14 (1966) 104-27.

2. Panjab, "Land of the Five Rivers": Avenue for Invasion, Trade, and Cultural Interchange

06929 BOSWORTH, C.E. The later Ghaznavids: splendour and decay. The dynasty in Afghanistan and Northern India, 1040-1186. NY: ColUP, 1977. 196p.

06930 FAUJA SINGH, ed. History of the Punjab; v. 3, AD 1000-1526. Patiala: Punjabi U., 1972. 420p.

06931 GOETZ, H. History of Chamba State in the later Middle Ages (c. AD 1190-1623/41). In his Studies in the history and art of Kashmir and the Indian Himalaya. Wiesbaden: Harrassowitz, 1969, 101-11. [1st pub. in JIH 30,3 (1952) 293-308]

06932 HABIB, M. Sultan Mahmud of Ghaznin. 2nd ed. Delhi: S. Chand, 1967. 128p. [1st ed. 1951]

06933 NAZIM, M. The life and times of Sultan Mahmud of Ghazna. ND: Munshiram, 1971. 271p. [Rpt. of 1931 ed.]

06934 NIJJAR, B.S. Panjāb under the sultāns, 1000-1526 A.D. Delhi: Sterling, 1968 . 253p.

06935 PRAKASH, BUDDHA. Evolution of heroic tradition in ancient Panjab. Patiala: Pubjabi U., 1971. 149p.

06936 SHARMA, S.R. The Ghaznavids in the Punjab. In JIH 46 (1968) 125-46.

3. Kashmir: Mountain Refuge of Hindu and Buddhist Culture during the Early Muslim Invasions; Beginning of Muslim Rule in 1339 AD

a. the Rājataraṅginī of Kalhaṇa (fl. 1148 AD): chronicle of the Hindu kings of Kashmir; other sources

06937 DHAR, K.N. Sanskrit chronicles and sultans of Kashmir. In Glimpses of Kashmiri Culture 3 (1977) 61-97.

06938 DHAR, S. Kalhana. ND: Sahitya Akademi, 1978. 85p.

06939 KOLVER, B., ed. Textkritische und philologische Untersuchungen zur Rājataraṅginī des Kalhaṇa. Wiesbaden: Steiner, 1971. 196p.

06940 PANDIT, R.S., tr. Rājataraṅginī; the saga of the kings of Kaśmir. Translated from the original Saṁskrita [of Kalhaṇa] and entitled The river of Kings. ND: Sahitya Akademi, 1968. 783p. [1st pub. 1935]

06941 STEIN, M.A., tr. Kalhaṇa's Rājataraṅginī: a chronicle of the kings of Kaśmīr. Delhi: Motilal, 1979. 2 v. [Rpt. 1900 ed.]

06942 VED KUMARI. The Nīlamata Purāṇa. Vol. I: A cultural and literary study of a Kaśmīrī Purāṇa. Srinagar: J. & K. Academy of Art, Culture and Languages, 1968. 256p.

06943 YASIN, M. Sources of the history of Kashmir. (10th-12th centuries). In QRHS 9,1 (1969-70) 33-40.

b. general studies of early medieval Kashmir

06944 GOETZ, H. The conquest of northern and western India by Lalitāditya-Muktāpīḍa of Kashmīr. In his Studies of the history and art of Kashmir and the Indian Himalaya. Wiesbaden: Harrassowitz, 1969, 8-22. [1st pub. in JBBRAS, 28,1 (1952) 43-58]

06945 HASAN, M. Kashmir under the Sultans. Calcutta: Iran Soc., 1959. 338p.

06946 KAPUR, M.L. Eminent rulers of ancient Kashmir: a detailed history of the life and rule of ten kings and queens of ancient Kashmir. Delhi: Oriental, 1975. 163p.

06947 ______. A history of medieval Kashmir, 1320-1586 A.D. Jammu: A.R.B. Pub., 1971. 266p.

06948 ______. Studies in the history and culture of Kashmir. Jammu: Trikuta, 1976. 256p. [8th-16th cent.]

06949 NAUDOU, J. L'autorité royale et ses limitations au Kaśmir medieval. In JA 251 (1963) 217-27.

06950 PARMU, R.K. A history of Muslim rule in Kashmir, 1320-1819. Delhi: PPH, 1969. 544p.

06951 RAY, S.C. Early history and culture of Kashmir. 2nd rev. ed. ND: Munshiram, 1970. 288p.

06952 SAXENA, K.S. Political history of Kashmir, B.C. 300-A.D. 1200. Lucknow: Upper India, 1974. 364p.

06953 TIKKU, G.L. Mysticism in Kashmir in the fourteenth and fifteenth centuries. In MW 53 (1963) 226-233.

06954 ZUTSHI, N.K. Sultan Zain-ul-Abadin of Kashmir; an age of enlightenment. Lucknow: Nupur Prakashan, 1976. 248p.

B. Religio-Philosophical Traditions: Buddhism, Hinduism, and Islam in the Early Medieval Indus Valley

1. Buddhism: Displacement by Śaivism and Islam, except for Lamaistic Remnants in Ladakh

06955 NAUDOU, J. Buddhists of Kaśmīr. 1st English ed. Delhi: Agam Kala, 1980. 308p. [Translation of Les bouddhistes kasmiriens au Moyen Age]

2. Kashmir Śaivism: Regional School Combining Monistic, Realistic, and Tantric Elements, Based on the Śaivāgamas and Śivasūtras

a. general studies of Kashmir Śaivism, called Trika ("Triad") School; the Śiva-sūtra

06956 CHATTERJI, J.C. Kashmir Shaivism. Srinagar: Govt. Res. and Publ Dept., 1962. 168p.

06957 JAIDEVA SINGH, tr. Śiva Sūtras: the yoga of supreme identity. Delhi: Motilal, 1979. 278p. [incl. Vimarsini commentary by Ksemaraja]

06958 ______,tr. Vijñānabhairava: or, Divine consciousness: a treasury of 112 types of yoga. Delhi: Motilal, 1979. 30 + 173p.

06959 KAW, R.K. The doctrine of recognition: (Pratyabhijñā philosophy); a study of its origin and development and place in Indian and western systems of philosophy. Hoshiarpur: VVRI, 1967. 398p. (VIS, 40)

06960 PANDIT, B.N. Aspects of Kashmir Śaivism. Srinagar: Utpal Pub., 1977. 239p.

06961 RASTOGI, N. Kālī as a metaphysical concept in the Karma system of Kashmir Shaivism. In JGJRI 22 (1965-66) 39-54.

06962 ______. The krama tantricism of Kashmir: historical and general sources. Delhi: Motilal, 1979-. v. 1, 283p.

06963 RUDRAPPA, J. Kashmir Śaivism. Mysore: U. of Mysore, 1969. 187p.

06964 SHARMA, L.N. Kasmir Śaivism. Varanasi: Bharatiya, 1972. 373p.

06965 TAIMNI, I.K., tr. The ultimate reality and realization: Śiva-sūtra. Madras: TPH, 1976. 215p.

b. Abhinavagupta (c. 1000): leading exponent and systematizer of Kashmir Śaivism. [for his work on poetics, see III. A. 2. e., above]; his teacher Utpaladeva, and his disciple, Kṣemarāja

06966 GNOLI, R., tr. Luce delle sacre scritture (Tantrāloka)... Torino: Unione tipografico-editrice torinese, 1972. 900p. (Classici delle religioni. Sezione 1: Le religioni orientali, 25) [by Abhinavagupta]

06967 JAIDEVA SINGH, tr. Pratyabhijñāhṛdayam [by Kṣemarāja]. 2nd rev. ed. Delhi: Motilal, 1977. 187p.

06968 KAW, R.K., tr. Pratyabhijñā Kārikā of Utpaladeva basic text of Pratyabhijña philosophy (the doctrine of recognition)... Srinagar: Sharada Peetha Res. Centre, 1975. v. 1, 92 + 84p. (Its Indological Res. ser., 12)

06969 LARSON, G.J. The aesthetic (rasasvāda) and the religious (brahmasvāda) in Abhinavagupta's Kashmir Śaivism. In PEW 36,4 (1976) 371-87.

06970 ______. The sources for sakti in Abhinavagupta's Kaśmir Śaivism: a linguistic & aesthetic category. In PEW 24,1 (1974) 41-56.

06971 LEIDECKER, K.F., tr. The secret of recognition (Pratyabhijñāhṛdayam), a reviving doctrine of salvation of medieval India. Madras: Adyar Library, 1938. 213p. [by Kṣemarāja, 11th cent.]

06972 PANDEY, K.C. Abhinavagupta: an historical and philosophical study. 2nd rev. & enl. ed. Varanasi: CSSO, 1963. 1014p. (CSS, 1)

06973 SHRINIVAS IYENGAR, P.T., tr. The Shiva-sūtra-vimarṣiṇī of Kṣemarāja. Allahabad: "Indian Thought", 1912. 90p.

06974 SILBURN, L., tr. Hymnes de Abhinavagupta. Paris: Boccard , 1970. 103p. (Pub. de l'Inst. de civilisation indienne, 31)

06975 ______,tr. Le Paramārthasāra [de Abhinavagupta]. Paris: Boccard, 1957. 105p. (Pub. de l'Inst. de civilisation indienne, 5)

c. Śaiva bhakti in Kashmir: the poetry of Lalla Ded and Bhaṭṭa Nārāyaṇa

06976 BHATNAGAR, I. Lal Ded--mystic poetess of Kashmir. In IAC 11 (1963) 361-66.

06977 GRIERSON, G. & L.D. BARNETT, tr. Lallā Vākyanī, or the wise sayings of Lalded, a mystic poetess of ancient Kashmir. London: RAS, 1920. 225p. (Its monograph, 25)

06978 KAUL, JAYALAL. Lal Ded. ND: Sahitya Akademi, 1973. 147p.

06979 KOUL, A. Life sketch of Laleshwari - a great hermitess of Kashmir. In IA 50 (1921) 302-08, 309-12.

06980 PARIMOO, B.N., tr. The ascent of self: a re-interpretation of the mystical poetry of Lalla-Ded. Delhi: Motilal, 1978. 217p.

06981 SILBURN, L., tr. Le stavacintāmaṇi; La bhakti. Paris: Boccard, 1964. 160p. (Études sur le śivaīsme du Kaśmir, 1) [text by Bhaṭṭa Nārāyaṇa]

06982 TEMPLE, R.C., tr. The word of Lalla, the prophetess; being the sayings of Lal Ded or Lal Diddi of Kashmir (Granny Lal) known also as Laleshwari, Lalla Yogishwari & Lalishri, between 1300 & 1400 A.D.... Cambridge: CamUP, 1924. 292p.

3. Earliest Development of Islam in the Indus Valley Area; Lives and Poetry of the Ṣūfī Mystics (beginning 11th cent. AD)

06983 ABDUR RASHID. The life and teachings of Hazrat Data Ganj Bakhsh (Shaikh Abul Hasan Ali bin Usman al-Hujwiri al-Jullabi al-Ghaznawi). Lahore: Central Urdu Development Board, 1967. 48p.

06984 ANAND, B.S. Baba Farid. ND: Sahitya Akademi, 1975. 95p.

06985 AZIZ AHMAD. Conversions to Islam in the Valley of Kashmir. In CAJ 23,1/2 (1979) 3-18.

06986 ELAHI, M., tr. Couplets of Baba Farīd. Lahore: Majlis Shah Hussain, 1967. 107p.

06987 INAM MOHAMMAD. Hazrat Lal Shahbaz Qalandar of Sehwan-Sharif. Karachi: Royal Book Co., 1978. 62 + 180p. + 12pl.

06988 KHAN, A.Z. Isma'ilism in Multan and Sind. In JPHS 1 (1975) 36-57.

06989 MACAULIFFE, M.A. The life of Shaikh Farīd I, and the compositions of Shaikh Farid II, contained in the Granth Sahib of the Sikhs. Lahore: Artistic Printing Works, 1903. 67p.

06990 NOOR NABI, M. Baba Farid Ganj-i-Shakar and his mystical philosophy. In IsC 48,4 (1974) 237-46.

06991 RAFIQI, A.Q. Sufism in Kashmīr, from the fourteenth to the sixteenth century. Varanasi: Bharatiya, 197-. 48 + 310p.

06992 SCHWERIN, K.G. Heiligenverehrung im indischen Islam: die legende des martyrers Sālār Mas'ud Gāzī. In ZDMG 126,2 (1976) 319-35.

06993 SHACKLE, C. Some categories for the comparative study of the medieval Muslim literatures of the Indus region. In J. of Medieval Indian literature 1,1 (1977) 3-14.

06994 TALIB, G.S. Baba Sheikh Farid: his life and teaching. Patiala: Punjabi U., 1973. 60p.

06995 ______,ed. Baba Sheikh Farid: life and teachings. Patiala: Baba Farid Mem. Soc., 1973. 288p.

C. Art and Architecture of the Indus Valley

06996 DWIVEDI, V.P. Ivories of North-west India. In P. Pal, ed. Aspects of Indian Art. Leiden: Brill, 1972, 70-77.

06997 ______. The Kashmir ivories. In Ananda Krishna, ed. Chhavi.... Banaras: BHU, Bharat Kala Bhavan, 1971, 322-26.

06998 FABRI, C. Akhnur terra-cottas. In Marg 8,2 (1955) 53-64.

06999 GOETZ, H. The beginnings of mediaeval art in Kashmir. In his Studies in the history and art of Kashmir and the Indian Himalaya. Wiesbaden: Harrassowitz, 1969, 37-67 + 10pl. [1st pub. in JUB 21,2 (1952) 63-93]

07000 MITRA, D. Pandrethan, Avantipur & Martand. ND: ASI, 1977. 128p. [9th cent. temples in Kashmir]

07001 TADDEI, M. An ekamukha-liṅga from the NWFP and some connected problems: a study in iconography and style. In E&W ns 13 (1962) 288-30.

IX. NORTH INDIA: THE UPPER AND MIDDLE GANGA PLAINS IN THE EARLY MEDIEVAL PERIOD (600-1526 AD)

A. General Histories

1. Harṣa-Vardhana (ruled 606-647 AD) of Kānyakubja/Kanauj: the Last Great Hindu Empire Builder of North India see also III. B. 1, 2, above]

07002 DEVAHUTI, D. Harsha: a political study. Oxford: OUP, 1970. 295p.

07003 MOOKERJI, RADHA KUMUD. Harsha. 3rd ed. Delhi: Motilal, 1965. 203p. [1st ed. 1926]

07004 SHARMA, B.N. Harsa and his times. Varanasi: Sushma Prakashan, 1970. 527p.

07005 SRIVASTAVA, B.N. Harsha and his times: a glimpse of political history during the seventh century A.D. Varanasi: CSSO, 1976. 294p. (CSS, 86)

2. Later Hindu Dynasties of North India, incl. General History of Kanauj

07006 MAJUMDAR, R.C. The Gurjara-Pratīhāras. In his Readings in political history of India. Delhi: B.R., 1976, 158-200. [1st pub. in CUDL 10 (1921) 1-70]

07007 ______. Some problems concerning Gurjara-Pratiharas. In his Readings in political history of India. Delhi: B.R., 1976, 201-14. [1st pub. in BV 10 (1949)]

07008 MISHRA, S.A. Yaśovarman of Kanauj: a study of political history, social, and cultural life of northern India during the reign of Yaśovarman. ND: Abhinav, 1977. 256p.

07009 MISHRA, V.B. The Gurjara-Pratiharas and their times. Delhi: S. Chand, 1966. 150p.

07010 NIYOGI, R. History of the Gāhadavāla dynasty. Calcutta: Oriental Book Agency, 1959. 283p.

07011 PRASAD, A.B.B. Political organisation of north India, A.D. 950-1194. Patna: Janaki Prakashan, 1979. 223p.

07012 PURI, B.N. The history of the Gurjara-Pratīhāras. Delhi: Oriental, 1975. 176p.

07013 TRIPATHI, R.S. History of Kanauj to the Moslem conquest. Delhi: Motilal, 1959. 420p.

3. The Delhi and Jaunpur Sultanates (1206-1526 AD): Muslim Dominance of North India

a. general studies

07014 HABIB, M. Introduction. In H.M. Elliot and J. Dowson. A history of India as told by its own historians. Rev. ed. of v.2. Aligarh: Cosmopolitan Pub., 1952, 1-102. [Rpt. of 1869 ed. with added intro., commentary by A.H. Hodiwala (p. 597-758) & supplement by K.A. Nizami (p. 763-855); only v. 2 revised]

07015 HABIB, M. & K.A. NIZAMI, ed. Delhi Sultanante. Delhi: PPH, 1970. 1189p. (Comprehensive history of India, 5)

07016 HAQ, S.M. A short history of the Sultanate of Delhi. 3rd rev. ed. Delhi: S. Chand, 1956. 293p.

07017 JOSHI, R. Facets of Delhi Sultanate. Allahabad: Kitab Mahal, 1978. 80p.

07018 KHAN, Y.H. Indo-Muslim polity: Turko-Afghan period. Simla: IIAS, 1971. 245p.

07019 MAHAJAN, V.D. & S. MAHAJAN. The Sultanate of Delhi. Rev. & enl. 2nd ed. Delhi: S. Chand, 1963. 264p.

07020 MAJUMDAR, R.C., ed. The Delhi sultanate. Bombay: BVB, 1960. 882p. (HCIP, v. 6) [1290-1526 AD]

07021 SAEED, M.M. The Sharqi sultanate of Jaunpur: a political and cultural history. Karachi: U. of Karachi, 1972. 380p., incl. 19pl. [1396-1495 AD]

07022 SRIVASTAVA, A.L. The Sultanate of Delhi, 711-1526 A.D.; including the Arab invasion of Sindh, Hindu rule in Afghanistan and causes of the defeat of the Hindus in early medieval age. 5th ed. Agra: Shiva Lal Agarwala, 1966. 369p.

b. the early Sultans: the Māmluks or "Slave" dynasty (1206-1290 AD), the Khaljīs (1290-1320 AD)

07023 AZIZ AHMAD, M. Political history and institutions of the early Turkish Empire of Delhi, 1206-1290 AD. ND: OBRC, 1972. 395p. [1st pub. 1969]

07024 BASU, S.P. Rise and fall of Khilji imperialism. Calcutta: U.N. Dhur, 1963. 143p.

07025 DAY, U.N. The North-West frontier under the Khalji sultans of Delhi. In IHQ 39,1/2 (1963) 98-108.

07026 FULLER, A.R. & A. KHALLAQUE, tr. The reign of 'Alāuddīn Khiljī. Calcutta: Pilgrim Pub., 1967. 162p. [tr. from Zia-ud-Din Barani's Tārīkh-i-Firūz Shāhī]

07027 HABIB, M., tr. The campaigns of 'Alā'ud-dīn Khiljī, being the Khazā'inul futūh (Treasures of victory) of Hazrat Amīr Khusrau. Bombay: Taraporevala, 1931. 39 + 131p.

07028 HABIBULLAH, A.B.M. The foundation of Muslim rule in India: a history of the establishment and progress of the Turkish Sultanate of Delhi, 1206-1290 A.D. 2nd rev. ed. Allahabad: Central Book Depot, 1961. 389p. [1st pub. 1945]

07029 HARDY, P. The growth of authority over a conquered political elite: the early Delhi Sultanate as a possible case study. In J.F. Richards, ed. Kingship and authority in South Asia. Madison: South Asian Studies, U. of Wisconsin, 1978, 192-214. (Its Pub. series, 3)

07030 JOSHI, R. Sultan Iltutmish. Varanasi: Bharatiya, 1979. 79p.

07031 LAL, K.S. History of the Khaljis, A.D. 1290-1320. Rev. ed. Bombay: Asia, 1967. 388p. [1st ed. 1967]

07032 NIGAM, S.B.P. Nobility under the Sultans of Delhi, A.D. 1206-1398. Delhi: Munshiram, 1968. 223p.

07033 SEN, A.K. People and politics in early mediaeval India, 1206-1398, AD. Calcutta: Indian Book Dist. Co., 1963. 168p.

07034 SIDDIQI, I.H. The nobility under the Khalji sultans. In IsC 37 (1963) 52-66.

07035 SRIVASTAVA, A.K. The life and times of Kutb-ud-din Aibak. Gorakhpur: Govind Satish Prakashan, 1972. 263p.

07036 AAKARIA, R. Razia: Queen of India. Bombay: Popular, 1966. 159p. [fictionalized biog.]

c. the later Sultāns: the Tughluqs (1320-1411 AD), the Sayyīds (1414-1451 AD), and the Lodīs (1451-1526 AD)

07037 AHMAD, M. Sultan Firoz Shah Tughlaq, 1351-1388 A.D. Allahabad: Chugh, 1978. 122p.

07038 ANSARI, H.N. Tirhut (north Bihar) and Bihar (south Bihar) under Muhammad Bin Tughluq. In JBRS 50 (1964) 59-72.

07039 ASKARI, S.H. Firuz Shah Tughlaq and his times: a study of the rare manuscript "Sīrat-i-Firūz Shāhī." In JIH 52,1 (1974) 127-46.

07040 BANERJEE, J.M. History of Firuz Shah Tughluq. Lahore: Progressive Books, 1976. 228p. [Rpt. 1968 ed.]

07041 BASU, K.K., tr. The Tārīkh-i-Mubārakshāhī, by Yāḥiya bin Ahmad bin ʿAbdullah Sirhindī. Karachi: Karimson's, 1977. 299p. [Rpt. 1932 ed.]

07042 BASU, S.P. The Tughluqs: years of experiments. Calcutta: U.N. Dhur, 197-. 178p.

07043 ELLIOT, H.M., tr. Tarikh-i Firoz Shahi of Zia-ud-Din Barni. Ed. by J. Dowson. Lahore: Sind Sagar Academy, 1974. 186p. [Rpt. of Chap. 15, v. 3, H.M. Elliot's The history of India..., 1871]

07044 HALIM, A. Foundation of the Sayyad Dynasty. In JIH 31 (1953) 199-212.

07045 ______. History of the Lodi sultans of Delhi and Agra. Dacca: U. of Dacca, 1961. 300p.

07046 HAQ, S.M. Barani's history of the Tughluqs. Karachi: Pakistan Historical Soc., 1959. 130p. [also in JPHS 7 (1959) 1-23, 68-89, 127-64]

07047 HUSAIN, A.M. The rise and fall of Muhammad bin Tughluq. London: Luzac, 1938. 274p.

07048 ______. Tughluq dynasty. Calcutta: Thacker, Spink, 1963. 675p.

07049 JAUHRI, R.C. Firoz Tughluq, 1351-1388 A.D. Agra: Shiva Lal Agarwala, 1968. 261p.

07050 LAL, K.S. Twilight of the sultanate; political, social & cultural history of the sultanate of Delhi, from the invasion of Timur to the conquest of Babur. London: Asia, 1963. 358p.

07051 PANDEY, A.B. The first Afghan empire in India, 1451-1526 AD. Calcutta: Bookland, 1956. 320p.

07052 PRASAD, I. A history of the Qaraunah Turks in India (based on original sources) by Ishwari Prasad... Allahabad: Indian Press, 1936. 367p.

07053 SIDDIQI, I.H. Afghan despotism in India, 1451-1555. ND: Indian Inst. of Islamic Studies, 1966. 257p.

07054 ______. Some aspects of Afghan despotism in India. Aligarh: Three Men Pub., 1969. 188p.

07055 ZAKI, M., tr. Tarikh-i-Muhammadi, by Muhammed Bihamad Khani; portion dealing with...Sultan Firoz Shah, his successor, and the minor kingdoms, 1351-1438 AD. Bombay: Asia, for Aligarh Muslim U., 1972. 110p.

B. Political, Economic and Social Life in Early Medieval North India (600-1526 AD)

1. Political and Military Organization

a. pre-Sultanate period (600-1206 AD)

07056 SINGH, R.C.P. Kingship in Northern India, c. 600 A.D.-1200 A.D. Delhi: Motilal, 1968. 151p.

07057 UDGAONKAR, P.B. The political institutions & administration of Northern India during medieval times, from 750 to 1200 A.D. Delhi: Motilal, 1969. 239p.

b. the Delhi Sultanate (1206-1526 AD)

07058 AHMAD, M.B. Judicial system of mediaeval India. In Legal History 1,1 (1975) 58-83.

07059 DAY, U.P. The government of the Sultanate. ND: Kumar Pub., 1972. 219p.

07060 DIGBY, S. War-horse and elephant in the Delhi Sultanate; a study of military supplies. Oxford: Orient Monographs, 1971. 100p.

07061 HABIB, M. & A.U. SALIM KHAN. The political theory of the Delhi Sultanate (incl. a translation of Ziauddin Barani's Fatawa-i Jahandari, c. 1358-9 A.D.) Allahabad: Kitab Mahal, 1961. 172p.

07062 KHAN, Y.H. Indo-Muslim polity (Turko-Afghan period). Simla: IIAS, 1971. 245p.

07063 QURESHI, I.H. The administration of the sultanate of Delhi. 5th rev. ed. ND: OBRC, 1971. 313p. [Rpt. 1944 ed.]

07064 SIDDIQUI, I.H. The army of the Afghan kings in north India--1451 A.D. - 1555 A.D. In IsC 39 (1965) 223-43.

07065 ______. The composition of the nobility under the Lodi sultans. In Medieval India, a Miscellany 4 (1977) 10-66.

07066 ______. Evolution of the Vilayat, the shiq and the sarkar in northern India, 1210-1555 A.D. In Medieval India Q.5 (1963) 10-32.

07067 TOPA, I.N. Politics in pre-Mughal times: a study in the political psychology of the Turkish kings of Delhi up to circa 1400 A.D. Delhi: IAD, 1976. 282p. [Rpt. 1938 ed.]

07068 TRIPATHI, R.P. Some aspects of Muslim administration. Allahabad: Central Book Depot, 1956. 408p.

07069 YUSUF, K.M. The judiciary in India under the sultans of Delhi and the Mughal emperors. In Indo-Iranica 18 (1965) 1-12.

2. Economic and Social Conditions

a. pre-Sultanate period (600-1206 AD)

07070 GOPAL, L. The economic life of northern India, c. AD 700-1200. Delhi: Motilal, 1965. 305p.

07071 MAJUMDAR, B.P. Socio-economic history of northern India. 1030-1194 A.D. Calcutta: KLM, 1960. 417p.

07072 NIYOGI, P. Contributions to the economic history of northern India; from the tenth to the twelfth century A.D. Calcutta: Progressive Pub., 1962. 335p.

07073 PRAKASH, BUDDHA. The genesis and character of landed aristocracy in ancient India. In JESHO 14,2 (1971) 106-22.

07074 SHARMA, B.N. Social life in Northern India, A.D. 600-1000. Delhi: Munshiram, 1966. 390p.

07075 SHARMA, B.N. Social and cultural history of northern India, c. 1000-1200 A.D. ND: Abhinav, 1972. 219p.

07076 VERMA, B.C. Socio-religious, economic and literary condition of Bihar (from ca. 319 A.D. to 1000 A.D.). Delhi: Munshiram, 1962. 209p.

b. period of the Delhi Sultanate (1206-1526 AD)

07077 ASHRAF, M. Life and conditions of the people of Hindustan. ND: Munshiram, 1970. 312p.

07078 CHOUDHARY, R.K. Social structure in medieval Mithila (c. AD 1200-1600). In R.S. Sharma, ed. Indian society: historical probings in memory of D.D. Kosambi. ND: PPH, 1974, 217-234.

07079 RASHID, A. Industry and industrial workers in medieval India. In JBRS 54 (1968) 245-54.

07080 SARKAR, J.N. Glimpses of medieval Bihar economy: thirteenth to mid-eighteenth century. Calcutta: Ratna Prakashan, 1978. 159p.

07081 SIDDIQUI, I.H. The agrarian system of the Afghans. In Studies in Islam 2,4 (1965) 229-53.

07082 SINGH, K.N. The territorial basis of medieval town and village settlement in eastern Uttar Pradesh, India. In Assn. of American Geographers, Annals 58 (1968) 203-20.

07083 SINGH, R.L. & K.N. SINGH. Evolution of the medieval towns in the Saryupar plain of the middle Ganga valley: a case study. In NGJI 9 (1963) 1-11.

C. Religio-Philosophical Traditions: the Meeting of Hinduism and Islam [for Buddhism in medieval Bihar see X. C. 2., below]

1. Studies of the General Religious Milieu

07084 BARTHWAL, P.D. Traditions of Indian mysticism based upon Nirguṇa school of Hindi poetry. ND: Heritage, 1978. 314p. [Rpt. 1936 ed.]

07085 MISHRA, V.B. Religious beliefs and practices of North India during the early mediaeval period. Leiden: Brill, 1973. 191p. (HO, 2:3)

07086 NIZAMI, K.A. Some aspects of religion and politics in India during the thirteenth century. Bombay: Asia, 1965. 421p. [Rpt. Delhi: IAD, 1978]

07087 SRIVASTAVA, A.L. Hindu-Muslim relations during the Sultanate period., 1206-1526 AD. In JIH 41,3 (1963) 577-93.

07088 UPADHYAY, V. The socio-religious condition of North India, 700-1200 A.D. Varanasi: CSSO, 1964. 388p. (CSS, 34)

2. Early Bhakti in North India: Egalitarian, Centered on Rāma Worship, and Expressed Exclusively in Hindī Vernacular

a. general studies

07089 HALIM, A. Religious movements in northern India, 1414-1526: Bhakti Cult. In JASP 7 (1962) 47-87.

07090 RAMSARAN, J.A. English and Hindi religious poetry: an analogical study. Leiden: E.J. Brill, 1973. 199p. (SHR, 23)

07091 RANADE, R.D. Pathway to God in Hindi literature. Sangli: Adhyatma Vidya Mandir, 1954. 405p.

07092 SEN, K. The mediaeval mystics of North India. In Cultural Heritage of India. Calcutta: RMIC, 1956, v. 4, 377-94.

b. Rāmānanda (1400-1470 AD) of Banāras: organizer and inspirer of North Indian Rāma-bhakti; his Camār disciple Ravidāsa/Rāidās

07093 DARSHAN SINGH. Saint Ravidas and his time. Delhi: Kalyani Pub., 1977. 84p.

07094 PANDEY, S.L. Existence, devotion and freedom; the philosophy of Ravidasa. Allahabad: Darshan Peeth, 1965. 165p.

07095 Ramanand to Ram Tirath: lives of the saints of northern India, including the Sikh gurus. 2nd ed. Madras: G.A. Natesan, 1947. 239p.

c. Kabīr (1440-1518); Muslim weaver of Banāras, and supposed disciple of Rāmānanda: Hindu-Muslim eclectic and reformer

i. Kabīr's poems in translation

07096 AHMAD SHAH, tr. The Bījak: or, The complete works of Kabīr. ND: Asian Pub., 1977. 236p. [Rpt. 1917 ed.]

07097 BLY, R., tr. The Kabir book: forty-four of the ecstatic poems of Kabir. Boston: Beacon Press, 1977. 71p.

07098 TAGORE, R.N. & E. UNDERHILL, tr. One hundred poems of Kabir. London: India Soc., 1914. 67p.

07099 VAUDEVILLE, C., tr. Granthāvalī. Pondicherry: IFI, 1957. 125p. [French translation]

07100 ______,tr. Kabīr. NY: OUP, 1974. 344p.

07101 ______,tr. Kabīr. Au cabaret de l'amour. Paris: Gallimard, 1959. 238p.

ii. studies of Kabīr and his followers, the Kabīr Panth

07102 EZEKIEL, I.A. Kabir, the great mystic. Beas: Radha Soami Satsang Beas, 1966. 440p.

07103 HEDAYETULLAH, M. Kabir, the apostle of Hindu-Muslim unity: interaction of Hindu-Muslim ideas in the formation of the bhakti movement with special reference to Kabir, the bhakta. Delhi: Motilal, 1977. 320p.

07104 JODH SINGH. Kabir. Patiala: Punjab U., 1971. 52p.

07105 KEAY, F.E. Kabir and his followers. Calcutta: Assn. Press, 1931. 156p.

07106 MACHWE, P.B. Kabir. ND: Sahitya Akademi, 1968. 59p.

07107 TOPA, I.N. The social philosophy of Kabir; a study of his thought-world. Gorakhpur: Sahitya Sansar Prakashan, 1975. 136p.

07108 VARMA, R.K. Kabir: biography and philosophy. ND: Prints India, 1977. 152p.

07109 VAUDEVILLE, C. Kabir and the interior Religion. In HR 3,2 (1964) 191-201.

07110 WESTCOTT, G.H. Kabir and the Kabir Panth. 2nd ed. Calcutta: Susil Gupta, 1953. 146p. [Rpt. 1907 ed.]

3. Sufism and Muslim literature in North India: Shaikh Nizām-ud-Dīn Awliyā (d. 1325 AD) and the Chishtī Order in Delhi

a. general studies

07111 ASKARI, S.H. The correspondence of two 14th century Sufi saints of Bihar with the contemporary sovereigns of Delhi and Bengal. In JBRS 42 (1956) 177-95. [Also in PIHC 19 (1956) 208-24]

07112 DAS, R.N. Shaikh Nizām-ud-Dīn Auliyā. In IsC 48,2 (1974) 93-104.

07113 DIGBY, S. ᶜAbd Al-Quddūs Gangōhī (1456-1537 AD): the personality and attitudes of a medieval Sufi saint. In Medieval India, a Miscellany 3 (1975) 1-66.

07114 ______. Sufis and travellers in the early Delhi sultanate: the evidence of the Fawāʾid al-Fuʾwād. In Attar Singh, ed. Socio-cultural impact of Islam on India. Chandigarh: Panjab U., 1976, 171-79.

07115 HABIB, M. Chishti mystics records of the Sultanate period. In his politics and society during the early medieval period. ND: PPH, 1974, 385-433. [1st pub. in Medieval India Q. 1,2 (1950)]

07116 HALIM, A. Mystics and mystical movements of the Saiyyad-Lodi period: 1414 A.D. to 1526 A.D. In JASP 8 (1963) 71-108.

07117 HAQ, S.M. Rise and expansion of the Chishtis in the subcontinent. In JPHS 22,3/4 (1974) 157-94, 207-48.

07118 KHAN, IQTIDAR ALAM. Shaikh ᶜAbdul Quddūs Gangōhī's relations with political authorities: a reappraisal. In Medieval India, a Miscellany 4 (1977) 73-90.

07119 PANDEY, S.M. Social relevance of mystic poetry - contribution of Hindi Sufi poet Maulānā Dāūd. In J. of Mediaeval Indian Literature 1,1 (1977) 28-43.

07120 WHITE, C.S.J. Sufism in medieval Hindi literature. In HR 5 (1966) 114-132.

b. Amīr Khusrau of Delhi (1253-1325): follower of Nizām-ud-Dīn Awliyā, and religious-secular literary genius in Persian and early Hindi

07121 Amir Khusrau: memorial volume. ND: PDMIB, 1975. 208p.

07122 ANSARI, A., ed. Life, times & works of Amīr Khusrau Dehlavī. ND: Seventh Centenary Natl. Amir Khusrau Soc., 1975. 360p. + 22pl.

07123 ASKARI, S.H. Amir Khusrau and music. In JIH 47 (1969) 313-28.

07124 HABIB, M. Hazrat Amir Khusrau of Delhi. Bombay: Taraporevala, 1927. 110p. [Rpt. in his Politics and society during the early medieval period. ND: PPH, 1974, 291-355]

07125 KHAN, A.H.J. Hazrat Amir Khusro. In JIMS 4,2 (1973) 1-20.

07126 MADHAVA ROA, P.S. Amir Khusrau as historian. In Indica 13,1/2 (1976) 75-82.

07127 MIRZA, M.W. The life and works of Amir Khusrau. Lahore: U. of the Panjab, 1962. 262p.

07128 QAMARUDDIN. Amir Khusrau & his Pandnama: lessons in socio-political morality. In IESHR 9,4 (1972) 349-366.

07129 SAMNANI, S.G. Amir Khusrau. ND: NBT, 1968. 78p.

07130 VATUK, V.P. Amir Khusrau and Indian riddle tradition. In J. of American folklore 82 (1969) 142-154.

D. Language: Emergence of the Earliest Forms of Hindi-Urdu

07131 BUKHARI, S.A.W. A brief history of the Hindi language and its Muslim poets. In JAU 25 (1964) 91-101.

07132 CHATTERJI, S.K. Indo-Aryan & Hindi. Rev. and enl. 2nd ed. Calcutta: KLM, 1969. 329p.

07133 HALIM, A. Growth and development of Hindi literature during the Sayyid-Lodi period. In JASP 2 (1957) 69-89.

07134 ______. Growth of Urdu language and literature during Sayyid-Lodi period. In JASP 3 (1958) 43-66.

07135 SINHA, M. The historical development of mediaeval Hindi prosody, Rāmānanda-Keśava, 1400-1600 A.D. Bhagalpur: Bhagalpur U., 1964. 178p.

E. Art and Architecture of North India in the Early Medieval Period (600-1526 AD)

1. Schools of Early North Indian Painting [see also Western Indian Painting, VII. C. 3. b., above]

07136 BHATTACHARYYA, A.K. A re-examination of the paintings of the Sultanate period. In RL 35,1/2 (1965) 24-29.

07137 BROWN, W.N. Early Vaishnava miniature paintings from Western India. In Eastern Art 2 (1930) 167-206.

07138 ______. A manuscript of the Sthānāṅga Sūtra illustrated in the early Western Indian style. In NIA 1,2 (1938) 127-9.

07139 CHAGHATAI, M.A. Painting during the Sultanate period, CE 712-1575. Lahore: Kitab Khana-i-Nauras, 1963. 62p.

07140 ______. Painting under the provincial sultanates. In Iqbal 12 (1963) 1-22.

07141 DIGBY, S. The literary evidence for painting in the Delhi Sultanate. In American Academy of Benares, Bulletin 1 (1967) 47-58.

07142 DOSHI, S. An illustrated Ādipurāṇa of 1404 A.D. from Yoginipur. In Anand Krishna, ed. Chhavi... Banaras: BHU, 1971, 382-391.

07143 FRAAD, I. & R. ETTINGHAUSEN. Sultanate painting in Persian style. In Anand Krishna, ed. Chhavi... Banaras: BHU, Bharat Kala Bhavan, 1971, 48-66.

07144 KHANDALAVALA, K.J. A "Gīta Govinda" series in the Prince of Wales Museum (in the style of the "Laur-Chandā" and "Chaurapañchāśikā" group). In PWMB 4 (1953-54) 1-18.

07145 ______. The Mṛigāvat of Bhārat Kalā Bhavan. In Anand Krishna, ed. Chhavi... Banaras: BHU, Bharat Kala Bhavan, 1971, 19-36.

07146 ______. A new document of Indian painting. In LK 10 (1961) 45-54.

07147 KHANDALAVALA, K. & MOTI CHANDRA. A consideration of an illustrated ms. from Maṇḍapadūrga (Maṇḍu) dated 1439 A.D. and its bearing on certain problems of Indian painting. In LK 6 (1959) 8-29.

07148 ______. An illustrated Kalpasūtra painted in Jaunpur in AD 1465. In LK 12 (1962) 9-15.

07149 ______. New documents of Indian painting -- a reappraisal. Bombay: PWM, 1969. 162p.

07150 ______. Three new documents of Indian painting. In PWMB 7 (1959-62) 23-34.

07151 KRISHNADASA, Rai. An illustrated Avadhī ms. of Laur-Chandā in the Bhārat Kalā Bhavan, Banāras. In LK 1/2 (1955-56) 66-71.

07152 MAJMUDAR, M.R. A dated ms. of the Kākarutaśāstra illustrated in the western Indian style. In LK 9 (1961) 55-56.

07153 ______. Two manuscripts illustrated in the western Indian style during Hīravijaya Surī's time: Abhidānanāmamālā and Uttarādhyayan sūtra. In Bull. of the Museum and Picture Gallery, Baroda 15 (1962) 13-19.

07154 MOTI CHANDRA. Costumes and textiles in the Sultanate period. In J. of Indian textile history 6 (1961) 5-61.

07155 ______. An illustrated ms. of Mahāpurāṇa in the collection of Śrī Digambar Nayā Mandir, Delhi. In LK 5 (1959) 68-81.

07156 MOTI CHANDRA & K. KHANDALAVALA. An illustrated manuscript of the Āraṇyaka Parvan in the collection of the Asiatic Society, Bombay. In JASBombay ns 38 (1963) 116-21.

07157 SHIVESHWARKAR, L. The pictures of the Chaurapañchāśikā, a Sanskrit love lyric. ND: Natl. Museum, 1967. 59p. + 18pl.

07158 TARAFDAR, M.R. Illustrations of the Chandāin in the Central Museum, Lahore. In JASP 8,2 (1963) 109-15.

2. Islamic Architecture of the Sultanate Period

07159 BLAKISTON, J.F. The Jami Masjid at Badaun and other buildings in the United Provinces. Calcutta: Govt. of India Central Pub. Branch, 1926. 9p. + 25pl. (ASI memoir, 19)

07160 BUKHARI, Y.K. Visnudhvaja or Qutb Minar. In ABORI 45 (1964) 87-104.

07161 BULLOCK, H. The architecture of the Delhi Sultanates. In Islamic Q. 1 (1954) 144-151.

07162 DIGBY, S. The tomb of Bahlol Lodi. In BSOAS 38,3 (1975) 550-61 + 4pl.

07163 FÜHRER, A.A. The Sharqi architecture of Jaunpur (N.-W.P.); with notes on Zafarabad, Sahet-Mahet and other places in the N.-W. Provinces and Oudh. Ed. by J. Burgess. Calcutta: Govt. Printing Press, 1889. 76p. (ASI new imperial series, 11)

07164 MOTI CHANDRA. An illustrated manuscript of the Kalpasūtra and Kālakāchāryakathā. In PWMB 4 (1953-54) 40-48.

07165 MUNSHI, R.N. The history of the Kutb Minar (Delhi). Bombay: Fort Printing Press, 1911. 94p.

07166 NATH, R. Concept of the Qutub Minar. In IsC 49,1 (1975) 43-62.

07167 ______. History of Sultanate architecture. ND: Abhinav, 1978. 121p. + 36pl. [On the architecture of Delhi, Ajmer, Badaon, Jaunpur, and Sasaram (Bihar), from 1192 AD to 1545 AD]

07168 ______. Panchmukhi mosques of the Afghan period. In IsC 50,2 (1976) 33-40 + 6pl.

07169 ______,tr. Monuments of Delhi: historical study. ND: Ambika, 1978. 107p. + 43pl. [Rev. tr. of Sir Syed Ahmad Khan's Āsāruṣṣanādīd]

07170 PAGE, J.A. Historical memoir on the Qutb, Delhi. Calcutta: Govt. of India Central Pub. Branch, 1926. 49p. (ASI memoirs, 22)

07171 ______. A memoir on Kotla Firoz Shah, Delhi with a translation of Sirat-i-Firozshahi by Mohammad Hamid Kuraishi. Delhi: MPGOI, 1937. 32p. (ASI memoir, 52)

07172 YAMAMOTO, T. & M. ARA & T. TSUMIKOWA. Delhi: architectural remains of the Delhi Sultanate period, detailed report of archaeological survey carried out by the Museum for Indian History and Archaeology, the U. of Tokyo. Tokyo: Inst. of Oriental Culture, 1967-70. 3 v., 440p. + 261pl. [Japanese text]

07173 ZAFAR HASAN, M. A guide to Nīzāmu-d Dīn. Calcutta: Supt. of Govt. Printing, 1922. 40p. (ASI memoirs, 10)

X. THE BENGAL AREA, INCL. BIHAR AND ASSAM, IN THE EARLY MEDIEVAL PERIOD (600-1538 AD): THE LOWER GANGA AND BRAHMAPUTRA VALLEYS

A. General and Political Histories

1. Buddhist and Hindu Dynasties: the Pālas (730-1197 AD), the Senas (1095-1204 AD) and Other Kingdoms

07174 BANERJI, R.D. The Palas of Bengal. Calcutta: Baptist Mission Press, 1915. 70p. [1st pub. in MASB 5,3 (1914) 43-113]

07175 BASAK, R.G. History of Northeast India, extending from the foundation of the Gupta empire to the rise of the Pala dynasty of Bengal (c. AD 320-760). Calcutta: Sambodhi Pub., 1967. 431p.

07176 CHOWDHURY, A.M. Dynastic history of Bengal, c. 750-1200 AD. Dacca: ASP, 1967. 310p. (ASP pub., 21)

07177 MORRISON, B.M. Political centers & cultural retions in early Bengal. Tucson: U. of Arizona Press, 1970. 189p. (AAS monograph, 25)

07178 RASHID, M.H. Pala rule in south-east Bengal. J. Varendra Res. Museum 3 (1974) 27-48.

07179 SINHA, B.P. The decline of the kingdom of Magadha, c. 455 AD-1000 AD. Patna: Motilal, 1954. 482p.

07180 ______. Dynastic history of Magadha, c. 450-1200 AD. ND: Abhinav, 1977. 275p.

07181 SINHA, C.P.N. Mithila under the Karnatas, c. 1097-1325 A.D. Patna: Janaki Prakashan, 1979. 192p.

2. Muslim Rule in Bengal up to the Mughal Period (1204-1538 AD)

07182 BHATTASALI, N.K. Coins and chronology of the early independent sultans of Bengal. Cambridge: W. Heffer, 1922. 184p.

07183 CHOUDHARY, R.K. History of Muslim rule in Tirhut, 1206-1765 A.D. Varanasi: CSSO, 1970. 295p. (CSS, 72)

07184 CHOWDHURY, A.M. New light on Sultan Firuz Shah Tughluq's first invasion of Bengal. In JASP 8 (1963) 47-54.

07185 DANI, A.H. Bibliography of the Muslim inscriptions of Bengal (down to A.D. 1538). Dacca: Paramount Press, 1957. 147p. [suppl. to JASP 2]

07186 ______. The conquest of Nudiya. In JIH 42 (1964) 229-39.

07187 KARIM, ABDUL. Aspects of Muslim administration in Bengal down to AD 1538. JASP 3 (1958) 67-103.

07188 ______. Early Muslim rulers in Bengal and their non-Muslim subjects (down to AD 1538). In JASP 4 (1959) 73-96.

07189 MONDAL, S. History of Bengal. Calcutta: Prakash Mandir, 1970-. v. 1, 1200-1526 AD, 236 + 52p.

07190 STEWART, C. The history of Bengal; from the first Mohammedan invasion until the virtual conquest of that country by the English, A.D. 1757. Delhi: Oriental Pub., 1971. 548p.

07191 TARAFDAR, M.R. Husain Shahi Bengal, 1494-1538 AD; a socio-political study. Dacca: ASP, 1965. 401p.

3. Early Medieval Assam (Kāmarūpa): Entry of Ahom People from Burma and Beginning of their Rule (13th cent. AD)

07192 ACHARYYA, N.N. The history of medieval Assam, from the thirteenth to the seventeenth century; a critical and comprehensive history of Assam during the first four centuries of Ahom rule.... Gauhati: Dutta Baruah, 1966. 308p.

07193 BHUYAN, S.K. Annals of the Delhi Badshahate = being a translation of the old Assamese chronicle Padshah-Buranji. Gauhati: Govt. of Assam, Dept. of Historical and Antiquarian Studies, 1947. 244p.

07194 CHOUDHURY, P.C. The history of civilisation of the people of Assam to the twelfth century A.D. 2nd ed. Gauhati: Dept. of Historical and Antiquarian Studies in Assam, 1966. 510p.

07195 GOGOI, P. The Tai and the Tai kingdoms; with a fuller treatment of the Tai-Ahom Kingdom in the Brahmaputra Valley. Gauhati: Gauhati U., 1968. 552p.

07196 GUHA, A. Ahom migration: its impact on rice economy of medieval Assam. In AV 9,2 (1967) 135-57.

B. Economic and Social Life in Early Medieval Eastern India (600-1538 AD)

07197 GUHA, A. Land rights and social classes in medieval Assam. In IESHR 3,3 (1966) 217-39.

07198 HUSSAIN, SHAHANARA. Everyday life in the Pāla Empire, with special reference to material remains. Dacca: ASP, 1968. 218p. + 81 pl.

07199 KARIM, ABDUL. Social history of the Muslims in Bengal (down to AD 1538). Dacca: ASP, 1959. 252p. (Its Pub., 2)

07200 INDEN, R.B. Marriage and rank in Bengali culture: a history of caste and clan in middle period Bengal. Berkeley: UCalP, 1976. 161p.

07201 MAJUMDAR, R.C. Expansion of Aryan culture in eastern India. Imphal: Atombapu Research Centre, 1968. 52p.

07202 NIYOGI, P. Brahmanic settlements in different subdivisions of ancient Bengal. Calcutta: ISPP, 1967. 90p.

07203 RAHIM, M.A. Social and cultural history of Bengal; 1201-1576. Karachi: Pakistan Pub. House, 1963. 453p. (Pakistan Hist. Soc. pub., 34)

C. Religio-Philosophical Traditions & their Literature in the Early Medieval Bengal Area (600-1538 AD): Developments in Buddhism, Hinduism, and Islam

1. The General Religious Milieu

07204 BANERJI, S.C. Tantra in Bengal: a study in its origin, development, and influence. Calcutta: Naya Prokash, 1977. 234 + 83p.

07205 CHAKRAVARTI, T. Some aspects of religious life as depicted in early inscriptions and literature of Bengal. In CUDL ns 1 (1957) 133-78.

07206 DAS GUPTA, S.B. Obscure religious cults. 2nd rev. ed. Calcutta: KLM, 1962. 436p. [1st pub. 1946]

07207 DASGUPTA, T.C. Some aspects of medieval Bengali literature. In CR 119 (1951) 69-82.

07208 KAKATI, B.K., ed. Aspects of early Assamese literature. Gauhati: Gauhati U., 1953. 315p.

07209 SASTRI, H.P. Bengali Buddhist literature. In CR no. 290 (1917) 390-407.

07210 SEN, D.C. Glimpses of Bengal life. Calcutta: Calcutta U., 1925. 313p.

2. Buddhism under Pāla Patronage: Dominance of Mahāyāna and Vajrayāna (Tantrism); the Buddhist Sahajiyā Cult

a. general studies

07211 CHOUDHARY, R.K. The University of Vikramaśīla. Patna: Bihar Res. Soc., 1975. 75p.

07212 DARIAN, S. Buddhism in Bihar from the 8th to the 12th century with special reference to Nālandā. In AS/EA 25 (1971) 335-52.

07213 GHOSH, A. A guide to Nālandā. Delhi: MPGOI, 1939. 51p. + 10pl.

07214 LING, T.O. Buddhism in Bengal; a changing concept of salvation? In E.J. Sharpe & J.R. Hinnells, eds. Man and his salvation. Manchester: Manchester U. Press, 1973, 171-88.

07215 SANKALIA, H.D. The University of Nālandā. 2nd rev. & enl. ed. Delhi: Oriental, 1972. 297p. [1st pub. 1934]

07216 SASTRI, HIRANANDA. Nālandā & its epigraphic material. Delhi: MPGOI, 1942. 133p. (ASI Memoir, 66)

07217 SINGH, B.P. Naropa: his life & activities. In JBRS 53 (1967) 117-29.

07218 UPASAK, C.S., ed. Nalanda, past and present: silver jubilee souvenir. Nalanda: Nava Nalanda Mahavihara, 1977. 210p.

b. Buddhist literature in Sanskrit and Old Bengali; dohās and caryā songs

07219 BAGCHI, P.C. Dohākosa with notes. In CUDL 28 (1935) 180p.

07220 BHATTACHARYYA, B. The date of the Baudha gān o dohā. In JBORS 14,3 (1928) 341-57.

07221 DE, S.K. The Buddhist Tantric (Sanskrit) literature of Bengal. In NIA 1 (1938) 1-23.

07222 KVAERNE, P., tr. An anthology of Buddhist tantric songs; a study of the Caryāgīti. Oslo: Universitetsforlaget, 1977. 255p.

07223 MOJUMDAR, A. The Caryāpadas: a treatise on the earliest Bengali songs. Calcutta: Naya Prokash, 1967. 192p.

07224 SEN, N. Early eastern New Indo-Aryan versification; a prosodical study of Caryāgītikoṣa. Simla: IIAS, 1973. 91p.

07225 ______,tr. Caryāgītikoṣa (facsimile ed.) Simla: IIAS, 1977. 39 + 160p.

07226 SEN, S., ed. & tr. Old Bengali texts: Caryāgīti-Vajragīti-Prahelikā. In Indian Linguistics 10 (1948) 1-55.

07227 SHAHIDULLAH, M. Les chants mystiques de Kānha et de Saraha: les Dohā-koṣa et Caryā. Paris: Adrien-Maisonneuve, 1928. 236p.

3. Vaiṣṇavism in the Bengal Area: the Culmination of the Bhakti-Vedānta Tradition in Caitanya (1486-1533 AD)

a. Bengal Vaiṣṇavism and its literature - general studies and translations

07228 BHATTACHARYA, D., tr. Songs of Kṛṣṇa. NY: Weiser, 1978. 191p.

07229 CHAKRAVARTI, S.C. Philosophical foundation of Bengal Vaiṣṇavism; a critical exposition. Calcutta: Academic Publishers, 1969. 437p.

07230 DASGUPTA, A.R. The lyric in Indian poetry; a comparative study in the evolution of Bengali lyric forms up to the seventeenth century. Calcutta: KLM, 1962. 152p.

07231 DE, S.K. Early history of the Vaiṣṇava faith and movement in Bengal, from Sanskrit and Bengali sources. 2nd ed. Calcutta: KLM, 1961. 703p.

07232 ______. Studies in Bengal Vaiṣṇavism. In his Bengal's contribution to Sanskrit literature; studies in Bengal Vaiṣṇavism. Calcutta: KLM, 1960, 84-153.

07233 DIMOCK, E.C., JR. Muslim Vaiṣṇava poets of Bengal. In D. Kopf, ed. Bengal regional identity. East Lansing: Michigan State U., 1969, 23-32.

07234 ______. Muslim Vaiṣṇava poets of Bengal. In Languages and areas: studies presented to George V. Bobrinskoy. Chicago: Division of the Humanities, U. of Chicago, 1967, 28-37.

07235 DIMOCK, E.C., JR. & D. LEVERTOV, tr. In praise of Krishna: songs from the Bengali. London: Cape, 1968. 92p. (UNESCO series)

07236 HARDY, F. Mādhavendra Puri: a link between Bengal Vaiṣṇavism and South Indian bhakti. In JRAS (1974) 23-41.

07237 MALLIK, G.N. The philosophy of the Vaiṣṇava religion, with special reference to the Kṛṣṇaite and Gourāngite cults. Lahore: Motilal, Punjab Sanskrit Book Depot, 1927. 377p. (Punjab or. ser., 14)

07238 MAZUMDAR, B.P. Vaiṣṇavism in mediaeval Mithilā (c. 1097-1530 AD). In JBRS 48,3 (1962) 19-33.

07239 MUKHERJI, S.C. A study of Vaiṣṇavism in ancient and medieval Bengal, up to the advent of Caitanya; based on archaeological & literary data. Calcutta: Punthi Pustak, 1966. 244p.

07240 SEN, D.C. The Vaiṣṇava literature of medieval Bengal. Calcutta: U. of Calcutta, 1917. 257p.

07241 SEN, S. History of Brajabulī literature: being a study of the Vaiṣṇava lyric poetry and poets of Bengal. Calcutta: U. of Calcutta, 1935. 600p.

b. the Bengali Rāmāyaṇas of Kṛttibās (15th cent.) and others

07242 MAZUMDAR, S., tr. Rāmāyaṇa. Bombay: Orient Longmans, 1958. 540p. [Kṛittibas]

07243 SEN, D.C. The Bengali Rāmāyaṇas. Calcutta: U. of Calcutta, 1920. 305p.

c. the Gīta-Govinda of Jayadeva (12th cent. AD): erotic-devotional poem on Rādhā and Kṛṣṇa

i. translations from the Sanskrit

07244 ARNOLD, E., tr. Indian poetry, containing a new edition of The Indian song of songs from the Gīta Govinda of Jayadeva. London: Trubner, 1881.

07245 BANKEY BEHARI, tr. The Geet Govind. Jodhpur: Radha Madhav Soc., 1964. 88p.

07246 GREENLEES, D., tr. The song of divine love, Gīta-Govinda. Madras: Kalakshetra Pub., 1962. 102p.

07247 KEYT, G., tr. Shri Jayadeva's Gīta govinda: the loves of Krshna & Radha. Bombay: Kutub, 1947. 103p.

07248 MILLER, B.S., tr. Love song of the dark lord: Jayadeva's Gītagovinda. NY: ColUP, 1977. 225p. (UNESCO series)

07249 VARMA, M., tr. The Gīta Govinda of Jayadeva. Calcutta: Writers Workshop, 1968. 107p.

ii. studies

07250 CHATTERJI, S.K. Jayadeva. ND: Sahitya Akademi, 1973. 67p.

07251 DASH, G.N. The king and the priests: an analysis of the Gīta-Govinda tradition. In VQ 40,3 (1975) 227-46.

07252 FORGUE, S.S. Le Gītagovinda; tradition et innovation dans le Kāvya. Stockholm: Almqvist and Wiksell Intl., 1977. 275p. (Stockholm or. studies, 11)

07253 KUPPUSWAMY, G. & M. HARIHARAN, ed. Jayadeva and Gītagovinda: a study. Trivandrum: College Book House, 1980. 202p.

07254 MILLER, B.S. Rādhā: consort of Kṛṣṇa's vernal passion. In JAOS 95,4 (1975) 655-71.

07255 MUKHERJI, A.D. Lyric metres in Jayadeva's Gīta Govinda. In JASB 9,3/4 (1947) 232-45.

07256 SIEGEL, L. Sacred and profane dimensions of love in Indian traditions, as exemplified in the Gītagovinda of Jayadeva. Delhi: OUP, 1978. 328p.

07257 VATSYAYAN, K. Gita-Govinda and the artistic traditions of India. In JMA 45,1/4 (1974) 131-46.

d. Rādhā-Kṛṣṇa bhakti; the poems of Vidyāpati in Maithilī, and of Caṇḍidāsa in Bengali

07258 BHATTACHARYA, D., tr. Love songs of Chandidas: the rebel poet-priest of Bengal. London: Allen & Unwin, 1967. 172p. (UNESCO series)

07259 ______,tr. Love songs of Vidyāpati. NY: Grove Press, 1979. 148p. [Rpt. 1970 ed.]

07260 COOMARASWAMY, A.K. & A. SEN, tr. Vidyāpati: Bangīya padābalī. Songs of the love of Rādhā and Krishṇa...with intro. and notes and illustrations from Indian paintings. London: Old Bourne Press, 1915. 192p.

07261 JHA, R.N. Vidyapati. ND: Sahitya Akademi, 1972. 75p.

07262 SEN, P.R. The story of Chandidas. In Folklore (C) 4 (1963) 313-60.

07263 SEN, S. Chandidas. ND: Sahitya Akademi, 1971. 58p.

e. Caitanya (1486-1533 AD), called Śrī Gaurāṅga, central figure of Gauḍiya (Gauḍ=Bengal) Vaiṣṇava bhakti, and founder of the Acintya-Bhedābheda school of Vedānta

i. general studies of the Caitanya movement

07264 CHAKRAVARTI, J. Bengal Vaisnavism and Sri Chaitanya. Calcutta: Asiatic Soc., 1975. 95p.

07265 DIMOCK, E.C., JR. Doctrine and practice among the Vaiṣṇavas of Bengal. In M. Singer, ed. Krishna: myths, rites, and attitudes. Honolulu: EWCP, 1966, 41-64.

07266 KAPOOR, O.B.L. The philosophy and religion of Sri Caitanya (the philosophical background of the Hare Krishna movement). ND: Munshiram, 1976. 248p.

07267 KENNEDY, M.T. The Chaitanya movement; a study of the Vaisnavism of Bengal. Calcutta: Assn. Press, 1925. 270p.

07268 MAJUMDAR, A.K. Gauḍiya-Vaiṣṇava studies. Calcutta: Jijñāsa, 1978. 96p.

07269 MUKHERJEE, D.K. Chaitanya. ND: NBT, 1970. 132p.

ii. the Śrī-Caitanya-caritāmṛta and later biographies of Caitanya

07270 BHAKTIVEDANTA SWAMI, A.C., tr. Śrī Caitanya-caritāmṛta of Kṛṣṇadāsa Kavirāja Gosvāmi. NY: Bhaktivedanta Book Trust, 1973-75. 3 pts. in 17 v. [Each v. has a different title]

07271 BON, B.H. Śrī Caitanya. 2nd ed. ND: Oxford & IBH, 1973. 218p. [1st pub. 1940]

07272 DAS, S. Sri Chaitanya Mahaprabhu. Madras: Shree Gaudiya Math, 1972. 266p.

07273 GHOSE, S.K. Lord Gauranga. Bombay: BVB, 1961. 196p.

07274 ROY, N.K., tr. Śrī Śrī Chaitanya charitāmṛita. 2nd ed. Puri: the translator, 1959. 3 v. [by Kavirāja Krishnadāsa Goswāmin]

07275 SANYAL, N.K. Sree Krishna Chaitanya. Royapettah, Madras: Tridandi Swami Bhakti Hridaya Bon, Sree Gaudiya Math, 1933. 2 v.

07276 SARKAR, J.N., tr. Chaitanya's life and teachings from his contemporary Bengali biography, the Chaitanya-charit-amrita [of Kṛṣṇadāsa Kavirāja Goswāmi]. Calcutta: M.C. Sarkar, 1922. 297p.

07277 ______,tr. Chaitanya's pilgrimages and teachings. From his contemporary biography, the Chaitanya-charit-āmṛita: Madhyalīlā. Calcutta: M.C. Sarkar, 1913. 319p.

iii. studies and expositions of Caitanya's teachings

07278 BHAKTIVEDANTA SWAMI, A.C. Teachings of Lord Chaitanya; a treatise on factual spiritual life. NY: International Soc. for Krishna Consciousness, 1968. 292p.

07279 CHAKRAVARTI, S. Caitanya et sa théorie de l'amour divin (prema). Paris: PUF, 1933. 185p.

07280 EIDLITZ, W. Kṛṣṇa-Caitanya: sein Leben und seine Lehre. Stockholm: Almqvist & Wiksell, 1968. 561p.

07281 HEIN, N.J. Caitanya's ecstasies and the theology of the name. In B.L. Smith, ed. Hinduism: new essays in the history of religions. Leiden: Brill, 1976, 15-32. (SHR, 33)

07282 MAJUMDAR, A.K. Caitanya, his life and doctrine; a study in Vaiṣṇavism. Bombay: BVB, 1969. 392p.

07283 SIDDHANTA SARASWATI. Shri Chaitanya's teachings. Ed. by Vilās Tīrtha Goswāmi. Madras: Sree Gaudiya Math, 1967. 434p.

iv. lives and works of Caitanya's disciples, the six Gosvāmins

07284 BHAKTIVEDANTA SWAMI, A.C. The nectar of devotion; the complete science of Bhakti Yoga. NY: Bhaktivedanta Book Trust, 1970. 439p. [summary study of Śrīla Rūpa Gosvāmi's Bhakti-rasāmṛta sindhu]

07285 ______,tr. The nectar of instruction; an authorized English presentation of Srīla Rūpa Gosvāmi's Sri Upadeśāmṛta. NY: Bhaktivedanta Book Trust, 1975. 130p.

07286 BON, BHAKTI HRDAYA, tr. Śrī Rūpa Gosvāmin's Bhaktirasāmṛtasindhuh. Vrindaban: Inst. of Oriental Philosophy, 1965. 426p.

07287 DIMOCK, E.C., JR. The place of Gauracandrikā in Bengali Vaiṣṇava lyrics. In JAOS 78 (1958) 153-169.

07288 MAHANAMBRATA, Brahmachari. Vaiṣṇava Vedānta: the philosophy of Śrī Jīva Gosvāmi. Calcutta: Das Gupta, 1974. 240p.

07289 O'CONNELL, J.T. Caitanya's followers & the Bhagavadgītā: case study in Bhakti & the secular. In B.L. Smith, ed. Hinduism: new essays in the history of religions. Leiden: Brill, 1976, 33-52. (SHR, 33)

07290 SEN, D.C. Chaitanya & his companions. Calcutta: U. of Calcutta, 1917. 309p.

07291 YATI, BHAKTI PRAJNAN, tr. Sri Bṛihat bhāgavatāmṛitam. 2nd ed. Madras: Sree Gaudiya Math, 1975. 320p. [by Sanātana Goswāmi, 1484-1558]

f. Śaṅkaradeva (1486-1568 AD) and the Vaiṣṇava movement in Assam

07292 BARUA, B.K. Śaṅkaradeva; Vaiṣṇava saint of Assam. Gauhati: Assam Academy for Cultural Relations, 1960. 138p.

07293 CHALIHA, BHABA PRASAD, ed. Sankaradeva: studies in culture. Gauhati: Srimanta Sankaradeva Sangha, 1978. 168p.

07294 NEOG, M. The bhakti cycle of Assamese lyrics: bargits and after. In Gauhati U. J. 1 (1950) 53-70.

07295 ______. Sankaradeva. ND: NBT, 1967. 111p.

07296 ______. Śaṅkaradeva and his times. Early history of Vaiṣṇava faith and movement in Assam. Gauhati: Gauhati U., 1965. 400p.

07297 SARMA, S.N. The Neo-Vaisnavite movement and the Satra institution of Assam. Gauhati: Gauhati U., 1966. 240p.

07298 SREENIVASA MURTHY, H.V. Vaiṣṇavism of Śaṁkaradeva and Rāmānuja: a comparative study. Delhi: Motilal, 1973. 254p.

4. Śaiva and Other Hindu Sects in the Bengal Area

a. general studies

07299 BHATTACHARYA, A. Early Bengali Śaiva poetry. Calcutta: Calcutta Book House, 1951. [1st pub. in

DUS 6 (1944)]

07300 CHATTERJEE, A. Vākreśvara--a centre of Śaivism in medieval Bengal. In IHQ 35 (1959) 57-64.

07301 CLARK, T.W. Evolution of Hinduism in medieval Bengali literature: Śiva, Caṇḍī, Manasā. In BSOAS 27,3 (1955) 503-18.

07302 SARKAR, A. Śiva in medieval Indian literature. Calcutta: Punthi Pustak, 1974. 221p.

b. the Nāthas: esoteric cult of Haṭhayoga (psychophysiological practices) and its Ādi Siddha, Gorakṣa/Gorakh Nātha (13th cent AD?)

07303 BANERJEA, A.K. Philosophy of Gorakhnath with Goraksha-Vacana-Sangraha. Gorakhpur: Mahant Dig Vijai Nath Trust, 1961. 343p.

07304 BRIGGS, G.W. Gorakhnāth and the Kānphaṭa yogīs. Delhi: Motilal, 1973. 380p.

07305 ELIADE, M. Yoga: immortality and freedom. Tr. from French by W.R. Trask. Princeton: PUP, 1973. 536p. (Bollingen series, 56) [1st ed. 1958; 301-318 on Nāthas]

07306 KARAMBELKAR, V.W. Matsyendranāth and his yoginī cult. In IHQ 31 (1955) 362-74.

07307 MOHAN SINGH, tr. Gorakhnath and medieval Hindu mysticism; incl. text and translation of Machhendra-Gorakhgoshti padas and shlokas of Gorakh: shlokas of Charpatnath. Lahore: the author, 1937. 178p.

07308 SEN, S. The Nātha cult. In Cultural Heritage of India. Calcutta: RMIC, 1956, v. 4, 280-90.

c. Manasā, goddess of snakes, adopted into Hinduism from tribal religion

07309 DIMOCK, E.C., JR. The goddess of snakes in medieval Bengali literature. In HR 1 (1962) 307-21; 3 (1964) 300-22. [pt. 2 with A.K. Ramanujan]

07310 DIMOCK, E.C., JR. Manasā, goddess of snakes; the Ṣaṣṭhī myth. In J.M. Kitagawa & C.H. Long, eds. Myths and symbols.... Chicago: UChiP, 1969, 217-226.

07311 MAITY, P.K. Historical studies in the cult of the goddess Manasā; a socio-cultural study. Calcutta: Punthi Pustak, 1966. 377p.

07312 RAMESHWAR RAO, S. The legend of Manasā Devī. Bombay: Orient Longmans, 1977. 41p.

07313 RAWSON, P.S. The iconography of the Goddess Manasā. In OA ns 1,4 (1955) 151-58.

07314 SMITH, W.L. The myth of Manasā: a study in popular Hinduism in medieval Bengal. Stockholm: Stockholm U., 1976. 201p.

07315 THIERRY, S. Présentation de la déesse indienne Manasā. In O&M 5 (1965) 3-20.

5. The Navya-Nyāya School of Hindu Logic in Mithilā and Bengal; Gaṅgeśa (13th cent.) and his Tattva-cintāmaṇi

07316 BANDYOPADHYAY, N. The concept of logical fallacies: problems of hetvābhāṣa in Navya-Nyāya in the light of Gangeśa and Raghunātha Śiromaṇi. Calcutta: SPB, 1977. 206p.

07317 BHATTACHARYA, T. The nature of vyāpti according to the Navya-nyāya. Calcutta: Sanskrit College, 1970. 306p. (Its res. ser., 49)

07318 BHATTACHARYYA, G. Navya-nyāya: some logical problems in historical perspective. Delhi: Bharatiya, 1978. 113p.

07319 BHATTACHARYYA, S.J. Some features of Navya-nyāya logic. In PEW 24,3 (1974) 329-342.

07320 FRAUWALLNER, E. Raghunātha Śiromaṇi. In WZKS 10 (1966) 86-207.

07321 GANGOPADHYAY, M.K. Gaṅgeśa on Vyāptigraha. The means for the ascertainment of invariable concomitance: the "Vyāptigrahopaya" section of "Tattvacintāmaṇi." In JIP 3,1/2 (1975) 167-208.

07322 GOEKOOP, C. The logic of invariable concomitance in the Tattvacintāmaṇi. Gaṅgeśa's Anumitinirūpana and commentary. Dordrecht: D. Reidel, 1967. 162p.

07323 GUHA, D.C. Navya nyāya system of logic: basic theories & techniques. 2nd rev. ed. Delhi: Motilal, 1979. 271p. [1st ed. 1968]

07324 INGALLS, D.H.H. Materials for the study of Navya-nyāya logic. Cambridge: HUP, 1951. 181p. (HOS, 40)

07325 MATILAL, B.K. The navya-nyāya doctrine of negation. The semantics & ontology of negative statements in navya-nyāya philosophy. Cambridge: HUP, 1968. 208p. (HOS, 46)

07326 MUKHERJEA, A.K. The definition of pervasion (vyāpti) in Navya-nyāya. In JIP 4,1/2 (1976) 1-50.

07327 MULLATTI, L.C. The Navya-Nyāya theory of inference. Dharwar: Karnatak U., 1977. 140p. (Its Res. pub., 30)

5. Early Development of Islam in the Bengal Area

07328 ALI, S.M. Saints of East Pakistan. Dacca: OUP, 1971. 61p.

07329 FUZLI RUBBEE, K. The origin of the Musalmans of Bengal. 2nd ed. Dacca: Soc. for Pakistan Studies, 1970. 96p.

07330 HAQ, M.E. A history of Sufi-ism in Bengal. Dacca: Asiatic Soc. of Bangladesh, 1975. 455p. (Its pub., 30)

07331 HAQ, M.M. The Shuttari order of Sufism in India and its exponents in Bihar and Bengal. In JASP 16 (1971) 167-75.

07332 RAHIM, A. The saints in Bengal: Sheikh Jalal al-Din Tabrizi and Shah Jalal. In JPHS 8 (1960) 206-26.

07333 ______. Shaykh Ākhi Sirāj al-Dīn ʿUthmān, a Bengali saint. In JPHS 9 (1961) 23-29. [Chishti Sufi d. 1335 AD]

07334 SARKAR, J.N. Islam in Bengal (thirteenth to eighteenth centuries). In JIH 48 (1970) 469-512.

D. Language: Old and Early Middle Bengali (c. 950-1500 AD) and Related Languages

07335 BANERJI, R.D. The origin of the Bengali script. Calcutta: Nababharat, 1973. 112p. [Rpt. 1919 ed.]

07336 BHUYAN, S.K. Assamese historical literature. In IHQ 5 (1929) 457-78.

07337 DASGUPTA, S.C., comp. A bibliography of Indology; v. 3, Bengali language and literature, part 1 (early period). Calcutta: National Library, 1964. 390p.

07338 MUKHERJI, T. The Old Bengali language and text. Calcutta: U. of Calcutta, 1963. 203p.

07339 TIWARI, U.N. The origin and development of Bhojpuri. Calcutta: ASB, 1960. 282p. (Its monograph, 10)

E. Art and Architecture of the Bengal Area in the Early Medieval Period (600-1538 AD) under the Pāla, Sena and Other Dynasties

1. General Studies

07340 FRENCH, J.C. The art of the Pal empire of Bengal. London: OUP, 1928. 15 + 26p. + 32pl.

07341 GROUSSET, R. L'art pāla et sena dans l'Inde extérieure. In Mélanges Linossier. Paris: Leroux, 1932, v. 1, 277-285.

2. Manuscript Illustration and Other Painting

07342 BHATTACHARYA, A.K. An early Pala ms. cover with Vessantara Jataka scene. In RL 34,1/2 (1964) 19-21.

07343 BHATTACHARYA, B. Krishna in the traditional painting of Bengal. Calcutta: Kamal Banerjee, 1972. 59p.

07344 CONZE, E. Remarks on a Pala MS in the Bodleian Library. In OA 1,7 (1948) 9-12.

07345 DAS GUPTA, R. Eastern Indian manuscript painting. Bombay: Taraporevala, 1972. 16 + 112p. + 26pl.

07346 GHOSH, D.P. Eastern school of mediaeval Indian painting. In Anand Krishna, ed. Chhavi... Banaras: BHU, Bharat Kala Bhavan, 1971, 91-103.

07347 PAL, P. Evidences of Buddhist painting in E. India in the 15th C. In JASCalcutta 8 (1866) 267-70.

07348 _____. A new document of Indian painting. In JRAS (1965) 103-11 + 6pl.

07349 SARASWATI, S.K. East Indian manuscript painting. In Anand Krishna, ed. Chhavi... Banaras: BHU, Bharat Kala Bhavan, 1971, 243-262.

3. Sculpture in Stone, Bronze, and Terracotta

07350 BANERJI, R.D. The eastern Indian school of medieval sculpture. Delhi: ASI, 1933. 203p. (ASI new imperial series, 47)

07351 BERNET KEMPERS, A.J. The bronzes of Nalanda and Hindu-Javanese art. Leiden: Brill, 1933. 88p.

07352 BHATTACHARJEE, A. Icons and sculptures of early and medieval Assam. Delhi: Inter-India, 1978. 76p. + 16pl.

07353 DANI, A.H. Buddhist sculpture in East Pakistan. Karachi: Dept. of Archaeology in Pakistan, 1959. 152p., incl. 46pl.

07354 DAS GUPTA, S.K. History of the Surya image in Bengal. In Folklore(C) 8 (1967) 423-27.

07355 HAQUE, Z. Terracotta decorations of late mediaeval Bengal: portrayal of a society. Dacca: Asiatic Soc. of Bangladesh, 1980. 178p. + 44pl.

07356 HUNTINGTON, S.L. The origin and development of sculpture in Bihar and Bengal, c. 8th-12th centuries. Ph.D. diss. UCLA, 1972. 920p. [UM 72-25,783]

07357 HUSSAIN, SHAHANARA. The terracotta plaques from Paharpur. In JASP 8 (1963) 5-11.

07358 KRAMRISCH, S. Pāla and Sena sculpture. In Rūpam 40 (1929) 107-26.

07359 SARASWATI, S.K. Early sculpture of Bengal. 2nd ed. Calcutta: Sambodhi, 1962. 128p. + 24pl.

07360 WEINER, S.L. From Gupta to Pāla sculpture. In ArtAs 25,2/3 (1962) 167-92 + 15pl.

4. Architecture: Buddhist, Hindu, and Muslim

07361 DIKSHIT, K.N. Excavations at Paharpur, Bengal. Delhi: MPGOI, 1938. 99p.

07362 FARID, G.S. The tombs and mausoleums of sultans of Bengal. In Indo-Iranica 31,3/4 (1978) 63-79.

07363 HASAN, S.M. The Adina Masjid, the largest mosque ever built in IndoPak sub-continent at Hazrat Pandua, A.H. 776/A.D. 1374-75; a monograph. Dacca: Soc. for Pakistan Studies, 1970. 76p.

07364 _____. Mosque architecture of pre-Mughal Bengal. 2nd rev. ed. Dacca: University Press, 1979. 217p. + 21pl.

07365 HUSAIN, A.B.M. A study of the Firozah Minar at Gaur. In JASP 8,2 (1963) 53-70.

07366 LOHUIZEN-DE LEEUW, J.E. VAN. The ancient Buddhist monastery at Paharpur. In Antiquity & Survival 2,1 (1957) 29-42.

07367 QADIR, M.A.A. A guide to Paharpur. Karachi: Dept. of Archaeology, 1963. 32p.

07368 SARASWATI, S.K. Architecture of Bengal. Book 1 (ancient phase). Calcutta: G. Bharadwaj, 1976. 176p. + 25pl.

XI. THE HIMALAYAN RIM: THE NEPAL AREA AND BHUTAN IN THE EARLY MEDIEVAL PERIOD (600-1530 AD)

A. General Histories

07369 ARIS, M. Bhutan: the early history of a Himalayan kingdom. Warminster, Wilts.: Aris & Phillips, 1978. 240p.

07370 CHOUDHARY, R.K. Nepal and the Karnatas of Mithila, 1097-1500 AD. In JIH 36 (1958) 123-30.

07371 JAYASWAL, K.P. Chronology and history of Nepal. Varanasi: Bharati-Prakashan, 1976. 112p. [1st pub. in JBORS 22,3 (1936) 147-264]

07372 PETECH, L. Mediaeval history of Nepal (c. 750-1480). Rome: IIMEO, 1958. 239p. (Serie orientale Roma, 10)

07373 RAY, H.C. Dynastic history of Nepal. In his (ed.) The dynastic history of northern India (early medieval period). Calcutta: U. of Calcutta, 1931, v. 1, 185-234.

07374 REGMI, D.R. Medieval Nepal. Calcutta: KLM, 1965-66. 4 v.

07375 _____. Medieval system of administration in Nepal, as it existed till the 15th century AD. In IAC 11,2 (1962) 152-76.

07376 _____. Sources for a history of Nepal (880-1680 AD). In JBORS 28 (1942) 24-42.

07377 THAKUR, U. Harisiṁhadeva and the Karnāṭa invasion of Nepal. In JAIH 3,1/2 (1969-70) 77-85.

07378 Vaṁśāvalī. History of Nepal. Tr. from Parbatiya by Shew Shunker Singh & Pandit Gunanand. E. by D. Wright. Kathmandu: Nepal Antiquated Book Pub., 1972. 320p. [1st pub. 1877]

B. Religio-Philosophical Traditions

07379 RAJENDRA RAM. A history of Buddhism in Nepal, A.D. 704-1396. Patna: Janabharati Prakashana, 1978. 249p.

C. Art and Architecture of Nepal

07380 GOETZ, H. Early Indian sculptures from Nepal. In ArtAs 18 (1955) 61-74.

07381 MONOD-BRUHL, O. Une peinture népalaise du Musée Guimet. In ArtsAs 6,4 (1959) 297-310.

07382 MOOKERJEE, M. An illustrated cover of a manuscript of the Ashṭasāhasrikā Prajñāparamitā in a private collection. In LK 6 (1959) 56-62.

07383 _____. Two illuminated manuscripts in the Asutosh Museum of Indian Art. In JISOA 15 (1947) 89-99.

07384 PAL, P. Umā-Maheśvara theme in Nepali sculpture. In Boston Museum of Fine Arts, Bulletin, 66 (1968) 85-100.

07385 SLUSSER, M. Nepali sculptures - new discoveries. In P. Pal, ed. Aspects of Indian art. Leiden: Brill, 1972, 93-104.

5

The Mughals, Marathas, and the Rise of British Power: South Asia in an Era of World Integration and Interaction, 1526–1818

I. REFERENCE WORKS, SOURCES, AND GENERAL HISTORIES OF SOUTH ASIA IN THE MUGHAL-MARATHA PERIOD (1526-1818)

A. Bibliography and Reference

07386 HABIB, I. An atlas of the Mughal Empire. Oxford: OUP, 1981? 160p. [forthcoming]

07387 KHAN, S.A. Sources for the history of British India in the seventeenth century. London: OUP, 1926. 395p. (Allahabad U. Studies in history, 4)

07388 MARSHALL, D.N. Mughals in India: a bibliographical survey. v. 1: Manuscripts. London: Asia, 1967. 634p. [no more pub.]

07389 SARKAR, J. Sir Jadunath Rachanāpañji. Comp. by A. De & A. Ray & B. Ray. Calcutta: Calcutta Hist. Soc., 1972. 107p. [Bibl. of J.N. Sarkar; most entries in English]

07390 SHARMA, G.N. A bibliography of mediaeval Rajasthan; social and cultural. Agra: Lakshmi Narain Agarwal, 1965. 96p.

07391 SHARMA, S.R. A bibliography of Mughal India (1526-1707 A.D.). Bombay: Karnatak Pub. House, 1938. 206p.

07392 TARAPOREVALA, V.D.B. & D.N. MARSHALL. Mughal bibliography; select Persian sources for the study of Mughals in India. Bombay: New Book Co., 1962. 164p.

B. Historiography and Sources; Numismatics

07393 DIEHL, K.S., ed. Primary sources for 16th-19th century studies in Bengal, Orissa, and Bihar libraries; seminar papers. Calcutta: AIIS, 1971. 280p.

07394 HODIVALA, S.H. Historical studies in Mughal numismatics. Calcutta: Numismatic Soc. of India, 1923. 376p.

07395 LANE-POOLE, S., comp. Coins of the Moghul Emperors of Hindustan in the British Museum. Ed. by R.S. Poole. London: British Museum, 1892. 553p.

07396 MAREK, J. Mughul miniatures as a source of history. In JPHS 11 (1963) 195-207.

07397 PRASHAD, B. & H. BEVERIDGE, ed. The Maāthir-ul-umarā... index to the English translation vols. I and II. Calcutta: Asiatic Soc., 1964. 443p.

07398 RODGERS, C.J. Catalogue of the coins in the Indian Museum. Calcutta: Panjab Govt., 1894-95. [v. 2, The Moghul Emperors]

07399 SARKAR, J.N. History of history writing in medieval India: contemporary historians: an introduction to medieval Indian historiography. Calcutta: Ratna Prakashan, 1977. 195p.

07400 ______. Sources for the study of medieval Indian history. In PPP 8,2 (1974) 382-403.

07401 SMITH, V.A. Coins of ancient India; catalogue of the coins in the Indian Museum, Calcutta. Delhi: IndBH, 1972. 3 v. [1st pub. 1906-19; v. 3, Mughal Emperors]

07402 SRIVASTAVA, K.P., ed. Mughal farmans. Lucknow: Uttar Pradesh State Archives, 1974-. v. 1, 82p. + 44 documents.

07403 WHITEHEAD, R.B. Catalogue of coins in the Panjab museum. Oxford: OUP, 1914-34. v. 2, Coins of the Mughal Emperors, 443p. + 21pl.; v. 3, Coins of Nādir Shah and the Durrani dynasty, 195p. + 14pl.

C. General Histories of the Mughal-Maratha Period

1. General Histories and Studies of "Muslim Rule in India," incl. the pre-Mughal Period

07404 ABDUL HAI, Syed. India during Muslim rule. Tr. by Mohiuddin Ahmad. Lucknow: Academy of Islamic Res. & Pub., 1977. 221p.

07405 ALAVI, R.A. Studies in the history of medieval Deccan. Delhi: IAD, 1977. 100p.

07406 ARSHAD, M. An advanced history of Muslim rule in Indo-Pakistan. Dacca: Ideal Pub., 1967. 201 + 174p.

07407 AL-BADAONI. Muntakhab-ut-tawarikh. Tr. from Persian by G.S.A. Ranking & W.H. Lowe & T. Wolseley Haig. Delhi: IAD, 1973. 3 v., 1873p. [1st pub. 1898-99]

07408 ELLIOT, H.M. & J. DOWSON, eds. The history of India, as told by its own historians: the Muhammadan period. Allahabad: Kitab Mahal, 1963-64. 8 v. [1st pub. 1867-77]

07409 FIRISHTAH, MUHAMMAD QASIM. The history of Hindostan. Tr. from Persian by A. Dow. 2nd rev. & enl. ed. ND: Today & Tomorrow's, 1973. 3 v. [1st pub. 1770-72; tr. of Tārīkh-i-Firishtah]

07410 ______. History of the rise of the Mahomedan power in India till the year AD 1612. Tr. from Persian by J. Briggs. Calcutta: Editions Indian, 1966. 4 v. [1st pub. 1908-10]

07411 GREWAL, J.S. Muslim rule in India - the assessment of British historians. NY: OUP, 1970. 218p.

07412 HANAFI, M.A. A short history of Muslim rule in Indo-Pakistan. Dacca: Ideal Library, 1964. 317p.

07413 HODIVALA, S.K. Studies in Indo-Muslim history: a critical commentary on Elliott and Dowson's History of India as told by its own historians. Bombay: 1939. 2 v., 727p.

07414 IKRAM, S.M. Muslim civilization in India. Ed. by A.T. Embree. NY: ColUP, 1964. 325p.

07415 JAFFAR, S.M. Some cultural aspects of Muslim rule in India. Delhi: IAD, 1972. 252p. [1st pub. 1939]

07416 KEENE, H.G. A sketch of the history of Hindustan from the first Muslim conquest to the fall of the Mughal Empire. Delhi: IAD, 1972. 476p.

07417 LANE-POOLE, S. Medieval India under Mohammedan rule (A.D. 712-1764). NY: Haskell House, 1970. 449p. [Rpt. 1903 ed.]

07418 MAHAJAN, V.D. Muslim rule in India. 2nd ed., rev. Delhi: S. Chand, 1965. 328 + 329p.

07419 MALIK, H. Moslem nationalism in India and Pakistan. Washington: Public Affairs Press, 1963. 355p. [also covers 1857 to the present]

07420 NIZAM AL-DIN AHMAD, Khvajah. The Ṭabaqāt-i-Akbarī of Khwājah Nīzāmuddīn Aḥmad: a history of India from the early Musalman invasions to the thirty-sixth year of the reign of Akbar. Tr. from Persian by B. De. Calcutta: Asiatic Soc., 1936-1973. 3 v. (BI, 225, 300)

07421 PRASAD, I. A short history of Muslim rule in India, from the advent of Islam to the death of Aurangzeb. Rev. ed. Allahabad: Indian Press, 1965. 694p.

07422 SHARMA, S.R. The crescent in India; a study in medieval history. Rev. 3rd ed. Bombay: Hind Kitabs,

1966. 747p.

07423 SYED MAHMUD, Dr. The India of yesterday. Tr. from Urdu by Syed Asadullah. Hyderabad: Inst. of Indo Middle East Cultural Studies, 1957. 185p.

2. General Studies of South Asia during the Period of Mughal Rule (1526-1707)

07424 CHAND, TARA. Society and state in the Mughal period. ND: PDMIB, 1965. 112p.

07425 EDWARDES, S.M. & H.L.O. GARRETT. Mughal rule in India. NY: AMS Press, 1976. 374p. + 15pl. [Rpt. 1930 ed.]

07426 HOLDEN, E.S. The Mogul emperors of Hindustan, A.D. 1398-A.D. 1707. Delhi: Metropolitan Book Co., 1975. 365p. + 10pl. [Rpt. 1895 ed.]

07427 JAFFAR, S.M. The Mughal Empire, from Babar to Aurangzeb. Delhi: Ess Ess, 1974. 441p. [Rpt. 1936 ed.]

07428 KEENE, H.G. The Turks in India; critical chapters on the administration of that country by the Chughtai, Babar, and his descendants. Delhi: IAD, 1972. 255p. [1st pub. 1879]

07429 KENNEDY, P. History of the great Moghuls, 1398 to 1739 AD. Calcutta: Thacker Spink, 1968. 556p.

07430 MAJUMDAR, R.C., ed. The Mughul Empire. Bombay: BVB, 1974. 1004p. (HCIP, 7)

07431 PANDEY, A.B. Later medieval India; a history of the Mughals. Allahabad: Central Book Dept., 1963. 537p.

07432 PRASAD, I. The Mughal Empire. Allahabad: Chugh, 1974. 694p.

07433 SHARMA, S.R. Mughal empire in India; a systematic study including source material. Rev. ed. Agra: Lakshmi Narain Agarwal, 1966. 655p.

07434 SHERWANI, H.K. Cultural trends in medieval India; architecture, painting, literature & language. Bombay: Asia, 1969. 111p.

07435 SRIVASTAVA, A.L. The Mughul Empire, 1526-1803 A.D. 5th rev. ed. Agra: S.L. Agarwala, 1966. 591p. [1st ed. 1952]

07436 TRIPATHI, R.P. Rise and fall of the Mughal empire. Allahabad: Central Book Depot, 1956. 527p.

3. General Studies of South Asia during the period of Maratha Supremacy (1674-1818)

07437 ABDUR RASHID, Sheikh. History of the Muslims of Indo-Pakistan sub-continent, 1707-1806. Lahore: Res. Soc. of Pakistan, 1978-.

07438 DUFF, J.G. History of the Mahrattas. Ed. by J.P. Guha. ND: Associated Pub. House, 1971. 2 v. [1st pub. 1876]

07439 JOSHI, V.V. Clash of three empires; a study of British conquest of India with special reference to the Maratha people. Allahabad: Kitabistan, 1941. 207p.

07440 KINCAID, C.A. & D.B. PARASNIS. History of the Maratha people. 2nd ed. London: OUP, 1931. 503p.

07441 OWEN, S. India on the eve of the British conquest; an analytical history of India (1627-1761). London: OUP, 1872. 204p. [Rpt. Calcutta: Susil Gupta, 1954]

07442 PRASAD, I. India in the eighteenth century. Allahabad: Chugh, 1973. 284p.

07443 RAO, V.D., ed. Studies in Indian history: Dr. A. G. Pawar felicitation volume. Kolhapur: Y.P. Powar, 1968. 444p.

07444 SARDESAI, G.S. The main currents of Maratha history. Rev. & enl. ed. Bombay: Phoenix Pub., 1959. 190p. [1st pub. 1926]

07445 ______. New history of the Marathas. Bombay: Phoenix Pub., 1957. 3 v. [1st pub. 1946-48]

07446 SARKAR, J.N. A study of eighteenth century India. Calcutta: Saraswat Library, 1976-. v. 1, 480p.

07447 VAISH, D.C.L. The rise of British power and the fall of Marathas. Lucknow: Upper India Pub. House, 1972. 703p.

II. THE MUGHAL EMPIRE: POLITICAL AND ADMINISTRATIVE UNIFICATION OF THE SUBCONTINENT UNDER MUSLIM RULE

A. The Rise and Consolidation of Mughal Rule: Babar to Shah Jahan

1. Bābar (1483-1530): Descendant of Chingīz Khān and Timur, and Founder of the Mughal Empire

07448 BABAR. Babur-nama (Memoirs of Bābur). Tr. from the original Turki text of Zahirud-dīn Muhammad Bābur Pādshāh Ghāzī by A.S. Beveridge. ND: OBRC, 1970. 880p. [1st pub. 1922]

07449 ______. Memoirs of Zehīr-ed-Dīn Muhammed Bābur. Tr. from Turkī by J. Leyden & W. Erskine. Rev. & ann. by L. King. London: OUP, 1921. 2 v. [1st pub. 1826; tr. of Bābar-nāma]

07450 EDWARDES, S.M. Babur: diarist and despot. London: A.M. Philpot, 1926. 138p.

07451 GRENARD, F. Baber, first of the Moguls. Tr. and adapted by H. White & R. Glaenzer. Dehra Dun: Natraj Pub., 1971. 253p. [1st pub. 1930]

07452 LAL, MUNI. Babar: life and times. ND: Vikas, 1977. 126p.

07453 LAMB, H.A. Babur, the Tiger; first of the great Moguls. Garden City, NY: Doubleday, 1961. 336p.

07454 LANE-POOLE, S. Babar. Delhi: S. Chand, 1964. 206p. (Rulers of India) [1st pub. 1899]

07455 RADHEY SHYAM. Babar. Patna: Janaki Prakashan, 1978. 567p.

07456 RUSHBROOK WILLIAMS, L.F. An empire builder of the sixteenth century; a summary account of the political career of Zahir-ud-din Muhammad, surnamed Babur, being the Allahabad University lectures for 1915-16. Delhi: S. Chand, 1962. 188p.

2. Humāyūn (1508-1556), and the Interregnum (1538-45) of the Afghan, Sher Shāh

07457 AVASTHY, R.S. The Mughal emperor Humayun. Allahabad: U. of Allahabad, 1967. 491p.

07458 GULBADAN, Begam. The history of Humayun. Tr. by A.S. Beveridge. London: RAS, 1902. 427p. [tr. of Humāyūn-nāma; rpt. Delhi: IAD, 1972]

07459 KHAN, IQTIDAR ALAM. Mirza Kamran, a biographical study. Bombay: Asia, 1964. 78p. [Humayun's brother]

07460 JAWHAR. The Tezkereh al vakiāt; or, Private memoirs of the Moghul Emperor Humāyūn. Tr. by C. Stewart. Kumar Bros., 1970. 127p. [1st ed. 1832]

07461 LAL, MUNI. Humayun. ND: Vikas, 1978. 242p.

07462 PRASAD, I. The life and times of Humayun. Allahabad: Central Book Depot, 1976. 422p. + 8pl. [Rpt. 1955 ed.]

07463 QANUNGO, K.R. Sher Shah, a critical study based on original sources. Calcutta: K. Majumdar, 1921. 452p.

07464 ______. Sher Shah and his times. An old story retold by the author after decades from a fresh standpoint. Bombay: Orient Longmans, 1965. 459p.

07465 RAY, S. Humayun in Persia. Calcutta: ASB, 1948. 113p. (Its monograph series, 6)

07466 SENSARMA, P. The military profile of Sher Shah Sur. Calcutta: dist. Naya Prokash, 1976. 160p.

07467 SIDDIQI, I.H. History of Sher Shah Sur. Aligarh: P.C. Dwadas Shreni, 1971. 171p.

3. Akbar (1542-1605): Indianization of Mughal Rule, Bureaucracy, and Cultural Rapprochement of Hindus and Muslims

a. original sources: Indian and European

07468 ABUL FAZL. Ain i Akbari. Tr. from Persian by H. Blochmann. Lahore: Qausain, 1975. 741p. + 17pl. (BI, 61) [Rpt. of 2nd ed., 1927; 1st pub. 1871]

07469 ______. Akbar-nama. Tr. from Persian by E. Mackenzie. Lahore: Sheikh Mubarak Ali, 1975. 155p. [Rpt. 1875 ed.; incl. Akbar-nama of Shaikh Illahdad Faizi Sirhindi, 122-155]

07470 ______. The Akbar nāma of Abu-l-Fazl: history of the reign of Akbar, including an account of his predecessors. Tr. from Persian by H. Beveridge. Delhi: Ess Ess, 1977. 3 v. [Rpt. of 1902-39 ed.]

07471 MONSERRATE, A. Commentary....on his journey to the Court of Akbar. Tr. from Latin by J.S. Hoyland & annot. by S.N. Banerjee. London: OUP, 1922. 288p.

07472 MUKHIA, H. Historians and historiography during the reign of Akbar. ND: Vikas, 1976. 197p.

b. biographies and political studies

07473 BINYON, L. Akbar. NY: D. Appleton, 1932. 158p.

07474 MALLESON, G.B. Akbar and the rise of the Mughal Empire. Ed. by W.W. Hunter. Lahore: Islamic Book Service, 1979. 204p. (Rulers of India) [Rpt. 1903 ed.]

07075 NOER, F.C.K.A., Graf von. The Emperor Akbar: a contribution towards the history of India in the 16th century. Tr. from German and rev. by A.S. Beveridge. Patna: Academica Asiatica, 1973. 2 v. [Rpt. 1890 ed.]

07476 QURESHI, I.H. Akbar: the architect of the Mughul empire. Karachi: Ma aref, 1978. 300p.

07477 SHELAT, J.M. Akbar. Bombay: BVB, 1959. 396p.

07478 SMITH, V.A. Akbar, the Great Mogul, 1542-1605. 2nd ed., rev. Delhi: A. Chand, 1966. 379p. [1st pub. 1919]

07479 SRIVASTAVA, A.L. Akbar the Great. Agra: Shiva Lal Agarwala, 1962-. v. 1, 375p.

4. Jahāngīr (1569-1627), Patron of the Arts; his Empress Nūr Jahān

07480 HASAN, S. NURUL. The theory of the Nur Jahan "junta": a critical examination. In PIHC 21 (1958) 324-35.

07481 JAHANGIR. Memoir of the Emperor Jahangueir. Tr. from Persian by D. Price. Delhi: Rare Books, 1970. 247p. [Rpt. 1904 ed.]

07482 ______. Memoirs of Jahangir. Tr. from Persian by H.M. Elliot. Ed. by J. Dowson. Lahore: Islamic Book Service, 1975. 240p. [Rpt. 1891 ed.]

07483 ______. The Tūzuk-i-Jahāngīrī; or, Memoirs of Jahangir. Tr. by A. Rogers. Ed. by H. Beveridge. 2nd ed. Delhi: Munshiram, 1968. 2 v. in 1. [1st pub. 1909-14]

07484 ______. Wakiᶜāt-i Jahāngīrī. Tr. from Persian by H.M. Elliot. Lahore: Sheikh Mubarak Ali, 1975. 124p. [Rpt. from Elliot's History of India...., v. 6, 1875; extracts from Jahāngīrnāmah]

07485 PANT, C. Nur Jahan and her family. Allahabad: Dandewal Pub. House, 1978. 199p.

07486 PELSAERT, F. Jahangir's India = The Remonstrantie of Francisco Pelsaret. Tr. from Dutch by W.H. Moreland & P. Geyl. Delhi: IAD, 1972. 88p. [Rpt. 1925 ed.]

07487 PRASAD, B. History of Jahangir. London: OUP, 1922. 501p.

07488 ROE, T. The embassy of Sir Thomas Roe to India 1615-19, as narrated in his journal and correspondence. Ed. by W. Foster. Rev. ed. London: OUP, 1926. 79 + 532p. [1st ed. 1899]

07489 SHUJAUDDIN, M. & R. SHUJAUDDIN. The life and times of Noor Jahan. Lahore: Caravan Book House, 1967. 146p.

5. Shāh Jahān (1592-1666): Imperial Expansion, and Patronage of Architecture and Scholarship; Builder of the Tāj Mahal

07490 ELLIOT, H.M., tr. Shah Jahan. Lahore: Sh. Mubarak Ali, 1975. 156p. [Rpt. of translated sources from Elliot's History of India..., 1867-77]

07491 JAHĀNĀRĀ. The life of a Mogul princess: Jahānārā Begam, daughter of Shāh Jahān. Tr. from Persian by A. Butenschön. London: G. Routledge, 1931. 221p.

07492 SAKSENA, B.P. History of Shahjahan of Dihli. Allahabad: Central Book Depot, 1962. 373p. [1st pub. 1932]

07493 VENKATARAMAIAH, S., ed. Mughal archives: a descriptive catalogue of the documents pertaining to the reign of Shah Jahan, 1628-1658. Hyderabad: State Archives, Govt. of Andhra Pradesh, 1977-.

B. Aurangzīb and his Successors: Decline of the Mughals

1. Aurangzīb (1619-1707): Rejection of Akbar's Religious Toleration, and Promotion of Sunni Orthodoxy; Wars with Sikhs, Rajputs, and Marathas

a. original sources, incl. European travellers' accounts

07494 AHMAD, TASNEEM. Ishwardas: a Hindu chronicler of Aurangzeb's reign. In IsC 49,4 (1975) 223-31.

07495 AURANGZIB. Rukaᶜāt-i-Ālamgīrī; or, Letters of Aurangzebe. Tr. from Persian by J.H. Bilimoria. Delhi: IAD, 1972. 184p. [1st pub. 1908]

07496 BERNIER, F. Travels in the Mogul empire, AD 1656-1668. Rev. 2nd ed. (based upon I. Brock's translation) by A. Constable. Delhi: S. Chand, 1968. 497p. [1st pub. 1934]

07497 BHIMSEN. Sir Jadunath Sarkar birth centenary commemoration volume; English translation of Tarikh-i-dil-kasha (Memoirs of Bhimsen relating to Aurangzib's Deccan campaigns). Tr. by V.G. Khobrekar. Bombay: Dept. of Archives, Maharashtra, 1972. 288p.

07498 DAS, H.H. The Norris embassy to Aurangzib, 1699-1702. Ed. by S.C. Sarkar. Calcutta: KLM, 1959. 339p.

07499 ISHWARDAS NAGAR. Ishwardas Nagar's Futūḥāt-i-Ālamgīrī. Tr. from Persian by Tasneem Ahmad. Delhi: IAD, 1978. 305p.

07500 KHĀFI KHĀN, MUHAMMAD HĀSHIM. Aurangzeb in Muntakhab-al lubāb. Tr. from Persian by Anees Jahan Syed. Bombay: Somaiya, 1977. 427p.

07501 MANUCCI, N. A Pepys of Mogul India 1653-1708... abridged ed. of Storia do Mogor. Tr. from Italian by W. Irvine. London: Murray, 1913. 310p.

07502 ______. Storia do Mogor, or Mogul India, 1653-1708. Tr. from Italian by W. Irvine. Calcutta: Editions Indian, 1965. 4 v., 1971p. [tr. 1st pub. 1907-8]

07503 SARKAR, JADUNATH, tr. Anecdotes of Aurangzeb. 3rd ed. Calcutta: M.C. Sarkar, 1949. 128p. [tr. of Ahkam-i-Ālamgīrī, ascribed to Hamīd al-Dīn Khān Bahādur; tr. 1st pub. 1912]

07504 TAVERNIER, J.B. Travels in India. Tr. by V. Ball. Ed. by W. Crooke. ND: OBRC, 1977. 2 v. [Rpt. of 2nd ed. 1925; 1st French ed. 1676]

b. biographies and studies of Aurangzīb; Dārā Shukoh, Sufi elder brother and rival for the throne

07505 FARUKI, Z. Aurangzeb & his times. Delhi: IAD, 1972. 596p. [Rpt. 1935 ed.]

07506 GHAURI, I.A. War of succession between the sons of Shah Jahan 1657-1658. Lahore: Pub. United, 1964. 177p.

07507 HASRAT, B.J. Dara Shikuh: life & works. Calcutta: Visvabharati, 1953. 304p.

07508 LANE-POOLE, S. Aurangzib and the decay of the Mughal Empire. Delhi: S. Chand, 1964. 212p. (Rulers of India) [1st pub. 1893]

07509 QANUNGO, K.R. Dara Shukoh. 2nd ed. Calcutta: S.C. Sarkar, 1952. 320p. [1st ed. 1935]

07510 SARKAR, JADUNATH. History of Aurangzib: mainly based on Persian sources. Bombay: Orient Longmans, 1972-1974. 5v. in 4. [1st pub. 1912-24]

07511 ______. A short history of Aurangzib, 1618-1707. 3rd ed., abr. Calcutta: M.C. Sarkar, 1962. 478p.

07512 ______. Studies in Aurangzib's reign. Calcutta: M.C. Sarkar, 1933. 302p.

2. Later Mughal Emperors - General Accounts

07513 DATTA, K.K. Shah Alam II and the East India Company. Calcutta: World Press, 1965. 148p.

07514 EDWARDES, M. King of the world: the life and times of Shah Alam, Emperor of Hindustan. London: Secker & Warburg, 1970. 279p.

07515 FRANCKLIN, W. The history of the reign of Shah-Aulum, the present Emperor of Hindostaun. Lucknow: Pustak Kendra, 1973. 139p. [1st pub. 1798]

07516 GHOLĀM HOSEYN KHĀN TABĀTABĀʿĪ. A translation of the Seir mutaqherin: or, View of modern times, being an history of India, from the year 1118 to the year 1194 (this year answers to the Christian year 1781-82) of the Hedjrah, containing, in general, the reigns of the seven last emperors of Hindostan, and in particular, an account of the English wars in Bengal... Lahore: Sheikh Mubarak Ali, 1975. 4 v. [1st pub. 1789]

07517 IRVINE, W. Later Mughals. Ed. and augmented with the History of Nadir Shah's invasion, by Jadunath Sarkar. ND: OBRC, 1971. 2 v. in 1. 855p. [1st pub. 1921-22]

07518 KEENE, H.G. The fall of the Moghul Empire of Hindustan. New ed. Lahore: al-Biruni, 1975. 299p. [Rpt. 1887 ed.]

07519 LAW DE LAURISTON, J. Memoirs sur quelques affairs de l'Empire Mogol 1756-61. Ed. by A. Martineau. Paris: Champion, 1913. 589p.

07520 LOCKHART, L. Nadir Shah. London: Luzac, 1938. 344p.

07521 MALIK, Z. The reign of Muhammad Shah, 1719-1748. Bombay: Asia, 1977. 472p.

07522 SARKAR, JADUNATH. Nadir Shah in India. Calcutta: Naya Prokash, 1973. 87p. [Rpt. 1925 ed.]

07523 SHIV DĀS LAKHNAVĪ. Ṣhāhnāma munawwar kalām. Tr. from Persian by Syed Hasan Askari. Patna: Janaki Prakashan, 1980. 232p.

3. The Fall of the Mughals: Analyses from Aligarh Muslim U. and Elsewhere

07524 ATHAR ALI, M. The passing of empire: the Mughal case. In MAS 9,3 (1975) 385-96.

07525 HABIB, IRFAN. Agrarian causes of the fall of the Mughal Empire. In Enquiry (ND) ns 3 (1960) 68-80.

07526 OWEN, S.J. The fall of the Mogul Empire. 2nd ed. Varanasi: CSSO, 1960. 206p. (CSS, 7) [1st ed. 1912]

07527 SARKAR, JADUNATH. Fall of the Mughal empire. 3rd ed. Bombay: Orient Longmans, 1964-72. 4 v. [1st ed. 1932-50]

07528 Symposium: Decline of the Mughal Empire. In JAS 35,2 (1976) 221-63. [essays by M.N. Pearson, J.F. Richards, P. Hardy]

C. Political Structure and Administrative System of the Mughal Empire

1. Political Thought and Concepts of Authority

07529 CHAUBE, J. The nature of sovereignty in medieval India. In Prajna 14,1 (1968) 97-111.

07530 NATH, R. The Mughal concept of sovereignty in the inscriptions at Fatehpur Sikri, Agra and Delhi (1570-1654). In Indica 11,2 (1974) 91-100.

07531 RICHARDS, J.F. The formulation of imperial authority under Akbar and Jahangir. In his (ed.) Kingship and authority in South Asia. Madison: South Asian Studies, U. of Wisconsin, 1978, 252-85. (Its Pub. ser, 3)

07532 USMANI, A.F. Political ideas of Abul Fazl Allami (1556-1602). In IJPS 24 (1963) 259-83.

2. General Studies of Politics and Administration

07533 ATHAR ALI, M. Presidential address. In PIHC 33 (1972) 175-88.

07534 DAY, U.N. The Mughal government, A.D. 1556-1707. ND: Munshiram, 197-. 249p.

07535 IBN HASAN. The central structure of the Mughal Empire and its practical working up to the year 1657. ND: Munshiram, 1970. 398p. [1st pub. 1936]

07536 PEARSON, M.N. Political participation in Mughal India. In IESHR 9,2 (1972) 113-131.

07537 QURESHI, I.H. The administration of the Mughul Empire. Karachi: U. of Karachi, 1966. 340p.

07538 SARKAR, JADUNATH. Mughal administration. Bombay: Orient Longmans, 1972. 179p. [Rpt. of 3rd ed., 1935]

07539 SATISH CHANDRA. Parties and politics at the Mughal court, 1707-1740. Aligarh: Aligarh Muslim U., 1959. 309p.

07540 SHARMA, S.R. Mughal government and administration. Bombay: Hind Kitabs, 1951. 290p.

07541 SRIVASTAVA, M.P. Policies of the great Mughals. Allahabad: Chugh, 1978. 214p.

07542 TRIPATHI, R.P. Some aspects of Muslim administration. Allahabad: Central Book Depot, 1964. 408p.

07543 YAR, MUHAMMAD KHAN. The Deccan policy of the Mughals. Lahore: United Book Corp, 1971. 334p.

3. Provincial and Local Government [see also regional sections in this chapter, below]

07544 ATHAR ALI, M. Provincial governors under Aurangzeb - an analysis. In Medieval India: a Miscellany 1 (1969) 96-133.

07545 ______. Provincial governors under Shah Jahan: an analysis. In Medieval India, a Miscellany 3 (1975) 80-112.

07546 DWIVEDI, R.D. Powers and functions of the Kotwal in Mughal India from 1526 to 1605 AD. In JIH 53,1 (1975) 57-62.

07547 SARAN, P. The provincial government of the Mughals, 1526-1658. 2nd ed. NY: Asia, 1973. 464p.

4. The Mughal Military Elite: the Mansabdārī System
a. general studies of the Mughal aristocracy

07548 ATHAR ALI, M. Foundation of Akbar's organisation of the nobility: an interpretation. In MIQ 3 (1961) 290-99.

07549 ______. The Mughal nobility under Aurangzeb. Bombay: Asia, 1966. 274p.

07550 KHAN, A.R. Chieftains in the Mughal empire in the reign of Akbar. Simla: IIAS, 1977. 271p.

07551 KHOSLA, R.P. Mughal kingship and nobility. Delhi: IAS, 1976. 311p. [Rpt. 1934 ed.]

07552 MOOSVI, SHIREEN. The magnitude of the land-revenue demand and the income of the Mughal ruling class under Akbar. In Medieval India, a Miscellany 4 (1977) 91-121.

07553 MORELAND, W.H. Rank (mansab) in the Mogul state service. In JRAS (1936) 641-65.

07554 RIZVI, S.A.A. The Mughal elite in the sixteenth and seventeenth century. In Abr-Nahrain 11 (1971) 69-104.

07555 UMAR, M. Life of the Mughal royalty in India during the 18th century. In MIQ 4 (1961) 137-153.

07556 ______. Mughal aristocracy during the 18th century. In MIQ 5 (1963) 88-112.

b. biographies of Mughal nobles, ministers, and generals

07557 AGRAWAL, C.M. Wazirs of Aurangzeb. Bodh-Gaya: Kanchan Pub., 1978. 141p.

07558 AHMAD, L. The prime ministers of Aurangzeb. Allahabad: Chugh, 1976. 160p.

07559 DAS, K.R. Raja Todar Mal. Calcutta: Saraswat Library, 1979. 325p.

07560 KHAN, IQTIDAR ALAM. The political biography of a Mughal noble: Munʿim Khān Khān-i Khānān, 1497-1575. ND: Orient Longmans, 1973. 20 + 188p.

07561 MALIK, Z. The Mughal Statesman of the eighteenth century; Khan-i-Dauran, Mir Bakshi of Muhammed Shah, 1719-1739. NY: Asia Pub. House, 1973. 120p. [1st pub. in Medieval India, a Miscellany 1 (1969) 134-232]

07562 PANDEY, R.K. Life and achievements of Muhammad Bairam Khan Turkoman. Bareilly: Prakash Book Depot, 1978. 287p.

07563 SARKAR, J.N. The life of Mir Jumla, the general of Aurangzeb. 2nd rev. and enl. ed. ND: Rajesh Pub., 1979. 452p.

07564 SINHA, P.P. Raja Birbal: life and times. Patna: Janaki Prakashan, 1980. 192p. + 8pl.

c. the Mughal military system and warfare

07565 AZIZ, ABDUL. The mansabdārī system and the Mughal army. Delhi: IAD, 1972. 242p.

07566 IRVINE, W. The army of the Indian Moghuls: its organization and administration. ND: Eurasia Pub. House, 1962. 324p. [1st pub. 1903]

07567 PHUL, R.K. Armies of the great Mughals, 1526-1707. ND: Oriental, 1978. 372p.

07568 ROY, A.C. A history of Mughal navy and naval warfares. Calcutta: World Press, 1972. 164p.

07569 SARKAR, JADUNATH. Military history of India. Calcutta: M.C. Sarkar, 1960. 179p.

07570 SARKAR, J.N. Some aspects of military thinking and practice in medieval India. Calcutta: Ratna Prakashan, 1974. 58p.

07571 ______. Some aspects of warfare in medieval India. In BPP 89 (1970) 153-71.

5. Law and Judicial Administration under the Mughals

07572 AHMAD, M.B. The administration of justice in medieval India. Karachi: Mgr. of Pub., 1951. 307p. [Rpt. 1941 ed.]

07573 AKBAR, M. The administration of justice by the Mughals. Lahore: Muhammad Ashraf, 1948. 71p.

07574 CALKINS, P.B. A note on lawyers in Muslim India. In Law & Society R. 3,2 (1968-69) 403-06.

07575 HUSAIN, W. Administration of justice during the Muslim rule in India: with a history of the origin of the Islamic legal institutions. Delhi: IAD, 1977. 185p. [Rpt. 1934 ed.]

07576 JAIN, B.S. Administration of justice in seventeenth century India (a study of salient concepts of Mughal justice). Delhi: Metropolitan Book Co., 1970. 153p.

07577 SANGAR, S.P. Crime and punishment in Mughal India. Delhi: Sterling, 1967. 249p.

07578 SMITH, G. & J.D.M. DERRETT. Hindu judicial administration in pre-British times and its lesson for today. In JAOS 95,3 (1975) 417-23.

6. Foreign Relations of the Mughals

07579 ABDUR RAHIM. Mughal relations with Persia and Central Asia; from Babur to Aurangzeb. In IsC 8,3 (1934) 457-73; 9,1 (1935) 113-30.

07580 DESAI, Z.A. Relations of India with Middle-Eastern countries during the 16-17th centuries. In JOIB 23,1/2 (1973) 75-106.

07581 GOREKAR, N.S. Indo-Iranian relations during the Mughal period. In Indica 12,1 (1975) 11-21.

07582 RAHIM, M.A. History of the Afghans in India, A.D. 1545-1631, with especial reference to their relations with the Mughals. Karachi: Pakistan Pub. House, 1961. 326p.

07583 RIAZUL ISLAM. Indo-Persian relations; a study of the political and diplomatic relations between the Mughul Empire and Iran. Teheran: Iranian Culture Foundation, 1970. 287p.

07584 VARMA, R.C. Foreign policy of the great Mughals, 1526-1727 A.D. Agra: Shiva Lal Agarwala, 1967. 243p.

D. Economic Activity and Institutions under the Mughals

1. General Economic Histories

07585 ALI, A.U. Medieval India: social and economic conditions. London: OUP, 1932. 55p.

07586 CHABLANI, H.L. The economic condition of India during the sixteenth century. Delhi: Oxford Book & Stationery Co., 1929. 113p.

07587 CHICHEROV, A.I. India: Economic development in the 16th-18th centuries: Outline history of crafts and trade. Moscow: Nauka, 1971. 281p. [Summarized as "A Soviet view on the economic development of India before the British conquest." In Central Asian R. 14 (1967) 57-61.]

07588 DESAI, A.V. Population & standards of living in Akbar's time. In IESHR 9,1 (1972) 43-62.

07589 GUPTA, S. Potential of industrial revolution in pre-British India. In EPW 14,9 (1980) 471-74.

07590 HABIB, I. Potentialities of capitalist development in the economy of Mughal India. In JEH 29,1 (1969) 32-78.

07591 KULSHRESHTHA, S.S. The development of trade and industry under the Mughals, 1526 to 1707 A.D., based upon original sources. Allahabad: Kitab Mahal, 1964. 276p.

07592 MORELAND, W.H. From Akbar to Aurangzeb; a study in Indian economic history. ND: OBRC, 1972. 364p. [1st pub. 1923]

07593 ______. India at the death of Akbar; an economic study. Delhi: Atma Ram, 1962. 306p. [Rpt. 1920 ed.]

07594 MUKERJEE, R.K. The economic history of India, 1600-1800. Allahabad: Kitab Mahal, 1967. 195p. [Rpt. 1941 ed.]

07595 RAYCHAUDHURI, T. Patterns of economic organization and activity in seventeenth century India. In Intl. Conf. of Econ. History, 2nd, Aix-en-Provence, 1962. Paris: Mouton, 1965, v. 2, 751-60.

07596 SARKAR, J.N. Studies in economic life in Mughal India. Delhi: Oriental, 1975. 433p.

2. The Agrarian System under the Mughals: Land Tenure and Revenue

07597 GROVER, B.R. Nature of dehat-i-taaluqu (Zamindari villages) and the evolution of the taaluqdari system during the Mughal age. In IESHR 2 (1965) 166-77, 259-90.

07598 ______. Nature of land-rights in Mughal India. In IESHR 1 (1963) 1-23.

07599 HABIB, IRFAN. The agrarian system of Mughal India, 1556-1707. NY: Asia, 1963. 453p.

07600 HASAN, S. NURUL. Zamindars under the Mughals. In R.C. Frykenberg, ed. Land control & social structure in Indian history. Madison: UWiscP, 1969, 17-31.

07601 MORELAND, W.H. The agrarian system of Moslem India: a historical essay with appendices. 2nd ed. Delhi: OBRC, 1968. 296p. [1st pub. 1929]

07602 RAYCHAUDHURI, T.K. The agrarian system of Mughal India. In Enquiry (ND) ns 2 (1965) 92-121.

07603 SHARMA, S.R. Assessment and collection of land

of land revenue under Akbar. In IHQ 14 (1938) 705-36.

07604 SIDDIQI, N.A. Land revenue administration under the Mughals (1700-1750). NY: Asia, 1970. 182p.

3. Public Finance; Money and Banking

07605 AZIZ, ABDUL. The imperial treasury of the Indian Mughals. Delhi: IAD, 1972. 572p. [1st pub. 1942, as v. 2 of his The Mughal Indian court and its institutions]

07606 HABIB, IRFAN. Banking in Mughal India. In T. Raychaudhuri, ed. Contributions to Indian economic history. Calcutta: KLM, 1960, 1-20.

07607 ______. Currency system of the Mughal empire 1556-1707. In MIQ 4 (1961) 1-21.

07608 ______. Usury in medieval India. In CSSH 6 (1964) 393-419. [with comment by J.J. Spengler, 420-23]

07609 HASAN, A. The silver currency output of the Mughal empire and prices in India during the 16th and 17th centuries. In IESHR 6,1 (1969) 85-116. [Critique by Om Prakash & J. Krishnamurty, with reply, in IESHR 7,1 (1970) 139-60]

07610 SATISH CHANDRA. Some aspects of the growth of a money economy in India during the seventeenth century. In IESHR 3 (1966) 321-31.

4. Transport and Communication under the Mughals

07611 AGARWAL, U. The roads from Surat to Agra in the seventeenth and eighteenth centuries. In QRHS 5,3 (1965-66) 148-55.

07612 FAROOQUE, A.K.M. Roads and communications in Mughal India. Delhi: IAD, 1977. 248p. (Its or. ser., 43)

07613 KOFFSKY, P.L. Postal systems of India (1600-1785). In BPP 90,1 (1971) 47-74.

07614 MUSTAFA, K. Travel in Mughal India. In MIQ 3 (1958) 270-84.

07615 QAISAR, A.J. Shipbuilding in the Mughal Empire during the seventeenth century. In IESHR 5 (1968) 149-70.

5. Trade and Commerce under the Mughals

07616 ARASARATNAM, S. Indian merchants and their trading methods, (circa 1700). In IESHR 3,1 (1966) 85-95.

07617 ASKARI, S.H. Mughal naval weakness and Aurangzeb's attitude toward the traders and pirates on the western coast. In JBRS 46 (1960) 1-15.

07618 COHN, B.S. The role of the Gosains in the economy of 18th and 19th century upper India. In IESHR 1,4 (1964) 175-82.

07619 PANT, D. The commercial policy of the Moguls. Delhi: IAD, 1978. 281p. [Rpt. 1930 ed.]

07620 QAISAR, A.J. Merchant shipping in India during the seventeenth century. In Medieval India, a Miscellany 2 (1972) 195-220.

07621 ______. The role of brokers in medieval India. In IHR 1 (1974) 220-46.

07622 SARKAR, J.N. Private trade in seventeenth century India. In JBRS 49 (1963) 200-52.

6. Industries and Urbanization under the Mughals

07623 CHAUDHURI, K.N. Some reflections on town and country in Mughal India. In MAS 12,1 (1978) 77-96.

07624 NAQVI, H.K. Capital cities of the Mughal Empire (1556-1803). In JPHS 13,3 (1965) 211-43.

07625 ______. Mughal Hindustan, cities and industries, 1556-1803. 2nd ed. Karachi: Natl. Book Foundation, 1974. 366p. [1st ed. 1968]

07626 ______. Progress of urbanization in United Provinces, 1550-1800. In JESHO 10 (1967) 81-101.

07627 ______. Urbanisation and urban centres under the great Mughals, 1556-1707; an essay in interpretation. Simla: IIAS, 1971-. v. 1, 210p.

07628 PRAKASH, I. Organization of industrial production in urban centers in India during the 17th century with special reference to textiles. In B.N. Ganguli, ed. Readings in Indian economic history. Bombay: Asia, 1964, 44-52.

E. Social and Cultural Life under the Mughal Empire

1. General Studies

07629 AZHAR, A.M. Social life of the Mughal emperors (1526-1707). Allahabad: Shanti Prakashan, 1975. 230p.

07630 CHOPRA, P.N. Life and letters under the Mughals. ND: Ashajanat Pub., 1976. 439p.

07631 DATTA, K.K. Survey of India's social life and economic condition in the eighteenth century, 1707-1813. ND: Munshiram, 1978. 264p. [1st ed. 1961]

07632 KHAN, Y.H. Glimpses of medieval Indian culture. 2nd ed. Bombay: Asia, 1959. 165p. [1st ed. 1957]

07633 OJHA, P.N. North Indian social life during Mughal period. Delhi: Oriental, 1975. 182p.

07634 RAGHUVANSHI, V.P.S. Indian society in the eighteenth century. ND: Associated Pub. House, 1969. 374p.

07635 SATISH CHANDRA. Writings on social history of medieval India: trends and prospects. In IHR 3,2 (1977) 267-85.

07636 SHARMA, R.C. Life of a middle-class man in the 17th century. In JIH 52,2/3 (1974) 389-403.

07637 SRIVASTAVA, A.L. Medieval Indian culture. 2nd ed. Agra: Shiva Lal Agarwala, 1975. 233p. [1st ed. 1964]

07638 SRIVASTAVA, M.P. Social life under the great Mughals, 1526-1700 A.D. Allahabad: Chugh, 1978. 148p.

07639 SURI, P. Social conditions in eighteenth century northern India. Delhi: U. of Delhi, 1977. 252p.

07640 YASIN, MOHAMMAD. A social history of Islamic India, 1605-1748. 2nd rev. ed. ND: Munshiram, 1974. 206p.

2. Caste and Social Stratification

07641 RAGHUVANSHI, V.P.S. The institution and working of caste in the latter part of the eighteenth century from European sources. In Horst Krüger, ed. Kunwar Mohammed Ashraf; an Indian scholar and revolutionary, 1903-1962. Delhi: PPH, 1966, 147-75.

07642 SINDER, L. Caste instability in Moghul India. Seoul, Korea: Intl. Culture Res. Center, Chung-Ang U., 1963. 294p.

07643 SMITH, W.C. The Mughal empire and the middle class: a hypothesis. In IsC 18,3 (1944) 349-63.

3. Social and Cultural Role of Women

07644 MISRA, R. Women in Mughal India: 1526-1748. Delhi: Munshiram, 1967. 177p.

07645 MUKHERJEE, I. Social status of North Indian women, 1526-1707 A.D. Agra: Shiva Lal Agarwala, 1972. 172p.

4. Education and Learning

07646 AZIZ, ABDUL. The imperial library of the Mughals. Lahore: Panjab U. Press, 1967. 62p.

07647 BEARCE, G.D. Intellectual and cultural characteristics of India in a changing era, 1740-1800. In JAS 25 (1965) 3-17.

07648 JAFFAR, S.M. Education in Muslim India; being an inquiry into the state of education during the Muslim period of Indian history, 1000-1800 A.C. Delhi: IAD, 1973. 261p. [Rpt. 1936 ed.]

07649 LAW, N.N. Promotion of learning in India during Muhammadan rule (by Muhammadans). London: Longmans, Green & Co., 1916. 259p.

07650 OHDEDAR, A.K. The growth of the library in modern India: 1498-1836. Calcutta: World Press, 1966. 268p.

07651 PRIOLKAR, A.K. The printing press in India, its

beginnings and early development; being a quatercentenary commemoration study of the advent of printing in India (in 1556). Bombay: Marathi Samshodhana Mandala, 1958. 363p.

07652 SAHAY, B.K. Education and learning under the great Mughals, 1526-1707 A.D., with a special reference to contemporary literatures. Bombay: New Literature Pub. Co., 1968. 238p.

F. Religions under the Mughals: Hinduism, Islam, and the State [see regional sections below for Christianity, Sikhism, etc.]

1. General Studies of the Religious Policy of the Mughals

07653 AZIZ AHMAD. Moghulindien und Dār al-Islām. In Saeculum 12,3 (1961) 266-290.

07654 ______. The role of ulemā in Indo-Muslim history. In Studia Islamica 31 (1970) 1-13.

07655 FANĪ, MUHAMMAD MUḤSIN. The Dabistan or School of Manners: the religious beliefs, observances, philosophic opinions and social customs of the nations of the East. Tr. from Persian by D. Shea; tr. & ed. by A. Troyler. Washington: M. Walter Dunne, 1901. 411p. [1st pub. 1843]

07656 GRAHAM, G.M. Akbar and Aurangzeb--syncretism and separatism in Mughal India, a reexamination. In MW 59 (1969) 106-26.

07657 HAQ, S.M. Influence of orthodoxy at the Mughal court (seventeenth century). In JPHS 25,3 (1977) 151-76.

07658 ______. Sufi Shaykhs and Sufi poets in the 17th, 18th and 19th centuries. In JPHS 25,2 (1977) 77-124.

07659 QURESHI, I.H. Ulema in politics; a study relating to the political activities of the ulema in the South-Asian subcontinent from 1556 to 1947. Karachi: Maᶜaref, 1972. 432p.

07660 ROY CHOUDHURY, M.L. The state and religion in Mughal India. Calcutta: India Publicity Soc., 1951. 386p.

07661 SATISH CHANDRA. Jizyah and the state in India during the 17th century. In JESHO 12 (1969) 322-40.

07662 SHARMA, S.R. The religious policy of the Mughal emperors. 3rd ed. NY: Asia, 1972. 245p. [2nd ed.: 1962. 206p.]

07663 SMITH, W.C. The ulama in Indian politics. In C.H. Philips, ed. Politics and society in India. London: Allen & Unwin, 1963, 39-51.

2. Akbar's Syncretic "Divine Faith," the Dīn-i-Ilāhī, and his Policy of Religious Tolerance

07664 AMBASHTHYA, B.P., ed. Contributions on Akbar and the Parsees. Patna: Janaki, 1976. 177p.

07665 AZIZ AHMAD. Akbar, hérétique ou apostat? In JA 249 (1961) 21-35.

07666 FAZLUR RAHMAN, A.K.M. Akbar's religion. In JASP 10 (1965) 121-34.

07667 KHAN, I.A. The nobility under Akbar and the development of his religious policy, 1560-80. In JRAS (1968) 29-36.

07668 KRISHNAMURTY, R. Akbar, the religious aspect. Baroda: MSUB, 1961. 184p.

07669 ROY CHOUDHURY, M.L. The Dīn-i-Ilāhī, or, The religion of Akbar. Calcutta: U. of Calcutta, 1941. 337p.

07670 WELLESZ, E. Akbar's religious thought, reflected in Mogul painting. London: Allen & Unwin, 1952. 47p. + 40pl.

3. Aurangzīb's Persecution of Hindus, Sikhs, and Shīᶜās in the Name of Sunni Orthodoxy

07671 AHUJA, A.M. & N.D. AHUJA. Persecution of Muslims by Aurangzeb. Chandigarh: Kirti Pub. House, 1975. 40p.

07672 BANERJEE, A.C. Aurangzeb and the Sikh Gurus. In Harbans Singh and N.G. Barrier, eds. Panjab past and present: essays in honour of Dr. Ganda Singh. Patiala: Punjabi U., 1976, 119-64.

07673 SARKAR, J.N. Rajasthani letter regarding temple destruction in Amber. In BPP 94,179 (1975) 89-105.

4. Developments within Indian Islam under the Mughals

a. general studies

07674 ABBOTT, F. Islam in India before Shah Waliullah. In Studies in Islam 1 (1964) 1-11, 101-16.

07675 RIZVI, S.A.A. Muslim revivalist movements in northern India in the sixteenth and seventeenth centuries. Agra: Agra U., 1965. 497p.

07676 ______. Religious and intellectual history of the Muslims in Akbar's reign, with special reference to Abūʾl Fazl, 1556-1605. ND: Munshiram, 1975. 564p.

b. Shaikh Aḥmad Sirhindī (1564-1625): Naqshbandīya Sufi, reconciler of Sufism and Sunni orthodoxy

07677 AZIZ AHMAD. Religious and political ideas of Shaikh Ahmad Sirhindi. In Rivista degli studi orientali (Rome) 36 (1961) 259-270.

07678 FARUQI, B.A. Imān-i-Rabbānī Mujaddid-i-Alf-i-Thānī Shaikh Aḥmad Sirhindī's conception of tawhīd; or the Mujaddid's conception of tawhīd. Lahore: Sh. Muhammed Ashraf, 1943. 182p.

07679 FRIEDMAN, Y. Shaykh Ahmad Sirhindi: an outline of his thought and a study of his image in the eyes of posterity. Montreal: McGill U. Inst. of Islamic Studies, 1971. 130p. (McGill Islamic Studies, 2)

c. Shāh Walīullāh of Delhi (1703-1763): premodern reformer and revitalizer of Indian Islam

07680 BALJON, M.S. Prophetology of Shah Wali Allah. In Islamic studies 9,1 (1970) 69-79.

07681 JALBANI, G.H. Teachings of Shāh Walīyullāh of Delhi. Lahore: Sh. Muhammad Ashraf, 1967. 199p.

07682 MUZTAR, A.D. Shah Wali Allah: a saint-scholar of Muslim India. Islamabad: Natl. Cmsn. on Historical and Cultural Res., 1979. 235p.

07683 WALIULLAH, Shah. al-Khair al-kathir. Tr. by G.N. Jalbani. Lahore: Sh. Muhammad Ashraf, 1974. 200p.

07684 ______. Shah Waliyullah's Taᶜwil al-ahadith. Tr. by G.N. Jalbani. Lahore: Sh. Muhammad Ashraf, 1973. 103p.

5. Christianity and the Mughal Empire

07685 CAMPOS, A. Jerome Zavier, S.J. and the Muslims of the Mughal Empire; controversial works and missionary activity. Schöneck-Bachenreid: Nouvelle revue de science missionaire Suisse (1957) 260p. (Its Suppl. 6)

07686 DU JARRIC, P. Akbar and the Jesuits: an account of the Jesuit missions to the court of Akbar. Tr. by C.H. Payne. ND: Tulsi Pub. House, 1979. 288p. + 8pl. [Rpt. 1926 ed.; 1st pub. 1614]

07687 MACLAGAN, E.D. The Jesuits and the Great Mogul. London: Burns, Oates & Washbourne, 1932. 433p.

G. Literatures of Court and Camp: Persian and Early Urdu under the Mughal Empire

1. Indo-Persian Literature: Blossoming of Verse, Letter-writing, and History

07688 ᶜABD AL-GHANI, M. A history of Persian language and literature at the Mughul court, with a brief survey of the growth of Urdu language (Babur to Akbar). Allahabad: The Indian Press, 1929-30. 3 v.

07689 ABIDI, S.A.H. The story of Padmāvat in Indo-Persian literature. In Indo-Iranica 15 (1962) 1-11.

07690 ARSHAD, A.D. A life sketch of Faizi: A.H. 955-1004. In JRSP 3,1/2 (1966) 139-57.

07691 BAUSANI, A. Indian elements in Indo-Persian poetry: the style of Ganīmat Kunğāhī. In J.M. Barral, ed. Orientalia Hispanica.... Leiden: Brill, 1974, v. 1, 105-19.

07692 BOWEN, J.C.E. The golden pomegranate: a selection from the poetry of the Mogul Empire in India, 1526-1858; rendered into English verse. London: Baker, 1966. 120p.

07693 NAIK, C.R. ʿAbduʾr-Rahim Khān-I-Khānān and his literary circle. Ahmedabad: Gujarat U., 1966. 583p.

07694 NANDA LĀLA. The Pilgrim's way; diwan of Bhai Nand Lal Goya... Tr. from Persian by B.P.L. Bedi. Patiala: Punjabi U., 1969. 129p.

07695 NIZAMI, K.A. Persian literature under Akbar. In MIQ 3 (1961) 300-28.

07696 RAHMAN, M.L. Persian literature in India during the time of Jahangir and Shah Jahan. Baroda: Dept. of Persian and Urdu, MSUB, 1970. 60 + 203p.

07697 RAHMAN, S.S.A. Kashmir in Indo-Persian literature. In Indo-Iranica 19,2 (1966) 1-22; 20,1 (1967) 1-20.

07698 SARKAR, J.N. Historical biography in Persian in medieval India. In Indo-Iranica 29 (1976) 29-56.

07699 SINGH, S.B. Rahim. ND: NBT, 1967. 116p.

07700 TIKKU, G.L. Muḥammad Ṭahir Ghanī; an Indian allegorist of the Persian language. In Studies in Islam 3,4 (1966) 185-200.

07701 UDHRAIN, S.D., tr. Star-lore; being an account of the disposition of the planets in the 12 houses of the horoscope, with the Persian-Sanskrit verses composed by Nawab Khan-i-Khan an Abdul Rahim of Akbar's Court. ND: Sagar, 1973. 161p.

07702 ZEB-UN-NISSA, Begum. The diwan of Zeb-un-Nissa, the first fifty ghazals. Tr. from Persian by Magan Lal & J.D. Westbrook. 2nd ed. Lahore: Orientalia, 1954. 100p.

2. Development of Literary Urdu out of the Dakhnī of the Provincial Sultanates

07703 BUKHARI, S.A.W. A brief history of the origin of Urdu & Hindu poets of the Urdu language. In J. of the Annamalai Univ. Part A, Humanities 25 (1964) 80-90.

07704 HASAN, M. Nazir Akbarabadi. ND: Sahitya Akademi, 1973. 72p.

07705 KHAN, Y.H. The origin and growth of the Urdu language in medieval times. In IsC 39 (1956) 351-64.

07706 LEHMAN, F. Urdu literature and Mughal decline. In Mahfil 6,2/3 (1970) 125-31.

07707 PRITCHETT, F.W. Convention in the classical Urdu ghazal; the case of Mīr. In JSAMES 3,1 (1979) 60-77.

07708 RUSSELL, R. An eighteenth century Urdu satirist. In IL 2 (1958-59) 36-45. [on Mīrzā Rafīʿ Saudā, 1707-1781]

07709 RUSSELL, R. & K. ISLAM. Three Mughal poets; Mir, Sauda, Mir Hasan. Cambridge: HUP, 1968. 290p. (UNESCO series)

07710 SAYED MOHAMED. The value of Dakhni language and literature. Mysore: U. of Mysore, 1968. 59p.

H. Art and Architecture under the Mughals

1. Indian Miniature-Painting - Collections from Mughal and Other Periods

07711 ARNOLD, T.W. The library of A. Chester Beatty; a catalogue of the Indian miniatures. London: E. Walker, 1936. 3 v.

07712 BINNEY, E. Persian and Indian miniatures from the collection of Edwin Binney, 3rd, exhibited at the Portland Art Museum, September 28-November 29, 1962. Portland, Oregon: Portland Art Assn., 1962. 48p.

07713 CHANDRA, PRAMOD, ed. Indian miniature paintings: the collection of Ernest C. Watson & Jane Werner Watson. Madison: Elvehjem Art Centre, U. of Wisconsin, 1971. 153p.

07714 ETTINGHAUSEN, R. Paintings of the sultans and emperors of India in American collections. ND: Lalit Kalā Akademi, 1961. 35p.

07715 GANGOLY, O.C. Critical catalogue of miniature paintings in the Baroda Museum. Baroda: The Museum and Picture Gallery, 1961. 192p.

07716 GOETZ, H. The Indian and Persian miniature paintings in the Rijkspretenkabinet (Rijksmuseum) Amsterdam. Amsterdam: Rijks-Museum, 1958. 67p.

07717 Indian painting: Mughal and Rajput and a Sultanate manuscript. London: P. & D. Colnaghi, 1978. 160p. incl. 73pl.

07718 KHANDALAVALA, K. & MOTI CHANDRA, ed. Miniatures and sculptures from the collection of the late Sir Cowasji Jehangir, Bart. Bombay: Prince of Wales Museum, 1965. 44p.

07719 KHANDALAVALA, K. & MOTI CHANDRA & PRAMOD CHANDRA. Miniature painting: a catalogue of the exhibition of the Sri Motichand Khajanchi Collection. ND: Lalit Kala Akademi, 1960. 64p.

07720 KÜHNEL, E. Indische Miniaturen aus dem Besitz der Staatlichen Museen zu Berlin. Berlin: Mann, 1937. 32p.

07721 Miniatures, Lahore Museum collections. Lahore: Panjabi Adabi Academy, 1964. v. 1, 28p., incl. 10pl.

07722 Painting for the Royal Courts of India: to be exhibited for sale by Spink & Son Ltd. London: Spink, 197-. 43p.

07723 SKELTON, R. Fondazione "Giorgio Cini", Venice. Centro di cultura e civiltà. Istituto di storia dell' arte. Catalogue of the exhibition. Venezia: N. Pozza, 1961. 119p. + 98pl. (Its Cataloghi di mostre, 13)

07724 SMITHSONIAN INSTITUTION. Indian miniatures from the collection of Mildred and W.G. Archer, London. Washington: Smithsonian Institution, 1963. 1 v. (Smithsonian pub., 4520)

07725 WELCH, S.C., JR. A flower from every meadow: Indian paintings from American collections. NY: Asia Society, 1973. 142p.

07726 ______. Mughal and Deccani miniature paintings from a private collection. In Ars Orientalis 5 (1963) 221-23 + 15pl.

07727 WELCH, S.C., JR. & M.C. BEACH. Gods, thrones & peacocks: northern Indian painting from two traditions, fifteenth to nineteenth centuries. NY: Asia Soc., 1965. 129p.

2. Painting under the Mughals [for regional traditions see below]
a. general surveys and studies

07728 ANAND KRISHNA. Early Mughal painting. ND: Lalit Kalā Akademi, 1971. 4p. + 6pl.

07729 ARDESHIR, A.C. Moghul miniature painting. In RL 1,2 (1940) 19-37 + 4pl.

07730 BEACH, M.C. The grand Mogul: imperial painting in India, 1600-1660. Williamstown, MA: Sterling and Francine Clark Art Inst., 1978. 199p. + 6pl.

07731 BINNEY, E., 3rd. Later Mughal painting. In P. Pal, ed. Aspects of Indian Art. Leiden: Brill, 1972, 118-23.

07732 BINYON, L. The court painters of the Grand Moguls; with historical introduction and notes by T.W. Arnold. London: OUP, 1921. 86p. + 40pl.

07733 BROWN, P. Indian painting under the Mughals, A.D. 1550 to A.D. 1750. Oxford: OUP, 1924. 204p. + 72pl.

07734 COOMARASWAMY, A.K. Catalogue of the Indian collections: pt. VI, Mughal painting. Boston: Museum of Fine Arts, 1930. 114p. + 74pl.

07735 DEVAPRIAM, E. The influence of Western art on Mughal painting. Ph.D. diss., Case Western Reserve U., 1972. 356p. [UM 73-6288]

07736 HÁJEK, L. Indian miniatures of the Mogul school. London: Spring Books, 1960. 88p.

07737 Indian painting, 15th-19th centuries, from the collections of Mrs. John F. Kennedy, John Kenneth Galbraith, Stuart Cary Welch and the Fogg Art Museum. Exhibition, March 10-April 20, 1965. Boston: 1965. 1 v.

07738 KHANDALAVALA, K. Some problems of Mughal painting. In LK 11 (1962) 9-13.

07739 KÜHNEL, E. Moghul-Malerei. Berlin: Mann, 195-. 63p.

07740 KURZ, O. A volume of Mughal drawings and miniatures. In London U., Warburg and Courtauld Institutes, Journal 30 (1967) 251-71.

07742 MOTI CHANDRA. The technique of Mughal painting. Lucknow: U.P. Hist. Soc., 1949. 108p.

07743 RAY, N.R. Mughal court painting: a study in social and formal analysis. Calcutta: Indian Museum, 1975. 226p.

07744 SARASVATI, S.K. Eighteenth century north Indian painting. Calcutta: Pilgrim Pub., 1969. 30p.

07745 STCHOUKINE, I.V. Les Miniatures indiennes de l'époque des grands Moghols au Musée du Louvre. Paris: E. Leroux, 1929. 106p. + 20pl.

07746 ______. La peinture indienne a l'époque des grands Moghols. Paris: E. Leroux, 1929. 214p. + 100pl.

07747 WELCH, S.C., JR. The art of Mughal India: painting and precious objects. NY: Asia Soc., 1963. 179p.

07748 ______. Early Mughal miniature paintings from two private collections shown at the Fogg Art Museum. In Ars Orientalis 3 (1959) 133-146.

07749 WILKINSON, J.V.S. Mughal painting. London: Faber & Faber, 1956. 24p. + 10pl.

2. Painters and Painting from the Courts of Humāyūn and Akbar

07750 ANAND KRISHNA. A study of the Akbari artist: Farrukh Chela. In his Chhavi.... Banaras: BHU, Bharat Kala Bhavan, 1971, 353-73.

07751 CHAGHATAI, M.A. The illustrated edition of the Razm Nama...at Akbar's court. In BDCRI 5 (1943-44) 281-329.

07752 ______. Khawajah ʾAbd al-Samad Shirīn Qalam. In JPHS 11,2 (1963) 155-81.

07753 FAROOQI, A. Art of India and Persia. Delhi: B.R., 1979. 104p.

07754 ______. Painters of Akbar's court. In IsC 48,2 (1974) 119-26.

07755 GLÜCK, H. Die indischen Miniaturen des Haemzaeromanes im Österreichischen Museum fur Kunst und Industrie in Wien und anderen Sammlungen. Zurich: Amalthea-verlag, 1925. 155p.

07756 LEE, S.E. & PRAMOD CHANDRA. A newly discovered Tuti-Nama and the continuity of the Indian tradition of manuscript painting. In Burlington magazine 105,729 (1963) 547-554, illus.

07757 MAREK, J. & H. KNIZKOVA. The Jenghiz Khan miniatures from the court of Akbar the Great. Tr. by Olga Kuthanova. London: Spring Books, 1963. 42p. + 56pl.

07758 SPINK, W.M. & D. LEVINE. Akbar-nama: catalogue. NY: U. of the State of New York, Foreign Area Materials Center, 1968. 24p.

07759 STAUDE, W. Les artistes de la cour d'Akbar et les illustrations du Dastān i-Amīr Hamzah. In ArtsAs 2 (1955) 47-65, 83-111.

07560 ______. Moghul-Maler der Akbar-Zeit. Vienna: C. Schneid, 1935. 82p.

07761 VERMA, S.P. Art and material culture in the paintings of Akbar's court. ND: Vikas, 1978. 38 + 150p. + 40pl.

07762 WELCH, S.C., JR. The paintings of Basāwan. In LK 10 (1961) 7-17.

c. the school of Jahāngīr, and later Mughal court painting

07763 AHMAD, NAZIR. The Mughal artist Farrukh Beg. In IsC 35 (1961) 115-29.

07764 ARDESHIR, A.C. Mughal miniature painting: the school of Jehangir. In RL 2,3 (1940) 19-42 + 5pl.

07765 ______. Mughal miniature painting: the school of Shah Jehan. In RL 2,4 (1940) 23-52 + 4pl.

07766 CLARKE, C. STANLEY. Indian drawings: thirty Mogul paintings of the school of Jahangir (17th century) and four panels of calligraphy in the Wantage bequest. Lahore: Qausain, 1977. 24p. + 24pl. [Rpt. 1922 ed.]

07767 DAS, A.K. Bishndās. In Anand Krishna, ed. Chhavi... Banaras: BHU, Bharat Kala Bhavan, 1971, 183-91.

07768 ______. Mughal painting during Jahangir's time. Calcutta: Asiatic Society, 1978. 278p. + 28pl.

07769 KÜHNEL, E. & H. GOETZ. Indische Buchmalereien aus dem Jahangir-album der Staatsbibliothek zu Berlin. Berlin: Scarabaeusverlag, 1924. 62p. + 63pl.

07770 SKELTON, R. The Mughal artist Farrokh Beg. In Ars Orientalis 2 (1957) 393-411.

07771 WILKINSON, J.V.S. An Indian manuscript of the Golestan of the Shah Jahan Period. In Ars Orientalis 2 (1957) 423-25.

d. "popular" schools of Mughal painting

07772 CHANDRA, PRAMOD. A series of Rāmāyaṇa paintings of the popular Mughal school. In PWMB 6 (1957-50) 64-70.

07773 ______. Ustād Śālivāhana and the development of popular Mughal art. In LK 8 (1960) 25-45.

07774 HÁJEK, L. Indische Miniaturen der lokalen Schulen aus den Ateliers der Mogulkaiser in Delhi. Prague: Artia Verlag, 1961. 137p.

3. Mughal Architecture: Forts, Palaces, Gardens; Mosques and Tombs

a. general studies

07775 ANSARI, M.A. Palaces and gardens of the Mughals. In IsC 33 (1959) 50-72.

07776 BROWN, P. Monuments of the Mughal period. In Cambridge History of India. Delhi: S. Chand, 1963, v. 4, 523-76. [Rpt. of 1939 ed.]

07777 CROWE, S. & S. HAYWOOD. The gardens of Mughal India. London: Thames & Hudson, 1972. 200p.

07778 FARUQI, H.A. Mughal architecture in India. In Iqbal R. 6,3 (1965) 97-110.

07779 GOETZ, H. Later Mughal architecture. In Mārg 11,4 (1958) 11-25.

07780 NATH, R. Colour decoration in Mughal architecture. Bombay: Taraporevala, 1970. 82p.

07781 ______. History of decorative art in Mughal architecture. Delhi: Motilal, 1976. 188p. + 35pl.

07782 ______. Some aspects of Mughal architecture. ND: Abhinav, 1976. 168p. + 24pl.

07783 SARASVATI, S.K. Glimpses of Mughal architecture. Calcutta: A. Goswami, 1953. 560p.+ 45pl.

b. the imperial capitals: Delhi, Āgrā, and Fatehpur Sīkrī

07784 Delhi, Agra and Sikri. Ed. by M.R. Anand. Bombay: Mārg Pub., 196-. 67p. [1st pub. in Mārg 20,4 (1967) 3-67]

07785 HAMBLY, G. Cities of Mughul India: Delhi, Agra and Fatehpur Sikri. NY: Putnam, 1968. 168p.

07786 KANWAR, H.I.S. Ustad Ahmed Lahori. In IsC 48,1 (1974) 11-32.

07787 MAZUMDAR, K.C. Imperial Agra of the Moghuls. Agra: Gaya Prasad, 1939. 212p.

07788 NATH, R. Agra and its monumental glory. Bombay:

Taraporevala, 1977. 104 + 34p.

07789 ______. Plan of Akbar's tomb at Sikandra (Agra) and a proposed dome over it. In Indica 4 (1967) 99-100.

07790 RIZVI, S.A.A. & V.J.A. FLYNN. Fathpur-Sīkrī. Bombay: Taraporevala, 1975. 175 + 48p.

07791 SMITH, E.W. The Moghul architecture of Fathpur-Sikri. Allahabad: Govt. Press, 1894-98. 180p. + 311p. (ASI new imperial series, 18:1-4) [Pt. 1 rpt. Delhi: IndBH, 1973]

c. the Tāj Mahal in Āgrā: Shāh Jahān's memorial to his empress, Mumtāz

07792 CARROLL, D. The Taj Mahal. NY: Newsweek, 1973. 172p.

07793 HAVELL, E.B. Handbook to Agra and the Taj, Sikandra, Fatehpur-Sikri and the neighbourhood. 2nd ed. rev. with appendix. Calcutta: Thacker & Spink, 1924. 147p. [1st pub. 1904]

07794 KANWAR, H.I.S. Harmonious proportions of the Taj Mahal. In IsC 49,1 (1975) 1-21.

07795 LAL, KANWAR. The Taj. Delhi: R & K Pub., 1965. 98p.

07796 NATH, R. The immortal Taj Mahal. Bombay: Taraporevala, 1972. 114p.

07797 QANUNGO, S.N. Architect of the Taj Mahal. In IAC 11 (1963) 367-70.

4. Other Arts under the Mughals

07798 AZIZ, ABDUL. Arms and jewellery of the Indian Mughuls. In his Mughul Indian court and its institutions. Lahore: 1947. 159p.

07799 MIRZA, A.H. Mughal jade carving. In Museums J. of Pakistan 17 (1965) 11-16.

07800 NATH, R. Calligraphic art in Mughal architecture. Calcutta: Iran Soc., 1979. 73p. + 24pl.

07801 RAHMAN, P.I.S.M. Islamic calligraphy in medieval India. Dacca: University Press, 1979. 117p. + 16pl.

07802 SANGAR, S.P. Ornaments of Hindu women in Mughal India. In JIH 44,1 (1966) 181-204.

III. THE EUROPEAN RE-DISCOVERY OF INDIA: TRAVELLERS, TRADERS, AND MISSIONARIES (FROM 1498)

A. General

1. Historical Interpretations of European Expansion and its Impact on South Asia

07803 CHAUDHURI, K.N. Towards an "inter-continental mode": some trends in Indo-European trade in the 17th century. In IESHR 6,1 (1969) 1-29. [with comm. by A.K. Bagchi 31-40]

07804 ______. The trading world of Asia and the English East India Company 1660-1760. Cambridge: CamUP, 1978. 628p.

07805 CRONE, G.R. The discovery of the East. London: H. Hamilton, 1972. 178p.

07806 FURBER, H. Rival empires of trade in the Orient, 1600-1800. Minneapolis: U. of Minnesota Press, 1976. 408p. (Europe and the World in the Age of Expansion, 2)

07807 HEESTERMAN, J.C. Was there an Indian reaction? Western expansion in an Indian perspective. In H.L. Wesseling, ed. Expansion and reaction. Leiden: Leiden U. Press, 1978, 31-58.

07808 NESS, G.D. & W. STAHL. Western imperialist armies in Asia. In CSSH 19,1 (1977) 2-29.

07809 PANIKKAR, K.M. Asia and Western dominance, 1498-1945: a survey of the Vasco da Gama epoch of Asian history. London: Allen & Unwin, 1953. 530p.

07810 STEENSGAARD, N. The Asian trade revolution of the seventeenth century: the East India Companies and the decline of the caravan trade. Chicago: UChiP, 1974. 441p. [Also pub. as Carracks, caravans & companies....]

2. General Histories of Political, Economic, and Cultural Contacts

07811 ANAND, I. The appearance of Ostenders in Indian waters. In IESHR 6 (1969) 133-50.

07812 DHARAMPAL. Indian science & technology in the eighteenth century: some contemporary European accounts. Delhi: Impex India, 1971. 282p.

07813 FELDBAEK, O. India trade under the Danish flag, 1772-1808. Copenhagen: Studentlitteratur, 1969. 359p. (Scandinavian Inst. of Asian Studies Monograph, 2)

07814 GOITEIN, S.D. Letters and documents on the India trade in medieval times. In IsC 37 (1963) 188-205.

07815 LACH, D.F. Asia in the making of Europe. Chicago: UChiP, 1965-77. v. 1, 1&2, The century of discovery, 957p.; v. 2, 1&2, The century of wonder [visual & literary arts], 257, 392p.

07816 MARSHALL, P.J. The British discovery of Hinduism in the eighteenth century. London: CamUP, 1970. 310p.

07817 MURRAY, H., comp. Historical account of discoveries and travels in Asia. Edinburgh: H. Constable, 1820. 3 v. [summaries of accounts]

07818 PARRY, J.H. The age of reconnaissance. Cleveland: World Pub. Co., 1963. 364p.

07819 SEN, A.K. Settlement of Europeans in India: the first phase (1766-1833). In CR 169 (Oct. 1963) 17-29; (Dec. 1963) 298-308.

07820 VICTORIA AND ALBERT MUSEUM. Art and the East India trade. London: HMSO, 1970. 2p. + 31 pl.

3. Travel Accounts by Europeans
a. general studies of early European travellers in South Asia

07821 ANSARI, M.A. European travellers under the Mughals, 1580-1627. Delhi: IAD, 1975. 152p.

07822 BIDWELL, S. Swords for hire: European mercenaries in 18th century India. London: J. Murray, 1970. 258p.

07823 HUTCHINSON, L. European freebooters in Moghul India. Bombay: Asia, 1964. 192p.

07824 OATEN, E.F. European travellers in India during the fifteenth, sixteenth & seventeenth centuries; the evidence afforded by them with respect to Indian social institutions, and the nature and influence of Indian governments. London: K. Paul, Trench, Trübner, 1909. 274p. [Rpt. NY: AMS Press, 1971]

07825 WHEELER, J.T. European travellers in India. Calcutta: S. Gupta, 1956. 119p.

b. major collections of travel accounts

07826 CHURCHILL, A. & J. CHURCHILL. A collection of voyages and travels.... 3rd ed. London: 1744-47. 8v. [1st pub. 1704]

07827 HAKLUYT, R. The principal navigations, voiages, traffiques and discoveries of the English nation. London: J.M. Dent, 1927-28. 10v. [1st pub. 1598-1600]

07828 HAKLUYT SOCIETY. Works issued. London. 1st series, v. 1-100 (1847-1898); 2nd series, v. 1-. [150 v. to 1976; many volumes of this series have been reprinted by various publishers]

07829 KERR, R., ed. A general history and collection of voyages and travels. Edinburgh: W. Blackwood, 1824. 18 v. [1st pub. 1811-14]

07830 PINKERTON, J., ed. A general collection of the best and most interesting voyages and travels in all parts of the world. London: Longman, Hurst, Rees & Orme, 1808-14. 17v.

07831 PURCHAS, S. Hakluytas posthumus; or Purchas, his Pilgrimes: contayning a history of the world in sea voyages & lande travells by Englishmen and others. Glasgow: J. MacLehose, 1905-07. 20v. [Rpt. 1625 ed.]

07832 WHEELER, J.T., ed. Early travels in India, 16th & 17th centuries: reprints of rare and curious narratives of old travellers in India in the sixteenth and seventeenth centuries. Delhi: Deep Pub., 1975. 228p.

[Rpt. 1864 ed.; accts. by S. Purchas, J.H. Van Linschoten]

07833 The World Displayed, or a curious collection of voyages and travels. London: J. Newberry, 1760-61.

c. accounts and studies by Italians, Spaniards and other Europeans (not included in sections below)

07834 FEDERICI, C. Voyages & travels of Cesar Frederick in India. In Robert Kerr. General history & collection of voyages & travels.... Edinburgh: Wm Blackwood, T. Cadell, 1824. v. 7, 142-210.

07835 FELDBAEK, O. Danish East India trade 1772-1807: statistics and structure. In Scandinavian Econ. History R. 26,2 (1978) 128-44.

07836 KONINCKX, C. The maritime routes of the Swedish East India Company during its first and second charter (1931-1766). In Scandinavian Econ. History R. 26,1 (1978) 36-65.

07837 LAET, JOANNES DE. The empire of the Great Mogol. A translation of De Laet's "Description and Fragment of Indian history". Tr. from Latin by J.S. Hoyland. Bombay: Taraporevala, 1928. 252p. [Orig. pub. 1631]

07838 SASSETTI, F. Lettere Indiane. Turin: Giulio Einaudi, 1961. 107p.

07839 VALLE, P. DELLA. The travels of Pietro della Valle in India. Tr. from Italian by G. Havers. Ed. by E. Grey. NY: B. Franklin, 1973. 2 v. [Rpt. 1892 ed. Hakluyt Soc., 1st ser., 84, 85]

07840 VARTHEMA, L. DE. Travels...1503-1508. Tr. & ed. by J.W. Jones. NY: B. Franklin, 1973. 442p. [Rpt. 1863 ed.; Hakluyt Soc., 1st ser. 32; orig. Italian ed. 1510]

B. The Portuguese Settlement of South Asia after Vasco da Gama's Arrival in 1498

1. Bibliography and Reference

07841 BOXER, C.R. A glimpse of the Goa archives. In BSOAS 14,2 (1952) 299-324.

07842 ______. Tentative checklist of Indo-Portuguese imprints, 1556-1674. Bastora, Goa: Tip. Rangel, 1956. 23p. [Separada do Boletim do Instituto Vasco da Gama, 73]

07843 ______. Three historians of Portuguese Asia: Barros, Conto & Bocarro. Macau: 1948. 32p. [16th-17th cent.]

07844 BURNELL, A.C. Tentative list of books & some mss. relating to the history of the Portuguese in India proper. Mangalore: Basel Mission Press, 1880.

07845 DANVERS, F.C. Report to the Secretary of State for India on the Portuguese records relating to the East Indies contained in the Archivo de Torre do Tomba and the public libraries at Lisbon and Evora. London: India Office, 1892. 209p.

07846 HARRISON, J.B. Five Portuguese historians. In C.H. Philips, ed. Historians of India, Pakistan, and Ceylon. London: OUP, 1961, 155-69.

07847 KOSHY, M.J. Sources for the study of Portuguese India. In JKS 2,1 (1975) 55-70.

07848 PISSURLENCAR, D.S.S. Roteiro dos arquivos da India Portuguesa. Bastora: 1955. 262p.

07849 PORTUGAL. AGÊNCIA GERAL DO ULTRAMAR. Catalogo bibliografico das Colonias. Lisboa: 1943. 302p.

07850 SCHURHAMMER, G. Die zeitgenössischen Quellen zur Geschichte Portugiesisch-Asiens und seiner Nachbarländer zur Zeit des He. Franz Zaver (1538-1552). Leipzig: Verlag Asia Major, 1932. 47, 521p.

07851 SEN, S.N. A preliminary report on the historical records at Goa. Calcutta: Calcutta U. Press, 1925. 86p. [Rpt. from CR May-Oct. 1925]

2. Document Collections (in Portuguese)

07852 ARQUIVO HISTORICO DO ESTADO DA ÍNDIA. Agentes da diplomacia portuguesa na Índia (Hindus, Muçulmanos, Judeus e Parses). Documentos... Bastora, Goa: Tip. Rangel, 1952. 656p.

07853 ARQUIVO PORTUGUES ORIENTAL. Nova ed. Bastorá, Goa: Tip. Rangel, 1936-. 2 v. [1,4 only]

07854 BOTELHO DE SOUSA, Alfredo. Subsídios para a história militar marítime da Índia (1585-1669). Lisboa: Impr. da Armada, 1930-56. 4 v.

07855 GODINHO, Vitorino de Magalhães. Documentos sobre a expansão portuguesa. Lisboa: Editorial "Gleba", 1943-54. 3 v.

07856 IRIA, A., ed. Da navegacão portuguesa no Índico no século XVII; documentos do Arquivo Histórico Ultramarino. Lisboa: Centro de Estudos Históricos Ultramarinos, 1963. 309p.

07857 PORTUGAL. Colescão de tratudos e concêrtos de pazes que o estado da India portuguieza fêz com os reis e senhores ... ao do século XVII. Lisboa: Imprensa nacional, 1881-87. 14v.

3. Biographies and Accounts of Portuguese Travelers and Administrators

07858 ALBUQUERQUE, AFFONSO DE. Commentaries.... Tr. & ed. by W. de G. Birch. NY: B. Franklin, 1973. (Hakluyt Soc., 1st ser., 53, 55, 62, 69) [Rpt. 1875-83 ed.]

07859 AQUARONE, J.B.D. João de Castro, gouverneur et vice-roi des Indes orientales, 1500-48. Paris: PUF, 1968. 2 v.

07860 CORREA, G. The three voyages of Vasco Da Gama, & his viceroyalty. In his Lendas da India. Tr. by H.E.J. Stanley. NY: B. Franklin, 1973. 430p. (Hakluyt Soc., 1st ser., 42) [Rpt. 1869 ed.; 1st Portuguese ed. 1561]

07861 GAMA, VASCO DA. Journal of the 1st voyage...1497-1499. Tr. by E.G. Ravenstein. NY: B. Franklin, 1973. 250p. (Hakluyt Soc., 1st ser., 99) [Rpt. 1898 ed.]

07862 MENDES PINTO, FERNÃO. Voyages and adventures of Ferdinand Mendez Pinto. Tr. by H. Cogan. London: Dawson's, 1969. 318p. [Rpt. 1653 ed.]

07863 SANCEAU, E. Indies Adventure; the amazing career of Alfonso De Albuquerque. London: Blackie, 1936. 308p.

07864 ______. Knight of the Ranaissance; D. Joao de Castro. London: Hutchinson, 1949. 235p.

07865 SMITH, R.B., ed. The first age of the Portuguese embassies, navigations, and peregrinations to the ancient kingdoms of Cambay and Bengal (1500-1521). Bethesda, MD: Decatur Press, 1969. 155p.

4. Early Portuguese Histories of the Estado da Índia, in Original or Translation

07866 BARROS, JÕAO DE & DIOGO DO COUTO. Da Ásia de João de Barros e de Diogo de Couto. Nova ed. Lisbon: Na Regia Officina Typografica, 1777-78. 24v. [Rpt. Lisbon: S. Carlos, 1973-75]

07867 CAMOENS, LUIZ DE. The Lusiad. Tr. from Portuguese by R. Fanshawe. Ed. by G. Bullough. Carbondale: S. Illinois U. Press, 1964. 352p.

07868 ______. The Lusiad; or, the discovery of India... Tr. from the original Portuguese... by W.J. Mickle. In Works of the English poets, Chaucer to Cowper. Oxford: 1776, v. 21, 517-783. [Rpt. by Greenwood, 1969]

07869 CASTANHEDA, F.L. DE. História do descobrimento & conquista da Índia pelos Portugueses. 3a. edicão. 9 livros. Coimbra: Imprensa da Univ., 1924-33. [1st pub. 1551-61;Scriptores Rerum Lusitanarum serie A]

07870 ______. The first book of the history of the discouerie and conquest of the East Indies enterprised by the Portingales.... London: T. East, 1582. 164p. [English tr.; rpt. NY: Da Capo Press, 1973]

07871 FARIA Y SOUSA, M. DE. The Portuguese Asia or, the history of the discovery and conquest of India by the Portuguese. Tr. by Capt. J. Stevens. London: C. Brome, 1695. 3 v. [orig. Portuguese ed., 1666-75]

07872 FREITHS, W.J. Camoens and his epic.... Stanford: Inst. of Hispanic American & Luso-Brazilian Studies, 1963. 227p.

07873 GOMES SOLIZ, DUARTE. Discursos sobre los comercios de las dos Indias. Lisbon: Gráfica Lisbonense, 1943. 29 + 263p.

5. Recent Histories of the Portuguese Enterprise in India

07874 BOXER, C.R. Four centuries of Portuguese expansion, 1415-1825; a succinct survey. Johannesburg: Witwatersrand U. Press, 1961. 102p.

07875 ______. The Portuguese seaborne empire, 1415-1825. London: Hutchinson, 1969. 426p.

07876 CORREIA-AFONSO, J., ed. International seminar on Indo-Portuguese history. Bombay: Heras Institute, St. Xavier's College, 1978. 124p.

07877 DANVERS, F.C. The Portuguese in India, being a history of the rise and decline of their Eastern empire. NY: Octagon Books, 1966. 2 v. [1st pub. 1894]

07878 DISNEY, A.R. The first Portuguese India Company, 1628-33. In EHR 30,2 (1977) 242-58.

07879 LUZ, F.P.M. DA. O Consêlho da Índia, contribuição ao estudo da história da administração e do comércio do ultramar português nos princípios do século XVII. Lisboa: Agência Geraldo Ultramar, 1952. 649p.

07880 PEARSON, M.N. Wealth and power: Indian groups in the Portuguese Indian economy. In SA 3 (1973) 36-44.

07881 PESCATELLO, A.M. The African presence in Portuguese India. In JAH 11,1 (1977) 26-48.

07882 WHITEWAY, R.S. The rise of Portuguese power in India, 1497-1550. Patna: Janaki Prakashan, 1979. 61 + 357p. [Rpt. 1899 ed.]

6. The Establishment of the Roman Catholic Church in India under the Portuguese

a. documents

07883 CORREIA-AFONSO, J. Jesuit letters and Indian history, 1542-1773. 2nd ed. Bombay: OUP, 1969. 211p.

07884 Documentos remittidos da India; ou, Livros das Monçoes. Lisboa: Classe de Sciencias Moraes, Politicas e Bellas-Lettras da Academia Real das Sciencias de Lisboa, 1880-1935. 5 v.

07885 MEERSMAN, A., comp. Annual reports of the Portuguese Franciscans in India, 1713-1833. Lisboa: Centro de Estudos Historicos Ultramarinos, 1972. 492p.

07886 REGO, ANTONIO DA SILVA. Documentação para a história das missoẽs do Padroado Portuguẽs do Oriente. Lisboa: Agência Geral das Colónias, 1947-53. 12 v.

07887 WICKI, J., ed. Documenta Indica, 1-7, 1540-1569. Rome: Society of Jesus, 1948-62. (Monumenta Missionum Societatis Iesu, 4,5,6,9,14,16,19)

b. studies

07888 DIEHL, K.S. Catholic religious orders in South Asia, 1500-1835. In JAS 37,4 (1978) 699-712. [review article]

07889 MEERSMAN, A. The ancient Franciscan Provinces of India, 1500-1835. Bangalore: CLS, 1971. 590p.

07890 WICKI, J. Ein vorbildlicher Missionar Indiens, P. Henriques (1520-1600). In Studia missionalia 13 (1963) 113-168.

C. The Vereenigde Oostindische Compagnie (V.O.C. - "United East Indies Company") of the Netherlands (founded 1602): Dutch Traders in South Asia

1. Bibliography and Reference

07891 Catalogue de Livres imprimés dans les possessions Neerlandaises aux Indes-Orientales. The Hague: Nijhoff, 1873. 17p. [Suppl., 1877]

07892 RAY, N.R., ed. Dutch activities in the East, seventeenth century; being a "Report on the records relating to the East in the state Archives in the Hague". Calcutta: Book Emporium, 1945. 81p.

2. Documents and Travellers' Accounts

07893 BALDAEUS, P. A true and exact description of the most celebrated East India coasts of Malabar and Coromandel; as also of the isle of Ceylon... Tr. from the High-Dutch. In A. Churchill & J. Churchill, eds. A collection of voyages and travels.... London: 1745, v. 3, 509-793.

07894 DAPPAR, O. Asia; oder, ausführliche Beschreibung des Reichs des grossen Mogols und eines grossen Theils von Indien. Tr. from Dutch by J.C. Beern. Nurnberg: J. Hoffmann, 1681. 2v. in 1.

07895 GRAAF, NIKOLAAS VAN. Voyages de... aux Indes Orientales.... Amsterdam: J.F. Bernard, 1719. 358p.

07896 LINSCHOTEN, J.H. VAN. The voyage... to the Indies. Ed. by A.C. Burrell & P.A. Tiele. NY: B. Franklin, 1973. (Hakluyt Soc., 1st ser., 70-71) [Rpt. 1885 ed.; orig. English tr. 1598]

07897 MADRAS (PRESIDENCY). Selections from the records of the Madras government. Dutch records... Madras: Govt. Press, 1908-11. 15v.

07898 NARAIN, BRIJ, tr. A contemporary Dutch chronicle of Mughal India. Calcutta: Susil Gupta, 1957. 104p.

3. Studies of Dutch Activities in South Asia

07899 BOXER, C.R. The Dutch seaborne empire, 1600-1800. London: Hutchinson, 1965. 326p.

07900 GLAMANN, K. Dutch-Asiatic Trade, 1620-1740. Copenhagen: Danish Science Press, 1958. 234p.

07901 RADWAN, A.B. The Dutch in Western India, 1601-1632: a study in mutual accommodation. Columbia, MO: South Asia Books, 1978. 159p.

D. The French in India: from Trade to Imperial Ambition

1. Bibliography and Reference

07902 GAUDART, E., ed. Catalogue des manuscrits des anciennes archives de l'Inde française. Paris: Leroux, 1926-36. 8 v. in 5.

07903 SCHOLBERG, H., ed. Bibliographie des Français dans l'Inde. Avec la collaboration d'E. Divien. Pondicherry: Hist. Soc. of Pondicherry, 1973. 216p.

07904 SEN, S.P. French historical writing on European activities in India. In C.H. Philips, ed. Historians of India, Pakistan, and Ceylon. London: OUP, 1961, 183-208.

2. Document Collections

07905 CHANDERNAGOR. CONSEIL. Correspondance du Conseil Superieur de Pondichéry avec le Conseil de Chandernagor. n.p.: pub. for A. Martineau, 1915-19. 3 v. [refers to period 1745-57]

07906 COMPAGNIE NOUVELLE DES INDES. Correspondance des agents à Pondichéry de la nouvelle Compagnie des Indes avec les administrateurs à Paris, 1788-1803. Pondicherry: Bibliothèque coloniale, 1931. 511p.

07907 MADRAS. CONSEIL PROVINCIAL. Resumé des lettres du Conseil provincial de Madras: avec Mahé de la Bourdonnais, Dupleix, le conseil supérieur et divers. Ed. by H. de Closets D'Errey. Pondichéry: Impr. moderne, 1936. 166p.

07908 PONDICHERRY. CONSEIL SUPERIEUR. Resumé des lettres du Conseil supérieur de Pondichéry à divers: du 1er août 1725 au 31 décembre 1742 et du 8 décembre 1749 au 14 novembre 1760. Ed. by H. de Closets d'Errey. Pondichéry: Bibliothèque publique, 1933. 222p.

3. French Traveller's Accounts

07909 BAMBOAT, Z. Les voyageurs français dans l'Inde aux XVII et XVIII siècles. NY: B. Franklin, 1972. 197p. [Rpt. 1933 ed.]

07910 BERNIER, F. Travels in the Mogul Empire, A.D. 1656-1668. Rev. ed. based upon I. Brock's tr. by A. Constable. Lahore: al-Biruni, 1976. 497p. [Rpt. 1891 ed.]

07911 GENTIL, J.B.J. Mémoire sur l'Indoustan ou empire mogol. Paris: Petit, 1822. 474p.

07912 PYRARD DE LAVAL, FRANCOIS. Voyage...to the E. Indies.... Tr. by A. Gray. NY: B. Franklin, 1973. 2 v. [Rpt. 1887 ed.; Hakluyt Soc., 1st ser., 76,77; orig. French ed. 1611]

07913 SEN, S.N., ed. Indian travels of Thevenot and Careri.... ND: NAI, 1949. 64 + 434p. + 20pl. (Indian records ser.) [Jean de Thevenot and Dr. Giovanni Francesco Gemelli-Careri]

07914 TAVERNIER, J.B. Les six voyages de Jean Baptiste Tavernier, ecuyer baron d'Aubonne, qu'il a fait en Turquie, en Perse, et aux Indes. Paris: G. Clouzier, 1676-1677. 2 v.

4. Histories of French Activities in India: Commercial and Military Policies Dictated by World-wide Anglo-French Rivalry

a. general studies

07915 D'ERREY, H. DE C. Précis chronologique de l'histoire de l'Inde Française (1665-1816). Pondicherry: Impr. du gouvernement, 1934. 102p.

07916 GLACHANT, R. Histoire de l'Inde des Français. Paris: Plon, 1965. 343p.

07917 RANGASWAMI, A. Political system of French India. In CR 3 (1900) 281-306.

b. La Compagnie Royale des Indes Orientales (founded 1664) and its successors; François Martin and the establishment of Pondicherry as the center of French India

07918 CARRE, H. ...François Martin, fondateur de l'Inde française, 1665-1706. Paris: Fontenelle, 1946. 235p.

07919 DUARTE, A. Les premières relations entre les Français et les princes indigènes dans l'Inde au XVIIe siècle (1666-1706). Paris: Jouve, 1932. 207p.

07920 KAEPPELIN, P. La Compagnie des Indes orientales et François Martin; étude sur l'histoire du commerce et des établissements français dans l'Inde sous Louis XIV, 1664-1719. NY: B. Franklin, 1967. 673p. [1st pub. 1908]

07921 MALLESON, G.B. History of the French in India, from the founding of Pondicherry in 1674 to the capture of that place in 1761. 2nd ed. London: W.H. Allen, 1893. 614p. [1st pub. 1868]

07922 MARTIN, F. Mémoire de François Martin sur l'établissement des colonies françaises aux Indes Orientales 1665-1696. Ed. by A.A. Martineau. Paris: Soc. d'Éditions Géographiques, Maritimes, et Coloniales, 1931-4. 3 v.

07923 SEN, S.P. The French in India, first establishment and struggle. Calcutta: U. of Calcutta, 1947. 360p.

07924 SOTTAS, J. Une escadre française aux Indes en 1690; Histoire de la Compagnie royale des Indes Orientales, 1664-1719. Paris: Plon-Nourrit, 1905. 496p.

07925 WEBER, H. La Compagnie française des Indes 1604-1875. Paris: A. Rousseau, 1904. 715p.

c. Joseph François Dupleix (1697-1764), and his challenge to British hegemony through alliance with native states; the diary of Ānanda Ranga Pillai, dubāsh of Dupleix

07926 ANANDARANGA PILLAI. The private diary... A record of matters political, historical, social, and personal. Tr. from the Tamil & ed. by J.F. Price and K. Rangachari. Madras: Govt. Press, 1904-08. 12 v. [Pillai was Dupleix's dubash, secretary-translator]

07927 CHASSAIGNE, M. Le comte de Lally. Paris: Soc. de l'histoire des colonies francaises, 1938. 334p.

07928 DALGLIESH, W.H. The Perpetual Company of the Indies in the days of Dupleix, 1722-1754. Philadelphia: 1933. 238p.

07929 DUPLEIX, J.F. Dupleix & his letters (1742-54). Ed. by V.M. Thompson. NY: R.O. Ballou, 1933. 920p. [extracts from Dupleix's letters in a connected narrative]

07930 HATALKAR, V.G. Relations between the French and the Marathas, 1668-1815. Bombay: U. of Bombay, 1958. 306p.

07931 MALLESON, G.B. Dupleix. Oxford: OUP, 1890. 188p. (Rulers of India)

07932 MARTINEAU, A.A. Bussy et l'Inde, 1720-1785. Paris: Société de l'histoire des colonies françaises, 1935. 459p.

07933 ______. Dupleix et l'Inde française. Paris: E. Champion, 1920. 4 v.

07934 NILAKANTA SASTRI, K.A. New pages from Ananda Ranga Pillai's diary. Madras: JMU Suppl. to 14,2 (1942) 1-49.

07935 SRINIVASACHARI, C.S. Ananda Ranga Pillai: the "Pepys" of French India. Madras: P. Varadachary, 1940. 512p.

d. after the defeat of French imperial aspirations: the War of the American Revolution, the French Revolution, and the Napoleonic era (1763-1815)

07936 CAVALIERO, R. Admiral Suffren in the Indies. In History Today 20,7 (1970) 472-80.

07937 KILLION, H.R. The Suffren expedition: French operations in India during the war of American independence. Ph.D. diss., Duke U., 1972. 533p. [UM 73-8084]

07938 LABERNADIE, M.V. La révolution et les établissements français dans l'Inde. Paris: E. Leroux, 1930. 343p.

07939 MALLESON, G.B. French struggles in India. Delhi: Inter-India, 1977. 286p. [Rpt. 1878 ed.]

07940 SEN, S.P. The French in India, 1763-1816. Calcutta: KLM, 1958. 621p.

E. The British in India: From Trade to Administration (1600-1818)

1. Early British Travellers

07941 BOWERY, T. Geographical account of countries round the Bay of Bengal, 1669 to 1679. Ed. by Sir R.C. Temple. Cambridge: Hakluyt Soc., 1905. 387p. (Hakluyt Soc., 2nd ser., 12)

07942 FOSTER, W. Early travels in India, 1583-1619. Delhi: S. Chand, 1968. 351p. [1st pub. 1921]

07943 FRYER, J. New account of East India and Persia... 1672-1681. Ed. by W. Crooke. London: Hakluyt Soc., 1909-15. 3 v. (Hakluyt Soc., 2nd ser., 19,20,39)

07944 HAMILTON, A. A new account of the East Indies. Ed. by W. Foster. London: Argonaut Press, 1930. 2 v. [1st pub. 1727]

07945 JOURDAIN, J. Journal... Ed. by W. Foster. London: Hakluyt Soc., 1905. 394p. (Hakluyt Soc., 2nd ser., 16)

07946 LOCKE, J.C., ed. The first Englishmen in India; letters and narratives of sundry Elizabethans written by themselves. NY: AMS Press, 1970. 229p. [Rpt. 1930 ed.]

07947 MUNDY, P. Travels of Peter Mundy in Europe & Asia, 1608-67. Ed. by R.C. Temple. London: Hakluyt Soc., 1907-36. 5 v. (Hakluyt Soc., 2nd ser., 17,35,45,55,78)

07948 ORME, R. Historical fragments of the Mogul Empire, of the Morattoes, and of the English concerns in Indostan, from the year M.DC.LIX. ND: Associated Pub. House, 1974. 319p.

07949 PRASAD, R.C. Early English travellers in India; a study in the travel literature of the Elizabethan and Jacobean periods with particular reference to India. Delhi: Motilal, 1965. 392p.

07950 RYLEY, J.H. Ralph Fitch, England's pioneer to India and Burma. London: T. Fisher Unwin, 1889. 264p.

2. The East India Company, Founded 1600 by Royal Charter under Elizabeth I. to Gain Access to the Eastern Spice Trade

a. general histories of the Company

07951 BRUSH, J.E. The growth of the Presidency towns. In R.G. Fox, ed. Urban India.... Durham: DUPCSSA, 1970, 91-114. (Its monograph, 10)

07952 CHAUDHURI, K.N. The English East India Company: the study of an early joint-stock company, 1600-1640. London: Cass, 1965.

07953 FOSTER, W. John Company. London: John Lane, 1926. 285p.

07954 GARDNER, B. The East India Company: a history. NY: McCall Pub., 1972. 319p.

07955 MARSHALL, P.J. British expansion in India in the eighteenth century: a historical revision. In History 60,198 (1975) 28-43.

07956 ______, ed. Problems of empire: Britain and India 1757-1813. NY: Barnes & Noble, 1968. 239p. (Hist. problems: studies and documents, 3) [extracts from sources, with intro.]

07957 MUKHERJI, R.K. The rise and fall of the East India Company; a sociological appraisal. NY: Monthly Review Press, 1974. 445p. [1st pub. 1958]

07958 NIGHTINGALE, P. Trade and empire in western India 1784-1806. Cambridge: CamUP, 1970. 264p.

07959 PHILIPS, C.H. The East India Company, 1784-1834. Manchester: Manchester U. Press, 1961. 374p. [Rpt. 1940 ed.]

07960 SCHOROWSKY, M. Die Englander in Indien: 1600-1773. Bochum: Studienverlag Brockmeyer, 1978. 153p.

07961 SPEAR, T.G.P. The Nabobs: a study of the social life of the English in eighteenth century India. New ed. London: OUP, 1963. 236p.

07962 WOODRUFF, P. The men who ruled India; v. 1, The founders. London: J. Cape, 1963. 402p. [1st pub. 1953]

b. sources: official documents and correspondence

07963 BIRDWOOD, G., ed. The register of letters, etc., of the governour and company of merchants of London trading into the East Indies, 1600-1619. London: B. Quaritch, 1893. 530p.

07964 BROWNE, J. Browne correspondence. Ed. by K.D. Bhargava. ND: NAI, 1960. 363p. (Indian records ser.) [Hastings' emissary to Shah Alam's court]

07965 COLLET, J. The private letter books of Joseph Collet. Ed. by H.H. Dodwell. London: Longmans, Green, 1933. 256p.

07966 DANVERS, F.C. & W. FOSTER, eds. Letters received by the East India company from its servants in the East, 1602-1617. London: Sampson Low, Marston, 1896-1902. 6 v.

07967 FAWCETT, C. The English factories in India, 1670-1684. Oxford: OUP, 1936-55. 4 v.

07968 FORREST, G.W., ed. Selections from the state papers of the Governors-General of India. Oxford: B.H. Blackwell, 1910-26. 4 v. [W. Hastings & Lord Cornwallis only]

07969 FOSTER, W., ed. The English factories in India, 1618-1669. Oxford: OUP, 1906-1927. 13v.

07970 KHAN, S.A. Sources for the history of British India in the seventeenth century. ND: Cosmo, 1978. 395p. [Rpt. 1925 ed.]

07971 SAINSBURY, E.B., ed. A calendar of the court minutes etc. of the East India Company, 1635-1679. Oxford: OUP, 1907-1938. 11v.

07972 WHEELER, J.T. Early records of British India, a history of the English settlements in India. London: Trübner, 1878. 391p.

c. politics and administration of the Company

07973 ALDER, G.J. Britain and the defence of India - the origins of the problem, 1798-1815. In JAH 6 (1972) 14-44.

07974 AUBER, P. An analysis of the constitution of the East India Company. London: Kingsbury, 1826. 804p. + 207p. suppl.

07975 BAKSHI, S.R. British diplomacy and administration in India 1807-13. ND: Munshiram, 1971. 227p.

07976 CALLAHAN, R. The East India Company and army reform, 1783-1798. Cambridge: HUP, 1972. 242p.

07977 CARDEW, A.G. The White Mutiny: a forgotten episode of the history of the Indian army. London: Constable, 1929. 264p. [Mutiny of British officers in 1809]

07978 COHN, B.S. From Indian status to British contract. In JEH 21 (1961) 613-628.

07979 DASGUPTA, A.P. The Central Authority in British India, 1774-1784. Calcutta: U. of Calcutta, 1931. 368p.

07980 ______. Studies in the history of the British in India. Calcutta: U. of Calcutta, 1942. 165p.

07981 FIRMINGER, W.K., ed. The fifth report from the Select Committee of the House of Commons on the affairs of the East India Company, 28th July, 1812. NY: A.M. Kelley, 1969. 3 v. [Rpt. 1917-18 ed.]

07982 FOSTER, W. The East India house. London: J. Lane, 1924. 250p.

07983 FURBER, H. Henry Dundas, administrator of British India. London: OUP, 1931. 331p.

07984 ______. John Company at work: a study of European expansion in India in the late eighteenth century. NY: Octagon, 1970. 407p. [1st pub. 1948]

07985 KAYE, J.W. The administration of the East India Company; a history of Indian progress. Allahabad: Kitab Mahal, 1966. 712p. [1st pub. 1853]

07986 LAWFORD, J.P. Britain's army in India: from its origins to the conquest of Bengal. Boston: Allen & Unwin, 1978. 342p.

07987 MALCOLM, J. The government of India. London: Murray, 1833. 258p.

07988 ______. The political history of India, 1784 to 1823. Ed. by K.N. Panikkar. ND: Associated Pub. House, 1970. 2 v. [Rpt. 1826 ed.]

07989 MISRA, B.B. The central administration of the East India Company, 1774-1834. Manchester: Manchester U. Press, 1959. 476p.

07990 MISRA, G.S. British foreign policy and Indian affairs, 1783-1815. Bombay: Asia, 1963. 110p.

07991 ORME, R. A history of the military transactions of the British nation in Indostan from the year 1659. London: J. Nourse, 1763-78. 2 v. [Rpt. ND: Today & Tomorrow's, 1973]

07992 PHILIPS, C.H. The secret committee of the East India Company. In BSOAS 19 (1940-42) 299-315, 699-716.

07993 RICHMOND, H.W. The Navy in India, 1763-1783. London: E. Benn, 1931. 432p.

07994 SUTHERLAND, L.S. The East India Company in eighteenth century politics. Oxford: OUP, 1952. 430p.

07995 ______. Lord Macartney's appointment as Governor of Madras, 1780: the treasury in East India Company elections. In English Historical R. 90, 3561 (1975) 523-35.

07996 VERELST, H. A view of the rise, progress, and present state of the English government in Bengal... London: J. Nourse, 1772. 401p.

07997 WELLER, J. Wellington in India. London: Longman, 1972. 338p.

d. trade activities of the Company

07998 BALKRISHNA. Commercial relations between India and England, 1601 to 1757. London: Routledge, 1924. 370p.

07999 CHAUDHURI, K.N. Treasure and trade balances: the East India Company's export trade, 1660-1720. In EHR 21,2 (1968) 480-502.

08000 FOSTER, W. England's quest of eastern trade. London: A. & C. Black, 1933. 354p.

08001 HAMILTON, C.J. Trade relations between England and India, 1600-1896. Calcutta: Thacker, Spink, 1919. 263p.

08002 KHAN, S.A. The East India trade in the XVIIth century in its political and economic aspects. ND: S. Chand, 1975. 325p. [Rpt. 1923 ed.]

08003 ROBINSON, F.P. The trade of the East India Company, 1709-1813. Cambridge: CamUP, 1912. 186p.

08004 WRETTS-SMITH, M. The business of the East Indian Company, 1680-1681. In IESHR 1 (1963) 91-121.

3. Lord Robert Clive (1725-74) and the Establishment of the British Indian State: Final Victory over the Mughals and French [see also Bengal and Assam, IX, below]

a. biographies and studies of Lord Robert Clive, Governor of Bengal and mansabdār of the Mughal Empire

08005 BENCE-JONES, M. Clive of India. London: Constable, 1974. 377p.

08006 CHATTERJI, N. Clive as an administrator. Allahabad: Indian Press, 1955. 239p.

08007 CHAUDHURI, N.C. Clive of India: a political and psychological essay. London: Barrie & Jenkins, 1975. 446p.

08008 DAVIES, A.M. Clive of Plassey. London: Nicholson & Watson, 1939. 522p.

08009 DODWELL, H.H. Dupleix and Clive; the beginning of empire. Gorakhpur: V. Prakashan, 1962. 302p. [Rpt. 1920 ed.]

08010 EDWARDES, A. The rape of India; a biography of Robert Clive and a sexual history of the conquest of Hindustan. NY: Julian Press, 1966. 350p.

08011 FORREST, G.W. The life of Lord Clive. London: Cassell, 1918. 2 v.

08012 GARRETT, R. Robert Clive. London: A. Barker, 1976. 224p.

08013 LAWFORD, J.P. Clive, Proconsul of India: a biography. London: Allen & Unwin, 1976. 432p.

08014 SPEAR, T.G.P. Master of Bengal: Clive and his India. London: Thames and Hudson, 1975. 224p.

08015 TURNBULL, P. Clive of India. Folkestone: Bailey and Swinfen, 1975. 163p.

08016 WATNEY, J.B. Clive of India. Farnborough, Hants: Saxon House, 1974. 226p.

b. the Battle of Plassey (1757) and other engagements

08017 BARBER, N. The Black Hole of Calcutta; a reconstruction. London: Collins, 1965. 254p. [1756]

08018 EDWARDES, M. Plassey: the founding of an empire. London: Hamilton, 1969. 209p.

08019 FURBER, H. & K. GLAMANN. Plassey: a new account from the Danish archives. In JAS 19 (1960) 177-87.

08020 GUPTA, B.K. Sirajuddaullah and the East India Company, 1756-1757; background to the foundation of British power in India. Leiden: Brill, 1962. 170p.

08021 MACFARLANE, I. The Black Hole: or, The makings of a legend. London: Allen & Unwin, 1975. 341p. + 8pl.

08022 PATRA, A.N. The Battle of Plassey. In BPP 92,1 (1973) 104-111.

08023 SARKAR, JADUNATH. Memoir of M. René Madec (after the battle of Buxar). In BPP 52 (1936) 61-66; 53 (1937) 69-80; 55 (1938) 1-10.

08024 SHEPPARD, E.W. Coote Bahadur, a life of Lieutenant-General Sir Eyre Coote. London: W. Laurie, 1956. 247p.

08025 WYLLY, H.C. Life of Lieutenant-General Sir Eyre Coote. Oxford: OUP, 1922. 468p.

4. The Rule of the Early Governors-General from Calcutta (1774-1813), under the Regulating Act of 1773

a. Warren Hastings, 1774-85

08026 BEVERIDGE, H. Warren Hastings in Bengal. Calcutta: SPB, 1978. 122p. [1st pub. in CR 65-82 (1877-86)]

08027 DAVIES, A.M. Strange destiny. NY: H. Fertig, 1971. 468p. [1st pub. 1935]

08028 EDWARDES, M. Warren Hastings: king of the Nabobs. London: Hart-Davis, MacGibbon, 1976. 208p.

08029 FEILING, K.G. Warren Hastings. NY: St. Martin's Press, 1954. 419p.

08030 FORREST, G.W. The administration of Warren Hastings, 1772-1785. Calcutta: Supt. of Govt. Pub., 1892. 317p.

08031 HASTINGS, W. Memoirs relative to the State of India. ND: Oxford & IBH, 1973. 196p. [1st pub. 1787]

08032 MONCKTON-JONES, M.E. Hastings in Bengal, 1772-1774. Oxford: OUP, 1918. 359p.

08033 MOON, P. Warren Hastings and British India. NY: Collier Books, 1962. 224p.

08034 PARKES, J. & H. MERIVALE, ed. Memoirs of Sir Philip Francis, K.C.B., with correspondence and journals. London: Longmans, Green, 1867. 2 v., 458 + 566p.

08035 TROTTER, L.J. Warren Hastings. Freeport, NY: Books for Libraries, 1972. 219p. [Rpt. 1890 ed.]

08036 TURNBULL, P. Warren Hastings. London: New English Library, 1975. 232p.

08037 WEITZMAN, S. Warren Hastings and Philip Francis. Manchester: Manchester U. Press, 1929. 400p.

b. Charles Cornwallis, First Marquess Cornwallis, 1786-93 and 1805

08038 ASPINALL, A. Cornwallis in Bengal. Manchester: Manchester U. Press, 1931. 210p.

08039 SETON-KARR, W.S. Marquess Cornwallis. Oxford: OUP, 1893. 202p. (Rulers of India)

c. Sir John Shore, Lord Teignmouth, 1793-98

08040 FURBER, H., ed. Private record of an Indian governor-generalship: the correspondence of Sir John Shore [Teignmouth] with Henry Dundas. Cambridge: HUP, 1933. 206p. (Harvard History monographs, 2)

08041 TEIGNMOUTH, C.J.S. Memory of the life of John, Lord Teignmouth. London: Hatchard, 1843. 2 v.

d. Richard Wellesley, Earl of Mornington, Marquess Wellesley, 1798-1805

08042 HUTTON, W.H. The Marquess Wellesley K.G. Delhi: S. Chand, 1978. 155p. (Rulers of India) [1st pub. 1897]

08043 INGRAM, E., ed. Two views of British India: the private correspondence of Mr. Dundas and Lord Wellesley, 1798-1801. Bath: Adams & Dart, 1970. 344p.

08044 ROBERTS, P.E. India under Wellesley. London: G. Bell, 1929. 323p.

08045 WELLESLEY, R.C.W. The despatches, minutes, and correspondence of the Marquess Wellesley. Ed. by M. Martin. London: W.H. Allen, 1836-40. 5 v.

e. Gilbert Elliot, Earl of Minto I, 1807-13

08046 BAKSHI, S.R. British diplomacy and administration in India, 1807-13. ND: Munshiram, 1971. 228p.

08047 MINTO, G.E., 1st Earl of. Lord Minto in India: life and letters... 1807-14, while Governor-General of India. London: Longmans, Green, 1880. 403p. [Sequel to his Life & letters pub. 1874]

IV. CEYLON: INDIGENOUS KINGDOMS AND EUROPEAN INVADERS (1505-1795)

A. Political, Economic, and Social History of Sri Lanka

1. Bibliography and Sources

08048 DE SILVA, C.R. & D. DE SILVA. The history of Ceylon (c. 1500-1658); a historiographical and bibliographical survey. In CJHSS ns 3,1 (1973) 52-77.

2. Accounts of Ceylon by Early European Travellers

08049 BALDAEUS, P. A true and exact description of the great Island of Ceylon. Tr. from Dutch by P. Brohier. Pub. as CHJ 8 (1958-59) 476p. [1st Dutch ed. 1672]

08050 HULUGALLE, H.A.J. Ceylon of the early travellers. 2nd ed. Colombo: Wesley Press, 1969. 130p.

08051 KNOX, R. An historical relation of Ceylon. 2nd ed. Dehiwala: Tisara Prakasakayo, 1966. 471p. [1st pub. 1681; also pub. as CHJ 6 (1956-57)]

08052 ______. Robert Knox in the Kandyan Kingdom. Ed. by E.F.C. Ludowyk. Bombay: OUP, 1948. 175p. [selections from Knox's 1681 acct.]

08053 LUDOWYK, E.F.C. Robert Knox and Robinson Crusoe. In UCR 19 (1952) 243-252.

08054 PERCIVAL, R. Account of the island of Ceylon. Dehiwala: Tisara Prakasakayo, 1975. 315p. [Pub. as CHJ 22]

3. The Kingdom of Kandy of the Central Ceylon Highlands (1593-1815)

08055 ARASARATNAM, S. The kingdom of Kandy: aspects of its external relations and commerce, 1648-1710. In CJHSS 3,2 (1960) 109-27.

08056 DA SILVA, O.M. Vikrama Bahu of Kandy; the Portuguese and the Franciscans (1542-1551). Colombo: Gunasena, 1967. 110p.

08057 DERRETT, J.D.M. The origins of the laws of the Kandyans. In UCR 14 (1956) 105-50.

08058 SEWARAJA, L.S. A study of the political, administrative and social structure of the Kandyan kingdom of Ceylon: 1707-1760. Colombo: LHI, 1972. 245p.

08059 (entry deleted)

08060 D'OYLY, J. Sketch of the constitution of the Kandyan Kingdom. Ed. by L.J.B. Turner. Dehiwala: Tisara Prakasakayo, 1975. 241p. [Pub. as CHJ 24]

08061 GUNASEKHARA, A. Rajakariya or the duty of a king in the Kandyan kingdom of Sri Lanka. In W.D. O'Flaherty and J.D.M. Derrett, eds. The concept of duty in South Asia. ND: Vikas, 1978, 119-43.

08062 NANAYAKKARA, V. A return to Kandy: over Balana and beyond. Colombo: 1971. 237p.

08063 PIERIS, R. Sinhalese social organization: the Kandyan Period. Peradeniya: Ceylon U. Press, 1956. 311p.

08064 SENEVIRATNE, H.L. Rituals of the Kandyan State. Cambridge: CamUP, 1978. 190p. (Cambridge Studies in Social Anthropology, 22)

4. The Tamil Kingdom of Jaffna in the Northern Coastal Region

08065 ARASARATNAM, S. Trade and agricultural economy of the Tamils of Jaffna during the latter half of the seventeenth century. In TC 9 (1961) 371-86.

08066 ______. The Vanniear of north Ceylon: a study of feudal power and central authority, 1660-1760. In CJHSS 9 (1966) 101-12.

08067 PATHMANATHAN, S. The Kingdom of Jaffna. Colombo: Arul M. Rajendran, 1978-. v. 1, 294p.

08068 PIERIS, P.E. The Kingdom of Jafanapatam 1645, being an account of its administrative organisation as derived from the Portuguese Archives. Colombo: Ceylon Daily News Printers, 1944. 36p.

5. The Coming of the Portuguese (1505) and their Rule in Coastal Ceylon (1594-1658)

08069 ABEYASINGHE, T. Portuguese rule in Ceylon, 1594-1612. Colombo: LHI, 1966. 247p.

08070 DE SILVA, C.R. The first Portuguese revenue register of the Kingdom of Kotte, 1599. In CJHSS ns 5,1/2 (1975) 71-153.

08071 ______. The Portuguese and pearl fishing off South India and Sri Lanka. In SA ns 1,1 (1978) 14-28.

08072 ______. The Portuguese in Ceylon, 1617-1638. Colombo: H.W. Cave, 1972. 267p.

08073 DON PETER, W.L.A. Education in Sri Lanka under the Portuguese. Bolawalana: Don Peter, 1978. 342p.

08074 PARANAVITANA, S. The emperor of Ceylon at the time of the arrival of the Portuguese in 1505. In UCR 19 (1961) 10-29.

08075 PIERIS, P.E. Ceylon and the Portuguese 1505-1658. Tellippalai: American Ceylon Mission Press, 1920. 290p.

08076 ______. Ceylon: the Portuguese era; being a history of the island for the period 1505-1658. Colombo: Colombo Apothecaries Co., 1913, 1914. 2 v.

08077 PEIRIS, P.S. & M.A.H. FITZLER. Ceylon and Portugal. Pt. 1. Kings and Christians 1539-1552, from the original documents at Lisbon. Leipzig: Verlag der Asia Major, 1927. 408p.

08078 QUEYROZ, F. DE. The temporal and spiritual conquest of Ceylon. Tr. by F.S.G. Perera. Colombo: Govt. Printer, 1930. 3 v., 1274p.

08079 RIBEIRO, J. The historic tragedy of the island of Ceilao. Dedicated to Dom Pedro the Second, King of Portugal. Tr. from Portuguese by P.E. Pieris in 1905. 4th ed. Colombo: Ceylon Daily News, 1948. 266p. [1st pub. 1685]

08080 SCHURHAMMER, G. & E.A. VORETZSCH. Ceylon zur Zeit des Königs Bhuvaneka Bahu und Franz Xavers 1539-1552. Quellen zur Geschichte der Portugiesen, sowie der Franziskaner und Jesuiten Mission auf Ceylon. Leipzig: Verlag der Asia Major, 1928. 2 v., 384, 726p.

08081 TRINIDADE, P. DA. Chapters on the introduction of Christianity to Ceylon, taken from the Conquista Spiritual do Oriente. Tr. from Portuguese by E. Peiris & A. Meersman. Chilaw, Ceylon: E. Peiris, 1972. 328p.

6. Dutch-Portuguese Rivalry and Dutch Rule in Ceylon (1658-1795)

08082 ANTHONISZ, R.G. The Dutch in Ceylon: an account of their early visits to the island, their conquests, & their rule over the maritime regions during a century & a half. Colombo: C.A.C. Press, 1929. 198p. [v. 1, Early visits & settlement on the island; no more pub.]

08083 ARASARATNAM, S. The administrative organisation of the Dutch East India Company in Ceylon. In CJHSS 8,1/2 (1965) 1-13.

08084 ______. Baron vom Imhoff and Dutch policy in Ceylon 1736-1740. In Bijdragen tot de taal-, land- en volkenkunde 118 (1962) 454-468.

08085 ______. Dutch commercial policy in Ceylon and its effects on the Indo-Ceylon trade (1690-1750). In IESHR 4 (1967) 109-30.

08086 ______. Dutch power in Ceylon (1658-1687). Amsterdam: Djambatan, 1958. 256p.

08087 ______. The indigenous ruling class in Dutch maritime Ceylon. In IESHR 8,1 (1971) 57-71.

08088 ______. Memoir of Julius Stein Van Gollenesse, Governor of Ceylon, 1743-1751. Colombo: Dept. of Natl. Archives, 1974. 154p.

08089 BROHIER, R.L. Links between Sri Lanka and the Netherlands: a book of Dutch Ceylon. Colombo: Netherlands Alumni Assoc. of Sri Lanka, 1978. 165p. + 35pl.

08090 DIEHL, K.S. The Dutch press in Ceylon, 1734-96. In Library Q. 42,3 (1972) 329-42.

08091 GOLLENESSE, J.S. VAN. Memoir of Julius Stein van Gollenesse, Governor of Ceylon, 1743-1751, for his successor Gerrit Joan Vreeland, 28th February 1751. Tr. by S. Arasaratnam. Colombo: Dept. of Natl. Archives, 1974. 154p.

08092 GOONEWARDENA K.W. The foundation of Dutch power in Ceylon. Amsterdam: Djambatan, 1958. 196p.

08093 JURRIAANSE, M.W. Catalogue of the archives of the Dutch Central Government of coastal Ceylon, 1640-1796. Colombo: 1943. 354p.

08094 NEDERLANDSCHE OOSTINDISCHE COMPAGNIE. Instructions from the Governor-General and Council of India to the Governor of Ceylon, 1656 to 1665. Tr. from Dutch by S. Pieters. Colombo: Govt. Printer, 1908. 126p. (Memoirs & instructions of Dutch Governors, Commandeurs, &c.)

08095 PIERIS, P.E. Ceylon and the Hollanders. Tellippalai: American Mission Press, 1924. 190p.

08096 ______. Some documents relating to the rise of the Dutch power in Ceylon, 1602-1670, from the translations at the India Office. NY: Barnes & Noble, 1973. 292p.

08097 WINIUS, G.D. The fatal history of Portuguese Ceylon; transition to Dutch rule. Cambridge: HUP, 1971. 215p.

B. Religions of Ceylon during the Period 1505-1795: Buddhism, Hinduism, Islam, Roman Catholic and Protestant Christianity

08098 BOUDENS, R. The Catholic Church in Ceylon under Dutch Rule. Rome: Officium Libri Catholici, 1957. 266p.

08099 FERNANDO, P.E.E. An account of the Kandyan mission sent to Siam in 1750 AD. In CJHSS 2,1 (1959) 37-83.

08100 MASCARENHAS, A. Father Joseph Vaz of Sancoale: the hero of a Christian epic in Sri Lanka. Vasco: Mascarenhas, 1977. 99p.

08101 PEIRIS, E. Sinhalese Christian literature of the XVII & XVIII centuries. In JRASCB 35,96 (1943) 163-81.

08102 PEIRIS, E. & A. MEERSMAN, tr. Chapters on the introduction of Christianity to Ceylon, taken from the Conquista Spiritual do Oriente of Friar Paulo da Trinidade, O.F.M. Colombo: Colombo Catholic Press, 1972. 328p.

08103 PERERA, S.G. Life of Father Jacome Goncalvez. Madras: De Nobili Press, 1942. 150p.

C. Literature

08104 ALAGIYAVANNA MUKAVETI. Alagiyavanna's Kustantinu Hatana (The campaign of Don Constantine). Tr. by S.G. Perera & M.E. Fernando. Colombo: Catholic Press, 1932. 99p. [attrib. to Alagiyavanna]

08105 ______. Dahamsonda jataka kavya. Tr. from Sinhalese by E.P. Wijetunge. Colombo: Colombo Apothecaries, 1954. 131p.

08106 ______. An Eastern love story: Kusa jātakaya, a Buddhistic legend. Tr. from Sinhalese by T. Steele. London: Trubner, 1871. 260p.

08107 ______. A translation of Alagiyavanna's Subhasitaya into English verse. Tr. by E.P. Wijetunge. Colombo: Ceylon Daily News Press, 1930. 26p.

08108 ______. Translation of Dahmsonda kāvya. Tr. by C.M. Austin de Silva. Colombo: W.E. Bastian, 1930. 34p.

D. Art and Architecture

08109 COOMARASWAMY, A.K. Kandyan art: what it meant and how it ended. In Ceylon Natl. R. 1 (1906) 1-12.

08110 ______. Medieval Sinhalese art. 2nd ed. NY: Pantheon, 1956. 344p. + 43pl. [1st ed. 1908]

08111 GUNASINGHE, S. Kandyan painting. In R. Pieris, ed. Some aspects of traditional Sinhalese culture. Peradeniya: Ceylon U. Conf. on Traditional Cultures, 1956, 47-52.

V. SOUTH INDIA IN THE MUGHAL-MARATHA PERIOD (1565-1818)

A. General and Political Histories of South India in the Mughal-Maratha Period

1. Bījāpur and Golkoṇḍa: the Ādil Shāhī and Qutb Shāhī Sultanates of the Southern Deccan

08112 FUKAZAWA, H. A study of the local administration of Adilshahi Sultanate (AD 1489-1688). In Hitotsubashi J. of Economics 3,2 (1963) 37-67.

08113 GHAURI, I.A. Central structure of the kingdom of Bijapur. In IsC 44 (1970) 19-33. [Also pub. in JPHS 18 (1970) 88-109]

08114 MORELAND, W.H. Relations of Golconda in the early seventeenth century. London: Hakluyt Soc., 1931. 109p. (Its 2nd ser., 66)

08115 NAYEEM, M.A. External relations of the Bijapur Kingdom, 1489-1686 A.D.: a study in diplomatic history. Hyderabad: Bright Pub., 1974. 321p.

08116 RICHARDS, F.J. The Hyderabad Karnatik 1687-1707. In MAS 9,2 (1975) 241-60.

08117 ______. The imperial crisis in the Deccan. In JAS 35,2 (1976) 237-56.

08118 ______. Mughal administration in Golconda. Oxford: OUP, 1975. 350p.

08119 ______. The seventeenth century concentration of state power at Hyderabad. In JPHS 23,1 (1975) 1-35.

08120 SHERWANI, H.K. History of the Qutb Shahi dynasty. ND: Munshiram, 1974. 739p. [Rpt. 1969 ed.]

08121 ______. Muhammad-Quli Qutb Shah, founder of Haidarabad. Bombay: Asia, 1967. 150p.

08122 ______. Political and military aspects of the reign of Muhammad-Quli Qutb Shah. In JIH 39,3 (1961) 503-33; 40,1 (1962) 85-128.

08123 ______. Some cultural aspects of the reign of Muhammad Quli Qutb Shah. In MIQ 3,3/4 (1958) 253-69.

08124 ______. Tilangana under Ibrahim Qutb Shah: diplomacy and military campaigns. In JIH 35 (1958) 247-69, 359-85; 36 (1958) 73-100.

08125 VERMA, D.C. History of Bijapur. ND: Kumar Bros., 1974. 306p.

2. Hyderabad under the Early Nizams: Āsaf Jāh I (1671-1748) Asserts Independence of the Declining Mughals

08126 KHAN, Y.H. The first Nizam; the life and times of Nizamu'l-Mulk Asaf Jah I. 2nd rev. and enl. ed. Bombay: Asia, 1963. 267p. [1st ed. 1936]

08127 MALIK, ZAHIRUDDIN. Chauth-collecting in the Subah of Hyderabad, 1726-1748. In IESHR 8,4 (1971) 395-414.

08128 NIZAM ALI KHAN. Diplomatic correspondence between Mir Nizam Ali Khan and the East India Company (1780-98). Ed. by Yusuf Husain Khan. Hyderabad, Deccan: Central Records Office, 1958. 206p.

08129 REGANI, S. Nizam-British relations, 1724-1857. Hyderabad: Booklovers, 1963. 323p.

3. The Malabar Coast: Portuguese, Dutch, and British Settlements; the Rise of Travancore; the Muslim Sea-power of the Zamorin at Calicut

08130 BOUCHON, G. Mamale de Cananor: un adversaire de l'Inde portugaise, 1507-1528. Paris: Champion, 1975. 228p.

08131 DALE, S.F. The Mappilas during Mysorean rule: agrarian conflict in 18th century Malabar. In SA 6 (1976) 1-13.

08132 GONCALVES, D. Historia do Malavar. Ed. by J. Wicki. Münster: Aschendorffsche Verlagsbuchhandlung, 1955. 142p. (Missionswissenschaftliche Abhandlungen und Texte, 20)

08133 IBRAHIM KUNJU, A.P. Expansion of Travancore in the 18th century. In JIH 53,3 (1975) 431-81.

08134 ______. Rise of Travancore: a study of the life and times of Mārtāṇḍa Varma. Trivandrum: Kerala Hist. Soc., 1976. 173p.

08135 ______. Studies in medieval Kerala history. Trivandrum: Kerala Hist. Soc., 1975. 156p.

08136 JACOB, H.K. 'S., ed. De Nederlanders in Kerala 1663-1701: de memories en instructies betreffende het Commandement Malabar van de Verenigde Oost-Indische Compagnie. The Hague: Nihoff, 1976. 437p.

08137 MADRAS (PRESIDENCY) DEPTS. OF STATE AND PUBLIC INSTITUTIONS, ARMY. An account of the origin, progress and consequences of the late discontents of the army of the Madras establishment. London: T. Cadell & W. Davies, 1810. 294p.

08138 NAMBIAR, O.K. The Kunjalis, admirals of Calicut. NY: Asia Pub. House, 1963. 155p. [1st pub. 1955 as ...Portuguese pirates and Indian seamen]

08139 PANIKKAR, K.M. A history of Kerala, 1498-1801. Annamalainagar: Annamalai U., 1960. 471p. (Its hist. ser., 15)

08140 ______. Malabar and the Dutch. Bombay: Taraporevala, 1931. 187p.

08141 POONEN, T.I. Dutch hegemony in Malabar and its collapse, A.D. 1663-1705. Trivandrum: U. of Kerala, 1978. 238p.

08142 ______. A survey of the rise of the Dutch power in Malabar, 1603-1678. Trichinopoly: St. Joseph's Industrial School Press, 1948. 303p.

08143 RAJAYYAN, K. Rise and fall of the poligars of Tamilnad. Madras: U. of Madras, 1974. 131p. [1st pub. in JMU 46,1 (1974) 83-206]

08144 RAJENDRAN, N. Establishment of British power in Malabar, 1664 to 1799. Allahabad: Chugh, 1979. 292p.

08145 SOBHANAN, B. Rama Varma of Travancore, his role in the consolidation of British power in South India. Calicut: Sandhya Pub., 1978. 120p.

08146 WOOD, C. The first Moplah rebellion against British rule in Malabar. In MAS 10,4 (1976) 543-56.

08147 ZAIN AL-DIN, AL-MAʾBARI. Tohfut-ul-Mujahideen. An historical work in the Arabic language. Tr. by M.J. Rowlandson. London: Oriental Translation Fund, 1830. 181p. (Its series, 30)

4. The Coromandel/Cōlamaṇḍalam Coast; the Nayaks of Madurai and Tanjore, Maratha Rule, and European Coastal Settlements

08148 ABDUL RAHIM, M. Nagapattinam region and the Portuguese. In JIH 53,3 (1975) 483-96.

08149 CALDWELL, R. A political and general history of the District of Tinnevelly, in the Presidency of Madras: from the earliest period to its cession to the English government in A.D. 1801. Madras: Govt. Press, 1881. 300p.

08150 HILL, S.C. Yusuf Khan, the rebel commandant. London: Longmans, Green, 1914. 320p.

08151 NARAYANAMPOULLE. Histoire detaillée des rois du Carnatic. Tr. from Tamil by M. Gnanou Diagou. Paris: E. Leroux, 1939. 223p.

08152 RAJAYYAN, K. Administration and society in the Carnatic, 1701-1801. Tirupati: Sri Venkateswara U., 1966. 170p. (their Historical ser., 7)

08153 ______. Fall of the Nayaks of Madurai. In JIH 45 (1968) 807-16.

08154 ______. A history of British diplomacy in Tanjore. Mysore: Rao & Raghavan, 1969. 124p.

08155 ______. History of Madurai, 1736-1801. Madurai: Madurai U., 1974. 467p.

08156 SATHYANATHA AIYAR, R. History of the Nayaks of Madura. Madras: OUP, 1924. 403p. (Madras U. hist. ser., 2)

08157 ______. Tamiḻaham in the 17th century. Madras: U. of Madras, 1956. 207p.

08158 SAULIERE, A. The revolt of the southern Nayaks. In JIH 42 (1964) 89-105; 44 (1966) 163-80.

08159 SRINIVASAN, C.K. Maratha rule in the Carnatic. Ed. by C.S. Srinivasachari. Annamalainagar: Annamalai U., 1944. 414p.

08160 SUBRAMANIAN, K.R. The Maratha rajas of Tanjore. Madras: the author, 1928. 105p.

08161 VRIDDHAGIRISAN, V. The Nayaks of Tanjore. Annamalainagar: Annamalai U., 1942. 241p.

5. Mysore/Karṇāṭaka: the Wadiyār Dynasty and the Interregnum under Haidar Alī (c. 1722-1782) and his son Tipū Sultān (1753-1799)

08162 ALI, B.S. British relations with Haidar Ali, 1760-1782. Mysore: Rao & Raghavan, 1963. 358p.

08163 BOWRING, L.B. Haidar Ali and Tipu Sultan and the struggle with the Musalman powers of the South. Dehra Dun: EBD Pub., 1969. 227p. [Rpt. 1893 ed.]

08164 CHITNIS, K.N. Keladi polity. Dharwar: Karnatak U., 1974. 270p.

08165 FERNANDES, P. Storm over Seringapatam; the incredible story of Hyder Ali & Tippu Sultan. Bombay: Thackers, 1969. 277p.

08166 FORREST, D.M. Tiger of Mysore: the life and death of Tipu Sultan. London: Chatto & Windus, 1970. 388p.

08167 HAYAVADANA RAO, C. History of Mysore, 1399-1799. Bangalore: Supt. Got. Press, 1943-46. 3 v.

08168 ḤUSAIN ʿALĪ, KIRMĀNĪ. The history of the reign of Tipu Sultan: being a continuation of the Neshari Hyduri. Tr. from Persian by W. Miles. ND: Oriental, 1980. 203p. [Rpt. 1844 ed.]

08169 IBRAHIM KUNJU, A.P. Mysore-Kerala relations in the eighteenth century. Trivandrum: Kerala Hist. Soc., 1975. 138p.

08170 KHAN, MOHIBBUL HASAN. The French in the second Anglo-Mysore War. In BPP 65 (1945) 55-65.

08171 ______. History of Tipu Sultan. 2nd ed. Calcutta: World Press, 1971. 442p. [1st ed. 1951]

08172 LOHUIZEN, J. VAN. The Dutch East India Company & Mysore, 1762-1790. The Hague: Nijhoff, 1961. 205p. (K. Instituut voor taal-, land- en volkenkunde. Verhandelingen, 31)

08173 MUDDHACHARI, B. The Mysore-Maratha relations in the 17th century. Mysore: U. of Mysore, 1969. 176p.

08174 ______. The resistance of Mysore to the Maratha expansion, 1726-1761. Mysore: U. of Mysore, 1970. 186p.

08175 PARSONS, C.E. Seringapatam. London: OUP, 1931. 168p.

08176 STUART, C. Life of Tipoo Sultaun. Extracted from Charles Stuart's catalogue and memoirs of Tipoo Sultaun. Lahore: Pakistan Admin. Staff College, 1964. 105p.

08177 SWAMINATHAN, K.D. The Nayaks of Ikkeri. Madras: P. Varadachary, 1957. 327p.

08178 WODEYAR, S.S. Rani Chennamma. ND: NBT, 1977. 153p.

6. The Beginnings of British Administration in South India: Fort St. George (built 1640) and the Presidency of Madras

a. selected records and correspondence

08179 DODWELL, H.H., ed. Calendar of the Madras despatches, 1744-1765. Madras: Govt. Press, 1920-30. 2 v.

08180 ______, ed. The Calendar of the Madras Records, 1740-44. Madras: Govt. Press, 1917. 550p.

08181 JACKSON, W.C. Memoir of the public conduct and services of William Collins Jackson, senior merchant on the Company's Madras establishment. London: B. McMillan, 1809. 79p.

08182 LOVE, H.D. Vestiges of Old Madras, 1640-1800; traced from East India Company Records. London: Murray,

1913. 4 v. (Indian records series)

08183 MACARTNEY, GEORGE MACARTNEY, 1st Earl. The private correspondence of Lord Macartney, Governor of Madras (1781-85). London: Royal Historical Soc., 1950. 236p.

08184 MADRAS (PRESIDENCY). RECORD OFFICE. Records of Fort St. George. Despatches from England. 1670-. Madras: Govt. Press, 1911-.

08185 ______. Records of Fort St. George. Despatches to England, 1694-1751. Madras: Govt. Press, 1916-32. 18v.

08186 MASTER, S. The diaries of Streynsham Master, 1675-1680. Ed. by R.C. Temple. London: Murray, 1911. 2 v.

b. general studies of early British policy and administration; early resistance to British rule

08187 ARASARATNAM, S. Trade and political dominion in South India, 1750-1790: Changing British-Indian relationships. In MAS 13,1 (1979) 19-40.

08188 FURBER, H. Madras Presidency in the mid-eighteenth century. In Readings on Asian topics... Lund: Scandinavian Inst. of Asian Studies, 1970, 108-21. (Its monograph ser., 1)

08189 RAJAYYAN, K. South Indian rebellion; the first war of independence, 1800-1801. Mysore: Rao & Raghavan, 1971. 315p.

08190 SRINIVASACHARI, C.S. The early development of the government of the Presidency of Fort St. George. In JMU 1,2 (1929) 227-245.

B. Economic and Social History of South India in the Mughal-Maratha period (1565-1818)

1. The Coromandel Coast and the Northern Circars: Tamil Nadu and Andhra

a. general studies

08191 ARASARATNAM, S. Aspects of the role and activities of South Indian merchants c. 1650-1750. In Intl. Conf. Seminar of Tamil Studies, 1st, Kuala Lumpur, 1966. Proceedings. 528-596.

08192 ______. The politics of commerce in the coastal kingdoms of Tamil Nad, 1650-1700. In SA 1 (1971) 1-19.

08193 BANERJI, R.N. Economic progress of the East India Company on the Coromandel Coast, 1702-1746. Nagpur: Nagpur U., 1974. 243p.

08194 BRENNIG, J.J. Chief merchants and the European enclaves of seventeenth-century Coromandel. In MAS 11,3 (1977) 321-40.

08195 LEWANDOWSKI, S.J. Changing form and function in the ceremonial and the colonial port city in India: an historical analysis of Madurai and Madras. In MAS 11,2 (1977) 183-212.

08196 RAYCHAUDHURI, T. Jan Company in Coromandel, 1605-1690; a study in the interrelations of European commerce and traditional economies. The Hague: Nijhoff, 1962. 230p. (Verhandelingen van het Koninklijk Instituut voor Taal-, Land- en Volkenkunde, 38)

08197 SRINIVASACHARI, C.S. Economic condition of the Madras Presidency on the eve of the British conquest. In Madras U. Journal 2,1 (1929) 68-81.

08198 WRIGHT, H.R.C. The East India Company and the economy in India: the Madras investment, 1795-1800. In Intl. Conf. of Economic History, 2nd, Aix-en-Provence, 1962. Paris: Mouton, 1965, v. 2, 761-780.

b. colonial life in early Fort St. George, Madras

08199 LAWSON, C. Memories of Madras. London: S. Sonnenschein, 1903. 313p.

08200 LEIGHTON, D. Vicissitudes of Fort St. George. Madras: 1902. 246p.

08201 PENNY, F.E. Fort St. George, Madras. London: S. Sonnenschein, 1900. 244p.

08202 WHEELER, J.T. Madras in the Olden Time. Madras: Higginbotham, 1882. 715p.

2. The Malabar Coast

08203 DAS GUPTA, A. Malabar in Asian trade 1740-1800. London: CamUP, 1967. 204p.

08203a DISNEY, A.R. Twilight of the pepper empire: Portuguese trade in southwest India in the early seventeenth century. Cambridge: HUP, 1978. 220p. (Harvard hist. ser., 95)

08204 KIENIEWICS, J. The Portuguese factory and trade in pepper in Malabar during the 16th century. In IESHR 6,1 (1969) 61-84.

08205 KUSUMAN, K.K. English trade in Travancore. Trivandrum: Kerala Hist. Soc., 1977. 101p.

3. Mysore and its Kanara Coast

08206 GOPAL, M.H. Tipu Sultan's Mysore, an economic study. Bombay: Popular, 1971. 112p.

C. Religion and Society in South India in the Mughal-Maratha Period (1565-1818)

1. Hinduism

08207 BHARATI, S. Voice of Tayumanar; the life of the saint and his song-offering. Madras: Shuddhananda Library, 1963. 134p.

08208 DERRETT, J.D.M. Modes of saṁnyāsīs and the reform of a South Indian maṭha carried out in 1584. In JAOS 94,1 (1974) 65-72.

08209 RAGHAVENDRA, Swami. Shri Raghavendra, his life, and works. Ed. by G.B. Joshi. Mantralaya, Dist. Dharwar: Shri Raghavendra Swami Brindavan Office, 1972-.

08210 SOURIRAJAN, P. A critical study of saint Tāyumāṉavar. Tirupati: Sri Venkateswara U., 1978. 268p.

08211 VENKAṬĀDHVARIN. Rāghavayādavīya. Tr. into French by M.-C. Porcher. Pondicherry: IFI, 1972. 130p. (Its pub., 46)

2. Islam: Sufis and the Mappila Shahīds (martyrs)

08212 DALE, S.F. The Islamic frontier in Southwest India: the Shahid as a cultural ideal among the Mappillas of Malabar. In MAS 11,1 (1977) 41-56.

08213 EATON, R.M. The court and the dargah in the seventeenth century Deccan. In IESHR 10,1 (1973) 50-63.

08214 ______. Sufi folk literature & the expansion of Indian Islam. In HR 14,2 (1974) 117-27.

08215 ______. Sufis of Bijapur, 1300-1700: social roles of Sufis in medieval India. Princeton: PUP, 1978. 358p.

3. Christian Churches: Syrian, Roman Catholic, and Protestant

08216 BERTRAND, J. Mémoires historiques sur les missions des ordres religieux et spécialment sur les questions du clergé indigène et des rites malabares, d'après des documents inédits. Paris: P. Brunet, 1862. 467p.

08217 ______. La Mission du Madure d'après des documents inédits. Paris: Poussielgue-Russand, 1847-48. 2 v., 380, 416p.

08218 BROU, A. Saint François Xavier, 1506-1552. Paris: G. Beauchesne, 1912. 2 v., 455, 487p.

08219 CRONIN, V. A pearl to India: the life of Roberto de Nobili. London: Longman & Todd, 1966. 288p.

08220 FERROLI, D. The Jesuits in Malabar. Bangalore: Bangalore Press, 1939-51. 2 v.

08221 GNANAPRAGASAM, V.M. Father Beschi, the missionary. In Studia missionalia 13 (1963) 169-180.

08222 KILLAPARAMBIL, J. Mar Dionysius the great of Malabar for the One True Fold. In Orientalia Christiana perioda 30 (1964) 148-192.

08223 KUSUMAN, K.K. The Syrian Christians of Kerala: a case study. In JKS 2,1 (1975) 25-36.

08224 MUNDADAN, A.M. The arrival of the Portuguese in India and the Thomas Christians under Mar Jacob, 1498-1552. Bangalore: Dharmaram College, 1967. 163p.

08225 ______. Sixteenth-century traditions of St. Thomas Christians. Bangalore: Dharmaram College, 1970. 190p.

08226 PEARSON, H.N. Memoirs of the life and correspondence of the Reverend Christian Frederick Swartz. 2nd ed. London: J. Hatchard, 1935. 2 v.

08227 RAJAMANICKAM, S. The first oriental scholar. Tirunelveli: De Nobili Res. Inst., 1972. 279p.

D. Languages and Literatures of South India: Late Medieval Developments in Sanskrit and the Dravidian Regional Languages (1565-1818)

08228 ACHYUTA MENON, C. Ezuttaccan and his age. Madras: U. of Madras, 1940. 198p. (Madras U. Malayalam Dept. ser., 6)

08229 PORCHER, M.-C. Un poème satirique sanskrit la Viśvaguṇadarśacampū de Venkaṭādhvarin. Pondicherry: IFI, 1972. 232p.

08230 VASUMATI, E. Telugu literature in the Qutub Shahi period. Hyderabad: Abul Kalam Azad Oriental Res. Inst., 196-. 276p.

08231 VENKATARAO, N. The Southern school in Telugu literature. 3rd ed. Madras: U. of Madras, 1978. 162p.

E. Art and Architecture of Late Medieval South India (1565-1818)

08232 COOMARASWAMY, A.K. Citra-laksana. In Sir Asutosh memorial volume. Patna: J.N. Samaddar, 1926-28, pt. 1, 49-61. [Tr. of chap. 64 of Silparatna by Sri Kumara of Kerala, 16th cent.]

08233 COUSENS, H. Bijapur and its architectural remains, with an historical outline of the Adil Shahi dynasty. Bombay: Govt. Central Press, 1916. 132p. (ASI, new imperial ser., 37)

08234 MARTIN-DUBOST, P. Lepakshi: joyau de l'architecture andhra. In Archeologia 51 (1972) 53-62.

08235 MITTAL, J. Andhra paintings of the Ramayana. Hyderabad: A.P. Lalit Kala Akademi, 1969. 69p. + 52pl.

08236 REA, A. Monumental remains of the Dutch East India Company in the Presidency of Madras. Madras: Govt. Press, 1897. 79p. (ASI, new imperial ser., 25)

08237 SHERWANI, H.K. Town planning and architecture of Haidarabad under the Qutb Shahis. In IsC 50,2 (1976) 61-80.

08238 THIAGARAJAN, K. Meenakshi Temple, Madurai. Madurai: Meenakshi Sundareswarar Temple Renovation Cmtee., 1965. 81p.

VI. MIDDLE INDIA DURING THE MUGHAL-MARATHA PERIOD (1565-1818)

A. General and Political History

1. The Ahmadnagar and Berār Sultanates of the Northern Deccan

a. Ahmadnagar; Muslim resistance to Mughal imperialism under Sultān Chānd Bībī (d. 1600) and Malik Ambar (1549-1626), the Abyssinian "slave" Prime Minister

08239 CHAUDHURY, J.N. Malik Ambar; a biography. Calcutta: M.C. Sarkar, 1934. 181p.

08240 GRIBBLE, J.D.B. The story of Queen Chand and the fall of Ahmadnagar. In his A history of the Deccan. London: Luzac, 1896, v. 1, 211-241.

08241 QADRI, S.A. Memoirs of Chand Bibi: the princess of Ahmednagar. Tr. from Urdu by M.H. Quraishi. Hyderabad: Tarikh Office, 1939. 128p. (Nawab Lutf ud-Daulah mem. series, 2)

08242 SHYAM, R. The Kingdom of Ahmadnagar. Delhi: Motilal, 1966. 440p.

08243 ______. Life and times of Malik Amber. Delhi: Munshiram, 1968. 169p.

08244 TAMASKAR, B.G. Historical geography of Malik Ambar's territory (1600-1626 A.D.). In JIH 53 (1975) 255-68, 393-413.

08245 ______. Life and work of Malik Ambar. Delhi: IAD, 1978. 403p.

b. Berar/Vidarbha: the ʾImād-Shāhī dynasty

08246 CHAUDHURI, J.N. The ʾImād-Shāhī dynasty of Berar. In R.C. Majumdar, ed. The Mughul Empire. Bombay: BVB, 1974, 463-66. (HCIP, 7)

2. The Marathas: from Anti-Mughal Guerrilla Warfare to India-Wide Supremacy

a. sources

08247 HATALKAR, V.G., tr. French records (relating to the history of the Marathas). Bombay: Maharashtra State Board for Literature and Culture, 1978-. v. 1, 214p.; v. 2, 194p. [to be 6 v.]

08248 PATWARDHAN, R.P. & H.G. RAWLINSON, eds. Source book of Maratha history. Calcutta: K.P. Bagchi, 1978. 322p. [1st pub. 1929]

08249 RANADE, M.G. Introduction to Peshwa's diaries. In R. Temple, et al. Sivaji and the rise of the Mahrattas. Calcutta: Susil Gupta, 1953, 53-86.

08250 SARDESAI, G.S., ed. Selections from the Peshwa Daftar. Bombay: Govt. Central Press, 1929-33. 45 v. [summaries in English]

08251 SARKAR, JADUNATH, ed. Persian records of Maratha history. Bombay: Dir. of Archives, 1953-54. 2 v., 213, 68p.

08252 SARKAR, JADUNATH & G.S. SARDESAI, eds. English records of Maratha history; Poona Residency Correspondence. Bombay: Govt. Central Press, 1936-58. 14 v.

b. general histories of the Maratha power, 17th - 19th cents.

08253 BEHERE, N.K. The background of Maratha renaissance in the seventeenth century: historical survey of the social, religious & political movements of the Marathas. Bangalore: Bangalore Press, 1946. 175p.

08254 KARANDIKAR, S.L. The rise and fall of the Maratha power. Vol. 1: 1620-1689 (Shahaji, Shivaji, Sambhaji). Poona: S.S. Karandikar, 1969. 346p.

08255 NADKARNI, R.V. The rise and fall of the Maratha Empire. Bombay: Popular, 1966. 410p.

08256 PISSURLENCAR, P.S.S. The Portuguese and the Marathas: translation of articles of the late Dr. Pandurang S. Pissurlenkar's Portugueses e Maratas in Portuguese language. Tr. by P.R. Kakodkar. Bombay: Maharashtra State Board for Literature and Culture, 1975. 644p.

08257 RANADE, M.G. & R.T. TELANG. Rise of the Maratha power and other essays and gleanings from Maratha chronicles. Bombay: Bombay U. Press, 1961. 236p. [1st pub. 1900]

08258 SARKAR, JADUNATH. House of Shivaji: studies and documents on Maratha history: royal period. Calcutta: Orient Longmans, 1978. 307p. [Rpt. of 3rd ed., 1955]

08259 SAVARKAR, V.D. Hindu-pad-padashahi; or, A review of the Hindu empire of Maharashtra. 4th ed. ND: Bharti Sahitya Sadan, 1971. 252p. [1st pub. 1925]

08260 SHARMA, S.R. The founding of Maratha freedom. Rev. ed. Bombay: Orient Longmans, 1964. 467p.

08261 ______. Maratha history re-examined, 1295-1707. Bombay: Karnatak Pub. House, 1944. 348p.

08262 TEMPLE, R.C., et al. Sivaji and the rise of the Mahrattas. Calcutta: Susil Gupta, 1953. 157p.

c. studies of Maratha institutions: administrative, fiscal, judicial, and military

08263 APTE, B.K. A history of the Maratha navy and merchantships. Bombay: State Board for Literature and Culture, 1973. 311p.

08264 DEOPUJARI, M.B. Shivaji and the Maratha art of war. Nagpur: Vidarbha Samshodhan Mandal, 1973. 276p.

08265 GUNE, V.T. The judicial system of the Marathas. Poona: DCPRI, 1953. 391p. (Its diss. ser., 12)

08266 NAYEEM, M.A. The working of the chauth and sardeshmukhi system in the Mughal provinces of the Deccan (1707-1803 AD). In IESHR 14,2 (1977) 153-206.

08267 SALETORE, B.A. The antiquity and justification of chauth. In JUB ns 30 (1961-62) 1-65.

08268 SEN, S.N. Administrative system of the Marathas. 3rd ed. Calcutta: K.P. Bagchi, 1976. 430p. [rpt. of 2nd ed., 1925]

08269 ______. The military system of the Marathas. 2nd rev. ed. Calcutta: K.P. Bagchi, 1979. 266p. [Rpt. 1958 ed.]

08270 VASHISHTA, H.B. Land revenue and public finance in Maratha administration. Delhi: Oriental, 1975. 196p.

d. Shivājī Chhatrapati (1627-1680): the Marāṭhā revolt against the Mughals
i. contemporary records and biographies

08271 English records on Shivaji (1659-82). Poona: Shiva Charitra Karyalaya, 1931. 779p.

08272 KHOBREKAR, V.G. Archival sources of Maratha history. In Indica 9,1 (1972) 31-44.

08273 ______, ed. Records of the Shivaji period. Bombay: Govt. Central Press, 1974. 250p. (Chhatrapti Shri Maharaj coronation tercentenary commem. vol., 1) [In Marathi; prefatory matter in English]

08274 MORRISON, B.M. A history of Shivaji (an 18th century French account). In JIH 42 (1964) 49-76.

08275 SARKAR, JADUNATH, tr. Rajasthani records: Shivaji's visit to Aurangzib at Agra; a collection of contemporary Rajasthani letters.... Calcutta: Indian History Congress, 1963. 55p. (its Research series, 1)

08276 SEN, S.N. Foreign biographies of Shivaji. 2nd rev. ed. Calcutta: K.P. Bagchi, 1977. 332p. [1st pub. 1930]

08277 ______, tr. Śiva Chhatrapati, being a translation of Sabhasad Bakhar with extracts from Chitnis & Sivadigvijaya, with notes. Calcutta: U. of Calcutta, 1920. 272p.

ii. later biographies and studies of Shivaji

08278 APTE, B.K., ed. Chhatrapati Shivaji: coronation tercentenary commemoration volume. Bombay: U. of Bombay, 1975. 251p.

08279 INDIAN INST. OF PUBLIC ADMIN. Shivaji and swarajya. Bombay: Orient Longmans, 1975. 94p.

08280 KARAKA, D.F. Shivaji; portrait of an early Indian. Bombay: Times of India Press, 1969. 167p.

08281 KELUSKAR, K.A. The life of Shivaji Maharaj, founder of the Maratha empire. Adapted from Marathi of N.S. Takakhav. Bombay: Manoranjan Press, 1921. 643p.

08282 KINCAID, D. The grand rebel; an impression of Shivaji, founder of the Maratha empire. London: Collins, 1937. 329p.

08283 KULKARNEE, N.H., ed. Chhatrapati Shivaji, architect of freedom: an anthology. Delhi: Chhatrapati Shivaji Smarak Samiti, 1975. 79 + 358p.

08284 KULKARNI, A.R. Maharashtra in the age of Shivaji. Poona: Deshmukh, 1969. 308p.

08285 KULKARNI, V.B. Shivaji, the portrait of a patriot. Bombay: Orient Longmans, 1963. 236p.

08286 PEARSON, M.N. Shivaji and the decline of the Mughal Empire. In JAS 35,2 (1976) 221-35.

08287 RAWLINSON, H.G. Shivaji the Maratha, his life and times. Oxford: OUP, 1915. 125p.

08288 SARDESAI, S.G. Shivaji: contours of a historical evaluation. ND: Perspective, 1974. 36p. [1st pub. in Mainstream June 8 & 15, 1974]

08289 SARKAR, JADUNATH. Shivaji and his times. 5th ed. Calcutta: M.C. Sarkar, 1952. 412p. [1st ed. 1919]

08290 SHARMA, S.L., ed. 300th anniversary of coronation of Chatrapati Shivaji Maharaj: souvenir. ND: Foreign Window, 1974. 82p.

08291 VAIDYA, C.V. Shivaji, the founder of Maratha Swaraj. Poona: Aryabhushan Press, 1931. 410p.

iii. Shivājī's descendants, Sāmbhājī I, Rājārām I and his queen Tārā Bāī; rival chhatrapatis at Sātārā and Kolhāpur

08292 GOKHALE, K.S. Chhatrapati Sambhaji. Poona: Navakamal, 1978. 438p.

08293 KISHORE, B. Tara Bai and her times. NY: Asia, 1964. 232p.

08294 MALGONKAR, M. Chhatrapatis of Kolhapur. Bombay: Popular, 1971. 613p.

08295 SARKAR, J.N. Mirza Rajah Jai Singh and Shivaji. In JIH 42 (1964) 251-64.

e. the Peshwās at Poona: Chitpāvan Brahman prime-ministers of the Chhatrapatis, and de facto rulers, 1713-1818
i. the peak of Maratha expansion: the first four Peshwās (1713-73); defeat by the Afghans at Panipat, 1761

08296 BANERJEE, A.C. Peshwa Madhav Rao I. 2nd ed., rev. & enl. Calcutta: A. Mukherjee, 1968. 204p. [1st pub. 1943]

08297 DAS GUPTA, A. Crisis at Surat, 1730-32. In BPP 86,2 Diamond jubilee no. (1967) 148-62.

08298 DESAI, W.S. Bombay and the Marathas up to 1774. ND: Munshiram, 1970. 248p.

08299 DIGHE, V.G. Peshwa Bajirao I and the Maratha expansion. Bombay: Karnatak Pub. House, 1944. 235p.

08300 GUPTA, H.R. Marathas and Panipat. Chandigarh: Panjab U., 1961. 378p.

08301 SHARMA, HIRA LAL. Ahilyabai. ND: NBT, 1969. 123p.

08302 SHEJWALKAR, T.S. Panipat: 1761. Poona: DCPRI, 1946. 141p. (Its monograph, 1)

08303 SINHA, H.N. Rise of the Peshwas. Allahabad: Indian Press, 1931. 255p.

08304 SRINIVASAN, C.K. Baji Rao I, the great Peshwa. NY: Asia, 1962. 152p.

ii. Maratha provincial feudatories, origin of later Princely States: the Bhonsles of Nagpur, Angres of Kolaba, Scindias/Shindes of Gwalior, Holkars of Indore, and Gaikwaḍs of Baroda

08305 GORDON, S.N. Legitimacy and loyalty in some successor states of the eighteenth century. In J.F. Richards, ed. Kingship and authority in South Asia. Madison: South Asian Studies, U. of Wisconsin, 1978, 286-303. (Its Pub. series, 3)

08306 ______. Old rights and new masters: Maratha conquest and control in eighteenth century Malwa. Ph.D. diss., U. of Michigan, 1972.

08307 ______. Scarf and sword: thugs, marauders, and state-formation in 18th century Malwa. In IESHR 6,4 (1969) 403-30.

08308 ______. The slow conquest: administrative integration of Malwa into the Maratha Empire, 1720-1760. In MAS 11,1 (1977) 1-40.

08309 KEENE, H.G. Mādhava Rāo Sindhia and the Hindu reconquest of India. Oxford: OUP, 1891. 207p. (Rulers of India)

08310 KOTHEKAR, S.V. The Gaikwads of Baroda and the East India Company, 1770-1820. Nagpur: Nagpur U., 1977. 254p.

08311 MALGONKAR, M. The sea hawk. ND: Vision Books, 1979. 293p. [Rpt. of 1959 ed., titled Kanhoji Angre...]

08312 QANUNGO, S.N. Jaswant Rao Holkar; the golden rogue. Lucknow: the author, 1965. 351p.

08313 SEN, S.N. Early career of Kanhoji Angria and other papers. Calcutta: U. of Calcutta, 1941. 225p.

08314 SINHA, R.M. Judicial administration under the Nagpur Bhonslas before the advent of British power in 1818. In JIH 47 (1969) 95-114.

08315 WILLS, C.U. British relations with the Nagpur state in the 18th century. An account mainly based on contemporary English records. Nagpur: Central Provinces Govt. Press, 1926. 272p.

iii. the Maratha Confederacy under the later Peshwas and the Regent Nānā Phadnīs (1741-1800): confrontations with growing British power, to 1818

08316 ABDUL ALI, A.F.M. Commercial and social intercourse between the East India Company and the Poona court in the 18th cent. In BPP 37 (Jan-June 1929) 19-34.

08317 BROUGHTON, T.D. Letters from a Mahratta camp during the year 1809: descriptive of the character, manners, domestic habits, and religious ceremonies of the Mahrattas. Calcutta: K.P. Bagchi, 1977. 252p. [Rpt. 1813 ed.]

08318 BURTON, R.G. The Mahratta and Pindari War. Delhi: Seema, 1975. 126p. + 8pl. [Rpt. 1910 ed.]

08319 CHAKRAVORTY, U.N. Anglo-Maratha relations and Malcolm, 1798-1830. ND: Associated, 1979. 200p.

08320 CHOKSEY, R.D. A history of British diplomacy at the court of the Peshwas, 1786-1818. Poona: R.D. Choksey, 1951. 399p.

08321 DEODHAR, Y.N. Nana Phadnis and the external affairs of the Maratha empire. Bombay: Popular, 1962. 247p.

08322 GHOSH, B.N. British policy towards the Pathans and the Pindaris in Central India, 1805-1818. Calcutta: Punthi Pustak, 1966. 364p.

08323 GUPTA, P.C. Baji Rao II and the East India Company, 1796-1818. 2nd rev. ed. Bombay: Allied, 1964. 239p.

08324 JHA, J.S. Suppression of the Pindaris. In JBRS 43 (1957) 251-84.

08325 MACDONALD, A. Memoir of the life of the late Nana Farnavis.... London: OUP, 1927. 184p.

08326 PEMBLE, J. Resources and techniques in the second Maratha War. In Historical J. 19,2 (1976) 375-404.

08327 ROY, M.P. Origin, growth, and suppression of the Pindaris. ND: Sterling, 1973. 355p.

08328 SEN, S.N. Anglo-Maratha relations during the administration of Warren Hastings, 1772-1785. Calcutta: KLM, 1961. 288p.

08329 SHAKESPEAR, L.W. A history of Poona and its battlefields. Lahore: Sheikh Mubarak Ali, 1976. 99p. [Rpt. 1912 ed.]

08330 SINHA, B.K. The Pindaris, 1798-1818. Calcutta: Bookland, 1971. 224p.

08331 SINHA, K.N. Studies in Anglo Maratha relations. Jabalpur: Lok Chetana Prakashan, 1969. 132p.

08332 VAIDYA, S.G. Peshwa Bajirao II and the downfall of the Maratha power. Nagpur: Pragati Prakashan, 1976. 357p.

08333 VARMA, S.P. A study in Maratha diplomacy: Anglo-Maratha Relations, 1772-1783. Agra: Shiva Lal Agarwala, 1956. 432p.

3. Goa: Portuguese presence on the Konkan coast, 1510-1961

08334 BOXER, C.R. Portuguese society in the tropics: the municipal councils of Goa, Macao, Bahia & Luanda, 1510-1800 AD. Madison: U. of Wisc. Press, 1965. 240p.

08335 FONSECA, J.N. DA. An historical and archaeological sketch of the city of Goa. Bombay: Thacker, 1878. 332p.

08336 PRIOLKAR, A.K. The Goa Inquisition, being a quatercentenary commemoration study of the Inquisition in India. Bombay: 1961. 310p.

08337 RAJAGOPALAN, S. Old Goa. ND: ASI, 1975. 50p. + 8pl.

08338 RAO, R.P. Portuguese rule in Goa, 1510-1961. NY: Asia, 1963. 242p.

08339 RENAULT-ROULIER, G. Goa, Rome de l'Orient. "By Remy". Paris: France-Empire, 1955. 319p.

4. Gujarat: from Muslim Kingdom to Mughal Province (1572); Maratha Raids and Occupation; Dutch Settlements [for Surat and the British see 7. b. below]

08340 ALI MUHAMMAD KHAN. Mirat-i-Aḥmadī. Tr. [from Persian] by C.N. Seddon. Baroda: Oriental Inst., 1928. 2 v. (GOS, 43, 50)

08341 ______. Mirat-i-Aḥmadī: a Persian history of Gujarat. Tr. from Persian by M.F. Lokhandwala. Baroda: Oriental Inst., 1965. 946p. (GOS, 146)

08342 CHAVDA, V.K. A select bibliography of Gujarat; its history and culture, 1600-1857. Ahmedabad: New Order Book Co., 1972. 232p.

08343 COMMISSARIAT, M.S. A history of Gujarat, including a survey of its chief architectural monuments and inscriptions. Bombay: Longmans, Green, 1957. v. 2, 1573-1758, 592p.

08344 ______. Madelslo's travels in western India (AD 1638-39). London: OUP, 1931. 115p.

08345 ______. Studies in the history of Gujarat. Bombay: Longmans, Green, 1935. 157p.

08346 MACMURDO, J. The peninsula of Gujarat in the early nineteenth century. Ed. by S.C. Ghosh. ND: Sterling, 1977. 163p. [his Journal of a route through the peninsula of Gujarat in the year 1809 and 1810]

08347 PEARSON, M.N. Merchants and rulers in Gujarat: the response to the Portuguese in the sixteenth century. Berkeley: UCalP, 1976. 178p.

08348 RADWAN, A.B. The Dutch in western India, 1601-1632: a study of mutual accommodation. Calcutta: KLM, 1978. 159p.

08349 SHAH, A.M. Political system in eighteenth century Gujarat. In Enquiry ns 1 (1964) 83-95.

5. Rajput Princes of Rajasthan: Hindu Martial Aristocracy, in Mughal Service, until Revolt against Aurangzīb; Relations with Marathas and British

a. general studies

08350 BANERJI, A.C. The Rajput states and the East India Company. Calcutta: A. Mukherjee, 1951. 456p.

08351 BHATTACHARYYA, S. The Rajput states and the East India Company, from the close of 18th century to 1820. ND: Munshiram, 1972. 278p.

08352 GUPTA, B. Maratha penetration into Rajasthan: through the Mukandara Pass. ND: Research, 1979. 141p.

08353 HALLISSEY, R.C. The Rajput rebellion against Aurangzeb: a study of the Mughal Empire in seventeenth-century India. Columbia: U. of Missouri Press, 1977. 119p.

08354 MATHUR, R.M. Rajput states and East India Company. Delhi: Sundeep, 1979. 268p.

08355 SAXENA, R.K. Maratha relations with the major states of Rajputana, 1761-1818 A.D. ND: S. Chand, 1973. 286p.

08356 SHARMA, G.C. Administrative system of the Rajputs. ND: Rajesh, 1979. 223p.

08357 ZIEGLER, N.P. Some notes on Rajput loyalties during the Mughal period. In J.F. Richards, ed. Kingship and authority in South Asia. Madison: South Asian Studies, U. of Wisconsin, 1978, 215-51. (Its Pub. ser., 3)

b. Mewāṛ/Udaipur: home of the Sisodia clan

08358 GUPTA, K.S. Mewar and the Maratha relations, 1735-1818 AD. ND: S. Chand, 1971. 230p.

08359 MANKEKAR, D.R. Mewar saga: the Sisodias' role in Indian history. ND: Vikas, 1976. 199p.

08360 MEHTA, B.S. & JODH SINGH MEHTA. Pratap, the patriot: with a concise history of Mewar and its missing links. Udaipur: Pratap Inst. of Hist. Res., 1971. 110p.

08361 MITRA, S.C. Pratap Singha, or a memoir of the great Maharana of Mewar. Calcutta: Chuckervertty, Chatterjee, 1928. 200p.

08362 SHARMA, G.N. Mewar and the Mughal emperors (1526-1707 A.D.). Agra: S.L. Agarwala, 1954. 265p.

08363 SHARMA, S.R. Maharana Pratap. Hoshiarpur: V.V.R. Inst., 1954. 156p. [Rpt. 1934 ed.]

08364 ______. Maharana Raj Singh and his times. Delhi: Motilal, 1971. 146p.

c. Mārwāṛ/Jodhpur: desert stronghold of the Rāṭhod clan

08365 BHARGAVA, V.S. Marwar and the Mughal emperors (A.D. 1526-1748). Delhi: Munshiram, 1966. 228p.

08366 PARIHAR, G.R. Marwar and the Marathas, 1724-1843 AD. Jodhpur: Hindi Sahitya Mandir, 1968. 316p.

08367 RAGHUBIR SINH. Durga Das Rathor. ND: NBT, 1975. 185p.

08368 RAHIM, M.A. Emperor Aurangzeb's annexation of Jodhpur and Rajput rebellion. In JASP 14 (1969) 65-90.

08369 SHARMA, G.D. Rajput polity, a study of politics and administration of the state of Marwar, 1638-1749. ND: Manohar, 1977. 333p.

08370 ______. Marwar War as depicted in Rajasthani sources (1678-79 A.D.). In JIH 53,1 (1975) 43-55.

d. Amber and Jaipur: the Kacchwāhs

08371 BHATNAGAR, V.S. Life and times of Sawai Jai Singh, 1688-1743. Delhi: Impex India, 1974. 386p.

08372 PRASAD, R.N. Raja Man Singh of Amber. Calcutta: World Press, 1966. 196p.

08373 RAJASTHAN STATE ARCHIVES. A descriptive list of the khatoot ahalkaran (Rajasthani), 1633 to 1796 A.D. Bikaner: 1975. 114p.

08374 REFAQAT ALI KHAN, Kunwar. The Kachwahas under Akbar and Jahangir. ND: Kitab, 1976. 243p.

08375 SRIVASTAVA, A.L. Amber's alliance with Akbar: an estimate of Raja Bharmal. In JIH 46 (1968) 27-34.

e. Ajmer

08376 TIRMIZI, S.A.I. Ajmer through inscriptions 1532-1852 A.D. ND: Indian Inst. of Islamic Studies, 1968. 87p.

6. Central India and Orissa

08377 GUPTA, B.D. Life and times of Maharaja Chhatrasal Bundela. ND: Radiant, 1980. 162p.

08378 PATTANAIK, P.K. A forgotten chapter of Orissan history: with special reference to the rajas of Khurda and Puri, 1568-1828. Calcutta: Punthi Pustak, 1979. 319p.

7. Growth of British Power in Middle India, 1608-1818

a. general studies

08379 ANDERSON, P. The English in western India. London: Smith, Elder, 1856. 403p.

08380 FURBER, H. Bombay Presidency in the mid-eighteenth century. NY: Asia, 1965. 76p.

08381 NIGHTINGALE, P. Trade and empire in Western India, 1784-1806. Cambridge: CamPU, 1970. 264p.

08382 OVINGTON, J. A voyage to Surat in the year 1689. London: OUP, 1929. 313p.

08383 RABITOY, N. System v. expediency: the reality of land revenue administration in the Bombay Presidency, 1812-1820. In MAS 9,4 (1975) 529-46.

08384 RAWLINSON, H.G. British beginnings in Western India, 1579-1657. Oxford: OUP, 1920. 158p.

b. East India Company headquarters at Surat in Gujarat (1613-1687) and Bombay in Maharashtra (from 1687)

08385 DA CUNHA, J.G. The origin of Bombay. In JBBRAS, extra no. (1900) 368p.

08386 DAVID, M.D. History of Bombay, 1661-1708. Bombay: U. of Bombay, 1973. 488p.

08387 DESAI, W.S. Bombay and the Marathas up to 1774. ND: Munshiram, 1970. 248p.

08388 SHAFAʿAT AHMAD KHAN. Anglo-Portuguese negotiations relating to Bombay, 1660-77. London: OUP, 1922. 156p.

08389 STRACHEY, R. & O. STRACHEY. Keigwin's rebellion; an episode in the history of Bombay. Oxford: Clarendon Press, 1916. 184p.

08390 WRIGHT, A. Annesley of Surat and his times; the true story of the mythical Wesley fortune. London: A. Melrose, 1918. 357p.

B. Economic and Social History of Middle India during the Mughal-Maratha Period (1526-1818)

1. General Economic and Social History

08391 BENJAMIN, N. Dr. Hove's travelogue: a document for the economic history of Western India. In JIH 52,1 (1974) 164-88.

08392 DAS, B.S. Studies in the economic history of Orissa from ancient times to 1833. Calcutta: KLM, 1978. 300p.

08393 DE SOUZA, T.R. Glimpses of Hindu dominance of Goan economy in the 17th century. In Indica 12,1 (1975) 27-35.

08394 FUKAZAWA, H. State and caste system (Jati) in the eighteenth century Maratha kingdom. In Hitotsubashi J. of Econ. 9,1 (1968) 32-44.

08395 GOKHALE, B.G. Ahmadabad in the 17th century. In JESHO 12 (1969) 187-97.

08396 ______. Burhanpur: notes on the history of an Indian city in the XVIIth century. In JESHO 15,3 (1972) 316-325.

08397 ______. Capital accumulation in 17th century western India. In JASBombay 39/49 (1964-65) 51-60.

08398 GOPAL, S. Commerce and crafts in Gujarat, 16th and 17th centuries: a study in the impact of European expansion on precapitalist economy. ND: PPH, 1975. 289p.

08399 MAHALEY, K.L. Estimated population of Shivaji's kingdom in Maharashtra. In QRHS 7 (1967-68) 250-54.

08400 QURAISHI, M. Muslim education and learning in Gujarat, 1297-1758. Baroda: Faculty of Educ. and Psychology, MSUB, 1972. 328p.

08401 SHARMA, G.N. Social life in medieval Rajasthan, 1500-1800 A.D., with special reference to the impact of Mughal influence. Agra: Lakshmi Narain Agarwal, 1968. 447p.

2. The Agrarian System and Village Life

08402 ALAM, M. The zamindars and Mughal power in the Deccan, 1685-1712. In IESHR 11,1 (1974) 74-91.

08403 CHAMBARD, J.-L. Les commencements d'une histoire agraire: implantation des castes dominantes dans une village de l'Inde Central ou le défrichement date du XVIe siècle. In Puruṣārtha 1 (1975) 5-15.

08404 EDWARDES, S.M. Side-lights on Dekkan village life in the 18th century. In IA (1926) 108-113.

08405 FUKAZAWA, H. Lands and peasants in the eighteenth century Marāṭhā Kingdom. In Hitotsubashi J. of Econ. 6 (1965) 32-61.

08406 ______. Rural servants in the 18th century Maharashtrian village - demiurgic or jajmani system? In Hitotsubashi J. of Econ. 12,2 (1972) 14-40.

08407 KULKARNI, A.R. Village life in the Deccan in the 17th century. In IESHR 4 (1967) 38-52.

08408 KULKARNI, G.T. Land revenue and agricultural policy of Shivaji: an appraisal. In BDCRI 35,3/4 (1976) 73-82.

08409 MANDLIK, V.N. [Account of the founding of the village Murud]. In his Writings and speeches of the late honourable Rao Saheb Visvanath Narayan Mandlik, C.S.I. Bombay: Native Opinion Press, 1896, 201-34.

08410 MANN, H.H. A Deccan village under the Peshwas. In IJE 4 (1923) 30-46.

08411 PEARSON, M.N. Indigenous dominance in a colonial economy; the Goa rendas, 1600-1670. In Mare Luso-Indicum 2 (1972) 61-73. [rendas=revenue rights]

08412 PERLIN, F. Of white whale and countrymen in the 18th century Maratha Deccan; extended class relations, rights, and the problem of rural autonomy under the old regime. In JPS 5,2 (1978) 172-237.

3. Trade and Commerce; the Ports of Surat and Bombay

08413 APTE, M.D. The nature and scope of the records from Peshwa Daftar with reference to Zakat system. In IESHR 6 (1969) 369-80.

08414 DAS GUPTA, A. The merchants of Surat, c. 1700-50. In E. Leach & S.N. Mukherjee, eds. Elites in South Asia. Cambridge: CamUP, 1970, 201-22.

08415 FURBER, H. The country trade of Bombay and Surat in the 1730's. In Indica 1,1 (1964) 39-46.

08416 GOKHALE, B.G. English trade with western India (1650-1700). In JIH 42 (1964) 329-42.

08417 ______. Some aspects of early English trade with western India, 1600-1650. In JIH 40 (1962) 269-86.

08418 ______. Surat in the seventeenth century: a study in urban history of pre-modern India. London: Curzon, 1977. 240p. (Scandinavian Inst. of Asian Studies, 28)

08419 GOPAL, S. Commerce and crafts in Gujarat, 16th and 17th centuries; a study in the impact of European expansion on precapitalist economy. ND: PPH, 1975. 289p.

08420 ______. Gujarati shipping in the seventeenth century. In IESHR 8,1 (1971) 31-39.

08421 PISSURLENCAR, P.S.S. Portuguese records on Rustamji Manockji the Parsi broker of Surat. Nova Goa: the author, 1933-36. 2 v. in 1. [vol. 2, English tr. by S.B. d'Silva]

08422 RABITOY, N. Sovereignty, profits, and social change: the development of British administration in Western India, 1800-1820. Ph.D. diss., U. of Pennsylvania, 1972. 399p. [UM 73-13,456]

08423 SINGH, O.P. Surat and its trade in the second half of the 17th century. Delhi: U. of Delhi, 1976. 223p.

08424 WRIGHT, A. Annesley of Surat and his times; the true story of the mythical Wesley fortune. London: A. Melrose, 1918. 357p.

C. Religion and Society in Middle India during the Mughal-Maratha Period (1526-1818)

1. Later Maharashtrian Santas (Poet-saints) [see also Chap. Four, VII. B. 2. for Early santas]

a. general studies; minor poet-saints

08425 ABBOTT, J.E., tr. Bahina Bai: a translation of her autobiography and verses. Poona: Scottish Mission Industries, 1929. 185p. (Poet-saints of Maharashtra, 5)

08426 ______, tr. Daśopanta-caritra. Poona: Scottish Mission Industries, 1928. 194p. (Poet-saints of Maharashtra, 4)

b. Ekanātha (c. 1548-c. 1609), Brahman bhakta in the Dnyāneśvara tradition

08427 DEMING, W.S. Eknath, a Marathi bhakta. Bombay: Karnatak Printing Press, 1931. 117p.

08428 DESHPANDE, M.S. Saint Ekanatha's light for life divine: or, Gospel of Goddevotion. Aurangabad: Sri Ekanath Sanshodhan Mandir, 1976. 222p.

08429 EKANATHA. Bhikshugīta; the mendicant's song, the story of a converted miser...the 23rd chapter of the Eknāthi Bhāgavata. Tr. by J.E. Abbott. Poona: Scottish Mission Indistries, 1928. 248p. (Poet-saints of Maharashtra, 3)

08430 KULKARNI, S.R. Saint Eknath. ND: Maharashtra Info. Centre, 1968. 28p.

08431 MAHIPATI. Eknath: a translation from the Bhaktalilamrita. Tr. by J.E. Abbott. Poona: Scottish Mission Industries, 1927. 295p. (Poet-saints of Maharashtra, 2) [Chs. 13-24]

c. Tukārāma (1608-1649), most popular of the santas

08432 BELSARE, K.V. Tukaram. ND: Maharashtra Info. Centre, 1967. 64p.

08433 DELEURY, G.A. Prier avec Toukārām. In Studia missionalia, 13 (1963) 53-63.

08434 FRASER, J.N. & J.F. EDWARDS. The life and teachings of Tukaram. Madras: CLS, 1922. 323p.

08435 MAHIPATI. Tukaram; translation from Mahipati's Bhaktalilamrita, chap. 25-40. Poona: Scottish Mission Industries, 1930. 346p. (The poet-saints of Maharashtra, 7)

08436 SHARMA, S.R. Focus on Tukaram from a fresh angle. Bombay: Popular, 1962. 106p.

08437 TUKĀRĀMA. Poems. Tr. from Marathi by J.N. Fraser & K.B. Marathe. Madras: CLS, 1909-15. 3 v.

08438 ______. Psaumes du pélerin; traduction, introduction et commentaires. Tr. by G.A. Deleury. Paris: Gallimard, 1956. 220p. (UNESCO series)

08439 ______. Tukaram, saint of Maharashtra. Tr. by C. Rajwade. Beas: Radha Soami Satsang Beas, 1978. 156p.

08440 ______. Tukaram's poems. Tr. from Marathi by Prabhakar Machwe. Calcutta: United Writer, 1977. 49p.

08441 ______. Twenty-five poems. Tr. from Marathi by P. Machwe. In Mahfil 5,1/2 (1968-69) 61-69.

08442 ______. Village songs of western India. Tr. by J.S. Hoyland... London: Allenson, 1934. 86p.

d. Rāmadāsa (1608-1681), supposed preceptor of Shivājī

08443 APTE, S.S. Shree Samartha Ramdas, life and mission. Bombay: Vora, 1965. 265p.

08444 BOKIL, V.P. Rajguru Ramdas. Poona: Kamalesh P. Bokil, 1979. 448p.

08445 DATE, V.H. Spiritual treasure of Saint Rāmadāsa. Delhi: Motilal, 1975. 242p.

08446 DEMING, W.S. Rāmdās and the Rāmdāsīs. Calcutta: Assn. Press, 1928. 223p.

08447 JOSHI, T.D. Social and political thought of Ramdas. Bombay: Vora, 1970. 176p.

08448 MAHIPATI. Ramdas... Mahīpati's Santavijaya. Tr. from Marathi by J.E. Abbott. Poona: N.R. Godbole, 1932. 409p. (Poet-saints of Maharashtra, 8)

08449 RAMADASA. Dāsabodha. Tr. by V.S. Kanvinde. Nagpur: Jayashree Prakashan, 1963. 216p.

2. Dādū (1544-1603) and the Dādū-Pantha: Bhakta Followers of Kabīr in Rajasthan

08450 CALLEWAERT, W.M. Key for understanding mystical literature. In Orientalia Lovaniensia Periodica 8 (1977) 309-30.

08451 ______. Life and works of the Dādū-Panthī Rajjab; North India, 16th-17th c. In Orientalia Lovaniensia Periodica 4 (1973) 141-53.

08452 ______. The Sarvāṅgi of the Dādūpanthī Rajab. Louvain: Dept. Orientalistiek, Katholieke U. Leuven, 1978. 446p. (Orientalia Lovaniensia analecta, 4)

08453 ______. Search for manuscripts of the Dādū-Panthī literature in Rajasthan [& Delhi and Benares]. In Orientalia Lovaniensia Periodica 4 (1973) 155-67; 8 (1977) 305-8.

08454 DĀDŪDAYĀLA. Dādū, the compassionate mystic. Tr. by K.N. Upadhyaya. Dera Baba Jaimal Singh: Radha Soami Satsang Beas, 1979. 232p.

08455 MUKHIA, HARBANS. The ideology of the Bhakti movement: the case of Dadu Dayal. In Debiprasad Chattopadhyaya, ed. History and society.... Calcutta: K.P. Bagchi, 1978, 445-54.

08456 ORR, W.G. A sixteenth-century Indian mystic. London: Lutterworth, 1947. 238p.

3. Islamic Religious Developments

08457 AZIZ AHMAD. Dār al-islām and the Muslim kingdoms of Deccan and Gujarat. In CHM 7 (1963) 787-93.

08458 IVANOW, W. The sect of Imām Shāh in Gujrat. In JASBombay ns 12 (1936) 19-70. [Shīʿi]

D. Languages and Literatures of Middle India in Mughal-Maratha Period (1526-1818)

08458a ACWORTH, H.A. Ballads of the Marathas. London: Longmans, Green, 1894. 129p.

08459 BELL, H.W. Some translations from the Marathi poets. Bombay: Times Press, 1913. 209p.

08460 BENDER, E., tr. The Nalarāyadavadantīcarita (Adventures of King Nala & Davadantī). In TAPS 40,4 (1950) 265-372.

08461 KANHERE, S.G. Wāman Pandit: scholar and Marathi poet (17th century). In BSOAS 4 (1927) 305-14.

08462 PRABHAKAR, M. A critical study of Rajasthani literature, with exclusive reference to the contribution of Cāraṇas. Jaipur: Panchsheel Prakashan, 1976. 195p.

E. Art and Architecture of Middle India in the Mughal-Maratha Period (1526-1818)

1. Painting
a. Deccani painting of the Five Sultanates; Mālwā and Bundelkhaṇḍ

08463 ARCHER, W.G. Central Indian painting. London: Faber & Faber, 1958. 24p. + 10pl.

08464 BANERJI, A. An illustrated Hindi manuscript of Śakuntalā dated 1789 A.D. In LK 1/2 (1955) 46-54.

08465 BARRETT, D.E. Painting at Bijapur. In R.H. Pinder-Wilson, ed. Paintings from Islamic lands. Oxford: B. Cassirer, 1969, 141-52.

08466 ______. Painting of the Deccan, XVI-XVII century. London: Faber & Faber, 1958. 24p. + 10pl.

08467 ______. Some unpublished Deccan miniatures. In LK 7 (1960) 9-13.

08468 GOSWAMY, B.N. Deccani painting. In LK 12 (1962) 41-44.

08469 Identification of the portraits of Malik Ambar. In LK 1/2 (1955) 23-31.

08470 KRAMRISCH, S. A survey of painting in the Deccan. London: India Soc., 1937. 234p. + 24pl.

08471 MITTAL, J. Some Deccani paintings in the Baroda Museum. In Baroda Museum and Picture Gallery, Bulletin 20 (1968) 19-24.

08472 MOTI CHANDRA. Some unpublished paintings from Bijapur in the Prince of Wales Museum of Western India. In Bombay Hist. Soc. 7 (1941) 34-47.

08473 NASIR AHMED. Farrukh Husain, the royal artist at the court of Ibrahim Adil Shah II. In IsC 30,1 (1956) 31-35.

08474 SKELTON, R. Documents for the study of painting at Bijapur in the late sixteenth and early seventeenth centuries. In ArtsAs 5 (1958) 97-125 + 6pl.

b. Gujarati painting

08475 SHAH, U.P. More documents of Jaina paintings and Gujarati paintings of sixteenth and later centuries. Ahmedabad: L.D. Inst. of Indology, 1976. 28p. + 19pl.

c. Rajasthani painting
i. general

08476 ARCHER, W.G. Indian paintings from Rajasthan. Catalogue of an exhibition of works from the collection of Sri Gopi Krishna Kanoria of Calcutta. London: Arts Council of Great Britain, 1957. 44p.

08477 ARCHER, W.G. & E. BINNEY III. Rajput miniatures from the collection of Edwin Binney III. Exhibition catalog. Portland: Portland Art Museum, 1968. 132p.

08478 COOMARASWAMY, A.K. Catalogue of the Indian collections in the Museum of Fine Arts, Boston; pt. V: Rajput paintings. Boston: Museum of Fine Arts, 1927. 276p. + 132pl.

08479 ______. Hindi Rāgmālā texts. In JAOS 43 (1924) 396-409.

08480 ______. Rajput painting. London: OUP, 1916. 2 v., incl. 77pl. [Rpt. Delhi: Motilal, 1977]

08481 EBELING, K. Rāgamālā painting. Paris: Ravi Kumar, 1973-74. 300p.

08482 GANGOLY, O.C. Masterpieces of Rajput painting. Calcutta: Rūpam, 1927. 8p. + 52pl.

08483 GRAY, B. Rajput painting... London: Faber & Faber, 1948. 24p. + 10pl.

08484 MONTGOMERY, G. Rajput painting. NY: Asia Soc., 1960. 84p.

08485 MUKHERJI, H. The origin of Rajasthani painting. In RL 33,1/2 (1962) 43-59.

08486 PAL, P. Rāgamālā paintings in the Museum of Fine Arts, Boston. Boston: 1967. 84p.

08487 SANYAL, A.N. Rāgas and Rāginīs. Bombay: Orient Longmans, 1959. 282p.

08488 SINGH, K.S. Rajasthani paintings. In Cultural forum 8/4 (1966) 46-50.

08489 SKELTON, R. Rajasthani temple hangings of the Krishna cult. NY: American Federation of Arts, 1973. 112p.

08490 WALDSCHMIDT, E. A contribution to Rāgamālā iconography. In J.H. Date, ed. Munshi indological felicitation volume. Bombay: BVB, 1963, 278-302. [Pub. as BV 20,21 (1960-61)]

08491 ______. Londoner Entsprechungen zu einer Berliner Serie musikinspirierter indischer Miniaturen. In Akademie der Wissenschaften, Göttingen, Philologisch-historische Klasse, Nachrichten 7 (1962) 175-201 + 15pl.

ii. Bundī and Koṭā schools

08492 ANDHARE, S.K. Bundi painting. ND: Lalit Kala Akademi, 1970. 4p. + 6pl. (Lalit Kala ser., portfolio, 7)

08493 ARCHER, W.G. Indian painting in Bundi and Kotah. London: HMSO, 1959. 58p. + 24pl. (Victoria and Albert Museum monograph, 13)

08494 BANERJI, A. Illustrations to the Rasikapriyā from Buṇḍi-Koṭah. In LK 3/4 (1956) 67-73.

08495 BEACH, M.C. Painting of the later eighteenth century at Bundi and Kota. In P. Pal, ed. Aspects of Indian Art. Leiden: Brill, 1972, 124-29.

08496 ______. Rajput painting at Bundi and Kota. Ascona: Artibus Asiae Pub., 1974. 58p. + 60pl. (ArtAs suppl., 32)

08497 CHANDRA, PRAMOD. Buṇḍi painting. ND: Lalit Kalā

Akademi, 1959. 27pl. (Lalit Kalā series of Indian art, 6)

08498 KHANDALAVALA, K.J. Five Bundi paintings of the late 17th century A.D. In PWMB 5 (1955-57) 50-56.

08499 ______. A group of Bundi miniatures. In PWMB 3 (1952-53) 23-35.

08500 RANDHAWA, M.S. Painting in Bundi. In RL 35,1/2 (1965) 6-14.

iii. Mewāṛ/Udaipur school

08501 CHANDRA, PRAMOD. A Rāgamālā set of the Mewar school in the National Museum of India. In LK 3/4 (1956) 46-54.

08502 GOETZ, H. The first golden age of Udaipur: Rajput art in Mewar during the period of Mughal supremacy. In Ars Orientalis 2 (1957) 427-437.

08503 MOTI CHANDRA. Mewar painting. ND: Lalit Kalā Akademi, 1971. 4p. + 6pl. (Lalit Kala series, portfolio, 9)

08504 ______. Mewar painting in the seventeenth century. ND: Lalit Kalā Akademi, 1957. 1 v.

08505 ______. Paintings from an illustrated version of the Rāmāyaṇa painted at Udaipur in A.D. 1649. In PWMB 5 (1955-57) 33-49.

08506 SHARMA, G.N. An approach to Mewar school of painting (13th-18th century AD). In JBRS 47 (1961) 276-89.

iv. other Rajasthani schools

08507 ANDHARE, S.K. A dated Āmber Rāgamalā and the problem of provenance of the eighteenth century Jaipuri painting. In LK 15 (1970) 47-51.

08508 ______. Painting from the Thikana of Deogarh. In PWMB 10 (1967) 43-53 + 13pl.

08509 BEACH, M.C. Painting at Devgarh. In Archives of Asian Art 24 (1970-71) 23-35.

08510 DICKINSON, E. Kishangarh painting. ND: Lalit Kalā Akademi, 1959. 50p. + 16 col. pl.

08511 KHANDALAVALA, K.J. Wall painting from Amber. ND: Lalit Kalā Akademi, 1974. 4p. + 8pl.

08512 MAJMUDAR, M.R. Two illustrated mss of the Bhāgavata Daśamaskandha. In LK 8 (1960) 47-54.

08513 MEHTA, R.N. Picchavāis: temple-hangings of the Vallabhācārya sect. In J. of Indian Textile History 3 (1959) 4-14.

08514 SHARMA, G.N. Nathdwara painting from 17th to 20th century A.D. In PIHC (1958) 558-64.

08515 SINGH, K.S. An early Rāgamālā ms. from Pāli (Mārwār school) dated 1623 A.D. In LK 7 (1960) 76-81.

v. the "Mālwā school", an extension of Rajasthani painting

08516 ANAND KRISHNA. Malwa painting. Varanasi: Bharat Kala Bhavan, BHU, 1968. 48p.

08517 ARCHER, W.G. Central Indian painting. London: Faber & Faber, 1958. 22p. + 10pl.

08518 BANERJI, A. Malwa school of painting. In RL 31 (1960) 32-42.

08519 MOTI CHANDRA. An illustrated set of the Amaruśataka. In PWMB 2 (1951-52) 1-63.

2. Architecture

08520 Homage to Jaipur (special issue). In Mārg 30,4 (1977) 1-94.

08521 HUSSAIN, A. Monuments of Muslim rule at Cuttack. In OHRJ 11,1 (1962) 1-8.

08522 MATE, M.S. Deccan woodwork. Poona: DCPRI, 1967. 61p. (DCBC, 49)

08523 ______. Maratha architecture (1650 A.D. to 1850 A.D.). Poona: U. of Poona, 1959. 128p.

08524 NUNES, J. The monuments in old Goa: a glimpse into the past and present. Delhi: Agam Kala, 1979. 128p.

08525 SILVA, M.M. DE CAGIGAL E. A arte indo-portuguesa. Lisboa: Edicoes Excelsior, 1966. 374p.

3. Decorative and Industrial Arts

08526 Deccani Kalams. In Mārg 16 (1963) 2-64. [by S.C. Welch, R. Ettinghausen, Jagdish Mittal, K. Khandalavala, R. Skelton, M. Ashraf, V.K. Bawa, Syed Mohiuddin]

08527 HENDLEY, T.H. Asian carpets; 16th and 17th century designs from Jaipur palaces. London: W. Griggs, 1905. 20p.

08528 IRWIN, J. The commercial embroidery of Gujarat in the 17th century. In Mārg 17 (1964) 71-2.

08529 ______. Golconda cotton paintings of the early seventeenth century. In LK 5 (1959) 11-48.

VII. THE INDUS VALLEY AND NORTHWEST MOUNTAIN FRONTIER IN THE MUGHAL-MARATHA PERIOD (1526-1799)

A. General and Political History

1. Sind and Baluchistan

08530 KHAN, ANSAR ZAHID. The Arbabs of Sind. In JPHS 22,1 (1974) 18-31.

2. Panjab and the Sikhs, from Guru Nanak (1469-1538) to the Rise of Ranjit Singh, 1799

a. sources

08531 FAUJA SINGH, ed. Historians and historiography of the Sikhs. ND: Oriental, 1978. 296p.

08532 GANDA SINGH. Some non-Muslim sources of the history of the Punjab during the medieval period. In Mohibbul Hasan, ed. Historians of medieval India. Meerut: Meenakshi Prakashan, 1968, 209-224.

08533 MADHAVA RAO, P.S. The Punjab (1758-1763): from the Tahmasnama abridged and translated. In JASBombay ns 38 (1963) 85-115.

08534 SURI, S.L. An outstanding original source of Panjab history: Umdat-ut-tawarikh. Tr. from Persian by V.S. Suri. Delhi: S. Chand, 1961-. v. 1-.

b. general histories of the Panjab and the Sikhs: from religious sect to military power between Mughals and Afghans

08535 AHMAD, R. Political and economic life of the Punjab between 1707 and 1849. In Punjab (Pak.) U. J. of Research (Humanities) 1,1 (1966) 57-84.

08536 AKBAR, M. The Punjab under the Mughals. Lahore: Ripon Printing Press, 1948. 325p.

08537 BANERJEE, I. Evolution of the Khalsa. 2nd ed. Calcutta: A. Mukherjee, 1963. 2 v.

08538 CHHABRA, G.S. Advanced history of the Punjab. 2nd rev. ed. Jullundur: New Academic Pub. Co., 1968-. 2 v. [v. 1; Guru & post Guru up to Ranjit Singh, 540p.]

08539 CUNNINGHAM, J.D. A history of the Sikhs, from the origin of the nation to the battles of the Sutlej. Delhi: S. Chand, 1966. 402p. [Rpt. 1849 ed.]

08540 GILL, P.S. History of Sikh nation: foundation, assassination, resurrection. Jullundur: New Academic Pub. Co., 1978. 380p.

08541 GORDON, J.J.H. The Sikhs. Patiala: Languages Dept., Punjab, 1970. 236p. [1st pub. 1904]

08542 GREWAL, J.S. From Guru Nanak to Maharaja Ranjit Singh: essays in Sikh history. Amritsar: Guru Nanak U., 1972. 195p.

08543 GUPTA, H.R. History of the Sikhs. Calcutta: S.C. Sarkar, 1939-44. 3 v. [v. 1, 3rd ed. ND: Munshiram, 1978]

08544 ______. Later Mughal history of the Panjab (1707-1793). Lahore: Sang-e-Meel, 1976. 348p. [Rpt. 1944 ed.]

08545 JAGJIT SINGH. The Jats and Sikh militarization. In J. of Sikh Studies 4,1 (1977) 36-54.

08546 KOHLI, S.R. The struggle over the Panjab (the Sikhs, Mughals and Afghans). In H.R. Gupta, ed. Sir Jadunath Sarkar Commemoration volume. Hoshiarpur: Panjab U., 1958, v. 2, 206-16.

08547 MALIK, A.D. An Indian guerilla war: the Sikh people's war, 1699-1768. ND: Wiley Eastern, 1975. 124p.

08548 MCLEOD, W.H. The evolution of the Sikh community: five essays. Delhi: OUP, 1975. 118p.

08549 NARANG, G.C. Transformation of Sikhism, or how the Sikhs became a political power. 5th rev. ed. ND: New Book Soc., 1963. 268p. [1st ed. 1912]

08550 NIJJAR, B.S. Panjab under the great Mughals, 1526-1707 AD. Bombay: Thacker, 1968. 244p.

08551 ______. Panjab under the later Mughals, 1707-1759. Jullundur: New Academic Pub. Co., 1972. 324p.

08552 PAYNE, C.H. A short history of the Sikhs. 2nd ed. Patiala: Dept. of Languages, Punjab, 1970. 248p. [1st pub. 1915]

08553 SIDDIQUI, I.H. The Afghan governors of the Punjab during the life-time of Guru Nanak. In J. of Sikh studies 1,2 (1974) 74-85.

08554 SINHA, N.K. Rise of the Sikh power. 3rd ed. Calcutta: A. Mukherjee, 1973. 135p. [1st ed. 1946]

c. Hindu states of the Panjab hills

08555 GOETZ, H. History of Chamba State in Mughal and Sikh times. In his Studies in the history and art of Kashmir and the Indian Himalayas. Wiesbaden: Harrassowitz, 1969, 112-26. [1st pub. in JIH 31,2 (1953) 135-56]

08556 HUTCHISON, J. & J.P. VOGEL. History of the Punjab hill states. Lahore: Supt. of Govt. Printing, 1933. 2 v.

d. Jammu and Kashmir

08557 CHARAK, S.D.S. Maharaja Ranjitdev and the rise and fall of Jammu Kingdom, from 1700 A.D. to 1820 A.D. Pathankot: Dogra-Pahari Itihas Kendra, 1971. 188p.

08558 MALIK, Z. The subah of Kashmir under the later Mughals 1708-1748. In Medieval India, a Miscellany 2 (1972) 249-62.

08559 PARMU, R.K. A history of Muslim rule in Kashmir 1320-1809. Delhi: PPH, 1969. 544p.

08560 SAIF-ud-DIN, M. Sources of the history of Kashmir (from Sultan Fateh Shah's reign 1505 to the time of Amir Zaman Shah's fall in 1801). In QRHS 9 (1969-70) 17-22.

B. Economic and Social History of the Indus Valley Area in the Mughal-Maratha Period (1526-1799)

08561 AHMAD, RAFIQ. Taxation and tenure of agricultural land in the Punjab between 1707 and 1849. In Punjab (Pak.) U. J. of research (Humanities) 1,2 (1966) 131-61.

08562 BANGA, I. Agrarian system of the Sikhs: late eighteenth and early nineteenth century. ND: Manohar, 1978. 260p.

08563 CHABLANI, S.P. Economic conditions in Sind, 1592-1843. Bombay: Orient Longmans, 1951. 209p.

08564 HABIB, IRFAN. Evidence for sixteenth-century agrarian conditions in the Guru Granth Sahib. In IESHR 1 (1964) 64-72.

C. Religious Traditions of the Sikhs: Syncretism of Hinduism and Islam in the Panjab (1469-1799)

1. General Studies of Sikhism
a. bibliography

08565 GANDA SINGH. A select bibliography of the Sikhs and Sikhism. Amritsar: Shiromani Gurdwara Parbankhak Cmtee., Sikh Itihas Res. Board, 1965. 439p.

08566 KHUSHWANT SINGH. The Sikhs. In C.J. Adams, ed. A reader's guide to the great religions. 2nd ed. rev. & enl. NY: Free Press, 1977, 223-30.

b. histories and surveys

08567 ARCHER, J.C. The Sikhs in relation to Hindus, Moslems, Christians, and Ahmadiyyas. A study in comparative religion. Princeton: PUP, 1946. 353p. [Rpt. NY: Russel & Russel, 1971]

08568 COLE, W.O. & P.S. SAMBHI. The Sikhs; their religious beliefs and practices. London: Routledge & Kegan Paul, 1978. 210p.

08569 DALIP SINGH. Sikhism: a modern and psychological perspective. Chandigarh: Bahri, 1979. 130p. (Series in Sikh history and culture, 1)

08570 FAUJA SINGH, et al. Sikhism. Patiala: Punjabi U., 1969. 161p.

08571 GILL, P.S. Trinity of Sikhism: philosophy, religion, state. Jullundur: New Academic Pub. Co., 1973. 303p.

08572 GOPAL SINGH. A history of the Sikh people, 1469-1978. ND: World Sikh U. Press, 1979. 762p. + 8pl.

08573 ______. The religion of the Sikhs. NY: Asia, 1971. 191p.

08574 HARBANS SINGH. The heritage of the Sikhs. Bombay: Asia, 1964. 219p.

08575 JOHAR, S.S. Handbook on Sikhism. Delhi: Vivak Pub. Co., 1977. 197p.

08576 KHUSHWANT SINGH. A history of the Sikhs. v. 1, 1469-1839. Princeton: PUP, 1963. 419p.

08577 ______. The Sikhs. London: Allen & Unwin, 1953. 215p.

08578 KOHLI, S.S. Outlines of Sikh thought. ND: Punjabi Prakashak, 1966. 166p.

08579 TEJA SINGH. Sikh religion; an outline of its doctrines. Amritsar: Shiromani Gurdwara Parbandhak Cmtee., 1963. 32p.

c. philosophy, ethics, and doctrine

08580 AVTAR SINGH. Ethics of the Sikhs. Patiala: Punjabi U., 1970. 288p.

08581 DALJEET SINGH. Sikhism, a comparative study of its theology and mysticism. ND: Sterling, 1979. 379p.

08582 JAINA, N.K. Sikh religion and philosophy. ND: Sterling, 1979. 119p.

08583 KOHLI, S.S. Sikh ethics. ND: Munshiram, 1975. 85p.

08584 SHER SINGH, Gyani. Philosophy of Sikhism. 2nd ed. Delhi: Sterling, 1966. 316p.

d. Sikh shrines and ritual

08585 GANDA SINGH. History of the Gurdwara Shahidganj, Lahore, from its origin to November 1935; compiled from original sources, judicial records, and contemporary materials. Amritsar: G. Singh, 1935. 115p.

08586 JOGENDRA SINGH. Sikh ceremonies. Bombay: International Book House, 1941. 96p.

08587 JOGINDER SINGH. Sikh ceremonies. Chandigarh: Sikh Religious Book Soc., 1968. 96p.

08588 JOHAR, S.S. The Sikh gurus and their shrines. Delhi: Vivek Pub. Col., 1976. 328p. + 8pl.

08589 MEHAR SINGH. Sikh shrines in India. ND: PDMIB, 1975. 47p. + 10pl.

08590 SAHI, J.S. Sikh shrines in India and abroad. Faridabad: Common World, 1978. 160p.

08591 Sikh sacred music. ND: Sikh Sacred Music Soc., 1967. 90p.

08592 TEJA SINGH. The Sikh prayer. Amritsar: Shiromani Gurdwara Parbandhak Cmtee., 1963. 22p.

08593 WALIULLAH KHAN, M. Sikh shrines in West Pakistan. Karachi: Dept. of Archaeology, Min. of Educ. and Info., 1962. 143p.

2. General Studies of the Ten Gurus, from Nanak to Gobind Singh

08594 BANERJEE, A.C. Guru Nanak to Guru Gobind Singh. Allahabad: Rajesh, 1978. 244p.

08595 GANDHI, S.S. History of the Sikh gurus: a comprehensive study. Delhi: Gur Das Kapur, 1978. 642p.

08596 PURAN SINGH. The ten masters. 4th ed. Amritsar: Chief Khalsa Diwan, 1969. 151p.

08597 RAY, N.R. The Sikh gurus and the Sikh society; a study in social analysis. Patiala: Punjabi U., 1970. 204p.

3. Guru Nānak (1469-1539): Follower of Kabīr and the North Indian Santas, and Founder of Sikhism

a. bibliography and sources on Guru Nānak

08598 BAL, S.S. Guru Nanak in the eyes on non-Sikhs. Chandigarh: Panjab U., 1969. 188p.

08599 FAUJA SINGH & KIRPAL SINGH. Atlas: travels of Guru Nanak. Patiala: Punjabi U., 1976. 72p. + 26pl.

08600 GANDA SINGH. Guru Nanak's works: a bibliography. In IL 12,2 (1969) 28-49.

b. works of Guru Nānak: translations and commentaries

08601 BHAVE, V. Commentary on Japuji, Guru Nanak's great composition. Tr. by G.S. Talib. Patiala: Punjabi U., 1973. 67p.

08602 GURSARAN SINGH. Guru Nanak's Japji, the morning prayer of the Sikhs, an interpretation in the light of modern thought. Delhi: Atma Ram, 1972. 291p.

08603 KIRPAL SINGH. Jap-ji: enseignement initiatique du Guru Nanak (XVI siècle). Chambery: Éditions Présences, 1970. 191p.

08604 MAJITHIA, S.S. & Y.G. KRISHNAMURTI, tr. Japjee, the universal hope. Sardarnagar: Lady Parsan Kaur Charitable Trust (Educational Society), 1967. 144p.

08605 NĀNAK. Guru Nānak in his own words. Ed. by H.S. Shan. Armitsar: Chief Khalsa Diwan, 1969-70. 120p.

08606 ______. Guru Nanak's Japji. Tr. from Panjabi by G.S. Randhawa & G. Singh. ND: Navayug Traders, 1970. 64p.

08607 ______. Hymns of Guru Nanak. Tr. from Panjabi by Khushwant Singh. ND: Orient Longmans, 1969. 192p.

08608 ______. The Jap-ji; fourteen religious songs. Tr. from Panjabi by P. Lal. Calcutta: Writers Workshop, 1967. 16p.

c. biographies of Guru Nānak

08609 BAL, S.S. Life of Guru Nanak. Chandigarh: Panjab U., 1969. 283p.

08610 BANERJEE, A.C. Guru Nanak and his times. Patiala: Punjabi U., 1971. 245p.

08611 GOPAL SINGH. Guru Nanak. ND: NBT, 1967. 134p.

08612 Guru Nanak. ND: PDMIB, 1969. 224p.

08613 KARTAR SINGH. Life of Guru Nanak Dev. Rev. ed. Ludhiana: Lahore Book Shop, 1958. 320p.[1st ed. 1937]

08614 TALIB, G.S. Guru Nanak, his personality and vision. Delhi: Gur Das Kapur, 1969. 32 + 327p.

08615 TRILOCHAN SINGH. Guru Nanak: founder of Sikhism: a biography. Delhi: Gurdwara Parbandhak Cmtee., 1969. 509p.

d. general studies of Guru Nānak's teachings

08616 ANAND, B.S. Guru Nanak: religion and ethics. Patiala: Punjabi U., 1968. 64p.

08617 GANDA SINGH, ed. Sources of the life and teachings of Guru Nanak. In PPP 3,1/2 (1969) 639p. [Guru Nanak's Birth Quincentenary Vol.; English 444p.; Panjabi 151p.; Urdu 44p.]

08618 GREWAL, J.S. Guru Nanak in history. Chandigarh: Panjab U., 1969. 348p.

08619 HARBANS SINGH. Guru Nanak and origins of the Sikh faith. Bombay: Asia, 1969. 247p.

08620 ISHAR SINGH. Nanakism: a new world order, temporal and spiritual. ND: Ranjit Pub. House, 1976. 288p.

08621 KOHLI, S.S. Philosophy of Guru Nanak. Chandigarh: Panjab U., 1969. 200p.

08622 ______. Travels of Guru Nanak. Chandigarh: Panjab U., 1969. 200p.

08623 MCLEOD, W.H. Guru Nanak and the Sikh religion. Oxford: OUP, 1968. 259p.

08624 NIHAL SINGH, G., ed. Guru Nanak, his life, time, and teachings; Guru Nanak Foundation quincentenary volume. Delhi: National, 1969. 305p.

08625 SRINIVASA IYENGAR, K.R., ed. Guru Nanak: a homage; [papers presented at the Sahitya Akademi seminars held at New Delhi, Calcutta, Madras, Bombay, and Ludhiana, December 1969-February 1970]. ND: Sahitya Akademi, 1973. 304p.

08626 TARAN SINGH, ed. Guru Nanak and Indian religious thought; Guru Nanak commemorative lectures. Patiala: Sri Guru Granth Sahib Studies Dept., Punjabi U., 1970. 2 v.

08627 ______, ed. Teachings of Guru Nanak Dev. Patiala: Punjabi U., 1977. 136p.

08628 VARMA, S.C. Guru Nānak and the logos of divine manifestation; with the Jap nishān in verse and an interpretation. Delhi: Gurdwara Prabandhak Cmtee., 1969. 425p.

08629 WAZIR SINGH. Humanism of Guru Nanak: a philosophic inquiry. Delhi: Ess Ess, 1977. 191p.

e. Guru Nānak and Islām, and other comparative studies

08630 AHUJA, N.D. The great Guru Nanak and the Muslims. Chandigarh: Kirti Pub. House, 1971. 214p.

08631 GURMIT SINGH. Islam & Sikhism; a comparative study. Sirsa: Usha Inst. of Religious Studies, 1966. 153p.

08632 ISHAR SINGH. The philosophy of Guru Nanak; a comparative study. ND: Ranjit Pub. House, 1969. 274p.

08633 LOEHLIN, C.H. Sufism and Sikhism. In MW 29 (1939) 351-58.

08634 MCLEOD, W.H. The influence of Islam upon the thought of Guru Nanak. In HR 7 (1968) 302-16.

08635 SIKKA, A.S. The philosophy of mind in the poetry of Guru Nanak; comparative study with European philosophy. Ludhiana: Bee Kay, 1973. 200p.

4. The Later Gurus: Transformation from Panth ("Sect") to Militant Khālsā (Brotherhood of the "Pure")

a. Guru Rām Dās (1534-1581), the fourth Guru

08636 MANSUKHANI, G.S. Guru Ramdas, his life, work, and philosophy. ND: Oxford & IBH, 1979. 185p.

b. Guru Har Gobind (1595-1644): sixth guru, and the beginnings of militarization

08637 GILL, P.S. Life story of first national hero, Guru Hargobind. In his History of Sikh nation: foundation, assassination, resurrection. Jullundur: New Academic Pub., 1978, 153-161.

08638 GOPAL SINGH. Guru Har Gobind (1595-1644 AD). In his A history of the Sikh people (1469-1978). ND: World Sikh U. Press, 1979, 212-35.

c. Guru Tegh Bahādur (1621-1675), ninth guru and martyr to Auranzīb's persecution

08639 ANAND, B.S. Guru Tegh Bahadur, a biography. ND: Sterling, 1979. 235p.

08640 DALJIT SINGH. Guru Tegh Bahadur. Paitiala: Language Dept., Punjab, 1971. 195p.

08641 GILL, P.S. Guru Tegh Bahadur, the unique martyr. Jullundur: New Academic Pub. Co., 1975. 123p.

08642 GREWAL, J.S. Guru Tegh Bahadur and the Persian chroniclers. Amritsar: Dept. of History, Guru Nanak Dev U., 1976. 138p.

08643 GUPTA, B.S. Guru Tegh Bahadur: a study. Chandigarh: Panjab U., 1978. 149p.

08644 TALIB, G.S., ed. Guru Tegh Bahadur: background and the supreme sacrifice: a collection of research articles. Patiala: Punjabi U., 1976. 250p.

08645 TEGH BAHADUR. Hymns of Guru Tegh Bahadur: songs of nirvana. Tr. from Panjabi by Trilochan Singh. Delhi: Delhi Sikh Gurdwara Mgmt. Cmtee., 1975. 257p.

08646 TRILOCHAN SINGH. Guru Tegh Bahadur, prophet and martyr; a biography. Delhi: Gurdwara Parbandhak Cmtee., 1967. 358p.

d. Guru Gobind Singh (1666-1708): the tenth and last human Guru, founder of the Khālsā

08647 BAAGHA, A.S. Banur had orders; a critical study, of an hitherto unknown Hukamnamah of Guru Gobind Singh. Delhi: Ranjit, 1969. 104p.

08648 FAUJA SINGH. Travels of Guru Gobind Singh. Patiala: Punjabi U., 1968. 32p. + 14pl.

08649 GANDA SINGH. Guru Gobind Singh's death at Nanded: an examination of succession theories. Faridkot: Guru Nanak Foundation, Bhatinda District, 1972. 136p.

08650 GOPAL SINGH. Guru Govind Singh. ND: NBT, 1966. 128p.

08651 GREWAL, J.S. & S.S. BAL. Guru Gobind Singh: a biographical study. Chandigarh: Dept. of History, Panjab U., 1967. 280p.

08652 HARBANS SINGH. Guru Gobind Singh. Chandigarh: Guru Gobind Singh Foundation, 1966. 183p.

08653 JOHAR, S.S. Guru Gobind Singh, a biography. Delhi: Sterling, 1967. 266p.

08654 ______. Guru Gobind Singh: a study. ND: Marwah Pub., 1979. 248p.

08655 KARTAR SINGH. Life of Guru Gobind Singh. Rev. and enl. 3rd ed. Ludhiana: Lahore Book Shop, 1968. 306p.

08656 KHUSHWANT SINGH & SUNEET VIR SINGH. Homage to Guru Gobind Singh. Bombay: Jaico, 1970. 100p. [1st pub. 1966]

08657 MANSUKHANI, G.S. & S.S. KOHLI. Guru Gobind Singh, his personality and achievement. ND: Hemkunt, 1976. 134p.

08658 RAMDEV, J.S. Guru Gobind Singh; a descriptive bibliography. Chandigarh: Panjab U., 1967. 260p.

08659 SEETAL, S.S. Prophet of man, Guru Gobind Singh. Ludhiana: Seetal Pustak Bhandar, 1968. 400p.

08660 SHER SINGH, Gyani. Social & political philosophy of Guru Gobind Singh. Delhi: Sterling, 1967. 283p.

5. The Guru Granth Sahib, or Ādi-Granth, the Sikh Scriptures: Installed in Gurdwārās as Guru after 1708

08661 GOPAL SINGH, tr. Sri Guru Granth Sahib. Chandigarh: World Sikh U. Press, 1978. 4 v., 1351p.

08662 KOHLI, S.S. A critical study of Ādi Granth, being a comprehensive and scientific study of Guru Granth Sāhib, the scripture of the Sikhs. 2nd ed. Delhi: Motilal, 1976. 391p.

08663 MACAULIFFE, M.A. The Sikh religion, its gurus, sacred writings, and authors. Delhi: S. Chand, 1963. 6 v. in 3. [1st pub. 1909; incl. translation of the Adi-Granth]

08664 MANMOHAN SINGH, tr. Sri Guru Granth Sahib. Amritsar: Shiromani Gurdwara Parbandhak Cmtee., 1962. 6 v. [English and Panjabi trans.]

08665 TRILOCHAN SINGH, et al., tr. Selections from the sacred writings of the Sikhs. Rev. by G.S. Fraser. London: Allen & Unwin, 1960. 288p. (UNESCO series)

08666 TRUMPP, E., tr. The Adi Granth; or, The holy scriptures of the Sikhs. 2nd ed. ND: Munshiram, 1970. 138p. + 715p. [1st pub. 1877]

D. Religious Traditions: Hinduism and Islam in the Indus Valley Area (1526-1799)

1. Hinduism: Survival in the Face of Islam and Sikhism

08667 DHAR, T.N. Rupa Bhawani, life, techings & philosophy. Srinagar: All India Saraswat Cultural Organization, Jammu & Kashmir Region, 1977. 167p.

08668 GOSWAMY, B.N. & J.S. GREWAL. The Mughal and Sikh rulers and the Vaishnavas of Pindori; a historical interpretation of 52 Persian documents. Simla: IIAS, 1969. 447p.

08669 ______, tr. The Mughals and the Jogis of Jakhbar; some madad-i-maʿāsh and other documents. Simla: IIAS, 1967. 200p.

08670 GOSWAMY, K. The Bathu Shrine and the Rajas of Guler: a brief study of a Vaishnava establishment. In JIH 43,2 (1965) 577-85.

2. Islam: Sufi Mysticism and Poetry
a. Sindh: Shāh Abdul Karīm (1536-1624), Shāh Abdul Laṭīf (1689-1752), and other Sufi poets

08671 ABD AL-LAṬĪF, Shāh. Risālo of Shāh Abdul Laṭīf (selections). Tr. by Elsa Kazi. Hyderabad: Sindhi Adabi Board, 1965. 252p.

08672 ADVANI, K.B. Sachal. ND: Sahitya Akademi, 1971. 46p.

08673 ______. Shah Latif. ND: Sahitya Akademi, 1970. 70p.

08674 GIDVANI, M.M. Shah Abdul Latif. London: India Soc., 1922. 47p.

08675 GULRAJ, J.P. Sind and its Sufis. Lahore: Sang-e-Meel, 1979. 224p.

08676 HOTCHAND, T.D. Shah Abdul Latif's immortal song: the Song of Kinjhar Lake. Hyderabad: Pardeep, 1963. 127p.

08677 JOTWANI, M.W. Risālo of Shāh ʿAbd al-Karīm. In Studies in Islam 7 (1970) 150-87.

08678 ______. Shah Abdul Karim; a mystic poet of Sindh. ND: Kumar Bros., 1970. 56p.

08679 KHALID, K.B., ed. Poet laureate of Sindhi. Hyderabad: Deputy Director of Public Relations, 1961. 154p.

08680 QURESHI, A.A., ed. Shah Latif, a poet for all times. Karachi: Sind Graduates Assoc., 1978. 145p.

08681 RAHI, K. Saint literature in Sindhi. In IL 19,5 (1976) 63-71.

08682 SCHIMMEL, A. Pain and grace; a study of two mystical writers of eighteenth-century Muslim India. Leiden: Brill, 1976. 310p. [Mir Daud & Shah Abdul Latif]

08683 ______. Šāh ʿAbdul Laṭīfs Beschreibung des wahren Sufi. In R. Gramlich, ed. Islamwissenschaftliche Abhandlungen. Fritz Meier zum sechzigsten Geburtstag. Wiesbaden: Steiner, 1974, 263-84.

08684 ______. Shāh ʿInāyat of Jhok; a Sindhi mystic of the early eighteenth century. In Liber Amicorum; studies in honour of Prof. C.J. Bleeker. Leiden: Brill, 1969, 151-70. (SHR, 17)

08685 SORLEY, H.T. Shah Abdul Latif of Bhit: his poetry, life and times; a study of literary, social and economic conditions in eighteenth century Sind. Lahore: OUP, 1966. 432p. [Rpt. 1940 ed.]

b. Panjabi Sufi poets

08686 RAMA KRISHNA, L. Pañjābī Sūfī poets, A.D. 1460-1900. ND: Ashajanak, 1973. 162p. [1st pub. 1938]

08687 SHAH HUSAIN. The paths unknown. Tr. from Punjabi by G.Y. Anwar. Lahore: Majlis Shah Hussain, 1966. 164p.

08688 SHARDA, S.R. Sufi thought: its development in Panjab and its impact on Panjabi literature, from Baba Farid to 1850 A.D. ND: Munshiram, 1974. 288p.

3. Buddhism in Ladakh

08689 NAWANG TSERING. Buddhism in Ladakh: a study of the life and works of the eighteenth century Ladakhi saint scholar. ND: Sterling, 1979. 102p.

E. Language and Literature of the Indus Valley Area in the Mughal-Maratha Period (1526-1799): Baluchi, Pashto, Panjabi

08690 BALUCH, M.S.K. Literary history of the Baluchis: the classical period, 1450-1650 A.D. Quetta: Baluchi Academy, 1977-. v. 1-.

08691 KAMIL, D.M.K. On a foreign approach to Khushhal; a critique of Caroe and Howell. Peshawar: Maktaba-i-Shaheen, 1968. 157p. [Pashto]

08692 KHWUSHHĀL KHĀN. The poems of Khusshāl Khān Khatak. Tr. by E. Howell & O. Caroe. Peshawar: Pashto Academy, 1963. 98p.

08693 WĀRIS SHĀH. The adventures of Hir & Ranjha. Tr. from Panjabi by C.F. Usborne. Ed. by Mumtaz Hasan. Karachi: Lion Art Press, 1966. 205p. [1st pub. 1905; Rpt. NY: P. Owen, 1973 (UNESCO series)]

08694 ______. The love of Hir and Ranjha. Tr. from Panjabi by S.S. Sekhon. Ludhiana: Old Boys' Assn., College of Agri., Punjab Agri. U., 1978. 269p.

F. Art and Architecture of the Indus Valley

1. Pahāṛī Painting of the Hindu Principalities of the Panjab Hills

a. general studies

08695 AIJAZUDDIN, F.S. Pahari paintings and Sikh portraits in the Lahore Museum. London: Sotheby Parke Bernet, 1977. 101p. + 64pl.

08696 ANAND, M.R. Some notes on the composition of Pahari murals. In Mārg 17 (1974) 8-14.

08697 ARCHER, W.G. Indian painting from the Punjab Hills: a survey and history of Pahari miniature painting. London: Sotheby Parke Bernet, 1973. 2 v., 448, 335p., incl. 900 ill.

08698 ______. Pahari miniatures: a concise history. In Mārg 28,2 (1975) 3-44.

08699 ______. Visions of courtly India: the Archer collection of Pahari miniatures. Washington: Intl. Exhibits Foundation, 1976. 156p.

08700 BEACH, M. Paintings from the Punjab Hills. In Asia 5 (1966) 25-38.

08701 GOSWAMY, B.N. The Islamic influence: a study of the terminology used by the Pahari painters. In Attar Singh, ed. Socio-cultural impact of Islam on India. Chandigarh: Panjab U., 1976, 147-58.

08702 ______. The Pahari artists: a study. In RL 32 (1961) 31-50.

08703 ______. Pahari painting: the family as the basis of style. In Mārg 21,4 (1968) 17-62.

08704 ______. Pahari paintings of the Nala-Damayanti theme in the Collection of Dr. Karan Singh. ND: Natl. Museum, dist. PDMIB, 1975. 158p.

08705 ______. Of patronage and Pahari painting. In Pratapaditya Pal, ed. Aspects of Indian art. Leiden: Brill, 1972, 130-38.

08706 ______. The technique of Pahari painting; a discussion of colour and pattern notes. In E&W ns 17 (1967) 287-94.

08707 ______. The traveller von Ujfalvy and Pahari painting. In RL 34,1/2 (1963) 10-18.

08708 KHANDALAVALA, K. Pahari miniature painting. Bombay: New Book Co., 1958. 409p.

08709 LAWRENCE, G. Indian art, paintings of the Himalayan states. London: Methuen, 1963. 16p. + 15pl.

08710 MITTAL, J. New studies in Pahari painting. In LK 12 (1962) 26-35.

08711 RANDHAWA, M.S. The Krishṇa legend in Pahāṛī paintings. ND: Lalit Kalā Akademi, 1956. 1 v., incl. 12pl. (Lalit kala series of Indian art, 2)

b. the Basohli school (c. 1650-1750)

08712 GOSWAMY, B.N. The problem of the artist "Nainsukh of Jasrota". In ArtAs 28 (1966) 205-10.

08713 Indian miniatures. ND: NBD Pub., 1977. 8p. + 40pl.

08714 PADMANABHAN TAMPY, K.P. Basohli paintings in the Sri Chitralayam, Trivandrum. In Modern review 108 (Oct. 1960) 312-317.

08715 RANDHAWA, M.S. Basohli painting. ND: PDMIB, 1959. 125p.

08716 ______. Basohli paintings of Bhanudatta's Rasamanjari. In RL 36,1/2 (1966) 1-124.

08717 ______. A note on Rasamanjari paintings from Basohli. In RL 31 (June 1960) 16-26.

08718 The Rasamanjari in Basohli painting. In LK 3/4 (1956) 26-38.

c. the Kāngrā school (c. 1750-1850)

08719 ARCHER, W.G. Kangra painting... London: Faber and Faber, 1952. 24p. + 10pl.

08720 FRENCH, F.C. Himalayan art. London: OUP, 1931. 116p. + 24pl.

08721 GOSWAMY, B.N. The "Basohli" Gita Govinda. In Cultural forum 9,1/2 (1967-68) 39-44.

08722 ______. Six Kangra paintings. ND: Lalit Kalā Akademi, 1968. 4p. + 6pl. (Lalit Kalā series portfolio, 6)

08723 KHANDALAVALA, K.J. The Bhāgavata Purāṇa in Kangra painting. ND: Lalit Kalā Akademi, 1965. 4p. + 6pl. (Lalit Kalā series, portfolio, 1)

08724 ______. Kangra paintings from the Bhagavat Purana in the Baroda museum. In Baroda Museum and Picture Gallery, Bulletin 19 (1966) 1-7.

08725 MORLEY, G. Kangra painting. In Portfolio 8 (1964) 42-47.

08726 RANDHAWA, M.S. Kangra paintings of the Bihārī Sat Sāi. ND: Natl. Museum, 1966. 87p.

08727 ______. Kangra paintings of the Gita Govinda. ND: Natl. Museum, 1963. 132p.

08728 ______. Kangra paintings on love... ND: Natl. Museum, 1962. 209p.

08729 ______. Kangra rāgamālā paintings. ND: Natl. Museum, 1971. 88p. + 19pl.

08730 ______. Kangra Valley painting. ND: PDMIB, 1954. 17p. + 40pl.

08731 VASWANI, A.S. Story of Dhruva Maharaj in Kangra Valley paintings. ND: 1963. 25pl. [From the art collections of Shri Tula Ram of Red Fort]

d. Pahāṛī art of particular hill-states: Jammū, Chambā, Guler, Kulu, Maṇḍī, Gaṛhwāl

08732 An Aniruddha-Ushā series from Chāmbā and the painter Rām Lāl. In LK 1/2 (1955) 37-44.

08733 ARCHER, W.G. Garhwal painting. London: Faber & Faber, 1954. 24p. + 10pl.

08734 ARYAN, K.C. Nurpur. In Mārg 17 (1964) 61-65.

08735 GOETZ, H. The art of Chamba in the Islamic period. In JOIB 11 (1961-62) 135-44, 217-36.

08736 GOSWAMY, B.N. The artist-family of Rajol: new light on an old problem. In RL 35,1/2 (1965) 15-23.

08737 ______. The Bhagavata paintings from Mankot. ND: Lalit Kalā Akademi, 1978. 4p. + 6pl. (Lalit Kala series; portfolio, 17)

08738 ______. Painting in Chamba: a study of new documents. In Asian Review ns 2 (Aug. 1965) 53-58.

08739 ______. Some early nineteenth century frescoes and the painter "Angad of Simur". In ArtAs 13 (1966) 99-110.

08740 KHANDALAVALA, K.J. Balvant Singh of Jammu--a patron of Pahari painting. In PWMB 2 (1951-52) 71-81.

08741 MITTAL, J. Chamba. In Mārg 17 (1964) 23-27.

08742 ______. An early Guler painting. In LK 11 (1962) 31-34.

08743 ______. An illustrated manuscript of Madhu-Malati and other paintings from Kulu. In LK 3/4 (1956) 90-95.

08744 ______. Kulu. In Marg 17 (1964) 48-54.

08745 MUKANDI LAL. Garhwal painting. ND: PDMIB, 1968. 110p.

08746 ______. Molaram: the poet and the painter of Garhwal. In A.K. Haldar, et al., eds. S.P. Shah memorial volume. Lucknow: Mrs. Shivlal Panacand Shah, 1940, 107-26.

08747 RANDHAWA, M.S. Chamba painting. In RL 37,1/2 (1967) 7-17.

08748 ______. Signed paintings of Jwala Ram, artist of Garhwal. In RL 32,2 (1961) 51-58.

08749 WALDSCHMIDT, E. Musikinspirierte Miniaturen.... v. 1. Rāgamālā-Bilder aus dem westlichen Himalaya-Gebiet von Ernst und Rose Leonore Waldschmidt. Wiesbaden: Harrassowitz, 1966. 218p. (Museum für indische Kunst, Berlin, Veroffentlichungen, 2)

2. Art under the Sikh Rulers; Pahāṛī Painters on the Panjab Plains

08750 ARCHER, W.G. Painting of the Sikhs. London: HMSO, 1966. 284p. (Victoria & Albert Museum monograph, 31)

08751 GOSWAMY, B.N. Painters at the Sikh court: a study based on twenty documents. Wiesbaden: Steiner, 1975. 146p. (SSI, 20)

08752 Homage to Amritsar [special issue]. In Marg 30,3 (1977) 1-74.

3. Islamic Art and Architecture of Lahore

08753 CHAGHTAI, M.A. The Badshahi Masjid, built by Aurangzeb in 1084/1674: history and architecture. Lahore: Kitab Khana-i-Nauras, 1972. 52p.

08754 VOGEL, J.P. Tile-mosaics of the Lahore fort. Karachi: Pakistan Pub., 1972. 69p. [Rpt. 1920 ed.]

VIII. NORTH INDIA: THE UPPER AND MIDDLE GANGA PLAINS IN THE MUGHAL-MARATHA PERIOD (1526-1801)

A. General and Political History [for Mughal Central Government, see II above]

1. The Upper Ganga Plains (Haryana, Delhi, and Western U.P., incl. Rohilkhand)

08755 BANERJI, B.N. Begam Samru. Calcutta: M.C. Sarkar, 1925. 228p.

08756 HENNESSY, M.N. The rajah from Tipperary. NY: St. Martins, 1972. 183p.

08757 MAHESHWAR DAYAL. Rediscovering Delhi: The story of Shahjahanabad. ND: S. Chand, 1975. 237p. + 12pl.

08758 PRASAD, BISHESHWAR. Rise of Daud Khan Rohilla. In JIH 5 (1926) 380-94.

08759 QANUNGO, K.R. History of the Jats: a contribution to the history of Northern India, v. 1. To the death of Mirza Najaf Khan, 1782. Calcutta: M.C. Sarkar, 1925. 377p.

08760 SPEAR, P. Twilight of the Mughuls: studies in late Mughul Delhi. Karachi: OUP, 1973. 269p. [1st pub. 1951]

08761 STRACHEY, J. Hastings and the Rohilla War. Oxford: OUP, 1892. 324p.

2. The Avadh/Oudh Area of Eastern U.P.

08762 BARNETT, R.B. North India between empires; Awadh, the Mughals, and the British 1720-1801. Berkeley: UCalP, 1980. 400p.

08763 BASU, P. Oudh and the East India Company, 1785-1801. Lucknow: Maxwell Co., 1943. 219p.

08764 COHN, B.S. The initial British impact on India; a case study of the Benares region. In JAS 19 (1960) 418-31.

08765 ______. Political systems in eighteenth century India: the Banaras region. In JAOS 82,3 (1962) 313-20.

08766 DAVIES, C.C. Warren Hastings and Oudh. London: OUP, 1939. 271p.

08767 FISHER, M.H. The imperial court and the province: a social and administrative history of pre-British Awadh (1775-1856). Ph.D. diss., U. of Chicago, 1978. 250p.

08768 HASTINGS, W. The Benares diary of Warren Hastings. Ed. by C.C. Davies. London: Royal Hist. Soc., 1948. 40p.

08769 ______. Narrative of the insurrection in the Zemeedary of Banaris. Calcutta: 1782. 70 + 213p.

08770 ______. A narrative of the late transactions at Benares. Calcutta: N. Roy, 1905. 150p.

08771 SANYAL, S. Benares and the English East India Company, 1764-1795. Calcutta: World Press, 1979. 249p.

08772 SINHA, S.N. The administrative setup of the subah of Allahabad under the great Mughals, 1526 to 1707. In IsC 39 (1965) 85-109.

08773 ______. The mid-Gangetic region in the eighteenth century, some observations of Joseph Tieffenthaler. Allahabad: Shanti Prakashan, 1976. 161p.

08774 ______. Subah of Allahabad under the great Mughals, 1580-1707. ND: Jamia Millia Islamia, 1974. 238p.

08775 SRIVASTAVA, A.L. The first two Nawabs of Oudh, a critical study based on original sources. 2nd ed., rev. Agra: S.L. Agarwala, 1954. 307p. [1st ed. 1933]

08776 ______. Shuja-ud-Daulah of Awadh. Calcutta: Midland Press, 1967. 2v. 313, 378p. [1st pub. 1939]

08777 WAERDEN, H. VAN DER. Warren Hastings und der Raja von Benares; ein Beitrag zur Klärung des Hastings-Prozesses. Zürich: Europa, 1964. 67p.

3. The Bihar Area: Mithila, Magadha, Tirhut

08778 MISHRA, R. History of Purnea, 1722-1793. Calcutta: India Book Exchange, 1978. 139p.

08779 MISHRA, S.G. History of Bihar, 1740-1772. ND: Munshiram, 1970. 187p.

08780 QEYAMUDDIN, A. A view of the provincial administration of Bihar under Farukhsiyar, 1712-19. In JBRS 50 (1964) 114-24.

08781 RAYE, N.N. The annals of the early English settlement in Bihar. Calcutta: Kamala Book Depot, 1927. 320p.

08782 THAKUR, U. Socio-economic life in Mithila under the Khandavalas. In JBRS 48,2 (1962) 64-89.

08783 VIROTTAM, B. The Nagbanshis and the Cheros. ND: Munshiram, 1972. 224p.

B. Economic and Social History of North India in the Mughal-Maratha Period (1526-1801)

08784 BAYLY, C.A. Town building in North India, 1790-1830. In MAS 9,4 (1975) 483-504.

08785 HABIB, I. Aspects of agrarian relations and economy in a region of Uttar Pradesh during the 16th century. In IESHR 4 (1967) 205-32.

08786 MARSHALL, P.J. Economic and political expansion: the case of Oudh. In MAS 9,4 (1975) 465-82.

08787 MUKHERJEE, R. Trade and empire in Awadh, 1765-1804. Calcutta: Centre for Studies in Social Sciences, 1977. 23p.

08788 SARKAR, J.N. Glimpses of medieval Bihar economy: thirteenth to mid-eighteenth century. Calcutta: Ratna Prakashan, 1978. 159p.

08789 SINHA, S.N. Economic condition of the Subah of Allahabad under the Mughals (1526-1707). In IsC 40,3 (1966) 151-70.

C. Religious Traditions and their Literatures in North India during the Mughal-Maratha Period (1565-1801); Emergence of Avadhī and Brajbhāṣā, Early Forms of Hindi [see also Chap. Four, II., F., above]

1. Rāma-bhakti in Avadh: Tulsīdās (1532-1623) and his Rāmāyaṇa in Avadhī, Rāmcaritmānas, "Holy Lake of the Acts of Rāma"

a. translations of the Rāmcaritmānas and other works of Tulsīdās

08790 ALLCHIN, F.R., tr. Kavitāvalī. London: Allen & Unwin, 1964. 229p.

08791 ______, tr. The petition to Rām; Hindi devotional hymns of the seventeenth century; a translation of the Vinaya-patrikā. London: Allen & Unwin, 1966. 335p.

08792 ATKINS, A.G., tr. The Rāmāyaṇa of Tulsīdās. Calcutta: Birla Academy of Arts & Culture, 1966. 2 v., 903p. [1st pub. 1954]

08793 BAHADUR, S.P., tr. Complete works of Gosvāmī Tulsīdās. Varanasi: Prachya Prakashan, 1978-. v. 1-.

08794 ______, tr. The Rāmāyaṇa of Goswāmī Tulsīdās. Bombay: Jaico, 1972. 414p.

08795 GROWSE, F.S., tr. The Ramayana of Tulsidas. 5th ed. Allahabad: NW Provinces & Oudh Govt. Press, 1887. 572p.

08796 HILL, W.D.P., tr. The holy lake of the acts of Rāma: a translation of Tulasī Dās's Rāmacaritamānasa. Bombay: OUP, 1971. 538p.

08797 KAPUR, B.L. Hanumān chālīsa: the descent of grace. ND: Trimurti Pub., 1974. 130p. [Includes the text of Tulasīdāsa's Hanumāna cālīsa in Hindi with explanatory notes in English]

08798 VAUDEVILLE, C., tr. Le lac spirituel: l'Ayodhya-kāṇḍa du Rāmāyaṇa. Paris: Librarie d'Amérique et d'Orient, 1955. 157p.

08799 ______, tr. Le Rāmāyaṇ de Tulsī-dās. Paris: "Les Belles Lettres", 1977. 211p. [about 1/7 of text]

b. studies

08800 ALLCHIN, F.R. The place of Tulsi Das in North Indian devotional tradition. In JRAS (1966) 123-40.

08801 BABINEAU, E.J. Love of God and social duty in the Rāmcaritmānas. Delhi: Motilal, 1979. 207p.

08802 BAHADUR, K.P. Rāmacharitmānasa: a study in perspective. Delhi: Ess Ess, 1976. 365p. + 8pl.

08803 BHARADWAJ, R. The philosophy of Tulsidas. ND: Munshiram, 1979. 359p.

08804 CHANDRA, S. Two aspects of Hindu social life and thought, as reflected in the works of Tulsīdās. In JESHO 19,1 (1976) 48-60.

08805 HANDOO, C.K. Tulasīdāsa; poet, saint and philosopher of the sixteenth century. Bombay: Orient Longmans, 1964. 300p.

08806 JONATHAN, K.F. The devotion of Tulsidas. In ICQ 24,1 (1967) 55-59.

08807 LAHIRI, B.K. A short biography of Goswami Tulsidas... Raniganj: S.S. Bazaj, 1961. 45p.

08808 MADAN GOPAL. Tulasi Das: a literary biography. ND: Bookabode, 1977. 118p.

08809 MCGREGOR, R.S. Tulsīdās' Śrīkṛṣṇagītāvalī. In JAOS 96 (1976) 520-27.

08810 SHANKAR RAJU NAIDU, S. Comparative study of Kamba Ramayanam and Tulasi Ramayan. Madras: U. of Madras, 1971. 591p.

08811 SINGH, DEVENDRA. Tulsidas. ND: NBT, 1971. 86p.

08812 VAUDEVILLE, C. Études sur les sources et la composition du Rāmāyaṇa de Tulsī-Dās. Paris: Librairie d'Amérique et d'Orient, 1955. 337p.

2. The Rādhā-Krishṇa Bhakti Sampradāyas (sects) of Braj, centered on Mathurā and Vrindāban

a. The Vallabha Sampradāya: Sūrdās (1483-1563) of the Aṣṭachāp ("eight signatures") group of poets

08813 BARZ, R. The Bhakti sect of Vallabhācārya. Delhi: Thomson Press, 1976. [pt. II, p. 97-256, is tr. of Caurāsī Vaiṣṇavam Kī Vārtā on Sūradāsa, Paramānandadāsa, Kumbhanadāsa, & Kṛṣṇadāsa]

08814 BRYANT, K.E. Poems to the child-god: structures and strategies in the poetry of Sūrdās. Berkeley: UCalP, 1978. 247p.

08815 HAWLEY, J.S. The early Sūr Sāgar and the growth of the Sūr tradition. In JAOS 99,1 (1979) 64-73.

08816 KINSLEY, D. "Without Kṛṣṇa there is no song." In HR 12,2 (1972) 149-80.

08817 MISRA, J. The religious poetry of Sūrdās. Patna: United Press, 1935. 161p.

08818 NAGENDRA, ed. Sūradāsa: a revaluation. ND: National, 1979. 294p.

08819 ______, ed. Sūradāsa, his mind and art. Chandigarh: Bahri, 1978. 57p.

08820 NANDDAS. The round dance of Krishṇa, and Uddhav's message. Tr. by R.S. McGregor. London: Luzac, 1974. 135p.

08821 NEHRU, S.S. Bhakt Sūrdās, the blind saint. 2nd ed. Mitcham, Surrey: West Brothers, 1949. 94p.

08822 PANDEY, S.M. & N. ZIDE. Sūrdās & his Krishna-bhakti. In M. Singer, ed. Krishna: Myths, rites, and attitudes. Honolulu: EWCP, 1966, 173-99.

08823 SURDAS. Pastorales, par Sour-Dās. Tr. from Braj by C. Vaudeville, Paris: Gallimard, 1971. 203p. (UNESCO series)

08824 WHITE, C.S.J. Kṛṣṇa as divine child. In HR 10,2 (1970) 156-77.

b. The Rādhāvallabha sampradāya: Goswāmī Hit Harivaṁś and his Caurāsī Pad

08825 Hita Harivaṁśa Gosvāmī. The Caurāsī pad of Śrī Hit Harivaṁś. Tr. from Braj by C.S.J. White. Honolulu: UPH, 1977. 199p. (ASH, 16)

c. The Nimbārka Sampradāya: Ghanānand (1719-1739)

08826 ĀNANDAGHANA. Love poems of Ghanānand. Tr. from Hindi by K.P. Bahadur. Delhi: Motilal, 1977. 202p. (UNESCO series)

3. Islam in North India

08827 AKHTAR, M.S. An introduction to the life and works of Sheikh ʿAbd Al-Ḥaqq Muḥaddith Dihlawī. In MW 68,3 (1978) 205-14.

08828 HAFIZ MOHD. TAHIR ALI. Shaikh Muḥibullah of Allahabad - life and times. In IsC 47 (1973) 241-56.

08829 SCHIMMEL, A. Mir Dards Gedanken über der Verhältnis von Mystik und Wort. In W. Eilers, ed. Festgabe deutscher Iranisten zur 2500 Jahrfeier Irans. Stuttgart: Hochwacht Druck, 1971, 117-32.

08830 SCHIMMEL, A. Pain and grace; a study of two mystical writers of eighteenth-century Muslim India. Leiden: Brill, 1976. 310p. [Mir Dard & Shah Abdul Latif]

08831 UMAR, M. Mirza Mazhar Jānjānān; a religious and social reformer of the eighteenth century. In Studies in Islam 6 (1969) 118-54.

D. Language and Literature in North India during the Mughal-Maratha Period (1526-1801)

08832 BAHL, K.C. The Hindi rīti tradition and the Rasikaprīyā of Keshavadāsa: an introductory review. In JSAL 10,1 (1974) 1-38.

08833 DWIVEDI, V.P. Bārahmāsā: the song of seasons in literature & art. Delhi: Agam, 1980. 183p.

08834 HALIM, S.A. Development of Hindi literature during Akbar's reign. In MIQ 3 (1957) 88-99.

08835 HOLLAND, B.G. The Satsaī of Bihārī: Hindi poetry of the early Rīti period; introduction, translation, and notes. Ph.D. thesis, U. of California, Berkeley, 1969. 394p. [UM 70-17,578]

08836 KEŚAVADĀSA. The Rasikaprīyā. Tr. from Sanskrit by K.P. Bahadur. Delhi: Motilal, 1972. 248p.

08837 MATHUR, R. Padmāvata: an etymological study. Delhi: National, 270p. (Intercultural Res. Inst. monograph, 1)

08838 MCGREGOR, R.S. The language of Indrajīt of Orchā: a study of early Braj Bhāsā prose. London: CamUP, 1968. 265p. (Its or. pub., 13)

08839 MILTNER, V. The Hindi sentence structure in the works of Tulsīdās. Delhi: Munshiram, 1967. 55p.

IX. BENGAL AND ASSAM: THE GANGA DELTA AND THE BRAHMAPUTRA VALLEY IN THE MUGHAL-MARATHA PERIOD (1538-1813)

A. General and Political Histories

1. General Studies of the Bengal Sūbah under the Mughals

08840 GHULAM HUSAIN ZAIDPURI. The Riyazu-s-salatīn; a history of Bengal. Tr. from Persian by Maulavi Abdus Salam. Calcutta: Asiatic Soc., 1902-04. 437p. (BI, 154)

08841 ROY, A.C. History of Bengal; Mughal period, 1526-1765 A.D. Calcutta: Nababharat, 1968. 525p.

08842 SARKAR, JADUNATH. Bengal Nawabs. Calcutta: Asiatic Soc., 1952. 156p. [translated sources]

2. Early Mughal Rule to 1707: Conquest of Afghan Successors of Sher Shah

08843 BHATTASALI, N.K. Bengal chiefs' struggle. Calcutta: 1928. 1 v. [Rpt. from BPP 35; on Hindu resistance to Mughals]

08844 CHATTERJEE, A.B. Bengal in the reign of Aurangzib, 1658-1707. Calcutta: Progressive, 1967. 284p.

08845 DAS GUPTA, J.N. Bengal in the sixteenth century. Calcutta: Calcutta U., 1914. 189p.

08846 GHOSH, J.M. Magh raiders in Bengal. Calcutta: Bookland, 1960. 145p.

08847 MĪRZĀ NATHAN. Bahāristān-i-Ghaybī: a history of the Mughal wars in Assam, Cooch Behar, Bengal, Bihar and Orissa during the reigns of Jahangir and Shahjahan. Tr. from Persian by M.I. Borah. Gauhati: Narayani Handqui Hist. Inst., Govt. of Assam, 1936. 2 v. 930p.

3. Northeast Kingdoms of Koch Bihar, Kamrup, and the Ahom State of Assam

08848 BARBARUA, S.D. Tungkhungia buranji; or, A history of Assam, 1681-1826 A.D.; an old Assamese chronicle of the Tungkhungia dynasty of Ahom sovereigns. Tr. by S.K. Bhuyan. Gauhati: Dept. of Hist. and Antiquarian Studies in Assam, 1968. 257p.

08849 BHATTACHARYA, S.N. A history of Mughal North-east Frontier policy; being a study of the political relation of the Mughal Empire with Koch Bihar, Kamrup and Assam. Calcutta: 1929. 434p.

08850 BHUYAN, S.K. Atan Butogohain and his times; a history of Assam, from the invasion of Nawab Mir Jumla in 1762-62, to the termination of Assam-Mogul conflicts in 1662. Gauhati: Lawyers Book Stall, 1957. 366p.

08851 ______. Lachit Barphukan and his times; a history of the Assam-Mogul conflicts of the period 1776 to 1671 A.D. Gauhati: Govt. of Assam, 1947. 221p.

08852 WADE, J.P. An account of Assam. Ed. by Benudhar Sharma. Gauhati: Asam Jyoti, 1972. 375p. [1st pub. 1927]

4. European Settlements in Bengal - Portuguese, Dutch, Danish, Belgian, and French

08853 CAMPOS, J.J.A. History of the Portuguese in Bengal. Patna: Janaki Prakashan, 1979. 388p. [Rpt. 1919 ed.]

08854 DATTA, K.K. The Dutch in Bengal and Bihar, 1740-1825 A.D. 2nd rev. ed. Delhi: Motilal, 1968. 200p.

08855 DUMONT, G.H. Banquibazar; la colonisation belge au Bengale au temps de la Compagnie d'Ostende. Bruxelles: Les Ecrits, 1942. 222p.

08856 KENNEDY, B.E. An Indian crisis and its European ramifications in the eighteenth century: the Chandernagore Ditch Affairs 1767-1771. In BPP 94,178 (1975) 1-24.

08857 PRAKASH, OM. The Dutch East India Company in Bengal: trade privileges & problems, 1633-1712. In IESHR 9,3 (1972) 258-287.

08858 ______. The Sobha Singh revolt: Dutch policy and response. In BPP 94,178 (1975) 31-6.

08859 RAY, I. The French company & the merchants of Bengal: 1680-1730. In IESHR 8,1 (1971) 41-56.

08860 SARKAR, JADUNATH. Picture of Chandernagore & subordinate French factories in Bengal - 1765-1778. In BPP 72 (1953) 63-71.

5. The Mughal Sūbah of Bengal, 1707-1757, and its Administrators

08861 CALKINS, P.B. The formation of a regionally oriented ruling group in Bengal, 1700-1740. In JAS 29,4 (1970) 799-806.

08862 CHATTERJI, N. Mir Qasim, Nawab of Bengal, 1760-1763. Allahabad: Indian Press, 1935. 332p.

08863 DATTA, K.K. Alivardi and his times. 2nd rev. ed. Calcutta: World Press, 1963. 249p. [1st pub. 1939]

08864 ______. Siraj-ud-Daulah. Bombay: Orient Longmans, 1971. 132p.

08865 DIMOCK, E.C. & P.C. GUPTA, tr. The Maharashta purana: an eighteenth-century Bengali historical text. Honolulu: EWCP, 1965. 22 + 86p.

08866 GHULAM HUSAIN KHAN, TABATABAʾI. Siyar-ul-Mutakherin; a history of the Mahomedan power in India during the last century. Tr. by Haji Mustefa [pseud.]. Rev. by J. Briggs. London: Oriental Translation Fund, 1832. v. 1, 467p. [no more pub.]

08867 GUPTA, BRIJEN K. Sirajuddaulah and the East India Company. Leiden: Brill, 1962. 172p.

08868 HILL, S.C. Bengal in 1756-7. London: Murray, 1905. 3 v.

08869 KARIM, A. Murshid Quli Khan and his times. Dacca: ASP, 1963. 284p. (Its pub., 12)

08870 MUKHOPADHYAY, S.C. The career of Rajah Durlabhram Mahindra (Rai-Durlabh), Diwan of Bengal, 1710-1770. Varanasi: Manisha Prakashan, 1974. 226p.

08871 SCRAFTON, L. A history of Bengal before and after the Plassey, 1739-1758. Calcutta: Editions Indian, 1975. 131p. [Rpt. 1763 ed.]

6. British Assumption of Political Power: Dyarchy of the East India Company and Mughal Provincial Governments [see also III. E. 3., above]

08872 CHAKRABORTY, R.L. Some aspects of the Anglo-Arakanese relations, 1760-1785. In JASBangla 20,3 (1975) 41-50.

08873 CHATTERJI, N. Some Anglo-French disputes in Bengal

during post-Diwany period. In IHQ 17 (1941) 324-39. [based on Bengal records]

08874 ______. Verelst's rule in India. Allahabad: Indian Press, 1939. 299p.

08875 CHAUDHURI, N.G. Cartier, Governor of Bengal, 1769-1772. Calcutta: KLM, 1970. 223p.

08876 DHAR, N. The administrative system of the East India Company in Bengal, 1714-1786. Calcutta: Eureka Publishers, 1964-68. 2 v.

08877 GOPAL, RAM. How the British occupied Bengal; a corrected account of the 1756-1765 events. NY: Asia, 1964. 373p.

08878 INDIA (REP.) NATIONAL ARCHIVES. Calendar of Persian correspondence; being letters, referring mainly to affiars in Bengal, which passed between some of the company's servants & Indian rulers & notables. Delhi: MPGOI, 1970. 12 v. [Rpt. of 1911 ed.]

08879 ______. Fort William-India House correspondence. Delhi: MPGOI, 1949-69. 21v. (Indian Records series)

08880 JAIN, P. Critical assessment of British relations with Mir Jafar. In JIH 52,2/3 (1974) 405-19.

08881 MAJEED KHAN, ABDUL. The transition in Bengal, 1756-1775; a study of Saiyid Muhammad Reza Khan. London: CamUP, 1969. 376p. (Its South Asian studies, 7)

08882 MAJUMDAR, N. Justice and police in Bengal, 1765-1793. A study of the Nizamat in decline. Calcutta: KLM, 1960. 351p.

08883 PANDEY, B.N. The introduction of English law into India: the career of Elijah Impey in Bengal, 1774-1783. London: Asia, 1967. 248p. (Asia hist. ser., 3)

08884 ROY, A.C. Career of Mir Jafar Khan (1757-65 A.D.). Calcutta: Das Gupta, 1953. 339p.

08885 ROY, B.K. The career and achievements of Maharaja Nanda Kumar, Dewan of Bengal, 1705-1775. Calcutta: Punthi Pustak, 1969. 276p.

08886 VANSITTART, H. A narrative of the transactions in Bengal, 1760-1764. Ed. by A.C. Banerjee & B.K. Ghosh. Calcutta: K.P. Bagchi, 1976. 591p. [Rpt. 1766 ed.]

08887 VERELST, H. A view of the rise, progress, and present state of the English government in Bengal. London: J. Nourse, 1772. 148p.

08888 WILSON, C.R. Early annals of the English in Bengal: being the Bengal Public Consultations for the first half of the eighteenth century. London: W. Thacker, 1895-1917. 3v. in 4 (v. 2 in 2 pts.)

B. Economic and Social History of the Bengal-Assam Area in the Mughal-Maratha Period (1538-1813)

1. General Economic History

08889 BHATTACHARYA, S. The East India Company and the economy of Bengal from 1704 to 1740. 2nd ed. Calcutta: KLM, 1969. 232p.

08890 DAS GUPTA, T.C. Aspects of Bengali society from old Bengali literature. Calcutta: U. of Calcutta, 1935. 371p.

08891 DATTA, K.K. Studies in the history of the Bengal subah, 1740-70; v. 1, Social and economic. Calcutta: U. of Calcutta, 1936. 567p.

08892 KARIM, K.M. Economic conditions in Bihar and Bengal under Shahjahan. In JPHS 14,3 (1966) 180-87.

08893 RAYCHAUDHURI, T. Bengal under Akbar and Jahangir; an introductory study in social history. Delhi: Munshiram, 1969. 268p.

2. The Agrarian Order: Peasants, Zamīndārs, and the Revenue System

a. land system and revenue under Mughal and early British rule (to 1793)

08894 BANERJEE, D.N. Early land revenue system in Bengal and Bihar; v. 1, 1765-1772. London: Longmans, Green, 1936. 228p.

08895 BLYN, G. Revenue administration of Calcutta in the first half of the 18th century. In IESHR 1 (1964) 120-42.

08896 CALKINS, P. Collecting the revenue in early eighteenth century Bengal: from the cultivator to the Zamindar. In R. Beech & M.J. Beech, eds. Bengal: change and continuity. East Lansing: Michigan State U., Asian Studies Center, 1970, 3-30. (Its occ. papers, S.A. ser., 16)

08897 HUQ, M. The East India Company's land policy and commerce in Bengal, 1698-1784. Dacca: ASP, 1964. 295p. + map. (Its Pub., 14)

08898 KAVIRAJ, NARAHARI. A peasant uprising in Bengal, 1783: the first formidable peasant uprising against the rule of the East India Company. ND: PPH, 1972. 111p.

08899 MAHMOOD, A.B.M. The revenue administration of Northern Bengal, 1765-1793. Dacca: Natl. Inst. of Public Admin., 1970. 244p.

08900 MALIK, Z.U. Agrarian structure of Bengal at the beginning of British conquest - a contemporary Persian account. In Medieval India, a miscellany 4 (1977) 177-202.

08901 RAMSBOTHAM, R.B. Studies in the land revenue history of Bengal (1769-1787). London: OUP, 1926. 205p.

08902 SERAJUDDIN, A.M. The revenue administration of the East India Company in Chittagong, 1761-1785. Chittagong: U. of Chittagong, 1971. 259p.

b. the 1793 permanent settlement of Lord Cornwallis, Governor General

08903 ASCOLI, F.D. Early revenue history of Bengal and the fifth report, 1812. Oxford: OUP, 1917. 272p.

08904 BHATTACHARYA, S. Permanent settlement revenue. In BPP 85 (1966) 159-82.

08905 GOPAL, S. The permanent settlement and its effect on Bengal. London: Allen & Unwin, 1949. 52p.

08906 GUHA, R. A rule of property for Bengal; an essay on the idea of permanent settlement. Paris: Mouton, 1963. 222p.

08907 ISLAM, S. The operation of the sun-set law and changes in the landed society of Dacca district, 1793-1817. In JASBangla 19,1 (1974) 49-68.

08908 PRASAD, R. Some aspects of British revenue policy in India, 1773-1833 (the Bengal Presidency). ND: S. Chand, 1970. 248p.

08909 RAY, R. Land transfer and social change under the permanent settlement: a study of two localities. In IESHR 11,1 (1974) 1-45.

3. Commerce and Industry; the Indigenous Economy and the East India Company

08910 CHAUDHURI, S. Bengal merchants and commercial organisation in the second half of the seventeenth century. In BPP 90,2 (1971) 182-216.

08911 ______. English trade in Bengal raw silk, 1650-1720. In JASBengal 13 (1971) 153-65.

08912 ______. The problem of financing East India Company's investments in Bengal: 1650-1720. In IESHR 8,2 (1971) 109-33.

08913 ______. Trade and commercial organization in Bengal, 1650-1720, with special reference to the English East India Company. Calcutta: KLM, 1975. 293p.

08914 COLEBROOKE, H.T. Remarks on the husbandry and internal commerce of Bengal. London: 1804. 204p.

08915 MARSHALL, P.J. British merchants in 18th century Bengal. In BPP 95,1 (1976) 151-64.

08916 ______. East Indian fortunes: the British in Bengal in the eighteenth century. Oxford: OUP, 1976. 284p.

08917 ______. Private British investment in eighteenth century Bengal. In BPP 86,2 (1967) 52-67.

08918 MITRA, D.B. The cotton weavers of Bengal, 1757-1833. Calcutta: KLM, 1978. 250p.

08919 PRAKASH, OM. The European trading companies and the merchants of Bengal 1650-1725. In IESHR 1 (1964) 37-63.

4. Urban Centers
a. traditional urban centers

08920 BHADRA, G. Social groups and relations in the town of Murshidabad, 1765-1793. In IHR 2,2 (1976) 312-38.

08921 CALKINS, P.B. The role of Murshidabad as a regional and subregional center in Bengal. In R.L. Park, ed. Urban Bengal. East Lansing: Michigan State U., Asian Studies Center, 1969, 17-28. (Its occ. papers, S.A. ser., 12)

08922 KARIM, A. Dacca, the Mughal capital. Dacca: ASP, 1964. 514p.

08923 SANYAL, H.R. Social aspects of temple building in Bengal: 1600 to 1900 AD. In MI 48 (1968) 201-24.

b. Fort William (estd. 1669) and the developing colonial city of Calcutta

08924 BUSTEED, H.E. Echoes from old Calcutta; being chiefly reminiscences of the days of Warren Hastings, Francis, and Impey. 4th ed. London: W. Thacker, 1908. 431p.

08925 CHAUDHURI, S. The rise and decline of Hugli - a port in medieval Bengal. In BPP 86,1 (1967) 33-67.

08926 FURBER, H. Glimpses of life and trade on the Hugli 1720-1770. In BPP 86,2 (1967) 13-23.

08927 GHOSH, S.C. The social condition of the British community in Bengal, 1757-1800. Leiden: Brill, 1970. 205p.

08928 MURPHEY, R. The city in the swamp: aspects of the site and early growth of Calcutta. In Geographical J. 130 (1960) 241-56.

08929 SETON-KARR, W.S., ed. The Calcutta gazette; or, the Oriental advertiser. Selections ... 1784-1823. Calcutta: O.T. Cutler, 1864-69. 5 v.

08930 THANKAPPAN NAIR, P., ed. Job Charnock, the founder of Calcutta: in facts and fiction: an anthology. Calcutta: Engineering Times Pub., 1977. 288p.

08931 WILSON, C.R. Old Fort William in Bengal. London: Murray, 1906. 2 v.

C. Religion and Religious Literature in the Bengal-Assam Area in the Mughal-Maratha Period (1538-1813)

1. General Developments in Religion and Philosophy

08932 CHAPMAN, J.A. Religious lyrics of Bengal. Calcutta: Book Company, 1926. 92p.

08933 GHOSH, J.M. Sannyāsī and fakīr raiders in Bengal. Calcutta: Bengal Secretariat Book Depot, 1930. 160p.

08934 LORENZEN, D. La rebelion de los Sannyāsīs. In EO 9,1-2 (1974) 2-13.

2. The Spread of Śakti Worship and Tantric Rituals; Rāmprasād Sen (1718-1775)

08935 CHAKRAVARTI, C. Śakti-worship and the Śākta saints. In Cultural Heritage of India. Calcutta: RMIC, 1956, v. 4, 408-18.

08936 RAMAPRASADA SENA. Chants à Kālī de Rāmprasād. Tr. from Bengali by M. Lupsa. Pondicherry: IFI, 1967. 169p. [Its pub., 30]

08937 ______. Rāma Prasāda's devotional songs: the cult of Shakti. Tr. from Bengali by J.N. Sinha. Calcutta: Sinha Pub. House, 1966. 175p.

08938 ______. Rāmprasād and western man. Tr. from Bengali by P.N. Chaudhuri. Calcutta: Gautam Mallick, 1976. 128p. [translations + study]

08939 THOMPSON, E.J. & M. SPENCER, tr. Bengali religious lyrics: Śākta. Calcutta: Assn. Press, 1933. 102p.

3. Vaiṣṇavism after Caitanya; the Sahajiya Cult; the Philosophy of Madhusūdana Sarasvatī (1540-1648)

08940 BOSE, M.M. The post-Caitanya Sahajiya cult of Bengal. Calcutta: U. of Calcutta, 1930. 320p.

08941 DIMOCK, E.C., JR. The place of the hidden moon; erotic mysticism in the Vaiṣṇavasahajiya cult of Bengal. Chicago: UChiP, 1966. 299p.

08942 GUPTA, S. Studies in the philosophy of Madhusūdana Sarasvatī. Calcutta: SPB, 1966. 230p.

08943 ELIOT, C.N.E. Hinduism in Assam. In JRAS (1910) 1155-86.

08944 MADHUSŪDANA SARASVATĪ. Madhusūdana Sarasvatī on the Bhagavad Gītā: being an English translation of his commentary, Gūḍhārtha dīpikā. Tr. by S.K. Gupta. Delhi: Motilal, 1977. 343p.

08945 SHUKLA, N.S., tr. Le Karṇānanda de Kṛṣṇadāsa. Pondicherry: IFI, 1971. 322p. (Its pub., 41)

4. The Bāuls, "Mad" Singers of Bengal: Hindu-Muslim Mysticism and Social Egalitarianism

08946 BYATTACHARYA, DEBEN, tr. The mirror of the sky: songs of the Bauls from Bengal. London: Allen & Unwin, 1969. 120p. (UNESCO series) [tr. from Bengali]

08947 CAPWELL, C.H. The esoteric beliefs of the Bauls of Bengal. In JAS 33,2 (1974) 255-264.

08948 CHAKRAVARTI, P., tr. Baul: Bengali mystic songs from oral traditions. Port Moresby: Papua Pocket Books, 1970. 28p.

08949 CHATTERJI, S.K. Hindu-Muslim Baul and Marafati songs in Bengali literature. In IL 15,3 (1972) 5-27.

08950 DIMOCK, E.C. The Bāuls of Bengal. In his The place of the hidden moon: erotic mysticism in the Vaiṣṇavasahajiya cult of Bengal. Chicago: UChiP, 1966, 249-70.

08951 PAUL, H.C. Baul poets on Chāri-Chandra (or four states of the mind). In JASBangla 18 (1973) 1-53.

08952 RAHIM, M.A. The Bāul mystic order. In JRSP 2,1 (1965) 49-61.

5. Islam in Bengal

08953 SARKAR, J.N. Islam in Bengal (thirteenth to nineteenth century). Calcutta: Ratna Prakashan, 1972. 92p.

6. Early Protestant Missions in Bengal: William Carey in the Danish Enclave of Serampore/Śrīrāmpur

08954 ABRAHAM, C.E. William Carey and the Indian church. Calcutta: Baptist Mission Press, 1964. 29p.

08955 DAVIS, W.B. William Carey, father of modern missions. Chicago: Moody Press, 1963. 160p.

08956 DREWERY, M. William Carey: a biography. Grand Rapids: Zondervan Pub. House, 1979. 224p.

08957 LAIRD, M.A. Missionaries and education in Bengal, 1793-1837. Oxford: OUP, 1972. 300p.

08958 MARSHMAN, J.C. The story of Carey, Marshman, and Ward. London: J. Heaton, 1864. 333p.

08959 MIDDLEBROOK, J.B. William Carey. London: Carey Kingsgate Press, 1961. 112p.

08960 POTTS, E.D. British Baptist missionaries in India, 1793-1837; the history of Serampore and its missions. Cambridge: CamUP, 1967. 276p.

08961 SEN GUPTA, K.P. The Christian missionaries in Bengal, 1793-1833. Calcutta: KLM, 1971. 245p.

D. Language and Literature of the Bengal-Assam Area in the Mughal-Maratha Period (1538-1813)

08962 BHATTACHARYYA, A. An introduction to the study of medieval Bengali epics. Calcutta: Calcutta Book House, 1943. 60p. [1st pub. in DUS 5,2 (1941-42) 69-128]

08963 ______. Mediaeval narrative Bengali poetry on historical themes. In IHQ 20,1 (1944) 21-35.

08964 GHOSHAL, S.N. Beginning of secular romance in Bengali literature. In VBA 9 (1959) 300p.

08965 KHAN, M. SIDDIQ. The early Bengali printed books. In Gutenberg Jahrbuch (1966) 200-208.

08966 MANNAN, Q.A. The emergence and development of Dobhasi literature in Bengal, up to 1855 A.D. Dacca: Dept. of Bengali and Sanskrit, U. of Dacca, 1966. 273p.

08967 SEN, S. A history of Brajabuli literature. 2nd ed. Calcutta: U. of Calcutta, 1935. 600p.

E. Art and Architecture of the Bengal-Assam Area in the Mughal-Maratha Period (1538-1813)

08968 AAL, I. Bengali terra-cotta temples: new lines of inquiry. In R. Beech & M.J. Beech, eds. Bengal: change and continuity. East Lansing: Michigan State U., Asian Studies Center, 1970, 69-83. (Its occ. papers, S.A. ser., 16)

08969 BANERJI, A. Temples of Tripura. Varanasi: Prithivi Prakashan, 1968. 22p. + 8 pl.

08970 MCCUTCHION, D.J. Late mediaeval temples of Bengal. In JASCalcutta 12 (1970) 1-80.

08971 SANYAL, H.R. Religious architecture in Bengal (15th-17th century): a study of the major trends. In S. Sinha, ed. Aspects of Indian culture and society.... Calcutta: AnthSI, 1972, 187-203.

08972 SKELTON, R. Murshidabad painting. In Mārg 10,1 (1956) 10-22.

X. NEPAL AND THE HIMALAYAN RIM IN THE MUGHAL-MARATHA (1559-1816)

A. General and Political History

08973 BURLEIGH, P. A chronology of the later kings of Patan. In Kailash 4,1 (1976) 21-71.

08974 BUCHANAN, F.H. An account of the Kingdom of Nepal and of the territories annexed to this dominion by the House of Gorkha. ND: Manjuśrī Pub. House, 1971. 364p. (Bibliotheca Himalayica, ser. 1, 10) [1st pub. 1819]

08975 CHAUDHURI, K.C. Anglo-Nepalese relations from the earliest times of the British rule in India till the Gurkha War. Calcutta: Modern Book Agency, 1960. 181p.

08976 HAMILTON, W.G. The campaign in Kumaon: an episode in the Nepal War. In JUSI 32 (1903) 256-98.

08977 KIRKPATRICK, W. An account of the Kingdom of Nepaul; being the substance of observations made during a mission to that country in the year 1793. ND: Manjuśrī Pub. House, 1969. 386p. (Bibliotheca Himalayica, ser. 1,3) [1st pub. 1811]

08978 KUNWAR, M.J. China and war in the Himalayas, 1792-1793. In English Historical R. 77 (1962) 283-97.

08979 PEMBLE, J. The invasion of Nepal: John Company at war. Oxford: OUP, 1971. 389p.

08980 PETECH, L. The rulers of Bhutan, c. 1650-1750. In Oriens Extremus 19,1/2 (1972) 203-13.

08981 RANA, N.R.L. The Anglo-Gorkha war, 1814-1816. Kathmandu: 1970. 133p.

08982 STILLER, L.F. Rise of the house of Gorkha; a study in the unification of Nepal, 1768-1816. ND: Manjusri, 1973. 390p. (Bibliotheca Himalayica, ser. 14,15)

08983 ______. The role of fear in the unification of Nepal. In CNS 1,2 (1974) 42-89.

08984 TUCCI, G. Nepal: the discovery of the Malla. Tr. from Italian by L. Edwards. NY: Dutton, 1962. 96p.

B. Art and Architecture

08985 An introduction to the Hanuman Dhoka. Kirtipur: Inst. of Nepal and Asian Studies, Tribhuvan U., 1975. 57p.

08986 MOTI CHANDRA. A painted scroll from Nepal. In Mārg 4,1 (1950) 42-49.

Part Three

Transformations in the Modern Age: National Level

6

The Raj: Princely and British India, from Company to Empire to Independence, 1818–1947

I. RESEARCH TOOLS AND GENERAL HISTORY OF THE BRITISH PERIOD

A. Bibliography, Historiography, and Reference

1. Bibliography

08987 AZIZ, K.K. The historical background of Pakistan, 1857-1947; an annotated digest of source material. Karachi: Pakistan Inst. of Intl. Affairs, 1970. 626p.

08988 CASE, M.H. South Asian history 1750-1950; a guide to periodicals, dissertations, and newspapers. Princeton: PUP, 1968. 561p.

08989 COHN, B.S. The development and impact of British administration in India: a bibliographic essay. ND: IIPA, 1961. 88p.

08990 DATTA, K.K. A survey of recent studies on modern Indian history. Calcutta: KLM, 1963. 115p. [1st pub. 1957]

08991 KOMAROV, E.N. Studies in the history of India in modern times by Soviet scholars. In ISPP 1,4 (1960) 651-61.

08992 MATTHEWS, W., ed. British diaries; an annotated bibliography of British diaries written between 1442 and 1942. Berkeley: UCalPress, 1955. 34 + 339p.

08993 PANDE, RAM, ed. An introduction to source material on modern Indian history. Jaipur: Shodhak, 1976. 97p.

08994 SHAFAᶜAT AHMAD KHAN. The history and historians of British India. Allahabad: Kitabistan, 1939. 107p.

08995 THATCHER, M., comp. & ed. The Cambridge South Asian archive. London: Mansell, 1973. 346p. [Records of the British period in S. Asia held in Centre of South Asian Studies, U. of Cambridge]

08996 WILSON, P. Government and politics in India and Pakistan 1885-1955; a bibliography of works in western languages. Berkeley: South Asia Studies, Inst. of East Asiatic Studies, U. of California, 1956. 356p.

2. Historiography

08997 BAYLY, C.A. English language historiography on British expansion in India and Indian reactions since 1945. In P.C. Emmer & H.L. Wesseling, eds. Reappraisals in overseas history. Leiden: Leiden U. Press, 1979. 248p. (Comp. studies in overseas history, 2)

08998 COHN, B.S. Notes on the history of the study of Indian society and culture. In M.B. Singer & B.S. Cohn, eds. Structure and change in Indian society. Chicago: Aldine, 1968, 3-28.

08999 HARRISON, J.B. The rulers and the ruled; a historiographical essay. In SAR 3,1 (1969) 59-71.

09000 LOW, D.A. Introduction. In his (ed.) Soundings in modern South Asian history. Berkeley: UCalP, 1968, 1-24.

09001 MAJUMDAR, R.C. Historiography in modern India. Bombay: Asia, 1970. 61p.

09002 PHILIPS, C.H. Historians of India, Pakistan and Ceylon. London: OUP, 1961. [155-496 cover "European dominance and Nationalist movement"]

09003 RAY, R.K. Political change in British India. In IESHR 14,4 (1977) 493-517.

09004 SEN, S.P., ed. Studies in modern Indian history; a regional survey. Calcutta: IHS, 1969. 221p.

09005 SPODEK, H. Pluralist politics in British India: the Cambridge cluster of historians of modern India. In American Historical R. 84,3 (1979) 688-707.

09006 WINKS, R.W., ed. The historiography of the British Empire-Commonwealth. Durham, NC: DUP, 1966. [India, by R.I. Crane, 357-95; Pakistan, by D.P. Singhal, 396-420; Ceylon, by K.W. Goonewardena, 421-47]

3. Chronologies, Handbooks, and Dictionaries

09007 MITRA, N.N., ed. The Indian annual register; an annual digest of public affairs of India. Calcutta: Annual Register Office, 1919-47. 29 v.

09008 SHARMA, J.S. India since the advent of the British; a descriptive chronology from 1600 to Oct. 2, 1969. Delhi: S. Chand, 1970. 817p.

09009 TARKALANKAR, G.C. & P.N. SARASWATI. Chronological tables,... from 1764-1900. Bhowanipore: S. Banerjee, 1910. 580p.

09010 WILSON, H.H. A glossary of judicial and revenue terms and of useful words occuring in official documents ... pub. under the authority of the East India Company. 2nd ed. Delhi: Munshiram, 1968. 728p. [1st ed. 1855]

09011 YULE, H. & A.C. BURNELL. Hobson-Jobson: a glossary of colloquial Anglo-Indian words and phrases.... Delhi: Munshiram, 1968. 1021p. [1st pub. 1903]

4. Biographical Sources

09012 BUCKLAND, C.E. Dictionary of Indian biography. Varanasi: IndBH, 1971. 494p. [Rpt. 1906 ed.]

09013 KABADI, W.P., ed. Indian who's who. Bombay: Yeshanand, 1935-. [Only 1935, 1937 vol. pub.]

09014 KAYE, J.W. Lives of Indian officers, illustrative of the history of the civil and military services of India. London: Strahan, 1867. 2 v.

09015 The Indian nation builders. Madras: Ganesh, 1921. 3 v.

09016 Makers of modern India. 2nd rev. ed. ND: ICHR, 1974. 125p.

09017 OSWELL, G.D. Sketches of rulers of India. Delhi: Researchco Publications, 1972-76. 4 v., 846p.

09018 PETERS, T., ed. The royal coronation number and Who's who in India, Burma and Ceylon. Poona Sun Pub. House, 1937. 615p.

09019 RADHAKRISHNAN, S. Great Indians. Ludhiana: Kalyani, 1973. 127p.

09020 SEN, S.P., ed. Dictionary of national biography. Calcutta: IHS, 1972-73. 4 v.

09021 SINHA, SACHCHIDANANDA. Some eminent Indian contemporaries. Patna: Janaki Prakashan, 1976. 257p.

09022 SMITH, G. Twelve Indian statesmen. London: Murray, 1897. 323p.

09023 TANDON, P.D. Leaders of modern India. Bombay: Vora, 1955. 159p.

09024 Who's who in India, containing lives and portraits of ruling chiefs, notables et al. Lucknow: Newul Kishore, 1911. 1610p. [Suppl. 1912, 206p.]

09025 WOODRUFF, P. The men who ruled India; v. 2, the guardians. London: J. Cape, 1963. 385p. [1st pub. 1954]

B. General History of the British Period

1. Overall Assessments and Thematic Interpretations

09026 ALI, A.Y. A cultural history of India during the British period. NY: AMS Press, 1976. 334p. [Rpt. 1940 ed.]

09027 AZIZ, K.K. The British in India: a study in imperialism. Islamabad: Natl. Cmsn. on Hist. and Cultural Res., 1976. 415p.

09028 BASU, B.D. Rise of the Christian power in India. Calcutta: R. Chatterjee, 1923-24. 5 v. [v. 1 pub. by M.C. Sarkar]

09029 CHAMBERLAIN, M.E. Britain and India: the interaction of two peoples. Hamden, CT: Archon Books, 1974. 272p.

09030 DUTT, R.P. India to-day. 2nd Indian ed. (with the original text restored). Calcutta: Manisha Granthalaya, 1970. 662p. [1st pub. 1940]

09031 DUTT, R.C. England and India; a record of progress during a hundred years, 1785-1885. London: Chatto & Windus, 1897. 166p.

09032 GRIFFITHS, P.J. The British impact on India. London: Cass, 1965. 520p. [Rpt. 1952 ed.]

09033 GROVER, B.L. & R.R. SETHI. A new look on modern Indian history; from 1707 to the present day. 2nd ed. Delhi: S. Chand, 1970. 495p. [1st ed. 1963]

09034 HUTCHINS, F.G. The illusion of permanence; British imperialism in India. Princeton: PUP, 1967. 217p.

09035 LAL, C. The vanishing empire. Tokyo: Kyodo Printing Co., 1937. 248p. [2nd ed., ND: N.K. Sagar, 1963. 293p.]

09036 LOW, D.A. Lion rampant: essays in the study of British imperialism. London: F. Cass, 1973. 230p.

09037 MASANI, R.P. Britain in India; an account of British rule in the Indian subcontinent. London: OUP, 1960. 278p.

09038 MURPHEY, R. The outsiders: the Western experience in India and China. Ann Arbor: UMichP, 1977. 299p.

09039 O'MALLEY, L.S.S. Modern India and the West; a study of the interaction of their civilizations. London: OUP, 1968. 834p. [1st pub. 1941]

09040 RAWLINSON, H.G. The British achievement in India: a survey. London: W. Hodge, 1948. 248p.

09041 RAM GOPAL. British rule in India, an assessment. Bombay: Asia, 1963. 364p.

09042 REYNOLDS, R. The white sahibs in India. Westport, CT: Greenwood, 1970. 410p. [Rpt. 1937 ed.]

09043 SUNDERLAL. British rule in India. Bombay: Popular, 1972. 472p. [Hindi ed. 1st pub. 1929; proscribed by British govt.]

09044 THOMPSON, E.J. & G.T. GARRATT. The rise and fulfillment of British rule in India. NY: AMS Press, 1971. 690p. [1st pub. 1934]

2. Introductory Surveys

09045 EDWARDES, M. British India, 1772-1947; a survey of the nature and effects of alien rule. NY: Taplinger, 1968. 396p.

09046 GRIFFITHS, P. Modern India. 3rd ed. London: Benn, 1962. 283p.

09047 GOLANT, W. The long afternoon: British India 1601-1947. NY: St. Martin's, 1975. 270p.

09048 HUTCHINSON, L. The empire of the Nabobs: a short history of British India. London: Allen & Unwin, 1937. 277p.

09049 MUDFORD, P. Birds of a different plumage: a study of British-Indian relations from Akbar to Curzon. London: Collins, 1974. 314p. + 24 pl.

09050 POUCHEPADASS, J. L'Inde au XXe siècle. Paris: PUF, 1975. 214p.

09051 SPEAR, T.G.P. India, Pakistan, and the West. 4th ed. London: OUP, 1967. 178p.

09052 WOODFORD, P. Rise of the Raj. NY: Humanities Press, 1978. 160p.

3. General Histories for Reference or Advanced Study

09053 BOSE, P.N. A history of Hindu civilization during British rule. ND: Asian Pub. Services, 1975. 3v. [1st pub. 1894-96]

09054 CHHABRA, G.S. Advanced study in the history of modern India. ND: Sterling, 1971. 3v.

09055 ELPHINSTONE, M. The rise of the British power in the East. London: Murray, 1887. 553p.

09056 LYALL, A.C. The rise and expansion of the British dominion in India. 5th ed. London: Murray, 1911. 397p. [1st pub. 1893]

09057 MAJUMDAR, R.C. & A.K. MAJUMDAR & D.K. GHOSE, eds. British paramountcy and Indian renaissance. Bombay: BVB, 1963-65. pts. 1 & 2, 1205, 688p. (HCIP, 9,10)

09058 MILL, J. The history of British India. 3 v. ND: Assoc. Pub. House, 1972. 3v., 730, 980, 859p. [Rpt. of 1840-48 ed.]

09059 ______. The history of British India. Abridged by W. Thomas. Chicago: UChiP, 1975. 599p.

09060 ROBERTS, P.E. History of British India under the Company and the Crown. 3rd ed. London: OUP, 1952. 707p. [1st ed. 1921]

09061 SPEAR, T.G.P. The Oxford history of modern India, 1740-1947. Oxford: OUP, 1965. 426p.

4. Essay Collections

09062 GALLAGHER, J. & G. JOHNSON & ANIL SEAL, eds. Locality, province and nation, essays on Indian politics, 1870-1940. Cambridge: CamUP, 1973. 325p. [Rpt. from MAS 7,3 (1973) 321-589]

09063 LOW, D.A., ed. Soundings in modern South Asian history. Berkeley: UCalP, 1968. 391p.

09064 METCALF, T.R., ed. Modern India: an interpretive anthology. NY: Macmillan, 1971. 291p.

09065 PRASAD, B., ed. Ideas in history; proceedings of a seminar on ideas motivating social and religious movements and political and economic policies during the 18th and 19th centuries in India. Bombay: Asia, 1968. 351p.

09066 WILLIAMS, D. & E. D. POTTS, ed. Essays in Indian history, in honour of Cuthbert Collin Davies. NY: Asia, 1973. 259p.

5. Documentary Histories

09067 DOBBIN, C.E., ed. Basic documents in the development of modern India and Pakistan, 1835-1947. London: Van Nostrand Reinhold, 1970. 167p.

09068 FORREST, G.W. Selections from letters, dispatches, & other state papers preserved in the Foreign Department of the Government of India, 1772-1785. Calcutta: Govt. Press, 1890. 3 v.

09069 KEITH, A.B., ed. Speeches & documents on Indian policy, 1750-1921. London: OUP, 1922. 2v.

09070 MUIR, R., ed. Making of British India, 1756-1858, described in a series of dispatches, treaties, statutes & other docs. Lahore: OUP, 1969. 398p. [Rpt. 1915 ed.]

09071 PHILIPS, C.H., ed. The evolution of India and Pakistan, 1858 to 1947; select documents. London: OUP, 1962. 786p. (Select documents on the history of India and Pakistan, 4)

09072 WHEELER, J.T. Early records of British India.... NY: Barnes & Noble, 1972. 395p. [Rpt. 1878 ed.]

II. POLITICAL AND ADMINISTRATIVE HISTORY OF BRITISH INDIA, AND RELATIONS WITH THE PRINCELY STATES

A. The Central Policy-making and Executive Organs in England and India

1. Constitutional History and Documents

09073 ARCHBOLD, W.A.J. Outlines of Indian constitutional history (British Period). NY: Barnes & Noble, 1973. 367p. [1st pub. 1926]

09074 BANERJI, A.C. The constitutional history of India. Delhi: Macmillan of India, 1977. 3 v. 543, 514, 475p. [v. 1, 1600-1858; v. 2, 1858-1919; v. 3, 1919-1977]

09075 ______. Indian constitutional documents, 1857-1947. 3rd ed. Calcutta: A. Mukherjee, 1961-65. 4v.

09076 KEITH, A.B. A constitutional history of India, 1600-1935. 2nd ed., rev. and enl. NY: Barnes & Noble, 1969. 581p. [Rpt. 1936 ed.]

09077 MAHAJAN, V.D. Constitutional history of India, including the nationalist movement. 8th ed., rev. and enl. Delhi: S. Chand, 1971. 435 + 309p.

09078 MUKHERJI, P., ed. Indian constitutional documents. 2nd ed. Calcutta: Thacker, Spink, 1918. 2v. [v. 1, 1600-1918; v. 2, Govt. of India Acts of 1915 and 1916]

09079 MUNSHI, K.M. Indian constitutional documents. Bombay: BVB, 1967-. v. 1,2, 621, 554. [v. 1, Pilgrimage to Freedom, 1902-1950; to be 4 v.]

09080 RANA, M.S. Writings on Indian constitution, 1861-1972. Delhi: Indian Bureau of Bibliography, 1973. 496p. [biblio.]

09081 ROY, S. Indian politics and constitutional development. ND: Meenakshi, 1976. 250p.

09082 SAHARAY, H.K. A legal study of the constitutional development of India (up to the Government of India Act, 1935). Calcutta: Nababharat, 1970. 297p.

09083 VISHNOO BHAGWAN. Indian constitutional development. 5th ed., rev. Delhi: Atma Ram, 1979-. v. 1-.

2. General History of Politics and Policies at the Center

09084 CHINTAMANI, C.Y. Indian politics since the mutiny; ... the development of public life and political institutions and of prominent political personalities. Allahabad: Kitabistan, 1947. 238p. [Rpt. 1935 ed.]

09085 CUMMING, J.G., ed. Political India, 1832-1932; a co-operative survey of a century. Delhi: S. Chand, 1968. 324p. [Rpt. 1932 ed.]

09086 GOPAL, S. British policy in India 1858-1905. London: CamUP, 1965. 423p.

09087 ILBERT, C.P. The government of India. Oxford: OUP, 1934. 269p. [1st ed. 1898]

09088 MACDONALD, J.R. The government of India. ND: Metropolitan Book Co., 1978. 291p. [Rpt. 1919 ed.]

09089 NAPIER, C.J. Defects, civil and military, of the Indian Government. Ajmer: Shabd Sanchar, 1977. 437p. [Rpt. of 2nd ed., 1853]

09090 RAM GOPAL & D. SINGH. Indian politics; from Crown rule to independence, 1858-1947. Aligarh: Bharat Pub. House, 1967. 464p.

09091 SCHRENK-NOTZLING, C. Hundert Jahre indien; die politische Entwicklung, 1847-1960; eine Einführung. Stuttgart: Kohlhammer, 1961. 247p.

09092 SINGH, H.L. Problems and policies of the British in India, 1885-1898. Bombay: Asia, 1963. 284p.

3. The Home Government in London

09093 CHATTERJI, P.K. The making of India policy, 1853-65: a study of the relations of the Court of Directors, the India Board, the India Office, and the Government of India. Burdwan: U. of Burdwan, 1975. 409p.

09094 MOORE, R.J. Liberalism and Indian politics: 1872-1922. London: Edward Arnold, 1966. 136p.

09095 ______. Sir Charles Wood's Indian policy, 1853-66. Manchester: Manchester U. Press, 1966. 284p.

09096 SETON, M.C. The India office. London: Putnam's, 1926. 299p.

09097 SINGH, S.N. The Secretary of State for India and his Council (1858-1919). Delhi: Munshiram, 1962. 186p.

09098 WEST, A.E. Sir Charles Wood's administration of Indian affairs, from 1859 to 1866. London: Smith, Elder, 1867. 179p.

09099 WILLIAMS, D. The Council of India and the relationship between the Home and Supreme Governments. In English Hist. R. 81,1 (1966) 56-73.

4. The Supreme Government of India: The Governors-General (and, after 1858, Viceroys) and their Administrations (to 1899)

a. general

09100 CAMPBELL, G.D. India under Dalhousie and Canning. London: Longman, 1865. 143p.

09101 CURZON, GEORGE NATHANIEL, Marquess of Kedleston. British government in India. London: Cassell, 1925. 2v.

09102 JAIN, R.S. The growth & development of Governor-General's Executive Council, 1848-1919. Delhi: S. Chand, 1962. 236p.

09103 KAMINSKY, A.P. Agents or autocrats: India's viceroys in the late nineteenth century. In AsProf 7,3 (1979) 249-64.

09104 KULKARNI, V.B. British statesmen in India. Bombay: Orient Longmans, 1961. 550p.

09105 MERSEY, CLIVE BINGHAM, Viscount. The Viceroys and Governors-General of India, 1757-1947. London: Murray, 1949. 179p.

09106 RUDRA, A.B. The Viceroy & Governor-General of India. London: H. Milford, 1940. 362p.

b. Earl of Moira, Marquess of Hastings, 1813-23 (Francis Rawdon)

09107 HASTINGS, FRANCIS RAWDON-HASTINGS, 1st Marquis of. The private journal of the Marquess of Hastings. Ed. by his daughter, the Marchioness of Bute. Allahabad: The Panini office, 1907. 395p. [1st pub. 1858]

09108 PRINSEP, H.T. History of the political and military transactions in India during the administration of the Marquess of Hastings, 1813-1823. NY: Harper & Row, 1972. 2 v., 484, 487p. [Rpt. 1825 ed.]

09109 ROSS-OF-BLADENSBURG, J.F.G., Sir. The Marquess of Hastings. Oxford: OUP, 1893. 226p. (Rulers of India, 13)

c. Earl Amherst, 1823-28 (William Pitt Amherst)

09110 RITCHIE, A.I., Lady. Lord Amherst and the British advance eastwards to Burma. Oxford: OUP, 1894. 220p. (Rulers of India, 17)

d. Lord William Bentinck, 1828-35 (William Cavendish-Bentinck)

09111 AHMED, MANAZIR. Lord William Bentinck. Allahabad: Chugh, 1978. 303p.

09112 BOULGER, D.C. Lord William Bentinck. Oxford: Clarendon Press, 1892. 214p. (Rulers of India, 12)

09113 PHILIPS, C.H., ed. The correspondence of Lord William Cavendish Bentinck, Governor-General of India, 1828-1835. Oxford: OUP, 1977. 2v., 1483p.

09114 ROSSELLI, J. Lord William Bentinck and his age. In BPP 94,179 (1975) 68-88.

09115 ______. Lord William Bentinck: the making of a liberal imperialist, 1774-1839. Berkeley: UCalP, 1974. 384p.

e. Earl of Auckland, 1835-42 (George Eden)

09116 SINHA, D.P. Some aspects of British social and administrative policy in India during the administration of Lord Auckland. Calcutta: Punthi Pustak, 1969. 336p.

f. Earl of Ellenborough, 1842-44 (Edward Law)

09117 ELLENBOROUGH, EDWARD LAW, 1st Earl of. History of the Indian administration of Lord Ellenborough.... Ed. by Lord Colchester. London: R. Bentley, 1874. 452p. [his letters to the Duke of Wellington and to the Queen]

09118 ______. India under Lord Ellenborough, March 1842-June 1844; a selection from the hitherto unpublished papers and secret despatches of Edward, earl of Ellenborough. Ed. by A. Law. London: Murray, 1926. 211p.

09119 IMLAH, A.H. Lord Ellenborough; a biography of Edward Law, earl of Ellenborough, governor-general of India. Cambridge: HUP, 1939. 295p.

g. Viscount Hardinge, 1844-48 (Henry Hardinge)

09120 HARDINGE, CHARLES STEWART, 2nd Viscount. Viscount Hardinge. Oxford: OUP, 1892. 200p. (Rulers of India)

h. Marquess of Dalhousie, 1848-56

09121 ARNOLD, E. Dalhousie's administration of British India. London: Saunders, Otley, 1862-65. 2v.

09122 BAIRD, J.G.A. Private letters of the Marquess of Dalhousie. Edinburgh: W. Blackwood, 1911. 448p.

09123 DAS, M.N. Studies in the economic and social development of modern India; 1848-56. Calcutta: KLM, 1959. 449p.

09124 GHOSH, S.C. Dalhousie in India, 1848-56; a study of his social policy as Governor-General. ND: Munshiram, 1975. 166p.

09125 HUNTER, W.W. The Marquess of Dalhousie and the final development of the company's rule. Delhi: S. Chand, 1961. 160p. (Rulers of India) [1st pub. 1895]

09126 JACKSON, C.R.M. A vindication of the marquis of Dalhousie's Indian administration. Allahabad: Chugh, 1975. 179p. [Rpt. of 1865 ed.]

09127 LEE-WARNER, W. The life of the Marquis of Dalhousie. London: Macmillan, 1904. 2v.

09128 RAHIM, M.A. Lord Dalhousie's administration of the conquered and annexed states. Delhi: S. Chand, 1963. 396p.

j. Earl Canning, 1856-62 - first Viceroy, from 1858 (Charles John Canning)

09129 CUNNINGHAM, H.S. Earl Canning. Oxford: OUP, 1892. 220p. (Rulers of India)

09130 MACLAGAN, M. "Clemency" Canning; Charles John, 1st earl Canning, Governor-General and Viceroy of India. London: Macmillan, 1962. 419p.

k. Earl of Elgin, 1862-63 (James Bruce)

09131 ELGIN, JAMES BRUCE, 8th Earl of. Letters and journal of James, eighth Earl of Elgin. Ed. by Theodore Walrond. London: Murray, 1873. 467p.

09132 MORISON, J.L. The eighth earl of Elgin; a chapter in nineteenth-century imperial history. Westport, Conn.: Greenwood, 1970. 312p. [1st pub. 1928]

09133 ______. Lord Elgin in India, 1862-63. In Cambridge Hist. J. 1,3 (1925) 178-96.

i. Lord Lawrence, 1863-69 (John Laird Mair Lawrence)

09134 AITCHISON, C.U. Lord Lawrence and the reconstruction of India under the Crown. Oxford: OUP, 1894. 216p. (Rulers of India)

09135 EDWARDES, M. The necessary hell; John and Henry Lawrence and the Indian Empire. London: Cassell, 1958. 213p.

09136 MALLESON, G.B. Recreations of an Indian official. London: Longmans, Green, 1872. 467p. [1-132 on Lord Lawrence]

09137 PAL, DHARM. Administration of Sir John Lawrence in India, 1864-1869. Simla: Minerva Book Shop, 1952. 284p.

09138 SMITH, R.B. Life of Lord Lawrence. London: Smith, Elder, 1883. 2v.

m. Earl of Mayo, 1869-72 (Richard Southwell Bourke)

09139 HUNTER, W.W. The Earl of Mayo. Oxford: OUP, 1892. 206p. (Rulers of India)

09140 ______. A life of the Earl of Mayo, fourth Viceroy of India. London: Smith, Elder, 1876. 2 v.

n. Earl of Northbrook, 1872-76 (Thomas George Baring)

09141 MALLET, BERNARD. Thomas George Earl of Northbrook, G.C.S.Q. A memoir. London: Longmans, Green 1908. 306p.

09142 MOULTON, E.C. Lord Northbrook's Indian administration, 1872-1876. Bombay: Asia, 1968. 313p.

o. Earl of Lytton, 1876-80 (Edward Robert Bulwer Lytton)

09143 BALFOUR, E. The history of Lord Lytton's Indian administration, 1876-1880. London: Longmans, Green, 1899. 551p.

p. Marquess of Ripon, 1880-84 (George Frederick Samuel Robinson)

09144 BLUNT, W.S. India under Ripon. London: T.F. Unwin, 1909. 343p.

09145 GOPAL, S. The viceroyalty of Lord Ripon 1880-1884. London: OUP, 1953. 245p.

09146 MATHUR, L.P. Lord Ripon's administration in India (1880-84 A.D.). ND: S. Chand, 1972. 257p.

q. Marquess of Dufferin, 1884-88 (Frederick Temple Blackwood)

09147 DUFFERIN AND AVA, Marchioness of. Our Viceregal life in India; selections from my journal, 1884-1888. New ed. London: J. Murray, 1893. 408p. [1st pub. 1889]

09148 MARTIN, B., JR. Lord Dufferin and the Indian National Congress, 1885-88. In J. of British Studies 7,1 (1967) 68-96.

r. Marquess of Lansdowne, 1888-94 (Henry Charles Keith Petty-Fitzmaurice)

09149 MISRA, J.P. The administration of India under Lord Lansdowne, 1888-1894. ND: Sterling, 1975. 260p.

09150 PERTI, R.K. South Asia: frontier policies, administrative problems, and Lord Lansdowne. ND: Oriental, 1976. 328p.

s. Earl of Elgin, 1894-99 (Victor Alexander Bruce)

09151 MALHOTRA, P.L. Administration of Lord Elgin in India, 1894-99. ND: Vikas, 1979. 216p.

5. Legislative Councils

09152 DESIKACHAR, S.V. Centralised legislation; a history of the legislative system of British India from 1834 to 1861. London: Asia, 1963. 359p.

09153 INDIA. The Indian Councils Acts, 1861 and 1892. Calcutta: Supt. of Govt. Printing, 1898. 59p.

09154 MAJUMDAR, B.B. Indian political associations and reform of legislature (1818-1917). Calcutta: KLM, 1965. 477p.

09155 NAG, S.K. Evolution of parliamentary privileges in India till 1947. ND: Sterling, 1978. 360p.

09156 SHARAN, P. The Imperial legislative council of India from 1861 to 1920. Delhi: S. Chand, 1961. 281p.

09157 SURI, P. Growth of committee system in the Central Legislature of India, 1920-1947. ND: Associated Pub. Co., 1979. 227p.

09158 YASIN, M. The Indian Councils Act of 1892; an analytical study. In JIH 55,1/2 (1977) 255-63.

B. Administrative Organization of British India

1. General Histories and Studies of Administration

09159 CAMPBELL, G. Modern India: a sketch of the system of civil government; To which is prefixed, some account of the natives and native institutions. London: Murray, 1852. 560p.

09160 CAPPER, J. The Three Presidencies of India: a history of the rise and progress of the British Indian possessions, from the earliest records to the present time. London: Ingram, Cooke, 1853. 492p.

09161 CHAILLEY-BERT, J. Administrative problems of British India. Tr. from French by W. Meyer. London: Macmillan, 1910. 590p.

09162 CHESNEY, G.T. Indian polity: a view of the system of administration in India. 3rd ed. London: Longmans, Green, 1894. 409p. [1st pub. 1868]

09163 GHOSE, A.K. Public administration in India (historical, structural and functional). Calcutta: U. of Calcutta, 1930. 743p.

09164 GREAT BRITAIN. PARLIAMENT. HOUSE OF COMMONS. SELECT COMMITTEE ON THE EAST INDIA COMPANY. Reports from the select committee[s] of the House of Commons appointed to enquire into the present state of the affairs of the East-India Company, together with the minutes of evidence, [appendixes] of documents, and [general indexes]. London: 1830-33. 14v.

09165 NAPIER, C.J. Defects, civil and military, of the Indian government. 2nd ed. Ajmer: Shabd Sanchar, 1977. 437p. [Rpt. 1853 ed.]

09166 MISRA, B.B. The administrative history of India, 1834-1947; general administration. Bombay: OUP, 1970. 672p.

09167 RUTHNASWAMY, M.D. Some influences that made the British administrative system in India. London: Luzac, 1939. 660p.

09168 STRACHEY, J. India, its administration & progress. 4th ed. London: Macmillan, 1911. 567p.

09169 SUBRAMANIAM, S. A brief history of the organisation of official statistics in India during the British period. In Sankhya 22 (1960) 85-118.

2. Biographies and Studies of Leading Administrators

09170 CAMPBELL, G. Memoirs of my Indian career. Ed. by C.E. Bernard. London: Macmillan, 1893. 2v.

09171 FRERE, H.B.E. The speeches and addresses. Ed. by B.N. Pitale. Bombay: 1870. 570p.

09172 KAYE, J.W. Life and correspondence of Metcalfe. London: Smith, Elder, 1858. 2 v.

09173 ______. Life and correspondence of Sir John Malcolm. London: Smith, Elder, 1856. 2 v.

09174 ______. Selections from the papers of Lord Metcalfe. London: Smith, Elder, 1855. 476p.

09175 LAWRENCE, W.R. The India we served. London: Cassell, 1928. 317p.

09176 MARTINEAU, J. The life and correspondence of the Right Hon. Sir Bartle Frere. 2nd ed. London: Murray, 1895. 2 v.

09177 TEMPLE, R. Journals kept in Hyderabad, Kashmir, Sikkim, and Nepal. Ed. by his son Richard Carnac Temple. ND: Cosmo, 1977. 2 v. [Rpt. 1887 ed.]

09178 THOMPSON, E.J. Life of Charles, Lord Metcalfe. London: Faber & Faber, 1937. 439p.

3. The Indian Civil Service (ICS) and Other Public Services of British India

a. general studies of the public services, and official reports

09179 BEAGLEHOLE, T.H. From rulers to servants: the I.C.S. and the British demission of power in India. In MAS 11,2 (1977) 237-56.

09180 BLUNT, E.A.H. The I.C.S.; the Indian Civil Service. London: Faber & Faber, 1937. 291p.

09181 CHAUDHURI, M.A. The growth of the civil service in British India and Pakistan. In JASP 5 (1960) 74-127.

09182 DE, BARUN. Brajendranath De and John Beames -- a study in the reactions of patriotism and paternalism in the I.C.S. at the time of the Ilbert Bill. In BPP 81 (1962) 1-31.

09183 DIVER, K.H.M.M. The unsung; a record of British services in India. Edinburgh: W. Blackwood, 1945. 296p.

09184 GREAT BRITAIN. ROYAL COMMISSION ON THE PUBLIC SERVICES IN INDIA. Report...[and appendices]. London: HMSO, 1914-17. 20v. (Cd. 8382, Parl. Pap. 1916:7; Cd. 7293-96, 7578-83, Parl. Pap. 1914:21-24; Cd. 7900-08, Parl. Pap. 1914-16:15-17) [Lord Islington, Chm.]

09185 GREAT BRITAIN. ROYAL COMMISSION ON THE SUPERIOR CIVIL SERVICES IN INDIA. Report. London: HMSO, 1924. 189p. (Cmd. 2128, Parl.Pap. 1924:8) [Viscount Lee, Chm.]

09186 INDIA. PUBLIC SERVICE CMSN., 1887-87. Report. Calcutta: 1888. 116p. (C. 5327; Parl. Pap. 1888:48) [Sir C.U. Aitchison, chm.: rpt. Delhi: Concept, 1977, as: British attitudes towards the employment of Indians in civil service..., with intro. by B. Spangenberg]

09187 JAIN, P.K. The Indian Agricultural Service: a study in technical personnel, 1906-1924. ND: Glorious Pub. House, 1978. 200p.

09188 MATHUR, P.N. The Civil Service of India (1731-1894). Jodhpur: Prabhash Prakashan, 1979. 239p.

09189 MISRA, H.B. The bureaucracy in India: an historical analysis of development up to 1947. Delhi: OUP, 1977. 421p.

09190 O'MALLEY, L.S.S. The Indian Civil Service, 1601-1930. 2nd ed. London: Cass, 1965. 310p. [1st ed. 1931]

09191 POTTER, D.C. Manpower shortage & the end of colonialism: the case of the Indian Civil Service. In MAS 7,1 (1973) 47-73.

09192 SPANGENBERG, B. British bureaucracy in India: status, policy and the I.C.S. in the late 19th century. ND: Manohar, 1976. 380p.

09193 THAKUR, R.N. The All India services; a study of their origin & growth. Patna: Bharati Bhawan, 1969. 298p.

b. recruitment and training for the ICS: Haileybury College, and the competitive system

09194 COHN, B.S. Recruitment and training of British civil servants in India, 1600-1860. In R. Braibanti, ed. Asian bureaucratic systems emergent from the British imperial tradition. Durham: DUP, 1966, 87-140.

09195 COMPTON, J.M. Open competition and the Indian civil service. In English Hist. R. 83 (1968) 265-284.

09196 DEWEY, C.J. Ruling elite: the Indian Civil Service in the era of competitive examination. In English Hist. R. 83 (1973) 262-85.

09197 MONIER-WILLIAMS, M. Memorials of old Haileybury College. Westminster: A. Constable, 1894. 668p.

09198 MOORE, R.J. The abolition of patronage in the Indian civil service and the closure of Haileybury College. In Historical J. 7 (1964) 246-57.

09199 SPANGENBERG, B. The problem of recruitment for the Indian civil service during the late nineteenth century. In JAS 30,2 (1971) 341-60.

c. accounts and memoirs by officials

09200 BELLEW, F.J. Memoirs of a griffin: or a cadet's first year in India. New ed. London: W.H. Allen, 1880. 373p. [1st ed. 1843]

09201 CAMPBELL, G. Memoirs of my Indian career. Ed. by C.E. Barnard. London: Macmillan, 1893. 2 v.

09202 COTTON, H.J.S. Indian and home memories. London: T.F. Unwin, 1911. 352p.

09203 D'OYLY, C. Tom Raw, the Griffin: a burlesque poem in twelve cantos: illustrated by twenty-five engravings, descriptive of the adventures of a cadet in the East India company's service.... London: R. Ackermann, 1828. 325p.

09204 FRASER, A.H.L. Among Indian rajahs and ryots: a civil servant's recollections & impressions of thirty-seven years of work & sport in the Central Provinces & Bengal. 3rd & rev. ed. Allahabad: Chugh, 1975. 375p. + 24 pl.

09205 HALLIDAY, J. A special India. London: Chatto & Windus, 1968. 248p.

09206 MACLEOD, R.D. Impressions of an Indian civil servant. London: Witherby, 1938. 233p.

09207 MACONOCHIE, E. Life in the Indian Civil Service. London: Chapman & Hall, 1926. 269p.

09208 MASON, P. A shaft of sunlight: memories of a varied life. London: Deutsch, 1978. 240p. + 8 pl.

09209 PANJABI, K.L., ed. The civil servant in India, by ex-Indian Civil Servants. Bombay: BVB, 1965. 356p.

09210 SMITH, W.H.S. A young man's country: letters of a subdivisional officer of the Indian Civil Service, 1936-7. Salisbury: M. Russell, 1977. 112p.

09211 TEMPLE, R. India in 1880. London: Murray, 1881. 524p.

09212 TREVELYAN, G.O. The competition wallah. NY: AMS Press, 1977. 355p. [Rpt. of 2nd ed., 1866]

09213 TREVELYAN, H. The India we left: Charles Trevelyan, 1826-65, Humphrey Trevelyan, 1929-47. London: Macmillan, 1972. 255p.

4. Provincial, District, and Local Government

09214 GREAT BRITAIN. INDIA OFFICE. East India (Local Government).... "Copy of or extracts from correspondence between the Secretary of State for India in Council, the government of India, and the various local governments, on the proposed measures for the extension of local government in India." .... London: 1883. 2 v. in 1.

09215 MATTHAI, J. Village government in British India. London: T.F. Unwin, 1915. 211p.

09216 RAHMAN, Q. Official ideas of representation in the local self-government bodies in the late nineteenth century. In JASBangla 20,2 (1975) 53-68.

09217 RAI, HARIDWAR. Politico-administrative bases of Indian field administration: the patterns of the district officer system under the British. In IJPA 16 (1970) 455-84.

09218 RUSSELL, T.B. Principles of a local government in England and their application in India. Madras: P. Varadachary, 1932. 71p.

09219 SHAH, K.T. & G.J. BAHADURJI. Constitution, functions and finance of Indian municipalities. Bombay: Indian Newspaper Co., 1925. 514p.

09220 SHARMA, M.P. Local self-government in India. 2nd ed. Bombay: Hind Kitabs, 1951. 129p. [1st ed. 1941]

09221 TINKER, H.R. The foundations of local self-government in India, Pakistan and Burma. London: Athlone Press, 1954. 376p. (U. of London hist. ser., 1)

5. Police Administration and Crime in British India

a. history, organization, and personal accounts

09222 COX, E.C. Police and crime in India. London: S. Paul, 1911. 328p.

09223 CURRY, J.C. The Indian police. London: Faber & Faber, 1932. 353p.

09224 DASGUPTA, U. Crime, law and the police in India, 1870-80. In IESHR 10,4 (1973) 333-70.

09225 GOULDSBURY, C.E. Life in the Indian police. ND: Manu Pub., 1977. 284p. + 24 pl.

09226 GRIFFITHS, P.J. To guard my people: the history of the Indian police. London: E. Benn, 1971. 444p.

09227 GUPTA, A.S. Crime and police in India, up to 1861. Agra: Sahitya Bhawan, 1974. 392p.

09228 ______. The police in British India, 1861-1947. ND: Concept, 1979. 579p.

09229 INDIA. POLICE CMSN. Report of the Indian Police Commission and resolution of the Government of India. London: HMSO, 1905. 276p. (Cd. 2478; Parl. Pap. 1905: 57)

09230 SINHA, A.K. Thirty-two years in the police and after. Patna: Sanjivan, 1952. 229p.

b. thugs/ṭhags, dacoits, and other underworld types

09231 BRUCE, G.L. The stranglers: the cult of Thuggee and its overthrow in British India. London: Longmans, 1968. 234p.

09232 EDWARDES, S.M. Crime in India. London: OUP, 1924. 169p.

09233 FLORIS, G.A. A note on dacoits in India. In CSSH 4 (1962) 467-72.

09234 MACMUNN, G.F. The underworld of India. London: Jarrold's, 1933. 284p.

09235 SIMHADRI, Y.C. Criminal tribes of India: a socio-historical analysis. In JSR 17,2 (1974) 22-30.

09236 SLEEMAN, J.L. Thug; or, a million murders. London: S. Low, Marston, 1933. 246p.

09237 SLEEMAN, W.H. Ramaseeana, or a vocabulary of the peculiar language used by the Thugs. Calcutta: G.H. Huttman, Military Orphan Press, 1836. 115p.

09238 ______. Report on Budhuk alias Bagree dacoits, and other gang robbers by hereditary profession, and on the measures adopted by the government of India for their suppression. Calcutta: J.C. Sherriff, 1849. 433p.

09239 TAYLOR, M. Confessions of a Thug. London: Blond, 1967. 338p. [1st pub. 1840]

09240 THORNTON, E. Illustrations of the history and practices of the Thugs. London: W.H. Allen, 1837. 475p.

09241 TUKER, F.I.S. The yellow scarf; the story of the life of Thuggee Sleeman, or Major-General Sir William Henry Sleeman, K.C.B., 1788-1856, of the Bengal Army and the Indian Political Service. London: Dent, 1961. 211p.

09242 WALSH, C.H. Crime in India, with an introduction on forensic difficulties and peculiarities. London: E. Benn, 1930. 287p.

09243 WIGHTMAN, A.J. No friend for travellers. London: R. Hale, 1959. 156p.

6. Law and Judicial Administration

a. history of the judicial system in British India

09244 CARTHILL, A. The company of Cain. Edinburgh: Blackwood, 1929. 316p. [Acct. by former Judicial Commissioner of Sind]

09245 CHOWDHURY, B.S. Studies in judicial history of British India. Calcutta: Eastern Law House, 1972. 264p.

09246 COWELL, H. History and constitution of the courts and legislative authorities in India. 6th ed., rev. by S.C. Bagchi. Calcutta: Thacker, Spink, 1936. 293p.

09247 FAWCETT, C. The first century of British justice in India. Oxford: OUP, 1934. 269p.

09248 GAUBA, K.L. Famous and historical trials. Delhi: Hind Pocket Books, 1972. 186p.

09249 Indian judges; biographical and critical sketches with portraits. Madras: G.A. Natesan, 1932. 509p.

09250 JAIN, M.P. Outlines of Indian legal history. 3rd ed. Bombay: N.M. Tripathi, 1972. 640p.

09251 MITTAL, J.K. An introduction to Indian legal history. 3rd ed. Allahabad: Allahabad Law Agency, 1970. 428p.

09252 MORLEY, W.H. The administration of justice in British India: its past history and present state, comprising an account of the laws peculiar to India. ND: Metropolitan Book Co., 1976. 357p. [Rpt. 1858 ed.]

09253 NOORANI, A.G. Indian political trials. ND: Sterling, 1976. 259p.

09254 RANKIN, G.C. Background to Indian law. Cambridge: CamUP, 1946. 223p.

09255 SINHA, B.S. The legal history of India. Lucknow: Eastern Book Co., 1953. 304p.

09256 SINHA, C.R. The Indian civil judiciary in making, 1800-33. ND: Munshiram, 1971. 209p.

09257 SRIVASTAVA, R.C. Development of judicial system in India under the East India Company, 1833-1858. Lucknow: Lucknow Pub. House, 1971. 232p.

09258 TREVELYAN, E.J. The constitution and jurisdiction of courts of civil justice in British India. Calcutta: Thacker, Spink, 1962. 702p.

09259 WOODRUFF, P. Call the next witness. London: J. Cape, 1945. 220p. [novel by former magistrate]

b. Hindu and Muslim personal and family law under British administration

09260 ALI, HAMID. Custom and law in Anglo-Muslim jurisprudence. Calcutta: Thacker, Spink, 1938. 127p.

09261 DERRETT, J.D.M. Administration of Hindu law by the British. In CSSH, 4 (1961-62) 10-52.

09262 ______. Essays in classical and modern Hindu law. v. 3, Anglo-Hindu legal problems. Leiden: Brill, 1977. 414p.

09263 ______. A juridical fabrication of early British India: the Mahanirvāṇa-Tantra. In Zeitschrift für vergleichende Rechtswissenschaft, 69 (1968) 138-81.

09264 GUPTE, S.V. Hindu law in British India. Bombay: N.M. Tripathi, 1945. 1148p.

09265 HASSAN, S.R. The reconstruction of legal thought in Islam: comparative study of the Islamic and the Western systems of law in the latter's terminology with particular reference to the Islamic laws suspended by the British rule in the subcontinent. Rev. and enl. ed. Lahore: Idara Tarjuman al-Quran, 1977. 440p.

09266 INDIA. HINDU LAW COMMITTEE. Report. Simla: Govt. of India Press, 1941. 49p.

09267 MAYNE, J.D. A treatise on Hindu law and usage. Madras: Higginbothams, 1938. 1057p.

09268 ROCHER, L. Indian response to Anglo-Hindu law. In JAOS 92,3 (1972) 419-24.

09269 SONTHEIMER, G.D. Religious endowments in India: the juristic personality of Hindu deities. In Zeitschrift für vergleichende Rechtswissenschaft 67 (1964) 45-100.

09270 WILSON, R.K. Introduction to the study of Anglo-Mohammedan law. London: Thacker, 1894. 151p.

09271 YADUVANSH, U. Decline of the Qazis (1793-1876). In IJPS 28 (1967) 216-28.

c. adaptation and effects of British law in India; law and caste

09272 COHN, B.S. Anthropological notes on disputes and law in India. In AA 67 (1965) 82-122.

09273 DOBBIN, C. The Ilbert Bill: a study of Anglo-Indian opinion in India, 1883. In Historical Studies: Australia and New Zealand 12 (1965) 87-102.

09274 GALANTER, M. The displacement of traditional law in India. In J. of Social Issues 24,4 (1968) 65-91.

09275 GLEDHILL, A. The reception of English law in India. In W.B. Hamilton, ed. The transfer of institutions. Durham: DUP, 1964, 165-91.

09276 KANE, P.V. Hindu law and modern custom. Bombay: U. of Bombay, 1950. 122p.

09277 KIKANI, L.T. Caste in courts, or rights and powers of castes in social and religious matters as recognized by Indian courts. Rajkot: Ganatra Printing Works, 1912. 180p.

09278 LIPSTEIN, K. The reception of western law in India. In Intl. Social Science Bull. 9,1 (1957) 85-95.

09279 MCCORMACK, W.C. Caste and the British administration of Hindu law. In JAAS(L) 1,1 (1966) 27-34.

09280 ROY, S.C. Customs and customary law in British India. Calcutta: Hare Press, 1911. 621p.

09281 RUDOLPH, L.I. & S.H. RUDOLPH. Barristers and Brahmans in India: legal cultures and social change. In CSSH 8 (1965) 24-49.

09282 SEN, S.P. Effects on India of British law and administration in the 19th century. In CHM 4 (1958) 849-80.

7. Military Organization and History

a. general history of the armed forces, British and Indian

09283 BEAUMONT, R. Sword of the Raj: the British Army in India, 1747-1947. NY: Bobbs-Merrill, 1977. 237p.

09284 BONARJEE, P.D. A handbook of the fighting races of India. ND: Asian Pub. Services, 1975. 228p. [Rpt. 1899 ed.]

09285 BOPEGAMAGE, A. The military as a modernizing agent in India. In EDCC 20,1 (1971) 71-79.

09286 GUTTERIDGE, W. The Indianization of the Indian army, 1918-1945. In Race 4 (1963) 39-48.

09287 HEATHCOTE, T.A. The Indian army: the garrison of British Imperial India, 1822-1922. London: David & Charles, 1974. 215p.

09288 JAIPUR, H.H. MAHARAJA OF. A history of the Indian State Forces. Bombay: Orient Longmans, 1967. 122p.

09289 KHERA, P.N. Role of the Indian army, 1900-1939. In JUSI 94 (1964) 277-89.

09290 LONGER, V. Red coats to olive green: a history of the Indian Army, 1600-1974. Bombay: Allied, 1974. 543p.

09291 MACMUNN, G.F. The armies of India. London: A. & C. Black, 1911. 224p. + 72 pl.

09292 ______. The martial races of India. Delhi: Mittal, 1979. 368p. + 17 pl. [Rpt. 1933 ed.]

09293 MASON, P. A matter of honour: an account of the Indian army, its officers and men. London: J. Cape, 1974. 580p.

09294 REDDY, K.N. Indian defence expenditure: 1872-1967. In IESHR 7 (1970) 467-88.

09295 SAXENA, K.M.L. The military system of India (1850-1900). ND: Sterling, 1974. 292p.

09296 SHIBLY, A.H. The "irregular" system in the British-Indian army. In JASBangla 20,1 (1975) 73-81.

09297 SINGH, R. History of the Indian Army. ND: Attar Singh, 1963. 283p.

b. selected unit histories

09298 BARAT, A. The Bengal Native Infantry; its organisation and discipline, 1796-1852. Calcutta: KLM, 1962. 341p.

09299 CADELL, P.R. History of the Bombay Army. London: Longmans, Green, 1938. 377p.

09300 CARDEW, F.G. A sketch of the services of the Bengal native army, to the year 1895. ND: Today & Tomorrow's, 1971. 576p. [1st pub. 1903]

09301 GREAT BRITAIN. MIN. OF DEFENCE. Nepal and the Gurkhas. London: HMSO, 1965. 158p.

09302 GULATI, Y.B. History of the Regiment of Artillery, Indian Army. Ed. by Maj. Gen. D.K. Palit. London: Leo Cooper, 1972. 342p.

09303 INDIA. OFFICE OF THE ADJUTANT GENERAL. Precis of the services of the Madras native army, with a note on its composition. Ootacamund: 1886. 58p. [largely an abstract of...W.J. Wilson's History of the Madras Army ....]

09304 JAMES, H.D. & D. SHEIL-SMALL. The Gurkhas. London: Macdonald, 1965. 211p.

09305 LAWFORD, J.P. & W.E. CATTO, eds. Solah Punjab: the history of the 16th Punjab Regiment. Aldershot: Gale & Polden, 1967. 302p.

09306 MOJUMDAR, K. Recruitment of Gurkhas in the Indian army, 1814-1877. In JUSI 93 (1963) 143-57.

09307 MYERS, M.A. Regimental histories of the Indian army: bibliography. London: 1957. 65p. [U. of London librarianship thesis]

09308 NORTHEY, W.B. & C.J. MORRIS. The Gurkhas: their manners, customs, and country. Delhi: Cosmo, 1974. 282p. [Rpt. 1928 ed.]

09309 SIMCOX, A.H.A. A memoir of the Khandesh Bhil Corps, 1825-1891; compiled from original records. Bombay: Thacker, 1912. 281p.

09310 STEVENS, G.R. Fourth Indian Division. Toronto: McLaren, 1968. 414p.

09311 TUKER, F. Gorkha, the story of the Gurkhas of Nepal. London: Constable, 1957. 319p.

09312 WILLIAMS, J. The Bengal Native Infantry, 1757 to 1796. London: Muller, 1970. 388p. [Rpt. 1817 ed.]

09313 YOUNGHUSBAND, G.J. The story of the Guides. London: Macmillan, 1908. 207p.

c. biographies, memoirs, and studies of British military men in India

09314 BADEN-POWELL, R.S.S. Memories of India; recollections of soldiering and sport. Philadelphia: D. McKay, 1915. 363p.

09315 BIRDWOOD, W.R. Khaki and gown, an autobiography. NY: R. Speller, 1957. 456p. [1st pub. 1941]

09316 CASSERLY, G. Life in an Indian outpost. London: T.W. Laurie, 1914. 320p.

09317 COOPER, L. Havelock. London: Bodley Head, 1957. 192p.

09318 HOLMAN, D. Sikander Sahib: the life of Colonel James Skinner, 1778-1841. London: Heinemann, 1961. 275p.

09319 HOLMES, T.R.E. Sir Charles Napier. Cambridge: CamUP, 1925. 183p. [1st pub. 1889]

09320 LAWRENCE, R., Lady. Charles Napier, friend and fighter, 1782-1853. London: Murray, 1952. 236p.

09321 LEWIN, T.H. A fly on the wheel: or, how I helped to govern India. Calcutta: KLM, 1977. 318p. [Rpt. 1912 ed.]

09322 LUMSDEN, P.S. & G.R. ELSMIE. Lumsden of the Guides, a sketch of the life of Lieut.-Gen. Sir Harry Burnett Lumsden.... London: Murray, 1899. 333p.

09323 MACMUNN, G.F. Vignettes from Indian wars. Quetta: Nisa Traders, 1978. 214p. [Rpt. 1932 ed.]

09324 MARSHMAN, J.C., ed. Memoirs of Major-General Sir Henry Havelock. London: Longmans, Green, 1902. 457p.

09325 NAPIER, W.F.P. The life and opinions of General Sir Charles James Napier, G.C.B. London: J. Murray, 1857. 4 v.

09326 ROBERTS, F.S. Forty-one years in India; from subaltern to commander-in-chief. New ed. London: Macmillan, 1904. 601p. [1st pub. 1898]

09327 SANDES, E.W.C. The military engineer in India. Chatham: Inst. of Royal Engineers, 1933-35. 2 v.

09328 SHORE, F.J. Notes on Indian affairs. London: J.W. Parker, 1837. 2 v.

09329 SITARAMA, Subahdar. From sepoy to subadar, being the life and adventures of a native officer of the Bengal Army. Written by himself. Tr. by J.T. Norgate. Ed. by B.C. Phillott. 3rd ed. Calcutta: Baptist Mission Press, 1911. 130p.

09330 SLEEMAN, W.H. Rambles and recollections of an Indian official. Rev. ed. Karachi: OUP, 1973. 667p. [1st pub. 1844]

09331 TROTTER, L.J. Life of Hodson of Hodson's Horse. NY: Dutton, 1927. 306p.

09332 ______. Life of John Nicholson, soldier and administrator. London: Murray, 1898. 333p.

09333 YEATS-BROWNE, F.C.C. Lives of a Bengal lancer. NY: Viking, 1930. 299p.

09334 YOUNGHUSBAND, G.J. A soldier's memories in peace and war. NY: E.P. Dutton, 1917. 355p.

C. Princely India: from Mughal Allegiance to British Paramount Power [For Individual States, see Index]

1. Biographical Guides and Other Reference Works

09335 The Coronation durbar, Delhi, 1903. Official directory. Delhi: Foreign Office Press, 1903. 208p.

09336 GRIFFITH, M. India's princes: short life sketches of the native rulers of India. London: W.H. Allen, 1894. 273p.

09337 INDIA. Memoranda on native states in India, 1915; together with a list of independent ruling chiefs, chiefs of frontier states, and other personages with their proper forms of address. Calcutta: Supt. Govt. Printing, 1916. [issued periodically]

09338 LETHBRIDGE, R. The golden book of India, a genealogical and bibliographical dictionary of the ruling princes, chiefs, and other personages, titled or decorated, of the Indian Empire. London: Macmillan, 1893. 584p.

09339 MEHTA, M.N. & M.N. MEHTA, comp. The Hind Rajasthan, or the annals of the native states of India. Bhadarwa (Rewa Kantha): A.G. Shah, 1896. 1331p.

09340 SUNDAR-ISANON, A.N. Indian states' register and directory. Madras: Indian States Register & Directory Office, 1929, 1932. 2 v. [no more pub.]

09341 VADIVELU, A. The ruling chiefs, nobles and zamindars of India. Madras: 1915. 771p.

09342 VENKOBA RAO, R. Ministers in Indian states. Trichinopoly: Wednesday R. Press, 1928. 189p.

2. General History and Studies of the Native States

09343 BARTON, W.P. The princes of India, with a chapter on Nepal. London: Nisbet, 1934. 327p.

09344 CHAKRAVARTI, J.C. The native states of India. Calcutta: S.K. Shaw, 1895. 264p.

09345 DIVER, K.H.M. Royal India, a descriptive and historical study of India's fifteen principal states and their rulers. NY: Appleton-Century, 1942. 317p.

09346 FORBES, R. (TORR). India of the Princes. London: The Right Book Club, 1939. 318p.

09347 JEFFREY, R., ed. People, princes, and paramount power: society and politics in the Indian princely states. Delhi: OUP, 1978. 396p.

09348 LEE-WARNER, W. The native states of India. London: Macmillan, 1910. 425p. [1st pub. 1877; rpt. NY: AMS Press, 1971]

09349 MACMUNN, G.F. The Indian states and princes. London: Jarrolds, 1936. 287p.

09350 MALLESON, G.B. Historical sketch of native states. London: Longmans, Green, 1875. 397p.

09351 NIHAL SINGH, S. The King's Indian allies: the rajas and their India. London: S. Low, Marston, 1916. 308p.

09352 The origin, rise, and consolidation of the Indian states: a British assessment, 1929. Delhi: B.R. Pub. Corp., 1975. 136p. [1st pub. by the Govt. of India in 1932.]

09353 PATHIK, B.S. What are Indian states? With illustrative documents. An introd. to the study of the problem of Indian states and the real conditions of their people. Ajmer: S.L. Verma, 1928. 238p.

09354 ROUSSELET, L. India and its native princes: travels in Central India and in the presidencies of Bombay and Bengal. Rev. & ed. by Lt. Col. Buckle. Delhi: B.R., 1975. 619p. [Rpt. 1882 ed.; tr. from French]

09355 THOMPSON, E.J. The making of the Indian princes. London: OUP, 1943. 304p.

3. Political Relations Between the Paramount Power and Princes; the Indian Political Service

09356 AITCHISON, C.U., comp. A collection of treaties, engagements and sanads. Calcutta: Supt. of Govt. Printing, 1892-93. 11 v.

09357 CHUDGAR, P.L. Indian princes under British protection: a study of their personal rule, their constitutional position and their future. London: Williams & Norgate, 1929. 240p.

09358 CLUNES, J. Historical sketch of the princes of India - stipendiary, subsidiary, protected and feudatory. Edinburgh: Smith, Elder, 1833. 209p.

09359 CORFIELD, C. The princely India I knew, from Reading to Mountbatten. Madras: Indo British Hist. Soc., 1975. 199p.

09360 CREAGH COEN, T. The Indian political service: a study in indirect rule. London: Chatto & Windus, 1971. 291p.

09361 DAS, T.N. Sovereign rights of the Indian princes. Madras: Ganesh, 1924. 104p.

09362 FITZE, K. Twilight of the maharajas. London: Murray, 1956. 180p.

09363 KNIGHT, L.A. The Royal Titles Act and India. In HJ 11,3 (1968) 488-507.

09364 MEHTA, M.S. Lord Hastings and the Indian States Bombay: D.B. Taraporevala, 1930. 275p.

09365 NEOGY, A.K. The paramount power and the princely states of India, 1858-1881. Calcutta: K.P. Bagchi, 1979. 323p.

09366 NICHOLSON, A.P. Scraps of paper: India's broken treaties, her princes, and the problem. London: E. Benn, 1930. 354p.

09367 PANIKKAR, K.M. Evolution of British policy towards Indian states, 1774-1858. Calcutta: S.K. Lahiri, 1929. 117p.

09368 ______. An introduction to the study of the relations of Indian states with the government of India. London: Hopkinson, 1927. 169p.

09369 Paramountcy in practice, by a retired Indian states officer. ND: New India, 1936. 224p.

09370 PRASAD, S.N. Paramountcy under Dalhousie. Being a thesis on the policy of Dalhousie towards the protected Indian states. Delhi: Ranjit, 1964. 222p.

09371 SASTRY, K.R.R. Treaties, engagements and sanads of the Indian states. Allahabad: author, 1942. 316p.

09372 SHARMA, H. Princes and paramountcy. ND: Arnold-Heinemann, 1978. 183p.

09373 SRINIVASACHARI, C.S. The inwardness of British annexation in India. Madras: U. of Madras, 1951. 221p.

09374 TUPPER, C.L., comp. Indian political practice; a collection of the decisions of the Government of India in political cases. Delhi: B.R., 1974. 4 v.

09375 ______. Our Indian protectorate: an introduction to the study of the relations between the British Government and its Indian feudatories. London: Longmans, Green, 1893. 426p.

4. Moves Toward Federation and Integration: the Chamber of Princes (Est. 1921), and the Govt. of India Act, 1935

09376 GREAT BRITAIN. INDIAN STATES CMTEE. Indian States Committee, 1928. Oral evidence recorded before the committee. n.p., 1929?. 794p.

09377 ______. Report of the Indian States committee, 1928-29. London: H.M.S.O., 1929. 74p. (Cmd. 3302; Parl. Pap. 1928/29:6) [Chm: H. Butler]

09378 HANDA, R.L. History of freedom struggle in princely states. ND. Central News Agency, 1968. 414p.

09379 INDIA. CHAMBER OF PRINCES. The British crown and the Indian states; an outline sketch drawn up on behalf of the standing committee of the Chamber of Princes by the directorate of the Chamber's special organization. London: P.S. King, 1929.

09380 PANIKKAR, K.M. The Indian princes in Council. A record of the Chancellorship of His Highness the Maharaja of Patiala, 1926-1931, and 1933-1936. London: University Press, 1936. 183p.

09381 PHADNIS, U. Towards the integration of Indian states, 1919-1947. London: Asia, 1968. 297p.

09382 RAMUSACK, B.N. The princes of India in the twilight of Empire: dissolution of a patron-client system, 1914-1939. Columbus: Ohio State U. Press, 1978. 322p.

09383 RICHTER, W.L. & B. RAMUSACK. The chamber and the consultation: changing forms of princely association in India. In JAS 34,3 (1975) 755-76.

D. Foreign Relations of the Government of India

1. General Diplomatic History; Relations with Western Nations

09384 ABUL KHAIR, M. United States foreign policy in the Indo-Pakistan subcontinent, 1939-1947. Dacca: ASP, 1968. 128p. (Its pub., 22)

09385 BAROOAH, N.K. India and the official Germany, 1886-1914. Frankfurt: P. Lang, 1977. 254p.

09386 BHAGAT, G. Americans in India, 1784-1860. NY: NYU Press, 1970. 195p.

09387 HESS, G.R. America encounters India, 1941-1947. Baltimore: Johns Hopkins Press, 1971. 211p.

09388 MANCHANDA, M.K. India and America: historical links, 1776-1920. Chandigarh: Young Men Harmilap Assn., 1976. 236p.

09389 PRASAD, BISHESHWAR. The foundations of India's foreign policy, 1860-1882. 2nd ed. Delhi: Ranjit, 1967. 277p. [1st pub. 1955]

09390 ______. Foundations of India's foreign policy: imperial era, 1882-1914. Calcutta: Naya Prokash, 1979. 596p.

09391 ______. Our foreign policy legacy: a study of British Indian foreign policy. ND: PPH, 1965. 89p.

09392 SHARMA, A.P. India's external relations under Lord Curzon, 1899-1905. Ranchi: Subodh Granthmala Karyalaya, 1978. 374p.

09393 VENKATARAMANI, M.S. & B.K. SHRIVASTAVA. America and the Indian political crisis, July-August 1942. In IS 6 (1964) 1-48.

09394 VERMA, D.N. India and the League of Nations. Patna: Bharati Bhawan, 1968. 350p.

2. India as a Part of the British Empire and Commonwealth; Relations with the Middle East

09395 ALDER, G.J. India and the Crimean War. In JICH 2,1 (1973) 15-37.

09396 BUSCH, B.C. Britain, India, and the Arabs, 1914-1921. Berkeley: UCalP, 1971. 522p.

09397 DOMIN, D. Aspects of India's position within the British Empire (1832-1917). In QRHS 15,2 (1975-76) 63-76.

09398 ELLINWOOD, D.C. The Round Table Movement and India, 1909-1920. In JComPolS 9,3 (1971) 183-209.

09399 KUMAR, RAVINDER. India and the Persian Gulf region, 1858-1907; a study in British imperial policy. Bombay: Asia, 1965. 259p.

09400 MEHROTRA, S.R. The Commonwealth and the nation. ND: Vikas, 1978. 168p.

09401 ______. India and the Commonwealth, 1885-1929. NY: Praeger, 1965. 287p.

09402 SHUKLA, R.L. Britain, India, and the Turkish Empire, 1853-1882. ND: PPH, 1973. 262p.

09403 TOMLINSON, B.R. India and the British Empire, 1880-1935. In IESHR 12 (1975) 337-80.

09404 WILBUR, M.K.E. The East India Company and the British Empire in the Far East. NY: Russell & Russell, 1970. 477p. [Rpt. 1945 ed.]

3. Relations with Burma: British Conquest and Annexation 1824-1886; a Province of India 1886-1935

09405 POLLACK, O.B. Empires in collision: Anglo-Burmese relations in the mid-nineteenth century. Westport, CT: Greenwood Press, 1980. 214p.

09406 SINGHAL, DAMODAR P. Annexation of Upper Burma. Singapore: Eastern Universities Press, 1960. 129p.

09407 STEWART, A.T.Q. The pagoda war: Lord Dufferin and the fall of the Kingdom of Ava, 1885-6. London: Faber, 1972. 223p.

4. The "Great Game" of British-Russian Rivalry in Central Asia

a. general studies

09408 ABROL, M. British relations with frontier states, 1863-1875. ND: S. Chand, 1974. 157p.

09409 BAJPAI, S.C. The northern frontier of India: central and western sector. Bombay: Allied, 1970. 223p.

09410 CHAKRAVARTI, P.C. The evolution of India's northern borders. NY: Asia Pub. House, 1971. 179p.

09411 CHAVDA, V.K. India, Britain, Russia; a study in British opinion, 1838-1878. Delhi: Sterling, 1967. 245p.

09412 CURZON, G.N. Russia in central Asia in 1889 and the Anglo-Russian question. NY: Barnes & Noble, 1967. 477p. [1st pub. 1889]

09413 EDWARDES, M. Playing the great game: a Victorian cold war. London: Hamilton, 1975. 167p.

09414 GREAVES, R. Persia and the defense of India; a study of the foreign policy of the 3rd Marquis of Salisbury. London: Athlone Press, 1959. 301p.

09415 HOGBEN, W.M. A century of British political-military friction on the North-west Frontier of India. In CAS 10 (1977) 94-103.

09416 INGRAM, E. The rules of the Game: a commentary on the defence of British India, 1798-1829. In JICH 3,2 (1975) 257-79.

09417 MACMUNN, G.F. The romance of the Indian frontiers. Quetta: Nisa Traders, 1978. 351p.+20pl. [Rpt. 1931 ed.]

09418 RAWLINSON, H.C. England and Russia in the East. A series of papers on the political and geographical condition of Central Asia. London: J. Murray, 1875. 393p.

09419 SOLOV'YEV, O.F. Russia's relations with India 1800-1917. In Central Asian R. 6 (1958) 448-64.

09420 TERWAY, V. East India Company and Russia, 1800-1857. ND: S. Chand, 1977. 232p.

b. Afghanistan and the north-west frontier

09421 BILGRAMI, A.H. Afghanistan and British India, 1793-1907; a study in foreign relations. ND: Sterling, 1972. 360p.

09422 BRUCE, R.I. The Forward Policy and its results; thirty-five years' work amongst the tribes on our north-western frontier of India. London: Longmans, Green, 1900. 28 + 382p. [Rpt. Quetta, 1977]

09423 DURAND, HENRY MARION. The First Afghan War and its causes. Ed. by Sir Henry Mortimer Durand. London: Longmans, Green, 1879.

09424 ELPHINSTONE, M. An account of the Kingdom of Caubul, and its dependencies in Persia, Tartary and India.... London: R. Bentley, 1842. 2 v. [1st pub. 1815]

09425 EYRE, V. The military operations at Cabul, which ended in the retreat and destruction of the British Army, January 1842: with a journal of imprisonment in Afghanistan. Peshawar: Qami Maktaba, 1977. 436p. [Rpt. 1843 ed.]

09426 FREDERICKS, P.G. The sepoy and the cossack. London: W.H. Allen, 1972. 279p.

09427 HANNA, H.B. The Second Afghan War, 1878-79-80; its causes, its conduct, and its consequences. Westminster: A. Constable, 1899-1904. 2 v.

09428 HARRIS, L. The frontier route from Peshawar to Chitral: political and strategic aspects of the forward policy, 1889-1896. In CAS 1 (1971) 81-108.

09429 HENSMAN, H. The Afghan war of 1879-80: being a complete narrative of the capture of Cabul.... Lahore: Sang-e-Meel, 1978. 567p. [Rpt. 1881 ed.]

09430 HUTTENBACK, R.A. The "Great Game" in the Pamirs and the Hindu-Kush: the British conquest of Hunza and Nagar. In MAS 9,1 (1975) 1-29.

09431 INDIA. ARMY. The third Afghan war, 1919; official account, comp. in the General staff branch, Army HQ India. Calcutta: Govt. of India Central Pub. Branch, 1926. 174p.

09432 INDIA. INTELLIGENCE BRANCH (ARMY). The second Afghan war, 1878-80. Abridged official account. London: Murray, 1908. 734p.

09433 JAECKEL, H. Die Nordwestgrenze in der Verteidigung Indiens 1900-1908, und der Weg Englands zum russisch-britischen Abkommen von 1907. Köln: Westdeutschen Verlag, 1968. 296p.

09434 MACRORY, P. The fierce pawns. NY: J.B. Lippincott, 1966. 352p.

09435 NORRIS, J.A. The first Afghan war: 1838-42. Cambridge: CamUP, 1967. 500p.

09436 SINGHAL, D.P. India and Afghanistan, 1876-1907. A study in diplomatic relations. Brisbane: U. of Queensland Press, 1963. 216p.

09437 SYKES, P.M. The Right Honourable Sir Mortimer Durand: a biography. Lahore: al-Biruni, 1977. 355p. [Rpt. 1926 ed.]

09438 TRIPATHI, G.P. Indo-Afghan relations, 1882-1907. ND: Kumar Bros., 1973. 203p.

c. Tibet and the Himalayan frontier

09439 BIDYA NAND. British India and Tibet. ND: Oxford & IBH, 1975. 166p.

09440 CHOUDHURY, D.P. The north-east frontier of India. In MAS 4,4 (1970) 359-65.

09441 ______. The north-east frontier of India, 1865-1914. Calcutta: Asiatic Soc., 1978. 186p.

09442 FLEMING, P. Bayonets to Lhasa: the first full account of the British invasion of Tibet in 1904. London: Hart-Davis, 1961. 319p.

09443 GHOSH, S. Tibet in Sino-Indian relations, 1899-1914. ND: Sterling, 1977. 228p.

09444 LAMB, A. Britain and Chinese central Asia. The road to Lhasa, 1767 to 1905. London: Routledge & Kegan Paul, 1960. 388p.

09445 ______. The McMahon line: a study in the relations between India, China and Tibet, 1904 to 1914. London: Routledge & Kegan Paul, 1966. 2 v.

09446 MEHRA, P. The McMahon line and after: a study of the triangular contest on India's north-eastern frontier between Britain, China, and Tibet, 1904-47. Delhi: Macmillan, 1974. 497p.

09447 ______. The north-eastern frontier: a documentary study of the internecine rivalry between India, Tibet, and China. Delhi: OUP, 1979.

09448 ______. Younghusband expedition: an interpretation. Bombay: Asia, 1968. 408p.

09449 SEAVER, G. Francis Younghusband, explorer and mystic. London: Murray, 1952. 391p.

09450 WOODCOCK, G. Into Tibet: the early British explorers. London: Faber & Faber, 1971. 277p.

09451 WOODMAN, D. Himalayan frontiers: a political review of British, Chinese, Indian and Russian rivalries. NY: Barrie & Jenkins, 1970. 423p.

09452 YOUNGHUSBAND, F.E. The heart of a continent, commemorating the fiftieth anniversary of his journey from Peking to India by way of the Gobi desert and Chinese Turkestan, and across the Himalaya by the Mustagh Pass. London: J. Murray, 1937. 246p. [First acct. pub. 1896]

09453 ______. India and Tibet; a history of the relations which have subsisted between the two countries from the time of Warren Hastings to 1910, with a particular account of the mission to Lhasa of 1904. Delhi: Oriental, 1971. 455p. [1st pub. 1910]

III. GROWTH OF INDIAN NATIONALISM IN RESPONSE TO EXPANDING BRITISH POWER (TO 1919)

A. Background to Nationalism: Early Civil and Military Discontent

1. Early Opposition to British Rule (to 1857)

09454 CHAUDHURI, S.B. Civil disturbances during the British rule in India (1765-1857). Calcutta: World Press, 1955. 231p.

09455 DATTA, K.K. Anti-British plots and movements before 1857. Meerut: Meenakshi, 1970. 152p.

09456 DHARAMPAL. Civil disobedience and Indian tradition; with some early nineteenth century documents. Varanasi: Sarva Seva Sangh Prakashan, 1971. 64+122p.

09457 GHOSH, S. & A. GHOSH. British India's first freedom movement, 1820-1830. Calcutta: KLM, 1979-. v. 1-

2. 1857: "Sepoy Mutiny" or "War of Independence"?

a. bibliography and historiography

09458 ADAS, M. Twentieth century approaches to the Indian mutiny of 1857-58. In JAH 5 (1971) 1-19.

09459 ASHRAF, KUNWAR MUHAMMED. Muslim revivalists and the revolt of 1857. Ed. by P.C. Joshi. ND: PPH, 1957.

09460 CHAUDHURI, S.B. English historical writings on the Indian mutiny, 1857-1859. Calcutta: World Press, 1979. 368p.

09461 ______. Theories of the Indian mutiny (1857-59); a study of the views of an eminent historian on the subject. Calcutta: World Press, 1965. 207p. [critique of R.C. Majumdar]

09462 CHAUDHURI, S. The literature on the rebellion in India in 1857-9: a bibliography. Calcutta: KLM, 1971. 29p.

09463 EMBREE, A.T., ed. 1857 in India: mutiny or war of independence? Boston: D.C. Heath, 1963. 101p. (Problems in Asian civilizations)

09464 MALIK, SALAHUDDIN. Nineteenth century approaches to the Indian "mutiny." In JAH 7 (1973) 95-127.

09465 LADENDORF, J.M. The revolt in India 1857-58. An annotated bibliography of English language materials. Zug: Inter Documentation Co., 1966. 191p.

09466 SEN, S.N. Writings on the mutiny. In C.H. Philips, ed. Historians of India, Pakistan, and Ceylon. London: OUP, 1961, 373-84.

09467 SEN GUPTA, K.K. Recent writings on the revolt of 1857: a survey. ND: ICHR, 1975. 70p.

09468 SINGH, S.D. Novels on the Indian mutiny. ND: Arnold-Heinemann, 1973. 248p.

b. document collections

09469 FORREST, G.W., ed. The Indian mutiny, 1857-58: selections from the letters, despatches and other state papers preserved in the Military Department of the Government of India, 1857-58. Calcutta: Govt. of India, 1893-1912. 4 v.

09470 GREAT BRITAIN. PARLIAMENT. HOUSE OF COMMONS. Papers on mutiny of native regiments.... London: 1857, (v. 30) sessional papers: C. 2252, 2254, 2264-66, 2277; and 1857-58 (v. 44): C. 2294-95, 2330, 2351, 2363, 2448-49.

09471 Mutiny reports from Punjab and N.W.F.P. Lahore: Al-Biruni, 1976. 2 v., 408, 371p. [Rpt. of 1911 ed.]

09472 RIZVI, S.A.A. & M.L. BHARGAVA, eds. Freedom struggle in Uttar Pradesh: source material. Lucknow: Pub. Bureau, Info. Dept., Uttar Pradesh, 1957-61. 6 v. [v. 1, 1857-59, nature and origin; v. 2, Awadh, 1857-59; v. 3, Bundelkhand and adjoining territories, 1857-59; v. 4, Eastern and adjoining districts, 1857-59; v. 5, Western districts and Rohilkhand, 1857-59; v. 6, consolidated index and chronology]

c. selected personal accounts and biographies [for more of this huge literature, see bibliographies in a. above]

09473 CAMPBELL, C. Narrative of the Indian revolt from its outbreak to the capture of Lucknow. London: G. Vickers, 1858. 452p.

09474 DUBERLY, F.I.L. Suppression of mutiny, 1857-1858. ND: Sirjana Press, 1974. 168p. [1st ed. 1859]

09475 EDWARDS, W. Personal adventures during the Indian rebellion in Rohilcund, Futtehghur, and Oude. 4th ed. Allahabad: Legend Pub., 1974. 206p.

09476 GHALIB, A.K. Dastanbūy; a diary of the Indian revolt of 1857. Tr. from Persian by Khwaja Ahmad Faruqi. NY: Asia, 1970. 96p.

09477 HUTCHINSON, D., ed. N.A. Chick: annals of the Indian rebellion 1857-58. London: C. Knight, 1974. 293p.

09478 JACOB, G.L. Western India before and during the mutinies: picture drawn from life. London: King, 1871. 262p.

09479 MAJENDIE, V.D. Up among the Pandies; or, a year's service in India. Allahabad: Legend Pub., 1974. 360p. [Rpt. 1859 ed.]

09480 METCALFE, C.T., tr. & ed. Two native narratives of the mutiny in Delhi. Delhi: Seema, 1974. 259p. [Rpt. 1898 ed.]

09481 PRICHARD, I.T. The mutinies in Rajpootana: being a personal narrative of the mutiny.... Ajmer: Shabd Sanchar, 1976. 312p. [1st pub. 1860]

09482 RAIKES, C. Notes on the revolt in the north-western provinces of India. London: Longman, Brown, Green, Longmans, & Roberts, 1858. 195p.

09483 RUSSELL, W.H. My India mutiny diary. Ed. by M. Edwardes. London: Cassel, 1957. 288p. [Abridgement of 2 v. 1860 ed.; Russell was correspondent for The Times, London]

09484 SHERER, J.W. Daily life during the Indian mutiny: personal experiences of 1857. Allahabad: Legend Pub., 1974. 197p. [1st pub. 1898]

09485 WILBERFORCE, R.G. An unrecorded chapter of the Indian mutiny: being the personal reminiscences of Reginald G. Wilberforce, late 52nd Light Infantry compiled from a diary and letters written on the spot. Gurgaon: Academic Press, 1976. 234p. [1st pub. 1894]

d. history of the revolt of 1857-59
i. nineteenth century British accounts

09486 BURNE, O.T. Clyde and Strathnairn: the suppression of the great revolt. Oxford: OUP, 1895. 194p. (Rulers of India)

09487 FORREST, G.W. A history of the Indian mutiny, reviewed and illustrated from original documents. London: Wm. Blackwood, 1904-1912. 3 v.

09488 HOLMES, T.R.E. History of the Indian mutiny. 5th ed. London: Macmillan, 1913. 659p. [1st pub. 1883]

09489 HUTCHINSON, G. Narrative of the mutinies in Oude, comp. from authentic records. London: Smith, Elder, 1859. 256p. [Done under British govt. auspices.]

09490 KAYE, J.W. & G.B. MALLESON. Kaye's and Malleson's history of the Indian mutiny, 1857-8. London: W.H. Allen, 1889-93. 6 v.

ii. reinterpretations by Marxists, nationalists, and twentieth century scholars

09491 AHMAD KHAN, SYED. The causes of the Indian revolt, written by Sir Syed Ahmed Khan Bahadur in Urdu in the year 1858 and translated into English by his two European friends. Lahore: Book House, 1970. 86p. [1st pub. 1875]

09492 BRODKIN, E.I. The struggle for succession: rebels and loyalists in the Indian mutiny of 1857. In MAS 6,3 (1972) 277-90.

09493 CHATTOPADHYAYA, H.P. The sepoy mutiny, 1857: a social study and analysis. Calcutta: Bookland, 1957. 234p.

09494 CHAUDHURY, N.A. Great rising of 1857 and the repression of Muslims. Lahore: Punjab Govt. Printing Press, 1970. 70p. (Punjab Govt. record office pub., monograph 22)

09495 CHAUDHURI, S.B. Civil rebellion in the Indian mutinies, 1857-1859. Calcutta: World Press, 1957. 367p.

09496 DATTA, K.K. Reflections on the "Mutiny." Calcutta: U. of Calcutta, 1967. 82p.

09497 DHARAIYA, R.K. Gujarat in 1857. Ahmedabad: Gujarat U., 1970. 180p.

09498 GUPTA, P.C. Nana Sahib and the rising at Cawnpore. Oxford: OUP, 1963. 227p.

09499 JOSHI, P.C., ed. Rebellion, 1857: a symposium. ND: PPH, 1957. 355p.

09500 LUTFULLAH, Syed. Azimullah Khan Yusufzai, the man behind the war of independence, 1857. 2nd ed. Karachi: Mohamedali Educ. Soc., 1970. 197p.

09501 MAJUMDAR, R.C. The sepoy mutiny and the revolt of 1857. 2nd ed. Calcutta: KLM, 1963. 503p.

09502 MALIK, H. & M. DEMBO. Sir Sayyid Ahmad Khan's history of the Bijnor rebellion. East Lansing: Asian Studies Center, Michigan State U., 1972. 163p. (South Asia series, occ. paper, 17)

09503 MALIK, SALAHUDDIN. The Panjab and the Indian "mutiny": a reassessment. In Islamic Studies 15,2 (1976) 81-110.

09504 MARX, KARL & F. ENGELS. The first Indian war of independence 1857-1859. Moscow: Progress, 1968. 226p.

09505 PALMER, J.A.B. The mutiny outbreak at Meerut in 1857. Cambridge: CamUP, 1966. 175p.

09506 QURESHI, I.H. Causes of the war of independence. In Pakistan Historical Society. History of the Freedom Movement.... Karachi: Pakistan Hist. Soc., 1957-61, v. 2 (1831-1905), pt. 1, 230-69.

09507 SAVARKAR, V.D. The Indian war of independence of 1857, by an Indian nationalist. Bombay: Phoenix Pub., 1947. 552p. [1st pub. 1909]

09508 SEN, S.N. Eighteen fifty-seven. ND: PDMIB, 1977. 468p. + 8 pl. [1st pub. 1957]

09509 SRIVASTAVA, M.P. The Indian mutiny, 1857. Allahabad: Chugh, 1979. 249p.

09510 STOKES, E. Traditional resistance movements and Afro-Asian nationalism: the context of the 1857 mutiny rebellion in India. In his The peasant and the Raj.... Cambridge: CamUP, 1978, 120-40. [1st pub. in P&P 48 (1970)]

09511 THOMPSON, E.J. The other side of the medal. NY: Harcourt, Brace, 1926. 142p.

09512 YADAV, K.C. The revolt of 1857 in Haryana. ND: Manohar Book Service, 1977. 192p.

iii. some recent popular narratives

09513 CARDWELL, P. The Indian mutiny. London: Longman, 1975. 112p.

09514 COSENS, F.R. & C.L. WALLACE. Fategarh and the mutiny. Karachi: Indus Pub., 1978. 276p. [Rpt. 1933 ed.]

09515 EDWARDES, M. Red year: the Indian rebellion of 1857. London: Hamilton, 1973. 251p.

09516 ______. A season in hell: the defence of the Lucknow Residency. London: Hamilton, 1973. 330p.

09517 HARRIS, J. The Indian mutiny. London: Hart-Davis MacGibbon, 1973. 205p.

09518 HIBBERT, C. The great mutiny: India, 1857. NY: Viking Press, 1978. 472p.

09519 LLEWELLYN, A. The siege of Delhi. London: MacDonald & Jane's, 1977. 182p.

09520 SINHA, S.N. Rani Lakshmi Bai of Jhansi. Allahabad: Chugh, 1980. 134p.

e. aftermath and effects

09521 METCALF, T.R. The aftermath of revolt: India, 1857-1870. Princeton: PUP, 1964. 352p.

09522 RAJ, JAGDISH. The mutiny and British land policy in North India, 1856-1868. Bombay: Asia, 1965. 191p.

09523 TINKER, H. 1857 and 1957. The mutiny and modern India. In Intl. Affairs 34 (1958) 57-65.

B. Indian Nationalism and the "Freedom Movement"--General Histories and Studies

1. Bibliography and Reference

09524 GHOSH, A. & R. GHOSH. Indian political movement, 1919-1971: a systematic bibliography. Calcutta: India Book Exchange, dist. K.P. Bagchi, 1976. 499p.

09525 INDIAN NATIONAL CONGRESS. Congress Handbook. Allahabad: Swaraj Bhawan, 1946. 294p.

09526 MCCULLY, B.T. Bibliographic article: the origin of Indian nationalism according to native writers. In J. of Modern History 7 (1970) 215-314.

09527 SEN, S.P., ed. Historical writings on the nationalist movement in India. Calcutta: IHS, 1977. 251p.

09528 SHARMA, J.S. AICC circulars, a descriptive bibliography (March 23, 1940 - July 28, 1950). ND: INC, 1957. 44p. (Natl. bibl., 4)

09529 ______. Indian National Congress: a descriptive bibliography of India's struggle for freedom. 2nd ed. Delhi: S. Chand, 1971. 816 + 131p. (Natl. bibl., 3)

2. Histories of Modern Indian Political Thought

09530 APPADORAI, A. Indian political thinking in the twentieth century, from Naoroji to Nehru; an introductory survey. Madras: OUP, 1971. 189p.

09531 ______, ed. Documents on political thought in Modern India. Bombay: OUP, 1973. 2 v., 892p.

09532 BROWN, D.M. The nationalist movement: Indian political thought from Ranade to Bhave. Berkeley: UCalP, 1970. 244p. [1st pub. 1960]

09533 BUCH, M.A. The development of contemporary Indian political thought. Baroda: Good Companions, 1938-40. 3 v.

09534 GHOSE, S. Political ideas and movements in India. Bombay: Allied, 1975. 558p.

09535 ______. Socialism, democracy, and nationalism in India. Bombay: Allied, 1973. 503p.

09536 JHA, M.N. Modern Indian political thought: Ram Mohan Roy to present day. Meerut: Meenakshi, 1975. 348p.

09537 KARUNAKARAN, K.P. Continuity and change in Indian politics; a study of the political philosophy of the Indian national movement, 1885-1921. ND: PPH, 1962. 204p.

09538 ______. Indian politics from Dadabhai Naoroji to Gandhi: a study of the political ideas of modern India. ND: Gitanjali, 1975. 226p.

09539 ______. Modern Indian political tradition. NY: Allied, 1962. 452p.

09540 MAJUMDAR, B.B. History of Indian social and political ideas, from Rammohan to Dayananda. Calcutta: Bookland, 1967. 332p. [1st pub. 1934]

09541 NARAVANE, V.S. Modern Indian thought. ND: Orient Longman, 1978. 300p.

09542 RAGHUVANSHI, V.P.S. Indian nationalist movement and thought. Agra: L.N. Agarwal, 1959. 335p.

09543 SAXENA, K. Modern Indian political thought: Gandhism and Roy's new humanism. ND: Chetana, 1978. 250p.

09544 SHARMA, G.N. & M. SHAKIR. Politics and society, Ram Mohan Roy to Nehru. Aurangabad: Parimal, 1976. 392p.

09545 VARMA, V.P. Modern Indian political thought. 4th rev. & enl. ed. Agra: Agarwal, 1971. 640p.

3. History of Indian Nationalism and the Independence Movement

a. interpretations by contemporaries, Indian and British

09546 BESANT, A. India, bond or free? A world problem. London: G.P. Putnam's, 1926. 126p.

09547 DAS, D. India from Curzon to Nehru and after. NY: John Day, 1970. 487p.

09548 LAJPAT RAI, Lala. Young India; an interpretation and a history of the nationalist movement from within. Delhi: PDMIB, 1965. 199p. [1st ed. 1916]

09549 LOVETT, H.V. A history of the Indian Nationalist movement. London: Cass, 1968. 303p. [Rpt. of 3rd ed., 1921]

09550 MOON, P. Strangers in India. Westport, CT: Greenwood, 1972. 212p. [1st pub. 1945]

09551 NEVINSON, H.W. The new spirit in India. Delhi: Metropolitan Book Co., 1975. 353p. + 35 pl. [Rpt. 1908 ed.]

09552 THOMPSON, E.J. Reconstruction of India. London: Faber & Faber, 1930. 320p.

09553 ZETLAND, LAWRENCE JOHN LUMLEY DUNDAS, 2nd marquis of. The heart of Aryavarta; a study of the psychology of Indian unrest.... London: Constable, 1925. 262p.

b. post-independence assessments of the nationalist movement

09554 AGGARWALA, R.N. Indian national movement, 1885-1947. Delhi: Metropolitan Book Co., 1971. 265p.

09555 VISHNOO BHAGWAN. Constitutional history of India and national movement. 3rd rev. ed. Delhi: Atma Ram, 1972. 322 + 354p.

09556 BOSE, N.S. The Indian national movement; an outline. Calcutta: KLM, 1974. 150p.

09557 CHAND, TARA. History of the freedom movement in India. Rev. ed. Delhi: PDMIB, 1965-72. 4 v.

09558 CHANDRA, BIPAN & A. TRIPATHI & BARUN DE. Freedom struggle. ND: National Book Trust, India, 1972. 228p.

09559 CHOUDHARY, S. Growth of nationalism in India. ND: Trimurti, 1973. 2 v.

09560 EMBREE, A.T. India's search for national identity. NY: Knopf, 1972. 138p.

09561 GANGADHARAN, K.K., ed. Indian national consciousness: growth and development. ND: Kalamkar, 1972. 330p.

09562 GHOSE, S. The western impact on Indian politics, 1885-1919. Bombay: Allied, 1967. 247p.

09563 GUPTA, D.C. Indian national movement. Delhi: Vikas, 1970. 270p.

09564 MCLANE, J.R., ed. The political awakening in India. Englewood Cliffs, NJ: Prentice-Hall, 1970. 182p.

09565 MAHAJAN, V.D. The nationalist movement in India. ND: Sterling, 1975-1976. 2 v.

09566 MAJUMDAR, B.B. Indian political associations and reform of legislature, 1818-1917. Calcutta: KLM, 1965. 477p.

09567 MAJUMDAR, R.C. History of the freedom movement in India. 2nd rev. ed. Calcutta: KLM, 1971-72. 3 v., 1739p. [1st ed. 1962-63]

09568 MASSELOS, J. Nationalism on the Indian subcontinent; an introductory history. Melbourne: T. Nelson, 1972. 227p.

09569 MEHROTRA, S.R. Towards India's freedom and partition. ND: Vikas, 1979. 322p.

09570 MUKHERJEE, S.N. The movement for national freedom in India. Oxford: OUP, 1966. 114p. (St. Anthony papers, 18, South Asian affairs, 2)

09571 PAKISTAN HISTORICAL SOCIETY. A history of the freedom movement (being the story of the Muslim struggle for the freedom of Hind-Pakistan, 1707-1947). Karachi: 1957-70. 4 v. in 6, 1612p.

09572 PANDEY, B.N., ed. The Indian nationalist movement, 1885-1947: select documents. NY: St. Martin's, 1978.

09573 POCHHAMMER, W. VON. Indiens Weg zur Nation. Bremen: Schünemann, 1973. 920p.

09574 RAM GOPAL. How India struggled for freedom; a political history. Bombay: Book Centre, 1967. 469p.

09575 RAY, N.R. Nationalism in India. An historical analysis of its stresses and strains. Aligarh: Aligarh Muslim U., 1973. 180p.

09576 ROTHERMUND, D. The phases of Indian nationalism and other essays. Bombay: Nachiketa, 1970. 270p.

09577 ROY, S. Indian politics and constitutional development. ND: Meenakshi, 1976. 250p.

09578 SEAL, A. The emergence of Indian nationalism: competition and collaboration in the later nineteenth century. London: CamUP, 1968. 416p.

09579 SMITH, W.R. Nationalism and reform in India. New Haven: YUP, 1938. 485p.

09580 SREEKUMARAN NAIR, M.P. Reappraisal: studies on Indian national movement. Trivandrum: Kerala Hist. Soc., 1972. 91p.

09581 SANTHANAM, K.I. British imperialism and Indian nationalism. Bombay: BVB, 1972. 62p.

09582 SUDHIR CHANDRA. Dependence and disillusionment: emergence of national consciousness in later 19th century India. ND: Manas, 1975. 195p.

c. role of women in the freedom movement

09583 AGNEW, V. Elite women in Indian politics. ND: Vikas, 1979. 163p.

09584 BASU, APARNA. The role of women in the Indian struggle for freedom. In B.R. Nanda, ed. Indian women: from purdah to modernity. ND: Vikas, 1976, 16-40.

09585 KAUR, M.M. Role of women in the freedom movement (1857-1947). ND: Sterling, 1968. 298p.

09586 ROY CHOWDHURY, B. Madame Cama: a short life-sketch. ND: PPH, 1977. 34p.

4. Collective and Comparative Biographies of National Leaders

09587 AMBEDKAR, B.R. Ranade, Gandhi, and Jinnah. Jullundur: Bheem Patrika Pub., 1964. 64p. [Rpt. of 1943 speech]

09588 GUPTA, S.K. Gandhi-Jawaharlal confluence. ND: Oriental, 1976. 295p.

09589 HUTHEESING, K.N. We Nehrus. NY: Holt, Rinehart & Winston, 1967. 343p.

09590 KULKARNI, V.B. The Indian triumvirate; a political biography of Mahatma Gandhi, Sardar Patel, and Pandit Nehru. Bombay: BVB, 1969. 728p.

09591 LAMB, B.P. The Nehrus of India; three generations of leadership. NY: Macmillan, 1967. 276p.

09592 MAJUMDAR, S.K. Jinnah and Gandhi; their role in India's quest for freedom. Calcutta: KLM, 1966. 310p.

09593 MURTHI, R.K. Foreigners who served India. ND: Allora, 1979. 160p. + 8 pl.

09594 NANDA, B.R. Gokhale, Gandhi, and the Nehrus: studies in Indian nationalism. NY: St. Martin's, 1974. 203p.

09595 ______. The Nehrus, Motilal and Jawaharlal. London: Allen & Unwin, 1962. 357p.

09596 PARAMESWARAN, P., ed. Gandhi, Lohia and Deendayal. ND: Deendayal Res. Inst., 1978. 165p.

09597 WOLPERT, S.A. Tilak and Gokhale: revolution and reform in the making of modern India. Berkeley: UCalP, 1962. 370p.

5. Social Background of Nationalists

09598 BASU, APARNA. The growth of education and political development in India, 1898-1920. ND: OUP, 1974. 258p.

09599 CHOPRA, P.N., ed. Role of Indian Muslims in the struggle for freedom. ND: Light & Life, 1979. 234p.

09600 DESAI, A.R. Social background of Indian nationalism. 4th ed. Bombay: Popular, 1966. 461p.

09601 GANGULI, B.N. Conceptualizing the Indian middle class. In K.S. Krishnaswamy et al., eds. Society and change.... Bombay: OUP, 1977, 20-33.

09602 KEMP, T. Leaders and classes in the Indian National Congress, 1918-1939. In Science & Society 28 (1964) 1-19.

09603 MCCULLY, B.T. English education and the origins of Indian nationalism. Gloucester, MA: P. Smith, 1966. 418p.

09604 ROTHERMUND, D. The role of the Western educated elite in political mass movements of India in the twentieth century. In his The phases of Indian nationalism and other essays. Bombay: Nachiketa, 1970, 144-62.

6. The Indian National Movement and the World: International Context and Relations

09605 BANDYOPADHYAY, J. Indian nationalism vs. international communism; role of ideology in international politics. Calcutta: KLM, 1966. 368p.

09606 BANERJEE, S.K. American interest in Indian independence. In IQ 24 (1968) 311-32.

09607 BIMLA PRASAD. The origins of Indian foreign policy; the Indian National Congress and world affairs, 1885-1947. 2nd ed. Calcutta: Bookland, 1962. 393p.

09608 BIRENDRA PRASAD. Indian nationalism and Asia, 1900-1947. Delhi: B.R., 1979. 260p.

09609 BOSE, A.C. Indian revolutionaries abroad, 1905-1922, in the background of international developments. Patna: Bharati Bhawan, 1971. 268p.

09610 CZEKUS, S., ed. The Great October, socialist community, and India. Bombay: Allied, 1978. 249p.

09611 DUA, R.P. The impact of the Russo-Japanese (1905) war on Indian politics. ND: S. Chand, 1966. 105p.

09612 HOPE. A.G. America and swaraj; the U.S. role in Indian independence. Washington: Public Affairs Press, 1968. 136p.

09613 IMAM, ZAFAR. Colonialism in East-West relations; a study of Soviet policy towards India and Anglo-Soviet relations, 1917-1947. ND: Eastman, 1969. 531p.

09614 JAUHRI, R.C. American diplomacy and independence for India. Bombay: Vora, 1970. 160p.

09615 JHA, M.R. Civil disobedience and after: the American reaction to political developments in India during 1930-1935. Meerut: Meenakshi, 1973. 300p.

09616 JOSHI, N. Foundations of Indo-Soviet relations: a study of non-official attitudes and contacts, 1917-1947. ND: Radiant, 1975. 204p.

09617 HARNAM SINGH. The Indian national movement and American opinion. Delhi: Central Electric Press, 1962. 400p.

09618 KEMP-ASHRAF, P.M. India and internationalism: a note on the early working class movement. In H. Krüger, ed. Kunwar Mohammed Ashraf; an Indian scholar and revolutionary, 1903-1962. Delhi: PPH, 1966, 187-223.

09619 KRASA, M. The idea of pan-Asianism and the nationalist movement in India. In AO 40 (1972) 238-260.

09620 ______. Relations between the Indian National Congress and the Wafd Party of Egypt in the thirties. In AO 41 (1973) 212-33.

09621 MEHROTRA, SRIRAM. The development of the Indian outlook on world affairs before 1947. In JDS 1 (1965) 269-94.

09622 MUZUMDAR, H.T. America's contributions to India's freedom. Allahabad: Central Book Depot, 1962. 51p.

09623 RAO, M.B., ed. Lenin and India. ND: PPH, 1970. 250p.

09624 SAREEN, T.R. Indian revolutionary movement abroad, 1905-1921. ND: Sterling, 1979. 300p.

09625 ______. Russian revolution and India: a study of Soviet policy towards Indian national movement, 1922-29. ND: Sterling, 1978. 164p.

09626 SINGH, D.P. American attitude towards the Indian nationalist movement. ND: Munshiram, 1974. 362p.

09627 SINHA, N.C. Asian relations and Gandhi. In IYIA 17 (1974) 510-23.

09628 SINHA, P.B. Indian national liberation movement and Russia, 1905-1917. ND: Sterling, 1975. 336p.

09629 SRIVASTAVA, N.M.P. Growth of nationalism in India; effects of international events. Meerut: Meenakshi, 1973. 207p.

C. The Indian National Congress (Est. 1885): The First All-India Organization for Political and Social Reform

1. General History of the INC

09630 AIYAR, R.P. & L.S. BHANDARE. The Congress caravan: the history of the Indian National Congress and of India's struggle for swaraj, 1885-1945. Bombay: Natl. Youth Pub., 1945. 151p.

09631 ANDREWS, C.F. & G.K. MOOKERJEE. The rise and growth of Congress in India, 1832-1920. 2nd ed. Meerut: Meenakshi, 1967. 204p. [1st pub. 1938]

09632 BESANT, A. How India wrought for freedom: the story of the National Congress told from official records. Adyar, Madras: TPH, 1915. 709p.

09633 DAS, M.N. Indian National Congress versus the British. Delhi: Ajanta, 1978-. v. 1, 424p.

09634 DAS GUPTA, H.N. Indian National Congress. Calcutta, J.K. Das Gupta, 1946. 288p.

09635 GHOSE, S. Indian National Congress, its history and heritage. ND: AICC, 1975. 390p.

09636 GHOSH, P.C. The development of the Indian National Congress, 1892-1909. Calcutta: KLM, 1960. 263p.

09637 INDIAN NATIONAL CONGRESS. Congress presidential addresses, 1911-34. Madras: Natesan, 1934-35. 2 v.

09638 ISWARA DUTT, K. Congress cyclopaedia; the Indian National Congress: 1885-1920. v. 1, the pre-Gandhi era. ND: K. Iswara Dutt, 1967. 388p. [Resolutions of first 35 Congress sessions, with analysis]

09639 KAUSHIK, H.P. The Indian National Congress in England, 1885-1920. Delhi: Research, 1972. 155p.

09640 KRIPALANI, J.B. Indian National Congress. Bombay: Vora, 1946. 65p.

09641 MAJUMDAR, B.B. & B.P. MAZUMDAR. Congress and congressmen in the pre-Gandhian era, 1885-1917. Calcutta: KLM, 1967. 527p.

09642 MEHROTRA, SRIRAM. The early organization of the Indian National Congress, 1885-1920. In IQ 22 (1966) 329-52.

09643 PATTABHI SITARAMAYYA, B. History of the Indian National Congress. Delhi: S. Chand, 1969. 2 v. [Rpt. of 1946-47 ed.] [The official history]

09644 ZAIDI, A.M. & S. ZAIDI. The encyclopedia of the Indian National Congress. ND: S. Chand, 1976-. [to be 18 v.]

2. The Founding (1885) and Early Years of Congress (to 1905): Emphasis on Moderation and Petition of Grievances

a. general studies

09645 CHATTERJI, N. The forgotten precursor of the Indian National Congress. In JIH 36 (1958) 9-14.

09646 CHAUDHARY, V.C.P. Imperial policy of British in India, 1876-1880; birth of Indian nationalism. Calcutta: Punthi Pustak, 1968. 398p.

09647 GUPTA, B.K. Connection with Britain as an issue in Indian nationalist politics, 1885-1905. In JIH 41 (1963) 489-516.

09648 MCLANE, J.R. Indian nationalism and the early Congress. Princeton: PUP, 1977. 404p.

09649 MARTIN, B. New India, 1885; British official policy and the emergence of the Indian National Congress. Berkeley: UCalP, 1969. 365p.

09650 MEHROTRA, SRIRAM. The emergence of the Indian National Congress. Delhi: Vikas, 1971. 461p.

b. early Congress leaders: A.O. Hume, W.C. Bonnerjee, Dadabhai Naoroji, Pherozeshah Mehta, Surendranath Banerjea

09651 BANERJEA, S.N. A nation in making; being the reminiscences of fifty years of public life. Bombay: OUP, 1963. 389p.

09652 BANERJEE, B. Surendranath Banerjea and history of modern India, 1848-1925. ND: Metropolitan, 1979. 256p.

09653 BONNERJEE, S. Life of W.C. Bonnerjee, first president of the Indian National Congress. Calcutta: Bhowanipore Press, 1944. 149p.

09654 BOSE, S.K. Surendranath Banerjea. ND: PDMIB, 1968. 224p.

09655 CUMPSTON, M. Some early Indian Nationalists and their allies in the British Parliament, 1851-1906. In English Hist. R. 76 (1961) 279-97.

09656 GOKHALE, B.G. Some aspects of Indian liberalism. In South Atlantic Q. 62 (1963) 275-85.

09657 MASANI, R.P. Dadabhai Naoroji. Delhi: PDMIB, 1960. 195p.

09658 ______. Dadabhai Naoroji: the grand old man of India. London: Allen & Unwin, 1939. 567p.

09659 NAOROJI, D. Dadabhai Naoroji correspondence. Ed. by R.P. Patwardhan. ND: Allied, 1977-. [v. 2, pt. 1&2, Corresp. with D.E. Wacha, 909p.]

09660 MEHTA, P.M. Some unpublished & later speeches & writings. Bombay: Commercial Press, 1918. 500p.

09661 ______. Speeches & writings. Ed. by C.Y. Chintamani. Allahabad: Indian Press, 1905. 826 + 79p.

09662 MODY, H. Pherozeshah Mehta. ND: PDMIB, 1963. 219p.

09663 ______. Sir Pherozeshah Mehta, a political biography. NY: Asia Pub. House, 1963. 400p. [Rpt. 1921 ed.]

09664 NAOROJI, D. Speeches and writings. Madras: Natesan, 1917. 686 + 216p.

09665 SHARMA, B. The concept of self government and the Indian liberals. In PSR 15 (1976) 62-84.

09666 SRINIVASA SASTRI, V.S. Life and times of Sir Pherozeshah Mehta. Ed. by S.R. Venkataraman. 2nd rev. ed. Bombay: BVB, 1975. 224p. [1st pub. 1945]

09667 WEDDERBURN, W. Allan Octavian Hume, C.B.: father of the Indian National Congress, 1829-1912. ND: Pegasus, 1974. 182p. [Rpt. 1913 ed.]

c. Gopal Krishna Gokhale (1866-1915), Congress Moderate leader, and member of Imperial Legislative Council: Disciple of M.G. Ranade and "political guru" of M.K. Gandhi

09668 DEOGIRIKAR, T.R. Gopal Krishna Gokhale. Delhi: PDMIB, 1964. 219p.

09669 GANDHI, M.K. Gokhale, my political guru. Ahmedabad: Navajivan, 1955. 67p.

09670 GOKHALE, G.K. Speeches and writings. Ed. by R.P. Patwardhan & D.V. Ambekar. Bombay: Asia, 1962-1967. 3 v.

09671 HOYLAND, J.S. Gopal Krishna Gokhale; his life and speeches. Calcutta: UMCA, 1947. 156p.

09672 MATHUR, D.B. Gokhale, a political biography; a study of his services and political ideas. Bombay: Manaktalas, 1966. 487p.

09673 NANDA, B.R. Gokhale: the Indian moderates and the British raj. Princeton: PUP, 1977. 520p.

09674 PARVATE, T.V. Gopal Krishna Gokhale. Ahmedabad: Navajivan, 1959. 484p.

09675 PATWARDHAN, R.P., ed. The select Gokhale. ND: Maharashtra Info. Centre, 1965. 423p.

09676 ROTHERMUND, D. Emancipation or re-integration. The politics of Gopal Krishna Gokhale and Herbert Hope Risley. In D.A. Low, ed. Soundings in modern South Asian history. Berkeley: UCalP, 1968, 131-58.

09677 SRINIVASA SASTRI, V.S. Life of Gopal Krishna Gokhale. Bangalore: Bangalore Printing and Pub., 1937. 138p.

09678 ______. My master Gokhale: selections from speeches and writings. Madras: Model, 1946. 276p.

D. The Politicization of Nationalism, 1905-19: From Lord Curzon's Raj to Gandhian Non-Cooperation; Rise of the Muslim League; the Great War, 1914-18

1. The Extremists and Revolutionaries: Religious Nationalism and Approval of Violence; Boycotts and the Swadeshi Movement

a. general studies

09679 ARGOV, D. Moderates and extremists in the Indian national movement, 1883-1920; with special reference to Surendranath Banerjea and Lajpat Rai. Bombay: Asia, 1967. 246p.

09680 CHAUDHRY, K.C. Role of religion in Indian politics, 1900-1925. Delhi: Sundeep, 1978. 347p.

09681 CHAUDHURI, K. The Mother and passionate politics. Calcutta: Vidyodaya Library, 1979. 174p.

09682 CHIROL, V. Indian unrest. London: Macmillan, 1910. 387p.

09683 GHOSE, S. The renaissance to militant nationalism in India. Bombay: Allied, 1969. 387p.

09684 GOYAL, O.P. Studies in modern Indian political thought (the moderates and the extremists). Allahabad: Kitab Mahal, 1964. 113p.

09685 GUHA, A.C. First spark of revolution; the early phase of India's struggle for independence, 1900-1920. Bombay: Orient Longmans, 1971. 528p.

09686 KER, J.C. Political trouble in India, 1907-1917. Delhi: Oriental Publishers, 1973. 550p. [Rpt. 1917 ed.]

09687 MAJUMDAR, B.B. Militant nationalism in India and its socio-religious background, 1897-1917. Calcutta: General Printers & Pub., 1966. 202p.

09688 MUKHERJEE, HARIDAS & UMA MUKHERJEE. India's fight for freedom; or, the Swadeshi movement. Calcutta: KLM, 1958. 256p.

09689 ______, comp. "Bande Mataram" and Indian nationalism... . Calcutta: KLM, 1947. 96p. [editorials by A. Ghose and B.C. Pal]

09690 O'DONNELL, C.J. India's freedom movement: the causes of discontents. ND: Tulsi, 1979. 119p. [1st pub. 1908]

09691 PUROHIT, B.R. Hindu revivalism and Indian nationalism. Gagar: Sathi Prakashan, 1965. 188p.

09692 SAGGI, P.D., ed. Life and work of Lal, Bal, and Pal, a nation's homage. ND; Overseas, 1962. 363p.

09693 SAXENA, V.K. Indian reaction to British policies, 1898-1911. Delhi: Sundeep, 1978. 202p.

09694 SIRDAR ALI KHAN, Sayyid. The unrest in India considered and discussed. Bombay: Bombay Gazette Steam Press, 1907. 87p.

09695 TRIPATHI, A. The extremist challenge: India between 1890 and 1910. Bombay: Orient Longmans, 1967. 246p.

09696 VAJPEYI, J.N. The extremist movement in India. Allahabad: Chugh, 1974. 378p.

b. Bal Gangadhar Tilak (1856-1920): Maharashtrian editor of Kesari and Mahratta, and pioneer of mass mobilization [see also Chap. Twelve, I. C. 2. b.]

09697 BROWN, D.M. The philosophy of Bal Gangadhar Tilak: Karma vs Jñāna in the Gītā Rahasya. In JAS 17 (1958) 197-206.

09698 JOG, N.G. Lokamanya Bal Gangadhar Tilak. Delhi: PDMIB, 1962. 208p.

09699 KARANDIKAR, S.L. Lokamanya Bal Gangadhar Tilak; the Hercules and Prometheus of modern India. Bombay: Siddhamohan Art Printery, 1957. 655p.

09700 KEER, D. Lokamanya Tilak, father of the Indian freedom struggle. 2nd ed. Bombay: Popular, 1969. 463p.

09701 KELKAR, N.C. Life and times of Lokamanya Tilak. Tr. from Marathi by D.V. Divekar. Madras: S. Ganesan, 1928. 564p.

09702 PARVATE, T.V. Bal Gangadhar Tilak. A narrative and interpretative review of his life, career and contemporary events. Ahmedabad: Navajivan, 1958. 550p.

09703 PRADHAN, G.P. & A.K. BHAGAT. Lokamanya Tilak; a biography. Bombay: Jaico, 1959. 380p.

09704 RAM GOPAL. Lokamanya Tilak: a biography. London: Asia, 1965. 481p.

09705 REISNER, I.M. & N.M. GOLDBERG, ed. Tilak and the struggle for Indian freedom. ND: PPH, 1966. 682p.

09706 SHAY, T.L. Legacy of the Lokamanya; the political philosophy of Bal Gangadhar Tilak. London: OUP, 1956. 215p.

09707 SREEKUMARAN NAIR, M.P. Bal Gangadhar Tilak: the moderate as extremist. In JIH 54 (1976) 567-88.

09708 TAHMANKAR, D.V. Lokamanya Tilak, father of Indian unrest and maker of modern India. London: Murray, 1956. 340p.

09709 TILAK, B.G. Bal Gangadhar Tilak: his writings and speeches. 3rd ed. Madras: Ganesh, 1922. 411p.

09710 ______. Letters of Lokamanya Tilak. Ed. by M.D. Vidwans. Poona: Kesari Prakashan, 1966. 287p.

09711 The Tilak trial. n.p., 192-?. 1 v. [Report of the Bombay Presidency treason trial, High Court of Judicature, Sept., 1897]

09712 VARMA, V.P. The life and philosophy of Lokamanya Tilak: with excerpts from original sources. Agra: Lakshmi Narain Agarwal, 1978. 525p.

c. Bipin Chandra Pal (1858-1932): Bengali editor of New India

09713 DEV, H.M. A short life-sketch of Bipin Chandra Pal. Calcutta: S.B. Dev, 1957. 164p.

99714 LIPSKI, A. Bipincandra Pal's synthesis of modernity and tradition. In JIH 50 (1972) 431-40.

09715 MOOKERJEE, A.P. Social and political ideas of Bipin Chandra Pal. Calcutta: Minerva, 1974. 184p.

09716 MUKHERJEE, H. & U. MUKHERJEE. Bipin Chandra Pal and India's struggle for swaraj. Calcutta: KLM, 1958. 140p.

09717 PAL, B.P. Memories of my life and times. 2nd rev. ed. Calcutta: Bipinchandra Pal Inst., 1973. 664p. [1st pub. 1932-51]

d. Aurobindo Ghose (1872-1950): Bengali editor of Bande Mataram [see also VII. C. 7, below]

09718 GHOSE, A. Bande Mataram: early political writings. Pondicherry: Sri Aurobindo Birth Centenary Library, 1970. [v. 1 of his Complete works]

09719 ______. New lamps for old. Pondicherry: Sri Aurobindo Ashram, 1974. 71p.

09720 ______. Tales of prison life. Calcutta: Sri Aurobindo Pathamandir, 1974. 124p.

09721 GORDON, L. Aurobindo Ghose: secrets of the self and revolution. In R.P. Beech & M.J. Beech, eds. Bengal: change and continuity. East Lansing: Asian Studies Center, Michigan State U., 1971, 31-68. (Its occ. papers, S.A. series, 16)

09722 GUHA, A.C. Aurobindo and Jugantar. Calcutta: Sahitya Sansad, 197-. 91p.

09723 MITRA, S.K. Sri Aurobindo. ND: Indian Book Co., 1972. 215p.

09724 MUKHERJEE, H. & U. MUKHERJEE. Sri Aurobindo and the new thought in Indian politics.... Calcutta: KLM, 1964. 393p.

09725 ______. Sri Aurobindo's political thought (1893-1908). 1st ed. Calcutta: KLM, 1958. 188p.

09726 SOUTHARD, B. The political strategy of Aurobindo Ghose. In MAS 14,3 (1980) 353-76.

e. Lajpat Rai (1865-1928): Panjabi lawyer and Arya Samajist

09727 BAINS, J.S. Lala Lajpat Rai's idealism and Indian national movement. In IJPS 30,4 (1969) 291-316.

09728 DHANPAT RAI, Lala. Life story of Lala Lajpat Rai. Written in Urdu by his brother... Tr. by I.D. Puri & R.C. Puri. ND: Metropolitan, 1976. 119p.

09729 DHARAMPAL. Lajpat Rai: a descriptive bibliography. Chandigarh: Punjab U., 1962. 31p.

09730 FEROZ CHAND. Lajpat Rai, life and work. ND: PDMIB, 1978. 590p.

09731 GANDA SINGH, ed. Deportation of Lala Lajpat Rai and Sardar Ajit Singh. Patiala: Dept. of Punjab Hist. Studies, Punjabi U., 1978. 353p. (History of the freedom movement in the Punjab, 4)

09732 LAJPAT RAI, Lala. Autobiographical writings. Delhi: University Pub., 1965. 256p.

09733 ______. The political future of India. NY: B.W. Huebsch, 1919. 237p.

09734 ______. The story of my life: an unknown fragment. ND: Gītanjali Prakashan, 1978. 120p.

09735 ______. Writings and speeches. Ed. by V.C. Joshi. Delhi: University Pub., 1966. 2 v.

09736 NAGAR, P. Lala Lajpat Rai, the man and his ideas. ND: Manohar, 1977. 325p.

09737 SHARMA, K.K. Life and times of Lala Lajpat Rai. Ambala Cantt.: Indian Book Agency, 1975. 321p.

f. the Revolutionaries: terrorism and armed conspiracy; the Lahore conspiracy, the Anusilan Samiti of Bengal, the Hindustan Ghadar Party among Punjabis overseas

09738 BHATTACHARYYA, BUDDHADEVA, ed. Freedom struggle and Anushilan Samiti. Calcutta: Anushilan Samiti, 1979-. to be 2 v.

09739 BROWN, E.C. Har Dayal: Hindu revolutionary and rationalist. Tucson: U. of Arizona Press, 1975. 321p.

09740 CHATTERJEE, S.P., ed. Rash Behari Basu, his struggle for India's independence. Calcutta: Biplabi Mahanayak Rash Behari Basu Smarak Samity, 1963. 596p.

09741 DATTA, V.N. Madan Lal Dhingra and the revolutionary movement. ND: Vikas, 1978. 115p.

09742 DEOL, G.S. The role of the Ghadar Party in the national movement. Delhi: Sterling, 1969. 244p.

09743 DHARMAVIRA. I threw the bomb. ND: Orient Paperbacks, 1979. 149p.

09744 ______. Lala Har Dayal and revolutionary movements of his times. ND: India Book Co., 1970. 363p.

09745 DIGNAN, D.K. The Hindu conspiracy in Anglo-American relations during World War I. In Pacific Hist. R. 40 (1971) 57-76.

09746 GANGULY, A.B. Ghadar revolution in America. ND: Metropolitan, 1980. 128p.

09747 JOHNSTON, H.J.M. The voyage of the Komagata Maru: the Sikh challenge to Canada's colour bar. Delhi: Oxford U. Press, 1979. 162p.

09748 JOSH, S.S. Hindustan Gadar Party: a short history. ND: PPH, 1977. 310p.

09749 ______. Tragedy of Komagata Maru. ND: PPH, 1975. 120p.

09750 JUERGENSMEYER, M. Ghadar sources: research on Punjabi revolutionaries in America. In Harbans Singh & N.G. Barrier, eds. Punjab past and present.... Patiala: Punjabi U., 1976, 302-22.

09751 ______. The Ghadar syndrome: nationalism in an immigrant community. In Punjab J. of Politics 1,1 (1977) 1-22.

09752 KHUSHWANT SINGH & SATINDRA SINGH. Ghadar, 1915, India's first armed revolution. ND: R & K Pub. House, 1966. 102p.

09753 MATHUR, L.P. Indian revolutionary movement in the United States of America. Delhi: S. Chand, 1970. 169p.

09754 MUKHERJEE, U. Two great Indian revolutionaries; Rash Behari Bose & Jyotindra Nath Mukherjee. Calcutta: KLM, 1966. 251p.

09755 SPELLMAN, J.W. The international extensions of political conspiracy as illustrated by the Ghadr party. In JIH 37 (1959) 23-45.

09756 SRIVASTAVA, N.M.P. Sachindra Nath Sanyal: a great Indian revolutionary. In J. of Hist. Res. (Ranchi) 15,1 (1972) 110-19.

09757 YAJNIK, I.K. Shyamaji Krishnavarma, life and times of an Indian revolutionary. Bombay: Lakshmi, 1950. 335p.

g. the Home Rule Leagues, founded 1916 by B.G. Tilak and Annie Besant: demand for self-rule at War's end

09758 OWEN, H. Towards nation-wide agitation and organisation: the Home Rule Leagues, 1915-18. In D.A. Low, ed. Soundings in modern Asian history. Berkeley: UCalP, 1968, 159-95.

09759 KELKAR, N.C. The case for Indian home rule, being a general introduction to the Congress-League scheme of political reforms in India. Poona: Aryabhusan, 1917. 125p.

09760 ROBB, P. The government of India and Annie Besant. In MAS 10,1 (1976) 107-30.

09761 SHIRSAT, K.R. Kaka Joseph Baptista: father of Home Rule Movement in India. Bombay: Popular, 1974. 179p.

2. The Indian Muslims between Nationalism and Communalism (1880's - 1919)

[For Muslim Religion and Thought, see VII. C. 2. c., below]

a. general studies of Muslims under the Raj: relations with the British and Hindus after the end of the Mughal Empire and the "Mutiny"

09762 ABDUL HAMID. Muslim separatism in India; a brief survey, 1858-1967. Lahore: DUP, 1967. 263p.

09763 AHMAD KHAN, SYED. Review on Dr. Hunter's Indian Musulmans: are they bound in conscience to rebel against the Queen? Lahore: Premier Book House, 1974. 77p. [1st pub. 1872]

09764 ASHRAF, K.M. Political history of Indian Muslims (1857-1947). In Zafar Imam, ed. Muslims in India. ND: Orient Longman, 1975, 23-55.

09765 AZIZ, K.K. Britain and Muslim India: a study of British public opinion vis-à-vis the development of Muslim nationalism in India, 1857-1947. London: Heinemann, 1963. 278p.

09766 AZIZ AHMAD. Les musulmans et le nationalisme indien. In Orient (Paris) 22 (1962) 75-94.

09767 DUMONT, L. Nationalism and communalism. In CIS 7 (1964) 30-70.

09768 HANAFI, Z.A. Die modernistische Denkbewegung im indischen Islam (1858-1940). Dargestellt an den Ideen dreier führender Gestalten. Freiburg: Arnold Bergstruesser Inst., 1963. 106p.

09769 HAQ, M.U. Muslim politics in modern India, 1857-1947. Meerut: Meenakshi, 1970. 171p.

09770 HARDY, P. Muslims of British India. Cambridge: CamUP, 1972. 306p. (Its South Asian studies, 13)

09771 HUNTER, W.W. The Indian Musulmans. 3rd ed. Delhi: IndBH, 1969. 208p. [1st pub. 1871]

09772 IKRAM, S.M. Modern Muslim India and the birth of Pakistan, 1858-1951. 2nd rev. ed. Lahore: Sh. Muhammad Ashraf, 1970. 506p.

09773 ISLAM, ZAFARUL & R.L. JENSEN. Indian Muslims and the public service 1871-1915. In JASP 9 (1964) 85-149.

09774 KABIR, HUMAYUN. Muslim politics, 1906-47, and other essays. Calcutta: KLM, 1969. 133p.

09775 MCDONOUGH, S. The religious legitimation of change among modernists in Indo-Pakistani Islam. In B.L. Smith, ed. Religion and the legitimation of power in South Asia. Leiden: Brill, 1978, 42-52.

09776 MATHUR, Y.B. Growth of Muslim politics in India. Delhi: Pragati, 1979. 359p.

09777 ______. Muslims and changing India. ND: Trimurti, 1972. 295p.

09778 MITTAL, S.K. Muslim attitudes towards Indian National Congress (1885-1900). In JIH 54 (1976) 143-62.

09979 NIZAMI, T.A. Muslim political thought and activity in India during the first half of the 19th century. Aligarh: Three Mens Pub., 1969. 123p. [1st pub. in Studies in Islam 4 (1967) 96-113, 139-62]

09780 PRASAD, ISHWARI & S.K. SUBEDAR. Hindu-Muslim problems. Allahabad: Chugh, 1974. 218p.

09781 RAM GOPAL. Indian Muslims; a political history, 1858-1947. 2nd ed. Bombay: Asia, 1964. 351p.

09782 RIZVI, S.A.A. The breakdown of traditional society. In P.M. Holt, ed. Cambridge History of Islam. Cambridge: CamUP, 1970, v. 2, 67-96.

09783 ROY, S. Freedom movement and Indian Muslims. ND: PPH, 1979. 157p.

09784 RUSSELL, R. Strands of Muslim identity in South Asia. In SAR 6,1 (1972) 21-32.

09785 SMITH, W.C. Modern Islam in India; a social analysis. NY: Russell & Russell, 1972. 366p. [Rpt. of 1946 rev. ed.; 1st ed. 1943]

09786 THORPE, C.L. Education and the development of Muslim nationalism in pre-partition India. In JPHS 13 (1965) 1-26, 131-53, 244-64.

09787 ZAIDI, A.M., ed. Evolution of Muslim political thought in India. v. 1, From Syed to the emergence of Jinnah. ND: Michiko & Panjathan, 1975. 623p. [documents]

09788 ZAKARIA, R. Rise of Muslims in Indian politics: an analysis of developments from 1885-1906. Bombay: Somaiya, 1970. 427p.

b. early Muslim leaders - biographies and studies

i. Sir Sayyid Ahmad Khan (1817-1898): advocate of Western education to restore Muslim political fortunes, opponent of the Indian National Congress [for his religious and educational views, see VII. D. 2., below]

09789 AHMAD KHAN, SYED. Writings and speeches of Sir Syed Ahmad Khan. Ed. by Shan Mohammad. Bombay: Nachiketa, 1972. 272p.

09790 AMEER ALI, Maulavi Saiyid. Memoirs. In IsC 5 (1931) 509-42; 6 (1932) 1-18, 163-82, 333-62, 503-25.

09791 ______. The spirit of Islam. Rev. ed. London: Christopher's, 1922. 71 + 515p. [1st pub. 1891]

09792 CASE, M.H. The Aligarh era: Muslim politics in north India, 1860-1910. Diss., U. of Chicago, 1970. 274p.

09793 MALIK, H. Sir Sayyid Ahmad Khan's contribution to the development of Muslim nationalism in India. In MAS 4,2 (1970) 129-47.

09794 MALIK, H. Sir Sayyid Ahmad Khan's doctrines of Muslim nationalism and national progress. In MAS 2,3 (1968) 221-44.

09795 NARAIN, P. Political views of Sayyid Ahmad Khan: evolution and impact. In JIH 53,1 (1975) 105-53.

09796 SHĀN MUHAMMAD. Sir Syed Ahmad Khan; a political biography. Meerut: Meenakshi, 1969. 272p.

ii. other early Muslim political leaders

09797 AHMAD, QEYAMUDDIN & J.S. JHA. Mazharul Haque. ND: PDMIB, 1976. 118p.

09798 ALI, MOHAMED, Maulana. My life, a fragment; an autobiographical sketch of Maulana Mohamed Ali. Ed. by Afzal Iqbal. Lahore: Sh. Muhammad Ashraf, 1966. 252p.

09799 ______. Select writings and speeches. Ed. by Afzal Iqbal. 2nd ed. Lahore: Sh. M. Ashraf, 1963. 2 v., 379, 217p.

09800 AZIZ, K.K. Ameer Ali: his life and work. Lahore: Publishers United, 1968. 119, 684p.

09801 IQBAL, AFZAL. The life and times of Mohamed Ali; an analysis of the hopes, fears and aspirations of Muslim India from 1778 to 1931. Lahore: Inst. of Islamic Culture, 1974. 443p.

09802 JAFRI, R.A., ed. Selections from Mohammad Ali's Comrade. Lahore: Mohammad Ali academy, 1965. 558, 100p. [weekly journal in English, 1911 +]

09803 KHALID, D. ʿUbayd-Allāh Sindhī: modern interpretation of Muslim universalism. In Islamic studies 8 (1969) 97-114.

09804 [Maulana Mohamed Ali Jauhar special issue] In JPHS 26,4 (1978) 207-312.

09805 SHAN MUHAMMAD. Freedom movement in India: the role of Ali brothers. ND: Associated, 1979. 284p. [On Maulana Mohamed Ali, 1878-1931, and Maulana Shaukat Ali, 1872-1936.]

09806 ______., ed. Unpublished letters of the Ali brothers. Delhi: IAD, 1979. 304p.

09807 SULTAN MUHAMMAD SHAH, AGA KHAN. The memoirs of Aga Khan: world enough and time. NY: Simon & Schuster, 1954. 367p.

09808 YUSUFI, A.B. Life of Maulana Mohamed Ali Jauhar. Karachi: Mohamedali Educ. Soc., 1970-. v. 1. 334p.

c. Muslim political organization (to 1919): loyalty to the British and protection of Muslim rights: rapprochement with Congress in the 1916 Lucknow Pact

09809 GOKHALE, B.G. The "Lucknow Pact"-a re-examination. In his (ed.) A collection of papers.... NY: Humanities Press, 1967. (Asian studies, 1)

09810 LAL BAHADUR. The Muslim League: its history, activities, and achievements. Lahore: Book Traders, 1979. 368p. [1st pub. 1954]

09811 NOMAN, M. Muslim India: rise and growth of the All-India Muslim League. Allahabad: Kitabistan, 1942. 433p.

09812 OWEN, H.F. Negotiating the Lucknow pact. In JAS 31,3 (1972) 561-88.

09813 PIRZADA, S., Syed. Foundations of Pakistan: All-India Muslim League documents, 1906-1947. Karachi: Natl. Pub. House, 1969-70. 2 v., 605, 636p.

09814 RAHMAN, M. From consultation to confrontation: a study of the Muslim League in British Indian politics, 1906-1912. London: Luzac, 1970. 313p.

09815 RAJPUT, A.B. Muslim League: yesterday and today. Lahore: Muhammad Ashraf, 1948. 288p.

3. British Reactions to Nationalist Petitions and Bombs: Repression and Constitutional Change

a. Lord Curzon, Marquess of Kedleston (Viceroy, 1899-1904, 1904-05), and his administration [for 1905 partition of Bengal, see Chap. Fifteen II. A. 5. c.]

09816 COHEN, S.P. Issue, role, and personality: the Kitchener-Curzon dispute. In CSSH 10,3 (1968) 337-55.

09817 CURZON, GEORGE NATHANIEL, Marquess of Kedleston. Leaves from a viceroy's notebook. London: Macmillan, 1926. 414p.

09818 DARLING, M. Apprentice to power; India 1904-1908. London: Hogarth, 1966. 256p.

09819 DIGHE, V.G. Lord Curzon and the national movement. In JASBombay 39/40 (1964-65) 125-42.

09820 DILKS, D. Curzon in India. NY: Taplinger, 1970. 2 v.

09821 FRASER, L. India under Curzon and after. London: W. Heinemann, 1911. 495p.

09822 ZETLAND, LAWRENCE JOHN LUMLEY DUNDAS, 2nd Marquis of. The life of Lord Curzon. London: E. Benn, 1928 3 v.

b. Earl of Minto II, Viceroy 1905-10 (Gilbert John Elliott-Murray-Kynynmound)

i. general studies of Lord Minto and his administration

09823 BUCHAN, J. Lord Minto: a memoir. London: Nelson, 1924. 352p.

09824 DAS, M.N. Political ideologies in Britain vis-a-vis problems of Indian empire: 1905-10. In QRHS 3,3 (1963-64) 135-41.

09825 GILBERT, M. Servant of India; a study of imperial rule from 1905 to 1910 as told through the correspondence and diaries of Sir James Dunlop Smith. London: Longmans, Green, 1966. 266p. [Smith was Minto's private secretary]

09826 MINTO, MARY CAROLINE, Countess of. India, Minto and Morley, 1905-1910; compiled from the correspondence between the Viceroy and the Secretary of State. London: Macmillan, 1934. 447p.

09827 PARDAMAN SINGH. Lord Minto and Indian nationalism, 1905-1910. Allahabad: Chugh, 1976. 247p.

09828 WASTI, S.R. Lord Minto and the Indian nationalist movement, 1905-1910. Oxford: OUP, 1964. 254p.

ii. the "Morley-Minto Reforms", or Indian Councils Act of 1909: increased Indian council membership and the beginning of communal representation

09829 DAS, M.N. India under Morley and Minto; politics behind revolution, repression and reform. Lond: Allen & Unwin, 1964. 279p.

09830 GREAT BRITAIN. ROYAL COMMISSION ON DECENTRALIZATION IN INDIA. Report...[with minutes of evidence]. London: HMSO, 1908-09. 10 vols. in 4. (Parl. Pap. 1908:XLIV-XLVI; Cmd. 4360-4369).

09831 GROVER, B.L. A documentary study of British policy towards Indian nationalism, 1885-1909. Delhi: Natl. Pub., 1967. 295p.

09832 JHA, P. Genesis of franchise in India. In JBRS 60 (1974) 160-82.

09833 KOSS, S.E. John Morley at the India Office, 1905-1910. New Haven: YUP, 1969. 231p.

09834 MORLEY, JOHN, Viscount. Recollections. NY: Macmillan, 1917. 2 v.

09835 The Reform proposals. Full text of Lord Morley's despatch, Govt. of India's despatch, speeches in the House of Lords by Lord Morley, Lord Lansdowne, Lord Macdonnell; Mr. Buchanan's speech in the Commons; with the Hon. Mr. Gokhale's note to Lord Morley and his speech at the Madras Congress. Madras: G.A. Natesan, 1909. 147p.

09836 SIRDAR ALI KHAN, Sayyid. The life of Lord Morley. London: I. Pitman, 1923. 340p.

09837 WOLPERT, S.A. Morley and India, 1906-1910. Berkeley: UCalP, 1967. 299p.

c. Lord Hardinge of Penshurst, Viceroy 1910-16 (Charles Hardinge)
i. general studies of Lord Hardinge and his administration

09838 KUMAR, VIRENDRA. India under Lord Hardinge. ND: Rajesh, 1978. 411p.

ii. the visit of King-Emperor George V, the Delhi Durbar of 1911, and the moving of the capital from Calcutta to Delhi, 1912

09839 The historical record of the imperial visit to India, 1911; comp. from the official records under the orders of the viceroy and governor-general of India. London: Pub. for the Govt. of India by J. Murray, 1914. 457p.

09840 REES, J.D. Coronation concessions in India. In FN 92 (1912) 303-15.

d. repressive measures in response to nationalist agitation and German support of conspirators
i. the Rowlatt Acts (March, 1919) and nationwide hartals (general strikes) called by M.K. Gandhi

09841 INDIA. SEDITION COMMITTEE. Report. Calcutta: New Age Pub., 1973. 226p. [President: S.A.T. Rowlatt. Rpt. 1918 ed.]

09842 KUMAR, RAVINDER, ed. Essays on Gandhian politics: the Rowlatt satyagraha of 1919. London: OUP, 1971. 347p. [essays from Nov. 1966 symposium at Australian Natl. U.]

ii. the massacre of civilians at Jallianwala Bagh, Amritsar (April, 1919)

09843 COLVIN, I.D. The life of General Dyer. London: Blackwood, 1929. 345p.

09844 DATTA, V.N. Jallianwala Bagh. Kurukshetra: Lyall Book Depot, 1969. 183p.

09845 ______., ed. New light on the Punjab disturbances in 1919: volumes VI and VII of the Disorders Inquiry Committee evidence. Simla: IIAS, 1975. 2 v., 1155p.

09846 FEIN, H. Imperial crime and punishment: the massacre at Jallianwala Bagh and the British judgment, 1919-1920. Honolulu: UPH, 1977. 250p.

09847 FURNEAUX, R. Massacre at Amritsar. London: Allen & Unwin, 1963. 183p.

09848 HORNIMAN, B.G. Amritsar and our duty to India. London: T.F. Unwin, 1920. 196p.

09849 INDIA. DISORDERS INQUIRY CMTEE., 1919-1920. Report.... London: HMSO, 1920. 176p. + 5 v. evidence. [Cmd. 681; Parl. Pap. 1920:14; President Lord Wm. Hunter]

09850 INDIAN NATIONAL CONGRESS. ALL INDIA CONGRESS CMTEE. PUNJAB SUB-CMTEE. Punjab disturbances, 1919-20. ND: Deep Pub., 1976. 2 v. [Rpt. 1920 ed.]

09851 MOHAN, PEARAY. An imaginary rebellion and how it was suppressed. An account of the Punjab disorders and the working of martial law. Lahore: Khosla, 1920. 691p.

09852 RAJA RAM. The Jallianwala Bagh massacre; a premeditated plan. Chandigarh: Panjab U., 1969. 208p.

09853 SWINSON, A. Six minutes to sunset; the story of General Dyer and the Amritsar affair. London: Peter Davies, 1964. 215p.

IV. NON-COOPERATION AND CONSTITUTIONAL PROGRESS TOWARDS INDEPENDENCE AND PARTITION, 1919-1947

A. Mohandās Karamchand Gāndhī (1869-1948), Called the Mahātmā ("Great Soul")

1. Bibliography and Reference

09854 DALAL, C.B. Gandhi: 1915-1948; a detailed chronology. ND: Gandhi Peace Foundation, 1971. 210p.

09855 DESHPANDE, P.G., comp. Gandhiana; a bibliography of Gandhian literature. Ahmedabad: Navajivan, 1948. 239p.

09856 DHARMA VIR. Gandhi bibliography. Chandigarh: Gandhi Smarak Nidhi, Punjab, Haryana & Himachal Pradesh, 1967. 575p.

09857 GOSWAMI, K.P. Mahatma Gandhi: a chronology. ND: PDMIB, 1971. 220p.

09858 Mohandas Karamchand Gandhi: a bibliography. ND: Orient Longman, 1974. 379p. (ICSSR pub., 53)

09859 SATYAPRAKASH, ed. Gandhiana, 1962-1976. Gurgaon: Indian Documentation Service, 1977. 184p.

09860 SHARMA, J.S. Mahatma Gandhi: a descriptive bibliography. 2nd ed. Delhi: S. Chand, 1968. 650p. (Natl. bibl., 1) [1st ed. 1955]

2. Gandhi's Writings

09861 BHATTACHARYA, B. Mahatma Gandhi. ND: Arnold Heinemann, 1977. 236p. (Indian writers series, 14) [1st pub. 1969]

09862 GANDHI, M.K. All men are brothers. Paris: UNESCO, 1958. 196p.

09863 ______. An autobiography; the story of my experiments with truth. Tr. from Gujarati by Mahadev Desai. Boston: Beacon Press, 1966. 528p. [1st ed. 1927-29]

09864 ______. The collected works of Mahatma Gandhi. Delhi: PDMIB, 1958-. [v. 74 (to Oct. 10, 1941) pub. 1978]

09865 ______. The essential Gandhi. Ed. by L. Fischer. London: Allen & Unwin, 1963. 369p.

09866 ______. The Gandhi reader; a source book of his life and writings. Ed. by H.A. Jack. NY: AMS Press, 1970. 532p. [1st pub. 1956]

09867 ______. Gandhiji's correspondence with the government, 1942-44. Ahmedabad: Navajivan, 1945. 360p. [Also: 1944-47, Navajivan, 1959. 375p.]

09868 ______. The selected works of Mahatma Gandhi. Ed. by Shriman Narayan. Ahmedabad: Navajivan, 1968. 6 v.

09869 ______. Selected writings of Mahatma Gandhi. Ed. by R. Duncan. London: Fontana, 1971. 288p. [1st pub. 1951]

09870 ______. Selections from Gandhi. Ed. by Nirmal Kumar Bose. Ahmedabad: Navajivan, 1948. 311p.

09871 ______. Young India, 1924-1926. NY: Viking Press, 1927. 984p.

09872 ______. The mind of Mahatma Gandhi. Ed. by R.K. Prabhu & U.R. Rao. Rev. & enl. ed. Ahmedabad: Navajivan, 1967. 589p.

3. General Biographical Studies of M. K. Gandhi
a. selected biographies and biographical studies

09873 DEVANESEN, C.D.S. The making of the Mahatma. Madras: Orient Longmans, 1969. 432p.

09874 ERIKSON, E.H. Gandhi's truth; on the origins of militant nonviolence. NY: Norton, 1969. 474p.

09875 FISCHER, L. The life of Mahatma Gandhi. NY: Macmillan-Collier, 1962. 500p. [1st pub. 1950]

09876 Gandhi centenary number. In MAS 3,4 (1969) 289-393.

09877 HORSBURGH, H.J.N. Mahatma Gandhi. London: Lutterworth, 1972. 62p.

09878 HUNT, J.D. Gandhi in London. ND: Promilla, 1978. 264p.

09879 KEER, D. Mahatma Gandhi: political saint and unarmed prophet. Bombay: Popular, 1973. 819p.

09880 KRIPALANI, J.B. Gandhi, his life and thought. ND: PDMIB, 1970. 508p.

09881 MANDELBAUM, D.G. The study of life history: Gandhi. In CA 14,3 (1972) 177-206.

09882 MUKERJEE, H.N. Gandhiji: a study. 3rd rev. ed. ND: PPH, 1979. 225p.

09883 PAYNE, R. The life and death of Mahatma Gandhi. NY: E.P. Dutton, 1969. 703p.

09884 NANDA, B.R. Mahatma Gandhi; a biography. London: Allen & Unwin, 1958. 542p.

09885 RAYCHAUDHURI, P.C. Gandhi, the man. Mysore: Geetha Book House, 1974. 264p.

09886 REYNOLDS, R. The true book about Mahatma Gandhi. London: F. Muller, 1960. 144p.

09887 SHEEAN, V. Lead, kindly light. NY: Random House, 1949. 374p.

09888 TENDULKAR, D.G. Mahatma, life of Mohandas Karamchand Gandhi. Rev. ed. Delhi: PDMIB, 1961-63. 8 v. [1st pub. 1951-54]

09889 WOODCOCK, G. Gandhi. London: Fontana, 1972. 108p.

b. personal accounts by Gandhi's associates

09890 BIRLA, G.D. Bapu, a unique association. Bombay: BVB, 1977. 2 v.

09891 ______. In the shadow of the Mahatma: a personal memoir. Bombay: Orient Longmans, 1953. 337p.

09892 BOSE, N.K. My days with Gandhi. Bombay: Orient Longman, 1974. 270p.

09893 DESAI, M.H. Day-to-day with Gandhi; secretary's diary. Tr. by H.G. Nilkanth. Varanasi: Sarva Seva Sangh Prakashan, 1968-. 9 v. to 1979 (covers up to March, 1927).

09894 GANDHI, MANUBEHN. Bapu - my mother. Tr. from Gujarati by Chitra Desai. Ahmedabad: Navajivan, 1949. 56p.

09895 ______. The end of an epoch. Tr. from Gujarati by G.K. Gandhi. Ahmedabad: Navajivan, 1962. 78p.

09896 ______. Last glimpses of Bapu. Tr. from Gujarati by Moti Lal Jain. Delhi: Shiva Lal Agarwala, 1962. 348p.

09897 GHOSH, P.C. Mahatma Gandhi as I saw him. ND: S. Chand, 1968. 236p.

09898 GHOSH, S. Gandhi's emissary. Boston: Houghton Mifflin, 1967. 351p.

09899 KALELKAR, D.B., "KAKA." Stray glimpses of Bapu. Tr. from Hindi by R. Tyabji. 2nd rev. ed. Ahmedabad: Navajivan, 1960. 166p.

09900 NAIR, PYARELAL. Mahatma Gandhi - the early phase. Ahmedabad: Navajivan, 1965-. v. 1, 854p.

09901 ______. Mahatma Gandhi - the last phase. Ahmedabad: Navajivan, 1956-58. 2 v., 750, 887p.

09902 NEHRU, JAWAHARLAL. Nehru on Gandhi. NY: John Day, 1948. 150p.

09903 PRASAD, RAJENDRA. At the feet of Mahatma Gandhi. Westport, CT: Greenwood Press, 1971. 335p. [1st pub. 1961]

09904 RAY, A.S. Yes, I saw Gandhi. ND: Bombay, BVB, 1976. 205p. [tr. from Bengali]

09905 SHRIMAN NARAYAN. Memoirs: window on Gandhi and Nehru. Bombay: Popular Prakashan, 1971. 339p.

09906 SLADE, M. Spirit's pilgrimage. NY: Coward-McCann, 1960. 318p. [autobiography of "Mira Behn," disciple of Gandhi]

09907 STERN, E.G. Women behind Mahatma Gandhi. London: Reinhart, 1954. 271p.

09908 TAGORE, R.N. Tagore and Gandhi argue. Ed. by J.P. Chander. Lahore: Indian Printing Works, 1945. 181p.

c. assessments of Gandhi's life and historic role

09909 ALEXANDER, H. Gandhi through western eyes. NY: Asia, 1970. 218p.

09910 AMBEDKAR, B.R. Gandhi and Gandhism. Jullundur: Bheem Patrika Pub., 1970. 160p.

09911 BANDYOPADHYAYA, J. Mao Tse-Tung and Gandhi: perspectives on social transformation. Bombay: Allied, 1973. 156p.

09912 BEDEKAR, D.K. Towards understanding Gandhi. Ed. by R. Gawande. Bombay: Popular, 1975. 172p.

09913 BISSOONDOYAL, B. Mahatma Gandhi: a new approach. Bombay: BVB, 1975. 123p.

09914 CHATFIELD, C., ed. The Americanization of Gandhi; images of the Mahatma. NY: Garland, 1976. 802p.

09915 FISHER, F.B. That strange little brown man Gandhi. ND: Orient Longmans, 1970. 251p. [Rpt. 1932 ed.]

09916 [Gandhi special issue]. In PSR 9 (1970) 1-126, 194-205.

09917 LEWIS, M.D. Gandhi: maker of modern India? Boston: Heath, 1965. 113p.

09918 MEHTA, VED. Mahatma Gandhi and his apostles. NY: Viking, 1977. 260p.

09919 MOON, P. Gandhi and modern India. NY: Norton, 1969. 312p.

09920 POWER, P.F., ed. The meanings of Gandhi. Honolulu: UPH, 1971. 199p.

09921 RAMACHANDRAN, G. & T.K. MAHADEVAN, eds. Quest for Gandhi. Delhi: Gandhi Peace Foundation, 1970. 458p.

09922 RAY, H. Soviet view of Mahatma Gandhi. In IAF 2,4 (1971) 476-89.

09923 RAY, S.N., ed. Gandhi, India and the world; an international symposium. Philadelphia: Temple U. Press, 1970. 336p.

09924 ROY, M.N. Gandhism, nationalism, socialism. Calcutta: Bengal Radical Club, 1940. 130p.

09925 SETHI, J.C.D. Gandhi today. 2nd ed. ND: Vikas, 1979. 230p.

09926 SHIRER, W.L. Gandhi; a memoir. NY: Simon & Schuster, 1980. 255p.

09927 TIDMARSH, K. The Soviet re-assessment of Mahatma Gandhi. In Raghavan Iyer, ed. South Asian affairs, no. 1. London: Chatto & Windus, 1960, 86-115.

4. The Transformation of Indian Politics under Gandhi's Leadership

a. general studies of Gandhi's political career

09928 BOSE, N.K. & P.H. PATWARDHAN. Gandhi in Indian politics. Bombay: Lalvani, 1967. 93p.

09929 BROWN, J.M. Gandhi's rise to power, Indian politics 1915-1922. Cambridge: CamUP, 1972. 384p.

09930 LAHIRY, A. Gandhi in Indian politics: a critical review. Calcutta: KLM, 1976. 221p.

09931 MAHADEVAN, T.K. Dvija: a prophet unheard. ND: Affiliated East-West Press, 1977. 181p.

09932 ROTHERMUND, D. Gandhi as a politician. In IQ 26 (1970) 362-67.

09933 RUDOLPH, L.I. & S.H. RUDOLPH. the traditional roots of charisma: Gandhi. In their The modernity of tradition. Chicago: UChiP, 1967, 155-249. [Comprises articles previously pub. in Conspectus, 3,2 (1967); American scholar 35 (1965-66); World politics 16 (1963)]

b. Gandhi's political and social thought - beginnings of "Gandhism"

09934 ANDREWS, C.F. Mahatma Gandhi's ideas. NY: Macmillan, 1930. 382p.

09935 BHATTACHARYYA, BUDDHADEVA. Evolution of the political philosophy of Gandhi. Calcutta: Calcutta Book House, 1969. 601p.

09936 BOSE, N.K. Studies in Gandhism. 3rd ed., rev. Calcutta: 1962. 316p.

09937 DALTON, D. Gandhi: ideology and authority. In MAS 3 (1969) 377-93.

09938 DHAWAN, G.N. The political philosophy of Mahatma Gandhi. Bombay: Popular Book Depot, 1941. 354p.

09939 DREVET, C. Pour connaître la pensée de Gandhi. Évreux: dist. le Cercle du bibliophile, 1970. 244p. [1st pub. 1946]

09940 GANDHI, M.K. Sarvodaya (the welfare of all). Ed. by B. Kumarappa. Ahmedabad: Navajivan, 1954. 200p.

09941 ______. Satyagraha: non-violent resistance. Ahmedabad: Navajivan, 1951. 406p.

09942 GANGULI, B.N. Gandhi's social philosophy: perspective and relevance. Delhi: Vikas, 1973. 453p.

09943 IYER, R. The moral and political thought of Mahatma Gandhi. NY: OUP, 1973. 449p.

09944 MATHUR, J.S. & P.C. SHARMA. Facets of Gandhian thought. Ahmedabad: Navajivan, 1975. 127p.

09945 MORRIS-JONES, W.H. Mahatma Gandhi--political philosopher? In IJPS 21 (1960) 203-24.

09946 MUKHERJI, H.C. Congress and the masses. Calcutta: Calcutta Book House, 1945. 260p.

09947 POWER, P.F. Toward a re-evaluation of Gandhi's political thought. In Western Political Q. 16 (1963) 99-108.

09948 PRASAD, M. Social philosophy of Mahatma Gandhi. Gorakhpur: Vishwavidyalaya Prakashan, 1958. 342p.

09949 RATTAN, R. Gandhi's concept of political obligation. Calcutta: Minerva, 1972. 346p.

09950 ROTHERMUND, I. The individual and society in Gandhi's political thought. In JAS 28 (1969) 313-20.

09951 RUTHNASWAMY, M. The political philosophy of Mr. Gandhi. Madras: Tagore, 1922. 99p.

09952 TEMPLIN, R.T. Gandhi on human power; democratic versus imperial uses. In J. of Human Relations 18,4 (1970) 1161-1176.

09953 TEWARI, S.M. The concept of democracy in the political philosophy of Mahatma Gandhi. In IPSR 6,2 (1972) 225-251.

09954 VERMA, S. Metaphysical foundation of Mahatma Gandhi's thought. ND: Orient Longmans, 1970. 177p.

c. Gandhi's new strategy of satyāgraha ("truth force"): reliance on moral force and ahimsa ("nonviolence")

09955 ASHE, G. Gandhi: a study in revolution. London: Heinemann, 1968. 404p.

09956 BONDURANT, J.V. Conquest of violence; the Gandhian philosophy of conflict. Rev. ed. Berkeley: UCalP, 1965. 271p. [1st pub. 1958]

09957 DIWAKAR, R.R. Saga of satyagraha. Rev. and enl. ed. ND: Gandhi Peace Foundation, 1969. 248p. [1st ed. 1946]

09958 GAUR, V.P. Mahatma Gandhi: a study of his message of non-violence. ND: Sterling, 1977. 144p.

09959 GHOSE, A. The doctrine of passive resistance. 2nd ed. Pondicherry: Sri Aurobindo Ashram, 1952. 87p.

09960 HORSBURGH, H.J.N. Non-violence and aggression: a study of Gandhi's moral equivalent of war. London: OUP, 1968. 207p.

09961 MAHALE, M.K.J. L'ahiṁsā de Gandhi devant l'opinion française. In JKU(H) 9 (1965) 150-63.

09962 On violence and nonviolence East and West [special issue]. In PEW 19,2 (1969) 121-94. [articles by A.L. Herman, K.N. Upadhyaya, H.J.N. Horsburgh, et al.]

09963 PANTER-BRICK, S. Gandhi against Machiavellism; non-violence in politics. Tr. from French by P. Leon. Bombay: Asia, 1966. 240p.

09964 ROTHERMUND, I. The philosophy of restraint; Mahatma Gandhi's strategy and Indian politics. Bombay: Popular, 1963. 195p.

09965 SHARP, G. Gandhi as a political strategist: with essays on ethics and politics. Boston: P. Sargent, 1979. 357p.

09966 ______. Gandhi wields the weapon of moral power: three case histories. Ahmedabad: Navajivan, 1960. 316p.

09967 ______. Nonviolence: moral principle or political technique? Clues from Gandhi's thought and experience. In IPSR 4,1 (1969-70) 17-36.

09968 SHRIDHARANI, K.J. War without violence: a study of Gandhi's method & its accomplishments. NY: Garland, 1972. 351p. [1st pub. 1939]

09969 SPODEK, H. On the origin of Gandhi's political methodology: the heritage of Kathiawad and Gujarat. In JAS 39,2 (1971) 361-372.

B. The Nationalist Movement: Proliferation of Strategies in Response to Devolution of Power by British, 1919-47

1. General Studies of the Nationalist Movement and its Context, 1919-47

09970 BALABUSHEVICH, V.V. & A.M. DYAKOV. A contemporary history of India. Delhi: PPH, 1964. 585p. [1st Russian ed. 1959]

09971 BOSE, S.C. The Indian struggle, 1935-1942. Calcutta: Chakerverty, Chatterjee, 1952. 122p.

09972 ______. The Indian struggle, 1920-1942. Comp. by Netaji Res. Bureau, Calcutta. Bombay: Asia, 1964. 476p.

09973 CRADDOCK, R.H. The dilemma in India. London: Constable, 1929. 378p.

09974 DWARKADAS, K. India's fight for freedom, 1913-1937; an eyewitness story. Bombay: Popular Prakashan, 1966. 480p.

09975 KAUSHIK, P.D. The Congress ideology and programme, 1920-47; ideological foundations of Indian nationalism during the Gandhian era. Bombay: Allied, 1964. 405p.

09976 LOW, D.A., ed. Congress and the Raj: facets of the Indian struggle, 1917-47. London: Heinemann, 1977. 513p.

09977 MISHRA, S.G. Constitutional development and national movement in India, 1919-47. Patna: Janaki Prakashan,

1978. 400p.

09978 MISRA, B.B. The Indian political parties: an historical analysis of political behaviour up to 1947. Delhi: OUP, 1976. 665p.

09979 MOORE, R.J. The crisis of Indian unity, 1917-1940. Oxford: OUP, 1974. 334p.

09980 MORAES, J.R. Witness to an era: India 1920 to the present day. London: Weidenfeld and Nicolson, 1973. 332p.

09981 ROTHERMUND, D. Constitutional reform vs. national agitation in India, 1900-1950. In his The phases of Indian nationalism and other essays. Bombay: Nachiketa, 1970, 116-44. [1st pub. JAS 21,4 (1962) 505-22]

09982 ______. Die politische Willensbildung in Indien, 1900-1960. Wiesbaden: Harrassowitz, 1965. 262p. (SSI, 1)

09983 SHAKIR, M. Khilafat to partition; a survey of major political trends among Indian Muslims during 1919-1947. ND: Kalamkar Prakashan, 1970. 300p.

09984 TINKER, H. The India conciliation group, 1931-50; dilemmas of the mediator. In JCCP 14,3 (1976) 224-41.

09985 TOMLINSON, B.R. The Indian National Congress and the Raj, 1929-1942: the penultimate phase. Toronto: Macmillan, 1976. 208p.

2. The Khilafat and Non-Cooperation Movements (1919-1924): High Tide of Hindu-Muslim Unity

09986 ASGAR KHAN, M. ALI. The Turkish nationalists and the Indian Khilafatists. In JASBangla 19,3 (1974) 39-50.

09987 AZIZ, K.K., comp. The Indian khilafat movement, 1915-1933; a documentary record. Karachi: Pak Pub., 1972. 400p.

09988 BAMFORD, P.C. Histories of the non-co-operation and Khilafat movements. Delhi: Deep, 1974. 270p. [1st pub. 1925]

09989 BHESANIA, N.C. The failure of Gandhism. Bombay: C.S. Deole, 1923. 58p.

09990 CHOUDHARY, S. Indian people fight for national liberation: non-co-operation, Khilafat & revivalist movements, 1920-22. ND: Srijanee Prakashan, 1972. 456p.

09991 GANDHI, M.K. Swaraj in one year. NY: AMS, 1972. 121p. [Rpt. 1921 ed.]

09992 GORDON, R. Non-cooperation and council entry 1919 to 1920. In J. Gallagher & G. Johnson & Anil Seal, ed. Locality, province and nation.... Cambridge: CamUP, 1973, 123-53. [Rpt. from MAS 7,3 (1973) 443-73]

09993 GUHA, C.C. Seven months with Mahatma Gandhi; being an inside view of the Non-Cooperation Movement (1921-22). Madras: S. Ganesan, 1928. 449p.

09994 KELKAR, N.C. A passing phase of politics. Poona: S.W. Awati, 1925. 266p.

09995 KRISHNA, G. The development of the Indian National Congress as a mass organization, 1918-1923. In JAS 25 (1966) 413-30.

09996 ______. The Khilafat movement in India: the first phase (September 1919-August 1920). In JRAS (1968) 37-53.

09997 LOW, D.A. The government of India and the first non-cooperation movement - 1920-1922. In JAS 25 (1966) 241-59.

09998 MCPHERSON, K. The Muslims of Madras and Calcutta: agitational politics in the early 1920's. In SA (1975) 32-47.

09999 MINAULT, G. Islam and mass politics: the Indian Ulema and the Khilafat Movement. In D.E. Smith, ed. Religion and political modernization. New Haven: YUP, 1974, 168-182.

10000 ______. The Khilafat Movement: a study of Indian Muslim leadership, 1919-24. Ph.D. diss., U. of Pennsylvania, 1972.

10001 ______. Urdu political poetry during the Khilafat Movement. In MAS 8,4 (1974) 459-71.

10002 NIEMEIJER, A.C. The Khilafat movement in India, 1919-1924. The Hague: Nijhoff, 1972. 263p.

10003 1921 movement reminiscences. ND: PDMIB, 1971. 227p.

10004 QURESHI, M.N. The Indian Khilāfat movement (1918-1924). In JAH 12 (1978) 152-68.

10005 ROY, M.N. & E. ROY. One year of non-cooperation; from Ahmedabad to Gaya. Calcutta: Communist Party of India, 1923. 184p.

10006 TAUNK, B.M. Non-co-operation movement in Indian politics, 1919-1924: a historical study. Delhi: Sundeep, 1978. 239p.

10007 WASTI, S.R. The Khilafat movement in the Indo-Pakistan subcontinent. In Iqbal 19,3 (1972) 14-33.

3. Responsive Cooperation: Political Parties Formed from Congress for Elections and Council Entry

a. National Liberal Federation (est. 1918); Tej Bahadur Sapru; V.S. Srinivasa Sastri; C.Y. Chintanami; H.N. Kunzru

10008 BOSE, S.K. Tej Bahadur Sapru. ND: PDMIB, 1978. 232p.

10009 JAGADISAN, T.N. V.S. Srinivasa Sastri. ND: PDMIB, 1969. 231p.

10010 KODANDA RAO, P. The Right Honourable V.S. Srinivasa Sastri, P.C., C.H., LL.D., D. Litt; a political biography. Bombay: Asia, 1963. 476p.

10011 NAIK, V.N. Indian liberalism. Bombay: Padma, 1945. 353p.

10012 RAJAN, M.S. Pandit Hriday Nath Kunzru: a memoir. In IQ 34 (1978) 441-56.

10013 The Rt. Hon. V.S. Srinivasa Sastri (1869-1946) centenary souvenir (22-9-1969). Madras: Right Honourable V.S. Srinivasa Sastri Centenary Committee, Servants of India Society, 1969. 104p.

10014 SAPRU, TEJ BAHADUR. Responsa: selected legal opinions. Ed. by K.N. Raina. Bombay: N.M. Tripathi, 1976-. v. 1-.

10015 SHUKLA, B.D. A history of the Indian liberal party. Allahabad: Indian Press, 1960. 508p.

10016 SIVASWAMI AIYAR, P.S. A great liberal; speeches and writings of Sir P.S. Sivaswami Aiyar. Ed. by K.A. Nilakanta Sastri. Bombay: Allied, 1965. 827p.

10017 SMITH, R.T. The role of India's "liberals" in the Nationalist Movement, 1915-1947. In AS 8 (1968) 607-24.

10018 ______. V.S. Srinivasa Sastri and the moderate style in Indian politics. In SA 2 (1972) 81-100.

10019 SRINIVASA SASTRI, V.S. Letters. Ed. by T.N. Jagadisan. 2nd ed. Bombay: Asia, 1963. 377p.

10020 ______. Speeches and writings of the Right Honourable V.S. Srinivasa Sastri. Madras: Right Honourable V.S. Srinivasa Sastri Birth Centenary Committee, 1969. 2 v.

b. the Swaraj Party (est. 1922): C.R. Das, Motilal Nehru, Vithalbhai Patel

10021 BAKER, D.E.U. The breakdown of Nationalist unity and the formation of the Swaraj parties, India, 1922 to 1924. In University Studies in History 4 (1970) 85-113.

10022 CHATTERJEE, D.K. C.R. Das and Indian national movement; a study in his political ideals. Calcutta: Post-Graduate Book Mart, 1965. 262p.

10023 DAS GUPTA, H.N. Deshbandhu Chittaranjan Das. 2nd ed. ND: PDMIB, 1969. 234p.

10024 JOSE, P.K. Responsivists and the Indian national movement. In JIH 54 (1976) 613-48.

10025 NANDA, B.R. Motilal Nehru. Delhi: PDMIB, 1964. 235p.

10026 NAYAK, R.K., ed. Vithalbhai Patel, patriot and president. ND: Natl. Forum of Lawyers and Legal Aid,

1976. 464p.

10027 NEHRU, MOTILAL. Pandit Motilal Nehru, his life and work. Ed. by U.C. Bhattacharyya & S.S. Chakravarty. 3rd ed., rev. and enl. Calcutta: Modern Book Agency, 1934. 175p.

10028 ______. The voice of freedom: selected speeches of Pandit Motilal Nehru. NY: Asia, 1961. 563p.

10029 PATEL, G.I. Vithalbhai Patel: life and times. Bombay: R.A. Moramkar, 1950. 2 v.

10030 RAY, P.C. Life and times of C.R. Das. London: OUP, 1927. 313p.

10031 ROY CHOUDHURY, P.C. C.R. Das and his times. Mysore: Geetha Book House, 1979. 187p.

10032 SRINIVASA IYENGAR, S. Swarāj constitution.... Madras: S. Ganesan, 1927. 76p.

4. The Rise of the Left: Communists and Socialists

a. general studies of leftist movements in India, 1919-47

10033 CHOUDHARY, S. Peasants' and workers' movement in India, 1905-1929. ND: PPH, 1971. 328p.

10034 NANDA, B.R., ed. Socialism in India. Delhi: Vikas, 1972. 299p. [selection of papers of two seminars on socialism in India, 1919-39, organized by the Nehru Memorial Museum and Library]

10035 NARAIN, B. Indian socialism. Lahore: Atma Ram, 1937. 158p.

10036 RAI CHOWDHURI, S. Leftist movements in India, 1917-1947. Calcutta: Minerva, 1977. 313p.

10037 SEMINAR ON SOCIALISM IN INDIA, 1919-1939. Delhi, 1968 and 1969. Proceedings. ND: Nehru Memorial Museum and Library, 1970. 2 v., 852p.

10038 SINHA, L.P. The left-wing in India, 1919-47. Muzaffarpur: New Publishers, 1965. 623p.

b. the Communist Party of India (est. 1925)

i. CPI documents and British official reports

10039 ADHIKARI, G.M., ed. Documents of the history of the Communist Party of India. ND: PPH, 1971-. [5 v. pub. to 1978]

10040 Communist papers; documents selected from those obtained on the arrest of the Communist leaders on the 14th and 21st Oct., 1925. London: HMSO, 1926. 132p. (Cmd. 2682; Parl. Pap. 1926:23)

10041 Communists challenge imperialism from the dock. Calcutta: Natl. Book Agency, 1967. 316p. [statement of Meerut conspiracy defendents]

10042 HALE, H.W. Political trouble in India, 1917-1937. Allahabad: Chugh, 1974. 285p. [1st pub. by Intelligence Bureau, GOI]

10043 NANDI, D., comp. Some documents relating to early Indian communists & controversies around them. ND: Eastern Pub., 1972. 136p.

10044 PETRIE, D. Communism in India, 1924-1927. Calcutta: Editions Indian, 1972. 384p. [1st pub. 1927]

10045 ROY, S., ed. Communism in India, by Sir Cecil Kaye; with unpublished documents from National Archives of India, 1919-1924. Calcutta: Editions Indian, 1971. 384p.

10046 ______, ed. Communism in India; unpublished documents, 1935-1945. Calcutta: S. Roy, 1976. 419p.

10047 WILLIAMSON, H. India and communism. Calcutta: Editions Indian, 1976. 407p. [1st pub. 1933 by Intelligence Bureau, GOI]

ii. general history of the CPI

10048 AHMAD, MUZAFFAR. The Communist Party of India and its formation abroad. Tr. from Bengali by H.N. Mukerjee. Calcutta: Natl. Book Agency, 1962. 177p.

10049 FAROOQU, M. India's freedom struggle and the Communist Party of India. ND: CPI, 1974. 53p.

10050 GHOSH, P. Meerut conspiracy case & the left-wing in India. Calcutta: Papyrus, 1978. 230p.

10051 Guidelines of the history of the Communist Party of India. ND: CPI, 1974. 134p.

10052 JOSH, S.S. The great attack: Meerut conspiracy case. ND: PPH, 1979. 110p.

10053 MASANI, M.R. The Communist Party of India; a short history. Bombay: BVB, 1967. 265p. [1st pub. 1954]

10054 OVERSTREET, G.D. & M. WINDMILLER. Communism in India. 2nd ed. Bombay: Perennial Press, 1960. 603p. [1st ed. 1959]

10055 SEN, M. Revolution in India: path & problems. ND: PPH, 1977. 164p.

iii. memoirs and biographies of Indian Communists and foreign agents

10056 AHMAD, MUZAFFAR. Myself and the Communist Party of India, 1920-1929. Tr. from Bengali by P.K. Sinha. Calcutta: Natl. Book Agency, 1970. 652p.

10057 CHARI, A.S.R. Memoirs of an unrepentant communist. Bombay: Orient Longmans, 1975. 172p.

10058 HUTCHINSON, L. Conspiracy at Meerut. NY: Arno, 1972. 190p. [Rpt. 1935 ed.]

10059 MURUGESAN, K. & C.S. SUBRAMANYAM. Singaravelu, first communist in South India. ND: PPH, 1975. 246p.

10060 NAMBOODIRIPAD, E.S.M. How I became a Communist. Tr. from Malayalam by P.K. Nair. Trivandrum: Chinta Pub., 1976. 211p. [autobiog. to 1938]

10061 RAO, M.B. & MOHIT SEN, eds. Our Doc; tributes to Comrade Gangadhar Adhikari on his seventieth birthday. ND: CPI, 1968. 63p.

10062 S.V. Ghate: our first general secretary; a memorial volume. ND: CPI, 1971. 122p.

10063 SAHA, P. Shapurji Saklatvala: a short biography. Delhi: PPH, 1970. 104p.

10064 SPRATT, P. Blowing up India; reminiscences and reflections of a former Comintern emissary. Calcutta: Prachi Prakashan, 1955. 117p.

c. M.N. Roy: from Communism to Radical Humanism

i. bibliography

10065 GANGULY, S.M. M.N. Roy: a bibliographical study. In The Indian Archives 24,2 (1975) 21-46.

10066 WILSON, P. A checklist of the writings of M.N. Roy. Rev. ed. Berkeley: South Asia Studies, Inst. of Intl. Studies, U. of California, 1957. (Modern India Project. Bibl. study no. 1 rev.)

ii. writings of M.N. Roy and of Ellen Roy

10066a ROY, ELLEN. The world her village: selected writings and letters of Ellen Roy. Ed. by S.N. Ray. Calcutta: Ananda, 1979. 376p.

10067 ROY, M.N. Fragments of a prisoner's diary. 2nd rev. ed. Calcutta: Renaissance, 1950-57. 2 v. 286, 307p. [1st pub. 1940]

10068 ______. The future of Indian politics. Calcutta: Minerva, 1971. 89p. [1st pub. 1926]

10069 ______. India in transition. Bombay: Nachiketa, 1971. 288p. [1st pub. 1922]

10070 ______. Memoirs. Sponsored by the Indian Renaissance Institute, Dehra Dun. Bombay: Allied, 1964. 627p.

10071 ______. New humanism; a manifesto. 2nd rev. ed. Calcutta: Renaissance, 1953. 111p.

10072 ______. Reason, romanticism and revolution. Calcutta: Renaissance, 1952-55. 2 v.

iii. studies of M.N. Roy, his political career, and thought

10073 AWASTHI, R.K. Scientific humanism: socio-political

ideas of M.N. Roy; a critique. Delhi: Research, 1973. 287p.

10074 BHATTACHARJEE, G.P. Evolution of political philosophy of M.N. Roy. Calcutta: Minerva, 1971. 266p.

10075 DALTON, D.G. M.N. Roy and radical humanism: the ideology of an Indian intellectual elite. In E. Leach & S.N. Mukherjee, eds. Elites in South Asia. Cambridge: CamUP, 1970, 152-71.

10076 DAS GUPTA, B.N. M.N. Roy: quest for freedom. Calcutta: KLM, 1970. 50p.

10077 DHAR, N. The political thought of M.N. Roy, 1936-1954. Calcutta: Eureka Pub., 1966. 270p.

10078 GORDON, L.A. Portrait of a Bengal revolutionary. In JAS 27 (1968) 197-216.

10079 GROVER, D.C. M.N. Roy: a study of revolution and reason in Indian politics. Calcutta: Minerva, 1973. 187p.

10080 HAITHCOX, J.P. Communism and nationalism in India; M.N. Roy and Comintern policy, 1920-1939. Princeton: PUP, 1971. 389p.

10081 ______. Left wing unity and the Indian nationalist movement: M.N. Roy and the Congress Socialist Party. In MAS 3 (1969) 17-56.

10082 KARNIK, V.B. M.N. Roy: political biography. Bombay: Nav Jagriti Samaj, 1978. 656p.

10083 RAY, S.N., ed. M.N. Roy: philosopher-revolutionary; a symposium. Calcutta: Renaissance Pub., 1959. 72p.

10084 ROY, S. The restless Brahmin; early life of M.N. Roy. Bombay: Allied, 1970. 148p.

10085 SHIVIAH. New humanism and democratic politics: a study of M.N. Roy's theory of the state. Bombay: Popular, 1977. 281p.

10086 TALWAR, S.N. Political ideas of M.N. Roy. Delhi: Khosla Pub. House, 1978. 171p.

d. the Congress Socialist Party (est. 1934): socialists within the Indian National Congress

10087 BHAMBHRI, C.P. Nehru and the Socialist movement in India (1920-47). In IJPS 30,2 (1969) 130-48.

10088 BHARGAVA, G.S. Acharya Kripalani: profile and personal views. ND: Popular Book Services, 1967. 78p.

10089 BRIGHT, J.S. President Kripalani and his ideas. Lahore: Indian Printing Works, 1947. 218p.

10090 DEVA, NARENDRA. Socialism and the national revolution. Ed. by Yusuf Meherally. Bombay: Padma, 1946. 208p.

10091 ______. Towards socialist society. ND: Centre of Applied Politics, 1979. 476p.

10092 KRIPALANI, J.B. Class struggle. Wardha: Akhil Bharat Sarva-Seva-Sangha, 1958. 94p.

10093 ______. Some stray thoughts. Ahmedabad: Navajivan, 1979. 370p.

10094 LAKHANPAL, P.L. History of the Congress Socialist Party. Lahore: National Pub., 1946. 158p.

10095 NANDA, B.R. Jawaharlal Nehru and socialism: the early phase. In his Gokhale, Gandhi and the Nehrus. NY: St. Martin's, 1973, 106-119.

10096 NARAYAN, J.P. Socialism to sarvodaya. Madras: Socialist Book Center, 1956. 128p.

10097 ______. Towards struggle. Ed. by Yusuf Meherally. Bombay: Padma Publications, 1946. 244p.

10098 ______. Why socialism? Benares: All India Congress Socialist Party, 1936. 160p.

10099 ROTHERMUND, D. Nehru and early Indian socialism. In his The phases of Indian nationalism and other essays. Bombay: Nachiketa Publications, 1970, 65-80.

10100 RUSCH, T.A. Role of the Congress Socialist Party in the Indian National Congress 1931-1942. Diss., U. of Chicago, 1955.

10101 SETH, H.L. The red fugitive: Sri Jayaprakash Narayan. 3rd rev. ed. Lahore: Indian Printing Works, 1946. 163p.

10102 SHANKAR, G. Rise of the socialist left-wing in the Indian National Congress. In JIH 52 (1974) 457-73.

10103 SINGH, H.K. The rise and secession of the Congress Socialist Party of India (1934-1948). In Raghavan Iyer, ed. South Asian Affairs, no. 1. London: Chatto & Windus, 1960, 116-40.

10104 TANDON, P.D. Acharya J.B. Kripalani (a symposium). Bombay: Hind Kitabs, 1948. 132p.

e. the Hindustan Socialist Republican Army and other terrorist groups

10105 BIPAN CHANDRA. The ideological development of the revolutionary terrorists in northern India in the 1920's. In Proceedings of the Seminar on Socialism in India, 1919-1939. ND: Nehru Memorial Museum and Library, 1970, 123-61.

10106 DEOL, G.S. Shaheed-e-Azam Sardar Bhagat Singh: the man and his ideology. Nabha: Deep Prakashan, 1978. 159p.

10107 FRIEND, C. The Hindustan Socialist Republican Army: a revolutionary arm of the Freedom Movement. In Harbans Singh & N.G. Barrier, eds. Panjab past and present: essay in honour of Dr. Ganda Singh. Patiala: Punjabi U., 1976, 363-88.

10108 GAUR, D. The Azad episode. Bangalore: IBH Prakashana, 1979. 118p. [On Chandra Sekhar Azad, 1906-34]

10109 GUPTA, M.N. Bhagat Singh and his times. Delhi: Lipi Prakashan, 1977. 223p.

10110 ______. History of the Indian revolutionary movement. Bombay: Somaiya, 1972. 258p. [1st pub. 1939 in Hindi]

10111 ______. They lived dangerously; reminiscences of a revolutionary. Delhi: PPH, 1969. 440p.

10112 ______. The executions of March 1931, Gandhi and Irwin. In BPP 90,1 (1971) 99-117.

10113 SINHA, B.K. In Andamans, the Indian Bastille. Cawnpore: Profulla C. Mittra, 1939. 207p.

10114 THAKUR, GOPAL. Bhagat Singh, the man and his ideas. Bombay: PPH, 1953. 44p.

5. Communalism and the Growth of Hindu-Muslim Tensions (1917-47): Religious Communities as the Basis of Politics

a. general studies

10115 DIXIT, P. Communalism - a struggle for power. ND: Orient Longman, 1974. 236p.

10116 GANDHI, M.K. Communal unity. Ahmedabad: Navajivan, 1949. 1006p.

10117 ______. The way to communal harmony. Ed. by U.R. Rao. Ahmedabad: Navajivan, 1963. 522p.

10118 HASAN, M. Nationalism and communal politics in India, 1916-1928. ND: Manohar, 1979. 372p.

10119 HUSAIN, A. Gandhiji and communal unity. Bombay: Orient Longmans, 1969. 151p.

10120 MAJUMDAR, A.K. British attitude to communal politics: last phase. In Quest 83 (1973) 25-33.

10121 MANSHARDT, C. The Hindu-Muslim problem in India. London: Allen & Unwin, 1936. 128p.

10122 MEHTA, A. & A. PATWARDHAN. The communal triangle in India. 2nd rev. ed. Allahabad: Kitabistan, 1942. 263p.

10123 PRASAD, B. India's Hindu-Muslim questions. Lahore: Book Traders, 1977. 152p. [Rpt. 1946 ed.]

10124 THURSBY, G.R. Hindu-Muslim relations in British India: a study of controversy, conflict, and communal movements in Northern India, 1923-1928. Leiden: Brill, 1975. 194p. (SHR, 35)

b. Muslims and the Congress, from the Lucknow Pact (1916) to the Nehru Report (1928): demand for separate electorates

10125 ALL PARTIES CONFERENCE, 1928. The Nehru report: an anti-separatist manifesto. ND: Michiko & Panjathan, 1975. 208p. [1st pub. 1928 by AICC; chm., Motilal Nehru]

10126 MAJUMDAR, B.B. The Congress and the Moslems. In QRHS 5,2 (1965-66) 65-77.

10127 Muslims and the Congress: select correspondence of Dr. M.A. Ansari, 1912-1935. Ed. by M. Hasan. ND: Manohar, 1979. 335p.

10128 UMAR, M. Muslims and the demand for separate electorates. In JPHS 14,4 (1966) 221-36.

10129 ZAIDI, A.M., ed. Evolution of Muslim political thought in India. v. 3, Parting of the ways. ND: S. Chand, 1977. 713p. [documents]

c. Hindu communalism: the politicization of orthodox Hindus; the Hindu Mahāsabhā; Pandit M. M. Mālavīya; Swāmī Shraddhānanda

10130 CHATURVEDI, S. Madan Mohan Malaviya. ND: PDMIB, 1972. 134p.

10131 GORDON, R. The Hindu Mahasabha and the Indian National Congress, 1915 to 1926. In MAS 9,2 (1975) 145-203. [All-India Hindu Mahasabha est. 1915]

10132 GUPTA, S.L. Pandit Madan Mohan Malaviya: a socio-political study. Allahabad: Chugh, 1978. 462p.

10133 JAMBUNATHAN, M.R., tr. & ed. Swami Shraddhanand [His autobiography, adapted from the Hindi]

10134 KAPUR, K.N. Swami Shraddhananda. Jullundur: Arya Pratinidhi Sabha, Punjab, 1978. 143p.

10135 INDRA PRAKASH. Hindu Mahasabha; its contribution to India's politics. ND: Akhil Bharat Hindu Mahasabha, 1966. 182p.

10136 ______. A review of the history and work of the Hindu Mahasabha and the Hindu Sangathan movement. ND: Hindu Mahasabha, 1938. 401p.

10137 MALAVIYA, M.M. Speeches and writings. Madras: Natesan, 1919. 534p.

10138 Malaviyana; a bibliography of Pandit Madan Mohan Malaviya. Varanasi: Sayaji Rao Gaekwad Library BHU, 1962. 550p. (Its bibliographical series, 3)

10139 SHANKAR, S. Political views of orthodox Hindus. Asiatic R. 24 (1928) 85-114.

10140 SRADDHANANDA, Swami. Hindu sangathan: saviour of the dying race. Delhi: Shraddhananda, 1926. 141p.

10141 ______. Inside Congress. Bombay: Phoenix Pub., 1946. 208p.

6. Gandhi's Resumption of Congress Leadership: the Civil Disobedience Movement - Salt Satyāgraha - of 1930

10142 BRAILSFORD, H.N. Why India followed Gandhi. In his Subject India. NY: John Day, 1943, 219-31.

10143 BROWN, J.M. Gandhi and civil disobedience: the Mahatma in Indian politics, 1928-34. Cambridge: CamUP, 1977. 414p.

10144 GANDHI, M.K. Salt satyagraha. In his Satyagraha: non-violent resistance. Ahmedabad: Navajivan, 1951, 220-70.

10145 LOW, D.A. "Civil martial law": the Government of India and the civil disobedience movements, 1930-39. In his Congress and the Raj. London: Heinemann, 1977, 165-98.

10146 MUZUMDAR, H.T. India's non-violent revolution. NY: 1930. 63p.

7. Other Major Congress Leaders
a. Jawaharlal Nehru, 1889-1964 [see also Chap. Eight, III. D. 2.]

10147 CHALAPATHI RAU, M. Gandhi and Nehru. Bombay: Allied, 1967. 152p.

10148 NEHRU, JAWAHARLAL. The first sixty years; presenting in his own words the development of the political thought of Jawaharlal Nehru and the background against which it evolved.... Ed. by D. Norman. NY: John Day, 1965. 2 v.

10149 ______. Important speeches; being a collection of most significant speeches delivered by Jawaharlal Nehru from 1922 to 1945. Ed. by Jagat S. Bright. Lahore: Indian Printing Works, 1945. 243p.

10150 ______. The unity of India; collected writings, 1937-1940. London: L. Drummond, 1941. 432p.

10151 ______. Toward freedom; the autobiography of Jawaharlal Nehru. NY: John Day, 1941. 445p.

10152 PATIL, V.T. Nehru and the freedom movement. ND: Sterling, 1977. 335p.

b. Subhas Chandra Bose, 1877-1945 [see also IV. D. 4. 3., below]

10153 BOSE, A.N. My uncle Netaji. Calcutta: Esem Pub., 1977. 254p.

10154 BOSE, S.C. Crossroads, being the works of Subhas Chandra Bose, 1938-1940. Compiled by Netaji Res. Bureau, Calcutta. Bombay: Asia, 1962. 367p.

10155 ______. Fundamental questions of Indian revolution. Calcutta: Netaji Res. Bureau, 1970. 91p.

10156 ______. An Indian pilgrim; an unfinished autobiography, and collected letters, 1897-1921. Tr. from Bengali by S.K. Bose. NY: Asia, 1965. 199p.

10157 ______. Life and times of Subhas Chandra Bose, as told in his own words. Ed. by Madan Gopal. ND: Vikas, 1978. 352p.

10158 ______. Netaji's life and writings. Calcutta: Thacker, Spink, 1948. 2 v.

10159 ______. Subhas Chandra Bose; correspondence 1924-1932. Ed. by S.K. Bose. Calcutta: Netaji Res. Bureau, 1967. 432p.

10160 BOSE, S.K., ed. Netaji and India's freedom: proceedings of the International Netaji Seminar, 1973. Calcutta: Netaji Res. Bureau, 1975. 472p.

10161 HAYASHIDA, T. Netaji Subhas Chandra Bose: his great struggle and martyrdom. English tr. Ed. by B.N. Chatterjee. Bombay: Allied, 1970. 183p.

10162 JOG, N.G. In freedom's quest; a biography of Netaji Subhas Chandra Bose. Bombay: Orient Longmans, 1969. 356p.

10163 KAR, J. The new horizon: Netaji's concept of leftism. Calcutta: K.P. Bagchi, 1978. 137p.

10164 KURTI, K. Subhas Chandra Bose as I knew him. Calcutta: KLM, 1966. 66p.

10165 LAHIRI, AMAR. Said Subhas Bose. Calcutta: Book House, 1947. 151p.

10166 MOOKERJEE, G.K. Europe at war, 1938-1946; impressions of war, Netaji and Europe. Meerut: Meenakshi, 1968. 296p.

10167 MUKERJEE, H.N. Bow of burning gold: a study of Subhas Chandra Bose. ND: PPH, 1977. 118p.

10168 MUKHERJI, G.K. Subhas Chandra Bose. ND: PDMIB, 1975. 156p.

10169 Report of the one-man Commission of Inquiry into the Disappearance of Netaji Subhas Chandra Bose. ND: Min. of Home Affairs, Govt. of India, 1974. 137p. [Chm., G.D. Khosla]

10170 ROY, D.K. Netaji, the man; reminiscences. Bombay: BVB, 1966. 214p.

10171 SETH, H.L. Personality and political ideals of Subhas Chandra Bose. Is he a fascist? 3rd ed. Lahore: Hero Pub., 1944. 133p.

10172 SINGH, D. Rebel president; a biographical study of S.C. Bose. 3rd ed. Lahore: Hero Pub., 1942. 152p.

10173 TALWAR, B.R. The Talwars of Pathan land and Subhas Chandra's great escape. ND: PPH, 1976. 267p.

10174 TOYE, H. The springing tiger; a study of a revolutionary. London: Cassell, 1959. 238p.

10175 WERTH, A., ed. Der Tiger Indiens. Subhas Chandra Bose. München: Bechtle, 1971. 272p.

c. Vallabhbhai Patel, 1875-1950

10176 AHLUWALIA, B.K. Sardar Patel: a life. ND: Sagar, 1974. 294p.

10177 HEREDIA, S. A patriot for me: a biographical study of Sardar Patel. Bombay: Orient Longman, 1972. 240p.

10178 KHAN, ABDUL MAJID. Life and speeches of Sardar Patel; a study of the career and character of Sardar Patel, as well as his ideas and ideals, including all his important speeches until his death. ND: Indian Printing Works, 1951. 376p.

10179 KSHIRSAGAR, S.K. The indomitable sardar and the triumph of Borsad. Vallabh Vidyanagar: Sardar Patel U., 1973. 251p.

10180 MURTHI, R.K. Sardar Patel: the man and his contemporaries. ND: Sterling, 1976. 220p.

10181 NANDURKAR, G.M., ed. Sardar Patel - in tune with the millions, I & II. Ahmedabad: Sardar Vallabhbhai Patel Smarak Bhavan, 1975-76. 2 v., 365, 416p. (Birth centenary vol., 2 & 3)

10182 ______., ed. Sardar's letters, mostly unknown. Ahmedabad: Sardar Vallabhbhai Patel Smarak Bhavan, 1977-. (Birth centenary vol., 4) [pt. 1, 1945-46, 332p.]

10183 ______., ed. This was Sardar: the commemorative volume. Ahmedabad: Sardar Vallabhbhai Patel Smarak Bhavan, 1974. 464p. (Birth centenary vol., 1)

10184 PANJABI, K.L. The indomitable Sardar. 4th ed. Bombay: BVB, 1977. 299p. [1st pub. 1962]

10185 PARIKH, N.D. Sardar Vallabhbhai Patel. Ahmedabad: Navajivan, 1978. 2 v. [Rpt. 1953-56 ed.; tr. from Gujarati]

10186 PATEL, VALLABHBHAI JHAVERBHAI. For a united India; speeches of Sardar Patel, 1947-1950. ND: PDMIB, 1967. 198p. [1st pub. 1949]

10187 ______. Sardar Patel's correspondence, 1945-50. Ed. by Durga Das; (principal collaborators: Shankara Prasad and others). Ahmedabad: Navajivan, 1971-74. 10 v.

10188 RAVINDRANATH, P.K., ed. Sardar Patel in new perspective. Bombay: Sardar Patel Birth Centenary Celebrations Committee, 1978. 104p.

10189 SHANKAR, V. My reminiscences of Sardar Patel. Delhi: Macmillan, 1974-75. 2 v.

10190 TAHMANKAR, D.V. Sardar Patel. London: Allen & Unwin, 1970. 299p.

10191 TIWARI, A.R.G. Making of the leader: Sardar Vallabhbhai Patel, his role in Ahmedabad Municipality, 1917-1922. Vallabh Vidyanagar: Sardar Patel U., 1967. 264p.

d. Abul Kalam Azad, 1888-1958

10192 DESAI, M.H. Maulana Abul Kalam Azad, the president of the Indian National Congress; a biographical memoir. 2nd Indian ed. Agra: S.L. Agarwala, 1946. 136p.

10193 KABIR, HUMAYUN, ed. Maulana Abul Kalam Azad; a memorial volume. NY: Asia, 1959. 241p.

10194 SHAKIR, MOIN, et al. Azad, Islam, and nationalism; essays. ND: Kalamkar Prakashan, 1969. 99p.

10195 SIDDIQI, M.M. The religious philosophy of Moulana Azad. Hyderabad, A.P.: Moulana Azad Oriental Res. Inst., 1965. 881p.

10196 SUBRAMONIA IYER, R. The role of Maulana Abul Kalam Azad: the Indian politics. Hyderabad, A.P.: Abul Kalam Azad Oriental Res. Inst., 1968. 239p.

e. Chakravarti Rajagopalachari, 1879-1972

10197 AHLUWALIA, B.K., ed. Facets of Rajaji. ND: Newman Group, 1978. 144p.

10198 AHLUWALIA, B.K. & S. AHLUWALIA. Rajaji and Gandhi. Shashi Ahluwalia. ND: Allora, 1978. 199p.

10199 COPLEY, A.R.H. The political career of C. Rajagopalachari, 1937-1954: a moralist in politics. Delhi: Macmillan, 1978. 337p.

10200 FELTON, M. I meet Rajaji. London: Macmillan, 1962. 193p.

10201 GANDHI, R.M. The Rajaji story. Madras: Bharathan 1978-. v. 1-

10202 MURTHI, R.K. Rajaji, life and work. ND: Allora, 1979. 204p.

10203 NARSIMHACHAR, K.T. C. Rajagopalachari: his life and mind. ND: Heritage, 1978. 184p.

10204 PERUMAL, N. Rajaji, a biographical study. Calcutta: Maya pub., 1948. 133p.

10205 RAJAGOPALACHARI, C. Jail diary; ... being notes made by him in Vellore jail from Dec. 1921 to Mar. 1922 Madras: Swarajya Printing & Pub. Co., 1922. 136p.

10206 ______. Rajaji's speeches. 2nd ed. Bombay: BVB, 1978. 2 v.

10207 VENGUSWAMY, N.S. Rajaji: the lone voice (1940-1947). Nellayi, Trichur Dt.: 1971. 167p.

10208 VENKATESA IYENGAR, M. Rajaji: a study of his personality. Bangalore: Jeevana Karyalaya, 1975. 2 v. in 1.

10209 WAGHORNE, J.P. Rajaji, the Brahmin - a style of power. In B.L. Smith, ed. Religion and the legitimation of power in South Asia. Leiden: Brill, 1978, 53-72.

f. Rajendra Prasad, 1884-1963
[see Chap. Eight, II. E. 2. b. i.]

C. Constitutional Developments, the Government of India Acts of 1919 and 1935: From Dyarchy to Federation

1. General History of Constitutional Changes, 1919-47

10210 BOLTON, G. Peasant and prince: modern India on the eve of the reforms. London: Routledge, 1937. 296p.

10211 BRIDGE, C. Conservatives and Indian reform (1929-39): towards a pre-requisites model of Imperial constitution-making. In JICH 4,2 (1976) 176-93.

10212 BROWN, J.M. Imperial façade: some constraints upon and contradictions in the British position in India, 1919-35. In Trans. of the Royal Hist. Soc., 5th ser. 26 (1976) 35-52.

10213 COATMAN, J. Years of destiny; India, 1926-32. London: J. Cape, 1932. 384p.

10214 COUPLAND, R. The constitutional problem of India. London: H. Milford, 1944. 716p. [1st pub. in 3 parts]

10215 ______. India: a re-statement. London: OUP, 1945. 311p.

10216 GHOSH, S.C. The British Conservative Party and the Indian problem, 1929-1934; a case study of a decision and the actual operation of powers. In CR 171 (1964) 55-71.

10217 GWYER, M.L. & A. APPADORAI, eds. Speeches and documents on the Indian Constitution, 1921-47. NY: OUP 1957. 2 v., 802p.

10218 JHA, M.R. Role of central legislature in the freedom struggle. ND: NBT, 1972. 342p.

10219 RASHIDUZZAMAN, M. The central legislature in British India, 1921-1947. Dacca: Mullick Bros., 1965. 282p.

10220 RUMBOLD, A. Watershed in India, 1914-1922. London: Athlone Press, 1979. 344p.

10221 SHARMA, A.P. Prelude to Indian federalism: a study of division of powers under the acts of 1919 and 1935. ND: Sterling, 1976. 303p.

10222 VEERATHAPPA, K. British Conservative Party and Indian independence, 1930-1947. ND: Ashish Pub. House, 1976. 336p.

2. The Montagu-Chelmsford ("Montford") Reforms, 1919

a. Edwin S. Montagu, Secretary of State for India; and Lord Chelmsford, Viscount (Frederick John Napier Thesiger): Viceroy 1916-21: biographical studies

10223 COTTON, H.E.A. The Viceroyalty of Lord Chelmsford. In Contemporary R. 119 (1921) 764-70.

10224 E.S. Montagu: a study in Indian polity. Madras: G.A. Natesan, 1925. 84p.

10225 Hon. Mr. Edwin S. Montagu on Indian affairs. Madras: Ganesh, 1917. 438p. [speeches]

10226 MONTAGU, E.S. An Indian diary. Ed. by V. Montagu. London: Heinemann, 1930. 410p.

10227 WALEY, S.D. Edwin Montagu: a memoir and account of his visits to India. NY: Asia, 1964. 343p. [Pt. 2 contains extracts from diary, 1912-13]

b. the Government of India Act, 1919: provincial dyarchy with increased Indian representation

10228 APPADORAI, A. Dyarchy in practice. London: Longmans, Green, 1937. 431p.

10229 CHIROL, V. India old and new. London: Macmillan, 1921. 319p.

10230 CURTIS, L., ed. Papers relating to the application of the principle of dyarchy to the government of India, to which are appended the Report of the Joint Select Committee and the Government of India Act, 1919. Oxford: OUP, 1920. 606p.

10231 DANZIG, R. The announcement of August 20th, 1917. In JAS 28,1 (1968) 19-37.

10232 ______. The many-layered cake: a case study in the reform of the Indian Empire. In MAS 3 (1969) 57-74.

10233 GREAT BRITAIN. INDIA OFFICE. Report on Indian constitutional reforms. London: HMSO, 1918. 300p. (Cmd. 9109; Parl. Pap. 1918:8)

10234 GREAT BRITAIN. INDIA OFFICE. FRANCHISE CMTEE. East India (consitutional reforms: Lord Southborough's committee)... London: HMSO, 1919. 3 v. (Cmd. 141,103, 176; Parl. Pap. 1919:16)

10235 HORNE, E.A. The political system of British India with special reference to the recent constitutional changes. Oxford: OUP, 1922. 184p.

10236 ILBERT, C.P. The new constitution of India; being three Rhodes lectures by Sir Courtenay Ilbert and three by Rt. Hon. Lord Meston, delivered at University of London, University College, session 1921-1922. London: U. of London Press, 1923. 212p.

10237 MEHROTRA, S.R. The politics behind the Montagu declaration of 1917. In C.H. Philips, ed. Politics and society in India. London: Allen & Unwin, 71-96.

10238 MENON, V.P. Montagu-Chelmsford reforms. Bombay: BVB, 1965. 60p.

10239 PANIKKAR, K.N. The working of dyarchy in India, 1919-28. Bombay: Taraporevala, 1928. 159p.

10240 RAO, V.D. Tilak's attitudes towards the Montagu-Chelmsford reforms. In JIH 53,2 (1975) 289-301.

10241 ROBB, P. The government of India and reform: policies towards politics and the constitution, 1916-1921. Oxford: OUP, 1976. 379p.

10242 RYLAND, S. Edwin Montagu in India 1917-1918: politics of the Montagu-Chelmsford Report. In SA (1973) 79-92.

10243 SMITH, V.A. Indian constitutional reform viewed in the light of history.... Oxford: OUP, 1919. 118p.

c. Lord Reading, 1st Marquess (Rufus Daniel Isaacs), Viceroy 1921-26: the Reforms Enquiry Committee, 1924 (Sir A.P. Muddiman, chm.)

10244 COATMAN, J. Report of the administration of Lord Reading, Vice-roy and Governor-General of India, 1921-1926; general summary. Simla: Govt. of India Press, 1927. 157p.

10245 HYDE, HARFORD MONTGOMERY. Lord Reading: the life of Rufus Isaacs, First Marquess of Reading. London: Heinemann, 1967. 454p.

10246 INDIA. REFORMS ENQUIRY COMMITTEE, 1924. Report. London: HMSO, 1925. 3v. in 4. (Cmd. 2360; Parl. Pap. 1924/5:10) [A.P. Muddiman, chm.]

10247 ISAACS, GERALD RUFUS, 2nd Marquess of Reading. Rufus Isaacs, First Marquess of Reading. NY: G.P. Putnam's, 1942-45. 2 v.

10248 PILCHER, G. Lord Reading's Indian viceroyalty. In Edinburgh Review 243 (1926) 224-39.

10249 SIRDAR ALI KHAN, Syed. The Earl of Reading: a sketch of a great career at the Bar, on the Bench, in diplomacy, in India, together with an authorized report of his speeches delivered in India. London: Pitman, 1924. 404p.

3. The Simon Commission, 1927, to evaluate the 1919 Reforms, and Plan New Constitution; Widespread Boycotts

10250 BAKSHI, S.R. Simon commission - a case study of its appointment. In JIH 50 (1972) 561-72.

10251 ______. Simon commission and Indian nationalism. ND: Munshiram, 1977. 238p.

10252 ______. Simon commission and political awakening in India. In JIH 52 (1974) 437-56.

10253 GREAT BRITAIN. INDIAN STATUTORY COMMISSION. Report. London: HMSO, 1930. 17 v. in 5. [Sir J.A. Simon, chm.]

10254 INDIA. INDIAN CENTRAL CMTEE. Report, 1928-29. London: HMSO, 1929. 428p. (Cmd 3451; Parl. Pap. 1929/30: 10) [appointed by Lord Irwin to work with Simon Cmsn.]

4. Lord Irwin, Earl of Halifax (Edward Wood) Viceroy 1926-31: British Offer of Dominion Status, Congress Demand for Pūrṇa Swarāj ("Complete Independence")

10255 ADENWALLA, M. British responses to Indian nationalism - the Irwin declaration on dominion status, 1929. In Studies on Asia (U. of Nebraska, Lincoln) 5 (1964) 121-41.

10256 ARGOV, D. The conflict between Gandhi and Nehru in 1928 over the issue of dominion status versus independence. In AAS(J) 10,1 (1974-75) 39-58.

10257 GOPAL, S. The viceroyalty of Lord Irwin, 1926-1931. Oxford: OUP, 1957. 152p.

10258 HALIFAX, EDWARD FREDERICK LINDLEY WOOD, 1st Earl of. Fulness of days. London: Collins, 1957. 319p.

10259 LOW, D.A. The purna swaraj decision 1929; new potentialities for Indian nationalist biography. In Gungwu Wang, ed. Self and biography.... Sydney: Sydney U. Press, 1975, 140-70.

5. The Round-Table Conference, 1930-32, in London: Federation, Position of the Princes, and Communal Questions

10260 FAZL-I HUSAIN, MIAN. Diary and notes of Mian Fazl-i-Husain. Ed. by Waheed Ahmad. Lahore: Research Soc. of Pakistan, 1977. 363p.

10261 Gandhiji in England and the proceedings of the second round table conference. Madras: B.G. Paul, 1932. 241p.

10262 GREAT BRITAIN. Proposals for Indian constitutional reform. London: HMSO, 1933. 127p. (Cmd. 4268; Parl. Pap. 1932/33:20)

10263 GREAT BRITAIN. INDIAN FRANCHISE CMTEE, 1932. Report. London: HMSO, 1932. 5 v., incl. memoranda and evidence. (Cmd. 4086; Parl. Pap. 1931/32:8) [Marquess of Lothian, Chm.]

10264 INDIAN ROUND TABLE CONF., 1ST, LONDON, 1930-31. Proceedings. London: HMSO, 1931. 513p. (Cmd. 3778; Parl. Pap. 1930/31:12) [Ramsay MacDonald, Chm.]

10265 ______, 2ND. Proceedings. HMSO, 1932. 426p. (Cmd. 3997; Parl. Pap. 1931/32:8) [Ramsay MacDonald, Chm.]

10266 ______, 3RD. [Agenda, general discussion, and memoranda]. London: HMSO, 1933. 207p. (Cmd. 4238; Parl. Pap. 1932/33:11)

10267 LOW, D.A. Sir Tej Bahadur Sapru and the first Round-Table Conference. In D.A. Low, ed. Soundings in modern South Asian history. Berkeley: UCalP, 1968, 294-329.

10268 The round table conference: India's demand for dominion status: speeches by the King, the Premier, the British party leaders, and the representatives of the princes and people of India. Madras: G.A. Natesan, 1931. 342p.

6. Lord Willingdon, Marquess of Willingdon (Freeman Freeman-Thomas) Viceroy 1931-36

10269 TRENCH, VICTOR [pseud.] Lord Willingdon in India. Bombay: S.A. Ezekiel, 1934. 333p.

10270 WILLINGDON, FREEMAN FREEMAN-THOMAS, Lord. Speeches. Simla: MPGOI, 1935-37. 2 v.

10271 ______. Thoughts on India. In United Empire 16 (1925) 11-23.

7. The Government of India Act of 1935: Elections under the Communal Award, Popular Provincial Ministries, Refusal of Princes to Accede to Federation

10272 AGARWALA, M.L. The new constitution, being an analytical study of the Government of India statute of 1935. Allahabad: R.N. Lal, 1939. 839p.

10273 ALL INDIA MUSLIM LEAGUE. Report of the inquiry committee appointed by the Council of the All India Muslim League to inquire into Muslim grievances in Congress provinces. Delhi: Liaquat Ali Khan, 1939. 96p. [Pirpur report]

10274 BOSE, S.M. The working constitution of India; a commentary on the Government of India Act, 1935.... London: OUP, 1940. 689p.

10275 CHINTAMANI, C.Y. & M.R. MASANI. India's constitution at work. Bombay: Allied, 1940. 212p.

10276 COATMAN, J. India, the road to self-government. London: Allen & Unwin, 1941. 146p.

10277 EDDY, J.P. & F.H. LAWTON. India's new constitution: a survey of the Government of India Act 1935. London: Macmillan, 1935. 239p.

10278 GANGULEE, N.N. The making of federal India.... London: J. Nisbet, 1936. 352p.

10279 GREAT BRITAIN. PARLIAMENT. JOINT CMTEE ON INDIAN CONSTITUTIONAL REFORM. Report. [Proceedings and record] London: HMSO, 1934. 2 v. in 3 (H.L. 6, H.C. 5; Parl. Pap. 1933/34:6-8) [Marquis of Linlithgow, chm.]

10280 INDIA. LAWS, STATUTES, ETC. Government of India act, 1935. London: HMSO, 1935. 430p. (25 + 26 George V. Ch. 42)

10281 KRISHNASWAMI, A. The new Indian constitution. London: Williams & Norgate, 1933. 230p.

10282 LELE, P.R. The federation of India. 2nd ed. rev. & enl. Bombay: Popular, 1937. 182p. [1st pub. 1936]

10283 RAGHUBIR SINGH. Indian states and the new regime. Bombay: Taraporewala, 1938. 469p.

10284 RANBIR SINGH, Sardar. The Indian states under the Government of India Act, 1935. Bombay: Taraporevala, 1938. 276p.

10285 SHAFAᶜAT AHMAD KHAN. The Indian federation; an exposition and critical review. London: Macmillan, 1937. 450p.

10286 SHAH, K.T. Federal structure (under the Government of India Act, 1935). Bombay: Vora, 1937. 546p.

10287 ______. Provincial autonomy (under the Government of India Act, 1935). Bombay: Vora, 1937. 444p.

D. The End of the Raj: World War II, Partition, Independence, and the Integration of the Princely States (1939-1948)

1. General Histories, Studies, and Documents

10288 ALI, C.M. The emergence of Pakistan. NY: ColUP, 1967. 418p.

10289 AZAD, ABUL KALAM, Maulana. India wins freedom; an autobiographical narrative. Bombay: Orient Longmans, 1959. 252p.

10290 BANERJEE, A.C. The making of the Indian Constitution 1939-1947. Calcutta: A. Mukherjee, 1948. 2 v.

10291 BARNS, M. India today and tomorrow. London: Allen & Unwin, 1937. 303p.

10292 BHAGAT, K.P. A decade of Indo-British relations, 1937-47. Bombay: Popular, 1959. 521p.

10293 DESAI, T. American role in the Indian freedom movement. In IPSR 11,1 (1977) 1-32.

10294 DWARKADAS, K. Ten years to freedom (1938-48). Bombay: Popular, 1968. 265p.

10295 EDWARDES, M. The last years of British India. London: Cassell, 1963. 250p.

10296 FISCHER, G. Le parti travailliste et la décolonisation de l'Inde. Paris: Maspero, 1966. 240p.

10297 HASAN, K.S., ed. The transfer of power. Karachi: Pakistan Inst. of Intl. Affairs, 1966. 464p. (Documents on the foreign relations of Pakistan series)

10298 HODSON, H.V. The great divide: Britain, India, Pakistan. London: Hutchinson, 1969. 563p.

10299 KHAN, ABDUL WAHEED. India wins freedom: the other side. Karachi: Pakistan Educ. Pub., 1961. 405p.

10300 MANSERGH, N., gen. ed. The transfer of power, 1942-7. London: HMSO, 1970-. (Constitutional relations between Britain and India) [documents; 8 v. to 1979; indiv. volumes in relevant sections below]

10301 MENON, V.P. The transfer of power in India. Princeton: PUP, 1957. 543p.

10302 MOON, P. Divide and quit. Berkeley: UCalP, 1962. 302p.

10303 MOORE, R.J. Churchill, Cripps, and India, 1939-1945. Oxford: OUP, 1979. 152p.

10304 MOSLEY, L.O. The last days of the British raj. NY: Harcourt, Brace & World, 1962. 263p.

10305 PHILIPS, C.H. & M.D. WAINWRIGHT, eds. The partition of India: policies and perspectives, 1935-1947. London: Allen & Unwin, 1970. 607p. [554-583, detailed political chronology, 1935-47]

10306 RAY, A. Inconsistencies in Azad. Howrah: Bangavarati Granthalaya, 1968. 40p. [on Abul Kalam Azad's India wins freedom....]

10307 RAZA KHAN, M. What price freedom? A historical survey of the political trends and conditions leading to independence and the birth of Pakistan and after. Madras: Nuri Press, 1969. 604p.

2. Indian Muslims between Nationalism and Separatism
a. general studies of the period, 1928-47

10308 ABDURRASHID, M. Islam in the Indo-Pakistan subcontinent: an analytical study of the Islamic movement. Lahore: Natl. Book Foundation, 1977. 149p.

10309 AZIZ, K.K., ed. The All India Muslim Conference, 1928-1935; a documentary record. Karachi: National Pub. House, 1972. 330p.

10310 ______. The road to Pakistan. The All India Muslim conference 1928-1935; its role in Indian Muslim politics. In Pakistan Q. 14 (1966) 2-12.

10311 KAURA, UMA. Muslims and Indian nationalism: the emergence of the demand for India's partition, 1928-40. ND: Manohar, 1977. 223p.

10312 ______. Provincial autonomy and the Congress-League Rift, 1937-1939. In IS 14,4 (1975) 587-606.

10313 MCDONOUGH, S. Iqbāl, Gāndhī, and Muḥammed ʿAlī: religious charisma and the nationalist Muslims, 1920-28. In D.P. Little, ed. Essay on Islamic civilization presented to Niyazi Berkes. Leiden: Brill, 1976, 211-23.

10314 MATHUR, Y.B. Growth of Muslim politics in India. Delhi: Pragati, 1979. 359p.

10315 PADMASHA. Indian National Congress and the Muslims, 1928-1947. ND: Rajesh, 1980. 288p.

10316 PANDEY, D. Congress-Muslim League relations 1937-39; 'the parting of the ways'. In MAS 12,4 (1978) 629-54.

10317 ROBINSON, F. Nation formation: the Brass thesis and Muslim separatism. In JCCP 15,3 (1977) 215-30. [reply by Paul R. Brass, 231-34]

10318 SHIV LAL. Sectarian politics in India and Pakistan since 1857. ND: Election Archives, 1971. 192p.

10319 ZAIDI, A. MOIN, ed. Evolution of Muslim political thought in India: v. 4, The communal award. ND: S. Chand, 1978. 762p. [documents]

b. origin of the idea of Pakistan and its realization

i. Sir Muhammad Iqbal and Choudhary Rahmat Ali [see also VII. D. 3. and VIII. C. 2. c. below, for Iqbal as philosopher and poet]

10320 AHMAD, S.H. Iqbal, his political ideas at crossroads: a commentary on unpublished letters to Professor Thompson, with photographic reproductions of the original letters. Aligarh: Printwell Pub., 1979. 98p.

10321 AZIZ AHMAD. Iqbal et la théorie du Pakistan. In Orient (Paris) 17 (1961) 81-90.

10322 GORDON-POLANSKAYA, L.R. Ideology of Muslim nationalism. In Hafeez Malik, ed. Iqbal: poet-philosopher of Pakistan. NY: ColUP, 1971, 108-15.

10323 HUSSAIN, R. The politics of Iqbal: a study of his political thoughts and actions. Lahore: Islamic Book Service, 1977. 159p.

10324 IQBAL, MUHAMMAD, Sir. Letters of Iqbal to Jinnah, a collection of Iqbal's letters to the Qaid-i-Azam conveying his views on the political future of Muslim India. Lahore: Sh. M. Ashraf, 1963. 32p.

10325 ______. Speeches and statements of Iqbal. Comp. by "Shamloo." 2nd enl. ed. Lahore: Al-Manar Academy, 1948. 239p.

10326 MASUDUL HASAN. Life of Iqbal: general account of his life. Lahore: Ferozsons, 1978. 2 v., 506, 446p.

10327 PARVEEN FEROZE HASSAN. The political philosophy of Iqbal. Lahore: Publishers United, 1970. 426p.

10328 RAHMAN, F. Some aspects of Iqbal's political thought. In Studies in Islam 5 (1968) 161-66.

10329 RAHMAT ALI, Choudhary. Complete works of Rahmat Ali. Ed. by K.K. Aziz. Islamabad: National Cmsn. on Hist. and Cultural Res., 1978-. v. 1, 301p.

10330 ______. Contribution à l'étude du problème hindou-musulman. Revue d'études Islamiques (1932) 269-414.

10331 ______. Pakistan, the fatherland of the Pak nation. Cambridge, England: Pakistan Natl. Liberation Movement, 1946. 392p.

ii. documents and sources

10332 ALLANA, GULAM ALI, ed. Pakistan movement: historical documents. 3rd ed. Lahore: Islamic Book Service, 1977. 607p. [1st ed. 1967]

10333 AHMAD, JAMIL-UD-DIN, comp. Historic documents of the Muslim freedom movement. Lahore: Publishers United, 1970. 575p.

10334 JINNAH, MAHOMED ALI. Congress leaders correspondence with Quaid-i-Azam. Ed. by S. Qaim Hussain Jafri. Lahore: Aziz Pub., 1977. 258p.

10335 ______. Jinnah-Nehru correspondence, including Gandhi-Jinnah and Nehru-Nawab Ismail correspondence. Lahore: Book House, 196-. 96p.

10336 PIRZADA, S.S. Evolution of Pakistan. Lahore: All-Pakistan Legal Decisions, 1963. 309p.

10337 WEST PAKISTAN. BUREAU OF NATL. RECONSTRUCTION. Struggle of independence: photograph album, 1905-1947. Lahore: 1970. 238p.

10338 ZAIDI, A. MOIN, ed. Evolution of Muslim political thought in India. v. 5 The demand for Pakistan. ND: S. Chand, 1978. 738p. [documents]

iii. the birth of Pakistan

10339 AHMAD, JAMIL-UD-DIN, comp. Creation of Pakistan. Lahore: Publishers United, 1976. 376p.

10340 AHMAD, N. The basis of Pakistan. Calcutta: Thacker, 1947. 203p.

10341 AMBEDKAR, B.R. Pakistan or the partition of India. 3rd ed. Bombay: Thacker, 1946. 481p.

10342 AZIZ, K.K. The making of Pakistan: a study in nationalism. London: Chatto & Windus, 1967. 223p.

10343 KHALIQUZZAMAN, Choudhry. Pathway to Pakistan. Lahore: Longmans, Pakistan Branch, 1961. 432p.

10344 KHURSHID, A.S. History of the idea of Pakistan. Islamabad: Natl. Cmtee. for Birth Centenary Celebrations of Quaid-i-Azam Mohammad Ali Jinnah, 1977. 179p.

10345 NAGARKAR, V.V. Genesis of Pakistan. Bombay: Allied Pub., 1975. 515p.

10346 NAIM, C.M., ed. Iqbal, Jinnah, and Pakistan: the vision and the reality. Syracuse: Maxwell School of Citizenship and Public Affairs, Syracuse U., 1979. 216p.

10347 PANDEY, B.N. The break-up of British India. London: Macmillan, 1969. 246p.

10348 QURESHI, I.H. The struggle for Pakistan. 2nd ed. Karachi: U. of Karachi, 1969. 389p.

10349 RAFIQUE AFZAL, M., ed. The case for Pakistan. Islamabad: Natl. Cmsn. on Hist. and Cultural Res., 1979. 191p. (Documentation series, 4)

10350 RAJENDRA PRASAD. India divided. 3rd ed. Bombay: Hind Kitabs, 1947. 427p.

10351 SAYEED, K.B. Pakistan, the formative phase, 1857-1948. 2nd ed. London: OUP, 1968. 341p. [1st pub. 1960]

10352 SEN, SACHIN. The birth of Pakistan. Lahore: Book Traders, 1978. 199p. [1st pub. 1955]

10353 SHAH, K.T. Why Pakistan? And why not? Bombay: Pratibha, 1944. 284p.

10354 SHERWANI, L.A., comp. Pakistan resolution to Pakistan, 1940-1947; a selection of documents presenting the case for Pakistan. Karachi: Natl. Pub. House, 1969. 287p.

10355 SYMONDS, R. The making of Pakistan. Islamabad: Jinnah Birth Centenary Cmtee., Min of Educ., 1976. 231p. [Rpt. 1950 ed.]

10356 WAHEED-UZ-ZAMAN. Towards Pakistan. 3rd ed. Lahore: Publishers United, 1978. 253p.

10357 ZAMAN, M. Students' role in the Pakistan movement. Karachi: Quaid-i-Azam Academy, 1978. 242p.

3. Mohamed Ali Jinnah (1876-1948): Qāʿid-i-Aʿẓam ("Great Leader") of the Muslims and Creator of Pakistan
a. bibliography and reference

10358 AKHTAR, A.H., ed. Analytical catalogue of books on Quaid-i-azam (in the Liaquat Memorial Library). Karachi: Dept. of Libraries, Min. of Educ., 1976. 191p.

10359 ANWAR, M. Quaid-e-Azam Jinnah; a selected bibliography. Karachi: Natl. Pub. House, 1970. 110p.

10360 KHURSHID, A. Quaid-i-Azam Mohammad Ali Jinnah: an annotated bibliography. Karachi: Quaid-i-Azam Academy, 1978-1979. 2 v.

10361 PAKISTAN. EDUC. DIV. QUAID-I-AZAM PAPERS CELL. Descriptive catalogue of Quaid-i-Azam papers. Islamabad: The Cell, 1971-. v. 1.

10362 USMANI, M.A., et al., eds. Books on Quaid-i-Azam in Dr. Mahmud Husain Library (Karachi University Library). Karachi: Dr. Mahmud Husain Library, U. of Karachi, 1976. 138p.

b. Jinnah's writings

10363 JINNAH, MAHOMED ALI. Jinnah, as a parliamentarian. Ed. by M. Jafar & I.A. Rehman & Ghani Jafar. Islamabad: Azfar Associates, 1977. 367p.

10364 ______. Mahomed Ali Jinnah, an ambassador of unity: his speeches and writings, 1912-1917, with a biographical appreciation by Sarojini Naidu. Madras: Ganesh, 1918. 324p.

10365 ______. Plain Mr. Jinnah: selections from Quaid-e-Azam's correspondence relating mainly to personal matters. Ed. by Syed Shamsul Hasan. Karachi: Royal Book Co., 1976. 350p.

10366 ______. Presidential addresses of Qaid-e-Azam M.A. Jinnah, delivered at the sessions of the All India Muslim League. Delhi: S. Shamsul Hasan, Muslim League Printing Press, 1946. 222p. [addresses to 1937-43 sessions]

10367 ______. Quaid-e-Azam Jinnah's correspondence. Ed. by S.S. Pirzada. 3rd rev. and enl. ed. Karachi: East and West Pub. Co., 1977. 425p.

10368 ______. Quaid-i-Azam Mohammad Ali Jinnah: rare speeches, 1910-1918. Ed. by M. Umar. Karachi: Al-Mahfooz Res. Academy, 1973. 252p.

10369 ______. Selected speeches and statements of the Quaid-i-Azam Mohammad Ali Jinnah, 1911-34 and 1947-48. Ed. by M. Rafique Afzal. Lahore: Res. Soc. of Pakistan, U. of the Punjab 1966. 475p. (Its pub., 3)

10370 ______. Speeches and writings of Mr. Jinnah. Ed. by Jamil-ud-Din Ahmad. 6th ed. Lahore: Sh. M. Ashraf, 1960-64. 2 v., 586, 572p. [1st pub. 1947]

c. biographies and studies

10371 AHMAD, ZIAUDDIN, ed. Mohammad Ali Jinnah, founder of Pakistan. Islamabad: Min. of Info. & Broadcasting, 1976. 177p.

10372 AHMAD SAEED. The green Titan: a study of Quaid-i-Azam Mohammad Ali Jinnah. Lahore: Sang-e-Meel, 1976. 263p.

10373 AKHTAR, RAFIQUE. The Quaid-e-Azam: a pictorial biography. Karachi: East & West Pub. Co., 1976. 200p.

10374 ALLANA, G.A. Quaid-e-Azam Jinnah: the story of a nation. Lahore: Ferozsons, 1967. 537p.

10375 BOLITHO, H. Jinnah, creator of Pakistan. London: John Murray, 1957. 244p.

10376 Faith, unity, discipline: special issue published on the occasion of the Quaid-i-Azam centenary celebrations, 1976. In JPHS 24,3/4 (1976) 313p.

10377 HARRIS, M.A., ed. Quaid-i-Azam. Karachi: Times Press, 1976. 176p. + 11 pl.

10378 ISPAHANI, M.A.H. Qaid-e-Azam Jinnah, as I knew him. 2nd rev. & enl. ed. Karachi: Forward Pub. Trust, 1967. 319p.

10379 KHAN, SHAFIQUE ALI. Mr. Jinnah as a political thinker. Hyderabad: Markaz-i-Shaoor-o-Adab, 1974. 230p.

10380 LATIF, SYED ABDUL. The great leader. Lahore: Lion Press, 1947. 200p.

10381 MCDONOUGH, S., comp. Mohammed Ali Jinnah, maker of modern Pakistan. Lexington, MA: Heath, 1970. 101p.

10382 MAHMUD ALI. Quaid-e-Azam and Muslim economic resurgence. Lahore: Amir Pub., 1977. 115p.

10383 MAJUMDAR, S.K. Jinnah and Gandhi; their role in India's quest for freedom. Calcutta: KLM, 1966. 310p.

10384 PANNU, N.A. Jinnah, the lawyer. Lahore: Mansoor Book House, 1976. 355p.

10385 SAIYID, M.H. Mohammad Ali Jinnah (a political study). 2nd ed. Lahore: Sh. M. Ashraf, 1953. 715p.

10386 SHEIKH, A.Z. & M.R. MALIK, eds. Quaid-e-Azam and the Muslim world: selected documents, 1937-1948. Karachi: Royal Book Co., 1978. 298p.

10387 SULERI, ZIAUDDIN AHMAD. My leader: being an estimate of Mr. Jinnah's work for Indian Mussalmans. Lahore: Lion Press, 1945. 174p.

10388 TOOSY, M.S. My reminiscences of Quaid-i-Azam: a collection of interviews and talks with Quaid-i-Azam during November 1942 to May 1943. Islamabad: Natl. Cmtee. for Birth Centenary Celebrations of Quaid-i-Azam Mohammad Ali Jinnah, Min. of Educ., 1976. 62p.

4. Other Muslim Organizations
a. the Khāksār Movement (1926-46): a militaristic Islamic nationalist group led by Ināyat Allāh Khān Mashriqī (1888-1963)

10389 MATHUR, Y.B. The Khaksar movement. In Studies in Islam 6,1 (1969) 27-62.

10390 SETH, H.L. The Khaksar movement - under searchlight and the life story of its leader Allama Mashraqi. Lahore: Hero Pub., 1943. 110p.

10391 SHAN MUHAMMAD. Khaksar movement in India. Meerut: Meenakshi Prakashan, 1973. 164p.

b. Jamʿīat al-ʿulamāʾ-i-Hind, a pro-Congress group of Muslim scholars

10392 FRIEDMANN, J. The attitude of the Jamʿ-iyat-i Ulamāʾ-i-Hind to the Indian national movement and the establishment of Pakistan. In AAS(J) 7 (1971) 157-80.

10393 HARDY, P. Partners in freedom - and true Muslims. The political thought of some Muslim scholars in British India 1912-1947. Lund: Student Litteratur, 1971. 63p. (Scandinavian Inst. of Asian Studies, Monograph, 5)

5. Indian Nationalism during World War II
a. Lord Linlithgow, Marquess of Linlithgow (Victor Alexander John Hope) Viceroy 1936-43: declared India at war, without consultation; Indian responses

10394 GLENDEVON, JOHN HOPE. Viceroy at bay: Lord Linlithgow in India. London: Collins, 1971. 288p.

10395 JINNAH, MAHOMED ALI. Jinnah-Linlithgow correspondence, 1939-1943. Ed. by Waheed Ahmad. Lahore: Res. Soc. of Pakistan, U. of the Punjab, 1978. 129p. [Its pub., 49]

10396 LINLITHGOW, VICTOR A.J. HOPE, Marquess of. Speeches and statements, 1936-43. ND: Bureau of Public Info., Govt. of India, 1945. 467p.

10397 RIZVI, G. Linlithgow and India: a study of British policy and the political impasse in India, 1936-43. London: Royal Hist. Soc., 1978. 261p.

b. India and the Indian Army in World War II

10398 ELLIOT, J.G. Unfading honour; the story of the Indian Army, 1939-45. NY: A.S. Barnes, 1965. 392p.

10399 MITROKHIN, L. Friends of the Soviet Union: India's solidarity with the USSR during the Second World War in 1941-1945. Bombay: Allied, 1977. 276p.

10400 Official history of the Indian Armed Forces in the Second World War, 1939-45. Gen. ed., Bisheshwar Prasad. ND: Combined Inter-services Hist. Section, India and Pakistan, dist. Delhi: MPGOI, 1952-66. 25 v. in 27. [Each vol. has separate title; v. 25, India and the War, is a general summary.]

10401 STEVENS, G.R. & W.G. HINGSTON. The tiger kills; India's fight in the Middle East and North Africa. Bombay: F. Borton, 1944. 354p.

10402 TINKER, H. A forgotten long march: the Indian exodus from Burma, 1942. In J. of Southeast Asian Studies 6 (1975) 1-15.

10403 VOIGT, J.H. Indien im Zweiten Weltkrieg. Stuttgart: Deutsche Verlags-Anstalt, 1978. 413p.

c. the Cripps Mission (March-April, 1942) to gain Indian support for war effort, backed by U. S. emissary Louis Johnson

10404 ALEXANDER, H.G. India since Cripps. London: Penguin, 1944. 93p.

10405 COUPLAND, R. The Cripps mission. London: OUP, 1942. 91p.

10406 MANSERGH, N. & E.W.R. LUMBY, eds. The transfer of power 1942-7; vol. 1, The Cripps Mission, Jan.-Apr. 1942. London: HMSO, 1970. 928p. [documents]

10407 MITCHELL, K.L. Cripps Mission to India. In Amerasia 6 (1942) 107-52.

10408 MOORE, R.J. The mystery of the Cripps mission. In JComPolSt 11,3 (1973) 195-213.

10409 SINGH, B.S. The Cripps Mission: a handiwork of British imperialism. ND: Usha, 1979. 112p.

10410 SPRY, G. Cripps Mission to India. In Intl. Conciliation 381 (1942) 305-59. [incl. text of draft declaration]

10411 SUBRAHMANYAN, M. Why Cripps failed. ND: Hindustan Times Press, 1943. 111p.

10412 VENKATARAMANI, M.S. & B.K. SHRIVASTAVA. The United States and the Cripps mission. In IQ 19 (1963) 214-65.

d. Gandhi's "Quit India" ultimatum, arrest of Congress leaders, "Revolt of 1942" and government repression

10413 BHUYAN, A.C. The Quit India movement: the Second World War and Indian nationalism. ND: Manas, 1975. 262p. (Studies in Asian history & politics, 4)

10414 CHAKRAVARTI, T.S., ed. India in revolt, 1942. Calcutta: T. Ganguly, 1946. 170p.

10415 DARBARA SINGH. Indian struggle, 1942. 2nd ed. Lahore: Hero Pub., 1946. 254p.

10416 GANDHI, M.K. Gandhiji's correspondence with the government, 1942-44. Ahmedabad: Navajivan, 1945. 360p.

10417 ______. Gandhiji's correspondence with the government, 1944-47. Ahmedabad: Navajivan, 1959. 375p.

10418 GUNTHER, F. Revolution in India. NY: Island Press, 1944. 122p.

10419 HUTCHINS, F.G. India's revolution; Gandhi and the Quit India movement. Cambridge: HUP, 1973. 326p. [1st pub. 1971 as: Spontaneous revolution: the Quit India movement.]

10420 INDIA. HOME DEPT. Congress responsibility for the disturbances, 1942-43. Delhi: MPGOI, 1943. 86p. (Cmd. 6430; Parl. Pap. 1942/43:9)

10421 India ravaged; being an account of atrocities committed, under British aegis ... in the latter part of 1942. n.p., 1943. 163p.

10422 MANSERGH, N. & E.W.R. LUMBY, eds. The transfer of power 1942-7; v. 2, 'Quit India,' 30 April-21 September 1942. London: HMSO, 1971. 1044p. [documents]

10423 MATHUR, Y.B. Quit India movement. Delhi: Pragati, 1979. 212p.

10424 MITRA, BEJAN, ed. Rebel India. Calcutta: Orient, 1946. 260p.

10425 PRASAD, AMBA. The Indian revolt of 1942. Delhi: S. Chand, 1958. 138p.

10426 SAHAI, G. '42 rebellion, an authentic review of the great upheaval of 1942. Delhi: Rajkamal, 1947. 451p.

10427 TAGORE, S.N. Revolution and Quit India. Calcutta: Ganavani, 1946. 40p.

10428 VENKATARAMANI, M.S. & B.K. SHRIVASTAVA. Quit India: the American response to the 1942 struggle. ND: Vikas, 1979. 350p.

10429 VIDYARTHI, R.S., ed. British savagery in India. Agra: Agarwala, 1946. 333p.

10430 WICKENDEN, T. Quit India movement: British secret report. Ed. by P.N. Chopra. Faridabad: Thomson Press, 1976. 407p. [orig. GOI report 1944]

10431 ZAIDI, A. MOIN. The way out to freedom; an inquiry into the Quit India movement conducted by participants. ND: Orientalia, 1973. 254p.

e. Āzād Hind ("Free India"), est. 1943 under Japanese auspices by Subhas Chandra Bose, and its Indian National Army (INA)

10432 BHATTACHARYA, S.N. Subhas Chandra Bose in self-exile, his finest hour. Delhi: Metropolitan, 1975. 130p.

10433 BOSE, S.C. Dissentient report. Calcutta: 1956. 234p.

10434 COHEN, S.P. Subhas Chandra Bose and the Indian National Army. In PA 36 (1963-64) 411-29.

10435 CORR, G.H. The war of the springing tigers. London: Osprey, 1975. 200p.

10436 GHOSH, K.K. The Indian National Army; second front of the Indian independence movement. Meerut: Meenakshi, 1969. 351p.

10437 JHAVERI, V.K. & S.S. BOTLIVALA, ed. Jai-Hind, the diary of a rebel daughter of India with the Rani of Jhansi Regiment. Bombay: Janmabhoomi Prakashan Mandir, 1945. 130p.

10438 KHOSLA, G.D. Last days of Netaji. Delhi: Thomson Press, 1974. 184p.

10439 LEBRA, J.C. Jungle alliance: Japan and the Indian National Army. Singapore: Asia Pacific Press, 1971. 255p.

10440 MOHAN SINGH. Soldiers' contribution to Indian independence: the epic of the Indian National Army. ND: Army Educational Stores, 1974. 408p.

10441 MOOKERJEE, N. Netaji through German lens. 2nd ed. Calcutta: Jayasree, 1974. 145p.

10442 Netaji inquiry committee report. ND: PDMIB, 71p. [Shah Nawaz Khan, Chm.]

10443 SENGUPTA, B. The mystery of Netaji's disappearance. Tr. from Bengali by S. Banerjee. Calcutta: Ananya Prokashan, 1979. 115p.

10444 SHAH NAWAZ KHAN. My memories of I.N.A. and its Netaji. Delhi: Rajkamal Publications, 1946. 296p.

10445 SIVARAM, M. The road to Delhi. Tokyo: Tuttle, 1967. 264p.

f. the Sapru Committee (1943-45): attempt to mediate communal and minority conflict

10446 BANERJEE, D.N. The Sapru committee and leading principles of a new constitution for India. In MR 78 (1946) 173-76.

10447 NON-PARTY POLITICAL CONF. CONCILIATION CMTEE. Constitutional proposals of the Sapru committee. Bombay: Padma, 1945. 448p. [Tej Bahadur Sapru, chm.]

g. Archibald Percival Wavell, 1st Earl Wavell (Viceroy, Oct. 1943 - March 1947)

10448 MANSERGH, N. & E.W.R. LUMBY, eds. The transfer of power 1942-7; v. 3, Reassertion of authority, Gandhi's fast and the succession to the Viceroyalty 21 Sept. 1942 - 12 June 1943. London: HMSO, 1971. 1095 p. [documents]

10449 ______., eds. The transfer of power 1942-7; v. 4, The Bengal famine and the new viceroyalty, 15 June 1943 - 31 August 1944. London: HMSO, 1973. 1295p. [documents]

10450 WAVELL, ARCHIBALD PERCIVAL WAVELL, 1st Earl. Wavell: the Viceroy's journal. Ed. by P. Moon. London: OUP, 1973. 528p.

6. Post-War Constitutional Negotiations: Congress, League, and Atlee's Labour Government (Elected July, 1945)

a. the Simla Conference (June-July 1945): Jinnah's intransigence prevents agreement on communal representation

10451 BANERJEE, D.N. The Wavell offer. In MR 78 (1945) 82-87.

10452 BARTON, W.P. The Wavell plan and after. In QR 284 (1946) 17-29.

10453 MANSERGH, N. & P. MOON, eds. The transfer of power, 1942-7; v. 6, The post-war phase: new moves by the Labour government 1 August 1945 - 22 March 1946. London: HMSO, 1976. 1280p. [documents]

10454 ______., eds. The transfer of power, 1942-7; v. 5, The Simla Conference; background and proceedings, 1 September 1944 - 28 July 1945. London: HMSO, 1974. 1346p. [documents]

10455 TINKER, H. Jawaharlal Nehru at Simla, May 1947. A moment of truth? In MAS 4,4 (1970) 349-58.

b. the INA trials (1945-46) and the Royal Indian Navy mutiny (Feb., 1946)

10456 DESAI, B.J. INA defence (subject peoples' right to fight for freedom). Bombay: Congress Pub. Board, 1945. 155p.

10457 DUTT, B.C. Mutiny of the innocents. Bombay: Sindhu Pub., 1971. 238p.

10458 A GROUP OF VICTIMISED R.I.N. RATINGS. The R.I.N. strike. Delhi: PPH, 1954. 167p.

10459 The INA speaks, being the statements of Major-General Shah Nawaz Khan...[and others] in the general courts of martial. Delhi: Rajkamal, 1946. 147p. (INA Enquiry & Relief Cmtee. ser., 2)

10460 SHAH NAWAZ KHAN & P.K. SAHGAL & G.S. DHILLON. The INA heroes; autobiographies.... Lahore: Hero, 1946. 266p.

c. the Cabinet Mission (March, 1946), to help Indians frame their constitutional future; Jinnah's rejection of the Mission's proposals and his call for Muslim "Direct Action"

10461 ASHRAF, M., ed. Cabinet Mission and after. Lahore: Sh. M. Ashraf, 1946. 429p. [documents]

10462 BANERJEE, A.N. & D.R. BOSE, eds. The cabinet mission in India. Calcutta: A. Mukherjee, 1946. 386p. [documents]

10463 GOKHALE, S.M. Indian states and the cabinet mission plan. Baroda: M.S. Gokhale, 1947. 94p.

10464 GREAT BRITAIN. CABINET MISSION TO INDIA. ...Correspondence and documents connected with the conference between the Cabinet mission and His Excellency the Viceroy and representatives of the Congress and the Muslim League, May 1946.... London: HMSO, 1946. 19p. (Cmd. 6829; Parl. Pap. 1945/46:19)

10465 ______. Statement by the Cabinet Mission and His Excellency the Viceroy. London: HMSO, 1946. 9p. (Cmd. 6821; Parl. Pap. 1945/46:19)

10466 MANSERGH, N. & P. MOON, eds. The transfer of power, 1942-7; v. 7, The Cabinet Mission, 23 March-29 June 1946. London: HMSO, 1977. 1130p. [documents]

d. the Interim Government, headed by J. Nehru (took office Sept. 1946), and the Constituent Assembly (met 20 Jan. 1947)

10467 MANSERGH, N. & P. MOON, eds. The transfer of power; 1942-7; v. 8, The interim government, 3 July-1 November 1946. London: HMSO, 1979. 899p. [documents]

7. Divide and Quit, 1947: Mountbatten's Mission to Transfer Power

a. Louis Mountbatten, 1st Earl Mountbatten of Burma: last Viceroy, and first Governor-General of the Dominion of India, 1947-48

10468 AUCHINLECK, C. The British-Indian army: the last phase. In AR ns 44 (1948) 356-71.

10469 DUTT, R.P. The Mountbatten plan for India. In Labour Monthly 29 (1947) 210-19.

10470 Lord Mountbatten on his viceroyalty. In AR ns 44 (1948) 345-55.

10471 MOUNTBATTEN, LOUIS MOUNTBATTEN, Earl. Mountbatten: eighty years in pictures. NY: Viking, 1979. 224p.

10472 ______. Time only to look forward.... London: N. Kaye, 1949. 276p. [speeches 1947-48]

10473 MURPHY, R.L. Last Viceroy; the life and times of Rear-Admiral the Earl Mountbatten of Burma. London: Jarrolds, 1948. 270p.

b. transfer of power and partition: the Independence of India Act, and the Dominions of Pakistan and India, August 14 and 15, 1947

10474 BIRDWOOD, C.B.B. India and Pakistan; a continent decides. NY: Praeger, 1954. 315p.

10475 CAMPBELL-JOHNSON, A. Mission with Mountbatten. New ed. London: Hale, 1962. 383p. [1st pub. 1951]

10476 COLLINS, L. & D. LAPIERRE. Freedom at midnight. NY: Simon & Schuster, 1975. 572p.

10477 DARLING, M.L. At freedom's door. Bombay: OUP, 1949. 369p.

10478 FRYKENBERG, R.E. The partition of India: a quarter century after. In American Hist. R. 77,2 (1972) 463-72.

10479 KHOSLA, G.D. Stern reckoning; a survey of the events leading up to and following the partition of India. ND: Bhawnani, 1949. 349p.

10480 LOHIA, RAMMANOHAR. Guilty men of India's partition. Hyderabad: Rammanohar Lokia Samata Vidyalaya Nyas, 1970. 103p.

10481 LUMBY, E.W.R. The transfer of power in India 1945-7. London: Allen & Unwin, 1954. 274p.

10482 MITTELSTEN SCHEID, J. Die Teilung Indiens. Zur Zwei-Nationen-Theorie. Köln: Verlag Wissenschaft und Politik, 1970. 160p.

10483 RIZVI, J.H. Pakistan story. Lahore: Zia H. Rizvi, 1973. 173p.

10484 SMITH, R.A. Divided India. NY: McGraw Hill, 1947. 259p. [NY Times reporter]

10485 TINKER, H. Experiment with freedom: India and Pakistan, 1947. London: OUP, 1967. 165p.

10486 ______. Pressure, persuasion, decision: factors in the partition of the Punjab, August 1947. In JAS 36,4 (1977) 695-704.

10487 TUKER, F.I.S. While memory serves; the last two years of British rule in India. London: Cassell, 1950. 668p.

10488 WALLBANK, T.W., ed. The partition of India; causes and responsibilities. Boston: Heath, 1966. 103p. (Problems in Asian civilizations)

10489 ZAIDI, A. MOIN, ed. Evolution of Muslim political thought in India; v. y, Freedom at last. ND: S. Chand, 1979. 704p. [documents]

8. Aftermath of Partition

a. transfer of populations and intercommunal violence among Muslims, Sikhs, and Hindus; resettlement of refugees

10490 ALEXANDER, H.G. New citizens of India. Bombay: OUP, 1951. 130p.

10491 ANAND, B.S. Cruel interlude. NY: Asia, 1962. 228p.

10492 BHASKAR RAO, U. The story of rehabilitation. Delhi: Dept. of Rehabilitation, Min. of Labour, Employment and Rehabilitation, 1967. 230p.

10493 DAVIS, K. Population and partition. In his The population of India and Pakistan. Princeton: PUP, 1951, 195-202.

10494 Evacuee property problem in India and Pakistan; Pakistan's case. Karachi: Dept. of Advertising, Films & Pub., 1959. 26p.

10495 GANDA SINGH. A diary of the partition days. In PPP 13,2 (1978) 439-97.

10496 INDIA (REP.). MINISTRY OF REHABILITATION. Rehabilitation retrospect. ND: 1957. 98p.

10497 JEFFREY, R. The Punjab Boundary Force and the problem of order, August 1947. In MAS 8,4 (1974) 491-520.

10498 JILLANI, M.S. Resettlement pattern of displaced persons in Pakistan. In Geografia 2 (1963) 77-98.

10499 JONES, G.E. Tumult in India. NY: Dodd, Mead, 1948. 227p.

10500 KHUSHDEVA SINGH. Love is stronger than hate; a remembrance of 1947. Patiala: Guru Nanak Mission, 1973. 117p.

10501 KIRPAL SINGH. The partition of the Punjab. Rev. by Sri Ram Sharma. Patiala: Punjabi U., 1972. 188p.

10502 Millions on the move; the aftermath of partition. Delhi: PDMIB, 1952. 80p.

10503 PAKISTAN. MIN. OF REFUGEES AND REHABILITATION. Refugees rehabilitation in Pakistan. 3 v. Karachi: 1951-52.

10504 RAI, S.M. Partition of the Punjab; a study of its effects on the politics and administration of the Punjab, 1947-56. London: Asia, 1965. 304p.

10505 RANDHAWA, M.S. Out of the ashes; an account of the rehabilitation of refugees from West Pakistan in rural areas of East Punjab. Punjab: Public Relations Dept., 1954. 229p.

10506 SAKSENA, R.N. Refugees: a study in changing attitudes. London: Asia, 1961. 119p.

10507 SCHECHTMAN, J.B. Evacuee property in India and Pakistan. In IQ 9,1 (1953) 3-35.

10508 SPATE, O.H.K. The partition of India and the prospects of Pakistan. In Geographical R. 38 (1948) 5-30.

10509 TAHILRAMANI, P.V. Why the exodus from Sind? being a brief resume of conditions responsible for exodus of Hindus, Sikhs and Harijans from Sind. n.p., 1947? 72p.

10510 VAKIL, C.N. & P.H. CABINETMAKER. Government and the displaced persons; a study in social tensions. Bombay: Vora, 1956. 144p.

b. economic and political consequences of partition

10511 AHMAD, M. RIAZUDDIN. Pakistan: an economic proposition. Allahabad: Kitabistan, 1948. 135p.

10512 COUPLAND, R. Note on the financial prospects of Pakistan. In his The Indian problem: report on the constitutional problem of India; v. 3, The future of India. NY: OUP, 1944, 189-203.

10513 MICHEL, A.A. The Indus rivers: a study of the effects of partition. New Haven: YUP, 1967. 595p.

10514 SPATE, O.H.K. The partition of the Punjab and Bengal. In GJ 110 (1947) 201-222.

10515 VAKIL, C.N. Economic consequences of divided India: a study of the economy of India and Pakistan. Bombay: Vora, 1950. 555p.

10516 ______. Economic consequences of the partition. Bombay: Natl. Info. and Pub., Ltd., 1948. 128p.

c. Mahatma Gandhi's final efforts in behalf of Hindu-Muslim peace

10517 BOSE, N.K. My days with Gandhi. Calcutta: A. Chatterjea, 1953. 309p.

10518 BOURKE-WHITE, M. Half-way to freedom, in words and pictures. Bombay: Asia, 1950. 192p.

10519 GANDHI, MANUBEHN. The lonely pilgrim [Gandhiji's Noakhali pilgrimage]. Ahmedabad: Navajivan, 1964. 273p. [tr. from Gujarati]

10520 SINHA, B.K. Pilgrim of Noakhali: a souvenir album of Gandhiji's peace mission to Noakhali. Calcutta: 1948. 15p. + 34pl.

d. Gandhi's assassination by a Chitpavan Brahman unreconciled to partition and Gandhi's alleged favoritism to Muslims; the murder trial

10521 ABHYANKAR, K. Karbala re-enacted by Godse or "Bapu sacrificed for Moslems". Madras: New World Pub., 1948. 59p.

10522 AGARWALA, N.N. India's savior crucified: a challenge for us to think and act. Agra: Shiva Lal Agarwal, 1948. 62p.

10523 Gandhi Murder Trial. 2nd ed. ND: Tagore Memorial Pub., 1949. 207p.

10524 GAUBA, K.L. Assassination of Mahatma Gandhi. Bombay: Jaico, 1969. 424p.

10525 GHOSH, T. The Gandhi murder trial. NY: Asia, 1975. 336p.

10526 GODSE, N.V. May it please your honour: statement of Nathuram Godse. Pune: Vitasta Prakashan, 1977. 122p. [deposition of the assassin]

10527 GOLWALKAR, M.S. Justice on trial; a collection of the historic letters between Sri Guruji and the government, 1948-49. 5th ed. Bangalore: Rashtriya Swayamsevak Sangh, 1969. 107p.

10528 INAMDAR, P.L. The story of the Red Fort trial, 1948-49. Bombay: Pouplar, 1979. 224p.

10529 INDIA (REP.). CMSN. OF INQUIRY INTO CONSPIRACY TO MURDER MAHATMA GANDHI. Report. ND: Min. of Home Affairs, 1970. 2 v. in 1. [J.L. Kapur, chm.]

10530 JAIN, J.C. I could not save Bapu. Tr. from Hindi. Banaras: Jagran Sahitya Mandir, 1947. 241p.

10531 ______. Murder of Mahatma Gandhi: prelude and aftermath. Bombay: Chetna, 1961. 176p.

10532 KHOSLA, G.D. The murder of the Mahatma, and other cases from a judge's notebook. London: Chatto & Windus, 1963. 254p.

10533 MALGONKAR, M. The men who killed Gandhi. Delhi: Macmillan, 1978. 184p.

e. the integration of the Princely States into the Dominions of India and Pakistan

10534 INDIA (DOMINION). White paper on Indian States. ND: MPGOI, 1948. 101p.

10535 INDIA (REP.). MIN. OF STATES. White paper on Indian States. Rev. ed. Delhi: MPGOI, 1950. 395p.

10536 MENON, V.P. The story of the integration of the Indian states. NY: Macmillan, 1956. 511p.

V. CHANGING PATTERNS OF SOCIAL AND CULTURAL ORGANIZATION AND COMMUNICATION, 1813-1947

A. Initial British Views of Indian Society and the Question of Interference vs. Cultural Laissez-faire

1. Rationales for Social and Educational Policy: Utilitarian and Evangelical

10537 EAST INDIA COMPANY. Memorandum of the improvements in the administration of India during the last thirty years; and, The Petition of the East-India company to Parliament by John Stuart Mill. Farnborough: Gregg, 1968. 129p. [Rpt. 1858 ed.]

10538 EMBREE, A.T. Charles Grant and British rule in India. NY: ColUP, 1962. 320p.

10539 GHOSH, S.C. The utilitarianism of Dalhousie and the material improvement of India. In MAS 12,1 (1978) 97-110.

10540 GRANT, C. Observations on the state of society among the Asiatic subjects of Great Britain, particularly with respect to morals; and on the means of improving it. London: printed by order of the House of Commons, 1792. 116p.

10541 IYER, RAGHAVAN. Utilitarianism and all that - (the political theory of British imperialism in India). In his (ed.) South Asian affairs, no. 1. London: Chatto & Windus, 1960, 9-71. (St. Anthony's papers, 8)

10542 MACAULAY, T.B.M. Lord Macaulay's legislative minutes. Ed. by C.D. Dharker. London: OUP, 1946. 312p.

10543 MORRIS, H. Life of Charles Grant. London: Murray, 1904. 404p.

10544 SPEAR, T.G.P. Stern daughter of the voice of God: ideas of duty among the British in India. In W.D. O'Flaherty and J.D.M. Derrett, eds. The concept of duty in South Asia. ND: Vikas, 1978, 166-189.

10545 STOKES, E. The English Utilitarians and India. Oxford: OUP, 1959. 350p.

2. Early Western Accounts of Indian Society

10546 COHN, B.S. Notes on the history of the study of Indian society and culture. In M.B. Singer and B.S. Cohn, eds. Structure and change in Indian society. Chicago: Aldine, 1968, 3-28.

10547 PEGGS, J. India's cries to British humanity, relative to infanticide; British connection with idolatry, ghaut murders, suttee, slavery, and colonization of India. 3rd ed. rev. & enl. London: Simpkin & Marshall, 1832. 500p.

10548 TENNANT, W. Indian recreations; consisting chiefly of strictures on the domestic and rural economy of the Mahomedans & Hindoos. 2nd ed., enl. London: Longman, Hurst, Rees, & Orme, 1804. 2 v.

B. Education under the Raj: Agency for Westernization and National Identity

1. Bibliography

10549 GREAVES, M.A. Education in British India 1698-1947: a bibliography and guide to the sources of information in London. London: Inst. of Educ., U. of London, 1967. 182p. (Educ. Libraries Bull., Suppl. 13)

10550 KHANDWALA, V., ed. Bibliography: women's education in India, 1850-1967. In G.B. Sardar, ed. Golden Jubilee commemoration volume. Bombay: Shrimati Nathibai Damodar Thackersey Women's U., 1968., 1-102.

2. General Histories, Studies, and Document Collections

10551 BHATT, B.D. & J.C. AGGARWAL, eds. Educational documents in India, 1813-1968; survey of Indian education. ND: Arya Book Depot, 1969. 328p.

10552 CRANE, R.I. The transfer of western education to India. In W.B. Hamilton, ed. The transfer of institutions. Durham: DUP, 1965, 108-138.

10553 GILBERT, I.A. The Indian academic profession: the origins of a tradition of subordination. In Minerva 10,3 (1972) 384-411.

10554 ______. Organization of the academic profession in India: the Indian Educational Services, 1864-1924. In S.H. Rudolph & L.I. Rudolph, eds. Education and politics in India.... Cambridge: HUP, 1972, 319-41.

10555 HARTOG, P.J. Some aspects of Indian education, past and present. London: OUP, 1939. 109p.

10556 JAMES, H.R. Education and statesmanship in India; 1797-1910. 2nd ed. London: Longmans, Green, 1917. 143p. [1st ed. 1911]

10557 MCGAVRAN, D.A. Education and the beliefs of popular Hinduism. Jubbulpore: Mission Press, 1935. 179p.

10558 MATHUR, Y.B. Women's education in India (1813-1966). NY: Asia, 1973. 208p.

10559 MAYHEW, A.I. Education in India, 1835-1920.... London: Faber & Gwyer, 1926. 306p.

10560 MAZUMDAR, V. Education & social change; three studies on nineteenth century India. Simla: IIAS, 1972. 88p.

10561 NURULLAH, SYED & J.P. NAIK. A history of education in India (during the British period). 2nd rev. ed. London: Macmillan, 1951. 953p. [1st ed. 1943]

10562 PARANJOTI, V. East and West in Indian education; with special reference to the work of Protestant missions. Lucknow: Lucknow Pub. House, 1969. 262p.

10563 Progress of Education in India; quinquennial review. Delhi: Bureau of Educ.,Govt. of India. [issued 1882-1947; 1937-47 issue subtitled Decennial review]

10564 SAIYIDAIN, K.G. The humanist tradition in Indian educational thought. Bombay: Asia, 1966. 237p.

10565 SHARP, H. & J.A. RICHEY, eds. Selections from the educational records of the government of India. Calcutta: Bureau of Educ., 1920-22. 2 v. [v. 1, 1781-1839; v. 2, 1840-59]

10566 Shri R.V. Parulekar felicitation volume. Bombay: A.N. Samant, 1956. 268p.

10567 VAKIL, K.S. & S. NATARAJAN. Education in India. 3rd rev. ed. Bombay: Allied, 1966. 216p. [1st pub. 1937]

3. Education under the East India Company (1813-1853): Search for an Educational Policy

10568 ADAM, W. Adam's reports on vernacular education. Ed. by J. Long. Calcutta: Home Secretariat Press, 1868. 342p.

10569 ______. Reports on the state of education (1835 and 1838).... Ed. by A.N. Basu. Calcutta: U. of Calcutta, 1941. 578p.

10570 BASU, A.N., ed. Indian education in Parliamentary Papers. Bombay: Asia, 1952-. [pt. 1 (1832) 306p; no more pub.?]

10571 BASU, B.D. History of education in India under the rule of the East India Company. Calcutta: The Modern review office, 192-. 108p.

10572 BOMAN-BEHRAM, B.K. Educational controversies in India; the cultural conquest of India under British imperialism. Bombay: Taraporevala, 1943. 633p.

10573 MAJUMDAR, B.P. First fruits of English education, 1817-1857. Calcutta: Bookland, 1973. 378p.

10574 SPEAR, T.G.P. Bentinck and education. In Cambridge Hist. J. 6 (1938) 79-101.

10575 TREVELYAN, C.E. On the education of the people of India. London: Longman, Orme, Brown, Green, 1838. 220p.

4. From Wood's Despatch on Education (1854) to the Hunter Commission Report (1882): Beginnings of University Education

10576 BHARGAVA, K.D., ed. Selections from the educational records of the Government of India; v. 1, Educational reports, 1859-71. Delhi: MPGOI, 1960. 584p.

10577 GILBERT, I.A. Autonomy and consensus under the Raj: Presidency (Calcutta); Muir (Allahabad); M.A.-O. (Aligarh). In S.H. Rudolph & L.I. Rudolph, eds. Education and politics in India; studies in organization, society, and policy. Cambridge, Mass: HUP, 1972, 172-206.

10578 INDIA. EDUC. CMSN. Report of the Indian Education Commission, appointed by the resolution of the Government of India, dated 3rd February 1882. Calcutta: Govt. Printing, 1883. 639p. [W.W. Hunter, President]

10579 JOHNSTON, J. Abstract and analysis of the report of the Indian Education Commission.... London: Hamilton & Adams, 1884. 184p.

10580 NAIK, J.P., ed. Selections from the educational records of the Government of India; v. 2. Development of university education, 1860-87. Delhi: MPGOI, 1963. 558p.

10581 NAIK, J.P. & S.C. GHOSH, eds. Development of educational service, 1859-1879. ND: Zakir Husain Centre for Educ. Studies, Jawaharlal Nehru U., 1976. 80 + 416p.

5. Expansion and Indianization (1884-1947): Prelude to Independence

a. general studies and documents

10582 BASU, A.N. Education in modern India; a brief review. 2nd ed., rev. & enl. Calcutta: Orient Book Co., 1947. 184p.

10583 GOEL, B.S. Development of education in British India, 1905-1929. ND: Central Inst. of Educ., 1969. 108p.

10584 GREAT BRITAIN. INDIAN STATUTORY CMSN. AUXILIARY CMTEE. ON GROWTH OF EDUCATION. ...Interim report.... (Review of growth of education in British India by the Auxiliary committee appointed by the commission)... London: HMSO, 1929. 401p. [Chm., Sir Philip Hartog]

10585 INDIA. CENTRAL ADVISORY BOARD OF EDUCATION. ... Post-war educational development in India. Delhi: MPGOI, 1944. 118p. [Chm., Sir John Sargent]

10586 Indian educational policy; being a resolution issued by the Governor General in Council, on the 11th March 1904. Calcutta: Supt. Govt. Printing, 1904. 51p. [Lord Curzon, Gov.-Genl.]

10587 MISRA, L. Education of women in India, 1921-1966. Bombay: Macmillan, 1966. 225p.

10588 PANDIT, S.S. A critical study of the contribution of the Arya Samaj to Indian education. ND: Sarvadeshik Arya Pratinidhi Sabha, 1975. 368p.

10589 SINHA, S.P. English in India: a historical study with particular reference to English education in India. Patna: Janaki Prakashan, 1978. 196p.

b. higher education

10590 BASU, A.N. University education in India, past and present. Calcutta: Book Emporium, 1944. 166p.

10591 BOSE, A. American missionaries and higher education. In Indica 11,2 (1974) 101-22.

10592 ______. Higher education in India in the 19th century: the American involvement, 1883-1893. Calcutta: Punthi Pustak, 1978. 411p.

10593 BRAISTED, P.J. Indian nationalism and the Christian colleges. NY: Assn. Press, 1935. 171p.

10594 CHIB, S.N. Language, universities, and nationalism in India. London: OUP, 1936. 59p.

10595 GHOSH, S.C., ed. Development of university education, 1916-20. Zakir Husain Centre for Educ. Studies, Jawaharlal Nehru U., 1977. 394p. (Selections from the educ. records of the Govt. of India, new series 2)

10596 INDIA. INDIAN UNIVERSITIES CMSN. Report. Simla: Govt. Central Printing Office, 1902. 93p. [Apptd. by Lord Curzon; president, T. Raleigh]

10597 JAMES, H.R. Problems of higher education in India. London: Longmans, Green, 1916. 87p.

10598 RAMASWAMI AIYAR, C.P. Indian universities, retrospect and prospects; comprising nineteen convocation addresses, 1924-1964. Annamalainagar: Annamalai U., 1964. 306p.

10599 SESHADRI, P. The universities of India. London: OUP, 1935. 58p.

c. primary and secondary education

10600 BASU, A. Indian primary education, 1900-1920. In IESHR 8,3 (1971) 284-297.

10601 BASU, A.N. Primary education in India: its future. Calcutta: Indian Associated Pub. Co., 1946. 64p.

10602 GORDON, C., ed. Teaching in Indian elementary schools. London: OUP, 1921. 123p.

10603 OLCOTT, M. Better village schools, a programme of action. Calcutta: Assn. Press, 1937. 235p.

10604 SEN, J.M. History of elementary education in India. 2nd ed. Calcutta: The Book Co., 1941. 313p. [1st ed. 1933]

10605 ______. Primary education Acts in India, a study. Calcutta: Assn. Press, 1925. 88p.

10606 Village education in India. The report of a commission of inquiry.... London: OUP, 1920. 210p.

d. vocational and technical education

10607 ABBOTT, A., & S.H. WOOD. Report on the vocational education in India. Delhi: MPGOI, 1937. 138p.

10608 BASU, A. Technical education in India, 1900-1920. In IESHR 4 (1967) 361-74.

10609 BHARGAVA, K.D., ed. Selections from educational records of the Government of India; v. 4, Technical education in India, 1886-1907. Delhi: MPGOI, 1968. 353p.

10610 BHATT, R.G. The role of vocational and professional education in the economic development of India, from 1918 to 1951. Baroda: Baroda Pub. House, 1964. 170p.

10611 CRANE, R.I. Technical education and economic development in India before World War I. In C.A. Anderson & M.J. Bowman, eds. Education and economic development. Chicago: Aldine, 1965, 167-201.

e. adult education and literacy

10612 CHAMPNESS, E. & H.B. RICHARDSON, eds. Indian adult education handbook. London: National Adult School Union of Great Britain, 194-. 152p.

10613 LAUBACH, F.C. Forty years with the silent billion; adventuring in literacy. Old Tappan, NJ: F.H. Revell, 1970. 501p. [1st pub. 1960 as Thirty years...]

10614 PARULEKAR, R.V. Literacy in India. London: Macmillan, 1939. 181p.

6. Indian Nationalist Educational Thought and Experiments

a. the National Education Movement (1905-22)

10615 GHOSE, A. A system of national education, some introductory essays. 3rd ed. Madras: Arya, 1948. 57p. [1st pub. 1924]

10616 GOKHALE, G.N. Practical education; a monograph on education in India. Madras: B.G. Paul, 1936. 225p.

10617 LAJPAT RAI, Lala. The problem of national education in India. Delhi: PDMIB, 1966. 122p. [1st pub. 1920]

10618 MUKHERJEE, H. A phase of the swadeshi movement (national education, 1905-1910). Calcutta: Chuckerverty, Chatterjee, 1953. 84p.

10619 MUKHERJEE, H. & U. MUKHERJEE. The origins of the national education movement, 1905-1910. Calcutta:

Jadavpur U., 1957. 440p.

10620 PARULEKAR, R.V. The educational writings of Shri R.V. Parulekar. Ed. by J.P. Naik. Bombay: Asia, 1957. 268p.

b. Rabindranath Tagore and Viśva-Bhāratī, his experimental institutions of Śāntiniketan and Śrīniketan

10621 BANERJI, N.C. At the cross-roads, 1885-1946: the autobiography of Nripendra Chandra Banerji (Mastarmahasaya). 2nd ed. Calcutta: Jijnasa, 1974. 282p. [1st pub. 1950]

10622 GHOSE, S.D. Music and dance in Rabindranath Tagore's education philosophy. ND: Sangeet Natak Akademi, 1978. 60p.

10623 KUMARAPPA, J.M. Rabindranath Tagore: India's schoolmaster; a study of Tagore's experiment in the Indianization of education in light of India's history. NY: 1928. 222p.

10624 MUKHERJEE, H.B. Education for fulness; a study of the educational thought and experiment of Rabindranath Tagore. NY: Asia, 1963. 495p.

10625 PEARSON, W.W. Shantiniketan, the Bolpur school of Rabindranath Tagore. London: Macmillan, 1916. 130p.

10626 SARKAR, B.N. Tagore, the educator. 2nd ed. Calcutta: Academic Pub., 1974. 100p.

10627 SURYANARAYANA, A.V. Tagore as educationist. Visakhapatnam: M.S.R. Murty, 1962. 64p.

10628 TAGORE, T.N. & L.K. ELMHIRST. Rabindranath Tagore, pioneer in education: essays and exchanges between Rabindranath Tagore and L.K. Elmhirst. London: Murray, 1961. 111p.

10629 Visva-Bharati and its institutions. Santiniketan: Visva-Bharati, 1961. 63p.

c. Gandhian educational ideas and the Wardha Scheme of Basic Education

10630 ALL INDIA EDUCATION BOARD. Basic national education syllabus. Prepared by Zakir Husain Cmtee. Wardha: 1938. 65 + 207p.

10631 ALL-INDIA NATIONAL EDUCATION CONF., Wardha, 1937. Basic national education; report of the Zakir Husain Cmtee. 3rd ed. Wardha: Hindustani Talimi Sangh, 1938. 202p.

10632 GANDHI, M.K. Basic education. Ahmedabad: Navajivan, 1951. 112p.

10633 ______. Educational reconstruction. Wardha: Hindustani Talimi Sangh, 1939. 296p.

10634 ______. The problem of education. 1st ed. Ahmedabad: Navajivan, 1962. 316p.

10635 GUPTA, B. Intelligent man's guide to the Wardha scheme of education (contains Gandhiji's latest doctrine...) Aligarh: Natl. Lit. Pub. Soc., 1939. 224p.

10636 Indian education. Lucknow: Hindustan Pub. House, 1939. 319p. [a survey with full text of Wardha Educ. Cmtee. & recommended syllabus]

10637 PATEL, M.S. The educational philosophy of Mahatma Gandhi. Ahmedabad: Navajivan, 1953. 288p.

10638 RAMANATHAN, G.K. Education from Dewey to Gandhi: the theory of basic education. Bombay: Asia, 1962. 308p.

10639 RAO, R.V. The Gandhian institutions of Wardha. Bombay: Thacker, 1947. 47p.

10640 VARKEY, C.J. The Wardha scheme of education, an exposition and examination. 2nd ed. London: OUP, 1940. 176p.

d. Muslim educational leaders

10641 ABDUHU, G.R. The educational ideas of Maulana Abul Kalam Azad. ND: Sterling, 1973. 171p.

10642 AHMAD, M.M.Z. Present day problems of Indian education (with special reference to Muslim education). Bombay: the author, 1935. 89p.

10643 ANDREWS, C.F. Zaka Ullah of Delhi. Lahore: Universal Books, 1976. 159p. [1st pub. 1929]

10644 Iqbal and education. Karachi: Jamia Inst. of Educ., 1966. 132p. [seminar papers]

10645 SAIYIDAIN, K.G. Iqbal's educational philosophy. 6th rev. ed. Lahore: Sh. M. Ashraf, 1965. 162p. [1st pub. 1938]

10646 SINGH, R.P. Zakir Husain: dynamics of indigenous education. Delhi: Sterling Pub., 1968. 114p.

10647 TUFAIL, M.M. Iqbal's philisophy and education. Lahore: Bazm-i-Iqbal, 1966. 144p.

10648 WASEY, A. Education of Indian Muslims: a study of the All-India Muslim Educational Conference, 1886-1947. ND: Press Asia International, 1977. 98p.

C. Science and Technology under the Raj

1. The Introduction and Development of Modern Science in India

10649 BURKILL, I.H. Chapters in the history of botany in India. Calcutta: Botanical Survey of India, 1965. 245p.

10650 FERMOR, L. The development of scientific research in India to the end of the nineteenth century. In Asiatic Soc. of Bengal, Yearbook 1 (1935) 9-22.

10651 Fifty years of science in India. Calcutta: Indian Science Congress Assn., 1963. 10v. [each on a science]

10652 HILL, A.V. Scientific research in India. London: Royal Society, 1945. 55p.

10653 LARWOOD, H.J.C. Western science in India before 1850. In JRAS (1962) 62-76.

10654 MACLEOD, R.M. Scientific advice for British India: imperial perceptions and administrative goals, 1898-1923. In MAS 9,3 (1975) 343-84.

10655 SEN, S.N. The character of the introduction of Western science in India during the eighteenth and nineteenth centuries. In IJHS 1,2 (1966) 112-122.

2. The Indian Scientific Community
a. institutions and associations for scientific research, from the founding of the Asiatic Society, Calcutta, 1784

10656 Centenary of the Geological Survey of India, 1851-1951. Calcutta: Geological Survey of India, 1951. 122p.

10657 GUPTA, S.P. Modern India and progress in science and technology. ND: Vikas, 1979. 164p.

10658 INDIA (REP.). GEOLOGICAL SURVEY. One hundred twentyfive years of the Geological Survey of India, 1851-1976: a short history. Calcutta: 1976. 58p.

10659 INDIA (REP.). METEOROLOGICAL DEPT. Hundred years of weather service, 1875-1975. ND: 1976. 207p.

10660 MUKERJI, B. & P.K. BOSE. Short history of the Indian Science Congress Association, 1914-63. Calcutta: Indian Science Congress Assn., 1963. 132p.

b. Indian and Western scientists

10661 BASU, S.N. Jagadis Chandra Bose. ND: NBT, 1970. 83p.

10662 CHATTERJI, S. & E. CHATTERJEE. Satyendra Nath Bose. ND: NBT, 1976. 127p.

10663 DHAR, N.R. Acharya P.C. Ray and his achievements. Calcutta: Indian Chemical Soc., 1972. 54p.

10664 GEDDES, P. The life and work of Sir Jagadis C. Bose. London: Longmans, Green, 1920. 259p.

10665 GUPTA, S.M. Birbal Sahni. ND: NBT, 1978. 87p.

10666 HOWARD, L. Sir Albert Howard in India. Emmaus, PA: Rodale Press, 1954. 272p.

10667 Indian scientists: biographical sketches.... Madras: Natesan, 1929. 280p.

10668 NANDY, A. Alternative sciences: creativity and authenticity in two Indian scientists. ND: Allied, 1980. 155p.

10669 ______. Indianized science: J.C. Bose's experiments with truth. In Quest 84 (1973) 19-34.

10670 RANGANATHAN, S.R. Ramanujan, the man and the mathematician. Bombay: Asia, 1967. 138p.

10671 RAY, P.C. Life and experiences of a Bengali chemist. Calcutta: Chuckervertty, Chatterjee, 1932. 2 v.

10672 RICHARDS, NORAH. Sir Shanti Swarup Bhatnagar, F.R.S.; a biographical study of India's eminent scientist. ND: New Book Soc., 1948. 239p.

D. Public Health and Medical Services under the Raj

10673 BALFOUR, M.I. & R. YOUNG. The work of medical women in India. London: OUP, 1929. 201p.

10674 BEATSON, W.B. Indian Medical Service, past and present. In AR 14 (1902) 272-319.

10675 BRADFIELD, E.W.C. Indian medical review. Delhi: MPGOI, 1938. 658p. (survey of medical establishment, education & research)

10676 BUCHANAN, W.J. Introduction and spread of Western medical science in India. In CR 278 (Oct. 1914) 419-54.

10677 CHANDRASEKHAR, S. Infant mortality in India: 1901-1951. London: Allen & Unwin, 1959. 175p.

10678 COTTON, H.E.A. Indian Medical Service. In BPP 41 (1931) 165-73.

10679 CRAWFORD, D.G. History of the Indian medical service, 1600-1913. London: W. Thacker, 1930. 710p. [1st pub. 1914]

10680 GANGULEE, N. Health and nutrition in India. London: Faber & Faber, 1938. 337p.

10681 HERIR, P. The medical profession in India. London: H. Frowde, 1923. 139p.

10682 INDIA. HEALTH SURVEY AND DEVELOPMENT CMTEE. Report. Delhi: MPGOI, 1946. 4 v. [J.W. Bhore, Chm.]

10683 JEFFERY, R. Recognizing India's doctors: the institutionalization of medical dependency, 1918-39. In MAS 13,2 (1979) 301-26.

10684 LEAGUE OF NATIONS, HEALTH ORGANISATION. Health organisation in India. Calcutta: the League, 1928. 388p.

10685 NIGHTINGALE, F. Life or death in India. London: Spottiswoode, 1874. 63p.

E. Cities and Urbanization under the Raj

10686 AHMED ALI, M. Historical aspects of town planning in Pakistan and India. Karachi: al-Ata Foundation, 1972. 100p.

10687 BAYLY, C.A. Town building in North India, 1790-1830. In MAS 9,4 (1975) 483-504.

10688 FORREST, G.W. Cities of India. Westminster: Archibald Constable, 1903. 356p.

10689 GEDDES, P. Patrick Geddes in India. Ed. by J. Tyrwhitt. London: L. Humphries, 1947. 103p.

10690 KING, A.D. Colonial urban development; culture, social power, and environment. London: Routledge, Kegan Paul, 1976. 344p.

10691 MELLER, H.E. Urbanization and the introduction of modern town planning ideas in India, 1900-25. In K.N. Chaudhuri & C.J. Dewey, eds. Economy and society. Delhi: OUP, 1979, 330-50.

10692 MURPHEY, R. City and countryside as ideological issues: India and China. In CSSH 14,3 (1972) 250-67.

F. Social Welfare and Reform under the Raj

1. General Studies

10693 APPASWAMY, P. Legal aspects of social reform. Madras: CLS, 1929. 256p.

10694 BLUNT, E.A.H., ed. Social service in India. London: HMSO, 1938. 446p.

10695 CARROLL, L. The temperance movement in India: politics and social reform. In MAS 10,3 (1976) 417-47.

10696 CASSELS, N.G. The "compact" and the pilgrim tax; the genesis of East India Company social policy. In Canadian J. of History 7,1 (1972) 37-49.

10697 CHINTAMANI, C.Y., ed. Indian social reform: a collection of essays.... Madras: Minerva Press, 1901. 2 v., 369, 390p.

10698 DATTA, K.K. Renaissance, nationalism, and social changes in modern India. 2nd ed. Calcutta: Bookland, 1973. 166p.

10699 DUA, R.P. Social factors in the birth and growth of the Indian National Congress movement...1885 to 1935. ND: S. Chand, 1967. 163p.

10700 DWIVEDI, H.P. Thakkar Bapa. Tr. from Hindi by K.K. Misra. ND: PDMIB, 1977. 157p.

10701 GANGULI, B.N. Concept of equality: the nineteenth century Indian debate. Simla: IIAS, 1975. 132p.

10702 HEIMSATH, C.H. Indian nationalism and Hindu social reform. Princeton: PUP, 1964. 379p.

10703 NATARAJAN, S. A century of social reform in India. 2nd ed., rev. & enl. Bombay: Asia, 1962. 223p.

10704 O'MALLEY, L.S.S. India's social heritage. Oxford: OUP, 1934. 194p.

10705 SANKARAN NAIR, C. Position of Hindu social reform associations. Madras: Indian Printing Works, 1913. 60p.

10706 SEN, S.P. Social and religious reform movements in the nineteenth and twentieth centuries. Calcutta: IHS, 1979. 520p.

10707 SINGH, S.R. Nationalism and social reform in India. Delhi: Ranjit, 1968. 391p.

2. Early British Social Intervention: Collision of Traditional Customs with Christian Morality (Up to 1857)

a. satī/suttee, "a woman who is true," used for the practice of widow-burning (outlawed 1829)

10708 MITRA, K. Suppression of suttee in the province of Cuttack. In BPP 46 (1933) 125-31.

10709 MUKHOPADHYAY, A. Sati as a social institution in Bengal. In BPP 75 (1957) 118-26.

10710 NANDY, A. Sati: a nineteenth century tale of women, violence and protest. In V.C. Joshi, ed. Rammohun Roy and the process of modernization in India. ND: Vikas, 1975, 168-94.

10711 SAXENA, R.K. Social reforms: infanticide and sati. ND: Trimurti, 1975. 155p.

10712 SHARMA, A. Suttee: a study in Western reactions. In his Thresholds in Hindu-Buddhist studies. Calcutta: Minerva, 1979. 231p.

10713 STEIN, D. Women to burn: suttee as a normative institution. In Signs 4,2 (1978) 253-68.

10714 THOMPSON, E.J. Suppression of suttee in Native States. In Edinburgh R. 245 (1927) 274-86.

10715 ______. Suttee; a historical and philosophical enquiry into the Hindu rite of widow-burning. Boston: Houghton Mifflin, 1928. 165p.

b. female infanticide

10716 CAVE-BROWNE, J. Indian infanticide: its origin, progress, and suppression. London: W.H. Allen, 1857. 234p.

10717 DAS, MANMATHA NATH. Movement to suppress the custom of female infanticide in the Punjab and Kashmir. In MI 37 (1957) 280-93.

10718 PANIGRAHI, L. British social policy and female infanticide in India. ND: Munshiram, 1972. 204p.

10719 WILSON, J. History of the suppression of infanticide in Western India under the government of Bombay.... London: 1855. 457p.

c. slavery

10720 FRERE, H.B.E. Abolition of slavery in India and Egypt. In Fortnightly R. 39 (1883) 349-68.

10721 INDIA. LAW CMSN. Report on Indian slavery. n.p., 1841. 379p.

3. Efforts to Raise the Status of Women in Indian Society (after 1857)

a. general

10722 CATON, A.R., ed. The key of progress: a survey of the status and conditions of women in India. London: OUP, 1930. 250p.

10723 KARVE, D.K. Professor Karve's work in the cause of Indian women as described by himself. In MR 18 (1915) 537-46.

10724 SESHADRI, P., ed. Har Bilas Sarda commemoration volume. Ajmer: Vedic Yantralaya, 1937. 554p.

b. child marriage, the "age of consent" controversy, and the problem of widow remarriage

10725 HEIMSATH, C.H. The origins and enactment of the Age of Consent bill. In his Indian nationalism and Hindu social reform. Princeton: PUP, 1964, 147-75. [1st pub. in JAS 21 (1962) 491-504]

10726 INDIA. AGE OF CONSENT CMTEE. Report, 1928-29. Calcutta: Govt. of India Central Pub. Branch, 1929. 353p. [Sir M.V. Joshi, chm.]

10727 INDIA. HOME DEPT. Papers relating to infant marriage and enforced widowhood. Calcutta: 1886. 303p.

10728 INDIA. LAWS, STATUTES. Child Marriage Restraint Act, 1929. (No. 19 of 1929) In Unrepealed Central Acts. Delhi: MPGOI, 1939, v. 8, 406-07. [Harbilas Sarda Act]

10729 MALABARI, B.M. Infant marriage and enforced widowhood in India, being a collection of opinions, for and against.... Bombay: Voice of India Printing Press, 1887. 109p.

10730 MAYO, K. Volume two. NY: Harcourt, Brace, 1931. 301p. [critique of 1928 Age of Consent Cmtee. report, dealing with child marriage.]

10731 VIDYASAGAR, ISHWARCHANDRA. Marriage of Hindu widows. Calcutta: K.P. Bagchi, 1856. 144p. [1st Bengali ed. 1855]

c. courtesans and temple prostitutes: dancing ("nautch") girls and devadāsīs

10732 CHATTERJEE, S. Devadasi: temple dancer. Calcutta: Book House, 1945. 128p.

10733 VENKATARATNAM NAIDU, R. Social purity and the anti-nautch movement. In C.Y. Chintamani, ed. Indian social reform. Madras: Minerva, 1909, pt. I, 249-81.

d. pardā/purdah ("curtain"): seclusion of women in the zenānā ("female quarters")

10734 DAS, F.M.H. Purdah, the status of Indian woman. ND: Ess Ess, 1979. 289p. [Rpt. 1932 ed.]

10735 PAPANEK, H. Purdah: separate worlds and symbolic shelter. In CSSH 15,3 (1973) 289-325.

10736 PITMAN, E.R. Indian zenana missions: [their need, origin, objects, agents, modes of working, and results]. London: J. Snow, 1903. 48p.

e. legal status of women - ownership and inheritance of property

10737 BANERJEE, G.D. The Hindu law of marriage and stridhana. 5th ed. Calcutta: S.K. Lahiri, 1923. [1st pub. 1878]

10738 INDIA. HINDU LAW CMTEE. Report. ND: MPGOI, 1947. 183p.

10739 MEHTA, R.V. A thesis on the legal rights of women under different communal laws in vogue in India. Bombay: G.G. Blat, 1933. 93p.

10740 SIRVYA, B.D. Hindu woman's estate; non-technical stridhana. Calcutta: Butterworth, 1913. 418p.

f. women's leaders and organizations: progress toward enfranchisement and equality

10741 ASTHANA, P. Women's movement in India. Delhi: Vikas, 1974. 135p.

10742 CHANDAVARKAR, G.L. Dhondo Keshav Karve. ND: PDMIB, 1970. 248p. [1st pub. 1958]

10743 DATTA, G.S. A woman of India; being the life of Saroj Nalini (founder of the Women's Institute movement in India) by her husband. 2nd ed. London: L. & Virginia Woolf, 1929. 149p. [1st pub. 1929]

10744 GANDHI, M.K. The role of women. Ed. by A.T. Hingorani. Bombay: BVB, 1964. 120p.

10745 KARVE, D.K. Looking back. Poona: Hindu Widows' Home Assn., 1936. 199p.

4. Stratification and Untouchability: Social and Economic Discrimination on the Basis of Caste

a. studies of social stratification

10746 AHMAD, I. Caste mobility movements in N. India. In IESHR 8,2 (1971) 164-91.

10747 BROOMFIELD, J.H. The regional elites: a theory of modern Indian history. In IESHR 3,3 (1966) 279-91.

10748 MISRA, B.B. The Indian middle classes: their growth in modern times. London: OUP, 1961. 438p.

b. general studies of problems of Untouchables, about 1/5 of all Hindus

10749 The depressed classes; a chronological documentation. Kurseong: St. Mary's College, 1931-37. 597p.

10750 MUKERJEE, RADHA KAMAL. Caste and social change in India. In AJS 43 (1937) 377-90.

10751 MUKERJI, D.G. Caste and outcaste. NY: E.P. Dutton, 1923. 303p.

10752 RAMANUJACHARI, K. The condition of low castes. In C.Y. Chintamani, ed. Indian social reform. Madras: Minerva Press, 1901, 312-34.

10753 SANJANA, J.E. Caste and outcaste. Bombay: Thacker, 1946. 249p.

10754 SINGH, M. The depressed classes, their economic and social condition. Bombay: Hind Kitabs, 1947. 213p.

10755 SUNDARANANDA, Swami. Hinduism and untouchability. Calcutta: Udbodhan Office, 1946. 130p.

10756 VENKATRAMAN, S.R. Temple entry legislation reviewed; with acts and bills. Madras: Bharat Devi, 1946. 128p.

10757 VENKATASWAMY, P.R. Our struggle for emancipation. Secunderabad: the author, 1955. 2 v., 663p.

c. early effort at "elevation of the depressed classes" by missionaries and Indian reformers

10758 CHAKRAVARTI, S.C. & S.N. RAY, eds. Brahmo Samaj, the depressed classes and untouchability. Calcutta: 1933. 87p.

10759 The depressed classes; an enquiry into their condition and suggestions for their uplift. Madras: Natesan, n.d. 268p. [statements by 23 prominent Indians and foreigners, originally published in The Indian Review, 1909-11]

d. Gandhi's work for the "Harijans" ("Children of God"): the first All-India movement for abolition of untouchability

10760 ALEXANDER, H.G. Mr. Gandhi and the untouchables. In Contemporary R. 147 (1935) 194-201.

10761 ANDREWS, C.F. Untouchable problem. In Contemporary R. 144 (1933) 152-60.

10762 BARTON, W.P. Indian federation and the untouchable. In Quarterly R. 268 (1937) 18-28.

10763 COATMAN, J. Reforms in India and the depressed classes. In AS ns 29 (1933) 41-70.

10764 DALTON, D. The Gandhian view of caste, and caste after Gandhi. In P. Mason, ed. India and Ceylon: unity and diversity. London: OUP, 1967, 159-81.

10765 FONTERA, R.M. Gandhi and the Poona pact. In PSR 6,1 (1967) 11-25.

10766 GANDHI, M.K. Caste must go and the sin of untouchability. Ed. by R.K. Prabhu. Ahmedabad: Navajivan, 1964. 108p.

10767 ______. My varnashrama dharma. Ed. by A.T. Hingorani. Bombay: BVB, 1965. 131p.

10768 ______. None high: none low. Ed. by A.T. Hingorani. Bombay: BVB, 1965. 135p.

10769 SORABJI, C. Temple-entry and untouchability. In Nineteenth Century 113 (1933) 689-702.

10770 VERMA, M.B. Crusade against untouchability: history of the Harijan Sevak Sangh, 1932-68. Delhi: Harijan Sevak Sangh, 1971. 245p.

e. Bhimrao Ramji Ambedkar (1892-1956): Mahar economist, lawyer, Constitution-framer, and Untouchable political leader; his confrontation with Gandhi

10771 AMBEDKAR, B.R. Annihilation of caste with a reply to Mahatma Gandhi; and Castes in India: their mechanism, genesis, and development. Jullundur: Bheem Patrika Pub., 1968. 160p.

10772 ______. Dr. Babasaheb Ambedkar, writings and speeches. Bombay: Educ. Dept., Govt. of Maharashtra, 1979-. v. 1-

10773 ______. Mr. Gandhi and the emancipation of the untouchables. Bombay: Thacker, 1943. 73p.

10774 ______. The untouchables. 2nd ed. Shravasti, U.P.: Bharatiya Bauddha Shiksha Parishad, 1969. 203p.

10775 ______. What Congress and Gandhi have done to the untouchables. Bombay: Thacker, 1946. 399p.

10776 BHARILL, C. Social and political ideas of B.R. Ambedkar: a study of his life, services, social and political ideas. Jaipur: Aalekh Pub., 1977. 347p.

10777 Dr. Ambedkar: pioneer of human rights. Ed. by R.D. Suman. ND: Bodhisattva Pub., Ambedkar Inst. of Buddhist Studies, 1977. 324p.

10778 JATAVA, D.R. Dr. Ambedkar's role in national movement, 1917-1947. ND: Bauddha Sahitya Sammelan, 1979. 216p.

10779 ______. The political philosophy of B.R. Ambedkar. Agra: Phoenix Pub. Agency, 1965. 256p.

10780 ______. The social philosophy of B.R. Ambedkar. Agra: Phoenix Pub. House, 1965. 277p.

10781 ______. To the critics of Dr. Ambedkar. ND: Bharatiya Shoshit Jan Utthan Parishad, 1975. 151p.

10782 KEER, D. Dr. Ambedkar, life and mission. 2nd ed. Bombay: Popular, Prakashan, 1962. 528p.

10783 KUBER, W.N. B.R. Ambedkar. ND: PDMIB, 1978. 178p.

10784 ______. Dr. Ambedkar; a critical study. ND: PPH, 1973. 332p.

10785 LOKHANDE, G.S. Bhimrao Ramji Ambedkar: a study in social democracy. ND: Sterling, 1977. 264p.

10786 RAJASEKHARIAH, A.M. B.R. Ambedkar, the politics of emancipation. Bombay: Sindhu Pub., 1971. 347p.

10787 ROBBIN, J. Dr. Ambedkar and his movement. Hyderabad: Dr. Ambedkar Pub. Soc., 1964. 180p.

10787a ZELLIOT, E.M. Dr. Ambedkar and the Mahar movement. Ph.D. diss., U. of Pennsylvania, 1969. 53 + 304p. [UM 69-21,466]

5. Later Western Censure of Indian Society in the Name of Reform: "Mother India" (1927) and its Critics

10788 BLUNT, W.S. Ideas about India - II: Race hatred. In Fortnightly R. 42 (1884) 445-59.

10789 EMERSON, G. Voiceless India. Westport, CT: Greenwood Press, 1971. 458p. [rpt. of 1930 ed.]

10790 FIELD, H.H. After Mother India.... London: J. Cape, 1929. 299p. [discussion of the book and its critics]

10791 JHA, M.R. Katherine Mayo and India. ND: PPH, 1971. 128p.

10792 LAJPAT RAI, Lala. Unhappy India. 2nd ed., rev. & enl. Calcutta: Banna Pub. Co., 1928. 70 + 565p. [1st ed. also 1928]

10793 MAYO, K. Mother India. NY: Harcourt Brace, 1927. 440p.

10794 NICHOLS, B. Verdict on India. NY: Harcourt Brace, 1944. 304p.

10795 WOOD, E.E. An Englishman defends Mother India; a complete constructive reply to "Mother India." Madras: Ganesh, 1930. 475p.

G. Journalism and the Press under the Raj

1. General Histories of the Indian Press, in Western and Regional Languages

10796 BARNS, M. The Indian press; a history of the growth of public opinion in India. London: Allen & Unwin, 1940. 491p.

10797 BHATNAGAR, R.R. The rise and growth of Hindi journalism, 1826-1945. Allahabad: Kitab Mahal, 1948. 780p.

10798 CARROLL, L. Kayastha Samāchār: from a caste - to a national newspaper. In IESHR 10,3 (1973) 280-92.

10799 CHALAPATHI RAU, M. The press in India. Bombay: Allied, 1968. 145p.

10800 DAS GUPTA, U. The Indian press, 1870-1880: a small world of journalism. In MAS 11,2 (1977) 213-36.

10801 DIGBY, WM. Native newspapers of India and Ceylon. In CR 65 no. 130 (1877) 356-94. [incl. lists of non-English publications by province]

10802 ______. The 'struggle for existence' of the English press in India. In CR 62 no. 124 (1876) 256-74.

10803 GHOSE, H.P. The newspaper in India. Calcutta: U. of Calcutta, 1952. 89p.

10804 GUPTA, A. Indian newspaper press and the national movement till 1920. In VQ 27 (1961) 150-62.

10805 100 years of the Statesman, 1875-1975. Calcutta: Statesman, 1975. 172p.

10806 IYER, V.N. The Indian press. Bombay: Padma, 1945. 72p.

10807 KASTURI, G., ed. The Hindu speaks. Bombay: Interpress, 1978. 319p. [selected editorials]

10808 KHARE, P.S. The growth of press and public opinion in India, 1857 to 1918. Allahabad: Piyush Prakashan, 1964. 151p.

10809 KHURSHID, A.S. Journalism in Pakistan: first phase, 1845 to 1857. Lahore: Publishers United, 1964. 122p.

10810 LAL, K.S. A short history of Urdu newspapers. Hyderabad: Inst. of Indo-Middle East Cultural Studies, 1964. 51p.

10811 LETHBRIDGE, R. Vernacular press in India. In Contemporary R. 37 (1880) 459-73.

10812 MAJUMDER, N. The Statesman: an anthology, 1875-1975. Calcutta: Statesman Ltd., 1975. 623p.

10813 MOITRA, M. A history of Indian journalism. Calcutta: Natl. Book Agency, 1969. 193p.

10814 MURTHY, N.K. Indian journalism; origin, growth and development of Indian journalism from Asoka to Nehru. Mysore: U. of Mysore, 1966. 506p.

10815 NARAIN, P. Press and politics in India 1885-1905. Delhi: Munshiram, 1970. 321p.

10816 NATARAJAN, J. History of Indian journalism. ND: PDMIB, 1955. 287p. [Pt. 2 of Press Cmsn. report]

10817 NATARAJAN, S. A history of the press in India. Bombay: Asia, 1962. 425p.

10818 PARTHASARATHY, R. A hundred years of The Hindu. Madras: Kasturi, 1978. 842p.

10819 RHODES, D.E. India, Pakistan, Ceylon, Burma and Thailand. NY: Schram, 1969. 95p. (The Spread of Printing: Eastern hemisphere)

10820 SANIAL, S.C. History of journalism in India. In CR 124-32 (1907-1911) passim.

10821 SEN, S.P., ed. Indian press (a collection of papers presented at the 4th annual conference of the Institute, Mysore, 1966). Calcutta: IHS, 1967. 166p.

2. Biographies and Memoirs of Leading Journalists in India

10822 BHATTACHARYYA, S.N. Mahatma Gandhi the journalist. Bombay: Asia, 1965. 195p.

10823 BOSE, N.S. Ramananda Chatterjee. ND: PDMIB, 1974. 165p. [editor of Modern Review]

10824 BUCKINGHAM, J.S. Autobiography.... London: Longman, Brown, Green, & Longmans, 1855. 2 v. [editor of Oriental Herald, Calcutta Journal]

10825 DAS, DURGA. India from Curzon to Nehru and after; with a foreword by Zakir Hussain. London: Collins, 1969. 487p. [editor of Hindustan Times]

10826 GHOSE, M.M. The life of Girish Chunder Ghose, the founder and first editor of "the Hindoo Patriot" and "the Bengalee," by one who knew him. Calcutta: R. Cambray, 1911. 239p.

10827 GHOSE, S.L. Motilal Ghose. ND: NBT, 1970. 134p.

10828 GOVINDARAJAN, S.A. G. Subramania Iyer. ND: PDMIB, 1969. 110p. [founder of The Hindu]

10829 Life of Shishir Kumar Ghosh, founder-editor of Amrita Bazar Patrika. Calcutta: T.K. Ghosh, 1946. 195p. [by "Wayfarer"]

10830 NARASIMHAN, V.K. Kasturi Srinivasan. Bombay: Popular, 1969. 164p. [editor of The Hindu]

10831 RAMA RAO, K. The pen as my sword; memoirs of a journalist. Bombay: BVB, 1965. 332p.

10832 REED, S. The India I knew, 1897-1947. London: Odhams, 1952. [editor of Times of India]

10833 SANIAL, S.C. Father of Indian journalism, Robert Knight - his life-work. In CR 19 (1926) 287-325; 20 (1926) 28-63, 305-49. [editor of Bombay Times]

10834 SAHNI, J.N. Truth about the Indian press. Bombay: Allied, 1974. 259p.

10835 SARAF, M.R. Fifty years as a journalist. Jammu: Raj Mahal Pub., 1967. 183p.

10836 SINHA, SACHCHIDANANDA. Recollections and reminiscences of a long life. In Hindustan R. (Patna) 80-85 (1946-1949). [autobiography of editor of Hindustan Review]

10837 TURNER, R.E. The relations of James Silk Buckingham with the East India Company, 1818-36. Pittsburgh: the author, 1930. 145p.

3. Government and the Press: Freedom of the Press vs. Censorship

10838 AGRAWAL, S. Press, public opinion, and government in India. Jaipur: Asha Pub. House, 1970. 249p.

10839 BARRIER, N.G. Banned: controversial literature and political control in British India, 1907-1947. Columbia: U. of Missouri Press, 1974. 324p.

10840 BISHUI, K. Lord Dufferin and the Indian press. In BPP 84 (1965) 38-48.

10841 DAS, M.N. Measures against the Indian press during the Bande Mataram movement. In JIH 41 (1936) 167-76.

10842 DASGUPTA, U. Indian public opinion and the Vernacular Press Act, 1878. In BPP 92,2 (1973) 201-19.

10843 ______. Rise of an Indian public: impact of official policy, 1870-1880. Calcutta: Rddhi, 1977. 332p.

10844 GHOSE, H.P. Press laws in India. Calcutta: D.K. Mittra, 1930. 102p.

10845 INDIA. ... Copy of the Indian press act, 1910, and proceedings of the Legislative council of the governor general of India relating thereto. London: HMSO, 1910. 67p. (Cd. 5269; Parl. Pap. 1910:68)

10846 ______. ... The India press ordinance, 1930. London: HMSO, 1930. 14p. (Cmd. 3578; Parl. Pap. 1929/30: 23)

10847 The native press of Bengal. In CR 43,86 (1866) 357-79.

10848 LETHBRIDGE, R. Government relations with the press; an Indian precedent. In Nineteenth Century (1918) 403-11.

10849 MENON, K.B. The Press laws of India. Bombay: K.B. Menon, 1937. 52p. (Indian Civil Liberties Union series, 1)

10850 PRADHAN, R.G. History of press legislation in India. In MR 14 (1913) 131-40; 256-62.

10851 Rammohun Roy and freedom of the press in India. In Muslim R. (1930) 24-38.

10852 ROY, G.K. Law relating to press and sedition. Calcutta: 1922. 203p.

VI. ECONOMIC HISTORY OF INDIA IN THE BRITISH PERIOD (1818-1947)

A. Bibliography and Reference

10853 Annotated bibliography on the economic history of India (1500 AD to 1947 AD). Poona: GIPE, 1977. 3 v., 1865p. [to be 4 v.]

10854 BENJAMIN, N. Economic history of India (1526-1900); a bibliographic essay. In AV 12,4 (1970) 594-626.

10855 KUMAR, DHARMA. Recent research in the economic history of modern India. In IESHR 9,1 (1972) 63-90. [bibl. essay]

10856 MORRIS, M.D. Trends and tendencies in Indian economic history. In IESHR 5,4 (1968) 319-88.

B. Economic History of the Raj

1. General Studies

10857 ANSTEY, V.P. The economic development of India. 4th ed. London: Longmans, Green, 1952. 677p.

10858 BANERJEA, P.N. A study of Indian economics. 5th rev. & enl. ed. London: Macmillan, 1940. 395p. [1st pub. 1911]

10859 BHATT, V.V. Aspects of economic change and policy in India, 1800-1960. Bombay: Allied, 1967. 140p.

10860 BHATTACHARYA, S. Cultural and social constraints on technological innovation and economic development: some case studies. In IESHR 3,3 (1966) 240-67.

10861 BUCHANAN, D.H. The development of capitalistic enterprise in India. London: Cass, 1966. 497p. [Rpt. 1934 ed.]

10862 CHAKRAVARTI, N.R. Hundred years of Japan and India, 1868-1968: a comparative study of development. Calcutta: Progressive, 1978. 393p.

10863 CHAUDHURI, K.N., comp. The economic development of India under the East India Company 1814-58; a selection of contemporary writings. Cambridge: CamUP, 1971. 319p.

10864 DEWEY, C. & A.G. HOPKINS, ed. The imperial impact: studies in the economic history of Africa and India. London: Athlone Press, 1978. 409p.

10865 GADGIL, D.R. The industrial evolution of India in recent times, 1860-1939. 5th ed. Bombay: OUP, 1971. 362p.

10866 GANGULI, B.N., ed. Readings in Indian economic history. NY: Asia, 1964. 190p. [proc. of 1961 seminar]

10867 GAUTAM, V. Aspects of Indian society and economy in the nineteenth century; a study based on an evaluation of the American Consular records. Delhi: Motilal, 1972. 201p.

10868 HABIB, I. Colonialization of the Indian economy, 1757-1900. In SocSci 3,8 (1975) 23-53.

10869 Indian economy in the nineteenth century; a symposium. Delhi: Indian Econ. and Social History Assn., 1969. 170p. [also in IESHR 5 (1968) 1-100; essays by M.D. Morris, Bipan Chandra, T. Matsui, T. Raychaudhuri]

10870 KAUSHAL, G. Economic history of India, 1757-1966. ND: Kalyani, 1979. 713p.

10871 LEVKOVSKY, A.I. Capitalism in India; basic trends in its development. Bombay: PPH, 1966. 663p.

10872 MADDISON, A. Class structure and economic growth; India and Pakistan since the Moghuls. NY: Norton, 1972. 181p.

10873 MORRIS, M.D. Values as an obstacle to economic growth in South Asia: an historical survey. In JEH 27 (1967) 588-607.

10874 RANADE, M.G. Essays on Indian economics.... 2nd ed. Madras: Natesan, 1906. 353p. [1st ed. 1899]

10875 RAYCHAUDHURI, T., ed. Contributions to Indian economic history. Calcutta: KLM, 1960-63. 2 v.

10876 RUDRA, ASHOK. Studies in the development of capitalism in India: essays. Lahore: Vanguard Books, 1978. 459p.

10877 SINGH, V.B. Indian economy, yesterday and today. 2nd enl. ed. Delhi: PPH, 1970. 182p.

10878 ______., ed. Economic history of India: 1857-1956. Bombay: Allied, 1965. 795p.

2. Demography and Population

10879 GEDDES, A. Social and psychological significance of variability in population change, with examples from India (1871-1941). In Human Relations 1 (1947) 181-205.

10880 INDIA (REP.). CENSUS OF INDIA, 1961. Report on the population estimates of India (1820-1930). Ed. by D.P. Bhattacharya & B. Bhattacharya. Delhi: 1963. 395p. (Census of India, 1961, v. 29)

10881 KLEIN, I. Population and agriculture in northern India 1872-1921. In MAS 8,2 (1974) 191-216.

10882 MAHALANOBIS, P.C. Growth of population of India and Pakistan 1801-1961. In AV 18,1 (1976) 1-10.

10883 ZACHARIAH, K.C. A historical study of internal migration in the Indian sub-continent, 1901-1931. London: Asia, 1965. 297p.

3. Secular Trends and Structural Changes; National Income

10884 BAGCHI, A.K. Reflections on patterns of regional growth in India during the period of British rule. In BPP 95,1 (1976) 247-89.

10885 BHATTACHARYA, D. Trend of wages in India, 1873-1900. In AV 7 (1965) 202-12.

10886 CHAUDHURI, M.K., ed. Seminar on trends of socio-economic change in India, 1871-1961. Simla: IIAS, 1969. 811p. (Its trans., 7)

10887 DESAI, R.C. Standard of living in India and Pakistan, 1931-32 to 1940-41. Bombay: Popular, 1953. 286p.

10888 KRISHNAMURTY, J. Secular changes in the occupational structure of the Indian union, 1901-1961. In IESHR 2 (1965) 42-51.

10889 Long-term trends in the employment pattern in India. In IEJ 7 (1960) 415-40.

10890 MUKHERJEE, M.A. National income of India: trends and structure. Calcutta: Statistical Pub. Soc., 1969. 521p.

10891 NARAIN, L. Price movements in India, 1929-1963. Meerut: Shri Prakashan, 1963. 396p.

10892 PALEKAR, S.A. Real wages in India, 1939-1950. Bombay: Intl. Book House, 1962. 378p.

10893 SAINI, K.G. Economic performance and institutional change: the experience of India, 1860-1913. In CAS 3 (1973) 83-95.

10894 RAO, V.K.R.V. The national income of British India, 1931-2. London: Macmillan, 1940. 240p.

10895 RAYCHAUDHURI, G.S. On some estimates of national income: Indian economy 1858-1947. In EPW 1,16 (1966) 673-79.

10896 REDDY, K.N. Growth of government expenditure and national income in India: 1872-1966. In Public Finance 25,1 (1970) 81-95.

10897 SHAH, K.T. & K.J. KHAMBATA. Wealth and taxable capacity of India. Bombay: Taraporevala, 1924. 347p.

10898 THORNER, A. The secular trend in the Indian economy, 1881-1951. In EW 14 (1962) 1156-65.

10899 THORNER, D. Long term trends in output in India. In S. Kuznets, J.J. Spengler, & W.E. Moore, eds. Economic growth: Brazil, India, Japan. Durham: DUP, 1955, 103-28.

C. Economic Thought: Indian and British Views

1. Surveys of Modern Indian Economic Thought

10900 BIPAN CHANDRA. The rise and growth of economic nationalism in India; economic policies of Indian national leadership, 1880-1905. ND: PPH, 1966. 783p.

10901 DATTA, B. Indian economic thought: twentieth century perspectives, 1900-1950. ND: Tata McGraw-Hill, 1978. 200p.

10902 DATTA, S.C. Conflicting tendencies in Indian economic thought. Calcutta: N.M. Raychowdhury, 1934. 225p. [on M.K. Gandhi & B.K. Sarkar]

10903 ______. Thirty-five years of Indian economic thought, 1898-1932. Calcutta: M.M. Moulik, 1932. 20p. [bibl.]

10904 GANGULI, B.N. Indian economic thought: nineteenth century perspectives. ND: Tata McGraw-Hill, 1977. 283p.

10905 GOPALAKRISHNAN, P.K. Development of economic ideas in India, 1880-1950. ND: PPH, 1959. 208p.

10906 MADAN, G.R. Economic thinking in India. ND: S. Chand, 1966. 399p.

10907 SINGH, V.B. From Naoroji to Nehru; six essays in Indian economic thought. ND: Macmillan, 1975. 174p.

2. The "Drain Theory," "Aborted Growth," and other Economic Critiques of British Rule

10908 BOSE, P.N. Survival of Hindu civilization. Part 1, the impoverishment of India and its remedy. Calcutta: W. Newman, 1918. 47 + 81p.

10909 BOULDING, K.E. & T. MUKERJEE. Unprofitable empire: Britain in India, 1800-1967, a critique of the Hobson-Lenin thesis on imperialism. In Peace Research Society, Papers, 16, The Rome Conference, 1970 (1971) 1-22.

10910 DIGBY, W. India for the Indians - and for England. London: Talbot Brothers, 1885. 261p.

10911 ______. 'Prosperous' British India, a revelation from official records. ND: Sagar, 1969. 661p. [Rpt. 1901 ed.]

10912 DUTT, R.C. The economic history of India. Critical intro. by D.R. Gadgil. ND: PDMIB, 1970. 2 v. [1st pub. 1902]

10913 GANGULI, B.N. Dadabhai Naoroji and the drain theory. Bombay: Asia, 1965. 152p.

10914 LAJPAT RAI, Lala. England's debt to India; a historical narrative of Britain's fiscal policy in India. ND: PDMIB, 1967. 48 + 242p. [Rpt. 1917 ed.]

10915 MCLANE, J.R. The drain of wealth and Indian nationalism at the turn of the century. In T. Raychauduri, ed.

Contributions to Indian economic history. Calcutta: KLM, 1960-63, v. 2, 21-40.

10916 NAOROJI, D. Poverty and un-British rule in India. London: Sonnenschein, 1901. 675p. [Rpt. Delhi: PDMIB, 1962]

10917 PAVLOV, V.I. India: economic freedom versus imperialism. ND: PPH, 1963. 247p. [tr. from Russian]

10918 ROSEN, G. A case of aborted growth: India, 1860-1900; some suggestions for research. In EW 14 (1962) 1299-1302. [comment by W.C. Neale in EW 14 (1962) 1862]

10919 ROY, M.N. India in transition. Bombay: Nachiketa, 1971. 288p.

10920 SAINI, K.G. A case of aborted economic growth: India, 1860-1913. In JAH 5 (1971) 89-118.

10921 SEN, S.K. Studies in economic policy and development of India (1848-1939). 2nd ed., rev. & enl. Calcutta: Progressive, 1972. 278p.

3. British Economic Thought and India Policy

10922 AMBIRAJAN, S. Classical political economy and British policy in India. Cambridge: CamUP, 1978. 301p. (Cambridge South Asian studies, 21)

10923 ______. Economic ideas and economic policy in British India. In IEJ 15 (1967) 188-208.

10924 BARBER, W.J. British economic thought and India, 1600-1858. Oxford: OUP, 1975. 264p.

10925 ______. James Mill and the theory of economic policy in India. In History of Political Economy 1 (1969) 85-100.

10926 BHATTACHARYA, S. Laissez-faire in India. In IESHR 2 (1965) 1-22.

10927 BLACK, R.D.C. Economic policy in Ireland and India in the time of J.S. Mill. In EHR 21 (1968) 321-36.

10928 HARNETTY, P. Imperialism and free trade, Lancashire and India in the mid-nineteenth century. Vancouver: U. of British Columbia Press, 1972. 137p.

10929 MOORE, R.J. Imperialism and "free trade" policy in India, 1853-4. In EHR 17 (1964) 135-45.

D. The Agrarian Base

1. General Studies of Agricultural Development

10930 ADAMS, J. Agriculture, growth and rural change in India in the 1900's. In PA 43,2 (1970) 189-202.

10931 BLYN, G. Agricultural trends in India, 1891-1947: output, availability, and productivity. Philadelphia: U. of Pennsylvania Press, 1966. 370p.

10932 DIONNE, R.J. Government directed agricultural innovation in India: the British experience. Diss., Duke U., 1973. 239p. [UM 74-7532]

10933 GANGULEE, N.N. The Indian peasant and his environment; the Linlithgow Commission and after. London: OUP, 1935. 230p.

10934 GHOSH, A.K. Cyclical trends in Indian agriculture 1861-1913. In IESHR 4 (1967) 177-202.

10935 GREAT BRITAIN. ROYAL CMSN. ON AGRICULTURE IN INDIA. Report. ND: Agricole Pub. Academy, 1979. 755p. [Rpt. 1928 ed.; V.A.J. Hope Linlithgow, chm.]

10936 MORRIS, M.D. Economic change and agriculture in nineteenth century India. In IESHR 3,2 (1966) 185-209.

10937 MUKERJEE, RADHAKAMAL. The rural economy of India. London: Longmans, Green, 1926. 262p.

10938 NARAIN, D. The impact of price movements on areas under selected crops in India, 1900-1939. London: CamUP, 1965. 234p.

10939 STOKES, E.T. Dynamism and enervation in North Indian agriculture: the historical dimension. In BPP 95,1 (1976) 227-46.

10940 VOELCKER, J.A. Report on the improvement of Indian agriculture. London: Eyre & Spottiswoode, 1893. 460p.

10941 THORNER, D. & A. THORNER. Land and labour in India. Bombay: Asia, 1962. 227p.

10942 WADHWA, D.C., ed. Agrarian legislation in India (1793-1966). Poona: GIPE, 1973-. v. 1, Andhra-Maharashtra. 868p. (Its Studies, 61) [guide to legislation and to administrative geography]

2. Land Tenure and Revenue Systems; Beginnings of Land Reform

10943 BADEN-POWELL, B.H. Administration of land revenue and tenure in British India. ND: Ess Ess, 1978. 262p. [Rpt. 1907 ed.]

10944 ______. The land systems of British India. Oxford: OUP, 1892. 3 v. [Rpt. NY: Johnson Rpt. Corp., 1972]

10945 BHUTANI, V.C. The apotheosis of imperialism: Indian land economy under Curzon. ND: Sterling, 1976. 191p.

10946 CHAUDHURI, B.B. Movement of rent in eastern India, 1793-1930. In IHR 3,2 (1977) 308-90. [Bengal, Bihar, Orissa, Assam]

10947 COHN, B.S. Comments on papers on land tenure. In IESHR 1,1 (1963) 177-83.[Comments on papers by Metcalf, McLane and Hauser appearing in previous issue]

10948 ______. From Indian status to British contract. In JEH 21 (1961) 613-28.

10949 FRYKENBERG, R.E., ed. Land control and social structure in Indian history. Madison: UWiscP, 1969. 256p.

10950 ______., ed. Land tenure and peasant in South Asia. Delhi: Orient Longman, 1977. 311p.

10951 GALLOWAY, A. Observations on the law and constitution, and present government of India, on the nature of landed tenures and financial resources. London: Parbury, Allen, 1832. 512p.

10952 GUPTA, S.C. Agrarian relations and early British rule in India, 1801-33. Bombay: Asia, 1963. 338p.

10953 METCALF, T.R. Laissez-faire and tenant right in mid-nineteenth century India. In IESHR 1,1 (1963) 74-81.

10954 ______. The struggle over land tenure in India, 1860-1868. In JAS 21 (1962) 295-307.

10955 MUKERJEE, RADHAKAMAL. Land problems of India. London: Longmans, Green, 1933. 369p.

10956 ROTHERMUND, D. Freedom of contract and the problem of land alienation in British India. In SA 3 (1973) 57-78.

10957 ______. Government, landlord and tenant in India. 1875-1900. In IESHR 6,4 (1969) 351-58.

10958 ______. The land revenue problem in British India. In BPP 95,1 (1976) 210-26.

10959 ______. The record of rights in British India. In IESHR 8,4 (1971) 443-61.

10960 SEN, B. Evolution of agrarian relations in India, including a study of the nature and consequences of post-independence agrarian legislation. ND: PPH, 1962. 295p.

10961 SEN, S.K. Agrarian relations in India, 1793-1947. ND: PPH, 1979. 249p.

3. The Indian Village and the Peasantry under the Raj [See also Chap. One, III. G., and Regional Chaps. Ten - Sixteen]

a. general studies of rural conditions

10962 BIPAN CHANDRA. Indian peasantry and national integration. In SocSci 5,2 (1976) 3-29.

10963 GANGULEE, N.N. Problems of rural India: being a collection of addresses.... Calcutta: U. of Calcutta, 1928. 155p.

10964 IYENGAR, S. KESAVA. Studies in Indian rural economics. London: P.S. King, 1927. 203p.

10965 MANN, H.H. The social framework of agriculture; India, Middle East, England. Ed. by D. Thorner. NY: A.M. Kelley, 1967. 501p.

b. early British views of the "Indian village community"

10966 BADEN-POWELL, B.H. The Indian village community. London: Longmans, Green, 1896. 456p.

10967 ______. The origin and growth of village communities in India. NY: Johnson Rpt. Corp., 1970. 155p. [Rpt. of 1899 ed.]

10968 DEWEY, C. Images of the village community: a study in Anglo-Indian thought. In MAS 6,3 (1972) 291-328.

10969 DUMONT, L. The "village community" from Munro to Maine. In CIS 9 (1965) 67-89.

10970 MAINE, H.J.S. Village communities in the East and West. NY: Henry Holt, 1889. 413p.

10971 MATTHAI, J. Village government in British India. London: T.F. Unwin, 1915. 211p.

10972 OOMMEN, T.K. Myth and reality in India's communitarian villages. In JComPolSt 4,2 (1966) 94-116.

10973 PHEAR, J.B. The Aryan village in India and Ceylon. ND: Asian Pub. Services, 1975. 295p. [Rpt. 1880 ed.]

10974 SRINIVAS, M.N. The Indian village; myth and reality. In J.H.M. Beattie & R.G. Lienhardt, ed. Studies in social anthropology: essays in memory of E.E. Evans-Pritchard.... Oxford: OUP, 1975, 41-85.

10975 SRINIVAS, M.N. & A.M. SHAH. The myth of self-sufficiency of the Indian village. In EW 12,37 (1960) 1375-78.

10976 ZAMORA, M.D. A historical summary of Indian village autonomy. In AsSt 3 (1965) 262-82.

c. rural reconstruction: Gandhian and other programs

10977 BRAYNE, F.L. Better villages. 3rd ed. London: OUP, 1951. 306p. [1st ed. 1937]

10978 DASGUPTA, S. A poet and a plan; Tagore's experiences in rural reconstruction. Calcutta: Thacker Spink, 1962. 149p.

10979 KUMARAPPA, J.C. Why the Village Movement? (a plea for a village centered economic order in India). Wardha: All India Village Industries Assn., 1946. 153p.

10980 LAL, P.C. Reconstruction and education in rural India in the light of the programme carried on at Sriniketan, the Institute of Rural Reconstruction. London: Allen & Unwin, 1932. 262p.

10981 PILLAI, A.P. Welfare problems in rural India. Bombay: Taraporevala, 1931. 195p.

10982 TARLOK SINGH. Poverty and social change; with a reappraisal. 2nd ed. Bombay: Orient Longmans, 1969. 352p. [1st pub. 1945]

d. peasant indebtedness, moneylenders, and the cooperative movement

10983 BENJAMIN, N. Some aspects of agricultural indebtedness in British India, 1850-1900. In IJE 51 (1971) 209-27.

10984 HOUGH, E.M. The co-operative movement in India. 5th ed., rev. & enl. by K. Madhava Das. London: OUP, 1966. 492p.

10985 KAJI, B.L., ed. Co-operation in India. Bombay: All-India Co-op. Inst. Assn., 1932. 501p.

10986 MCLANE, J.R. Peasants, money-lenders and nationalists at the end of the 19th century. In IESHR 1,1 (1963) 66-73.

10987 METCALF, T.R. The British and the money lender in nineteenth-century India. In J. of Modern History 34 (1962) 390-97.

10988 MUKHERJI, P. The Cooperative Movement in India. Calcutta: Thacker, Spink, 1923. 468 + 80p.

10989 RAY, S.C. Agricultural indebtedness in India and its remedies. Calcutta: Calcutta U., 1915. 468p. [selections from official documents]

10990 RESERVE BANK OF INDIA. Review of the cooperative movement in India, 1939-1946. Bombay: 1948. 111p.

10991 WOLFF, H.W. Cooperation in India. London: W. Thacker, 1919. 352p.

e. agricultural laborers

10992 BHATIA, B.M. Famine and agricultural labour in India: a historical perspective. In IJIR 10,4 (1975) 575-94.

10993 GHOSE, K.K. Agricultural labourers in India: a study in the history of their growth and economic condition. Calcutta: Indian Pub., 1969. 296p.

10994 KRISHNAMURTHY, J. The growth of agricultural labour in India: a note. In IESHR 9,3 (1972) 327-32. [on S.J. Patel's Agricultural labourers...]

10995 PATEL, S.J. Agricultural labourers in India and Pakistan. Bombay: Current Book House, 1952. 169p.

f. peasant movements and unrest

10996 DESAI, A.R., ed. Peasant struggles in India. Bombay: OUP, 1979. 772p.

10997 DHANAGARE, D.N. Agrarian movements and Gandhian politics. Agra: Inst. of Social Sciences, Agra U., 1975. 128p.

10998 ______. The politics of survival: peasant organizations and the left wing in India, 1925-46. In SB 24,1 (1975) 29-54.

10999 GOUGH, K. Indian peasant uprisings. In EPW 9,32-34 (1974) 1391-1412.

11000 HARDIMAN, D. Politicisation and agitation among dominant peasants in early twentieth century India. In EPW 11,9 (1976) 365-71.

11001 FUCHS, S. Messianic and chiliastic movements among Indian aboriginals. In Studia missionalia 13 (1963) 85-103.

11002 ______. Messianic movements in primitive India. In AFS 24,1 (1965) 11-62.

11003 ______. Rebellious prophets; a study of messianic movements in Indian religions. NY: Asia, 1965. 304p.

11004 NATARAJAN, L. Peasant uprisings in India, 1850-1900. Bombay: PPH, 1953. 80p.

11005 PANDEY, S.M. The emergence of peasant movement in India: an area study. In IJIR 7,1 (1971) 59-104.

11006 RANGA, N.G. Indian peasants' struggle and achievements. In A.R. Desai. Peasant struggles in India. Bombay: OUP, 1979, 66-84.

11007 ______. Kisans and communists. Bombay: Pratibha, Pub., 19--. 127p.

11008 RASUL, M.A. A history of the All India Kisan Sabha. Calcutta: Natl. Book Agency, 1974. 368p.

11009 SHIVE KUMAR. Peasantry and the Indian national movement, 1919-1933. Meerut: Anu Prakashan, 1979. 274p.

11010 STOKES, E.T. The peasant and the Raj: studies in agrarian society and peasant rebellion in colonial India. Cambridge: CamUP, 1978. 308p.

11011 ______. The return of the peasant to South Asian history. In SA 6 (1976) 96-111.

4. Famine and Famine Policy

11012 AMBIRAJAN, S. Political economy and Indian famines. In SA 1 (1971) 20-28.

11013 BHATIA, B.M. Famines in India; a study in some aspects of the economic history of India, 1860-1965. 2nd ed. Bombay: Asia, 1967. 389p.

11014 BLAIR, C. Indian famines; their historical, financial and other aspects.... Edinburgh: Blackwood, 1874. 240p.

11015 DIGBY, W. The famine campaign in southern India (Madras and Bombay presidencies and province of Mysore) 1876-1878. London: Longmans, Green, 1878. 2 v.

11016 DUTT, R.C. Open letters to Lord Curzon on famines and land assessments in India. London: K. Paul, Trench, Trübner, 1900. 322p.

11017 GEDDES, J.C. Administrative experience, recorded in former famines; extracts from official papers.... Calcutta: Bengal Secretariat Press, 1874. 441p.

11018 GREAT BRITAIN. INDIA OFFICE. East India (famine). Papers regarding the famine and the relief operations in India during 1900-1902. London: HMSO, 1902. 2 v.

11019 ______. East India (Madras and Orissa) famine. London: 1867. 281p.

11020 INDIA. FAMINE CMSN., 1878-80. Report. London: HMSO, 1881. 3 v., + 5 append.

11021 INDIA. FAMINE CMSN., 1898. Report. Calcutta: Supt. Govt. Printing, 1898. 371p. + 7 v. of evidence. [Chm. J.B. Lyall]

11022 INDIA. FAMINE CMSN., 1901. Report of the Indian Famine Commission. ND: Agricole Pub. Academy, 1979. 132p. [Rpt. 1901 ed.; Chm., A.P. MacDonell]

11023 LOVEDAY, A. The history and economics of Indian famines. London: G. Bell, 1914. 163p.

11024 SRIVASTAVA, H.S. The history of Indian famines and development of famine policy, 1858-1918. Agra: Sri Ram Mehra, 1968. 417p.

5. Water Supply: Irrigation and Flood Control

11025 BUCKLEY, R.B. The irrigation works of India. 2nd ed. London: E. & F.N. Spon, 1905. 336p. [1st ed. 1880]

11026 COTTON, A.T. Lectures on irrigation works in India. Vijayawada: 1968. 60p.

11027 INDIA. IRRIGATION CMSN., 1901. Report. London: HMSO, 1903. 4 v. (Cd. 1851-4; 1904) [Chm., Sir C. Scott-Moncrieff]

11028 KANETKAR, B.D. Pricing of irrigation service in India (1854-1959). In AV 2,2 (1960) 158-68.

6. Crops: Field and Plantation; Forestry

11029 BORPUJARI, J.G. Indian cottons and the cotton famine, 1860-65. In IESHR 10,1 (1973) 37-49.

11030 GRIFFITHS, P.J. The history of the Indian tea industry. London: Weidenfeld & Nicolson, 1967. 730p. + 24 pl.

11031 HARNETTY, P. Cotton exports and Indian agriculture, 1861-1870. In EHR 24,3 (1971) 414-29.

11032 RIBBENTROP, B. Forestry in British India. Calcutta: Supt. Govt. Printing, 1900. 245p.

11033 SILVER, A.W. Manchester men and Indian cotton, 1847-1872. Manchester: Manchester U. Press, 1966. 349p.

E. Transportation and Commerce under the Raj

1. General Studies

11034 BANERJI, T. History of internal trade barriers in British India; a study of transit and town duties. Calcutta: Asiatic Soc., 1972-. v. 1 -

11035 ______. Internal market of India, 1834-1900. Calcutta: Academic Pub., 1966. 358p.

11036 GORMAN, M. Sir William O'Shaughnessy, Lord Dalhousie and the establishment of the telegraph system in India. In Technology and Culture 12 (1971) 581-601.

11037 SHAH, K.T. Trade, tariffs and transport in India. London: P.S. King, 1923. 450p.

11038 SHRIDHARANI, K.J. Story of the Indian telegraphs; a century of progress. ND: Posts and Telegraphs Dept., 1956. 172p.

11039 VERGHESE, K.E. The development and significance of transport in India, 1834-1882. ND: N.V. Pub., 1976. 234p.

2. Indian Railways and Shipping

11040 ASHTA, M.C. Passenger fares on the Indian railways, 1849-1869. In IESHR 4,1 (1967) 53-89.

11041 BATRA, S. The major ports of India. 3rd rev. ed. Adipur: Kandla Commercial Pub., 1970. 269p.

11042 BERNSTEIN, H.T. Steamboats on the Ganges; an exploration in the history of India's modernization through science and technology. Bombay: Orient Longmans, 1960. 239p.

11043 GRAHAM, G.S. Great Britain and the Indian Ocean; a study of maritime enterprise, 1810-50. Oxford: OUP, 1967. 479p.

11044 GREAT BRITAIN. INDIAN RAILWAY CMTEE., 1920. Report. London: HMSO, 1921. 4 v. [Chm., Sir Wm. Acworth]

11045 HURD, J., II. Railways and the expansion of markets in India, 1861-1921. In Explorations in Econ. History 12,3 (1975) 263-88.

11046 JOHNSTON, J. Inland navigation of Gangetic rivers. Calcutta: Thacker, Spink, 1947. 167p.

11047 MCALPIN, M.B. Railroads, prices, and peasant rationality: India 1860-1900. In JEH 34,3 (1974) 662-84.

11048 MACPHERSON, W.J. Investment in Indian railways. In EHR 8 (1955) 177-86.

11049 MALIK, M.B.K. 100 years of Pakistan railways.... Karachi: Min. of Railways & Comm., 1962. 226p.

11050 SAHNI, J.N. Indian railways, 100 years (1853 to 1953). ND: Ministry of Railways (Railway Board), 1953. 200p.

11051 SANJEEVA RAO, T.S.A. A short history of modern Indian shipping. Bombay: Popular, 1965. 278p.

11052 SANYAL, N. Development of Indian railways. Calcutta: U. of Calcutta, 1930. 397p.

11053 STAPLES, A.C. Indian maritime transport in 1840. In IESHR 7,1 (1970) 61-90.

11054 THORNER, D. Investment in empire: British railway and steam shipping enterprise in India, 1825-1849. Philadelphia: UPaP, 1950. 197p.

11055 ______. The pattern of railway development in India. In FEQ 14,2 (1955) 201-16.

3. Foreign Economic Relations and Tariffs; Balance of Payments

11056 ADAMS, J. The impact of the Suez canal on India's trade. In IESHR 8,3 (1971) 229-40.

11057 BANERJEE, A.K. India's balance of payments; estimates of current and capital accounts from 1921-22 to 1938-39. London: Asia, 1963. 255p.

11058 BHATIA, B.M. Terms of trade and economic development: a case study of India - 1861-1939. In IEJ 16 (1969) 414-33.

11059 CHAUDHURI, K.N. India's international economy of the nineteenth century: an historical survey. In MAS 2 (1968) 31-50.

11060 CHUNG, T. The Britain-China-India trade triangle (1771-1840). In IESHR 11,4 (1974) 411-31.

11061 DURGA PARSHAD, I. Some aspects of India's foreign trade, 1757-1893. London: P.S. King, 1932. 238p.

11062 GANGULI, B.N. India's economic relations with the Far Eastern and Pacific countries in the present century. Calcutta: Orient Longmans, 1956. 348p.

11063 GREENBERG, M. British trade and the opening of China, 1800-42. Cambridge: CamUP, 1951. 238p.

11064 GURTOO, D.H.N. India's balance of payments, 1920-1960. Delhi: S. Chand, 1961. 241p.

11065 HAMILTON, C.J. The trade relations between England and India, 1600-1896. Calcutta: Thacker, Spink, 1919. 263p.

11066 HARNETTY, P. The imperialism of free trade: Lancashire and the Indian cotton duties, 1859-62. In EHR 2nd ser. 18,2 (1965) 333-49.

11067 ______. India and British commercial enterprise: the case of the Manchester Cotton Company, 1960-64. In IESHR 3,4 (1966) 396-421.

11068 ______. The Indian cotton duties controversy, 1894-1896. In English Historical R. 77 (1962) 684-702.

11069 KLEIN, I. English free traders and Indian tariffs, 1875-1896. In MAS 5,3 (1971) 251-72.

11070 MANI, V. Foreign capital and economic development: a case study of an overpopulated backward export economy with special reference to India up to 1950. ND: Vidya Vahini, 1978. 180p.

11071 PANDIT, Y.S. India's balance of indebtedness, 1898-1913. London: Allen & Unwin, 1937. 210p.

11072 RAY, P. India's foreign trade since 1870. London: G. Routledge, 1934. 300p.

11073 SHAH, N.J. History of Indian tariffs. Bombay: Thacker, 1924. 433p.

11074 SOVANI, N.V. Economic relations of India with South East Asia and the Far East. ND: Indian Council of World Affairs, 1949. 137p.

11075 TOMLINSON, J.D. The First World War and British cotton piece exports to India. In EHR 32,4 (1979) 494-506.

11076 VENKATASUBBIAH, H. Foreign trade of India, 1900-1940; a statistical analysis. Bombay: OUP, 1946. 83p.

F. Indian Industry under the Raj

1. The Decline of Traditional Handicrafts

11077 BAGCHI, A.K. Deindustrialization in gangetic Bihar, 1809-1901. In B. De, ed. Essays in honour of Prof. Susobhan Chandra Sarkar. ND: PPH, 1976, 499-522.

11078 ______. De-industrialization in India in the nineteenth century: some theoretical implications. In JDS 7,2 (1976) 135-64.

11079 BASU, B.D. The ruin of Indian trade and industries. 2nd ed., rev. & enl. Calcutta: R. Chatterjee, 1929. 206p.

11080 CHATTOPADHYAY, R. De-industrialization in India reconsidered. In EPW 10,12 (1975) 523-30.

11081 KRISHNAMURTY, J. Changes in the composition of the working force in manufacturing, 1901-51: a theoretical and empirical analysis. In IESHR 4,1 (1967) 1-16.

11082 THORNER, D. & A. THORNER. "De-industrialization" of India. In their Land and labour in India. Bombay: Asia, 1962, 70-81.

11083 VICZIANY, M. The deindustrialization of India in the nineteenth century: a methodological critique of Amiya Kumar Bagchi. In IESHR 16,2 (1979) 105-46. [Bagchi's reply, 147-62]

2. Origins and Growth of India's Modern Industry

11084 DEWEY, C.J. The government of India's "New Industrial Policy," 1900-25: formation and failure. In K.N. Chaudhury & C.J. Dewey, eds. Economy and society. Delhi: OUP, 1979, 215-57.

11085 INDIA. INDUSTRIAL CMSN. Indian Industrial Commission, 1916-18: report. ND: Agricole Pub. Academy, 1980. 355p. [Rpt. 1918 ed.; Chm., T.H. Holland]

11086 LOKANATHAN, P.S. Industrial organization in India. London: Allen & Unwin, 1935. 413p.

11087 RAY, R.K. Industrialization in India: growth and conflict in the private corporate sector, 1914-47. Delhi: OUP, 1979. 384p.

11088 ROSEN, G. Industrial change in India: industrial growth, capital requirements and technical change 1937-1955. London: Asia, 1962. 202p. [1st pub. 1958]

11089 RUNGTA, R.S. Promotion and finance of Indian companies before 1850. In IJE 46,4 (1966) 477-86.

11090 SIVASUBRAMONIAN, S. Income from the secondary sector in India, 1900-47. In IESHR 14,4 (1977) 427-93.

11091 SOCIO-ECONOMIC RES. INST. BIBLIOGRAPHY UNIT. Industrialization in India, 1919-1939: a bibliography: draft. Calcutta: 1969. 133p.

3. The Indian Business Community
a. indigenous business groups: transformation to industrial entrepreneurship

11092 KANNANGARA, A.P. Indian millowners and Indian nationalism before 1914. In P&P 40 (1968) 147-64.

11093 TIMBERG, T.A. The Marwaris, from traders to industrialists. ND: Vikas, 1978. 268p.

b. businessmen, firms, and the managing agency system

11094 HAMIED, K.A. K.A. Hamied: an autobiography: a life to remember. Bombay: Lalvani, 1972. 390p.

11095 HARRIS, F.R. Jamsetji Nusserwanji Tata; a chronicle of his life. 2nd ed. Bombay: Blackie, 1958. 339p. [1st ed. 1925]

11096 HARRISON, G. Bird and Company of Calcutta: a history produced to mark the firm's centenary, 1864-1964. Calcutta: 1964. 340p.

11097 KLING, B.B. The origin of the managing agency system in India. In JAS 26,1 (1966) 37-47.

11098 MODY, JEHANGIR R.P. Jamsetjee Jejeebhoy; the first Indian knight and baronet. Bombay: 1959. 188p.

11099 MORAES, F.R. Sir Purshotamdas Thakurdas. Bombay: Asia, 1957. 316p.

11100 RUNGTA, R.S. Rise of business corporations in India 1851-1900. Cambridge: CamUP, 1970. 332p. (Cambridge South Asian studies, 8)

11101 RUSSELL, W. Indian summer. Bombay: Thacker, 1951. 250p. [memoir of an English businessman]

11102 SEN, S.K. The house of Tata, 1839-1939. Calcutta: Progressive, 1975. 173p.

11103 TIMBERG, T.A. A North Indian firm as seen through its business records, 1860-1914: Tarachand Ghanshyamdas, a "great" Marwari firm. In IESHR 8,3 (1971) 264-83.

11104 TOWNEND, H.D. A history of Shaw Wallace and Co.... London: 1965. 256p.

11105 WACHA, D.E. Life and life work of J.N. Tata. 3rd ed. Madras: Ganesh, 1918. 202p.

4. Studies of Specific Industries

11106 DESAI, M. Demand for cotton textiles in nineteenth century India. In IESHR 8,4 (1971) 337-61.

11107 GHOSH, A.B. Coal industry in India: an historical and analytical account. ND: S. Chand, 1977-. v. 1, Pre-independence period.

11108 JONES, G.G. The state and economic development in India, 1890-1947: the case of oil. In MAS 13,3 (1979) 353-75.

11109 MEHTA, S.D. The cotton mills of India, 1854 to 1954. Bombay: Textile Assn. of India, 1954. 308p.

11110 SIMMONS, C.P. Vertical integration and the Indian steel industry: the colliery establishment of the Tata Iron and Steel Company 1907-56. In MAS 11,1 (1977) 127-48.

5. The Industrial Worker in India
a. general studies

11111 AGARWALA, A.N., ed. Indian labour problems. Allahabad: East End Pub., 1947. 406p.

11112 BROUGHTON, G.M. Labour in Indian industries. Oxford: Milford, 1924. 214p.

11113 CHAKRAVARTY, L. Emergence of an industrial labour force in a dual economy - British India, 1880-1920. In IESHR 15,3 (1978) 249-328.

11114 GREAT BRITAIN. ROYAL CMSN. ON LABOUR, 1891. Report. London: HMSO, 1893. 2 v. (C. 6795; Parl. Pap. 1892:11) [v. 2 on India and colonies]

11115 GREAT BRITAIN. ROYAL CMSN. ON LABOUR IN INDIA. Report [with evidence]. London: HMSO, 1931. 12 v. (Cmd. 3883, 1930/31) [Chm., J.H. Whitley]

11116 INTERNATIONAL LABOUR OFFICE. Industrial labour in India. Geneva: 1938. 335p.

11117 KAKKAR, N.K. India and the International Labour Office: story of 50 years. Delhi: S. Chand, 1970. 127p.

11118 KELMAN, J.H. Labour in India; a study of the conditions of Indian women in modern industry. London: Allen & Unwin, 1923. 277p.

11119 MORRIS, M.D. Caste and the evolution of the industrial workforce in India. In PAPS 104 (1960) 124-33.

11120 ______. The emergence of an industrial labor force in India; a study of the Bombay cotton mills, 1854-1947. Berkeley: UCalP, 1965. 263p.

11121 MUKERJEE, RADHAKAMAL. The Indian working class. 3rd rev. & enl. ed. Bombay: Hind Kitabs, 1951. 407p. [1st ed. 1945]

11122 MUKHTAR, A. Factory labour in India. Madras: Annamalai U., 1930. 328p.

11123 RASTOGI, T.N. Indian industrial labour: with special reference to textile labour. Bombay: Hind Kitabs, 1949. 236p.

11124 READ, M. The Indian peasant uprooted; a study of the human machine. London: Longmans, Green, 1931. 256p.

11125 SHIVA RAO, B. The industrial worker in India. London: G. Allen & Unwin, 1939. 263p.

11126 THORNER, D. Casual employment of a factory labour force; the case of India, 1850-1939. In EW 9,3/4/5 (1957) 121-24.

b. the trade union movement and its leaders

11127 AITUC - fifty years: documents. ND: AITUC, 1973-. v. 1, 233p. [proc. of the annual sessions of the All India Trade Union Congress; v. 1: 1920 & 1921.]

11128 BHARGAVA, G.S. V.V. Giri. Bombay: Popular, 1969. 122p.

11129 DAS, R.K. The labour movement in India. Berlin: W. De Gruyter, 1923. 112p.

11130 DWARKADAS, K. Forty-five years with labour. London: Asia, 1962. 315p.

11131 GIRI, V.V. Labour problems in Indian industry. 3rd ed. rev. & enl. NY: Asia, 1972. 564p. [1st ed. 1958]

11132 JHA, S.C. The Indian trade union movement; an account and an interpretation. Calcutta: KLM, 1970. 341p.

11133 KARNIK, V.B. N.M. Joshi, servant of India. Bombay: United Asia, 1972. 280p.

11134 LAKSHMAN, P.P. Congress and the labour movement in India. Allahabad: AICC, 1947. 174p.

11135 MUKERJEE, RADHAKAMAL. Labour and planning; essays in honour of Shri V.V. Giri. Bombay: Allied, 1964. 267p.

11136 MUKHTAR, A. Trade unionism and labour disputes in India. London: Longmans, Green, 1935. 251p.

11137 PRASADA RAO, P.D.P. Strikes in India, 1860-1970. Hyderabad: Ravi, 1972. 156p.

11138 PUNEKAR, S.D. Trade unionism in India. Bombay: New Book Co., 1948. 407p.

11139 RAMANUJAM, G. From the babul tree; story of Indian labour. ND: Indian Natl. Trade Union Congress, 1967. 252p.

11140 REVRI, C.L. The Indian trade union movement; an outline history, 1880-1947. ND: Orient Longman, 1972. 295p.

c. labor policy and legislation

11141 DAS, R.K. History of Indian labour legislation. Calcutta: Calcutta U. Press, 1941. 378p.

11142 A decade of labour legislation in India 1937-1948. In Intl. Labour R. 59 (1949) 394-424, 506-36.

11143 GADGIL, D.R. Regulation of wages and other problems of industrial labour in India. Poona: GIPE, 1943. 93p.

11144 KYDD, J.C. History of Indian factory legislation. Calcutta: U. of Calcutta, 1920. 190p.

11145 MAITY, A.B. Labour administration in India. In IJPA 31,4 (1975) 745-61.

11146 MATHUR, A.S. Labour policy and industrial relations in India. Agra: Ram Prasad, 1968. 590p.

11147 SIMMONS, C. Working conditions, accidents, and "protective" labour legislation in the Indian coal mining industry in the pre-independence period. In BPP 95,1 (1976) 184-201.

G. Government Economic Policy, Investment, and Currency

1. Public Finance and Taxation

11148 AMBEDKAR, B.R. The evolution of provincial finance in British India. London: P.S. King, 1925. 285p.

11149 BANERJEA, P.N. A history of Indian taxation. London: Macmillan, 1930. 541p.

11150 ______. Indian finance in the days of the East India Company. London: Macmillan, 1928. 392p.

11151 ______. Provincial finance in India. London: Macmillan, 1929. 367p.

11152 BHATTACHARYYA, S. Financial foundations of the British Raj, men and ideas in the post-mutiny period of reconstruction of Indian public finance, 1858-1872. Simla: IIAS, 1971. 355p.

11153 ______. Trevelyan, Wilson, Canning and the foundations of Indian financial policy. In BPP 80 (1961) 65-73.

11154 BORPUJARI, J.G. The impact of the transit duty system in British India. In IESHR 10,3 (1973) 218-43.

11155 INDIA. FINANCE DEPT. TAXATION ENQUIRY CMTEE., 1924. Report [with evidence]. Delhi: MPGOI, 1926. 7 v. [Chm., Sir C. Todhunter]

11156 INDIA. FISCAL CMSN., 1921. Report [with evidence]. Delhi: MPGOI, 1922-23. 4 v. [Chm., Ibrahim Rahimtoola]

11157 KLEIN, I. Wilson vs. Trevelyan: finance and modernization in India after 1857. In IESHR 7,2 (1970) 179-209.

11158 NIYOGI, J.P. The evolution of the Indian income tax. London: P.S. King, 1929. 326p.

11159 SHAH, K.T. Review of Indian finance (1927-1934): Supplement to Sixty years of Indian finance. Bombay: Popular Book Depot, 1934. 48p.

11160 ______. Sixty years of Indian finance. 2nd ed. Bombay: Taraporevala, 1927. 534p. [1st pub. 1921]

11161 STRACHEY, J., & R. STRACHEY. The finances and public works of India from 1869 to 1881. London: Kegan Paul, 1882. 467p.

11162 THOMAS, P.J. The growth of Federal finance in India, being a survey of India's public finance from 1833 to 1939. London: OUP, 1939. 558p.

2. Banking and Monetary Policy; the Reserve Bank of India

11163 AMBEDKAR, B.R. History of Indian currency and banking. Bombay: Thacker, 1947. 285p.

11164 BARBER, W.J. British economic thought and the Indian monetary system during the period of East India Company rule. In J. of Oriental Studies (Hong Kong) 8,1 (1970) 113-26.

11165 COOKE, C.N. The rise, progress and present condition of banking in India. Calcutta: P.M. Cranenburgh, 1863. 424p.

11166 GHOSH, A.K. Prices and economic fluctuations in India, 1861-1947. ND: S. Chand, 1979. 100p.

11167 GREAT BRITAIN. ROYAL CMSN. ON INDIAN CURRENCY AND FINANCE, 1913. Interim and final reports [with evidence]. London: HMSO, 1913-14. 9 v. (Cd. 7068-72 of 1913; Cd. 7036-39 of 1914)

11168 GUPTA, O.P. Central banking in India, 1773-1934. Delhi: Hindustan Times Press, 1934. 290p.

11169 INDIA. CENTRAL BANKING ENQUIRY CMTEE., 1929. Report [with evidence]. Delhi: MPGOI, 1931. 4 v. [Chm., Sir B.N. Mitra]

11170 JAIN, L.C. Indigenous banking in India. London: Macmillan, 1929. 274p.

11171 ______. The monetary problems of India. London: Macmillan, 1933. 222p.

11172 KEYNES, J.M. Indian currency and finance. NY: B. Franklin, 1971. 263p. [Rpt. of 1913 ed.]

11173 RAMACHANDRA RAO, B. Present-day banking in India. 4th ed., enl. Calcutta: U. of Calcutta, 1938. 784p. [1st ed. 1922]

11174 ______. Reserve Bank of India. Contemporary R. 1 (1935) 157-86.

11175 RAMANA, D.V. Determinants of money supply in India 1914-50. In IER 3,4 (1957) 1-33.

11176 RAO, V.K.R.V. India and international currency plans. Delhi: S. Chand, 1944. 102 + 68p. [1st pub. 1943]

11177 ROTHERMUND, D. The monetary policy of British imperialism. In IESHR 7,1 (1970) 91-107.

11178 SIMHA, H. Early European banking in India. London: Macmillan, 1927. 274p.

11179 SIMHA, S.L.N. History of the Reserve Bank of India, 1935-51. [Prepared by S.L.N. Simha, under the guidance of an editorial committee comprising C.D. Deshmukh, chairman, and others.] Bombay: the Bank, 1970. 878p.

11180 SINGH, H.L. The Indian currency problem 1885-1900. In BPP 80 (1961) 16-37.

11181 TOMLINSON, B.R. Britain and the Indian currency crisis, 1930-2. In EHR 32,1 (1979) 88-99.

11182 VAKIL, C.N. & S.K. MURANJAN. Currency and prices in India. Bombay: Taraporevala, 1927. 549p.

3. Public and Private Investment

11183 BAGCHI, A.K. Foreign capital and economic development in India: a schematic view. In K. Gough & H.P. Sharma, eds. Imperialism and revolution in South Asia. NY: Monthly Review Press, 1973, 43-76.

11184 ______. Private investment in India, 1900-39. Cambridge: CamUP, 1972. 482p. (Cambridge South Asian Studies, 10)

11185 JENKS, L.H. The migration of British capital to 1875. NY: A. Knopf, 1927. 442p.

11186 MUKERJI, K.M. Levels of economic activity and public expenditure in India; a historical and quantitative study. NY: Asia, 1965. 140p. (GIPE studies, 45)

11187 SEN, AMARTYA KUMAR. The commodity pattern of British enterprise in early Indian industrialization, 1854-1914. In Intl. Conf. of Economic History, 2nd, Aix-en-Provence, 1962. Paris: Mouton, 1965, v. 2, 781-808.

11188 ______. The pattern of British enterprise in India 1854-1914: a causal analysis. In Baljit Singh & V.B. Singh, eds. Social and economic change.... Bombay: Allied, 1967, 409-29.

11189 THAVARAJ, M.K. Pattern of public investment in India, 1900-1939. In IESHR 1,1 (1963) 36-56.

11190 ______. Public investment in India, 1898-1914: some features. In IER 2,4 (1955) 37-52.

11191 TOMLINSON, B.R. Foreign private investment in India 1920-1950. In MAS 12,4 (1978) 655-77.

4. Beginnings of National Economic Planning

11192 INDIA. RECONSTRUCTION CMTEE. OF COUNCIL. Report on the progress of reconstruction.... [1st & 2nd]. Delhi: MPGOI, 1944. 2 v. [Policy cmtee. reports on various topics also pub. by MPGOI, 1944-45]

11193 INDIAN FEDERATION OF LABOUR. Peoples' plan for economic development of India; being the report of the Post-war Reconstruction Committee of the Indian Federation of Labour. Released ... by M.N. Roy. 2nd ed. Delhi: A.K. Mukherjee, 1944. 44p. [1st ed. also 1944]

11194 INDIAN NATL. CONGRESS. NATL. PLANNING CMTEE., 1938. Report. Ed. by K.T. Shah. Bombay: Vora, 1949. 257p. [Chm., Jawaharlal Nehru; sub-cmtee. reports on various topics also pub. by Vora, 1947-49.]

11195 ROY, M.N. Planning a new India. Calcutta: Renaissance Pub., 1944. 64p.

11196 SHRIMAN NARAYAN. The Gandhian plan of economic development for India. Bombay: Padma, 1944. 115p.

11197 THAKURDAS, PURSHOTAMDAS. Memorandum outlining a plan of economic development for India. NY: Penguin, 1945. 105p.

11198 ______. A plan of economic development for India. Bombay: S. Ramu, 1944-45. 2 v. [the "Bombay plan"]

VII. SOCIO-RELIGIOUS REVIVAL AND REFORM, 1818-1947: NATIONAL AND TRANSREGIONAL LEADERS AND MOVEMENTS

A. General Studies of Social and Religious Change

11199 BISHOP, D.H. Religious humanism in modern India. In Indian Horizons 25,1/2 (1976) 42-60.

11200 COHN, B.S. Recruitment of elites in India under British rule. In L. Plotnikov & A. Tuden, eds. Essays in comparative social stratification. Pittsburg: U. of Pittsburg Press, 1970, 121-47.

11201 ______. Society and social change under the raj. In SAR 4,1 (1970) 27-49.

11202 ESCHMANN, A. Der Avataragedanke im Hinduismus des neuenzehnten und zwanzigsten Jahrhunderts. In NUMEN 19,2/3 (1972) 229-40.

11203 FARQUHAR, J.N. Modern religious movements in India. Delhi: Munshiram, 1967. 471p. [1st pub. 1915]

11204 HACKER, P. Aspects of Neo-Hinduism as contrasted with surviving traditional Hinduism. In his Kleine Schriften. Wiesbaden: Franz Steiner, 1978, 580-609.

11205 HEIMSATH, C.H. Indian nationalism and Hindu social reform. Princeton: PUP, 1964. 379p.

11206 KARUNAKARAN, K.P. Religion and political awakening in India. Meerut: Meenakshi, 1965. 262p.

11207 KUMAR, J. India unbound: essays in national consciousness. ND: Indian Films & Pub., 1977. 162p.

11208 LIPSKI, A. Some methodological problems encountered by Western scholars in the study of modern Indian religious history. In JIH 48,2 (1970) 276-86.

11209 MALHOTRA, S.L. Social and political orientations of Neo-Vedantism; study of the social philosophy of Vivekananda, Aurobindo, Bipin Chandra Pal, Tagore, Gandhi, Vinoba, and Radhakrishnan. Delhi: S. Chand, 1970. 178p.

11210 NARAIN, V.A. Social history of modern India: nineteenth century. Meerut: Meenakshi, 1972. 206p.

11211 NARAVANE, V.S. Modern Indian thought; a philosophical survey. Bombay: Asia, 1964. 310p.

11212 SARKAR, S. Bibliographical survey of social reform movements in the eighteenth and nineteenth centuries. ND: ICHS, 1975. 54p.

11213 SARMA, D.S. Renascent Hinduism. Bombay: BVB, 1966. 261p.

11214 SCOTT, R.W. Social ethics of modern Hinduism. Calcutta: YMCA, 1953. 243p.

11215 SMITH, W.R. Nationalism and reform in India. New Haven: YUP, 1938. 485p.

11216 STOKES, E. The first century of British colonial rule in India: social revolution or social stagnation? In P&P 58 (1973) 136-60.

11217 TANGRI, S.S. Intellectuals and society in nineteenth century India. In CSSH 3 (1961) 368-94.

11218 VYAS, K.C. The social renaissance in India. Bombay: Vora, 1957. 206p.

B. Hindu Response to British Culture and Reforms

1. General Studies of the "Hindu Renaissance"

11219 BHARATI, A. The Hindu renaissance and its apologetic patterns. In JAS 29,2 (1970) 267-88.

11220 GHOSE, AUROBINDO. Bankim - Tilak - Dayananda. Calcutta: Arya Pub. House, 1947. 68p.

11221 NAGARAJA RAO, P. Contemporary Indian philosophy. Bombay: BVB, 1970. 188p.

11222 NARAVANE, V.S. Modern Indian thought. ND: Orient Longman, 1978. 300p.

11223 RANADE, M.G. Religious and social reform. Ed. by M.B. Kolaskar. Bombay: G. Narayan, 1902. 304p.

11224 SARMA, D.S. Studies in the renaissance of Hinduism in the nineteenth and twentieth centuries. Benares: BHU, 1944. 686p.

11225 SHARMA, N. Twentieth century Indian philosophy: nature and destiny of man. Varanasi: Bhāratīya Vidyā Prakāśana, 1972. 292p.

11226 SRIVASTAVA, R.S. Contemporary Indian philosophy. Delhi: Munshiram, 1965. 398p.

11227 SRIVASTAVA, R.P. Contemporary Indian idealism (with special reference to Swami Vivekananda, Sri Aurobindo, and Sarvepalli Radhakrishnan). Delhi: Motilal, 1973. 212p.

2. Ram Mohan Roy and the Brāhmo Samāj: An Ethical Hinduism Purified of Idolatry and Other 'Abuses'

a. Raja Ram Mohan Roy (1772? - 1833)

i. works

11228 HAY, S., ed. Dialogue between a theist and an idolater.... An 1820 tract probably by Rammohan Roy. Calcutta: KLM, 1963. 200p. [Bengali & English]

11229 MITTRA, K.C. Rammohun Roy and Tuhfatul Muwahhiddin. Calcutta: K.P. Bagchi, 1975. 48 + 22p. [1st pub. 1866 & 1883]

11230 RAMMOHUN ROY, Raja. The English works of Raja Rammohun Roy. Ed. by Kalidas Nag & Debajyoti Burman. Calcutta: Sadharan Brahmo Samaj, 1945-51. 7 v. in 1.

11231 ______. Selected works of Raja Rammohun Roy. ND: PDMIB, 1977. 332p.

11232 RAY, A.K. The religious ideas of Rammohun Roy: a survey of his writings on religion particularly in Persian, Sanskrit, and Bengali. ND: Kanak Pub., 1976. 112p.

ii. biographies and studies

11233 BISWAS, D.K. Rammohan Roy and Horace Hayman Wilson. In BPP 92,2 (1973) 125-47.

11234 CARPENTER, M. The last days in England of the Rajah Rammohun Roy. Ed. by S. Majumdar. Calcutta: Riddhi, 1976. 159p. [1st pub. 1866]

11235 COLLET, S.D. The life and letters of Raja Rammohun Roy. Ed. by D.K. Biswas & P.C. Ganguli. 3rd ed. Calcutta: Sadharan Brahmo Samaj, 1962. 562p.

11236 IQBAL SINGH. Rammohun Roy; a biographical enquiry into the making of modern India. Bombay: Asia, 1958-. v. 1, 328p.

11237 JOSHI, V.C., ed. Rammohun Roy and the process of modernization in India. Delhi: Vikas, 1975. 234p.

11238 KOPF, D. Rammohun Roy's historical quest for an identity in the modern world: the puritanization of a Hindu tradition in Bengal. In his (ed.) Bengal regional identity. East Lansing: Asian Studies Center, Michigan State U., 1969, 51-60.

11239 KOTNALA, M.C. Raja Ram Mohun Roy and Indian awakening. ND: Gitanjali Prakashan, 1975. 240p.

11240 MAJUMDAR, R.C. On Rammohan Roy. Calcutta: Asiatic Soc., 1972. 67p.

11241 MUKERJI, H.N. Indian renaissance and Raja Rammohun Roy. Poona: U. of Poona, 1975. 44p.

11242 NAG, J. Raja Rammohun Roy: India's great social reformer. ND: Sterling, 1972. 167p.

11243 RAY, A.K. Religious ideas of Rammohun Roy. ND: Kanak, 1976. 112p.

11244 SEN, A.K. Raja Rammohun Roy, the representative man. Calcutta: Calcutta Text Book Soc., 1967. 450 + 79p.

11245 SINHA, NIRMAL. Indian nationalism - Rammohun and the Derozians. In BPP 92,2 (1973) 148-56.

11246 TAGORE, S.N. Raja Rammohun Roy. ND: Sahitya Akademi, 1966. 63p.

11247 ______. Rammohun Roy: his role in Indian renaissance. Calcutta: Asiatic Soc., 1975. 101p.

b. the Brāhmo Samāj (est. 1828 as Brāhmo Sabhā): Ram Mohan's religious organization

11248 Leaders of the Brahmo Samaj; being a record of the lives and achievements of the pioneers of the Brahmo movement. Madras: G.A. Natesan, 1926. 248p.

11249 LEONARD, G.S. A history of the Brahmo Samaj, from its rise to 1878 A.D. 2nd ed. Calcutta: Adi Brahmo Samaj Press, 1934. 343p.

11250 SASTRI, S.N. History of the Brahmo Samaj. 2nd ed. Calcutta: Sadharan Brahmo Samaj, 1974. 642p. [1st pub. 1911-12]

c. the later Brāhmo Samāj: leaders and factions, the turn to social and political activity

11251 BORTHWICK, M. Keshub Chunder Sen: a search for cultural synthesis. Calcutta: Minerva, 1977. 243p.

11252 CHAUDHURI, NARAYAN. Maharshi Devendranath Tagore. ND: Sahitya Akademi, 1973. 74p.

11253 GHOSE, BENOY. Selections from English periodicals of 19th century Bengal. v. 7, 1878-80 Brahmo Public Opinion. Calcutta: Papyrus, 1978. 260p.

11254 MOZOOMDAR, P.C. The faith and progress of the Brahmo Somaj. 2nd ed. Ed. by K.S. Ghosh. Calcutta: Navavidhan Pub. Cmtee., 1934. 209p.

11255 MÜLLER, F. MAX. Keshub Chunder Sen. Ed. by Nanda Mookerjee. Calcutta: S. Gupta, 1976. 117p.

11256 SARKAR, H.C. Life of Ananda Mohan Bose. Calcutta: A.C. Sarkar, 1910. 208p.

11257 SEN, K.C. Jeevan veda; being sixteen discourses in Bengali on life, its divine dynamics. Tr. from Bengali by J.K. Koar. 3rd ed. Calcutta: Nababidhan Trust, 1969. 153p.

11258 ______. Keshub Chunder Sen: a selection. Ed. by D.C. Scott. Madras: CLS, 1979. 361p.

11259 ______. Keshub Chunder Sen's lectures in India. London: Cassell, 1901. 492p.

11260 ______. Life and works of Brahmananda Keshav. Comp. by P.S. Basu. Calcutta: Navavidhan Pub. Cmtee., 1940. 591p.

11261 SRINIVASAN, R. The Brahmo Samaj in Tamilnad. In JUB 44/45 (1975-76) 213-29.

11262 TAGORE, D.N. The autobiography of Maharshi Devendranath Tagore. Tr. from Bengali by S.N. Tagore & Indira Devi. Calcutta: S.K. Lahiri, 1909. 195p.

3. The Dev Samāj of Satyānand Agnihotri, 1850-1929: Offshoot of the Brāhmo Samāj in North India

11263 KANAL, P.V. Dev Atma. Lahore: Dev Samaj Book Depot, 1942. 693p.

11264 ______. Dev Dharma in the service of man. Chandigarh: Dev Samaj Pub., 1979. 55p.

11265 ______. In thy light. Chandigarh: Dev Samaj Pub., 1979. 103p.

11266 ______. My Bhagwan; what I saw of him. Delhi: Panchal Press, 1959. 138p.

11267 KANAL, S.P. The ethics of Devatma. ND: Munshiram, for Dev Samaja, 1974. 350p.

11268 SATYANAND AGNIHOTRI. The Dev shastra, by the founder of Dev Dharma. 2nd ed. ND: Dev Samaj, 1975-. v. 1-

4. Swāmī Dayānanda and the Ārya Samāj: Revival of the Vedas in the Service of Social and Religious Reform

a. Swāmī Dayānand Saraswatī (1824-1883): Gujarati Brahman, from sannyāsī to social reformer

i. works

11269 DAYANANDA SARASVATI, Swami. Autobiography of Dayanand Saraswati. Ed. by K.C. Yadav. 2nd rev. ed. ND: Manohar, 1978. 136p. [This tr. 1st pub. 1976]

11270 ______. Devotional texts of the Aryans; English tr. of 'Aaryaabhivinaya.' Tr. & ed. by Satyaananda Saastrii. Ghaziabad, U.P.: Virajaananda Vaidika Samsthanna, 1972. 212p.

11271 ______. An English translation of the Satyārth Prakāsh; literally, Expose of right sense (of Vedic religion). Tr. from Hindi by Durga Prasad. 2nd ed. ND: Jan Gyan Prakashan, 1970. 68 + 570p. [1st pub. 1908]

11272 ______. Light of truth: or, An English translation of the Satyārth prakāsh. Tr. from Hindi by Chiranjiva Bharadwaja. New ed. ND: Sarvadeshik Arya Pratinidhi Sabha, 1975. 732p.

11273 ______. The Sanskār vidhi = The procedure of sacraments of Swami Dayanand Saraswati. Tr. by V.N. Shastri. ND: Sarvadeshik Arya Pratinidhi Sabha, 1976. 359p.

11274 PATHAK, R.P. Teachings of Swami Dayanand: talks and sermons. Hoshiarpur: VVRI, 1973. 83p. (WIS, 17)

11275 SARDA, HAR BILAS. Works of Maharshi Dayanand and Paropkarini Sabha: a reply to P. Amar Singh's Views on meat diet and forgeries suppressing Swami Dayanand's opinions. Ajmer: Vedic Yantralaya, 1942. 129p.

ii. biographies and studies

11276 BAWA, A.S. Dayananda Saraswati, founder of Arya Samaj. ND: Ess Ess, 1979. 87p.

11277 CHHAJU SINGH. Life and teachings of Swami Dayanand Saraswati. ND: Jan Gyan Prakashan, 1971. 171 + 182p. [1st ed. 1903]

11278 MAL, B. Dayanand; a study in Hinduism. Hoshiarpur: 1962. 238p. (Sarvadanand universal series, 40)

11279 JORDENS, J.T.F. Dayānanda Saraswatī and Vedānta: a comparison of the first and second editions of his Satyārth Prakāsh. In IESHR 9,4 (1972) 367-79.

11280 ______. Dayānanda Sarasvatī, his life and ideas. Delhi: OUP, 1978. 368p.

11281 KLIMKEIT, H.-J. Dayānanda Saraswatī: ein indischer nativistischer Prophet. In Anthropos 74,5/6 (1979) 889-907.

11282 SARDA, HAR BILAS. Life of Dayanand Saraswati, world teacher. Ajmer: Vedic Yantralaya, 1946. 622p.

11283 SINGH, B.K. Swami Dayanand. ND: NBT, 1970. 143p.

11284 UPADHYAYA, G.P. Philosophy of Dayananda. 2nd ed. Allahabad: Vedic Prakashan Mandir, 1968. 550p.

11285 VISHWA PRAKASH. Life and teachings of Swami Dayanand. 2nd ed. Allahabad: Kala Press, 1969. 228p.

b. the Ārya Samāj (est. 1875): movement for change in Punjab and North India, stimulated by the Brāhmos and in reaction to Christian missionaries

11286 CAMPATARAYA. Ten commandments; principles of Arya Samaj. ND: Jan Gyan Prakashan, 1970. 104p.

11287 JONES, K.W. Arya Dharm: Hindu consciousness in 19th century Punjab. Berkeley: UCalP, 1976. 343p.

11288 ______. Sources for Arya Samaj history. In W.E. Gustafson & K.W. Jones, eds. Sources on Punjab history. Delhi: Manohar, 1975, 130-70.

11289 LAJPAT RAI, Lala. A history of the Arya Samaj; an account of its origin, doctrines and activities, with a biographical sketch of the founder. Rev. & ed. by Sri Ram Sharma. Bombay: Orient Longmans, 1967. 217p.

11290 PANDEY, D. The Arya Samaj and Indian nationalism, 1875-1920. ND: S. Chand, 1972. 203p.

11291 PAREEK, R.S. Contribution of Arya Samaj in the making of modern India, 1875-1947. ND: Sarvadeshik Arya Pratinidhi Sabha, 1973. 374p.

11292 SHARMA, U. Status striving and striving to abolish status: the Arya Samaj and the low castes. In SocAct 26,3 (1976) 214-36.

11293 SHASTRI, V.N. The Arya Samaj; its cult and creed. 2nd ed. ND: Sarvadeshik Arya Pratinidhi Sabha, 1967. 269p.

5. Śrī Rāmakrishṇa and his Disciples: Vedānta for the Modern World

a. Rāmakrishṇa Paramahaṅsa (1834-86): from Bengali Kālī bhakta to Advaita Vedāntin

11294 APURVANANDA, Swami. Sri Ramakrishna and Sarada Devi. Madras: Sri Ramakrishna Math, 1961. 245p.

11295 CHATTERJEE, S.C. Classical Indian philosophies: their synthesis in the philosophy of Sri Ramakrishna. Calcutta: U. of Calcutta, 1963. 152p.

11296 DEVDAS, N. Sri Ramakrishna. Bangalore: CISRS, 1966. 115p.

11297 GAMBHIRANANDA, Swami. Holy Mother Shri Sarada Devi. 2nd ed. Madras: Sri Ramakrishna Math, 1969. 540p.

11298 ISHERWOOD, C. Ramakrishna and his disciples. NY: Simon & Schuster, 1965. 348p.

11299 Life of Sri Ramakrishna; compiled from various authentic sources. 2nd ed. Calcutta: Advaita Ashrama, 1964. 619p.

11300 MOOKERJEE, NANDA, ed. Sri Ramakrishna, in the eyes of Brahma and Christian admirers. Calcutta: KLM, 1976. 141p.

11301 MÜLLER, F. MAX. Ramakrishna, his life and sayings. Ed. by Nanda Mookerjee. Calcutta: S. Gupta, 1974. 148p. [1st pub. 1898]

11302 NEEVEL, W.G., JR. The transformation of Śrī Rāmakrishna. In B.L. Smith, ed. Hinduism: new essays in the history of religions. Leiden: Brill, 1976, 53-97. (SHR, 33)

11303 NIKHILANANDA, Swami. Holy Mother: being the life of Sri Sarada Devi, wife of Sri Ramakrishna and helpmate in his mission. NY: Ramakrishna-Vedanta Center, 1962. 334p.

11304 ______. Sri Ramakrishna. Madras: Sri Ramakrishna Math, 1968. 184p.

11305 PANGBORN, C.R. The Rāmakrishṇa maṭh and mission: a case study of a revitalization movement. In B.L. Smith, ed. Hinduism: new essays in the history of religions. Leiden: Brill, 1976, 98-119. (SHR, 33)

11306 RAMAKRISHNA. Gospel of Sri Ramakrishna. (Originally recorded in Bengali by M....). Trans. by Swami Nikhilananda. NY: Ramakrishna-Vivekananda Center, 1942. 1063p.

11307 ______. Tales and parables of Sri Ramakrishna. 3rd ed. Madras: Sri Ramakrishna Math, 1967. 272p. [1st ed. 1943]

11308 ROLLAND, R. Ramakrishna, the man-gods, and the universal gospel of Vivekananda (a study of mysticism and action in living India). Tr. from French by E.F. Malcolm-Smith. Mayavati, Almora, Himalayas: Advaita Ashrama, 1954. v. 1, Life of Ramakrishna, 325p.

11309 SARADANANDA, Swami. Sri Ramakrishna, the great master. Tr. from Bengali by Swami Jagadananda. 3rd ed. Madras: Sri Ramakrishna Math, 1963. 960p.

11310 SCHNEIDERMAN, L. Ramakrishna: personality and social factors in the growth of a religious movement. In JSSR 8 (1969) 60-71.

11311 Sri Ramakrishna: a biography in pictures. Calcutta: Advaita Ashrama, 1976. 108p.

11312 STARK, C.A. God of all; Sri Ramakrishna. Hartford, VT: C.A. Stark & Co., 1974. 236p.

b. Swāmī Vivekānanda (1863-1902): Bengali apostle to India and the West, founder of Ramakrishna Mission and Vedanta Societies
i. works and sources

11313 BASU, S.P., ed. Vivekananda in Indian newspapers, 1893-1902. Ed. by S.P. Basu & S.B. Ghosh. Calcutta: Basu Bhattacharyya, 1969. 735p.

11314 BURKE, M.L. Swami Vivekananda in America; new discoveries. Calcutta: Advaita Ashrama, 1958. 639p. [sources]

11315 VIVEKANANDA, Swami. The complete works of Swami Vivekananda. Calcutta: Advaita Ashrama, 1970-73. 8 v. [1st pub. 1926-36]

11316 ______. The science and philosophy of religion; a comparative study of Samkhya, Vedanta, and other systems of thought. 8th ed. Calcutta: Udbodhan Office, 1964. 112p.

11317 ______. What religion is in the words of Swami Vivekananda. Ed. by J. Yale. London: Phoenix House, 1962. 224p.

ii. biographies and studies

11318 ATHALYE, D.V. Swami Vivekananda: a study. ND: Ashish, 1979. 286p.

11319 BANHATTI, G.S. The quintessence of Vivekananda. Nagpur: Suvichar Prakashan Mandal, 1963. 296p.

11320 DEVDAS, N. Swāmī Vivekānanda. Bangalore: CISRS, 1968. 224p.

11321 DHAR, S.N. A comprehensive biography of Swami Vivekananda. Madras: Vivekananda Prakashan Kendra, 1975-76. 2 v.

11322 GHANANANDA, Swami & G. PARRINDER, eds. Swami Vivekananda; East and West. London: Ramakrishna Vedanta Center, 1968. 224p.

11323 GUPTA, K.P. Swami Vivekananda: a case study of the Hindu religious tradition and the modern secular ideal. In Quest 80 (1973) 9-24. [Discussion and response in Quest 81 (1973) 75-81]

11324 The life of Swami Vivekananda, by his Eastern and Western disciples. 4th ed. Calcutta: Advaita Ashrama, 1965. 765p.

11325 MAHADEVAN, T.M.P. Swāmī Vivekānanda and the Indian renaissance. Periyanayakkanpalaiyam: Sri Ramakrishna Mission Vidyalaya Teachers College, 1967. 114p.

11326 MAJUMDAR, A.K. Understanding Vivekananda. Calcutta: SPB, 1972. 97p.

11327 MAJUMDAR, R.C. Swāmī Vivekānanda; a historical review. Calcutta: General Printers & Publishers, 1965. 182p.

11328 ______., ed. Swami Vivekananda centenary memorial volume. Calcutta: Swami Vivekananda Centenary, 1963. 617p.

11329 MITAL, S.S. The social and political ideas of Swami Vivekananda. ND: Metropolitan, 1979. 338p.

11330 NIVEDITA, Sister [M.E. NOBLE]. The Master as I saw him.... 3rd ed. Calcutta: Udbodhan Office, 1923. 510p.

11331 RAO, V.K.R.V. Swami Vivekananda, the prophet of Vedantic socialism. ND: PDMIB, 1979. 281p.

11332 ROLLAND, R. The life of Vivekananda and the universal gospel. Tr. from French by E.F. Malcolm-Smith. Calcutta: Advaita Ashrama, 1965. 382p.

11333 SATPRAKASHANANDA, Swami. Swami Vivekananda's contribution to the present age. St. Louis: Vedanta Soc., 1978. 249p.

11334 Seminar on Swami Vivekananda's Teaching, May 1 to May 7, 1964. Coimbatore: Sri Ramakrishna Mission Vidyalaya, 1965. 133p.

11335 SHARMA, B.S. Swami Vivekananda; a forgotten chapter of his life. Calcutta: Oxford Book & Stationery Co., 1963. 229p.

11336 Vivekananda: a biography in pictures. Rev. 3rd ed. Calcutta: Advaita Ashrama, 1977. 119p.

11337 WILLIAMS, G.M. The quest for meaning of Svāmī Vivekānanda; a study of religious change. Chico, CA: New Horizons Press, 1974. 148p.

c. Sister Niveditā (Margaret Noble, 1867-1911): British disciple of Swami Vivekānanda

11338 CHAKRAVARTY, BASUDHA. Sister Nivedita. ND: NBT, 1975. 84p.

11339 FOXE, B. Long journey home: a biography of Margaret Noble (Nivedita). London: Rider, 1975. 239p.

11340 MAZUMDAR, A.K., ed. Nivedita commemorative volume. Calcutta: Vivekananda Janmotsava Samiti, 1968. 321p.

11341 NIVEDITA, Sister [M.E. NOBLE]. Complete works.... Calcutta: Ramakrishna Sarada Mission, Sister Nivedita Girls' School, 1967-68. 4 v.

11342 ______. Sister Nivedita's lectures and writings... Calcutta: Ramakrishna Sarada Mission, Sister Nivedita Girl's School, 1975. 427p. ["hitherto unpublished"]

11343 REYMOND, L. The dedicated: a biography of Nivedita. NY: John Day, 1953. 374p. [tr. from French]

d. the Rāmakrishṇa movement: modern missionaries of Indic culture and social service

11344 ABHEDANANDA, Swami. Abhedananda in India in 1906. Calcutta: Ramakrishna Vedanta Math, 1968. 276p. [lectures]

11345 BISHOP, D.H. Indian religion in the modern period: the Ramakrishna movement. In VK 56 (1970) 390-98.

11346 FRENCH, H.W. The swan's wide waters: Ramakrishna and Western culture. Port Washington, NY: Kennikat, 1974. 220p.

11347 GAMBHIRANANDA, Swami. History of the Ramakrishna math and mission. Calcutta: Advaita Ashrama, 1957. 452p.

11348 ______., ed. The apostles of Shri Ramakrishna. Calcutta: Advaita Ashrama, 1967. 401p.

11349 JNANATMANANDA, Swami. Invitation to holy company: being the memoirs of ten direct disciples of Sri Ramakrishna. Tr. from Bengali by J.N. Dey. Madras: Sri Ramakrishna Math, 1979. 131p. + 8 pl.

11350 LEMAÎTRE, S. Ramakrishna and the vitality of Hinduism. Tr. from French by C.L. Markmann. NY: Funk & Wagnalls, 1969. 244p.

11351 MUPPATHYIL, C. Meditation as a path to God-realization: a study in the spiritual teachings of Swami Prabhāvānanda and his assessment of Christian spirituality. Rome: Università gregoriana, 1979. 159p.

11352 PRAJNANANANDA, Swami. The philosophical ideas of Swami Abhedananda: a critical study; a guide to the complete works of Swami Abhedananda. Calcutta: Ramakrishna Vedanta Math, 1971. 584p.

6. The Theosophical Society [Est. 1875]: Amalgam of Westernized Sanskritic Hinduism and Occultism
a. general histories and studies of the Theosophical movement in India

11353 BARBORKA, G.A. H.P. Blavatsky, Tibet and Tulku. Madras: Theosophical Pub. House, 1966. 476p.

11354 BLAVATSKY, H.P. The secret doctrine; the synthesis of science, religion, and philosophy. 5th ed. Wheaton,

IL: Theosophical Press, 1946. 6 v. [1st pub. 1893-97]

11355 CODD, C.M. The ageless wisdom of life. 4th ed. Madras: TPH, 1967. 269p.

11356 EEK, S., comp. Damodar and the pioneers of the theosophical movement. Compiled and annotated by Sven Eek. Madras: TPH, 1965. 720p.

11357 FARQUHAR, J.N. Theosophy. In his Modern religious movements in India. Delhi: Munshiram Manoharlal, 1967, 208-90.

11358 JINARĀJADĀSA, C. The golden book of the Theosophical Society; a brief history of the Society's growth 1875-1925. Adyar, Madras: TPH, 1925. 421p.

11359 MÜLLER, F. MAX. Theosophy; or, psychological religion. NY: AMS Press, 1975. 585p. (His Collected works, 4) [Rpt. 1903 ed.]

b. Annie Besant (1847-1933) and Theosophical involvement in politics and social problems

11360 BESANT, ANNIE. The ancient wisdom: an outline of theosophical teachings. Adyar, Madras: TPH, 1949. 396p. [1st pub. 1897]

11361 ______. An autobiography. London: Allen & Unwin, 1920. 368p.

11362 ______. Essays and addresses. Madras: TPS, 1911-13. 4 v.

11363 NETHERCOT, A.H. The first five lives of Annie Besant. Chicago: UChiP, 1960. 418p.

11364 ______. The last four lives of Annie Besant. Chicago: UChiP, 1963. 483p.

11365 PRAKASA, SRI. Annie Besant as woman and leader. Bombay: BVB, 1962. 231p.

11366 RAMASWAMI AIYAR, C.P. Annie Besant. Delhi: PDMIB, 1963. 152p.

7. Sri Aurobindo (Aravinda Ghose, 1872-1950): from England-returned Intellectual to Bengali Extremist to Mystic-Philosopher and Super-Man

a. bibliography and reference

11367 GHOSE, A. Dictionary of Sri Aurobindo's yoga, compiled from the writings of Sri Aurobindo. Pondicherry: Dipti Pub., 1966. 315p.

11368 Glossary of terms in Sri Aurobindo's writings. Pondicherry: Sri Aurobindo Ashram, 1978. 300p.

11369 KAUL, H.K. Sri Aurobindo: a descriptive bibliography. ND: Munshiram, 1972. 222p.

11370 MANMOHAN REDDY, V., comp. Sri Aurobindo: a bibliography. Hyderabad: Inst. of Human Study, 1973. 48p.

11371 ______, comp. Subject index to Mother India, 1949-1972. Hyderabad: Inst. of Human Study, 1973. 154p.

11372 ______, comp. Subject-index to Sri Aurobindo Mandir annual, 1942-1972. Hyderabad: Inst. of Human Study, 1973. 23p.

11373 ______, comp. Subject-index to the Advent, 1944-1972. Hyderabad: Inst. of Human Study, 1973. 39p.

b. writings of Sri Aurobindo

11374 GHOSE, AUROBINDO. The life divine. Pondicherry: Sri Aurobindo Birth Centenary Library, 1970. 1070p. [1st pub. 1939-40]

11375 ______. Sri Aurobindo. Pondicherry: Sri Aurobindo Birth Centenary Library, 1970-75. 30v. [his complete works; v. 30, Index & glossary]

c. studies of Sri Aurobindo and his philosophy of Integral Yoga

11376 BOLLE, K.W. The persistence of religion: an essay on Tantrism and Sri Aurobindo's philosophy. Leiden: Brill, 1971. 134p. (SHR, 8) [Rpt. 1965 ed.]

11377 BRUTEAU, B. Worthy is the world; the Hindu philosophy of Sri Aurobindo. Rutherford, N.J.: Fairleigh Dickenson U. Press, 1971. 288p.

11378 CHAUDHURI, H., ed. The integral philosophy of Sri Aurobindo; a commemorative symposium. London: Allen & Unwin, 1960. 350p.

11379 DEUTSCH, E.S. Sri Aurobindo's interpretation of spiritual experience: a critique. In Intl. Philosophical Q. 4 (1964) 581-94.

11380 DIWAKAR, R.R. Mahayogi Sri Aurobindo; life, sadhana and teachings of Sri Aurobindo. 3rd rev. & enl. ed. Bombay: BVB, 1962. 298p.

11381 DOCKHORN, K. Tradition und Evolution; Untersuchungen zu Sri Aurobindos Auslegung autoritätiver Sanskritschriften mit einer Einführung in sein Leben und Werk. Gütersloh: Gütersloher Verlaghaus Gerd Mohn, n.d. 231p.

11382 FEYS, J. Life of a yogi. Calcutta: KLM, 1976. 54p.

11383 GEORGE, N. Realization of God according to Sri Aurobindo: a study of a neo-Hindu vision on the divinization of man. Bangalore: Claretian Pub., 1979. 308p.

11384 GUPTA, N.K. The yoga of Sri Aurobindo. Pondicherry: Sri Aurobindo Ashram, 1950-72. 6 v.

11385 GUPTA, N.K. & K. AMRITA. Reminiscences. Pondicherry: Sri Aurobindo Ashram, 1969. 190p.

11386 JOHNSON, D.L. The task of relevance: Aurobindo's synthesis of religion and politics. In PEW 23,4 (1973) 507-16.

11387 JOSHI, V.C., ed. Sri Aurobindo; an interpretation. Delhi: Vikas, 1973. 174p.

11388 MAITRA, S.K. An introduction to the philosophy of Sri Aurobindo. 2nd ed. Banaras: BHU, 1945. 112p. [1st pub. 1941]

11389 ______. The meeting of East and West in Sri Aurobindo's philosophy. Pondicherry: Sri Aurobindo Ashram, 1956. 451p.

11390 MCDERMOTT, R.A. Six pillars: introductions to the major works of Sri Aurobindo. Chambersburg, PA: Conococheague Associates, 1974. 198p.

11391 MINOR, R.N. Sri Aurobindo, the perfect and the good. Calcutta: Minerva, 1978. 191p.

11392 MITRA, S.K. The liberator Sri Aurobindo, India, and the world. 2nd ed. Bombay: Jaico Pub. House, 1970. 307p. [1st pub. 1954]

11393 ______. Sri Aurobindo. ND: Indian Book Co., 1972. 215p.

11394 O'NEIL, L.T. Towards the life divine: Sri Aurobindo's vision. ND: Manohar, 1979. 103p.

11395 ROARKE, J. Sri Aurobindo. Pondicherry: Sri Aurobindo Ashram, 1973. 189p.

11396 SHARMA, R.N. The social philosophy of Sri Aurobindo. Delhi: Vineet, 1980. 230p.

11397 SRINIVASA IYENGAR, K.R. Sri Aurobindo; a biography and a history. 3rd rev. and enl. ed. Pondicherry: Sri Aurobindo International Centre of Education, 1972. 2 v. [1st pub. 1945]

11398 TRIVEDI, R.C. The philosophy of Sri Aurobindo: its epistemological & conceptive significance. In E&W 21, 1/2 (1971) 121-36.

11399 ZAEHNER, R.C. Evolution in religion: a study in Sri Aurobindo & Pierre Teilhard de Chardin. Oxford: OUP, 1971. 121p.

d. The Mother/La Mère: Sri Aurobindo's French śakti and successor at the Pondichery Ashram

11400 THE MOTHER [LA MÈRE]. Collected works, centenary edition. Pondicherry: Sri Aurobindo Ashram, 1976-. [to be 15v.]

11401 NANDAKUMAR, PREMA. The Mother (of Sri Aurobindo Ashrama). ND: NBT, 1977. 136p.

11402 RAVINDRA. The white lotus: at the feet of the Mother. ND: S. Chand, 1978. 214p.

11403 SATPREM. Mother: or, The divine materialism. Tr.

from French by M. de La Forêt. Madras: Macmillan, 1977. 3 v.

11404 SRINIVASA IYENGAR, K.R. On the Mother: the chronicle of a manifestation and ministry. 2nd rev. and enl. ed. Pondicherry: Sri Aurobindo Intl. Centre of Education, 1978. 2 v. 847p.

8. Ramana Mahārṣi (1879-1950): Jīvanmukta, Living Exemplar of Advaitic Self-Realization in Modern Tamilnadu

11405 ANANTHA MURTHY, T.S. Life and teachings of Shree Ramana Maharshi. Bangalore: T.S. Anantha Murthy, 1972. 176p.

11406 BRUNTON, P. A search in secret India. NY: E.P. Dutton, 1935. 312p.

11407 BURGI-KYRIAZI, M. Ramana Mahārṣhi et l'expérience de l'être. Paris: Librairie d'Amérique et d'Orient, 1975. 224p.

11408 COHEN, S.S. Guru Ramana; memories and notes. 3rd rev. & enl. ed. Tiruvannamalai: Sri Ramanasramam, 1967. 164p.

11409 DEVARAJA MUDALIAR, A. Day by day with Bhagavan: from a diary of A. Devaraja Mudaliar, covering March 16, 1945 to January 4, 1947. Tiruvannamalai: Sri Ramanasramam, 1977. 318p. [Rpt. 1968 ed.]

11410 MOUNI SADHU. In days of great peace; the highest yoga as lived. London: Allen & Unwin, 1957. 213p.

11411 NARASIMHA SWAMI, B.V. Self realisation; life and teachings of Sri Ramana Maharshi. 5th ed., rev. Tiruvannamalai: T.N. Venkataraman, 1953. 272p.

11412 OSBORNE, A. Ramana Maharshi and the path of self knowledge. NY: S. Weiser, 1970. 207p. [Rpt. 1954 ed.]

11413 RAMANA, Maharshi. The collected works of Ramana Maharshi. Ed. by A. Osborne. 34d ed. Tiruvannamalai: Sri Ramanasramam, 1968. 293p.

11414 ______. The spiritual teaching of Ramana Maharshi. Berkeley: Shambala, 1972. 125p.

11415 SADHU OM. The path of Shri Ramana; an exposition of the method of self-enquiry taught by Shri Ramana Maharshi. Kanpur: City Book House, 1971. 176p.

11416 SWAMINATHAN, K. Ramana Maharshi. ND: NBT, 1975. 156p.

11417 Talks with Sri Ramana Maharshi. 3rd ed. Tiruvannamalai: Sri Ramanasramam, 1963. 748p.

11418 ZIMMER, H. Der Weg zum Selbst; Lehren und Leben des indischen Heiligen Shri Ramana Maharshi aus Tiruvannamalai. Zurich: Rascher, 1944. 262p.

9. Swāmī Sivānanda Saraswatī (1887-1963): Vedāntin and Āyurvedic Physician, Founder of the Divine Life Society

11419 ANANTHANARAYANAN, N. From man to God-man; the inspiring story of Swami Sivananda. ND: 1970. 270p.

11420 FORNARO, R.J. Sivananda and the Divine Life Society; a paradigm of the secularism, puritanism, and cultural dissimulation of a neo-Hindu religious society. Ph.D. Diss., Syracuse U., 1969. 247p. [UM 70-12,772]

11421 RAMASWAMI SASTRI, K.S. Sivananda, the modern world-prophet. Rishikesh: Yoga-Vedanta Forest U., 1953. 594p.

11422 SIVANANDA, Swami. Mind: its mysteries and control. 8th ed. Sivanandanagar: Divine Life Soc., 1974. 504p.

11423 ______. Religious education. 2nd ed. Sivanandanagar: Divine Life Soc., 1970. 367p.

11424 ______. Voice of the Himalayas. 3rd ed. Sivanandanagar: Divine Life Soc., 1968. 334p.

10. Academic Philosophers: Blending of Hindu Tradition and Western Scholarship

a. general studies

11425 BHATTACHARYA, KALIDAS. The fundamentals of K.C. Bhattacharyya's philosophy. Calcutta: Saraswat Library, 1975. 239p.

11426 DASGUPTA, SURAMA. An ever-expanding quest of life and knowledge. ND: Orient Longman, 1971. 290p. [on S.N. Dasgupta]

11427 KADANKAVIL, K.T. The philosophy of the absolute; a critical study of Krishnachandra Bhattacharya's writings. Bangalore: Dharmaram College, 1972. 222p.

11428 JHA, G.N. The philosophical discipline. Varanasi: Bharatiya, 1979. 166p. [Rpt. 1928 ed.]

11429 LAL, B.K. Contemporary Indian philosophy. 2nd rev. ed. Delhi: Motilal, 1978. 346p.

11430 NAGARAJA RAO, P. Contemporary Indian philosophy. Bombay: BVB, 1970. 188p.

11431 SHARMA, NILIMA. Twentieth century Indian philosophy: nature and destiny of man. Varanasi: Bharatiya Vidya Prakasana, 1972. 292p.

b. Sir Sarvepalli Radhakrishnan (1888-1975): interpreter of Hindu philosophy to the world

11432 ARAPURA, J.G. Radhakrishnan and integral experience; the philosophy and world vision of Sarvepalli Radhakrishnan. NY: Asia, 1966. 211p.

11433 ATREYA, B.L., ed. Dr. S. Radhakrishnan souvenir volume; collection of 76 articles by scholars of international fame. Moradabad: Darshana Intl., 1964. 600p.

11434 JOAD, C.E.M. Counter-attack from the East; the philosophy of Radhakrishnan. Bombay: Hind Kitabs, 1951. 228p. [1st pub. 1933]

11435 MCDERMOTT, R.A. Radhakrishnan's contribution to comparative philosophy. In Intl. Philosophical Q. 10,3 (1970) 420-440.

11436 MICHAEL, A. Radhakrishnan on Hindu moral life and action. Delhi: Concept, 1979. 226p.

11437 RADHAKRISHNAN, S. Radhakrishnan; an anthology. Ed. by A.N. Marlow. London: Allen & Unwin, 1952. 148p.

11438 ______. Radhakrishnan reader; an anthology: selections from the world-famous philosopher-statesman's 40 and odd books written over a period of 60 years. Ed. by P. Nagaraja Rao & K. Gopalaswami & S. Ramakrishnan. Bombay: BVB, 1969. 680p.

11439 ______. Radhakrishnan; selected writings on philosophy, religion and culture. Ed. by R.A. McDermott. NY: E.P. Dutton, 1970. 344p.

11440 SAMARTHA, S.J. Introduction to Radhakrishnan: the man and his thought. ND: YMCA Pub. House, 1964. 110p.

11441 SCHLIPP, P.A. The philosophy of Sarvepalli Radhakrishnan. NY: Tudor, 1952. 883p.

11442 SINGH, R.P. Radhakrishnan: the portrait of an educationist. Delhi: Sterling, 1967. 147p.

C. Islam and the Muslims under the Raj: Crisis of Belief and Identity (1818-1947)

1. Pre-Mutiny Muslim Revivalist Movements: Attempts to Restore Islamic Orthodoxy and Muslim Rule

a. Sayyid Ahmad of Rae Bareli (1786-1831): adaptation of Arabian Wahhabism to the tradition of Shah Wali-ullah

11443 AHMAD, MOHIUDDIN. Saiyid Ahmad Shahid: his life and mission. Lucknow: Academy of Islamic Res. and Pub., 1975. 427p.

11444 AHMAD, QEYAMMUDIN. The Wahabi movement in India. Calcutta: KLM, 1966. 391p.

11445 ANSARI, A.S.B. Sayyid Ahmad Shahid in the light of his letters. In Islamic Studies 15,4 (1976) 231-45.

11446 HEDAYETULLAH, M. Sayyid Ahmad: a study of the religious reform movement of Sayyid Ahmad of Ra'e Bareli. Lahore: Sh. Muhammad Ashraf, 1970. 180p.

b. the Farāʾidī Movement

[see Chap. Fifteen, I. E. 3.]

2. Post-Mutiny Islamic Modernists: Accommodation to Secular British Rule and Western Science and Culture

a. general studies

11447 AHMAD KHAN, MUIN-UD-DIN. A bibliographic introduction to modern Islamic developments in India and Pakistan, 1700-1955. Suppl. to JASP 6 (1959) 170p.

11448 AZIZ AHMAD. Islamic modernism in India and Pakistan, 1857-1964. London: OUP, 1967. 294p.

11449 AZIZ AHMAD & G.E. VON GRUNEBAUM, ed. Muslim self-statement in India and Pakistan 1857-1968. Wiesbaden: Harrassowitz, 1970. 240p.

11450 BALJON, J.M.S. Modern Muslim Koran interpretation 1880-1960. Leiden: Brill, 1961. 135p.

11451 GIBB, H.A.R. Modern trends in Islam. Chicago: UChiP, 1947. 317p.

11452 HARDY, P. Partners in freedom - and true Muslims. The political thought of some Muslim scholars in British India 1912-1947. Lund: Scandinavian Inst. of Asian Studies, 1971. 63p.

11453 HASAN, MUSHIRUL. Aspects of the problems of Muslim social reform. In Zafar Imam, ed. Muslims in India. ND: Orient Longman, 1975, 217-30.

11454 JAWED, N.A. Principles of movement in modern Islam: an analysis of some ideas developed in the 19th and 20th centuries by Indo-Pakistan Muslims in justification of change in religious thought and structure. In Islamic studies 9,4 (1970) 295-315.

11455 MCDONOUGH, S. The authority of the past; a study of Muslim modernists. Chambersburg, PA: American Academy of Religion, 1970. 56p.

11456 MAY, L.S. The evolution of Indo-Muslim thought after 1857. Lahore: Sh. Muhammad Ashraf, 1970. 488p.

11457 MIR HASAN ALI, Mrs. B. Observations on the Mussulmauns of India. Ed. by W. Crooke. Karachi: OUP, 1974. 442p. [1st pub. 1832]

11458 MURAD, M.A. Intellectual modernism of Shiblī Nuʾmānī: an exposition of his religious and socio-political ideas. Lahore: Inst. of Islamic Culture, 1976. 135p.

11459 NAVDĪ, ABULHASAN ALĪ. Religion and civilization. Tr. from Urdu by Mohiuddin Ahmad. Lucknow: Academy of Islamic Res. and Pub., 1970. 120p. [1942 lectures]

11460 POWELL, A.A. Maulānā Raḥmat Allāh Kairānawī and Muslim-Christian controversy in India in the mid-nineteenth century. In JRAS (1976) 42-63.

11461 QURESHI, I.H. Ulemā in politics; a study relating to the political activities of the ulemā in the South-Asian subcontinent from 1556 to 1947. Karachi: Maᶜaref, 1972. 432p.

11462 RAHMAN, R. Muslim modernism in the Indo-Pakistan subcontinent. In BSOAS 21 (1958) 82-99.

11463 RIZVI, S.A.A. Muhammad in South Asian biographies; changes in Islamic perceptions of the individual in society. In Gungwu Wang, ed. Self and biography.... Sydney: Sydney U. Press, 1975, 99-122.

11464 SIDDIQI, M. Intellectual bases of Muslim modernism, I. In Islamic Studies 9,2 (1970) 149-71.

11465 YANUCK, M. The Indian Muslim self-image: nine historians in search of a past. In Islam and the Modern Age 4,4 (1973) 78-94.

b. Sir Sayyid Aḥmad Khān (1817-98): modernizing theologian and educator in opposition to orthodox ulama

11466 AHMAD KHAN, SYED. A series of essays on the life of Muhammad and subjects subsidiary thereto, by Syed Ahmed Khan Bahador. Lahore: Premier Book House, 1968. 394p.

11467 BALJON, J.M.S. The reforms and religious ideas of Sir Sayyid Ahmad Khan. 3rd rev. ed. Lahore: Sh. Muhammad Ashraf, 1964. 160p. [1st ed. 1949]

11468 AZIZ AHMAD. Sayyid Aḥmad Khān, Jamāl al-dīn al-Afghānī and Muslim India. In Studia Islamica 13 (1960) 55-78.

11469 DAR, B.A. Religious thought of Sayyid Ahmad Khan. Lahore: Inst. of Islamic Culture, 1957. 304p.

11470 GRAHAM, G.F.I. The life and work of Syed Ahmed Khan, C.S.I. Delhi: IAD, 1974. 412p.

11471 ḤALĪ, K.A.H. Hayat-i-Javed: a biographical account of Sir Sayyid. Tr. by K.H. Qadiri & D.J. Matthews. Delhi: IAD, 1979. 251p.

11472 HADI HUSAIN, M. Syed Ahmed Khan: pioneer of Muslim resurgence. Lahore: Inst. of Islamic Culture, 1970. 259p.

11473 NIZAMI, K.A. Sayyid Ahmad Khan. Delhi: PDMIB, 1967. 184p.

11474 TROLL, C.W. Sayyid Ahmad Khan: a reinterpretation of Muslim theology. ND: Vikas, 1978. 384p.

c. the Muhammadan Anglo-Oriental College (after 1920, Aligarh Muslim University), founded 1875 by Sayyid Ahmad Khan, and the Aligarh Movement

11475 BHATNAGAR, S.K. History of the M.A.O. College, Aligarh. Bombay: Asia, 1969. 373p. (Sir Syed Hall publication, no. 1)

11476 JAIN, M.S. The Aligarh movement; its origin and development, 1858-1906. Agra: Sri Ram Mehra, 1965. 201p.

11477 LELYVELD, D. Aligarh's first generation: Muslim solidarity and English education in northern India, 1875-1900. Ph.D. Diss., U. of Chicago, 1975. 441p.

11478 ______. Three Aligarh students: Aftab Ahmad Khan, Ziauddin Ahmad and Muhammad Ali. In MAS 9,2 (1975) 227-40.

11479 MINAULT, G. & D. LELYVELD. The campaign for a Muslim university 1898-1920. In MAS 8,2 (1974) 145-90.

11480 MUMTAZ MOIN. The Aligarh movement: origin and early history. Karachi: Salman Academy, 1976. 273p.

11481 SHAN MUHAMMAD, ed. The Aligarh movement: basic documents, 1864-1898. Meerut: Meenakshi, 1978. 3 v., 1130p.

3. ᶜAllāma Dr. Muḥammad Iqbāl (1877-1938): Foremost Philosophical Thinker of Modern Islam in South Asia; between Fundamentalism and Westernism

a. bibliography

11482 AKHTAR, A.H. Analytical catalogue of books on Allama Mohammad Iqbal, 1877-1977. Karachi: Dept. of Libraries, Min. of Educ., 1978. 97 + 182p.

11483 AZHAR, M.M.N. A bibliography of articles on Iqbal, 1900-1977. Lahore: Islamic Book Service, 1978. 63p.

11484 RIZVI, S.J.A., comp. Theses on Iqbal: a bibliographical survey of the theses on Iqbal, submitted to the University of the Punjab, Lahore, 1950-1976. Lahore: Aziz Pub., 1977. 148p.

11485 USMANI, M.A. & N. FATIMA. Books on Allama Iqbal in university libraries of Pakistan. Karachi: Dr. Mahmud Husain Library, U. of Karachi, 1977. 24 + 62p.

11486 WAHEED, K.A. A bibliography of Iqbal. Karachi: Iqbal Academy, 1965. 224p.

b. religious and philosophical writings of Iqbal

11487 IQBAL, MUHAMMAD. Letters and writings of Iqbal. Ed. by B.A. Dar. Karachi: Iqbal Academy, 1967. 129p.

11488 ______. Letters of Iqbal. Ed. by B.A. Dar. Lahore: Iqbal Academy, 1978. 270p.

11489 ______. The reconstruction of religious thought in Islam. Oxford: OUP, 1934. 205p.

11490 ______. The secrets of the self. Lahore: S.M. Ashraf, rev. ed., 1944. 147p.

11491 ______. Speeches, writings, and statements of

Iqbal. Ed. by L.A. Sherwani. 3rd rev. & enl. ed. Lahore: Iqbal Academy, 1977. 263p.

11491 ______. Stray reflections; a note-book of Allama Iqbal. Ed. by Javid Iqbal. Lahore: Sh. Ghulam Ali, 1962. 161p.

11493 ______. Thoughts and reflections of Iqbal. Ed. by Syed Abdul Vahid. Lahore: Sh. M. Ashraf, 1964. 381p.

11494 ______. What should then be done, O people of the East. Tr. by B.A. Dar. Lahore: Iqbal Academy, 1977. 146p.

c. studies of Iqbal's religio-philosophical ideas

11495 DAR, B.A. A study of Iqbal's philosophy. Lahore: Ghulam Ali, 1970. 329p.

11496 Iqbal as a thinker; essays by eminent scholars. 3rd ed. Lahore: Sh. M. Ashraf, 1960. 304p.

11497 IQBAL SINGH. The ardent pilgrim: an introduction to the life and work of Mohammed Iqbal. London: Longmans, Green, 1951. 246p.

11498 KAMAL, RAHIMUDDIN. Iqbal's concept of man. In IsC 37 (1963) 30-48.

11499 MEMON, M.U., ed. Iqbal: poet and philosopher between East and West. Madison: UWiscP, 1979. 119p. (South Asian studies pub., 4)

11500 MAÎTRE, L.-C. Un grand humaniste oriental: Mohammad Iqbal. In Orient 4,13 (1960) 81-94.

11501 MALIK, HAFEEZ, ed. Iqbal: poet-philosopher of Pakistan. NY: ColUP, 1971. 441p.

11501a MARUF, M. Iqbal's philosophy of religion: a study in the cognitive value of religious experience. Lahore: Islamic Book Service, 1977. 267p.

11502 ______., ed. Contributions to Iqbal's thought. Lahore: Islamic Book Service, 1977. 148p.

11503 MAY, L.S. Iqbal: his life and times, 1877-1938. Lahore: Sh. M. Ashraf, 1974. 347p.

11504 NADVĪ, ABULHASAN ALĪ. Glory of Iqbal. Tr. from Urdu by M.A. Kidwai. Lucknow: Academy of Islamic Res. and Pub., 1973. 220p.

11505 NURUDDIN, ABU SAYEED. Allama Iqbal's attitude toward Sufism and his unique philosophy of khudi (self). Dacca: Islamic Foundation Bangladesh, 1978. 64p.

11506 RAFIUDDIN. Iqbal's idea of the self. In Iqbal R. 4 (1963) 1-31.

11507 RAHMAN, FAZLUR. Iqbal's idea of the Muslim. In Islamic Studies 2 (1963) 439-45.

11508 RASHID, K.A. Iqbal, Quran, and the Western world. Lahore: Progressive, 1978. 100p.

11509 SCHIMMEL, A. Gabriel's wing. A study into the religious ideas of Sir Muhammad Iqbal. Leiden: Brill, 1963. 431p. (SHR, 6)

11510 ______. Muhammad Iqbal as seen by a European historian of religion. In Studies in Islam 5,2 (1968) 53-82.

11511 SIDDIQI, M.M. Concept of Muslim culture in Iqbal. Islamabad: Islamic Research Inst., 1970. 144p.

11512 VAHID, S.A. Iqbal: his art and thought. London: John Murray, 1959. 254p.

11513 ______. Studies in Iqbal. Lahore: Sh. Muhammad Ashraf, 1967. 364p.

11514 VAHIDUDDIN, SYED. Iqbal and mysticism. In Studies in Islam 5 (1968) 180-87.

11515 VALIUDDIN, MIR. Iqbal's concepts of love and reason. In Studies in Islam 5 (1968) 83-113.

4. Islamic Conservatism in Modern India: The Network of Madrasas (Religious Schools) Centered on Deoband, U.P.

11516 FARUQI, ZIYA-UL-HASAN. The Deoband school and the demand for Pakistan. Bombay: Asia, 1963. 148p.

11517 METCALF, B. The madrasa at Deoband: a model for religious education in modern India. In MAS 12,1 (1978) 111-34.

5. Mirzā Ghulām Aḥmad of Qadiyan, Punjab (1835-1908) and the Aḥmadiyah Movement: Progressive, Heterodox Interpretation of Islam

11518 ADDISON, JAMES T. The Ahmadiya Movement and its Western propaganda. In Harvard Theological R. 22 (1929) 1-32.

11519 AḤMAD, BASHĪR AL-DĪN MAḤMŪD. The Ahmadiyya movement. Qadian: Book Depot, Talif-o Isha at, 1924. 97p.

11520 ______. Aḥmadiyyat; or, the true Islam. Qadian: Book Depot, Talif-o-Isha at, 1924. 429p.

11521 GHULAM AHMAD, MIRZA. Our teaching; translated from Kashti-Nuh. Qadian: Ahmadiyya Community, 1966. 68p.

11522 ______. The teachings of Islam: a solution of five fundamental religious problems from the Muslim point of view. Delhi: Inter-India, 1978. [Rpt. 1910 ed.]

11523 IQBAL, MUHAMMAD. Islam and Ahmadism, with a reply to questions raised by Pandit Jawahar Lal Nehru. Lahore: Anjuman-i-khuddam-ud-Din, 1934. 47p.

11524 LAVAN, S. The Ahmadiyah movement: a history and perspective. ND: Manohar, 1974. 220p.

11525 NADVĪ, ABULHASAN ALĪ. Qadianism; a critical study. Tr. from Urdu by Z.I. Ansari. 2nd ed. Lucknow: Academy of Islamic Res. and Pub., 1967. 152p.

11526 RAJEKE, B.A. Ahmadiyya movement in India. 7th ed., rev. & enl. Qadian: Nazir Dawato Tabligh, 1968. 56p.

11527 WALTER, H.A. The Ahmadiya movement. Calcutta: Assn. Press, 1918. 185p.

D. Christianity under the Raj (1813-1947): From Foreign Missionary Dominance to Indianization

1. General Histories and Studies of Churches and Missions

11528 ANDREWS, C.F. North India. London: Mowbray, 1908. 243p.

11529 BAAGØ, K. A history of the National Christian Council of India, 1914-1964. Nagpur: Natl. Christian Council, 1965. 88p.

11530 ______. Pioneers of indigenous Christianity. Bangalore: CISRS & CLS, 1969. 214p.

11531 GIBBS, M.E. The Anglican Church in India, 1600-1970. Delhi: ISPCK, 1972. 437p.

11532 HUNTER, R. History of the missions of the Free Church of Scotland, in India and Africa. London: T. Nelson, 1873. 387p.

11533 LAPP, J.A. The Mennonite Church in India, 1897-1962. Scottdale, PA: Herald, 1972. 278p.

11534 MAYHEW, A.I. Christianity and the government of India; an examination of the Christian forces at work in the administration of India and of the mutual relations of the British government and Christian missions, 1600-1920. London: Faber & Gwyer, 1929. 260p.

11535 PICKETT, J.W. Christian mass movements in India: a study with recommendations. Lucknow: Lucknow Pub. House, 1969. 370p. [Rpt. 1933 ed.]

11536 ORR, J.E. Evangelical awakenings in India in the early twentieth century. ND: Masihi Sahitya Sanstha, 1970. 177p.

11537 RICHTER, J.A. A history of missions in India. Tr. by S.H. Moore. Edinburgh: Oliphant, Anderson & Ferrier, 1908. 469p.

11538 SEYBOLD, T.C. God's guiding hand; a story of the Central India Mission, 1868-1967. NY: United Church Board for World Ministries of the United Church of Christ, 1967. 179p.

11539 WHERRY, E.M. Our missions in India, 1834-1924. Boston: Stratford, 1926. 356p. [Presbyterian]

2. Major Church Leaders - Biographies and Studies

11540 Andrews number. In VQ 36,1/4 (1970-71) 3-283. [on C.F. Andrews]

11541 CHATURVEDI, B. & M. SYKES. Charles Freer Andrews: a narrative. ND: PDMIB, 1971. 334p. [1st pub. 1949]

11542 CLARK, I.D.L. C.F. Andrews (Deenabandhu). Delhi: ISPCK, 1970. 79p.

11543 GODWIN, C.J. Spend and be spent: a reflection on missionary vocation, spirituality, and formation, with particular reference to India. Bangalore: Asian Trading Corp., 1977. 209p.

11544 HANSEN, L.E. The double yoke; the story of William Alexander Noble, M.D., Fellow of the American College of Surgeons, Fellow of the International College of Surgeons, Doctor of Humanities, medical missionary extraordinary to India, his adopted land. NY: Citadel Press, 1968. 288p.

11545 HOLCOMB, H.H.H. Men of might in Indian missions; the leaders and their epochs, 1706-1899. Chicago: F.H. Revell, 1901. 346p.

11546 LEFROY, G.A. The life and letters of George Alfred Lefroy, Bishop of Calcutta, and Metropolitan. London: Longmans, Green, 1920. 265p.

11547 PARANJOTI, V. As evangelist on the Indian scene, Dr. E. Stanley Jones. Bombay: Bombay Tract & Book Soc., 1970. 120p.

11548 PARKER, R.J. Children of the light in India; biographies of noted India Christians. NY: H. Revell, 1920. 192p.

11549 PORTER, G. The letters of the late Father George Porter, S.J., Archbishop of Bombay. London: Burns & Oates, 1891. 484p.

11550 ROY CHOUDHURY, P.C. C.F. Andrews: his life and times. Bombay: Somaiya, 1971. 200p.

11551 SHARPE, E.J. John Nicol Farquhar, a memoir. Calcutta: YMCA Pub. House, 1963. 143p.

11552 THOMAS, T.K. The witness of S.K. George. Madras: CLS, 1970. 151p. (Confessing the faith in India series, 6)

11553 TINKER, H. The ordeal of love: C.F. Andrews and India. Delhi: OUP, 1979. 334p.

11554 VERGHESE, H.G. K.E. Abraham, an apostle from modern India: a brief life story of Rev. Dr. K.E. Abraham. Kadambanad: Christian Literature Service of India, 1974. 129p.

3. Christianity and Hinduism: Mutual Views and Interactions

11555 ANDREWS, C.F. The renaissance in India, its missionary aspect. London: Church Missionary Soc., 1912. 310p.

11556 BOWMAN, A.H. Christian thought and Hindu philosophy; a treatise. London: Religious Tract Soc., 1917. 2 v.

11557 DAS, S.K. The shadow of the cross; Christianity and Hinduism in a colonial situation. ND: Munshiram, 1974. 181p.

11558 FALLON, P. Catholicism and Hinduism in modern times. In Studia Missionalia 13 (1963) 188-206.

11559 FARQUHAR, J.N. The crown of Hinduism. ND: OBRC, 1971. 468p. [1st pub. 1913]

11560 GANDHI, M.K. Christian missions: their place in India. Ahmedabad: Navajivan, 1941. 311p.

11561 MATTAM, J. Land of the Trinity; a study of modern Christian approaches to Hinduism. Bangalore: Theological Publications in India, 1975. 200p.

11562 MINZ, NIRMAL. Mahatma Gandhi and Hindu-Christian dialogue. Madras: CLS, 1970. 202p.

11563 PATHAK, S.M. American missionaries and Hinduism; a study of their contacts from 1813 to 1910. Delhi: Munshiram, 1967. 283p.

4. Christians in Social Welfare and Reform

11564 INGHAM, K. Reformers in India, 1793-1833; an account of Christian missionaries on behalf of social reform. Cambridge: CamUP, 1956. 149p.

11565 ODDIE, G.A. Protestant missions, caste and social change in India, 1850-1914. In IESHR 6 (1969) 259-91.

11566 ______. Social protest in India: British Protestant missionaries and social reforms, 1850-1900. ND: Manohar, 1979. 283p.

VIII. MODERN LITERATURES UNDER THE RAJ: GENERAL STUDIES AND LITERATURES IN TRANSREGIONAL LANGUAGES (HINDI, URDU, ENGLISH) 1800-1947

A. General Surveys and Studies

1. Studies of Modern Indian Literatures

11567 CHATTERJI, S.K. Languages and literatures of modern India. Calcutta: Bengal Pub., 1963. 380p.

11568 CLARK, T.W., ed. The novel in India; its birth and development. Berkeley: UCalP, 1970. 239p.

11569 Contemporary Indian literature; a symposium. 2nd ed. ND: Sahitya Akademi, 1959. 338p. [1st ed. 1957]

11570 GOKAK, V.K., ed. Literatures in modern Indian languages. Delhi: PDMIB, 1957. 332p.

11571 GRIERSON, G.A. The modern vernacular literature of Hindustan. Calcutta: Asiatic Soc., 1889. 170p.

11572 KRIPALANI, K. Modern Indian literature; a panoramic glimpse. Bombay: Nirmala Sadanand Pub., 1968. 131p.

11573 KUMARAPPA, B., ed. The Indian literatures of today, a symposium. Bombay: Intl. Book House, 1947. 181p.

11574 MACHWE, P.B. Four decades of Indian literature: a critical evaluation. ND: Chetana Pub., 1976. 160p.

11575 NAGENDRA. Literary criticism in India. Meerut: Sarita Prakashan, 1976. 320p.

11576 NARASIMHAIAH, C.D., ed. Indian literature of the past fifty years, 1917-1967. Mysore: U. of Mysore, 1970. 371p.

11577 Problems of modern Indian literature. Calcutta: Statistical Pub. Soc., 1975. 202p.

11578 QAMAR RAIS, ed. October Revolution: impact on Indian literature. ND: Sterling, 1978. 136p.

11579 VATSYAYAN, S.H. [AGYEYA]. Conflict as a bridge: some aspects of the fiction of modern India. In Diogenes 45 (1964) 49-65.

11580 YAJNIK, R.K. The Indian theatre, its origins and its later developments under European influence, with special reference to western India. NY: Haskell House, 1970. 284p.

2. Collections and Anthologies

11581 ANAND, M.R., ed. Indian short stories. London: New India Pub. Co., 1946. 193p.

11582 NATWAR SINGH, K., ed. Tales from modern India. NY: Macmillan, 1966. 274p.

11583 RAJESVARARAV, A.V., ed. Modern Indian poetry, an anthology. ND: Kavitā, 1958. 140p.

B. Hindi Literature under the Raj

1. Bibliography and General Studies of the Development of Modern Hindi and its Literature

11584 GAEFFKE, H.P.T. On the conception of the dialogue in Hindi narratives. In WZKS 14 (1970) 33-38.

11585 GARCIN DE TASSY, J.H. Histoire de la littérature hindoui et hindoustani. Paris: A. Labitte, 1870-71. 3 v. (Oriental Translation Fund) [1st pub. 1839-47]

11586 MADAN, I.N. Modern Hindi literature; a critical analysis. Lahore: Minerva Book Shop, 1939. 241p.

11587 MCGREGOR, R.S. Hindi literature of the nineteenth and early twentieth centureis. Wiesbaden: Harrassowitz, 1974. p. 62-121. (HIL, 8:1:2)

11588 MISHRA, J.P. Shakespeare's impact on Hindi literature. ND: Munshiram, 1970. 231p.

11589 ROADARMEL, G.C. A bibliography of English source materials for the study of modern Hindi literature. Berkeley: U. of California Center for South & Southeast Asia Studies, 1969. 96p. (Its occ. papers, 4)

11590 SARIN, D.P. Influence of political movements on Hindi literature, 1906-1947. Chandigarh: Panjab U. Pub. Bureau, 1967. 222p.

11591 SIDDIQUI, M.A. Origins of modern Hindustani literature; source material: Gilchrist letters. Aligarh: Naya Kitab Ghar, 1963. 191p.

11592 VEDALANKAR, S.D. The development of Hindi prose literature in the early nineteenth century, 1800-1856 A.D. Allahabad: Lokbharti Pub., 1969. 270p.

2. The Making of Modern Hindi, based on North Indian Dialects: Developed as an Administrative Language by Fort William College and Serampore Mission

11593 BAILEY, T.G. Does Kharī Bolī mean nothing more than rustic speech? In BSOAS 8 (1935-37) 363-71.

11594 BARANNIKOV, A. Modern literary Hindi. In BSOAS 8 (1935-37) 373-90.

11595 KING, C.R. The Nagarī Prachāriṇī Sabhā (Society for the Promotion of the Nāgarī script and language) of Benares 1893-1914: a study in the social and political history of the Hindi language. Ph.D. diss., U. of Wisconsin, 1974. 518p. [UM 74-19,924]

11596 MCGREGOR, R.S. Bengal and the development of Hindi, 1850-1880. In SAR 5,2 (1972) 137-46.

11597 ______. The rise of standard Hindi & early Hindi prose fiction. In T.W. Clark, ed. The novel in India. Berkeley: UCalP, 1970, 142-78. [1st pub. in JRAS (1967) 114-32]

3. Hariścandra (1850-85), called Bhāratendu ("Moon of India"): Journalist, Dramatist, and Poet from Benares

11598 GOPAL, MADAN. Bharatendu Harishchandra. ND: Sahitya Akademi, 1971. 41p.

11599 ______. The Bharatendu: his life & times. ND: Sagar, 1972. 219p.

4. Premchand, pseud. of Dhanapat Rai Srivāstava (1880-1936): Pioneer Urdu and Hindi Novelist and Short Story Writer

a. biographies and studies

11600 GOPAL, MADAN. Munshi Premchand: a literary biography. London: Asia, 1964. 462p.

11601 ______. Premchand. Lahore: Bookabode, 1944. 130p.

11602 GOVIND NARAIN. Munshi Prem Chand. Boston: Twayne, 1978. 178p.

11603 GUPTA, P.C. Prem Chand. ND: Sahitya Akademi, 1968. 56p.

11604 MADAN, I.N. Premchand (an interpretation). Lahore: Minerva Book Shop, 1946. 177p.

11605 ORR, I.C. Premchand's use of folklore in his short stories. In AFS 36,1 (1977) 31-56.

11606 RAHBAR, H.R. Prem Chand: his life and work. Delhi: Atma Ram, 1957. 188p.

11607 SWAN, R.O. Munshi Premchand of Lamhi village. Durham: DUP, 1969. 149p. (DUPCSSA series, 3)

11608 THOMAS, C. Le village dans la forêt: sacrifice et renoncement dans le Godan de Premchand. In Puruṣārtha 2 (1975) 205-52.

b. translations of Premchand's works

11609 PREMCHAND. The chess player and other stories. Tr. by Gurdial Mallik. Delhi: Hind Pocket Books, 1967. 174p.

11610 ______. The gift of a cow; a translation of the Hindi novel Godan. Tr. by G.C. Roadarmal. Bloomington: Indiana U. Press, 1968. 442p. (UNESCO series)

11611 ______. A handful of wheat and other stories by Prem Chand. ND: PPH, 1955. 230p. [tr. by P.C. Gupta]

11612 ______. The shroud and 20 other stories. Tr. by Madan Gopal. ND: Sagar, 1972. 278p.

11613 ______. Le suaire: récits d'une autre Inde. Tr. from Hindi by C. Thomas. Paris: Pub. orientalistes de France, 1975. 137p. (UNESCO series)

11614 ______. The world of Premchand; selected stories.... Tr. by D. Rubin. Bloomington: Indiana U. Press, 1969. 215p. (UNESCO Asian fiction series)

5. Twentieth Century Hindi Poetry: Mystic-Romanticism (chāyāvād), Nationalism, and Progressivism

11615 GAEFFKE, H.P.T. Grundbegriffe moderner indischer Erzählkunst aufgezeigt am Werke Jayasankara Prasads 1889-1937. Leiden: Brill, 1970. 248p. (HO, 2: suppl. 2)

11616 MISRA, V.N., ed. Modern Hindi poetry; an anthology. Bloomington: Indiana U. Press, 1965. 126p.

11617 PANT, S.N. Fifty poems from Chidambara. Tr. by D.B. Mukhopadhyaya, et al. Ed. by A.R. Dasgupta & L.C. Jain. Calcutta: Bharatiya Jnanpith Pub., 1969. 127p.

11618 PRASAD, J.S. Kamayani. Tr. by B.L. Sahney. Delhi: Yugbodh Prakashan, 1971. 215p.

11619 ______. Kamayani. Tr. by M. Bandopadhyay. ND: Ankur Pub. House, 1978. 304p.

11620 RUBIN, D. Nirala and the renaissance of Hindi poetry. In JAS 31 (1972) 111-26.

11621 SHAH, R.C. Jaishankar Prasad. ND: Sahitya Akademi, 1978. 84p.

11622 TRIPATHI, S.K. [Nirala]. A season on the earth: selected poems of Nirala. NY: ColUP, 1977. 152p. (UNESCO series)

16623 VATSYAYAN, S.H. [Agyeya]. First person, second person: a selection of peoms from the work of Agyeya. Tr. by the author & L. Nathan. Berkeley: UCalP, 1971. 104p.

11624 ______. Selected poems of Agyeya; The unmastered lute and other poems. Tr. from Hindi by the author in collaboration with L. Nathan. Calcutta: Rina Nandy, 1969. 16p.

6. Other Major Hindi Writers of Fiction, Drama, Poetry - Studies and Translations

11625 GOPAL, MADAN. Mahavir Prasad Dwivedi, a maker of modern Hindi. In IL 15,1 (1972) 27-37.

11626 MACHWE, P.B. Rahul Sankrityayan. ND: Sahitya Akademi, 1978. 60p.

16627 MISHRA, K.P. Forms & themes in early Hindi novels. In E&W 23,1/2 (1973) 171-85.

11628 ROADARMEL, G.C. The theme of alienation in the modern Hindi short story. Ph.D. diss., U. of California, Berkeley, 1969. 445p. [UM 60-18,963]

11629 ______, tr. Modern Hindi short stories. Berkeley: UCalP, 1974. 211p. (UNESCO series) [1st pub. 1972 as A death in Delhi...]

11630 YASHPAL. Short stories of Yashpal, author and patriot. Tr. by C. Friend. Philadelphia: UPaP, 1969. 143p.

C. Urdu Literature under the Raj

1. General Studies of Modern Urdu Literature

11631 LATIF, SYED ABDUL. The influence of English literature on Urdu literature. London: F. Groom, 1924. 141p.

11632 QADIR, ABDUL. Famous Urdu poets and writers. 2nd ed. ND: Seemant Prakashan, 1977. 200p. [1st pub. 1947]

11633 SADIQ, M. Twentieth century Urdu literature, a review. Baroda: Padmaja Pub., 1947. 95p.

2. Urdu Poetry: the Ghazal and Other Forms
a. general studies

11634 GHĀLIB. Selections from Ghālib & Muhammad Iqbāl. Tr. by K.N. Sud. ND: Sterling, 1978. 110p.

11635 JHA, A.N. Urdu poets and poetry (Essays, Urdu verses in Devanagari script). Allahabad: Leader Press, 1956. 350p.

11636 MAHDI, S.A., ed. Parallelism in English and Urdu poets. Lucknow: 1965. 285p.

11637 NAIM, C.M. Yes, the poem itself. In LEW 15,1 (1971) 7-16.

11638 NARANG, G.C. Some social and cultural aspects of Urdu masnawiis. In Mahfil 3,2/3 (1966) 55-64.

11639 QURESHI, R. Tarannum: the chanting of Urdu poetry. In Ethnomusicology 13 (1969) 425-68.

11640 RUSSELL, R. The pursuit of the Urdu Ghazal. In JAS 29,1 (1969) 107-24.

11641 ______. The Urdu ghazal in Muslim society. In SAR 3,2 (1970) 141-49.

b. Mīrzā Asadullāh Khān Ghālib (1797-1869): poet and letter-writer in Persian and Urdu
i. bibliography

11642 SILVER, B.Q. A bibliography of English sources on Ghalib. In Mahfil 5,4 (1968/69) 115-25.

ii. works in translation

11643 GHALIB. Ghalib, 1797-1869. Volume I: Life and Letters. Tr. by R. Russell & Khurshidul Islam. Cambridge: HUP, 1969. 404p. (UNESCO series) [no more pub.]

11644 ______. Ghazals of Ghalib; versions from the Urdu. Tr. by Aijaz Ahmad, et al. NY: ColUP, 1971. 174p.

11645 ______. Hundred ghazals of Mirza Ghalib. Tr. by P. Bandyopadhyay. Calcutta: United Writers, 1975. 33p.

11646 ______. Persian ghazals of Ghalib. Tr. by Yusuf Husain. ND: Ghalib Inst., 1980. 188 + 160p.

11647 ______. Persian letters of Ghalib. Ed. by S.A.I. Tirmizi. Bombay: Asia, 1969. 69 + 122p. [Persian text; English foreword, preface and intro.]

11648 ______. Twenty-five verses. Tr. from Urdu by C.M. Naim. Calcutta: Writers Workshop, 1970. 46p.

iii. biographies and studies

11649 AHMAD, AIJAZ. Ghalib: "The dew drop on the red poppy--". In Mahfil 5,4 (1968-69) 59-69.

11650 ALI, AHMED & A. BAUSANI. Ghalib: two essays by Ahmed Ali and Alessandro Bausani. Roma: IIMEO, 1969. 167p.

11651 Aspects of Ghalib; five essays. Karachi: Pakistan American Cultural Centre, 1970. 94p.

11652 BAUSANI, A. The position of Ghālib (1796-1869) in the history of Urdu and Indo-Persian poetry. In Der Islam 34 (1959) 99-127.

11653 GILANI, A.C., Sayyid. Ghalib; his life and Persian poetry. Karachi: Azam Books Corp., 1962. 296p.

11654 HASAN, M. Some important critics of Ghalib. Tr. from the Urdu by M.U. Memon. In Mahfil 5,4 (1968-69) 31-43.

11655 JAFRI, A.S. & Q. HYDER. Ghalib and his poetry. Bombay: Popular, 1970. 92p.

11656 LAKHANPAL, P.L. Ghalib, the man and his verse. Delhi: Intl. Books, 1960. 263p.

11657 LALL, I.J. Candle's smoke; Ghalib's life and verse. Delhi: Saluja Prakashan, 1970. 64p.

11658 LATIF, S.A. Ghalib, a critical appreciation of his life and Urdu poetry. Hyderabad, Deccan: Chandra-Kanth Press, 1929. 104p.

11659 MAHMUD, S.F. Ghalib, a critical introduction. Lahore: U. of the Punjab, 1969. 518p. (Pub. of the Majlis-i-Yadgar-i-Ghalib, 16)

11660 MALIK, R. Mirza Ghalib. ND: NBT, 1968. 93p.

11661 MUJEEB, M. Ghalib. ND: Sahitya Akademi, 1969. 80p.

11662 NAIM, C.M. The poem (Ghalib's) itself. In Mahfil 5,4 (1968-69) 97-114.

11663 RIZVI, S.E.H. The elements of Ghalib's thought. Tr. from Urdu by C.M. Naim & M.U. Memon. In Mahfil 5,4 (1968-69) 7-29.

11664 RUSSELL, R., ed. Ghalib: the poet & his age; papers read at the centenary celebrations at SOAS, U. of London. London: Allen & Unwin, 1972. 131p.

11665 ______. On translating Ghalib. In Mahfil 5,4 (1968-69) 71-87.

11666 SAIYIDAIN, K.G. Tagore lecture, 1969, on Ghalib. Ahmedabad: Gujarat U., 1971. 78p.

11667 SARAN, S. Mirza Ghalib: the poet of poets. ND: Munshiram, 1976. 231p.

11668 SCHIMMEL, A. A dance of sparks: imagery of fire in Ghalib's poetry. ND: Vikas, 1979. 141p.

11669 ______. Ghalib's Qasida in honour of the prophet. In A.T. Welch & P. Cachia, eds. Islam: past influence and present challenge. Albany: State U. of N.Y. Press, 1979, 188-209.

11670 SUD, K.N. Eternal flame; aspects of Ghalib's life and works. Delhi: Sterling, 1969. 136p.

11671 WARIS KIRMANI, M. Evaluation of Ghalib's Persian poetry. Aligarh: Dept. of Persian, Aligarh Muslim U., 1972. 120p.

c. Sir Muḥammad Iqbāl (1877-1938): Urdu and Persian poet [for his role in politics and philosophy, see IV. D. 2. b. i. and VII. D. 3., above]
i. works in translation

11672 IQBAL, MUHAMMAD. Gabriel's wing (Bal-i-Gibril). Tr. from Urdu by Syed Akbar Ali Shah. Islamabad: Modern Book Depot, 1979. 162p.

11673 ______. Longer poems of Iqbal. Tr. by A.R. Tariq. Lahore: Sh. Ghulam Ali, 1978. 206p.

11674 ______. A message from the East: a translation of Iqbal's Payam-i Mashriq. Tr. by M. Hadi Hussain. 2nd ed. Lahore: Iqbal Academy, 1977. 189p.

11675 ______. The pilgrimage of eternity, being an English translation of Muhammad Iqbal's Javid nama by Shaikh Mahmud Ahmad. Lahore: Inst. of Islamic Culture, 1961. 187p.

11676 ______. Rubayiat of Iqbal. Tr. by A.R. Tariq. Lahore: Sh. Ghulam Ali, 1973. 220p.

11677 ______. Secrets of the self: a philosophical poem. Tr. from Persian by R.A. Nicholson. ND: Arnold-Heinemann, 1978. 131p.

ii. critical studies

11678 BUKHARI, S.A.W. Iqbal, his poetry & philosophy. In JAU 25 (1964) 102-12.

11679 CLAVEL, L.S. Islamic allusions in the poetry of Iqbal. In AsSt 8 (1970) 378-85.

11680 DICKIE, J. Muhammad Iqbal: a reappraisal. In Iqbal R. 9 (1968) 67-74.

11681 HABIB, K. Studies in Iqbal's longer poems. In Iqbal R. 6,1 (1965) 1-32.

11682 FYZEE RAHAMIN, ATIYA BEGUM. Iqbal. Lahore: Aina-i-Adab, 1969. 93p.

11683 HASSAN, RIFFAT, comp. The sword and the sceptre: a collection of writings on Iqbal, dealing mainly with his life and poetical works. Lahore: Iqbal Academy Pakistan, 1977. 56 + 394p.

11684 IQBAL, M. The poet's vision and magic of words: an approach to Iqbal's poetry. Lahore: Islamic Book Service, 1978. 142p.

11685 MALIK, H. An appreciation of Guru Nanak in Iqbal's poetry. In Studies in Islam 5 (1968) 146-60.

11686 MASUD-UL-HASAN. Life of Iqbal: general account of his life. Lahore: Ferozsons, 1978-. [to be 4 v.]

11687 NAIM, C.M. The "pseudo-dramatic" poems of Iqbal. In M.U. Memon, ed. Iqbal: poet and philosopher between East and West. Madison: UWiscP, 1979, 82-104. (South Asian studies, Pub. 4)

11688 NAIMUDDIN, S. The concept of love in Rumi and Iqbal. In IsC 42 (1968) 185-210.

11689 SIDDIQUI, MISBAH-UL-HAQ, comp. Iqbal; a critical study. Lahore: Farhan Pub., 1977. 257p.

11690 SINHA, SACHCHIDANANDA. Iqbal: the poet & his message. Allahabad: Ram Narain Lal, 1947. 512p.

11691 TASEER, M.D. Iqbal: the universal poet. Lahore: Munib Pub., 1977. 75p.

d. modernist and nationalist poets

11692 CASE, M.H. The social and political satire of Akbar Ilāhābādī (1846-1921). In Mahfil 1,4 (1964) 11-20.

11693 FAIZ, FAIZ AHMAD. Poems by Faiz. Tr. from Urdu by V.G. Kiernan. London: Allen & Unwin, 1971. 288p.

11694 RUSSELL, R. & KHURSHIDUL ISLAM. The satirical verse of Akbar Ilahabadi (1846-1921). In MAS 8,1 (1974) 1-58.

3. Modern Urdu Prose: Development of the Novel and Short Story

a. Urdu fiction in translation

11695 MIRZA, AGHA IQBAL, tr. Modern Urdu stories. Calcutta: Writers Workshop, 1975. 94p.

11696 RUSWA, M.M.H. The courtesan of Lucknow (Umrao Jan Ada). Tr. by Khushwant Singh & M.A. Husaini. Delhi: Hind Pocket Books, 1970. 240p. (UNESCO series) [1st pub. 1899]

b. studies of Urdu fiction

11697 CHANDAR, KRISHAN. Flame and the flower. Bombay: Current Book House, 1951. 99p.

11698 ______. I cannot die, a story of Bengal. Tr. from Urdu by K.A. Abbas. Poona: Kutub, 1943. 52p.

11699 NARANG, G.C. Major trends in the Urdu short story. In IL 16,1/2 (1973) 113-32.

11700 RUSSELL, R. The development of the modern novel in Urdu. In T.W. Clark, ed. The novel in India.... Berkeley: UCalP, 1970, 102-41.

11701 SUHRAWARDY, S.A.B. Critical survey of the development of the Urdu novel and short story. London: Longmans, Green, 1945. 316p.

11702 ZAMAN, M. The Urdu novel. In Pakistan Q. 15 (1968) 82-89.

D. English Literature by South Asian Writers (to 1947) [see also Chap. Eight, X. C. 5]

1. Bibliography

11703 ALPHONSO-KARKALA, J.B. Bibliography of Indo-English literature: a checklist of works by Indian authors in English, 1800-1966. Bombay: Nirmala Sadanand Pub., 1974. 167p.

17704 Indian English literature. In A bibliography of Indian English. Hyderabad: Central Inst. of English & Foreign Languages, 1972. pt. 1, 218p.

11705 JAIN, S.K. Indian literature in English: a bibliography... of poetry, drama, fiction, autobiography, and letters written by Indians in English, or translated from modern Indian languages into English. Tenterden, Kent: Sushil Jain Pub., 1967. 179p. [available from University Microfilms, Ann Arbor, 1972]

11706 NAQVI, R.A. Indian response to literature in English (British, American, and Indo-Anglian); an annotated bibliography. Gurgaon: Indian Documentation Service, 1974. 191p.

11707 PIET, D. Bibliography: secondary sources on Indian fiction in English. In LEW 15,1 (1972) 74-82.

11708 SPENCER, D.M. Indian fiction in English; an annotated bibliography. Philadelphia: UPaP, 1960. 98p.

11709 SRINATH, C.N. Annual bibliography of Commonwealth literature 1967: India. In J. of Commonwealth Literature 6 (1960) 67-76. [appears annually since 1964]

2. General Studies of Indo-Anglian Literature

11710 ALPHONSO-KARKALA, J.B. Indo-English literature in the nineteenth century. Mysore: Literary Half-yearly, U. of Mysore, 1970. 168p.

11711 BADAL, R.K. Indo-Anglian literature: an outline. 1st ed. Bareilly: Prakash Book Depot, 1975. 56p.

11712 BELLIAPPA, N.M. East-West encounter: Indian women writers of fiction in English. In Literary Criterion 7,3 (1966) 18-27.

11713 MCCUTCHION, D. Indian writing in English; critical essays. Calcutta: Writers Workshop, 1969. 120p.

11714 MELWANI, M.D. Critical essays on Indo-Anglian themes. Calcutta: Writers Workshop, 1971. 45p.

11715 ______. Themes in Indo-Anglian literature. Bareilly: Prakash Book Depot, 1977. 119p.

11716 MOHAN, RAMESH, ed. Indian writing in English: papers read at the Seminar on Indian English held at the Central Institute of English and Foreign Languages, Hyderabad, July 1972. Bombay: Orient Longman, 1978. 260p.

11717 MOKASHI-PUNEKAR, S. Theoretical & practical studies in Indo-English literature. Dharwar: Karnatak U., 1978. 265p.

11718 MUKHERJEE, M., ed. Considerations. Bombay: Allied, 1977. 152p.

11719 NARASIMHAIAH, C.D. Indian literature of the past fifty years, 1917-1967. Mysore: Prasaranga, U. of Mysore, 1970. 371p.

11720 RAGHAVACHARYULU, D.V.K., ed. The two-fold voice; essays on Indian writing in English. Vijayawada: Navodaya Pub., 1971. 184p.

11721 SHARMA, K.K., ed. Indo-English literature: a collection of critical essays. Ghaziabad: Vimal Prakashan, 1977. 273p.

11722 SINHA, R.C.P. The Indian autobiographies in English. ND: S. Chand, 1978. 223p.

11723 SRINIVASA IYENGAR, K.R. Indian writing in English. NY: Asia, 1962. 440p.

11724 VERGHESE, C.P. Essays on Indian writing in English. ND: N.V. Pub. 1975. 151p.

11725 WILLIAMS, H.M. Indo-Anglian literature, 1800-1970; a survey. Madras: Orient Longmans, 1976. 137p.

3. Indo-English Fiction: Novels and Short Stories

11726 DERRETT, M.E. The modern Indian novel in English; a comparative approach. Brussels: Editions de l'Inst. de sociologie, U. libre de Bruxelles, 1966. 195p.

11727 FISKE, A.M. Karma in five Indian novels. In LEW 10,1/2 (1966) 98-111.

11728 HARREX, S.C. The fire and the offering: the English-language novel of India, 1935-1970. Calcutta: Writers Workshop, 1977-78. 2 v.

11729 HEMENWAY, S.I. The novel of India. Calcutta: Writers Workshop, 1975. 2 v.

11730 KRISHNA RAO, A.V. The Indo-Anglian novel and the changing tradition; a study of the novels of Mulk Raj Anand, Kamala Markandaya, R.K. Narayan, and Raja Rao, 1930-64. Mysore: Rao and Raghavan, 1972. 146p.

11731 MEHTA, P.P. Indo-Anglian fiction; an assessment. Bareilly: Prakash Book Depot, 1968. 298p.

11732 MUKHERJI, M. The twice born fiction; themes and techniques of the Indian novel in English. ND: Heinemann Educ. Books, 1971. 239p.

11733 NAIK, M.K. The political novel in Indian writing in English. In CAS 6 (1975) 6-15.

11734 NARASIMHAN, R. Sensibility under stress: aspects of Indo-English fiction. ND: Ashajanak Pub., 1976. 144p.

11735 PARAMESWARAN, UMA. A study of representative Indo-English novelists. ND: Vikas, 1976. 179p.

11736 RIEMENSCHNEIDER, D. Der moderne englishsprachige Roman Indiens. Darmstadt: Thesen-Verlag, 1974. 161p.

11737 SARMA, G.P. Nationalism in Indo-Anglian fiction. ND: Sterling, 1978. 391p.

11738 SHIRWADKAR, M. Image of woman in the Indo-Anglian novel. ND: Sterling, 1979. 169p.

11739 SINGH, R.S. Indian novel in English: a critical study. ND: Arnold-Heinemann Pub., 1977. 206p.

11740 SPEIGHT, E.E., ed. Indian masters of English, an anthology of English prose.... Calcutta: Longmans, Green, 1934. 177p.

11741 VENUGOPAL, C.V. The Indian short story in English: a survey. Bareilly: Prakash Book Depot, 1976. 132p.

11742 VERGHESE, C.P. Indian English and man in Indo-Anglian fiction. In IL 13,1 (1970) 6-25.

4. Indo-Anglian Poetry and Drama
a. general studies and anthologies

11743 BASU, L. Indian writers of English verse. Calcutta: U. of Calcutta, 1935. 156p.

11744 BHUSHAN, V.N., ed. The Peacock Lute: an anthology of poems in English by Indian writers. Bombay: Padma, 1945. 29 + 155p.

11745 BOSE, A. Modern Indian poetry in English. In IL 13,1 (1970) 51-59.

11746 DASGUPTA, M.A. Hers: Indian perspectives: an anthology of poetry in English by Indian women. Calcutta: Writers Workshop, 1978. 106p.

11747 DESHPANDE, G., ed. An anthology of Indo-English poetry. Delhi: Hind Pocket Books, 1974. 162p.

11748 DUNN, T.O.D. Bengali writers of English verse. Calcutta: Thacker, 1918. 27p.

11749 GHOSE, AUROBINDO. Collected plays and short stories. Pondicherry: Sri Aurobindo Ashram, 1971. 2 v.

11750 GOKAK, V.K., ed. The golden treasury of Indo-Anglian poetry, 1828-1965. ND: Sahitya Akademi, 1970. 323p.

11751 ______, ed. Twenty-one Indo-Anglian poems. Madras: M. Seshachalam, 1975. 42p.

11752 KOTOKY, P.C. Indo-English poetry; a study of Sri Aurobindo and four others. Gauhati: Gauhati U., 1969. 203p.

11753 LAHIRI, K.C., ed. Indo-English poetry in Bengal. Calcutta: Writers Workshop, 1974. 171p.

11754 LAL, P. & K. RAGHAVENDRA RAO, eds. Modern Indo-Anglian poetry, an anthology. ND: A. Chaya Deir, 1959. 51p.

11755 MEHTA, K.A. English drama on the Bombay stage towards the turn of the century, 1880-1900. In JASBombay 39/40 (1964-65) 205-24.

11756 NAIK, M.K. Echo and voice in Indian poetry in English. In Indian Writing Today 4 (1970) 32-40.

11757 ______, ed. Indian response to poetry in English. Bombay: Macmillan, 1970. 285p.

11758 NANDY, P., ed. Strangertime: an anthology of Indian poetry in English. Delhi: Hind Pocket Books, 1977. 218p.

11759 SAHA, S.C. Insights. Calcutta: Writers Workshop, 1972. 116p.

11760 ______. Modern Indo-Anglian love poetry. Calcutta: Writers Workshop, 1971. 47p.

11761 SINHA, R.P.N. The birth and development of Indo-English verse. ND: Dev Pub. House, 1971. 203p.

b. early imitative Indo-English poetry of the Bengal Renaissance

11762 DAS, H. Life and letters of Toru Dutt. London: OUP, 1921. 364p.

11763 DASGUPTA, M.A., ed. Henry Louis Vivian Derozio (1808-31), Anglo-Indian patriot and poet; a memorial volume. Calcutta: Derozio Commemorative Cmtee., 1973. 25 + 31p.

11764 DEROZIO, HENRY. Poems. Calcutta: Writers Workshop, 1972. 23 + 44p.

11765 DOVER, C. Henry Derozio: Eurasian poet and preceptor. In The Poetry R. 27,2 (1936) 105-17.

11766 DUTT, TORU. Ancient ballads and legends of Hindustan. Allahabad: Kitabistan, 1969. 175p. [1st pub. 1941]

11767 DWIVEDI, A.N. Toru Dutt. ND: Arnold-Heinemann, 1977. 168p.

11768 MADGE, E.W. Henry Derozio, the Eurasian poet and reformer. Ed. by S.R. Choudhuri. Calcutta: Metropolitan Book Agency, 1967. 58p. [1st pub. 1905]

11769 SENGUPTA, P. Toru Dutt. ND: Sahitya Akademi, 1968. 94p.

c. poetry of Hindu and nationalist inspiration

11770 BAIG, T.A. Sarojini Naidu. ND: PDMIB, 1974. 175p.

11771 DAS, MANOJ. Sri Aurobindo. ND: Sahitya Akademi, 1972. 82p.

11772 GHOSE, AUROBINDO. Collected poems; the complete poetical works. Pondicherry: Sri Aurobindo Ashram, 1972. 625p.

11773 GHOSE, S.K. The poetry of Sri Aurobindo; a short survey. Calcutta: Chatuskone, 1969. 124p.

11774 GUPTA, RAMESHWAR. Sarojini: the poetess. Delhi: Doaba House, 1975. 142p.

11775 PURANI, A.B. Sri Aurobindo's Savitri; an approach and a study. Pondicherry: Sri Aurobindo Soc., 1970. 397p.

11776 SEETARAMAN, M.V. Studies in Sri Aurobindo's dramatic poems. Annamalainagar: Annamalai U., 1964. 99p.

11777 SENGUPTA, P. Sarojini Naidu; a biography. Bombay: Asia, 1966. 359p.

11778 SETHNA, K.D. The poetic genius of Sri Aurobindo. Rev. 2nd ed. Pondicherry: Sri Aurobindo Ashram, 1974. 141p.

11779 ______. Sri Aurobindo -- the poet. Pondicherry: Sri Aurobindo Inst. Centre of Educ., 1970. 472p.

11780 SINHA, A.K. The dramatic art of Sri Aurobindo. ND: S. Chand, 1979. 227p.

IX. ART AND ARCHITECTURE UNDER THE RAJ

A. General Studies

11781 APPASAMY, J. The development of modern Indian art. In Indian Inst. of Advanced Study, Bull. 4,3 (1970) 33-38.

11782 ARCHER, W.G. India and modern art. London: Allen & Unwin, 1959. 143p.

11783 COOMARASWAMY, A.K. Art and Swadeshi. Madras: Ganesh, 191-. 150p. + 18pl.

11784 MOOKERJEE, A.C. Modern art in India. Calcutta: Oxford Book and Stationery, 1956. 137p.

11785 NANDI, S.K. Studies in modern Indian aesthetics. Simla: IIAS, 1975-.

11786 PARIMOO, R. Baroda painters and sculptors - a school and a movement. In LKC 4 (1966) 13-18.

11787 ______. Studies in modern Indian art: a collection of essays. ND: Kanak Publications, 1975. 147p.

B. Painting

1. General

11788 FURTADO, R. DE L. Three painters. ND: Dhoomimal Ramchand, 1960. 23p. + 48pl. [on Amrita Sher-Gil, Maqbool Fida Husain, George Keyt]

11789 RAMACHANDRA RAO, P.R. Modern Indian painting. Madras: Rachana, 1953. 1 v.

11790 SHELLIM, M. Engravings of old Calcutta. In BPP 87 (1968) 27-44.

11791 WELCH, S.C. & G.D. BEARCE. Painting in British India 1757-1857; exhibition. Brunswick, ME: Bowdoin College Museum of Fine Arts, 1963. 31p. + 11p. of ill.

2. "Company Painting" by Indian Artists for British Patrons

11792 ARCHER, M. Company painting in South India: the early collections of Niccolas Manucci. In Apollo 92 (1970) 104-13.

11793 ARCHER, M. & W.G. ARCHER. Indian painting for the British, 1770-1880. London: OUP, 1955. 147p. + 24 pl.

3. "Bazaar" Painting of Calcutta

11794 ARCHER, M. Bazaar style. In Mārg 20,1 (1966-67) 53-54.

11795 ARCHER, W.G. Bazaar paintings of Calcutta: the style of Kalighat. London: HMSO, 1953. 76p.

11796 ______. Kalighat paintings, Victoria and Albert Museum: a catalogue and introduction. London: HMSO, 1971. 127p.

11797 BIRLA, B.K. Kalighat drawings, from the Basant Kumar Birla collection, formerly Ajit Ghosh collection. Bombay: Mārg Pub., 1962. 1 v.

11798 GHOSH, P. Kalighat pats; annals and appraisal. Calcutta: Shilpayan Artists Soc., 1967. 35p.

11799 SEN GUPTA, S., ed. The patas and the Patuas of Bengal. Calcutta: Indian Pub., 1973. 144p.

4. Modern Painting of India (1808-1930)
a. the Bengal School

11800 AMRITA. Jaimini Roy. In LKC 2 (1964) 15-26.

11801 ANAND, M.R. Paintings of Rabindranath Tagore. In Mārg 14 (1961) 3-44.

11802 APPASAMY, JAYA, ed. Binode Behari Mukherjee. ND: Lalit Kalā Akademi, 1965. 6p. + 26 pl.

11803 BHATTACHARYYA, N.C. Paintings of Rabindranath Tagore. In RL 128 (1958) 66-74.

11804 DAW, P., ed. The two great Indian artists. Calcutta: KLM, 1978. 114p.

11805 DEY, B. The paintings of Rabindranath Tagore. In VQ 23 (1957) 89-99.

11806 DEY, BISHNU & J. IRWIN. Jaimini Roy. Calcutta: Indian Soc. of Oriental Art, 1944. 30p.

11807 GUHA, A. Abanindranath in Government School of Art. In BPP 91,2 (1972) 166-75.

11808 INDIAN SOC. OF ORIENTAL ART. Abanindranath Tagore. Calcutta: 1961. 115p. [Pub. as v. 20 of JISOA]

11809 KRAMRISCH, S. Form elements in the visual work of Rabindranath Tagore. In LKC 2 (1964) 37-44.

11810 MAJUMDAR, KSHITINDRANATH. Kshitindranath Majumdar. Ed. by Jaya Appasamy. ND: Lalit Kalā Akademi, 1967. 1v.

11811 MITRA, A. Gaganendranath Tagore. In LKC 2 (1964) 7-13.

11812 ______. Four painters. Calcutta: New Age Publishers, 1965. 74 p.

11813 Nandalal number. In VQ 34,1/4 (1968-69) 3-196. [on Nandalal Bose]

11814 PARIMOO, R. The paintings of the three Tagores: Abanindranath, Gaganendanath, Rabindranath; chronology and comparative study. Baroda: MSUB, 1973. 182p.

11815 SEN, S.M. Art of Sunil Madhav Sen. Calcutta: Mrs. Aruna Sen, dist. Oxford Book & Stationery Co., 1971. 16p.

11816 TAGORE, ABANINDRANATH. Abanindranath Tagore: his early work. Ed. by R.N. Chakravorty. 2nd ed., rev. by A. Sarkar. Calcutta: Indian Museum, 1964. 19p. + 13pl.

11817 TAGORE, G.N. Gaganendranath Tagore. Calcutta: Rabindra-Bharati Soc. & Assam Book Depot, 1964. 26p.

11818 ______. Gaganendranath Tagore. ND: Lalit Kala Akademi, 1964. 1 v. 14p. + 20 pl.

11819 ______. The humorous art of G.T. (Gogonendranath Tagore). Calcutta: Birla Academy of Art & Culture, 197-. 24p. + 24 pl.

11820 TAGORE, RABINDRANATH. Drawings and paintings of Rabindranath Tagore. ND: Lalit Kala Akademi, 1961. 10p. + 40 pl.

b. Amrita Sher-Gil (1913-1941): confluence of Western and Indian styles

11821 Amrita Sher-Gil; essays. Bombay: Marg Pub., 1972. 144p.

11822 FABRI, C. Notes towards a biography of Amrita Sher-Gil. In LKC 2 (1964) 17-36.

11823 KHANDALAVALA, K. Amrita Sher-gil. Bombay: New Book Co., nd.

11824 SHER-GIL, A. Sher-Gil. ND: Lalit Kalā Akademi, 1965. 31p.

c. leading painters of other schools

11825 CHUGHTAI, M.A.R. Chughtai's paintings. 2nd ed. Lahore: Print Printo Press, 1970. 101p., incl. 45 pl.

11826 JAMES, J. The Madras school. In LKC 6 (1967) 31-36.

11827 RAMA RAO, D. Damerla Rama Rao: masterpieces. Rajamundry: Damerla Rama Rao Memorial Art Gallery and School, 1969. 36p.

11828 VARMA, RAVI. Ravi Varma. ND: Lalit Kala Akademi, 1960. 15p. + 21 pl.

11829 VENKATAPPA, K. K. Venkatappa. ND: Lalit Kalā Akademi, 1968. 1 v.

C. Architecture: Uniformity of Style through Hybridization of European and Indian Elements

11830 ARCHER, M. Indian architecture and the British 1780-1830. Feltham: Country Life Books, 1968. 64p.

11831 BENCE-JONES, M. Palaces of the Raj: magnificence and misery of the Lord Sahibs. London: Allen & Unwin, 1973. 225p.

11832 MCCUTCHION, D. European impact on the art and architecture of temples in Bengal. In Quest 54 (1967) 12-18.

11833 NILSSON, S.A. European architecture in India, 1750-1850. Tr. from Swedish by A. George & E. Zettersten. London: Faber, 1968. 215p.

11834 SANDERSON, G. Types of modern Indian buildings at Delhi, Agra, Allahabad, Lucknow, Ajmer, Bhopal, Bikanir, Gwalior, Jaipur, Jodhpur and Udaipur, with notes on the craftsmen employed on their design and execution.

Allahabad: Supt., Govt. Press, 1913. 1 v.

11835 SHARMA, B.B. European sepulchral architecture in India. In Indica 12,1 (1975) 36-40, pls.

X. INDIA AND THE WEST: MUTUAL ENCOUNTERS DURING THE PERIOD OF BRITISH RULE

A. Orientalism: The Western Discovery of India's Great Tradition

1. General Studies

11836 BEARCE, G.D. British attitudes towards India, 1784-1858. London: OUP, 1961. 315p.

11837 DUBOIS, J.A. Hindu manners, customs and ceremonies. Oxford: OUP, 1906. 741p.

11838 HOCKINGS, P. The Abbé Dubois, an early French ethnographer. In CIS 11,2 (1977) 330-43.

11839 MADAN, G.R. Western sociologists on Indian society: Marx, Spencer, Weber, Durkheim, Pareto. Bombay: Allied, 1979. 398p.

11840 MITTER, P. Much maligned monsters: history of European reactions to Indian art. Oxford: OUP, 1977. 351p.

11841 ______. Western bias in the study of South Indian aesthetics. In SAR 6,2 (1973) 125-36.

11842 ROŞU, A. Eminescu et l'indianisme romantique. In ZDMG 119 (1970) 241-50.

11843 ROWLAND, B. The world's image of Indian architecture. In Royal Soc. of Arts J. 112 (1964) 795-809.

11844 ROY, S.N. Indian archaeology from Jones to Marshall. In AI 9 (1953) 4-28.

11845 SCHWAB, R. La renaissance orientale.... Paris: Payot, 1950. 526p.

11846 SINGER, M.B. Passage to more than India. In his When a great tradition modernizes.... NY: Praeger, 1972, 11-39.

2. Sir William Jones (1746-1794), Founder of the Asiatic Society of Bengal in 1786

11847 CANNON, G.H. Oriental Jones; a biography of Sir William Jones, 1746-1794. Bombay: Asia, 1964. 215p.

11848 ______. The Indian affairs of Sir William Jones, 1746-94. In Asian Affairs (London) 10 (1979) 27-41.

11849 ______. Sir William Jones's translation-interpretation of Sanskrit literature. In LEW 15,3 (1971) 358-70.

11850 JONES, W. The letters of Sir William Jones. Ed. by G.H. Cannon. Oxford: OUP, 1970. 2 v.

11851 MUKHERJI, S.N. Sir William Jones: a study in eighteenth-century British attitudes to India. London: CamUP, 1968. 199p.

3. Friedrich Max Müller (1823-1900), Editor of Sacred Books of the East

11852 CHAUDHURI, N.C. Scholar extraordinary: the life of Professor the Rt. Hon. Friedrich Max Müller. NY: OUP, 1974. 393p.

11853 VOIGT, J.H. Max Mueller; the man and his ideas. Calcutta: KLM, 1967. 101p.

4. Ananda Kentish Coomaraswamy (1877-1947): Anglo-Ceylonese Apostle of Indian Art and Culture

11854 JAG MOHAN. Ananda K. Coomaraswamy. ND: PDMIB, 1979. 118p.

11855 NARAVANE, V.S. Ananda K. Coomaraswamy. Boston: Twayne, 1978. 188p.

11856 RAPHAEL, R. Ananda Coomaraswamy: spiritual frontiers of art, literature, and culture. Madras: Rayappa, 1977. 229p.

11857 SASTRI, P.S. Ananda K. Coomaraswamy. ND: Arnold-Heinemann, India, 1974. 203p.

B. Indian Inspiration in Western Philosophy and Literature

11858 DEBIDOUR, A. L'Indianisme de Voltaire. In R. de littérature comparée 4 (1924) 26-40.

11859 DESHMUKH, D.G. Thoreau and Indian thought.... In NUJ 23,1/2 (1972-73) 1-102.

11860 DWIVEDI, A.N. Indian thought and tradition in American literature. ND: Oriental, 1978. 280p.

11861 GHOSH, D. Indian thought in T.S. Eliot: an analysis of the works of T.S. Eliot in relation to the major Hindu-Buddhist religious and philosophical texts. Calcutta: SPB, 1978. 127p.

11862 GLASENAPP, H. VON. Das Indienbild deutscher Denker. Stuttgart: K.F. Koehler, 1960. 241p.

11863 ______. Kant und die Religionen des Ostens. Kitzingen-Main: Holzner, 1954. 198p.

11864 MARSHALL, P.J., ed. The British discovery of Hinduism in the eighteenth century. London: CamUP, 1970. 310p.

11865 MEESTER, M.E. DE. Oriental influences in the English literature of the nineteenth century. Heidelberg: C. Winter, 1915. 80p.

11866 MOJUMDER, M.A.T. Sir William Jones, the Romantics, and the Victorians. Dacca: University Press, Ltd., 1976. 104p.

11867 RAYAPATI, J.P.R. Early American interest in Vedanta; pre-Emersonian interest in Vedic literature and Vedantic philosophy. NY: Asia, 1973. 133p.

11868 RIEPE, D.M. The philosophy of India and its impact on American thought. Springfield, IL: Thomas, 1970. 339p.

11869 WILLSON, A.L. A mythical image: the ideal of India in German romanticism. Durham: DUP, 1964. 261p.

C. The Indian Discovery of the West: Travellers to Europe and America

11870 ABU TALEB KHAN, MIRZA. Travels of Mirza Abu Taleb Khan in Asia, Africa, and Europe during the years 1799 to 1803. Tr. from Persian by C. Stewart. ND: Sona Publications, 1972. 351p. [1st pub. 1814]

11871 CHAUDHURI, N.C. A passage to England. London: Macmillan, 1959. 229p.

11872 GAUBA, K.L. Uncle Sham; the strange tale of a civilization run amuck. NY: C. Kendall, 1929. 261p.

11873 MOHAN LAL. Travel in the Punjab, Afganistan, and Turkistan to Balk, Bokhara, and Herat, and a visit to Great Britain and Germany. 2nd rev. ed. Calcutta: K.P. Bagchi, 1977. 324p. [1st pub. 1846]

11874 VIVEKANANDA, Swami. Memoirs of European travel. Calcutta: Advaita Ashram, 1963. 108p.

D. Images of India in Western Fiction [Individual Works of Fiction not Included]

1. General Studies and Reference Works

11875 BISSOONDOYAL, B. India in French literature. London: Luzac, 1967. 94p.

11876 DUNN, T.D., ed. India in song: eastern themes in English verse by British and Indian poets. Bombay: OUP, 1920. 96p.

11877 GEORGE, R.E.G. India in English literature. London: Simpkin, Marchall, Hamilton, Kent, 1925. 468p.

11878 GOKHALE, B.G., ed. Images of India. Bombay: Popular, 1971. 196p. (Asian Studies, 2)

11879 GOONETILLEKE, D.C.R.A. Difficulties of connection in India: Kipling and Forster. In his Developing countries in British fiction. Totowa, NJ: Rowman and Littlefield, 1977, 134-69.

11880 GREENBERGER, A.J. The British image of India; a study in the literature of imperialism, 1880-1960. London: OUP, 1969. 234p.

11881 GUPTA, B.K. India in English fiction, 1800-1970; an annotated bibliography. Metuchen, NJ: Scarecrow Press, 1973. 296p.

11882 HOWE, S. Novels of empire. NY: ColUP, 1949. 186p.

11883 OATEN, E.F. A sketch of Anglo-Indian literature. London: K. Paul, Trench, Trubner, 1908. 215p.

11884 PARRY, B. Delusions and discoveries: studies on India in the British imagination, 1880-1930. London: Allen Lane, 1972. 369p.

11885 SATIN, N. India in modern English fiction: with special reference to R. Kipling, E.M. Forster, and A. Huxley. Norwood, PA: Norwood Editions, 1976. 274p.

11886 SENCOURT, R. India in English literature. Port Washington, NY: Kennikat, 1970. 468p. [1st pub. 1923]

11887 SHAMSUL ISLAM. Chronicles of the Raj: a study of literary reaction to the imperial idea towards the end of the Raj. Totowa, NJ: Rowman and Littlefield, 1979. 130p.

11888 SINGH, B. A survey of Anglo-Indian fiction. London: Curzon Press, 1975. 344p. [Rpt. 1934 ed.]

11889 VISWANATHAM, K. India in English fiction. Waltair: Andhra University Press, 1971. 253p.

11890 WOODCOCK, G. A distant and a deadly shore: notes on the literature of the Sahibs. In PA 46,1 (1973) 94-110.

2. Flora Annie Steel (1847-1929)

11891 PATWARDHAN, D. A star of India: Flora Annie Steel, her works and times. Bombay: A.V. Griha Prakashan, 1963. 219p.

11892 STEEL, F.A. The garden of fidelity, being the autobiography of Flora Annie Steel, 1847-1929. London: Macmillan, 1929. 293p.

3. Rudyard Kipling (1865-1936): "Voice of Anglo-India"

a. bibliographies and collections

11893 KIPLING, R. In the vernacular: the English in India. Ed. by R. Jarrell. Garden City: Doubleday, 1963. 291p.

11894 ______. The writings in prose and verse of Rudyard Kipling. NY: Scribner's, 1897-1899. 23 v.

11895 LIVINGSTON, F.V. Bibliography of the works of Rudyard Kipling. NY: E.H. Wells, 1927. 523p.

11896 Rudyard Kipling: an annotated bibliography of writings about him. In English Fiction in Transition 3,3/4/5 (1960) 1-235; English Lit. in Transition 8,3/4 (1965) 136-241.

11897 STEWART, J.M. Rudyard Kipling, a bibliographical catalogue. Ed. by A.W. Yeats. Toronto: Dalhousie U. Press, 1959. 673p.

b. biographies and studies

11898 CARRINGTON, C.E. Rudyard Kipling; his life and work. Harmondsworth: Penguin, 1970. 634p. [1st pub. 1955]

11899 CORNELL, L.L. Kipling in India. London: Macmillan, 1966. 224p.

11900 DEUTSCH, K.W. & N. WIENER. The lonely nationalism of Rudyard Kipling. In Yale R. 52 (1963) 499-517.

11901 HUSSAIN, S.S. Kipling and India; an inquiry into the nature and extent of Kipling's knowledge of the Indian sub-continent. Dacca: U. of Dacca, 1964. 181p.

11902 JAMILUDDIN, K. The tropic sun: Rudyard Kipling and the Raj. Lucknow: Dept. of English & Modern European Languages, Lucknow U., 1974. 224p.

11903 MARQUARDT, H. Kipling und Indien. Breslau: Priebatsch, 1931. 167p.

11904 MASON, P. Kipling: the glass, the shadow, and the fire. London: J. Cape, 1975. 334p.

11905 RAO, K.B. Rudyard Kipling's India. Norman: U. of Oklahoma Press, 1967. 190p.

11906 SHAHANE, V.A. Rudyard Kipling: activist and artist. Carbondale: Southern Illinois U. Press, 1973. 157p.

11907 SHAMSUL ISLAM. Kipling's "law": a study of his philosophy of life. London: Macmillan, 1975. 174p.

11908 WILSON, A. The strange ride of Rudyard Kipling: his life and works. NY: Viking Press, 1978. 370p. + 28 pl.

4. E.M. Forster (1879-1970): Symbolic Interpretations of India and Anglo-India

11909 DAS, G.K. E.M. Forster's India. London: Macmillan, 1977. 170p.

11910 FORSTER, E.M. The hill of Devi. London: E. Arnold, 1953. 267p.

11911 ______. Only connect: letters to Indian friends. Ed. by Syed Hamid Husain. ND: Arnold Heinemann, 1979. 127p.

11912 GARDNER, P., ed. E.M. Forster: a critical heritage. London: Routledge & K. Paul, 1973. 498p.

11913 LEWIS, R.J. E.M. Forster's passages to India. NY: ColUP, 1979. 157p.

11914 MCDOWELL, F.P.W. E.M. Forster: an annotated secondary bibliography. In English Lit. in Transition 13,2 (1970) 93-173.

11915 NATWAR-SINGH, K., ed. E.M. Forster: a tribute. With selections from his writings on India. NY: Harcourt, Brace & World, 1964. 145p.

11916 PRADHAN, S.V. Anglo-Indian fiction and E.M. Forster. In M. Manuel & K. Ayyappa Paniker, eds. English and India. Madras: Macmillan, 1978, 42-61.

11917 SHAHANE, V.A. E.M. Forster, A Passage to India: a study. Delhi: OUP, 1977. 67p.

11918 ______. E.M. Forster, a reassessment. Allahabad: Kitab Mahal, 1962. 160p.

11919 ______. E.M. Forster: a study in double vision. ND: Arnold-Heinemann, 1975. 130p.

11920 ______., ed. Focus on Forster's A Passage to India: Indian essays in criticism. Bombay: Orient Longman, 1975. 137p.

11921 ______., ed. Perspectives on E.M. Forster's A Passage to India: a collection of critical essays. NY: Barnes & Noble, 1968. 174p.

11922 STALLYBRASS, O., ed. The manuscripts of A Passage to India. London: E. Arnold, 1978. 589p.

5. Other Significant Writers

11923 BANTOCK, G.H. L.H. Myers: a critical study. London: J. Cape, 1956. 157p.

11924 GODDEN, R. Rungli-Rungliot means in Paharia, thus far and no further. Boston: Little, Brown, 1946. 196p.

11925 GODDEN, R. & J. GODDEN. Two under the Indian sun. London: Macmillan, 1966. 240p.

11926 HARDING, D.W. The works of L.H. Myers. In Scrutiny 3 (1934) 44-63.

11927 HARTLEY, L. The Indian novels of Rumer Godden. In Mahfil 3,2/3 (1966) 65-75.

11928 NAIDIS, M. G.A. Henty's idea of India. In Victorian Studies 8 (1964) 49-58.

11929 SIMPSON, H.A. Rumer Godden. NY: Twayne, 1973. 160p.

E. The European Experience in India under the Raj

1. Journals and Reminiscences of Residents and Travellers

11930 ACKERLY, J.R. Hindoo holiday; an Indian journal. London: Chatto & Windus, 1932. 341p.

11931 BUTLER, I. The viceroy's wife: letters of Alice, Countess of Reading, from India, 1921-25. London: Hodder & Stoughton, 1969. 190p. + 8 pl.

11932 CAREY, W.H., comp. The good old days of Honorable John Company; being curious reminiscences during the rule of the East India Company, 1600-1858.... New abridged ed. Calcutta: Quins Book Co., 1964. 287p.

11933 DUFFERIN AND AVA, HARIOT GEORGINA, Marchioness of. Our Viceregal life in India. London: Murray, 1890. 2 v.

11934 DYSON, K.K. A various universe: a study of the journals and memoirs of British men and women in the Indian subcontinent, 1765-1856. Delhi: OUP, 1978. 406p. + 8 pl.

11935 FITZROY, Y.A.G. Courts and camps of India; impressions of Viceregal tours, 1921-1924. London: Methuen, 1926. 243p.

11936 GRAHAM, M. Journal of a residence in India. 2nd ed. Edinburgh: A. Constable, 1812. 211p.

11937 GRANT, C. Anglo-Indian domestic life; a letter from an artist in India to his mother in England. 2nd ed., rev. and enl. Calcutta: Thacker, Spink, 1862. 181p.

11938 HEBER, R. Narrative of a journey through the upper provinces of India, from Calcutta to Bombay, 1824-25. London: Murray, 1928. 3 v.

11939 JACQUEMONT, V. État politique et social de l'Inde du nord en 1830; extraits de son journal de voyage. Paris: E. Leroux, 1933. 467p.

11940 LAIRD, M.A., ed. Bishop Heber in northern India: selections from Heber's journal. Cambridge: CamUP, 1971. 324p. [1824-25]

11941 LEAR, E. Edward Lear's Indian journal; water colours and extracts from the diary ... (1873-75). London: Jarrolds, 1953. 240p.

11942 LOTI, P. L'Inde (sans les Anglais). Paris: Calmann-Levy, 1903. 458p.

11943 MUTALIK, K. Mark Twain in India. Bombay: Noble Pub. House, 1978. 151p. + 9 pl.

11944 NEWCOMBE, A.C. Village, town, and jungle life in India. ND: Tulsi, 1979. 417p. + 30 pl.

11945 ORLICH, L. VON. Travels in India, including Sinde and the Punjab. Tr. from German by H. Evans Lloyd. Lahore: East & West Pub. Co., 1976. 2 v. [Rpt. 1845 ed.]

11946 PRICHARD, I. The chronicles of Budgepore or sketches of life in Upper India. Delhi: Manohar, 1972. 344p. [Rpt. 1872 ed.]

11947 RAVEN-HILL, L. An Indian sketch-book. London: "Punch" Office, 1903. 103p.

11948 THAPAR, RAJ, ed. The invincible traveller. ND: Vikas, 1980. 218p.

2. Sahibs and Memsahibs: British Life in India
a. general studies

11949 ALLEN, C. Raj, a scrapbook of British India, 1877-1947. NY: St. Martin's, 1978. 142p.

11950 ______., ed. Plain tales from the Raj: images of British India in the twentieth century. NY: St. Martin's Press, 1976. 240p.

11951 ATKINSON, G.F. "Curry and rice" on forty plates, or the ingredients of social life at "our station" in India. London: John B. Day, 1859. 90p. + 39 pl.

11952 BARR, P. The Memsahibs: the women of Victorian India. London: Secker & Warburg, 1976. 210p.

11953 BHATIA, H.S. European women in India: their life and adventures. ND: Deep & Deep, 1979. 224p.

11954 BROOK-SHEPHERD, G. Where the lion trod. London: Macmillan, 1960. 176p.

11955 BROWN, H., ed. The sahibs; the life and ways of the British in India as recorded by themselves. London: W. Hodge, 1948. 266p.

11956 HUNTER, W.W. The Thackerays in India and some Calcutta graves. London: H. Frowde, 1897. 191p.

11957 KINCAID, D. British social life in India, 1608-1937. London: Routledge & K. Paul, 1973. 344p. [Rpt. 1938 ed.]

11958 PEARSE, H.W. The Hearseys; five generations of an Anglo-Indian family. Edinburgh: Blackwood, 1905. 410p.

11959 STANFORD, J.K. Ladies in the sun: the Memsahibs' India, 1790-1860. London: Gallay Press, 1945. 145p.

11960 STOCQUELLER, J.H. The handbook of British India: a guide to the stranger, the traveller, the resident, and all who may have business with or opportunity to India. 3rd ed. London: W.H. Allen, 1854. 512p. [1st pub. 1844]

11961 ______. India; its history, climate, productions, and field sports, with notices of European life and manners.... London: G. Routledge, 1857. 219p.

11962 ______. The Oriental interpreter, and treasury of East India knowledge. London: C. Cox, 1848. 334p.

11963 WILKINSON, T. Two monsoons. London: Duckworth, 1976. 240p.

11964 WILLIAMSON, T. The East-India vade-mecum; or, Complete guide to gentlemen intended for the civil, military, or naval service of the hon. East India Company. London: Black, Parry & Kingsbury, 1910. 2 v.

11965 WORSWICK, C. & A. EMBREE. The Last Empire: photography in British India, 1855-1911. Millerton, NY: Aperture, 1976. 146p.

b. the Hill Station: retreat from the tropics, and islands of British social life

11966 BARR, P. & R. DESMOND. Simla: a hill station in British India. London: Scolar Press, 1978. 108p.

11967 CLARKE, W.H. English stations in the hill regions of India, their value and importance.... London: Truebner, 1881. 48p.

11968 KING, A.D. Culture, social power and environment: the hill station in colonial urban development. In Social Action 26,3 (1976) 195-213.

11969 MITCHELL, N. The Indian hill-station: Kodaikanal. Chicago: U. of Chicago, Dept. of Geography, 1972. 199p. (Its Res. paper, 14)

11970 Pachmarhi, queen of Satpuras: a visitors' guide. Gwalior: Dir. of Info. and Publicity, Madhya Pradesh, 1962. 110p.

11971 PANTER-DOWNES, M. Ooty preserved: a Victorian hill station. London: H. Hamilton, 1967. 134p.

11972 PRICE, J.F. Ootacamund. A history. Madras: The Supt., Govt. Press, 1908. 281p.

11973 SHROFF, B.K.F. A handbook of Mahableshwar and Panchgani. Bombay: Taraporevala, 1949. 85p. + 8 pl.

c. British artists of the Indian scene

11974 ARCHER, M. British drawings in the India Office Library. London: HMSO, 1969. 2 v., 712p. + 113 pl.

11975 ______. British painters of the Indian scene. Royal Soc. of Arts J. 115 (1967) 863-79.

11976 ______. Picturesque India with the Daniells. In Connoisseur 152 (1963) 171-75.

11977 DANIELL, T. & W. DANIELL. Oriental scenery. One hundred and fifty views of the architecture, antiquities, and landscape scenery of Hindoostan. London: the authors, 1812-16. 6 pt. in 3 v.

11978 HARDIE, M. Thomas Daniell, RA...Wm. Daniell, RA... London: Walker's Galleries, 1932. 106p.

11979 RAY, N.R. A descriptive catalogue of Daniells work in the Victoria Memorial. Calcutta: Victoria Memorial, 1976. 76p. + 9 pl.

11980 SHELLIM, M. India and the Daniells. London: Inchcape & Spink, 1979. 144p. + 151 pl.

11981 SUTTON, T. The Daniells, artists and travellers. London: Bodley Head, 1954. 200p.

7

The Present-Day South Asian Subcontinent in Its Global Context, 1947–

I. BIBLIOGRAPHY AND REFERENCE

11982 Asian recorder; a weekly digest of Asian events. 1955-.

11983 Asian social science bibliography, with annotations and abstracts, 1969. ND: Inst. of Economic Growth, 1952-. v. 1-18, to 1979. [Formerly UNESCO's Social science bibliog., India, etc.]

11984 Documentation on Asia. ND: Indian Council of World Affairs, 1960-. v. 1-5, to 1976. [Formerly Documents on Asian affairs, and select articles on current affairs.]

11985 South Asia and the strategic Indian Ocean. Washington: Dept. of the Army, 1973. 373p. (Pamphlet No. 550-15) [bibl. survey]

II. THE INDIAN OCEAN AREA: ITS GEOPOLITICAL AND ECONOMIC SIGNIFICANCE

11986 ADIE, W.A.C. Oil, politics, and seapower: the Indian Ocean vortex. NY: Crane, Russak, 1975. 98p.

11987 BEZBORUAH, M. U.S. strategy in the Indian Ocean: the international response. NY: Praeger, 1977. 268p.

11988 BURT, R. Strategic politics and the Indian Ocean. In PA 47,4 (1974-75) 509-14.

11989 COTTRELL, A.J. & R.M. BURRELL. Soviet-U.S. naval competition in the Indian Ocean. In Orbis 18 (1975) 1109-28.

11990 ______., eds. The Indian Ocean: its political, economic and military importance. NY: Praeger, 1973. 457p.

11991 Defence and security in the Indian Ocean area, by a study group of the Indian Council of World Affairs. ND: 1957. 178p. (Institute of Pacific Relations. 13th Conf., Lahore, 1958. Indian paper, 4)

11992 GUPTA, R. The Indian Ocean; a political geography. ND: Marwah, 1979. 184p.

11993 HÖPKER, W. Wetterzone der Weltpolitik: der Indische Ozean im Kraftespiel der Mächte. Stuttgart-Degerloch: Seewald, 1975. 187p.

11994 India and the geopolitics of the Indian Ocean: seminar organised by the Institute of Asian Studies and the Osmania Graduates Association, Hyderabad, March 1972. Hyderabad: Inst. of Asian Studies, 1974. 53p.

11995 JUKES, G. The Indian Ocean in Soviet naval policy. London: Intl. Inst. for Strategic Studies, 1972. 30p. (Adelphi papers, 86)

11996 KAUSHIK, D. The Indian Ocean: towards a peace zone. Delhi: Vikas, 1972. 225p.

11997 KHAN, RAHMATULLAH. Indian Ocean fisheries: the 200-mile economic zone. ND: Ankur Pub. House, 1977. 264p.

11998 KOHLI, S.N. Sea power and the Indian Ocean: with special reference to India. ND: Tata McGraw-Hill, 1978. 168p.

11999 MILLAR, T.B. Soviet policies in the Indian Ocean area. Canberra: ANUP, 1970. 22p.

12000 MISRA, K.P. Quest for an international order in the Indian Ocean. Bombay: Allied, 1977. 159p.

12001 PATRA, S., ed. Indian Ocean and great power. ND: Sterling, 1979. 82p.

12002 Indian Ocean power rivalry. ND: Young Asia Pub., 1974. 317p. [seminar papers]

12003 RAJENDRA SINGH, K. The Indian Ocean: big power presence and local response. ND: Manohar, 1977. 336p.

12004 ______. Politics of the Indian Ocean. ND: Thomson Press, 1974. 252p.

12005 SETH, S.P. The Indian Ocean and Indo-American relations. In AS 15,8 (1975) 645-55.

12006 STUDY CONFERENCE ON THE INDIAN OCEAN IN INTERNATIONAL POLITICS. Collected papers. Southampton: U. of Southampton, Dept. of Extra-Mural Studies, 1973. 236p.

12007 THOMSON, G.G. Problems in the Indian Ocean. In Pacific Community 3,1 (1971) 126-41.

12008 U.S. CONGRESS HOUSE CMTEE. ON FOREIGN AFFAIRS. SUBCMTEE. ON NATL. SECURITY POLICY AND SCIENTIFIC DEVELOPMENTS. The Indian Ocean: political and strategic future. Hearings, 92nd Congress, first session. Washington: U.S. Govt. Printing Office, 1971. 242p.

12009 VALI, F.A. Politics of the Indian Ocean region: the balances of power. NY: Free Press, 1976. 272p.

12010 VARMA, RAVINDRA. Strategic importance of the Indian Ocean. In IJPS 28 (1967) 51-61.

12011 VIBHAKAR, J. Afro-Asian security and Indian Ocean. ND: Sterling, 1974. 100p.

III. THE SOUTH ASIAN NATIONS IN WORLD POLITICS

A. General

12012 AIYAR, S.P. The Commonwealth in South Asia. Bombay: Lalvani, 1969. 409p.

12013 APPADORAI, A. Foreign policies of South Asian states: more issues for consideration. In SAS 3,2 (1968) 15-26.

12014 AYOOB, M. India as a factor in Sino-Pakistani relations. In IS 9 (1968) 279-300.

12015 BARNDS, W.J. India, Pakistan and the Great Powers. NY: Praeger, 1972. 388p.

12016 BHANEJA, B. The politics of triangles: the alignment patterns in South Asia, 1961-71. Delhi: Research, 1973. 192p.

12017 BURKE, S.M. Mainsprings of Indian and Pakistani foreign policies. Minneapolis: U. of Minnesota Press, 1974. 308p.

12018 CHOUDHARY, L.K. Pakistan as a factor in Indo-Iranian relations. In IJPS 35,4 (1974) 352-62.

12019 CHOUDHURY, G.W. India, Pakistan, Bangladesh, and the major powers: politics of a divided subcontinent. NY: Free Press, 1975. 276p.

12020 COHEN, S.P. Security issues in South Asia. In AS 15,3 (1975) 202-14.

12021 GANGAL, S.C. The Commonwealth and Indo-Pakistani relations. In IS 8,2 (1966) 134-49.

12022 HYDER, K. Strategic balance in South and Southeast Asia. In Pakistan Horizon 24,4 (1971) 11-29.

12023 KENNEDY, D.E. The security of southern Asia. NY: Praeger, 1965. 308p.

12024 KHAN, Z.R. Japanese relations with India, Pakistan and Bangladesh. In PA 48,4 (1975-6) 541-57.

12025 MALAVIYA, H.D., ed. Asian security for world peace: documents of Delhi and Baghdad conferences on peace and security in Asia. Bombay: Allied, 1975. 186p.

12026 PALMER, N.D. The defense of South Asia. In Orbis (Philadelphia) 9 (1966) 899-929.

12027 ______. Recent Soviet and Chinese penetration in India and Pakistan: guidelines for political-military policy. McLean, VA: Res. Analysis Corp., Strategic Studies Dept., 1970. (Report, RAC-R-85)

12028 PRASAD, BIMAL. The superpowers and the subcontinent. In IS 13,4 (1974) 719-49.

12029 SEN GUPTA, B. The fulcrum of Asia: relations among China, India, Pakistan and the USSR. NY: Pegasus, 1970. 383p.

12030 ZIRING, L., ed. The subcontinent in world politics: India, its neighbors and the great powers. NY: Praeger, 1978. 238p.

B. China and the Subcontinent

12031 HASAN, K.S., comp. China, India, and Pakistan. Karachi: Pakistan Inst. of Intl. Affairs, 1966. 441p. (Documents on the Foreign Relations of Pakistan)

12032 HUSSAIN, T.K. Sino-Indian conflict and international politics in the Indian sub-continent, 1962-66. Faridabad: Thomson Press, 1977. 190p.

12033 JAIN, J.P. & R.K. JAIN, comp. China, Pakistan, and Bangladesh. ND: Radiant, 1974-76. 2 v.

12034 KAUSHIK, D. Soviet relations with India and Pakistan. Delhi: Vikas, 1971. 119p.

12035 ROY, A.K. Domestic compulsions and foreign policy: Pakistan in Indo-Soviet relations, 1947-1958. Delhi: Manas, 1975. 254p.

12036 SHARMA, B.L. The Pakistan-China axis. Bombay: Asia, 1968. 226p.

12037 SHARMA, P.K. India, Pakistan, China, and the contemporary world. Delhi: National, 1972. 213p.

12038 SHERWANI, L.A. India, China and Pakistan. Karachi: Council for Pakistan Studies, 1967. 140p.

12039 SIDKY, M.H. Chinese world strategy and South Asia: the China factor in Indo-Pakistani relations. In AS 16,10 (1976) 965-80.

12040 STAHNKE, A.A. Diplomatic triangle: China's policies toward India and Pakistan in the 1960's. In J.A. Cohen, ed. The dynamics of China's foreign relations. Cambridge: HUP, 1970, 21-40.

12041 TRIVEDI, R.N. Sino-Indian border dispute and its impact on Indo-Pakistan relations. ND: Associated Pub. House, 1977. 329p.

12042 WILCOX, W.A. India, Pakistan and the rise of China. NY: Walker, 1964. 144p.

C. USSR and the Subcontinent

12043 JAIN, J.P. Soviet policy towards Pakistan and Bangladesh. ND: Radiant, 1974. 258p.

12044 JAIN, R.K., comp. Soviet South Asian relations, 1947-1978. ND: Radiant, 1978. 2 v. [documents]

12045 BRAUN, D. Die Sowjetunion und Südasien. In Indo-Asia 17,1 (1975) 29-40.

12046 BUDHRAJ, V.S. Soviet Russia and the Hindustan subcontinent. Bombay: Somaiya, 1973. 296p.

12047 KAUSHIK, D. Soviet relations with India and Pakistan. Delhi: Vikas, 1971. 119p.

12048 RIZVI, H.A. The Soviet Union and the Indo-Pakistan sub-continent. Lahore: Progressive, 1974. 32p.

12049 SEN GUPTA, B. Soviet-Asian relations in the 1970's and beyond: an interperceptional study. NY: Praeger, 1976. 368p.

12050 SETH, S.P. Russia's role in Indo-Pakistani politics. In AS 9 (1969) 614-24.

D. USA and the Subcontinent

12051 COHEN, S.P. U.S. weapons and South Asia: a policy analysis. In PA 49,1 (1976) 49-69.

12052 GANGULY, S. The United States and South Asia: a study of policy and process. Ph.D. Diss., U. of Illinois, 1977. 362p. [UM 78-03998]

12053 GUPTA, R.C. U.S. policy towards India and Pakistan. ND: B.R., 1977. 184p.

12054 KAUL, K.K. U.S.A. and the Hindustan Peninsula, 1952-1966. Lucknow: Pustak Kendra, 1977. 170p.

12055 MUTTAM, J. U.S., Pakistan, and India; a study of U.S. role in the India-Pakistan arms race. ND: Sindhu, 1974. 112p.

12056 NAYAR, B.R. American geopolitics and India. ND: Manohar, 1976. 246p.

12057 PALMER, N.D. South Asia and United States policy. Boston: Houghton Mifflin, 1966. 332p.

12058 SINHA, J. Pakistan and the Indo-US relations, 1947-1958. Patna: Associated Book Agency, 1978. 206p.

IV. RELATIONS AMONG THE SOUTH ASIAN NATIONS

A. General Studies

12059 AYOOB, MUHAMMED. India, Pakistan, and Bangladesh: search for a new relationship. ND: Indian Council of World Affairs, 1975. 185p.

12060 AZIZ, M.A. Can there be durable peace in the subcontinent? Dacca: Dahuk Pub., 1978. 31p.

12061 HECKER, H. Das Staatsangehörigkeitsrecht von Indien, Pakistan, Nepal. Frankfurt am Main: A. Metzner, 1965. 187p.

12062 MISHRA, P.K. India, Pakistan, Nepal, and Bangladesh: India as a factor in the intra-regional interaction in South Asia. Delhi: Sundeep, 1979. 286p.

12063 NAYAR, K. Distant neighbors; a tale of the subcontinent. ND: Vikas, 1972. 253p.

12064 PHADNIS, U. & S.D. MUNI. Emergence of Bangladesh: responses of Ceylon and Nepal. In SAS 7,2 (1972) 173-92.

12065 VARMA, S.P. & K.P. MISRA, eds. Foreign policies in South Asia. Bombay: Orient Longmans, 1969. 403p.

B. India-Pakistan Relations

1. General Studies

12066 BEG, A. Pakistan faces India. Lahore: Babur and Amer Pub., 1966. 282p.

12067 BLINKENBERG, L. India-Pakistan: the history of unsolved conflicts. Copenhagen: Munksgaard, 1972. 440p.

12068 CHOUDHURY, G.W. Pakistan's relations with India. Meerut: Meenakshi, 1971. 264p. [1st pub. 1968]

12068a DAS GUPTA, J.B. Indo-Pakistan relations, 1947-1955. Amsterdam: Djambatan, 1958. 254p.

12069 FREY, H. Der indisch-pakistanische Konflikt und seine wirtschaftlichen und sozialen Kosten für Pakistan in den Jahren 1958-1968. Wiesbaden: Steiner, 1978. 234p. (BSAF, 38)

12070 GHAZNAWI, K. Story of Indian aggressions against Pakistan. Lahore: Natl. Book House, 1966. 328p.

12071 JAI SINGH. Tanot Longanwala and other battles of the Rajasthan desert, 1965 and 1971. Ed. by D.K. Palit. Dehra Dun: Palit & Palit Pub., 1973. 193p.

12072 JHA, D.C. Indo-Pakistan relations (1960-1965). Patna: Bharati Bhawan, 1972. 418p.

12073 KAK, B.L. The fall of Gilgit: the untold story of Indo-Pak affairs from Jinnah to Bhutto, 1947 to July 1977. ND: Light & Life, 1977. 122p.

12074 RAJAN, M.S. India and Pakistan as factors in each other's foreign policy and relations. In IS 3 (1962) 349-94.

12075 RAY, J.K. India and Pakistan as factors in each other's foreign policies. In IS 8,1/2 (1966) 49-63.

12076 SAXENA, K.C. Pakistan, her relation with India 1947-1966. ND: Vir Pub. House, 1966. 267p.

2. The Kashmir Conflict over Accession to India (October 1947)

a. documents of India, Pakistan, and the United Nations

12077 CHAGLA, M.C. Kashmir, 1947-1965. Delhi: PDMIB, 1965. 124p. [Speeches delivered ... in the U.N. Security Council in 1964 and 1965.]

12078 HASAN, K.S., comp. The Kashmir question. Karachi: Pakistan Inst. of Intl. Affairs, 1966. 484p.

12079 INDIA (DOMINION). White paper on Jammu and Kashmir. ND: 1948. 89p.

12080 LAKHANPAL, P.L. Essential documents and notes on Kashmir dispute. 2nd rev. ed. Delhi: International Books, 1965. 326p. [1st pub. 1958]

12081 MOHAMMAD ABDULLAH, Sheikh. Kashmir, India and Pakistan. In Foreign Affairs 43 (1965) 528-35.

12082 PAKISTAN. MIN. OF FOREIGN AFFAIRS. White paper on Jammu and Kashmir dispute. Islamabad: 1977. 137p.

12083 UNITED NATIONS. SECURITY COUNCIL. REPRESENTATIVE FOR INDIA AND PAKISTAN. Reports on Kashmir by United Nations representatives. Karachi: Govt. of Pakistan, 1958. 289p.

b. studies of the Kashmir conflict

12084 AGARWAL, H.O. Kashmir problem: its legal aspects. Allahabad: Kitab Mahal, 1979. 194p.

12085 AUSTIN, G. History past and history present: report on Kashmir. NY: Inst. of Current World Affairs, 1965. 59p.

12086 BAZAZ, P.N. The history of struggle for freedom in Kashmir. ND: Kashmir Pub. Co., 1954. 744p.

12087 BIRDWOOD, C.B. Two nations and Kashmir. London: R. Hale, 1956. 237p.

12088 BRECHER, M. The struggle for Kashmir. NY: OUP, 1953. 211p.

12089 CHOPRA, S. UN mediation in Kashmir; a study in power politics. Kurukshetra: Vishal Pub., 1971. 290p.

12090 DAS GUPTA, J.B. Jammu and Kashmir. The Hague: Nijhoff, 1968. 430p.

12091 GEIGER, R. Die Kaschmirfrage im Lichte des Völkerrechts. Berlin: Duncker & Humblot, 1970. 288p.

12092 GUPTA, S. Kashmir: a study in India-Pakistan relations. Bombay: Asia, 1967. 511p. (Indian Council of World Affairs Pub.)

12093 KORBEL, J. Danger in Kashmir. Rev. ed. Princeton: PUP, 1966. 401p.

12094 LAMB, A. The Kashmir problem; a historical survey. NY: Praeger, 1967. 163p. [1st pub. 1963 as Crisis in Kashmir....]

12095 MAHAJAN, S. Debacle in Baltistan. ND: A.K. Corp., 1973. 148p.

12096 MISRA, K.K. Kashmir and India's foreign policy. Allahabad: Chugh, 1979. 605p.

12097 MULLIK, B.N. My years with Nehru: Kashmir. Bombay: Allied, 1971. 320p.

12098 NOORANI, A.G. The Kashmir question. Bombay: Manaktalas, 1964. 125p.

12099 SAXENA, H.L. The tragedy of Kashmir. ND: Nationalist Pub., 1975. 580p.

3. The 1965 Indo-Pakistan War, U.N. Ceasefire Resolution, and the Tashkent Accord (January 1966)

12100 BANERJI, A.K. The triumph and tragedy in Tashkent. Calcutta: Benson's, 1966. 58p.

12101 BHASKARA RAO, N. Indo-Pak conflict: controlled mass communication in inter-state relations. ND: S. Chand, 1971. 200p.

12102 BRINES, R. The Indo-Pakistani conflict. London: Pall Mall, 1968. 486p.

12103 INDIAN SOC. OF INTL. LAW. The Kutch-Sind border question; a collection of documents with comments. ND: 1965. 213p.

12104 KAUL, B.M. Confrontation with Pakistan. Delhi: Vikas, 1971. 338p.

12105 RAJAN, M.S. The Tashkent Declaration: retrospect and prospect. In IS 8,1/2 (1966) 1-28.

12106 SAEED AHMAD. The Indo-Pak clash in the Rann of Kutch. Rawalpindi: Army Educ. Press, 1973. 149p.

12107 SAVARA, S.K., ed. The fight for peace; the long road to Tashkent. ND: Hardy & Ally, 1966. 573p.

12108 SHARMA, D. Tashkent, the fight for peace; a study in foreign relations with documents. Varanasi: Gandhian Inst. of Studies, 1966. 247p.

12109 SHARMA, S.P. The Indo-Pakistan maritime conflict, 1965; a legal appraisal. Bombay: Academic Books, 1970. 130p.

12110 SYED, ANWAR. China and the Indo-Pakistan war of 1965. In Orbis 10 (1966) 859-80.

12111 TIRIMAGNI-HURTIG, C. La fin de la guerre indo-pakistanaise de 1965: épuisement ou impasse? In Revue Française de Science Politique 24,2 (1974) 309-27.

12112 The War and after; a symposium on the implications and involvements of the present conflict. In Seminar 75 (1965) 10-50. [Articles by S. Ghosh, R. Khan, P.N. Dhar, M. Kumaramangalam, F. Moraes, T.N. Srinivasan and V.K. Krishna Menon]

4. The Breakup of Pakistan, the Birth of Bangladesh, and the Indo-Pak War of 1971

a. reference works and document collections

12113 Bangla Desh documents. ND: Ministry of External Affairs, 1971. 719p.

12114 GANDHI, INDIRA. India and Bangla Desh; selected speeches and statements, March to December, 1971. Delhi: Orient Longman, 1972. 195p.

12115 ______. Indira speaks on genocide war and Bangladesh. Ed. by D. Mullick. Calcutta: Academic Pub., 1972. 96p.

12116 KAYASTHA, V.P., ed. The crisis on the Indian subcontinent and the birth of Bangladesh: a selected reading list. Rev. & enl. ed. Ithaca, NY: South Asia Program, Cornell University, 1972. 142p. (South Asia occ. papers and theses, 1)

12116a PAKISTAN. MIN. OF INFO. AND NATL. AFFAIRS. White paper on the crisis in East Pakistan. Islamabad: 1971. 125p.

12117 SWARAN SINGH. Bangla Desh and Indo-Pak war: India speaks at the U.N.; speeches by India's External Affairs Minister Shri Swaran Singh and India's permanent representative Shri S. Sen at the United Nations. ND: PDMIB, 1972. 129p.

12118 SWARAN SINGH & S. SEN. Bangla Desh and Indo-Pak war: India speaks at the U.N. ND: PDMIB, 1972. 129p.

12119 TEWARY, I.N., ed. War of independence in Bangla Desh: a documentary study. Varanasi: Navachetna Prakashan, 1971. 180p.

b. general studies of the Bangladesh liberation movement and its international context

12120 ALI, MEHRUNNISA. East Pakistan crisis: international reactions. In Pakistan Horizon 24,2 (1971) 31-58.

12121 AYOOB, M., et al. Bangla Desh; a struggle for nationhood. Delhi: Vikas, 1971. 194p.

12122 BUDHRAJ, V.S. Moscow and the birth of Bangladesh. In AS 13,5 (1973) 482-95.

12123 CHATTERJEE, S. Bangladesh: the birth of a nation. Calcutta: The Book Exchange, 1972. 191p.

12124 CHAUDHURY, KABIR, et al., eds. A nation is born. Calcutta: Calcutta U. Bangladesh Sahayak Samiti, 1974. 386p.

12125 DIL, S. The extent and nature of Soviet involvement in the Bangladesh crisis. In Asia Q. 3 (1973) 243-59.

12126 KASHYAP, S.C., ed. Bangla Desh: background and perspectives. Delhi: National, 1971. 187p.

12127 KHANDAKER, A.M. Fall of General Niazi and birth of Bangladesh. Dacca: Rangpur Pub., 1977. 86p. + 8 pl.

12128 LINDE, G. Bangla Desh; Indien und die Grossmächte im Pakistanischen Konflikt. Stuttgart: W. Kohlhammer, 1972. 153p.

12129 MCKINLEY, J. Death to life, Bangladesh: the experience of an American missionary family. Dacca: Immanuel Baptist Church, 1979. 136p.

12130 MASSA, F. Bengale, histoire d'un conflit. Paris: A. Moreau, 1972. 295p.

12131 MISRA, K.P. The role of the U.N. in the Indo-Pakistani conflict, 1971. Delhi: Vikas, 1973. 197p.

12132 NAIK, J.A. India, Russia, China and Bangla Desh. ND: S. Chand, 1972. 163p.

12133 NICHOLAS, M.R. & P. OLDENBURG, comp. Bangladesh: the birth of a nation; a handbook of background information and documentary sources. Madras: M. Seshachalam, 1972. 156p.

12134 ROY CHOWDHURY, S. The genesis of Bangladesh: a study in international legal norms and permissive conscience. London: Asia, 1972. 357p.

12135 SHARMA, S.R. Bangladesh crisis and Indian foreign policy. ND: Young Asia, 1978. 485p.

12136 WILLIAMS, L.F.R. The East Pakistan tragedy. NY: Drake, 1972. 142p.

12137 ZAMAN, H., comp. East Pakistan crisis and India. Dacca: Pakistan Academy, 1971. 504p.

c. Pakistan Army repression and genocide in East Bengal, and the exodus of 6,000,000 refugees to India

12138 ABUL HASANAT. Bangladesh, sufferings, surfacing, survival: let humanity not forget the ugliest genocide: being a resume of inhuman atrocities in East Pakistan, now Bangladesh, and a plea for welfare states all over. Dacca: Muktadhara, 1978. 66p.

12139 ______. Let humanity not forget - the ugliest genocide in history: being a resume of inhuman atrocities in East Pakistan, now Bangladesh. Dacca: Muktadhara, 1974. 381p.

12140 BHATTACHARJEA, A., comp. Dateline Bangla Desh. Bombay: Jaico, 1971. 252p.

12141 CHOPRA, PRAN, ed. The challenge of Bangla Desh; a special debate. Bombay: Popular, 1971. 159p.

12142 Crisis in East Pakistan. Hearings, 92nd Congress, 1st Session. May 11-25, 1971. Washington: Govt. Printing Office, 1971. 50p. [House Subcmtee. on Asian and Pacific Affairs]

12143 FRANDA, M.F. Population politics in South Asia. In American U. Field Staff Reports Service, South Asia series 16,2 (1972) 1-13; 16,3 (1972) 1-14.

12144 GLASS, R. Bengal notes. In Monthly R. 23,5 (1971) 17-42.

12145 GUPTA, R. & K.S. RADHAKRISHNA. World meet on Bangla Desh; report of the International Conference on Bangla Desh, held in New Delhi from Sept. 18 to 20, 1971. Delhi: Impex, 1972. 304p.

12146 JAG MOHAN, comp. The black book of genocide in Bangla Desh; a documentary book. ND: Geeta Book Centre, 1971. 124p.

12147 KABIR, MAFIZULLAH. Experiences of an exile at home; life in occupied Bangladesh. Dacca: Rezina Nazli Kabir, 1972. 216p.

12148 KENNEDY, E.M. Crisis in South Asia: a report to the subcommittee to investigate problems connected with refugees and escapees.... Washington: U.S. Govt. Printing Office, 1971. 73p.

12149 MAITRAYE DEVI. Exodus. Calcutta: S. Das, 1974. 75p.

12150 MASCARENHAS, A. The rape of Bangladesh. Delhi: Vikas, 1971. 168p.

12151 MEHRISH, B.N. War crimes and genocide; the trial of Pakistani war criminals. Delhi: Oriental Pub., 1972. 349p.

12152 MISRA, K.P. The role of the United Nations in the Indo-Pakistani conflict, 1971. ND: Vikas, 1973. 197p.

12153 MORAES, D.F. The tempest within; an account of East Pakistan. Delhi: Vikas, 1971. 103p.

12154 NAIR, B.N. The Indian presence in the Indian Ocean: some considerations. In J. of African and Asian Studies 3,1 (1969) 27-48.

12155 QUADERI, F.Q., comp. Bangladesh genocide and world press. 2nd rev. ed. Dacca: Begum Dilafroz Quaderi, 1972. 455p.

12156 Relief problems in Bangladesh. Hearing, 92nd Congress, 2nd session, Feb. 2, 1972. Washington: U.S. Govt. Printing Office, 1972. 188p. [Senate Subcmtee. to Investigate Problems Connected with Refugees & Escapees]

12157 WAHAB, ABDUL. One man's agony; a sketch book of the Yahyan oppression. Dacca: Purbolekh Prokashanee, 1972. 117p.

d. Indian intervention and the 1971 war

12158 AHMAD, K.U. Breakup to Pakistan: background and prospects of Bangladesh. London: Social Science Pub., 1972. 153p.

12159 ANDERSON, JACK. The Anderson papers. NY: Random House, 1973. 275p. [5th section on Bangladesh]

12160 ARORA, J.S.B. War with Pakistan, 1971. Delhi: Army Pub., 1972. 208p.

12161 AYOOB, M. & K. SUBRAHMANYAM. The liberation war. ND: S. Chand, 1972. 292p.

12162 BHARGAVA, G.S. "Crush India" -- Gen. Yahya Khan; or, Pakistan's death wish. Delhi: Indian School Supply Depot, 1972. 207p.

12163 ______. Their finest hour: saga of India's December victory. Delhi: Vikas, 1972. 169p.

12164 BOIS, P. Les révoltés du Bengale; un an de feu et de sang au Pakistan. Paris: Hachette, 1972. 140p.

12165 CHOPRA, PRAN. India's second liberation. ND: Vikas, 1973. 270p.

12166 CHOUDHARY, S. Indo-Pak war and big powers. ND: Trimurti, 1972. 195p.

12167 DINESH, D. Indira wins the war. Delhi: Oriental, 1972. 214p.

12168 GUPTA, VINOD. Anderson papers; a study of Nixon's blackmail of India. ND: Indian School Supply Depot, 1972. 236p.

12169 HESS, P. Bangla Desh - Tragödie einer Staatsgründung. Stuttgart: Huber, 1972. 227p.

12170 ______. Hintergründe des pakistanischen Bürgerkrieges. In IAF 2,5 (1971) 546-59.

12171 The India-Paksitan War [special issue] . In Pakistan Horizon 25,1 (1972) 1-186.

12172 JACKSON, R.V. South Asian crisis: India, Pakistan, and Bangla Desh; a political and historical analysis of the 1971 war. NY: Praeger, 1975. 240p.

12173 KRISHNAN, N. No way but surrender: an account of the Indo-Pakistan War in the Bay of Bengal, 1971. ND: Vikas, 1980. 75p.

12174 LACHMAN SINGH. Indian sword strikes East Pakistan. ND: Vikas, 1979. 218p.

12175 MANKEKAR, D.R. Pakistan cut to size, the authentic

story of the 14-day Indo-Pak war. ND: Indian Book Co., 1972. 175p.

12176 MARWAH, O. India's military intervention in East Pakistan, 1971-72. In MAS 13,4 (1979) 549-80.

12177 MOSSÉ, C. Mourir pour Dacca. Paris: R. Laffort, 1972. 219p.

12178 MUKHERJEE, S.K. Bangla Desh and international law. Calcutta: West Bengal Political Science Assn., 1971. 55p.

12179 NAWAZ, M.K. Bangla Desh and international law. In Indian J. of Intl. Law 11,2 (1971) 251-66.

12180 PALIT, D.K. The lightning campaign; the Indo-Pakistan war, 1971. ND: Thomson Press, 1972. 166p.

12181 SAADULLAH KHAN. East Pakistan to Bangla Desh. Lahore: Lahore Law Times Pub., 1975. 204p.

12182 SAXENA, J.N. Self determination: from Biafra to Bangla Desh. Delhi: U. of Delhi, 1978. 151p.

12183 SHARMA, S.R. Bangladesh crisis and Indian foreign policy. ND: Young Asia, 1978. 485p.

e. the Simla Agreement, 1972, and its aftermath

12184 BHARGAVA, G.S. Success or surrender? The Simla summit. ND: Sterling, 1972. 160p.

12185 BHUTTO, Z.A. The great tragedy. Karachi: Pakistan People's Party, 1971. 107p.

12186 ______. The Simla accord. In Pakistan Horizon 25,3 (1972) 3-16.

12187 BURKE, S.M. India's offer of a no-war declaration to Pakistan: its history & import. In Pakistan Horizon 25,3 (1972) 23-37.

12188 ______. The postwar diplomacy of the Indo-Pakistani war of 1971. In AS 13,11 (1973) 1036-49.

12189 MUSTAFA, Z. The Kashmir dispute and the Simla agreement. In Pakistan Horizon 25,3 (1972) 38-52.

12190 SALUNKE, S.P. Pakistani POW's in India. ND: Vikas, 1977. 145p.

5. India-Pakistan-Bangladesh Relations after 1972; Normalization?

12191 AYOOB, M. India and Pakistan: prospects for detente. In Pacific Community 8 (1976) 149-69.

12192 HEGINBOTHAM, S.J. In the wake of Bangla Desh: a new role for India in Asia? In PA 45,3 (1972) 372-86.

12193 KHAN, A.R. India, Pakistan, and Bangladesh: conflict or co-operation? Dacca: Sindabad, 1976. 143p.

12194 MUGHAL, N.A. Inching together or a mile apart: India and Pakistan towards detente. In Pakistan Horizon 29,3 (1976) 20-32.

12195 PAKISTAN. Pakistan-Bangladesh relations: issues and non-issues. Islamabad: Print. Corp. of Pakistan Press, 1975. 68p.

12196 RAJAN, M.S. Bangladesh and after. In PA 45,2 (1972) 191-205.

12197 TIRIMAGNI-HURTIG, C. The Indo-Pakistan war and the ending of a power balance in South Asia. In IJPS 35,3 (1974) 201-19.

12198 VERGHESE, B.G. An end to confrontation (Bhutto's Pakistan). ND: S. Chand, 1972. 172p.

C. Sri Lankan Relations with Other South Asian States

12199 COELHO, V.H. Across the Palk Straits: India-Sri Lanka relations. Dehra Dun: Palit & Palit, 1976. 188p.

12200 KODIKARA, S.U. Indo-Ceylon relations since independence. Colombo: Ceylon Inst. of World Affairs, 1965. 262p.

12201 LALIT KUMAR. India and Sri Lanka: Sirimavo-Shastri pact. ND: Chetana Pub., 1977. 132p.

12202 PHADNIS, U. Indo-Ceylonese relations. In JUSI 93 (1963) 158-72.

V. POLITICS AND GOVERNMENT - SUBCONTINENTAL AND COMPARATIVE STUDIES

12203 AZIZ AHMAD. Islam and democracy in the Indo-Pakistan subcontinent. In Religion & change in contemporary Asia. Minneapolis: U. of Minnesota Press, 1971, 123-42.

12204 ______. Problems of Islamic modernism with special reference to Indo-Pakistan sub-continent. In Archives de sociologie des religions 12,23 (1966) 107-16.

12205 BRAIBANTI, R.J.D. Asian bureaucratic systems emergent form the British Imperial tradition. Durham: DUP, 1966. 733p.

12206 BRASS, P.R. & M.F. FRANDA. Radical politics in South Asia. Cambridge: MIT Press, 1973. 439p.

12207 BROEKMEIJER, M.W.J.M. The future of communism in South Asia. In Asia Q 1 (1974) 43-64.

12208 CHOPRA, PRAN. Political re-alignment in India. In PA 44,4 (1971-72) 511-26.

12209 GOUGH, K. & H.P. SHARMA. Imperialism and revolution in South Asia. NY: Monthly R. Press, 1973. 470p.

12210 KEARNEY, R.N. Politics and modernization in South and Southeast Asia. Cambridge: Schenkman, 1975. 277p.

12211 MINATTUR, J. Martial law in India, Pakistan and Ceylon. The Hague: Nijhoff, 1962. 99p.

12212 OMVEDT, G. Marxism and the analysis of South Asia. In J. of Contemporary Asia 4,4 (1974) 481-501.

12213 PALMER, N.D. Elections and political development: the South Asian experience. ND: Vikas, 1976. 340p.

12214 PANDEY, B.N., ed. Leadership in South Asia. ND: Vikas, 1977. 731p.

12215 RAI, H.A.K. Political development in India & Pakistan, from 1947 to 1958: a study in comparative politics. Lahore: Nzarsons, 1978. 54p.

12216 ROSE, S. Socialism in southern Asia. London: OUP, 1959. 278p.

12217 ______, ed. Politics in Southern Asia; papers. London: Macmillan, 1963. 386p.

12218 SMITH, B.L., ed. Special number on religion and social conflict in South Asia. In JAAS(L) 11,1/2 (1976) 112p.

12219 SMITH, D.E. Religion and political development, an analytical study. Boston: Little, Brown, 1970. 298p.

12220 ______, ed. South Asian politics and religion. Princeton: PUP, 1966. 563p.

12221 TAMBIAH, S.J. Politics of language in India and Ceylon. In MAS 1,3 (1967) 215-40.

12222 TAYLOR, D. & M. YAPP, eds. Political identity in South Asia. London: Curzon Press, 1979. 266p.

12223 TINKER, H. The foundations of local self-government in India, Pakistan and Burma. NY: Praeger, 1968. 376p. [1st pub. 1954]

12224 ______. India and Pakistan; a political analysis. Rev. ed. NY: Praeger, 1968. 248p. [1st ed. 1962]

12225 ______. India and Pakistan; a short political guide. London: Pall Mall Press, 1962. 228p.

12226 Turmoil and political change in south Asia: Bangladesh, Sri Lanka, India, and Pakistan. Jaipur: Aalekh, 1978. 203p.

12227 WEINER, M. Political change in South Asia. Calcutta: KLM, 1963. 285p.

12228 WILCOX, W.A. India and Pakistan. NY: Foreign Policy Assn., 1967. 79p.

12229 ______. Political modernization in South Asia. Santa Monica, CA: RAND Corp., 1968. 42p. (P-3845)

12230 WRIGGINS, W.H. & J.F. GUYOT, eds. Population, politics, and the future of southern Asia. NY: ColUP, 1973. 402p.

VI. ECONOMIC INSTITUTIONS AND DEVELOPMENT - SUBCONTINENTAL AND COMPARATIVE STUDIES

A. General Studies

12231 ALAMGIR, M. Famine in South Asia: the political economy of mass starvation. Cambridge, MA: Oelgeschlager, Gunn, & Hain, 1980.

12232 FAROOQ, G.M. Dimensions and structure of labour force in relation to economic development: a comparative study of Pakistan and Bangladesh. Islamabad: PIDE, 1975. 185p.

12233 HOGAN, W.P. Exports of manufacturers: the South Asian experience in the 1960's. In SA 3 (1973) 45-56.

12234 LAMBERT, R.D. & B.F. HOSELITZ, eds. The role of savings and wealth in southern Asia and the West. Paris: UNESCO, 1963. 432p.

12235 NILSSON, S. The new capitals of India, Pakistan and Bangladesh. Lund: Studentlitteratur, 1973. 230p.

12236 SCHAMS, M.R. Die Bedeutung der Kompensatorischen Finanzierung für die Entwicklungslander: eine Untersuchung am Beispiel von Indien, Ceylon und Ghana. Hamburg: Verlag Weltarchiv, 1974. 265p.

12237 VAKIL, C.N. & G. RAGHAVA RAO. Economic relations between India and Pakistan; need for international cooperation. Bombay: Vora, 1968. 214p.

B. Economic Resources

1. General Studies

12238 BROWN, J.C. & A.K. DEY. The mineral and nuclear fuels of the Indian subcontinent and Burma: a guide to the study of the coal, oil, natural gas, uranium and thorium resources of the area. Delhi: OUP, 1975. 517p.

2. Water Resources; Dispute over Use of Indus and Ganga Rivers

12239 AHMAD, K.S. Some geographical aspects of the Indus waters treaty and development of irrigation in West Pakistan. In Pakistan Geographical R. 20 (1965) 1-30.

12240 BANGLADESH. White paper on the Ganges water dispute. Dacca: 1976. 26p. + 6pl.

12241 BERBER, F.J. The Indus water dispute. In IYIA 6 (1957) 46-62.

12242 GULHATI, N.D. Indus Waters Treaty; an exercise in international mediation. Bombay: Allied, 1973. 472p.

12243 HASAN, M. The Farakka Barrage dispute: Pakistan's case. In Pakistan Horizon 21 (1968) 356-60.

12244 KHAN, Z.A., ed. Basic documents on Farakka conspiracy from 1951 to 1976. Dacca: Khoshroz Kitab Mahal, 1976. 197p.

12245 KÜLZ, H.R. Further water disputes between India and Pakistan. In Intl. & Comparative Law Q. 18 (1969) 718-38.

12246 MICHEL, A.A. The Indus Rivers; a study of the effects of partition. New Haven: YUP, 1967. 595p.

C. Economic Development and International Economic Cooperation

12247 AGGARWAL, M.R. Regional economic co-operation in South Asia. ND: S. Chand, 1979. 155p.

12248 BHUYAN, A.R. Economic integration in South Asia: an exploratory study. Dacca: U. of Dacca, 1979. 224p.

12249 CHANANA, C., ed. South Asia, the changing environment. ND: MERB Bookshelf, 1979. 266p.

12250 COLOMBO PLAN CONSULTATIVE CMTEE. The Colombo Plan for Co-operative, Economic, and Social Development in Asia and the Pacific: the special topic, the transfer and adaptation of technology: country papers, the consultants; working paper, and the special topic chapter of the 26th Consultative Committee Meeting, Nepal, 29 November-December 1977. Colombo: Colombo Plan Bureau, 1978. 274p.

12251 ______. The Colombo Plan for Cooperative Economic and Social Development in Asia and the Pacific: development perspectives: country issues papers submitted by member governments to the twenty-seventh Consultative Committee Meeting, Washington, D.C., 28 November-6 December 1978. Colombo: Colombo Plan Bureau, 1979. 156p.

12252 ELIAS, J. Die Aussenwirtschaftsbeziehungen des Comecon mit den Entwicklungslandern unter besonderer Berüchsichtigung Südasiens. Bern: P. Lang 1977. 204p.

12253 ÉTIENNE, G. De Caboul à Pékin; rythmes et perspectives d'expansion économique. Paris: Librairie Minard, 1959. 268p.

12254 JAYARAMAN, T.K. Economic cooperation in the Indian sub-continent: a customs union approach. Bombay: Orient Longmans, 1978. 161p.

12255 LEFEBER, L. Regional development experiences and prospects in South and Southeast Asia. Paris: Mouton, 1971. 278p.

12256 MASON, E.S. Economic development in India and Pakistan. Cambridge: Center for Intl. Affairs, Harvard U., 1966. 67p.

12257 MORRISON, B.M. Asian drama, act II: development prospects in South Asia. In PA 48,1 (1975) 5-26.

12258 MYRDAL, G. Asian drama; an inquiry into the poverty of nations. NY: Twentieth Century Fund, 1968. 3v., 2284p.

12259 ______. Asian drama; an inquiry into the poverty of nations. An abridgement by Seth S. King. NY: Pantheon, 1972. 464p.

12260 PAREKH, H.T. Indian and regional development: the case for a common market. Bombay: Vora, 1969. 90p.

12261 ROBINSON, E.A.G. & M. KIDRON, ed. Economic development in South Asia: proceedings of a conference held by the International Economic Association at Kandy, Ceylon [during July, 1969]. London: Macmillan, 1970. 585p.

12262 SPARKS, S. & A. SHOURIE, & J.A. WESTCOTT. Bibliography on development administration; India and Pakistan. Syracuse: Centre for Overseas Operations & Res., Maxwell Graduate School of Citizenship and Public Affairs, 1964. 51p.

12263 TOMLINSON, J.W.C. The joint venture process in international business: India and Pakistan. Cambridge, MA: MIT Press, 1970. 227p.

12264 VAKIL, C.N. & G. RAGHAVA RAO. Economic relations between India and Pakistan; need for international cooperation. Bombay: Vora, 1968. 214p.

VII. SOCIAL CHANGE AND DEVELOPMENT

12265 CHOUDHURY, L.H. Social change and development administration in South Asia. Dacca: Natl. Inst. of Public Admin., 1979. 152p.

12266 CRANE, R. I., ed. Transition in South Asia: problems of modernization. Durham: Duke U., 1970. 178p. (South Asia monograph series, 9)

12267 JAHAN, ROUNAQ & H. PAPANEK, eds. Women and development: perspectives from South and Southeast Asia. Dacca: Bangladesh Inst. of Law and Intl. Affairs, 1979. 439p.

12268 SARKAR, N.K. Social structure and development strategy in Asia. ND: People's Pub. House, 1978. 298p.

12269 ULLRICH, H.E., ed. Competition and modernization in South Asia. ND: Abhinav, 1975. 243p.

8

India as Nation-State: The Challenge of Development in the World's Largest Democracy, 1947–

I. THE DOMINION OF INDIA, 1947-1950: TRANSITION FROM EMPIRE TO REPUBLIC WITHIN THE COMMONWEALTH [see also Chap. Six, IV. D. 7.]

A. General Studies and Document Collections

12270 Chief Ministers speak; being resumes of the activities of the governments, central and states, during the three years, 1947-1950. ND: AICC, 1950. 241p.

12271 PATEL, V.J. On Indian problems. Delhi: PDMIB, 1949. 117p.

12272 POPLAI, S.J. Indian 1947-1950. Bombay: OUP, 1959. 2v., 666, 672p. [documents]

12273 SARKAR, B.J. Dominion India in world perspectives, economic and political. Calcutta: Chuckervertty Chatterjee, 1949. 176p.

B. The Constituent Assembly, 1946-1950

12274 AHIR, D.C. Dr. Ambedkar and Indian Constitution. Lucknow: Buddha Vihara, 1973. 202p.

12275 AMBEDKAR, B.R. States and minorities; what are their rights and how to secure them in the Constitution of free India. Hyderabad, India: Baba Saheb Dr. Ambedkar Memorial Soc., 1970. 88p.

12276 BANERJEE, A.C., comp. The Constituent Assembly of India. Calcutta: A. Mukherjee, 1947. 48, 350p.

12277 GADGIL, D.R. Some observations on the draft Constitution. Poona: GIPE, 1948. 112p. [Its pub. 1948]

12278 INDIA (DOMINION). CONSTITUENT ASSEMBLY. (Legislative) Debates Official Report, 1947-49. ND: Lok Sabha Secretariat, 1967. 12v. [Rpt. of 1947-51 ed; orig. ed. had 21 appendices in 1 v., 354p.]

12279 KODANDA RAO, P. Language issue in the Indian Constituent Assembly, 1946-1950: rational support for English and non-rational support for Hindi. Bombay: dist. Intl. Book House, 1969. 68p.

12280 MISRA, P. The making of the Indian Republic; some aspects of India's constitution in the making. Calcutta: Scientific Book Agency, 1966. 255p.

12281 PANIKKAR, K.M. Indian Constituent Assembly. Bombay: Bombay Book Depot, 1947. 116p.

12282 RAU, B.N. India's constitution in the making. Ed. by B. Shiva Rao. Rev. & enl. ed. Bombay: Allied, 1963. 541p.

12283 SHIVA RAO, B., et al., eds. The framing of India's constitution; a study. ND: IIPA, 1968. 894p.

12284 ______., eds. The framing of India's constitution; select documents. ND: IIPA, 1966-1968. 4 v., 3322p.

12285 TIWARY, U.K. The making of the Indian constitution. Allahabad: Central Book Depot, 1967. 376p.

II. THE REPUBLIC OF INDIA, 1950 - : POLITICAL SYSTEM AND INSTITUTIONS

A. Bibliography and Reference

1. Bibliography

12286 GHOSH, A. & R. GHOSH. Indian political movement, 1919-1971: a systematic bibliography. Calcutta: India Book Exchange, 1976. 499p.

12287 INDIA (REP.). PARLIAMENT. HOUSE OF THE PEOPLE. Abstracts and index of reports and articles. ND: Jan. 1963-. [quarterly; replaces its Abstracts of reports and Abstracts and index of articles, 1951-.]

12288 RANA, M.S. Writings on Indian Constitution, 1861-1972. Delhi: Indian Bureau of Bibliography, 1973. 496p.

12289 A select bibliography on Indian government and politics. Jaipur: U. of Rajasthan Library, 1965. 196p.

12290 SHARMA, R.N. & S. BAKSHI, eds. Political science in India: an index to twelve political science journals of India. Delhi: Concept, 1978. 266p.

12291 A survey of research in political science. ND: Allied, 1979-. [to be 5 v.; sponsored by ICSSR]

12292 VIRENDRA KUMAR, ed. Committees and commissions in India, 1947-73. Delhi: D.K., 1975-. [8 v. (1947-73) pub. to 1979; summaries of recommendations]

12293 WILSON, P. Government and politics in India and Pakistan 1885-1955; a bibliography of works in western languages. Berkeley: Inst. of East Asiatic studies, U. of California, 1956. 356p.

2. The Study of Indian Politics, and Political Science in India - Trends and Methodology

12294 ELKINS, D.J. The American science of Indian politics. In PA 52,3 (1979) 491-99.

12295 HAJJAR, S.G. The professional literature of Indian political science: a comparative study. In IPSR 11,1 (1977) 67-85.

12296 JAIN, C.M. Current trends and issues in Indian political science. In Political Scientist 7/8, 1/2/1 (1970-71) 77-88.

12297 SHARMA, S.K., ed. Political science in independent India: presidential addresses delivered at the All India Political Science Conferences. Chandigarh: Godwin Pub., 1976. 2 v.

12298 SINHA, N.K.P. Study of government and politics of the different parts of India: a review of articles published in the Indian Journal of Political Science (Vols. I-XXV). In IJPS 26,4 (1965) sect. 3, 1-12.

12299 SUBRAMANIAM, V. & N. SRINIVASAN. The Indian political system: need for new research angles. In EPW 6,17 (1971) 867-73.

B. General Studies of India's Political System

12300 ADAMS, J. & W.C. NEALE. India, the search for unity, democracy, and progress. NY: D. Van Nostrand Co., 1976. 165p.

12301 BHATIA, H.S. Origin and development of legal and political system in India. ND: Deep & Deep, 1976-. [2 v. to 1980]

12302 DAS, B.C. Indian government and politics: a critical commentary. Meerut: Pragati Prakashan, 1979. 598p.

12303 DORÉ, F. La République indienne. Paris: Librairie générale de droit et de jurisprudence, 1969. 501p.

12304 GOYAL, O.P. India: government and politics. ND: Light & Life, 1977. 226p.

12305 GUPTA, D.C. Indian government and politics. 4th rev. & enl. ed. ND: Vikas, 1978. 758p.

12306 HANSON, A.H. & J. DOUGLAS. India's democracy. London: Weidenfeld & Nicolson, 1972. 236p.

12307 HARDGRAVE, R.L., JR. India: government and politics of a developing nation. 3rd ed. NY: Harcourt, Brace & World, 1980. 285p.

12308 KOTHARI, R. Politics in India. Boston: Little, Brown, 1970. 461p.

12309 KRISHNA MURTHY, P. The constitutional and administrative system in India. 2nd ed. Hyderabad: 1967. 253p.

12310 MORRIS-JONES, W.H. The government and politics of India. 3rd rev. ed. London: Hutchinson, 1976. 280p.

12311 NOORANI, A.G. India's constitution and politics. Bombay: Jaico Pub. House, 1970. 588p.

12312 PALMER, N.D. The Indian political system. 2nd ed. Boston: Houghton, Mifflin, 1971. 325p.

12313 PARK, R.L. India's political system. Englewood Cliffs, NJ: Prentice-Hall, 1967. 116p.

12314 PYLEE, M.V. Constitutional government of India. Rev. ed. Bombay: Asia, 1965. 824p. [1st pub. 1960]

12315 SANTHANAM, K.I. Conventions and proprieties of parliamentary democracy in India. ND: IIPA, 1966. 101p.

12316 SESHADRI, K. Indian politics, then and now: essays in historical perspective. Delhi: Pragatee Prakashan, 1976. 167p.

12317 SETHI, J.C.D. India's static power structure. Delhi: Vikas, 1969. 53 + 212p.

12318 SHARMA, B.M. The Republic of India: constitution and government. Bombay: Asia, 1966. 655p.

C. The Constitution of India, Adopted 26 January, 1950

1. Texts of the Constitution

12319 INDIA (REPUBLIC). CONSTITUTION. The Constitution of India: as modified up to the 15th January 1980. ND: Govt. of India, Ministry of Law, Justice, and Company Affairs, 1980. 453p.

2. Commentaries on the Constitution

12320 BASU, D.D. Shorter Constitution of India. 7th ed. Calcutta: S.C. Sarkar, 1976-.

12321 DIWAN, P. & P. RAJPUT. Constitution of India. 2nd ed. ND: Sterling, 1979. 486p.

12322 KAGZI, M.C.J. The constitution of India. 3rd ed. Delhi: Metropolitan Book Co., 1975. 898p.

12323 MAHAJAN, V.D. The constitution of India. 5th ed. Lucknow: Eastern Book Co., 1971. 607p.

12324 RAJU, V.B. Commentaries on the constitution of India. Lucknow: Eastern Book Co., 1976. 899p.

12325 TOPE, T.K. The constitution of India. 3rd ed. Bombay: Popular, 1971. 567p.

3. General Studies of the Constitution, Constitutional Law, and Constitutional History

12326 ALEXANDROWICZ, C.H. Constitutional developments in India. Bombay: OUP, 1957. 255p.

12327 AUSTIN, G. The Indian constitution: cornerstone of a nation. Oxford: OUP, 1966. 390p.

12328 BASU, D.D. Constitutional law of India. ND: Prentice-Hall, 1977. 564p.

12329 ______. Introduction to the constitution of India. Calcutta: S.C. Sarkar, 1971. 383p.

12330 DASH, S.C. The constitution of India; a comparative study. 2nd ed. Allahabad: Chaitanya Pub. House, 1968. 610p.

12331 DHAVAN, R. & A. JACOB, ed. Indian constitution: trends and issues. Bombay: N.M. Tripathi, 1978. 448p.

12332 DOUGLAS, W.O. We the judges: studies in American and Indian constitutional law from Marshall to Mukherjea. Garden City, NY: 1956. 480p.

12333 GAJENDRAGADKAR, P.B. The constitution of India: its philosophy and basic postulates. NY: OUP, 1970. 107p.

12334 GLEDHILL, A. The Republic of India, the development of its laws and constitution. Westport, CT: Greenwood Press, 1970. 309p. [1st pub. 1951]

12335 GUPTA, R.N. Development and working of the Indian constitution. Allahabad: Kitab Mahal, 1958. 504p.

12336 JACOB, A., ed. Constitutional development since Independence. Bombay: N.M. Tripathi, 1975. 691p.

12337 JAIN, M.P. Indian constitutional law. 3rd ed. Bombay: N.M. Tripathi, 1978. 759p.

12338 JENNINGS, W.I. Some characteristics of the Indian constitution. Madras: Oxford University Press, 1953. 86p.

12339 JOSHI, R. & M. PINTO & L. D'SILVA. The Indian constitution and its working. 2nd rev. ed. Bombay: Orient Longman, 1979. 233p.

12340 MASTER, M.K. Citizenship of India; dual nationality and the constitution. Calcutta: Eastern Law House, 1970. 332p.

12341 MUKHARJI, P.B. Three elemental problems of the Indian constitution. Delhi: Natl. Pub. House, 1972. 102p.

12342 PYLEE, M.V. India's constitution. 3rd rev. ed. Bombay: Asia, 1979. 471p.

12343 SETALVAD, M.C. The Indian constitution, 1950-1965. Bombay: U. of Bombay, 1967. 239p.

12344 SHAH, J.C. The rule of law and the Indian constitution. Bombay: N.M. Tripathi, 1972. 95p.

12345 SHARMA, S.R. Constitutional history of India. 3rd rev. ed. Bombay: Orient Longman, 1974. 480p.

12346 SINGH, M.M. The constitution of India: studies in perspective. Calcutta: World Press, 1975. 1257p.

12347 SUBBA RAO, K. Some constitutional problems. Bombay: U. of Bombay, 1970. 318p.

12348 VENKATA SUBBARAO, G.C. Indian constitutional law. 2nd ed. Madras: C. Subbiah Chetty, 1971. 2 v.

12349 VENKATARAMA AIYAR, T.L. The evolution of the Indian constitution. Bombay: U. of Bombay, 1970. 132p.

4. Central Provisions of the Constitution
a. fundamental rights

12350 AIYAR, S.P. & S. VENKATARAM RAJLI, eds. Fundamental rights and the citizen. Bombay: Academic Books, 1972. 242p.

12351 CHATTERJI, S.K., ed. The people, the Parliament, and the fundamental rights. Madras: CIS, for CISRS, 1969. 96p.

12352 CHAWLA, V.N., ed. Fundamental rights: a re-interpretation. Jullundur: Intl. Book Co., 1977. 227p.

12353 GAJENDRAGADKAR, P.B. The Indian Parliament and the fundamental rights. Calcutta: Eastern Law House, 1972. 211p.

12354 GLEDHILL, A. Fundamental rights in India. London: Stevens, 1955. 134p.

12355 KHANNA, H.R. Constitution and civil liberties. ND: Radha Krishna, for ICPS, 1978. 94p.

12356 MAHINDRU, K.C. Public protests and civil liberties in India. In PSR 13,1/4 (1974) 195-208.

12357 MALIK, S., ed. Fundamental rights case: the critics speak. Lucknow: Eastern Book Co., 1975. 158 + 115p. [Kesavananda Bharati v. State of Kerala, (1973)]

12358 MUKHARJI, P.B. Civil liberties. Bombay: N.M. Tripathi, 1968. 170p.

12359 RAJA, C.K.N. Freedom of speech and expression under the constitutions of India and the United States. Dharwad: Karnatak U., 1979. 317p.

12360 SANTHANAM, K. Fundamental rights and the Indian

constitution. Ahmedabad: Harold Laski Inst. of Political Science, 1969. 62p.

12361 SAROJINI REDDY, P. Judicial review of fundamental rights. ND: Natl. Pub. House, 1976. 394p.

12362 SATHE, S.P. Fundamental rights and amendment of the Indian constitution. Bombay: U. of Bombay, 1968. 68p.

12363 SINGHVI, L.M. Fundamental rights and constitutional amendment. Delhi: Natl. Pub. House, for ICPS, 1971. 740p.

12364 SUBBA RAO, K. Fundamental rights under the constitution of India. Madras: U. of Madras, 1966. 86p.

12365 SWARUP, J. Human rights and fundamental freedoms. Bombay: N.M. Tripathi, 1975. 408p.

12366 TRIPATHI, P.K. Some insights into fundamental rights. Bombay: U. of Bombay, 1972. 313p.

12367 WADHWA, K.K. Minority safeguards in India: constitutional provisions and their implementation. Delhi: Thomson Press, 1975. 273p.

b. directive principles of state policy

12368 HEGDE, K.S. The directive principles of state policy in the constitution of India. Delhi: Natl. Pub. House, 1972. 89p.

12369 MARKANDAN, K.C. Directive principles in the Indian constitution. NY: Allied, 1966. 447p.

12370 PARANJAPE, N.V. The role of directive principles under the Indian constitution. Allahabad: Central Law Agency, 1975. 196p.

12371 SHARMA, G.S. Concept of leadership implicit in the directive principles of state policy in the Indian constitution. In JILI 7,4 (1965) 173-88.

12372 SHARMA, R. Conflict of fundamental rights and directive principles. Jodhpur: Usha Pub. House, 1977. 144p.

c. emergency provisions, incl. President's Rule in the States

12373 CHATTERJEE, N.C. & P. PARAMESWARA RAO. Emergency and law, with special reference to India. Bombay: Asia, 1966. 132p.

12374 DHAVAN, R. President's rule in the states. Bombay: N.M. Tripathi, 1979. 240p.

12375 DUA, B.D. Presidential rule in India, 1950-1974: a study in crisis politics. ND: S. Chand, 1979. 414p.

12376 MAHESHWARI, S.R. President's rule in India. ND: Macmillan, 1977. 223p.

12377 President's rule in the states. ND: Lok Sabha Secretariat, 1976. 40p.

12378 SCHOENFELD, B.N. Emergency rule in India. In PA 36 (1963) 221-37.

12379 VERMA, P.M. Constitutional validity of emergency laws. Allahabad: Indian Natl. Renaissance Soc., 1978. 66p.

d. amendment procedures

12380 CHAND, HARI. The amending process in the Indian constitution. Delhi: Metropolitan, 1972. 242p.

12381 Constitution amendment in India. 4th ed., rev. ND: Lok Sabha Secretariat, 1974. 334p.

12382 GROVER, K.L. Constitution versus Parliament: a treatise on the amendment of the constitution. Allahabad: Legend Publications, 1976. 224p.

12383 KUMARAMANGALAM, M. Constitutional amendments: the reason why. ND: AICC, 1971. 30p.

12384 MARKANDAN, K.C. The amending process and constitutional amendments in the Indian constitution. ND: Sterling, 1972. 840p.

12385 SINGHVI, L.M., ed. Parliament and constitutional amendment. Delhi: Natl. Pub. House, for ICPS, 1970. 191p.

D. Indian Democracy and the Problems of National Integration

1. General Studies

12386 ALL-INDIA COLLOQUIUM ON ETHICAL AND SPIRITUAL VALUES AS THE BASIS OF NATIONAL INTEGRATION, BOMBAY, 1966-1967. Record of proceedings. Bombay: BVB, 1967. 739p.

12387 BOSE, N.K. Problems of national integration. Simla: IIAS, 1967. 77p.

12388 BRASS, P.R. Language, religion and politics in North India. NY: CamUP, 1974. 467p.

12389 EMBREE, A.T. India's search for national identity. NY: Knopf, 1972. 138p.

12390 ______. Pluralism and national integration: the Indian experience. In J. of Intl. Affairs 27,1 (1973) 41-52.

12391 GAJENDRAGADKAR, P.B. Indian democracy: its major imperatives. Bombay: B.I. Pub., 1975. 112p.

12392 ______. The philosophy of national integration: its broad imperatives. Delhi: Natl., for ICPS, 1974. 84p.

12393 HARRISON, S.S. India: the most dangerous decades. Princeton: PUP, 1960. 352p.

12394 INDIA. (REP.). CMTEE. ON EMOTIONAL INTEGRATION. Report. Delhi: Min. of Educ., 1962. 277p.

12395 KABIR, HUMAYUN. Minorities in a democracy. Calcutta: KLM, 1968. 94p.

12396 KOTHARI, R. Politics of fragmentation and political integration. In PSR 6,1 (1967) 1-10.

12397 KULKARNI, V.B. Problems of Indian democracy. Bombay: BVB, 1972. 372p.

12398 MASON, P., ed. India and Ceylon: unity and diversity. London: OUP, for Inst. of Race Relations, 1967. 311p.

12399 MUKHERJI, N. Standing at the cross-roads; an analytical approach to the basic problems of psychosocial integration. Bombay: Allied, 1964. 204p.

12400 NAMBOODRIPAD, E.M.S. Problems of national integration. Calcutta: National Book Agency, 1966. 129p.

12401 NARAIN, IQBAL. Cultural pluralism, national integration and democracy in India. In AS 16,10 (1976) 903-17.

12402 National integration. Hyderabad: Inst. of Indo-Middle East Cultural Studies, 1972. 302p.

12403 RAMACHANDRASEKHARA RAO, R.V., comp. Indian unity; a symposium. ND: PDMIB, 1969. 152p.

12404 SAGGI, P.D., ed. We shall unite; a plea for national integration. ND: Overseas, 1968. 121p.

12405 SEMINAR ON NATIONAL INTEGRATION, DELHI, 1958. Report. ND: University Grants Cmsn., 1961. 127p.

12406 SIDDIQI, A.H. National integration in India; a sociological approach. Aligarh: Three Men Pub., 1971. 158p.

12407 SINHA, M.R., ed. Integration in India. Bombay: Asian Studies Press, 1969. 256p.

12408 SUBBA RAO, K. Conflicts in Indian polity. Delhi: S. Chand, 1970. 120p.

12409 SRINIVAS, M.N. The nature of the problem of Indian unity. In EW 10 (1958) 571-77.

12410 SUKHWAL, B.L. India: a political geography. Bombay: Allied, 1971. 288p.

2. Secularism as the Answer to Religious Conflict

a. general studies of India as a secular state; freedom of religion

12411 AGGARWAL, S.N. The law on religious and charitable endowments. Chandigarh: Khurana Law Agency, 1977. 134p.

12412 AHMAD, IMTIAZ. Secularism and communalism. In EPW 4,28-30 (1969) 1137-58.

12413 BACHAL, V.M. Freedom of religion and the Indian judiciary: a critical study of judicial decisions,

26-1-1950 to 26-1-1975. Poona: Shubhada Saraswat, 1975. 361p.

12414 BAIRD, R.D. Religion and the legitimation of Nehru's concept of the secular state. In B.L. Smith, ed. Religion and the legitimation of power in South Asia. Leiden: Brill, 1978, 73-87.

12415 CHUNKATH, A. & P.M. GIDWANI. Bibliography: on secularism. In JCPS 10,2 (1976) 221-49.

12416 CREEL, A.B. Secularisation and Hindu tradition. In R&S 22,4 (1975) 77-92.

12417 DE, K.P. Religious freedom under the Indian constitution. Calcutta: Minerva, 1977. 143p.

12418 DERRETT, J.D.M. Examples of freedom of religion in modern India. In CAS 10 (1977) 42-51.

12419 ______. Religion, law and the state in India. NY: Free Press, 1968. 615p.

12420 GAJENDRAGADKAR, P.B. Secularism and the constitution of India. Bombay: Bombay U. Press, 1971. 181p.

12421 GALANTER, M. Hinduism, secularism, and the Indian judiciary. In PEW 21,4 (1971) 467-88.

12422 ______. Secularism, East and West. In CSSH 7 (1965) 113-72.

12423 GHOUSE, M. Secularism, society, and law in India. Delhi: Vikas, 1973. 254p.

12424 LANKA SUNDARAM. A secular state for India; thoughts on India's political future. Delhi: Raj Kamal, 1944. 114p.

12425 LING, TREVOR OSWALD. Religious change and the secular state. Calcutta: Research India, 1978. 107p.

12426 LUTHERA, V.P. The concept of the secular state and India. London: OUP, 1964. 187p.

12427 SETALVAD, M.C. Secularism. Delhi: PDMIB, 1965. 54p.

12428 SHAH, A.B. Challenges to secularism. 2nd enl. ed. Bombay: Nachiketa, 1969. 184p.

12429 SHARMA, G.S., ed. Secularism: its implications for law and life in India. Bombay: N.M. Tripathi, 1966. 257p. [seminar papers]

12430 SHELAT, J.M. Secularism: principles and application. Bombay: N.M. Tripathi, 1972. 144p.

12431 SINHA, V.K., ed. Secularism in India. Bombay: Lalvani, 1968. 207p.

12432 SMITH, D.E. India as a secular state. Princeton: PUP, 1967. 518p. [1st pub. 1963]

12433 TRIPATHI, P.K. Secularism: constitutional provision and judicial review. In JILI 8,1 (1966) 1-29.

12434 VENKATARAMAN, T.S. A treatise on secular state. Madras: 1950. 200p.

b. survivals of communalism in Indian political life

12435 AGARWALLA, N.D. The Hindu-Muslim question. Calcutta: A. Chakrabarti, 1951. 80p.

12436 FELDMAN, H. The communal problem in the Indo-Pakistan subcontinent: some current implications. In PA 42 (1969) 145-63.

12437 GHURYE, G.S. Social tensions in India. Bombay: Popular, 1969. 552p.

12438 GOPAL KRISHNA. Religion in politics. In IESHR 8,4 (1971) 362-94.

12439 GUPTA, R. Hindu-Muslim relations. Lucknow: Ethnographic and Folk Culture Soc., U.P., 1976. 208p.

12440 MURPHY, G. In the minds of men; the study of human behaviour and social tensions in India. NY: Basic Books, 1953. 306p.

12441 NANAVATI, M.B., ed. Group prejudices in India. Bombay: Vora, 1951. 223p.

12442 PURANIK, S.N. The problem of communal harmony in India. In IPSR 9,1 (1975) 50-67.

12443 SHIV LAL. Sectarian politics in India and Pakistan since 1857. ND: Election Archives, 1971. 192p.

12444 WATSON, V.C. Communal politics in India and United States. In PSR 5 (1966) 209-29.

c. the Indian Muslim community - political expectations

12445 AHMAD, IMTIAZ. Muslim politics in India: a re-evaluation. In Islam and the Modern Age 2,4 (1971) 71-95.

12446 DALWAI, H.U. Muslim politics in India. Bombay: Nachiketa, 1969. 110p.

12447 DATTA, D. Humayun Kabir: a political biography. Bombay: Asia, 1969. 80p.

12448 GANI, H.A. Muslim political issues and national integration. ND: Sterling, 1978. 230p.

12449 GOPAL KRISHNA. Piety and politics in Indian Islam. In CIS ns 6 (1972) 142-71.

12450 GUPTA, S.K. Moslems in Indian politics, 1947-60. In IQ 18 (1962) 355-81.

12451 HASSNAIN, S.E. Indian Muslims; challenge and opportunity. Bombay: Lalvani Pub. House, 1968. 144p.

12452 KHAN, R.N. La communauté musulmane indienne et les problèmes de la partition. In Politique étrangère 31 (1966) 44-64.

12453 AL-MUJAHID, SHARIF. Indian secularism; a case study of the Muslim minority. Karachi: Dept. of Journalism, U. of Karachi, 1970. 313p.

12454 Muslim minority and the Communist Party. ND: CPI, 1975. 27p.

12455 NAIM, C.M. The "Muslim problem" in India. In Quest 75 (1972) 51-63.

12456 SHAKIR, MOIN. Muslim attitudes: a trend report and bibliography. Aurangabad: Primal Prakashan, 1974. 199p.

12457 ______. Muslims in free India. ND: Kalamkar Prakashan, 1972. 156p.

12458 WRIGHT, T.P., JR. Muslim legislators in India: profile of a minority elite. In JAS 23 (1964) 253-67.

12459 ______. Muslims as candidates and voters in 1967 general election. In PSR 8 (1969) 23-40.

d. bans of cow slaughter: collision of Hindu and Muslim values

12460 Ban on cow slaughter: the other view. Trivandrum: Dept. of Public Relations, Govt. of Kerala, 1979. 42p.

12461 Ban on cow slaughter, why? Madurai: Tamilnad Gandhi Smarak Nidhi, 1979. 46p.

12462 The cow: a symposium on the many implications of a current agitation. In Seminar 93 (1967) 12-41. [Articles by H.D. Sankalia, Prodipto Roy, Surendra Singh, Sanjoy Sen, Vishnu Dutt, K.R. Malkani, P. Kesava Dev]

12463 Cow problem and Indian economy. ND: Communist Party of India, 1979. 43p.

12464 JAIN, D.C. & K.C. JOSHI. Constitutional aspect of the ban on cow slaughter. In Intl. J. of Legal Res. 2 (1967) 1-10.

12465 LODRICK, DERYCK O. Sacred cows, sacred places; origins and survivals of animal homes in India. Berkeley: UCalP, 1980. 350p.

12466 PAREL, A. The political symbolism of the cow in India. In JCPS 7,3 (1969) 179-203.

12467 SHAH, A.B., ed. Cow-slaughter: horns of a dilemma. Bombay: Lalvani, 1967. 82p.

12468 VERMA, P.M. Fundamentals of secular democracy: cow-worship and Ramrajya. Allahabad: Indian Natl. Renaissance Soc., 1966. 56p.

3. Regionalism and Language Problems
a. general studies of India's language problems

12469 BHAVE, V. Language problem. Varanasi: Sarva Seva Sangh Prakashan, 1965. 46p.

12470 DASGUPTA, A. The language problem. IN MI 48 (1968) 18-28.

12471 DASGUPTA, J. Language conflict and national development; group politics and national language policy in India. Berkeley: UCalP, 1970. 293p.

12472 GANDHI, M.K. Our language problem. Ed. by A.T. Hingorani. Bombay: BVB, 1965. 133p.

12473 KARAT PRAKASH. Language and nationality politics in India. Bombay: Orient Longmans, 1973. 180p.

12474 MATHUR, P.C. Dilemmas and decision in India's language policy. IN PSR 13,1/4 (1974) 394-414.

12475 MAZUMDAR, S.N. Marxism and the language problem in India. ND: PPH, 1970. 146p.

12476 PANDIT, P.B. Language in a plural society. ND: Dev Raj Chanana Memorial Cmtee., 1977. 65p.

12477 PRASAD, N. K. The language issue in India. Delhi: Leeladevi, 1979. 126p.

12478 RAM GOPAL. Linguistic affairs of India. Bombay: Asia Pub., 1966. 270p.

12479 RAO, V.K.R.V. Many languages and one nation: the problem of integration. Bombay: Mahatma Gandhi Memorial Res. Centre, Hindustani Prachar Sabha, 1979. 93p.

12480 SHRIVASTAVA, G. The language controversy and the minorities. Delhi: Atma Ram, 1970. 160p.

12481 SUNDARA REDDI, G., ed. The language problem in India. Delhi: National, 1973. 90p.

12482 TAMBIAH, S. J. The politics of language in India and Ceylon. In MAS 1 (1967) 215-40.

12483 VENKATA RAO, V. Language politics in India. In IJPS 31 (1970) 203-221.

12484 YADAV, R.K. The Indian language problem, a comparative study. Delhi: National, 1966. 181p.

b. the official language: continued use of English, or Hindi only?

12485 AHMAD, Z.A., comp. National language for India (a symposium). Allahabad: Kitabistan, 1941. 299p.

12486 ANAND, M.R. The King-Emperor's English; or the role of the English language in free India. Bombay: Hind Kitabs, 1948. 70p.

12487 Modern India rejects Hindi, report of the All-India Language Conference. Calcutta: Assn. for the Advancement of the Natl. Languages of India, 1958. 150p.

12488 GOPAL SHARMA, P. & SURESH KUMAR, eds. Indian bilingualism: proceedings of the symposium held under the joint auspices of Kendriya Hindi Sansthan and Jawaharlal Nehru University, February 1976. Agra: Kendriya Hindi Sansthan, 1977. 242p.

12489 INDIA (REP.). OFFICIAL LANGUAGE COMMISSION. Report, 1956. ND: Govt. of India Press, 1957. 495p.

12490 INDIA (REP.). OFFICAL LANGUAGE COMMISSION. Report, 1958. ND: Govt. of India Press, 1959. 122p.

12491 KESAVA MENON, K.P., ed. Retain English for unity and progress. Calicut: Powra Sangham, 1968. 198p.

12492 KUMARAMANGALAM, S.M. India's language crisis; an introductory study. Madras: New Century Book House, 1965. 122p.

12493 MAJUMDAR, A.K. Problem of Hindi; a study. Bombay: BVB, 1965. 156p.

12494 MATHAI, I., ed. India demands English language, from the speeches and writings of C.P. Ramaswami Iyer (and others). Bombay: Mathai's Pub., 1960. 95p.

12495 NAYAR, B.R. National communication and language policy in India. NY: Praeger, 1969. 310p.

12496 RAGHUVIRA. India's national language; a collection of articles. ND: IAIC, 1965. 351p.

12497 RAJAGOPALACHARI, C. The question of English. Madras: Bharathan Publications, 1962. 82p.

12498 RAM, MOHAN. Hindi against India; the meaning of DMK. ND: Rachna Prakashan, 1968. 137p.

12499 SATYANARAYANA, M. The place and position of a link language in the multilingual set up of India. Bombay: Mahatma Gandhi Memorial Res. Centre, Hindustani Prachar Sabha, 1977. 64p.

12500 SATYANARAYANAMURTI, V. The language revolution: let my language rule. Madras: M. Seshachalam, 1974. 167p.

12501 SHUKLA, R.S. Lingua Franca for India (Hind). Lucknow: Oudh Pub. House, 1947. 398p.

12502 VENU, A.S. Why South opposes Hindi. Madras: Justice Pub., 1979. 88p.

12503 WADIA, A. The future of English in India. Bombay: Asia Pub., 1954. 166p.

c. linguism: cultural-linguistic regionalism as the basis of political units

12504 AMBEDKAR, B.R. Thoughts on linguistic states. Aurangabad: 1955. 65p.

12505 ANNAMALAI, E., ed. Language movements in India. Mysore: CIIL, 1979. 134p.

12506 BONDURANT, J.V. Regionalism versus provincialism; a study in problems of Indian national unity. Berkeley: Inst. of Intl. Studies, U. of California, 1958. 150p. (Indian press digests, monograph 4)

12507 BRETON, R.J.L. Les langues de l'Inde depuis l'indépendance; étude de géographie culturelle du monde indien: Inde, Pakistan, Népal, Ceylan. Aix-en-Provence: La Pensée universitaire, 1968. 285p.

12508 RICKETT, L.P. The politics of regionalism in India. In PA 44,2 (1971) 193-210.

12509 INDIAN NATIONAL CONGRESS. LINGUISTIC PROVINCES CMTEE. Report of the Linguistic Provinces Committee appointed by the Jaipur Congress, (Dec. 1948). ND: 1949. 16p.

12510 KACHRU, B.B. Linguistic schizophrenia and language census: a note on the Indian situation. In Linguistics 186 (1977) 17-32.

12511 KODESIA, K. The problems of linguistic states in India. Delhi: Sterling, 1969. 132p.

12512 MORRIS-JONES, W.H. Language and region within the Indian Union. In P. Mason, ed. India and Ceylon: unity and diversity. London: OUP, 1967, 51-66.

12513 RAY, N.C. Federalism and linguistic states. Calcutta: KLM, 1962. 279p.

12514 SATISH CHANDRA & K.C. PANDE & P.C. MATHUR, eds. Regionalism and national integration: proceedings of a seminar. Jaipur: Aalekh Pub., 1976. 247p.

12515 WINDMILLER, M.L. Linguistic regionalism in India. In PA 27 (1954) 291-310.

4. Indian Federalism: Division of Powers between the Union and the States

a. general studies

12516 AIYAR, S.P. The structures of power in the Indian federal system. In JCPS 3,4 (1969) 55-67.

12517 BOMBWALL, K.R. The foundations of Indian federalism. Bombay: Asia Pub., 1967. 384p.

12518 ______, ed. National power and state autonomy. Meerut: Meenakshi, 1978. 219p.

12519 ETIENNE, G. Démocratie, fédéralism et planification en Inde. In Politique étrangère 31 (1966) 173-94.

12520 FRANDA, M. Federalising India: attitudes, capacities and constraints. In SAR 3,3 (1970) 199-213.

12521 GADGIL, D.R. The Federal problem in India. Bombay: 1947. 201p. (GIPE pub., 15)

12522 KRISHNASWAMI, A. The Indian union and the states; a study in autonomy and integration. NY: Pergamon Press, 1965. 89p.

12523 LEONARD, T.J. Federalism in India. In W.S. Livinston, ed. Federalism in the Commonwealth; a bibliographic commentary. London: Cassell, 1963, 87-143.

12524 MAHESHWARI, S.R. Zonal councils in the Indian federal system: a case study. In EW 17 (1965) 1131-38.

12525 NARAIN, IQBAL & A.K. SHARMA. The emerging issues and ideas in Indian federalism. In JCPS 3,4 (1969) 173-93.

12526 RADHAKRISHNAN, N. Zonal councils - an experiment in federalism. In IYIA 11 (1962) 188-218.

12527 RAY, A. Tension areas in India's federal system. Calcutta: World Press, 1970. 160p.

12528 RAY, B. Evolution of federalism in India. Calcutta: Progressive Publishers, 1967. 229p.

12529 SHARMA, P.K. Federalism and political development: developed and developing areas. Delhi: Pragati, 1979. 233p.

12530 SHARMA, S.R. The Indian federal structure; a comparative study. Allahabad: Central Book Depot, 1967. 91p.

12531 VENKATARANGAIYA, M. & M. SHIVIAH. Indian federalism. ND: Arnold-Heinemann, 1975-. v. 1-

b. the process of states reorganization: consolidation and rationalization on cultural-linguistic lines

12532 ALEXANDROWICZ, C.H. India before and after reorganisation. In Yearbook of World Affairs (1958) 133-55.

12533 MUKERJI, K.P. & S. RAMASWAMY. Reorganization of Indian states. Bombay: Popular, 1955. 91p.

12534 INDIA (REP.). MIN. OF STATES. White paper on Indian states. Rev. ed. ND: 1950. 395p.

12535 INDIA (REP.). PART B STATES (SPECIAL ASSISTANCE) ENQUIRY CMTEE. Report. Delhi: MPGOI, 1953. 61p.

12536 INDIA (REP.). STATES REORGANIZATION CMSN. Report. Delhi: MPGOI, 1955. 266p.

12537 SHARMA, P.K. Political aspects of states reorganization in India. ND: Mohuni Pub., 1969. 333p.

c. the Princes as pensioners of the Republic; the privy purses and their final abolition in 1971

12538 CHATURVEDI, S.C. The privy purses case: a critique. In JILI 11,3 (1971) 481-90.

12539 GOPALKRISHNA, D. Privileges of rulers of the former Indian states. In Supreme Court J. 38 (1968) 48-60.

12540 HARICHAND. The question of jurisdiction in the privy purses case. In Supreme Court J. 45,9 (1971) 1-5.

12541 IMAM, MOHAMMED. The privy purse case - a critique. In JILI 13,3 (1971) 385-435.

12542 KASLIWAL, R.R. The privileges and privy purses of the former rulers of Indian states. In Political Scientist 4 (1967-68) 57-62.

12543 MAHENDRU, K.C. The politics of privy purses; India's parliamentary system examined in privy purses issue. Ludhiana: Kalyani, 1971. 215p.

12544 Question of privy purse. In Intl. J. of Legal Res. 2 (1967) 195-215.

12545 VOLLMER, F.-J. Die Streichung der Fürstenabfindungen: ein Beitrag zum indischen "Socialist pattern of society". In IAF 6,1 (1975) 55-65.

E. The Union Executive

1. General Studies - the Central Policy-Making Offices

12546 CHATURVEDI, R.G. The President and the Council of Ministers. ND: ICPS, 1971. 51p.

12547 DAYAL, ISHWAR. Dynamics of formulating policy in Government of India: machinery for policy development. Delhi: Concept, 1976. 94p.

12548 INDIA (REP.). WORKING GROUP ON DEVELOPMENTAL, CONTROL AND REGULATORY ORGANIZATIONS. Report, March, 1968. Delhi: MPGOI, 1968. 108p.

12549 JAIN, H.M. The union executive. Allahabad: Chaitanya Pub. House, 1969. 327p.

12550 KHERA, S.S. The central executive. ND: Orient Longman, 1975. 334p.

12551 MISRA, R.N. The President and the Parliament. Bombay: Vora, 1978. 112p.

2. The President and Vice-President

a. the offices: their powers and functions

12552 DAS, B.C. Prelude to the Presidency in India. ND: Ashish Pub., 1977. 142p.

12553 ______. The President of India. ND: S. Chand, 1977. 499p.

12554 DATTA, C.L. With two presidents: the inside story. Delhi: Vikas, 1970. 149p.

12555 GUNJAL, S.R. BDJ, a portrait of the Vice-President. ND: Sterling, 1979. 90p. [on Basappa Danappa Jatti]

12556 LAL, J.N. The vice-president of India. In IJPS 28 (1967) 104-16.

12557 MISRA, R.N. The president of the Indian Republic. Bombay: Vora, 1965. 243p.

12558 MUNSHI, K.M. The president under the Indian constitution. Bombay: BVB, 1963. 54p.

12559 PANDIT, H.N. The PM's President: a new concept on trial. ND: S. Chand, 1974. 104p.

12560 The powers of the president under the constitution. Proceedings of the seminar. In Indian Advocate 10 (1970) 4-56.

12561 QURAISHI, Z.M. The presidential election in India. In IPSR 2 (1967-68) 23-56.

12562 ______. Struggle for Rashtrapati Bhawan; a study of presidential elections. Delhi: Vikas, 1973. 190p.

12563 SHIV LAL. India-America election handbook on head of state. ND: Election Archives, 1975. 106 + 160p.

12564 SIWACH, J.R. The Indian presidency. Delhi: Hariyana Prakashan, 1971. 377p.

b. India's Rashtrapatis: documents, biographies, studies of the presidents

i. Rajendra Prasad (1884-1963), Pres. 1950-62

12565 CHATTERJEE, B. The presidential predicament: Rajendra Prasad remembered. ND: Affiliated East-West Press, 1974. 119p.

12566 DATTA, K.K. Rajendra Prasad. ND: PDMIB, 1970. 355p.

12567 HANDA, R.L. Rajendra Prasad: twelve years of triumph and despair. ND: Sterling, 1978. 239p.

12568 PANJABI, K.L. Rajendra Prasad, first president of India. London: Macmillan, 1960. 215p.

12569 RAJENDRA PRASAD. Autobiography. Bombay: Asia, 1957. 624p.

12570 ______. Portrait of a president: letters of Dr. Rajendra Prasad written to Mrs. Gyanwati Darbar. Delhi: Vikas Pub. House, 1974-76. 2 v.

12571 ______. Speeches.... Delhi: PDMIB, 1955. 2 v.

12572 ______. Speeches of President Rajendra Prasad. ND: PDMIB, 1973-77. 3 v., 998p.

12573 ______. The unity of India (selected speeches, 1951-1960). Delhi: PDMIB, 1961. 84p.

12574 WASI, S.M. President Prasad, a biography. Calcutta: Thacker, Spink, 1962. 363p.

ii. Sarvepalli Radhakrishnan (1888-1975), Pres. 1962-67

12575 AHLUWALIA, B.K., ed. Facets of Radhakrishnan. ND: Newman Group, 1978. 157p.

12576 ISWARA DUTT, ed. Sarvepalli Radhakrishnan; a study of the President of India. ND: Popular Book Services, 1966. 128p.

12577 RADHAKRISHNAN, SARVEPALLI. President Radhakrishnan's speeches and writings; May 1962-May 1964. Delhi: PDMIB, 1965. 459p.

12578 ______. President Radhakrishnan's speeches and writings, May 1964-May 1967. 2nd series. ND: PDMIB, 1970. 520p.

12579 RAY, S.K. The political thought of President Radhakrishnan. Calcutta: KLM, 1966. 204p.

iii. Zakir Husain (1897-1969), Pres. 1967-69

12580 AHLUWALIA, B.K. Zakir Husain; a study. ND: Sterling, 1971. 127p.

12581 CHISHTI, A. President Zakir Husain; a study. ND: Rachna Prakashan, 1967. 125p.

12582 Dr. Zakir Husain; a special issue in memory of Dr. Zakir Husain. Ed. H.N. Trivedi. Bombay: Industrial Advertisers, 1970. 102p.

12583 HUSAIN, ZAKIR. President Zakir Husain's speeches. ND: PDMIB, 1974. 386p.

12584 MOHAN, RADHEY, ed. Dr. Zakir Husain as I saw him. ND: Indiana Pub., 1974. 215p.

12585 MUJEEB, M. Dr. Zakir Husain; a biography. ND: NBT, 1972. 248p.

12586 NOORANI, A.G. President Zakir Husain: a quest for excellence. Bombay: Popular Prakashan, 1967. 128p.

iv. V.V. Giri (1894-1980), Pres. 1969-74

12587 GIRI, V.S. The voice of conscience. Madras: Vyasa, 1971. 245p.

12588 GIRI, V.V. My life and times. Delhi: Macmillan, 1976-. v. 1, 219p.

12589 ______. President speaks; a compilation of the speeches made by President V.V. Giri from May 1969 to March 1970. Ed. by Nagendra Singh. Delhi: S. Chand, 1970. 208p.

12590 ______. Speeches of President V.V. Giri. ND: PDMIB, 1974. 2 v.

v. Fakhruddin Ali Ahmed (1905-1977), Pres. 1974-77

12591 NAIDU, M.A. Fakhruddin Ali Ahmed. Hyderabad: 1975. 78p.

12592 REHMANEY, F.A.A. My eleven years with Fakhruddin Ali Ahmed. ND: S. Chand, 1979. 254p.

vi. N. Sanjeeva Reddy (1913-), Pres. 1977-

3. The Prime Minister and the Council of Ministers (the Cabinet and Ministers of State) [For Individual PM's, see III. D., below]

12593 GANGAL, S.C. Prime Minister and the Cabinet in India; a political study. Varanasi: Navachetna, 1972. 102p.

12594 JHA, S.N. The Union Council of Ministers in India 1952-71: a study in elite composition. In PSR 13,1/4 (1974) 40-58.

12595 KHILNANI, N.M. Salient features of the cabinet government in India. In JCPS 11,1 (1977) 83-101.

12596 Names and portfolios of the members of the Union Council of Ministers; from August 15, 1947 to June 30, 1978. ND: Lok Sabha Secretariat, 1978. 157p.

12597 NICHOLSON, N.K. Factionalism and the Indian Council of Ministers. In JCPS 10,3 (1972) 179-91.

12598 ROBINS, R.S. Institutional linkages with an elite body: a correlational analysis of the institutional representation in the Indian Council of Ministers, 1952-1960. In Comparative Politics 4,1 (1971) 109-15.

12599 SHARMA, L.N. The Indian prime minister: office and powers. Delhi: Macmillan, 1976. 207p.

12600 VENKATESWARAN, R.J. Cabinet government in India. London: Allen & Unwin, 1967. 200p.

4. The Attorney-General for India: a separate Office Coequal with the Council of Ministers

12601 SETALVAD, M.C. My life: law and other things. Bombay: N.M. Tripathi, 1970. 636p.

5. Public Administration and the Bureaucracy

a. bibliography and reference

12602 Documentation in public administration. ND: IIPA, 1973-. [quarterly]

12603 INDIAN INST. OF PUBLIC ADMIN. The organisation of the government of India. 2nd rev. ed. Bombay: Somaiya, 1971. 539p. [1st ed. 1958]

12604 MENGE, P.E. Government administration in South Asia: a bibliography. Washington: Comp. Admin. Group, American Soc. for Public Admin., 1968. 100p.

12605 A survey of research in public administration. Bombay: Allied, 1973-75. 2 v. [sponsored by ICSSR]

b. general studies of Indian administration

12606 APPLEBY, P.H. Public administration in India: report of a survey. Delhi: MPGOI, 1953. 66p.

12607 ARORA, R.K., ed. Administrative change in India. Jaipur: Aalekh Pub., 1974. 364p.

12608 BHAMBHRI, C.P. Bureaucracy and politics in India. Delhi: Vikas, 1971. 349p.

12609 CHANDA, A.K. Indian administration. London: Allen & Unwin, 1958. 274p.

12610 DUBE, S.C., ed. Public services and social responsibility. ND: Vikas, 1979. 277p.

12611 GUPTA, B.B. Problems of Indian administration. Allahabad: Chugh, 1975. 186p.

12612 INDIA (REP.). STUDY TEAM ON MACHINERY OF THE GOVERNMENT OF INDIA AND ITS PROCEDURES OF WORK. Report. Delhi: MPGOI, 1967-68. 2 v. [Team appt. by Admin. Reforms Cmsn.]

12613 INDIAN POLITICAL SCIENCE ASSN. Indian administration: organisation and working. Ed. by Harmandar Singh. Jullundur: Books Intl., 1967. 139p.

12614 INST. OF SECRETARIAT TRAINING AND MANAGEMENT. Organisational set-up and functions of the ministries/departments of the Government of India. 5th ed. ND: 1975. 425p.

12615 JAIN, R.B. Contemporary issues in Indian administration. Delhi: Vishal Pub., 1976. 491p.

12616 MAHESHWARI, S.R. The evolution of Indian administration. Agra: Lakshmi Narain Agarwal, 1970. 324p.

12617 MANGAT RAI, E.N. Patterns of administrative development in independent India. London: U. of London, 1976. 167p.

12618 MURUGESA MUDALIAR, N. Indian administration: today and tomorrow. Madras: Orient Longmans, 1969. 188p.

12619 PAI PANANDIKAR, V.A. & S.S. KSHIRSAGAR. Bureaucracy in India: an empirical study. In IJPA 17,2 (1971) 187-208.

12620 POTTER, D.C. Bureaucratic change in India. In R. Braibanti, ed. Asian bureaucratic systems emergent from the British imperial tradition. Durham: DUP, 1966, 141-208.

12621 RAI, H. & S.P. SINGH. Current ideas and issues in Indian administration: a developmental perspective. ND: Uppal, 1979. 234p.

12622 RAMACHANDRAN, V.G. Administrative law: origin, development, process, powers, procedure, justice and tribunals. Lucknow: Eastern Book Co., 1969. 693p.

12623 SHARAN, P. Public administration in India. Meerut: Meenakshi, 1078. 732p.

12624 SHARMA, S.K. Studies in Indian administration. Jullundur: Intl. Book Co., 1967. 204p.

12625 VARMA, R.S. Bureaucracy in India. Bhopal: Progress Pub., 1973. 106p.

12626 VEPA, R.K. Change and challenge in Indian administration. ND: Manohar, 1978. 288p.

c. the All-India Services (Administrative, Police, Forest, Medical and Health) and other public services
i. general studies

12627 BANSAL, P.L. Administrative development in India. ND: Sterling, 1974. 196p.

12628 BHAMBHRI, C.P. The administrative elite and political modernization in India: a study of the value-attitudes of IAS probationers 1970-71. In IJPA 17,1 (1971) 47-64.

12629 ______. The Indian administrative service: milieu, challenges, and responses. In J. of Admin. Overseas 9,4 (1970) 262-72.

12630 CHOPRA, D.S. Law relating to government servants, with reference to provisions of the Indian Constitution. Calcutta: Eastern Law House, 1975. 295p.

12631 DWARKADAS, R. The role of the higher civil service in India. Bombay: Popular, 1958. 260p.

12632 INDIA (REP.). STUDY TEAM ON PROMOTION POLICIES, CONDUCT RULES, DISCIPLINE, AND MORALE. Report, December 1967. Delhi: MPGOI, 1967. 528p. [Team appt. by Admin. Reforms Cmsn.]

12633 MAHESHWARI, S.R. The all-India services. In Public Admin. 49,3 (1971) 291-308.

12634 POTTER, D.C. Relevance of training for Indian administrative service. In PSR 8 (1969) 325-46.

12635 PRASAD, B.N. The Indian Administrative Service. Delhi: S. Chand, 1968. 290p.

12636 RAY, S.K. Indian bureaucracy at the crossroads. ND: Sterling, 1979. 407p.

12637 ROY, N.C. The civil service in India. Calcutta: KLM, 1958. 328p.

12638 SRIVASTAVA, G.P. The Indian Civil Service; a study in administrative personnel. Delhi: S. Chand, 1965. 281p.

12639 TYAGI, A.R. The civil servant in a developing society. ND: Sterling, 1969. 426p.

ii. the Public Services Commissions, recruitment and training

12640 ARORA, R.K. & G.C. KUKAR, eds. Training and administrative development. Jaipur: HCM State Inst. of Public Admin., 1979. 179p.

12641 CHOWDHRY, K. Union public service commission: some comments on selectors and selection methods. In IJPA 13 (1967) 716-28.

12642 Civil services examination: report of the Committee on Recruitment Policy and Selection Methods. ND: Union Public Service Cmsn., 1976. 235p.

12643 HAZARIKA, N. Public service commissions: a study. Delhi: Leeladevi, 1979. 200p.

12644 INDIA (REP.). STUDY TEAM ON RECRUITMENT, SELECTION, U.P.S.C./STATE P.S.C.'S AND TRAINING. Report (June 1967). ND: Admin. Reforms Cmsn., 1969. 103p.

12645 MUTTALIB, M.A. The Union Public Service Commission. ND: IIPA, 1967. 251p.

12646 Public service commissions in India: review of the role and functions. ND: Union Public Service Cmsn., 1978. 193p.

12647 SAXENA, A.P. Training and development in government. ND: IIAP, 1974. 108p.

iii. the Indian bureaucrat - sociological studies of background and behavior

12648 GOYAL, S.K. Bureaucracy: a sociological study of clerks. In Inter-discipline 6 (1969) 254-64.

12649 ______. Bureaucracy: a sociological study of levels of orientation of clerks towards the norms of bureaucracy. In SB 5 (1968) 248-60.

12650 HEGINBOTHAM, S.J. Cultures in conflict: the four faces of Indian bureaucracy. NY: ColUP, 1975. 236p.

12651 PAI PANANDIKAR, V.A. Values, attitudes and motivation of civil servants. In IJPA 7,3 (1966) 544-58.

12652 PRASAD, G.K. Bureaucracy in India: a sociological study. ND: Sterling, 1074. 152p.

12653 RAMANATHAN, G.K. Indian babu; a study in social psychology. ND: Sudha Pub., 1965. 284p.

12655 ______. Social background of India's administrators; a socio-economic study of the higher civil services of India. ND: PDMIB, 1971. 180p.

12656 TAUB, R.P. Bureaucrats under stress; administrators and administration in an Indian state. Berkeley: UCalP, 1969. 235p.

iv. personal accounts and biographies of public servants

12657 BONARJEE, N.B. Under two masters. Calcutta: OUP, 1970. 317p.

12658 CHETTUR, S.K. The crystal years; the I.C.S. in free India. Madras: dist. Higginbothams, 1965. 114p.

12659 DESHMUKH, C.D. The course of my life. ND: Orient Longmans, 1974. 367p.

12660 DESHMUKH, D. Chintaman and I. ND: Allied, 1980. 121p.

12661 DHARMA VIRA. Memoirs of a civil servant. ND: Vikas, 1975. 154p.

12662 DUBHASHI, P.R. The profession of public administration. Pune: Shubhada-Saraswat, 1980. 140p.

12663 KRISHEN, P. A bureaucrat's diary. ND: Vikas, 1977. 234p.

12664 MANGAT RAI, E.N. Commitment, my style: career in the Indian Civil Service. Delhi: Vikas, 1973. 275p.

12665 MUKERJI, M. Ham in the sandwich: lighter side of life in the IAS. ND: Vikas, 1979. 111p.

12666 PULLA REDDI, O. Autumn leaves. Bombay: BVB, 1978. 176p.

12667 RAO, P.V.R. Red tape and white cap. ND: Orient Longmans, 1970. 344p.

12668 SINHA, S.K. From dusk to dawn. Hyderabad: Hyderabad Paperbacks, 1977. 181p.

12669 VANMIKANATHAN, G. Random recollections: an autobiography with a difference. Bombay: MMC School of Mgmt., 1978. 282p.

d. administrative problems, corruption, reform
i. general studies of corruption; the Santhanam Committee Report, 1964

12670 BHAMBHRI, C.P. Corruption in public administration; some observations in the Indian context. In PSR 3 (1964) 48-62.

12671 BHARGAVA, G.S. India's Watergate: a study of political corruption in India. ND: Arnold-Heinemann, 1974. 226p.

12672 DWIVEDY, S.N. & G.S. BHARGAVA. Political corruption in India. ND: Popular Book Services, 1967. 180p.

12673 INDIA (REP.). MIN. OF HOME AFFAIRS. CMTEE. ON PREVENTION OF CORRUPTION. Report. ND: 1964. 303p. [Chm., K. Santhanam]

12674 JAGANNADHAM, V. Sociological aspect of administrative reforms. In IJPA 12,3 (1966) 673-85.

12675 KOHLI, S., ed. Corruption in India. ND: Chetana, 1975. 128p.

12676 MANSUKHANI, H.L. Corruption and public servants. ND: Vikas, 1979. 346p.

12677 MATHUR, J.S. Civil service ethics in a developing society: India. In JNAA 15,2/3 (1970) 41-54.

12678 MONTEIRO, J.B. Corruption; control of maladministration. Bombay: Manaktalas, 1966. 303p.

12679 MUHAR, P.S. Corruption in the public services in

India. In IJPS 26 (1965) 1-18.

12680 PANDA, B. Indian bureaucracy: an inside story. ND: Uppal Pub. House, 1978. 213p.

12681 VARMA, S.P. Corruption and political development in India. In PSR 13 (1974) 157-79.

ii. commissions of inquiry and advisory committees

12682 GUPTA, S.C. The law relating to commissions of inquiry. Delhi: Indian Law Centre, 1977. 341p.

12683 MAHESHWARI, S.R. Government through consultation; advisory committees in Indian Government. ND: IIPA, 1972. 380p.

iii. the Administrative Reforms Commission (1966-69) and other efforts at reform

12684 INDIA (REP.). ADMIN. REFORMS CMSN. The Administrative Reforms Commission and its work: a brief survey. Ed. by S.P. Vittal & A.V. Seshanna. Delhi: MPGOI, 1970. 68p.

12685 ______. Recommendations and conclusions of Administrative Reforms Commission; a compendium, July 1970. ND: 1970. 172p.

12686 JAIN, R.B. Innovations and reforms in Indian administration. In IPSR 9,2 (1975) 91-118.

12687 KHAN, M.M. Failure to reform an elite bureaucracy: a study of the impact of Administrative Reforms Commission on Indian Administrative Service. In JASBangla 21,1 (1976) 21-37.

12688 KRISHNA KUMAR, T. The ambiguity of ideology and administrative reform. Bombay: Allied, 1979. 367p.

12689 MAHESHWARI, S.R. The Administrative Reforms Commission. Agra: Lakshmi Narain Agarwal, 1972. 570p.

12690 MOHARIR, V.V. Administrative reforms in India. In Development and Change (The Hague) 2 (1970-71) 83-97.

iv. the citizen vs. the bureaucracy; proposals for a Lokpal and Lokayukta ("people's protector, advocate") or ombudsman

12691 AGRAWALA, S.K. The proposed Indian ombudsmen; a comparative study of the Lokpal and Lokayuktas bill, 1968. Bombay: N.M. Tripathi, 1971. 81p.

12692 BARNABAS, A.P. Citizens' grievances and administration; a study in participation and alienation. ND: IIPA, 1969. 163p. [study for Admin. Reforms Cmsn.]

12693 Citizen and administration (special number). In IJPA 21,3 (1975) 289-615.

12694 JAGANNADHAM, V. & H.R. MAKHIJA. Citizen administration and lokpal. Delhi: S. Chand, 1969. 214p.

12695 JAIN, M.P. Lokpal: ombudsman in India. Bombay: Academic Books, 1970. 332p.

12696 The Lokpal and Lokayuktas bill, 1968; report of the joint committee [of Parliament], presented on the 26th March 1969. ND: Lok Sabha Secretariat, 1969. 33 + 82p.

12697 Ombudsman - a select bibliography. In JCPS 11,2 (1977) 98-138.

12698 VERMA, S.L. Lokpal, bureaucracy, and the common man. In IJPA 24,4 (1978) 1130-44.

12699 WADE, H.W.R. Government and citizens' rights: new problems, new institutions. Delhi: National, for ICPS, 1974. 78p.

e. police administration and operations; paramilitary forces

12700 BAYLEY, D.H. The police and political development in India. Princeton: PUP, 1969. 482p.

12701 ______. The police in India. In EPW 6,45 (1971) 2287-90.

12702 ______. Preventive detention in India; a case study in democratic social control. Calcutta: KLM, 1962. 144p.

12703 BHARDWAJ, R.K. Indian police administration. ND: National, 1978. 349p.

12704 GHOSH, S. Indian police at crossroads. Calcutta: Eastern Law House, 1975. 160p.

12705 ______. Police and the public. Bhubaneswar: Govt. of Orissa, Home Dept. 1965. 108p.

12706 India's silent force: BSF. In The States (8 Jan 1972) 8-28. [4 articles on the Border Security Force]

12707 LAHIRI, B.N. Leaves from a policeman's diary. Meerut: Meenakshi, 1967. 245p.

12708 MULLIK, B.N. A philosophy for the police. Rev. ed. Bombay: Allied, 1969. 162p.

12709 NIGAM, S.R. Scotland Yard and the Indian police. Allahabad: Kitab Mahal, 1963. 218p.

12710 PANDE, D.C. Police coercion in India; a study of legal limits on it and comparative study with U.S.A. Lucknow: Pacific Pub., 196-. 142p.

12711 Police administration special number . In IJPA 24,1 (1978) 1-354.

12712 RAM REDDY, G. & K. SESHADRI, ed. Developing society and police. Hyderabad: Osmania U., 1972. 206p.

12713 RUSTAMJI, K.F. India's paramilitary forces. In JIDSA 10,1 (1977) 1-12.

12714 SHARMA, P.D. Indian police: a developmental approach. ND: Research Pub. in Social Sciences, 1977. 334p.

12715 SINGHVI, G.C. A case for induction of railway police in the union list. In JCPS 6,3 (1972) 82-93.

12716 VOHRA, B. BSF: they patrol our border. In IWI 93,27 (2 July 1972) 20-25. [Border Security Force]

6. The Armed Forces of Independent India: Generals and Jawans

a. general studies in military history and administration

12717 CHATURVEDI, M.S. History of the Indian Air Force. ND: Vikas, 1978. 215p.

12718 COHEN, S.P. Officer tradition in the Indian army. In JUSI 94, (1964) 32-38.

12719 DHARAM PAL. Traditions of the Indian army. 3rd rev. ed. ND: NBT, 1978. 170p.

12720 MACMILLAN, M. The Indian army since independence. In SAR 3,1 (1969) 45-58.

12721 PRAVAL, K.C. India's paratroopers: a history of the Parachute Regiment of India. Delhi: Thomson Press, 1974. 366p. + 17pl.

12722 PRASAD, S.N. History of the Custodian Force (India) in Korea, 1953-54. ND: Historical Section, Min. of Defence, 1976. 182p.

12723 PUSHPINDAR SINGH. Aircraft of the Indian Air Force, 1933-73. ND: English Book Store, 1974. 180p.

12724 RAJENDRA SINGH. Organization and administration in the Indian army. 2nd ed. ND: Army Educational Stores, 1964. 442p.

12725 SHARMA, M.M. The National Cadet Corps of India. ND: Vision Books, 1980. 215p.

12726 SHASHI, S.S. Jawan: pride of the nation. Delhi: Indian School Supply Depot, 1973. 197p. + 8pl.

12727 STRETTELL, D. The Indian Army before and after 1947. In J. of the Royal Central Asian Soc. 35 (1948) 116-30.

12728 THOMAS, R.G.C. The Indian navy in the Seventies. In PA 48,4 (1975-6) 500-18.

12729 VENKATESWARAN, A.L. Defence organisation in India; a study of major developemnts in organisation and administration since independence. ND: PDMIB, 1967. 385p.

b. the military and society

12730 COHEN, S.P. The Indian Army; its contribution to the development of a nation. Berkeley: UCalP, 1971. 216p.

12731 ______. The Indian military and social change. In JIDSA 2,1 (1969) 12-29.

12732 ______. The untouchable soldier: caste, politics, and the Indian Army. In JAS 28 (1969) 453-68.

12733 RAO, M.S.A. Caste and the Indian army. In EW 16, 35 (1964) 1439-43.

12734 RUDOLPH, L.I. & S.H. RUDOLPH. Generals and politicians in India. In PA 37 (1964) 3-19.

c. memoirs and biographies of "Old Soldiers"

12735 CHAUDHURI, J.N. Arms, aims and aspects. Bombay: Manaktalas, 1966. 280p.

12736 ______. General J.N. Chaudhuri: an autobiography, as narrated to B.K. Narayan. ND: Vikas, 1978. 207p.

12737 EVANS, H. Thimayya of India; a soldier's life. NY: Harcourt, Brace, 1960. 307p.

12738 HARJINDER SINGH. Birth of an air force: the memoirs of Air Vice Marshal Harjinder Singh. ND: Palit & Palit, 1977. 307p.

12739 MUTHANNA, I.M. General Cariappa (the first Indian commander-in-chief). Mysore: Usha Press, 1964. 148p.

12740 ______. General Thimayya. Bangalore: Orient Power Press, 1972. 242p.

12741 SUKHWANT SINGH. India's wars since independence. ND: Vikas, 1980-. v. 1-.

12742 ______. Three decades of Indian army life, autobiography of Brigadier Sukhwant Singh. Delhi: Sterling, 1967. 191p.

12743 THAPAR, D.R. The morale builders; forty years with the military medical services of India. NY: Asia, 1965. 343p.

7. The Indian Foreign Service
a. studies of Foreign Service administration

12744 BHAMBHRI, C.P. The Indian Foreign Service. In J. of Admin. Overseas 7 (1968) 528-37.

12745 BHARGAVA, G.S. The ills of the Indian Foreign Service. In EPW 1,10 (1966) 407-10. [also in Janata 21,29 (1966) 9-11]

12746 Choosing our envoys. In Thought 23,31 (31 July 1971) 4-5.

12747 INDIA (REP.). CMTEE. TO REVIEW THE STRUCTURE AND ORGANISATION OF THE INDIAN FOREIGN SERVICE. Report of the Committee on the Indian Foreign Service. ND: Min. of External Affairs, 1966. 157p.

12748 MAITRA, S. Ills of the Indian Foreign Service: a comment. In EPW 1,13 (1966) 549-51.

b. memoirs and biographies of India's diplomats

12749 ANDREWS, R.D. A lamp for India: the story of Madame Pandit. Englewood Cliffs, NJ: Prentice-Hall, 1967. 406p.

12750 BRECHER, M. India and world politics; Krishna Menon's view of the world. NY: Praeger, 1968. 390p.

12751 BRITTAIN, V.-M. Envoy extraordinary; a study of Vijaya Lakshmi Pandit and her contribution to modern India. London: Allen & Unwin, 1965. 178p.

12752 GEORGE, T.J.S. Krishna Menon, a biography. NY: Taplinger Pub. Co., 1965. 272p.

12753 GOYAL, N. Krishna Menon, profile and personal views. ND: Popular Book Services, 1967. 94p.

12754 JENSEN, I.K.K. The men behind the woman: case study of the political career of Mme. Vijaya Lakshmi Pandit. In CAS 10 (1977) 76-93.

12755 KAUL, T.N. Diplomacy in peace and war: recollections and reflections. ND: Vikas, 1979. 251p.

12756 LENGYEL, E. Krishna Menon. NY: Walker, 1962. 253p.

12757 MENON, K.P.S. Memories and musings. Bombay: Allied, 1979. 361p.

12758 ______. Yesterday and today. Bombay: Allied, 1976. 223p.

12759 PANDIT, V.L.N. The scope of happiness: a personal memoir. NY: Crown Pub., 1979. 333p.

12760 PANT, A. Mandala: an awakening. Bombay: Orient Longmans, 1978. 210p.

12761 ______. A moment in time. Bombay: Orient Longmans, 1974. 190p.

F. Parliament

1. General Studies of India's Parliament

12762 FARTYAL, H.S. Role of the opposition in the Indian Parliament. Allahabad: Chaitanya Pub. House, 1971. 260p.

12763 JAIN, R.B. The Indian Paliament: innovations, reforms, and development. Calcutta: Minerva, 1976. 144p.

12764 KASHYAP, S.C. Human rights and parliament. ND: Metropolitan, 1978. 409p.

12765 KAUL, M.N. Parliamentary institutions and procedures. ND: National, 1978. 449p.

12766 LAL, A.B. The Indian Parliament. Allahabad: Chaitanya, 1956. 296p.

12767 MALLYA, N.N. Indian Parliament. ND: NBT, 1970. 203p.

12768 MORRIS-JONES, W.H. Parliament in India. Westport, CT: Greenwood Press, 1975. 417p. [Rpt. 1957 ed.]

12769 MUKHERJI, H.N. India and Parliament. ND: PPH, 1962. 163p.

12770 RAJAGOPALA IYENGAR, T.S. Indian Parliament: a critical study. Mysore: Prasaranga, U. of Mysore, 1972. 216p.

12771 SHAKDHER, S.L. Glimpses of the working of Parliament. ND: Metropolitan Book Co., 1977. 396p.

12772 ______, ed. The Constitution and the Parliament in India: the 25 years of the Republic. Delhi: National, for Lok Sabha Secretariat, 1975. 694p.

12773 UPRETI, N. Provisional Parliament of India: a case study in the development of parliamentary democracy. Agra: L.N. Agarwal, 1975. 315p.

2. The Rajya Sabha (Council of States)

12774 BHALERAO, S.S., ed. The Second Chamber: its role in modern legislatures: the twenty-five years of Rajya Sabha. ND: National, for Rajya Sabha Secretariat, 1977. 467p.

12775 BHATNAGAR, A.K. The Rajya Sabha: a critical study. Allahabad: Chugh, 1977. 334p.

12776 SINGH, B. Council of States in India; a structural and functional profile. Meerut: Meenakshi, 1973. 360p.

12777 SRIVASTAVA, S. Constitution and functioning of Rajya Sabha. Allahabad: Chugh, 1979. 360p.

3. The Lok Sabha (House of the People)

12778 INDIA (REP.). PARLIAMENT. HOUSE OF THE PEOPLE. Parliament of India, the Fifth Lok Sabha, 1971-1977: a study. Ed. by S.L. Shakdher, secretary general, Lok Sabha. ND: Indus Intl. for Lok Sabha Secretariat, 1977. 401p.

12779 ______. Rules of procedures and conduct of business in Lok Sabha. 6th ed. ND: Lok Sabha Secretariat, 1977. 250p.

12780 SHAKDHER, S.L. Secretary-general of Lok Sabha: functions & responsibilities. ND: Lok Sabha Secretariat, 1976. 22p.

12781 SIVA DHARMA SASTRY, B. A comparative study of the Speaker: India, Britain, and the U.S.A. ND: Sterling, 1978. 314p.

12782 YADAV, J.N. SINGH. The Speaker and his rulings. In JCPS 11,1 (1977) 1-16.

4. Parliamentary Procedure

12783 AGRAWAL, VEENA. Parliamentary procedure. In IJPS 27 (1966) 37-54.

12784 KAUL, M.N. & S.L. SHAKDHER. Practice and procedure of Parliament: with particular reference to Lok Sabha. 3rd rev. ed. ND: Metropolitan, 1978-79. 2 v., 998p.

12785 MUKHERJEA, A.R. Parliamentary procedure in India. Calcutta: OUP, 1967. 497p. [1st ed. 1958]

12786 SEEVANAYAGAM. Legislative procedures in the parliaments of India and Ceylon: a comparison. In JCPS 3,3 (1969) 21-63.

5. MP's and Parliamentary Privileges; Who's Whos and Biographies

12787 CHATTERJEE, A.P. Parliamentary privileges in India. Calcutta: New Age Pub., 1971. 181p.

12788 HANS RAJ. Privileges of members of Parliament in India: including the members of state legislatures. Delhi: Surjeet, 1979. 287p.

12789 KARNIK, D.B. This was a man. Bombay: Janata Pub., 1978. 28p.

12790 KOCHANEK, S.A. The relation between social background and attitudes of Indian legislators. In JComPolSt 6 (1968) 34-53.

12791 JAIN, D.C. Parliamentary privileges under the Indian constitution. ND: Sterling, 1975. 232p.

12792 Lok Sabha who's who. ND: Lok Sabha Secretariat, 1952-.

12793 MASANI, M.R. Bliss was it in that dawn: a political memoir up to independence. ND: Arnold-Heinemann, 1977. 220p.

12794 MENON, P.G. Parliamentary privileges and their codification. ND: ICPS, 1968. 28p. 1st pub. in JCPS 2,3 (1968) 1-28.

12795 MUKHERJEE, H.N. Portrait of parliament; reflection and recollection: 1952-77. ND: Vikas, 1978. 165p.

12796 Rajya Sabha who's who. ND: Rajya Sabha Secretariat, 1955-.

12797 SINGH, T. Indian Parliament 1952-1957...biographical dictionary of the two houses of Parliament. ND: Arunam and Sheel, 1954. 304 + 92p.

12798 SWAMMIKANNU, S. Parliamentary privilege. In Madras Law J. 124,4 (1963) 31-61.

6. Committees and Parliamentary Control of Finance and Administration

12799 AGGARWALA, R.N. Financial committees of the Indian Parliament; a study in parliamentary control over public expenditure. Delhi: S. Chand, 1966. 490p.

12800 BALAKRISHNAN NAIR, A. Parliamentary control of the administrative function in India: a study in procedure. Trivandrum: 1973. 276p.

12801 BHAMBHRI, C.P. Parliamentary control over state enterprise in India: a study in public administration. Delhi: Metropolitan, 1960. 115p.

12802 GADHOK, D.N. Accountability of public enterprises to Parliament: working & impact of Parliamentary Committee on Public Undertakings. ND: Sterling, 1980. 147p.

12803 ______. Parliamentary control over government expenditure. ND: Sterling, 1976. 292p.

12804 JENA, B.B. Parliamentary committees in India. Calcutta: Scientific Book Agency, 1966. 339p.

12805 MAHESHWARI, S.R. Informal consultative committees of Parliament. In JCPS 2,1 (1968) 27-53.

12806 NARAIN, LAXMI. Parliament and public enterprise in India: report of a seminar on the Parliamentary Committee on Public Undertakings. ND: S. Chand, 1979. 224p.

12807 POTTER, D.C. Public enterprises: parliamentary control or accountability? In IJPA 5 (1959) 320-32.

12808 PREMCHAND, A. Control of public expenditure in India. A historical and analytical account of the administrative, audit, and parliamentary processes. ND: Allied, 1963. 480p.

12809 SESHADRI, S. Parliamentary control over finance: a study of the Public Accounts Committee of Parliament. Bombay: Allied, 1975. 295p.

12810 SHAKDHER, S.L. The budget and the Parliament. ND: National, 1979. 166p.

12811 ______. The system of parliamentary committees. ND: Lok Sabha Secretariat, 1974. 276p. [comparative study]

12812 SINGHVI, L.M., ed. Parliament and administration in India. Delhi: Metropolitan Book, 1972. 278p.

12813 WATTAL, P.K. Parliamentary financial control in India. 2nd rev. & enl. ed. Bombay: Minerva, 1962. 329p.

G. The Union Judiciary and the Legal System

1. Bibliography

12814 DAS, VEENA. Sociology of law: trend report. In Survey of research in sociology and social anthropology. Bombay: Popular, 1974, v. 2, 367-400. [sponsored by ICSSR]

12815 JAIN, H.C. Indian legal materials: a bibliographic guide. Bombay: N.M. Tripathi, 1970. 123p.

2. General Studies of the Indian Judiciary

12816 CHATURVEDI, R.G. Judiciary under constitution. Allahabad: Law Book Co., 1967. 263p.

12817 GADBOIS, G.H., JR. Indian judicial behavior. In EPW 5,3/4/5 (1970) 149-66.

12818 INDIA (REP.). LAW CMSN. Reform of judicial administration. Delhi: MPGOI, 1958. 2 v., 1282p. [Chm., M.C. Setalvad]

12819 Judges of the Supreme Court and the high courts: as on 1-4-77. Delhi: Min. of Law, Justice and Company Affairs, Dept. of Justice, Govt. of India, 1977. 277p.

12820 SEERVAI, H.M. The position of the judiciary under the Consitution of India. Bombay: U. of Bombay, 1970. 164p.

3. The Supreme Court
a. general studies and reference

12821 AGARWALA, B.R. Practice and procedure of the Supreme Court of India. 3rd ed. Bombay: N.M. Tripathi, 1978. 427p.

12822 AGARWALA, S.K. & S.G. SINGH. Supreme Court on criminal law; twenty-one years Supreme Court criminal digest, 1950-70. Allahabad: Law Book Co., 1971. 1045p.

12823 BAKSHISH SINGH. The Supreme Court of India as an instrument of social justice. ND: Sterling, 1976. 303p.

12824 BAXI, U. The Indian Supreme Court and politics. Lucknow: Eastern Book Co., 1980. 272p.

12825 DHAVAN, R. Justice on trial: the Supreme Court today. Allahabad: Wheeler, 1980. 292p.

12826 ______. The Supreme Court of India: a socio-legal critique of its juristic techniques. Bombay: N.M. Tripathi, 1977. 524p.

12827 ______. The Supreme Court of India and parliamentary sovereignty: a critique of its approach to the recent constitutional crisis. ND: Sterling, 1976. 404p.

12828 GADBOIS, G.H., JR. The Supreme Court of India. In JCPS 4 (1970) 33-54.

12829 HIRSH, H. & G.L. MASON. A system analysis of the Indian Supreme Court. In EPW 6,42/43 (1971) 2201-07.

12830 IMAM, MOHAMMED. The Indian Supreme Court and the Constitution; a study of the process of construction. Lucknow: Eastern Book Co., 1968. 571p.

12832 SATHE, S.P. Supreme court, parliament and constitution. In EPW 6,34 (1971) 1821-28; 6,35 (1971) 1873-80.

12833 SHARMA, A. The Supreme Court of India, as the guardian of fundamental rights. Muzaffarpur: Manisha, 1977. 196p.

12834 SHARMA, S.R. The Supreme Court in the Indian constitution. 2nd rev. ed. Calcutta: S.C. Sarkar, 1972. 2 v. [1st pub. 1958]

b. Justices of the Supreme Court - studies and biographies

12835 ANTULAY, A.R. Appointment of a chief justice; perspectives on judicial independence, rule of law, and political philosophy underlying the Constitution. Bombay: Popular Prakashan, 1973. 243 p. [on 1973 appointment of Ajit Nath Ray]

12836 CHAUDHURI, A.K. Appointment of a Chief Justice - the study of a controversy in a new perspective. In JCPS 11,4 (1977) 1-38.

12837 DHAVAN, R. & A. JACOB. Selection and appointment of Supreme Court judges: a case study. Bombay: N.M. Tripathi, 1978. 125p.

12838 HIDAYUTULLAH, M. A judge's miscellany. Bombay: N.M. Tripathi, 1972. 324p.

12839 KUMARAMANGALAM, S.M. Judicial appointments; an analysis of the recent controversy over the appointment of the Chief Justice of India. ND: Oxford & IBH, 1973. 96p.

12840 MAHAJAN, M.C. Looking back; the autobiography of Mehr Chand Mahajan, former chief justice of India. Bombay: Asia, 1963. 299p.

12841 MAHAJAN, V.D. Chief Justice Gajendragadkar: his life, ideas, papers and addresses. Delhi: S. Chand, 1966. 350p.

12842 ______. Chief Justice K. Subba Rao: defender of liberties. Delhi: S. Chand, 1967. 128p.

12843 ______. Chief Justice Mehr Chand Mahajan; the biography of the great jurist. Lucknow: Eastern Book Co., 1969. 280p.

4. Judicial Review, and Relations of the Judiciary with other Branches

12844 BASU, D.D. Tagore law lectures on limited government and judicial review. Calcutta: S.C. Sarkar, 1972. 575p.

12845 DUGVEKAR, T.G. The problem of separation of judicial from executive functions. In IPSR 3 (1968-69) 31-54.

12846 FAZAL, M.A. Judicial control of administrative action in India and Pakistan: a comparative study of principles and remedies. Oxford: OUP, 1969. 345p.

12847 HIDAYATULLAH, M. Democracy in India and the judicial process. NY: Asia, 1966. 89p.

12848 JHA, C. Judicial review of legislative acts. Bombay: N.M. Tripathi, 1974. 459p.

12849 MARKOSE, A.T. Judicial control of administrative action in India; a study in methods. Madras: Madras Law J. Office, 1956. 752p.

12850 RAY, S.N. Judicial review and fundamental rights. Calcutta: Eastern Law House, 1974. 346p.

5. The Indian Legal System

12851 BEHARI, C. The principles of administration of criminal justice in India. Allahabad: Hind Pub. House, 1968. 282p.

12852 DATTA GUPTA, S. Justice and the political order in India: an inquiry into the institutions and ideologies, 1950-1972. Calcutta: K.P. Bagchi, 1979. 299p.

12853 DERRETT, J.D.M. Essays in classical and modern Hindu law. v. 4, Current problems and the legacy of the past. Leiden: Brill, 1978. 454p.

12854 GALANTER, M. The aborted restoration of "indigenous" law in India. In CSSH 14,1 (1972) 53-70.

12855 ______. Indian law as an indigenous conceptual system. In Items (Social Science Research Council) 32, 3/4 (1978) 42-46.

12856 KHARE, R.S. Indigenous culture & lawyer's law in India. In CSSH 14,1 (1972) 71-96.

12857 KIDDER, R.L. Law and political crisis: an assessment of the Indian legal system's potential role. In AS 16.9 (1976) 879-97.

12858 KRISHNA IYER, V.R. Law and the people; a collection of essays. ND: PPH, 1972. 173p.

12859 MINATTUR, J., ed. The Indian legal system. Bombay: N.M. Tripathi, 1978. 683p.

12860 PATHAK, G.S. Some reflections on the civil revolution in India. Delhi: National, for ICPS, 1972. 75p.

12861 RAINA, S.M.N. Law, judges, and justice. Indore: Vedpal Law House, 1979. 264p.

12862 SETALVAD, M.C. The common law in India. Bombay: N.M. Tripathi, 1970. 251p.

12863 ______. The role of English law in India. London: OUP, 1967. 76p.

12864 SHELAT, N.G. Law, lawyers, and judiciary. Ahmedabad: New Gujarat House, 1972. 128p.

6. The Indian Legal Profession - Studies and Biographies of Lawyers and Judges

12865 CHARI, A.S.R. Trials of strength. Bombay: Orient Longman, 1975. 101p.

12866 GAJENDRAGADKAR, P.B. Law, lawyers, and social change. ND: Natl. Forum of Lawyers and Legal Aid, 1976. 22 + 40p.

12867 GAUBA, K.L. Friends and foes: an autobiography. ND: Indian Book Co., 1974. 296p.

12868 KHANNA, H.R. Liberty, democracy, and ethics. ND: Radha Krishna, 1979. 75p.

12869 KHOSLA, G.D. Memories and opinions. Delhi: Research, 1973. 146p.

12870 ______. A taste of India. Bombay: Jaico, 1970. 200p.

12871 KRISHNASWAMI NAYUDU, W.S. My memoirs. Madras: Krishnaswami Nayudu, 1977. 589p.

12872 Lawyers in developing societies, with particular reference to India: a symposium. In Law and Society R. 3,2 (1968-69) 201-406. [articles by M. Galanter, C. Morrison, S. Schmitthener, et al.]

12873 MATHEW, K.K. K.K. Mathew on democracy, equality, and freedom. Lucknow: Eastern Book Co., 1978. 86 + 364p.

12874 MORRISON, C. Munshis and their masters: the organization of an occupational relationship in the Indian legal system. In JAS 31,2 (1972) 309-28.

12875 SHELAT, N.G. Reminiscences of a judge. Ahmedabad: Gujarat Law Reporter Office, 1970. 282p.

H. The Twenty-two States and the Nine Union Territories [For Individual States and Territories, see Regional Chapters]

1. General Studies of State Government and Administration

12876 INDIA (REP.). ADMIN. REFORMS CMSN. Report on state administration, Nov. 1969. ND: 1970. 155p. [K. Hanumanthaiya, Chm.]

12877 INDIA (REP.). STUDY TEAM ON STATE LEVEL ADMIN. Report, October 1968. Delhi: MPGOI, 1970. 187p. [Team appt. by Admin. Reforms Cmsn.]

12878 MAHESHWARI, S.R. State governments in India. Delhi: Macmillan, 1979. 328p.

12879 MEHTA, B. Dynamics of state administration. Allahabad: Chugh, 1975. 167p.

12880 SHUKLA, J.D State and district administration in India. ND: National, for ICPS, 1976. 387p.

12881 SINGH, J. The administrative reform reports of the states: a content analysis. In IJPA 9 (1963) 491-513.

12882 State Administration in India [special number]. In IJPA 22,3 (1976) 307-618.

2. The Office of the State Governor

12883 DAHIYA, M.S. Office of the governor in India: a critical commentary. Delhi: Sundeep Prakashan, 1979. 324p.

12884 Forum: the role of State Governors in India. In IPSR 2 (1968) 155-222.

12885 GEHLOT, N.S. The office of the governor, its constitutional image and reality. Allahabad: Chugh, 1977. 321p.

12886 NARAIN, IQBAL. The office of the Governor. In J. of African and Asian Studies 1 (1968) 171-82.

12887 [Office of the Governor - special section]. In JCPS 2,4 (1968) 77-184.

12888 SEN, A.K. Role of governors in the emerging pattern of centre-state relations in India. Delhi: National, for ICPS, 1975. 75p.

12889 SINGH, P. Governor's office in independent India. Baidyanath-Deoghar: Navayug Sahitya Mandir, 1968. 269p.

12890 SIWACH, J.R. Office of the Governor: a critical study. Delhi: Sterling, 1977. 292p.

12891 SRI PRAKASA. State governors in India. 2nd rev. and enl. ed. Meerut: Meenakshi, 1975. 131p.

3. The State Legislature and the Chief Minister

12892 FORRESTER, D.B. Indian state ministers and their roles. In AS 10,6 (1970) 472-82.

12893 JAIN, R.B. Comparative legislative behaviour: research explorations in Indian perspective. ND: Uppal, 1980. 137p.

12894 JHA, D. State legislature in India: legislature in the Indian political system. ND: Abhinav, 1977. 347p.

12895 NARASAIAH, P. Social background of state chief ministers. In PSR 18,2 (1979) 121-32.

12896 NARASIMHA RAO, P.V. Change with stability: the chief minister's burden. In B.N. Pandey, ed. Leadership in South Asia. ND: Vikas, 1977, 262-89.

12897 PARANJPE, H.G. Financial committees in state legislatures. In Indian J. of Parliamentary Information 17,1 (1971) 28-43.

4. The High Courts and State Judiciaries

12898 BANERJEE, D.N. Supreme Court on the conflict of jurisdiction between the Legislative Assembly and the High Court of Uttar Pradesh. Calcutta: World Press, 1966. 124p.

12899 [High Courts and subordinate judiciary.] In India (rep.) Law Cmsn., 14th report (reform of judicial admin.) ND: Min. of Law, 1958, v. 1, 64-251.

12900 IMAM, MOHAMMED. Jurisdiction and powers of the High Courts: interpretation of article 226 of the Constitution. In All India Reporter 54 (1967) 6-11.

12901 NAMBYAR, M.K. Article 226 of the Constitution and the Law Commission's questionnaire. In Lawyer 1,4 (1956) 15-21.

12902 [State judiciaries and judicial administrations in 13 states]. In India (Rep.) Law Cmsn., 14th report (reform of judicial admin.) ND: Min. of Law, 1958, v. 2, 926-1221.

12903 VIJIA KUMAR, N. Constitution of India and the High Courts. In Lawyer 4,5 (1972) 68-72.

5. The Union Territories, under Presidentially-Appointed Administrators

12904 INDIA (REP.). ADMIN. REFORMS CMSN. Report on administration of Union Territories and NEFA. Delhi: MPGOI, 1969. 56p.

12905 INDIA (REP.). STUDY TEAM ON ADMIN. OF UNION TERRITORIES AND NEFA. Report. ND: Admin. Reforms Cmsn., 1970. 2 v., 369, 206p. [Chm., R.R. Morarka]

12906 SHARMA, S.K. Union territory administration in India; an analysis of constitutional, administrative, and political trends. Chandigarh: Chandi Pub., 1968. 260p.

6. Inter-governmental Relations in India
a. bibliography and general studies

12907 GARDE, D.K. & M.R. VAKIL. Bibliography of Centre-State relations in India (1952-1967). In JUP 29 (1969) 103-50.

12908 RAY, A. Inter-governmental relations in India; a study of Indian federalism. Bombay: Asia, 1966. 184p.

12909 SHIVIAH. Inter-governmental relations in India. In IJPS 28 (1967) 62-69.

12910 SRINIVASAN, N. Union-state relations; a trend report. In A survey of research in public administration. Bombay: Allied, 1973, v. 1, 92-125. [sponsored by ICSSR]

12911 WADHWA, O.P. Centre-state and inter-state relations in India, 1919-1970: a bibliography. Delhi: Vidya Mandal, 1973. 148p.

b. Centre-State relations

12912 BOMBWALL, K.R., ed. National power and state autonomy. Meerut: Meenakshi, 1977. 219p.

12913 CHANDA, A.K. Federalism in India; a study of union-state relations. London: Allen & Unwin, 1965. 347p.

12914 HAQQI, A.H., ed. Union-state relations in India. Meerut: Meenakshi, 1967. 216p.

12915 INDIA (REP.). ADMIN. REFORMS CMSN. Report on Centre-State relationships. Delhi: MPGOI, 1969. 54p.

12916 INDIA (REP.). STUDY TEAM ON CENTRE-STATE RELATIONSHIPS. Report. Delhi: MPGOI, 1968. 3 v. [Team appt. by Admin. Reforms Cmsn.]

12917 JAIN, S.N. & S.C. KASHYAP & N. SRINIVASAN, eds. The Union and the states. Delhi: National, 1972. 522p.

12918 KASHYAP, S.C., ed. Union-state relations in India. ND: ICPS, 1969. 292p. [pub. as JCPS 3,4]

12919 MAHESHWARI, B.L., ed. Centre-state relations in the seventies. Calcutta: Minerva, 1973. 357p. [1971 seminar, Hyderabad]

12920 NIGAM, K.K. Constitutional law: a study of Indian federalism through cases. Allahabad: Allahabad Law Agency, 1975. 279p.

12921 NOORANI, A.G., ed. Centre-state relations in India; proceedings of a seminar held in Agra, March 1972. Bombay: Leslie Sawhny Programme of Training for Democracy, 1972. 152p.

12922 SANTHANAM, K. Union-state relations in India. Bombay: Asia, 1960. 71p.

12923 SARKAR, S. The centre and the states. Calcutta: Academic Pub., 1972. 239p.

12924 SETALVAD, M.C. Union and state relations under the Indian Constitution. Calcutta: Eastern Law House, 1974. 247p.

c. inter-state relations, incl. boundary and water disputes

12925 ANTULAY, A.R. Mahajan report uncovered. Bombay: Allied, 1968. 192p.

12926 BASHEER HUSSAIN, M. The Cauvery water dispute; an analysis of Mysore's case. Mysore: Rao and Raghavan, 1972. 142p.

12927 CHATURVEDI, B.N. The Godavari Krishna water dispute-a geographic appraisal. In Deccan Geographer 5, 1/2 (1967) 30-58.

12928 HALAPPA, G.S. & R.T. JANGAM. The Mahajan Commission and after; a study of elite response. In JKU(SS) 4 (1968) 9-17.

12929 HART, H.C. New India's rivers. Bombay: Orient Longmans, 1956. 301p.

12930 INDIA (REP.). CMSN. ON MAHARASHTRA-MYSORE-KERALA BOUNDARY DISPUTES. Report. Delhi: Manager of Publications, 1967. 2v. [Chm., Mehr Chand Mahajan]

12931 INDIA (REP.). KRISHNA GODAVARI CMSN. Report. ND: Min. of Irrigation and Power, 1962. 336p. + 37 pl. [Chm., N.D. Gulhati]

12932 JAIN, S.N. & A. JACOB & S.C. JAIN. Interstate water disputes in India; suggestions for reform in law. Bombay: N.M. Tripathi, 1971. 176p. [study for Min. of Irrigation & Power.]

12933 KRISHNASWAMY, S. An approach to interstate river water disputes in India. In IYIA 17 (1974) 373-459.

12934 LINCOLN INST. OF SOCIAL RESEARCH AND PUBLIC OPINION, DHARWAR. RES. UNIT. The moving frontiers of Maharashtra; an objective analysis of the border disputes between Maharashtra & Mysore. Dharwar: 1967. 63p.

12935 MAHARASHTRA. Memorandum on Maharashtra-Mysore border dispute to the Commission on Maharashtra-Mysore-Kerala boundary disputes, 1967. Bombay: 1967. 256p.

12936 MALIK, Y.K. Conflict over Chandigarh: a case study of an interstate dispute in India. In CAS 3 (1973) 51-64.

12937 RAMA RAO, T.S. Inter-state water disputes in the Indian Union. In IYIA 11 (1962) 147-87.

J. Local Government: District, Municipal, Village

1. General Studies

12938 BHARGAVA, B.S. & S. RAMA RAO. Indian local government: a study. Calcutta: Minerva, 1978. 247p.

12939 BHATNAGAR, S. Rural local government in India. ND: Light & Life Publishers, 1978. 278p.

12940 BHOGLE, S.K. Local government and administration in India. Aurangabad: Parimal Prakashan, 1977. 329p.

12941 CHAWLA, V.N. Studies in local self-government in India. Jullundur: Intl. Book Co., 1967. 208p.

12942 DAS, R.B. & D.P. SINGH, eds. Deliberative and executive wings in local government. Lucknow: Inst. of Public Admin., Lucknow U., 1968. 168p.

12943 GUPTA, B.B. Local government in India. Allahabad: Central Book Depot, 1968. 190p.

12944 MAHESHWARI, S.R. Local government in India. ND: Orient Longman, 1971. 392p.

12945 SHARIB, Z.H. Local self-government in relation to development in India and Pakistan. Bombay: All-India Inst. of Local Self-Government, 1962. 124p.

12946 VENKATARANGAIYA, M. & M. PATTABHIRAM, eds. Local government in India; select readings. Bombay: Allied, 1969. 515p.

2. District Administration

12947 DAYAL, ISHWAR & K. MATHUR & M. BHATTACHARYA. District administration: a survey for reorganization. Delhi: Macmillan, 1976. 91p.

12948 DUBHASHI, P.R. The division commissioner in Indian administration. In Intl. R. of Admin. Sciences 43,3 (1977) 255-58.

12949 INDIA (REP.). STUDY TEAM ON DISTRICT ADMIN. February 1967. ND: Admin. Reforms Cmsn., 1968. 169p. [Chm., Takhatmal Jain]

12950 KHERA, S.S. District administration in India. 2nd rev. ed. ND: National, 1979. 359p. [1st pub. 1964]

12951 KOTHARI, S. & R. ROY. Relations between politicians and administrators at the district level. ND: Centre of Applied Politics, 1969. 215p. [study for Admin. Reforms Cmsn.]

12952 KRISHNAMACHARI, V.T. Report on Indian and state administrative services and problems of district administration. ND: Planning Cmsn., 1962. 108p.

12953 MILLER, D.F. Pervasive politics: a study of the Indian district. Melbourne: Dept. of Political Science, U. of Melbourne, 1972. 226p.

12954 PAI PANANDIKAR, V.A. District administration: a trend report. In A survey of research in public administration. Bombay: Allied, 1973, v.1, 177-92. [sponsored by ICSSR]

12955 POTTER, D.C. Government in rural India; an introduction to contemporary district administration. London: London School of Econ. and Political Science, 1964. 91p.

12956 RAI, HARIDWAR. District magistrate and police superintendent in India: the controversy of dual control. In J. of Admin. Overseas 6 (1967) 192-99.

12957 ______. The district officer in India today. In J. of Admin. Overseas 6 (1967) 13-27.

12958 ______. Dual control of law and order administration in India-a study in magistracy and police relationship. In IJPA 13 (1967) 43-64.

12959 ______. Local government, local administration and development: role adaptation of the district officer in India. In IJPA 14 (1968) 89-104.

12960 SHUKLA, J.D. State and district administration in India. ND: National, for IIPA, 1976. 387p.

3. Municipal Administration

12961 ALL INDIA COUNCIL OF MAYORS. Decennial report, 1962-63 to 1971-72. Comp. by Hira Lall. Delhi: 1973. 140p.

12962 ARGAL, R. Municipal government in India. Rev. and enl. 3rd ed. Allahabad: Agarwal Press, 1967. 245p.

12963 ASHRAF, ALI. Government and politics of big cities: an Indian case study. Delhi: Concept, 1977. 201p.

12964 AVASTHI, A., ed. Municipal administration in India. Agra: L.N. Agarwal, 1972. 539p.

12965 BHARDWAJ, R.K. The municipal administration in India; a sociological analysis of rural and urban India. Delhi: Sterling, 1970. 296p.

12966 BHATTACHARYA, M. Essays in urban government. Calcutta: World Press, 1970. 170p.

12967 ______. Management of urban government in India. ND: Uppal Book Store, 1976. 216p.

12968 ______. Municipal government: problems and prospects. Delhi, Research, 1974. 124p.

12969 ______. State directorates of municipal administration. ND: Centre for Training & Res. in Municipal Admin., IIPA, 1969. 113p.

12970 ______. State-municipal relations; a functional analysis. ND: Centre for Training and Res. in Municipal Admin., IIPA, 1972. 61p.

12971 BOSE, A. Administration of urban areas: a trend report. In A survey of research in public administration. Bombay: Allied, 1973, v.1, 193-248. [sponsored by ICSSR]

12972 Cabinet system in municipal government; proceedings of the seminar, September 15-15, 1969, New Delhi. ND: Centre for Training & Res. in Municipal Admin., IIPA, 1970. 84p.

12973 DAS, R.B., ed. Conference on the role of local authorities in urban planning, Lucknow University, 1968. Urban planning and local authorities. Lucknow: Regional Centre for Res. & Training in Municipal Admin., Lucknow U., 1970. 137p.

12974 DATTA, A. Urban government, finance, and development. Calcutta: World Press, 1970. 174p.

12975 Growing cities and priorities: proceedings of the seminar on January 31, 1972, Bombay-1. Bombay: AIILSG, 1972. 92p.

12976 KHANNA, R.L. Municipal government and administration in India. Chandigarh, Mohindra Capital Pub., 1967. 212p.

12977 SHAH, R.M. Municipal election laws in India. Bombay: AIILSG, 1976. 948p.

12978 SHARMA, S.K. & V.N. CHAWLA. Municipal administration in India: some reflections. Jullundur: Intl. Book Co., 1975. 439p.

12979 State machinery for municipal supervision; proceedings of the seminar, May 7 to 8, 1970, New Delhi. ND: Centre for Training & Res. in Municipal Admin., IIPA, 1971. 58p.

4. Panchayati Raj: Democratic Decentralisation for Self-government and Community Development

a. bibliography and reference

12980 INDIA (REP.). DEPT. OF RURAL DEV. ADMIN. INTELLIGENCE DIV. Panchayati raj at a glance; statistics. ND: 1973/74-. [annual]

12981 A select bibliography on panchayati raj, planning and democracy. Jaipur: U. of Rajasthan Library, 1964. 70p.

b. reports from the Government and the Indian National Congress

12982 BHARGAVA, B.S. Panchayati raj institutions: an analysis of issues, problems, and recommendations of Asoka Mehta Committee. ND: Ashish, 1979. 79p.

12983 INDIA (REP.). CMTEE. ON PANCHAYATI RAJ INSTITUTIONS. Report. ND: Min. of Agri. and Irrigation, 1978. 301p. [Asoka Mehta, Chm.]

12984 INDIA (REP.). DEPT. OF COMMUNITY DEV. Panchayati raj; a comparative study on legislations. ND: Min. of Comm. Dev. and Coop., 1962. 37p.

12985 INDIAN NATL. CONGRESS. VILLAGE PANCHAYAT CMTEE. Report. ND: AICC, 1954. 60 + 80p.

12986 MAHESHWARI, S.R. New perspectives on rural local government in India: The Asoka Mehta Committee report. In AS 19, 11 (1979) 1110-15.

12987 MALAVIYA, H.D. Village panchayats in India. ND: AICC, 1956. 843p.

12988 SHUKLA, K.B. Panchayati raj revisited. In IJPA 24, 4 (1978) 1159-76. [on Asoka Mehta Cmtee.]

c. general studies of gram panchayats ("village councils") and Panchayati Raj

12989 ASSN. OF VOLUNTARY AGENCIES FOR RURAL DEV. Panchayati raj as the basis of Indian polity; an exploration into the proceedings of the Constituent Assembly. ND: AVARD, 1962. 80p.

12990 Case studies in panchayati raj. ND: IIPA, 1972. 161p.

12991 DAYAL, R. Panchayati raj in India. Delhi: Metropolitan, 1970. 315p.

12992 DUBEY, S.N. & R. MURDIA. Structure and process of decision-making in panchayati raj institutions. Bombay: Somaiya, 1976. 166p.

12993 HALDIPUR, R.M. & V.R.K. PARAMAHAMSA, eds. Local government institutions in rural India: some aspects; proceedings of the Seminar on Panchayati Raj held at the NICD, Hyderabad, 13-16 October 1969. Hyderabad: NICD, 1970. 346p.

12994 JACOB, G., comp. Readings on panchayati raj. Hyderabad: NICD, 1967. 166p.

12995 KHAN, ILTIJA. Government in rural India. Calcutta: Asia Pub. Co., 1971. 185p.

12996 KHANNA, R.L. Panchayati raj in India. Ambala Cantt.: English Book Depot, 1972. 231p.

12997 KIHLBERG, M. The panchayati raj of India: debate in a developing country. ND: Young Asia Pub., 1976. 123p.

12998 MADDICK, H. Panchayati raj: a study of rural local government in India. London: Longman Group, 1970. 402p.

12999 MATHUR, M.V. & IQBAL NARAIN, eds. Panchayati raj, planning, and democracy. Bombay: Asia, 1969. 530p. [1964 seminar papers]

13000 NARAIN, IQBAL, et al. Panchayati raj administration: old controls and new challenges. ND: IIPA, 1970. 222p.

13001 [Panchayati raj special number] In IJPA 8 (1962) 443-528.

13002 PRASAD, R.C. Democracy and development; the grass-roots experience in India. ND: Rachna Prakashan, 1971. 336p.

13003 RAM REDDY, G., ed. Patterns of panchayati raj in India. Delhi: Macmillan, 1977. 312p.

13004 RAMAN RAO, A.V. Structure and working of village panchayats; a survey based on case studies in Bombay & Madras. Poona: GIPE, 1954. 218p. [Its pub., 58]

d. nyaya panchayats ("judicial councils"): village-level courts

13005 INDIA (REP.). STUDY TEAM ON NYAYA PANCHAYATS. Report. Delhi: Min. of Law, Govt. of India, 1962. 226p.

13006 [Panchayats] In India (Rep.). Law Cmsn., 14th Report. (Reform of Judicial Admin.) ND: Min. of Law, 1958, v.2, 874-925.

III. The Indian Political Process, 1947- : Parties, Elections, Leaders

A. Bibliography and Reference

13007 BAVISKAR, B.S. Sociology of politics: a trend report. In A survey of research in sociology and social anthropology. Bombay: Popular, 1974, v.2, 431-507. [sponsored by ICSSR]

13008 A select bibliography on electoral and party behaviour in India. Jaipur: U. of Rajasthan Library, 1966. 159p.

B. General Studies

1. General History of Indian Politics since Independence

13009 AIYAR, S.P. & R. SRINIVASAN, eds. Studies in Indian democracy. Bombay: Allied, 1965. 779p.

13010 APPADORAI, A. Essays in Indian politics and foreign policy. Delhi: Vikas, 1971. 252p.

13011 ______. India: studies in social and political development, 1947-1967. Bombay: Asia, 1968. 342p.

13012 BHARDWAJ, R.K. Democracy in India. ND: National, 1980. 346p.

13013 BHATIA, K. The ordeal of nationhood; a social study of Indian since independence, 1947-1970. NY: Atheneum, 1971. 390p.

13014 BOMBWALL, K.R. & L.P. CHOUDHRY. Aspects of democratic government and politics in India; presented to Dr. B.M. Sharma, retired professor of political science, Lucknow University, on his seventieth birthday. Delhi: Atma Ram, 1968. 631p.

13015 CHAKRABARTI, A., comp. India since 1947. Bombay: Allied, 1967. 487p.

13016 CHANDA, A.K. Under the Indian sky. Bombay: Nachiketa, 1971. 232p.

13017 CHOPRA, PRAN. Uncertain India: a political profile of two decades of freedom. Cambridge: MIT Press, 1971. 402p. [Rpt. of 1968 ed.]

13018 DAS, B.C. Political development in India. ND: Ashish, 1978. 392p.

13019 DESAI, A.R. Recent trends in Indian nationalism. Supplement to Social background of Indian nationalism. Bombay: Popular Book Depot, 1960. xii, 149p.

13020 DEY, S.K. Power to the people? a chronicle of

India, 1947-67. Bombay: Orient Longmans, 1969. 338p.

13021 DUNBAR, W. India in transition. Beverly Hills, CA: Sage Pub., 1976. 80p.

13022 JAIN, B.S. The ordeals India has been through. ND: Trimurti, 1978. 300p.

13023 KAMAL, K.L. & R.C. MEYER. Democratic politics in India. ND: Vikas, 1977. 288p.

13024 KARUNAKARAN, K.P. Democracy in India. ND: Intellectual Book Corner, 1978. 256p.

13025 KOTHARI, R. Politics in India. Boston: Little, Brown, 1970. 461p.

13026 MOHAN, K.T.J. Independence to Indira and after. 4th ed. ND: S. Chand, 1977. 190p.

13027 MORAES, F.R. Witness to an era; India 1920 to the present day. NY: Holt, Rinehart and Winston, 1974. 332p.

13028 MORRIS-JONES, W.H. Politics mainly Indian. Bombay: Orient Longman, 1978. 392p.

13029 MURTHI, V.K. In the larger personal interest: an investigation into Indian politics since 1947. ND: Allora Pub., 1978. 206p.

13030 NARAIN, IQBAL. Twilight or dawn; the political change in India, 1967-71. Agra: S.L. Agarwala, 1972. 244p.

13031 NIMBKAR, K. A political dissenter's diary, 1970-1978. Pune: Intl. Book Service, 1978-79. 2 v.

13032 PARK, R.L., ed. Change and persistence of tradition in India: five lectures. Ann Arbor: UMCSSAS, 1971. 85p. [Its Papers, 2]

13033 SHRIMALI, K.L. The prospects for democracy in India. Carbondale, IL: Southern Illinois U. Press, 1970. 142p.

13034 SINGH, L.P. Political development or political decay in India? In PA 44,1 (1971) 65-80.

13035 THARYAN, P. India: the critical decade after Nehru. ND: Sterling, 1974. 212p.

13036 YUNUS, M. Persons, passions and politics. ND: Vikas, 1980. 333p. + 14 pl.

2. Politics and Society

a. general studies of political culture and participation

13037 BHASKARAN, R. Sociology of politics: tradition and politics in India. Bombay: Asia, 1967. 282p.

13038 BONDURANT, J.V. & M.W. FISHER. Ethics in action: contrasting approaches to social and political problems in modern India. In Australian J. of Politics and History 12 (1966) 177-93.

13039 CRANE, R.I., ed. Aspects of political mobilization in South Asia. Syracuse: Maxwell School of Citizenship and Public Affairs, Syracuse U., 1976. 159p. (Foreign and comp. studies; South Asian series, 1)

13040 ELDERSVELD, S.J. & BASHIRUDDIN AHMED. Citizens and politics; mass political behavior in India. Chicago: UChiP, 1978. 351p.

13041 FADIA, B. Pressure groups in Indian politics. ND: Radiant, 1980. 295p.

13042 GUPTA, S.K. Citizen in the making: socialization for the citizenship role in a democratic society. Delhi: National, 1975. 302p.

13043 GUSFIELD, J.R. Political community and group interests in modern India. In PA 38 (1965) 123-41.

13044 JOHN, V.V. & C. KULSHRESTHA. Not by politics alone!: the non-political roots of a free society. ND: Arnold-Heinemann, 1978. 72p.

13045 KHARE, B.B. India, political attitudes and social change. ND: Light & Life, 1974. 264p.

13046 KURIAN, K.M. India - state and society; a Marxian approach. Bombay: Orient Longman, 1975. 308p.

13047 LAKSHMANA RAO, G. Internal migration and political change in India: a study based on the analysis of aggregate socio-economic and demographic data and election statistics of 88 traditional cities and 22 modern cities all over India combined with a sample survey of one modern city and one traditional city in central India. ND: National, 1977. 212p.

13048 MORRIS-JONES, W.H. India's political idioms. In C.H. Philips, ed. Politics and society in India. London: Allen & Unwin, 1963, 133-54.

13049 MUKHOPADHYAY, A.K., ed. Society and politics in contemporary India. Calcutta: Council for Political Studies, 1974. 239p.

13050 NANDY, A. The culture of Indian politics: a stock taking. In JAS 30,1 (1970) 57-80.

13051 ______. The making and unmaking of political cultures in India. In Daedalus 102,1 (1973) 115-37.

13052 PHILIPS, C.H., ed. Politics and society in India. London: Allen & Unwin, 1963. 190p.

13053 RUDOLPH, S.H. Consensus and conflict in Indian politics. In World Politics 13,4 (1961) 385-99.

13054 SHAKIR, MOIN. Politics of minorities: some perspectives. Delhi: Ajanta, 1980. 172p.

13055 SOOD, P. Politics of socio-economic change in India. ND: Marwah, 1979. 255p.

13056 SURI, S. Politics and society in India. Calcutta Naya Prokash, 1974. 338p.

13057 VANDERBOK, W. Political culture and development: some pervasive themes in the study of Indian politics. In MAS 12,1 (1978) 145-55.

13058 WEINER, M. India: two political cultures. In L.W Pye & S. Verba, eds. Political culture and political development. Princeton: PUP, 1965, 199-244.

13059 ______. The politics of scarcity; public pressure and political response in India. Chicago: UChiP, 1962. 251p.

b. political elites and leadership

13060 ARORA, S.K. & H.C. LASSWELL. Political communication; the public language of political elites in India and the United States. NY: Holt, Rinehart and Winston, 1969. 312p.

13061 BHATT, A.H. Caste, class, and politics: an empirical profile of social stratification in modern India. Delhi: Manohar, 1975. 224p.

13062 BRECHER, M. Political leadership in India: an analysis of elite attitudes. NY: Praeger, 1968. 195p. (McGill U. studies in development, 2)

13063 DE SOUZA, A., ed. The politics of change and leadership development: the new leaders in India and Africa. ND: Manohar, 1978. 290p.

13064 ______. Some social and economic determinants of leadership in India. In SA 26,4 (1976) 329-50.

13065 NICHOLSON, N.K. India's modernizing faction and the mobilization of power. In Intl. J. of Comp. Sociology 9 (1968) 302-17.

13066 PANDEY, B.N., ed. Leadership in South Asia. ND: Vikas, 1977. 731p.

13067 PARK, R.L., ed. Leadership and political institutions in India. Princeton: PUP, 1959. 469p.

13068 SHILS, E.A. Rulers and intellectuals: some genera observations and some particular references to India. In G. Wijeyewardene, ed. Leadership and authority. Singapore: U. of Malaya Press, 1968, 309-21.

13069 SRIVASTAVA, H.C. Dysfunctional para-politics and elite action in India. Varanasi: Bharatiya Vidya Prakashan, 1967. 132p.

13070 VAJPEYI, D.A. Conceptual analysis of opinion leadership, opinion leaders and elites. In IJPS 31,2 (1970) 138-52.

13071 VIDYARTHI, L.P., comp. Leadership in India. Bombay: Asia, 1967. 375p.

c. caste and Indian politics

13072 AHMED, BASHIRUDDIN. Caste and electoral politics. In AS 10,11 (1970) 979-92.

13073 BHATT, ANIL. Caste, class and politics: an empirical profile of social stratification in India. In PSR 13 (1974) 363-93.

13074 DUSHKIN, L. Scheduled caste politics. In J.M. Mahar, ed. The Untouchables in contemporary India. Tucson: U. of Arizona Press, 1972, 165-26.

13075 FURER-HAIMENDORF, C. VON. Caste and politics in South Asia. In C.H. Philips, ed. Politics and society in India. London: Allen & Unwin, 1963, 52-70.

13076 KOTHARI, R. Caste in Indian politics. ND: Orient Longman, 1970. 380p.

13077 LYNCH, O. The politics of untouchability. NY: ColUP, 1969. 251p.

13078 MATHUR, P.C. Levels and limits of casteism in Indian politics. In IJPS 32,2 (1971) 195-212.

13079 RUDOLPH, L.I. The modernity of tradition: the democratic incarnation of caste in India. In American Political Science Review 59 (1965) 975-89.

13080 RUDOLPH, L.I. & S.H. RUDOLPH. The political role of India's caste associations. In PA 33 (1960) 1-22.

13081 SHETH, D.L. Caste and politics: a survey of literature. In Gopal Krishna, ed. Contributions to South Asian Studies 1. Delhi: OUP, 1979, 161-97.

13082 VERBA, S. & BASHIRUDDIN AHMED & ANIL BHATT. Caste, race and politics: a comparative study of India and the United States. Beverly Hills: Sage Pub., 1971. 279p.

d. political protest and violence
i. general

13083 AIYAR, S.P., comp. The politics of mass violence in India. Bombay: Manaktalas, 1967. 164p.

13084 ARORA, S. Political participation: deprivation and protest. In EPW 6,3/4/5 (1971) 341-50.

13085 BAYLEY, D.H. Public protest and the political process in India. In PA 42 (1969) 5-16.

13086 ______. Violent public protest in India: 1900-1960. In IJPS 24 (1963) 309-25.

13087 CHANDRA SHEKHAR. Social protest in the Indian political system. ND: Yuva Bharati Trust, 1975. 24p.

13088 DHANGARE, D.N. Urban-rural differentials in election violence. In PSR 7 (1968) 747-59.

13089 INDIA (REP.). CMSN. OF INQUIRY ON COMMUNAL DISTURBANCES. Report. ND: 1969. 2 v. [Chm., Raghubir Dayal]

13090 PRACHAND, S.L.M. Mob violence in India. Chandigarh: Abhishek Publications, 1979. 144p.

13091 WEINER, M. Urbanization and political protest. In Civilisations 17 (1967) 44-52.

13092 WOOD, J.R. Extra-parliamentary opposition in India: an analysis of populist agitations in Gujarat and Bihar. In PA 48,2 (1975) 313-34.

ii. student political unrest

13093 ALTBACH, P.G. The transformation of the Indian student movement. In AS 6 (1966) 448-60.

13094 ______., ed. The student revolution: a global analysis. Bombay: Lalvani, 1970. 408p.

13095 ______., ed. Turmoil and transition; higher education and student politics in India. NY: Basic Books, 1969. 277p.

13096 COPLEY, A. Student protest: a sense of life's demands. In SAR 7,4 (1974) 291-306.

13097 EAKIN, T.C. Students and politics: a comparative study. Bombay: Popular, 1972. 222p.

13098 KATZ, A.N. Changing student perceptions of the Indian government. In AS 17,3 (1977) 264-74. [Survey of Indian students in U.S.]

13099 MANSUKHANI, G.S., ed. Student power in India. ND: Oxford & IBH Pub. Co., 1975. 110p.

13100 OOMMEN, T.K. Student power in India: a political analysis. In PSR 14,1/2 (1975) 10-38.

13101 RUDOLPH, L.I. & S.H. RUDOLPH & KARUNA AHMED. Student politics and national politics in India. In J. Di Bona, ed. The context of education in Indian development. Durham, NC: DUPCSSA, 1974. 203p. (Its monograph & occ. papers series, 13) [1st pub. in EPW 6,30/32 (1971) 1655-68]

13102 SARDESAI, S.G. Student upsurge and Indian revolution. ND: All India Youth Federation, 1974. 30p.

13103 SHAH, B.V. Students' unrest - a sociological hypothesis. In SB 17 (1968) 55-64.

13104 SINGHAL, S. Academic leadership and student unrest. ND: Newman Group, 1977. 208p.

3. Journalistic Accounts of Indian Politics

13105 HIRO, DILIP. Inside India today. London: Routledge & K. Paul, 1976. 331p.

13106 KHUSHWANT SINGH. Good people, bad people. Ed. by Rahul Singh. ND: Orient Paperbacks, 1977. 191p.

13107 MIRCHANDANI, G.G., ed. Reporting India. ND: Abhinav Pub., 1975. 340p.

13108 MORAES, F.R. India today. NY: Macmillan, 1960. 248p.

13109 ______. Without fear or favour; a selection of articles. Ed. by R.C. Cooper. Delhi: Vikas, 1974. 155p.

13110 NAYAR, KULDIP. Between the lines. Bombay: Allied, 1969. 231p.

13111 ______. India, the critical years. Delhi: Vikas, 1971. 280p.

13112 PURI, RAJINDER. India, the wasted years: 1969-1975. ND: Chetana, 1975. 240p.

13113 SAHNI, J.N. The lid off; fifty years of Indian politics, 1921-1971. Bombay: Allied, 1971. 529p.

4. Political Cartoons and Satire

13114 ABU ABRAHAM. The games of emergency: a collection of cartoons and articles. ND: Vikas, 1977. 132p.

13115 LAXMAN, R.K. You said it. 5th series. Bombay: IBH, 1975. 100p.

13116 MIRANDA, M. & RAJAN NARAYAN. Elections Indian style. Bombay: Jaico, 1980. 69p.

13117 PILLAI, K.S., ed. Shankar's weekly souvenir. ND: Shankar's weekly, 1975. 255p.

13118 RAGHU RAM, N.V. Games bureaucrats play. Ill. by Abu. ND: Vikas, 1978. 77p.

13119 RAO, AMIYA & B.G. RAO, ed. A report to the nation, July, 1969 - June, 1970. ND: Orient Longman, 1971. 1 v.

13120 Shankar, his cartoons, and his weekly. Ed. by S. Dewan. ND: Dewan, 1979. 31p.

13121 SINHA, R. Three jeers for bureaucracy. ND: Sangam Books, 1978. 116p.

13122 SUNDARARAJAN, P. The coffee break: satirical musings on Indian attitudes to life. Madras: Bikram Pub., 1975. 56p.

13123 UNNI, K.P.K. Sparks: a pack of socio-politico-satirical pieces. Nagercoil: Krishna Press, 1976. 150p.

C. Political Parties, Movements, and Ideologies

1. Bibliography and Reference

13124 Indian political parties: select bibliography. In JCPS 6,4 (1972) 103-39.

13125 SHARMA, J.S. Indian socialism: a descriptive bibliography. Delhi: Vikas, 1975. 349p.

2. General Studies of the Party System - at the All-India Level
a. the working of the party system

13126 BHATTACHARJEE, K.S. The party system in India: one-party dominance. In IPSR 9,2 (1975) 189-202.

13127 CENTER FOR THE STUDY OF DEVELOPING SOCIETIES. Party system and election studies. Bombay: Allied, 1967. 294p. (Its occ. papers, 1)

13128 DAVEY, H. Polarization and consensus in Indian party politics. In AS 12,8 (1972) 701-16.

13129 GRAVES, D.R. Political mobilization in India: the first party system. In AS 16,9 (1976) 864-78.

13130 HARTMANN, H. Political parties in India. 2nd ed. Meerut: Meenakshi, 1980. 320p. [1st pub. 1971]

13131 INDIA (REP.). CMTEE ON DEFECTIONS. Report of the Committee; report of the lawyers-group and explanatory/dissenting notes by members. ND: Min. of Home Affairs, 1969. 54p. [Chm., Y.B. Chavan]

13132 JHA, P. Political representation in India. Meerut: Meenakshi, 1976. 203p.

13133 KASHYAP, S.C., ed. Indian parties and politics. ND: ICPS, 1972. 171p. [1st pub. in JCPS 6,1 (1972) 1-171]

13134 KOTHARI, R. Continuity and change in India's party system. In AS 10,11 (1970) 937-48.

13135 MITAL, N.S. Crisis of political parties in India. In JCPS 6,1 (1972) 82-100.

13136 SADASIVAN, S.N. Party and democracy in India. ND: Tata McGraw-Hill, 1977. 537p.

13137 SHETH, D.L., ed. Citizens and parties: aspects of competitive politics in India. Bombay: Allied, 1975. 205p.

13138 STERN, R.W. The process of opposition in India; two case studies of how policy shapes politics. Chicago: UChiP, 1970. 173p.

13139 WEINER, M. Party politics in India.... Port Washington, NY: Kennikat, 1972. 319p. [Rpt. 1957 ed.]

13140 ______. Traditional role performance and the development of modern political parties: the Indian case. In J. of Politics 26 (1964) 830-49.

b. party ideologies - general and comparative studies

13141 BHATKAL, R.G., ed. Political alternatives in India. Bombay: Popular, 1967. 443p.

13142 GHOSE, S. Political ideas and movements in India. Bombay: Allied Pub., 1975. 558p.

13143 ______. Socialism and communism in India. Bombay: Allied, 1971. 468p.

13144 GOEL, M.L. Social bases of party support and political participation in India. (Social bases of Indian political parties). In PSR 13,1/4 (1974) 59-88.

13145 JHANGIANI, M.A. Jana Sangh and Swatantra; a profile of the rightist parties in India. Bombay: Manaktalas, 1967. 223p.

13146 KASHYAP, S.C., ed. Indian political parties: programmes, promises, and performances. Delhi: Research, for ICPS, 1971. 356p. [1st pub. in JCPS 5,4 (1971) 377-732]

13147 ROLNICK, P.L. Political ideology: reality and myth in India. In AS 2 (1962) 19-32.

13148 SHIV LAL. National parties of India. ND: Election Archives, 1971. 240p.

13149 ______. National parties of India. Rev. and enl. ed. ND: Election Archives, 1972. 252p.

13150 SINHA, SACHCHIDANANDA. The permanent crisis in India: after Janata what? ND: Heritage, 1978. 145p.

3. The Indian National Congress (Est. 1885) after Independence
a. general studies of the Congress Party

13151 GHOSE, S. Indian National Congress, its history and heritage.... ND: AICC, 1975. 390p.

13152 KOCHANEK, S.A. The Congress party of India; the dynamics of one-party democracy. Princeton: PUP, 1968. 516p.

13153 MISHRA, R.S. The Congress in power. Patna: Jnanada Prakashan, 1976. 275p.

13154 MORRIS-JONES, W.H. The Indian Congress Party: a dilemma of dominance. In MAS 1 (1967) 109-32.

13155 NAMBOODIRIPAD, E.M.S. India under Congress rule. Calcutta: National Book Agency, 1967. 229p.

13156 RASTOGI, S.K. The Congress crucible: role of Indian National Congress in Indian politics, 1966-1980. Meerut: Anu, 1980. 426p.

13157 ROY, R. Factionalism and "stratarchy": the experience of the Congress Party. In AS 7 (1967) 896-908.

13158 WEINER, M. Party building in a new nation; the Indian National Congress. Chicago: UChiP, 1967. 509p.

b. INC organization

13159 Constitution of the Indian National Congress. ND: AICC, 1965. 28p.

13160 Forum: relationship between the organisational and Parliamentary wings of the Congress party. In IPSR 4 (1970) 265-96.

13161 FRANDA, M.F. The organizational development of India's Congress party. In PA 35 (1962) 248-60.

13162 RAJMUKAR, N.V. Development of the Congress constitution. ND: AICC, 1949. 147p.

13163 RAMANA RAO, M.V. The development of the Congress constitution. ND: AICC, 1958. 242p.

c. Congress programme and ideology: "a socialistic pattern of society"

13164 INDIAN NATL. CONGRESS. ALL INDIA CONGRESS CMTEE. Resolutions on economic policy, programme and allied matters, 1924-1969. ND: AICC, 1969. 190p.

13165 KOCHANEK, S.A. Political recruitment in the Indian National Congress: the fourth general election. In AS 7 (1967) 292-304.

13166 MAHAJAN, V.S. Socialistic pattern in India: an assessment. ND: S. Chand, 1974. 151p.

13167 MALAVIYA, H.D. Socialist ideology of Congress; a study in its evolution. ND: Socialist Congressman, 1966. 74p.

13168 SEN, MOHIT. Congress socialism: appraisal and appeal. ND: CPI, 1976. 51p.

13169 SHRIMAN NARAYAN. A plea for ideological clarity. ND: INC, 1957. 92p.

13170 ______. Socialist pattern of society. 3rd rev. & enl. ed. ND: INC, 1957. 57p.

4. Socialism and the Socialist Parties: Successors to the Congress Socialist Party after 1948
a. general studies of socialism in India

13171 ADVANI, B.T. Influence of socialism on policies, legislation, and administration of India since independence, 1947-'62. ND: Sterling, 1975. 195p.

13172 APPADORAI, A. Recent socialist thought in India. In R. of Politics 30 (1968) 349-62.

13173 BANERJEE, M. Democratic socialism. Calcutta: Katyayani, 1968. 238p.

13174 BHASIN, P. Socialism in India. ND: Young Asia Pub., 1968. 269p.

13175 FISHER, M.W. & J.V. BONDURANT. Indian approaches to a socialist society. Berkeley: Inst. of Intl.

Studies, U. of California, 1956. 105p. (Indian press digests, monograph series, 2)

13176 NANDA, B.R., comp. Socialism in India. Delhi: Vikas, 1972. 299p.

13177 NARENDRA DEVA, Acarya. Towards socialist society. Ed. by Brahmanand. ND: Centre of Applied Politics, 1979. 476p.

13178 SAMPURNANAND. Indian socialism. NY: Asia, 1961. 131p.

b. the Socialist Parties

13179 FERNANDES, G. What ails the Socialists? ND: New Society, 1972. 112p.

13180 FICKETT, L.P. The major socialist parties of India: a study in leftist fragmentation. Syracuse: Maxwell School of Citizenship and Public Affairs, Syracuse U., 1976. 185p.

13181 The merger; how and why. Bombay: Praja Socialist Pub., 1952. 47p.

13182 PRAJA SOCIALIST PARTY. [Reports of the 1st, 2nd and 3rd national conference.] ND: 1953-56. 3 v. 211, 247, 240p.

13183 SCHOENFELD, B.N. The birth of India's Samyukta Socialist Party. In PA 38 (1965/66) 245-68.

13184 SINGH, H.K. A history of the Praja Socialist Party. Lucknow: Narendra Prakashan, 1959. 239p.

13185 SINHA, PHULGENDA. The Praja Socialist Party of India. Diss., American U., 1968. 444p. [UM 68-14,624]

c. Socialist leaders - biographies, studies, and writings
i. Rammanohar Lohia (1910-1967)

13186 ARUMUGAM, M. Socialist thought in India; the contribution of Rammanohar Lohia. ND: Sterling, 1978. 166p.

13187 LOHIA, RAMMANOHAR. Interval during politics. Hyderabad: Navahind, 1965. 197p.

13188 ______. Marx, Gandhi and socialism. Hyderabad: Navahind, 1963. 550p.

13189 MEHROTRA, N.C. Lohia: a study. Delhi: Atma Ram, 1978. 254p.

13190 SHARAD, ONKAR. Lohia. Lucknow: Prakashan Kendra, 1972. 312p.

13191 VARMA, R.K. Lohia. Allahabad: Rashmi Prakashan, 1969. 109p.

ii. other socialist leaders

13192 JOSHI, S.M. Socialist's quest for the right path. Bombay: Sindhu, 1971. 187p.

13193 MEHTA, A. Democratic socialism. Hyderabad: Chetana Prakashan, 1954. 208p.

13194 ______. Reflections on socialist era. ND: S. Chand, 1977. 497p.

13195 ______. Socialism and peasantry. Bombay: Socialist Party, 1953. 88p.

13196 ______. Studies in Asian socialism. Bombay: BVB, 1959. 241p.

13197 NARAIN, DHIRENDRA & S.H. DESHPANDE, eds. Remembering G.D. Parikh. Bombay: Centre for the Study of Social Change, Mumbai Marathi Grantha Sangrahalaya, 1979. 371p.

5. The Communist Parties of India after Independence
a. general studies of Indian Communism

13198 ALTBACH, P.G. The two Indian communist parties. In Government & Opposition 2 (1967) 289-95.

13199 BALARAM, N.E. A short history of the Communist Party of India. Trivandrum: Prabhath Book House, 1967. 72p.

13200 CHATTOPADHYAY, G. Abani Mukherji, a dauntless revolutionary and pioneering Communist. ND: PPH, 1976. 56p.

13201 DANGE, S.A. When communists differ. Bombay: Indian Inst. of Socialist Studies, 1970. 96p.

13202 Immortal heroes: lives of Communist leaders. ND: CPI, 1975. 165p.

13203 KAUTSKY, J.H. Moscow and the Communist Party of India. NY: MIT Press & J. Wiley, 1956. 220p.

13204 LOOMIS, C.P. & J. RYTINA. Marxist theory and Indian Communism; a sociological interpretation. East Lansing: Michigan State U. Press, 1970. 148p.

13205 MASANI, M.R. The Communist Party of India; a short history. With an introduction by G. Wint and an appendix by V.B. Karnik. Bombay: BVB, 1967. 265p. [1st pub. 1954]

13206 NIZAMI, T.A. The divided left. Allahabad: P.C. Dwadash Shreni, 1971. 132p.

13207 OVERSTREET, G.D. & M. WINDMILLER. Communism in India. 2nd ed. Bombay: Perennial Press, 1960. 603p. [1st ed. 1959]

13208 PANIKKAR, K.N., ed. Prospects of left unity: proceedings of K. Damodaran Memorial Seminar. ND: Envee Pub., 1979. 143p.

13209 RAM, M. Indian communism. Split within a split. Delhi: Vikas, 1969. 293p.

13210 RAY, H. Peking and the Indian Communist movement. In IAF 3,1 (1972) 64-74.

13211 RAY, S. Communism in India: ideological and tactical differences among four parties. In Studies in Comp. Communism 5,2/3 (1972) 163-233.

13212 RETZLAFF, R.H. Revisionists and sectarians: India's two Communist Parties. In R.A. Scalapino, ed. The Communist revolution in Asia. 2nd ed. Englewood Cliffs, NJ: Prentice-Hall, 1969, 329-61. [1st pub. as Revisionism and dogmatism, in 1st ed., 1965]

13213 ROTHERMUND, I. Die Spaltung der Kommunistischen Partei Indiens: Ursachen und Folgen. Wiesbaden: Harrassowitz, 1969. 109p.

13214 SEN GUPTA, B. Communism in Indian politics. NY: ColUP, 1972. 455p.

13215 SHARMA, T.R. Electoral imperatives in the Indian Communist Party split. In MAS 10,3 (1976) 349-60.

13216 WOOD, J.B. Observations on the Indian Communist Party split. In PA 38 (1965) 47-63.

13217 ZAGORIA, D.S. The social bases of Indian communism. In R. Lowenthal, ed. Issues in the future of Asia.... NY: Praeger, 1969, 97-124.

b. the Communist Party of India (CPI, est. 1925): Soviet-oriented, ally of Congress since 1970

13218 FIC, V.M. Peaceful transition to communism in India; strategy of the Communist Party. Bombay: Nachiketa Pub., 1969. 478p.

13219 JOSHI, P.C., ed. Balraj Sahni: an intimate portrait. Delhi: Vikas, 1974. 132p.

13220 RAJSEKHAR REDDY, N. What is CIP's programme? ND: CPI, 1975. 31p.

13221 SARDESAI, S.G. India's path to socialism. ND: CPI, 1966. 53p.

13222 STERN, R.W. The Sino-Indian border controversy and the Communist Party of India. In J. of Politics 27 (1965) 66-86.

c. the CPI(M): Peking-oriented up to 1964 split, later independent

13223 ADHIKARI, G.M. Communist Party and India's path to national regeneration and socialism; a review and comment on Comrade E.M.S. Namboodiripad's Revisionism & dogmatism in the Communist Party of India. ND: CPI, 1964. 204p.

13224 COMMUNIST PARTY OF INDIA (MARXIST). Political resolution adopted by the eighth congress, Cochin, December 23-29, 1968. Calcutta: 1968. 53p.

13225 COMMUNIST PARTY OF INDIA (MARXIST). CENTRAL CMTEE. The new situation and the new tasks confronting our party; report of the Central Committee - adopted at its session in Calcutta from April 10 to 16, 1967. Calcutta: dist. National Book Agency, 1967. 90p.

13226 ______. Political-organisational report of the Central Committee to the Eighth Congress of the Communist Party of India (Marxist). Calcutta: 1969. 317p.

13227 COMMUNIST PARTY OF INDIA (MARXIST). POLIT BUREAU. Ideological debate summed up. Calcutta: 1968. 183p.

13228 INDIA (REP.). MIN. OF HOME AFFAIRS. Anti-national activities of pro-Peking communists and their preparations for subversion and violence. ND: 1965. 45p.

13229 NAMBOODIRIPAD, E.M.S. Conflicts and crisis: political India, 1974. Bombay: Orient Longman, 1974. 160p.

13230 ______. Revisionism and dogmatism in the Communist Party of India. ND: New Age, 1963. 128p.

13231 RAIS, J.P. Political stance of the Communist Party of India (Marxist). In IJPS 30 (1969) 177-84.

13232 SEN, C. CPI-M, promises, prospects, problems. ND: Young Asia Pub., 1979. 296p.

13233 SEN, B. The truth about CPM; a critique of the ideological-political line of the Communist Party of India (Marxist). ND: CPI, 1972. 35p.

13234 SEN, MOHIT & BHUPESH GUPTA. CPM's politics X-rayed. ND: CPI, 1978. 31p.

d. the Naxalbari (W. Bengal) peasant uprising, 1967: Maoist revolutionary violence

13235 CPI's defence of Naxalite prisoners. ND: CPI, 1978, 63p.

13236 CHOPRA, PRAN. Three waves of Indian terrorism: a first hand report on the Naxalite movement. In Dissent 17,5 (1970) 433-38.

13237 DASGUPTA, B. Naxalite armed struggles and the annihilation campaign in rural areas. In EPW 8,4/5/6 (1973) 173-88.

13238 ______. The Naxalite movement: an Indian experiment in Maoist revolution. In China Report 10,4 (1974) 25-43.

13239 MOHANTY, M.R. Revolutionary violence: a study of the Maoist movement in India. ND: Sterling, 1977. 267p.

13240 RAY, A.K. The spring thunder and after: a survey of the Maoist and ultra-leftist movements in India, 1962-75. Calcutta: Minerva, 1975. 303p.

13241 SEN, MOHIT. Naxalites and naxalism. In EPW 6, 3/4/5 (1971) 195-98.

13242 STIEBLER, K. Wie gefährlich sind die Naxaliten? In IAF 2,1 (1971) 112-117.

13243 TIWAR, J.G. Analysis of Naxalite behaviour. In Indian Communist 2,1/2 (1969) 3-28; 2,3 (1969) 29-49.

13244 RAI, HARIDWAR & K.M. PRASAD. Naxalism: a challenge to the proposition of peaceful transition to socialism. In IJPS 33,4 (1972) 455-80.

13245 ZAGORIA, D.S. The ecology of peasant communism in India. In APSR 65,1 (1971) 144-160.

e. the Communist Party of India (Marxist-Leninist): Naxalite split from CPI(M) in 1969

13246 BANERJEE, S. In the wake of Naxalbari: a history of the Naxalite movement in India. Calcutta: Subarnarekha, 1980. 436p.

13247 FRANDA, M.F. India's third Communist party. In AS 9 (1969) 797-817.

13248 KROEF, J.M. VAN DER. India's Maoists: organizational patterns & tactics. In CAS 1 (1971) 49-63.

13249 JAWAID, SOHAIL. The Naxalite movement in India; origin and failure of the Maoist revolutionary strategy in West Bengal, 1967-71. ND: Associated, 1979. 140p.

13250 JOHARI, J.C. Naxalite politics in India. Delhi: Research, 1972. 188p.

13251 RAM, MOHAN. Maoism in India. Delhi: Vikas, 1971. 196p.

13252 SEN, SAMAR, et al., eds. Naxalbari and after: a Frontier anthology. Calcutta; Kathashilpa, 1978-. [to be 2v.]

6. Communal (Religio-centric) Parties and Supporting Groups

a. general studies of Hindu communal political groups

12353 GANGADHARAN, K.K. Sociology of revivalism; a study of Indianization, Sanskritization, and Golwalkarism. ND: Kalamkar Prakashan, 1970. 166p.

13254 JOHNSON, E.W., II. Comparative approaches to the study of the Hindu communal political parties in contemporary India.... Unpub. Ph.D. diss., New York U., 1970. 234p. [UM 71-2359]

13255 LAMBERT, R.D. Hindu communal groups in Indian politics. In R.L. Park & I. Tinker, eds. Leadership and political institutions in India. Princeton: PUP, 1959, 211-224.

13256 SMYTH, D.C. The social basis of militant Hindu nationalism. In J. of Developing Areas 6,3 (1972) 323-44.

13257 VARSHNEY, M.R. Jana Sangh - R.S.S. and Balraj Madhok. Aligarh: 1973. 172p.

b. Akhil Bharat ("All-India") Hindu Mahasabha (est. 1915) and its ideologue, Veer Savarkar (1883-1966) [see also Chap. Six, IV. B. 5. c.]

13258 GUPTA, C. Life of barrister Savarkar. Rev. by Indra Prakash. ND: Hindu mission Pustak Bhandar, 1939. 259p.

13259 INDRA PRAKASH. Hindu Mahasabha, its contribution to India's politics. ND: Akhil Bharat Hindu Mahasabha, 1966. 182p.

13260 KEER, D. Veer Savarkar. 2nd ed. Bombay: Popular 1966. 569p.

13261 SAVARKAR, V.D. Hindu Rashtra Darshan: a collection of the presidential speeches delivered from the Hindu Mahasabha platform. Bombay: L.G. Khare, 1949. 309p.

13262 ______. Hindu Rashtravad; being an exposition of the ideology and immediate programme of Hindu Rashtra. Ed. by Satya Parkash. Rohtak: S. Parkash, 1945. 218p.

13263 ______. Hindutva. ND: Central Hindu Yavak Sabha, 1938. 184p.

13264 ______. The story of my transportation for life. Bombay: Sadbhakti Pub., 1950. 572p. [1st pub. in Marathi, 1927]

c. Bharatiya Jana Sangh ("Indian People's Party," est. 1951)

13265 ANDERSEN, W.K. The Jana Sangh: ideology and organization in party behavior. Ph.D. diss. U. of Chicago, 1975. 432p.

13266 BHARATIYA JAN SANGH. Bharatiya Jana Sangh: party documents 1951-1972. ND: 1973. 5v.

13267 BAXTER, C. The Jana Sangh; a biography of an Indian political party. Philadelphia: UPaP, 1969. 352p.

13268 BHANDARI, S.S., ed. Jana Sangh souvenir; a publication brought out on the occasion of the 15th annual session of Bharatiya Jana Sangh, Bombay, April 25-27, 1969. Delhi: 1969. 144p.

13269 DAVEY, H.T., JR. The transformation of an ideological movement into an aggregative party: a case study of the Bharatiya Jana Sangh. Ph.D. diss., U. of California, Los Angeles, 1969. 425p. [UM 70-8129]

13270 GRAHAM, BRUCE D. The Jana Sangh and party alliances: 1967-70. In SAR 4,1 (1970) 9-26.

13271 ______. Syama Prasad Mookerjee and the communalist alternative. In D.A. Low, ed., Soundings in modern South Asian history, Berkeley: UCalP, 1968, 330-366.

13272 INDIA (REP.). CMSN. OF INQUIRY TO ENQUIRE INTO THE FACTS AND CIRCUMSTANCES RELATING TO THE DEATH OF SHRI DEEN DAYAL UPADHYAYA. Report regarding the facts and circumstances relating to the death of Shri Deen Dayal Upadhyaya, by Y.V. Chandrachud (Commission of Inquiry). ND: Min. of Home Affairs, 1970. 160p.

13273 MADHOK, BALRAJ. Indian nationalism. ND: Bharati Sahitya Sadan, 1969. 99p. [Pub. in 1946 as Hindusthan on the crossroads; rev. ed., 1955, Hindu rashtra....]

13274 _____. Indianisation? What, why, and how. Delhi: S. Chand, 1970. 135p.

13275 _____. Portrait of a martyr; biography of Dr. Shyama Prasad Mookerji. Bombay: Jaico, 1969. 255p.

13276 RAJE, S., ed. Destination: nation's tribute to Deendayal Upadhyaya. ND: Deendayal Res. Inst., 1978. 104p.

13277 _____. Pt. Deendayal Upadhyaya; a profile. ND: Deendayal Res. Inst., 1972. 212p.

13278 UPADHYAYA, DEENDAYAL. The integral approach. ND: Deendayal Res. Inst., 1979. 116p.

d. the Rashtriya Swayamsevak Sangh ("National Volunteer Organization," est. 1925): not a party, but a self-syled "cultural organization" with great political influence

13279 ANDERSEN, W.K. The Rashtriya Swayamsevak Sangh. In EPW 7,11-14 (1972) 589-597, 633-630, 673-682, 724-727.

13280 CURRAN, J.A. Militant Hinduism in Indian politics: a study of the R.S.S. Ed. by N. Damodaran Nayar. ND: All-India Qaumi Ekta Sammelan, 1979. 204p. [1st ed. 1951, 94p.]

13281 DESHMUKH, N. RSS, victim of slander: a multidimensional study of RSS, Jana Sangh, Janata Party, and the present political crisis. ND: Vision Books, 1979. 168p.

13282 DHOORIA, R.L. I was a swayamsewak; an inside view of the RSS. ND: Sampradayikta Virodhi Cmtee, 1969. 59p.

13282 GOLWALKAR, M.S. Bunch of thoughts. Bangalore: Vikrama Prakashan, 1966. 437p.

13284 _____. We; or Our nationhood defined. 4th ed. Nagpur: Bharat Prakashan, 1947. 83p.

13285 GOYAL, D.R. Rashtriya Swayamsewak Sangh. ND: Radha Krishna, 1979. 232p.

13286 JOSHI, S., ed. RSS: A danger to democracy. ND: Sampradayikta Virodhi Cmtee., 1967. 104p.

13287 MAHENDRA, K.L. Defeat the RSS fascist designs. 2nd enl. ed. ND: CPI, 1977. 83p.

13288 MISHRA, D.N. RSS, myth and reality. Tr. from Hindi by D.P. Pandey. ND: Vikas, 1980. 219p.

13289 SAHAI, G. A critical analysis of Rashtriya Swayamsevak Sangh. ND: 1956. 64p.

e. the Indian Union Muslim League and other Muslim political groups

13290 HYDER, G. Politics of Jamaat-e-Islami-e-Hind. ND: CPI, 1974. 42p.

13291 QURAISHI, Z.M. Electoral strategy of a minority pressure group: the Muslim Majlis-e-Mushawarat. In AS 8 (1968) 976-87.

13292 _____. Emergence and eclipse of Muslim Majlis-e-Mushawarat. In EPW 6,25 (1971) 1229-34.

13293 SHAKIR, MOIN. Theory and practice of Jamaat-e-Islami (Hind). ND: Sampradayikta Virodhi Cmtee., 1970. 19p.

13294 WRIGHT, T.P., JR. The Muslim League in South India since independence: a study in minority group political strategies. In American Political Science R. 60 (1966) 579-99.

f. the Shiromani Akali Dal (est. 1920): Sikh communal party

13295 DHAMI, M.S. Minority leaders' image of the Indian political system: an exploratory study of the attitude of Akali leaders. ND: Sterling, 1975. 72p.

13296 GULATI, K.C. The Akalis - past and present. ND: Ashajanak, 1974. 259p.

13297 MEHTA, I.M. The Shiromani Akali Dal. In JCPS 5,4 (1971) 706-27.

7. The Swatantra Party (est. 1959): Voice of Economic Conservatism and the Private Sector

13298 ERDMAN, H.L. The Swatantra Party and Indian conservatism. London: CamUP, 1967. 356p. (Cambridge South Asian Studies, 5.)

13299 MASANI, M.R. Congress misrule and the Swatantra alternative. Bombay: Manaktalas, 1966. 196p.

13300 RANGA, N.G. Fight for freedom, autobiography of N.G. Ranga. Delhi: S. Chand, 1968. 560p.

8. The Republican Party of India (est. 1957): Heir to Dr. B.R. Ambedkar's Movement of Former Untouchables

13301 DUSHKIN, L. Scheduled caste politics. In J.M. Mahar, ed. The untouchables in contemporary India. Tucson: U. of Arizona Press, 1972, 165-226. [discusses Republican Party of India]

13302 GAIKWAD, B.K. & B.P. MAURYA & B.D. KHOBRAGADE. The Charter of Demands submitted to Shri Lal Bahadur Shastri, the Hon'ble. Prime Minister of India. ND: Republican Party of Inida, 1964. 32p.

13303 REPUBLICAN PARTY OF INDIA. Election manifesto... 1967. Chanda: B.D. Khobragade, 1967. 24p.

9. The Heritage of Gandhism

13304 BOSE, N.K. Gandhism and modern India. Gauhati: U. of Gauhati, 1970. 118p.

13305 DAS, B.C. & G.P. MISHRA, eds. Gandhi in to-day's India. ND: Ashish, 1979. 232p.

13306 DOCTOR, A.H. Sarvodaya; a political and economic study. Bombay: Asia, 1967. 229p.

13307 MEHTA, V.P. Mahatma Gandhi and his apostles. NY: Viking Press, 1977. 260p.

13308 MUKHERJEE, D. The towering spirit: Gandhian relevance assessed. ND: Chetana Publications, 1978. 152p.

13309 NAMBOODIRIPAD, E.M.S. The Mahatma and the ism. 2nd ed. Delhi: PPH, 1959. 136p. [1st ed. 1958]

13310 RAO, V.K.R.V. The Gandhian alternative to Western socialism. Bombay: BVB, 1970. 83p.

13311 SETHI, J.P. Gandhi today. ND: Vikas, 1978. 211p.

13312 SHRIMAN NARAYAN. India needs Gandhi. ND: S. Chand, 1976. 150p.

13313 TANDON, V.N. The social and political philosophy of sarvodaya after Gandhiji. Varanasi, Sarva Seva Sangh Prakashan, 1965. 252p.

13314 TINKER, H. Magnificent failure? The Gandhian ideal in India after sixteen years. In Intl. Affairs 40 (1964) 262-76.

13315 UNNITHAN, T.K.N. Gandhi in free India. Groningen: J.B. Wolters, 1956. 266p.

D. Politics at the Centre: Elections, Prime Ministers and Their Administrations

1. The Indian Electoral System
a. bibliography and reference

13316 BAXTER, C., comp. District voting trends in India; a research tool. NY: Southern Asian Inst. School of Intl. Affairs, Columbia U., 1969. 378p.

13317 BRASS, P.R. Indian election studies. In SA ns 1,2 (1978) 91-108. [review article]

13318 CHANDIDAS, R., et al., eds. India votes, a source book on Indian election. Bombay: Popular, 1968-70. 2 v., 717, 107p.

13319 The election archives. Ed. by Shiv Lal. ND: Election Archives, 1969-. [quarterly]

13320 Elections and electoral reforms: a select bibliography. In JCPS 4 (1970) 785-812.

13321 GRAHAM, B.D. Studies on Indian elections: a review article. In JCCP 13,2 (1975) 193-205.

13322 NARAIN, IQBAL, et al. Election studies in India: an evaluation: report of an ICSSR project. Bombay: Allied, 1978. 181p.

b. election law and procedures

13323 INDIA (REP.). Manual of election law; a compilation of the statutory provisions governing elections to Parliament and the state legislatures. 6th ed. ND: MPGOI, 1971. 438p.

13324 INDIA (REP.). ELECTION CMSN. Delimitation of parliamentary and assembly constituencies order, 1966. ND: 1967. 419p.

13325 ______. Delimitation of parliamentary and assembly constituencies order, 1976. ND: 1976. 665p.

13326 ______. Instructions to presiding officers. ND: 1980. 111p.

13327 ______. A hand book for candidates for election to the House of the People and the legislative assemblies. ND: 1968. 146p.

13328 INDIA (REP.). PARLIAMENT. JOINT CMTEE. ON AMENDMENTS TO ELECTION LAW. Report. ND: Lok Sabha Secretariat, 1972. 2 v. in 1.

13329 INDIA (REP.). SUPREME COURT. The Supreme Court on election law....1966 to 1971. Ed. by B.A. Masodkar. Agra: Wadhwa, 1972. 460p.

13330 JHA, L.K. & MUSHTAQ AHMAD. Encyclopedia of election laws, rules and petitions. 2nd ed. Allahabad: Allahabad Law Pub., 1962. 456p.

13331 SHIV LAL. Supreme court on elections. 2nd enl. ed. ND: Election Archives, 1975. 2 v.

c. general studies of India's national elections

13332 ARORA, N.D. The Lok Sabha elections in India: a study in statistics. Delhi: Pragatee Prakashan, 1977. 199p.

13333 BHALLA, R.P. Elections in India, 1950-1972. ND: S. Chand, 1973. 485p.

13334 BHAMBHRI, C.P. General elections and political competition in India. In PSR 7 (1968) 760-79.

13335 BHARADVAJA, B. Election symbols in politics. In IPSR 6,1 (1971-72) 56-74.

13336 DASGUPTA, B. & W.H. MORRIS-JONES. Patterns and trends in Indian politics: an ecological analysis of aggregate data on society and elections. Bombay: Allied, 1975. 364p.

13337 Elections and electoral reforms in India. In JCPS 4 (1970) 457-631. [Articles by L.K. Advani, B. Shiva Rao, J.D. Sethi, K. Santhanam, et al.]

13338 FISHER, M.W. & J.V. BONDURANT. The Indian experience with democratic elections. Berkeley: Inst. of Intl. Studies, U. of California, 1956. 200p. (Indian press digests, monograph 3)

13339 KASHYAP, S.C., ed. Elections and electoral reforms in India. ND: ICPS, 1971. 385p.

13340 KRISHNA MANI, P.N. Elections, candidates and voters. ND: ICPS, 1967. 100p.

13341 MCDONOUGH, P. Electoral competition and participation in India: a test of Huntington's hypothesis. In Comp. Politics 4,1 (1971) 77-87.

13342 MEHTA, P. Election campaign: anatomy of mass influence. Delhi: National, 1975. 230p. + 17 pl.

13343 MOREHOUSE, W. Voter rationality and Indian elections: a commentary and hypothesis. In East-West Center Review 4 (1967) 17-32.

13344 NARAIN, IQBAL & MOHAN LAL. Election politics in India: notes toward an empirical theory. In AS 9 (1969) 202-20.

13345 PALMER, N.D. Elections and political development; the South Asian experience. Durham: DUP, 1975. 340p.

13346 SHIV LAL. Elections in India: an introduction. ND: Election Archives, 1978. 196p.

13347 ______. Indian elections since independence. ND: Election Archives, 1972. 447p.

2. Pandit Jawaharlal Nehru (1889-1964): India's First Prime Minister, 1947-64

a. bibliography

13348 SHARMA, J.C. Jawaharlal Nehru; a descriptive bibliography. ND: S. Chand, 1969. 541p. [1st ed. 1955]

b. Nehru's writings and speeches

13349 NEHRU, JAWAHARLAL. A bunch of old letters, written mostly to Jawaharlal Nehru and some written by him. Bombay: Asia, 1958. 511p.

13350 ______. Jawaharlal Nehru's speeches [1946-64]. ND: PDMIB, 1958-1968. 5 v.

13351 ______. The philosophy of Mr. Nehru: as revealed in a series of intimate talks with R.K. Karanjia. London: Allen & Unwin, 1966. 162p.

13352 ______. Selected works of Jawaharlal Nehru. Ed. by S. Gopal. ND: Orient Longman, 1972-. [11 v. issued to 1978; to be 20 v.]

c. biographical studies

13353 CHALAPATHI RAU, M. Jawaharlal Nehru. ND: PDMIB, 1973. 428p.

13354 GOPAL, S. Jawaharlal Nehru: a biography. Cambridge: HUP, 1976-. [to be 3 v.]

13355 MATHAI, M.O. My days with Nehru. ND: Vikas, 1979. 270p.

13356 ______. Reminiscences of the Nehru age. ND: Vikas Pub. House, 1977. 299p.

13357 MORAES, F.R. Jawaharlal Nehru; a biography. NY: Macmillan, 1956. 511p.

13358 ______. Nehru: sunlight and shadow. Bombay: Jaico, 1964. 208p.

13359 MUKHERJEE, H.N. The gentle colossus; a study of Jawaharlal Nehru. Calcutta: Manisha Granthalaya, 1964. 239p.

13360 PANDEY, B.N. Nehru. London: Macmillan, 1976. 499p.

13361 SETON, M. Panditji: a portrait of Jawaharlal Nehru. NY: Taplinger, 1967. 515p.

d. political studies of Nehru's thought and administration

13362 AHLUWALIA, B.K., ed. Jawaharlal Nehru, India's man of destiny. ND: Newman Group, 1978. 200p.

13363 BRECHER, M. Nehru: a political biography. London: OUP, 1959. 682p.

13364 ______. Nehru; a political biography. Abridged ed. Boston: Beacon Press, 1962. 267p.

13365 CROCKER, W. Nehru; a contemporary's estimate. NY: OUP, 1966. 186p.

13366 DAS, M.N. The political philosophy of Jawaharlal Nehru. London: Allen & Unwin, 1961. 256p.

13367 EDWARDES, M. Nehru: a political biography. London: Penguin, 1971. 352p.

13368 JAGANNARAYANAN, S. India under Nehru. Delhi: Motilal, 1967. 118p.

13369 PATEL, B. Burning words: a critical history of nine years of Nehru's rule from 1947 to 1956. Bombay: Sumati Pub., 1956. 609p.

13370 PILAT, JAN. The political thought of Jawaharlal Nehru. In AO 34,3 (1966) 350-74.

13371 RAO, AMIYA & B.G. RAO. Six thousand days: Jawaharlal Nehru, Prime Minister. ND: Sterling, 1974. 522p.

13372 PRASHAD, G. Nehru: a study in colonial liberalism. ND: Sterling, 1976. 218p.

13373 SMITH, D.E. Nehru and democracy; the political thought of an Asian democrat. Bombay: Orient Longmans, 1958. 194p.

13374 TYSON, G.W. Nehru: the years of power. London: Pall Mall, 1966. 206p.

e. Panditji's legacy and the problem of succession

13375 BRECHER, M. Succession in India: a study in decision-making. London: OUP, 1966. 269p. [pub. in US as Nehru's mantle...]

13376 _____. Succession in India 1967: the routinization of political change. In AS 7 (1967) 423-43.

13377 HANGEN, W. After Nehru, who? NY: Harcourt, Brace & World, 1963. 303p.

13378 RAO, V.K.R.V. The Nehru legacy. Bombay: Popular, 1971. 92p.

13379 SUNDER RAO, M. & HERBERT JAI SINGH, et al. Indian politics after Nehru. Bangalore: CISRS, 1967. 193p.

3. India's Elections during the Nehru Years

a. 1952: the first election under universal franchise

13380 INDIA (REP.). ELECTION CMSN. Report on the first general elections in India 1951-52. ND: Govt. of India Press, 1955. 2 v.

13381 KOGEKAR, S.V. & R.L. PARK, eds. Reports on the Indian general elections, 1951-52. Bombay: Popular, 1956. 322p.

13382 MEHTA, ASHOK. The political mind of India; analysis of the results of the general elections. Bombay: Socialist Party, 1952. 88p.

13383 MORRIS-JONES, W.H. Indian Elections. In Political Q. 23 (1952) 235-49.

13384 PARK, R.L. Indian democracy and the general election. In PA 25 (1952) 130-39.

b. 1957 election: Communist victory in Kerala challenges Congress monopoly

13385 INDIA (REP.). ELECTION CMSN. Report on the second general elections in India, 1957. ND: 1959. 2 v.

13386 POPLAI, S.L., ed. National politics and 1957 elections in India. Delhi: Metropolitan, 1957. 172p.

13387 ROACH, J.R. India's 1957 elections. In Far Eastern Survey 26 (1957) 65-78.

c. 1962: India's third Lok Sabha election

13388 DASTUR, A.J. Menon vs. Kripalani; North Bombay election, 1962. Bombay: U. of Bombay, 1967. 138p.

13389 Election analysis: a symposium on the trends revealed by the results of the third general election. In Seminar 34 (1962) 10-55.

13390 INDIA (REP.). ELECTION CMSN. Report on the third general election in India, 1962. ND: 1962. 2 v., 126, 478p.

13391 MAHESHWARI, S.R. The general election in India. Allahabad: Chaitanya Pub. House, 1963. 228p.

13392 MAYER, A.C. Rural leaders and the Indian general election. In AS 1 (1961) 23-29.

13393 POPLAI, S.L. 1962 general elections in India; issued under the auspices of the Diwan Chand Indian Information Centre, New Delhi. Bombay: Allied, 1962. 420p.

13394 SURI, S. 1962 elections; a political analysis. ND: Sudha Pub., 1962. 201p.

13395 WEINER, M. & R. KOTHARI, ed. Indian voting behaviour: studies of the 1962 general elections. Calcutta: KLM, 1965. 219p.

13396 _____. India's third general elections. In AS 2 (1962) 3-18.

13397 Your vote: a symposium which covers the election appeal of our major political parties. In Seminar 29 (1962) 10-57.

13398 ZINKIN, M. The Indian elections. In Asian R. 58 (1962) 141-51.

4. Lal Bahadur Shastri (1904-1966): Prime Minister, 1964-66

a. writings and speeches

13399 SHASTRI, L.B. Selected speeches of Lal Bahadur Shastri, June 11, 1964 to January 10, 1966. ND: PDMIB, 1974. 363p.

13400 _____. Speeches, June 1964 - May 1965. Delhi: PDMIB, 1965. 156p.

13401 _____. When freedom is menaced; speeches of Lal Bahadur Shastri, August 13 - September 26, 1965. Delhi: PDMIB, 1965. 79p.

b. biographies and studies

13402 ALEXANDER, M.K. Lal Bahadur Shastri; an illustrated biography. ND: New Light, 1967. 100p.

13403 GUPTA, R.C. Lal Bahadur Shastri, the man and his ideas; an analysis of his socio-political and economic ideas. Delhi: Sterling, 1966. 156p.

13404 MANKEKAR, D.R. Lal Bahadur, a political biography. Bombay: Popular, 1964. 168p.

13405 _____. Lal Bahadur Shastri. ND: PDMIB, 1973. 232p.

13406 SATISH CHANDER, et al., eds. Shastri memorial souvenir. Delhi: S.M.S. Committee, Cultural Meet Pub., 1966. 252p.

13407 SAVARA, S.K., ed. Shri Lal Bahadur Shastri commemoration souvenir. ND: 1967. 220p.

13408 YADAV, J.N.S. Lal Bahadur Shastri; a biography. Delhi: Hariyana Prakashan, 1971. 220p.

5. Indira Nehru Gandhi (1917-): Prime Minister 1966-77, 1980-

a. bibliography

13409 MOODGAL, H.M.K. & S. MAJUMDAR & R.K. SHARMA. Indira Gandhi; a select bibliography. ND: Gitanjali Prakashan, 1976. 275p.

b. writings and speeches

13410 GANDHI, INDIRA. Freedom is the starting point: a collection of memorable words by Indira Gandhi. ND: INC, 1976. 111p.

13411 _____. India: the speeches and reminiscences of Indira Gandhi. Calcutta: Rupa, 1975. 221p.

13412 _____. Selected speeches of Indira Gandhi, January 1966 - August 1969. ND: PDMIB, 1971. 497p.

c. biographies and studies

13413 ABBAS, K.A. Indira Gandhi; return of the red rose. Bombay: Popular, 1966. 189p.

13414 ALEXANDER, M.K. Madame Gandhi; a political biography. North Quincy, MA: Christopher Pub. House, 1969. 226p.

13415 BHATIA, KRISHAN. Indira: a biography of Prime Minister Gandhi. NY: Praeger, 1974. 290p.

13416 CARRAS, M.C. Indira Gandhi: in the crucible of leadership: a political biography. Boston: Beacon Press, 1979. 289p.

13417 CHALAPATHI RAU, M., et al. Indira Priyadarshini. ND: Popular Book Services, 1966. 90p.

13418 DESAI, B. Indira Gandhi, call to greatness. Bombay: Popular, 1966. 117p.

13419 DRIEBERG, T. Indira Gandhi; a profile in courage. Delhi: Vikas, 1972. 221p.

13420 HUTHEESING, KRISHNA. Dear to behold; an intimate portrait of Indira Gandhi. NY: Macmillan, 1969. 221p.

13421 MASANI, ZAREER. Indira Gandhi: a biography. NY: T.Y. Crowell, 1976. 341p.

13422 MOHAN, ANAND. Indira Gandhi, a personal and political biography. NY: Meredity Press, 1967. 303p.

13423 MURTHI, R.K. The cult of the individual: a study of Indira Gandhi. ND: Sterling, 1977. 152p.

13424 SAHGAL, N.P. Indira Gandhi's emergence and style. ND: Vikas, 1978. 215p.

13425 SAHOTA, S.S. Indira Gandhi; a political biography. Jullundur: New Academic, 1972. 193p.

13426 SHASHI BHUSHAN. Feroze Gandhi, [socialist, democrat, secular]: a political biography. ND: Progressive People's Sector Pub., 1977. 220p.

13427 TEWARI, V.N. 12 Willingdon Crescent: Indian politics at the crossroads. Delhi: Ajanta, 1979. 142p.

13428 VASUDEV, UMA. Indira Gandhi: revolution in restraint. ND: Vikas, 1974. 582p.

13429 ______. Two faces of Indira Gandhi. ND: Vikas, 1977. 208p.

6. Indira vs. the Congress Organization, 1966-75

a. the 1967 Lok Sabha elections: post-Nehru surfacing of ideological differences

13430 ELDERSVELD, S.J. Elections and the party system: patterns of party regularity and defection in 1967. In AS 10,11 (1970) 1015-30.

13431 Election outcome; a symposium analysing the results of the fourth general elections. In Seminar 94 (1967) 10-47. [Articles by Ranjit Gupta, R. Kothari, J.D. Sethi, Surindar Suri, Mohan Kumaramangalam, E.P.W. da Costa]

13432 FICKETT, L.P., JR. The major Socialist parties of India in the 1967 election. In AS 8 (1968) 489-98.

13433 The fourth general elections; a statistical analysis. ND: N. Balakrishnan, for AICC, 1967. 110p.

13434 Fourth general elections; an analysis. ND: Min. of Info. and Broadcasting, 1967. 297p.

13435 GENA, C.B. Party manifestos - a review. In PSR 6,3/4 & 7,1/2 (1967-68) 1-37.

13436 INDIA (REP.). ELECTION CMSN. Report on the fourth general elections in India (1967). ND: 1967. 2 v., 121, 629p.

13437 Indian political opinion after the 1967 elections. In IIPO, Monthly Public Opinion Survey 12,11/12 (1967) 3-62.

13438 KOTHARI, R., et al. Context of electoral change in India: general elections, 1967. Bombay: Academic Books, 1969. 185p.

13439 PALMER, N.D. India's fourth general election. In AS 7 (1967) 275-91.

13440 PATTABHIRAM, M., ed. General election in India 1967; an exhaustive study of main political trends. Bombay: Allied, 1967. 403p.

13441 RUDOLPH, L.I. & S.H. RUDOLPH. New era for India. In PSR 7 (1968) 585-601.

13442 RUSCH, T.A. Socialists in fourth general elections. In PSR 7 (1968) 653-85.

13443 Studies in the fourth general elections. ND: Allied Pub. House, 1972. 295p. [sponsored by ICSSR]

13444 VARMA, S.P. & IQBAL NARAIN, eds. Fourth general election in India. Bombay: Orient Longmans, 1968-70. 2 v.

13445 Your vote; a symposium which covers the election appeal of our major political parties. In Seminar 89 (1967) 10-41. [Articles by Ranjit Gupta, Sadiq Ali, N.K. Krishnan, N. Dandekar, Deendayal Upadhyaya, & Jyoti Basu]

b. the 1969 Presidential election of V.V. Giri over N. Sanjeeva Reddy: conflict of P.M. and Congress "Syndicate"

13446 QURAISHI, Z.M. The Indian Presidential election (1969). In IJPS 31,1 (1970) 32-59.

13447 SATHYAMURTHY, T.V. The crisis in the Congress Party: the Indian Presidential election. In World Today 25 (1969) 478-87.

13448 Voting pattern in Presidential election. In J. of Society for Study of State Govts. 2,3 (1969) 174-78.

c. the Congress split, Nov. 1969, into Cong(R), the "ruling" Congress headed by Smt. Gandhi, and Cong(O), the "organisation" Congress headed by Morarji Desai

13449 CHATTERJI, B.K. The Congress splits; the blow-by-blow account of the bloodless battle which culminated in the parting of the bullocks. Delhi: S. Chand, 1970. 355p.

13450 GHOSE, ATULYA. The split. Calcutta: Jayanti, 1970. 86p.

13451 HARDGRAVE, R.L. The Congress in India: crisis and split. In AS 10,3 (1970) 256-62.

13452 RAHMAN, M.M. The Congress crisis. ND: Associated Pub. House, 1970. 164p.

13453 RAO, R.P. The Congress splits. Bombay: Lalvani, 1971. 304p.

13454 ZAIDI, A. MOIN. The great upheaval, 1969-1972; the case of the Indian National Congress in ferment, based on documents emanating from official sources. ND: Orientalia, 1972. 606p.

d. the fifth Lok Sabha elections 1971: Indira's populist appeal for socio-economic reform, Garibi Hatao! ("Abolish poverty!")

13455 BHAMBHRI, C.P. Fifth Lok Sabha elections: ideas and issues. In JCPS 6,1 (1972) 64-75.

13456 CHATTERJI, S.K. Political prospects in India; a post-election enquiry. Madras: CLS, for CISRS, 1971. 192p.

13457 COMMUNIST PARTY OF INDIA. NATIONAL COUNCIL. On the general election of March 1971; resolutions and review report of the National Council of the Communist Party of India, New Delhi, 23 to 28 April 1971. ND: CPI, 1971. 105p.

13458 GOYAL, O.P. The rise of the middle castes and the Indian parliamentary elections of 1971. In JCPS 6,4 (1972) 39-46.

13459 GUPTA, R.L. Politics of commitment; a study based on fifth general elections in India. ND: Trimurti, 1972. 264p.

13460 INDIA (REP.). ELECTION CMSN. Report on the fifth general election in India, 1971-72. ND: 1973. 2 v., 245, 598p.

13461 MEHTA, H., ed. Election manifestos, 1971: Akali Dal, BKD, CPI, (PICM), Congress (O), Congress (R), DMK, Jan Sangh, PSP, SSP, Swatantra, and statistics of the last general elections and bye-elections held thereafter. Bombay: Awake India Pub., 1971. 1 v.

13462 MORRIS-JONES, W.H. India elects for change and stability. In AS 11,8 (1971) 719-41.

13463 The 1971 Indian Parliamentary elections: a symposium. In AS 11,12 (1971) 1119-66. [essays by L.I. Rudolph, S.J. Heginbotham, M. Weiner]

13464 SARKAR, S.C. & S. BISWAS, ed. Elections, 1971. Calcutta: M.C. Sarkar, 1971. 135p.

13465 SHAM LAL, et al. General elections, 1971; a study. ND: PDMIB, 1971. 25p.

e. the "Indira Wave" (1971-73): triumph in elections and in Bangladesh

13466 BHASIN, PREM. Riding the wave; the first authentic account of the recent struggle for power in India. ND: Ashajanak, 1972. 165p.

13467 ROY, AJIT. Economics and politics of garibi hatao. Calcutta: Naya Prokash, 1973. 144p.

13468 ROY, RAMASHRAY. India 1972: fissure in the fortress. In AS 13,2 (1973) 231-45.

13469 RUDOLPH, S.H. The writ from Delhi: the Indian government's capabilities after the 1971 election. In AS 11,10 (1971) 958-69.

f. Jayaprakash Narayan's call for "total revolution" (the J.P. Movement): focus of growing socio-economic unrest and opposition to Indira

i. J.P.'s writings and speeches

13470 NARAYAN, JAYAPRAKASH. Communitarian society and panchayati raj. Ed. by Brahmanand. Varanasi: Navachetna Prakashan, 1970. 155p.

13471 ______. Nation building in India. Ed. by Brahmanand. Varanasi: Navachetna Prakashan, 1975. 430p.

13472 ______. A picture of Sarvodaya social order. Tanjore: Sarvodaya Prachuralaya, 1957. 139p.

13473 ______. Prison diary, 1975. 2nd ed. Bombay: Popular, 1977. 144p.

13474 ______. Socialism, Sarvodaya, and democracy; selected works of Jayaprakash Narayan. Ed. by Bimla Prasad. NY: Asia, 1964. 287p.

13475 ______. Towards a new society. ND: Office for Asian Affairs, Congress for Cultural Freedom, 1958. 170p.

13476 ______. Towards fair and free elections. ND: Lok Niti Parishad, 1975. 96p.

13477 ______. Towards total revolution. Ed. by Brahmanand. Bombay: Popular, 1978. 4 v.

ii. biographies and political studies

13478 BARIK, R.K. Politics of the JP movement. ND: Radiant, 1977. 120p.

13479 BHATTACHARJEA, AJIT. Jayaprakash Narayan: a political biography. Rev. ed. ND: Vikas, 1978. 229p. [1st pub. 1975]

13480 CHATTERJI, B. J.P., profile of a non-conformist. Calcutta: Minerva, 1979. 58p.

13481 DASGUPTA, S., ed. Total revolution: a symposium. Calcutta: Naya Prokash, 1978. 126p.

13482 DATTA-RAY, S.K. Bihar shows the way. Bombay: Nachiketa Pub., 1977. 134p., mostly plates.

13483 FAZAL-E RAB, SYED. The J.P. movement and the emergence of Janata Party: a select bibliography. Gurgaon: Indian Documentation Service, 1977-. v. 1, pre-Emergency phase, 232p.

13484 KARANJIA, R.K. Indira-JP confrontation: the great debate. ND: Chetana, 1975. 128p.

13485 MAHADEVAN, T.K., ed. Jayaprakash Narayan and the future of Indian democracy. ND: Affiliated East-West Press, 1975. 143p.

13486 MASANI, M.R. JP, mission partly accomplished. Delhi: Macmillan, 1977. 155p. [1st pub. 1975 as Is J.P. the answer?]

13487 NARGOLKAR, V.S. JP vindicated! ND: S. Chand, 1977. 170p.

13488 ______. JP's crusade for revolution. ND: S. Chand, 1975. 215p.

13489 SCARFE, A. & W. SCARFE. J. P., his biography. ND: Orient Longmans, 1975. 462p.

13490 SHARAD, ONKAR. J.P. = Jayaprakash Narayan: biography, thoughts, letters, documents. 2nd rev. ed. Allahabad: Sahitya Bhawan, 1977. 199p.

13491 THAKUR, H.K. Jayaprakash Narayan analysed through the Gandhian prism. ND: AICC, 1975. 32p.

g. the High Court's conviction of the P.M. for 1971 election law violations

13492 GROVER, K.L. The verdict: inside story of Shrimati Indira Gandhi's case with unabridged judgment. Allahabad: Legend Pub., 1975. 288p.

13493 PRASHANT BHUSHAN. The case that shook India. ND: Vikas, 1978. 294p.

12494 SHIV LAL. The Prime Minister's poll case and other judgments. ND: Election Archives, 1975. 296p.

7. The Emergency (25 June 1975-20 Mar., 1977)

a. why Emergency?: rationales for and against

13495 BRIGHT, J.S. One year of emergency in India and 20-point programme. ND: Pankaj Pub., 1976. 142p.

13496 The crisis of democracy and the implementation of 20-point program. [special issue]. In R&S 23,2 (1976) 1-108.

13497 DHARIA, M. Fumes and the fire. ND: S. Chand, 1975. 184p.

13498 DRIEBERG, T. Four faces of subversion. ND: Drieberg, 1975. 80p.

13499 DUTT, V.P. The Emergency in India: background and rationale. In AS 16,12 (1976) 1124-38.

13500 GANDHI, D.V., ed. Era of discipline: documents on contemporary reality. ND: Samachar Bharati, 1976. 361p.

13501 LAL, KANWAR. Emergency, its need and gains. ND: Hittashi Pub., 1976. 270p.

13502 MAVALANKAR, P.G. "No, Sir": being the collection of 24 speeches (with background notes) in the Lok Sabha (House of the People), between July 21, 1975 and November 5, 1976, during the internal emergency in India. Ahmedabad: Sannishtha Prakashan, 1979. 314p.

13503 PARK, R.L. Political crisis in India, 1975. In AS 15,11 (1975) 996-1013.

13504 PURI, BALRAJ. Revolution, counter-revolution. ND: Newman Group, 1978. 144p.

13505 RAJESWARA RAO, C. & B. GUPTA & MOHIT SEN. Emergency and the Communist Party. ND: CPI, 1975. 38p.

13506 SAVARA, S.K., ed. Fight against poverty: the socio-economic revolution. ND: Commercial Pub. Bureau, 1977. 116p.

13507 THAKUR, R.C. The fate of India's parliamentary democracy. In PA 49,2 (1976) 263-93.

13508 Timely steps. ND: PDMIB, 1975. 77p.

13509 Why emergency? ND: Min. of Home Affairs, 1975. 59p.

b. the 20-Point Economic Programme

13510 GUPTA, J.P. 20-point economic programme - a bibliographic study. In Administrator 21,3 (1976) 801-24.

13511 HANIF, M.W. 25-point socio-economic programme. ND: S. Chand, 1977. 148p.

13512 INDIAN NATL. CONGRESS. India's twenty point programme: a review. ND: AICC, 1976. 20p.

13513 KWATRA, R.D. Programme and progress: towards richer life. ND: PDMIB, 1977. 106p.

13514 MISHRA, G., et al. Twenty-point programme and democratic advance. ND: CPI, 1976. 55p.

13515 NAIK, J.A. An alternative polity for India. ND: S. Chand, 1976. 143p.

13516 REGE, P.W., ed. Legislation on the 20-point economic programme. Bombay: U. of Bombay, 1976. 256p.

c. fundamental Rights and the debate over constitutional amendment
i. general studies of Emergency and the Constitution

13517 DWIVEDI, G.C. Supreme Court on enforcement of fundamental rights during emergency: latest Supreme Court decision of April 28, 1976, right of a detenu to challenge his detention barred. Allahabad: Law Pub. House, 1976. 267p.

13518 GANDHI, INDIRA. Constitution is for the people. ND: Indraprastha Press, 1976. 31p.

13519 GUPTA, BHUPESH. Some comments on constitutional changes. ND: CPI, 1976. 58p.

13520 MIRCHANDANI, G.G. Subverting the Constitution. ND: Abhinav, 1977. 264p.

13521 SEYID MUHAMMAD, V.A. Our Constitution for haves or have-nots? Delhi: Lipi Prakashan, 1975. 175p.

ii. 42nd Amemdment: attempt to institutionalize and perpetuate Emergency Rule - passed 18 Dec. 1976, repealed 28 March, 1977

13522 DHAVAN, R. The amendment: conspiracy or revolution? Allahabad: Wheeler, 1978. 235p.

13523 DIWAN, P. Abrogation of Forty-second amendment: does our Constitution need a second look. ND: Sterling Pub., 1978. 194p.

13524 JAIN, D.C. Forty-second amendment as culmination of the socio-economic aspirations of the people: an evaluation. In JCPS 11,2 (1977) 1-23.

13525 RAMAN, SUNDER. Fundamental rights and the 42nd Constitutional amendment. Calcutta: Minerva, 1977. 104p.

13526 SHESHADRI, P. & K.R. ACHARYA. Constitution forty-second amendment act, 1976: a critical study. Hyderabad: Osmania U., 1977. 161p.

iii. detention under Emergency provisions, and accounts by detenus

13527 ADVANI, L.K. A prisoner's scrap-book. ND: Arnold-Heinemann, 1978. 327p.

13528 HAKSAR, U. That case of Pandit Brothers. ND: Perspective Pub., 1978. 87p.

13529 HARDWARI LAL. 555 days in jail: recollections of a MISA detenu. Chandigarh: Printing Promoters, 1977. 128p.

13530 LEWIS, P. Reason wounded: an experience of India's emergency. ND: Vikas, 1978. 207p.

13531 MADHOK, B. Reflections of a detenu. ND: Newman Group, 1978. 140p.

13532 MALKANI, K.R. The midnight knock. ND: Vikas Pub. House, 1978. 98p.

13533 NARGOLKAR, V.S. A nonentity fasts for freedom. Kainad, Dist. Thane: Vijnanashram, 1978. 121p.

13534 NAYAR, KULDIP. In jail. ND: Vikas, 1978. 152p.

13535 REDDY, C.G.K. Baroda dynamite conspiracy: the right to rebel. ND: Vision Books, 1977. 176p.

13536 SAHGAL, N.P. A voice for freedom. Delhi: Hind Pocket Books, 1977. 115p.

13537 VARKHEDKAR, V. The four documents. Nagpur: Citizens for Democracy Nagpur Pub., 1977. 44p.

d. Indira vs. the Press; censorship and the underground journals

13538 BASU, SAJAL, ed. Underground literature during Indian emergency. Calcutta: Minerva, 1978. 242p.

13539 DESAI, M., ed. The smugglers of truth: selections from Satyavani. Baroda: Friends of India Soc. Intl., 1978. 103p.

13540 MANKEKAR, D.R. The press vs. the government, before and during emergency. Rev. ed. Delhi: Clarion Books, 1978. 185p.

13541 The Pen in revolt: souvenir: underground literature published during the emergency. ND: Press Inst. of India, 1978. 23p.

13542 RAO, AMIYA & B.G. RAO, eds. The Press she could not whip: emergency in India as reported by the foreign press. Bombay: Popular, 1977. 399p.

13543 SORABJEE, S.J. The emergency, censorship, and the press in India, 1975-77. ND: Central News Agency, 1977. 63p.

e. the National Population Policy (April, 1976) and charges of "forced sterilization" [see also V. B. 5. a., below]

13544 HENDRE, S.L. Undeclared civil war in India. Bombay: Supraja Prakashan, 1975. 462p.

13545 PAI PANANDIKAR, V.A. & R.N. BISHNOI & O.P. SHARMA. Family planning under the emergency: policy implications of incentives and disincentives. ND: Radiant, 1978. 176p.

f. Sanjay Gandhi (1946-1980), the P.M.'s son, and his Youth Congress

13546 INDIA (REP.). CMSN. OF INQUIRY ON MARUTI AFFAIRS. Report, May 31, 1979. Delhi: Controller of Pub., 1979. 2 v.

13547 JAGAT SINGH. Sanjay Gandhi and the awakening of youth power. ND: Pankaj Pub., 1977. 160p.

13548 MEHTA, V. The Sanjay story: from Anand Bhavan to Amethi. Bombay: Jaico, 1978. 192p.

13549 RAO, M.J. Youth resurgence. ND: Progressive Writers & Publishers, 1976. 123p.

g. the sixth Lok Sabha elections, 1977, one year later than scheduled
i. general studies and election results

13550 AIYAR, S.P. & S.V. RAJU. When the wind blows: India's ballot-box revolution. Bombay: Himalaya Pub. House, 1978. 482p.

13551 ARORA, N.D. The Lok Sabha elections in India: a study in statistics. Delhi: Pragatee Prakashan, 1977. 199p.

13552 DEVADAS PILLAI, S. The Incredible elections, 1977: a blow-by-blow document as reported in the Indian Express. Bombay: Popular, 1977. 439p.

13553 GUPTA, A. Revolution through ballot; India, January-March 1977. ND: Ankur Pub. House, 1977. 163p.

13554 JAIN, P.K. The glorious revolution in India: an analysis of historical foundations, 1947-77. ND: Gitanjali Prakashan, 1978. 196p.

13555 MATHEW, G. Religion, politics and the 1977 Lok Sabha elections in India. In Asia Q. (1979) no. 1, 35-49.

13556 MIRCHANDANI, G.G. 320 million judges: analysis of 1977 Lok Sabha and state elections in India. ND: Abhinav, 1977. 270p.

13557 PAUL, S. 1977 general elections in India. ND: Associated, 1977. 236p.

13558 We the people. ND: Educ. Resources Center, U. of the State of New York, 1978. 115p.

13559 WEINER, M. India at the polls; the parliamentary elections of 1977. Washington: American Enterprise Inst. for Public Policy Res., 1978. 150p.

ii. manifestoes of the contesting parties

13560 COMMUNIST PARTY OF INDIA (MARXIST). CENTRAL CMTEE. Manifesto on elections to Lok Sabha, March 1977. Calcutta: CPI(M), 1977. 16p.

13561 GHOSE, S.K. The crusade and end of Indira raj. ND: Intellectual Book Corner, 1978. 262p.

13562 INDIAN NATL. CONGRESS. 1977 Congress election manifesto. ND: AICC, 1977. 20p.

13563 JANATA PARTY. Election manifesto, 1977. ND:

The Party, 1977. 26p.

13564 SHAKDER, S.L. The Sixth general election to Lok Sabha. ND: Oxford & IBH Pub., for Lok Sabha Secretariat, 1977. 186p.

h. the Shah Commission of Inquiry, and other investigations of abuses during Emergency

13565 BHARGAVA, G.S. Indira's India Gate: latest study of political corruption in India. ND: Arnold-Heinemann, 1977. 143p.

13566 DAYAL, J. & AJOY BOSE. The Shah Commission begins. ND: Orient Longmans, 1978. 351p.

13567 GANGADHARAN, K. The inquisition: revelations before the Shah Commission. ND: Path Pub., 1978. 259p.

13568 HARDWARI LAL. Bansi Lal and his associates. Panipat: West's Associates, 1977. 141p.

13569 INDIA (REP.). P. JAGANMOHAN REDDY CMSN. OF INQUIRY. P. Jaganmohan Reddy Commission of Inquiry regarding Shri Bansi Lal: report. Delhi: Cont. of Pub., 1978. 343p.

13570 INDIA (REP.). SHAH CMSN. OF INQUIRY. Interim report. Delhi: Cont. of Pub., 1978. 3 v., 94, 147, 284p.

13571 KAPUR, JAGGA. What price perjury: facts of the Shah Commission. ND: Arnold-Heinemann, 1978. 330p.

13572 LEKHI, P.N. Witness for prosecution: sedition unmasked. ND: Allied, 1979. 272p.

13573 Memorandum of action taken on the first and second reports of the commission of inquiry headed by Justice J.C. Shah. ND: Min. of Home Affairs, 1978. 68p.

13574 NAMBOODIRIPAD, E.M.S. Put them in the dock: the Shah Commission report and after. ND: CPI(M), 1978. 22p.

13575 Trial of a dictator. ND: Janata Party, 1977. 42p.

j. overall assessments of the Emergency and "Indira Raj"

13576 ABBAS, K.A. 20th March 1977: a day like any other day. ND: Vikas, 1978. 134p.

13577 BRIGHT, J.S. Allahabad High Court to Shah Commission. ND: Deep & Deep, 1979. 172p.

13578 CHATTERJI, S.K., ed. The meaning of the Indian experience: the emergency. Madras: CLS, for CISRS, 1978. 117p.

13579 Christians and the Emergency. [special issue]. In R&S 24,2/3 (1977) 1-260.

13580 COMMUNIST PARTY OF INDIA. CIP's fight agaist the caucus, sterilisation, and demolition. ND: CPI, 1977. 61p.

13581 DARBARA SINGH. Indian politics. Delhi: Sundeep, 1978. 182p.

13582 GHURYE, G.S. India recreates democracy. Bombay: Popular, 1978. 414p.

13583 HART, H.C., ed. Indira Gandhi's India; a political system reappraised. Boulder, CO: Westview Press, 1976. 313p.

13584 HENDERSON, M. Experiment with untruth: India under emergency. Delhi: Macmillan, 1977. 250p.

13585 KALHAN, P. Black Wednesday: power politics, emergency, and elections. ND: Sterling, 1977. 152p.

13586 KANWAR LAL. Thank you, Mrs. Gandhi. ND: Anupam Pub., 1977. 332p.

13587 KARANTH, K.S. Fascism dethroned: a critical analysis of emergency and its aftermath. Bombay: Parivartan Prakashan, 1977. 80p.

13588 KRIPALANI, J.B. The nightmare and after. Bombay: Popular, 1980. 264p.

13589 MANKEKAR, D.R. & K. MANKEKAR. Decline and fall of Indira Gandhi. ND: Vision Books. 1977. 208p.

13590 MEHTA, VED. The new India. NY: Viking Press, 1978. 174p.

13591 MENDELSOHN, O. The collapse of the Indian National Congress. In PA 51,1 (1978) 41-66.

13592 MITRA, ASHOK. The hoodlum years. ND: Orient Longmans, 1979. 186p.

13593 NARAWANE, K. The great betrayal, 1966-1977. Foreword by Atal Behari Vajpayee. Bombay: Popular, 1980. 192p.

13594 NAYAR, K. The judgement: inside story of the emergency in India. ND: Vikas, 1977. 228p.

13595 NIHAL SINGH, S. Indira's India: a political notebook. Bombay: Nachiketa Pub., 1978. 428p.

13596 PANDIT, C.S. End of an era; the rise and fall of Indira Gandhi. ND: Allied, 1977. 196p.

13597 PRASAD, B.K. India regained: a dynastic rule and the '77 democratic revolution. ND: Oriental, 1978. 245p.

13598 PURI, BALRAJ, ed. Revolution, counter-revolution. ND: Newman Group, 1978. 144p.

13599 SELBOURNE, D. An eye to India: the unmasking of a tyranny. NY: Penguin, 1977. 561p.

13600 SHIV LAL. The she-Tughlaq of India. ND: Newman Group, 1977. 232p.

13601 SHOURIE, A. Symptoms of fascism. ND: Vikas, 1978. 322p.

13602 THAKUR, J. All the Prime Minister's men. ND: Vikas, 1977. 182p.

13603 THAKUR, J. Indira Gandhi and her power game. ND: Vikas, 1979. 165p.

13604 THOMAS, M.M. Response to tyranny: writings between July 1975 and February 1977. ND: Forum for Christian Concern for People's Struggle, 1979. 127p.

8. The Janata Party in Power (March 1977-Aug. 1979): Coalition of Indira's Opposition led by Jayaprakash Narayan

a. general studies of Janata and its administration

13605 ABBAS, K.A. Janata in a jam? Bombay: Jaico, 1978. 123p.

13606 ADVANI, L.K. The people betrayed. ND: Vision Books, 1979. 160p.

13607 BHANDARI, A. India under Janata. Bombay: Jaico, 1978. 176p.

13608 BRAHM DUTT. Five headed monster: a factual narrative of the genesis of Janata Party. ND: Surge Pub., 1978. 158p.

13609 GHOSE, S.K. The betrayal: politics as if people mattered. ND: Sterling, 1979. 215p.

13610 Janata era: first year. ND: Janata Party, 1978. 172p.

13611 JANATA PARTY. Constitution of the Janata Party: as amended by the Working Committee of the Janata Party on December 21, 1977. ND: Janata Party, 1977. 43p.

13612 NAIK, J.A. From total revolution to total failure. ND: National, 1979. 187p.

13613 SENGUPTA, B. Last days of the Morarji Raj. Calcutta: Ananda, 1979. 180p.

13614 SHARMA, D. The janata (people's) struggle: the finest hour of the Indian people: with underground documents, resistance literature, and correspondence relating to advent of Janata Party. ND: Philosophy and Social Action, 1977. 391p.

13615 SHARMA, U., ed. Violence erupts. ND: Radha Krishna, 1978. 148p.

13616 SHIV LAL. Elections under the Janata rule. ND: Election Archives, 1978. 292p.

13617 SHOURIE, A. Institutions in the Janata phase. Bombay: Popular, 1980. 300p.

13618 SOOD, P. Towards new horizons: India after emergency. ND: Qaumi Ekta Trust, 1976. 175p.

13619 THAKUR, J. All the Janata men. ND: Vikas, 1978. 175p.

13620 VARMA, S. India's second explosion: Janata victory. ND: Bharatiya Prakashan, 1977. 168p.

b. Morarji Ranchodji Desai (1896-): Prime Minister 1977-79

13621 BHARGAVA, G.S. Morarji Desai: Prime Minister of India. Delhi: Hind Pocket Books, 1977. 176p.

13622 CHATTERJEE, B.K. The mind of Morarji Desai, as revealed in the replies to a series of penetrating and provocative questions put to him between January and June 1969. Bombay: Orient Longmans, 1969. 111p.

13623 DESAI, M.R. In my view. Bombay: Thacker, 1966. 239p.

13624 ______. The story of my life. Delhi: Macmillan, 1974. 2 v.

13625 DHAR, M.K. Morarji, the truth. Poona: Harshad Prakashan, 1978. 98p.

9. Charan Singh (1899-), P.M. Aug. 1979-Jan. 1980, the defeat of Janata, and the 1980 Mid-Term Election of the Seventh Lok Sabha

13626 A Black paper on conspiracy against the people. ND: Janata Party, 1979. 72p.

13627 CHAUBEY, H.L. The lust for power: an inside story of the fall of the Morarji government and thereafter. ND: Vindhyachal Prakashan, 1979. 151p.

13628 HOODA, R.K. Man of the masses, Chaudhry Charan Singh: first peasant prime minister of India. ND: Chaudhry Hari Ram, 1979. 78p.

13629 INDIA (REP.). ELECTION CMSN. Parliamentary elections in India, 1979-80: a guide. Delhi: 1979. 59p.

13630 KHUSHWANT SINGH. Indira Gandhi returns. ND: Vision Books, 1979. 184p.

13631 MIRCHANDANI, G.G. The people's verdict: DCM computer-based study. ND: Vikas, 1980. 194p.

13632 MURTHI, V.K. Politics of survival: fall of Janata government. ND: Allora, 1979. 192p.

13633 PAUL, S. 1980 general elections in India: a study of the mid-term poll. ND: Associated Pub. House, 1980. 335p.

13634 ROY, AJIT. Seventh Lok Sabha elections. In EPW 15,5/6/7 (1980) 227-28.

13635 SHAKIR, MOIN. Electoral participation of minorities and Indian political system. In EPW 15,5/6/7 (1980) 221-26.

10. The Return to Power of Indira Gandhi (Jan. 1980-)

13636 GOULD, H.A. The second coming: the 1980 elections in India's Hindi belt. In AS 20,6 (1980) 595-616.

13637 NAIK, J.A. The meaning of her victory. Kolhapur: Avinash Pub., 1980. 122p.

13638 RUDOLPH, S.H. & L.I. RUDOLPH. The centrist future of Indian politics. In AS 20,6 (1980) 575-94.

13639 VISHNU DUTT. Indira Gandhi: promises to keep. ND: National, 1980. 223p.

11. Other Recent Contenders for the Prime Ministership

13640 CHANCHREEK, K. Jagjivanram: a select bibliography, 1908-1975. ND: S. Chand, 1975. 186p.

13641 ______. Jagjivan Ram's crusade for democracy. ND: S. Chand, 1978. 176p.

13642 CHAVAN, Y.B. Winds of change. Bombay: Somaiya, 1973. 235p.

13643 Four decades of Jagjivan Ram's parliamentary career. ND: S. Chand, 1977. 256p.

13644 KALE, B.B. Man of crisis. Bombay: Sindhu, 1969. 118p. [Y.B. Chavan]

13645 KALHAN, P. Jagjivan Ram and power politics. ND: Allora, 1980. 104p.

13646 KARNIK, D.B. Y.B. Chavan; a political biography. Bombay: United Asia Pub., 1972. 164p.

13647 KUNHI KRISHNAN, T.V. Chavan and the troubled decade. Bombay: Somaiya, 1971. 420p.

13648 SHAH, C.M. Yeshwantrao Chavan. Bombay: Vidya Pub. House, 1963. 107p.

13649 SHARMA, D.P. Jagjivan Ram: the man and the times. ND: Indian Book Co., 1974. 191p.

13650 SINGH, N.N. Jagjivan Ram: symbol of social change. Delhi: Sundeep, 1977. 139p.

E. State and Local Politics, 1947- [see also Regional Chaps. Ten-Sixteen]

1. General Studies of State Politics

13651 AIYAR, J.S. The politics of coalition governments. In JCPS 4 (1970) 371-93.

13652 BARNETT, M.R., et al. Electoral politics in the Indian states: party systems and cleavages. Delhi: Manohar, 1975. 209p.

13653 BHAGWATI, J.N. Electoral politics in the Indian states: three disadvantaged sectors. Delhi: Manohar, 1975. 199p.

13654 CHATTERJI, S.K., ed. The coalition government: a critical examination of the concept of coalition, the performance of some coalition governments, and the future prospects of coalition in India. Madras: CLS, for CISRS, 1974. 145p.

13655 GOYAL, O.P. & H. HAHN. The nature of party competition in five Indian states. In AS 6,10 (1966) 580-88.

13656 KASHYAP, S.C. The politics of power: defections and state politics in India. Ed. by Savita Kashyap. Delhi: National, 1974. 709p. [1st pub. 1969]

13657 MITRA, S.K. Governmental instability in Indian states: West Bengal, Bihar, Uttar Pradesh, and Punjab. Delhi: Ajanta, 1978. 150p.

13658 NARAIN, I. Coalition politics in India and the political system: the crisis of compatibiblity. In PSR 10,1/2 (1971) 30-50.

13659 ______, ed. State politics in India. Meerut: Meenakshi, 1976. 620p.

13660 ______, ed. State politics in India; papers. Meerut: Meenakshi, 1967. 671p.

13661 NARAIN, I. & M.L. SHARMA. The fifth state assembly elections in India. In AS 13,3 (1973) 318-335.

13662 PALMER, N.D. Elections and the political system in India: the 1972 State assembly elections and after. In PA 45,4 (1972-73) 535-55.

13663 ROY, RAMASHRAY. The uncertain verdict; a study of the 1969 elections in four Indian states. ND: Orient Longmans, 1973. 288p.

13664 SAHNI, N.C., comp. Coalition politics in India. Jullundur: New Academic Pub. Co., 1971. 148p.

13665 SINGH, BALJIT & D.K. VAJPEYI. Political stability and continuity in the Indian states during the Nehru era, 1947-1964: a statistical analysis. East Lansing: Asian Studies Center, Michigan State U., 1973. 53p. (Its Occ. papers, South Asia series, 19)

13666 WEINER, M., ed. State politics in India. Princeton: PUP, 1968. 520p.

2. Politics at the Local Level: District, Municipal, Village
a. urban politics

13667 MISHRA, S.N. Politics and leadership in municipal government. Delhi: Inter-India Pub., 1979. 123p.

13668 ROSENTHAL, D.B. Factions and alliances in Indian city politics. In Midwest J. of Political Science, 10,3 (1966) 320-49.

13669 ______. The limited elite: politics and government

in two Indian cities. Chicago: UChiP, 1970. 360p. [Agra and Poona]

13670 ______, ed. The city in Indian politics. Faridabad: Thomson Press, 1976. 256p.

13671 ROSENTHAL, D.B., et al. Symposium on Indian urban politics. In AS 13,4 (1973) 380-438.

13672 Urban politics in a plural society: a symposium. In JAS 29 (1961) 265-97. [essays by M. Singer, H. Hart, M. Weiner, L.I. Rudolph]

b. politics of panchayati raj and rural leadership

13673 ABRAHAM, M.F. Dynamics of leadership in village India. Allahabad: Indian Intl. Pub., 1974. 116p.

13674 BAXTER, C. District voting trends in India: a research tool. NY: ColUP, 1969. 378p.

13675 BHARGAVA, B.S. Panchayati raj system and political parties. ND: Ashish Pub. House, 1979. 536p.

13676 Emerging patterns of rural leadership in southern Asia; report on an international round table conference. Hyderabad: NICD, 1965. 237p.

13677 The impact of Panchayati Raj on political attitudes: a survey in Andhra Pradesh, Madras and Rajasthan with special reference to the 1962 general elections. In IIPO, Monthly Public Opinion Survey 8,6-9 (1963) 1-128.

13678 LAL, A.K. Dynamics of village factionalism: a study of conflict between tradition and emerging leadership. In J. of Social and Econ. Studies 1,2 (1973) 217-31.

13679 MEHTA, R.R.S. Rural leadership and panchayat: a behavioural approach. Chandigarh: Bahri Pub., 1978. 277p.

13680 MILLER, D.F. Factions in Indian village politics. In PA 38 (1965) 17-31.

13681 PANT, NIRANJAN. The politics of panchayati raj administration: a study of official-non-official relations. Delhi: Concept, 1979. 95p.

13682 SESHADRI, K. Political linkages and rural development: a comparative study of the political processes and interactions between different levels of government in two Indian states. ND: National, 1976. 233p.

IV. INDIA'S INTERNATIONAL RELATIONS, 1947- [For relations within the subcontinent, see Chap. Seven]

A. General

1. Bibliography, Reference, and Document Collections

13683 Foreign affairs record. ND: Min. of External Affairs, 1955-. [monthly]

13684 Foreign policy of India: texts of documents, 1947-64. ND: Lok Sabha Secretariat, 1966. 634p. [1st pub. 1958]

13685 India and world affairs. An annual bibliography. In International Studies (Bombay). 1959-.

13686 India in world affairs. ND: ICWA, 1952-
- v.1 (Aug. 1949-Jan.1950), by K.P. Karunakaran, 1952, 407p.
- v.2 (Feb. 1950-Dec.1953), by K.P. Karunakaran, 1958, 266p.
- v.3 (1954-1956), by M.S. Rajan, 1964, 675p.
- v.4 (1957-58), by V.K. Arora & A. Appadorai, 1975, 358p.

13687 SAMUEL, C.M., ed. India treaty manual, 1972; containing information about 1600 treaties and related documents concerning India. Mysore: Wesley Press, 1972. 307p. [1st pub. 1966]

13688 SATISH KUMAR, ed. Documents on India's foreign policy. 1972- ND: Macmillan, 1975. [pub. annually; vols. for 1973, 1974 pub. to 1977]

13689 SHARMA, S.R. Indian foreign policy; annual survey. 1971-. ND: Sterling, 1977. 364p. [vols. for 1972, 1973, 1974 pub. to 1980]

13690 VIDYA SAGAR. India in world affairs: chronology of events, 1947-72. ND: Swastik Prakashan, 1973. 248p.

2. General Studies of India's Foreign Policy

13691 APPADORAI, A. Essays in politics and international relations. Bombay: Asia, 1969. 288p.

13692 ______. Impact of federalism on India's foreign relations. In IS 13,3 (1974) 389-423.

13693 BANERJI, J. The making of India's foreign policy: determinants, institutions, processes, and personalities. Bombay: Allied, 1970, 286p.

13694 BIMAL PRASAD, ed. India's foreign policy: studies in continuity and change. ND: Vikas, 1979. 540p.

13695 COHEN, S.P. & R.L. PARK. India: emergent power? NY: Crane, Russak, 1978. 95p.

13696 DOCTOR, A.H. Essays on India's foreign policy. ND: National, 1977. 127p.

13697 HEIMSATH, C.H. & S. MANSINGH. A diplomatic history of modern India. Bombay: Allied, 1971. 559p.

13698 ILCHMAN, W.F. Political development and foreign policy: the case of India. In JComPolSt 4 (1966) 216-30.

13699 India's foreign policy; continuity and change. [special double issue]. In IS 17,3/4 (1978) 379-909.

13700 MADAN GOPAL. India as a world power; aspects of foreign policy. ND: Sagar Pub., 1974. 165p.

13701 MEHRISH, B.N. India's recognition policy towards the new nations. Delhi: Oriental, 1972. 228p.

13702 MELLOR, J.W., ed. India, a rising middle power. Boulder, CO: Westview Press, 1979. 374p.

13703 MISRA, K.P. Foreign policy and its planning. NY: Asia, 1970. 88p.

13704 ______. India's policy of recognition of states and governments. Bombay: Allied, 1966. 214p.

13705 ______, comp. Studies in Indian foreign policy. Delhi: Vikas, 1969. 346p.

13706 NARAIN, IQBAL. The political system and external crisis: notes towards a theoretical framework of study. In SAS 3,2 (1968) 54-69.

13707 NOORANI, A.G. Aspects of India's foreign policy. Bombay: Jaico, 1970. 400p.

13708 Parliament and foreign policy; a study. ND: Lok Sabha Secretariat, 1972. 127p.

13709 Parliament and international treaties. ND: Lok Sabha Secretariat, 1976. 50p.

13710 PATWANT SINGH. India and the future of Asia. NY: Knopf, 1966. 264p.

13711 PILLAI, K.R. India's foreign policy: basic issues and political attitudes. Meerut: Meenakshi, 1969. 247p.

13712 SHAH, A.B., ed. India's defence and foreign policies. Bombay: Manaktalas, 1966. 169p.

13713 SHARMA, S.P. India's boundary and territorial disputes. Delhi: Vikas, 1971. 198p.

13714 SINGH, BALJIT. Indian foreign policy: an analysis. Bombay: Asia, 1975. 111p.

13715 SONDHI, M.L. Non-appeasement: a new direction for Indian foreign policy. ND: Abhinav, 1972. 291p.

3. Political Parties and India's Foreign Policy

13716 ERDMAN, H.L. Foreign policy views of the Indian right. In PA 29 (1966) 5-18.

13717 GUPTA, SISIR. Foreign policy in the 1967 election manifestos. In IQ 23 (1967) 28-46.

13718 KISHORE, M.A. Jana Sangh and India's foreign policy. ND: Associated, 1969. 248p.

13719 LIMAYE, MADHU. India and the world. ND: New Literature, 1979. 58p.

13720 LOHIA, RAMMANOHAR. Foreign policy. Aligarh: P.C. Dwadesh Shreni, 1964. 381p.

13721 MADHOK, B. Balraj Madhok on India's foreign policy & national affairs; collection of some speeches delivered in the Lok Sabha. ND: Bharati Sahitya Sadan, 1969. 156p.

13722 NIZAMI, T.A. The Communist Party and India's foreign policy. ND: Associated, 1971. 282p.

13273 Political parties on foreign policy in the inter-election years 1962-1966. In IQ 23 (1967) 47-75.

13724 RAJKUMAR, N.V., ed. The background of India's foreign policy. ND: AICC, 1952. 110p.

13725 [entry deleted]

4. Epochs of India's Foreign Policy
a. the Nehru years, 1947-64
i. general studies

13726 BHATTACHARYA, S. Pursuit of national interests through neutralism: India's foreign policy in the Nehru era. Calcutta: KLM, 1978. 280p.

13727 BRECHER, M. India and world politics: Krishna Menon's view of the world. NY: Praeger, 1968. 390p.

13728 DUTT, SUBIMAL. With Nehru in the Foreign Office. Calcutta: Minerva, 1977. 326p.

13729 GUPTA, K. India in world politics; a period of transition, fall 1956 to spring 1960 (from Suez crisis to Paris summit). Calcutta: Scientific Book Agency, 1969. 324p.

13730 NANDA, B.R. Indian foreign policy, the Nehru years. Delhi: Vikas, 1976. 279p.

13731 NASENKO, Y.P. Jawaharlal Nehru and India's foreign policy. ND: Sterling, 1977. 351p. [tr. from Russian]

13732 NEHRU, J. India's foreign policy: selected speeches, September 1946-April 1961. Delhi: PDMIB, 1961. 612p.

13733 POWER, P.F. Indian foreign policy: the age of Nehru. In R. of Politics 26 (1964) 257-86.

13734 RAJAN, M.S. ed. India's foreign relations during the Nehru era: some studies. Bombay: Asia, 1976. 351p.

13735 RANA, A.P. The imperatives of nonalignment: a conceptual study of India's foreign policy strategy in the Nehru period. Delhi: Macmillan, 1976. 322p.

13736 RANGE, W. Jawaharlal Nehru's world view; a theory of international relations. Athens: U. of Georgia Press, 1961. 139p.

ii. the Asian Relations Conference (1947) and the Bandung Asian-African Conference, 1955, and its Five Principles (Panchasheel)

13737 ASIAN-AFRICAN CONF., BANDUNG, JAVA, 1955. Prime Minister Jawaharlal Nehru's speeches. The final communiqué. ND: PDMIB, 1955. 38p.

13738 ______. Selected documents of the Bandung Conference.... NY: Inst. of Pacific Relations, 1955. 35p.

13739 Asian relations, being report of the proceedings and documentation of the First Asian Relations Conference, New Delhi, March-April, 1947. ND: Asian Relations Organization, 1948. 314p.

13740 KAHIN, G.M. The Asian-African Conference, Bandung, Indonesia, April 1955. Ithaca: CornellUP, 1956. 88p.

b. Lal Bahadur Shastri's foreign policy, 1964-66

13741 SINGH, L.P. India's foreign policy: the Shastri period. ND: Uppal, 1980. 167p.

c. Indira Gandhi's foreign policy, 1966-1977

13742 CHAVAN, Y.B. India's foreign policy. Bombay: Somaiya, 1979. 246p.

13743 PANT, H.G. Indian foreign policy under Mrs. Indira Gandhi, 1966-71. In PSR (Jaipur) 13,1/4 (1974) 327-62.

d. the Janata Party's foreign policy, 1977-79

13744 GANGAL, S.C. Indian foreign policy: a documentary study of India's foreign policy since the installation of the Janata Government on 24 March 1977. ND: Young Asia, 1980. 502p.

13745 MISRA, K.P., ed. Janata's foreign policy. ND: Vikas, 1979. 240p.

13746 PANDA, K.K. & P.K. MISHRA. New perspectives in India's foreign policy: the Janata phase. Delhi: Sundeep, 1980. 347p.

13747 VAJPAYEE, A.B. New dimensions of India's foreign policy. ND: Vision Books, 1979. 256p.

5. Neutralism and Non-Alignment: Continuation of Nehru's Major Foreign Policy Principles

13748 CRABB, C.V., JR. The elephants and the grass: a study of non-alignment. NY: Praeger, 1965. 237p.

13749 DUTTA, P. Neutralism: theory & practice, with special reference to India, Burma, Ceylon, Egypt & Ghana. Calcutta: World Press, 1978. 327p.

13750 HEIMSATH, C.H. Nonalignment reassessed: the experience of India. In R. Hilsman & R.C. Good, ed., Foreign policy in the sixties: the issues and the instruments. Baltimore: Johns Hopkins Press, 1965, 47-66.

13751 KAMALANATHAN, K. ed. National Seminar on Non-alignment; seminar proceedings, February 24-26, 2977. Tirupati: Centre for Studies in Peace and Non-Violence, Sri Venkateswara U., 1977. 239p.

13752 MALLIK, D.N. The development of non-alignment in India's foreign policy. Allahabad: Chaitanya Pub. House, 1967. 342p.

13753 POWER, P.F., comp. India's nonalignment policy; strengths and weaknesses. Boston: Heath, 1967. 114p. (Problems in Asian civilizations)

13754 RAHMAN, M.M. The politics of non-alignment. ND: Associated, 1969. 267p.

13755 RAJAN, M.S. Non-alignment: India and the future. Mysore: U. of Mysore, 1970. 116p.

13756 RUBINOFF, A.G. Neutralism and national interest: India's foreign relations with Egypt and Yugoslavia. Ph.D. diss., U. of Chicago, 1977. 315p.

13757 SEN GUPTA, J. Non-alignment: search for a destination. Calcutta: Naya Prokash, 1979. 208p.

13758 SHASHI BHUSHAN. Non-alignment: legacy of Nehru. ND: Progressive Peoples Sector Pub., 1976. 223p.

B. India's Security and Defense

1. General Studies

13759 ABHYANKAR, M.G. Defence: principles and organisation. Poona: Usha Prakashan, 1974. 223p. [tr. from Marathi]

13760 BHAGAT, P.S. The shield and the sword; India 1965 and after, the new dimension. Calcutta: Statesman, 1967. 111p.

13761 Defence of India. Delhi: Vikas, 1969. 102p. [1966 seminar papers]

13762 KAUL, RAVI. India's strategic spectrum. Allahabad: Chanakya Pub. House, 1969. 223p.

13763 KAVIC, L.J. India's quest for security; defence policies, 1947-1965. Berkeley: UCalP, 1967. 263p.

13764 KHERA, S.S. India's defence problem. Bombay: Orient Longmans, 1968. 329p.

13765 RAO, P.V.R. Defence without drift. Bombay: Popular, 1970. 351p.

13766 RAY, J.K. Security in the missile age. Bombay: Allied, 1967. 156p.

13767 SARHADI, A.J. India's security in resurgent Asia. ND: Heritage, 1979. 338p.

13768 SUBRAHMANYAM, K. Our national security. ND: Economic & Scientific Res. Foundation, 1972. 65p.

13769 ______. Perspectives in defence planning. ND: Abhinav, 1972. 202p.

13770 THOMAS, R.J.C. The defense of India; a budgetary perspective of strategy and politics. Delhi: Macmillan, 1978. 245p.

13771 ______. Indian defense policy: continuity and change under the Janata government. In PA 53,2 (1980) 223-44.

2. Nuclear Weapons Policy, before and after India's First Nuclear Explosion (18 May 1974) at Pokharan, Rajasthan

13772 BHATIA, S. India's nuclear bomb. ND: Vikas, 1979. 169p.

13773 FISCHER, G. L'Inde et la bombe. In Politique étrangère 39,3 (1974) 307-330.

13774 JAIN, J.P. Nuclear India. ND: Radiant Pub., 1974. 2v.

13775 KAPUR, A. India's nuclear option; atomic diplomacy and decision making. NY: Praeger, 1976. 295p.

13776 KAUL, RAVI. India's nuclear spin-off. Allahabad: Chanakya Pub. House, 1974. 191p.

13777 KAUSHIK, B.M. India's nuclear policy. In SAS 3,1 (1968) 67-82.

13778 MIRCHANDANI, G.G. India's nuclear dilemma. ND: Popular Book Services, 1968. 264p.

13779 NANDY, A. Between two Gandhis: psychopolitical aspects of the nuclearization of India. In AS 14,11 (1974) 966-970.

13780 PALSOKAR, R.D. Minimum deterrent: India's nuclear answer to China. Bombay: Thacker, 1969. 158p.

13781 POULOSE, T.T. Perspectives of India's nuclear policy. ND: Young Asia, 1978. 252p.

13782 RIZVI, H.A. Politics of the bomb in South Asia. Lahore: Progressive Publishers, 1975. 40p.

13783 SAMPOORAN SINGH. India and the nuclear bomb. ND: S. Chand, 1971. 180p.

13784 SESAGIRI, N. The bomb!: fallout of India's nuclear explosion. Delhi: Vikas, 1975. 147p.

13785 SINGH, R.N. India, the sixth nuclear power: a comparative account of her potentials & nuclear policy. Patna: Chintamani Prakashan, 1978. 182p.

13786 SUBRAHMANYAM, K. The Indian nuclear test in a global perspective: lecture delivered on 1 August 1974 at the India International Centre. ND: IIC, 1974. 25p.

3. Indian Attitudes toward the Non-Proliferation Treaty and Arms Control

13787 ABDEL-AZIZ, M. Nuclear proliferation and national security. ND: Lancers, 1978. 238p.

13788 BHABHA, H.J. Safeguards and the dissemination of military power. In Disarmament & Arms Control 2,4 (1964) 433-440.

13789 JAIN, J.P. India and disarmament. ND: Radiant, 1974. v.1- [v.1, Nehru era; an analytical study]

13790 KAUSHIK, B.M. International safeguards in India's nuclear policy. In Strategic Analysis 1, 10 (1978) 8-19.

13791 ______. Nuclear arms control, a study with reference to South Asia. In SAS 4,1 (1969) 98-123.

13792 RUSCH, T.A. Indian socialists and the nuclear non-proliferation treaty. In JAS 28 (1969) 755-70.

13793 SULLIVAN, M.J., III. Indian attitudes on international atomic energy controls. In PA 43,4 (1970) 353-69.

C. India in the World Economy

1. Foreign Exchange and Balance of Payments
a. general

13794 DALAYA, C. The external debt of the Government of India. Bombay: Vora, 1970. 117p.

13795 GURTOO, D.H.N. India's balance of payments, 1920-1960. ND: S.Chand, 1961. 241p.

13796 A historical analysis of India's external payments: 1950-1966. In QER 14,1 (1967) 26-36.

13797 MACDOUGALL, D. India's balance of payments problem. In P.N. Rosenstein-Rodan, ed. Pricing and fiscal policies; a study in method. Cambridge, MA: MIT Press, 1964, 175-212.

13798 MAJUMDAR, N. Analysis of India's terms of trade, 1948-1960. In Economic Affairs 7 (1972) 289-99, 306-09, 404-10, 460-62, 492-96.

13799 PANCHMUKHI, V.R. The terms-of-trade effects and the balance of payments (a factual analysis for 1949-63). In IER 3,1 (1968) 15-31.

13800 RESERVE BANK OF INDIA. India's balance of payments 1948-49 to 1961-62. Bombay: 1963. 149p. [1st pub. 1953]

13801 Rethinking on India's international payments: 1968-1971. In QER 14,3 (1969) 38-46.

13802 TANEJA, S.K. India and international monetary management. ND: Sterling, 1976. 480p.

13803 WADHVA, C.D. & S. PAUL. The dollar devaluation and India's balance of payments. In EPW 8,10 (1973) 517-22.

b. the rupee: devaluation in 1949 and 1966, and delinking from Sterling in 1975

13804 GANGULI, B.N. Devaluation of the rupee. Delhi: Ranjit Printers & Pub., 1966. 112p.

13805 INDIA. MIN. OF INDUSTRIAL DEV. AND COMPANY AFFAIRS. Bibliography on devaluation. ND: 1967. 35p.

13806 IYENGAR, S. KESAVA. Devaluation. In his Devaluation and after: vicissitudes of the Fourth plan. Bombay: Asia, 1970, 3-86.

13807 KOTHARI, M.M. The Indian rupee: from devaluations to delinking. Allahabad: Chaitanya, 1978. 200p.

13808 MISHRA, S.K. Devaluation and fourth plan. Bombay: Vora, 1966. 103p.

13809 SARDESAI, S.G. Devaluation: the great betrayal. ND: CPI, 1966. 65p.

13810 SINGHVI, L.M., ed. Devaluation of the rupee: its implications and consequences. 2nd rev. ed. Delhi: S. Chand, for ICPS, 1968. 272p.

13811 SRIVASTAVA, B.L. Impact of devaluation of rupee (1966) on India's foreign trade. Meerut: Pragati Prakashan, 1977-78. 258p.

13812 VAKIL, C.N. The devaluation of the rupee: a challenge and an opportunity. Bombay: Lalvani, 1966. 78p.

2. India's Foreign Trade
a. bibliography, reference, and statistics

13813 Documentation on foreign trade: a select list of articles. ND: Indian Inst. of Foreign Trade, 1972-. [semi-annual]

13814 GUHA, C.R., ed. Sources of information: basic bibliography on foreign trade. ND: Indian Inst. of Foreign Trade, 1970. 39p.

13815 INDIA (REP.). DEPT. OF COMMERCIAL INTELLIGENCE AND STATISTICS. A guide to official statistics of trade, shipping and customs and excise revenue of India. Calcutta: 1965. 150p.

13816 INDIA (REP.). DIR. OF RES. AND STATISTICS. Brochure of foreign trade statistics of India (countrywise by major commodities): third five year plan. ND: 1967. 213p.

13817 INDIA (REP.). TREATIES. India's trade agreements with other countries, as in force on January 1, 1968.

ND: Dir. of Commercial Publicity, Min. of Commerce, 1968. 364p.

13818 THANAWALA, K.H. Statistics relating to India's foreign trade, 1948-1949 to 1959-1960. Bombay: Popular, 1967. 117p.

b. general studies of India's foreign trade

13819 BHAGWATI, J.N. & T.N. SRINIVASAN. India. NY: Natl. Bureau of Econ. Res., 1975. 261p.

13820 BHARADWAJ, R.N. Structural basis of India's foreign trade; a study suggested by the input-output analysis. Bombay: U. of Bombay, 1962. 121p. (Bombay University, series in monetary and intl. econ., 6)

13821 DAYAL, E. The changing patterns of India's international trade. In Economic Geography 44 (1968) 240-69.

13822 Foreign trade problems: an analysis: proceedings of the Seminar held at Bombay from May 8 to 13, 1978. Bombay: Bankers Training College, 1978. 225p.

13823 GURDIP SINGH. India's economic ties with the non-aligned countries. ND: Sumeet Publishers, 1978. 168p.

13824 HASAN, MASOOD. India's trade relations with rupee payments countries. Aligarh: Intl. Book Traders, 1972. 154p.

13825 INDIAN INST. OF FOREIGN TRADE. India's joint ventures abroad. ND: 1977. 146p.

13826 ______. Trading with the world; country profiles. ND: 1968. 560p.

13827 MALENBAUM, W. Foreign trade in India's development. In Foreign Trade R. 5,4 (1971) 424-37.

13828 PANCHAMUKHI, V.R. Trade policies of India: a quantitative analysis. Delhi: Concept, 1978. 317p.

13829 SAINY, H.C. India's foreign trade, its nature and problems. ND: National, 1979. 352p.

13830 VERGHESE, S.K. India's foreign trade, organisational and financial aspects. ND: Allied, 1964. 328p.

c. imports and tariff policy

13831 DASGUPTA, B. World oil, development, and India. In SocSci 5,6/7 (1977) 49-72.

13832 DESAI, A.V. Evolution of import control. In EPW 5,29/30/31 (1970) 1271-77.

13833 DESAI, P. Tariff protection and industrialization; a study of the Indian Tariff Commissions at work, 1946-1965. Delhi: Hindustan Pub. Corp., 1970. 106p.

13834 ECON. AND SCIENTIFIC RES. FOUNDATION, DELHI. Structure of Indian imports, 1957-1964. ND: 1966. 72p.

13835 INDIA (REP.). IMPORT AND EXPORT POLICY CMTEE. Report. ND: Min. of Commerce and Industry, 1962. 111p. [A. Ramaswami Mudaliar, chm.]

13836 INDIA (REP.). MIN. OF COMMERCE. Kennedy round of trade negotiations, 1964-67; analysis of results with reference to India's trade. ND: 1967. 166p.

13837 MANSUKHANI, H.L. The jungle of import trade law. Bombay: Times of India Press, 1970. 675p.

13838 TANZER, M. India: a case study. In his The political economy of international oil and the underdeveloped countries. Boston: Beacon Press, 1969, 163-274.

13839 VERMA, Y.P. Growth of protectionism in India: a critical appraisal of the policy of protection in India. ND: S. Chand, 1974. 245p.

d. India's exports and export markets

13840 AGARWALA, P.N. India's export strategy. ND: Vikas, 1978. 384p.

13841 BISWAS, B. An economic analysis of India's export performance, 1950-70. Diss., U. of Chicago, 1976. 103p.

13842 CHITALE, V.P. & V. SRI RAM. The exporting mills; a review of the investment, technology and export performance of the textile industry. ND: Econ. & Scientific Res. Foundation, 1970. 112p.

13843 CHOPRA, V.P. India's industrialization and mineral exports: 1951-52 to 1960-61 and projections to 1970-71. NY: Asia, 1965. 95p. (Studies in econ. growth, 7)

13844 COHEN, B.I. The stagnation of Indian exports, 1951-1961. In Quarterly J. of Econ. 78 (1964) 604-20.

13845 DEB, K. Export strategy in India since Independence. ND: S. Chand, 1976. 344p.

13846 HALDER, A. India's export pattern: analysis on potential diversification. Calcutta: Minerva, 1976. 157p.

13847 INDIAN CHAMBER OF COMMERCE, CALCUTTA. WORLD TRADE DEPT. Survey of India's exports. Calcutta: The Chamber, 1979. 31 + 86p.

13848 INDIAN INST. OF FOREIGN TRADE. Role of shipping policy in the export strategy of India. ND: 1977. 108p.

13849 MANMOHAN SINGH. India's export trends and the prospects for self-sustained growth. Oxford: OUP, 1964. 369p.

13850 NCAER. India's export potential in selected countries. ND: 1970. 2 v.

13851 NAYYAR, D. India's exports and export policies in the 1960's. Cambridge: CamUP, 1976. 392p.

13852 SAXENA, V.K. & A. HONE. India's spice trade: prospects and policies. In SAR 4,2 (1971) 145-55.

13853 THOMPSON (J. WALTER) CO. MARKET RES. DEPT. Major Indian export markets. Bombay: 1966. 263p.

13854 UNITED NATIONS. INDUSTRIAL DEV. ORGANISATION. SPECIAL INDUSTRIAL SERVICES TEAM. Report to the government of India by Mission to India concerning export production and promotion under the UNIDO Special Industrial Services Programme. ND: Dir. of Commercial Publicity, Min. of Commerce, 1967. 165p.

3. Foreign Aid and Investment
a. bibliography, reference, and statistics

13855 Directory of foreign collaborations in India. Delhi: De Indiana Overseas Pub., 1968-69. 2 v.

13856 MISHRA, SUDHAKANTA. Economics of foreign aid: bibliography on foreign aid with special reference to India. Allahabad: Kitab Mahal, 1978-. v. 1-

13857 SRIVASTAVA, B.L. & KANHAIYA LAL, eds. Bibliography of investment finance, foreign aid, technical assistance. ND: Min. of Industry and Supply, 1965. 150p.

b. general studies of foreign investment (public and private)

13858 BOLZ, K. Die Rolle des ausländischen Kapitals in der indischen Entwicklungsplanung, dargestellt am Beispiel der indischen Funfjahrpläne. Hamburg: Hamburgisches Welt-Wirtschafts-Archiv, 1969. 208p.

13859 CHITALE, V.P. Foreign technology in India. ND: Econ. and Scientific Res. Foundation, 1973. 200p.

13860 DESAI, A.V. Foreign technology and investment: a study of their role in India's industrialization. ND: NCAER, 1971. 176p.

13861 ECON. AND SCIENTIFIC RES. ASSN., CALCUTTA. Foreign capital and industrial growth. Calcutta: 1977. 118p.

13862 INDIA (REP.). CMTEE. ON UTILISATION OF EXTERNAL ASSISTANCE, 9163. Report. ND: Min. of Finance, 1963. 59p.

13863 KHAN, M.S. India's economic development and international economic relations. 2nd rev. ed. Bombay: Asia, 1966. 229p. [1st pub. 1961]

13864 KURIAN, K.M. Impact of foreign capital on Indian economy. ND: PPH, 1966. 354p.

13865 KURK, N.M. Foreign collaboration agreements: policy as law. In JILI 9,1 (1967) 1-70.

13866 PRASAD, D.N. External resources in economic development of India. ND: Sterling, 1972. 432p.

13867 RESERVE BANK OF INDIA. Foreign collaboration in Indian industry; survey report. Bombay: 1968. 140p.

c. foreign aid

13868 CHANDRA, N.R. Western imperialism and India today. In EPW 8,4/5/6 (1973) 221-44; 8,7 (1973) 403-08.

13869 COLUMBIA U. SCHOOL OF LAW. Public international development financing in India. NY: 1964. 256p. (Its Public intl. dev. financing, 9)

13870 ELDRIDGE, P.J. The politics of foreign aid in India. Delhi: Vikas, 1969. 289p.

13871 Foreign aid; a symposium, a survey and an appraisal by the Research Committee on Foreign Aid of the Indian Economic Centre, Indian International Group and Indian Council on Current Affairs, Calcutta. Calcutta: Indian Council on Current Affairs, 1968. 544p.

13872 HAZARI, R.K. & S.D. MEHTA. Public international development financing in India. Bombay: Asian Studies Press, 1968. 337p. (Columbia U. School of Law, Public intl. dev. financing, 9)

13873 KATZ, S.S. External assistance and Indian economic growth. London: Asia, 1968. 104p. (Asia monograph series, 19)

13874 KRISHNANATH. Impact of foreign aid on India's foreign policy, economic and political development, and cultural change. Hyderabad: Rammanohar Lohia Samata Vidyalaya Nyas, 1971. 359p.

13875 ILCHMAN, W.F. A political economy of foreign aid: the case of India. In AS 7 (1967) 667-88.

13876 RAO, V.K.R.V. & DHARM NARAIN. Foreign aid and India's economic development. NY: Asia, 1963. 111p.

13877 ROY, K.C. & A.L. LOUGHEED. India's foreign aid experience since 1956: some observations. In SA 6 (1976) 66-74.

13878 SHARMA, R.K. Foreign aid to India: an economic study. ND: Marwah Pub., 1977. 176p.

d. private foreign investment
i. general

13879 BARANSON, J. Manufacturing problems in India; the Cummins diesel experience. Syracuse: Syracuse U. Press, 1967. 146p.

13880 HAZARI, R.K., ed. Foreign collaboration; report and proceedings of the seminar held by the Centre of Advanced Studies, Dept. of Economics, U. of Bombay, February 1-3, 1965. Bombay: U. of Bombay, 1967. 271p.

13881 Industrial licensing and foreign collaboration. Rev. ed. ND: Indian Investment Centre, 1976. 81p.

13882 KACKER, M.P. Marketing adaptation of U.S. business firms in India. ND: Sterling, 1974. 160p.

13883 KAPOOR, A. International business negotiations: a study in India. NY: NYU Press, 1970. 361p.

13884 KIDRON, M. Foreign investments in India. London: OUP, 1965. 368p.

13885 KUST, M.J. Foreign enterprise in India: laws and policies. Chapel Hill: U. of N. Carolina Press, 1964. 498p.

13886 MARKENSTEN, K. Foreign investment and development. Swedish companies in India. Lund: Studentlitteratur, 1972. 295p.

13887 NEGANDHI, A.R. The foreign private investment climate in India. Bombay: Vora, 1966. 159p.

13888 SINGHAL, H.K. Taxing for development: incentives affecting foreign investment. In Harvard Intl. Law R. 14,1 (1973) 50-88.

13889 SRIVASTAVA, P.K. Foreign collaboration: its significance in India's industrial progress. Agra: S.L. Agarwala, 1975. 245p.

13890 SUBRAHMANIAN, K.K. Import of capital and technology; a study of foreign collaborations in Indian industry. ND: PPH, 1972. 248p.

13891 TOMLINSON, J.W.C. The joint venture process in international business: India and Pakistan. Cambridge: MIT Press, 1970. 227p.

13892 VEDAVALLI, R. Private foreign investment and economic development: a case study of petroleum in India. Cambridge: CamUP, 1976. 222p.

ii. the role of multinational corporations

13893 GAURI SHANKAR, V. The performance of transnational corporations in India. In IQ 33,2 (1977) 181-97.

13894 Menace of multinationals. ND: PPH, 1977. 78p.

13895 Multinationals and underdevelopment [special issue]. In SocSci 7,80/81 (1979) 3-112.

13896 PAUL, S. Transnational corporations and developing countries: some issues in industrial policy. In EPW 14,30-32 (1979) 1315-30.

13897 SANGAL, P.S. Multinationals and their impact on India. In R&S 23,4 (1976) 29-41.

13898 SARKAR, P.L. Transfer of technology to less developed countries: Indian experience with multinational corporations. In IEJ 26,2 (1978) 131-52.

13899 SINGH, V.B. Multinational corporations and India. ND: Sterling, 1979. 161p.

13900 SUBRAHMANIAN, K.K. & P. MOHANAN PILLAI. Multinationals and Indian export: a study of foreign collaboration and export performance in selected Indian industries. ND: Allied, 1979. 115p.

D. India's Relations with Specific Countries and Areas

1. General Studies (Multilateral)

13901 DATAR, A.L. India's economic relations with the U.S.S.R. and Eastern Europe, 1953 to 1969. Cambridge: CamUP, 1972. 278p.

13902 GUPTA, SISIR. Sino-U.S. detente and India. In IQ 27,3 (1971) 179-84.

13903 KAPUR, H. The embattled triangle: Moscow-Peking-New Delhi. Delhi: Abhinav, 1973. 175p.

13904 KAUL, T.N. India, China, and Indochina: reflections of a liberated diplomat. ND: Allied, 1980. 163p.

13905 MILLER, J.D.B., ed. India, Japan, Australia, partners in Asia? Canberra: ANUP, 1968. 214p.

13906 SHARMA, S.P. India's boundary and territorial disputes. Delhi: Vikas, 1971. 198p.

13907 WOODMAN, D. Himalayan frontiers; a political review of British, Chinese, Indian, and Russian rivalries. NY: Barrie & Jenkins, 1970. 423p.

2. China-India Relations
a. general studies

13908 DUNCAN, G.T. & R.M. SIVESON. Markov chain models for conflict analysis; results from Sino-Indian relations, 1959-1964. In Intl. Studies Q. 14,3 (1975) 343-74.

13909 HU, CHI-HSI. Pekin et le mouvement communiste indien. Paris: A. Colin, 1972. 152p.

13910 JETLY, N. India-China relations, 1947-1977: a study of Parliament's role in the making of foreign policy. ND: Radiant, 1979. 344p.

13911 KAPUR, A. India-China dialogue: changing perceptions. In China Report 11,1 (1975) 13-26.

13912 MATHUR, G. New Delhi - Peking: a study in relationship. ND: Kalamkar Prakashan, 1978. 88p.

13913 MOHAN RAM. Politics of Sino-Indian confrontation. Delhi: Vikas, 1973. 241p.

13914 ROWLAND, J. A history of Sino-Indian relations; hostile co-existence. Princeton: Van Nostrand, 1967. 248p.

13915 SREEDHAR. Problems and prospects of Sino-Indian trade. In IQ 32,2 (1976) 142-52.

b. Sino-Indian border disputes and the 1962 War
i. documents

13916 Chinese aggression in war and peace; letters of the Prime Minister of India. ND: PDMIB, 1962. 44p.

13917 INDIA (REP.). MIN. OF EXTERNAL AFFAIRS. Notes, memoranda and letters exchanged and agreements signed between the Governments of India and China, white paper. ND: 1959-64. 10 v. in 8.

13918 ______. Report of the officials of the governments of India and the People's Republic of China on the boundary question. ND: 1961. 342 + 213p.

13919 Prime Minister on Chinese aggression. ND: Min. of External Affairs, 1963. 118p.

13920 Prime Minister on Sino-Indian relations. ND: Min. of External Affairs, 1961-62. 2 v. in 4, 741p.

13921 The Sino-Indian boundary question. Enl. ed. Peking: Foreign Languages Press, 1962. 134p.

13922 The Sino-Indian boundary; texts of treaties, agreements and certain exchange of notes... ND: Indian Soc. of Intl. Law, 1962. 49p.

ii. general studies of the Sino-Indian border dispute

13923 CAROE, O. The Sino-Indian question. In Royal Central Asian Soc. J. 50 (1963) 238-51.

13924 CHAKRAVARTI, P.C. The evolution of India's northern borders. NY: Asia, for ICWA, 1971. 179p.

13925 CONNELL, J. The India-China frontier dispute. In Royal Central Asian Soc. J. 47,3/4 (1960) 270-285.

13926 EEKELEN, W.F. VAN. Indian foreign policy and the border dispute with China. 2nd rev. ed. The Hague: Nijhoff, 1967. 230p. [1st ed. 1964]

13927 FISHER, M.W. & J.V. BONDURANT. Indian views of Sino-Indian relations. Berkeley: Inst. of Intl. Studies, U. of California, 1956. 195p. (Indian press digests, monograph 1)

13928 INDIAN SOC. OF INTL. LAW. The India-China boundary question, a legal study with a brief historical introduction. ND: 1963. 68p.

13929 LAMB, A. The China-India border; the origins of the disputed boundaries. London: OUP, 1964. 192p.

13930 ______. The Sino-Indian border in Ladakh. Canberra: ANUP, 1973. 113p.

13931 LINUS, J. The Sino-Indian border dispute. Singapore: Malaysia Pub., 1965. 62p.

13932 MULLIK. B.N. The Chinese betrayal; my years with Nehru. Bombay: Allied, 1971. 650p.

13933 MUNAWWAR KHAN. Sino-Indian border dispute. Sialkot Cantt.: Modern Book Depot, 1972. 72p.

13934 RANA, S.P., ed. Our northern borders, India-China border dispute. ND: Book Times Co., 1963. 158p.

13935 STAHNKE, A.A. The place of international law in Chinese strategy and tactics: the case of the Sino-Indian boundary dispute. In JAS 30,1 (1970) 95-119.

13936 VARKEY, O. At the crossroads: the Sino-Indian border dispute and the Communist Party of India, 1959-1963. Calcutta: Minerva, 1974. 304p.

13937 VARMA, S.P. Struggle for the Himalayas: a study in Sino-Indian relations. 2nd ed., rev. and enl. ND: Sterling, 1971. 316p. [1st ed. 1965]

iii. India, China, and the problem of Tibet

13938 GOPAL, RAM. India-China-Tibet triangle. Lucknow: Pustak Kendra, 1964. 225p.

13939 JAIN, G. Panchsheela and after; a reappraisal of Sino-Indian relations in the context of the Tibetan insurrection. NY: Asia, 1961. 241p.

13940 KANT, R. Tibet in Indian foreign policy. In PSR 8 (1969) 213-25.

13941 SINHA, N.C. India and the Tibet region of China. In BPP 92,1 (1973) 58-72.

iv. the 1962 War in Ladakh and NEFA: Indian military debacle

13942 BHARGAVA, G.S. The battle of NEFA; the undeclared war. Bombay: Allied, 1964. 187p.

13943 COMMUNIST PARTY OF INDIA. The Indian-China border dispute and the Communist Party of India; resolutions, statements and speeches, 1959-1963. ND: CPI, 1963. 127p.

13944 DALVI, J.P. Himalayan blunder; the curtain-raiser to the Sino-Indian War of 1962. 2nd ed. Bombay: Thacker, 1969. 506p.

13945 FISHER, M.W. & L.E. ROSE & R.A. HUTTENBACK. Himalayan battleground; Sino-Indian rivalry in Ladakh. NY: Praeger, 1963. 205p.

13946 FRIEDMAN, E. Some political constraints on a political science: quantitative content analysis and the Indo-Chinese border crisis of 1962. In China Q. 63 (1975) 528-38.

13947 HANSEN, G.E. The impact of the border war on Indian perceptions of China. In PA 40,3/4 (1967-68) 235-49.

13948 JOHRI, S. Chinese invasion of Ladakh. Lucknow: Himalaya Pub., 1969. 221p.

13949 ______. Chinese invasion of NEFA. Lucknow: Himalaya Pub., 1968. 260p.

13950 KARNIK, V.B., ed. China invades India; the story of invasion against the background of Chinese history and Sino-Indian relations. Bombay: Allied, 1963. 316p.

13951 KAUL, B.M. The untold story. Bombay: Allied, 1967. 507p.

13952 KRISHNA MENON, V.K. India and the Chinese invasion. Bombay: Contemporary Pub., 1963. 91p.

13953 LIMAYE, MADHU. The Sino-Indian war; its historical and international background and pre-conditions of victory. Bombay: H. Jhaveri, 1962. 62p.

13954 LOHIA, RAMMANOHAR. India, China and northern frontiers. Hyderabad: Navahind, 1963. 272p.

13955 MANKEKAR, D.R. The guilty men of 1962. Bombay: Tulsi Shah Enterprises, 1968. 184p.

13956 MAXWELL, N. India's China war. London: Cape, 1970. 475p.

13957 PATTERSON, G.N. Peking versus Delhi. NY: Praeger, 1964. 310p.

13958 SAIGAL, J.R. The unfought war of 1962: the NEFA debacle. Bombay: Allied, 1979. 180p.

13959 SINHA, SATYANARAYAN. China strikes. London: Blandford Press, 1964. 160p.

3. USSR-India Relations
a. bibliography

13960 ATTAR CHAND. Bibliography of Indo-Soviet relations, 1947-77: a book of readings with selected abstracts. ND: Sterling, 1978. 152p.

13961 KUMAR, L.C. Indian view of Soviet Russia: bibliography of Indian literature on USSR, 1947-1977. ND: Tulsi, 1979. 384p.

b. general studies of Indo-Soviet relations

13962 ANAND, J.S. Indo-Soviet relations: a more glorious future. ND: Sterling, 1979. 83p.

13963 ANWER AZEEM. Deep are the roots. ND: PPH, 1969. 148p.

13964 BALABUSHEVICH, V.V. & BIMLA PRASAD, eds. India and the Soviet Union; a symposium. Delhi: PPH, 1969. 228p.

13965 BIMAL PRASAD. Indo-Soviet relations 1947-1972: a documentary study. Bombay: Allied Pub., 1973. 494p.

13966 CHATTERJI, B.K. Indo-Soviet friendship: an analytical study. ND: S. Chand, 1974. 259p.

13967 GHOSH, P.C. India's foreign policy and the Soviet Union. Calcutta: Classical, 1973. 146p.

13968 IMAM, ZAFAR. Ideology and reality in Soviet policy in Asia: Indo-Soviet relations, 1947-60. Delhi:

Kalyani Publishers, 1975. 260p.

13969 KHAN, RASHEEDUDDIN, et al., eds. India and the Soviet Union: cooperation and development. Bombay: Allied, 1975. 392p.

13970 KULKARNI, M. Indo-Soviet political relations since the Bandung Conference of 1955. Bombay: Vora, 1968. 216p.

13971 MENON, K.P.S. A diplomat speaks. Bombay: Allied, 1974. 140p.

13972 NEELKANT, K. Partners in peace; a study in Indo-Soviet relations. Delhi: Vikas, 1972. 192p.

13973 OVERSTREET, G.D. India and Pakistan. In T.H. Hammond, ed. Soviet foreign relations and world communism; a selected, annotated bibliography. Princeton: PUP, 1965, 824-36.

13974 PARDESI, G. Indo-Soviet relations: chances of peace in South Asia. In IAF 5,3 (1974) 335-52.

13975 ROTHERMUND, D. Indien und die Sowjetunion. Tübingen: Arbeitsgemeinschaft für Osteuropaforschung, 1968. 128p.

13976 STEIN, A.B. India and the Soviet Union: the Nehru era. Chicago: UChiP, 1969. 320p.

13977 ______. India and the USSR: the post-Nehru period. In AS 7 (1967) 165-75.

c. Soviet policy towards India - perceptions and strategies

13978 BANERJEE, J. India in Soviet global strategy: a conceptual study. Calcutta: Minerva, 1977. 201p.

13979 CHICHEROV, A. The tendencies in the development of national relations in independent India. In AS 14,3 (1974) 279-88.

13980 DONALDSON, R.H. India: the soviet stake in stability. In AS 12,6 (1972) 475-92.

13981 ______. Soviet policy toward India: ideology and strategy. Cambridge: HUP, 1974. 338p.

13982 IMAM, ZAFAR, ed. Soviet view of India, 1957-1975. Delhi: Kalyani, 1977. 211p.

13983 KAPUR, H. The Soviet Union and the emerging nations: a case study of Soviet policy towards India. London: Joseph, for the Grad. Institute of Intl. Studies, Geneva, 1972. 124p.

13984 NAIK, J.A. Soviet policy towards India from Stalin to Brezhnev. Delhi: Vikas, 1970. 201p.

13985 SAGER, P. Moscow's hand in India; an analysis of Soviet propaganda. Bombay: Lalvani, 1967. 224p.

13986 Soviet scholars view South Asia [special issue]. In AS 14,3 (1974) 205-306.

d. the 1971 Indo-Soviet Treaty of Peace, Friendship, and Cooperation: alliance without alignment?

13987 CHAUDHURI, S. Indo-Soviet treaty; a close-up view. ND: Kalamkar, 1973. 187p.

13988 CHOPRA, PRAN. Before & after the Indo-Soviet treaty. ND: S. Chand, 1971. 175p.

13989 GHATATE, N.M. Indo-Soviet treaty; reactions and reflections. ND: Deendayal Res. Inst., 1972. 300p.

13990 KAPUR, A. Indo-Soviet treaty and the emerging Asian balance. In AS 12,6 (1972) 463-74.

13991 JAIN, A.P. Shadow of the bear: the Indo-Soviet treaty. ND: P.K. Deo, 1971. 176p.

13992 MENON, K.P.S. The Indo-Soviet treaty; setting and meaning. Delhi: Vikas, 1971. 83p.

13993 SETHI, J.D. Indo-Soviet treaty and non-alignment. In IQ 27,4 (1971) 327-36.

e. Indo-Soviet economic relations

13994 DAGLI, V., ed. Indo-Soviet economic relations; a survey. Bombay: Vora, 1971. 159p.

13995 GRANOVSKY, A. & V. KOPTEVSHY & L. RAITSIN. Indo-Soviet economic cooperation and trade relations. ND: Sumeet Pub., 1977. 54p.

13996 Indo-Soviet economic cooperation, 1955-1968. ND: Econ. Coop. Study Group, 1968. 106p.

13997 MEHTA, Vinod. Soviet Union and India's industrial development. ND: Manas Pub., 1975. 89p.

13998 MUKHERJI, R. Economics of Soviet trade and aid: a critique. Calcutta: Subarnarekha, 1978. 256p.

13999 SEBASTIAN, M. Industrial development in India: some political objectives of Soviet aid. In SocAct 24, 3 (1974) 248-59.

14000 SHARMA, R.K. Indo-Soviet relations: economic analysis. ND: Allied, 1980. 112p.

14001 ______, ed. The economics of Indo-Soviet trade. Bombay: Allied, 1979. 125p.

14002 STANISLAUS, M.S. Soviet economic aid to India: an analysis and evaluation. ND: N.V. Pub., 1975. 388p.

4. United States-India Relations
a. general studies

14003 American policy in India. In Central Asian R. 10, 3 (1962) 185-93. [summary of Soviet works]

14004 BARNDS, W.J. Indian and America at odds. In Intl. Affairs (London) 49,3 (1973) 371-384.

14005 BHARGAVA, G.S. Indo-U.S. Relations: an analysis of three periods. In JIDSA 6 (1974) 483-526.

14006 HARRISON, S., ed. India and the United States. NY: Macmillan, 1961. 244p.

14007 DINESH SINGH. Indo-U.S. relations. In JIDSA 6,1 (1973) 1-14.

14008 HEIMSATH, C.H. American images of India as factors in U.S. foreign policy planning. In ATS 2 (1977) 271-89.

14009 KUNHI KRISHNAN, T.V. The unfriends, India and America. Thompson, CT: InterCulture Associates, 1974. 271p.

14010 MALAVIYA, H.D. India - U.S.: a blunt and cold relationship. ND: Malaviya, 1978. 122p.

14011 NATARAJAN, L. American shadow over India. Rev. ed. Delhi: PPH, 1956. 305p.

14012 NAYAR, B.R. American geopolitics and India. ND: Manohar, 1977. 246p.

14013 RAHAMATHULLA, B. Indo-American politics, 1970-78. Delhi: Surjeet Pub., 1980. 155p.

14014 SETH, S.P. The Indian Ocean and Indo-American relations. In AS 15,8 (1975) 645-55.

14015 TALBOT, P. & S.L. POPLAI. India and America, a study of their relations. NY: Harper, 1958. 200p.

14016 TEWARI, S.C. Indo-U.S. relations, 1947-1976. ND: Radiant, 1977. 179p.

b. memoirs of U.S. and Indian diplomats

14017 BOWLES, C. Ambassador's report. NY: Harper, 1954. 415p.

14018 ______. Promises to keep: my years in public life, 1941-1969. NY: Harper & Row, 1971. 657p.

14019 ______. A view from New Delhi; selected speeches and writings, 1963-1969. Bombay: Allied, 1969. 276p.

14020 CHAGLA, M.C. An ambassador speaks. London: Asia, 1962. 152p.

14021 GALBRAITH, J.K. Ambassador's journal; a personal account of the Kennedy years. Boston: Houghton Mifflin, 1969. 656p.

14022 GOODFRIEND, A. The twisted image. NY: St. Martin's Press, 1963. 264p. [by USIA official]

14023 KAUL, T.N. The Kissinger years; Indo-American relations. ND: Arnold Heinemann, 1980. 112p.

14024 MOYNIHAN, D.P. Indo-U.S. relations. In IQ 30,1 (1974) 5-11.

c. major issues of U.S.-India relations

14025 Academic colonialism: a symposium on the influences which destroy intellectual independence. In Seminar 112 (1968) 10-43.

14026 ADEL, D.S. Danger of CIA. ND: Progressive Peoples Sector Pub., 1976. 164p.

14027 BRECHER, M. India's decisions on the Voice of America: a study in irresolution. In AS 14,7 (1974) 637-650.

14028 KAUSHIK, R.P. The crucial years of non-alignment: U.S.A., Korean War, India. ND: Kumar Bros., 1972. 264p.

14029 MCCORMACK, W. Problems of American scholars in India. In AS 16,11 (1976) 1064-80.

14030 SINGH, L.P. Regional power vs. global power in arms control: India, America, and nuclear affairs. In IQ 35,3 (1979) 351-61.

14031 STEINBERG, B.S. The Korean war: a case study in Indian neutralism. In Orbis 8 (1975) 837-954.

14032 SUBRAMANIAM, V. American academics and India. In EPW 7,51 (1972) 2449-51.

d. U.S.-India economic relations - trade and general studies

14033 DAGLI, V., comp. Two decades of Indo-U.S. relations. Bombay: Vora, 1969. 231p.

14033a DESAI, ASHOK V. U.S. corporations as investors in India: a study of their experience, 1955-1978. In EPW 14,49 (1979) 2015-21.

14034 SALVI, P.G. Aid to collaboration: a study in Indo-U.S. economic relations. Bombay: Popular, 1978. 173p.

14035 SHOURIE, H.D. Prospects of trade with U.S.A. In EE 53 (1969) 10-19.

e. U.S. economic assistance to India
i. general studies: Point Four (1950), Technical Cooperation Mission (1952), and other development programs

14036 BAUER, P.T. Indian economic policy and development. Bombay: Popular, 1965. 152p. [1st pub. 1959 as U.S. aid and Indian economic development]

14037 CHANDRASEKHAR, S. American aid and India's economic development. NY: Praeger, 1965. 243p.

14038 DESAI, T. Indo-American wheat negotiations of 1950-1951. In IPSR 9,2 (1975) 119-51.

14039 INDIA (REP.). DEPT. OF ECON. AFFAIRS. Report on the Indo-U.S. technical co-operation programme. Jan. 1952 - March 1954-. ND: MPGOI, 1955-1969.

14040 JOHANSEN, R.C. United States foreign aid to India: a case study of the impact of U.S. foreign policy on the prospects for world order reform. Princeton: Woodrow Wilson School of Public & Intl. Studies, Princeton U., 1975. 136p.

14041 LOOMBA, J.F. U.S. aid to India; 1951-1967: a study in decision-making. In IQ 28,4 (1972) 304-331.

14042 MAHESHWARI, B. Bokaro: the politics of American aid. In IS 10 (1969) 163-80.

14043 PAVLOV, V.I. India: economic freedom versus imperialsim. ND: PPH, 1963. 247p. [1st Russian ed. 1962]

14044 RAY, AJIT. Economics and politics of U.S. foreign aid. Calcutta: National Pub., 1966. 76p.

14045 SINGH, A.K. Impact of American aid on Indian economy. Bombay: Vora, 1973. 175p.

ii. PL480: sale of U.S. surplus agricultural commodities for rupees

14046 BILGRAMI, S.A.R. The farm surplus problem in the United States: the case for Public Law 480. In Indian J. of American Studies 3,1 (1973) 58-70.

14047 DESAI, T. Indo-American wheat negotiations of 1950-1951. In IPSR 9,2 (1975) 119-50.

14048 GUPTA, S.C. Freedom from foreign food: pernicious effects of PL480. Delhi: Blitz Natl. Forum, 1965. 53p.

14049 Indo-U.S. agreement on Public Law 480 and other funds. In Foreign Affairs Report 23,3 (1974) 33-42.

14050 NICHOLSON, N.K. Politics and food policy in India. Ph.D. diss. Cornell U., 1966. 432p. [UM 66-11,029]

14051 RATH, N. & V.S. PATVARDHAN. Impact of assistance under P.L. 480 on Indian economy. Poona: GIPE, 1967. 204p.

14052 SHENOY, B.R. PL480 aid and India's food problem. ND: Affiliated East-West Press, 1974. 342p.

14053 U.S. GENERAL ACCOUNTING OFFICE. Opportunities for better use of United States-owned excess foreign currency in India; report to the Congress by the Comptroller General of the United States. Washington: 1971. 210p.

iii. private foreign assistance through foundations and voluntary agencies

14054 HERTA, W.J. Roots of change; the Ford Foundation in India. NY: Ford Foundation, 1961. 52p.

14055 STREETER, C.P. A partnership to improve food production in India. NY: Rockefeller Foundation, 1969. 137p.

5. United Kingdom-India Relations Since Independence

14056 BANERJI, A.K. India and Britain, 1947-68: the evolution of post-colonial relations. Calcutta: Minerva, 1977. 341p.

14057 ______. The quest for a new order in Indo-British relations. In IQ 33,3 (1977) 292-307.

14058 BAROOH, D.P. Indo-British relations 1950-1960. ND: Sterling, 1977. 336p.

14059 FABIAN, P., ed. Delhi post, dak edition: the bedside Delhi post. ND: Fabian, McGurk, and McGuigan, 1977. 221p. [selected items from the Delhi post, 1971-1976, house magazine of the British High Commission in India]

14060 GUPTA, R.L. Conflict and harmony, Indo-British relations: a new perspective. Delhi: Trimurti, 1971. 174p.

14061 LIPTON, M. & J. FIRN. The erosion of a relationship: India and Britain since 1960. NY: OUP, 1975. 427p.

14062 ZINKIN, M. & T. ZINKIN. Britain and India: requiem for Empire. London: Chatto & Windus, 1964. 191p.

6. India in the British Commonwealth, and Relations with Commonwealth Nations

14063 BRECHER, M. India's decision to remain in the Commonwealth. In JComPolSt 12,1 (1974) 63-90. [suppl. In 12,2 (1974) 228-30]

14064 GANGAL, S.C. India and the Commonwelath. Agra: S.L. Agarwala, 1970. 152p.

14065 HAUSE, E.M. India and the Commonwelath of nations: a study in contemporary political thought. In IJPS 23 (1962) 225-39.

14066 MAPRAYIL, C. Nehru and the Commonwealth. ND: Radiant, 1976. 109p.

14067 RAJAN, M.S. India and the commonwelath. In Australian J. of Politics & History 12 (1966) 229-40.

14068 ______. The Indo-Canadian entente. In Intl. J. (Toronto) 17 (1962) 358-84.

14069 THOMSON, D.C. India and Canada: a decade of cooperation 1947-1957. In Islamic Studies 9 (1968) 404-430.

7. India and Europe
a. the European Economic Community (Common Market)

14070 BIERWIRTH, G. Die Kulturpolitik der Bundesrepublik in Indien. In IAF 4,4 (1973) 572-586.

14071 DAGLI, V. India and Germany: a survey of economic relations. Bombay: Vora, 1970. 232p.

14072 DHARMA KUMAR. India and the European Economic Community. Bombay: Asia, 1966. 272p.

14073 DRURY, M. The Eruopean Economic Community: its relations with South and South-East Asia. In Asian Affairs 10,1 (1979) 9-19.

14074 HUNCK, J.M. India tomorrow; pattern of Indo-German future. Tr. fr. German. Düsseldorf: Verlag Handelsblatt, 1963. 307p.

14075 ______. India's silent revolution, a survey of Indo-German cooperation. Tr. fr. German. Düsseldorf: Verlag Handelsblatt, 1958. 172p.

14076 INDIAN CHAMBER OF COMMERCE, CALCUTTA. WORLD TRADE DEPT. India's trade with ECM countries. Calcutta: 1966. 70-.

14077 LOKRE, S.L. The OEEC countries and India, 1948-61. In NUJ 23,3/4 (1972-73) 1-165.

14078 RANGNEKAR, D.K. India, Britain and European Common Market. ND: R. & K., 1963. 236p.

14079. TANDON, J.K. Indo-German economic relations. ND: National, 1978. 241p.

b. the Comecon nations of Eastern Europe

14080 CHISHTI, S. India's trade with East Europe. ND: Indian Inst. of Foreign Trade, 1973. 118p.

14081 India's economic relations with East European countries; a special number by the Alumni Association of India Institute of Foreign Trade. ND: the Assn., 1973. 215p.

14082 JAG MOHAN. 25 years GDR, 1949-1974. ND: Himala Publishers, 1974. 96p.

14083 KALMAR, G., ed. India and Hungary: decades of cooperation. ND: Sterling, 1979. 111p.

14084 20 years of India-GDR relations: an anthology. ND: All India Indo-GDR Friendship Assn., 1974. 140p.

8. India and the Middle East

14085 ALI, MEHRUNNISA. Changing pattern of India-Iran relations. In Pakistan Horizon 28,4 (1975) 53-66.

14086 BHARGAVA, G.S., ed. India and West Asia; a survey of public opinion. ND: Popular Book Services, 1967. 109p.

14087 HAMID, M. The unholy alliance: Indo-Israel collaboration against the Muslim world. Lahore: Islamic Book Centre, 1978. 263p.

14088 India and Palestine; the evolution of a policy. ND: Min. of External Affairs, 1968. 74p.

14089 Indo-Israel relations; a study of India's posture on Arab-Israel conflict. Karachi: Maᶜaref, 1969. 36p.

14090 KOZICKI, R.J. Indian policy toward the Middle East. In Orbis 11 (1967) 786-97.

14091 RAO, S.V. The Arab-Israeli conflict: the Indian view. ND: Orient Longman, 1972. 69p.

14092 SHUKLA, M. Indo-Egyptian relations. Jodhpur: Usha Pub. House, 1979. 108p.

9. India and Southeast Asia

14093 DAS, P.K. India and the Vietnam War. ND: Young Asia, 1972. 176p.

14094 INDIAN CHAMBER OF COMMERCE, CALCUTTA. WORLD TRADE DEPT. India's trade with ECAFE countries. Calcutta: 1967. 30 + 93p.

14095 NOORANI, A.B. India, South-east Asia and Vietnam. Bombay: Democratic Res. Service, 1967. 24p.

14096 PANCHAMUKHI, V.R. Revealed comparative advantage: India's trade with the countries of the ECAFE region. In EPW 8,2 (1973) 65-74.

14097 SARDESAI, D.R. Indian foreign policy in Cambodia, Laos and Vietnam, 1947-1964. Berkeley: UCalP, 1968. 336p.

14098 SINGH, K.R.K. India's trade with South East Asia: a study. Allahabad: Chugh, 1976. 160p.

14099 SINGH, U.S. Burma and India, 1948-1962: a study in the foreign policies of Burma and India and Burma's policy towards India. ND: Oxford & IBH, 1979. 256p.

14100 SUBRAHMANYAM, K., ed. Self-reliance and national resiliences. [Papers from] India-Indonesia Seminar, Delhi 1975. ND: Abhinav, 1975. 192p.

14101 THIEN, T.T. India and South East Asia, 1947-1960; a study of India's policy towards the South East Asian countries in the period 1947-1960. Genève: Droz, 1960. 384p.

10. Japan-India Relations

14102 AGARWAL, B. Indo-Japanese trade relations: a diagnosis. Jaipur: Aalekh Pub., 1974. 196p.

14103 India and Japan: the emerging balance of power in Asia and opportunities for arms control, 1970-1975. NY: Southern Asian Inst., East Asian Inst., Columbia U., 1971. 4v.

14104 Round Table Conference of the India and Japan Committees, November 4-8, 1968. Proceedings. ND: Planning Commission, 1969. 39p.

11. India's Relations with Africa and Latin America

14105 HARDEV SINGH. India and Africa. In EE (Annual number) 1974, 1316-28.

14106 ______. India and Latin America. In EE (Annual number) 1974, 1329-34.

14107 SAHOTA, G.S. An analysis of trade between India and Brazil: nominal and effective tariffs. In Foreign Trade R. (New Delhi) 3,2 (1968) 198-228.

14108 SUBRAMANIAM, V. Styles of Africanisting: an Indian viewpoint. In Africa R. 12,1 (1972) 9-15.

12. India in the United Nations

14109 ASHRAF, SHAUKAT. India and the United Nations: a select bibliography, 1945-1963. In IS 7 (1965) 363-400.

14110 BERKES, R.N. & M.S. BEDI. The diplomacy of India: Indian foreign policy in the U.N. Stanford: Stanford U. Press, 1958. 221p.

14111 BILGRAMI, J.R. India's role in the U.N., with special reference to trust and non-self-governing territories. ND: Jamia Millia, 1969. 243p.

14112 CHAMLING, D.R. India and the United Nations. ND: Associated, 1978. 248p.

14113 DHILLON, N.S. In pursuit of freedom: India's policy at the United Nations. Washington: University Press of America, 1977. 227p.

14114 GUPTA, A. India and UN peace-keeping activities: a case study of Korea, 1947-53. ND: Radiant, 1977. 164p.

14115 India and the United Nations; report of a study group set up by the Indian Council of World Affairs. NY: Manhattan Pub. Co., 1957. 229p.

14116 KOCHANEK, S.A. India's changing role in the United Nations. In PA 53,1 (1980) 48-68.

14117 NAND LAL. From collective security to peacekeeping: a study of India's contribution to the United Nations Emergency Force, 1956-67. Calcutta: Minerva, 1975. 248p.

14118 PARAKATIL, F. India and United Nations peacekeeping operations. ND: S. Chand, 1975. 223p.

14119 RAMAKRISHNA REDDY, T. India's policy in the United Nations. Rutherford: Farleigh Dickinson U. Press, 1968. 164p.

14120 RANA, S. The changing Indian diplomacy at the United Nations. In Intl. Organization 24,1 (1970) 48-73.

14121 SCHLEICHER, C.P. & J.S. BAINS. The administration

of Indian foreign policy through the United Nations. Dobbs Ferry, NY: Oceana Pub., 1969. 130p.

V. PLANNING FOR INDIA'S DEVELOPMENT: STRUCTURE AND INSTITUTIONS OF THE ECONOMY

A. Bibliography and Reference

1. Bibliographies and Reference Works

14122 Basic statistics relating to the Indian economy, 1950-51 to 1972-73. ND: Central Stat. Org., Dept. of Statistics, Min. of Planning, 1976. 132p.

14123 Data India. ND: Press Institute of India. v.1-. 1976- [weekly digest of political & economic affairs]

14124 GUHA, P.S. Directory of economic research centres in India. Calcutta; Info. Res. Academy, 1972. 426p.

14125 GUPTA, G.P. Economic investigations in India; a bibliography of researches in commerce and economics approved by Indian universities, with supplement, 1966. Agra: Ram Prasad, 1966. 170p.

14126 RATH, VIMAL. Index of Indian economic journals, 1916-1965. Poona: Orient Longman, 1971. 302p. [GIPE studies, 57]

14127 A survey of research in economics. Bombay: Allied, 1977-78. 7 v. [v. 1, Methods and techniques, 135p.; v. 7, Econometrics, 385p.; other vols. in appropriate sections below; sponsored by ICSSR]

2. The State of Economic Research on India: Trends and Methodology

14128 BHAGWATI, J.N. & S. CHAKRAVARTY. Contributions to Indian economic analysis: a survey. In American Econ. R. 59,4:2 (1969) 1-73.

14129 DANDEKAR, V.M. Dhananjaya Ramchandra Gadgil (1901-1971). In AV 8,2 (1971) i-xxiv.

14130 NATL. COUNCIL OF APPLIED ECON. RES. Current problems of planned economy; five years of research by NCAER. ND: 1962. 115p.

14131 RAO, C.R., ed. Data base of Indian economy: review and reappraisal. Calcutta: Statistical Pub. Soc., 1972. 253p. (Data base of Indian economy, 1)

B. Demography and Population Policy

1. Bibliography, Statistics; Status of Population Studies

14132 BHENDE, ASHA A. & T. KANITKAR & G. RAMA RAO, eds. Teaching and research in population studies: seventeen years of IIPS. Bombay: Intl. Inst. for Population Studies, 1976. 294p.

14133 BOSE, ASHISH & D.B. GUPTA & G. RAYCHAUDHURI, eds. Population statistics in India. ND: Vikas, 1977. 445p. (Data base of Indian economy series, 3)

14134 BOSE, ASHISH & P.B. DESAI & S.P. JAIN. Studies in demography. Chapel Hill: U. of N. Carolina Press, 1970. 579p.

14135 DESAI, P.B. A survey of research in demography. Bombay: Popular, 1975. 440p. [sponsored by ICSSR]

14136 HUSAIN, I.Z. State and status of demographic research in the country; seminar papers. Lucknow: Demographic Res. Centre, Lucknow U., 1970. 326p.

14137 INDIA (REP.). CENSUS OF INDIA, 1971. Bibliography of census publications in India. Delhi: MPGOI, 1972. 520p. [Census centenary pub., 5]

14138 ROY BURMAN, B.K. Social demography in India; a trend report. In A survey of research in sociology and social anthropology. Bombay: Popular, 1974, v. 1, 1-81. [sponsored by ICSSR]

14139 A status study on population research in India. ND: Tata McGraw-Hill, 1974-75. 3 v., 261, 265, 501p.

14140 TEXAS UNIV. POPULATION RES. CENTER. International population census bibliog.: Asia. Austin: U. of Texas, 1966. (Census bibliog. #5) [Ceylon, India, Nepal, Pakistan; 130p.]

2. General Studies of India's Population; Population and Economic Development

14141 AGARWALA, S.N. India's population problems. 2nd ed. Bombay: Tata McGraw-Hill, 1977. 231p. [1st ed. 1972]

14142 ______. Population. 2nd rev. ed. ND: NBT, 1977. 168p. (India, the land and the people; 1st ed. 1968)

14143 BAHADUR, K.P. Population crisis in India. ND: National, 1977. 180p.

14144 BHENDE, A.A. & T. KANITKAR. Principles of population studies. Bombay: Himalaya Pub. House, 1978. 578p.

14145 BOSE, ASHISH, ed. Population in India's development. Delhi: Vikas, 1974. 437p.

14146 CASSEN, R. India, population, economy and society. NY: Holmes & Meier, 1978. 419p.

14147 CHANDRASEKHAR, S. India's population; facts, problem and policy. Meerut: Meenakshi, 1967. 76p.

14148 COALE, A.J. & E.M. HOOVER. Population growth and economic development in low-income countries: a case study of India's prospects. Princeton: PUP, 1958. 389p.

14149 DAVIS, K. The population of India and Pakistan. NY: Russell & Russell, 1968. 283p. [1st pub. 1951]

14150 GANGULI, B.N. Population and development. ND: S. Chand, 1973. 132p.

14151 GYAN CHAND. Population in perspective; study of population crisis in India in the context of new social horizons. ND: Orient Longman, 1972. 380p.

14152 INDIA (REP.). CENSUS OF INDIA, 1971. Intercensal growth of population; analysis of extracts from all India census reports. ND: Office of the Registrar General, 1972. 255p. (Census centenary monograph, 3)

14153 KUPPUSWAMY, B. Population and society in India. Bombay: Popular, 1975. 136p.

14154 MITRA, ASOK. India's population: aspects of quality and control. ND: Abhinav, 1978. 2 v., 929p.

14155 RELE, J.R. & M.K. JAIN, eds. Population change and rural development in India. Bombay: Intl. Inst. for Population Studies, 1978. 309p.

14156 SANYAL, R.K. & A.K. NANDA & A.D. TRIPATHI. Demographic situation in India. ND: NIFP, 1975. 130p.

14157 SINHA, V.C. Dynamics of India's population growth. ND: National, 1979. 506p.

14158 SRINIVASAN, K. & S. MUKERJI, eds. Dynamics of population and family welfare in India. Bombay: Popular, 1979. 399p.

14159 SUBBIAH, B.V. The world population crisis; a case study of India. Allahabad: Kitab Mahal, 1972. 156p.

14160 VIG, O.P. India's population: a study through extension of stable population techniques. ND: Sterling, 1976. 144p.

3. Distribution and Composition of the Population: Sex Ratio, Regional Differences, and Migration

14161 BHATTACHARJEE, P.J. & G.N. SHASTRI. Population in India; a study of interstate variations. ND: Vikas, 1976. 131p.

14162 BHATTACHARYYA, A. Population geography of India. ND: Shree Pub. House, 1978. 68p.

14163 BOSE, ASHISH, ed. Patterns of population change in India, 1951-61. Bombay: Allied, 1967. 403p. [seminar on inter-state and intra-state variations]

14164 EAMES, E. Urbanization and rural-urban migration in India. In Population R. 9,1/2 (1965) 38-47.

14165 GUPTA, S.K. Interstate migration as an indicator of national integration. In Indian Anthropologist 2,1 (1972) 7-26.

14166 INDIA (REP.). CENSUS OF INDIA, 1961. Sex ratio of the population of India, by Pravin M. Visaria. ND: Office of the Registrar-general, 1971. 83p. (v. 1, monograph 10)

14167 INDIA (REP.). CENSUS OF INDIA, 1971. The changes in the sex ratio. ND: Office of the Registrar General, 1972. 105p. (Census centenary monograph, 6)

14168 INDIA (REP.). VITAL STATISTICS DIV. Sex composition in India. ND: 1972. 42p.

14169 KSHIRSAGAR, S. Pattern of internal migration of males in India - inter-state and intra-state flows. In AV 15,2 (1973) 161-79.

14170 RAMACHANDRAN, K.V. & V.A. DESHPANDE. The sex ratio at birth in India by regions. In Milbank Memorial Fund Q. 42 (1964) 84-94.

14171 ZACHARIAH, K.C. & J.P. AMBANNAVAR. Population redistribution in India: inter-state and rural-urban. In Ashish Bose, ed. Patterns of population change in India, 1951-61. ND: Allied, 1967, 93-106.

14172 ZACHARIAH, K.C. & K.S. SEETHARAM. Inter-state migration in India, 1951-1961. In Indian J. of Public Health 12 (1968) 47-63.

4. Studies of Fertility and Mortality in India

14173 DUBEY, D.C. & A. BARDHAN. Status of women and fertility in India. ND: NIFP, 1972. 49p.

14174 KOHLI, K.L. Mortality in India: a state-wise study. ND: Sterling, 1977. 296p.

14175 KURUP, R.S., ed. Studies on fertility in India. Gandhigram, Madurai Dist.: Gandhigram Inst. of Rural Health and Family Planning, 1975. 510p.

14176 MANDELBAUM, D.G. Human fertility in India; social components and policy perspectives. Berkeley: UCalP, 1974. 132p.

14177 ______. Social components of Indian fertility. In EPW 8,4/5/6 (1973) 151-72.

14178 PAULUS, C.R. The impact of urbanization on fertility in India. Mysore: U. of Mysore, 1966. 106p.

14179 SEN GUPTA, S.K. & P.N. KAPOOR. Principal causes of deaths in India. ND: Central Bureau of Health Intelligence, 1970. 110p.

14180 SRINIVAS, M.N. & E.A. RAMASWAMY. Culture and human fertility in India. Delhi: OUP, 1977. 32p.

14181 VAIDYANATHAN, K.E., ed. Studies on mortality in India. Gandhigram, Madurai Dist.: Gandhigram Inst. of Rural Helath and Family Planning, 1972. 400p.

14182 VISARIA, L. Religious and regional differences in mortality and fertility in the Indian subcontinent. Ph.D. Diss., Princeton U., 1972. 251p. [UM 72-24,709]

5. Population Policy and Population Control [See also VIII. G. 4., below]

14183 ARNIM, B. VON. Bevölkerungsentwicklung, Bevölkerungspolitik und Wirtschaftsplanung in Indien. Stuttgart: G. Fischer, 1969. 214p.

14184 BARNABAS, A.P. Population control in India: policy-administration-spread. ND: IIPA, 1977. 121p.

14185 CHANDRASEKHAR, S. Infant mortality, population growth, and family planning in India. Chapel Hill: U. of N. Carolina Press, 1972. 399p.

14186 DASGUPTA, B. Population policy; the crucial factor. In SAR 3,4 (1970) 331-46.

14187 INDIA (REP.). SMALL FAMILY NORM CMTEE. Report, 1968. ND: Dept. of Family Planning, GOI, 1969. 98p. [Chm., Govind Narain]

14188 MITRA, ASOK. National population policy in relation to national planning. Ahmedabad: Ajit Bhagat Memorial Trust, 1977. 42p.

14189 RAM, N.V.R. Management and population: a systems view and review of family planning programme in India. Delhi: D.K., 1974. 130p.

14190 Recommendations and documents: National Conference on Population Control, New Delhi, September 19-21, 1975. ND: Indian Medical Assoc., 1976. 186p.

14191 REITZ, J. Use of social research in population programs: a case study of a policy debate among social science experts. In S.R. Ingman & A.E. Thomas, eds. Topias and Utopias in health. The Hague: Mouton, 1975. 548p.

14192 SIMMONS, G.B. The Indian investment in family planning. NY: Population Council, 1971. 213p.

14193 Towards a population policy. ND: Council for Social Development, 1970-71. 4 v., 690p. [Proc. of four regional conferences]

C. Economic Geography and Natural Resources

14194 BHAT, L.S. & A.T.A. LEARMONTH. Recent contributions to the economic geography of India: some current preoccupations. In Economic Geography 44 (1968) 189-209.

14195 BOSE, S.C. Economic geography of India. Calcutta: Annapurna, 1974. 216p.

14196 CHAUDHURI, M.R. An economic geography of India. 2nd ed. Calcutta: Oxford & IBH, 1971. 222p.

14197 DAGLI, V., ed. Natural resources in the Indian economy. Bombay: Vora, 1971. 366p.

14198 GANANATHAN, V.S. Economic geography of India. ND: NBT, 1967. 135p.

14199 HUSAIN, M. Agricultural geography. Delhi: Inter-India Pub., 1979. 232p.

14200 INDIA (REP.). GEOLOGICAL SURVEY. Geology and mineral resources of the States of India. Delhi: Cont. of Pub., 1974-. v. 1-

14201 LAHIRI, A. & R. NAGARAJAN. India in perspective; development issues. ND: Arnold-Heinemann. 1977 [v. 2 on natural resources, 307p.]

14202 The wealth of India; a dictionary of Indian raw materials and industrial products. Delhi: Council of Scientific and Industrial Res., 1948-76. 21 v.

D. Output, Income, and Standards of Living

1. National Product and National Income: Estimates and Studies

14203 BRAHMANANDA, P.R. Determinants of real national income and price level in India. Bombay: U. of Bombay, 1977. 96p.

14204 CHAVAN, B.W. & A. CHAVAN. National income in India: concepts and methods. Bombay: Sindhu, 1970. 88p.

14205 INDIA. NATL. INCOME CMTEE. Final report, 1954. ND: Min. of Finance, 1954. [P.C. Mahalanobis, chm.]

14206 INDIAN CONF. ON RES. IN NATL. INCOME. Papers on national income and allied topics. London: Asia, 1963-. v. 1, 2, 3-

14207 KUZNETS, S. Observations on national income estimates and related measures in India, January 1957. In Sankhya ser. B 26,3/4 (1964) 337-56.

14208 MUKHERJEE, M. National income of India: trends and structure. Calcutta: Statistical Pub. Soc., 1969. 521p.

14209 National income of India, growth and distribution, 1950-51 to 1960-61; facts and problems. Bombay: IMC Econ. Res. and Training Foundation, 1963. 271p. (Res. pub. series, 4)

14210 RAMANA, D.V. National accounts and input-output accounts of India. Bombay: Asia, 1969. 100p.

14211 RAO, V.K.R.V. Changing structure of Indian economy as seen through national accounts data. In EPW 14,50 (1979) 2049-58.

2. Income Distribution and Standard of Living

14212 INDIA (REP.). CMTEE. ON DISTRIBUTION OF INCOME AND LEVELS OF LIVING, 1960. Report. Pt. 1, Distribution of income and wealth and concentration of economic power; Pt. 2, Changes in levels of living. ND: Planning Cmsn., 1964-69. 2 v., 107, 114p. [Chm., P.C. Mahalanobis]

14213 KANSAL, S.M. Changes in the per capita income and the per capita availability of essential commodities in India since 1931, and their projections in future. ND: Econ. and Scientific Res. Foundation, 1974. 46p.

14214 LOKANATHAN, P.S. Patterns of income distribution and saving. ND: NCAER, 1967. 46p.

14215 NCAER. Household income and its disposition. ND: 1980. 218p.

14216 OJHA, P.D. A configuration of Indian poverty: inequality and levels of living. In SocAct 20 (1970) 103-22.

14217 OJHA, P.D. & V.V. BHATT. Pattern of income distribution in an underdeveloped economy: a case study of India. In American Econ. R. 54 (1964) 711-20.

14218 RANADIVE, K.R. Pattern of income distribution in India, 1953-54 to 1959-60. In Bull. of the Oxford U. Inst. of Econ. and Stat. 30,3 (1968) 231-61.

14219 RUDRA, ASHOK. The rate of growth of the Indian economy. In E.A.G. Robinson & M. Kidron, eds. Economic development in South Asia. London: Macmillan, 1970, 35-53.

14220 SARMA, I.R.K. Changes in the distribution of income and levels of living. In Economic development, issues and policies; Dr. P.S. Lokanathan seventh-second birthday commemoration volume. Bombay: Vora, 1966, 204-22.

3. Regional and State Differences in Income and Living Levels

14221 CHAUDHRY, M.D. Regional income accounting in an underdeveloped economy; a case study of India. Calcutta: KLM, 1966. 144p.

14222 The course of state incomes: 1960-1968: unequal growth in India's states. In QER 15,4 (1969) 15-28.

14223 GANGULI, B.N. & D.B. GUPTA. Levels of living in India: an inter-state profile. ND: S. Chand, 1976. 273p.

14224 HESTON, A. Regional income differences in India and the "historical" pattern. In IEJ 15 (1967) 222-31.

14225 INDIA (REP.). PLANNING CMSN. PROGRAMME EVALUATION ORGANISATION. Regional variations in social development and levels of living: a study of the impact of plan programmes. ND: 1968. 2 v. (PEO pub. 52 & 59)

14226 MAJUMDAR, A.G. Distribution of national income by states 1960-61. ND: NCAER, 1965. 216p.

14227 NCAER. Estimates of state income; 1950-51, 1955-56 and 1960-61 at 1960-61 prices. ND: 1967. 71p.

E. Economic Development and the Planning Process

1. Economic History of India since Independence

14228 ALAVI, HAMZA. India and the colonial mode of production. In EPW 10,33-35 (1975) 1235-62.

14229 BETTELHEIM, C. India independent. Tr. from French by W.A. Caswell. NY: Monthly Review Press, 1969. 410p. [1st French ed., 1962]

14230 BHATT, V.V. Two decades of development - the Indian experiment. Bombay: Vora, 1973. 107p.

14231 BHULESHKAR, A.V., ed. Growth of Indian economy in socialism. Bombay: Oxford & IBH, 1975. 607p.

14232 DAGLI, V. Twenty-five years of independence: a survey of Indian economy. Bombay: Vora, 1973. 245p.

14233 DAS, S.K. The changing image of India. ND: Abhinav, 1977. 123p.

14234 FRANKEL, F.R. India's political economy, 1947-1977; the gradual revolution. Princeton: PUP, 1978. 600p.

14235 GUJRAL, M.L. Economic failures of Nehru and Indira Gandhi: a study of three decades of deprivation and disillusionment. ND: Vikas, 1979. 255p.

14236 MALENBAUM, W. Modern India's economy; two decades of planned growth. Columbus, OH: C.E. Merrill, 1971. 230p.

14237 MISHRA, M.L. Performance and problems of Indian economy, 1947-1971 (Indian economy since Independence). In PSR 13,1/4 (1974) 254-77.

14238 SHETTY, S.L. Structural retrogression in the Indian economy since the mid-sixties. Bombay: Econ. and Political Weekly, 1978. 79p. [1st pub. in EPW, annual no. (Feb. 1978)]

14239 SHIV LAL, ed. Aspects of Indian progress. ND: Archive Pub., 1975. 220p.

14240 VENKATASUBBIAH, H. Indian economy since Independence. Bombay: Asia, 1958. 343p.

2. Economic Growth and Development
a. general studies

14241 BASU, D.N., ed. India in perspective; development issues. ND: Arnold-Heinemann, 1978. 3 v.

14242 CHAUDHURI, P. The Indian economy: poverty and development. ND: Vikas, 1978. 279p.

14243 CLARKSON, S. L'analyse soviétique des problèmes indiens du sous-développement, 1955-1964. Paris: Mouton, 1970. 270p.

14244 FAULWETTER, H. & P. STIER. Indien; Bilanz und Perspektive. Bilanz und Perspektive einer kapitalistischen Entwicklung. Innere und äussere Bedingungen der ökonomischen Reproduktion. Berlin: Akademie-Verlag, 1970. 246p.

14245 KHUSRO, A.M. The Indian economy: stability and growth. ND: Prachi Prakashan, 1979. 126p.

14246 KURIEN, C.T. Indian economic crisis: a diagnostic study. Bombay: Asia, 1969. 120p.

14247 LEWIS, J.P. Quiet crisis in India. NY: Doubleday, 1963. 383p.

14248 ______. Wanted in India: a relevant radicalism. Princeton: Center of Intl. Studies, Princeton U., 1969. 49p. [Also in EPW 5, special no. (July, 1970) 1211-26.]

14249 MELLOR, A. The new economics of growth; a strategy for India and the developing world. Ithaca: Cornell UP, 1976. 335p.

14250 ROSEN, G. Democracy and economic change in India. Berkeley: UCalP, 1966. 326p.

14251 REDDAWAY, W.B. The development of the Indian economy. London: Allen & Unwin, 1962. 216p. (Studies in the econ. dev. of India, 1)

14252 SINGH, M.L. Sectoral terms of trade and economic growth in India. ND: Sterling, 1976. 336p.

14253 THAKUR, S.Y. Indian economic development: retrospect and prospect. ND: Sterling, 1978. 180p.

14254 VEIT, L.A. India's second revolution: the dimensions of development. NY: McGraw-Hill, 1976. 402p.

b. essay collections

14255 BRAHMANANDA, P.R. & D.M. NANJUDAPPA & B.K. NARAYAN, eds. Indian economic development and policy: essays in honour of Professor V.L. D'Souza. ND: Vikas, 1978. 352p.

14256 CHAUDHURI, P., ed. Aspects of Indian economic development: a book of readings. London: Allen & Unwin, 1971. 288p.

14257 GADGIL, D.R. Selected writings and speeches of Professor D.R. Gadgil on planning and development, 1967-1971. Ed. by A.R. Kamat. Poona: GIPE, 1973. 372p. (Its studies, 62)

14258 JOSHI, N.C. Readings in applied economics: India's critical issues analysed. Delhi: Vivek Pub. Co., 1977. 272p.

14259 LAHIRI, A. & R. NAGARAJAN. India in perspective: development issues. ND: Arnold-Heinemann, 1977-. [to be 3 v.]

14260 MEYER-DOHM, P., ed. Economic and social aspects of Indian development: an A.B.O.C.S. symposium. Bombay: Shakuntala, 1975. 293p.

14261 SREENIVASAN, K. Growth and development: selected speeches. Coimbatore: Kalaikathir Achchagam, 1977. 221p.

14262 VAKIL, C.N. Poverty, planning, and inflation. Bombay: Allied, 1978. 316p.

14263 YOGENDRA SINGH. Essays on modernization in India. ND: Manohar, 1978. 196p.

c. models and projections of economic growth

14264 CLARKSON, S. In search of a communist development model; the Soviet's political economy of India. In EPW 7,12 (1971) 623-30.

14265 ECKAUS, R.S. & K.S. PARIKH. Planning for growth: multisectoral, intertemporal models applied to India. Cambridge: MIT Press, 1968. 408p. (Studies in the econ. dev. of India, 6)

14266 EZEKIEL, H. Second India studies: overview. Delhi: Macmillan, 1978. 215p.

14267 GUPTA, S.P. Planning models in India: with projections to 1975. NY: Praeger, 1971. 400p.

14268 KAPUR, J.C. India in the year 2000. ND: IIC, 1975. 54p.

14269 MAHALANOBIS, P.C. The approach of operational research to planning in India. NY: Asia, 1963. 168p.

14270 PANI, P.K. A macroeconomic model of the Indian economy. Delhi: Macmillan, 1977. 301p.

14271 PATEL, S.J. The India we want; its economic transition. Bombay: Manaktalas, 1966. 223p.

d. comparisons with other developing nations

14272 BECHTOLDT, H. Indien oder China. Die Alternative in Asien. Berlin: Deutsche Buch-Gemeinschaft, 1962. 331p.

14273 BERGMANN, T. The development models of India, the Soviet Union and China: a comparative analysis. Assen: Van Gorcum, 1977. 255p. (Pub. of the European Soc. for Rural Sociology, 1)

14274 CHEN, KUAN-I & J.S. UPPAL, eds. India and China: studies in comparative development. NY: Free Press, 1971. 404p.

14275 China and India: development during the last twenty-five years. In American Econ. R. 65,2 (1975) 345-71.

14276 KUZNETS, S., et al., eds. Economic growth; Brazil, India and Japan. Durham: DUP, 1955. 613p.

e. poverty and the social context of development

14277 DANDEKAR, V.M. & N. RATH. Poverty in India. Poona: Indian School of Political Economy, 159p. [1st pub. in EPW 6,1&2 (1971)]

14278 GUPTA, R.K. Essays in economic anthropology: essays in advocacy of change. Calcutta: Inst. of Social Res. & Applied Anthropology, 1979. 193p.

14279 JOSHI, N. The challenge of poverty. ND: Arnold-Heinemann, 1978.

14280 KURIEN, C.T. Poverty and development. Madras: CLS, for CISRS, 1974. 209p. (CISRS social concerns series, 17)

14281 ______. Poverty, planning, and social transformation. Bombay: Allied, 1978. 174p.

14282 NANJUNDAPPA, D.M. Development with social justice. ND: Oxford & IBH, 1976. 158p.

14283 SACHCHIDANANDA & A.K. LAL, eds. Elite and development. ND: Concept, 1980. 276p.

14284 SUBRAMANIAM, C. War on poverty. Bombay: Interpress, 1975. 220p.

14285 URFF, W. VON. Das Problem der Armut in der indischen Entwicklungsplanung. In IAF 5,4 (1974) 460-79.

3. Economic Philosophies and Ideologies of India after 1947

a. general studies

14286 BARDHAN, K. Diagnosis of India's development problems and approaches to an alternative path. ND: ICSSR, 1977. 41p.

14287 BHULESHKAR, A.V., ed. Indian economic thought and development. London: C. Hurst, 1969. 445p.

14288 BIMLA PRASAD, ed. Socialism, sarvodaya, and democracy: selected works of Jayaprakash Narayan. Bombay: Asia, 1964. 287p.

14289 GHOSE, S. Changing India. Bombay: Allied, 1978. 298p.

14290 SHARMA, K.D. & M.A. QURESHI, eds. Alternative technology: proceedings of the seminar held in September 1975 under the joint auspices of the IIAS, Simla and CSIR, New Delhi. Simla: IIAS, 1979. 331p.

14291 SPENGLER, J.J. Indian economic thought: a preface to its history. Durham, NC: DUP, 1971. 192p.

b. Gandhian economic thought - Sarvodaya ("uplift of all"): utopian vision or viable alternative?

i. general studies

14292 CHARAN SINGH. India's economic policy - the Gandhian blueprint. ND: Vikas, 1978. 127p.

14293 DAS, A. Foundations of Gandhian economics. Bombay: Allied, 1979. 146p.

14294 DEVADOSS, T.S. Sarvodaya and the problem of political sovereignty. Madras: U. of Madras, 1974. 651p.

14295 GANDHI, M.K. Economic thought of Mahatma Gandhi. Ed. by J.S. Mathur & A.S. Mathur. Allahabad: Chaitanya, 1962. 666p.

14296 ______. Industrialize - and perish! Comp. by R.K. Prabhu. Ahmedabad: Navajivan, 1966. 120p.

14297 GUPTA, S.S. The economic philosophy of Mahatma Gandhi. Delhi: Ashok Pub., 1968. 223p.

14298 HETTEN, B. & G. TAMM. The development strategy of Gandhian economics. In JIAS 6,1 (1971) 51-66.

14299 KLEIN, I. Indian nationalism and anti-industrialization: the roots of Gandhian economics. In SA 3 (1973) 93-104.

14300 MATHUR, J.S., ed. Gandhian thought and contemporary society. Bombay: BVB, 1974. 273p. [Proc. of a seminar at U. of Allahabad]

14301 MEHTA, V.L. Equality through trusteeship: an alternative for full employment along Gandhian lines. ND: Tata McGraw-Hill, 1977. 24 + 408p.

14302 OSTERGAARD,G.N. & M. CURRELL. The gentle anarchists: a study of the leaders of the Sarvodaya movement for non-violent revolution in India. Oxford: Clarendon Press, 1971. 421p.

14303 PANDAY, R. Gandhi and modernisation. Meerut: Meenakshi, 1979. 304p.

14304 SETHI, J.C.D. Gandhi today. ND: Vikas, 1978. 211p.

14305 SHRIMAN NARAYAN. India needs Gandhi. ND: S. Chand, 1976. 150p.

14306 ______. Principles of Gandhian planning. Allahabad: Kitab Mahal, 1960. 342p.

14307 ______. Towards the Gandhian plan. ND: S. Chand, 1978. 187p.

14308 SINHA, ARCHANA. The social and political philosophy of Sarvodaya. Patna: Janaki Prakashan, 1978. 235p.

14309 SWARUP, RAM. Gandhian economics: a supporting technology. ND: Swarup, 1977. 32p.

14310 TANDON, VISHWANATH. The social and political philosophy of sarvodaya after Gandhiji. Varanasi: Sarva Seva Sangh Prakashan, 1965. 252p.

14311 VAKIL, C.N. Janata economic policy: towards Gandhian socialism: aspirations and limitations. Delhi: Macmillan, 1979. 28 + 133p.

ii. Acharya Vinoba Bhave, leading practitioner of Gandhian economics

14312 BHAVE, VINOBA. Revolutionary Sarvodaya; a philosophy for the remaking of man. Comp. & tr. by V. Nargolkar. Bombay: BVB, 1964. 53p.

14313 ______. Swarāj Śāstra; the principles of a non-violent political power. 5th ed. Tr. by Bharatan Kumarappa. Varanasi: Sarva Seva Sangh Prakashan, 1963. 95p.

14314 ______. Third power. Tr. by M. Sykes & K.S. Acharlu. Varanasi: Sarva Seva Sangh Prakashan, 1972. 131p. [Tr. of Tīsarī śaktī]

14315 ______. Vinoba on Gandhi. Ed. by K. Shah. Varanasi: Sarva Seva Sangha Prakashan, 1973. 187p. [tr. from Hindi]

14316 LANZA DEL VASTO, J.J. Gandhi to Vinoba; the new pilgrimage. NY: Schocken Books, 1974. 231p. [Rpt. 1956 ed.; tr. of Vinoba; ou, Le nouveau pélerinage]

14317 NARGOLKAR, VASANT. The creed of saint Vinoba. Bombay: BVB, 1963. 307p.

14318 SATISH KUMAR, ed. School of non-violence: a handbook by Vinoba Bhave [and others]. London: Christian Action, Housemans, 1969. 72p.

14319 SHARMA, J.S. Vinoba and bhoodan; a selective descriptive bibliography in Hindi, English and other Indian languages. ND: Indian National Congress, 1956. 92p.

14320 SHRIMAN NARAYAN. Vinoba: his life and work. Bombay: Popular, 1970. 370p.

14321 TANDON, P.D. Vinoba Bhave; the man and his mission. Bombay: Vora, 1952. 107p.

14322 TENNYSON, H. India's walking saint; the story of Vinoba Bhave. Garden City, NY: Doubleday, 1955. 224p.

c. "socialistic pattern of society" advocated by the Indian National Congress, and other socialists

14323 BHULESHKAR, A.V., ed. Towards socialist transformation of Indian economy. Bombay: Popular, 1972. 422p. (Jawaharlal Nehru memorial volumes, 2)

14324 DATTA, A. Socialism, democracy and industrialization: a collection of essays. London: Allen & Unwin, 1962. 118p.

14325 GYAN CHAND. Socialist transformation of Indian economy; a study in social analysis, critique, and evaluation. Bombay: Allied, 1965. 628p.

14326 KAMARAJ, K. Towards socialism; a compilation. ND: Congress Forum of Socialist Action, 1966. 108p.

14327 MEHTA, ASOKA. Reflections on socialist era. ND: S. Chand, 1977. 497p.

14328 ______. Studies in socialism. 2nd ed. Bombay: BVB, 1964. 208p. [1st ed. 1954]

14329 MISRA, OM PRAKASH. The economic philosophy of Pt. Jawaharlal Nehru. Allahabad: Chugh, 1978. 218p.

14330 NEHRU, JAWAHARLAL. Nehru on socialism: selected speeches and writings. ND: Perspective Pub., 1964. 120p.

14331 PRICE, R.B. Ideology and Indian planning. In American J. of Econ. and Sociology 26 (1967) 47-64.

14332 SAMPURNANAND. Indian socialism. London: Asia, 1961. 131p.

14333 SHRIMAN NARAYAN. Socialism in Indian planning. Bombay: Asia, 1964. 185p.

14334 ______. Towards a socialist economy. ND: INC, 1956. 142p.

d. economic ideas of Indian Marxists

14335 DANGE, S.A. Gadgil and the economics of Indian democracy. ND: PPH, 1971. 54p.

14336 NAMBOODRIPAD, E.M.S. Economics and politics of India's socialist pattern. ND: PPH, 1966. 419p.

14337 ______. Indian planning in crisis. Trivandrum: Deshabhimani Book House, 1974. 136p.

14338 ROY, AJIT. A Marxist commentary on economic developments in India, 1951-1965; a selection of articles and notes. Calcutta: National Pub., 1967. 160p.

14339 ______. Planning in India; achievements and problems. Calcutta: National Pub., 1965. 523p.

e. economic conservatism: advocates of free enterprise and the private sector

14340 CHINAI, B.M. India's march towards democratic socialism; a businessman's perspective. Ed. by M.P. Pai. Bombay: Shri Brihad Bharatiya Samaj, 1972. 427p.

14341 MEHTA, G.L. Dilemmas in planning. Bombay: Vora, 1972. 138p.

14342 NAYAR, B.R. Business attitudes towards economic planning in India. In AS 11,9 (1971) 850-65.

14343 PAI, M.R., ed. A decade of planning in India; second and third five-year plans, a commentary. A collection of Forum of Free Enterprise publications. Bombay: Popular, 1969. 244p.

14344 ______, ed. Planning in India; a commentary. A collection of Forum of Free Enterprise publications. Bombay: Popular, 1966. 234p.

14345 ______, ed. Socialism in India: a commentary. A collections of Forum of Free Enterprise publications. Bombay: Popular, 1967. 247p.

14346 SHROFF, P.J. Statism in India: a critique. Bombay: Lalvani, 1973. 154p.

4. Traditional Values in Economic Modernization: the Weber Thesis and Other Analyses

14347 BHARATI, A. Hinduism and modernization. In R.F. Spencer, ed. Religion and change in contemporary Asia. Minneapolis: U. of Minnesota Press, 1971, 67-104.

14348 BRAIBANTI, R. & J.J. SPENGLER, eds. Tradition, values, and socio-economic development. Durham, NC: DUP, 1961. 305p.

14349 DASGUPTA, S. Hindu ethos and the challenge of change. Rev. 2nd ed. ND: Arnold-Heinemann, 1977. 317p.

14350 DRAGUHN, W. Entwicklungsbewusstsein und wirtschaftliche Entwicklung in Indien. Wiesbaden: Harrassowitz, 1970. 288p. (Schriften des Instituts für Asienkunde in Hamburg, 28)

14351 GANGULY, S.N. Tradition, modernity and development. Delhi: Macmillan, 1977. 182p.

14352 GOHEEN, J., et al. India's cultural values and economic development: a discussion. In EDCC 7 (1958) 1-12.

14353 KAPP, K.W. Hindu culture, economic development and economic planning in India; a collection of essays. London: Asia, 1963. 228p.

14354 KOLLER, J.M. Values and development in India. In ATS 1,2 (1976) 111-29.

14355 LOOMIS, C.P. & Z.K. LOOMIS, eds. Socio-economic change and the religious factor in India: an Indian symposium of views on Max Weber. ND: Affiliated East-West Press, 1969. 140p.

14356 MISHRA, V. Hinduism and economic growth. Bombay: OUP, 1962. 219p.

14357 MODDIE, A.D. The Brahmanical culture and modernity. London: Asia, 1968. 143p.

14358 MURUGESA MUDALIAR, N. Traditional Hinduism and social development: an enquiry. Madras: CLS, 1978. 48p.

14359 NANDY, S.K. A critique of Max Weber's conception of the ethic of India. In VQ 32 (1966-67) 277-304.

14360 RAO, M.S.A. Religion and economic development. In SB 18 (1969) 1-15.

14361 RAO, V.K.R.V. Values and economic development; the Indian challenge. ND: Vikas, 1971. 182p.

14362 SHARMA, A. Hindu scriptural value system and the economic development of India. ND: Heritage, 1980. 113p.

14363 SINGER, M.B. Industrial leadership, the Hindu ethic, and the spirit of socialism. In his When a great tradition modernizes. NY: Praeger, 1972, 272-380.

14364 ______. Religion and social change in India: the Max Weber thesis. Phase three. In EDCC 4 (1966) 497-505.

14365 ______. Religion and traditional values in relation to modernization. In ATS 1,3 (1976) 258-65.

14366 STERN, H. Réligion et société en Inde selon Max Weber; analyse critique de l'Hindouisme et du Bouddhisme. In Social Science Information 10,6 (1971) 69-112.

14367 TAMBIAH, S.J. Buddhism & this-worldly activity. In MAS 7,1 (1973) 1-20.

5. Indian Planning: Process and Experience
a. general studies

14368 ALI, MANSOOR. Missing links in Indian planning. ND: Light & Life, 1979. 316p.

14369 BETTELHEIM, C. Some basic planning problems. NY: Asia, 1961. 68p. (Indian statistical series, 12)

14370 BHAGWATI, J.N. & PADMA DESAI. India: planning for industrialization: industrialization and trade policies since 1951. London: OUP, 1970. 537p.

14371 BREUER, H. Die Industrialisierung Indiens unter dem Druck der steigenden Auslandverschuldung. Eine Konflictanalyse der bisherigen Planstrategien. Berlin: Duncker & Humblot, 1967. 162p.

14372 DASGUPTA, A.K. A framework of planning for India. In IEJ 16 (1969) 265-76.

14373 DESAI, P.B. Planning in India, 1951-1978. ND: Vikas, 1979. 194p.

14374 DHAR, P.N. The Indian economic experiment. In JDS 3,1 (1966) 42-62.

14375 DIVEKAR, V.D. Planning process in Indian polity. Bombay: Popular, 1978. 398p.

14376 GADGIL, D.R. Planning and economic policy in India. 3rd ed. London: Asia, 1965. 354p. (GIPE studies, 39) [1st pub. 1961]

14377 IYENGAR, S. KESAVA. Fifteen years of democratic planning. London: Asia, 1968-66. 2 v.

14378 KRISHNAMACHARI, V.T. & S. VENU. Planning in India: theory and practice. Rev. ed. Bombay: Orient Longmans, 1977. 191p. [1st ed. 1962]

14379 NAYAR, B.R. The modernization imperative and Indian planning. Delhi: Vikas, 1972. 246p.

14380 PATANKAR, M. Economic planning: principles & practice, with special reference to India. ND: S. Chand, 1977. 456p.

14381 RAJ, K.N. Indian economic growth, performance, and prospects. ND: Allied, 1965. 28p.

14382 REPETTO, R.C. Time in India's development programmes. Cambridge: HUP, 1971. 237p.

14383 SHENOY, B.R. Indian economic policy. Bombay: Popular, 1968. 354p.

14384 SHENOY, S.R. Central planning in India: a critical review. ND: Wiley Eastern, 1975. 124p.

14385 ______. India: progress or poverty? A review of the outcome of central planning in India, 1951-69. London: The Inst. of Econ. Affairs, 1971. 122p.

14386 VASUDEVAN, A. The strategy of planning in India. Meerut: Meenakshi, 1970. 330p.

14387 VENKATASUBBIAH, H. The anatomy of Indian planning. Bombay: Vora, 1969. 218p.

14388 VENUGOPAL REDDY, Y. Multilevel planning in India. ND: Vikas, 1979. 193p.

b. essay collections on planning

14389 CHAUDHURI, S. Economic planning and social organisation: selected writings of Sachin Chaudhuri. Bombay: Econ. and Political Weekly, 1969. 176p.

14390 DATTA, B. Essays in plan economics; a commentary on Indian planning experience. Calcutta: World Press, 1963. 190p.

14391 IENGAR, H.V.R. Business and planned economy. Bombay: Vora, 1968. 191p.

14392 ______. Planning in India. Delhi: Macmillan, 1974. 84p.

14393 JALAN, B. Essays in development policy. Delhi: Macmillan, 1975. 156p.

14394 MAHALANOBIS, P.C. Talks on planning. Bombay: Asia, 1961. 159p. (Indian stat. series, 14)

14395 MOHNOT, S.R. New economic deal. Calcutta: Oxford & IBH, 1968. 149p.

14396 MUKERJEE, RADHAKAMAL, ed. Social sciences and planning in India. Bombay: Asia, 1970. 208p.

14397 TANDON, B.K. Essays on planning. Calcutta: Asha Pub. House, 1967. 76p.

14398 ______. Topical essays. Calcutta: Asha Pub. House, 1967. 138p.

14399 VAIDYA, M.J. Objectives of planning in India and other essays; some writings of Murarji J. Vaidya. Bombay: Popular, 1969. 161p.

c. the machinery of planning: the Planning Commission and the bureaucracy

14400 AVASTHI, A. & ARORA, R.K. Bureaucracy and development: Indian perspectives. ND: Associated, 1978. 267p.

14401 BHALERAO, C.N. Administration, politics & development in India. Bombay: Lalvani, 1972. 510p.

14402 BHATTACHARYA, M. Bureaucracy and development administration. ND: Uppal, 1979. 152p.

14403 BRAIBANTI, R. & J.J. SPENGLER, eds. Administration and economic development in India. Durham: DUP, 1963. 312p.

14404 DUBHASHI, P.R. Economics, planning, and public administration. Bombay: Somaiya Pub., 1976. 153p.

14405 INDIA (REP.). ADMIN. REFORMS CMSN. Report (final) on machinery for planning. Delhi: MPGOI, 1968. 63p.

14406 ______. Report on economic administration. Delhi: MPGOI, 1968. 98p.

14407 INDIA (REP.). ADMIN. REFORMS CMSN. STUDY TEAM ON THE MACHINERY FOR PLANNING. Final report, December, 1967. Delhi: MPGOI, 1968. 183p. [apptd. by Admin. Reforms Cmsn.]

14408 INDIA (REP.). PLANNING CMSN. PROGRAMME EVALUATION ORGANISATION. Structure, functions, and activities. ND: 1979. 47p.

14409 KHANNA, B.J. Bureaucracy and development in India. In E.W. Weidner, ed. Development administration in Asia. Durham: DUP, 1970, 219-250.

14410 KRISHNA IYER, V.R. The integral yoga of public law and development in the context of India. ND: N.M. Tripathi, for ICPS, 1979. 154p.

14411 MUTHAYYA, B.C. & I. GNANAKANNAN. Developmental personnel; a psycho-social study across three states in India. Hyderabad: NICD, 1973. 185p.

14412 NAYAR, P.K.B. Leadership, bureaucracy, and planning in India; a sociological study. ND: Associated, 1969. 176p.

14413 PAI PANANDIKAR, V.A. & S.S. KSHIRSAGAR. Bureaucracy and development administration. ND: Centre for Policy Res., 1978. 208p.

14414 PARANJAPE, H.K. Planning commission, a descriptive account. ND: IIPA, 1964. 216p.

14415 ______. The reorganised Planning Commission; a study in the implementation of administrative reforms. ND: IIPA, 1970. 58p.

d. the Five-Year Plans - documents and studies
i. general studies of the Plans, their implementation and results

14416 GHOSH, A. New horizons in planning: a study of planning techniques with special reference to India's first and second five year plans. Calcutta: World Press, 1956. 141p.

14417 HANSON, A.H. The process of planning; a study of India's five-year plans, 1950-1964. London: OUP, 1966. 560p.

14418 MALLIK, K. The resource mobilisation and Indian five-year plans. Patna: Bihar Granth Kutir, 1979. 227p.

14419 PATEL, V.G. An analysis of plan implementation in India. Ahmedabad: Balgovind Prakashan, 1969. 163p.

14420 PATHAK, H.N. Select bibliography of articles on India's five year plans. Ahmedabad: New Order Book Co., 1962. 50p.

14421 SARMA, N.A. Economic development in India: the first and second five year plans. In Intl. Monetary Fund Staff Papers 6 (1958) 180-238.

14422 STREETEN, P. & M. LIPTON. The crisis of Indian planning: economic planning in the 1960's. London: OUP, 1968. 416p.

ii. the First Five-Year Plan, 1951-55

14423 GADGIL, D.R. Notes on the Government of India's first five year plan: July 1951. In EDCC 1,1 (1952) 57-72.

14424 INDIA (REP.). PLANNING CMSN. The first five year plan. ND: 1953. 671p.

14425 ______. First five year plan. (People's edition). Delhi: PDMIB, 1953. 263p.

14426 ______. Review of the first five year plan. Delhi: MPGOI, 1959. 479p.

14427 RANADIVE, B.T. India's five-year plan: what it offers. Bombay: Current Book House, 1953. 259p.

14428 RAO, V.K.R.V. India's first five year plan -- a descriptive analysis. In PA 25 (1952) 3-23.

14429 SINGH, BALJIT. Economic planning in India, 1951-56. Bombay: Hind Kitabs, 1953. 155p.

14430 WADIA, P.A. The five-year plan: a criticism. Bombay: Popular, 1951. 84p.

iii. the Second Five-Year Plan, 1956-60

14431 GADGIL, D.R. Prospects for the second five year plan period. In IQ 13,1 (1957) 5-23.

14432 INDIA (REP.). PLANNING CMSN. Appraisal and prospects of the Second Five Year Plan. Delhi: MPGOI, 1958. 97p.

14433 ______. Second five-year plan. ND: Govt. of India Press, 1956. 653p.

14434 KRISHNASWAMY, K.S. India's Second Plan: the background. In EDCC 7,3 (1959) 194-205.

14435 NURKSE, R. Reflections on India's development plan. In Quarterly J. of Economics 71,2 (1957) 188-204.

iv. the Third Five-Year Plan, 1961-65

14436 BETTELHEIM, C. India's third Five-year Plan, some problems of realisation. In Pacific viewpoint 4 (1963) 139-54.

14437 Draft outline of the third five-year plan; a symposium. ND: AICC, 1960. 292p.

14438 INDIA (REP.). PLANNING CMSN. Problems in the third plan, a critical miscellany. ND: Govt. of India Press, 1962. 200p.

14439 ______. Third five year plan: a draft outline. ND: 1960. 265p.

14440 ______. Third five-year plan. ND: MPGOI, 1961. 774p.

14441 ______. The third plan mid-term appraisal. Delhi: MPGOI, 1963. 179p.

14442 ______. Towards a self-reliant economy; India's third plan 1961-66. Delhi: PDMIB, 1962. 320p.

14443 INDIAN STATISTICAL INST. Economic strategy and the third plan. London: Asia, 1964. 132p. (Indian stat. series, 21)

14444 JACKSON, B. The plan under pressure; an observer's view. NY: Asia, 1963. 60p.

14445 LITTLE, I.M.D. A critical examination of India's third five-year plan. In Oxford Economic Papers ns 14 (1962) 1-24.

14446 MALENBAUM, W. The role of government in India's third plan. In EDCC 8 (1960) 225-36.

14447 NCAER. Indian economy, 1961-66. ND: 1966, 1961-66. 116p.

v. the "Plan Holiday," 1966-68: three annual plans during reconstitution of the Planning Commission

14448 ARTHA GNANI [pseud]. Decline of Planning Commission. In EPW 1,4 (10 Sep. 1966) 162-63.

14449 CHAKRAVARTI, P. On the postponement of the 4th five-year plan. In Econ. Studies 8,11/12 (1968) 675-76, 667.

14450 CHATTERJEE, P. Pause in planning. In AICC Econ. R. 19,11/13 (1968) 100-102.

14451 SETHI, J.D. Scuttling again. In Seminar 105 (May 1968) 26-30.

vi. the Fourth Five-Year Plan, 1969-74

14452 GUPTA, R., ed. Planning for self reliance; proceedings of a seminar on fourth five year plan, held by the Gandhian Institute of Studies. ND: Impex India, 1966. 196p.

14453 A hard core for the fourth plan: a reassessment of development with defence. In QER 12 (1965) 19-34.

14454 HONE, A. India's fourth plan; the missing steps. In SAR 3,1 (1969) 11-21.

14455 INDIA (REP.). PLANNING CMSN. Fourth five year plan, a draft outline. ND: 1966. 430p.

14456 ______. Fourth five year plan, 1969-74; draft. Delhi: MPGOI, 1969. 357p.

14457 ______. Fourth five year plan, 1969-74. ND: 1970. 452p.

14458 MINHAS, B.S. The poor, the weak and the Fourth Plan. In A.J. Fonseca, ed. Challenge of poverty in India. Delhi: Vikas, 1971, 69-71.

14459 RAJ, K.N. The Fourth Plan and future economic policy. In EPW 2,11 (1967) 555-63.

14460 RUDRA, A. An overconsistent plan. In EPW 2,3/4/5 (1967) 279-84.

vii. the Fifth Five-Year Plan, 1974-78

14461 INDIA (REP.). PLANNING CMSN. Approach to the Fifth Plan, 1974-79. ND: 1973. 62p.

14462 ______. Draft Fifth five year plan, 1974-79. ND: 1973-74. 2v. in 1.

14463 ______. Fifth five-year plan, 1974-79. ND: 1976. 162p.

14464 RAJ, K.N. Approach to the Fifth Plan: first impressions. In EPW 8,4/5/6 (1973) 309-14.

14465 RAKSHIT, G. India's Fifth plan: a critical assessment. Calcutta: World Press, 1977. 134p.

v. the Draft Five-Year Plan, 1978-83: the Sixth Plan in the making

14466 BRAHMANANDA, P.R. Planning for a futureless economy: a critique of the 6th plan and its development strategy. Bombay: Himalaya Pub. House, 1978. 224p.

14467 [Draft five-year plan 1978-83 - special number]. In EPW 12,31/32/33 (1978) 1245-1452.

14468 HALLIKERI, R.K. Highlights of the sixth five-year plan. In Maharashtra Cooperative Q. 62,4 (1979) 269-73.

14469 INDIA (REP.). PLANNING CMSN. Draft five year plan, 1978-83. ND: 1978. 276p.

14470 The Sixth Plan. In Seminar 228 (1978) 1-48.

e. subnational aspects of planning in India: zones, regions, states, and districts
i. regional development and planning

14471 AHMAD, ENAYAT & D.K. SINGH. Regional planning, with particular reference to India. ND: Oriental, 1980. 2 v.

14472 BALAKRISHNA, R.C. Regional planning in India. Bangalore: Bangalore Printing and Pub., 1948. 458p.

14473 BHAT, L.S. Regional planning in India. Calcutta: Statistical Pub. Soc., 1972. 153p.

14474 BHATTACHARYYA, A.K. Economic regions in the context of development: some basic considerations. In AV 15,1 (1973) 57-90.

14475 HANSON, A.H. Power shifts and regional balances. In P. Streeten & M. Lipton, eds. The crisis of Indian planning. London: OUP, 1968, 19-62.

14476 INDIA (REP.). CENSUS OF INDIA, 1961. Economic regionalization of India: problems and approaches, by P. Sen Gupta & G. Sdasyuk. ND: 1968. 257p. (Census of India, 1961, v. 1 monograph 8)

14477 LAHIRI, T.B., ed. Balanced regional development: concepts, strategy, and case studies. Calcutta: Oxford & IBH, 1972. 154p.

14478 LEFEBER, L. Regional allocation of resources in India. In P.N. Rosenstein-Rodan, ed. Pricing and fiscal policies: a study in method. Cambridge, MA: MIT Press, 1964, 18-30. (Studies in the econ. dev. of India, 3)

14479 MENON, K.S.V. Development of backward areas through incentives: an Indian experiment. ND: Vidya Vahini, 1979. 477p.

14480 MISRA, R.P. Regional planning; concepts, techniques, policies, and case studies. Mysore: U. of Mysore, 1969. 631p.

14481 NATH, V. Regional development in Indian planning. In EPW 5,3/4/5 (1970) 247-60.

14482 ______. Regional development policies. In EPW 6, 30-32 (1971) 1601-08.

ii. planning at the state and district levels

14483 District planning special issue. In J. of the Lal Bahadur Shastri Natl. Academy of Admin. 29,1 (1975) 1-242.

14484 MEHTA, ASHOK. Indian federalism and economic development. In JCPS 3,4 (1969) 124-35.

14485 PARANJAPE, H.K. Centre-state relations in planning. In IJPA 16 (1970) 47-83.

14486 RAGHAVAIAH, Y. District planning and development administration: a case for unified and integrated approach. In IJPA 13,4 (1967) 729-44.

14487 RAJ, K.N. "Planning from below" with reference to district development and state planning. In EPW 6,30-32 (1971) 1609-18.

14488 UPPAL, J.S. Economic development of Indian states: a study in development contrast. In CAS 3 (1973) 65-82.

F. India's Financial and Monetary System since 1947

1. General Studies

14489 ARUMUGAM, M. The role of non-banking financial institutions in Indian economy. In AV 14 (1972) 404-45.

14490 AVADHANI, V.A. Studies in Indian financial system. Bombay: Jaico, 1978. 375p.

14491 BHOLE, L.M. Investment, interest, and monetary policy in India. Bombay: U. of Bombay, 1974. 154p.

14492 DAGLI, V. Financial institutions of India. Bombay: Vora, 1976. 338p. (Commerce econ. studies, 12)

14493 GOYAL, O.P. Financial institutions & economic growth of India. ND: Light & Life, 1979. 658p.

14494 Organizational framework for the implementation of social objectives; report of a study group of the National Credit Council, October 1969. Bombay: Bank of India, 1969. 645p. [D.R. Gadgil, Chm.]

14495 SETHURAMAN, T.V. Institutional financing of economic development in India. Delhi: Vikas, 1970. 166p.

14496 SUBRAMANIAN, V.K. The Indian financial system. ND: Abhinav, 1979. 233p.

2. Public Finance
a. general studies

14497 AGARWALA, S.N. Indian public finance. Bombay: Vora, 1967. 419p.

14498 BHARGAVA, P.K. Current problems of Indian public finances. Mysore: Geetha Book House, 1974. 193p.

14499 CHELLIAH, R.J. Fiscal policy in underdeveloped countries: with special reference to India. 2nd ed. London: Allen & Unwin, 1969. 216p. [1st ed. 1960]

14500 KULKARNI, R.G. Deficit financing and economic development, with special reference to Indian economic development. Bombay: Asia, 1966. 399p.

14501 LAL, S.N. Problems of public borrowing in underdeveloped countries. Allahabad: Chugh, 1978. 286p.

14502 LALL, G.S. Public finance and financial administration in India. ND: H.P.J. Kapoor, 1976. 360p.

14503 MATHEW, T. Economic objectives and tax-expenditure policies of India, 1950-70. ND: Econ. and Scientific Res. Foundation, 1974. 56p.

14504 MISRA, B. Economics of public finance. Delhi: Macmillan, 1978. 284p.

14505 PREMCHAND, A. Control of public expenditure in India; a historical and analytical account of the administrative, audit and parliamentary processes. 2nd rev. ed. Bombay: Allied, 1966. 475p. [1st ed. 1973]

14506 ROSENSTEIN-RODAN, P.N., ed. Pricing and fiscal policies: a study in method. Cambridge: MIT Press, 1964. 216p. (Studies in the econ. dev. of India, 3)

14507 TRIPATHY, R.N. Fiscal policy and economic development in India. 2nd rev. ed. Calcutta: World Press, 1970. 475p.

14508 ZAHIR, M. Public expenditure and income distribution in India. ND: Associated, 1972. 191p.

b. finances of the Central Government

14509 BARMAN, K. India's public debt and policy since Independence. Allahabad: Chugh, 1978. 284p.

14510 BHARGAVA, R.N. The theory and working of union finance in India. 3rd ed., rev. and enl. Allahabad: Chaitanya Pub. House, 1971. 424p.

14511 DALAYA, C. Internal debt of the Government of India. Bombay: Vora, 1966. 144p.

14512 GHUGE, V.B. "Real" burden of internal national debt. In Economic Affiars 13 (1968) 452-66.

14513 GUPTA, B.N. Indian federal finance and budgetary policy. Allahabad: Chaitanya Pub. House, 1970. 467p.

14514 INDIA (REP.). ADMIN REFORMS CMSN. Report of the study team on financial administration. ND: MPGOI, 1967. 402p.

14515 INDIA (DOMINION). FISCAL CMSN., 1949-50. Report. Delhi: MPGOI, 1950. 4 v. [V.T. Krishnamachari, chm.]

14516 MUKHERJI, S.K. Recent trends in union finance; a critique of the budgetary policy of the Government of India since 1935. Calcutta: Bookland, 1964. 514p.

14517 NCAER. Management of public debt in India. ND: 1965. 158p.

14518 A review of trends in budgetary transactions of the central government: 1951-52 to 1968-69. In Reserve Bank of India Bull. 22 (Oct. 1968) 1275-1300.

14519 SINGH, G.N. Public debt and Indian economic development. Calcutta: Blackie Employees' Coop. Industrial Soc., 1976. 200p.

14520 SREEKANTARADHYA, B.S. Public debt and economic development in India. ND: Sterling, 1972. 232p.

c. Centre-state financial relations
i. general studies

14521 BHARGAVA, M. Inter-governmental financial relations in India since independence. Allahabad: Chaitanya Pub. House, 1976. 256p.

14522 BHATIA, H.L. Centre-state financial relations in India. ND: Abhinav, 1979. 176p.

14523 CHATTERJI, A. The central financing of state plans in the Indian federation. Calcutta: KLM, 1971. 214p.

14524 DOSS, V. Impact of planning on centre-state financial relations in India. ND: National, 1978. 239p.

14525 GREWAL, B.S. Centre-state financial relations in India. Paliala: Punjabi U., 1975. 268p.

14526 LAKDAWALA, D.T. Union-state financial relations. Bombay: Lalvani, 1967. 120p.

14527 PHUL CHAND, ed. Federal financial relations in India. ND: ICPS, 1974. 251p.

14528 SHARMA, J.N. The Union and the states; a study in fiscal federalism. ND: Sterling, 1974. 248p.

14529 THIMMAIAH, G. An approach to centre-state financial relations in India. Mysore: Ganga Tharanga, 1968. 325p.

14530 VEERARAGHAVACHAR, S.M. Union-State financial relations in India. Delhi: Sterling, 1970. 306p.

ii. the Finance Commissions, established by the Constitution to allocate certain taxes between Centre and the states

14531 BHARGAVA, R.N. The Finance Commission. In IJE 34,4 (1954) 285-95. [on First FC]

14532 BHATNAGAR, S. Union state financial relations and finance commissions. Allahabad: Chugh, 1979. 355p.

14533 CHELLIAH, R.J. Report of the Finance Commission, 1978. In IER ns 14,1 (1979) 51-64. [Seventh FC]

14534 The Finance Commission Act. In JCPS 8,4 (1974) 608-10.

14535 GOVINDA RAO, M. Federal fiscal transfers in India: performance of six Finance Commissions. In EPW 12,31 (1977) 1226-33.

14536 INDIA (REP.). FINANCE CMSN., 1951. Report. Delhi: MPGOI, 1952. 1 v. [First FC]

14537 ______, 1956. Report. ND: Min. of Finance, 1958. 215p. [K. Santhanam, chm., Second FC]

14538 ______, 1961. Report. ND: MPGOI, 1962. 118p. [Ashok Kumar Chanda, chm., Third FC]

14539 ______, 1964. Report. ND: MPGOI, 1965. 234p. [Dr. P.V. Rajamannar, chm., Fourth FC]

14540 ______, 1968. Report. ND: MPGOI, 1970. 282p. [Mahavir Tyagi, chm., Fifth FC]

14541 ______, 1972. Report. ND: MPGOI, 1973. 1 v. [K. Brahmananda Reddi, chm., Sixth FC]

14542 ______, 1977. Report. ND: MPGOI, 1978. 300p. [J.M. Shelat, chm., Seventh FC]

14543 JHAVERI, N.J. The Sixth Finance Commission; an evaluation of its recommendations. In JCPS 8,4 (1974) 480-500. [also pub. in EPW 9,5 (1974) 137-50]

14544 LAKDAWALA, D.T. The four Finance Commissions in India. In IEJ 13,4 (1966) 498-522.

14545 MATHUR, P.C. The Fourth Finance Commission. In IJPA 11 (1965) 750-66.

14546 SASTRI, K.V.S. Federal-State fiscal relations in India: a study of the Finance Commission and the techniques of fiscal adjustment. Bombay: OUP, 1967. 143p.

14547 Seventh Finance Commission: Recommendations. In Yojana 22,23 (1978) 11-14.

14548 SINHA, R.K. The fifth Finance Commission: a comparative study. In Economic Affairs 15 (1970) 97-114.

14549 THIMMAIAH, B. Some neglected aspects of the Finance Commission. In IJPA 20,1 (1974) 15-31. [the Sixth cmsn.]

14550 VANJARI, S. Finance commissions in retrospect. In EE 53,8 (1969) 254-60.

d. state finance

14551 Finances of state governments, 1976-77. In RBI Bull. 30,12 (1976) 863-1020.

14552 JAIN, R.K. State finances in India. Bhopal: Progress Pub., 1978. 222p.

14553 JOSHI, M.D., ed. Mobilisation of state resources. ND: Impex India, 1967. 240p.

14554 PATEL, H. Growing indebtedness of states: a case against statutory debt limit on states' debt. In JCPS 11,4 (1977) 70-85.

14555 Problems of resource mobilisation in the states; conference proceedings, April 21, 1969. ND: IIPA, 1970. 130p.

14556 VENKATARAMAN, K. States' finances in India: a perspective study for the plan periods. London: Allen & Unwin, 1968. 244p.

e. local and municipal finance

14557 Finances of local authorities, 1951/52 to 1961/62. In RBI Bull. 19 (1965) 686-711.

14558 INDIA (REP.). CENTRAL COUNCIL OF LOCAL SELF-GOVT. Augmentation of financial resources of urban local bodies. Delhi: MPGOI, 1965. 566p.

14559 INDIA (REP.). LOCAL FINANCE ENQUIRY CMTEE, 1949. Report. Delhi: MPGOI, 1951. 617p. [P.K. Wattal, chm.]

14560 INDIA (REP.). MIN. OF COMMUNITY DEVELOPMENT & COOPERATION. Report of the study team on Panchayati Raj finances. ND: 1963. 2v. in 1. [K. Santhanam, chm.]

14561 TRIPATHY, R.N. Local finance in a developing economy. Delhi: 1967. 496p. [study sponsored by Planning Cmsn.]

14562 VENKATARAMAN, K. Local finance in perspective. Bombay: Asia, 1965. 63p.

2. Taxation and Tax Reform in India since 1947
a. documents

14563 BHOOTHALINGAM, S. Final report on rationalisation and simplification of the tax structure. ND: Min. of Finance, 1968. 196p.

14564 Chokshi Committee report on direct tax laws. In EE 70,20 (1978) 1005-14.

14565 INDIA (REP.). DIRECT TAXES ADMIN. ENQUIRY CMTEE., 1958. Report. Delhi: MPGOI, 1960. 578p. [Mahavir Tyagi, chm.]

14566 ______. Final report, Dec. 1971. ND: Min. of Finance, 1972. 315p. [K.N. Wanchoo, chm.]

14567 INDIA (REP.). DIRECT TAX LAWS CMTEE. Interim report. ND: Min. of Finance, 1978. 74p. [C.C. Chokshi, chm.]

14568 INDIA (REP.). TAXATION ENQUIRY CMSN. Report, 1953-54. ND: Min. of Finance, 1955. 3 v.

14569 Jha Committee's proposals for rationalisation of taxes. In Commerce 135,3474 (1977) 1279-80.

14570 KALDOR, N. Indian tax reform: report of a survey. ND: Min. of Finance, 1956. 139p.

b. general studies of Indian taxation

14571 AMBIRAJAN, S. The taxation of corporate income in India. Bombay: Asia, 1964. 315p.

14572 BISHNOI, U. Union taxes in India. Allahabad: Chugh, 1980. 232p.

14573 BORKAR, V.V. Income tax reform in India. Bombay: Popular, 1971. 234p.

14574 CHAWLA, O.P. Personal taxation in India, 1947-1970. Bombay: Somaiya, 1972. 242p.

14575 CHELLIAH, R.J. & R.N. LAL. Incidence of indirect taxation in India, 1973-74. ND: Natl. Inst. of Public Finance and Policy, 1978. 103p.

14576 CUTT, J. Taxation and economic development in India. NY: Praeger, 1969. 415p.

14577 GANDHI, V.P. Some aspects of India's tax structure: an economic analysis. Bombay: Vora, 1970. 202p.

14578 GOPAL, M.H. Wealth tax in India: its burden and impact. ND: Econ. and Scientific Res. Foundation, 1970. 172p.

14579 GUPTA, A. A study of personal income taxation in India. Calcutta: Progressive, 1975. 190p.

14580 GUPTA, A.P. Central government taxes: have they reduced inequality? In EPW 12,4 (1977) 88-100.

14581 HARVARD U. INTL. PROGRAM IN TAXATION. Taxation in India. Boston: Little, Brown, 1960. 555p.

14582 JAIN, A.K. Taxation of income in India: an empirical study since 1939. Delhi: Macmillan, 1975. 257p.

14583 LAKDAWALA, D.T. & K.V. NAMBIAR. Commodity taxation in India. Ahmedabad: Sardar Patel Inst. of Econ. & Social Res., 1972. 189p.

14584 MAHLER, W.R. Sales and excise taxation in India. Bombay: Orient Longmans, 1970. 426p.

14585 PANDYA, J.F., comp. Studies in Indian taxation; a survey of eleven years' literature (1960-70). Ahmedabad: Balgovind, 1971. 180p.

14586 RAO, V.G. The responsiveness of the Indian tax system, 1960-61 to 1973-74. Bombay: Allied, 1979. 122p.

14587 SRIVASTAVA, G.K. Commercial taxes in India. Jaipur: Pitaliya Pustak Bhandar, 1975. 223p.

14588 SUMAN, H.N.P.S. Direct taxation and economic growth in India. ND: Sterling, 1974. 300p.

c. agricultural taxation

14589 ANGRISH, A.C. Direct taxation of agriculture in India, with special reference to land revenue & agricultural income tax. Bombay: Somaiya, 1972. 339p.

14590 BHARGAVA, P.K. Taxation of agriculture in India. Bombay: Vora, 1976. 111p.

14591 GANDHI, V.P. Tax burden on Indian agriculture. Cambridge: Law School of Harvard U., 1966. 240p.

14592 INDIA (REP.). CMTEE. ON TAXATION OF AGRICULTURAL WEALTH AND INCOME. Report. ND: Min. of Finance, 1972. 165p. [K.N. Raj, chm.]

14593 JOSHI, T.M. Studies in the taxation of agricultural land and income in India. Bombay: Asia, 1970. 392p.

14594 MANSINGHKA, S. & R.S. DANI. Agriculture and direct taxes. Allahabad: Central Law Agency, 1977. 144p.

14595 MATHEW, E.T. Agricultural taxation and economic development in India. Bombay: Asia, 1968. 204p.

14596 Taxation of agriculture in India; a critical survey of agricultural taxes on land, income, and wealth. Bombay: Indian Merchants' Chamber Econ. Research & Training Foundation, 1970. 125p.

d. state and local taxation

14597 GHUGE, V.B. States' taxation in Indian federation. Poona: Mehta Pub. House, 1979. 191p.

14598 JAIN, R.K. State taxation in India. Bhopal: Progress Pub., 1972. 339p.

14599 MISHRA, B.S. Municipal taxation in a developing economy. Delhi: New Heights, 1974. 155p.

14600 NANJUNDAPPA, D.M. & M.V. NADKARNI. Local taxation in urban areas. In JKU(SS) 3 (1967) 41-83.

14601 SINHA, K.K. Local taxation in a developing economy. Bombay: Vora, 1968. 198p.

e. tax avoidance and evasion

14602 Black money voluntary disclosure scheme: editorial. In Management Accountant 10,11 (1975) 721-22.

14603 DAS, BABA GOPAL. Curbing inflation, tax evasion and black money. In Capital (Annual Number 1972) 121-24.

14604 GAUR, K.D. Judicial attitude to tax avoidance in the United Kingdom and India. In JILI 15,2 (1973) 217-52.

14605 GULATI, I.S. HUF tax avoidance revisited. In EPW 8,7 (1973) 397-402. [taxation of Hindu Undivided Family]

14606 ______. The undivided Hindu family: a study of its tax privileges. Bombay: Asia, 1962. 96p.

14607 SUJAN, M.A. & V.D. TRIVADI. Smuggling, the inside story: an account of the world's second oldest profession. Bombay: Jaico, 1976. 203p.

14608 SUKH DEO, ed. Tax axe v. tax resistance. Jodhpur: Sona Law House, 1978. 160p.

14609 UMAMAHESHWARA RAO, T. Voluntary disclosure scheme [VDS]: an overview. In SE 14,18 (1976) 11-14.

3. Banking and Monetary Policy, and Other Financial Institutions

a. general studies

14610 GHOSH, D.N. Banking policy in India: an evaluation. Bombay: Allied, 1979. 385p.

14611 HASAN, K.S. Banking in India. Ed. by L.N. Blythe. Tr. from German by R. North. Plymouth: Macdonald, 1979. 106p.

14612 INDIA (REP.). BANKING CMSN. Report. Delhi: MPGOI, 1972. 760p. [R.G. Saraiya, chm.]

14613 INDIA (REP.). STUDY GROUP ON NON-BANKING FINANCIAL INTERMEDIARIES. Report. Bombay: Banking Cmsn., 1972. 285p. [Bhabatosh Datta, chm.]

14614 JOSHI, M.S. Financial intermediaries in India. Bombay: U. of Bombay, 1965. 285p.

14615 KARKAL, G. Perspectives in Indian banking. Bombay: Popular, 1977. 127p.

14616 MUTALIK DESAI, V.R. Banking development in India. Bombay: Manaktalas, 1967. 184p.

14617 PANANDIKAR, S.G. Banking in India. 12th ed., rev. by D.M. Mithani. Bombay: Orient Longmans, 1975. 655p.

14618 PATHAK, D.S. Working of the monetary system in India. Baroda: Dept. of Business Econ., MSUB, 1979. 104p.

14619 RAO, B.S.R. Functioning of the LIC: an appraisal. Madras: Inst. for Financial Mgmt. and Res., 1976. 391p. [Life Insurance Corp. of India, Ltd.]

14620 RESERVE BANK OF INDIA. STUDY GROUP ON NON-BANKING COMPANIES. Report. Bombay: RBI, 1975. 150p. [J.S. Raj, chm.]

14621 ROY, A.K. The structure of interest rates in India. Calcutta: World Press, 1975. 130p.

14622 SHUKLA, M.M., ed. Banks and banking in India, with special reference to bank nationalization: a select list of articles. Delhi: New Star, 1970. 283p.

b. the Reserve Bank of India (est. 1935), India's central bank, and its monetary management

14623 BASU, C.R. Central banking in a planned economy: the Indian experiment. ND: Tata-McGraw Hill, 1977. 371p.

14624 BHATTACHARYYA, P.C. Central banking in a developing economy. Bombay: Vora, 1971. 283p.

14625 GHOSH, A. Control techniques in Indian monetary management. Calcutta: World Press, 1971. 119p.

14626 GUPTA, G.P. The Reserve Bank of India and monetary management. 2nd ed., rev. Bombay: Asia, 1962. 391p.

14627 GUPTA, S.B. Monetary planning for India. Delhi: OUP, 1979. 240p.

14628 HAJELA, P.D. Problems of monetary policy in underdeveloped countries, with special reference to India. Bombay: Lalvani, 1969. 298p.

14629 IENGAR, H.V.R. Monetary policy and economic growth. Bombay: Vora, 1962. 295p.

14630 INDIA (REP.). WORKING GROUP ON THE RESERVE BANK OF INDIA. Report, August 1969. ND: Admin. Reforms Cmsn., 1970. 42p.

14631 JOSHI, V. Monetary policy in a developing economy; a study with special reference to the role of the Reserve Bank of India in Indian economic development, 1960-71. Hyderabad: Vivek Vardhini Educ. Soc. Res. Inst., 1979. 43p.

14632 MAJUMDAR, B. Central banks and treasuries. Bombay: Vora, 1974. 160p.

14633 MANAKTALA, T.R. Economic development and monetary management in India. Bombay: Vora, 1966. 251p.

14634 MITRA, S. Monetary politics in India. Bombay: Vora, 1972. 250p.

14635 The monetary policy of the Reserve Bank of India; papers read at the Indian Economic Conference, Bombay, 1963. Bombay: Popular, 1964. 233p.

14636 RESERVE BANK OF INDIA. The Reserve Bank of India: functions and working. Bombay: 1970. 251p.

14637 ROY, H.N. The role of monetary policy in economic development; a study of the activities of Reserve Bank of India, 1949-56. Calcutta: World Press, 1962. 229p.

14638 SHAH, M. The new role of Reserve Bank in India's economic development. Bombay: Vora, 1970. 142p.

14639 SHARMA. K.K. Indian monetary policy; a study in recent developments. Meerut: Meenakshi, 1968. 264p.

14640 SHRIVASTAVA, N.N. Evolution of the techniques of monetary management in India. Bombay: Somaiya, 1972. 415p.

14641 SIMHA, S.L.N. History of the Reserve Bank of India, 1935-51. Bombay: RBI, 1970. 878p.

c. prices and inflation

14642 AGRAWAL, S.B. Price trends in India since 1951. Delhi: S. Chand, 1972. 234p.

14643 AHLUWALIA, I.J. Behaviour of prices and outputs in India: a macro-econometric approach. Delhi: Macmillan, 1979. 120p.

14644 ______. An analysis of price and output behaviour in the Indian economy, 1951-73. In J. of Dev. Econ. 6 (1979) 363-90.

14645 CHAKRAVARTI, S.K. The behaviour of prices in India, 1952-70. Delhi: Macmillan, 1977. 202p.

14646 CHANDHOK, H.L. Wholesale price statistics, India, 1947-1978. ND: Econ. and Scientific Res. Foundation, 1978. 2 v.

14647 GHOSH, A.B. Price trends and policies in India. Delhi: Vikas, 1974. 255p.

14648 HAJRA, S. Inflation and Indian economy, 1951-52 to 1973-74. ND: Econ. and Scientific Res. Foundation, 1975. 69p.

14649 PAI PANANDIKAR, D.H. Anatomy of inflation. ND: Centre for Monetary Res., 1974. 111p.

14650 RAJ, K.N. Price behaviour in India, 1949-66; an explanatory hypothesis. In IER 1,2 (1966) 56-80.

14651 RAO, V.K.R.V., et al. Inflation and India's economic crisis. Delhi: Vikas, 1973. 64p.

14652 SAMANT, D.R. Inflation and development: some reflections. Bombay: Popular, 1975. 128p.

14653 SREENIVAS, M.A. Price behaviour in India, 1948-49 to 1965-66: a comparative study of three macro-approaches. Bangalore: Sreenivas; Bombay: dist., Vora, 1974. 186p.

14654 TRIVEDI, M.L. Price levels and economic growth: with special reference to India. Bombay: Somaiya, 1978. 350p.

14655 VAKIL, C.N. War against inflation: the story of the falling rupee, 1943-77. Delhi: Macmillan, 1978. 338p.

d. development banking and industrial finance

14656 BASU, S.K. Industrial finance in India: a study in investment banking and state-aid to industry with special reference to India. 3rd ed. Calcutta: U. of Calcutta, 1953. 467p.

14657 NIGAM, B.M.L. Banking and economic growth; with special reference to India. Bombay: Vora, 1967. 207p.

14658 ROSEN, G. Some aspects of industrial finance in India. London: Asia, 1962. 144p.

14659 SAKSENA, R.M. Development banking in India. Bombay: Vora, 1970. 309p.

14660 SINGH, P.N. Role of development banks in a planned economy. Delhi: Vikas, 1974. 161p.

14661 SINGH, S.N. Industrialization in modern perspective. ND: Classical, 1979. 119p.

e. commercial banking
i. general studies

14662 GHOSAL, S.N. & M.D. SHARMA. Economic growth and commercial banking in a developing economy: India, a case study. Calcutta: Scientific Book Agency, 1965. 227p.

14663 HESTER, D.D. Indian banks, their portfolios, profits, and policy. Bombay: U. of Bombay, 1964. 101p. (U. of Bombay Series in monetary and intl. econ., 7)

14664 INDIAN BANKS' ASSN. Financial analysis of banks, 1973-1976; with a supplement analysing data for 1976 of public sectors banks and foreign banks operating in India. Bombay: 1977. 2 v.

14665 MATHUR, O.P. Public sector banks in India's economy: a case study of the State Bank. ND: Sterling, 1978. 211p.

14666 MEHTA, R.R.S. Sociology of banking: a study of the branch bank. Chandigarh: Bahri Pub., 1979. 200p.

14667 RESERVE BANK OF INDIA. Banking profile. Bombay: 1972. 53p.

14668 SHARMA, B.P. The role of commercial banks in India's developing economy. ND: S. Chand, 1974. 414p.

14669 VAISH, M.C. An analysis of investments and advances of scheduled banks in India during 1951-1966. Agra: Ratan Prakashan Mandir, 1969. 288p.

ii. nationalization of banks, 1969

14670 BANERJEE, G.L. Nationalisation and social control of banks. Calcutta: KLM, 1968. 51p.

14671 [Bank nationalisation - special issue]. In Indian J. of Commerce 22,4 (1969) 83-142.

14672 KHAN, G. Nationalised banking and economic development. Bombay: Vora, 1978. 253p.

14673 KUMAR, NARENDRA, ed. Bank nationalisation in India; a symposium. Bombay: Lalvani, 1969. 272p.

14674 MOHINDER SINGH, ed. Facets of social control and nationalisation of banks in India; a selected annotated bibliography. Ahmedabad: Balgovind Prakashan, 1970. 136p.

14675 NCAER. Operation of credit policies of nationalised banks since 1969. ND: 1978. 284p.

14676 Nationalisation of banks; a symposium. ND: PDMIB, 1970. 178p.

14677 QUDDUS, M. Control of commercial banks in India. Agra: Sahitya Bhawan, 1976. 175p.

14678 SHARMA, H.C. Nationalisation of banks in India: retrospect and prospect. Agra: Sahitya Bhawan, 1970. 86p.

14679 SHUKLA, M.M. & J.S. CHAUHAN & V.K. MAHESHVARI, eds. Banks and banking in India, with special reference to bank nationalisation; a select list of articles. Delhi: New Star Pub., 1970. 283p.

14680 TORRI, M. Factional politics and economic policy: the case of India's bank nationalization. In AS 15,12 (1975) 1077-96.

f. indigenous financial agencies

14681 INDIA (REP.). STUDY GROUP ON INDIGENOUS BANKERS. Report. Bombay: Banking Cmsn., 1971. 139p. [H.T. Parekh, chm.]

14682 KARKAL, G. Unorganized money markets in India. Bombay: Lalvani, 1967. 138p.

g. savings and capital formation
i. general studies

14683 GORE, M.S. India. In R.D. Lambert & B.F. Hoselitz, eds. The role of savings and wealth in southern Asia and the West. Paris: UNESCO, 1963, 178-218.

14684 HEALEY, J.M. The development of social overhead capital in India 1950-60. Oxford: Blackwell, 1965. 180p.

14685 MALHOTRA, P.C. & A.C. MINOCHA, eds. Studies in capital formation, savings, and investment in a developing economy. Bombay: Somaiya, 1971. 256p.

14686 MEHROTRA, G.N. National savings movement in India. Delhi: Atma Ram, 1978. 444p.

14687 MINOCHA, A.C. Estimates of saving and capital formation in India--a review of existing estimates and methodology. In Economic Affairs 12 (1967) 229-38, 269-80.

14688 PRASAD, BRAHMANAND. Planned capital formation in India: a critique of Keynesian fiscal monetary policies. Bombay: Vora, 1965. 224p.

14689 ROSENSTEIN-RODAN, P.N., ed. Capital formation and economic development. London: Allen & Unwin, 1964. 164p. (Studies in the econ. dev. of India, 2)

14690 SAHNI, B.S. Saving and economic development, with special reference to India. Calcutta: Scientific Book Agency, 1967. 149p.

ii. India's capital markets

14691 BHATIA, B. New issue market of India. Bombay: Vora, 1976. 125p.

14692 CHAKRABORTY, S.K. Corporate capital structure and cost of capital: a preliminary study of the Indian private sector. Calcutta: Inst. of Cost and Works Accountants of India, 1977. 294p.

14693 INDIA (REP.). CMTEE. ON FINANCE FOR THE PRIVATE SECTOR, 1953. Report. Bombay: RBI, 1954. 162p. [A.D. Shroff, chm.]

14694 KHAN, M.Y. New issue market and finance for industry in India. Bombay: Allied, 1978. 149p.

14695 MAITIN, T.P. Institutional financing in India. Agra: Sahitya Bhawan, 1971. 283p.

14696 MEHTA, R.C. Capital market in India for planned growth. Gwalior: Kitab Ghar, 1965. 278p.

14697 NCAER. Capital market in a planned economy. ND: 1966. 135p.

14698 NADDA, N.L. Capital market in India. Patna: Bharati Bhawan, 1965. 460p.

14699 SIMHA, S.L.N. The capital market of India. Bombay: Vora, 1960. 300p.

G. The Cooperative Movement in India since Independence [for rural cooperatives, see VI. E. 5., below]

1. Bibliography and Reference

14700 BASAL, S.C., ed. Documentation on co-operative development. Jaipur: Co-op. Dept. Rajasthan, 1968. 117p.

14701 INTERNATIONAL CO-OPERATIVE ALLIANCE. REGIONAL OFFICE & EDUC. CENTRE FOR SOUTH-EAST ASIA. Research in cooperation in India; a review. ND: 1965. 116p.

2. general studies

14702 DARLING, M.L. Report on certain aspects of co-operative movement in India. ND: Planning Cmsn., 1957. 53p.

14703 DEY, S.K. Sahakari samaj; the cooperative commonwealth. Bombay: Asia, 1967. 138p.

14704 GADGIL, D.R. Writings and speeches of Professor D.R. Gadgil on co-operation. Poona: GIPE, 1975. 296p. [Its studies, 64]

14705 HOUGH, E.M. The cooperative movement in India. 5th ed., rev. and enl. by K. Madhava Das. London: OUP, 1966. 492p.

14706 IYENGAR, A.S.K. A study in the co-operative movement in India; facts, theory, polemics. Bombay: Current Book House, 1962. 253p.

14707 KAMAT, G.S. New dimensions of cooperative management. Bombay: Himalaya Pub. House, 1978. 503p.

14708 KULKARNI, K.R. Theory and practice of co-operation in India and abroad. 2nd ed., rev. and enl. Bombay: Co-operator's Book Depot, 1958-62. 4 v. in 5.

14709 MATHUR, B.S. Co-operation in India; a critical analysis of the co-operative movement in India's planned economy. Agra: Sahitya Bhawan, 1971. 684p.

14710 MEHTA, S.C. Consumer co-operation in India. Delhi: Atma Ram, 1964. 324p.

14711 NATL. COOPERATIVE UNION OF INDIA. Cooperative developments in India, 1956-62; report to the Fourth Indian Cooperative Congress, November 1963, New Delhi. ND: 1964. 158p.

14712 Role of cooperatives in the development of hill areas and hill states: proceedings of All India Conference, January 30-31, 1976. ND: Natl. Coop. Union, 1976. 238p.

14713 SHAIKH, A.U., ed. Doyen of cooperation: reminiscences of Vaikunth L. Mehta. Bombay: Shad Adam Shaikh Trust, 1978. 270p.

14714 SHRISHRIMAL, W.C. Co-operative economy: problems and potentialities. Bombay: Maharashtra State Co-op. Bank, 1978. 381p.

14715 SINHA, B.K. Co-operatives in India. ND: Cmtee. for Coop. Training, Natl. Coop. Union of India, 1968. 261p.

14716 TYAGI, R.B. Recent trends in the cooperative movement in India. Bombay: Asia, 1969. 476p.

3. Cooperative Banks, and Credit in the Non-Agricultural Sector

14717 INDIA (REP.). SPECIAL WORKING GROUP ON FINANCING OF INDUSTRIAL COOPERATIVES BY COOPERATIVE BANKS. Report, July 1966. ND: Min. of Industry, 1967. 59p.

14718 INDIA (REP.). STUDY GROUP ON CREDIT COOPERATIVES IN THE NON-AGRICULTURAL SECTOR. Report. Delhi: Min. of Community Development & Cooperation, 1964. 118p.

14719 INDULE, C.B. Co-operative banking in India. Poona: Continental Prakashan, 1968. 206p.

14720 Industrial cooperative banks in India; proceedings of the All-India Seminar on Industrial Cooperative Banks held at Sholapur (Maharashtra) on 24th and 25th February, 1965. ND: National Cooperative Union of India, 1965. 141p.

14721 NAKKIRAN, S. Co-operative banking in India. Coimbatore: Rainbow, 1980. 552p.

14722 RESERVE BANK OF INDIA. WORKING GROUP ON INDUSTRIAL FINANCING THROUGH CO-OPERATIVE BANKS. Report. Bombay: RBI, 1968-. v. 1-.

VI. RECONSTRUCTING RURAL INDIA: AGRICULTURAL DEVELOPMENT AND SOCIAL CHANGE SINCE 1947

A. Bibliography and Reference

1. Bibliographies and Atlases

14723 ICAR. New vistas in crop yields. ND: 1970. 710p.

14724 INDIA (REP.). AGRICULTURAL METEOROLOGY DIV. Agro-climatic atlas of India. Pune: India Meteorological Dept., 1978. 91p.

14725 INDIA (REP.). DIR. OF ECON. & STAT. A bibliography of Indian agricultural economics. Delhi: MPGOI, 1952. 194p. [2nd ed. (covers 1952-59), 1960. 342p.; Suppl. (covers 1960-66), 1967. 164p.]

14726 ______. Indian agricultural atlas. 3rd ed. ND: Min. of Agriculture, 1971. 76p.

14727 JAIN, T.C. Survey of Indian agro-bio-economic and allied literature, 1947-1975: a bibliography. ND: Agricole Pub. Academy, 1978. 2 v., 966p.

14728 JASBIR SINGH. An agricultural atlas of India: a geographical analysis. Kurukshetra: Vishal, 1974. 356p.

14729 MOHINDER SINGH & R.N. SHARMA, eds. Rural development: a select bibliography. ND: Uppal, 1978. 336p.

14730 SATYAPRAKASH. Agriculture: a bibliography. Gurgaon: IDS, 1977. 384p.

14731 SHAH, C.H. A survey of research in agricultural economics in India. Bombay: U. of Bombay Dept. of Econ., 1971. 281p.

14732 SHARMA, R.N., ed. Thirty years of Indian journal of agricultural economics: cumulative index to volumes I-XXX, 1946-1975. Delhi: Concept, 1977. 257p.

14733 A survey of research in economics; v. 3, 4, Agriculture. Bombay: Allied, 1975. 2 v., 264, 345p. [sponsored by ICSSR]

2. Statistical Collections and Guides to Statistics

14734 BANSIL, P.C. Agricultural statistics in India. 2nd rev. ed. ND: Arnold Heinemann, 1974. 454p. [1st ed. 1970; study of their scope, development, and availability]

14735 KALIA, D.R. & M.K. JAIN & T.D. GULIANI. Statistical sources on Indian agriculture. ND: Marwah, 1978. 279p. [Annotated bibliography, chiefly of official documents arranged in broad subject categories.]

14736 NAIDU, I.J. An introduction to the agricultural census operations in India, 1970-71. ND: Dept. of Agriculture, 1973. 132p.

3. Research in Indian Agriculture - Surveys and Reviews

14737 CHOWDHRY, K. & V.R. GAIKWAD & S.K. BHATTACHARYYA. An organisation study of the Indian Council of Agricultural Research. Ahmedabad: Centre for Mgmt. in Agri., Indian Inst. of Mgmt., 1972. 71p.

14738 ICAR. Agricultural research in India: new horizons and perspectives. ND: 1971. 34p.

14739 ______. ICAR handbook. ND: 1972. 119p.

14740 INDIA (REP.). COUNCIL OF SCIENTIFIC AND INDUSTRIAL RES. CSIR in the service of rural society. ND: 1978. 77p.

14741 National index of agricultural field experiments. 1948/53-. ND: Inst. of Agri. Res. Stat., ICAR, 1954-. [quinquennial]

14742 RANDHAWA, M.S. Agricultural research in India, institutes and organisations. 2nd rev. ed. ND: ICAR, 1958. 448p.

B. Agricultural Development Through Planning

1. Indian Agriculture and its Problems - Descriptive Studies

14743 BANSIL, P.C. Agricultural problems of India. 2nd rev. and enl. ed. Delhi: Vikas, 1975. 608p.

14744 BHALLA, G.S. & V.K. ALAGH. Performance of Indian agriculture: a districtwise study. ND: Sterling, 1979. 239p.

14745 BHARADWAJ, K. Production conditions in Indian agriculture: a study based on farm management surveys. London: CamUP, 1974. 128p.

14746 DAGLI, V., ed. Foundations of Indian agriculture. Bombay: Vora, 1968. 378p. (Commerce econ. series, 1)

14747 ______., ed. Regional profile of Indian agriculture. Bombay: Vora, 1974. 311p.

14748 ÉTIENNE, G. Studies in Indian agriculture; the art of the possible. Tr. from French by M. Mothersole. Berkeley: CalUP, 1968. 343p.

14749 INDIA (REP.). NATL. CMSN. ON AGRICULTURE. National Commission on Agriculture, 1976: abridged report. ND: Min. of Agri. & Irrigation, 1977. 748p.

14750 ______. Report, 1976. ND: Min. of Agri. & Irrigation, 1976-1977. 15 v. [Chm. Nathu Ram Mirdha]

14751 JOHN, P.V. Some aspects of the structure of Indian agricultural economy, 1947-48 to 1961-62. NY: Asia, 1968. 325p.

14752 MAMORIA, C.B. Agricultural problems of India. 9th ed., rev. & enl. Allahabad: Kitab Mahal, 1979. 1064p.

14753 NCAER. Agricultural income by states, 1960-1961. ND: 1963. 88p. (Its occ. paper, 7)

14754 ______. Changes in rural income in India, 1968-69, 1969-70, 1970-71. ND: 1975. 155p.

14755 SHARMA, D.P. & V.V. DESAI. Rural economy of India. ND: Vikas, 1980. 382p.

14756 SHARMA, P.S. Agricultural regionalisation of India. Delhi: New Heights, 1973. 190p.

2. Agricultural Development
a. general studies

14757 ALI MOHAMMAD, ed. Dynamics of agricultural development in India. Delhi: Concept, 1979. 209p.

14758 ARORA, R.C. Development of agriculture and allied sectors: an integrated area approach. ND: S. Chand, 1976. 212p.

14759 ______. Industry and rural development. ND: S. Chand, 1978. 227p.

14760 BANDYOPADHYAY, K. Agricultural development in China and India: a comparative study. ND: Wiley Eastern, 1976. 204p.

14761 BERGMANN, T. Resource mobilisation and obstacles to development in Indian farming. In Pacific Viewpoint 14,1 (1973) 1-23.

14762 DASGUPTA, A.K. Agriculture and economic development in India. ND: Associated, 1973. 117p.

14763 ÉTIENNE, G. Les Chances de l'Inde. Paris: Ed. du Seuil, 1969. 254p.

14764 GUHA, S. Rural manpower and capital formation in India. Bombay: Academic Books, 1969. 186p.

14765 INDIA (REP.). DIR. OF ECON. & STATISTICS. Growth rates in agriculture, 1949-50 to 1964-65. ND: 1968. 283p. [1st ed. 1964]

14766 JAIN, S.C. Agricultural development in India. Allahabad: Kitab Mahal, 1967. 384p.

14767 LIPTON, M. India's agricultural performance: achievements, distortions, and ideologies. In AAS(J) 6 (1970) 127-48.

14768 SHAH, C.H., ed. Agricultural development of India: policy and problems: R.P. Nevatia felicitation volume. Bombay: Orient Longman, 1979. 688p. [honoring Rameshwar Prasad Nevatia, b. 1907, Indian industrialist]

14769 SWAMINATHAN, M.S. Agricultural evolution, productive employment, and rural prosperity. Mysore: U. of Mysore, 1974. 48p.

14770 TEWARI, R.N. Agricultural development and population growth. Delhi: S. Chand, 1970. 226p.

b. the "Green Revolution," beginning 1965 with the use of high-yielding varieties (HYV's)

14771 BYRES, T.J. The dialectic of India's green revolution. In SAS 5,2 (1972) 99-116.

14772 DAYA KRISHNA. The new agricultural strategy; the vehicle of green revolution in India. Delhi: 1971. 226p.

14773 FRANKEL, F.R. India's green revolution: economic gains and political costs. Princeton: PUP, 1971. 232p.

14774 INDERJIT SINGH & R.H. DAY. Microeconometric chronicle of the Green Revolution. In EDCC 23,4 (1975) 661-86.

14775 LADEJINSKY, W. Ironies of India's green revolution. In Foreign Affairs 48,4 (1970) 758-68.

14776 MANDAL, G.C. & M.G. GHOSH. Economics of the Green Revolution: a study in east India. Bombay: Asia, 1976. 113p.

14777 MOTOOKA, T. Some observations on the green revolution in India: a brief report of the invitation trip of Indian government in Nov. and Dec. of 1971. Kyoto: Center for Southeast Asian Studies, Kyoto U., 1972. 46p.

14778 OOMMEN, T.K. Impact of the Green Revolution on the weaker sections. In R&S 21,3 (1974) 26-43.

14779 SINHA, S.K. Green Revolution and breakthrough in food production in India. In IJAE 28,2 (1973) 26-42.

14780 SUBRAMANIAM, C. The new strategy in Indian agriculture: the first decade and after. ND: Vikas, 1979. 91p.

14781 TORRI, M. Economic policy and political gains; the first phase of India's Green Revolution (1966-71). In Asia Q. 1 (1976) 3-34. [also in AsSt 12 (1974) 45-75]

3. Agricultural Planning
a. strategies and administration

14782 Alternatives in agricultural development: an ICSSR working group report. ND: Allied, 1980. 136p.

14783 BARNABAS, A.P. & D.C. PELZ. Administering agricultural development; coordination, initiative, and communication in three north Indian states. ND: IIPA, 1970. 145p.

14784 DUBHASHI, P.R. Rural development administration in India. Bombay: Popular, 1970. 343p.

14785 HUNTER, G. The administration of agricultural development: lessons from India. London: OUP, 1970. 160p.

14786 INDIA (REP.). ADMIN. REFORMS CMSN. Report of the Parliamentary Seminar on Agricultural Administration. Delhi: MPGOI, 1967. 333p. [chm., H.M. Channabasappa]

14787 INDIA (REP.). ADMIN. REFORMS CMSN. STUDY TEAM ON AGRICULTURAL ADMIN. Report, Sept. 1967. Delhi: MPGOI, 1969. 2 v. in 1. [chm., H.M. Channabasappa]

14788 LIPTON, M. Strategy for agriculture: urban bias and rural planning. In P. Streeten & M. Lipton, eds. The crisis of Indian planning. London: OUP, 1968, 83-148.

14789 MELLOR, J.W., ed. Developing rural India: plan and practice. Ithaca: CornellUP, 1968. 411p.

14790 MISRA, R.P. & K.V. SUNDARAM. Rural area development: perspectives and approaches. ND: Sterling, 1979. 428p.

14791 MUTTALIB, M.A. Development administration in rural government for agricultural production: an appraoch in comparative administration. Hyderabad: Osmania U., 1973. 268p.

14792 NICHOLSON, N.K. Rural development policy in India: elite differentiation and the decision making process. Dekalb: Center for Governmental Studies, Northern Illinois U., 1974. 78p.

14793 RAY, S.K. & R.W. CUMMINGS & R.W. HERDT. Policy planning for agricultural development. ND: Tata McGraw-Hill, 1979. 237p.

14794 SEN, S.R. The strategy for agricultural development and other essays on economic policy and planning. London: Asia, 1963. 244p.

14795 SHENOI, P.V. Agricultural development in India: a new strategy in management. Delhi: Vikas, 1975. 373p.

14796 SRINIVASAN, N., ed. Agricultural administration in India. ND: IIPA, 1969. 399p. [1966 seminar papers]

b. the Intensive Agricultural District Program (IADP)

14797 BROWN, D.D. Agricultural development in India's districts. Cambridge: HUP, 1971. 169p.

14798 DESAI, D.K. IADP - analysis of results. In EPW 4,26 (1969) A83-A90.

14799 INDIA (REP.). EXPERT CMTEE. ON ASSESSMENT AND EVAL. OF THE INTENSIVE AGRICULTURAL DISTRICT PROGRAMME. Report, 1961-63. ND: Dept. of Agri., 1963. 216p. [chm., S.R. Sen]

14800 ______. Second report, 1960-65. ND: Dept. of Agri., 1966. 437p. [chm., S.R. Sen]

14801 ______. Modernising Indian agriculture; report on the Intensive agricultural district programme, 1960-68. ND: Dept. of Agri., 1969-71. 2 v. [chm., S.R. Sen]

14802 ______. Intensive agricultural district programme, 1968-69 - 1970-71.... ND: Dept. of Agri., 1975. 2 v. [chm., M.V. Mathur]

14803 RANDHAWA, M.S. Intensive agricultural programme. ND: Farm Info. Unit, GOI, 1965. 114p.

14804 SHAH, S.M. Growth centers as a strategy for rural development: Indian experience. In EDCC 22,2 (1974) 215-28.

14805 SHANMUGASUNDARAM, V., ed. Agricultural development of India; a study of the Intensive Agricultural District Program. Madras: U. of Madras, 1972. 300p. [1967 seminar papers]

c. food policy and supply
i. general studies

14806 BHATIA, B.M. India's food problems and policy since independence. Bombay: Somaiya, 1970. 251p.

14807 DAYAL, R. India's new food strategy. Delhi: Metropolitan, 1968. 208p.

14808 GARG, V.K. State in foodgrain trade in India: a study of policies and practices of public distribution system. ND: Vision Books, 1980. 104p.

14809 GHOSH, A. Market structure of Indian agriculture, an analysis. Calcutta: World Press, 1963. 47p.

14810 ICAR. Emergency food production drive, 1972-73: steps for maximizing production from the available inputs and working for a farm-management revolution. ND: 1972. 57p.

14811 INDIA (REP.). FOODGRAINS POLICY CMTEE. Report, 1966. ND: Ministry of Good, Agri., Community Dev. & Coop., 1966. 103p.

14812 JASDANWALLA, Z.Y. Marketing efficiency in Indian agriculture. Bombay: Allied, 1966. 132p.

14813 MADALGI, S.S. Population and food supply in India. Bombay: Lalvani, 1970. 160p.

14814 MUTALIK DESAI, V.R., ed. The strategy of food and agriculture in India. Bombay: Lalvani, 1969. 223p.

14815 NICHOLSON, N.K. Political aspects of Indian food policy. In PA 41 (1968) 34-50.

14816 ______. Politics and food policy in India. Diss., Cornell U., 1966. 432p. [UM 66-11,029]

14817 SEN, SUDHIR. Turning the tide: a strategy to conquer hunger and poverty. Delhi: Macmillan, 1978. 195p.

14818 SUKHATME, P.V. Feeding India's growing millions. Bombay: Asia, 1965. 172p.

ii. the Food Corporation of India and government marketing

14819 FOOD CORPORATION OF INDIA. The Food Corporation of India; review of activities since inception. ND: 1967. 25p.

14820 GULATI, I.S. & T.N. KRISHNAN. Public distribution and procurement of foodgrains: a proposal. In EPW 10,21 (1975) 829-42. [discussion in EPW 11,8 (1976) 332-37]

14821 GUPTA, ARVIND. Public distribution of foodgrains in India. Ahmedabad: Centre for Mgmt. in Agri., Indian Inst. of Mgmt., 1977. 249p.

14822 HARRISS, B. Policies pertaining to the marketing of food grains in India: the experience of 1973. In MCS 5,2 (1974) 138-51.

14823 KHUSRO, A.M. Buffer stocks and storage of foodgrains in India. ND: Tata McGraw-Hill, 1973. 144p.

14824 LELE, UMA J. Food grain marketing in India: private performance and public policy. Ithaca: CornellUP, 1971. 264p.

14825 RAJ KRISHNA. Government operations in foodgrains. In EPW 2,37 (1967) 1695-1706.

iii. famines and famine policy

14826 DANDEKAR, V.M. & V.P. PETHE. A survey of famine conditions in the affected regions of Maharashtra and Mysore. Poona: GIPE, 1972. 203p. (Its mimeograph ser., 13)

14827 MORRIS, M.D. Needed - a new famine policy. In EPW 10,5-7 (1975) 283-94.

14828 ______. What is a famine? In EPW 9,44 (1974) 1855-64.

14829 Famine relief and reconstruction: report of the Workshop, January 12-16, 1971. ND: Central Inst. of Res. & Training in Public Coop., 1971. 154p.

14830 SURESH SINGH, K. The Indian famine 1967; a study in crisis and change. ND: PPH, 1975. 312p.

d. agricultural price policy

14831 BATRA, M.M. Agricultural production: prices and technology. ND: Allied, 1978. 170p.

14832 DANDEKAR, V.M. Agricultural price policy: a critique of Dantwala. In EPW 3,11 (1968) 454-59. [with M.L. Dantwala, Agricultural price policy: reply, 459-61]

14833 ______. Food and freedom. Dharwar: Karnatak U., 1967. 53p.

14834 DANTWALA, M.L. Incentives and disincentives in Indian agriculture. In IJAE 22,2 (1967) 1-25.

14835 INDIA (REP.). AGRI. PRICES CMSN. Reports, 1965-. ND: Min. of Agri. [periodic reports on various commodities]

14836 INDIA (REP.). FOODGRAINS PRICES CMTEE. Report of Jha Committee ... for 1964-65 season. ND: Min. of Food & Agri., 1968. 25p.

14837 JAIN, S.C. Price behaviour and resource allocation in Indian agriculture. Bombay: Allied, 1968. 158p.

14838 JHA, B.V. Agricultural price-stabilization in India. Calcutta: Shot Pub., 1971. 312p.

14839 NADKARNI, M.V. Agricultural prices and development with stability. ND: National Pub., 1973. 335p.

14840 SIDHU, D.S. Price policy for wheat in India: an economic analysis of production and marketing problems. ND: S. Chand, 1979. 127p.

14841 TYAGI, D.S. Farmers' response to agricultural prices in India: a study in decision making. Delhi: Heritage Pub., 1974. 239p.

4. Agricultural Technology and Innovation

a. modernization and its effects - general studies

14842 HANUMANTHA RAO, C.H. Technological change and distribution of gains in Indian agriculture. Delhi: Macmillan, 1975. 249p.

14843 MALONE, C.C. & B.D. SHASTRY & T.S. FRANCIS. A guid to agricultural modernization. ND: Ford Foundation, 1970. 110p.

14844 Technological change in Indian agriculture [special issue]. In IJAE 21,1 (1966) 1-131.

b. innovation and the peasant

14845 AIYER, A.K.Y.N. Village improvement and agricultural extension. Bangalore: Bangalore Printing, 1954. 222p

14846 BHARAT KRISHAK SAMAJ. Dr. Punjabrao Deshmukh and his team of workers. Madras: Bharat Krishak Samaj, 197 153p.

14847 BLANCKENBURG, P. VON. Who leads agricultural modernisation: a study of some progressive farmers in Mysor and Punjab. In EPW 7,40 (1972) A94-A112.

14848 BROEHL, W.C., JR. The village entrepreneur; change agents in India's rural development. Cambridge: HUP, 1978. 228p.

14849 CHAUDHRI, D.P. Education, innovations, and agricultural development: a study of north India, 1961-72. ND: Vikas, 1979. 127p.

14850 DEB, P.C. & H. SINGH & M.L. SHARMA. Sources of information used in the adoption of improved practices. In MI 48 (1968) 167-73.

14851 FLIEGEL, F.C., et al. Agricultural innovations in Indian villages. Hyderabad: NICD, 1968. 119p.

14852 MUTHAYYA, B.C. Farmers and their aspirations: influence of socio-economic status and work orientation. NY: OUP, 1971. 113p.

14853 MUTHAYYA, B.C. & S. VIJAYAKUMAR. Psycho-social dimensions of agricultural development: an analysis. Hyderabad: NICD, 1980. 103p.

14854 NAIR, KUSUM. In defense of the irrational peasant: Indian agriculture after the Green Revolution. Chicago: UChiP, 1979. 154p.

14855 ______. The lonely furrow: farming in the United States, Japan, and India. Ann Arbor: UMichP, 1969. 314p

14856 ROCHIN, R.I. The subsistence farmer as innovator: a field survey. In SAR 6,4 (1973) 289-302.

14857 ROY, P., et al. Agricultural innovation among Indian farmers. Hyderabad: NICD, 1968. 112p.

c. high yielding varieties and other seed programs

14858 CHAKRAVARTI, A.K. The impact of the high-yielding varieties program on foodgrain production in India. In Canadian Geographer 20,2 (1976) 199-223.

14859 Economic aspects of high-yielding varieties programme. In IJAE 23,4 (1968) 48-151. [ISAE, 28th Conf.]

14860 HARRISS, B. Innovation adoption in Indian agriculture - the high yielding varieties programme. In MAS 6,1 (1972) 71-98.

14861 INDIA (REP.). PLANNING CMSN. PROGRAMME EVAL. ORG. Evaluation study of the high yielding varieties programme; report for rabi 1967-68: wheat, paddy, and jowar ND: 1971. 128p.

14862 INDIAN INST. OF MASS COMMUNICATION. Agro-information flow at the village level; a survey of communication sources in the adoption process of high-yielding varieties of crops in 33 villages. ND: 1968. 39p.

14863 LOCKWOOD, B. & P.K. MUKHERJEE & R.T. SHAND. The high yielding varieties programme in India. ND: Planning Cmsn., Programme Eval. Org., 1971-1977. 2 v.

14864 Progress report of the All-India Coordinated Rice Improvement Project: Kharif 1970. Hyderabad: Rockefelle Foundation, 1971. 3 v.

14865 SINGH, K.N. & P.N. JHA. A concept of communication sensitivity and its measurement with reference to High-Yielding Varieties Programme. In IJSR 12,2 (1971) 116-22.

d. fertilizers

14866 ALEXANDER, T.M., et al. Seminar on Fertiliser Production and Technology; proceedings. ND: Fertilizer Assn. of India, 1970. 753p.

14867 DESAI. G.M. The growth of fertilizer use in Indian agriculture - past trends and future demand. Ithaca NY: Dept. of Agric. Econ., Cornell U., 1969. 197p. (Its Occasional paper)

14868 INDIA (REP.). CMTEE. ON FERTILISERS. Report. Delhi: Min. of Food and Agri., 1965. 204p.

14869 INDIA (REP.). PLANNING CMSN. PROGRAMME EVAL. ORG. Study on the use of fertilizers and manures in agricultural production. ND: 1967. 212p.

14870 NCAER. Factors affecting fertilizer consumption: problems and policies. ND: 1964. 104p.

e. mechanization of agriculture

14871 BERGMANN, T. Mechanization of Indian farming: obstacles and prospects. Bombay: Popular, 1978. 132p.

14872 INDIA (REP.). MIN. OF FOOD & AGRI. Report of the committee on large-sized mechanized farms: first report, 1961; second report, 1964. Delhi: 1961 and 1964. 2v.

14873 Seminar on Problems of Farm Mechanization. Bombay: ISAE, 1972. 179p. (Its Seminar ser., 9)

f. irrigation and water management
i. general studies

14874 ANSARI, N. Economics of irrigation rates: a study in Punjab and Uttar Pradesh. London: Asia, 1968. 360p.

14875 CLARK, C. The economics of irrigation. In IJAE 19, 3/4 (1964) 25-32.

14876 ______. The economics of irrigation. Oxford: Pergamon Press, 1967. 116p.

14877 Command area development; its concept, constraints, and course of action. [special number]. In Kurukshetra 26,23 (1978) 1-56.

14878 GULHATI, N.D. Administration and financing of irrigation works in India. ND: Central Board of Irrigation and Power , 1965. 104p.

14879 INDIA (REP.). CENTRAL BOARD OF IRRIGATION AND POWER. Water resources research in India. ND: 1979. 249p. (Its pub., 78 rev.)

14880 INDIA (REP.). CENTRAL WATER AND POWER CMSN. Pocket book on major and medium irrigation. ND: 1976. 231p.

14881 JAISWAL, P.L., ed. Desertification and its control. ND: ICAR, 1977. 358p.

14882 KUMAR, P. Economics of water management. Delhi: Heritage, 1977. 117p.

14883 Labour intensive technology in water resources development: Indian experience. ND: Central Board of Irrigation and Power, 1979. 221p. (Its pub., 139)

14884 RAO, S.K. Inter-regional variations in agricultural growth, 1952-53 to 1964-65: a tentative analysis in relation to irrigation. In EPW 6, 27 (1971) 1333-46.

14885 Rao, K.L. India's water wealth: its assessment, uses and projections. ND: Orient Longman, 1975. 155p.

14886 SINGH, T. Drought prone areas in India: aspects of identification and development strategy. ND: People's Pub. House, 1978. 124p.

14887 WADE, R. The social response to irrigation: an Indian case study. In JDS 16,1 (1979) 3-26.

ii. irrigation policies and projects

14888 DHAWAN, B.D. Trends in tubewell irrigation, 1951-78. In EPW 14, 51-52 (1979) A143-54.

14889 INDIA (REP.). CENTRAL BOARD OF IRRIGATION AND POWER. Development of irrigation in India. ND: 1965. 231p.

14890 INDIA (REP.). CENTRAL WATER & POWER CMSN. India: irrigation and power projects; five year plans (revised). ND: 1970, 407p.

14891 INDIA (REP.). IRRIGATION CMSN. Report, 1972. ND: Min. of Irrigation and Power, 1972. 2v. [A.P. Jain, chm.]

14892 INDIA (REP.). NARMADA WATER RESOURCES DEV. CMTEE. Report of the Narmada Water Resources Development Committee. ND: Min. of Irrigation and Power, 1965. 224p. [Chm., A.N. Khosla]

14893 PUTTASWAMAIAH, K. Irrigation projects in India: towards a new policy. Bangalore: Nrusimha Pub., 1977. 96p.

14894 WADE, R. Water to the fields: India's changing strategy. In SAR 8,4 (1975) 301-21.

iii. land reclamation and colonization

14895 FARMER, B.H. Agricultural colonization in India since Independence. ND: OUP, 1974. 372p.

14896 SINGH, A.L. Economics and geography of agricultural land reclamation. Delhi: B.R., 1978. 163p.

C. The Land and Its Agricultural Products

1. Land Use and Crops - general studies

14897 DABADGHAO, P.M. & K. SHANKARNARAYAN. The grass cover of India. ND: ICAR, 1973. 713p.

14898 Hot-spots of diseases and pests of major field and horticultural crops. ND: ICAR, 1975. 63p.

14899 INDIA (REP.). NATL. CMSN. ON AGRICULTURE. Rainfall and cropping patterns. ND: 1977-79. 16v.

14900 MOHAMMAD, NOOR. Agricultural land use in India: a case study. Delhi: Inter-India, 1978. 231p.

14901 MATHUR, R.S. Plant diseases. ND: NBT, 1969. 132p.

14902 PRADHAN, S. Insect pests of crops. ND: NBT, 1969. 208p. (India - the land & people)

14903 RAYCHAUDHURI, S.P. Land and soil. ND: NBT, 1969. 190p. (India - the land & people)

2. Food and Commercial Crops

14904 CHANDRASEKHARAN, S. & K.T. ACHAYA. Profile of Indian vegetable oil industry. In EPW 15,8 (1980) 441-445; 15,9 (1980) 475-82.

14905 CHAUDHURI, M.R. The tea industry in India; a diagnostic analysis of its geo-economic aspects. Calcutta: Oxford Book and Stationery Co., 1978. 66p.

14906 CHOPRA, KUSUM & GURUSHRI SWAMY. Pulses: an analysis of demand and supply in India, 1951-1971. ND: Sterling, 1975. 132p.

14907 CHOUDHURY, B. Vegetables. ND: NBT, 1967. 193p. (India - the land & people)

14908 GEORGE, P.S. & UMA K. SRIVASTAVA & B.M. DESAI. The oilseeds economy of India: an analysis of past supply and projections for 1985. Madras: Macmillan, 1978. 174p.

14909 GORADIA, P. Profiles of tea. ND: Oxford & IBH, 1979. 99p.

14910 HAJRA, S. Jute industry: problems and prospects. ND: Econ. and Scientific Res. Foundation, 1978. 63p.

14911 HALAYYA, M. An economic analysis of the Indian tea industry and public policy. Dharwar: Karnatak U., 1972. 245p.

14912 INDIA (REP.). CMTEE. ON TEA MARKETING. Report, November 1978. Calcutta: Tea Board, 1979. 185p. [Chm. Prakash Tandon]

14913 INDIA (REP.). STUDY GROUP FOR PLANTATIONS (TEA). Report. Delhi: MPGOI, 1969. 105p.

14914 INDIA (REP.). TARIFF CMSN. Report on the biennial

review of the sericulture industry, Bombay, June 1973. Delhi: MPGOI, 1974. 83p.

14915 JAIN, S.K. Medicinal plants. ND: NBT, 1968. 176p. (India - the land & people)

14916 RANJIT SINGH. Fruits. ND: NBT, 1969. 213p. (India - the land & people)

3. Forestry

14917 Forestry in India. Dehra Dun: Indian Forester, 1967. 91p.

14918 Indian forest utilization. Comp. at the Forest Research Inst. & Colleges, Dehru Dun. Delhi: MPGOI, 1970-72.

14919 100 years of Indian forestry, 1861-1961. Issued on the occasion of the celebration of Indian forest centenary, 18 Nov. 1961. Dehra Dun: Forest Research Inst., 1961. 2v.

14920 SAGREIYA, K.P. Forests and forestry. ND: NBT, 1967. 218p. (India - the land & people)

14921 SHARMA, L.C. Development of forests and forest-based industries. Dehra Dun: Bishen Singh Mahendra Pal Singh, 1978. 237p.

14922 SONI, R.C. Afforestation in India's economy. ND: Econ. and Scientific Res. Foundation, 1975. 119p.

14923 THAPAR, S.D. India's forest resources. Delhi: Macmillan, 1975. 75p.

4. Animal Husbandry, Fishing, and Wildlife

14924 CHANDY, M. Fishes. ND: NBT, 1970. 166p. (India - the land & people)

14925 Cow problem and Indian economy. ND: CPI, 1979. 43p.

14926 DANDEKAR, V.M. Sacred cattle and more sacred production functions. In EPW 5,12 (1970) 527-31.

14927 Development of fisheries: economic aspects. In IJAE 23,4 (1968) 204-68. [ISAE, 28th Conf.]

14928 Fish processing industry in India: symposium. Mysore: Assn. of Food Scientists & Technologists, 1976. 156p.

14929 HANUMANTHA RAO, C.H. India's surplus cattle: some empirical results. In EPW 4,52 (1969) A225-27.

14930 HARBANS SINGH. Domestic Animals. ND: NBT, 1966. 155p. (India - the land & people)

14931 ______, ed. Cattle keeping in India. ND: Central Council of Gosamvardhana, 1967. 195p.

14932 HARBANS SINGH & Y.M. PARNERKAR. Basic facts about cattle wealth and allied matters. ND: Central Council of Gosamvardhana, 1966. 221p.

14933 INDIA (REP.). INDIAN BOARD FOR WILD LIFE. Conservation in India: proceedings of the special meeting, New Delhi, 24 Nov. 1965. Morges: Intl. Union for Conservation of Nature and Natural Resources, 1969. 60p.

14934 INDIA (REP.). STUDY GROUP ON WILD LIFE AND WILD LIFE PRODUCTS, 1964. Report. ND: Dept. of Agri., 1967. 42p. [Hari Singh, chm.]

14935 Indian fisheries, 1947-1977. Cochin: Central Marine Fisheries Res. Inst., 1977. 96p.

14936 JHINGRAN, V.G. Fish and fisheries of India. Delhi: Hindustan Pub., 1975. 954p.

14937 JOHN, P. Economics of dairy development in India. Patna: Prabhat Prakashan, 1975. 335p.

14938 LALL, H.K. The resurrection of the cow in India. Hoshiarpur: Vishveshvaranand Inst., 1973. 322p.

14939 MISHRA, S.N. Livestock planning in India. ND: Vikas, 1978. 278p. (Studies in econ. dev. & planning; no. 21)

14940 MOORE, M.P. Secular aspects of the sacred cow: the productivity of some Indian farm animals. Brighton: Inst. of Development Studies, U. of Sussex, 1974. 26p. (IDS discussion paper, 58)

14941 SHASHI, S.S. The shepherds of India: a socio-cultural study of sheep and cattle-rearing communities. Delhi: Sundeep Prakashan, 1978. 122p.

14942 WHYTE, R.O. The grassland and fodder resources of India. ND: ICAR, 1957. 437p.

14943 ______. Land, livestock, and human nutrition in India. NY: Praeger, 1968. 309p.

14944 ______. The nature and utilization of the grazing resources of India. In L.S. Leshnik & G.D. Sontheimer, eds., Pastoralists and nomads in South Asia. Wiesbaden: Harassowitz, 1975, 220-34.

14945 WHYTE, R.O. & M.L. Mathur. The planning of milk production in India. Bombay: Orient Longmans, 1968. 221p.

D. Land Tenure and Reform since Independence

1. Bibliographies and Reviews of Research

14946 BALASUBRAMANIAN, K. Bibliography on agrarian tensions and land reforms. ND: Documentation Centre, Gandhi Peace Foundation, 1972. 68p.

14947 DANDEKAR, B.M. A review of the land reform studies sponsored by the Research Programs Committee of the Planning Commission. In AV 4,4 (1962) 291-329.

14948 JHA, S.C. A critical analysis of Indian land reform studies. Bombay: Asian Studies Press, 1971. 119p.

14949 JOSHI, P.C. Land reforms; a trend report. In A survey of research in economics, v.4, Agriculture. Bombay: Allied, 1975, 1-172. [sponsored by ICSSR]

2. General Studies of Land Tenure and Agrarian Reforms

14950 BHATTACHARYA, D. & A.L. SEN. A note on sub-infeudation of land and fragmentation of rights: with a brief outline of tenancy legislation, 1973-1976. Calcutta: Socio-Economic Res. Inst., 1977. 26p.

14951 DAS, A.N. & V. NILAKANT, eds. Agrarian relations in India. ND: Manohar, 1979. 273p.

14952 DRIVER, P.N. Problems of zamindari and land tenure reconstruction in India. Bombay: New Book Co., 1949. 310p.

14953 DUBEY, S.N. & R. MURDIA, eds. Land alienation and restoration in tribal communities in India. Bombay: Himalaya Pub. House, 1977. 213p. [Tata Inst. of Social Sciences Seminar]

14954 HERRING, R.J. Land tenure and credit-capital tenure in contemporary India. In R.E. Frykenberg, ed. Land tenure and peasant in South Asia. ND: Orient Longman, 1977, 120-60.

14955 LADEJINSKY, W.I. A study on tenurial conditions in package districts. Delhi: Planning Cmsn., 1965. 59p.

19456 MERILLAT, H.C.L. Land and the constitution in India. NY: ColUP, 1970. 321p.

14957 NANAVATI, M.B. & J.J. ANJARIA. The Indian rural problem. 7th rev. ed. Bombay: ISAE, 1970. 622p.

14958 PATEL, G. D. The Indian land problem and legislation. Bombay: N.M. Tripathi, 1954. 534p.

14959 RAJ, K.N. Ownership and distribution of land. In IER ns 5 (1970) 1-42.

14960 SEN, BHOWANI. Evolution of agrarian relations in India; including a study of the nature and consequences of post-independence agrarian legislation. ND: PPH, 1962. 295p.

14961 SUBBARAYAN, G.E. The agricultural land under the Constitution. Hyderabad: Asia Law House, 1978. 216p.

14962 WADHWA, D.C. Agrarian legislation in India, 1793-1966. Poona: GIPE, 1973. v.1, Andhra-Maharashtra, 868p. (Its studies, 61) [guide to legislation & admin. geography]

3. Land Reform, by Legislation, Persuasion, and Direct Action

a. documents

14963 INDIA (REP.). CENSUS OF INDIA, 1961. Land tenures in India. ND: 1961-. v.1. pt. 11-A(i) & (ii); 223, 425p. [state-wise surveys]

14964 INDIA (REP.). CMTEE. ON LAND REFORMS. Report. ND: Min. of Agriculture and Irrigation, 1978. 10p. [Raj Krishna, Chm.]

14965 INDIA (REP.). LAND REFORMS IMPLEMENTATION CMTEE. Implementation of land reforms; a review by the Land Reforms Implementation Committee of the National Development Council. ND: Planning Cmsn., 1966. 285p.

14966 INDIA (REP.). PLANNING CMSN. Implementation of land reforms; a review. ND: 1966. 404p.

14967 ______. Progress of land reform. Delhi: MPGOI, 1963. 276p.

14968 ______. Reports of the committees of the Panel on Land Reforms. Delhi: MPGOI, 1959. 226p.

14969 INDIA (REP.). STUDY TEAM OF COMMUNITY DEVELOPMENT AGENCY AND PANCHAYATI RAJ INSTITUTIONS IN THE IMPLEMENTATION OF BASIC LAND REFORM MEASURES, 1967. Report. ND: Min. of Food, Agri., Comm. Dev. & Coop., 1969. 42p. [V. Ramanathan, chm.]

14970 MALAVIYA, H.D. Land reforms in India. 2nd ed. ND: AICC, 1955. 461p.

b. studies of land reforms and land reform legislation, enacted by the states under Central guidance

14971 MALJIT SINGH. Next step in village India: a study of land reform and gorup dynamics. Bombay: Asia, 1961. 135p.

14972 DANTWALA, M.L. & C.H. SHAH. Evaluation of land reforms. Bombay: U. of Bombay, 1971. 196p.

14973 JOSHI, P.C. Land reforms in India: trends and perspectives. Bombay: Allied, 1975. 181p.

14974 KHUSRO, A.M. The economics of land reform and farm size in India. Madras: Macmillan, 1973. 162p.

14975 KOTOVSKY, G.G. Agrarian reforms in India. Tr. from Russian by K.J. Lambkin. ND: PPH, 1964. 182p.

14976 LEHMANN, D. Agrarian reform and agrarian reformism: studies of Peru, Chile, China, and India. London: Faber & Faber, 1974. 320p.

14977 MICHIE, A.N. Land reforms policies in India: a comparative perspective (Politics of land reforms in India). In PSR 13, 1/4 (1974) 278-304.

14978 MINHAS, B.S. Rural poverty, land redistribution and development strategy: facts and policy. In IER ns 5 (1970) 97-128.

14979 RAJ KRISHNA. Agrarian reform in India: the debate on ceilings. In EDCC 7,3 (1959) 302-17.

14980 RAO, N.P. Progress of land reform; a critical review. ND: CPI, 1960. 107p.

14981 SIDHU, B.S. Land reform, welfare, and economic growth. Bombay: Vora, 1976. 271p.

14982 SUNDARAYYA, P. The land question. ND: All India Kisan Sabha, 1976. 79p.

14983 SWAMY, SUBRAMANIAN. Land reforms: an economist's approach. ND: Deendayal Res. Inst., 1973. 40p.

14984 THORNER, D. The agrarian prospect in India: five lectures on land reform delivered in 1955 at the Delhi School of Economics. 2nd ed. Bombay: Allied, 1976. 82p. [1st ed. 1956]

14985 WUNDERLICH, G.L. Land reform in India. Washington: AID, 1970. 92p.

c. Bhoodan ("land-gift") and Gramdan ("Village-gift"): Gandhian reform from below through moral persuasion, led by Vinoba Bhave

14986 BARRATT, B.B. The alternative village. In SAR 7,4 (1974) 267-290.

14987 BERGMANN, T. The Bhoodan and Gramdan movement in India: a critical assessment of achievement and failure. In IAF 5.3 (1974) 316-334.

14988 BHAVE, V.N. Bhoodan yajna (land-gifts mission). Ahmedabad: Navajivan, 1954. 134p.

14989 BHAVE, V. & J.P. NARAYAN. Gramdan for gramswaraj. Varanasi: Sarva Seva Sangh Prakashan, 1967. 104p. [Hindi speeches tr. by Suresh Ram]

14990 DASGUPTA, S. A great society of small communities; the story of India's land gift movement. Varanasi: Sarva Seva Sangh Prakashan, 1968. 75p.

14991 A dream takes shape: Anand Niketan's twenty-three years, 1949-1971. ND: Soc. for Developing Gramdans, 1972. 49p.

14992 LINTON, E. Fragments of a vision: a journey through India's gramdan villages. Varanasi: Sarva Seva Sangh Prakashan, 1971. 267p.

14993 MISRA, BABU RAM. V for Vinoba; the economics of the Bhoodan movement. Calcutta: Orient Longmans, 1956. 67p.

14994 MISRA, R.N. Bhoodan movement in India; an economic assessment. ND: S. Chand, 1972. 227p.

14995 OOMMEN, T.K. Charisma, stability and change; an analysis of the Bhoodan-Gramdan movement in India. ND: Thomson Press, 1972. 183p.

14996 SHARMA, J.S. Vinoba and Bhoodan, a selected descriptive bibliography of Bhoodan.... ND: INC, 1956. 92p.

14997 SURESH RAM. Vinoba and his mission; being an account of the rise and growth of the Bhoodan Yajna movement. 3rd ed., rev. & enl. Kashi: Akhil Bharat Sarva Seva Sangh, 1962. 516p.

E. Peasant Society and Rural Social Change

1. Bibliography

14998 CHAUHAN, B.R. Rural studies: a trend report. In A survey of research in sociology and social anthropology. Bombay: Popular, 1974, v.1, 82-114. [sponsored by ICSSR]

14999 HALDIPUR, R.N. Sociology of community development and Panchayati Raj; a trend report. In A survey of research in sociology and social anthropology. Bombay: Popular, 1974, v.2, 30-165. [sponsored by ICSSR]

15000 MOHINDER SINGH & R.N. SHARMA. Rural development: a select bibliography. ND: Uppal, 1978. 336p.

2. The Indian Village in an Era of Planned Social Change - General Studies

15001 DESAI, A.R., comp. Rural sociology in India. 4th rev. ed. Bombay: Popular, 1969. 968p. [1st ed. 1953]

15002 ENSMINGER, D. Rural India in transition. ND: All India Panchayat Parishad, 1972. 115p.

15003 Farmers of India. ND: ICAR, 1959-1968. 4 v., 1477p.
- v. 1 Punjab, Himachal Pradesh, Jammu & Kashmir.
- v. 2 Madras, Andhra Pradesh, Mysore, Kerala.
- v. 3 Assam, Orissa, W. Bengal, Andamans & Nicobars, Manipur, NEFA, Tripura.
- v. 4 Madhya Pradesh, Rajasthan, Gujarat, Maharashtra.

15004 GOULD, H.A. The peasant village: centrifugal or centripetal? In EA 13 (1959) 3-16.

15005 History of rural development in modern India. Genl. ed., S. Dasgupta. ND: Impex India, 1967-. [Sponsored by Gandhian Inst. of Studies & Assoc. of Voluntary Agencies for Rural Dev.; to be 5 v.]

15006 ISHWARAN, K. Change and continuity in India's villages. NY: ColUP, 1970. 296p.

15007 MAZUMDAR, VINA, ed. Role of rural women in development: report of an international study seminar held at the Institute of Development Studies, University of Sussex, U.K., 5th January to 10th February 1977. Bombay: Allied, 1978. 125p.

15008 PUNIT, A.E. Social systems in rural India. ND: Sterling, 1978. 160p.

15009 ROSEN, G. Peasant society in a changing economy: comparative development in Southeast Asia and India. Urbana: U. of Illinois Press, 1975. 256p.

15010 Rural development in India: some facets. Hyderabad: NICD, 1979. 560p.

15011 SENGUPTA, P.R. Community organisation process in India: a sociological study of village community, its socio-economic institutions and groups. Lucknow: Kiran Pub., 1976. 126p.

15012 SHARMA, R.N. Indian rural sociology: a sociological analysis of rural community, rural social change, rural social problems, community development projects and rural welfare in India. ND: Munshiram, 1979. 319p.

15013 TADA, H. Disintegration of the peasantry in India: some issues. In Developing Economies 13,1 (1975) 94-106.

15014 TAYLOR, C.C., et al. India's roots of democracy; a sociological analysis of rural India's experience in planned development since independence. NY: Praeger, 1966. 694p.

15015 THIMMAIAH, G., ed. Studies in rural development. Allahabad: Chugh, 1979. 223p.

15016 WINDEY, M.A. Rural reconstruction: the village community as agent of change. In SocAct 25,2 (1975) 145-63.

3. Planning for Rural India: from Community Development to Integrated Rural Development

a. the Community Development Programme (est. 1952)

i. bibliography

15017 Bibliography on Community Development. Mussoorie (later Hyderabad): NICD, 1961-63. No. 1-7.

ii. studies

15018 ARORA, R.C. Integrated rural development. ND: S. Chand, 1979. 462p.

15019 BHATTACHARYYA, S.N. Community development; an analysis of the programme in India. Calcutta: Academic Pub., 1970. 171p.

15020 BJORKMAN, J.W. Politics of administrative alienation in India's rural development programs. Delhi: Ajanta, 1979. 368p.

15021 DEY, S.K. Community development. 2nd rev. ed. Allahabad: Kitab Mahal, 1962. 199p. [1st ed. 1961]

15022 ENSMINGER, D. A guide to community development. Rev. ed. Calcutta: Min. of Community Dev. & Coop., 1962. 180p.

15023 INDIA (REP.). TEAM FOR THE STUDY OF COMMUNITY PROJECTS AND NATL. EXTENSION SERVICE, 1956. Report. ND: Planning Cmsn., 1957. 175p. [B.G. Mehta, chm.]

15024 JAIN, S.P. & V. KRISHNAMURTHY REDDY. Role of women in rural development: a study of mahila mandals. Hyderabad: NIRD, 1979. 93p.

15025 MANN, H.S. Analysis of some problems of community development in India. Delhi: Atma Ram, 1967. 103p.

15026 MISRA, R.P. & K.V. SUNDARAM. Multi-level planning and integrated rural development in India. ND: Heritage, 1980. 234p.

15027 MUKHERJI, B. Community development in India. Rev. ed. Bombay: Orient Longmans, 1967. 383p.

15028 NAIR, KUSUM. Blossoms in the dust; the human element in Indian development. London: G. Duckworth, 1961. 201p.

15029 NEALE, W.C. The evaluation of community development projects. In AV 8 (1966) 431-44.

15030 PANDE, V.P. Village community projects in India; origin, development and problems. Bombay: Asia, 1967. 258p.

15031 PRASAD, N. Change strategy in a developing society: India. Meerut: Meenakshi, 1970. 344p.

15032 SEN, L.K. & V.R. GAIKWAD & G.L. VERMA. People's image of community development and panchayati raj. Hyderabad: NICD, 1967. 31p.

15033 SHARMA, S.K. & S.L. MALHOTRA. Integrated rural development: approach, strategy and perspectives. ND: Abhinav, 1977. 104p.

iii. collections of essays and case studies

15034 Action for rural change; readings in Indian community development. ND: Munshiram, 1970. 507p.

15035 CHATTERJEE, B.B. Micro-studies in community development, panchayati raj, and co-operation. Delhi: Sterling, 1969. 213p.

15036 CHATTERJEE, U.N., ed. Developing village India; studies in village problems. Rev. ed. Bombay: Orient Longmans, 1951. 290p.

15037 CHEKKI, D.A., ed. Community development: theory and method of planned change. ND: Vikas, 1979. 258p.

15038 KAUFMAN, H.F. & AVTAR SINGH & S. DASGUPTA. Villages upward bound: community structure and technological development in selected Indian villages. Calcutta: Editions Indian, 1975. 188p.

15039 KRISHNAMACHARI, V.T. Community development in India; speeches and articles. Rev. ed. Delhi: PDMIB, 1962. 192p.

15040 Kurukshetra, a symposium. Rev. Delhi: PDMIB, 1967. 548p.

15041 MEHTA, S. Working with village people; a collection of case studies. ND: Natl. Fundamental Educ. Centre, Natl. Council of Educ. Res. and Training, 1965. 111p.

15042 PARAMAHAMSA, V.R.K. Development with social justice: proceedings of the seminar held at NICD, Hyderabad, 26-28 Nov., 1973. Hyderabad: NICD, 1974. 110p.

15043 SEN, L.K., ed. Readings on micro-level planning and rural growth centres. Hyderabad: NICD, 1972. 350p.

b. Community Development and local government: dual control by bureaucracy and elected panchayats

i. panchayati raj - agency for integrated development?

15044 DAYAL, R. Community development, panchayati raj and sahakari samaj. Delhi: Metropolitan, 1965. 224p.

15045 JAIN, S.C. Community development and panchayati raj in India. NY: Allied, 1967. 656p.

15046 MAMORIA, C.B. Cooperation, community development and village panchayats in India. Allahabad: Kitab Mahal, 1966. 125p.

15047 NEHRU, JAWAHARLAL. Jawaharlal Nehru on community development, panchayati raj and co-operation. Delhi: PDMIB, 1965. 165p.

15048 SINGH, B.P. Development administration in India. Patna: Jnanada Prakashan, 1969. 310p.

15049 VALSAN, E.H. Community development programs and rural local government comparative studies of India and the Philippines. NY: Praeger, 1970. 485p.

ii. district, block, and village level development administration

15050 BEERS, H.W. The development block as a social system. In IJPA 5 (1959) 135-52.

15051 ______. Relationships among workers in C.D. blocks. Hyderabad: NICD, 1962. 38p.

15052 GANGRADE, K.D. The change agent in community development: India's village level worker. In Intl. R. of Community Dev. 19/20 (1968) 309-26.

15053 JAIN, C.M. Dynamics of development administration:

an enquiry into the office of vikas adhikari. Delhi: Research Pub. in Social Sciences, 1978. 92p.

15054 MATHUR, K. Bureaucratic response to development; a study of block development officers in Rajasthan and U.P. Delhi: National, 1972. 121p.

15055 PRASAD, A. The block development officer: a portrait of bureaucracy in India. Patna: Associated Book Agency, 1976. 265p.

15056 SESHADRI, K. Co-ordination of development programmes at the block level. In IJPA 12,1 (1966) 60-87.

15057 SINHA, P.R.R. & T.K. CHAKRAVARTY & H.P.S. ARYA. Village-level workers: a study of factors influencing their performance. Hyderabad: NICD, 1976. 111p.

c. communication and education in rural development

15058 ATWAL, A.S., ed. New concepts in agricultural education in India. Ludhiana: Punjab Agri. U. Press, 1969. 683p.

15059 BOSE, J. Educational techniques in community development. Bombay: Orient Longmans, 1965. 246p.

15060 DAHAMA, O.P. Extension and rural welfare. 4th ed. Agra: Ram Prasad, 1966. 708p.

15061 DASGUPTA, S. & M.G. BHAGAT, eds. New agricultural technology and communication strategy. Bombay: Natl. Inst. of Bank Mgmt., 1976. 310p.

15062 ILCHMAN, A.S. Agricultural education in Indian development. In AS 9 (1969) 765-75.

15063 KAMATH, M.G. Writing for farm families. Bombay: Allied, 1969. 196p.

15064 MAKHIJA, H.R. Training for community development personnel in India. ND: IIPA, 1968. 170p.

15065 MATHUR, J.C. Adult education for farmers in a developing society. ND: Indian Adult Educ. Assn., 1972. 233p.

15066 ROY, P. & F.B. WAISANAN & E.M. ROGERS. The impact of communication on rural development; an investigation in Costa Rica and India. Hyderabad: UNESCO & NICD, 1969. 160p.

15067 RUDRAMOORTHY, B. Extension in planned social change; the Indian experience. Bombay: Allied, 1964. 263p.

15068 SEN, L.K. Opinion leadership in India; a study of interpersonal communication in eight villages. Hyderabad: NICD, 1969. 61p.

15069 SINGH, K.N. & C.S.S. RAO & B.N. SAHAY. Research in extension education for accelerating development process; papers and recommendations. ND: Indian Soc. of Extension Educ., 1970. 496p.

15070 The village and the communicator. In Seminar 235 (1979) 10-43.

d. rural electrification

15071 Economics of rural electrification. [special issues] In IJAE 24,4 (1969) 145-200.

15072 SEN, L.K. The role of Rural Electrification Corporation in the development of backward areas. In IJPA 23,2 (1977) 570-78.

15073 SINHA, R.K. Some aspects of rural electrification in India. In Economic Affairs 15 (1970) 221-28.

15074 VENKATAPPIAH, B. Electricity and rural India: a developmental approach. ND: Rural Electrification Corp., 1975. 25p.

4. Rural Labor in India

a. the Agricultural Labour Enquiry, and other government reports

15075 INDIA (REP.). ALL-INDIA AGRICULTURAL LABOUR ENQUIRY. Report on intensive survey of agricultural labour. Delhi: MPGOI, 1955. 7 v.

15076 INDIA (REP.). LABOUR BUREAU. Rural labour enquiry, 1974-75: final report on indebtedness among rural labour households. Chandigarh: Labour Bureau, Min. of Labour, 1978. 332p.

15077 INDIA (REP.). MIN. OF LABOUR EMPLOYMENT. Agricultural labour in India; report on the Second Agricultural Labour Enquiry, 1956-57. Delhi: 1961-62. 14 v.

15078 INDIA (REP.). PLANNING CMSN. PROGRAMME EVAL. ORG. Resettlement programme for landless agricultural labourers; case studies of selected colonies. ND: 1968. 182p.

15079 INDIAN STATISTICAL INST. Tables with notes on rural employment and unemployment. Delhi: MPGOI, 1969. 135p. (National Sample Survey, 156)

15080 RAO, V.K.R.V. Second agricultural labour enquiry: review and suggestions. In EW 13,30 (1961) 1217-25.

15081 RAJ, K.N. Second agricultural labour enquiry: a futile and misleading investigation. In EW 13,12 (1961) 505-12.

15082 THORNER, D. The agricultural labour enquiry; reflections on concepts and methods. In EW 8,24-26 (1956) 759-66.

b. general studies of rural labor

15083 AHUJA, K. Idle labour in village India. ND: Manohar, 1978. 160p.

15084 BHATTY, I.Z. Technological change and employment: a study of plantations. Delhi: Macmillan, 1978. 221p.

15085 BILLINGS, M.H. & ARJAN SINGH. Mechanisation and rural employment. In EPW 5,26 (1970) A61-72.

15086 DASGUPTA, B. Village society and labour use. Delhi: OUP, 1977. 229p.

15087 GHOSE, K.K. Agricultural labourers in India; a study in the history of their growth and economic condition. Calcutta: Indian Pub., 1969. 296p.

15088 Labour market in rural areas. In IJAE 25,3 (1970) 1-66. [ISAE 30th Conf.]

15089 MENCHER, J.P. Agricultural labor unions: some socioeconomic and political considerations. In K. David, ed. The new wind: changing identities in South Asia. The Hague: Mouton, 1977, 309-36. (WA)

15090 MITRA, ASHOK K. Surplus labour in agriculture: some estimates. In EPW 11,28 (1976) 1041-45.

15091 PANDEY, S.M., ed. Rural labour in India: problems and policy perspectives. ND: Shri Ram Centre for Industrial Relations and Human Resources, 1976. 300p.

15092 RAO, V.K.R.V., ed. Agricultural labour in India. London: Asia, 1963. 196p.

15093 SANGHVI, P. Surplus manpower in agriculture and economic development, with special reference to India. Bombay: Asia, 1969. 343p.

15094 SCHWARTZBERG, J.E. Agricultural labor in India: a regional analysis with particular reference to population growth. In EDCC 11 (1963) 337-52.

15095 SINGH, R.P. Employment of family labour and its productivity in agriculture. Varanasi: BHU, 1969. 123p.

15096 SUNDA, K. Structure of the work force in rural India: 1950-51 to 1971. In IER 12,1 (1977) 15-41.

15097 TOBIAS, G. The labour force explosion versus the new technology in agriculture. In IJIR 5 (1970) 350-66.

15098 VYAS, V.S. Rural labour utilization and agricultural development: the case of India. In AV 6,1 (1970) 50-65.

15099 VYAS, V.S. & H.V. SHIVAMAGGI. Agricultural labour; a trend report. In A survey of research in economics; v. 4, agriculture, pt. 2. Bombay: Allied, 1975, 172-273. [sponsored by ICSSR]

c. bonded labor

15100 ARORA, U.P. & M.K. PATRA & N.P. CHAUBEY, eds. Social cost of bonded labour. Allahabad: Indian Academy of Social Sciences, 1977. 94p.

15101 National survey on the incidence of bonded labour: preliminary report: an action research project of Gandhi

Peace Foundation, National Labour Institute. ND: The Institute, 1979. 93p.

15102 SEMINAR ON CULTURAL ACTION FOR SOCIAL CHANGE, DELHI, 1974. Bonded labour in India. Calcutta: India Book Exchange, 1976. 136 + 96p.

5. Rural Financial Institutions, Credit, and Cooperatives

a. rural credit - general studies

15103 BANERJEE, P.K. Indian agricultural economy: financing small farmers. ND: Chetana, 1977. 200p.

15104 BHAGAT, M.G. & S. DASGUPTA. Developing adivasis and small farmers. Bombay: Natl. Inst. of Bank Mgmt., 1975. 103p.

15105 DATEY, C.D. Loan policy and procedural arrangements in relation to the institutional credit system in India. Bombay: Reserve Bank of India, Agri. Credit Dept., 1976. 86p.

15106 GHATAK, S. Rural money markets in India. Delhi: Macmillan, 1976. 230p.

15107 HOSELITZ, B.F. Capital formation, saving and credit in Indian agricultural society. In R. Firth & B.S. Yamey, ed. Capital, saving and credit in peasant societies. Chicago: Aldine, 1964, 347-75.

15108 KODESIA, J., ed. Agricultural credit in India: an appraisal. ND: World Agri. Fair Mem. Farmers Welfare Trust Soc., 1974. 287p.

15109 PANIKAR, P.G.K. Rural savings in India. Bombay: Somaiya, 1970. 179p.

15110 RESERVE BANK OF INDIA. All-India rural credit survey; district monographs. Bombay: 1957-1960. 14 v.

15111 ______. All-India rural credit survey; report of the Committee of Direction. Bombay: 1954-56, 3 v. in 4, 3400p.
- v. 1, pt. 1, survey report (credit agencies)
- v. 1, pt. 2, survey report (rural families)
- v. 2, general report
- v. 3, technical report

15112 ______. The general report of the Committee of Direction, All-India rural credit survey. Abridged ed. Bombay: 1959. 301p. [Rpt. 1959 ed.]

15113 ______. Rural credit follow-up survey, 1956-7. Bombay: 1960. 740p.

15114 ______. Rural credit follow-up survey, 1959-60. Bombay: 1962. 296p.

15115 ______. Studies in agricultural credit. Bombay: 1970. 209p.

15116 RESERVE BANK OF INDIA. ALL-INDIA RURAL CREDIT REVIEW CMTEE. Report. Bombay: 1969. 1073p. [Chm., B. Venkatappiah]

15117 SURENDRANATHAN, P.K. The small farmers development agencies, 1972-73: a field study. Bombay: RBI, 1975. 214p.

b. banking in the rural economy

15118 BASU, S.K. Commercial banks and agricultural credit: a study in regional disparity in India. Bombay: Allied, 1979. 201p.

15119 CHANANA, C., ed. Agricultural finance in India: role of commercial banks. ND: Marketing and Econ. Res. Bureau, 1969. 165p.

15120 DESAI, S.S.M. Rural banking in India. Bombay: Himalaya Pub. House, 1979. 387p.

15121 Financing of the primary agricultural credit societies by commercial banks. Bombay: RBI, 1976. 313p.

15122 GEORGE, P.S. & U.K. SRIVASTAVA. Planning and implementation of rural development projects by a banking organization. Ahmedabad: Centre for Mgmt. in Agri., Indian Inst. of Mgmt., 1975. 140p. (CMA monograph, 55)

15123 GHOSAL, S.N. Agricultural financing in India, with special reference to land mortgage banks. Bombay: Asia, 1966. 199p.

15124 INDIA (REP.). RURAL BANKING ENQUIRY CMTEE. Report. Delhi: MPGOI, 1953. 214p. [Chm. Purshotamdas Thakurdas]

15125 MATHUR, B.S. Land development banking in India. Delhi: National, 1974. 315p.

15126 PADHY, K.C. Commercial banks and rural development: a study of India. ND: Asian Pub. Services, 1980. 111p.

15127 PENDHARKAR, V.G. & V.M. JAKHADE & A. RAMAN, eds. Financing of agriculture by commercial banks; report of a seminar held on December 6 to 8, 1968. 2nd rev. ed. Bombay: RBI, 1971. 352p.

15128 Rural Banking [special issue]. In Kurukshetra 26,2 (1977) 1-21.

c. rural credit cooperatives

15129 Conference on the Impact of Cooperative Agricultural Credit on Weaker Sections, 20th and 21st December, 1976: report. ND: Natl. Coop. Union of India, Agri. Coop. Div., 1977. 135p.

15130 INDIA (REP.). CMTEE. ON TAKAVI LOANS AND COOP. CREDIT, 1961. Report. ND: Min. of Community Dev. & Coop., 1963. 113p. [B.P. Patel, chm.]

15131 INDIA (REP.). MIN. OF COMMUNITY DEV. AND COOP. Report of the Committee on cooperative credit, 1959. ND: 1960. 256p. [chm., V.L. Mehta]

15132 KRISHNASWAMY, O.R. Co-operative democracy in action: an empirical study of democratic control and management in agricultural co-operative credit structure in a state in India. Bombay: Somaiya, 1976. 271p.

15133 MAMORIA, C.B. Role of Reserve Bank of India in promoting agricultural cooperative credit. In Indian Coop. R. 5 (1967) 43-57.

15134 MOULTON, A.D. Political and bureacratic determinants of public policy: Indian agricultural credit programs. Ph.D. diss., U. of Chicago, 1977. 324p.

15135 NCAER. Effectiveness of cooperative credit for agricultural production. ND: 1972. 396p.

15136 Role of co-operative credit in increasing farm production: a survey report. Bombay: RBI, 1974. 214p.

15137 TIRUPATI NAIDU, V. Farm credit and co-operatives in India. Bombay: Vora, 1968. 231p.

d. other cooperative institutions, and general studies of rural cooperation

15138 HALSE, M., ed. Studies in block development and cooperative organisation. Ahmedabad: Indian Inst. of Mgmt., 1967. 382p.

15139 INDIA (REP.). CMTEE. OF DIRECTION ON COOP. FARMING. Report. ND: Min. of Community Dev. & Coop., 1966. 236p. [chm. D.R. Gadgil]

15140 INDIA (REP.). CMTEE. ON COOP. MARKETING, 1964. Report. ND: 1966. 383p. [chm. M.L. Dantwala]

15141 INDIA (REP.). EXPERT CMTEE. ON ASSESSMENT & EVALUATION OF THE INTENSIVE AGRICULTURAL DISTRICT PROGRAMME. Report of the working group on co-operatives in IADP districts. ND: 1966. 177p.

15142 LAXMINARAYAN, H. & K. KANUNGO. Glimpses of cooperative farming in India. Bombay: Asia, 1967. 144p.

15143 MATHUR, B.S. Co-operative marketing in India. Jaipur: Pitaliya Pustak Bhandar, 1973. 264p.

15144 RAY, A.C. Co-operative farming in India. Calcutta: P. Ghosh, 1978. 164p.

15145 SINHA, B.K. Cooperatives in package districts. ND: Natl. Union of India, 1968. 121p.

15146 THORNER, D. Agricultural cooperatives in India; a field report. Bombay: Asia, 1964. 119p.

e. small and marginal farmers - special problems

15147 BANERJEE, P.K. Indian agricultural economy: financing small farmers. ND: Chetana, 1977. 200p.

15148 KHAN, M.A. Sociological analysis of the working of

Small Farmers Development Agency. Simla: Indian Inst. of Advanced Study, 1978. 175p.

15149 RESERVE BANK OF INDIA. DIV. OF RURAL SURVEYS. The small farmers, 1967-69; a field study. Bombay: RBI, 1975. 147p.

15150 VYAS, V.S., et al. Significance of the new strategy of agricultural development for small farmers. Vallabh Vidyanagar: Agro-econ. Res. Centre, Sardar Patel U., 1969. 95p.

6. Rural Industrialization; Khādī (Handloom) and other Cottage Industries

15151 BEHARI, B. Rural industrialization in India. ND: Vikas, 1976. 232p.

15152 CHAKRAVARTI, N.C. Surveys and plans for rural industries. Bombay: Asia, 1965. 161p.

15153 DAGLI, V., ed. Khadi and village industries in the Indian economy. Bombay: Commerce Pub., 1976. 140p. + 22pl.

15154 FELDSIEPER, M. Rural industrialisation and industrial dispersion with the help of modern small-scale industries: past experience and future prospects in India. In IAF 2,2 (1971) 219-231.

15155 HOSELITZ, B.F. Economic growth and rural industrialization. In EW 10,8 (1958) 291-301.

15156 INDIA (REP.). KHADI & VILLAGE INDUSTRIES CMSN. Patterns of assistance: khadi and village industries. Bombay: 1965. 187p.

15157 INDIA (REP.). KHADI & VILLAGE INDUSTRIES CMTEE. Report, Feb. 1968. ND: 1968. 190p. [chm. Asoka Mehta]

15158 INDIA (REP.). KHADI EVAL. CMTEE. Report. ND: Min. of Commerce and Industry, 1960. 387p.

15159 INDIA (REP.). VILLAGE & SMALL SCALE INDUSTRIES CMTEE. Report. Delhi: MPGOI, 1956. 89p.

15160 INDIA (REP.). WORKING GROUP ON SMALL SCALE INDUSTRIES, HANDICRAFTS AND SERICULTURE. SUB-GROUP ON SMALL SCALE INDUSTRIES. Report, July 1965. ND: Dept. of Industry, 1966. 347p.

15161 MEHTA, V.L. Decentralized economic development. Bombay: Khadi & Village Industries Cmsn., 1964. 439p.

15162 PRASAD, K. Technological choice under developmental planning; a case study of the small industries of India. Bombay: Popular, 1963. 385p.

15163 RAO, R.V. Problems of rural industrialisation and reconstruction. Mysore: U. of Mysore, 1978. 83p.

15164 ______. Rural industrialisation in India: the changing profile. Delhi: Concept, 1978. 151p.

7. Rural Settlements and Housing

15165 BRAYNE, F.L. The peasant's home and its place in national planning. London: Village Welfare Assn., 1949. 24p.

15166 CHANANA, C., ed. Rural settlements in South Asia. ND: MERB Bookshelf, 1980. 265p.

15167 MANDAL, R.B. Introduction to rural settlements. ND: Concept, 1979. 312p.

15168 OAKLEY, D. & K. RAMAN UNNI, eds. The rural habitat; dimensions of change in village homes and house groupings. ND: School of Planning & Architecture, 1965. 122p.

15169 SEMINAR ON RURAL HOUSING AND VILLAGE-PLANNING, VALLABH VIDYANAGAR, INDIA, 1960. Proceedings. Ed. by G.C. Mathur. ND: Natl. Buildings Org., 1962. 356p.

15170 SINGH, R.L. & R.P.B. SINGH. Transformation of rural habitat in Indian perspective, a geographic dimension. Varanasi: International Geog. Union, Working Group, Transformation of Rural Habitat in Developing Countries & Intl. Centre for Rural Habitat Studies, 1978. 200p.

VII. INDIAN INDUSTRY, COMMERCE, AND LABOR SINCE 1947

A. Industry and Industrialization

1. Bibliography and Reference

15171 SETHI, N.K. A bibliography of Indian management; with reference to the economic, industrial, international, labor, marketing, organizational, productivity, and the public administration perspectives. Bombay: Popular, 1967. 116p.

15172 A survey of research in economics; v.5, Industry. Bombay: Allied, 1975. 362p. [sponsored by ICSSR]

15173 A survey of research in management. ND: Vikas, 1973-77. 2v., 502, 683p. [bibl. essays; sponsored by ICSSR]

15174 Thapar's Indian Industrial Directory. 9th ed. Calcutta: 1978.

2. General Studies of Indian Industry and Its Development

15175 AHMAD, JALEEL. Import substitution and structural change in Indian manufacturing industry, 1950-1966. In JDS 4 (1968) 352-79.

15176 BAGCHI, A.K. Long-term constraints on India's industrial growth, 1951-1968. In E.A.G. Robinson & M. Kidron, eds., Economic development in South Asia. London: Macmillan, 1970, 170-192.

15177 DAGLI, V.J. A profile of Indian industry. Bombay: Vora, 1970. 403p.

15178 DESAI, P. Growth and structural change in the Indian manufacturing sector: 1951-1963. In IEJ 17 (1969) 205-33.

15179 GUPTA, K.R. Issues in Indian industry. ND: Atlantic Pub. & Dist., 1980. 264p.

15180 GUPTA, N.S. & A. SINGH. Industrial economy of India. ND: Light & Life, 1978. 460p.

15181 Handbook of information on industrial development of backward regions. Bombay: Industrial Dev. Bank of India, 1974. 544p.

15182 INDIA (REP.). DEPT. OF INDUSTRY. Industrial development in India. Delhi: PDMIB, 1965. 76p.

15183 KAPOOR, T.N., ed. Industrial development in the states of India. Delhi: Sterling, 1967. 581p.

15184 KULKARNI, M.R. Industrial development. ND: NBT, 1971. 327p. (India - the land & peoples)

15185 MANNE, A.S., ed. Investments for capacity expansion: size, location, and time-phasing. London: Allen & Unwin, 1967. 329p. (Studies in the econ. dev. of India, 5)

15186 MEDHORA, P.B. Industrial growth since 1950: an assessment. Bombay: U. of Bombay, 1968. 118p.

15187 MEHTA, M. Structure of Indian industries (a statistical study in the size, location and integration of industrial units in the seven selected industries of India). Bombay: Popular, 1955. 340p.

15188 NCAER. Under-utilization of industrial capacity. ND: 1966. 117p.

15189 ROY, S.K. Corporate image in India: a study of elite attitudes towards private and public industry. ND: Shri Ram Centre for Industrial Relations & Human Resources, 1974. 343p.

15190 SOMAYAJULU, V.V.N. Structural changes and growth in Indian industries: 1946-1970. In Asian Econ. R. 16, 3 (1974) 131-84.

15191 STANFORD RES. INST. Costs of urban infrastructure for industry as related to city size in developing countries; India case study. Menlo Park, CA: 1968. 435p.

3. Industrial Geography and Interstate Differences

15192 ALAGH, Y. & K.K. SUBRAHMANIAN & S.P. KASHYAP. Regional industrial diversification in India. In EPW 6,15 (1971) 795-802.

15193 DHAR, P.N. & D.V. SASTRY. Inter-state variations in industry, 1951-61. In EPW 4,12 (1969) 535-38.

15194 LAKDAWALA, D.T. & Y.K. ALAGH & A. SARMA. Regional variations in industrial development. Ahmedabad: Sardar Patel Inst. of Econ. & Social Res., 1974. 316p.

15195 PATNI, R.L. & S. HAJRA. Changes in the locational pattern of select Indian industries, 1950-65. ND: 1969. 148p.

15196 NCAER. A study on regional differences in industrial pattern (1960). ND: 1964. 76p. (Its Occ. paper, 10)

15197 SINHA, B. Industrial geography of India. Calcutta: World Press, 1972. 320p.

4. Industrial Policy and Planning
a. documents

15198 INDIA (REP.). PLANNING CMSN. Programmes of industrial development, 1851-56. Delhi: MPGIO, 1953. 275p.

15199 ______. Programmes of industrial development, 1956-61. Delhi: MPGIO, 1956. 439p.

15200 ______. Programmes of industrial development, 1961-66. Delhi: MPGIO, 1962. 706p.

b. studies

15201 BARANWAL, R., ed. Guide to new industrial policy of Government of India. ND: Guide Pub., 1978. 102p.

15202 BHAGWATI, J. & P. DESAI. India: planning for industrialization and trade policies since 1951. NY: OUP, 1970. 536p.

15203 GOPAL, M.H. The evolution and basis of Indian industrial policy. Mysore: Rao & Raghavan, 1967. 56p.

15204 INDIAN INVESTMENT CENTRE. Scope for industries in different states: incentives and facilities for industrial promotion. Rev. ed. ND: Indian Investment Centre, 1976. 314p.

15205 MALGAVKAR, P.D. & V.A. PAI PANANDIKAR. Towards an industrial policy, 2000 A.D. ND: Centre for Policy Res., 1977. 68p.

15206 SIDDHARTHAN, N.S. Industrial houses, multinationals and industrial policy. In EPW 14,29 (1979) 1197-1203.

5. The Public Sector: Government Ownership of Key Industries and Services
a. bibliography and reference

15207 CHATTOPADHYAY, P. Public enterprises; a trend report. In A survey of research in economics. Bombay: Allied, 1975, v.5, 147-281. [sponsored by ICSSR]

15208 DAGLI, V.J. Commerce yearbook of public sector, 1976-77. Bombay: Commerce Ltd., 34 + 480p.

15209 IIPA. A bibliography on public enterprises in India. New ed. ND: 1968. 135p.

15210 INDIA (REP.). BUREAU OF PUBLIC ENTERPRISES. A handbook of information on public enterprises. 1969- ND: Min. of Finance, 1970-. [annual]

15211 NAYAR, M.P. & D. KUMAR. Public enterprise in India: a select bibliography. ND: Budua's Press, 1980. 256p.

b. documents

15212 INDIA (REP.). ADMIN. REFORMS CMSN. Report on public sector undertakings, Oct. 1967. Delhi: MPGIO, 1967. 123p.

15213 INDIA (REP.). PARLIAMENT. HOUSE OF THE PEOPLE. CMTEE. ON PUBLIC UNDERTAKINGS. Personnel policies and labour-management relations in public undertakings. ND: Lok Sabha Secretariat, 1972. 149p. [chairman M.B. Rana]

15214 INDIA (REP.). STUDY TEAM ON PERSONNEL PLANNING, STAFFING OF PUBLIC SECTOR UNDERTAKINGS, AND PERSONNEL MANAGEMENT. Report, August, 1967. Delhi: MPGOI, 1969. 333p. [apptd. by Admin. Reforms Cmsn.]

15215 INDIA (REP.). STUDY TEAM ON PUBLIC SECTOR UNDERTAKINGS. Report. Delhi: PMGOI, 1967. 342p. [for Admin. Reforms Cmsn.]

15216 INDIA (REP.). STUDY TEAM ON REFORMS IN ACCOUNTS AND ROLE OF AUDIT. Report, Sept. 1967. ND: Admin. Reforms Cmsn., 1968. 149p. [chm. S. Ratnam]

c. general studies of the public sector

15217 DAGLI, V., ed. The public sector in India; a survey. Bombay: Vora, 1969. 296p. (Commerce econ. studies, 2)

15218 DAS, N. The public sector in India. 3rd ed. Bombay: Asia, 1966. 143p.

15219 FAROOQI, I.H. Macro structure of public enterprise in India. Aligarh: Faculty of Commerce, Aligarh Muslim U., 1968. 258p.

15220 The future of public sector in India. ND: Documentation Centre for Corporate & Business Policy Res., 1979. 210p.

15221 GEORGE, P.V., et al. Performance of Indian public enterprises: macro report: a research study. ND: Standing Conf. of Public Enterprises, 1978. 262p.

15222 GUPTA, R.K. Public enterprises in India. Agra: Sahitya Bhawan, 1978. 324p.

15223 KHAN, ZIAUDDIN & R.K. ARORA, eds. Public enterprises in India: a study of the state government undertakings. ND: Associated, 1975. 216p.

15224 KHERA, S.S. Government in business. 2nd rev. ed. ND: National, 1977. 464p. [1st pub. 1963]

15225 NARAIN, LAXMI. Public enterprise in India: a study of public relations and annual reports. ND: S. Chand, 1975. 249p. [1st ed. 1967]

15226 PRAKASH, OM. The theory and working of state corporations, with special reference to India. London: Allen & Unwin, 1962. 272p.

15227 RAJASEKHARIAH, A.M. & S.Y. GUBBANNAVAR. Problems of public undertakings in India - a review. In JKU (SS) 13 (1977) 13-22.

15228 RAMASWAMY, T. Public enterprises in India: objectives & performance. Meerut: Meenakshi, 1972. 169p.

15229 SHARMA, T.R. The working of state enterprises in India. Bombay, Vora, 1961. 232p.

d. management and control of public enterprises

15230 ARORA, R.S. Administration of government industries; three essays on the public corporation. ND: IIPA, 1969. 132p.

15231 GANGULY, M. Nature and control of public corporations in India. Calcutta: Progressive, 1968. 288p.

15232 GUPTA, K.R., ed. Organisation and management of public enterprises. ND: Atlantic, 1978. 2v.

15233 GUPTA, L.N. A study into the profitability of government companies: with reference to selected running concerns. ND: Oxford & IBH, 1977. 169p.

15234 INST. OF PUBLIC ENTERPRISE, HYDERABAD. Incentives in public enterprise; seminar papers and proceedings. Ed. by: V.V. Ramanadham. Bombay: N.M. Tripathi, 1967. 252p.

15235 MALLYA, N.N. Public enterprises in India: their control and accountability. Delhi: National, 1971. 292p.

15236 NAWAB, A.W. Political administration of Indian economy. Delhi: IAD, 1973. 351p.

15237 NIGAM, R.K., comp. Management of public sector in India. Bombay: Vora, 1971. 333p.

15238 PARANJAPE, H.D. The flight of technical personnel in public undertakings. ND: IIPA, 1964. 191p.

15239 RAJ, A.B.C. Public enterprise investment decisions in India, a managerial analysis. Delhi: Macmillan, 1977. 235p.

15240 RAMANADHAM, V.V. The control of public enterprises in India. NY: Asia, 1964. 304p.

15241 SATYANARAYANA, J. Incentives and productivity in public enterprises. Bombay: Popular, 1974. 153p.

15242 SHARMA, A.K. & H.R. ISSARANI. Recruitment of managerial personnel to public undertakings in India: a diagnosis of ideas and issues. In Intl. J. of Admin. Sciences 38,1 (1972) 72-84.

15243 STANDING CONF. OF PUBLIC ENTERPRISES. Government policy for the management of public enterprises. 2nd ed. ND: 1979. 2v.

15244 TANDON, BHARAT CHANDRA. Management of public enterprises. Allahabad: Chaitanya, 1978. 200p.

e. financing of public sector undertakings

15245 BHALLA, G.S. Financial administration of nationalised industries in the United Kingdom and India. Meerut: Meenakshi, 1968. 392p.

15246 MATHUR, B.P. The financing of public enterprises in India and the question of private equity participation. In IJE 50,196 (1969) 55-75.

15247 MISHRA, R. Problems of working capital with reference to selected public undertakings in India. Bombay: Somaiya, 1975. 304p.

15248 RAMANADHAM, V.V. The finances of public enterprises. Bombay: Asia, 1963. 139p.

15249 ______. Financial organisation in public enterprise. Bombay: N.M. Tripathi, 1967. 253p.

15250 SHARMA, B.S. Financial planning in the Indian public sector: a management approach. Delhi: Vikas, 1974. 212p.

6. The Joint Sector: Mixed Participation of Public and Private Firms

15251 CHAKRABORTI, A.M., ed. The joint sector. ND: Inst. of Company Secretaries, 1974. 116p.

15252 GHOSH, A. Joint sector and "control" of Indian monopoly. In EPW 9,23 (1974) 906-16.

15253 MOHSIN, M. Rationale of joint sector. In J. of the Indian Inst. of Bankers 44,4 (1973) 297-302.

15254 SPENCER, D.L. India, mixed enterprise and Western business: experiments in controlled change for growth and profit. The Hague: Nijhoff, 1959. 252p.

7. The Private Sector
a. general studies of private business and its management

15255 ALEXANDER, K.C. Participative management: the Indian experience. ND: Shri Ram Center for Industrial Relations and Human Resources, 1972. 132p.

15256 BAUMGARTEL, H. The penetration of modern management technology and organizational practices in Indian business organizations. In Indian Admin. & Mgmt. R. 3,2 (1971) 1-13.

15257 CHAKRABORTY, S.K. Managerial development and appraisal: empirical perspectives. Delhi: Macmillan, 1978. 385p.

15258 CHOWDHRY, K. Social and cultural factors in management development in India and role of the expert. In Intl. Labour R. 94 (1966) 132-47.

15259 DASGUPTA, A. Business and management in India. ND: Vikas, 1974. 291p.

15260 DAVE, M. & G. MURTHY. Control practices in Indian industry. Bombay: U. of Bombay, 1972. 157p.

15261 GAUTAM, V. Enterprise and society: a study of some aspects of entrepreneurship and management in India. Delhi: Concept, 1979. 118p.

15262 GUPTA, L.C. The changing structure of industrial finance. Oxford: OUP, 1969. 182p.

15263 NIGAM, R.K. & N.D. JOSHI. The pattern of company directorships in India. ND: Res. & Stat. Div., Dept. of Company Law Admin., Min. of Commerce & Industry, 1963. 66p.

15264 PRASAD, S.B. & A.R. NEGANDHI, eds. Managerialism for economic development: essays on India. The Hague: Nijhoff, 1968. 188p.

15265 RESERVE BANK OF INDIA. Financial statistics of joint stock companies in India, 1960-61 to 1970-71. Bombay: RBI, 1975. 497p.

b. private economic power and its social control
i. problems of economic concentration and monopolies

15266 BAIG, N. Big business in India and the U.K. ND: Atlantic, 1980. 104p.

15267 CHAUDHURI, A. Private economic power in India: a study in genesis and concentration. ND: PPH, 1975. 318p.

15268 DASGUPTA, A. & N.K. SENGUPTA. Government and business in India. Calcutta: Allied Book Agency, 1978. 438p.

15269 GHOSH, A. Concentration in Indian industries, 1948-1968. Ph.D. Diss., City U. of New York, 1972. 285p. [UM 73-2837]

15270 HAZARI, R.K. The structure of the corporate private sector; a study of concentration, ownership and control. Bombay: Asia, 1966. 400p.

15271 INDIA (REP.). HIGH-POWERED EXPERT CMTEE. ON COMPANIES AND MRTP ACTS. Report. ND: Min. of Law, Justice and Company Affairs, 1978. 368p. [MRTP = Monopolies & Restrictive Trading Practices; Cmtee. chm., R. Sachar]

15272 INDIA (REP.). MONOPOLIES INQUIRY CMSN. Report. Delhi: MPGOI, 1965. 2 v. in 1, 438p. [K.C. Dasgupta, chm.]

15273 JOSHI, L.A. The control of industry in India: a study in aspects of combination and concentration. Bombay: Vora, 1965. 265p.

15274 KOTHARI, M.L. Industrial combinations; a study of managerial integration in Indian industries. Allahabad: Chaitanya Pub. House, 1967. 235p.

15275 MOHNOT, S.R. Concentration of economic power in India; a statistical study of concentration and diffusion of economic power in India. Allahabad: Chaitanya Pub. House, 1962. 275p.

15276 NAMJOSHI, M.V. Monopolies in India; policy proposals for a mixed economy. Bombay: Lalvani, 1966. 176p.

ii. the Managing Agency System and its abolition in 1970

15277 BASU, S.K. Managing agency system, in prospect and retrospect. Calcutta: World Press, 1958. 222p.

15278 The eclipse of the managing agency system. In Commerce 120,3075 (1970) 748-52.

15279 HAZARI, R.K. The implications of the managing agency system in Indian development. In A.V. Bhuleshkar, ed. Indian economic thought and development. London: 1969, 193-213.

15280 INDIA (REP.). MANAGING AGENCY ENQUIRY CMTEE. Report. ND: Dept. of Company Affairs, Min. of Law, 1966. 61p. [I.G. Patel, chm.]

15281 NCAER. The managing agency system; a review of its working and prospects for its future. London: Asia, 1959. 147p.

15282 NIGAM, R.K. Managing agencies in India; first round: basic facts. ND: Issued by Res. & Stat. Div., Dept. of Company Law Admin., Min. of Commerce & Industry, 1957. 102p.

iii. government regulation and licensing of business

15283 CHAUDHURI, A. Industrial licensing policy and prevention of concentration of economic power in India: a critical review. In AV 14 (1972) 333-73.

15284 HAZARI, R.K. Industrial planning and licensing policy; final report. Delhi: Planning Cmsn., 1967-68. 2 v. in 4, 2009p.

15285 INDIA (REP.). INDUSTRIAL LICENSING POLICY INQUIRY CMTEE. Report. ND: Dept. of Industrial Dev., 1969. 4 v.

15286 MERCHANT, B.B. Monopoly laws: a comparative study, India and U.S.A. Bombay: N.M. Tripathi, 1976. 175p.

15287 MOHNOT, S.R. Monopoly, concentration, and industrial licensing. Calcutta: Oxford & IBH, 1968. 171p.

15288 PANDE, D.C., ed. Government regulation of private enterprise. Bombay: N.M. Tripathi, 1971. 388p. [1969 seminar by Indian Law Inst.]

c. business communities of independent India
i. Indian entrepreneurs and managers - social and economic studies

15289 AGARWAL, V.K. Initiative, enterprise and economic choices in India: a study of the patterns of entrepreneurship. ND: Munshiram, 1975. 236p.

15290 BAIG, N. Pattern of company management in India. Aligarh: Navman Prakashan, 1971. 202p.

15291 GAUTAM, V. Enterprise and society: a study of some aspects of entrepreneurship and management in India. Delhi: Concept, 1979. 118p.

15292 JAIN, S.C. Indian manager: his social origin and career. Bombay: Somaiya, 1971. 263p.

15293 LOKANATHAN, P.S. Entrepreneurship: supply of entrepreneurs and technologists with special reference to India. In K. Berrill, ed. Economic development with special reference to East Asia. NY: St. Martin's, 1964, 156-90.

15294 NAFZIGER, E.W. Indian entrepreneurship: a survey. In P. Kilby, comp. Entrepreneurship and economic development. NY: Free Press, 1971, 287-316.

15295 NOBORU, T. Indian entrepreneurs at the cross roads: a study of business leadership. Tokyo: Inst. of Developing Economies, 1970. 98p.

15296 SHARMA, K.L. & H. SINGH. Entrepreneurial growth and development programmes in northern India: a sociological analysis. ND: Abhinav, 1980. 194p.

15297 SHARMA, R.A. Emerging patterns of industrial entrepreneurship in India. In Oriental Economist 11,1 (1973) 39-61.

15298 SINGER, M.B., ed. Entrepreneurship and modernization of occupational cultures in South Asia. Durham: DUPCSSA, 1973. 328p. (Its Monograph & occ. papers series, 12)

15299 SINGH, P. Occupational values and styles of Indian managers. ND: Wiley Eastern, 1979. 152p.

15300 SUBRAMANIAM, V. The managerial class of India. ND: All India Mgmt. Assn., 1971. 91p.

15301 TANDON, B.C. Environment and entrepreneur. Allahabad: Chugh, 1975. 131p.

ii. studies of individuals or groups important in transregional business

15302 GUPTA, B.R. The Aggarwals: a socio-economic study. ND: S. Chand, 1975. 146p.

15303 JOSHI, ARUN. Lala Shri Ram: a study in entrepreneurship and industrial management. ND: Orient Longman, 1975. 708p.

15304 KHUSHWANT SINGH & ARUN JOSHI. Shri Ram: a biography. London: Asia, 1968. 240p.

15305 MICHIE, B.H. Baniyas in the Indian agrarian economy: a case of stagnant entrepreneurship. In JAS 37,4 (1978) 637-52.

15306 TANDON, P. Beyond Punjab, 1937-1960. Berkeley: UCalP, 1971. 222p.

15307 TANDON, P.L. Management as an Indian tradition. In SAR 3,3 (1970) 241-48.

15308 TIMBERG, T.A. The Marwaris: from traders to industrialists. ND: Vikas, 1978. 268p.

15309 WACHA, D.E. The life and life work of J.N. Tata. 2nd ed. Madras: Ganesh, 1915. 204p.

iii. business organizations

15310 DHEKNEY, M.R. Chambers of commerce and business associations in India. Bombay: Popular, 1971. 170p.

15311 KOCHANEK, S.A. Interest groups and interest aggregation: changing patterns of oligarchy in the FICCI. In EFW 5,29-31 (1970) 1271-1301.

15312 NAMJOSHI, M.V. & B.R. SABADE. Chambers of commerce in India. Poona: GIPE, 1967. 143p. (Its studies, 50)

15313 VENKATASUBBIAH, H. Enterprise and economic change: 50 years of FICCI. ND: Vikas, 1977. 176p.

iv. Indian business and politics

15314 BURMAN, D.J. Mystery of Birla House. Calcutta: Jugabani Sahitya Chakra, 1950. 114p.

15315 ______. T.T.K. and Birla House. Calcutta: Jugabani, 1957. 205p.

15316 KOCHANEK, S. Business and politics in India. Berkeley: UCalP, 1975. 382p.

15317 Politics and Indian business: a symposium. In AS 11,9 (1971) 841-915. [essays by W. Malenbaum, B.R. Nayar, S.A. Kochanek, R.W. Hunt, R.N. Blue]

15318 ROY, N.C. Mystery of Bajoria-Jalan House; story of a private empire within the Republic of India. Calcutta: dist. by Alpha Pub. Concern, 1972. 255p.

8. Small Industries and Industrial Cooperatives
a. general studies of modern small-scale industries (non-cottage)

15319 FELDSIEPER, M. Zur Problematik der Entwicklung und Förderung des Kleinindustriellen Sektors in Entwicklungslandern. (Untersuchungen am Beispiele Indiens.) Wiesbaden: Harrassowitz, 1968. 282p. (DSI, 4)

15320 HOSELITZ, B.F. & M. SHINOHARA & D. FISHER. The role of small industry in the process of economic growth. The Hague: Mouton, 1968. 218p.

15321 INDIA (REP.). ADMIN. REFORMS CMSN. Report on small scale sector, Dec. 1969. ND: 1970. 79p.

15322 INDIA (REP.). OFFICE OF THE DEVELOPMENT COMMISSIONER, SMALL SCALE INDUSTRIES. Small scale industries. ND: 1971. 842p.

15323 INDIA (REP.). WORKING GROUP ON SMALL SCALE SECTOR. Report, June 1968. ND: Admin. Reforms Cmsn., 1969. 164p. [Chm., A.C. Guha]

15324 INTL. PLANNING TEAM ON SMALL INDUSTRY IN INDIA. Development of small scale industries in India: prospects, problems, and policies. Delhi: Min. of Industry, 1968. 144p. [1st ed. 1954]

15325 KHAN, R.R. Management of small-scale industries. ND: S. Chand, 1979. 220p.

15326 MEHAN, K.K. Small industry procedures handbook; or, How to plan and start/expand a small scale industry enterprise in India. Bombay: Productivity Services Intl., 1971. 208p.

15327 NCAER. Study of selected small industrial units. ND: 1972. 75p.

15328 RAO, R.V. Small industries and the developing economy in India. ND: Concept, 1979. 210p.

15329 RAO, T.V. & T.K. MOULIK, eds. Identification and selection of small scale entrepreneurs. Ahmedabad: Indian Inst. of Mgmt., 1975. 173p.

15330 SANDESARA, J.C. Size and capital-intensity in Indian industry. Bombay: U. of Bombay, 1969. 163p.

15331 Small industries in India: commemorative volume. ND: Dev. Commissioner, Small Scale Industries, Min. of Industry, 1978. 348p.

15332 SUBRAHMANIAN, K.K. & S.P. KASHYAP. Small-scale industry; a trend report. In A survey of research in economics. Bombay: Allied, 1975, v. 5, 75-112.

15333 VEPA, R.K. Small industry in the seventies. Delhi: Vikas, 1971. 307p.

15334 Small industries and social change; four studies in India. Delhi: UNESCO Res. Centre on Social and Econ. Dev. in Southern Asia, 1966. 186p.

b. industrial estates: government-supported areas for facilitating industrial enterprises

15335 ALEXANDER, P.C. Industrial estates in India. Bombay: Asia, 1963. 103p.

15336 All India Seminar on Cooperative Industrial Estates Report of the proceedings, recommendations and background papers. ND: Natl. Coop. Union, 1964. 105p.

15337 BHARTI, R.K. Industrial estates in developing economies. ND: National, 1978. 312p.

15338 MATHUR, O.P. Manual on industrial estate planning. Hyderabad: Small Industry Extension Training Inst., 1971. 187p.

15339 NAGAIYA, D. Industrial estates programme: the Indian experience. Hyderabad: Small Industry Extension Training Inst., 1971. 242p.

15340 SANGHVI, R.L. Role of industrial estates in a developing economy. Bombay: Multi-Tech, 1979. 285p.

c. industrial cooperatives

15341 BERGMANN, T. The industrial activities of the cooperative movement in India. In Indian Coop. R. 12,3 (1975) 202-27.

15342 INDIA (REP.). WORKING GROUP ON INDUSTRIAL CO-OPERATIVES. Report of the second working group on industrial co-operatives. ND: Min. of Commerce & Industry, 1963. 236p.

15343 MEHTA, S.C. Industrial cooperatives in India. Delhi: Atma Ram, 1975. 323p.

15344 SEMINAR ON INDUSTRIAL CO-OPERATION, DELHI, 1961. Report of the proceedings, background papers, and working groups' reports. Delhi: Min. of Commerce & Industry, 1961. 197p.

15345 SINGH, R.S. Progress of cooperative sugar industry in India and its managerial problems. In Indian Coop. R. 15,4 (1978) 550-65.

9. Studies of Specific Industries

a. mining and mineral resources - general studies

15346 KRISHNASWAMY, S. India's mineral resources. ND: Oxford & IBH, 1972. 503p.

15347 MADAN, A.K. Problems, progress and prospects of mineral production. ND: Inst. of Econ. & Industrial Survey, 1979. 208p.

15348 ROY, B.C. Indian mineral resources, industries, and economics. Calcutta: Editions Indian, 1973. 626p.

15349 SYMPOSIUM ON BASE METALS, CALCUTTA, 1966. Base metals. Delhi: MPGOI, 1971-72. 2 v., 822p. (Geol. Survey of India. Misc. pub., 16)

15350 WADIA, M.D.N. Minerals of India. ND: NBT, 1966. 199p.

b. energy resources and production

i. surveys of energy resources and demand

15351 BROWN, J.C. & A.K. DEY. The mineral and nuclear fuels of the Indian subcontinent and Burma: a guide to the study of the coal, oil, natural gas, uranium, and thorium resources of the area. Delhi: OUP, 1975. 517p.

15352 CHAUDHRI, D.B.R., ed. Power for growth. Enl. ed. ND: Punjab, Haryana & Delhi Chamber of Commerce and Industry, 1975. 2 v.

15353 CHAUDHURI, M.R. Power resources of India; an economic-geographic appraisal. Calcutta: Oxford & IBH, 1970. 116p.

15354 INDIA (REP.). CENTRAL WATER & POWER CMSN. POWER WING. Power atlas of India. Rev. and enl. ed. ND: PDMIB, 1970. 1 v.

15355 INDIA (REP.). ENERGY SURVEY OF INDIA CMTEE. Report. ND: 1965. 441p.

15356 KASHKARI, C. Energy: resources, demand, and conservation, with special reference to India. ND: Tata-McGraw Hill, 1975. 231p.

ii. energy policy

15357 CHITALE, V.P. & M. ROY. Energy crisis in India. ND: Econ. & Scientific Res. Foundation, 1975. 102p.

15358 HENDERSON, P.D. India: the energy sector. Delhi: OUP, for World Bank, 1975. 191p.

15359 LOKANATHAN, P.S. India's energy problems. ND: Punjab: Haryana & Delhi Chamber of Commerce and Industry, 1967. 53p.

15360 POWER, P.F. The energy crisis and Indian development. In AS 15,4 (1975) 328-45.

15361 ROBINSON, E.A.G. The case of energy investment. In P. Streeten & M. Lipton, eds. The crisis of Indian planning. London: OUP, 1968, 173-86.

15362 WAGLE, D.M. & N.V. RAO. The power sector in India. Bombay: Popular, 1978. 133p.

iii. coal resources and production

15363 GUPTA, A.B. Whither coal: a study of post-nationalisation coal industry. ND: Vision Books, 1979. 124p.

15364 PARIKH, S.S., ed. Coal after nationalisation. Calcutta: Coal Consumers Assn., 1977. 898p.

iv. petroleum resources and production

15365 DASGUPTA, B. The oil industry in India: some economic aspects. London: F. Cass, 1971. 257p.

15366 KHERA, S.S. Oil: rich man, poor man. ND: National, 1979. 240p.

15367 The Indian petroleum handbook, 1969. ND: Petroleum Info. Service, 1969. 378p.

15368 India's oil potential. Dehra Dun: Himachal Times, 1976. 121p. [pub. as Himachal Times 27,29 (1976)]

v. atomic energy development

15369 DESAI, B.A., ed. Atoms for peace: an exposition of India's nuclear policy. ND: AICC, 1975. 56p.

15370 GOLD, N.L. Regional economic development and nuclear power in India. Washington: Natl. Planning Assn., 1957. 132p.

15371 HASSON, J.A. Nuclear power in India. In IJE 45 (1964) 1-29.

15371a INDIA (REP.). DEPT. OF ATOMIC ENERGY. 10 years of atomic energy in India, 1954-1964. Bombay: 1965. 36p.

15372 JAIN, J.P. Nuclear India. ND: Radiant, 1974. 2 v.

15373 JAISHANKER, S. & C. RAJA MOHAN. Civil nuclear power: technological and socio-political risks. In JIDSA 9,3 (1977) 237-55.

15374 RAMANNA, R. The atomic power programme of India. Mysore: U. of Mysore, 1969. 35p.

vi. new energy alternatives: bio-gas (gobar), solar and geothermal power

15375 GUHA, S.K. Geothermal energy: myth and reality. In Commerce 135,3475 (1977) 111-14.

15376 JAIN, B.C. Solar energy for rural development. In Commerce (Annual Number) 137,3256 (1978) 121-25.

15377 MOULIK, T.K. & U.K. SRIVASTAVA & P.M. SHINGI. Biogas system in India: a socio-economic evaluation. Ahmedabad: Centre for Mgmt. in Agri., Indian Inst. of Mgmt., 1978. 174p.

15378 RELE, S.J. Solar energy for rural India. In KG 24,11 (1978) 527-30.

15379 RESERVE BANK OF INDIA. INTER-INSTITUTIONAL GROUP ON FINANCING GOBER GAS PLANTS BY BANKS. Report. Bombay: RBI, 1976. 152p.

15380 SATHIANATHAN, M.A. Bio-gas: achievements and challenges. ND: AVARD, 1975. 192p.

15381 SOOTHA, C.D. Solar energy: the untapped abundance. In Yojana (Annual Number) 18,1 (1974) 72-74.

c. iron and steel industry

15382 AGARWAL, G.C. Public sector steel industry in India. Allahabad: Chaitanya, 1976. 258p.

15383 CHAUDHURI, M.R. The iron and steel industry of India: an economic-geographic appraisal. 2nd ed., rev. and enl. Calcutta: Oxford & IBH, 1975. 252p. [1st ed. 1964]

15384 HAFIZUDDIN. Executive performance in Indian public enterprises, with a case study of H.S.L. Aligarh: Faculty of Commerce, Aligarh Muslim U., 1969. 231p.

15385 INDIA (REP.). DEPT. OF STEEL. White paper on steel industry: presented to Parliament in May 1976 in pursuance of recommendation of Estimates Committee, Fifth Lok Sabha, twentieth report. Delhi: Cont. of Pub., 1976. 81p.

15386 JOHNSON, W.A. The steel industry of India. Cambridge: HUP, 1966. 340p.

15387 LIEDHOLM, C. The Indian iron and steel industry; an analysis of comparative advantage. East Lansing: Div. of Res., Graduate School of Business Admin., Michigan State U., 1972. 150p.

15388 PATHAK, M.C. Industrial relations in the steel industry of India: a case study of Hindustan Steel Limited. Bhagalpur: Bharat Book Depot, 1979. 244p.

15389 STANG, F. Die indischen Stahlwerke und ihre Städte. Eine wirtschafts- und siedlungsgeographische Untersuchung zur Industrialisierung und Verstädterung eines Entwicklungslandes. Wiesbaden: Steiner, 1970. 169p.

15390 Steel industry in India: a new perspective: reports of the six study groups constituted by Steel Authority of India on various problems facing the steel industry to-day. Calcutta: India Book Exchange, 1978. 119p.

d. the textile industries

15391 AIYER, H.R. Economics of textile trade and industry in India. Bombay: Vora, 1977. 108p.

15392 GAUR, M. The textiles: woes and echoes of an ailing industry. Bombay: PPSI, 1977. 239p.

15393 INDIAN INST. OF FOREIGN TRADE. Readymade garment industry in India: a study of problems and prospects. ND: 1978. 111p.

15394 KULKARNI, V.B. History of the Indian cotton textile industry. Bombay: Millowners' Assn., 1979. 400p.

15395 MEHTA, S.D. The Indian cotton textile industry, an economic analysis. Bombay: Textile Assn., 1953. 232p.

15396 MOHOTA, R.D. Textile industry and modernisation. Bombay: Current Book House, 1976. 204p.

e. tourism

15397 ACHARYA, RAM. Tourism in India. ND: National, 1977. 114p.

15398 AHUJA, S.P. & S.R. SARNA, eds. Tourism in India: a perspective to 1990. ND: Inst. of Econ. & Market Res., 1977. 180p.

15399 ANAND, M.M. Tourism and hotel industry in India: a study in management. ND: Prentice-Hall, 1976. 260p.

15400 BENDRE, V.P. Tourism in India. Aurangabad: Parimal, 1979. 295p.

15401 BHATIA, A.K. Tourism in India: history and development. ND: Sterling, 1978. 188p.

15402 Destination - India. In J. of Industry and Trade 26,2 (1976) 17-24.

15403 MUTHIAH, S. In quest of the tourist. In Indian R. 73,10 (1978) 58-64.

15404 THANGAMANI, K. Behavioral pattern of foreign tourist related economy and area development. In Deccan Geographer 14,2 (1976) 135-44.

f. other Indian industries

15405 DOSHI, R.T. Mixed fertiliser industry. Bombay: Popular, 1969. 178p.

15406 INDIA (REP.). CMTEE. TO REVIEW THE PROGRESS OF THE TANNING AND LEATHER INDUSTRIES AND TO RECOMMEND LONG TERM EXPORT POLICY. Report. ND: 1966. 254p. [Chm., Y. Nayudamma]

15407 INDIA (REP.). ELECTRONICS CMTEE. Electronics in India; report, Feb. 1966. Bombay: 1966. 396p. [Chm., H.J. Bhabha]

15408 INDIA (REP.). PARLIAMENT. HOUSE OF THE PEOPLE. CMTEE. ON PUBLIC UNDERTAKINGS. Hindustan Machine Tools Limited (Ministry of Heavy Industry). ND: Lok Sabha Secretariat, 1973. 346p.

15409 INDIA (REP.). PETRO-CHEMICAL CMTEE. Report of the Petro-Chemical Committee. ND: Min. of Commerce and Industry, 1963. 120p. [Chm., G.P. Kane]

15410 MAJUMDAR, A.G. Aluminium industry in India: problems and prospects. ND: Econ. & Scientific Res. Foundation, 1970. 85p.

15411 NIJHAWAN, B.R. & A.B. CHATTERJEA. Non-ferrous metal industry in India: a symposium held at the National Metallurgical Laboratory on February 1, 2, 3, 1954. Jamshedpur: Council of Scientific & Industrial Res., Natl. Metallurgical Laboratory, 1957. 297p.

15412 PODDER, V.P. Cement industry in India. Dalmianagar: Rohtas Industries, 1962-66. 2 v.

15413 ______. Paper industry in India: a study. ND: Oxford & IBH, 1979. 223p.

15414 SINGH, R.K., ed. India's engineering industry. Calcutta: Engineering Export Promotion Council, 1968. 78p.

B. India's Transport and Communication System

1. General Studies

15415 BHATNAGAR, K.P. Transport in modern India. Rev. & enl. ed. Kanpur: Kishore Pub. House, 1970. 749p. [1st pub. 1953]

15416 INDIA (REP.). CMTEE. ON TRANSPORT POLICY & CO-ORDINATION. Final report. ND: Planning Cmsn., 1966. 340p.

15417 INDIA (REP.). JOINT TECHNICAL GROUP FOR TRANSPORT PLANNING. Regional transport surveys: summary. ND: 1972. 551p.

15418 MATHEW, M.O. Rail and road transport in India, a study in optimum size and organisation. Calcutta: Scientific Book Agency, 1964. 226p.

15419 NANJUNDAPPA, D.M., ed. Transport planning and finance: proceedings of an all-India seminar organised by the Dept. of Econ. of Karnatak U. Dharwar: Karnatak U., 1973. 441p.

15420 OWEN, W. Distance and development; transport and communications in India. Washington: Brookings Inst., Transport Res. Program, 1968. 170p.

15421 PAVASKAR, M.G. & R.R. KULKARNI. Communications: second India studies. Bombay: Popular, 1978. 100p.

15422 PAVASKAR, M.G. Transport: second India studies. Bombay: Popular, 1978. 103p.

2. Railways

15423 INDIA (REP.). ADMIN. REFORMS CMSN. Report on railways. ND: 1970. 88p.

15424 INDIA (REP.). RAIL TARIFF ENQUIRY CMTEE. Interim report. ND: Min. of Railways, 1978. 130p. [Chm., H.K. Paranjape]

15425 INDIA (REP.). RAILWAY CORRUPTION ENQUIRY CMTEE., 1953. Report. ND: Min. of Railways, 1955. 180p.

15426 INDIA (REP.). STUDY TEAM ON RAILWAYS. Report, Nov. 1968. ND: Admin. Reforms Cmsn., 1970. 267p. [Chm., H.N. Kunzru]

15427 INDIA (REP.). RAILWAY BOARD. History of Indian railways constructed and in progress. Corrected up to 31 March 1964. ND: 1966. 222p.

15428 JOHNSON, J. The economics of Indian rail transport. Bombay: Allied, 1963. 457p.

15429 PRASAD, A. Indian railways; a study in public utility administration. Bombay: Asia, 1960. 435p.

15430 SARASWATHY RAO, Y. The Railway Board: a study in administration. ND: S. Chand, 1978. 333p.

3. Road Transport

15431 CENTRAL ROAD RES. INST. History of road development in India; a brief account of the genesis and development of the Indian road system. ND: Council of Scientific and Industrial Res., 1963. 115p.

15432 ______. 25 years of road research: Seminar on Role of Research in Road Development, 10 March 1978. ND: 1978. 58p.

15433 ______. CRRI silver jubilee souvenir, March 1978. ND: 1978. 64p.

15434 HINDUSTAN MOTORS, LTD. DEPT. OF ECON. AND MARKET RES. Road transport in India; a study. Calcutta: 1968. 107p.

15435 INDIA (REP.). STUDY GROUP ON WAYSIDE AMENITIES. Report of the Study Group on Wayside Amenities, Sept. 1972. ND: Min. of Shipping & Transport, 1974. 77p. [Chm., S.N. Sinha]

15436 NCAER. Road transport industry: a review. ND: 1979. 99p.

15437 NANJUNDAPPA, D.M. Road user taxation and road finance in Indian economy. Bombay: Jawaharlal Nehru Mem. Inst. of Dev. Studies, 1973. 253p.

4. Urban Mass Transit

15438 FERNANDES, B.G. Review of mass transportation system in metropolitan cities of India. In URPT 13 (1970) 226-42.

15439 INDIA (REP.). CMTEE. ON PLAN PROJECTS. STUDY TEAM ON METROPOLITAN TRANSPORT. Traffic & transportation problems in metropolitan cities; interim report. ND: Planning Cmsn., 1967. 109p.

15440 INDIA (REP). WORKING GROUP ON METROPOLITAN TRANSPORT SERVICES. Report. ND: Planning Cmsn., 1970. 108p. [Chm., G.C. Baveja]

15441 Mass transport.... In Seminar 171 (1973) 10-42.

15442 ROY, S.K. Urban transportation in India. In IJPA 14 (1968) 716-35.

15443 Traffic and transportation [special issue]. In J. of Inst. of Town Planners 84/85 (1974-75) 1-39.

5. Water Transport: Inland and Maritime Shipping

15444 MASTER, M.A. So I rest on my oars: collection of writings and speeches, 1947-1970 of M.A. Master. Ed. by K.V. Hariharan. Bombay: M.A. Master Mem. Trust, 1977. 2 v.

15445 MESSEGEE, G.H. Seafaring in the Indian Ocean; an analysis of the first eight years of maritime development after independence in India, Pakistan, Burma, and Ceylon. Bangkok: Tiranasar Press, 1962. 256p.

15446 MISRA, R.P. Inland water transport in India. Mysore: U. of Mysore, for Inst. of Dev. Studies, 1972. 224p.

15447 SANKLECHA, S.N. Tramp shipping in India. Bombay: U. of Bombay, 1966. 319p.

6. Air Transport

15448 ACHARYA, Ram. Civil aviation and tourism administration in India: a study in management. ND: National, 1978. 252p.

15449 DHEKNEY, M.R. Air transport in India: growth and problems. Bombay: 1953. 247p.

15450 DHINGRA, M.M., et al. Studies on civil air transportation in India. Kanpur: Dept. of Aeronautical Engineering, Indian Inst. of Technology, 1969. 132p.

15451 INDIA (REP.). AIR TRANSPORT ENQUIRY CMTEE., 1950. Report. Delhi: MPGOI, 1950. 335p. [Chm., Justice Rajadhyaksha]

15452 INDIA (REP.). PARLIAMENT. HOUSE OF THE PEOPLE. CMTEE. ON PUBLIC UNDERTAKINGS. Report on Air India: commercial and staff matters, Ministry of Tourism and Civil Aviation. ND: Lok Sabha Secretariat, 1979. 65p.

15453 NAWAB, A.W. Economic development of Indian air transport. Delhi: National, 1967. 460p.

15454 SEN, A. Five golden decades of Indian aviation: Tata's memorable years. Bombay: Aeronautical Pub. of India, 1978. 134p.

7. Posts and Telecommunications

15455 INDIA (REP.). ADMIN. REFORMS CMSN. Report on posts and telegraphs, May 1970. Delhi: MPGOI, 1970. 82p.

15456 INDIA (REP.). WORKING GROUP ON POSTS AND TELEGRAPHS. Report, May 1968. Delhi: MPGOI, 1969. 102p. [apptd. by Admin. Reforms Cmsn.]

15457 SINGH, R.C. Indian P & T employees' movement. Allahabad: Indian Intl. Pub., 1974. 182p.

15458 SRIVASTAVA, R.S. Economics of telecommunications in India, with reference to telephones. ND: Tech India Pub., 1968. 428p.

15459 SYMPOSIUM ON TELECOMMUNICATIONS IN INDIA - GROWTH AND GAPS, CALCUTTA, 1971. Proceedings. ND: Institution of Telecommunication Engineers, 1972. 83p.

C. India's Internal Commerce

1. Commercial Policy and General Studies

15460 CHAKRAVARTY, S. On the question of home market and prospects for Indian growth. In EPW 14,30-32 (1979) 1229-42.

15461 TAIMNI, K.K. Studies in retailing, consumers' cooperation & public distribution system. Poona: Harshad Prakashan, 1975. 201p.

15462 VARTIKAR, V.S. Commercial policy and economic development in India. NY: Praeger, 1969. 168p.

15463 WALI, B.M. Some aspects of trade and growth: an Indian experience. Dharwar: Karnatak U., 1976. 225p.

2. Marketing and Distribution; the State Trading Corporation

15464 DHINGRA, H.L. Market structure of Indian industry. In Indian J. of Commerce 18,2 (1965) 169-96.

15465 GUPTA, K.R. Working of state trading in India. ND: S. Chand, 1970. 343p.

15466 GUPTA, R. Retailing in metropolitan India. ND: Indian cooperative union, 1964. 90p.

15467 INDIA (REP). CMTEE. TO REVIEW THE STATE TRADING CORPORATION OF INDIA. Final report. ND: State Trading Corp. of India, 1969. 49p.

15468 MAMORIA, C.B. & R.L. JOSHI. Principles and practice of marketing in India. 2nd ed. Allahabad: Kitab Mahal, 1968. 788p.

15469 RAO, S.B. Distribution of consumer goods in rural areas. Pune: Pushpak Prakashan, 1979. 211p.

15470 RASTOGI, T.N. Marketing of Indian manufactured goods at home and abroad. Bombay: Orient Longmans, 1965. 500p.

15471 SAXENA, B.S. & S.P. SAXENA & O.P. NIGAM. A study of marketing in India. Kanpur: Kishore Pub. House, 1969. 624p.

15472 SINGH, V.B. An evaluation of fair price shops. ND: Oxford & IBH, 1973. 141p.

3. Interstate Trade

15473 JARIWALA, C.M. Freedom of interstate trade in India. ND: Sterling, 1975. 271p.

4. The Indian Consumer

15474 BHATTACHARYA, N. & B. MAHALANOBIS. Regional disparities in household consumption in India. In American Stat. Assoc. J. 62 (1967) 143-61.

15475 The changing pattern of Indian consumption: 1966-67. In QER 14,1 (1967) 10-25.

15476 The changing pattern of Indian standards of living and comfort, 1950-1970: an analysis of shifts in durables consumption. In QER 12 (1965) 18-33.

15477 GOYAL, S.K. Consumers' cooperative movement in India. Meerut: Meenakshi, 1972. 228p.

15478 GUPTA, D.B. Consumption patterns in India; a study of inter-regional variations. Bombay: Tata McGraw-Hill, 1973. 156p.

15479 HAZARI, B.R. Import intensity of consumption in India. In IER ns 2,2 (1967) 155-76.

15480 NCAER. All India consumer expenditure survey. ND: 1966-. v. 1-.

15481 ROY CHOWDHURY, U.D. Study of trends in consumer expenditure, 1953-54 to 1960-61. In IER ns 1,2 (1966) 13-41.

15482 SREENIVASA IYENGAR, N. & L.R. JAIN. Changes in the pattern of consumption in India. In AV 16,3 (1974) 231-66.

D. Labor in the Indian Economy

1. Bibliography and Reference

15483 Index to periodical articles on industrial relations in India. In IJIR [index appears quarterly].

15484 INDIA (REP.). DEPT. OF LABOUR AND EMPLOYMENT. LIBRARY. Bibliography on industrial relations in India, 1951-1968. ND: 1968. 264p.

15485 INDIA (REP.). LABOUR BUREAU. An annotated bibliography of labour research in India 1956-62. Simla: 1963. 140p.

15486 INDIAN SOC. OF LABOUR ECON. Labour research in India. Ed. by V.B. Singh. Bombay: Popular, 1970. 225p.

15487 INST. OF APPLIED MANPOWER RES. DOCUMENTATION CENTRE. Employment, unemployment, and underemployment in India: an annotated bibliography. ND: 1972. 200p.

15488 KANNAPPAN, S. Review article: unlimited labour supply and the problems of shaping an industrial labour force in India. In EDCC 16,3 (1968) 451-69.

15489 SHETH, N.R. Industrial sociology; trend report. In A survey research in sociology and social anthropology. Bombay: Popular, 1974, v. 1, 148-232. [sponsored by ICSSR]

15490 SRIVASTAVA, S. Research on human relations in industry in India; annotated bibliography. Bombay: Progressive Corp., 1968. 91p.

15491 VISARIA, P. Employment; a trend report. In A survey of research in economics. Bombay: Allied, 1976, v. 2, 125-246. [sponsored by ICSSR]

2. The Labor Market
a. general studies of employment and unemployment

15492 BASU, S.K. Labour market behaviour in a developing economy. Calcutta: New Age, 1969. 126p.

15493 BATRA, V.P. The economy and human resources. Delhi: B.R., 1978. 216p.

15494 GULATI, J.S. The changing occupational pattern. ND: Natl. Council of Educ. Res. and Training, 1975. 104p.

15495 INDIA (REP.). CMTEE. OF EXPERTS ON UNEMPLOYMENT ESTIMATES. Report. ND: Planning Cmsn., 1970. 203p.

15496 INDIA (REP.). CMTEE. ON UNEMPLOYMENT. Report. Delhi: Controller of Publications, 1974. 410p. [Chm., B. Bhagavati]

15497 INDIA (REP.). CMTEE. ON UNEMPLOYMENT. WORKING GROUP ON INDUSTRIES. Report. Delhi: Controller of Publications, 1973. 82p. [Chm., A.G. Kulkarni]

15498 INDIA (REP.). STUDY GROUP ON EMPLOYMENT AND TRAINING. Report. ND: Natl. Cmsn. on Labour, 1969. 163p.

15499 INDIAN STAT. INST. Tables with notes on urban employment and unemployment. Delhi: MPGOI, 1969. 221p. (National Sample Survey, 157)

15500 INTL. ECON. CONF. ON PROBLEMS OF UNEMPLOYMENT IN INDIA, LONDON, 1971. Problems of unemployment in India. Ed. by Mansur Hoda. Bombay: Allied, 1974. 89p.

15501 KHUSRO, A.M. Economic development with no population transfers; a study in demand for and supply of labour in the non-agricultural sector of the Indian economy: 1951-76. Bombay: Asia, 1962. 47p.

15502 MORRIS, M.D. The labour market in India. In W.E. Moore & A.S. Feldman, eds. Labour commitment and social change in developing areas. NY: Social Science Res. Council, 1960, 172-200.

15503 NARAYANA, D.L. Employment and economic growth in India: I.L.O. fiftieth anniversary lectures. Madurai: Madurai U., 1970. 126p.

15504 PUTTASWAMAIAH, K. Unemployment in India: policy for manpower. ND: Oxford & IBH, 1977. 196p.

15505 RAJ, K.N. Employment and unemployment in the Indian economy: problems of classification, measurement, and policy. In EDCC 7,3 (1959) 258-78.

15506 SCHWARTZBERG, J.E. Occupational structure and level of economic development in India; a regional analysis. ND: Registrar Genl., 1969. 267p. (CI, 1969, mono. 4)

15507 SINHA, J.N. Comparability of 1961 and 1951 census economic data. In AV 6 (1964) 273-88.

15508 THORNER, A. How to use the 1961 Census working force data. In EPW 1,12 (Nov. 5, 1966) 495-502.

15509 ______. Working force size and structure in India, 1951: a regional analysis of census and sample survey data. In Sankhya 25, series B, 1 & 2 (1963) 121-94.

15510 TOBIAS, G. Human resources in India. ND: Meenakshi, 1971. 95p.

15511 VISARIA, P. Unemployment in India in perspective. In EPW 5, 29-31 (1970) 1251-58.

b. educated manpower & unemployment

15512 BLAUG, M. & R. LAYARD & M. WOODHALL. The causes of graduate unemployment in India. London: Allen Lane, 1969. 312p.

15513 CHANDER, R. Pattern of internal migration of scientific and technical manpower in India. In Manpower U. 4,1 (1968) 111-54.

15514 DHAR, T.N. The politics of manpower planning: graduate unemployment and the planning of higher education in India. Calcutta: Minerva, 1974. 284p.

15515 The educated unemployed: a symposium on the crisis facing our trained personnel. In Seminar 129 (1969) 19-31. (articles by J.P. Naik, R.P. Sinha, S. Kannappan, V.V. John, R.G. d'Mello, K.R. Sivaramakrishnan)

15516 Education and manpower: a select bibliography. In Manpower 1,3/4 (1965/66) 296-312.

15517 FORUM OF EDUC. CMTEE. ON EDUC. AND TOTAL EMPLOYMENT. Educated unemployment in India: challenge and responses. ND: Hindustan Pub. Corp, 1972. 103p. [Chm., B.K. Bhan]

15518 ILCHMAN, W.F. "People in plenty": educated unemployment in India. In AS 9,10 (1969) 781-95.

15519 ILCHMAN, W.F. & T.N. DHAR. Student discontent and educated unemployment. In EPW 5,29-31 (1970) 1259-66.

15520 INDIA (REP.). DIR. GENERAL OF EMPLOYMENT AND TRAINING. Report on the employment pattern of graduates. ND: Dir. Genl. of Employment & Training, Min. of Labour, 1977. 111p.

15521 PANDIT, H.N. Nature and dimensions of unemployed educated manpower in India, 1953 to 1964. In Manpower 1,3/4 (1965-66) 119-76.

15522 RAY, KAMALESH. Scientific manpower--review of characteristics of stock and problems of utilisation. In Manpower Journal 3,4 (1968) 29-42.

15523 SAXENA, J.P. Educated unemployment in India; problems and suggestion. ND: Commercial Pub. Bureau, 1972. 194p.

15524 SUNDARAM, K.N. Engineering manpower - a study of our resources and requirements. In Manpower 1,3/4 (1966) 42-87.

c. the "brain drain"

15525 ABRAHAM, P.M. Regaining high level Indian manpower from abroad - a review of policies, programmes and problems. In Manpower J. 3,4 (1968) 83-112.

15526 DANDEKAR, V.M. Brain drain: the Indian situation. In EPW 2,33-35 (1967) 1573-86.

15527 DAS, M.S. Brain drain controversy and utilization of returning Indian scholars trained abroad. In Population R. 21,1/2 (1977) 28-36.

15528 KABRA, K.N. Political economy of brain drain: reverse transfer of technology. ND: Arnold-Heinemann, 1976. 190p.

15529 MERRIAM, M.F. Brain drain study at IIT Kanpur. In Manpower J. 5,1 (1969) 52-82.

15530 Our brain drain; a symposium on the use of the talent available to us. In Seminar 92 (1967) 10-35. (Articles by P.S. Ray, Mahendra Kumar, A.D. Moddie, J. Bhagwati, Surindar Suri, Raj Krishna & S. Ghosh)

d. women in the labor force

15531 AHMED, KARUNA. Studies of educated working women in India: trends and issues. In EPW 14,33 (1979) 1435-40.

15532 ANDIAPPON, P. Public policy and sex discrimination in employment in India. In IJIR 14,3 (1979) 395-415.

15533 BOSERUP, E. Women in the labour market. In Devaki Jain, ed. Indian women. ND: PDMIB, 1975, 99-111.

15534 DHOLAKIA, B.H. & R.H. DHOLAKIA. Interstate variation in female labour force participation rates in India. In IJLE 20,4 (1978) 290-307.

15535 GULATI, L. Female labour in the unorganised sector: profile of a brick worker. In EPW 14,16 (1979) 744-52.

15536 ______. Female work participation: a study of inter-state differences. In EPW 10,1/2 (1975) 35-42. [Discussion by: J.N. Sinha in EPW 10,16 (1975) 672-74; D. Narasimha Reddy in EPW 10,23 (1975) 902-05; reply by L. Gulati in EPW 10,23 (1975) 1215-18]

15537 ______. Occupational distribution of working women; an inter-state comparison. In EPW 10,43 (1975) 1692-1704.

15538 ______. Profile of a female agricultural labourer. In EPW 13,12 (1978) A-27-47.

15539 KAPUR, P. The changing status of the working woman in India. Delhi: Vikas, 1974. 178p.

15540 NATH, KAMLA. Female work participation and economic development: a regional analysis. In EPW 5,21 (1970) 846-49.

15541 ______. Urban women workers: a preliminary study. In EW 17,37 (1965) 1405-12.

15542 ______. Women in the working force in India. In EPW 3,31 (1968) 1205-18.

15543 PANDEY, R.N. Women: status, employment and wage disparity. In ILJ 17,1 (1976) 1-18.

15544 RANADIVE, V. Women workers of India. Calcutta: National Book Agency, 1976. 100p.

15545 SINHA, G.P. & S.N. RANADE. Women construction workers. Bombay: Allied, 1977. 92p.

15546 SRIVASTAVA, V. Employment of educated married women in India: its causes and consequences. ND: National, 1978. 192p.

15547 Women in industry. ND: Min. of Labour & Employment, 1975. 241p.

3. Labor and Manpower Policy

15548 DAS, N. Unemployment and employment planning. Bombay: Orient Longmans, 1968. 100p.

15549 DHYANI, S.N. International Labour Organisation and India: in pursuit of social justice. ND: National, 1977. 315p.

15550 GUPTA, A.P. Fiscal policy for employment generation in India: a study prepared for the International Labour Office within the framework of the World Employment Programme. ND: Tata McGraw-Hill Pub. Co., 1977. 142p.

15551 INDIA (REP.). DEPT. OF LABOUR AND EMPLOYMENT. Tripartite conclusions, 1942-1967. 2nd ed. Delhi: MPGOI, 1968. 353p.

15552 INDIA (REP.). LABOUR BUREAU. Silver jubilee souvenir, 1946-71. Simla: Labour Bureau, Min. of Labour and Rehabilitation, 1972. 365p.

15553 INDIA (REP.). NATL. CMSN. ON LABOUR. Report. ND: Min. of Labour & Employment & Rehabilitation, 1969. 503 + 178p. [Chm., P.B. Gajendragadkar]

15554 INDIA (REP.). STUDY GROUP ON LABOUR PROBLEMS IN THE PUBLIC SECTOR. Report. ND: Natl. Cmsn. on Labour, 1968. 104p.

15555 INDIA (REP.). WORKING GROUP ON LABOUR ADMIN. (EASTERN REGION). Report. ND: Natl. Cmsn. on Labour, 1969. 126p.

15556 ______ (NORTHERN REGION). Report. Delhi: MPGOI, 1969. 157p.

15557 ______ (SOUTHERN REGION). Report. Delhi: MPGOI, 1969. 162p.

15558 ______ (WESTERN REGION). Report. Delhi: MPGOI, 1969. 190p.

15559 INDIAN NATL. TRADE UNION CONGRESS. Conclusions & recommendations of National Commission on Labour: a digest with minutes of dissent, August 1969. ND: 1969. 89p.

15560 ______. Labour policies and programmes in the Fourth Five Year Plan. ND: 1965. 66p.

15561 JOHRI, C.K. Issues in Indian labour policy; papers and conclusions of the fourth National Seminar on Industrial Relations in a Developing Economy, 1968. ND: Shri Ram Centre for Industrial Relations, 1969. 344p.

15562 MATHUR, K. & N.R. SHETH. Tripartitism in labour policy; the Indian experience. ND: Shri Ram Centre for Industrial Relations, 1969. 183p.

15563 MUKERJEE, RADHAKAMAL, ed. Labour and planning: essays in honour of V.V. Giri. Bombay: Allied, 1964. 267p.

15564 PUTTASWAMAIAH, K. Unemployment in India: policy for manpower. ND: Oxford & IBH, 1977. 196p.

15565 SINHA, M.R., ed. The economics of manpower planning. Bombay: Asian Studies Press, 1965. 194p.

15566 TOBIAS, G. India's manpower strategy revisited, 1947-1967. Bombay: N.M. Tripathi, 1968. 265p.

15567 VAID, K.N., ed. Contours of labour policy, being a report of the seminar...held at New Delhi in February-March 1965. ND: Shri Ram Centre Press, 1965. 74p.

15568 ______. State and labour in India. Bombay: Asia, 1965. 279p.

4. Labor Legislation

15569 AGARWAL, S.L. Labour relations law in India. Delhi: Macmillan, 1978. 659p.

15570 AGGARWAL, A.P. Indian and American labor legislation and practices: a comparative study. London: Asia, 1967. 329p.

15571 DAWSON, W.A. An introductory guide to central labour legislation. Bombay: Asia, 1967. 240p.

15572 KOTHARI, G.M. Labour law and practice. 2nd ed., as amended up to date. Calcutta: Intl. Law Book Centre, 1980. 3 v.

15573 KULSHRESHTHA, J.C. Child labour in India. ND: Ashish, 1978. 145p.

15574 SONARIKAR, S.S. Implementation of labour enactments. Bombay: Popular, 1976. 349p.

15575 VIDYARTHI, R.D. Growth of labour legislation in India since 1939, and its impact on economic development. Calcutta: Star Printing Works, 1961. 335p.

5. Wages, Wage Policy, and Productivity
a. wage determination and productivity

15576 CHATTERJEE, A.K. Productivity and earnings in Indian manufacturing industries, 1946-58. In IJLE 10 (1967) 28-52.

15577 FONSECA, A.J. Wage determination and organized labour in India. Bombay: OUP, 1964. 241p.

15578 GUJARATI, D. Money wage and employment in a labour surplus economy: Indian experience, 1951-1968. In IJLE 19 (1967) 198-208.

15579 INDIA (REP.). LABOUR BUREAU. Wage fixation in industry and agriculture in India. Delhi: Cont. of Pub., 1974. 106p.

15580 KANSAL, S.M. Changes in value added per person in selected industries in India, 1946 to 1969. ND: Econ. and Scientific Res. Foundation, 1975. 54p.

15581 MEHTA, S.S. Productivity, production function, and technical change: a survey of some Indian industries. ND: Concept, 1980. 184p.

15582 NATH, R. Occupational pattern and wage structure in Indian industries. ND: Sterling, 1976. 248p.

15583 PAPOLA, T.S. Principles of wage determination; an empirical study. Bombay: Somaiya, 1970. 243p.

15584 SINGH, R. The movement of industrial wages in India. Bombay: Asia, 1975. 352p.

15585 SINHA, J.N. & P.K. SAWHNEY. Wages and productivity in selected Indian industries. Delhi: Vikas, 1970. 190p.

b. wage policy

15586 FONSECA, A.J. Incomes and wages policy in India: a study of its major objectives. In SocAct 25,2 (1975) 114-31.

15587 ______. Wage issues in a developing economy: the Indian experience. Bombay: OUP, 1975. 264p.

15588 INDIA (REP.). STUDY GROUP FOR WAGE POLICY. Report. Delhi: MPGOI, 1969. 125p.

15589 INDIA (REP.). STUDY GROUP ON WAGES, INCOMES, AND PRICES. Report. ND: Bureau of Public Enterprises, 1978. 146p.

15590 MENON, K.S.V. Foundations of wage policy; with special reference to the Supreme Court's contribution. Bombay: N.M. Tripathi, 1969. 311p.

15591 PALEKAR, S.A. Problems of wage policy for economic development with special reference to India. London: Asia, 1963. 343p.

15592 SANDESARA, J.C. & L.K. DESHPANDE, eds. Wage policy and wage determination in India; papers and proceedings of the seminar held by the Centre of Advanced Study in Economics, U. of Bombay, during March 19-21, 1969. Bombay: U. of Bombay, 1970. 313p.

6. The Indian Industrial Worker
a. general studies

15593 GHOSH, S. Indian labour in the phase of industrialization. Calcutta: New Age, 1966. 194p.

15594 GIRI, V.V. Labour problems in Indian industry. 2nd ed. London: Asia, 1959. 456p.

15595 INDIA (REP.). CMTEE. ON LABOUR WELFARE. Report, 1969. Delhi: MPGOI, 1970. 501p.

15596 INDIA (REP.). NATL. CMSN. ON LABOUR. Indian worker: a changing profile, 1947-1967. ND: 1969. 232p.

15597 ______. Indian worker: an industry-wise review, 1947-1968, August 1969. ND: 1969. 209p.

15598 MEHROTRA, G.N. Studies in industrial sociology: the Indian context. Delhi: Atma Ram, 1975. 126p.

15599 ORNATI, O.A. Jobs and workers in India. Ithaca, NY: Inst. of Intl. Industrial and Labor Rel., Cornell U., 1955. 215p.

15600 PANT, S.C. Indian labour problems. 2nd ed. Allahabad: Chaitanya Pub. House, 1970. 468p.

15601 SINGH, V.B., ed. Industrial labour in India. 2nd rev. and enl. ed. Bombay: Asia, 1963. 664p.

15602 ______. An introduction to the study of Indian labour problems. Agra: S.L. Agarwala, 1967. 194p.

15603 VAID, K.N. Labour welfare in India. ND: Shri Ram Centre for Industrial Relations, 1970. 392p.

b. problems of recruitment, commitment, and absenteeism

15604 KANNAPPAN, S. Labour force commitment in early stages of industrialisation. In IJIR 5 (1970) 290-349.

15605 KAPOOR, K.D. Anti-management employees in industry. Kanpur: Alka Prakashan, 1978. 207p.

15606 MORRIS, M.D. The recruitment of an industrial labor force in India, with British and American conparisons. In CSSH 2 (1960) 304-28.

15607 SHARMA, B.R. Absenteeism: a search for correlates. In IJIR 5 (1970) 267-89.

15608 ______. Commitment to industrial work: the case of the Indian automobile worker. In IJIR 4 (1968) 3-32.

15609 SHETH, N.R. Commitment to industrial work: a methodological note. In IJIR 4 (1968) 215-47.

15610 ______. The problem of labour commitment. In EPW 6,9 (1971) M35-39.

15611 VAID, K.N. Contract labour in manufacturing industries: a report and an analysis. ND: Shriram Centre for Industrial Relations, 1966. 93p.

15612 ______. Papers on absenteeism. Bombay: Asia, 1967. 109p.

7. Industrial Relations
a. general studies

15613 AGARWAL, R.D., comp. Dynamics of labour relations in India; a book of readings. Bombay: Tata McGraw-Hill, 1972. 296p.

15614 AGNIHOTRI, V. Industrial relations in India. Delhi: Atma Ram, 1970. 216p.

15615 BHASKARA RAO, V. Employer-employee relations: a critical study of Government of India and its employees. Delhi: Concept, 1978. 264p.

15616 DUFTY, N.F. Industrial relations in India. Bombay: Allied, 1964. 168p.

15617 GANGADHARA RAO, M. Industrial relations in Indian railways. Waltair: Andhra U. Press, 1978. 352p.

15618 INDIA (REP.). STUDY GROUP ON SOCIOLOGICAL ASPECTS OF LABOUR-MANAGEMENT RELATIONS. Report. ND: Natl. Cmsn. on Labour, 1968. 54p.

15619 MEHROTRA, G.N. Industrial relations in a changing India. Meerut: Jai Prakash Nath, 1970. 391p.

15620 MYERS, C.A. & S. KANNAPPAN. Industrial relations in India. 2nd rev. & enl. ed. NY: Asia, 1970. 426p. [1st ed. 1958]

15621 PUNEKAR, S.D. & M.S. SAVUR. Management white-collar relations. Bombay: Popular, 1969. 362p.

15622 RAMASWAMY, E.A., ed. Industrial relations in India: a sociological perspective. Delhi: Macmillan, 1978. 146p.

15623 SHETH, J. A survey of research on personnel management and industrial relations; a trend report. In A survey of research in management. Delhi: Vikas, 1973, v. 1, 284-489. [sponsored by ICSSR]

b. personnel management and policies

15624 DAVAR, R.S. Personnel management and industrial relations in India. Delhi: Vikas, 1976. 369p.

15625 DESAI, K.G. Human problems in Indian industries. Bombay: Sindhu, 1969. 113p.

15626 GHOSH, P. Personnel administration in India. ND: Sudha Pub., 1969. 408p.

15627 HUMAN RESOURCES FOUNDATION. Personnel managers at work; comparative survey of personnel policies of major companies in India. Madras: 1968. 52 + 202p.

15628 INDIAN INST. OF PERSONNEL MGMT. Personnel management in India: the practical approach to human relations in industry. Bombay: Asia, 1961. 316p.

15629 KAPOOR, T.N., ed. Personnel management and industrial relations in India. Bombay: N.M. Tripathi, 1968. 287p.

15630 RUDRABASAVARAJ, M.N. Personnel administration practices in India. Poona: Vaikunth Mehta Natl. Inst. of Coop. Mgmt., 1969. 467p.

c. workers' participation in management: towards industrial democracy

15631 ALEXANDER, K.C. Participative management: the Indian experience. ND: Shri Ram Centre for Industrial Relations and Human Resources, 1972. 132p.

15632 BOGAERT, M. VAN DEN. Industrial democracy and its future in India. In Inter-discipline 6 (1969) 13-40.

15633 DAS, N. Experiments in industrial democracy. Bombay: Asia, 1964. 175p.

15634 INDIA (REP.). MIN. OF LABOUR AND EMPLOYMENT. Reports on the working of joint management councils. ND: 1965. 179p.

15635 MHETRAS, V.G. Labour participation in management; an experiment in industrial democracy in India. Bombay: Manaktalas, 1966. 247p.

15636 PYLEE, M.V. Worker participation in management; myth and reality. ND: N.V. Pub., 1975. 278p.

15637 SHETH, N.R. The joint management council: problems and prospects. ND: Shri Ram Centre for Industrial Relations and Human Resources, 1972. 173p.

15638 TANIĆ, Z. Workers' participation in management: ideal and reality in India. ND: Shri Ram Centre for Industrial Relations, 1969. 132p.

15339 WORKSHOP ON BIPARTISM, NEW DELHI, INDIA, 1976. Bipartism: concept and role: being the proceedings of a Workshop on Bipartism. Bombay: Employers' Federation of India, 1977. 84p.

d. the trade union movement: All-India Trade Union Congress, Indian National Trade Union Congress, and other unions

i. general studies of the labor movement

15640 BOGAERT, M. VAN DEN. Trade unionism in Indian ports; a case study at Calcutta and Bombay. ND: Shri Ram Centre for Industrial Relations, 1970. 196p.

15641 GOYAL, R.C. Trade unionism among white collar workers in India. In IJLE 11 (1968-69) C137-55.

15642 JOHRI, C.K. Unionism in a developing economy; a study of the interaction between trade unionism and government policy in India, 1950-1965. Bombay: Asia, 1967. 303p.

15643 KARNIK, V.B. Indian labour: problems and prospects. Calcutta: Minerva, 1974. 286p.

15644 ______. Indian trade unions: a survey. 3rd rev. ed. Bombay: Popular, 1978. 431p. [1st ed. 1960]

15645 KENNEDY, V.D. Unions, employers and government: essays on Indian labour questions. Bombay: Manaktalas, 1966. 227p.

15646 MAST, M.K. Trade union movement in Indian railways. Meerut: Meenakshi, 1969. 210p.

15647 MATHUR, J.S. Indian working-class movement. Allahabad: 1964. 415p.

15648 MUNSON, F.C. Indian trade unions; structure and function. Ann Arbor: Inst. of Intl. Commerce, U. of Michigan, 1970. 132p.

15649 RAMAN RAO, A.V. Indian trade unions. Honolulu: UPH, 1967. 98p.

15650 SHARMA, G.K. Labour movement in India: its past and present. 2nd ed. ND: Sterling, 1971. 296p.

15651 TRIVEDI, H.N., ed. Thirty years of the Indian National Trade Union Congress, 1947 to 1977: review of the services rendered to Indian workers by the INTUC during three decades since its foundation on May 3, 1947. Bombay: INTUC, 1977. 138p.

ii. Indian labor leadership

15652 ACHARJI, N. Trade union leadership profile. ND: Ambika, 1980. 116p.

15653 PUNEKAR, S.D. & S. MADHURI. Trade union leadership in India; a survey. Bombay: Lalvani Pub. House, 1967. 192p. (Tata Institute of Social Sciences series, no. 16)

15654 SHETH, N.R. & S.P. JAIN. The status role of local union leaders. In IJIR 4 (1968) 70-88.

iii. the Gandhian approach to labor relations

15655 ANJANEYULU, V. Gandhian concept of industrial relations and its influence on Indian labour policy. In IJIR 5(1969) 123-46.

15656 KANNAPPAN, S. The Gandhian model of unionism in a developing economy: the TLA in India. In Industrial and Labor Relations R. 16 (1962) 86-110.

15657 Social responsibilities of trade unions; proceedings of seminar convened by the India International Centre, New Delhi, and the Gandhian Institute of Studies, Varanasi, at New Delhi from March 29-31, 1966. ND: IIC, 1966. 110p.

e. labor disputes and collective bargaining; strikes, lockouts, and gheraos ("surrounding" an employer to enforce demands)

15658 AGGARWAL, A.P. Gheraos and industrial relations. Bombay: N.M. Tripathi, 1968. 187p.

15659 ______. Strikes in the United States and India: a comparative analysis. In JILI 5 (1963) 237-70.

15660 Industrial disputes in India during 1965. In Indian Labour Journal 8 (1967) 11-53. [appears periodically]

15661 KARNIK, V.N. Strikes in India. Bombay: Manaktalas: 1967. 436p.

15662 RAMAN RAO, A.V. Mediation, conciliation and arbitration: U.S.A. and India, a comparative study. Bombay: Popular, 1963. 232p.

15663 SETHI, A.S. Role of collective bargaining in industrial relations in India. Delhi: Atma Ram, 1962. 200p.

15664 SRIVASTAVA, G. Collective bargaining and labour-management relations in India. Allahabad: Bookland, 1962. 407p.

15665 SUR, MARY. Collective bargaining; a comparative

study of development in India and other countries. Bombay: Asia, 1965. 192p.

15666 VAID, K.N. Industrial disputes in India. ND: Shri Ram Centre Press, 1965. 36p. (SRC Industrial relations stat. series, 5)

f. trade unions and politics

15667 BAVISKAR, B.S. Union politics and management politics. In IJIR 3 (1968) 300-15.

15668 BOGAERT, M. VAN DEN Dynamics of political unionism: the present Indian context. In SocAct 19 (1969) 211-28.

15669 CROUCH, H.A. Trade unions and politics in India. Bombay: Manaktalas, 1966. 315p.

15670 KARNIK, V.B. Trade unions and politics. Bombay: U. of Bombay, 1968. 73p.

15671 PATTABHI RAMAN, N. Political involvement of India's trade unions; a case study of the anatomy of the political labor movement in Asia. Bombay: Asia, 1967. 203p.

15672 RAMASWAMY, E.A. Politics and organized labor in India. In AS 13,10 (1973) 914-928.

15673 ______. Trade unions and politics. In SB 18 (1969) 138-47.

15674 ______. Trade unions and the electoral process: general elections in a working class area. In IJIR 7,2 (1971) 205-227.

15675 SEMINAR ON INDUSTRIAL RELATIONS IN A DEVELOPING ECONOMY, 3RD, CHANDIGARH, 1967. Trade unions and politics in India. Delhi: Shri Ram Centre for Industrial Relations, 1968. 2v., 557p.

15676 TRIPATHI, S.D. Politics of a multi-union plant: the Swadeshi experience. In IJIR 3 (1968) 441-58.

VIII. CONTEMPORARY INDIAN SOCIETY: STRUCTURE AND CHANGE SINCE 1947

A. The Study of Indian Society: Sources and Trends in the Behavioral Sciences

1. Bibliography

15677 ICSSR journal of abstracts and reviews; sociology and social anthropology. ND: ICSSR, 1971- [semi-annual]

15678 ICSSR research abstracts quarterly. ND: Orient Longman, 1971-.

15679 INDIA (REP.). CENSUS OF INDIA, 1961. Bibliography on scheduled castes, scheduled tribes and selected marginal communities of India. Ed. by B.K. Roy Burman. ND: 1966. 7v.

15680 Indian behavioural sciences abstracts. Delhi: Behavioural Sciences Centre, Jan. 1970-. [quarterly]

15681 PAREEK, U.N., ed. Behavioural science research in India, a directory, 1925-65. Delhi: Behavioural Science Centre, 1966. 574p.

15682 ______. Foreign behavioural research on India. Delhi: Achran Sahkar, 1970. 159p.

15683 A survey of research in psychology. Bombay: Popular, 1972. 454p. [sponsored by ICSSR]

15684 A survey of research in sociology and social anthropology. Bombay: Popular, 1972-74. 3v., 1404p. [sponsored by ICSSR]

2. Trends and Methodology in Anthropology, Sociology, and Psychology

15685 ATAL, Y. Social sciences: the Indian scene. ND: Abhinav, 1976. 281p.

15686 CHEKKI, D.A. The sociology of contemporary India. ND: Sterling, 1978. 216p.

15687 CLINARD, M.B. & J.W. ELDER. Sociology in India: a study in the sociology of knowledge. In American Sociological R. 30,4 (1965) 581-87.

15688 DAMLE, Y.B. Sociology in India: its teaching and status. In Intl. Social Science J. 26,2 (1974) 343-8.

15689 DE, B. & D. SINHA. A perspective on psychology in India: Dr. S.M. Mohsin felicitation volume. Allahabad: Sinha, 1977. 279p.

15690 INDIA (REP.). CMTEE. ON SOCIAL SCIENCE RES. Report. ND: Planning Cmsn., 1968. 132p.

15691 JOSHI, P.C. Reflections on social science research in India. In SB 24,2 (1975) 139-62.

15692 KURIAN, K.M., ed. India, state and society: a Marxian approach. Bombay: Orient Longman, 1975. 308p.

15693 LAKSHMANA, C. Teaching and research in sociology in India. In SB 23,1 (1974) 1-13.

15694 MOTWANI, K. Towards Indian sociology. Agra: Satish Book Enterprise, 1971. 138p.

15695 MUKHERJEE, R.K. Data inventory on social sciences: India: first phase, 1967-68. Calcutta: Stat. Pub. Soc., 1971. 160p.

15696 ______. Social indicators. Delhi: Macmillan, 1975. 146p.

15697 ______. Sociology of Indian sociology. Bombay: Allied, 1979. 199p.

15698 RAMALINGASWAMI, P. Psychology in India: challenges and opportunities. ND: Prachi Prakashan, 1980. 56p.

15699 ROY BURMAN, B.K. A critique of Maurice Freedman's report on sociology and social anthropology. In MI 54,2 (1974) 129-44.

15700 SEMINAR ON METHODOLOGY OF SOCIAL SCIENCE RES., GANDHIAN INST. OF STUDIES, 1964. Methodology of social science research. ND: Impex India, 1967. 172p.

15701 SRINIVAS, M.N. Sociology and sociologists in India today. In SB 19,1 (1970) 1-10.

15702 UNNITHAN, T.K.N. Sociology for India; papers. ND: Prentice Hall, 1967. 219p.

3. Applied Social Science and Problems of Indian Society

15703 ABBI, B.L. & S.SABERWAL, Eds. Urgent research in social anthropology. Simla: IIAS, 1969. 235p. (Its Transactions, 10)

15704 BOSE, N.K. Anthropology & some Indian problems. Calcutta: Inst. of Social Res. & Applied Anthropology, 1972. 284p. [collected essays]

15705 DUBE, S.C. Explanation and management of change. Bombay: Tat McGraw-Hill, 1971. 99p.

15706 MUKERJEE, RADHAKAMAL. Social sciences and planning in India. Bombay: Asia, 1970. 208p.

15707 MUKHERJEE, RAMKRISHNA. The sociologist and social change in India today. ND: Prentice-Hall of India, 1965. 229p.

15708 NAIK, T.B. Applied anthropology in India; a trend report. In A survey of research in sociology and social anthropology. Bombay: Popular, 1972, v.3, 240-81.

15709 SINHA, S.C. Urgent problems for research in social and cultural anthropology: perspectives and suggestions. In SB 17 (1968) 123-41.

15710 VIDYARTHI, L.P., ed. Applied anthropology in India; principles, problems, and case studies. Allahabad: Kitab Mahal, 1968. 543p.

15711 ______, ed. Indian anthropology in action. Ranchi: the editor, 1960. 144p.

15712 VIDYARTHI, L.P. & B.N. SAHAY, ed. Applied anthropology and development in India. ND: National, 1980. 291p.

B. Social Change and Social Policy Since Independence

1. general studies of social change

15713 DUBE, S.C. Contemporary India and its modernization. Delhi: Vikas, 1974. 145p.

15714 ______, ed. India since independence: social report on India, 1947-1972. ND: Vikas, 1977. 277p.

15715 GHOSH, B. Profiles of social change. ND: Oxford & IBH, 1979. 198p.

15716 KUPPUSWAMY, B. Social change in India. ND: Vikas, 1972. 355p.

15717 MADAN, G.R. Indian social problems: social disorganization and reconstruction. Bombay: Allied, 1966-67. 2v., 396, 452p.

15718 ______. India's social transformation. 2nd ed., rev. and enl. ND: Allied, 1979-. [to be 3v., 1st pub. 1971-75 under different titles]

15719 MANN, R.S. Social structure, social change, and future trends: Indian village perspective. Jaipur: Rawat, 1979. 264p.

15720 MATHUR, J.S., ed. Non-violence and social change. Ahmedabad: Navajivan, 1977. 287p. [1971 seminar papers]

15721 MATHUR, K.S. & B.R.K. SHUKLA & BANVIR SINGH. Studies in social change. Lucknow: Ethnographic & Folk Culture Soc., 1973, 217p.

15722 RAMU, G.N. Family and caste in urban India: a case study. ND: Vikas, 1977. 224p.

15723 RAO, M.S.A., ed. Social movements in India. ND: Manohar, 1978-79. 2v., 250, 198p.

15724 ______. Tradition, rationality, and change; essays in sociology of economic development and social change. Bombay: Popular, 1972. 182p.

15725 ______. Role analysis and social change: with special reference to India. In K. David, ed. The new wind: changing identities in South Asia. The Hague: Mouton, 1977, 287-308. (WA)

15726 ROY, G.C. Indian culture: the tradition of non-violence and social change in India. Delhi: Ajanta Pub., 1976. 198p.

15727 SHAH, A.B. & C.R.M. RAO, eds. Tradition and modernity in India. Bombay: Manaktalas, 1965. 219p.

15728 SMITH, T.L. & M.S. DAS, ed. Sociocultural change since 1950. ND: Vikas, 1978. 379p.

15729 SRINIVAS, M.N. Social change in modern India. Berkeley: UCalP, 1970. 196p. [1st pub. 1966]

15730 SRINIVAS, M.N. & S. SESHAIAH & V.S. PARTHASARATHY, eds. Dimensions of social change in India. Bombay: Allied, 1977. 518p.

15731 VIDYARTHI, L.P., ed. Conflict, tension, and cultural trend in India. Calcutta: Punthi Pustak, 1969. 312p.

15732 YOGENDRA SINGH. Modernization of Indian tradition; a systemic study of social change. Delhi: Thomson Press, 1973. 267p.

2. Social Policy and Planning

15733 AGARWAL, R.D. Economic aspects of welfare state in India. Allahabad: Chaitanya Pub. House, 1967. 264p.

15734 AMRIT KAUR, Rajkumari. Selected speeches and writings. Ed. by G. Borkar. ND: Archer Pubs., 1961. 341p.

15735 BANERJI, B.N. Essays in social reconstruction. Calcutta: Jijnasa, 1978. 112p.

15736 DESAI, A.R. State and society in India: essays in dissent. Bombay: Popular, 1975. 184p.

15737 DHAR, D.P. Planning and social change. ND: Arnold-Heineman, 1976. 210p.

15738 JAGANNADHAM, V. Administration and social change. ND: Uppal, 1978. 214p.

15739 KOTHARI, R. Democratic polity and social change in India: crisis and opportunities. Bombay: Allied, 1976. 124p.

15740 KULKARNI, P.D. Social policy and social development in India. Madras: Assn. of Schools of Social Work in India, 1979. 137p.

15741 PATWARDHAN, A. Ideologies and the perspective of social change in India. Bombay: U. of Bombay, 1971. 42p.

15742 SAVITA. Gandhi and social policy in India; a sociological analysis. Delhi: Nation, 1970. 186p.

15743 TARLOK SINGH. Towards an integrated society; reflections on planning, social policy, and rural institutions. Bombay: Orient Longmans, 1969. 554p.

3. Law and Social Change

15744 CHATTERJEE, B.B. & S.S. SINGH & D.R. YADAV. Impact of social legislation on social change. Calcutta: Minerva, 1971. 261p.

15745 GANGRADE, K.D. Social legislation in India. Delhi: Concept, 1978. 2v.

15746 INDIA (REP.). PLANNING CMSN. Social legislation; its role in social welfare. ND: 1956. 418p.

15747 KRISHNA IYER, V.R. Law and social change: an Indian overview. Chandigarh: Panjab U., 1978. 134p.

15748 RAMA RAO, T.S. Law and social change: historical perspective: independence and after. In IYIA 17 (1974) 460-84.

15749 SUBBA RAO, K. Social justice and law. Delhi: National, 1974. 133p.

C. Social Categories in Contemporary India

1. Changing Patterns of Social Stratification - General Studies

15750 AHMAD, M.T. Systems of social stratification in India and Pakistan. Lahore: Punjab U. Press, 1972. 144p.

15751 BÉTEILLE, A. Castes: old and new; essays in social structure and social stratification. Bombay: Asia, 1969. 254p.

15752 BHATT, A.H. Caste, class, and politics: an empirical profile of social stratification in modern India. Delhi: Manohar, 1975. 224p.

15753 Caste, class, and power structure [special issue]. In R&S 21,3 (1974) 1-86.

15754 CHHIBBAR, Y.S. From caste to class; a study of the Indian middle classes. ND: Associated, 1967. 142p.

15755 Class and caste in India [annual number]. In EPW 14,7/8 (1979) 221-484.

15756 GANGRADE, K.D. Social mobility in India: a study of depressed class. In MI 55,3 (1975) 248-72.

15757 SINGH, V.P. Caste, class, and democracy: changes in a stratification system. Cambridge, MA: Schenkman Pub. Co., 1976. 158p.

15758 YOGENDRA SINGH. Caste and class: some aspects of continuity and change. In SB 17 (1968) 165-86.

15759 ______. Social stratification and change in India. ND: Manohar, 1977. 157p.

15760 ______. Sociology of social stratification; trend report. In A survey of research in sociology and social anthropology. Bombay: Popular, 1974, v.1, 311-82. [sponsored by ICSSR]

2. Caste (jati): Hierarchical Structure in Context of Change
a. general studies

15761 ATAL, Y. The changing frontier of caste. Delhi: National, 1968. 288p.

15762 BARNABAS, A.P. & S.C. MEHTA. Caste in changing India. ND: IIPA, 1965. 84p.

15763 GOULD, H.A. The adaptive functions of caste in contemporary Indian society. In AS 3 (1963) 427-38.

15764 ______. Castes, outcastes and the sociology of stratification. In Intl. J. of Comp. Sociology 1 (1960) 220-38.

15765 LOHIA, RAMMANOHAR. The caste system. Hyderabad: Navahind, 1964. 147p.

b. "Untouchables" in post-Independence India
i. general studies

15766 BANDOPADHYAYA, J., et al. The Harijans. Varanasi: Gandhian Inst. of Studies, 1978. 66p.

15767 DUSHKIN, L. Scheduled caste policy in India: history, problems, prospects. In AS 7 (1967) 626-36.

15768 INDIA (REP.). CMTEE. ON UNTOUCHABILITY, ECON. AND EDUC. DEV. OF THE SCHEDULED CASTES. Report, 1969. ND: Dept. of Social Welfare, 1969. 431p. [Chm. L. Elayaperumal]

15769 ISAACS, H.R. India's ex-Untouchables. NY: John Day, 1965. 188p.

15770 MAHAR, J.M., ed. The Untouchables in contemporary India. Tucson: U. of Arizona Press, 1972. 496p.

15771 MALIK, S. Social integration of scheduled castes. ND: Abhinav, 1979. 190p.

15772 RUDOLPH, L.I. & SUZANNE H. RUDOLPH. Untouchability: the test of fellow feeling. In their The Modernity of Tradition. Chicago: UChiP, 1967, 132-154.

15773 SACHCHIDANANDA. Research on scheduled castes with special reference to change. In A survey of research in sociology & social anthropology. Bombay: Popular, 1974, v.1, 276-310. [sponsored by ICSSR]

15774 Scheduled castes [special issue]. In JSR 18,2 (1975) 156p.

15775 SEMINAR ON CASTEISM AND REMOVAL OF UNTOUCHABILITY, DELHI, 1955. Report. Bombay: Indian Conf. of Social Work, 1955. 285p.

15776 SRINIVAS, M.N. Caste in modern India and other essays. Bombay: Asia, 1970. 171p. [1st pub. 1962]

15777 SRIVASTAVA, S.N. Harijans in Indian society: a cultural study of the status of Harijans and other backward classes from the earliest times to the present day. Lucknow: Upper India Pub. House, 1980. 304p.

ii. Untouchability and the law; constitutional abolition under Article 17

15778 BORALE, P.T. Segregation and desegregation in India; a socio-legal study. Bombay: Manaktalas, 1968. 310p.

15779 GALANTER, M. The abolition of disabilities: untouchability and the law. In J. Michael Mahar, ed. The Untouchables in contemporary India. Tucson: U. of Arizona Press, 1972, 227-314. [earlier version in EPW 4, 1/2 (annual number 1969) 131-70]

15780 ______, Changing legal conceptions of caste. In M.B. Singer & B.S. Cohn, eds., Structure and change in Indian society. Chicago: Aldine, 1968, 299-36.

15781 ______. Law and caste in modern India. In AS 3 (1963) 544-59.

15782 INDIA (REP.). PARLIAMENT. JOINT CMTEE. ON THE UNTOUCHABILITY (OFFENCES) AMENDMENT & MISCELLANEOUS PROVISION BILL, 1972. Report. ND: Lok Sabha Secretariat, 1974. 57p. [Chm., S.M. Siddhayya]

15783 SHARMA, G.B. Enforcement of Untouchability Offences Act in India. In PSR 13,1/4 (1974) 305-26.

15784 ______. Legislation and cases on untouchability and scheduled castes in India. Bombay: Allied, 1975. 157p.

3. The Adivasis ("aboriginals"): Tribal Peoples in Independent India [see also Chap. One, III. M. & regional chaps. below]

15785 BARDHAN, A.B. The tribal problem in India. Rev. & enl. ed. ND: CPI, 1976. 96p.

15786 BHUPINDER SINGH & J.S. BHANDARI, ed. The tribal world and its transformation. ND: Concept, 1980. 276p.

15787 ELWIN, V., ed. A new deal for tribal India. ND: Min. of Home Affairs, 1963. 146p.

15788 FÜRER-HAIMENDORF, C. VON. Morals and merit: a study of values and social controls in South Asian societies. London: Weidenfeld & Nicholson, 1967. 239p.

15789 ______. The position of the tribal populations in modern India. In P. Mason, ed. India and Ceylon: unity and diversity. London: OUP, 1967, 182-222.

15790 GARDNER, P.M. India's changing tribes: identity and interaction in crises. In G.R. Gupta, ed. Cohesiveness and conflict in modern India. ND: Vikas, 1978, 289-318.

15791 INDIA (REP.). DEPT. OF SOCIAL WELFARE. A statistical handbook of tribal welfare and development. ND: 1968. 113p.

15792 INDIA (REP.). MIN. OF HOME AFFAIRS. TRIBAL DEV. DIV. Scheduled tribes and scheduled areas in India. ND: Ministry of Home Affairs, 1978. 62p. (Background papers on tribal development, 4)

15793 INDIA (REP.). STUDY TEAM ON TRIBAL DEV. PROGRAMMES. Report. ND: Planning Commission, 1969-70. 21 v. in 11. [Chm., P. Shilu Ao]

15794 INDIA (REP.). STUDY GROUP FOR TRIBAL LABOUR (AGRICULTURAL AND INDUSTRIAL). Report. ND: National Commission on Labour, 1969. 120p.

15795 RAGHAVIAH, V. Tribal revolts. Nellore: Andhra Rashtra Adimajati Sevak Sangh, 1971. 269p.

15796 SCHERMERHORN, R.A. Tribal integration in India. In CAS 10 (1977) 107-115.

15797 SEMINAR ON PROBLEMS OF DEVELOPMENT OF TRIBAL AREAS, WARORA, INDIA, 1979. Problems of development of tribal areas. Delhi: Leeladevi, 1980. 182p.

15798 SINHA, SURAJIT & B.D. SHARMA. Primitive tribes: the first step. ND: Min. of Home Affairs, 1977. 191p.

15799 SURESH SINGH, K., ed. Tribal situation in India: proceedings of a seminar. Simla: IIAS, 1972. 632p. (Its Trans., 13)

15800 Tribal women in India. Calcutta: IAS, 1978. 199p.

15801 VIDYARTHI, L.P., ed. Anthropology and tribal welfare in India. Ranchi: L.P. Vidyarthi, 1959. 106p.

15802 ______. Cultural change in the tribes of modern India. In JSR 11,1 (1968) 1-36. [rpt. in R. Srivastava, ed. Social Anthropology in India. ND: Books Today, 1979, 47-83]

15803 ______. Studies on social change in tribal India: a methodological review. In L.P. Vidyarthi, ed. Conflict, tension, and cultural trend in India. Calcutta: Punthi Pustak, 1969, 312p.

15804 ______. Tribal development in independent India and its future. In MI 54,1 (1974) 45-72.

15805 VYAS, N.N. & R.S. MANN, eds. Indian tribes in transition. Jaipur: Rawat, 1980. 187p.

4. The "Backward Classes", including Scheduled Castes and Scheduled Tribes, in Public Policy and Law
a. general studies

15806 ARLES, J.P. Economic and social promotion of the scheduled castes and tribes in India. In Intl. Labour R. 103,1 (1971) 29-64.

15807 BÉTEILLE, A. & M.N. SRINIVAS. The future of the backward classes, the competing demands of status and power. In P. Mason, ed. India and Ceylon: unity and diversity. London: OUP, 1967, 83-120. [1st pub. in Perspectives, suppl. to IJPA 11 (1965) 1-39]

15809 BOSE, N.K. Scheduled castes and tribes: their present condition. In MI 50 (1970) 319-49.

15810 GALANTER, M. Who are the Other Backward Classes? An introduction to a constitutional puzzle. In EPW 13,43/44 (1978) 1812-28.

15811 GHOSH, S. Protection of minorities and scheduled castes. ND: Ashish, 1980. 181p.

15812 HAVANUR, L.G. Specifying backward classes without the caste basis. Bangalore: T.V. Venkataswamy, 1965. 122p.

15813 INDIA (REP.). ADVISORY CMTEE. ON THE REV. OF THE LISTS OF SCHEDULED CASTES & SCHEDULED TRIBES, 1965.

Report. ND: Dept. of Social Security, 1965. 115p. [B.N. Lokur, chm.]

15814 INDIA (REP.). BACKWARD CLASSES CMSN. Report. Delhi: Manager of Pub., Civil Lines, 1956. 3 v. [D.B. Kalelkar, chm.]

15815 INDIA (REP.). COMMISSIONER FOR SCHEDULED CASTES & SCHEDULED TRIBES. Report. ND: GOI Press, 1951-. [annual]

15816 INDIA (REP.). SPECIAL WORKING GROUP ON COOP. FOR BACKWARD CLASSES. Report, Sept. 1962. ND: Min. of Home Affairs, 1964-65. 2 v.

15817 INDIA (REP.). STUDY TEAM ON SOCIAL WELFARE AND WELFARE OF BACKWARD CLASSES, 1958. Report. Delhi: MPGOI, 1959. 2 v. [Smt. Renuka Ray, leader]

15818 KAMBLE, J.R. Rise and awakening of depressed classes in India. ND: National, 1979. 327p.

15819 REVANKAR, R.G. The Indian constitution - a case study of backward classes. Rutherford, NJ: Fairleigh Dickinson U. Press, 1971. 361p.

15820 SANYAL, S. & B.K. ROY BURMAN, eds. Social mobility movements among scheduled castes and scheduled tribes of India. ND: Office of Registrar Genl., 1970. 31p.

b. "protective discrimination" in legislatures, jobs, and education

15821 GALANTER, M. Compensatory discrimination in political representation: a preliminary assessment of India's thirty-year experience with reserved seats in legislatures. In EPW 14,7/8 (1979) 437-54.

15822 GUPTA, S.S. Preferential treatment in public employment and equality of opportunity. Lucknow: Eastern Book Co., 1979. 228p.

15823 IMAM, M. Reservation of seats for backward classes in public services and educational institutions. In JILI 8,3 (1966) 441-49.

15824 INDIA (REP.). DEPT. OF PERSONNEL AND ADMIN. REFORMS. Brochure on reservation for scheduled castes and scheduled tribes in services. 5th ed. ND: Min. of Home Affairs, 1978. 353p.

15825 NAIK, J.P. Education of the Scheduled Tribes, 1965-66. ND: ICSSR, 1971. 40p.

15826 NAUTIYAL, K.C. & Y.D. SHARMA. Equalisation of educational opportunities for scheduled castes and scheduled tribes. ND: Natl. Council of Educ. Res. and Training, 1979. 68p.

15827 RADHAKRISHNAN, N. Reservation to the Backward Classes. In IYIA 13 (1964) 293-345.

15828 VERMA, G.P. Caste reservation in India: law and the Constitution. Allahabad: Chugh, 1980. 164p.

15829 ZACHARIAH, M. Positive discrimination in education for India's scheduled castes: a review of the problem, 1950-1970. In Comp. Educ. R. 16,1 (1972) 16-29.

5. Elites and Other Socio-Economic Groups

a. general studies of India's elites

15830 BÉTEILLE, A. Elites, status groups and caste in modern India. In P. Mason, ed. India and Ceylon: unity and diversity. London: OUP, 1967, 223-43. [Rpt. in his Castes old and new. London: Asia, 1969, 204-28]

15831 BOTTOMORE, T.B. Cohesion and division in Indian elites. In P. Mason, ed. India and Ceylon: unity and diversity. London: OUP, 1967, 244-59.

15832 DE, N.R. & R. TANDON. The Indian urban elites: an exploratory study. In IJIR 12,2 (1976) 117-46.

15833 EHRENFELS, U.R. VON. Prestigesymbole und Prestige in den Wandlungen der neuen indischen Elite. In Zeitschrift für Ethnologie 87 (1962) 217-26.

b. the Indian intellectual

15834 CHAUDHURI, N.C. The intellectual in India. ND: Vir Pub. House, 1967. 80p.

15835 Indian intellectuals [special issue]. In Seminar 222 (1978) 10-58.

15836 JHA, A. Intellectuals at the crossroads; the Indian situation. ND: Vikas, 1977. 112p.

15837 KHATKHATE, D.R. Intellectuals and the Indian polity. In AS 17,3 (1977) 251-63.

15838 ______. Intellectuals, power, and change in India. In K.S. Krishnaswamy, et al., eds. Society and change. Bombay: OUP, 1977, 186-208.

15839 MALIK, Y. North Indian intellectuals' perceptions of their role and status. In AS 17,6 (1977) 565-80.

15840 SANDHU, H.S. Intellectuals and social change in India. In CAS 3 (1973) 128-37.

15841 SHILS, E.A. The intellectual between tradition and modernity: the Indian situation. The Hague: Mouton, 1961. 120p. (CSSH, suppl. 1)

15842 SRIVASTAVA, H.C. Intellectuals in contemporary India. ND: Heritage, 1978. 160p.

6. India's Minority Communities [For Minorities in Regions, see Chaps. 10-16]

a. general studies

15843 GHURYE, G.S. Social tensions in India. Bombay: Popular, 1968. 552p.

15844 IMAM, M., ed. Minorities and the law. Bombay: N.M. Tripathi, 1972. 476p.

15845 SCHERMERHORN, R.A. Ethnic plurality in India. Tucson: U. of Arizona Press, 1978. 369p.

15846 SHARMA, J.S. India's minorities: a bibliographical study. Delhi: Vikas, 1975. 192p.

15847 WEINER, M. Sons of the soil: migration and ethnic conflict in India. Princeton: PUP, 1978. 383p.

b. India's 80 million Muslims: a conspicuous and diverse minority

15848 ABID HUSAIN, S. The destiny of Indian Muslims. London: Asia, 1965. 276p.

15849 AZAM, K.J. The Indian Muslims; the quest for identity. In IJPS 37,3 (1976) 24-42.

15850 BAIG, M.R.A. The Muslim dilemma in India. Delhi: Vikas, 1974. 169p.

15851 GAUBA, K.L. Passive voices; a penetrating study of Muslims in India. ND: Sterling, 1973. 396p.

15852 IMAM, ZAFAR, ed. Muslims in India. ND: Orient Longmans, 1975. 216p.

15853 KHAN, RASHEEDUDDIN. Minority segments in Indian polity: Muslim situation and plight of Urdu. In EPW 13,35 (1978) 1509-15. [Comment by A.B. Shah in EPW 13,46 (1978) 1910-12]

15854 KUMEDAN, B.S. Modernization and social reforms among the Muslims: a select bibliography. Delhi: Delhi School of Social Work, U. of Delhi, 1978. 56p.

15855 NADWI, S. ABUL HASAN ALI. The Musalman. Tr. from Urdu by Mohiuddin Ahmad. Lucknow: Academy of Islamic Res. & Pub., 1972. 119p. [Urdu ed. also 1972]

15856 PURI, B. Autonomy and participation; dimensions of Indian Muslim identity. In EPW 13,40 (1978) 1706-12.

15857 SIDDIQUI, N.A. Population geography of Muslims of India. ND: S. Chand, 1976. 189p.

c. India's Christian communities: about 15,000,000 souls

15858 BEAGLEHOLE, J.H. The Indian Christians - a study of a minority. In MAS 1 (1967) 59-80.

15859 D'SOUZA, S. Some demographic characteristics of Christianity in India. In Social Compass 13 (1966) 415-429.

15860 HAYWARD, V.E.W., ed. The Church as Christian community; three studies of North Indian Churches. London: Lutterworth Press, 1966. 353p.

d. Anglo-Indians (Eurasians): culturally ambivalent All-India minority of 100,000 - 300,000

15861 ANTHONY, F. Britain's betrayal in India; the story of the Anglo-Indian community. Bombay: Allied, 1969. 484p.

15862 GAIKWAD, V.R. The Anglo-Indians: a study in the problems and processes involved in emotional and cultural integration. Bombay: Asia, 1967. 300p.

15863 GIST, N.P. Anglo-Indians: an urban minority in India. In J.V. Ferreira & S.S. Jha, eds. The Outlook Tower... Bombay: Popular, 1976, 318-38.

15864 GIST, N.P. & R.D. WRIGHT. Marginality and identity; Anglo-Indians as a racially-mixed minority in India. Leiden: Brill, 1973. 161p.

15865 GRIMSHAW, A.D. The Anglo-Indian community: the integration of a marginal group. In JAS 18 (1959) 227-40.

15866 GUPTA, S.K. Marriage among the Anglo-Indians. Lucknow: Ethnographic & Folk Culture Soc., 1968. 86p.

15867 WRIGHT, R.D. & S.W. WRIGHT. Anglo-Indian community in contemporary India. In Midwest Quarterly 12 (1971) 175-85.

7. Women in Changing India

15868 ALEMENAS-LIPOWSKY, A.J., ed. The position of women in the light of legal reform; a socio-legal study of the position of Indian women as interpreted and enforced by the Law Courts compared and related to their position in the family and at work. Wiesbaden: Steiner, 1975. 217p.

15869 DASGUPTA, K., ed. Women on the Indian scene: an annotated bibliography. ND: Abhinav, 1976. 391p.

15870 DESAI, N. Woman in modern India. 2nd ed. Bombay: Vora, 1977. 334p.

15871 DE SOUZA, A., ed. Women in contemporary India: traditional images and changing roles. Delhi: Manohar, 1975. 264p.

15872 INDIA (REP.). WOMEN'S WELFARE DIV. Women in India: a compendium of programmes. ND: Dept. of Social Welfare, 1975. 118p.

15873 INDIAN COUNCIL OF SOCIAL SCIENCE RES. ADVISORY CMTEE. ON WOMEN'S STUDIES. Critical issues on the status of women: suggested priorities for action. ND: 1977. 32p.

15874 KAPUR, P. The changing status of the working woman in India. Delhi: Vikas, 1974. 178p.

15875 KHANNA, G. & M.A. VARGHESE. Indian women today. ND: Vikas, 1978. 212p.

15876 MANKEKAR, K. Women in India. ND: Central Inst. of Res. & Training in Public Coop., 1975. 76p.

15877 MAPPILAPARAMBIL, A. Die indische Frau zwischen traditioneller Familienbildung und moderner Arbeitswelt. In Jahrbuch des Instituts für christliche Sozialwissenschaften der Westfälischen Wilhelms-Universität, Münster 5 (1964) 141-64.

15878 MAZUMDAR, V., ed. Symbols of power: studies on the political status of women in India. Bombay: Allied, 1979. 373p. (Women in a changing society, 1)

15879 MEHTA, R. The western educated Hindu woman. NY: Asia, 1970. 216p.

15880 MIES, M. Indian women and patriarchy: conflicts and dilemmas of students and working women. Tr. from German by S.K. Sarkar. ND: Concept, 1980. 311p.

15881 MITRA, A. & A.K. SHRIMANY & L.P. PATHAK. The status of women: household and non-household economic activity. Bombay: Allied, 1979. 78p. (ICSSR programme of women's studies, 3)

15882 NANDA, BAL RAM, ed. Indian women: from purdah to modernity. ND: Vikas, 1976. 187p.

15883 NATL. FEDERATION OF INDIAN WOMEN. Ninth Congress. Jullundur, Oct. 8-11, 1976. ND: The Federation, 1976. 111p.

15884 Role and status of women in Indian society. Calcutta: KLM, 1978. 167p.

15885 SHARMA, S. Women students in India: status and personality. ND: Concept, 1979. 171p.

15886 VASHISHTA, B.K. Encyclopedia of women in India. ND: Praveen Encyclopaedia Pub., 1976. 548p.

D. Kinship and the Family: Changing Structures and Relationships since 1947

1. General Studies

15887 CHEKKI, D.A. Modernization and kinship in urban India. In JKU(SS) 5 (1969) 35-47.

15888 CONKLIN, G.H. The family formation process in India: an overview. In J. of Family Welfare 14,3 (1968) 28-37.

15889 DEVADOSS, T.S. Hindu family and marriage: a study of social institutions in India. Madras: Dr. S. Radhakrishnan Inst. for Advanced Study in Philosophy, U. of Madras, 1979. 150p.

15890 GUPTA, G.R., ed. Family and social change in modern India. ND: Vikas, 1971. 263p. (Main currents in Indian sociology, 2)

15891 KHATRI, A.A. Social change in the caste Hindu family and its possible impact on personality and mental health. In SB 11 (1962) 146-65.

15892 KURIAN, G. Problems of socialization in Indian families in a changing society. In E. Fuchs, ed. Youth in a changing world. The Hague: Mouton, 1976, 259-72.

15893 NARAIN, D., ed. Explorations in the family and other essays: Professor K.M. Kapadia commemoration volume. Bombay: Thacker, 1975. 662p.

15894 SHAH, V.P. Attitudinal change and traditionalism in the Hindu family. In SB 14 (1965) 77-89.

2. Family Structure: the Trend from Joint to Nuclear Family

15895 CONKLIN, G.H. Social change and the joint family: the causes of research biases. In EPW 4,36 (1969) 1445-48.

15896 DERRETT, J.D.M. Law and the predicament of the Hindu joint family. In EW 12,7 (1960) 305-11.

15897 DEVANANDAN, P.D. & M.M. THOMAS, eds. The changing pattern of family in India. Enl. and rev. ed. Bangalore: CISRS, 1966. 228p.

15898 D'SOUZA, V.S. Family types and industrialization in India. In G. Kurian, ed. The family in India: a regional view. The Hague: Mouton, 1974, 151-62. [1st pub. SocAct 19 (1969) 100-12]

15899 EHRENFELS, U.R. VON. Matrilineal joint family patterns in India. In G. Kurian, ed. The family in India. The Hague: Mouton, 1974, 91-106.

15900 The Indian family in the change and challenge of the seventies. ND: Sterling, 1971. 267p. [Selected papers from seminar organized by Family Life Centre of Indian Social Inst., ND]

15901 KOLENDA, P.M. Region, caste, and family structure: a comparative study of the Indian "joint" family. In M.B. Singer & B.S. Cohn, eds. Structure and change in Indian society. Chicago: Aldine, 1968, 339-96.

15902 ORENSTEIN, H. & M. MICKLIN. The Hindu joint family: the norms and the numbers. In PA 39 (1966-67) 314-25.

15903 SONTHEIMER, G.-D. The joint Hindu family: its evolution as a legal institution. ND: Munshiram, 1977. 272p.

3. Marriage: Changing Patterns and Attitudes

a. general studies

15904 AVASTHI, ABHA. Hindu marriage in continuity and change. Lucknow: Pradeep Prakashan Kendra, 1979. 244p.

15905 KAPUR, P. Marriage and the working woman in India. Delhi: Vikas, 1970. 528p. [Abridged ed. Vikas, 1972]

15906 REDDY, V. NARAYAN KARAN. Marriages in India: a psycho-sociological study. Gurgaon: Academic Press, 1978. 132p.

b. age at marriage

15907 ABEILLE, M. Age at marriage: historical obstacles to needed reforms. In G. Kurian, ed. The family in India: a regional view. The Hague: Mouton, 1974, 263-75.

15908 AGARWALA, S.N. Age at marriage in India. London: Probsthain, 1963. 296p.

15909 BASAVARAJAPPA, K.G. & M.I. BELVALGIDAD. Changes in age at marriage of females and their effect on the birth rate in India. In Eugenics Q. 14 (1967) 14-26.

15910 INDIA (REP.). CENSUS OF INDIA, 1971. Age and marital status. By D. Natarajan. ND: Office of the Registrar General, 1972. 170p. (Census centenary monograph, 8)

15911 JAIN, P.K. Marriage age patterns in India. In AV 11 (1969) 662-97.

15912 KALE, B.D. Education and age at marriage of females in India. In J. of the Inst. of Econ. Res. 4 (1969) 59-74.

15913 KARKAL, M. Annotated bibliography of studies on age at marriage in India. Bombay: Intl. Inst. for Population Studies, 1971. 25p.

15914 YADAV, S.S. Trends in marriage age of girls in India. In AV 13,1 (1971) 119-37.

c. reform of dowry and brideprice customs; the Dowry Prohibition Act, no. 28 of 1961

15915 INDIA (REP.). LAWS, STATUTES. Dowry Prohibition Act: containing an illuminating commentary on the act and states' notifications. By M.R. Achar & T. Venkanna. Allahabad: Law Book Company, 1962. 80p.

15916 ______. The prohibition of dowry act (act 28 of 1961). By M.L. Anand & Gargi Sethi. Allahabad: Law Publishers, 1962. 136p.

15917 VERGHESE, J. Her gold and her body. ND: Vikas, 1980. 228p.

d. marriage arrangements: love-marriage, arranged marriage, matrimonial advertisement

15918 ANAND, K. An analysis of matrimonial advertisements. In SB 14 (1965) 57-71.

15919 CORWIN, L.A. Caste, class and the love-marriage: social change in India. In J. of Marriage & the Family 39,4 (1977) 823-31.

15920 GIST, N.P. Mate selection and mass communication in India. In Public Opinion Q. 17 (1954) 481-95.

15921 GUPTA, G.R. Love, arranged marriage, and the Indian social structure. In J. of Comp. Family Studies 7,1 (1976) 75-85.

15922 KAPUR, PROMILLA. Love marriage and sex. Delhi: Vikas, 1973. 302p.

15923 REYES-HOCKING, A. The newspaper as surrogate marriage broker in India. In SB 15,1 (1966) 25-39.

15924 UPRETI, H.C. Matrimonial advertisements: a brief sociological analysis. In J. of Family Welfare 14,1 (1967) 33-43.

15925 VREEDE-DE STUERS, C. The relevance of matrimonial advertisements for the study of mate selection in India. In Bijdragen tot de taal-, land-, en volkenkunde 125,1 (1969) 103-17.

e. intercaste and other intergroup marriages

15926 BHUTANI, K. Attitude change: towards mixed marriages: as affected by some cognitive and personality factors. ND: Research Foundation, 1979. 192p.

15927 DAS, M.S. An exploratory study of touchable-untouchable intercaste marriage in India. In IJS 1 (1970) 130-38.

15928 GUPTA, B.N. Inter-caste marriages and emotional integration. In J. of Social Sciences 4,2 (1967) 38-49.

15929 KANNAN, C.T. Intercaste and inter-community marriages in India. Bombay: Allied, 1963. 236p.

f. divorce

15930 AGRAWALA, RAJKUMARI. Changing basis of divorce and the Hindu law. In JILI 14,3 (1972) 431-42.

15931 FONSECA, M.B. Family disorganisation and divorce in Indian communities. In SB 12 (1963) 14-33.

15932 ______. 'Marital separations' - disorganisation as seen through an agency. In SB 13 (1964) 47-60.

15933 KUMAR, V. The changing concept of divorce under Hindu law. In Law R. (Punjab) 19,2 (1967) 18-32.

15934 KUPPUSWAMY, B. A study of opinion regarding marriage and divorce. Bombay: Asia, 1957. 71p.

15935 MEHTA, R. Divorced Hindu women. Delhi: Vikas, 1975. 173p.

4. Childhood and Youth: Growing Up in Indian Society

a. child-rearing and socialization

15936 BAIG, T.A. Our children. ND: PDMIB, 1979. 390p.

15937 DAYKIN, D.S. & B.R. HERTEL. The bearing of urbanism and socio-economic status on individual modernity in India. In EA 31,4 (1978) 379-92.

15938 DE SOUZA, A., ed. Children in India: critical issues in human development. ND: Manohar, 1979. 262p.

15939 GOKULANATHAN, K.S. & K.P. VERGHESE. Child care in a developing community; a preliminary survey. Ernakulam: Ernakulam Polyclinic, 1967. 72p.

15940 GORE, M.S. Indian youth: processes of socialization. ND: Vishwa Yuvak Kendra, 1977. 73p.

15941 HERTEL, B.R. & D.S. DAYKIN. The relative impact of early and late socialization on individual modernity in India. In JAAS(L) 11,3/4 (1976) 194-202.

15942 KAKAR, S. Indian childhood: cultural ideals and social reality. Delhi: OUP, 1979. 47p.

15943 ______. The inner world: a psycho-analytic study of childhood and society in India. Delhi: OUP, 1978. 213p.

15944 MINTURN, L. & W.W. LAMBERT. Mothers of six cultures: antecedents of child rearing. NY: Wiley, 1964. 351p.

15945 MISTRY, D.K. The Indian child and his play. In SB 7 (1958) 137-47; 8 (1959) 86-96; 9 (1960) 48-55.

15946 NARAIN, D. Growing up in India. In Family Process 3 (1964) 127-54.

15947 PANDEY, R.S. Our adolescents: their interests and education. Agra: L.N. Agarwal, 1963. 387p.

15948 PAREEK, U.N. Developmental patterns in reactions to frustration. Bombay: Asia, 1964. 182p.

15949 SRINIVASAN, K. & P.C. SAXENA & T. KANITKAR, ed. Demographic and socio-economic aspects of the child in India. Bombay: Himalaya Pub. House, 1979. 662p.

15950 UNICEF study on the young child: Indian case study. ND: Natl. Inst. of Public Coop. & Child Dev., 1976. 201p.

b. Indian youth and the generation gap: attitudes and values

15951 AGOCHIYA, D. Youth leadership in India. ND: Vishwa Yuvak Kendra, 1978. 111p.

15952 ESWARA REDDY, V. The out of school youth. ND: Sterling, 1977. 299p.

15953 GANGRADE, K.D. Crisis of values: a study in generation gap. ND: Chetana, 1975. 295p.

15954 ______. Inter-generational conflict: a sociological study of Indian youth. In AS 10,10 (1970) 924-36.

15955 GARG, P.K. & I.J. PARIKH. Profiles in identity: a study of Indian youth at the crossroads. ND: Vision Books, 1978. 292p.

15956 INDIA (REP.). DIR. OF ADULT EDUC. An inventory of Central Government's programmes with relevance for youth work. ND: The Directorate, 1974. 170p.

15957 KAKAR, S. & K. CHOWDHRY. Conflict and choice: Indian youth in a changing society. Bombay: Somaiya, 1970. 174p.

15958 KATTIKARAN, K. & C. VETTICKATHADAM, ed. Youth quest: an exploration into values. Bangalore: KJC Pub., 1978. 208p.

15959 KIRPAL, P. Youth and established culture (dissent and cooperation): an Indian study sponsored by UNESCO. ND: Sterling, 1976. 96p.

15960 MEHRA, L.S. Youth in modern society. Allahabad: Chugh, 1977. 205p.

15961 MEHTA, PRAYAG, ed. The Indian youth: emerging problems and issues. Bombay: Somaiya, 1971. 194p.

15962 PANDEY, R. India's youth at the crossroads: a study of the values and aspirations of college students. Varanasi: Vani Vihar, Res. Div., 1975. 414p.

15963 ROKADIYA, B.C., et al., ed. An inventory of Central Government's programmes with relevance for youth work: a brief description of Central Government's schemes for social and economic progress with relevance for promoting the well-being of youth and their involvement in the national development. ND: Dir. of Adult Educ., Min. of Education & Social Welfare, 1975. 189p.

15964 SHINGI, P.M. & N.P. SINGH & D. JADHAV. Rural youth: education, occupation, and social outlook. Ahmedabad: Centre for Mgmt. in Agri., Indian Inst. of Mgmt., 1977. 153p.

15965 SINGHVI, L.M., ed. Youth unrest: conflict of generations. Delhi: Natl., 1972. 451p.

15966 SUDARSHAN KUMARI. Aspirations of Indian youth: a study in sociology of youth. Varanasi: Chaukhambha Orientalia, 1978. 282p. (CORS, 10)

15967 Youth in India today: a report of the survey on the attitudes of youth and the values to which they remain attached / issued under the auspices of the World Assembly of Youth. Bombay: Allied, 1963. 232p.

5. Aging and the Aged: Growing Old in India Today

15968 BILLIMORIA, H.M. Welfare services for the aged. In Social Welfare 16,3 (1969) 13, 22-23.

15969 ROWE, W.L. The middle and later years in Indian society. In R.W. Kleemerer, ed. Aging and leisure. NY: OUP, 1961, 104-109.

15970 D'SOUZA, V.S. Changes in social structure and changing roles of older people in India. In Sociology & Social Res. 55,3 (1971) 297-304.

15971 SOODAN, K.S. Aging in India. Calcutta: Minerva, 1975. 204p.

15972 VATUK, S. The aging woman in India; self-perceptions and changing roles. In A. DeSouza, ed. Women in contemporary India. Delhi: Manohar, 1975, 142-63.

6. Family and Personal Law: Towards a Uniform Civil Code?

a. general studies across community lines

15973 AGRAWALA, RAJKUMARI. Uniform civil code: a formula not a solution. In Tahir Mahmood, ed. Family law and social change. Bombay: N.M. Tripathi. 1975, 110-144.

15974 CHEKKI, D.A. Social legislation and kinship in India; a socio-legal study. In Journal of Marriage and the Family 31 (1969) 165-72.

15975 GOPALAKRISHNAN, T.P. Family laws. Madras: Vimala, 1969. 478p.

15976 MAHMOOD, T., ed. Family law and social change; a Festschrift for Asaf A.A. Fyzee. Bombay: N.M. Tripathi, 1975. 172p.

15977 PERAL, D. Modernising the personal laws in India. In SAR 5,2 (1972) 147-154.

15978 SIVARAMAYYA, B. Women's rights of inheritance in India; a comparative study of equality and protection. Madras: Madras Law J. Office, 1973. 215p.

15979 VENKATA SUBBARAO, G.C. Family law in India: Hindu law, Mahomedan law, and personal law of Christians, Parsis, etc., including law of testamentary and intestate succession .... 3rd ed. Madras: C. Subbiah Chetty, 1979. 494p.

b. Hindu law in secular India

i. general studies of Hindu law since Independence

15980 DERRETT, J.D.M. The contribution of Mr. Justice Subba Rao to Hindu law. In JILI 9 (1967) 547-67.

15981 ______. A critique of modern Hindu law. Bombay: N.M. Tripathi, 1970. 460p.

15982 ______. Hindu law, past and present. Calcutta: A. Mukherjee and Co., 1957. 408p.

15983 ______. Introduction to modern Hindu law. Bombay: OUP, 1963. 94 + 653p.

15984 MEGHE, D.R. Uniform civil code and Hindu law.... Nagpur: Pathik Prakashan, 1973. 227p.

ii. the Hindu Code Bill (passed 1955), and other attempts at codification and reform

15985 DESHPANDE, V.V. Dharma-shastra and the proposed Hindu code. Kashi: S.M. Parande, 1943. 157p.

15986 DERRETT, J.D.M. The codification of personal law in India: Hindu law. In IYIA 1 (1957) 189-211.

15987 ______. Hindu law past and present; being an acacount of the controversy which preceded the enactment of the Hindu Code, the text of the code as enacted, and some comments thereon. Calcutta: A. Mukherjee, 1957. 408p.

15988 GAJENDRAGADKAR, P.B. The Hindu code bill; two lectures delivered under the auspices of the Karnatak U. at Dharwar on the 12th and 13th April, 1951. Dharwar: 1951. 52p.

15989 Hindu law reform: a short introduction. Delhi: PDMIB, 1965. 47p.

15990 INDIA (REP.). LAWS, STATUTES. The Hindu code; being a commentary on Hindu succession act, Hindu adoptions and maintenance act, Hindu minority and guardianship act, Hindu marriage act, Hindu Mitakshara coparcenary, Dayabhaga joint family and Hindu endowments, by Gyan Prakash. 2nd ed. Allahabad: Hind Pub. House, 1958. 500 + 101p.

15991 KHETARPAL, S.P. Codification of Hindu law. In D.C. Buxbaum, ed. Family law and customary law in Asia. The Hague: Nijhoff, 1968, 202-233.

15992 LEVY, H.L. Indian modernization by legislation: the Hindu code bill, Ph.D. diss., U. of Chicago, 1973. 536p.

15993 OVERSTREET, G.D. The Hindu Code Vill. In J.B. Christoph, ed. Cases in comparative politics. Boston: Little, Brown, 1965, 413-440.

15994 ______. The Hindu code bill. In L.W. Pye, ed. Cases in comparative politics: Asia. Boston: Little, Brown, 1970, 161-219.

15995 RAY, RENUKA. The background of the Hindu Code Bill. In PA 25(1952) 268-77.

iii. Hindu law relating to kinship and succession

15996 AGARWAL, M.G. Supreme Court on taxation of Hindu undivided families with important cases of High Courts and methods of tax planning. ND: Taxation, 1977. 346p.

15997 INDIA (REP.). LAWS, STATUTES. Hindu Adoptions and Maintenance Act (Act 28 of 1956). By T.P. Gopalakrishnan. 3rd ed., rev. by J.P. Singhal. Allahabad: Law Book Co., 1969. 230p.

15998 ______. Hindu Minority and Guardianship Act (Act 23 of 1956). With exhaustive commentary.... by D.C.

15999 ______. Hindu Succession Act (Act 30 of 1956). By R.B. Sethi. Rev. & enl. by E.S. Subrahmanyan. 4th ed. Allahabad: Law Book Co., 1970. 344p.

16000 ______. The law of succession. Ed. by L.S. Sastri. Allahabad: Law Book Co., 1950. 90p.

iv. Hindu law of marriage

16001 BAGGA, V., ed. Studies in the Hindu marriage and the Special Marriage Acts. Bombay: N.M. Tripathi, 1978. 352p. (1975 seminar by Indian Law Inst.)

16002 DERRETT, J.D.M. The death of a marriage law: epitaph for the rishis. ND: Vikas, 1978. 228p.

16003 DESAI, KUMUD. Indian law of marriage and divorce. 3rd ed. Bombay: N.M. Tripathi, 1978. 576p. [1st ed. 1964]

16004 INDIA (REP.). LAWS, STATUTES. Hindu law of marriage. by S.V. Gupte. 2nd ed. Bombay: N.M. Tripathi, 1976. 468p.

16005 ______. Hindu Marriage Act (Act 25 of 1955). As amended up to date by P. Deolalkar. 2nd ed. Allahabad: Law Book Co., 1964. 347p.

16006 ______. Hindu marriage act, Act no. 25 of 1955, by R.N. Sarkar. Calcutta: S.C. Sarkar, 1956. 141p.

16007 ______. Special marriage act (Act 43 of 1954). by D.J. Chaudhari. 2nd ed. Calcutta: Eastern Law House, 1958. 340p.

16008 LATIFI, D. Indian marriage laws and the rights of women. In Enquiry 2,3 (1965) 103-18.

c. Muslim law in secular India

16009 CARROLL, L. The Muslim Family Laws Ordinance, 1961: provision and procedures - a reference paper for current research. In CIS ns 13 1 (1979) 117-42.

16010 DIWAN, P. Muslim law in modern India. Allahabad: Allahabad Law Agency, 1977. 302p.

16011 FYZEE, A.A.A. Cases in the Muhammadan law of India and Pakistan. Oxford: OUP, 1965.

16012 ______. The reform of Muslim personal law in India. In Humanist R. 2 (1970) 369-403.

16013 HAQ, MUSHIR UL. Indian Muslims and personal law. In Islam and the modern age 2,1 (1971) 75-93.

16014 LATIFI, D. Muslim personal law reform. In JCPS 4,1 (1970) 111-18.

16015 LOKHANDWALLA, S.T. Islamic law and Ismaili communities (Khojas and Bohras). In IESHR 4,2 (1967) 155-76.

16016 ______. Muslim personal law and the problem of uniform civil code for India. In Quest 73 (Nov.-Dec. 1971) 67-74.

16017 MAHMOOD, T. An Indian civil code and Islamic law. Bombay: N.M. Tripathi, 1976. 119p.

16018 ______. Islamic law in modern India. Bombay: N.M. Tripathi, 1972. 259p.

16019 ______. Muslim personal law: role of the state in the Subcontinent. ND: Vikas, 1977. 219p.

16020 TYABJI, R.H.B. Muslim law; the personal law of Muslims in India and Pakistan. 4th ed. Bombay: N.M. Tripathi, 1968. 1061p.

E. Urbanization: Cities and Towns in Independent India

1. Bibliography

16021 BOSE, A. Bibliography on urbanization in India, 1947-1976. ND: Tata McGraw-Hill, 1976. 179p.

16022 ______. Urbanization in India; an inventory of source materials. Bombay: Academic Books, 1970. 389p.

16023 CARROLL,J.J. Field research on urbanization and family change in India. In MI 55,4 (1975) 339-54.

16024 D'SOUZA, V.S. Urban studies; a trend report. In A survey of research in sociology and social anthropology. Bombay: Popular, 1974, v.1, 115-57. [sponsored by ICSSR]

16025 GOSAL, G.S. Urban geography; a trend report. In A survey of research in geography. Bombay: Popular, 1972, 203-25. [sponsored by ICSSR]

16026 SINGH, R.L. The concept of umland with reference to Indian cities; a trend report. In A survey of research in geography. Bombay: Popular, 1972, 225-34. [sponsored by ICSSR]

2. General Studies of Urbanization

16027 BANERJI, S. The spatial dimension of urbanization in relation to development planning in India. ND: Associated, 1969. 104p.

16028 BOSE, A. India: the urban context. In S.C. Dube, ed., India since Independence. ND: Vikas, 1977, 85-130.

16029 ______. India's urbanization, 1901-2001. ND: Tata McGraw-Hill, 1978. 567p.

16030 ______. Studies in India's urbanization, 1901-1971. Bombay: Tata McGraw-Hill, 1973. 449p.

16031 BULSARA, J.F. Problems of rapid urbanisation in India. Being a memorandum based on the findings of the socio-economic surveys of nine Indian cities. Bombay: Popular, 1964. 215p. [surveys for Planning Cmsn]

16032 FERREIRA, J.V. & S.S. JHA, eds. The Outlook tower: essays on urbanization in memory of Patrick Geddes. Bombay: Popular, 1976. 475p.

16033 HOSELITZ, B.F. Urbanization in India. In Kyklos 13 (1960) 361-72.

16034 INDIA (REP.). CENSUS OF INDIA, 1961. An approach to urban studies in India. Ed. by B.K. Roy Burman. ND: Office of the Registrar-genl., 1971. 530p. (Census of India, misc. monograph; proc. of seminar)

16035 JAKOBSON, L. & VED PRAKASH. Urbanization and national development. Beverly Hills, CA: Sage, 1971. 320p.

16036 MISRA, R.P. & B.S. BHOOSHAN. Habitat Asia; issues and responses. v.1 India. ND: Concept, 1979. 288p.

16037 MOOKHERJEE, D. & R.L. MORRILL. Urbanization in a developing economy: Indian perspectives and patterns. Beverly Hills, CA: Sage, 1973. 74p.

16038 PANDEY, S.M. Nature & determinants of urbanization in a developing economy: the case of India. In EDCC 25, 2 (1977) 265-78.

16039 ROSSER, C. Urbanization in India. NY: Urbanization Survey, 1973. 106p.

16040 SABERWAL, SATISH, ed. Process and institution in urban India: sociological studies. ND: Vikas, 1978. 251p.

16041 SIVARAMAKRISHNAN, K.C. Indian urban scene. Simla: IIAS, 1978. 152p.

16402 SOVANI, N.V. Urbanization and urban India. NY: Asia, 1966. 160p.

16043 TURNER, R., ed. India's urban future; selected studies.... Berkeley: UCalP, 1962. 47op.

3. Morphology and Functions of Indian Urban Centers; Land Use

16044 AHMAD, QAZI S. Indian cities; characteristics and correlates. Chicago: U. of Chicago Dept. of Geog., 1965. 184p. (Its res. paper, 102)

16045 BRUSH, J.E. Spatial patterns of population in Indian cities. In Geographical R. 58 (1968) 362-91.

16046 GANGULI, B.N. Classification of Indian cities, town groups and towns. In M.R. Chaudhuri, ed. Essays in geography (S.P. Chatterjee volume). Calcutta: Geog. Soc. of India, 1965, 82-93.

16047 HAZLEHURST, L.W. The middle-range city in India. In AS 8,7 (1968) 539-52.

16048 INDIA (REP.). CMTEE. ON URBAN LAND POLICY. Report. ND: Min. of Health, 1965. 98p.

16049 KULSHRESTH, S.K. Land use patterns of urban centres of India. In URPT 11 (1968) 192-235.

16050 Land use patterns of India's cities and towns. In URPT 11 (1968) 145-91.

16051 MITRA, ASOK. A functional classification of India's towns. Delhi: Inst. of Econ. Growth, 1974. 76p.

16052 NCAER. Market towns and spatial development in India. ND: 1965. 162p.

16053 PETHE, V.P. & V.S. BADARI. Cities of India: functional and locational spects. In AV 13,4 (1971) 381-90.

16054 SEMINAR ON MARKET TOWNS AND SPATIAL DEV., NEW DELHI, 1971. Market towns and spatial development. ND: NCAER, 1972. 203p.

16055 TANEJA, K.L. Morphology of Indian cities. Varanasi: NGSI, 1971. 169p.

4. Urban Society and Its Problems
a. general studies

16056 CHERUKUPALLE, N.D. Urban social structure and economic development policy: some hypotheses & empirical results. In MI 52,2 (1972) 131-149.

16057 DE SOUZA, A., ed. The Indian city: poverty, ecology, and urban development. ND: Manohar, 1978. 243p.

16058 Environmental pollution and urban administration: seminar proceedings. ND: Centre for Urban Studies, 1977. 69p.

16059 FISCHER, H.J., ed. Problems of urbanisation: proceedings of a seminar held in Bombay, November 1971. Bombay: Leslie Sawhny Programme of Training for Democracy, 1972. 80p.

16060 MISRA, R.P., ed. Million cities of India. ND: Vikas, 1978. 405p.

16061 RAO, M.S.A., ed. Urban sociology in India: reader and source book. ND: Orient Longman, 1974. 542p.

16062 ROWE, WILLIAM L. Caste, kinship, and association in urban India. In A. Southall, ed. Urban anthropology: cross-cultural studies of urbanization. London: OUP, 1973, 211-249. [study of Bangalore and Bombay]

16063 TRIVEDI, H.R. Urbanism: a new outlook. Delhi: Atma Ram, 1976. 209p.

16064 ______. Urbanization and macro-social change. Allahabad: Chugh, 1975. 182p.

b. housing

16065 BHASKARA RAO, B. Housing and habitat in developing countries. ND: Newman Group, 1979. 291p.

16065a HAJRA, S. & ASHOK KUMAR. Housing India's millions. ND: Econ. & Scientific Res. Foundation, 1977. 37p.

16066 Housing for the poor [workshop papers]. In J. of the Inst. of Town Planners 88/89 (1975-76) 1-58.

16067 INDIA (REP.). NATL. CMTEE. ON SCIENCE AND TECHNOLOGY. PANEL ON HOUSING, URBANISATION, AND CONSTRUCTION TECHNOLOGY. Draft status report on housing and construction technology: research design development & extension requirements. ND: 1976. 880p.

16068 KHANDEKAR, M. Social housing in India with particular reference to industrial housing. In IJSW 31 (1970) 229-42.

16069 Mass Housing: a symposium on how to provide shelter for our people. In Seminar 162 (1973) 7-44.

16070 MOHSIN, M. LIC & urban housing. Aligarh: Aligarh Muslim U., 1969. 186p. [Life Insurance Corporation]

16071 PATEL, S.B. A research programme for urban housing. In EPW 8,14 (1973) 671-76.

16072 SINHA, B.D. Housing growth in India. ND: Arnold-Heinemann, 1976. 159p.

16073 TANGRI, S.S. Urban growth, housing and economic development: the case of India. In AS 8 (1968) 519-38.

16074 Urban Land Ceiling Act [special issue]. In J. of Inst. of Town Planners 90 (1976) 1-31.

16075 VARGHESE, K.V. Housing problem in India. ND: Eureka Pub., 1980. 361p.

c. slums

16076 CLINARD, M.B. Slums and community development; experiments in self-help. NY: Free Press, 1970. 395p. [1st pub. 1966]

16077 DESAI, A.R. & S. DEVADAS PILLAI. Slums and urbanization. Bombay: Popular, 1970. 356p.

16078 INDIAN CONF. OF SOCIAL WORK. Report of the seminar on slum clearance. Bombay: 1957. 324p.

16079 JAGMOHAN. Housing and slum clearance. In IJPA 14, 3 (1968) 691-708.

16080 SINGH, A.M. Slum and pavement dwellers in urban India; some urgent research and policy considerations. In SocAct 28,2 (1978) 164-87.

16081 Slums: housing for the poor [issue]. In J. of Inst. of Town Planners 79 (1974) 1-54.

5. Urban Planning and Development

16082 BHARDWAJ, R.K. Urban development in India. Delhi: National, 1974. 456p.

16083 BILJANI, H.U. Urban problems. ND: Centre for Urban Studies, IIPA, 1977. 171p.

16084 DATTA, A., ed. Municipal and urban India: selections from Nagarlok. ND: Centre for Urban Studies, IIPA, 1980. 259p.

16085 DE SOUZA, A., ed. The Indian city: poverty, ecology, and urban development. ND: Manohar, 1978. 245p.

16086 DOXIADĒS, K.A. The human settlements that we need. ND: Tata McGraw-Hill, 1976. 84p.

16087 GANDHI, N.K. Study of town and country planning in India: a pragmatic approach to planning and development. Bombay: Indian Town and Country Planning Assn., 1973. 348p.

16088 INDIA (REP.). TASK FORCE TO EXAMINE THE PLANNING AND DEVELOPMENT OF SMALL AND MEDIUM TOWNS AND CITIES. Report. ND: Min. of Works & Housing, 1977. 2v. [chm., Bijit Ghosh]

16089 KABRA, K.N. Urban land and housing policies: ceiling and socialisation. ND: PPH, 1975. 64p.

16090 ______. Urban land ceiling and socialisation of the urban land. In R & S 23,2 (1976) 76-99.

16091 MODAK, N.V. & V.N. AMBEDKAR. Town and country planning and housing. With a foreword by Albert Mayer. Bombay: Orient Longman, 1971. 252p.

16092 NOBLE, A.G. & A.K. DUTT. Indian urbanization and planning: vehicles of modernization. ND: Tata McGraw-Hill, 1977. 366p.

16093 POULOSE, K.T. Experiences and experiments in town and country planning. Trivandrum: C. Mathews, 1979. 192p.

16094 RAHEJA, B.D. Urban India and public policy. Bombay: Somaiya, 1973. 323p.

16095 SEMINAR ON LAW AND URBANIZATION IN INDIA, ALLAHABAD, 1967. Law and urbanization in India; papers. Bombay: N.M. Tripathi, 1969. 399p.

16096 SINGH, S.R. Urban planning in India: a case study of urban improvement trusts. ND: Ashish, 1979. 432p.

16097 SUBHASH CHANDRA & S.P. PUNALEKAR. Urban community development programme in India. ND: Natl. Inst. of Public Coop. and Child Dev., 1975. 106p.

16098 Urban and regional planning legislation [issue]. In J. of the Inst. of Town Planners 80 (1974) 1-57.

16099 Urban development; papers and proceedings of the seminar held in Bombay. Bombay: TISS, 1976. 396p. [pub. as IJSW 36, 3/4]

16100 Urban planning and development authorities. ND: Centre for Urban Studies, IIPA, 1978. 223p. [1974 seminar]

16101 VED PRAKASH. New towns in India. Durham: DUPCSSA, 169. 149p. (Its monograph & occ. papers, 8)

6. Rural-Urban Relationships

16102 ALI ASHRAF. Report of the rural-urban relationship committee, 1966 - a critical review. In IJPA 14,3 (1968) 816-29.

16103 CHATTERJEE, M. The town/village dichotomy in India. In MI 48 (1968) 193-200.

16104 INDIA (REP.). RURAL URBAN RELATIONSHIP CMTEE. Report. ND: Min. of Health & Family Planning, 1966. 3v.

16105 LAKSHMANA RAO, G. Internal migration and political change in India: a study based on the analysis of aggregate socio-economic and demographic data and election statistics of 88 traditional cities and 22 modern cities all over India combined with a sample survey of one modern city and one traditional city in central India. ND: National, 1977. 212p.

16106 LYNCH, O.M. Rural cities in India: continuities and discontinuities. In P. Mason, ed. India and Ceylon: unity and diversity. London: OUP, 1967, 142-158.

16107 MANDAL, R.B. The concept of rurban centres. In R.B. Mandal & V.N.P. Sinha, eds. Recent trends and concepts in geography. ND: Concept, 1979, 157-78.

16108 MISRA, R.P. & P.D. MAHADEV & D.C. JAYASHANKAR, eds. Urban systems and rural development; a seminar. Mysore: U. of Mysore, 1972. 2v.

16109 OOMMEN, T.K. The rural-urban continuum re-examined in the Indian context. In Sociologia ruralis 7,1 (1967) 30-48.

16110 PATEL, J.P. The rurban community. Varanasi: Sarvodaya Sahitya Prakashan, 1969. 214p.

16111 POCOCK, D.F. Sociologies: urban and rural. In CIS 4 (1960) 63-81.

16112 SHETH, N.R. Modernization and the urban-rural gap in India: an analysis. In SB 18 (1969) 16-34.

F. Social Problems and Social Service in Independent India

1. Bibliography and Reference

16113 Encyclopaedia of social work in India. Delhi: PDMIB, 1968. 3v., 1514p.

16114 NAGPAUL, H. Sociological analysis of social welfare in Indian society: a bibliographical essay. In IJSW 31 (1970) 303-18.

16115 RANADE, S.N. Social work research; a trend report. In A survey of research in sociology and social anthropology. Bombay: Popular, 1974, v.2, 531-563. [sponsored by ICSSR]

2. General Studies of Social Welfare

16116 BANSAL, U.R. Social welfare activities of the Government of India: from 1947-1957. Varanasi: Kishor Vidya Niketan, 1980. 250p.

16117 GANGULI, B.N., ed. Social development; essays in honour of Smt. Durgabai Deshmukh. ND: Sterling, 1977. 303p.

16118 INDIA (REP.). PLANNING CMSN. Plans and prospects of social welfare in India 1951-61. Delhi: PDMIB, 1963. 254p.

16119 ______. Social welfare in India. Rev. & abridged ed. ND: MPGOI, 1960. 380p. [1st ed. 1955]

16120 JAGANNADHAM, V. Social welfare organisation. ND: IIPA, 1967. 149p.

16121 MAMORIA, C.B. Social problems and social disorganization. Allahabad: Kitab Mahal, 1960.

16122 MUZUMDAR, AMMU. Social welfare in India: Mahatma Gandhi's contributions. Bombay: Asia, 1964. 179p.

16123 NAGPAUL, H. The study of Indian society; a sociological analysis of social welfare and social work education. ND: S. Chand, 1972. 510p.

16124 PATHAK, S. Social welfare, health, and family planning in India. ND: Marwah, 1979. 296p.

16125 PATIL, B.R. Economics of social welfare in India. Bombay: Somaiya, 1978. 158p.

3. The Central Social Welfare Board and other Organizations, Public and Private

16126 CHOWDHRY, D.P. Voluntary social welfare in India. ND: Sterling, 1971. 320p.

16127 DUBEY, S.N. Administration of social welfare programmes in India. Bombay: Somaiya, 1973. 214p. (TISS series, 27)

16128 GANDHI SMARAK NIDHI. In memory of Mahatma Gandhi: 27 years of Gandhi Smarak Nidhi. ND: 1976. 161p.

16128a GOKHALE, S.D. Social welfare, legend and legacy: silver jubilee commemoration volume of the Indian Council of Social Welfare. Bombay: Popular, 1975. 432p.

16129 INDIA (REP.). CMSN. OF INQUIRY INTO THE AFFAIRS OF THE BHARAT SEVAK SAMAJ, 1969. Report. ND: Min. of Agri., Dept. of Com. Dev., 1973. 15v. [J.L. Kapur, chm.]

16130 KULKARNI, P.D. The Central Social Welfare Board: a new experiment in welfare administration. Bombay: Asia, 1961. 92p.

16131 LALITHA, N.V. Voluntary work in India: a study of volunteers in welfare agencies. ND: Natl. Inst. of Public Coop. & Child Dev., 1975. 344p.

16132 LE JOLY, E. We do it for Jesus: Mother Teresa and her Missionaries of Charity. Calcutta: OUP, 1977. 182p.

16133 OOMMEN, T.K. The theory of voluntary associations in a cross-cultural perspective. In SB 24,2 (1975) 163-80.

16134 RATH, S. Centre-state relations in the field of social services: 1950-70. ND: Oriental, 1978. 356p.

4. Public Assistance and Social Insurance Schemes

16135 BHATTACHARYA, V.R. Some aspects of social security measures in India. Delhi: Metropolitan, 1970. 309p.

16136 MEHTA, USHA & A.D. NARDE. Health insurance in India and abroad. Bombay: Allied, 1965. 228p.

16137 RAJAN, V.N. Medical care under social insurance in India. In Intl. Labour R. 98 (1968) 141-55.

16138 SHARMA, K.M. Social assistance in India. Delhi: Macmillan, 1976. 119p.

16139 SINHA, P.K. Social security measures in India. ND: Classical, 1980. 248p.

16140 Social security and national development: report of a national seminar in India, New Delhi, 19-30 September 1977. ND: Intl. Labour Office, 1978. 380p.

5. Professional Social Work and Education

16141 BANERJI, G.R. Papers on social work; an Indian perspective. Bombay: TISS, 1973. 296p. (TISS series, 23)

16142 DASGUPTA, S., ed. Towards a philosophy of social work in India. ND: Popular Book Services, for the Gandhian Inst. of Studies, 1967. 272p.

16143 GANGRADE, K.D. Dimensions of social work in India: case studies. ND: Marwah, 1976. 188p.

16144 JACOB, K.K. Methods and fields of social work in India. 2nd rev. ed. NY: Asia, 1965. 264p. [1st ed. 1958]

16145 KRISHNAN NAIR, T., ed. Social work education and development of weaker sections. Madras: Assn. of Schools of Social Work in India, 1975. 197p. [proc. of seminar]

16146 RAMACHANDRAN, P. Professional social workers in India; a study of their employment position and functions. Bombay: United Asia, 1969. 167p.

16147 WADIA, A.R. History and philosophy of social work in India. 2nd ed. Bombay: Allied, 1968. 464p. (TISS series, 4)

16148 YASAS, F.M. Gandhian values in professional social work education in India. In IJSW 25 (1964) 1-28.

16149 YELAJA, S.A. Schools of social work in India: historical development 1936-1966. In IJSW 29 (1969) 361-78.

6. Social Problems and Services
a. child welfare

16150 Adoption and foster care [special issue]. In IJSW 37,2 (1976) 109-86.

16151 CENTRAL INST. OF RES. & TRAINING IN PUBLIC COOP. Perspectives on the child in India. ND: 1975. 146p.

16152 CHATURVEDI, T.N. Administration for child welfare. ND: IIPA, 1979. 428p.

16153 GOKHALE, S.D. & N.K. SOHONI, ed. Child in India. Bombay: Somaiya, 1979. 320p.

16154 GUPTA, SATYA, ed. The child in India: commemorative volume, XVth International Congress of Pediatrics, 1977, New Delhi, India. ND: Indian Academy of Pediatrics, 1977. 117p.

16155 JAIN, S.N., ed. Child and the law. Bombay: N.M. Tripathi, 1979. 218p.

16156 KAPADIA, K.M. & S. DEVADAS PILLAI. Young runaways; a study of children who desert home. Bombay: Popular, 1971. 124p.

16157 KULSHRESHTHA, J.C. Child labour in India. ND: Ashish, 1978. 145p.

16158 MATANI, P.R. A study of the destitute children discharged from children's homes in Delhi. ND: Natl. Inst. of Public Coop. & Child Dev., 1975. 59p.

16159 MOHINDER SINGH & R.N. SHARMA, eds. Administration for child welfare: a select bibliography. In IJPA 25, 3 (1979) 961-86.

16160 PANDHE, M.K. Child labour in India: based on official & semi-official reports. Calcutta: India Book Exchange, 1979. 179p.

16161 PANT, I.P. Child welfare in India; an integrated approach. Delhi: MPGOI, 1963. 145p.

16162 SADHU, S.N. & V. DIXIT. Child welfare in India: a bibliography. ND: Sagar, 1980. 152p.

16163 SHAH, J.H. Child welfare in India. In IJSW 29 (1968) 289-309.

b. prostitution and "immoral traffic in women"

16164 D'SOUZA, A.A. Prevention of prostitution: a strategy of social change. In SocAct 23,1 (1973) 41-51.

16165 HUSAIN, M. The Suppression of Immoral Traffic in Women and Girls Act, 1956; with critical commentary.... 3rd ed., rev. & enl. Lucknow: Eastern Book Co., 1978. 210p. [1st ed. 1958]

16166 INDIA (REP.). ADVISORY CMTEE. ON SOCIAL & MORAL HYGIENE, 1954. Report. ND: Central Social Welfare Board, 1956. 175p. [Dhanwanthi Rama Rau, chm.]

16167 JAYAKAR, R.B.K. Prostitution and immoral traffic in India. In Durgabai Deshmukh, ed. Social welfare in India. ND: PDMIB, 1955, 353-71.

16168 KAPUR, P. The life and world of call-girls in India: a socio-psychological study of the aristocratic prostitute. ND: Vikas, 1973. 368p.

16169 NEHRU, R. Recovery of abducted women. In IJSW 9,4 (1949) 303-09.

16170 Regional training course in suppression of immoral traffic. In Social Defence 12,47 (1977) 39-48.

16171 SURENDRA SINGH. The problem of prostitution in contemporary Indian society. In Social Defence 11,44 (1976) 16-21.

16172 TRIBHUWAN, J. Suppression of Immoral Traffic in Women and Girls Act, 1956: a critical study. Ahmednagar: the author, 1966. 26p.

16173 Women and girls in moral and social danger. ND: Central Bureau of Correctional Services, 1971. 127p.

c. the physically handicapped - the blind, deaf, crippled

16174 AGARWAL, L.P. Prevention and control of visual impairment and blindness. In Yojana 19,19 (1975) 4-11.

16175 All-India directory of welfare agencies for the blind. ND: Central Inst. of Res. & Training in Public Coop., 1972. 270p.

16176 BHATT, U. The physically handicapped in India; a growing national problem. Bombay: Popular, 1963. 376p.

16177 FAZELBHOY, R.S. What are we doing for our 5,100,000 blind? In IWI 97,6 (1976) 28-31.

16178 Towards a fuller life: education and rehabilitation of the handicapped. ND: Dept. of Social Security, 1967. 224p.

16179 YADAV, R.S. Organisational problems of work for the deaf. In Social Welfare 17.9 (1970) 8-10.

d. beggars and beggary

16180 BHATTACHARYYA, S.K. Beggars and the law. In JILI 19,4 (1977) 498-502.

16181 ______. Prevention of begging. In Social Defense 10,39 (1975) 9-13.

16182 GORE, M.S. Society and the beggar. In SB 7 (1958) 23-48.

16183 PRASAD, C. The problem of beggary in an urban community. In J. of Social Studies 1 (1958) 47-58.

e. juvenile delinquency, crime, and corrections

16184 ATTAR, A.D. Juvenile delinquency; a comparative study. Bombay: Popular, 1964. 192p.

16185 CHANDRA, S. Sociology of deviation in India. Bombay: Allied, 1967. 264p.

16186 GHOSH, S.K. Crime on the increase. 2nd ed., rev. and enl. Calcutta: Eastern Law House, 1969. 170p.

16187 INDIA (REP.). ADVISORY CMTEE. ON AFTER-CARE PROGRAMMES, 1954. Report. ND: Central Social Welfare Board, 1955. 2 v.

16188 INDIA (REP.). CENTRAL BUREAU OF CORRECTIONAL SERVICES. Juvenile delinquency; a challenge. ND: 1970. 76p.

16189 ______. Probation and prisons; a statistical analysis. ND: 1972. 77p.

16190 KERAVALA, P.C. A study in Indian crime. Bombay: Popular, 1959. 215p.

16191 MUKHERJI, S.K. Administration of juvenile correctional institutions: a comparative study in Delhi and Maharashtra. ND: Sterling, 1974. 304p.

16192 NARULA, R.K. Jail or bail: justice to undertrials: law and procedure of bail in India and U.K. Bombay: Himalaya Pub. House, 1979. 126p.

16193 NAYAR, B.R. Violence and crime in India: a quantitative study. Delhi: Macmillan, 1975. 150p.

16194 SETHNA, M.J. Society and the criminal; with special reference to the problems of crime and its prevention, the personality of the criminal, the treatment of the criminal, prison reform, and juvenile delinquency in India. 3rd rev. ed. Bombay: N.M. Tripathi, 1971. 508p.

16195 SHETH, H. Juvenile delinquency in an Indian setting. Bombay: Popular, 1961. 295p.

16196 SINGH, I.J. Indian prison: a sociological enquiry. Delhi: Concept, 1979. 179p.

16197 TYLER, M. My years in an Indian prison. ND: B.I. Pub., 1977. 191p.

16198 VARMA, P. Sex offences in India and abroad. Delhi: B.R., 1979. 235p.

16199 ______, ed. Juvenile delinquency: its problem and treatment in India: report of the All India Seminar on Juvenile Delinquency, Lucknow, September 29-30, 1973. 43p.

16200 VENUGOPALA RAO, S. Facets of crime in India. 2nd rev. ed. Bombay: Allied, 1967. 275p. [1st ed. 1963]

f. alcohol and drug abuse; prohibition and control

16201 CHOPRA, R.N. & I.C. CHOPRA. Drug addiction, with special reference to India. ND: Council of Scientific & Industrial Res., 1965. 264p.

16202 GANDHI, M.K. Drink, drugs, and gambling. Ahmedabad: Navajivan, 1952. 173p.

16203 INDIA (REP.). PLANNING CMSN. PROHIBITION ENQUIRY COMMITTEE. Report, 1954-55. Delhi: MPGOI, 1955. 183p.

16204 ______. State governments' memoranda and other documents. Delhi: MPGOI, 1956. 269p.

16205 NAYYAR, S. History of prohibition in India. Rev. ed. ND: All India Prohibition Council, 1977. 13p.

16206 Prohibition; a symposium on a controversial policy now under review. In Seminar 60 (1964) 10-54. (Contributions by S. Natarajan, Pitambar Kaushik, U.N. Dhebar, R.K. Karanjia, P. Kodanda Rao, A.M. Khusro)

G. Health Services and Medical Systems in Independent India

1. Bibliography and Reference

16207 AHLUWALIA, A. Sociology of medicine; a trend report. In A survey of research in sociology and social anthropology. Bombay: Popular, 1974, v. 2, 401-30. [sponsored by ICSSR]

16208 CENTRAL COUNCIL FOR RES. IN INDIAN MEDICINE AND HOMOEOPATHY. Hand book of domestic medicine and common ayurvedic remedies. ND: Min. of Health and Family Welfare, 1978. 538p. (CCRIMH pub., 196)

16209 INDIA (REP.). AYURVEDIC PHARMACOPOEIA CMTEE. The ayurvedic formulary of India. ND: Min. of Health and Family Planning, 1978-. v. 1, 324p. [Chm. A.N. Namjoshi]

16210 INDIA (REP.). CENTRAL BUREAU OF HEALTH INTELLIGENCE. Health atlas of India, 1962. ND: 1964. 89p.

16211 INDIA (REP.). MIN. OF HEALTH. Pharmacopoeia of India; the Indian pharmacopoeia. 2nd ed. Delhi: MPGOI, 1966. 1124p.

16212 ______. Supplement, 1975, to the Pharmacopoeia of India, 1966. ND: Cont. of Pub., 1976. 244p.

16213 JAIN, D.P. References in nutrition and related subjects: India, 1967-1974. ND: USAID, 1975. 432p.

16214 KAKAR, D.N. Primitive, folk, and modern medicine: a selected bibliography with special reference to community nutrition. Chandigarh: Punjab Nutrition Dev. Project, Govt. of Punjab-CARE, 1973. 263p.

16215 Public health: select review of literature published in India. Calcutta: All India Institute of Hygiene and Public Health, 1965-. [annual]

16216 UMMAL FAZAL & M.A. RAZZACK, eds. A hand book of common remedies in unani system of medicine. ND: Central Council for Res. in Indian Medicine and Homoeopathy, Min. of Health and Family Planning, 1967. 173p.

2. General Studies of Health Services and Administration

16217 AHUJA, M.M.S., ed. Progress in clinical medicine in India. ND: Arnold-Heinemann, 1976. 600p. + 21pl.

16218 Alternative approaches to health care: report of a symposium. ND: Indian Council of Medical Res., 1977. 242p.

16219 GANDHI, H.S., et al. Report of the political actions in the field of health in India from 1947-1975. ND: Natl. Inst. of Health Admin. & Educ., 1976. 78p.

16220 GANDHIGRAM INST. OF RURAL HEALTH & FAMILY PLANNING. Bulletin...research activities 1964-1976: major findings & implications. Ambathurai: The Inst., 1977. 131p.

16221 INDIA (REP.). CMTEE. ON INTEGRATION OF HEALTH SERVICES. Report, March 1967. ND: Dir. Genl. of Health Services, 1968. 46p. [Chm., N. Jungalwalla]

16222 INDIA (REP.). HEALTH SURVEY & PLANNING CMTEE. Report. Aug. 1959 - Oct. 1961. Delhi: Min. of Health, 1962. 2 v. [Chm., A.L. Mudaliar]

16223 MAHAJAN, B.K. Health services in India. Jamnagar: Aruna B. Mahajan, 1969. 164p.

16224 ______. Preventive medicine in India. Jamnagar: Aruna B. Mahajan, 1968. 300p.

16225 NAIK, J.P. An alternative system of health care services in India: some proposals. Bombay: Allied, 1977. 81p.

16226 NATIONAL INST. OF HEALTH & FAMILY WELFARE. Health sector of India: an overview. ND: 1977. 83p.

16227 OGALE, S.L. Health and population. Bombay: S.S. Ogale, 1976. 319p.

16228 PANIKAR, P.G.K. Health care delivery system in India; alternative approaches. In EPW 11,22 (1976) 817-19. [reply by R. Jefferey, EPW 11,28 (1976) 1046-47]

16229 PATEL, A.J., ed. In search of diagnosis: analysis of present system of health care. Vadodara: Medico Friend Circle, 1977. 174p.

16230 PATHAK, S.H. Medical social work in India. Delhi: Delhi School of Social Work, 1961. 76p.

16231 SANJIVI, K.S. Planning India's health. Bombay: Orient Longmans, 1971. 119p.

16232 SEAL, S.C. Health administration in India. Calcutta: Dawn Books, 1975. 638p.

16233 SEMINAR ON HEALTH INFO. SYSTEM, NEW DELHI, 1973. Report. ND: Natl. Inst. of Health Admin. and Educ., 1974. 177p.

16234 SINGH, C.M. Role of veterinary public health in India. Madras: U. of Madras, 1974. 51p.

16235 VENKATARATNAM, R. Medical sociology in an Indian setting. Madras: Macmillan, 1979. 273p.

3. Major Public Health Problems
a. sanitation and pollution control

16236 ALL INDIA SEMINAR ON ENVIRONMENTAL POLLUTION, BOMBAY, INDIA, 1975. The hazards of environmental pollution: a scientific view: proceedings.... Bombay: Max Mueller Bhavan, 1976. 123p.

16237 DESH BANDHU & EKLAVYU CHAUHAN, eds. Current trends in Indian environment: proceedings of the Workshop on Environmental Education, held at the Indian National Science Academy, New Delhi on July 11-12, 1977. ND: Today & Tomorrow's, 1977. 232p.

16238 INDIA (REP.). ENVIRONMENTAL HYGIENE CMTEE., 1948. Report. Delhi: MPGOI, 1950. 208p. [B.C. DasGupta, chm.]

16239 INDIA (REP.). NATL. WATER SUPPLY & SANITATION CMTEE. Report, 1960-61. ND: Min. of Health, 1962. 167p.

16240 INDIA (REP.). PARLIAMENT. JOINT CMTEE. ON AIR (PREVENTION AND CONTROL OF POLLUTION) BILL, 1978. Report, presented on the 18th May 1979. ND: Lok Sabha Secretariat, 1979. 78p. [Chm., Karan Singh]

16241 KAWATA, K. Environmental sanitation in India. Ludhiana: Christian Medical College, Dept. of Social and Preventive Medicine, 1963. 217p.

16242 KHARE, R.S. A study of social resistance to sanitation programmes in rural India. In EA 17 (1964) 86-94.

16243 LEE, T. & I. BURTON. Future water supply for Indian cities. In Deccan Geographer 3/4,2/1 (1965-66) 129-43.

16244 MALKANI, N.R. Clean people and an unclean country. Delhi: Harijan Sevak Sangh, 1965. 144p.

16245 SARAF, R.K., ed. Symposium on environment pollution; proceedings. Nagpur: Central Public Health Engineering Res. Inst., 1973. 372p.

16246 SEMINAR ON ENVIRONMENTAL POLLUTION IN THE CONTEXT

OF PRESENT INDUSTRIAL DEVELOPMENTS IN INDIA, TRIVANDRUM, 1974. Proceedings. Calcutta: Institution of Engineers, Public Health Engineering Div., 1974. 187p.

16247 SEMINAR ON POLLUTION AND HUMAN ENVIRONMENT, BOMBAY, 1970. Proceedings. Bombay: Bhabha Atomic Res. Centre, 1971. 585p.

16248 TIAGI, B. & GOPAL, B. Teaching of ecology and environmental sciences in India. Jaipur: Intl. Scientific Pub., 1978. 187p.

b. nutrition and malnutrition

16249 AURORA, G.S. Toward a sociology of foods and nutrition in India. In SocAct 19 (1969) 124-35.

16250 BERG, A. The nutrition factor; its role in national development. Washington: Brookings Inst., 1973. 290p.

16251 GOPALAN, C. Diet atlas of India. Hyderabad: Natl. Inst. of Nutrition, 1969. 102p.

16252 GOPALAN, C. & B.V. RAMA SASTRI & S.C. BALASUBRAMANIAN. Nutritive value of Indian foods. Hyderabad: Natl. Inst. of Nutrition, 1972. 204p.

16253 GOPALAN, C. & K. VIJAYA RAGHAVAN. Nutrition atlas of India. Hyderabad: Natl. Inst. of Nutrition, 1971. 188p.

16254 MUTHAYYA, B.C., et al. Evaluation of Applied Nutrition Programme: a study across the six states. Hyderabad: NIRD, 1978. 142p.

16255 NATL. INST. OF NUTRITION. A decade of progress, 1961-1970. ND: Indian Council of Medical Res., 1970. 145p.

16256 NATL. SEMINAR ON SPECIAL NUTRITION PROGRAMME, SRINAGAR, INDIA, 1978. Report and recommendations. ND: Natl. Inst. of Public Coop. & Child Dev., 1978. 161p.

16257 SUKHATME, P.V. Assessment of adequacy of diets and different income levels. In EPW 13,31-33 (1978) 1378-84.

16258 ______. The incidence of protein deficiency in India. In Indian J. of Medical Res. 57 (1969) 2170-85.

16259 TASKAR, A.D. Regional variation and adequacy of Indian diets: statistical evaluation of diet surveys. In Indian J. of Medical Res. 44 (1956) 519-37; 46 (1958) 485-92.

c. studies of major diseases

16260 BASU, R.N. Evolution of smallpox eradication programme in India. In IJPH 20,2 (1976) 51-61.

16261 CHATTERJEE, B.R., ed. A window on leprosy: Gandhi Memorial Leprosy Foundation silver jubilee commemorative volume. Wardha: The Foundation, 1978. 395p.

16262 GOKHALE, S.D. Valley of shadows: problem of leprosy in India. Bombay: Popular, 1979. 132p.

16263 INDIA (REP.). MIN. OF HEALTH AND FAMILY PLANNING. National smallpox eradication programme in India; planning, organization and execution, problems encountered, approach to their solution. ND: 1966. 330p.

16264 INDIA (REP.). SPECIAL CMTEE. TO REVIEW THE WORKING OF THE NATL. MALARIA ERADICATION PROGRAMME AND TO RECOMMEND MEASURES FOR IMPROVEMENT. Report. ND: Min. of Health, Family Planning & Urban Dev., 1969. 121p. [Chm., R.N. Madhok]

16265 MISRA, R.P. Medical geography of India. ND: NBT, 1970. 205p.

16266 MUTATKAR, R.K. Society and leprosy. Pune: Shubhada-Saraswat, 1979. 297p.

16267 PATNAIK, K.C. & P.N. KAPOOR. Statistical review of cholera problem in India, with particular reference to endemicity and epidemicity. ND: Central Bureau of Health Intelligence, 1967. 181p.

16268 ______. Statistical review of smallpox problem in India; with particular reference to endemicity and epidemicity. ND: Central Bureau of Health Intelligence, 1968. 103p.

d. mental health & hygiene

16269 INDIA (REP.). PARLIAMENT. JOINT COMMITTEE ON THE MENTAL HEALTH BILL, 1978. Report, 24th Nov. 1978. ND: Lok Sabha Secretariat, 1978. 86p. [Chm. Sushila Nayar

16270 Mental health in India. Bangalore: CISRS, 1979. 98p. [pub. as R&S 26,2]

16271 MOHAN, BRIJ. Social psychiatry in India: a treatis on the mentally ill. Calcutta: Minerva, 1973. 226p.

16272 PANDEY, R.E. The suicide problem in India. In Intl. Journal of Social Psychiatry 14 (1968) 193-200.

16273 SEN GUPTA, S.K. & D.R. CHAWLA. Mental health in India. ND: Central Bureau of Health Intelligence, 1970. 82p.

16274 TAYLOR, W.S. Behavior disorders and the breakdown of the Hindu family. In IJSW 4 (1943) 163-70.

4. Family Planning: Knowledge, Attitudes, and Practice (KAP) [see also V. B. 5., above]

a. bibliographies and surveys of research

16275 Bibliography of cost benefit studies on family planning in India and IUCD studies in India. Bombay: Demographic Training and Res. Centre, 1970. 21p.

16276 CHANDRASEKARAN, C. Recent trends in family planning research in India. In Intl. Conf. on Family Planning Programs, Geneva, 1965. Proceedings: family planning and population programs. Chicago: UChiP, 1966, 545-59.

16277 DESAI, P.B. Nuptiality, fertility, and family planning. In his A survey of research in demography. Bombay: Popular, 1975, 211-332. [sponsored by ICSSR]

16278 DUTT MULLICK, V. & D.C. DUBEY. A review of studie in family planning communication. ND: Natl. Inst. of Family Planning, 1974. 32p.

16279 KUMAR, A. An over-view of IUCD studies in India. Bombay: Intl. Inst. for Population Studies, 1971. 94p.

16281 KRISHNA MURTHY, K.G. Research in family planning in India. Delhi: Sterling, 1968. 108p.

16282 RAINA, B.L. Research in family planning. In EE 52,7 (1967) 521-28.

b. general studies of family planning

16283 ALL INDIA SEMINAR ON FAMILY PLANNING PROBLEMS IN INDIA, BOMBAY, 1972. A report. Bombay: Intl. Inst. for Population Studies, 1972. 244p.

16284 AMONKER, R.G. Family planning performance in India In AS 15,7 (1975) 586-97.

16285 BANERJI, D. Family planning in India; a critique and a perspective. ND: PPH, 1971. 84p.

16286 CHATTERJEE, B. & NAVREKHA SINGH. A guide to voluntary action in family planning. ND: Population Council of India, 1972. 193p.

16287 Family planning and the status of women in India; report of a seminar held on Aug. 10-14, 1969 in New Delhi. ND: Central Inst. of Res. and Training in Publi Coop., 1972. 207p.

16288 INDIA (REP.). CENSUS OF INDIA, 1961. Family planning in rural India. Ed. by B.K. Roy Burman. ND: 1968 264p. (Census of India, 1961, monograph)

16289 Integration of health and family planning in village sub-centres: report on the Fifth Narangwal Conference, Nov. 1970. Narangwal: Rural Health Res. Centre, 1971. 95 + 102p.

16290 MANKEKAR, K. Voluntary effort in family planning: a brief history. ND: Abhinav, 1974. 97p.

16291 MUKHERJEE, RAMKRISHNA. Family and planning in India. Bombay: Orient Longmans, 1976. 88p.

16292 NATL. CONF. ON POPULATION CONTROL, NEW DELHI, 1975 Recommendations and documents. ND: Indian Medical Assoc., 1976. 186p.

16293 PAI PANANDIKAR, V.A. & R.N. BISHNOI & O.P. SHARMA. Family planning under the emergency: policy implication of incentives and disincentives. ND: Radiant, 1978. 176p. [On new population policy, April 1976-]

16294 PATHAK, S. Social welfare, health, and family planning in India. ND: Marwah, 1979. 296p.

16295 PATHARE, R. The family planning programme: a sociological analysis. In SB 15,2 (1966) 44-62.

16296 ROY BURMAN, B.K. Family planning from the point of view of cultural anthropology. In IJSW 30 (1970) 343-54.

16297 SATYA PRAKASH & K. SHARMA. Administering family planning. Rohtak: Rachna, 1979. 128p.

16298 SURJIT KAUR. Wastage of children. ND: Sterling, 1978. 282p.

16299 UNITED NATIONS. TECHNICAL ASSISTANCE PROGRAM. Report on the family planning programme in India. NY: 1966. 123p. (Report no. TAO/IND/48)

c. attitudes and acceptance: family planning education and communication

16300 BANERJEE, S. Family planning communication: a critique of the Indian programme. ND: Radiant, 1979. 210p.

16301 BHANDARI, L. Communications for social marketing: a study in family planning. Delhi: Macmillan, 1978. 193p.

16302 DUBEY, D.C. Family planning communications studies in India; a review of findings and implications of studies on communications. ND: Central Family Planning Inst., 1969. 96p.

16303 KHAN, M.E. Family planning among Muslims in India: a study of the reproductive behaviour of Muslims in an urban setting. ND: Manohar, 1979. 198p.

16304 MASCARENHAS, M.M. Population education for quality of life. Bangalore: Family Welfare Centre, 1974. 547p.

16305 MOHANTY, S.P. Attempts at measuring family planning attitudes in India: an assessment of traditional and emerging techniques. In AV 13,3 (1971) 298-318.

16306 NAGDA, S., ed. Proceedings of the National Seminar on Population Education. Tirupati: Population Studies Centre, Sri Venkateswara U., 1976. 436p.

16307 PATANKAR, P. & L. DEY. Social communication in family planning: a case book. ND: Orient Longmans, 1973. 219p.

16308 POHLMAN, E. & K. SESHAGIRI RAO. Children, teachers, and parents view birth planning; a preliminary report of the Central Family Planning Institute and Carolina Population Center Collaborative Project. ND: Central Family Planning Inst., 1970. 101p.

16309 SANYAL, S.N. Attitudes towards contraceptive methods. In MI 42 (1962) 126-38.

16310 SHARMA, R.C. Population trends, resources, and environment: handbook on population education. Delhi: Dhanpat Rai, 1975. 296p.

d. selected studies of birth control methods in India; abortion, sterilization, IUCD

16311 BENJAMIN, V. The Indian imperatives for the legalisation of abortion. In R&S 19,2 (1972) 56-61.

16312 BHATIA, J.C. & S.R. MEHTA. Induced abortion, opinions of indigenous medicine practitioners. In IJSW 32,4 (1972) 435-43.

16313 CHANDRASEKHAR, S. Abortion in a crowded world: the problem of abortion with special reference to India. Seattle: UWashP, 1974. 184p.

16314 CHATTERJI, S.K., ed. Legislation of abortion. Madras: CLS, for CISRS, 1971. 71p. (Studies on natl. legislation, 3)

16315 DANDEKAR, K. & V. BHATE. Prospects of population control: evaluation of contraception activity (1951-1964). ND: Orient Longmans, 1971. 253p.

16316 GANDHI, M.K. Through self-control. Ed. by A.T. Hingorani. Bombay: BVB, 1964. 108p.

16317 HUSAIN, I.Z. Liberalisation of abortion law: a survey of opinions. In EPW 4,45/46 (1969) 1777-80.

16318 INDIA (REP.). CMTEE. TO STUDY THE QUESTION OF LEGALISATION OF ABORTION, 1964-. Report. ND: Min. of Health & Family Planning, 1967. 143p. [Shantilal H. Shah, chm.]

16319 KASHAPPAGOUDER, N.B. Legalization of abortion: some points of new. In Interdiscipline 7,3 (1970) 289-305.

16320 KUMAR, ASHOK. An overview of IUCD studies in India. Bombay: Intl. Inst. for Population Studies, 1971. 123p.

16321 LAUMAS, K.R., ed. Review of research work in India on intra-uterine contraceptive devices: proceedings of a seminar. ND: Indian Council of Medical Res., 1969. 227p.

16322 Medical Termination of Pregnancy Act, 1971 special issue . In JILI 16,4 (1974) 549-709. [Articles by Alice Jacob, R.V. Kelkar, Savithri Chattopadhyay, Joseph Minattur, D.C. Pande]

16323 NAYAK, V.T. Birth-control and Gandhian morality. In IJSW 21 (1961) 373-86.

16324 A review of some selected studies on abortion in India. In J. of Family Welfare 14,4 (1968) 38-48.

16325 Seminar on medical and socio-economic aspects of abortion, Calcutta, November 25-27, 1972. Calcutta: Family Planning Assoc. of India, 1973. 172p.

16326 SINGH, S.K. & R.K. RAIZADA. Abortion law in India: past and present. Chandigarh: Family Planning Assoc. of India, Haryana Branch, 1976. 171p.

16327 Studies in sterilization. Bangalore: P.C.B., India Population Project, Karnataka, 1976. 75p.

5. Indigenous and Cosmopolitan Systems of Medicine: Competition and Collaboration

a. general studies

16328 DUNN, F.L. Traditional Asian medicine and cosmopolitan medicine as adaptive systems. In C. Leslie, ed. Asian medical systems: a comparative study. Berkeley: UCalP, 1976, 133-58.

16329 LESLIE, C. The ambiguities of medical revivalism in modern India. In his (ed.) Asian medical systems: a comparative study. Berkeley: UCalP, 1976, 356-67.

16330 MANDELBAUM, D.G. Curing and religion in South Asia. In Surajit Sinha, ed. Aspects of Indian culture and society.... Calcutta: IAS, 1972, 171-82.

16331 RAMASWAMI, S. Medicine indigenous and modern, a judicious synthesis. In BITCM (1966) pt. 2, 251-58.

16332 VALUNJKAR, T.N. & H.R. CHATURVEDI. Religion and illness in Hindu society. In JMSUB 13-16,2 (1967) 45-52.

b. indigenous medical systems in contemporary India

16333 ATHAVALE, V.B. Bala-veda: pediatrics & ayurveda. Bombay: Athavale, for Pediatric Clinics of India, 1977. 191p.

16334 DESAI, M.R. Nature cure. ND: S. Chand, 1978. 36p.

16335 GARDE, R.K. Principles and practice of yoga therapy. Bombay: Taraporevala, 1972. 131p.

16336 HAMSANANDA, Swami. Naturopathie et yoga; santé, guérison, bonheur. Brussels: Dereume, 1966. 290p.

16337 INDIA (DOMINION). CMTEE. ON INDIGENOUS SYSTEMS OF MEDICINE. Report. Delhi: Min. of Health, Govt. of India, 1948. 2 v. in 1. [Chm., R.N. Chopra]

16338 INDIA (REP.). CMTEE. TO ASSESS & EVALUATE THE PRESENT STATUS OF AYURVEDIC SYSTEM OF MEDICINE, 1958. Report. Delhi: Min. of Health, 1958. 246p. [Chm., K.N. Udupa]

16339 INDIA (REP.). CMTEE. TO STUDY THE QUESTION OF FORMULATING UNIFORM STANDARDS IN RESPECT OF EDUCATION AND REGULATION OF PRACTICE OF VAIDYAS, HAKIMS, & HOMEOPATHS, 1955. Interim Report. Delhi: MPGOI, 1956. 144p.

[D.T. Dave, chm.]

16340 INDIA (REP.). SHUDDHA AYURVEDIC EDUC. CMTEE. Report. Delhi: MPGOI, 1963. 89p. [Chm., Mohanlal P. Vyas]

16341 JUSSAWALLA, J.M. Healing from within; a treatise on the philosophy and theory of nature cure. Bombay: Manaktalas, 1966. 147p.

16342 KERALA. EXPERT CMTEE. ON AYURVEDA. Report. Trivandrum: Govt. Press, 1965. 66p.

16343 KURUP, P.N.V. Bird's-eye-view on indigenous systems of medicine in India. Rev. ed. ND: Kurup, 1979. 68p.

16344 RAO, J. Principles and practice of medical astrology. Rev. ed. ND: Sagar, 1972. 208p.

16345 UDUPA, K.N., ed. Advances in research in Indian medicine. Varanasi: BHU, 1970. 406p.

6. Health Professionals and Institutions
a. physicians, vaidyas, hakims, and other practitioners

16346 ATHALYE, V.V. Forty-four years' practice in homeopathy; therapeutic experiences with useful hints and observations. Poona: Anath Vidyarthi Griha Prakashan, 1962. 341p.

16347 AURORA, G.S. Medical scientists in India: institutional framework. In SocAct 26,1 (1976) 27-51.

16348 An evaluation of community health workers' scheme: a collaborative study. ND: Natl. Inst. of Health & Family Welfare, 1978. 172p. (Its technical report, 4)

16349 KAKAR, D.N. Dais, the traditional birth attendants in village India. Delhi: New Asian Pub., 1980. 151p.

16350 LESLIE, C. The professionalization of indigenous medicine. In M.B. Singer, ed. Entrepreneurship and modernization of occupational cultures in South Asia. Durham: DUPCSSA, 1973, 216-242. (Its monographs & occ. papers, 12)

16351 NANDI, P.K. & C.P. LOOMIS. Professionalization of nursing in India; determining and facilitating aspects of the culture. In JAAS(L) 9,1/2 (1974) 43-59.

16352 NATL. CONF. ON WOMEN DOCTORS IN INDIA, NEW DELHI, INDIA, 1975. Proceedings. ND: Indian Medical Assoc., 1975. 96p.

16353 OOMMEN, T.K. Doctors and nurses: a study in occupational role structures. Delhi: Macmillan, 1978. 258p.

16354 SRIVASTAVA, A.L. Human relations in social organizations. Allahabad: Chugh, 1979. 196p.

16355 TAKULAI, H.S., et al. The health center doctor in India. Baltimore: Johns Hopkins Press, 1967. 67p.

16356 TAYLOR, C.E. The place of indigenous medical practitioners in the modernization of health services. In C. Leslie, ed. Asian medical systems: a comparative study. Berkeley: UCalP, 1976, 285-99.

b. medical education

16357 ALL INDIA WORKSHOP ON HEALTH EDUCATION IN HOSPITAL SERVICES, CHANDIGARH, 1977. Report. Chandigarh: State Health Educ. Bureau, Haryana, 1977. 53p.

16358 BANERJI, D. Social orientation of medical education in India. In EPW 8,9 (1973) 485-88.

16359 BRASS, P.R. The politics of Ayurvedic education: case study of revivalism and modernization in Inida. In S.H. Rudolph & L.I. Rudolph, eds. Education and politics in India.... Cambridge: HUP, 1972, 342-71.

16360 CHITKARA, H.L., ed. Papers on homeopathic education in India. ND: All India Homeopathic Medical Assoc., 1973. 130p.

16361 CONF. ON THE TEACHING OF PREVENTATIVE AND SOCIAL MEDICINE IN RELATION TO THE HEALTH NEEDS OF THE COUNTRY, DELHI, 1965. Report and recommendations. ND: Natl. Inst. of Health Admin. & Educ.,1966. 48p.

16362 Handbook of medical education, 1978. ND: Assn. of Indian Universities, 1978. 179p.

16363 INDIA (REP.). MEDICAL EDUC. CMTEE. Report, 1969. ND: Dir. Genl. of Health Services, 1970. 141p. [Chm., Govind Narain]

16364 INDIA (REP.). REVIEW CMTEE. ON UPGRADED AND POSTGRADUATE DEPARTMENTS IN MEDICAL COLLEGE. Postgraduate medical education; report. ND: Min. of Health Dir. Genl. of Health Services, 1965. 1 v.

16365 INDIA (REP.). SUDDHA UNANI EDUC. CMTEE. Report. Delhi: MPGOI, 1966. 100p.

16366 JAGGI, O.P. Western medicine in India: medical education and research. Delhi: Atma Ram, 1979. 335p. (History of science, technology and medicine in India, 13)

16367 JAYARAM, N. Social implications of medical education. In J. of Higher Educ. 3,2 (1977) 207-20.

16368 NAYAR, D.P. An approach to medical education in India. In Manpower J. 4,4 (1969) 7-26.

16369 TAYLOR, C.E. Doctors for the villages: study of rural internships in seven Indian medical colleges. Bombay: Asia Pub. House, 1976. 197p.

16370 TRAINING CAPABILITIES OF PRIMARY HEALTH CENTRES IN INDIA. ND: Natl. Inst. of Health & Family Welfare, 1978. 69p. (Its technical report, 1)

16371 VENKATESWARA RAO, T. Doctors in making. Ahmedabad: Sahitya Mudranalaya, 1976. 231p.

c. hospitals and other institutions

16372 ANAND, K.K. Studies in hospital management. Bombay: Bombay Mgmt. Assn., 1976.

16373 Directory of hospitals, 1975. ND: Central Bureau of Health Intelligence, 1977. 104p.

16374 Directory of para medical institutions in India, 1976. ND: Central Bureau of Health Intelligence, 1978. 119p.

16375 HOUTART, F. & G. LEMERCINIER & M. LEGRAND. The Catholic hospital system in India. Bombay: Shakuntala, 1979. 76p.

16376 HUSS, C.A. Study of planned organisational change in the structure and functioning of Indian hospitals. ND: Voluntary Health Assn. of India, 1975. 357p.

H. Education in India since 1947

1. Bibliography and Reference

16377 AGGARWALA, D.V. & GURBACHAN SINGH, eds. All India educational directory. Chandigarh: All India Directories Pub., 1972. 1262p.

16378 BISWAS, A. & SUREN AGRAWAL, eds. Indian educational documents since independence: committees, commissions, conferences. ND: Academic Pub., 1971. 639p.

16379 BREMBECK, C.S. & E.W. WEIDNER. Education and development in India and Pakistan; a select and annotated bibliography. East Lansing: Michigan State U., College of Educ. & Intl. Programmes, 1963. 221p.

16380 BUCH, M.B. Second survey of research in education 1972-1978. Baroda: Soc. for Educ. Res. & Dev., 1979. 614p.

16381 ______. A survey of research in education. Baroda: M.S.U. of Baroda, Centre for Advanced Study in Education, 1974. 618p.

16382 CHITNIS, S. Sociology of education; a trend report. In A survey of research in sociology and social anthropology. Bombay: Popular, 1974, v. 2, 166-232.

16383 INDIA (REP.). MIN. OF EDUC. & SOCIAL WELFARE. STAT. & INFO. DIV. Education in India since Independence: a statistical review. ND: 1972. 58p.

16384 SHARMA, R.C. Educational innovation and change in India: trends and bibliography. In University Admin. 3,1 (1976) 76-86.

2. General Studies of Indian Education since Independence

16385 ADISESHIAH, M.S. Let my people awake. ND: Orient Longmans, 1970. 375p.

16386 BISWAS, A. & J.C. AGGARWAL. Education in India, 1971. ND: Arya Book Depot, 1972. 255p.

16387 Educational research: an inter-disciplinary approach; report of a seminar sponsored by the University Grants Commission. Delhi: Central Inst. of Educ., 1969. 163p.

16388 HUSAIN, ZAKIR. Educational reconstruction in India. ND: PDMIB, 1969. 74p.

16389 INDIA (REP.). MIN. OF EDUC. & SOCIAL WELFARE. Educational developments in India, 1971-77. ND: 1977. 72p.

16390 KIRPAL, PREM. A decade of education in India. Delhi: Indian Book Co., 1968. 212p.

16391 ______. Education. ND: PDMIB, 1973. 55p.

16392 NAIK, J.P. Policy and performance in Indian education, 1947-74. ND: Dr. K.G. Saiyidain Mem. Trust, 1975. 112p.

16393 OAD, L.K., et al. Perspectives of Indian education: an interdisciplinary approach. Agra: Sri Ram Mehra, 1975. 262p.

16394 PASRICHA, P. Guidance and counselling in Indian education. ND: Natl. Council of Educ. Res. & Training, 1976. 350p.

16395 RUHELA, S.P., ed. Educational challenges in socialist India. Delhi: Kalyani Pub., 1975. 220p.

16396 SARGENT, J. Society, schools, and progress in India. Oxford: Pergamon Press, 1968. 233p.

16397 SARKAR, S. Education in India: a perspective. Calcutta: World Press, 1978. 140p.

16398 SHARMA, S.R. American influence on Indian education. ND: Raaj Prakashan, 1979. 175p.

16399 VAKIL, K.S. & S. NATARAJAN. Education in India. 3rd rev. ed. NY: Allied, 1966. 216p.

3. Educational Policy and Planning
a. general studies

16400 AGGARWAL, J.C. Evaluation of the new pattern and the report of the Review Committee, 1977. ND: Arya Book Depot, 1978. 104p. [1st pub. 1974]

16401 AIRAN, J.W. & T. BARNABAS & A.B. SHAH. Climbing a wall of glass; aspects of educational reform in India. Bombay: Manaktalas, 1965. 176p.

16402 BISWAS, A. & S. DUTT & R.P. SINGHAL. The new educational pattern in India. Delhi: Vikas, 1975. 164p.

16403 GRIFFIN, W.H. & UDAI PAREEK. The process of planned change in education. Bombay: Somaiya, 1970. 269p.

16404 INDIA (REP.). MIN. OF EDUC. Educational activities of the Government of India. Delhi: MPGOI, 1963. 599p.

16405 INDIA (REP.). MIN. OF EDUC. & SOCIAL WELFARE. Draft national policy on education, 1979. ND: 1979. 22p.

16406 INDIA (REP.). WORKING GROUP ON EDUC. TECHNOLOGY. Report. ND: Min. of Educ. & Social Welfare, 1978. 145p. [Chm., P. Sabanayagam]

16407 LASKA, J.A. Planning and educational development in India. NY: Teachers College Press, Columbia U., 1968. 129p.

16408 MAHANTA, D. Our education in the making: a strategy to build up new Indian education. Calcutta: West Bengal Headmasters' Assoc., 1977. 144p.

16409 NAIK, J.P. Educational planning in India. Bombay: Allied, 1965. 197p.

16410 PREMI, M.K. Educational planning in India: implications of population trends. ND: Sterling, 1972. 284p.

16411 SAXENA, S. Educational planning in India: a study in approach & methodology. ND: Sterling, 1979. 202p.

16412 SHARMA, G.S., ed. Educational planning: its legal and constitutional implications in India. Bombay: N.M. Tripathi, 1967. 279p. [seminar]

16413 SHUKLA, P.D. Towards the new pattern of education in India. ND: Sterling, 1976. 215p.

16414 THOMAS, T.M. Indian educational reforms in cultural perspective. Delhi: S. Chand, 1970. 312p.

b. the Education Commission of 1965-66: report and critiques

16415 AGGARWAL, J.C. Major recommendations of the Education Commission, 1965-66, including selected passages and comments. ND: Arya Book Depot, 1966. 168p.

16416 BHATNAGAR, S. Kothari Commission; recommendations and evaluation. Meerut: Intl. Pub. House, 1967. 208p.

16417 INDIA (REP.). CMTEE. OF MEMBERS OF PARLIAMENT ON EDUCATION. Report, 1967: National policy on education. Delhi: Min. of Educ., 1967. 56p. (Its pub. 807)

16418 INDIA (REP.). EDUC. CMSN. Education and national development; report of the Education Commission, 1964-66. ND: Natl. Council of Educ. Res. & Training, 1971. 992 + 88p. [Chm., D.S. Kothari; 1st ed. 1966, 692p.]

16419 INDIA (REP.). PARLIAMENT. HOUSE OF THE PEOPLE. Report of the Education Commission; comments and reactions, a study. ND: Lok Sabha Secretariat, 1967. 90p.

16420 NAIK, J.P. The main recommendations of the Education Commission; a summary. ND: Natl. Council of Educ. Res. & Training, 1969. 111p.

c. education and national goals of development and national integration

16421 AVINASHILINGAM, T.S., ed. Education for national integration, a symposium. Periyanaikanpalayam: Sri Ramakrishna Mission Vidyalaya, 1967. 165p.

16422 DI BONA, J., ed. The context of education in Indian development. Durham: DUPCSSA, 1972. 229p. (Its monographs & occ. papers, 13)

16423 Higher education and development: a selection of papers presented to the Golden Jubilee Seminar. ND: Assoc. of Indian Universities, 1975. 166p.

16424 KARVE, D.D. The universities and the public in India. In A.B. Shah, ed. Education, scientific policy and developing societies. Bombay: Manaktalas, 1967, 151-76.

16425 KOTHARI, D.S. Education, science, and national development. Bombay: Asia, 1970. 96p.

16426 MEHTA, T.S. & PRABHAKAR SINGH & R.S. VASHISHT, eds. Teaching of geography and national integration. ND: Natl. Council of Educ. Res. & Training, 1973. 157p.

16427 SAINI, S.K. Development of education in India: socio-economic and political perspectives. ND: Cosmo, 1980. 428p.

16428 SODHI, T.S. Education and economic development: a treatise on the problems of economics of education. Ludhiana: Mukand, 1978. 244p.

16429 VERMA, R. Educational planning & poverty of India: a comparative study, 1944-77. ND: Lancers Pub., 1978. 202p.

d. educational finance, economics, and administration

16430 ABU BAKER, M. The union and the states in education: a study in educational finance and planning. ND: Shabd Sanchar, 1976. 258p.

16431 INDIA (REP.). STUDY GROUP ON SUPERVISION & INSPECTION. Report. ND: Natl. Council of Educ. Res. & Training, 1969. 162p. [Chm., M.V. Rajagopal]

16432 MISRA, A. The financing of Indian education. Bombay: Asia, 1967. 312p.

16433 MUKHERJI, S.N., ed. Administration of education in India. Baroda: Acharya Book Depot, 1962. 679p.

16434 PADMANABHAN, C.B. Economics of educational planning in India. ND: Arya Book Depot, 1971. 176p.

16435 PRAKASH, SHRI. Educational system of India: an econometric study. Delhi: Concept, 1978. 269p.

16436 Research in economics of education - India. ND: Assoc. of Indian Universities, 1979. 66p.

16437 Some basic facts about educational administration in India. ND: Natl. Inst. of Educ. Planning and Admin., 1979. 110p.

c. manpower policy and education

16438 BURGESS, T. & R. LAYARD & P. PANT. Manpower and educational development in India, 1961-1986. Toronto: U. of Toronto Press, 1968. 89p.

16439 DHAR, T.N. & A.S. ILCHMAN & W.F. ILCHMAN. Education and employment in India: the policy nexus. Calcutta: Minerva, 1976. 137p.

16440 ILCHMAN, W.F. & T.N. DHAR. Optional ignorance and excessive education: educational inflation in India. In AS 11,6 (1971) 523-43.

16441 INDIA (REP.). EXPERT CMTEE. ON UNEMPLOYMENT. WORKING GROUP ON EDUC. Report of the Working Group on Education, 19th Nov. 1972. ND: 1974. 55p. [Chm., L.S. Chandrakant]

4. Sociology of Education; Education and Social Change

16442 AHMAD, KARUNA. Towards a study of education and social change. In EPW 14,4 (1979) 157-64.

16443 CHAUHAN, B.R. & G. NARAYANA & T.R. SINGH. Scheduled castes and education. Meerut: Anu Pub., 1975. 154p.

16444 GORE, M.S. & I.P. DESAI & S. CHITNIS. Field studies in the sociology of education; all India report; v. 1, general report. ND: Natl. Council of Educ. Res. & Training, 1970. 671p.

16445 ______, eds. Papers in the sociology of education in India. ND: Natl. Council of Educ. Res. & Training, 1967. 363p.

16446 MEHTA, S. The school and the community in India. ND: S. Chand, 1974. 250p.

16447 MISRA, P.K. University and society. In MI 53,4 (1973) 333-46.

16448 NATIONAL SEMINAR ON TRIBAL EDUC. IN INDIA, UDAIPUR, 1965. Tribal education in India; report. ND: Tribal Educ. Unit, Dept. of Adult Educ., 1967. 221p.

16449 NEELSEN, J.P. The impact of education on the social stratification in India. In IAF 2,4 (1971) 497-514. [Also in JSR 15,2 (1972) 51-76]

16450 RUHELA, S.P., ed. Contributions to sociology of education in India. ND: Jain Bros., 1969. 152p. [v. 1. University education in India]

16451 ______, ed. Social determinants of educability in India; papers in the sociological context of Indian education. ND: Jain Bros., 1969. 267p.

16452 RUHELA, S.P. & K.C. VYAS. Sociological foundations of education in contemporary India. Delhi: Dhanpat Rai, 1970. 342p.

16453 SALAMATULLAH & S.P. RUHELA, ed. Sociological dimensions of Indian education. ND: Raaj Prakashan, 1971. 159p.

16454 SHAH, A.B., ed. The social context of education: essays in honour of Professor J.P. Naik. Bombay: Allied, 1978. 276p.

5. Indian Educators and Educational Thought

16455 AHUJA, R.L. The problems of teachers in India. Ambala Cantt.: Assoc. Pub., 1975. 170p.

16456 ARORA, K. Differences between effective and ineffective teachers. ND: S. Chand, 1978. 175p.

16457 BHAVE, V. Thoughts on education. Tr. from Hindi by M. Sykes. 2nd ed. Varanasi: Sarva Seva Sangh Prakashan, 1964. 276p.

16458 DE SOUZA, A. Public school headmasters. In SocAct 24,2 (1974) 145-57.

16459 DOWSETT, N.C. & S.R. JAYASWAL. Education of the child. Pondicherry: Sri Aurobindo Soc., 1974. 70p.

16460 GANDHI, M.K. To the students. Ed. by A.T. Hingorani. Bombay: BVB, 1965. 224p. [1st pub. 1949]

16461 GHOSH, Y.K. Two great educationists, Mohsin and Mookherjee. Calcutta: KLM, 1972. 28p.

16462 GUPTA, K.L. & S.K. KAPOOR, ed. Heads of the educational institutions in India: who's who; an illustrated biographical directory of administrative educationists in India. Delhi: Tradesman & Men India, 1964. 321p.

16463 INDIA (REP.). MIN. OF EDUC. The teacher today and tomorrow. ND: 1966. 150p.

16464 JOHN, V.V. The great classroom hoax & other reflections on India's education. ND: Vikas, 1978. 229p.

16465 KABIR, HUMAYUN. Education for tomorrow. Calcutta: KLM, 1969. 72p.

16466 KHOSLA, C.L., comp. Men of education in India; distinguished who's who. ND: Premier Pub., 1965. 364p.

16467 PARIKH, P.C. Educational thinking in modern India. Ahmedabad: Shree Mudranalaya, 1976. 462p.

16468 RAMAN NAYAR, R. Philosophical and sociological bases of education. 2nd ed. Trivandrum: College Book House, 1971. 115p.

16469 RUHELA, S.P., ed. Sociology of the teaching profession in India. ND: NCERT, 1970. 330p.

16470 SAIYIDAIN, K.G. Education, culture and the social order. Bombay: Asia, 1963. 284p. [1st pub. 1958]

16471 Shri S. Natarajan, a great educationist: commemoration volume. Madras: S. Natarajan Mem. Cmtee., 1978. 146p.

16472 SINGH, R.P. The Indian teacher. Delhi: National, 1969. 186p.

16473 THOMAS, T.M. Indian educational reforms in cultural perspective. Delhi: S. Chand, 1970. 312p.

6. Higher Education
a. bibliography and reference

16474 HINGWE, K.S. Higher education in India: a select bibliography (1947-1969). In JPU (Humanities) 33 (1970) 79-93.

16475 INDIA (REP.). UNIV. GRANTS CMSN. Third All India Educational Survey: higher education, 1973-74. ND: 1978. 502p.

16476 KAMALAVIJAYAN, D. Problems of higher education in India: an annotated bibliography of source material. Gurgaon: IDS, 1979. 116p.

16477 RAO, M.L. & T.V. RAO. Higher education in India: trends and bibliography. Ahmedabad: Indian Inst. of Mgmt., 1976. 28p.

16478 Universities handbook; India. ND: Assoc. of Indian Univ., 1958-. [annual; title varies]

16479 VIJAI GOVIND & C. LAL. Higher education in India: a bibliography. ND: Ess Ess, 1978. 229p.

b. government reports on higher education

16480 INDIA (DOMINION). UNIV. EDUC. CMSN. Report, Dec. 1948-Aug. 1949. Delhi: MPGOI, 1949-50. 3 v. [Chm., S. Radhakrishnan]

16481 INDIA (REP.). CMTEE. ON COLLEGES. Report. ND: Univ. Grants Cmsn., 1976. 44p.

16482 INDIA (REP.). UNIV. GRANTS CMSN. Centres of advanced study in Indian universities. Delhi: MPGOI, 1967. 81p.

16483 ______. Development of higher education in India: a policy frame. ND: 1978. 16p.

16484 ______. University development in India: basic facts and figures 1967-68. ND: MPGOI, 1971. 324p.

c. general studies of higher education in India

16485 AIRAN, J.W., ed. College education in India. Bombay: Manaktalas, 1967. 226p.

16486 ALTBACH, P.G. Problems of university reform in India. In Comp. Educ. R. 16,2 (1972) 251-66.

16487 AMRIK SINGH & P.G. ALTBACH, eds. The higher learning in India. Delhi: Vikas, 1974. 451p.

16488 BHANDARKAR, S.S. Association of Indian Universities (formerly the Inter-University Board of India): a short history, 1925-75. ND: Assoc. of Indian Univ., 1975. 227p.

16489 DICKINSON, R.D.N. The Christian college in developing India: a sociological inquiry. London: OUP, 1971. 370p.

16490 DONGERKERY, S.R. University education in India. Bombay: Manaktalas, 1967. 360p.

16491 GANDHI, K. Issues and choices in higher education: a sociological analysis. Delhi: B.R., 1977. 195p.

16492 GAUDINO, R.L. The Indian university. Bombay: Popular, 1965. 268p.

16493 GAUTAM, G. Crisis in the temples of learning. ND: S. Chand, 1972. 136p.

16494 HAGGERTY, W.J. Higher and professional education in Inida. Washington: Office of Educ., 1969. 181p.

16495 JOHN, V.V. Misadventures in higher education. ND: Young Asia, 1973. 253p.

16496 KAUL, J.N. Higher education in India, 1951-71: two decades of planned drift. Simla: IIAS, 1974. 203p.

16497 ______, ed. Higher education, social change, and national development.... Simla: IIAS, 1975. 232p.

16498 MANSUKHANI, G.S., ed. Crises in Indian universities. ND: Oxford & IBH, 1972. 211p.

16499 PARIKH, G.D. General education and Indian universities. NY: Asia, 1959. 203p.

16500 RAJ, K.N. Crisis of higher education in India. ND: PDMIB, 1971. 30p.

16501 REDDY, D.J. Challenges in higher education. Tirupati: Sri Venkateswara U., 1972. 494p.

16502 SHAH, A.B. Higher education in India. Bombay: Lalvani, 1967. 237p.

16503 SHARMA, G.D. Enrolment in higher education: a trend analysis, 1961-75. ND: Res. Cell in Econ. of Educ., Assn. of Indian Univ., 1977. 115p. (AIU occ. papers, 1)

16504 SHARMA, S.L. Modernizing effects of university education. ND: Allied, 1979. 236p.

16505 SURI, M.S. American influence on higher education in India: a study of post-independence era. ND: Sterling, 1979. 88p.

16506 U. OF MADRAS. CMSN. ON HIGHER EDUC. FOR WOMEN. Report. Madras: U.of Madras, 1979. 250p. [Chm., R.P. Devadas]

16507 VERBENKO, V.A. & BATUK DESAI. IIT, symbol of new India: 20 years of Indian Institute of Technology. ND: USSR Embassy, 1979. 57p.

d. administration of higher education; the University Grants Commission

16508 AZAD, J.L. Financing of higher education in India .... ND: Sterling, 1975. 236p.

16509 DONGERKERY, S.R. University autonomy in India. Bombay: Lalvani, 1967. 128p.

16510 INDIA (REP.). CMTEE. ON GOVERNANCE OF UNIVERSITIES & COLLEGES, 1969. Report. ND: Univ. Grants Cmsn., 1971-. v. 1, 96p. [Chm., P.B. Gajendrahadkar; to be 3 v.?]

16511 JOHN, V.V. Freedom to learn: the challenge of the autonomous college. Delhi: Vikas, 1976. 108p.

16512 JOSHI, K.L. Problems of higher education in India: an approach to structural analysis and reorganization. Bombay: Popular, 1977. 312p.

16513 MALIK, S.C., ed. Management and organisation of Indian universities. Simla: IIAS, 1971. 283p.

16514 MATHAI, S. The University Grants Commission. In Amrik Singh & P.G. Altbach, eds. The higher learning in India. ND: Vikas, 1974, 25-37.

16515 University finance: a statistical profile. ND: Assoc. of Indian Univ., 1978. 181p.

16516 WOOD, G. Planning university reform: an Indian case study. In Comp. Educ. R. 16,2 (1972) 267-80.

e. university teachers and teaching

16517 CHITNIS, S. & P.G. ALTBACH, eds. The Indian academic profession: crisis and change in the teaching community. Delhi: Macmillan, 1979. 192p.

16518 INDIA (REP.). UNIV. GRANTS CMSN. Psychology in Indian universities. ND: 1968. 71p.

16519 ______. Report on the status of teaching of sociology and social anthropology. ND: 1978-79. 2 v.

16520 ______. Sociology in Indian universities; report of the University Grants Commission Review Committee. ND: 1966. 72p.

16521 KABIR, HUMAYUN, et al. The teaching of social sciences in India, 1947-67. Rev. and enl. ed. Delhi: Universal Book & Stationery Co., 1968. 727p.

16522 MACPHAIL, J.R. Reflections from a Christian college. Madras: CLS, 1966. 50p.

16523 SAINI, B.S. Library organisation for higher education: the status and role of university librarian. Delhi: Ess Ess, 1976. 116p.

16524 SHAH, A.B., ed. Modernization of university teaching: teaching of natural and social sciences in India. Bombay: Nachiketa, 1969. 196p.

16525 SHILS, E. The academic profession in India. In E. Leach & S.N. Mukherjee, eds. Elites in South Asia. Cambridge: CamUP, 1970, 172-200. [1st pub. in Minerva 7 (1969) 345-72]

f. examination system and education standards

16526 DAVE, R. & W. HILL. Educational and social dynamics of an examination system: a case study of India. In Comp. Educ. R., 18,1 (1974) 24-38.

16527 Examination reform: a plan of action and the recommendations of the zonal workshops. ND: Univ. Grants Cmsn., 1976. 44p.

16528 Examinations in higher education; report of a seminar...Jan. 27-31, 1971 at New Delhi. ND: Inter-Univ. Board of India & Ceylon, 1971. 84p.

16529 INDIA (REP.). UNIV. GRANTS CMSN. Evaluation in higher education, a report of the seminars on examination reform organised by the University Grants Commission under the leadership of Dr. Benjamin S. Bloom. ND: 1961. 272p.

16530 ______. Report on examination reform. ND: 1962. 115p.

16531 ______. Report on standards of university education. ND: 1965. 282p.

16532 NARAIN, R. Falling educational standards; an analysis. Agra: L.N. Agarwal, 1970. 134p.

16533 NATARAJAN, V. Monograph on internal assessment for universities. ND: Assoc. of Indian Univ., 1977. 177p.

16534 RAYCHAUDHURI, T. Standards of university education in India: some neglected questions. In Conspectus 2,1 (1966) 13-24.

16535 RUDOLPH, L.I. & S.H. RUDOLPH. "Standards" in democratised higher education: an analysis of the Indian experience. In EPW 5,3/4/5 (1970) 209-18.

16536 SAIYIDAIN, K.G. & H.C. GUPTA. Access to higher education in India, a depth study of university admission procedures. Prepared for the International Study of University Admissions, sponsored by United Nations Educational, Scientific and Cultural Organisation and International Association of Universities. ND: UNESCO & Intl. Assoc. of Universities, 1962. 101p.

16537 SINGH, A. & H.S. SINGHAL, eds. The management of examinations. ND: Assoc. of Indian Univ., 1977. 258p.

16538 SRIVASTAVA, H.S. & PRITAM SINGH & V.S. ANAND. Reforming examinations: some emerging concepts. ND: Natl. Council of Educ. Res. & Training, 1978. 92p.

g. post-graduate and professional education
i. teacher education

16539 CHAURASIA, G. Challenges and innovations in education. ND: Sterling, 1977. 244p.

16540 DEVE GOWDA, A.C. Teacher education in India. Bangalore: dist. Bangalore Book Bureau, 1973. 233p.

16541 LIPKIN, J.P. Secondary school teacher education in transition. London: Asia, 1970. 123p. (Indian educ. series, 1)

16542 MEHRA, C. National survey of elementary teacher education in India. ND: NCERT, 1970. 181p.

16543 PANDEY, B.N. & C. MEHRA & N. SABHARWAL. A decade of state institutes of education. ND: NCERT, 1974.

16544 SABHARWAL, N. & D.N. KHOSLA. Teacher education in India at secondary level: report on affiliation terms & conditions. ND: NCERT, 1974. 59p.

16545 SHUKLA,R.S. Emerging trends in teacher education. Allahabad: Chugh, 1977. 228p.

16546 SRIVASTAVA, R.C. & K. BOSE. Theory and practice of teacher education in India. Allahabad: Chugh, 1978. 344p.

16547 Teacher education curriculum: a framework prepared for National Council for Teacher Education. ND: NCERT, 1978. 67p.

16548 VASISHTHA, K.K. Teacher education in India: a study in new dimensions. ND: Concept, 1979. 259p.

ii. commerce, management, and public administration education

16549 AGARWALA, A.N. Education for business in a developing society. East Lansing, MI: Inst. for Intl. Business & Econ. Dev. Studies, Michigan State U., 1969. 124p.

16550 CHANDRAKANT, L.S. Management education and training in India. Bombay: Taraporevala, 1973. 91p.

16551 Commerce education [special issue]. In Indian J. of Commerce 29,2 (1976) 21-70.

16552 FAROOQUEE, Q.H. Some problems of commerce and management education in India analysed. Aligarh: Faculty of Commerce, Aligarh Muslim U., 1963. 17p.

16553 HILL, T.M., et al. Institution building in India: a study of international collaboration in management education. Boston: Div. of Res., Harvard Business School, 1973. 384p.

16554 JAIN, R.K. Higher education for business in India; a critique of commerce education in Indian universities. Nagpur: Vishwa Bharati Prakashan, 1966. 117p.

16555 MAHESHWARI, S., ed. The teaching of public administration in India. ND: IIPA, 1979. 97p.

16556 SINGH, C.D. Graduate education in commerce. Calcutta: Naya Prokash, 1979. 273p.

iii. legal education

16557 ALEXANDROWICZ, C.H. Legal education (1947-1956). In Humayun Kabir, et al. The teaching of the social sciences in India. Delhi: Universal Book & Stationery Co., 1968, 191-200.

16558 EKBOTE, G.R. Educational system in India and legal education. Waltair: Andhra U. Press, 1973. 68p.

16559 GETMAN, J.G. Development of Indian legal education: the impact of the language problem. In J. of Legal Educ. 21 (1969) 513-22.

16560 KULSHRESHTHA, V.D. Directory of law colleges in India. 2nd ed. Bombay: N.M. Tripathi, 1971. 373p.

16561 OJHA, G.K. Legal education (1956-67). In Humayun Kabir, et al. The teaching of the social sciences in India (1947-1967). Delhi: Universal Book & Stationery Co., 1968, 389-410.

16562 VON MEHREN, A.T. Law and legal education in India: some observations. In Harvard Law R. 78 (1965) 1180-89.

iv. engineering education

16563 DE, A.K. Engineering education and its challenges. In Commerce 137,3526 (1978) 205-09.

16564 EISEMON, T. U.S. educated engineering faculty in India. Bombay: TISS, 1974. 129p. (TISS series, 33)

16565 RAGHAVAN, K. & L. MANOCHA. Educational cost functions - a study of engineering educational institutions in India. In Manpower J. 11,3 (1975) 50-87.

v. agricultural education: universities and rural institutes

16566 DIONNE, R. The historical foundations of Indian agricultural universities. In J. Di Bona, ed. The context of education in Indian development. Durham: DUPCSSA, 1972, 10-20. (Its monograph & occ. papers series, 13)

16567 INDIA (REP.). CMTEE. ON HIGHER EDUC. FOR RURAL AREAS. Rural Institutes; report on the committee on higher education for rural areas. ND: 1955. 77p.

16568 INDIA (REP.). CMTEE. ON PLAN PROJECTS. STUDY TEAM ON SELECTED EDUC. SCHEMES. Report on rural institutes. ND: 1963. 73p.

16569 INDIA (REP.). CMTEE. ON RURAL HIGHER EDUC., 1967. Report. ND: Min. of Educ. & Youth Services, 1970. 126p. [G. Ramachandran, Chm.]

16570 A method of assessing progress of agricultural universities in India; Joint Indo-American Study Team report. ND: ICAR, 1970. 2 v.

16571 NAIK, K.C. Agricultural education in India; institutes and organizations. ND: ICAR, 1961. 178p.

16572 NAIK, K.C. & A. SANKARAM. A history of agricultural universities. Rev. and enl. ed. ND: Oxford & IBH, 1972. 296p.

16573 READ, H. Partners with India; building agricultural universities. Champaign-Urbana: U. of Illinois College of Agriculture, 1974. 157p.

16574 SINGH, Y.P. & U. PAREEK & D.R. ARORA. Diffusion of an interdiscipline: social sciences in agricultural education. Delhi: New Hights, 1974. 191p.

vi. medical education [see VIII. G. 6. b., above]

7. Students in Indian Higher Education [for students in politics, see III. B. 2. d. ii., above]

16575 CHATTERJI, S.K., ed. Student participation. Madras: CLS, for CISRS, 1970. 90p. [student involvement in educ. admin.]

16576 CORMACK, M.L. She who rides a peacock; Indian students and social change. NY: Praeger, 1962. 264p.

16577 EYDE, L.D. Characteristics and problems of Indian universities and their students. In Intl. R. of Educ. 9 (1963-64) 461-76.

16578 GANGULI, H.C. Foreign students: the Indian experience. ND: Sterling, 1974. 126p.

16579 GUPTA, R.C., ed. Youth in ferment. Delhi: Sterling, 1968. 143p.

16580 KING, A.D. The IIT Graduate: 1970; aspirations, expectations, and ambitions. In EPW 5,36 (1970) 1497-1510.

16581 MISRA, D.K. & C.M. JAIN & S.L. DOSHI. Youth, university and community. ND: S. Chand, 1975. 133p.

16582 NEELSEN, J.P. Student unrest in India, a typology and a socio-structural analysis. Munich: Weltforum, 1973. 101p.

16583 ROSS, R.D. Student unrest in India; a comparative approach. Montreal: McGill-Queen's U. Press, 1969. 301p.

16584 SARKAR, S.N. Student unrest: a socio-psychological study. Calcutta: India Book Exchange, 1974. 191p.

16585 SHRINIVAS RAO, K. University discipline & law: a socio-legal analysis. Hyderabad: Osmania U., 1978. 116p.

16586 SINGHAL, S. Academic leadership and student unrest. ND: Newman Group, 1977. 208p.

16587 Student unrest: problems and perspectives. ND: ICPS, 1966. 120p.

8. Elementary and Secondary Education
a. elementary education (ages 6-14), mandated under Directive Principles of the Constitution
i. general studies; primary and middle schools

16588 DESAI, D.M. Major obstacles to universal elementary education in India. In JMSUB 14 (1965) 105-23.

16589 GUPTA, R.K. A review of the recommendations of the nine national seminars on elementary education, 1961-69. ND: Natl. Inst. of Educ., 1971. 48p.

16590 INDIA (REP.). PLANNING CMSN. PROGRAMME EVAL. ORG. Problems of extension of primary education in rural areas. ND: 1967. 254p.

16591 NAIK, J.P. Elementary education in India; the unfinished business. Bombay: Asia, 1966. 165p.

16592 Primary education in rural India; participation and wastage. Bombay: Tata McGraw-Hill, 1971. 86p.

16593 SHARMA, R.C. & C.L. SAPRA. Wastage and stagnation in primary and middle schools in India. ND: NCERT, 1969. 166p.

16594 Wastage and stagnation in primary education; nine articles on the theme. In Educ. Q. 20,3 (1968) 1-46.

ii. Basic Education and Work-Experience: the Gandhian heritage

16595 HIREMATH, N.R. Basic syllabus in practice. Dharwar: Karnatak U., 1966. 304p.

16596 INDIA (REP.). ASSESSMENT CMTEE. ON BASIC EDUC. Basic education in India; report. Delhi: MPGOI, 1962. 87p. [1st pub. 1956]

16597 NATL. INST. OF BASIC EDUC. Craft education in Indian school system. Delhi: 1965. 222p.

16598 ______. Difficulties of basic school teachers. ND: 1960. 60p.

16599 ______. Research in education. 2nd ed. ND: NCERT, 1966. 136p.

16600 RAO, R.V. Sevagram; Gandhiji's ashram and other institutions in Wardha. 3rd ed. Wardha: Sevagram Ashram Pratishthan Pub., 1969. 69p. [1st pub. 1947]

16601 SHRIMALI, K.L. The future of basic education. Chandigarh: Panjab U., 1966. 63p.

16602 Special issue on basic education -- a fresh look. In Buniyadi Talim 8,1 (1965) 1-48.

16603 ULLAH, S. Thoughts on basic education. Bombay: Asia, 1963. 112p.

16604 VARMA, E. Basic education in India: its origins and development. Patna: Nagari Prakashan, 1962. 240p.

16605 VERMA, I.B. Basic education; a reinterpretation. Agra: Sri Ram Mehra, 1969. 374p.

16606 ZACHARIAH, M. Public authority and village reconstruction: the case of basic education in India. In J. of Educ. Thought 4 (1970) 94-106.

b. secondary education
i. general studies

16607 AHLUWALIA, S.P. Secondary education in India, 1947-1961: some discernible trends. In Paedagogica Historica 6,2 (1966) 343-63.

16608 CHAUBE, S.P. Secondary education for India. 2nd enl. ed. With critical evaluations of the Mudaliar Commission and second Narendra Deva Committee reports. Delhi: Atma Ram, 1956. 227p.

16609 INDIA (REP.). MIN. OF EDUC. Reconstruction of secondary education. Recommendations of the Central Advisory Board of Education, the Education Ministers' Conference, and the All India Council for Secondary Education. Delhi: 1967. 109p.

16610 INDIA (REP.). SECONDARY EDUC. CMSN. Report, October 1952-June 1953. ND: Min. of Educ. and Social Welfare, 1973. 334p. [1st pub. 1953; Chm., A. Lakshmanswami Mudaliar]

16611 MANSUKHANI, G.S. & G.S. DHILLON, eds. Whither secondary education. ND: Oxford & IBH, 1973. 252p.

16612 MUKERJI, S.N. Secondary education in India. ND: Orient Longmans, 1972. 220p.

16613 Recommendations on secondary education; a compilation prepared by the National Council of Educational Research and Training, at the request of the Education Commission. ND: NCERT, 1966. 107p.

16614 SAIYIDAIN, K.G., ed. The fourth Indian year book of education: secondary education. ND: NCERT, 1973. 530p.

16615 ZACHARIAH, M. The durability of academic secondary education in India. In Comp. Educ. R. 14,2 (1970) 152-61.

16616 ______. India: government strategies for secondary education reform, 1952-1965. In R.M. Thomas, et al., eds. Strategies for curriculum change. Scranton, PA: Intl. Textbook Co., 1968, 177-212.

2. vocational and technical education

16617 AGGARWAL, J.C. Plus 2 Committee, 1978: recommendations and observations: Adiseshiah report. ND: Arya Book Depot, 1978. 79p.

16618 CHANDRAKANT, L.S. Polytechnic education in India. Bombay: Taraporevala, 1971. 124p.

16619 ______. Technical education in India today. ND: Min. of Scientific Res. & Cultural Affairs, 1963. 107p.

16620 INDIA (REP.). MIN. OF EDUC. Facilities for technical education in India. 3rd rev. ed. ND: 1965. 2 v., 443, 227p.

16621 INDIA (REP.). NATL. REVIEW CMTEE. ON HIGHER SECONDARY EDUC. Learning to do: towards a learning and working society: report of the National Review Committee on Higher Secondary Education with special reference to vocationalisation. ND: Min. of Educ. & Social Welfare, 1978. 60p. [Chm., M.S. Adiseshiah]

16622 INDIA (REP.). SPECIAL CMTEE. ON REORGANISATION & DEV. OF POLYTECHNIC EDUC. IN INDIA. Report, 1970-71. ND: Min. of Educ. & Social Welfare, 1971. 245p. [G.R. Damodaran, chm.]

16623 INDIA (REP.). WORKING GROUP ON VOCATIONALISATION OF EDUC. & WORK EXPERIENCE. Report, Jan. 1968. ND: Planning Cmsn., 1968. 80p.

16624 NATL. INST. OF EDUC. Survey of high/higher secondary/multipurpose schools offering technical (engineering) stream/group/subject under elective/optional/diversified course, 1968. ND: 1968. 414p. [Second All-India Educational Survey, conducted by K.N. Hiriyanniah]

c. "Public Schools" and other private institutions

16625 DE SOUZA, A. Indian public schools; a sociological study. ND: Sterling, 1974. 304p.

16626 D'SOUZA, A.A. Anglo-Indian education: a study of its origin and growth in Bengal up to 1960. Delhi: OUP, 1976. 344p.

16627 INDIAN PUBLIC SCHOOLS CONF. A handbook of the Indian public schools. Issued on the 25th anniversary of the founding of the Indian Public Schools (Headmasters') Conference. ND: 1964. 124p.

16628 Judgements on minority educational rights. ND: Catholic Bishops' Conf. of India, 1974. 360p.

16629 PATEL, K. & A. VERSTRAETEN. What they think; a survey of opinions and attitudes of students in Jesuit schools and colleges in India. Delhi: Jesuit Educ. Assoc. of India, 1972. 508p.

16630 SINGH, R.P. The Indian public school. ND: Sterling, 1972. 138p.

9. Curriculum and Textbook Questions [see also VIII. H. 6. e., above]

16631 DAVE, J.P. Our changing schools; a research profile. Ahmedabad: dist. New Order Book Co., 1969. 247p. [on high school social studies teaching]

16632 INDIAN PARLIAMENTARY & SCIENTIFIC CMTEE. Science education in schools; report. ND: NCERT, 1965. 56p.

16633 KALIA, N.N. Sexism in Indian education: the lies we tell our children. ND: Vikas, 1979. 193p.

16634 Position of mathematics in India: an analysis of current syllabuses. ND: NCERT, 1965. 80p.

16635 Position of science teaching in Indian schools; a factual report. Delhi: NCERT, 1965. 155p.

16636 Position of social studies in India; an analysis of current syllabuses. ND: NCERT, 1964. 148p.

16637 RASTOGI, K.G. Preparation and evaluation of textbooks in mother tongue: principles and procedures. ND: NCERT, 1976. 103p. [1st pub. 1970]

16638 RUHELA, S.P. Sociology of sex education in India. Delhi: Dhanpat Rai, 1969. 45p.

10. Language Problems in Multilingual India
a. general studies

16639 CHATURVEDI, M.G. & B.V. MOHALE. Position of languages in school curriculum in India. ND: NCERT, 1976. 290p.

16640 DESAI, M.P. Language study in Indian education. Ahmedabad: Navajivan, 1957. 54p.

16641 JOHN, V.V. Education and language policy. Bombay: Nachiketa, 1969. 79p.

16642 KHUBCHANDANI, L.M. Study of languages in a multilingual nation: comments on Education Commission's recommendations. In BDCRI 27 (1966-67) 32-50.

16643 MAHMOOD, M. Language politics and higher education in India. In IJPS 35,3 (1974) 277-88.

16644 PATTANAYAK, D.P. Language curriculum: an approach to and structure of curriculum in Indian languages. 2nd ed., rev. and enl. Mysore: CIIL, 1977. 59p.

16645 ______. Language policy and programmes. ND: Min. of Educ. & Youth Services, 1971. 96p.

16646 SHAH, A.B., ed. The great debate; language controversy and university education. Bombay: Lalvani, 1968. 211p.

16647 SRIVASTAVA, A.K. & RAJ SHEKHAR & B.D. JAYARAM. The language load: report of the survey of the opinions of the students, parents, and teachers on the various aspects of the problem of load of learning several languages. Mysore: CIIL, 1978. 153p. (CIIL occ. monographs ser., 13)

b. problems of medium of instruction at various levels: Hindi, English, regional languages, mother tongue?

16648 CHICKERMANE, D.V. Impact of bilingualism on the progress of children in primary schools in rural areas. ND: NCERT, 1971. 53p.

16649 GAJENDRAGADKAR, P.B. The medium of instruction in Indian higher education: the language question. In Minerva 6,2 (1968) 257-67.

16650 GOEL, B.S. & S.K. SAINI. Mother tongue and equality of opportunity in education. ND: NCERT, 1972. 114p.

16651 INDIA (REP.). WORKING GROUP TO CONSIDER ALL ASPECTS OF THE QUESTION PERTAINING TO THE CHANGE OF THE MEDIUM OF INSTRUCTION FROM ENGLISH TO AN INDIAN LANGUAGE. Medium of instruction; report. ND: Univ. Grants Cmsn., 1961. 123p.

16652 THIRTHA, N.V. Babel; language dilemma in Indian schools: a study in the social foundations of Indian education. Masulipatnam: M. Seshachalam, 1962. 127p.

c. English in independent India: function and status

16653 CHATTERJI, K.K. English education in India: issues and opinions. Delhi: Macmillan, 1976. 203p.

16654 CONF. ON THE TEACHING OF ENGLISH IN SCHOOLS, DELHI, 1963. The teaching of English in schools, report. ND: NCERT, 1963. 56p.

16655 India: further steps towards the displacement of English. In Minerva 7 (1968-69) 178-234.

16656 INDIA (REP.). ENGLISH REVIEW CMTEE. Report. ND: Univ. Grants Cmsn., 1965. 56p.

16657 INDIA (REP.). STUDY GROUP ON THE TEACHING OF ENGLISH AT THE SCHOOL STAGE. Report. ND: Min. of Educ. & Youth Services, 1971. 158p. [Chm., V.K. Gokak]

16658 ______. The study of English in India; report of a study group appointed by the Ministry of Education, submitted to the Education Commission in 1965. Delhi: Min. of Educ., 1967. 271p.

16659 SINHA, S.P. English in India: a historical study with particular reference to English education in India. Patna: Janaki Prakashan, 1978. 196p.

11. Illiteracy (65% in 1981) and its Eradication

16660 GOSAL, G.S. Literacy in India: an interpretative study. In Rural Sociology 29 (1964) 261-77.

16661 INDIA (REP.). CENSUS OF INDIA, 1971. Extracts from the all India census reports on literacy, by D. Natarajan. ND: Office of the Registrar Genl., 1972. 118p. (Census centenary monograph, 9)

16662 INDIA (REP.). DIR. OF ADULT EDUC. Farmers functional literacy project; a review of fourth plan and progress in 1973. ND: 1974. 137p.

16663 INDIA (REP.). PANEL ON LITERACY AMONG INDUSTRIAL WORKERS. Report on literacy among industrial workers. ND: Cmtee. on Plan Projects, 1964. 56p.

16664 KRISHAN, GOPAL & MADHAV SHYAM. Pattern of city literacy. In EPW 9,20 (1974) 795-800.

16665 RAY, P. & J.M. KAPOOR. The retention of literacy. Delhi: Macmillan, 1975. 119p.

16666 SOPHER, D.E. Sex disparity in Indian literacy. In his An exploration of India. Ithaca: CornellUP, 1980, 130-88.

16667 TILAK, J.B.G. Regional inequality in literacy in India. In Indian J. of Adult Educ. 39,1 (1978) 14-22.

16668 TIRTHA, R. Areal patterns of literacy in India. In Manpower 1,3/4 (1965-66) 88-118.

16669 VAIDYANATHAN, K.E. Some analysis of the trends in literacy in India based on the provisional results of the 1971 census. In AV 14 (1972) 446-56.

12. Social, i.e., Adult, Education

16670 ALL INDIA ADULT EDUC. CONF., 24TH, BHUBANESWAR, 1970. Adult education in the seventies: report.... ND: Indian Adult Educ. Assn., 1970. 90p.

16671 ______., 26TH, JAIPUR, 1973. Adult education and national development: report.... ND: Indian Adult Educ. Assn., 1976. 55p.

16672 ______., 28TH, JABALPUR, 1975. Non-formal education: a remedy and a restorer: report.... ND: Indian Adult Educ. Assn., 1976. 43p.

16673 ANAND, SATYAPAL. University without walls: the Indian perspective in correspondence education. ND: Vikas, 1979. 204p.

16674 CHIB, S.S. Teaching by correspondence in India. ND: Light & Life, 1977. 188p.

16675 CONF. ON UNIV. ADULT EDUC., BHOPAL, 1965. Report. Jaipur: U. of Rajasthan, 1965. 80p.

16676 DEVADAS, R.P. Planning and programming adult education: report of the Workshop of Principals on the University's Participation in the National Adult Education Programme. Madras: U. of Madras, 1978. 140p.

16677 DIRECTORY OF VOLUNTARY ORGANISATIONS WORKING IN THE FIELD OF ADULT EDUCATION IN INDIA. ND: Min. of Educ. & Social Welfare, 1974. 232p.

16678 DUTTA, S.C. India. In J. Lowe, ed. Adult education and nation-building.... Edinburgh: Edinburgh U. Press, 1970, 137-49.

16679 INDIA (REP.). CMTEE. ON PLAN PROJECTS. STUDY TEAM FOR SELECTED EDUC. SCHEMES. Report on social education. ND: 1963. 77p.

16680 INDIA (REP.). DIR. OF ADULT EDUC. Adult education components in the development schemes of Government of India. ND: Min. of Educ. & Social Welfare, 1979. 251p.

16681 INDIA (REP.). MIN. OF EDUC. All India report of social education, for 1947-1951. Delhi: 1954. 195p.

16682 INDIA (REP.). MIN. OF EDUC. & SOCIAL WELFARE. National Adult Education Programme: an outline. ND: 1978. 25p.

16683 KAKKAR, N.K. Workers' education in India. ND: Sterling, 1973. 404p.

16684 NAIK, J.P. Some perspectives on non-formal education. Bombay: Allied, 1977. 116p.

16685 STYLER, W.E. Adult education in India. Bombay: OUP, 1966. 114p.

13. Special Problems of Women and Girls in Indian Education

16686 DESAI, C. Girls' school education and social change. Bombay: A.R. Sheth, 1976. 288p.

16687 INDIA (REP.). CMTEE. TO LOOK INTO THE CAUSES FOR LACK OF PUBLIC SUPPORT ... FOR GIRLS' EDUC. AND TO ENLIST PUBLIC COOP. Report. ND: Min. of Educ., 1965. 97p.

16688 INDIA (REP.). EDUC. CMSN. Recommendations on women's education. ND: 1965. 112p.

16689 INDIA (REP.). NATL. CMTEE. ON WOMEN'S EDUC. Report, May 1958 to Jan. 1959. Delhi: Min. of Educ., 1959. 335p. [chm., Durgabai Deshmukh]

16690 NATL. SEMINAR ON ADULT EDUC. OF WOMEN IN THE CHANGING PATTERN OF SOCIETY, DELHI, 1968. Adult education of women in the changing pattern of society: report.... ND: Indian Adult Educ. Assn., 1973. 96p.

16691 PANANDIKAR, S. & N. DESAI & K. BHANSALI, eds. Future trends in women's higher education and the role of the S.N.D.T. Women's University: report of the Round Table Discussion. Bombay: Srimati Nathibai Damodara Thakarasi Mahila Vidyapitha, 1975. 170p.

IX. RELIGIO-PHILOSOPHICAL TRADITIONS IN SECULAR INDIA

A. Contemporary Indian Philosophy

16692 ANIKEEV, N.P. Modern ideological struggle for the ancient philosophical heritage of India. Calcutta: ISPP, 1969. 68p. (Soviet Indology series, 1)

16693 BURCH, G. Contemporary Vedanta philosophy. In R. of Metaphysics 9 (1955-56) 485-504, 662-80; 10 (1956-57) 122-57.

16694 CHATTERJEE, M., ed. Contemporary Indian philosophy, series two. London: Allen & Unwin, 1974. 323p.

16695 CHATTOPADHYAY, D. What is living and what is dead in Indian philosophy. ND: PPH, 1976. 656p.

16696 DAYA KRISHNA. Philosophy in India. In R. Klibansky, ed. Contemporary philosophy: a survey. Firenze: La Nuova Italia Editrice, 1971, v. 4, 564-77.

16697 DEVARAJA, N.K. Indian philosophy today. Delhi: Macmillan, 1975. 286p.

16698 ______. What is living and what is dead in traditional Indian philosophy. In PEW 26,4 (1976) 427-42.

16699 GOPALAN, S. The Hindu philosophy of social reconstruction. Madras: Centre for Advanced Study in Philosophy, U. of Madras, 1970. 108p.

16700 MOHANTY, J.N. & S.P. BANERJEE. Self, knowledge, and freedom: essays for Kalidas Bhattacharyya. Calcutta: World Press, 1978. 233p.

16701 RIEPE, D. Indian philosophy since Independence. Calcutta: Res. India Pub., 1979. 397p.

16702 SCHREINER, P. Concepts of philosophy: K.C. Bhattacharya and G.R. Malkani. In WZKS 21 (1977) 239-56.

16703 SINGH, S.P. Revival of Upaniṣadic thought in contemporary Indian philosophy. Patna: Delhi Pustak Sadan, 1974. 324p.

16704 SRIVASTAVA, R.S., ed. The philosophy of Dr. B.L. Atreya. ND: Oriental, 1977. 196p.

16705 VARMA, V.P. Philosophical humanism and contemporary India. Delhi: Motilal, 1979. 203p.

B. Hinduism: Transregional Trends and Movements

16706 ASHBY, P.H. Modern trends in Hinduism. NY: ColUP, 1974. 143p.

16707 BECKER, R. DE. L'Hindouisme et la crise du monde moderne. Paris: Éditions Planète, 1966. 255p.

16708 BHAKTI PRAJNAN YATI MAHARAJ, ed. Renaissance of Gaudiya Vaishnava movement. Madras: Sree Gaudiya Math, 1978. 374p.

16709 BOWES, PRATIMA. Hindu intellectual tradition. ND: Allied, 1977. 218p.

16710 COOKE, G.B. Neo-Hindu ashrama in South India. Bangalore: CISRS, 1966. 52p.

16711 DEVARAJA, N.K. Hinduism and the modern age. ND: Islam & Modern Age Soc., 1975. 154p.

16712 GARG, R.K. Upaniṣadic challenge to science. Delhi: Sundeep, 1978. 316p.

16713 KLOSTERMAIER, K. Der moderne Hinduismus und die soziale Neuordnung Indiens. Rome: Pontificia Universitas Gregoriana, 1961. 71p.

16714 Modernism and traditional values of the Hindus - a report of a seminar. In BITCM (1966) pt. 2, 277-340.

16715 MOFFITT, J. Varieties of contemporary Hindu monasticism. In VK 57 (1970) 91-99, 128-36.

16716 PANIKKAR, R. Contemporary Hindu spirituality. In Philosophy Today 3 (1959) 112-27.

16717 ______. The unknown Christ of Hinduism. London: Darton, Longman and Todd, 1964. 165p.

16718 RANGANATHANANDA, S. Science and religion. Calcutta: Advaita Ashrama, 1978. 223p.

16719 SCOTT, R.W. Social ethics in modern Hinduism. Calcutta: YMCA, 1953. 243p.

16720 SINHA, A.K. Vedanta and modern science. Bombay: Somaiya, 1978. 284p.

16721 YUSAFJI, HABIB. Bazaar brochures. In ICQ 21,2 (1964) 21-30. [continued in subsequent issues]

C. Sects and Cults Deriving from Hinduism, in India and the West, Using English and Modern Media

1. The Export of "Hinduism" to the West - General Studies

16722 BHARATI, A. The light at the center; context and pretext in modern mysticism. Santa Barbara: Ross-Erikson, 1976. 254p.

16723 DE KALBERMATTEN, G. The advent. Bombay: Life Eternal Trust Pub., 1979. 419p.

16724 DOWNTON, J.V. Sacred journeys; the conversion of young Americans to Divine Light Mission. NY: ColUP, 1979. 304p.

16725 EBON, M., comp. Maharishi, the Guru; an international symposium. Indian ed. Bombay: Pearl Books, 1968. 164p.

16726 HARPER, M.H. Gurus, swamis, and avatars: spiritual masters and their American disciples. Philadelphia: Westminster, 1972. 271p.

16727 HUMMEL, R. Indische Mission und neue Frömmigkeit im Western. Stuttgart: Kohlhammer, 1980. 312p.

16728 HUTTEN, K. & S. VON KORTZFLEISCH, eds. Asien missioniert im Abendland. Stuttgart: Kreuz-Verlag, 1962. 296p.

16729 MCDERMOTT, R.A. Indian spirituality in the West: a bibliographical mapping. In PEW 25,2 (1975) 213-39.

16730 MAHESH YOGI, Maharishi. The science of being and art of living. ND: Allied, 1963. 365p.

16731 MEHTA, GITA. Karma Cola. London: Cape, 1980. 201p.

16732 NAYAR, T.N.K., Mrs. Mother and Bhagawan. Mangalore: Rama Sakti Mission, 1977. 178p.

16733 TRIVEDI, P. Swami Muktananda Paramahansa: the saint and his mission. Ganeshpuri: Shree Gurudev Ashram, 1971. 90p.

16734 VARMA, M.M. A saint's call to mankind: a plea for a spiritual revaluation of life. Vrindaban: Manav Sewa Sangh, 197-. 174p. [Rpt. 1957 ed.]

16735 WHITE, C.S.J. Ramakrishna's Americans: a report on intercultural monasticism. Delhi: Yugantar, 1979. 106p.

16736 WIENER, SITA. Swami Satchidananda. San Francisco: Straight Arrow, 1970. 194p.

2. Sathya Sai Baba: Popular "Miracle Man" (1926-)

16737 BALASINGHAM, C. Sai Baba and the Hindu theory of evolution. Delhi: Macmillan, 1974. 71p.

16738 BROOKE, R.T. Sai Baba, lord of the air. ND: Vikas, 1979. 414p.

16739 GOKAK, V.K. Bhagavan Sri Sathya Sai Baba: an interpretation. ND: Abhinav, 1975. 308p.

16740 MURPHET, H. Sai Baba: a man of miracles. London: Muller, 1971. 211p.

16741 ______. Sai Baba avatar: a new journey into power and glory. Delhi: Macmillan, 1978. 288p.

16742 RUHELA, S.P. & D. ROBINSON, ed. Sai Baba and his message: a challenge to behavioural sciences. Delhi: Vikas, 1976. 330p.

16743 SANDWEISS, S.H. Sai Baba, the holy man ... and the psychiatrist. San Diego, CA: Birth Day Pub. Co., 1975. 240p.

16744 SCHULMAN, A. Baba. NY: Viking Press, 1971. 177p.

3. Meher Baba (1894-1969): Parsi Spiritual Leader in the Yogic Tradition

16745 ADRIEL, J. Avatar, the life story of the Perfect Master Meher Baba. Santa Barbara: J.F. Rowny Press, 1947. 284p.

16746 HOPKINSON, H.T. Much silence: Meher Baba, his life and work. NY: Dodd, Mead, 1975. 191p.

16747 MEHER BABA. God speaks; the theme of creation and its purpose. 2nd ed. NY: Dodd, Mead, 1973. 334p.

16748 ______. The mastery of consciousness: an introduction and guide to practical mysticism and methods of spiritual development. Ed. by A.Y. Cohen. NY: Harper & Row, 1977. 202p.

16749 ______. Messages of Meher Baba, delivered in the East and West. Ahmednagar: Meher Baba Universal Spiritual Centre, 1945. 101p.

16750 ______. The path of love. NY: S. Weiser, 1976. 102p.

16751 NATU, BAL, ed. Avatar Meher Baba bibliography: 1928 to February 25, 1978: works by and about Meher Baba in English and other European languages. ND: Kris, 1978. 82p.

16752 PURDOM, C.B. The Godman. London: Allen & Unwin, 1964. 463p.

4. Ācārya Rajneesh (1931 -): Poona Magnet for Foreign Spiritual Seekers

16753 KARKARIA, B.J. Dance your way to God. In IWI 99,47 (1978) 36-41.

16754 PRASAD, R.C. The mystic of feeling; a study in Rajneesh's religion of experience. Delhi: Motilal, 1970. 229p.

16755 RAJANEESH, Acharya. I am the gate. Bombay: Jeevan Jagriti Kendra, 1972. 244p.

5. The Hare Kṛṣṇa Movement: Modern Followers of Caitanya Vaiṣṇavism

16756 DANER, F.J. The American children of Kṛṣṇa; a study of the Hare Kṛṣṇa Movement. NY: Holt, Rinehart & Winston, 1976. 118p.

16757 JUDAH, J.S. Hare Krishna and the counterculture. NY: Wiley, 1974. 301p.

16758 LEVINE, F. Strange world of Hare Krishnas. Greenwich, CT: Fawcett, 1974. 189p.

16759 MOODY, J.F. Ethic and counterculture: an analysis of the ethics of Hare Kṛṣṇa. Ph.D. Diss., Claremont Graduate School, 1978.

16760 SHARMA, A. The Hare-Krishna movement: a study. In VQ 40,2 (1974) 154-78.

D. The Buddhist Revival in Contemporary India

16761 AHIR, D.C. Buddhism in modern India. Nagpur: Bhikkhu Niwas Prakashan, 1972. 138p.

16762 FISKE, A.M. Buddhistische Bewegungen in Indien. In H. Dumoulin, ed. Buddhismus der Gegenwart. Freiburg: Herder, 1970, 72-88.

16763 HUMPHREYS, C. Sixty years of Buddhism in England (1907-1967); a history and a survey. London: Buddhist Society, 1968. 84p. + 8 pl.

16764 JATAVA, D.R. The Buddha and Karl Marx. Agra: Phoenix Pub. House, 1968. 236p.

16765 MACY, J.R. & E. ZELLIOT. Tradition and innovation in contemporary Indian Buddhism. In A.K. Narain, ed. Studies in history of Buddhism... Delhi: BR, 1980, 133-53.

16766 ZELLIOT, E. The Indian rediscovery of Buddhism 1855-1956. In A.K. Narain, ed. Studies in Pali and Buddhism. Delhi: B.R., 1979, 389-406.

16767 ______. The revival of Buddhism in India. In Asia 10 (1968) 33-45.

E. Jainism in Contemporary India

16768 BURCH, G.B. Jain philosophy and modern science. In Aryan Path 34,2 (1963) 57-61.

16769 DIWAKER, S.C. Religion and peace. 2nd ed., rev. Mathura: All India Digamber Jain Sangh, 1962. 326p.

16770 JAIN, S.K. Progressive Jains of India. ND: Shraman Sahitya Sansthan, 1975. 319p.

16771 NAIR, V.G. Jainism and Terehpanthism. Bangalore: Shri Adinath Jain Svetambar Temple, 1970. 138p.

16772 NATHAMAL, Muni. Acharya Tulasi, his life and philosophy: English version of Acharya Tulasi, jeewandarshan. Tr. N. Sahal. Churu: Adarsh Sahitya Sangh, 1968. 202p.

16773 SANGAVE, V.A. Jaina community, a social survey. Bombay: Popular, 1959. 480p.

F. Islam in Secular India

16774 DESAI, ZIYAUD-DIN A. Centres of Islamic learning in India. ND: PDMIB, 1978. 154p.

16775 HAQ, MUSHIR UL. Islam in secular India. Simla: IIAS, 1972. 106p.

16776 KARANDIKAR, M. Islam in India's transition to modernity. Bombay: Orient Longmans, 1968. 414p.

16777 LOKHANDWALLA, S.T., ed. India and contemporary

Islam. Simla: IIAS, 1971. 512p. (Its trans., 6)

16778 MATHUR, Y.B. Muslims and changing India. ND: Trimurti, 1972. 295p.

16779 SHAKIR, MOIN. Muslims in free India. ND: Kalamkar Prakashan, 1972. 156p.

G. Judaism in India Today

16780 ROLAND, J.G. The Jews of India: communal survival or the end of a sojourn? In Jewish Social Studies 42,1 (1980) 75-90.

H. Christianity: Continuing Indigenization in Theology and Personnel

1. Bibliography and Reference

16781 HAMBYE, E.R. A bibliography on Christianity in India. s.l.: Church History Association of India, 1976. 183p.

16782 List of publications on religion and society, 1953-1974. Bangalore: CISRS, 1975. 184p.

16783 VARGHESE, V.E. Review of literature on Indian Christian theology published in India during the past twenty-five years. In Indian J. of Theology 25,3/4 (1976) 133-47.

2. General Studies

16784 BANERJEE, B.N. Management of Christian organisations in India. ND: Masihi Sahitya Sanstha, 1973. 229p.

16785 THANGASAMY, D.A. India and the ecumenical movement. Madras: CLS, 1973. 56p.

16786 THOMAS, A.V. Christians in secular India. Rutherford, N.J. Fairleigh Dickinson U. Press, 1974. 246p.

3. Indian Christian Theology and the Dialogue with Hinduism

16787 AMALORPAVADASS, D.S. Towards indigenisation in the liturgy: theological reflection, policy, programme, and texts. Bangalore: Natl. Biblical, Catechetical & Liturgical Centre, 1972. 176p.

16788 AMIRTHAN, S., ed. A vision for man: essays on faith, theology, and society in honour of Joshua Russell Chandran, principal of the United Theological College, Bangalore, presented on the occasion of his Shastiabdapoorthi celebrations. Madras: CLS, 1978. 416p.

16789 BOYD, R.H.S. An introduction to Indian Christian theology. Madras: CLS, 1969. 285p.

16790 BÜRKLE, H., ed. Indische Beiträge zur Theologie der Gegenwart. Stuttgart: Evangelisches Verlagswerk, 1966. 284p.

16791 CHETHIMATTAM, J.B. Unique and universal: fundamental problems of an Indian theology. Bangalore: Centre for the Study of World Religions, Dharmaram College, 1972. 230p. (Dharmaram College studies, 11)

16792 DOCKHORN, K. Christ in Hinduism as seen in recent Indian theology. In R&S 21,4 (1974) 39-57.

16793 FAKIRBHAI, D. Khristopanishad (Christ-Upanishad). Bangalore: CISRS, 1965. 44p. (Indian Christian thought series, 3)

16794 IMMANUEL, R.D. The influence of Hinduism on Indian Christians. Jabalpur: Leonard Theological College, 1950. 251p.

16795 Indian christian theology and self identity. Bangalore: CISRS, 1978. 100p. [pub. as R&S 25,3]

16796 KLOSTERMAIER, K. Hindu and Christian in Vrindaban. Tr. from German by A. Fonseca. London: Student Christian Movement Press, 1969. 118p.

16797 LE SAUX, H. [Swami ABHISHIKTANANDA] Hindu-Christian meeting point within the cave of the heart. Tr. by S. Grant. Rev. ed. Delhi: ISPCK, 1976. 139p. [French ed. 1966]

16798 MOFFITT, J. Journey to Gorakhpur; an encounter with Christ beyond Christianity. NY: Holt, Rinehart & Winston, 1972. 304p.

16799 MOOKENTHOTTHAM, A. Indian theological tendencies. Berne: P. Lang, 1978. 320p.

16800 PAREKH, M.C. & D. FAKIRBHAI. Manilal C. Parekh, 1885-1967, Dhanjibhai Fakirbhai, 1895-1967: a selection. Madras: CLS, for the Dept. of Res. and Post-graduate Studies, United Theological College, Bangalore, 1974. 303p. (Library of Indian Christian theology, 2)

16801 PERINGALLOOR, J. Salvation through Gita and Gospel. Bombay: Inst. of Indian Culture, 1972. 109p.

16802 SAMARTHA, S.J. The Hindu response to the unbound Christ. Madras: CLS, 1974. 202p.

16803 STEWART, W. India's religious frontier; Christian presence amid modern Hinduism. London: SCM Press, 1964. 183p.

16804 SUNDER RAO, M. Concerning Indian Christianity. ND: YMCA Pub. House, 1973. 129p.

16805 Theology - from dialogue and for dialogue [special issue]. In R&S 24,4 (1977) 1-81.

4. Christian Evangelization and Resistance: the Niyogi Committee (1956) and Legislation on Conversion

16806 AMALORPAVADASS, D.S. L'Inde à la rencontre du Seigneur. Paris: Éditions Spes, 1964. 367p.

16807 HOEFER, H. Debate on mission. Madras: Gurukul Lutheran Theological College & Res. Inst., 1979. 470p.

16808 KAROKARAN, A. Evangelization and diakonia: a study in the Indian perspective. Bangalore: Dharmaram Pub., 1978. 285p.

16809 LE JOLY, E. Proclaiming Christ. Allahabad: St. Paul Pub., 1970. 416p.

16810 MCGAVRAN, D.A. Ethnic realities and the church: lessons from India. South Pasadena, CA: Wm. Carey Library, 1979. 262p.

16810a Truth shall prevail (Satyameva Jayate); reply to Niyogi Cmtee. Bombay: Catholic Assn., 1957. 276p.

5. The Roman Catholic Church in India

16811 The Catholic Directory of India. ND: St. Paul Pub. [latest v. 1972, 877p.; pub. irregularly]

16812 GODWIN, C.J. Indian religious at the cross-roads. Bombay: St. Paul Pub., 1975. 153p.

16813 GRACIAS, VALERIAN, Cardinal. Cardinal Gracias speaks: a selection of speeches, addresses, sermons, articles, broadcasts by the Cardinal during the last 48 years. Bombay: St. Paul Pub., 1977. 825p.

16814 ______. To revive old memories. Bombay: Examiner Press, 1977. 306p.

16815 ALL INDIA SEMINAR ON CHURCH IN INDIA TODAY, BANGALORE, 1969. Report. ND: Catholic Bishops' Congerence of India Centre, 1969. 167p.

16816 LE SAUX, H. [Swami Abhishiktananda] Towards the renewal of the Indian Church. Bangalore, Dharmaram College, 1970. 99p.

16817 PINTO, C.D. Indian Catholic reference book. Bombay: Catholic Assn. of Bombay, 1864. 338p.

16818 POTHACAMURY, T. The Church in Independent India. Maryknoll, NY: Maryknoll Pub., 1958. 90p.

16819 PLATTNER, F. Visage de l'église - L'Inde. Paris: Desclée, 1965. 284p.

6. Protestant and Other Denominations

16820 APPASAMY, A.J. A bishop's story. Madras: CLS, 1969. 185p. [Church of S. India]

16821 BAYNE, S.F. Ceylon, North India, Pakistan; a study in ecumenical decision. London: SPCI, 1960. 249p.

16822 Cathedrals in modern India; a report of the conference held in March 1968 under the auspices of Synod Theological Cmsn. of the Church of South India. Bangalore: 1968. 55p.

16823 CHURCH OF INDIA, PAKISTAN, BURMA, AND CEYLON. The

constitution, canons, and rules of the Church of India, Pakistan, Burma, and Ceylon. Rev. according to the decisions of the General Council, 1960. Delhi: ISPCK, 1962. 315p. [with Index 1962, 24p.]

16824 PAUL, R.D. Ecumenism in action: a historical survey of the Church of South India. Madras: CLS, 1972. 370p.

16825 ______. First decade and account of the Church of South India. Madras: CLS, 1958. 294p.

16826 PAUL, R.D. & J. KUMARESON. Church of South India - Lutheran Conversation; a historical sketch. Madras: CLS, 1970. 72p.

16827 LAVAN, S. Unitarians and India: a study in encounter and response. Boston: Beacon Press, 1977. 217p.

16828 RAWLINSON, A.E.J. The Church of South India. London: Hodder and Stoughton, 1951. 127p.

X. CULTURE AND COMMUNICATION IN INDEPENDENT INDIA

A. Mass Media and Communication

1. Bibliography and Reference

16829 MEHROTRA, R.K., ed. Mass communication in India; an annotated bibilography. Singapore: Asian Mass Communication Res. & Inf. Centre, 1976. 216p.

16830 Press and advertisers year book. ND: India News & Features Alliance. 1962-.

2. General Studies

16831 AHUJA, B.N. & S. BATRA. Mass communications: press, radio, T.V., films, advertising, and other media: with special reference to Indian conditions. ND: Varma Bros., 1978. 329p.

16832 APTE, M.L., ed. Mass culture, language and arts in India: Papers presented at a symposium at Duke U., Durham, N. Carolina. Bombay: Popular, 1978. 202p.

16833 CHATTERJEE, R.K. Mass communications. 2nd ed., rev. ND: NBT, 1978. 198p. (India, the land & people) [1st ed. 1973]

16834 DESAI, A.V. Economic aspects of the Indian press. ND: Press Inst. of India, 1971. 51p.

16835 INDIA (REP.). CMTEE. ON BROADCASTING & INFO. MEDIA, 1966. Report on coordination of media of mass communication. ND: MIB, 1966. 41p. [Chm. Ashok K. Chanda]

16836 Mass media in India 1978. ND: PDMIB, 1978. 285p. [annual]

16837 MEHTA, D.S. Mass communication and journalism in India. Bombay: Allied, 1979. 313p.

16838 NARAYANA MENON, V.K. The communications revolution. ND: NBT, 1976. 89p.

16839 PARMAR, S. Folk music and mass media. ND: Communication Pub., 1977. 112p.

16840 ______. Traditional folk media in India. ND: Gekha Books, 1975. 176p.

16841 ROBERGE, G. Mediation: the action of the media in our society. ND: Manohar, 1980. 210p.

16842 SARKAR, C. Challenge and stagnation: the Indian mass media. ND: Vikas, 1969. 116p.

16843 SEMINAR ON MASS COMMUNICATION MEDIA & ADULT LITERACY, NEW DELHI, 1966. Mass media and adult literacy, report. ND: Indian Inst. of Mass Communication, 1966. 135p.

16844 SRINIVASA RAO, R. Multi media communication: report of the seminar held at Tirupati.... Tirupati: Dept. of Edu., Sri Venkateswara U., 1973. 160p.

16845 TEWARI, I.P. Mass communication in India: a review. ND: Indian Inst. of Mass Communication, 1971. 48p.

16846 Women and the reluctant media. [special issue] In Vidura 13,1 (1976) 1-48.

3. Government and the Media: Law, Censorship, and Press Freedom

16847 DESAI, M.V. Communication policies in India. Paris: UNESCO, 1977. 88p.

16848 KHOSLA, G.D. Pornography and censorship in India. ND: Indian Book Co., 1976. 168p.

16849 MANKEKAR, D.R. The press vs the government, before and during emergency. Delhi: Clarion Books, 1978. 182p.

16850 MINATTUR, J. Freedom of the press in India: constitutional provisions and their application. The Hague: M. Nijhoff, 1961. 136p.

16851 MUDHOLKAR, J.R. Press law. Calcutta: Eastern Law House, 1975. 180p.

16852 NARASIMHAN, V.K. The press, the public, and the administration. ND: IIPA, 1961. 68p.

16853 NATARAJAN, S. Democracy and the press. Bombay: Manaktalas, 1965. 38p.

16854 NOORANI, A.G., ed. Freedom of the press in India; proceedings of a seminar held in Srinagar, May 1970. Bombay, Nachiketa, 1971. 143p.

16855 The press and the law; papers from a seminar.... ND: Press Inst. of India, 1968. 90p.

16856 RADHAKRISHNAMURTI, B. Indian press laws. Guntur: India Law House, 1976. 295p.

16857 SARKAR, C. The government and the press. In JNAA 14,1 (1969) 100-12.

16858 SEN, SACHIN. The press and democracy. Calcutta: General Printers & Pub., 1957. 162p.

16859 SHAH, A.B. The roots of obscenity; obscenity, literature and the law. Bombay: Lalvani, 1968. 148p.

16860 SORABJI, S.J. Law of press censorship in India. Bombay: N.M. Tripathi, 1976. 272p.

4. Journalism and the Indian Press since Independence

a. general studies

16861 AHUJA, B.N. Theory & practice of journalism: set to Indian context. Delhi: Surjeet, 1979. 375p.

16862 BASU, J.N. Romance of Indian journalism. Calcutta: Calcutta U., 1979. 617p.

16863 BHATTACHARJEE, A. The Indian press, profession to industry. Delhi: Vikas, 1972. 216p.

16864 CHALAPATHI RAU, M. The press. ND: NBT, 1974. 211p.

16865 EAPEN, K.E. Daily newspapers in India: their status and problems. In Journalism Q. 44 (1967) 520-532.

16866 ______. India: an overview. In John A. Lent, ed. The Asian newspapers' reluctant revolution. Ames: Iowa State U. Press, 1971, 282-298.

16867 INDIA (REP.). ENQUIRY CMTEE. ON SMALL NEWSPAPERS. Report, 1965. ND: PDMIB, 1966. 308p. [chm. R.R. Diwakar]

16868 INDIA (REP.). FACT-FINDING CMTEE. ON NEWSPAPER ECONOMICS, 1972. Report. ND: PDMIB, 1975. 698p. [chm. Bhabatosh Datta]

16869 INDIA (REP.). PARLIAMENT. ADVISORY CMTEE. ON THE PRESS COUNCIL, 1968. Report. ND: PDMIB, 1969. 102p.

16870 INDIA (REP.). PRESS CMSN., 1952. Report. Delhi: MPGOI, 1954. 3v. v.1, 540p.; v.2, 287p.; v.3, 453p. [chm. G.S. Rajadhyaksha; v.2 also issued as: J. Natarajan, History of Indian Journalism. ND: MPGOI, 1954]

16871 JAGANNATHAN, N.S. Mass communication - the press: proceedings of a seminar held in Bangalore, December 1973. Bombay: Leslie Sawhny Programme of Training for Democracy, 1973. 59p.

16872 KOSCHWITZ, H. Publizistik in der Entwicklungs - demokratie: Situationen und Probleme der modernen indischen Press. In IAF 4,4 (1973) 587-598.

16873 LUIZ, T. Indian Catholic press: a survey. Bombay:

Communications Coordination Centre, 1972. 105p.

16874 NARASIMHAN, V.K. The making of editorial policy; a study of the Indian press. Madras: dist. P. Varadachari, 1956. 88p.

16875 PRESS INST. OF INDIA. Emerging estate; papers from seminars held by the Press Institute of India and the International Press Institute. ND: Orient Longmans, 1966. 178p.

16876 SARKAR, C. The changing press. Bombay: Popular, 1967. 126p.

16877 ______. Press councils and their role. Delhi: Press Inst. of India, 1965. 18p. (Its pub., 4)

16878 ______. What ails the Indian Press? a multiplicity of diseases. In Vidura 6,2 (1969) 18-21.

16879 SEMINAR ON EDITORIAL CONTENT, DELHI, 1965. The newspaper and the community. ND: Press Inst. of India, 1966. 63p.

16880 What ails the Indian press? diagnosis and remedies. ND: Somaiya, 1970. 128p.

16881 WOLSELEY, R.E., ed. Journalism in modern India. 2nd rev. ed. Bombay: Asia, 1964. 279p. [1st ed. 1953]

b. memoirs and biographies of Indian journalists

16882 BHATIA, P. All my yesterdays. Delhi: Vikas, 1972. 179p.

16883 CHALAPATHI RAU, M. MC: selected editorials and other writings of M. Chalapathi Rau, editor, 'National Herald' for 30 years from 1946 onwards. ND: Young Asia, 1976. 448p.

16884 ______. Magnus & muses: off the record musings of 'MC' (M. Chalapathi Rau). Ed. by H.Srivastava. Gurgaon: Academic Press, 1980. 240p.

16885 GHOSH, K. No apology. Bombay: Orient Longman, 1971. 128p.

16886 KARAKA, D.F. Then came Hazrat Ali; autobiography, 1972. Bombay: 1972. 354p.

16887 MORAES, F.R. Without fear or favour; a selection of articles. Ed. by R.C. Cooper. Delhi: Vikas, 1974. 155p.

16888 ______. Witness to an era: India 1920 to the present day. London: Weidenfeld & Nicolson, 1973. 332p.

16889 NAYAR, KULDIP. In jail. ND: Vikas, 1978. 152p.

16890 SAHNI, J.N. Truth about the Indian press. Bombay: Allied, 1974. 259p.

c. news agencies and news management

16891 CHANDRA, J.P., ed. Proceedings of the Seminar on Non-Aligned News Pool held in New Delhi on February 12, 1978. ND: All India Newspaper Editors Conf., 1978. 146p.

16892 CHOWDHURY, NEERJA. The news agencies. In Vidura 15,3 (1978) 145-52.

16893 INDIA (REP.). CMTEE. ON NEWS AGENCIES. Report, August 1977. ND: PDMIB, 1977. 165p. [chm. Kuldip Nayar]

16894 INDIAN INST. OF MASS COMMUNICATION. A manual for news agency reporters. ND: Allied, 1980. 144p.

16895 MANKEKAR, D.R. One-way free flow: neo-colonialism via news media. Delhi: Clarion Books, 1978. 171p.

16896 REDDY, C.G.K. Does Samachar need restructuring? A critique of Kuldip Nayar Committee's report. In EPW 12,30 (1977) 1705-09.

5. The Indian Publishing Industry: Books and Periodicals

16897 ALTBACH, P.G. Publishing in India: an analysis. Delhi: OUP, 1975. 115p.

16898 DASH, B.K., ed. Indian publishing in the seventies. ND: NBT, 1978. 97p.

16899 DUGGAL, K.S. Book publishing in India. ND: Marwah, 1980. 267p.

16900 ISRAEL, S. Indian publishing: the changing scene. In Quest 68 (1971) 50-58.

16901 KANJILAL, S. The university press in India. In Scholarly publishing 4 (1972) 72-80.

16902 PRAKASH, OM & C. FYLE. Books for the developing countries: South Asia and Africa. Paris: UNESCO, 1966.

16903 Publishing: getting ready for the boom. In Business India (Jul. 24-Aug. 6, 1978) 21-33.

16904 SANKARANARAYANAN, N. Book distribution and promotion problems in South Asia. Madras: UNESCO, 1964.

16905 SEMINAR ON BOOK PUBLISHING, NEW DELHI, 1969. Report. Delhi: Fed. of Pub. & Booksellers Assoc. in India, 1969. 182p.

16906 SINGH, ATTAR, et al. National Book Trust. In Round Table 1,19 (1972) 28-42.

16907 STC and the booktrade. In Indian Publisher & Bookseller 23 (1973) 195-226.

16908 VINOD KUMAR, ed. Book industry in India: problems and prospects. ND: Fed. of Pub. & Booksellers Assoc. in India, 1980. 164p.

6. Libraries and Information Services

16909 ATHERTON, P. Putting knowledge to work; an American view of Ranganathan's Five laws of library science. Delhi: Vikas, 1973. 158p.

16910 BHATTACHARJEE, K.K. Modern trends in librarianship in India. Calcutta: World Press, 1979. 203p.

16911 GHOSH, G.B. & B.N. BANERJEE. Trends of information service in India. Calcutta: World Press, 1974. 286p.

16912 GOYAL, S.P., ed. Indian librarianship; essays in honour of S.R. Bhatia. Delhi: Scientific Book Store, 1972. 207p.

16913 GUJRATI, B.S. Library organization and its growth in India. 2nd rev. ed. ND: Hemkunt Press, 1970. 134p.

16914 INDIA (REP.). PLANNING CMSN. WORKING GROUP ON LIBRARIES. A survey of public library services in India. Delhi: Indian Library Assoc., 1965. 66p.

16915 INDIA (REP.). UNIV. GRANTS CMSN. Universities and college libraries. ND: 1965. 228p. [report & seminar proc.]

16916 KAULA, P.N., ed. Library movement in India. Delhi: Delhi Library Assn., 1958. 158p.

16917 ______. The National Library of India; a critical study. Bombay: Somaiya, 1970. 175p.

16918 KESAVAN, B.S. India's National Library. Calcutta: Natl. Library, 1961. 300p.

16919 MISRA, J. History of libraries and librarianship in modern India since 1850. Delhi: Atma Ram, 1979. 188p.

16920 MOOKERJEE, S.K. Development of libraries and library science in India. Calcutta: World Press, 1969. 534p.

16921 PRASHER, R.G. Indian library literature; an annotated bibliography. ND: Today & Tomorrow's, 1971. 504p.

16922 RANGANATHAN, S.R. Documentation: genesis and development. Delhi: Vikas, 1973. 310p.

16923 ______. New education and school library: experience of half a century. Delhi: Vikas, 1973. 510p.

16924 ______, ed. Documentation and its facets. Bombay: Asia, 1963. 639p.

16925 SAHA, J. Special libraries and information services in India and the U.S.A. Metuchen, NJ: Scarecrow Press, 1969. 216p.

16926 SAHAI, SHRINATH. Library and the community. ND: Today & Tomorrow's, 1973. 282p.

16927 SEN, N.B., ed. Development of libraries in New India.... ND: New Book Soc., 1965. 355p.

16928 ______, ed. Progress of libraries in New India. ND: New Book Soc., 1967. 247p.

16929 SRIVASTAVA, A.P. Ranganathan, a pattern maker: a syndetic study of his contributions. ND: Metropolitan, 1977. 137p.

16930 UMAPATHY SETTY, K. Librarianship: change or status quo? ND: Vikas, 1977. 192p.

7. Public Relations and Advertising

16931 DHEKNEY, V.M. Public relations in business and public administration in India. Poona: Vaishali Prakashan, 1972. 253p.

16932 KAUL, J.M. Public relations in Inida. Calcutta: Naya Prokash, 1976. 216p.

16933 PANDYA, I.H. English language in advertising: a linguistic study of Indian press advertising. Delhi: Ajanta, 1977. 192p.

16934 SENGUPTA, S. Cases in advertising and communication management in India. Ahmedabad: Indian Inst. of Mgmt., 1976. 240p.

8. Radio and Television Broadcasting
a. general studies

16935 AWASTHY, G.C. Broadcasting in India. Bombay: Allied, 1965. 268p.

16936 DUGGAL, K.S. What ails Indian broadcasting? ND: Marwah, 1980. 183p.

16937 INDIA (REP.). CMTEE. ON BORADCASTING & INFORMATION MEDIA, 1966. Radio & television; report. ND: MIB, 1966. 249p. [chm. Ashok K. Chanda]

16938 INDIA (REP.). WORKING GROUP ON AUTONOMY FOR AKASHVANI & DOORDARSHAN. Akash Bharati, National Broadcast Trust: report. ND: MIB, 1978. 2v.

16939 MASANI, M. Broadcasting and the people. ND: NBT, 1976. 179p. (India, the land & people)

16940 MULLICK, K.S. Tangled tapes; the inside story of Indian broadcasting. ND: Sterling, 1974. 159p.

b. radio (ākāshvāṇi): All-India Radio government monopoly

16941 BHARGAWA, R. Radio broadcasting in India - a bibliography. In Vidura 12,3 (1975) 199-203.

16942 NARENDRA KUMAR. Educational radio in India. ND: Arya Book Depot, 1967. 116p.

16943 NEURATH, P.M. Radio farm forum as a tool of change in Indian villages. In CDCC 10 (1962) 175-83.

c. television: Doordarshan government network

16944 DHAWAN, B.D. Economics of television in India. ND: S. Chand, 1974. 182p.

16945 DUA, M.R. Programming potential of Indian television: with special reference to education, economic growth, and social change. ND: Communication Pub., 1979. 167p.

16946 INDIA (REP.). ALL INDIA RADIO. Social education through television; an All India Radio - UNESCO pilot project. Paris: UNESCO, 1963. 44p.

16947 NARENDRA KUMAR & JAI CHANDIRAM. Educational television in India. ND: Arya Book Depot, 1967. 119p.

16948 Television; how far - how fast? [special issue] In Vidura 13,3 (1976) 63-107.

d. Satellite Instructional Television Experiment (SITE) for rural development

16949 AGRAWAL, B.C. Television comes to village: an evaluation of SITE. Ahmedabad: Space Applications Centre, Software Systems Group, Res. & Evaluation Cell, 1978. 207p.

16950 ______, et al. Satellite Instructional Television Experiment: social evaluation: impact on adults. Bangalore: India Space Res. Org., 1977. 2v.

16951 Another TV, a reportage on the experiences of the space applications centre. In Seminar 232 (1978) 10-40.

16952 BOROOAH, R. & J.S. JHALA. Television goes to village India. In Indian Horizon 24,1 (1975) 13-22.

16953 DASGUPTA, K. & B.K. PRASAD, eds. SITE: a select bibliography. In Vidura 13,3 (1976) 129-31.

16954 RAHMAN, SAULAT. Educational television (Udayabhanu): an exploratory study of educational satellite broadcast television programme in Orissa. ND: Min. of Educ. & Social Welfare, 1977. 173p.

16955 Satellite Instructional Television Experiment. [special issue]. In Vidura 11,2 (1974) 526-79.

16956 Satellite Instructional Television Experiment: SITE Winter School, January 16-28, 1976. Ahmedabad: Space Applications Centre, Indian Space Res. Org., 1976. 449p.

16957 SINHA, B.P. Television in diffusion of farm information; a motivational study. Delhi: New Heights, 1974. 148p.

16958 UN-UNESCO PANEL ON SITE EXPERIENCES, AHMEDABAD, 1977. Satellite instructional television experiment. Oct. 31-Nov. 5, 1977. Ahmedabad: Space Applications Centre, Indian Space Res. Org., 1978. 61p.

9. Indian Cinema: World's Largest Film Industry
a. bibliography and reference

16959 ADARSH, B.K. Film industry of India. Bombay: Adarsh, 1963. 1129p.

16960 DHARAP, B.V., ed. Indian films, 1977 & 1978. Poona: Motion Picture Enterprises, 1979. 660p. [annual editions from 1972]

16961 GULAWANI, V.N., ed. Films Division catalogue of films, 1949-1972. Bombay: Films Div., MIB, 1974. 655p.

16962 RANGOONWALLA, R. Indian filmography; silent & Hindi films, 1897-1969. Bombay: J. Udeshi, 1970. 471p.

16963 ______. Indian films index: 1912-1967. Bombay: J. Udeshi, 1968. 130p.

b. general studies of Indian cinema

16964 BARNOUW, E. & S. KRISHNASWAMY. Indian film. NY: ColUP, 1963. 301p.

16965 BHARATI, A. Anthropology of Hindi films. In Folklore(C) 18,9 (1977) 288-300.

16966 DIRECTORATE OF FILM FESTIVALS. Retrospective, 1954-1978. ND: MIB, 1979. 88p.

16967 Documentary in national development; report of a Seminar on the Role of Documentary Films in National Development held at Vigyan Bhawan on May 1-4, 1967. Delhi: Indian Inst. of Mass Communication, 1968. 161p.

16968 Films and films; a symposium on the present state of our film industry. In Seminar 9 (1960) 12-45.

16969 Films in India: symposium. In Cultural Forum 12,1/2 (1969-70) 9-95.

16970 GARGI, B.D. Screen adaptation of Indian literature. In J.R. Brandon, ed. The performing arts in Asia. Paris: UNESCO, 1971, 113-21.

16971 GAUR, MADAN. Other side of the coin (an intimate study of the Indian film industry). Bombay: Trimurti, 1973. 347p.

16972 INDIA. INDIAN CINEMATOGRAPH CMTEE. Report, 1927-1928. Madras: Supt., Govt. Press, 1928. 226p.

16973 INDIA (REP.). FILM ENQUIRY CMTEE., 1949. Report. ND: PDMIB, 1951. 339p. [S.K. Patil, chm.]

16974 Indian cinema - what are we missing? [special issue]. In Vidura 14,1 (1977) 3-56.

16975 JANKI DASS. My misadventures in filmland. ND: Newman Group, 1980. 223p.

16976 JAIN, R.D. The economic aspects of the film industry in India. Delhi: Atma Ram, 1960. 327p.

16977 JOSHI, P.C. Balraj Sahni: an intimate portrait. Delhi: Vikas, 1974. 132p.

16978 MAHMOOD, H. The kaleidoscope of Indian cinema. ND: Affiliated East-West Press, 1974. 219p.

16979 MENON, R.R. K.L. Saigal, the pilgrim of the swara. Delhi: Clarion Books, 1978. 111p.

16980 PARRAIN, P. Regards sur le cinema indien. Paris: Ed. du Cerf, 1969. 400p.

16981 RANGOONWALLA, F. Guru Dutt, 1925-1965; a monograph. Poona: Natl. Film Archive, 1974. 133p.

16982 ______. 75 years of Indian cinema. ND: Indian Book Co., 1975. 168p.

16983 RAY, R.M. Film seminar report, 1955. ND: Sangeet Natak Akademi, 1956. 271p.

16984 RAY, S. Our films, their films. Bombay: Orient Longman, 1976. 219p.

16985 ROBERGE, G. Chitra bani; a book on film appreciation. Calcutta: Chitra Bani, 1974. 274p.

16986 SARKAR, K. Indian cinema to-day: an analysis. ND: Sterling, 1975. 167p.

16987 SETON, M. The Indian cinema. In Indian Horizon 24,2/3 (1975) 54-79.

c. film censorship

16988 INDIA (REP.). ENQUIRY CMTEE. ON FILM CENSORSHIP. Report. ND: MIB, 1969. 202p. [Chm., G.D. Khosla]

16989 INDIA (REP.). LAWS, STATUTES. Law relating to cinemas in India. Ed. by C.L. Bafna. Jaipur: Bafna Law Pub., 1978. 800p.

16990 VASUDEV, A. Liberty and licence in the Indian cinema. ND: Vikas, 1978. 221p.

B. The Arts in India; The New Role of Government as Patron Since 1947

16991 INDIA (REP.). REVIEWING CMTEE. FOR THE THREE AKADEMIES (SAHITYA, LALIT KALA AND SANGEET NATAK) & THE INDIAN COUNCIL FOR CULTURAL RELATIONS. Report. ND: Min. of Educ., 1964. 124p.

16992 INDIAN COUNCIL FOR CULTURAL RELATIONS. I.C.C.R., 1950-68. ND: 1969. 103p.

C. Literatures of Independent India - the Pan-Indian Languages and General Literary Scene

1. General Studies of Indian Literatures in Various Languages

a. surveys and studies

16993 COPPOLA, C., ed. Marxist influences and South Asian literatures. East Lansing: Asian Studies Center, Michigan State U., 1974. 2 v.

16994 JOSHI, V. Contemporary Indian literature: 1950-1970. In LEW 15,1 (1972) 38-54.

16995 JOTWANI, M.W., ed. Contemporary Indian literature and society. ND: Heritage, 1979. 251p.

16996 KOHLI, S., ed. Aspects of Indian literature: the changing pattern. Delhi: Vikas, 1975. 179p.

16997 Language and literature survey (1975-76). In IL 20,3 (1977) 128p.

16998 The literary journal in India. In IWT 3,4 (1969) 3-75.

16999 MACHWE, P.B. Four decades of Indian literature; a critical evaluation. ND: Chetana, 1976. 160p.

17000 ______. Modernity and contemporary Indian literature. ND: Chetana, 1978. 186p.

17001 ______. Renaissance in Indian literature. Calcutta: United Writers, 1979. 172p.

17002 MALIK, HAFEEZ. The Marxist literary movement in India and Pakistan. In JAS 26 (1967) 649-64.

17003 Modernity and contemporary Indian literature. Simla: IIAS, 1968. 443p.

17004 NARASIMHAIAH, C.D., ed. Indian literature of the past fifty years, 1917-1967. Mysore: U. of Mysore, 1970. 371p.

17005 NARASIMHAIAH, G.D. & S. NAGARAJAN, eds. Studies in Australian and Indian literature: proceedings of a seminar. ND: ICCR, 1971. 280p.

17006 Problems of modern Indian literature. Calcutta: Stat. Pub. Soc., 1975. 202p.

17007 PATTANAYAK, D.P. Trends in juvenile literature in India: papers submitted to the 14th Session of the All-India Juvenile Literary Conference, Mysore, March 8-10, 1975. Mysore: CIIL, 1976. 212p.

17008 SAHITYA AKADEMI. Contemporary Indian literature; a symposium. Delhi: PDMIB, 1957. 299p.

17009 SINGH, MAHEEP. Social change as depicted in the contemporary Indian literature. In J. of Intercultural Studies 4 (1977) 21-50.

17010 SRINIVASA IYENGAR, K.R., ed. Indian literature since independence; a symposium. ND: Sahitya Akademi, 1973. 372p.

17011 VATSYAYAN, S.H. The role of the writer in contemporary Indian society. In IAF 2,4 (1971) 526-34.

b. anthologies - prose and poetry

17012 BANDYOPADHYAY, P., ed. Hundred Indian poets: an anthology of modern poetry by one hundred Indian poets. Calcutta: Oxford & IBH, 1977. 112p.

17013 BHARATI, S., ed. Indian poetry today. Calcutta: Rupambara Prakashan, 1969-. v. 1,2,3-.

17014 CEVET, D., ed. The shell and the rain; poems from new India. London: Allen & Unwin, 1973. 107p.

17015 DARUWALLA, K.N., ed. Two decades of Indian poetry, 1960-1980. ND: Vikas, 1980. 176p.

17016 Fragrant flowers: a literary collection from some Sahitya Akademi award winners; authors' own selection. ND: PDMIB, 1969. 175p.

17017 GABRIEL, M.C. & G. GABRIEL, eds. Call it a day; a selection of modern Indian stories. Delhi: Siddhartha Pub., 1968. 200p.

17018 Indian poetry today. ND: ICCR, 1974-75. 3 v., 658p.

17019 JUSSAWALLA, A.J., ed. New writing in India. Harmandsworth: Penguin, 1974. 320p.

17020 KHUSHWANT SINGH & QURRATULAIN HYDER, eds. Stories from India. ND: Sterling, 1974. 206p.

17021 KOHLI, S., ed. Modern Indian short stories. ND: Arnold Heinemann, 1974. 164p.

17022 Modern Indian short stories. ND: ICCR, 1975-77. 3 v., 558p.

17023 NANDY, P., ed. Modern Indian poetry. ND: Arnold Heinemann, 1974. 231p.

17024 SAHITYA AKADEMI. Contemporary Indian short stories, series 1. ND: Sahitya Akademi, 1959. 132p.

c. fiction: studies of novels and short stories

17025 MALIK, Y.K., ed. Politics and the novel in India. In CAS 6 (1975) 155p.

17026 NARASIMHAIAH, C.D., ed. Fiction and the reading public in India. Mysore: U. of Mysore, 1967. 239p. [1965 seminar]

17027 SRINIVASA IYENGAR, K.R. Contemporary Indian short story. In IL 13,3 (1970) 36-44.

d. poetry - studies

17028 Indian poetry today: poetry in translation from nineteen Indian languages and Indo-English. In IL 23,1/2 (1980) 593p.

17029 LEWIS, D. Past and present in modern Indian and Pakistani poetry. In LEW 10 (1966) 69-85; 11 (1967) 301-12.

17030 MAHAPATRA, S. Barefoot into reality. The relevance of myth and archetype for Indian poetry. In IWT 4,2 (1970) 64-74.

17031 Modern Indian fiction and the "new morality" [special issue]. In IL 21,5 (1978) 1-108.

17032 Post-Independence Indian poetry. In I. Monani, ed. Indian writers meet. Bombay: P.E.N. All-India Centre, 1966, 34-104.

17033 Trends in the Indian short story [special section]. In IL 21,1 (1978) 33-114.

e. studies of contemporary Indian theatre

17034 Aspects of theatre in India today. In Cultural Forum 2 (1960) 41-66.

17035 CHALAPATHI RAO, I.V. Mimicry and monoacting: world renowned Venumadhav. Hyderabad: Trust Pub. Co., 1978. 39p. + 32 pl.

17036 RANGACHARYA, A. Towards a professional theatre. In SN 10 (1968) 48-53.

17037 SRINIVASA IYENGAR, K.R., ed. Drama in modern India, and the writer's responsibility in a rapidly changing world. Symposia at the fourth P.E.N. All-India Writer's Conf., Baroda, 1957. Bombay: P.E.N. All-India Centre, 1961. 201p.

2. Hindi Literature of Independent India

a. general studies

17038 GAEFFKE, H.P.T. Hindi literature in the twentieth century. Wiesbaden: Harrassowitz, 1978. 118p. (HIL, 8:5)

17039 MACHWE, P.B. Stylistics and literary criticism in Hindi. In Triveni 38,2 (1969) 21-33.

b. fiction

17040 ANSARI, D. Changes in the Hindi new short story of the 1960's. In AO 43,1 (1975) 33-52.

17041 ______. Die Frau im modernen Hindi-Roman nach 1947. Berlin: Akademie-Verlag, 1970. 238p. (Deutsche Akademie der Wissenschaften zu Berlin. Inst. für Orientforschung. Veröffentlichung, 68) [with English summary]

17042 ______. Indian social reality of the early 1960's as reflected in Hindi new short story. In AO 42 (1974) 289-99.

17043 JAI RATAN, tr. Contemporary Hindi short stories. Calcutta: Writers Workshop, 1962. 103p.

17044 MCGREGOR, R.S. Aspects of Hindi fiction since independence. In SAR 8,2 (1975) 117-32.

17045 MALIK, Y.K. Contemporary political novels in Hindi: an interpretation. In CAS 6, Leiden: Brill (1975) 16-42.

17046 Mohan Rakesh issue (1925-1972). In JSAL 9,2-3 (1973) 267p.

17047 SHRAWAN KUMAR & P.B. MACHWE, tr. Hindi short stories. Bombay: Jaico, 1970. 175p.

17048 SINHA, R. Social change in contemporary literature: a new approach to criticism in sociology of literature. ND: Munshiram, 1979. 88p.

c. poetry

17049 DAVE, R. Recent trends in Hindi poetry. In ATS 3,9 (1978) 322-29.

17050 MADHUKARA, M. The poetry of Mani Madhukar. Tr. by M. Ryan. ND: Lipi Prakashan, 1980. 76p.

17051 SHAH, R.C. Hindi poetry: a decade in perspective. In IWT 5,3 (1971) 124-30.

17052 VAJPEYI, K., ed. Visions and myths: contemporary Hindi poetry. ND: Indian Literary Review Editions, 1979. 132p.

17053 ZAHRA, I., tr. Seufzend streift der Wind durch Land: moderne Hindilyrik. Berlin: Verlag Volk & Welt, 1976. 202p.

3. Urdu Literature in India since 1947

17054 COPPOLA, C. Interview with Ismat Chughtai. In Mahfil 8,2/3 (1972) 169-88.

17055 ______. Interview with Rajinder Singh Bedi. In Mahfil 8,2/3 (1972) 139-55.

17056 COPPOLA, C. & M.H.K. QURESHI. A note on Sahir Ludhianvi; poems by Sahir Ludhianvi. In LEW 10 (1966) 86-97.

17057 HASSAN, M. Urdu. In K.R. Srinivasa Iyengar, ed. Indian literature since Independence.... ND: Sahitya Akademie, 1973, 346-58.

17058 NAIM, C.M. The consequences of Indo-Pakistani war for Urdu language and literature. In JAS 28 (1968) 269-83.

17059 PAUL, J. The contemporary Urdu short story. In IWT 5,2 (1971) 82-89.

17060 SAHIR LUDHIANVI, A.H. The bitter harvest: selections from Sahir Ludhianvi's verse. Tr. by Riffat Hassan. Lahore: Aziz Pub., 1977. 196p.

17061 Twenty years of the Urdu short story. In IL 19,6 (1976) 225p.

4. Sanskrit and Its Literature in Modern India

17062 INDIA (REP.). MIN. OF EDUC. & SOCIAL WELFARE. Sanskrit in India. ND: Rashtriya Sanskrit Sansthan, 1972. 498p.

17063 INDIA (REP.). SANSKRIT CMSN., 1956. Report. Delhi: MPGOI, 1958. 439p. [Suniti Kumar Chatterji, chm.]

17064 JANI, A.N. Sanskrit: its past, present and future. In JOIB 24,3/4 (1975) 373-90.

17065 RAGHAVAN, V. Sanskrit. In K.R. Srinivasa Iyengar, ed. Indian literature since Independence.... ND: Sahitya Akademi, 1973, 266-81.

17066 ______. Sanskrit writings in the first half of the present century. In JASCalcutta 9 (1967) 212-31.

17067 SATYAVRAT, U. Sanskrit dramas of the twentieth century. Delhi: dist. Meharchand Lachhmandas, 1971-. v. 1, 441p.

17068 SHARMA, N.K. Linguistic and educational aspirations under a colonial system: a study of Sanskrit education during the British rule in India. Delhi: Concept, 1976. 242p.

17069 SHUKLA, H.L. Renaissance in modern Sanskrit literature. Raipur, M.P.: Alok Prakashan, 1969-. v. 1, 126p.

5. Indo-English Literature Since Independence

a. general studies

17070 FISKE, A.M. Karma in five Indian novels. In LEW 10 (1966) 98-111.

17071 GOKAK, V.K. English in India, its present and future. NY: Asia, 1964. 183p.

17072 HARREX, S.C. The fire and the offering; the English-language novel of India, 1935-70. Calcutta: Writers Workshop. 2 v.

17073 HEMENWAY, S.I. The novel in India. Calcutta: Writers Workshop, 1975. v. 1, The Anglo-Indian novel, 163p.; v. 2, The Indo-Anglian novel, 125p.

17074 MEHTA, P.P. Indo-Anglian fiction: an assessment. 2nd rev. and enl. ed. Bareilly: Prakash Book Depot, 1979. 394p.

17075 MOHAN, RAMESH, ed. Indian writing in English: papers read at the Seminar on Indian English held at the Central Inst. of English and Foreign Languages, Hyderabad, July 1972. Bombay: Orient Longman, 1978. 260p.

17076 MOKASHI-PUNEKAR, S. Theoretical and practical studies in Indo-English literature. Dharwad: Karnatak U., 1978. 265p.

17077 NAIK, M.K., ed. Aspects of Indian writing in English: essays in honour of Professor K.R. Srinivasa Iyengar. Delhi: Macmillan, 1979. 319p.

17078 NAIK, M.K. & S.K. DESAI & G.S. AMUR, ed. Critical essays on Indian writing in English: presented to Armando Menezes. 2nd rev. and enl. ed. Dharwar: Karnatak U., 1972. 461p. [1st ed. 1968]

17079 NARASIMHAIAH, C.D. The swan and the eagle. Simla: IIAS, 1969. 202p.

17080 NARASIMHAN, R. Indo-English: criticism without criteria. In Indian Horizon 124,1 (1975) 45-71.

17081 NICHOLSON, K. A presentation of social problems in the Indo-Anglian and the Anglo-Indian novel. Bombay: Jaico, 1972. 272p.

17082 REDDY, G.A., ed. Indian writing in English and its audience. Bareilly: Prakash Book Depot, 1979. 306p.

17083 SHIRWADKAR, M. Image of woman in the Indo-Anglian novel. ND: Sterling, 1979. 169p.

17084 SINHA, K.N., ed. Indian writing in English. ND: Heritage, 1979. 237p.

17085 STEINBORTH, K. The Indo-English novel; the impact of the West on literature in a developing country. Wiesbaden: Steiner, 1975. 149p.

17086 VERGHESE, C.P. Problems of the Indian creative writer in English. Bombay: Somaiya, 1971. 203p.

b. linguistic studies of Indian English

17087 DUSTOOR, P.E. Missing and intrusive articles in Indian English. In Allahabad U. Studies 31 (1954) 1-70.

17088 Indian English. In A bibliography of Indian English. Hyderabad: Central Inst. of Eng. & Foreign Languages, 1972, pt. 2, 23p.

17089 KACHRU, BRAJ B. English in South Asia. In M.B. Emeneau & C.A. Ferguson, eds. Linguistics in South Asia. The Hague: Mouton, 1969, 627-78. (CTL, 5)

17090 SPENCER, J. The Anglo-Indians and their speech: a socio-linguistic essay. In Lingua 16 (1966) 57-70.

17091 SUBBA RAO, G. Indian words in English: a study in Indo-British cultural and linguistic relations. Oxford: OUP, 1954. 139p.

17092 VERMEER, H.J. Das Indo-Englische. Situation und linguistische Bedeutung, mit Bibliographie. Heidelberg: Julius Groos Verlag, 1969. 98p.

c. Indo-English poetry - anthologies and general studies

17093 ANNIAH GOWDA, H.H. The use of images in contemporary Indian verse in English. In WLWE 20 (1971) 61-76.

17094 DARUWALLA, K.N., ed. Two decades of Indian poetry, 1960-1980. ND: Vikas, 1980. 176p.

17095 DESHPANDE, G., ed. An anthology of Indo-English poetry. Delhi: Hind Pocket Books, 1974. 163p.

17096 GOKAK, V.K., ed. The golden treasury of Indo-Anglian poetry, 1828-1965. ND: Sahitya Akademi, 1970. 323p.

17097 LAL, P., ed. Modern Indian poetry in English: the Writers Workshop selection; an anthology and a credo. Calcutta: Writers Workshop, 1969. 594p.

17098 NAIK, M.K. The Indianness of Indian poetry in English. In JIWE 1,2 (1973) 1-7.

17099 NANDY, P. Indian poetry in English: the dynamics of a new sensibility. In IL 14,1 (1971) 9-18.

17100 NANDY, P., ed. Indian poetry in English 1947-1972. ND: OUP, 1972. 164p.

17101 PARTHASARATHY, R., ed. Ten twentieth-century Indian poets. NY: OUP, 1976. 114p.

17102 PEERADINA, S., ed. Contemporary Indian poetry in English: an assessment and selection. Bombay: Macmillan, 1972. 130p.

17103 SARADHI, K.P. Three Indo-Anglian women poets: Gauri Deshpande, Roshen Alkazi and Kamala Das. In JIWE 2,1 (1974) 29-35.

17104 Special English poetry in India number. In Mahfil 8,4 (1972) 146p.

d. Indian writers in English - studies of individuals

i. Mulk Raj Anand (1905 -)

17105 ANAND, MULK RAJ. Apology for heroism: a brief autobiography of ideas. 3rd ed. ND: Arnold-Heinemann, 1975. 203p.

17106 ______. Author to critic: the letters of Mulk Raj Anand. Ed. by S. Cowasjee. Calcutta: Writers Workshop, 1973. 125p.

17107 BALARAMA GUPTA, G.S. Mulk Raj Anand: a study of his fiction in humanist perspective. Bareilly: Prakash Book Depot, 1974. 163p.

17108 BERRY, M. Mulk Raj Anand: the man and the novelist. Amsterdam: Oriental, 1971. 114p.

17109 Bibliography of the novels and stories by Mulk Raj Anand in various world languages. In Contemporary Indian Literature 5,11/12 (1965) 35-41.

17110 COWASJEE, S. So many freedoms: a study of the major fiction of Mulk Raj Anand. Delhi: OUP, 1977. 205p.

17111 KULSHRESTHA, C. The hero as survivor: reflections on Anand's Untouchable. In WLWE 19,1 (1980) 84-91.

17112 LINDSAY, J. The elephant and the lotus; a study of the novels of Mulk Raj Anand. 2nd rev. ed. Bombay: Kutub Popular, 1965. 35p.

17113 MUKHERJEE, M. The tractor and the plough: the contrasted visions of Sudhin Ghose and Mulk Raj Anand. In IL 13,1 (1970) 88-101.

17114 NAIK, M.K. Mulk Raj Anand. ND: Arnold-Heinemann, 1973. 199p. (Indian writers series, 1)

17115 NIVEN, A. The yoke of pity: a study in the fictional writings of Mulk Raj Anand. ND: Arnold Heinemann, 1978. 128p.

17116 SHARMA, K.K., ed. Perspectives on Mulk Raj Anand. Ghaziabad: Vimal, 1978. 188p.

17117 SINHA, K.N. Mulk Raj Anand. NY: Twayne, 1972. 154p.

ii. R.K. Narayan (1906 -)

17118 ANNIAH GOWDA, H.H. R.K. Narayan. In Literary Half-Yearly 6 (1965) 25-39.

17119 BADAL, R.K. R.K. Narayan: a study. Bareilly: Prakash Book Depot, 1976. 84p.

17120 BERRY, M. Ramayana and Narayana: epic transformed. In AsProf 7,2 (1979) 131-40.

17121 GEROW, E. The quintessential Narayan. In LEW 10,1/2 (1960) 1-18.

17122 HARREX, S.C. R.K. Narayan's the printer of Malgudi. In LEW 13,1/2 (1969) 68-82.

17123 HOLMSTROM, L. The novels of R.K. Narayan. Calcutta: Writers Workshop, 1973. 130p.

17124 PANDURANGA RAO, V. The art of R.K. Narayan. In JCL 5 (1968) 29-40.

17125 RAIZADA, H. R.K. Narayan: a critical study of his works. ND: Young Asia, 1969. 204p.

17126 SINGH, R.S. R.K. Narayan: The guide; some aspects. Delhi: Doaba House, 1971. 91p.

17127 SUNDARAM, P.S. R.K. Narayan. ND: Arnold-Heinemann, 1973. 164p. (Indian writers series, 6)

17128 VENKATACHARI, K. R.K. Narayan's novels: acceptance of life. In IL 13,1 (1970) 73-87.

17129 VENUGOPAL, C.V. The master of comedy: R.K. Narayan as a short story writer. In JKU(H) 13 (1969) 177-87.

17130 WESTBROOK, P.D. The short stories of R.K. Narayan. In JCL 5 (1968) 41-51.

iii. Raja Rao (1909 -)

17131 NAIK, M.K. Raja Rao. NY: Twayne, 1972. 163p.

17132 ______. "The serpent and the rope": the Indo-Anglian novel as epic legend. In M.K. Naik & S.K. Desai & G.S. Amur, eds. Critical essays on Indian writing in

English. Dharwar: Karnatak U., 1968, 214-48.

17133 NARASIMHAIAH, C.D. Raja Rao. ND: Arnold-Heinemann, 1973. 170p. (Indian writers series, 4)

17134 ______. Raja Rao's "Kantapura" - an analysis. In M.K. Naik & S.K. Desai & G.S. Amur, eds. Critical essays on Indian writing in English. Dharwar: Karnatak U., 1968, 270-95.

17135 RAO, K.R. The fiction of Raja Rao. Aurangabad: Parimal, 1980. 164p.

iv. Nissim Ezekiel (1924 -)

17136 GARMAN, M. Nissim Ezekiel - pilgrimage and myth. In M.K. Naik & S.K. Desai & G.S. Amur, eds. Critical essays on Indian writing in English. Dharwar: Karnatak U., 1968, 106-21.

17137 KARNANI, CHETAN. Nissim Ezekiel. ND: Arnold Heinemann, 1974. 192p. (Indian writers, 9)

17138 KHER, I.N., ed. Nissim Ezekiel Issue. In JSAL 11,3/4 (1976) 288p.

17139 TARANATH, R. Nissim Ezekiel. In Quest 74 (1972) 1-17.

17140 TARANATH, R. & M. BELLIAPA. The poetry of Nissim Ezekiel. Calcutta: Writers Workshop, 1966. 19p.

17141 VERGHESE, C.P. The poetry of Nissim Ezekiel. In IL 15,1 (1972) 63-75.

v. Dom Moraes (1938 -)

17142 LAL, P. Dom Moraes: stray notes on his poetry. In M.K. Naik & S.K. Desai & G.S. Amur, eds. Critical essays on Indian writing in English. Dharwar: Karnatak U., 1969, 160-63.

17143 MORAES, D.F. From east and west: a collection of essays. Delhi: Vikas, 1971. 207p.

17144 ______. Gone away; an Indian journey. Boston: Little, Brown, 1960. 239p.

vi. A.K. Ramanujan (1929 -)

17145 NAGAJARAN, S. A.K. Ramanujan. In Quest 74 (1972) 18-37.

17146 PARTHASARATHY, R. How it strikes a contemporary: the poetry of A.K. Ramanujan. In Literary Criterion 12,2/3 (1976) 187-97.

vii. Manohar Malgonkar (1913 -)

17147 AMUR, G.S. Manohar Malgonkar. ND: Arnold-Heinemann India, 1973. 155p. (Indian writers series, 3)

17148 DAYANAND, Y.J. Initiatory motifs in Manohar Malgonkar's The Princes. In Mahfil 8,2-3 (1972) 223-35.

17149 ______. Interview with Manohar Malgonkar. In WLWE 12 (1973) 260-87.

17150 ______. Rhythm in M. Malgonkar's The Princes. In LEW 15,1 (1972) 55-73.

17151 MALHOTRA, M.L. Manohar Malgonkar: a novelist with an old-world air. In his Bridges of literature: twenty-three critical essays in literature. Ajmer: Sunanda Pub., 1971, 193-204.

viii. Anita Desai (1937 -)

17152 BELLIAPPA, M. Anita Desai: a study of her fiction. Calcutta: Writers Workshop, 1971. 52p.

17153 MALHOTRA, M.L. Anita Desai: a writer with a promise. In his Bridges of literature: twenty-three critical essays in literature. Ajmer: Sunanda Pub., 1971, 205-11.

17154 RAMACHANDRA RAO, B. The novels of Mrs. Anita Desai: a study. ND: Kalyani Publishers, 1977. 65p.

ix. Kamala Markandaya (1924 -)

17155 CHANDRASEKHARAN, K.R. East and West in the novels of Kamala Markandaya. In M.K. Naik & S.K. Desai & G.S. Amur, eds. Critical essays on Indian writing in English. Dharwar: Karnatak U., 1968, 62-85.

17156 HARREX, S.C. A sense of identity: the novels of Kamala Markandaya. In JCL 6 (1971) 65-78.

17157 NARAYANA RAO, K.S. Kamala Markandaya: the novelist as craftsman. In IWT 8 (1969) 32-40.

17158 ______. The novels of Kamala Markandaya: a contemporary Indo-Anglian novelist. In LEW 15,2 (1972) 209-18.

17159 PARAMESWARAN, U. India for the western reader - a study of Kamala Markandaya's novels. In Texas Q. 11,2 (1968) 231-47.

17160 VENKATESWARAN, S. The language of Kamala Markandaya's novels. In Literary Criterion 9,3 (1970) 57-67.

x. Khushwant Singh (1915 -)

17161 DULAI, S.S. The legacy of paternalism: the sociopolitical syndrome in Khushwant Singh's fiction. In Mahfil 5,1/2 (1968-69) 1-8.

17162 KULSHRESTHA, C. Khushwant Singh's fiction: a critique. In IWT 4,1 (1970) 19-26.

17163 KHUSHWANT SINGH. Khushwant Singh's India; a mirror for its monsters and monstrosities. Ed. by Rahul Singh. Bombay: IBH Pub. Co., 1970. 232p.

17164 SHAHANE, V.A. Khushwant Singh. NY: Twayne, 1972. 176p.

17165 ______. Theme, title and structure in Khushwant Singh's train to Pakistan. In Literary Criterion 9,3 (1970) 68-76.

xi. Ruth Prawer Jhabvala (1927 -)

17166 BELLIAPPA, M. A study of Jhabvala's fiction. In Miscellany 43 (1971) 24-40.

17167 HARTLEY, L. R. Prawer Jhabvala, novelist of urban India. In LEW 9 (1966) 265-73.

17168 JHABVALA, R.P. An experience of India. NY: W.W. Norton, 1972. 220p.

17169 SHAHANE, V.A. Ruth Prawer Jhabvala. ND: Arnold-Heinemann, 1976. 198p. (Indian writers series, 11)

17170 VARMA, P.N. A note on the novels of R. Prawer Jhabvala. In Rajasthan U. Studies in English 5 (1971) 87-96.

17171 WILLIAMS, H.M. The fiction of Ruth Prawer Jhabvala. Calcutta: Writers Workshop, 1973. 60p.

17172 ______. Strangers in a backward place: modern India in the fiction of Ruth Prawer Jhabvala. In JCL 6,1 (1971) 53-64.

xii. other prominent Indo-Anglian writers, including Overseas Indians

17173 CHANDRASEKHARAN, R.K. Bhabani Bhattacharya. ND: Arnold-Heinemann, 1974. 179p. (Indian writers ser., 7)

17174 CHAUDHURI, N.C. The autobiography of an unknown Indian. Berkeley: UCalP, 1968. 506p. [1st pub. 1951]

17175 DASGUPTA, S. Pritish Nandy. ND: Arnold-Heinemann, 1976. 184p. (Indian writers series, 12)

17176 DESAI, S.K. Santha Rama Rau. ND: Arnold-Heinemann, 1976. 96p. (Indian writers series, 13)

17177 FISHER, M. The women in Bhattacharya's novels. In WLWE 11,2 (1972) 95-108.

17178 JAIN, J. Nayantara Sahgal. ND: Arnold-Heinemann, 1978. 176p. (Indian writers series, 16)

17179 KOHLI, D. Kamala Das. ND: Arnold-Heinemann, 1975. 128p.

17180 NARAYAN, S.A. Sudhin N. Ghose. ND: Arnold-Heinemann, 1973. 156p. (Indian writers series, 5)

17181 SHARMA, K.K. Bhabani Bhattacharya, his vision and themes. ND: Abhinav, 1979. 156p.

17182 THEROUX, P. V.S. Naipaul, an introduction to his work. London: Deutsch, 1972. 144p.

17183 VERGHESE, C. Nirad C. Chaudhuri. ND: Arnold-Heinemann, 1973. 118p.

D. Contemporary Art in India

1. General Studies

17184 ANAND KRISHNA. A living hereditary artist of the Mughal school. In LK 1/2 (1955) 77-78.

17185 ANAND, M.R. The four initiators of the contemporary experimentalism. In LKC 2 (1964) 1-5.

17186 APPASAMY, J. An intorduction to modern Indian sculpture. ND: ICCR, 1970. 40p. + 60p. of ill.

17187 ______. Portfolio of contemporary paintings. ND: Lalit Kala Akademi, 1969-.

17188 ______. Portfolio of contemporary sculpture. ND: Lalit Kala Akademi, 1970-.

17189 ______, ed. 25 years of Indian art; painting, sculpture & graphics in the post-independence era. ND: Lalit Kala Akademi, 1972. 32p. + 32p. of ill.

17190 ASIA FOUNDATION. Ten contemporary painters from India. San Francisco: 1963. 28p.

17191 Contemporary Indian painters. Delhi: PDMIB, 195_. 4p. + 26pl.

17192 CRAVEN, R.C., Jr. Contemporary art in India. In RL 34, 1/2 (1964) 28-33.

17193 Drawings by fourteen contemporary artists of Bengal. Calcutta: Mukherjee & Mullick, 1970. 35p.

17194 GOSWAMY, B.N. Indian painting today: the subverted tradition. In SAR 5,1 (1971) 19-28.

17195 Indian art since the early 40s: a search for identity. Madras: Artists' Handicrafts Assoc. of Cholamandal Artists' Village & Progressive Painters' Assoc., 1974. 171p.

17196 KAPUR, G. Contemporary Indian artists. ND: Vikas, 1978. 225p.

17197 ______. Pictorial space: a point of view on contemporary Indian art: an exhibition, December 14, 1977 to January 3, 1978. ND: Lalit Kala Akademi, 1978. 80p.

17198 ______. Some characteristic attitudes in contemporary Indian painting. In IAC 15,2 (1966) 145-54.

17199 KHANNA, K. Trends in modern Indian art. In Conspectus 2,1 (1966) 34-40.

17200 MITRA, ASOK. Four painters. Calcutta: New Age Pub., 1965. 74p.

17201 NARAYAN, BADRI. Artists of the third epoch. In LKC 3 (1965) 21-23.

17202 NATL. GALLERY OF MODERN ART, NEW DELHI. Selected expressionist paintings from the collection of the National Gallery of Modern Art. ND: The Gallery, 1975. 48p.

17203 RAMACHANDRA RAO, P.R. Contemporary Indian art. Hyderabad: the author, 1969. 49p.

17204 Some modern Indian painters. ND: Info. Services, GOI, 1965. 60p.

2. Studies of Individual Artists

17205 ALKAZI, E. M.F. Husain, the modern artist & tradition. ND: Art Heritage, 1978. 38p.

17206 BARTHOLEMEW, R.L. & S.S. KAPUR. Husain. NY: Abrams, 1971. 200p.

17207 BHAGAT, D. Bhagat. ND: Lalit Kala Akademi, 1965. 10p. + 29pl.

17208 BRUNNER, E. A painter's pilgrimage: Elizabeth Brunner's Buddhist paintings from India, Nepal, Burma, Sri Lanka, and Thailand. ND: Hungarian Info. & Cultural Center, 1978. 31 + 16pl.

17209 BRUNNER, E.F. A vision of India: the art of Elizabeth Sass Brunner and Elizabeth Brunner. Bombay: Allied, 1979. 85p.

17210 CHAUDHURI, S. Sankho Chaudhuri. Ed. by J. Appasamy. ND: Lalit Kala Adademi, 1970. 9p. + 13pl.

17211 DALLAS, C. Painting of Cumi Dallas. Bombay: J.V. Navlakhi, 1964. 17 + 40p.

17212 DAVIERWALLA, A.M. A.M. Davierwalla. ND: Lalit Kala Akademi, 1971. 40p.

17213 HEBBAR, K.K. An artist's quest. ND: Abhinav, 1974. 11p. + 15pl.

17214 HUSAIN, M.F. Husain. ND: Lalit Kala Akademi, 1961. 8p. + 21pl.

17215 ______. Husain. Bombay: Vakil, 1969. 44p.

17216 KAR, C. Chintamoni Kar. ND: Lalit Kala Akademi, 1965. 1v.

17217 KRISHNA REDDY, N. Krishna Reddy. Ed. by J. Appasamy. ND: Lalit Kala Akademi, 1974. 40p.

17218 MOOKERJEA, S. Sailoz Mookherjea. Ed. by J. Appasamy. ND: Lalit Kala Akademi, 1966. 1v.

17219 MULLINS, E.B. F.N. Souza, an introduction. London: Blond, 1962. 108p.

17220 PAUL, A. Ashit Paul, paintings and drawings. Calcutta: Dasgupta, 1973. 6p. + 17pl.

17221 RAM KUMAR. Ram Kumar. ND: Lalit Kala Akademi, 1968. 25p.

17222 ROY CHOWDHURY, D.P. Devi Prosad Roy Chowdhury. Ed. by J. Appasamy. ND: Lalit Kala Akademi, 1973. 40p.

17223 SABAVALA, J. Sabavala. Bombay: Vakils, 1966. 48p.

17224 SANYAL, B.C. Bhabesh Chandra Sanyal. Ed. by J. Appasamy. ND: Lalit Kala Akademi, 1967. 1v.

17225 SEGHAL, A.N. Amarnath Sehgal. Bombay: Marg Pub., 1964. 31p.

17226 SEN, P. Paritosh Sen. Ed. by J. Appasamy. ND: Lalit Kala Akademi, 1975. 12 + 23p.

17227 SHAMLAL. Padamsee. Bombay: Vakil, 19__. 43p.

17228 SOUZA, F.N. Words and lines. London: Villiers, 1959. 27p.

17229 SHIRGAONKAR, S.B. Artist A.H. Muller and his art. Bombay: Siragavakara, 1975. 50p.

17230 SREENIVASULU, K. K. Sreenivasulu. Ed. by J. Appasamy. ND: Lalit Kala Akademi, 1966. 1v.

E. Music, Dance, and the Performing Arts in Independent India [see Chap. One, VII.]

XI. SCIENCE AND TECHNOLOGY IN INDIA SINCE 1947

A. General Studies

17231 BHATIA, M. Science in India. ND: Survey & Planning of Scientific Res. Unit, Council of Scientific & Industrial Res., 1965. 67p.

17232 BHIDE, V.G. Aspects of science and technology in India. In Indian Horizon 24,4 (1975) 35-52.

17233 CHATTERJEE, S.P. Fifty years of science in India: progress of geography. Calcutta: Indian Science Congress Assn., 1964. 277p.

17234 GUPTA, S.P. Modern India and progress in science and technology. ND: Vikas, 1978. 164p.

17235 KHANOLKAR, V.R. Fifty years of science in India: progress of medical science. Calcutta: Indian Science Congress Assn., 1963. 50p.

17236 MOREHOUSE, W., ed. Understanding science and technology in India and Pakistan; problems of research in the social sciences and humanities. Delhi: Foreign Area Materials Center, U. of the State of N.Y., 1967. 70p.

17237 MUKERJI, B. & S.N. PRADHAN. Fifty years of science in India: Progress of physiology. Calcutta: Indian Science Congress Assn., 1963. 168p.

17238 NANDA, B.R., ed. Science and technology in India. ND: Vikas, 1977. 179p.

17239 Profiles of science [special issue]. In Seminar 238 (1979) 10-42.

17240 RAHMAN, ABDUR, ed. Science and technology in India. ND: ICCR, 1973. 535p.

17241 RAY, P. Fifty years of science in India: progress of chemistry. Calcutta: Indian Science Congress Assn., 1964. 296p.

17242 SETH, B.R. Fifty years of science in India; progress of mathematics. Calcutta: India Science Congress Assn., 1963. 44p.

17243 SUNDARA RAJAN, M. India in space. ND: PDMIB, 1976. 92p.

B. Science Policy and Development

17244 AHMAD, AQUIEL. Science and technology in development policy options for India and China. In EPW 51/52 (1978) 1079-90.

17245 BHABHA, H.J. Science and the problems of development. Bombay: Atomic Energy Establishment Trombay, 1966. 11p.

17246 GOPAL, M.H. Science, universities, and research in India: an introductory essay. Mysore: Geetha Book House, 1976. 71p.

17247 INDIA (REP.). COUNCIL OF SCIENTIFIC & INDUSTRIAL RES. CSIR in the service of rural society. ND: Council of Scientific & Industrial Res., 1978. 77p.

17248 MOREHOUSE, W. Analytical elegance or relevant analysis: institution building and public policy for science in Inida. In J. DiBona, ed. The context of education in Indian development. Durham: DUPCSSA, 1972, 21-62. (Its monograph & occ. papers series, 13)

17249 ______. Science in India; institution-building and the organizational system for research & development. Bombay: Popular, 1971. 144p.

17250 PULPARAMPIL, J.K. Science and society: a perspective on the frontiers of science policy. Delhi: Concept, 1978. 209p.

17251 RAHMAN, ABDUR. Science policy studies in India: a status report. ND: Centre for the Study of Science, Technology & Dev., ICSSR, 1977. 137p.

17252 SARABHAI, V. Science policy and national development. Delhi: Macmillan, 1974. 174p.

17253 SEMINAR ON SCIENCE IN INDIA'S BASIC PROBLEMS, DELHI, 1967. Science in India's future. Delhi: Vikas, 1969. 116p.

17254 SHAH, A.B., ed. Education, scientific policy and developing societies. Bombay: Manaktalas, 1967. 506p.

17255 SINGH, H.K. Science and our age. Bombay: Allied, 1978. 100p.

C. Science and Indian Society

17256 HALDANE, J.B.S. Science and Indian culture. Calcutta: New Age, 1965. 194p.

17257 MENON, M.G.K. Science and society. ND: PDMIB, 1973. 41p.

17258 MOREHOUSE, W. Confronting a four-dimensional problem: science, technology, society, and tradition in India and Pakistan. In Technology & Culture 8 (1967) 363-75.

17259 ______, ed. Science and the human condition in India and Pakistan. NY: Rockefeller U. Press, 1968. 230p.

17260 RAHMAN, ABDUR. Anatomy of science. Delhi: National, 1972. 94p.

17261 ______. Trimurti; science, technology, and society; a collection of essays. ND: PPH, 1972. 315p.

17262 Science and its impact on society: Indian experience: proceedings of a seminar organised by the Indian National Science Academy, New Delhi, April 22-23, 1978. ND: The Academy, 1978. 264p.

D. The Indian Scientist

1. Science as a Profession in India

17263 BHATTACHARYA, K.R. A rational scheme of recruitment and promotion for scientific personnel. In EPW 8, 1 (1973) 31-36.

17264 CHOWDHURY, P.N. & R.K. NANDY. Towards better utilisation of scientific manpower. In EPW 6,25 (1971) 1241-49.

17265 RAHMAN, ABDUR. Scientists in India: the impact of economic policies and support in historical and social perspective. In Intl. Social Science J. 22,1 (1970) 54-79.

17266 SRI CHANDRA. Scientists: a social-psychological study; report on the research project entitled 'A social-psychological study of frustration among Indian scientists.' ND: Oxford & IBH, 1970. 272p. [sponsored by Planning Commission]

2. Scientific Societies and Research Organizations

17267 ANDERSON, R.S. The life of science in India; a comparative ethnography of two research institutes. Unpub. Ph.D. diss., U. of Chicago, 1971. 395p.

17268 Our research institutions. Rev. and enl. ed. ND: PDMIB, 1974. 150p.

17269 JOSHI, N. Manpower planning in scientific research institutes. ND: Centre for the Study of Science, Technology and Dev., Council of Scientific and Industrial Res., 1979. 76p.

17270 MUKHERJI, B. & P.K. Bose, ed. A short history of the Indian Science Congress Association, with life-sketches of general presidents, 1914-1963. Calcutta: Indian Science Congress Assn., 1963. 132p.

17271 25 years of CSIR. ND: Council of Scientific and Industrial Research, 1968. 76p.

3. Biographies and Studies of Indian Scientists

17272 BAGAL, J.C. Pramatha Nath Bose. ND: P.N. Bose Centenary Cmtee., 1955. 155p.

17273 BROWN, M. Satyen Bose: a life. Calcutta: Annapurna Pub. House, 1974. 119p.

17274 C.P. Ramanujam: a tribute. ND: Narosa Pub. House, 1973. 361p. (Tata Inst. of Fundamental Res., studies in mathematics, 8)

17275 JAGJIT SINGH. Some eminent Indian scientists. Delhi: PDMIB, 1966. 131p.

17276 KANWAR SAIN. Reminiscences of an engineer. ND: Young Asia, 1978. 493p.

17277 KOTHARI, M., ed. Self-immolation of a scientist: a memoir to Dr. Vinod H. Shah, M.Sc., Ph.D. Bombay: J.H. Shah, 1973. 317p.

17278 KULKARNI, R.P. & V. SARMA. Homi Bhabha: father of nuclear science in India. Bombay: Popular, 1969. 73p.

17279 MISHRA, D.K. Five eminent scientists: their lives and work. Delhi: Kalyani, 1976. 214p.

17280 NATL. INST. OF SCIENCES OF INDIA. Biographical memoirs of fellows. ND: The Inst., 1966-70. 2v.

17281 Reminiscences of retired officers and staff of the Geological Survey of India and eminent geoscientists from the country and abroad. Calcutta: Geological Survey of India, 1976. 197p.

17282 RIPLEY, S.D., II, ed. A bundle of feathers: proffered to Salim Ali for his 75th birthday in 1971. Delhi: OUP, 1978. 241p. [Festschrift honoring Indian ornithologist Salim A. Ali]

9

The Islamic State of Pakistan: Genesis, Division, and Development, 1947–71, 1971–

I. REFERENCE AND GENERAL

A. Bibliography and Reference

17283 BAHADUR, KALIM. Survey of recent research: recent developments in Pakistan's internal and external affairs. In IS 13,1 (1974) 105-27.

17284 EBERHARD, W. Studies on Pakistan's economic and social conditions: a bibliographic note. In his Settlement and social change in Asia. Hong Kong: Hong Kong U. Press, 1967, 340-83.

17285 GUSTAFSON, W.E. Pakistan and Bangladesh: bibliographic essays in social science. Islamabad: U. of Islamabad Press, 1976. 364p.

17286 JONES, G.N. & SHAUKAT ALI, eds. Pakistan government & administration; a comprehensive bilbiography. Peshawar: PARD, 1970-74. 3v., 104, 253, 245p.

17287 Pakistan. Chronology of important events during six years of the revolutionary government in Pakistan, October 1958- June 1964. Karachi: Pakistan Pub., 1965. 159p.

17288 Pakistan central government and quasi-governmental organizations: a preliminary directory and list of IDS library holdings, 1947-71. Brighton: U. of Sussex, Inst. of Dev. Studies Library, 197-. 1v.

17289 SATYAPRAKASH, ed. Pakistan: a bibliography, 1962-74. Gurgaon: IDS, 1975. 338p. [incl. 6,500 articles from 109 Indian journals & the Times of India]

17290 SIDDIQUI, A.H. A guide to Pakistan Government publications, 1958-70. Karachi, Natl. Book Centre, 1973. 276p.

17291 ______. Social science bibliography for Pakistan, 1947-53. Karachi: PIDE, 1958. 153p.

17292 SIDDIQUI, A.H. & QAMAR AFROZ. A guide to Pakistan government publications, 1971-76. Karachi: Natl. Book Council, 1978. 131p.

B. General Histories since 1947

17293 GANKOVSKII, I.V. & L. GORDON-POLONSKAIIA. History of Pakistan, 1947-1958. Moscow: Nauka, 1964. 334p. [Rpt; Lahore: PPH, n.d.]

17294 IKRAM AZAM, R.M. Pakistan: yesterday, today, and tomorrow. Lahore: Student Services, 1976. 436p.

17295 KHALIQ, S.A. Pakistan - peace and war. London: Regency Press, 1973. 168p.

17296 MUNIR, M. From Jinnah to Zia. Lahore: Vanguard Books, 1979. 183p.

17297 Pakistan: past & present: a comprehensive study published in commemoration of the centenary of the birth of the founder of Pakistan. London: Stacey Intl., 1977. 288p.

17298 PIRZADA, S.S. Evolution of Pakistan. Lahore: All-Pakistan Legal Decisions, 1963. 309p.

17299 SINGHAL, D.P. Pakistan. Englewood Cliffs, NJ: Prentice-Hall, 1972. 214p.

17300 TEPPER, E. Pakistan in retrospect. In Intl. J. 27,3 (1972) 357-380.

17301 Twenty years of Pakistan, 1947-67. Karachi: Pakistan Pub., 1967. 850p.

17302 WILLIAMS, L.F.R. The state of Pakistan. London: Faber and Faber, 1962. 254p.

17303 WRIGGINS, W.H., ed. Pakistan in transition. Islamabad: U. of Islamabad Press, 1975. 175p.

17304 YUSUF, HAMID. Pakistan in search of democracy, 1947-77. Lahore: Afrasia Pub., 1980. 189p.

17305 ZIRING, L. & R. BRAIBANTI & W.H. WRIGGINS, eds. Pakistan: the long view. Durham, NC: DUP, 1977. 485p.

II. PAKISTAN GOVERNMENT AND POLITICS, 1947 - : ALTERNATION OF CIVIL AND MILITARY RULE, AND THE SEARCH FOR A VIABLE CONSTITUTION

A. Government Structure: Administration, Legislatures, and Judiciary

1. General Studies of Pakistan's Political System

17306 AHMAD, MUSHTAQ. Government and politics in Pakistan. 3rd rev. ed. Karachi: Space Pub., 1970. 392p.

17307 ALI, TARIQ. Pakistan: military rule or people's power. NY: Morrow, 1970. 270p.

17308 CALLARD, K. Pakistan: a political study. NY: Macmillan, 1957. 355p.

17309 ______. Political forces in Pakistan, 1947-1959. NY: Inst. of Pacific Relations, 1959. 48p.

17310 KHUHRO, H. Pakistan's experiments in democracy. In G.F. Hudson, ed. Reform and revolution in Asia. London: Allen & Unwin, 1972, 191-224. (St. Antony's Pub., 7)

17311 MAHMOOD, SAFDAR. Political study of Pakistan. Lahore: S.M. Ashraf, 1972. 395p.

17312 RAI, HAMEED ALI KHAN. Pakistan: a study in political system. Lahore: Kazi Sons, 1972. 208p.

17313 RASHIDUZZAMAN, M. Pakistan: a study of government and politics. Dacca: Ideal Library, 1967. 284p.

17314 SAYEED, K.B. The political system of Pakistan. Lahore: OUP, 1967. 321p.

17315 SHARAN, P. Government of Pakistan: development and working of the political system. Meerut: Meenakshi, 1975. 348p.

2. Constitutional History and Law - General Studies

17316 AHMAD, MASUD. Pakistan: a study of its constitutional history, 1857-1975. Lahore: Res. Soc. of Pakistan, 1978. 302p.

17317 CHOUDHURY, G.W. Constitutional development in Pakistan. 2nd ed. rev. and enl. Vancouver: U. of British Columbia, 1969. 277p. [1st pub. 1959]

17318 ______. Documents and speeches on the constitution of Pakistan. Dacca: Green Book House, 1967. 999p.

17319 GLEDHILL, A. Fundamental rights in Pakistan. In JILI 7,1/2 (1965) 70-81.

17320 MAHMOOD, SAFDAR. The constitutional foundations of Pakistan. Lahore: Publishers United, 1975. 951p.

17321 MISRA, K.P. & M.V. LAKHI & V. NARAIN. Pakistan's search for constitutional consensus. ND: Impex India, 1967. 269p. (South Asian studies, 1)

17322 PIRZADA, S.S. Fundamental rights and constitutional remedies in Pakistan. Lahore: All Pakistan Legal Decisions, 1966. 626p.

17323 WHEELER, R.S. The politics of Pakistan: a constitutional quest. Ithaca, NY: CornellUP, 1970. 346p.

2. Executive Offices: President (Governor-General before 1956), Prime Minister, and Council of Ministers

17324 CHOWDHURY, K.A. Civil service and the ministers under the Dyarchical reform. Dacca: Bureau of Natl. Reconstruction, East Pakistan, 1970. 52p.

17325 HABIB, HASSAN. Public policy: formulation and review, with particular reference to Pakistan. Lahore: Wajidalis, 1976. 188p.

3. Administration and Bureaucracy
a. general studies

17326 AHMAD, MUNEER. Aspects of Pakistan's politics and administration: five papers. Lahore: South Asian Inst., U. of Punjab, 1974. 190p.

17327 BHAMBHRI, C.P. & M. BHASKARAN NAIR. Bureaucracy in authoritarian political system: the case of Pakistan. In SAS 7,1 (1972) 79-94.

17328 BIRKHEAD, G.S., ed. Administrative problems in Pakistan. Syracuse: Syracuse U. Press, 1966. 223p.

17329 BRAIBANTI, R.J.D. Research on the bureaucracy of Pakistan; a critique of sources, conditions, and issues, with appended documents. Durham, NC: DUP, 1966. 569p.

17330 EGGER, R.A. The improvement of public administration in Pakistan. Karachi: Inter Services Press, 1953. 134p.

17331 GOODNOW, H.F. The civil service of Pakistan; bureaucracy in a new nation. New Haven: YUP, 1964. 328p.

17332 HAIDER, S.M. Public administration and administrative law. Lahore: Pakistan Law Times Pub., 1973. 296p.

17333 INAYATULLAH, M., ed. Bureaucracy and development in Pakistan. Peshawar: PARD, 1963. 453p.

17334 NIAZ, A. & AYYAZ MAHMOOD. Public administration in Pakistan; a select bibliography - Karachi. Karachi: Natl. Inst. of Public Administration, 1966. 75p.

17335 RAJA, IRFAN-UR-REHMAN. Administration: its theory, history, and practice, with special reference to Pakistan. Lahore: Catapult Publishers, 1976. 235p.

17336 RAY, J.K. Political development in Pakistan, 1947-71: role of the bureaucracy. In JIDSA 6,1 (1973) 92-124.

17337 ZIRING, L. & R. LAPORTE. The Pakistan bureaucracy: two views. In AS 14,12 (1974) 1086-1103.

b. the Civil Service

17338 ABBAS, M.B.A. Public administration training in Pakistan: a critical appraisal. In Intl. R. of Admin. Sciences 36,3 (1970) 256-76.

17339 AHMAD, MUNEER. The civil servant in Pakistan, a study of the background and attitudes of public servants in Lahore. Karachi: OUP, 1964. 288p.

17340 ______. Demokratische Entwicklungen in der pakistanischen Beamtenschaft. Dortmund: Sozialforschungsstelle, U. Muenster, 1966. 158p.

17341 ALI AHMED. Role of higher civil servants in Pakistan. Dacca: NIPA, 1968. 502p.

17342 ANISUZZAMAN, M. Training for public service; papers presented and circulated at the Seminar on Training, July 19-20, 1968. Dacca: NIPA, 1969. 134p.

17343 BRAIBANTI, R. The civil service of Pakistan: a theoretical analysis. In South Atlantic Q. 58 (1959) 258-304.

17344 ______. The higher bureaucracy of Pakistan. In R. Braibanti, ed. Asian bureaucratic systems emergent from the British imperial tradition. Durham: DUP, 1966, 209-353.

17345 ______. Public bureaucracy and judiciary in Pakistan. In J. LaPalombara, ed. Bureaucracy and political development. Princeton: PUP, 1963, 360-440.

17346 BURKI, S.J. Twenty years of the civil service of Pakistan: a reevaluation. In AS 9 (1969) 239-54.

17347 CHAUDHURI, M.A. The civil service in Pakistan: the centrally recruited civil services. 2nd rev. ed. Dacca: NIPA, 1969. 393p.

17348 GORVINE, A. The civil service under the revolutionary government in Pakistan. In Middle East J. 19 (1965) 321-36.

17349 HAIDER, S.M. Public service: the new imperatives. Lahore: Book House, 1979. 486p.

17350 HAMID, S.M. Administrative in-service training in Pakistan. In J. of Admin. Overseas 8,3 (1969) 169-77.

17351 SAYEED, K.B. Political role of Pakistan's civil service. In PA 31 (1958) 131-46.

c. corruption and administrative reform

17352 BHAMBHRI, C.P. & M. BHASKARAN NAIR. Corruption in Pakistan Civil Service: an analytical study. In SAS 6,2 (1971) 30-40.

17353 FAZAL, M.A. Judicial control of administrative action in India and Pakistan: a comparative study of principles and remedies. Oxford: OUP, 1969. 345p.

17354 HAIDER, S.M. Judicial review of administrative discretion in Pakistan. Lahore: All Pakistan Legal Decisions, 1967. 278p.

17355 ______., ed. Administrative reforms and administrative justice. Lahore: Pakistan Law Times Pub., 1973. 286p.

17356 INAYATULLAH & A.T. KHAN, ed. Administrator and the citizen. Lahore: NIPA, 1964. 100p.

17357 KAYANI, M.R. Half truths. Lahore: Pakistan Writers' Co-op. Soc., 1966. 102p.

17358 KUREISHY, M.A. Reforms in financial management in Pakistan. In Intl. J. of Admin. Sciences 39,3 (1973) 236-46.

17359 MAHESHWARI, S.R. Administrative reforms in Pakistan. In IJPS 35,2 (1974) 144-56.

17360 PAKISTAN. PAY AND SERVICES CMSN. Report, 1959-1962. Karachi: MPGOP, 1969. 478p. [Chm., A.R. Cornelius]

17361 RAHMAN, M.A., ed. Administrative reforms in Pakistan; an annotated bibliography. Lahore: PASC, 1969. 124p.

17362 RASHID, A. Corruption in Pakistan. Karachi: Naseem Pub. Corp., 1965. 68p.

17363 SHAMSUL HOQUE, A. Administrative reform in Pakistan; an analysis of Reform Commission reports in the light of United Nations doctrine. Dacca: NIPA, 1970. 380p.

4. Pakistan's Armed Forces and Their Political Role

17364 ATTIQUR RAHMAN, M. The wardens of the marches: a history of the Piffers, 1947-1971. Lahore: Wajidalis, 1980. 255p.

17365 AYOOB, MOHAMMED. The military in Pakistan's political development: its growing strength and implications. In SAS 7,1 (1972) 14-29.

17366 COHEN, S.P. Arms and politics in Pakistan. In IQ 20 (1964) 403-20.

17367 GILL, A. Army reforms. Lahore: PPH, 1979. 97p.

17368 KHAN, F.M. The story of the Pakistan Army. 2nd ed. Karachi: OUP, 1964. 250p.

17369 MOORE, R.A. Nation building and the Pakistan army, 1947-1969. Lahore: Aziz Pub., 1979. 384p.

17370 RIZVI, H.A. The military and politics in Pakistan. 2nd rev. ed. Lahore: Progressive, 1976. 378p.

17371 ROSCHMANN, H. Zur Struktur der pakistanischen

Armee. In IAF 4,4 (1973) 639-52.

17372 SAYEED, K.B. The role of the military in Pakistan. In J. Van Doorn, ed. Armed forces in society: sociological essays. The Hague: Mouton, 1968, 274-97.

17373 SHER ALI KHAN, Nawabzada. The story of soldiering and politics in India and Pakistan. Lahore: Wajidalis, 1978. 430p.

17374 WILCOX, W.A. Political role of army in Pakistan: some reflections. In SAS 7,1 (1972) 30-44.

5. The Police Service of Pakistan (PSP) and Other Security Forces

17375 HAIDER, S.M., ed. Public administration and police in Pakistan; incorporating report of a Seminar on Police Administration inaugurated by President Field Marshal Mohammad Ayub Khan. Peshawar: PARD, 1968. 331p.

17376 SEMINAR ON THE POLICE & THE CITIZEN, LAHORE, 1961. Report. Lahore: Supt., Govt. Print., West Pakistan, 1962. 282p.

6. Parliament

17377 AHMAD, MUNEER. Legislatures in Pakistan, 1947-58. Lahore: Dept. of Political Science, U. of the Punjab, 1960. 160p.

17378 ZAKARIA, N. Parliamentary government in Pakistan. Lahore: New Pub., 1958. 222p.

7. The Judiciary and the Legal System: Interaction of Parliamentary Legislation and Islamic Law

17379 AHMAD, BASHIR. Justice Shah Din; his life and writings. Lahore: 1962. 449p.

17380 AHMED, SHEIKH, ed. Some salient features of the Islamic law and constitution. Pakistan: Inst. of Arts and Design, 1970. 96p.

17381 ASHRAF, M. Supreme court of Pakistan. Lahore: Mahmood & Co., 1964. 116p.

17382 CERULLI, E. Questions actuelles de droit musulman au Pakistan: les Uṣūl al-fiqh; la donation; le contrôle des naissances. In Studia Islamica 29 (1969) 103-17.

17373 HOEBEL, E.A. Fundamental cultural postulates and judicial lawmaking in Pakistan. In AA ns 67,6 (1965) 43-56.

17384 JAFAR, M.M. Future of Islamic law in Pakistan - judicial process. In Iqbal 16,3 (1968) 3-25.

17385 KAYANI, M.R. A judge may laugh and even cry. Lahore: Pakistan Writers' Coop. Soc., 1970. 165p.

17386 KAZI, F.H. Law and politics in Pakistan. Karachi: Royal Book Co., 1976. 426p.

17387 MAUDOODI, SYED ABULʿALA, Maulana. The Islamic law and its introduction in Pakistan. Tr. from Urdu & ed. by Khurshid Ahmad. 2nd ed. Lahore: Islamic Pub., 1960. 66p.

17388 NAJIBULLAH KHAN, M. Legislation in conflict with fundamental law: a study of validity of laws in Pakistan. Karachi: Indus Pub., 1971-73. 2 v.

17389 PAKISTAN. LAW REFORM CMSN. Report, 1967-70. Karachi: MPGOP, 1970. 491p.

17390 SHAHBUDDIN, M. Recollections and reflections; being a summary of views on religious and social life in the sub-continent of Indo-Pakistan. Lahore: Supreme Court of Pakistan, 1972. 263p.

17391 TANZIL-UR-RAHMAN. Islamization of Pakistan law: surveying from Islamic point of view... Karachi: Hamdard Academy, 1978. 95p. (Islamization of Pakistan law series, 1)

8. Islam and the Political System

17392 ABBOTT, F. Islam and Pakistan. Ithaca, NY: CornellUP, 1968. 242p.

17393 AHMED, MANZOORUDDIN. Pakistan, the emerging Islamic state. Karachi: Allies Book Corp., 1966. 313p.

17394 AZIZ, K.K. Religion and politics in Pakistan (1947-1958). In JRSP 3,1/2 (1966) 74-119.

17395 AZIZ AHMAD, ed. Religion and society in Pakistan. In CAS 2 (1971) 1-104.

17396 BINDER, L. Pakistan and modern Islamic nationalist theory. In Middle East J. 11 (1957-8) 382-96.

17397 ______. Religion and politics in Pakistan. Berkeley: UCalP, 1961. 440p.

17398 CONN, H.M. Islamic socialism in Pakistan: an overview. In Islamic Studies 15,2 (1976) 111-21.

17399 IQBAL, JAVID. Ideology of Pakistan. Karachi: Ferozsons, 1971. 178p.

17400 JAWED, N.A. Islamic socialism: an ideological trend in Pakistan in the 1960's. In MW 65 (1975) 196-215.

17401 KARUNAKARAN, K.P. Interrelation between religion and politics in Pakistan. In IQ 14 (1958) 43-62.

17402 LAKHI, M.V. Islamic state controversy in Pakistan. In PSR 6,1 (1967) 79-95.

17403 MCDONOUGH, S. Some leading ideas constitutive of Pakistan's nationhood. In Islamic studies 7 (1968) 9-31.

17404 MASIH, INAYAT. The place of religion in the Islamic state of Pakistan. In M.M. Thomas & M. Abel, eds. Religion, state and ideologies in East Asia. Mysore: The East Asia Christian Conf., Cmtee. on Church & State, 1965, 127-42.

17405 MAUDOODI, SYED ABUL ʿALA, Maulana. The Islamic law and constitution. Tr. by Khurshid Ahmad. 2nd ed. Lahore: Islamic Pub., 1960. 439p.

17406 Pakistan: the politics of Islamic identity. In D.E. Smith, ed. South Asian politics and religion. Princeton: PUP, 1966, 337-449.

17407 QURESHI, I.H. The Pakistan way of life. Melbourne: W. Heinemann, 1956. 81p.

17408 ______. Perspectives of Islam and Pakistan. Karachi: Ma'aref, 1979. 222p.

17409 RAHMAN, FAZLUR. Implementation of the Islamic concept of state in the Pakistani milieu. In Islamic Studies 6,3 (1967) 205-24.

17410 SAYEED, K.B. Religion and nation building in Pakistan. In Middle East J. 17 (1963) 279-91.

9. Federalism and National Integration

17411 BAXTER, C. Constitution making: the development of Federalism in Pakistan. In AS 14,12 (1974) 1074-1085.

17412 LAKHI, M.V. Language and regionalism in Pakistan. In SAS 3,1 (1968) 47-54.

17413 MALIK, HAFEEZ. The emergence of the federal pattern in Pakistan. In JAAS(L) 8,3/4 (1973) 205-15.

17414 NATL. SEMINAR ON PAKISTANI NATIONHOOD, DACCA, PAKISTAN, 1961. Pakistan nationhood. Dacca: Bureau of Natl. Reconstruction, Govt. of East Pakistan, 1962. 155p.

17415 QURESHI, S.M.M. Pakistani nationalism reconsidered. In PA 45,4 (1972-73) 556-72.

17416 SHARIF, M.M. National integration, and other essays. Lahore: Inst. of Islamic Culture, 1965. 153p. (His Collected papers, 4)

17417 TAYYEB, A. Pakistan: a political geography. London: OUP, 1966. 250p.

17418 WHEELER, R.S. Federalism in Pakistan. In W.S. Livingston, ed. Federalism in the commonwealth; a bibliographical commentary. London: Cassell, 1963, 145-58.

17419 WILCOX, W.A. Pakistan; the consolidation of a nation. NY: ColUP, 1963. 276p.

17420 ZIRING, L. Politics and language in Pakistan. In CAS 1 (1971) 109-22.

B. The Political Process

1. General Histories and Studies of Pakistan Politics

17421 AHMAD, MUSHTAQ. Politics without social change. Karachi: Space Pub., 1971. 275p.

17422 AKHTAR, J.D. Political conspiracies in Pakistan: Liaquat Ali's murder to Ayub Khan's exit. Delhi: Punjabi Pustak Bhandar, 1969. 380p.

17423 BERINDRANATH, D. Power politics in Pakistan. In JUSI 98 (1968) 99-115.

17424 CHOUDHURY, G.W. Democracy in Pakistan. Dacca: Green Book House, 1963. 309p.

17425 DAS, TAPAN. Pakistan politics. Delhi: PPH, 1969. 74p.

17426 HUSAIN, AHMED. Politics and people's representation in Pakistan. Karachi: Ferozsons, 1972. 243p.

17427 HUSSAIN, S.S. Lengthening shadows; the story of Pakistan's politics and politicians from advent of Pakistan to fall of Ayub. Rawalpindi: Mujahid, 1970. 216p.

17428 IKRAM AZAM, R.M. Pakistan's security and national integration: a study in opinions and points of view. Rawalpindi Cantt.: London Book Co., 1974. 145p.

17429 JUNAID, M.M. The resurgence of Pakistan. Karachi: Natl. Book Foundation, 1975. 187p.

17430 KHAN, F.M. Pakistan's crisis in leadership. Karachi: Natl. Book Foundation, 1973. 285p.

17431 LAPORTE, R. Power and privilege: influence and decision-making in Pakistan. ND: Vikas, 1976. 225p.

17432 MILLER, J.M. Political change in Pakistan; an evaluation. In SAS 3,1 (1968) 1-20.

17433 NAYAK, P. Laporte's thesis - where does it fall short? In SAS 11,1/2 (1976) 127-44.

17434 QAMARUL AHSAN. Politics and personalities in Pakistan. Rev. and enl. ed. Dacca: Mohiuddin, 1969. 211p.

17435 SAHNI, N.C. Political struggle in Pakistan. Jullundur: New Academic Pub. Co., 1969. 239p.

17436 SULERI, Z.A. Pakistan's lost years, being a survey of a decade of politics, 1948-1958. Lahore: Progressive Papers, 1962. 148p.

17437 ______. Politicians and Ayub; being a survey of Pakistani politics from 1948 to 1964. Lahore: Lion Art Press, 1964. 212p.

17438 VORYS, K. VON. Political development in Pakistan. Princeton: PUP, 1965. 341p.

17439 WILCOX, W.A. Political change in Pakistan: structures, functions, constraints and goals. In PA 41,3 (1968) 341-54. [Rpt. in C.E. Welch, Jr., ed. Political modernization.... 2nd ed. Belmont, CA: Wadsworth Pub., 1971, 278-92.]

17440 ZIRING, L. Pakistan: a political perspective. In AS 15,7 (1975) 629-44.

2. Politics and Society

17441 AHMAD, MUNEER. Political sociology: perspectives on Pakistan. Lahore: Punjabi Adbi Markaz, 1978. 176p.

17442 AHMED, AKBAR S. Pieces of green, the sociology of change in Pakistan, 1964-1974. Karachi: Royal Book Co., 1977. 259p.

17443 HUSSAIN, ASAF. Elites and political development in Pakistan. In Developing Economies 14,3 (1976) 224-38.

17444 ______. Ethnicity, national identity and praetorianism: the case of Pakistan. In AS 16,10 (1976) 918-30.

17445 LINDHOLM, C. The segmentary linkage system: its applicability to Pakistan's political structure. In A.T. Embree, ed. Pakistan's western borderlands: the transformation of a political order. ND: Vikas, 1977, 41-66.

17446 MANIRUZZÀMAN, T. Group interests in Pakistan politics, 1947-1958. In PA 39,1/2 (1966) 83-98.

17447 WRIGHT, T.P. Indian Muslim refugees in the politics of Pakistan. In JCPS 12,2 (1974) 189-205.

3. Pakistan's Political Parties
a. general studies of political parties

17448 AFZAL, M. RAFIQUE. Political parties in Pakistan, 1947-1958. Islamabad: Natl. Cmsn. on Hist. and Cultural Research, 1976. 270p.

17449 DITTMER, K. Zur Geschichte der Parteien Pakistans. In IAF 4,2 (1973) 193-214.

17450 MIZANUR RAHMAN SHELLY. Pakistan, the Second Republic: politics and parties. Dacca: Concept, 1970. 144p.

17451 Political parties: their policies and programmes. Lahore: Ferozsons, 1971. 267p.

17452 QURESHI, S.M. Party politics in the Second Republic of Pakistan. In Middle East J. 20 (1966) 456-72.

b. the Pakistan Muslim League

17453 AYUB KHAN, MOHAMMED, Field-Marshal. Ideology and objectives. Ed. by Syed Shabbir Hussain. Lahore: Pakistan Muslim League, 1968. 173p.

17454 CHAUDHORY, FAZLUL QUADER. Pakistan Muslim League. In Pakistan R. 18,12 (1970) 39-43. [followed by statements of Muslim League (Council) & Qaiyum Group 44-52]

17455 Pakistan - eclipse of the Muslim League. In Round Table (1956) 83-86.

c. the Awami League, founded 1949 by Sheikh Mujibur Rahman

17456 Awami League stands for democratic socialism. In Econ. Affairs 16,8/9 (1971) 256-65.

17457 KAMAL, KAZI AHMED. Sheikh Mujibur Rahman: man and politician. 2nd ed., enl. Dacca: Kazi Giasuddin Ahmed, 1970. 182p. [1st ed. also 1970]

17458 MUJIBUR RAHMAN, Sheikh. 6-point program: our right to live. Dacca: East Pakistan Awami League, 1966. 20p.

17459 RASHIDUZZAMAN, M. The Awami league in the political development of Pakistan. In AS 10,7 (1970) 574-87.

d. the National Awami Party, founded 1957 by Maulana Abdul Hamid Bashani, in split from Awami League

17460 BAKHTIAR, Y. Attorney General Yahya Bakhtiar's opening address in the Supreme Court of Pakistan in the reference by the Islamic Republic of Pakistan on dissolution of National Awami Party, Rawalpindi, June 19, 20, and 23, 1975. Islamabad: Info. & Broadcasting Division, Govt. of Pakistan, 1975. 55p.

17461 RASHIDUZZAMAN, M. The National Awami Party of Pakistan: leftist politics in crisis. In PA 43,3 (1970) 394-409.

e. the Pakistan People's Party, founded 1967 by Zulfiqar Ali Bhutto

17462 BHUTTO, Z.A. Let the people judge. Lahore: Pakistan People's Party, 1969. 58p.

17463 ______. Political situation in Pakistan. 2nd ed. Lahore: Pakistan People's Party, 1969. 48p. [1st pub. 1968]

17464 RIZVI, H.A. Pakistan People's Party: the first phase, 1967-71. Lahore: Progressive, 1973. 30p.

17465 SAYEED, K.B. How radical is the Pakistan People's Party? In PA 48,1 (1975) 42-59.

17466 SYED, A.H. The Pakistan People's Party: phases one and two. In L. Ziring & R. Braibanti & W.H. Wriggins, eds. Pakistan: the long view. Durham: DUP, 1977, 70-116.

f. the Jamāʿāt-i-Islāmī, founded 1949 by Maulānā Syed AbūlʿAlā Maudoodi

17467 ABBOTT, F. The Jamāʿāt-i-Islāmī of Pakistan. In Middle East J. 11 (1957) 37-51.

17468 ADAMS, C.J. The ideology of Mawlana Mawdudi. In D.E. Smith, ed. South Asian politics and religion. Princeton: PUP, 1966, 371-97.

17469 AHMAD, SAYED RIAZ. Maulana Maududi and the Islamic state. Lahore: PPH, 1976. 192p.

17470 BAHADUR, K. The Jamaᶜat-i-Islami of Pakistan: political thought and political action. ND: Chetana, 1977. 228p.

17471 MAUDOODI, SYED ABULᶜALA, Maulana. Our message. Lahore: Islamic Pub., 1979. 48p.

17472 SAYEED, K.B. The Jamaᶜat-i-Islami movement in Pakistan. In PA 30 (1957) 59-68.

4. Elections and Election Law - General Studies

17473 CHAUDHARY, M.I. New election laws. Lahore: Lahore Law Times Pub., 1970. 135p.

17474 HUQ, M. MAHFUZUL. Electoral problems in Pakistan. Dacca: ASP, 1966. 222p. (ASP pub., 18)

17475 MAHMOOD, SHAUKAT. Election laws for 1970. Lahore: Pakistan Law Times Pub., 1970. 272p.

17476 PAKISTAN. LAWS, STATUTES. Election laws in Pakistan.... By Syed Anwer Ali. Karachi: Syed Pub., 1965. 1 v.

17477 PAKISTAN. MIN. OF LAW. Report of the Franchise Commission, 1963; an analysis. Karachi: 1964. 63p.

C. Phases of Pakistan's Political Development, 1947 -

1. 1947-58: Founding, Consolidation, and Constitution-making

a. general studies

17478 ALI, CHAUDHRI MUHAMMAD. Speeches of Chaudhri Muhammad Ali in the Constituent and National Assemblies of Pakistan, 1952-58. Ed. by Salahuddin Khan. Lahore: Res. Soc. of Pakistan, 1975. 386p.

17479 ______. The task before us: selected speeches and writings of Chaudhri Muhammad Ali, formerly Prime Minister of Pakistan. Ed. by Salahuddin Khan. Lahore: Res. Soc. of Pakistan, 1974. 437p.

17480 LLEWELYN, B. From the back streets of Bengal. London: Allen & Unwin, 1955. 286p.

17481 NEWMAN, K.J. Essays from Pakistan: some national and international problems in the era of Constitution-making. Lahore: Publishers United, 1959. 130p.

17482 QURESHI, SALEEM. Elite politics: the initial phase of the politics of Pakistan, 1947-1958. In ATS 4,12 (1979) 268-85.

17483 SAYEED, K.B. Pakistan: the formative phase. Karachi: Pakistan Pub. House, 1960. 492p.

17484 SEN, S. The birth of Pakistan. Lahore: Book Traders, 1978. 199p.

b. Quaid-i-Azam Mahomed Ali Jinnah (1876-1948): founder and first Governor-General [see Chap. Six, IV. D. 3.]

c. Liaquat Ali Khan (1895-1951): first Prime Minister of Pakistan

17485 LIAQUAT ALI KHAN. Pakistan; the heart of Asia: speeches in the United States and Canada, May and June 1950. Cambridge: HUP, 1950. 150p.

17486 ______. Speeches and statements of Quaid-i-Millat Liaquat Ali Khan, 1941-51. Ed. by M. Rafique Afzal. Lahore: Res. Soc. of Pakistan, U. of the Panjab, 1967. 657p.

17487 PAKISTAN. The assassination of Mr. Liaquat Ali Khan. Report of the commission of enquiry. Karachi: MPGOP, 1952. 64p.

17488 ZIAUDDIN AHMAD, ed. Quaid-i-Millat Liaquat Ali Khan, leader and statesman. Karachi: Oriental Academy, 1970. 295p.

d. the Constituent Assemblies and the Constitution of 1956

17489 CALDER, G.J. Constitutional debates in Pakistan. In MW 46 (1956) 40-60, 144-56, 253-71.

17490 FELDMAN, H. A constitution for Pakistan. Karachi: OUP, 1956. 102p.

17491 GLEDHILL, A. Pakistan: the development of its law and constitution. 2nd ed. London: Stevens & Sons, 1967. 393p. [1st pub. 1957]

17492 HUQ, MAHFUZUL. Some reflections on Islam and constitution making in Pakistan: 1947-56. In Islamic Studies 5,1 (1966) 207-20.

17493 JENNINGS, W.I., ed. Constitutional problems in Pakistan. Westport, CT: Greenwood, 1972. 378p. [Rpt. 1957 ed.]

17494 MAHMUD, HASSAN. A nation is born. Lahore: Feroz Printing Works, 1958. 607p.

17495 NEWMAN, K.J. Essays on the Constitution of Pakistan, including the Draft and Final Constitutions of Pakistan with comments. Dacca: Pakistan Coop. Book Soc., 1956. 395p.

17496 PAKISTAN. CONSTITUENT ASSEMBLY. Debates: official reports, 1st - 16th sessions, Aug. 10, 1947 - Sept. 21, 1954. Karachi: MPGOP, 1947-54? 9v.

17497 ______. Debates: official reports, 1st - 83rd sessions, July 7, 1955 - Mar. 22, 1956. Karachi, MPGOP, 1955-56? 4v.

17498 PAKISTAN, CONSTITUTION. The constitution of the Islamic republic of Pakistan. Karachi: MPGOP, 1956. 224p.

17499 SHAFQAT, C.M. The new Pakistan constitution. Lahore: All-Pakistan Legal Decisions, 1957. 348p.

2. 1958-62: Martial Law Under Army-Bureaucratic Rule

a. general studies

17500 CHOUDHURY, G.W. Failure of parliamentary government in Pakistan. In Parliamentary Affairs 11 (1957-58) 79-91.

17501 FELDMAN, H. Revolution in Pakistan: a study of the martial law administration. London: OUP, 1967. 242p.

17502 KAYANI, M.R. Not the whole truth. 2nd ed. Lahore: Pakistan Writer's Coop. Soc., 1963. 211p.

17503 SAYEED, H.B. Collapse of parliamentary democracy in Pakistan. In Middle East J. 13 (1959) 389-406.

17504 MINATTUR, J. Martial law in India, Pakistan, and Ceylon. The Hague: Nijhoff, 1962. 99p.

17505 NEWMAN, K.J. Pakistan's preventive autocracy and its causes. In PA 32 (1959) 18-33.

17506 WILCOX, W.A. The Pakistan coup d'état of 1958. In PA 38,2 (1965) 142-63.

17507 WINT, G. The 1958 revolution in Pakistan. In Raghavan Iyer, ed., South Asian affairs, no. 1, London: Catto & Windus, 1960, 72-85.

b. Field Marshal Mohammad Ayub Khan, leader of the 1958 "Revolution"

17508 AHMAD, MOHAMMAD. My chief. Lahore: Longmans, Green, 1960. 111p.

17509 AYUB KHAN, MOHAMMAD. Ayub, soldier and statesman: speeches and statements (1958-1965) of Field Marshal Mohammad Ayub Khan, president of Pakistan & a detailed account of the Indo-Pakistan War, 1965. Ed. by Rais Ahmad Jafri. Lahore: Mohammad Ali Academy, 1966. 243 + 576p.

17510 ______. Friends not masters: a political autobiography. London: OUP, 1967. 275p.

17511 ______. Speeches and statements. Karachi: Pakistan Pub., 1961-64. 6v.

17512 DOBELL, W.M. Ayub Khan: a de Gaulle in Asia? In CAS 1 (1971) 64-80.

17513 JAHAN, ROUNAQ. Ten years of Ayub Khan and the problem of national integration. In J. of Comp. Admin. 2,3 (1970) 261-76.

17514 SAEED, S.A. President without precedent; a brilliant account of Ayub and his regime. Lahore: Lahore Book Depot, 1960. 129p.

17515 ZULFI, SAHBA. President Ayub. Lahore: Ashraf Pub. House, 1964. 156p.

3. 1962-69: Presidency of Ayub Khan under the New Constitution

a. the Constitution of 1962: from parliamentary to presidential government

17516 AHMED, MANZOORUDDIN. Islamic aspects of the new constitution of Pakistan. In Islamic Studies 2 (1963) 249-86.

17517 ______. Sovereignty of God in the Constitution of Pakistan: a study in the conflict of traditionalism and modernism. In Islamic Studies 4,1 (1965) 201-12.

17518 BHAMBHRI, C.P. Pakistan's new constitution and its working: a survey. In IJPS 26 (1965) 25-57.

17519 CONRAD, D. Die Grundrechtsnovelle von 1964 sur pakistanischen Verfassung. In Zeitschrift für ausländisches offentliches Recht und Volkerrecht 24 (1964) 738-48.

17520 COURBE, N. La constitution de la République du Pakistan du 1er mars 1962. In Revue du droit public et de la science politique en France et à l'étrangère 79 (1963) 453-76.

17521 MAHMOOD, SHAUKAT. The second republic of Pakistan an analytical and comparative evaluation of the constitution of Pakistan, 1962. 2nd rev. ed. Lahore: Ilmi Kitab Khana, 1963. 179p.

17522 PAKISTAN. CONSTITUTION. The Constitution of the Islamic Republic of Pakistan with appendices and index, as modified up to the 10th April, 1968. Karachi: MPGOP, 1968. 337p.

17523 ______. The Constitution of Pakistan (as amended up to date). By Sh. Shaukat Mahmood. Lahore: Pakistan Law Times Pub., 1965. 647p.

17524 PAKISTAN. CONSTITUTION CMSN. Report, 1961. Karachi: MPGOP, 1962. 178p.

17525 PAKISTAN. ELECTION CMSN. Pakistan general elections, 1962. Karachi: Govt. of Pakistan Press, 1963. 327p.

17526 PAKISTAN. MIN. OF LAW & PARLIAMENTARY AFFAIRS. LAW DIV. The Constitution of the Republic of Pakistan, as modified up to the 9th Oct. 1962. Karachi: MPGOP, 1963. 92p.

17527 SCHULER, E.A. & K.R. SCHULER. Public opinion and constitution making in Pakistan, 1958-1962. East Lansing: Michigan State U. Press, 1967. 286p.

17528 WHEELER, R.S. Pakistan: new constitution, old issues. In AS 3,2 (1963) 107-15.

b. the general elections of 1965

17529 AL-MUJAHID, SHARIF. The assembly elections in Pakistan. In AS 5,11 (1965) 538-551.

17530 ______. Pakistan's first presidential elections. In AS 5,6 (1965) 280-94.

17531 JAFRI, A.B.S. From the gallery, a record of the first two sessions of the National Assembly of Pakistan, being a collection of the column "From the Gallery" written for the Pakistan Times, Lahore and Rawalpindi. Lahore: Progressive Papers, 1963. 163p.

17532 MISRA, K.P. & M.V. LAKHI & V. NARAIN. Pakistan's search for constitutional consensus. ND: Impex India, 1967. 269p. (South Asian series, 1)

17533 PAKISTAN. ELECTION CMSN. Presidential election result, 1965. Rawalpindi: 1965. 25p.

17534 ______. Report on general elections in Pakistan, 1964-65. Rawalpindi: 1967-. v.1-

17535 ______. Results of elections to provincial assemblies of East and West Pakistan, 1965. Karachi, MPGOP, 1966. 109p.

17536 RASHIDUZZAMAN, M. The National Assembly of Pakistan under the 1962 constitution. In PA 42 (1969) 481-93.

17537 SAYEED, K.B. 1965 - an epoch-making year in Pakistan - general elections and war with India. In AS 6 (1966) 76-85.

c. the Presidency of Ayub Khan, 1965-69, and his "Basic Democracies" program

17538 DOBELL, W.M. Ayub Khan as president of Pakistan. In PA 42,3 (1969) 294-310.

17539 FELDMAN, H. From crisis to crisis: Pakistan 1962-1969. London: OUP, 1972. 340p.

17540 MOORE, R.A., Jr. The role of the Army in Pakistan's development during the Ayub years; a retrospective appraisal. In Indian J. of Politics 8, 1/2 (1974) 29-48.

17541 SAYEED, K.B. Pakistan's constitutional autocracy. In PA 36 (1964-65) 365-77.

17542 WILCOX, W.A. Pakistan: a decade of Ayub. In AS 9, 2 (1969) 87-93.

17543 ZIRING, L. The Ayub Khan era: politics in Pakistan 1958-1969. Syracuse: Syracuse U. Press, 1971. 234p.

d. 1969: political crisis and the resignation of Ayub Khan

17544 ANWAR, M.R. Presidential government in Pakistan. Lahore: Caravan Book House, 1967. 342p.

17545 BHARGAVA, G.S. Pakistan in crisis. Delhi: Vikas, 1969. 222p.

17546 BURKI, S.J. Ayub's fall: a socio-economic explanation. In AS 12,3 (1972) 201-12.

17547 ______. Social and economic determinants of political violence: a case study of the Punjab. In Middle East J. 25,4 (1971) 465-80.

17548 LAPORTE, R., Jr. Succession in Pakistan: continuity and change in a garrison state. In AS 9,11 (1969) 842-61.

17549 MANIRUZZAMAN, T. Crisis of political development and the collapse of the Ayub regime in Pakistan. In Journal of Developing Areas 5,1 (1971) 221-38.

17550 WILCOX, W.A. Pakistan in 1969: once again at the starting point. In AS 10,2 (1970) 73-81.

4. 1969-1971: Martial Law Under General Agha Muhammad Yahya Khan

a. general studies

17551 BERINDRANATH, D. Private life of Yahya Khan. ND: Sterling, 1974. 139p.

17552 FELDMAN, H. The end and the beginning: Pakistan, 1969-1971. London: OUP, 1975. 210p.

17553 IKRAM, M. The martial law regulations and orders, 1969 and 1958. Lahoure: Lahore Law Times Pub., 1969. 94p.

17554 ZIRING, LAWRENCE. Militarism in Pakistan: the Yahya Khan interregnum. In W.H. Wriggins, ed. Pakistan in transition. Islamabad: U. of Islamabad Press, 1975, 198-233.

b. the general election of 1970: victories of Zulfiqar Ali Bhutto and Mujibur Rahman in West and East wings

17555 BAXTER, C. Pakistan votes, 1970. In AS 11,3 (1971) 197-218.

17556 BUDRUDDIN, S.G.M. Election handbook, 1970. Karachi: Pub. & Marketing Assoc., 1970. 197p.

17557 IFTIKHAR AHMAD. Pakistan general elections, 1970. Lahore: South Asian Inst., Punjab U., 1976. 159p.

17558 PAKISTAN. ELECTION CMSN. Report on general election, Pakistan, 1970-71. Karachi: MPGOP, 1972-. 2v.

17559 Political parties; their politics and programmes [special issue]. In Pakistan R. 18,12 (1970) 1-69. [pre-election statements by 15 parties]

c. the culmination of tensions between East and West Pakistan [for 1971 war and creation of Bangladesh see Chap. Seven, IV. B. 4]

17560 CHOUDHURY, G.W. The last days of united Pakistan. Bloomington: Indian U. Press, 1974. 239p.

17561 JAHAN, ROUNAQ. Pakistan: failure in national integration. NY: ColUP, 1972. 248p.

17562 LAPORTE, R. Pakistan in 1971: the disintegration of a nation. In AS 12,2 (1972) 97-108.

17563 QURESHI, KHALIDA. An overview of the East Pakistan situation. In Pakistan Horizon 24,3 (1971) 32-60.

17564 RASHIDUZZAMAN, M. Leadership, organization, strategies and tactics of the Bangla Desh movement. In AS 12,3 (1972) 185-200.

17565 SCHUMAN, H. A note on the rapid rise of mass Bengali nationalism in East Pakistan. In AJS 78,2 (1972) 290-98.

17566 STIETENCRON, H. VON Zur Rolle der Religion in der pakistanischen Staatskrise, 1970/71. In IAF 4,2 (1973) 332-341.

17567 VARMA, S.P. & VIRENDRA NARAIN. Pakistan political system in crisis: emergence of Bangladesh. Jaipur: South Asia Studies Center, 1972. 252p.

5. 1972-77: Rule of Zulfiqar Ali Bhutto and his Pakistan People's Party, and its Program of "Islamic Socialism"
a. general studies

17568 AYOOB, M. Pakistan's new political structure: change and continuity. In IS 12,2 (1973) 183-206.

17569 BURKI, S.J. Pakistan under Bhutto, 1971-1977. NY: St. Martin's Press, 1980. 245p.

17570 GOPINATH, M. Pakistan in transition: political development and rise to power of Pakistan People's Party. Delhi: Manohar, 1975. 162p.

17571 HERRING, R.J. Zulfikar Ali Bhutto and "eradication of feudalism" in Pakistan. In EPW 15,12 (1980) 599-614.

17572 KORSON, J.H., ed. Contemporary problems of Pakistant. Leiden: Brill, 1974. 151p.

17573 ______, ed. Special number on contemporary problems of Pakistan. In JAAS(L) 8,3/4 (1973) 161-306.

17574 KUMAR, S. The new Pakistan. ND: Vikas, 1978. 387p.

17575 PAKISTAN. Promises and performance: a report by the Government of Pakistan on the implementation of the 1970 manifesto of the Pakistan People's Party. Islamabad: Dir. of Res. Reference & Pub., Min. of Info. & Broadcasting, 1977. 261p.

17576 ______. White paper on the performance of the Bhutto regime. Islamabad: Print. Corp. of Pakistan Press, 1979. 4v. in 2.

17577 TEPPER, E.L. The new Pakistan: problems & prospects. In PA 47,1 (1974) 56-68.

17578 VERGHESE, B.G. An end to confrontation: Bhutto's Pakistan; restructuring the sub-continent. ND: S. Chand, 1972. 158p.

b. Zulfiqar Ali Bhutto (1928-1979): sources and studies [see also 6. b. below]

17579 BHUTTO, Z.A. "I have kept my pledge with God & man;" collection of President Bhutto's speeches. Karachi: Natl. Forum, 1972. 83p.

17580 ______. The myth of independence. London: OUP, 1969. 188p.

17581 ______. Speeches and statements, December 20, 1971-March 31, 1972. Karachi: Dept. of Films and Pub., Govt. of Pakistan, 1972. 164p.

17582 ______. The Third World, new directions. London: Quartet Books, 1977. 144p.

17583 FAKHAR ZAMAN & AKHTAR ZAMAN. Z.A. Bhutto: the political thinker. Lahore: People's Pub., 1973. 101p.

17584 KAUSHIK, S.N. Bhutto's leadership: some issues and challenges. In SAS 12, 1/2 (1977) 20-30.

17585 KUMAR, SATISH. The new Pakistan. ND: Vikas, 1978. 387p.

17586 MAHMUD DHAM. Larkana to Peking: some travels with Mr. Bhutto. Karachi: Natl. Book Foundation, 1976. 151p.

17587 MUKERJEE, D. Zulfiqar Ali Bhutto: quest for power. Delhi: Vikas, 1972. 240p.

17588 Pakistan and Ali Bhutto. Colombo: Friends of Pakistan, 1078. 110p.

17589 RASA, M.S.R. The architect of new Pakistan. Peshawar: Sarhad Pub., 1977. 108p.

17590 SINHA, K. Zulfiqar Ali Bhutto: six steps to summit. Delhi: Indian School Supply Depot, 1972. 272p.

17591 TASEER, S. Bhutto, a political biography. ND: Vikas, 1980. 208p.

c. the Constitution of 1973: return to parliamentary government

17592 AHMAD, QADEERUDDIN & S.M. ZAFAR. The Constitution of the Islamic Republic of Pakistan. Karachi: East and West Pub. Co., 1974. 164p.

17593 MAHMOOD, M. The Constitution of the Islamic Republic of Pakistan, 1973; a comprehensive and detailed commentary with a comparative study of the Constitutions of Pakistan, 1956 and 1962. Lahore: Pakistan Law Times Pub., 1973. 500p.

17594 MAHMOOD, SHAUKAT. Constitution of the Islamic Republic of Pakistan, 1973. Lahore: Legal Res. Centre, 1973. 584p.

17595 MUNIR, M. Constitution of the Islamic Republic of Pakistan: being a commentary on the Constitution of Pakistan, 1973. Lahore: Law Pub. Co., 1975. 680p.

17596 PAKISTAN. CONSTITUTION. The Constitution of the Islamic Republic of Pakistan. Karachi: MPBOP, 1973. 179p.

17597 ______. The Constitution of the Islamic Republic of Pakistan: as modified up to the 4th January 1977. Karachi: MPGOP, 1977. 193p.

17598 ______. The Interim Constitution of the Islamic Republic of Pakistan. Karachi: MPGOP, 1972. 114p.

17599 PAKISTAN. NATL. ASSEMBLY. Constitution-making in Pakistan. Karachi: MPGOP, 1973. 172p.

17600 RAHMAN, FAZLUR. Islam and the new Constitution of Pakistan. In JAAS(L) 8,3/4 (1973) 190-205.

6. 1977- : Reimposition of Martial Law under Gen. Mohammad Zia ul-Haq
a. general studies

17601 BROHI, A.K. Mr. A.K. Brohi, Counsel for Federation, statement in the Supreme Court of Pakistan, Rawalpindi, Oct. 10, 1977. Islamabad: Govt. of Pakistan, 1977. 93p. + 17pl.

17602 Framework for Pakistan's general elections scheduled for November 17, 1979. In JSAMES 3,2 (1978) 70-97.

17603 KARIM, A.S. Pakistan, search for political participation. Karachi: Maktaba-e-Faridi, 1978. 64p.

17604 KAUSHIK, S.N. Aftermath of the March 1977 general elections in Pakistan. In SAS 13,1 (1978) 70-78.

17605 PAKISTAN. White paper on the conduct of the general elections in March 1977. Rawalpindi: Govt. of Pakistan, 1978. 1449p.

17606 PAKISTAN. LAWS, STATUTES. The Martial Law proclamation: with CMLA's & zonal Martial Law regulations and

Martial Law orders, 1978.... Lahore: Natl. Law Pub., 1978. 130p.

17607 ZIA-UL-HAQ, M. Accountability should precede the elections: address to the nation, October 1, 1977. Islamabad: DPMIB, 1977. 16p.

17608 ______. General Mohammad Zia-ul-Haq, Chief of the Army Staff and Chief Martial Law Administrator meets the press, September 1, 1977, Rawalpindi. Islamabad: DPMIB, 1977. 62p.

17609 ______. Introduction of Islamic laws: address to the nation. Islamabad: DPMIB, 1979. 77p.

b. the trial and execution of former Prime Minister Bhutto on the charge of murder

17610 BATRA, J.C. The trial and execution of Bhutto. Delhi: Kunj, 1979. 184p.

17611 BHATIA, H.S. Portrait of a political murder. ND: Deep & Deep, 1979. 176p.

17612 BHUTTO, ZULFIQAR ALI. Chairman Bhutto's reply to Gen. Zia's 2nd statement in the Supreme Court. Karachi: Mussawat Press, 1977. 104p.

17613 ______. If I am assasinated. ND: Vikas, 1979. 36 + 234p.

17614 ______. My execution. ND: Biswin Sadi Pub., 1980. 130p.

17615 KAK, B.L. Z.A. Bhutto: notes from the death cell. ND: Radha Krishna Press, 1979. 95p.

17616 PAKISTAN. SUPREME COURT. The State vs Z.A. Bhutto: Lahore High Court judgment and two Supreme Court judgements. Karachi: Maz Pub., 1978. 351p.

17617 ______. Supreme Court judgement on Begum Nusrat Bhutto's petition challenging detention of Mr. Z.A. Bhutto and others under Martial Law order 12 of 1977. Islamabad: MPGOP, 1977. 12op.

17618 QURESHI, S.A. Analysis of contemporary Pakistani politics: Bhutto versus the military. In AS 19,9 (1979) 910-21.

17619 SHAH, MOWAHID H. The death of Bhutto and the future of Pakistan: from the grave Bhutto may pose a larger threat to General Zia's regime. In Worldview 22 (June 1979) 25-28.

D. Provincial and Local Government and Politics in Pakistan

1. Provincial Government and Politics

17620 HAIDER, HUSAIN. Working of provincial governments in Pakistan. In NIPA J. 7 (Jan.-Mar. 1968) 158-64.

2. Local Government

a. general studies

17621 KIZILBASH, H.H. Local government: democracy at the capital and autocracy in the villages. In Pakistan Econ. & Social R. 11,1 (1973) 104-24.

17622 MUMTAZ AHMAD. Unfinished revolution: studies in local government and rural development in Pakistan. Karachi: Book Land, 1976. 148p.

17623 RIZVI, S.A. Changing patterns of local government in Pakistan, 1688-1975. Karachi: Pakistan Hist. Soc., 1976. 140p.

17624 ______. Local bodies in Pakistan. In Pakistan Q. 14 (Winter 1966) 50-57, 77.

17625 ______. Local government in Pakistan; a study in clash of ideas. Karachi: Centre for Res. in Local Govt., 1980. 314p.

17626 ______. Modernisation of local government in Pakistan. In JPHS 21,3/4 (1973) 191-204, 241-94; 24,1 (1976) 31-50.

17627 SEMINAR ON PROBLEMS & PROSPECTS OF LOCAL GOVT., ISLAMABAD, 1972. Local government: problems and prospects. Rawalpindi: Lansdowne Cantonment Trust, 1972. 83p.

17628 SINGH, R.P. Decision making and rural elites: a study of rural-urban elites interaction in decision making process. Delhi: Research Pub. in Social Sciences, 1975. 123p.

b. the Basic Democracies program 1959-1969, under Ayub Khan - general studies

17629 BEG, AZIZ, ed. Grass roots government, essays on the genesis, philosophy and working of basic democracies in Pakistan. Rawalpindi: Pakistan Patriotic Pub., 1962. 223p.

17630 HASAN, MASUDUL. Text book of basic democracy and local government in Pakistan. Lahore: All Pakistan Legal Decisions, 1968. 551p.

17631 MAHMOOD, AFZAL. Basic democracies; being an exclusive commentary on Basic democracies order, 1959. Lahore: All Pakistan Legal Decisions, 1964. 545p.

17632 MUHITH, A.M.A. Political and administrative roles in East Pakistan's districts. In PA 40,3/4 (1967-68) 279-93.

17633 NARAIN, IQBAL. Basic democracies in Pakistan - some conceptual and empirical hypotheses. In PSR 4 (April 1965) 79-96.

17634 OMER, S. The judicial role of basic democracies in Pakistan. In J. of Local Admin. Overseas 5(1966) 115-123.

17635 PAKISTAN. BUREAU OF NATL. RECONSTRUCTION. An analysis of the working of basic democracy institutions in East Pakistan. Comilla: PARD, 1963. 106p.

17636 PAKISTAN. LAWS, STATUTES. The basic democracies order, 1959. Karachi: MPGOP, 1959. 51p.

17637 RAHMAN, HABIBUR. Basic democracies as institutions of local government in Pakistan. In J. of Local Admin. Overseas 1 (1962) 231-38.

17638 RASHIDUZZAMAN, M. Indirect elections in Pakistan. In Zeitschrift für Politik 15 (1968) 326-36.

17639 ______. Politics and administration in the local councils; a study of union and district councils in East Pakistan. Karachi: OUP, 1968. 124p.

17640 RIZVI, S.A. Facets of local government in Pakistan: a critical study of basic democracies. Karachi: Pakistan Group for the Study of Local Govt., 1974. 71p.

17641 RIZVI, S.M.A., ed. A reader in basic democracies. Peshawar: West Pakistan Academy for Village Dev., 1961. 234p.

17642 TEPPER, E. Changing patterns of administration in rural East Pakistan. Syracuse, NY: Maxwell School, Syracuse U., 1966. 140p. (Michigan State U., Asian Studies Center, occ. papers, 5)

17643 WILLIAMS, L.F. RUSHBROOK. Basic democracies as institutions of local government in Pakistan - II. In J. of Local Admin. Overseas 1 (1962) 247-56.

17644 ZIRING, L. The administration of basic democracies: the working of democracy in a Muslim state. In Islamic Studies 4,4 (1965) 393-440.

c. Divisional and District government

17645 MAHMOOD, KHALID. District and divisional administration. In NIPA J. 9 (March 1970) 1-16.

17646 ASLAM, A.H. The Deputy Commissioner: a study in public administration. Lahore: Punjab U., 1957. 58p. (Its Studies in Political Science, etc., no. 2)

17647 INAYATULLAH, ed. Basic democracies, district administration, and development. Peshawar: PARD, 1962. 327p.

17648 ______. District administration in West Pakistan: its problems and challenges. Peshawar: PARD, 1964. 336p.

d. municipal government

17649 HASAN, MASUDUL. Manual of municipal administration, law, and practice; being a commentary on the Municipal Administration Ordinance, 1960. Lahore: All

Pakistan Legal Decisions, 1967. 2v.

17650 SHAUKAT ALI, C. & M.M. SIDDIQ. Municipal administration in West Pakistan: a survey of its evolution, reorganization, processes, and problems. Lahore: Dept. of Basic Democracies & Local Govt., 1970. 1v.

e. sub-district government: village and tehsil/thana

17651 ANISUZZAMAN, M. The circle officer; a study of his role. Dacca: NIPA, 1963. 97p.

17652 AQUILA KIANA, et al. Emerging patterns of rural leadership in West Pakistan. Peshawar: PARD, 1971. 259p.

17653 HAIDER, S.M. Expanding role of patwaris in revenue administration. Peshawar: PARD, 1966. 218p.

17654 PAKISTAN. West Pakistan union councils; evaluation report, 1964-65. Karachi: MIB, 1965. 133p.

17655 RASHIDUZZAMAN, M. Election politics in Pakistan villages. In JComPolSt 4 (1966) 191-200.

E. Pakistan's Foreign Relations [for Relations Within South Asia, see Chap. Seven]

1. Bibliography and Reference

17656 WASAN, R.P. Pakistan-International relations: a select bibliography. In JIDSA 2 (1969) 219-39.

2. Documents and Sources

17657 BHUTTA, Z.A. Foreign policy of Pakistan; a compendium of speeches made in the National Assembly of Pakistan 1962-64. Karachi: Pakistan Inst. of Intl. Affairs, 1964. 125p.

17658 ______. The quest for peace: selections from speeches and writings, 1963-65. Karachi: Pakistan Inst. of Intl. Affairs, 1966. 106p.

17659 PAKISTAN. MIN. OF FOREIGN AFFAIRS. RESEARCH DIRECTORATE. Joint communiques. Islamabad: The Directorate, 1975-1977. 3v.

17660 PAKISTAN. TREATIES. Pakistan treaty series, 1964. Islamabad: Min. of Foreign Affairs, 1967. 2v.

3. General Studies of Pakistan's Foreign Relations

17661 AHMAD, MUSHTAQ. Pakistan's foreign policy. Karachi: Space Pub., 1968. 191p.

17662 AKHTAR AMAN. Pakistan: new trends in foreign policy. Lahore: Progressive, 1974. 95p.

17663 BHUTTO, BENAZIR. Foreign policy in perspective. Lahore: Classic, 1978. 120p.

17664 BHUTTO, Z.A. Bilateralism: new directions. In Pakistan Horizon 19,4 (1976) 3-59.

17665 BURKE, S.M. Mainsprings of Indian and Pakistani foreign policies. Minneapolis: U. of Minnesota Press, 1974. 308p.

17666 ______. Pakistan's foreign policy: an historical analysis. London: OUP, 1973. 432p.

17667 CHAUDHRI, M.A. Pakistan and the great powers. Karachi: Council for Pakistan Studies, 1970. 140p.

17668 HASAN, MASUMA, ed. Pakistan in a changing world: essays in honour of K. Sarwar Hasan. Karachi: Pakistan Inst. of Intl. Affairs, 1978. 250p.

17669 IKRAM AZAM, R.M. Pakistan's geopolitical and strategic compulsions. Lahore: Progressive Pub., 1980. 443p.

17670 IQBAL, MEHRUNNISA H. Survey of Pakistan's foreign relations: 1973. Pakistan's relations with Western Europe. In Pakistan Horizon 27,3 (1974) 70-80.

17671 KHAN, M. ZAFRULLAH. Pakistan's foreign relations. Karachi: Pakistan Inst. of Intl. Affairs, 1951. 24p.

17672 KIZILBASH, H.H. & KHAWAR MUMTAZ. Pakistan foreign policy and the legislature. Lahore: South Asian Inst., U. of the Punjab, 1976. 97p.

17673 LAKHI, M.V. Pakistan's foreign policy under Ayub, continuity and change. In SAS 4,1 (1969) 26-42.

17674 QURESHI, KHALIDA & MEHRUNNISA ALI. Survey of Pakistan's foreign relations: 1973. Pakistan and the USSR, Pakistan and the United States, Pakistan and Canada. In Pakistan Horizon 27,1 (1974) 61-79.

17675 QURESHI, M. ASLAM. Glimpses of Quaid-i-Azam's foreign policy. In JRSP 13,4 (1976) 119-38.

17676 RAZVI, MUJTABA. The frontiers of Pakistan: a study of frontier problems in Pakistan's foreign policy. Karachi: National Pub. House, 1971. 339p.

17677 SANGAT SINGH. Pakistan's foreign policy. Bombay: Asia, 1970. 260p.

17678 SAYEED, KHALID B. Preliminary analysis of Pakistan's foreign policy. In SAS 3,2 (1968) 70-80.

17679 SIDDIQUI, KALIM. The functions of international conflict: a socio-economic study of Pakistan. Karachi: Royal Book Co., 1975. 232p.

17680 TAHIR-KHELI, SHIRIN. The foreign policy of the "new" Pakistan. In Orbis 20,3 (1976) 733-59.

17681 ZIRING, L. Bhutto's foreign policy, 1972-1973. In JAAS(L) 8,3/4 (1973) 216-40.

4. Islam as a Factor in Foreign Policy

17682 CHAUDHRI, NAZIR AHMAD KHAN. Thoughts on Pakistan and Pan-Islamism. Lahore: al-Ahibba, dist. Ferozsons, 1977. 322p.

17683 GUPTA, S.K. Islam as a factor in Pakistani foreign relations. In IQ 18 (1962) 230-53.

17684 HUSSAIN, ARIF. Pakistan: its ideology and foreign policy. London: Cass, 1966. 188p.

5. Defense and Security
a. general studies

17685 BHUTTO, Z.A. Pakistan and the alliances. Lahore: Pakistan People's Party, 1969. 64p.

17686 CHAUDHRI, M. AHSAN. Pakistan and the regional pacts. Karachi: East Pub., 1958. 144p.

17687 ISPAHANI, M.A.H. Pakistan and the new regional arrangements. In Pakistan Horizon 22,3 (1969) 199-207.

17688 ROYAL INST. OF INTL. AFFAIRS. Collective defense in South Asia: the Manila treaty and its implications. London: OUP, 1956. 197p.

17689 SIDDIQUI, ASLAM. Pakistan seeks security. Lahore: Longmans, Green & Co., 1960. 201p.

b. Pakistan's nuclear policy

17690 CHARI, P.R. Pakistan's nuclear option. In Indian J. of Asian Studies 1,1 (1977) 77-91.

17691 ______. Pakistan nuclear purpose and India option? In EPW 15,3 (1980) 117-22.

17692 KAUSHIK, B.M. & O.N. MEHROTRA. Pakistan's nuclear bomb. ND: Sopan Pub. House, 1980. 228p.

17693 KHALILZAD, ZALMAY. Pakistan: the making of a nuclear power. In AS 16,6 (1976) 580-92.

17694 NAMBOODIRI, P.K.S. Pakistan's bomb and India's options. In Strategic Analysis 3,4 (1979) 127-30.

17695 PALIT, D.K. & P.K.S. NAMBOODIRI. Pakistan's Islamic bomb. ND: Vikas, 1979. 150p.

17696 SUBRAMANIAN, R.R. Pakistan's nuclear option: open or closed? In Strategic Analysis 3,8 (1978) 286-88.

6. International Economic Relations of Pakistan
a. foreign exchange and balance of payments

17697 AZIZ, SARTAJ & B. GLASSBURNER. The balance of payments and external resources in Pakistan's third five year plan. In PDR 6 (1966) 567-79.

17698 CHILD, F.C. Liberalization of the foreign exchange market. In PDR 8 (1968) 167-91.

17699 GLASSBURNER, B. The balance of payments and external resources in Pakistan's third five year plan. In PDR 5 (1965) 496-524.

17700 HASAN, PARVEZ. Balance of payments problems of Pakistan. In PDR 1 (1961) 15-48.

17701 KAZMI, AQDAS ALI. Rupee devaluation of Pakistan: problems and prospects. Lahore: Progressive, 1972. 34p.

17702 MIAN, NURUL-ISLAM. Pakistan's balance of payments. In Zeitschrift für die gesamte Staatswissenschaft 123 (1967) 296-321.

b. foreign trade

17703 BRUTON, H.J. & S.R. BOSE. The Pakistan export bonus scheme. Karachi: PIDE, 1963. 110p. (Its Monographs in the econ. of dev., 11)

17704 ISLAM, NURUL. Imports of Pakistan; growth and structure, a statistical study. Karachi: PIDE, 1967. (Its Stat. papers, 3)

17705 ______. Tariff protection, comparative costs, and industrialization in Pakistan. Karachi: PIDE, 1967. (Its Res. report, 57)

17706 KARACHI. CHAMBER OF COMMERCE & INDUSTRY. Pattern of foreign trade of Pakistan. Karachi: Royal Book Co., 1977. 287p.

17707 KHAN, GHANI MOHAMMAD. Afghanistan's transit trade through Pakistan and the unrecorded transactions at Laudikotal. Peshawar: U. of Peshawar, 1972. 29p.

17708 SIDDIQUI, A.H. Foreign trade of Pakistan; a select bibliography. Karachi: Royal Book Co., 1968. 57p.

17709 SOLIGO, R. & J.J. STERN. Tariff protection, import substitution and investment efficiency. In K. Griffin & Azizur Rahman Khan, eds. Growth and inequality in Pakistan. London: Macmillan, 1972, 132-48. [Also in PDR 5,2 (1965) 249-70]

17710 STERN, J.J. A note on the structure of Pakistan's foreign trade. In PDR 9,2 (1969) 212-23.

17711 SYED, HASAN ALI. Exports of manufactured goods: costs and policies. Lahore: Board of Econ. Enquiry, 1970. 75p.

c. foreign aid and investment

17712 BHARGAV, ABHAY. Pakistan: pattern of foreign aid. In SAS 11,1/2 (1976) 92-109.

17713 BRECHER, I. & S.A. ABBAS. Foreign aid and industrial development in Pakistan. Cambridge: CamUP, 1972. 271p.

17714 CHAUDHRY, S.A. Private foreign investment in Pakistan. In PDR 10,1 (1970) 100-11.

17715 CHENERY, H.B. & A. MACEWAN. Optimal patterns of growth and aid: the case of Pakistan. In PDR 6,2 (1966) 209-42.

17716 GHULAM ALI. Elimination of foreign aid; a case study of Pakistan. In AV 19,3 (1977) 259-72.

17717 GRIFFIN, K. & AZIZUR RAHMAN KHAN. Note on the degree of dependence on foreign assistance. In K. Griffin &. Azizur Rahman Khan, eds. Growth and inequality in Pakistan. London: Macmillan, 1972, 188-98.

17718 IQBAL, MEHRUNNISA. Pakistan: foreign aid and foreign policy. In Pakistan Horizon 15,4 (1972) 54-71.

17719 MUSTAFA, SAMI. Pakistan: a study in underdevelopment. Lahore: South Asian Inst., U. of the Punjab, 1975. 74p.

17720 PAPANEK, G.F. Foreign advisers and planning agencies. In M. Faber & D. Seers, eds. The crisis in planning, v. 1. London: Chatto & Windus, 1972, 172-87.

17721 RADHU, G.M. Transfer of technical know-how through multinational corporations in Pakistan. In PDR 7,4 (1973) 361-75.

17722 RAHMAN, MANISUR. The welfare economics of foreign aid. In PDR 7,2 (1965) 141-57.

17723 UHRENBACHER, W.J. Pakistan: Studie zur Entwicklungshilfe. Horn: Berger, 1972. 250p.

7. Pakistan's Relations with Specific Countries and Areas
a. United States - Pakistan relations
i. general studies

17724 HASAN, K. SARWAR. The background of American arms aid to Pakistan. In Pakistan Horizon 20,2 (1967) 20-6.

17725 IRSHAD KHAN, SHAHEEN. Rejection alliance? A case study of U.S. - Pakistan relations, 1947-1967. Lahore: Ferozsons, 1972. 186p.

17726 KIZILBASH, H.H. & KHAWAR MUMTAZ. Changes in United States foreign policy and Pakistan's options: a perspective. Lahore: South Asian Inst., U. of the Punjab, 1974. 75p.

17727 LERSKI, G.J. The Pakistan-American alliance; a reevaluation of the past decade. In AS 8 (1968) 400-15.

17728 RAHMAN, M. ATAUR. Dependency theory reconsidered: consequences for public policy of Pakistan-U.S. relations, 1958-1968. Diss., U. of Chicago, 1978. 122p.

17729 TRAGER, F.N. The United States and Pakistan: a failure of diplomacy. In Orbis 9 (1965) 613-29.

17730 VENKATARAMANI, M.S. & H.C. ARYA. America's military alliance with Pakistan: the evolution and course of an uneasy partnership. In IS 8,1/2 (1966) 73-125.

ii. American economic and military assistance

17731 ALAVI, HAMZA & AMIR KHUSRO. Pakistan: the burden of U.S. aid. In R.I. Rhodes, ed. Imperialism and underdevelopment; a reader. NY: Praeger, 1970, 62-78.

17732 AYOOB, M. U.S. economic assistance to Pakistan 1954-65: a case study in the politics of foreign aid. In IQ 23 (1967) 127-44.

17733 BABER, SATTAR. United States aid to Pakistan; a case study of the influence of the donor country on the domestic and foreign policies of the recipient. Karachi: Pakistan Inst. of Intl. Affairs, 1974. 150p.

17734 MAHFOOZ ALI. The United States economic aid programmes in Pakistan: 1952-62. In PEJ 20,2 (1969-70) 1-38.

17735 MUSTAFA, SAMI. Pakistan: development of underdevelopment. In Pakistan Horizon 28,2 (1975) 48-58.

17736 SHRIVASTAVA, B.K. U.S. military assistance to Pakistan; a reappraisal. In IQ 32,1 (1976) 26-41.

b. China - Pakistan relations

17737 DOBELL, W.M. Ramifications of the China-Pakistan border treaty. In PA 37 (1964) 283-95.

17738 GOSWAMI, B.N. Pakistan and China; a study of their relations. Bombay: Allied, 1971. 160p.

17739 MEHROTRA, O.N. Sino-Pak relations; a review. In China Report 12,5/6 (1976) 54-75.

17740 RAIS, R.B. China and Pakistan: a political analysis of mutual relations. Lahore: Progressive, 1977. 163p.

17741 SHARMA, B.L. The Pakistan-China axis. Bombay: Asia, 1968. 226p.

17742 SYED, ANWAR HUSSAIN. China and Pakistan: diplomacy of an Entente Cordiale. Amherst: U. of Massachusetts Press, 1974. 259p.

c. USSR - Pakistan relations

17743 AYOOB, M. Pakistan's trade relations with the Soviet Union. In IS 11 (1969) 44-69.

17744 BUDHRAJ, V.S. The evolution of Russia's Pakistan policy. In The Australian J. of Politics & History 16,3 (1970) 343-60.

17745 CHAWLA, V. Soviet-Pakistan relations; changing perspectives. In SAS 7,1 (1972) 95-113.

17746 HASAN, Z. Soviet arms aid to Pakistan and India. In Pakistan Horizon 21,4 (1968) 344-55.

17747 RAGHUNATH RAM. Soviet economic cooperation with Pakistan, 1947-71. In IS 15,3 (1976) 427-38.

17748 SHARMA, B.L. Soviet arms for Pakistan. In JUSI 98 (1968) 223-38.

d. Pakistan's relations with the United Kingdom and the Commonwealth (withdrew from Commonwealth, 1971)

17749 ALI, MEHRUNNISA. Pakistan's withdrawal from the Commonwealth. In Pakistan Horizon 25,4 (1972) 40-53.

17750 AZIZ, K.K. Britain and Pakistan; a study of British attitude towards the East Pakistan crisis of 1971. Islamabad: U. of Islamabad Press, 1974. 402p.

17751 HASAN, K. SARWAR. Pakistan and the Commonwealth. Karachi: Pakistan Inst. of Intl. Affairs, 1950. 36p.

17752 QURESHI, M. ASLAM. Anglo-Pakistan relations, 1947-1976. Lahore: Res. Soc. of Pakistan, 1976. 395p.

e. Pakistan and the Middle East

17753 ALI, MEHRUNNISA. The attitude of the new Afghan regime toward its neighbors. In Pakistan Horizon 27,3 (1974) 43-69.

17754 ASOPA, S.K. Military alliance and regional cooperation in West Asia; a study of the politics of the northern tier. Meerut: Meenakshi, 1971. 268p.

17755 BHUTTO, Z.A. RCD: challenge and response. In Pakistan Horizon 29,2 (1976) 3-12.

17756 MONTAGNO, G.L. The Pak-Afghan detente. In AS 3,12 (1963) 616-24.

17757 MUSTAFA, Z. Recent trends in Pakistan's policy towards the Middle East. In Pakistan Horizon 28,4 (1975) 1-18.

17758 QURESHI, K. Pakistan and Iran - a study in neighbourly diplomacy. In Pakistan Horizon 21,1 (1968) 33-39.

17759 ______. Pakistan and the Middle East. In Pakistan Horizon 19,2 (1966) 156-66.

17760 SINHA, P.B. Pak perception of the coup in Kabul. In Strategic Analysis 2,3 (1978) 82-87.

17761 TAHIR-KHELI, S. Iran and Pakistan: cooperation in an area of conflict. In AS 17,5 (1977) 474-90.

f. Pakistan's relations with other nations

17762 KIDRON, M. Pakistan's trade with eastern bloc countries. NY: Praeger, 1972. 130p.

17763 MEHDI, S.S. The new Pakistan and the Asian-Pacific region. In Pakistan Horizon 27,4 (1974) 21-58.

17764 POONAWALA, R. Pakistan's relations with Japan. In Pakistan Horizon 24,1 (1971) 26-34.

g. Pakistan and the United Nations

17765 AHMAD, MUSHTAQ. The United Nations and Pakistan. Karachi: Pakistan Inst. of Intl. Affairs, 1955. 162p.

17766 BHUTTO, Z.A. Peace-keeping by the United Nations. Karachi: Pakistan Pub. House, 1967. 80p.

17767 HASAN, K. SARWAR. Pakistan and the United Nations. NY: Manhattan Pub. Co., 1960. 328p.

17768 RAI, HAMEED A.K., ed. Pakistan in the United Nations: speeches delivered in the General Assembly by the heads of Pakistan delegations, 1948-1978. Lahore: Aziz Pub., 1979. 524p.

17769 United Nations in Pakistan. Islamabad: U.N. Info. Centre for Pakistan, 1975. 60p.

III. THE PAKISTAN ECONOMY: PROBLEMS OF DEVELOPMENT

A. Bibliography and Reference

17770 ALI, SHAUKAT & G.N. JONES. Planning development and change: an annotated bibliography on development administration. Lahore: Punjab U. Press, 1966. 217p. (Public admin. series no. 1)

17771 EBERHARD, W. Studies on Pakistan's economic and social conditions: a bibliographic note. In his Settlement and social change in Asia. Hong Kong: Hong Kong U. Press, 1967, 340-83.

17772 NATL. SCIENCE COUNCIL. Review of scientific research in major fields related to economic & social development. Islamabad: National Science Council of Pakistan, 1978-79. 3 v.

17773 PAKISTAN. ECON. ADVISOR'S WING. Pakistan economic survey, 1977-78. Islamabad: 1978. 174p. [issued irregularly]

17774 PEACH, W.N. Basic data of the economy of Pakistan. Karachi: OUP, 1959. 235p.

17775 PIDE. An abstract of economic and demographic research: past, present, and planned. Islamabad: PIDE, 1974. 51p.

17776 SIDDIQUI, A.H. Devindex Pakistan: index to 1976 Pakistani literature on economic and social development. Islamabad: PIDE, 1978. 28p.

17777 ______. Economic planning in Pakistan: a select bibliography. Karachi: Pak Pub., 1970. 62p.

17778 ______, ed. The economy of Pakistan: a select bibliography, 1947-1962. Karachi: PIDE, 1963. 162p.

17779 ______, ed. The economy of Pakistan; a select bibliography, 1963-1965. Karachi: PIDE, 1967. 42p.

17780 TALUKDER, ALAUDDIN, ed. Cumulative index of PIDE publications, 1961-1968. Karachi: PIDE, 1969. 75p.

B. Demography and Population Policy

1. Bibliography

17781 BHATTI, A.D., ed. A bibliography of Pakistan demography. Karachi: PIDE, 1965. 59p.

17782 SIDDIQUI, A.H. & ABDUL HAMEED. Demographic studies on Pakistan: a select bibliography. Islamabad: PIDE, 1977. 79p.

2. General Studies of Pakistan's Population

17783 AFZAL, M. The population of Pakistan. Islamabad: PIDE, 1974. 112p.

17784 BEAN, L.L. & A.D. BHATTI. Pakistan's population in the 1970's: problems and prospects. In JAAS(L) 8,3/4 (1973) 259-78.

17785 ÉTIENNE, G. La population et le développement économique de Pakistan. In Population 20 (1965) 851-64.

17786 HOOVER, E.M. & M. PERLMAN. Measuring the effects of population control on economic development: a case study of Pakistan. In PDR 6 (1966) 545-66.

17787 KROTKI, K.J. Pakistan's population size and growth in the light of the 1972 census evaluation survey. In PDR 15,2 (1976) 181-94.

17788 KROTKI, K.J. & KHALIDA PARVEEN. Population growth and size in Pakistan based on early reports of the 1972 census. In PDR 15,3 (1976) 290-318.

17789 NAZIR AHMAD. Population in Pakistan. Karachi: Central Stat. Office, 1965. 50p.

17790 QURESHI, A.I. Pakistan's population problem. In S. Chandrasekhar, ed. Asia's population problems. NY: Praeger, 1967, 146-64.

17791 ROBINSON, W.C. Studies in the demography of Pakistan. Karachi: PIDE, 1967. 225p.

3. Population Structure and Distribution; Fertility and Mortality

17792 BEAN, L.L. & MASIHUR RAHMAN KHAN. Mortality patterns in Pakistan. Karachi: PIDE, 1967. 8p.

17793 GUSTAFSON, E. Existing birth and death registration systems in East and West Pakistan, 1964; a summary report. Karachi: Population Growth Estimation, Govt. of Pakistan, 1966. 35p.

17794 KHAN, MASIHUR RAHMAN & L.L. BEAN. Interrelationships of some fertility measures in Pakistan. Karachi: PIDE, 1967. 16p.

17795 KROTKI, K. Population size, growth and age distribution: fourth release from the 1961 census of Pakistan. In PDR 3 (1963) 279-305.

17796 KROTKI, K. & NAZIR AHMED. Vital rates in East and West Pakistan--tentative results from the PGE experiment. In PDR 4 (1964) 734-59. [Population Growth Estimation]

17797 SHAW, D.C. An analysis of the age structure of Pakistan. Washington: Intl. Demographic Stat. Center, Population Division, U.S. Bureau of the Census, 1970. 51p.

17798 SYED, SABIHA HASSAN. Female status and fertility in Pakistan. In PDR 17,4 (1978) 408-30.

17799 WORLD FERTILITY SURVEY. Pakistan fertility survey: first report. Lahore: Population Planning Council of Pakistan, 1976. 312p.

4. Population Policy and Control

17800 KROTKI, K.J. The feasibility of an effective population policy for Pakistan. In PDR 4 (1964) 283-333.

17801 PAKISTAN INTL. FAMILY PLANNING CONF., DACCA, 1969. Population control: implications, trends, and prospects. Ed. by Nafis Sadik et al. Islamabad: Pakistan Family Planning Council, 1969. 686p.

17802 PAKISTAN. MIN. OF HEALTH, LABOUR & SOCIAL WELFARE. Family planning scheme for Pakistan during the third Five Year Plan period, 1965-1970. Rawalpindi: 1965? 192p.

17803 ROBINSON, W.C. Family planning in Pakistan 1955-1977: a review. In PDR 17,2 (1978) 233-47.

17804 ______. Family planning in Pakistan's third Five Year Plan. In PDR 6,2 (1966) 255-81.

C. Output, Income, and Standards of Living

17805 BERGAN, A. Personal income distribution and personal savings in Pakistan, 1963-64. Karachi: PIDE, 1966. 35p.

17806 ______. Personal income distribution and personal savings in Pakistan. In K. Griffin & Azizur Rahman Khan, eds. Growth and inequality in Pakistan. London: Macmillan, 1972, 208-23. [Also in PDR 7,2 (1967) 160-212]

17807 KHAN, TAUFIQ M., comp. Studies on national income and its distribution. Karachi: PIDE, 1970. 191p.

17808 Living standards in Pakistan; a group study. Karachi: Inst. of Intl. Affairs, 1954. 82p.

17809 PAKISTAN. NATL. INCOME CMSN. Final report, November 1965. Karachi: 1965. 124p.

D. Economic Development and Planning

1. General Studies of Pakistan's Economy since 1947

17810 AHMAD, S.J. An approach to economic problems of Pakistan. 2nd ed. Karachi: Kifayat Academy, 1970. 656p.

17811 AKHTAR, S.M. Economics of Pakistan. 7th rev. ed. Lahore: Publishers United, 1963-64. 2 v.

17812 International economic issues and Pakistan. [special issue] In Pakistan Horizon 15,4 (1972) 161p.

17813 MALATHVI, M.H. Fundamentals of Pakistan economics. Karachi: Farooq Kitab Ghar, 1977. 552p.

17814 MUSTAFA, SAMI. Pakistan: a study in underdevelopment. Lahore: South Asian Inst., U. of Punjab, 1975. 74p.

17815 NATL. INST. OF SOCIAL & ECON. RES. Problems and prospects of development in Pakistan; an analysis of pressing socio-economic problems and their possible solutions. Karachi: Pak Pub., 1972. 98p.

19816 NAYAK, PANDAV. Political economy of Islamic Pakistan. In SAS 13,1 (1978) 1-24.

17817 Pakistan essays on economic problems. Lahore: Progressive, 1979. 1 v.

17818 PAKISTAN. OFFICE OF THE ECON. ADVISER. Economy of Pakistan, 1948-68. Islamabad: 1968. 378p.

17819 PAKISTAN. PLANNING CMSN. Pakistan. Islamabad: MIB, 1975. 127p.

17820 QURESHI, A.I. Economic history of Pakistan. Lahore: Islamic Book Service, 1978. 466p.

17821 SAEED, KHAWAJA AMJAD. Economic structure of Pakistan. Lahore: Accountancy & Taxation Services Inst., 1977. 396p.

17822 SEMINAR ON THE CURRENT ECON. PROBLEMS OF PAKISTAN, KARACHI, 1967. A report. Karachi: 1967. 52p.

2. Economic Growth and Development

17823 AKHTAR, S.M. Economic development of Pakistan. New ed. Lahore: Publishers United, 1978-. v. 1 -

17824 DIL, ANWAR S., comp. Toward developing Pakistan. Abbottabad: Bookservice, 1970. 272p.

17825 FALCON, W.P. & G.F. PAPANEK, eds. Development policy II - the Pakistan experience. Cambridge: HUP, 1971. 267p.

17826 GHOUSE, AGHA M., ed. Pakistan in the development decade: problems and performance. Lahore: 1968. 406p. [proc. of 3rd Econ. Dev. Seminar, Karachi, 1968]

17827 GRIFFIN, K.B. & AZIZUR RAHMAN KHAN, eds. Growth and inequality in Pakistan. London: Macmillan, 1972. 282p.

17828 HABIB, HASSAN & G.S. BIRKHEAD, eds. Selected papers on development economics and administration by members of session 5, September-December 1962. Lahore: Pakistan Admin. Staff College, 1963. 163p.

17829 HEALY, D.T. Development policy: new thinking about an interpretation. In J. of Econ. Literature 10 (1972) 757-97.

17830 JAMIL AHMAD. An approach to economic problems of Pakistan, with an appendix on People's Government reforms. 3rd rev. ed. Karachi: Kifayat Academy, 1974. 786p.

17831 MACEWAN, A. Contradictions in capitalist development: the case of Pakistan. In R. of Radical Political Econ. 3 (1971) 40-57.

17832 MIRZA, MANZOOR. Economic development in theory and practice, with special reference to Pakistan. Rawalpindi: Punjab Religious Book Soc., 1969. 301p.

17833 NORBYE, O.D.K. Development prospects of Pakistan. Oslo: Universitets-forlaget, 1968. 336p.

17834 PAPANEK, G.F. Pakistan's development: social goals and private incentives. Cambridge: HUP, 1967. 354p.

17835 STERN, J.J. & W.P. FALCON. Growth and development in Pakistan, 1955-1969. Cambridge, MA: Center for Intl. Affairs, Harvard U., 1970. 94p.

3. Economic Thought; Islam and Modernization

17836 AHMAD, BASHIRUDDIN MAHMUD. The economic structure of Islamic society. Rabwah: Ahmadiyya Muslim Foreign Missions Office, 1962. 152p.

17837 ALI, AUSAF. Studies towards an understanding of the developmental perspective. Karachi: Royal Book Co., 1979. 607p.

17838 EISTER, A.W. Perspectives sur les fonctions de la religion dans un pays en voie de développement: l'Islam au Pakistan. In Archives de sociologie des religions 8 (1963) 35-42.

17839 IMRAN, M. An outline of the economic system of Islam. Lahore: Islamic Book Centre, 1978. 70p.

17840 MAHMUD ALI. Quaid-e-Azam and Muslim economic resurgence. Lahore: Amir Pub., 1977. 115p.

17841 MALIK, H. The spirit of capitalism and Pakistani Islam. In CAS 2 (1971) 59-78.

7842 MAUDOODI, SYED ABULᶜALA, Maulana. Economic problem of man and its Islamic solution. 4th ed. Lahore: Islamic Pub., 1968. 40p.

7843 MUSLEHUDDIN, M. Economics and Islam. Lahore: Islamic Pub., 1974. 112p.

7844 ROY, ASIM. Islam and aspects of modernity in India and Pakistan. In JASBangla 20,1 (1975) 25-45.

7845 SIDDIQUI, M. NEHJATULLAH. The economic enterprise in Islam. Lahore: Islamic Pub., 1972. 179p.

4. Pakistan's Economic Planning
a. general studies

7846 AHMAD, RAFIQ & S.M. NASEEM & AGHA M. GHOUSE, eds. Economic reconstruction in Pakistan: problems, policies and prospects: papers presented to the 16th annual All Pakistan Econ. Conf., Islamabad U., Islamabad, Feb. 18-20, 1973. Karachi: Pakistan Econ. Assn., 1973. 323p.

7847 AHMED, EMAJUDDIN. Development strategy: class and regional interests of the ruling elites in Pakistan. In IESHR 15,4 (1978) 421-50.

7848 BHATIA, B.M. Pakistan's economic development, 1948-78: the failure of a strategy. ND: Vikas, 1979. 282p.

7849 BOSE, S.R. Pakistan's development - the role of government and private enterprise. In PDR 8 (1968) 265-80.

7850 GHOUSE, AGHA M., ed. Economic planning and development in Pakistan. Karachi: Trade and Industry Pub., 1965. 246p. [proc. of 2nd Econ. Dev. Seminar, Lahore, 1964]

7851 GRIFFIN, K.B. Financing development plans in Pakistan. In K. Griffin & Azizur Rahman Khan, eds. Growth and inequality in Pakistan. London: Macmillan, 1972, 31-64. [Also in PDR 4 (1965) 601-30]

7852 HAQ, MAHBUBUL. The strategy of economic planning: a case study of Pakistan. Karachi: OUP, 1966. 266p.

7853 KHAN, AZIZUR RAHMAN, ed. Symposium on planning experience in Pakistan. Karachi: PIDE, 1968. 102p. [Rpt. from PDR 8,3 (1968)]

7854 MACEWAN, A. Development alternatives in Pakistan; a multisectoral and regional analysis of planning problems. Cambridge: HUP, 1971. 211p.

7855 MANIRUZZAMAN, TALUKDER. The politics of development: the case of Pakistan, 1947-1958. Dacca: Green Book House, 1971. 191p.

7856 RAHIM, A.M.A. The development strategy of Pakistan: the case for revision. In AS 13,6 (1973) 577-86.

7857 WATERSTON, A. Planning in Pakistan; organization and implementation. Baltimore: Johns Hopkins Press, 1963. 150p.

b. the Plans
i. the Two-Year Development Plan (1949-50) and the Six-Year Development Programme (1951-57)

7858 PAKISTAN. MIN. OF ECON. AFFAIRS. Report of the first meeting of the Planning Advisory Board held at Karachi, 1949. Karachi: MPGOP, 1949. 108p.

7859 ______. Six-year development programme of Pakistan, July 1951 to June 1957. Karachi: 1951. 67p.

ii. the First Five-Year Plan, 1955-60

7860 ABBAS, S.A. An appraisal of Pakistan's first five year plan. Rotterdam: Netherlands Econ. Inst., Div. for Balanced Intl. Growth, 1956. 23p.

7861 PAKISTAN. PLANNING CMSN. The First Five Year Plan, 1955-60. Karachi: MPGOP, 1958. 652p.

7862 ______. The first five year plan 1955-60 (Draft). Karachi: MPGOP, 1956. 2 v.

iii. the Second Five-Year Plan, 1960-65

7863 ECONOMIC CONF. ON SECOND FIVE YEAR PLAN, RAWALPINDI, 1961. Economic Conference on second five year plan. Lahore: Bureau of Natl. Reconstruction, 1962. 183p.

17864 KHAN, A.R. Financing the Second Five-Year Plan. In PDR 1 (1961) 52-63.

17865 PAKISTAN. PLANNING CMSN. Final evaluation of the second five-year plan, 1960-65. Karachi: 1966. 239p.

17866 ______. Mid-plan review; evaluation of progress during the first three years of the second five-year plan. Karachi: 1964. 145p.

17867 ______. Mid-plan review of progress in 1960/61-1961/62 under the second five-year plan. Rev. and enl. ed. Karachi: 1963. 136p.

17868 ______. Outline of the second five year plan, 1960-65. Karachi: MPGOP, 1960. 103p.

17869 ______. Preliminary evaluation of progress during the second five year plan. Karachi: 1965. 168p.

17870 ______. The second five year plan (1960-65). Karachi: MPGOP, 1960. 414p.

iv. the Third Five-Year Plan, 1965-70

17871 PAKISTAN. PLANNING CMSN. Evaluation of the first year, 1965-66, of the third five year plan, 1965-70. Karachi: 1967. 199p.

17872 ______. Guidelines for the Third Five Year Plan (1965-70). Karachi: 1963.

17873 ______. Outline of the third five-year plan, 1965-70. Karachi: Govt. of Pakistan, 1964. 248p.

17874 ______. The third five-year plan, 1965-70. Karachi: MPGOP, 1967. 517p.

17875 QURESHI, ANWAR IQBAL, ed. Third five-year plan and other papers. Papers read at the 12th Pakistan Economic Conference held at Peshawar from March 1 to 3, 1965. Lahore: Pakistan Econ. Assn., 1965. 325p.

17876 TIMS, W. Analytical techniques for development planning: a case study of Pakistan's third five-year plan. Karachi: PIDE, 1968. 210p.

v. the Fourth Five-Year Plan, 1970-75

17877 BURKI, S.J. Politics of economic decision making during the Bhutto period. In AS 14,12 (1974) 1126-40.

17878 GUSTAFSON, W.E. Economic problems of Pakistan under Bhutto. In AS 16,4 (1976) 364-80.

17879 GUSTAFSON, W.E. Economic reforms under the Bhutto regime. In JAAS(L) 8,3/4 (1973) 241-58.

17880 PAKISTAN. ADVISORY PANELS FOR THE FOURTH FIVE-YEAR PLAN. Reports. Islamabad: 1970. 2 v.

17881 PAKISTAN. PLANNING CMSN. The fourth five year plan, 1970-75. Islamabad: 1970. 574p.

17882 ______. Socio-economic objectives of the fourth five-year plan, 1970-75. Karachi: 1968. 23p.

vi. the Fifth Five-Year Plan, 1978-83

17883 PAKISTAN. PLANNING CMSN. The fifth five year plan, 1978-83. Karachi: MPGOP, 1978. 266p.

e. economic disparities of East and West Pakistan
[see Chap. Fifteen, II. C. 3. b.]

E. Pakistan's Financial and Monetary System

1. Public Finance

17884 ANDRUS, J.R. & AZIZALI F. MOHAMMED. Trade, finance, and development in Pakistan. Stanford, CA: Stanford U. Press, 1966. 289p.

17885 BOSE, S.R., comp. Studies on fiscal and monetary problems. Karachi: PIDE, 1970. 275p.

17886 Financial problems of local government: a report and technical papers of symposium organized in Karachi on 2-3 Nov. 1975. Karachi: Pakistan Group for the Study of Local Govt., 1976. 112p.

17887 LEWIS, S.R. Aspects of fiscal policy and resource

mobilization in Pakistan. In PDR 4 (1964) 261-82.

17888 PAKISTAN. MIN. OF FINANCE. Fiscal policy in Pakistan: a historical perspective. Islamabad: 1972. 2 v.

2. Taxation

17889 CHAUDHRY, M.G. The problem of agricultural taxation in West Pakistan and an alternative solution. In PDR 12 (1973) 93-122; comment by Sarfaraz Khan Qureshi in 12 (1973) 433-7.

17890 LEWIS, S.R. & SARFARAZ KHAN QURESHI. The structure of revenues from indirect taxes in Pakistan. In PDR 4 (1964) 491-526.

17891 PAKISTAN. FINANCE DIV. Taxation structure of Pakistan. Islamabad: 1977. 57p.

17892 PAKISTAN. TAXATION CMSN. Interim report. Karachi: MPGOP, 1971. 76p.

17893 PAKISTAN. TAXATION ENQUIRY CMSN. Report. Karachi: 1960-64. 2 v.

3. Banking and Monetary Policy
a. the State Bank of Pakistan (est. 1948), and commercial banks

17894 MEENAI, SAEED AHMED. An appraisal of the credit and monetary situation in Pakistan. Karachi: State Bank of Pakistan, 1964. 127p.

17895 ______. Money and banking in Pakistan. 2nd ed. Karachi: Royal Book Co., 1977. 272p. [1st ed. 1966]

17896 MINHAS, ILYASIB. Analysis of banking practices and policies in Pakistan. Karachi: Natl. Inst. of Social & Econ. Res., 1973. 149p.

17897 MUSLEHUDDIN, M. Banking and Islamic law. Karachi: Islamic Res. Academy, 1974. 153p.

17898 NATL. BANK OF PAKISTAN. The story of the National Bank of Pakistan. Karachi: United Advertisers, 1966. 100p. [1949-66]

17899 PANJATAN, S. GHULAM. Banking law and practice in Pakistan. Karachi: Sir Sayyed Academy, 1977. 611p.

17900 PORTER, R.C. Liquidity and lending; the volume of bank credit in Pakistan. Karachi: PIDE, 1963. 143p. (Monographs in the econ. of dev., 10)

17901 SIDDIQUI, M. NEJATULLAH. Banking without interest. Lahore: Islamic Pub., 1973. 207p.

17902 STATE BANK OF PAKISTAN. DEPT. OF RESEARCH. The State Bank of Pakistan: its growth, functions, and organization. Karachi: 1961. 75p.

b. prices and inflation

17903 DESPRES, E. Price, distortions and development planning: Pakistan. In his International economic reform: collected papers of Emile Despres. NY: OUP, 1973, 133-45.

17904 LEWIS, S.R., JR. Effects of trade policy on domestic relative prices: Pakistan, 1951-64. In American Econ. R. 58 (1968) 60-78.

17905 LEWIS, S.R., JR. & S. MUSHTAQ HUSSAIN. Relative price changes and industrialization in Pakistan, 1951-1964. Karachi: PIDE, 1967. 77p.

17906 A measure of inflation in Pakistan, 1951-60. Karachi: PIDE, 1961. 113p.

17907 PAKISTAN. EXPERTS' CMTEE. OF ECONOMICS ON PRICES. Report. Islamabad: Min. of Industries & Natl. Resources, 1969.

c. savings and capital formation

17908 BAQAI, MOINUDDIN. A study of savings in the corporate sector in Pakistan, 1959-1963. Karachi: PIDE, 1967. 36p.

17909 HASAN, PARVEZ. Deficit financing and capital formation: the Pakistan experience 1951-59. Karachi: PIDE, 1962. 97p.

17910 HUSAIN, A.F.A. Pakistan. In R.D. Lambert & B.F. Hoselitz, eds. The role of savings and wealth in southern Asia and the West. Paris: UNESCO, 1962, 245-315.

17911 LEWIS, S.R. & M. IRSHAD. Estimates of noncorporate private saving in Pakistan: 1949-62. In PDR 4 (1964) 1-50.

17912 SAFIULLAH, M. Corporate saving in Pakistan, 1959-63. Dacca: Bureau of Econ. Res., Dacca U., 1967. 82p.

4. The Cooperative Movement in Pakistan

17913 OWENS, J.E. Cooperatives in Pakistan. In Sociology & Social Res. 44 (1960) 251-56.

17914 WEST PAKISTAN. COOPERATIVE INQUIRY CMTEE. Report, 1955. Lahore: Supt., Govt. Press, 1956. 227p.

F. Agriculture and Rural Development

1. Bibliography, Reference, and Statistics

17915 AZIM, M. A bibliography of Academy publications, 1959-69. Peshawar: PARD, 1970. 48p.

17916 BHATTI, K.M. Bibliography on rural development in Pakistan. Peshawar: PARD, 1973. 127p.

17917 PAKISTAN. MIN. OF AGRI. & WORKS. PLANNING UNIT. Agricultural statistics of Pakistan. Karachi: 1970. 200p.

17918 PAKISTAN. OFFICE OF THE CENSUS COMMISSIONER. 196[illegible] Pakistan census of agriculture. Pakistan: Agri. Census Organization, Min. of Food & Agri., 1962. 1218p.

17919 PAKISTAN. PLANNING CMSN. AGRI. & FOOD SECTION. Handbook of agricultural statistics. Karachi: 1964. 203p.

17920 PAKISTAN MANPOWER INST. Annotated bibliography on rural poverty and employment, internal migration, agriculture mechanization and employment, rural manpower development, international migration, resettlement of returning migrants. Islamabad: PMI, 1978. 200p.

17921 SHARMA, P.C. Planning for agricultural and rural development in Pakistan (1950-1970): a selected research bibliography. Monticello, IL: Council of Planning Librarians, 1975. 12p.

17922 SIDDIQUI, AKHTAR H. Agriculture in Pakistan; a selected bibliography, 1947-1969. Rawalpindi: USAID, 1969. 88p.

2. General Studies of Pakistan's Agriculture

17923 AFZAL, M. Farming in Pakistan. Islamabad: Pakistan Academy of Sciences, 1976. 277p.

17924 FALCON, W.P. Farmer response to price in a subsistence economy: the case of Pakistan. In American Economic Review, Papers and Proceedings, May 1964, 580-91.

17925 HUSSAIN, MUSHTAQ & M. IRSHAD KHAN, eds. Empirical studies on Pakistan agriculture. Karachi: PIDE, 1970. 373p.

17926 KAHNERT, F., et al. Agriculture and related industries in Pakistan: prospects and requirements until 1975. Paris: Dev. Centre, OECD, 1970. 452p.

17927 KHAN, SHAMS-UL-ISLAM. Development of agriculture in Pakistan. In J. of the U. of Peshawar 10 (1965) 38-66.

17928 SAEED HAFEEZ. Pakistan agriculture, 1975. Karachi: Project Div., Press Corp. of Pakistan, 1975. 100p

17929 SEMINAR ON AGRI. MARKETING, WEST PAKISTAN AGRI. U. 1967. 577p.

17930 U.S. AID MISSION TO PAKISTAN. FOOD & AGRI. DIV. Pakistan agriculture: resources, progress and prospects Karachi: 1966. 206p.

3. Agricultural Development and the "Green Revolution"

17931 ALAVI, HAMZA. Elite farmer strategy and regional disparities in the agricultural development of Pakistan In EPW 8,13 (1973) A31-A39.

17932 ANWAR, ABDUL AZIZ & M. AHMAD KHAN. A survey of the sugar industry of West Pakistan with special reference to its socio-economic benefits. Lahore: Board of Econ. Inquiry, 1965. 300p. (Its Pub., 132)

17933 FALCON, W.P. The green revolution: generations of problems. In American J. of Agri. Econ. 52 (1970) 698-710.

17934 GOTSCH, C.H. Regional agricultural growth: the case of West Pakistan. In AS 8 (1968) 188-205.

17935 HAFEEZ, SAEED. Pakistan agricultural revolution. Karachi: Press Corp. of Pakistan, Project Div., 1974. 114p.

17936 ______., ed. Ten years of agricultural development in Pakistan, 1958-68. Karachi: Press Corp. of Pakistan, 1968. 227p.

17937 KHAN, MAHMOOD HASAN. The economics of the Green Revolution in Pakistan. NY: Praeger, 1975. 229p.

17938 ______. The role of agriculture in economic development. A case study of Pakistan. Wageningen: Centre for Agri. Pub. & Documentation, 1966. 161p.

17939 KUHNEN, F. Agriculture and beginning industrialization: West Pakistan; socio-economic investigations in five Pakistani villages. Tr. from German by A. Lamp. Opladen: Leske, 1968. 274p. (Pub. of the German Orient-Institute)

17940 SHARIF, C.M., comp. Food production increase in West Pakistan: problems and effects. Peshawar: PARD, 1971. 365p.

17941 STEVENS, R.D. & HAMZA ALAVI & P.J. BERTOCCI, eds. Rural development in Bangladesh and Pakistan: past achievements and present challenges. Honolulu: UPH, 1976. 399p.

4. Agricultural Planning

17942 ALVI, SHAHIRUDDIN, ed. Bureaucracy and rural development: selected papers presented in the seminars on rural development at the Pakistan Academy for Rural Development. Peshawar: PARD, 1968. 92p.

17943 BURKI, S.J. West Pakistan's rural works program: a study in political and administrative response. In Middle East J. 23,3 (1969) 321-42.

17944 GOTSCH, C.H. & W.P. FALCON, eds. Agricultural price policy and the development of West Pakistan. Cambridge, MA: Org. for Social & Technical Innovation, 1970. [v. 1, Final Report; v. 2, Working Papers]

17945 IMDAD ALI KHAN. A report on evaluation of ulema project. Peshawar: PARD, 1972. 68p.

17946 KANEDA, H. Economic implications of the "green revolution" and the strategy of agricultural development in West Pakistan. Karachi: PIDE, 1969. 50p. [Also in K. Griffin & Azizur Rahman Khan, ed. Growth and inequality in Pakistan. London: Macmillan, 1972, 94-122; also in PDR 9,2 (1969) 111-43]

17947 KHAN, AKHTER HAMEED. Four rural development programmes: an evaluation. Peshawar: PARD, 1974. 92p.

17948 SCHULER, E.A. & RAGHU SINGH. Pakistan academies for rural development. Comilla and Peshawar, 1959-64. East Lansing: Asian Studies Center, Michigan State U., 1965. 116p. [an annotated bibliography prepared by the Asian Studies Center]

17949 TIRMIZI, F.A.M. Ulema project, 1967-68. Peshawar: PARD, 1968. 34p.

5. Agricultural Technology and Innovation [See also F. 3., above]

17950 BOSE, S.R. & E.H. CLARK. Some basic considerations on agricultural mechanization in West Pakistan. Karachi: PIDE, 1969. 110p. [also in PDR 9,3 (1969) 273-309]

17951 BURKI, S.J. Interest group involvement in West Pakistan's rural works program. In Public Policy 19 (1971) 167-206.

17952 COWNIE, J. & B.F. JOHNSON & B. DUFF. The quantitative impact of the seed-fertilizer revolution in West Pakistan: an exploratory study. In Food Res. Inst. Studies 9 (1970) 57-95.

17953 GOTSCH, C.H. Tractor mechanization and rural development in Pakistan. In Intl. Labour R. 197 (1973) 133-66.

17954 INAYATULLAH. Diffusion and adoption of improved practices, a study of agricultural practices in a village. Peshawar: Pakistan Academy for Village Dev., 1962. 81p.

17955 KANEDA, H. Mechanization, industrialization and technical change in rural West Pakistan. In R.T. Shand, ed. Technical change in Asian agriculture. Canberra: ANUP, 1973, 161-82.

17956 NIAZ, SHAFI. Agriculture mechanization in Pakistan. In Journal of R. Dev. & Admin. 7,2 (1970) 57-69.

17957 NULTY, L. The green revolution in West Pakistan; implications of technological change. NY: Praeger, 1972. 150p.

6. Irrigation and Water Management

17958 CARRUTHERS, I.D. Irrigation development planning: aspects of Pakistan experience. Ashford: Wye College (Econ. Dept.), 1968. 67p.

17959 DORFMAN, R. & R. REVELLE & H. THOMAS. Waterlogging and salinity in the Indus plain: some basic considerations. In PDR 5 (1965) 331-70.

17960 ÉTIENNE, G. Progrès agricole et maîtrise de l'eau. Le cas du Pakistan. Paris: PUF, 1967. 188p.

17961 GHULAM MOHAMMAD. Private tubewell development and cropping patterns in West Pakistan. In PDR 5,1 (1965) 1-53.

17962 ______. Programme for the development of irrigation and agriculture in West Pakistan; a preliminary analysis of some of the major recommendations in the Bank Consultants report. Karachi: PIDE, 1967. 63p.

17963 ______. Waterlogging and salinity in the Indus Plain: a critical analysis of the major conclusions of the Revelle Report. In PDR 4,3 (1964) 356-403.

17964 GHULAM MOHAMMAD & C. BERINGER. Waterlogging and salinity in West Pakistan: an analysis of the Revelle Report. In PDR 3 (1963) 250-78.

17965 KANEDA, H. Tubewells and the green revolution in West Pakistan's agriculture. In Keizai Kenkyu 21 (1970) 353-62.

17966 KARPOV, A.V. Indus Valley: West Pakistan's life line. In J. of the Hydraulics Div., Proc. of the American Soc. of Civil Engineers 90 (Jan. 1964) 207-42. [comments in 90 (July & Sept. 1964) 371-89, 431-51; repply in 91 (March 1965) 300-14]

17967 MICHEL, A.A. The Indus rivers; a study of the effects of partition. New Haven: YUP, 1967. 595p.

17968 NASRI, S.NAVAID. Bibliography on waterlogging and salinity problems in Pakistan. 2nd ed. Lahore: Planning and Coordination Cell, Irrigation, Drainage and Flood Control Res. Council, 1976. 283p.

17969 NATL. INST. OF SOCIAL & ECON. RES. Water & power development in West Pakistan, 1947-72. Karachi: 1972. 45p.

17970 PAKISTAN. WATERLOGGING & SALINITY STUDY CELL. Waterlogging and salinity problems in Pakistan. Ed. by Nazir Ahmad. Lahore: The Cell, 1974. 5 v.

17971 SNELGROVE, A.K. Geohydrology of the Indus River of West Pakistan. Hyderabad: Sind U. Press, 1967. 200p.

17972 U.S. WHITE HOUSE - DEPT. OF INTERIOR PANEL ON WATERLOGGING & SALINITY IN WEST PAKISTAN. Report on land and water development in the Indus Plain. Washington: Govt. Printing Office, 1964. 454p. [the Revelle report]

17973 Water and power resources of West Pakistan: a study in sector planning. Prepared by a World Bank Study Group headed by Pieter Lieftinck. Baltimore: Johns Hopkins Press, 1968-69. 3 v.

7. Land Use and Agricultural Products

17974 CHAMPION, H.G. & S.K. SETH & G.M. KHATTAK. Forest types of Pakistan. Peshawar: Pakistan Forest Inst., 1965. 238p.

17975 Ecology, environment, and afforestation. Islamabad: Govt. of Pakistan, Environment and Urban Affairs Div., 1974. 168p.

17976 HUSAIN, KHALIFA AMJAD. History of fisheries research & development in West Pakistan, 1870-1963. 2nd ed., rev. & enl. Lahore: 1964. 158p.

17977 WEST PAKISTAN. DIR. OF FISHERIES. A decade of progress in fisheries. Lahore: 1969. 142p.

8. Land Tenure and Reforms; Agricultural Credit

17978 AKRAM, C.M. Manual of land reforms.... Lahore: National Law Pub., 1973. 106p.

17979 BASHIR, M. Land reforms regulation, MLR 115. Lahore: Khyber Law Pub., 1980. 80p.

17980 ESPOSITO, B.J. The politics of agrarian reform in Pakistan. In AS 14,5 (1974) 429-38.

17981 HERRING, R. & M. GHAFFAR CHAUDHRY. The 1972 land reforms in Pakistan and their economic implications: a preliminary analysis. In PDR 13,3 (1974) 245-79.

17982 JAHANIAN, CH. MOHAMMAD HUSAIN. The colonization of government lands. Lahore: Caravan Book House, 1965. 201p.

17983 KHAN, AKHTER HAMEED. Land reforms in Pakistan, 1947-72. Karachi: Natl. Inst. of Social & Econ. Res., 1972. 20p.

17984 KHAN, M. IRSHAD. The development of institutional agricultural credit in Pakistan. In PDR 3 (1963) 66-97.

17985 KHURSHID, M. IDRIS. Land reforms, a selected bibliography (annotated). 2nd ed. Dacca: Govt. of Pakistan Press, 1962. 28p.

17986 MIAN, INAM-UL-HAQ. Manual of land reforms with rules; containing Martial Law regulation no. 115, all relevant noficiations & amendments of Punjab, Sind, Baluchistan & N.W.F.P. Lahore: Mansoor Book House, 1973. 176p.

17987 PAKISTAN. LAND REFORMS CMSN. FOR WEST PAKISTAN. Report, January 1959. Lahore: Supt., Govt. Printing, West Pakistan, 1961. 74p.

17988 SANDERATNE, N. Landowners and land reform in Pakistan. In SAR 7,2 (1974) 123-36.

17989 SIDDIQUI, S.I. Land tenure as a factor in land use in West Pakistan. In Pakistan Geographical R. 13 (1958) 18-23.

17990 STATE BANK OF PAKISTAN. Agricultural credit in Pakistan. Karachi: 1962. 145p.

17991 ______. Report on rural banking: expansion of the commercial banking system in rural areas. Karachi: 1968. 67p.

9. Peasant Society and Rural Social Change

17992 FALCON, W.P. & C.H. GOTSCH. Paths of rural change: two approaches with the same result. In Asian R. 1 (1968) 239-55.

17993 JONES, G.N. Community associations in Pakistan: a survey of organizational development. In NIPA J. 8 (1968) 2-86,

17994 KHAN, AKHTER HAMEED. Community and agricultural development in Pakistan. East Lansing: Asian Studies Center, Michigan State U., 1969. 34p.

17995 KHAN, SHOAIB SULTAN. Rural development in Pakistan. ND: Vikas, 1980. 161p.

17996 QADEER, MOHAMMAD A. An evaluation of the integrated rural development programme. Islamabad: PIDE, 1977. 95p.

17997 RAUF, ABDUR. West Pakistan: rural education and development. Honolulu: EWCP, 1970. 173p.

G. Pakistan's Industry

1. Bibliography and Reference

17998 AKHTAR, ABDUL HAFEEZ. Small and medium industries of Pakistan; a select bibliography 1948-62. Karachi: PIDE, 1963. 34p.

17999 PAKISTAN. DEPT. OF INVESTMENT PROMOTION & SUPPLIES. Directory of industrial establishments in Pakistan. Karachi: MPGOP, 1970-1976. 4 v.

18000 SIDDIQUI, AKHTAR H., ed. Industrial Pakistan; a select bibliography, 1948-1966. Karachi: Editions Mystique, 1968. 131p.

18001 Trade directory. Karachi: Chamber of Commerce & Industry, 1971-. [pub. irreg.]

2. General Studies of Industrialization

18002 AHMAD, NAFIS. Some aspects of economic development of Pakistan with special reference to industrialization 1947-1968. In Oriental Geographer 13,1 (1969) 1-24.

18003 AZIZ, SARTAJ. Industrial location policy in Pakistan. Karachi: National Publishing House, 1969. 71p.

18004 CHEEMA, AFTAB AHMAD. Productivity trends in the manufacturing industries. In PDR 17,1 (1978) 44-65.

18005 FALCON, W.P. Agriculture and industrial interrelationship in West Pakistan. In J. of Farm Economics 49 (Dec. 1967) 1139-54. [comment by S.R. Lewis, 1154-7]

18006 HUQ, SAYEEDUL. Patterns of industrialisation in Pakistan. In E.A.G. Robinson & M. Kidron, ed. Economic development in South Asia. London: Macmillan, 1970, 153-69.

18007 LEWIS, S.R., Jr. Economic policy and industrial growth in Pakistan. London: Allen & Unwin, 1969. 191p.

18008 ______. Pakistan: industrialization and trade policies. London: OUP, 1970. 214p.

18009 NATL. INST. OF SOCIAL & ECON. RES. West Pakistan's industrial production: impact of loss of East Pakistan market. Karachi: Pakistan Pub., 1972. 71p.

18010 NURUL ISLAM. Comparative costs, factor proportions and industrial efficiency in Pakistan. In K. Griffin & Azizur Rahman Khan, eds. Growth and inequality in Pakistan. London: Macmillan, 1972, 149-68. [Also in PDR 7,2 (1967) 213-46]

18011 PAPANEK, G.F. Industrial production and investment in Pakistan. In PDR 4 (1964) 462-90.

18012 ______. The location of industry. In PDR 10,3 (1970) 291-309.

18013 SAQI, M.F. Industrial Pakistan, history of the first decade, 1947-1957. Karachi: Sind Zamindar Hotel, 1958. 164p.

18014 West Pakistan Industrial Development Corporation; an introduction. Karachi: Public Relations Dept., WPIDC, 1971. 36p.

3. The Public Sector

18015 BAQAR, S. ALI & TANVIR AHMAD, ed. Report on the performance of the industries taken-over by the Government of Pakistan on 2nd January 1972 under the Economic reforms order, 1972. Karachi: Pakistan Econ. Res. Unit, 1972. 65p.

18016 RAHMAN, M. AKHLAQUR. The role of the public sector in the economic development of Pakistan. In E.A. Robinson & M. Kidron, ed. Economic development in South Asia. London: Macmillan, 1970, 69-89.

18017 SIDDIQUI, ANWAR H. Management of public enterprises in Pakistan. Lahore: Wajidalis, 1979. 538p.

18018 SYED, REZA H. Role and performance of public enterprises in the economic growth of Palistan. Karachi: Investment Advisory Centre of Pakistan, 1977. 156 + 83p.

18019 Taken-over industries and the need for de-nationalisation. Karachi: Chamber of Commerce & Industry, 1979. 175p.

4. The Private Sector and the Pakistani Business Communities

18020 AMJAD, RASHID. Industrial concentration and economic power in Pakistan: a preliminary report. Lahore: South Asian Inst., U. of the Punjab, 1974. 137p.

18021 ASLAM, M.M. Some memories are sweet: an autobiographical sketch. Karachi: Asia Printers & Pub., 1977. 200p.

18022 THE BUSINESSMEN'S CONF., KARACHI, 1973. Economic revival and private enterprise in Pakistan; proceedings. ... Karachi: Chamber of Commerce & Industry, 1973. 353p.

18023 PAPANEK, G.F. The development of entrepreneurship. In American Econ. R. 52,2 (1962) 46-58. [comments by E. Hagen, A.N. Kamarek and F.C. Shorter, 59-66; rpr. in P. Kilby, ed. Entrepreneurship and economic development. NY: Free Press, 1971, 317-29.]

18024 PAPANEK, H. Pakistan's big businessmen: Muslim separatism, entrepreneurship, and partial modernization. In EDCC 21,1 (1972) 1-32.

18025 WHITE, L.J. Industrial concentration and economic power in Pakistan. Princeton: PUP, 1974. 212p.

5. Industrial Management and Finance

18026 AHMED, RAJIQ, ed. The role of management in Pakistan; proceedings of the Management Convention held at Karachi, November 17-18, 1966. Karachi: West Pakistan Mgmt. Assn., 1967. 181p.

18027 KHAN, M. AKRAM, ed. Management and national growth; proceedings of the Second Management Convention held at Karachi, April 25 and 25, 1968. Karachi: West Pakistan Mgmt. Assn., 1968. 218p.

18028 MEGGINSON, L.C. & AGHA M. GHOUSE, eds. Management cases of Pakistan. Karachi: West Pakistan Inst. of Mgmt., 1969. 350p.

18029 UZAIR, M. Some thoughts on economy, finance, and management. Karachi: Khusrow Academy, 1974. 301p.

6. Energy Resources and Production

18030 AHMAD, MANSOOR. Nuclear power planning study for Pakistan. Vienna: Atomic Energy Agency, 1975. 177p.

18031 INTL. ATOMIC ENERGY AGENCY. MISSION TO STUDY PROSPECTS OF NUCLEAR POWER IN PAKISTAN, 1962. Prospects of nuclear power in Pakistan: report.... Vienna: 1962. 52p.

18032 PAKISTAN ATOMIC ENERGY CMSN. Atomic energy in Pakistan, 1958-68. Karachi: 1968. 31p.

7. Studies of Specific Industries

18033 ANWAR, ABDUL AZIZ. Fruit processing industry in West Pakistan. Lahore: Board of Economic Inquiry, West Pakistan, 1967. 160p.

18034 ______. Production of sugar: policies and problems. Lahore: Board of Econ. Inquiry, Punjab, Pakistan, 1971. 397p.

18035 FAZILI, M.A. Pharmaceutical industries in West Pakistan. Lahore: Dir. of Industries & Commerce, Govt. of West Pakistan, 1969. 55p.

18036 INDUSTRIAL DEV. BANK OF PAKISTAN. A survey of the cotton textile industry of Pakistan. Dacca: 1965. 231p.

18037 MIAN, NURUL-ISLAM. Tobacco industry in Pakistan, with special reference to the N.W.F. region. Peshawar: Board of Economic Enquiry, N.W.F., Peshawar U., 1966. 44p.

18038 PAKISTAN. TEXTILE ENQUIRY CMSN. Report. Karachi: MPGOP, 1960. 199p.

18039 PAKISTAN. TEXTILE INDUSTRY CAPACITY CMTEE. Report, Feb. 1968. Karachi: MPGOP, 1970. 83p.

18040 A study of structure and capacity of construction industry in Pakistan. Karachi: Nasiruddeen Associates, 1978-. v. 1-. [for Planning Cmsn.]

18041 WERNER INTL. MGMT. CONSULTANTS. Study of the cotton textile industry in Pakistan. Karachi: All Pakistan Textile Mills Assoc., 1979. 6v. in 1, 613p.

H. Labor in Pakistan's Economy

1. Labor Force, Wages, and Unemployment

18042 ANWAR, ABDUL AZIZ. Problems of unemployment of the educated manpower. Lahore: Board of Econ. Inquiry, Punjab, 1973. 212p.

18043 BEAN, L.L. & D.M. FAROOZ & M.R. KHAN. The labour force of Pakistan: a note on the 1961 census. In PDR 6 (1966) 587-91.

18044 BHATTI, FAIZ MUHAMMAD. Minimum wages in West Pakistan. Lahore: Zarreen Book Agency, 1968. 140p.

18045 FAROOQ, GHAZI MUMTAZ. Labour force participation rates in Pakistan: 1901-1961. In PDR 8 (1968) 74-103.

18046 GUISINGER, S. & M. IRFAN. Real wages of industrial workers in Pakistan: 1954-1970. In PDR 13,4 (1974) 363-88.

18047 HAIDER, S.M. Rural manpower resources; a study of patterns of employment in rural Pakistan. Peshawar: PARD, 1962. 36p. (Its monograph, 11)

18048 KHAN, AZIZUR RAHMAN. What has been happening to real wages in Pakistan? In K. Griffin & Azizur Rahman Khan, eds. Growth and inequality in Pakistan. London: Macmillan, 1972, 224-49. [Also in PDB 7,3 (1967) 317-47]

18049 JOZEFOWICZ, A. Unemployment among the educated youth. Karachi: Planning Cmsn., 1970. 128p.

18050 RAHMAN, M. AKHLAGUR. The analysis of relative wage and salary structure in Pakistan. Karachi: MPGOP, 1971. 114p.

2. Labor and Manpower Policy and Legislation

18051 ANDREWS, E.W. Labor law and practice in Pakistan. Washington: U.S. Dept. of Labor, Bureau of Labor Statistics; for sale by the Superintendent of Documents, U.S. Govt. Print. Office, 1964. 68p. (BLS report, 271)

18052 AQUILA KIANI, ed. Sociology of development in Pakistan. Karachi: Social Res. Centre, U. of Karachi, 1971. 265p.

18053 NAWAZ, MOHAMMED. Manpower problem of Pakistan. In Econ. J. (Lahore) 8,1 (1975) 21-46.

18054 PARVIZ, N. Labour policy and planning in Pakistan. Karachi: Pakistan Inst. of Personnel Admin., 1962. 56p.

18055 SEMINAR ON A POLICY FOR SKILLED MANPOWER, DACCA, 1967. Report. Dacca: Mgmt. Dev. Centre, Govt. of East Pakistan, 1968? 96p.

18056 SHAFI, M. Eleven years of labour policy. Karachi: Bureau of Labour Pub., 1959. 128p.

18057 ______. Labour policy of Pakistan. Karachi: Bureau of Labour Pub., 1969. 108p.

18058 WEATHERFORD, W.D. Pakistan. In W. Galenson, ed. Labor in developing economies. Berkeley: UCalP, 1962, 11-70.

3. Industrial Relations and Trade Unions

18059 HAFEEZ, SABEEHA. Influence of the perceived problems of the trade unions on their perceived functions in Pakistan: an empirical assessment. In Pakistan Mgmt. R. 17,3 (1976) 75-92.

18060 ______. The problems of trade unions in Pakistan; an assessment of perceived interdependence. In Pakistan Mgmt. R. 16,4 (1975) 73-85.

18061 ______. The trade unions of Pakistan as change agent: an empirical assessment. In Pakistan Political Science R. 1,2 (1973), 28-41.

18062 KHAN, BADIUDDIN A. Growth of trade unionism in Pakistan; an analytic study of the statistics. In Pakistan Mgmt. R. 19,4 (1978) 15-27.

18063 ______. Notes on trade unionism in Pakistan. In Pakistan Mgmt. R. 16,3 (1975) 21-30.

18064 RAZA, M. ALI. The industrial relations system of Pakistan. Karachi: Bureau of Labour Pub., 1963. 174p.

18065 RIZVI, S.A. SARWAR. Industrial labour relations in Pakistan. Karachi: Natl. Inst. of Social & Econ. Research, 1973. 73p.

18066 SCHREGEL, J. Labour relations in Pakistan - some major issues. In Pakistan Mgmt. R. 19,1 (1978) 63-87.

J. Transportation and Internal Commerce

18067 AHMAD, KAMALUDDIN. Pakistan trade. Karachi: Pub. Intl., 1966. 111p.

18068 ISLAM, NURUL. Studies in consumer demand. Dacca: Bureau of Econ. Res., Dacca U., 1965-66. 2 v.

18069 MALIK, RASHID A. Pakistan's intra-regional pattern of transportation. In J. of Geography 61 (1962) 209-14.

18070 NAQVI, SYED NAWAB HAIDER. The structure of commercial policy in Pakistan. Karachi: PIDE, 1967. 25p.

18071 RAHMAN, M. AKHLAQUR. Partition, integration, economic growth, and interregional trade; a study of interwing trade in Pakistan: 1948-1959. Karachi: PIDE, 1963. 206p.

18072 SETH, K.L. Interwing trade in Pakistan, causes, consequences and prospects. Delhi: Sterling, 1968. 88p.

IV. SOCIETY AND SOCIAL CHANGE IN PAKISTAN

A. General Studies of Pakistan Society

18073 AHMED, AKBAR S. Pieces of green: the sociology of change in Pakistan, 1964-1974. Karachi: Royal Book Co., 1977. 259p.

18074 ALL PAKISTAN SOCIOLOGY SEMINAR, 1ST, DACCA, 1963. Sociology and social research in Pakistan. Ed. by M. Afsaruddin. Dacca: East Pakistan Unit, Pakistan Sociological Assn., 1963. 140p.

18075 BAQAI, M. SABIHUDDIN. Social order in Pakistani society. Karachi: Natl. Book Foundation, 1975. 379p.

18076 CHAUDHARI, H. A. et al., eds. Pakistan sociological perspectives: collected papers of the Pakistan Sociological Association's 2nd, 3rd and 4th conferences. Lahore: Pakistan Sociological Assn., 1968. 277p.

18977 CHOUDHRY, M. IQBAL. The socio-cultural problems of Pakistan; a selection of articles. Lahore: Zarreen Book Agency, 1967. 163p.

18078 CHOUDHRY, M. IQBAL & MUSHTAQ AHMAD KHAN. Pakistani society; a sociological analysis. 2nd ed. Lahore: Noorsons, 1968. 391p.

18079 FAYYAZ, M., ed. Pakistan sociological writings. Lahore: Punjab U. Sociologists Alumni Assn., Dept. of Sociology, U. of the Punjab, 1970-. v. 1 -

18080 GARDEZI, HASSAN NAWAZ, comp. Sociology in Pakistan. Lahore: Dept. of Sociology, Panjab U., 1966. 149p.

18081 HASHMI, SULTAN, ed. Pakistan sociological studies. Lahore: Pakistan Sociological Assn., 1965.

18082 HUSAIN, A.F.A. Human and social impact of technological change in Pakistan; a report on a survey conducted by the University of Dacca. Dacca: OUP, 1956. 2 v.

18083 KHAN, FAZLUR RASHID. Sociology of Pakistan. Dacca: Shirin Pub., 1966. 265p.

18084 QURESHI, I.H. The Pakistani way of life. 2nd ed. London: Heinemann, 1957. 83p.

18085 Sociology today in Pakistan. Karachi: Pakistan Sociological Assn., 1975. 126p.

B. Social Categories in Pakistan: Class, Caste, and Tribe

1. Social Stratification and Minorities

18086 BHATTACHARYA, S.S. Elite sub-systems and operational ideology in Pakistan. In Interdiscipline 5 (1969) 228-34.

18087 KHAN, N.A.G. Development of the middle class in Pakistan. In Development of a middle class in tropical and subtropical countries. Brussels: 1956, 314-23. [Proc. of Intl. Inst. of Differing Civilizations. 29th Session, London, 1955.]

18088 Minorities in Pakistan. 2nd ed. Karachi: Pakistan Pub., 1964. 52p. [1st ed., 1955]

18089 NATL. INST. OF SOCIAL & ECON. RES. Growth of middle class in Pakistan. Karachi: 1971. 70p.

18090 WESTPHAL-HELLBUSCH, S. & H. WESTPHAL. The Jat of Pakistan. Berlin: Duncker & Humblot, 1964. 110p.

2. Women in Pakistan Society

18091 BEAN, L.L. Utilization of human resources: the case of women in Pakistan. In Intl. Labour R. 9,4 (1968) 391-410.

18092 KHAN, MAZHAR-UL-HAQ. Social pathology of the Muslim society. Delhi: Amar Prakashan, 1978. 196p.

18093 NIGHAT AYUB. Women in Pakistan and other Islamic countries: a selected bibliography with annotations. Karachi: Women Resource Centre, 1978. 203p.

C. Kinship and the Family: Changing Structures and Relationships

1. General Studies

18094 KHAN, FAZAL MUQEEM. Pakistani youth at the crossroads. Karachi: OUP, 1972. 166p.

18095 KORSON, J.H. Some aspects of social change in the Muslim family in West Pakistan. In CAS 3 (1973) 138-55.

18096 ZAIDI, S.M. HAFEEZ. Sociocultural change and value conflict in developing countries: a case study of Pakistan. In Conf. on Mental Health Res. in Asia and the Pacific, East-West Center, 1966. Mental health research in Asia and the Pacific. Honolulu: EWCP, 1969, 415-30.

2. Marriage: Changing Patterns and Attitudes

18097 ABBOTT, F. Pakistan's new marriage law: a reflection of Qur'anic interpretation. In AS 1 (1962) 26-32. [in re Muslim Family Laws Ordinance of 1961]

18098 AHMED, FEROZ. Age at marriage in Pakistan. In J. of Marriage & the Family 31 (1969) 799-807.

18099 DAS, VEENA. The structure of marriage preferences: an account from Pakistani fiction. In Man 8,1 (1973) 30-45.

18100 KORSON, J.H. The roles of dower and dowry as indicators of social change in Pakistan. In J. of Marriage & the Family 30,4 (1968) 696-707.

18101 ______. Student attitudes toward mate selection in a Muslim society: Pakistan. In J. of Marriage & the Family 31 (1969) 153-65.

3. Family and Personal Law

18102 AHMAD, KHURSHID, ed. Marriage commission report x-rayed: a study of the family laws of Islam and a critical appraisal of the modernist attempts to "reform" it. Karachi: Chiragh-e-Rah, 1959. 315p. [contrib. by Maudoodi et al.; incl. text of 1956 Marriage Cmsn. Report, see 18109 below]

18103 ______., ed. Studies in the family law of Islam. 2nd ed. Karachi: Chiragh-e-Rah, 1961. 254p. [Marriage Cmsn. Report reprod. as Chap. 3, 35-86]

18104 ANWARI, KHAWAJA ARSHAD MUBEEN. The manual of family laws: as amended up-to-date. Rev. & enl. ed. Lahore: Khyber Law Pub., 1978. 58p.

18105 COULSON, N.J. Islamic family law: progress in Pakistan. In J.N.D. Anderson, ed. Changing law in developing countries. London: Allen & Unwin, 1963, 240-57.

18106 ______. Reform of family law in Pakistan. In Studia Islamica 7 (1957) 135-55.

18107 FARUKI, K.A. Islamic family law in Pakistan in the context of modern reformist movements in the world of Islam. In Islamic R. 53,5 & 6 (1965) 5-8, 8-12.

18108 MIRZA, MUKARRAM. Muslim family laws. Lahore: National Law Pub., 1978. 95p.

18109 PAKISTAN. COMMISSION ON MARRIAGE AND FAMILY LAWS OF 1956. Report. In Gazette of Pakistan, Extraordinary No. F. 9(4)/56-Leg., dated 20 June 1956. Dissenting note by Maulana Ehteshamul Haq Thanvi in Gazette (Extra.) of 30 June 1956. [Text of Report reproduced in Khurshid Ahmad, ed., 18102 above]

18110 RAHMAN, FAZLUR. The controversy over the Muslim family laws. In D.E. Smith, ed. South Asian politics and religion. Princeton: PUP, 1966, 414-27.

D. Urbanization in Pakistan

1. General Studies

18111 AHMAD, QAZI SHAKIL. Distribution of city sizes in Pakistan. In Pakistan Geographical R. 22,2 (1967) 77-85.

18112 ______. Distribution pattern of urban centres in Pakistan. In Pakistan Geographical R. 22 (1967) 1-8.

18113 ______. Urban growth in Pakistan. In Geografia 5,1/2 (1966) 1-16.

18114 ______. Urbanization trends in West Pakistan: a geographical analysis. In Pakistan Geographical R. 21,1 (1966) 1-20.

18115 BABAR, IFTIKHARULLAH. Report based on urban socio-economic survey, Rawalpindi, 1977. Islamabad: PIDE, 1977. 161p.

18116 BELOKRENITSKY, V. The urbanization processes and the social structure of the urban population in Pakistan. In AS 14,3 (1974) 244-57.

18117 BURKI, S.J. Development of towns: the Pakistan experience. In AS 14,8 (1974) 751-62.

18118 HASHMI, SHAFIK H. & G.N. JONES. Problems of urbanization in Pakistan; proceedings. Karachi: NIPA, 1967. 294p.

18119 RUDDUCK, G. Towns and villages of Pakistan, a study. Karachi: MPGOP, 1964. 229p.

2. Urban Society and Its Problems

18120 HUSSAIN, S. MANZOOR. Housing problem of the low income groups in urban areas of Pakistan. In Pakistan Admin. Staff College Q. 4 (1966) 108-16.

18121 PAKISTAN. PLANNING CMSN. PHYSICAL PLANNING AND HOUSING SECTION. Incentives for housing. Karachi: 1964. 33p.

18122 Seminar on Metropolitan Area Problems in Pakistan, NIPA, KARACHI, 1963. Proceedings. Karachi: 1965. 161p.

18123 SEMINAR ON SOCIAL PROBLEMS OF URBANIZATION IN PAKISTAN, KARACHI, 1962. Social problems of urbanization in Pakistan. Karachi: Social Services Coordinating Council, 1963. 83p.

E. Social Problems and Social Service in Pakistan

18124 ABBAS, RABEYA. Social welfare administration in Pakistan. Lahore: Alhamra Academy, 1969. 83p.

18125 KHALID, M. Welfare state; a case study of Pakistan. Karachi: Royal Book Co., 1968. 327p.

18126 NASEEM, S.M. Mass poverty in Pakistan: some preliminary findings. In PDR 7,4 (1973) 317-60.

18127 PAKISTAN. CMSN. FOR ERADICATION OF SOCIAL EVILS. Report. Karachi: Min. of Health, Labour & Social Welfare, 1965. 102p.

18128 QAISER ALI KHAN. Concept and administration of social welfare in West Pakistan. Lahore: Pub. Cell, Dir. Genl. of Social Welfare, West Pakistan, 1969. 96p.

18129 SEMINAR ON THE ERADICATION OF SOCIAL EVILS, LAHORE, 1961. Report. Karachi: Supt. Govt. Printing, West Pakistan, 1963. 407p.

18130 WEST PAKISTAN. DIR. GENERAL OF SOCIAL WELFARE. PUBLIC RELATIONS WING. Facts and figures about social welfare in West Pakistan. Lahore: 1969. 1 v.

F. Health Services and Medical Systems

1. General Studies

18131 AWAN, AKHTAR HUSSAIN. The system of local health services in rural Pakistan and planned administrative and technical support. Lahore: Public Health Assoc. of Pakistan, 1969. 189p.

18132 AWAN, ASGHARI K. Maternal and child health. Lahore: Muzaffar Medical Pub., 1979. 160p.

18133 ISLAM, NURUL, ed. Symposium on Post-graduate Medical Education in Pakistan; transactions, held on May 13-15, 1966, at Institute of Post-Graduate Medicine. Dacca: Inst. of Postgraduate Medicine, 1967. 75p.

18134 NATL. CONF. ON CONTROL OF COMMUNICABLE DISEASES, 3RD, LAHORE, 1968. Report. Lahore: 1969. 144p.

18135 NATL. CONF. ON MUNICIPAL HEALTH, 2ND, LAHORE, 1968. Report. Lahore: Health Assn. of Pakistan, 1968. 119p.

18136 THREE-DAY SEMINAR ON MENTAL HEALTH IN PAKISTAN, KARACHI, 1960. Mental health in Pakistan; a report of the proceedings and recommendations. Karachi: Social Services Coordinating Council, 1961. 58p.

2. Family Planning

18137 AQUILA KIANI. The effectiveness of the social welfare approach to clients for the adoption of family planning: an action research project in selected areas of Pakistan. Karachi: Social Research Centre, U. of Karachi, 1977. 246p.

18138 AZHAR, M. & J.G. HARDEE. Change and differentials in men's knowledge of, attitude towards, and practice of family planning in Pakistan during 1960's. Islamabad: PIDE, 1977. 50p.

18139 BEAN, L.L. & A.D. BHATTI. Three years of Pakistan's new national family-planning programme. In PDR 9 (1969) 35-57.

18140 BEAN, L.L. & D.M. FAROOQ & QAMAR FATIMA. Family planning in Pakistan: a review of selected service statistics, 1966-67. Karachi: PIDE, 1968. 2 v.

18141 EGER, G. Familienplanung in Pakistan. Saarbrücken: Verlag der SSIP-Schriften Breitenbach, 1973. 146p. (SSIP-Schriften, 15)

18142 Family planning in Pakistan. Karachi: Pakistan Family Planning Council, 1969. 52p.

18143 FAYYAZ, M. The impact of motivational campaigns on family planning knowledge, attitudes, and practices. Lahore: West Pakistan Family Planning Assoc., 1971. 81p.

18144 GARDEZI, HASSAN NAWAZ & ATTIYA INAYATULLAH. The Dai study; the dai, midwife, a local functionary and her role in family planning. Lahore: West Pakistan Family Planning Assn., 1969. 106p.

18145 GREEN, L.W. & YASMIN AZRA JAN. Family planning knowledge and attitude surveys in Pakistan. In PDR 4 (1964) 332-55. [review article]

G. Education in Pakistan

1. Bibliography and Statistics

18146 BREMBECK, C.S. & E.W. WEIDNER. Education and development in India and Pakistan; a select and annotated bibliography. East Lansing: Michigan State U. College of Educ., 1962. 221p.

18147 PUNJAB UNIV. INSTITUTE OF EDUC. & RES. Statistical profile of education in West Pakistan. Karachi: Manager of Publications, 1973. 289p. (Natl. Cmsn. on Manpower & Educ., res. study, 14)

18148 WEST PAKISTAN. BUREAU OF EDUC. Bibliography on education in Pakistan. Lahore: 1970. 112p.

18149 ZAKI, WALI MUHAMMAD & M. SARWAR KHAN, eds. Pakistan education index. Islamabad: Central Bureau of Educ., 1970. 204p.

2. General Studies of Education

18150 COMMONWEALTH EDUC. CONF., 5TH, CANBERRA, 1971. Education in Pakistan, before and after the New Education Policy, 1970. Islamabad: Min. of Educ. & Scientific Res., 1971. 26p.

18151 INST. OF EDUC. & RES., U. OF PANJAB, LAHORE. A study on teachers in West Pakistan. Islamabad: Planning Cmsn., 1970. 440p. [Natl. Cmsn. on Manpower and Educ., Res. study, 9]

18152 JILLANI, M.S. Changes in levels of educational attainment in Pakistan: 1951-1961. In PDR 4 (1964) 69-92.

18153 KALIM, M. SIDDIQ. Pakistan, an educational spectrum. Lahore: Arslan Pub., 1978. 223p.

18154 PAKISTAN. CURRICULUM WING. Development of education in Pakistan 1973/75. Islamabad: Min. of Educ., 1975. 97p.

18155 QURESHI, I.H. Education in Pakistan: an inquiry into objectives and achievements. Karachi: Maʿaref, 1975. 301p.

18156 SASSANI, ABUL HASSAN K. Education in Pakistan. Washington: Office of Education, 1954. 92p. (U.S. Office of Educ., Bull. 1954,2)

18157 SHAMI, PARWAIZ. Education in search of fundamentals. Karachi: Natl. Book Foundation, 1976. 368p.

18158 ZINGEL, W.-P. Das Erziehungswesen in Pakistan. In IAF 4,2 (1973) 306-331.

3. Educational Policy and Planning
a. general studies

18159 AYUB KHAN, MOHAMMAD. President Ayub on educational revolution. Rawalpindi: Sardar Mohammad Aslam Khan, 1968. 114p.

18160 BALOCH, N.B., comp. The education policy, 1972: implications and implementation. Hyderabad: Inst. of Educ., U. of Sind, 1972. 107p. [documents & seminar papers]

18161 BENSON, C.S. Finance of education, training, and related service in the public sector. Karachi: Planning Cmsn., 1970. 83p. (Natl. Cmsn. on Manpower & Educ., Res. study, 3)

18162 CURLE, A. Educational problems of developing societies; with case studies of Ghana and Pakistan. NY: Praeger, 1969. 170p.

18163 ______. Planning for education in Pakistan: a personal case study. London: Tavistock, 1966. 208p.

18164 End of misery (nationalization of schools and colleges) [special issue]. In Pakistan Educ. R. 12 (1972) 1-84.

18165 HAMIED, KHWAJA ABDUL. Addresses and speeches. 2nd ed. Rawalpindi: Dir. of Educ., 1966. 309p.

18166 HUSAIN, M.A. Report of the Commission on National Education. In Pakistan J. of Science 12 (Mar. 1960) 59-67.

18167 KORSON, J.H. Bhutto's educational reform. In JAAS(L) 8,3-4 (1973) 279-306.

18168 The New Education Policy [special section]. In Pakistan Educ. R. 2 (1970) 1-41.

18169 PAKISTAN. CMSN. ON NATL. EDUC. Report, Jan.-Aug. 1959. Karachi: MPGOP, 1960. 360p.

18170 PAKISTAN. EDUC. DIV. Six-year national plan of educational development for Pakistan. Karachi: Govt. of Pakistan Press, 1952. 2 pts. in 1.

18171 PAKISTAN. MIN. OF EDUC. The education policy, 1972-1980. Islamabad: 1972. 45p.

18172 QUDDUS, SYED ABDUL. Education and national reconstruction of Pakistan. Lahore: S.I. Gilani, 1979. 270p.

18173 RAHMAN, FAZLUR. New education in the making of Pakistan; its ideology and basic problems. London: Cassell, 1953. 166p.

18174 RAHMAN, FAZLUR. The Quranic solution of Pakistan's educational problems. In Islamic Studies 6 (1967) 315-26.

18175 RAUF, ABDUR. Religious education in West Pakistan. Lahore: West Pakistan Bureau of Educ., 1964. 62p.

b. education and manpower planning

18176 AHMAD, SHAIKH MAHMUD & S.M. HASAN. Estimation of brain drain. Karachi: MPGOP, 1971. 37p.

18177 FLØYSTAD, G. The labour market and training programmes for diploma holders from the polytechnic institutes in Pakistan. Karachi: Pakistan Inst. of Dev. Econ., 1968. 45p.

18178 KARWANSKI, R.A. Education and the supply of manpower in Pakistan. Karachi: MPGOP, 1970. 188p. (Natl. Cmsn. on Manpower & Educ., Res. study, 1)

18179 KHAN, SYED AHMED. The whys and hows of National Commission on Manpower and Education: a sociological perspective. In Aquila Kiani, ed. Sociology of Development in Pakistan. Karachi: Social Res. Centre, U. of Karachi, 1971, 49-60.

18180 RUUD, K. Manpower and educational requirements of Pakistan. Karachi: Planning Cmsn., 1970. 89p.

18181 ZAKI, WALI MUHAMMAD. Educational development in Pakistan; a study of educational development in relation to manpower requirements and resource availability. Islamabad: West Pakistan Pub. Co., 1968. 99p.

4. Higher Education

18182 CHOUDHURY, A.H. Economic aspects of higher education and student unrest in Pakistan. Dacca: Soc. for Pakistan Studies, 1971. 56p.

18183 Handbook to the universities of Pakistan. Karachi: Academy of Educ. Res., All Pakistan Educ. Conf., 1963. 138p.

18184 KIBBEE, R.J. Higher education in Pakistan. In J. of Higher Educ. 23,6 (1962) 179-89.

18185 PAKISTAN. CURRICULUM WING. The changing role of the teacher and its influence on the preparation for the profession and on in-service training. Islamabad: Min. of Educ., 1975. 78p.

18186 ______. Teacher education in Pakistan. Islamabad: Min. of Education, 1977. 61p.

18187 PAKISTAN. STUDY GROUP ON EXAMINATIONS IN UNIV. Report. Islamabad: Univ. Grants Cmsn., 1975. 230p.

18188 PFEFFER, K.H. Foreign training for Pakistanis; a study of Pakistanis returned from training in Germany. Lahore: Social Sciences Research Centre, U. of the Panjab, 1961. 64p.

18189 SHARAFUDDIN, A.M. & H.C. ALLISON, eds. Improvement of teacher education; proceedings of teacher education; proceedings of the Seminar on Teacher Education, October 15-22, 1968. Dacca: Educ. Extension Centre, 1969. 128p.

18190 Teacher education [special issue]. In Pakistan Educ. R. 9 (1972) 1-111.

18191 WEST PAKISTAN. BUREAU OF EDUC. Universities in West Pakistan. Lahore: 1967. 124p.

18192 ZAKI, WALI MUHAMMAD. Education of the people. Islamabad: People's Open U., 1975. 141p.

18193 ______. The People's Open University, the concept, programme, structure, and physical facilities. Islamabad: People's Open U., 1975. 71p.

5. Elementary and Secondary Education

18194 DIL, ANWAR S. & AFIA DIL, eds. Developing secondary education in West Pakistan. Lahore: Educ. Extension Centre, 1964. 214p.

18195 HUQ, M. SHAMSUL. Compulsory education in Pakistan. Paris: UNESCO, 1954. 169p.

18196 NAMDAR KHAN. Some aspects of planning for primary education in Pakistan. Lahore: West Pakistan Educ. Extension Centre, 1969. 32p.

18197 RAUF, ABDUR. West Pakistan: rural education and

development. Honolulu: EWCP, 1970. 173p.

6. Literacy and Adult Education (1972 Literacy 21.7%)

18198 AKHTAR, JAMILA. Literacy and education: fifth release from the 1961 census of Pakistan. In PDR 3 (1963) 424-42.

18199 MAHMOOD, NAUSHIN. Literacy and educational attainment levels in Pakistan, 1951-1973. In PDR 17,3 (1978) 267-301.

7. Special Problems of Female Education

18200 SALIMA HASHMI. Education of rural women in West Pakistan [a study in development framework]. Lyallpur: West Pakistan Agri. U. Press, 1968. 142p.

8. Pakistani Students: Problems, Attitudes, and Unrest

18201 ABBAS, S. ZIA. Students and the nation. Karachi: 1970. 200p.

18202 EISTER, A.W. Evaluations of selected jobs and occupations by university students in a developing country: Pakistan. In Social Forces 44 (Sept. 1965) 66-73.

18203 KHAN, SHAFIQUE ALI. The age of rage: an academic study of the universal youth unrest, with particular reference to Pakistan. Hyderabad, Sind: Markez-i-Shaoorb-Adab, 1974. 320p.

18204 MANIRUZZAMAN, TALUKDER. Political activism of university students in Pakistan. In JComPolSt. 9,3 (1971) 234-45.

18205 PAKISTAN. CMSN. ON STUDENT PROBLEMS AND WELFARE. Report. Karachi: MPGOP, 1966. 234p.

V. RELIGIO-PHILOSOPHICAL TRADITIONS IN THE ISLAMIC STATE OF PAKISTAN

A. Islam in Pakistan: Continued Conflict of Orthodoxy and Modernism (In 1980, 98.2% of Pakistanis were Muslim)

1. General Studies

18206 AZIZ AHMAD. Das Dilemma von Modernismus und Orthodoxie in Pakistan. In Saeculum 18 (1967) 1-12.

18207 BROHI, A.K. Islam in the modern world. Ed. by Khurshid Ahmad. Karachi: Chiragh-e-Rah pub., 1968. 163p.

18208 CERULLI, E. Problèmes actuels de l'Islam pakistanais. In Studia Islamica 23 (1965) 137-147.

18209 EBERHARD, W. Modern tendencies in Islam in Pakistan. In Sociologus Ns 10,2 (1960) 139-52.

18210 MCDONOUGH, S. The social import of Parwez's religious thought. In CAS 1 (1971) 79-92.

18211 MARYAM JAMEELA. Islam and modernism. Lahore: Mohammad Yusuf Khan, 1966. 162p.

18212 PAKISTAN. MIN. OF RELIGIOUS AFFAIRS. Haj statistics, Zilhaj 1394 (Dec. 1974). Islamabad: Central Haj Org., 1975. 187p.

18213 PARWEZ, GHULAM AHMAD. Islam: a challenge to religion. Lahore: Idara-e-Tulu-e-Islam, 1968. 392p.

18214 RAHMAN, FAZLUR. Currents of religious thought in Pakistan. In Islamic studies 7 (1968) 1-7.

18215 ______. Some reflections on the reconstruction of Muslim society in Pakistan. In Islamic studies 6 (1967) 103-20.

18216 RASHID, KHWAJA ABDUL. Re-evaluation of Islamic thought and other essays. Lahore: Universal Books, 1975. 194p.

18217 RAUF, ABDUR. Renaissance of Islamic culture and civilization in Pakistan. Lahore: Sh. Muhammad Ashraf, 1965. 320p.

2. Maulana Sayyid Abulᶜalā Maudūdi (1903-79): Foremost Exponent of Islamic Fundamentalism

18218 AZIZ AHMAD. Mawdudi and orthodox fundamentalism in Pakistan. Middle East J. 21 (1967) 369-80.

18219 GILANI, A. Maududi: thought and movement. Tr. by Hasan Muizuddin Qazi. 5th ed. Lahore: Farooq Hasan Gilani, 1978. 414p.

18220 MAUDOODI, SYED ABULᶜALĀ, Maulana. Correspondence between Maulana Maudoodi and Maryam Jameela. Lahore: Mohammad Yusuf Khan, 1969. 88p.

18221 ______. Islam today. Tr. by Khurshid Ahmad. Karachi: Chiragh-e-Rah Pub., 1968. 64p.

18222 ______. A short history of the revivalist movement in Islam. Tr. by al-Ashᶜari. 2nd ed., rev. Lahore: Islamic Pub., 1972. 156p.

18223 ______. Towards understanding Islam. Tr. & ed. by Khurshid Ahmad. 14th ed. Lahore: Idara Tarjuman-ul-Quran, 1974. 179p.

B. The Ahmadiyyas: Are They Muslim?

18224 AHMED, MUNIR D. Ausschluss der Ahmadiyya aus dem Islam. Eine umstrittene Entscheidung des Pakistanischen Parlaments. In Orient (Hamburg) 16,1 (1975) 112-43.

18225 BASHIR AHMAD, MIRZA. Future of Ahmadiyya movement. 2nd ed. Qadian: Nazir Dawat-o-Tabligh, 1970. 46p.

18226 BRUSH, S.E. Ahmadiyyas in Pakistan. In MW 54 (1959) 275-86.

18227 ______. Ahmadiyyat in Pakistan. In MW 45 (1955) 145-71.

18228 MAUDOODI, SYED ABULᶜALĀ, Maulana. Finality of prophethood. Lahore: Islamic Pub., 1975. 71p.

18229 MUBARAK AHMAD, MIRZA. Our foreign missions; a brief account of the Ahmadiyya work to push Islam in various parts of the world. 4th rev. ed. Rabwah: West Pakistan, Ahmadiyya Muslim Foreign Missions, 1965. 105p.

18230 MUNEER, NUR-UD-DIN. Some misunderstandings about the Ahmadiyya movement in Islam. In Review of Religions (Rabwah) 71,8 (1976) 220-36.

18231 NASIR AHMAD, MIRZA. Are Ahmadis Muslims: pronouncement of the head of the Ahmadiyya movement. Qadian: Nazir Dawat-o-Tabligh, 1973. 33p.

18332 PUNJAB. COURT OF ENQUIRY TO ENQUIRE INTO THE PUNJAB DISTURBANCES OF 1953. Report. Lahore: Supt., Govt. Printing, 1954. 387p.

18233 Qadianism on trial: the case of the Muslim ummah against Qadianis presented before the National Assembly of Pakistan. Comp. by Mohammad Taqi Usmani in Urdu. Tr. by Mohammad Wali Raʾzi. Karachi: Maktaba Darul Uloom, 1977. 191p.

18234 ZAHEER, EHSAN ELAHI. Qadiyaniat; an analytical survey. Lahore: Idara Tarjuman al-Sunnah, 1972. 360p.

C. Religious Minorities: Chirstian, Zoroastrian, Hindu

18235 DHALLA, M.N. Dastur Dhalla, the saga of a soul: an autobiography of Shams-ul-ulama Dastur Dr. Maneckji Nusserwanji Dhalla, high priest of the Parsis of Pakistan. Tr. by Gool & Behram Sohrab H.J. Rustomji. Karachi: Dastur Dr. Dhalla Mem. Inst., 1975. 739p.

18236 PFEFFER, K.H. Eine sozio-ethno-religiöse Minderheit: die Christen West-Pakistans. In Sociologus ns 12, 2 (1962) 113-27.

18237 WEBSTER, W. Pakistan. In Donald E. Hoke, ed. The Church in Asia. Chicago: Moody Press, 1975, 475-99.

D. Contemporary Philosophy in Pakistan

18238 QUADIR, C.A., ed. The world of philosophy; studies prepared in honour of Professor M.M. Sharif. Lahore: Sharif Presentation Volume Cmtee., 1965. 367p.

18239 SAID, H.M., comp. & ed. Main currents of contemporary thought in Pakistan. Karachi: Hamdard Natl. Foundation, 1978. 2v.

18240 SMET, R.V. Philosophical activity in Pakistan. Lahore: Pakistan Philosophical Congress, 1961. 132p.

VI. CULTURE AND COMMUNICATION IN PAKISTAN

A. Mass Media and Communication

1. Government and the Media: Law Censorship, and Press Freedom

18241 PAKISTAN. White paper on misuse of media, December 20, 1971-July 4, 1977. Islamabad: Print. Corp. of Pakistan Press, 1978. 363p.

18242 PAKISTAN. PRESS CMSN. Report. Karachi: MPGOP, 1959. 138p.

18243 The Press and Publications Ordinance (XV of 1960). Lahore: All-Pakistan Legal Decisions, 1964.

18244 Press curbs in Pakistan. In Intl. Cmsn. of Jurists, Bull. 17 (Dec. 1963) 30-34.

18245 SARKAR, PABITRA. Five "Dangerous" Books: on the question of censorship in East Pakistan. In Mahfil 7 (Spring-Summer 1971) 31-42.

18246 VARMA, S.P. Press and public opinion in Pakistan. In SAS 3,1 (1968) 55-66.

2. Journalism and the Press

18247 KHURSHID, ABDUS SALAM. Pakistan. In John A. Lent, ed. The Asian newspapers' reluctant revolution. Ames, IA: Iowa State U. Press, 298-316.

18248 NIZAMI, MAJID. The press in Pakistan. Lahore: U. of Punjab Dept. of Pol. Sci., 1958. 89p. (Its studies in Pol. Sci., Pub. Admin., & Intl. Affairs, 3)

18249 SHARIF AL MUJAHID. After decline during Ayub Era, Pakistan press thrives, improves. Ed. by J.W. Markham. In Journalism Q. 48,3 (1971) 526-34.

3. Book Publishing and Libraries

18250 ALI, S.A. The book world of Pakistan. In Pakistan Q. 12,3 (1964) 56-65.

18251 FARUQUI, J.A. Reading habits in Pakistan: report. Karachi: Natl. Book Centre of Pakistan, 1974. 131p.

18252 KHURSHID, ZAHIRUDDIN. Librarianship in Pakistan: ten years' work, 1963-1972. Karachi: Dept. of Library Science, U. of Karachi, 1974. 214p.

18253 SIDDIQUI, AKHTAR H. Library development in Pakistan. 2nd ed. Islamabad: English Book House, 1974. 137p.

18254 SOCIETY FOR THE PROMOTION & IMPROVEMENT OF LIBRARIES. Plan for development of libraries in Pakistan. Karachi: 1972. 121p.

4. Radio and Television, Cinema

18255 ALI, S. AMJAD Rise of film-making in Pakistan. In Pakistan Q. 13 (Spring 1964) 41-55.

18256 KABIR, ALAMGIR. The cinema in Pakistan. Dacca: Sandhani Pub., 1969. 194p.

18257 ______. A study of the Pakistani cinema. In James R. Brandon, ed. The performing arts in Asia. Paris: UNESCO, 144-152.

18258 KALIMULLAH, A.F. Television in Pakistan. In Pakistan Q. 15 (1967) 267-72.

18259 PAKISTAN. RADIO PAKISTAN. Ten years of development, 1958-68. Karachi: 1968. 52p.

18260 RAHMAN, I.A. Pakistan cinema poised for a leap. In Pakistan Pictorial 6 (1973) 118-122.

B. Literatures of Pakistan in Urdu and English [for Bengali Literature of E. Pakistan, see Chap. Fifteen, II. G. 1., below]

18261 ALLANA, GULAM ALI. Presenting Pakistani poetry. Karachi: Pakistan Writers' Guild, 1961. 206p.

18262 ANDERSON, D.D. Ahmed Ali and Twilight in Delhi: the genesis of a Pakistani novel. In Mahfil 7,1/2 (1971) 81-86.

18263 ______. Pakistani literature today. In LEW 10 (1966) 235-44.

18264 ANIS NAGI, tr. Modern Urdu poems from Pakistan. Lahore: Swad Noon Pub., 1974. 220p.

18265 AZIM, S. VIQAR, ed. Modern Urdu short stories from Pakistan. Islamabad: Pakistan Branch, E.C.D. Cultural Inst., 1977. 216p.

18266 BRANDER, L. Two novels by Ahmed Ali. In JCL 3 (1967) 76-86.

18277 FAIZ, FAIZ AHMED. Poems. ND: PPH, 1958. 85p.

18268 ______. Poems by Faiz. Tr. from Urdu by V.G. Kiernan. London: Allen & Unwin, 1971. 288p. (UNESCO series)

18269 FAROOKI, N.A. Pakistani short stories. Lahore: Ferozsons, 1955. 264p.

18270 FARRUKHI, ASLAM. Urdu poetry since independence. In Pakistan Q. 15 (1967) 272-79.

18271 HASHMI, ALAMGIR. Some directions of contemporary Urdu poetry in Pakistan: from 1965 to the present. In SA ns 1,2 (1978) 67-79.

18272 MEMON, MUHAMMED UMAR. Partition literature: a study of Intiẕār Husain. In MAS 14,3 (1980) 377-410.

18273 NIAZ, A.Q., ed. Cries in the night, an anthology of modern Pakistani Urdu poetry. 2nd ed., rev. & enl. Lahore: Mahmaʾ-el-Bahrain, 1957. 287p.

18274 RAHMAN, MUNIBUR. Political novels in Urdu. In CAS 6 (1975) 140-53.

18275 TAHIR, NAEEM. The theatre in Pakistan. In Pakistan Q. 17,3/4 (1970) 45-66.

C. Contemporary Art and Music of Pakistan

18276 AHMED, JALAL UDDIN. Art in Pakistan. 2nd rev. & enl. ed. Karachi: Pakistan Pub., 1962. 151p.

18277 ALI, S.A. Abstract painting in Pakistan. In Pakistan Q.5,1 (1955) 29-38.

18278 DEHLAVI, S.A. Music in Pakistan. In Pakistan Q. 6,1 (1956) 43-50.

18279 ENAYETULLAH, ANWAR. Two decades of music in Pakistan. In Pakistan Q. 15 (1967) 253-66.

18280 HASHIM, M. Modern trends in Pakistani art. In Scintilla 5 (April-July 1964) 39-44.

18281 KHAN, INAYAT. Music. Lahore: Sh. Muhammad Ashraf, 1971. 101p.

18282 Paintings from Pakistan. Karachi: Ferozsons, 1972. 68p.

18283 SADEQUAIN. Sadequain; sketches & drawings. Karachi: Editions Mystique, 1966. 151p.

VII. SCIENCE AND TECHNOLOGY IN PAKISTAN

18284 AHMAD, NAZIR. Development of science and technology in Pakistan. Karachi: Pakistan Assn. of Scientists and Scientific Professions, 1963. 28p.

18285 CHUGHTAI, M.I.D. Pakistan Association for the Advancement of Science: its history and achievements, 1947-1975. Lahore: Pakistan Assn. for the Advancement of Science, 1977. 95p.

18286 MOREHOUSE, W. Science and the human condition in India and Pakistan. NY: Rockefeller U. Press, 1968. 230p.

18287 PAKISTAN ASSN. OF SCIENTISTS & SCIENTIFIC PROFESSIONS. Scientists and technologists of Pakistan: a directory. Karachi: 1966. 367p.

Part Four

Transformations in the Modern Age: The Eight Geo-Cultural Areas

10

Ceylon to Sri Lanka: Cosmopolitan Island, Colony to Nation-State, 1796–1948, 1948–; The Maldives

I. GENERAL HISTORIES AND STUDIES OF SRI LANKA SINCE 1796

18289 DE SILVA, K.M. Sri Lanka: a survey. Honolulu: UPH, 1977. 496p.

18290 LUDOWYK, E.F.C. The modern history of Ceylon. NY: Praeger, 1966. 308p.

18291 MUKHERJEE, S. Ceylon: island that changed. ND: PPH, 1971. 135p.

18292 NANAYAKKARA, V. A return to Kandy: over Balana and beyond. Colombo: 1971. 237p.

18293 PERERA, L.H.H. Ceylon under Western rule. Madras: Macmillan, 1955. 343p.

18294 WIJETUNGA, W.M.K. Sri Lanka in transition. Colombo: Wijetunga, 1974. 146p.

II. GOVERNMENT AND POLITICS OF SRI LANKA SINCE 1796

A. British Rule in Ceylon, 1796-1948

1. General Histories

18295 DE SILVA, K.M., ed. University of Ceylon history of Ceylon. Vol. 3: from the beginning of the 19th century to 1948. Peradeniya: U. of Ceylon Press, 1974. 579p.

18296 HULUGALLE, H.A.J. British governors of Ceylon. Colombo: Associated Newspapers, 1963. 252p.

18297 MENDIS, G.C. Ceylon under the British. 2nd ed. Colombo: Colombo Apothecaries' Co., 1946. 132p.

18298 MILLS, L.A. Ceylon under British rule, 1795-1932; with an account of the East India Company's embassies to Kandy, 1762-1795. London: Cass, 1964. 312p. [Rpt. 1933 ed.]

18299 WICKREMERATNE, L.A. Kandyans and nationalism in Sri Lanka: some reflections. In CJHSS ns 5,1/1 (1975) 49-67.

2. Foundation of British rule, 1796-1833

a. capture of the Maritime Provinces from the Dutch and conquest of the Kandyan Kingdom

18300 ALEXANDER, A. The life of Alexander Alexander. Ed. by J. Howell. Edinburgh: W. Blackwood, 1830. [v.1, 102-212 on his 8 years military service in Ceylon]

18301 BRYNN, E. The Marquess Wellesley and Ceylon, 1798-1803; a plan for imperial consolidation. In CJHSS 3,2 (1973) 1-13.

18302 DOLAPIHILLA, P. In the days of Sri Wickramarajasingha, last King of Kandy; traditionary material about men & matters of the last phase of Sinhala rule narrated in story form. Maharagama: Saman Press, 1959. 301p.

18303 MARSHALL, H. Ceylon: a general description of the island and its inhabitants, with an historical sketch of the conquest of the colony by the English. Kandy: Kandy Printers, 1954. 222p. [Rpt. 1846 ed.]

18304 MENDIS, V.L.B. The advent of the British to Ceylon 1762-1803. Dehiwela: Tisara Prakasakayo, 1971. 226p.

18305 PERCIVAL, R. An account of the Island of Ceylon. Dehiwala: Tisara Prakasakayo, 1975. 446p. [1st pub. 1803]

18306 PIERIS, P.E. Tri Sinhala: the last phase, 1796-1815. 3rd ed. Colombo: Colombo Apothecaries, 1945. 154p. [1st ed. 1939; on Sri Vikrama Raja Simha, last King of Kandy]

18307 POWELL, G. The Kandyan Wars: the British army in Ceylon, 1803-1818. London: Leo Cooper, 1973. 320p.

18308 SAMARAWEERA, V. Ceylon's trade relations with Coromandel during early British times, 1796-1957. In MCS 3,1 (1972) 1-18.

18309 VIMALANANDA, T., ed. The British intrigue in the Kingdom of Ceylon; the full narrative of the commencement of British political connection in Ceylon - the details of the sinister political manoeuvres to gain supremacy over the Kingdom of Kandy. Colombo: M.D. Gunasena, 1973. 173 + 560p. (Gunasena hist. series, 2) [sources]

18310 ______. The great rebellion of 1818; the story of the first war of independence and betrayal of the nation. Colombo: M.D. Gunasena, 1970. 79 + 482p. (Gunasena hist. series, 5:1) [documents]

b. colonial government, to the Colebrooke-Cameron Reforms, 1833

18311 DAVY, J. An account of the interior of Ceylon and of its inhabitants with travels in that island. Dehiwala: Tisara Prakasakayo, 1969. 399p. (CHJ, 16) [1st pub. 1821]

18312 DE SILVA, C.R. Ceylon under the British occupation, 1795-1833: its political, administrative and economic development. Colombo: Colombo Apothecaries, 1941-42. 2v.

18313 DE SILVA, K.M. The Colebrooke-Cameron Reforms. In CJHSS 2 (1959) 244-256.

18314 HARDY, S.M. Wilmot-Horton's government of Ceylon, 1831-1837. In U. of Birmingham Historical J. 7,2 (1960) 180-99.

18315 MENDIS, G.C., ed. The Colebrooke-Cameron papers: documents on British colonial policy in Ceylon, 1796-1833. London: OUP, 1956. 2v.

18316 SAMARAWEERA, V. Governor Sir Robert Wilmot Horton and the reforms of 1833 in Ceylon. In Historical J. 15 (1972) 33-42.

18317 ______. The judicial administration of the Kandyan provinces of Ceylon, 1815-1833. In CJHSS 1 (1971) 123-50.

18318 ______. Land tax in Ceylon: doctrinal influences in the controversy between William Colebrooke and Charles Cameron. In MCS 1,2 (1970) 133-45.

3. Consolidation of British rule, 1834-1910

18319 BAKER, S.W. Eight years in Ceylon. Dehiwala: Tisara Prakasakayo, 1966. 221p. [Rpt. 1855 ed]

18320 BALASINGHAM, S.V. The administration of Sir Henry Ward, Governor of Ceylon, 1855-60. Dehiwala: Tisara Prakasakayo, 1968. 142p. [pub. as CHJ, 11]

18321 BASTIAMPILLAI, B. The administration of Sir William Gregory, Governor of Ceylon 1872-77. Dehiwala: Tisara Prakasakayo, 1969. 188p. [pub. as CHJ, 12]

18322 ______. The Colonial Office and Sir William Gregory, Governor of Ceylon, 1872-77; a study in British imperial administration. In CJHSS 9,1 (1966) 20-34.

18323 DE SILVA, K.M. The abortive project of a land tax for Ceylon, 1846-8. In JRAS(CB) ns 11 (1967) 46-77.

18324 ______. The 1848 "Rebellion" in Ceylon: the British Parliamentary post-mortem. In MCS 5,1/2 (1974) 40-76, 117-37.

18325 ______. "Rebellion" of 1848 in Ceylon. In CJHSS 7 (1964) 144-70.

18326 ______., ed. Letters on Ceylon, 1846-50, the administration of Viscount Torrington and the "rebellion" of 1848; the private correspondence of the Third Earl Grey and Viscount Torrington. Kandy: K.V.G. de Silva, 1965. 240p.

18327 DIGBY, W. Forty years of official and unofficial life in an oriental crown colony; being the life of Sir Richard F. Morgan, Kt., Queen's Advocate and Acting Chief Justice of Ceylon. Madras: Higginbotham, 1879. 2 v., 391, 373p.

18328 DOIG, R.P. Lord Torrington's government of Ceylon, 1847-1850. In Durham U. J. 54 (1962) 49-58.

18329 GREY, H.G. The colonial policy of Lord John Russell's administration. 2nd ed. London: R. Bentley, 1853. [v. 2, 161-97 on Ceylon]

18330 HAECKEL, ERNST. Visit to Ceylon. Tr. by Clara Bell. Dehiwala: Tisara Prakasakayo, 1975. 229p. (CHJ, 23) [1st pub. 1883]

18331 ROBERTS, M.W. Facets of modern Ceylon history through the letters of Jeronis Pieris. Colombo: Hansa Pub., 1975. 108p.

18332 TENNENT, J.E. Ceylon: an account of the island, physical, historical, and topographical, with notices of its natural history, antiquities, and production. 6th ed. Dehiwala: Tisara Prakasakayo, 1977-78. 643, 663p. [Rpt. 4th ed., 1860; 1st pub. 1859]

18333 WOOLF, L.S. Growing; an autobiography of the years 1904-1911. NY: Harcourt, Brace & World, 1962. 256p.

4. Constitutional Reform and the National Movement, 1911-1948

a. communal riots of 1915 between Buddhists and Muslims

18334 BLACKTON, C.S. The 1915 riots in Ceylon; a survey of the action phase. In CJHSS 10,1/2 (1967) 27-69.

18335 DE SOUZA, A. Hundred days in Ceylon: under martial law in 1915. 2nd ed. Colombo: Ceylon Morning Leader, 1919. 318 + 51p. [1st ed. London, 1916]

18336 FERNANDO, P.T.M. The British raj and the 1915 communal riots in Ceylon. In MAS 3,3 (1969) 245-56.

18337 KARUNATILAKE, H.N.S. Life and times of Edward Henry Pedris, national hero. Colombo: P. Gangodagedara, 1978. 24p.

18338 The 1915 riots in Ceylon: a symposium. In JAS 29,2 (1970) 219-66. [Articles by C.S. Blackton, R.N. Kearney, P.T.M. Fernando, V.K. Jayawardena]

18339 PERERA, E.W. Memorandum on recent disturbances in Ceylon. London: E. Hughes, 1915. 75p.

18340 RAMANATHAN, P. Riots and martial law in Ceylon. London: St. Martin's, 1916. 314p.

18341 RUTNAM, J.T. The Rev. A.G. Fraser and the riots of 1915. In CJHSS ns 1 (1971) 151-96.

b. the Ceylon nationalist movement

i. general studies

18342 ARUNACHALAM, P. Speeches and writings. Colombo: H.W. Cave, 1936. 332p.

18343 BANDARANAIKE, S.D. Remembered yesterdays; being the reminiscences of Maha Mudaliyar Sir Solomon Dias Bandaranaike. London: J. Murray, 1929. 300p.

18344 FERNANDO, T. Arrack, toddy and Ceylonese nationalism: some observations on the temperance movement, 1912-1921. In MCS 2,2 (1971) 123-50.

18345 ______. Buddhist leadership in the nationalist movement of Ceylon: the role of the temperance movement. In Social Compass 20,2 (1973) 333-36.

18346 RANASINGE, D.D. The lion of Kotte - his life and times. Colombo: M.D. Gunasena, 1976. 201p. [on E.W. Perera]

18347 ROBERTS, M.W. Elites, nationalisms and the nationalist movement in Ceylon. In his Documents of the Ceylon National Congress and nationalist politics in Ceylon, 1929-1950. Colombo: Dept. of Natl. Archives, 1977, xxi-ccxxii.

18348 ______. Nationalism in economic and social thought. In his (ed.) Collective identities, nationalisms and protest in modern Sri Lanka. Columbo: Marga Inst., 1979, 386-419.

18349 VYTHILINGAM, M. The life of Sir Ponnambalam Ramanathan. v. 1. Colombo: Ramanathan Commemoration Soc., 1971. 605p. + 16 pl.

ii. the Ceylon National Congress, founded 1919

18350 BANDARANAIKE, S.W.R.D., ed. The handbook of the Ceylon National Congress, 1919-28. Colombo: Ceylon Natl. Congress, 1928. 912p.

18351 CEYLON NATL. CONGRESS. Documents of the Ceylon National Congress and nationalist politics in Ceylon, 1929-1950. Ed. by M.W. Roberts. Colombo: Dept. of Natl. Archives, 1977. 4 v., 3430p.

18352 DE SILVA, K.M. The Ceylon National Congress in disarray, 1920-21; Sir Ponnambalam Arunachalam leaves the Congress. In CJHSS ns 2,2 (1972) 97-117.

18353 ______. The Ceylon National Congress in disarray II: the triumph of Sir William Manning, 1921-1924. In CJHSS ns 3,1 (1973) 16-39.

18354 ______. The formation and character of the Ceylon National Congress, 1917-19. In CJHSS 10 (1967) 70-102.

iii. other nationalist parties

18355 LERSKI, G.J. Origins of Trotskyism in Ceylon: a documentary history of the Lanka Sama Samaja Party, 1935-1942. Stanford, CA: Hoover Inst. on War, Revolution, and Peace, 1968. 288p.

c. the Donoughmore Commission, 1928 and the 1931 Constitution

18356 CEYLON. CONSTITUTION. Constitution of Ceylon... London: HMSO, 1931. 102p. (Cmd. 3862)

18357 COLLINS, C.H. The significance of the Donoughmore Constitution in the political development of Ceylon. In Parliamentary Affairs 4,1 (1950) 101-10.

18358 FISCHER, G. Le travaillisme anglais et la réforme constitutionnelle de 1931 à Ceylan. In Civilisations 13 (1963) 136-60.

18359 GREAT BRITAIN. COLONIAL OFFICE. Report of the Special Commission on the (Ceylon) Constitution. London: HMSO, 1928. 188p. (Cmd. 3131) [Chm., the Earl of Donoughmore]

d. Ceylon government and politics, 1931-48

18360 WEERAWARDANA, I.D.S. Government and politics in Ceylon (1931-46). Colombo: Ceylon Econ. Res. Assn., 1951. 207p.

18361 WIJESEKERA, N. Sir D.B. Jayatilaka: a biography and assessment of the man and his works. Colombo: Dept. of Cultural Affairs, 1973. 230p.

e. the Soulbury Constitutional Commission, 1944-45

18362 GREAT BRITAIN. CMSN. ON CONSTITUTIONAL REFORM IN CEYLON. Report of the Commission on Constitutional Reform. Colombo: Ceylon Govt. Press, 1969. 211p. [Chm., Lord Soulbury; 1st pub. London: HMSO, 1945, 159p. (Cmd. 7667)]

B. Independent Ceylon/Sri Lanka - Government and Politics, 1948-

1. Constitutional Law and History - General Studies

18363 AMERASINGHE, C.F. The doctrines of sovereignty and separation of powers in the law of Ceylon. Colombo: LHI, 1970. 284p.

18364 COORAY, J.A.L. Constitutional government and human rights in a developing society. Colombo: Colombo Apothecaries, 1969. 81p.

18365 COORAY, L.J.M. Operation of conventions in the constitutional history of Ceylon - 1948 to 1965. In MCS 1,1 (1970) 1-42.

18366 ______. Reflections on the Constitution and the Constituent Assembly; an analysis of the law, the underlying problems, and concepts of the Constitution, 1796-1971, with special reference to 1948-1971 and the Constituent Assembly of Sri Lanka. Colombo: Hansa Pub., 1971. 130p.

18367 COORAY, L.J.M. & J. JUPP. The Constitutional system in Ceylon. In PA 43,1 (1970) 73-83.

18368 JUPP, J. Constitutional developments in Ceylon since independence. In PA 41 (1968) 169-83. [comment by L.J.M. Cooray in PA 43 (1970) 73-78]

2. The Constitution of 1948

18369 CEYLON. CONSTITUTION. The Constitution of Ceylon, Feb. 1948. Colombo: Ceylon Govt. Press, 1948. 42p. [Rpt. 1960]

18370 JENNINGS, W.I. The Constitution of Ceylon. 3rd ed. London: OUP, 1953. 294p.

3. Political Process in Ceylon/Sri Lanka, 1948-
a. general studies

18371 DE SILVA, M. Sri Lanka: the end of welfare politics. In SAR 6,2 (1973) 91-110.

18372 FERNANDO, T. Elite politics in the new states: the case of post-independence Sri Lanka. In PA 46,3 (1973) 361-83.

18373 JEFFRIES, C. Ceylon - the path to independence. London: Pall Mall, 1962. 148p.

18374 JUPP, J. Sri Lanka: third world democracy. London: F. Cass, 1978. 423p.

18375 KEARNEY, R.N. A documentary guide to research on contemporary politics in Sri Lanka. In M.L.P. Patterson & M. Yanuck, eds. South Asian library resources in North America. Zug: Interdocumentation Co., 1975, 211-21.

18376 ______. Political mobilization in contemporary Sri Lanka. In R.I. Crane, ed. Aspects of political mobilization in South Asia. Syracuse: Maxwell School of Citizenship & Public Affairs, Syracuse U., 1976, 35-66. (Foreign & Comp. Studies; South Asian series, 1)

18377 ______. The politics of Ceylon (Sri Lanka). Ithaca: CornellUP, 1973. 249p.

18378 MATTHEWS, B. Recent developments in Sri Lanka politics. In PA 51,1 (1978) 84-100.

18379 NAMASIVAYAM, S. Parliamentary government in Ceylon, 1948-1958. Colombo: K.V.G. de Silva, 1959. 126p.

18380 SINGER, M.R. The emerging elite; a study of political leadership in Ceylon. Cambridge, MA: M.I.T. Press, 1964. 203p.

18381 Sri Lanka since independence. [special issue] In CJHSS ns 4,1/2 (1974) 157p.

18382 TYAGI, A.R. & K.K. BHARDWAJ. The working of parliamentary democracy in Ceylon. Delhi: Chand, 1969. 223p.

18383 WILSON, A.J. The Cabinet system in Ceylon, 1947-1959. In IYIA 8 (1959) 397-431.

18384 ______. Ceylonese cabinet ministers 1947-1959: their political, economic and social background. In Ceylon Economist 5,1 (1960) 1-54.

18385 ______. Politics in Sri Lanka, 1947-1973. NY: St. Martin's, 1974. 347p.

18386 ______. The role of governor-general in Ceylon. In MAS 2,3 (1968) 193-220.

18387 WISWA WARNAPALA, W.A. The formation of the cabinet in Sri Lanka; a study of the 1970 United Front cabinet. In PSR 12,1 (1973) 121-32.

18388 WRIGGINS, W.H. Ceylon: dilemmas of a new nation. Princeton: PUP, 1960. 505p.

b. political parties
i. general studies

18389 KARALASINGHAM, V. Politics of coalition. Colombo: Intl. Pub., 1964. 84p.

18390 PHADNIS, U. Parties and politics in Ceylon. In PSR 3,1 (1964) 26-42.

18391 WOODWARD, C.A. The growth of a party system in Ceylon. Providence: Brown U. Press, 1969. 338p.

ii. Marxist parties

18392 BLACKTON, C.S. Sri Lanka's Marxists. In Problems of Communism 22,1 (1973) 28-43.

18393 CEYLON COMMUNIST PARTY. 25 years of the Ceylon Communist Party, 1943-1968. Colombo: PPH, 1968. 109p.

18394 GERMAIN, E. Peoples' Frontism in Ceylon: from wavering to capitulation. In Intl. Socialist R. 25 (Fall 1964) 104-17.

18395 GOONEWARDENE, L. The history of the L.S.S.P. in perspective. Goonewardene, 1978. 24p.

18396 ______. A short history of the Lanka Sama Samaja Party [18 Dec. 1935 - 18 Dec. 1960] Colombo: Gunaratne, 1961. 66p.

18397 JAYAWARDENA, V.K. The origins of the Left movement in Sri Lanka. In MCS 2,2 (1971) 195-221.

18398 KARALASINGHAM, V. Senile leftism; a reply to Edmund Samarakkody. Colombo: Intl. Pub., 1966. 64p.

18399 KEARNEY, R.N. Communist Parties of Ceylon. In R.A. Scalapino, ed. Communist revolution in Asia. Englewood Cliffs, NJ: 1969, 391-416. [1st pub. 1965]

18400 ______. The Marxist parties of Ceylon. In P.R. Brass & M.F. Franda, eds. Radical politics in South Asia. Cambridge: MIT Press, 1973, 401-40.

18401 VAN DER KROEF, J.M. Ceylon's political left: its development and aspirations. In PA 40,3/4 (1967-68) 250-78.

iii. communal parties

18402 WILSON, A.J. The Tamil Federal Party in Ceylon politics. In JCPS 4 (1966) 117-37.

c. the electoral system and elections

18403 DE SILVA, G.P.S.H. A statistical survey of elections to the legislatures of Sri Lanka, 1911-1977. Colombo: Marga Inst., 1979. 439p.

18404 FERNANDO, B.J.P. Mandate '70; a journalist's view of Ceylon's general election of 1970. Moratuwa: D.P. Dodangoda, 1970. 88p.

18405 FRETTY, R.E. Ceylon: election-oriented politics. In AS 9 (1969) 99-103.

18406 JIGGINS, J. Dedigama 1973: a profile of a by-election in Sri Lanka. In AS 14,11 (1974) 1000-13.

18407 WEERAWARDANA, I.D.S. Ceylon general election 1956. Colombo: M.D. Gunasena, 1960. 262p.

18408 ______. The general elections in Ceylon, 1952. In CHJ 2,1/2 (1952) 109-78.

18409 WILSON, A.J. Electoral politics in our emergent state: the Ceylon general election of May 1970. London: CamUP, 1975. 240p.

18410 WOODWARD, C.A. Sri Lanka's electoral experience: from personal to party politics. In PA 47,4 (1974-75) 455-71.

d. political leaders of Sri Lanka

18411 BANDARANAIKE, S.W.R.D. Speeches and writings. Colombo: MIB, 1963. 609p.

18412 ______. Towards a new era: selected speeches ... made in the legislature of Ceylon 1931-1959. Colombo: Govt. of Ceylon, 1961. 948p.

18413 DE SILVA, E.P. A short biography of Dr. N.M. Perera, Ph.D., D.S.c., B.Sc. Moratuwa: De Silva, 1975. 131p.

18414 DISSANAYAKE, T.D.S.A. Dudley Senanayake of Sri Lanka. Colombo: Swastika, 1975. 153p. + 10 pl.

18415 FERNANDO, J.L. Three prime ministers of Ceylon. London: Luzac, 1963. 113p. + 10 pl.

18416 HULUGALLE, H.A.J. The life and times of Don Stephen Senanayake, Sri Lanka's first Prime Minister. Colombo: M.D. Gunasena, 1975. 306p. + 25 pl.

18417 J.R. Jayewardene, the President of the Republic of Sri Lanka: felicitation volume. Colombo: M.D. Gunasena, 1978. 104p. + 18 pl.

18418 JAYEWARDENE, J.R. A new path. Colombo: MIB, 1978. 88p.

18419 ______. Selected speeches, 1944-1973. Colombo: H.W. Cave, 1974. 101p.

18420 JEFFRIES, C. 'O.E.G.': a biography of Sir Oliver Ernest Goonetilleke. London: Pall Mall, 1969. 176p.

18421 KOTELAWALA, J.L. An Asian prime minister's story. London: Harrap, 1956. 203p.

18422 ______. Ceylon and Kotelawala: a selection of speeches made in the Legislature of Ceylon...1931-56. Ed. by G.E.P. de S. Wickramaratna. Maharagama: Saman, 1964. 328p.

18423 Maithripala Senanayake felicitation volume. Colombo: Maithripala Senanayake Felicitation Cmtee., 1972. 186p.

18424 MUKHERJI, K.P. Madame Prime Minister Sirimavo Bandaranaike. Colombo: M.D. Gunasena, 1960. 75p.

18425 NADESAN, P., ed. This man Kotelawala; reflections on his life and work. Colombo: Nadaraja Press, 1956. 247p.

18426 RANASINGHA, A. Memories and musings. Colombo: M.D. Gunasena, 1972. 408p.

18427 SENEVIRATNE, M. Sirimavo Bandaranaike, the world's first woman Prime Minister: a biography. Colombo: Hansa Pub., 1975. 209p.

18428 THALGODAPITIYA, W. Portraits of Ten Patriots of Sri Lanka. Kandy: Godamune, 1966. 192p.

18429 WEERAMANTRY, L.G. Assassination of a Prime Minister; the Bandaranaike Murder Case. Geneva: the author, 1969. 312p.

4. The Insurrection of April 1971 by the Janatha Vimukthi Peramuna (People's Liberation Front), Ceylon's "Guevarists"

a. bibliography

18430 GOONETILEKE, H.A.I. The April 1971 insurrection in Ceylon: a select bibliography (July 1973). Louvain: C.R.S.R., 1973. 89p.

18431 ______. The Sri Lanka insurrection of 1971: a select bibliographical commentary. In B.L. Smith, ed. Religion and the legitimation of power in South Asia. Leiden: Brill, 1978, 134-83.

b. studies

18432 ALLES, A.C. Insurgency, 1971: an account of the April insurrection in Sri Lanka. 2nd ed. Colombo: Colombo Apothecaries, 1977. 256p.

18433 ARASARATNAM, S. The Ceylon insurrection of April 1971: some causes and consequences. In PA 45,3 (1972) 356-71.

18434 BHARATI, A. Monastic and lay Buddhism in the 1971 Sri Lanka insurgency. In JAAS(L) 11,1/2 (1976) 102-12.

18435 DUBEY, S.R. Insurgency threat in Sri Lanka. In SAS 10,1/2 (1975) 121-33.

18436 IZZAT MAJEED. The 1971 insurrection in Sri Lanka: historical background. Lahore: South Asian Inst., U. of the Panjab, 1974. 38p.

18437 JEYASINGHAM, S.J. Janatha Vimukthi Peramuna. In SAS 9,1/2 (1974) 1-16.

18438 KEARNEY, R.N. Educational expansion and political volatility in Sri Lanka: the 1971 insurrection. In AS 15,9 (1975) 727-44.

18439 KEARNEY, R.N. & J. JIGGINS. The Ceylon insurrection of 1971. In JComPolSt 13,1 (1975) 40-64.

18440 OBEYESEKERE, G. Some comments on the social backgrounds of the April 1971 insurgency in Sri Lanka (Ceylon). In JAS 33,3 (1974) 367-85.

18441 PHADNIS, U. Insurgency in Ceylonese politics: problems and prospects. In JIDSA 3,4 (1971) 582-616.

18442 VAN DER KROEF, J.M. The Sri Lanka insurgency of April 1971: its development and meaning. In Asia Q. 2 (1973) 111-30.

18443 WILSON, A.J. Ceylon: the People's Liberation Front and the "revolution" that failed. In Pacific Community 3,2 (1972) 364-77.

18444 WISWA WARNAPALA, W.A. The Marxist parties of Sri Lanka and the 1971 insurrection. In AS 15,9 (1975) 745-57.

5. The 1972 Constitution: Ceylon Becomes the Republic of Sri Lanka

18445 COORAY, J.A.L. Constitutional and administrative law of Sri Lanka (Ceylon); a commentary on the Constitution and the law of public administration of Sri Lanka. Colombo: Hansa Pub., 1973. 646p.

18446 COORAY, L.J.M. The law, the Constituent Assembly and the new Constitution. In MCS 2,1 (1971) 1-13.

18447 NADESAN, S. Some comments on the Constituent Assembly and the draft basic resolutions. Colombo: Nadaraja, 1971. 129p.

18448 PHADNIS, U. & L.M. JACOB. The new Constitution of Sri Lanka. In IQ 28,4 (1972) 291-303.

18449 SRI LANKA. CONSTITUTION. The Constitution of Sri Lanka (Ceylon). Colombo: Govt. Pub. Bureau, 1972. 56p.

18450 WISWA WARNAPALA, W.A. The new constitution of Sri Lanka. In AS 13,12 (1973) 1179-92.

6. The 1978 Constitution: from Parliamentary to Presidential System

18451 DE SILVA, C.R. The new Constitution of Sri Lanka (1978): implications of a break from the Westminster model. In ATS 4,11 (1979) 180-88.

18452 PERERA, N.M. Critical analysis of the new Constitution of the Sri Lanka Government, promulgated on 31-8-78. Colombo: V.S. Raja, 1979. 112p.

18453 SRI LANKA. CONSTITUTION. The Constitution of the Democratic Socialist Republic of Sri Lanka: certified on 31st August 1978. Colombo: Govt. Pub. Bureau, 1978. 135p.

18454 WISWA WARNAPALA, W.A. Sri Lanka's new Constitution. In AS 20,9 (1980) 914-30.

C. Political System and Institutions - British and Independent Ceylon

1. Religion, Nationalism, and the State

a. general studies

18455 Ceylon: the politics of Buddhist resurgence. In D.E. Smith, ed. South Asian politics and religion. Princeton: PUP, 1966, 451-546.

18456 HOUTART, F. Religion and ideology in Sri Lanka. Colombo: Hansa Pub., 1974. 541p.

18457 OBEYESEKERE, G. Religious symbolism and political change in Ceylon. In B.L. Smith, ed. The two wheels of dhamma.... Chambersburg, PA: American Academy of Religion, 1972, 58-78. [Its monograph, 3; 1st pub. in MCS 1,1 (1970) 43-63]

18458 SMITH, D.E. The political monks of Burma and Ceylon. In Asia 10 (1968) 3-10.

18459 VIMALANANDA, T., ed. The state and religion in Ceylon since 1815... Colombo: M.D. Gunasena, 1971. 269p.

b. Buddhism under Christian - secular British rule

18460 DE SILVA, K.M. Buddhism and the British government in Ceylon 1840-55. In CHJ 10,1/4 (1960-61) 91-159.

18461 EVERS, H.-D. Buddhism and British colonial policy in Ceylon, 1815-1875. In AsSt 2,3 (1964) 323-33.

18462 FERNANDO, T. The Western-educated elite and Buddhism in British Ceylon: a neglected aspect of the nationalist movement. In CAS 4 (1973) 18-29.

18463 VIMALANANDA, T., ed. Buddhism in Ceylon under the Christian powers, and the educational and religious policy of the British government in Ceylon, 1797-1832. Colombo: M.D. Gunasena, 1963. 190p. [chiefly documents]

18464 ______, ed. The state and religion in Ceylon since 1815, with an introduction explaining the culture and civilization of the people, together with the findings of the Parliamentary Select Committee which included three former British prime ministers, who acknowledged that the British Crown was solemnly bound by the convention of 1815 to protect Buddhism in this country above all other religions. Colombo: M.D. Gunasena, 1970. 269p. [evidence before 1848 Cmtee.]

18465 WICKREMERATNE, L.A. Religion, nationalism, and social change in Ceylon, 1865-1885. In JRAS (1969) 123-50.

c. Buddhism in independent Sri Lanka, and the Constitutional directive to "protect and foster the Buddhist Sāsana"

18466 BECHERT, H. Buddhism and mass politics in Burma and Ceylon. In D.E. Smith, ed. Religion and political modernization. New Haven: YUP, 1974, 147-67.

18467 ______. S.W.R.D. Bandaranaike and the legitimation of power through Buddhist ideals. In B.L. Smith, ed. Religion and legitimation of power in Sri Lanka. Chambersburg, PA: Conococheague Associates, 1978, 199-211.

18468 BUDDHIST CMTEE. OF INQUIRY. The betrayal of Buddhism; an abridged version of the Report. Balangoda: Dharmavijaya Press, 1956. 124p. [Full Report in Sinhala]

18569 CEYLON. BUDDHIST SĀSANA CMSN. Report. Colombo: Ceylon Govt. Press, 1959. 352p.

18470 JAYEWARDENE, J.R. Buddhism, Marxism, and other essays. London: East & West, 1957. 93p.

18471 PHADNIS, U. Religion and politics in Sri Lanka. ND: Manohar, 1976. 376p.

18472 VIJAYAVARDHANA, D.C. The revolt in the temple; composed to commemorate 2500 years of the land, the race and the faith. Colombo: Sinha, 1953. 700p.

2. Language, Communalism, and National Integration

a. general studies

18473 ARASARATNAM, S. Nationalism, communalism, and national unity in Ceylon. In P. Mason, ed. India and Ceylon: unity and diversity. Oxford: OUP, 1967, 260-278.

18474 DE SILVA, K.M. Discrimination in Sri Lanka. In W.A. Veenhaven, ed., Case studies on human rights and fundamental freedoms: a world survey. The Hague: Nijhoff, 1975-76, v.3, 71-119.

18475 FARMER, B.H. Ceylon: a divided nation. London: OUP, 1963. 74p.

18476 ______. The social basis of nationalism in Ceylon. In JAS 24 (1965) 431-39)

18477 JAIN, B.K. The problem of citizenship rights of persons of Indian origin in Ceylon. In IJPS 24 (1963) 65-78.

18478 JENNINGS, W.I. Nationalism and political development in Ceylon. In CHJ 3 (1953) 62-84, 99-114, 197-206.

18479 KEARNEY, R.N. Communalism and language in the politics of Ceylon. Durham, NC: DUP, 1967. 165p.

18480 ______. Sinhalese nationalism and social conflict in Ceylon. In PA 37 (1964) 125-36.

18481 KODIKARA, S.U. Communalism and political modernisation in Ceylon. In MAS 1,1 (1970) 94-114.

18482 MATTHEWS, B. The problem of communalism in contemporary Burma and Sri Lanka. In Intl. J. 34,3 (1979) 430-456.

18483 Race relations in Sri Lanka. Colombo: Centre for Society and Religion, 1977. 3v.

18484 ROBERTS, M.W. Ethnic conflict in Sri Lanka and Sinhalese perspectives: barriers to accommodation. In MAS 12,3 (1978) 353-376.

18485 ______, ed. Collective identities, nationalisms, and protest in modern Sri Lanka. Colombo: Marga Inst., 1979. 573p.

18486 SIRIWEERA, W.I. Recent developments in Sinhala-Tamil relations. In AS 20,9 (1980) 903-13.

18487 THANI NAYAGAM, S.X. Language rights in Ceylon. In TC 5,3 (1956) 217-230.

18488 VITTACHI, T. Emergency '58: the story of the Ceylon race riots. London: A. Deutsch, 1958. 123p.

b. the Tamils of Ceylon (22% of tot. pop.): problems of citizenship and official language

18489 BASTIAMPILLAI, B. Social conditions of the Indian immigrant labourer to Ceylon in the 19th century, with special reference to the 'seventies, and some comparisons in other colonies. In Intl. Conf. Seminar of Tamil Studies, 1st, 1966. Proceedings. Kuala Lumpur, 1968, 678-725.

18490 CEYLON INDIAN CONGRESS. Memorandum of the Ceylon Indian Congress on the joint report of the delegations from India and Ceylon. n.p., 1941. 51p.

18491 DE SILVA, K.M. Indian immigration to Ceylon, the first phase, c. 1840-55. In CJHSS 4,2 (1961) 106-37.

18492 DEVILLERS, P. Minorités ethniques et conflits internationaux: les Indiens à Ceylan. In R. française de science politique 17 (1967) 726-37.

18493 GUPTA, B.L. Political and civil status of Indians in Ceylon. Agra: Agra U. Press, 1963. 245p.

18494 HARNAM SINGH. The Indo-Ceylon Agreement of 1964: The question of separate electoral registers. In Indian J. of Intl. Law 5,1 (1965) 9-22.

18495 JAYARAMAN, R. Indian emigration to Ceylon: some aspects of the historical and social background of the emigrants. In IESHR 4 (1967) 319-60.

18496 KARALASINGHAM, V. The way out for the Tamil speaking people: including postscript, 1977. 2nd ed. Colombo: Intl. Pub., 1978. 87p.

18497 KRISHNA SHETTY, K.P. The law of citizenship for Indian and Pakistani residents of Ceylon. In IYIA 7 (1958) 165-185.

18498 PHADNIS, U. The Indo-Ceylon pact and the "stateless" Indians in Ceylon. In AS 7 (1967) 226-36.

18499 RAGHAVAN, M.D. Ceylon and her immigrants. In IAC 11 (1962) 387-403.

18500 ROBERTS, M. The master-servant laws of 1841 and the 1860's and immigrant labour in Ceylon. In CJHSS 8, 1/2 (1965) 24-37.

18501 SCHWARZ, W. The Tamils of Sri Lanka. London: Minority Rights Group, 1975. 16p.

18502 SILVA, N. The problem of Indian immigration to Ceylon. In Raghavan Iyer, ed., South Asian affairs, no. 1, London: Chatto & Windus, 1960, 141-153.

18503 VANDENDRIESEN, I.H. Indian immigration to Ceylon, the first phase c. 1840-1855 - a comment. In CJHSS 7 (1964) 218-29.

3. Public Administration and Bureaucracy
a. general studies

18504 COLLINS, C.H. Ceylon: the imperial heritage. In R. Braibanti, ed. Asian bureaucratic systems emergent from the British imperial tradition. Durham, NC: DUP, 1966, 444-84.

18505 ______. Public administration in Ceylon. London: Royal Inst. of Intl. Affairs, 1951. 162p.

18506 HENSMAN, C.R., ed. The public services and the people. Colombo: Community Inst., 1963. 153p.

18507 KEARNEY, R.N. Ceylon: the contemporary bureaucracy. In R. Braibanti, ed. Asian bureaucratic systems emergent from the British imperial tradition. Durham: DUP, 1966, 485-549.

18507a KEARNEY, R.N. & R.L. HARRIS. Bureaucracy and environment in Ceylon. In JCPS 2 (1964) 253-66.

18508 WILSON, A.J. Public administration in Ceylon. In S.S. Hsueh, ed. Public administration in South and Southeast Asia. Brussels: Intl. Inst. of Admin. Sciences, 1962, 199-240.

18509 ______. The Public Service Commission and ministerial responsibility: the Ceylonese experience. In Public Admin. 46 (1968) 81-93.

b. the Ceylon Civil Service, and other government services

18510 CEYLON. POLICE CMSN. Final report. Colombo: 1970. 404p. (SP21, 1970)

18511 The Ceylon Light Infantry: history of the First Battalion (Regular Force), 1949-1975. n.p., 1976. 425p.

18512 FERNANDO, P.T.M. The Ceylon Civil Service: a study of recruitment policies, 1880-1920. In MCS 1,1 (1970) 64-83.

18513 A history of the Ceylon police. Colombo: Times of Ceylon, 19--. 2v.

18514 KANNANGARA, P.D. The history of the Ceylon civil service, 1802-1833; a study of administrative change in Ceylon. Dehiwala: Tisara Prakasakayo, 1966. 287p.

18515 SANDERATNE, A.E.H. Glimpses of the public services of Ceylon during a period of transition, 1927-1962. Colombo: Sam Printing Works, 1975. 116p.

18516 SYMONDS, R. Ceylon. In his The British and their successors, a study in the development of the government services in the new states. London: Faber, 1966, 98-115.

18517 WISWA WARNAPALA, W.A. Civil service administration in Ceylon: a study in bureaucratic adaptation. Colombo: Dept. of Cultural Affairs, 1974. 411p.

18518 ______. The triumph of competition in the Ceylon Civil Service. In CJHSS ns 1,1 (1971) 62-77.

4. The Legislature in Ceylon

18519 BALASINGHAM, C. Parliamentary control of finance. Colombo: Ceylon Branch, Commonwealth Parliamentary Assn., 1968. 63p.

18520 JAYARATNE, B.C.F. Abolition of the Senate of Ceylon. In Parliamentarian 53,2 (1972) 104-12.

18521 NAMASIVAYAM, S. The legislatures of Ceylon, 1928-48. London: Faber & Faber, 1951. 185p.

18522 WISWA WARNAPALA, W.A. Parliamentary opposition in Sri Lanka: some aspects of the behavior of Marxists. In JCPS 9,4 (1975) 451-67.

18523 ______. Parliamentary supervision of administration in Ceylon, 1947 to 1956: problems and issues. In CJHSS 3,1 (1973) 40-51.

5. The Multiple Legal Systems of Ceylon

18524 ALLES, A.C. Famous criminal cases of Sri Lanka. Colombo: Colombo Apothecaries, 1977. 115p.

18525 COORAY, J.A.L. The Supreme Court of Ceylon. In Intl. Cmsn. of Jurists, J. 9 (1968) 96-113.

18526 COORAY, L.J.M. An introduction to the legal system of Ceylon. Colombo: LHI, 1972. 263p.

18527 DISSANAYAKE, T.B. & A.B. COLIN DE SOYSA. Kandyan law and Buddhist ecclesiastical law. Colombo: Dharmasamaya Press, 1963. 310p.

18528 HAYLEY, F.A. A treatise on the laws and customs of the Sinhalese including the portions still surviving under the name Kandyan law. Colombo: H.W. Cave, 1923. 617p.

18529 JAYAWICKRAMA, N. Human rights in Sri Lanka. Colombo: Dept. of Govt. Pringint, 1976. 77p.

18530 JENNINGS, W.I. & H.W. TAMBIAH. The Dominion of Ceylon, the development of its laws and constitution. Westport, CT: Greenwood Press, 1970. 319p.

18531 MODDER, F.H. Principles of Kandyan law. 2nd ed. London: Stevens & Haynes, 1914. 640p. [1st ed. 1902]

18532 NADARAJA, T. The legal system of Ceylon in its historical setting. Leiden: Brill, 1972. 46 + 311p.

18533 PEIRIS, L.L.T. The citizenship law of the Republic of Sri Lanka (Ceylon): a study of the Citizenship act. Colombo: Govt. Pub. Bureau, 1974. 102p.

18534 RAJANAYAGAM, M.J.L. The reception and restriction of English commercial law in Ceylon. In Intl. & Comp. Law Q. 18 (1969) 378-91.

18535 SAMARAWEERA, V. The Ceylon Charter of Justice of 1883: a Benthamite blueprint for judicial reform. In JICH 2,3 (1974) 263-78.

18536 TAMBIAH, H.W. The laws and customs of the Tamils of Ceylon. Colombo: Tamil Cultural Soc., 1954. 180p.

18537 ______. The laws and customs of the Tamils of Jaffna. Colombo: Times of Ceylon, 1951. 339 + 67p.

18538 ______. The law of Thesawalamai. In TC 7 (1958) 386-408. [Tamil law]

18539 ______. Principles of Ceylon law. Colombo: H.W. Cave, 1972. 571p.

18540 ______. Sinhala laws and customs. Colombo: LHI, 1968. 356p.

D. Local Government in Ceylon

18541 CEYLON. CMTEE. OF INQUIRY ON LOCAL GOVT. Report. Colombo: 1972. 197p. (SP 7, 1972) [chm. V.C. Jayasuriya]

18542 CEYLON. LOCAL GOVT. CMSN. Report. Colombo: 1955. 501p. (SP 33, 1955) [chm. N.K. Choksy]

18543 CEYLON. STATE COUNCIL. Report of the Commission on the Headmen System, Nov. 1935. Colombo: 1935. (SP 27, 1935)

18544 Choksy report (a commission on local government appointed by the Govt. of Ceylon): an appreciation and a summary of the recommendations. In QJLSGI 27 (1957) 197-244.

18545 FERNANDO, E. Local government elections in Ceylon; including local government institutions. Kuliyapitiya, Ceylon: 1967. 274p.

18546 FERNANDO, N. Regional administration in Sri Lanka. Colombo: Academy of Admin. Studies, 1973. 69p.

18547 KANESALINGAM, V. A hundred years of local government in Ceylon, 1865-1965. Colombo: Modern Plastic Works, 1971. 198p.

18548 LEITAN, G.R.T. Local government and decentralized administration in Sri Lanka. Colombo: LHI, 1979. 279p.

18549 MENDIS, M.W.J.G. Local government in Sri Lanka. Colombo: Colombo Apothecaries, 1976. 126p.

18550 ROBINSON, M.S. Political structure in a changing Sinhalese village. Cambridge: CamUP, 1975. 376p.

18551 WISWA WARNAPALA, W.A. District agencies of government departments in Ceylon. In Intl. J. of Admin. Sciences 38,2 (1972) 133-40.

18552 ______. Kachcheri system of district administration in Ceylon. In IJPA 16,4 (1970) 539-54.

E. Sri Lanka's Foreign Relations

1. General Studies; the Policy of Non-Alignment

18553 BANDARANAIKE, S.W.R.D. The foreign policy of Sri Lanka: extracts from statements by the late Prime Minister Mr. S.W.R.D. Bandaranaike. 3rd ed. Colombo: Info. Dept., 1976. 122p.

18554 DUTTA, P. Neutralism, theory and practice, with special reference to India, Burma, Ceylon, Egypt and Ghana. Calcutta: World Press, 1978. 327p.

18555 JAYAWARDENE, J.R. D.S. Senanayake's foreign policy. In CHJ 5 (1955) 49-61.

18556 KODIKARA, S.U. Continuity and change in Sri Lanka's foreign policy: 1974-79. In AS 20,9 (1980) 879-91.

18557 ______. Major trends in Sri Lanka's non-alignment policy after 1956. In AS 13,12 (1973) 1121-1136.

18558 KRISHNA SHETTY, K.P. Ceylon's foreign policy: emerging patterns of non-alignment. In PSR 5,1 (1966) 1-32. [Also in SAS 1,2 (1966) 1-32]

18559 NISSANKA, H.S.S. The foreign policy of Sri Lanka under S.W.R.D. Bandaranaike: a turning point in the history of a newly independent country in Asia. Colombo: Dept. of Info., 1976. 193p.

18560 PHADNIS, U. Ceylon's foreign policy: survey of research & source materials. In IS 6 (1965) 454-63.

18561 ______. Non-alignment as a factor in Ceylon's foreign policy. In IS 3 (1962) 425-42.

18562 PRASAD, D.M. Ceylon's foreign policy under the Bandaranaikes (1956-65); a political analysis. ND: S. Chand, 1973. 465p.

18563 ______. Ceylon's foreign policy under the Bandaranaikes 1956-65: a study in the emergence and role of non-alignment. In IJPS 33,3 (1972) 271-290.

18564 TRANCHELL, C.L. A doodled self-portrait. Colombo: Times of Ceylon, 1974. 201p.

2. Relations with specific nations and areas [for Indo-Ceylon Relations, see Chap. Seven, IV. C.]

18565 ANAND, J.P. Sino-Ceylonese relations. In JIDSA 3 (1971) 325-52.

18566 JACOB, L.M. Sri Lanka from dominion to republic; a study of the changing relations with the United Kingdom. Delhi: National, 1973. 247p.

18567 NAVARATNE, G. The Chinese connexion: a study of Sri Lanka-Chinese relations in the modern period. Colombo: Sandesa News Agency, 1976. 165p.

18568 WICKREMASINGHE, S. Ceylon's relations with South-East Asia, with special reference to Burma. In CJHSS 3 (1960) 38-58.

3. Sri Lanka in the World Economy since 1948
a. foreign trade; balance of payments

18569 DUTTA, A. International migration, trade, and real income; a case study of Ceylon, 1920-38. Calcutta: World Press, 1973. 171p.

18570 GAGZOW, B. Aussenwirtschaftsorientierte Entwicklungspolitik kleiner Länder; das Beispiel Ceylon. Stuttgart: G. Fischer, 1969. 224p.

18571 IMFELD, AL. Sri Lanka setzt auf Freihandelszonen; gefährliche Entwicklungsillusionen; eine Kleine Fallstudie. In IAF 9, 1/2 (1978) 113-29.

18572 INTL. BANK FOR RECONSTRUCTION & DEV. Review of the economic situation and foreign exchange problem of Ceylon. Colombo: Min. of Planning & Econ. Affairs, 1968. 132p.

18573 KARUNATILAKE, H.N.S. The impact of import and exchange controls and bilateral trade agreements on trade and production in Ceylon. In T. Morgan & N. Spoelstra, eds. Economic interdependence in Southeast Asia. Madison: UWiscP, 1969, 285-303.

18574 LIM, YOUNGIL. Trade and growth: the case of Ceylon. In EDCC 16,2 (1968) 245-60.

18575 NEWMAN, P. Studies in the import structure of Ceylon. Colombo: Planning Secretariat, 1958. 108p.

b. foreign investment and aid

18576 ANTHONISZ, B.V.A. The role and impact of external assistance on the economy of Sri Lanka 1960-1970. In Staff Studies, Central Bank of Ceylon 3,1 (1973) 91-120.

18577 CEYLON. MIN. OF PLANNING & ECON. AFFAIRS. Foreign aid. Colombo: Govt. Press, 1966. 41p.

18578 CEYLON. TREASURY. External economic assistance; (a review, 1950-64). Colombo: Govt. Press, 1964. 91p.

18579 COREA, G. Aid and the economy. In Marga 1,1 (1971) 19-54.

18580 KANESATHASAN, S. Foreign capital in the economic development of Ceylon. In CJHSS 6,1 (1963) 84-98.

III. THE CEYLON ECONOMY: FROM PLANTATION COLONY TO SOCIALIST WELFARE STATE

A. Bibliography and Reference

18581 CEYLON. The Ceylon economic atlas. Colombo: Dept. of Census & Statistics, 1969. 69p.

18582 Quarterly Economic Review (QER); Sri Lanka (Ceylon). London: The Economist Intelligence Unit Ltd. 1976-. [quarterly]

18583 RANASINGHE, W. & S.M.K. MILEHAM & C. GUNATUNGA. A Bibliography of socio-economic studies in the agrarian sector of Sri Lanka. Colombo: Agrarian Res. & Training Inst., 1977. 208p.

B. Economic History of Ceylon since 1796

18584 BERTOLACCI, A. A view of the agricultural, commercial and financial interests of Ceylon. London: Black, Parbury & Allen, 1817. 577p.

18585 CRAIG, J.E., Jr. Ceylon. In W.A. Lewis, ed. Tropical development 1880-1913. London: Allen & Unwin, 1970, 221-49.

18586 DUTTA, A. Inter-war Ceylon: trade and migration. In IESHR 7 (1970) 1-23.

18587 GUNEWARDENA, E. External trade and the economic structure of Ceylon, 1900-1955. Colombo: Central Bank of Ceylon, 1965. 234p.

18588 INDRARATNA, A.D.V. DE S. The Ceylon economy, from the Great Depression to the Great Boom; an analysis of cyclical fluctuations and their impact (1930-1952). Colombo: M.D. Gunasena, 1966. 116p.

18589 MEYER, É. De la dette interne à la dette externe. Observations sur les mutations du crédit à Sri Lanka à la période coloniale. In Puruṣārtha 4 (1980) 207-26.

18590 ______. Impact de la dépression des années 1930 sur l'économie et la société rurale de Sri Lanka. In Puruṣārtha 2 (1975) 31-66.

18591 NICHOLAS, S.E.N. Commercial Ceylon. Colombo: Times of Ceylon, 1933. 310p.

18592 PEEBLES, P. Land use and population growth in colonial Ceylon. In CAS 9 (1976) 64-79.

18593 RASAPUTRAM, W. Influence of foreign trade on the level and growth of national income of Ceylon, 1926-1957. Colombo: Central Bank of Ceylon, 1964. 187p.

18594 STAHL, K.M. The metropolitan organization of British colonial trade: four regional studies. London: Faber & Faber, 1951. 313p. [Pt. 3, Ceylon, 125-75]

18595 VANDENDRIESEN, I.H. Some aspects of the financing of commercial enterprize in 19th century Ceylon. In UCR 18 (1960) 213-21.

18596 ______. Some trends in the economic history of Ceylon in the 'modern' period. In CJHSS 3,1 (1960) 1-17.

18597 WIJESINGHE, MALLORY E. The economy of Sri Lanka, 1948-1975. Colombo: the author, RANCO Printers, 1976. 245p.

C. Demography and Population Policy

1. General Studies of Ceylon's Population; Population and Economic Development

18598 IMMERWAHR, G. How many people in Sri Lanka? Colombo: Immerwahr, 1979. 58p.

18599 JONES, G.W. & S. SELVARATNAM. Population growth and economic development in Ceylon. Colombo: Hansa Pub. & Marga Inst., 1972. 249p.

18600 Population of Sri Lanka. Bangkok: U.N. Econ. & Social Cmsn. for Asia & the Pacific, 1976. 397p.

18601 SANDERATNE, N. Socio-economic variables in Sri Lanka's demographic transition, an analysis of recent trends. In Staff Studies, Central Bank of Ceylon 5,1 (1975) 157-90.

18602 SELVARATNAM, S. Some implications of population growth in Ceylon. In CJHSS 4 (1961) 33-49.

18603 SRI LANKA. DEPT. OF CENSUS & STAT. The population of Sri Lanka. Colombo: Dept. of Census and Statistics, 1974. 128p.

18604 WIJEWARDANA, D. Population growth and economic development in Sri Lanka. In Staff Studies, Central Bank of Ceylon 5,1 (1975) 21-44.

2. Fertility and Mortality; Distribution of Population

18605 ABHAYARATNE, O.E.R. & C.H.S. JAYAWARDENE. Fertility trends in Ceylon. Colombo: Colombo Apothecaries, 1967. 421p.

18606 ______. Internal migration in Ceylon. In CJHSS 8 (1965) 68-90.

18607 RYAN, B. Institutional factors in Sinhalese fertility. In Milbank Memorial Fund Q. 30 (1952) 359-81.

18608 VAMATHEVAN, S. Some aspects of internal migration in Ceylon. In World Population Conf., 2nd, Belgrade, 1965. Proc. NY: United Nations, 1967, v. 4, 542-49.

18609 WRIGHT, N.H. Recent fertility change in Ceylon and prospects for the national family planning program. In Demography 5 (1968) 745-56.

3. Population Policy and Control

18610 ABHAYARATNE, O.E.R. & C.H.S. JAYEWARDENE. Family planning in Ceylon. Colombo: Colombo Apothecaries, 1968. 188p.

18611 AMUNUGAMA, S. Social science research on family planning in Sri Lanka. Colombo: Family Planning Communication Strategy Project, Min. of Info. & Broadcasting, 1976. 28p.

18612 KINCH, A. National programs: achievements and problems. Ceylon. In Intl. Conf. on Family Planning Programs, Geneva, 1965. Proceedings: family planning and population programs. Chicago: UChiP, 1966, 105-10.

18613 SELVARATNAM, S. & S.A. MEEGAMA. Towards a population policy for Ceylon. In Marga 1,2 (1971) 65-82.

D. Output, Income, and Standards of Living

18614 CEYLON. DEPT. OF CENSUS & STAT. National accounts of Ceylon, 1963-68. Colombo: 1969. 20p. [latest ed., National accounts of Sri Lanka, 1970-77. Colombo: 1977. 45p.]

18615 ______. Socio-economic survey of Sri Lanka, 1969-70, rounds 1-4: statistical tables. Colombo: Dept. of Census and Statistics, 1973-.

18616 KARUNATILAKE, H.N.S. Changes in income distribution in Sri Lanka. In Staff St. 4,1 (1974) 87-109.

18617 RASAPUTRAM, WARNASENA. Changes in the pattern of income inequality in Ceylon. In Marga 1,4 (1972) 60-91.

18618 SAUNDRANAYAGAM, TERRENCE. Sri Lanka's gross national product, 1950-58. In Staff St. 6,1 (1976) 1-30.

18619 WILLIAMS, K. The national income of Ceylon. Colombo: Min. of Finance, 1952. 27p.

E. Natural Resources

18620 FERNANDO, S.N.U. Ceylon soils. Colombo: Swabhasha Printers, 1967. 76p.

18621 HERATH, J.W. Mineral resources of Sri Lanka. Colombo: Geological Survey Dept., 1975. 72p.

F. Economic Development and Planning in Sri Lanka

1. General Studies of Development

18622 BALAKRISHNAN, N. Economic policies and trends in Sri Lanka. In AS 20,9 (1980) 891-902.

18623 CEYLON. MIN. OF PLANNING & ECON. AFFAIRS. Economic development, 1966-68: review and trends. Colombo: 1967. 105p.

18624 CEYLON. NATL. PLANNING COUNCIL. Papers by visiting economists (J.R. Hicks, N. Kaldor, J. Robinson, O. Lange, J.K. Galbraith, U. Hicks & G. Myrdal). Colombo: Ceylon Govt. Press, 1959. 123p.

18625 COREA, G. The instability of an export economy. Colombo: Marga Inst., 1975. 374p.

18626 DESAUVAGE, A. & M. VAN DE WIELE. Tableau d'une économie en voie de développement: Sri Lanka. Tournai: Arts et idees, 1976. 176p.

18627 The economy of Ceylon: trends and prospects. Colombo: Min. of Finance, 1971. 79p.

18628 GAMBURD, G. Patrons and profits: hierarchy and competition in Sri Lanka. In H.E. Ullrich, ed. Competition and modernization in South Asia. ND: Abhinav, 1975, 103-50.

18629 INTL. BANK FOR RECONSTRUCTION & DEV. The economic development of Ceylon; report of a mission.... Baltimore: Johns Hopkins Press, 1953. 829p.

18630 ______. Recent economic trends, Ceylon. Colombo: Min. of Planning & Econ. Affairs, 1966. 95p.

18631 JENNINGS, W.I. The economy of Ceylon. 2nd ed. Madras, London: OUP, 1951. 194p. [1st ed. 1948]

18632 KARUNATILAKE, H.N.S. Economic development in Ceylon. NY: Praeger, 1971. 378p.

18633 PYATT, G. & A. ROE. Social accounting for development planning with special reference to Sri Lanka. Cambridge: CamUP, 1977. 190p.

18634 SNODGRASS, D.R. Ceylon: an export economy in transition. Homewood, IL: R.D. Irwin, 1966. 416p.

18635 STEIN, B. Problems of economic development in Ceylon. In CHJ 3 (1954) 286-330.

2. Buddhist Values and Economic Modernization; the Weber Thesis

18636 KALANSURIYA, A.D.P. Empirical Buddhism: a novel aspect of Sinhalese Buddhism made explicit. In Social Compass 25,2 (1978) 251-65.

18637 KARUNATILAKE, H.N.S. This confused society. Colombo: Buddhist Info. Center, 1976. 120p.

18638 PIERIS, R. Economic development and ultramondaneity. In Archives de sociologie des religions 15 (1963) 95-100.

18639 SARAM, P.A.S. Weberian Buddhism and Sinhalese Buddhism. In Social Compass 23,4 (1976) 355-83.

18640 SARATHCHANDRA, E.R. Traditional values and the modernisation of a Buddhist society: the case of Ceylon. In R.N. Bellah, ed. Religion and progress in modern Asia. NY: Free Press, 1965, 109-23.

3. Economic Policy and Planning
a. general studies

18641 HENSMAN, C.R., ed. Organising for development:

progress and reaction in Ceylon, 1947-1963. Colombo: 1964.

18642 HEWAVITHARANA, B. Choice of techniques in Ceylon. In E.A.G. Robinson & M. Kidron, eds. Economic development in South Asia. London: Macmillan, 1970, 431-48.

18643 JAYAWARDENA, L. Recent approaches to planning in Ceylon. In E.A.G. Robinson & M. Kidron, eds. Economic development in South Asia. London: Macmillan, 1970, 391-430.

18644 MÖLLER, BIRGER. Employment approaches to economic planning in developing countries with special reference to Ceylon. Lund: Studentlitteratur, 1972. 159p. (Scandinavian Inst. of Asian Studies monograph series, 9)

18645 OLIVER, H.M., JR. Economic opinion and policy in Ceylon. Durham, NC: DUP, 1957. 145p.

18646 WEERASOORIA, W.S. Credit and security in Ceylon (Sri Lanka); the legal problems of development finance. NY: Crane, Russak, 1973. 303p.

18647 WEIJLAND, H. Development policy in Ceylon and Ghana; the application of a medium-term planning model. In Development & Change 2,1 (1970-71) 4-59.

b. development plans

18648 BALAKRISHNAN, N. The five year plan and development policy in Sri Lanka: socio-political perspectives and the plan. In AS 13,12 (1973) 1155-68.

18649 CEYLON. NATL. PLANNING COUNCIL. First interim report. Colombo: Planning Secretariat, 1957. 192p.

18650 ______. The Ten Year Plan. Colombo: Ceylon Govt. Press, 1959. 490p.

18651 FARMER, B.H. The Ceylon Ten-year plan, 1959-1968. In Pacific Viewpoint 2,2 (1961) 123-36.

18652 The Five-Year Plan, 1972-1976. Colombo: Min. of Planning and Employment, 1971. 137p.

18653 GUNAWARDENE, C.A. Ceylon's ten year development plan. In Asian R. 56 (1960) 57-68.

G. Sri Lanka's Financial and Monetary System

1. Public Finance and Taxation

18654 CEYLON. DEPT. OF INLAND REVENUE. The new tax structure, 1969-70. Colombo: 1969. 117p.

18655 GOODE, R. New system of direct taxation in Ceylon. In National Tax J. 13 (1960) 329-40.

18656 HEWAVITHARANA, B. The management of external and internal finances in Sri Lanka: problems and policies. In AS 13,12 (1973) 1137-54.

18657 HICKS, J.R. & U.K. HICKS. Local government and finance in Ceylon. In Ceylon, Natl. Planning Council. Papers by visiting economists. Colombo: 1959, 107-18.

18658 INST. OF CHARTERED ACCOUNTANTS OF CEYLON. The Constitution and public finance in Ceylon. Colombo: 1964. 271p.

18659 JAYAMAHA, G. The growth of public expenditure in Sri Lanka, 1960-1975. In Staff Studies, Central Bank of Ceylon 6,2 (1976) 71-88.

18660 RAMACHANDRAN, N. Ceylon's tax system: some recent experiments. In Public Finance 22 (1967) 316-32.

18661 SELVAJAYAM, S. & M. AMARASINGHAM, eds. Rates of direct taxes in Ceylon. Colombo: Income Tax Payers' Assoc. of Ceylon, 1965. 81p.

18662 SILVA, M. The evasion of taxation in Ceylon. In Staff Studies, Central Bank of Ceylon 2,2 (1972) 1-24.

2. Banking and Monetary Policy; Other Financial Institutions

18663 Central Bank of Ceylon, 1950-1975. Colombo: Central Bank of Ceylon, 1975. 103p.

18664 GREENBERG, M. Central banking in Ceylon. In G. Davies, ed. Central banking in South and East Asia. Hong Kong: Hong Kong U. Press, 1960, 9-26.

18665 GUNASEKERA, H.A. DE SILVA. Ceylon. In W.F. Crick, ed. Commonwealth banking systems. Oxford: OUP, 1965, 279-302.

18666 ______. From dependent currency to central banking in Ceylon: an analysis of monetary experience 1825-1957. London: G. Bell, 1962. 324p.

18667 ______. A review of central banking in Ceylon. In CJHSS 2 (1959) 125-47.

18668 INST. OF CHARTERED ACCOUNTANTS OF CEYLON. Banking in Ceylon. Colombo: 1963. 175p.

18669 KAHAGALLE, S. An estimate of savings and its determinates in the Sri Lanka economy, 1960-1972. In Staff Studies, Central Bank of Ceylon 5,2 (1975) 33-74.

18670 KANNANGARA, D.M. The growth of branch banking in Ceylon. In CJHSS 9 (1966) 134-54.

18671 KARUNATILAKE, H.N.S. Banking and financial institutions in Ceylon. Colombo: Central Bank of Ceylon, 1968. 270p.

18672 ______. Central banking and monetary policy in Sri Lanka. Colombo: LHI, 1973. 209p.

18673 SANMUGANATHAN, M. Incentives to save and an appraisal of their effectiveness in Sri Lanka. In Econ. Bull. for Asia & the Pacific 26,1 (1975) 153-69.

18674 SHENOY, B.R. Ceylon currency and banking. London: Longmans, Green, 1941. 300p.

18675 TAMBIAH, S.J. Ceylon. In R.D. Lambert & B.F. Hoselitz, eds. The role of savings and wealth in southern Asia and the West. Paris: UNESCO, 1963, 44-125.

3. The Cooperative Movement

18676 CEYLON. ROYAL CMSN. ON THE COOP. MOVEMENT IN CEYLON. Report. Colombo: Govt. Pub. Bureau, 1970. 391p. (SP 2, 1970)

18677 Cooperative movement and national development. Colombo: Dept. of Coop. Dev., 1973. 102p.

18678 The cooperative system and rural credit in Sri Lanka. Colombo: Marga Inst., 1974. 216p.

18679 GOONERATNE, T.E. Fifty years of co-operative development in Ceylon through consumer societies. Colombo: LHI, 1966. 83p.

18680 KURUKULASURIYA, G. Cooperation: its rise and growth in Ceylon. Colombo: Coop. Federation of Ceylon, 1971. 320p.

18681 TAMBIAH, S.J. The co-operatives in relation to the economic needs of the Ceylonese peasant. In CJHSS 1 (1958) 36-61.

H. Restructuring Agriculture and Rural Society in Sri Lanka

1. General Studies of Ceylon Agriculture

18682 APPADURAI, R.R. Grassland farming in Ceylon. Kandy: T.B.S. Godamunne, 1968. 135p.

18683 BANSIL, P.C. Ceylon agriculture: a perspective. Delhi: Dhanpat Rai, 1971. 407p.

18684 CEYLON. DEPT. OF CENSUS & STAT. Census of agriculture, 1962. Colombo: 1965. 3 v. in 1.

18685 RICHARDS, P. & E. STOUTJESDIJK. Agriculture in Ceylon until 1975. Paris: OECD, 1970. 228p.

18686 SENEWIRATNE, S.T. & R.R. APPADURAI. Field crops of Ceylon. Colombo: LHI, 1966. 376p.

2. Agricultural Planning and Development

a. general studies

18687 ANDARAWEWA, A.B. Agricultural development in Ceylon. In R. Weitz & Y.H. Landau, ed. Rural development in a changing world. Cambridge, MA: MIT Press, 1971, 554-75.

18688 APPADURAI, R.R., ed. The development of the cattle industry in Ceylon; proceedings of a symposium organised by the Dept. of Animal Husbandry, U. of Ceylon, with support from the Min. of Agriculture and Food. Kandy:

T.B.S. Godamunne, 1970. 164p.

18689 BROHIER, R.L. D.S. Senanayake as Minister of Agriculture and Lands. In CHJ 5 (1955-56) 68-80.

18690 CEYLON. MIN. OF AGRI. & FOOD. Agricultural development proposals, 1966-1970. Colombo: Min. of Planning and Econ. Affairs, 1966. 351p.

18691 ______. Agricultural plan; first report of the Ministry Planning Committee. Colombo: Ceylon Govt. Press, 1958. 381p.

18692 COREA, G. Economic planning, the Green Revolution, and the "food drive" in Ceylon. In D.L. David, ed. Public finance, planning and economic development... London: Macmillan, 1973, 273-303.

18693 DE SILVA, L. A critical evaluation of agricultural policy 1960-68. In Staff Studies, Central Bank of Ceylon 1,1 (1971) 93-111.

18694 PEIRIS, G. Agricultural growth through "decentralization and popular participation": a survey of DDC farm projects in Kandy District, 1971-73. In MCS 3,1 (1972) 60-94.

18695 SRI LANKA. DEPT. OF RURAL DEV. RES. COUNCIL. The role of rural development societies in Sri Lanka: a report of a research study. Colombo: 1976. 120p.

18696 Symposium on the Dev. of Agriculture in the Dry Zone, 1967. Proceedings. Ed. by O.S. Peries. Colombo: Swabhasha Printers, 1967. 236p.

b. agricultural technology and innovation

18697 ALEXANDER, P. Innovation in a cultural vacuum: the mechanization of Sri Lanka fisheries. In HO 34,3 (1975) 333-44.

18698 DIEDERICH, G. Probleme der landwirtschaftlichen Beratung und der Ubernahme von Neuerungen in Ceylon. Frankfurt/Main: DLG-Verlag, 1970. 261p. (Zeitschrift fur auslandische Landwirtschaft. Materialiensammlung, 12)

c. irrigation and water management

18699 ARUMUGAM, S. Water resources of Ceylon: its utilisation and development. Colombo: Water Resources Board, 1969. 415p.

18700 BROHIER, R.L. Food and the people. Colombo: LHI, 1975. 199p.

18701 FAO. Report of the irrigation program review: Ceylon. Colombo: Min. of Planning & Econ. Affairs, 1968. 117p.

18701a GOONETILLEKE, L.P. D.J. Wimalasurendra and his pioneer role in the development of hydro-electricity in Sri Lanka. Ratmalana: Sri Lanka Sisyopakara Samitiya, 1976. 144p.

18702 KEANE, J. Report on irrigation in Ceylon. Colombo: George J.A. Skeen, Govt. printer, 1905. 81p. (SP 45, 1905)

18703 PEIRIS, W. Wimalasurendra: story of our water power resources. Maharagama: Peiris, 1976. 64p. [biog. of D.J. Wimalasurendra, 1874-1953, electrical engineer]

18704 ROBERTS, M.W. Irrigation policy in British Ceylon during the nineteenth century. In SA 2 (1972) 47-63.

d. integrated river basin schemes

18705 BROHIER, R.L. The Gal Oya Valley project in Ceylon. Colombo: Dept. of Info., 1951. 44p.

18706 CEYLON. GAL OYA PROJECT EVAL. CMTEE. 1969. Report. Colombo: 1970. 203p. (SP, 1, 1970)

18707 CEYLON. MAHAWELI DEV. BOARD. Mahaweli Ganga Development Project 1: feasibility study for stage 11. Mahaweli Development Board, Sogreah. Colombo: 1972. 8 v.

18708 IRIYAGOLLE, G. The truth about the Mahaweli. Nugegoda: Iriyagolle, 1978. 88p.

18709 Mahaweli, projects and programme: review of progress under the Accelerated Programme of Mahaweli Development and programme, 1980. Colombo: Min. of Lands & Land Dev. & Mahaweli Dev., 1979. 124p. + 38 pl.

18710 MENDIS, M.W.J.G. The planning implications of the Mahaweli development project in Sri Lanka. Colombo: LHI, 1973. 149p.

18711 PIERIS, R. The effects of technological development on the population of Gal Oya valley. In CJHSS 8,1/2 (1965) 163-72.

3. The Plantation Sector

a. history of plantation agriculture and export economy

18712 BASTIANPILLAI, B. From coffee to tea in Ceylon - the vicissitudes of a colony's plantation economy. In CJHSS 7,1 (1964) 43-66.

18713 RAJARATNAM, S. The growth of plantation agriculture in Ceylon, 1886-1931. In CJHSS 4 (1961) 1-20.

18714 RAMACHANDRAN, N. Foreign plantation investment in Ceylon, 1889-1958. Colombo: Central Bank of Ceylon, 1963. 200p.

18715 ROBERTS, M.W. Indian estate labour in Ceylon during the coffee period - 1830-1880. In IESHR 3 (1966) 1-52, 101-36.

18716 VANDENDRIESEN, I.H. Plantation agriculture and land-sales policy in Ceylon - the first phase 1836-86. In UCR 14,1/2 (1956) 6-25.

18717 WIMALADHARMA, K.P., ed. Agricultural diversification in Sri Lanka: an annotated bibliography on the publications of the Agricultural Diversification Project. Peradeniya: UNDP/FAO Agricultural Diversification Project, Min. of Plantation Industries, 1977. 34p.

b. major plantation crops: tea, rubber, coconut

18718 AMEER ALI, A.C.L. Cinchona cultivation in nineteenth-century Ceylon. In MCS 5,1 (1974) 93-106.

18719 FARRINGTON, J. Cotton: the economics of expansion in Sri Lanka. Colombo: Agrarian Res. & Training Inst., 1979. 83p.

18720 FORREST, D.M. A hundred years of Ceylon tea, 1867-1967. London: Chatto & Windus, 1967. 320p.

18721 LIM, YOUNGIL. Impact of the tea industry on the growth of the Ceylonese economy. In Social and economic studies (Kingston, Jamaica) 17 (1968) 453-67.

18722 MARBY, H. Tea in Ceylon - an attempt at a regional and temporal differentiation of the tea growing areas in Ceylon. Wiesbaden: Steiner, 1972. 238p.

18723 MOORE, M.P. The state and the cinnamon industry in Sri Lanka. Colombo: Agrarian Res. & Training Inst., 1978. 51p.

18724 RAJARATNAM, S. The Ceylon tea industry, 1886-1931. In CJHSS 4 (1961) 169-202.

18725 SAMARAWEERA, V. The cinnamon trade of Ceylon in the early nineteenth century. In IESHR 8,4 (1971) 415-442.

18726 VANDENDRIESEN, I.H. The history of coffee culture in Ceylon. In CHJ 3,1 (1953) 31-61; 3,2 (1953) 156-72.

18727 WICKRAMARATNE, L.A. The establishment of the tea industry in Ceylon: the first phase 1870 to 1900. In CJHSS 11,2 (1972) 131-55.

4. The Peasant Sector

a. general studies

18728 BRAYNE, C.V. The problem of peasant agriculture in Ceylon. In Ceylon Econ. J. 6 (1934) 34-46.

18729 FARMER, B.H., ed. Green revolution? Technology and change in rice-growing areas of Tamil Nadu and Sri Lanka. London: Macmillan, 1977. 429p.

18730 GUNADASA, J.M. A review of planning for paddy production in Sri Lanka, 1947-70. In MCS 3,2 (1972) 159-93.

18731 KELEGAMA, J.B. The economy of rural Ceylon and the problem of the peasantry. In Ceylon Economist 4,4 (1959) 341-70.

18732 SAMARASINGE, S.W.R. DE A. Agriculture in the

peasant sector of Sri Lanka. Colombo: Sri Lanka U. Press, 1977. 202p.

18733 SATHASIVAMPILLAI, K. & G.A.C. DE SILVA. Farm business management in the intermediate zone of Sri Lanka during 1973/74. Peradeniya: Div. of Agri. Econ., Farm Mgmt. & Stat., 1976. 106p.

18734 UNITED NATIONS. RES. INST. FOR SOCIAL DEV. Rice revolution in Sri Lanka. Geneva: 1977. 282p.

b. pioneer peasant colonization: a continuing development from the 19th century

18735 AMERASINGHE, N. Efficiency of resource utilisation in paddy production on settlement farms in Sri Lanka. In MCS 5,1 (1974) 77-92.

18736 ______. The impact of high yielding varieties of rice on a settlement scheme in Ceylon. In MCS 3,1 (1972) 19-32.

18737 ______. Overview of settlement schemes in Sri Lanka. In AS 16,7 (1976) 620-36.

18738 AMUNUGAMA, S. Chandrikawewa: a recent attempt at colonization on a peasant framework. In CJHSS 8,1/2 (1965) 130-62.

18739 ELLMAN, A.O., et al. Land settlement in Sri Lanka, 1840-1975: a review of the major writings on the subject. Colombo: Agrarian Res. & Training Inst., 1976. 94p.

18740 ELLMAN, A.O. & D. DE S. RATNAWEERA. New settlement schemes in Sri Lanka: a study of twenty selected youth schemes, cooperative farms, DDC agricultural projects, and land reform settlements. Colombo: Agrarian Res. & Training Inst., 1974. 234p.

18741 ______. Thannimurrippu Paripalana Sabai: case study, the transfer of administration of an irrigated settlement scheme from government officials to a people's organisation. Colombo: Agrarian Res. & Training Inst., 1973. 28p.

18742 ELLMAN, A.O. & K.P. WIMALADHARMA. Settlement development in the wet zone of Sri Lanka: a training handbook on institutions, policies, and procedures concerning settlements. Peradeniya: UNDP/FAO Agri. Diversification Project, Min. of Plantation Industries, 1976. 40p.

18743 FARMER, B.H. Pioneer peasant colonization in Ceylon: a study in Asian agrarian problems. London: OUP, 1957. 387p.

18744 ______. The pioneer peasant in India: some comparisons with Ceylon. In Ceylon Geography 17,1 (1963) 49-63.

18745 FONSEKA, H.N.C. Unnichchai colony: the agricultural geography of a peasant colonisation scheme in the dry zone. In CJHSS 9 (1966) 120-33.

18746 GOONERATNE, W., et al. Kurundankulama dry farming settlement: a socio-economic appraisal. Colombo: Agrarian Res. & Training Inst., 1977. 40p.

18747 RAJENDRA, M. The Rajangana colonization project: a study of the implementation of a development project. In G.U. Iglesias. Implementation: the problem of achieving results. Manila: Eastern Regional Org. for Public Admin., 1976, 62-94.

18748 RATNAWEERA, D. DE S. New agricultural settlement schemes. Colombo: Colombo Apothecaries, 1977. 107p.

18749 WANIGARATNE, R.D. The Minipe colonisation scheme: an appraisal. Colombo: Agrarian Res. & Training Inst., 1979. 60p.

18750 WIKKRAMATILEKE, R. Southeast Ceylon: trends and problems in agricultural settlement. Chicago: UChiP, 1963. 163p.

5. Land Tenure and Reform

a. land policy under British rule; the Land Commission of 1927

18751 CEYLON. LAND CMSN. Final report. Colombo: 1929. 35p. (SP 18, 1929)

18752 CEYLON. VIHARAGAM, DEWALAGAM, AND NINDAGAM LAND TENURE CMSN. Report. Colombo: Govt. Printers, 1956. 173p. (SP 1, 1956)

18753 DE SILVA, K.M. The development of British policy on temple lands in Ceylon, 1840-1855. In JRASCB ns 8,2 (1963) 312-29.

18754 ______. The third Earl Grey and the maintenance of an Imperial policy on the sale of Crown lands in Ceylon, c. 1832-1852. In JAS 27 (1967) 5-20.

18755 ______. Studies in British land policy in Ceylon. In CJHSS 7,1 (1964) 28-42.

18756 FERGUSON, A.M. Taxation in Ceylon: with special reference to the grain taxes: the import duty on rice balanced by a local excise levy; and the proposal to substitute a general land tax. Colombo: Ceylon Observer Press, 1890. 161p.

18757 MOORE, M.P. & G. WICKRAMASINGHE. Thattumaru, kattimaru systems of land tenure. Colombo: Agrarian Res. & Training Inst., 1978. 52p.

18758 ROBERTS, M.W. Grain taxes in British Ceylon, 1832-1878. In JAS 27 (1968) 809-34.

18759 ______. Grain taxes in British Ceylon, 1832-1878; problems in the field. In JAS 27,4 (1968) 809-34.

18760 ______. Grain taxes in British Ceylon, 1832-1978: theories, prejudices and controversies. In MCS 1,1 (1970) 115-46.

18761 VANDENDRIESEN, I.H. Land sales policy and some aspects of the problem of tenure - 1836-1886. In UCR 15,1/2 (1957) 36-52.

b. land tenure in Independent Ceylon; the Land Reform Act of 1972

18762 ABEYSINGHE, A. Land reform in Sri Lanka, 1505-1975: oppression to liberation. Colombo: Centre for Society & Religion, 1976. 51p.

18763 AGRARIAN RES. & TRAINING INST. Land reform and the development of coconut lands: a case study of selected villages and estates in the class II coconut lands of Colombo District. Colombo: Agrarian Res. & Training Inst., 1977. 76p.

18764 ALEXANDER, P. Sea tenure in southern Sri Lanka. In Ethnology 16,3 (1977) 231-53.

18765 CEYLON. DEPT. OF CENSUS & STAT. Report on the survey of landlessness, July 1952. Colombo: Ceylon Govt. Press, 1952. 38p. (SP 13, 1952)

18766 CEYLON. LAND CMSN. Report. Colombo: 1958. 234p. (SP 10, 1958)

18767 GUNASINGHE, N. Agrarian relations in the Kandyan countryside in relation to the concept of extreme social disintegration. In Social Sciences R. (Colombo) 1 (1979) 1-41.

18768 HERRING, R.J. The forgotten 1953 Paddy Lands Act in Ceylon: ideology, capacity, and response. In MCS 3,2 (1972) 99-124.

18769 LEACH, E.R. Transition from group landholding to individual landholding. An example from dry-zone Ceylon. In Intl. Conf. of Econ. History, 2nd, Aix-en-Provence, 1962. Paris: Mouton, 1965, v. 2, 313-322.

18770 OBEYESEKERE, G. Land tenure in village Ceylon: a sociological and historical study. London: CamUP, 1967. 320p.

18771 PEIRIS, G.H. The current land reforms and peasant agriculture in Sri Lanka. In SA 5 (1975) 78-89.

18772 ______. Land reform and agrarian change in Sri Lanka. In MAS 12,4 (1978) 611-28.

18773 ______. Share tenancy and tenurial reform in Sri Lanka. In CJHSS 6,1 (1976) 24-54.

18774 SANDERATNE, N. Sri Lanka's new land reform. SAR 6,1 (1972) 7-19.

18775 ______. Tenancy in Ceylon's paddy lands: the 1958 reform. In SAR 5,2 (1972) 117-36.

J. Industry in Sri Lanka

1. General Studies

18776 Directory of industrial products and manufacturing establishments in Ceylon. Colombo: Industrial Dev. Board, 1969. 488p.

18777 EVERS, H.-D. Kulturwandel in Ceylon; eine Untersuchung uber die Entstehung einer Industrie-Unternehmerschicht. Baden-Baden: A. Lutzeyer, 1964. 206p.

18778 KARUNARATNE, N.D. Techno-economic survey of industrial potential in Sri Lanka. Colombo: Industrial Dev. Board, 1973. 398p.

18779 PANDITRATNA, B.L. The trend of industrialization in Colombo city, the capital of Ceylon. In Pakistan Geographical R. 20,2 (1965) 143-55.

18780 Research and industry. Colombo: Industrial Dev. Board, 1970. 304p.

18781 THIAGARAJAH, A. The economic development of Ceylon with special reference to industrialisation. Jaffna: Sri Sanmuganatha Press, 1966. 220p.

2. Public Corporations

18782 AMERASINGHE, A.R.B. Public corporations in Ceylon. Colombo: LHI, 1971. 349p.

18783 CEYLON. MIN. OF FINANCE. Public sector progress, 1973.... Colombo: Min. of Finance, 1974. 52p.

18784 MINKES, A.L. & R.M. WITHANA. Management training in Sri Lanka: a brief study of the public sector. Colombo: Sri Lanka Academy of Admin. Studies, 1977. 91p.

18785 NAYLOR, G.W. Report of reconnaissance mission to Ceylon in connection with state industrial corporations, February 16-March 16, 1966. Colombo: Min. of Planning & Econ. Affairs, 1966. 147p.

18786 Public enterprises in economic development of Sri Lanka. Colombo: Natl. Inst. of Mgmt., 1976. 298p.

K. Transport and Communication

18787 CEYLON GOVT. RAILWAY. Ceylon Government Railway: one hundred years, 1864-1964. Colombo: 1964. 174p.

18788 GUNARATNE, M.H. A concept of countervailing power in maritime affairs, Central Freight Bureau of Sri Lanka. Colombo: The Bureau, 1978. 124p.

18789 HOGG, V.W. & G.P.C. MACKAY & E.S. SCHAEFER. Report of a Bank transportation mission. Colombo: Min. of Planning & Econ. Affairs, 1966. 77p. [study by World Bank]

18790 PERERA, G.F. The Ceylon railway: the story of its inception and progress. Colombo: Ceylon Observer Press, 1925. 286p.

L. Labor in Ceylon's Economy

1. General studies: Labor Force and Employment

18791 LIPTON, M. Ceylon: the role of the inter-agency mission. In SAR 5,3 (1972) 195-105.

18792 Matching employment and expectations: a program of action for Ceylon. Geneva: Intl. Labour Office, 1971. 2v., 251, 251p.

18793 RICHARDS, P.J. Employment and unemployment in Ceylon. Paris: Dev. Centre of the OECD, 1971. 211p.

18794 A survey of employment, unemployment and underemployment in Ceylon. In Intl. Labour R. 87 (1963) 247-254.

18795 WALL, D. The new missionaries. In SAR 5,3 (1972) 181-194.

18796 WILSON, P. Economic implications of population gtowth: Sri Lanka labour force, 1946-81. Canberra: Dept. of Demography, Inst. of Advanced Studies, ANU, 1975. 240p.

2. Labor Policy and Legislation

18797 BANDARANAIKE, S.W.R.D. Speeches on labour. Colombo: Labour Secretariat, 1976. 190p.

18798 CEYLON. CMSN. ON PROFIT SHARING. Report. Colombo: 1967. 345p. (SP 27, 1967)

18799 CEYLON. DEPT. OF LABOUR. Twenty-five years of labour progress in Ceylon. Colombo: Ceylon Printers, 1948. 86p.

18800 ROBERTS, M.W. Labour and the politics of labour in the late nineteenth and early twentieth centuries. In MCS 5,2 (1974) 179-208.

18801 Workers participation in management. Colombo: Sri Lanka Foundation Inst., 1977. 104p. [Its Seminar report, 5]

3. Industrial Relations and Trade Unions

18802 CENTRE FOR SOCIETY & RELIGION. An analysis of the White paper on employment relations. Colombo: 1978. 24p.

18803 CEYLON. CMSN. ON INDUSTRIAL DISPUTES. Report, 1966-69. Colombo: Govt. Pub. Bureau, 1970. 482p. (SP 4, 1970) [Chm. H.W. Jayawardene]

18804 D'COSTA, R. The role of the trade-union in developing countries: a study in India, Pakistan and Ceylon. Nivelles: Inst. of Economic, Social, & Political Res. Press, Catholic U. of Louvain, 1963. 182p.

18805 DE SILVA, C.R. White paper, black law: a critical analysis of the white paper on employment relations, issued by the Ministry of Labour of Sri Lanka. Colombo: Ceylon Federation of Labour, 1978. 41p.

18806 DE SILVA, W.P.N. Industrial conflict: a study of trade union strategy and the law. Colombo: LHI, 1978. 179p.

18807 JAYAWARDENA, V.K. The rise of the labor movement in Ceylon. Durham, NC: DUP, 1972. 382p.

18808 KEARNEY, R.N. Militant public service trade unionism in a new state: the case of Ceylon. In JAS 25 (1966) 397-412.

18809 ______. The partisan involvement of trade unions in Ceylon. In AS 8 (1968) 576-88.

18810 ______. Trade unions and politics in Ceylon. Berkeley: UCalP, 1971. 195p.

18811 PIERIS, R. The role of the government in labour relations in Ceylon. In Intl. Conf. on Industrial Relations, 2nd; Tokyo, 1967. Labour relations in the Asian countries. Tokyo: 1967. 222-236.

18812 ROBERTS, M.W. Fissures and solidarities: weaknesses within the working class movement in the early twentieth century. In MCS 5,1 (1974) 1-31.

18813 SRI LANKA. DEPT. OF LABOUR. LIBRARY. State intervention in labour relations in Sri Lanka: labour dispute awards, 1940-1950. Colombo: 1977. 607p.

18814 SRI LANKA. MIN. OF LABOUR. White paper on employment relations. Colombo: 1978. 48p.

IV. SOCIETY AND SOCIAL CHANGE IN CEYLON

A. Social Categories in Ceylon

1. Social Stratification: Caste and Class

18815 FERNANDO, T. Aspects of social stratification. In T. Fernando & R.N. Kearney, eds. Modern Sri Lanka: a society in transition. Syracuse, NY: Maxwell School of Citizenship & Public Affairs, Syracuse U., 1979, 29-43. (Its Foreign & comp. studies, South Asia ser., 4)

18816 JAYARAMAN, R. Caste continuities in Ceylon: a study of the social structure of three tea plantations. Bombay: Popular Prakashan, 1975. 240p.

18817 PIERIS, R. New elites in Ceylon. In World Congress of Sociology, 5th, Washington, D.C., Sept. 2-8, 1962. Transactions. Louvain: Intl. Sociological Assn., 1964, v.3 295-302.

18818 ROBERTS, M.W. Problems of social stratification and the demarcation of national and local elites in British Ceylon. In JAS 33,4 (1974) 549-578.

2. Ethnic, Religious, and Linguistic Groups [incl. Kinship and Marriage Patterns]
a. general studies

18819 MEYER, W. & É. Meyer. Sri Lanka, Ceylan et ses populations. Brussels: Éd. Complexe, 1979. 240p. (Pays & populations)

18820 PEIRIS, E. Marriage customs and ceremonies of Ceylon. In JRASCB ns 8,1 (1962) 1-28.

18821 ROBERTS, M.W. Ethnic conflict in Sri Lanka and Sinhalese perspectives: barriers to accommodation. In MAS 12,3 (1978) 353-376.

18822 RYAN, B.F. Sociocultural regions of Ceylon. In Rural Sociology 15 (1950) 3-19.

18823 SCHWEINFURTH, U. Landschaftsökologische Forschungen auf der Insel Ceylon. Wiesbaden: Steiner, 1971. 232p.

18824 SELVADURAI, A.J. Kinship and land rights in the context of demographic change. In CAS 9 (1976) 97-112.

18825 STRAUS, M.A. & S. CYTRYNBAUM. Support and power structure in Sinhalese, Tamil, and Burgher student families. In Intl. J. of Comp. Sociology 3,1 (1962) 138-153. [also in J. Mogey, ed. Family and marriage. Leiden: Brill, 1963, 138-153.]

18826 WEERAWARDANA, I.D.S. Minority problems in Ceylon. In PA 25,3 (1952) 278-87.

18827 YALMAN, N.O. Sinhalese-Tamil intermarriage on the east coast of Ceylon. In Sociologus ns 12,1 (1962) 36-53.

18828 ______. Under the Bo tree; studies in caste, kinship, and marriage in the interior of Ceylon. Berkeley: UCalP, 1967. 406p.

b. the Veddas: Ceylon's disappearing aborigines

18829 BROW, J. The impact of population growth on the agricultural practices and settlement patterns of the Anuradhapura Veddahs. In CAS 9 (1976) 80-96.

18830 ______. Vedda villages of Anuradhapura: the historical anthropology of a community in Sri Lanka. Seattle: UWashP, 1978. 268p.

18831 DERANIYAGALA, P.E.P. The hybridization of the Veddas with the Sinhalese. In Spolia Zeylanica 30,1 (1963) 111-47.

18832 GOONETILEKE, H.A.I. Bibliography of the Veddah: the Ceylon aboriginal. In CJHSS 3,1 (1960) 96-106.

18833 SELIGMANN, C.G. & B.Z. SELIGMANN. The Veddas. Oosterhout: Anthropological Pub., 1969. 463p. (Cambridge archaeol. & ethnological series) [1st pub. 1911]

18834 SPITTEL, R.L. Vanished trails: the last of the Veddas. Bombay: OUP, 1950. 258p.

c. the Kandyan and Low-Country Sinhalese: the "paradox" of a Buddhist caste society

18835 CONF. ON TRADITIONAL CULTURES, CEYLON U., 1956. Some aspects of traditional Sinhalese culture. Peradeniya: 1956. 113p.

18836 FERNANDO, P.T.M. Factors affecting marital selection - a study of matrimonial advertisements by middle class Sinhalese. In CJHSS 7 (1964) 171-88.

18837 JIGGINS, J. Caste and family in the politics of the Sinhalese, 1947-1976. Cambrdige: CamUP, 1979. 189p.

18838 LEACH, E.R. Polyandry, inheritance, and the definition of marriage with particular reference to Sinhalese customary law. In his Rethinking anthropology. London: Athlone Press, 1961, 105-113.

18839 ______. The Sinhalese of the dry zone of northern Ceylon. In G.P. Murdock, ed. Social structure in Southeast Asia. Chicago: Quadrangle Books, 1960, 116-126.

18840 RAGHAVAN, M.D. The Karāva of Ceylon; society and culture. Colombo: K.V.G. de Silva, 1961. 216p.

18841 ROBERTS, M.W. Facets of modern Ceylon history through the letters of Jeronis Pieris. Colombo: Hansa, 1975. 108p.

18842 ROBINSON, M.S. Some observations on the Kandyan Sinhalese kinship system. In Man ns 3 (1968) 402-23.

18843 RYAN, B.F. Caste in modern Ceylon; the Sinhalese system in transition. New Brunswick, NJ: Rutgers U. Press, 1953. 371p.

18844 ______. The Sinhalese family system. In EA 6 (1953) 143-63.

18845 TAMBIAH, S.J. Kinship fact and fiction in relation to the Kandyan Sinhalese. In JRAI 95,2 (1965) 131-73.

18846 ______. Polyandry in Ceylon - with special reference to the Laggala region. In C. von Fürer-Haimendorf, ed. Caste and kin in Nepal, India and Ceylon. Bombay: Asia, 1966, 164-358.

18847 ______. The structure of kinship and its relationship to land possession and residence in Pata Dumbara, central Ceylon. In JRAI 8 (1958) 21-44.

18848 YALMAN, N.O. The flexibility of caste principles in a Kandyan community. In E.R. Leach, ed. Aspects of caste in South India, Ceylon, and North-West Pakistan. Cambridge: CamUP, 1960, 78-112.

18849 ______. The structure of Sinhalese kindred: a reexamination of the Dravidian terminology. In AA 64,3 (1962) 548-75.

d. the Hindu Tamils, native and Indian immigrant [see also II. C. 2. b., above]

18850 AZEEZ, A.M.A. Arumuga Navalar. In his The west reappraised. Maharagama: Saman, 1964, 51-64.

18851 BANKS, M. Caste in Jaffna. In E.R. Leach, ed. Aspects of caste in South India, Ceylon, and North-West Pakistan. Cambridge: CamUP, 1960, 61-77.

18852 CHATTOPADHYAYA, H.P. Nattukottai Chettiars in the economy of Sri Lanka. In Calcutta Hist. J. 1,2 (1977) 179-97.

18853 DAVID, K. Hierarchy and equivalence in Jaffna, North Sri Lanka: normative codes as mediator. In K. David, ed. The new wind: changing identities in South Asia. The Hague: Mouton, 1977, 179-226. (WA)

18854 MUTTUCUMARASWAMY, V. Sri La Sri Arumuga Navalar, the champion reformer of the Hindus, 1822-1879. Rev. ed. Colombo: Ranjana Printers, 1965. 124p.

18855 RAGHAVAN, M.D. Tamil culture in Ceylon; a general introduction. Colombo: Kalai Nilayam, 1971. 316p.

18856 Rajaraththinam, A. The history of Thamiraparani. Madras: Chelvanayagam Pub., 1976. 176p.

18857 THANI NAYAGAM, X.S. Tamil culture - its past, its present and its future with special reference to Ceylon. In TC 4 (1955) 341-64.

18858 WEERASOORIA, W.S. The Nattukottai Chettiar merchant bankers in Ceylon. Dehiwala: Tisara Prakasakayo, 1973. 170p.

e. Ceylon's Muslims ("Moors"): Arabs, Indians, and Malays

18859 HASSAN, M.C.A. Sir Razik Fareed: the political and personal life of Sir Razik Fareed, O.B.E., M.P., J.P.U.M., the Ceylon Moor leaders, with a biographical sketch of his father and grandfather. Colombo: Sir Razik Fareed Foundation, 1968. 242p.

18860 MARIKAR, A.I.L. & A.L.M. LAFIR & A.H. MACAN MARKAR, ed. Glimpses from the past of the Moors of Sri Lanka. Colombo: Moors' Islamic Cultural Home, 1976. 224p.

18861 MAUROOF, M. Aspects of religion, economy and society among the Muslims of Ceylon. In CIS 6 (1972) 66-83.

18862 PHADNIS, U. Political profile of the Muslim minority of Sri Lanka. In IS 18,1 (1979) 27-48.

18863 SAMARAWEERA, V. ʿArabi Pasha in Ceylon, 1883-1901. In IsC 50,4 (1976) 219-27.

18864 ______. The Muslim revivalist movement, 1880-1915. In M.W. Roberts, ed. Collective identities, nationalisms, & protest in modern Sri Lanka. Colombo: Marga Inst., 1979, 243-78.

18865 ______. Some sociological aspects of the Muslim revivalism in Sri Lanka. In Social Compass 25,3/4 (1978) 465-75.

18866 THAWFEEQ, M.M. Muslim mosaics. Colombo: Al Eslam and the Moors Islamic Cultural Home, 1972. 152p.

f. the Burghers and Euro-Ceylonese

18867 FERNANDO, T. The Burghers of Ceylon. In N.P. Gist and A.G. Dworkin. The blending of races.... NY: Wiley, 1972, 61-78.

18868 STIRRAT, R.L. Compadrazgo in Catholic Sri Lanka. In Man ns 10,4 (1975) 589-606.

g. women

18869 JAYAWEERA, S. Aspects of the role and position of women. In T. Fernando & R.N. Kearney, eds. Modern Sri Lanka: a society in transition. Syracuse, NY: Maxwell School of Citizenship & Public Affairs, Syracuse U., 1979, 165-80. (Its Foreign and comp. studies, South Asia ser., 4)

18870 NAYAR, U. Women of Sri Lanka. In Social Change 7,3/4 (1977) 31-45.

18871 SIRIWARDENA, B.S. The life of Ceylon women. In B.E. Ward, ed., Women in the new Asia.... Paris: UNESCO, 1963, 150-72.

B. Rural Society and Social Change

1. General Studies

18872 The disintegrating village: a socio-economic survey conducted by the University of Ceylon. Pt. 1. Peradeniya: Ceylon U. Press, 1957. 83p. [preface by N.K. Sarkar & S.J. Tambiah]

18873 MORRISON, B.M. & M.P. MOORE & M.U. ISHAK LEBBE, ed. The disintegrating village: social change in rural Sri Lanka. Colombo: LHI, 1979. 273p.

18874 WANIGARATNE, R.D. Family dominance in a village society: the Mahantegama Village, Beminiwatte Agricultural Productivity Area. Colombo: Agrarian Res. and Training Inst., 1977. 27p.

18875 ______. A study of communication flow in selected villages in Sri Lanka: case study. Colombo: Agrarian Res. & Training Inst. & the Communication Strategy Project, MIB, 1975-1978. 4v.

18876 WOOD, A.L. Political radicalism in changing Sinhalese villages. In HO 23 (1964) 99-107.

2. Village Studies

18877 CHANDRASOMA, M. Five to eight. Colombo: Gunasena, 1979. 141p. [life in a village in southern Sri Lanka]

18878 FELLENBERG, T. VON. Social relations in a Sinhalese village. In CJHSS 8,1/2 (1965) 119-29.

18879 LEACH, E.R. Pul Eliya, a village in Ceylon; a study of land tenure and kinship. Cambridge: CamUP, 1961. 344p.

18880 RYAN, B.F. Sinhalese village. Coral Gables, FL: U. of Miami Press, 1958. 229p.

18881 WOOLF, L.S. The village in the jungle. Delhi: V.R., 1975. 301p. [Rpt. 1913 ed.]

3. Rural and Community Development

18882 ABEYABOONASEKERA, J. & A. GUNAWARDANA. Some aspects of community development. Colombo: Sri Lanka Academy of Admin. Studies, 1973. 78p.

18883 ARIYARATNE, A.T. Sarvodaya shramadana: growth of a people's movement. Colombo: Kularatne, 1970. 39p.

18884 FELLENBERG, T. VON. The process of dynamisation in rural Ceylon, with special reference to a Kandyan village in transition. Bern: A.E. Bruderer, 1966. 242p.

18885 GUNARATNE, S.A. Modernisation and knowledge; a study of four Ceylonese villages. Singapore: Asian Mass Communication Res. & Info. Centre, 1976. 92p.

18886 KRAUSE, G. & J. PERERA. The role of local groups in rural development: a case study of a village in the class II coconut area, Colombo District. Colombo: Agrarian Res. & Training Inst., 1977. 33p.

18887 NATL. SYMPOSIUM ON THE TRADITIONAL RURAL CULTURE OF SRI LANKA, COLOMBO NATL. MUSEUM, 1977. Proceedings. Colombo: 1977. 192p.

18888 PIERIS, R. The influence of community development work on the cultural traditions of the people of Ceylon. In Traditional cultures in South-east Asia. Bombay: Orient Longmans, 1958, 76-111.

4. Agricultural Credit

18889 AMUNUGAMA, S. Rural credit in Ceylon - some sociological observations. In CJHSS 7,2 (1964) 135-43.

18890 MARGA INST. The co-operative system and rural credit in Sri Lanka: a study. Colombo: Marga Inst. for USAID. 1974. 174p.

18891 SANDERATNE, N. Agricultural credit: Ceylon's experience. In SAR 3,3 (1970) 215-26.

18892 TILAKARATNA, W.M. Agricultural credit in a developing economy - Ceylon. Colombo: Central Bank of Ceylon, 1963. 234p.

C. Cities and Urbanization

1. General Studies

18893 GUNATILLEKE, G. Development and the rural-urban balance: the experience in Ceylon. In Asia 28 (1972-73) 10-60.

18894 JONES, G.W. & S. SELVARATNAM. Urbanization in Ceylon, 1946-63. In MCS 1,2 (1970) 199-212.

18895 PANDITHARATNA, B.L. A geographical description and analysis of Ceylonese towns. In CJHSS 4 (1961) 71-95.

18896 ______. Some sources of data and aids for a study of the towns of Ceylon. In UCR 20 (1962) 222-43.

18897 ______. Trends of urbanization in Ceylon 1901-1953. In CJHSS 7,2 (1964) 203-17.

2. Colombo: Ceylon's Cosmopolitan Capital and Cultural Center (1977 est. pop. 800,000)

18898 HULUGALLE, H.A.J. Centenary volume of the Colombo Municipal Council 1865-1965. Colombo: Colombo Municipal Council, 1965. 261p.

18899 PANDITHARATNA, B.L. Colombo City, its population growth and increase from 1824-1954. In Ceylon Geographer 14 (1960) 5-16.

18900 ______. The Colombo townscape: some aspects of its morphology. In UCR 19 (1961) 45-60.

18901 ______. A critical review of plans for the development of Colombo City and some trends in planning. In CJHSS 6 (1973) 111-23.

18902 ______. Functional zones of Colombo. In UCR 19 (1961) 138-66.

18903 ______. The harbour and port of Colombo; a geographical appraisal of its historical and functional aspects. In CJHSS 3 (1960) 128-43.

18904 ______. The urban field of Colombo. In Ceylon Geographer 16 (1962) 26-36.

18905 PEIRIS, K.R.S. & C. DOIDGE. Portrait of a shanty town. Moratuwa: Dept. of Architecture, U. of Sri Lanka, Katubedda Campus, 1976. 32p.

18906 SILVA, P. & K. GUNAWARDENA. The urban fringe of Colombo: some trends and problems concerning its land use. In MCS 2,1 (1971) 39-68.

3. Other Cities and Towns

18907 Centennial volume of the Galle Municipal Council, 1867-1967. Colombo: Colombo Apothecaries, 1968. 110p.

18908 DE SILVA, G.P.S.H. Nuwara Eliya, the beginnings and its growth. Colombo: Dept. of Info., 1978. 122p. [hill station]

D. Social Problems and Social Welfare in Sri Lanka

18909 JAYASURIYA, W.F. The rescue of the prisoner; a study in conditions obtaining in the Ceylon prisons. Colombo: Ceylon Prison Reform Soc., 1969. 57p.

18910 JAYEWARDENE, C.H.S. & H. RANASINGHE. Criminal homicide in the southern province. Colombo: Colombo Apothecaries, 1963. 181p.

18911 KARUNATILAKE, H.N.S. The impact of welfare services in Sri Lanka on the economy. In Staff Studies, Central Bank of Ceylon 5,1 (1975) 1-32.

18912 MARGA INST. Housing in Sri Lanka. Colombo: 1976. 255p. (Marga res. studies, 6)

18913 Needs of children and adolescents: a case study of Sri Lanka. Colombo: Marga Inst., 1975. 166p.

18914 OBEYESEKERE, G. Sorcery, premeditated murder and the canalization of aggression in Sri Lanka. In Ethnology 14,1 (1975) 1-24.

18915 RATNAPALA, N. The beggar in Sri Lanka. Colombo: World Vision Intl., 1979. 63p.

18916 STRAUS, J.H. & M.A. STRAUS. Suicide, homicide, and social structure in Ceylon. In AJS 63,5 (1953) 461-69.

18917 Welfare and growth: a case study of Sri Lanka prepared for the UNRISD project; the unified approach to development planning and analysis. Colombo: Marga Inst., 1974. 130p.

18918 WOOD, A.L. Crime and aggression in changing Ceylon: a sociological analysis of homicide, suicide and economic crime. Philadelphia: American Philosophical Soc., 1961. 132p. (TAPS 51:8)

18919 Youth, land, and employment. Colombo: Marga Inst., 1974. 185p.

E. Health Services and Medical Systems

18920 ALL CEYLON BUDDHIST CONGRESS. NATL. DEV. ENQUIRY CMTEE. HEALTH ENQUIRY CMTEE. A national health plan for Ceylon; report.... Colombo: 1964. 128p.

18921 AMUNUGAMA, S. Social science research on family planning in Sri Lanka. Colombo: Family Planning Communication Strategy Project, MIB, 1978. 28p.

18922 DE SILVA, C.C., ed. A history of family planning in Sri Lanka: silver jubilee souvenir of the Family Planning Association of Sri Lanka. Colombo: Family Planning Assoc. of Sri Lanka, 1978. 215p.

18923 JAYASUNDERA, M.G. Mental health surveys in Ceylon. In Conference on Mental Health Research in Asia and the Pacific, East-West Center, 1966. Mental health research in Asia and the Pacific. Honolulu: UPH, 1969, 54-65.

18924 JAYASURIYA, D.C. Narcotics and drugs in Sri Lanka: socio-legal dimensions. Mount Lavinia: Associated Educ. Pub., 1978. 219p.

18925 MADAN, T.N., et al. Doctors and society: three Asian case studies: India, Malaysia, Sri Lanka. ND: Vikas, 1980. 311p.

18926 OBEYESEKERE, G. Āyurveda and mental illness. In CSSH 12 (1970) 292-96.

18927 ______. The impact of Āyurvedic ideas on the culture and the individual in Sri Lanka. In Charles Leslie, ed. Asian medical systems: a comparative study. Berkeley: UCalP, 1976, 201-26.

18928 RYAN, B.F. Hinayana Buddhism and family planning in Ceylon. In The interrelations of demographic, economic, and social problems in selected underdeveloped areas. NY: Milbank Memorial Fund, 1954, 90-102.

18929 SIMEONOV, L.A. Better health for Sri Lanka: report on a health manpower study. ND: WHO, Regional Office for SE Asia, 1975. 315p.

F. Education in Ceylon (78% literacy in 1971)

1. Bibliography

18930 Bibliography on education in Ceylon. In Education in Ceylon (from the sixth century BC to the present day). Colombo: Min. of Educ. & Cultural Affairs, 1969, v. 3, 1273-1318.

2. History of Education since 1796

18931 A.E. Tamber, 26-10-1904 - 18-2-1971: a memorial volume. Ed. by Tamber Commemoration Cmtee. Jaffna: Eelanadu, 1972. 96p. + 8 pl.

18932 AMES, M.M. The impact of Western education on religion and society in Ceylon. In PA 40 (1967) 19-42.

18933 COREA, J.C.A. One hundred years of education in Ceylon. In MAS 3,2 (1969) 151-76.

18934 JAYASURIYA, J.E. Education in Ceylon before and after independence: 1939-1968. Colombo: Associated Educ. Pub., 1969. 218p.

18935 JAYAWEERA, S. British educational policy in Ceylon in the nineteenth century. In Pedagogica Historica 9 (1969) 68-90.

18936 ______. Religious organizations and the state in Ceylonese education. In Comp. Educ. R. 12 (1968) 159-70.

18937 LEVY, ARIEH. Youth in Ceylon. Pt. 1, Analysis of youth needs in Ceylon; Pt. 2, The National Youth Organisation. Colombo: Govt. Pub. Bureau, 1967. 233p. (SP 3, 1967)

18938 MAHROOF, M.M.M. Muslim education in Ceylon (Sri Lanka) 1881-1901. In IsC 47,4 (1973) 301-25.

18939 RUBERU, T.R. Education in colonial Ceylon, being a research study on the history of education in Ceylon for the period 1796 to 1834. Kandy: Kandy Printers, 1962. 260p.

18940 RYAN, B.F. Status, achievement and education in Ceylon: an historical perspective. In JAS 20 (1961) 463-76.

18941 SUMATHIPALA, K.H.M. History of education in Ceylon 1796-1965, with special reference to the contribution made by C.W.W. Kannangara... Dehiwala: Tisara Prakasakayo, 1969. 416p. (Pub. as CHJ, 13)

18942 WICKREMERATNE, L.A. 1865 and the change in education policies. In MCS 1,1 (1970) 84-93.

3. Educational Policy and Development

18943 ARIYADASA, K.D. Management of educational reforms in Sri Lanka. Paris: UNESCO, 1976. 41p.

18944 CEYLON. NATL. EDUC. CMSN., 1961. Final report. Colombo: Govt. Press, 1962. 241p. (SP 17, 1962) [Chm., J.E. Jayasuriya; Interim report, 1962, 95p. (SP 1, 1962)]

18945 CEYLON. SPECIAL CMTEE. ON EDUCATION. Colombo: Ceylon Govt. Press, 1943. 160p. (SP 24, 1943) [Chm., C.W.W. Kannangara]

18946 HALLAK, J. Financing and educational policy in Sri Lanka (Ceylon). Paris: UNESCO, Intl. Inst. for Educ. Planning, 1972. 159p.

18947 JAYASURIYA, J.E. Some issues in Ceylon education, 1964. Peradeniya: Associated Educ. Pub., 1964. 87p.

18948 JAYAWEERA, S. Recent trends in educational expansion in Ceylon. In Intl. R. of Educ. 15 (1969) 277-94.

18949 MARGA INST. Non formal education in Sri Lanka: a study undertaken by the Marga Institute for ICED/UNICEF. Colombo: 1974. 242p. (Marga Res. studies, 1)

18950 MUELDER, W.R. Schools for a new nation, the development and administration of the educational system of Ceylon. Colombo: K.V.G. de Silva, 1962. 216p.

18951 SIRISENA, U.D.I. Education legislation and educational development: compulsory education in Ceylon. In History of Educ. Q. 7 (1967) 329-48.

18952 WALATARA, D. The teaching of English as a complementary language in Ceylon. Colombo: LHI, 1965. 240p.

4. Higher Education

18953 CEYLON. CMSN. ON HIGHER EDUC. IN THE NATL. LANGUAGES. Final report... Colombo: 1956. 218p. (SP 10, 1956) [Chm., E.A.L. Wijeyewardena]

18954 CEYLON. CMTEE. OF INQUIRY ON THE UNIV. OF COLOMBO. Report. Colombo: Govt. Pub. Bureau, 1968. 55p. (SP 8, 1968)

18955 CEYLON. CMTEE. OF INVESTIGATION INTO THE WORKING OF TEACHER TRAINING COLLEGES. Report. Colombo: Govt. Pub. Bureau, 1966. 129p. (SP 11, 1966)

18956 CEYLON. CMSN. APPOINTED TO INQUIRE INTO THE INCIDENTS AT THE PEREDENIYA CAMPUS OF THE UNIV. OF SRI LANKA ON 11TH & 12TH NOV. 1976. Report. Colombo: Govt. Pub. Bureau, 1977. 103p. (SP 1, 1977) [Chm., D. Wimalaratne]

18957 CEYLON. UNIVERSITIES CMSN., 1962. Report. Colombo: Govt. Pub. Bureau, 1962. 232p. (SP 16, 1963) [Chm., D.C.R. Gunawardena]

18958 CEYLON. UNIVERSITY CMSN., 1929. Report. Colombo: Govt. Printer, 1929. 134p. (SP 4, 1929)

18959 CEYLON. UNIVERSITY CMSN., 1959. Report. Colombo: Govt. Pub. Bureau, 1959. 306p. (SP 23, 1959) [Chm., J. Needham]

18960 CHELLIAH, J.V. A century of English education. The story of Batticotta Seminary and Jaffna College. Tellippalai: American Ceylon Mission Press, 1922. 117p.

18961 DE SILVA, C.R. Weightage in University admissions: standardisation and district quotas in Sri Lanka 1970-75. In MCS 5,2 (1974) 151-78.

18962 JAYASURIYA, D.L. Developments in university education: the growth of the University of Ceylon (1942-1965). In UCR 23 (1965) 83-153.

18963 PEIRIS, H.S.A.T. The Wesley College centenary souvenir, 1874-1974. Colombo: The College, 1975. 150p.

18964 PIERIS, R. Universities, politics and public opinion in Ceylon. In Minerva 2 (1964) 435-54. [Rpt. in A.B. Shah, ed. Education, scientific policy and developing societies. Bombay: Manaktalas, 1967, 177-201.]

18965 Report of the Ceylon Universities Commission. In Minerva 2 (1964) 492-518.

18966 THISTLETHWAITE, F. Report on the establishment of the University of Colombo. Colombo: Govt. Pub. Bureau, 1967. 59p. (SP 26, 1967)

18967 USWATTE-ARATCHI, G. University admissions in Ceylon: their economic and social background and employment expectations. In MAS 8,3 (1974) 289-318.

5. Elementary and Secondary Education

18968 CEYLON. CMSN. OF INQUIRY ON TECHNICAL EDUCATION IN CEYLON. Report. Colombo: Govt. Pub. Bureau, 1963. 349p. (SP 10, 1963) [Chm., T.P. de S. Munasinghe]

18969 CEYLON. CMSN. ON ELEMENTARY EDUC. IN CEYLON. Colombo: Govt. Pub. Bureau, 1905. 40p. (SP 28, 1905) [Chm., H. Wace]

18970 CEYLON. CMTEE. OF INQUIRY INTO THE TEACHING OF ENGLISH IN CEYLON SCHOOLS. Report. Colombo: Govt. Pub. Bureau, 1960. 58p. (SP 5, 1960) [Chm., S.F. de Silva]

18971 MUNASINGHE, V.G.B. Elementary education. In Education in Ceylon... Colombo: Min. of Educ. & Cultural Affairs, 1969, v. 3, 795-809.

18972 WARNASURIYA, W.M.A. Secondary education. In Education in Ceylon... Colombo: Min. of Educ. & Cultural Affairs, 1969, v. 3, 811-24.

V. RELIGIO-PHILOSOPHICAL TRADITIONS IN BUDDHIST CEYLON, 1796 -

A. The Resurgence and Dominance of Theravada Buddhism

1. Bibliography

18973 REYNOLDS, F.E. Tradition and change in Theravada Buddhism: a bibliographic essay focused on the modern period. In CAS 4 (1973) 94-104.

2. General Studies of Buddhism in Modern Ceylon since 1796

18974 BECHERT, H. Contradictions in Sinhalese Buddhism. In CAS 4 (1973) 7-17.

18975 FERNANDO, A. Buddhismus im heutigen Ceylon. In H. Dumoulin, ed. Buddhismus der Gegenwart. Freiburg: Herder, 1970, 58-65.

18976 HALVERSON, J. Religion and psychosocial development in Sinhalese Buddhism. In JAS 37,2 (1978) 221-32.

18977 MALALGODA, K. Buddhism in Sinhalese society, 1750-1900: a study of religious revival and change. Berkeley: UCalP, 1976. 300p.

18978 OBEYESEKERE, G. The fire-walkers of Kataragama: the rise of bhakti religiosity in Buddhist Sri Lanka. In JAS 37,3 (1978) 457-76.

18979 ______. Sinhalese-Buddhist identity in Ceylon. In G. De Vos & L. Romanucci-Ross, eds. Ethnic identity. Palo Alto: Mayfield, 1975, 231-58.

18980 PERNIOLA, V. Buddhism in modern Ceylon. In Studia Missionalia 12 (1962) 68-80.

18981 REYNOLDS, C.H.B. Religion and social position in British Ceylon. In H. Bechert, ed. Buddhism in Ceylon and studies on religious syncretism in Buddhist countries. Göttingen: Vandenhoeck & Ruprecht, 1978, 134-45.

18982 SIRIWARDENE, C.D.S. Buddhist reorganization in Ceylon. In D.E. Smith, ed. South Asian politics and religion. Princeton: PUP, 1966, 531-46.

3. The Buddhist Revival in the Mid-19th Century; Olcott and the Theosophical Society; Anagārika Dharmapāla (1864-1933)

18983 DHARMADASA, K.N.O. A nativistic reaction to colonialism: the Sinhala-Buddhist revival in Sri Lanka. In AsSt 12 (1974) 159-79.

18984 DHARMAPALA, Anagarika. Return to righteousness, a collection of speeches, essays and letters... Ed. by Ananda Guruge. Colombo: Anagarika Dharmapala Birth Centenary Cmtee., Min. of Educ. & Cultural Affairs, Ceylon, 1965. 89 + 875p.

18985 GOKHALE, B.G. Anagarika Dharmapala: toward modernity through tradition in Ceylon. In CAS 4 (1973) 30-39.

18986 NILES, D.T. Resurgent Buddhism in Ceylon and the Christian Church. In Intl. R. of Missions 32 (1943) 258-63.

18987 SANGHARAKSITA, Bhikshu. Anagarika Dharmapala; a biographical sketch. 3rd ed. Kandy: Buddhist Pub. Soc., 1964. 98p.

18988 WICKREMERATNE, L.A. Annie Besant, Theosophism, and Buddhist nationalism in Sri Lanka. In CJHSS 6,1 (1976) 62-79.

4. Traditional Buddhist Monasticism in Modern Ceylon

18989 BAREAU, A. La vie et l'organisation des communautés bouddhiques modernes de Ceylan. Pondicherry: IFI, 1957. 90p. [Its pub., 10]

18990 CRAWFORD, H.L. Papers on the Buddhist Temporalities Ordinance of 1905. Colombo: 1910. (SP 23, 1910)

18991 EVERS, H.-D. Kinship and property rights in a Buddhist monastery in central Ceylon. In AA 69,6 (1967) 703-10.

18992 ______. "Monastic landlordism" in Ceylon: a traditional system in a modern setting. In JAS 28,4 (1969) 685-92.

18993 ______. Monks, priests and peasants; study of Buddhism and social structure in Ceylon. Leiden: Brill, 1972. 136p.

18994 TAMBIAH, H.W. Buddhist ecclesiastical law. In JRASCB 8,1 (1962) 71-107.

18995 YALMAN, N.O. The ascetic Buddhist monks of Ceylon. In Ethnology 1 (1962) 315-28.

5. Resurgence of Monastic and Lay Buddhism after 1956

18996 AMES, M. Ideological and social change in Ceylon. In HO 22,1 (1963) 45-53.

18997 BUDDHIST COUNCIL OF CEYLON. An event of dual significance. Colombo: Lanka Bauddha mandalya, 1956. 60p.

18998 LEACH, E. Buddhism in the post-colonial political order in Burma and Ceylon. In Daedalus 102,1 (1973) 29-54.

18999 MALALGODA, K. Millenialism in relation to Buddhism. In CSSH 7,4 (1970) 421-41.

19000 OBEYESEKERE, G. Religious symbolism and political change in Ceylon. In B.L. Smith, ed. The two wheels of Dhamma.... Chambersburg, PA: AAR, 1972, 58-78. (AAR studies in religion, 3)

19001 RAHULA, W. The heritage of the bhikkhu: a short history of the bhikkhu in educational, cultural, social, and political life. Tr. by K.P.G. Wijayasurendra, & rev. by the author. NY: Grove Press, 1974. 176p.

19002 SMITH, B.L. Sinhalese Buddhism and the dilemmas of reinterpretation. In his (ed.) The two wheels of Dhamma.... Chambersburg, PA: AAR, 1972, 79-106. (AAR monograph, 3) [Also in CAS 3 (1973) 1-25]

19003 SWEARER, D.K. Lay Buddhism and the Buddhist revival in Ceylon. In JAAR 38 (1970) 255-75.

6. Buddhism and Folk Religion: Interactions and Syncretism

a. Buddha and the Sinhalese pantheon

19004 AMES, M.M. Ritual presentations and the structure of the Sinhalese pantheon. In M. Nash, ed. Anthropological studies in Theravada Buddhism. New Haven: YUP, 1966, 27-50.

19005 BECHERT, H. On the popular religion of the Sinhalese. In his (ed.) Buddhism in Ceylon and studies on religious syncretism in Buddhist countries. Göttingen: Vandenhoeck & Ruprecht, 1978, 217-33.

19006 EVERS, H.-D. Buddha and the seven gods: the dual organization of a temple in central Ceylon. In JAS 27,3 (1968) 541-50.

19007 HIATT, L.R. The Pattini cult of Ceylon: a Tamil perspective. In Social Compass 20,2 (1973) 231-50.

19008 LEACH, E.R. Pulleyar and the Lord Buddha: an aspect of religious syncretism in Ceylon. In Psychoanalysis & the Psychoanalytic R. 49,2 (1962) 81-102.

19009 MEERWARTH-LEVINA, L. The Hindu goddess Pattini in the Buddhist popular beliefs of Ceylon. In Ceylon Antiquary and Literary Register 1 (1915-16) 29-37.

19010 OBEYESEKERE, G. The Buddhist pantheon in Ceylon and its extensions. In M. Nash, ed. Anthropological studies in Theravada Buddhism. New Haven: YUP, 1966, 1-26.

19011 ______. The goddess Pattini and the Lord Buddha. In Social Compass 20,2 (1973) 217-30.

19012 ______. The great tradition and the little tradition in the perspective of Sinhalese Buddhism. In JHS 22,2 (1963) 139-53.

b. Sinhalese rituals of exorcism and healing

19013 AMES, M.M. Buddha and the dancing goblins: a theory of magic and religion. In AA 66 (1964) 75-82.

19014 ______. Magical-animism and Buddhism: a structural analysis of the Sinhalese religious system. In JAS 23 (1964) 21-52. [Rpt. in E.B. Harper, ed. Aspects of religion in South Asia. Seattle: UWashP, 1964, 21-52]

19015 GOMBRICH, R.F. Food for seven grandmothers. In Man 6,1 (1971) 5-17.

19016 ______. Precept and practice: traditional Buddhism in the rural highlands of Ceylon. Oxford: OUP, 1971. 366p.

19017 GRÜNWEDEL, A. Singhalesische Masken. In Intl. Archives for Ethnography 7 (1893) 71-130.

19018 LUCAS, H. Ceylon-Masken; der Tanz der Krankheits-Dämonen. Eisenach: E. Roth, 1958. 234p.

19019 OBEYESEKERE, G. Psycho-cultural exegesis of a case of spirit possession from Sri Lanka. In CAS 8 (1975) 41-89.

19020 ______. The ritual drama of the Sanni demons: collective representations of disease in Ceylon. In CSSH 11 (1969) 174-216.

19021 ______. The structure of Sinhalese ritual. In CJHSS 1 (1958) 192-202.

19022 PERTOLD, O. The ceremonial dances of the Sinhalese; an inquiry into Sinhalese folk religion. In CHJ 20 (1973) 142p. [1st pub. in AO 2 (1930)]

19023 ______. A protective ritual of the Southern Buddhists. In JAnthSB 12,6 (1923) 744-89.

19024 SAMARASINGHE, S.G. Methodology for the collection of the Sinhala ritual. In AFS 36,2 (1977) 105-30.

19025 SELVADURAI, A.J. Land, personhood, and sorcery in a Sinhalese village. In JAAS(L) 11,1/2 (1976) 82-96.

19026 WIRZ, P. Exorcism and the art of healing in Ceylon. Leiden: Brill, 1954. 255p. + 51 pl. [1st pub. in German, 1941]

19027 YALMAN, N.O. The structure of Sinhalese healing rituals. In JAS 23 (1964) 115-50. [Rpt. in E.B. Harper, ed. Aspects of religion in South Asia. Seattle: UWashP, 1964, 115-50.

B. Hinduism in Modern Ceylon; the Saiva Murugan Cult among the Tamils

19028 ARUNACHALAM, P. Light from the East, being letters on Gnanam, the divine knowledge. Ed. by E. Carpenter. London: Allen & Unwin, 1927. 157p.

19029 CARTMAN, J. Hindusim in Ceylon. Colombo: M.D. Gunasena, 1957. 191p.

19030 NAVARATNAM, C.S. A short history of Hinduism in Ceylon, and three essays on the Tamils. Jaffna: 1964. 211p.

19031 NAVARATNAM, T.C. Saint Yogaswami and the testament of truth.... Jaffna: Thiru Kasipillai Navaratnam, 1972. 449p.

19032 YOGASWAMI. Words of our Master. Jaffna: Jaffna Cooperative Tamil Books Pub. & Sale Soc., 1972. 134p.

C. Christianity in Modern Ceylon: Missionary Dominance and "Ceylonization"

1. General Studies

19033 ABEYRATNA, O.M. Sidelights on Christianity in Sri Lanka. Rajagiriya: Abeyratna, 1977. 56p.

19034 CASPERSZ, P. The role of Sri Lanka Christians in a Buddhist majority system. In CJHSS ns 4 (1974) 104-110.

19035 DE SILVA, K.M. Social policy and missionary organizations in Ceylon, 1840-1855. London: Longmans, 1965. 318p. (Royal Commonwealth Soc., Imperial studies, 26)

19036 MALALGODA, K. The Buddhist-Christian confrontation in Ceylon, 1800-1880. In Social Compass 20,2 (1973) 171-200.

19037 SIVATHAMBY, K. Hindu reaciton to Christian proselytization and westernization in 19th century Sri Lanka. In Social Science R. (Colombo) 1 (1979) 41-75.

19038 TENNENT, J.E. Christianity in Ceylon ... under the Portuguese, the Dutch, the British and American missions.... London: J. Murray, 1950. 348p.

19039 Twenty-five years of the Christa Seva Ashram, Jaffna, Ceylon 1939-1964. Manipay: American Ceylon Mission Press, 1964. 67p.

19040 WILSON, D. The Christian Church in Sri Lanka: her problems & her influence. Colombo: Study Centre for Religion & Soc., 1975. 144p.

2. The Roman Catholic Church

19041 ANANDAPPA, J.B.C. The Catholic directory of Sri Lanka, 1975-1976. Colombo: Anandappa, 1976. 520p.

19042 ARASARATNAM, S. Oratorians and Predikants: the Catholic Church in Ceylon under Dutch rule. In CJHSS 1, 2 (1958) 216-22.

19043 HOUTART, F. & G. LEMERCINIER. Modèles culturels socio-religieux des groupes élitiques catholiques à Sri Lanka. In Social Compass 20,2 (1973) 303-20.

19044 The Houtart survey of Catholics in Ceylon: socio-religious research 1969/70. Quest (Colombo) 43 (1971) 1-52.

19045 TAMBIMUTTU, F. A profile of Ceylon's Catholic heritage. Maryknoll, NY: Maryknoll, 1961. 103p.

3. The Anglicans and Other Protestants

19046 BALDING, J.W. One hundred years in Ceylon, or the centenary volume of the Church Missionary Society in Ceylon, 1818-1918. Madras: Diocesan Press, 1922. 237p.

19047 BEVEN, F.L., ed. History of the diocese of Colombo, a centenary volume. Colombo: Times of Ceylon, 1946. 426p.

19048 FURTADO, C.L. The contribution of Dr. D.T. Niles to the church universal and local. Madras: CLS, 1978. 246p.

19049 KULANDRAN, S. A life sketch of Canon S.S. Somasundaram. Manipay: A.C.M. Press, 1970. 155p.

19050 NEGOTIATING CMTEE. FOR CHURCH UNION IN CEYLON. Proposed scheme of church union in Ceylon. Madras: CLS, 1966. 112p. [1st pub. 1964]

19051 ROOT, H.I. A century in Ceylon (1816-1916); a brief history of the American Board in Ceylon. Jaffna: American Ceylon Mission Press, 1916. 87p.

19052 SMALL, W.J.T., ed. A history of the Methodist Church in Ceylon 1814-1964. Colombo: Wesley Press, 1971. 666p.

19053 VELUPILLAI, C.D. A history of American Ceylon Mission. Tellippalai: American Ceylon Mission Press, 1922. 231p.

19054 WICKREMESINGHE, P. Rev. Canon Ekanayake of Colombo: priest, missionary and theologian. Colombo: Church of Ceylon Defense League, 1949. 260p.

D. Islam in Ceylon since 1796 [see also IV. A. 2. e., above]

19055 MAHROOF, M.M.M. The faqirs of Ceylon. In IsC 41 (1967) 99-109.

VI. MEDIA AND THE ARTS

A. The Mass Media: Press, Broadcasting, Cinema

19056 AMUNUGAMA, S. The cinema. In Education in Ceylon.... Colombo: Min. of Educ. & Cultural Affairs, 1969, 1229-36.

19057 BANDARA, H.H. Cultural policy in Sri Lanka. Paris: UNESCO, 1972. 70p.

19058 CEYLON. CMSN. OF INQUIRY INTO THE FILM INDUSTRY IN CEYLON, 1962. Report. Colombo: Govt. Pub. Bureau, 1965. 133p. (SP 2, 1965) [Chm. Jotiyasena Wickramasinghe]

19059 CEYLON. CMSN. OF INQUIRY ON THE CEYLON BROADCASTING COPORATION. Inquiry on the Ceylon Broadcasting Corporation. Colombo: 1972. 217p. (SP 10, 1972)

19060 CEYLON. CMSN. ON BROADCASTING & INFO. Report. Colombo: 1966. (SP 12, 1966)

19061 CEYLON. PRESS CMSN. Final report. Colombo: Govt. Pub. Bureau, 1964. 137p. SP 11, 1964) [chm., K.D. de Silva; Interim report, 1964, 169p. (SP 9, 1964)]

19062 DE SILVA, M.A. & R. SIRIWARDENE. Communication policies in Sri Lanka. Paris: UNESCO, 1977. 59p.

19063 DUBEY, S.R. Government control over the press in Sri Lanka. In SAS 9, 1/2 (1974) 58-77.

10964 FERNANDO, W.L. The press in Ceylon. Colombo: Trade Exchange, 1973. 63p.

19065 GUNARATNE, S.A. Government - press conflict in Ceylon: freedom versus responsibility. In Journalism Q. 47 (1970) 530-43.

19066 ______. The taming of the press in Sri Lanka. Lexington, KY: Assoc. for Educ. in Journalism, 1975. 42p.

19067 HULUGALLE, H.A.J. Ceylon. In J.A. Lent, ed. The Asian newspapers' reluctant revolution. Ames: Iowa State U. Press, 1971, 259-267.

19068 ______. Life and times of D.R. Wijewardene (founder of the Ceylon Daily News). Colombo: Associated Newspapers of Ceylon, 1960. 261p.

19069 JAYAWEERA, N.D. Mass media. In Education in Ceylon (from the sixth century BC to the present day). Colombo: Min. of Educ. & Cultural Affairs, 1969, 1217-1228.

19070 MARGA INST. The Sinhala reading public: a study. Colombo: 1974. 70 + 44p. (Marga res. studies, 4)

19071 WISWA WARNAPALA, W.A. Press and politics in Sri Lanka (Ceylon). In JCPS 9,2 (1975) 125-55.

B. Literatures of Modern Ceylon

1. Sinhala, Tamil, and English

19072 BANDARANAIKE, N.Y.D. The literature of Ceylon. In A.L. McLeod, ed. The Commonwealth pen.... Ithaca, NY: CornellUP, 1961, 100-14.

19073 COATES, W.A. The languages of Ceylon in 1946 and 1953. In UCR 19,1 (1961) 81-91.

19074 DERANIYAGALA, P.E.P. Sinhala verse (kavi), collected by the late Hugh Nevill, 1869-1886. Colombo: Ceylon Natl. Museums Dept., 1954-55. 3v., 1031p.

19075 DHARMADASA, K.N.O. Language and Sinhalese nationalism: the career of Munidasa Cumaratunga. In MCS 3,2 (1972) 125-43.

19076 GOONERATNE, Y. English literature in Ceylon, 1815-1878. Dehiwala: Tisara Prakasakayo, 1968. 234p. [pub. as CHJ 14]

19077 GOONETILEKE, H.A.I. Bibliography of Ceylonese literature in English 1964 and 1965. In JCL 2 (1966) 55-58, 90-100.

19078 OBEYESEKERE, R. Sinhala writing and the new critics. Colombo: M.D. Gunasena, 1974. 119p.

19079 PROCTOR, R. Forever life; short stories from Ceylon. Lahore: Afro-Asian Book Club, 1967. 191p.

19080 SIVAKUMARAN, K.S. Contemporary Tamil writing in Sri Lanka. Colombo: Vijeyaluckshmi, 1974. 64p.

19081 WICKRAMASINGHE, M. Sinhala language and culture. Dehiwala: Tisara Prakasakayo, 1975. 155p.

2. Folk Literature

19082 GOONETILEKE, H.A.I. A bibliography of Sinhalese folklore: stories, songs, proverbs and riddles. In CJHSS 3 (1960) 208-15.

19083 KEYT, G. Folk stories of Sri Lanka. Colombo: LHI, 1974. 75p.

19084 PARKER, H. Village folk-tales of Ceylon. Dehiwala: Tisara Prakasakayo, 1971-73. 3v. [1st pub. 1910]

19085 RATNATUNGA, M. Folk tales of Sri Lanka. ND: Sterling, 1979. 119p.

19086 ROBINSON, M.S. "The house of the mighty hero" or "The house of enough paddy?" Some implications of a Sinhalese myth. In E.R. Leach, ed. Dialectic in practical religion. Cambridge: CamUP, 1968, 122-52. (Cambridge Papers in Social Anthropology, 5)

19087 VIJAYATUNGA, J. The glass princess and other Singhala folk tales. Colombo: Gunasena, 1949. 57p.

19088 WALATARA, D. The princess of the well: tales from Sri Lanka. Colombo: LHI, 1975. 42p.

C. Art and Architecture of Modern Sri Lanka

19089 Contemporary artists of Ceylon. In Mārg 5,3 (1952) 69-77.

19090 COOMARASWAMY, A.K. Notes on painting, dyeing, lacwork, dumbara mats, and paper in Ceylon. In JRASCB 19, 58 (1907) 103-121.

19091 George Keyt: a felicitation volume. Colombo: George Keyt Felicitation Cmtee., 1977. 125p.

19092 GOONETILEKE, H.A.I. George Keyt: the Indian ethos in a Ceylonese studio. In Arts of Asia 3,1 (1973) 16-23.

19093 ______, ed. George Cluessen drawings. Colombo: Jataka, 1946. 24p. + 20pl.

19094 JAYEWARDENE, E.D.W. Sinhala masks. Kandy: T.B.S. Godamunne, 1970. 93p.

19095 KELLER, D. & P. KELLER. Report on the handcrafts of Ceylon. Colombo: Ceylon Tourist Board, 1968. 121p.

19096 MOHAN, JAG. The modern movement in Sinhalese art. In Mārg 5,3 (1952) 59-61.

19097 RUSSELL, M. George Keyt: Introduction and biographical note. Bombay: Mārg Pub., 1950. 56p.

19098 VANGEYZEL, L.C. The painting of George Keyt. In Mārg 1,3 (1947) 43-65.

D. Science in Modern Sri Lanka

19099 CISIR contribution to science and industry: proceedings of the 21st anniversary seminar, May 4-6, 1976. Colombo: Ceylon Inst. of Scientific & Industrial Res., 1977. 221p.

19100 CEYLON. CMTEE. APPOINTED TO INVESTIGATE AND REPORT ON THE ESTABLISHMENT IN CEYLON OF AN INST. OF THEORETICAL STUDIES. Report. Colombo: Govt. Pub. Bureau, 1979. 146p. (SP 2, 1979) [Chm. A.W. Mailvaganam]

19101 NATIONAL SCIENCE COUNCIL OF SRI LANKA. Scientific and technical institutions in Sri Lanka, 1976. Colombo: 1977. 87p.

VII. THE MALDIVE ISLANDS: ISLAMIC REPUBLIC IN THE INDIAN OCEAN; FORMER BRITISH PROTECTORATE ADMINISTERED FROM CEYLON TO 1965

19102 ADENEY, M. & W.K. CARR. The Maldive Republic. In J.M. Ostheim, ed. The politics of the Western Indian Ocean Islands. NY: Praeger, 1975, 139-60.

19103 ANAND, J.P. The Maldives: a profile. In JIDSA 9,2 (1976) 116-29.

19104 BELL, H.C.P. Maldive Islands: an account of the physical features, climate, history, inhabitants, productions, and trade. Colombo: F. Luker, Acting Govt. Printer, 1882. 133p.

19105 ______. The Maldive Islands; monograph on the history, archaeology and epigraphy. Colombo: Ceylon Govt. Press, 1940. 204p.

19106 Constitution of the Republic of the Maldives. In A.P. Blaustein & G.H. Flanz, ed. Constitutions of the countries of the world. Dobbs Ferry, NY: Oceana Pub., 1976. 32p. [unofficial tr. by Adnan Hussain; ed. by H. Hecker]

19107 CROWE, P.K. Diversions of a diplomat in Ceylon. London: Macmillan, 1957. [280-304 on Maldives]

19108 FORBES, A. & FANZIA ALI. Republic of 100 islands. In Geographical Magazine 50,4 (1978) 264-68.

19109 HECKER, H. Die Republik im Indischen Ozean: Verfassungsentwicklung und Rechtstellung der Maldiven. In Mitteilungen des Inst. für Asienkunde (Hamburg), 1970, 46p.

19110 HOCKLEY, T.W. The two thousand isles; a short account of the poeple, history and customs of the Maldive archipelago. London: Witherby, 1935. 101p.

19111 MALONEY, C. The Maldives: new stresses in an old nation. In AS 16,7 (1976) 654-71.

19112 ______. People of the Maldive Islands. Madras: Orient Longman, 1978. 432p.

19113 PHILLIPS, W.W.A. The Maldivian tangle. In J. of the Royal Commonwealth Soc., ns 3,1 (1960) 15-18.

19114 REYNOLDS, C.H.B. Linguistic strands in the Maldives. In CAS 11 (1978) 155-66.

19115 STODDARD, T.L. The Republic of the Maldives. In his (ed.). Area handbook for the Indian Ocean Territories. Washington: American U., 1971, 21-48.

11

The Dravidian South of India: Cultural Distinctness versus National Integration, 1800–

I. OVERALL STUDIES OF SOUTH INDIA

A. Political Studies

19116 APPA RAO, T. Municipal corporations in South India. Waltair: Andhra U. Press, 1974. 234p.

19117 ELKINS, D.J. Electoral participation in a South Indian context. Durham, NC: Carolina Academic Press, 1975. 251p.

19118 HARDGRAVE, R.L. Essays in the political sociology of South India. ND: Usha, 1979. 262p.

19119 RAJPUROHIT, J., ed. Official language problems analysed: papers read in the Southern States Official Language Seminar, 1976 at Mysore. Bangalore: Govt. of Karnataka, Dir. of Languages & Dev. of Kannada, 1976. 325p.

19120 ROCHER, L. South Indian "letters to the editor" and the Indian language problem. In Revue du sud-est asiatique 3 (1963) 125-82.

19121 WALCH, J. Faction and front: party systems in South India. ND: Young Asia, 1976. 464p.

B. Economic Studies

19122 BALDWIN, G.B. Industrial growth in south India: case studies in economic development. Glencoe, IL: Free Press, 1959. 339p.

19123 KOPPEL, B. & R.E. PETERSON. Industrial entrepreneurship in India: a reevaluation. In Developing Economies 13,3 (1975) 318-30.

19124 KRISHNAN, V. Indigenous banking in South India. Bombay: Bombay Co-op. Union, 1959. 208p. (Its pub., 18)

19125 NARAYAN, B.K. Southern states through plans; a regional analysis. Delhi: Sterling, 1970. 168p.

19126 NCAER. Demand for energy in southern India. ND: 1962. 203p.

C. Social and Cultural Studies

19127 ASHER, R.E. Social comment in South Indian prose fiction. In SAR 5,3 (1972) 207-220.

19128 JAGADISA AYYAR, P.V. South Indian customs. With a foreword by K.S. Ramaswami Sastry. Madras: Diocesan Press, 1925. 169p.

19129 MENCHER, J.P. Kerala and Madras: a comparative study of ecology and social structure. In Ethnology 5 (1966) 135-71.

19130 NAIR, A.A. Peeps at the press in South India; a short survey of the achievements of editors and publishers. Madras: 1966. 171p.

19131 Supplement on southern writing. In IL 17,1/2 (1974) 141-290.

19132 THURSTON, E. Castes and tribes of southern India. Madras: Govt. Press, 1909. 7 v. [Rpt. Delhi: Cosmo, 1975. 4 v.]

19133 ______. Ethnographic notes in Southern India. Delhi: Cosmo, 1975. 580p. [Rpt. 1906 ed.]

II. MADRAS PRESIDENCY TO MADRAS STATE TO TAMILNADU

A. Government and Politics since 1800

1. The British Raj in the South, 1800 - 1947
a. accounts by officials and travellers

19134 BELL, T.E. The empire in India: letters from Madras and other places. London: Trubner, 1864. 412p.

19135 BUCHANAN, F.H. A journey from Madras through the countries of Mysore, Canara, and Malabar. London: T. Cadell & W. Davies, 1807. 3 v.

19136 BUTTERWORTH, A. Southlands of Siva. London: J. Lane, 1923. 258p.

19137 LAWSON, C.A. Memories of Madras. London: S. Sonnenschein, 1905. 313p.

19138 NORTON, J.B. A letter to Robert Lowe ... from John Bruce Norton ... on the condition and requirements of the Presidency of Madras... Madras: Pharoah, 1854. 325p.

19139 PLAYNE, S.S. Southern India; its history, people, commercial and industrial resources. London: Foreign & Colonial Pub., 1914-15. 766p.

19140 THURSTON, E. Madras Presidency with Mysore, Coorg and associated states. Cambridge: CamUP, 1913. 293p. (Prov. geog. of India)

19141 WILKS, M. Historical sketches of the south of India. London: Longman, Hurst, Rees, & Orme, 1810-17. 3 v.

b. government and politics of the Madras Presidency

19142 ARNOLD, D. The armed police and colonial rule in South India, 1914-47. In MAS 11,1 (1977) 101-26.

19143 BAKER, C.J. The politics of South India, 1920-1937. NY: CamUP, 1976. 363p.

19144 BAKER, C.J. & D.A. WASHBROOK. South India: political institutions and political change, 1880-1940. Delhi: Macmillan, 1975. 238p.

19145 BALIGA, B.S. Studies in Madras administration. Rev. ed. Madras: Govt. Press, 1960. 2 v., 390, 372p. [1st ed. 1949]

19146 BOAG, G.T. The Madras Presidency, 1881-1931. Madras: Supt. Govt. Press, 1933. 140p.

19147 GOPALRATNAM, V.C. A century completed: a history of the Madras High Court, 1862-1962. Madras: Madras Law J. Office, 1962. 476p.

19148 MADRAS (PRESIDENCY). Handbook of information on the administration of the presidency of Madras. Madras: Govt. Press, 1939. 252p.

19149 ______. Manual of the administration of the Madras Presidency. Madras: Govt. Press, 1885-1893. 3 v.

19150 MARKANDAN, K.C. Madras legislative council: the constitution and working between 1861 and 1909. ND: S. Chand, 1964. 199p.

19151 MUDALIAR, A.L. Searchlight on Council debates; speeches in the Madras Legislative Council. Bombay: Orient Longmans, 1960. 492p.

19152 PARAMESVARA PILLAI, G. Representative men of Southern India. Madras: Price Current Press, 1896. 213p.

19153 SLATER, G. Southern India, its political and economic problems. London: Allen & Unwin, 1936. 383p.

19154 WASHBROOK, D.A. The emergence of provincial politics: the Madras Presidency, 1870-1920. Cambridge: CamUP, 1976. 358p. (Cambridge South Asian studies, 18)

19155 ______. The influence of government institutions on provincial politics and leadership in Madras, 1880-1925. In B.N. Pandey, ed. Leadership in South Asia. ND: Vikas, 1977, 232-61.

c. local government and politics

19156 MURTON, B.J. Key people in the countryside: decision makers in interior Tamilnadu in the late eighteenth century. In IESHR 10,2 (1973) 157-80.

19157 PILLAI, K.K. History of local self-government in the Madras Presidency. Bombay: Local Self-govt. Inst., 1953. 240p.

19158 STODDART, B. The unwanted Commission: national agitation and local politics in Madras City, 1928. In SA 5 (1975) 48-66.

19159 SUNTHARALINGAM, R. The Salem riots, 1882. Judiciary versus executive in the mediation of a communal dispute. In MAS 3,3 (1969) 193-208.

19160 VENKATA RAO, V. The administration of district boards in the Madras Presidency, 1884-1945. Bombay: Local Self-Govt. Inst., 1953. 533p.

19161 VENKATARANGAIYA, MAMIDIPUDI. Development of local boards in the Madras Presidency. Bombay: Local Self-govt. Inst., 1938. 242p.

19162 WASHBROOK, D.A. Country politics: Madras 1880 to 1930. In J. Gallagher & G. Johnson & Anil Seal, eds. Locality, province, and nation.... Cambridge: CamUP, 1973, 155-211. [Rpt. from MAS 7,3 (1973) 475-531]

2. The Nationalist Movement in the Madras Presidency

19163 ARNOLD, D. The Congress in Tamilnad: nationalist politics in South India, 1919-1937. ND: Manohar, 1977. 252p. (ANU monographs on South Asia, 1)

19164 ______. The Gounders and the Congress: political recruitment in South India, 1920-1937. In SA 4 (1974) 1-20.

19165 BAKER, C.J. The Congress at the 1937 elections in Madras. In MAS 10,4 (1976) 557-89.

19166 IRSCHICK, E.F. Civil disobedience in Tamil Nadu, 1930-32. In SA 6 (1976) 34-50.

19167 MCPHERSON, K.I. Yakub Hasan: Communalist or Patriot? In Univ. Studies in History 5,4 (1970) 72-84.

19168 MUTHULAKSHMI REDDY, S. My experience as a legislator. Madras: Current Thought Press, 1930. 246p.

19169 PADMANABHAN, R.A. V.O. Chidambaram Pillai. ND: NBT, 1977. 103p.

19170 PARTHASARATHI, R. S. Satyamurti. ND: PDMIB, 1979. 234p. [Biog. of a parliamentarian]

19171 SADASIVAN, D. The growth of public opinion in the Madras Presidency, 1858-1909. Madras: U. of Madras, 1974. 157p.

19172 SASTRY, K.R.R. S. Srinivasa Iyengar. ND: PDMIB, 1972. 105p.

19173 SIVAGNANAM, M.P. The great patriot V.O. Chidambaram Pillai. Tr. from Tamil by S. Mahadevan. Madras: Inbha Nilayam, 1972. 80p.

19174 SUNTHARALINGAM, R. The "Hindu" and the genesis of nationalist politics in South India, 1878-1885. In SA 2 (1972) 64-80.

19175 ______. The Madras Native Association: a study of an early Indian political organization. In IESHR 4 (1967) 233-54.

19176 ______. Politics and nationalist awakening in South India, 1852-1891. Tucson: U. of Arizona Press, 1974. 396p. (AAS monographs, 27)

19177 Who's who of freedom fighters. Madras: Stree Seva Mandir Press, 1973. 3 v.

3. The Justice Party, Anti-Brahmanism, and the Dravidian Movement

a. general studies

19178 CHAKRAVARTHY, P. Emergence of the Justice Party. In JIH 55 (1977) 283-306.

19179 HARDGRAVE, R.L., JR. The Dravidian movement. Bombay: Popular, 1965. 88p.

19180 IRSCHICK, E.F. Politics and social conflict in South Asia: the non-Brahmin movement and Tamil separatism, 1916-1929. Berkeley: UCalP, 1969. 414p.

19181 JACOB-PANDIAN, E.T. Dravidianization: a Tamil revitalization movement. Diss., Rice U., 1972. 235p. [UM 72-26,427]

19182 Justice Party golden jubilee souvenir, 1968. Madras: Justice Party, 1968. 404 + 182p.

19183 KLIMKEIT, H.-J. Anti-religiöse Bewegungen in modernen Südindien, eine religionssoziologische Untersuchung zur Säkularisierungsfrage. Bonn: Ludwig Röhrscheid Verlag, 1971. 155p.

19184 ______. Indigenous elements in modern Tamil secularism. In R&S 23,3 (1976) 77-98.

19185 PATRO, A.P. Justice movement in India. In Asiatic R. ns 28 (1932) 27-49.

19186 RAM, N., et al. The Dravidian movement: a historical perspective. In Mainstream 16,25 (1978) 15-20; 16,26 (1978) 11-22, 34.

19187 Sir P.T. Rajan's eighty second birthday souvenir, 1973. Madras: Justice Party, 1973. 382p. + 82 pl.

b. E.V. Ramaswami Naicker (1878-1973): founder of the Self-Respect Movement (1925) and the Dravida Kazhagam (DK, 1944)

19188 BAKER, C.J. Leading up to Periyar: the early career of E.V. Ramaswami Naicker. In B.N. Pandey, ed. Leadership in South Asia. ND: Vikas, 1977. 731p.

19189 BALASUBRAMANIAM, K.M. Periyar E.V. Ramasami. 2nd ed. Trichy: Periyar Self-Respect Propaganda Institution Pub., 1973. 46p.

19190 DEVANANDAN, P.D. The Dravida Kazhagam: a revolt against Brahminism. Bangalore: CISRS, 1959. 30p.

19191 DIEHL, A. Periyar E.V. Ramaswami: a study of the influence of a personality in contemporary South India. Bombay: B.I. Pub., 1978. 146p.

19192 MOHAN RAM. Ramaswami Naicker and the Dravidian Movement. In EPW 9,6-8 (1974) 217-24.

19193 Periyar, the man and the revolutionary! n.p.: 1972. 43p.

19194 VISWANATHAN, E.S. E.V. Ramaswami Naicker and the Tamilnad Congress: a study of social conflict between Brahman and Non-Brahman. In JIH 54,1 (1976) 173-218.

4. Pondicherry: French Enclave Ceded to India 1954, Now a Union Territory

19195 Treaty of succession of the French establishments of Pondicherry, Karikal, Mahé, and Yanam. In IYIA 5 (1956) 175-88.

B. Post-Independence Government and Politics in Madras State and Tamilnadu

1. General Studies; Political System and Administration

19196 HEGINBOTHAM, S.J. Cultures in conflict: the four faces of Indian bureaucracy. NY: ColUP, 1975. 236p.

19197 JAYAKANTHAN, D. A literary man's political experiences; Tamil Nadu politics since 1946. ND: Vikas, 1976. 270p.

19198 MENON, S. Responses to class and caste oppression in Thanjavur district 1940-72. In SocSci 7,6 (1979) 14-31; 7,7 (1979) 57-68.

2. The Period of Congress Rule, 1946-1967; K. Kamaraj, Congress Leader

19199 FORRESTER, D.B. Kamaraj: a study in percolation of style. In MAS 4,1 (1970) 43-61.

19200 KAPUR, R.P. Kamaraj, the iron man. ND: Deepak Assoc., 1966. 287p.

19201 MADRAS (STATE). Report on general elections, 1962. Madras: 1963. 307p.

19202 NARASIMHAN, V.K. Kamaraj, a study. Bombay: Manaktalas, 1967. 176p.

19203 RUDOLPH, L.I. Urban life and populist radicalism: Dravidian politics in Madras. In JAS 20 (1961) 283-97.

19204 Sri K. Kamaraj 60th birthday commmemoration volume. Madras: Sri Kamaraj 60th Birthday Commem. Cmtee., 1962.

19205 SUBBARAMAN, P.S. Kamaraj; symbol of Indian democracy. Bombay: Popular, 1966. 47p.

3. DMK Rule, 1967 -
a. the Dravida Munnetra Kazhagam (DMK), the party of Tamil regionalism
i. general studies

19206 BARNETT, M.R. The politics of cultural nationalism in south India. Princeton: PUP, 1976. 368p.

19207 HARDGRAVE, R.L., JR. The DMK and the politics of Tamil nationalism. In PA 37 (1964-65) 396-411.

19208 KARUNANITHI, M. Reply to the memoranda presented to the President of India. Madras: Govt. of Tamil Nadu, 1972. 286p.

19209 RAM, N. Pre-history and history of the DMK. In SocSci 6,5 (1977) 59-91. [Review of M.R. Barnett, The politics of cultural nationalism in S. India]

19210 RAMANUJAM, K.S. The big change. Madras: Higginbothams, 1967. 282p.

19211 SATHYAMURTHY, T.V. The Dravida Munnetra Kazhagam in the politics of Tamil Nadu, 1949-1971. In B.N. Pandey, ed. Leadership in South Asia. ND: Vikas, 1977, 395-425.

19212 SRINIVASAN, R. Tamil regionalism. In Seminar 224 (1978) 31-35.

19213 SWAMINATHAN, S. Karunanidhi: man of destiny. ND: Affiliated East-West Press, 1974. 89p.

ii. C.N. Annadurai (1908-1969): founder of DMK and Chief Minister of Tamil Nadu, 1967-69

19214 AHLUWALIA, S. Anna: the tempest and the sea. ND: Young Asia, 1969. 240p. [polit. biog.]

19215 ANNADURAI, C.N. Assembly speeches of Anna. Thanjavur: Anna Pub. House, 1975. 139p.

19216 ______. Convocation addresses of Anna. Rev. ed. Thanjavur: Anna Pub. House, 1975. 78p.

19217 ______. Inaugural and presidential addresses of Anna. Thanjavur: Anna Pub. House, 1975. 166p.

19218 ______. Occasional speeches of Anna. Thanjavur: Anna Pub. House, 1975. 299p.

19219 ______. Radio talks of Anna. Thanjavur: Anna Pub. House, 1975. 51p.

19220 JANARTHANAM, A.P., ed. The Anna commemoration volume. Madras: 1970. 111p.

19221 ______., ed. The Anna sixtieth birthday souvenir. Madras: 1968. 167p.

19222 SIVASWAMY, T.C. Anna, leader of the South. Madras: Poompukar Pub., 1968. 112p.

b. Tamilnadu politics under DMK rule, 1967-

19223 FORRESTER, D.B. Factions and filmstars: Tamil Nadu politics since 1971. In AS 16,3 (1976) 283-96.

19224 ______. State legislators in Madras. In JCPS 7 (1969) 36-57.

19225 HARDGRAVE, R.L., JR. The celluloid god: MGR and the Tamil film. In SAR 4,4 (1971) 307-14.

19226 ______. When stars displace the gods: the folk culture of cinema in Tamil Nadu. Austin, TX: Center for Asian Studies, U. of Texas, 1975. 25p. (Its Occ. paper series, 3)

19227 INDIA (REP.). SARKARIA CMSN. OF INQUIRY. First report. Madras: Govt. of Tamil Nadu, 1977. 271p. [Justice R.S. Sarkaria Inquiry into State official misconduct]

19228 NIMBKAR, K. Trends in Tamilnad politics during the emergency. Madurai: Koodal Pub., 1977. 40p.

19229 RAMANUJAM, K.S. Challenge and response; an intimate report of Tamil Nadu politics, 1967-1971. Madras: Sundara Prachuralayam, 1971. 225p.

19230 SPRATT, P. D.M.K. in power. Bombay: Nachiketa Pub., 1970. 164p.

19231 TAMIL NADU. CENTRE-STATE RELATIONS INQUIRY CMTEE. Report, 1971. Madras: Govt. of Tamil Nadu, 1971. 282p. [P.V. Rajamannar, Chm.]

19232 VISWANATHAN, E.S. The politics of Tamil populism. In JTS 6 (1974) 78-89.

4. Language and Politics; Anti-Hindi Agitation

19233 ANDRONOV, M.S. Problems of the national language in Tamilnad. In Anthropos 70,1/2 (1975) 180-93.

19234 FORRESTER, D.B. The Madras anti-Hindi agitation, 1965: political protest and its effects on language policy in India. In PA 29 (1966) 19-36.

19235 HARDGRAVE, R.L., JR. The riots in Tamilnad: problems and prospects of India's language crisis. In AS 5 (1965) 399-407.

19236 MOHAN RAM. Hindi against India - the meaning of DMK. ND: Rachna Prakashan, 1968. 137p.

19237 SINGH, B.N. Language politics in multilingual states: a case study of the D.M.K. in India. In Afro-Asian & World Affairs 5,1 (1968) 38-53.

5. Local Government and Panchayati Raj

19238 ALL INDIA PANCHAYAT PARISHAD. STUDY & RES. UNIT. The Madras panchayat system. Delhi: Impex India, 1972-73. 2 v., 327, 231p.

19239 JAYARAMAN, K. A study of panchayats in Madras. Bombay: ISAE, 1947. 157p.

19240 KUMAR, S. & K. VENKATARAMAN. State-panchayati raj relations; a study of supervision and control in Tamil Nadu. NY: Asia, 1974. 160p.

19241 MADRAS (STATE). RURAL DEV. & LOCAL ADMIN. DEPT. Guide book on Panchayat development in Madras State. Rev. & enl. Madras: 1961. 2 v.

19242 VENKATARAMAN, K. Panchayat unions in Tamil Nadu. In EE 53 (1969) 343-51.

C. The Economy of Madras Presidency and Tamilnadu

1. Bibliography and Reference

19243 MADRAS (PRESIDENCY). Statistical atlas of the Madras Presidency... Madras: Supt. Govt. Press, 1924. 760p.

19244 MADRAS (STATE). STAT. DEPT. A statistical atlas of the Madras state, rev. and brought up to the end of Fasli 1360 (1950-51). Madras: Dir. of Stat., 1963. 803p.

19245 MADRAS INST. OF DEV. STUDIES. A manual of sources of data on the Tamil Nadu economy. Madras: 1979. 92p.

19246 NCAER. Economic atlas of Madras state. ND: 1962. 138p.

2. General Economic History

19247 AMBIRAJAN, S. Laissez-faire in Madras. In IESHR 2,3 (1966) 238-58.

19248 DUPUIS, J. Madras et le Nord du Coromandel; étude des conditions de la vie indienne dans un cadre géographique. Paris: Adrien-Maisonneuve, 1960. 558p.

19249 FOLKE, S. Evolution of plantations, migration and population growth in Nilgiris and Coorg (South India). In Geografisk Tidsskrift (Copenhagen) 65 (1966) 198-239.

19250 HJEJLE, B. Slavery and agricultural bondage in South India in the nineteenth century. In Scandinavian Econ. History R. 15 (1967) 71-126.

19251 KUMAR, DHARMA. Land and caste in South India; agricultural labour in the Madras Presidency during the nineteenth century. Cambridge: CamUP, 1965. 211p.

19252 RATNAM, R. Agricultural development in Madras State prior to 1900. Madras: New Century Book House, 1966. 444p.

19253 SARADA RAJU, A. Economic conditions in the Madras Presidency, 1800-1850. Madras: Madras U. Press, 1941. 322p. [Its Econ. series, 5]

19254 SRINIVASA RAGHAVAIYANGAR, S. Memorandum on the progress of the Madras Presidency during the last forty years of British administration. Madras: Govt. Press, 1893. 340p.

19255 SUBRAMANIAN, P. The economic condition of the peasantry in the Tamil country in the latter part of the nineteenth century. In BITCM (1977) pt. 2, 57-67.

19256 THOMAS, P.J. & B. NATARAJAN. Economic depression in the Madras Presidency, 1825-54. In EHR 7 (1936-37) 67-75.

3. Demography (1981 pop. 48,297,456)

19257 INDIA (REP.). CENSUS OF INDIA, 1971. Portrait of population; Tamil Nadu, by K. Chockalingam. Delhi: Cont. of Pub., 1978. 159p.

19258 MAHADEVAN, K. Sociology of fertility: determinants of fertility differentials in South India. ND: Sterling, 1979. 158p.

4. Economic Development and Planning

19259 CHANDRASEKARA NAIDU, V. Regional patterns of development in Tamil Nadu. In BMDSS 9,4 (1979) 220-27.

19260 KURIEN, C.T. & J. JAMES. Economic change in Tamil Nadu, 1960-1970: a regionally and functionally disaggregated analysis. Bombay: Allied, 1979. 374p.

19261 MADRAS (STATE) FINANCE DEPT. Fourth five-year plan: programme. Madras: 1966-. 2 v.

19262 ______. Third five-year plan; mid-term review. Madras: 1964. 137p.

19263 NCAER. Techno-economic survey of Madras; economic report. Madras: Dept. of Industries, Labour, & Coop., 1960. 286p.

19264 ______. Techno-economic survey of Pondicherry. ND: 1965. 147p.

19265 RAO, G.R., ed. Progressive Madras State, a saga of integrated development. Madras: Hindustan Chamber of Commerce, 1967. 272p.

19266 SHANMUGASUNDARAM, Y. A review of Tamil Nadu economy, 1970-77. In BMDSS 9,2 (1979) 99-113.

19267 SONACHALAM, K.S. Electricity and economic development of Madras State. Annamalainagar: Annamalai, 1968. 256p.

19268 TAMIL NADU. FINANCE DEPT. Tamil Nadu; an economic appraisal, 1971-72. Madras: Govt. Pub. Depot, 1971. 326p.

19269 Tamil Nadu aiming high. In EE 55, special suppl. (Oct. 18, 1970) 3-94.

5. Agriculture in Madras/Tamilnadu since 1818
a. general studies of agricultural development

19270 HARRISS, B. Paddy and rice marketing in northern Tamil Nadu. Madras: Sangam Pub. for MIDS, 1979. 269p. (MIDS pub., 19)

19271 HASWELL, M.R. Economics of development in village India. London: Routledge & K. Paul, 1967. 105p. [re-survey of G. Slater's villages, 19279]

19272 KRISHNASWAMY, S.Y. Rural problems in Madras. Madras: Govt. Press, 1947. 545p.

19273 MADRAS (PRESIDENCY). Famine code. Madras: Supt. Govt. Press, 1905. 247p.

19274 MADRAS (STATE). CMTEE. ON AGRI. PRODUCTION. Report. Madras: 1966. 346p.

19275 MENCHER, J.P. Agriculture and social structure in Tamil Nadu: past origins, present transformations, and future prospects. Bombay: Allied, 1978. 314p.

19276 NORR, K.F. The organization of coastal fishing in Tamilnadu. In Ethnology 14,4 (1975) 357-72.

19277 SAMPATH, R.K. & J. GANESAN. Economics of dry farming in Tamil Nadu. Madras: Sangam, for MIDS, 1972. 128p. (MIDS pub., 2)

19278 SAYANA, V.V. The agrarian problems of Madras Province. Madras: Business Week Press, 1949. 332p.

19279 SLATER, G. Some south Indian villages. London: OUP, 1918. 265p. (U. of Madras Econ. studies, 1)

19280 SUDAN, M.L. Package programme in Thanjavur - an appraisal. In JNAA 14,2 (1969) 63-125.

19281 SWENSON, G.C. The distribution of benefits from increased rice production in Thanjavur District, South India. In IJAE 31,1 (1976) 1-12.

19282 TAMIL NADU. DEPT. OF AGRICULTURE. Agriculture compendium: Tamil Nadu, 1971-72. Madras: 1971. 387p.

19283 ______. A note book of agricultural facts and figures. 7th ed. Madras: 1970. 440p. [1st pub. 1915]

19284 TAMIL NADU. LEGISLATURE. JOINT SELECT CMTEE. ON THE TAMIL NADU AGRICULTURISTS RELIEF (AMENDMENT) BILL, 1972 (L.A. BILL NO. 22 OF 1972). Report and proceedings.... Madras: Legislative Assembly Dept., 1972. 47p.

19285 THOMAS, P.J. & K.C. RAMAKRISHNAN. Some South Indian villages; a re-survey. Madras: U. of Madras, 1940. 460p. (Madras U. Econ. series, 4) [re-survey of Slater's villages, 19279]

b. agricultural technology and innovation

19286 ADICEAM, E. La géographie de l'irrigation dans la Tamilnad. Paris: EFEO, 1966. 522p.

19287 FARMER, B.H., ed. Green Revolution? Technology and change in rice-growing areas of Tamil Nadu and Sri Lanka. London: Macmillan, 1977. 429p.

19288 KRAMER, F.A. Paddy dryers for Thanjavur: case of agricultural development. In AS 11,8 (1971) 787-802.

19289 LUDDEN, D. Patronage and irrigation in Tamil Nadu: a long-term view. In IESHR 16,3 (1979) 347-65.

19290 MALONE, C.C. Some responses of rice farmers to package program in Tanjore district, India. In J. of Farm Econ. 47 (1965) 256-69.

19291 MENCHER, J.P. Conflicts and contradictions in the "Green Revolution": the case of Tamil Nadu. In EPW 9, 6-8 (1974) 309-23.

19292 RAMACHANDRAN, R. Spatial diffusion of innovations in rural India: a case study of the spread of irrigation pumps in Coimbatore Plateau. Mysore: Inst. of Dev. Studies, U. of Mysore, 1975. 138p.

19293 SONACHALAM, K.S. Benefit-cost analysis of the Cauvery-Mettur project. ND: Planning Cmsn., 1963. 233p.

c. land tenure and reform
i. the ryotwari and other tenure systems of Madras Presidency

19294 AROKIASWAMI, M. Land system in South India in the early nineteenth century. In Intl. Conf. Seminar of Tamil Studies, 1st, 1966. Proceedings. Kuala Lumpur: 1968, 625-34.

19295 BAKER, C.J. Tamil Nadu estates in the twentieth century. In IESHR 13,1 (1976) 1-44.

19296 GEORGE, P.T. Land system and legislation in Madras. In AV 12 (1970) 16-74.

19297 KUMAR, DHARMA. Landownership and inequality in Madras Presidency: 1853-54 to 1946-47. In IESHR 12,3 (1975) 229-61.

19298 MADRAS (STATE). LAND REVENUE REFORM CMTEE. Report. Madras: Govt. Press, 1951. 2 v. in 1.

19299 MUKHERJEE, N. The ryotwari system in Madras, 1792-1827. Calcutta: KLM, 1962. 397p.

19300 MUKHERJEE, N. & R.E. FRYKENBERG. The ryotwari system and social organization in the Madras Presidency. In R.E. Frykenberg, ed. Land control and social structure in Indian history. Madison: UWiscP, 1969, 217-26.

19301 MURTON, B.J. Changing land categories in interior Tamilnadu, 1750-1850: propositions and implications for the agricultural system. In R.C. Eidt & K.N. Singh & Rana P.H. Singh, eds. Man, culture, and settlement.... ND: Kalyani, 1977, 31-40. (NGSI res. pub., 17)

19302 SIVASWAMY, K.G. The Madras ryotwari tenant. Madras: S. Indian Fed. of Agri. Workers Unions, 1948. 229p.

19303 SUNDARAJ IYENGAR, S. Land tenures in Madras Presidency. Madras: Modern Printing Works, 1916. 487p.

ii. land reform

19304 ALEXANDER, K.C. Agrarian tension in Thanjavur. Hyderabad, India: NICD, 1975. 192p.

19305 NAGARAJAN, N. & K. SUBRAMANIAN. History of land revenue settlement and abolition of intermediary tenures in Tamil Nadu. Madras: Govt. of Tamil Nadu, 1977. 585p.

19306 PADMAVALLI, R. & C. SETHU. A study of the changes in the structural distribution of land ownership and use (since Independence) in Tamil Nadu. In SER 5,4 (1977) 241-51.

19307 PARTHASARATHY, G. The Madras land reform bill: a critical study. In EW 12,21 (1960) 771-76.

19308 SONACHALAM, K.S. Land reforms in Tamil Nadu; evaluation of implementation. ND: Oxford & IBH, 1970. 201p.

19309 TAMIL NADU. LAWS, STATUTES. Tamil Nadu land reforms: containing Madras land reforms (fixation of ceiling on land) act and other tenancy reform acts, with rules, by K. Venkoba Rao. Madras: Madras Law Journal Office, 1975. 519p.

19310 VENKATARAMANI, G. Land reform in Tamil Nadu. Madras: Sangam, for MIDS, 1973. 160p.

d. rural credit and cooperatives

19311 KRISHNA RAO, B. Six agricultural credit societies; a case study in Madurai and Salem Districts. Madras: Madras U., 1964. 216p.

19312 RESERVE BANK OF INDIA. Review of agricultural development and co-operative credit in Tamil Nadu, 1961-1975. Bombay: Reserve Bank of India, 1978. 125p.

19313 ROBERT, B.L., JR. Agricultural credit cooperatives in Madras, 1893-1937: rural development and agrarian politics in pre-independence India. In IESHR 16,2 (1979) 163-84.

19314 TAMIL NADU. CMTEE. ON CO-OPERATION. Report, May 1969. Madras: 1969. 3 v. in 1. [Chm., K. Santhanam]

19315 VICTOR, M.A. Co-operation in Madras State. Madras: Palaniappa Bros., 1964. 321p.

6. Industry and Transportation

19316 BERNA, J.J. Industrial entrepreneurship in Madras State. NY: Asia, 1960. 239p.

19317 BROWN, H. Parrys of Madras; a story of British enterprise in India. Madras: 1954. 347p.

19318 LOBLIGEOIS, M. Ateliers publics et filatures privées a Pondichéry après 1816. In BEFEO 59 (1972) 3-99.

19319 MINES, M. Tamil Muslim merchants in India's industrial development. In M.B. Singer, ed. Entrepreneurship and modernization of occupational cultures in South Asia. Burham, NC: DUPCSSA, 1973, 37-60. (Its monograph & occ. papers series, 12)

19320 NCAER. Regional transport survey of Madras and Pondicherry. ND: 1967. 280p.

19321 ORR (P.) & SONS. The turn of a century, 1849-1949. Madras: 1949. 79p.

19322 RENGARAJAN, V. Link roads in Tamil Nadu. Madras: Sangam, for MIDS, 1977. 116p. (MIDS pub., 115)

19323 SINGER, M.B. The Indian joint family in modern industry. In M.B. Singer & B.S. Cohn, eds. Structure and change in Indian society. Chicago: Aldine, 1968, 423-52.

19324 SUBRAMANIAN, R. & K. SHIVAKUMAR & M. PALANISAMI. Entrepreneurship in small-scale industries in Madurai City and its environs. Madras: Sangam, for Gandhigram Inst. of Rural Higher Educ., 1975. 114p.

19325 TAMIL NADU. EXPERT CMTEE. ON HANDLOOM INDUSTRY. Report, Feb. 1973. Madras: Govt. of Tamil Nadu, 1975. 106p.

7. Labor and Trade Unions

19326 ARNOLD, D. Industrial violence in colonial India. In CSSH 22,2 (1980) 234-55. [S. Indian Railway strike]

19327 INDIA (REP.). NATL. EMPLOYMENT SERVICE. Occupational pattern of employees in the public sector in Madras State, September 1962. Madras: Dir. of Employment & Training, State Employment Market Info. Unit, 1964. 108p.

19328 MADRAS (STATE). DEPT. OF STAT. Fact book on manpower in Madras State. Madras: 1966-71. 3 v. in 1. [based on 1961 Census]

19329 MADRAS (STATE). STATE EMPLOYMENT MARKET INFO. UNIT. Short term study of the utilisation pattern of educated persons produced during the third plan period in Madras State. Madras: 1968. 98p.

19330 RAMASWAMY, E.A. Trade unionism and caste in South India. In MAS 10,3 (1976) 361-73.

19331 ______. The worker and his union: a study in south India. Bombay: Allied, 1977. 204p. [Coimbatore]

19332 VISWANATHAMURTHI, J. Rural employment in Tamil Nadu. Madras: Sangam, for MIDS, 1976. 232p. (MIDS pub., 19)

D. Society and Social Change in Madras Presidency and Tamil Nadu since 1818

1. General Studies

19333 BECK, B.E.F., ed. Perspectives on a regional culture: essays about the Coimbatore Area of South India. ND: Vikas, 1979. 211p.

19334 BHATIA, B.M. Growth and composition of the middle class in South India in the 19th century. In IESHR 2,4 (1965) 341-56.

19335 INDIA (REP.). CENSUS OF INDIA, 1961. Madras; scheduled castes and tribes. Madras: Supt. of Census Operations, 1964. 455p. (Census of India 1961, v. 9, pt. 5A)

19336 OLIVIER, G. Anthropologie des Tamouls du sud de l'Inde. Précédé de: Les divisions sociales de l'Inde, par Jean Filliozat. Paris: EFEO, 1961. 339p.

19337 RAMANUJAN, A.K. Language and social change; the Tamil example. In R.I. Crane, ed. Transition in South Asia: problems of modernization. Durham, NC: DUPCSSA, 1970, 61-84. (Its monographs and occ. papers series, 9)

19338 SARASWATI, S. Minorities in Madras state: group interests in modern politics. ND: Impex India, 1974. 247p.

19339 SHANMUGASUNDARAM, Y. The role of women - a Tamilnadu perspective. In BMDSS 7,12 (1977) 714-34.

2. Castes and the Caste System in Madras
a. general studies

19340 BARNETT, S.A. Identity choice and caste ideology in contemporary South India. In K. David, ed. The new wind: changing identities in South Asia. The Hague: Mouton, 1977, 393-416. (WA)

19341 ______. The process of withdrawal in a South Indian caste. In M.B. Singer, ed. Entrepreneurship and modernization of occupational cultures in South Asia. Durham, NC: DUPCSSA, 1973, 179-204. (Its monographs and occ. papers, 12)

19342 BECK, B.E.F. Peasant society in Konku; a study of right and left subcastes in South India. Vancouver: U. of Brit. Columbia Press , 1972. 334p.

19343 ______. The right-left division of South Indian society. In JAS 29,4 (1970) 779-98.

19344 BECK, B.E.F. A sociological sketch of the major castes in the Coimbatore district. In Intl. Conf. Seminar of Tamil Studies, 1st, 1966. Proceedings. Kuala Lumpur, 1968, 635-649.

19345 BETEILLE, A. Caste and political group formation in Tamilnad. In R. Kothari, ed. Caste in Indian politics. ND: Orient Longmans, 1970, 259-98.

19346 BOPEGAMAGE, A. & P.V. VEERARAGHAVAN. Status images in changing India. Bombay: Manaktalas, 1967. 212p. [studies of Coimbatore & Poona]

19347 GOUGH, K. Caste in a Tanjore village. In E.R. Leach, ed. Aspects of caste in South India, Ceylon, and North-west Pakistan. Cambridge: CamUP, 1960, 11-60. (Cambridge papers in social anthropology, 2)

19348 GOULD, H.A. Priest and contrapriest: a structural analysis of jajmani relationships in the Hindu plains and the Nilgiri hills. In CIS ns 1 (1967) 26-55.

19349 OUDEN, J.H.B. DEN. Social stratification as expressed through language: a case study of a South Indian village. In CIS ns 13,1 (1979) 33-59.

19350 PILLAY, K.P.K. The caste system in Tamil Nadu. Madras: U. of Madras, 1977. 89p. [1st pub. in JMU 49,2 (1977)]

19351 SELVARAJ, C. Small fishermen in Tamil Nadu. Madras: Sangam, for MIDS, 1975. 67p.

19352 TAMIL NADU. BACKWARD CLASSES CMSN. Report, 1970. Madras: 1974-1975. 3 v. [Chm., A.N. Sattanathan]

b. Brahman castes

19353 GOUGH, K. Brahman kinship in a Tamil village. In AA 58 (1956) 826-53.

19354 NAIR, B.N. The dynamic Brahmin, a study of the Brahmin's personality in Indian culture with special reference to South India. Bombay: Popular, 1959. 251p.

19355 RANGACHARI, K. The Sri Vaisnava Brahmans. Madras: Govt. Press, 1931. 158p. (Madras Govt. Museum, Bull. 2)

19356 SUBRAMANIAM, K. Brahmin priest of Tamil Nadu. ND: Wiley Eastern, 1974. 183p.

19357 SUBRAMANIAM, V. Emergence and eclipse of Tamil Brahmins: some guidelines to research. In EPW 4,28-30 (1969) 1133-36.

c. non-Brahman castes

19358 HARDGRAVE, R.L. The Nadars of Tamilnad; the political culture of a community in change. Berkeley: UCalP, 1969. 314p.

19359 ______. Political participation and primordial solidarity: the Nadars of Tamilnad. In R. Kothari, ed. Caste in Indian politics. ND: Orient Longmans, 1970, 102-28.

19360 ______. Varieties of political behaviour among the Nadars of Tamilnad. In AS 6 (1966) 614-21.

19361 OUDEN, J.H.B. DEN. The Komutti Chettiyar; position and change of position of a merchant caste in a South-Indian village. In Tropical Man 2 (1970) 45-59.

19362 ROCHER, L. Jacob Mossel's treatise on the customary laws of the Vellalar Chettiyars. In JAOS 89 (1969) 27-50.

d. Adi-Dravida, or "untouchable", castes

19363 EHRENFELS, U.R. VON. Parayer in Indien. In Zeitschrift fur Ethnologie 89 (1964) 180-89.

19364 INDIA (REP.). CENSUS OF INDIA, 1971. Scheduled castes of Tamil Nadu. Madras: Office of Dir. of Census Operations, 1971. 2 v., 392, 505p. (Census of India 1971, series 19, part 5B)

19365 KUMARASWAMI, T.J. Adi-Dravidas of Madras. In MI 3 (1923) 59-64.

19366 MENCHER, J.P. Continuity and change in an ex-Untouchable community of South India. In J.M. Mahar, ed. The Untouchables in comtemporary India. Tucson: U. of Arizona Press, 1972, 37-57.

19367 MOFFATT, M. An untouchable community in South India, structure and consensus. Princeton: PUP, 1979. 323p.

19368 ______. Untouchables and the caste system: a Tamil case study. In CIS ns 9,1 (1975) 111-22.

19369 OUDEN, J.H.B. DEN. De onaanraakbaren van Konkunad: een onderzoek naar veranderingen in de sociale positie van de scheduled castes in een dorp van het district Coimbatore, India. Wageningen: H. Veenman, 1975-. v. 1-.

19370 VAGISWARI, A. Income-earning trends and social status of the Harijan community in Tamil Nadu. Madras: Sangam, for MIDS, 1972. 150p. (MIDS pub., 1)

3. Adivasis (Tribals) of Tamilnad
a, general studies

19371 AGESTHIALINGOM, S. & S. SAKTHIVEL. A bibliography for the study of Nilagiri hill tribes. Annamalainagar: Annamalai U., 1973. 60p.

19372 AIYAPPAN, A. Report on the socio-economic conditions of the aboriginal tribes of the province of Madras. Madras: Govt. Press, 1948. 185p. [Report of Aboriginal Tribes Welfare Cmtee.]

19373 BLACKBURN, S.H. The Kallars: a Tamil "criminal" tribe reconsidered. In SA ns 1,1 (1978) 38-51.

19374 DUMONT, L. Une sous-caste de l'Inde du Sud: organisation et religion des Pramalai Kallar. Paris: Mouton, 1957. 460p.

19375 HOCKINGS, P. Ancient Hindu refugees: Badaga social history, 1550-1975. ND: Vikas, 1980. 285p.

19376 ______. A bibliography for the Nilgiri Hills of southern India. New Haven: HRAF, 1978. 2 v., 303p.

19377 ______. On giving salt to buffaloes: ritual as communication. In Ethnology 7 (1968) 411-26.

19378 INDIA (REP.). CENSUS OF INDIA 1961. Madras: ethnological notes on scheduled tribes. Madras: Supt. of Census Operations, 1964. 268p. (Census of India 1961, v. 9, part 5B-1)

19379 KING, W.R. The aboriginal tribes of the Nilgiri hills. London: Longmans, Green, 1870. 52p.

19380 MANDELBAUM, D.G. Culture change among four Nilgiri tribes. In AA 43 (1941) 19-26.

19381 MISRA, R.L. Inter-tribal relations in Erumad. In EA 25,2 (1972) 135-48.

19382 MORRIS, B. Tappers, trappers and the Hill Pandaram (South India). In Anthropos 72,1/2 (1977) 225-41.

19383 RAMANATHAN, S. Tribal welfare in Kalrayan Hills, South Arcot District: role of government and voluntary agencies. Madras: MIDS, 1977. 82p.

19384 ______. Tribal welfare in Salem District: role of government and voluntary welfare agencies. Madras: Sangam, for MIDS, 1977. 240p. (MIDS pub., 13)

b. the Todas of the Nilgiri Hills

19385 EMENEAU, M.B. Oral poets of south India: the Todas. In M.B. Singer, ed. Traditional India: structure and change. Philadelphia: American Folklore Soc., 1959, 313-25. (J. of American Folklore 71, 281)

19386 ______. Personal names of the Todas. In AA 40 (1938) 205-23.

19387 ______. Toda culture thirty-five years after: an acculturation study. In ABORI 19 (1938) 101-21.

19388 entry deleted

19389 ______. Toda dream songs. In JAOS 85 (1965) 39-44.

19390 ______. Toda marriage regulations and taboos. In AA 39 (1937) 103-12.

19391 ______. Toda songs. Oxford: OUP, 1971. 1004p.

19392 ______. Toda verbal art and Sanskritization. In JOIB 14 (1965) 273-79.

19393 INDIA (REP.). CENSUS OF INDIA 1961. Todas. Madras: Supt. of Census Operations, 1965. 147p. (Census of India, 1961, v. 9, part 5C)

19394 MUDALIAR, N.M. Toda God names. In BITCM (1974) pt. 1, 37-51.

19395 NOBLE, W.A. Toda dwellings and temples. In Anthropos 61 (1966) 727-36.

19396 RIVERS, W.H.R. The Todas. London: Macmillan, 1906. 755p.

19397 ROOKSBY, R.L. W.H.R. Rivers and the Todas. In SA 1 (1971) 109-22.

c. the Kotas of the Nilgiri Hills

19398 EMENEAU, M.B. Kota texts. Berkeley: UCalP, 1944. 4 v.

19399 MANDELBAUM, D.G. A reformer of his people. In J.B. Casagrande, ed. In the company of man. NY: Harper, 1960, 273-308.

19400 ______. The world and the world-view of the Kota. In M. Marriott, ed. Village India. Chicago: UChiP, 1955, 223-54.

19401 SMITH, M.W. Kota texts: a review of the primitive in Indic folklore. In J. of American Folklore 61 (1948) 283-336.

19402 VERGHESE, I. Is the Kota society polyandrous? In CAS 3 (1973) 156-66.

19403 ______. Polyandry in the Kota society: an appraisal. In JIAS 3 (1968) 141-52.

19404 ______. Priesthood among the Kota of Nilgiri hills. In Vanyajati 13 (1965) 64-71.

4. Religious Minorities of Tamilnad
[See also E. 3. below]

a. Christians

19405 CAPLAN, L. Social mobility in metropolitan centers: Christians in Madras city. In CIS 11,1 (1977) 193-218.

19406 ESTBORN, S. Our village Christians; a study of the life and faith of village Christians in Tamilnad. Madras: CLS, for Tamilnad Christian Council, 1959. 69p.

19407 PONNIAH, J.S. An enquiry into the economic and social problems of the Christian community of Madura, Ramnad and Tinnevelly districts. Madura: Dept. of Res. & Extension, American College, 1938. 222p.

19408 ROCHE, P. The marriage ceremonies of the Christian Paraiyans of the Kumbakonam area, India. In AFS 36,1 (1977) 83-95.

19409 WIEBE, P.D. & S. JOHN-PETER. The Catholic Church and caste in rural Tamil Nadu. In EA 25,1 (1972) 1-12.

b. Muslims

19410 MCPHERSON, K. The social background and politics of the Muslims of Tamil Nad, 1901-1937. In IESHR 6,4 (1969) 381-402.

19411 MINES, M. Islamisation and Muslim ethnicity in South India. In Man ns 10,3 (1975) 404-19.

19412 ______. Muslim merchants; the economic behaviour of an Indian Muslim community. ND: Shri Ram Centre for Industrial Relations and Human Resources, 1972. 136p.

19413 ______. Social stratification among the Muslim Tamils in Tamilnadu. In Imtiaz Ahmad, ed. Caste and social stratification among the Muslims. ND: Manohar, 1973, 61-72.

19414 ______. Urbanization, family structure and the Muslim merchants of Tamilnadu. In Imtiaz Ahmad, ed. Family, kinship and marriage among the Muslims of India. ND: Manohar, 1976, 298-318.

19415 MOSES, S.T. The Muhammadans of Pulicat. In MI 3 (1923) 74-87.

19416 Tamilnadu Muslim Educational Conference, 1973: souvenir. Madras: Tamilnadu Muslim Educ. Standing Cmtee., 1973. 128p.

5. Villages and Rural Society

19417 BARNETT, M.R. & S.A. BARNETT. A contemporary peasant and post-peasant alternatives in Tamil Nadu, South India: the ideas of a militant South Indian Untouchable. In Annals of the N.Y. Academy of Science 222 (1974) 385-410.

19418 BÉTEILLE, A. Caste, class, and power; changing patterns of stratification in a Tanjore village. Berkeley: UCalP, 1971. 240p. [1st pub. 1965]

19419 DJURFELDT, G. & S. LINDBERG. Behind poverty: the social formation in a Tamil village. Lund: Studentlitteratur, 1975. 340p. (Monograph series - Scandinavian Inst. of Asian Studies, 22)

19420 GOUGH, K. Agrarian change in Thanjavur. In K.S. Krishnaswamy, et al., eds. Society and change. Bombay: OUP, 1977, 258-91.

19421 ______. The social structure of a Tanjore village. In M.N. Srinivas, ed. India's villages. 2nd ed. Bombay: Asia, 1960, 82-92. [also in M. Marriott, ed. Village India. Chicago: UChiP, 1955, 36-52]

19422 NAKAMURA, H. Accumulation and interchange of labor: an inquiry into the non-market economy in a South Indian village. Tokyo: Inst. of Developing Economies, 1976. 138p.

19423 NORR, K.F. Factions and kinship: the case of a South Indian village. In AS 16,12 (1976) 1139-50.

19424 SIVERTSEN, D. When caste barriers fall; a study of social and economic change in a South Indian village. NY: Humanities Press, 1963. 141p.

19425 SREENIVASAN, K. Climbing the coconut tree: a partial autobiography. Delhi: OUP, 1980. 163p.

6. Cities and Urbanization in Madras

a. general studies

19426 ANANTAPADMANABAN, N. Functional classification of urban centres in Madras State. In Bombay Geographical Magazine 13,1 (1965) 85-95.

19427 LEWANDOWSKI, S.J. Changing form and function in the ceremonial and colonial port city in India: an historical analysis of Madurai and Madras. In K.N. Chaudhury & C.J. Dewey. Economy and society.... Delhi: OUP, 1979, 299-330.

19428 SUBRAHMANYAM, N. Regional distribution and relative growth of the cities of Tamil Nad. In IGJ 16,1 (1941) 71-83.

19429 THIRUNARANAN, B.M. Tiruttani: study of a temple town. In IGJ 32 (1957) 33-56.

19430 VASANTHA DEVI, M.N. Functional classification of towns in Tamilnadu. In IGJ 14,3/4 (1969) 1-14.

b. Madras: metropolis of the South (1981 pop. 4,276,635)

i. history and general studies

19431 CHANDRASEKHAR, S. Growth of population in Madras city 1639-1961. In Population R. 8 (1964) 17-45.

19432 LEWANDOWSKI, S.J. Kerala migrants in Madras city, 1880-1970: an analysis of social and cultural change. Diss., U. of Chicago, 1972. 308p.

19433 ______. Urban growth and municipal development in the colonial city of Madras, 1860-1900. In JAS 34,2 (1975) 341-60.

19434 Madras on the move. [special issue] In Civic Affairs 25,5 (1977) 1-191.

19435 MADRAS TERCENTENARY CELEBRATION CMTEE. The Madras

tercentenary commemoration volume. London: H. Milford, 1939. 457p.

19436 NCAER. Traffic survey of Madras Port. ND: 1968. 99p.

19437 NARAYANASWAMY, S.R. Demographic structure in metropolitan cities: Madras, a case study. In IGJ 51,2 (1976) 28-38.

19438 NEILD, S.M. Colonial urbanism: the development of Madras city in the eighteenth and nineteenth centuries. In MAS 13,2 (1979) 217-46.

19439 RAMADAS, R. Role of co-operatives in the public distribution system in Madras City. Madras: 1976. 95p.

19440 SINGER, M.B. Beyond tradition and modernity in Madras. In CSSH 13,2 (1971) 160-95.

19441 ______. The great tradition in a metropolitan center: Madras. In M.B. Singer, ed. Traditional India; structure and change. Philadelphia: American Folklore Soc., 1959, 141-82.

19442 SOMASUNDARA RAO, B. Madras, a Telegu city. Madras: 1953. 102p.

19443 SRINIVASACHARI, C.S. History of the city of Madras, written for the tercentenary celebration committee, 1939. Madras: P. Varadachary, 1939. 363p.

ii. slums, urban problems, and development

19444 ABRAHAM, C.M. Slums in and around Madras city. In BMDSS 9,9 (1979) 423-36.

19445 BARNETT, S.A. Urban is as urban does: two incidents on one street in Madras City, South India. In Urban Anthropology 2,2 (1973) 129-60.

19446 CHANDRAN, C.S. An approach to Madras metropolitan development. In BMDSS 9,7 (1979) 325-38.

19447 INDIA (REP.). CENSUS OF INDIA, 1961. The slums of Madras. Madras: Supt. of Census Operations, 1965. 435p. (v. 9, pt. 11-c)

19448 LEWANDOWSKI, S.J. Urban planning in the Asian port city: Madras, an overview, 1920-1970. In SA ns 2,1/2 (1979) 30-45.

19449 MADRAS METROPOLITAN DEV. AUTHORITY. URBAN NODE DIVISION. Master plan for Alandur, 1991. Madras: 1973. 50p. [suburb of Madras]

19450 ______. Master plan for Manali, 1971-1991. Madras: 1973. 43p. [village in Saidapet Taluka, Chingleput Dist.]

19451 ______. Master plan for Avadi, 1991. Madras: 1974. 47p. [township in Chingleput Dist.]

19452 TAMIL NADU SLUM CLEARANCE BOARD. Socio-economic survey of Madras slums. Madras: 1975. 179p.

19453 WIEBE, P.D. Social life in an Indian slum. Delhi: Vikas, 1975. 179p.

7. Social Problems and Social Welfare

19454 FELTON, M. A child widow's story. NY: Harcourt, Brace & World, 1967. 192p.

19455 MADRAS (STATE). JAIL REFORMS CMTEE. Report of the Jail Reforms Committee, Madras, 1950-51. Madras: Govt. of Madras, 1952. 2 v. [K.S. Krishnaswamy Iyengar, Chm.]

19456 RAMA, K.G. Women's welfare in Tamil Nadu. Madras: Sangam, for MIDS, 1974. 55p. (MIDS pub., 7)

19457 RAMAMURTHY, M. Poverty and supply of wage goods in Tamil Nadu. Madras: Sangam, for MIDS, 1974. 115p. (MIDS pub., 6)

8. Health Services and Medicine

19458 DEVADAS, R.P. Nutrition in Tamil Nadu. Madras: Sangam, for MIDS, 1972. 164p. (MIDS pub., 3)

19459 JEFFREY, M.P. Ida S. Scudder of Vellore.... Mysore: Wesley Press, 1951. 273p. [1st pub. 1938]

19460 MATTHEWS, C.M.E. Health and culture in a South Indian village. ND: Sterling, 1979. 498p. [N.Arcot Dist.]

19461 MONTGOMERY, E. Social structuring of nutrition in southern India. In L.S. Greene, ed. Malnutrition, behavior, and social organization. NY: Academic Press, 1977, 143-72.

19462 ______. Systems and the medical practitioners of a Tamil town. In C. Leslie, ed. Asian medical systems.... Berkeley: UCalP, 1976, 272-84.

19463 NATARAJAN, T.S. Concurrent field training in the professional preparation of health educators: issues and experiences. Gandhigram, Madurai Dist.: Gandhigram Inst. of Rural Health & Family Planning, 1973. 80p.

19464 NATL. SEMINAR ON THE ROLE OF VOLUNTARY AGENCIES IN THE IMPLEMENTATION OF PUBLIC HEALTH, MEDICAL CARE, & FAMILY PLANNING PROGRAMMES UNDER FIVE YEAR PLANS, MADRAS, 1965. National health seminar. Madras: Andhra Mahila Sabha, 1966. 60 + 205p.

19465 REDDY, D.V.S. The beginning of modern medicine in Madras. Calcutta: Thacker, Spink, 1947. 244p.

19466 ______. Medical relief in South India; centers of medical aid and types of medical institutions. In BIHM 9 (1941) 385-400.

19467 WILSON, D.C. Dr. Ida: the story of Dr. Ida Scudder of Vellore. NY: McGraw-Hill, 1959. 358p.

19468 ______. Take my hands: the remarkable story of Dr. Mary Verghese. NY: McGraw-Hill, 1963. 216p.

9. Education (Literacy 45.78% in 1981)
a. general studies

19469 ADISESHIAH, M.S., ed. Backdrop to the learning society: education perspective for Tamil Nadu. Madras: MIDS & ICSSR, 1978. 395p.

19470 JOSHUA, A. Rural primary education and adult literacy in Tamilnadu. Madras: Published by Sangam, for MIDS, 1978. 156p. (MIDS pub., 17)

19471 MADRAS. UNIVERSITY. Reorganising of education in Madras Presidency. Report of the special committee appointed by the syndicate to examine problems of post-war educational reconstruction. Madras: G.S. Press, 1945. 115p.

19472 NORTON, G. Native education in India; comprising a review of its state and progress within the Presidency of Madras. Madras: Pharoah, 1848. 82p.

19473 SARGUNAM, M.J. An autobiography. Coimbatore: Sargunam, 1978. 168p. [Autobiog. of Tamil Christian educationist]

19474 SATTHIANADHAN, S. A history of education in the Madras Presidency. Madras: Srinivasa, Varadachari, 1894. 441p.

19475 VENKATASUBRAMANIAN, K. Education and economic development in India: Tamil Nadu, a case study. Delhi: Frank Bros, 1980. 287p.

b. higher education; Universities of Madras (1857), Annamalai (1929), Madurai (1966)

19476 ADISESHIAH, M.S. The University in 1976. Madras: U. of Madras, 1977. 44p. (U. of Madras monograph, 9)

19477 Annamalai University, 1929-1979: golden jubilee. Annamalainagar: Annamalai U., 1979. 68p.

19478 BROCKWAY, K.N. & G.R. SAMUEL. A new day for Indian women; the story of St. Christopher's training college, Madras 1923-1963. Madras: CLS, 1963. 226p.

19479 Centenary celebrations [of the U. of Madras]. Commemoration souvenir. 1857-1957. Madras: 1957. 1 v.

19480 History of higher education in South India. Madras: Associated Printers, 1957. 2 v., 226, 398p. [centenary of U. of Madras]

19481 LAKSHMINARAYANA, H.D. Caste, class, sex, and social distance among college students in South India. In SB 24,2 (1975) 181-92.

19482 MADRAS (PRESIDENCY). Report of the Tamil University committee, 1927. Madras: Supt., Govt. Press, 1927. 2 v.

19483 MADRAS. UNIVERSITY. Report of the Inspection Commission, appointed under section 53 of the Madras

University Act of 1923; 1928-29. Madras: Minerva Press, 1929. 1 v.

19484 NAGARAJAN, K. The Annamalai University, 1929-1979: a short history. Annamalainagar: Annamalai U., 1979. 186p.

19485 VAIDYANATHAN, P.S. University of Madras; a record of twenty-five years, 1942-1967. Madras: Higginbothams, dist., 1967. 71p.

E. Religio-Philosophical Traditions of Tamil Nadu Since 1818

1. General Studies; Interactions of Hinduism and Christianity

19486 DIEHL, C.G. Church and shrine; intermingling patterns in the life of some Christian groups in South India. Uppsala: Acta Universitatis Upsaliensis, 1965. 203p. (Historia religionum, 2)

19487 DIETRICH, G. Religion and people's organisation in east Thanjavur. Madras: CLS, for CISRS, 1977. 169p.

19488 HIRUDAYAM, I. Christianity and Tamil culture. Madras: Dr. S. Radhakrishnan Inst. for Advanced Study in Philosophy, U. of Madras, 1977. 85p.

19489 HUDSON, D.D. The life and times of H.A. Krishna Pillai (1827-1900): a study of the encounter of Tamil Sri Vaishnava Hinduism and Evangelical Protestant Christianity in nineteenth century Tirunelveli District. Diss., Claremont Graduate School, 1970. 534p. [UM 71-13,702]

19490 MANICKAM, S. The social setting of Christian conversion in South India: the impact of the Wesleyan Methodist missionaries on the Trichy-Tanjore Diocese with special reference to the Harijan communities of the mass movement area 1820-1947. Wiesbaden: Steiner, 1977. 296p. (BSAF, 36)

19491 TILIANDER, B. Christian and Hindu terminology: a study in their mutual relations with special reference to the Tamil area. Uppsala: Almqvist & Wiksell, 1974. 311p.

2. Hinduism
a. general studies

19492 BALASUBRAMANIAM, K.M. The life of J.M. Nallaswami Pillai; the centenary memorial to a champion of Saiva siddhanta. Annamalainagar: J.M. Somasundaram Pillai, 1965. 152p.

19493 BECK, B.E.F. Colour and heat in South Indian ritual. In Man 4,4 (1969) 553-72.

19494 BURKHART, G. Equal in the eyes of God: a South Indian devotional group in its hierarchical setting. In CAS 5 (1974) 1-14.

19495 FERRO-LUZZI, G.E. The logic of South Indian food offerings. In Anthropos 72,3/4 (1977) 529-56.

19496 ______. Ritual as language: the case of South Indian food offerings. In CA 18,3 (1977) 507-14.

19497 GOVINDA RAJULU CHETTY, T.V. Sri Chidambaram Ramalinga Swamiji: his life, mission and studies. Madras: Central Coop. Printing Works, 1935. 177p. [devotee of Murugan; 1823-74]

19498 JACOB-PANDIAN, E.T. The goddess of chastity and the politics of ethnicity in the Tamil society of South Asia. In CAS 10 (1977) 52-63.

19499 ______. Nadu Veedu rituals and family shamanism in Tamil society: a cult institution of Hinduism. In MI 55,1 (1975) 67-77.

19500 KASINATHAN, N. Hero-stones in Tamilnadu. Madras: Arun Pub., 1978. 88p. + 6 pl.

19501 LE SAUX, HENRI. [Swami ABHISHIKTANANDA] Gnanānanda; un maître spirituel du pays tamoul. Chambery: Éditions Presence, 1970. 157p.

19502 MARTIN, J.L. Hindu orthodoxy in a South Indian village. In JAAR 35 (1967) 362-71.

19503 ______. Variations on Tengalai belief in a South Indian village. In ICQ 26 (1970) 109-16.

19504 RAMALINGA, Swami. English renderings of Thiru Arutpa; selected verses. Tr. from Tamil by A. Balakrishnan. Pollachi: Nachimuthu Industrial Assn., 1966. 291p. [devotee of Murugan; 1823-74]

19505 REINICHE, MARIE-LOUISE. Les "demons" et leur culte dans le structure du panthéon d'un village du Tirunelveli. In Puruṣārtha 2 (1975) 173-203.

19506 ______. Les dieux et les hommes: étude des cultes d'un village du Tirunelveli, Inde du Sud. Paris: Mouton, 1979. 283p.

19507 SINGER, M.B. The Radhakrishna bhajanas of Madras city. In his (ed.) Krishna: myths, rites, and attitudes. Honolulu: EWCP, 1966, 90-138. [1st pub. in HR 2 (1963) 183-226; also in his When a great tradition modernizes.... NY: Praeger, 1972, 199-244]

19508 SRINIVASAN, C. An introduction to the philosophy of Ramalinga Swami. Tiruchi: Ilakkia Nilayam, 1968. 112p. [devotee of Murugan; 1823-74]

19509 TAPASYANANDA, Swami. Swami Ramakrishnananda, the apostle of Sri Ramakrishna to the South. Madras: Sri Ramakrishna Math, 1972. 270p.

19510 VEDACHALAM PILLAI, N.R.S. The Saiva Siddhanta as a philosophy of practical knowledge, by Swami Vedachalam, alias Maraimalai Adigal. With a sympathetic note by F.C.S. Schiller. 2nd ed. Tirunelveli: SISSWPS, 1966. 133p.

19511 VENKATESWARAN, T.K. Radha-Krishna bhajanas of South India: a phenomenological, theological, and philosophical study. In M.B. SINGER, ed. Krishna: Myths, rites, and attitudes. Honolulu: EWCP, 1966, 139-72.

19512 VIMOCHANANANDA, Swami. Ever blossoms: selections from the sayings of H.H. Sri Swami Vimochananandaji. Comp. by D. Jayaramulu Naidu. Namakkal: Sri Sathya Sai Press, 1973. 85p. [exponent of Ayyappa cult]

19513 WADLINGTON, T.C. Yogi Ramsuratkumar, the godchild, Tiruvannamalai. Madras: Diocesan Press, 1972. 92p. [yogi, 1919 -]

b. temples and endowments - their political and economic role

19514 BÉTEILLE, A. Social organization of temples in a Tanjore village. In HR 5,1 (1965) 74-92.

19515 BRECKENRIDGE, C.A. From protector to litigant - changing relations between Hindu temples and the Raja of Ramnad. In IESHR 14,1 (1978) 75-107.

19516 ______. The Sri Minaksi Sundaresvarar temple: worship and endowments in South India, 1833 to 1975. Diss., U. of Wisconsin, 1976. [UM 77-8082]

19517 CHIDAMBARAM PILLAI, P. Right of temple-entry. Nagercoil: Chidambaram Pillai, 1933. 270p.

19518 MARTIN, J.L. The economy of the Tiru Jeer Math and the Alagianambirayar Temple. In Studies on Asia (U. of Nebraska) 7 (1966) 15-37.

19519 MUDALIAR, C. The secular state and religious institutions in India; a study of the administration of Hindu public religious trusts in Madras. Wiesbaden: Steiner, 1974. 261p. (SSI, 19)

19520 ______. State and religious endowments in Madras. Madras: U. of Madras, 1976. 396p.

19521 PRESLER, F.A. The legitimation of religious policy in Tamil Nādu: a study of the 1970 Archaka legislation. In B.L. Smith, ed. Religion and the legitimation of power in South Asia. Leiden: Brill, 1978, 106-33.

19522 ______. Religion under bureaucracy; policy and administration for Hindu temples in Tamil Nadu, South India. Diss., U. of Chicago, 1978. 375p.

3. Christianity: from Missionary to Indian Direction

19523 ANTON, R. The far-off hills. Garden City, NY: Doubleday, 1979. 287p. [Kodaikanal Catholic mission]

19524 CARMICHAEL, A.W. Lotus buds. London: Morgan & Scott, 1910. 341p. [at Dohnavur, Tinnevelly Dist.]

19525 ______. Things as they are; mission work in southern India. London: Morgan & Scott, 1903. 303p. [later ed. 1921]

19526 ______. Walker of Tinnevelly... London: Morgan & Scott, 1916. 458p.

19527 The Church of South India, the Indian Missionary Society, Madras, and the National Missionary Society of India jointly celebrate the birth centenary of Bishop Azariah, the first Indian Bishop and founder of the Indian Missionary Society and the National Missionary Society, on 5th and 6th October 1974 in Madras. Madras: Diocesan Press, 1974. 87p.

19528 DETTMAN, P.R. The forgotten man: the C.S.I. laity in historic perspective. Madras: CLS, 1967. 74p. [Church of S. India]

19529 GRAHAM, C. Azariah of Dornakal. Rev. ed. Madras: CLS, 1972. 118p.

19530 HOLLIS, M. Paternalism and the church: a study of south Indian church history. London: OUP, 1962. 114p.

19531 HOOLE, E. Madras, Mysore, and the South of India: or, a personal narrative of a mission to those countries from 1820 to 1828. 2nd ed. London: Longman, Brown, 1844. 443p. [1st ed. 1829]

19532 LEHMANN, E.A. It began in Tranquebar; a history of the first Protestant mission in India. Madras: CLS, 1956. 185p.

19533 LING, C.F. Dawn in Toda land: a narrative of missionary effort on the Nilgiri hills, South India. London: Morgan & Scott, 1910. 90p. + 11 pl.

19534 MONEY, N. & G.V.I. SAMA. The history of St. Mary's Tope...the Catholic Brahmin colony, Tiruchi. Bangalore: Asian Trading Corp., 1977. 217p.

19535 MORRIS, H. The life of John Murdoch, L.L.D., the literary evangelist of India. London: CLS for India, 1906. 285p.

19536 NELSON, A. A new day in Madras: a study of Protestant churches in Madras. Pasadena, CA: William Carey Library, 1974. 340p.

19537 NEWBIGIN, J.E.L. A South India diary. Rev. ed. London: SCM Press, 1960. 129p. [Bishop of Church of S. India]

19538 PAUL, R.D. Neelakantan Devadasan, first pastor of the Nagercoil congregation. Madras: CLS, 1971. 83p. [19th century Hindu convert]

19539 PEROWNE, T.T. A memoir of the Rev. Thomas Gajetan Ragland, B.D. London: Seeley, Jackson, and Halliday, 1861. 356p. [Missionary in Tinnevelly]

19540 SANTOS, S.R. The Shrine Basilica of Our Lady of Health, Vailankanni. 10th ed., rev. & enl. Thanjavur: Don Bosco Press, 1978. 120p. + 17 pl.

19541 SARGANT, N.C. The dispersion of the Tamil Church. Rev. & enl. ed. Delhi: ISPCK, 1962. 140p.

19542 SARGUNAM, M.E. Multiplying churches in modern India: an experiment in Madras. Madras: Fed. of Evangelical Churches in India, 1974. 183p.

19543 SHARROCK, J.A. South Indian missions: containing glimpses into the lives and customs of the Tamil people. Westminster: Soc. for the Propagation of the Gospel in Foreign Parts, 1910. 312p. + 48 pl.

19544 SUNDKLER, B.G.M. Church of South India: the movement towards union, 1900-47. 2nd ed., rev. London: Lutterworth Press, 1954. 547p.

F. Media and the Arts in Tamilnadu

1. Journalism and the Press

19545 LAKSHMANAN CHETTIAR, S.L. Brief survey of the Tamil press. In TC 4,2 (1955) 158-68.

19546 NARASIMHAN, V.K. Kasturi Ranga Iyengar. Delhi: PDMIB, 1963. 239p. [Editor, The Hindu]

19547 NIRMAL, C.J. The press in Madras under the East India Company. In JIH 44,2 (1966) 483-515.

19458 SUBBA RAU, K. Revived Memories. Madras: Ganesh, 1933. 518p.

2. Cinema of Tamil Nadu and its Political role [See also II. B. 3. b., above]

19549 Films and society in Tamil Nadu. In IIPO, Monthly Public Opinion Survey 15, 6/7 (1970)3-62.

19550 HARDGRAVE, R.L. Politics and the film in Tamilnadu: the stars and the DMK. In AS 13,3 (1973) 288-305.

19551 HARDGRAVE, R.L. & ANTHONY C. NEIDHART. Films and political consciousness in Tamil Nadu. In EPW 10,1/2 (1976) 27-35.

3. Modern Tamil Literature; the "Pure Tamil" Movement

a. general studies

19552 ANNAMALAI, E. Changing society and modern Tamil literature. In Mahfil 4,3/4 (1968) 21-36.

19553 KAILASAPATHY, K. The Tamil Purist Movement: a re-evaluation. In SocSci 82 (May 1979) 23-51. [the "Tanittamil" movement]

19554 MEENAKSHISUNDARAM, T.P. Tamil literature. In Contemporary Indian literature: a symposium. ND: Sahitya Akademi, 1959, 269-283.

19555 NANNITHAMBY, L. Women in modern Tamil literature. Kuala Lumpur: Dept. of India Studies, U. of Malaya, 1969. 184p.

19556 RAGHAVAN, T.S. Makers of modern Tamil. 1st ed. Tirunelveli: SISSWPS, 1965. 131p.

19557 SIVATHAMBY, K. The politics of a literary style. In SocSci 6,8 (1978) 16-33.

19558 SOUTHWORTH, F.C. Linguistic masks for power: some relationships between semantic and social change. In Anthropological Linguistics 16,5 (1974) 177-91. [adoption of pure-Tamil pen names]

19559 SUBRAMANYAM, K.N. Tamil writing today: the wasted heritage. In Asian R. 2,3 (1969) 203-14.

19560 SWAMINATHAN, V. Little magazines in Tamil. In IWT 3,4 (1969) 58-65.

19561 Tamil literature number. In IL 21,3 (1978) 5-161.

19562 Tamil literature special issue. In CIL 5,8 (1965) 1-58.

19563 THANI NAYAGAM, X.S. Regional nationalism in twentieth century Tamil literature. In TC 10 (1963) 1-23.

b. modern Tamil prose

19564 ARUMUGHAM, B. Dr. M. Varadarajan - as a novelist. In CIL 5,10 (1965) 6-7, 24-26.

19565 ASHER, R.E. Littérature en prose en tamoul et en malayalam jusqu'à la fin du XIXe siècle. In BEFEO 59 (1972) 124-43.

19566 ______. Pandit S.M. Natesa Sastri (1859-1906), pioneer Tamil novelist. In Second Intl. Conf.-Seminar on Tamil Studies, Madras, 1968. Madras: IATR, 1971, 107-15.

19567 ______. The Tamil renaissance and the beginnings of the Tamil novel. In T.W. Clark, ed. Novel in India. Berkeley: UCalP, 1970. 179-204. [1st pub. in JRAS (1969) 13-28]

19568 BANGARUSWAMI, R. Early Classics of Tamil Fiction. In IL 11,2 (1968) 48-52.

19569 CHENGALVARAYA PILLAI, V.S. History of the Tamil prose literature. Tirunelveli: 1966. 77p.

19570 DEVA SANGEETHAM, D. The fiction of Dr. M. Varadarajan. Tirupati: Sri Venkateswara U., 1978. 269p.

19571 DHANDAYUDHAM, R. A study of the sociological novels in Tamil. Madras: U. of Madras, 1977. 258p.

19572 MANUEL, V. Man in modern Tamil fiction. Madras: CLS, for CISRS, 1973. 57p.

19573 MUTHIAN, A.R. Origin and development of Tamil prose. In BITCM (1974) pt. 2, 119-40.

19574 SUBRAMANYAM, KA NAA. Tamil short stories. ND: Author's Guild of India Coop. Soc., 1978. 202p.

19575 SUNDARAJAN, P.G. The short story in Tamil. In IWT 2 (1968) 58-64.

19576 SWAMINATHAN, K., et. al, eds. The plough and the stars; stories from Tamilnad. NY: Asia, 1963. 205p.

19577 THANI NAYAGAM, X.S. The novelist of the city of Madras. In TC 10,2 (1963) 1-18.

19578 VARADARAJAN, M. The spoken and literary language in modern Tamil literature. In IL 8,1 (1965) 82-89.

19579 ZVELEBIL, K. The Tamil short story today: Jeyakanthan, Janakiraman, Ramamirtham. In Mahfil 4,3/4 (1968) 37-45.

c. modern Tamil poetry
i. general studies

19580 DAYANANDAN FRANCIS, T. Christian poets and Tamil culture. Madras: Dr. S. Radhakrishan Inst. for Advanced Study in Philosophy, U. of Madras, 1978. 68p.

19581 JOHN SAMUEL, G. Studies in Tamil poetry. Madras: Mani Pathippakam, 1978. 190p.

19582 ZVELEBIL, K. New voices in Tamil poetry. In IL 16, 1/2 (1973) 153-163.

ii. C. Subramanya Bharati (1882-1921)

19583 BHOOTHALINGAM, M. The finger on the lute; the story of Mahakavi Subramania Bharati. ND: NCERT, 1970. 130p.

19584 Essays on Bharati. Calcutta: Bharati Tamil Sangam, 1958-1962. 2v.

19585 NANDAKUMAR, P. Bharati. ND: Sahitya Akademi, 1978. 86p.

19586 ______. Subramania Bharati. Mysore: Rao & Raghavan, 1964. 88p.

19587 ______. Subramania Bharati. ND: NBT, 1968. 127p.

19588 ROY, K.K. Subramanya Bharati. NY: Twayne, 1974. 157p.

19589 SACHITHANANDAN, V. The impact of Western thought on Bharathi. Annamalainagar, Annamalai U., 1970. 218p.

19590 ______. Whitman and Bharati: a comparative study. Bombay: Macmillan, 1978. 234p.

19591 SUBRAHMANYA BHARATI, C. Bharati in English. 2nd ed. Calcutta: Bharati Tamil Sangham, 1966. 103p.

19592 ______. Poems of Subramanya Bharati: a selection.... Tr. by Prema Nandakumar. ND: Sahitya Akademi, 1977. 232p. (UNESCO series)

19593 ______. Songs to Krishna. Tr. by D. Bruce. Calcutta: Writers Workshop, 1973. 40p.

19594 ______. The vow of Panchali.... Tr. by H.K. Valam. Madras: Mohana Trust Pattippagam, 1972. 127p. [tr. of Panchali sapatham]

19595 VIJAYA BHARATI, S. C. Subramanya Bharati. ND: PDMIB, 1972. 67p.

19596 ______. Subramanya Bharati: Personality and poetry. ND: Munshiram, 1975. 183p.

4. Folk Literature of Tamil Nadu

19597 BLACKBURN, S.H. The folk hero and class interests in Tamil heroic ballads. In AFS 37,1 (1978) 131-149.

19598 GOVER, C.E. The folk-songs of Southern India. Madras: SISSWPS, 1959. 300p.

19599 KINGSCOTE, G. Tales of the sun, or folklore of southern India. London: W.H. Allen, 1890. 308p.

19600 SEETHALAKSHMI, K.A. Folk tales of Tamilnadu. Delhi: Sterling, 1969. 119p.

19601 SRINIVAS, M.N. Some Tamil folk-songs. In JUB 12, 1 (1943-44) 48-80; 12, 4 (1943-44) 55-86.

19602 VANAMAMALAI, N. Studies in Tamil folk literature; papers read in International Conf. Seminar of Tamil Studies I and II. 1st ed. Madras: New Century Book House, 1969. 152p.

19603 VARADARAJAN, M. The influence of folklore on Tamil literature. In Annals of Oriental Res. (Madras) 23,1 (1970) 1-17.

III. ANDHRA PRADESH: THE TELUGU-SPEAKING AREA OF MADRAS PRESIDENCY AND HYDERABAD STATE

A. General and Political History of Andhra since 1818

1. general studies

19604 KESAVANARAYANA, B. Political and social factors in Andhra, 1900-1956. Vijayawada: Navodaya Pub., 1976. 355p.

19605 LEONARD, J.G. Politics and social change in South India: a study of the Andhra movement. In JComPolSt 5 (1967) 60-77.

19606 NARAYANA RAO, K.V. The emergence of Andhra Pradesh. Bombay: Popular, 1973. 350p.

19607 RAGHUNATHA RAO, P. History of modern Andhra. ND: Sterling, 1978. 138p.

19608 REDDY, V.M. & P. RAGHUNATHA RAO. Andhra under British rule. Hyderabad: Andhra Pradesh Sahitya Akademi, 1975. 70p.

19609 RUSSELL, G.E. Reports on the disturbances in Purla Kimedy, Vizagapatnam and Goomsoor in 1832-36. Madras: Fort St. George Gazette Press, 1856. 2v. (Selections from the records of the Madras Govt., 24)

19610 SUBBA RAO, G.V. Life and times of K.V. Reddi Naidu. Rajahmundry: Saraswathi Power Press, 1957. 305p. [member of ICS]

2. The Nizam's Dominions to 1949, and Hyderabad State to 1956
a. general studies

19611 AGHA MIRZA BEG. My life: being the autobiography of Nawab Server-Ul-Mulk Bahadur. Tr. from Urdu by his son Nawab Jiwan Yar Jung Bahadur. London: A.H. Stockwell, 1897. 342p.

19612 AHMED, ZAHIR. Life's yesterdays: glimpses of Sir Nizamat Jung and his times. Bombay: Thacker, 1945. 287p.

19613 BILGRAMI, SAIYID HUSAIN. Historical and descriptive sketch of his Highness the Nizam's dominions. Bombay: Times of India Steam Press, 1883-84. 2v.

19614 BRIGGS, H.G. The Nizam, his history and his relations with the British government. London: B. Quaritch, 1861. 2v. [Nizam Ali Khan, 1732-1803]

19615 CHAUDHURI, N.G. British relations with Hyderabad, 1798-1843. Calcutta: U. of Calcutta, 1964. 328p.

19616 CHHABRA, H.S. Hyderabad personalities; a unique, authentic, and comprehensive biographical directory of Hyderabad and its people. Delhi: New Pub., 1954. 107p.

19617 DATE, S.R. Bhaganagar struggle: a brief history of the movement led by Hindu Maha Sabha in Hyderabad State in 1938-39. Pune: Date, 1940. 249p.

19618 DAYAL, DEEN. Princely India; photographs... 1884-1910. NY: Knopf, 1980. 151p.

19619 HYDERABAD. Correspondence regarding the claim of the Nizam of Hyderabad to the restoration of the province of Berar. London: HMSO, 1925. 90p.

19620 HYDERABAD. CENTRAL RECORDS OFFICE. Chronology of modern Hyderabad, 1720-1890. Hyderabad: 1954. 1v.

19621 INDIA (DOMINION). White paper on Hyderabad, 1948. Delhi: MPGOI, 1948. 79p. [suppl., Delhi: MPGOI, 1948. 55p.]

19622 KARAKA, D.F. Fabulous Mogul: Nizam VII of Hyderabad. London: D. Verschoyle, 1955. 176p.

19623 KHAN, M. FATHULLA. A history of administrative reforms in Hyderabad state. Secunderabad: New Hyderabad Press, 1935. 160p.

19624 LEONARD, K.I. Cultural change and bureaucratic modernization in nineteenth century Hyderabad: Mulkis, non-Mulkis, and the English. In P.M. Joshi, ed. Studies the foreign relations of India.... Hyderabad: State Archives, 1975. 601p.

19625 ______. The Deccani sunthesis in old Hyderabad: an historiographic essay. In JPHS 21,4 (1973) 205-18.

19626 ______. The Hyderabad political system and its participants. In JAS 30 (1971) 569-82.

19627 ______. The Mulki - non-Mulki conflict in Hyderabad State. In R. Jeffrey, ed. People, princes, and paramount power. Delhi: OUP, 1978, 65-106.

19628 LYNTON, H.R. & MOHINI RAJAN. The days of the beloved. Berkeley: UCalP, 1974. 279p.

19629 MCAULIFFE, R.P. The Nizam; the origin and future of the Hyderabad state. London: C.J. Clay, 1904. 86p.

19630 MUNSHI, K.M. The end of an era; Hyderabad memories. Bombay: BVB, 1957. 291p.

19631 SHERWANI, H.K. The evolution of the legislature in Hyderabad. In IJPS 1 (1940) 424-38.

19632 YAZDANI, Z. Hyderabad during the residency of Henry Russell, 1811-1820: a case study of the subsidiary alliance system. Hyderabad: Yazdani, 1976. 141p.

b. Communist-led peasant uprising against Nizam and landlords, 1946-51

19633 AGRICULTURISTS' ASSN. HYDERABAD STATE. Immediate agrarian problems, Hyderabad State. Hyderabad: 1949. 80p.

19634 DHANAGARE, D.N. Social origins of the peasant insurrection in Telangana (1946-1951). In CIS ns 8 (1974) 190-234.

19635 ELLIOTT, C.M. Decline of a patrimonial regime: the Telengana Rebellion in India, 1946-1951. In JAS 34,1 (1974) 27-48.

19636 GOUR, R.B., et al. Glorious Telangana armed struggle. ND: CIP, 1973. 162p.

19637 KHODWE, A., ed. The People's movement in Hyderabad. Nanded, Nizam State: Chanda Prakashan, 1947. 175p.

19638 NARAYAN REDDY, R. Heroic Telengana; reminiscences and experiences. ND: CPI, 1973. 88p.

19639 SMITH, W.C. Hyderabad: Muslim tragedy. In Middle East J. 4,1 (1950) 27-51.

19640 SUNDARAYYA, P. Telangana people's struggle and its lessons. Calcutta: CPI (Marxist), 1972. 592p.

3. The Nationalist Movement in Andhra and Provincial Politics

19641 PRASANNA KUMAR, A. Dr. B. Pattabhi Sitaramayya: a political study. Waltair: Andhra U. Press, 1978. 295p.

19642 RANGA, N.G. Fight for freedom; an autobiography. ND: S. Chand, 1968. 560p.

19643 REGANI, S. Highlights of the freedom movement in Andhra Pradesh. Hyderabad: Min. of Cultural Affairs, Govt. of Andhra Pradesh, 1972. 234p.

19644 ______, ed. Who's who of freedom struggle in Andhra Pradesh. Hyderabad: State Cmtee. for the Compilation of the History of the Freedom Struggle in Andhra Pradesh, Min. of Educ. & Cultural Affairs, 1978-. v.1-

19645 RUDRAYYA CHOWDARI, G. Prakasam; a political study. Madras: Orient Longman, 1971. 237p.

19646 RAMANANDA TIRTHA, Swami. Memoirs of Hyderabad freedom struggle. Bombay: Popular, 1967. 247p.

19647 STODDART, B. The structure of Congress politics in coastal Andhra, 1925-37. In D.A. Low, ed. Congress and the Raj. London: Heinemann, 1977, 109-32.

19648 VENKATARANGAIYA, M., ed. The freedom struggle in Andhra Pradesh. Hyderabad: State Cmtee. for the Compilation of a History of the Freedom Struggle in Andhra Pradesh, 1965-74. 4v., 2465p.

4. Andhra Politics after Independence: the Demand for Vishala ("Greater") Andhra versus Subregionalisms

a. the formation of Andhra State, 1953, from the Madras Telugu districts

19649 Communist Party memorandum to Justice Wanchoo. Vijayawada: Visalaandhra Pub. House, n.d. 47p.

19650 INDIA (REP.). MIN. OF HOME AFFAIRS. Report of the Hon'ble Mr. Justice Wanchoo on the formation of Andhra State. ND: 1953. 66p.

19651 MADRAS. PARTITION CMTEE. Formation of Andhra Province: report of the Partition Committee. Madras: 1950. 64p. [Chm. P.S. Kumaraswami Raja]

19652 SUNDARAYYA, P. Vishala Andhra. Bombay: PPH, 1946. 76p.

b. general studies of politics: Andhra State, 1953-56, Andhra Pradesh (Hyderabad + Andhra States) 1956-

19653 ANDHRA PRADESH. OFFICIAL LANGUAGE REVIEW CMTEE. Report. Hyderabad: Govt. of Andhra Pradesh, General Admin. Dept., 1971. 126p.

19654 BERNSTORFF, D. Eclipse of "Reddy-raj?" The attempted restructuring of Congress Party leadership in Andhra Pradesh. In AS 13,10 (1973) 959-978.

19655 ______. Political leadership in Andhra Pradesh, 1956-73. In B.N. Panday, ed., Leadership in South Asia. ND: Vikas, 1977, 290-320.

19656 BHASKARA RAO, N. The politics of leadership in an Indian state: Andhra Pradesh. Vijayawada: Bharat Pub., 1968. 163p.

19657 COHEN, S.P. & C.V. RAGHAVULU. The Andhra cyclone of 1977: individual and institutional responses to mass death. ND: Vikas, 1979. 131p.

19658 ELLIOTT, C.M. Caste and faction among the dominant caste: the Reddis and Kammas of Andhra. In R. Kothari, ed. Caste in Indian politics. ND: Orient Longmans, 1970, 129-71.

19659 ______. Participation in an expanding polity: a study of Andhra Pradesh, India. Ph.D. diss., Harvard U., 1968. 752p.

19660 HARRISON, S.S. Caste and the Andhra Communists. In APSR 50,2 (1956) 378-404.

19661 INDIA (REP.). VIMADALAL CMSN. OF INQUIRY. Report. ND: 1978. v.- [Chm. J.R. Vimadalal; on Vengal Rao ministry in AP, 1975-77]

19662 IYENGAR, S. Political agitation and childhood political learning: the case of Andhra Pradesh. In J. of Developing Areas 12,1 (1977) 3-16.

19663 KASIPATI, K. Tryst with destiny. Hyderabad: K.V. Rao, 1970. 153p. [on K. Brahmananda Reddy]

19664 KHAN, RASHEEDUDDIN. Charminar: communal politics and electoral behaviour in Hyderabad city. In PSR 8 (1969) 59-90.

19665 ______. Muslim leadership and electoral politics in Hyderabad: a pattern of minority articulation. In EPW 6,15 (1971) 783-93; 6,16 (1971) 833-40.

19666 RAM, MOHAN. The Communist movement in Andhra Pradesh. In P.R. Brass & M.F. Franda, eds., Radical politics in South Asia. Cambridge, MA: MIT Press, 1973, 281-324.

19667 RAM REDDY, G. & B.A.V. SHARMA. State government and politics: Andhra Pradesh. ND: Sterling, 1979. 684p.

19668 Two score and ten. Hyderabad: Dr. N. Sanjiva Reddy Golden Jubilee Celebrations Cmtee., 1963. 92p. + 25pl.

19669 WRIGHT, T.P., Jr. Revival of the Majlis Ittihad-ul-Muslimin of Hyderabad. In MW 53 (1963) 234-43.

c. election studies

19670 ACHARYA, K.R. The critical elections. Hyderabad: Acharya, 1979. 326p. [A.P., 1978]

19671 ANDHRA PRADESH, GENL. ADMIN. (ELECTIONS) DEPT. Report on the bye-elections in Andhra Pradesh, 1967-1972. Hyderabad: 1972. 69p.

19672 ______. Report on the sixth general elections (House of the People) in Andhra Pradesh, 1977. Hyderabad: 1977. 2v.

19673 AZAM, K.J. Assembly elections in Andhra Pradesh, 1978. In J. of State Politics & Admin. 1,2 (1978) 39-63.

19674 BERNSTORFF, D. Candidates for the 1967 general election in Hyderabad, Andhra Pradesh. In E.R. Leach & S.N. Mukherjee, eds. Elites in South Asia. London: CamUP, 1970. 136-51.

19675 ______., ed. Wallkampf in Indien: Untersuchung der allgemeinen Wahlen 1967 und 1971 in Andhra Pradesh. Dusseldorf: Bertelswann Universitäts verlag, 1971. 380p.

19676 GRAY, H. The 1962 general election in a rural district of Andhra. In AS 2,9 (1962) 25-35.

19677 ______. The 1962 Indian general election in a communist stronghold of Andhra Pradesh. In JComPolSt 1 (1963) 296-311.

19678 ______. The 1962 Indian general election in Musheerabad, Andhra Pradesh. In J. of Local Admin. Overseas 2 (1963) 195-203.

19679 INDIA (REP.). ELECTION CMSN. Report on the general election to the Andhra legislative assembly, 1955. Delhi: MPGOI, 1956. 55p.

19680 SUNDARAYYA, P. For victory in Andhra. ND: CPI, 1955. 43p.

d. subregionalism of Telangana (Telugu districts of former Hyderabad State), 1968-

19681 Crisis in Andhra Pradesh: from safeguards to separation. Hyderabad, Pemmaraju Pub., 1973. 159p.

19682 FORRESTER, D.B. Subregionalism in India; the case of Telangana. In PA 43,1 (1970) 5-21.

19683 GRAY, H. The demand for a separate Telangana state in India. In AS 11,5 (1971) 463-74.

19684 ______. The failure of the demand for a separate Andhra state. In AS 14,4 (1974) 338-49.

19685 KISTAIAH, M. Sub-regionalism in India: a study of elite reaction towards the six-point formula for Andhra Pradesh. Hyderabad: Book Links Corp., 1977. 109p.

19686 KULKE, E. Telangana: eine neue Variante des Regionalismus in Indien. In IAF 1,2 (1970) 250-67.

19687 NARAYANA RAO, K.V. Telangana; a study in the regional committees in India. Calcutta: Minerva, 1972. 422p.

19688 PARTHASARATHY, G. & K.V. RAMANA & G. DASARADHA RAMA RAO. Separatist movement in Andhra Pradesh: shadow and substance. In EPW 8,11 (1973) 560-63.

19689 RAJESWARA RAO, C. Defeat separatist conspiracy in Andhra. ND: CPI, 1973. 38p.

19690 RAM REDDY, G. & B.A.V. SHARMA. Regionalism in India: a study of Telangana. ND: Concept, 1979. 347p.

19691 RAO, G.R.S. Regionalism in India: a case study of Telangana issue. ND: S. Chand, 1975. 194p.

19692 RAO, K.V.N. Separate Telangana state: background to the current agitation. In J. of the Soc. for the Study of State Govt. 2,3 (1969) 129-43.

19693 SESHADRI, K. The Telengana agitation and the politics of Andhra Pradesh. In IJPS 31 (1970) 60-81.

e. Maoist armed uprisings by Naxalite peasants in Srikakulam District and elsewhere, and their suppression

19694 The Bhargava Commission. In EPW 12,30 (1977) 1169. [judicial probe into anti-Naxalite actions]

19695 "Encounters" are murders: a documentation of the "Naxalite" policy of the Andhra Pradesh Government. Hyderabad: Civil Rights (Tarkunde) Cmtee., 1977. 50p.

19696 "Encounters" are murders: interim report of civil rights committee. In EPW 12,21 (1977) 827-29.

19697 Killings in Guntur. In EPW 12,25 (1977) 971-73. [anti-Naxalite actions]

19698 SHARMA, RAJIV. Red sickle over Srikakulam. In Administrator 22,1 (1977) 307-12.

19699 SURENDRA, L. Srikakulam tribal uprising. In R&S 22,2 (1975) 39-48.

5. Administration, State and Local
a. state, district, and municipal administration

19700 ANDHRA PRADESH. ADMIN. REFORMS CMTEE. Report, 1964-65. Hyderabad: 1965. 193p.

19701 APPA RAO, T. Municipal government in Visakhapatnam. Visakhapatnam: Arsha Printing Industrial School & Press, 1974. 150p.

19702 FRYKENBERG, R.E. Guntur district 1788-1848: a history of local influence and central authority in South India. Oxford: OUP, 1965. 294p.

19703 JAMES, P.A. Forms of municipal government in Andhra Pradesh: a study in the organizational analysis and evaluation. In JNAA 16,2 (1971) 97-109.

19704 LEONARD, J.G. Urban government under the Raj: a case study of municipal administration in nineteenth-century South India. In MAS 7,2 (1973) 227-51. [Rajahmundry, Godavari Dist.]

19705 PAI, M.R. & G. RAM REDDY. Secretariat and heads of departments, a study of their relationship. Hyderabad: IIPA, A.P. Regional Branch, 1964. 181p.

19706 PRASAD, D.R. & V.M.M.M. REDDY. Changing pattern of district administration in Andhra Pradesh. In QJLSGI 39 (1969) 289-99.

19707 VEPA, R.K. New pattern of district administration in Andhra Pradesh. In IJPA 14 (1968) 105-16.

b. Panchayati Raj, introduced in 1959

19708 ANDHRA PRADESH. HIGH POWER CMTEE. ON PANCHAYATI RAJ. Report, 1972. Hyderabad: Panchayati Raj Dept., 1973. 251p. [Chm., C. Narasimham]

19709 ANDHRA PRADESH. LAWS, STATUTES. Law of panchayats in Andhra Pradesh, corrected up to 31st October, 1976.... Ed. by D.M. Raju. Machilipatnam: Aurora, 1976. 839p.

19710 ANDHRA PRADESH. PANCHAYATI RAJ DEPT. A brief report on the gram panchayat elections, held in Andhra Pradesh during 1964. Hyderabad: 1967. 347p.

19711 ANDHRA PRADESH. VILLAGE OFFICERS ENQUIRY CMTEE. Report. Hyderabad: Stamps Press, 1958. 152p.

19712 MUTHAYYA, B.C. Panchayat taxes: factors influencing their mobilisation; a study in three panchayats in East Godavari, Andhra Pradesh. Hyderabad: NICD, 1972. 146p.

19713 RAMAREDDI, P. The law of local self govt. services in Andhra Pradesh. Hyderabad: Panchayat Pub., 1970. 623p.

19714 RAM REDDY, G. & K. SESHADRI. The voter and panchayati raj; a study of the electoral behaviour during panchayat elections in Warangal District; Andhra Pradesh. Hyderabad: NICD, 1972. 113p.

19715 RAMASWAMY NAIDU, Y. Local finances in Andhra Pradesh. Tirupati: Bhargavi Pub., 1974. 508p.

19716 SESHADRI, K. Panchayati raj and political perceptions of electorate; a study of electoral behaviour in the mid-term poll of 1971 in Hyderabad constituency. Hyderabad: NICD, 1972. 99p.

19717 SESHADRI, K. The principle of unanimity in Panchayat elections in the state of Andhra Pradesh, India. In J. of Local Admin. Overseas 3 (1964) 214-20.

19718 VENKATARANGAIYA, M. & G. RAM REDDY. Panchayati raj in Andhra Pradesh. Hyderabad: A.P. State Chamber of Panchayati Raj, 1967. 292p.

19719 VEPA, R.K. Official-non-official relations in

Panchayati Raj - the experience of Andhra Pradesh. In IJPA 8 (1962) 186-99.

19720 WEINER, M. Village and party factionalism in Andhra. In EW 14,38 (1962) 1509-18.

19721 WIEBE, P. Elections in Peddur: democracy at work in an Indian town. In HO 28 (1969) 140-47.

B. The Andhra Economy since 1818

1. General Economic History

19722 QURESHI, ANWAR IQBAL. The economic development of Hyderabad. Bombay: Orient Longmans, 1947. [v. 1 Rural economy, 358p.]

19723 RAMAN RAO, A.V. Economic development of Andhra Pradesh, 1766-1957. Bombay: Popular, 1958. 384p.

19724 VITTAL RAO, Y. Socio-economic conditions in Andhra in the Company period till 1858. In JAHRS 31 (1966) 9-30.

2. Economic Development and Planning

19725 ANDHRA PRADESH. PLANNING & COOP. DEPT. Perspective plan for coastal Andhra. Hyderabad: 1974-. 671p. + 47 maps.

19726 ______. Perspective plan for Telangana. Hyderabad: 1972-. v. 1, 2, 272, 230p.

19727 ANDHRA PRADESH. PLANNING DEPT. Economic development of Andhra Pradesh, 1951-1968; the three plans in retrospect. Hyderabad: 1968. 309p.

19728 Andhra Pradesh Congress Committee souvenir, AICC session, 1938. Hyderabad: Gandhi Bhavan, 1958. 528p.

19729 BRONGER, D. Formen räumlicher Verflechtung von Regionen in Andhra Pradesh / Indien als Grundlage einer Entwicklungsplanung.... Paderborn: Schöningh, 1976. 267p.

19730 CHATURVEDI, B.N. Hyderabad State, a regional and economic survey. Hyderabad: Hyderabad Geography Assn., 1956. 152p.

19731 IYENGAR, S. KESAVA. Rural economic enquiries in the Hyderabad State. Hyderabad: Govt. Press, 1951. 700p.

19732 NCAER. Survey of backward districts of Andhra Pradesh. ND: 1970. 124p.

19733 ______. Techno-economic survey of Andhra Pradesh. ND: 1962. 333p.

19734 RAMANADHAM, V.V. The economy of Andhra Pradesh. NY: Asia, 1959. 302p.

19735 RAO, R.V. Industrial wealth and prospects in Andhra Pradesh; a study in regional, economic, and commercial geography. Hyderabad: Dist. Industrial Consultation Bureau, 1970. 116p.

19736 SARMA, P.V. Regional integration in Andhra Pradesh. In AV 16,3 (1974) 298-313.

19737 SEN, L.K., et al. Planning rural growth centers for integrated area development: a study of Miryalguda Taluka. Hyderabad: NICD, 1971. 245p.

3. Agriculture
a. general studies

19738 ANDHRA PRADESH. BUREAU OF ECON. & STAT. World agricultural census report, 1970-71: Andhra Pradesh. Hyderabad: 1974. 223p.

19739 ANDHRA PRADESH. IRRIGATION CMTEE. Andhra Pradesh Irrigation Committee report, September 1973. Hyderabad: 1974. 612p. [Chm. K.N. Anantaraman]

19740 ANDHRA PRADESH. RAYALASEEMA DEV. BOARD. SUB-CMTEE. ON IRRIGATION. Report.... Fourth five-year plan schemes. Hyderabad: Planning & Panchayati Raj Dept., Planning Wing, 1970. 143p.

19741 FLIEGEL, F.C. & C.R. PRASAD RAO. Caste dominance, traditional farming castes and agricultural modernization in Andhra Pradesh. In CIS ns 12,2 (1978) 240-51.

19742 GOPALAKRISHNAN, M.D. & T. RAMAKRISHNA RAO. Regional variations in agricultural productivity in Andhra Pradesh. In IJAE 19 (1964) 227-36.

19743 JUSSAWALLA, M.F. Evaluation of the benefits of the Nizamsagar irrigation project. Hyderabad: Osmania U., 1965. 139p.

19744 LAKSHMANA RAO, Y.V. Communication and development: a study of two Indian villages. Minneapolis: U. of Minnesota Press, 1966. 145p.

19745 MURTHY, A.S. & S.N. SINGH. Communication behaviour of farmers. Delhi: New Heights, 1974. 216p.

19746 NARAYANA, D.L. Economics of tractor cultivation, Chittoor District. Tirupati: Sri Venkateswara U., 1977. 119p.

19747 PARTHASARATHY, G. Agricultural development and small farmers; a study of Andhra Pradesh. Delhi: Vikas, 1971. 123p.

19748 PARTHASARATHY, G. & G. DASARADHA RAMA RAO. Employment and unemployment of rural labour and the crash programme: a study of West Godavari District. Waltair: Andhra University Press, 1974. 180p.

19749 PATEL, K.V. Farm structure and resource use in drought-prone area. Bombay: Natl. Inst. of Bank Mgmt., 1978. 2 v.

19750 RAGHUNADHA RAO, L. Rural co-operatives: a study with reference to Andhra Pradesh. Delhi: S. Chand, 1974. 220p.

19751 RAO, G.N. Stagnation and decay of the agricultural economy of coastal Andhra. In AV 20,3 (1978) 221-43.

19752 RAVINDRA PRASAD, D. Cooperatives and rural development: a case study of a district cooperative central bank in Andhra Pradesh. Hyderabad: Osmania U., 1978. 205p.

19753 SESHADRI, K. Agricultural administration in Andhra Pradesh: a study of the process of implementation of intensive agricultural development programmes. Bombay: Popular, 1974. 302p.

19754 SUBBARAO, K. Rice marketing system and compulsory levies in Andhra Pradesh: a study of public intervention in foodgrain marketing. Bombay: Allied, 1978. 173p.

19755 VENKATA REDDY, K. Agricultural productivity in Andhra Pradesh: a study in trends, problems, and prospects. Tirupati: Sri Venkateswara U., 1977. 226p.

b. land tenure and reform

19756 ANDHRA PRADESH. JOINT SELECT COMMITTEE ON THE ANDHRA PRADESH (ANDHRA AREA) TENANCY (AMENDMENT) BILL, 1970. Report. Hyderabad: Andhra Pradesh Legislature, Assembly Secretariat, 1970. 70p. [Chm., K. Brahmananda Reddy]

19757 ______. Oral evidence and written representations. Hyderabad: Andhra Pradesh Legislature (Assembly Secretariat), 1970-73. 3 v.

19758 ANDHRA PRADESH. JOINT SELECT COMMITTE ON THE ANDHRA PRADESH LAND REFORMS. (CEILING ON AGRICULTURAL HOLDINGS) BILL, 1971 (L.A. BILL NO. 20 OF 1972). Report. Hyderabad: Andhra Pradesh Legislature, Assembly Secretariat, 1972. 117p.

19759 GEORGE, P.T. Impact of the implementation of land reforms in Andhra Pradesh. In AV 11,1 (1969) 1-21.

19760 ______. Land reforms in Andhra Pradesh: some problems of implementation of tenancy reforms. In AV 12 (1970) 467-506.

19761 GEORGE, P.T. & V.B.R.S. SOMASEKHARA RAO. Land reforms: production-productivity: a study in Andhra Pradesh. Hyderabad: NICD, 1979. 82p.

19762 HANUMANTHA RAO, C.H. Taxation of agricultural land in Andhra Pradesh. London: Asia, 1966. 171p.

19763 KHUSRO, A.M. Economic and social effects of jagirdari abolition and land reforms in Hyderabad. Hyderabad: Osmania U., 1958. 240p.

19764 PARTHASARATHY, G. & B. PRASADA RAO. Implementation of land reforms in Andhra Pradesh; a study sponsored by the R.P.C., Planning Commission. Calcutta: Scientific Book Agency, 1969. 392p.

19765 RAO, T.V.S. Land legislation in Andhra Pradesh (1800-1950). In AV 8,3 (1966) 320-49; 8,4 (1966) 355-81.

19766 SARVESWARA RAO, B. The economic and social effects of zamindari abolition in Andhra. Delhi: MPGOI, 1964. 100p.

4. Industry in Andhra

19767 ANDHRA PRADESH. BUREAU OF ECON. & STAT. Brochure on industries and infrastructure in Andhra Pradesh. Hyderabad: 1975. 220p.

19768 ______. Public sector undertakings in Andhra Pradesh, owned, managed, and with shares by the Government of Andhra Pradesh, 1969-70 and 1970-71. Hyderabad: 1973. 119p.

19769 DE, N.R. Towards effective coordination of public enterprises: case study in an Indian state. ND: Natl. Labour Inst., 1976. 75p.

19770 Emerging investors: a rural profile; a study based around a coastal district in Andhra Pradesh. Hyderabad: Admin. Staff College of India & Dir. of Industries, Govt. of Andhra Pradesh, 1969. 151p.

19771 GAIKWAD, V.R. & R.N. TRIPATHY. Socio-psychological factors influencing industrial entrepreneurship in rural areas; a case study in Tanuku region of West Godavari. Hyderabad: NICD, 1970. 139p.

19772 NAFZIGER, E.W. Class, caste, and entrepreneurship: a study of Indian industrialists. Honolulu: UPH, 1978. 188p.

19773 NARAYAN, B.K. A survey of industries in Telangana. Secunderabad: Keshav Prakashan, 1962. 122p.

19774 UPADHYAY, M.N. Economics of handicrafts industry. ND: S. Chand, 1973. 149p.

19775 VEPA, R.K. Industrial development in Andhra Pradesh and general problems. Machilipatnam: M. Seshachalam, 1968. 216p.

5. Labor in the Andhra Economy

19776 ANDHRA PRADESH. JOINT SELECT CMTEE. ON THE ANDHRA PRADESH INDUSTRIAL RELATIONS CMSN. BILL, 1971 (L.A. BILL NO. 13 OF 1970). The Andhra Pradesh industrial relations commission bill... Report. Hyderabad: Andhra Pradesh Legislature (Assembly) Secretariat, 1971. 165p. [Chm., G. Sanjeeva Reddy]

19777 ANDHRA PRADESH. PLANNING AND COOP. DEPT. Unemployment and registrations in employment exchange: a case study of civil engineers in Andhra Pradesh, 1973. Hyderabad: 1973. 56p.

19778 INST. OF APPLIED MANPOWER RES. Working force in Andhra Pradesh, 1951-71. ND: 1977-78. 2 v.

19779 SIVAYYA, K.V. Industrial relations in shipbuilding industry; a study of the personnel and management-union problems at the Hindustan Shipyard Ltd., Visakhapatnam. Waltair: Andhra U. Press, 1967. 292p. [sponsored by Planning Cmsn.]

19780 ______. Industrial relations in the Visakhapatnam Port, Visakhapatnam. Waltair: Andhra U. Press, 1968. 241p. [sponsored by Planning Cmsn.]

19781 ______. Trade union movement in Visakhapatnam. Waltair: Andhra U., 1966.

6. Commerce and Transportation

19782 HARNETTY, P. "India's Mississippi": the River Godavari Navigation Scheme, 1853-71. In JIH 43,3 (1965) 699-732.

19783 RAO, B.P. Internal and external relations of the port of Visakhapatnam. In NGJI 12 (1966) 114-27.

C. Society and Social Change in Andhra

1. General Studies

19784 ABBASAYULU, Y.B. Sociology of depressed groups. Hyderabad: Centre for Harijan Studies, Osmania U., 1979. 74p.

19785 ANDHRA PRADESH. BACKWARD CLASSES CMSN. Report. Hyderabad: 1970. 203p. [K.N. Anantaraman, Chm.]

19786 AL-HASSAN, SIRAJ. The castes and tribes of H.E.H. the Nizam's dominions. Bombay: Times Press, 1920. 651p.

19787 CHANDRAMANI, G.Y. Profiles of women in A.P. In Vina Mazumdar, ed. Symbols of power.... Bombay: Allied, 1979. 373p.

19788 DESHMUKH, DURGABAI. The stone that speaketh. Hyderabad: Andhra Mahila Sabha, 1979-80. 2 v. [on the Andhra Mahila Sabha]

19789 LAKSHMANNA, C. The study of scheduled caste and scheduled tribe high school students in Andhra Pradesh. Hyderabad: Dept. of Sociology, Osmania U., 1974. 128p.

19790 MUDIRAJ, G.N.R. Caste-sect dichotomy in Telangana villages. In MI 55 (1970) 280-88.

19791 SASTRY, S.A.R. Inequality, welfare, and ranking: a study of Andhra Pradesh. In AV 20,4 (1978) 353-67.

2. Social Categories
a. castes in Andhra

19792 ABBASAYULU, Y.B. Scheduled caste elite: a study of scheduled caste elite in Andhra Pradesh. Hyderabad: Dept. of Sociology, Osmania U., 1978. 136p.

19793 FISHMAN, A.T. Culture change and the underprivileged; a study of Madigas in south India under Christian guidance.... Madras: CLS, 1941. 207p.

19794 LAKSHMANNA, C. Caste dynamics in village India. Bombay: Nachiketa, 1973. 144p.

19795 LEONARD, K.I. Social history of an Indian caste: the Kayasths of Hyderabad. Berkeley: UCalP, 1978. 353p.

19796 NICHOLSON, S. Social organization of the Malas - an outcaste Indian people. In JRAI 56 (1926) 91-103.

19797 RAMASWAMY, UMA. Scheduled castes in Andhra: some aspects of social change. In EPW 9,29 (1974) 1153-58.

19798 ______. Self identity among scheduled castes: a study of Andhra. In EPW 9,47 (1974) 1959-64.

19799 RANGA RAO, K. & K. RADHAKRISHNA MURTY. Cultural matrix and reference group behavior: a case of desanskritization and Islamization of the Telangana Brahmins. In EA 25,3 (1972) 241-47.

19800 SINGH, T.R. The Madiga; a study in social structure and change. Lucknow: Ethnographic & Folk Culture Soc., U.P., 1969. 77p.

19801 SURYANARAYANA, M. Marine fisherfolk of north-east coastal Andhra Pradesh. Calcutta: AnthSI, 1977. 147p. (Its Memoir, 47)

19802 VENKATSWAMY, P.R. Our struggle for emancipation. Secunderabad: 1955. 2 v. 663p.

b. tribes of Andhra

19803 ANDHRA PRADESH. CMTEE. ON WELFARE OF SCHEDULED TRIBES. Report on educational facilities, representation in services, medical facilities, and other socio-economic schemes implemented for the welfare of scheduled tribes...28th June, 1977. Hyderabad: Andhra Pradesh Legislature, Assembly Secretariat, 1977. 178p. [Chm., K. Bheem Rao]

19804 ______. Report on the welfare of scheduled tribes in plain areas...27th Dec., 1977. Hyderabad: Andhra Pradesh Legislature, Assembly Secretariat, 1978. 94p. [Chm., K. Bheem Rao]

19805 BOSE, N.K. Integration of tribes in Andhra Pradesh. In MI 44 (1964) 97-104.

19806 FÜRER-HAIMENDORF, C. VON. The aboriginal tribes of Hyderabad. London: Macmillan, 1943-48. 3 v. [v. 1, the Chenchus; v. 2, the Reddis of the Bison hills; v. 3, the Raj Gonds of Adilabad]

19807 ______. Beliefs concerning human sacrifice among the Hill Reddis. In MI 24,1 (1944) 11-28.

19808 ______. The Gonds of Andhra Pradesh: tradition and change in an Indian tribe. ND: Vikas, 1979. 569p.

19809 KAMALAMANOHAR RAO, P. A report on the working of

the T.D. Blocks in Andhra Pradesh. Hyderabad: Tribal Welfare Dept., Govt. of Andhra Pradesh, 1968. 2 v. in 1.

19810 PAGDI, S.R. Among the Gonds of Adilabad. 2nd ed. Bombay: Popular, 1952. 122p.

19811 PAREEK, R.N. Tribal culture in flux: the Jatapus of Eastern Ghats. Delhi: B.R., 1977. 288p.

19812 PRATAP, D.R. Tribes of Andhra Pradesh. Hyderabad: World Telugu Conf. Office, 1975. 78p.

19813 RAGHAVIAH, V. The Yanadis. ND: Bharatiya Adimjati Sevak Sangh, 1962. 451p.

19814 SIMHADRI, Y.C. The ex-criminal tribes of India. ND: National, 1979. 185p. [Yerukula of A.P.]

19815 ______. Institutional factors and tribal criminality: an analysis of an Yerukula tribe in Andhra village. In EA 27,1 (1974) 45-60.

19816 YORKE, M. Kinship, marriage, and ideology among the Raj Gonds: a tribal system in the context of south India. In CIS ns 13,1 (1979) 85-117.

3. Villages and Rural Society

19817 BRONGER, D. Jajmani system in southern India. In JIAS 10,1 (1975) 1-38.

19818 CHAILLEUX, J.-Y. Les castes dominantes du village de Peravali face à la modernisation de l'agriculture (Andhra Pradesh). In Puruṣārtha 2 (1975) 17-30.

19819 DUBE, S.C. Indian village. Ithaca: CornellUP, 1955. 248p. [Shamirpet]

19820 FRYKENBERG, R.E. British society in Guntur during the early nineteenth century. In CSSH 4 (1962) 200-08.

19821 ______. Elite groups in a South Indian district: 1788-1858. In JAS 24 (1965) 261-81.

19822 ______. Village strength in south India. In his Land control and social structure in Indian history. Madison: UWiscP, 1969, 227-47.

19823 GALLAIS, J. Villages d'Inde centrale: Andhra Pradesh; étude graphique. Rouen: Université de Rouen, Faculté des lettres et sciences humaines, 1972. 54p.

19824 GRAY, H. The landed gentry of Telengana, Andhra Pradesh. In E.R. Leach & S.N. Mukherjee, eds. Elites in South Asia. London: CamUP, 1970, 119-35.

19825 HIEBERT, P.G. Konduru: structure and integration in a South Indian village. Minneapolis: U. of Minnesota Press, 1971. 192p.

19826 KAMESHWARA RAO, N.V. Impact of drought on the social system of a Telangana village. In EA 27,4 (1974) 299-314.

19827 LAKSHMANA RAO, Y.V. Communication and development; a study of two Indian villages. Minneapolis: U. of Minnesota Press, 1966. 145p.

19828 NAGABHUSHANAM, K. & B. SARVESWARA RAO. Report on the socio-agro economic survey of the Nagarjunasagar Project area. Waltair: Andhra U., 1972. 2 v. in 4.

19829 PARTHASARATHY, G. Changes in rural society, 1955-56 and 1960-61; a case study of Pathikonda Village, Chittoor District, Andhra Pradesh. Madras: Agri. Econ. Res. Centre, U. of Madras, 1965. 164p.

19830 SARVESWARA RAO, B. A study of rural poverty and inequalities in a developed district. Madras: Sangam, MIDS, 1978. 152p. (MIDS pub., 18) [East Godavari]

19831 SEN, L.K. & G.K. MISRA. Regional planning for rural electrification (a study in Suryapet Taluk, Nalgonda District, Andhra Pradesh). Hyderabad: NICD, 1974. 144p.

19832 SUBRAHMANYAM, Y.S. Social change in village India: an Andhra case study. ND: Prithvi Raj Pub., 1975. 213p.

19833 SUNDARAYYA, P. Class differentiation of the peasantry: results of rural surveys in Andhra Pradesh. In SocSci 5,8 (1977) 51-83; 5,9 (1977) 45-60.

4. Cities and Urbanization

19834 ALAM, SHAH MANZOOR. Hyderabad-Secunderabad, twin cities; a study in urban geography. Bombay: Allied, 1965. 159p.

19835 ______. Metropolitan Hyderabad and its region; a strategy for development. Bombay: Asia, 1972. 315p.

19836 ANDHRA PRADESH. DEPT. OF TOWN PLANNING. Report on the delineation of Hyderabad Metropolitan District. Hyderabad: Dir. of Town Planning, Govt. of A.P., 1972. 76p.

19837 ______. Vijayawada by the River Krishna; outline development plan (general town planning scheme) 1967. Hyderabad: 1969. 135p.

19838 ANDHRA PRADESH. HEALTH, HOUSING, & MUNICIPAL ADMIN. DEPT. Development plan for the area comprising the Municipal Corporation of Hyderabad. Hyderabad: 197-. 50p.

19839 AUFDERLANDWEHR, W. Mobilität in Indien: Stadtgerichtete und innerstädtische Wanderungen im südlichen Indien untersucht am Beispiel der drei Städte Vijayawada, Guntur und Tenali. Tübingen: H. Erdmann, 1976. 205p.

19840 BERRY, B.J.L. & V.I.S. PRAKASA RAO. Urban-rural duality in the regional structure of Andhra Pradesh: a challenge to regional planning and development. Wiesbaden: Steiner, 1968. 49p.

19841 COUSINS, W.J. & C. GOYDER. Changing slum communities: urban community development in Hyderabad. ND: Manohar, 1979. 110p.

19842 GOPI, K.N. Process of urban fringe development: a model. Delhi: Concept, 1978. 120p. [study of Uppal, a Hyderabad suburb]

19843 IYENGAR, S. KESAVA. A socio-economic survey of Hyderabad-Secunderabad city area. Hyderabad: Indian Inst. of Econ., 1957. 390p.

19844 RAO, B.P. Visakhapatnam; a study in geography of port town. Varanasi: NGSI, 1971. 139p.

19845 REDDY, N.B.K. Distributional aspects of urbanism in the Krishna and Godavari deltas. In Deccan Geographer 8,1-2 (1970) 101-18.

19846 ______. Urban evolution, growth pattern and urbanization trends in the Krishna and Godavari deltas. In NGJI 16 (1970) 270-87.

19847 VISWANADHAM, G. Urban demography and ecology: a case study of an Indian city (Hyderabad). ND: Light & Life, 1979. 170p.

5. Health and Social Welfare

19848 ANDERSON, R.T. Voluntary associations in Hyderabad. In Anthropological Q. 37 (1964) 175-90.

19849 ANDHRA PRADESH. LEGISLATIVE COUNCIL. CMTEE. ON THE WORKING OF THE SOCIAL WELFARE HOSTELS IN ANDHRA PRADESH. Report. Hyderabad: A.P. Legislature, Council Secretariat, 1972. 75p. [Chm., A. Chengal Reddy]

19850 BALKRISHNA, S. Family planning, knowledge, attitude and practice: a sample survey in Andhra Pradesh. Hyderabad: NICD, 1971. 139p.

19851 MUNSON, A. Jungle days: being the experiences of an American woman doctor in India. NY: Appleton, 1913. 297p. [Medah district]

19852 MUTHAYYA, B.C. Child welfare: existing conditions and parental attitudes; a purposive study in Andhra Pradesh. Hyderabad: NICD, 1972. 184p.

19853 NAGDA, S. & V.K. REDDY. Report of fertility and family planning survey of Kotala Village, Chandragiri Taluk, Chittoor District.... Tirupati: Population Studies Centre, Sri Venkateswara U., 1976. 61p.

19854 RANGA RAO, M. & J.V. RAGHAVENDER RAO. The prostitutes of Hyderabad; a study of the sociocultural conditions of the prostitutes of Hyderabad. Hyderabad: Assoc. for Moral & Social Hygiene in India, A.P. Branch, 1970. 79p.

19855 REDDY, P.R. Food and nutrition. Tirupati: Sri Venkateswara U., 1977. 133p.

19856 SURYANARAYANA MURTI, C. A doctor's log. Madras: M. Seshachalam, 1973. 124p.

6. Education (Literacy 29.94% in 1981)

19857 ANDHRA PRADESH. CMTEE. ON NATIONALISED TEXTBOOKS. Report of the Committee on Nationalised Textbooks. Hyderabad: Andhra Pradesh Govt. Text-book Press, 1973. 157p. [Chm. S.R. Ramamurthy]

19858 ANDHRA PRADESH. EDUC. DEPT. Two decades of growth in education. Hyderabad: 1976. 28p.

19859 ANDHRA PRADESH STATE SEMINAR ON EDUC. PLANNING & ADMIN., HYDERABAD, INDIA, 1970. Report. ND: Natl. Staff College for Educ. Planners and Administrators, 1973. 57p.

19860 ELLIOTT, C.M. The problem of autonomy: the Osmania University case. In S.H. Rudolph & L.I. Rudolph, eds. Education and politics in India.... Cambridge: HUP, 1972, 173-309.

19861 IMADI, SAIDUL HAQ. Nawab Imad-ul-Mulk: social and cultural activities of Nawab Imad-ul-Mulk Syed Husain Bilgrami in Hyderabad. Hyderabad: State Archives, 1978. 143p. (Its monograph series, 5)

19862 KRISHNA MURTY, S. A critical study of reforms in educational administration introduced in Andhra Pradesh during 1956-1966. Hyderabad: Rajeswari Pub., 1972.

19863 MANOHAR RAO, G. Report of the second educational survey in Andhra Pradesh, 1956-66. Hyderabad: Dir. of Public Instruction, 1970. 387p.

19864 NAGAIAH, S. Memoirs of a principal. Tirupati: Nagaiah, 1979. 235p.

19865 RAJAGOPAL, M.V. Education in Andhra Pradesh; a study in qualitative development. Hyderabad: Vidyarthi Pub., 1969. 123p.

19866 SHERWANI, H.K. The Osmania University first phase: the Urdu medium (1917-48). In H.K. Sherwani, ed. Dr. Ghulam Yazdani Commemoration Volume. Hyderabad: Maulana Abul Kalam Azad Oriental Res. Inst., 1966, 237-47. (Studies in Indian culture)

19867 VENKATAIAH, N. Impact of Farmers' Functional Literacy Programme on the participants in Andhra Pradesh. Tirupati: Sri Venkateswara U., 1978. 189p.

19868 SRI VENKATESWARA U. REVIEW CMTEE. Report. Anantapur: Sri Venkateswara U. Post Graduate Centre, 1972. 189p. [B.R. Seshachar, Chm.]

19869 VITTAL RAO, Y. Education and learning in Andhra under the East India Company. Secunderabad: N. Vidyaranya Swamy, 1979. 324p.

D. Religions of Modern Andhra: Hinduism, Islam, and Christianity

19870 AKHMEDZYANOV, A.V. The rebirth of a Muslim communal organization in Andhra. In Central Asian R. 13 (1965) 232-238. [Tr. from Russian]

19871 ANNA RAO, C. Administration of temples. Tirupati: Tirumala Tirupati Devasthanams, 1974. 183p.

19872 BHARADWAJA, E. The life and teachings of the Mother. Bapatla, A.P.: Matrusri Pub., 1968. 110p. [on Anasuya Devi]

19873 CHAMBERLAIN, J. The cobra's son: and other stories of missionary work among the Telugus of India. ND: H. Revell, 1900. 270p.

19874 DRACH, G. & C.F. KUDER. The Telugu mission of the General Council of the Evangelical Lutheran Church in North America, containing a biography of the Rev. Christian Frederick Heyer, M.D. Philadelphia: Genl. Council Pub. House, 1914. 399p.

19875 LAMB, F. The story of Haidarabad. London: Wesleyan Methodist Missionary Soc. & Women's Auxiliary, 1920. 63p.

19876 LUKE, P.Y. & J.B. CARMAN. Village Christians and Hindu culture: study of a rural church in Andhra Pradesh. London: Lutterworth, 1968. 246p.

19877 ODDIE, G.A. Christian conversion among non-Brahmans in Andhra Pradesh, with special reference to the Dornakal Diocese, c. 1900-1936. In his (ed.) Religion in South Asia. ND: Manohar, 1977, 67-99.

19878 ______. Christian conversion in the Telugu country, 1860-1900: a case study of one Protestant movement in the Godavery-Krishna Delta. In IESHR 12,1 (1975) 61-79.

19879 RAMA, K.S. The history of Sri Rama Nama Kshetram, from its inception in 1926 to the golden jubilee, 1975. Guntur: S.S.R.N.S. Sangham, 1978. 228p. [on a Vaiṣṇava institution at Guntur]

19880 SACKETT, F.C. Posnett of Medak. London: Cargate Press, 1951. 138p. [Methodist missionary]

19881 SUBBARAMAIAH, S. Finances of an Indian temple; a case study of the finances of the Tirumala-Tirupati devasthanams (1951-1963). Jullundur: Intl. Book Co., 1968. 121p.

19882 TAPPER, B.E. Widows and goddesses: female roles in deity symbolism in a South Indian village. In CIS ns 13, 1 (1979) 1-31.

E. Media and the Arts in Andhra

1. Journalism and the Press

19883 SESHAGIRI RAO, K.R. Studies in the history of Telugu journalism; presented to V.R. Narla on the occasion of his shashtyabdapurti. Delhi: Narla Shashtyabdapurti Celebration Cmtee, 1968. 170p. [Venkatesvara Rao Narla]

19884 THAKUR, B.S. & E.G. PARAMESWARAN. Newspaper reading habits in Hyderabad-Secunderabad. Hyderabad: Dept. of Journalism, Osmania U., 1966. 97p.

2. Telugu and Urdu Literatures of Modern Andhra
a. general studies

19885 ANJANEYULU, D. Dr. C.R. Reddy. ND: Sahitya Akademi, 1973. 75p.

19886 ______. The little review in Telugu. In IWT 3,4 (1969) 66-75.

19887 BROWN, C.P. Literary autobiography of C.P. Brown. Tirupati: Sri Venkateswara U., 1978. 168p.

19888 CHOWDARY, P.U.C., ed. World Telugu Conference, Hyderabad, April 12-18, 1975: souvenir. Delhi: North Regional Cmtee., World Telugu Conference, 1975. 168p.

19889 Current concerns of contemporary Telugu novelists: a synoptic introduction. Madras: M. Seshachalam, 1970. 155p.

19890 INNAIAH, N. & A. KHUNDMIRI, eds. Tradition and modernity in Telugu and Urdu literature. Hyderabad: Indian Cmtee. for Cultural Freedom, Hyderabad Chapter, 1967. 38p.

19891 NARAYANA RAO, V. The political novel in Telugu. In CAS 6 (1975) 94-105.

19892 SASTRY, S.M.Y. Modern Telugu literature and theatre: two studies. Bombay: Bombay Andhra Mahasabha & Gymkhana, 1975. 75p.

19893 SHRIDEVI, S. Luminaries of Andhra Pradesh. Hyderabad: Andhra Pradesh Sahitya Akademi, 1976. 156p.

19894 Telugu novel: a collection of essays introducing twelve selected Telugu novels. Secunderabad: Yuvabharathi, 1975-. v.1, 122p.

19895 VENKATARAYA SASTRY, V. Vedam Venkataraya Sastry. ND: Sahitya Akademi, 1976. 72p.

b. Swāmī Tyāgarāja (1767-1847): Vaiṣṇava dramatist and composer of South Indian music

19896 BHARATI, SHUDDHANANDA. St. Tyāgarāja, the divine singer: his life and teachings. Madras: Shuddhananda Library, 1968. 79p.

19897 KRISHNASWAMY, S.Y. Thyagaraja - saint and singer. Bombay: Orient Longmans, 1968. 200p.

19898 PURUSHOTHAMAN, E.N. Tyagopanishad. Hyderabad: A.P. Sangeeta Nataka Akademi, 1975. 376p.

19899 RAMANUJACHARIAR, C., tr. The spiritual heritage of Tyagaraja. 2nd ed. Madras: Sri Ramakrishna Math, 1966. 759p.

19900 SAMBAMOORTHY, P. Tyaga. ND: NBT, 1967. 94p.

19901 TYAGARAJA, Swami. The pancaratna kritis of Sri Tyagaraja.... Tr. by T.S. Parthasarathy. ND: Music Club, 1969. 24p.

19902 Tyagaraja Bi-Centenary Conference (41st Madras Music Conference). In JMA 39,1/4 (1968) 43-168.

c. Kandukuri Viresalingam (1848-1919): Brahmo social reformer and pioneer of Telugu prose

19903 ANJANEYULU, D. Kandukuri Veeresalingam. ND: PDMIB, 1976. 163p.

19904 NARLA, V.R. Veeresalingam. ND: Sahitya Akademi, 1968. 96p.

19905 VIRESALINGAM, K. Autobiography of Kandukuri Veeresalingam Pantulu. Tr. by V. Ramakrishna Rao & T. Rama Rao. Rajahmundry: Addepally, 1970. 116p.

d. Gurazada Venkata Apparao (1861-1915): innovative poet in the colloquial language

19906 RAMANUJA RAO, D., ed. The Gurazada souvenir. Hyderabad: Gurazada Centenary Cmtee., Andhra Pradesh, 1962. 77p.

19907 SITAPATI, G.V. Mahakavi Guruzada Apparao. Hyderabad: Sagar Pub., 1978. 148p.

19908 SURYANARAYANA, P. A critical estimate of Sri G.V. Apparao's works. Vijayawada: Vijnana Sahiti Pub., 1968. 140p.

19909 ______. The life and greatness of Sri Gurajada Venkata Apparao. Vijayawada: Vignana Sahiti Pub., 1968. 104p.

3. Folk Literature

19910 RAMARAJU, B. Folk tales of Andhra Pradesh. ND: Sterling, 1974. 111p.

19911 ______. Folklore of Andhra Pradesh. ND: NBT, 1978. 176p.

IV. KERALA AND LAKSHADWEEP/LACCADIVES: THE MALAYALAM-SPEAKING REGION OF SOUTHWEST SOUTH INDIA

A. Government and Politics since 1800

1. Malabar District under the Madras Presidency

19912 KURUP, K.K.N. The Ali Rajas of Cannanore. Trivandrum: College Book House, 1975. 132p.

19913 LOGAN, W. Malabar. Madras: Govt. Press, 1951. 3v. [1st pub. 1887]

19914 RAVINDRAN, T.K. Cornwallis system in Malabar. Calicut: Parasparasahayi Co-op. Printing & Pub. Works, 1969. 139p.

19915 ______. Malabar under Bombay Presidency; a study of the early British judicial system in Malabar, 1792-1802. Calicut: Mascot Press, 1969. 89p.

19916 ______. Towards a liberal policy; a study of the Munro system in Malabar. Calicut: Asoka Printing Press, 1969. 206p.

2. The Princely States of Travancore and Cochin up to 1949

19917 "C.P." by his contemporaries: being a commemoration volume issued on the occasion of the eighty-first birthday of Dr. C.P. Ramaswami Aiyar. Madras: Dr. C.P.'s 81st Birthday Celebration Cmtee., 1959. 315p.

19918 CHIDAMBARAM, S. With profound respects. Madras: Higginbothams, 1967. 153p. [on C.P. Ramaswami Aiyar, 1879-1966]

19919 DAY, F. The land of the Permauls; or Cochin; its past and its present. Madras: Gantz, 1863. 577p.

19920 DESAI, M.H. The epic of Travancore. Ahmedabad: Navajivan, 1937. 251p.

19921 ELENKATH, K.R. Dewan Nanoo Pillay: biography with his select writings and letters. Neyyoor: Dewan Nanoo Pillay Memorial Reading Room, 1974. 202p.

19922 GEORGE, K.C. Immortal Punnapra-Vayalar. ND: CPI, 1975. 171p.

19923 JEFFREY, R. The decline of Nayar dominance: society and politics in Travancore, 1847-1908. NY: Holmes & Meier, 1976. 376p.

19924 ______. The politics of "indirect rule:" types of relationship among rulers, ministers and residents in a "native state." In JComPolSt 13,3 (1975) 261-81.

19925 KARUNAKARAN NAIR, K. Genesis of the Travancore State Congress. In JKS 1,2/3 (1974) 327-44.

19926 KOSHY, M.J. Constitutionalism in Travancore and Cochin. Trivandrum: Kerala Hist. Soc., 1972. 215p.

19927 ______. Last days of monarchy in Kerala. Trivandrum: Kerala Hist. Soc., 1973. 302p.

19928 MOOSS, N.S. The Travancore Anchal. Kottayam: Vaidya Sarathy, 1973. 221p.

19929 RAMNATH AIYER, S. Brief sketch of Travancore, the model state of India; the country, its people, and its progress under the Maharajah. Trivandrum: Western Star Press, 1903. 242p.

19930 RAVINDRAN, T.K. Vaikkam satyagraha and Gandhi. Trichur: Sri Narayana Inst. of Social and Cultural Dev., 1975. 372p.

19931 Selections from the writings and speeches of Sachivottama Sir C.P. Ramaswami Aiyar, Dewan of Travancore. Trivandrum: Supt. Govt. Press, 1945. 2v. in 1.

19932 SOBHANAN, B. Cochin under subsidiary alliance. In JKS 4,2 (1977) 413-27.

19933 ______. Dewan Velu Tampi and the British. Trivandrum: Kerala Hist. Soc., 1978. 197p.

19934 YESUDAS, R.N. British policy in Travancore, 1805-1859. Trivandrum: Kerala Hist. Soc., 1977. 110p.

19935 ______. Colonel John Munro in Travancore. Trivandrum: Kerala Hist. Soc., 1977. 118p.

19936 ______. Colonel John Munro in Travancore. In JKS 4,2 (1977) 363-411.

3. The Nationalist Movement in Kerala

19937 The history of freedom movement in Kerala. Trivandrum: Govt. of Kerala, 1970-. v. 1 (1600-1885), 126p.; v. 2 (1885-1933), 522p. [to be 3 v.]

19938 JEFFREY, R. A sanctified label - "Congress" in Travancore politics, 1938-48. In D.A. Low, ed. Congress and the Raj. London: Heinemann, 1977, 435-72.

19939 KARUNAKARAN NAIR, K., ed. Who is who of freedom fighters in Kerala. Ernakulam: S.G.P., Govt. Press, 1975. 632p.

19940 KOSHY, M.J. Genesis of political consciousness in Kerala. Trivandrum: Kerala Hist. Soc., 1972. 210p.

19941 KURUP, K.K.N. The Kayyur riot: a terrorist episode in the nationalist movement in Kerala. Calicut: Sandhya Pub., 1978. 122p.

19942 KUSUMAN, K.K. The extremist movement in Kerala. Trivandrum: Kerala Hist. Soc., 1977. 104p.

19943 NAMBOODRIPAD, E.M.S. Kerala: yesterday, today and tomorrow. Calcutta: Natl. Book Agency, 1967. 251p.

19944 RAVINDRAN, T.K. Asan and social revolution in Kerala; a study of his assembly speeches. Trivandrum: Kerala Hist. Soc., 1972. 206p.

4. Politics of Post-Independence Kerala: Multipartism Based on Castes/Communities

a. the Travancore-Cochin Union, 1949-56, and the establishment of Kerala State, 1956

19945 NAMBOODRIPAD, E.M.S. The national question in Kerala. Bombay: PPH, 1952. 178p.

b. general studies of Kerala politics

19946 AHMED, BASHIRUDDIN. Communist and Congress prospects in Kerala. In AS 6,7 (1966) 389-99. [also in

Centre for the Study of Developing Societies. Party system and election studies. ND: Allied, 1967. 294p.]

19947 GIRI, V.V. Selected speeches and addresses of V.V. Giri, Governor of Kerala. Trivandrum: Govt. Press, 1963. 291p.

19948 ______. Speeches and addresses. Trivandrum: Govt. Press, 1965. 451p.

19949 JOHN, K.C. The melting pot: Kerala, 1950's-1970's. Trivandrum: Prasanthi Printers, 1975. 158p.

19950 KERALA. ADMIN. REORG. & ECONOMY CMTEE., 1965-67. Report. Trivandrum: Govt. Press, 1967. 238p.

19951 KERALA. CMSN. FOR ENQUIRY INTO THE SCALES OF PAY AND RELATED MATTERS. Report. Trivandrum: The Govt., 1969. 443p. [Chm., V.K. Velayudhan]

19952 LIETEN, G.K. Education, ideology, and politics in Kerala, 1957-59. In SocSci 6,2 (1977) 3-21.

19953 PRASANNAN, R., ed. Fourth Kerala Legislative Assembly: souvenir. Trivandrum: Secretariat of the Kerala Legislative Assembly, 1979. 540p. + 32 pl.

19954 RAMAKRISHNAN NAIR, R. Constitutional experiments in Kerala. Trivandrum: Kerala Academy of Political Science, 1964. 219p.

19955 ______. Social structure and political development in Kerala. Trivandrum: Kerala Academy of Political Science, 1976. 34p.

19956 SUKUMARAN NAYAR, V.K., ed. Kerala society and politics; a souvenir of the 31st Indian Political Science Conference held at Trivandrum in Dec. 1969. Trivandrum: the Conf., 1969. 82p.

19957 TURLACH, M. Kerala; politisch-soziale Struktur und Entwicklung eines indischen Bundeslandes. Wiesbaden: Harrassowitz, 1970. 386p. (SIAK, 26)

c. election studies

19958 BHAGAT, K.P. The Kerala mid-term election of 1960; the Communist Party's conquest of new positions. Bombay: Popular, 1962. 208p.

19959 GIDWANI, N.N. The 1965 mid-term election in Kerala. In PSR 4 (1965) 135-51.

19960 GOUGH, K. Kerala politics and the 1965 elections. In Intl. J. of Comp. Sociology 8 (1967) 55-88.

19961 HARDGRAVE, R.L., JR. Caste and the Kerala elections. In EW 17,16 (1965) 669-72.

19962 HARTMANN, H. Changing political behavior in Kerala. In EPW 3,1/2 (1968) 163-77.

19963 INDIA (REP.). ELECTION CMSN. Report on the general election to the Kerala Legislative Assembly, 1965. Delhi: 1965. 51p.

19964 JAYARAJ, D. Majority rule in Kerala: a study of five elections, 1957-1970. Trivandrum: Dept. of Politics, U. of Kerala, 1974. 38p.

19965 KRISHNA MURTHY, K.G. & G. LAKSHMANA RAO. Political preferences in Kerala; an electoral analysis of the Kerala general elections, 1957, 1960, 1965 & 1967. Delhi: Radha Krishna, 1968. 99p.

19966 PYLEE, M.V. & N.C. JOHN. The fourth general elections in Kerala. In PSR 6/7 (1967-68) 251-66.

19967 RAMAKRISHNAN NAIR, R. The verdict of the Kerala electorate in 1967. In Political Science Review 6,3/4 & 7,1/2 (1967/1968) 267-280.

19968 SHETH, BHANU. 1965 election in Kerala: an analysis. In Political Scientist 2,1 (1965) 53-63.

d. Kerala Communists and experiments in coalition

19969 AUSTIN, H. Anatomy of the Kerala coup. ND: PPH, 1959. 150p.

19970 FIC, V.M. Kerala: Yenan of India, rise of communist power, 1937-1969. Bombay: Nachiketa, 1970. 555p.

19971 GOPALAN, A.K. Kerala; past and present. London: Lawrence & Wishart, 1959. 128p.

19972 ______. In the cause of the people; reminiscences. Madras: Orient Longman, 1973. 294p.

19973 HARDGRAVE, R.L., JR. The Kerala Communists: contradictions of power. In P.R. Brass & M.F. Franda, eds. Radical politics in South Asia. Cambridge: MIT Press, 1973, 119-82.

19974 ______. The Marxist dilemma in Kerala: administration and/or struggle. In AS 10,11 (1970) 993-1003.

19975 HUNTER, T. Indian Communism and the Kerala experience of coalition government, 1967-69. In JComPolSt 10,1 (1972) 45-70.

19976 INDIAN CMSN. OF JURISTS, KERALA ENQUIRY CMTEE. Report. ND: 1960. 146p. [also in J. of the Intl. Cmsn. of Jurists 2 (1959-60) 139-214]

19977 JULLIEN, F. & E. SCHMEITS. Stratégies communistes au Kerala. In France-Asie/Asia 196 (1969) 59-82.

19978 LAKSHMANA RAO, G. & R. SEETALAKSHMI. Socio-economic support bases of communists in Kerala. In IJPS 29 (1968) 342-58.

19979 MALAVIYA, H.D. Kerala: a report to the nation. ND: People's Pub. House, 1959. 128p.

19980 MANKEKAR, D.R. The red riddle of Kerala. Bombay: Manaktalas, 1965. 178p.

19981 NOSSITER, T.J. Communist leadership in Kerala: the business of the many, the art of the few. In B.N. Pandey, ed. Leadership in South Asia. ND: Vikas, 1977, 461-83.

19982 PANIKKAR, C.V.K. What is happening in Kerala? Delhi: Revolutionary Socialist Party, 1957. 79p.

19983 SINGH, J. Communist rule in Kerala. ND: Diwan Chand Indian Info. Centre, 1959. 136p.

19984 SPIELMANN, K.F., JR. Regionalism, nationalism and revolution: a profile of communist tactics in Kerala. In Public Policy 15 (1966) 139-75.

19985 VARUGHESE, K.V. The United Front government in Kerala, 1967-1969: a study of the Marxist-led coalition. Madras: CLS, for CISRS, 1978. 247p. (Its Studies in Indian Marxism, 3)

5. Local Government and Politics

19986 GOUGH, K. Communist rural councillors in Kerala. In JAAS(L) 3 (1968) 181-202.

19987 ______. Village politics in Kerala. In EW 17,8&9 (1965) 363-72, 413-20.

19988 NEELAKANTAN NAIR, K. Growth and development of local bodies in Kerala. Bombay: All-India Inst. of Local Self-Govt., 1962. 102p.

19989 SUKUMARAN NAIR, K. Rural politics and government in Kerala. Trivandrum: Kerala Academy of Political Science, 1976. 304p.

6. Lakshadweep/Laccadives: Indian Ocean Union Territory since 1956

19990 FORBES, A.D.W. Sources towards a history of the Laccadive Islands. In SA ns 2,1/2 (1979) 130-50.

19991 KURUP, K.K.N. Sequestration of Laccadive Islands. In JIH 50 (1972) 195-202. [British seizure from Arakkal Raj of Malabar, 1854-61, 1875]

19992 MUKUNDAN, T.K. Laksha Dweep: a hundred thousand islands. Gurgaon: Academic Press, 1979. 225p.

B. The Kerala Economy since 1800

1. General Economic History

19993 KUSUMAN, K.K. Slavery in Travancore. Trivandrum: Kerala Hist. Soc., 1973. 183p.

19994 SIVASWAMY, K.G. Famine, rationing and food policy in Cochin. Madras: Servindia Kerala Relief Centre, 1946. 112p.

2. Demography (1981 pop. 25,403,217)

19995 Demographic report of Kerala 1901-61, with addendum for 1971. Trivandrum: Demographic Res. Centre, Bureau of Econ. & Stat., 1976. 184p.

19996 GORE, N.Y. Growth of population of Kerala 1901-1961. In Population R. 12 (1968) 39-47.

19997 INDIA. CENSUS OF INDIA, 1961. Changing population of Kerala, 1901-61, by N.K. Namboodiri. ND: MPGOI, 1968. 123p. (v. 1, monograph 2)

19998 INDIA (REP.). CENSUS OF INDIA, 1971. A portrait of population; Kerala. Trivandrum: Dir. of Census Operations, 1971. 197p.

19999 KRISHNAN, T.N. Demographic transition in Kerala: facts and figures. In EPW 11,31-33 (1976) 1203-24.

20000 KURUP, R.S. & K.A. GEORGE, eds. Population growth in Kerala. Trivandrum: Govt. Press, 1965. 330p.

20001 KURUP, R.S. & P.S.G. NAIR, eds. Research needs on the population problems of Kerala. Trivandrum: Demographic Res. Centre, Bureau of Econ. & Stat., 1969. 120p.

3. Economic Development and Planning

20002 Inward remittances, Kerala: a survey. Bombay: Bombay Chamber of Commerce and Industry, 1978. 58p.

20003 KANNAN, K.P. Kuttunad development project: an economic evaluation. In IJAE 30,4 (1975) 49-73.

20004 KERALA. BUREAU OF ECON. & STAT. Basic statistics relating to Kerala economy, 1956-57 to 1973-74. Trivandrum: Bureau of Econ. & Stat., 1975. 72p.

20005 ______. State income of Kerala; 1960-61 to 1968-69. Trivandrum: 1972. 107p.

20006 NCAER. Techno-economic survey of Kerala. ND: 1962. 367p.

20007 NAYAR, P.K.B., ed. Development of Kerala: problems and promises. Trivandrum: Dept. of Sociology, U. of Kerala, 1972. 277p. (1970 seminar)

20008 OOMMEN, M.A. Kerala economy since independence. ND: Oxford & IBH, 1979. 187p.

20009 PILLAI, V.P.R. & P.G.K. PANIKKAR. Monetisation in Kerala. ND: Planning Cmsn., 1970. 176p.

20010 THORNER, A. Kerala: a strange case of poverty. In Puruṣārtha 3 (1977) 141-54.

20011 UNITED NATIONS. DEPT. OF ECON. & SOCIAL AFFAIRS. Poverty, unemployment, and development policy: a case study of selected issues with reference to Kerala. NY: 1975. 235p.

4. Agriculture in Kerala
a. general studies

20012 CHILDS, J.N. Acceptance of innovations in a South Indian fishing village. In J. of Family Welfare 21,3 (1975) 3-15.

20013 CHIRAYATH, J.T. A study on the cashew industry in Kerala. Trivandrum: Labour & Industrial Bureau, 1965. 114p.

20014 KERALA. AGRIC. CENSUS DIV. The third decennial world census of agriculture, 1970-71: report for Kerala State. Trivandrum: 1976. 2 v.

20015 KERALA. BUREAU OF ECON. & STAT. Findings of agricultural field experiments in Kerala, 1959-60 to 1974-75. Trivandrum: 1976. 96p.

20016 KERALA. PUBLIC WORKS DEPT. Water resources of Kerala. Trivandrum: The Dept., 1974. 143p.

20017 KERALA. STATE PLANNING BOARD. EVAL. DIV. Report on intensive agricultural district programme in Kerala. Trivandrum: 1971. 145p.

20018 KLAUSEN, A.M. Kerala fishermen and the Indo-Norwegian pilot project. Oslo: Universitets-forlaget, 1968. 201p.

20019 NOBLE, A. & V.A. NARAYANAN KUTTY. Economics of the indigenous fishing units at Cochin: a case study. Cochin: Central Marine Fisheries Res. Inst., 1978. 24p.

b. land tenure and reform

20020 ALEXANDER, K.C. Emerging farmer-labour relations in Kuttanad. In EPW 8,34 (1973) 1551-60.

20021 ______. Land reform legislation in Kerala since independence. In Behavioural Science & Community Dev. 8,1 (1974) 40-54.

20022 GANGADHARAN, A. Gangadharan on laws on land in Kerala. 5th ed. Ed. by N. Sugathan. Cochin: KVKM Press, 1977. 484p.

20023 MAYER, A.C. Land and society in Malabar. NY: OUP, 1952. 158p.

20024 MENCHER, J.P. Agrarian relations in two rice regions of Kerala. In EPW 13,6-7 (1978) 349-66.

20025 OOMMEN, M.A. Land reforms and socio-economic change in Kerala; an introductory study. Madras: CLS, for CISRS, 1971. 106p.

20026 PANIKKAR, K.N. Agrarian legislation and social classes: a case study of Malabar. In EPW 13,21 (1978) 880-88.

20027 RAO, T.V.S. Land legislation in Kerala State (1800-1960). In AV 12 (1970) 75-116.

20028 SARADAMONI, K. Agrestic slavery in Kerala in the nineteenth century. In IESHR 10,4 (1973) 371-85.

20029 ______. Abolition of slavery in Kerala in the nineteenth century. In JKS 2,2 (1975) 217-36.

20030 SHEA, T.W., JR. Travancore-Cochin land tenure reform. In EW 6,38 (1954) 1041-47.

20031 TURLACH, M. Das Agrarprogramm der Kommunisten in Kerala und seine Verwirklichung. In Friedrich-Ebert-Stiftung, Forschungsinstitut, Vierteljahresberichte 33 (1968) 247-70.

20032 VARGHESE, T.C. Agrarian change and economic consequences; land tenures in Kerala, 1850-1960. Foreword by K.N. Raj. Bombay: Allied Pub., 1970. 275p.

c. agrarian unrest and peasant movements

20033 ALEXANDER, K.C. Agrarian unrest in Kuṭṭanāḍ, Kerala. In Behavioural Science and Community Dev. 7,1 (1973) 1-16.

20034 ______. The nature and background of agrarian unrest in Kuṭṭanāḍ, Kerala. In JKS 2,2 (1975) 157-91.

20035 GOUGH, K. Peasant resistance and revolt in South India. In PA 41 (1968-69) 526-44.

20036 JOSE, A.V. The origin of trade unionism among the agricultural labourers in Kerala. In SocSci 5,12 (1977) 24-43.

20037 KARAT, PRAKASH. Organized struggle of Malabar peasantry, 1934-40. In SocSci 5,8 (1977) 3-17.

20038 ______. The peasant movement in Malabar, 1934-40. In SocSci 5,2 (1976) 30-44.

20039 NAYAR, P.K.B. A case study of two peasant organizations in Palghat district, Kerala. In JKS 4,2-3 (1977) 239-49.

20040 OOMMEN, T.K. Agrarian tension in a Kerala district: an analysis. In IJIR 7,2 (1971) 230-68.

20041 SACHIDANAND. Sarvodaya in a Communist state; a socio-economic study of gramdan movement in Kerala. Bombay: Popular, 1961. 206p.

5. Industry and Transportation in Kerala

20042 CHIRAYATH, J.T. A study on the plywood industry in Kerala. Trivandrum: Labour & Industrial Bureau, 1966. 157p.

20043 GANGADHARAN PILLAI, V. State enterprises in Kerala. Trivandrum: Kerala Academy of Political Science, 1970. 112p.

20044 IBRAHIM, R. The development of transport facilities in Kerala: a historical review. In SocSci 6,8 (1978) 34-48.

20045 INDIA (REP.). OFFICE OF THE DEV. COMMISSIONER, SMALL SCALE INDUSTRIES. Entrepreneurship development programme: Kerala. ND: 1980. 53p.

20046 KERALA. STATE PLANNING BOARD. Industries, industrial labour, and infrastructure. Trivandrum: 1975. 167p.

20047 KERALA. STATE PLANNING BOARD. EVAL. DIV. Industrial estates in Kerala: an evaluation study. Trivandrum: 1973. 66p.

20048 Mineral resources of Kerala and their utilisation: proceedings of the symposium.... Trivandrum: State Planning Board, 1976. 166p.

20049 NCAER. Regional transport survey of Kerala. ND: 1969. 416p.

20050 OOMMEN, M.A. Small industry in Indian economic growth; a case study of Kerala. Delhi: Research Pub. in Social Sciences, 1972. 193p.

6. Labor in the Kerala Economy

20051 KERALA. BUREAU OF ECON. & STAT. EMPLOYMENT DIV. Factbook on manpower. Trivandrum: 1966. 116p.

20052 RAMACHANDRA RAJ, G. Industrial conflict: a study of industrial conflict in the context of conflicts in the larger society. ND: Light & Life, 1980. 168p. [Study conducted in Kerala]

20053 RAMACHANDRAN NAIR, K. Industrial relations in Kerala. ND: Sterling, 1973. 437p.

20054 SUGATHAN, N. Law of industrial disputes in Kerala. Ernakulam: Bharatheeya Mazdoor Sangh, 1977. 200p.

C. Society and Social Change in Kerala since 1800

1. General Studies of Kerala's Elaborate Social Structure

20055 ALEXANDER, K.C. Social mobility in Kerala. Poona: DCPRI, 1968. 258p. (Its diss. ser., 29)

20056 ANANTHA KRISHNA IYER, L.K. Social history of Kerala. Madras: Book Centre Pub., 1968-70. 2 v.

20057 D'SOUZA, V.S. Sociological significance of systems of names with special reference to Kerala. In SB 4 (1955) 28-44.

20058 HOUTART, F. & G. LEMERCINIER. Socio-religious movements in Kerala: a reaction to the capitalist mode of production. In SocSci 6,11 (1978) 3-35; 6,12 (1978) 25-43.

20059 KURIAN, G. Comments on the experiences of couples who married before the age of fourteen in Kerala State. In his The family in India: a regional view. The Hague: Mouton, 1974, 277-89.

20060 ______. Modern trends in mate selection and marriage with special reference to Kerala. In his The family in India: a regional view. The Hague: Mouton, 1974, 351-67.

20061 MATEER, S. Native life in Travancore. London: W.H. Allen & Co., 1883. 434p.

20062 MATHUR, P.R.G. Socio-economic changes among the weaker sections of the population of Kerala. In JKS 4,1 (1977) 137-75.

20063 NAIR, P.K.B. & G. NARAYANA PILLAI. Trivandrum City: report of a household survey. Trivandrum: Dept. of Sociology, U. of Kerala, 1975. 100p.

20064 RAO, M.S.A. Social change in Malabar. Bombay: Popular Book Depot, 1957. 228p.

20065 THULASEEDHARAN, K. Studies in traditional Kerala society. Trivandrum: College Book House, 1977. 150p.

20066 ______., ed. Conflict and culture: sociological essays. Trivandrum: College Book House, 1977. 91p.

2. Social Categories in Kerala
a. general studies, incl. kinship and marriage

20067 ANANTHA KRISHNA IYER, L.K. The Cochin tribes and castes. Madras: Higginbotham, for Govt. of Cochin, 1909-12. 2 v.

20068 ______. The Travancore tribes and castes. Trivandrum: Supt., Govt. Press, 1937-41. 3 v.

20069 GOUGH, K. Kinship and marriage in southwest India. In CIS ns 7 (1973) 104-34.

20070 ______. The modern disintegration of matrilineal descent groups. In D. Schneider & K. Gough, eds. Matrilineal kinship. Berkeley: UCalP, 1971, 631-52.

20071 JACOB, L. Profiles of women in Kerala. In Vina Mazumdar, ed. Symbols of power.... Bombay: Allied, 1979, 226-45.

20072 KERALA. BACKWARD CLASSES RESERVATION CMSN., 1970. Report. Trivandrum: Govt. Press, 1971. 2 v. in 1. [Chm., Nettur P. Damodaran]

20073 KERALA. BUREAU OF ECON. AND STAT. Report on the socio-economic survey on castes/communities, Kerala, 1968. Trivandrum: 1969. 579 + 62p. [chiefly tables]

20074 ______. Women in Kerala. Trivandrum: 1978. 85p.

20075 MENCHER, J.P. Growing up in South Malabar. In HO 22 (1963) 54-65.

20076 PANIKKAR, K.N. Land control, ideology and reform: a study of the changes in family organization and marriage system in Kerala. In IHR 4,1 (1977) 30-46.

20077 PUTHENKALAM, J. Family organization in the Southwest of India. In SB 15 (1966) 1-26.

20078 ______. Marriage and the family in Kerala, with special reference to matrilineal castes. Calgary: J. of Comp. Family Studies, 1977. 246p.

20079 RAMACHANDRA RAJ, G. Ideological conflict: an analysis of Nair-Catholic relations in Kerala. In SocAct 26,1 (1976) 8-26.

20080 SREEDHARA VARIAR, K. Marumakkathayam and allied systems of law in the Kerala State. Ernakulam: 1969. 412p.

b. Nāmbūdiri Brahmans (1% of Kerala's pop.)

20081 ABRAHAM, C.M. Nambuthiri Brahmins of Kerala. In Vikram (Arts) 5,4 (1960) 15-28.

20082 MATHUR, P.R.G. Caste council among the Namputiri Brahmans of Kerala. In EA 22 (1969) 207-24.

20083 MENCHER, J.P. & H. GOLDBERG. Kinship and marriage regulations among the Namboodiri Brahmans of Kerala. In Man 2,1 (1967) 87-106. [also in G. Kurian, ed. The family in India.... The Hague: Mouton, 1974, 291-316]

20084 ______. Namboodiri Brahmins: an analysis of a traditional elite in Kerala. In JAAS(L) 1,3 (1966) 183-96.

20085 ______. Social and economic change in India: the Namboodiri Brahmans. In American Philosophical Society Yearbook 1964. Philadelphia: 1965, 398-402.

c. the Nayars (16% of Kerala's pop.)
i. general studies

20086 ABRAHAM, C.M. Social change among the Nairs of Kerala. In JSR 8,2 (1965) 25-34.

20087 BALAKRISHNAN, V. An epoch in Kerala history: biography. Kottayam: Auroville Publishers, 1977. 67p. + 12pl. [Mannath Padmanabhan, 1878-1970, Nair Service Society worker]

20088 FULLER, C.J. The internal structure of the Nayar caste. In J. of Anthropological Res. 31,4 (1975) 283-312.

20089 ______. The Nayars today. Cambridge: CamUP, 1976. 173p.

20090 GOUGH, K. Cults of the dead among the Nayars. In M.B. Singer, ed. Traditional India: structure and change. Philadelphia: American Folklore Soc., 1959, 446-78. (J. of American Folklore, 71, 281)

20091 MENCHER, J.P. The Nayars of South Malabar. In M.F. Nimkoff, ed. Comparative family systems. Boston: Houghton Mifflin, 1965, 163-191.

20092 PANIKKAR, K.M. Some aspects of Nayar life. In JRAI 48 (1918) 254-93.

20093 RAMACHANDRA RAJ, G. Ideological conflict: an analysis of Nair - Catholic relations in Kerala. In SocSci 26,1 (1976) 8-26.

ii. kinship and marriage

20094 ABRAHAM, C.M. The custom of polyandry as practised in Travancore. In EA 12 (1958-59) 107-18.

20095 DUMONT, L. Les mariages Nayar comme faits indiens. In L'Homme 1 (1961) 11-36.

20096 GOUGH, K. Changing kinship usages in the setting of political and economic change among the Nayars of Malabar. In JRAI 82 (1952) 71-88.

20097 ______. A comparison of incest prohibitions and the rules of exogamy in three matrilineal groups of the Malabar coast. In Intl. Archives of Ethnography 46 (1952) 82-105.

20098 ______. Female initiation rites on the Malabar coast. In JRAI 85 (1955) 45-80.

20099 ______. A note on Nayar marriage. In Man 65 (1965) 8-11.

20100 ______. The Nayars and the definition of marriage. In JRAI 89,1 (1959) 23-34.

20101 MENCHER, J.P. Changing familial roles among south Malabar Nayars. In SWJA 18 (1962) 230-45.

20102 PETER, H.R.H. Prince of Greece and Denmark. The polyandry of the Thandons (Tiyas), Kammalans, and other artisan castes of Kerala. In his A study of polyandry. The Hague: Mouton, 1963, 159-239.

20103 RAMAN UNNI, K. Polyandry in Malabar. In SB 7 (1958) 62-79, 123-33.

20104 UNNITHAN, T.K.N. Contemporary Nayar family in Kerala. In G. Kurian, ed. The family in India: a regional view. The Hague: Mouton, 1974, 191-203.

d. the Ezhava/Ilavas: an "untouchable" caste group (22% of Kerala's pop.)

20105 AIYAPPAN, A. Iravas and culture change. Madras: Supt. Govt. Press, 1944. 204p. (Bull. of the Madras Govt. Museum, 1942)

20106 HARDGRAVE, R.L. The breast-cloth controversy: caste consciousness and social change in southern Travancore. In IESHR 5 (1968) 171-87.

20107 MATHUR, P.R.G. Caste councils of the Ilavas of Kerala. In JKS 4,2 (1977) 261-87.

20108 PULLAPILLY, C.K. The Izhavas of Kerala and their historic struggle for acceptance in the Hindu society. In JAAS(L) 11,1/2 (1976) 24-46.

20109 RAJENDRAN, G. The Ezhava community and Kerala politics. Trivandrum: Kerala Academy of Political Science, 1964. 82p.

20110 RAO, M.S.A. Sri Narayana Paripalana Movement, I & II. In his Social movements and social transformation. Delhi: Macmillan, 1979, 21-122.

20111 RAVINDRAN, T.K. Asan and social revolution in Kerala; a study of his assembly speeches. Trivandrum: Kerala Hist. Soc., 1972. 95p.

20112 TEMPLE ENTRY ENQUIRY CMTEE., TRIVANDRUM. Report. Trivandrum: Supt. Govt. Press, 1935. 413p.

20113 YESUDAS, R.N. A people's revolt in Travancore: a backward class movement for social freedom. Trivandrum: Kerala Historical Society, 1975. 281p.

e. Kerala Christians: the Syrian, Roman Catholic, and other communities (21% of Kerala's pop.)

20114 ALEXANDER, K.C. The problem of the neo-Christians of Kerala. In MI 47 (1967) 317-30.

20115 ANANTHA KRISHNA IYER, L.K. Anthropology of the Syrian Christians. Ernakulam: Cochin Govt. Press, 1926. 338p.

20116 FULLER, C.J. Kerala Christians and the caste system. In Man 11,1 (1976) 53-70.

20117 JOHN, P.J. The church of South India and the modernization of Kerala. In KJS 3,2 (1976) 209-27.

20118 KURIAN, G. The Indian family in transition; a case study of Kerala Syrian Christians. The Hague: Mouton, 1961. 147p.

20119 PLACID, Father. The Malabar Christians: a souvenir of the 19th century of the martyrdom of St. Thomas, 72-1972. Alleppey: Prakasam Pub., 1972. 75p.

20120 POTHAN, S.G. The Syrian Christians of Kerala. NY: Asia, 1963. 119p.

f. the Māppiḷḷas of Malabar and other Muslims (19% of Keṛala's pop.); the Moplah rebellions

20121 CHOUDHARY, S. Moplah uprising, 1921-23. Delhi: Agam Prakashan, 1977. 120p.

20122 DALE, S.F. Islamic society on the South Asian frontier: the Mappilas of Malabar 1498-1922. NY: OUP, 1980. 290p.

20123 ______. The Mappilla outbreaks: ideology and social conflict in nineteenth century Kerala. In JAS 35,1 (1975) 85-98.

20124 DHANAGARE, D.N. Agrarian conflict, religion, and politics: the Moplah rebellions of Malabar in the 19th and early 20th centuries. In P&P 74 (1977) 112-41.

20125 D'SOUZA, V.S. Kinship organization and marriage customs among the Moplahs on the southwest coast of India. In Imtiaz Ahmad, ed., Family, kinship and marriage among the Muslims in India. ND: Manohar, 1976, 141-68.

20126 ______. Social organization and marriage customs of the Moplahs on the Southwest coast of India. In Anthropos 54 (1959) 487-516.

20127 ______. Status groups among the Moplahs on the south-west coast of India. In Imtiaz Ahmad, ed. Caste and social stratification among the Muslims. ND: Manohar, 1973, 45-60.

20128 GOPALAN NAIR, C. The Moplah rebellion, 1921. Calicut: Norman Printing Bureau, 1923. 214p.

20129 HARDGRAVE, R.L. The Mappilla Rebellion, 1921: peasant revolt in Malabar. In MAS 11,1 (1977) 57-100.

20130 ______. Peasant mobilization in Malabar: the Mappilla rebellion, 1921. In R.I. Crane, ed. Aspects of political mobilization in South Asia. Syracuse: Maxwell School of Citizenship & Public Affairs, Syracuse U., 1976, 67-108. (Foreign & Comp. Studies, South Asian series, 1)

20131 HOLLAND-PRYOR, P. Mappillas or Moplahs. Calcutta: Supt., Govt. Printing, 1903. 62p. (caste handbooks for the Indian Army)

20132 MATHUR, P.R.G. The Mappila fisherfolk of Kerala: a study in inter-relationship between habitat, technology, economy, society, and culture. Trivandrum: Kerala Hist. Soc., 1977. 434p.

20133 SINDERBY, DONALD [pseud.] The jewel of Malabar, a story of the Moplah rebellion in India, 1921. London: Murray, 1927. 320p. [fiction]

20134 WOOD, C. Historical background of the Moplah Rebellion: outbreaks, 1836-1919. In SocSci 3,1 (1974) 5-34.

g. Muslim islanders of Lakshadweep

20135 DUBE, LEELA. Caste analogues among the Laccadive Muslims. In Imtiaz Ahmad, ed., Caste and social stratification among the Muslims. ND: Manohar, 1973, 195-234.

20136 ______. Matriliny and Islam: religion and society in the Laccadives. Delhi: Natl. Pub. House, 1969. 125p.

20137 FORBES, A.D.W. Studies in Indian Ocean Islam: caste and matriliny in the Laccadive Islands. In Religion 8,1 (1978) 15-39.

20138 ITTAMAN, K.P. Amini Islanders: social structure and change. 1st ed. ND: Abhinav, 1976. 284p.

20139 KUTTY, A.R. Marriage and kinship in an island society. Delhi: National Pub. House, 1972. 227p.

h. the Cochin Jews

20140 FISCHEL, W.J. The exploration of the Jewish antiquities of Cochin on the Malabar coast. In JAOS 87 (1967) 230-48.

20141 GURUKKAL, P.M. RAJAN. The ethnical dichromatism of the Jewry in Kerala: a new interpretation. In JKS 3,2 (1976) 195-201.

20142 MANDELBAUM, D.G. The Jewish way of life in Cochin. In Jewish Social Studies 1 (1939) 423-60.

20143 THANKAPPAN NAIR, P. Jews of Cennamangalam and Paṟavūr. In JKS 2,4 (1975) 479-510.

j. Adivasis (Tribals) of Kerala (1.25% of Kerala's pop.)

20144 AIYAPPAN, A. Social and physical anthropology of the Nayadis of Malabar. Madras: Govt. Press, 1937. 141p. (Bull. of the Madras Govt. Museum, 2,4)

20145 ALEXANDER, K.C. Changing religious beliefs and practices of the Pulayas of Kerala. In SocAct 18 (1968) 390-98.

20146 EHRENFELS, U.R. VON. Kadar of Cochin. Madras: U. of Madras, 1952. 319p.

20147 GUSINDE, M. Die Kadar in südwestlichen Indien. In Homo (Göttingen) 13 (1962) 26-37.

20148 HATCH, W.J. The land pirates of India: an account of the Kuraver, a remarkable tribe of hereditary criminals, their extraordinary skill as thieves, cattle-lifters and highwaymen, etc., and their manners and customs. London: Seeley Service & Co., 1928. 272p.

20149 LUIZ, A.A.D. Tribes of Kerala. ND: Bharatiya Adimjati Sevak Sangh, 1962. 257p.

20150 MATHUR, P.R.G. Transfer and alienation of tribal land and indebtedness in Kerala. In JKS 2,2 (1975) 193-215.

20151 ______. Tribal situation in Kerala. Trivandrum: Kerala Hist. Soc., 1977. 218p.

20152 NANDI, S.B. & C.R. RAJALAKSHMI & I. VERGHESE. Life and culture of the Mala Ulladan. Calcutta: AnthSI 1971. 94p.

3. Villages and Rural Society

20153 AIYAPPAN, A. Social revolution in a Kerala village; a study in culture change. Bombay: Asia, 1965. 183p.

20154 MATHEW, E.T. & P.R. GOPINATHAN NAIR. Socio-economic characteristics of emigrants and emigrant's households: a case study of two villages in Kerala. In EPW 13,28 (1978) 1141-53.

20155 PANIKKAR, K.K. Community development administration in Kerala. ND: S. Chand, 1974. 242p.

20156 UNNI, K. RAMAN. Toward comprehending Kerala: some social perspectives for planning settlements. In URPT 12,3/4 (1969) 163-173.

4. Cities and Urbanization

20157 ANSARI, J.H. A study of settlement pattern in Kerala. In URPT 12,3/4 (1969) 101-162.

20158 KERALA. TOWN PLANNING DEPT. Development plan for Cochin Region. Trivandrum: 1977-. v.1

20159 VINOD KUMAR, T.M. The urban threshold theory and its application to the Cochin urban complex. In URPT 14,4 (1971) 171-240.

5. Education in Kerala (69.2% literacy in 1981)

20160 AIKARA, J. Ideological orientation of student activism. Poona: Dastane Ramchandra, 1977. 133p.

20161 ARASARKADAVIL, D.J. The secondary school leaving examination in India; a case study of the validity of the examination in Kerala State. London: Asia, 1963. 203p.

20162 GOUGH, K. Literacy in Kerala. In J. Goody, ed. Literacy in traditional society. Cambridge: CamUP, 1968, 132-60.

20163 KERALA. CMSN. FOR RESERVATION OF SEATS IN EDUC. INSTITUTIONS. Report. Trivandrum: 1966. 142p.

20164 KERALA. LAWS, STATUTES. The Kerala University Act, 1957 (no. 14 of 1957). Trivandrum: Govt. Press, 1958. 20p.

20166 TRAVANCORE EDUC. REORG. CMTEE. Report. Trivandrum: Govt. Press, 1945. 140p.

20166 TRAVANCORE UNIV. CMTEE. Report. Trivandrum: Supt. Govt. Press, 1925. 466p. [discussion of possible establishment of a new university]

D. Religio-Philosophical Traditions of Modern Kerala

1. Hinduism

a. general studies

20167 AYROOKUZHIEL, A.N. ABRAHAM. A study of the religion of the Hindu people of Chirakkal (Kerala). In R&S 24,1 (1977) 5-54.

20168 KERALA. HIGH LEVEL CMTEE. FOR UNIFICATION OF LAWS RELATING TO HINDU RELIGIOUS INSTITUTIONS AND ENDOWMENTS. Report. Trivandrum: Govt. Press, 1966. 374p.

20169 MYLIUS, K. Durchführung eines grossen vedischen Somaopfers, Kerala 1975. In Ethnographische-Archälogische Zeitschrift 17,1 (1976) 111-26.

20170 NAIR, B.N. Toward a typological phenomenology of society and religion in Kerala. In JKS 4,1 (1977) 81-120.

20171 NAYAR, S.K. Ayyappa cult. In Annals of Oriental Res. 24,1 Malayalam Section (1972) 1-19.

b. Narayana Guru Swami (1840-1928): Ezhava Vedantin and social reformer [see also C. 2. d., above]

20172 NATARAJA GURU. An integrated science of the absolute: based on the "Darsana mala" (Garland of visions) by Narayana Guru. Tr. from Sanskrit by Nataraja Guru. Varkala: East West U. of Brahmavidya, 1977-. v.1-.

20173 ______. The word of the Guru; an outline of the life and teachings of the Guru Narayana. 2nd ed. Erankulam: Paico Pub. House, 1968. 442p.

20174 PARAMESWARAN, P. Narayana Guru, the prophet of renaissance. ND: Suruchi Sahitya, 1979. 179p.

20175 SAMUEL, V.T. One caste, one religion, one God: a study of Sree Narayana Guru. ND: Sterling, 1977. 220p.

20176 SANOO, M.K. Narayana Guru: a biography. Tr. by M. Ayyappath. Bombay: BVB, 1978. 237p.

2. Christianity (21% of Kerala's pop.): Indigenous and Missionary Churches [see also C. 2. e., above]

20177 ANDRÉ DE SAINTE MARIE, Father, ed. Dans l'Inde malabare; souvenirs et récits de nos missionnaires belges. Ypres: J. Tyberghein-Frayes, 1905. 247p.

20178 APREM, Mar. From relief to development: a profile of CASA. Kottayam: Jaffe Books, 1979. 261p. [on Church's Auxiliary for Social Action]

20179 ______. Mar Thoma Darmo: a biography. Cochin: Mar Sliwa Church, 1974. 214p.

20180 DALTON, E. The Baker family in India. Kottayam: C.M.S. Press, 1963. 78p.

20181 EDWIN, P.G. The first Protestant mission in Travancore. In JIH 52,1 (1974) 189-207.

20182 HOUTART, F. & G. LEMERCINIER. Church and development in Kerala. Bangalore: Theological Pub. of India, 1979. 355p.

20183 NIDHIRY, A.M. Father Nidhiry, 1842-1904; a history of his times. Kuravilangad: G.J. Nidhiry, 1971. 386p.

20184 THOMAS, M.M. Towards an evangelical social gospel: a new look at the reformation of Abraham Malpan. Madras: CLS, 1977. 39p.

20185 THOMAS, S. Behold a saint: the life and times of Parumala Mar Gregorios. ND: 1977. 49p.

20186 VERGHESE, H.G. K.E. Abraham, an apostle from modern India: a brief life story of Rev. Dr. K.E. Abraham. Kadambanad: Christian Literature Service of India, 1974. 129p.

3. Islam (18% of Kerala's pop.) [see also C. 2. f. above]

20187 MILLER, R.E. Mappila Muslims of Kerala: a study in Islamic trends. Madras: Orient Longman, 1976. 350p.

E. Media and the Arts in Modern Kerala

1. Journalism and the Press

20188 KOSHY, M.J. K.C. Mammen Mappilai: the man and his vision. Trivandrum: Kerala Hist. Soc., 1976. 673p.

20189 The press in Kerala. Trivandrum: Dept. of Public Relations, Kerala, 1977. 45p.

20190 SHREEDHARAN, G. A survey of Malayalam publishing. In IL 20,2 (1977) 89-96.

2. Modern Malayalam Literature
a. general studies

20191 [G. Sankara Kurup special number.] In Mahfil 8,1 (1972) 1-122.

20192 GEORGE, K.M. A.R. Rajaraja Varma. ND: Sahitya Akademi, 1979. 68p.

20193 ______. Malayalam. In K.R. Srinivasa Iyengar, ed. Indian literature since independence. ND: Sahitya Akademi, 1973, 140-68.

20194 ______. Western influence on Malayalam language and literature. Delhi: Sahitya Akademi, 1972. 287p.

20195 JOSEPH, C.A., ed. The Jnanapitha and Central Sahitya Akademi literary award winners of Kerala. In Malayalam Literary Survey 1,3/4 (1977) 27-40.

20196 Malayalam anthology, parts 1 & 2. Ed. by K.A. Panikar & Z.P. Thundy. In JSAL 15,1&2 (1980) 246, 294.

20197 SHREEDARAN, G. Malayalam poetry: a kaleidoscopic view. In IL 18,4 (1975) 12-26.

20198 THAKARAN, K.M. Malayalam: towards unconventionalism. In IL 19,1 (1976) 36-51.

b. modern Malayalam fiction

20199 ASHER, R.E. Three novelists of Kerala. In T.W. Clark, ed. The novel in India. Berkeley: UCalP, 1970, 205-34.

20200 CHANDU MENON, O. Crescent moon. Tr. by R. Leela Devi. ND: Pankaj, 1979. 195p. [tr. of Indulekha]

20201 ______. Indulekha: a Malayalam novel. Tr. by W. Dumergus. Madras: Addison, 1890. 304p.

20202 ITTIAVIRA, V. Social novels in Malayalam. Bangalore: CISRS, 1968. 75p.

20203 LEELADEVI, R. Influence of English on Malayalam novels. Trivandrum: College Book House, 1978. 200p.

20204 NAAYAR, S.G. Malayalam: the novel's pride of place. In IL 11,4 (1968) 53-59.

20205 SANKARA MENON, T.C. Chandu Menon. ND: Sahitya Akademi, 1974. 84p.

c. modern Malayalam poetry
i. Vallathol Narayana Menon (1878-1958): nationalist and poetic innovator

20206 HRDAYAKUMARI, B. Vallathol Narayana Menon. ND: Sahitya Akademi, 1974. 95p.

20207 NARAYANA MENON, VALLATHOL. Selected poems. Tr. by Ayyappa Panicker. Ed. by K.M. Tharakan. Trichur: Kerala Sahitya Akademi, 1978. 163p.

20208 SARMA, S., et al., eds. Vallathol: a centenary perspective. Trivandrum: Intl. Vallathol Birth Centenary Festival Cmtee., 1978. 126p.

20209 VARIAR, K.M.P., ed. Poetry and national awakening. Madras: Mahakavi Vallathol Birth Centenary Celebrations Cmtee., 1978. 148p.

ii. Kumaran Asan (1873-1924): Ezhava poet and social reformer

20210 GEORGE, K.M. Kumaran Asan. ND: Sahitya Akademi, 1972. 82p.

20211 GOVINDAN, M., ed. Poetry and renaissance: Kumaran Asan birth centenary volume. Madras: Sameeksha, 1974. 500p.

20212 KUMARAN ASAN. Selected poems of Kumaran Asan. Ed. by K. Ramachandran Nair. Trivandrum: U. of Kerala, 1975. 152p.

iii. Ulloor S. Paramesvara Iyer (1877-1949)

20213 GEORGE, K.M., ed. Mahakavi Ulloor: a centenary volume. Trivandrum: Mahakavi Ulloor Memorial Library & Research Inst., 1977. 172p.

20214 PARAMESWAR IYER, ULLOOR S. English essays and poems of Mahakavi Ulloor. Ed. by N. Viswanathan. Trivandrum: U. of Kerala, 1978. 304p.

20215 SUKUMAR AZHICODE. Mahakavi Ulloor. ND: Sahitya Akademi, 1979. 103p.

iv. G. Sankara Kurup (1901-)

20216 [G. Sankara Kurup special number.] In Mahfil 8,1 (1972) 1-122.

20217 SANKARA KURUP, G. Otakkuzhal and other poems. Tr. by V.V. Menon. Madras: 1966. 66p.

20218 ______. Selected poems of G. Sankara Kurup. Tr. by A.K. Ramanujan. Calcutta: Dialogue Calcutta, 1969. 16p.

3. Folk Literature

20219 CHOONDAL, CHUMMAR. Studies in folklore of Kerala. Trivandrum: College Book House, 1978. 86p. + 10 pl.

20220 JACOB, K. Folk tales of Kerala. ND: Sterling, 1972. 119p.

20221 KURUP, K.K.N. Aryan and Dravidian elements in Malabar folklore: a case study of Rāmavilliam Kalakam. Trivandrum: Kerala Historical Society, dist. College Book House, 1977. 67p.

20222 SHANTHA, K. Ballads of North Malabar. In Folklore (C) 17,3 (1975) 91-107.

V. KARNATAKA: THE KANNADA-SPEAKING NORTHWEST REGION OF SOUTH INDIA

A. General and Political Histories, 1799-

1. Mysore State under the Wadiyar Maharajas (1799-1831, 1881-1947) and under Direct British Rule (1831-1881)
a. general studies

20223 BELL, T.E. The Mysore reversion, "an exceptional case." 2nd ed. London: Trübner, 1966. 292p.

20224 ______. The rajah and principality of Mysore.... London: T. Richards, 1865. 56p.

20225 DUSHKIN, L. The Nonbrahman movement in princely Mysore. Diss., U. of Pennsylvania, 1974. 340p. [UM 74-22,833]

20226 GOPAL, M.H. The finances of Mysore State, 1799-1831. Madras: Orient Longmans, 1960. 267p.

20227 GUSTAFSON, D.R. Mysore 1881-1902: the making of a model state. Diss., U. of Wisconsin, 1969. 347p. [UM 69-9681]

20228 HETTNE, B. The political economy of indirect rule; Mysore 1881-1947. London: Curzon Press, 1978. 402p. (Scandinavian Inst. of Asian Studies, monograph 32)

20229 MANOR, J. Political change in an Indian state: Mysore, 1917-1955. ND: Manohar, 1977. 261p. (ANU monographs on South Asia, 2)

20230 ______. Princely Mysore before the storm: the state-level political system of India's model state, 1920-1936. In MAS 9,1 (1975) 31-58.

20231 RAO, M. SHAMA. Modern Mysore. Bangalore: Higginbothams, 1936. 2 v.

b. administrators: Princes, Diwans, and British Chief Commissioners

20232 BOWRING, L.B. Eastern experiences. 2nd ed. London: H.S. King, 1872. 475p. [Mysore & Coorg]

20233 ISMAIL, MIRZA MAHOMED. My public life: recollections and reflections of Sir Mirza Ismail. London: Allen & Unwin, 1954. 179p.

20234 ______. Speeches. Bangalore: Govt. Press, 1930-42. 4 v.

20235 JAYA CHAMARAJA WADIYAR BAHADUR, Maharaja of Mysore. Speeches, 1940-44. Mysore: Govt. Press, 1944. 255p.

20236 KANTIRAVA NARASIMHARAJA WADIYAR, Yuvaraja of Mysore. Speeches by His Highness Yuvaraja Sri Kantirava Narasimharaja Wadiyar Bahadur, G.C.I.E., Yuvaraja of Mysore, 1910-1939. Mysore: Govt. Branch Press, 1942. 557p.

20237 KNIGHT, L. British paramountcy and the education of the Mysore prince. In BPP 92,1 (1973) 37-57.

20238 KRISHNARAJA WADIYAR BAHADUR, Maharaja of Mysore. Speeches. Mysore: Govt. Press, 1934-40. 2 v.

20239 NARASIMHA MURTHY, N.K. Purniah. Bangalore: R. Purniah, 1976. 170p. [Biography of Purniah, 1732-1812, first dewan of the state of Mysore]

20240 RAMAKRISHNAN, R. & S. MALINI. The career and achievements of Dewan Purniah (1732-1812). In QRHS 16,2 (1976-77) 94-101.

20241 SESHADRI IYER, K. Papers of K. Seshadri Iyer, Dewan of Mysore, 1883-1901. Bangalore: Govt. of Karnataka, 1978. 253p.

20242 Sir Mirza M. Ismail; views and opinions on his retirement from the office of Dewan of Mysore. Bangalore: Bangalore Press, 1942. 172p.

20243 VENKATASUBBA SASTRI, K.N. The administration of Mysore under Sir Mark Cubbon (1834-1861). London: Allen & Unwin, 1932. 322p.

2. Coorg: A British Chief Commissioner's Province, 1834-1947; District of Karnataka, 1956-

20244 CONNOR, Lieut. Memoir of the Codugu survey, commonly written Koorg. Bangalore: Central Jail Press, 1870. 2 v., 137, 119p.

20245 MUTHANNA, I.M. A tiny model state of South India. Pollibetta, Coorg: "Tiny Spot", 1953. 362p.

20246 PLAYNE, S., comp. Province of Coorg. In his Southern India, its history, people, commerce, and industrial resources. London: Foreign & Colonial Compiling & Pub. Co., 1914-15, 427-58. [inventory of towns and plantations]

3. The Nationalist Movement in Karnataka

20247 GUBBANNAVAR, S. Political ideas of Hardekar Manjappa. Dharwar: Karnatak U., 1977. 222p.

20248 KRISHNA RAO, M.V. & G.S. HALAPPA. History of freedom movement in Karnataka. Bangalore: Govt. of Mysore, 1962-64. 2 v.

20249 MANOR, J. Gandhian politics and the challenge to princely authority in Mysore, 1936-47. In D.A. Low, ed. Congress and the Raj. London: Heinemann, 1977, 405-34.

20250 ______. The lesser leader amid political transformation: the Congress Party in Mysore State in 1941 and 1951. In W.H. Morris-Jones, ed. The making of politicians. London: Athlone Press, 1976, 140-55. (Commonwealth papers, 20)

4. Government and Politics after Independence: from Mysore State to United Karnataka

20251 BADA, C.R. The study of voting behaviour in Gulbarga District. Gulbarga: Inst. of Vichar Bharati Adhyayana Vedike, 1974. 34p.

20252 HALAPPA, G.S., ed. Studies in state administration. Dharwar: Karnatak U., 1963. 668p.

20253 KARNATAKA. PAY CMSN., 1976. Report. Bangalore: 1976. 611p. [Chm. A. Narayana Pai]

20254 MANOR, J. Kengal Hanumanthaiah in Mysore: the style and strategy of individual leadership in the integration of a region's politics. In SA 4 (1974) 21-38.

20255 ______. Structural changes in Karnatak politics. In EPW 12,44 (1977) 865-69.

20256 A summary of the salient points contained in the report of the Mysore Pay Commission, 1966-68. Bangalore: Govt. Press, 1969. 201p.

20257 THOTAPPA, K.B.Y. & R.T. JANGAM. General elections in Mysore state. In PSR 6/7 (1967-68) 325-48.

20258 VISWANATHAIAH, K.V. Public personnel administration: a study of its origin and growth in Mysore state up to 1967. In IJPA 20,1 (1974) 187-209.

5. Local Government and Politics

20259 FRITZ, D.A. The roles and relationship of local politicians and administrators in Mysore State, India. Diss., American U., 1973. 395p. [UM 73-28,759]

20260 KARNATAKA. CMSN. FOR REORG. OF DISTRICTS AND TALUKS IN KARNATAKA STATE. Report. Bangalore: The Commission, 1975. 187p. [M. Vasudeva Rao, one-man Cmsn.]

20261 KARNATAKA. MUNCIPAL FINANCE ENQUIRY CMTEE. Report. Bangalore: 1975. 681p. [Chm., M.M. Kharge]

20262 LAKSHMINARAYANA, H.D. Democracy in rural India: problems and process. ND: National, 1980. 128p. [Study of two panchayats in Mandya District]

20263 MYSORE. CMTEE. ON PANCHAYATI RAJ. Report, 1963. Bangalore: 1963. 212p.

20264 PARVATHAMMA, C. Elections and "traditional leadership" in a Mysore village. In EW 16,10 (1964) 475-81; 16,11 (1964) 511-18.

20265 SIEGEL, B. & A.R. BEALS. Pervasive factionalism. In AA 62 (1960) 394-417.

20266 VISWANATHAIAH, K.V. A study of report of the Committee on Panchayati raj in Mysore State, 1963. In QJLSGI 34,2 (1963) 137-60.

B. The Karnataka Economy since 1799

1. General Economic History

20267 CHOKSEY, R.D. Economic life in the Bombay Karnatak (1818-1939). Bombay: Asia, 1968. 299p.

20268 D'SOUZA, V.L. Economic development of the Mysore State. Bangalore: Bangalore Press, 1937. 49p.

2. Demography (1981 pop. 37,043,451)

20269 INDIA (REP.). CENSUS OF INDIA 1971. Portrait of population; Mysore. Mysore: Dir. of Census Operations, 1973. 214p.

20270 KALE, B.D. Population growth in Mysore State; regional variations. In JIER 3,1 (1968) 38-57.

20271 KALE, B.D. & T.B. JORAPUR. Demographic report of Mysore State, 1901-1961. Dharwar: Demographic Res. Centre, Inst. of Econ. Res., 1969. 265p.

20272 KOTESHWAR, R.K. A demographic study of a Malenad village in Mysore State: Kogilgeri. Dharwar: Demographic Res. Centre, Inst. of Econ. Res., 1968. 76p.

20273 LEARMONTH, A.T.A. & L.S. BHAT, eds. Mysore State. Bombay: Asia, 1961-62. 2 v. (Indian Stat. series, 13)

20274 PATIL, R.L. The sex ratio of population of Karnataka state (1901-1971). In JIER 11,1/2 (1976) 52-9.

20275 MYSORE. DIR. OF EVAL. & MANPOWER. Demographic and employment trends in Mysore State; a short review. Bangalore: 1969. 52p.

20276 SHIVAMURTHY, M. Regional disparities in population growth in Mysore State. In JIER 8,1-2 (1973) 54-66.

20277 SIVAMURTHY, M. Demography of Mansur. Dharwar: Karnatak U., 1974. 155p. [Study in Dharwar taluka]

20278 SRINIVASAN, K. & P.H. REDDY & K.N.M. RAJU. Changes over a generation in fertility levels and values in Karnataka: a comparison of salient findings from the Mysore population study (1951) and the Bangalore population study (1975). Bangalore: India Population Project, Karnataka, 1977. 61p.

20279 UNITED NATIONS. SECRETARIAT. The Mysore population study: report of a field survey carried out in selected areas of Mysore State, India; a cooperative project of the United Nations and the Government of India. NY: 1961. 444p.

3. Economic Development and Planning

20280 GAJARAJAN, C.S. Planned rehabilitation and economic change; a case study of Tungabhadra River Project Rehabilitation Colonies at H. B. Halli. Poona: GIPE, 1970. 169p. (Its mimeograph ser., 10)

20281 KARNATAKA. DIR. OF EVAL., MANPOWER, & PROJECT FORMULATION. PROJECT FORMULATION UNIT. Economic development of Bijapur District under drought prone areas programme with World Bank assistance. Bangalore: 1973. 346p. + 11 pl.

20282 KARNATAKA. PLANNING DEPT. Karnataka, 1972-1977. Bangalore: 1978. 295p. + 26 pl.

20283 METI, T.K. The economy of Karnataka: an analysis of development and planning. ND: Oxford & IBH, 1976. 80p.

20284 ______. Economy of scarcity areas; report of the economic survey of scarcity areas in Bijapur District with special reference to Bijapur Taluka. Dharwar: Karnatak U., 1966. 113p.

20285 ______., ed. Economic development and social change in Mysore State. Dharwar: Karnatak U., 1971. 554p.

20286 MYSORE. BUREAU OF ECON. & STAT. Economic development of Mysore, 1956-69. Bangalore: 1970. 292p.

20287 NANJUNDAPPA, D.M. Review of regional development: the economy of Karnataka: growth and potential. In SER 4,2 (1974) 105-28.

20288 NCAER. Techno-economic survey of Mysore. ND: 1965. 384p.

20289 PARAMAHAMSA, V.R.K. Growth centres in Raichur: an integrated area development plan for a district in Karnataka. Hyderabad: NICD, 1975. 416p.

20290 PUTTASWAMAIAH, K. Economic development of Karnataka: a treatise in continuity and change. ND: Oxford & IBH, 1980. 2 v., 1566p.

20291 ______. Indicators of development with reference to Mysore's economy. Bangalore: Dir. of Eval. & Manpower, 1972. 86p.

20292 RAO, V.K.R.V. Planning in perspective: policy choices in planning for Karnataka 1973-74 to 1988-89. Bombay: Allied, 1978. 119p.

20293 SITARAMIAH, V. M. Visvesvaraya. ND: PDMIB, 1971. 160p.

20294 SOMASEKHARA, N. Planning and development in Karnataka: targets, allocations, and perspectives. Mysore: Geetha Book House, 1978. 186p.

4. Finance, Taxation, and Banking

20295 KARNATAKA. DIR. OF EVAL. & MANPOWER. Report on the growth of development expenditure in Karnatak State. Bangalore: 1974. 95p.

20296 KHER, S.P. The finances of the Mysore State. Bombay: Popular, 1967. 265p.

20297 MYSORE. DEPT. OF CO-OPERATION. Co-operative movement in Mysore; important statistics, 1961-65. Bangalore: Mysore State Co-op. Union, 1967. 50p.

20298 ______. Co-operative movement in Mysore State: trend of progress; a brief narration. Bangalore: Mysore State Co-op. Union, 1967. 39p.

20299 NCAER. Incidence of taxation in Mysore State. ND: 1972. 57p.

20300 PEETHAMBARA RAO, B.T., ed. Resume of the cooperative movement in Mysore. Bangalore: Mysore State Co-op. Union, 1964. 130p.

20301 RAJAGOPALA RAO, N. Finances of municipalities in North Kanara District; a monograph study of local finance. Kumta: 1968. 104p.

20302 ______., ed. Urban co-operative banks: a study: seminar papers on urban banks in North Kanara District. Kumta: Dr. A.V. Baliga College of Commerce, 1978. 131p.

20303 SIMHA, S.L.N. Development banking in India, with special reference to a state level institution, Karnataka. Madras: Inst. for Financial Mgmt. & Res., Vora, 1976. 340p.

20304 SREEKANTARADHYA, B.S. Direct taxation of agriculture and resource mobilisation in Karnataka. In SER 5,1 (1975) 51-75.

5. Agriculture in Karnataka
a. general studies of agricultural development

20305 ADAMS, J. Regional patterns of development in Karnataka. In J. of Developing Areas 12,4 (1978) 439-48.

20306 DESAI, D.K. & S.B. TAMBAD. Farm finance by a commercial bank; a case study of the Syndicate Bank. Ahmedabad: Faculty for Mgmt. in Agri. & Co-op., Indian Inst. of Mgmt., 1973. 84p.

20307 EPSTEIN, T.S. Economic development and social change in South India. London: JK Pub., 1979. 353p. [1st pub. 1962]

20308 FOLKE, S. & I. JØRGENSEN & J. KJAER. An evaluation of the Danish Mysore project. An Indo-Danish agricultural-educational scheme; v. 1, general report. Copenhagen: Mellemfolkeligt Samvirke, D.B.K., 1969. 255p.

20309 GONDI, M.G. Development of agriculture in Karnataka, 1969-1973. Bangalore: Stat. Section, Dept. of Agri., 1973. 190p.

20310 KARNATAKA. DIR. OF EVAL. & MANPOWER. Report on land utilisation in Karnataka. Bangalore: Eval. Unit, Planning Dept., Govt. of Karnataka, 1975. 169p.

20311 ______. Report on the evaluation study of arecanut development programme. Bangalore: 1973. 182p.

20312 KARNATAKA. DIR. OF EVAL., MANPOWER & PROJECT FORMULATION. Dairy and dairy cattle development. Bangalore: 1975. 179p.

20313 ______. Project for the development of the off-shore and deep sea fishing off the Mysore coast. Bangalore: 1973. 160p.

20314 KARNATAKA. PLANNING DEPT. PROJECT FORMUALTION DIV. Small Farmers Development Agency, Bangalore District: supplementary project report, 1976-1979. Bangalore: 1976. 76p.

20315 KRISHNASWAMY, O.R. Co-operative democracy in action: an empirical study of democratic control and management in agricultural co-operative credit structure in a state in India. Bombay: Somaiya, 1976. 271p.

20316 MUTALIK DESAI, V.R. Agricultural development: a case study. Bombay: Popular, 1976. 156p.

20317 MYSORE. BUREAU OF ECON. & STAT. Bidar District; a survey of backward area. Bangalore: 1972. 69p.

20318 MYSORE. DEV., HOUSING, PANCHAYATRAJ, & CO-OP DEPT. Pilot Intensive Rural Employment Project (PIREP), Harihar. Bangalore: 1972. 42p.

20319 MYSORE. DIR. OF EVAL. & MANPOWER. Report on the Kharland reclamation schemes in North Kanara district of Mysore State. Bangalore: 1971. 90p. [reclamation of saltwater encroachment area]

20320 NAIB, V.P. The Land Army: an experiment in rural development. ND: Vikas, 1978. 156p.

20321 NANJUNDAPPA, D.M. Surplus rural manpower and economic development in Mysore; an evaluation report on rural manpower programme. Dharwar: Dept. of Econ., Karnatak U., 1971. 199p.

20322 NANJUNDAPPA, D.M. & M. BASAVANA GOUD. A note on rural economy of Raichur district: a scheme for agricultural estates. In JIER 3,2 (1968) 26-43.

20323 NYHOLM, K., et al. Socio-economic aspects of dairy development: report of the Bangalore milkshed area. In EPW 9,52 (1974) A127-A136.

20324 RAO, V.G. & P. MALYA. Agricultural finance by commercial banks. ND: Ashish, 1980. 220p.

20325 THINGALAYA, N.K. Marginal farmers and agricultural labourers in South Kanara District: an economic analysis. Manipal: Syndicate Bank, 1976. 111p.

20326 ______., ed. Studies in Kanara agriculture. Manipal: Econ. Res. Dept., Syndicate Bank, 1968. 51p.

b. agricultural technology and innovation, irrigation

20327 BHARGAVA, B.S. Minor irrigation development administration: a study in an Indian state. ND: Ashish, 1980. 128p.

20328 BISALIAH, S. & K.C. HIREMATH. Technical change in agricultural economy in Karnataka. In Southern Economist 18,13 (1979) 21-33.

20329 NCAER. Dry farming in Mysore State. ND: 1970. 156p.

20330 NADKARNI, M.V., et al. Impact of irrigation: studies of canal, well, and tank irrigation in Karnataka. Bombay: Himalaya Pub. House, 1979. 369p.

20331 PATTANSHETTI, C.C. Economics of lift irrigation using electric power in South Kanara District. Dharwar: Karnatak U., 1972. 223p.

20332 SINGH, J.P., et al. New seeds: adoption and yield. ND: Sterling, 1979. 362p.

c. land tenure and reform

20333 GEORGE, P.T. Land system and laws in Mysore State. In AV 12 (1970) 117-92.

20334 HILL, P. Comparative agrarian relations in Karnataka (S. India) and Hausaland (Northern Nigeria). In IESHR 16,3 (1979) 243-71.

20335 MISRA, R.P. & V.K. NATRAJ, eds. Land reforms in Mysore State: a seminar. Mysore: Inst. of Dev. Studies, U. of Mysore, 1972. 113p.

20336 MYSORE. CMTEE. FOR THE REVISION OF THE LAND REVENUE SYSTEM. Report. Bangalore: 1950. 472p.

20337 PARVATHAMMA, C. Landholding pattern and power relations in a Mysore village. In SB 17 (1968) 203-24.

20338 PATIL, N.P. Land tenure reforms in Mysore and ceiling on holdings. In IJAE 17 (1962) 169-74.

20339 RAJAN, M.A.S. The land reforms law in Karnataka: a descriptive account. Bangalore: Govt. of Karnataka, 1979. 50p.

20340 SHETTY, V.V. Consolidation of holdings in Mysore state. In IJAE 18 (1963) 46-54.

6. Industry in Karnataka

20341 BALAKRISHNA, R. Industrial development of Mysore. Bangalore: the author, 1940. 319p.

20342 KALE, B.D. A survey of handicrafts in South Mysore; a study of the economics of twelve crafts being pursued at certain important centres in eleven southern districts of Mysore State. Dharwar: Inst. of Econ. Res., 1963. 501p.

20343 KARENNAVAR, M.F. Industries of Bhadravati town. In DG 9,1 (1971) 1-16.

20344 LAKSHMAN, T.K. Cottage and small-scale industries in Mysore; a case study of their pattern and role in the context of a developing economy. Mysore: Rao & Raghavan, 1966. 390p.

20345 MAHAJAN, Y.S. Industrialisation of Karnatak; report of the industrial survey of Karnatak conducted by the Karnatak chamber of commerce, Hubli. Hubli: R.V. Sirur, 1950. 240p.

20346 MUNSHI, M.C. Location of industries in Mysore State. Calcutta: Indian Statistical Institute, 1962. 172p.

20347 Mysore industrial directory. Bangalore: Mysore Chamber of Commerce and Industry, 1971. 674p.

20348 NCAER. Industrial programmes for the fourth plan: Mysore. ND: 1969. 166p.

20349 ______. Small-scale industries of Mysore. ND: 1963. 215p.

20350 SOMASEKHARA, N. The efficacy of industrial estates in India, with particular reference to Mysore. Delhi: Vikas, 1975. 157p.

7. Labor and Trade Unions

20351 AZIZ, ABDUL. Industrial wage structure in Mysore State. Mysore: U. of Mysore, 1972. 164p.

20352 REINDORP, J. Leaders and leadership in the trade unions in Bangalore. Madras: CLS, 1971. 239p.

20353 SATYAPRIYA, V.S. Dimensions of agricultural labour in Karnataka. ND: Sterling, 1979. 165p.

20354 THOMAS, M.M. & H.F.J. DANIEL, eds. Human problems of industry in Bangalore. Bangalore: CISRS & St. Mark's Cathedral Industrial Team Service, 1964. 65p.

8. Transport and Communication

20355 HULLUR, S.I. & B.N. SINHA. Accessibility of roads in Mysore State. In NGJI 17,2-3 (1971) 77-89.

20356 KARNATAKA. PUBLIC WORKS DEPT. Road development in Karnataka State. 5th ed., rev. & enl. Bangalore: 1975. 124p. [1st ed. 1970]

20357 MYSORE. DEPT. OF PUBLICITY & INFO. Mysore ports. Bangalore: 1964. 99p.

20358 NCAER. Regional transport survey of Mysore State. ND: 1970. 570p.

20359 Traffic survey of Karwar, Honavar, and Coondapur ports. ND: NCAER, 1962. 276p.

20360 VISWANATHAIAH, K.V. Mysore State Road Transport Corporation - a case study. In IPSR 5,1 (1970-71) 23-44.

C. Society and Social Change

1. Social Categories, incl. Kinship and Marriage
a. general studies

20361 ANANTHA KRISHNA IYER, L.K. The Coorg tribes and castes. Madras: Gordon Press, 1948. 74p.

20362 ANANTHA KRISHNA IYER, L.K. & H.V. NANJUNDAYYA. The Mysore tribes and castes. Mysore: Mysore U., 1928-36. 4 v. + index, 2426p.

20363 CARSTAIRS, G.M. & R.L. KAPUR. The great universe of Kota: stress, change, and mental disorder in an Indian village. Berkeley: UCalP, 1976. 176p. [on Brahmans, Bants, and Mogers in S. Kanara Dist.]

20364 CLAUS, P.J. Determinants of household organization among tenants and landowners in the Bant caste. In CIS ns 9,1 (1975) 89-110.

20365 CONKLIN, G.H. Muslim family life and secularization in Dharwar, Karnataka. In Imtiaz Ahmad, ed. Family, kinship and marriage among the Muslims in India. ND: Manohar, 1976, 127-40.

20366 D'SOUZA, V.S. The Navayats of Kanara. Dharwar: Kannada Res. Inst., 1955. 224p. [a Muslim group]

20367 GOLDSTEIN, R.L. Indian women in transition: a Bangalore case study. Metuchen, NJ: Scarecrow Press, 1972. 172p.

20368 HARPER, J.W. Divarus of the Malnad: a study of kinship and land tenure in a paddy cultivating caste in South India. Seattle: UWashP, 1971. 180p.

20369 HAVANUR, L.G. Specifying the backward classes without a caste basis. Bangalore: T.V. Venkataswamy, 1965. 122p.

20370 HOLLAND, T.H. The Coorgs and the Yeruvas, an ethnological contrast. In JASBengal 10,3 (1901) 59-98.

20371 KAKADE, R.G. Depressed classes of South Kanara. Poona: Servants of Indian Soc., 1949. 151p.

20372 KARNATAKA. BACKWARD CLASSES CMSN. Report. Bangalore: 1975. 4v. in 5. [L.G. Havanur, Chm.]

20373 KUPPUSWAMY, B. Backward class movement in Karnataka. Banglaore: Bangalore U., 1978. 141p.

20374 LAKSHMINARAYANA, H.D. Dominant caste and power structure. In Behavioural Science & Community Dev. 4,2 (1970) 146-60.

20375 MYSORE. BACKWARD CLASSES CMTEE. Final report. Bangalore: Govt. Press, 1961. [Chm. R. Nagan Gowda]

20376 PALAKSHAPPA, T.C. The Siddhis of North Kanara. ND: Sterling, 1976. 110p.

20377 ______. Tibetans in India: a case study of Mundgod Tibetans. ND: Sterling, 1977. 119p.

20378 SARKAR, J. Occupational mobility among the Kumbars of Mysore city. In MI 53,1 (1973) 7-12.

20379 ULLRICH, H.E. Etiquette among women in Karnataka: forms of address in the village and family. In SocAct 25,3 (1975) 235-48.

b. kinship and marriage (not specific to one group)

20380 CHEKKI, D.A. Kalyan and Gokul: kinship and modernization in Northern Mysroe. In CAS 1 (1971) 1-15.

20381 ______. Modernization and kin network in a developing society: India. In Sociologus ns 23,1 (1973) 22-40.

20382 ______. Modernization and social change: the family and kin network in urban India. In George Kurian, ed. The family in India: a regional view. The Hague: Mouton, 1974, 205-231.

20383 CLAUS, P.J. Kinship organization of the Bant-Nadava caste complex. Ph.D. diss., Duke U., 1970. [UM 71-10, 437]

20384 CONKLIN, G.H. The household in urban India. In J. of Marriage and the Family 38,4 (1976) 771-79.

20385 D'SOUZA, V.S. The marriage customs of the Christians in South Canara (India). In AFS 31,1 (1972) 71-87.

20386 KARVE, I. Kinship terms and kinship uses of Karnatak. In BDCRI 10,1 (1950) 49-60.

20387 KULKARNI, M.G. Family patterns in Gokak taluka. In SB 9 (1960) 60-81.

20388 LAKSHMINARAYANA, H.D. Analysis of family patterns through a century. Poona: DCPRI, 1968. 168p.

20389 MCCORMACK, W.C. Sister's daughter's marriage in a Mysore village. In MI 38 (1958) 34-48.

20390 ROSS, A.D. The Hindu family in its urban setting. Toronto: U. of Toronto Press, 1967. 325p. [1st pub. 1961]

20391 SRINIVAS, M.N. Marriage and family in Mysore. Bombay: New Book Co., 1942. 218p.

20392 SILVA, S. & S.FUCHS. The marriage customs of the Christians in South Canara, India. In AFS 24,2 (1965) 1-52.

c. Gauḍa Sāraswat Brāhmaṇs of N. and S. Kanara districts

20393 CONLON, F.F. Caste by association: the Gauḍa Sārasvata Brāhmaṇa unification movement. In JAS 33,3 (1974) 351-366.

20394 ______. A caste in a changing world: the Chitrapur Saraswat Brahmans, 1700-1935. Berkeley: UCalP, 1977. 255p.

20395 DUTT, K.G. Chitrapur Saraswat retrospect, historical and sociological study. Bangalore: B.B. Power Press, 1955. 295p.

20396 KUDVA, V.N. History of the Dakshinatya Saraswats. Madras: Samyukta Gowda Saraswata Sabha, 1972. 367p.

20397 MAVINKURVE, B.S., ed. Portrait of a community. Chitrapur Saraswat census report. Comp. by Census Working Cmtee. of Kanara Saraswat Assoc. Bombay: Popular, 1972. 151p.

20398 MENEFEE, S.C. The Pais of Manipal. Bombay: Asia, 1969. 249p.

20399 WAGLE, N.K. The history and social organization of the Gauda Sarasvata Brahmanas of the West Coast of India. In JIH 48 (1970) 7-25, 295-333.

d. Vokkaligas (20%) and Lingayats/Vīraśaivas (13%): rival dominant groups of Karnataka

20400 BANERJEE, B. Marriage and kinship of the Gangadikara Vokkaligas of Mysore. 1st ed. Poona: DCPRI, 1966. 211p. (Its diss. ser. 27)

20401 CHEKKI, D.A. Mate selection, age at marriage, and propinquity among the Lingayats of India. In J. of Marriage & the Family 30 (1968) 707-11.

20402 ______. Some aspects of marriage among the Lingayats. In MI 48 (1968) 124-32.

20403 ISHWARAN, K. Lingayat kinship. In JAAS 1,2 (1966) 147-60.

20404 MCCORMACK, W. On Lingayat culture. In A.K. Ramanujan, Speaking of Siva. Baltimore: Penguin Books, 1973, 175-87.

20405 MANOR, J. The evolution of political arenas and units of social organization: the Lingayats and Okkaligas of Mysore. In M.N. Srinivas & S. Seshaiah & V.S. Parthasarathy, eds. Dimensions of social Change in India. Bombay: Allied, 1977, 69-87.

20406 PARVATHAMMA, C. Politics and religion: a study of historical interaction between socio-political relationships in a Mysore village. ND: Sterling, 1971. 276p.

20407 ______. Sociological essays on Veerasaivism. Bombay: Popular, 1972. 144p.

e. the Coorgs/Kodagus: the ruling warrior caste of Coorg

20408 EMENEAU, M.B. Kinship and marriage among the Coorgs. In his Collected papers. Annamalainagar: Annamalai U., 1967, 333-56. [1st pub. in JASBengal 4 (1938) 123-47]

20409 ______. Personal names of the Coorgs. In JAOS 96 (1976) 7-14.

20410 FORRESTER, D.B. Political culture of the Coorgs. In EPW 5,18 (1970) 748-51.

20411 GANAPATHY, B.D. Kodavas (Coorgs), their customs and culture. Mercara: Kodagu, 1967. 224p.

20412 HUSSAIN KHAN, C.G. Okka: the basic unit of Kodava social organization. In EA 30,1 (1977) 1-14.

20413 MUTHANNA, I.M. The Coorg memoirs (the story of the Kodavas); Muthanna speaks out. Mysore: Usha Press, 1971. 615p.

20414 SRINIVAS, M.N. Religion and society among the Coorgs of South India. Bombay: Asia, 1965. 269p. [1st pub. 1952]

f. scheduled castes of Karnataka, the Adi Karnatakas

20415 KADETOTAD, N.K. Caste hierarchy among the untouchables of Dharwar. In EA 19 (1966) 205-14.

20416 ______. Religion and society among the Harijans. Dharwar: Karnatak U., 1977. 149p.

20417 KHAN, MUMTAZ ALI. Place of economic schemes in the development of the scheduled castes: with special reference to Karnataka State. In R&S 21,3 (1974) 5-25.

20418 ______. Seven years of change: a study of some scheduled castes in Bangalore District. Madras: CLS, for CISRS, 1979. 232p. (Caste-class series, 2)

20419 MYSORE. DEPT. OF PLANNING, HOUSING, & SOCIAL WELFARE. The welfare of scheduled castes in Mysore State. Bangalore: 1962. 131p.

20420 RAMU, G.N. Migration, acculturation, and social mobility among the untouchable gold miners in South India: a case study. In HO 30,2 (1971) 170-78.

20421 WIEBE, P. D. & G.N. RAMY. Caste and religion in urban India: a case study. In CIS ns 9,1 (1975) 1-17.

20422 ______. Christian and Hindu Harijans: a study of the effects of Christian programs in India. In EA 28,3 (1975) 215-30.

g. Adivasis (tribals) of Karnataka

20423 LUIZ, A.A.D. Tribes of Mysore. Bangalore: G.S. Viswa, 1963. 192p.

20424 MORAB, S.G. The Soliga of Biligiri Rangana Hills. Calcutta: AnthSI, 1977. 121p. (Its memoirs, 45) [tribe in Mysore District]

2. Villages and Rural Society
a. village studies

20425 BEALS, A.R. Gopalpur, a south Indian village. NY: Holt, Rinehart and Winston, 1962. 99p.

20426 ______. Village life in South India: cultural design and environmental variation. Chicago: Aldine, 1974. 183p.

20427 BEALS, A.R. & B.J. SIEGEL. Divisiveness and social change; an anthropological approach. Stanford: Stanford U. Press, 1966. 185p.

20428 DESAI, M.N. Life and living in the rural Karnatak. Sirsi: Anand Pub., 1945. 409p.

20429 DESHPANDE, C.D. Market villages and periodic fairs of Bombay Karnatak. In IGJ 16,4 (1941) 327-339.

20430 EPSTEIN, T.S. Economic development and social change in south India. London: JK Pub., 1979. 353p. [Rpt. 1962 ed.]

20431 ______. South India: yesterday, today, and tomorrow; Mysore villages revisited. BY: Holmes & Meier, 1973. 273p.

20432 HANCHETT, S.L. Changing economic, social, and ritual relationships in a modern South Indian village. Ph.D. diss., Columbia U., 1971. 306p. [UM 71-17, 499]

20433 HARPER, E.B. Moneylending in the village economy of the Malnad. In EW 13,4/6 (1961) 169-77.

20434 ______. Two systems of economic exchange in village India. In AA 61 (1959) 760-78.

20435 ISHWARAN, K. A populistic community and modernization in India. Delhi: Vikas, 1978. 122p.

20436 ______. Shivapur: a South Indian village. London: Routledge & K. Paul, 1968. 205p.

20437 ______. Tradition and economy in village India. London: Routledge & K. Paul, 1966. 169p.

20438 MENEFEE, S.C. & A.G. MENEFEE. Communications in village India; a social experiment. Tiptur: Kalpataru College, 1964. 154p.

20439 PARVATHAMMA, C. Landholding patterns and power relations in a Mysore village. In SB 17 (1968) 203-24.

20440 ______. The logic and limits of tradition and economy in village India. In Indian J. of Social Res. 10,1 (1969) 55-70.

20441 RAMBOUSEK, W.H. Indian agriculture between isolation and integration; a theoretical review and an analysis of the economic and social geography of four villages of South India. Bern: P. Lang, 1978. 171p.

20442 A review symposium on M.N. Srinivas's The remembered village. In CIS ns 12,1 (1978) 1-152.

20443 SRINIVAS, M.N. The case of the potter and the priest. IN MI 39 (1959) 190-205.

20444 ______. A caste dispute among washermen of Mysore. In EA 7 (1954) 149-68.

20445 ______. The dominant caste in Rampura. In AA 61 (1959) 1-16.

20446 ______. The remembered village. Berkeley: UCalP, 1976. 356p. [Rampura]

20447 ______. The social structure of a Mysore village. In EW 3,1 (1951) 19-32. [Rpt. in his (ed.) India's villages. Calcutta: Dev. Dept., W. Bengal, 1955, 19-35.]

20448 ______. The social system of a Mysore village. In M. Marriott, ed. Village India. Chicago: UChiP, 1955, 1-35.

b. community development and rural social change

20449 FRITZ, D. Bureaucratic commitment in rural India: a psychological application. In AS 16,4 (1976) 338-54.

20450 ______. Community development and panchayat: raj leadership in Mysore. In IJPS 35,1 (1974) 60-74.

20451 KAMBLE, N.D. Rural growth and decline: a case study of selected villages. ND: Ashish, 1979. 143p.

20452 KARNATAKA. RURAL DEV. & COOP. DEPT. Rural development with social justice in Karnataka. Bangalore: 1975. 121p.

20453 PARVATHAMMA, C. Under the impact of directed change. ND: National, 1978. 154p.

20454 RAGHAVA RAO, D.V. Panchayats and rural development. ND: Ashish, 1980. 96p.

20455 RAJAPUROHIT, A.R. Business organization, caste and technical change in a fishing community. In AV 5,2 (1963) 112-32.

20456 VENKATARAYAPPA, K.N. Rural society and social change; a study of some villages in Mysore. Bombay: Popular, 1973. 264p.

3. Cities and Urbanization in Karnataka
a. general studies

20457 D'SOUZA, V.S. Inequality and integration in an industrial community. Simla: IIAS, 1977. 254p.

20458 KALE, B.D. Growth of towns in Mysore state. In JIER 2,2 (1967) 47-67.

20459 KATTI, A.P. & J.B. HASALKAR. History of rural in-migrants; a survey of the rural migration profiles, conducted in a high growth-rate area. Dharwar: Demographic Res. Centre, J.S.S. Inst. of Econ. Res., 1971. 91p.

20460 NCAER. Traffic survey of Karwar, Honavar, and Coondapur ports. ND: 1962. 276p.

20461 PRAKASA RAO, V.L.S. Towns of Mysore State. Bombay: Asia, 1964. 120p.

20462 SINHA, B.N. Sirsi: an urban study in application of research models. Dharwar: Karnatak U., 1970. 243p.

20463 VISHWANATH, M.S. Growth pattern and hierarchy of urban centres in Mysore. In IGJ 47,1/2 (1972) 1-11.

20464 WIEBE, P.D. & G.N. RAMU. Caste and religion in urban India: a case study. In CIS ns 9,1 (1975) 1-17.

b. Bangalore, capital of Karnataka (1981 pop. 2,913,537)

20465 Bangalore on the move [special issue]. In Civic Affairs 24,5 (1976) 1-159.

20466 CENTRAL ROAD RES. INST. Comprehensive traffic and transportation studies of Greater Bangalore. ND: Council of Scientific & Industrial Res., 1973. 297p.

20467 FAZLUL HASAN, M. Bangalore through the centuries. Bangalore: Hist. Pub., 1970. 254p.

20468 GIST, N.P. The ecology of Bangalore, India. In S.F. Fava, ed. Urbanism in world perspective. NY: T.Y. Crowell, 1968, 177-88.

20469 ______. Selective migration in south India. In SB 4 (1955) 147-60.

20470 KIDDER, R.L. Courts and conflict in an Indian city: a study in legal impact. In JComPolSt 11,2 (1973) 121-39.

20471 ______. Litigation as a strategy for personal mobility: the case of urban caste association leaders. In JAS 33,2 (1974) 177-192.

20472 MYSORE. BANGALORE METROPOLITAN PLANNING BOARD. The outline development plan for the Bangalore metropolitan region. Bangalore: Govt. Press, 1963. 128p.

20473 POTT, J. Old bungalows in Bangalore, South India. London: Pott, 1977. 72p.

20474 PRAKASA RAO, V.L.S. & V.K. TEWARI. The structure of an Indian metropolis: a study of Bangalore. ND: Allied, 1979. 448p.

20475 PUNEKAR, V.B. Assimilation: a study of north Indians in Bangalore. Bombay: Popular, 1974. 160p.

20476 RAMA RAO, S. Finances of Bangalore Municipal Corporation. Bombay: Allied, 1979. 119p.

20477 SINGH, R.L. Bangalore: an urban survey. Varanasi: Tara Pub., 1964. 165p.

20478 SURI, K.B. Impact of an expanding metropolis: Bangalore. In EPW 5,1 (1970) 16-20.

20479 VENKATARAYAPPA, K.N. Bangalore; a socio-ecological study. Bombay: U. of Bombay, 1957. 157p.

20480 WOODRUFF, G.M. Family migration into Bangalore. In EW 12,4/5/6 (1960) 163-72.

c. Mysore City, princely capital of Mysore (1971 pop. 355,685)

20481 Handbook of the City of Mysore. Mysore City: Wesleyan Mission Press, 1915. 158p.

20482 MAHADEV, P.D. People, space, and economy of an Indian city: an urban morphology of Mysore City. Mysore: Inst. of Dev. Studies, U. of Mysore, 1975. 193p.

20483 PARSONS, C.E. Mysore city. London: OUP, 1930. 208p.

20484 SWAMY, G.L. Mysore city. Mysore: G.L. Swamy, 1941. 100p.

20485 VENKATARAYAPPA, K.N. Slums; a study in urban problem. ND: Sterling, 1972. 105p.

d. Hubli and Dharwar, twin cities of NW Karnataka (1971 pop. 379,166)

20486 DHEKNEY, B.R. Hubli City: a study in urban economic life. Dharwar: Karnatak U., 1959. 281p.

20487 INST. OF ECON. RES., DHARWAR. DEMOGRAPHIC RES. CENTRE. Demographic survey of Dharwar: a survey conducted in Dharwar Town and 20 villages of Dharwar Taluka. Dharwar: 1968. 314p.

20488 KATTI, A.P. & R.K. KOTESHWAR. A district town resurveyed; a demographic resurvey of a district town: Dharwar (Mysore State), 1962-1969. Dharwar: Demographic Res. Centre, J.S.S. Inst. of Econ. Res., 1971. 89p.

e. Mangalore, port city of South Kanara District (1971 pop. 215,122)

20489 AGNES, M. Mangalore: a developing port on the west coast of Mysore. In Deccan Geographer 7,2 (1969) 146-153.

20490 HARIHARAN, K.V. The new Mangalore port: inauguration of the ninth major port.... In Indian Shipping 27, 2 (1975) 54-55.

20491 Mangalore: bustling centre of enterprise: diversified industries, distinctive culture. In Commerce (Suppl.) 133 (3419) (4 Dec 1976) 9-13.

20392 MYSORE. DEPT. OF PUBLICITY & INFO. Mysore ports. Bangalore: 1964. 99p.

20493 PANDITARADHYA, J.K. Our major ports: Mangalore - the new all-weather port. In Yojana 19,1 (1975) 54-55.

20494 NCAER. Traffic survey of Mangalore and Malpe ports. Bangalore: Public Works Dept., 1961. 125p.

20495 PEREIRA, A.B.M. Mangalore and environs. In JMGA 13,4 (1938) 373-394.

20496 VENN, T.W. Mangalore. Cochin: the author, 1945. 153p.

4. Social Problems and Social Welfare

20497 GODBOLE, N.H. Dr. N.H. Godbole: an autobiography and life sketch. Gadag: Navodaya Printers, 1979? 157p. + 34pl. [medical practitioner and social activist from Karnataka]

20498 INDIA (REP.). CENTRAL SOCIAL WELFARE BOARD. RES., EVALUATION, AND STAT, DIV. Directory of social welfare agencies in India, Karnataka. ND: 1980. 3v., 1463p.

20499 KHAN, MUMTAZ ALI. Sociological aspects of child development: a study of rural Karnataka. ND: Concept, 1980. 212p.

20500 MAHAPATRA, L.K. & H.M. MARULASIDDAIAH. The contours of social welfare: a survey of social welfare activities in Hubli-Dharwar Municipal Corporation area. Darwar: Karnatak U., 1974. 175p.

20501 MARULASIDDIAH, H.M. Old people of Makunti. Dharwar: 1962. 223p.

20502 PUTTE GOWDA, K. Social reforms in the princely state of Mysore (1900-1920). In J. of Hist. Studies 11 (1975) 39-47.

20503 THIMMIAH, G. & J.V.M. SHARMA. Socio-economic impact of drinking in Karnataka. Calcutta: Inst. of Social Studies, 1978. 59p.

5. Health Services and Family Planning

20504 BASKARA RAO, N. Family planning in India: a case study of Karnataka. ND: Vikas, 1977. 72p.

20505 BEALS, A.R. Strategies of resort to curers in South India. In C. Leslie, ed. Asian medical systems.... Berkeley: UCalP, 1976, 184-200.

20506 BHATIYA, S.L. Report on reorganization of medical education and health services in Mysore state. Bangalore: Govt. of Mysore, 1961. 393p.

20507 Family planning in Mysore state (proceedings of the seminar organised by the Demographic research centre of the Institute of economic research on 10th & 11th Jan., 1970). In JIER 5,1 (1970) 1-80.

20508 KALE, B.D. Family planning enquiry in Dharwar Taluka, Mysore State; a survey conducted in Dharwar town and twenty villages of Dharwar Taluka. Dharwar: Demographic Res. Centre, J.S.S. Inst. of Econ. Res., 1966. 195p.

20509 ______. Family planning enquiry in rural Shimoga, Mysore State; a survey conducted in a region currently experiencing a high rate of growth in population. Dharwar: Demographic Res. Centre, J.S.S. Inst. of Econ. Growth, 1966. 166p.

20510 ______. Family planning resurvey in Dharwar. Dharwar: Demographic Res. Centre, Inst. of Econ. Res., 1969? 129p.

20511 KARNATAKA. PLANNING DEPT. MANPOWER & EMPLOYMENT UNIT. An assessment of the medical and para-medical manpower in Karnataka, 1974-79. Bangalore: 1978. 38p.

20512 KATTI, A.P., ed. Seminar on Family Planning in Mysore State. Dharwar: Demographic Res. Centre, Inst. of Econ. Res., 1970. 204p.

20513 KRISHNA RAO, H., et al. The attitude of Muslim women towards family planning in Bangalore. In JIER 7,2 (1972) 1-22.

20514 March of Mysore in family planning programme. Bangalore: 1969. 79p.

20515 NICHTER, M. The language of illness in South Kanara (India). In Anthropos 74,1/2 (1979) 181-201.

20516 REDDY, P.H. & K.N.M. RAJU & J.M. SHAH. Family structure and desired number of children in rural Karnataka. In Asian Econ. R. 18,1 (1976) 19-35.

6. Education in Karnataka (1981 Literacy 38.41%)

20517 ALSE, A.J., ed. Adventure of ideas: story of Dr. T.M.A. Pai and his work. Manipal: Academy of General Educ., 1979. 67p. + 13pl.

20518 CHITRA, M.N. A student strike in Mysore - a sociological analysis. In J. Univ. Educ. 3 (1966) 149-61.

20519 FANEUFF, C.T. Population, education, and attitude change in the schools of Mysore. In J. DiBona, ed. The context of education in Indian development. Durham, NC: DUPCSSA, 1972, 146-52. (Its monograph & occ. papers series, 13)

20520 HALBAR, B.G. & T.N. MADAN. Caste and educational institutions in Mysore State. In JKU(SS) 3 (1967) 132-54.

20521 JAYARAM, N. Higher education as status stabilizer: students in Bangalore. In CIS ns 11,1 (1977) 169-91.

20522 JEVOOR, S.V. A history of education in Karnataka. Mysore: Mohana Prakashana, 1966. 212p.

20523 MADAN, T.N. & B.G. HALBAR. Caste and community in the private and public education of Mysore State. In S.H. Rudolph & Lloyd I. Rudolph, eds. Education and politics in India.... Cambridge: HUP, 1972, 121-147.

20524 MYSORE. EDUC. DEPT. Progress of education in Mysore State in the third five year plan period. Bangalore: 1967. 93p.

20525 MYSORE. CMTEE. FOR EDUC. REFORM. Report. Bangalore: Govt. Press, 1953. 500p.

20526 NATL. STAFF COLLEGE FOR EDUCATIONAL PLANNERS & ADMINISTRATORS. Educational administration in Karnataka: a survey report, 1977. ND: 1977? 92p.

20527 SHIVAKUMAR, C. Social behavior of students: a woman's college in Mysore. In EPW 10,22 (1975) 859-66.

20528 UNIV. OF AGRICULTURAL SCIENCES. The first ten years, 1965-1975. Bangalore: 1975? 455p.

20529 WOOD, G. Egalitarian and technocratic goals in educational growth: the view from Mysore. In CAS 5 (1974) 87-102.

20530 ______. National planning and public demand in Indian higher education: the case of Mysore. In Minerva 10 (1972) 83-106.

20531 ______. Planning and private initiative: the case of technical education in an Indian state. In J. Di Bona, ed. The context of education in Indian development. Durham, NC: DUPCSSA, 1972, 189-202. (Its monograph & occ. papers series, 13)

20532 ______. Planning university reform - an Indian case study. In Comp. Educ. R. 16,2 (1972) 267-80.

D. Religions of Modern Karnataka

1. Hinduism, incl. Vīraśaivism and Folk Religion

20533 BEALS, A.R. Conflict and interlocal festivals in a south Indian region. In E.B. Harper, ed. Aspects of Religion in South Asia. Seattle: UWashP, 1964, 99-114. [1st pub. in JAS 23 (1964) 99-114]

20534 BURNELL, A.C. Devil worship of Tuluvas from the papers of the late A.C. Burnell, ed. by Maj. R.C. Temple. In IA 23/26 (1894-97) passim.

20535 CLAUS, P.J. Mayndala: a legend and possession cult of Tulunad. In AFS 38,2 (1979) 95-130.

20536 ______. Possession, protection and punishment as attributes of the deities in a South Indian village. In MI 53 (1973) 231-42.

20537 ______. The Siri myth and ritual: a mass possession cult of South India. In Ethnology 14,1 (1975) 47-58.

20538 DESHPANDE, M.S. Sri Bhausaheb Maharaj: life-sketch and nama-yoga. Belgaum: Academy of Comp. Philosophy & Religion, 1978. 52p. [disciples of Nimbargi Maharaj, 1789-1884, Kannada saint]

20539 EPSTEIN, T.S. A sociological analysis of witch beliefs in a Mysore village. In EA 12 (1959) 234-51.

20540 GOSWAMI, B.B. & S.G. MORAH. Chamundesvari Temple in Mysore. Calcutta: AnthSI, 1975. 72p. (Its Memoirs, 35)

20541 GOWDRA, G.K. Ritual circles in a Mysore village. In SB 20,1 (1971) 24-38.

20542 HANCHETT, S.L. Festivals and social relations in a Mysore village: mechanics of two processions. In EPW 7,31/33 (1972) 1517-22.

20543 HARPER, E.B. A Hindu village pantheon. In SWJA 15 (1959) 227-34.

20544 ______. Hoylu: a belief relating justice and the supernatural. In AA 59 (1957) 801-16.

20545 ______. Shamanism in South India. In SWJA 13 (1957) 267-87.

20546 KRISHNASWAMY, S.Y., ed. The Saint of Sringeri in sacred India. Madras: Sringeri Jagadguru Sanatana Dharma Vidya Samiti, 1969. 436p.

20547 MCCORMACK, W.C. The forms of communication in Virasaiva religion. In M.B. Singer, ed. Traditional India: structure and change. Philadelphia: American Folklore Soc., 1957, 119-29.

20548 MAHADEVI, MATE. A guide to Lingayatism: a prose composition. Dharwar: Suyidhana Sugrantha Maale, 1973. 165p.

20549 NICHTER, M. The joga and maya of the Tuluva Buta. In EA 30,2 (1977) 139-56.

20550 PARVATHAMMA, C. A study of functional aspect of temple ceremonies. In EA 25,2 (1972) 123-133.

20551 SADASIVAIAH, H.M. A comparative study of two Virasaiva monasteries; a study in sociology of religion. Mysore: U. of Mysore, 1967. 303p.

20552 Sri Nimbargi Maharaj, his life and teaching. Belgaum: Academy of Comp. Philosophy & Religion, 1978. 46p. [Kannada saint, 1789-1884]

20553 SUBRAMANIAM, P.S. The call of Sringeri. Madras: Sri Abhinava Vidyathirtha Mahaswamigal Pattabisheka Silver Jubilee Celebrations Souvenir Cmtee., 1979. 328p.

20554 WALHOUSE, M.J. On the belief in bhutas - devil and ghost worship in western India. In JRAI 5 (1976) 408-23.

2. Christianity

20555 GIERTH, R. Christian life and work at the pastorate level and practical theology in South India: an inquiry based on 16 field studies of selected church of South India pastorates in Bangalore and the Kolar Gold Fields (Karnataka Central Diocese) and a survey of Indian publications on the field of practical theology. Madras: CLS, 1977. 396p.

20556 SHIRI, G. Karnataka Christians and politics. Madras: CLS for CISRS, 1978. 95p.

E. Kannada Literature of Modern Karnataka

1. General Studies

20557 DESAI, S.K. Literary magazines in Kannada. In IWT 3,4 (1969) 29-32.

20558 LUTZE, L. Srikrishna Alanahally: a literary self-portrait. In IAF 6,2 (1975) 180-189.

20559 MOKASHI-PUNEKAR, SHANKAR. Vinayak Krishna Gokak. Mysore: U. of Mysore, Inst. of Kannada St., 1974. 77p.

20560 NAYAK, G.H. Kannada. In K.R. Srinivasa Iyengar, ed. Indian literature since Independence. ND: Sahitya Akademi, 1973, 93-113.

20561 NAYAK, H.M. Kannada literature: a decade. Tr. by M. Rama Rao. Mysore: Rao & Raghavan, 1967. 97p.

20562 SESHAGIRI RAO, L.S. Trends in literary criticism in Kannada. In IL 20, 2 (1977) 78-84.

20563 SITARAMIAH, V. Panje Mangesha Rau. ND: Sahitya Akademi, 1978. 107p.

20564 SREEKANTHAIYA, T.N. Literary and spoken language in modern Kannada writing. In IL 6,2 (1963) 40-48.

2. Modern Kannada Fiction and Drama

20565 AMUR, G.S. Modern Kannada Drama. In IWT 5,1 (1971) 21-27.

20566 ANANTHA MURTHY, U.R. Samskara = A rite for a dead man. Tr. by A.K. Ramanujan. Delhi: OUP, 1976. 153p.

20567 KURTAKOTY, K.D. Modern Kannada short story: two significant writers. In IWT 2 (1968) 27-30.

20568 MOKASHI-PUNEKAR, S. The Kannada political novel. In CAS 6 (1975) 121-39.

20569 SESHAGIRI RAO, L.S., ed. Sixty years of Kannada prose. Bangalore: Kannada Sahitya Parishat, 1978. 68p.

20570 SITARAMIAH, V. Panje Mangesha Rau. ND: Sahitya Akademi, 1978. 107p.

3. Modern Kannada Poetry

20571 ADIGA, M. GOPALA KRISHNA. The song of the earth, and other poems. Tr. by A.K. Ramanujan, et al. Calcutta: Writers Workshop, 1968. 33p.

20572 BENDRE, D.R. D.R. Bendre's Four strings: selections from "Naku tanti," the anthology of Kannada poems. Tr. by K. Raghavendra Rao, V.D. Bendre, and K.S. Sharma. Dharwar: Kavyadhara Prakashana, 1974. 31p.

20573 GOKAK, V.K. Bendre: poet and seer. Bombay: Somaiya, 1970. 209p.

20574 MOORTHY RAO, A.N. B.M. Srikantayya. ND: Sahitya Akademi, 1974. 63p.

20575 PUTTAPPA, K. VENKATAPPA GOWDA. Kuvempu, his voice and vision: fifty poems tr. by Shyama. Mysore: Sri Kuvempu Vidyavardhaka Trust, 1978. 84p.

4. Folk Literature

20576 CHANDRAN, P.S. Folk tales of Karnataka. ND: Sterling, 1973. 119p.

20577 SINGH, T.G. Folk songs of Mysore. In Folklore(C) 4 (1963) 426-33.

20578 SUMITRA, L.G. The folklore of Karnataka. Collection, documentation and research work done so far: a critical survey. In JIMS 5,1 (1974) 8-18.

12

Middle India: Contrasts of Tradition and Modernity in an Area of Transition between North and South; Persistence of Tribal Cultures, Princely Conservatism and Urban Progress, 1818–

I. MIDDLE INDIA IN THE BRITISH PERIOD; 1818-1947: ADMINISTRATIVE DIVERSITY

A. General Studies and Accounts

20579 DOUGLAS, J. Glimpses of old Bombay and Western India. London: S. Low, Marston, 1900. 342p.

20580 FORREST, G.W. Selections from the travels and journals preserved in the Bombay secretariat. Bombay: Govt. Central Press, 1906. 361p.

20581 GUTHRIE, K.B. Life in Western India. London: Hurst & Blackett, 1881. 2 v.

20582 MALCOLM, J. A memoir of Central India, including Malwa and adjoining provinces.... ND: Sagar Pub., 1970. 2 v. [1st pub. 1832]

20583 ROUSSELET, L. India and its native princes; travels in Central India and in the Presidency of Bombay and Bengal. London: Chapman & Hall, 1876. 599p.

B. Princely States of Middle India

1. Princely States of Maharashtra (Integrated in 1948)

a. general studies

20584 BURKE, R.C., ed. Notes on the Sangli State. Kolhapur: Mission Press, 1909. 448p.

20585 CHOKSEY, R.D., ed. Malwan residency; Sawantvadi affairs, 1812-1819. Select documents from Ratnagiri collector's files, Peshwa Daftar. Poona: R.D. Choksey, 1956. 154p.

20586 COURTNEY, W. & J.W. AULD. Memoir on the Sawunt Waree State; [together with] Statistical report on the Portuguese settlements in India, by Capt. Kol. Bombay: 1855. 408p. (Selections from records of the Bombay Govt., 10)

20587 LIMAYE, P.M. Sangli State, 1910-1948: or, monograph on the rule of Captain His Highness Raja Shrimant Sir Chintamanrao Dhundirao alias Appasaheb Patwardhan, Raja of Sangli... Sangli: Limaye, 1955. 444p.

20588 RANADE, V.G. Life of His Highness Raja Shreemant Sir Raghunathrao S., alias Babasaheb Pandit Pant Sachiv, Raja of Bhor. Poona: V.G. Ranade, 1951. 386 + 126p.

20589 RANADE, V.G. & V.N. JOSHI. A short history of the Bhor State. Poona: R.K. Deshpande, 1930. 84p.

20590 WEST, E.W. Memoir of the States of the Southern Maratha country. Bombay: 1869. 452p. (Selections from records of the Bombay Govt., 113)

b. Kolhapur and its feudatories; the Non-Brahman movement [see also I. C. 2. d., below]

20591 COPLAND, I. The Maharaja of Kolhapur and the non-Brahman movement, 1902-1910. In MAS 7,2 (1973) 209-225.

20592 FRANKS, H.G. Story of Ichalkaranji. Poona: Scottish Mission Industries, 1929. 138p.

20593 GRAHAM, D.C., comp. Statistical report on the principality of Kolhapoor.... Bombay: 1854. 597p. (Selections from records of the Bombay Govt., 8)

20594 KAVLEKAR, K.K. Shri Shahu Maharaja of Kolhapur and his contribution to the Non-Brahmin movement. In J. of Shivaji U. 7,13 (1974) 73-88.

20595 KEER, D. Shahu Chhatrapati: a royal revolutionary. Bombay: Popular, 1976. 536p.

20596 LATTHE, A.B. Memoirs of H.H. Shri Shahu Chhatrapati - Maharaja of Kolhapur. Bombay: Times of India Press, 1924. 2 v.

20597 MALGONKAR, M. Chhatrapatis of Kolhapur. Bombay: Popular, 1971. 613p.

20598 MUDALIAR, C.Y. Die Kolhapur-Bewegung. Eine Sozialreformbewegung in Indien. In Saeculum 24,1/2 (1973) 154-66.

20599 ______. The Non-Brahmin movement in Kolhapur. In IESHR 15,1 (1978) 1-20.

20600 PAWAR, A.G., ed. Rajarshi Shahu Chhatrapati papers. Kolhapur: Shahu Research Inst., 1978-. v. 1, 1884-94, 391p.

20601 ROSENTHAL, D.B. From reformist princes to "co-operative kings"; pt. 1, Political change in pre-Independence Kolhapur. In EPW 8,20 (1973) 903-10.

20602 SABNIS, R.V. Notes on Kolhapur. Bombay: Times Press, 1928. 88p.

c. Satara, lapsed to British administration, 1849

20603 BASU, B.D. The story of Satara. Calcutta: Modern Review Office, 1922. 574p.

20604 CHOKSEY, R.D., comp. Raja Pratapsingh of Satara, 1818-1839; select documents from the Satara Residency papers, Peshwa Daftar, Poona, and the Elphinstone papers, India Office Library, London. Poona: Bharata Itihasa Samskodhaka Mandala, 1970. 226p.

20605 ______., comp. Raja Shahji of Satara, 1839-1848; select documents from the Satara Residency records, Peshwa Daftar, Poona. Poona: dist. Dastane Ramchandra, 1974. 192p.

20606 HUGHES, T.R. Memoir of the Satara territory. Bombay: Bombay Educ. Soc. Press, 1857. 268p. (Selections from records of the Bombay Govt., 41)

20607 PARASNIS, D.B. Satara; brief notes. Bombay: Tukaram Javaji, 1909. 64p.

20608 Satara - and British connection therewith. In CR 10 (1848) 437-95.

d. Nagpur, lapsed to British, 1853

20609 CENTRAL PROVINCES & BERAR. Collection of correspondence relating to the escape and subsequent adventures of Appa Sahib, ex-Rajah of Nagpur, 1818-1840. Nagpur: Govt. of the Central Provinces and Berar, 1939. 133p.

20610 JENKINS, R. Report on the territories of the Raja of Nagpur submitted to the Supreme Government of India. Calcutta: G.H. Huttmann, 1827. 357p.

20611 SINHA, R.M. Bhonslas of Nagpur: the last phase, 1818-1854. Delhi: S. Chand, 1967. 256p.

2. Princely States of Present-day Gujarat

a. general studies of Kathiawad and other states

20612 DEVADAS PILLAI, S. Rajahs and prajas: an Indian princely state, then and now. Bombay: Popular, 1976. 136p.

20613 DUMASIA, N.M. Jamnagar, a sketch of its ruler and its administration. Bombay: Dumasia, 1927. 261p. + 98 pl.

20614 Gondal's cherished treasures: an account of Shree Bhagvat Sinhjee golden jubilee celebrations. Gondal: Shree Bhagvat Sinhjee Golden Jubilee Cmtee., 1934. 215p. + 42 pl.

20615 HARILAL SAVAILAL. Samaldas Parmananddas. Bombay: B.H. Shinde, 1912. 300p.

20616 KINCAID, C.A. The land of "Ranji" and "Duleep." Edinburgh: Blackwood, 1931. 137p.

20617 MEHTA, M.S. A short biographical sketch of Namdar Shaikh Shree Jehangeermian Saheb of Mangrol (Kathiawar). n.p., n.d. 20p.

20618 Nawanagar State and its critics... Bombay: Times of India Press, 1929. 213p. [reply to criticisms from Indian States' People's Conf.]

20619 NIHAL SINGH. Shree Bhagvat Sinhjee, the maker of modern Gondal. Gondal: Golden Jubilee Cmtee., 1934. 380p.

20620 SHARPE, E. Thakore Sahib Shri Sir Daulat Singh of Limbdi, Kathiawar: a biography. London: Murray, 1931. 187p.

20621 SPODEK, H. Urban politics in the local kingdoms of India: a view from the princely capitals of Saurashtra under British rule. In MAS 7,2 (1973) 253-75.

20622 WESTERN INDIA STATES AGENCY. The ruling princes, chiefs and leading personages in the Western India States Agency. Rajkot: 1928. 442p.

20623 WILD, R. The biography of Colonel H.H. Shri Sir Ranjitsinhji Vibhaji, Maharaja Jamsaheb of Nawanagar. London: Rich and Cowan, 1934. 330p.

b. Baroda under the Gaikwads

20624 CHAVDA, V.K. Gaekwads and the British; a study of their problems, 1875-1920. Delhi: University Pub., 196-. 188p.

20625 COPLAND, I.F.S. The Baroda Crisis of 1873-77: a study in governmental rivalry. In MAS 2 (1968) 97-123.

20626 DESAI, G.H. Forty years in Baroda: being reminiscences of forty years' service in the Baroda State. Baroda: Pustakalaya Sahayak Sahakari Mandal, 1929. 226p.

20627 GENSE, J.H. & DADY RUSTOMJI BANAJI, eds. The Gaikwads of Baroda; English documents... Bombay: Taraporevala, 1936-45. 10 v.

20628 GUPTE, B.A., ed. Selections from the historical records of the hereditary minister of Baroda, consisting of letters from Bombay, Baroda, Poona and Satara governments. Calcutta: U. of Calcutta, 1922. 127p.

20629 MOULTON, E.C. British India and the Baroda crisis, 1874-75: a problem in princely state. In Canadian J. of History 3 (1968) 58-94.

20630 PANEMANGLOR, K.N. The viceregal visit to Baroda, 1926. Baroda: Panemanglor, 1927. 186p.

20631 RICE, S.P. Life of Sayaji Rao III, Maharaja of Baroda. London: OUP, 1931. 2 v.

20632 The rulers of Baroda. Bombay: Education Soc. Press, Byculla, 1879. 392p.

20633 SAYAJI RAO GAEKWAR III, Maharaja of Baroda. Speeches and addresses of H.H. Sayaji Rao III, 1877-1927. London: Macmillan, 1928. 519p.

3. Rajputana: Princely States of Present-day Rajasthan (Unified in 1949)

a. general studies

20634 ABDUL HAYE, CHOWDHRY. The Freedom Movement in Mewat and Dr. K.M. Ashraf. In H. Krüger, ed. Kunwar Mohammed Ashraf; an Indian scholar and revolutionary, 1903-1962. Delhi: PPH, 1966, 291-339.

20635 CHOUDHRY, P.S. Rajasthan between the two world wars, 1919-1939. Agra: Sri Ram Mehra, 1968. 248p.

20636 DARDA, R.S. From feudalism to democracy; a study in the growth of representative institutions in Rajasthan, 1908-1948. ND: S. Chand, 1971. 358p.

20637 FUTTEH SING, BAHADUR, Raja of Khetri. Autobiography of the chief of Khetree, [in Rajputana]. Calcutta: E.M. Lewis, 1869. 328p.

20638 HAYNES, E.S. Imperial impact on Rajputana: the case of Alwar, 1775-1850. In MAS 12,3 (1978) 419-53.

20639 LAXMAN SINGH. Political and constitutional development in the princely states of Rajasthan, 1920-49. ND: Jain Bros., 1970. 169p.

20640 MEHTA, Y.S. A study of some aspects of administration and reforms (Jaipur, Jodhpur, and Bikaner), 1901-1940. Jaipur: Chinmaya Prakashan, 1973. 200p.

20641 RUDOLPH, L.I. & S.H. RUDOLPH. Rajputana under British paramountcy: the failure of indirect rule. In J. of Modern History 38 (1966) 138-60.

20642 RUDOLPH, S.H. The princely states of Rajputana: ethic, authority and structure. In IJPS 24 (1963) 14-32

20643 SAXENA, K.S. The political movements and awakening in Rajasthan, 1857 to 1947. ND: S. Chand, 1971. 284p.

20644 VASHISHTHA, V.K. Rajputana Agency, 1832-1858: a study of British relations with the states of Rajputana during the period with special emphasis on the role of Rajputana Agency. Jaipur: Aalekh, 1978. 316p.

b. Mewar/Udaipur: the premier Rajput state

20645 PALIWAL, D.L. Mewar and the British, 1857-1921 A.D.; a history of the relations of the Mewar State with the British Government of India from 1857 to 1921 A.D. Jaipur: Bafna Prakashan, 1971. 304p.

20646 TIWARI, R.G. Historiography of Mewar: its sources, problems and difficulties. In PO 22 (1957) 12-36.

c. Marwar/Jodhpur

20647 SHARMA, PADMAJA. Maharaja Man Singh of Jodhpur and his times (1803-1843 A.D.) Agra: S.L. Agarwala, 1972. 304p.

20648 UPADHYAYA, N.M. The administration of Jodhpur State, 1800-1947 A.D. Jodhpur: Intl. Pub., 1973. 258p.

20649 VAN WART, R.B. The life of Lieut.-General H.H. Sir Pratap Singh. London: OUP, 1926. 237p.

20650 VYAS, R.P. Role of nobility in Marwar, 1800-1873 A.D. ND: Jain Bros, 1969. 266p.

d. Jaipur

20651 BATRA, H.C. The relations of Jaipur State with the East India Company, 1803-1858. Delhi: S. Chand, 1958. 204p.

20652 KAMAL, K.L. & R.W. STERN. Jaipur's freedom struggle and the bourgeois revolution. In JComPolSt 11,2 (1973) 231-50.

20653 Pictorial Jaipur directory, 1948-49: or, Silver-Jubilee book: His Highness of Jaipur and his twenty-five years rule. Jaipur: Silver-Jubilee Pub., 195-. 181p.

20654 RUDOLPH, S.H. & L.I. RUDOLPH, with MOHAN SINGH. A bureaucratic lineage in princely India: elite formation and conflict in a patrimonial system. In JAS 34,3 (1975 717-54.

20655 ______. Rajput adulthood; reflections on the Amar Singh diary. In Proc. of the American Academy of Arts & Sciences 105,2 (1976) 145-68.

20656 SHARMA, M.L. History of the Jaipur State. Jaipur: Rajasthan Inst. of Hist. Res., 1969. 286p.

e. Bikaner

20657 KARNI SINGH. The relations of the House of Bikaner with the central powers, 1465-1949. ND: Munshiram, 1974 432p.

20658 PANIKKAR, K.M. His Highness the Maharaja of Bikaner. London: OUP, 1937. 412p.

f. the Jat state of Bharatpur

20659 GUPTA, K.B.L. The evolution of administration of the former Bharatpur State, 1722-1947. Jaipur: Vidya Bhawan, 1969. 207p.

20660 PANDE, R. Bharatpur up to 1826; a social and political history of the Jats. Jaipur: Rama, 1970. 192p.

20661 SAHAI, JAWALA. History of Bhurtpore. Lahore: Tribune Press, 1896. 106p. [Bharatpur]

4. Princely States of Present-day Madhya Pradesh (Integrated in 1948, Unified in 1956)
a. general studies

20662 ABERIGH-MACKAY, G.R. Chiefs of Central India. Calcutta: Thacker, Spink, 1879. 458p.

20663 DHAR, S.N. The Indore State and its vicinity. Indore: Indian Science Congress, 23rd session, 1936. 104p.

20664 DICKINSON, J. Dhar not restored; in spite of the House of Commons and of public opinion. London: P.S. King, 1864. 110p.

20665 FORSTER, E.M. The hill of Devi. London: E. Arnold, 1953. 176p. [Dewas Sr.]

20666 GUPTA, S.K. Maharaja as I saw him: a brief history of Bastar, its people, and its royal family. Delhi: Ganpat Lal Sao 'Bilaspuri', 1965. 111p. [On Pravir Chandra Bhanjdeo Katatiya, Maharaja of Bastar, 1929-1966]

20667 LUARD, C.E. A bibliography of the literature dealing with the Central India Agency, to which is added a series of chronological tables. London: 1908. 118p.

20668 MALGONKAR, M. The Puars of Dewas Senior. Bombay: Orient Longmans, 1963. 332p.

20669 PHADKE, R.K. Lt. Col. His Highness Maharaja Sir Udaji Rao Puar...of Dhar; a life sketch. Dhar: 1940. 83p.

20670 Rulers, leading families, and officials in the states of Central India. 5th ed. Delhi: MPGOI, 1935. 168p. [issued irregularly]

b. Gwalior under the Scindia/Shinde family

20671 BROWN, M.H., ed. Gwalior today. Gwalior: Publicity Dept., Govt. of Gwalior, 1940. 250p. + 10 pl.

20672 BURWAY, M.W. Life of the Honorable Sir Dinkar Rao, Musheer-i-Khas Muntazim Bahadur, Prime Minister of Gwalior. Bombay: Tatva-Vivechaka Press, 1907. 255p.

20673 GUPTA, V.K. A handbook on Gwalior postal history and stamps, 1837-1950. Delhi: 1980. 218p.

20674 MADHO RAO SINDHIA, Maharaja of Gwalior, 1876-1925. His Highness the Maharaja Sindhia's Speeches. Ed. by Ramji Das Vaishya. Gwalior: 1915-24. 5 v. [Hindi or English]

20675 MANDELBAUM, D.G. Ceremony in Gwalior. In Pacific Spectator 2,3 (1948) 262-77.

c. the Muslim state of Bhopal and its Nawabs

20676 SULTAN JAHAN BEGAM, Nawab of Bhopal. An account of my life. Tr. by C.H. Payne & Abdus Samad Khan. London: Murray, 1910-27. 3 v., 919p.

20677 ______. Hayat-i-Shajehani; life of Her Highness the late Nawab Shahjehan Begum of Bhopal. Tr. by B. Ghosal. Bombay: Times Press, 1926. 301p.

20678 ______. Taj-ul-iqbal tarikh Bhopal; or, The history of Bhopal. Tr. by H.C. Barstow. Calcutta: Thacker, Spink, 1876. 240p.

20679 YADUVANSH, UMA. Administrative system of Bhopal under Nawab Sikandar Begum 1844-1868. In IsC 41 (1967) 205-32.

5. Princely States of Present-day Orissa (Integrated in 1949)

20680 COBDEN-RAMSAY, L.E.B. Feudatory states of Orissa. Calcutta: Bengal Secretariat Book Depot, 1910. 381p. (Bengal Dist. Gazetteers, 21)

20681 MAHTAB, H.K. Beginning of the end. Cuttack: Cuttack Students' Store, 1972. 316p. [1st ed. 1950, 203p.]

20682 ORISSA STATE'S PEOPLE'S CONF. ORISSA STATES ENQUIRY CMTEE. Report. Cuttack: Orissa Mission Press, 1939. 290p.

20683 RATH, R. The story of freedom movement in Orissa states. Cuttack: the author, 1964. 32p.

20684 Sucharu Devi, Maharani of Mayurbhanj: a biography. Calcutta: Writers Workshop, 1979. 55p. + 8 pl.

C. The British Raj in Middle India

1. Bombay Presidency (Parts of Karnataka, Maharashtra, Gujarat, and Sind): Government and Administration
a. reference and sources

20685 CHOKSEY, R.D. Twilight of the Maratha Raj, 1818: queries from Mr. Mountstuart Elphinstone...to the collectors in the Deccan and Political Agent, Satara. Poona: the author, 1976. 106p.

20686 ______, ed. Ratnagiri collectorate, 1821-29. Poona: R.D. Choksey, 1958. 221p.

20687 DOUGLAS, J. Bombay and Western India, series of state papers. London: S. Low Marston, 1893. 2 v.

20688 ELPHINSTONE, M. Selections from the minutes and other official writings of the Honourable Mountstuart Elphinstone, governor of Bombay. Ed. by G.W. Forrest. London: R. Bentley, 1884. 578p.

20689 KUNTE, B.G., ed. Maps of India, 1795-1935. Bombay: Maharashtra State Archives, 1979. 31p.

20690 Representative men of the Bombay Presidency; a collection of biographical sketches, with portraits of the princes, chiefs, philanthropists, statesmen and other leading residents of the Presidency. 2nd ed. Philadelphia: Hist. Pub. Co., 1900. 229p.

b. general studies of administration

20691 ABDUL ALI, A.F.M. Phases of early British administration in Bombay. In BPP 40 (1930) 18-26.

20692 Administrative reforms in the Bombay Presidency. In Q. J. of the Poona Sarvajanik Sabha 4 (1881) 1-56.

20693 CHAPLIN, W. A report exhibiting a view of the fiscal and judicial system of administration introduced into the conquered territory above the Ghauts under the authority of the Commissioner in the Dekhan. Bombay: Courier Press, 1824. 266p.

20694 COX, E.C. A short history of the Bombay presidency. Bombay: Thacker, 1887. 419p.

20695 CRAWFORD, A.T. Our troubles in Poona and the Deccan. Westminster: Archibald Constable & Co., 1897. 253p.

20696 ELPHINSTONE, M. Territories conquered from the Paishwa; a report. Delhi: Oriental Pub., 1973. 179p. [Rpt. 1838 ed.]

20697 GUPTA, A.K. Between a tory and a liberal: Bombay under Sir James Fergusson, 1880-85. Calcutta: K.P. Bagchi, 1978. 269p.

20698 HUNTER, W.W. Bombay, 1885-1890: a study in Indian administration. London: H. Frowde, 1892. 504p.

20699 RABITOY, N. Administrative modernization and the Bhats of British Gujarat, 1800-1820. In IESHR 11,1 (1974) 46-73.

20700 ______. Sovereignty, profits, and social change: the development of British administration in western India, 1800-1820. Ph.D. diss., U. of Pennsylvania, 1972. 439p. [UM 73-13,456]

c. British administrators

20701 CHOKSEY, R.D. Mountstuart Elphinstone: the Indian years, 1796-1827. Bombay: Popular, 1971. 465p.

20702 COLEBROOKE, T.E. Life of the Hon. Mountstuart Elphinstone. London: J. Murray, 1884. 2 v.

20703 COTTON, J.S. Mountstuart Elphinstone. Oxford: OUP, 1892. 222p. (Rulers of India, 14)

20704 Five years' administration of Sir James Fergusson. In Q. J. of Poona Sarvajanik Sabha 7 (1884) 44-66. [Governor of Bombay]

20705 FRERE, H.B.E. The speeches and addresses of Sir H.B.E. Frere, G.C.S.I., K.C.B., D.C.L. Comp. by Balkrishna Nilaji Pitale. Bombay: 1870. 570p. [Governor of Bombay]

20706 Sir John Malcolm. In CR 29 (1857) 157-206, 305-53.

20707 SYDENHAM, G.S.C. Speeches delivered by Lord Sydenham as governor of Bombay, 1908-1913. Comp. by M.G. Dongre. Kolhapur: Mission Press, 1913. 1 v.

d. law and the judiciary

20708 GUNTHORPE, E.J. Notes on criminal tribes residing in or frequenting the Bombay Presidency, Berar and the central provinces. Bombay: 1882. 111p.

20709 MAHARASHTRA. HIGH COURT OF JUDICATURE. High court at Bombay, 1862 to 1962. Bombay: Govt. Central Press, 1962. 169p.

20710 MULLA, D.F. Jurisdiction of courts in matters relating to the rights and powers of castes. Bombay: Caxton Printing Works, 1901. 85p.

20711 ROBINSON, F.B. Adaptation to colonial rule by the "wild tribes" of the Bombay Deccan, 1818-1880: from political competition to social banditry. Ph.D. diss, U. of Minnesota, 1978. 247p. [UM 78-13,450]

20712 STEELE, A.H. The law and customs of Hindoo castes within the Dekhun provinces subject to the presidency of Bombay, chiefly affecting civil suits. London: W.H. Allen, 1868. 460p.

20713 VACHHA, P.B. Famous judges, lawyers and cases of Bombay; a judicial history of Bombay during the British period. Bombay: N.M. Tripathi, 1962. 367p.

e. local government

20714 BARFIVALA, C.D. Directory of local self-government in India with special reference to Bombay Province. Bombay: Local Self-Govt. Inst., 1951. 1092p.

20715 DESAI, N.B. Report on the administrative survey of the Surat District. Bombay: ISAE, 1958. 336p.

20716 MASANI, R.P. Evolution of local self-government in Bombay. London: OUP, 1929. 421p.

20717 NAYAK, B.J. An analytical study of the Bombay Local Boards Act, 1923 (Act VI of 1923). In QJLSGI 28 (1957) 128-96, 369-414.

20718 THAKORE, J.M. Development of local self-government in Bombay and Saurashtra, with an appendix on principles of local self-government. Bombay: C.D. Barfivala, 1957. 158p.

2. Nationalism in Bombay Presidency [see also Chap. Six, III. C.]

a. the rise of regionalism and nationalism; Congress in Bombay (after 1885)

20719 BOMBAY. CMTEE. FOR A HISTORY OF THE FREEDOM MOVEMENT IN INDIA. Source material for a history of the Freedom Movement in India. Bombay: Govt. Central Press, 1957-78. [v. 1, 1818-85, 397p.; v. 2, 1885-1920, 1015p.; v. 3, pts. 1-7, Mahatma Gandhi, 1915-45, 3956p.; v. 4, Congress Activities, 1942-46, 212p.; v. 5, Non-cooperation movement in Sind, 1919-24; v. 6, Non-cooperation movement in Bombay City, 1919-24; v. 7, Corresp. & diary of G.S. Khaparde, 1897-34, 519p.; v. 8, pts. 1 & 2, Goa freedom struggle; after 1960, author is Govt. of Maharashtra]

20720 CHANDRA, S. The Indian League & the Western India Association. In IESHR 8,1 (1971) 73-98.

20721 DIGHE, V.G. The renaissance in Maharashtra: first phase (1818-1870). In JASBombay ns 36/37 (1961-62) 23-31.

20722 HAMBLY, G.R.G., ed. Mahratta nationalism before Tilak: two unpublished letters of Sir Richard Temple on the state of the Bombay Deccan, 1879. In Royal Central Asian Soc. J. 49 (1962) 144-60.

20723 JOHNSON, G. Chitpavan Brahmins and politics in Western India in the late nineteenth and early twentieth centuries. In E. Leach & S.N. Mukherjee, eds. Elites in South Asia. Cambridge: CamUP, 1970, 95-118.

20724 JOSHI, V.S. Vasudeo Balvant Phadke: first Indian rebel against British rule. Bombay: D.S. Marathe, 1959. 200p.

20725 KUMAR, RAVINDER. The new Brahmans of Maharashtra. In D.A. Low, ed. Soundings in modern South Asian history. Berkeley: UCalP, 1968, 95-130.

20726 MCDONALD, E.E. The growth of regional consciousness in Maharashtra. In IESHR 5 (1968) 223-43.

20727 MASSELOS, J.C. Power in the Bombay "Moholla", 1904-1915: an initial exploration into the world of the Indian urban Muslim. In SA 6 (1976) 75-95.

20728 ______. Towards nationalism: public institutions and urban politics in the nineteenth century. Bombay: Popular Prakashan, 1975. 332p.

20729 MEHROTRA, S.R. The Poona Sarvajanik Sabha: early phase (1879-1880). In IESHR 6 (1969) 293-321.

20730 NOORANI, A.G.A.M. Badruddin Tyabji. ND: PDMIB, 1969. 210p.

20731 PANSE, M.G. Regional individuality of Maharashtra. In QJHS 9,4 (1969-70) 219-29.

20732 ROY CHOWDHURY, B. Madame Cama: a short life-sketch. ND: PPH, 1977. 34p.

20733 SHETH, P.N. Political awakening in Surat (19th century). In JGRS 27,1 (1965) 40-51.

20734 TELANG, K.T. Selected writings and speeches. Bombay: K.R. Mitra, 1916. v. 1, 310p.

20735 ______. Telang's Legislative Council speeches with Sir Raymond West's essay on his life. Ed. by D.W. Pilgamker. Bombay: Indian Printing Press, 1895. 98p.

20736 TUCKER, R.P. Hindu traditionalism and nationalist ideologies in nineteenth century Maharashtra. In MAS 10,3 (1976) 321-48.

20737 ______. Ranade and the roots of Indian nationalism. Bombay: Popular, 1977. 352p.

20738 TYABJI, H.B. Badruddin Tyabji: a biography. Bombay: Thacker, 1952. 410p.

b. Bal Gangadhar Tilak (1856-1920): the Shivaji and Ganapati festivals and mass nationalism

20739 CASHMAN, R.I. The myth of the Lokamanya: Tilak and mass politics in Maharashtra. Berkeley: UCalP, 1975. 246p.

20740 ______. The political recruitment of God Ganapati. In IESHR 7 (1970) 347-73.

20741 GOKHALE, J.B. The "Mahratta" and nationalism in Maharashtra. In IPSR 9,1 (1975) 1-26.

20742 KHOBREKAR, V.G. Shivaji memorials: the British attitude (A.D. 1885-1926): source material from Bombay archives. Bombay: Govt. Central Press, 1974. 154p.

20743 MCDONALD, E.E. & C.M. STARK. English education, nationalist politics and elite groups in Maharashtra, 1885-1915. Berkeley: Center for South & Southeast Asia Studies, 1969. 83p. (Its occ. papers, 5)

20744 SAMARTH, A. Shivaji and the Indian national movement; saga of a living legend. Bombay: Somaiya, 1975. 160p.

c. post-Tilak nationalism: Gandhian non-cooperation and participation in constitutional reform

20745 DESAI, MAHADEV. The story of Bardoli. Ahmedabad: Navajivan, 1929. 363p.

20746 GILLION, K. Gujarat in 1919. In Ravinder Kumar, ed. Essays on Gandhian politics. Oxford: OUP, 1971,

126-45.

20747 GOPALASWAMI, K. Gandhi and Bombay. Bombay: Gandhi Smarak Nidhi & BVB, 1969. 566p.

20748 JAYAKAR, M.R. The story of my life. Bombay: Asia, 1958-59. 2 v., 627, 724p.

20749 KULKARNI, V.B. M.R. Jayakar. ND: PDMIB, 1976. 336p.

20750 KUMAR, RAVINDER. From Swaraj to Purna Swaraj: nationalist politics in the city of Bombay, 1920-32. In D.A. Low, ed. Congress and the Raj. London: Heinemann, 1977, 77-109.

20751 ROTHERMUND, I. Gandhi and Maharashtra: nationalism and the provincial response. In SA 1 (1971) 56-73.

d. socio-political protest movements by Non-Brahmans and "untouchable" Mahars [see also I. B. 1. b., above]

20752 JOHNSON, G. Provincial politics and Indian nationalism: Bombay and the Indian national Congress, 1880-1915. Cambridge: CamUP, 1974. 207p.

20753 KEER, D. Mahatma Jotirao Phooley, father of our social revolution. Bombay: Popular, 1964. 288p.

20754 MATTHEW, A.V. Karmaveer Bhaurao Patil: an amazing story of leadership and organization in rural education. Satara: Rayat Shikshan Sanstha, 1957. 361p. + 16pl.

20755 OMVEDT, G. Cultural revolt in colonial society - the Non-Brahman Movement in Western India, 1873-1930. Bombay: Scientific Socialist Educ. Trust, 1976. 389p.

20756 ______. Jotirao Phule and the ideology of social revolution in India. In EPW 6,37 (1971) 1969-1979.

20757 ______. Non-Brahmans and Communists in Bombay. In EPW 8,16-17 (1973) 749-59, 800-05.

20758 ______. Non-Brahmans and nationalists in Poona. In EPW 9,6-8 (1974) 201-216.

20759 ______. The Satyashodhak Samaj and peasant agitation. In EPW 8,44 (1973) 1971-82.

20760 PATTERSON, M.L.P. A preliminary study of the Brahman versus non-Brahman conflict in Maharashtra. Philadelphia: U. of Pennsylvania, M.A. Thesis, 1952. 153p.

20761 RANADIVE, B.T. Towards an understanding of the Non-Brahman movement. [review of G. Omvedt's "Cultural revolt in colonial society - the Non-Brahman movement in Western India, 1873-1930] In SocSci 6,8 (1978) 77-94.

20762 ZELLIOT, E.M. Learning the use of political means: the Mahars of Maharastra. In R. Kothari, ed. Caste in Indian politics. Delhi: Orient Longmans, 1970, 29-69.

20763 ______. Mahar and Non-Brahman movements in Maharashtra. In IESHR 7,3 (1970) 397-415.

3. Central Provinces and Berar/Vidarbha (British Districts of Madhya Pradesh and Parts of Maharashtra)
a. history and administration under the Raj

10764 DURAND, H.M. Life of the Rt. Hon. Sir Alfred Comyn Lyall. London: Blackwood, 1913. 492p.

20765 FULLER, J.B. Review of the progress of the Central Provinces during the past 30 years, and of the present and past condition of the people. Nagpur: Supt. Govt. Printing, 1842. 59p.

20766 KHAN, M. ASHIQULLAH. History of British administrative system in India: the formation and administration of the Central Provinces, 1858-1870. Raipur: Library Pub., 1979. 170p.

20767 MILLER, J.O. The Central Provinces. In Royal Soc. of Arts, 60 (1912) 611-30.

20768 SIL, J.N. History of the Central Provinces & Berar. Calcutta: 1917. 193p.

b. nationalism and politics in C.P. and Berar

20769 BAKER, D.E.U. The changing leadership of the Congress in the Central Provinces and Berar, 1919-39. In D.A. Low, ed. Congress and the Raj. London: Heinemann, 1977, 225-58.

20770 ______. Changing political leadership in an Indian province: the Central Provinces and Berar, 1919-1939. Delhi: OUP, 1979. 233p.

20771 ______. The Rowlatt Satyagraha in the Central Provinces and Berar. In Ravinder Kumar, ed. Essays in Gandhian politics... Oxford: OUP, 1971, 93-125.

20772 DIXIT, N.G., ed. Dharmaveer Dr. B.S. Moonje commemoration volume: birth centenary celebration, 1872-1972. Nagpur: Centenary Celebration Cmtee., 1972? 143p.

20773 MADHYA PRADESH. The history of the freedom movement in Madhya Pradesh. Nagpur: Govt. Printing, 1956. 419p.

4. The British Raj in Orissa, 1803-1947
a. general histories

20774 DE, S.C. Orissa in 1871 & -72: compiled from the Utkal Dipika. Bhubaneswar: Orissa State Archives, Govt. of Orissa, 1964. 44p.

20775 PATRA, K.M. Orissa under the East India Company. ND: Munshiram, 1971. 351p.

20776 RAY, B.C. Foundations of British Orissa. Cuttack: New Student's Store, 1959. 383p.

20777 SAMAL, J.K. Orissa under the British Crown, 1858-1905. ND: S. Chand, 1977. 379p.

20778 STIRLING, A. Orissa: its geography, statistics, history, religion and antiquities. London: John Snow, 1846. 416p. [Including a History of the General Baptist Mission estab. in the Province, by J. Peggs]

b. formation of Orissa Province in 1936 from Oriya-speaking districts of Bihar, Central Provinces, and Madras Presidency

20779 DASH, S.C. Emergence of modern Orissa. In Iqbal Narain, ed. Seminar on state politics. Meerut: Meenakshi, 1967, 203-08.

20780 INDIA. ORISSA ADMIN. CMTEE. Report. Delhi: MPGOI, 1933. 45p. [Chm. J.A. Hubback]

20781 INDIA. ORISSA CMTEE. Report. Calcutta: 1932. 2 v. [Chm., S.P. O'Donnell]

20782 MAJUMDAR, S.N. Report on the general elections in Orissa - 1937. Cuttack: Orissa Govt. Press, 1937. 32p.

20783 MAZUMDAR, B.C. Orissa in the making. Calcutta: U. of Calcutta, 1925. 247p.

20784 The Oriya movement, being a demand for a united Orissa, by two Bachelors of Arts. Ganjam: Oriya Samaj, 1919. 349p.

20785 PATNAIK, L.M. Resurrected Orissa. Cuttack: the author, 1941. 395p.

10786 PATRA, S.C. Formation of the Province of Orissa: the success of the first linguistic movement in India. Calcutta: Punthi Pustak, 1979. 292p.

20787 RAY, B.C. British attempt to settle the boundary line between Bengal and Orissa. In JBRS 43,3/4 (1957) 285-90.

c. nationalism and constitutional change

20788 BIHAR & ORISSA. Memorandum for the Indian Statutory Commission on the working of the reforms in Bihar and Orissa. Patna: Supt., Govt. Printing, 1930. 439p.

20789 BIHAR & ORISSA. FRANCHISE CMTEE. Memorandum. Patna: 1932. 65p.

20790 DAS, GOPABANDHU. Gopabandhu in legislature; speeches of Pandit Gopabandhu Dash in Bihar and Orissa Legislative Council. Comp. by R.N. Mahapatra. Cuttack: Inst. of Social Science Res., 1973. 184p.

20791 DASH, G.N. Jagannatha and Oriya nationalism. In A. Eschmann, H. Kulke, G.C. Tripathi, eds. The cult of Jagannath and the regional tradition of Orissa. ND: Manohar, 1978, 359-74.

20792 DASH, S.C. Pandit Gopabandhu, a biography. Cuttack: Gopabandhu Sahitya Mandir, 1964. 191p.

20793 MAHANTY, S. Madhusudan Das. NB: NBT, 1972. 153p.

20794 MISHRA, P.K. The political history of Orissa, 1900-1936. ND: Oriental, 1979. 263p.

20795 Pandit Gopabandhu Das. Cuttack: Gopabandhu Birth Centenary Celebration Cmtee., 1976. 103p.

20796 PATRA, K.M. Orissa State Legislature and freedom struggle, 1912-47. ND: ICHR, 1979. 311p.

20797 RATH, R.N. Late Utkalmoni Pandit Gopabandhu Das. Cuttack: 1964. 27p.

II. ADIVASIS OF MIDDLE INDIA: TRIBAL PEOPLES OF THE HILLS AND FORESTS, SINCE 1818

A. Tribes of Western Middle India

1. The Bhils of the Malwa Plateau

20798 AHUJA, RAM. Family pattern among Bhils. In EA 19,1 (1966) 29-43.

20799 ______. Religion of the Bhils -- a sociological analysis. In SB 14 (1965) 21-33.

20800 CARSTAIRS, G.M. Bhil villages of western Udaipur: a study in resistance to social change. In M.N. Srinivas, ed. India's villages. Calcutta: Dev. Dept. W. Bengal, 1955, 62-69. [1st pub. in EW]

20801 ______. The Bhils of Kotra Bhomat. In EA 7 (1954) 169-81.

20802 BHURIYA, M. Folk-songs of the Bhils. Indore: Mahipal Pub., 1979. 174p.

20803 DOSHI, J.K. Social structure & cultural change in a Bhil village. Delhi: New Heights, 1974. 184p.

20804 DOSHI, S.L. Bhils: between societal self-awareness and cultural synthesis. ND: Sterling, 1971. 284p.

20805 ______. Processes of tribal unification and integration: a case study of the Bhils. Delhi: Concept, 1978. 170p.

20806 JUNGBLUT, L.J. Magic songs of the Bhils of Jhabua State, C.I. In Intl. Archiv für Ethnographie 43 (1943) 1-136.

20807 KARVE, I. The Bhils of West Khandesh: a social and economic survey. Bombay: Bombay Anth. Soc., 1961. 85p.

20808 KONRAD, P. Im Lande der Bhagoria Bhils. Kaldenkirchen: Steyler, 1962. 291p.

20809 KOPPERS, W. Die Bhil in Zentralindien. Horn: F. Berger, 1948. 353p.

20810 KOPPERS, W. & L.J. YUNGBLUT. Bowmen of Mid-India: a monograph of the Bhils of Jhabua, M.P., and adjoining territories. Wien: Maria Enzersdorf; Elisabeth Stiglmayr, 1976. 2 v. (Acta ethnologica et linguistica; Nr. 33: Series Indica, 6)

20811 LUARD, C.E. The jungle tribes of Malwa.... Lucknow: M.L. Bhargava, 1909. 104p. (The Ethnographical Survey of the Central India Agency, Monograph, 2)

20812 MCCURDY, D.W. A Bhil village of Rajasthan. Ph.D. diss., Cornell U., 1964. 501p. [UM 65-3132]

20813 NAIK, T.B. The Bhils: a study. Delhi: Bharatiya Adimjati Sevak Sangh, 1956. 367p.

20814 ______. Impact of education on the Bhils; cultural change in the tribal life of Madhya Pradesh. ND: Res. Programmes Cmtee., Planning Cmsn., 1969. 337p.

20815 NATH, Y.V.S. Bhils of Ratanmal; an analysis of the social structure of a western Indian community. Foreword by C. von Fürer-Haimendorf. Baroda: MSUB, 1960. 229p.

20816 SINGH, R.Y. Bhils of Malwa region - their habitat, economy and society. In NGJI 18,3/4 (1972) 223-39.

20817 VARMA, S.C. Tha Bhil kills. Delhi: Kunj Pub. House, 1978. 386p. [homicides in this tribe]

20818 VYAS, N.N. & R.S. MANN & N.D. CHAUDHARY, eds. Rajasthan Bhils. Udaipur: Manikyalal Verma Tribal Res. Training Inst., Social Welfare Dept., Govt. of Rajasthan, 1978. 143p.

2. Tribes of Maharashtra

20819 CHAPEKAR, L.N. Thakurs of the Sahyadri. 2nd ed. Bombay: U. of Bombay, 1966. 238p. [1st ed. 1960]

20820 GHURYE, G.S. The Mahadev Kolis. Bombay: Popular, 1957. 267p.

20821 JAMES, V. Marriage customs of Christian Son Kolis. In AFS 36,2 (1977) 131-48.

20822 KULKARNI, M.G. Problems of tribal development: a case study. Aurangabad: Parimal Prakashan, 1974. 344p.

20823 PARULEKAR, G. Adivasis revolt: the story of Warli peasants in struggle. Calcutta: National Book Agency, 1975. 188p.

20824 PUNEKAR, V.B. The Son Kolis of Bombay. Bombay: Popular, 1959. 307p.

20825 SANGAVE, V.A. Phanse-Paradhis of Kolhapur: rehabilitation of the tribe. In SB 16,1 (1967) 81-87; 16,2 (1967) 67-76.

20826 SAVE, K.J. The Warlis. Bombay: Padma, 1945. 280p.

20827 SONTHEIMER, G.D. The Dhangars; a nomadic pastoral community in a developing agricultural environment. In L.S. Leshnik & G.-D. Sontheimer, eds. Pastoralists and nomads in South Asia. Wiesbaden: Harrassowitz, 1975, 139-70.

20828 WELING, A.N. The Katkaris: a sociological study of an aboriginal tribe of the Bombay Presidency. Bombay: Bombay Book Depot, 1934. 156p.

3. Tribes of Gujarat

20829 FISCHER, E. & HAKU SHAH. Vetra ne khambha, memorials for the dead: wooden figures and memorial slabs of Chodhri, Gamit, and Vasava tribes, South Gujarat, India. Ahmedabad: Gujarat Vidyapith, 1973. 60p. + 14pl.

20830 GUJARAT. BUREAU OF ECON. & STAT. Study on scheduled tribes area, Gujarat State. Ahmedabad: 1967. 77p.

20831 KOPPAR, D.H. Tribal art of Dangs. Baroda: Dept. of Museums, 1971. 166p.

20832 MEHTA, B.H. A summary survey of the economic life of an aboriginal tribe of Gujarat (Chodhra). In JUB 2 (1934) 311-64.

20833 SHAH, GHANSHYAM. Socio-economic condition of Chodras: a restudy. Surat: Centre for Social Studies, 1977. 207p.

20834 SHAH, P.G. The Dublas of Gujarat. Delhi: Bharatiya Adimjati Sevak Sangh, 1958. 333p.

20835 ______. Naikas-Naikdas. In JGRS 21 (1959) 123-68; 228-63.

20836 ______. Tribal life in Gujarat; an analytical study of the cultural changes with special reference to the Dhanka tribe. Bombay: Gujarat Res. Soc., 1964. 344p.

20837 SINHA, S.P. Tribal Gujarat: some impressions. Gandhinagar: Govt. of Gujarat, 1967. 100p.

4. Tribes of Rajasthan

20838 BHADURI, M.B. The Korwas of the Udaipur State. In MI 17 (19707) 324-36.

20839 MISRA, P.K. The nomadic Gadulia Lohar of eastern Rajasthan. Calcutta: AnthSI, 1977. 218p. (Its Memoirs, 41)

20840 RAJASTHAN. DEMOGRAPHIC & EVALUATION CELL. Tribal attitude towards family planning, Rajasthan. Jaipur: 1975. 79p.

20841 ROOP SINGH. Labels and tribal identity in S. Rajasthan. In EA 27,4 (1974) 325-35.

20842 RUHELA, S. The Gaduliya Lohars of Rajasthan; a study in the sociology of nomadism. ND: Impex India, 1968. 296p. [English and Hindi]

B. Tribes of Central Middle India

1. General Studies

20843 AURORA, G.S. Tribe-caste-class encounters; some aspects of folk-urban relations in Alirajpur Tehsil. Hyderabad: Admin. Staff College of India, 1972. 293p. [Bhilalas in Jhabua Dist., M.P.]

20844 BAGCHI, D. Alirajpur - a study in urban-tribal relationship. In DG 8,1/2 (1970) 129-40. [Jhabua Dist., M.P.]

20845 BHAGVAT, DURGA. The folk songs of Central India. In AFS 35,2 (1976) 43-80.

20846 DUBE, B.K. & F. BAHADUR. A study of the tribal people and tribal areas of Madhya Pradesh. In BTRI 6,2 (1966) 1-177.

20847 DUBE, S.C. The Kamar. Lucknow: Universal Pub., 1951. 216p.

20848 ELWIN, V. Specimens of the oral literature of Middle India. London: OUP, 1944-54. 5 v. [v. 1. Folk tales of Mahakoshal; v. 2. Folk-songs of the Maikal hills (with Shamrao Hivale); v. 3. Folk-songs of Chhattisgarh (with comment by W.G. Archer); v. 4. Myths of Middle India; v. 5. Tribal myths of Orissa]

20849 FORSYTH, J. Highlands of central India: notes on their forests and wild tribes, natural history & sports. London: Chapman & Hall, 1919. 398p. [1st pub. 1889]

20850 FUCHS, S. The children of Hari: a study of the Nimar Balahis. Vienna: V. Herold, 1950. 463p.

20851 GRIGSON, W.V. Aboriginal problem in the Central Provinces and Berar. Nagpur: Supt. Govt. Printing, 1944. 510p.

20852 HAEKEL, J. Some aspects of the social life of the Bhilala in central India. In Ethnology 2 (1963) 190-206.

20853 HERMANNS, M. Die religiös-magische Weltanschauung der Primitivstamme Indiens. v. 1. Die Bhagoria Bhil. v. 2. Die Bhilala, Korku, Gond, Baiga. Wiesbaden: Franz Steiner, 1964, 1966. 2 v.

20854 JAISWAL, H.K. Demographic structure of tribal society. Meerut: Meenakshi, 1979. 168p.

20855 NAIK, T.B. The changing tribes of Madhya Pradesh. In BTRI 2,4 & 3,1 (1959) 1-126.

20856 ______. The tribes of Madhya Pradesh. Bhopal: Dept. of Tribal Welfare, Govt. of M.P., 1964. 78p.

20857 NCAER. Socio-economic survey of primitive tribes in Madhya Pradesh. ND: 1963. 206p.

20858 SAXENA, R.P. Tribal economy in central India. Calcutta: KLM, 1964. 312p.

20859 SINHA, S.C. Tribe-caste and tribe-peasant continua in Central India. In MI 45 (1965) 57-83.

20860 ______. State formation and Rajput myth in tribal central India. In MI 42,1 (1962) 35-80.

20861 STIGLMAYR, E. & F. FODERMAYR. The Barela-Bhilala & their songs of creation: musical analysis of the songs. Vienna: Engelbert Stiglmayr, 1970. 246p.

2. The Gond Group of Dravidian-speaking Tribes (1971 pop. 4,000,000+)

20862 BHADRA, R.K. Revitalization movements among the Gond of Madhya Pradesh. In EA 30,2 (1977) 131-37.

20863 BHAGVAT, DURGA. Dances and charms of the tribes of Central India. In AFS 31,1 (1972) 41-70.

20864 BURADKAR, M.P. Kinship among the Gonds. In NUJ 6 (1940) 147-80.

20865 ELWIN, V. I married a Gond. In MI 20 (1940) 228-55.

20866 ______. The kingdom of the young; abridged from The Muria and their ghotul. Bombay: OUP, 1968. 261p.

20867 ______. Leaves from the jungle: life in a Gond village. London: OUP, 1958. 193p. [1st pub. 1936]

20868 ______. Maria murder and suicide. Bombay: OUP, 1950. 259p.

20869 ______. The Muria and their ghotul. Bombay: OUP, 1947. 730p.

20870 ELWIN, V. & S. HIVALE, comp. & tr. Songs of the forest; the folk poetry of the Gonds. London: Allen & Unwin, 1935. 170p.

20871 FUCHS, S. The Gond and Bhumia of eastern Mandla. 2nd ed. Bombay: New Literature Pub. Co., 1968. 608p.

20872 GRIGSON, W.V. The Maria Gonds of Bastar. London: OUP, 1949. 427p.

20873 HERRENSCHMIDT, O. Le cycle de Lingal: essai d'étude textuelle de mythologies: les mythologies des tribus de langue gondi (Inde Centrale). Paris: École Pratiques des Hautes Études, 1966. 353p.

20874 INDRAJIT SINGH. The Gondwana and the Gonds. Lucknow: Universal Pub., 1944. 201p.

20875 JAY, E.J. A tribal village of middle India. Calcutta: AnthSI, 1970. 300p. (Its Memoirs, 21) [On the Hill Maria Gonds of Orcha, Bastar Dist., M.P.]

20876 JOSHI, M.M. Bastar, India's sleeping giant. ND: PPH, 1967. 156p.

20877 KADUSKAR, M.R. Bibliography on the Gonds. In BTRI 2,4 & 3,1 (1959) 99-108.

20878 NAIK, T.B., ed. The Abujhmarhias; socio-economic aspects of a little known culture. Chhindwara: Tribal Res. Inst., 1963. 167p.

20879 WILKINSON, T.S. Ghotul school of the Muria Gonds of Bastar: a case study of a village Ghotul. Bangalore: CISRS, 1961. 44p.

20880 YADAV, K.S. Changes in the tribal economy of the Gonds in Madhya Pradesh. In Agricultural Situation in India 24,11 (1970) 985-92.

3. Other Major Tribes of Gondwana

20881 AGARWAL, P.C. Human geography of Bastar District. Allahabad: Garga Bros., 1968. 448p.

20882 ELWIN, V. The Agaria. London: OUP, 1942. 292p.

20883 ______. The Baiga. London: Murray, 1939. 550p.

20884 FUCHS, S. Folktales of the Gond and Baiga in eastern Mandla. In AFS 24,2 (1965) 53-116.

20885 FÜRER-HAIMENDORF, C. VON. The Pardhans: the bards of the Raj Gonds. In EA 4 (1951) 172-84.

20886 HAJRA, D. The Dorla of Bastar. Calcutta: AnthSI, 1970. 218p. (Its Memoirs, 17)

20887 HIVALE, S. The Pardhans of the upper Narbada valley. Bombay: OUP, 1946. 230p.

20888 NAG, D.S. Tribal economy (an economic study of the Baiga). Delhi: Bharatiya Adimjati Sevak Sangh, 1958. 418p.

20889 PATEL, M.L. Agro-economic survey of tribal Mandla. Delhi: PPH, 1969. 132p.

20890 THUSU, K.N. The Dhurwa of Bastar. Calcutta: AnthSI, 1968. 243p. (Its Memoirs, 16)

20891 ______. The panchayat system of the Dhruwas of Bastar, M.P. In MI 45 (1965) 134-51.

C. Tribes of the Chota Nagpur Plateau (Bihar, Orissa, and M.P.)

1. General Studies

20892 BILUNG, A. Religious and moral aspects of the Munda, Oraon and Kharia tribes of Chotanagpur. Leuven: Katholieke U., 1972. 102p.

20893 BRADLEY-BIRT, F.B. Chota-Nagpore: a little-known province of the empire. London: Smith, Elder, 1903. 310 + 40p.

20894 MACDOUGALL, J. Agrarian reform vs. religious revitalization: collective resistance to peasantization among the Mundas, Oraons, and Santals, 1858-95. In CIS ns 11,2 (1977) 295-327.

20895 MAHAPATRA, S. The empty distance carries...; Oraon & Mundari tribal songs transcreated. Calcutta: Writers Workshop, 1972. 59p.

20896 MAHTO, S. Hundred years of Christian missions in Chotanagpur since 1845. Ranchi: Chotanagpur Christian Pub. House, 1971. 268p.

20897 PRASAD, NARMADESHWAR. Land and people of tribal Bihar. Ranchi: Bihar Tribal Res. Inst., 1961. 378p.

20898 PRASAD, SAILESHWAR. Where the three tribes meet; a study in tribal interaction. Allahabad: Indian Intl. Pub., 1974. 232p.

20899 SA, FIDELIS DE. Crisis in Chota Nagpur: with special reference to the judicial conflict between Jesuit missionaries and British government officials, November 1889-March 1890. Bangalore: Redemptorist Publications, 1975. 357p.

20900 SACHCHIDANANDA. Cultural change in tribal Bihar; Munda and Oraon. Calcutta: Bookland, 1964. 158p.

20901 ______. Profiles of tribal culture in Bihar. Calcutta: KLM, 1965. 236p.

20902 ______. The tribal village in Bihar; a study in unity and extension. Delhi: Munshiram, 1968. 218p.

20903 SARAN, A.B. Murder and suicide among the Munda and the Oraon. Delhi: National, 1974. 266p.

20904 SCHWERIN, D. Von Armut zu Elend: Kolonialherrschaft und Agrarverfassung in Chota Nagpur, 1858-1908. Wiesbaden: Steiner, 1977. 551p. (BSAF, 31)

20905 SHARMA, P. DASH, ed. The passing scene in Chotanagpur: Sarat Chandra Roy commemorative volume. Ranchi: Maitryee, 1980. 171p.

20906 SINHA, B.B. Socio-economic life in Chotanagpur. Delhi: B.R., 1979. 215p.

20907 SINHA, S.C. & J. SEN & S. PANCHBHAI. The concept of diku among the tribes of Chotanagpur. In MI 49,2 (1969) 121-38.

20908 SRIVASTAVA, R. Ecology, population, and work in the three villages of Chotanagpur in North Central India. In JSR 17,2 (1974) 31-49.

20909 VARMA, P. Social organisation of Amnari: a village study in Chotanagpur. Calcutta: Inst. of Social Res. & Applied Anthropology, 1977. 276p.

20910 VIDYARTHI, L.P. Cultural contours of tribal Bihar. Calcutta: Punthi Pustak, 1964. 308p.

2. The Santals: The Largest Mundari-speaking Tribal Group (1971 pop. 3,786,899)

a. bibliography and reference

20911 BODDING, P.O. A Santal dictionary.... Oslo: A.W. Broggers Boktrykkeri, 1932-36. 5 v., 3406p.

20912 TROISI, J. The Santals: a classified and annotated bibliography. ND: Manohar Book Service, 1976. 234p.

b. general studies

20913 ARCHER, W.G. The hill of flutes: life, love, and poetry in tribal India: a portrait of the Santals. Pittsburgh: U. of Pittsburgh Press, 1974. 375p. + 10pl.

20914 BISWAS, P.C. Santals of the Santal Parganas. Delhi: Bharatiya Adimjati Sevak Sangh, 1956. 230p.

20915 BODDING, P.O., tr. Traditions and institutions of the Santals. Ed. by Sten Konow. Oslo: Etnografiske Museum, 1942. 198p. (Its Bull., 6)

20916 CULSHAW, W.J. Tribal heritage: a study of the Santals. London: Lutterworth, 1949. 211p.

20917 MARTEL, G. La culture du riz chez les Santals du Bengale. In BEFEO 52,2 (1965) 314-58.

20918 MUKHERJI, C.L. The Santals. Rev. 2nd ed. Calcutta: A. Mukherjee, 1962. 459p.

20919 ORANS, M. The Santal, a tribe in search of a great tradition. Detroit: Wayne State U. Press, 1965. 154p.

20920 PEDERSON, M.A. Sketches from Santalistan. 2nd ed. Minneapolis: Lutherske Missioneer, 1913. 187p.

c. social and psychological studies

20921 CULSHAW, W.J. Four Santal autobiographies. In Practical Anthropology 11 (1964) 77-89.

20922 HOCK, E.M. From green pastures to grey prisons: a study of emotional trouble in three Santhali tribals. In JSR 8 (1965) 50-70.

20923 KOCHAR, V.K. Social organization among the Santal. Calcutta: Editions Indian, 1970. 128p.

20924 ______. Socio-cultural denominators of domestic life in a Santal village. In EA 16 (1963) 167-80.

20925 RAY, P.C. Socio-cultural process and psychological adaptation of the Santal. Calcutta: AnthSI, 1975. 900p. (Its Memoirs, 33)

20926 SAHA, N.K. On role analysis; a study of inter personal relation among the Santals in a West Bengal village. Calcutta: Prantik, 1972. 60p.

20927 TROISI, J. Social organization of a Santal village: expanding socio-economic frontiers. In SocAct 24,4 (1974) 331-44.

d. cultural change and social unrest; the 1855 Santal Insurrection and the Kharwar Movement of 1871

20928 ARCHER, W.G. & W.J. CULSHAW. The Santal Rebellion. In MI 25,4 (1945) 218-39.

20929 BODDING, P.O. The Kharwar Movement among the Santals. In MI 1,3 (1921) 222-32.

20930 DAS GUPTA, N.K. Problems of tribal education and the Santals. ND: Bharatiya Adimjati Sevak Sangh, 1963. 152p.

20931 DATTA, K.K. The Santal insurrection of 1855-57. Calcutta: U. of Calcutta, 1940. 103p.

20932 DATTA-MAJUMDER, N. The Santal; a study in culture-change. Calcutta: MPGOI, 1956. 150p.

20933 GAUTAM, M.K. The santalization of the Santals. In K. David, ed. The new wind: changing identities in South Asia. The Hague: Mouton, 1977, 369-82. (WA)

20934 GHOSH, S.C. Dalhousie and the Santal insurrection of 1855. In BPP 90,1 (1971) 85-98.

20935 GUPTA, RANJAN. The aboriginal world of Birbhum from the Ghatwal Revolt to the Santal Insurrection of 1855-56. In BPP 93,1 (1974) 59-73.

20936 JHA, A.P. Nature of the Santal unrest of 1871-75 and origin of the Sajha Hor movement. In Indian Hist. Records Cmsn., Proc. 35,2 (1960) 103-13.

20937 MAHAPATRA, S. Ecological adaptation to technology: ritual conflict and leadership change: the Santal experience. In K. David, ed. The new wind: changing identities in South Asia. The Hague: Mouton, 1977, 357-68. (WA)

20938 SCHMITT, E. "Sonat Santal Samaj": eine soziale Bewegung der Santals im Dhanbad Distrikt, Bihar, Indien. In Sociologus ns 23,1 & 2 (1973) 3-21, 97-115.

20939 TROISI, J. Social movement among the Santals. In SocAct 26,3 (1976) 253-66.

e. Santal religion and folklore

20940 ARCHER, W.G. The Santal treatment of witchcraft. In MI 27,2 (1947) 103-21.

20941 BODDING, P.O., ed. Santal folk tales. Oslo: Aschchoug, 1925-29. 3 v., 369, 403, 411p.

20942 CAMPBELL, A., tr. Santal folk tales. Pokhuria: Santal Mission Press, 1891. 127p.

20943 CULSHAW, W.J. Some notes on Bongaism. In JASBengal 5 (1939) 427-31.

20944 KRAMRISCH, S. Mahavira vessel and the plant Putika. In JAOS 95,2 (1975) 222-35.

20945 MAHAPATRA, S. Bakhen: ritual invocation songs of a primitive community. ND: Prachi Prakashan, 1979. 73p. [Santals from the Mayurbhanj Dist., Orissa]

20946 ROY CHAUDHURY, I. Folk tales of the Santals. ND: Sterling, 1973. 120p. (Folk tales of India series, 13)

20947 TROISI, J. Tribal religion: religious beliefs and practices among the Santals. ND: Manohar, 1978. 294p.

3. The Mundas: a Mundari-speaking Tribal Group (1971 pop. 1,080,546)

a. reference

20948 HOFFMANN, J. & A. VAN EMELEN, eds. Encyclopaedia Mundarica. Patna: Supt., Govt. Printing, 1950. 13 v., 4149p. [Rpt. 1930-41 ed.; incomplete, A-S]

b. general studies

20949 CHOUDHURY, N.C. Munda social structure. Calcutta: KLM, 1977. 137p.

20950 PONETTE, P., ed. The Munda world: Hoffmann commemoration volume. Ranchi: Catholic Press, 1978. 148p.

20951 ROY, S.C. The Mundas and their country. NY: Asia, 1970. 391p. [1st pub. 1912]

20952 SACHCHIDANANDA. The changing Munda. ND: Concept, 1979. 361p.

20953 SUGIYAMA, K. A study of the Mundas' village life in India. Tokyo: Tokai U. Press, 1969. 292p.

20954 YAMADA, R. Cultural formation of the Mundas; hill peoples surrounding the Ganges Plain. Tokyo: Tokai U. Press, 1970. 433p.

c. Munda political and social movements: from Birsa Munda to Jaipal Singh

20955 AYYANGAR, M.A. Tribal and rural leadership in Bihar. In L.P. Vidyarthi, ed. Leadership in India. Bombay: Asia, 1967, 80-98.

20956 DEVALLE, S.B.C. El movimiento Birsaíta: un movimiento milenario en una sociedad tribal. In P.C. Mukherjee, et al. Movimientos agrarios y cambio social en Asia y Africa. Mexico, D.F.: Colegio de Mexico, 1974, 129-79.

20957 JHA, J.C. The Kol insurrection of Chota-Nagpur 1831-32. Calcutta: Thacker, Spink, 1964. 242p.

20958 SACHCHIDANANDA. Political consciousness in tribal Bihar. In MI 39 (1959) 301-08.

20959 SINHA, S.P. Life and times of Birsa Bhagwan. Ranchi: Bihar Tribal Res. Inst., 1964. 179p. (Studies in tribal Bihar, 1)

20960 SURESH SINGH, K. The dust-storm and the hanging mist; a study of Birsa Munda and his movement in Chhotanagpur, 1874-1901. Calcutta: KLM, 1966. 208 + 178p.

20961 VARMA, V.P. Political system of tribal Bihar. In IJPS 33,4 (1972) 381-400.

20962 VIDYARTHI, L.P. & K.N. SAHAY. The dynamics of tribal leadership in Bihar: research project on changing leadership in a tribal society, 1967-1971. Allahabad: Kitab Mahal, 1976. 630p.

20963 ZIDE, N.H. & RAM DAYAL MUNDA. Revolutionary Birsa and the songs related to him. In JSR 12,2 (1969) 37-60.

d. Munda religion and folklore

20964 HOFFMAN, J. Mundari poetry, music and dances. Calcutta: Baptist Mission Press, 1907. 35p. [MASB 2,5 (1907) 85-120]

20965 MAHAPATRA, S. The wooden sword. Cuttack: Utkal Sahitya Bikash, 1973. 48p. [Munda songs]

20966 MAJUMDAR, D.N. Bongaism. In J.P. Mills, et al., eds. Essays in anthropology. Lucknow: Maxwell, 1942, 60-79.

20967 PRASAD, DINESHWAR, ed. Hoffmann on Mundari poetry. Patna: Jyoti, 1979. 97p.

20968 SPENCER, D.M. The recruitment of shamans among the Mundas. In HR 10,1 (1970) 1-31.

4. The Bhumij: A Hinduized Munda Tribe, Claiming Rajput Descent

20969 DEVALLE, S.B.C. La rebelión de Ganga Narain en 1832. In Estudios orientales 9,1/2 (1974) 14-44.

20970 JHA, J.C. The Bhumij revolt, 1832-33: Ganga Narain's hangama or turmoil. Delhi: Munshiram, 1967. 208p.

20971 RAYCHOWDHURY, T.C. The Bhumij of Mayurbhanj. In MI 9 (1929) 95-115.

20972 SINHA, SURAJIT. Bhumij Kshatriya movement in South Manbhum. In BAnthSI 8,2 (1959) 9-32.

20973 ______. Changes in the cycle of festivals in a Bhumij village. In JSR 1 (1958) 24-53.

20974 ______. The media and nature of Hindu-Bhumij interactions. In JASBengal 23,1 (1957) 23-37.

20975 ______. Some aspects of changes in Bhumij religion. In MI 33,2 (1953) 148-64.

20976 ______. Training of a Bhumij medicine-man. In MI 38 (1958) 111-28.

5. The Hos and Kols: Munda Tribes

20977 CHATTERJEE, A.N. & T.C. DAS. The Hos of Seraikella. Calcutta: U. of Calcutta, 1927. 94p. + 23 pl. (Anthropological papers, ns 1)

20978 CHATTOPADHYAY, G. Kinship and marriage among the Hos. In Bull. of the Cultural Res. Inst. 3,2 (1964) 13-25.

20979 GRIFFITHS, W.G. The Kol tribe of central India. Calcutta: ASB, 1946. 333p.

20980 HASAN, AMIR. The Kols of Patha. Allahabad: Kitab Mahal, 1972. 254p.

20981 MAJUMDAR, D.N. The affairs of a tribe. Lucknow: Ethnographic and Folk-Culture Soc., U.P., by Universal Pub., 1950. 367p. [Ho]

20982 SINGH, C.P. The Ho tribe of Singhbhum. ND: Classical Pub., 1978. 168p.

6. The Oraons/Kurukhs: A Dravidian-speaking Tribal Group

20983 ARCHER, W.G. The blue grove: the poetry of the Uraons. London: Allen & Unwin, 1940. 210p.

20984 ______. The dove and the leopard: more Uraon poetry. Calcutta: Orient Longmans, 1948. 175p.

20985 DAS, A.K. & M.K. RAHA. The Oraons of Sunderban. Calcutta: Tribal Welfare Dept., Govt. of W. Bengal, 1963. 476p. (Bull. of the Cultural Res. Inst., special ser., 3)

20986 DEHON, P.S. The religion and customs of the Oraons. In MASB 1,9 (1906) 121-81.

20987 DHAN, R.O. These are my tribesmen: the Oraons. Ranchi: 1967. 143p.

20988 LALL, R.B. Changing economy of the Oraons. In JSR 3 (1960) 82-92.

20989 ROY, S.C. The Oraons of Chotanagpur: their history, economic life, and social organisation. Ranchi: the author, 1915. 491p.

20990 ______. Oraon religion and customs. Calcutta: Editions Indian, 1972. 303p. [Rpt. of 1928 ed., 418p.]

20991 SACHCHIDANANDA. Leadership and culture change in Kullu. In MI 44,2 (1964) 116-31.

20992 SAHAY, K.N. Under the shadow of the cross: a study of the nature and processes of Christianization among the Uraon of central India. Calcutta: Inst. of Social Res. & Applied Anthropology, 1976. 539p.

20993 SINGH, P.N. Sources of Hindu influence on Oraons living in Purnea District. In JSR 7 (1964) 79-86.

7. Other Tribes of Chota Nagpur

20994 BAINBRIDGE, R.B. The Saorias of the Rajmahal Hills. In MASB 2,4 (1907) 43-84.

20995 CHANDHOKE, S.K. The Tana Bhagats of Chota Nagpur. In Vanyajati 20,3/4 (1972) 128-44.

20996 DANDA, A.K. Agricultural economy of the Kawar of Surguja. In JSR 15,1 (1972) 71-91.

20997 DAS GUPTA, S.B. Birjhia: a section of the Asurs of Chota Nagpur. Calcutta: K.P. Bagchi, 1978. 227p.

20998 DHAN, R.O. The problems of the Tana Bhagats of Ranchi District. In BBTRI 2,1 (1960) 136-86.

20999 GUPTA, S.P. The Asur: ethno-biological profile. Ranchi: Bihar Tribal Welfare Res. Inst., 1976. 173p. + 15 pl. (Its monograph, 15)

21000 HARI MOHAN. The Chero: a study in acculturation. Patna: Bihar Tribal Welfare Res. Inst., 1973. 109p.

21001 ______. The Parhaiya: a study in culture change. Ranchi: Bihar Tribal Welfare Res. Inst., 1975. 144p.

21002 ______. Socio-economic organisation and religion among the hill Kharia of Dhalbhum. In BBTRI 3,1 (1961) 180-212.

21003 LEUVA, K.K. The Asur, a study of primitive iron-smelters. ND: Bharatiya Adimjati Sevak Sangh, 1963. 234p.

21004 ROY, S.C. The Birhors, a little-known jungle tribe of Chota Nagpur. Ranchi: Man in India Office, 1978. 298p. [Rpt. 1925 ed.]

21005 ROY, S.C. & R.C. ROY. The Kharias. Ranchi: Man in India Office, 1937. 2 v.

21006 VIDYARTHI, L.P. The Maler; a study in nature-man-spirit complex of a hill tribe in Bihar. Calcutta: Bookland, 1963. 261p.

D. Tribes of the Orissa Highlands

1. General Studies

21007 DAS, M.N. Suppression of human sacrifice among the hill tribes of Orissa. In MI 36 (1956) 21-48.

21008 ELWIN, V. Tribal myths of Orissa. Bombay: OUP, 1954. 700p.

21009 MAHAPATRA, L.K. Social movements among tribes in eastern India, with special reference to Orissa. In Sociologus 18 (1968) 46-63.

21010 MOHAPATRA, K. Growth of population and occupational pattern among the scheduled tribes of Orissa; an analysis of inter-census data 1961-71. In Adibasi 14,2-3 (1972) 1-23.

2. The Saoras/Savaras

21011 DUMONT, L. & D. POCOCK. Possession and priesthood. In CIS 3 (1959) 55-74. [Discussion of V. Elwin, The religion of an Indian tribe, 21012]

21012 ELWIN, V. The religion of an Indian tribe. Bombay: OUP, 1955. 597p.

21013 ______. The Saora priestess. In BDA 1,1 (1952) 59-85.

21014 PARIDA, G. Acculturation of Saura children into Ariya society. Cuttack: 1968. 115p.

21015 ROY, S.N. The Savaras of Orissa. In MI 7 (1927) 277-336.

21016 SRIVASTAVA, L.R.N. Identification of educational problems of the Saora of Orissa. ND: NCERT, 1971. 134p.

21017 TURNER, V.W. Aspects of Saora ritual and shamanism: an approach to the data of ritual. In A.L. Epstein, ed. The craft of social anthropology. London: Tavistock, 1967, 81-204.

3. The Juangs

21018 BOSE, N.K. Marriage and kinship among the Juangs. In his Cultural anthropology and other essays. Calcutta: Indian Associated Pub. Co., 1953, 136-46.

21019 ELWIN, V. Notes on the Juang. In MI 28,1/2 (1948) 1-146.

21020 MCDOUGAL, C. Juang categories and joking relations. In SWJA 20,4 (1964) 319-45.

21021 PATNAIK, N. Caste in formation among the Juang of Orissa. In MI 44 (1964) 22-30.

21022 ROUT, S.P. Handbook on the Juang. In Adibasi 11,1/2 (1969-70) 1-95.

4. Other Tribes of Highland Orissa

21023 BANERJEE, S. Ethnographic study of the Kuvi-Kandha. Calcutta: AnthSI, 1969. 113p. (Its Memoirs, 24) [tribe of Koraput Dist.]

21024 DUBEY, K.C. Possible origin of the Bhunjias and their ethnic relationship: a new hypothesis. In EA 14,1 (1961) 48-58.

21025 ELWIN, V. Bondo highlander. London: OUP, 1950. 290p.

21026 MAHAPATRA, L.K. The Cerenga Kulha of Bonai, Orissa; their changing economy. In Baessler-Archiv, Beiträge zur Volkerkunde ns 11 (1964) 347-59.

21027 ______. A hill Bhuiyan village; an empirical socio-economic study. Diss., U. of Hamburg, 1959. 257p.

21028 MAZUMDAR, B.C. Note on the Bhuiyas of Utkala and Jharkhanda. In MI 12 (1932) 320-24.

21029 MOHAPATRA, P.K. Handbook on Koya. In Adibasi 11,4 (1970) 1-66.

21030 NIGGEMEYER, H. Kuttia Kond, Dschungelbauern in Orissa. Haar bei München: Klaus Renner Verlag, 1964. 257p.

21031 ROY, S.C. The Hill Bhuiyas of Orissa. Ranchi: Man in India Office, 1935. 320p.

21032 SAHU, L.N. The hill tribes of Jeypore. Cuttack: E.R. Lazarus for Sahu, 1942. 205p.

21033 SHARMA, KRISHAN. The Konds of Orissa; an anthropometric study. ND: Concept, 1976. 112p.

21034 THUSU, K.N. The Pengo Porajas of Koraput: an ethnographic survey. Calcutta: AnthSI, 1977. 94p. (Its Memoirs, 39)

III. GOA: FROM PORTUGUESE COLONY TO UNION TERRITORIES

A. General and Political History

1. Portuguese Rule, 1818-1961 [see also Chap. 5], and the Liberation Movement

21035 Aqui é Portugal. Panjim: Repartição Central de Estatistica e Informação, 1950. 112p. (Colecção de divulgacão e cultura, 14)

21036 CUNHA, TRISTÃO DE BRAGANÇA. Goa's freedom struggle: selected writings. Bombay: Dr. T.B. Cunha Mem. Cmtee., 1961. 551p.

21037 DA CRUZ, A. Goa: men and matters. Vasco da Gama: Ashok Print. Press, 1974. 369p.

21038 A India portuguesa, v. 2. Nova Goa: Imprensa Nacional, 1923. 593p. + 37 pl.

21039 JORGE, E. Goa's awakening: reminiscences of the 1946 civil disobedience movement. Panjim: 18th Kune (Goan Revolution Day) Silver Jubilee Celebrations, 1971. 84p.

21040 MASCARENHAS, T. DE. When the mango-trees blossomed: quasi-memoirs. Bombay: Orient Longman, 1976. 291p. [Autobiography of Goan freedom fighter]

21041 MENEZES BRAGANÇA, LUIS DE. Prosas dispersas. Pangim: Comissão de Homenagem a Memória de Menezes Bragança, 1965-. v. 1, 520p. [journalist and nationalist leader, 1878-1938]

21042 Menezes Braganza: biographical sketch. Panaji: Tip. Sadananda, 1972. 107p.

2. The Union Territory of Goa, Daman, & Diu (1962 -); the U.T. of Dadra and Nagar Haveli (Liberated 1954)

a. India-Portugal struggle over Goa

21043 GAITONDE, P. & A.D. MANI. The Goa problem. ND: ICWA, 1956. 30p.

21044 Is Goa Portuguese? In United Asia 9,5 (1957) 307-78.

21045 LUTHERA, V.P. Goa and the Portuguese Republic. In IJPS 17 (1956) 261-80.

21046 NARAYANA RAO, K. The problem of Goa. In IYIA 5 (1956) 46-69.

21047 NEHRU, JAWAHARLAL. Nehru on Goa. ND: F.M. George for Goa Freedom Pub., 1956. 42p.

21048 PATWARDHAN, D. Nizam-Portuguese negotiations, 1947-48. In JIH 52,2/3 (1974) 475-92; 53,2 (1975) 303-22.

21049 SALAZAR, ANTONIO DE OLIVEIRA. Goa and the Indian Union - the Portuguese view. In Foreign Affairs 34 (1956) 418-31.

21050 WEINER, M. Struggle against power. In World Politics 8 (1956) 392-403.

b. Indian Army's liberation of Goa, 1961

21051 DHAR, P. India's foreign policy and the liberation of Goa, Daman, and Diu. In MR 111 (1962) 376-82.

21052 FISHER, M.W. Goa in wider perspective. In AS 2,4 (1962) 3-10.

21053 KHERA, P.N. Operation Vijay; the liberation of Goa and other Portuguese colonies in India (1961). ND: Min. of Defense, 1974. 253p.

21054 LAWRENCE, L. Nehru seizes Goa. NY: Pageant Press, 1963. 226p.

21055 MANKEKAR, D.R. The Goa action. Bombay: Popular, 1962. 51p.

21056 PORTUGAL. NATL. SECRETARIAT FOR INFO. The invasion and occupation of Goa in the world press. Lisbon: 1962. 636p.

21057 RUBINOFF, A.G. India's use of force in Goa. Bombay: Popular, 1971. 134p.

21058 TELKAR, S. Goa yesterday and today. Bombay: Telkar's Feature Service, 1962. 160p.

c. politics and elections of G.D.&D., 1962-

21059 D'MELLO, R.G. Goa, a new ideal. Bombay: Chetana, 1963. 102p.

21060 ______. Panchayat elections in Goa, Daman & Diu. In Kurukshetra 11,11 (1963) 4-6.

21061 ESTEVES, S. Goa and its future. Bombay: Manaktalas, 1966. 146p.

21062 ______. Parties and politics in 1972 legislative assembly elections in Goa. In PSR 11,2/3 (1972) 138-65.

21063 Goa; a symposium on the many facets of this territory's crisis of transition. In Seminar 69 (1965) 10-42. [by B.M. Braganza, P. Alvares, G. Vaz, R. D'Mello, F. Moraes, E.P.W. da Costa]

21064 GOA, DAMAN & DIU. DEPT. OF INFO. & TOURISM. Ten years of liberation, 1961-71. Panaji: 1971. 155p.

21065 HALAPPA, G.S. & K. RAGHAVENDRA RAO & A.M. RAJASEKHARIAH. The first general elections in Goa. Dharwar: Karnatak U., 1964. 119p.

21066 JOSHI, RAM. The general elections in Goa. In AS 4,10 (1964) 1093-1101.

d. the question of merger: rival claims of Karnataka and Maharashtra

21067 DESAI, N. Goa's merger, why and how? Colvate: Kumud Desai, 1966. 106p.

21068 KOWDI, A.V. Spotlight on Goa. Dharwar: Lincoln Inst. of Social Res. & Public Opinion, 1965. 30p.

21069 SAKSENA, R.N. Goa: into the mainstream. ND: Abhinav, 1974. 147p.

21070 SEMINAR ON THE PROBLEM OF GOA'S INTEGRATION WITH INDIA, MARGAO, 1964. Goa: the problems of transition. Ed. A.B. Shah. Bombay: Manaktalas, 1965. 100p.

B. The Goan Economy

1. General Studies; Development and Planning

21071 ALMEIDA, J.C. Some demographic aspects of Goa, Daman & Diu. Panjim: Govt. Print. Press, 1965. 363p. [Portuguese & English]

21072 Goa, Daman, and Diu; industrial potential survey. Bombay: Industrial Dev. Bank of India, 1974. 96p.

21073 GOA, DAMAN & DIU. Sixth five year plan, 1978-83. Panaji: 1980. 503p.

21074 GOA, DAMAN & DIU. BUREAU OF ECON., STAT., & EVAL. An economic review of Goa, Daman. & Diu, 1961-71. Panaji: 1973. 222p.

21075 ______. Report on the survey of potentialities of tourism in Goa. Panaji: 1972. 197p.

21076 GOA, DAMAN, & DIU. GENL. STAT. DEPT. Fact book on manpower for Goa, Daman & Diu. Panaji: 1968. 170p. (Manpower series, 1)

21077 ______. Report on the middle class family living survey in Panaji Town, 1964-65. Panaji: 1967. 84p.

21078 INDIA (REP.). CENSUS OF INDIA, 1971. A portrait of population: Goa, Daman, & Diu. Delhi: Cont. of Pub., 1976. 186p.

21079 LOBO, C. Portuguese India: its commerce and industries. Bombay: Times Press, 1927. 139p.

21080 NCAER. Development programmes for Goa, Daman, and Diu. ND: 1970. 171p.

21081 ______. Techno-economic survey of Goa, Daman, and Diu. ND: 1964. 275p.

21082 PADKI, M.B. & S.H. PORE & S.W. MURANJAN. Utilization of local resources: a case study of Goa. Poona: GIPE, 1967. 301p.

21083 TALUKDAR, S.C. Economic development of Goa, problem and prospects. In EW 14,23 (1962) 917-20.

2. Goan Agriculture

a. general studies

21084 ALMEIDA, J.C. Aspects of the agricultural activity in Goa, Daman and Diu. Panaji: Govt. Printing Press, 1967. 333 + 319p. [English & Portuguese]

21085 GOA, DAMAN & DIU. BUREAU OF ECON., STAT., & EVAL. Agricultural census, 1970-71: Union Territory of Goa, Daman & Diu. Panaji: 1976. 231p.

21086 GOA, DAMAN & DIU. DIR. OF FISHERIES. A survey of the fishing industry in Goa. Panaji: 1969. 41p.

21087 INDIA (REP.). CENTRAL BOARD FOR THE PREVENTION & CONTROL OF WATER POLLUTION. Union Territory of Daman, Dadra & Nagar Haveli (abridged). ND: 1979. 32p.

21088 VANJARI, S.K. Agriculture in Goa. In EE 52 (1969) 1125-31.

b. land tenure and reform

21089 GOA, DAMAN & DIU. CMTEE. OF THE PROBLEMS OF MUNDKARS IN THE UNION TERRITORY OF GOA, DAMAN & DIU. Report. Panjim: 1966. 90p. [farm tenants]

21090 GOA, DAMAN & DIU. LAND REFORM CMSN. Report. Panjim: 1964. 66p.

21091 GOA, DAMAN & DIU. LAND REFORMS CMTEE. Report... Nov. 1970. Panaji: 1971. 58p.

C. Society and Religion in Modern Goa

21092 DE SOUZA, R. Goa and the continent of Circe. Bombay: Wilco Pub. House, 1973. 215p.

21093 D'SOUZA, B.G. Goan society in transition: a study in social change. Bombay: Popular, 1975. 364p.

21094 GOA, DAMAN & DIU. DIR. OF EDUC. Report of the Second All India Educational Survey, 1965-66. Panaji: 1969. 143p.

21095 GOA, DAMAN & DIU. UNIVERSITY CMTEE. Report. Panaji: 1969. 68p. [Chm. G.D. Parikh]

21096 SALDANDA, J.A. The Indian caste. Bombay: Anglo-Lusitano Press, 1904-. 122p. [v. 1 Konkani, or Goan castes]

21097 SARASWATI, B.N. Temple organisation in Goa. In MI 43,2 (1963) 131-40.

21098 VARDE, P.S. History of education in Goa, from 1510 to the present day. Panaji: Goa Vidya Pratishthan, 1977. 159p.

D. Literatures of Modern Goa

1. Modern Literature in Konkani and Portuguese

21099 DESAI, S.R. Konkani: quality and quantity. In IL 21,6 (1978) 201-41.

21100 GOMES, F.L. Os brahmanes: romance. 3rd ed. Panaji: Comissão do Centenário de Falecimento do Dr. F.L. Gomes, 1969. 177p.

21101 LUPI, NITA. The music and spirit of Portuguese India. Lisbon: Editorial Imperio, 1960. 171p.

21102 MASCARENHAS, T. DE. Poemas de desespero e consolação. Panjim: Ediçoes Oriente, 1971. 149p.

21103 PANDIT, R.V. The moon...the moon: poems. Tr. from Konkani by T. Gay. Panji: Bhagawati Prakashan, 1969. 47p.

21104 ______. My Goa and other poems: poems. Tr. from Konkani by T. Gay. Panaji: Antonio Caetano Fernandes, 1971. 136p.

21105 PEREIRA, J. Konkani: a language; a history of the Konkani Marathi controversy. Dharwar: Karnatak U., 1971. 145p.

21106 VAS, L.S.R., comp. Modern Goan short stories. Bombay: Jaico, 1971. 179p.

2. Folk Literature

21107 RODRIGUES, L. Konkani folk-songs of Goa: Durpod, the song of joy. In Folklore (C) 2 (1961) 114-27, 178-82.

21108 ______. Of soil and soul and Konkani folk tales. Bombay: Laura D'Souza Rodrigues, 1974. 254p.

21109 SUKHTHANKER, V.S. Tales and tellers of Goa. Bangalore: dist. Asia Trading Corp., 1974. 121p.

IV. MAHARASHTRA: THE MARATHI-SPEAKING REGION OF WESTERN AND CENTRAL INDIA, 1818 -

A. General and Political History

1. Bombay State, 1947-60

21110 BOMBAY (STATE). LEGISLATURE. Bombay Legislature directory. Bombay: Bombay Legislature Congress Party, 1953. 4 pts. in 1v.

21111 DANGE, S.A. Report on the general elections in Bombay. Bombay: Samyukta Maharashtra Election Samiti, 1957. 24p.

21112 DASTER, A.J. & U. MEHTA. Congress rule in Bombay, 1952 to 1956. Bombay: Popular, 1958. 205p.

21113 KULKARNI, A.R. Second general election in Sholapur. Sholapur: Inst. of Public Admin., 1958. 38p.

21114 PATTERSON, M.L.P. Caste and political leadership in Maharashtra. In EW 6,39 (1954) 1065-67.

2. The Samyukta ("United") Maharashtra Movement and the Establishment of Maharashtra State, 1960

21115 AMBEDKAR, B.R. Maharashtra as a linguistic province. Statement submitted to the Linguistic Provinces Cmsn. Bombay: Thacker, 1948. 41p.

21116 Justice shall prevail; the struggle for Samyukta Maharashtra. Poona: J.S. Tilak, 1958. 107p. [by "Quaerens Veritatem," pseud.]

21117 MAHARASHTRA. DIR. OF PUBLICITY. Maharashtra state is launched; artist's view of events... Apr. 27-May 1, 1960. Bombay: Govt. Press, 1960. 89p.

21118 MUNSHI, K.M. Linguistic provinces and the future of Bombay. Bombay: National Info. & Pub., 1948. 62p.

21119 PHADE, Y.D. Politics and language. 1st ed. Bombay: Himalaya Pub. House, 1979. 359p.

21120 Problems of Maharashtra; report of a seminar held under the auspices of the Indian Committee for Cultural Freedom, the Asian Office, Congress for Cultural Freedom, and the Sadhana Weekly. Bombay: 1960. 197p.

21121 SAMYUKTA MAHARASHTRA PARISHAD. Reorganization of states in India with particular reference to the formation of Maharashtra. Bombay: 1954. 113p.

21122 SINGH, G.S. Maratha geopolitics of the Indian nation. Bombay: Manaktalas, 1966. 220p.

21123 SOVANI, Y.K., ed. A case for the formation of a new province - "United Maharashtra." Poona: Samyukta Maharashtra Parishad, 1947? 124p.

21124 STERN, R.W. Maharashtrian linguistic provincialism and Indian nationalism. In PA 37 (1964) 37-49.

21125 WINDMILLER, M.L. Politics of states reorganization in India: the case of Bombay. In Far Eastern Survey 25 (1956) 129-43.

3. General Studies of Maharashtra Politics, 1960-

21126 EAKIN, T.C. Students and politics; a comparative study, with a prospective set from past survey research on political behaviour. Bombay: Popular, 1972. 222p.

21127 KARNIK, D.B. This was a man. Bombay: Janata Pub., 1978. 28p. [on Nath Pai, 1924-71]

21128 POLLOCK, J. The new political leaders in Maharashtra. In School of Advanced Intl. Studies R. (Johns Hopkins U.) 11,4 (1967) 19-25.

21129 ROSENTHAL, D.B. Sources of district Congress factionalism in Maharashtra. In EPW 7,34 (1972) 1725-1746.

21130 SIRSIKAR, V.M. A study of political workers in Poona. Poona: Poona U. Press, 1961. 83p.

21131 SRINIVASAN, R. Maharashtra and the Congress Party 1962-67. In JUB 37 (1968) 254-77.

4. Election Studies, 1960-

21132 ESTEVES, S. Elections and one-party dominance: the pattern and causes of Congress triumph in Maharashtra. In PSR 13,1/4 (1974) 126-56.

21133 KINI, N.G.S. The city voter in India: a study of 1967 general elections in Nagpur. ND: Abhinav, 1974. 355p.

21134 KINI, N.G.S. & K.S. KSHIRSAGAR. The non-voter or political apathy. In NUJ 24,1/2 (1973-74) 1-79.

21135 SIRSIKAR, V.M. Nomination process in the Congress Party of Maharashtra: 1967 general elections. In JUP 37 (1972) 167-86.

21136 ______. Political behaviour in India; a case study of the 1962 general elections. Bombay: Manaktalas, 1965. 276p. [Report on Poona constituencies]

21137 ______. Sovereigns without crowns: a behavioral analysis of the Indian electoral process. Bombay: Popular, 1973. 414p.

21138 SRINIVASAN, R. Elections in Maharashtra and Congress dominance. In PSR 6,3/4 & 7,1/2 (1967-68) 447-61.

5. The Shiv Sena ("Army of of Shivaji"): Urban Middle-Class Party of Maharashtrian Nativism

21139 GANGADHARAN, K.K. Shiv Sena. In Seminar 151 (March 1972) 26-32.

21140 GUPTA, DIPANKAR. The causes and constraints of an urban social movement. In CIS 11,1 (1977) 69-90.

21141 JOHARI, J.C. Militant and protective regionalism in India - a case study of Shiv Sena in Maharashtra. In IPSR 7,1 (1972-73) 52-75.

21142 JOSHI, RAM. The Shiv Sena: a movement in search of legitimacy. In AS 10,11 (1970) 967-978.

21143 KATZENSTEIN, M.F. Ethnicity and equality: the Shiv Sena party and preferential politics in Bombay. Ithaca: CornellUP, 1979. 237p.

21144 ______. Politics of population movements: the case of Bombay. In EPW 10,51 (1975) 1955-59.

21145 MOHANTY, S.P. Sons of the soil and their socio-economic problems in greater Bombay. In JGRS 36 (1974) 66-72.

21146 RAO, VASANT D. Shiv Sena - a case study in regionalism in India. In QRHS 13,3 (1973-74) 133-43.

21147 SARKAR, C. Mr. Thackeray of Bombay: fanatical local nationalism. In RT 231 (1968) 275-82. [Bal Thakare, Shiv Sena leader]

6. Administration and Reorganization

21148 INDIAN INST. OF PUBLIC ADMIN. MAHARSHTRA REGIONAL BRANCH. Organisation of government in Maharashtra. Bombay: Popular, 1965. 473p.

21149 MAHARASHTRA. ADMIN. REORG. CMTEE. Report. Bombay: Printed at the Govt. Central Press, 1968. 367p.

21150 MAHARASHTRA. OFFICE OF THE COMMISSIONER (ADMIN. REORG). Reorganisation of Maharashtra administration; report, by M.N. Heble, Commissioner (Administrative Reorganisation). Bombay: Govt. Central Press, 1971. 2 v.

21151 VAKIL, A.K. Relations between the legislature and administration in Maharashtra State from 1957-1967. Pune: U. of Poona, 1978. 289p.

7. Local Government and Politics
a. general studies

21152 ALL-INDIA INST. OF LOCAL SELF-GOVT. The directory of local self-government in Maharshtra State. Bombay: All-India Institute of Local Self-Government, 1962. 544p. + 18pl.

21153 BHAT, K.S. Panchayati raj administration in Maharashtra: a study of supervision and control. Bombay: Popular, 1974. 167p.

21154 CARTER, A.T. Elite politics in rural India: political stratification and alliances in Western Maharashtra. Cambridge: CamUP, 1974. 207p.

21155 ______. Political stratification and unstable alliances in rural western Maharashtra. In MAS 6,4 (1972) 423-442.

21156 DARSHANKAR, A.Y. Leadership in panchayati raj: a study of Beed District. Jaipur: Panchsheel Prakashan, 1979. 202p.

21157 GAIKWAD, V.R. Panchayati raj and bureaucracy; a study of the relationship patterns. Hyderabad: Natl. Inst. of Community Dev., 1969. 77p.

21158 MAHARASHTRA. CMTEE. ON DEMOCRATIC DECENTRALISATION. Report. Bombay: Co-op. & Rural Dev. Dept., 1961. 304p. [chm., V.P. Naik]

21159 MAHARASHTRA. CMTEE. ON PANCHAYATI RAJ. Report. Bombay: 1971. 462p. [chm., L.N. Bongirwar]

21160 SIRSIKAR, V.M. The rural elite in a developing society; a study in political sociology. ND: Orient Longmans, 1970. 227p.

b. district administration and the zilla parishad

21161 CARRAS, M.C. The dynamics of Indian political factions: a study of district councils in the state of Maharashtra. NY: CamUP, 1972. 297p.

21162 ______. The economic determinants of political factionalism: a case study of an Indian rural district. In EDCC 21,1 (1972) 118-241.

21163 NANDEDKAR, V.G. Local government, its role in development administration. Delhi: Concept, 1979. 203p. [study of Nasik Zilla Parishad]

21164 ROSENTHAL, D.B. The expansive elite: district politics and state policy-making in India. Berkeley: UCalP, 1977. 348p.

21165 ______. From reformist princes to "co-operative kings," pt. 2, Personalization of Kolhapur politics, 1947-67; pt. 3, Trends toward routinization in Kolhapur politics. In EPW 8,21 & 22 (1973) 951-56, 995-1000.

21166 SHRADER, L.L & RAM JOSHI. Zilla Parishad elections in Maharashtra and the district political elite. In AS 3 (1963) 143-56.

c. village panchayats and local officials

21167 INAMDAR, N.R. Functioning of village panchayats. Bombay: Popular, 1970. 368p.

21168 MULEY, D.S. Working of village panchayats in Bhandara district. In QJLSGI 39 (1968-69) 156-89, 324-32.

21169 NANEKAR, S.R. Panchayati raj in Maharashtra: experience, problems and trends. In JNAA 16,3 (1971) 87-102.

21170 SAMANT, S.V. Village panchayats; with special reference to Bombay State. Bombay: C.D. Barfivala, 1957. 192p.

21171 SCHLESINGER, L.I. The emergency in an Indian village. In AS 17,7 (1977) 627-47.

d. urban administration and politics - general studies

21172 JANGAM, R.T. & B.A.V. SHARMA. Leadership in urban government. ND: Sterling, 1972. 128p.

21173 PANDE, V.K. Municipal finance in Marathwada. Aurangabad: Marathwada U., 1969. 401p.

21174 RAJADHYAKSHA, N.D. Municipal councils in Maharashtra. Bombay: All-India Inst. of Local Self-Govt., Regional Centre for Res. & Training in Municipal Admin., 1975. 203p.

21175 ROSENTHAL, D.B. Deurbanization, elite displacement, and political change in India. In Comp. Politics 2,2 (1970) 169-201. [Poona & Kolhapur]

21176 ______. The limited elite: politics and government in two Indian cities. Chicago: U. of Chicago Press, 1970. 360p. [Poona & Agra]

21177 WIRSING, R.G. Socialist society and free enterprise politics: a study of voluntary associations in urban India. ND: Vikas, 1977. 214p. [Nagpur]

e. Bombay City - government and politics
i. historical studies, 1818-1947

21178 DOBBIN, C. Competing elites in Bombay city politics in the mid-nineteenth century (1852-83). In E.R. Leach & S.N. Mukherjee, eds. Elites in South Asia. Cambridge: CamUP, 1970, 79-94.

21179 ______. Urban leadership in Western India: Politics and communities in Bombay City 1840-1885. London: OUP, 1972. 305p.

21180 DREWITT, F.G.D. Bombay in the days of George IV; memoirs of Sir Edward West, chief justice of the King's court during its conflict with the East India company, with hitherto unpublished documents. 2nd ed., rev. and enl. London: Longmans, Green, 1935. 342p. [1st ed. 1907]

21181 EDWARDES, S.M. The Bombay city police, 1672-1916. London: OUP, 1923. 223p.

21182 JEEJEEBHOY, J.R.B. Bribery and corruption in Bombay; being an historical account from the earliest to very recent times.... Bombay: 1952. 314p.

21183 MASSELOS, J.C. Bombay in the 1870's; a study of changing patterns in urban politics. In SAI (1971) 29-55.

21184 WACHA, D.E. Rise and growth of the Bombay municipal

government. Madras: G.A. Natesan, 1913. 455p.

ii. Bombay municipal administration and politics - general studies

21185 ALTBACH, P.G. Student politics in Bombay. London: Asia, 1968. 218p.

21186 [Bombay special issue]. In QJLSGI 47,1 (1976) 1-101.

21187 MASSELOS, J.C. Some aspects of Bombay city politics. In Ravinder Kumar, ed. Essays on Gandhian politics. Oxford, OUP, 1971, 145-188.

21188 SASTRY, S.M.Y. Studies in municipal administration of Greater Bombay. Bombay: All-India Inst. of Local Self-Govt., 1969. 87p.

iii. election studies

21189 BHADE, G.S. & M.U. RAO. The Bombay civic election of 1968. Bombay: Regional Centre for Res. & Training in Municipal Admin., All-India Inst. of Local Self-Govt., 1970. 246p.

21190 BILLIMORIA, R.N. Women and the Bombay municipal elections (1973). In JGRS 37,4 (1975) 20-31.

21191 DASTUR, A.J. Menon vs. Kripalani; North Bombay election, 1962. Bombay: U. of Bombay, 1967. 138p.

21192 MEHTA, USHA. A study in the voting behavior of the minorities in Greater Bombay. In JGRS 30 (1968) 84-89.

21193 PALMER, N.D. Election and by-election in North-East Bombay. In PSR 6,3/4 & 7,1/2 (1967-68) 521-42.

21194 ______. The 1962 election in North Bombay. In PA 36 (1963) 120-37.

21195 SHARMA, B.A.V. & R.T. JANGAM. The Bombay municipal corporation; an election study. Bombay: Popular, 1962. 170p.

B. The Economy of Maharashtra Since 1818

1. General Economic History, 1818-1947

21196 BAPAT, N.G. Economic development of Ahmednagar District, 1881-1960. Bombay: Progressive Corp., 1973. 492p.

21197 Bombay, the gateway to India: the advantages it offers to industrialists. Bombay: Rotary Club of Bombay, 1936. 111p.

21198 CHOKSEY, R.D. The aftermath (based on original records) 1818-1826. With select documents from the Deccan Commissioner's files, Peshwa Dafter, on the administrative and judicial organization of Maharashtra by the British. Bombay: New Book Co., 1950. 360p.

21199 ______. Economic history of the Bombay Deccan and Karnatak (1818-1868). Poona: R.D. Choksey, 1945. 369p.

21200 ______. Economic life in the Bombay Deccan, 1818-1938. Bombay: Asia, 1955. 227p.

21201 ______. Economic life in the Bombay Konkan 1818-1939. London: Asia, 1960. 215p.

21202 DESAI, A.V. The origins of Parsi enterprise. In IESHR 5 (1968) 307-17.

21203 GORDON, A.D.D. Businessmen and politics: rising nationalism and modernising economy in Bombay, 1918-1933. ND: Manohar, 1978. 323p. (ANU monographs on South Asia, 3)

21204 PANDIT, Y.S. Economic conditions in Maharashtra and Karnatak. Poona: Tilak Swarajya Sangh, 1936. 213p.

2. Demography (1981 pop. 62,693,898)

21205 AMBANNAVAR, J.P. A demographic study of Maharashtra State. ND: Natl. Inst. of Family Planning, 1975. 334p. (Its report ser., 16)

21206 DANDEKAR, V.M. & K. DANDEKAR. Survey of fertility and mortality in Poona District. Poona: GIPE, 1953. 191p.

21207 PETHE, V.P. Demographic profiles of an urban population. Bombay: Popular, 1964. 144p. [Sholapur]

21208 SOVANI, N.V. & K. DANDEKAR. Fertility survey of Nasik, Kolaba, and Satara (North) districts. Poona: GIPE, 1955. 167p. (Its pub., 31)

3. Surveys of Economic Conditions since 1947

21209 ARUNACHALAM, B. Maharashtra; a study in physical and regional setting and resource development. Bombay: A.R. Sheth, 1967. 308p.

21210 Economic atlas of Maharashtra. In Commerce (Suppl.) 129,3300 (10 Aug. 1974) 29-44.

21211 INDIAN MERCHANTS' CHAMBER. Techno-economic survey of Konkan Region, an underdeveloped area of Maharashtra. Bombay: 1964. 142p.

21212 Maharashtra: an economic review. Bombay: Maharashtra Econ. Dev. Council, 1967. 244p.

21213 NCAER. Techno-economic survey of Maharashtra. ND: 1963. 295p.

21214 PATIL, P.C. Regional survey of economic resources. India, Kolhapur; a typical study of resources and utility services of a region of the Indian Dominion. Bombay: 1950. 425p.

21215 RANBHISE, N.P. Regional economic disparities in Bombay state (a study based on 1951 census reports). Aurangabad: 1960. 75p.

21216 Regional imbalances in Maharashtra. Bombay: Maharashtra Econ. Dev. Council, 1976. 95p. (Its pub., 40)

21217 SAHASRABUDDHE, V.G. The economy of Maharashtra. Bombay: Admin. Staff College of Maharashtra State, 1972. 267p.

21218 SOVANI, N.V. Economic conditions in Maharashtra: data paper. In JUP 9 (1958) 105-16.

4. Economic Development and Planning

21219 DESHPANDE, S.H., ed. Economy of Maharastra; Shri C.V. Joag felicitation volume. Poona: Samaj Prabodhan Sanstha, 1973. 511p.

21220 KOLHAPUR. A development plan for the Kolhapur State 1946. Bombay: 1946. 184p.

21221 MAHARASHTRA. PLANNING DEPT. Eco-system plan for the development of Chandrapur District: document. Bombay: 1977. 209p. [former Chanda Dist.]

21222 MAHARASHTRA ECON. DEV. COUNCIL. MEDC, 1957-1977. Bombay: MEDC, 1978. 189p.

21223 ______. State planning and industrial development in Maharashtra. Bombay: MEDC, 1975. 286p.

21224 NAGAIYA, D. The identification of growth centers - a study of the Vidarbha region. In SIET Studies (Win. 1972) 1-17.

21225 NCAER. Industrial programmes for the Fourth Plan: Maharashtra. ND: 1966. 189p.

21226 TATA ECON. CONSULTANCY SERVICES. Second Maharashtra by 2005; a study in futurology. Bombay: Popular, 1977. 527p.

5. Finance and Banking

21227 BOMBAY (PRES.). PROVINCIAL BANKING ENQUIRY CMTEE. Report..., 1929-30. Bombay: Govt. Central Press, 1930. 4 v. [v. 1, Report. v. 2-4, Evidence; April 1937-Jan. 1950 = Bombay Prov., prior to 1937 = Pres.]

21228 JOSHI, T.M. Bombay finance (1921-46). Poona: GIPE, 1947. 220p. (Its pub., 16)

21229 PAREKH, H.T. The Bombay money market. Bombay: OUP, 1953. 226p.

21230 PARVATE, T.V. V.G. Kale: pioneer of banking in Maharashtra. In Commerce 132,3385 (1976) 510.

21231 RAMACHANDRA RAO, B. Early history of the Presidency Bank of Bombay. In CR 42 (1932) 89-107, 177-200.

21232 SHAH, A.C. & M.V. KULKARNI. Development of banking. In Economy of Maharashtra; Shri C.V. Joag felicitation volume. Poona: Samaj Prabodhan Sanstha, 1973. 511p.

21233 WACHA, D.E. A financial chapter in the history of Bombay city. 2nd ed. Bombay: A.J. Combridge, 1910. 224p.

6. Agriculture
a. agriculture in the Bombay Presidency, 1818 - 1947

21234 GUHA, A. Raw cotton of Western India: output, transportation and marketing, 1750-1850. In IESHR 9,1 (1972) 1-42.

21235 KEATINGE, G.F. Agricultural progress in western India. London: Longmans, Green, 1921. 253p.

21236 ______. Rural economy in the Bombay Deccan. London: Longmans, Green, 1912. 212p.

21237 KLEIN, I. Utilitarianism and agrarian progress in Western India. In EHR 18 (1965) 576-95.

21238 RAGHAVA RAO, G. The growth of agricultural production in the Bombay Presidency. In JUB 7 (1939) 98-117.

21239 TUCKER, R. Forest management and imperial politics: Thana District, Bombay, 1823-1887. In IESHR 16,3 (1979) 273-300.

b. agricultural development since 1947

21240 CHAUHAN, K.S., et al. Small farmers, problems and possibilities of development: a study in Sangli District of Maharashtra State. Ahmedabad: Centre for Mgmt. in Agri., Indian Inst. of Mgmt., 1973. 192p.

21241 KHARE, M.P. A study of income, saving and investment in agriculturally progressive areas in Ahmednagar District. In AV 15,3 (1973) 231-80.

21242 MAHARASHTRA. FINANCE DEPT. PLANNING DIV. Report of the evaluation enquiry into the working of intensive cultivation of food crops and pulses in the State of Maharashtra. Bombay: 1968. 93p.

21243 MAHARASHTRA ECON. DEV. COUNCIL. Agro-industries in Maharashtra - problems and prospects. Bombay: MEDC, 1969. 320p.

21244 NAMJOSHI, M.V. & M.D. SATHE. Planning for weaker sections. Pune: Centre of Studies in Social Sciences, 1978. 275p.

21245 SHINDE, S.D. Agriculture in an underdeveloped region: a geographical survey. Bombay: Himalaya Pub. House, 1980. 143p. + 16 pl. [Konkan]

21246 THORAT, S.S., ed. Report of a seminar on agricultural production and productivity in Maharashtra state, Mahatma Phule Agricultural University, July 1975. Rahuri: the University, 1976. 388p.

c. agricultural technology and innovation; irrigation

21247 BORKAR, V.V. & M.D. PADHYE. Purna River-Valley Project; a study of the socio-economic benefits. Aurangabad: Marathwada U., 1971. 202p.

21248 GADGIL, D.R. Economic benefits of irrigation, report of a survey of the direct and indirect benefits of the Godavari and Pravara Canals. Poona: GIPE, 1948. (Its pub., 17)

21249 INDIA (REP.). KRISHNA GODAVARI CMSN. Report of Krishna-Godavari Commission: summary of chapters I to XVII and full text of chapter XVIII. Bombay: Govt. Central Press, Govt. of Maharashtra, 1963. 60p.

21250 KARVE, I. & J. NIMBKAR. A survey of the people displaced through the Koyna Dam, July 1965 to January 1967. Poona: DCPRI, 1969. 148p.

21251 KHANDEWALE, S.V. Economics of cultivators and marketing of cotton in Vidarbha. Nagpur: Suvichar Prakashan Mandal, 1971. 188p.

21252 KULKARNI, D.G. People and irriculture. ND: Orient Longmans, 1970. 160p.

21253 ______. River basins of Maharashtra. ND: Orient Longmans, 1970. 60p.

21254 LAL, D. Wells and welfare: an exploratory cost-benefit study of the economics of small-scale irrigation in Maharashtra. Paris: Dev. Centre of the OECD, 1972. 162p.

21255 PATIL, R.K., et al. Appraisal of rural development project through systems analysis; a case study of rural electrification programme. Bombay: National Inst. of Bank Mgmt., 1976. 102p.

21256 SAPRE, S.G. Changes in land utilization and in cropping pattern in an irrigated village over two decades ending in 1960. In AV 6 (1964) 106-15.

d. land tenure and reform

21257 DANDEKAR, G.K. Law of land tenures in Bombay Presidency. Bombay: 1912. 2 v.

21258 DANDEKAR, V.M. & G.J. KHUDANPUR. Working of Bombay Tenancy Act, 1948: report of investigation. Poona: GIPE, 1957. (Its pub., 35)

21259 DANTWALA, M.L. & C.H. SHAH. Evaluation of land reforms; with special reference to the western region of India. Bombay: Dept. of Econ., U. of Bombay, 1971-72. 2 v.

21260 DESHPANDE, V.D. History of tenancy relations in the State of Maharashtra since 1900. In AV 12 (1970) 193-236.

21261 KUMAR, R. The rise of the rich peasants in Western India. In D.A. Low, ed. Soundings in modern South Asian history. Berkeley: UCalP, 1968, 25-58.

21262 MAHARASHTRA. CMTEE. APPOINTED BY THE GOVT. OF MAHARASHTRA FOR EVAL. OF LAND REFORMS. Report. Bombay: 1974. 407p. [Chm., M.P. Pande]

21263 MODAK, D.S. The Bombay land system and village administration. In six parts. Poona: Oriental Watchman Pub. House, 1932. 2 v., 287, 185p.

21264 NANEKAR, K.R. Land reforms in Vidarbha; an enquiry into the implementation of land reforms in the Vidarbha region. Calcutta: Oxford & IBH, 1968. 334p.

21265 NANEKAR, K.R. & S.V. KHANDEWALE. Bhoodan and the landless. Bombay: Popular, 1973. 125p. [study in Vidarbha]

21266 PATEL, G.D. The land problem of reorganized Bombay state. Bombay: N.M. Tripathi, 1957. 466p.

21267 ROGERS, A. The land revenue of Bombay; a history of its administration, rise, and progress. London: W.H. Allen, 1892. 2 v., 353, 424p.

e. rural credit and cooperatives

21268 BANK OF INDIA. ECON. & STAT. DEPT. Impact of agricultural finance: a case study of bank finance in Malsiras Taluka of Sholapur District. Bombay: 1975. 58p.

21269 CATANACH, I.J. Rural credit in western India, 1875-1930; rural credit and the co-operative movement in the Bombay Presidency. Berkeley: UCalP, 1970. 269p.

21270 KAJI, H.L. Cooperation in Bombay: short studies. Bombay: Taraporevala, 1930. 373p.

21271 MAHARASHTRA STATE CO-OP. UNION. Fifty years of co-operation; golden jubilee souvenir, 1904-54. Bombay: Bombay Provincial Co-op. Inst., 1954. 300p.

21272 NAIK, K.N. The cooperative movement in the Bombay State. Bombay: Popular, 1953. 282p.

f. agrarian unrest; the Deccan Riots of 1875

21273 BOMBAY (PRESIDENCY). CMTEE. ON THE RIOTS IN POONA & AHMEDNAGAR. Report..., 1875. Bombay: 1876. 2 v., 187, 188p.

21274 CATANACH, I.J. Agrarian disturbances in nineteenth century India. In IESHR 3,1 (1966) 65-84.

21275 CHARLESWORTH, N. The myth of the Deccan Riots of 1875. In MAS 6,4 (1972) 401-21.

21276 GHUGE, V.B. Review of regional development: early agrarian revolution in Kolhapur. In SER 4,4 (1975) 269-84.

21277 INDIAN NATL. CONGRESS. MAHARASHTRA PROVINCIAL

CONGRESS CMTEE. Report of the Peasant Enquiry Committee. Poona: S.D. Deo, 1936. 107p.

21278 JHIRAD, J.F.M. The Khandesh survey riots of 1852: government policy and rural society in Western India. In JRAS (1968) 151-65.

21279 KUMAR, R. The Deccan Riots of 1875. In JAS 24 (1965) 613-35.

21280 NEIL, J.W. The ryots of the Dekhan, and the legislation for their relief. In Asiatic R. 7 (1894) 396-419.

21281 PARULEKAR, G. Adivasis revolt: the story of Warli peasants in struggle. Calcutta: Natl. Book Agency, 1975. 188p. [Thana Dist.]

21282 Representation on the Deccan Agriculturist's relief bill. In Q.J. of the Poona Sarvajanik Sabha 2,3 (1879) 103-19.

g. famines and famine relief

21283 AUTI, V.B. & S.N. PAWAR. Famine: a study of a famine-stricken village in Maharashtra. In J. of Shivaji U. 7,13 (1974) 37-48.

21284 BOMBAY (PRESIDENCY). Famine relief code. Bombay Presidency, 1912. Bombay: Govt. Central Press, 1912. 225p.

21285 ______. Report on the famine in the Bombay Province, 1899-1902. Bombay: 1903. 2 v.

21286 ETHERIDGE, A.T., comp. Report on past famines in the Bombay Presidency. Bombay: Govt. of Bombay, 1868. 156 + 107p.

21287 The Indian famine: how dealt with in Western India. In Westminster R. 109 (Jan. 1878) 139-58.

21288 LADEJINSKY, W. Drought in Maharashtra: (not in a hundred years). In EPW 8,7 (1973) 683-96.

21289 MANN, H.H. Rainfall and famine; a study of rainfall in the Bombay Deccan, 1865-1938. Bombay: ISAE, 1955. 47p.

21290 PATVARDHAN, V.S. Food control in Bombay Province, 1939-1949. Poona: GIPE, 1958. 208p. (Its pub., 36)

7. Industry in Maharashtra since 1818
a. general studies

21291 GODBOLE, M.D. Industrial dispersal policies. Bombay: Himalaya Pub. House, 1978. 256p.

21292 MAHARASHTRA ECON. DEV. COUNCIL. Maharashtra, a guide to entrepreneurs. Bombay: MEDC, 1978. 267p. (Its pub., 50)

21293 ______. Power development in Maharashtra. Bombay: MEDC, 1975. 143p.

21294 PALSAPURE, P.Z. Industrial development of Vidarbha. Bombay: Popular, 1975. 236p.

21295 Recent trends in industrial production in India. Bombay: MEDC, 1977. 159p. (MEDC pub., 42)

b. studies of specific industries and industrialists

21296 Art in industry through the ages: monograph series on Bombay Presidency. ND: Navrang, 1976. 349 + 78p.

21297 HAMIED, K.A. K.A. Hamied: an autobiography; a life to remember. Bombay: Lalvani, 1972. 390p.

21298 INDIA (REP.). TEXTILE ENQUIRY CMTEE., 1952. Report. Delhi: MPGOI, 1955. 3 v. [Chm., Nityananda Kanungo]

21299 KAJI, H.L. Life and speeches of Sir Vithaldas Thackersey. Bombay: Taraporevala, 1934. 565p.

21300 MORRIS, M.D. Modern business organisation and labour administration; specific adaptations to Indian conditions of risk and uncertainty, 1850-1947. In EPW 14,40 (1979) 1680-87.

21301 MUDHOLKAR, G.G. Entrepreneurial and technical cadres of the Bombay cotton textile industry between 1854 and 1914. Diss., U. of N. Carolina, 1969. 389p. [UM 70-12,087]

21302 RUTNAGAR, S.M., ed. Bombay industries: the cotton mills... Bombay: Indian Textile J., Ltd., 1927. 744p.

21303 SHENDE, K.K. Salt industry of Bombay Province. Bombay: the author, 1947. 128p.

21304 VIJAYANAGAR, R.L.N., ed. Millowners' Association, Bombay: Centenary souvenir, 1875-1975. Bombay: The Assn., 1979. 573p.

21305 WADIA, R.A. Bombay dockyard and the Wadia master builders. Bombay: the author, 1957. 401p.

c. small-scale and cottage industries

21306 BOMBAY (PROVINCE). PROVINCIAL INDUSTRIES CMTEE. COTTAGE & SMALL-SCALE INDUSTRIES SUB-CMTEE. Report. Bombay: 1947. 177p.

21307 JOSHI, N.M. Urban handicrafts of the Bombay Deccan. Poona: D.R. Gadgil, 1936. 207p. (GIPE pub., 5)

21308 LAKDAWALA, D.T. & J.C. SANDESARA. Small industry in a big city: a survey in Bombay. Bombay: U. of Bombay, 1961. 403p. (Its Econ. series, 10)

8. Labor in Maharashtra since 1854
a. general studies

21309 AWCHAT, ANIL. Hamals of Poona: beasts of burden. In EPW 11,24-26 (1976) 862-64, 896-98, 942-43.

21310 BURNET-HURST, A. Labour and housing in Bombay; a study in the economic conditions of the wage-earning classes in Bombay. London: P.S. King, 1925. 160p.

21311 DEVADAS PILLAI, S. Men and machines. Bombay: Popular, 1968. 176p.

21312 GOKHALE, R.G. The Bombay cotton mill worker. Bombay: Millowners' Assn., 1957. 125p.

21313 JOSHI, H. & V. JOSHI. Surplus labour and the city: a study of Bombay. Delhi: OUP, 1976. 189p.

21314 LAMBERT, R.D. Workers, factories, and social change in India. Princeton: PUP, 1963. 247p.

21315 MEHTA, A.B. The domestic servant class. Bombay: Popular, 1960. 324p.

21316 MORRIS, M.D. The emergence of an industrial labor force in India; a study of the Bombay cotton mills, 1854-1947. Berkeley: UCalP, 1965. 263p.

21317 PATEL, KUNJ. Rural labour in industrial Bombay. Bombay: Popular, 1963. 191p.

21318 RAMACHANDRAN, P. Some aspects of labour mobility in Bombay City. Bombay: Somaiya, 1974. 139p. (TISS series, 30)

21319 THAKKER, G.K. Labour problems of textile industry; a study of the labour problems of the cotton mill industry in Bombay. Bombay: Vora, 1962. 175p.

b. wages and employment

21320 APTE, M.D. Wage scales and employment conditions; an analytical study. Poona: Industrial & Mgmt. Services, 1967. 1 v.

21321 MUKERJI, K. Trend in real wages in cotton textile mills in Bombay City and Island, from 1900 to 1951. In AV 1 (1959) 82-95.

21322 ______. Trend in textile mill wages in western India, 1900-1951. In AV 4 (1962) 156-65.

21323 NAIR, P.A. Employment market in an industrial metropolis; a survey of educated unemployment in Bombay. Bombay: Lalvani, 1968. 110p.

c. labor policy and legislation

21324 BOMBAY (PRESIDENCY). LABOUR OFFICE. Wages and employment in the Bombay cotton textile industry. Bombay: 1934. 220p.

21325 MAHARASHTRA. BADLI LABOUR INQUIRY CMTEE. COTTON TEXTILE INDUSTRY. Report, 1967. Bombay: 1968. 55p.

21326 MAHARASHTRA. NORMS CMTEE. Report. Bombay: 1961. 278p.

d. labor movement and trade unions

21327 AUTI, V.B. The working class movement in the nineteenth century Maharashtra. In J. of Shivaji U. 5,9-10 (1972) 39-48.

21328 DURAND-DASTES, F. Entrepreneurs et ouvriers d'industrie à Poona (Maharashtra). In Puruṣārtha 3 (1977) 109-40.

21329 KULKARNI, P.D. Textile trade unionism in Bombay. In IJSW 7 (1946) 224-38.

21330 KUMAR, RAVINDER. The Bombay textile strike, 1919. In IESHR 8,1 (1971) 1-30.

9. Commerce and Transportation

21331 BHOYMEEAH, TYABJEE. The autobiography of Tyabjee Bhoymeeah, merchant prince of Bombay, 1803-1863. Ed. by Asaf A.A. Fyzee. Bombay: Asiatic Soc. of Bombay, 1964. 75p. [Issued as JASBombay ns 36/37 (1961/62) Suppl.] [English, Urdu & Hindi]

21332 GUHA, A. The comprador role of Parsi seths, 1750-1850. In EPW 5,48 (1970) 1933-36.

21333 ______. Parsi seths as entrepreneurs, 1750-1850. In EPW 5,35 (1970) M107-M115.

21334 JOG, N.G. Narottam Morarjee, architect of modern Indian shipping. Bombay: Scindia Steam Navigation Co., 1977. 151p.

21335 KHANOLKAR, G.D. Walchand Hirachand; man, his times and achievements. Bombay: Walchand & Co., 1969. 679p.

21336 LELE, U.J. The traders of Sholapur. In J.W. Mellor, et al., eds. Developing rural India.... Ithaca, NY: Cornell UP, 1968, 237-94.

21337 RAO, S.B. Distributive trade in Poona. Bombay: Vaikunth Mehta Inst. of Coop. Mgmt., 1973. 310p. (Its Consumer studies, 9)

21338 SAWANT, S.B. & T.M. VARAT. Shopping areas in the city of Poona. In GRI 40,2 (1978) 155-63.

21339 SHEJWALKAR, P.C. Transport in Maharashtra. In JUP 15 (1962) 144-50.

21340 Shipowners' problems at the Port of Bombay: analysis and recommendations. ND: Indian Inst. of Foreign Trade, 1968. 130p.

21341 TAWDE, M.D. Report on a project entitled the Post-independence trends in weekly markets and fairs in South Ratnagiri District. Kolhapur: Shivaji U., 1977. 51p.

C. Society and Social Change in Maharashtra since 1818

1. Social Reform and Reformers in Maharashtra and Bombay Presidency

a. general studies

21342 BALLHATCHET, K. Social policy and social change in India, 1817-30. London: OUP, 1957. 335p.

21343 GUMPERZ, E.M. English education and social change in late nineteenth century Bombay. Diss., U. of California, Berkeley, 1965. 500p. [UM 65-13,499]

21344 ______. English education and social reform in late nineteenth century Bombay: a case study in the transmission of a cultural ideal. In JAS 25 (1966) 453-70.

21345 KUMAR, RAVINDER. Western India in the nineteenth century; a study in the social history of Maharashtra. London: Routledge & Kegan Paul, 1968. 347p.

21346 TUCKER, R.P. From dharmashashtra to politics: aspects of social authority in nineteenth century Maharashtra. In IESHR 7,3 (1970) 325-45.

b. Mahadev Govind Ranade (1842-1901): High Court Justice and founder of the National Social Conference, 1887 -

21347 JAGIRDAR, P.J. Mahadeo Govind Ranade. ND: PDMIB, 1971. 219p.

21348 KARVE, D.G. Ranade: the prophet of liberated India. Poona: Aryabhushan Press, 1942. 215p.

21349 KELLOCK, J. Mahadev Govind Ranade. Calcutta: Assn. Press, 1926. 204p.

21350 MANKAR, G.A. A sketch of the life and works of the late Mr. Justice M.G. Ranade. Bombay: Caxton Printing Works, 1902. 2 v.

21351 PARVATE, T.V. Mahadev Govind Ranade, a biography. NY: Asia, 1964. 326p.

21352 RANADE, MAHADEV GOVIND. Religious and social reform. A collection of essays and speeches. Ed. by M.B. Kolasker. Bombay: G. Narayen, 1902. 304p.

21353 RANADE, RAMABAI. Ranade: his wife's reminiscences. Tr. by K. Deshpande. Delhi: PDMIB, 1963. 232p.

21354 TUCKER, R.P. The proper limits of agitation; the crisis of 1879-80 in Bombay Presidency. In JAS 28 (1969) 339-55.

21355 ______. Ranade and the roots of Indian nationalism. Bombay: Popular, 1972. 352p.

c. women's reform movements

21356 ATHAVALE, P. My story; the autobiography of a Hindu widow. Tr. by J.E. Abbott. NY: Putnam's, 1930. 149p.

21357 CHANDAVARKAR, G.L. Dhondo Keshav Karve. ND: MPGOI, 1970. 248p.

21358 ______. Maharshi Karve. Bombay: Popular, 1958. 233p.

21359 DONGRE, R.K. & J.E. PATTERSON. Pandita Ramabai; a life of faith and prayer. Madras: CLS, 1963. 116p.

21360 DYER, H.S. Pandita Ramabai: her vision, her mission, and triumph of faith. London: Pickering & Inglis, 1923. 173p.

21361 HINGNE STREE-SHIKSHAN SAMSTHA. Maharshi Karve, his 105 years. Poona: 1963. 108p.

21362 KARVE, D.K. Looking back. Poona: Hindu Widow's Home Assn., 1936. 199p.

21363 ______. My life story. In D.D. Karve, ed. & tr. The new Brahmans... Berkeley: UCalP, 1963, 17-57.

21364 LIMAYE, P.N. Politicization of women in Maharashtra. In Vina Mazumdar, ed. Symbols of power... Bombay: Allied, 1979, 119-39.

21365 MACNICOL, N. Pandita Ramabai. Calcutta: Assn. Press, 1926. 154p.

21366 MADHAVADASA RAGHUNATHADASA. Story of a widow remarriage: being the experiences of Madhowdas Rugnathdas, merchant of Bombay. Bombay: S.K. Khambata, 1890. 118p.

21367 RAMABAI SARASVATI. The high-caste Hindu woman. NY: F.H. Revell, 1901. 42p. [1st pub. 1887]

21368 RAMABAI SARASVATI. The letters and correspondence of Pandita Ramabai. Comp. by Sister Geraldine. Ed. by A.B. Shah. Bombay: Maharashtra State Board for Literature & Culture, 1977. 435p.

21369 TAWALE, S.N. Profiles of women in Maharashtra [state politics]. In Vina Mazumdar, ed. Symbols of power.... Bombay: Allied, 1976, 246-63.

d. other social reformers

21370 CHANDAVARKAR, G.L. A wrestling soul: story of the life of Sir Narayan Chandavarkar. Bombay: Popular, 1955. 229p.

21371 JAMBHEKAR, G.G. Memories and writings of Acharya Bal Shastri Jambhekar. Poona: Lokashikshana Karyalaya, 1950. 3 v.

21372 JOGENDRA SINGH. B.M. Malabari: rambles with the pilgrim reformer. London: G. Bell, 1914. 202p.

21373 KARKARIA, R.P. India, forty years of progress and reform; a sketch of the life and times of Behramji M. Malabari. London: H. Frowde, 1896. 151p.

21374 KSHIRE, V.K. Lokahitawadi's thought: a critical study. Poona: U. of Poona, 1977. 170p. [Gopal Hari Deshmukh, 1823-1892]

21375 PRADHAN, G.P. Gopal Ganesh Agarkar, 1856-1895, rationalist of Maharashtra. Calcutta: Indian Renaissance Inst., 1962. 44p.

21376 SHAHANI, D.G. Un Reformateur Parsi - Behramji M. Malabari. Tr. from the English of M. Dayaram Gidumal. Paris: E. Flammarion, 1898. 300p.

2. Social Categories in Maharashtra, incl. Kinship and Marriage [see also II. A. above]

a. general studies

21377 BHATTACHARYA, D.K. The Anglo-Indians in Bombay: an introduction to their socio-economic and cultural life. In Race 10 (1968) 163-72.

21378 BOPEGAMAGE, A. & P.V. VEERARAGHAVAN. Status images in changing India. Bombay: Manaktalas, 1967. 212p. [studies of Coimbatore & Poona]

21379 ENTHOVEN, R.E. The tribes and castes of Bombay. Delhi: Cosmo, 1975-. [Rpt. 1920-22 ed., 3 v., 1299p.]

21380 KANNAN, C.T. Intercaste and inter-community marriages in India. Bombay: Allied, 1963. 236p.

21381 KARVE, I. Kinship terminology and kinship usages of the Maratha country. In BDCRI 1 (1939) 327-89; 2 (1940) 9-33.

21382 ______. Maharashtra; land and its people. Bombay: Dir. of Govt. Printing, 1968. 230p. (Maharashtra State Gazetteer)

21383 OMVEDT, G. Development of the Maharashtrian class structure, 1818-1931. In EPW 8,31-33 (1973) 1417-32.

21384 PARANJPE, A.C. Caste, prejudice, and the individual. Bombay: Lalvani, 1970. 236p.

21385 PATTERSON, M.L.P. Intercaste marriage in Maharashtra. In EW 10,4-6 (1958) 139-42.

21386 SANGAVE, V.A. Changing pattern of caste organization in Kolhapur City. In SB 11,1/2 (1961) 36-59.

21387 STRAUS, M.A. Some social class differences in family patterns in Bombay. In G. Kurian, ed. The family in India.... The Hague: Mouton, 1974, 233-48.

21388 STRAUS, M.A. & D. WINKELMANN. Social class, fertility, and authority in nuclear and joint households in Bombay. In JAAS(L) 4 (1969) 61-74.

b. Brahman castes: Chitpavan and Deshastha [for Saraswats, see Chap. Eleven, V. C. 1. b]

21389 PATTERSON, M.L.P. Changing patterns of occupation among Chitpavan Brahmans. In IESHR 7,3 (1970) 375-96.

21390 ______. Chitpavan Brahman family histories: sources for a study of social structure and social change in Maharashtra. In M.B. Singer & B.S. Cohn, eds. Structure and change in Indian society. Chicago: Aldine, 1968, 397-411.

21391 KARVE, D.D., ed. & tr. The new Brahmans. Five Maharashtrian families. Berkeley: UCalP, 1963. 303p.

21392 KARVE, I. A family through six generations. In L.K. Bala Ratnam, ed. Anthropology on the march. Madras: Book Centre, 1963, 241-62.

c. Non-Brahman castes: Marathas and others

21393 BETHAM, R.M. Marathas and Dekhani Musalmans. Calcutta: Supt. Govt. Printing, 1908. 196p. (Handbooks for the Indian army)

21394 CARTER, A.T. Caste "boundaries" and the principle of kinship amity: a Maratha caste Purāṇa. In CIS ns 9,1 (1975) 123-37.

21395 GULATI, R.K. Inter-group differences in an artisan caste of Maharashtra. Miami, FL: Field Research Projects, 1971. 114p.

21396 GUPTE, B.A. Kayastha Prabhus of Bombay, Baroda, Central India, and Central Provinces. Calcutta: Bee Press, 1913. 82p.

21397 ______. A Prabhu marriage; customary and religious ceremonies performed in the marriage of a member of the Chandraseni Kayasth Prabhus of Bombay.... Calcutta: Supt. Govt. Printing, 1911. 76p.

21398 KAKADE, R.G. A socio-economic survey of weaving communities in Sholapur. Poona: D.R. Gadgil, 1947. 221p. (GIPE pub., 14)

21399 KALE, D.N. Agris: a socio-economic survey. Bombay: Asia, 1952. 411p.

21400 MORAB, S.G. Caste council of the Bhandari of Dapoli. In MI 46,2 (1966) 154-63.

21401 ORENSTEIN, H. Caste and the concept "Maratha" in Maharashtra. In EA 16 (1963) 1-9.

21402 SAMANTA, D.K. Tradition and migrant group - a case from Maharashtra. In EA 32,1 (1979) 25-36. [Rajputs in Vidarbha]

d. Mahars and other "Untouchables"

i. general studies

21403 BHAGAT, M.G. The untouchable classes of Maharashtra. Bombay: U. of Bombay, 1955. 45p.

21404 Children of God become Panthers. In EPW 8,31/33 (1973) 1395-98. [on Dalit Panthers]

21405 CHINCHUNSURE, B.S. Rights-social equality and riots: a study with reference to the recent riots in Marathwada. Bombay: Maharashtra Sarvodaya Mandal, 1978. 31p.

21406 CHITNIS, S. Literacy and educational enrolment among the scheduled castes of Maharashtra. Bombay: Unit for Res. in the Sociology of Educ., TISS, 1974. 191p. (TISS Series, 31)

21407 The Dalit Panthers and their manifesto. In R & S 22,2 (1975) 24-38.

21408 DESHPANDE, V.D. Towards social integration: problems of adjustment scheduled caste elite. Pune: Shubhada-Saraswat, 1978. 224p.

21409 LYNCH, OWEN M. Some aspects of political mobilization among Adi-Dravidas in Bombay City. In R.I. Crane, ed. Aspects of political mobilization in South Asia. Syracuse: Maxwell School of Citizenship & Public Affairs, Syracuse U., 1976, 7-34. (Its Foreign & Comp. Studies; South Asian series, 1)

21410 MILLER, R.J. & PRAMODH KALE. The burden on the head is always there. In J.M. Mahar, ed. The Untouchables in contemporary India. Tucson: U. of Arizona Press, 1972, 317-60.

21411 PATWARDHAN, S. Change among India's Harijans: Maharashtra - a case study. ND: Orient Longman, 1973. 239p.

21412 ROBERTSON, A. The Mahar folk: a study of untouchables in Maharashtra. Calcutta: YMCA Pub. House, 1938. 101p.

ii. conversion of the Mahars to Buddhism under Dr. Ambedkar (1956) and its political consequences

21413 AMBEDKAR, B.R. The Buddha and his dhamma. Bombay: People's Educ. Soc., 1957. 599p.

21414 BHANDARE, R.D. The problems of the Indian Buddhists. Bombay: 1966. 68p.

21415 FINDLY, E.B. B.R. Ambedkar and the neo-Buddhist movement in India. In IAF 7,3/4 (1976) 289-321.

21416 FISKE, A.M. Buddhistische Bewegungen in Indien. In H. Dumoulin, ed. Buddhismus der Gegenwart. Freiburg: Herder, 1970, 72-88. [1st pub. in Saeculum 20 (1969) 236-52]

21417 ______. Religion and Buddhism among India's new Buddhists. In Social Research 36 (1969) 123-57.

21418 GOKHALE, B.G. Dr. Bhimrao Ramji Ambedkar: rebel against Hindu tradition. In JAAS(L) 11,1/2 (1974) 13-23.

21419 KARVE, I. & HEMALATA ACHARYA. Neo-Buddhism in Maharashtra. In JUP 15 (1962) 130-33.

21420 MILLER, B.D. Revitalization movements: theory and practice, as evidenced among the Buddhists of Maharashtra. In M.C. Pradhan, ed. Anthropology and Archaeology. London: OUP, 1969, 108-126.

21421 MILLER, R.J. Button, Button ... Great Tradition, Little Tradition, whose tradition? In Anthropological Q. 39 (1966) 26-42.

21422 ______. "They will not die Hindus": the Buddhist conversion of Mahar ex-untouchables. In AS 7 (1967) 637-44.

21423 PATWARDHAN, S. Social mobility and conversion of the Mahars. In SB 17 (1968) 187-202.

21424 PRESLER, H.H. The Neo-Buddhist stir in India. In ICQ 21,4 (1964) 1-29.

21425 WILKINSON, T.S. & M.M. THOMAS, eds. Ambedkar and the neo-Buddhist movement. Madras: CLS for CISRS, 1972. 163p.

21426 ZELLIOT, E.M. Background of the Mahar Buddhist conversion. In Studies on Asia (U. of Nebraska) 7 (1966) 49-63.

21427 ______. Buddhism and politics in Maharashtra. In D.E. Smith, ed. South Asian Politics and Religion. Princeton: PUP, 1966, 191-212.

21428 ______. The psychological dimension of the Buddhist movements in India. In G.A. Oddie, ed. Religion in South Asia.... ND: Manohar, 1977, 119-44.

21429 ______. Religion and legitimation in the Mahar movement. In B.L. Smith, ed. Religion and the legitimation of power in South Asia. Leiden: Brill, 1978, 88-105.

21430 ______. The revival of Buddhism in India. In AS 10 (Winter 1968) 33-45.

e. religious minorities
i. the Parsis: Zoroastrians of Bombay and other cities

21431 DAVAR, S.R. The history of the Parsi punchayet of Bombay. Bombay: New Book Co., 1949. 80p.

21432 DESAI, S.F. A community at the cross-road. Bombay: New Book Co., 1948. 201p.

21433 ______. Survival value of the Parsi: a socio-anthropological approach. In JASBombay 4 (1950) 40-48.

21434 DOBBIN, C. The Parsi Panchayat in Bombay city in the nineteenth century. In MAS 4,2 (1970) 149-64.

21435 EDWARDES, S.M. Kharshedji Rustamji Cama, 1831-1909; a memoir. London: OUP, 1923. 156p.

21436 Famous Parsis; biographical and critical sketches of patriots, philanthropists, politicians, reformers, scholars and captains of industry. Madras: G.A. Natesan, 1930. 488p.

21437 JOSHI, A.N. Life and times of Chevalier Framroze Dinshaw. Bombay: Brihad Gujarat Pub. House, 1950. 198p.

21438 KULKE, E. The Parsees in India: a minority as agent of social change. München: Weltforum Verlag, 1974. 300p.

21439 MANKEKAR, D.R. Homi Mody, a many splendoured life; a political biography. Bombay: Popular, 1968. 255p.

21440 MODI, J.J., ed. The K.R. Cama masonic jubilee volume: containing papers on masonic subjects. Bombay: Fort Printing Press, 1907. 293p.

21441 NANAVUTTY, P. The Parsis. ND: NBT, 1977. 191p.

21442 WADIA, P.A. Parsis ere the shadows thicken. Bombay: 1949. 170p.

ii. Muslim groups of Maharashtra

21443 ENGINEER, ASGHAR ALI. The Bohras. ND: Vikas, 1980. 332p.

21444 GREENWALL, H.J. His Highness the Aga Khan, Imam of the Ismailis. London: Cresset Press, 1952. 240p.

21445 ISHVANI. The brocaded sari. NY: J. Day, 1946. 205p. [Khoja autobiog.]

21446 MASSELOS, J.C. The Khojas of Bombay: the defining of formal membership criteria during the nineteenth century. In Imtiaz Ahmad, ed. Caste and social stratification among the Muslims. ND: Manohar, 1973, 1-20.

21447 SAIYED, A.R. Purdah, family structure, and the status of woman: a note on a deviant case. In Imtiaz Ahmad, ed. Family, Kinship and marriage among the Muslims in India. ND: Manohar, 1976, 235-64.

21448 SYED, MUJTABA ALI. The origin of the Khojas and their religious life today. Würzburg: R. Mayr, 1936. 209p.

21449 WRIGHT, T.P., JR. Muslim kinship and modernization: the Tyabji clan of Bombay. In Imtiaz Ahmad, ed. Family, kinship and marriage among the Muslims in India. ND: Manohar, 1976, 217-38.

iii. Christians of Maharashtra

21450 BAPTISTA, E.W. The East Indians; Catholic community of Bombay, Salsette and Bassein. Bombay: Bombay East Indian Assn., 1967. 255p. (Pub. of the Anthropos Inst., Indian Branch, 3)

21451 GODWIN, C.J. Change and continuity; a study of two Christian village communities in suburban Bombay. Bombay: Tata McGraw-Hill Pub. Co., 1972. 248p.

21452 MOULTON, J.L. Faith for the future; the American Marathi Mission, India sesquicentennial, 1963. NY: United Church Board for World Ministries, 1967. 228p.

21453 READ, H. The Christian Brahmun, or memoirs of the life, writings, and character of the converted Brahmun, Babajee. NY: Leavitt, Lord, 1836. 2v.

21454 TILAK, LAKSHMIBAI. From Brahma to Christ, the story of Narayan Waman Tilak and Lakshmibai, his wife. London: United Soc. for Christian Literature, 1956. 95p.

21455 WINSLOW, J.C. Narayan Vaman Tilak: the Christian poet of Maharashtra. Calcutta: Assn. Press, 1923. 137p.

iv. the Bene Israel: an indigenous Jewish community

21456 GUSSIN, C.M. The Bene Israel of India: politics, religion, and systemic change. Ph.D. Diss., Syracuse U., 1973. 214p. [UM 73-9527]

21457 ISRAEL, B.J. Religious evolution among the Bene Israel of India since 1750. Bombay: 1963. 22p.

21458 STRIZOWER, S. The Bene Israel of Bombay: a study of a Jewish community. NY: Schocken, 1971. 190p. [also issued as: Children of Israel: Bene Israel of Bombay. Bombay: OUP, 1971. 170p.]

v. "Neo-Buddhists" (Nava-Bauddhas): see C.2.d.ii above

3. Villages and Rural Development
a. villages of the Konkan Coast

21459 CHAPEKAR, L.N. Community development project blocks in Badlapur. In SB 7 (1958) 111-32.

21460 MORRISON, W.A. Family types in Badlapur: an analysis of a changing institution in a Maharashtrian village. In SB 8 (1959) 45-67.

21461 PUNEKAR, S.D. & A.R. GOLWALKAR. Community development, panchayat raj, and change in rural Konkan. In IJSW 33,4 (Jan 1973) 347-60.

21462 ______. Rural change in Maharashtra: an analytical study of change in six villages in Konkan. Bombay: Popular, 1973. 138p. (TISS series, 30A)

21463 RANADE, V.G. A social and economic survey of a Konkan village. Bombay: Provincial Coop. Inst., 1927. 113p.

b. villages of the Deccan Plateau (Desh, Marathwada, and Nag-Vidarbha)

21464 BADEN-POWELL, B.H. Study of the Dakhan villages, their origin and development. In JRAS (1897) 239-79.

21465 COATS, T. Account of the present state of the township of Lony. In Literary Society of Bombay, Trans. 3 (1823) 183-280. [see 21470 below]

21466 DANDEKAR. K. & V. BHATE. Socio-economic change during three five-year plans: based on a study of rural communities during 1953-66. In AV 17,4 (1975) 305-453.

21467 DELFENDAHL, B. Parenté, fonction, et territoire dans les cultes champêtres d'un village de l'Inde. In L'Homme 11,1 (1971) 52-67.

21468 DESHPANDE, U.G. & R.S. SAVALE. Nhavari; a socio-economic study. Poona: Maharashtra Dept. of Agri., 1967. 85p. (Its Socio-econ. studies, 3) [Dhulia district]

21469 DISKALKAR, P.D. Resurvey of a Deccan village: Pimple Saudagar. Bombay: ISAE, 1960. 160p.

21470 GHURYE, G.S. After a century and a quarter; Lonikand then and now. Bombay: Popular, 1960. 126p. [restudy of Coats' village, Lony, 21465 above]

21471 HIRAMANI, A.B. Social change in rural India: a study of two villages in Maharashtra. Delhi: B.R., 1977. 320p. [Marathwada]

21472 JAGALPURE, L.B. & K.D. KALE. Sarola Kasar. A study of a Deccan village in the famine zone. Ahmednagar: L.B. Jagalpure, 1938. 459p.

21473 JOSHI, V.H. Dongargaon: a socio-economic study. Poona: Maharashtra State Dept. of Agri., 1967. 131p. [Akola district]

21474 KAMBLE, N.D. Poverty within poverty: a study of the weaker sections in a Deccan village. ND: Sterling, 1979. 134p.

21475 KARVE, I. The role of weekly markets in the tribal, rural, and urban setting. Poona: DCPRI, 1970. 148p. (DCBC, 70)

21476 KARVE, I. & Y.B. DAMLE. Group relations in village community. Poona: DCPRI, 1963. 483p.

21477 MAHARASHTRA. DEPT. OF AGRI. Natambi; a socio-economic study. Poona: 1966. 114p. (Its Socio-econ. studies, 1) [Poona district]

21478 MANN, H.H. Land and labor in a Deccan village. Bombay: OUP, 1917. 184p. (U. of Bombay econ. series, 1)

21479 MANN, H.H. & N.V. KANITKAR. Land and labor in a Deccan village, study no. 2. Bombay: OUP, 1921. 182p. (U. of Bombay econ. series, 3)

21480 ORENSTEIN, H. Gaon: conflict and cohesion in a Maharashtrian village. Princeton: PUP, 1965. 341p. [Poona district]

21481 SHAHANI, S. Kinship in an Indian village. In G. Kurian, ed. The family in India.... The Hague: Mouton, 1974, 139-150.

21482 SRIVASTAVA, U.K. & P.S. GEORGE. Rural development in action: the experience of a voluntary agency. Bombay: Somaiya, 1977. 205p.

21483 UDESHI, J.J. Community development: costs and benefits: a study based on Purandhar Taluka of Maharashtra. Bombay: U. of Bombay, 1974. 237p. [Poona district]

21484 VALUNJKAR, T.N. Social organization, migration and change in a village community. Poona: DCPRI, 1966. 85p. [Satara district]

4. Cities and Urbanization
a. general studies

21485 AMLADI, D.R. & P.N. NARKHEDE. Aurangabad, queen of the Deccan. Bombay: Dir. of Archives, Govt. of Maharashtra, 1977. 24p.

21486 GADGIL, D.R. Sholapur city: socio-economic studies. Poona: GIPE, 1965. 337p. (GIPE pub. 46)

21487 GUMPERZ, E.M. City-hinterland relations and the development of a regional elite in nineteenth century Bombay. In JAS 33,4 (1974) 581-602.

21488 INDIAN SCIENCE CONGRESS, 1920. Nagpur and its environs. Nagpur: Govt. Press, 1920. 44p.

21489 KARVE, I. & J.S. RANADIVE. The social dynamics of a growing town and its surrounding area. Poona: DCPRI, 1965. 323p. (DCBC, 29) [Phaltan, Satara district]

21490 KULKARNI, M.G. Spatial distribution of some population characteristics in Aurangabad City. In J.V. Ferreira & S.S. Jha, ed. The outlook tower.... Bombay: Popular, 1976, 339-361.

21491 KULKARNI, S. Urbanising role of some cities in Maharashtra. In Interdiscipline 10,3 (1973) 67-84.

21492 MAHARASHTRA. TOWN PLANNING & VALUATION DEPT. Town planning in Maharashtra, 1914-1964; with special reference to new trends and future developments. Poona: 1965. 79p.

21493 MAHARASHTRA. URBAN DEV., PUBLIC HEALTH & HOUSING DEPT. Urban development in Maharashtra; progress and prospect. Bombay: 1967. 165p.

21494 PRABHAVALKAR, B.H. & K.S. BAHULEYAN. Trends of urbanisation in a new township: problems and prospects: a case study of Khopoli industrial complex. Bombay: Regional Centre for Training & Res. in Municipal Admin., All-India Inst. of Local Self-Govt., 1977. 148p. [Kolaba district]

21495 Selected papers in urban and regional planning. Bombay: Bombay Regional Chapter, Inst. of Town Planners, 1977. 135p.

21496 SOVANI, N.V. Social survey of Kolhapur City. Poona: D.R. Gadgil, 1952. 3v. (GIPE pub., 23, 24)

b. Bombay City, capital of Maharashtra (1981 pop. 8,202,759) [for govt. and politics, see IV.A.7.e, above]
i. historical studies since 1818

21497 BULSARA, J.F. Bombay, a city in the making. Bombay: Natl. Info. & Pub., 1948. 136p.

21498 EDWARDES, S.M. By-ways of Bombay. With illustrations by M.V. Dhurandhar. 2nd ed. Bombay: Taraporevala, 1912. 139p.

21499 ______, comp. Gazetteer of Bombay City and Island. Bombay: Times Press, 1909-10. 3v. [extensive historical sections; based on materials assembled by Sir James McNabb Campbell]

21500 LEIFER, W., ed. Bombay and the Germans. Bombay: Shakuntala Pub. House, 1975. 245p.

21501 LEWIS, R. Three faces has Bombay. Sketches by K.K. Hebbar. Bombay: Popular, 1957. 234p.

21502 Life in Bombay and the neighbouring out-stations. London: R. Bentley, 1852. 350p.

21503 MALABARI, B.M. Bombay in the making. London: T.F. Unwin, 1910. 507p.

21504 PUSALKER, A.D. & V.G. DIGHE. Bombay, story of the island city. Bombay: All India Oriental Conf., 1949. 125p.

21505 SULIVAN, R.J.F. One hundred years of Bombay: history of the Bombay Chamber of Commerce, 1836-1936. Bombay: Times of India Press, 1938. 319p.

21506 UJAGIR SINGH. Bombay: a study in historical geography 1667-1900 A.D. In NGJI 6 (1960) 19-29.

ii. the Bombay metropolitan area and problems of migration

21507 BULSARA, J.F. Patterns of social life in metropolitan areas; with particular reference to Greater Bombay. ND: Planning Cmsn., 1970. 456p.

21508 CHATTERJEE, M. Stabilization of immigrants in Indian towns: the case of Bombay. In SB 20,2 (1971) 145-158.

21509 FERREIRA, J.V. Socio-cultural analysis of greater Bombay and adjoining districts. In JAnthSB ns 13,1 (1968) 69-107.

21510 GORE, M.S. Inmigrants and neighbourhoods; two aspects of life in a metropolitan city. Bombay: TISS, 1970. 303p. (TISS series, 21)

21511 PADKI, M.B. Outmigration from a Konkan village to

Bombay. In AV 6 (1964) 27-35.

21512 RAJAGOPALAN, C. An ecological analysis of the growth of Bombay City. In Geografia 2 (1963) 99-105.

21513 ______. The Greater Bombay; a study in suburban ecology. Bombay: Popular, 1962. 211p.

21514 ZACHARIAH, K.C. The Maharashtrian and Gujarati migrants in greater Bombay. In SB 15,2 (1966) 68-87.

21515 ______. Migrants in Greater Bombay. Bombay: Asia, 1968. 355p.

iii. urban planning and economic development

21516 The Bombay Chamber of Commerce & Industry: directory of members. Bombay: 1976. 1023p.

21517 BOMBAY METROPOLITAN REGIONAL PLANNING BOARD. Regional plan for Bombay metropolitan region, 1971-91. Bombay: 1970. v.-

21518 Bombay: planning and dreaming. In Mārg 18,3 (1965) 1-56.

21519 Bombay's development and master plan: a 20 years' perspective. Bombay: Bombay Civic Trust, 1970. 394p. [1968 seminar]

21520 CHATTERJEE, A.K. Contemporary urban architecture: a design approach: a study of Bombay. Delhi: Macmillan, 1977. 133p.

21521 GANDHI, N.K. A brief study of the Bombay Town Planning Act of 1954. In QJLSGI 30 (1960) 459-78.

21522 HARRIS, N. Economic development, cities, and planning: the case of Bombay. Bombay: OUP, 1978. 93p.

21523 INDIAN STAT. INST. BOMBAY BRANCH. Report on the survey into the economic conditions of middle class families in Bombay city. Bombay: 1955. 63p.

21524 LAKDAWALA, D.T. Work, wages and well-being in an Indian metropolis; economic survey of Bombay city. Bombay: U. of Bombay, 1963. 863p. (Its Ser. in econ., 11)

21525 MAHARASHTRA ECON. DEV. COUNCIL. Twin city for Bombay; development prospects and problems. Bombay: Govt. Press, 1970. 226p. [seminar]

21526 PATEL, S.B. Regional planning for Bombay. In EPW 5,26 (1970) 1011-18.

iv. urban mass transportation

21527 INDIA (REP.). METROPOLITAN TRANSPORT TEAM. Report on existing mass transportation system, Bombay. 1968. 55p.

21528 MAHARASHTRA. TOWN PLANNING & VALUATION DEPT. TRAFFIC CELL. The mass transportation study, Bombay. Bombay: 1969. 139p. + 32pl.

21529 PATANKAR, P.G. Urban mobility in developing countries. Bombay: Popular Prakashan, 1978. 152p.

21530 PENDSE, S.N. The B.E.S.T. story. Tr. from Marathi by M.V. Rajadhyaksha. Bombay: Bombay Electric Supply & Transport Undertaking, 1972. 229p. + 10pl.

v. housing and slums

21531 DESAI, A.R. & S.D. PILLAI. A profile of an Indian slum. Bombay: U. of Bombay, 1972. 272p.

21532 LYNCH, O.M. Political mobilisation and ethnicity among Adi-Dravidas in a Bombay slum. In EPW 9,39 (1974) 1657-1668.

21533 SRINIVASAN, K.S., ed. Benefits of subsidized housing to industrial workers. ND: Natl. Buildings Org., Govt. of India & UN Regional Housing Centre, ECAFE, 1972. 115p. [study by TISS]

21534 RAMACHANDRAN, P. Housing situation in Greater Bombay. Bombay: Somaiya, 1977. 118p. (TISS series, 38)

21535 ______. Pavement dwellers in Bombay City, by P. Ramachandran. Bombay: TISS, 1972. 58p. (TISS series, 26)

21536 ______. Social and economic rents and subsidies for low-income groups in Greater Bombay. Bombay: Lalvani, 1967. 79p. (TISS series, 18)

vi. urban social problems and welfare

21537 BALAKRISHNA, K. A portrait of Bombay's underworld. Bombay: Manaktalas, 1966. 168p.

21538 DESAI, K.G. & R.D. NAIK. Problems of retired people in Greater Bombay. Bombay: TISS, 1973. 180p. (TISS series, 27)

21539 KHANDEKAR, M. Utilization of social and welfare services in Greater Bombay. Bombay: TISS, 1974. 262p. (TISS series, 34)

21540 MAYUR, RASHMI. Problmes of metropolises with special reference to Bombay. [workshop papers]. In JITP 88/89 (1975-76) 19-121.

21541 PUNEKAR, S.D. A study of prostitutes in Bombay, with reference to family background. 2nd rev. ed. Bombay: Lalvani, 1967. 244p.

21542 RAMACHANDRAN, P. Social welfare manpower in Greater Bombay. Bombay: Somaiya, 1977. 112p. (TISS series, 37)

c. Poona/Pune: Maharashtra's cultural center (1981 pop. 1,685,266)

21543 APHALE, C. Growing up in an urban complex: a study of upbringing of children in Maharashtrian Hindu families in Poona. ND: Natl. Pub. House, 1976. 175p.

21544 BAPAT, M. & N. CROOK. Housing and slums in Poona reconsidered: the possible alternatives. In EPW 14,33 (1979) 1425-31.

21545 BRAHME, S. & P. GOLE. Deluge in Poona; aftermath and rehabilitation. Poona: GIPE, 1967. 144p. (GIPE studies, 51)

21546 CHITALE, K. Health of school children in Pune: statistical analysis. Pune: Shree Prakashan, 1977. 108p.

21547 GADGIL, D.R. Poona; a socio-economic survey. Poona: D.R. Gadgil, 1945-52. 2 v. (GIPE pub., 12, 25)

21548 GHURYE, G.S. Anatomy of a rururban community. Bombay: Popular, 1963. 232p.

21549 JOSHI, R.V. Urban structure in western India: Poona, a sample study. In GRI 14,1 (1952) 7-19.

21550 MEHTA, S.K. Patterns of residence in Poona, India, by caste and religion: 1822-1965. In Demography 6 (1969) 473-91.

21551 ______. Patterns of residence in Poona (India) by income, education, and occupation (1937-65). In AJS 73 (1968) 496-508.

21552 NAIR, K.S. Ethnic identity in the Indian urban setting. In EA 32,1 (1975) 13-24.

21553 ______. Ethnicity and urbanization: a case study of the ethnic identity of south Indian migrants in Poona. Delhi: Ajanta, 1978. 224p.

21554 PETHE, V.P. Industrialization of a town (Poona's new economic role). In IJE 49 (1968) 167-75.

21555 RAMANAMMA, A. Graduate employed women in an urban setting. Poona: Dastane Ramchandra, 1979. 159p.

21556 SAWANT, S.B. The City of Poona: a study in urban geography. Poona: U. of Poona, 1978. 176p.

21557 SHAKESPEAR, L.W. A history of Poona and its battlefields. Lahore: Sheikh Mubarak Ali, 1976. 99p. + 6 pl. [Rpt. 1912 ed.]

21558 SOVANI, N.V. & D.P. APTE & R.G. PENDSE. Poona: a re-survey; the changing pattern of employment and earnings. Poona: GIPE, 1956. 555p. (Its pub., 34)

5. Social Problems and Social Welfare

21559 DATIR, R.N. Prison as a social system: with special reference to Maharashtra State. Bombay: Popular, 1978. 438p.

21560 DESAI, M.B. & V.M. RAO. Survey of drink habit and socio-economic conditions in Vidarbha and Marathwada. Bombay: Dept. of Econ., U. of Bombay, 1960. 95p.

21561 PUNEKAR, S.I. & P. RAMACHANDRAN. Socio-economic

survey of drink problem in urban Vidarbha and Marathwada. Bombay: Director, Govt. Printing, 1962. 162p. [study by TISS]

6. Health Services and Family Planning

21562 CHANDRASEKARAN, C. & K. KUDER & V.C. CHIDAMBARAM. Family planning through clinics; report of a survey of family planning clinics in greater Bombay. Bombay: Allied, 1965. 272p.

21563 DANDEKAR, K. Communication in family planning; report on an experiment. Poona: GIPE, 1967. 109p. (GIPE studies, 49)

21564 DANDEKAR, K. & V. BHATE. Contraceptive practice and its impact on birth rates of Maharashtra. In JGRS 40,3 (1978) 2-29.

21565 ______. Family planning in the city of Poona. In JIER 3,1 (1968) 1-21.

21566 MORRISON, W.A. Family planning attitudes of industrial workers of Ambarnath, a city of western India: a comparative analysis. In Population Studies 14 (1961) 235-48.

21567 RAM, E.R. & B.K. DATTA. A study of the utilization of primary health centre and sub-centre health services by the rural people of Miraj Taluka, Maharashtra. In IJPH 22,3 (1976) 134-43.

21568 SONI, V. Impact of the family planning programme in Greater Bombay. In EPW 6,35 (1971) 1867-80.

7. Education in Maharashtra since 1818 (47.4% literacy in 1981)

a. general history of education, 1818-1947

21569 BOMBAY (STATE). EDUC. DEPT. A review of education in Bombay State, 1855-1955. A volume in commemoration of the centenary of the Department of Education, Bombay. Poona: 1958. 542p.

21570 KARVE, D.D. The Deccan Education Society. In JAS 20 (1961) 205-12.

21571 LIMAYE, P.M. The history of the Deccan Education Society. Poona: M.K. Joshi, Deccan Educ. Soc., 1935. 3 v., 1730p.

21572 PARASNIS, N.R. The history and survey of education in Thana District, former Bombay State, now Maharashtra State. Bombay: U. of Bombay, 1967. 476p.

21573 PARULEKAR, R.V. Educational writings: selected and with an introductory essay on his life and work by J.P. Naik. Bombay: Asia, 1957. 268p.

21574 ______. Survey of indigenous education in the province of Bombay (1820-1830). 2nd ed. Bombay: Asia Pub., 1951. 195p. (Indian Inst. of Educ., Narayanrao Topiwala Mem. Educational Series, 1) [1st pub. 1945]

21575 Selections from the records of the govt. of Bombay: education. Bombay: Asia Pub., 1953-57. 3 v.
Pt. 1, 1819-1852. Ed. by R.V. Parulekar, 1953. 238p.
Pt. 2, 1815-1840. Ed. by R.V. Parulekar & C.L. Bakshi, 1955. 264p.
Pt. 3, 1826-1840. Ed. by R.V. Parulekar & C.L. Bakshi, 1957. 273p.
(Indian Inst. of Educ., Narayanrao Topiwala Mem. Educational Res. Series, 3, 4, 5)

21576 Shri R.V. Parulekar felicitation volume. Bombay: Shri R.V. Parulekar's 71st Birthday Celebration Cmtee., 1956. 268p.

b. educational policy and development since 1947

21577 AGASHE, D. The story of the Buldana School experiment in new education. Bombay: Paragon, 1979. 80p.

21578 INAMDAR, N.R. Educational administration in the zilla parishads in Maharashtra. Bombay: Popular, 1974. 273p.

21579 KAMAT, A.R. Progress of education in rural Maharashtra (Post-independence period). Bombay: Asia, 1968. 348p.

21580 MAHARASHTRA. EDUC. & SOCIAL WELFARE DEPT. Educational development in Maharashtra State, 1950-51 to 1965-66. Bombay: 1968. 101p.

21581 MAHARASHTRA. DIR. OF EDUC. RES. UNIT. Evaluation of gram shikshan mohim. Poona: 1964. 322p. [adult mass literacy drive launched in Satara District, 1961]

21582 NATL. STAFF COLLEGE FOR EDUC. PLANNERS & ADMINISTRATORS. Educational administration in Maharashtra: a survey report, 1977. ND: 1977. 117p.

21583 PAVATE, DADAPPA CHINTAPPA. Memoirs of an educational administrator. ND: Prentice-Hall, 1964. 337p.

21584 ROSENTHAL, D.B. Educational politics and policy-making in Maharashtra. In Comp. Educ. R. 18,1 (1974) 79-95.

c. elementary and secondary schools and teachers

21585 DESAI, I.P. High school students in Poona. Poona: DCPRI, 1953. 123p. [1st pub. in BDCRI 12 (1962) 271-393]

21586 KALE, P. The career of the secondary school teacher in Poona. Bombay: Nachiketa, 1972. 157p.

21587 ______. The guru and the professional: the dilemma of the secondary school teacher in Poona, India. In Comp. Educ. R. 14,3 (1970) 371-76.

21588 KHANOLKAR, V.P., ed. Indigenous elementary education in the Bombay Presidency in 1855 and thereabouts (being a departmental survey of indigenous education). Bombay: Indian Inst. of Educ., 1965. 638p.

21589 MAHARASHTRA. NIGHT HIGH SCHOOL CMTEE. Committee report on the night high schools. Bombay: 1965. 56p.

21590 PATWARDHAN, C.N. Education in the State of Maharashtra, India. Bombay: Dept. of Services to Schools, St. Xavier's Inst. of Educ., 1964. 50p.

21591 PETHE, V.P. Living and working conditions of primary school teachers, a Sholapur survey. Bombay: Popular, 1962. 70p.

21592 SHARPE, B. Bombay teachers and the cultural role of cities. Berkeley: U. of California Center for S. and SE Asia Studies, 1973. 132p. (Its monograph, 10)

d. higher education

i. general studies

21593 AHMEDNAGAR COLLEGE. Profile of a college: a self-study of Ahmednagar College.... 2nd rev. ed. Bombay: Nachiketa, 1972. 247p.

21594 ALTBACH, P.G. The university in transition; an Indian case study. Bombay: Sindhu, 1972. 136p. [U. of Bombay]

21595 DONGERKERY, S.R. A history of the University of Bombay, 1857-1957. Bombay: U. of Bombay, 1957. 313p.

21596 ______. Memories of two universities. Bombay: Manaktalas, 1966. 276p. [Bombay & Marathwada]

21597 FRASER, J.N. Deccan College: a retrospect, 1851-1901. Poona: the author, 1902. 160p.

21598 GOLAY, W.H. The University of Poona, 1949-1974. Poona: U. of Poona, 1974. 448p.

21599 JOAG, V.K. The first twelve years; a short history of the origin and growth of the Nowrosjee Wadia College and the Modern Education Society, Poona, 1932-1944. Poona: 1944-45. 118 + 27p.

21600 UNIV. OF BOMBAY. Centenary souvenir, 1857-1957. Bombay: T.V. Chidambaran, 1957. 301p.

ii. university students

21601 CHITNIS, S. Drugs on the college campus. Bombay: Unit for Res. in the Sociology of Educ., TISS, 1974. 68p. (TISS series, 32)

21602 COUNCIL ON WORLD TENSIONS. Report on a survey of the attitudes, opinions and personality traits of a sample of 1706 students of the University of Bombay, sponsored by World Brotherhood, Bombay. Bombay: Orient Longmans, 1960. 77p.

21603 KAMAT, A.R. Wastage in college education; two

studies about students of the University of Poona. London: Asia, 1963. 202p. (GIPE studies, 43)

21604 SHINDE, A.B. Political consciousness among college students. Bombay: G.V. Bhave, 1972. 283p.

21605 SIRSIKAR, V.M. Social and political attitudes of post-graduate students of the University of Poona, 1960-61. In JUP 17 (1963) 1-66.

D. Religio-Philosophical Traditions of Maharashtra since 1818

1. Hinduism
a. general studies

21606 BARNOUW, V. The changing character of a Hindu festival. In AA 56 (1954) 74-86.

21607 DAMLE, Y.B. Harikathā - a study in communication. In N.G. Kalelkar, ed. Sushil Kumar De felicitation volume. Poona: DCPRI, 1960, 63-107. [pub. as BDCRI 20,1-4]

21608 KLOSTERMAIER, K. Hinduism in Bombay. In Religion 2 (1972) 83-91.

21609 MEHTA, M. Maharaj libel case: a study of social change in western India in the nineteenth century. In IAC 19 (1970) 28-39.

21610 PANDE, D.K. The Paramahansa of Pawas. Pawas: Swami Swaroopananda Seva Mandal, 1973. 243p.

21611 SONTHEIMER, G.-D. Birobā, Mhaskobā und Khaṇḍobā: Ursprung, Geschichte und Umwelt von pastoralen Gottheiten in Mahārāṣhṭra. Wiesbaden: Steiner, 1976. 279p.

21612 STANLEY, J.M. Special time, special power: the fluidity of power in a popular Hindu festival. In JAS 37,1 (1977) 37-48.

21613 TIPNIS, S.N. Contribution of Upasani Baba to Indian culture. Sakuri: Shri Upasani Kanya Kumari Sthan, 1966. 250p.

21614 WHITE, C.S.J. Swāmi Muktānanda and the enlightenment through Śakti-pāt. In HR 13,4 (1974) 306-22.

b. Ramchandra Dattatraya Ranade (1886 - 1957): a modern mystic

21615 LEDERLE, M. R.D. Ranade's philosophy of God-realisation. In Studia Missionalia 13 (1963) 64-84.

21616 RANADE, R.D. Essays and reflections. Comp. by B.R. Kulkarni. Bombay: BVB, 1964. 194p.

21617 SANGORAM, K.D. & M.S. DESHPANDE. Silver jubilee souvenir: Academy of Comparative Philosophy & Religion, Belgaum. Belgaum: The Academy, 1978-. [to be 2 v.]

21618 SHARMA, SHRIPAD RAMA. Ranade; a modern mystic. Tr. by S.G. Tulpule. Poona: Venus Prakashan, 1961. 227p.

c. the cult of Sai Baba (d. 1918), Muslim-Hindu saint

21619 GUNAJI, N.V. Shri Sai Satcharita; or, The wonderful life and teachings of Shri Sai Baba. Adapted from the Marathi of Hemadpant. Bombay: Cmtee. of Shirdi Sansthan of Shri Sai Baba, 1947. 273p.

21620 NARASIMHA SWAMI, B.V. Life of Sai Baba. Madras: All India Sai Samaj, 1955. 366p.

21621 ______. Sai Baba's apostles and mission. Madras: All India Sai Samaj, 1956. 424p.

21622 OSBORNE, A. The incredible Sai Baba. London: Rider, 1958. 128p.

21623 SHAM RAO, D.P. Five contemporary gurus in the Shirdi (Sai Baba) tradition. Madras: CLS, for CISRS, 1972. 46p.

21624 WHITE, C.S.J. The Sai Baba movement: approaches to the study of Indian saints. In JAS 31,4 (1972) 863-78.

2. Christianity in Maharashtra

21625 ASHLEY-BROWN, W. On the Bombay coast of Deccan; the origin and history of the Bombay diocese, a record of 300 years work for Christ in western India. London: SPCK, 1937. 288p.

21626 KAMOJI, D.C. The Christian missions in Bombay, 1870-1885. In JIH 44 (1966) 839-52.

21627 MITCHELL, J.M. In Western India; recollections of my early missionary life. Edinburgh: D. Douglas, 1899. 417p.

21628 MODAK, M.R. The world is my family; biography of Rev. Ram Krishna Shahu Modak. Bombay: Thackers, 1970. 276p.

21629 PADMANJI, BABA. An autobiography. Ed. by J.M. Mitchell. Madras: 1892. 107p.

21630 SHIRSAT, K.R. Narayan Vaman Tilak: poet and patriot. Bombay: Bombay Tract and Book Society, 1979. 100p.

21631 TILAK, L.G. "Agadi step by step": testimony of Lakshmibai Tilak in her own words. Nasik: Mayawati A. Tilak, 1968. 46p. [Autobiographical reminiscences of a convert]

21632 ______. I follow after; an autobiography. Trans. by E.J. Inkster. Bombay: OUP, 1950. 353p.

E. Literature and Media in Maharashtra since 1818

1. Modern Marathi Literature
a. general studies

21633 APTE, M.L. Lokahitavadi and V.K. Chiplunkar: spokesmen of change in nineteenth-century Maharashtra. In MAS 7 (1973) 193-208.

21634 BHATE, G.C. History of modern Marathi literature, 1800-1938. Mahad: the author, 1939. 745p.

21635 DAVTAR, V. The literary scene in Marathi in 1968. In IL 13,2 (1970) 67-75.

21636 NADKARNI, D.G. Marathi. In K.R. Srinivasa Iyengar, ed. Indian literature since independence. ND: Sahitya Akademi, 1973, 186-200.

b. modern Marathi fiction

21637 APTE, M.L. Contemporary Marathi fiction: obscenity or realism? In JAS 29,1 (1969) 55-66.

21638 ______. The political novel in Marathi. In CAS 6 (1975) 75-85.

21639 GOLE, R.M. N.C. Kelkar. ND: Sahitya Akademi, 1976. 90p.

21640 JOSHI, R.B. H.N. Apte. ND: Sahitya Akademi, 1978. 93p. [1864-1919]

21641 KARANDIKAR, M. Hari Narayan Apte. ND: Natl. Book Trust, 1968. 85p.

21642 RAESIDE, I. Early prose fiction in Marathi. In T.W. Clark, ed. Novel in India. Berkeley: UCalP, 1970, 75-101. [In JAS 27 (1968) 791-808]

21643 ______., ed. The rough and the smooth: short stories tr. from Marathi. London: Asia, 1967. 178p.

21644 SHINDE, B.G., ed. Modern Marathi short stories. Madras: Jupiter Press, Madras, n.d. 127p.

21645 Sixteen modern Marathi short stories. Bombay: Kutub Popular, 1961. 236p.

c. modern Marathi poetry

21646 CHITRE, D., comp. An anthology of Marathi poetry, 1945-65. Bombay: Nirmala Sadanand, 1967. 197p. (Centre for Indian writers, Contemporary Indian poetry, 1)

21647 NEMADE, B. Towards a definition of modernity in modern Marathi poetry; a perspective on contemporary Marathi verse. In Mahfil 6,2/3 (1970) 71-82.

21648 MACHWE, P.B. Keshavsut. ND: Sahitya Akademi, 1966. 64p.

21649 SHAHANE, V.A. B.S. Mardhekar, a modern Marathi poet. In IIJ 6 (1962) 141-50. [also in Quest 28 (1961) 42-48]

d. modern Marathi drama and theatre

21650 MARATHI N.P. Marathi theatre: 1943 to 1960. Bombay: Popular, 1961. 78p.

21651 NADKARNI, D.G. New directions in the Marathi theatre. ND: Chief Info. Officer, Maharashtra Info. Centre, 1967. 53p.

2. Folk Literature

21652 BABAR, S.K. Folk literature of Maharashtra. ND: Maharashtra Info. Centre, 1968. 39p.

21653 BHAGVAT, DURGA. A critical bibliography of Folklore of Maharashtra 1950-1966. In JASBombay 41/42 (1966-67) 203-40.

21654 ______. Some folk-tales from Maharashtra: Sarjerao and Bhalerao. In Folklore (C) 5 (1964) 406-19.

21655 DEXTER, W.E. Marathi folk tales. London: G.G. Harrap, 1938. 190p.

21656 ENTHOVEN, R.E. The folklore of Bombay. Oxford: OUP, 1924. 353p.

21657 JACKSON, A.M.T. Folklore of the Konkan. Delhi: Cosmo, 1976. 92 + 37p. [1st pub. 1914-15]

21658 SHEOREY, I. Folk tales of Maharashtra. ND: Sterling, 1973. 117p.

3. Publishing and the Press in Maharashtra

21659 GUMPERZ, E.M. The modernizing of communication: vernacular publishing in nineteenth century Maharashtra. In AS 2 (1968) 589-606.

21660 INAMDAR, N.R. Political thought in journals in Maharashtra during 1818-1873. In JUP 30 (1968) 37-55.

21661 PARVATE, T.V. Marathi journalism. ND: Maharashtra Info. Center, 1969. 38p.

4. The Film Industry in Maharashtra: Center of Hindi and Marathi Cinema

21662 MUJAWAR, I. Maharashtra, birthplace of Indian film industry. ND: Maharashtra Info. Center, 1969. 156p.

V. GUJARAT: THE GUJARATI-SPEAKING REGION OF WESTERN MIDDLE INDIA

A. Political History [For Bombay Pres. and Princely States, see I, above]

1. From Independence to the Formation of Gujarat State (1947-1960)

21663 MUNSHI, KANAIYALAL MANEKLAL. Linguistic provinces and the future of Bombay. Bombay: Natl. Info. & Pub., 1948. 62p.

21664 WOOD, J.R. The political integration of British and princely Gujarat: the historical-political variable in Indian state politics. Diss., Columbia U., 1971. 473p. [UM 73-16,252]

2. General Studies of Gujarat Politics since 1960

21665 DESAI, K.D. Emergence of the Swatantra Party in Gujarat. In JGRS 25 (1963) 143-51.

21666 JONES, D.E. & R.W. JONES. The scholars' rebellion: educational interests and agitational politics in Gujarat. In JAS 36,3 (1977) 457-76.

21667 ______. Urban upheaval in India: the 1974 Nav Nirman riots in Gujarat. In AS 16,11 (1976) 1012-33.

21668 KOTHARI, R. & R. MARU. Caste and secularism in India: case study of a caste federation. In JAS 15,1 (1965) 33-50.

21669 ______. Federating for political interests: the Kshatriyas of Gujarat. In R. Kothari, ed. Caste in Indian politics. Bombay: Orient Longman, 1970, 70-101.

21670 PANTHAM, T. The social bases of party recruitment: a study of party organisational activists in an Indian city. In JCPS 13,2 (1975) 113-31.

21671 POCOCK, D.F. The bases of faction in Gujerat. In British J. of Sociology 8 (1957) 295-306.

21672 SHAH, AMITA, ed. Youth power in Gujarat: diary of events, December 1973-March 1974. ND: Vishwa Yuvak Kendra, 1977. 113p.

21673 SHAH, GHANSHYAM. Caste association and political process in Gujarat: a study of Gujarat Kshatriya Sabha. Bombay: Popular, 1975. 218p.

21674 ______. Communal riots in Gujarat: report of a preliminary investigation. In EPW 5,3/5 (1970) 187-200.

21675 ______. Politics of scheduled castes and tribes: adivasi and Harijan leaders of Gujarat. Bombay: Vora, 1975. 164p.

21676 SHETH, P.N. Nav Nirman and political change in India: from Gujarat 1974 to New Delhi 1977. Bombay: Vora, 1977. 192p.

21677 ______. Patterns of political behavior in Gujarat. Ahmedabad: Sahitya Mudranalaya, 1976. 324p.

21678 SHRIMAN NARAYAN. Those ten months: President's rule in Gujarat. Delhi: Vikas, 1973. 204p.

21679 COMJEE, A.H. Caste and the decline of political homogeneity. In APSR 67,3 (1973) 199-816.

21680 SPODEK, H. "Injustice to Saurashtra:" a case study of regional tensions and harmonies in India. In AS 12,5 (1972) 416-428.

3. Election Studies

21681 GUJARAT. CHIEF ELECTORAL OFFICER. Report on the general elections to the Gujarat Legislative Assembly, June 1975: statistical review. Gandhinagar: 1975. 253p.

21682 ______. Report on the sixth general elections to the House of the People, March 1977 (statistical). Gandhinagar: 1977. 60p.

21683 KOTHARI, R. & T. SHETH. Extent and limits of community voting: the case of Baroda East. In EW 14,37 (1962) 1473-86.

21684 MARU, RUSHIKESH. Fall of a traditional Congress stronghold [Rajkot]. In EW 17,25 (1965) 987-1000.

21685 PANTHAM, T. Voting behaviour in Baroda City; a 1967 general election study. Baroda: Dept. of Political Science, MSUB, 1968. 92p.

21686 PATHAK, D.N. & M.T. PAREKH & K.D. DESAI. Three general elections in Gujarat; development of a decade, 1952-1962. Ahmedabad: Gujarat U., 1966. 267p.

21687 SHAH, GHANSHYAM. The 1975 Gujarat assembly election in India. In AS 16,3 (1976) 270-82.

21688 SHETH, P.N. Elections in Gujarat: the emerging pattern. In PSR 6,3/4 & 7,1/2 (1968) 169-200.

21689 ______. Gujarat in the poll of 1971: some significant aspects. In JGRS 33,3 (1971) 207-10.

4. Local Government and Politics
a. general studies

21690 BHATT, ANIL. Panchayati Raj and the mobilisation of the periphery: the case of the location of a primary health centre. In JCPS 10,2 (1972) 130-48.

21691 PANTHAM, T. The formation of the politically active stratum: evidence from the career origins of party activists in an Indian city. In W.H. Morris-Jones, ed. The making of politicians.... London: Athlone Press, 1976, 207-26. [Baroda]

21692 PATEL, G.D. Report on the Sabarkantha field study project. Ahmedabad: Govt. Central Press, 1964. 276p.

21693 PATHAK, D.N. The Ahmedabad Municipal Corporation election (1960). Ahmedabad: Gujarat U., 1962.

21694 PULPARAMPIL, J. Nation building from below: a historical study of the municipal government system of an Indian state. ND: Amarko Book Agency, 1977. 143p.

21695 SOMJEE, A.H., ed. Politics of a periurban community in India. Bombay: Asia, 1964. 57p. [Baroda]

b. district administration

21696 GUJARAT. HIGH LEVEL TEAM ON DISTRICT ADMIN. Report. Ahmedabad: General Admin. Dept., Govt. of Gujarat, 1972. 280p.

21697 NANAVATI, M. Ideals of a District Officer. In JGRS 23 (1961) 122-38.

21698 SHAH, M.M. Impact of the changes in the district administration since independence on Kheda District. Vallabh Vidyanagar: Sardar Patel U., 1969. 200p.

c. village government and panchayats

21699 CHOKSHI, H.P. A study of mobilisation of resources for village panchayats in Baroda District, 1951-1965. Baroda: 1971. 226p.

21700 DESAI, K.S. Problems of administration in two Indian villages. Baroda: Dept. of Political Science, MSUB, 1961. 387p.

21701 GUJARAT. PANCHAYAT & HEALTH DEPT. Panchayati raj in Gujarat. Gandhinagar: 1973. 59p.

21702 SOMJEE, A.H. Democracy and political change in village India; a case study. ND: Orient Longman, 1971. 189p.

21703 ______. Groups and individuals in the politics of an Indian village. In AS 2,6 (1962) 13-18.

21704 ______. Political dynamics of a Gujarat village. In AS 12,7 (1972) 602-08.

21705 ______. Voting-behaviour in an Indian village. Baroda: Dept. of Political Science, MSUB, 1959. 64p.

B. The Gujarat Economy since 1818

1. General Economic History to 1947

21706 BARODA. ECON. DEV. CMTEE. Report. Bombay: Times Press, 1920. 297p.

21707 CHOKSEY, R.D. Economic life in the Bombay Gujarat, 1800-1939. Bombay: Asia, 1968. 288p.

21708 TRIVEDI, A.B. Wealth of Gujarat. Bombay: 1943. xvii, 447p.

2. Demography (1981 pop. 33,960,905)

21709 INDIA (REP.). CENSUS OF INDIA, 1971. Gujarat: a portrait of population. Delhi: Cont. of Pub., 1975. 280p.

21710 SAVLA, CHANDAN. Salient features of out migration from Kutch. In JGRS 36,3 (1974) 13-65.

3. Surveys of Economic Conditions after 1947

21711 NCAER. Techno-economic survey of Gujarat. ND: 1963. 260p.

21712 Statistical abstract of Maha Gujarat. In JGRS 9,3 (1947) 155-99.

21713 TRIVEDI, A.B. Post-war Gujarat: an economic survey after World War II. Bombay: A.B. Trivedi, 1949. 287p.

21714 VAKIL, C.N. & D.T. LAKDAWALA & M.B. DESAI. Economic survey of Saurashtra. Bombay: School of Econ. & Sociology, U. of Bombay, 1953. 664p.

4. Economic Development and Planning

21715 BHATT, M. & V.K. CHAWDA. The economic growth of Gujarat; deceleration in the third plan: some reasons. In EW 17,39 (1965) 1481-86.

21716 Economic development of backward regions: problems and prospects ... with special reference to Gujarat. Vallabh Vidyanagar: Sardar Patel U., 1974. 260p. [1972 seminar proc.]

21717 GUJARAT. GENL. ADMIN. DEPT. Perspective plan of Gujarat, 1974-1984. Ahmedabad, 1972. 3v.

21718 JAYARAMAN, T.K. & V.B. SAVDASIA. Development of backward areas in Gujarat state. In IJPA 23,3 (1977) 668-87.

21719 NEW INDIA INDUSTRIES LTD. MARKET RES. DIV. Inward remittances, Gujarat: a survey. Bombay: The Chamber of Commerce & Industry, 1979. 48p.

5. Finance and Taxation

21720 NCAER. Incidence of taxation in Gujarat. ND: 1970. 118p.

21721 PATHAK, M. & A.S. PATEL. Agricultural taxation in Gujarat. NY: Asia, 1970. 93p.

6. Agriculture in Gujarat
a. surveys and descriptive studies

21722 Agricultural census, 1970-71. Gandhinagar: Gujarat Govt. Central Press, 197-. v.-

21723 BARODA (STATE). Rural Baroda. Bombay: ISAE, 1949. 119p.

21724 DESAI, D.K. & D.A. PATEL. Regional differentials in agricultural productivity in Gujarat State. In JGRS 24,2 (1962) 100-08.

21725 DESAI, M.B. The rural economy of Gujarat. Bombay: OUP, 1948. 352p.

21726 DESAI, M.B. & C.H. SHAH. Rural economy of reconstituted Gujarat. In JGRS 14,3 (1952) 111-48.

21727 DESAI, N.B. Report on the administrative survey of Surat district. Bombay: ISAE, 1958. 336p.

21728 GUJARAT. AGRI. DEPT. Basic agricultural statistics of Gujarat State for the period 1949-50 to 1961-62. Baroda: 1968. 138p.

21729 ______. Gujarat State agricultural atlas. Ahmedabad: Dir. of Agri., 1968. 114p.

21730 KUMARAPPA, J.C. A survey of Matar taluka (Kaira district). Ahmedabad: D. Parikh, 1931. 179p.

21731 PATEL, G.A. Gujarat's agriculture. Admedabad: Overseas Book Traders, 1977. 363p.

21732 SAMBRANI, S. & K.R. PICHHOLIYA. An inquiry into rural poverty and unemployment. Ahmedabad: Centre for Mgmt. in Agri., Indian Inst. of Mgmt., 1975. 167p.

21733 SHAH, GHANSHYAM. Agricultural labourers: are they bonded? Surat: Centre for Social Studies, 1978. 41p.

21734 SHAH, VIMAL & C.H. SHAH. Resurvey of Matar Taluka. Bombay: Vora, 1974. 336p. [Kaira Dist.]

b. agricultural development and planning

21735 ASOPA, V.N. & B.L. TRIPATHI. Command area development in Mahi-Kadana. Ahmedabad: Centre for Mgmt. in Agri., Indian Inst. of Mgmt., 1978. 112p. (CMA monograph, 76)

21736 DESAI, B.M. & M.D. DESAI. The new strategy of agricultural development in operation: a case study of Kaira district in Gujarat. Bombay: Thacker, 1969. 148p.

21737 DESAI, M.B. & R.S. MEHTA. Green revolution in agriculture in Gujarat. In JMSUB, 20 2 (1971) 1-18.

21738 DESAI, M.B. & S.K. VARMA. Changing farm production and organisation in developing agriculture: a case study of the impact of the developmental effort in agriculture in a district in Gujarat, 1967-72. Baroda: Dept. of Agri. Econ., MSUB, 1978. 501p.

21739 DESAI, M.D. Green revolution and farm labour use: the case of the Kaira district. In AV 6,2 (1970) 51-59.

21740 GUJARAT. BUREAU OF ECON. AND STAT. Evaluation survey of agricultural demonstration plots. Ahmedabad: 1963. 127p.

21741 HIRWAY, I. Intergenerational occupational changes in a green revolution area: a study of Matak taluka. In IJLE 21,4 (1979) 27-36. [Kaira district]

21742 INDIAN INST. OF MGMT., AHMEDABAD. CENTRE FOR MGMT. IN AGRI. Rural development for rural poor: Dharampur Project. Ahmedabad: 1975-76. 2v. in 1.

21743 JOSHI, V.R. Regulated markets in Gujarat. Nadiad: Kaira District Coop. Union, 1971? 407p.

21744 VYAS, V.S., et al. New agricultural strategy and small farmers: a case study in Gujarat. In EPW 4,13 (1969) A49-A53.

21745 VYAS, V.S. & D.S. TYAGI & V.N. MISRA. Significance of the new strategy of agricultural development for small farmers; a cross-sectional study of two areas of Gujarat. Vallabh Vidyanagar: Agro-Economic Res. Centre, Sardar Patel U., 1969. 95p.

c. agricultural technology and innovation

21746 AMIN, R.K. Radio rural forums in Gujarat; an observation study. Vallabh Vidyanagar: Sardar Vallabhbhai Vidyapeeth, 1966? 63p.

21747 ASOPA, V.N. & B.L. TRIPATHI. Irrigation agriculture in Gujarat: problems and prospects. Ahmedabad: Centre for Mgmt. in Agri, Indian Inst. of Mgmt., 1975. 154p.

21748 MOULIK, T.K. & S.K. BASU & M.S. PATEL. Rural entrepreneurship: motivations and constraints: a study in Anand Taluka, Gujarat. Ahmedabad: Centre for Mgmt. in Agri., Indian Inst. of Mgmt., 1978. 130p.

21749 PATEL, A.S. Fertiliser use in Gujarat, a micro view: a study of Baroda and Junagadh Districts. Vallabh Vidyanagar: Dept. of Econ., Sardar Patel U., 1973. 141p.

21750 PATEL, S.M. & K.V. PATEL. Studies on economics of rural electrification and lift irrigation (Gujarat State). Ahmedabad: Faculty for Mgmt. in Agri. & Coop., Indian Inst. of Mgmt., 1969. 172p.

21751 PATEL, S.M. & P.P. MADAPPA & B.M. DESAI. Management of lift irrigation; report on a pilot research project in Gujarat. Ahmedabad: Faculty for Mgmt. in Agri. and Coop., Indian Inst. of Mgmt., 1969. 153p.

21752 SHARAN, G. & D.P. MATHUR & M. VISWANATH. Characterization of the process of mechanization and farm power requirement. Ahmedabad: Centre for Mgmt. in Agri., Indian Inst. of Mgmt., 1974. 153p. (CMA monograph, 45)

d. agricultural cooperatives in Gujarat

21753 CHOUDHARY, K.M. et al. An assessment of co-operative farming societies in Gujarat and Rajasthan. Vallabh Vidyanagar: Agro-econ. Res. Centre, 1972. 377p.

21754 DESAI, D.K. & A.V.S. NARAYANAN. Impact of modernization of dairy industry on the economy of Kaira district. In IJAE 22,3 (1967) 54-67.

21755 ELAVIA, B.H. The study of co-operative land development banking in Gujarat. Baroda: Dept. of Coop., Faculty of Commerce, MSUB, 1979. 151p.

21756 IRWIN, P.G. The dairying industry of Kaira, Western India. In SA 1,1 (1971) 123-131.

21757 NANAVATI, M.B. Fifty years of co-operation in Kodinar Taluka; a case study. Bombay: Indian Soc. of Agri. Econ., 1964. 37p. [Amreli district]

21758 PATEL, S.M. & D.S. THAKUR & M.K. PANDEY. Impact of the milk co-operatives in Gujarat. Allahabad: United, 1977. 191p.

21759 RESERVE BANK OF INDIA. Review of agricultural development and co-operative credit in Gujarat. Bombay: RBI, 1977. 116p.

21760 SHAH, C.H. Cooperation, development and socio-economic force: a case study of Kodinar Taluka. In SB 15,2 (1966) 36-43.

21761 SHAH, M.M. Integration of district dairy cooperatives in Gujarat. Vallabh Vidyanagar: Sardar Patel U., 1977. 276p.

e. land tenure and reform

21762 BARMEDA, J.N. Agrarian classes and the growth of tenancy in Gujarat. In IJAE 6,1 (1951) 78-103.

21763 BREMEN, J. Patronage and exploitation; changing agrarian relations in South Gujarat, India. Tr. by W. Van Gulik. Berkeley: UCalP, 1974. 287p. [tr. from Dutch]

21764 DESAI, M.B. Report on an enquiry into the working of the Bombay Tenancy and Agricultural Lands Act, 1948 (as amended up to 1953) in Gujarat excluding Baroda District). Bombay: ISAE, 1958. 96p. (ISAE pub., 27)

21765 ______. Tenancy abolition and the emerging pattern in Gujarat. Baroda: Dept. of Agri. Econ., MSUB, 1971. 194p.

21766 GUJARAT DIR. OF EVAL. Evaluation study of impact of land reform measures in Gujarat State. Gandhinagar: 1976. 131p.

21767 HARDIMAN, D. The crisis of the lesser Patidars: peasant agitations in Kheda District, Gujarat, 1917-34. In D.A. Low, ed. Congress and the Raj. London: Heinemann, 1977, 47-77. [Kaira district]

21768 MISHRA, R.R. Effects of land reforms in Saurashtra; report of a survey sponsored by Research Programmes Committee, Planning Commission. Bombay: Vora, 1961. 240p.

21769 OZA, U.K. The serfs of Kathiawar, being studies in the land revenue administration of smaller states in Kathiawar. Rajkot: Sadhana Services, 1945. 146p.

21770 PATEL, G.D. The land revenue settlements and the British rule in India. Ahmedabad: Gujarat U., 1969. 524p.

21771 SHARMA, J.N. Patterns of land holding in a Gujarat village. In JMSUB 11,2 (1962) 17-30.

21772 VYAS, V.S. Tenancy in a dynamic setting. In EPW 5,27 (1970) A73-A80.

7. Industry in Gujarat

21773 CHAUHAN, A.B. Organisation and working of public enterprises in Gujarat. Vallabh Vidyanagar: Sardar Patel U., 1978. 580p.

21774 CHOWDHRY, K. Institution building and social change: the Ahmedabad Textile Industry's Research Association. In IJPA 14,4 (1968) 943-61.

21775 ERDMAN, H.L. Political attitudes of Indian industry: a case study of the Baroda business elite. London: Athlone Press, 1971. 62p.

21776 ______. Politics and economic development in India: the Gujarat State Fertilizers Company as a joint sector enterprise. Delhi: D.K. Pub., 1973. 148p.

21777 GUJARAT. BUREAU OF ECON. AND STAT. Locations of industries in Gujarat State, 1956-1960. Ahmedabad: 1963. 186p.

21778 GUJARAT. DIR. OF INDUSTRIES. Industries in Gujarat; handbook of information. rev. & enl. Ahmedabad: 1971. 289p.

21779 KAPADIA, K.M. Industrial evolution of Navsari. In SB 15,1 (1966) 1-24.

21780 MEHTA, J.D. Regional industrial development in Gujarat (performance of developed and backward districts). In JGRS 35,3 (1973) 155-212.

21781 ______. The textile machinery industry in Ahmedabad city - an economic analysis. In JGRS 37,3 (1975) 64-78.

21782 PATHAK, H.N. State policy and industrial development in Baroda: a case study. In JGRS 31,2 (1969) 106-17.

21783 PATIL, R.K. Gold and silver thread industry of Surat; a socio-economic study. Surat: Chunilal Gandhi Vidyabhavan, 1956. 158p. (Its studies, 6)

21784 SHAH, M.M. Industrial co-operatives in Kaira District: a depth study. Nadiad: Kaira District Co-op. Union, 1975. 214p.

21785 SPODEK, H. The "Manchesterisation" of Ahmedabad. In EW 17,11 (1965) 483-90.

8. Labor and Trade Unions in Gujarat

21786 The Ahmedabad experiment in labour-management relations. In Intl. Labour R. 79 (1959) 343-79, 511-36. [study by E. Daya]

21787 BREMEN, J. Seasonal migration and cooperative capitalism: crushing of cane and of labour by sugar factories of Bardoli. In EPW 13, 31/33 (1978) 1317-60.

21788 DHOLAKIA, J.L. Labour commitment in a developing economy - a case study of five factories in Gujarat. In JGRS 28 (1966) 9-14.

21789 GUJARAT. BUREAU OF ECON. & STAT. Fact book on manpower. Ahmedabad: 1966. 63p.

21790 ______. Study of utilisation pattern of educated persons. Ahmedabad: 1967. 125p. (Its Monograph, 8)

21791 MADLANI, S.S. Socio-economic condition and industrial relations of workers of Porbandar. In JGRS 34,2 (1972) 117-54.

21792 MAJMUNDAR, P. An anatomy of peaceful industrial relations. Bombay: N.M. Tripathi, 1973. 291p. [Ahmedabad]

21793 PANDIT, D.P. Earning one's livelihood in Mahuva. NY: Asia, 1965. 92p. (MSUB, Dept. of Sociology, pub. 5)

21794 PAPOLA, T.S. & K.K. SUBRAHMANIAN. Wage structure and labour mobility in a local labour market: a study in Ahmedabad. Ahmedabad: Sardar Patel Inst. of Econ. & Social Res., 1975. 214p. (Its Monograph series, 4)

21795 SHETH, N.R. The social framework of an Indian factory. Manchester: Manchester U. Press, 1968. 220p.

21796 VERMA, PRAMOD. Labour in a textile city: a study of workers' needs and welfare in Ahmedabad. Ahmedabad: Verma, 1973? 71p.

9. Commerce and Transportation in Gujarat

21797 BATRA, S., ed. Port of Kandla: the gateway of Northwest India. Adipur: Kandla Commercial, 1964. 56p.

21798 ______. The ports of Gujarat: west coast of India. 3rd ed., rev. Adipur: Kandla Commercial Pub., 1974. 111p.

21799 DAFTARY, G.D. & H.B. PARIKH. Road communications in greater Gujarat. In JGRS 5,4 (1943) 183-96.

21800 GUJARAT. BUREAU OF ECON. & STAT. The report of the transport survey of Gujarat State. Ahmedabad: 1969. 212p.

21801 JANAKI, V.A. Kandla, the gateway of north west India. Baroda: MSUB, 1973. 140p.

21802 Shipping and port information of Gujarat. Bombay: Western India Shippers' Assn., 1978. 121p.

C. Society and Social Change in Gujarat since 1818

1. Social Reform in the 19th Century

21803 COOKE, H.R. Repression of female infanticide in Bombay Presidency...the measures taken to repress the crime in Gujarat and some of the neighbouring native states, and the result of the measures. Bombay: 1875. 102p. (Selections from the records of the Bombay Govt., ns 147)

21804 DESAI, N. Ideas which influenced the movement for changing the status of women in India in the 19th century, with spec. reference to the Gujarati Society. In B. Prasad, ed. Ideas in history: proceedings of a seminar. Bombay: Asia, 1968, 110-24.

21805 ______. Social change in Gujarat: a study of nineteenth century Gujarati society. Bombay: 1978. 479p.

21806 MEHTA, M.J. A study of the practice of female infanticide among the Kanbis of Gujarat. In JGRS 28, 1/4 (1966) 57-66.

21807 MEHTA, M.J. & S.M. MEHTA. The caste system and social reform movement in Gujerat in nineteenth century. In JGRS 27 (1965) 315-21.

21808 NATH, V. Female infanticide and the Lewa Kanbis of Gujarat in the nineteenth century. In IESHR 10,4 (1973) 386-404.

21809 PAKRASI, K.B. Female infanticide in India. Calcutta: Editions Indian, 1970. 304p.

21810 WILSON, J. History of the supression of infanticide in western India under the government of Bombay; including notices of the provinces and tribes in which the practice has prevailed. Bombay: Smith, Taylor, 1855. 457p.

2. Social Categories in Gujarat
a. general studies

21811 GUJARAT. CMSN. OF INQUIRY ON COMMUNAL DISTURBANCES AT AHMEDABAD AND AT VARIOUS PLACES IN THE STATE OF GUJARAT (ON OR AFTER 18th SEPT. 1969). Report. Gandhinagar: 1971. 337p.

21812 GUJARAT. LABOUR, SOCIAL WELFARE, & TRIBAL DEV. DEPT. Brochure on reservation for scheduled castes and scheduled tribes in services. Gandhinagar: 1977. 99p.

21813 GUJARAT. SOCIALLY & EDUCATIONALLY BACKWARD CLASS CMSN. Report. Ahmedabad: 1976. 2 v. [Chm., A.R. Bakshi]

21814 MAJUMDAR, D.N. Race realities in cultural Gujarat; report on the anthropometric, sereological and health survey of Maha Gujarat. Bombay: Gujarat Res. Soc., 1950. 87p.

21815 NAIK, T.B. Family in Gujarat. In JGRS 15,3/4 (1953) 117-37.

21816 PATEL, S.D. Rural community of South Gujarat. In JGRS 27,1 (1965) 52-62.

21817 POCOCK, D.F. Inclusion and exclusion: a process in the caste system of Gujerat. In SWJA 13 (1956) 19-31.

21818 SHAH, P.G. Ethnic history of Gujarat. Bombay: Gujarat Res. Soc., 1968. 122p.

21819 SHETH, P.N. Profiles of women in Gujarat [state politics]. In Vina Mazumdar, ed. Symbols of power... Bombay: Allied, 1979, 201-20.

21820 SHUKLA, D.M. Politicization of women in Gujarat. In Vina Mazumdar, ed. Symbols of power.... Bombay: Allied, 1979, 85-118.

b. kinship and marriage (not specific to one group)

21821 ACHARYA, H. Some possible variations in family types in Gujarat. In G. Kurian, ed. The family in India.... The Hague: Mouton, 1974, 179-90.

21822 DESAI, I.P. Some aspects of family in Mahuva; a sociological study of jointness in a small town. Bombay: Asia, 1964. 239p. (MSUB, Dept. of Sociology, Pub., 4)

21823 DESAI, N.C. Report on the joint family system. Baroda: Baroda State Press, 1936. 101p.

21824 KAPADIA, K.M. Rural family patterns: a study in urban-rural relations. In SB 5 (1956) 111-26.

21825 KARVE, I. Kinship terminology and kinship usages in Gujarat and Kathiawad. In BDCRI 4 (1943) 208-26.

21826 KHATRI, A.A. The adaptive extended family in India today. In J. of Marriage & the Family 37,3 (1975) 633-42.

21827 ______. Heterosexual friendships and involvement in mate selection process of primary and secondary teacher trainees in Ahmedabad. In G. Kurian, ed. The family in India.... The Hague: Mouton, 1974, 335-49.

21828 SHAH, A.M. The household dimension of the family in India: a field study in a Gujarat village and a review of other studies. Berkeley: UCalP, 1973. 281p.

21829 SHAH, V.B. Child rearing practices obtained in four cultural groups. In JMSUB 17,2 (1968) 27-40.

21830 Social change and perception of change in child rearing practices in a suburban Indian village. Baroda: MSUB, 1970. 121p.

c. Brahman castes

21831 DESAI, URMIBEN. Anthropological significance of aja padva as a custom in patriarchal society (a form of ancestor worship in Nagars). In JGRS 38-39,4/1 (1976-77) 3-17.

21832 NAIK, C.R. Cultivation of the Persian language and literature by the Nāgaras of Gujarat. In JOIB 14 (1964) 125-33.

21833 NAIK, T.B. The strains of a social system. In JGRS 20,2 (1958) S1-S11. [Anavils]

21834 VAN DER VEEN, K.W. I give thee my daughter; a study of marriage and hierarchy among the Anavil Brahmans of South Gujarat. Tr. from Dutch by N. Jockin. Assen: Van Gorcum, 1972. 297p.

d. Patidars and other intermediate castes

21835 POCOCK, D.F. The hypergamy of the Patidars. In K.M. Kapadia, ed. Professor Ghurye felicitation volume. Bombay: Popular, 1954, 195-204.

21836 ______. Kanbi and Patidar: a study of the Patidar community of Gujarat. Oxford: OUP, 1972. 190p.

21837 SHAH, A.M. & R.G. SCHROFF. The Vahivanca Barots of Gujarat: a caste of genealogists and mythographers. In M.B. Singer, ed. Traditional India: structure and change. Philadelphia: American Folklore Soc., 1959, 246-76.

21838 SHAHANI, S. The joint family: a case study. In EW 13,49 (1961) 1823-28.

21839 STEED, G.P. Notes on an approach to a study of personality formation in a Hindu village in Gujarat. In M. Marriott, ed. Village India. Chicago: UChiP, 1955, 102-44.

21840 TRIVEDI, H.R. The Mers of Saurashtra; an exposition of their social structure and organization. Baroda: MSUB, 1961. 114p.

e. "untouchable" castes of Gujarat

21841 DESAI, I.P. Untouchability in rural Gujarat. Bombay: Popular, 1976. 265p.

21842 GUJARAT. ZANZMER INQUIRY CMSN. Report of the Commission of Inquiry on the alleged failure or lapse on the part of police persons in giving protection to deceased Harijan Karsan Duda of Village Zanzmer, District Bhavnagar, 31st August 1978, by H.C. Shah. Gandhinagar: Govt. of Gujarat, 1978. 88p.

21843 KOTHARI, V.N. A study of economic profiles of the scheduled castes in Gujarat. Baroda: MSUB, 1976. 43p.

21844 Removal of untouchability in Gujarat: a seminar, March 5 & 6, 1973. Ahmedabad: Dept. of Sociology, Gujarat U., 1974. 111p.

21845 SHAH, GHANSHYAM. Growth of group identity among the adivasis of Dangs. In JGRS 34,2 (1972) 164-83.

21846 STEVENSON, M. Without the pale: the life story of an outcaste. Calcutta: Assn. Press, 1930. 87p. [Dheds of Gujarat]

f. Muslims of Gujarat [see also IV. C. 2. e. ii., above]

21847 ABDUL HUSAIN. Gulzare Daudi for the Bohras of India: a short note on the Bohras of India, their 21 Imams & 51 Dais, with their customs and tenets. Surat: Progressive Pub., 1977. 148p. [Rpt. 1920 ed.]

21848 CITIZENS FOR DEMOCRACY. NATHWANI CMSN. Dawoodi Bohra Commission (Nathwani Commission): report of investigation conducted by the Commission appointed by the Citizens for Democracy into the alleged infringement of human rights of reformist members of the Dawoodi Bohras in the name of the High Priest. Ahmedabad: 1979. 168p. [Chm., N.P. Nathwani]

21849 LAMBAT, I.A. Marriage among the Sunni Surati Vohras of South Gujarat. In Imtiaz Ahmad, ed. Family, kinship and marriage among the Muslims in India. ND: Manohar, 1976, 49-82.

21850 ______. A study of rural Muslims. In S. Devadas Pillai, ed. Aspects of changing India.... Bombay: Popular, 1976, 262-76.

21851 LOKHANDWALLA, S.T. The Bohras, a Muslim community of Gujarat. In Studia Islamica 3 (1955) 117-35.

21852 WRIGHT, T.P., JR. Competitive modernization within the Daudi Bohra sect of Muslims and its significance for Indian political development. In H.E. Ullrich. Competition and modernization in South Asia. ND: Abhinav, 1975, 151-70.

g. tribals of Gujarat [see II. A., above]

3. Villages and Rural Society
a. village studies

21853 AMIN, R.K. Mogri; socio-economic study of a Charotar village. Vallabh Vidyanagar: Sardar Vallabhbhai Vidyapeeth, 1965. 170p. (Studies in rural problems, 2)

21854 ______. Valasan; socio-economic study of a Charotar village. Vallabh Vidyanagar: Sardar Vallabhbhai Vidyapeeth, 1965. 72p. (Studies in rural problems, 1)

21855 Bhadkad; social and economic survey of a village, a comparative study, 1915 and 1955. Bombay: ISAE, 1957. 71p. (Its Pub., 24)

21856 DESAI, I.P. The patterns of migration and occupation in a South Gujarat village. Poona: DCPRI, 1964. 166p. (DCBC, 19)

21857 JANAKI, V.A. Vanadha-Chalamli; a study in rural dynamics (with a note on ancient village patterns in India). Baroda: MSUB, 1971. 151p. [Baroda Dist.]

21858 MUKHTYAR, G.C. Life and labour in a south Gujarat village. Calcutta: Longmans, 1930. 303p.

21859 PAI, D.N. Socio-economic and health survey of Narli-Agripada village; a preliminary report. In JGRS 25,3 (1963) 189-220.

21860 POFFENBERGER, T. & S.B. POFFENBERGER. Reaction to world news events and the influence of mass media in an Indian village. Ann Arbor: UMCSSAS, 1971. 44p. (MPSSA, 1)

21861 SHAH, A.M. & R.G. SHROFF & A.R. SHAH. Early nineteenth century village records in Gujarat. In JGRS 25 (1963) 126-34.

21862 SHAH, V. & S. SHAH. Bhuvel: socio-economic survey of a village. Bombay: Vora, 1949. 154p.

21863 SHUKLA, J.B. Life and labour in a Gujarat taluka. Bombay: Longmans, 1937. 291p.

b. community development and modernization

21864 DESAI, M.B. & R.S. MEHTA. Community development and change: a case study of a block in Gujarat. Hyderabad: NICD, 1967. 133p.

21865 DEVADAS PILLAI, S. & C. BAKS, eds. Winners and losers: styles of development and change in an Indian region. Bombay: Popular, 1979. 407p.

21866 JOSHI, V.H. Economic development and social change in a south Gujarat village; social consequences of industrialization and urbanization in a village in south Gujarat with special reference to tensions between groups and classes. Baroda: MSUB, 1966. 124p.

21867 KAPADIA, K.M. Industrialization and rural society; a study of Atul-Bulsar region. Bombay: Popular, 1972. 269p.

21868 PANCHANADIKAR, K.C. & J. PANCHANADIKAR. Rural modernization in India: a study in developmental infrastructure. Bombay: Popular, 1978. 398p.

4. Cities and Urbanization
a. general studies

21869 JANAKI, V.A. & Z.A. SAYED. The geography of Padra town. Baroda: MSUB, 1962. 139p. (Its Geog. ser., 1)

21870 JANAKI, V.A. Some aspects of the historical geography of Surat. Baroda: Dept. of Geography, MSUB, 1974. 103p.

21871 ______. Some aspects of the population patterns in the different functional groups of towns in Gujarat. Baroda: Dept. of Geography, MSUB, 1967. 80p.

21872 KAPADIA, K.M. The growth of townships in south Gujarat: Maroli Bazar. In SB 10 (1961) 69-87.

21873 PANDYA, N.M. Growth characteristics of South

Gujarat towns. In JMSUB 19,2 (1972) 79-85.

21874 SPODEK, H. Urban-rural integration in regional development: a case study of Saurashtra, India, 1800-1960. Chicago: U. of Chicago, Dept. of Geography, 1976. 144p. (Its Research paper, 171)

b. Ahmedabad: industrial city and center of Gandhism (1981 pop. 2,515,195)

21875 BHATT, M. & V.K. CHAWDA. Housing the poor in Ahmedabad. In EPW 11,19 (1976) 706-12.

21876 ______. Some aspects of co-operative housing societies in Ahmedabad City. Ahmedabad: Gujarat U., 1970. 68p.

21877 BOMAN-BEHRAM, B.K., ed. The rise of municipal government in the city of Ahmedabad. Bombay: Taraporevala, 1937. 438p.

21878 DOSHI, H.C. Industrialization and neighborhood communities in a Western Indian city - challenge and response. In SB 17 (1968) 19-34.

21879 DOSHI, H. Traditional neighbourhood in a modern city. ND: Abhinav Pub., 1974. 154p.

21880 DUCAT, W.M. Report on the water supply and sewerage of the city of Ahmedabad: submitted to the municipal Commissioners of that city. Ahmedabad: Aryodaya Press, 1885. 106p.

21881 GILLION, K.L.O. Ahmedabad, a study in Indian urban history. Berkeley: UCalP, 1968. 195p.

21882 SHUKLA, H.S. Ahmedabad guide. Ahmedabad: The Standard Trading Co., 1941. 296p.

21883 VERMA, P. Labour in a textile city: a study of workers' needs and welfare in Ahmedabad. Ahmedabad: Verma, 1973. 71p.

c. Baroda/Vadodara: former Maratha princely capital (1971 pop. 1,980,065)

21884 ABRAHAMSON, J. Involving people in community development: the Baroda project. In Community Dev. J. 5,1 (1970) 17-25.

21885 BHATT, ANIL. Baroda's experiment in urban decentralization: a study of some administrative aspects. Baroda: Dept. of Political Science, MSUB, 1978. 28p.

21886 MALKANI, H.C. A socio-economic survey of Baroda city. Baroda: MSUB, 1958. 179p.

21887 Profiles of a growing city: socio-economic studies of Baroda City. Baroda: Dept. of Econ., MSUB, 1971. 143p. (Its econ. series, 1)

21888 SOMJEE, A.H., ed. Politics of a periurban community in India. London: Asia, 1965. 57p.

5. Social Welfare and Health Services

21889 BHATT, L.J. & K.R. ADVANI. Conformity and deviation among adolescents; a sociopsychological study. ND: NCERT, 1970. 88p.

21890 DESAI, B.G. The emerging youth. Bombay: Popular, 1967. 199p. [study in Baroda]

21891 DESAI, M.D. & K.N. AMIN. A report on health survey of middle class families in Ahmedabad, 1953-54. In JGRS 17,2 (1955) 109-56.

21892 PATEL, TARA. Some reflections on the attitude of married couples towards family planning in Ahmedabad. In SB 12 (1963) 1-13.

21893 POFFENBERGER, T. Motivational aspects of resistance to family planning in an Indian village. In Demography 5 (1968) 757-66.

21894 POFFENBERGER, T. & H.G. PATEL. The effect of local beliefs on attitudes toward vasectomy in two Indian villages in Gujarat State. In Population R. 8 (1964) 37-44.

6. Education in Gujarat since 1818
a. general studies (1981 literacy 43.95%)

21895 ACHARYA, M.A. Article Thirty of the Indian Constitution and the Gujarat Secondary Education Act of 1972. In Progress of Educ. 48,5 (1973) 144-47.

21896 DESAI, D.M. Some problems of education in the Gujarat State. Baroda: MSUB, 1967. 64p.

21897 HEREDERO, J.M. Rural development and social change: an experiment in non-formal education. ND: Manohar, 1977. 181p.

21898 LAKDAWALA, D.T. & K.R. SHAH. Optimum utilization of educational expenditure in Gujarat. Ahmedabad: Sardar Patel Inst. of Econ. & Social Res., 1978. 269p.

21899 MEHTA, M.J. The British rule and the educational changes in Gujarat in the first half of the nineteenth century. In JGRS 32,1 (1970) 9-18.

21900 ______. Educational changes in Gujarat in the first half of the nineteenth century. In QRHS 8,4 (1968-69) 253-61.

21901 PANDYA, T.R. Education in Baroda. Bombay: the author, 1915. 178p.

21902 QURAISHI, M.A. Historical survey of language medium of instruction controversy in Gujarat. In Progress of Educ. 42 (1968) 398-404.

21903 SULLIVAN, E.E. Education in social change: a comparison of selected teacher training colleges in Gujarat. London: Asia, 1968. 103p. (Indian educ. series, 2)

b. higher education

21904 BENNETT, R.G. United States educational practices in faculties of the Maharaja Sayajirao Univ. of Baroda, India. Ann Arbor: U. of Michigan, School of Educ., 1971. 325p. (Comp. educ. diss. series, 20)

21905 DESAI, D.M. & S.S. PANDIT. Growth and development of the Maharaja Sayajirao University of Baroda, 1949-1967. Baroda: Dept. of Educ. Admin., MSUB, 1968. 126p.

21906 GUJARAT. CMSN. ON MODERNIZATION OF UNIV. ACTS. Report. Ahmedabad: Educ. & Labour Dept., 1971. 200p. [Chm., S.R. Dongerkery]

21907 GUJARAT. CMTEE. TO REVIEW THE STATE OF HIGHER EDUC. IN GUJARAT. Report. Gandhinagar: 1976. 67p. [Chm., V.V. John]

21908 RUDOLPH, S.H. & L.I. RUDOLPH. Parochialism and cosmopolitanism in university government: the environments of Baroda University. In their (ed.) Education and politics in India.... Cambridge: HUP, 1972, 207-72.

21909 SHAH, B.V. Gujarati college students and caste. In SB 10 (1961) 41-60.

21910 ______. Social change and college students of Gujarat. Baroda: MSUB, 1964. 228p.

21911 SHAH, B.V. & J.D. THAKER. Scheduled caste and scheduled tribe college students in Gujarat: a sociological study. Vallabh Vidyanagar: Sardar Patel U., 1978. 330p.

21912 TRIVEDI, A.K., ed. The Baroda College golden jubilee: commemoration volume. Baroda: Baroda College, 1933. 179p. + 13 pl.

D. Religions of Modern Gujarat

1. General Studies of Gujarati Hinduism

21913 DESAI, B.L. Mevlo: a rain-invoking ritual of south Gujarat. In Folklore(C) 3 (1962) 153-60.

21914 ERIKSON, J. Mata ni pachedi; a book on the temple cloth of the Mother Goddess. Ahmedabad: Natl. Inst. of Design, 1968. 74p.

21915 HAEKEL, J. Totenrituale und Ahnenkult bei den Rathwakoli in Gujerat (West Zentral-Indien). In Anthropos 63/64 (1968-69) 753-92.

21916 MULJI, KARSONDAS. History of the sect of Maharajas, or Vallabhacharyas, in Western India. London: Kegan Paul, Trench, Trubner, 1865. 182 + 183p.

21917 NAIK, T.B. Religion of the Anavils of Surat. In M.B. Singer, ed. Traditional India: structure and change. Philadelphia: American Folklore Soc., 1959, 389-96. (J. of American Folklore 71, 281)

21918 POCOCK, D.F. Mind, body, and wealth; a study of belief and practice in an Indian village. Totowa, NJ: Rowman & Littlefield, 1973. 187p.

21919 SOPHER, D.E. Pilgrim circulation in Gujarat. In Geographical R. 58 (1958) 392-425.

21920 THOOTHI, N.A. The Vaishnavas of Gujarat, being a study in methods of investigation of social phenomena. London: Longmans, 1935. 489p.

2. The Svāminārāyaṇa sect: reformist Vaishṇavism founded by Swāmi Sahajānanda, 1781 - 1830

21921 DAVE, H.T. Life and philosophy of Shree Swaminarayan. Bochasan, Gujarat: Shree Aksharpurushottam Sanstha, 1967. 184p.

21922 DAVE, R.M. Sahajanand charitra. Ahmedabad: Bochasanvasi Shri Aksharpurushottam Sanstha, 1978. 218p.

21923 ______. Yogiji Maharaj. Tr. by Swami Tyagvallabhdas. Bombay: Bochasanvasi Shri Aksharpurushottama Sanstha, 1975. 69p.

21924 ISHWARCHARANDAS. Gunatitanand Swami. Ahmedabad: Bochasanvasi Shri Aksharpurushottam Sanstha, 1979. 110p.

21925 MALLISON, F. La secte Krichṇaite des Svāmi-Nārayaṇi au Gujarāt. In JA 262 (1974) 435-71.

21926 MUKTĀNANDA, Swāmi. L'épouse idéale = La Satī-gītā de Muktānanda. Tr. from Gujarati by F. Mallison. Paris: Inst. de civilisation indienne, 1973. 184p. (Its pub., 35)

21927 PAREKH, M.C. Shri Swami Narayana: a gospel of Bhagavatadharma: or, God in redemptive action. 3rd ed. Bombay: BVB, 1980. 256p. [1st ed. 1936]

21928 PATEL, D.N. The real essence of tantra. Bombay: Yogi Divine Soc., 1978. 233p.

21929 SAHAJĀNANDA, Swāmi. Shree Swaminarayan's Vachanamritam. Tr. by H.T. Dave. Bombay: BVB, 1977. 680p.

21930 SCHUBRING, W. Sahajānanda und die Svāmi-Nārāyaṇīyas, eine reformierte bramanische Gemeinde. In Nachrichten der Akademie der Wissenschaften (Göttingen), Phil.-Hist. Klasse 1,2 (1962) 95-133.

21931 YAJNIK, J.A. The philosophy of Śri Svāminārāyaṇa. Ahmedabad: L.D. Inst. of Indology, 1972. 83p.

E. Literature and Media in Modern Gujarat

1. Modern Gujarati Literature

21932 BAKSHI, C. Gujarati novel - a genesis. In IWT 5,3 (1971) 144-47.

21933 BROKER, G.D. Narmadashankar. ND: Sahitya Akademi, 1977. 86p. [on Narmadashankar Lalshankar Dave, 1833-86]

21934 GOPALAN, G.V. The political novel in Gujarat. In CAS 6 (1975) 106-20.

21935 JAG MOHAN, SARLA, ed. & tr. Selected stories from Gujarat. Bombay: Jaico, 1961. 212p.

21936 JHAVERI, K.M. The present state of Gujarati literature; lectures. Bombay: U. of Bombay, 1934. 214p.

21937 JOSHI, RAMANLAL. Govardhanram. ND: Sahitya Akademi, 1979. 54p. [Govardhanram Madhavram Tripathi, 1855-1907]

21938 JOSHI, SURESH. Gujarati. In K.R. Srinivasa Iyengar, ed. Indian literature since Independence. ND: Sahitya Akademi, 1973, 71-78.

21939 ______. Life against death: the poetry of Ravji Patel. In IWT 12 (1970) 78-83.

21940 MANIAR, U.M. The influence of English on Gujarati poetry. Baroda: MSUB, 1969. 250p.

21941 ______. Nanalal. Sahitya Akademi, 1977. 88p. [Nanalal Dalpatram, 1877-1946]

21942 PARIKH, B.C. Nanalal, poet-laureate of modern Gujarat; a study in creative interpretation. Bombay: Hind Kitabs, 1953. 98p.

21943 Poet Nanalal (1877-1946) number. In IL 21,2 (1978) 5-72.

21944 SHETH, J. Munshi, self-sculptor. Bombay: BVB, 1979. 252p.

21945 TRIVEDI, V.J. Meghani. ND: Sahitya Akademi, 1977. 54p. [Zaverchand Kalidas Meghani, 1897-1947]

21946 Umashankar Joshi issue. In JSAL 9,1 (1973) 117p. [Gujarati poet, b. 1911]

2. Folk Literature of Gujarat

21947 BOSE, TARA. Folk tales of Gujarat. ND: Sterling, 1971. 119p.

21948 PATEL, M. Folksongs of south Gujarat. Bombay: Indian Musicological Soc., 1974. 121p. [1st pub. in JIMS 5,3 & 5,4 (1974) 1-74, 79-121.

21949 ______. Some aspects of Gujarati folk-songs. In Folklore(C) 2 (1961) 353-67.

3. Journalism and the Press in Modern Gujarat

21950 PARIKH, R.D. The press and society, a sociological study. Bombay: Popular, 1965. 154p.

VI. RAJASTHAN: THE FORMER PRINCELY STATES OF NORTHWEST MIDDLE INDIA

A. Political History since 1949 [For Princely States, see I. B., above]

1. General Studies

21951 JAIN, C.M. Centre-State relations in India: a case study of Rajasthan. In IJPS 31 (1970) 281-90.

21952 ______. State legislatures in India: the Rajasthan Legislative Assembly; a comparative study. ND: S. Chand, 1972. 263p.

21953 KAMAL, K.L. Party politics in an Indian state; a study of the main political parties in Rajasthan. Delhi: S. Chand, 1969. 270p.

21954 ______. Spot light on Rajasthan politics; traditional challenge in an Indian state. Alwar: Prakash Pub., 1967. 155p.

21955 NARAIN, IQBAL & MOHAN LAL. Rajasthan politics after 1967: trends and projections. In EPW 4,51 (1969) 1947-54.

21956 NARAIN, IQBAL & P.C. MATHUR. Union-state relations in India: a case study in Rajasthan. In JComPolSt 2 (1964) 120-40.

21957 PURI, S.L. Legislative elite in an Indian state: a case study of Rajasthan. ND: Abhinav, 1978. 281p.

21958 SINHA, V.M. Governor's invitation to form the government - the Rajasthan case. In PSR 6,1 (1967) 26-38.

21959 SISSON, R. Caste and political factions in Rajasthan. In R. Kothari, ed. Caste in Indian politics. Bombay: Orient Longman, 1969, 175-227.

21960 ______. The Congress Party in Rajasthan; political integration and institution-building in an Indian state. Berkeley: UCalP, 1971. 347p.

21961 SISSON, R. & L.L. SHRADER. Legislative recruitment and political integration: patterns of political linkage in an Indian state. Berkeley: Center for South Asian Studies, U. of Californai, 1972. 54p. (Center for South Asia Studies res. monograph, 6)

21962 UPRETI, N. Political consciousness of the elites: a case study in Rajasthan in the pre-fourth general election period. In JCPS 2,3 (1968) 116-30.

2. Election Studies

21963 BHARGAVA, K. Rajasthan politics and princely rulers: an analysis of electoral processes. In IJPS 33,4 (1972) 413-30.

21964 CHAKRAVARTI, A. General elections of 1967 in a Rajasthan village. In EPW 6,33 (1971) 1775-80.

21965 CHAKRAVARTI, A. The mid-term poll in a Rajasthan village. In SocAct 26,2 (1976) 134-47.

21966 KUMAR, SUSHIL. Nomination politics in the Congress party: a case study in Rajasthan. In PSR 7 (1968) 698-711.

21967 MATHUR, P.C. Dynamics of tandem voting in Indian general elections: the case of Alwar Lok Sabha constituency. In PSR 6,3/3 & 7,1/2 (1967/68) 553-84.

21968 MODI, S. & I.P. MODI & D.B. MATHUR. Independent candidates in Alwar assembly constituency. In PSR 7 (1968) 712-32.

21969 NARAIN, IQBAL & MOHAN LAL SHARMA. Election politics, secularization and political development: the 5th Lok Sabha elections in Rajasthan. In AS 12,4 (1972) 294-309.

21970 PANDE, K.C. The poll verdict in Rajasthan: an overview. In PSR 6,3/4 & 7,1/2 (1968) 462-94.

21971 RAJASTHAN. BUREAU OF STATISTICS. A statistical study of the general elections in Rajasthan, 1952. Jaipur: Bureau of Statistics, Rajasthan, 1952. 105p.

21972 TINKER, I. Rajasthan. In S.V. Kogekar & R.L. Park, eds. Reports on the Indian general elections, 1951-52. Bombay: Popular, 1956, 222-34.

21973 VARMA, S.P. & C.P. BHAMBHRI, eds. Elections and political consciousness in India, a study. Meerut: Meenakshi, 1967. 186p.

21974 VARMA, S.P. & IQBAL NARAIN. Voting behaviour in a changing society; a case study of the fourth general election in Rajasthan. Delhi: National, 1973. 385p.

3. Administration

21975 RAJASTHAN. ADMIN. REFORMS CMTEE. Report. Jaipur: 1963. 235 + 146p.

21976 SINGHI, N.K. Bureaucracy, positions and persons: role structures, interactions, and value-orientations of bureaucrats in Rajasthan. ND: Abhinav, 1974. 398p.

21977 SINGHVI, G.C. The lokayukta institution: Rajasthan experience. In IJPA 24,4 (1978) 1145-58.

21978 VERMA, S.L. The Board of Revenue for Rajasthan; an organisational and administrative study. ND: S. Chand, 1974. 308p.

4. Local Government and Politics
a. general studies of democratic decentralization/panchayati raj

21979 BHARGAVA, B.S. Politico-administrative dynamics in panchayati raj system. ND: Ashish Pub. House, 1978. 77p. [in Jhunjhunu Dist.]

21980 CHAUDHURI, P.K. Decentralisation or delegation of power? the Rajasthan Panchayat Samitis and Zila Parishads Act, 1959. In EW 11,40 (1959) 1365-68.

21981 GROVER, V.P. Panchayati raj administration in Rajasthan: a study of the media of supervision and control. Agra: N. Agarwal, 1973. 215p.

21982 MATHUR, M.V., et al. Panchayati raj in Rajasthan; a case study in Jaipur District. ND: Impex India, 1966. 323p.

21983 NARAIN, IQBAL. Developmental administration and panchayati raj: the Rajasthan experience. In IJPA 14 (1968) 56-74.

21984 NARAIN, IQBAL & K.C. PANDE & MOHAN LAL. Linkage elite and elections: a study of the role of P.R. functionaries in the context of electoral politics of Rajasthan. Meerut: Meenakshi, 1978. 172p.

21985 ______. Rural elite and elections in an Indian state: a study of panchayati raj leadership in the context of Rajasthan electoral politics. ND: National, 1976. 188p.

21986 PAPACHRISTOU, G.C. The inter-play of local and state politics: the Rajasthan case. In PSR 7,3/4 (1968) 733-46.

21987 RAJASTHAN. PANCHAYATI RAJ STUDY TEAM. Report, 1964. Jaipur: Panchayat & Dev. Dept., Govt. of Rajasthan, 1964. 433p.

21988 SHARIB, ZAHURUL HASSAN. Organization of rural self-government in Rajasthan. Bombay: C.D. Barfivala, 1957. 67p.

21989 SHARMA, P.D. Decision-making in Panchayati Raj: the Rajasthan experiment. In Canadian Public Admin. 11 (1968) 163-85.

21990 ______. Police - Panchayati Raj relations: a case study in Rajasthan. In PSR 13 (1974) 209-39.

b. district administration and zila parishads

21991 ADAMS, J. & BALU BUMB. The economic, political and social dimensions of an Indian state: a factor analysis of district data for Rajasthan. In JAS 33,1 (1973) 5-24.

21992 ALVI, S.S.N. The development role of the district collector: a case study of Jaipur District. Jaipur: Dept. of Public Admin., U. of Rajasthan, 1973. 60p.

21993 BHAMBHRI, C.P. Establishment of zila parishads in Rajasthan: a case study. In PSR 5 (1966) 292-303.

21994 DARDA, R.S. Government by committees; a case study of the committees of the zila parishads in Rajasthan. Chittorgarh: Sanjya Res. Pub., 1972. 52p.

21995 PLUNKETT, H.S. Leadership and social change in a district of Rajasthan, India. Diss., U. of California, Berkeley, 1972. 249p.

c. village panchayats and politics

21996 BHARGAVA, B.S. Politico-administrative dynamics in panchayati raj system. ND: Ashish Pub. House, 1978. 77p. [Jhunjhunu Dist.]

21997 BOSE, A.B. Studies in group dynamics I: factionalism in a desert village. In MI 44 (1964) 311-28.

21998 CHAKRAVARTI, A. Contradiction and change: emerging patterns of authority in a Rajasthan village. Delhi: OUP, 1975. 234p.

21999 MATHUR, P.L. The village panchayats in the former state of Jodhpur. In QJLSGI 38 (1968) 465-81.

22000 NARAIN, IQBAL. Political behaviour in rural India: the case of a Panchayat election in Rajasthan. In JComPolSt 5 (1967) 109-29.

22001 RETZLAFF, R.H. Village government in India; a case study. Bombay: Asia, 1962. 140p.

22001 SHARMA, RAVINDRA. Village panchayats in Rajasthan: an administrative profile. Jaipur: Aalekh Pub., 1974. 138p.

d. municipal politics and administration

22003 BASRAO, S. Municipal government in Rajasthan: a study of evolution, organization, and working. ND: S. Chand, 1975. 353p.

22004 BHAMBHRI, C.P. Municipalities and their finances; an empirical study of the municipalities of Rajasthan. Jaipur: Padam Book Co., 1969. 144p.

22005 BHAMBHRI, C.P. & P.C. MATHUR. Elections to the Jaipur Municipal Council: a case study against the Rajasthan perspective. In PSR 3 (1964) 70-88.

22006 GUPTA, B.P. Municipal administration in Rajasthan; a case study. Pilani: Jain Bros., 1971. 208p.

22007 MAHESHWARI, B. Municipal election in Jaipur. In EW 14,1 (1962) 15-19.

22008 PLUNKETT, H.S. Pragmatic politics in a Rajasthan town: case study of a municipal election. In EPW 6,49 (1971) 2442-46.

22009 SHARMA, G.D. Financing urban governments: a study of patterns and determinants of urban government expenditure by size of cities. Bombay: Himalaya Pub. House, 1978. 111p.

B. The Economy of Rajasthan

1. Demography (1981 pop. 34,102,912)

22010 BHARARA, L.P., et al. Impact of irrigation on the changes in population characteristics of beneficiary and non-beneficiary in a desert region. In IJSR 14,2 (1973) 137-45.

22011 MEHTA, B.C. Regional population growth: a case study of Rajasthan. Jaipur: dist. Research Books, 1978. 315p.

22012 NAND, NITYA. Distribution and spatial arrangement of rural population in East Rajasthan, India. In Assn. of American Geographers, Annals 56 (1966) 205-219.

22013 SEN, A.K. Settlement patterns in Rajasthan. In MI 46,3 (1966) 215-25.

22014 SHARMA, R.C. Settlement geography of the Indian desert. ND: Kumar Bros., 1972. 199p.

2. Economic Development and Planning

22015 HOOJA, RAKESH. State level planning: the Rajasthan case. In IJPA 22,3 (1976) 549-62.

22016 NCAER. Perspective plan of Rajasthan, 1974-1989. ND: 1980. 2 v.

22017 ______. Techno-economic survey of Rajasthan. ND: 1963. 316p.

22018 POTTER, D.C. Area planning in Rajasthan. In JAS 23 (1964) 571-79.

22019 PUROHIT, M.C. Identification of backward areas and its policy imperatives: a case study of Rajasthan. In IJPA 23,3 (1977) 653-67.

22020 RAJASTHAN. DIR. OF ECON. & STAT. Twenty-one years of Rajasthan's economy. Jaipur: 1975. 202p.

22021 ROONWAL, M.L., ed. The natural resources of Rajasthan. Jodhpur: U. of Jodhpur, 1977. 2 v., 1211p.

22022 SETHI, M.L. Economic and industrial minerals of Rajasthan. Udaipur: Rajasthan Dept. of Mines & Geology, 1966. 90p.

3. Finance and Banking

22023 PORWAL, L.S. State finances in India; a case of Rajasthan. Delhi: S. Chand, 1971. 237p.

22024 SARMA, H.C. Growth of banking in a developing economy; a case study of evolution, growth, and future prospects of banking in Rajasthan in relation to other states of India. Agra: Sahitya Bhawan, 1969. 316p.

4. Agriculture: Problems of a Desert Region
a. general studies

22025 ABICHANDANI, C.T. & B.B. ROY. Rajasthan desert - its origin and amelioration. In IGJ 41,3/4 (1966) 35-43.

22026 AHUJA, K. Idle labour in village India. ND: Manohar, 1978. 160p.

22027 BOSE, A.B. & S.P. MALHOTRA. Economic structure in a village in arid part of Rajasthan. In JSR 5 (1962) 81-94.

22028 DESAI, M.D. Hasteda; economic life in a Rajasthan village. Vallabh Vidyanagar: Agro-Econ. Res. Centre, Sardar Vallabhbhai Vidyapeeth, 1966. 224p. (Studies in rural problems, 5)

22029 DIGHE, A. Agricultural labourers in Jaipur District: a study of their needs and problems. ND: Council for Social Dev., 1978. 68p.

22030 GUPTA, N.L. & S.L. HIRAN. Agricultural regions of Rajasthan. In DG 11,1/2 (1973) 57-74.

22031 JODHA, N.S. & V.S. VYAS. Conditions of stability and growth in arid agriculture. Vallabh Vidyanagar: Agro-Econ. Res. Centre, Sardar Patel U., 1969. 127p.

22032 NCAER. Agriculture and livestock in Rajasthan. ND: 1964. 103p.

22033 SEN, A.K. Agricultural atlas of Rajasthan. ND: ICAR, 1972. 52p.

22034 SWAROOP, BHAGWAT. Trends in land utilization in Rajasthan, 1951-62. In AV 8,2 (1966) 186-235.

22035 TANDON, B.K. & B.S. MURDIA. Economic viability of farms in Udaipur District, Rajasthan; report of a study. Udaipur: U. of Udaipur, 1972. 249p.

22036 YADAV, J.P.S. Crop land-use patterns in Rajasthan. In Bombay Geog. Magazine 13,1 (1965) 97-115.

b. agricultural development and innovation; irrigation, and the Rajasthan Canal

22037 BOSE, A.B. The process of adoption of agricultural innovation in West Rajasthan. In IJSW 27 (1966) 263-68.

22038 CHATTERJEE, N.N. Rajasthan Canal: the man-made river that will make the desert bloom. In Yojana 21,12 (1977) 16-20.

22039 INDIA (REP.). PLANNING CMSN. RES. PROGRAMMES CMTEE. Evaluation of benefits of irrigation: Gang Canal, Rajasthan. ND: 1967. 226p.

22040 RAKHRAL, K.R. Economics of well irrigation in a Rajasthani village. In Artha-Vikas 3,1 (1967) 63-83.

22041 TEWARI, R.N. Agricultural planning and cooperatives. Delhi: S. Chand, 1972. 100p.

22042 VAGALE, L.R. The Rajasthan Canal area: a settlement structure. In URPT 16,3 (1973) 148-86.

c. land tenure and reform

22043 DOOL SINGH. Land reforms in Rajasthan; a study of evasion, implementation and socio-economic effects of land reforms. ND: Res. Programmes Cmtee., Planning Cmsn., 1964. 452p.

22044 DUTT, S.K. Land revenue law in Rajasthan. Jaipur: Bafna Law Pub., 1977. 368 + 304p.

22045 MATHUR, H.M., ed. Agrarian reform and rural development. Jaipur: HCM State Inst. of Public Admin., 1976. 219p.

22046 OOMMEN, T.K. Problems of gramdan; a study in Rajasthan. In EW 17,26 (1965) 1035-40.

22047 PANDE, RAM. Agrarian movement in Rajasthan. Delhi: University Pub., 1974. 108p.

22048 PANT, G.B. Report on Rajasthan Jagirdari abolition. Jaipur: Govt. Printing, 1953. 57p.

22049 PAREEK, S.N. Land reforms legislation in Rajasthan; with special reference to the Rajasthan zamindari and biswedari abolition act, 1959.... Ajmer: Bhanu Law Publishers, 1968. 366p.

22050 RAJASTHAN. DIR. OF PUBLIC RELATIONS. Land reforms in Rajasthan. Jaipur: 1959. 22p.

22051 RAJASTHAN. KHUDKASHT ENQUIRY CMTEE. Report. Jaipur: 1952. 28p.

22052 RAJASTHAN. STATE LAND CMSN. Report. Jaipur: Govt. Central Press, 1959. 119p.

22053 RAJASTHAN. ZAMINDARI ABOLITION CMTEE. Report. Jaipur: Govt. Central Press, 1958. 18p.

5. Industrial Development of Rajasthan
a. general studies

22054 KIRLOSKAR CONSULTANTS LTD. Industrial potential survey of Kota District. Jaipur: Rajasthan State Industrial & Mineral Dev. Corp., 1971. 86p. (District survey, 2)

22055 MATHUR, H.M. Industrial economy of a developing region; a case study of Rajasthan in relation to other states of India. Alwar: Prakash Pub., 1968. 359p.

22056 MATHUR, K.S. Mica industry in Rajasthan. Jaipur: Asha Pub. House, 1968. 320p.

22057 RAJASTHAN. DIR. OF INDUSTRIES & CIVIL SUPPLIES. Industrial potentials of Rajasthan: prospective industries based on minerals, live stock, forest products, agricultural products, etc. Jaipur: 1965. 96p.

22058 ______. Industrialisation in Rajasthan: growth, potential and prospects. Jaipur: 1969. 42p.

22059 RAJASTHAN CHAMBER OF COMMERCE & INDUSTRY. Prospects of industrial development in Rajasthan. Jaipur: 1969. 218p.

22060 RAJASTHAN STATE INDUSTRIAL & MINERAL DEV. CORP.

Survey of industrial potential in Rajasthan Canal area. Jaipur: 1972. 150p.

22061 SHARMA, G.D. Working of state enterprises in Rajasthan. ND: Sterling, 1975. 319p.

b. small-scale industry

22062 PAREEK, H.S. Financing of small scale industries in a developing economy. ND: National, 1978. 279p.

22063 RAJASTHAN. DIR. OF ECON. & STAT. Report on survey of small scale industries in Rajasthan (rural), 1972. Jaipur: 1975. 53p.

22064 RAJASTHAN. DIR. OF INDUSTRIES & CIVIL SUPPLIES. Hand-book on small scale industries in Rajasthan. Jaipur: 1969. 230p.

22065 SMALL INDUSTRIES SERVICE INST., JAIPUR. Industrial potential survey of Jaipur District: survey. Jaipur: Rajasthan State Industrial & Mineral Dev. Corp., 1973. 130p.

6. Labor in Rajasthan

22066 BAJAJ, R.K. Personnel problems of large scale industries: with special reference to Rajasthan. Jaipur: Panchsheel Prakashan, 1976. 198p.

22067 DOOL SINGH & K.S. PORWAL. Industrial relations in Rajasthan; case studies of industrial relations in selected industrial units in Rajasthan. Pilani: dist. Students Agency, 1969. 308p.

22068 MATHUR, D.C. Wage structure in a developing economy. Jaipur: The Students' Book Co., 1974. 182p.

22069 VAID, K.N. & GURDIAL SINGH. Contract labour in construction industry; a study in Rajasthan. ND: Shri Ram Centre for Industrial Relations, 1966. 72p.

22070 VAID, K.N. The new worker: a study at Kota. London: Asia, 1968. 196p.

7. Commerce and Transportation

22071 SAXENA, H.M. Geography of transport and market centres; a case study of Hadaoti Plateau. ND: S. Chand, 1975. 211p.

22072 SHARMA, K.K. Motor transport in Rajasthan. ND: Sterling, 1975. 348p.

22073 TRIPATHI, P.C. Rural transport and economic development. Delhi: S. Chand, 1972. 200p.

C. Society and Social Change in Modern Rajasthan

1. Social Categories

a. general studies, incl. kinship and marriage

22074 BOSE, A.B. Rural family organisation in Western Rajasthan. In EA 19 (1966) 163-76.

22075 CARSTAIRS, G.M. The twice-born; a study of a community of high-caste Hindus. London: Hogarth Press, 1957. 343p.

22076 DANDIYA, C.K., ed. Women in Rajasthan: proceedings of a Seminar on Women, the Untapped Potential of Rajasthan. Jaipur: Dept. of Adult Educ., U. of Rajasthan, 1975. 231p.

22077 DUBEY, B.R. Profiles of women in Rajasthan [state politics]. In Vina Mazumdar, ed. Symbols of power... Bombay: Allied, 1979, 291-304.

22078 ENGINEER, ASHGAR ALI. The revolt in Udaipur and its aftermath. In his The Bohras. ND: Vikas, 1980, 218-81.

22079 INDIA (REP.). SUPT. OF CENSUS OPERATIONS, RAJASTHAN. Ethnographic atlas of Rajasthan; with reference to scheduled castes and scheduled tribes. Delhi: MPGOI, 1969. 138p.

22080 JOSHI, S.L. Towards cultural interpretation: a comparative study of caste Hindus and tribals of South Rajasthan. In JSR 18,1 (1975) 43-52.

22081 KATIYAR, T.S. Social life in Rajasthan (a case study). Allahabad: Kitab Mahal, 1964. 127p.

22082 MALHOTRA, S.P. & M.L.A. SEN. A comparative study of the socio-economic characteristics of nuclear and joint house-holds. In Journal of Family Welfare 11 (1964) 21-32.

22083 STERN, H. Power in modern India: caste or class? An approach and case study. In CIS ns 13,1 (1979) 61-84.

b. the Rajputs

22084 BADEN-POWELL, B.H. Notes on the origin of the "Lunar" and "Solar" Aryan tribes and on the Rajput clans. In JRAS (1899) 295-328.

22085 BAHADUR, K.P., ed. Caste, tribes and culture of Rajputs. Delhi: Ess Ess, 1978. 190p.

22086 BINGLEY, A.H. Caste, tribes and culture of Rajputs. Ed. by K.P. Bahadur. Delhi: E s Ess, 1978. 190p. [1st pub. 1898, under title: Rajputs]

22087 HITREC, J.G. Son of the moon. NY: Harper Bros., 1948. 383p.

22088 PLUNKETT, F.T. Royal marriages in Rajasthan. In CIS ns 7 (1973) 64-80.

22089 RUDOLPH, L.I. & S.H. RUDOLPH. The political modernization of an Indian feudal order: an analysis of Rajput adaptation in Rajasthan. In Journal of Social Issues 24 (1968) 93-128.

c. Jats and other Hindu castes

22090 BHATTACHARYA, A.N. & R.N. VYAS. Habitat economy and society: a study of the Dangis. ND: Concept, 1979. 160p.

22091 BOSE, A.B. & S.P. MALHOTRA. Some characteristics of occupational castes in central and lower Luni in western Rajasthan. In EA 17 (1964) 137-56.

22092 ______. Studies in agricultural sociology at the Central Arid Zone Research Inst.: some characteristics of lower, middle and upper class farmers. In IJSR 2 (1964) 201-12.

22093 SISSON, R. Peasant movements and political mobilization: the Jats of Rajasthan. In AS 9,12 (1969) 946-63.

d. "Untouchables": Bhangis and other scheduled castes

22094 SHYAMLAL. Social reform movement among the Bhangis of West Rajasthan. In EA 32,2 (1979) 99-106.

e. the Meos: a Muslim caste of Mewat, in NE Rajasthan

22095 AGGARWAL, P.C. Caste hierarchy in a Meo village in Rajasthan. In Imtiaz Ahmad. Caste and social stratification among the Muslims. ND: Manohar, 1973, 74-88.

22096 ______. Caste, religion and power: an Indian case study. ND: Shri Ram Centre for Industrial Relations, 1971. 270p.

22097 ______. Kinship and marriage among the Meos of Rajasthan. In Imtiaz Ahmad, ed. Family, kinship and marriage among the Muslims in India. ND: Manohar, 1976, 265-96.

22098 ______. The Meos of Rajasthan and Haryana. In Imtiaz Ahmad, ed. Caste and social stratification among the Muslims. ND: Manohar, 1973, 21-44.

22099 AMIR ALI, HASHIM. The Meos of Mewat. ND: Oxford & IBH, 1970. 200p.

22100 MARWAH, I.S. Tabligh movement among the Meos of Mewat. In M.S.A. Rao, ed. Social movements in India. ND: Manohar, 1979, v. 2, 79-100.

f. tribals of Rajasthan [see also II. A., above]

22101 DOSHI, S.L. A sociological analysis of political unification among the scheduled tribes of Rajasthan. In SB 27,2 (1979) 231-44.

22102 MISRA, P.K. The Gadulia Lohars: their nomadism and economic activities. In L.S. Leshnik & G.-D. Sontheimer, eds. Pastoralists and nomads in South Asia. Wiesbaden: Harassowitz, 1975, 235-46.

22103 RUHELA, S.P. The Gaduliya Lohars of Rajasthan: a study in the sociology of nomadism. ND: Impex India, 1968. 296p.

22104 VETSCHER, T. Betrothal and marriage among the Minas of S. Rajasthan. In MI 53,4 (1973) 387-413.

2. Villages and Rural Social Development

22105 BOSE, A.B. & N.S. JODHA. The Jajmani system in a desert village. In MI 45 (1965) 105-26.

22106 BOSE, A.B. & S.P. MALHOTRA. Anthro-geographical study of the settlement pattern of a desert village. In MI 43 (1963) 233-49.

22107 CHATURVEDI, H.R. Bureaucracy and the local community: dynamics of rural development. Bombay: Allied Pub., 1977. 199p. (Centre for the Study of Developing Societies monograph series, 2)

22108 CHAUHAN, B.R. A Rajasthan village. ND: Vir Pub. House, 1967. 330p.

22109 NARAIN, IQBAL & K.C. PANDE & M.L. SHARMA. The rural elite in an Indian state: a case study of Rajasthan. ND: Manohar, 1976. 256p.

22110 OOMMEN, T.K. Myth and reality in India's communitarian villages. In JComPolSt 4 (1966) 94-116.

22111 ______. Rural community power structure in India. In Social Forces 49,2 (1970) 226-39.

22112 RAJASTHAN. EVAL. ORG. The pattern of rural development in Rajasthan; a report based on a study of the working of panchayati raj institutions and rural development programmes particularly during the year, 1962-63. Jaipur: 1963. 158p.

22113 SAXENA, J.C. Profile of a village in semi-arid part of Rajasthan. In EA 17 (1964) 49-61.

22114 SHARMA, K.L. The changing rural stratification system: a comparative study of six villages in Rajasthan, India. ND: Orient Longman, 1974. 226p.

22115 ______. Social stratification in rural Rajasthan. In PSR 14,3/4 (1975) 45-64.

22116 SINGH, R.P. Decision making and rural elites: a study of rural-urban elites interaction in decision making process. Delhi: Res. Pub. in Social Sciences, 1975. 123p.

3. Cities and Urbanization

22117 ARORA, R.K. & R. HOOJA & S. MATHUR. Jaipur, profile of a changing city. Jaipur: IIPA, Rajasthan Branch: HCM State Inst. of Public Admin., 1977. 137p.

22118 CHAUHAN, B.R. Towns in the tribal setting. Delhi: National, 1970. 207p.

22119 GHOSH, B. Jaisalmer: urban form and pattern of a medieval Indian town. In URPT 11 (1968) 5-55.

22120 JAIN, K.A. & J. JAIN, eds. The Jaipur album; or, All about Jaipur. Jaipur City: Rajasthan Directories Pub. House, 1935. 1 v.

22121 LAL, S.K. The urban elite. Delhi: Thomson Press, 1974. 147p.

22122 LODHA, R.M. Bhilwara and its umland. Delhi: New Heights, 1974. 155p.

22123 MATHUR, M.V. & D.L. GUPTA & R.J. CHELLIAH. Economic survey of Jaipur City. Jaipur: Dept. of Econ., U. of Rajasthan, 1965. 97p.

22124 MEHTA, B.C. Urbanisation in Rajasthan: a study of differential rates of urban growth. In Soc Act 26,1 (1976) 52-65.

22125 RAJASTHAN. TOWN PLANNING DEPT. Master plan for Ajmer. 1976. 62p.

22126 ROY, A.K. History of the Jaipur City. ND: Manohar, 1978. 260p.

22127 SARDA, HAR BILAS. Ajmer: historical and descriptive. Ajmer: Scottish Mission Industries, 1911. 176p.

4. Social Welfare and Health Services

22128 ADWANI, N.H. Perspectives on adult crime and correction: a comparative study of adult prisoners and probationers. ND: Abhinav, 1978. 222p.

22129 AGRAWAL, B.L. & K.M. MATHUR. A study of rural family planning welfare centres. Jaipur: Demographic & Eval. Cell, Govt. of Rajasthan, 1972. 61p.

22130 BEDI, M.S. Socially handicapped children: a study of their institutional services. Jodhpur: Jain Bros., 1978. 223p.

22131 CARSTAIRS, G.M. The case of Thakur Khuman Singh: a culture-conditioned crime. In British J. of Delinquency 4 (1953) 14-25.

22132 ______. Daru and bhang: cultural factors in the choice of intoxicants. In J. of Studies in Alcohol 15 (1954) 220-37.

22133 ______. Medicine and faith in rural Rajasthan. In B.D. Paul, ed. Health, culture and community. NY: R. Sage Foundation, 1955, 107-34.

22134 VARMA, S.C. The Ajmer-Pushkar project: a new approach to the problem of begging. In SocAct 18 (1968) 239-43.

5. Education in Modern Rajasthan (24.1% literacy in 1981)

22135 NARAIN, IQBAL. Rural local politics and primary school management. In S.H. Rudolph & L.I. Rudolph, eds. Education and politics in India.... Cambridge: HUP, 1972, 148-64.

22136 RAJASTHAN. DIR. OF EDUC. Education in the districts of Rajasthan, 1957-58; a statistical survey. Bikaner: 1960. 218p. (Its pub., 3)

22137 RAJASTHAN. EDUC. DEPT. Educational development in Rajasthan. Jaipur: 1965. 110p.

22138 RAJASTHAN. STATE PRIMARY EDUC. CMTEE. Report, 1963-64. Bikaner: Govt. Press, 1965. 177p.

22139 UNIV. OF RAJASTHAN. DEPT. OF ADULT EDUC. Continuing education at the university, a plan for the University of Rajasthan; report of a survey, January-April, 65. Jaipur: 1965. 141p.

22140 VENKATESWARA RAO, T. & ANIL BHATT & T.P. RAMA RAO. Adult education for social change: a study of the national adult education programme in Rajasthan. ND: Manohar, 1980. 192p.

22141 VREEDE-DE STUERS, C. Girl students in Jaipur: a study in attitudes towards family life, marriage, and career. NY: Humanities Press, 1970. 141p.

D. Religions of Modern Rajasthan

22142 ANWARUL HAQ, M. The Faith Movement of Mawlana Muhammad Ilyas. London: Allen & Unwin, 1972. 210p. [Sufism in Mewat]

22143 CARSTAIRS, G.M. Patterns of religious observance in three villages of Rajasthan. In L.P. Vidyarthi, ed. Aspects of religion in Indian society.... Meerut: Kedar Nath Ram Nath, 1961, 59-113.

22144 SHARMA, N.K. "Marwar Pancha" - Jaina tirtha. In JRIHR 11,3 (1974) 17-28.

E. Modern Literatures of Rajasthan

1. Rajasthani and its Emergence as a Literary Language

22145 KOTHARI, K. Rajasthani. In K.R. Srinivasa Iyengar, ed. Indian literature since Independence. ND: Sahitya Akademi, 1973, 252-65.

22146 SARASWAT, R. Rajasthani: in new dress. In IL 22,6 (1979) 73-84.

22147 ______. Rajasthani literature: a new consciousness. In IL 21,6 (1978) 178-89.

22148 SHARMA, I.K., tr. Contemporary Rajasthani poetry. Bikaner: Rajasthani Bhasha Sahitya Sangam (Academy), 1979. 247p.

22149 SHARMA, V.D. Surya Mall Mishran. ND: Sahitya Akademi, 1976. 37p.

2. Folk Literature

22150 BIRLA, L.N. Popular tales of Rajasthan. Bombay: BVB, 1967. 174p.

22151 BRYCE, L.W., ed. Women's folk-songs of Rajputana. Delhi: PDMIB, 1964. 187p.

22152 DINESH, K. Folk tales of Rajasthan. Jodhpur: Jainsons, 1979. 119p.

22153 MATHUR, U.B. The sound of music in Rajasthan. Jaipur: Music Lovers, 1976. 92p.

22154 ROY CHAUDHURY, B. Folk tales of Rajasthan. ND: Sterling, 1972. 119p. (Folk tales of India series, 9)

VII. MADHYA PRADESH: INDIA'S LARGEST STATE, IN THE UPLANDS OF CENTRAL MIDDLE INDIA

A. Political History [For British Period, see I. B. 4 and I. C. 3, above]

1. Politics of Madhya Pradesh (est. 1956)

22155 KAUSHIK, P.D. The government and politics of Madhya Pradesh. In Journal of the Soc. for Study of State Govts. 5,2 (1972) 113-45.

22156 MAHAKOSHAL PROVINCIAL CONGRESS CMTEE. Memorandum of the Mahakoshal Pradeshik Committee submitted to the States Reorganisation Commission. Nagpur: 1954. 48p. [Chm., Ghanshyam Singh Gupta]

22157 NORONHA, R.P. A tale told by an idiot. ND: Vikas, 1976. 182p.

22158 SINGH, K.P. S.V.D. rule in M.P. - an interview with G.N. Singh. In J. of the Soc. for Study of State Govts. 6 (1973) 55-62.

22159 WILCOX, W.A. Madhya Pradesh. In M. Weiner, ed. State politics in India. Princeton: PUP, 1968, 128-74.

2. Election Studies

22160 AHMED, BASHIRUDDIN & V.B. SINGH. Dimensions of party system change: case of Madhya Pradesh. In EPW 10,5-7 (1975) 295-318.

22161 AVASTHI, A. Madhya Pradesh. In S.V. Kogekar & R.L. Park, eds. Reports on the Indian general elections 1951-52. Bombay: Popular, 1956, 68-86.

22162 CHANDIDAS, R. The fourth general elections: Madhya Pradesh: a case study. In EPW 33-35 (1967) 1503-14.

22163 MORRIS-JONES, W.H. & B. DAS GUPTA. Fourth general elections in Madhya Pradesh. In EPW 3,1/2 (1968) 178-80.

22164 PUROHIT, B.R. Bharatiya Jan Sangh and the fourth general elections in Madhya Pradesh. In JCPS 2,3 (1968) 47-63.

22165 ______. General elections in M.P. In PSR 6,3/4 & 7,1/2 (1967-68) 303-24.

22166 SHARMA, S.R. Madhya Bharat. In S.V. Kogekar and R.L. Park, eds. Reports on the Indian general elections, 1951-52. Bombay: Popular, 1956, 188-203.

3. Local Government and Politics

22167 AGRAWAL, B.C. Cultural factors in political decision-making: a small town election in India. In EPW 6,8 (1971) 495-502.

22168 AVASTHI, A. Abolition of the posts of commissioners in Madhya Pradesh and their revival. ND: IIPA, 1967. 51p.

22169 DUGVAKAR, T.G. Village panchayat in Madhya Pradesh. In JNAA 16,3 (1971) 25-41.

22170 JONES, R.W. Urban politics in India: area, power, and policy in a penetrated system. Berkeley: UCalP, 1974. 420p. [study of Indore]

22171 MAYER, A.C. Local government elections in a Malwa village. In EA 11 (1958) 189-202.

22172 ______. Caste and local politics in India. In Philip Mason, ed. India and Ceylon: unity and diversity. London: CamUP, 1967, 121-41.

22173 ______. Some political implications of community development in India. In Archives européenes de sociologie 4,1 (1963) 86-106.

22174 MINOCHA, A.C. Finances of urban local bodies in Madhya Pradesh; a case study of Bhopal, Mahakoshal and Vindhya Pradesh regions. Bombay: C.D. Barfivala, Dir. Genl., All-India Inst. of Local Self-govt., 1965. 266p.

22175 PRASAD, RAMAYAN. Local self-government in Vindhya Pradesh. Bombay: C.D. Barfivala, 1963. 220p.

22176 PRAVIR CHANDRA BHANJDEO KATATIYA. I, Pravir, the Adivasi God. Bastar: 1965. 192p. [Maharaja of Bastar, former tribal princely state]

B. The Madhya Pradesh Economy

1. Demography (1981 pop. 52,131,717)

22177 AYYAR, N.P. & R.S. DUBE. Some aspects of the rural population of Madhya Pradesh. In Geographical Outlook 5 (1968) 29-41.

22178 DRIVER, E.D. Differential fertility in Central India. Princeton: PUP, 1963. 152p.

22179 LOEBNER, H.G. A path analysis of fertility in central India. Ph.D. diss., U. of Massachusetts, 1972. 265p. [UM 73-7118]

2. Surveys of Economic Conditions

22180 MADHYA PRADESH. DIR. OF ECON. & STAT. Changing economy of the states. Bhopal: 1966. 302p.

22181 ______. Districtwise indicators of regional development in Madhya Pradesh, 1960-61 to 1963-64. Bhopal: 1965? 58p.

22182 ______. Economic and statistical atlas of Madhya Pradesh. Bhopal: 1958. 44p.

22183 ______. Regional income atlas of Madhya Pradesh. Gwalior: 1960. 746p.

22184 ______. Socio-economic survey of Bhilai region. Bombay: Popular, 1959-68. 3 v.

22185 NCAER. Techno-economic survey of Madhya Pradesh. Bombay: Asia, 1960. 323p.

22186 PATEL, M.L. Agro-economic survey of tribal Mandla. ND: PPH, 1969. 136p.

22187 Report on the socio-economic survey of Geedam Block, Bastar District, M.P. In Administrator 22,1 (1977) 1-62. [Report on Kuakonda Block, Bastar Dist. in 22,1 (1977) 63-130; Reports on Kusmi Block, Sarguja Dist. & on Bagicha Block, Raigarh Dist. in 21,1 (1976) 185-368]

3. Economic Development and Planning

22188 ASHFAQ ALI. Economic development of Bhopal: a socio-economic survey, 1901-1975. Enl. ed. Bhopal: Jai Bharat Pub. House, 1976. 781p. + 19pl.

22189 AVARD. Socio-economic development of a dacoit affected area in Chambal Valley, Joura Block, Morena District, M.P. (India)... 1976. ND: Lakshmi Book Store, 1976. 109p.

22190 MADHYA PRADESH. PLANNING, ECON. & STAT. DEPT. Approach to the Fifth five year plan: Madhya Pradesh. Bhopal: 1972. 118p.

22191 ______. Fourth five year plan of Madhya Pradesh: mid-term appraisal. Bhopal: 1971. 113p.

22192 MINOCHA, A.C. Economic growth in Madhya Pradesh, 1950/51 to 1959/60. In Vikram 5 (1961) 67-76.

22193 ______. Role of commercial banks in regional development - a case study of Madhya Pradesh. In IEJ 22,5 (1974) 269-81.

22194 NAG, D.S., ed. Development potential of Madhya Pradesh. Bhopal: Kailash Pustak Sadan, 1966. 186p.

22195 SHRI PRAKASH & R. RAJAN. Economic development and structural changes in the economy of Madhya Pradesh. In IEJ 58,2 (1977) 203-38.

22196 SINGH, R.L. et al. Baghelkhand region: a study in population, resources regionalization and development models. In NGJI 22,1/2 (1976) 7-14.

22197 SUNDARAM, K.V. et al. Spatial planning for a tribal region, a case study of Bastar District, Madhya Pradesh. Mysore: Inst. of Dev. Studies, U. of Mysore, 1972. 49p. (Its Dev. Studies, 4)

4. Agriculture
a. general studies

22198 CHHIBBER, H.L. The development of landforms, soils and life in the neighborhood of Jubbulpore and Bhereghat, Madhya Pradesh. Banaras: NGSI, 1950, 1-64. (Its Bull., 14)

22199 GUPTA, R.P. Agricultural prices in a backward economy. Delhi: National, 1973. 238p.

22200 HARNETTY, P. Crop trends in the Central Provinces of India, 1861-1921. In MAS 11,3 (1977) 341-78.

22201 LESHNIK, L.S. The system of dry-farming in the West Nimar District of Central India. In Heidelberg U., Südasien-Inst., Jahrbuch (1966) 56-74.

22202 MADHYA PRADESH, DIR. OF LAND RECORDS. Agro-economic atlas of Madhya Pradesh. Rev. ed. Gwalior: 1966. 198p.

22203 ______. Report on agricultural census in Madhya Pradesh, 1970-71. Gwalior: 1975-79. 2 v., 125, 634p.

22204 ______. Standard outturn per acre of crops in Madhya Pradesh for decennium, 1942-43 to 1951-52. Gwalior: 1957. 121p.

22205 RATNAWAT, B.P. Agricultural manpower and economic development, with special case study of Madhya Pradesh. Bombay: Popular, 1975. 290p.

22206 SHARMA, H.S. The physiography of the Lower Chambal Valley and its agricultural development: a study in applied geomorphology. ND: Concept, 1979. 243p.

22207 SHUKLA, V.P. An economic analysis of farm resource use, Jabalpur District, Madhya Pradesh, India, 1967-68. Ithaca: Cornell U., Dept. of Agri. Econ., 1970. 75p.

22208 SINGH, K.N. & S.N. SINGH. Effective communication media for rural audiences: an experimental study. Bombay: Dharamsi Morarji Chemical Co., 1976. 98p.

22209 SRIVASTAVA, U.K. Management of drought prone areas programme: analyses and case studies from Jhabua District. Ahmadabad: Centre for Mgmt. in Agri., Indian Inst. of Mgmt., 1978. 250p. (CMA monograph, 71)

22210 VENKATARATNAM, L. Horticulture in central India. ND: Farm Info. Unit, Dir. of Extension, Min. of Agri., 1973. 168p.

22211 WAKE, W.H. The causal role of transportation improvements in agricultural changes in Madhya Pradesh, India, 1854-1954; a type study. In IGJ 37 (1962) 133-52.

22212 WEAVER, T.F. The farmers of Raipur. In J.W. Mellor, et al. Developing rural India: plan and practice. Ithaca: CornellUP, 1968, 143-236.

b. agricultural cooperatives

22213 CENTRAL PROVINCES & BERAR. BERAR CO-OP. ENQUIRY CMTEE. Report. Nagpur: Govt., C.P. & Berar, 1939. 139p.

22214 MUTHIAH, C. Assessment of progress and evaluation of cooperative farming societies in pilot project areas in Madhya Pradesh. Gwalior: Agro-Econ. Res. Centre for Madhya Pradesh, 1964. 297p. (Its Ad-hoc study, 6)

22215 RESERVE BANK OF INDIA. Review of agricultural development and co-operative credit in Madhya Pradesh. Bombay: RBI, 1977. 143p.

c. land tenure and reform

22216 AGARWAL, D.C. Land reforms in Vindhya Pradesh. In Indian J. of Commerce 23,2 (1970) 71-79.

22217 DUBE, S.L. Tenancy laws in Madhya Bharat with short notes. Agra: Wadhwa, 1959. 134p.

22218 HARNETTY, P. Curious exercise of political economy: some implications of British land revenue policy in the Central Provinces of India, 1861-1900. In SA 6 (1976) 14-33.

22219 JAIN, H. Land reforms in Madhya Pradesh. In EE 61,12 (1973) 543-46.

22220 JAIN, R.K. Classes and classification among the peasants of Central India: relations of production in village Parsana, M.P. In SB 26,1 (1977) 91-115.

5. Industry, Labor, and Transportation in Madhya Pradesh

22221 CHOUBEY, H.K. Bhilai steel project & its impact on the towns of Chhattisgarh. Secunderabad: Indian Inst. of Geography, 1975. 241p.

22222 DRAVID, V.V. Labour problem and policy in Madhya Pradesh. In ILJ 1 (1960) 217-30.

22223 KHERA, S.S. The establishment of the heavy electrical plant at Bhopal. ND: IIPA, 1963. 128p.

22224 MADHYA PRADESH. DIR. OF ECON. AND STAT. Report on the regional transport survey of Madhya Pradesh (1964-67). Indore: 1971. 430p.

22225 MADHYA PRADESH. DIR. OF INDUSTRIES. Industrial statistics, 1973. Bhopal: 1974. 111p.

22226 ______. Survey of footwear industry in Greater Gwalior. Indore: Govt. Regional Press, 1965. 69p.

22227 NANEKAR, K.R. Handloom industry in Madhya Pradesh. Nagpur: Nagpur U., 1968. 186p.

22228 SHUKLA, S.K. Location of industries in Madhya Bharat Plateau. Kanpur: Sahitya Ratnalaya, 1979. 164p.

C. Society and Social Change (1981 literacy 27.82%)

1. Social Categories [for Tribals, see II. B., above]

22229 AURORA, G.S. Tribe-caste-class encounters: some aspects of folk-urban relations in Alirajpur Tehsil. Hyderabad: Admin. Staff College of India, 1972. 293p.

22230 CHAMBARD, J.-L. Le mariage chez les Kirār (Madhya Pradesh) en tant que système de prévention de l'alliance. In Puruṣārtha 2 (1975) 107-145.

22231 ______. Mariages secondaires et foires aux femmes en Inde centrale. In L'Homme 1,2 (1961) 51-88. [in Gwalior]

22233 FUCHS, S. The scavengers of the Nimar District in Madhya Pradesh. In JASBombay 27,1 (1951) 86-98. [Mehtar caste]

22234 JACOBSON, D. The veil of virtue: purdah and the Muslim family in the Bhopal region of Central India. In Imtiaz Ahmad, ed. Family, kinship and marriage among the Muslims in India. ND: Manohar, 1976, 169-216.

22235 ______. The women of N. and central India: goddesses and wives. In C.J. Matthiasson, ed. Many sisters: women in cross-cultural perspective. NY: Free Press, 1974, 99-175.

22236 JAIN, R.K. Bundela genealogy and legends: the past of an indigenous ruling group of Central India. In J.H.M. Beattie & R.G. Lienhardt, eds. Studies in social anthropology.... London: OUP, 239-72.

22237 MAYER, A.C. The dominant caste in a region of central India. In SWJA 14 (1958) 407-27.

22238 MUKHERJEE, M. Gharuas: a metal artisan group and their art. In MI 54,4 (1974) 287-302.

22239 MUTATKAR, R.K. & A. ANSARI. Muslim caste in an Indian town: a caste study. In BDCRI 25 (1966) 163-90. [Sagar, M.P.]

22240 PANDEY, K.L. Report on the disturbances which took place at Jagdalpur on the 25th and 26th March, 1966. Bhopal: Govt. Central Press, 1967. 156p. [in former

Bastar State]

22241 RUSSELL, R.V. & HIRA LAL. The tribes and castes of the Central Provinces of India. Delhi: Cosmo, 1975. 4 v., 1963p. [1st pub. 1916]

22242 THALIATH, J. Notes on the Kurmis of northeastern Madhya Pradesh. In Anthropos 5,1/2 (1962) 121-66.

2. Villages and Rural Society

22243 CHANDRA, PRABHAT. Communication of some new ideas in a Madhya Pradesh village: a sociological study conducted in a mixed village. In EA 17 (1964) 183-214.

22244 GAIKWAD, V.R. &. B.L. TRIPATHI. Social interaction and communication in an Indian village. Ahmedabad: Centre for Mgmt. in Agri., Indian Inst. of Mgmt., 1974. 145p.

22245 GAIKWAD, V.R. & B.L. TRIPATHI & G.S. BHATNAGAR. Opinion leaders and communication in Indian villages. Ahmedabad: Centre for Mgmt. in Agri., Indian Inst. of Mgmt., 1972. 147p.

22246 LESHNIK, K.S. A village community in Central India. In Anthropos 61 (1966) 813-30. [W. Nimar Dist.]

22247 MATHUR, K.S. An aspect of village economy in Malwa. In EA 17 (1964) 98-113.

22248 ______. Caste and ritual in a Malwa village. London: Asia, 1964. 215p.

22249 MAYER, A.C. Caste and kinship in central India: a village and its region. Berkeley: UCalP, 1970. 320p. [1st pub. 1960]

22250 ______. Development projects in an Indian village. In PA 29 (1956) 37-45.

22251 ______. An Indian community development block revisited. In PA 30 (1957) 35-46.

22252 SINGH, K.N. & S.N. SINGH. Effective communication media for rural audiences: an experimental study. Bombay: Dharamsi Morarji Chemical Co., 1976. 98p. [Dewas Dist.]

22253 SINGH, R.Y. The Malwa Region: rural habitat system, structure, and change. Varanasi: Intl. Geographical Union, Working Group, Transformation of Rural Habitat in Developing Countries & Intl. Centre for Rural Habitat Studies, 1978. 196p.

3. Cities and Urbanization

22254 ASHFAQ ALI. Bhopal: past and present; a brief history of Bhopal from the hoary past up to the present time. Bhopal: Jai Bharat Pub. House, 1969. 218p.

22255 GEDDES, P. Town planning towards city development: a report to the Durbar of Indore. Indore: Holkar State Press, 1918. 2 v.

22256 GOYAL, R.K. The social grading of occupations with reference to the city of Indore. In EA 30,1 (1977) 22-32.

22257 MADHYA PRADESH. TOWN & COUNTRY PLANNING DEPT. Bhopal development plan, 1991 (draft). Bhopal: 1974. 302p.

22258 ______. Jabalpur development plan, 1977-91: draft. Bhopal: 1977. 315p.

22259 ______. Ujjain development plan, draft. Bhopal: 1975. 283p.

22260 MALHOTRA, P.C. Socio-economic survey of Bhopal City and Bairagarh. Bombay: Asia, 1964. 404p.

22261 MEHROTRA, S.N. Urbanisation in M.P. In GRI 23,4 (1961) 29-46.

22262 TIWARI, P.S. Functional pattern of towns in Madhya Pradesh. In NGJI 14,1 (1968) 41-54.

4. Social Problems and Social Welfare, incl. Dacoity in the Chambal Valley

22263 BHADURI, T.C. Chambal, the valley of terror. Delhi: Vikas, 1972. 212p.

22264 BHATTA, S.D. And they gave up dacoity! Varanasi: A.B. Sarva Seva Sangh, 1962. 301p.

22265 GARG, R.P. Dacoit problem in Chambal valley: a sociological study. Varanasi: Gandhian Inst. of Studies, 1965. 78p.

22266 JATAR, D.P. & M.Z. KHAN. The problem of dacoity in Bundelkhand and the Chambal Valley. ND: S. Chand, 1980. 114p.

22267 KATARE, S.S. Patterns of dacoity in India; a case study of Madhya Pradesh. ND: S. Chand, 1972. 213p.

22268 MADHYA PRADESH. PROHIBITION ENQUIRY CMTEE., 1951. Report. Nagpur: Govt. Press, 1952. 120p. [bound with P. Kodanda Rao, Separate report, 1952. 85p.]

22269 NARGOLKAR, V.S. Crime and non-violence: story of the conversion of the dacoits in Central India. Poona: Sulabha Rashtriya Granthamala Trust, 1974. 287p.

22270 SHUKLA, K.S. Adolescent thieves: a study in socio-cultural dynamics. Delhi: Leeladevi, 1979. 223p.

22271 SINGH, R.G. Terror to reform: a study of dacoits of central India. ND: Intellectual Pub. House, 1980. 206p.

22272 WINTHER, P.C. Chambal River dacoity: a study of banditry in north central India. Ph.D. diss., Cornell U., 1972. 270p. [UM 73-10,154]

D. Religions of Madhya Pradesh

1. Hinduism

22273 AGRAWAL, B.C. Cultural contours of religion and economics in Hindu universe. ND: National, 1980. 216p.

22274 BABB, L.A. The divine hierarchy: popular Hinduism in central India. NY: ColUP, 1975. 266p.

22275 ______. The food of the gods in Chhattisgarh: some structural features of Hindu ritual. In SWJA 26 (1970) 287-304.

22276 ______. Heat and control in Chhattisgarhi ritual. In EA 26,1 (1973) 11-28.

22277 MATHUR, K.S. The meaning of Hinduism in rural Malwa. In L.P. Vidyarthi, ed. Aspects of religion in Indian society.... Meerut: Kedar Nath Ram Nath, 1961, 114-28.

22278 PARGANIKA, B.L. The Satnami Movement. In JSR 10,1 (1967) 1-16.

22279 ROSNER, V. The bhak katek ritual in use among the Sadans of Jashpur, Madhya Pradesh, India. In Anthropos 56 (1961) 77-113.

2. Christianity and its Missionary Activity

22280 COFFIN, M.M. Friends in Bundelkhand India. Mysore: 1926. 53p.

22281 HERMANNS, M. Hinduism and tribal culture; an anthropological verdict on the Niyogi report. Bombay: K.L. Fernandes, 1957. 59p.

22282 MADHYA PRADESH. CHRISTIAN MISSIONS' ACTIVITIES ENQUIRY CMTEE. Report. Nagpur: Govt. Press, 1956. 2 v. [Report by Justice Niyogi]

22283 PUMPHREY, C.W. Samuel Baker of Hoshangabad: a sketch of Friends' missions in India. London: Headley Bros., 1900. 228p.

22284 SOARES, A., ed. Truth shall prevail; reply to Niyogi Committee. Bombay: Catholic Assn. of Bombay, 1957. 276p.

3. Tribal Religions [see II. B., above]

E. Literatures of Madhya Pradesh

1. Hindi Literature [see Chap. Six, VIII. B., and Chap. Eight, X. C. 2.]

2. Folk Literature

22285 PARMAR, SHYAM. Folk tales of Madhya Pradesh. ND: Sterling, 1973. 104p. (Folk tales of India series, 12)

22286 ______. Folklore of Madhya Pradesh. ND: NBT, 1972. 205p.

VIII. ORISSA (UTKAL): THE ORIYA-SPEAKING REGION OF EASTERN MIDDLE INDIA

A. Political History [for British Period, see I. B. 5. and I. C. 4., above]

1. General Studies of Orissa Politics

22287 BAILEY, F.G. Parliamentary government in Orissa, 1947-1959. In JComPolSt 1 (1962) 112-22.

22288 ______. Politics and social change: Orissa in 1959. Berkeley: UCalP, 1963. 241p.

22289 DAS, B.C. Government and politics in Orissa since independence: a bird's eye view. In IPSR 12,2 (1978) 161-78.

22290 DASH, S.C. Government and politics in Orissa. In IJPS 26,4 (1965) 83-100.

22291 GHOSH, S. Orissa in turmoil: a study in political developments. Calcutta: Sankha, 1978. 200p.

22292 JENA, B.B. The President's rule in Orissa: a case study. In PSR 2,1 (1963) 1-10.

22293 MOHAPATRA, M.K. Dimensions of social representation in a state cabinet in India; a case study of Orissa ministries, 1952-1972. In Interdiscipline 9,4 (1972) 9-26.

22294 ______. Political socialization of legislators in Orissa: an empirical study of the 1967 assembly. In JCPS 5,1 (1971) 116-127.

22295 NANDA, S. Coalition politics in Orissa. ND: Sterling, 1979. 374p.

22296 ORISSA. HOME (BOUNDARY) DEPT. Memorandum submitted to the States Reorganisation Commission. Cuttack: 1954. 270p.

22297 RAO, K.V. Politics in Orissa (social ecology and constitutional compulsions). In IJPS 26,4 (1965) 101-20.

22298 RAY, AMAL. Sub-regional politics & elections in Orissa. In EPW 4,49 (1974) 2033-36.

2. Election Studies

22299 DAS, B.C. The dynamics of factional conflict: a study of the dimensions of electoral conflict in an assembly constituency in Orissa. In IPSR 11,1 (1977) 60-66.

22300 JENA, B.B. General elections in Orissa. In PSR 6,3/4 & 7,1/2 (1967-68) 349-70.

22301 JENA, B.B. & J.K. BARAL & B.C. CHOUDHARY. Electoral behavior of an Orissan scheduled caste assembly constituency: Jagannathprasad. In Political Change 2,1 (1979) 30-46.

22302 ORISSA. HOME (ELECTIONS) DEPT. Report on the Fifth general elections in Orissa, 1971. Bhubaneswar: 1972. 137p.

22303 ______. Report on the sixth general elections to Lok Sabha, 1977. Bhubaneswar: 1978. 85p.

22304 ______. Report on the seventh general elections to state assembly, 1977. Bhubaneswar: 1978. 180p.

22305 RATH, S.N. Fourth general elections in Orissa. In Political Scientist 4 (1967) 139-52.

3. Administration and the Judiciary

22306 BARMAN, J. The judiciary in Orissa: evolution of the High Court at Cuttack. In JILI 15,1 (1973) 74-93.

22307 GHOSH, S. Challenge. Calcutta: Academic Pub., 1967. 250p. [on the Police]

22308 TAUB, R.P. Bureaucrats under stress; administrators and administration in an Indian state. Berkeley: UCalP, 1969. 235p.

4. Local Government and Politics

22309 BAILEY, F.G. Political change in the Kondmals. In EA 11 (1957) 88-106.

22310 ______. Tribe, caste, and nation: a study of political activity and political change in highland Orissa. Manchester: Manchester U. Press, 1960. 279p.

22311 DAS, G.C. Laxmisagar: leadership and factions: factions in a sub-urban village. In Adibasi 19,4 (1967-68) 37-42.

22312 PATNAIK, N. Profile of leadership in Ruruban, a peasant community in Orissa. In Behavioural Science & Community Dev. 3,2 (1969) 83-100.

22313 ______. Story of a village faction in Orissa. In MI 36 (1956) 17-20.

22314 PATNAIK, N. & H.D. LAKSHMINARAYANA. Factional politics in village India. In MI 49 (1969) 161-87.

B. The Orissa Economy

1. General Economic History, 1818-1947

22315 CHOUDHURY, S. Economic history of colonialism: a study of British salt policy in Orissa. Delhi: Inter-India, 1979. 229p.

22316 HUNTER, W.W. Orissa, or the vicissitudes of an Indian province under native and British rule. Calcutta: Thacker, Spink, 1872. 2 v., 330, 273p. [being the 2nd & 3rd vs. of Hunter's Annals of Rural Bengal]

22317 JENA, K.C. Socio economic conditions of Orissa [during the 19th century]. Delhi: Sundeep Prakashan, 1978. 171p.

22318 PATNAIK, G. The famine and some aspects of the British economic policy in Orissa, 1866-1905. Cuttack: Vidyapuri, 1980. 224p.

2. Demography (1981 pop. 26,272,054)

22319 GOPAL KRISNAN. Distribution and density of population in Orissa. In NGJI 14 (1968) 250-57.

22320 INDIA (REP.). CENSUS OF INDIA, 1971. A portrait of population, Orissa: census of India, 1971, series 16. Delhi: Cont. of Pub., 1973. 371p.

22321 SINHA, B.N. The bearing of population growth on the economy of Orissa. In DG 1,1 (1962) 1-27.

3. Surveys of Economic Conditions since 1947

22322 DASH, P.C. State income of Orissa: an economic appraisal, 1960-61 to 1969-70. In Orissa Econ. J. 4,2 & 5,1 (1971-72) 45-54.

22323 MISRA, SADASIV. Economic survey of Orissa. Cuttack: Finance Dept., Govt. of Orissa, 1961. 2 v.

22324 NCAER. Survey of backward districts of Orissa. ND: 1969. 176p.

22325 ______. Techno-economic survey of Orissa. ND: 1962. 309p.

22326 ORISSA. BUREAU OF STAT. & ECON. The economic base of Orissa for the Fifth plan. Cuttack: 1972. 78p.

4. Economic Development and Planning

22327 NCAER. Development of Dandakaranya. ND: 1963. 148p.

22328 PATNAIK, S.C. Orissa finances in perspective, 1951-52 to 1965-66; a regional study of the finances of Orissa in the context of a federal structure. ND: PPH, 1970. 356p.

5. Agriculture
a. general studies

22329 BOSE, S. Two important aspects of Orissa's agriculture with reference to crop rice. In Economic Affairs 12 (1967) 135-44.

22330 INDIA (REP.). CMTEE. ON PLAN PROJECTS. MINOR IRRIGATION TEAM. Report on minor irrigation works, Orissa State. ND: 1965. 91p.

22331 KUMAR, P. Economics of water management: a study of field channels. ND: Heritage Pub., 1977. 117p. [Sambalpur Dist.]

22332 MISRA, B. & A.K. MITRA & B. MISRA. A study of farm investment in three villages in Orissa. In IJAE 20 (1965) 216-21.

22333 MISRA, B.N. Studies in the economics of farm management in Cuttack District (Orissa). ND: Dir. of Econ. & Stat., Govt. of India, 1973. 3 v.

22334 ORISSA. BUREAU OF STAT. & ECON. Report on the benefits of Hirakud irrigation; a socioeconomic study. Cuttack: 1968. 415p.

22335 ______. Report on economic characteristics of weaker section in Orissa (small cultivator). Bhubaneswar: 1977. 82p.

22336 ORISSA. FOREST DEPT. Forests of Orissa. Cuttack: n.d., 43p.

22337 PATNAIK, N. Tribes and their development: a study of two tribal development blocks in Orissa. Hyderabad: NICD, 1972. 117p.

22338 SAHU, B. Land utilisation in Orissa. Cuttack: Orissa Govt. Press, 1951. 309p.

22339 SOVANI, N.V. & N. RATH. Economics of a multiple-purpose river dam: report of an inquiry into the economic benefits of the Hirakud Dam. Poona: Gokhale Institute of Politics and Economics, 1960. 389p.

b. land tenure and reform

22340 BHARADWAJ, K. & P.K. DAS. Tenurial conditions and mode of exploitation: a study of some villages in Orissa. In EPW 10,5-7 (1975) 221-40.

22341 JENA, K.C. Land revenue administration in Orissa during the nineteenth century. Delhi: S. Chand, 1968. 249p.

22342 MADDOX, S.L. Final report on the survey settlement of the Province of Orissa, 1890-1900. Calcutta: Bengal Secretariat Press, 1900. 675p.

22343 ORISSA. BOARD OF REVENUE. Land tenure and land reforms in Orissa, 1962. Cuttack: 1962. 147p.

22344 SAHASRABUDHE, A.W. Reports on Koraput Gramdans. Sevagram: A.W. Sahasrabudhe, 1960. 117p.

22345 SATAPATHY, B. Land reforms administration in Orissa: a case study of Sambalpur District. Bodhgaya: Inst. of Behavioural Sciences, 1977. 263p.

22346 SINGH, T.P., ed. Bhoodan & gramdan in Orissa; a social scientist's analysis (the first inter-disciplinary study of India's famous land gift movement). Varanasi: Sarva Seva Sangh Prakashan, 1973. 144p.

22347 SINHA, B.N. Fragmentation of holdings in Orissa: a regional analysis. In DG 1,2 (1963) 107-24.

6. Industry in Orissa

22348 ORISSA. INDUSTRIES DEPT. Orissa, guide to industrial development possibilities in Orissa State. Bhubaneswar: 1969. 86p.

22349 ORISSA. STATE EVAL. ORG. Evaluation of industrial estates in Orissa. Bhubaneswar: 1976. 131p.

22350 RÖH, K. Rourkela als Testfall für die Errichtung von Industrieprojekten in Entwicklungslandern. Hamburg: Verlag Weltarchiv, 1967. 514p.

22351 ______. Zum Arbeitsverhalten der indischen Belegschaft in Rourkela. In IAF 2,2 (1971) 203-18.

22352 SINHA, B. Heavy industries, their problems & possibilities in Orissa. In GRI 21,1 (1959) 17-29.

22353 ______. Large-scale, medium and cottage industries, their problems and possibilities in Orissa. In GRI 22 (1960) 34-47.

22354 SPERLING, J.B. The human dimension of technical assistance; the German experience at Rourkela, India. Tr. from German by G. Onn. Ithaca: CornellUP, 1969. 227p.

22355 ______. Rourkela; sozio-ökonomische Probleme eines Entwicklungsprojekts. Bonn: Eichholz-Verlag, 1963. 79p.

22356 TAUB, D.L. & R.P. TAUB. Cuttack entrepreneurs. In S. Seymour, ed. The transformation of a sacred town. Boulder: Westview, 1980, 235-53.

C. Society and Social Change

1. Social Categories [for Tribals, see II. D., above]

22357 BEHURA, N.K. Peasant potters of Orissa: a sociological study. ND: Sterling, 1978. 320p.

22358 BOSE, N.K., ed. Data on caste, Orissa. Calcutta: AnthSI, 1960. 192p. (Its Memoirs, 7)

22359 CHATTERJEE, B.B. & P.N. SINGH & G.R.S. RAO. Riots in Rourkela; a psychological study. ND: Popular Book Services, for Gandhian Inst. of Studies, 1967. 144p.

22360 FREEMAN, J.M. Occupational changes in an urbanizing Hindu temple village. In MI 54,1 (1974) 1-20.

22361 ______. Untouchable: an Indian life history. Stanford: Stanford U. Press, 1979. 421p.

22362 KULTA JATI MAHASABHA. Regulations of the Kulta caste of Orissa. In MI 37,1 (1957) 54-77.

22363 MAHAPATRA, M.M. The Badu: a service-caste at the Lingaraj temple at Bhubaneswar. In CIS 3 (1973) 96-108.

22364 PATNAIK, N. Assembly of barbers in Dimiria, Puri District. In MI 41 (1961) 194-203.

22365 ______. Caste and occupation in rural Orissa. In MI 34 (1954) 257-70.

2. Village and Rural Society

22366 BAILEY, F.G. Caste and the economic frontier: a village in highland Orissa. Manchester: U. of Manchester Press, 1957. 292p.

22367 ______. An Oriya village. In M.N. Srinivas, ed. India's Villages. Bombay: Asia, 1960, 122-46.

22368 CHANDOLA, L.M. Perspective of change in a gramdan village cluster in Orissa. In Interdiscipline 7,4 (1970) 6-26.

22369 DAS, H.C. Resources and responses in two Orissan villages: the influence of the new state capital, 1950-1970. Calcutta: Punthi Pustak, 1979. 327p. (Orissan studies project, 6)

22370 FRASER, T.M. Culture & change in India; the Barpali experiment. Amherst: U. of Massachusetts Press, 1968. 460p. [Quaker-led project]

22371 MOHANTI, P. My village, my life; Nanpur - portrait of an Indian village. London: Davis-Poynter, 1973. 232p.

22372 PATNAIK, N. Caste and social change; an anthropological study of three Orissa villages. Hyderabad: Natl. Inst. of Community Dev., 1969. 76p.

22373 RAY, AJIT. A Brahmin village of the sasana type in the district of Puri, Orissa. In MI 36 (1956) 7-15.

22374 Report on socio-economic survey of Lephripara block, Sundargarh district, Orissa. In Administrator 21,1 (1976) 369-409.

3. Cities and Urbanization

22375 GRENELL, P. The new city. In S. Seymour, ed. The transformation of a sacred town. Boulder: Westview, 1980, 9-66.

22376 JHA, M. Rising India: an urban anthropological approach to Puri. ND: Classical, 1978. 118p.

22377 SEYMOUR, S., ed. The transformation of a sacred town: Bhubaneswar, India. Boulder: Westview, 1980. 283p.

22378 SINHA, B. Urban geography of Orissa. In IGJ 32 (1957) 86-94.

4. Social Welfare and Health Services

22379 MISRA, B. & A.K. MOHANTY. A study of the beggar problem at Cuttack. Bhubaneswar: Dept. of Rural Econ.

& Sociology, Utkal U., 1963. 90p.

22380 ORISSA. STATE FAMILY PLANNING BUREAU. Family planning in Orissa, 1969. Bhubaneswar: 1970. 73p.

22381 RATH, S.N. The development of the welfare state in Orissa, 1950-60. ND: S. Chand, 1977. 315p.

5. Education (literacy 27.82% in 1981)

22382 NATL. STAFF COLLEGE FOR EDUC. PLANNERS & ADMINISTRATORS. Educational administration in Orissa: a survey report, 1977. ND: 1967. 71p.

22383 ORISSA. CMTEE. OF ENQUIRY: ORISSA STUDENTS' DISQUIETUDE. Report, 1967-68. Bhubaneswar: Education Dept., 1969. 277p. [Chm., Biswonath Das]

22384 RATH, R. & A.K. MOHANTY. Occupational stereotypes and preferences of a group of post-graduate students of Orissa. In Indian J. of Psychology 47,3 (1972) 197-211.

22385 SABLE, A. Paths through the labyrinth: a study of educational selection and allocation in an Indian State capital. ND: S. Chand. 281p. [Bhubaneswar]

D. Religious Traditions of Modern Orissa

1. Purī and the Vaishṇava Cult of Jagannāth [see also Chap. One, IV. C. 3. d. ii.]; Religious Endowments

22386 KULKE, H. Kings without a kingdom: the rajas of Khurda and the Jagannatha cult. In SA (1974) 60-77.

22387 LAURIE, W.F.B. Orissa, the garden of superstition and idolatry: including an account of British connexions with the temple of Jagannatha. London: Johnstone & Hunter, 1850. 306p.

22388 MAHAPATRA, L.K. Gods, kings, and the caste system in India. In K. David, ed. The new wind: changing identities in South Asia. The Hague: Mouton, 1977, 159-78. (WA)

22388a The Orissa Hindu Religous Endowments Act, 1951, as amended up to date. Cuttack: Cuttack Law Times, 1957. 88p.

22389 PATNAIK, N. Administration of Jagannath temple in the 18th century. In MI 43 (1963) 214-17.

22390 ______. Puri: impact of socio-economic changes on a religious complex. In EW 15,10 (1963) 1361-62.

22391 ______. The recent kings of Puri; a study in secularization. In Surajit Sinha, ed. Aspects of Indian culture and society.... Calcutta: AnthSI, 1972, 87-114. [1st pub. in JIAS 5,1/2 (1970) 87-114, as "The recent rajas...."]

22392 PATRA, K.M. The management of Jagannath temple during the East India Company's administration of Orissa. In BPP 88 (1969) 61-81.

22393 RÖSEL, J. Pilger und Tempelpriester: indische Wallfahrtsorganisation, dargestellt am Beispiel der südostindischen Tempelstadt Puri. In IAF 7,3/4 (1976) 322-54.

2. Mahimā Dharma (Alekha): a Reformist Hindu Sect, est. mid-19th Century

22394 ESCHMANN, A. Mahimā Dharma: an autochthonous Hindu reform movement. In A. Eschmann & H. Kulke & G.C. Tripathi, eds. The cult of Jagannath and the regional tradition of Orissa. ND: Manohar, 1978, 375-410.

22395 Impact of Satya Mahima Dharma on scheduled castes an scheduled tribes in Orissa. In Adibasi 10,1 (1968-69) 44-75. [by "T.R.B."]

22396 PANDA, D. Inter-disciplinary seminar on Mahima Dharma and Darshan. Koraput: Shamkar Philosophy Assn., D.A.V. College, 1972. 103p.

22397 PATRA, K.M. Religious movement in modern Orissa; "Satya Mahima Dharma." In JIH 55,1/2 (1977) 273-82.

22398 SENAPATI, N. Mahima Dharma. Cuttack: Dharma Grantha Store, 1975. 39p. + 10pl.

22399 VASU, N.N. The modern Buddhism and its followers in Orissa. Calcutta: The author, 1911. 181p.

3. Śākta and Śaiva Cults

22400 BOSE, N.K. & N. PATNAIK & AJIT K. RAY. Organisation of services in the temple of Lingaraj in Bhubaneswar. In JASBengal 24 (1958) 85-129.

22401 PRESTON, J.J. Commercial economy of an urban temple in India: a shift from inheritance to consignment rights. In J.J. Preston & B. Misra, ed. Community, self, and identity. The Hague: Mouton, 1978, 27-36. (WA) [on Chandi Temple in Cuttack]

22402 ______. The cult of the Goddess: social and religious change in a Hindu Temple. ND: Vikas, 1980. [Chandi Temple, Cuttack]

4. Christian Missionary Activities

22403 BOAL, B.M. The church in the Kond Hills: an encounter with animism. Nagpur: Natl. Christian Council of India, 1963. 149p.

E. Literatures of Modern Orissa

1. Oriya Literature

22404 BARIK, S. Literary magazines in Oriya. In IWT 3,4 (1969) 44-47.

22405 BOULTON, J.V. Phakirmohana Senapati and his times. Bhubaneswar: Orissa Sahitya Akademi, 1976. 28p. [Oriya novelist, 1843-1918]

22406 MAHAPATRA, S. Old man in summer and other poems. Calcutta: United Writers, 1975. 40p.

22407 ______. The other silence. Calcutta: Writers Workshop, 1973. 38p.

22408 ______. Quiet violence. Calcutta: Writers Workshop, 1970. 59p.

22409 MANSINHA, M. Fakirmohan Senapati. ND: Sahitya Akademi, 1976. 86p.

22410 ______. Ripples of the Mahanadi. Calcutta: Minerva, 1971. 133p.

22411 MOHANTY, G.N. Radhanath Ray. ND: Sahitya Akademi, 1978. 71p.

22412 MOHANTY, S. Oriya. In K.R. Srinivasa Iyengar, ed. Indian literature since Independence. ND: Sahitya Akademi, 1973, 201-21.

22413 NARASIMHA DAS, C.V. The stubble under the cloven hoof; an imaginative recast of Fabir Mohan Senapati's masterpiece in Oriya fiction, Cho mano atho guntho, by C.V. Narasimha Das. Cuttack: Sahitya Samsad, 1967. 365p.

22414 Oriya literature [special issue]. In IL 22,1 (1979) 5-135.

22415 RAUT RAY, S. Short stories. Cuttack: J. Mohapatra, 1972. 119p.

22416 ROUT, S. Women pioneers in Oriya literature: a monograph. Cuttack: Manorama Rout, 1971. 136p.

22417 SATPATHY, N. Song of the evening [and other stories]. Tr. by J.B. Mohanty. ND: Orient Paperbacks, 1975. 109p.

22418 SEN, P.R. Modern Oriya literature. Calcutta: 1947. 159p.

22419 SUBUDHI, N.S., comp. Long march. Balugaon, Dt. Puri: Bela Prakashani, 1971-. 3 v. [revolutionary Oriya poetry]

2. Folk Literature

22420 DAS, K.B. A study of Orissan folk-lore. Santiniketan: Visvabharati, 1953. 183p.

22420a DAS, K.B. & L.K. MAHAPATRA. Folklore of Orissa. ND: NBT, 1979. 160p.

22421 MAHAPATRA, S. Forgive the words: the poetry in the life of the Kondhs in Orissa. Calcutta: United Writers, 1978. 56p.

22422 ______. Similes and metaphors in Oriya folk ballads. In Folklore(C) 16,10/11 (1974) 315-329.

22423 ______. Staying is nowhere: an anthology of Kondh and Paraja poetry. Calcutta: Writers Workshop, 1975. 31 & 41p.

22424 MOHANTI, PRAFULLA. Indian village tales. London: Davis-Poynter, 1975. 123p.

22425 MOHANTY, S. Folk tales of Orissa. ND: Sterling, 1970. 119p. (Folk tales of India series, 4)

13

The Northwest: The Indus Valley and Mountain Frontier, 1799–

I. GENERAL STUDIES OF THE NORTHWEST

A. The British Period: Accounts by Officials and Travellers

22426 BURNES, A. Travels into Bokhara, and A Voyage on the Indus. Oxford: OUP, 1974. 3 v., 356, 473, 356p. [Rpt. 1834-39 ed.]

22427 DOUIE, J.M. The Panjab, North-West Frontier Province, and Kashmir. Delhi: Seema Pub., 1974. 373p. [Rpt. 1916 ed.]

22428 HOLDICH, T.H. Tha Indian Borderland, 1880-1900. 2nd ed. London: Methuen, 1909. 402p. [1st pub. 1901]

22429 HUGEL, C.A.A. Travels in Kashmir & the Panjab. Lahore: Qausain, 1976. 423p. [Rpt. 1845 ed.]

22430 MASSON, C. Narrative of various journeys in Balochistan, Afghanistan, and the Panjab. Karachi: OUP, 1974. 4 v. [Rpt. 1842 ed.]

22431 MOORCROFT, W. & G. TREBECK. Travels in the Himalayan provinces of Hindustan and the Panjab, in Ladakh and Kashmir, in Peshawar, Kabul, Kunduz, and Bokhara from 1819 to 1825. Ed. by H.H. Wilson. ND: Sagar Pub., 1971. 2 v. [1st pub. 1841]

22432 MURRAY, J. Handbook of the Panjab, Western Rajputana, Kashmir and Upper Sindh. London: Murray, 1883. 334p.

22433 OLIVER, E.E. Across the border: or Pathan and Biloch. Lahore: al-Biruni, 1977. 344p. [Rpt. 1890 ed.]

22434 POTTINGER, H. Travels in Beloochistan and Sinde, accompanied by a geographical and historical account of those countries.... Karachi: Indus Pub., 1976. 423p. [Rpt. 1816 ed.]

22435 ROSS, D. The land of the five rivers and Sindh: sketches historical and descriptive. Lahore: al-Biruni, 1976. 322p. [Rpt. 1883 ed.]

22436 STEIN, M.A. On Alexander's track to the Indus: personal narrative of explorations on the north-west frontier of India carried out under the orders of H.M. Indian Government. Karachi: Indus Pub., 1975. 182p. [Rpt. 1929 ed.]

22437 THOMSON, T. Western Himalayas and Tibet: a narrative on Ladakh and mountains of northern India. ND: Cosmo, 1978. 501p. [Rpt. 1852 ed.]

22438 WORKMAN, F.B. & W.H. WORKMAN. In the ice world of Himālaya, among the peaks and passes of Ladakh, Nubra, Suru, and Baltistan. 2nd ed. NY: Cassell, 1900? 204p.

B. Post-1947 Studies and Accounts

22439 EMBREE, A.T., ed. Pakistan's western borderlands: the transformation of a political order. Durham: Carolina Academic Press, 1977. 158p.

II. SIND: THE SINDHI-SPEAKING LOWER INDUS VALLEY, A PROVINCE OF PAKISTAN SINCE 1947

A. General and Political History

1. The British Period in Sind (annexed 1843, part of Bombay Presidency until 1936)

a. general studies and accounts

22440 ABBOTT, J. Sind: a re-interpretation of the unhappy valley. Karachi: Indus Pub., 1977. 113p. [1st pub. 1924]

22441 BURNES, J. A visit to the court of Sinde. Karachi: OUP, 1974. 146p. [1st pub. 1829]

22442 BURTON, R.F. Scinde, or the Unhappy Valley. London: Bentley, 1851. 2 v.

22443 ______. Sind revisited: with notices of the Anglo-Indian army; railroads.... London: Bentley, 1877. 2 v.

22444 ______. Sindh and the races that inhabit the valley of the Indus.... London: W.H. Allen, 1851. 422p.

22445 EASTWICK, E.B. A glance at Sind before Napier; or, Dry leaves from young Egypt. Karachi: OUP, 1973. 377p. [rev. of 2nd ed. 1851]

22446 HUTTENBACK, R.A. British relations with Sind, 1799-1843; an anatomy of imperialism. Berkeley: UCalP, 1962. 161p.

22447 ______. British relations with Sind during the first Afghan crisis, 1838-1841: a study in imperial foreign policy. In IHQ 36 (1960) 209-26.

22448 ______. The French threat to India and British relations with Sind, 1799-1809. In English Hist. Rev. 76 (1961) 590-99.

22449 ______. Lord Ellenborough, Sir Charles Napier and the annexation of Sind--the role of communications and personality in imperial expansion in India. In JIH 36 (1958) 15-23.

22450 INDIA. SIND ADMIN. CMTEE. Report, 1934. Delhi: MPGOI, 1934. 90p. [Chm., H. Dow]

22451 KHERA, P.N. British policy towards Sindh up to its annexation, 1843. 2nd ed. Delhi: Ranjit Printers & Pub., 1963. 152p.

22452 KHUHRO, H. The making of modern Sind: British policy and social change in the nineteenth century. Karachi: Indus Pub., 1978. 351p.

22453 LAMBRICK, H.T. Sir Charles Napier and Sind. Oxford: OUP, 1952. 402p.

22454 ______, tr. The terrorist. London: Benn, 1972. 246p. [native account of 2nd Hur rebellion, 1942-47]

22455 NAPIER, W.F.P. The conquest of Scinde, with some introductory passages in the life of Major-General Sir Charles James Napier. 2nd ed. London: T. & W. Boone, 1845. 531p.

22456 OUTRAM, J. The conquest of Scinde: a commentary. Quetta: Gosha-e Adab: sole distributors Nisa Traders, 1978-. [1st pub. 1846, 2 v.]

22457 PITHAWALLA, M.B., ed. Sind's changing map; an album containing 51 old and rare maps of Sind with critical and explanatory notes on them. Karachi: the editor, 1938. 12p.

22458 POSTANS, T. Personal observations on Sindh. London: Longman, Brown, Green & Longmans, 1843. 402p.

22459 SHAND, A.I. General John Jacob, commandant of the Sind irregular horse and founder of Jacobabad. London: Seeley, 1901. 320p.

22460 THAIRANI, K. British political missions to Sind; a narrative of negotiations from 1799 to 1843 leading up to the state's annexation. ND: Orient Longman, 1973. 193p.

b. politics and nationalism, 1937-47

22461 JONES, A.K. Muslim politics and the growth of the Muslim League in Sind, 1935-1941. Ph.D. diss., Duke U., 1977. 283p. [UM 78-7608]

22462 SAYED, G.M. Struggle for new Sind: a brief narrative of the working of provincial autonomy in Sind during a decade (1937-1947). Karachi: Sind Observer Press, 1949. 231p.

2. Sind Politics since 1947: A Province of Pakistan

22463 HYDERABAD, PAKISTAN (DIVISION). DIR. OF BASIC DEMOCRACIES. Towards fulfilment; report on working of basic democracies in Hyderabad Division during 1963-64. Hyderabad: 1965. 102p.

22464 JATOI, H.B. Shall Sindhi language stay in Karachi or not? Hyderabad: Sind Hari Office, 1957. 18p.

22465 TUNIO, M.M. Jiye Pakistan, jiye Sind. Larkana: Tunio, 1974? 32p.

B. The Sind Economy

1. General Studies

22466 KAMAL AZFAR. Modernising Sind: problems and prospects. Karachi: Dept. of Public Relations, Govt. of Sind, 1973. 128p.

22467 LEVIN, S. The upper bourgeoisie from the Muslim commercial community of Memons in Pakistan, 1947 to 1971. In AS 14,3 (1974) 231-43.

22468 MEMONS INTL. Memons International directory. Bombay: Memons Intl., 1971. 125 + 105p.

22469 PAKISTAN. SPECIAL CMTEE. ON COTTAGE INDUSTRIES FOR THE REHABILITATION OF REFUGEES OF KARACHI. Report. Karachi: 1949. 62p.

22470 PAPANEK, H. Pakistan's new industrialists & businessman: focus on the Memons. In M.B. Singer, ed. Entrepreneurship and modernization of occupational cultures in South Asia. Durham, NC: DUPCSSA, 1973, 61-106. (Its monograph & occ. papers ser., 12)

22471 PITHAWALLA, M.B. An introduction to Sind: its wealth and welfare. Karachi: Sind Observer Press, 1951. 150p.

22472 UNITED NATIONS. CENTRE FOR REGIONAL DEV. Regional development in Sind: a comprehensive planning report. Nagoya: UNCRD, 1977? 4 v. in 6.

22473 WEST PAKISTAN. INDUSTRIAL DEV. CORP. Report on the industrial potential of Upper Sind. Karachi: 1973. 54p.

2. Agriculture

22474 AMBEKAR, G.R. The crops of Sind: their geography and statistics. Bombay: Dept. of Agri., Govt. of Bombay, 1928. 158p. (Its Bull., 150)

22475 DEVRAJANI, B.T. Efficacy of various machines towards increased agricultural production in Sind province of Pakistan: annual report 1 (phase II). Tandojam: Sind Agri. U., 1978. 149p.

22476 KHOSO, A.W. Crops of Sind. Karachi: Khoso, 1977. 181p.

22477 MAIN, T.F. Agriculture in Sind under the barrage canals system. Bombay: Govt. Central Press, 1929. 72p. (Dept. of Agri. Bull., 159)

22478 MUSTO, A.A. Lloyd barrage and the future of Sind. In Asiatic R. 31 (1935) 1-36.

22479 QURESHI, A.A. Canal irrigation in Sind and its economic significance, 1900-1940. Hyderabad: Sind Geographers Assn., 1975. 48p.

22480 QURESHI, M.T. Impact of technological changes on per unit cost and returns in agriculture in Sind Province of Pakistan: final report, 1974. Tandojam: Dept. of Agri. Econ. & Rural Sociology, Sind Agri. College, 1974. 366p.

22481 ROCHIN, R.I. The subsistence farmer as innovator: a field survey. In SAR 6 (1973) 289-302.

22482 SIDDIQUI, S.A. To study the role of migratory farm labour in agricultural production in Sind province of Pakistan. Tandojam: Dept. of Agri. Econ. & Rural Sociology, Sind Agri. U., 1977. 211p.

22483 SIND, PAKISTAN. HARI ENQUIRY CMTEE. Report, 1947-48. Karachi: 1948. 141p. [Chm., Sir Roger Thomas; land tenure]

22484 SUMMERS, T. Development of cotton in India; Sind, a second Egypt. In Asiatic R. ns 5 (1914) 289-364.

22485 THOMAS, R. Notes on agricultural development in Sind. Karachi: Govt. Press, 1945. 72p.

C. Society and Social Change

1. General Studies

22486 ADVANI, G. La vie rurale dans le Sind. In Societé Languedocienne de Géographie, Bulletin 49 (1926) 1-95.

22487 BALOCH, N.B. Education in Sind before the British conquest and the educational policies of the British government. Hyderabad: Pakistan Inst. of Educ., U. of Sind, 1971. 70p.

22488 GREEN, L.W. & K.J. KROTKI. Class and parity biases in family planning programs: the case of Karachi. In Eugenics Q. 15 (1968) 235-51.

22489 KORSON, J.H. Age and social status at marriage: Karachi, 1961-64. In PDR 5 (1965) 586-600.

22490 ______. Dower and social class in an urban Muslim community. In J. of Marriage & the Family 29 (1969) 527-33.

22491 ______. Residential propinquity as a factor in mate selection in an urban Muslim society. In J. of Marriage & the Family, 30,3 (1968) 518-27.

22492 THAKUR, U.T. Sindhi culture. Bombay: U. of Bombay, 1959. 250p. (Its Pub., Sociology ser., 9)

2. Karachi: Pakistan's Largest City and Major Port, Capital of Sind Province (1978 pop. 3,500,000)

22493 AHSAN ULLAH & IZZAT ULLAH KHAN. The port of Karachi and its traffic. Karachi: Karachi Geographers Assn., 1964. 65p.

22494 BAILLIE, A.F. Kurachee: past, present, and future. Karachi: OUP, 1975. 269p. [1st pub. 1890]

22495 FAROOQ, MUMTAZ. The people of Karachi, economic characteristics. Karachi: PIDE, 1966. 179p. (MED, 15)

22496 FELDMAN, H. Karachi through a hundred years; the centenary history of the Karachi Chamber of Commerce and Industry, 1860-1960. 2nd ed. Karachi: OUP, 1970. 258p.

22497 HAIDER, AZIMUSSHAN. History of Karachi: with special reference to educational, demographical, and commercial developments, 1839-1900. Karachi: Haider, 1974. 100p.

22498 HASHMI, SHAFIK H. The slums of Karachi: a case study. Lahore: Aziz Pub., 1975. 120p.

22499 HASHMI, S.S. The people of Karachi; demographic characteristics. Karachi: PIDE, 1965. 152p. (MED, 13)

22500 HASHMI, S.S., MASIHUR RAHMAN KHAN & K.J. KROTKI. The people of Karachi; data from a survey. Karachi: PIDE, 1964. 368p. (Its Stat. papers, 2)

22501 HUSAIN, IMTIAZUDDIN & MOHAMMAD AFZAL & SYED AMJAD ALI BAHADUR RIZVI. Social characteristics of the people of Karachi. Karachi: PIDE, 1965. 155p. (MED, 14)

22502 KARACHI DEV. AUTHORITY. MASTER PLAN DEPT. Master Plan for Karachi Metropolitan Region. Karachi: 1972. 3v.

22503 Karachi encyclopaedia. Karachi: Reference Book Pub. Centre, 1969-. v. 1, 257p.

22504 MEHTA, J.N.R. Karachi municipality: its administration, activities and its future. Karachi: Jamshed N.R. Mehta, 1925. 144p.

22505 MUNIR, M. An annotated bibliography on urban and metropolitan affairs with special reference to Karachi-Pakistan. Karachi: NIPA, 1964. 15p.

22506 The socio-economic trends of the middle class of Karachi. Karachi: Associated Surveyors, 1976. 189p.

22507 Usmania Mohajir Colony: research in the socio-economic and physical conditions, recommendations for the upgrading of the colony. Karachi: Joint Res. Project for Slum Improvement & Urban Dev., 1975. 134p.

D. Modern Sindhi Literature in Pakistan and India

22508 CHANA, MAHBOOB ALI. Various trends in Sindhi literature. Hyderabad: Idara-i-Saleh Series, 1971. 38p.

22509 Desert blooms; an anthology of Sindhi stories and poems. ND: PDMIB, 1972. 230p.

22510 MALKANI, M.U. Western influence on Sindhi drama. In Indian P.E.N. 31 (1965) 199-206.

22511 RAMANI, H.K., tr. Sindhi short stories. 2nd ed., rev. & enl. ND: Hashmat Pub., 1963?. 151p.

22512 SADARANGANI, H.I. Modernity in contemporary Sindhi poetry. In IL 10,2 (1967) 81-100.

22513 ______. Sindhi. In K.R. Srinivasa Iyengar, ed. Indian literature since Independence. ND: Sahitya Akademi, 1973, 282-96.

22514 SCHIMMEL, A. The activities of the Sindhi Adabi Board. In Die Welt des Islams ns 6 (1961) 223-43.

III. BALUCHISTAN: THE ARID BASINS AND HILLS OF SOUTH-WESTERN PAKISTAN

A. General and Political History

1. The British Period (1839-1947): the Khanate of Kalat, Other Chiefdoms, and British Baluchistan

22515 AHMAD YAR KHAN. Inside Baluchistan: a political autobiography of His Highness Biglar Baigi, Khan-e-Azam-XIII Mir Ahmad Yar Khan Baluch, Khan-e-Baluch, ex-ruler of Kalat State. Karachi: Royal Book Co., 1975. 352p.

22516 FERRIER, J.P. Caravan journeys and wanderings in Persia, Afghanistan, Turkistan, and Beloochistan: with historical notices of the countries lying between Russia and India. Karachi: OUP, 1976. 534p. [Rpt. 1857 ed.]

22517 FLOYER, E.A. Unexplored Baluchistan. Quetta: Gosha-e-Adab, 1977. 507p. [Rpt. 1882 ed.]

22518 HOLDICH, T.H. The gates of India, being an historical narrative.... London: Macmillan, 1910. 555p.

22519 HUGHES, A.W. The country of Baluchistan: its geography, topography, ethnology, and history. Quetta: Gosha-e-Adab, 1977. 294p. [Rpt. of 1878 ed.]

22520 SWIDLER, N.B. The development of the Kalat Khanate. In JAAS(L) 7 (1972) 115-21.

22521 TATE, G.P. The frontiers of Baluchistan: travels on the borders of Persia and Afghanistan. Lahore: East & West Pub. Co., 1976. 261p. + 34pl.

22522 THORNTON, T.H. Colonel Sir Robert Sandeman. Quetta: Gosha-e-Adab, 1977. 392p.

2. Government and Politics after 1947

22523 AHMED, FEROZ. Focus on Baluchistan & Pushtoon question. Lahore: PPH, 1975. 116p.

22524 PAKISTAN. White paper on Baluchistan. Islamabad: 1974. 53p.

22525 PASTNER, S. & C.M. PASTNER. Adaptations to state-level politics by the Southern Baluch. In L. Ziring & R. Braibanti & W.H. Wriggins, eds. Pakistan: the long view. Durham: DUP, 1977, 117-39.

22526 SWIDLER, N. Brahui political organization and the national state. In A.T. Embree, ed. Pakistan's western borderlands: the transformation of a political order. ND: Vikas, 1977, 109-25.

B. The Baluchistan Economy

22527 Draft post-war development plan of Baluchistan. Delhi: Govt. of India Press, 1945. 75p.

22528 New face of Baluchistan. Islamabad: Pakistan Pub., 1979? 104p.

22529 PICKERING, A.K. Rural development in Baluchistan. In J. of Admin. Overseas 7 (1968) 444-53.

22530 PITHAWALLA, M.B. The problem of Baluchistan: development and conservation of water resources, soils and natural vegetation. Karachi: Min. of Econ. Affairs, 1953. 166p.

22531 SWIDLER, W. Economic change in Baluchistan: processes of integration in the larger economy of Pakistan. In A.T. Embree, ed. Pakistan's western borderlands: the transformation of a political order. ND: Vikas, 1977, 85-108.

C. Society and Social Change

22532 BRAY, D. DE SAUMAREZ. The Jat of Baluchistan. In IA 54 (1925) 30-33.

22533 ______. The life-history of a Brahui. Karachi: Royal Book Co., 1977. 180p. [Rpt. 1913 ed.]

22534 DAMES, M.L. The Baloch race. London: RAS, 1904. 90p. (Its monographs, 4)

22535 Education in Baluchistan [special issue]. In Pakistan Educ. R. 13 (1973) 1-92.

22536 JAFFREY, A.A. The confusion over Kuch and Baluch. In JASP 12 (1967) 305-20.

22537 JAMIAT RAI. The domiciled Hindus. Delhi: B.R., 1974. 98p. [1st pub. 1913]

22538 PASTNER, C.M. A social, structural and historical analysis of honor, shame and purdah. In Anthropological Q. 45,4 (1972) 248-61.

22539 PASTNER, S.L. Co-operation in crisis among Baluch nomads. In Asian Affairs 62 (ns 6),2 (1975) 165-76.

22540 ______. The man who would be anthropologist: dilemmas of fieldwork on the Baluchistan frontier of Pakistan. In JSAMES 3,2 (1978) 44-52.

22541 PASTNER, S.L. & C.M. PASTNER. Aspects of religion in Southern Baluchistan. In Anthropologica 14 (1972) 231-41.

22542 PEHRSON, R.N. The social organization of the Marri Baluch. Comp. from his notes by Fredrik Bart. Chicago: Aldine, 1966. 127p. [Viking Fund pub. in anthro., 43]

22543 ROOMAN, A. Education in Baluchistan. Quetta: Gosha-e-Adab, 1979. 247p.

22544 SCHOLZ, F. Belutschistan (Pakistan); eine socialgeographische Studie des Wandels in einem Nomadenland seit Beginn der Kolonialzeit. Göttingen: Erich Golze, 1974. 332p. (Göttinger Geographische Abhandlungen, 63)

22545 ______. Beobachtungen über künstliche Bewässung und Nomadismus in Belutschistan. In E. Ehlers & F. Scholz & G. Schweitzer, eds. Strukturwandlungen in nomadisch-bauerlichen Lebensraum des Orients. Wiesbaden: Steiner, 1970, 53-79.

22546 ______. Der moderne Wandel in den nomadischen Belutschen-und-Brahui-Stämmen der Gebirgsprovinz Belutschistan. In Sociologus 24 (1974) 117-37.

22547 SPOONER, B. Nomadism in Baluchistan. In L.S. Leshnik & G.D. Sontheimer, eds. Pastoralists and Nomads in South Asia. Wiesbaden: Harrassowitz, 1975, 171-82.

22548 SWIDLER, N.B. The political context of Brahui sedentarization. In Ethnology 12 (1973) 299-314.

22549 SWIDLER, W.W. Some demographic factors regulating the formation of flocks and camps among the Brahui of Baluchistan. In W. Irons & N. Dyson-Hudsons, eds. Perspectives on nomadism. Leiden: Brill, 1972, 69-192. [1st pub. as JAAS(L) 7,1/2 (1972)]

D. Languages and Literatures of Modern Baluchistan: Baluchi and Brahui

22550 AL-QADIR, S.M. KAMIL. Jām Durrak. In JPHS 19,2 (1971) 101-119. [20th cent. Baluchi poet]

22551 DAMES,M.L. Popular poetry of the Beloches. London: D. Nutt, for Folklore Soc., 1907. 2 v.

22552 KAMIL AL-QADRI, S.M. All about Brahui. In Pakistan Q. 17,1 (1969) 68-75.

22553 ROOMAN, M.A. A brief survey of Baluchi literature and language. In JPHS 16 (1968) 62-80.

IV. THE PUNJAB: THE PLAINS AND FOOTHILLS OF THE MIDDLE INDUS VALLEY

A. General and Political History since 1799

1. Bibliography and Sources

22554 BARRIER, N.G. Punjab history in printed British documents; a bibliographic guide to parliamentary papers and select nonserial publications, 1843-1947. Columbia: U. of Missouri Press, 1969. 109p.

22555 ______. The Punjab in nineteenth century tracts: an introduction to the Pamphlet collections in the British Museum and India Office. East Lansing: Asian Studies Center, Michigan State U., 1969. 76p. (Its Occ. papers, South Asia series, Research series on the Punjab, 1)

22556 CHAUDHRY, NAZIR AHMAD, comp. Calendar of Persian correspondence; collection of treaties, sanads, letters, etc., which passed between the East India Company, Sikhs, Afghans, and other notables. Lahore: Supt. Govt. Print., 1972-. v. 1, 374p.

22557 GUSTAFSON, W.E. & K.W. JONES, eds. Sources on Punjab history: a study sponsored by the Research Committee on the Punjab. Delhi: Manohar, 1975. 454p.

22558 MALIK, I.A., comp. A bibliography of the Punjab and its dependencies, 1849-1910. Lahore: Res. Soc. of Pakistan, U. of the Punjab, 1968. 309p. (Its Pub., 8)

2. General Histories of Modern Punjab since 1977

22559 BAJWA, H.S. Fifty years of Punjab politics, 1920-1970. Chandigarh: Modern Pub., 1979. 104p.

22560 BAL, S.S. A brief history of the modern Punjab. Ludhiana: Lyall Book Depot, 1974. 48p.

22561 CHHABRA, G.S. Advanced history of the Punjab. 2nd rev. ed. Jullundur: New Academic Pub. Co., 1968-72. 2 v., 540,552p.

22562 KHUSHWANT SINGH. A history of the Sikhs. v. 2, 1839-1964. Princeton: PUP, 1967. 395p.

22563 MALIK, IKRAM ALI, comp. A book of readings on the history of Punjab, 1799-1947. Lahore: Res. Soc. of Pakistan, U. of the Punjab, 1970. 740p. (Its pub., 20)

3. The Sikh Kingdom of the Punjab, 1799-1849
a. general studies

22564 AIJAZUDDIN, F.S. Sikh portraits by European artists. London: Sotheby Parke Bernet, 1979. 160p. + 8pl.

22565 BHAGAT SINGH. Sikh polity in the eighteenth and nineteenth centuries. ND: Oriental, 1978. 379p.

22566 CHOPRA, G.L. The Punjab as a sovereign state, 1799-1839. Lahore: al-Biruni, 1977. 365p. [Rpt. 1929 ed.]

22567 FAUJA SINGH. Military system of the Sikhs, during the period, 1799-1949. Delhi: Motilal, 1964. 382p.

22568 GOUGH, C.J.S. & A.D. INNES. The Sikhs and the Sikh wars: the rise, conquest, and annexation of the Punjab State. Patiala: Languages Dept., Punjab, 1970. 304p. [1st pub. 1897]

22569 SMYTH, G.C., ed. A history of the reigning family of Lahore.... Lahore: Govt. of West Pakistan, 1961. 279p. [Rpt. 1847 ed.]

b. Maharaja Ranjit Singh (1780-1839) and the consolidation of the Sikh Khālsā

22570 GARRETT, H.L.O. & G.L. CHOPRA, eds. Events at the court of Ranjit Singh, 1819-1817; tr. from the papers in the Alienation Office, Poona. Patiala: Languages Dept., Punjab, 1970. 288p.

22571 GRIFFIN, L.H. Life of Ranjit Singh. London: OUP, 1892. 223p. (Rulers of India)

22572 OSBORNE, W.G. The court and camp of Ranjeet Sing. Delhi: Heritage, 1973. 236p. [Rpt. 1840 ed.]

22573 ______. Ranjit Singh: the lion of the Punjab. Calcutta: Susil Gupta, 1952. 90p.

22574 PRINSEP, H.T. Origin of the Sikh power in the Punjab and political life of Maharaj Ranjit Singh; with an account of the religion, laws and customs of Sikhs. Patiala: Languages Dept., Punjab, 1970. 187p. [1st pub. 1834]

22575 SEETAL, S.S. Rise of the Sikh power and Maharaja Ranjeet Singh. Jullundur: Dhanpat Rai, 1971. 667p.

22576 ______. The Sikh Empire and Maharaja Ranjeet Singh. Jullundur: Dhanpat Rai, 1971. 187p.

22577 SETHI, R.R. The mighty and shrewd maharaja; Ranjit Singh's relations with other powers. Delhi: S. Chand, 1960. 255p.

22578 SHAHĀMAT ᶜALI. The Sikhs and Afghans, in connexion with the India and Persia, immediately before and after the death of Ranjeet Singh; from the journal of an expedition of Kabul, through the Panjab and the Khaibar Pass, by Shahamat Ali. Patiala: Languages Dept., Punjab, 1970. 550p. [1st pub. 1847]

22579 SINHA, N.K. Ranjit Singh. Calcutta: 1933. 216p.

22580 SOOD, D.R. Ranjit Singh. ND: NBT, 1968. 110p.

c. the Anglo-Sikh wars, and annexation of the Punjab in 1849

22581 AHLUWALIA, M.L. Sant Nihal Singh, alias Bhai Maharaj Singh: a saint-revolutionary of the 19th century Punjab. Patiala: Punjabi U., 1972. 117p.

22582 AJUDHIA PARSHAD. Waqai-jang-i-Sikhan: events of the (first) Anglo-Sikh War, 1845-46: eye-witness account of the battles of Pheroshahr & Sobraon. Tr. by V.S. Suri. Chandigarh: Punjab Itihas Prakashan, 1975. 59p.

22583 ALEXANDER, M. & SUSHILA ANAND. Queen Victoria's Maharaja; Duleep Singh 1838-93. NY: Taplinger, 1980. 326p.

22584 BAL, S.S. British policy towards the Punjab, 1844-49. Calcutta: New Age, 1971. 340p.

22585 BELL, E. The annexation of the Punjaub and the Maharajah Duleep Singh. Ludhiana: Lyall Book Depot, 1969. 175p. [1st pub. 1882]

22586 CHOPRA, B.R. Kingdom of the Punjab, 1839-45. Hoshiarpur: VVRI, 1969. 497p. (VIS, 43)

22587 DHULEEP SINGH. Maharaja Duleep Singh correspondence. Ed. by Ganda Singh. Patiala: Punjabi U., 1977. 108 + 732p.

22588 FAUJA SINGH, ed. Maharaja Kharak Singh, June 27, 1839-November 5, 1840: select records preserved in the National Archives of India, New Delhi. Patiala: Dept. of Punjab Hist. Studies, Punjabi U., 1977. 63 + 458p.

22589 GANDA SINGH. The British occupation of the Punjab. Patiala: Sikh Hist. Soc., 1955. 154p.

22590 ______, ed. Private correspondence relating to the Anglo-Sikh wars, being private letters of Lords Ellenborough, Harding, Dalhousie and Gough...to Sir Frederick Currie as British Resident at Lahore. Patiala: Sikh History Soc., 1955. 515p.

22591 ______, ed. The Punjab in 1839-40; selections from the Punjab Akhbars, Punjab Intelligence etc. preserved in the Natl. Archives of India, N. Delhi. Amritsar: Sikh Hist. Soc., 1952. 43 + 311p.

22592 GUPTA, H.R., ed. Punjab on the eve of the first Sikh War. Hoshiarpur: Punjab U., 1956. 397p.

22593 HASRAT, B.J. Anglo-Sikh relations, 1799-1849; a reappraisal of the rise and fall of the Sikhs. Hoshiarpur: VVRI, 1968. 411p.

22594 ______. The Punjab papers: selections from the private papers of Lord Auckland, Lord Ellenborough, Viscount Hardinge, and the Marquis of Dalhousie,1836-1849, on the Sikhs. Hoshiarpur: VVRI, 1970. 288p.

22595 HENTY, G.A. Through the Sikh war; a tale of the conquest of the Punjaub. Patiala: Languages Dept., Punjab, 1970, 373p. [1st pub. 1893]

22596 KHUSHWANT SINGH. The fall of the kingdom of the Punjab. Bombay: Orient Longmans, 1962. 172p.

22597 KOHLI, S.R. Sunset of the Sikh empire. Ed. by Khushwant Singh. Bombay: Orient Longmans, 1967. 203p.

22598 LOGIN, L.C. Sir John Login and Duleep Singh. Delhi: Neesa Books, 1978. 580p. [Rpt. 1890 ed.]

22599 MAHAJAN, J. Circumstances leading to the annexation of the Punjab, 1846-1849 (a historical revision). Allahabad: Kitabistan, 1949. 136p.

22600 NIJJAR, B.S. Anglo-Sikh wars, 1845-1849. ND: K.B., 1976. 126p.

22601 RAY, N.R. The Sikh gurus and the Sikh society: a study in social analysis. Patiala: Punjabi U., 1970. 209p.

4. The Princely States of the Punjab, 1799 - 1947

22602 ARORA, A.C. British rule and minority arrangements: the Phulkian States, 1858-1905. In BPP 92,1 (1973) 89-103.

22603 FAROOQI, MIAN BASHIR AHMED. British relations with the Cis-Sutlej States, 1809-23. Patiala: Languages Dept., Punjab, 1971. 58p. (Punjab Govt. Record Office pub., monograph 19)

22604 GRIFFIN, L.H. The rajas of the Punjab, being the history of the principal states in the Punjab and their political relations with the British government. Patiala: Languages Dept., Punjab, 1970. 630p. [Rpt. 1873 ed.]

22605 HUTCHISON, J. & J.P. VOGEL. History of the Panjab hill states. Lahore: Supt., Govt. Printing, Punjab, 1933. 2 v., 729p.

22606 INDIAN STATES' PEOPLE'S CONF. PATIALA ENQUIRY CMTEE. Indictment of Patiala: being a report of the Patiala Enquiry Committee appointed by the Indian States' People's Conference. Bombay: Indian States' People's Conf., 1930. 326p.

22607 MAN MOHAN. A history of the Mandi State. Lahore: Mandi Durbar, 1930. 166p. + 18 pl.

22608 RAMUSACK, B.N. Incident at Nabha; interaction between Indian states and British Indian politics. In JAS 28 (1969) 563-77. [on abdication of Nabha raja in 1923; rpt. in Harbans Singh & N.G. Barrier, eds. Punjab past and present.... Patiala: Punjabi U., 1967, 433-53]

22609 ______. The Princely States of Punjab: a bibliographic essay. In W.E. Gustafson & K.W. Jones, eds. Sources on Punjab history. ND: Manohar, 1975, 374-449.

22610 SHAH, NAZEER ALI. Sadiqnamah; the history of Bahawalpur State. Lahore: Maktaba Jadeed, 1959. 148p.

5. The British Province of the Punjab, 1849 - 1947

a. general studies of British rule

22611 BROADFOOT, W. Career of Major George Broadfoot in Afghanistan and the Punjab. London: Murray, 1888. 445p.

22612 ELSMIE, G.R. Thirty-five years in the Punjab, 1858-1893. Lahore: al-Biruni, 1975. 368p. [Rpt. 1908 ed.]

22613 GRIFFIN, L.H. Chiefs and families of the Punjab... Lahore: Supt. Govt. Printing, 1940. 2 v.

22614 KHILNANI, N.M. British power in the Punjab, 1839-1858. NY: Asia, 1972. 288p.

22615 ______. The Punjab under the Lawrences (1846-1858). Simla: Punjab Govt. Record Office, 1951. 163p. (Punjab Govt. Record Office, monograph 2)

22616 NIJJAR, B.S. Panjab under the British rule, 1849-1947. ND: K.B. Pub., 1974. 3 v.

22617 REINHART, W.W. The legislative council of the Punjab. Durham, NC: DUPCSSA, 1972. 160p. (Its monograph & occ. papers series, 11)

22618 RICHARDS, P.E. Indian dust: being letters from the Punjab. London: Allen & Unwin, 1932. 272p.

22619 THORBURN, S.S. The Punjab in peace and war. Patiala: Languages Dept., Punjab, 1970. 364p. [1st pub. 1904]

22620 WYLLY, H.C. The military memoirs of Lt. General Sir Joseph Thackwell. London: John Murray, 1908. 424p.

22621 YADAV, K.C. British policy towards Sikhs, 1849-57. In Harbans Singh & N.G. Barrier, eds. Punjab past and present.... Patiala: Punjabi U., 1976, 185-203.

b. administrative studies

22622 KALIA, B.R. A history of the development of the police in the Punjab, 1849-1905. Lahore: Punjab Govt. Record Office, 1929. (Its Monograph, 6)

22623 KAPUR, D.K. A history of the development of the judiciary in the Punjab, 1884-1926. Lahore: Punjab Govt. Record Office, 1928. (Its Monograph, 4)

22624 MATHUR, Y.B. British administration of Punjab, 1849-75. Delhi: Surjeet Book Depot, 1973. 248p.

22625 ______. Judicial administration of the Punjab, 1849-75. In JIH 44 (1966) 707-36.

22626 ______. Police administration in the Punjab, 1849-75. In JIH 41 (1963) 731-48; 42 (1964) 195-217.

22627 SMITH, R.B. John Lawrence in Haryana, 1831-45; a study of administration and society. In JHS 3,1/2 (1971) 1-38. (Its monograph, 2)

c. district and local government

22628 EMERSON, H.W., comp. Customary law of the Multan District: attested at the revised settlement, 1923-1924. Lahore: Supt., Govt. Printing, Punjab, 1924. 417p.

22629 IVER, G.G.B. In an Indian district; an enlarged edition of Police notes. Lahore: Civil and Military Gazette Press, 1919. 130p.

22630 MAGSI, M.A.K. Development of local self-government in the Punjab, 1919-1932. Ed. by M. Aslam Qureshi. Lahore: Res. Soc. of Pakistan, 1973. 86p. (Its pub., 31)

22631 ROSEBERRY, J.R. The administration of Multan, 1818-1881: a study of local society and imperial rule in Punjab. Diss., U. of Wisconsin, 1977. 391p. [UM 77-25,840]

d. Nationalist politics in the Punjab

i. general studies

22632 AHLUWALIA, M.L. & KIRPAL SINGH. The Punjab's pioneer freedom fighters. Bombay: Orient Longmans, 1963. 115p.

22633 BARRIER, N.G. The Arya Samaj and Congress politics in the Punjab, 1894-1908. In JAS 26 (1967) 363-79.

22634 FAUJA SINGH. Eminent freedom fighters of Punjab. Patiala: Punjabi U., 1972. 246p.

22635 GANDHI, M.K. Gandhiji and Haryana: a collection of his speeches and writings pertaining to Haryana. ND: Usha Pub., 1977. 158p.

22636 JOSH, B. Communist movement in Punjab, 1926-47. Delhi: Anupama Pub., 1979. 224p.

22637 KUMAR, RAVINDER. The Rowlatt satyagraha in Lahore. In his Essays on Gandhian politics. Oxford: OUP, 1971, 236-98.

22638 MALHOTRA, S.L. From civil disobedience to quit

India: Gandhi and the freedom movement in Punjab and Haryana, 1932-1942. Chandigarh: Panjab U., 1979. 188p.

22639 MUL RAJ, Rai Bahadur. Beginning of Punjabi nationalism; autobiography of R.B. Mul Raj. Hoshiarpur: VVRI, 1975. 327p.

22640 PANDEY, D. The Arya Samaj and Indian nationalism (1875-1920). ND: S. Chand, 1972. 220p.

22641 RAI, S.M. Punjabi heroic tradition, 1900-1947. Patiala: Punjabi U., 1978. 190p.

22642 SEN, N.B. Punjab's eminent Hindus, being biographical sketches of twenty Hindu ministers, judges, politicians, educationists and legislators.... 2nd ed. Lahore: New Book Society, 1944. 333p.

22643 SHARMA, S.R. Punjab in ferment. ND: S. Chand, 1971. 3 v.

ii. parties and leaders: the Unionist Party, Congress, Muslim League, and the Sikh Akali Dal

22644 AGNIHOTRI, H.L. & S.L. MALIK. A profile in courage: a biography of Ch. Chhotu Ram. ND: Light & Life Publishers, 1978. 144p.

22645 ALI, IMRAN. Relations between the Muslim League and the Panjab National Unionist Party 1935-1947. In SA 6 (1976) 51-65.

22646 BARKAT ALI, MALIK. Malik Barkat Ali: his life and writings. Ed. by M. Rafique Afzal. Lahore: Res. Soc. of Pakistan, U. of the Punjab, 1969. 63 + 378p. (Its pub., 16)

22647 BAXTER, C. Union or partition; some aspects of politics in the Punjab, 1936-45. In L. Ziring & R. Braibanti & W.H. Wriggins, eds. Pakistan: the long view. Durham: DUP, 1977, 40-69.

22648 GOPAL, MADAN. Sir Chhotu Ram: a political biography. Delhi: B.R., 1977. 179p.

22649 GULATI, K.C. The Akalis, past and present. ND: Ashajanak, 1974. 259p.

22650 HEEGER, G. The growth of the Congress movement in Punjab, 1920-1940. In JAS 32,1 (1972) 39-52.

22651 HUSAIN, AZIM. Fazl-i-Husain, a political biography. Bombay: Longmans Green, 1946. 388p.

22652 HUSAIN, FAZLI, Mian Sir. Diary and notes of Mian Fazl-i-Husain. Ed. by Waheed Ahmad. Lahore: Research Soc. of Pakistan, 1977. 363p. (Its pub., 47)

22653 KHAZAN SINGH. A correspondence on Akali movement. Ed. by S. Manjeet Singh. ND: Manjeet Singh, 1975. 80p.

22654 ______. Correspondence with Lord Hailey, former Governor of Punjab and U.P. Ed. by Manjeet Singh. ND: Manjeet Singh, 1975. 30p.

22655 LAKSHMAN SINGH. Autobiography. Ed. by Ganda Singh. Calcutta: Sikh Cultural Centre, 1965. 323p.

22656 OREN, S. The Sikhs, Congress, and the Unionists in British Punjab, 1937-1945. In MAS 8,3 (1974) 397-418.

22657 SHAH NAWAZ, JAHAN ARA, Begum. Father and daughter: a political autobiography. Lahore: Nigarishat, 1971. 304p. [Feminist leader & Muslim Leaguer]

22658 TIKA RAM. Sir Chhotu Ram: a biography. 2nd ed. Ed. by Karan Singh. Hissar: Ritu, 1979. 115p.

iii. communalism and partition: conflict of Sikhs, Muslims, and Hindus

22659 ALI, IMRAN. Panjab politics in the decade before partition. Lahore: South Asian Inst., U. of the Punjab, 1975. 55p. (Its Res. monograph, 8)

22660 BARRIER, N.G. The Punjab government and communal politics, 1870-1908. In JAS 27 (1968) 523-39.

22661 DARLING, M.L. At freedom's door. London: OUP, 1949. 369p.

22662 JONES, K.W. Communalism in the Punjab; the Arya Samaj contribution. In JAS 28 (1968) 39-54.

22663 MALHOTRA, S.L. Gandhi, an experiment with communal politics: a study of Gandhi's role in Punjab politics, 1922-1931. Chandigarh: Panjab U., 1975. 248p.

22664 RAI, S.M. Partition of the Punjab; a study of its effects on the politics and administration of the Punjab: 1947-56. London: Asia, 1965. 304p.

22665 ROSEBERRY, J.R. The beginning of Hindu-Muslim conflict in British Punjab (Pakistan). In JSAMES 3,1 (1979) 31-59.

22666 UPRETY, P. The Sikh disturbances of 1922-25; the response of the British government in India to a religious unrest. In PP&P 13,2 (1978) 359-69.

6. The Indian Punjab - Government and Politics since 1947

a. general studies

22667 DAR, ABDUL GHANI. Historic enquiry after Warren Hastings; rejoinders by memorialists. Delhi: 1964. 539p. [On Dass Cmsn. Enquiry on Kairon]

22668 GROVER, V. The Punjab legislative council. In IPSR 10,1 (1976) 68-96. [first proposed in 1933, functioned 1952-1969]

22669 HEEGER, G.A. Discipline vs. mobilization: party building and the Punjab Jana Sangh. In AS 12,10 (1972) 864-878.

22670 INDIA (REP.). CMSN. OF ENQUIRY ON CERTAIN ALLEGATIONS AGAINST S. PRATAP SINGH KAIRON, CHIEF MINISTER OF PUNJAB, 1963. Report. Delhi: Min. of Punjab, 1964. 298p. [S.R. Dass, one-man Cmsn.]

22671 PETTIGREW, J. Robber noblemen: a study of the political system of the Sikh Jats. London: Routledge & Kegan Paul, 1975. 272p.

22672 RAJPUT, P. Profiles of women in Punjab [state politics]. In Vina Mazumdar, ed. Symbols of power... Bombay: Allied, 1979, 265-90.

22673 VERMA, M. The coalition ministries in Punjab. Patiala: Sonu Sales Agency, 1978. 161p.

b. the Sikh demand for a Punjabi-speaking state, and the partition into Punjab and Haryana States

22674 BAR ASSN. OF INDIA. CMSN. OF ENQUIRY ON ALLEGED POLICE EXCESSES IN PUNJAB DURING ANTI-SUBA AGITATION IN MARCH 1966. Report. ND: 1966. 52p.

22675 BRASS, P.R. The politics of language and religion in the Punjab: Sikhs, Hindus, and the Punjabi language. In his Language, religion and politics in North India. NY: CamUP, 1974, 275-400.

22676 CHAUDHRY, R.S. Genesis of the demand for Vishal Haryana. In J. of the Soc. for the Study of State Govt. 1,1/2 (1968) 13-20.

22677 DHILLON, G.S. Evolution of the demand for a Sikh homeland. In IJPS 35,4 (1974) 362-73.

22678 GUPTA, G.S. The case of Arya Samaj (regarding language problem in Punjab). Delhi: Sarvadeshik Arya Pratinidhi Sabha, 1957. 54p.

22679 GURNAM SINGH. A unilingual Punjabi state and the Sikh unrest - a statement. ND: Sardar Gurnam Singh, 1960. 95p.

22680 HARBIR SINGH. Sant Fateh Singh's role in the creation of Punjabi Suba: a study in charismatic leadership. In IPSR 8,1 (1974) 151-69.

22681 INDIA (REP.). PARLIAMENTARY CMTEE. ON THE DEMAND FOR PUNJABI SUBA. Report, 18th March 1966. ND: Lok Sabha Secretariat, 1966. 90p. [Chm., Hukam Singh]

22682 INDIA (REP.). PUNJAB BOUNDARY CMSN. Report presented on the 31st May, 1966. Delhi: MPGOI, 1966. 150p.

22683 INDIA (REP.). PUNJAB CMSN., 1961. Report. ND: MPGOI, 1962. 16p. [Chm., S.R. Das]

22684 KAHOL, O.P. Hindus and the Punjabi State: a psycho-political discussion on the conception and rationale of Punjabi State. Ambala Cantt.: Hindu Prachara Sabha, 1955. 112p.

22685 NAYAR, B.R. Minority politics in the Punjab. Princeton: PUP, 1966. 373p.

22686 PETTIGREW, J. The influence of urban Sikhs on the development of the movement for a Punjabi speaking state. In JSS 5,1 (1978) 152-76.

22687 Punjabi Suba, a symposium. ND: Natl. Book Club, 1966. 171p.

22688 SARHADI, A.S. Punjabi Suba; the story of the struggle. Delhi: U.C. Kapur, 1970. 529p.

c. election studies, 1947 -

22689 ANAND, J.C. General elections in Punjab. In PSR 6,3/4 & 7,1/2 (1968) 412-46.

22690 CHANDIDAS, R. Fluctuating voter loyalties: Budhlada assembly constituency in 1969. In EPW 6,10 (1971) 583-94.

22691 DUA, VEENA. Elections in a scheduled caste neighborhood: a Punjab town. In EPW 6,46 (1971) 2323-27.

22692 ______. The mid-term poll in the Punjab: electoral alliances and voting behaviour in a scheduled caste locality. In SocAct 26,3 (1976) 237-52.

22693 HARCHARAN SINGH. Mid-term elections in Punjab: emerging trends. In IPSR 4 (1970) 207-32.

22694 KHANNA, B.S. Third general elections in the Panjab. (1962). In IJPS 24 (1963) 51-64.

22695 KOGEKAR, S.V. PEPSU. In S.V. Kogekar & R.L. Park, eds. Reports on the Indian general elections, 1951-52. Bombay: Popular, 1956, 213-21. [Patiala and Eastern Punjab States Union]

22696 PUNJAB, INDIA. ELECTIONS DEPT. Report on general elections in Punjab, 1967. Chandigarh: 1968. 101p.

22697 ______. Report on the mid-term general election to the Punjab Vidhan Sabha, 1969. Chandigarh: 1971. 69p.

22698 SHARMA, B.R. Punjab. In S.V. Kogekar & R.L. Park, eds. Reports on the Indian general elections, 1951-52. Bombay: Popular, 1956, 135-50.

d. administrative studies

22699 MANGAT RAI, E.N. Civil administration in the Punjab; an analysis of a state government in India. Cambridge: Center for Intl. Affairs, Harvard U., 1963. 82p.

22700 MANN, T.K. Administration of justice in India: a case study of Punjab. ND: Concept, 1979. 211p.

22701 PAVATE, D.C. My days as governor. Delhi: Vikas, 1974. 240p.

22702 PUNJAB, INDIA. PAY CMSN. Report, 1977-79. Chandigarh: 1979. 470p. [Chm., D.K. Mahajan]

e. local government and politics

22703 ALAVI, HAMZA. Politics of dependence - a village in West Punjab. In SAR 4,2 (1971) 111-28.

22704 BHATNAGAR, S. Panchayati Raj in the Punjab. In QJLSGI 38 (1968) 411-22.

22705 BURKI, S.J. Agricultural growth and local government in Punjab, Pakistan. Ithaca: Rural Dev. Cmtee., Center for Intl. Stud., Cornell U., 1974. 68p. (Spec. series on rural local govt., RLG 11)

22706 GANGRADE, K.D. & C.G. SANON. Panchayat elections in a Punjab village: changing political status of a depressed caste. In EA 3,1 (1969) 37-54.

22707 HARJINDAR SINGH. Village leadership; a case study of village Mohali in Punjab. Delhi: Sterling, 1968. 82p.

22708 IZMIRLIAN, H., JR. Dynamics of political support in a Punjab village. In AS 6 (1966) 125-33.

22709 KAPUR, K. Municipal elections in a small Punjab town: a case study of Chheharta municipal elections. In QJLSGI 36 (1965) 157-76.

22710 KHANNA, R.L. Local government in Punjab. 2nd rev. & enl. ed. Chandigarh: English Book Shop, 195-. 276p.

22711 ______. Panchayati raj in Punjab. Chandigarh: Mohindra Capital Pub., 1966. 202p.

22712 SHARMA, S.K. Deputy commissioner in Punjab. ND: IIPA, 1971. 340p.

22713 TEWARI, A.C. Municipalities and city fathers in the Punjab, 1963. Delhi: Adarsh Pub. House, 1964. 259p.

22714 YADAVA, J.S. Group dynamics and panchayat elections in a Punjab village. In JSR 11,2 (1968) 58-72.

7. The Pakistani Punjab - government and politics since 1947

22715 BAXTER, C. The People's Party vs. the Punjab "feudalists." In JAAS(L) 8,3/4 (1973) 166-89.

22716 BURKI, S.J. & C. BAXTER. Socio-economic indicators of the People's Party vote in the Punjab: a study at the Tehsil level. In JAS 34,3 (1975) 913-30.

22717 CHAUDHARI, H.A. Union councils; a study of Sahiwal and Lyallpur districts. Karachi: Planning & Eval. Unit, Basic Democracies Wing, MIB, Govt. of Pakistan, 1967. 117p.

22718 HAMID-UD-DIN, C. The Punjab local government laws: being a comprehensive book containing the Punjab local government ordinance, 1979.... Lahore: Hamid-ud-Din, 1979. 551p.

22719 HASHMI, RIAZ. Brief for Bahawalpur Province. Karachi: Bahawalpur Subah Mahaz, 1972. 235p.

22720 KHAN, SALEH MOHAMMED & MANSOOR MAHMOOD. Union councils at work: an assessment. Lahore: NIPA, 1968. 143p.

22721 WAHEED, ZUHRA. Contacts between villagers and public officials in three villages of Lyallpur tehsil. Lahore: Pakistan Admin. Staff College, 1964. 78p. (Its Res. study, 1)

B. The Punjab Economy

1. The Economy of British Punjab, 1849 - 1947
a. bibliography

22722 FAZAL, C.P.K. A bibliography of economic literature relating to the Punjab. Lahore: 1941. 112p. (Punjab Board of Econ. Inquiry, Pub., 73)

22723 ______. Guide to Punjab government reports and statistics. Lahore: Board of Econ. Inquiry, 1939. 256p. (Its Pub., 10)

b. general studies, incl. industry

22724 LATIFI, A. Industrial Punjab: a survey of facts, conditions, and possibilities. Bombay: Longmans, Green, 1911. 304p.

22725 MATHUR, Y.B. Revenue and financial administration of Punjab, (1849-75). In JIH 45 (1967) 695-726.

22726 PAUSTIAN, P.W. Canal irrigation in the Punjab. NY: ColUP, 1930. 179p.

22727 SAINI, B.S. The social and economic history of the Punjab, 1901-1939, including Haryana and Himachal Pradesh. Delhi: Ess Ess, 1975. 381p.

22728 SHAH, K.T. Industrialisation of the Punjab. Lahore: Supt., Govt. Printing, Punjab, 1941. 295p.

22729 TREVASKIS, H.K. The land of the five rivers: an economic history of the Punjab from the earliest times to the year of grace 1890. London: OUP, 1928. 372p.

22730 ______. The Punjab today: an economic survey of the Punjab in recent years, 1890-1925. Lahore: Civil & Military Gazette Press, 1931-32. 2 v.

c. agriculture
i. general studies

22731 CALVERT, H. The wealth and welfare of the Punjab: being some studies in Punjab rural economies. Lahore: Civil & Military Gazette Press, 1922. 224p.

22732 GORRIE, R.M. Soil and water conservation in the Punjab. Simla: 1946. 290p.

22733 KHAN, MUKHTAR AHMAD. Cooperative movement in the Punjab. Aligarh: Aligarh Printing, 1923. 127p.

22734 KRISHNA, RAJ. Farm supply response in India-Pakistan: a case study of the Punjab region, 1914-15 to 1945-46. In Economic J. (London) 73 (1963) 477-87.

22735 NARAIN, DHARM. Impact of price movements on areas under selected crops in India, 1900-1939. Cambridge: CamUP, 1965. 234p.

22736 THOMPSON, W.P. Punjab irrigation. Lahore: Civil & Military Gazette Press, 1925. 119p.

ii. land tenure, revenue and reform; agrarian unrest

22737 BARRIER, N.G. The Punjab alienation of land bill of 1900. Durham, NC: DUPCSSA, 1966. 125p. (Its monograph & occ. papers series, 2)

22738 ______. The Punjab disturbances of 1907: the response of the British Government in India to agrarian unrest. In MAS 1,4 (1967) 353-83. [Rpt. in PPP 8,2 (1974) 444-76.]

22739 CHOWDHRY, PREM. Rural relations prevailing in the Punjab at the time of enactment of the so-called "Golden Laws" or agrarian legislation of the late thirties. In PPP 10,1 (1976) 461-80.

22740 DARLING, M.L. The Punjab peasant in prosperity and debt. With new intro. by C.J. Dewey. ND: Manohar, 1977. 48 + 277p. [1st pub. 1925]

22741 DOMIN, D. Some aspects of British land policy in Panjab after its annexation in 1849. In PPP 8,1 (1974) 12-32.

22742 HAMBLY, G.R.G. Richard Temple and the Punjab Tenancy Act of 1868. In English Hist. R. 79 (1964) 47-66.

22743 NAIDIS, M. John Lawrence and the origin of the Punjab system, 1849-57. In BPP 80 (1961) 38-46.

22744 SARJIT SINGH & J. LINDAUER. The tax bases of an Indian land tax. In IESHR 7,4 (1970) 511-23.

22745 THORBURN, S.S. Report on peasant indebtedness and land alienations to money-lenders in part of the Rawalpindi Division. Lahore: Civil & Military Gazette Press, 1896. 80p.

22746 VAN DEN DUNGEN, P.H.M. The Punjab tradition; influence and authority in nineteenth-century India. London: Allen & Unwin, 1972. 366p.

2. The Economy of the Indian Punjab since 1947

a. demography (1981 pop. 16,669,755)

22747 KRISHAN, GOPAL. Regionalism in growth of population in Punjab's border districts of Amritsar and Gurdaspur: 1951-61. In GRI 30,2 (1968) 6-23.

22748 SINGH, K.P. Status of women and population growth in India. ND: Munshiram, 1976. 165p.

22749 VARMA, S.D. Density and patterns of population in the Punjab. In NGRI 2 (1956) 193-202.

22750 WYON, J.B. & J.E. GORDON. The Khanna study; population problems in the rural Punjab. Cambridge: HUP, 1971. 437p.

b. economic development and planning

22751 JAIN, H.R. Punjab economy. Patiala: Jainco, 1964. 111p.

22752 NCAER. Techno-economic survey of Punjab. ND: 1962. 234p.

22753 PRITAM SINGH. Emerging pattern of economic life in Punjab. Bombay: Thacker, 1975. 198p.

22754 PUNJAB, INDIA. ECON. & STAT. ORG. Study of impact of plan programmes; report. Chandigarh: 1967-. v. 1 -.

22755 ______. Compendium of the evaluation studies in Punjab, 1964-65 to 1970-71. Chandigarh: 1972. 244p. (Its pub., 149)

c. agriculture in the Punjab, "the granary of India"

i. agricultural development and planning

22756 AGGARWAL, P.C. The green revolution and rural labour; a study in Ludhiana. ND: Shri Ram Centre for Industrial Relations & Human Resources, 1973. 148p.

22757 BEDI, K.S., comp. & tr. Agricultural proverbs of the Punjab. Chandigarh: Public Relations Dept., Punjab, 1962. 144p.

22758 CHANDER, P. District-wise measurement and decomposition of the growth of agricultural output in the Punjab during the post-independence period. In IER ns 6 (1969) 333-50.

22759 DUGGAL, S.L. Agricultural atlas of Punjab. Hissar: Dir. of Res., Punjab Agri. U., 1966. 90p.

22760 GHOSH, R.N. Agriculture in economic development: with special reference to Punjab. ND: Vikas, 1977. 164p.

22761 GILL, M.S. The green revolution: successes and failures, success in the Indian Punjab. In JSS 4,1 (1977) 99-112.

22762 GOSAL, G.S. & B.S. OJHA. Agricultural land-use in Punjab; a spatial analysis. ND: IIPA, 1967. 87p.

22763 GOYAL, S.K. Some aspects of co-operative farming in India, with special reference to the Punjab. London: Asia, 1967. 210p.

22764 GREWAL, S.S. & D.S. SIDHU. Prosperity of Punjab farmer: reality or myth? Ludhiana: Dept. of Econ. & Sociology, Punjab Agri. U., 1980. 40p.

22765 GUPTA, S.S. Agriculture in Punjab. Chandigarh: Public Relations Dept., Punjab, 1977. 72p.

22766 GURBACHAN SINGH. Transformation of agriculture: a case study of Punjab. Kurukshetra: Vishal, 1979. 372p.

22767 HANUMANTHA RAO, C.H. Growth of agriculture in the Punjab during the decade 1952-62. In IJAE 20 (1965) 20-32.

22768 KAHLON, A.S. et al. The dynamics of Punjab agriculture. Ludhiana: Dept. of Econ. & Sociology, Punjab Agri. U., 1972. 109p. [1st pub. 1966]

22769 KAHLON, A.S. & A.C. SHARMA. Organizational and institutional implications of rapid growth and commercialization of Punjab agriculture. Ludhiana: Punjab Agri. U., 1974. 59p.

22770 LADEJINSKY, W. The green revolution in Punjab: a field trip. In EPW 4,26 (1969) A73-A82.

22771 NCAER. Cropping pattern in Punjab. ND: 1966. 95p.

22772 PUNJAB, INDIA. AGRI. CENSUS WING. The third decennial world agricultural census, 1970-71, report for Punjab State: general report and tables. Chandigarh: 1974. 112 + 325p.

22773 RANDHAWA, M.S. et al. Green revolution; a case study of Punjab. Delhi: VIkas, 1974. 207p.

ii. agricultural technology and innovation

22774 AVATAR SINGH. Community factors in farm practice adoption: a study of four Indian villages. In MI 53,4 (1973) 368-386.

22775 BILLINGS, M.H. & ARJAN SINGH. Mechanisation and rural employment: with some implications for rural income distribution. In EPW 5,26 (1970) A61-A72.

22775a ______. Mechanisation and the wheat revolution: effects on female labour in Punjab. In EPW 5,52 (1970) 169-173.

22776 CHAUDHARI, H.A. & E.C. ERICKSON & IJAZ BAJWA. Social characteristics of agricultural innovators in two Punjabi villages in West Pakistan. In Rural Sociology 32 (1967) 468-73.

22777 CHOPRA, KUSUM. Tractorisation and changes in factor inputs: a case study of Punjab. In EPW 9,52 (1974) A119-A127.

22778 KAHLON, A.S. Impact of mechanisation on Punjab agriculture with special reference to tractorisation. In IJAE 31,4 (1976) 54-70.

22779 LEAF, M.J. Peasant motivation, ecology, and economy in Panjab. In CAS 3 (1973) 40-50.

22780 MANN, K.S. & C.V. MOORE & S.S. JOHL. Estimates of the potential effects of new technology on agriculture In Punjab, India. In American J. of Agri. Econ. 50 (1968) 278-91.

22781 NCAER. Impact of rural electrification in Punjab. ND: 1967. 59p.

22782 SHARMA, A.C. Partial mechanisation of peasant farms: a case study. In IJE 56,4 (1976) 457-86.

iii. irrigation

22783 ANSARI, NASIM. Economics of irrigation rates, a study in Punjab and Uttar Pradesh. Bombay: Asia, 1968. 360p.

22784 CLARK, E.H. The development of tubewell irrigation in the Punjab: an investigation into alternative modes of groundwater development. Ph.D. diss., Princeton U., 1972. 283p. [UM 72-39, 770]

22785 MINHAS, B.S. & K.S. PARIKH & T.N. SRINIVASAN. Scheduling the operations of the Bhakra system; studies in technical and economic evaluation. Calcutta: Stat. Pub. Soc., 1972. 89p.

22786 PUNJAB, INDIA. BOARD OF ECON. INQUIRY. Effects of Bhakra Dam irrigation in the economy of the Barani villages, Hissar District. Chandigarh: 1964. (Its pub., 102)

22787 RAJ, K.N. Some economic aspects of the Bhakra Nangal Project; a preliminary analysis in terms of selected investment criteria. Bombay: Asia, 1960. 140p.

iv. land tenure and reform

22788 KRISHNA, RAJ. The optimality of land allocation: a case study of the Punjab. In IJAE 18 (1963) 63-73.

22789 LINDAUER, J. & SARJIT SINGH. Land taxation and Indian economic development. ND: Kalyani Pub., 1979. 396p.

22790 SONI, R.N. Ceiling on land holdings - a case study of the Punjab. In IJAE 24,3 (1969) 19-34.

22791 UPPAI, J.S. Implementation of land reform legislation in India - a study of two villages in Punjab. In AS 9 (1969) 359-72.

d. industry

22792 DHIMAN, R., ed. Punjab industries. 2nd ed. Ludhiana: Dhiman Press, 1962. 106p.

22793 NCAER. Industrial programmes for the fourth plan, Punjab. ND: 1967. 182p.

22794 PATHAK, H.N. Small-scale industries in Ludhiana. In EPW 5,28 (1970) 1091-97.

e. labor

22795 BHARDWAJ, S.M. & M.E. HARVEY. Occupational structure of the scheduled castes and general population of the Punjab: a comparative multivariate analysis. In NGJI 31,2 (1975) 75-97.

22796 PUNJAB, INDIA. PLANNING DEPT. Fact book on manpower. Chandigarh: 1968-69. 3 v. in 1.

22797 SHARMA, A.C. Employment and wage structure of farm labour in Punjab. In Manpower J. 2,4 (1967) 75-90.

22798 UPPAL, J.S. Measurement of disguised unemployment in Punjab agriculture. In Canadian J. of Econ. and Political Science 33 (1967) 590-96.

f. commerce and transportation

22799 INDIA (REP.). DIR. OF ECON. & STAT. Market directory for Punjab. ND: 1973. 87p.

22800 KAHLON, A.S. Impact of changing conditions on grain marketing institutions and the structure of grain markets in the erstwhile Punjab. Ludhiana: Punjab Agri. U., 1970. 128p.

22801 NEALE, W.C., et al. Kurali market: a report on the economic geography of marketing in Northern Punjab. In EDCC 13 (1965) 129-68.

22802 PUNJAB, INDIA. ECON. & STAT. ORG. Report on the pilot study of distributive trade of Patiala, Batala, and Hoshiarpur towns. Chandigarh: 1970. 343p. (Its pub., 110)

22803 RANGNEKAR, S.B. Regional transport survey of Punjab, Haryana, Himachal Pradesh, and Delhi. Chandigarh: Panjab U., Dept. of Econ., 1970. 214p.

22804 TOMAR, D.S. Rail race to Jammu. Delhi: Metropolitan, 1974. 92p.

3. The Economy of the Pakistani Punjab since 1947

22805 BUKHARI, SHAUKAT ALI. Evaluation report on cotton production in the Punjab. Lahore: Econ. Res. Inst., 1979. 55p. (Its pub., 174)

22806 CHILD, F.C. & H. KANEDA. Links to the Green Revolution: a study of small scale, agriculturally related industry in the Pakistan Punjab. In EDCC 23,2 (1975) 249-75.

22807 HUFBAUER, G.C. Occupational trends and social mobility in the Punjab. In Pakistan Econ. & Social R. 11 (1973) 83-103.

22808 IMTIAZI, I.A. Punjab development; review and prospects. Lahore: Planning & Dev. Dept., Punjab, 1971. 213p.

22809 MAY, B. Der Einfluss von Produktionstechniken auf die Produktion der Hauptfruchtarten im pakistanischen Punjab. Methodische Probleme der Erfassung und Quantifizierung. Wiesbaden: Steiner, 1976. 403p.

22810 RAHMAN, MUSHTAQUR. Deh Dali Nandi, West Pakistan; a study of cultural factors in land use. Karachi: Pakistan Inst. of Geography, 1965. 43p.

22811 REGIONAL SEMINAR ON PLANNING AND DEV., BAHAWALPUR, 1963. Proceedings. Lahore: 1963. 92 + 243p.

22812 SYED, HASAN ALI. Working of co-operative marketing societies in the Punjab. Lahore: Board of Econ. Inquiry, Punjab (Pakistan), 1958. 85p. (Its pub., 120)

22813 WASEEM, M.T. Regional economic scene in Pakistan: an academic study. Lahore: Progressive Pub., 1975. 72p.

22814 ZEUNER, T.H. Entwicklung der Betriebsgrossenstruktur und der Landbewirtschaftung in Kanalsiedlungen des Lyallpur-Distrikts im pakistanischen Panjab. In Heidelbert, U., Südasien-Inst., Jahrbuch (1966), 75-90.

C. Society and Social Change in the Punjab Region Since 1800

1. General Studies of Punjabi Society

22815 HAZLEHURST, L. Ceremony and social structure in nineteenth century Punjab. In EPW 11, 25 (1976) 1430-1435.

22816 KELLER, S.L. Uprooting and social change: the role of refugees in development. ND: Manohar, 1975. 357p.

22817 MEHTA, VED PARKASH. Mamaji. NY: OUP, 1979. 334p.

22818 SMITH, M.W. The misal: a structural village-group of India and Pakistan. In AA 54 (1952) 41-56.

22819 TANDON, PRAKASH. Punjabi century, 1857-1947. Berkeley: UCalP, 1968. 274p. [1st pub. 1961]

22820 ______. Return to Punjab. Berkeley: UCalP, 1981.

22821 VAN DEN DUNGEN, P.H.M. Changes in status and occupation in nineteenth-century Panjab. In D.A. Low, ed. Soundings in modern South Asian history, Berkeley: UCalP, 1968, 59-94.

2. Social Categories in the Punjab

22822 BINGLEY, A.H. History, caste and culture of Jāts and Gūjars. 2nd ed. ND: Ess Ess, 1978. 128p. [1st pub. 1899]

22823 DAHIYA, B.S. Jats, the ancient rulers: a clan study. ND: Sterling, 1980. 358p.

22824 D'SOUZA, V.S. Scheduled castes and urbanization in Punjab: an explanation. In SB 24,1 (1975) 1-12.

22825 HERSHMAN, P. Hair, sex and dirt. In MAN ns 9,2 (1974) 274-98.

22826 IBBETSON, D.C.J. Panjab castes. Patiala: Languages Dept., Punjab, 1970. 338p. [1st pub. 1916; Rpt. from 1883 Census]

22827 JONES, K.W. The Bengali elite in post-annexation Punjab: an example of inter-regional influence in nineteenth-century India. In Harbans Singh & N.G. Barrier, eds., Punjab, Past and Present.... Patiala: Punjabi U., 1976, 234-51. [1st pub. in IESHR 3 (1966) 376-95]

22828 MARENCO, E.K. The transformation of Sikh society. Portland, OR: HaPi Press, 1974. 342p.

22829 MCLEOD, W.H. Ahluwalias and Ramgarhias: two Sikh castes. In SA 4 (Oct. 1974) 78-90.

22830 PUNJAB, INDIA. EVAL. CMTEE. ON WELFARE. Report of the Evaluation Committee on Welfare, regarding the welfare of scheduled castes, backward classes and denotified tribes in Punjab State for the period commencing from 15th August, 1947 (December, 1965-August, 1966). Chandigarh: 1966. 319p.

22831 ROSE, H.A. A glossary of the tribes and castes of the Punjab and North-West Frontier Province.... Patiala: Languages Dept., Punjab, 1970. 3v. [1st pub. 1911-19; based on 1883 + 1892 Censuses]

22832 RUSTOMJI, K.J. A treatise on customary law in the Punjab: being an exhaustive and critical commentary on Punjab custom. Lahore: U. Book Agency, 1929. 738p.

22833 SABERWAL, S. Mobile men, limits to social change in urban Punjab. ND: Vikas, for IIAS, 1976. 267p.

22834 SHER SINGH. The Sansis of Punjab; a gypsy and denotified tribe of Rajput origin. Delhi: Munshiram, 1965. 367p.

22835 ______. The Sikligars of Punjab, a gypsy tribe. Delhi: Sterling, 1966. 415p.

22836 STREEFLAND, P.H. The Christian Punjabi sweepers: their history and their position in present-day Pakistan. Amsterdam: Anthropological-Sociological Center, U. of Amsterdam, 1973. 41p.

22837 THAPAR, P.N. General code of tribal custom in the Jhelum District, Punjab. Lahore: Supt., Govt. Printing, 1946. 146p.

22838 THORBURN, S.S. Mussalmans and moneylenders in the Punjab. London: Blackwood, 1886. 198p.

22839 WESTPHAL-HELLBUSCH, S. & H. WESTPHAL. The Jat of Pakistan. Berlin: Duncker & Humbolt, 1964. 110p.

22840 WIKELEY, J.M. Punjabi Musalmans. Calcutta: Supt. Govt. Printing, 1915. 130p.

3. Kinship and Marriage Patterns

22841 ALAVI, HAMZA A. Kinship in West Punjab Villages. In CIS ns 6 (1972) 1-27.

22842 DAS, VEENA. Masks and faces: an essay on Punjabi kinship. In CIS ns 10,1 (1976) 1-30.

22843 GIDEON, H. A baby is born in the Punjab. In AA 64 (1962) 1220-34.

22844 MAHAJAN, A. Changes in Punjabi marriage: a study of a displaced community. In J. of Family Welfare 13,4 (1967) 15-19.

22845 MORRISON, C. Kinship in professional relations: a study of North Indian district lawyers. In CSSH 14,1 (1972) 100-25.

22846 RAJAGOPALAN, C. & JASPAL SINGH. Changing trends in Sikh marriage. In J. of Family Welfare 14,2 (1967) 24-32.

22847 WAKIL, P.A. Explorations into the kin-networks of the Punjabi society: a preliminary statement. In J. of Marriage & the Family 32,4 (1970) 700-06.

22848 WYON, J.B., et al. Delayed marriage and prospects for fewer births in Punjab villages. In Demography 3 (1966) 209-217.

4. Villages and Rural Society
a. villages of pre-partition British Punjab

22849 BRAYNE, F.L. The remaking of Village India. London: OUP, 1929. 262p.

22850 DARLING, M.L. Rusticus loquitur; or the old light and the new in the Punjab village. London: OUP, 1930. 400p.

22851 ______. Wisdom and waste in the Punjab village. London: OUP, 1934. 368p.

22852 LUCAS, E.D. The economic life of a Punjab village. Lahore: Civil and Military Gazette Press, 1921. 138p.

22853 PUNJAB. BOARD OF ECON. ENQUIRY. Punjab village surveys. Lahore: 1928-40. 12 v. (Its pubs. 16-18, 27, 30, 31, 43, 35, 38, 51, 54, 69)

22854 YOUNG, M. Seen and heard in a Punjab village. London: Student Christian Movement Press, 1931. 225p.

b. villages of the Indian Punjab

22855 AVTAR SINGH. Community structure and technological development. In CAS 10 (1977) 25-41.

22856 DEB, P.C. Social stratification and mobility in rural setting. Delhi: Researchco, 1975. 120p.

22857 DEB, P.C. & B.K. AGARWAL. Rural leadership in green revolution. Delhi: Researchco, 1974. 96p.

22858 HARJINDAR SINGH. Authority and influence in two Sikh villages. ND: Sterling, 1976. 219p.

22859 ______. Village leadership; a case study of village Mohali in Punjab. Delhi: Sterling, 1968. 82p.

22860 IZMIRLIAN, H. Structure and strategy in Sikh society: the politics of passion. ND: Manohar, 1979. 221p.

22861 JAMMU, P.S. Changing social structure in rural Panjab. ND: Sterling, 1974. 207p.

22862 KAUSHAL, M.P. Dynamics of planned social change; a comparative approach. Ludhiana: Bee Kay Pub., 1973. 384p.

22863 KESSINGER, T.G. Vilyatpur 1848-1968: social and economic change in a north Indian village. Berkeley: UCalP, 1974. 244p.

22864 LEAF, M.J. Information and behavior in a Sikh village; social organization reconsidered. Berkeley: UCalP, 1972. 296p.

22865 MAMDANI, MAHAMOOD. The myth of population control: family, caste and class in an Indian village. NY: Monthly Review Press, 1973. 173p.

22866 MARRIOTT, M. Village structure and the Punjab government: a restatement. In AA 55 (1953) 137-43.

22867 NATH, V. The new village. In EPW 17, 16-19 (1965) 679-84, 713-22, 745-50, 777-80.

22868 PUNJAB, INDIA. COMMUNITY DEV. ORG. Regionwise progress of community development programme up to 31st March 1959. Chandigarh: 1960. 454p.

22869 PUNJAB, INDIA. ECON. & STAT. ORG. Family budgets of thirty-two cultivators in the Punjab for the year 1971-72, being the accounts of thirty-two peasant-proprietors of different agricultural zones in the state. Chandigarh: 1974. 108p. (Its pub., 108)

22870 RANDHAWA, M.S. National extension service and community projects in Punjab. Chandigarh: Community Projects Admin., Punjab, 1955. 303p.

22870a RAULET, H.M. & J.S. UPPAL. The social dynamics of economic development in rural Punjab. In AS 10,4 (1970) 336-47.

22870b SINGH, I.P. A Sikh village. In M.B. Singer, ed. Traditional India: structure and change. Philadelphia: American Folklore Society, 1959, 479-503. (J. of American Folklore 71, 281)

22870c SMITH, M.W. Social structure in the Punjab. In M.N. Srinivas, ed. India's Villages. Calcutta: West Bengal Dev. Dept., 1955, 144-60.

c. villages of the Pakistani Punjab

22871 AHMAD, S. SAGHIR. Class and power in a Punjabi village. NY: Monthly Review Press, 1977. 174p.

22872 ______. Social stratification in a Punjabi village. In CIS ns 4 (1970) 105-25.

22873 AKHTAR, S.M. & A.R. ARSHAD. Village life in Lahore District (a study of selected economic aspects). Lahore: Social Sciences Res. Centre, U. of the Panjab., 1860. 113p.

22874 ALAVI, HAMZA A. The politics of dependence: a village in West Panjab. In SAR 4 (1971) 111-28.

22875 ______. The rural elite and agricultural development in Pakistan. In R.D. Stevens, Hamza Alavi, & P.J. Bertocci, eds. Rural development in Bangladesh and Pakistan. Honolulu: UPH, 1976, 317-53.

22876 CAMBRDIGE U. ASIAN EXPEDITION. The Budhopur report, a study of the forces of tradition and change in a Punjabi village in the Gujranwala District, West Pakistan. Lahore: Social Sciences Res. Centre, U. of the Panjab, 1962. 82p.

22877 EGLAR, Z.S. A Punjabi village in Pakistan. NY: ColUP, 1960. 240p.

22878 HAIDER, AGHA SAJJAD. Village in an urban orbit; Shah-di-Khui, a village in Lahore urban area. Lahore: Social Sciences Res. Centre, U. of the Panjab, 1960. 35p.

22879 HONIGMANN, J.J. A case study of community development in Pakistan. In EDCC 8 (1960) 288-303. [Lyallpur District]

22880 ________. Three Pakistani villages. Chapel Hill, NC: Inst. for Res. in Social Change, 1958. 28p.

22881 INAYATULLAH. Caste, patti and faction in the life of a Punjab village. In Sociologus ns 8,2 (1958) 170-186.

22882 ______. Weltanschauung of the Punjab villager. In Baesler-Archiv ns 7 (1959) 165-80.

22883 INAYATULLAH & Q.M. SHAFI. Dynamics of development in a Pakistani village. Peshawar: PARD, 1963. 2v.

22884 QURESHI, JAMIL A. & QAMAR JABEEN. A study of social change in rural Punjab. Lahore: Econ. Res. Inst. 1980. 53p. (Its pub., 178)

22885 RAZA, M. RAFIQUE. Two Pakistani villages; a study in social stratification. Lahore: Dept. of Sociology, U. of the Punjab, 1969. 104p. [Lyallpur District]

22886 SLOCUM, W.L. & J. AKHTAR & A.F. SAHI. Village life in Lahore district, a study of selected sociological aspects. Lahore: Social Sciences Res. Centre, U. of the Punjab, 1960. 50p.

5. Cities and Urbanization

a. general studies

22887 FAUJA SINGH & R.C. RABRA. The city of Faridkot: past and present. Patiala: Punjabi U., 1976. 159p. + 14pl.

22888 GOSAL, G.S. Urbanization in Punjab (India): 1881-1961. In Punjab U. Res. Bull. ns Science 17, 1/2 (1966) 1-26.

22889 Multan: past and present. Karachi: Finance & Industry Pub., 1968. 179p.

22890 PRABHA, K. Towns, a structural analysis: a case study of Punjab. Delhi: Inter-India, 1979. 214p.

22891 PUNJAB, INDIA. BOARD OF ECON. INQUIRY. Report on pace of urbanisation in the Punjab. Chandigarh: Econ. & Stat. Org., Punjab, 1964. 63p. (Its Pub., 97)

22892 SAIDOOKHAIL, AYUB KHAN. Campbellpur: ancient and modern: the British role, the Pakistani role. Ghorghoshti, Distt. Campbellpur: Saidookhail Traders, 1978. 128p.

b. Lahore: Mughal city and capital of Pakistani Punjab (1972 pop. 2,200,000)

22893 LAHORE MUNICIPAL CORPORATION. Lahore city perspective: developments, prospects and problems. Lahore: 1975. 92p.

22894 MUHAMMAD LATIF, Saiyid. Lahore, its history, architectural remains and antiquities. Lahore: New Imperial Press, 1892. 426p.

22895 MUSHTAQ, M. Lahore: major urban regions. In Pakistan Geog. R. 22 (1967) 24-41.

c. Islamabad, city and capital territory, and its twin-city Rawalpindi (Pakistan) - 1972 pop., 235,000 + 615,392

22896 JAFRI, ZAMIR, ed. Islamabad takes shape; first three years of development, October 61-64. Rawalpindi: Director of Public Relations, Capital Dev. Authority, 1967? 1v.

22897 PAKISTAN. CENTRAL STAT. OFFICE. Socio-economic survey, Rawalpindi. Karachi: 1969. 146p.

22898 STEPHENSON, G.V. Two newly-created capitals: Islamabad and Brasilia. In Town Planning R. 41,4 (1970) 317-332.

d. Chandigarh: a Union Territory and capital of both India's Punjab and Haryana states (1971 pop. 257,251)

22899 Chandigarh: a new planned city. In Mārg 15 (Dec. 1961) 2-37.

22900 D'SOUZA, V.S. Problems of housing in Chandigarh. In URPT 16,4 (1973) 254-66.

22901 ______. Social structure of a planned city, Chandigarh. Bombay: Orient Longmans, 1968. 408p.

22902 EVENSON, N. Chandigarh. Berkeley: UCalP, 1966. 116p. + 121 pl.

22903 FRY, M. Chandigarh and development in India. In Asian R. 41 (1955) 110-25.

22904 GOPAL KRISHAN. Umland of a planned city: Chandigarh. In NGJI 16,1 (1970) 31-46.

22905 JAIN, K.S.S. Chandigarh - 1951-1964. In URPT 7 (1964) 86-109.

22906 JEANNERET-GRIS, C.É. [LE CORBUSIER] Chandigarh, the new capital of Punjab, India, 1951-. Tokyo: A.D.A. EDITA Tokyo, 1974. 63p. [Text in Japanese]

22907 MATHUR, B.P. Chandigarh and town planning. In RL 38 (1969) 267-75.

22908 MAYER, A. The new capital of the Punjab. In American Inst. of Architects J. 14 (1950) 166-75.

22909 SHARMA, S.R. Administrative set-up at Chandigarh. Una: Inst. of Public Admin., 1964. 99p.

e. Amritsar: sacred city of the Sikhs (1971 pop. 1,835,500)

22910 DATTA, V.N. Amritsar: past and present. Amritsar: Municipal Cmtee., 1967. 207p.

22911 FAUJA SINGH. The city of Amritsar: an introduction Patiala: Dept. of Punjab Hist. Studies, Punjabi U., 1977. 127p.

22912 ______., ed. The city of Amritsar: a study of historical, cultural, social, and economic aspects. ND: Oriental, 1978. 424p.

22913 JOHAR, S.S. The heritage of Amritsar. Delhi: Sundeep, 1978. 144p.

6. Social Welfare and Health Services

22914 DEB, P.C. Liquor in a green revolution setting. Delhi: Researchco, 1977. 96p.

22915 KIRKPATRICK, J. Primary and secondary institutions in the delivery of hospital services in South Asia: a case study and model. In J. of the Inst. of Bangladesh Studies 1,1 (1976) 169-90. [Ludhiana]

22916 ______. The sociology of an Indian hospital ward. Calcutta: KLM, 1979. 156p.

22917 PRASAD, RAJESHWAR. ACE: alcoholism, causes and effects; project report. Rajpura, Punjab: Kasturba

Rural Inst., 1968-. v. 1, 82p.

22918 SOHAN SINGH & J.E. GORDON & J.B. WYON. Medical care in fatal illnesses of a rural Punjab population: some social, biological and cultural factors and their ecological implication. In Indian J. of Medical Res. 50 (1962) 865-880.

7. Education
a. education in the British Punjab

22919 BRUCE, J.F. A brief history of the University of the Panjab. In JPUHS 2,2 (1933) 97-116.

22920 CHANDAVARKAR, G.A. The Dayanand Anglo-Vedic college, Lahore. In Hindustan R. 31 (1915) 516-21.

22921 GARRETT, H.L.O. & ABDUL HAMID. A history of Government College, Lahore, 1864-1964. Lahore: Govt. College, 1964. 309p.

22922 HARBANS SINGH. Beginning of modern Sikh education. In PPP 8,1 (1974) 127-44.

22923 KHALSA COLLEGE. A history of the Khalsa College, Amritsar, published on the occasion of its golden jubilee. Amritsar: G. Singh, 1949. 145p.

22924 LEITNER, G.W. History of indigenous education in the Punjab since annexation and in 1882. Calcutta: Supt. Govt. Printing, 1882. 179p.

22925 MATHUR, Y.B. Development of Western education in the Punjab 1849-75. In JIH 44,1 (1966) 223-53.

22926 MEHTA, H.R. A history of the growth and development of Western education in the Punjab, 1846-1884. Patiala: Languages Dept., Punjab, 1971. 96p.

22927 MIRZA, S.H., ed. The Punjab Muslim Students Federation: an annotated documentary survey, 1937-1947. Lahore: Res. Soc. of Pakistan, 1978. 555p. (Its pub., 53)

22928 PERRILL, J.P. Punjab orientalism: the Anjuman-i-Punjab and Punjab University, 1865-1888. Diss., U. of Missouri, 1976. 2 v., 712p. [UM 77-4946]

22929 PUNJAB. EDUC. DEPT. PUNJAB U. ENQUIRY CMTEE. Report. Lahore: Supt., Govt. Printing, Punjab, 1933. 387p.

22930 SHARMA, S.R. Mahatma Hansraj, maker of the modern Punjab. 2nd ed. Una, Punjab: Inst. of Public Admin., 1965. 171p. [1st ed. 1941, 291p.]

b. education in the Indian Punjab (literacy 40.8% in 1981)

22931 BHATNAGAR, G.S. Education and social change; a study in some rural communities in Panjab. Calcutta: Minerva, 1972. 150p.

22932 DI BONA, J. Gurus and graduates: the ruralization of higher education in the Punjab. In his (ed.) The context of education in Indian development. Durham, NC: DUPCSSA, 1972, 155-88. (Its monograph & occ. papers series, 13)

22933 MALIK, Y.K. & J.F. MARQUETTE. Changing social values of college students in the Punjab. In AS 14,9 (1974) 795-806.

22934 SETHI, R.R. & J.L. MEHTA. A history of the Panjab University, Chandigarh, 1947-1967. Chandigarh: Panjab U., 1968. 441p.

22935 SINGH, B.P. Educational progress and economic development in Punjab. Patiala: Punjab Econ. Res. Unit, Punjabi U., 1974. 144p.

c. education in the Pakistani Punjab

22936 LIESCH, J.R. Islamabad: profile of Pakistan's new university. In J. of Higher Educ. 39 (1968) 254-60.

22937 PUNJAB, PAKISTAN. BUREAU OF EDUC. Directory of colleges in Punjab. Lahore: The Bureau, 1973. 27p.

22938 USMANI, ABID HASAN. Census of colleges, high schools and middle schools of the Punjab Province, 1975-76. 3rd rev. ed. Lahore: Punjab Textbook Board, 1977. 194p.

22939 ______. Census of primary schools of the Punjab Province, 1975-76. Lahore: Punjab Textbook Board, 1977. 580p.

22940 WASIULLAH KHAN, M., ed. Teacher education. Lahore: Alumni Assoc. of Inst. of Educ. & Res., U. of the Panjab, 1967. 220p. (Seminar proceedings)

D. Religious Traditions of the Modern Punjab

1. General Studies

22941 GANDA SINGH, ed. The Singh Sabha and other socio-religious movements in the Punjab 1850-1925 [special issue]. In PPP 7,1 (1973) 1-279.

22942 GOSAL, G.S. Religious composition of Punjab's population changes, 1951-61. In EW 17,4 (1965) 119-24.

22943 WEBSTER, J.C.B., ed. Popular religion in the Punjab today. Delhi: ISPCK, 1974. 149p. [Christian Inst. of Sikh Studies Seminar, 1973]

2. Sikhism
a. general studies

22944 BARRIER, N.G. The Sikhs and their literature: a guide to books, tracts, and periodicals (1848-1919). Delhi: Manohar, 1970. 153p.

22945 DILGEER, H.S. The Akal Takht. Jullundur: Punjabi Book Co., 1980. 112p.

22946 GUR RATTAN PAL SINGH. The illustrated history of the Sikhs, 1947-78: containing chapters on PEPSU, AISSF, evolution of the demand for Sikh homeland, and the Princess Bamba collection. Chandigarh: Gur Rattan Pal Singh, 1979. 344p.

22947 KHUSHWANT SINGH. The Sikhs today; their religion, history, culture, customs and way of life. Rev. ed. Bombay: Orient Longmans, 1964. 133p.

22948 KOMMA. The Sikh situation in the Punjab. In PPP 13,2 (1978) 425-38. [1st pub. Fortnightly R. (Sept. 1923)]

22949 SINGH, I.P. Religion in Daleke, a Sikh village. In L.P. Vidyarthi, ed. Aspects of religion in Indian society... Meerut: Kedar Nath Ram Nath, 1961, 191-219.

b. the Akali movement for reformation of Gurdwaras, 1920-25

22950 GANDA SINGH, ed. Struggle for reform of Sikh shrines. Amritsar: Sikh Itihas Res. Board, 1965. 266p.

22951 The Gurdwara reform movement and the Sikh awakening. Jullunder: Desh Sewak Book Agency, 1922. 480p.

22952 KHAZAN SINGH. Warnings to the Panth. Ed. by Manjeet Singh. ND: Manjeet Singh, 1972. 1 v.

22953 MOHINDER SINGH. The Akali movement. Delhi: Macmillan, 1978. 245p.

22954 PEACE, M.L. S. Kartar Singh Jhabbar, the spearhead of the Akali movement. Jullundur: Peace and Rattan Kaur, 1968. 148p.

c. the Namdhari (Kuka) sect

22955 AHLUWALIA, M.M. Kukas, the freedom fighters of the Panjab. Bombay: Allied, 1965. 211p.

22956 FAUJA SINGH. Kuka movement, an important phase in Punjab's role in India's struggle for freedom. Delhi: Motilal, 1965. 235p.

22957 GANDA SINGH. Was the Kuka (Namdhari) movement a rebellion against the British government? In PPP 8,2 (1974) 325-41.

22958 GURMIT SINGH. Sant Khalsa. Sirsa: Usha Inst. of Religious Studies, 1978. 105p.

22959 MACLEOD, W.H. The Kukas: a millenarian sect of the Punjab. In G.A. Wood & P.S. O'Connor, eds. W.P. Morrell: a tribute. Dunedin: U. of Otago Press, 1973, 85-104.

d. the Nirankari sect and the conflict with the Akali orthodoxy

22960 BHATI, G.S. & C.L. GULATI. Baba Avtar Singh, his life and teachings. Delhi: Sant Nirankari Mandal, 1977. 229p. [Nirankari leader, 1899-1969]

22961 CHADHA, K.R. Nirankari Baba awakening the world. Delhi: Sant Nirankari Mandal, 1972. 111p.

22962 GARGI, B. Nirankari Baba. Delhi: Thomson Press, 1973. 172p.

22963 LABH SINGH. All the glory to master lord. Tr. from Punjabi by G.S. Bhatia. Delhi: Sant Nirankari Mandal, 1969. 104p.

22964 Sikhism and the Nirankari Movement. In PPP 13,2 (1978) 370-401.

22965 WEBSTER, J.C.B. The Nirankari Sikhs. Delhi: Macmillan, for Christian Inst. of Sikh Studies, 1979. 104p.

3. the Hindu tradition
a. the Arya Samaj in Punjab

22966 DUA, VEENA. Arya Samaj and Punjab politics. In EPW 5,43/44 (1970) 1787-90.

22967 ______. Social organisation of Arya Samaj: a study of two local Arya centres in Jullundur. In SB 19,1 (1970) 32-48.

22968 JONES, K.W. Arya Dharm: Hindu consciousness in nineteenth century Punjab. Berkeley: UCalP, 1976. 343p.

22969 ______. Ham Hindū Nahīn: Arya-Sikh relations, 1877-1905. In JAS 32,3 (1973) 457-76.

b. Swami Ram Tirth (1873-1906): modern Punjabi yogi

22970 ARORA, R.K. Swami Ram Tirath: his life and works. ND: Rajesh Pub., 1978. 128p.

22971 MAHESHWARI, H. The philosophy of Swami Rāma Tīrtha. Agra: S.L. Agarwala, 1969. 192p.

22972 PURAN SINGH. The story of Swami Rama, the poet monk of the Punjab. Ludhiana: Kalyani, 1974. 280p. + 16 pl.

22973 SHARMA, S.R. Swami Rama Tirtha. Bombay: BVB, 1961. 199p.

22974 SOOD, D.R. Swami Ram Tirth. ND: NBT, 1970. 119p.

4. Islam in modern Punjab

22975 CHURCHILL, E.D., JR. Muslim societies of the Punjab, 1860-90. In PPP 8,1 (1974) 69-91.

22976 EATON, R.M. The profile of popular Islam in the Pakistani Punjab. In JSAMES 2,1 (1978) 74-91.

22977 HARDY, P. Wahābis in the Panjab, 1876. In JRSP 1,2 (1964) 1-7.

22978 MAYER, A.C. Pir and Murshid: an aspect of religious leadership in West Pakistan. In Middle Eastern Studies 3 (1967) 160-69.

22979 SHACKLE, C. The pilgrimage and the extension of sacred geography in the poetry of Khwājā Ghulām Farīd. In Attar Singh, ed. Socio-cultural impact of Islam on India. Chandigarh: Panjab U., 1976. 197p.

4. Christianity and missionary activity in modern Punjab

22980 ANDREWS, C.F. Sadhu Sundar Singh; a personal memoir. London: Hodder & Stoughton, 1934. 255p.

22981 APPASAMY, A.J. Sundar Singh, a biography. Madras: CLS, 1966. 250p. [1st pub. 1948]

22982 BLONDEEL, E. A short history of the Catholic Diocese of Lahore. Lahore: 1977. 41p.

22983 CAMPBELL, E.Y. The Church in the Punjab: some aspects of its life and growth. In V.E.W. Hayward, ed. The church as Christian community. London: Lutterworth, 1966, 137-220.

22984 EWING, J.C.R. A prince of the church in India, being a record of the life of the Rev. Kali Charan Chatterjee, for forty-eight years a missionary at Hoshyarpur, Punjab, India. NY: F.H. Revell, 1918. 128p.

22985 GANDA SINGH. Christianity in the Punjab: a bibliographical survey. In PPP 1,2 (1957) 368-88.

22986 PARKER, R.J. Sadhu Sundar Singh, called of God. Madras: CLS, 1968. 121p. [Rpt. 1918 ed.]

22987 STOCK, F. & M. STOCK. People movements in the Punjab; with special reference to the United Presbyterian Church. South Pasadena, CA: Wm. Carey Library, 1974. 364p.

22988 SUNDAR SINGH, Sadhu. At the Master's feet. Tr. from Urdu by A. Parker. NY: F.H. Revell, 1922. 90p.

22989 ______. The cross is Heaven; the life and writings of Sadhu Sundar Singh. London: United Soc. for Christian Literature, 1956. 93p.

22990 WHITEHEAD, H. The mass movement towards Christianity in the Punjab. In Intl. R. of Missions 2 (1913) 442-53.

E. Literature and Media in Modern Punjab

1. Languages of Modern Punjab: Punjabi, Urdu, Siraiki

22991 CHAUDHRY, N.A. Development of Urdu as official language in the Punjab, 1849-1974. Lahore: Punjab Govt. Record Office, 1977. 444p.

22992 ROSSI, A.V. La posizione del "lahndi" e la situazione linguistica nel Panjab pakistan. In Annali dell' Istituto di Napoli 34 (1974) 347-65.

22993 SHACKLE, C. Language and cultural identity in the Pakistan Punjab. In Gopal Krishna, ed. Contributions to South Asian Studies 1. Delhi: OUP, 1979, 137-60.

22994 ______. Punjabi in Lahore. In MAS 4,3 (1970) 239-67.

22995 ______. Siraiki: a language movement in Pakistan. In MAS 11,3 (1977) 379-403.

2. Modern Punjabi literature in India and Pakistan
a. general studies

22996 AHLUWALIA, J.S. Punjabi literature in perspective: a Marxist approach. Ludhiana: Kalyani Pub., 1973. 174p.

22997 ______., ed. Tradition and experiment in modern Punjabi poetry. Ferozepore: Bawa Pub. House, 1960. 106p.

22998 ATTAR SINGH. Punjabi. In K.R. Srinivasa Iyengar, ed. Indian literature since independence. ND: Sahitya Akademi, 1973, 222-51.

22999 DULAI, S.S. Experimentalism and its impact on Punjabi literature. In JSAL 10,1 (1974) 145-66.

23000 ______. The political novel in Punjabi. In CAS 6 (1975) 43-74.

23001 GHULĀM FARĪDUDDĪN. Kafees. Tr. by Gilani Kameran & Aslam Ansarie. Multan: Bazm-e-Saqafat, dist. Ferozsons, 1969. 104p.

23002 HARBANS SINGH. Punjabi magazines. In IWT 3,4 (1969) 48-57.

23003 KOHLI, M.P. The influence of the West on Panjabi literature. Ambala City: Lyall Book Depot, Ludhiana, 1969. 258p.

23004 KHUSHWANT SINGH & JAYA THADANI, eds. Land of the five rivers. Bombay: Jaico Pub. House, 1965. 181p.

23005 MAINI, D.S. Studies in Punjabi poetry. ND: Vikas, 1979. 158p.

23006 PRITAM SINGH, comp. & tr. The voices of dissent: modern Punjabi poetry. Jullundur: Seema Prakashan, 1972. 93p.

23007 SHARMA, O.P. Shiv Batalvi, a solitary and passionate singer. ND: Sterling, 1979. 119p.

23008 SINGH, B.K. Reminiscences of Puran Singh. Patiala: Punjabi U., 1980. 78p.

23009 TASNEEM, N.S. Studies in modern Punjabi literature. ND: Avishkar, 1980. 163p.

23010 UPPAL, S.S. Panjabi short story; its origin and development. ND: Pushp Prakashan, 1966. 340p.

b. Bhai Vir Singh (1872-1957): poet and novelist of Sikh nationalism

23011 GANDA SINGH, ed. Bhai Vir Singh birth-centenary volume. In PPP 6,2 (1972) 239-489. [English and Panjabi]

23012 GULERIA, J.S., ed. Bhai Vir Singh: the sixth river of Punjab. ND: Guru Nanak Vidya Bhandar Trust, 1972. 132p.

23013 HARBANS SINGH. Bhai Vir Singh. ND: Sahitya Akademi, 1972. 102p.

23014 PARKASH SINGH. Continuing influence of Bhai Vir Singh. Amritsar: Singh Bros., 1972. 100p.

23015 RAJINDER SINGH, ed. Bhai Vir Singh, a critical appraisal. Patiala: Languages Dept., Panjab, 1973. 82p.

23016 VIR SINGH, Bhai. Bhai Vir Singh, poet of the Sikhs. Tr. by G.S. Talib & Harbans Singh. Delhi: Motilal, 1976. 155p. (UNESCO series)

23017 ______. Nargas, songs of a Sikh. Tr. by Puran Singh. London: J.M. Dent, 1924. 104p.

c. Amrita Pritam (1919-): poetess and novelist

23018 AMRITA PRITAM. The revenue stamp: an autobiography. Tr. by Krishna Gorowara. ND: Vikas, 1977. 130p.

23019 ______. Selected poems. Ed. by Pritish Nandy. Tr. by Khushwant Singh. Calcutta: Dialogue Calcutta Pub., 1970. 23p.

23020 Amrita Pritam number. In Mahfil 5,3 (1968-69) 1-134.

3. Hindi and Urdu Literature of the Punjab [See Hindi and Urdu Literature, Chap. Six, VIII. B. & C., and Chap. Eight, X. C. 2 & 3]

4. Folk Literature

23021 ANAND, M.R. Folk tales of Punjab. ND: Sterling, 1974. 112p.

23022 BEDI, S.S. Folklore of the Punjab. ND: NBT, 1971. 165p.

23023 MUKHERJI, K.K., tr. Rose-garden of the Punjab; English renderings from Punjabi folk poetry. Ed. by G.S. Talib. Patiala: Punjabi U., 1973. 114p.

23024 SAEED, AHMAD. Punjabi folk poetry. In Pakistan R. 13,11 (1965) 26-38.

23025 SETH, VEENA. The theme of separation in the folksongs of Punjab. In Folklore(C) 3 (1962) 41-47.

23026 STEEL, F.A., comp. Tales of the Punjab told by the people. London: Bodley Head, 1973. 310p. [Rpt. 1894]

23027 SWYNNERTON, C. Romantic tales from the Panjab. Lahore: Qausain, 1976. 483p. [Rpt. 1903 ed.]

23028 TEMPLE, R.C. The legends of the Punjab. Bombay: Educ. Soc. Press, 1884-1900. 3 v.

23029 VATUK, V.P. & S. VATUK. The lustful stepmother in the folklore of northwestern India. In JASL 11,1/2 (1975) 19-44.

5. Journalism and the Press in Modern Punjab

23030 BARRIER, N.G. & P. WALLACE. The Punjab press, 1880-1905. East Lansing: Res. Cmtee. on the Punjab & Asian Studies Center, Michigan State U., 1970. 201p.

23031 MALIK, I.A. Punjab Muslim press and the Muslim world, 1888-1911. Lahore: South Asian Inst., U. of the Punjab, 1974. 66p.

23032 ROTHERMUND, D. The Punjab press and non-cooperation in 1920. In his The phases of Indian nationalism and other essays. Bombay: Nachiketa, 1970, 93-104.

V. THE NORTHWEST FRONTIER PROVINCE (NWFP) AND TRIBAL AREAS SINCE THE MID-1800'S

A. General and Political History

1. General Histories of the Period

23033 CAROE, O.K. The Pathans 550 B.C.-A.D. 1957. Karachi: OUP, 1976. 521p. [1st pub. 1958]

23034 SPAIN, J.W. The Pathan borderland. The Hague: Mouton, 1963. 293p.

2. The British Raj after 1849: NWFP (est. 1901), Tribal Agencies, and Princely States
a. accounts by officials, soldiers, travellers

23035 ANNAND, A.M., ed. Cavalry surgeon: the recollections of John Henry Sylvester. London: Macmillan, 1971. 336p.

23036 CHURCHILL, WINSTON. Young Winston's wars; the original despatches of Winston S. Churchill, war correspondent, 1897-1900. Ed. by F. Woods. NY: Viking Press, 1973. 350p.

23037 DAVEY, C.J. A handbook of the North-West Frontier... Madras: Diocesan Press, 1942. 92p.

23038 ENRIQUEZ, C.M.D. The Pathan borderland...from Chitral to Dera Ismail Khan. Calcutta: Thacker, Spink, 1910. 141p.

23039 KEPPEL, A. Gun-running and the Indian North-West Frontier. Quetta: Gosha-e-Adab, 1977. [Rpt. 1911 ed.]

23040 NEVILL, H.L. Campaigns on the North-West Frontier. Lahore: Sang-e-Meel Publications, 1977. 413p. [1st pub. 1912]

23041 PENNELL, A.M. Pennell of the Afghan Frontier: the life of Theodore Leighton Pennell. Lahore: Sang-e-Meel Pub., 1972. 2 v. in 1. [1st pub. 1914]

23042 PENNELL, T.L. Among the wild tribes of the Afghan frontier. 2nd ed. Karachi: OUP, 1975. 323p. + 24 pl. [Rpt. 1909 ed.]

23043 ROBERTSON, G.S. Chitral, the story of a minor siege. Karachi: OUP, 1977. 368p. + 32 pl. [Rpt. 1898 ed.]

23044 SCHOMBERG, R.C.F. Kafirs and glaciers: travels in Chitral. London: Martin Hopkinson, 1938. 278p.

23045 THOMPSON, H.C. The Chitral campaign; a narrative of events in Chitral, Swat, and Bajour. London: Heinemann, 1895. 312p.

23046 THORBURN, S.S. Bannú; or our Afghan frontier. London: Trubner, 1876. 480p.

23047 YOUNGHUSBAND, F.E. & G.J. YOUNGHUSBAND. The relief of Chitral. London: Macmillan, 1895. 183p.

b. political studies of British rule

23048 ABDUL WADUD, Wali of Swat. The story of Swat as told by the founder Miangul Abdul Wadud Badshah Sahib to Muhammad Asif Khan. Tr. by Ashruf Altaf Husain. Peshawar: 1963. 143p.

23049 BARTON, W.P. India's north-west frontier. London: Murray, 1939. 308p.

23050 DAVIES, C.C. The problem of the North-west frontier, 1890-1908, with a survey of policy since 1849. 2nd ed., rev. and enl. London: Curzon Press, 1975. 220p. [1st ed. 1932]

23051 ELLIOTT, J.G. The frontier, 1839-1947: the story of the North-west frontier of India. London: Cassell, 1968. 306p.

23052 HOWELL, E.B. Mizh: a monograph on government's relations with the Mahsud tribe. Karachi: OUP, 1979. 119p. [1st pub. 1931]

23053 LAL BAHA. N.W.F.P. administration under British rule, 1901-1919. Islamabad: National Cmsn. on Hist. & Cultural Res., 1978. 297p.

23054 MEHRA, P., ed. North-Western Frontier and British India, 1839-42: being text of newsletters from the Foreign Department, Govt. of India.... Chandigarh: Panjab U., 1978-. [to be 2 v.]

23055 MILLER, C. Khyber, British India's northwest frontier: the story of an imperial migraine. NY: Macmillan, 1977. 393p. + 12 pl.

23056 OBHRAI, D.C. Evolution of NWFP, being a survey of the history and constitutional development. Peshawar: London Book Co., 1938. 362p.

23057 RITTENBERG, S. Continuities in borderland politics. In A.T. Embree, ed. Pakistan's western borderlands: the transformation of a political order. ND: Vikas, 1977, 67-84.

23058 SPAIN, J.W. Political problems of a borderland. In A.T. Embree, ed. Pakistan's western borderlands: the transformation of a political ofder. ND: Vikas, 1977, 1-23.

23059 SWINSON, A. North-west frontier; people and events, 1839-1947. London: Corgi, 1969. 413p. [1st pub. 1967]

c. Indian nationalism; Abdul Ghaffar Khan (1891-), "the Frontier Gandhi"

23060 AHMED, AKBAR S. Colonial encounter on the North-West Frontier Province; myth and mystification. In EPW 14,51/52 (1979) 2092-97.

23061 ANDREWS, C.F. The challenge of the north-west frontiers: a contribution to world peace. London: Allen & Unwin, 1937. 208p.

23062 GUPTA, A.K. North West Frontier Province: legislature and freedom struggle. ND: ICHR, dist. PPH, 1976. 239p.

23063 KHAN, ABDUL GHAFFAR, Khan. My life and struggle; autobiography of Badshah Khan as narrated to K.B. Narang. Tr. by H.H. Bouman. Delhi: Hind Pocket Books, 1969. 248p.

23064 NAIR, PYARELAL. A pilgrimage for peace. Gandhi and frontier Gandhi among NWF Pathans. Ahmadabad: Navajivan, 1950. 216p.

23065 ______. Thrown to the wolves: Abdul Ghaffar. Calcutta: Eastlight Book House, 1966. 164p.

23066 QAIYUM, ABDUL. Gold and guns on the Pathan frontier. Bombay: Hind Kitabs, 1945. 77p.

23067 TENDULKAR, D.G. Abdul Gaffar Khan: faith is a battle. Bombay: Popular, for Gandhi Peace Foundation, 1967. 540p.

23068 Unrest in the Peshawar District, 1930-1932. In J. of the Royal Central Asian Soc. 19 (1932) 624-42. [signed "H.R.S."]

23069 YUNUS, MOHAMMAD. Frontier speaks. 2nd ed. Bombay: Hind Kitabs, 1947. 204p.

23070 ZUTSHI, G.L. Frontier Gandhi; the fighter, the politician, the saint. Delhi: National, 1970. 167p.

3. NWFP and Centrally Administered Tribal Areas of Pakistan since 1947
a. general studies

23071 BERRY, W. Aspects of the Frontier Crimes Regulation in Pakistan. Durham, NC: DUPCSSA, 1966. 122p. (Its monograph & occ. papers series, 3)

23072 MIAN, NURUL-ISLAM. Municipal finance in the North-West Frontier region. Peshawar: Board of Econ. Enquiry, NW Frontier, Peshawar U., 1969. 53p. (Its pub., 43)

23073 RASHID, ABDUR. Civil service on the frontier. Peshawar: Khyber Printers, 1977. 215p. + 12 pl.

b. agitation for "Pakhtunistan/Pushtunistan," Pathan separatism supported by Afghanistan

23074 CARRÈRE D'ENCAUSSE, H. Les Pouchton au Pakistan. In Revue française de science politique 17 (1967) 760-69.

23075 CHOPRA, S. Afghan Pakistan relations: the Pakhtoonistan issue. In IJPS 35,4 (1974) 310-31.

23076 FRANCK, D.S. Pakhtunistan - disputed disposition of a tribal land. In Middle East J. 6 (1952) 49-68.

23077 POULLADA, L.B. Pushtunistan: Afghan domestic politics and relations with Pakistan. In A.T. Embree, ed. Pakistan's western borderlands.... ND: Vikas, 1977, 126-51.

23078 QURESHI, S.M.M. Pakhtunistan: the frontier dispute between Afghanistan and Pakistan. In PA 29 (1966) 99-114.

23079 SANKHDER, M.M. The Pakhtoon demand: fiction and reality. In Shakti 6,3 (1969) 68-74.

23080 SAYEED, KHALID BIN. Pathan regionalism. In South Atlantic Q. 63 (1964) 478-506.

B. The Economy of the Northwest Frontier

23081 AHMAD KHAN, M. Unemployment among the educated manpower in Northwest Frontier Province. Peshawar: Board of Economic Enquiry, NWFP, U. of Peshawar, 1972. 107p. (Its pub. 87)

23082 AHMED, AKBAR S. Social and economic change in the Tribal Areas, 1972-1976. Karachi: OUP, 1977. 81p.

23083 ASHRAF, KHALID. Some land problems in tribal areas of West Pakistan; a study of the selected farms in Kurram, North Waziristan, Malakand, Kalam, and Swat. Peshawar: Board of Econ. Enquiry, NWFP, Peshawar U., 1963. 191p.

23084 ______. Wool-weaving in Swat. Peshawar: Board of Econ. Enquiry, NWFP, Peshawar U., 1963. 54p.

23085 BERINGER, C. & ABDUL HADI. Land fragmentation and size of agricultural holdings in the former North-West Frontier Province of West Pakistan. Peshawar: Board of Econ. Enquiry, 1962. 47p.

23086 BERRIDGE, P.S.A. Couplings to the Khyber: the story of the North Western Railway. NY: Kelley, 1969. 320p.

23087 HUSSAIN, M. A socio-economic survey of village Baffa in the Hazara district. Peshawar: Board of Econ. Enquiry, NWFP, U. of Peshawar, 1958. 393p. (Its pub., 5)

23088 IBRAHIM BEG. M. Mechanization of agriculture in the North-West Frontier Province. Peshawar: Board of Econ. Enquiry, NWFP, U. of Peshawar, 1971. 195p. (Its pub., 65)

23089 JAVED, GHUFRANULLAH. Growth of financial institutions in NWFP. Peshawar: Board of Econ. Enquiry, NWFP, U. of Peshawar, 1972. 66p. (Its pub., 81)

23090 MIAN, NURUL-ISLAM. The agricultural economy of North-West Frontier. Peshawar: Board of Econ. Enquiry, NWFP, Peshawar U., 1970. 194p. (Its pub., 52)

23091 ______. Selected research papers on Pakistan economy with special reference to NWFP. Peshawar: Board of Econ. Enquiry, NWFP, U. of Peshawar, 1972. 230p. (Its pub., 90)

23092 MOHAMMAND, TILA. Price movements of agricultural commodities in Mardan, 1961-70. Peshawar: Board of Econ. Enquiry, NWFP, U. of Peshawar, 1972. 128p.

23093 PESHAWAR. UNIV. BOARD OF ECON. ENQUIRY. Causes, effects and remedies of poppy cultivation in Swabi-Gadoon area. Peshawar: The Board, 1978-79. 2v. (Its pub., 120)

23094 PESHAWAR. UNIV. DEPT. OF ECON. Resource base and economic progress of the Peshawar Valley. Peshawar: 1970. 284p.

23095 QURESHI, M. ANWAR A. Livestock industry in North-West Frontier Province. Peshawar: Board of Econ. Enquiry, NWFP, U. of Peshawar, 1971. 47p. (Its pub., 56)

C. Society and Social Change on the Northwest Frontier

1. Social Categories
a. general studies

23096 BARTH, F. Ecologic relationships of ethnic groups in Swat, North Pakistan. In AA 58 (1956) 1079-89.

23097 ______. Indus and Swat Kohistan: an ethnographic survey. In Studies honouring the centennial of Universitetets Ethnografiske Museum, Oslo, 1857-1957. Oslo: Forenede Trykkerier, 1956, v.2, 97p.

23098 HÖRHAGER, H. Die Volkstumsgrundlagen der indischen nordwest-grenzprovinz.... Deidelberg: K. Vowinckel, 1943. 130p.

23099 KHAN, GHULAM JILANI. Development of tribal areas. Peshawar: U. of Peshawar, Board of Econ. Enquiry, 1972. 152p.

23100 ROSE, H.A. A glossary of tribes and castes of Punjab and NW Province. Lahore: Govt. of India, 1911-1919.

23101 SCOTT, G.B. Afghan and Pathan: a sketch. London: Mitre Press, 1929. 188p.

23102 WESTPHAL-HELLBUSCH, S. Einige Nomadengruppen West-Pakistans in der Anpassung an die moderne Zeit. In Sociologus ns 12,2 (1962) 97-112.

b. the Pathans: Pushtu-speaking tribal group

23103 AHMAD, MAKHDUM TASADDUQ. Social organization of Yusufzai Swat; a study in social change. Lahore: Panjab U. Press, 1962. 94p.

23104 AHMED, AKBAR S. Millenium and charisma among Pathans: a critical essay in social anthropology. London: Routledge & Kegan Paul, 1976. 173p.

23105 ______. Pukhtun economy and society: traditional structure and economic development in a tribal society. London: Routledge & Kegan Paul, 1980. 406p. + 12pl.

23106 ASHRAF, KHALID. Tribal people of West Pakistan; a demographic study of a selected population. Peshawar: Board of Econ. Enquiry, NWFP, Peshawar U., 1962. 197p. (Its pub., 9)

23107 ANDERSON, J. Tribe and community among the Ghilzai Pashtun. In Anthropos 70,3/4 (1975) 575-601.

23108 BARTH, F. Political leadership among Swat Pathans. London: U. of London, Athlone Press, 1965. 143p. [1st pub. 1959]

23109 ______. Segmentary opposition and the theory of games: a study of Pathan organization. In JRAI 89,1 (1959) 5-22.

23110 ______. The system of social stratification in Swat, north Pakistan. In E.R. Leach, ed. Aspects of caste in South India, Ceylon, and northwest Pakistan. Cambridge: CamUP, 1960, 113-46.

23111 A dictionary of the Pathan tribes of the Northwest Frontier of India; prepared by the General Staff Army Headquarters, India. Calcutta: Supt. Govt. Printing, India, 1910. 262p.

23112 FAUTZ, B. Sozialstruktur und Bodennutzung in der Kulturlandschaft des Swat (Nordwesthimalaya). Giessen: W. Schmitz, 1963. 119p.

23113 GOODWIN, B. Life among the Pathans (Khattaks). London: 1969. 156p. [memoir of official in NWFP, 1930's]

23114 NEWMAN, R.E. Pathan tribal patterns; an interim study of authoritarian family process and structure. Ridgewood, NJ: Foreign Studies Inst., 1965. 111p.

23115 SPAIN, J.W. People of the Khyber; the Pathans of Pakistan. NY: Praeger, 1963. 190p.

c. Kafirs and other peoples of Chitral

23116 AFZAL KHAN, M. Chitral and Kafiristan: a personal study. Peshawar: Ferozsons, 1975. 101p.

23117 HUSSAM-UL-MULK, S. & J. STALEY. Houses in Chitral: tradition design and function. In Folklore(L) 79 (1968) 92-110.

23118 ISRAR-UD-DIN. Settlement pattern and house-types in Chitral State. In Pakistan Geog. R. 21,2 (1966) 21-38.

23119 PALWAL, A. RAZIQ. The Kafir status and hierarchy and their economic, military, political, and ritual foundations. Ph.D. diss., Pennsylvania State U., 1977. 338p. [UM 77-23, 264]

23120 QUENTRIC, N. Note sur les coutumes vestimentaires des Kalash du Pakistan. In O&M 13,2 (1973) 91-98.

23121 RAJPUT, A.B. Le monde perdu des Kalash (Kafiristan). In O&M 4,1 (1964) 3-28.

23122 ROBERTSON, G.S. The Kafirs of the Hindu Kush. Karachi: Civil & Military Press, 1974. 667p. [Rpt. 1896 ed.]

23123 SIDDIQI, M. IDRIS. Kafir gods and shrines. In Museums J. of Pakistan 17 (1965) 30-42.

2. Peshawar, capital of NWFP (1972 pop. 268,368)

23124 BEG, M. IBRAHIM. Low cost urban housing in the NWFP. Peshawar: Board of Econ. Enquiry, NWFP, Peshawar U., 1970. 82p.

23125 DANI, A.H. Peshawar: historic city of the frontier. Peshawar: Khyber Mail Press, 1969. 253p.

23126 PESHAWAR. UNIV. BOARD OF ECON. ENQUIRY. Factors influencing migration to urban areas in Pakistan: a case study of Peshawar city. Islamabad: PIDE, 1977. 92p.

23127 REGIONAL DEV. PLAN FOR PESHAWAR VALLEY. PROJECT OFFICE. Socio economic study of urban centres, Peshawar Division, Govt. of Pakistan. Karachi: 1969. 190p.

3. Education on the Northwest Frontier

23128 JANBAZ KHAN. Education, health, and social-welfare statistics of NWFP. Peshawar: Board of Econ. Enquiry, NWFP, U. of Peshawar, 1973. 133p. (Its pub., 93)

23129 MOEENUD-DIN, SYED. Employment pattern of Peshawar University graduates, 1965-61. Peshawar: Board of Econ. Enquiry, NWFP, U. of Peshawar, 1975. 84p. (Its pub., 102)

23130 QURASHI, SALMA MUSTAFA. Female education in the Peshawar District, West Pakistan. Peshawar: Board of Econ. Enquiry, NWFP, Peshawar U., 1960. 135p. (Its Pub., 7)

VI. THE KASHMIR REGION: THE UPPER INDUS VALLEY AND THE KARAKORAM MOUNTAINS

A. General and Political History since 1819

1. Ranjit Singh's Conquest of the Sultanate (1819) and Sikh Rule of Kashmir until 1846

23131 BAMZAI, P.N.K. Kashmir under the Sikhs, 1819-1846; an economic survey. In IJE 13 (1932) 35-58.

23132 PARMU, R.K. A history of Sikh rule in Kashmir, 1819-1846. Srinagar: Dept. of Educ., J&K Govt., 1977. 428p.

2. The Princely State of Jammu & Kashmir under the British Raj, 1846-1947
a. Gulab Singh (1792-1857): Dogra Maharaja of Jammu, and his conquest of Kashmir with British backing; his successors

23133 CHARAK, S.S. Indian conquest of the Himalayan territories: military exploits of General Zorawar Singh Dogra. Pathankot: Ajaya, 1978. 218p.

23134 DATTA, C.L. Ladakh and western Himalayan politics, 1819-1848; the Dogra conquest of Ladakh, Baltistan, and West Tibet, and reactions of other powers. ND: Munshiram, 1973. 239p.

23135 HUTTENBACK, R.A. Gulab Singh and the creation of the Dogra state of Jammu, Kashmir and Ladakh. In JAS 20 (1961) 477-88.

23136 ______. Kashmir as an imperial factor during the reign of Gulab Singh (1846-1857). In JAH 2,2 (1968) 77-108.

23137 INDIA. CMSN. OF ENQUIRY AGAINST MAHARAJA GULAB SINGH. Commission of enquiry against Maharaja Gulab Singh for his role in second Anglo-Sikh war. ND: Oriental, 1978. 183p. [Chiefly documents of 1850 enquiry]

23138 KIRPA RAM. Gulabnama of Diwan Kirpa Ram: a history of Maharaja Gulab Singh of Jammu and Kashmir. Tr. from Persian by S.S. Charak. ND: Light & Life, 1977. 462p.

23139 PANIKKAR, K.M. The founding of the Kashmir State; a biography of Maharajah Gulab Singh, 1782-1858. Mystic,

CT: Verry, 1964. 172p. [1st pub. 1930]

23140 SINGH, B.S. Gulab Singh of Jammu, Ladakh, and Kashmir, 1792-1846. Ph.D. diss. U. of Wisconsin, 1966. 311p. [UM 66-13, 450]

23141 ______. Raja Gulab Singh's role in the first Anglo-Sikh War. In MAS 5,1 (1971) 35-60.

b. accounts by officials and travellers

23142 CUNNINGHAM, A. Ladak, physical, statistical, and historical; with notices of the surrounding countries. ND: Sagar, 1970. 485p. [1st pub. 1854]

23143 DREW, F. The Jummoo and Kashmir territories: a a geographical account. Calcutta: K.P. Bagchi, 1971. 568p. [1st ed. 1875]

23144 DURAND, A. The making of a frontier: five years' experiences and adventures in Gilgit, Hunza, Nagar, Chitral, and the eastern Hindu-Kush. Karachi: Indus Pub., 1977. 298p. + 36pl. [1st pub. 1899]

23145 GANESHI LAL. Siyahat-i-Kashmir = Kashmir nama: or, Tarikh-i Kashmir: stage-wise account of journey from Ludhiana to Srinagar and return to Simla via Mandi.... Tr. by Vidya Sagar Suri. 2nd ed. Chandigarh: Punjab Itihas Prakashan, 1976. 66p. [1st pub. 1955]

23146 KEAY, J. The Gilgit game: the explorers of the western Himalayas, 1865-95. Hamden, CT: Archon Books, 1979. 277p. + 10pl,

23147 KNIGHT, E.F. Where three empires meet: a narrative of recent travel in Kashmir, Western Tibet, Gilgit and the adjoining countries. Karachi: Indus Pub., 1978. 158p. [1st pub. 1893]

23148 LAWRENCE, W.R. The valley of Kashmir. Srinagar: Kesar Pub., 1967. 478p. [1st pub. 1895]

23149 LEITNER, G.W. Results of a tour of Dardistan, Kashmir, Little Tibet, Ladak.... London: Trubner, 1868-73. 4v.

23150 NEVE, A. Thirty years in Kashmir. London: E. Arnold, 1913. 316p.

23151 ______. The tourist's guide to Kashmir, Ladakh, Skardo, etc. 16th ed. rev. by E.F. Neve. Lahore: Civil & Military Gazette Press, 1938. 200p. [1st pub. 188-]

23152 NEVE, E.F. A crusader in Kashmir, being the life of Dr. Arthur Neve, with an account of the medical missionary work of two brothers.... London: Seeley, Service, 1928. 218p.

23153 ______. Things seen in Kashmir.... London: Seeley, Service, 1931. 160p.

23154 TYNDALE-BISCOE, C.E. Kashmir in sunlight and shade; a description of the beauties of the country, the life, habits, and humour of its inhabitants and an account of the gradual but steady rebuilding of a once down-trodden people. ND: Sagar, 1971. 315p. [1st pub. 1922]

23155 YOUNGHUSBAND, F.E. Kashmir. Painted by E. Molyneux. ND: Sagar, 1970. 283p. [Rpt. 1909 ed.]

23156 ______. The northern frontier of Kashmir. Delhi: Oriental, 1973. 127p. [1st pub. 1890]

c. J&K relations with the Government of India, 1847-1947

23157 ALDER, G.J. British India's northern frontier, 1865-95: a study in imperial policy. London: Longmans for Royal Commonwealth Soc., 1963. 392p.

23158 GHOSE, D.K. Kashmir in transition, 1885-1893. Calcutta: World Press, 1975. 261p.

23159 HASSNAIN, F.M. British policy towards Kashmir (1846-1921) (Kashmir in Anglo-Russian politics). ND: Sterling, 1974. 148p.

23160 HUTTENBACK, R.A. The emasculation of a Princely State: the case of Kashmir. In JAH 7 (1973) 1-29.

23161 ______. The "Great Game" in the Pamirs and the Hindu-Kush: the British conquest of Hunza and Nagar. In MAS 9,1 (1975) 1-30.

23162 KAPUR, M.L. History of Jammu and Kashmir State. Jammu: Kashmir History Pub., 1980-. v.1-. [v.1, The Making of the State]

23163 ______. Kashmir sold and snatched. Jammu Tawi: the author, 1968. 180p.

d. nationalism and communalism; a Hindu Maharaja in a Muslim-majority state

23164 BAKSHI, G.M. Kashmir today through many eyes. Bombay: Bombay Provincial Congress Cmtee., 1946. 135p.

23165 BARJOR DAYAL. Jammu and Kashmir Assembly: first session. In Asiatic R. 31,105 (1935) 137-47.

23166 BAZAZ, P.N. The history of struggle for freedom in Kashmir: cultural and political, from the earliest times to the present day. Islamabad: Natl. Cmtee. for Birth Centenary Celebrations of Quaid-i-Azam Mohammad Ali Jinnah, Min. of Education, 1976. 774p. [Rpt. 1954 ed., New Delhi]

23167 ______. Inside Kashmir. Srinagar: Kashmir Pub., 1941. 412p.

23168 ______. Kashmiri Pandit agitation and its aftermath. ND: Pamposh, 1967. 40p.

23169 FAZILI, MANZOOR A. Socialist ideas and movements in Kashmir, 1919-1947. ND: Eureka Pub., 1980. 218p.

23170 Kashmir on trial: state vs. Sheikh Abdullah. Lahore: Lion Press, 1947. 224p.

23171 SARAF, M.Y. Kashmiris fight for freedom. Lahore: Ferozsons, 1977-. v.1, 708p.

23172 SETHI, R.R. Trial of Raja Lal Singh (the Lahore Minister). Patiala: Languages Dept., Punjab, 1971. 80p. [1st pub. 1932]

23173 TIKKU, S. Sheikh Abdulla, the saviour of Kashmir. Srinagar: Kashmir Mercantile Press, 194-. 141p.

3. Post-Independence Kashmir

a. the question of Maharaja Hari Singh's accession to India or Pakistan and the resulting conflict [see also Chap. Seven, IV. B. 2.]

23174 MENON, V.P. Jammu and Kashmir State. In his The story of the integration of the Indian States. NY: Macmillan, 1956, 390-514.

b. the Indian state of Jammu and Kashmir
i. special consitutional status and integration

23175 BHAGWAN SINGH. Political conspiracies of Kashmir. Rohtak: Light & Life, 1973. 158p.

23176 GAJENDRAGADKAR, P.B. Kashmir, retrospect and prospect. Bombay: U. of Bombay, 1967. 147p.

23177 JAMMU & KASHMIR. CONSTITUTION. The constitution. Jammu: Rambir Govt. Press, 1956. 71p.

23178 ______. Constitution of Jammu and Kashmir, including certain related provisions and rules and orders issued thereunder. Srinagar: Law Dept., 1970-1971. 2v.

23179 PURI, B.R. Jammu - a clue to Kashmir tangle. ND: 1966. 107p.

23180 SHARMA, B.R. Special position of Jammu and Kashmir in the Indian constitution. In IJPS 19 (1958) 282-90.

23181 TENG, K.M. & R.K.K. BHATT & S. KAUL. Kashmir: constitutional history and documents. ND: Light & Life, 1977. 689p.

23182 TENG, K.M. & S. KAUL. Kashmir's special status. Delhi: Oriental, 1975. 244p.

ii. Sheikh Mohammad Abdullah (1905-): charismatic leader of Kashmir since 1930

23183 ABDULLAH, MOHAMMAD, Sheikh. Interviews and speeches, after his release on 2nd January, 1968. Ed. by G.M. Shah. Srinagar: 1968. 2v., 79, 70p.

23184 BEG, MOHAMMAD AFZAL. Sheikh Abdullah defended. Srinagar: Jammu & Kashmir Legal Defence Cmtee., 1961. 347p.

23185 LOCKWOOD, D.E. Sheikh Abdullah and the politics of Kashmir. In AS 9,5 (1969) 382-96.

23186 PURI, B.R. & A.G. NOORANI. A debate on Sheikh Abdullah and Kashmir. Delhi: 1968. 50p.

23187 SHARMA, B.L. Kashmir awakes. Delhi: Vikas, 1971. 292p.

23188 The testament of Sheikh Abdullah. Dehra Dun: Palit & Palit; dist. Abhinav, 1974. 155p.

23189 VASHISHTH, S. Sheikh Abdullah, then and now. Delhi: Maulik Sahitya Prakashan, 1968. 234p.

iii. general studies of Kashmir government and politics since 1947

23190 BAZAZ, P.N. Democracy through intimidation and terror: the untold story of Kashmir politics. ND: Heritage, 1978. 222p.

23191 ______. Kashmir in crucible. ND: Pamposh Pub., 1967. 318p.

23192 HARI OM. Administration of justice in Jammu and Kashmir. ND: Light & Life, 1979. 241p.

23193 JAMMU & KASHMIR. Jammu and Kashmir, 1947-50: an account of the activities of the first three years of Sheikh Abdullah's government. Jammu: Ranbir Govt. Press, 1951. 191p.

23194 JAMMU & KASHMIR. CMSN. OF INQUIRY: JAMMU FIRING. Report. Srinagar: Govt. Press, 1967. 175p. [chm., B. Mukerji]

23195 JAMMU & KASHMIR. CMSN. OF INQUIRY TO INQUIRE INTO CERTAIN CHARGES OF MISCONDUCT AGAINST SHRI BAKHSHI GHULAM MOHAMMAD. Report. Srinagar: 1967. 1v.

23196 JOSHI, D.K. A new deal in Kashmir. ND: Ankur Pub. House, 1978. 178p.

23197 KAULA, P.N. & K.L. DHAR. Kashmir speaks. Delhi: S. Chand, 1950. 203p.

23198 KORBEL, JOSEF. The National Conference Administration, 1949-54. In Middle East J. 8,3 (1954) 287-94.

23199 LOCKWOOD, D.E. Challenge to Congress in Jammu and Kashmir. In SAR 3,2 (1970) 131-39.

23200 PARIHAR, R.R. Fourth general elections in Jammu and Kashmir. In PSR 6,3/4 & 7,1/2 (1967-68) 235-50.

23201 QURAISHI, Z.M. Elections and state politics of India: a case-study of Kashmir. Delhi: Sundeep, 1979. 256p.

23202 SARAF, M.R. Fifty years as a journalist. Jammu: Raj Mahal Pub., 1967. 183p.

c. "Azad Kashmir:" the Pakistan administered area of J&K

23203 BAZAZ, P.N. Azad Kashmir (Free Kashmir); a democratic socialist conception. Lahore: Ferozesons, 1950. 160p.

23204 HAFIZULLAH, M. Towards Azad Kashmir. Lahore: Bazam-i-Frogh-i-Adab, 1948. 170p.

23205 IBRAHIM KHAN, M., Sardar. The Kashmir saga. Lahore: Ripon Printing Press, 1965. 228p.

23206 KHALIFA, ABDUL MANNAN. Kashmir story. Lahore Cantt.: Abko Pub., 1970. 224p.

23207 SHARMA, P.N. Inside Pak-occupied Kashmir. ND: Delhi Press, n.d. 146p.

B. The Economy of the Kashmir Region

23208 AITCHISON, J.E.T. Handbook of the trade products of Leh; with statistics of the trade from 1867 to 1872. Calcutta: Wyman, 1874. 405p.

23209 ASBOE, W. Farmers and farming in Ladakh. In J. of the Royal Central Asian Soc. 34,2 (1947) 186-92.

23210 ASLAM, M. Land reforms in Jammu and Kashmir. In SocSci 6,4 (1977) 59-64.

23211 BARKER, A.F. The textile industries of Kashmir. In Royal Soc. of Arts J. 80 (1932) 309-26. [also pub. in Indian Textile J. 43,508 (1933)]

23212 BHAN, R.K. Economic potentialities of Kashmir. In Asiatic R. 35,123 (1939) 427-54.

23213 GANJU, M. Textile industries in Kashmir. Delhi: Premier, 1945. 252p.

23214 INDIA (REP.). CENSUS OF INDIA, 1971. Jammu and Kashmir: a portrait of population. Delhi: Cont. of Pub., 1974. 125p. + 14 pl.

23215 JAMMU & KASHMIR. JAMMU & KASHMIR CMSN. OF INQUIRY. Report, December 1968. Jammu: Ranbir Govt. Press, 1969. 142p. [Chm., P.B. Gajendragadkar]

23216 JAMMU & KASHMIR. PLANNING & DEV. DEPT. Fifth five-year plan, 1974-79. Srinagar: 1974. 308p.

23217 KAUL, S.N. Kashmir economics. Srinagar: Normal Press, 1954. 163p.

23218 LADAKH NATL. CONGRESS. The echo of Ladakh. Leh: Pleading Cmtee., Ladakh Natl. Congress, 1968. 51p.

23219 MUTHOO, M.K. Impact analysis of a renewable natural resource plan with reference to Kashmir. In AV 12,1/2 (1970) 270-99.

23220 NCAER. Techno-economic survey of Jammu and Kashmir. ND: 1969. 268p.

23221 NISAR ALI. Deteriorating agrarian situation in Jammu and Kashmir. In EE 71,24 (1978) 1227-73.

23222 RAHMAN, MAHFOOZUR. Co-operative credit and agricultural development: a study with reference to Jammu and Kashmir. Delhi: S. Chand, 1974. 216p.

23223 SHARMA, B.D. Problems and prospects of consumers cooperation in Jammu and Kashmir: a case study. In Cooperator's Bull. 15,21/22 (1972) 61-78.

23224 STALEY, J. Economy and society in the high mountains of Northern Pakistan. In MAS 3,3 (1969) 225-43.

C. Society and Social Change

23225 BAMZAI, A.K., Pandit. The Kashmiri pandit. Calcutta: Thacker, Spink, 1924. 105p.

23226 BINGLEY, A.H. & W.B. CUNNINGHAM. Introduction to the history and culture of the Dogras. Rev. and enl. by Sukhdev Singh Charak. Jammu: Ajaya, 1979. 194p. [1st pub. 1899 & 1932]

23227 ISENBERG, S.B. Srinagar's changing houseboats. In Cultural Forum 12,3/4 (1970) 91-96.

23228 JAMMU & KASHMIR. Report of the Committee constituted for examination of removal of defects in the Jammu and Kashmir scheduled castes and backward classes (reservation) rules, 1970, the Jammu and Kashmir scheduled castes and backward classes (reservation of appointment by promotion) rules, 1970, and the allied matters relating to backward classes. Srinagar: Govt. of J&K, 1977. 285p.

23229 JAMMU & KASHMIR. BACKWARD CLASSES CMTEE. Report. Srinagar: Govt. Press, 1969. 181p. [Chm., J.N. Wazir]

23230 JAMMU & KASHMIR. CMTEE. ON DEV. OF EDUC. IN THE STATE OF JAMMU & KASHMIR. Development of education in the State of Jammu and Kashmir: report. Srinagar: Govt. of J&K, 1973. 147p. [Chm., Bhagwan Sahay]

23231 JAMMU & KASHMIR. DIR. OF EDUC. All India Second Education Survey: Jammu & Kashmir State, ending December 1965. Srinagar: 1966. 87p.

23232 JAMMU & KASHMIR. EDUC. DEPT. Third All-India Educational Survey...school education: Jammu & Kashmir. Srinagar: 2975. 127p.

23233 KAK, B.L. Chasing shadows in Ladakh. ND: Light & Life, 1978. 151p.

23234 KHAN, GHULAM HASSAN. The Kashmiri Mussulman. Srinagar: Khan, 1973. 342 + 181p.

23235 KHAN, M. ISHAQ. History of Srinagar, 1846-1947: a study in socio-cultural change. Srinagar: Aamir Pub., 1978. 231p.

23236 KHATANA, R.P. Marriage and kinship among the Gujar Bakarwals of Jammu and Kashmir. In Imtiaz Ahmad, ed. Family, kinship and marriage among the Muslims in India. ND: Manohar, 1976, 83-126.

23237 KILAM, J.L. A history of Kashmiri pandits. Srinagar: Gandhi Mem. College, 1955. 340p.

23238 KOUL, S.C. Srinagar and its environs. 3rd ed. Srinagar: the author, 1962. 87p. [1st ed. 1946]

23239 MADAN, T.N. Family and kinship; a study of the pandits of rural Kashmir. Bombay: Asia, 1965. 259p.

23240 MODI, J.J. The pandits of Kashmir. In JAnthSB 10,6 (1913) 461-85.

23241 SANYAL, S. The boats and the boatmen of Kashmir. ND: Sagar, 1979. 115p. + 18 pl.

D. Religions of the Kashmir Region: Islam, Hinduism, Buddhism

23242 JAMMU & KASHMIR. CMTEE. OF ENQUIRY ON AMARNATH YATRA, 1970. Report. Srinagar: Govt. of J&K, 1970. 55p. [Chm., M.N. Kaul]

23243 MADAN, T.N. Religious ideology in a plural society: the Muslims and Hindus of Kashmir. In CIS ns 6 (1972) 106-41.

23244 MÜLLER-STELLRECHT, I. Feste in Dardistan: Darstellung und kulturgeschichtliche Analysen. Wiesbaden: Steiner, 1973. 354p.

23245 SUFI, GHULAM MUHIUDDIN. Islamic culture in Kashmir. ND: Light & Life, 1979. 393p.

23246 WALTER, H.A. Islam in Kashmir. In MW 4,4 (1914) 340-52.

E. Literatures of the Kashmir Area

1. Modern Kashmiri Literature

23247 KAUL, J.L. Kashmiri. In K.R. Srinivasa Iyengar, ed. Indian literature since independence. ND: Sahitya Akademi, 1973, 114-27.

23248 ______. Kashmiri literature (1962). In IL 6,2 (1963) 92-96.

23249 RAINA, A.N. Zinda Kaul. ND: Sahitya Akademi, 1974. 50p. [poet, 1884-1966]

23250 RAINA, T.N., tr. An anthology of modern Kashmiri verse, 1930-1960. Poona: Suresh Raina, 1972. 280p.

23251 TIKU, M.K. Problems of literary criticism in Kashmiri. In Humanist R. 2 (1970) 481-85.

2. Modern Dogri Literature of Jammu

23252 ALL INDIA DOGRI WRITERS CONF. Souvenir. ND: 1970-. [irregular]

23253 And quiet flows the stream. Jammu: Dogri Sanstha, 1966. 59p. [biographies of Dogri writers]

23254 SHARMA, N.D. An introduction to modern Dogri literature. Jammu: Jammu and Kashmir Academy of Art, Culture and Languages, 1965. 283p.

23255 SHIVANATH. Dogri. In K.R. Srinivasa Iyengar, ed. Indian literature since independence. ND: Sahitya Akademi, 1973, 27-41.

3. Hindi

23256 RAZDAN, PRITHVE NATH. Hindi in Kashmir; a survey. Srinagar: Mahanoor Pub., 1969. 372p.

4. Folk Literatures of Jammu, Kashmir, and Ladakh

23257 DHAR, S. Folklore of Kashmir. In Folklore(C) 2 (1961) 265-71.

23258 GRIERSON, G.A., ed. Hatim's tales; Kashmiri stories and songs. London: Murray, 1923. 86 + 527p.

23259 MEHTA, VEENA. Folk tales of Ladakh. Bombay: India Book House Educ. Trust, 1975. 84p.

23260 NARAIN, L. & S. CHAND. An introduction to Dogri folk literature and Pahari art. Jammu: Jammu and Kashmir Academy of Art, Culture and Languages, 1965. 170p.

23261 ROY CHOUDHURY, B. Folk tales of Kashmir. Delhi: Sterling, 1969. 118p. (Folk tales of India series, 2)

23262 SADHU, S.L. Folk tales from Kashmir. Bombay: Asia, 1962. 184p.

14

North India: The Populous Hindi-Speaking Ganga Plains, India's Political and Cultural Heartland, 1801–

I. HARYANA: HINDI-SPEAKING STATE CREATED FROM PUNJAB IN 1966 [see also Chap. THIRTEEN, IV. A.]

A. Government and Politics since 1966

1. General Studies

23263 CHAUDHRY, R.S. Genesis of the demand for Vishal Haryana. In J. of the Soc. for the Study of State Govt. 1,1/2 (1968) 13-20.

23264 HARYANA. DIR. OF PUBLIC RELATIONS. Haryana: diary of events: June 77 to June 78. Chandigarh: 1978. 32p.

23265 ______. One year of Janata government in Haryana. Chandigarh: 1978. 16p.

23266 LAL, M. Profile of a chief minister: a biography of Bansi Lal. Delhi: Vikas, 1975. 124p.

23267 RANBIR SINGH. Political developments in Haryana; a study of interaction between society and politics. In JHS 9,1/2 (1977) 63-70.

23268 YADAV, J.N. SINGH. The political scene in Haryana; a round-up. In his (ed.) Haryana; studies in history and politics. Gurgaon: Viros Prakashan, 1976, 143-99.

2. Election Studies

23269 AMANI, K.Z. Election in Haryana (India): a study in electoral geography. In Geographer 17 (1970) 27-39.

23270 JAIN, K. Impact of the defections in the mid-term elections in Haryana - an insight of voting behaviour. In IPSR 4 (1970) 233-44.

23271 SINHA, B.B. The fourth general election in Haryana. In PSR 6,3/4 & 7,1/2 (1967-68) 201-20.

3. Local Government and Politics

23272 PARTAP SINGH. Urban government in India: a study of grassroots institutions in Haryana. ND: Uppal, 1978. 157p.

23273 VISHNOO BHAGWAN. Municipal government and politics in Haryana: a study of Rohtak City. ND: S. Chand, 1974. 367p.

23274 YADAVA, J.S. Factionalism in a Haryana village. In AA 10 (1968) 898-910.

B. The Haryana Economy

1. Demography

23274a CHANDNA, R.C. Growth of rural population in Rohtak and Gurgaon districts (Haryana): 1951-61. In Panjab U. Res. Bull. 5,1 (1974) 75-89.

23275 HARYANA. DIR. OF HEALTH SERVICES. Demographic characteristics, Haryana state. Chandigarh: 1967. 113p.

2. Economic Development and Planning

23276 AGARWAL, K.K., ed. Karnal District, 1975. Karnal: N.K. Tandon, 1975. 301p. + 83 pl.

23277 BHAT, L.S., et al. Micro level planning: a case study of Karnal area, Haryana-India. ND: K.B. Pub., 1976. 137p.

23278 HARYANA. ECON. & STAT. ORG. Report on the estimates of gross capital formation in public sector in Haryana, 1970-71/1973-74. Chandigarh: 1978. 15p.

23279 HARYANA. PLANNING DEPT. Five year plan, 1978-83: draft proposals. Chandigarh: 1978. 501p.

23280 LAL, MUNI. Haryana; on high road to prosperity. ND: Vikas, 1974. 150p.

23281 NCAER. Techno-economic survey of Haryana. ND: 1970. 247p.

3. Agriculture in Haryana
a. general studies

23282 GUPTA, S.L. The cropping pattern of Haryana. In GRI 33,1 (1971) 23-55.

23283 HARYANA. ECON. & STAT. ORG. Cropping pattern in Haryana, 1950-51 to 1967-68. Chandigarh: 1970. 94p.

23284 ______. Evaluation study of the working of Agro-industries Corporation, Haryana, a state government public undertaking. Chandigarh: 1973. 56p. (Its pub., 132)

23285 ______. Evaluation report on the working of Small Farmers' Development Agency, Ambala. Chandigarh: 1978. 106p. (Its pub., 208)

23286 JAIN, P.C. Agricultural taxation in Haryana. Kurukshetra: Kurukshetra U., 1974. 205p.

23287 JASBIR SINGH. An agricultural geography of Haryana. Kurukshetra: Vishal Pub., 1976. 457p.

23288 MARKETING & ECON. RES. BUREAU. Economic impact of drought in Haryana; a survey. ND: 1971. 140p.

23289 SINGH, I.J. & A.C. GANGWAR & R. CHAKRAVARTY. Economics of milk production in Haryana State. Hissar: Dept. of Agri. Econ., Haryana Agri. U., 1979. 109p. (Its Res. bull., 4)

23290 SINGH, I.J. & K. CHOUDHRY. Economic analysis of potato production and marketing in Haryana. Hissar: Dept. of Econ., Haryana Agri. U., 1977. 68p. (Its Res. bull., 2)

23291 SINGH, I.J. & K. CHOUDHRY & R.C. GOEL. Dynamics of cotton production and marketing in Haryana. Hissar: Dept. of Agri. Econ., Haryana Agri. U., 1979. 92p. (Its Res. bull., 3)

b. land tenure and reform

23292 BHALLA, S. Changes in acreage and tenure structure of land holdings in Haryana, 1962-72. In EPW 12,13 (1977) A2-A15.

23293 RAM CHANDER. The systems of landholdings in Haryana: a cost-output analysis. Kurukshetra: Kurukshetra U., 1977. 115p.

4. Industry, Labor, and Commerce

23294 GUPTA, S.L. Faridabad: a study in industrial growth. In IGJ 42 (1967) 22-28.

23295 HARYANA. DEPT. OF INDUSTRIES. Report on industrial potentialities in Karnal District, Haryana. Chandigarh: 1969. 55p.

23296 HARYANA. DIR. OF INDUSTRIES. Directory of large and medium scale industries in Haryana. Chandigarh: 1968. 50p.

23297 HARYANA. ECON. & STAT. ORG. Employment trends and

manpower situation in Haryana. Chandigarh: 1969. 86p.

23298 HAZLEHURST, L.W. Entrepreneurship and the merchant castes in a Punjabi city. Durham, NC: DUPCSSA, 1966. 151p. (Its Monograph and occasional papers series, 1) [now in Haryana]

23299 PANINI, M.N. Networks and styles: individual entrepreneurs in Faridabad. In CIS ns 11,1 (1977) 91-115.

C. Society and Social Change

1. Social Categories; Kinship and Marriage

23300 MORRISON, C. Kinship in professional relations: a study of North Indian district lawyers. In CSSH 14,1 (1972) 100-25. [Ambala City]

23301 TIEMANN, G. Cattle herds and ancestral land among the Jat of Haryana in Northern India. In Anthropos 65,3/4 (1970) 480-504.

23302 YADAVA, J.S. Kinship groups in a Haryana village. In Ethnology 8 (1969) 494-502.

2. Villages and Rural Society; Urbanization

23303 BRAYNE, F.L. The remaking of village India; being the second ed. of Village uplift in India. London: OUP, 1929. 262p. [Gurgaon]

23304 ______. Socrates in an Indian village. 10th ed. London: OUP, 1954. 140p. [1st pub. 1931]

23305 DEY, S.K. Nilokheri. Bombay: Asia, 1962. 128p. [Karnal Dist.]

23306 MILLER, D.B. From hierarchy to stratification: changing patterns of social inequality in a north Indian village. Delhi: OUP, 1975. 229p.

23307 SINGH, I.P. & H.L. HARIT. Effects of urbanisation in a Delhi suburban village. In JSR 3 (1960) 38-43.

3. Health and Family Planning

23308 District health administration research project, 1969-1974: phase II, study-report, sponsored by NIHAE, WHO & UNICEF. ND: Natl. Inst. of Health Admin. & Educ., 1974. 151p. (Its Res. report, 24) [Rohtak Dist.]

23309 HARYANA. ECON. & STAT. ORG. Requirement and availability of medical and health personnel in Haryana, 1969-70. Chandigarh: 1970. 27p. (Its pub., 47)

23310 HENLEY, N.S. & S.C. JAIN. Family planning in Haryana: analysis of a state program in India. Chapel Hill: Carolina Population Center, U. of North Carolina, 1977. 181p.

23311 RAMACHANDRAN, L. Study on district health administration, Rohtak: a WHO/UNICEF assisted research project, conducted by the National Institute of Health Administration and Education, New Delhi, 1970-71. Gandhigram, Madurai Dist.: Gandhigram Inst. of Rural Health & Family Planning, 1980. 289p. (Its monograph, 9)

23312 SURJIT KAUR. Family planning in two industrial units: a study. ND: Sterling, 1976. 256p. [in Faridabad]

4. Education (Literacy 35.8% in 1981)

23313 Community effort in educational development. In Haryana R. 3,4 (1969) 39-41.

23314 GOEL, D.R. Students and school broadcasts. In Progress of Education 54,3 (1979) 50-58.

23315 RAJ SINGH & M.L. SHARMA. Impact of compulsory primary education legislation on the rural society of Haryana. In Education Q. 31,2 (1979) 23-25.

23316 SHANKER, U. & C.L. KUNDU. Education in Haryana; retrospect and prospect. Kurukshetra: Dept. of Educ., Kurukshetra U., 1971. 246p.

23317 YADAV, K.C. A brief history of the development of education in Haryana during the nineteenth century. In JHS 1,2 (1969) 7-20.

D. Literatures of Haryana: Hindi [see Chap. Six, VIII. B., & Chap. Eight, X. C. 2.] and Folk

23318 RANA, N.S. North Indian folklore: a research report. n.p.: 1975. 46p.

23319 ROY CHAUDHURY, I. & V. SRIVASTAVA. Folk tales of Haryana. ND: Sterling, 1974. 112p. (Folk tales of India series, 17)

II. DELHI, PERENNIAL SITE OF INDIA'S CAPITALS: FROM BRITISH DISTRICT TO UNION TERRITORY

A. General and Political History

1. The British Period, 1803 - 1947

23320 CHOPRA, P., ed. Who's who of Delhi freedom fighters. Delhi: Gazetteer Unit, Delhi Admin., 1974. 428p.

23321 FERRELL, D.W. Localization of national issues: non-cooperation and the Delhi municipal elections of 1922. In SA 5 (1975) 20-31.

23322 PANIKKAR, K.N. British diplomacy in north India; a study of the Delhi Residency, 1803-57. ND: Assoc. Pub. House, 1968. 200p.

23323 SANGAT SINGH. Freedom movement in Delhi, 1858-1919. ND: Associated Pub. House, 1972. 341p.

23324 SPEAR, T.G.P. The British administration of the Delhi territory, 1803-57. In JIH 19 (1940) 235-48.

2. Delhi Politics since 1947

23325 CHANDER, J.P. Delhi; a political study. Delhi: Metropolitan Book Co., 1969. 135p.

23326 DAYAL, J. & A. BOSE. Delhi under Emergency; for reasons of state. Delhi: Ess Ess, 1977. 239p.

23327 MEHTA, P. Election campaign: anatomy of mass influence. Delhi: National, 1975. 230p. [1971 study in South Delhi constituency]

23328 PARK, R.L. & GOPAL KRISHNA. Delhi. In S.V. Kogekar & R.L. Park, eds. Reports on the Indian general elections, 1951-52. Bombay: Popular Book Depot, 1956, 279-95.

23329 PURI, GEETA. Bharatiya Jana Sangh, organisation and ideology: Delhi, a case study. ND: Sterling, 1980. 292p.

23330 SAINI, M.K. & W. ANDERSEN. The Congress split in Delhi: the effect of factionalism on organizational performance and system level interactions. In AS 11,11 (1971) 1084-1100.

23331 SANKHDER, M.M. General elections in Delhi. In PSR 6,3/4 & 7,1/2 (1967-68) 152-68.

23332 SETHI, K. Second general elections in Delhi. In IJPS 19 (1958) 148-50.

3. Administrative Studies

23333 BHALLA, R.P. Electoral administration: Union Territory of Delhi. In IPSR 6,1 (1971-72) 1-28.

23334 ELDERSVELD, S.J. & V. JAGANNADHAM & A.P. BARNABAS. The citizen and the administrator in a developing democracy; an empirical study in Delhi State. ND: IIPA, 1968. 188p.

4. Local Government and Politics
a. Delhi and New Delhi

23335 CHANDIDAS, RAJ. Elections to Delhi Metropolitan Council: an analysis of electoral and ecological variables. In EPW 10,25/26 (1975) 964-73.

23336 DHARMENDRA. Municipal government of Delhi: a historical perspective. In QJLSGI 41 (1970) 177-88.

23337 JAGANNADHAM, V. & N.S. BAKSHI. Citizen and the municipal bureaucracy; a survey of the Building Department of the Delhi Municipal Corporation. ND: IIPA, 1971. 124p.

23338 NATH, D. The governmental set-up of Delhi: problems, views, and experiments. In IPSR 5,2 (1971) 135-58.

23339 OLDENBURG, P.K. Big city government in India; councilor, administrator, and citizen in Delhi. Tucson: U. of Arizona Press, for AAS, 1976. 400p. (AAS monograph, 31)

23340 PERSHAD, M., ed. The history of the Delhi municipality 1863-1921. Allahabad: Pioneer Press, 1921. 245p.

b. panchayati raj and village government in Delhi U.T.

23341 GANGRADE, K.D. Emerging patterns of leadership; comparative study of leadership and social structure. Delhi: Rachana, 1974. 263p.

23342 ______. Panchayat elections of 1959 & 1963. In MI 46,2 (1966) 135-53.

B. The Delhi Economy

1. Demography (1981 pop. 6,196,414)

23343 AGARWALA, S.N. A demographic study of six urbanising villages. Bombay: Asia, 1970. 195p.

23344 FREED, S.A. & R.S. FREED. The relationship of fertility and selected social factors in a north Indian village. In MI 51,4 (1971) 274-89.

23345 INDIA (REP.). CENSUS OF INDIA, 1971. A portrait of population, Delhi: Census of India, 1971, series 27. Delhi: Cont. of Pub., 1978. 61p.

2. Economic Development and Planning

23346 CHAUDHRY, M.D & B.F. HOSELITZ. State income of Delhi State 1951-52 and 1955-56. In EDCC 11,3 (1963) 1-126.

23347 DELHI (U.T.). BUREAU OF ECON. & STAT. Report on the family living conditions of the households in Delhi (Urban), 1971-72. Delhi: 1973. 36p.

23348 DELHI (U.T.). DIR. OF PUBLIC RELATIONS. Second five year plan of Delhi Union Territory. Delhi: 1957. 321p.

23349 ______. Two years of Delhi's second five year plan. Delhi: 1958. 48p.

23350 MATHUR, R.B. Spatial planning for development: a study of the Delhi region. Diss., U. of Minnesota, 1972. 253p. [UM 73-10,607]

3. Agriculture

23351 FREED, S.A. & R.S. FREED. Cattle in a north Indian village. In Ethnology 11,4 (1972) 399-408.

23352 JHA, DAYANATHA & PRADUMAN KUMAR. Effect of price changes on cost structure and factor demand: a case study on selected farms in Delhi Territory. In IJAE 31,3 (1976) 63-71.

23353 PURI, B.R. Land reforms in Delhi. In EW 11,10 (1959) 385-88.

23354 SINGH, U.S. & DAYANATHA JHA. A note on efficiency in transitional agriculture: a study of farms in rural Delhi. In IJAE 28,3 (1973) 61-65.

23355 SIROHI, A.S. & B.M. SHARMA. Maximization of returns through farm planning under fertilizer constraint in Alipur Block of the Union Territory of Delhi. In IJAE 33,2 (1978) 47-56.

4. Industry and Labor

23356 DHAR, P.N. Small-scale industries in Delhi: a study in investment, output and employment aspects. Bombay: Asia, 1958. 277p.

23357 INDIAN COUNCIL FOR CHILD WELFARE. Working children in urban Delhi: a study of their life and work: report submitted to the Dept. of Social Welfare, Govt. of India. ND: 1977. 173p.

23358 JOHRI, C.K. & S.M. PANDEY. Employment relationship in the building industry; a study in Delhi. ND: Shri Ram Centre for Industrial Relations and Human Resources, 1972. 208p.

23359 KUMAR, TEJ B. Fifty years of Delhi industry. In EE 58,4 (1972) 165-66.

23360 THAKUR, C.P. & F.C. MUNSON. Industrial relations in printing industry; a study in the context of technology and markets in Delhi area. ND: Shri Ram Centre for Industrial Relations, 1969. 152p.

23361 VAID, K.N. Growth and practice of trade unionism; an area study. Delhi: U. of Delhi, Delhi School of Social Work, 1962. 200p. (Studies in social work, 15)

C. Society and Social Change

1. Social Categories; Kinship and Marriage

23362 CHANNA, V.C. Caste, identity and continuity. Delhi: B.R., 1979. 180p. [Aggarwal community]

23363 FREED, S.A. Fictive kinship in a north India village. In Ethnology 2 (1963) 86-103.

23364 HOOJA, S.L. Dowry system in India; a case study. Delhi: Asia Press, 1969. 236p.

23365 INDIA (REP.). CMSN. OF INQUIRY INTO THE SADAR BAZAR DISTURBANCES. Report. ND: Govt. of India Press, 1974. 219p. [R. Prasad, one-man Cmsn.]

23366 KAPOOR, S. Family and kinship groups among the Khatris in Delhi. In SB 14 (1965) 54-63.

23367 RATAN, RAM. The changing religion of the Bhangis of Delhi: a case of Sanskritisation. In L.P. Vidyarthi, ed. Aspects of religion in Indian society.... Meerut: Kedar Nath Ram Nath, 1961, 172-90.

23368 RIZVI, S.M. AKRAM. Kinship and industry among the Muslim Karkhanedars in Delhi. In Imtiaz Ahmad, ed. Family, kinship, and marriage among the Muslims in India. ND: Manohar, 1976, 27-48.

2. Villages and Rural Society

23369 FREED, S.A. Caste ranking and the exchange of food and water in a north Indian village. In Anthropological Q. 43,1 (1970) 1-13.

23370 FREED, S.A. & R.S. FREED. Urbanization and family types in a north Indian village. In SWJA 25,4 (1969) 342-59.

23371 ______. Shanti Nagar: the effects of urbanization in a village in north India. NY: American Museum of Natural History, 1976-78. 2 v., 254, 152p.

23372 LEWIS, O. Group dynamics in a north-Indian village, a study of factions. ND: Program Eval. Org., Planning Cmsn., 1954. 48p.

23373 ______. Village life in northern India; studies in a Delhi village. NY: Vintage Books, 1965. 384p. [1st pub. 1958]

23374 MANN, R.S. Social structure, social change, and future trends: Indian village perspective. Jaipur: Rawat, 1979. 264p.

23375 MOULIK, T.K. From subsistence to affluence: socio-psychological aspects of developmental change in Delhi villages. Bombay: Popular, 1975. 180p.

23376 PANDEY, S.M. & J.S. SODHI. Developing the rural poor; a study of Marginal Farmers and Agricultural Labourers Development Agency in Delhi. ND: Shri Ram Centre for Industrial Relations & Human Resources, 1977. 192p.

23377 PAREEK, U. & T.K. MOULIK. Sociometric study of a north Indian village. In Intl. J. of Sociometry & Sociatry 3 (1963) 6-17.

23378 RAO, M.S.A. Urbanization and social change; a study of a rural community on a metropolitan fringe. ND: Orient Longmans, 1970. 254p.

3. Urbanization and Urban Problems: Delhi Urban Area (1981 pop. 5,227,730)

a. historical studies

23379 All about Delhi; an exhaustive handbook. Madras: G.A. Natesan, 1911. 264p.

23380 AZIZ, A. Origin and growth of Delhi. In Geographer 14 (1967) 101-18.

23381 BHATIA, S.S. Historical geography of Delhi. In Indian Geographer 1 (Aug. 1956) 17-43.

23382 BHATTACHARYA, V.R. The saga of Delhi. ND: Metropolitan, 1977. 156p.

23383 GUPTA, N. Military security and urban development: a case study of Delhi 1857-1912. In MAS 5,1 (1971) 61-78.

23384 HEARN, G.R. The seven cities of Delhi. Delhi: Ram Nath, 1974. 319p. [Rpt. 1906 ed.]

23385 SHARP, H. Historic Delhi. ND: Asian Pub., 1980. 148p. + 12pl. [Rpt. 1921 ed.]

b. urbanization and social change

23386 BOPEGAMAGE, A. Delhi: a study in urban sociology. Bombay: U. of Bombay, 1957. 235p. (Its Sociology ser., 7)

23387 ______. Neighborhood relations in Indian cities - Delhi. In SB 6 (1957) 34-42.

23388 DESHMUKH, M.B. Delhi: a study of floating migration. In UNESCO research centre on the social implications of industrialization in southern Asia. The social implications of industrialization and urbanization; five studies of urban populations of recent rural origin in cities of southern Asia. Calcutta: 1956, 143-225.

23389 GHOSH, B.R. Changes in the size and composition of the household brought about by urbanization in Delhi area. In G. Kurian, ed. The family in India: a regional view. The Hague: Mouton, 1974, 249-261.

23390 GORE, M. The impact of industrialization and urbanization in the Aggarwal family in Delhi area. Ph.D. diss., Columbia U., 1961. 472p.

23391 ______. Urbanization and family change. Bombay: Popular, 1968. 273p. [on Aggarwals]

23392 MITRA, A. Delhi: capital city. ND: Thomson Press, 1970. 129p.

23393 NANGIA, S. Delhi metropolitan region; a study in settlement geography. ND: K.B. Pub., 1976. 209p.

23394 RAO, V.K.R.V. & P.B. DESAI. Greater Delhi; a study in urbanisation, 1940-1957. Bombay: Asia, 1965. 479p.

23395 SINGH, A.M. Neighbourhood and social networks in urban India. ND: Marwah, 1976. 230p. [S. Indian migrants in Delhi]

23396 ______. South Indian voluntary associations in Delhi: an historical perspective. In SocAct 25,2 (1975) 101-13.

23397 TRIVEDI, H.R. Housing and community in old Delhi: the katra form of urban settlements. Delhi: Atma Ram, 1980. 120p.

c. urban problems

23398 BHARAT SEVAK SAMAJ. DELHI PRADESH. Slums of Old Delhi. Report of the socio-economic survey of the slum dwellers of Old Delhi City. Delhi: Atma Ram, 1958. 238p.

23399 GORE, M.S. Beggar problem in metropolitan Delhi. Delhi: Delhi School of Social Work, 1959. 320p.

23400 GUPTA, D.B. & G.A. BOSE. Housing Delhi's millions: a study of the rent structure, 1958-73. ND: Govt. of India, Natl. Buildings Organisation and UN Regional Housing Centre, ESCAP, 1978. 76p.

23401 INDIA (REP.). FACT FINDING CMTEE.: SLUM CLEARANCE, DEMOLITIONS, ETC. & FIRING IN TURKMAN GATE DURING THE EMERGENCY. Report. ND: Min. of Home Affairs, 1977. 426p.

23402 JAGMOHAN. Island of truth. ND: Vikas, 1978. 208p. [resettlement of squatters]

23403 MAJUMDAR, P.S. & I. MAJUMDAR. Rural migrants in an urban setting: a study of two shanty colonies in the capital city of India. Delhi: Hindustan Pub. Corp., 1978. 176p.

23404 MAJUMDAR, T.K. The urban poor and social change: a study of squatter settlements in Delhi. In SocAct 27, 3 (1977) 216-40.

23405 MISHRA, V.M. Communication and modernization in urban slums. NY: 1972. 128p.

23406 MISRA, G.K. & K.S.R.N. SARMA. Distribution and differential location of public utilities in urban Delhi. ND: Centre for Urban Studies, Indian Inst. of Public Admin, 1979. 456p.

23407 PAYNE, G.K. A case study of Delhi. In his Urban housing in the third world. London: Leonard Hill, 1977, 85-184.

23408 RAO, D.V.R. Re-housing of squatters: a case study of Delhi. In URPT 15,4 (1972) 1-47.

23409 RAO, M.S.V., et al. Transportation studies for metropolitan city centre of Delhi. In URPT 16,4 (1973) 187-233.

23410 SINGH, A.M. Women and the family: coping with poverty in the bastis of Delhi. In SocAct 27,3 (1977) 241-69.

23411 YADAV, C.S. Land use in big cities: a study of Delhi. Delhi: Inter-India, 1979. 272p.

d. urban planning and development

23412 ANAND, M. Master plan for Delhi. In Ekistics 2 (1961) 361-72.

23413 CULLEN, G. The ninth Delhi. ND: Min. of Health, Town Planning Org., 1961. 72p.

23414 DELHI. DEV. AUTHORITY. Master plan for Delhi. Delhi: 1957. 108p.

23415 DELHI, MUNICIPAL CORP. DEPT. OF URBAN COMMUNITY DEV. Evaluation study of the formation and working of the Vikas Mandals (Agency for Urban Community Development). Delhi: 1962. 46p.

23416 DOTSON, A. The Delhi Corporation: posers and prospects. In QJLSGI 24,1 (1958) 99-207.

23417 FERNANDES, B.G. National capital and the surrounding towns: problems and prospects. In J. of the Inst. of Town Planners 58 (1969) 62-68.

23418 GHOSH, B. & R. SABIKHI. City without a centre: New Delhi. In Civic Affairs 11 (1964) 23-31.

23419 HOWLAND, M. Delhi's large-scale land acquisition, development and disposal policy: an appraisal. In URPT 18,1 (1975) 23-52.

23420 JAGMOHAN. Rebuilding Shahjahanabad, the walled city of Delhi. Delhi: Vikas, 1975. 144p.

23421 PATWANT SINGH. The ninth Delhi. In Royal Soc. of Arts J. 119,5179 (1971) 461-475.

23422 RAHEJA, B.D. Delhi master plan. In QJLSGI 34,4 (1964) 475-97.

23423 RAO, D.V.R. & H.P. BAHRI. An urban renewal study of Motia Khan, Delhi. In URPT 15,4 (1972) 48-92.

4. Health Services and Family Planning

23424 AGARWALA, S.N. Fertility control through contraception; a study of family planning clinics of Metropolitan Delhi. ND: Dir. Genl. of Health Services, Min. of Health, 1962. 85p.

23425 BANERJEE, A.K. Health insurance in urban India; a preliminary study. In IJPH 13,1 (1969) 16-24.

23426 BANERJEE, U. Health administration in a metropolis. ND: Abhinav, 1976. 256p.

23427 DUBEY, D.C. Adoption of a new contraceptive in urban India. ND: Central Family Planning Inst., 1969. 132p. (Its monograph series, 6)

23428 FREED, S.A. & R.S. FREED. Shanti Nagar: the effect of urbanization in a village in north India; pt. 3 sickness and health. In Anthro. Papers of the American Museum of Natural History 55,5 (1979) 285-353.

23429 ______. Spirit possession as illness in a North Indian village. In Ethnology 3 (1964) 152-71.

23430 JEFFERY, ROGER. Estimates of doctors in Delhi: a

note. In EPW 12,5 (1977) 132-35.

23431 MADAN, T.N. Doctors and society: three Asian case studies: India, Malaysia, Sri Lanka. ND: Vikas, 1980. 311p.

23432 MANN, R.S. Concepts of disease and change in a Delhi village. In IJSW 27 (1967) 353-60.

23433 SANDHU, S.K. & K.S. BHARDWAJ. Study of sterilization units in the Union Territory of Delhi. ND: Central Family Planning Inst., 1970. 44p. (Its Monograph series, 13)

5. Education (61.06% literacy in 1981)

23434 DELHI UNIV. Report of the committee on the re-organization of legal education in the University of Delhi. Delhi: 1964. 73p. (chm., P.B. Gajendragadkar)

23435 INDIA (REP.). PARLIAMENT. JOINT CMTEE. ON THE DELHI SECONDARY EDUC. BILL, 1964. Report, 1st April 1966. ND: Lok Sabha Secretariat, 1966. 69p.

23436 KHUSRO, A.M. A survey of living and working conditions of students of the University of Delhi. Bombay: Asia, 1967. 183p.

23437 OOMMEN, T.K. Student politics in India: the case of Delhi University. In AS 14,9 (1974) 777-94.

23438 SHARMA, K.D. Education of a national minority: a case of Indian Muslims. ND: Kalamkar Prakashan, 1978. 263p.

23439 A study in campus designs: national competition for the master plan of Jawaharlal Nehru University Campus, New Delhi. ND: JNU, 1974. 271p.

23440 WHITE, C.M. A survey of the University of Delhi Library. Delhi: Planning Unit, U. of Delhi, 1965. 184p.

III. UTTAR PRADESH: THE GANGA-YAMUNA DOAB AND THE PLAINS OF ROHILKHAND AND AWADH/OUDH

A. General and Political History since 1801

1. The Nawabs of Oudh from 1801 to Company Annexation in 1856 [for 1857 "Mutiny", see Chap. Six, III. A. 2]

23441 BHATNAGAR, G.D. Awadh under Wajid Ali Shah. Varanasi: Bharatiya Vidya Prakashan, 1968. 270p.

23442 EDWARDES, M. The orchid house; splendours and miseries of the kingdom of Oudh, 1827-1857. London: Cassell, 1960. 216p.

23443 KNIGHTON, W. The private life of an eastern king, by a member of the household of His late Majesty, Nussir-u-Deen, king of Oude. NY: J.S. Redfield, 1856. 246p.

23444 MARSHALL, P.J. Economic and political expansion: the case of Oudh. In MAS 9,4 (1975) 465-482.

23445 MASIH UDDIN KHAN, M. British aggression in Avadh; being the treatise of M. Mohammad Masih Uddin Khan Bahadur entitled, Oude, its princes, and its government vindicated. Ed. by Safi Ahmad. Meerut: Meenakshi, 1969. 179p. [1st pub. 1857]

23446 PEMBLE, J. The raj, the Indian mutiny, and the Kingdom of Oudh, 1801-1859. Rutherford, NJ: Fairleigh Dickenson U. Press, 1977. 303p.

23447 SAFI AHMAD. Two kings of Awadh: Muhammad Ali Shah and Amjad Ali Shah, 1837-1847. Aligarh: P.C. Dwadash Shreni, 1971. 224p.

2. Rohilkhand: Ceded to the Company by Oudh in 1801

23448 BRENNAN, L. Social change in Rohilkhand: 1801-1833. In IESHR 7,4 (1970) 443-65.

23449 BRODKIN, E.I. British India and the abuses of power: Rohilkhand under early company rule. In IESHR 10,2 (1973) 129-56.

3. British Rule: the United Provinces of Agra and Oudh (formerly North-Western Provinces and Oudh)

a. accounts by officials and travellers

23450 GROWSE, F.S. Mathura; a district memoir. Ahmedabad: New Order Book Co., 1978. 434p. [Rpt. of 1883 ed.]

23451 IRWIN, H.C. The garden of India; or Chapters on Oudh history and affairs. Lucknow: Pustak Kendra, 1973. 2v. [Rpt. 1880 ed.]

23452 RAIKES, C. Notes on the North-western Provinces of India. London: Chapman & Hall, 1852. 270p.

23453 REEVES, P.D., ed. Sleeman in Oudh: an abridgement of W.H. Sleeman's a Journey through the Kingdom of Oude in 1849-50. Cambridge: CamUP, 1971. 330p.

23454 SLEEMAN, W.H. Rambles and recollections of an Indian official. Rev. ed. by V.A. Smith. Karachi: OUP, 1973. 667p.

23455 VEERASWAMY, E. Enugula Veeraswamy's journal (Kasiyatra charitra). Comp. by K. Srinivasa. Tr. by P. Sitapati & V. Purushottam. Hyderabad: Andhra Pradesh Govt. Oriental Manuscripts Library & Res. Inst., State Archives, 1973. 250p.

b. British administration

23456 AWASTHI, D. Administrative history of modern India: Sir Spencer Harcourt Butler's ideas, policies, and activities in the United Provinces of Agra and Awadh, 1918-1922. Delhi: National, 1973. 168p.

23457 ______. The dawn of modern administration (Thomasonian era, 1843-53). ND: S. Chand, 1972. 278p. [James Thomason, 1804-53, Lt.-Gov., NW Prov.]

23458 ______. Sir Spencer Harcourt Butler and his "Eastern Oxford." In JASP 10 (June 1965) 159-66. ["architect" of modern Lucknow]

23459 CHAND, T.P. The administration of Avadh, 1858-1877. Varanasi: Vishwavidyalaya Prakashan, 1971. 283p.

23460 COHN, B.S. The British in Benares: a nineteenth century colonial society. In CSSH 4 (1962) 169-99.

23461 ______. Some notes on law and change ... in North India. In EDCC 8 (1959-60) 79-93.

23462 FOX, R.G. Kin, clan, raja and rule; state-hinterland relations in preindustrial India. Berkeley: UCalP, 1971. 187p.

23463 ROBINSON, F.C.R. Consultation and control: the United Provinces government and its allies 1960-1906. In MAS 5,4 (Oct. 1971) 313-336.

23464 SRIVASTAVA, D.B. The Province of Agra, its history and administration. 2nd rev. ed. ND: Concept, 1979. 307p. [1st pub. 1957]

23465 TEMPLE, R. James Thomason. Oxford: Clarendon Press, 1893. 215p. (Rulers of India) [Lt. Gov., NW Prov.]

23466 WHISH, C.W. A district office in northern India with suggestions on administration. Calcutta: Thacker, Spink, 1892. 352p.

c. Indian nationalism and U.P. provincial politics, to 1947

23467 BAYLY, C.A. Patrons and politics in northern India. In J. Gallagher & G. Johnson & Anil Seal, eds. Locality, province, and nation.... Cambridge: CamUP, 1973, 29-68. [Rpt. from MAS 7,3 (1973) 349-88]

23468 BHARGAVA, M.L. First martyr to constitutional freedom: Pandit Ajudhianath. Allahabad: Rajesh Pub., 1978. 160p.

23469 BRENNAN, L. The local face of nationalism: Congress politics in Rohilkhand in the 1920's. In SA 5 (1975) 9-19.

23470 CHOPRA, P.N. Rafi Ahmad Kidwai; his life and work. Agra: S.L. Agarwala, 1960. 224p. [Congress Nationalist Muslim leader]

23471 GOULD, H.A. The emergence of modern Indian politics: political development in Faizabad (part 1: 1884-1935 and part 2: 1935-independence). In JCPS 12,1 & 2 (1974) 20-41, 157-88.

23472 HEITLER, R. The Varanasi House Tax Hartal of 1810-1811. In IESHR 9,3 (1972) 239-257.

23473 HILL, J.L. Congress and representative institutions in the United Provinces, 1886. Unpub. Ph.D. diss. Duke U., 1967. [UM 68-2725]

23474 JAIN, A.P. Rafi Ahmad Kidwai; a memoir of his life and times. NY: Asia, 1965. 130p.

23475 LOVE, D.E. Rebellion in southern Oudh, 1857-8. In BPP 91,1 (1972) 31-46.

23476 LÜTT, J. Hindu-Nationalismus in Uttar Pradeś, 1867-1900. Stuttgart: Klett, 1970. 171p.

23477 MASALDAN, P.N. The evolution of provincial autonomy in India 1858-1950, with special reference to Uttar Pradesh. Bombay: Hind Kitabs, 1953. 215p.

23478 PANDEY, G. The ascendancy of the Congress in Uttar Pradesh, 1962-34: a study in imperfect mobilization. Delhi: OUP, 1978. 245p.

23479 ______. Mobilization in a mass movement: Congress "propaganda" in the United Provinces (India), 1930-34. In MAS 9,2 (1975) 205-26.

23480 REEVES, P.D. Changing patterns of political alignment in the general elections to the U.P. Legislative Assembly, 1937 and 1946. In MAS 5,2 (1971) 111-142.

23481 ______. Landlords and party politics in the United Provinces, 1934-7. In D.A. Low, ed. Soundings in modern South Asian history. London: Weidenfeld & Nicholson, 1968. 261-93.

23482 ______. The politics of order. "Anti-noncooperation" in the United Provinces, 1921. In JAS 25,2 (1966) 261-74.

23483 REEVES, P.D. & B.D. GRAHAM & J.M. GOODMAN. A handbook on elections in Uttar Pradesh, 1920-1951. Delhi: Manohar, 1975. 504p.

23484 VERMA, G.L. Hindi journalism and the socio-political awakening in the North West Province and Oudh in the last three decades of the 19th century. In JIH 52,2/3 (1974) 377-87.

23485 ______. Party politics in U.P., 1901-1920. Delhi: Sundeep Prakashan, 1978. 296p.

d. the growth of Muslim separatism in U.P. [see also Chap. Six, III. D. 2]

23486 BRASS, P.R. Muslim separatism in United Provinces: social context and political strategy before partition. In EPW 5,3/4 (1970) 167-86.

23487 DITTMER, K. Die indischen Muslims und die Hindi-Urdu Kontroverse in den United Provinces. Wiesbaden: Harassowitz, 1972. 272p. (SSI,12)

23488 ROBINSON, F. Municipal government and Muslim separatism in the United Provinces 1883 to 1916. In J. Gallagher & G. Johnson & Anil Seal, eds. Locality, province, and nation.... Cambridge: CamUP, 1973, 69-121. [Rpt. from MAS 7,3 (1973) 389-441]

23489 ______. Separatism among Indian Muslims: the politics of the United Provinces' Muslims, 1860-1923. London: CamUP, 1974. 469p.

23490 YANUCK, M. The Kanpur Mosque affair of 1913. In MW 64 (1974) 307-21.

4. Uttar Pradesh Government and Politics Since 1947

a. general studies of politics

23491 AHMED, BASHIRUDDIN. Power patterns in Uttar Pradesh. In Seminar 95 (1967) 42-49. [Rpt. in Context of electoral changes in India; general elections, 1967. Bombay: Academic Books, 1969, 169-85]

23492 BRASS, P.R. Factional politics in an Indian state; the Congress Party in Uttar Pradesh. Berkeley: UCalP, 1965. 262p.

23493 ______. Uttar Pradesh. In M. Weiner, ed. State politics in India. Princeton: PUP, 1968, 61-124.

23494 BURGER, A.S. Opposition in a dominant-party system; a study of the Jan Sangh, the Praja Socialist Party, and the Socialist Party in Uttar Pradesh, India. Canberra: ANU Press, 1969. 306p.

23495 GUPTA, C.B. A collection of speeches. Lucknow: Info. Dept., U.P., 1963. 74p.

23496 KRIPALANI, S. Sucheta: an unfinished autobiography. Ed. by K.N. Vaswani. Ahmedabad: Navajivan, 1978. 265p.

23497 PANDEY, G. The shastris of Kashi and Lahore: the making of Congress leaders. In W.H. Morris-Jones, ed. The making of politicians.... London: Athlone Press, 1976, 116-26.

23498 SAMPURNANAND. Memories and reflections. London: Asia, 1962. 188p.

23499 SARIN, L.N. Chandra Bhanu Gupta; a profile in courage. Delhi: S. Chand, 1967. [UP Chief Minister]

23500 SHARMA, M.L. Pattern of party competitiveness: a case study of U.P. up to 1967. In IJPS 33,1 (1972) 75-98.

23501 SINGH, V.B. Jan Sangh in UP: fluctuating fortunes. In EPW 6,3/5 (1971) 307-16.

23502 SRIVASTAVA, S. Continuity and change in patterns of leadership recruitment at the subnational level in India: a case study of political leadership in Uttar Pradesh. In J. of State Politics & Admin. 1,2 (1978) 64-99.

23503 TEWARY, I.N. Profiles of women in Uttar Pradesh. [state politics]. In Vina Mazumdar, ed. Symbols of power.... Bombay: Allied, 1979, 305-

23504 U.P. Politics and elections [special issue]. In R&S 21,2 (1974) 1-92.

23505 UTTAR PRADESH. BHASHA VIBHAG. Facilities provided for linguistic minorities in Uttar Pradesh. Lucknow: 1966. 41p.

23506 UTTAR PRADESH. LANGUAGE CMTEE. Report (August, 1962). Lucknow: 1963. 91p.

23507 VERMA, M.S. Coalition government; U.P.'s first experiment. Lucknow: Dept. of Public Admin., Lucknow U., 1971. 112p.

b. election studies

23508 AHMED, BASHIRUDDIN. Congress defeat in Amroha - a case study in one party dominance. In EW 17,21 (1965) 847-58. [Rpt. in Party system and election studies. Bombay: Allied, 1967, 164-89]

23509 BRASS, P.R. Coalition politics in North India. In APSR 62,4 (1968) 1174-91.

23510 CHATURVEDI, H.R. & G. SHAH. Fusion and fission of castes in elections: a case study of Chhata, U.P. In EPW 5,40 (1970) 1642-48.

23511 GRAHAM, B.D. A report on some trends in Indian elections: the case of Uttar Pradesh. In JComPolst 5,3 (1967) 179-99.

23512 IMTIAZ AHMAD. General elections of 1967 in a rural constituency. In EPW 6,36 (1971) 1915-26.

23513 KOGEKAR, S.V. & R.L. PARK. Uttar Pradesh. In their (ed.) Reports on the Indian general election, 1951-52. Bombay: Popular, 1956, 151-66.

23514 ROY, R. Congress defeat in Farrukhabad: a failure of party organization. In EPW 17,22 (1965) 893-99. [Rpt. in Party systems and election studies. Bombay: Allied, 1967, 190-216]

c. mob violence and police firings

23515 CHAKRAVARTTY, N. & A.K. ROY & S. SABERWAL. Report on Kanpur killing. ND: Citizens' Cmtee. for Enquiry into Kanpur Massacre, 1978. 14p.

23516 MOORE, S.J. Rioting in northern India. Ph.D. diss., U. of Pennsylvania, 1976. 247p. [UM 77-10, 197]

23517 UTTAR PRADESH. BANDA POLICE FIRING INQUIRY CMSN.

Report. Allahabad: 1970. 59p.

23518 UTTAR PRADESH. CMSN. OF INQUIRY FOR RENUKOOT. Report. Lucknow: 1978. 105p.

23519 UTTAR PRADESH. MODINAGAR FIRING INQUIRY CMSN. Report, 1968: District Meerut. Allahabad: 1969. 63p.

d. administration and judiciary

23520 UTTAR PRADESH. HIGH COURT OF JUDICATURE. Centenary: High Court of Judicature at Allahabad, 1866-1966. Allahabad: 1966-. 2 v., 563p. + 37 pl., 488p. + 29 pl.

23521 UTTAR PRADESH. POLICE CMSN. Report of the Uttar Pradesh Police Commission, 1970-71. Allahabad: 1972. 287p.

23522 ZAHEER, M. & J. GUPTA. The organization of the Government of Uttar Pradesh; a study of state administration. Delhi: S. Chand, 1970. 770p.

e. local government and politics
i. general studies

23523 ATAL, Y. Local communities and national politics; a study in communication links and political involvement. Delhi: National, 1971. 428p.

23524 GOULD, H.A. Changing political behavior in rural Indian society. In EPW 2,33-35 (1967) 1515-24.

23525 OPLER, M.E. Factors of tradition and change in a local election in rural India. In R.L. Park & I. Tinker, ed. Leadership and political institutions in India. Princeton: PUP, 1959, 137-50.

23526 PAREEK, U.N., ed. Studies in rural leadership. Delhi: Behavioural Sciences Center, 1966. 116p.

23527 PURWAR, V.L. Panchayats in Uttar Pradesh; a critical study in the establishment and working of panchayats in U.P. Lucknow: the author, 1960. 442p.

23528 SAMIUDDIN, A. A critique of panchayati raj: with special reference to Uttar Pradesh. Agra: Sahitya Bhawan, 1976. 391p.

23529 SHARMA, M. Evolution of rural local self-government in Uttar Pradesh. Bombay: All India Inst. of Local Self-govt., 1957. 267p. [1st pub. in QJLSGI 25 (1954) 369-429, 431-89, 675-760; 26 (1955) 34-81, 253-70]

ii. district administration and politics; Zila parishads

23530 DUTTA, V.R. Emerging power patterns at the zila parishad level: a case study of Varanasi zila parishad. In IJPS 31 (1970) 291-300.

23531 ______. Micro level political elite; a study of the social background of Varanasi Zila Parishad members. Varanasi: Gandhian Inst. of Studies, 1973. 62p.

23532 JHA, S.N. Leadership and local politics: a study of Meerut District in Uttar Pradesh, 1923-1973. Bombay: Popular, 1979. 175p.

iii. municipal government

23533 BAYLY, C.A. The local roots of Indian politics: Allahabad, 1880-1920. Oxford: OUP, 1975. 314p.

23534 CHURCH, R. Authority and influence in Indian municipal politics: administrators and councillors in Lucknow. In SA 13,4 (1973) 421-37.

23535 DHAPOLA, T.S. Mid-term parliamentary election in Varanasi: a behavioural study. Varanasi: Rupa Psychological Centre, 1979. 150p.

23536 Ghaziabad: a study in local government. Lucknow: Regional Centre for Research & Training in Municipal Admin., Inst. of Public Admin., U. of Lucknow, 1978. 88p.

23537 GOULD, H.A. Local government roots of contemporary Indian politics. In EPW 6,7 (1971) 457-64.

23538 GUPTA, K.A. Politics of a small town: a sociological study. ND: Impex India, 1976. 179p.

23539 HAQQI, ANWARUL HAQUE. Urban political behaviour. Aligarh: Dept. of Political Science, Aligarh Muslim U., 1978. 59p.

23540 ROSENTHAL, D.B. The limited elite; politics and government in two Indian cities. Chicago: UChiP, 1970. 360p. [Agra & Poona]

23541 SHARMA, M.P. Local self-government and finance in Uttar Pradesh. 2nd ed., rev. Allahabad: Kitab Mahal, 1954. 224p.

23542 SRIVASTAVA, O.P. Municipal government and administration in India. Allahabad: Chugh, 1980. 420p.

23543 SRIVASTAVA, S. Power structure in urban India - a case study of Varanasi city. In Civic Affairs 25,3 (1977) 9-20; 25,4 (1977) 15-28.

23544 SWARUP, H. Growth and functioning of municipalities in Rohilkhand Division, U.P. In QJLSGI 33 (1962) 129-71.

iv. village panchayats and administration

23545 DUBEY, S.M. Role of kinship and ideology in rural factionalism: study of factions in a village of eastern U.P. with special reference to the role of Patti. In EA 18 (1965) 22-33.

23546 GUPTA, R. Decision-makers in a gramdan village. Lucknow: Planning Research & Action Inst., 1971. 87p. (Its Pub., 342)

23547 HITCHCOCK, J.T. Leadership in a north Indian village: two case studies. In R.L. Park & I. Tinker, eds. Leadership and political institutions in India. Princeton: PUP, 1959, 395-414.

23548 KANTOWSKY, D. Patterns of influence, power, and canvassing in a village of eastern Uttar Pradesh, India. In JComPolSt 6 (1968) 219-28.

23549 KEDAR SINGH. Rural democratisation x-rayed. Ghaziabad: Vimal Prakashan, 1974. 165p.

23550 KHARE, R.S. Groups and processes of political change in North Indian Gopalpur. In MI 49 (1969) 188-210.

23551 MADAN, T. Changing pattern of rural administration in Uttar Pradesh. Bombay: All-India Inst. of Local Self-Govt., 1969. 322p.

23552 RANGNATH. The changing pattern of rural leadership in Uttar Pradesh. ND: Indian Academy of Social Sciences, 1971. 164p.

23553 RASTOGI, P.N. Factionalism, politics and crime in a U.P. village. In EA 17 (1964) 168-82.

23554 ROBINS, R.S. Political elite formation in rural India: the Uttar Pradesh Panchayat elections of 1949, 1956, and 1961. In J. of Politics 29 (1967) 838-60.

v. nyaya panchayats (village courts)

23555 KANTOWSKY, D. Indische Laiengerichte: die Nyaya Panchayats in Uttar Pradesh. In Verfassung und Recht in Übersee 1 (1968) 140-61.

23556 KUSHAWAHA, R. Working of nyaya panchayats in India: a case study of Varanasi District. ND: Young Asia, 1977. 149p.

23557 ROBINS, R.S. India: judicial panchayats in Uttar Pradesh. In American J. of Comp. Law 11,2 (1962) 239-46.

B. The Economy of Uttar Pradesh since 1801

1. General Economic History to 1947

23558 HOEY, W. A monograph on the trade and manufactures in northern India. Lucknow: American Methodist Mission Press, 1880. 215p.

23559 TIWARI, S.G. Economic prosperity of the United Provinces; a study in the provincial income...1921-39. Bombay: Asia, 1951. 367p.

23560 United Provinces Chamber of Commerce: 1914-1939. Cawnpore: United Provinces Chamber of Commerce, 1939. 130p.

2. Demography of India's Most Populous State (1981 pop. 110,858,019)

23561 HUSAIN, ISHRAT ZAFAR. An urban fertility field; a report on city of Lucknow. Lucknow: Demographic Res. Centre, Lucknow U., 1970. 154p.

23562 MATHUR, J.K. The pressure of population: its effects on rural economy in Gorakhpur district. Allahabad: Govt. Press, 1931. 55p.

23563 ONKAR SINGH. Distribution and growth of population in Uttar Pradesh. In Geographical Viewpoint 1,2 (1970) 25-38.

23564 PRASAD, U. & R.M. DUBEY. Trends of population in Uttar Pradesh. In IJE 48 (1968) 443-51.

23565 SAKSENA, D.N. Differential urban fertility - Lucknow. Lucknow: Demographic Res. Centre, 1973. 157p.

23566 VARMA, K.N. Population problem in the Ganges valley. Agra: Shiva Lal Agarwala, 1970. 301p. [1st pub. 1967]

23567 VERMA, J.M.S. Dynamics of population growth. Lucknow: Jyotsna Pub., 1977. 208p.

3. Surveys of Economic Conditions since 1947

23568 KANCHAN, M.R., ed. Economic backwardness of Uttar Pradesh. ND: Arjun Arora, 1972. [1971 seminar papers]

23569 NCAER. Techno-economic survey of Uttar Pradesh. ND: 1965. 368p.

23570 SINGH, L.R. The Tarai region of U.P.; a study in human geography. Allahabad: Ram Narain Lal Beni Prasad, 1965. 145p.

4. Economic Development and Planning

23571 BALJIT SINGH. A non-developing economy: Uttar Pradesh. In IJE 51 (1971) 345-68.

23572 INDIA. PLANNING CMSN. Report of a joint study team. Uttar Pradesh. (Eastern Districts), Ghazipur, Azamgarh, Deoria, Jaunpur. Delhi: MPGOI, 1964. 300p.

23573 MASALDAN, P.N. Planning and the people; a study of public participation in planning in Uttar Pradesh. Bombay: Asia, 1964. 102p.

23574 ______. Planning in Uttar Pradesh; a study of machinery for coordination at the state level. Bombay: Vora, 1962. 49p.

23575 NCAER. District planning: Moradabad. ND: 1968. 217p.

23576 ______. Rehabilitation and development of Basti district; a case study in the economics of depressed areas. Bombay: Asia, 1959. 151p.

23577 SHANKAR, K. Growth process in Ghazipur. Allahabad: Arthik Anusandhan Kendra, 1979. 98p.

23578 ______. Economic development of Uttar Pradesh. Allahabad: Arthik Anusandhan Kendra, 1970. 224p.

23579 SINGH, H.P. Resource appraisal and planning in India: a case study of a backward region. ND: Rajesh, 1979. 183p.

23580 SINGH, S.K. Impact of electrification on agricultural and industrial developments of the Rihand Grid Area, Uttar Pradesh. Varanasi: Bhoogol Parishad, Dept. of Geography, Udai Pratap College, 1978. 228p.

23581 UTTAR PRADESH. PLANNING DEPT. Draft fifth five year plan, 1974-79. Allahabad: 1973-. v. 1-

23582 ______. Second five year plan; a review of progress. Lucknow: 1962. 212p.

23583 ______. Third five year plan; progress report. Lucknow: 1963-65. 3 v.

5. Finance and Banking

23584 BHARGAVA, P.K. Uttar Pradesh's finances since independence. Bombay: Vora, 1969. 193p.

23585 GOVIL, R.K. Mobilization of resources through agricultural taxation in Uttar Pradesh. Allahabad: Oriental, 1977. 216p.

23586 INDIA. U.P. PROVINCIAL BANKING ENQUIRY CMTEE. Report, 1929-30. Allahabad: Supt. Printing & Stationery, 1930-36. 4 v. [Chm., E.A.H. Blunt]

23587 KAPOOR, B.P. The place of octroi duties in the finance of municipal boards in Uttar Pradesh. Bombay: All-India Inst. of Local Self-Govt., 1967. 180p.

23588 TRIPATHI, S.D. The Kanpur money market; a study into the problems of a regional money market. Delhi: University Pub., 1966. 261p.

23589 VATUK, V.P. & S.J. VATUK. System of private savings among North Indian village women. In his ed. Studies in Indian folk traditions. ND: Manohar, 1979, 161-76.

5. Agriculture in the U.P. since 1801
a. surveys and descriptive studies

23590 ALI MOHAMMAD. Situation of agriculture, food, and nutrition in rural India. Delhi: Concept, 1978. 229p.

23591 GUPTA, S.C. & ABDUL MAJID. Producers' response to changes in prices and marketing policies; a case study of sugarcane and paddy in eastern Uttar Pradesh. NY: Asia, 1965. 79p.

23592 MORELAND, W.H. The agriculture of the United Provinces; an introduction for the use of land holders and officials.... 2nd ed. Allahabad: F. Luker, 1912. 239p.

23593 MUKERJEE, RADHAKAMAL, ed. Fields and farmers in Oudh. Calcutta: Longmans, Green, 1929. 302p.

23594 SINGH, V.R. Land use patterns in Mirzapur and environs. Varanasi: BHU, 1970. 151p.

23595 TIWARI, P.S. Agricultural atlas of Uttar Pradesh. Pantnagar (Nainital): Dir. of Translation & Pub., G.B. Pant U. of Agri. and Technology, 1973. 136p.

23596 UPADHYAY, M.D. Progress of the resin industry in Uttar Pradesh. In Indian Forester 83,1 (1957) 26-33.

23597 UTTAR PRADESH. DEPT. OF FISHERIES. Fisheries activities in Uttar Pradesh. Lucknow: Dept. of Fisheries, Uttar Pradesh, 1974. 48p.

b. agricultural development and planning

23598 BHATIA, S.S. Dynamic approach to the analysis of change: a case study of cropland use in U.P., India. In Geographia Polonica 19 (1970) 227-47.

23599 ______. Spacial variations, changes and trends in agricultural efficiency in Uttar Pradesh, 1953-1963. In IJAE 22,1 (1967) 66-80.

23600 DWIVEDI, D.N. Problems and prospects of agricultural taxation in U.P. ND: PPH, 1973. 228p.

23601 GANGULI, B.N. Land use and agricultural planning - with special reference to eastern Uttar Pradesh. In GRI 26 (1964) 53-72.

23602 JHA, D.N. Planning and agricultural development: a study with reference to Bihar. Delhi: S. Chand, 1974. 232p.

23603 LAVANIA, G.S. Studies in economics of farm management in Deoria, Uttar Pradesh. ND: Dir. of Econ. & Stat., Govt. of India, 1973. 3 v.

23604 MOHSIN, M., ed. Agro-industries in the economy of Uttar Pradesh. Aligarh: Faculty of Commerce, Aligarh Muslim U., 1970. 223p. [1969 seminar proc.]

23605 PRAKASA RAO, V.L.S. Development strategy for an agricultural region: a case study of Muzaffarnagar District, U.P. Mysore: Inst. of Dev. Studies, U. of Mysore, 1976. 198p.

23606 SAMIUDDIN. Co-operative farming and its impact on rural industries of India. Aligarh: Faculty of Commerce, Aligarh Muslim U., 1972. 242p.

23607 SHANKAR, K. Growth process in Ghazipur. Allahabad Arthik Anusandhan Kendra, 1979. 98p.

23608 TEWARI, R.N. Agricultural development and population growth; an analysis of regional trends in U.P. Delhi: S. Chand, 1970. 226p.

23609 TYAGI, B.N. & R.M. GANGWAR. A study on wheat production in Uttar Pradesh. Lucknow: Dir. of Agri., Uttar Pradesh, 1976. 41p.

c. agricultural technology and innovation; irrigation

23610 BALJIT SINGH & S.D. MISRA. Benefit-cost analysis of the Sarda Canal system. NY: Asia, 1965. 275p.

23611 CHAUBEY, N.P. Motivational dimensions of rural development: a study of risk-taking, risk-avoidance, and fear of failure in villagers. Allahabad: Chaitanya, 1974. 266p.

23612 GUPTA, S.S. Utilisation of electricity in the villages of the District of Aligarh. Aligarh: Dept. of Econ., Dharam Samaj College, 1969. 133p.

23613 GUPTA, V.K. & P.S. GEORGE & V.R. GAIKWAD. Water utilization and agricultural development in western Uttar Pradesh: a study of problems involved in tubewell irrigation for high cropping intensity. Bombay: Agro-Industrial Complex Study Group, Bhabha Atomic Res. Centre, 1971. 271p.

23614 MARTIN, L.J. The impact of improved technology on regional production and prices of major food commodities in U.P., India. Diss., U. of Illinois, 1972. 162p. [UM 72-19,879]

23615 MISRA, S.D. A comparative study of the economics of minor sources of irrigation in Uttar Pradesh; report. Calcutta: Oxford & IBH, 1968. 269p.

23616 SINGH, A.L. Economics and geography of agricultural land reclamation. Delhi: B.R., 1978. 163p. + 18 pl.

23617 SINGH, S.N. Modernisation of agriculture: a case study in eastern Uttar Pradesh. ND: Heritage Pub., 1976. 238p.

d. agricultural labor

23618 ALLAN, J.A. & C.P. SINGH. Agricultural labor in Chirchita village, Bulandshahr, U.P.: labour availability and peak demand. In IJAE 30,1 (1975) 77-85.

23619 PANDEY, S.M. Development of marginal farmers and agricultural labourers. ND: Shri Ram Centre for Industrial Relations & Human Resources, 1974. 116p.

23620 PANDEY, V.K. et al. Surplus farm family labour in Uttar Pradesh and its mobilization for economic development. In IJAE 30,3 (1975) 37-42.

23621 SAXENA, R.C. Agricultural labour, wages and living conditions in Meerut. Delhi: Elite Pub., 1969. 480p.

23622 SHRIVASTVA, R.S. Agricultural labour in eastern districts of Uttar Pradesh. Varanasi: 1966. 198p.

e. agricultural credit and cooperatives

23623 CHAUHAN, D.S. Changes in the role of cooperative credit. In AUJR(L) 16,2 (1968) 1-14.

23624 GARG, J.S. et al. Institutional credit - its impact on agricultural production and income. In Indian Cooperative R. 7,3 (1970) 477-82.

23625 LAVANIA, G.S. et al. Commercial bank finance to agriculture in U.P. - a study. In Indian Cooperative R. 14,3 (1977) 241-52.

23626 NEHRU, S.S. Caste and credit in the rural area. Calcutta: Longmans, Green, 1932. 174p.

23627 SHUKLA, B.D. & S.P. MISRA. Divergence in crop loan system: a case from U.P. In Maharashtra Cooperative Q. 58,1 (1974) 46-55.

23628 SINGH, G.N. et al. An economic appraisal of coop. agricultural finance in Unnao, U.P. In Indian Cooperative R. 16,2 (1979) 155-67.

f. land tenure, revenue and reform in British India

i. general studies of the land system

23629 BATESON, W.M. The agrarian system of the upper Gangetic plain, 1870-1910. Diss., U. of Wisconsin, 1974. 359p. [UM 74-26,478]

23630 JAFRI, S.N.A. The history and status of landlords and tenants in the United Provinces. Allahabad: Pioneer Press, 1931. 136p.

23631 METCALF, T.R. Land, landlords, and the British Raj: northern India in the nineteenth century. Berkeley: UCalP, 1979. 436p.

23632 MISRA, B.R. Land revenue policy in the United Provinces under British rule. Banaras: Nand Kishore, 1942. 274p.

23633 MORELAND, W.H. The revenue administration of the United Provinces. Allahabad: Pioneer Press, 1911. 203p.

23634 MUSGRAVE, P.J. Landlords and lords of the land: estate management and social control in U.P. 1860-1920. In MAS 6,3 (1972) 257-75.

23635 NEALE, W.C. Economic change in rural India; land tenure and reform in Uttar Pradesh, 1800-1955. New Haven: YUP, 1962. 333p.

23636 WHITCOMBE, E. Agrarian conditions in northern India. v. 1, The United Provinces under British rule, 1860-1900. Berkeley: UCalP, 1972. 343p.

ii. the Taluqdari system in Oudh: predominance of great landlords

23637 METCALF, T.R. From raja to landlord: the Oudh talukdars, 1850-1870. In R. Frykenberg, ed. Land control and social structure in Indian history. Madison: UWiscP, 1969, 123-41.

23638 ______. Social effects of British land policy in Oudh. In R. Frykenberg, ed. Land control and social structure in Indian history. Madison: UWiscP, 1969, 143-62.

23639 RAJ, JAGDISH. Economic conflict in north India: a study of landlord-tenant relations in Oudh, 1870-1890. Bombay: Allied, 1978. 259p.

23640 ______. The revenue system of the nawabs of Oudh. In JESHO 2 (1959) 92-104.

23641 THOLAL, B.N. History of the Sombansi raj and estate of Partabgarh in Oudh. Cawnpore: Printed at the Job Press, 1900. 109p.

iii. the NW Provinces and the Land Settlement of 1833

23642 BRENNAN, L. Agrarian policy and its effects on land-holders in Rohilkhand, 1833 to 1870. In Univ. Studies in History 5,4 (1970) 1-32.

23643 COHN, B.S. Structural change in Indian rural society, 1596-1885. In R. Frykenberg, ed. Land control and social structure in Indian history. Madison: UWiscP, 1969, 53-121.

23644 GUPTA, S.C. Agrarian relations and early British rule in India; a case study of ceded and conquered provinces: Uttar Pradesh, 1801-1833. Bombay: Asia, 1963. 338p.

23645 HUSAIN, I. Land revenue policy in North India, the ceded & conquered provinces, 1801-33. Calcutta: New Age Pub., 1967. 298p.

23646 ROSELLI, J. Theory and practice in North India; the background to the land "settlement" of 1833. In IESHR 8,2 (1971) 134-63.

23647 SIDDIQI, ASIYA. Agrarian change in a northern Indian state: Uttar Pradesh 1819-1833. London: OUP, 1973. 212p.

23648 ______. Agrarian depression in Uttar Pradesh in 1828-33. In IESHR 6 (1969) 166-78.

g. land tenure and reform since Independence

23649 BALJIT SINGH. Next step in Village India; a study of land reforms and group dynamics. Bombay: Asia, 1961. 135p.

23650 BALJIT SINGH & S.D. MISRA. A study of land reforms in Uttar Pradesh. Calcutta: Oxford Book Co., 1964. 266p.

23651 MISRA, S.D. Land reforms and the structure of holdings in U.P. In IJE 54,4 (1974) 447-59.

23652 MOORE, F.J. & C.A. FREYDIG. Land tenure legislation in Uttar Pradesh. Berkeley: U. of California, Inst.

of East Asiatic Studies, 1955. 124p. (Its Modern India Project, 1)

23653 NEWELL, R.S. Ideology and realities: land redistribution in U.P. In PA 45,2 (1972) 220-39.

23654 SIDDIQUI, NURUL HASAN. Landlords of Agra and Avadh. Lucknow: Pioneer Press, 1950. 386p.

23655 UNITED PROVINCES. ZAMINDARI ABOLITION CMTEE. Report. Allahabad: Supt. of Printing & Stationery, 1948. 2 v.

h. peasant movements and agrarian unrest in the U.P. since 1801

23656 CRAWLEY, W.F. Kisan Sabhas and agrarian revolt in the United Provinces, 1920 to 1921. In MAS (1971) 95-110.

23657 DHANAGARE, D.N. Congress and agrarian agitation in Oudh, 1920-22 and 1930-32. In SA 5 (1975) 67-77.

23658 KELKAR, G.S. Kisan unrest and the Congress in Uttar Pradesh, 1920-1922. In EPW 10,52 (1975) 1987-94.

23659 MOORE, F.J. & C.A. FREYDIG. Land tenure legislation in Uttar Pradesh. Berkeley: South Asia Studies, Inst. of East Asiatic Studies, U. of California, 1955. 124p. (South Asia studies monograph, 1)

23660 RAJENDRA SINGH. Agrarian social structure and peasant unrest: a study of land-grab movement in District Basti, East U.P. In SB 23,1 (1974) 44-69.

23661 SIDDIQI, M.H. Agrarian unrest in north India: the United Provinces, 1918-22. ND: Vikas, 1978. 247p.

23662 ______. The peasant movement in Pratapgarh, 1920. In IESHR 9,3 (1972) 305-26.

23663 STOKES, E. Traditional elites in the great rebellion of 1857: some aspects of rural revolt in the Upper and Central Doab. In E.R. Leach & S.N. Mukherjee, eds. Elites in S. Asia. Cambridge: CamUP, 1970, 16-32.

7. Industry of the U.P. since 1801
a. general studies

23664 HIRSCH, L.V. Marketing in an underdeveloped economy: the North Indian sugar industry. Englewood Cliffs, NJ: Prentice-Hall, 1961. 392p.

23665 INDIA (REP.). EXPERT CMTEE. ON THE ENVIRONMENTAL IMPACT OF MATHURA REFINERY. Report of the Expert Committee on the Environmental Impact of Mathura Refinery, December 1977. ND: Min. of Petroleum, Chemicals and Fertilizers, Govt. of India, 1978. 93p. [Chm. S. Varadarajan]

23666 KAYASTHA, S.L. & M.B. SINGH. A spatial analysis of manufacturing industry in Uttar Pradesh. In GRI 41,2 (1979) 93-104.

23667 KHANNA, S.S. The brass industry in Uttar Pradesh: investigations into the reorganisation on scientific lines of the brass industry of Varanasi, Moradabad and Mirzapur. Bombay: Asia, 1963. 64p.

23668 KUPPUSWAMY, B. Industrialization and social change; report of the research project. ND: Res. Council for Cultural Studies, India Intl. Centre, 1967. 99p.

23669 PANT, Y.P. A study in industrial location; with special reference to the problems of UP. Bombay: New Book Co., 1957. 226p.

23670 TEJVIR SINGH. Tourism and tourist industry in U.P. Delhi: New Heights, 1975. 263p.

23671 UPADHYAYA, K.K. Financing of industrial growth in a developing region. Allahabad: Chugh, 1980. 112p.

23672 UTTAR PRADESH, INDIA. SARVAJANIK UDYOG BUREAU. A handbook of U.P. State public sector enterprises. Rev. and enl. ed., corrected up to October 1978. Lucknow: 1979. 185p.

23673 UTTAR PRADESH. INDUSTRIES DEPT. Industrial programmes in Uttar Pradesh during fourth plan. Kanpur: Dir. of Industries, 1965. 285p.

b. small-scale industry

23674 BALJIT SINGH. The economics of small-scale industries; a case study of small-scale industrial establishments of Moradabad. London: Asia, 1961. 144p.

23675 JOSHI, P.C. The decline of indigenous handicrafts in Uttar Pradesh. In IESHR 1 (1963) 24-35.

23676 MCCRORY, J.T. Small industry in a north Indian town; case studies in latent industrial potential. Delhi: Min. of Commerce & Industry, 1956. 145p.

23677 MATHUR, S.P. Economics of small-scale industries. Delhi: Sundeep, 1979. 277p. [Agra Dist.]

8. Labor and Trade Unions

23678 AGNIHOTRI, V. Factory workers in Kanpur: a socio-economic study. Kanpur: Avantika Prakashan, 1957. 261p.

23679 MISRA, H.M. Un-bonded and after. Kanpur: Research & Pub. Branch, Office of the Labour Commissioner, U.P., 1977. 62p.

23680 MISRA, K.K. Labour welfare in Indian industry; a study of the problem in sugar industry of eastern Uttar Pradesh. Meerut: Meenakshi, 1971. 149p.

23681 PANDEY, S.M. Government employees' strike; a study in white collar unionism in India. Meerut: Meenakshi, 1969. 106p.

23682 ______. As labour organizes; a study of unionism in the Kanpur cotton textile industry. ND: Shri Ram Centre for Industrial Relations, 1970. 243p.

23683 RASTOGI, J.L. Industrial relations in Uttar Pradesh. Lucknow: 1965. 266p.

23684 SHUKLA, H.N. The growth of the trade union movement in Uttar Pradesh. In IJLE 11 (1968-69) C177-C187.

23685 SINGH, V.B. Climate for industrial relations; a study of Kanpur cotton mills. Bombay: Allied, 1968. 220p.

9. Commerce and Transportation

23686 MEHROTRA, H.C. & D.K. KULSHRESHTA. Economics of bus operation in U.P.: problems and suggestions. In AUJR(L) 23,2 (1975) 19-25.

23687 SINGH, R.B. Transport geography of Uttar Pradesh. Varanasi: NGSI, 1966. 168p.

C. Society and Social Change in the U.P. since 1801

1. Social Categories
a. general studies

23688 ANANT, S.S. The changing concept of caste in India. Delhi: Vikas, 1972. 153p. [study in Agra, Delhi, & Varanasi]

23689 BLUNT, E.A.H. The caste system of northern India, with special reference to the United Provinces of Agra and Oudh. Delhi: S. Chand, 1969. 374p. [1st pub. 1931]

23690 COHN, B.S. The pasts of an Indian village. In CSSH 3 (1961) 241-49.

23691 CROOKE, W. Tribes and castes of the Northwestern Provinces and Oudh. Calcutta: Supt. of Govt. Printing, 1906. 4 v.

23692 FOX, R.G. Family, caste, and commerce in a north Indian market town. In EDCC 15,3 (1967) 297-314.

23693 GOULD, H.A. Lucknow rickshawalas: the social organization of an occupational category. In Intl. J. of Comp. Sociology 6 (1965) 24-47.

23694 GUHA, U. & N.N. KAUL. A group distance study of the castes of U.P. In BDA 2 (1954) 85-98.

23695 JAIN, S.P. The social structure of a Hindu-Muslim community. Delhi: National, 1975. 194p.

23696 MAJUMDAR, D.N., et al. Inter-caste relations in Gohanakallan. In EA 8 (1955) 191-214.

23697 MISRA, S.D. Social geography of Mathura. In IGJ 34,1/2 (1959) 1-24.

23698 NANDI, P.K. A study of caste organizations in Kanpur. In MI 45 (1965) 84-99.

23699 OPLER, M.E. & SHALIGRAM SHUKLA. Palanquin symbolism: the special vocabulary of the palanquin-bearing castes of North Central India. In J. of American Folklore 81 (1968) 216-234.

23700 PRASAD, B. Socio-economic study of urban middle classes. Delhi: Sterling, 1968. 85p.

23701 ROWE, W.L. The new Cauhans: a caste mobility movement in North India. In J. Silverberg, ed. Social mobility in the caste system in India. The Hague: Mouton, 1968, 66-77.

23702 SCHWARTZBERG, J.E. Caste regions of the North Indian plain. In M.B. Singer & B.S. Cohn, eds. Structure and change in Indian society. Chicago: Aldine, 1968, 81-114.

23703 ______. The distribution of selected castes in the North Indian plain. In Geographical R. 55 (1965) 477-95.

23704 SHERRING, M.A. Hindu tribes and castes as represented in Benares. Delhi: Cosmo, 1974. 3v. [Rpt. 1872-81 ed.]

23705 SINGH, K.K. Patterns of caste tension; a study of inter-caste tension and conflict. Bombay: Asia, 1967. 118p.

23706 SINHA, D.P. Caste dynamics: a case from Uttar Pradesh. In MI 40 (1960) 19-29.

b. kinship and marriage (not specific to one group)

23707 GOULD, H.A. A further note on village exogamy in north India. In SWJA 17 (1961) 297-300.

23708 ______. The micro-demography of marriages in a North Indian area. In SWJA 16 (1960) 476-91.

23709 ______. True structural change and the time dimension in the North Indian kinship system. In Studies on Asia (U. of Nebraska) 6 (1965) 179-91.

23710 KHARE, R.S. On hypergamy and progeny rank determination in Northern India. In MI 50 (1970) 350-76.

23711 NIEHOFF, A. A study of matrimonial advertisements in North India. In EA 12 (1959) 73-86.

23712 REDDY, N.S. Rites and customs associated with marriage in a north Indian village. In EA 9 (1956) 77-91.

23713 ROWE, W. The marriage network and structural change in a North Indian community. In SWJA 16 (1960) 299-311.

23714 VATUK, S.J. Gifts and affines in north India. In CIS ns 9,2 (1975) 155-96.

23715 ______. Reference, address, and fictive kinship in urban North India. In Ethnology 8,3 (1969) 255-272.

23716 ______. A structural analysis of the Hindi kinship terminology. In CIS ns 3 (1969) 94-115.

23717 ______. Trends in North Indian urban kinship: the 'matrilateral asymmetry' hypothesis. In SWJA 27,3 (1971) 287-307.

c. Brahman castes of U.P.

23718 ELDER, J.W. Brahmans in an industrial setting: a case study. In W.B. Hamilton, ed., the transfer of institutions. Durham: DUP, 1964, 139-64.

23719 KHARE, R.S. A case of anomalous values in Indian civilization: meat-eating among the Kanya-Kubja Brahmans of Katyayan Gotra. In JAS 25 (1966) 229-40.

23720 ______. The changing Brahmans; associations and elites among the Kanya-Kubjas of North India. Chicago: UChiP, 1970. 251p.

23721 ______. Home and office: some trends of modernization among the Kanya-Kubja Brahmans. In CSSH 13,2 (1971) 196-215.

23722 ______. The Kanya-Kubja Brahmins and their caste organization. In SWJA 16 (1960) 348-67.

23723 ______. One hundred years of occupational modernization among Kanya-Kubja Brahmans: a genealogical reconstruction of social dynamics. In M.B. Singer, ed. Entrepreneurship and modernization of occupational cultures in South Asia. Durham, NC: DUPCSSA, 1973. 243-74. (Its monograph & occ. papers, 12)

23724 entry deleted

d. the Kayasthas: a high-caste scribal group

23725 CARROLL, L. Caste, community and caste(s) association: note on the organization of the Kayastha Conference and the definition of a Kayastha community. In CAS 10 (1977) 3-24.

23726 ______. Caste, social change and the social scientist: a note on the ahistorical approach to Indian social history. In JAS 35,1 (1975) 63-84.

23727 ______. Ideological factions in a caste(s) association - the Kayastha Conference: educationists and social reformers. In SA ns 1,2 (1978) 11-26.

23728 ______. The seavoyage controversy and the Kayasthas of North India, 1901-1909. In MAS 13,2 (1979) 265-299.

23729 HUSAIN, YUSUF. Les Kayasthas, ou 'scribes,' caste hindoue iranisée, et la culture musulmane dans l'Inde. In Revue des études Islamiques 1 (1927) 455-58.

23730 KANE, P.V. The Kayasthas. In NIA 1 (1929) 739-43.

23731 SHASTRI, R.M. A comprehensive study into the origin and status of the Kayasthas. In MI 2 (1931) 116-59.

e. Rajputs of U.P.

23732 HITCHCOCK, J.T. The idea of the martial Rajput. In M.B. Singer, ed. Traditional India: structure and change. Philadelphia: American Folklore Society, 1959, 216-223. (J. of American Folklore 71,281)

23733 MINTURN, L. & J.T. HITCHCOCK. The Rajputs of Khalapur, India. NY: Wiley, 1966. 158p. (Six cultures series, 3) [Also in B.B. Whiting, ed. Six cultures, studies in child rearing. NY: Wiley, 1965, 203-361.]

23734 SINGH, R.B. Rajput clan-settlements in Varanasi District. Varanasi: NGSI, 1975. 134p. (Its Res. pub., 12)

f. merchant castes of U.P.

23735 FOX, R.G. Parjah capitalism and traditional Indian merchants, past and present. In M.B. Singer, ed. Entrepreneurship and modernization of occupational cultures in South Asia. Durham, NC: DUPCSSA, 1973, 16-36. (Its Monograph & occ. papers, 12)

23736 ______. Resiliency and change in the Indian caste system: The Umar of U.P. In JAS 26 (1967) 575-87.

23737 SAHAI, INDU. The Rastogis of Lucknow - a case study of modernization. In EA 32,1 (1979) 37-44.

g. Jats and other agricultural castes

23738 MUKERJI, A.B. The Jats of the upper Ganga-Jamuna Doab; some ethno-geographic considerations. In DG 6 (1958) 22-50.

23739 PANDE, RAM. Studies in history: the Jats. Jaipur: Chinmaya, 1974. 67p.

23740 PRADHAN, M.C. The political system of the Jats of Northern India. Bombay: OUP, 1966. 275p.

23741 SHARMA, S.P. Marriage, family and kinship among the Jats and Thakurs: some comparisons. In CIS ns 7 (1973) 81-103.

23742 TIEMANN, G. The four-gotra rule among the Jat of Haryana in northern India. In Anthropos 65 (1970) 166-177.

h. scheduled castes: Chamars, Bhangis and others

23743 BHANDARI, J.S. Kinship, marriage and family among the Korwa of Dudhi (Mirzapur, U.P.). In EA 16 (1963) 79-106.

23744 BHATT, G.S. Urban impact and the trends of intra-caste solidarity and dissociability as measures of status mobility among the Chamar. In JSR 5 (1962) 97-108.

23745 BRIGGS, G.W. The Chamars. London: OUP, 1920. 270p.

23746 CHATTERJEE, M. Kinship in an urban low caste locality. In EA 27,4 (1974) 337-49. [Bhangis in Varanasi]

23747 COHN, B.S. Chamar family in a north Indian village: a structural contingent. In EW 13,27-29 (1961) 1051-55.

23748 ______. The changing status of a depressed caste. In M. Marriott, ed. Village India. Chicago: UChiP, 1955, 53-77. [Chamars]

23749 ______. Changing traditions of a low caste. In M.B. Singer, ed. Traditional India: structure and change. Philadelphia: American Folklore Society, 1959, 207-215. (J. of American Folklore 71,281) [Chamars]

23750 HARIJAN SEVAK SANGHA. CAWNPORE BRANCH. HARIJAN SURVEY CMTEE. Report of the committee appointed by the Cawnpore Harijan Sevak Sangha in May, 1933, to make a survey of the social and religious disabilities, working conditions, and the standard of life of the Harijans of Cawnpore. Cawnpore: 1934. 100p.

23751 JUYAL, B.N. The politics of untouchability in Uttar Pradesh. In R&S 21,3 (1974) 62-81.

23752 LYNCH, O.M. The politics of untouchability: a case from Agra, India. In M.B. Singer & B.S. Cohn, eds. Structure and change in Indian society. Chicago: Aldine, 1968, 209-40.

23753 ______. The politics of untouchability; social mobility and social change in a city of India. NY: ColUP, 1969, 251p.

23754 MAHAR, P.M. Changing caste ideology in a North Indian village. In J. of Social Issues 14 (1958) 51-65.

23755 ______. Changing religious practices of an untouchable caste. In EDCC 8 (1960) 179-87.

23756 MALIK, M.A. ["HAZARI"] I was an outcaste: the autobiography of an 'untouchable' in India. ND: Hindustan Times, 1957. 183p.

23757 MUKERJI, A.B. The Chamars of Uttar Pradesh: a study in social geography. Delhi: Inter-India, 1980. 155p.

23758 REDDY, N.S. Functional relations of Lohars in a north Indian village. In EA 8 (1955) 129-40.

j. Muslims of U.P. (15.5% of 1971 pop.)

23759 AHMAD, IMTIAZ. Caste and kinship in a Muslim village of Eastern Uttar Pradesh. In his (ed.) Family, kinship and marriage among the Muslims in India. ND: Manohar, 1976, 318-346.

23760 ______. Endogamy and status mobility among the Siddique Sheikhs of Allahabad, Uttar Pradesh. In his Caste and social stratification among the Muslims. ND: Manohar, 1973, 157-194.

23761 AHMAD, ZARINA. Muslim caste in Uttar Pradesh. In EW 14 (1962) 325-36.

23762 ANSARI, GHAUS. Muslim caste in Uttar Pradesh; a study of culture contact. Lucknow: Ethnographic & Folk Culture Soc., 1960. 83p. [pub. as EA 13 (Dec. 1959-Jan. 1960)]

23763 BHATTY, ZARINA. Status and power in a Muslim dominated village of Uttar Pradesh. In Imtiaz Ahmad, ed. Caste and social stratification among the Muslims. ND: Manohar, 1973, 89-106.

23764 GUPTA, R. Caste ranking and inter-caste relations among the Muslims of a village in north western U.P. In EA 10 (1956) 30-42.

23765 HAQQI, S.A.H. Polygamy among Indian Muslims: a case study. In Indian J. of Politics 8,1/2 (1974) 143-152.

23766 HUSAIN, SHEIKH ABRAR. Marriage customs among Muslims in India: a sociological study of the Shia marriage customs. ND: Sterling, 1976. 226p.

23767 JAIN, S.P. Caste stratification among the Muslims. In EA 28,3 (1975) 255-70.

23768 MEER HASAN ALI, MRS. B. Observations on the Mussulmauns of India: descriptive of their manners, customs, habits, and religious opinions; made during a twelve years' residence in their immediate society. Delhi: IAD, 1973. 2v. [1st pub. 1832, Lucknow]

23769 MUKERJI, A.B. The Muslim population of Uttar Pradesh, India: a spatial interpretation. In IsC 47,3 (1973) 213-30.

23770 ROY, S. Status of Muslim women in north India. Delhi: B.R., 1979. 241p.

23771 SINHA, A. Shia-Sunni conflict. In EPW 13,45 (1978) 1841-42.

23772 WRIGHT, T.P., JR. The politics of Muslim sectarian conflict in India. In JSAMES 3,3 (1980) 67-74. [Lucknow study]

k. Adivasis (tribals) of U.P. [for tribals of the Terai, see Chap. Sixteen, III. C.]

23773 BRIGGS, G.W. The Doms and their relations. Mysore: Wesley Press, 1953. 680p.

23774 FUCHS, S. Nomadic tribes in the plains of North India. In JGRS 31 (1969) 92-101.

23775 GOSWAMI, B.B. Tribal panchayats in rural and urban settings. In BAnthSI 13 (1964) 1-8.

23776 MAJUMDAR, D.N. The Korwas of the United Provinces. In MI 9 (1929) 237-250.

23777 MATHUR, K.S. Sorcery and witchcraft among the tribes of Dudhi. In EA 5 (1951-52) 79-86. [Mirzapur District]

23778 SANKHDHER, L.M. Caste interaction in a village tribe: an anthropological case study of the tribes in Dhanaura Village in Mirzapur District of Uttar Pradesh. ND: K.B. Pub., 1974. 63p.

23779 SINGH, B.P. A view on the Kols of Mirzapur. In Indian Sociological Bull. 2,2 (1964-65) 93-97.

2. Villages and Rural Society

a. village studies of "Senapur," "Karimpur," etc.

23780 DASGUPTA, S. & G.R. MADAN. Community and agriculture in two Indian villages. Calcutta: Editions Indian, 1978. 188p.

23781 EAMES, E. Urban migration and the joint family in a north Indian village. In J. of Developing Areas 1 (1967) 163-77.

23782 GOULD, H.A. The Indian village: a sociological perspective. In Baljit Singh & V.B. Singh, eds. Social and economic change.... Bombay: Allied, 1967. 178-207.

23783 ______. A Jajmani system of North India: its structure, magnitude, and meaning. In Ethnology 3 (1964) 12-41.

23784 GUPTA, S.C. An economic survey of Shamaspur village (District Shamaspur, U.P.): a case study in the structure and functioning of a village economy. Bombay: Asia, 1959. 148p.

23785 KHARE, D.S. Group dynamics in a north Indian village. In HO 21 (1962) 201-13.

23786 KROPP, E.W. Zur Mobilisierung ländlicher Arbeitskräfte im anfanglichen Industrialisierungsprozess; ein Verleich der Berufsstruktur in ausgewählten industrienahen und industriefernen Gemeinden Nordindiens. Wiesbaden: Steiner, 1975. 231p. (BSAF, 12) [U.P. & Punjab]

23787 LUSCHINSKY, M.S. Problems of culture change in the Indian village. In HO 22 (1963) 66-74.

23788 MARRIOTT, M. Little communities in an indigenous civilization. In his (ed.) Village India. Chicago: UChiP, 1955, 171-222.

23789 OPLER, M.E. & R.D. SINGH. The division of labor in an Indian village. In C.S. Coon, ed. A reader in general anthropology. NY: Henry Holt, 1948, 464-497.

23790 ______. Two villages of eastern Uttar Pradesh. In AA 54 (1952) 179-90.

23791 RASTOGI, P.N. Polarization at Thakurpur: the process and the pattern. In SB 15,1 (1966) 61-74.

23792 SIMON, S.R. The village of Senapur. In J.W. Mellor, et al. Developing rural India: plan and practice. Ithaca, NY: CornellUP, 1968, 297-228.

23793 SINGH, R.D. The unity of an Indian village. In JAS 16 (1956) 10-19.

23794 SINGH, S.P. Dholri Village (Meerut District). Varanasi: NGSI, 1971. 112p. (Rural studies in geography series, 1)

23795 SINGH, T.R. Glimpses of village life in Northern India. Calcutta: Thacker Spink, 1926. 132p.

23796 SRIVASTAVA, S.L. Impact of emigration on structure and relations in a village in eastern U.P. In JSR 11,2 (1968) 73-86.

23797 WISER, C. Four families of Karimpur. Syracuse: Syracuse U., Maxwell School Foreign & Comp. Stud. Program, 1978. 24 + 229p. (Its South Asian series, 3)

23798 WISER, C.M. & W.H. WISER. Behind mud walls, 1930-1960; with a sequel: The village in 1980. Rev. & enl. Berkeley: UCalP, 1971. 287p. [1st pub. 1930]

b. rural change and community development
i. general studies

23799 BARNABAS, A.P. Social change in a north Indian village. ND: IIPA, 1969. 179p.

23800 BLUNT, E.A.H. Government and rural development: U.P. experiments. In Asiatic R. 32 (1936) 509-40.

23801 DUBE, S.C. India's changing villages; human factors in community development. Ithaca: CornellUP, 1958. 230p.

23802 HALE, S.M. Development and underdevelopment at village level. In EA 28,1 (1975) 23-58.

23803 JETLEY, S. Modernizing Indian peasants: a study of six villages in eastern Uttar Pradesh. ND: Asian Educ. Services, 1977. 182p.

23804 KANTOWSKY, D. Dorfentwicklung und Dorfdemokratie in Indien: Formen und Wirkungen von Community Development und Panchayati Raj detailliert am Beispiel eines Entwicklungsblocks und dreier Dorfer in östlichen Uttar Pradesh. Freiburg: Bertelsmann, 1970. 171p.

23805 MARRIOTT, M. Changes in an Indian village. In EE 52 (1969) 719-24.

23806 ______. New farmers in an old village. In M.B. Singer, ed. Entrepreneurship and modernization of occupational cultures in South Asia. Durham, NC: DUPCSSA, 1973, 205-215. (Its Monograph & occ. papers series, 12)

23807 PANDEY, P.S. Impact of undustrialization on the rural community: a study of social change in some villages surrounding the sugar factories of Deoria District. ND: Research Pub. in Social Sciences, 1976. 154p.

23808 SHARIB, A.H. Problems of rural reconstruction in India; with special reference to Uttar Pradesh. Bombay: Local Self-Govt. Inst., 1953? 238p.

23809 SHARMA, K.N. Institutions, networks and social change. Simla: IIAS, 1974. 202p.

23810 SINHA, D. Indian villages in transition; a motivational analysis. ND: Associated Pub. House, 1969. 232p.

23811 SINHA, D. Motivation and rural development. Calcutta: Minerva, 1974. 151p.

23812 UNITED NATIONS ECON. CMSN. FOR ASIA AND THE FAR EAST. Community development and economic development, case study of the Ghosi community development block, Uttar Pradesh, India. Bangkok: ECAFE/FAO Agri. Div., 1960. 100p.

ii. the Pilot Project at Etawah, 1948-54

23813 AGRAWAL, A.L. Some aspects of rural employment; a statistical village study in Etawah, U.P. In IJE 48,4 (1968) 365-85.

23814 JAIN, S.K. An Indian experiment in rural development, the Etawah project. In Intl. Labour R. 68,4-5 (1953) 393-406.

23815 MAYER, ALBERT & M. MARRIOTT & RICHARD L. PARK. Pilot Project, India: the story of rural development at Etawah, Uttar Pradesh. Westport, CT: Greenwood Press, 1978. 367p. [1st pub. 1958]

23816 SUSSMAN, G.E. The road from Etawah: integrated rural development in India. Unpub. Ph.D. diss., U. of Michigan, 1975. 402p. [UM 75-20,460]

23817 THORNER, DANIEL. Dropping the Pilot: a review. In EDCC 7 (1959) 377-80. [With Albert Mayer's comment on the review, 477-78.]

23818 U.P. PLANNING RES. & ACTION INST. Pilot development project Etawah. Lucknow: Kalakankar House, 1960. 103p. (PRAI pub. 207)

c. language, communication, and rural development

23819 GUMPERZ, J.J. Dialect differences and social stratification in a north Indian village. In AA 60 (1958) 668-82.

23820 ______. Language problems in the rural development of north India. In JAS 16 (1957) 251-59.

23821 ______. Religion and social communication in village North India. In E.B. Harper, ed. Aspects of Religion in South Asia. Seattle: UWashP, 1964, 89-77. [1st pub. in JAS 23 (1964) 89-97]

23822 MAJUMDAR, D.N. Caste and communication in an Indian village. Bombay: Asia, 1958. 358p.

23823 VAJPEYI, D.K. The role of mass communications in modernization and social change in U.P. In IJPS 34 (1973) 129-156.

3. Cities and Urbanization
a. general studies

23824 AHMAD, ENAYAT. Social and geographical aspects of human settlements. ND: Classical, 1979. 298p.

23825 BAYLY, C.A. Town building in North India, 1790-1830. In MAS 9,4 (1975) 483-504.

23826 GANGULI, B.N. Some aspects of urbanisation in Uttar Pradesh. In GRI 25 (1963) 99-107.

23827 MUKERJI, A.B. Urbanization in the Avadh region, Uttar Pradesh. In Geographical Viewpoint 6,1-2 (1975) 1-30.

23828 ONKAR SINGH. Functions and functional classification of towns in Uttar Pradesh. In NGJI 15 (1969) 179-95.

23829 ______. The trend of urbanization in Uttar Pradesh. In NGJI 13 (1967) 141-57.

23830 SAXENA, S. Trends of urbanisation in Uttar Pradesh. Agra: Satish Book Enterprise, 1970. 275p.

23831 SINGH, O.P. Central place regions for planning in Uttar Pradesh. In NGJI 31,2 (1975) 98-197.

23832 ______. Functions and functional classes of places in Uttar Pradesh. In NGJI 14 (1968) 83-127.

23833 SINGH, R.P. & M.P. DABRAL. An analysis of the functional characteristics of the towns of the Ganga-Yamuna Doab. In DG 10,2 (1972) 15-22.

23834 SINGH, S.C. Changes in the course of rivers and their effects on urban settlements in the Middle Ganga Plain. Varanasi: NGSI, 1973. 166p.

23835 VATUK, S.J. Kinship and urbanization in North India. Berkeley: UCalP, 1972. 219p. [Meerut City]

b. the "KAVAL towns": Kanpur, Agra, Varanasi, Allahabad, Lucknow

23836 CHAND, M. Employment and migration in Allahabad City. Calcutta: Oxford & IBH, 1969. 277p.

23837 CHAUHAN, D.S. Trends of urbanization in Agra. Bombay: Allied, 1966. 459p.

23838 DESAI, P.B., ed. Regional perspective of industrial and urban growth: the case of Kanpur. Bombay: Macmillan, 1969. 406p. [1967 seminar papers]

23839 DUBE, K.K. Use and misuse of land in the KAVAL towns, U.P. Varanasi: NGJI, 1976. 150p. + 10 pl.

23840 DWIVEDI, R.L. Origin and growth of Allahabad. In IGJ 38 (1963) 16-32.

23841 MAJUMDAR, D.N. Social contours of an industrial city; social survey of Kanpur, 1954-56. Bombay: Asia, 1960. 447p.

23842 MUKERJEE, RADHAKAMAL & BALJIT SINGH. Social profiles of a metropolis: social and economic structure of Lucknow, capital of Uttar Pradesh 1954-56. London: Asia, 1961. 210p. tables.

23843 NIGAM, M.N. Evolution of Lucknow. In NGJI 6 (1960) 30-46.

23844 ______. Functional regions of Lucknow. In NGJI 10,1 (1964) 38-52.

23845 OLDENBURG, V.T. Peril, pestilence, and perfidy: the making of colonial Lucknow, 1856-1877. Diss., U. of Illinois, Urbana-Champaign, 1979. 285p. [UM 80-18,193]

23846 Prayag or Allahabad; a handbook. Calcutta: Modern Review office, 1910. 190p.

23847 SHARAR, ABDUL HALIM. Lucknow: the last phase of an oriental culture. Tr. from Urdu by E.S. Harcourt & Fakhir Hussain. Boulder, CO: Westview Press, 1976. 295p. + 8 pl.

23848 SINGH, A.N. The economics of a religious city: a case study of Varanasi. In JSR 15,1 (1972) 58-70.

23849 SINGH, H.H. Kanpur; a study in urban geography. Varanasi: Indrasini Devi, 1972. 152p.

23850 SINGH, R.L. Banaras: a study in urban geography. Banaras: Nand Kishore, 1955. 184p.

23851 SINHA, D. Motivation of rural population in a developing country. Bombay: Allied, 1969. 51p.

23852 TIWARI, A.R. Urban regions of Agra. In AUJR(L) 6 (1958) 101-14.

23853 UJAGIR SINGH. Allahabad; a study in urban geography. Varanasi: Banaras Hindu U., 1966. 265p.

23854 ______. Evolution of Allahabad. In NGJI (1958) 109-29.

c. other urban centers of U.P.

23855 FOX, R.G. From zamindar to ballot box; community change in a north Indian market town. Ithaca, NY: CornellUP, 1969. 302p. [Mirzapur]

23856 MUKERJEE, RADHAKAMAL & BALJIT SINGH. A district town in transition; social and economic survey of Gorakhpur. NY: Asia, 1965. 187p.

23857 NIGAM, M.N. Gorakhpur: a study in historical geography. In Geographical Thought 3,1 (1967) 36-49.

23858 RAM, PARS. A UNESCO study of social tensions in Aligarh, 1950-1951. Ed. by G. Murphy. Ahmedabad: New Order Book Co., 1955. 206p.

23859 SARIKWAL, R.C. Sociology of a growing town. Delhi: Ajanta, 1978. 350p. [Ghaziabad]

23860 SAXENA, D.P. Rururban migration in India: causes and consequences. Bombay: Popular, 1977. 225p. [Gorakhpur Dist.]

23861 SINGH, R.L. Gorakhpur: a study in urban morphology. In NGJI 1 (1953) 1-10.

23862 ______. Mirzapur: a study in urban geography. In Geographical Outlook 1 (1956) 16-57.

23863 SINHA, R.K. & M. HASAN. Glimpses of Faizabad. Delhi: Idara-i-Tasnif, 1975. 86p.

4. Social Problems and Social Welfare

23864 AGNIHOTRI, V. Housing condition of factory workers in Kanpur. Kanpur: Avantika Prakashan, 1954. 63p.

23865 CHATTERJEE, B.B. & S.S. SINGH & D.R. YADAV. Impact of social legislation on social change. Calcutta: Minerva, 1971. 261p. [Varanasi Dist.]

23866 SINHA, D. The Mughal syndrome; a psychological study of intergenerational differences. Bombay: Tata McGraw-Hill, 1972. 195p. [Allahabad U.]

23867 SRIVASTAVA, S.S. Juvenile vagrancy; a socio-ecological study of juvenile vagrants in the cities of Kanpur and Lucknow. Bombay: Asia, 1963. 254p.

23868 VAJPEYI, D.K. Modernization and social change in India. ND: Manohar, 1979. 298p.

23869 VARMA, S.C. The young delinquents; a sociological inquiry. Lucknow: Pustak Kendra, 1970. 105p. [in Kanpur & Lucknow]

23870 YOGENDRA SINGH. Cultural integration and changing values; a study of value system of educated youth. In SB 13 (1964) 49-66.

5. Health Services and Family Planning

23871 ALI MOHAMMAD. Food and nutrition in India. ND: K.B. Pub., 1977. 163p.

23872 ELDER, R.E. Development administration in a north Indian state: the family planning program in U.P. Chapel Hill: U. of N. Carolina, Carolina Population Center, 1972. 195p. (Its Monograph, 18)

23873 GOULD, H.A. Modern medicine and folk cognition in rural India. In HO 25 (1965) 201-08. [Faizabad Dist.]

23874 HASAN, K.A. The cultural frontier of health in village India. Bombay: Manaktalas, 1967. 233p. [Lucknow Dist.]

23875 HOCH, E.M. Indian children on a psychiatrist's playground; observations on Indian children examined and treated at Nur Manzil Psychiatric Centre, Lucknow, 1956-61. ND: Indian Council of Medical Res., 1967. 488p.

23876 KAKAR, D.N. Folk and modern medicine: a north Indian case study. Delhi: New Asian, 1977. 218p.

23877 KHAN, M.E. Family planning among Muslims in India: a study of the reproductive behaviour of Muslims in an urban setting. ND: Manohar, 1979. 198p. [Kanpur]

23878 MADAN, T.N. Doctors in a north Indian city: recruitment, role perception, and role performance. In S. Saberwal, ed. Beyond the village. Simla: IIAS, 1972, 77-110. [Ghaziabad]

23879 MARRIOTT, M. Western medicine in a village of northern India. In B.D. Paul & W.B. Miller, eds. Health, culture and community. NY: R. Sage Foundation, 1955, 239-68.

23880 PLANALP, J.M. Heat stress and culture in north India. U.S. Army Medical Res. & Dev. Command, 1971. 557p.

23881 PLANNING RES. & ACTION INST. Induced change in health behaviour; a study of a pilot environmental sanitation project in Uttar Pradesh. Lucknow: 1968. 176p. (P.R.A.I. pub., 356)

23882 PRASAD, HANUMAN. Health and development; a study of health conditions of thirteen villages in Mirzapur District, Uttar Pradesh. Banwasi Seva Ashram, Dist. Mirzapur: Agrindus, 1969. 62p.

23883 RAINA, B.L. et al. A study in family planning communication, Meerut district. ND: Central Family Planning Inst., 1967. 82p.

23884 SOODAN, K.S. Aging in India. Calcutta: Minerva, 1975. 204p. [Lucknow]

23885 Uttar Pradesh Jal Nigam [special issue]. In Civic Affairs 25,11 (1978) 1-119. [on water supply & sewerage]

23886 WISER, C.V. The foods of an Indian village of

north India. In Annals of the Missouri Botanical Garden 42 (1955) 301-412.

6. Education in U.P. since 1801 (27.4% literacy in 1981)
a. general studies

23887 CHATTERJEE, B.B. & SUDARSHAN KUMARI & A.B. SINGH. Voluntary action for adult literacy; report of Gramdan Shikshan Yojana at Darbhanga and Mirzapur. Varanasi: Navachetna Prakashan, 1969. 128p.

23888 FENNER, P. Education in Uttar Pradesh, 1843-54: James Thomason's role in vernacular indigenous education. In JIH 53,3 (1975) 523-60.

23889 GOULD, H.A. Educational structures and political processes in Faizabad District, U.P. In S.H. Rudolph & L.I. Rudolph, eds. Education and politics in India.... Cambridge: HUP, 1972, 94-120.

23890 JOSHI, P.C. & M.R. RAO. Changes in literacy and education: study of villages in U.P. and Punjab. In EW 17,27 (1965) 1061-68.

23891 ______. Social and economic factors in literacy and education in rural India. In EW 16,1 (1964) 21-27.

23892 TEWARI, D.D. Primary education in U.P. Allahabad: Ram Narain Lal Beni Madho, 1967. 532p.

d. higher education
i. Banaras Hindu University (est. 1915)

23893 BANARAS HINDU U. LIBRARY. DOCUMENTATION UNIT. Students unrest in the Banaras Hindu University: classified documentation list based on the periodical literature. Varanasi: 1969. 5 v. in 1. (Its Documentation series, 5-9)

23894 DAR, S.L. Agitation of 1958. Varanasi: BHU, 1958. 154p.

23895 DAR, S.L. & S. SOMASKANDAN. History of the Banaras Hindu University. Varanasi: BHU, 1966. 2 v.

23896 INDIA (REP.). BANARAS HINDU U. ENQUIRY CMTEE., 1958. Report. Delhi: MPGOI, 1958. 44p. [Chm., A.L. Mudaliar]

23897 INDIA (REP.). BANARAS HINDU U. INQUIRY CMTEE., 1969. Report, Jan.-July 1969. ND: Min. of Educ. & Youth Services, 1969. 238p. [P.B. Gajendragadkar, Chm.]

23898 INDIA (REP.). PARLIAMENT. JOINT CMTEE. ON THE BANARAS HINDU U. (AMENDMENT) BILL. Report, 16th August, 1965. ND: Rajya Sabha Secretariat, 1965. 112p.

23899 RAY, A.B. Students and politics in India: the role of caste, language, and region in an Indian university. ND: Manohar, 1977. 232p.

23900 SRIVASTAVA, H.C. The genesis of campus violence in Banaras Hindu University, Varanasi. Allahabad: Indian Intl. Pub., 1974. 106p.

23901 SUNDARAM, V.A., ed. Benares Hindu University, 1905-1935. Benares: 1936. 632p.

ii. Aligarh Muslim University [see also Chap. Six, VII. C. 2. c.]

23902 GHOUSE, M. A minority University and the Supreme Court. In JILI 10,3 (1968) 521-30.

23903 HAQQI, S.A.H. Proposals for amending A.M.U. Act. In Secular Democracy 11,7 (1978) 31-33.

23904 WRIGHT, T.P., JR. Muslim education in India at the cross roads: the case of Aligarh. In PA 29 (1966) 50-63.

iii. Allahabad University

23905 ALLAHABAD U. ENQUIRY CMTEE., 1953. Report. Lucknow: Supt. Printing & Stationery, U.P., 1953. 267p. [Chm., H.P. Mootham]

23906 ALTBACH, P.G. The university in transition; an Indian case study. Bombay: Sindhu, 1972. 136p.

23907 ANDERSEN, W. & ALOK PANT. Student politics at Allahabad university. In EPW 5,23 (1970) 910-16; 5,24 (1970) 941-48.

23908 DI BONA, J.R. Change and conflict in the Indian University. Durham, NC: DUPCSSA, 1969. 206p. (Its Monograph & occ. papers series, 7)

23909 MEHROTRA, K.K., ed. Seventieth anniversary souvenir, University of Allahabad. Allahabad: 1958. 221p.

D. Religious Traditions of the U.P. since 1801 [See also Sacred Centers, Chap. One, IV. B. 2. e.]

23910 ALTER, J.P. & H. JAI SINGH. The Church in Delhi. In V.E.W. Hayward, ed. The Church as Christian community. London: Lutterworth, 1966, 3-138.

23911 ARYA, S.P. The folk religion of western U.P. In Folklore(C) 14,7/8/10 (1973) 257-77, 292-311, 371-85.

23912 ______. The Ghuggal fair, in Saharanpur in Uttar Pradesh. In Folklore(C) 8 (1967) 428-32.

23913 ASHBY, P.H. Popular esoteric religion: Rādhā Soāmī Satsang. In his Modern trends in Hinduism. NY: Columbia, 1974, 71-91. (Lectures on the history of religions, 10)

23914 BISHNOI, D.P. A gigantic project handled on a gigantic scale; a report on arrangements at Kumbh Mela. In Civic Affairs 24,10 (1977) 25-29.

23915 BONAZZOLI, G. Kumbh Mela: a way to moksa. In Hindutva 7, 9/10 (1976-77) 74-80.

23916 CHARAN SINGH. Light on Sant Mat, consisting of discourses and excerpts from letters. 3rd ed. Beas: Radhi Soami Satsang, 1964. 442p.

23917 CROOKE, W. The popular religion and folklore of northern India. 2nd ed., rev. Delhi: Munshiram, 1968. 2 v., 294, 359p. [1st pub. 1894]

23918 FRIPP, P. The mystic philosophy of Sant Mat; as taught by the present spiritual master at the Radha Soami Colony, Beas, India. London: Spearman, 1964. 174p.

23919 GOPAL, K. The religion of the middle class. Meerut City: Anu Prakashan, 1977. 98p.

23920 GUHA, K. Bhairon; a saivite deity in transition. In Folklore(C) 1 (1960) 207-22.

23921 HAWLEY, J.S. Pilgrims' progress through Krishna's playground. In Asia 3,3 (1980) 12-19, 45.

23922 KIRPAL SINGH. Godman. Delhi: Ruhani Satsang, 1967. 186p. [on Sawan Singh, 1858-1948]

23923 MATHUR, A.P. Radhasoami faith; a historical study. Delhi: Vikas, 1974. 189p.

23924 MISRA, B.S., Maharaj Saheb. Discourses on Radhasoami faith. 2nd ed. Benares: R.S. Satsang, 1929. 330p.

23925 OPLER, M.E. The place of religion in a North Indian village. In SWJA 15 (1959) 219-26.

23926 ______. Spirit possession in a rural area of northern India. In W.A. Lessa & E.Z. Vogt, eds. Reader in comparative religion. NY: Harper & Row, 1965, 553-66.

23927 PLANALP, J.M. Religious life and values in a North Indian village. Ithaca: Diss., Cornell U., 1956.

23928 RADHASOAMI SATSANG SABHA. Dayalbagh (Agra); a brief description of the origin, early history, and development of the colony and its institutions. 11th ed. Dayalbagh: 1963. 60p.

23929 RAM CHANDRA, Guru. Truth eternal; the original writings of Samarth Guru Shri Ram Chandraji Maharaj of Fatehgarh, U.P. Tr. from Urdu by S.A. Sarnad. Shahjahanpur, U.P.: Shri Ram Chandra Mission, 1973. 146p.

23930 TRIPATHI, B.D. Sadhus of India: the sociological view. Bombay: Popular, 1978. 258p.

23931 TULSI SAHIB. Tulsi Sahib, saint of Hathras: poems. Dera Baba Jaimal Singh, Punjab: Radha Soami Satsang Beas, 1978. 112p.

23932 UNITED PROVINCES OF AGRA & OUDH. HINDU RELIGIOUS AND CHARITABLE ENDOWMENTS CMTEE. Report. Allahabad: Govt. Press, 1931. 131 + 168p. [Pres., Sir Rampal Singh]

E. Literatures of U.P.

1. Hindi and Urdu Literature
[For Hindu & Urdu Literature, see Chap. Six, VIII. B.&C., and Chap. Eight X. C. 2.&3.]

2. Folk Literature

23933 ARYA, S.P. The institution of "marriage" in folklore of western U.P. In Folklore(C) 13 (1972) 281-307.

23934 ______. The caste in folklore of western U.P. In Folklore(C) 14,4&5 (1973) 150-60, 182-98.

23935 ______. Riddles, proverbs and magical practices of western U.P. In Folklore(C) 13,6 (1972) 218-32.

23936 ______. A sociological study of folklore: projected research in Kuru region (Saharanpur, Muzaffarnagar, Meerut, Bulandshahar, and Bijnor Districts of western Uttar Pradesh). Calcutta: Indian Pub., 1975. 188p. (Its folklore series, 25)

23937 ______. A sociological study of folklore in western U.P.: the folk-poetry. In Folklore(C) 13,5 (1972) 161-79.

23938 BAHADUR, K.P. Folk tales of Uttar Pradesh. ND: Sterling, 1972. 117p. (Folk tales of India series, 10)

23939 PARMAR, S. Bibliography of Hindi folktales. In Folklore(C) 5 (1964) 365-70.

23940 TEWARI, L.G. Folk music of India: Uttar Pradesh. Diss., Wesleyan U., 1974. 292p. [UM 74-23,028]

23941 VATUK, V.P. The Bhajnopdeshak as an agent of social change. In his (ed.) Studies in Indian folk traditions. ND: Manohar, 1979, 137-60. [professional folk composer-singers]

23942 ______. "Malhor": a type of work song in western U.P., India. In AFS 29 (1970) 251-74.

23943 VATUK, V.P. & S. VATUK. The ethnography of Sāng, a North Indian folk opera. In AFS 26 (1967) 29-51.

IV. BIHAR: THE MIDDLE GANGA PLAINS AND THE CHOTA NAGPUR PLATEAU

A. General and Political History since 1801

1. Bihar under the Raj: Part of Bengal Pres. to 1912; 1912-35 Bihar & Orissa Prov.; 1935-47 Bihar Prov. - General Studies and Sources

23944 BRASS, P.R. The Maithili movement in North Bihar. In his Language, religion and politics in North India. NY: CamUP, 1974, 51-116.

23945 DATTA, K.K. Biography of Kunwar Singh and Amar Singh. Patna: K.P. Jayaswal Res. Inst., 1957. 231p.

23946 ______. Catalogue of Patna Commissioner's records, 1813-1853. Patna: Political Dept., State Central Record Office, 1963. 358p.

23947 ______. Unrest against British rule in Bihar, 1831-1859. Patna: State Central Records Office, 1957. 85p.

23948 GOPAL, S. Social changes in Bihar in the second half of the nineteenth century. In MI 47 (1967) 81-91.

23949 JHA, J.S. History of Darbhanga Raj. Patna: Res. Soc. of Bihar, 1966. 91p. [1st pub. JBRS 48,1 (1962) 14-104]

23950 RAYE, N.N. The annals of the early English settlement in Bihar. Calcutta: Kamala Book Depot, 1927. 320p.

23951 RAYCHAUDHURI, P.C. Gaya old records. Patna: Supt. Secretariat Press, Bihar, 1958. 323p.

23952 SINHA, K.G. The Bihar earthquake and the Darbhanga Raj. Calcutta: Darbhanga Raj, 1963. 107p.

23953 SOHONI, S.V. Notes on the revenue history of Darbhanga Raj. In JBRS 48,1 (1962) 105-42.

2. Nationalism and Provincial Politics in British Bihar
a. general studies

23954 BASU, M.K. Regional patriotism: a study in Bihar politics (1907-1912). In IHR 3,2 (1977) 286-307.

23955 DATTA, K.K. History of the freedom movement in Bihar. Patna: Govt. of Bihar, 1957-58. 3 v.

23956 INDIA. CORRUPTION ENQUIRY CMTEE., BIHAR. Report. 30th Nov. 1938. Patna: Supt., Govt. Printing, Bihar, 1939. 90p. [Chm., Syed Abdul Aziz]

23957 JHA, J.S. Biography of an Indian patriot, Maharaja Lakshmishwar Singh of Darbhanga. Patna: Maharaja Lakshmishwar Singh Smarak Samiti, 1972. 363p.

23958 ______. Early revolutionary movement in Bihar, 1906-1920. Patna: K.P. Jayaswal Res. Inst., 1977. 280p. + 16 pl. (Its Hist. res. series, 16)

23959 NAGENDRA KUMAR. Indian national movement, with special reference to the District of Old Saran, Bihar, 1857-1947. Patna: Janaki Prakashan, 1979. 270p.

23960 NATH, S. Terrorism in India. ND: National, 1980. 350p. [events in Bihar, 1902-35]

23961 ROBB, P. Officials and non-officials as leaders in popular agitations: Shahabad 1917 and other conspiracies. In B.N. Pandey, ed. Leadership in South Asia. ND: Vikas, 1977, 179-210.

23962 SINHA, B.P. Sachchidananda Sinha. ND: PDMIB, 1969. 167p.

23963 SINHA, SACHCHIDANANDA. Some eminent Behar contemporaries. Patna: Himalaya Pub., 1944. 218p.

b. Gandhi at Champaran, 1917: the first test of satyagraha

23964 DATTA, K.K. Gandhiji in Bihar. Patna: Govt. of Bihar, 1969. 244p.

23965 MISHRA, G. Socio-economic background of Gandhi's Champaran movement. In IESHR 5 (1968) 245-75.

23966 ______. Agrarian problems of permanent settlement: a case study of Champaran. ND: PPH, 1978. 354p.

23967 MISRA, B.B., ed. Select documents on Mahatma Gandhi's movement in Champaran, 1917-18. Patna: Govt. of Bihar, 1963. 597p.

23968 MITTAL, S.K. Peasant uprisings and Mahatma Gandhi in north Bihar: a politico-economic study of indigo industry, 1817-1917, with special reference to Champaran. Meerut: Anu Prakashan, 1978. 283p.

23969 POUCHEPADASS, J. Local leaders and the intelligentsia in the Champaran Satyagraha (1917): a study in peasant mobilization. In CIS ns 8 (1974) 67-88.

23970 ______. Mouvement paysan et mouvement national: le cas du Champaran, 1917. In Puruṣārtha 2 (1975) 3-30.

23971 RAJENDRA PRASAD. Satyagraha in Champaran. Ahmedabad: Navajivan, 1949. 224p.

23972 ROY CHOUDHURY, P.C. Gandhiji's first struggle in India. 2nd rev. & enl. ed. Ahmedabad: Navajivan, 1963. 203p. [1st pub. 1955]

23973 TENDULKAR, D.G. Gandhi in Champaran. ND: PDMIB, 1957. 115p.

3. Bihar Government and Politics since 1947
a. general studies

23974 AHUJA, RAM. Political elites and modernisation: the Bihar politics. Meerut: Meenakshi, 1975. 144p.

23975 BIHAR. MUDHOLKAR CMSN. OF INQUIRY. Report on the charges against fourteen ex-United Front ministers. Patna: 1970. 286p. [J.R. Mudholkar, one-man Cmsn.]

23976 BIHAR. PUBLIC RELATIONS DEPT. The States Reorganisation Commission's visit to Bihar. Patna: Supt. Secretariat Press, Bihar, 1955. 136p.

23977 BIHAR. T.L. VENKATARAMA AIYAR CMSN. OF INQUIRY. Report of the T.L. Venkatarama Aiyar Commission of Inquiry, constituted by the Government of Bihar to inquire into charges against Krishna Ballabh Sahay, Mahesh

Yadav, Raghvendra Narain Singh, Ambika Sharan Singh, February 5, 1970. Patna: Secretariat Press, 1970. 561p.

23978 HEIDENREICH, H. Caste, class, and voting power: a study of changing political organizations in North Monghyr. In R. Beech & M.J. Beech, eds. Bengal: change and continuity. East Lansing: Asian Studies Center, Michigan State U., 1975, 255-62. (Its occ. papers, South Asia series, 16)

23979 JHA, C. & S.N. JHA. Some aspects of Bihar politics. In IQ 20,3 (1964) 312-29.

23980 JHA, L. Mithila will rise. Darbhanga: Mithila Mandal, 1955. 57p.

23981 JHA, NAGESH. Caste in Bihar politics. In EPW 5,7 (1970) 341-44.

23982 JHA, S.S. Political elite in Bihar. Bombay: Vora, 1972. 332p.

23983 ______. Tribal leadership in Bihar. In EPW 3,15 (1968) 603-08.

23984 MISHRA, D.N. Legislatures and Indian democracy: a procedural study of questions in Bihar Legislative Assembly, 1952-62. Delhi: Concept, 1978. 205p.

23985 RAI, H.D. & J.L. PANDEY. The party system and mass behaviour: the Indian experience. In IJPS 35,3 (1974) 220-38.

23986 ______. Politics of coalition governments: the experience of the first United Front government in Bihar. In JCPS 6,2 (1972) 48-82.

23987 ROY, R. Caste and political recruitment in Bihar. In R. Kothari, ed. Caste in Indian politics. Bombay: Orient Longmans, 1970, 228-58.

23988 ______. Dynamics of one-party dominance in an Indian state. In AS 8 (1968) 553-75.

23989 ______. Intra-party conflict in the Bihar Congress. In AS 6,12 (1966) 707-15. [Rpt. in Party systems and election studies. Bombay: Allied, 1967, 99-113]

23990 ______. Politics of immobilism - selecting Congress candidates in Bihar. In PSR 6,3/4 & 7,1/2 (1968) 41-58.

23991 ROY, S. Recent historical studies about modern Bihar. Calcutta: J. Roy, 1978. 56p.

23992 RUTHS, G.W. Regionale Entwicklung und Abhängigkeit; zur Theorie des internen Kolonialismus in Entwicklungsländern am Beispiel des Bergbaudistriktes Dhanbad, Bihar in Indien. Wiesbaden: Steiner, 1977. 317p.

23993 SEN, JYOTI. The Jharkhand Movement. In K. Suresh Singh, ed. Tribal situation in India. Simla: IIAS, 1972, 432-37.

23994 SHARMA, K.L. Jharkhand Movement in Bihar. In EPW 11,1/2 (1976) 37-43.

23995 SINGH, M.P. Cohesion in a predominant party: the Pradesh Congress and party politics in Bihar. ND: S. Chand, 1975. 148p.

23996 SINHA, J.K.P. Emerging trends in Bihar politics. In IJPS 34,4 (1973) 471-81.

23997 VIDYARTHI, L.P. The historic march of Jharkhand Party. In Indian Sociological Bull. 1,2 (1964) 5-10.

23998 Who killed L.N. Mishra?: an Indian Express investigation. Bombay: Popular, 1979. 79p.

b. election studies

23999 BIHAR. HOME (ELECTION) DEPT. Report on the fourth general elections in Bihar, 1967. Patna: Secretariat Press, 1968. 302p.

24000 BLAIR, H.W. Minority electoral politics in a North Indian state: aggregate data analysis and the Muslim community in Bihar, 1952-1972. In APSR 67,4 (1973) 1275-1287.

24001 ______. Voting, caste, community, society: explorations in aggregate data analysis in India and Bangladesh. ND: Young Asia, 1979. 199p.

24002 JHA, C. Election panorama in Bihar. In PSR 6,3/4 & 7,1/2 (1967-68) 139-51.

24003 PRASAD, R. Report on the third general elections in Bihar, 1962. Patna: Supt., Secretariat Press, Bihar, 1963. 311p.

24004 PRASAD, R.C. The mature electorate: an empirical reconnaissance. ND: Ashish, 1975. 167p.

24005 SACHCHIDANANDA. The tribal voter in Bihar. ND: National, 1976. 127p.

24006 VARMA, V.P. A study of the fourth general elections in Bihar, 1967. Patna: Inst. of Public Admin., Patna U., 1968. 240p. (J. of Admin. Sciences, 13)

24007 ______. A study of the mid-term parliamentary elections in Bihar, 1971. Patna: Inst. of Public Admin., Patna U., 1975. 272p. (J. of the Admin. Sciences, 18, 1-3)

c. riots and communal violence

24008 GEORGE, T.J.S. Revolt in Bihar; a study of the August 1965 uprising. ND: Perspective, 1965. 28p.

24009 HEIDENREICH, H. The anatomy of a riot: a case study from Bihar, 1965. In JComPolSt 6 (1968) 107-24.

24010 INDIA (REP.). CMSN. OF INQUIRY ON COMMUNAL DISTURBANCES, RANCHI-HATIA, AUGUST 22-29, 1967. Report. ND: 1968. 203p.

d. administrative studies

24011 KUMAR, N. Patna High Court. Patna: Govt. of Bihar, 1967. 52p.

24012 SINGH, S.D. Provincial bureaucracy. Patna: Bihar Granth Kutir, 1978. 196 + 56p.

24013 SINHA, A.K. Thirty two years in the police and after. Patna: Sanjivan Press, 1952. 229p.

e. local government and politics

24014 BLAIR, H.W. Primary and secondary characteristics in peasant politics at the micro-level in an Indian constituency: a statistical odyssey. In CIS ns 9,1 (1975) 55-87.

24015 MAJUMDAR, B.B. Civic life in Bihar. Patna: Motilal, 1952. 96p.

24016 MISHRA, S.N. Pattern of emerging leadership in rural India. Patna: Associated Book Agency, 1977. 264p.

24017 ______. Politics and society in rural India: a case study of Darauli Gram Panchayat, Siwan District, Bihar. Delhi: Inter-India, 1980. 184p.

24018 PANT, N. The politics of panchayati raj administration: a study of official-non-official relations. Delhi: Concept, 1979. 95p.

24019 PRASAD, R.C. Democracy and development; the grass-roots experience in India. ND: Rachna Prakashan, 1971. 336p.

24020 PRASAD, V. Administrative tribunals in action: a study of administrative tribunals and authorities at the district level in Bihar. ND: Oxford & IBH, 1974. 240p.

24021 RAI, H.D. The separation of the executive and judicial functions of the district magistrate: an aspect of the criminal administration in a district of Bihar. In JNAA 11,1 (1966) 1-22.

24022 RAI, H.D. & AWADHESH PRASAD. Reorganising panchayati raj in Bihar: a critique of the reform proposals. In IJPA 21,1 (1975) 19-47.

24023 RAI, H.D. & S.P. SINGH. Village judiciary at work: a case study in the working of gram cutcherries in Bihar. In PSR 10,1/2 (1971) 65-80.

24024 SAHAY, B.N. Dynamics of leadership. ND: Bookhive, 1969. 227p.

24025 SARAN, P. Rural leadership in the context of India's modernization. ND: Vikas, 1978. 151p.

24026 TRIVEDI, R.N. Report on a comparative study of the working of traditional and statutory panchayats in the tribal areas of Ranchi District. Delhi: Motilal, 1970. 287p.

24027 VERMA, N.K.P. Civic administration of cantonments in Bihar. In QJLSGI 36 (1965) 185-94.

24028 ______. Local franchise in Bihar: a short history. Bombay: All-India Inst. of Local Self-Govt., 1965. 44p.

24029 VIDYARTHI, L.P. & K.N. SAHAY. The dynamics of tribal leadership in Bihar: research project on changing leadership in a tribal society, 1967-1971. Allahabad: Kitab Mahal, 1967. 630p.

B. The Bihar Economy since 1801

1. Demography (1981 pop. 69,823,154)

24030 BANERJEE, S.N. Effect of changes in age-patterns of marriage on fertility rates in Bihar, 1961-86. In MI 53,3 (1973) 262-78.

24031 BOSE, S.R. Bihar population problems. Calcutta: KLM, 1969. 87p.

24032 CASTRO LOPO, L. DE. An analysis of internal migration in Bihar, North India. In Geografisk Tidsskrift 66 (1967) 1-23.

2. Economic Development and Planning
a. general studies

24033 AGARWAL, P.C. Human geography of Bastar district. Allahabad: Garga, 1968. 448p.

24034 ARICKAL, G. Die Non-Governmental Organisations (NGOs) als Partner des Staates im Rahmen einer geplanten sozialökonomischen Entwicklung. Berlin: Duncker & Humboldt, 1976. 192p.

24035 BIHAR. FINANCE DEPT. Fourth five-year plan. Patna: Supt., Secretariat Press, Bihar, 1966-73. 7 v.

24036 BOSE, S.R. Economy of Bihar. Calcutta: KLM, 1971. 167p.

24037 JOY, J.L. & E. EVERITT, eds. The Kosi symposium: the rural problem in north-east Bihar: analysis of policy and planning in the Kosi area. Brighton: U. of Sussex, Inst. of Dev. Studies, 1976. 272p.

24038 KARAN, P.P. Economic regions of Chota Nagpur, Bihar, India. In Econ. Geography 29,3 (1953) 216-50.

24039 MISHRA, J.N. Co-operative banking in Bihar. Patna: Lalit Narayan Mishra Inst. of Econ. Dev. & Social Change, 1977. 311p.

24040 NCAER. Techno-economic survey of Bihar. Bombay: Asia, 1960. 276p. [1st pub. 1959]

24041 PRASAD, K.N. The economics of a backward region in a backward economy; a case study of Bihar in relation to other states of India. Calcutta: Scientific Book Agency, 1967. 2 v.

24042 RODGERS, G.B. Effects of public works on rural poverty: some case studies from the Kosi area of Bihar. In EPW 8,4-6 (1973) 255-68.

24043 SINGH, J.K. Regional economics. Varanasi: Bharati Prakashan, 1978. 90p.

24044 SINGH, R.P. & A. KUMAR. Monograph of Bihar; a geographical study. Patna: Bharati Bhawan, 1970. 193p.

24045 SINGH, P.N. Some aspects of rural life in Bihar: an economic study, 1793-1833. Patna: Janaki Prakashan, 1980. 304p.

24046 SINHA, B.B. Socio-economic life in Chotanagpur. Delhi: B.R., 1979. 215p.

24047 SINHA, D.P. Socio-economic implications of economic development in Banari: the case of Birhor resettlement. In EA 20,2 (1967) 109-32.

24048 SINHA, SACHCHIDANAND. The internal colony; a study in regional exploitation. ND: Sindhu, 1973. 159p.

24049 SRIVASTAVA, V.K. Habitat and economy in the Upper Son Basin. Gorakhpur: Uttar Bharat Bhoogol Parishad, 1973. 179p. + 16pl.

b. the Damodar Valley Corporation (est. 1948)

24050 BASU, S.K. & S.B. MUKHERJEE. Evaluation of Damodar canals, 1959-60; a study of the benefits of irrigation in the Damodar region. Bombay: Asia, 1963. 152p.

24050a BOSE, S.C. The Damodar Valley Project. Calcutta: Phoenix Press, 1948. 139p.

24051 HAMILTON, R.E. Damodar Valley Corporation: India's experiment with the TVA model. In IJPA 15 (1969) 86-109.

24052 INDIA (REP.). DAMODAR VALLEY CORP. ENQUIRY CMTEE., 1952. Report. ND: Min. of Irrigation & Power, 1953. 152p. [Chm., P.S. Rau]

24053 Indian Journal of Power and River Valley Development; DVC special number: 20 years of DVC. Calcutta: P.K. Menon, 1968. 103p.

24054 JOINT CMTEE. FOR DIAGNOSTIC SURVEY OF THE DAMODAR VALLEY REGION. Report on the lower Damodar Valley region. Calcutta: Damodar Valley Corp., 1969. v. 2, 190p. [to be 6v.]

24055 PRASAD, PARMANAND. The Damodar Valley Corporation: a brief study. ND: IIPA, 1963. 96p.

3. Agriculture in Bihar since 1801
a. agricultural development and planning

24056 BHATTACHARJEE, J.P. Under-employment among Indian farmers: an analysis of its nature and extent based on data for Bihar. In AV 3 (1961) 246-78.

24057 BIHAR. AGRI. CENSUS. Report on Agricultural Census, 1970-71, Bihar. Patna: Dept. of Revenue, 1975. 496p.

24058 BOSE, S.R. The changing face of Bihar agriculture. In IJE 51 (1970) 169-84.

24059 ______. A study in Bihar agriculture. Patna: 1967. 61p.

24060 DESAI, D.K. & HARI PRAKASH. Planning and implementation of financing agriculture through area approach: a case study in Bihar State. Ahmedabad: Centre for Mgmt. in Agri., Indian Inst. of Mgmt., 1973. 148p.

24061 FAHIM-UD-DIN, M. Animal production in Bihar. Bombay: Asia, 1963. 166p.

24062 JANNUZI, F.T. Agrarian crisis in India. The case of Bihar. Austin: U. of Texas Press, 1974. 233p.

24063 JHA, B.N. Problems of land utilization: a case study of Kosi Region. ND: Classical, 1979. 251p.

24064 JHA, D.N. Planning and agricultural development: a study with reference to Bihar. Delhi: S. Chand, 1974. 232p.

24065 LADEJINSKY, W. Green revolution in Bihar. In EPW 4,39 (1969) A147-A162.

24066 MISHRA, M. Changing agrarian economy of Purnea district: 1765-1950. In JBRS 58 (1972) 197-223.

24067 Notes on the ryot of Behar. In CR 69,138 (1879) 332-47.

24068 O'DONNELL, C.J. The wants of Behar. In CR 69,137 (1879) 146-66.

24069 RAI, B.K. Man and forest in Chotanagpur. In Vanyajati 16,3 (1968) 85-92.

24070 SACHCHIDANANDA. Social dimensions of agricultural development. Delhi: National, 1972. 197p.

24070a SENGUPTA, S.C. Santal rural economy: a study based on village survey in Santal Parganas. Santiniketan: AgroEcon. Res. Centre, 1973. 108p.

24071 SINHA, S.P. Marginal and small farmers: perspectives, problems, and prospects: a study with reference to north Bihar. Muzaffarpur: Manisha, 1978. 194p.

24072 VIDYARTHI, L.P. The future of traditional "primitive" societies: a case study of an Indian shifting cultivation society. In EA 28,4 (1975) 313-26.

b. agricultural technology and innovation; irrigation and water control

24073 CLAY, E.J. Equity and productivity effects of a package of technical innovations and changes in social institutions: tubewells, tractors, and high-yielding varieties. In IJAE 30,4 (1975) 74-87.

24074 HÄNSCH, H. Innovationsfaktoren in der Landwirtschaft Indiens: gezeigt am Beispiel ausgewählter Dörfer des Dhanbad Distrikts, Bihar, Indien. Wiesbaden: Steiner, 1977. 327p. (BSAF, 37)

24075 INDIA (REP.). CMTEE. ON PLAN PROJECTS. MINOR IRRIGATION TEAM. Report on minor irrigation works in Bihar State. ND: 1965. 64p.

24076 JHA, D. Evaluation of benefits of irrigation: Tribeni Canal report. Bombay: Orient Longmans, 1967. 601p.

24077 PANDEY, M.P. The impact of irrigation on rural development: a case study. ND: Concept, 1979. 191p.

24078 SHASTRI, C.P. Investment on farm and capital formation in agriculture with particular reference to Bihar. In IJAE 20 (1965) 175-83.

c. famines and famine relief

24079 BIHAR. Bihar famine report, 1966-1967. Patna: Supt., Secretariat Press, Bihar, 1973. 473p.

24080 CENTRAL INST. OF RES. & TRAINING IN PUBLIC CO-OPERATION. Famine relief in Bihar; a study. ND: 1969. 385p.

24081 GANGRADE, K.D. & S. DHADDA. Challenge and response; a study of famines in India. Delhi: Rachana, 1973. 124p. [special reference to Bihar famine of 1966-67]

24082 SCARFE, W. & A. SCARFE. Tiger on a rein: report on the Bihar famine. London: G. Chapman, 1969. 216p.

24083 SINGH, K. SURESH. The Indian famine, 1967: a study in crisis and change. ND: PPH, 1975. 312p.

24084 VERGHESE, B.G. Beyond the famine; an approach to regional planning for Bihar. ND: Super Bazar, for Bihar Relief Cmtee., 1967. 42p.

d. land tenure, land reform, and agrarian relations

24085 HAUSER, W. The Indian National Congress and land policy in the twentieth century. In IESHR 1 (1963) 57-65.

24086 JAIN, K.B. The Haryana ceiling on land holdings act, 1972: Haryana act no. 26 of 1972 with rules, amended up to date and also contains the scheme for utilisation of surplus land with detailed comments, notes, and case-law. Rohtak: Law Home, 1978. 268p.

24087 JHA, H. Lower-caste peasants and upper-caste zamindars in Bihar (1921-1925): an analysis of Sanskritization and contradiction between the two groups. In IESHR 14,4 (1977) 549-60.

24088 JHA, J.C. History of land revenue of Chota Nagpur in the first half of the nineteenth century. In JBRS 50 (1964) 105-13.

24089 MISHRA, G. Agrarian problems of permanent settlement: a case study of Champaran. ND: PPH, 1978. 354p.

24090 ______. Indigo plantation and agrarian relations in Champaran during the nineteenth century. In IESHR 3,4 (1966) 332-57.

24091 MISHRA, J.N., ed. Land reforms in Bihar. Patna: Bihar Inst. of Econ. Dev., 1974. 149p.

24092 MUNDLE, S. Backwardness and bondage: agrarian relations in a south Bihar district. ND: Indian Inst. of Public Admin., 1979. 184p.

24093 OJHA, G. Land problems and land reforms: a study with reference to Bihar. ND: S. Chand, 1977. 327p.

24094 POUCHEPADASS, J. L'endettement paysan dans le Bihar colonial. In Puruṣārtha 4 (1980) 165-206.

24095 ROBB, P. Hierarchy and resources: peasant stratification in late nineteenth century Bihar. In MAS 13 (1979) 97-126.

24096 SARASWATI, SAHAJANAND, Swami. Abolition of zamindari; how to achieve it. Patna: Orient Press, 1946. 33p.

24097 SCHWERIN, D. Von Armut zu Elend; Kolonialherrschaft und Agrarverfassung in Chota Nagpur, 1858-1908. Wiesbaden: Steiner, 1977. 551p.

24098 SINHA, R.N. Bihar tenantry, 1783-1833. Bombay: PPH, 1968. 190p.

24099 YANG, A.A. Control and conflict in an agrarian society: a study of Saran district, 1888-1920. Diss., U. of Virginia, 1976. 370p. [UM 77-28,597]

24100 ______. An institutional shelter: the court of wards in late nineteenth-century Bihar. In MAS 13,2 (1979) 247-64.

e. peasant movements and organizations

24101 CHAUDHURI, B.B. Agrarian movements in Bengal and Bihar, 1919-39. In A.R. Desai, ed. Peasant struggles in India. Bombay: OUP, 1979, 337-74.

24102 HAUSER, W. The Bihar provincial Kisan Sabha, 1929-1942; a study of an Indian peasant movement. Diss., U. of Chicago, 1961. 214p.

24103 MISHRA, RAMNANDAN. Kisan problems. Patna: Bihar Provincial Kisan Sabha, 1948. 116p.

24104 REID, D.N. The disaffection in Behar. In Fortnightly R. 61 (1894) 808-16.

24105 VIDYARTHI, L.P. The peasant organisation in India: a case study of a voluntary-organisation in tribal Bihar. Ranchi: Council of Social & Cultural Res., Dept. of Anthro., Ranchi U., 1977. 144p.

4. Industry in Bihar

24106 BIHAR INST. OF ECON. DEV. Industrial financing in Bihar. Patna: 1974. 186p.

24107 BOGAERT, M. VAN DEN. Entrepreneurial patterns in the urban informal sector: the case of tribal entrepreneurs in Ranchi. In SocAct 27,3 (1977) 306-23.

24108 DAS GUPTA, P.K. Impact of industrialisation on a tribe in south Bihar. Calcutta: AnthSI, 1978. 188p. (Its memoir, 48)

24109 DESAI, P. The Bokaro steel plant; a study of Soviet economic assistance. Amsterdam: North-Holland, 1972. 108p.

24110 ELWIN, V. The story of Tata steel. Bombay: 1958. 117p.

24111 KEENAN, J.L. A steel man in India. NY: Duell, Sloan & Pearce, 1943. 224p.

24112 KROPP, E.W. Einfluss des Bergbaus auf die Beschäftigungsstruktur in ländlichen Gemeinden gezeigt am Beispiel des Dhanbad Distriktes, Bihar, Indien. Wiesbaden: Steiner, 1976. 184p.

24113 MANDAL, B. Manufacturing regions of North Bihar. In NGJI 17,1 (1971) 51-62.

24114 NCAER. Industrial programmes for the fourth plan: Bihar. ND: 1967. 205p.

24115 ______. Perspective plan of industrial development of Bihar, 1979-80 to 1988-89. ND: 1979. 268p.

24116 PRASAD, A. Industries of Chotanagpur: a study in regional pattern of distribution, growth, and amplitudes. In Geographical Outlook 7 (1970-71) 71-83.

24117 PRASAD, KEDARNATH. The strategy of industrial dispersal and decentralized development; a case study. ND: Wedoli Advertisers, 1974. 516p.

24118 ROTHERMUND, D. & D.C. WADHWA, ed. Zamindars, mines, and peasants: studies in the history of an Indian coalfield and its rural hinterland. ND: Manohar, 1978. 236p. (South Asian studies, 9a)

24119 SHARMA, M.L. Institutional finance and industrial development: a case study of Bihar. Calcutta: Scientific Book Agency, 1977. 262p.

24120 SINHA, P.B. Development of the mineral industries of Bihar: 1833-1918. In J. of Hist. Res. 16,1 (1973) 74-86.

24121 THAKAR, J.N. Silk industry in Bihar. In JBRS 58 (1972) 285-313.

24122 VIDYARTHI, L.P. Socio-cultural implications of industrialisation in India; a case study of tribal Bihar. Ranchi: Council of Social & Cultural Res., Dept. of Anthro., Ranchi U., 1969. 552p.

5. Labor and Trade Unions in Bihar

24123 BIHAR. LABOUR DEPT. Indebtedness amongst industrial workers in Bihar; a survey report. Patna: Supt., Secretariat Press, Bihar, 1961. 43p.

24124 MORRIS, M.D. Order and disorder in the labour force: the Jamshedpur crisis of 1958. In EW 10,44 (1958) 1387-95.

24125 ROTHERMUND, I. Women in a coal-mining district. In EPW 10,31 (1975) 1160-65.

24126 SHUKLA, H.N. A study of trade unions in Bihar. In IJLE 11,3/4 (1969) C165-176.

24127 SRIVASTAVA, V.L. A socio-economic survey of the workers in the coalmines of India; with particular reference to Bihar. Calcutta: Scientific Book Agency, 1970. 643p.

24128 The story of a strike, May 1958. The Communist bid for power at Jamshedpur. Jamshedpur: Tata Iron and Steel Co., 1958. 67p.

6. Commerce and Transportation

24129 JAGDISH SINGH. Railroad traffic densities and patterns in South Bihar: a geographical analysis. In NGJI 7,3 (1961) 137-49.

24130 ______. Transport geography of South Bihar. Varanasi: BHU, 1964. 271p.

24131 LAL, R.S. Transport and accessibility in lower Ghaghara Gandak Duab. In DG 7,1 (1969) 14-34.

24132 SINGH, B.N. Trade and industrial markets of Bihar. Patna: Arvind Pub., 1974. 168p.

C. Society and Social Change in Bihar since 1801

1. Social Categories; Kinship and Marriage
a. general studies

24133 BRADLEY-BIRT, F.B. The story of an Indian upland. London: Smith, Elder, 1905. 354p. [Rajmahal hills & their inhabitants]

24134 SACHCHIDANANDA & K. GOPAL IYER. Caste tension in Patna. In EA 22,3 (1969) 327-48.

24135 SINGH, RANA P.B. Clan settlements in the Saran Plain (Middle Ganga Valley): a study in cultural geography. Varanasi: NGSI, 1977. 174p. (NGSI res. pub., 18)

24136 ______. Distribution of castes and search for a new theory of caste ranking: case of the Saran plain. In NGJI 21,1 (1975) 20-46.

24137 ______. Mechanism of the diffusion of clan settlements in the Saran Plain, a spatio-temporal analysis. In NGJI 21,3/4 (1975) 172-96.

24138 SINHA, D.P. Culture change in an intertribal market; the role of the Banari inter-tribal market among the hill peoples of Chotanagpur. Bombay: Asia, 1968. 117p.

b. Brahman castes: Maithil, Gayawal, Bhumihar, and others

24139 JHA, MAKHAN. Death rites among Maithil Brahmans. In MI 46 (1966) 241-47.

24140 ______. Spirit possession among the Maithil Brahmans. In EA 22 (1969) 363-68.

24141 JHA, U.N. The genealogies and genealogists of Mithila: a study of the panji and the panjikars. Varanasi: Kishor Vidya Niketan, 1980. 187p.

24142 ______. The origin of Panji system. In EA 19 (1966) 190-204.

24143 PRASAD, NARMADESHWAR. The Gayawals of Bihar. In AA 54 (1952) 279-83.

24144 SARASWATI, B.N. The institution of panji among Maithil Brahmans. In MI 42 (1962) 263-76.

24145 ______. The web of Maithil clanship. In EA 11 (1957-58) 31-35.

24146 SHASTRI, J.G. The mode of appraoch of the Mithila Smartas to various social problems. In JBRS 48 (1962) 34-49.

24147 VIDYARTHI, L.P. Origin and development of the Gayawal. In JBRS 40 (1954) 232-48.

24148 ______. The extensions of an Indian priestly caste. In MI 39 (1959-60) 28-35.

c. intermediate castes
[for Kayasthas, see III. C. 1. d., above]

d. scheduled castes (14% of Bihar pop. 1971)

24149 MISHRA, N. Some aspects of the Dusadh of Darbhanga. In JSR 18,2 (1975) 9-28.

24150 SACHCHIDANANDA. Emergent scheduled caste elite in Bihar. In R&S 21,3 (1974) 55-61.

24151 ______. The Harijan elite. Delhi: Thomson Press, 1977. 214p.

24152 SENGUPTA, N. Destitutes and development: a study of the Bauri community in the Bokaro region. ND: Concept, 1979. 123p.

24153 VIDYARTHI, L.P. & N. MISHRA. Economic problems of the scheduled castes of Bihar: some preliminary observations. In JRS 18,2 (1975) 126-41.

24154 ______. Harijan today: sociological, economic, political, religious, and cultural analysis. ND: Classical Publications, 1977. 232p.

e. Muslims of Bihar

24155 AHMAD, ZEYAUDDIN. Caste elements among the Muslims of Bihar. In K. David, ed. The new wind: changing identities in South Asia. The Hague: Mouton, 1977, 337-56. (Its World Anthropology series)

24156 ______. Marriage and family among the Muslims of Bihar. In G. Kurian, ed. The family in India: a regional view. The Hague: Mouton, 1974, 317-333.

24157 ALI, HASAN. Elements of caste among the Muslims in a district in southern Bihar. In MI 54,3 (1973) 190-212.

f. Adivasis (tribals) [for tribes of Chota Nagpur area, see Chap. Twelve, II. C.]

2. Villages and Rural Development

24158 ANSARI, A.W. The changing village India. ND: Chetana, 1980. 341p.

24159 GRIERSON, G.A. Bihar peasant life, being a discursive catalogue of the surroundings of the people of that province.... Delhi: Cosmo, 1975. 431p. + 16 pl. [1st pub. 1885]

24160 KHADI & VILLAGE INDUSTRIES CMSN. The Deora village plan. Bombay: 1959. 104p.

24161 MISHRA, N. Cultural persistence and change: a rural profile of Anjan. ND: Classical, 1978. 210p. [Ranchi Dist.]

24162 PRASAD, AWADESH. The block development officer - a portrait of Indian bureaucracy. Patna: Associated Book Agency, 1976. 265p.

24163 PRASAD, AYODHYA. Chotanagpur; geography of rural settlements. Ranchi: Ranchi U., 1973. 467p.

24164 SACHCHIDANANDA. Caste and conflict in a Bihar village. In EA 20,2 (1967) 143-50.

24165 SAHAY, K.N. Caste and occupation in a village in Bihar. In MI 47,3 (1967) 178-88.

24166 SCARFE, W. & A. SCARFE. A mouthful of petals. NY:

Taplinger, 1967. 211p. [on Sarvodaya Movement]

24167 SEN, JYOTI. Community development in Chota Nagpur. Calcutta: Asiatic Soc., 1968. 100p.

24168 SHUKLA, N.K. The social structure of an Indian village. ND: Cosmo, 1976. 185p.

24169 SINHA, D.P. Innovation, response and development in Banari. In MI 48,3 (1968) 225-43.

24170 WOOD, G. From raiyat to rich peasant. In SAR 7,1 (1973) 1-16.

3. Cities and Urbanization
a. general studies

24171 BIHAR. TOWN PLANNING ORG. Draft master plan: Dhanbad-Jharia-Sindri complex. Dhanbad: Dhanbad Town Planning Authority, 1968. 120p.

24172 GAUNTIA, R. & V.N.P. SINHA. Trends in the urbanization of the Chota Nagpur plateau. In DG 8,2 (1969) 117-28.

24173 GAYA IMPROVEMENT TRUST. Draft master plan. Gaya: 1965. 60p.

24174 KARAN, P.P. Patna and Jamshedpur. In GRI 14 (1956) 25-32.

24175 MUKHERJI, M. Function and functional classification of towns in Bihar. In DG 8 (1970) 56-66.

24176 PANDEYA, P. Impact of industrialisation on urban growth; a case study of Chhotanagpur. Allahabad: Central Book Depot, 1970. 258p.

24177 SINGH, K.N. Urban development in India. ND: Abhinav, 1978. 231p.

24178 SINHA, V.N.P. Chota Nagpur Plateau: a study in settlement geography. ND: K.B. Pub., 1976. 222p.

24179 THAKUR, B. Evolution of the townscape of Darbhanga. In JBRS 54 (1968) 345-58.

b. Patna, site of ancient Pataliputra, and capital of Bihar (1971 pop. 490,265)

24180 ABDUL ALI, A.F.M. Patna - her relations with John Company Bahadur. In BPP 41 (1931) 30-40.

24181 BEVERIDGE, H. The city of Patna. In CR 76,152 (1883) 211-33.

24182 BIHAR. CMSN. TO INQUIRE INTO THE AFFAIRS OF THE PATNA IMPROVEMENT TRUST, THE PATNA MUNICIPAL CORP. & THE PATNA WATER BOARD.... Report. Patna: Supt., Secretariat Press, 1970. 179p. [Chm., S.P. Varma]

24183 KUMAR, N. Image of Patna. Patna: Govt. of Bihar, Gazetteers Branch, 1972. 210p.

24184 PATNA IMPROVEMENT TRUST. Master plan. Patna: 1962. v. 1, Text and photos, 136p.; v. 2, Drawings, 20 pl.

24185 SAMI, ABDUS. Intra urban market geography: a case study of Patna. ND: Concept, 1980. 219p.

24186 SINHA, M.M.P. The impact of urbanization on land use in the rural-urban fringe: a case study of Patna. ND: Concept, 1980. 258p.

c. Jamshedpur: Tata Iron and Steel Co. (TISCO) center in Singhbum Dist. (1971 pop. 465,200)

24187 AMES, M.M. Structural dimensions of family life in the steel city of Jamshedpur, India. In M.B. Singer, ed. Entrepreneurship and modernization of occupational cultures in South Asia. Durham, NC: DUPCSSA, 1973, 107-131. (Its Monographs & occ. papers series, 12)

24188 BIHAR. LABOUR DEPT. Report on the industrial housing survey at Jamshedpur. Patna: Supt., Secretariat Press, Bihar, 1959. 81p.

24189 DUTT, A.K. Evolution of Jamshedpur city, a historical approach to urban study. In IGJ 41 (1966) 19-28.

24190 DUTTA, M. Jamshedpur: the growth of the city and its regions. Calcutta: Asiatic Soc., 1977. 177p.

24191 MISRA, B.R. Report on socio-economic survey of Jamshedpur City. Patna: B.R. Misra, for Dept. of Applied Econ. & Commerce, Patna U., 1959. 2 v. in 1.

24192 SHARMA, T.R. A tribal community in an industrial context. (A case study in Jamshedpur City). In JSR 5 (1962) 114-23.

d. Ranchi: political center of Chota Nagpur tribal region (1971 pop. 256,011)

24193 KULDIP SINGH. Ranchi: an appraisal of an extended town. In URPT 7,1/2 (1964) 3-13.

24194 MUKHERJEE, B. Ranchi: a study in urban morphology. In NGJI 2,2 (1956) 97-105.

24195 RANCHI IMPROVEMENT TRUST. Draft master plan for Greater Ranchi. Ranchi: 196-. 92p. + 6 maps.

24196 SINHA, S.K. Ranchi: physical and socio-economic characteristics. In URPT 7 (1964) 14-39.

24197 VIDYARTHI, L.P. Cultural configuration of Ranchi; survey of an emerging industrial city of tribal India, 1960-62. Calcutta: J.N. Basu, 1969. 412p.

4. Social Welfare and Health Services

24198 IVERN, F. Chotanagpur survey; a study of socio-economic and health development. Delhi: Indian Social Inst., 1969. 524p.

24199 MANDAL, B.B. The physically handicapped in Bihar. Calcutta: Inst. of Social Res. & Applied Anthropology, 1979. 119p.

24200 MATHUR, B.L. & G.P.L. SRIVASTAVA. Some aspects of the Bihar mass vasectomy camps. In J. of Family Welfare 20,3 (1974) 73-83.

24201 RAO, T.S. & M.V.D. BOGAERT. The beggar problem in Ranchi. In IJSW 31,3 (1970) 285-302.

24202 SAKSENA, D.N. Vasectomy: field experience of a district hospital in Bihar. In J. of Family Welfare 18,2 (1971) 9-19.

24203 VIDYARTHI, L.P. & R.K. PRASAD & V.S. UPADHYAY. Changing dietary patterns and habits: a socio-cultural study of Bihar. ND: Concept, 1979. 191p.

5. Education in Bihar since 1801 (26.0% literacy in 1981)

24204 AMBASHT, N.K. A critical study of tribal education, with special reference to Ranchi District. Delhi: S. Chand, 1970. 173p.

24205 BANERJEE, M. Literacy in Singhbhum. In GRI 37,2 (1975) 151-57.

24206 BASTEDO, T.G. Law colleges and law students in Bihar. In Law & Society R. 3,2 (1968-69) 269-94.

24207 BIHAR. EDUC. RE-ORGANISATION CMTEE., 1938. Report. Patna: Govt. Press, 1940-41. 3 v. in 1.

24208 BIHAR. SECONDARY EDUC. CMTEE. Report. Patna: Supt., Secretariat Press, 1963. 128p.

24209 BIHAR STATE SEMINAR ON EDUC. PLANNING & ADMIN., PATNA, 1970. Report of the Bihar State Seminar on Educational Planning and Administration, Patna, January 20-24, 1970. ND: Natl. Staff College for Educ. Planners & Administrators, 1972. 71p.

24210 BLASCHKE, D. Probleme interdisziplinärer Forschung: Organisations- und forschungssozialogische Untersuchung der Erfahrung mit interdisziplinärer Zusammenarbeit im SFB 16 unter besonderer Betonung des Dhanbad-Projekts. Wiesbaden: Steiner, 1976. 201p.

24211 JHA, J.S. Beginnings of modern education in Mithila; selections from educational records, Darbhanga Raj, 1860-1930. Patna: K.P. Jayaswal Res. Inst., 1972. 78 + 256p. (Its Hist. res. series, 9)

24212 ______. Sanskrit education in Bihar (1860-1937). In JBRS 47 (1961) 89-105.

24213 ______. State of Sanskrit education in Bihar, 1813-1859. In JBRS 45 (1959) 265-96.

24214 SACHCHIDANANDA. Education and changes in social values. In MI 48 (1968) 71-85.

24215 SARKAR, JAGADISH NARAYAN & J.C. JHA. A history of the Patna College, 1863-1963. Patna: Patna College, 1963. 170p.

24216 SINHA, N. University administration in India: with special reference to the universities in Bihar. Patna: Janaki Prakashan, 1979. 331p.

24217 SINHA, N.K. Governors' functions as the Chancellor of the Universities: a case study in Bihar during the period 1952-60. In IJPS 23,1 (1962) 72-82.

24218 SRIVASTAVA, L.R.N. The role of education in the modernization of Chotanagpur. In Indian Educ. R. 6,1 (1971) 162-82.

24219 VIDYARTHI, L.P. Students unrest in Chotanagpur, 1969-70. Calcutta: Punthi Pustak, 1976. 409p.

24220 ______. University youths in Chotanagpur: a study in campus life. In JSR 15,2 (1972) 1-23.

D. Religious Traditions of Modern Bihar
[For Tribal Religions, see Chap. Twelve, II. C.]

24221 CHATTOPADHYAY, K. Rites and rituals: media of rural integration. In EA 23,2 (1970) 217-33.

24222 CHAUBEY, G. An unique organisation of Shaiva pilgrims. In Indian Folklore 1 (1958) 49-59.

24223 MAHTO, S. Hundred years of Christian missions in Chotanagpur since 1845. Ranchi: Chotanagpur Christian Pub. House, 1971. 268p.

24224 MATTHEWS, D.S. The joyful kingdom of Raj Anandpur. Maryknoll, NY: Maryknoll Pub., 1967. 114p.

24225 SAHAY, K.N. Hindu shrines of Chotanagpur: case study of Tanginath. Simla: IIAS, 1975. 101p.

E. Literatures and Media in Modern Bihar

1. Maithili Literature of North Bihar
[See also Chap. One, VI. F. 5; for Hindi and Urdu Literature, see Chap. Six, VIII. B. & C. and Chap. Eight, X. C. 2. & 3.]

24226 MISHRA, J.K. Maithili. In K.R. Srinivasa Iyengar, ed. Indian literature since Independence. ND: Sahitya Akademi, 1973, 128-39.

24227 ______. Maithili: struggling against great odds. In IL 11,4 (1968) 46-52.

2. Folk Literature

24228 JHA, M. Folk-lore, magic, and legends of Mithila. Patna: Jyoti, 1979. 96p.

24229 MISHRA, S.D. Elements of culture in Bhojpuri folksongs. In Folklore(C) 6 (1965) 28-39.

24230 PAKRASI, M. Folk tales of Bihar. ND: Sterling, 1973. 120p. (Folk tales of India series, 14)

24230a PRASAD, H.C. A bibliography of folklore of Bihar: books, articles, reports, and monographs in English and Hindi. Calcutta: Indian Pub., 1971. 96p. (Its Folklore series, 17) [draft pub. in Folklore(C) 11 (1970) 258-71, 334-40, 369-83, 452-71.]

24231 ROY CHOUDHURY, P.C. Folk tales of Bihar. ND: Sahitya Akademi, 1968. 132p.

24232 ______. Folklore of Bihar. ND: NBT, 1976. 203p.

24233 SINGH, D.P. Kumar Singh in Bhojpuri folksongs and dance. In Folklore(C) 5,10 (1964) 378-98.

24234 ______. Mysticism and high poetic expressions and ideas in folk songs of Bhojpuri. In Folklore(C) 3 (1962) 304-18.

24234a UPADHYAYA, H.S. Indian family structure and the Bhojpuri riddles. In Folklore(L) 81 (1970) 115-31.

24235 VIDYARTHI, L.P. Bihar in folklore study; an anthology. Calcutta: Indian Pub., 1971. 312p.

3. Journalism and the Press

24236 DATTA, K.K., ed. Souvenir: Dr. Sachchidananda Sinha birth centenary. Patna: Shrimati Radhika Sinha Inst. & Sachchidananda Sinha Library, 1972. 125p.

24237 JHA, J.S. Early printing presses and newspapers in Bihar. In JBRS 50 (1964) 98-104.

24238 NAGENDRA KUMAR. Journalism in Bihar; a supplement to Bihar State gazetteer. Patna: Govt. of Bihar, Gazetteers Branch, 1971. 215p. (Gazetteer of India: Bihar)

24239 SARKAR, S.C. What ails the Bihar press? In Vidura 7,2 (1970) 17-20.

24240 SINHA, SACHCHIDANANDA. Recollections and reminiscences of a long life. In Hindustan R. 80-85 (1946-49) passim.

15

The Northeast: The Bengal-Bangladesh and Assam Area of the Ganga Delta and Brahmaputra Valley, 1813–

I. BENGAL: THE BENGALI-SPEAKING GANGA DELTA

A. Bengal Presidency: General and Political History, 1813 - 1947

1. Sources and Reference Works

24241 CHATTOPADHYAY, G., ed. Bengal, early nineteenth century: selected documents. Calcutta: Research India Pub., 1978. 281p.

24242 DAS, S., ed. Selections from the Indian journals. Calcutta: KLM, 1963-1965. 2 v., 376, 528p. [from Calcutta J., 1818-20]

24243 DIEHL, K.S. Early Indian imprints. NY: Scarecrow Press, 1964. 533p. [based on W. Carey Historical Library, Serampore College]

24244 GHOSE, B., comp. Selections from English periodicals of nineteenth century Bengal. Calcutta: Papyrus, 1978-. v. 1-.

24245 HUNTER, W.W. Statistical account of Bengal. Delhi: D.K. Pub. House, 1973. 20 v. [Rpt. 1875-77 ed.]

24246 KOPF, D. A bibliographic essay on Bengal studies in the U.S. In R. Van M. Baumer, ed. Aspects of Bengali history and society. Honolulu: UPH, 1975, 200-42.

24247 LAKSHMINARASIAH, P., comp. The encyclopaedia of Bengal, Behar and Orissa. Madras: Indian Encyclopaedias Compiling & Publishing, 1924-25. 320p.

24248 MOITRA, S.C., comp. Selections from Jnananessan. Calcutta: Prajna, 1979. 175 + 121p. [from Bengali-English bilingual weekly Jñānānveshaṇa (Gyananneshun), 1831-1840]

24249 SINHA, N., comp. Freedom movement in Bengal, 1818-1904: who's who. Calcutta: Educ. Dept., Govt. of W. Bengal, 1968. 495p.

2. General Histories of Bengal, incl. Local Histories

24250 BAUMER, R. VAN M., ed. Aspects of Bengali history & society. Honolulu: UPH, 1975. 246p. (Asian Studies at Hawaii, 12)

24251 BHUPENDRA CHANDRA SINHA, MAHARAJA OF SUSANGA. Changing Times. Calcutta: AnthSI, 1965. 182p.

24251a BUCHANAN, F.H. Geographical, statistical and historical description of the district, or Zila, of Dinajpur in the province...of Bengal.... Calcutta: Baptist Mission Press, 1833. 342p.

24252 CONF. ON BENGAL STUDIES, 1st-7th. East Lansing: Asian Studies Center, Michigan State U., 1967-1975. (Its occ. papers, South Asia series 6,9,12,13,16,18,21 25, 26)
- 6. Bengal: literature and history. Ed. by E.C. Dimock, 1967. 177p.
- 9. Bengal regional identity. Ed. by D. Kopf, 1969. 150p.
- 12. Urban Bengal. Ed. by R.L. Park, 1970. 127p.
- 13. Bengal: East and West. Ed. by A. Lipski, 1970. 149p.
- 16. Bengal: change and continuity. Ed. by R. & M.J. Beech, 1971. 270p.
- 18. Prelude to crisis: Bengal and Bengal studies in 1970. Ed. by P. Bertocci, 1972. 111p.
- 21. West Bengal and Bangladesh: perspectives from 1972. Ed. by B. Thomas & S. Lavan, 1973. 327p.
- 25. Bengal in the 19th and 20th centuries. Ed. by J.R. McLane, 1975. 219p.
- 26. Studies on Bengal. Ed. by W.M. Gunderson, 1976. 145p.

24253 MAJUMDAR, P.C. The Musnud of Murshidabad (1704-1904), being a synopsis of the history of Murshidabad. Murshidabad: Saroda Ray, 1905. 322p.

24254 MAJUMDAR, R.C. Glimpses of Bengal in the nineteenth century. Calcutta: KLM, 1960. 112p.

24255 ______. History of modern Bengal. Calcutta: G. Bharadwaj, 1978-. [to be 2v; v. 1, 1765-1905]

24256 O'MALLEY, L.S.S. History of Bengal, Bihar & Orissa under British rule. Calcutta: Bengal Secretariat Book Depot, 1925. 779p.

24257 PRICE, J.C. Notes on the history of Midnapore, as contained in records extant in the Collector's Office. Calcutta: Bengal Secretariat Press, 1876. 1 v.

24258 REID, R. Years of change in Bengal and Assam. London: E. Benn, 1966. 170p.

24259 SINHA, N.K., ed. The history of Bengal, 1757-1905. Calcutta: U. of Calcutta, 1967. 627p.

24260 TAYLOR, J. Sketch of the topography and statistics of Dacca. Calcutta: G.H. Huttman, Military Orphan Press, 1840. 371p.

24261 WALSH, J.H.T. A history of Murshidabad District, with biographies of some of its noted families. London: Jarrold, 1902. 261p.

3. Administration and Judiciary; the Rule of the Lieutenant Governors

24261a BANERJEE, S. Studies in administrative history of Bengal, 1880-1898. ND: Rajesh Pub., 1978. 306p.

24262 BEAMES, J. Memoirs of a Bengal civilian. London: Chatto & Windus, 1961. 311p.

24263 BENGAL. RETRENCHMENT CMTEE. Report. Calcutta: Bengal Govt. Press, 1932. 180p.

24264 BUCKLAND, C.E. Bengal under the Lieutenant Governors, 1854-1898. Calcutta: S.K. Lahiri, 1901. 2 v.

24265 BURMAN, D.J. History of Bengal's shifting boundary and population. In MR 79 (1946) 264-75.

24266 EDWARDS, W. Reminiscences of a Bengal civilian. London: Smith, Elder, 1866. 352p.

24267 Government and politics in Bengal: Andrew Fraser. Delhi: Mittal Pub., 1979. 203p. [Rpt. 1908 ed.; Lt-Gov. 1903-08]

24268 HUNTER, W.W. Thackerays in India. London: H. Frowde, 1897. 191p.

24269 KABEER, R.R. Administrative policy of the Government of Bengal, 1870-1890. Dacca: NIPA, 1965. 174+146p.

24270 MOORE, C. The sheriffs of Fort William, 1775-1926. 2nd ed. Calcutta: Thacker, Spink, 1926 516p.

24271 PANDEY, B.N. The introduction of English law into India; the career of Elijah Impey in Bengal, 1774-1783. Bombay: Asia, 1967. 248p.

24272 ROY, N.C. A critical study of some aspects of public administration in Bengal. Calcutta: U. of Calcutta Press, 1945. 99p.

24273 SINHA, C.R. A judiciary at odds with the executive -- the Calcutta Supreme Court and the Bengal Administration 1781-1833. In JASCalcutta 9 (1967) 25-48.

24274 WAVERLEY, J.A. Speeches and addresses...1932-37. London: Macmillan, 1939. 394p.

24275 WHEELER-BENNETT, J.W. John Anderson, Viscount Waverley. NY: St. Martin's Press, 1962. 430p.

24276 ZETLAND, L. (LORD RONALDSHAY). Lord Ronaldshay in Bengal; being a selection from his speeches as Governor of Bengal, 1917-1922. Calcutta: Art Press, 1929. 399p.

4. Local Government in Bengal, 1813-1947 [for Calcutta, see I. D. 5., below]

24277 ABEDIN, NAJMUL. Local administration in Bengal: the first half of the 20th century. In BHS 1 (1976) 112-30.

24278 CARSTAIRS, R. The little world of an Indian district officer. London: Macmillan, 1912. 381p.

24279 ______. Plea for the better local government of Bengal. London: Macmillan, 1904. 166p.

24280 HART, S.G. Self-government in rural Bengal, by a district officer. 2nd ed. Calcutta: 1927. 2 v.

24281 ROY, N.C. Rural self-government in Bengal. Calcutta: U. of Calcutta, 1936. 202p.

24282 TOYNBEE, G. Sketch of the administration of Hooghly district from 1795 to 1845.... Calcutta: Bengal Secretariat Press, 1888. 177p.

5. Nationalism and Bengal Provincial Politics
a. general studies

24283 DAS, N.N. History of Midnapur. Calcutta: Midnapur Samskriti Parishad, v. 2, 1962. 258p. [mainly Freedom Movement, 1905-1942]

24284 GORDON, L.A. Bengal: the nationalist movement, 1876-1940. NY: ColUP, 1974. 407p.

24285 MAITY, S.K. Freedom movement in Midnapore. Calcutta: KLM, 1975-. v. 1, 183p.

b. early nationalist organizations

24286 BAGAL, J.C. History of the Indian Association, 1876-1951. Calcutta: Indian Assoc., 1953. 262p.

24287 SARKAR, H.C. A life of Ananda Mohan Bose. Calcutta: A.C. Sarkar, 1910. 208p.

24288 SINGH ROY, P.N. Chronicle of the British Indian Association, 1851-1952. Calcutta: British Indian Assoc., 1965. 549p.

c. Partition of Bengal 1905, India-wide nationalist protest, and reunification 1912

24289 BAIG, M.R.A. The Partition of Bengal and its aftermath. In IJPS 30,2 (1969) 103-29.

24290 BROOMFIELD, J.H. The partition of Bengal: a problem in British administration, 1830-1912. In PIHC 23 (1961) 13-24.

24291 CRONIN, R.P. British policy and administration in Bengal, 1905-1912; partition and the new province of Eastern Bengal and Assam. Calcutta: KLM, 1977. 236p.

24292 CHAKRABARTI, H. The how and the why of the creation of a new Bengal, 1911. In BPP 92,2 (1973) 171-200.

24293 GHOSH, Y.K., ed. The Barisal District Conference, 1908. Calcutta: Barisal Seva Samiti, 1979. 71p.

24294 ______, ed. Bengal Provincial Conference, 1905, Mymensingh session. Calcutta: Adhyayan; dist. KLM, 1974. 168p.

24295 ______, ed. Bengal Provincial Conference, 1906, Barisal Session. Calcutta: Ghosh: dist. KLM, 1978. 168p.

24296 ______, ed. Echo of Aswanikumar's deportation. Calcutta: Barisal Seva Samiti, 1980. 252p. [Aswini Kumar Dutt, 1856-1923]

24297 EUSTIS, F.A. & Z.H. ZAIDI. King, Viceroy and Cabinet: the modification of the Partition of Bengal, 1911. In History 49 (1964) 171-84.

24298 JOHNSON, G. Partition, agitation and Congress: Bengal 1904 to 1908. In J. Gallagher & G. Johnson & Anil Seal, eds. Locality, province, and nation.... Cambridge: CamUP, 1973, 213-68. [1st pub. in MAS 7,3 (1973) 533-88]

24299 MCLANE, J.C. The decision to partition Bengal in 1905. In IESHR 2,3 (1965) 221-37.

24300 PARDAMAN SINGH. The annulment of the partition of Bengal. In BPP 92,1 (1973) 73-83.

24301 ______. Lord Minto and the partition agitation. In BPP 85,2 (1966) 141-58.

24302 RAY, A.B. Communal attitudes to British Policy: the case of the Partition of Bengal, 1905. In SocSci 6,5 (1977) 34-46.

24303 SARKAR, S. The Swadeshi Movement in Bengal, 1903-1908. ND: PPH, 1973. 552p.

24304 ZAIDI, Z.H. The political motive in the partition of Bengal, 1905. In JPHS 7 (1964) 113-49.

d. later Bengal nationalism: extremism, Gandhism, constitutionalism

24305 BANERJI, N.C. At the crossroads, 1885-1946; the autobiography of Nripendra Chandra Banerji (Mastarmahasaya). 2nd ed. Calcutta: Jijnasa, 1974. 282p. [1st pub. 1950]

24306 BASAK, B. Bankshall Court: some memorable trials. Calcutta: Naya Prokash, 1977. 158p.

24307 BHATTACHARYA, B. Satyagrahas in Bengal, 1921-39. Calcutta: Minerva, 1977. 351p.

24308 ______, ed. Freedom struggle and Anushilan Samiti. Calcutta: Anushilan Samiti, 1979-. v. 1, 335p.

24309 BOSE, A. Inside Bengal, 1941-44; Forward Bloc and its allies vs. Communist Party. Bombay: PPH, 1945. 65p.

24310 BOSE, S.C. I warned my countrymen; being the collected works, 1945-50. Ed. by S.K. Bose. Calcutta: Netaji Res. Bureau, 1968. 354p.

24311 ______. The voice of Sarat Chandra Bose: selected speeches, 1927-1941. Ed. by S.K. Bose. Calcutta: Netaji Res. Bureau, 1979. 149p.

24312 BROOMFIELD, J.H. The non-cooperation decision of 1920: a crisis in Bengal politics. In D.A. Low, ed. Soundings in modern South Asian history. Berkeley: UCalP, 1968, 225-60.

24313 CHAKRABARTI, H. Government and Bengal terrorism 1912-18. In BPP 90,2 (1971) 165-181.

24314 CHAKRABORTY, T.N. Thirty years in prison; sensational confessions of a revolutionary. Tr. from Bengali by N. Datta. Enl. English ed. Calcutta: Alpha-Beta Pub., 1963. 359p.

24315 CHATTOPADHYAYA, G. Communism and Bengal's freedom movement. ND: PPH, 1970-. v. 1, 1917-29, 179p.

24316 DAS, K. Profile of a martyr, Jatin Das. Chandigarh: Public Relations, Haryana, 1979? 90p. [Jatindra Nath Das, 1904-1929]

24317 DUTT, K. Chittagong Armoury raiders: reminiscences. 2nd rev. ed. ND: PPH, 1979. 90p.

24318 GHOSH, Y.K., ed. Bengal Provincial Conference, 1928, Basirhat session. Calcutta: Y. Ghosh: dist. KLM, 1979. 167p.

24319 GORDON, L.A. Bengal's Gandhi: a study in modern Indian regionalism, politics and thought. In D. Kopf, ed. Bengal regional identity. East Lansing: Asian Studies Center, Michigan State U., 1969, 87-132.

24320 LAUSHEY, D.M. Bengal terrorism & the Marxist left: aspects of regional nationalism in India, 1905-1942. Calcutta: KLM, 1975. 187p.

24321 Law and order in Midnapur, 1930: as contained in the reports of the non-official enquiry committee. Calcutta: D.C. Lodh, 1930. 27p. + 9pl.

24322 MAJUMDAR, R.C. The revolutionary movement in Bengal

and the role of Surya Sen. Calcutta: U. of Calcutta, 1978. 27p. [1892-1934]

24323 RAY, R.K. Masses in politics: the non-cooperation movement in Bengal 1920-22. In IESHR 11,4 (1974) 343-410.

24324 SARKAR, T. The first phase of civil disobedience in Bengal, 1930-1. In IHR 4,1 (1977) 75-95.

24325 SENGUPTA, P. Deshapriya Jatindra Mohan Sengupta. ND: PDMIB, 1968. 180p. [1885-1933]

e. Bengal provincial politics - general studies

24326 BROOMFIELD, J.H. Elite conflict in a plural society; twentieth-century Bengal. Berkeley: UCalP, 1968. 349p.

24327 ______. The social and institutional bases of politics in Bengal, 1906-1946. In R. Van M. Baumer, ed. Aspects of Bengali history and society. Honolulu: UPH, 1975, 132-46.

24328 ______. The vote and the transfer of power; a study of the Bengal general election, 1912-1913. In JAS 21 (1962) 163-81.

24329 GALLAGHER, J. Congress in decline: Bengal 1930 to 1939. In J. Gallagher & G. Johnson & Anil Seal, ed. Locality, province, and nation.... Cambridge: CamUP, 1973, 269-325.

24330 GOSWAMI, T.C. Footprints of liberty; selections from the speeches and writings.... Serampore: Tulsi-Beena Trust, 1971. 430p.

24331 MCLANE, J.R. Calcutta and the mofussilization of Bengali politics. In R.L. Park, ed. Urban Bengal. East Lansing: Asian Studies Center, Michigan State U., 1969, 63-86. (Its occ. papers, South Asia series, 12)

f. Muslims in Bengal politics, 1813-1947

24332 ABDUL LATIF. Autobiography and other writings of Nawab Abdul Latif Dhan Bahadur. Ed. by M. Mohar Ali. 2nd ed., rev. and enl. Chittagong: Mehrub Pub., 1968. 321p.

24333 BROOMFIELD, J.H. The forgotten majority: the Bengal Muslims and September 1918. In D.A. Low, ed. Soundings in modern South Asian history. Berkeley: UCalP, 1968, 196-224.

24334 DE, A. Roots of separatism in nineteenth century Bengal. Calcutta: Ratna Prakashan, 1974. 190p.

24335 KAMAL, KAZI AHMED. Politicians and inside stories; a glimpse mainly into lives of Fazlul Huq, Shaheed Suhrawardy and Moulana Bhashani. Dacca: Kazi Giasuddin Ahmed, 1970. 232p.

24336 MCPHERSON, K. The Muslim microcosm, Calcutta, 1918 to 1935. Wiesbaden: Steiner, 1974. 162p. (BSAF, 8)

24337 QURESHI, M.S. Étude sur l'évolution intellectuelle chez les musulmans du Bengale 1857-1947. The Hague: Mouton, 1971. 208p.

24338 RAHIM, M. ABDUR. The Muslim society and politics in Bengal, A.D. 1757-1947. Dacca: U. of Dacca, 1978. 388p.

24339 SARKAR, S. Hindu-Muslim relations in Swadeshi Bengal, 1903-1908. In IESHR 9,2 (1972) 161-216.

24340 SEN, S. Muslim politics in Bengal, 1937-1947. ND: Impex India, 1976. 310p.

g. A.K. Fazlul Huq (1873-1962), leader of the Krishak Praja Party and the first Premier of Bengal, 1937-42

24341 ABDUR RAB, A.S.M. A.K. Fazlul Haq; life and acheivements. Lahore: Ferozsons, 1967. 211p.

24342 DE, A. Fazlul Huq and his reaction to the two-nation theory. In BPP 93,1 (1974) 23-38.

24343 FAZLUL HUQ, ABDUL KASEM. Bengal today. Barisal: al-Helal Pub. House, 1978. 60p. [1st pub. 1944]

24344 ______. Fazlul Huq speaks in Council, 1913-1916: new style in Muslim politics. Ed. by Sirajul Islam. Dacca: Bangladesh Itihas Samiti, 1976. 78p.

24345 ______. Memorable speeches of Sher-e-Bangla. Ed. by A.K. Zainul Abedin. Barisal: al-Helal Pub. House, 1978. 196p.

24346 Fazlul Haq special number . In BHS 1 (1976) 1-208.

24347 GHOSH, S. Fazlul Haq and Muslim politics in pre-partition Bengal. In IS 13,3 (1974) 441-64.

24348 MOMEN, H. Muslim politics in Bengal; a study of Krishak Praja Party and the elections of 1937. Dacca: Sunny House, 1972. 94p.

B. The Indian State of West Bengal - General and Political History since 1947

1. West Bengal Politics - Surveys and General Studies

24349 BANERJEE, N. Politicization of women in West Bengal. In Vina Mazumdar, ed. Symbols of power.... Bombay: Allied, 1979, 140-70.

24350 CHAKRABORTY, S.R. Pressure groups in West Bengal. In IJPS 35,2 (1974) 172-84.

24351 FRANDA, M.F. Electoral politics in West Bengal: the growth of the united front. In PA 42,3 (1969) 279-93.

24352 ______. Intra-regional factionalism and coalition-building in West Bengal. In JCPS 8,3 (1970) 187-205.

24353 ______. West Bengal and the federalizing process in India. Princeton: PUP, 1968. 257p.

24354 GANGULY, B. Profiles of women in West Bengal state politics . In Vina Mazumdar, ed. Symbols of power.... Bombay: Allied, 1979, 319-49.

24355 GHOSH, S. Alliance and misalliance in West Bengal. In SAR 3,4 (1970) 285-91.

24356 ______. The disinherited state; a study of West Bengal, 1967-70. Bombay: Orient Longman, 1971. 323p.

24357 LAMBERT, R.D. Religion, economics and violence in Bengal. In Middle East J. 4 (1950) 307-28.

24358 NICHOLAS, R.W. West Bengal's united front. In Asian R. 2,4 (1969) 303-12.

24359 ROY, R. The agony of West Bengal. 2nd enl. ed. Calcutta, New Age, 1972. 170p.

24360 STANDING CMTEE. IN DEFENCE OF DEMOCRACY, WEST BENGAL. Police action under Sri P.C. Ghosh; a report. Calcutta: 1968. 46p.

24361 WEST BENGAL. Memorandum before States Reorganisation Commission. Alipore: Bengal Govt., 1954. 285p.

24362 WEST BENGAL. PRADESH CONGRESS CMTEE. Memorandum submitted to the States Reorganisation Commission. Calcutta: 1954. 184p. [Suppl. memorandum. Calcutta: 1955. 47p.]

2. Chief Ministers and Other Politicians

24363 CHAKRABARTI, S. With Dr. B.C. Roy and other Chief Ministers; a record up to 1962. Calcutta: Benson's, 1974. 534p.

24364 ______. With West Bengal chief ministers: memoirs, 1962-1977. Calcutta: Chakrabarty, 1978. 520p.

24365 CHAKRAVARTY, M. Personality and state politics: first four years of B.C. Roy's premiership. In PSR 6 (1969) 231-35.

24366 FRANDA, M.F. The political idioms of Atulya Ghosh. In AS 6,8 (1966) 420-33.

24367 ROY, B.C. Towards a prosperous India: speeches and writings of Bidhan Chandra Roy. Calcutta: Pulinbihari Sen, 1964. 462p.

24368 THOMAS, K.P. Dr. B.C. Roy. Calcutta: West Bengal Pradesh Congress Cmtee., 1955. 279p.

3. West Bengal Communist Parties: CPI, CPM, CPML (Naxalites) [See also Chap. Eight, III. C. 5.]

24369 CHANDRA, N.K. Industrialisation and the Left movement: on several questions of strategy in West Bengal. In SocSci 7,3 (1978) 57-73.

24370 FIELD, J.O, & M.F. FRANDA. Electoral politics in the Indian states: the Communist parties of West Bengal. Delhi: Manohar Book Service, 1974. 158p.

24371 FRANDA, M.F. Radical politics in West Bengal. Cambridge: MIT Press, 1971. 287p.

24372 GHOSH, S. The Naxalite movement (a Maoist experiment). Calcutta: KLM, 1974. 183p.

24373 GUPTA, B. & R. SEN & P. DAS GUPTA. CPM terror in West Bengal. ND: CPI, 1970. 47p.

24374 IRANI, C.R. Bengal; the communist challenge. Bombay: Lalvani, 1968. 168p.

24375 JAI GOPAL. Class character of communist influence in rural Bengal. In Indian Communist 1,1 (1968) 3-11.

24376 JAWAID, S. The Naxalite movement in India: origin and failure of the Maoist revolutionary strategy in West Bengal, 1967-1971. ND: Associated Pub. House, 1979. 140p.

4. Election Studies

24377 BANERJEE, D.N. West Bengal. In S.V. Kogekar & R.L. Park, eds. Reports on the Indian general elections, 1951-52. Bombay: Popular Book Depot, 1956, 167-76.

24378 The decline of the Left in a Calcutta suburb: Behala Constituency. In EW 14, 35 (1962) 1413-17.

24379 GANGULY, B. 1967 general elections in West Bengal. In PSR 6,3/4 & 7,1/2 (1967-68) 390-411.

24380 GANGULY, B. & M. GANGULY. Voting behavior in a developing society; West Bengal: a case study. ND: Sterling, 1975. 199p.

24381 GHOSAL, A.K. Second general election in West Bengal; an analysis. In MR 103 (1958) 374-80.

24382 GHOSE, S. West Bengal polls, its results, and analysis. Calcutta: North Calcutta Book House, 1971. 148p.

24383 MITRA, A. West Bengal elections. In EW 14,4-6 (1962) 155-162.

24384 ______. West Bengal elections - a further note. In EW 14,19 (1962) 781-87.

24385 MUKHERJEE, S.K. Last general election in West Bengal. In CR 146 (1958) 134-46.

24386 RAY, A. Elections and political development in West Bengal: a case-study of the 1972 elections. In PSR 13,1/4 (1974) 113-25.

5. Administrative Studies

24387 CHATTERJEE, B. A study in the police administration of West Bengal. Calcutta: Apurba, 1973. 184p.

24388 GHOSH, P.K. Position of governor in relation to his council of ministers - with special reference to constitutional impasse in West Bengal. In IJPS 28 (1967) 250-52.

24389 GHOSH, S. Legislative committees in West Bengal. Calcutta: SPB, 1974. 208p.

6. Local Government and Politics [for Calcutta, see I. D. 5., below]

24390 CHAUDHURI, R. Panchayats and interest groups: study of a Bengali village. In EW 16,38 (1964) 1527-30.

24391 ______. Pattern of leadership in a West Bengal village. In EW 16,14 (1964) 641-44.

24392 DATTA, A.K. Politics in Village India; an enquiry into the structure of power in Jagannathbarh. In Tropical Man 3 (1970) 88-159. [Midnapore district]

24393 MUKHERJEE, S.K. Local self-government in West Bengal. Calcutta: Dasgupta, 1974. 204p.

24394 ______. Some aspects of the panchayat system in West Bengal. In IJPA 13 (1967) 313-37.

24395 MUKHOPADHYAY, A.K. The panchayat administration in West Bengal: a study of West Bengal's unhappy utopia. Calcutta: World Press, 1977. 215p.

24396 NICHOLAS, R.W. Village factions and political parties in rural West Bengal. In JComPolSt 2 (1963) 17-32.

C. The Economy of Bengal Presidency and West Bengal State since 1813

1. General Economic History

24397 BARUI, B.C. The smuggling trade of opium in the Bengal Presidency: 1793-1817. In BPP 94,179 (1975) 123-136.

24398 CHATTOPADHYAYA, A.K. Slavery in the Bengal Presidency. London: Golden Eagle Press, 1977. 178p.

24399 GHOSAL, H.R. Economic transition in the Bengal presidency, 1793-1833. 2nd ed. Calcutta: KLM, 1966. 322p. [1st pub. 1950]

24400 GHOSH, G. Ramdoolal Dey, the Bengalee millionaire. Calcutta: Riddhi-India, 1978. 43p.

24400a INDIA. BANKING ENQUIRY CMTEE. (BENGAL) 1929-30. Report. Calcutta: Bengal Govt. Press, 1930. 3v.

24401 JACK, J.C. The economic life of a Bengal district: a study. Delhi: Agam Prakashan, 1975. 158p. [Rpt. 1916 ed.]

24402 LITTLE, J.H. House of Jagatseth. Calcutta: Calcutta Hist. Soc., 1967. 264p. [1st pub. in BPP, 1920-1921.]

24403 MITTER, S.C. A recovery plan for Bengal. Calcutta: The Book Co., 1934. 699p.

24404 MOHSIN, KHAN MOHAMMAD. A Bengal district in transition: Murshidabad, 1765-1793. Dacca: Asiatic Soc. of Bangladesh, 1973. 306p. (Its pub., 27)

24405 PALIT, C.B. Indigenous business enterprise and its failure in Bengal, 1780-1880. In QRHS 6 (1966-67) 213-23.

24406 PANANDIKAR, S.G. The wealth and welfare of the Bengal delta. Calcutta: U. of Calcutta, 1926. 364p.

24407 SINGH, S.B. Bengal's cotton trade with China, 1800-1833. In JBRS 46 (1960) 233-40.

24408 ______. European agency houses in Bengal, 1783-1833, Calcutta: KLM, 1966. 331p.

24409 SINHA, J.C. Economic annals of Bengal. London: Macmillan, 1927. 301p.

24410 SINHA, N.K. The economic history of Bengal, from Plassey to the Permanent Settlement. Calcutta: KLM, 1961-62. 3v., 264, 300, 172p. [covers 1757-1848]

24411 ______. European banking in Bengal 1793-1848. In BPP 88,1 (1969) 18-32.

24412 ______. Indian business enterprise: its failure in Calcutta (1800-1848). In BPP 86,2 (1969) 112-23.

24413 TIMBERG, T.A. A North Indian firm as seen through its business records, 1860-1914; Tarachand Ghanshyamdas, a "great" Marwari firm. In IESHR 8,3 (1971) 264-83.

24414 ______. A note on the arrival of Calcutta Marwaris. In BPP 90,1 (1971) 75-84.

24415 TRIPATHI, A. Trade and finance in the Bengal Presidency, 1793-1833. New & rev. ed. Calcutta: OUP, 1979. 340p. [1st ed. 1956]

24416 TYSON, G.W. The Bengal Chamber of Commerce & Industry, 1853-1953; a centenary survey. Calcutta: D.A. Lakin, 1953. 203p.

2. Demography (West Bengal 1981 pop. 54,485,560)

24417 BHOWMICK, K.L., et al. Fertility of Muslim women in lower Bengal. Calcutta: Inst. of Social Studies, 1974. 175p.

24418 INDIA (REP.). CENSUS OF INDIA, 1961. Demographic

trends in West Bengal during 1901-51. ND: MPGOI, 1967. 40p. (V.1, monograph 5)

24419 MAJUMDAR, D.N. & C.RADHAKRISHNA RAO. Race elements in Bengal; a quantitative study. NY: Asia, 1960. 200p. (Indian stat. series, 3)

24420 MUKHERJEE, S.B. Studies on fertility rates in Calcutta based on the socio-economic survey 1954/55 to 1957/58. Calcutta: Bookland, 1961. 143p.

24421 PATEL, A.M. Population of north Bengal. In Oriental Geographer 10 (1966) 73-91.

3. Surveys of Economic Condition since 1947

24422 CHATTERJEE, A.B. & AVIJIT GUPTA & P.K. MUKHOPADHYAY, eds. West Bengal. Calcutta: KLM, 1970. 213p.

24423 CHATTERJI, S.P. Bengal in maps, a geographical analysis of resource distribution in West Bengal and Eastern Pakistan. Bombay: Orient Longmans, 1949. 105p.

24424 GHOSE, S. West Bengal today. Calcutta: State Planning Board, West Bengal, 1976. 134p.

24425 NCAER. Techno-economic survey of West Bengal. ND: 1962. 284p.

24426 RAYCHOUDHURY, P. West Bengal: a decade 1965-75. Calcutta: Boipatra, 1977. 278p.

24427 West Bengal: an analytic study, sponsored by the Bengal Chamber of Commerce and Industry. ND: Oxford & IBH, 1971. 208p.

24428 West Bengal: the travail continues, sponsored by the Bengal Chamber of Commerce and Industry. ND: Oxford & IBH, 1975. 74p.

4. Economic Development and Planning

24429 BHATTACHARYA, D., ed. Focus on West Bengal: problems and prospects. Calcutta: Samatat Prakashan, 1972. 207p.

24430 BHATTACHARYYA, A.K. Economic regions in the context of development: some basic considerations. In AV 15,1 (1973) 57-90.

24431 GANGULY, D.S. Regional economy of West Bengal: a study of urbanisation, growth potential, and optimisation of industrial location. ND: Orient Longman, 1979. 314p.

24432 Growth centres in West Bengal. Calcutta: Econ. & Scientific Res. Assn., 1977. 77p.

24433 GUPTA, R.K. Essays in economic anthropology: essays in advocacy of change. Calcutta: Inst. of Social Res. & Applied Anthro., 1979. 193p.

24434 WEST BENGAL. CALCUTTA METROPOLITAN PLANNING ORG. Regional planning for West Bengal; a statement of needs, prospects and strategy. Calcutta: 1965. 96p.

24435 WEST BENGAL. STATE PLANNING BOARD. West Bengal's approach to Fifth five-year plan, 1974-79. Calcutta: 1972. 147p.

5. Agriculture since 1813
a. agriculture in Bengal under the Raj
i. general studies

24436 CHAUDHURI, B.B. Agriculture growth in Bengal and Bihar, 1770-1860: Growth of cultivation since the famine of 1770. In BPP 95,1 (1976) 290-340.

24437 ______. Agricultural production in Bengal; 1850-1900: Co-existence of decline and growth. In BPP 88 (1969) 152-206.

24438 GUPTA, R.K. Agricultural developments in a Bengal district: Birbhum, 1793-1852. In IHR 4,1 (1977) 47-74.

24439 ISLAM, M.M. Bengal agriculture 1920-46; a quantitative study. Cambridge: CamUP, 1979. 283p. (Cambridge S. Asian studies, 22)

24440 RAY, R.K. The crisis of Bengal agriculture, 1870-1927 - the dynamics of immobility. In IESHR 10,3 (1973) 244-279.

24441 RAY, R.K. & R.RAY. The dynamics of continuity in rural Bengal under the British imperium: a study of quasi-stable equilibrium in underdeveloped societies in a changing world. In IESHR 10,2 (1973) 103-127.

24442 WEST BENGAL. AGRI. & COMMUNITY DEV. DEPT. A short note on agricultural development in West Bengal, 1965-66. Calcutta: 1966. 123p.

ii. plantation and commercial crops: tea, jute, indigo, opium, forests

24443 BENGAL. INDIGO CMSN. Report, 1860. Calcutta: Bengal Govt. Press, 1860. 4v., 755p. [Pres., W.S. Seton-Karr]

24444 CHAUDHURI, B.B. Growth of commercial agriculture in Bengal, 1757-1900. Calcutta: R.K. Maitra, for ISPP, 1964. 217p.

24445 ______. Growth of commercial agricultre in Bengal. 1859-1885. In IESHR 7 (1970) 25-60, 211-51.

24446 CHAUDHURI, N.C. Jute in Bengal. New ed. Calcutta: W. Newman, 1921. 288p. [1st pub. 1908]

24447 DAS, A.K. & H.N. BANERJEE, ed. Impact of tea industry on the life of the tribals of West Bengal. Calcutta: Tribal Welfare Dept., Govt. of W. Bengal, 1964. 88p.

24448 DESHPANDE, S.R. Report on an enquiry into the cost and standard of living of plantation workers in Assam and Bengal. Delhi: Labour Bureau, Min. of Labour, Govt. of India, 1948. 112p. (Its pub., 4)

24449 WEST BENGAL. FOREST DIR. West Bengal forests. Calcutta: 1964. 344p.

iii. famines and famine control - incl. 1943 famine

24450 GHOSH, K.C. Famines in Bengal, 1770-1943. Calcutta: Indian Associated Pub., 1944. 204p.

24451 GHOSH, T.K. The Bengal tragedy. Lahore: Hero Pub., 1944. 107p. [1943]

24452 GREENOUGH, P. Prosperity and misery in modern Bengal: the Bengal famine of 1943-44. Ph.D. diss., U. of Chicago, 1977. 525p.

24453 HUNTER, W.W. Annals of rural Bengal. 7th ed. NY: Johnson Rpt. Corp., 1970. 475p. [Rpt. 1897 ed.]

24454 ______. Famine aspects of Bengal districts. London: Trübner, 1874. 204p.

24455 INDIA. FAMINE INQUIRY CMSN. ... Report on Bengal. Delhi: MPGOI, 1945. 236p.

24456 MAHALANOBIS, P.C. & R.K. MUKHERJEE & A. GHOSH. A sample survey of the after-effects of the Bengal famine of 1943. Calcutta: Statistical Pub. Soc., 1946. 56p. [also pub. in Sankhya 7,4 (1946)]

24457 MANSERGH, N. & E.W.R. LUMBY, eds. The transfer of power, 1942-47; constitutional relations between Britain and India; v.4, Bengal famine and the new viceroyalty June-Aug. 1943. London: HMSO, 1973. 1295p. [India Office documents]

24458 NARAYAN, T.G. ... Famine over Bengal. Calcutta: The Book Co., 1944. 234p.

24459 VENKATARAMANI, M.S. Bengal Famine of 1943: the American response. Delhi: Vikas, 1973. 137p.

b. agricultural development in West Bengal since 1947
i. general studies

24460 BANERJEE, B. Changing cropland of West Bengal. In GRI 26 (1964) 11-22.

24461 BHATTACHARYA, R. & G.L. SAHA. Changes of agricultural pattern in Bongaon sub-division. In GRI, 32,4 (1970) 223-242.

24462 BOSE, S.P. Eadpur, a study into rice yields of a West Bengal village. Calcutta: Dept. of Agri., Govt. of W. Bengal, 1963. 68p.

24463 DAS, A. Food problem of West Bengal. In Econ. Affairs 13 (1968) 235-46.

24464 GUPTA, R.K. Agrarian West Bengal: three field studies. Calcutta: Inst. of Social Res. & Applied Anthro.,

Dept. of Anthro., Calcutta U., 1977. 199p.

24465 MUKHERJI, S.N. A brief agricultural geography of West Bengal. Calcutta: Dir. of Agri., W. Bengal, 1956. 163p.

24466 PAL, B.K. Agricultural finance in West Bengal. Calcutta: KLM, 1973. 112p.

24467 THAPAR, S.D. Fringe areas of Calcutta: development of three rural situations. ND: AVARD, 1978. 167p. (AVARD micro-level planning studies, 11)

ii. agricultural technology and innovation

24468 BHATTACHARYA, R. Social and cultural constraints in agriculture in three villages (Hindu, Moslem, and tribal). In JIAS 3,1/2 (1968) 78-108.

24469 DANDA, A.K. & D. G. DANDA. Adoption of agricultural innovations in a West Bengal village. In MI 52,4 (1972) 303-319.

24470 DAS, K.K. Attitude, information sources, and the adoption of agro-cultural practices by Indian farmers. In Interdiscipline 8,3 (1971) 28-47.

24471 DASGUPTA, S. Innovation and innovators in an Indian village. In MI 43,1 (1963) 27-34.

24472 FRANKEL, F. Agricultural modernization and social change. In Mainstream 8,15 (1969) 17-23.

24473 NCAER. Impact of Indo-German Fertilizer Educational Project in West Bengal: an evaluation. ND: NCAER, 1979. 223p.

c. rural credit and cooperatives

24474 CHAUDHURI, B. Rural credit relations in Bengal; 1859-1885. In IESHR 6 (1969) 204-57.

24475 RUDRA, A. Loans as a part of agrarian relations: some results of a preliminary survey in West Bengal. In EPW 10,28 (1975) 1049-53.

24476 SEN, S.N. Co-operative movement in West Bengal. Calcutta: Bookland, 1966. 63p.

24477 VISVA-BHARATI U. AGRO-ECON. RES. CENTER. Experiments in co-operative farming: a study in east India. Santiniketan: 1961. 71p.

d. land tenure, land revenue, and reform
i. land tenure and revenue under the British

24478 ASCOLI, F.D. Revenue history of the Sunderbans from 1870 to 1920. Calcutta: Bengal Secretariat Book Depot, 1921. 159p.

24479 BENGAL. LAND REVENUE CMSN., 1938. Report. Calcutta: Bengal Govt. Press, 1940-41. 6v., 2366p. [Chm., Sir Francis Floud]

24480 CHATTERJI, S.C. Bengal ryots, their rights and liabilities: being an elementary treatise on the law of landlord and tenant. Calcutta: K.P. Bagchi, 1977. 54 + 139p.

24481 CHAUDHURI, H.N., comp. The Cooch Behar State and its land revenue settlements: Cooch Behar: Cooch Behar State Press, 1903. 705p.

24482 CHAUDHURI, K.C. The history and economics of the land system in Bengal. Calcutta: the Book Co., 1927. 148p.

24483 GUPTA, M.N. Land system of Bengal. Calcutta: U. of Calcutta, 1940. 300p.

24484 GUPTA, R.K. Permanent settlements in Birbhum: impact on landed interests (1793-1856). In Calcutta Hist. J. 3,2 (1979) 1-39.

24485 KABIR, LUTFUL. The rights and liabilities of the raiyats under the Bengal tenancy act, 1885, and the State acquisition and tenancy act, 1950, with amendments. Dacca: Law House Pub., 1972. 548p.

24486 MUKERJI, K.M. Land transfers in Birbhum, 1928-1955: some implications of the Bengal Tenancy Act, 1885. In IESHR 8,3 (1971) 241-263.

24487 ______. The problems of land transfer; a study of the problems of land alienation in Bengal. Santiniketan: Santiniketan Press, 1957. 274p.

24488 ______. Rents and forms of tenancy in Birbhum since the permanent settlement. In IESHR 14,3 (1977) 363-76.

24489 NIGHTINGALE, F. Florence Nightingale's Indian letters, a glimpse into the agitation for tenancy reform, Bengal, 1878-82. Ed. by P.R. Sen. Calcutta: S.M. Sen, 1937. 67p.

24490 PALIT, C.B. Tensions in Bengal rural society: landlord, planters, and colonial rule, 1830-1860. Calcutta: Progressive Pub., 1975. 226p.

24491 PARGITER, F.E. Revenue history of the Sundarbans from 1765 to 1870. Alipore: Bengal Govt. Press, 1934. 156p.

24492 RAY, R.K. & R. RAY. Zamindars and Jotedars: a study of rural politics in Bengal. In MAS 9,1 (1975) 81-102.

24493 RAYCHAUDHURI, T. Permanent settlement in operation: Bakarganj district, East Bengal. In R. Frykenberg, ed. Land control and social structure in Indian history. Madison: UWiscP, 1969, 163-174.

24494 ROTHERMUND, D. The Bengal tenancy act of 1885 and its influence on legislation in other provinces. In BPP 86,2 (1967) 90-105.

ii. land reform since 1947

24495 BASU, S.K. & S. BHATTACHARYA. Land reforms in West Bengal; a study in implementation. ND: Oxford, 1963, 126p.

24496 DUTT, K. Changes in land relations in West Bengal. In EPW 12,53 (1977) A106-A110.

24497 GHOSH, R. Effect of agricultural legislation on land distribution in W. Bengal. In IJAE 31,3 (1976) 40-46.

24498 GHOSH, R. & K. NAGARAJ. Land reforms in West Bengal. In SocSci 6,6/7 (1978) 50-67.

24499 VISVA-BHARATI. AGRO-ECON. RES. CENTRE. Land reforms and the changing rural economic structure, Coochbehar: a case study. Santiniketan: 1973-1974. 2v.

e. peasant movements and revolts in Bengal

24500 BHATTACHARYA, J. An examination of leadership entry in Bengal peasant revolts, 1937-47. In JAS 37,4 (1978) 611-36.

24501 CHAUDHURI, B.B. The story of a peasant revolt in a Bengal district. In BPP 92,2 (1973) 220-278.

24502 GHOSH, S.K. Peasant revolution in Bengal. Ed. by J.C. Bagal. Calcutta: Bharati Library, 1953. 50p.

24503 KLING, B.B. The blue mutiny; the indigo disturbances in Bengal, 1859-1862. Philadelphia: UPaP, 1966. 243p.

24504 NAHAR, S. The agrarian uprising of Titu Mir 1831; the economics of a revivalist movement. In J. of the Inst. of Bangladesh Studies 1,1 (1976) 104-15.

24505 SARKAR, K.K. Kakdwip tebhaga movement. In A.R. Desai, ed. Peasant struggles in India. Bombay: OUP, 1979, 469-85.

24506 SEN, S.K. Agrarian struggle in Bengal, 1946-47. ND: People's Pub. House, 1972. 111p.

24507 SENGUPTA, K.K. Agrarian disturbances in Eastern and Central Bengal in the late nineteenth century. In IESHR 8,2 (1971) 192-212.

24508 ______. The agrarian league of Pabna, 1873. In IESHR 7,2 (1970) 253-69.

24509 ______. Pabna disturbances and the politics of rent, 1873-1885. ND: PPH, 1974. 212p.

6. Industry in Bengal since 1813
a. general and historical studies

24510 BANDYOPADHYAYA, K. Industrialization through industrial estates; a pattern of economic decentralization. Calcutta: Bookland, 1969. 254p.

24511 BANERJEE, B. & D. ROY. Industrial profile of the Calcutta metropolitan district. Calcutta: Indian Pub., 1967. 191p.

24512 BASU, S.K. & A. GHOSH & S. RAY. Problems and possibilities of ancillary industries in a developing economy: a study based on the survey of ancillary units in West Bengal. Calcutta: World Press, 1965. 161p.

24513 CHATTERJEE, A.B. Industrial landscape of Howrah. In GRI 25 (1963) 211-41.

24514 CHAUDHURI, M.R. Durgapur - future Ruhr of India. In his (ed.) Essays in geography. Calcutta: Geog. Soc. of India, 1965, 165-80.

24515 ______. The industrial landscape of West Bengal; an economic-geographic appraisal. Calcutta: Oxford & IBH, 1971. 205p.

24516 DAS, A.K. & S.K. BANERJEE. Impact of industrialisation on the life of the tribals of West Bengal. Calcutta: Tribal Welfare Dept., Govt. of West Bengal, 1962. 88p.

24517 KLING, B.B. Entrepreneurship and regional identity in Bengal. In D. Kopf, ed. Bengal regional identity. East Lansing: Asian Studies Center, Michigan State U., 1969, 75-84. (Its occ. papers, S.A. series, 9)

24518 LAHIRI, N.K. Industries in West Bengal: a survey. In India in Industries 6,3 (1964) 30-43.

24519 SANYAL, HITESRANJAN. The indigenous iron industry of Birbhum. In IESHR 5,1 (1968) 101-08.

24520 SIVARAMKRISHNAN, K.C., et al. Planning for a coal-steel-complex: a case study of Chittaranjan-Asansol-Durgapur region. In R.P. Misra, ed. Regional planning. Mysore: U. of Mysore, 1969, 449-64.

b. studies of specific industries - incl. small-scale

24521 AHMED, RAKIBUDDIN. The progress of the jute industry and trade, 1855-1966. Dacca: Pakistan Central Jute Cmtee., 1966. 526p.

24522 BANERJEE, R.M. Employment in small industry in West Bengal. In Manpower J. 8,1 (1972) 100-19.

24523 COTTON, H.E.A. A famous Calcutta firm [Thacker Spink & Co.]. In BPP 41 (1938) 157-64.

24524 FELDVAECK, I. Cloth production and trade in late eighteenth century Bengal: a report from the Danish factory in Serampore. In BPP 86,2 (1967) 124-49.

24525 LETHBRIDGE, R. Dundee and Calcutta jute industry and the new export duty on jute. In Asiatic Q.R. 33 (1912) 1-20.

24526 RAY, B. Growth of small-scale industries in West Bengal: a study. In Socialist Perspective 4,4 (1977) 12-41.

24527 SANYAL, H.R. The indigenous iron industry of Birbhum. In IESHR 5,1 (1968) 101-08.

24528 TULPULE, B. Amidst heat and noise: Durgapur recalled. ND: All India Mgmt. Assn., 1977. 133p.

24529 WALLACE, D.R. Romance of jute: a short history of the Calcutta jute mill industry, 1855-1909. London: W. Thacker, 1928. 129p. [1st pub. 1909]

24530 WEST BENGAL. STATE STAT. BUREAU. Brass and bell-metal industry; a type study. Alipore: W. Bengal Govt. Press, 1965. 241p.

24531 ______. A short note on tanning industry. Alipore: W. Bengal Govt. Press, 1964. 47p.

24532 ______. Silk and matka weaving industry; a type-study. Alipore: W. Bengal Govt. Press, 1966. 122p.

7. Labor and Trade Unionism in Bengal
a. general studies

24533 CALCUTTA UNIV. DEPT. OF COMMERCE. Study of the problem of unemployment in some selected urban and rural areas of West Bengal, May 1973. ND: Cmtee. on Unemployment, Min. of Labour & Rehabilitation, 1975. 96p.

24534 CALCUTTA UNIV. DEPT. OF ECONOMICS. A study of the employment pattern of the post-graduate students of University of Calcutta, May 1972. ND: Cmtee. on Unemployment, Min. of Labour & Rehabilitation, 1975. 72p.

24535 KIDDER, D.E. Private industry and manpower planning in India: a study of the Calcutta engineering industry. In IJIR 5 (1970) 440-52.

b. industrial relations

24536 DE, N. & S. SRIVASTAVA. Gheraos in West Bengal. In EPW 2,45-49 (1967) 2015-22, 2062-68, 2099-2104, 2169-76.

24537 GEORGE, C.M. Industrial relations in West Bengal. ND: Shri Ram Centre for Industrial Relations, 1968. 103p.

24538 SEN, S.N. & T. PIPLAI. Industrial relations in the jute industry in West Bengal; a case study. Calcutta: Bookland, 1968. 242p.

24539 VAID, K.N. Gheraos and labour unrest in West Bengal. ND: Shri Ram Centre for Industrial Relations & Human Resources, 1972. 252p.

c. trade unions and the labor movement

24540 CHAKRABARTY, D. Communal riots and labour: Bengal's jute mill hands in the 1890's. Calcutta: Centre for Studies in Social Sciences, 1976. 70p.

24541 GHOSH, M. Our struggle; a short history of trade union movement in Tisco industry at Jamshedpur. 2nd ed. rev. and enl. Calcutta: KLM, 1973. 278p.

24542 MUKHERJEE, R. & T. PARMANAND & G.B. SUKHEE. Mao's shadow over West Bengal; a report on the Communist bid to subvert and destroy the democratic trade union movement in the industrial belt of eastern India. Bombay: Co-ordinating Cmtee. of Independent Trade Unions, 1967. 48p.

24543 SAHA, P. History of the working-class movement in Bengal. ND: PPH, 1978. 239p.

24544 SENGUPTA, A.K. Trade unions, politics, and the state: a case from West Bengal. In CIS ns 11,1 (1977) 45-68.

8. Commerce and Transportation in Bengal

24545 BANERJEE, T. History of internal trade barriers in British India: a study of transit and town duties: Bengal presidency 1765-1838. Calcutta: Asiatic Soc., 1972. 156p. (Its monograph, 21)

24546 FUREDY, C. Development of modern elite retailing in Calcutta, 1880-1920. In IESHR 16,4 (1979) 377-94.

24547 INDIA (REP.). REGIONAL TRANSPORT SURVEY UNIT, EASTERN REGION, CALCUTTA. Eastern region transport survey. Calcutta: 1967. 7 v.

24548 KLING, B. Partner in Empire: Dwarkanath Tagore and the age of enterprise in eastern India. Berkeley: UCalP, 1976. 276p.

24549 NCAER. Transport requirements of the iron and steel belt. ND: NCAER, 1964. 222p.

24550 REED, W. Areal interaction in India: commodity flows of the Bengal-Bihar industrial area. Chicago: U. of Chicago, Dept. of Geography, 1967. 209p. (Its res. paper, 110)

D. Society and Social Change since 1813

1. Social Reform and Intellectual Awakening in Nineteenth-century Bengal
a. general studies

24551 BANERJI, A.R. An Indian pathfinder; being the memoirs of Sevabrata Sasipada Banerji, 1840-1924. Oxford: Kemp Hall Press, 192-. 143p.

24552 BHATTACHARYA, B. Socio-political currents in Bengal: a nineteenth century perspective. ND: Vikas, 1980. 147p.

24553 CHUNDER, P.C. The sons of mystery: a Masonic miscellany from old Calcutta. Calcutta: Jayanti, 1973. 182p.

24554 DUTT GUPTA, B. Sociology in India; an enquiry into sociological thinking and empirical social research in the nineteenth century, with special reference to Bengal. Calcutta: Centre for Sociological Res., 1972. 308 + 449p.

24555 FORBES, G.H. Positivism in Bengal: a case study in the transmission and assimilation of an ideology. Calcutta: Minerva, 1975. 181p.

24556 KARIM, A.K. NAZMUL. Changing society in India and Pakistan; a study in social change and social stratification. Dacca: Ideal, 1961. 178p. [1st pub. 1956]

24557 MAJUMDAR, R.C. Renascent India: first phase. Calcutta: G. Bharadwaj, 1976. 290p.

24558 MUKHERJEE, S.N. Class, caste and politics in Calcutta, 1815-38. In E.R. Leach & S.N. Mukherjee, eds. Elites in South Asia. Cambridge: CamUP, 1970, 33-79.

24559 SINHA, P. Nineteenth century Bengal, aspects of social history. A study in some new pressures on society and in relation between tradition and change. Calcutta: KLM, 1965. 203p.

24560 TATTVABHUSHAN, S. Social reform in Bengal, a side sketch. Calcutta: City Book Soc., 1904. 98p.

b. the "Bengal Renaissance" [see also Chap. Six, VII. B.]

24561 BAUMER, R. VAN M. The reinterpretation of dharma in nineteenth-century Bengal: righteous conduct for man in the modern world. In her (ed.) Aspects of Bengali history and society. Honolulu: UPH, 1975, 82-98.

24562 BOSE, N.S. Indian awakening and Bengal. 3rd rev. and enl. ed. Calcutta: KLM, 1976. 408p.

24563 CHAKRABARTY, D. The colonial context of the Bengal Renaissance: a note on early railway-thinking in Bengal. In IESHR 11,1 (1974) 92-111.

24564 CHATTOPADHYAYA, G., ed. Awakening in Bengal in early nineteenth century; selected documents. Calcutta: Progressive, 1965. 415p.

24565 GUPTA, A.C., ed. Studies in the Bengal renaissance. 2nd rev. and enl. ed. Calcutta: Natl. Council of Educ., Bengal, 1977. 606p.

24566 KOPF, D. British orientalism and the Bengal renaissance; the dynamics of Indian modernization, 1773-1835. Berkeley: UCalP, 1969. 324p.

24567 KOPF, D. & S. JOARDER, eds. Reflections on the Bengal renaissance. Rajshahi, Bangladesh: Rajshahi U., Inst. of Bangladesh Studies, 1977. 190p.

24568 MUKHERJEE, A. Reform and regeneration in Bengal, 1774-1823. Calcutta: Rabindra Bharati U., 1968. 392p.

24569 MUKHOPADHYAY, A.K., ed. The Bengali intellectual tradition: from Rammohun Ray to Dhirendranath Sen. Calcutta: K.P. Bagchi, 1979. 288p.

24570 PODDAR, A. Renaissance in Bengal; quests and confrontations, 1800-1860. Simla: IIAS, 1970. 254p.

24571 _____. Renaissance in Bengal: search for identity. Simla: IIAS, 1977. 252p.

24572 SALAHUDDIN AHMED, A.F. Social ideas and social change in Bengal, 1818-1835. Leiden: Brill, 1965. 204p.

24573 SANYAL, R. Societies for acquiring general knowledge in Calcutta in the first half of the nineteenth century. In BPP 94,1 (1975) 37-56.

24574 SARKAR, S.C. Bengal renaissance and other essays. ND: PPH, 1970. 285p.

24575 _________. On the Bengal Renaissance. Calcutta: Papyrus, 1979. 166p.

24576 SEMINAR ON RENASCENT BENGAL, 1817-1857, CALCUTTA, 1971. Renascent Bengal, 1817-1857. Calcutta: Asiatic Soc., 1972. 86p.

24577 SIVANATHA SASTRI. A history of the renaissance in Bengal: Ramtanu Lahiri, Brahman and reformer. Ed. by Sir R. Lethbridge. Calcutta: Editions Indian, 1972. 185p. [1st pub. 1907, tr. from Bengali]

2. Social Categories in Bengal; Kinship and Marriage

a. general studies

24578 BHOWMICK, P.K. Caste and service in a Bengal village. In MI 43 (1963) 277-327.

24579 ______. Occupational mobility and caste structure in Bengal; study of rural market. Calcutta: Indian Pub., 1969. 98p.

24580 ______. Socio-cultural profile of frontier Bengal. Calcutta: Punthi Pustak, 1976. 416p. + 8 pl.

24581 BOSE, N.K. Modern Bengal. Calcutta: Vidyodaya Library Private, 1959. 98p.

24582 ______. Some aspects of caste in Bengal. In MI 38 (1958) 73-97.

24583 BOSE, S.C. The Hindoos as they are: a description of the manners, customs and inner life of Hindoo society in Bengal. Calcutta: W. Newman, 1881. 305p.

24584 CHATTOPADHYAY, G. Caste dominance and disputes in a village in West Bengal. In MI 46,4 (1966) 287-318.

24585 CHATTOPADHYAY, K.A. & S. BANDYOPADHYAY. Caste ranking in some West Bengal villages - an exploratory formulation. In JIAS 2 (1967) 169-74.

24586 DAVIS, M. Philosophy of Hindu rank from rural West Bengal. In JAS 36,1 (1976) 5-24.

24587 DUTT, N.K. Origin and growth of caste in India; v. 2, Castes in Bengal. Calcutta: KLM, 1965. 169p.

24588 MITRA, A. The tribes and castes of West Bengal. Alipore: W. Bengal Govt. Press, 1953. 413p. (1951 census)

24589 MOOKHERJEE, H.N. & S. DASGUPTA. Caste status and ritual observances in a West Bengal village. In MI 50 (1970) 390-401.

24590 Pilot survey of socio-economic conditions of the Anglo-Indian community, 1957-58. Calcutta: Anglo-Indian Survey Cmtee., nd. 33p. [in Calcutta]

24591 RAY, P.C. Stereotypes and tensions among the Muslims and Hindus in a village in Bengal. In L.P. Vidyarthi, ed. Conflict, tension, and cultural trend in India. Calcutta: Punthi Pustak, 1969, 228-53.

24592 RISLEY, H.H. The tribes and castes of Bengal. Calcutta: Bengal Secretariat Press, 1891. 2 v.

24593 SAKHAROV, I.V. Ethnic community, class and occupation in a multi-ethnic environment in India: a case study of West Bengal. In JSR 18,1 (1975) 8-42.

24594 SENGUPTA, S. Caste, status, group, aggregate, and class: an inquiry into the social stratification in rural West Bengal. Calcutta: KLM, 1979. 182p.

24595 SINHA, S. Levels of economic initiative and ethnic groups in Pargana Barabhum. In EA 16 (1963) 65-74.

24596 SUR, A.K. Folk elements in Bengali life. Calcutta: Indian Pub., 1975. 112p. (Its Folklore series, 24)

24597 WISE, J. Notes on the races, castes, and tribes of eastern Bengal. London: Harrison, 1883. 427p.

b. kinship and marriage (not specific to one group)

24598 BEECH, M.J. Family cycle in three urban Bengali neighborhoods. In R. Beech & M.J. Beech, eds. Bengal: change and continuity. East Madison: Asian Studies Center, Michigan State U., 1970, 185-203. (Its occ. papers, S.A. series, 16)

24599 BHOWMICK, P.K. Artificial relationships in Midnapur. In MI 41,2 (1961) 111-28.

24600 CHAKRAVARTY, S.C. A study of the Kulinism in Bengal. In Folklore(C) 3 (1962) 366-70, 384; 393-415.

24601 DAVIS, M. The politics of family life in rural West Bengal. In Ethnology 15,2 (1976) 189-200.

24602 ______. Rank and rivalry in a Bengali Hindu family. In EA 30,1 (1977) 67-87.

24603 GANGOPADHYAY, B. Marriage regulations among certain castes of Bengal. Poona: DCPRI, 1964. 121p.

24604 INDEN, R.B. & R.W. NICHOLAS. Kinship in Bengali culture. Chicago: UChiP, 1977. 139p.

24605 KLASS, M. Marriage rules in Bengal. In AA 68 (1966) 951-70.

24606 MUKHERJEE, R.K. West Bengal family structures, 1946-1966: an example of viability of joint family. Delhi: Macmillan, 1977. 267p.

24607 NICHOLAS, R.W. Economics of family types in two West Bengal villages. In EW 13 (1961) 1057-60.

24608 OWENS, R.L. Industrialization and the Indian joint family. In Ethnology 10,2 (1971) 223-50.

24609 PAKRASI, K. A study of some aspects of household types and family organization in rural Bengal, 1946-47. In EA 15 (1962) 55-63.

24610 SARMA, J. Formal and informal relations in the Hindu joint household of Bengal. In MI 31 (1951) 51-71.

24611 SENGUPTA, S. Family organisation in West Bengal: its nature and dynamics. In EW 10 (1958) 384-89.

c. the bhadralok ("respectable people") and other elites

24612 CHAKRABARTI, S. Concept of Bhadralok and Chhotolok in Bengali Hindu society: some observations. In BAnthSI 19,1 (1970) 66-74.

24613 DAY, L.B. Bengal peasant life. Folk tales of Bengal. Recollections of my school-days. Ed. by M. Saha. Calcutta: Editions Indian, 1969. 555p. [1st pub. 1874]

24614 GHOSE, B. The crisis of Bengali gentility in Calcutta. In EW 9 (1957) 821-26.

24615 ______. The economic character of the urban middle class in nineteenth century Bengal. In B.N. Ganguli, ed. Readings in Indian economic history. Bombay: Asia, 1964, 137-47.

24616 MAHTAB, P.C. The Bengal nobles: a status group, 1911-19. In BPP 92,1 (1973) 23-36.

24617 ______. Bengal nobles: an assessment of their influence, 1911-1919. In BPP 94,2 (1975) 106-22.

24618 MUKHERJEE, N. A Bengal zamindar in 1857. In BPP 91,1 (1972) 47-63.

24619 ______. A Bengal zamindar, Jaykrishna Mukherjee of Uttarpara, and his times, 1808-1888. Calcutta: KLM, 1975. 589p.

24620 SINHA, S. & R. BHATTACHARYA. Bhadralok and chhotolok in a rural area of West Bengal. In SB 18 (1969) 50-66.

d. Brahman castes of Bengal

24621 CHAKRAVARTI, N. An ethnic analysis of the culture-traits in the marriage customs as found among the Rāḍhiya Brahmins of Mymensingh. In CUDL 26 (1935) 1-80.

24622 DATTA, J.M. Influence of religious beliefs on the geographical distribution of Brahmans in Bengal. In MI 42,2 (1962) 89-103.

24623 RAY CHAUDHURI, T.C. The Varendra Brahmanas of Bengal. In MI 13 (1933) 85-96.

24624 SARMA, J.M. The nuclearization of joint family households in West Bengal. In MI 44 (1964) 193-206.

24625 ______. Three generations in my Calcutta family. In B.E. Ward, ed. Women in the new Asia. Paris: UNESCO, 1963, 216-228.

e. intermediate groups: professional, commercial, agricultural, and artisan castes

24626 BASU, D. The Banian and the British in Calcutta, 1800-1850. In BPP 92,2 (1973) 157-170.

24627 ______. The early Banians of Calcutta. In BPP 90,1 (1971) 30-46.

24628 BROOMFIELD, J.H. The rural parvenu: a report of research in progress. In SAR 6,3 (1973) 181-95. [Ugra Kshatriya caste]

24629 MUKHOPADHYAY, T. Some aspects of caste organization among the potters in eastern Midnapore. In JIAS 1 (1966) 177-84.

24630 OWENS, R.L. & A. NANDY. The new vaisyas. Bombay: Allied, 1977. 205p.

24631 SANYAL, H.R. Continuities of social mobility in traditional and modern society in India: two case studies of caste mobility in Bengal. In JAS 30,2 (1971) 315-40. [Tili & Sadgopa castes]

24632 ______. Social aspects of temple building in Bengal, 1600-1900 AD. In MI 48,3 (1968) 215-17. [Tili caste]

f. scheduled castes and tribes of Bengal [for Santals, see Chap. Twelve, II. C. 2.]

24633 BANERJEE, G. A note on the dancing girl (nachni) of Purulia. In MI 53,3 (1973) 279-93.

24634 BHAGBATI, A. & P.K. BHOWMICK. The Lodhas of West Bengal: a socio-economic study. Calcutta: Punthi Pustak, 1963. 618p. [Mundari speaking tribe]

24635 BOSE, S.K. & R.N. SAHA. On educational and economic achievements; a study on intercommunity differences in twenty-four villages of West Bengal. Calcutta: Cultural Res. Inst., 1971. 209p.

24636 DALTON, E.T. Tribal history of eastern India. ND: Cosmo, 1978. 327p. [rpt. of 1872 ed., Descriptive ethnology of Bengal]

24637 DAS, A.K. The Koras and some little known communities of West Bengal. Calcutta: Tribal Welfare Dept., 1964. 112p. (Bull. of the Cultural Res. Inst., Spec. series, 5)

24638 DAS, A.K., et al. Scheduled tribes and scheduled castes of West Bengal: programmes, facts, and figures. Calcutta: Cultural Res. Inst., Scheduled Castes and Tribes Welfare Dept., Govt. of W. Bengal, 1978. 194p. + 8 pl.

24639 DAS, A.K. & B.K. ROY CHOWDHURY & M.K. RAHA. Handbook on scheduled castes and scheduled tribes of West Bengal. Calcutta: Tribal Welfare Dept., Govt. of W. Bengal, 1966. 224p. (Bull. of the Cultural Res. Inst., Spec. series, 8)

24640 ______. The Malpaharias of West Bengal. Calcutta: Tribal Welfare Dept., Govt. of W. Bengal, 1966. (Bull. of the Cultural Res. Inst., Spec. series, 7)

24641 ROY, A.K. Some notes on the Ksatriya movement in North Bengal. In JASBangla 20,1 (1975) 47-71.

24642 RAY, P.C. The Lodha and their spirit-possessed man; a psychosocio-cultural study. Calcutta: AnthSI, 1969. 138p. [Midnapur Dist.]

24643 SANYAL, T.K. ...And keeping the flame alive: a study on food habits and dietaries with nutritional efficiency of West Bengal tribes. Calcutta: Scheduled Castes & Tribes Welfare Dept., Govt. of W. Bengal, 1979. 208p. (Bull. of the Cultural Res. Inst., Spec. series, 23)

24644 SENGUPTA, S. Social profiles of the Mahalis. Calcutta: KLM, 1970. 204p.

24645 SHASMAL, K.C. The Bauris of West Bengal; a socio-economic study. Calcutta: Indian Pub., 1972. 260p.

24646 WEST BENGAL. TRIBAL WELFARE DEPT. Backward classes welfare in West Bengal, 1952-56. Calcutta: 1957. 115p.

g. Muslims of Bengal

24647 AHMED, SUFIA. Muslim community in Bengal, 1884-1912. Dacca: S. Ahmed, dist. OUP, 1974. 425p.

24648 BHATTACHARYA, R.K. The concept and ideology of caste among the Muslims of rural West Bengal. In Imtiaz Ahmad, ed. Caste and social stratification among the Muslims. ND: Manohar, 1973, 107-32.

24649 FRUZZETTI-OSTOR, L. The idea of community among West Bengal Muslims. In P.J. Bertocci, ed. Prelude to crisis. East Lansing: Michigan State U., Asian Studies Centre, 1972, 79-90. (Its occ. papers, S.A. series, 18)

24650 GUHA, UMA. Caste among rural Bengali Muslims. In MI 45,2 (1965) 167-69.

24651 MCPHERSON, K. The Muslim microcosm: Calcutta 1918-1935. Wiesbaden: Steiner, 1974. 162p. (BSAF, 8)

24652 MONDAL, SEKH RAHIM. Structure of kinship among Muslims in a West Bengal village. In Man & Life 3,3/4 (1977) 80-90.

24653 SIDDIQUI, M.K.A. Caste among the Muslims of Calcutta. In Imtiaz Ahmad, ed. Caste and social stratification among the Muslims. ND: Manohar, 1973, 133-56.

24654 ______. Muslims of Calcutta: a study in aspects of their social organisation. Calcutta: AnthSI, 1974. 144p. (Its Memoirs, 36)

h. Europeans, Jews, and Armenians

24655 ELIAS, F. & J.E. COOPER. The Jews of Calcutta: the autobiography of a community, 1798-1972. Calcutta: Jewish Assn. of Calcutta, 1974. 243p.

24656 MUSLEAH, E.N. On the banks of the Ganga: the sojourn of Jews in Calcutta. North Quincy, MA: Christopher, 1975. 568p.

24657 PEARSON, R. Eastern interlude; a social history of the European community in Calcutta. Calcutta: Thacker, Spink, 1954. 238p.

24658 SETH, M.J. Khojah Tetrus, the Armenian merchant-diplomat of Calcutta. In BPP 36 (1928?) 110-26.

24659 TIMBERG, T.A. The Jews of Calcutta. In BPP 93,1 (1974) 7-22.

j. women in Bengal

24660 CHAKRABORTY, USHA. Condition of Bengali women around the second half of the nineteenth century. Calcutta: the author, 1963. 232p.

24661 FORBES, G. The ideals of Indian womanhood: six Bengali women during the independence movement. In J.R. McLane, ed. Bengal in the nineteenth and twentieth centuries. East Lansing: Asian Studies Center, Michigan State U., 1975, 159-74. (Its occ. papers, S.A. series, 25)

24662 MAZUMDAR, S. A pattern of life: the memoirs of an Indian woman. ND: Manohar, 1977. 246p.

24663 ROY, M. Bengali women. Chicago: UChiP, 1975. 205p. [1st pub. 1972]

24664 URQUHART, M.M. Women of Bengal: a study of the Hindu Pardanasins of Calcutta. 2nd ed. Calcutta: Assn. Press, 1926. 165p.

3. Villages and Rural Society in Bengal since 1813

a. rural society and change under the Raj

24665 BHATTACHARYYA, N.C. & L.A. NATESAN. Some Bengal villages, an economic survey. Calcutta: U. of Calcutta, 1932. 225p.

24666 DUTT, R.C. The peasantry of Bengal. Calcutta: Manisha, 1980. 194p. [1st pub. 1874]

24667 GEDDES, A. Au pays de Tagore. La civilisation rurale du Bengale occidental et ses facteurs geographiques. Paris: A. Colin, 1927. 235p.

24668 GHOSE, B. Aspects of social change in rural Bengal in the nineteenth century. In S. Sinha, ed. Aspects of Indian culture and society.... Calcutta: IAS, 1972, 57-63.

24669 LAL, P.C. Reconstruction and education in rural India in the light of the programme carried on at Sriniketan, the institute of rural reconstruction, founded by Rabindranath Tagore. London: Allen & Unwin, 1932. 262p.

24670 RAY, RATNALEKHA. Change in Bengal agrarian society, c1760-1850. ND: Manohar, 1979. 339p.

b. general studies of rural society, and village studies in W. Bengal since 1947

24671 BANERJEE, TARASANKAR. Panchagram (Five villages). Tr. from Bengali by M.F. Franda & S.K. Chatterjee. Delhi: Manohar, 1973. 352p. [novel]

24672 BASU, T.K. The Bengal peasant from time to time. NY: Asia, 1963. 205p. (Indian stat. series, 15)

24673 BHATTACHARJEE, J.P. Shajapur: socio-economic study of a West Bengal village. Shantiniketan: B.R. Bose, for Agro-Econ. Res. Centre, Visva-Bharati U., 1958. 145p.

24674 BHOWMICK, P.K. Kasba Narayangarh: a Muslim village In MI 45 (1965) 201-22.

24675 CHAKRABORTI, B. & P. ROY. Twenty villages of West Bengal: a socio-economic study on intercommunity differences. Calcutta: Cultural Res. Inst., Govt. of W. Bengal, 1972. 294p.

24676 CHATTOPADHYAY, G. Ranjana: a village in West Bengal. Calcutta: Bookland, 1964. 262p. [Midnapur Dist.]

24677 DAS, A.K. Trends of occupation pattern through generations in rural areas of West Bengal. Calcutta: Scheduled Castes and Tribes Welfare Dept., Govt. of W. Bengal, 1961. 103p. (Bull. of the Cultural Res. Inst., Spec. series, 10)

24678 GUPTA, R.K. Agrarian West Bengal: three field studies. Calcutta: Inst. of Social Res. & Applied Anthro., Dept. of Anthro., Calcutta U., 1977. 199p.

24679 MANDAL, G.C. & S.C. SENGUPTA. Kashipur, West Bengal, 1959-60; a report on re-survey of a village. Santiniketan: Agro-Econ. Res. Centre, Visva-Bharati, 1962. 104p.

24680 MUKHERJEE, RAMKRISHNA. The dynamics of a rural society; a study of the economic structure in Bengal villages. Berlin: Akademie-Verlag, 1957. 134p.

24681 ______. Six villages of Bengal. Bombay: Popular, 1971. 303p. [1st pub. in JASBengal, 1971]

24682 NICHOLAS, R.W. Ecology and village structure in deltaic West Bengal. In EW 15 (1963) 1185-96.

24683 ______. Villages of the Bengal Delta: a study of ecology and peasant society. Diss., U. of Chicago, 1962. 198p.

24684 SARMA, JYOTIRMOYEE. A village in West Bengal. In M.N. Srinivas, ed. India's villages. Calcutta: W. Bengal Dev. Dept., 1955, 161-79.

24685 SENGUPTA, S. Social interaction and status groups in Bengal villages. Calcutta: KLM, 1970. 82p.

24686 ______. The social system of a Bengal village. Calcutta: Editions Indian, 1973. 137p.

24687 SINHA, S. & R. BHATTACHARYA. Bhadralok and chhotolok in a rural area of West Bengal. In SB 18 (1969) 50-66.

c. rural community development in W. Bengal since 1947

24688 BANERJEE, H. Experiments in rural reconstruction. Calcutta: Visva-Bharati, 1966. 157p.

24689 BASU, S.K. & R.N. SAHA. On educational and economic achievements; a study on intercommunity differences in twenty-four villages of West Bengal. Calcutta Cultural Res. Inst., Govt. of W. Bengal, 1971. 209p. (Its Bull., spec. ser., 13)

24690 COUSINS, W.T. Community development in West Bengal In Community Dev. R. 4,3 (1953) 37-77.

24691 DANDA, A.K. & D.G. DANDA. Development and change in Basudha; study of a West Bengal village. Hyderabad: NICD, 1971. 132p.

24692 DASGUPTA, S. Communication and innovation in Indian villages. In Social Forces 43 (1965) 330-37.

24693 DASGUPTA, S. Social work and social change; a case study in Indian village development. Boston: P. Sargent, 1968. 222p. [Birbhum Dist.]

24694 MUKHARJEE, K.K. & K. DUTTA. Mandra experiment: a case study. ND: People's Action for Dev. with Justice, 1980. 42p. (Its series, 2) [Hooghly District]

4. Cities and Urbanization - General Studies

24695 BASU, D.N. New towns in West Bengal - a demographic and economic appraisal. In AV 13,2 (1971) 246-260.

24696 BHATTACHARYA, N.D. Murshidabad: a study in urban geography. In NGJI 5,1 (1959) 33-51.

24697 DATTA, J.M. Urbanization in Bengal. In GRI 18,4 (1956) 19-23.

24698 GUHA, M. Urban regions of West Bengal: a few examples. In GRI 19,3 (1956) 31-44.

24699 JANA, M.M. Decennial growth and functional characteristics of urban areas in Midnapur district. In GRI 37,4 (1975) 364-77.

24700 KHAN, S. MD. REZA ALI. The Murshidabad guide: a brief historical survey of Murshidabad, from 1704 to 1969. Calcutta: Sk. Pear Mohammed, 1975. 56p.

24701 MOHSIN, M. Chittaranjan; a study in urban sociology. Bombay: Popular, 1964. 198p.

24702 MUKHERJEE, C. Growth pattern of a "rural" town (1851-1961); a case study. In IESHR 4 (1967) 375-400.

24703 ______. Trend of urbanization in West Bengal. In MR 124 (1969) 847-65.

24704 ______. Urban growth in a rural area: a case study of a town in West Bengal. Santiniketan: Visva-Bharati, 1972. 333p.

24705 PARK, R.L., ed. Urban Bengal. East Lansing: Michigan State U., Asian Studies Center, 1969. 123p. (Its occ. papers, S.A. series, 12)

24706 SAHAI, J. Urban complex of an industrial city. Allahabad: Chugh, 1980. 155p. [Durgapur]

24707 WEST BENGAL. ASANSOL PLANNING ORG. Interim development plan, Asansol-Durgapur. Calcutta: 1966. 73p.

5. Calcutta (1981 pop. 9,165,650)
a. historical studies and descriptions

24708 BAGCHI, P.C. Calcutta, past and present. Calcutta: Calcutta U. Press, 1939. 127p.

24709 BLAISE, C. & B. MUKHERJEE. Days and nights in Calcutta. NY: Doubleday, 1977. 300p.

24710 BLECHYNDEN, K. Calcutta, past and present. New ed. Calcutta: Genl. Printers & Pub., 1978. 206p. + 13pl.

24711 CHATTERJEE, A.B. The Hooghly river and its west bank: a study in historical geography. In GRI 25 (1963) 164-82.

24712 CHATTERJI, S.K. The changing culture of Calcutta. In BPP 87 (1968) 1-26.

24713 CHAUDHURI, P. & N.S. BOSE, eds. Calcutta: people and empire; gleanings from old journals. Calcutta: India Book Exchange, 1975. 254p.

24714 CHOUDHURY, R.R., ed. Glimpses of old Calcutta, period 1836-50. Bombay: Nachiketa, 1978. 114p.

24715 CLARK, T.W. The languages of Calcutta: 1760-1840. In BSOAS 18 (1956) 453-74.

24716 BEN, B.K. The early history and growth of Calcutta. Calcutta: Rddhi, 1977. 255p. [1st pub. 1905]

24717 DOIG, D. Calcutta; an artist's impression. Calcutta: Statesman, 1968. 1v.

24718 KIPLING, R. City of dreadful night and other places. Allahabad: A.H. Wheeler, 1891. 96p.

24719 LONG, J. Calcutta in the olden time; its localities and its people. Calcutta: SPB, 1974. 136p. [1st pub. in CR 18 (1852) & 35 (1960)]

24720 MITRA, A. Calcutta: India's city. ND: New Age, 1963. 99p.

24721 MUKHERJEE, N. The Port of Calcutta; a short history. Calcutta: Commissioners for the Port of Calcutta, 1968. 276p.

24722 MUKHERJEE, S.N. Calcutta; myths and history. Calcutta: Subarnarekha, 1977. 108p.

25723 RAY, A., ed. Calcutta. Calcutta: Rddhi-India, 1977. 299p.

24724 ______, ed. Calcutta keepsake. Calcutta: Rddhi-India, 1978. 322p.

24725 RAY, N.R. The city of Job Charnock. Calcutta: Victoria Memorial, 1979. 47p.

24726 RAY, R.K. Historical roots of the crisis of Calcutta, 1876-1939. In EPW 14,29 (1979) 1206-12.

24727 SINHA, P. Approaches to urban history: Calcutta (1750-1850). In BPP 87 (1968) 106-19.

24728 ______. Calcutta in urban history. Calcutta: KLM, 1978. 168p.

24729 ______. Social forces and urban growth - Calcutta from the mid-eighteenth to the mid-nineteenth century. In BPP 92,2 (1973) 288-302.

24730 VICTORIA MEMORIAL (MUSEUM). Calcutta, 1690-1930: a catalogue of objects on Calcutta in the collection of the Victoria Memorial. Calcutta: Victoria Memorial, 1976. 119p.

b. municipal government and politics

24731 ASHRAF, ALI. The city government of Calcutta; a study of inertia. NY: Asia, 1966. 126p.

24732 BHATTACHARYA, M. Rural self-government in metropolitan Calcutta. NY: Asia, for Inst. of Public Admin., 1965. 106p. (Calcutta res. studies, 5)

24733 BHATTACHARYA, M. & M.M. SINGH & F.J. TYSEN. Government in metropolitan Calcutta; a manual. NY: Asia, for Inst. of Public Admin., 1965. 238p. (Calcutta res. studies, 1)

24734 CHAKRAVORTI, R. The personality factor in local politics; a study of the Calcutta municipal election. In EW 17,26 (1965) 1027-30.

24735 CHATTERJI, M. An econometric study of municipal finances in the Calcutta metropolitan district. In IJPA 16,1 (1970) 97-114.

24736 CHOUDHURI, K. Calcutta: story of its government. Bombay: Orient Longman, 1973. 378p.

25837 DATTA, A. Inter-governmental grants in metropolitan Calcutta. NY: Asia, for Inst. of Public Admin., 1965. 50p.

24738 DATTA, A. & D.C. RANNEY. Municipal finances in the Calcutta metropolitan district: a preliminary study. NY: Asia, for Inst. of Public Admin, 1965. 123p. (Calcutta res. studies, 3)

24739 FUREDY, C. Muslim participation in colonial local administration: the case of Calcutta, 1876-1900. In Indian J. of Politics 9,2 (1975) 163-80.

24740 GOODE, S.W., ed. Municipal Calcutta, its institutions in their origin and growth. Edinburgh: Constable, 1916. 410p.

24741 MUKHERJEE, S.N. Daladali in Calcutta in the nineteenth century. In MAS 9,1 (1975) 59-80. [faction feuds]

24742 RAY, R.K. Urban roots of Indian nationalism: pressure groups and conflict of interests in Calcutta City politics, 1875-1939. ND: Vikas, 1979. 246p.

24743 SAMADDAR, S. Calcutta is. Calcutta: Corporation of Calcutta, 1978. 324p. + 23pl. [On the management of the Calcutta Corp., 1975-77.]

24744 SINGH, M.M. Municipal government in the Calcutta Metropolitan District; a preliminary survey. NY: Asia, for Inst. of Public Admin., 1965. 44p. (Calcutta res. studies, 2)

24745 TYSEN, F.J. District administration in Metropolitan Calcutta. NY: Asia, for Inst. of Public Admin., 1965. 53p. (Calcutta res. studies, 4)

24746 WEINER, M. Violence and politics in Calcutta. In JAS 20 (1961) 275-81.

c. the Calcutta conurbation (1971 pop. 7,040,345)
i. Howrah and other contiguous cities

24747 BAGCHI, K. The Howrah conurbation - a study in urban sprawl. In GRI 28,1 (1966) 16-31.

24748 BONNERJEE, J., ed. Howrah civic companion. Calcutta: Calcutta Pub., 1955. 1v.

24749 CHATTERJEE, A.B. Howrah: a study in social geography. Calcutta: U. Chatterjee, 1967. 191p.

24750 ______. Industrial landscape of Howrah. In GRI 25,4 (1963) 211-42.

24751 WEST BENGAL. CALCUTTA METROPOLITAN PLANNING ORG. Howrah area development plan, 1966-1986. Calcutta: 1967. 66p.

ii. relations of city and hinterland

24752 BANERJEE, P. Calcutta and its hinterland: a study in economic history of India, 1833-1900. Calcutta: Progressive, 1975. 240p.

24753 BOSE, A.N. Calcutta and rural Bengal: small sector symbiosis: a study prepared for the Intl. Labour Office. Calcutta: Minerva, 1978. 171p.

24754 DUTT, A.K. & S.C. CHAKRABORTY. Reality of Calcutta and conurbation. In NGJI 9 (1963) 161-74.

24755 GUHA, M. The urban fringe of Calcutta. In JIAS 1 (1966) 191-96.

24756 KAR, N.R. Economic character of metropolitan sphere of influence of Calcutta: a study in functional classification of towns and typology of economic activities around Calcutta. In GRI 25 (1963) 108-37.

24757 ______. Urban hierarchy and central functions around Calcutta and lower West Bengal, India, and their significance. In Proc. of the Intl. Geog. Union Symposium on Urban Geography. Lund: Univ. Lund, 1962, 253-74. (Lund studies in Geography; series B, 24)

24758 ______. On the economy of Calcutta region; a study of the basic-nonbasic activity of Calcutta and its conurbation. In GRI 28,2 (1966) 1-28.

d. socio-economic studies

24759 BERRY, B.J. & P.H. REES. The factorial ecology of Calcutta. In AJS 74 (1969) 445-91.

24760 BISWAS, A., et al. The ethnic composition of Calcutta and the residential pattern of minorities. In GRI 39,2&3 (1976) 140-66, 307-10.

24761 BOSE, N.K. Calcutta: a premature metropolis. In Scientific American 213 (1965) 90-102.

24762 ______. Calcutta, 1964; a social survey. Bombay: Lalvani, 1968. 328p.

24763 CHAKRABORTTY, K. The conflicting worlds of working mothers: a sociological enquiry. Calcutta: Progressive, 1978. 305p.

24764 GHOSH, M. & A.K. DUTTA & B. RAY. Calcutta: a study in urban growth dynamics. Calcutta: KLM, 1972. 120p.

24765 GUHA, M. Concentration of communities in Burrabazar, Calcutta. In MI 44 (1964) 289-97.

24766 INDIA (REP.). CENSUS OF INDIA, 1961. Calcutta - the primate city. ND: MPGOI, 1966. 149p. (V.1, monograph 2)

24767 MOORHOUSE, G. Calcutta. London: Weidenfeld, 1971. 376p.

24768 MUNSHI, SUNIL K. Calcutta metropolitan explosion: its nature and roots. ND: PPH, 1975. 175p.

24769 SEN, S.N. The city of Calcutta; a socio-economic survey, 1954-55 to 1957-58. Calcutta: Bookland, 1960, 271p.

24770 SINHA, S. Scope for urban anthropology and the city of Calcutta. In his (ed.) Aspects of Indian culture and society.... Calcutta: IAS, 1972. 65-72.

24771 ______, ed. Cultural profile of Calcutta. Calcutta: IAS, 1972. 283p. [1970 seminar]

e. urban planning and development; the Calcutta Metropolitan Planning Organization

24772 BHATTACHARYYA, M.K. Local government and Calcutta metropolitan plan. In QJLSGI 38 (1968) 169-95.

24773 CHAKRAVARTY, B. Interventions and the organisational perspective of urban development authorities: the case of CMDA. In Nagarlok 12,1 (1980) 52-64.

24774 FORD FOUNDATION. Drafting a new blueprint for India's largest urban center: Calcutta metropolitan plan project. ND: Ford Foundation, 1964. 24p.

24775 GREEN, L. & A. DATTA. Special agencies in metropolitan Calcutta: a comparative study. London: Asia, for the Inst. of Public Admin, 1968. 141p.

24776 LUBELL, H. Calcutta: its urban development and employment prospects. Geneva, ILO, 1974. 143p.

24777 MITRA, A. Planning and provision of services in Calcutta: a test case of societal responses to population change. In M.F. Franda, ed. Responses to population growth in India. NY: Praeger, 1975, 223-64.

24778 MUKHERJEE, C. Land utilization planning in metropolitan Calcutta. In Economic Affairs 7 (1962) 375-86.

24779 MUKHERJEE, R.N. Urban development and planning: Calcutta metropolis. Calcutta: Intl. Pub., 1978. 221p.

24780 Proceedings of workshop series on Calcutta 2000, some imperatives for action now. Calcutta: Civic Affairs & Tourism Sub-Cmtee., Indian Chamber of Commerce, 1978. 277p.

24781 ROSSER, C. Action planning in Calcutta; the problem of community participation. In J. of Dev. Studies 6,4 (1970) 21-39.

24782 Towards a better Calcutta, proceedings of the seminar held in April, 1965. Calcutta: Indian Chamber of Commerce, 1965. 202p.

24783 WEST BENGAL. CALCUTTA METROPOLITAN PLANNING ORG. Basic development plan for the Calcutta Metropolitan District, 1966-1986. Calcutta: 1966. 176p.

f. urban problems and services
i. general studies

24784 GUHA, M. Social institutions in a municipal ward in Calcutta. In MI 42 (1962) 181-94.

24785 SEMINAR ON CALCUTTA AND ITS PROBLEMS, CALCUTTA, 1970. Calcutta today; a comprehensive survey. Calcutta: Sales & Display Pub., 1980. 200p.

ii. slums (bustees/bastis) and housing

24786 MAITRA, M.S. Calcutta slums: public intervention and prospects. In Nagarlok 11,2 (1979) 34-60.

24787 MITRA, A. Housing the urban poor: case of Calcutta. In EPW 6, 30-32 (1971) 1627-34.

24788 SENGUPTA, B.K. Bustee improvement programme in CMD area. In Civic Affairs 20,10 (1973) 115-22.

24789 SIDDIQUI, M.K.A. The slums of Calcutta: a problem and its solution. In IJSW 29 (1968) 173-82.

24790 SIVARAMAKRISHNAN, K.C. The slum improvement programme in Calcutta; the role of the CMDA. In SocAct 27, 3 (1977) 292-305.

iii. transportation and water supply

24791 CHAKRAVARTI, A.K. Construction of underground railway in Calcutta: Progress and problems. In Indian Railways 21,4 (1976) 59-63.

24792 ______. Metro railway keeps its pace. In Indian Railways 24,1 (1979) 159-92.

24793 CHATTERJIA, P.K. Water for metropolitan Calcutta. In Civic Affairs 20,11 (1973) 15-20.

24794 DUTTA, S.J. & T.R. BHASKARAN. Sewage treatment for Howrah-Calcutta. In Civic Affairs 20,10 (1973) 107-13.

24795 HALDER, D.K. Impact of rapid transit system on land use and environment: the case of Calcutta tube rail. In Nagarlok 10,3 (1978) 33-43.

24796 HALDER, D.K. & S. BASU. Financial performance of the CSTC vis-a-vis private operators: a comparative study. In Nagarlok 11,2 (1979) 98-133.

24797 INDIA (REP.). METROPOLITAN TRANSPORT TEAM. Report on mass transportation system in Calcutta. ND: 1969. 72p.

24798 MITRA, P.C. Our major ports: the Calcutta-Haldia complex. In Yojana 19,1 (1975) 28-31.

24799 RAO, M.S.V. Traffic and transportation plan for Calcutta metropolitan district. In URPT 13,3 (1970) 191-200.

24800 SAHA, LEENA. The port that won't say die. In IWI 94, 25 (1973) 20-25.

24801 VENKATACHALAM, S.K. Calcutta port centenary. In Indian Shipping 22,10 (1970) 3-5.

24802 WEST BENGAL. CALCUTTA METROPOLITAN PLANNING ORG. Traffic and transportation plan for the Calcutta metropolitan district, 1966-1986. Calcutta: 1967. 178p.

24803 WORLD HEALTH ORG. Survey of water supply resources of Greater Calcutta. Geneva: 1969. 51p.

6. Social Problems and Social Welfare in West Bengal
a. general studies

24804 INDIA (REP.). CENTRAL SOCIAL WELFARE BOARD. RES., EVAL. & STAT. DIV. Directory of social welfare agencies in India: West Bengal. ND: 1979. 5v., 2041p.

24805 MALLIK, B.P. Language of the underworld of West Bengal. Calcutta: Sanskrit College, 1972. 129p.

24806 MUKHOPADHYAY, S. Juvenile delinquency in Calcutta. In MI 43,4 (1963) 315-22.

24807 NAG, MONI. Beggar problem in Calcutta and its solution. In IJSW 24,3 (1965) 243-52.

24808 OWENS, R.L. & A. NANDY. Organizational growth and organizational participation: voluntary associations in a West Bengal city. In CIS ns 9,1 (1975) 19-53.

24809 PRABARTAK SAMGHA. Message and mission of Prabartak Samgha. Chandernagore: Prabartak Samgha, 1970. 92p.

b. refugees from E. Bengal - problems of resettlement

24810 DE, S.L. & A.K. BHATTACHARJEE. The refugee settlement in the Sunderbans, West Bengal; a socio-economic study. Calcutta: India Stat. Inst., 1973. 35p.

24811 GUHA, B.S. Studies in social tensions among the refugees from eastern Pakistan. Delhi: MPGOI, 1959. 130p. (Dept. of Anthro., Memoirs, 1)

24812 GUPTA, S.K. Dandakaranya: a survey of rehabilitation. In EW 16, 1-3 (1965) 15-26, 59-65, 89-96. [resettlement area in M.P.]

24813 PAKRASI, K.B. On some aspects of family structures of the refugees of West Bengal 1947-48. In SB 14,1 (1965) 13-20.

24814 ______. The uprooted; a sociological study of the refugees of West Bengal. Calcutta: Editions Indian, 1971. 172p.

7. Health Services and Family Planning

24815 BAGAL, J.C. Early years of the Calcutta Medical College. In MR 82 (1947) 210-15.

24816 BASU, R. Cholera in Calcutta: a case study in medical geography. In GRI 31,3 (1969) 1-12.

24817 DE, S.L. & A.K. BHATTACHARJEE. Social consciousness and fertility patterns of refugee settlers in West Bengal. In J. of Family Welfare 21,2 (1974) 63-81.

24818 GUPTA, B. Indigenous medicine in nineteenth- and twentieth-century Bengal. In C. Leslie, ed. Asian medical systems: a comparative study. Berkeley: UCalP, 1976, 368-82.

23819 KLEIN, I. Malaria and mortality in Bengal, 1840-1921. In IESHR 9,2 (1972) 132-160.

24820 ROGERS, L. A short historical note on medical societies and medical journals in Calcutta. In JASBengal ns 2 (1906) 393-97.

24821 SAHA, H. An evaluation of a family planning programme in a rural area in West Bengal. In J. of Family Welfare 18,1 (1971) 10-15.

24822 SEAL, S.C. Planning of health services in West Bengal till 2000 A.D., vis-a-vis population growth. Calcutta: Dawn Books, 1975. 112p.

24823 SEAL, S.C. & K.K. MODAK. A study of plague epidemic in West Bengal. In IJPS 19,3 (1975) 126-46; 20 (1976) 25-38, 122-33.

8. Education in Bengal since 1813
[see also: Rabindranath Tagore, Visvabharati Chap. Six, V. B. 6. b. and Vidyasagar (Ishwar Chandra Sarma) I. F. 2. d., below]
a. general histories and studies

24824 ADAM, W. Report on the state of education in Bengal (1835 and 1838). Ed. by Anathnath Basu. Calcutta: U. of Calcutta, 1941. 578p.

24825 BHATTACHARYA, R., ed. David Hare bicentenary volume, 1975-76. Calcutta: David Hare Bicentenary of Birth Celebration Cmtee., dist. KLM, 1976. 271p.

24826 CHATTERJI, B. Indo-British cultural confrontation: Gooroodass Banerjee and his times. Calcutta: Minerva, 1979. 232p.

24827 EAST PAKISTAN. BUREAU OF EDUC. INFO. & STAT. Chronology of the growth of education, 1600-1966. Dacca: East Pakistan Govt. Press, 1966. 49p.

24828 KIDDER, D.E. Education and manpower planning in India. Bombay: Progressive Corp., 1973. 182p. [study of engineering graduates, Calcutta]

24829 MAZUMDAR, V. Education and social change; three studies on nineteenth century India. Simla: IIAS, 1972. 88p.

24830 MUKHERJEE, N.C. An examination of education in Bengal between 1920 and 1947. In CR 179 (1966) 57-70.

24831 NATL. STAFF COLLEGE FOR EDUCATIONAL PLANNERS & ADMINISTRATORS. Educational administration in West Bengal: a survey report, 1977. ND: 1977. 86p.

24832 SEN, P.R. Education as a channel of Western influence in Bengal. In CR 18 (1926) 118-34.

24833 SINHA, D.P. The educational policy of the East India Company in Bengal to 1854. Calcutta: Punthi Pustak, 1964. 320p.

24834 STARK, H.A. Vernacular education in Bengal from 1813 to 1912. Calcutta: Calcutta Genl. Pub., 1916. 208p.

24835 WEST BENGAL. EDUC. DEPT. Septennial review on the progress of education in West Bengal for the period 1957-58 to 1963-64. Alipore: 1970. 178p.

b. higher education
i. general studies

24836 GHOSH, J. Higher education in Bengal under British rule. Calcutta: The Book Co., 1926. 142p.

24837 The National Council of Education; Bengal; a history and homage. Calcutta: Jadavpur U., 1956? 114p.

24838 SENGUPTA, P. Harendra Coomar Mookerjee. ND: NBT, 1977. 73p.

ii. the University of Calcutta (est. 1857); Sir Asutosh Mukherjee (1864-1924), High Court judge and educator

24839 CALCUTTA UNIV. Hundred years of the University of Calcutta: a history of the University issued in commemoration of the centenary celebrations. Calcutta: U. of Calcutta, 1957. 539p. [with Suppl., 732p.]

24840 CALCUTTA. UNIV. DEPT. OF ECON. A study of the employment pattern of the post-graduate students of University of Calcutta, May 1972. ND: Cmtee. on Unemployment, Min. of Labour & Rehabilitation, 1975. 72p.

24841 DASGUPTA, A.P. Asutosh Mukherjee. ND: NBT, 1973. 127p.

24842 INDIA. CALCUTTA UNIV. CMSN., 1917-19. Report [with evidence]. Calcutta: Supt. Govt. Printing, 1919. 13v. [Also pub. London: HMSO, 1919, Cmd. 386-; Chm., Sir M.E. Sadler]

24843 MUKERJI, K.M. Study of the finances of the Calcutta University. Calcutta: KLM, 1976. 87p.

24844 PAL, B.C. Sir Ashutosh Mookherjea: a character study. Calcutta: D.P. Datta, 19__. 88p.

24845 SINHA, N.K. Asutosh Mookerjee; a biographical study. Calcutta: Asutosh Mukerjee Centenary Cmtee., 1966. 192p.

24846 SINHA, S. Asutosh Mookerjee. ND: PDMIB, 1970. 88p.

iii. other universities and colleges

24847 BENGAL. DACCA UNIV. CMTEE., 1912. Report. Calcutta: Supt. Govt. Printing, 1912. 283p. + 35pl.

24848 DAS, S.K. Sahibs and munshis: an account of the College of Fort William. ND: Orion Pub., 1978. 192p.

24849 PRESIDENCY COLLEGE, CALCUTTA. Centenary Volume, 1955. Alipore: W. Bengal Govt. Press, 1956. 372p. 70p. of port.

24850 RANKING, G.S.A. History of the College of Fort William from its first foundation. In BPP 7 (1911) 1-29; 21 (1920) 160-200; 22 (1921) 120-58; 23 (1921) 1-37, 84-153; 24 (1922) 112-38.

24851 SERAMPORE COLLEGE. The story of Serampore and its college. 3rd ed. Serampore: Serampore College, 1961. 121p.

24852 ZACHARIAH, K. History of Hoogly College, 1836-1936. Alipore: Supt. Govt. Printing, 1936. 144p.

iv. student attitudes and unrest

24853 CHATTOPADHYAY, K.P. & P.K. BOSE & A. CHATTERJI. Undergraduate students in Calcutta: how they live and work. In CR 132 (1954) 1-42.

24854 DASGUPTA, S. The great gherao of 1969: a case study of campus violence and protest methods. ND: Orient Longman, 1974. 156p.

c. elementary and secondary education

24855 BAGAL, J.C. Primary education in Calcutta, 1818-33, mainly based on the manuscript proceedings of the Calcutta School Society. In BPP 81 (1962) 83-95.

24856 D'SOUZA, A.A. Anglo-Indian education: a study of its origins and growth in Bengal up to 1960. Delhi: OUP, 1976. 344p.

24857 HARRISON, J.L. The Midnapore system of primary education. In CR 63, 125 (1876) 25-76.

24858 MITRA, R.L. Raja Rajendralal Mitra and elementary education in Bengal. In CR 17 (1925) 127-38.

24859 Ninety-five years of secondary education under the University of Calcutta. In CR 156 (1960) 193-213.

d. education of Muslims in Bengal, 1813 - 1947

24860 BENGAL. MOSLEM EDUC. ADVISORY CMTEE. Report. Alipore: 1935. 172p.

24861 HAQUE, ENAMUL. Nawab Bahadur Abdul Latif, his writings and related documents. Dacca: Samudra Prokashani, 1968. 309p.

24862 HENA, A. Reactions and reconcilement. Chittagong: Pak. Coop. Book Soc., 1969. 392p.

24863 HUSSAIN, S.M. Islamic education in Bengal. In IsC 8 (1934) 439-47.

24864 MALLICK, AZIZUR RAHMAN. British policy and the Muslims in Bengal, 1757-1856. 2nd ed. Dacca: Bangla Academy, 1977. 408p. [1st pub. 1961]

24865 RAHMAN, M. FAZLUR. The Bengali Muslims and English education, 1965-1835. Dacca: Bengali Academy, 1973. 136p.

24866 SANIAL, S.C. History of the Calcutta Madrassa. In BPP 8 (1914) 83-111, 225-50.

24867 SUHRAWARDY, H. Muhammedan education. In CR 8 (1923) 229-38.

e. education of women in Bengal

24868 BAGAL, J.C. Female education in mid-nineteenth century: origin of the Bethune School. In MR 74,1 (1943) 65-9.

24869 ______. Women's education in eastern India, the first phase: mainly based on contemporary records. Calcutta: World Press, 1956. 132p.

24870 BANERJI, B.N. Ishwarchandra Vidyasagar as a promoter of female education in Bengal. In JASBengal ns 23 (1927) 381-97.

24871 DE, S.K. Women's education in Bengal from the Battle of Plassey to Sepoy Mutiny. In CR 161,3 (1961) 255-65.

24872 NAG, K. & L. GHOSH, eds. Bethune School and College centenary volume, 1849-1949. Calcutta: Bethune College, 1950. 237p.

E. Religious Traditions of Modern Bengal

[See also:
Brahmo Samaj, Chap. Six, VII. C. 2.;
Ramakrishna, Vivekananda, Chap. Six, VII. B. 5.;
Sacred Centers, Chap. One, IV. C. 3. g.]

1. General Studies; Folk Religion

24873 BHATTACHARYA, A. The cult of the village gods of West Bengal. In MI 35 (1955) 19-30.

24874 BHATTACHARYA, B. The deified saints of Bengal: a profile. In Folklore(C) 12,11&12 (1971) 399-410, 439-56.

24875 BHOWMICK, P.K. Occultism in fringe Bengal. Calcutta: Subarnarekha, 1978. 168p.

24876 FUCHAS, Mother. Fairs and festivals of Bengal. In Folklore(C) 16,10 (1975) 334-61.

24877 ______. Folk religion, magic and cults. In Folklore(C) 16,8 (1975) 258-91.

24878 MAHAPATRA, P.K. Minor folk cults of Bengal. In Folklore(C) 13,11 (1972) 428-39.

24879 NICHOLAS, R.W. Vaiṣṇavism and Islam in rural Bengal. In D. Kopf, ed. Bengal regional identity. East Lansing: Asian Studies Center, Michigan State U., 1969, 33-50. (Its occ. papers, S.A. series, 9)

24880 RAY, B.G. Religious movements in modern Bengal. Santiniketan: Visva-Bharati, 1965. 244p. [includes Hindu movements and gurus, Chittagong Buddhism, Islam, Christianity, Theosophy]

2. Hinduism
a. Vaiṣṇava, Śākta, and other sects

24881 BHATTACHARYYA, A. The rites of the serpent-goddess. In Folklore (C) 2 (1961) 41-48.

24882 BHOWMICK, P.K. Four temples in Midnapur, West Bengal. In MI 40,2 (1960) 81-102.

24883 ______. Gajan: a regional festival. In Folklore(C) 5 (1964) 321-33.

24884 CHAKRABARTY, R. Vaisnavism, the Chaitanya movement and the "Renaissance" in Bengal (1800-1900). In Jadavpur J. of Comp. Literature 13 (1975) 112-38.

24885 DAS, S.R. A study of the vrata rites of Bengal. In MI 32 (1952) 207-45.

24886 DIMOCK, E.C., JR. Doctrine and practice among the Vaisnavas of Bengal. In M.B. Singer, ed. Krishna: myths, rites and attitudes. Honolulu: EWCP 1966, 41-64. [1st pub. in HR 3 (1963) 106-27]

24887 DUTT, K.L. & K.M. PURKAYASTHA. The Bengal Vaishnavism and modern life. Calcutta: Sribhumi Pub. Co., 1963. 97p.

24888 LIPSKI, A. Bipinchandra Pal and reform Hinduism.

In P.J. Bertocci, ed. Prelude to crisis.... East Lansing: Michigan State U., Asian Studies Center, 1972, 99-111. (Its occ. papers, S.A. series, 18)

24889 ______. Vijay Kṛṣṇa Gosvāmi: reformer and traditionalist. In JIH 52,1 (1974) 209-35.

24890 MUKHERJEE, K.L. Birth of a cult: Chandi in Barbhanda. In MI 52,1 (1972) 82-86.

24891 OSTOR, A. The play of the gods: locality, ideology, structure, and time in the festivals of a Bengali town. Chicago: UChiP, 1980. 241p. [Bishnupur]

24892 PAL, B.C. Saint Bijayakrishna Goswami. Calcutta: Bipinchandra Pal Inst., 1964. 106p.

24893 RAY, S.K. The ritual art of the Bratas of Bengal. Calcutta: KLM, 1961. 74p.

24894 ROY, S.K. A study of Brata rituals of Bengal. In Folklore(C) 1 (1960) 83-96.

24895 SARMA, J. Puja associations in West Bengal. In JAS 28 (1968) 579-94.

24896 SINHA, S. Vaisnava influence on a tribal culture. In M.B. Singer, ed. Krishna: myths, rites, and attitudes. Honolulu: EWCP, 1966, 64-89.

b. Lord Dharma and his cult: admixture of Hindu, Buddhist, and tribal elements, appealing to lower castes

24897 BHATTACHARYA, A. The Dharma-cult. In BDA 1 (1952) 117-53.

24898 MAHAPATRA, P.K. The cult of Dharma Thakur. In Folklore(C) 13,2 (1972) 41-70.

24899 MAITY, P.K. Dharma Thakur of Bengal and his association with human fertility. In Folklore(C) 12,3 (1971) 81-94.

24900 ROBINSON, S.P. The Dharmapūjā: a study of rites and symbols associated with the Bengali deity Dharmaraj. Diss., U. of Chicago, 1980. 422p.

24901 SEN, S. Is the cult of Dharma a living relic of Buddhism in Bengal? In D.R. Bhandarkar, ed. B.C. Law volume, pt. 1. Calcutta: Indian Res. Inst., 1945, 669-674.

c. Śrī Ānandamayī Mā and her āshram

24902 ĀNANDAMAYĪ. Aux sources de la joie. Tr. by Jean Herbert. 5th ed. Lyons: P. Derain, 1963. 75p.

24903 ______. Matri vani. Tr. by Atmananda. 4th ed. Varanasi: Shree Shree Anandamayee Charitable Society, 1977. 2 v.

24904 ______. Words of Sri Anandamayi Ma. Tr. by Atmananda. 3rd ed. Varanasi: Shree Shree Anandamayee Charitable Society, 1978. 242p.

24905 BANERJEE, S. A mystic sage: Ma Anandamayi. Calcutta: 1973. 217p.

24906 JOSHI, H.R. Mā Ānandamayī līlā: memoirs of Śrī Hari Ram Joshi. Varanasi: Shree Shree Anandamayee Charitable Society, 1974. 199p.

24907 LIPSKI, A. Life and teaching of Śrī Ānandamayī Mā. Delhi: Motilal, 1977. 74p.

24908 ______. Some aspects of the life and teachings of the East Bengal saint Anandamayi Ma. In HR 9 (1969) 59-77.

24909 Ma Anandamayi by devotees. Benares: Ma Anandamayi Ashram, 1946. 253p.

3. Islam in Modern Bengal; the Farāʿidī/Ferazi Movement

24910 AHMAD, RAFIUDDIN. Islamization in nineteenth century Bengal. In Gopal Krishna, ed. Contributions to South Asian Studies 1. Delhi: OUP, 1979, 88-120.

24911 AHMAD KHAN, MUIN-UD-DIN. History of the Farāʿidī movement in Bengal, 1818-1906. Karachi: Pakistan Hist. Soc., 1965. 117 + 165p.

24912 ______., ed. Selections from Bengal government records on Wahhabi trials, 1863-70. Dacca: ASP, 1961. 418p.

24913 KARIM, A.K. NAZMUL. Some aspects of popular beliefs among Muslims of Bengal. In EA 9 (1955) 29-41.

24914 SUBHAN, ABDUS. Social and religious reform movement in the nineteenth century among the Muslims - a Bengali reaction to the Wahhabi movement. In S.P. Sen, ed. Social and religious reform movements.... Calcutta: Inst. of Historical Studies, 1979, 484-491.

4. Christianity in Modern Bengal

24915 ALI, M. MOHAR. The Bengali reaction to Christian missionary activities, 1833-1857. Chittagong: Mehrub Pub., 1965. 243p.

24916 DAS, S.K. The shadow of the Cross: Christianity and Hinduism in a colonial situation. ND: Munshiram, 1974. 181p.

24917 MAJUMDAR, R.C. Christian missionaries and renaissance in Bengal. In BPP 86,2 (1967) 1-12.

24918 ODDIE, G.A. Protestant missionaries and social reform: the indigo planting question in Bengal, 1850-1860. In J. of Religious History 3 (1965) 314-26.

F. Literature and Media in Modern Bengal

1. Bengali Literature - General Studies and Anthologies

a. surveys

24919 BOSE, B. An acre of green grass; a review of modern Bengali literature. Bombay: Orient Longmans, 1948. 107p.

24920 ______, ed. An anthology of Bengali writing. Bombay: Macmillan, 1971. 180p.

24921 DASGUPTA, A. Bengali. In K.R. Srinivasa Iyengar, ed. India literature since Independence. ND: Sahitya Akademi, 1973, 10-26.

24922 GHOSE, S.K. Bengali writing today: a fractured pride. In SAR 3,2 (1970) 151-60.

24923 KABIR, HUMAYUN, ed. Green and gold; stories and poems from Bengal. Westport, CT: Greenwood Press, 1958. 288p.

24924 MUKHERJI, J. Bengali literature in English; a bibliography. Calcutta: M.C. Sarkar, 1970. 130p. [bibl. of Bengali works trans. into English]

24925 SEN, P.R. Western influence in Bengali literature. Rev. ed. Calcutta: Saraswaty Library, 1947. 298p.

24926 SINHA, M. The little magazines of Calcutta - a preliminary exploration. In IWT 3,4 (1969) 13-18.

b. fiction

24927 BISWAS, D.K. Sociology of major Bengali novels. Gurgaon: Academic Press, 1974, 331p.

24928 CHATTERJEE, E., ed. & tr. An anthology of modern Bengali short stories. Calcutta: Prayer Books, 1977. 99p.

24929 CHAUDHURI, N. Social changes as reflected in Bengali literature. In IL 14,2 (1971) 41-52.

24930 FELDSIEPER, M. Bengalische Erzählungen. Tr. from Bengali by A. Datta & M. Feldsieper. Stuttgart: Reclam, 1971. 102p.

24931 GHOSE, B. & P. SEN. Bengali fiction: a panoramic view. Calcutta: Prima Pub., 1975. 95p.

24932 GHOSE, S., comp. Contemporary Bengali literature: fiction. Calcutta: Academic Pub., 1972. 166p.

24933 GUPTA, B.S. The political novel in Bengal. In CAS 6 (1975) 86-93.

24934 KENNEDY, R.S. Attitudes toward the "independent woman" in five Bengali novels. In IL 22,4 (1979) 145-67.

24935 RAY, L. ed. & tr. Broken bread; short stories of modern Bengal. Calcutta: M.C. Sarkar, 1957. 260p.

c. poetry

24936 Bengali poetry issue. In JSAL 9,4 (1974) 181p.

24937 CHATTERJEE, D.P., ed. Modern Bengali Poems. Calcutta: The Signet Press, 1945. 111p.

24938 DASGUPTA, S.R. & S. CHAKRAVARTY, eds. & tr. Bengali poems on Calcutta. Calcutta: Writers Workshop, 1972. 129p.

24939 DE, S. & A. GHOSE, eds. 20th century Bengali poetry. Calcutta: Arindam Ghose, dist. KLM, 1973. 95p.

24940 GHOSE, B. & S.K. GHOSH, ed. Glimpses of modern peotry from Bengal. Calcutta: Sanyal Prakasan, 1978. 64p.

24941 GHOSE, N., ed. Studies in modern Bengali poetry. Calcutta: Novela, 1968. 224p.

24942 GHOSH, S., comp. Contemporary Bengali literature: poetry. Calcutta: Academic Pub., 1972. 139p.

24943 KABIR, HUMAYUN. Studies in Bengali poetry. Bombay: BVB, 1962. 123p.

24944 MADDERN, M. Bengali poetry into English: an impossible dream? Calcutta: Editions Indian, 1977. 104p. (U. of Melbourne Indian studies, 1)

24945 RASHID, M. HARUNUR, ed. Three poets: Shamsur Rahman, Al Mahmud, Shaheed Quaderi. Dacca: Bangladesh Books Intl., 1976. 73p.

24946 RAY, S.M. & M. MADDERN, ed. I have seen Bengal's face: a selection of modern Bengali poetry in English translation. Calcutta: Editions Indian, 1974. 203p.

d. drama and theatre

24947 BANDYOPADHYAY, S.K. Trends in modern Bengali drama. In IWT 4,3 (1970) 149-55.

24948 GUHA-THAKURTA, P.C. Bengali drama, its origin and development. Westport, CT: Greenwood Press, 1974. 244p. [Rpt. of 1930 ed.]

24949 MAHANTY, S. Madhusudan Das. ND: NBT, 1972. 153p.

24950 MOOKERHEE, S.P. The Bengali theatre. In CR 10 (1924) 109-36.

24951 RAHA, K. Bengali theatre. ND: NBT, 1978. 164p. (India, the land and the people)

2. Modern Bengali Literature - The Formative Period

a. general studies

24952 AL-AZAD, ALAUDDIN. A study of life and short poems of Iswarchandra Gupta. Dacca: Asiatic Soc. of Bangladesh, 1979. 278p. (Its pub., 34)

24953 AWWAL, M. ABDUL. The prose works of Mir Masarraf Hosen, 1869-1899. Chittagong: U. of Chittagong, 1975. 329p.

24954 BANERJEE, B.N. Bengali stage, 1793-1873. Calcutta: Ranjan Pub. House, 1943. 58p.

24955 CLARK, T.W. Bengali prose fiction up to Bankincandra. In his The Novel in India. Berkeley: UCalP, 1970, 21-74.

24956 DAS, S.K. Early Bengali Prose: Carey to Vidyasagar. Calcutta: Bookland, 1966. 256p.

24957 DAS GUPTA, H.M. Studies in western influence on nineteenth century Bengali poetry, 1857-1887. 2nd ed. Calcutta: Semushi, dist KLM, 1969. 248p.

24958 DATTA, R.C. Romesh Chunder Dutt. ND: PDMIB, 1968. 258p.

24959 DE, S.K. Bengali literature in the nineteenth century, 1757-1857. 2nd rev. ed. Calcutta: KLM, 1962. 650p. [1st pub. 1919]

24960 DIMOCK, E.C. Literary and colloquial Bengali in modern Bengali prose. In Intl. J. of American Linguistics 16,3 (1960) 43-63.

24961 GHOSE, L. Manmohan Ghose. ND: Sahitya Akademi, 1975. 96p. [1869-1924]

24962 GHOSE, MANMOHAN. Collected poems. Ed. by Lotika Ghose. Calcutta: Calcutta U., 1970. 3v. [1869-1924]

24963 ______. Selected poems. Ed. by Lotika Ghose. ND: Sahitya Akademi, 1974. 257p.

24964 MITRA, DINABANDHU. Nil durpan; or The indigo planting mirror. Ed. with an introd. by S. Sen Gupta. Calcutta: Indian Pub., 1972. 216p. (Masterpiece of Bengali literature, 1) [1st pub. 1861]

24965 MUKHOPADHYAY, M.M. Early history of the Bengali stage. In CR 9 (1923) 380-87.

24966 PANDHE, P., ed. Suppression of drama in nineteenth century India: including text of two Bengali dramas Gaekwar durpan and Chakar durpan rendered into English by official translator in the year 1875. Calcutta: Indian Book Exchange, 1978. 132p.

24967 SARKAR, K. Nabin Sen, the poet: a comprehensive study of the poet's contribution to world-literature in the perspective of his romanticism, patriotism, and social reform. Calcutta: Prabhat (Bengali Monthly), 1975. [1847-1909]

b. Vidyasagar (Ishwar Chandra Sarma, 1820-91): social and educational reformer, and artificer of modern literary Bengali

24968 BANERJI, H. Iswarchandra Vidyasagar. ND: Sahitya Akademi, 1968. 87p.

24969 BOSE, S.K. Ishwar Chandra Vidyasagar. ND: NBT, 1969. 82p.

24970 GHOSE, B. Iswar Chandra Vidyasagar. Delhi: PDMIB, 1965. 174p.

24971 HALDAR, G. Vidyasagar; a reassessment. ND: PPH, 1972. 94p.

24972 MITRA, S.C. Isvar Chandra Vidyasager: a story of his life and work. ND: Ashish Pub. House, 1975. 675p.

24973 SEN, A. Iswar Chandra Vidyasagar and his elusive milestones. Calcutta: Riddhi-India, 1977. 194p.

24974 TRIPATHI, A. Vidyasagar, the traditional moderniser. Bombay: Orient Longmans, 1974. 112p.

24975 VIDYASAGAR, ISWAR CHANDRA. Unpublished letters of Vidyasagar. Ed. by A. Guha. Calcutta: Ananda Pub., 1971. 236p.

c. Bankim Chandra Chatterji/Chattopadhyay (1838-94): government official and leading nationalist novelist

24976 BAGCHEE, M. Vande Mataram. Bombay: BVB, 1977. 74p.

24977 BANERJI, S.K. Bankim Chandra; a study of his craft. Calcutta: KLM, 1968. 204p.

24978 BOSE, S.K. Bankim Chandra Chatterji. ND: PDMIB, 1974. 152p.

24979 CHATTERJI, BANKIM CHANDRA. The abbey of bliss. Tr. by N.C. Sengupta. Calcutta: P.M. Neogi, 1906. 201p. [tr. of Anandamath]

24980 ______. Bankim rachanavali. Ed. by Jogesh Chandra Bagal. Calcutta: Sahitya Samsad, 1969. 294p.

24981 ______. Essays and letters. Ed. by B.N. Banerji & S.K. Das. Calcutta: Bangiya Sahitya Parishad, 1940. 204p.

24982 ______. Essentials of dharma; translation of the Dharmatattva, or: Anusilan. Tr. by Manomohan Ghosh. Calcutta: Sribhumi Pub. Co., 1977. 239p.

24983 ______. Krishna Kanta's will. Tr. by M.S. Knight. London: T.F. Unwin, 1895. 264p.

24984 ______. Rajmohan's wife; a novel. Ed. by B.N. Banerji & S.K. Das. Calcutta: Bangiya Sahitya Parishad, 1940. 100p.

24985 ______. Renaissance & reaction in nineteenth century Bengal. Tr. by M.K. Haldar. Calcutta: Minerva, 1977. 236p. [tr. of his essay Samya]

24986 DASGUPTA, J.K. A critical study of the life and novels of Bankimcandra. Calcutta: Calcutta U., 1937. 187p.

24987 GHOSE, AUROBINDO. Bankim Chandra Chatterji. Pondicherry: Sri Aurobindo Ashram, 1954. 50p.

24988 RANGARAJAN, V. Vande Mataram. Madras: Sister Nivedita Academy, 1977. 55p.

24989 SENGUPTA, S.C. Bankim Chandra Chatterjee. ND: Sahitya Akademi, 1977. 60p.

24990 SINHA, N.K. Bankim Chandra Chatterjee in the little world of a civil servant. In BPP 90,2 (1971) 133-45.

24991 VAN METER, R.R. Bankimchandra Chatterji and the Bengali Renaissance. Ph.D. diss., U. of Pennsylvania, 1964. 256p.

3. Gurudev Rabindranath Tagore (1861-1949): Multifaceted Creative Genius, Patriot-Internationalist, and Nobel Laureate

a. bibliography

24992 BIBLIOTHÈQUE NATIONALE, PARIS. Rabindranath Tagore, 1861-1941. Paris: 1961. 152p. [bibl.]

24993 DAS GUPTA, N. Lodestar; or, A guide to English translations of some of Tagore's poems. ND: Sudha Pub., 1968. 219p.

24994 SEN, P.B., ed. Books about Rabindranath Tagore. Santiniketan: Viswa-Bharati, 1957. 31p.

24995 ______, ed. Rabindranath Tagore; contributions and translations pub. in periodicals. Santiniketan: Viswa-Bharati, 1961. 155p.

24996 SEN, P.B. & S.L. GANGULI. Works of Rabindranath Tagore: English. In Jadavpur J. of Comp. Literature 8 (1968) 111-25.

24997 Tagore bibliography. ND: Lalit Kala Akademi, 1961. 72p.

b. anthologies and collected works

24998 TAGORE, RABINDRANATH. Boundless sky. Calcutta: Visva-Bharati, 1964. 470p.

24999 ______. Gesammelte Werke. Ed. by Heinrich Meyer-Benfey & Helene Meyer-Frank. Munich: K. Wolff, 1920-21. 6 v.

25000 ______. The housewarming and other selected writings. Ed. by Amiya Chakravarty. Tr. by Mary Lago & Tarun Gupta & the ed. NY: New American Library, 1965. 318p.

25001 ______, A Tagore reader. Ed. by Amiya Chakravarty. NY: Macmillan, 1961. 401p.

25002 ______. A Tagore testament; tr. from Bengali by Indu Dutt. London: Meridian Books, 1953. 117p.

25003 ______. Toward universal man. NY: Asia, 1961. 387p.

c. poems and plays in translation

25004 TAGORE, RABINDRANATH. Anthology of one hundred songs of Rabindranath Tagore. ND: Sangeet Natak Akademi, 1961. 107p.

25005 ______. Collected poems and plays. NY: Macmillan, 1965. 466p. [1st pub. 1936]

25006 ______. Gitanjali. Tr. by the author. NY: Macmillan, 1971. 123p. [1st English ed. 1912]

25007 ______. Later poems. Tr. by A. Bose. London: Owen, 1974. 142p.

25008 ______. L'Offrande lyrique. Tr. from English by André Gide... [and] La Corbeille de fruits. Tr. by H. Du Pasquier. Paris: Gallimard, 1971. 256p. [1st pub. 1963; tr. of Gitanjali & Fruit-gathering]

25009 ______. Love poems of Tagore. Tr. by R.N. Choudhury. ND: Orient Paperbacks, 1975. 188p.

25010 ______. Shesh lekha; the last poems of Rabindranath Tagore. Tr. from Bengali by P. Nandy. Calcutta: Dialogue Pub., 1973. 20p.

25011 ______. Svaralipi: Anthology of one hundred songs, in staff notation. ND: Sangeet Natak Akademi, 1961-67. 2 v.

d. philosophical works and letters

25012 BANERJEE, H. The humanism of Tagore; special lectures. Mysore: U. of Mysore, 1968. 69p.

25013 Rabindranath Tagore et Romain Rolland; lettres et autres écrits. Paris: Albin Michel, 1961. 205p. (Cahiers Romain Rolland, 12)

25014 RADHADRISHNAN, S. The philosophy of Rabindranath Tagore. Baroda: Good Companions, 1961. 180p.

25015 RAY, B.G. The philosophy of Rabindranath Tagore. 2nd ed., rev. & enl. Calcutta: Progressive, 1970. 144p.

25016 ROTHENSTEIN, W. Imperfect encounter; letters of William Rothenstein and Rabindranath Tagore, 1911-1941. Ed. by M.M. Lago. Cambridge: HUP, 1972. 402p.

25017 SEN, SACHIN. The political thought of Tagore. Calcutta: Genl. Printers & Pub., 1947. 360p.

25018 SINHA, S. Social thinking of Rabindranath Tagore. NY: Asia, 1962. 192p.

25019 TAGORE, RABINDRANATH. Creative unity. NY: Macmillan, 1922. 195p.

25020 ______. Glimpses of Bengal: selected from letters, 1885-95. Tr. by S.N. Tagore. London: Macmillan, 1921. 166p.

25021 ______. Letters to a friend, ed. with two introductory essays by C.F. Andrews. London: G. Allen & Unwin, 1931. 195p.

25022 ______. On art and aesthetics. Calcutta: Orient Longmans, 1961. 113p.

25023 ______. The religion of man... NY: Macmillan, 1931. 244p.

25024 ______. Sadhana; the realization of life. Tucson: Omen Press, 1972. 164p. [Rpt. 1913 ed.]

25025 ______. Talks in China; lectures delivered in April and May, 1924. Calcutta: Visva-Bharati Book-Shop, 1924. 157p.

e. biography and autobiography

25026 ARONSON, A. Rabindranath through western eyes. 2nd ed. Calcutta: Rddhi-India, 1978. 134p.

25027 BANERJEE, H. Rabindranath Tagore. ND: PDMIB, 1972. 195p.

25028 CHANDRASEKHARAN, K. Tagore: a master spirit. Madras: Triveni, 1961. 164p.

25029 HAY, S.H. Asian ideas of east and west: Tagore and his critics in Japan, China, and India. Cambridge: HUP, 1970. 480p.

25030 KHANOLKAR, G.D. The lute and the plough; a life of Rabindranath Tagore. Tr. by T. Gay. Bombay: Book Centre, 1963. 376p.

25031 KRIPALANI, K. Rabindranath Tagore; a biography. NY: OUP, 1962. 417p.

25032 ______. Tagore: a life. 2nd and rev. ed. Calcutta: Kripalani, sole dist. Orient Longmans, 1971. 280p. [abridgement of 1962 ed.]

25033 MAHALANOBIS, P.C. Rabindranath Tagore's visit to Canada. Brooklyn: Haskell House, 1977. 73p. [Rpt. 1929 ed.]

25034 MUKHERJEE, S. Passage to America; the reception of Rabindranath Tagore in the United States, 1912-1941. Calcutta: Bookland, 1964. 239p.

25035 MUKHOPADHYAY, P.K. Life of Tagore. Tr. from Bengali by S.S. Ghosh. ND: Indian Book Co., 1975. 208p.

25036 NARAVANE, V.S. An introduction to Rabindranath Tagore. Delhi: Macmillan, 1977. 180p.

25037 RAY, K. Rabindranath Tagore; a life story. Tr. from Bengali by L. Ray. Delhi: PDMIB, 1961. 92p.

25038 ROTHERMUND, D., ed. & tr. Rabindranath Tagore in Germany; a cross-section of contemporary reports. 2nd ed. ND: Max Mueller Bhavan, German Cultural Inst., 1962. 70p.

25039 RHYS, E. Rabindranath Tagore: a biographical

study. NY: Haskell House, 1970. 157p. [Rpt. 1915 ed.]

25039 RHYS, E. Rabindranath Tagore: a biographical study. NY: Haskell House, 1970. 157p. [Rpt. 1915 ed.]

25040 SINGH, D. The sentinel of the East, a biographical study of Rabindra Nath Tagore. NY: Haskell House, 1974. 155p. [Rpt. 1941 ed.]

25041 TAGORE, RABINDRANATH. My boyhood days. Tr. by M. Sykes. Calcutta: Visva-Bharati, 1945. 87p.

25042 ______. My reminiscences. Tr. by S.N. Tagore. NY: Macmillan, 1917. 273p.

f. commemorative volumes

25043 GHOSE, S., ed. The centenary book of Tagore. Calcutta: Grantham, 1961. 245p.

25044 Hommage de la France à Rabindranath Tagore; pour le centenaire de sa naissance, 1961. Paris: Inst. de civilisation indienne, 1962. 109p.

25045 KULASRESTHA, M., ed. Tagore centenary volume. Hoshiarpur: VVRI, 1961. 2v. (WIS, 2A-2B)

25046 Rabindranath Tagore birth centenary celebrations. Proceedings of conferences. Santiniketan: Visva-Bharati, 1961-62. 7 v. [v. 1, Educ.; v. 2, All-India Literary Conf.; v. 3, Philos. Conf.; v. 4, Confs. on Rural Reconstruction; v. 5, Bengali Lit. & Natl. Reawakening; v. 6, Music & Drama; v. 7, Human Factor in Rural Econ.]

25047 Rabindranath Tagore 1861-1961: a centenary volume. ND: Sahitya Akademi, 1961. 531p.

25048 SEN GUPTA, S.C., ed. Rabindranath Tagore; homage from Visva-Bharati. Santiniketan: Visva-Bharati, 1962. 236p.

g. critical studies of Tagore's works

25049 BAKE, A. Tagore: the man and the artist. In Arts & Letters 35,1 (1961) 10-20.

25050 BANERJI, S.K. Phases of Tagore's poetry. Mysore: U. of Mysore, 1973. 49p.

25051 BOSE, B. Tagore; portrait of a poet. Bombay: U. of Bombay, 1962. 114p.

25052 CHAKRAVORTY, B.C. Rabindranath Tagore: his mind and art; Tagore's contribution to English literature. ND: Young India, 1971. 304p.

25053 CHATTERJI, S.K. World literature and Tagore: Viśva-Bhāratī, Ravindra-Bhāratī. Santiniketan: Visva-Bharati, 1971. 233p.

25054 CHATTOPADHYAYA, S. Art and the abyss: six essays in interpretation of Tagore. Calcutta: Jijnasa, 1977. 106p.

25055 DIMOCK, E.C. Rabindranath Tagore -- the greatest of the Bāuls of Bengal. In JAS 19 (1959) 33-52.

25056 GHOSE, S.K. The later poems of Tagore. London: Asia, 1961. 304p.

25057 KABIR, HUMAYUN. Rabindranath Tagore. London: SOAS, 1962. 72p. (Tagore lectures, 1961)

25058 LAGO, M.M. The parting of the ways: a comparative study of Yeats and Tagore. In Indian Literature 6,3 (1963) 1-34. [also in Mahfil 3,1 (1966) 32-57]

25059 ______. Rabindranath Tagore. Boston: Twayne, 1976. 176p.

25060 MAJUMDAR, B.B. Heroines of Tagore, a study in the transformation of Indian society, 1875-1941. Calcutta: KLM, 1968. 345p.

25061 MUKHERJI, S.B. The poetry of Tagore. ND: Vikas, 1977. 236p.

25062 NARASIMHAIAH, C.D. The reputation of English Gitanjali: Tagore & his critics. In Literary Criterion 9,4 (1971) 1-22.

25063 RAY, N.R. An artist in life; a commentary on the life's works of Rabindranath Tagore. Trivandrum: U. of Kerala, 1967. 473p.

25064 ROY, B.K. Rabindranath Tagore, the man and his poetry. Folcroft, PA: Folcroft Library Editions, 1977. 223p. [1st ed. 1915]

25065 THOMPSON, E.J. Rabindranath Tagore, his life and work. Rev. by Kalidas Nag. Calcutta: YMCA Pub. House, 1961. 96p. [1st pub. 1921]

25066 ______. Rabindranath Tagore: poet and dramatist. Westport, CT: Greenwood, 1974. 330p. [1st pub. 1926, 327p.; rpt. of 1948 rev. ed.]

25067 ZBAVITEL, D. Rabindranath Tagore in 1887-1891 [in 1891-1905,1905-13..1941]. In AO 24 (1956) 581-90; 25 (1957) 405-25; 26 (1958) 101-13, 336-84; 27 (1959) 60-75, 251-71.

4. Saratchandra Chatterji (1876-1938): Novelist of Social Realism

25068 BAPAT, VASANT. Saratchandra and the Marathi novel. In IL 22,4 (1979) 5-11.

25069 BASU, TARAPADA. La société bengalie du vingtième siècle dans l'oeuvre de Sarat Chandra Chatterji. Paris: Impr. artistique moderne, A. Lapied, 1940. 174p.

25070 CHATTERJI, SARATCHANDRA. The drought and other stories. Tr. by Sasadhar Sinha. ND: Sahitya Akademi, 1970. 122p.

25071 ______. The eldest sister and other stories. Allahabad: Central Book Depot, 1950. 125p.

25072 ______. Srikanta. Tr. by K.C. Sen & T. Thompson. Benares: Indian Pub., 1945. 4 v.

25073 ______. Srikanta, the autobiography of a wanderer. Tr. by K.C. Sen. Benares: Indian Pub., 1945. 154p. [tr. of the 1st of 4 pts.]

25074 The golden book of Saratchandra; a centenary commemorative volume. Calcutta: All Bengal Sarat Centenary Cmtee., 1977. 511p.

25075 KABIR, HUMAYUN. Sarat Chandra Chatterjee. Calcutta: Silpee Samstha Prakasani, 1963. 60p.

25076 MADAN, I.N. Saratchandra Chatterji, his mind and art. Lahore: Minerva Book-shop, 1944. 159p.

25077 NARAVANE, V.S. Sarat Chandra Chatterji; an introduction to his life and work. Delhi: Macmillan, 1976. 182p.

25078 SEN GUPTA, S.C. Saratchandra: man and artist. ND: Sahitya Akademi, 1975. 110p.

5. Kazi Nazrul Islam (1899-1976): Nationalist Muslim Poet of Undivided Bengal

25079 CHAKRAVARTI, B. Kazi Nazrul Islam. ND: NBT, 1968. 101p.

25080 CHOUDHURY, S.I. Introducing Nazrul Islam. 2nd ed. Dacca: Muktadhara (Swadhin Bangla Sahitya Parishad), 1974. 96p. [1st pub. 1965]

25081 HALDAR, G. Kazi Nazrul Islam. ND: Sahitya Akademi, 1973. 82p.

25082 NAZRUL ISLAM, KAZI. The fiery lyre of Nazrul Islam. Tr. by Abdul Hakim. Dacca: Bangla Academy, 1974. 175p.

25083 ______. Nazrul Islam. Tr. by Mizanur Rahmad. 3rd ed., rev. & enl. Dacca: 1966. 210p.

25084 ______. The Rebel and other poems. Tr. by B. Chakravarty. ND: Sahitya Akademi, 1974. 98p.

25085 SEN, P.C. Kazi Nazrul Islam, the Muslim poet of Bengal. In VQ 24 (1958) 52-68.

6. Post-Tagore Bengali Writers

25086 BANERJEA, P., comp. Some post-independence Bengali poems. Tr. by Pradeep Banerjea. Calcutta: Writers Workshop, 1969. 1 v.

25087 BANERJEE, B.B. Pather panchali. Tr. by M. Varma. Calcutta: Writers Workshop, 1973. 3v.

25088 ______. Pather panchali. Song of the road: a Bengali novel; tr. by T.W. Clark & T. Mukherji. London: Allen & Unwin, 1968. 326p. (UNESCO series)

25089 BHATTACHARYA, M. Tarashankar Bandyopadhyay. ND: Sahitya Akademi, 1975. 68p. [1898-1971]

25090 BHATTACHARYA, S. Sukanta Bhattacharya: a selection of his poems. Tr. by K. Roy. Calcutta: Saraswat Library, 1978. 95p.

25091 DAS, JIBANANANDA. Banalata Sen, & other poems. Tr. from Bengali. Calcutta: Writers Workshop, 1962. 24p.

25092 DAS GUPTA, C. Jibanananda Das. ND: Sahitya Akademi, 1972. 56p.

25093 DASGUPTA, A.R. Buddhadeva Bose. ND: Sahitya Akademi, 1977. 70p.

25094 DASGUPTA, S., ed. Water my roots; essays by and on Bishnu Dey. Calcutta: Writers Workshop, 1973. 75p. [1909-]

25095 DATTA, SUDHINDRANATH. The world of twilight; essays and poems. Bombay: OUP, 1971. 292p.

25096 DEY, BISHNU. In the sun and the rain: essays on aesthetics. ND: PPH, 1972. 253p.

25097 ______. Selected poems. Tr. from Bengali; ed. by S. Dasgupta. Calcutta: Writers Workshop, 1972. 94p. [1909-]

25098 DIMOCK, E.C., JR. The poet as mouse & owl: reflections on a poem by Jībanānanda Dās. In JAS 33,4 (1974) 603-10.

25099 GHOSH, T.C. Geeta-manjari = The buds of songs: a selection of poems translated by the author from the original Bengali. Chinsurah: Pratima Prakashani, 1980. 57p.

25100 GUHA, N. The poet as exponent of culture. In IL 14,2 (1971) 11-21. [on Sudhindranath Datta, 1901-60]

25101 JASIMUDDIN. Selected poems of Jasim Uddin. Tr. by Hasna Jasimuddin Moudud. Dacca: Moudud, dist. by OUP, 1975. 54p.

25102 LAGO, M.M., ed. Modern Bengali poetry issue. In JSAL 3,4 (1967) 1-119.

25103 LAGO, M.M. & T. GUPTA. Pattern in the imagery of Jivanananda Das. In JAS 24 (1965) 637-44.

25104 MITRA, S.M. Manik Bandyopadhyay. ND: Sahitya Akademi, 1974. 84p. [1908-1956]

25105 MUKHERJEE, SUBHAS. Poet of the people: poems of Subhas Mukhopadhyay. Tr. by P. Nandy. Calcutta: Dialogue, 1970. 26p.

25106 RAY, A.S. A writer speaks. Calcutta: United Writers, 1977. 98p.

25107 SEELY, C.B. Doe in heat: a critical biography of the Bengali poet Jibanananda Das (1899-1954) with relevant literary history from the mid-1920's to the mid-1950's. Ph.D. diss., U. of Chicago, 1976. 761p.

25108 SEN, S.R. The complete poems of Samar Sen. Tr. by P. Nandy. Calcutta: Writers Workshop, 1970. 192p.

7. Folk Literature of Bengal
a. folklorists and folklore studies

25109 BHATTACHARYYA, A. Serpent stories in Bengal and its comparative study. In Folklore(C) 2 (1961) 97-104, 169-77, 329-43.

25110 FUCHAS, Mother. Folklore of Bengal: region and people. In Folklore 16,5 (1975) 149-78.

25111 ______. Study of Bengali myth and mythology. In Folklore 16,6 (1975) 185-203.

25112 HALDAR, GOPAL. Studies in Bengali language & literature: the legend of Rājā Gopichānd. In ISPP 5 (1965) 133-44.

25113 ROY, B. Evolution of folk songs and factors that made the folk songs differ from region to the other in Bengal. In Folklore(C) 3 (1962) 217-24.

25114 SEN GUPTA, S. Folklore of Bengal: a projected study. Calcutta: Indian Pub., 1976. 248p. (Its folklore series, 26)

25115 ______. Folklorists of Bengal; life-sketches and bibliographical notes. Calcutta: Indian Pub., 1965. 180p. (Indian folklore series, 2)

25116 ______. Saratchandra Roy's approach to anthropo-folklorology and the progress of folklore scholarship in Bengal. In L.P. Vidyarthi, ed. Essays in Indian Folklore.... Calcutta: Indian Pub., 1973, 108-50.

25117 SEN GUPTA, S. A survey of folklore study in Bengal: West Bengal and East Pakistan. Calcutta: Indian Pub., 1967-. v. 1, 149p.

25118 SIDDIQUI, ASHRAF. Sarat Chandra Mitra and his contribution to Bengali folklore. In Folklore(C) 14,4-6 (1973) 125-35, 164-77, 204-16.

25119 TROGER, R. A comparative study of a Bengal folktale, underworld beliefs and underworld helpers; an analysis of the Bengal folktale type, The pursuit of blowing cotton - AT-480. Tr. from German & intro. by Heinz Mode. Calcutta: Indian Pub., 1966. 96p. (Its folklore series, 8)

25120 ZIDE, N.H. & R.D. MUNDA. Structural influence of Bengali Vaisnava songs on traditional Mundari songs. In JSR 13,1 (1970) 36-48.

b. collections of folktales and folksongs

25121 BHATTACHARYA, A. Folklore of Bengal. ND: NBT, 1978. 191p.

25122 CHATTERJEE, SILA & SANTA CHATTERJEE. Tales of Bengal. London: OUP, 1922. 110p.

25123 DAY, LAL BEHARI. Folktales of Bengal. London: Macmillan, 1883. 248p. [Rpt. with his Bengal peasant life; Calcutta: Editions Indian, 1969]

25124 MAJUMDAR, G. Folk tales of Bengal. ND: Sterling, 1971. 120p. (Folk tales of India series, 6)

25125 MODE, H., tr. Bengalische Märchen. Frankfurt: Insel-Verlag, 1967. 506p.

25126 SEN, D.C. The folk-literature of Bengal. Calcutta: U. of Calcutta, 1920. 362p.

8. Journalism and the Press in Modern Bengal

25127 BANERJEE, S. National Awakening and the Bangabasi. Calcutta: Amitava-Kalyan, 1968. 251p. [Bengali weekly]

25128 BOSE, P.N. & H.W.B. MORENO. A hundred years of the Bengali press. Calcutta: Moreno, 1920. 129p.

25129 CHAKRABORTI, S. The Bengali press, 1818-1868: a study in the growth of public opinion. Calcutta: KLM, 1976. 252p.

25130 DUTT, P. Memoirs of Moti Lal Ghose. Calcutta: Amrita Bazar Patrika Office, 1935. 386p.

25131 EDWARDS, T. The press of Calcutta. In CR 77,153 (1883) 58-71.

25132 GHOSH, S.L. Motilal Ghose. ND: NBT, 1970. 134p.

25133 KAMAL, ABU HENA MUSTAFA. The Bengali press and literary writing. Dacca: University Press, 1977. 210p.

25134 MOITRA, M. Hindu patriot: India's first "National" newspaper. In CR 169 (1963) 135-44.

25135 The native press of Bengal. In CR 43,86 (1866) 357-79.

25136 NURUL ISLAM, M. Bengali Muslim public opinion as reflected in the Bengali press, 1901-1930. Dacca: Bangla Academy, 1973. 341p.

25137 SINHA, SACHCHIDANANDA. The Calcutta Press under the East India Company (1780-1858). In CR 91 (1944) 26-34.

9. The Bengali Cinema

25138 DAS GUPTA, C. The cinema of Satyajit Ray. ND: Vikas, 1980. 88p. + 40pl.

25139 SETON, M. Portrait of a director: Satyajit Ray. Bloomington: Indiana U. Press, 1971. 350p.

25140 WOOD, R. The Apu trilogy. NY: 1971. 96p.

II. THE PEOPLE'S REPUBLIC OF BANGLADESH (THE FORMER EAST PAKISTAN, 1947-71), 1971-

A. Bibliography and Reference

25141 BHASKARAN NAIR, M. Survey of source material on Bangladesh. In IS 13,2 (1974) 324-46.

25142 GUSTAFSON, W.E., ed. Pakistan and Bangladesh: bibliographic essays in social science. Islamabad: U. of Islamabad Press, 1976. 364p.

25143 JANIK, B. Bangladesh- ein Bericht über die deutschsprachige Literatur. In IAF 7,1/2 (1976) 157-59.

25144 MOMEN, N. Bangladesh, the first four years: from 16 December 1971 to 15 December 1975. Dacca: Bangladesh Inst. of Law & Intl. Affairs, 1980. 184p. [chronology]

25145 NAJMIR NUR BEGUM. Social and administrative research in Bangladesh; an annotated bibliography. Dacca: NIPA, 1973. 74p.

25146 NICHOLAS, M. & P. OLDENBURG, comps. Bangladesh: the birth of a nation; a handbook of background information and documentary sources. Madras: M. Seshachalam, 1972. 156p.

25147 SERAJUL HAQUE & SHAMSUL ISLAM KHAN. Spatial distribution, rural and urban: a select bibliography. Dacca: Bangladesh Inst. of Dev. Studies, 1976. 11p.

25148 SATYAPRAKASH, comp. & ed. Bangla Desh: a select bibliography. Gurgaon: IDS, 1976. 218p.

25149 SCHENDEL, W. VAN, ed. Bangladesh: a bibliography with special reference to the peasantry. Amsterdam: Afdeling Zuid-en Zuidoost-Azië Antropologisch-Sociologisch Centrum, U. of Amsterdam, 1976. 227p.

B. Government and Politics, 1947-

1. General Surveys

25150 ABUL HASHIM. In retrospection. Dacca: Subarna Pub., 1974. 194p. [memoirs of a political leader, 1905-74]

25151 AHMED, MOUDUD. Bangladesh: constitutional quest for autonomy, 1950-1971. Wiesbaden: Steiner, 1978. 373p. [also pub. Dacca U. Press, 1979. 333p.]

25152 CHAKRABARTI, S.K. The evolution of politics in Bangladesh,1947-1978. ND: Associated, 1978. 304p.

25153 CHATTERJEE, S. Bangladesh: the birth of a nation. Calcutta: The Book Exchange, 1972. 191p.

25154 DREYFUS, P. Du Pakistan au Bangladesh. Paris: Arthaud, 1972. 251p.

25155 KAMRUDDIN AHMAD. A socio political history of Bengal and the birth of Bangladesh. 4th ed. Dacca: Zahiruddin Mahmud Inside Library, 1975. 420p.

25156 MUHITH, A.M.A. Bangladesh, emergence of a nation. Dacca: Bangladesh Books Intl., 1978. 358p.

25157 SEN GUPTA, J. History of freedom movement in Bangladesh, 1943-1973; some involvement. Calcutta: Naya Prokash, 1974. 506p.

25158 UMAR, BADRUDDIN. Politics and society in East Pakistan and Bangladesh. Dacca: Nowla Bros., 1973. 2 v., 344, 344p.

2. East Pakistan, 1947-71: An Unequal and Uneasy Partnership with West Pakistan [for Pakistan National Politics, see Chap. Nine]

a. general studies of provincial politics

25159 AHMAD, NAFIS. The evolution of the boundaries of East Pakistan. In Oriental Geographer 2 (1958) 97-106.

25160 BANERJI, D.N. East Pakistan; a case-study in Muslim politics. Delhi: Vikas, 1969. 204p.

25161 CHOUDHURY, G.W. The East Pakistan political scene, 1955-57. In PA 30 (1957) 312-20.

25162 ______. Roles and careers of middle-rank politicians; some cases from East Bengal. In W.H. Morris-Jones, ed. The making of politicans. London: Athlone Press, 1976, 195-206.

25163 FRANDA, M.F. Communism and regional politics in East Pakistan. In AS 10,7 (1970) 588-606.

25164 JILANI, S.G. Fifteen governors I served with: untold story of East Pakistan. Lahore: Bookmark, 1979. 235p.

b. the demand for provincial autonomy, the 1971 War, and Independence [see also Chap. Seven, IV. B. 4.]

25165 AHMAD, NAZIRUDDIN. Trial of collaborators. Dacca: Book Society, 1972. 124p. [on 1972 special tribunals]

25166 AKANDA, S.A. The national language issue; potent force for transforming East Pakistani regionalism into Bengali nationalism. In J. of the Inst. of Bangladesh Studies 1,1 (1976) 1-29.

25167 BHATTACHARJEE, G.P. Renaissance and freedom movement in Bangladesh. Calcutta: Minerva, 1973. 361p.

25168 DATZA, S. Eyeless in the urn. Dacca: Lalan Prakashani, 1975. 45p. [Poems on murder of political leader Dhirendranath Datta, 1886-1971, by Pakistan Army.]

25169 HUSSAIN, SERAJUDDIN. Look in to the mirror. Dacca: M. Ahmed, 1974. 123p. [1st pub. 1970]

25170 ISLAM, M.R. A tale of millions. Dacca: Adeylbros, 1974. 254p.

25171 KHAN, ZILLUR R. March movement of Bangladesh; Bengali struggle for political power. In IJPS 33,3 (1972) 291-322.

25172 LAMBERT, R.D. Factors in Bengali regionalism in Pakistan. In Far Eastern Survey 28 (1959) 49-58.

25173 MANIRUZZAMAN, TALUKDER. Radical politics and the emergence of Bangladesh. In P.R. Brass & M.F. Franda, eds. Radical politics in South Asia. Cambridge: MIT Press, 1973, 223-80.

25174 MASWANI, A.M.K. Subversion in East Pakistan. Lahore: Amir, 1979. 304p.

25175 SRIVASTAVA, P. The discovery of Bangla Desh. ND: Sanjay Pub., 1972. 171p.

c. Sheikh Mujibur Rahman (1922-1975): Awami League leader and first President of Bangladesh

25176 BLAIR, H.W. Sheikh Mujib and dejà vu in East Bengal: the tragedies of March 25. In EPW 6,52 (1971) 2555-62.

25177 DASGUPTA, S.R. Midnight massacre in Dacca. ND: Vikas, 1978. 139p.

25178 HUQ, OBAIDUL. Voice of thunder. Dacca: Anjam Maroof, 1973. 213p.

25179 KAMAL, KAZI AHMED. Sheikh Mujibur Rahman and birth of Bangladesh. Dacca: K.G. Ahmed, 1972. 204p.

25180 MUJIBUR RAHMAN, Sheikh. Bangladesh, my Bangladesh; selected speeches and statements, Oct. 28, 1970, to Mar. 26, 1971. Ed. with notes by R. Majumdar. ND: Orient Longman, 1972. 166p.

25181 SEDERBERG, P.C. Sheikh Mujib and charismatic politics in Bangladesh. In Asian Forum 4,3 (1972) 1-10.

25182 TOFAYELL, Z.A. Mujib and Bangladesh revolution; flashback journal. Panchgaon, Noakhali Dist.: Atikullah, 1973. 115p.

2. The Constitution and Formation of the Nation of Bangladesh

25183 AMINULLAH. Right to property in Bangla Desh. In JCPS 8,3 (1974) 269-90.

25184 BANGLADESH. CONSTITUTION. The Constitution of the People's Republic of Bangladesh: as modified up to 28th February 1979. Dacca: Min. of Law and Parliamentary Affairs, 1979. 198p.

25185 BARUA, R.P. Philosophy of the Bangla Desh constitution. In JCPS 8,2 (1974) 220-34.

25186 HUQ, ABUL FAZL. Constitution-making in Bangladesh. In PA 46,1 (1973) 59-76.

25187 JAHAN, ROUNAQ. Bangladesh in 1972: nation building in a new state. In AS 13,2 (1973) 199-210.

25188 KHAN, ZILLUR RAHMAN & A.T.R. RAHMAN. Provincial autonomy and constitution making: the case of Bangladesh. Dacca: Green Book House, 1973. 298p.

25189 LING, T.O. Creating a new state: the Bengalis of Bangladesh. In SAR 5,3 (1972) 231-38.

25190 MUKHERJEE, R.K. Nation-building and state formation in Bangladesh. In SAS 7,2 (1972) 137-63.

25191 MUNIM, F.K.M.A. Rights of the citizen under the constitution and law. Dacca: Bangladesh Inst. of Law & Intl. Affairs, 1975. 343p.

25192 RAHIM, SYED BAZLUR. Constitutional law in Bangladesh. Dacca: Pub. Intl., 1973. 190p.

25193 TRIPATHI, R.N. Travails of democracy: emergence of jantantrik Bangla Desh. Kanpur: Pustak Bhawan, 1972. 62p.

4. Bangladesh Politics since 1971
a. general political studies, incl. elections

25194 ALI, S.M. After the dark night - problems of Sheikh Mujibur Rahman. ND: Thomson Press, 1973. 196p.

25195 ANDERSON, R.S. Impressions of Bangladesh: the rule of arms and the politics of exhortation. In PA 49,3 (1976) 443-75.

25196 BANGLADESH. LAWS, STATUTES. Jatiya rakkhi bahini Act. Ed. H. Hossain; rev. by Kamrul Islam. Dacca: Khoshroz Kitab Mahal, 1974. 68p. [on a para-military group]

25197 BARUA, T.K. Political elite in Bangladesh; a socio-anthropological and historical analysis of the processes of their formation. Bern: P. Lang, 1978. 354p.

25198 DUBEY, S.R. Elections in Bangla Desh. In SAS 8,2 (1973) 62-69.

25199 ISLAM, A.K.M. AMINUL. Victorious victims; political transformation in a traditional society. Boston: G.K. Hall, 1978. 158p.

25200 JAHAN, ROUNAQ. Bangladesh in 1973: management of factional politics. In SA 14,2 (1974) 125-35.

25201 KABIR, M. GHULAM. Minority politics in Bangladesh. ND: Vikas, 1980. 167p. [1947-71 period]

25202 LIFSCHULTZ, L. Bangladesh: the unfinished revolution. London: Zed Press, 1979. 221p.

25203 MANIRUZZAMAN, T. Bangladesh: an unfinished revolution? In JAS 34,4 (1975) 891-912.

25204 RASHIDUZZAMAN, M. Changing political patterns in Bangladesh: internal constraints and external fears. In AS 17 (1977) 793-808.

25205 SHAMS-UD-DIN, ABU ZAFAR. Sociology of Bengal politics and other essays. Dacca: Bangla Academy, 1973. 152p.

25206 SINGAMMAL, M.A. 1978 presidential election in Bangla Desh. In IJPS 40,1 (1979) 97-110.

25207 TIPU SULTAN, K.M. Government and citizens in politics and development: an Asian case. Comilla: BARD, 1978. 122p.

b. the 1975 coups, assassination of President Mujib, and the martial law regime of Gen. Ziaur Rahman (1936-81)

25208 BERTOCCI, P.J. Bangladesh: transition to democracy amid the gathering storm. In ATS 4,11 (1979) 250-53.

25209 BLAIR, H.W. Voting, caste, community, society: explorations in aggregate data analysis in India and Bangladesh. ND: Young Asia, 1979. 199p.

25210 DASGUPTA, S.K. Midnight massacre in Dacca. ND: Vikas, 1978. 139p.

25211 JAHAN, ROUNAQ. Bangabandhu and after: conflict and change in Bangladesh. In RT 261 (1976) 73-84.

25212 KHAN, ZILLUR R. Leadership, parties and politics in Bangladesh. In Western Political Q. 29,1 (1976) 102-25.

25213 LIFSCHULTZ, L. Abu Taher's last testament; Bangladesh: the unfinished revolution. In EPW 12,33-34 (1977) 1303-54.

25214 LIFSCHULTZ, L. & K. BIRD. Bangladesh: anatomy of a coup. In EPW 14,49&50 (1979) 1999-2014, 2059-68.

25215 MANIRUZZAMAN, TALUKDER. Bangladesh in 1975; the fall of the Mujib regime and its aftermath. In AS 16,2 (1976) 119-29.

25216 MATHIEU, G.K. Palace revolution continued. In EPW 11,17 (1976) 623-27.

25217 RAHMAN, MOFAKHKHAR. Gang politics in Bangla Desh. In SAS 13,1 (1978) 36-43.

c. dilemmas of secularism in a Muslim nation

25218 O'CONNELL, J.T. Dilemmas of secularism in Bangladesh. In JAAS 11,1/2 (1976) 64-81.

25219 PEARL, D. Bangladesh: Islamic laws in a secular state. In SAR 8,1 (1974) 33-43.

25220 SIDDIQUI, S.A. The pattern of secularism in India and Bangladesh. Chittagong: Siddiqui, 197-. 72p.

5. Administrative Studies, 1947 -

25221 AHMED, EMAJUDDIN. Dominant bureaucratic elites in Bangla Desh. In IPSR 13,1 (1979) 30-48.

25222 BANGLADESH. NATL. PAY CMSN. Report. Dacca: Bangladesh Govt. Press, 1973-. v. 1-

25223 CHOUDHURY, LUTFUL HOQ. Social change, development, and public administration. In DUS 25,A (1976) 81-98.

25224 GIASUDDIN AHMED, S. The image of public service in Bangladesh: a study of attitudes of students towards public service and public employees in Bangladesh. Dacca: Centre for Admin. Studies, Dept. of Public Admin., U. of Dacca, 1975. 140p. (Its monograph series, 1)

25225 KIBRIA, A.B.M.G. Police administration in Bangladesh. Dacca: Khoshroz Kitab Mahal, 1976. 324p.

25226 MAHESHWARI, S.R. Problems of public administration in Bangladesh. In IJPS 36,4 (1975) 385-98.

25227 RAHMAN, A.T.R. Administration and its political environment in Bangladesh. In PA 47,2 (1974) 171-191.

25228 SINHA, P.B. Armed Forces of Bangladesh. ND: Inst. for Defence Studies & Analyses, 1979. 60p. (Its occ. papers, 1)

6. Local Government and Politics since 1947

25229 ABEDIN, NAJMUL. Local administration and politics in modernising societies, Bangladesh and Pakistan. Dacca: NIPA, 1973. 458p.

25230 ALAM, BILQUIS ARA. Tax collection of Dacca Pourashava: an enquiry into selected aspects. Dacca: Local Govt. Inst., 1977. 131p.

25231 ALI, QAZI AZHER. District administration in Bangladesh. Dacca: NIPA, 1978. 75p.

25232 AMINUL ISLAM, A.K.M. A Bangladesh village; conflict and cohesion; an anthropological study of politics. Cambridge, MA: Schenkman, 1974. 196p.

25233 AMINUR RAHMAN, A.H.M. Adequacy of the union parishad in the fulfilment of its role. In DUS 29,A (1978) 66-77.

25234 AMINUZZAMAN, SALAHUDDIN M. Local government and administration in Bangladesh: a selected bibliography. Dacca: Center for Admin. Studies, U. of Dacca, 1979. 57p.

25235 GIASUDDIN AHMED, S. The emergent leadership pattern in pourashavas in Bangladesh. In SAS 10,1/2 (1975) 1-32.

25236 HUQ, ABU NASAR HUSAIN. District administration in East Pakistan; its classical form and emerging pattern. In Administrative Sciences R. 4 (1970) 21-48.

25237 HUSSAIN, SAJJAD, ed. Urban affairs.... Dacca: Local Govt. Inst., 1972. 94p. [1969-70 seminar]

25238 LÖFFLER, L.G. Basic democracies in den Chittagong Hill Tracts, Ostpakistan. In Sociologus 18,2 (1968) 152-71.

25239 MAHTAB, NAZMUNNESSA. Local government in France and Bangladesh: a descriptive analysis of executive action. Dacca: Center for Admin. Studies, U. of Dacca, 1978. 24p. (CENTAS occ. paper, 2)

25240 MANJUR-UL-ALAM, M. Characteristics of newly elected representatives (chairman, vice-chairman, and members) of Union Parishads of Kotwali Thana, Comilla. Comilla: BARD, 1974. 25p.

25241 ______. Financial strength of local government in Bangladesh: a study on financial administration of three union parishads in Comilla Kotwali Thana. Comilla: BARD, 1976. 28p.

25242 ______. Leadership pattern, problems, and prospects of local government in rural Bangladesh. Comilla: BARD, 1976. 19p.

25243 MUHITH, A.M.A. The deputy commissioner in East Pakistan. Dacca: PARD, 1968. 120p.

25244 NURUZZAMAN, Syed. Survey of training needs of pourashava and zilla board in Bangladesh. Dacca: Local Govt. Inst., 1973. 87p.

25245 RAFIQUR RAHMAN, A.T. Basic democracies at the grass roots; a study of three union councils of Kotwali Thana, Comilla. Comilla: Pakistan Academy for Village Dev., 1962. 103p. (Its tech. pub., 13)

25246 SHAFIQUR RAHMAN, A.B.M. Bangladesh pourashava (municipality) statistics. Dacca: Local Govt. Inst., 1977. 374p.

25247 SHAFIQUR RAHMAN, A.B.M., et al. Who wants to lead our cities?: a sociological study on Chittagong municipal election, 1977. Chittagong: Dept. of Sociology, U. of Chittagong, 1977. 62p.

25248 SOLAIMAN, M. & M. MANJUR-UL-ALAM. Characteristics of candidates for election in three union parishads in Comilla Kotwali Thana. Comilla: BARD, 1977. 13p.

25249 TIPU SULTAN, K.M. Problems of rural administration in Bangladesh. Comilla: BARD, 1974. 58p.

25250 WHEELER, R.S. Divisional councils in East Pakistan, 1960-1965: an evaluation. Durham, NC: DUPCSSA, 1967. 78p. (Its monograph & occ. papers series, 4)

7. Bangladesh Foreign Relations, 1971 - [see also Chap. Seven]
a. general studies

25251 BATEMAN, C.H. National security and nationalism in Bangladesh. In AS 19 (1979) 780-88.

25252 CHAKRAVARTY, S.R. & V. NARAIN. Foreign policy of Bangladesh - trends and issues. In SAS 12,1/2 (1977) 77-85.

25253 HAQUE, MAHMUDUL & M. GUHA. Bangladesh and non-alignment, 1971-75 [and] Change and continuity in foreign policy: Bangladesh, a case study. Dacca: Forum for Intl. Affairs, 1978. 24p. (Its occ. papers, 3)

25254 LYON, P. Bangladesh: fashioning a foreign policy. In SAR 5,3 (1972) 231-36.

25255 RAY, J.K. The Farakka agreement. In Intl. Stud. 17 (1978) 235-46.

b. foreign economic relations: dependence on foreign aid and rebuilding of the export economy

25256 AHMED, RAQUIBUDDIN, ed. Six years on seven seas, February 1972-February 1978: souvenir. Dacca: Bangladesh Shipping Corp., 1978. 54p.

25257 ALAM, AHMED FAKHRUL. Problems of export financing in Bangladesh. Dacca: Bureau of Econ. Res., U. of Dacca, 1974. 185p.

25258 EAST PAKISTAN. BUREAU OF STAT. Foreign trade of East Pakistan, 1961-62 & 1962-63. Dacca: 1965. 514p.

25259 HONE, A. A strategy for exports from Bangladesh. In SAR 6,4 (1973) 303-10.

25260 JAYARAMAN, T.K. Import demand function of Bangla Desh: 1956-57 to 1970-71. In Asian Econ. R. 18,2/3 (1976) 152-66.

25261 MUKHERJI, I.N. Import policy of Bangla Desh. In Foreign Trade R. 10,1 (1975) 52-67.

25262 RAHMAN, SULTAN HAFEEZ. An analysis of terms of trade of Bangladesh, 1959/60 to 1974/75. In BDS 4,3 (1976) 375-98.

25263 REZA, SADREL. Break-up of erstwhile Pakistan: implications for the exports of Bangla Desh. In SAS 13,2 (1978) 41-65.

25264 SETH, K.L. Export prospects in Bangladesh. In IQ 29,1 (1973) 32-44.

25265 ______. The infant economy: trade and debt servicing. ND: Trimurti, 1974. 163p.

25266 TALUKDER, ALAUDDIN. Bangladesh international economics: a select bibliography. Dacca: BIDS, 1975. 11p.

C. The Bangladesh Economy since 1947

1. Bibliography and Reference

25267 EAST PAKISTAN. BUREAU OF STAT. Handbook of economic indicators of East Pakistan, 1965. Dacca: 1966. 183p.

25268 TALUKDER, ALAUDDIN. BDS articles and BIDS publications: a cumulative index, 1971-1975. Dacca: BIDS, 1976. 33p.

25269 ______. Bangladesh economy: a select bibliography. Dacca: BIDS, 1976. 211p.

25270 ______., ed. Ten years of BER articles and BIDE publications; a cumulative index, 1961-1970. Dacca: BIDE, 1972. 65p.

25271 TALUKDER, ALAUDDIN & HASHMAT ARA BEGUM. Ten years of BDS articles and BIDS publications: a cumulative index: supplement, 1971-1979. Dacca: BIDS, 1980. 71p.

2. Demography (1974 pop. 76,398,000)
a. bibliography

25272 SERAJUL HAQUE & ALAUDDIN TALUKDER & M. SHAMSUL ISLAM KHAN. Bangladesh demography: a select bibliography. Dacca: BIDS, 1976. 59p.

25272a SERAJUL HAQUE. Popindex Bangladesh: Bangladesh literature on population control and its allied subjects. Dacca: Haque, 1978. 125p.

b. general studies of the Bangladesh population

25273 ARTHUR, W.B. & G. MCNICOLL. An analytical survey of population and development in Bangladesh. In Population and Development R. 4 (1978) 23-80.

25273a BADRUD DUZA, M. Cultural consequences of population change in Bangladesh. Dacca: Asfia Duza, 1977. 160p.

25274 BALDWIN, S.C. Catastrophe in Bangladesh: an examination of alternative population growth possibilities 1975-2000. In AS 17,4 (1977) 345-57.

25275 BANGLADESH. CENSUS, 1974. Population census of Bangladesh, 1974: national volume: reports and tables. Dacca: Bureau of Stat., 1977. 673p.

25276 ______. Projection and estimate of population of Bangladesh. Dacca: Census Org., Min. of Home Affairs, 1973. 104p.

25277 D'SOUZA, S. Large scale computerisation of the 1981 census: implications of the 1974 census of Bangla Desh. In SocAct 28,1 (1978) 18-36.

25278 D'SOUZA, S. & S. RAHMAN. Intercensal population growth rates of Bangla Desh. In SocAct 27,2 (1977) 1-18.

25279 JANIK, B. & L. BIGLER & P. WIRTH. Probleme der Bevölkerung und Bevölkerungsstruktur und der Nahrungsmittelversorgung in Bangladesh. In IAF 6,1 (1975) 4-24.

25280 KHAN, MASIHUR RAHMAN. Pattern of external migration to and from Bangladesh, 1901-61. In BER 2,2 (1974) 599-632.

25281 SCHULTZ, T.P. & J. DA VANZO. Analysis of demographic change in East Pakistan: a study of retrospective survey data. Santa Monica, CA: Rand Corp., 1970. 72p. (Rand report R-564-AID)

25282 SHARIFA BEGUM. Birth rate and death rate in Bangladesh, 1951-74. Dacca: BIDS, 1979. 28p. (Its res. reports, ns 28)

c. population policy and control

25283 BANGLADESH. POPULATION CONTROL & FAMILY PLANNING DIV. Bangladesh national population policy: an outline. Dacca: 1977. 14p.

25284 ______. Population control and family planning programme: the Two Year Plan, 1978-80 and the second Five-Year Plan, 1980-85. Dacca: 1977. 2 v., 364p.

25285 FRANDA, M.F. Bangladesh: perceptions of a population policy. In American Universities Field Staff. Population perspective, 1973. San Francisco: Freeman, Cooper, 1973, 227-39.

25286 Islam and family planning. Dacca: Dir. of Population Control & Family Planning, 1977. 43p.

3. Surveys of Economic Conditions since 1947
a. general studies

25287 AHMAD, NAFIS. An economic geography of East Pakistan. 2nd ed. London: OUP, 1968. 401p. [1st pub. 1958]

25288 ______. A new economic geography of Bangla Desh. ND: Vikas, 1975. 213p.

25289 ALAMGIR, MOHIUDDIN. Economy of Bangladesh: which way are we moving? Dacca: Bangladesh Econ. Assn., 1976. 90p.

25290 ALAMGIR, MOHIUDDIN & L. BERLAGE. An analysis of national accounts of Bangladesh, 1949/50-1968/69. Dacca: BIDE, 1972. 85p. (Its Res. reports, ns 7)

25291 ______. Bangladesh: national income and expenditure, 1949/50-1969/70. Dacca: BIDS, 1974. 240p. (Its Res. monographs, 1)

25292 BERTOCCI, P.J. East Pakistan: the harvest of strife. In SAR 5,1 (1971) 11-18.

25293 CHAKRAVARTY, S.R. The state of economy in Bangla Desh (1971-74). In SAS 10,2 (1975) 94-111.

25294 CHANANA, C. Economics of Bangla Desh. ND: Marketing & Econ. Res. Bureau, 1971. 88p.

25295 INTL. BANK FOR RECONSTRUCTION AND DEV. Land and water resources sector study; Bangladesh. Washington: IBRD, 1972. 9 v.

25296 KHAN, AZIZUR RAHMAN. The economy of Bangladesh. London: Macmillan, 1972. 196p.

25297 KLATT, W. Bangladesh: an economic survey. In Quest 83 (1973) 15-24.

25298 MUKHERJI, I.N. Economic problems and prospects of Bangladesh. In IS 13,2 (1974) 278-308.

25299 RAHIM, A.M.A., ed. Bangladesh economy: problems and issues. Dacca: Univ. Press, 1977. 286p.

25300 ______., ed. Current issues of Bangladesh economy. Dacca: Bangladesh Books Intl., 1978. 246p.

25301 RAO, V.K.R.V. Bangla Desh economy: problems and prospects. Delhi: Vikas, 1972. 199p.

25302 SETH, K.L. Economic prospects of Bangla Desh. ND: Trimurti, 1972. 103p.

b. economic inequality of East Pakistan, 1947 - 71

25303 AHRENS, H. Umfang und Ursacher der wirtschaftlichen Disparitäten zwischen Ost- und Westpakistan. In IAF 4 (1973) 239-78.

25304 BOSE, S.R. East-west contrast in Pakistan's agricultural development. In E.A.G. Robinson & M. Kidron, ed. Economic development in South Asia. London: Macmillan, 1970, 127-46.

25305 ______. East-West contrast in Pakistan's agricultural development. In K. Griffin & Azizur Rahman Khan, eds. Growth and inequality in Pakistan. London: Macmillan, 1972, 69-93.

25306 FAROOQI, M. Pakistan: policies that led to a break-up. ND: PPH, 1972. 105p.

25307 KHAN, KHUSHI MOHAMMED. Regionale Wirtschaftsentwicklung in Pakistan; eine kritische Analyse. Stuttgart: G. Fischer, 1971. 179p.

25308 MACEWAN, A. Problems of interregional and intersectoral allocation: the case of Pakistan. In PDR 10,1 (1970) 1-23.

25309 NATL. INST. OF SOCIAL & ECON. RES. West Pakistan assets in East Pakistan; a study on investment in companies located in East Pakistan by entrepreneurs considered to be West Pakistanis. Karachi: Pakistan Pub., 1972. 20p.

25310 ______. Basic facts about East and West Pakistan; comparative statistics on pace of economic development in the two wings of Pakistan, 1959-60 to 1969-70. Karachi: Pakistan Pub., 1972. 32p.

25311 RAHMAN, MUHAMMAD ANISUR. East and West Pakistan: a problem in the political economy of regional planning. Cambridge: Harvard U., Center for Intl. Affairs, 1968. 38p. (Its occ. papers, 20)

25312 SOBHAN, R. The problem of regional imbalance in the economic development of Pakistan. In AS 2 (1962) 31-37.

25313 URFF, W. VON. Das Ost-West-problem in der pakistanischen Entwicklungsplanung. In IAF 4,2 (1973) 215-38.

4. Economic Development and Planning since 1947

25314 ALAMGIR, MOHIUDDIN & ATIQUR RAHMAN. Saving in Bangladesh, 1959/60-1969/70. Dacca: BIDE, 1974. 260p. (Its Res. monograph, 2)

25315 ALAMGIR, MUHIUDDIN KHAN. Development strategy for Bangladesh. Dacca: Centre for Social Studies, 1980. 477p.

25316 BANGLADESH. PLANNING CMSN. The First five year plan, 1973-78. Dacca: 1973. 549p.

25317 ______. The Two-year plan. Dacca: 1978. 295p. [draft]

25318 FAALAND, J. & J.R. PARKINSON. Bangladesh, the test case of development. Dacca: Univ. Press, 1976. 203p.

25319 FAROUK, A. Economic development of Bangladesh: some lessons from Meiji Japan. Dacca: U. of Dacca, Bureau of Business Res., 1974. 51p. (Its Res. monographs, 1)

25320 HAROUN ER-RASHID. East Pakistan; a systematic regional geography and its development planning aspects. Lahore: Sh. Ghulam Ali, 1965. 387p.

25321 ISLAM, NURUL. Development planning in Bangladesh: a study in political economy. Dacca: Univ. Press, 1979. 267p. [Rpt. 1977 ed.]

25322 KHAN, AZIZUR RAHMAN. Bangladesh: economic policies since Independence. In SAR 8,1 (1974) 13-32.

25323 ______. The possibilities of the East Pakistan economy during the fourth five-year plan. In PDR 9,2 (1969) 144-211.

25324 KUHNEN, F. Agriculture and beginning industrialization: West Pakistan. Opladen: C.W. Leske, 1968. 274p.

25325 PAKISTAN. DEPT. OF FILMS & PUB. Economic development in East Pakistan; role of Central Government. Karachi: 1971. 55p.

25326 ROBINSON, E.A.G. & K. GRIFFIN, eds. The economic development of Bangladesh within a socialist framework: proceedings of a conference held by the International Economic Association at Dacca. NY: Wiley, 1974. 330p.

25327 SHAMSUL ISLAM. Public corporations in Bangladesh. Dacca: Local Govt. Inst., 1975. 507p.

25328 SHARIF, M. RAIHAN. Planning with social justice: the Bangladesh case. Dacca: Bangladesh Books Intl., 1979. 324p.

25329 URFF, W. VON & H. AHRENS. Zur Realisierung des ersten Fünfjahresplanes von Bangladesh (1973-78) - unter besonderer Berücksichtigung der Landwirtschaft. In IAF 8,1 (1977) 4-29.

25330 YUNUS, MUHAMMAD. Planning in Bangladesh: format, technique, and priority, and other essays. Chittagong: Rural Studies Project, Dept. of Economics, Chittagong U., 1976. 82p.

5. Agriculture in Bangladesh since 1947
a. bibliography

25331 SERAJUL HAQUE. A select bibliography on agricultural, rural labour: employment, unemployment and underemployment. Dacca: BIDS, 1976. 18p.

25332 SERAJUL HAQUE & M. SHAMSUL ISLAM KHAN & NILUFAR AKHTER. Green revolution: a select bibliography, 1950 to 1977. Dacca: BIDS, 1978. 42p.

25333 CLAY, E.J. & M.N. CLAY. A select bibliography on agricultural economics and rural development, with special reference to Bangladesh. Dacca: Bangladesh Agri. Res. Council, 1977. 100p. [suppl. 1978, 138p.]

25334 TALUKDER, ALAUDDIN. Bangladesh agricultural economics: a select bibliography. Dacca: BIDS, 1975. 59p.

b. agricultural conditions
i. general studies

25335 ALIM, A. An introduction to Bangladesh agriculture. Dacca: M. Alim, 1974. 432p.

25336 AMINUL ISLAM, M. Changes in cropping patterns in East Pakistan. In Oriental Geographer 13,1 (1968) 1-23.

25337 BANGLADESH. AGRO-ECON. RES. STATION. Basic statistics of Bangladesh agriculture. Dacca: 1975. 203p.

25338 BANGLADESH. BUREAU OF STAT. Agricultural production levels in Bangladesh, 1947-1972. Dacca: Bangladesh Bureau of Stat., Min. of Planning, 1976. 305p.

25339 BOSE, S.R. Trend of real income of the rural poor in East Pakistan, 1949-66: an indirect estimate. Karachi: PIDE, 1968. 39p. (Its res. report 68) [1st pub. in PDR 8,3 (1968) 452-88; also pub. in K. Griffin & Azizur Rahman Khan, eds. Growth and inequality in Pakistan. London: Macmillan, 1972, 250-76]

25340 HUQ, M. NURUL. Institutions for rural development in Bangladesh. Bogra: Rural Dev. Academy, 1979. 50p.

25341 KALIMUDDIN AHMED. Agriculture in East Pakistan. Dacca: Ahmed Bros., 1965. 428p.

25342 KAMALUDDIN AHMED. Bangladesh agriculture and field crops. Dacca: Mumtaj Kamal, 1980. 137p.

25343 PATEL, AHMED M. Populations, food and agriculture in East Pakistan. In Pakistan Geog. R. 23 (1968) 61-77.

ii. floods, cyclones, and famines

25344 BANGLADESH INST. OF DEV. STUDIES. Famine, 1974: political economy of mass starvation in Bangladesh: a statistical annex. Dacca: BIDS, 1977-. v. 1,2-.

25345 BOSE, S.R. Food grain availability and possibilities of famine in Bangladesh. In EPW 7, 5-6 (1972) 293-96.

25346 CHOWDHURY, A.K.M. ALAUDDIN & L.C. CHEN. The dynamics of contemporary famine. Dacca: Ford Foundation, 1977. 26p. (Its Report, 47)

25347 DODGE, P. & P.D. WIEBE. Famine relief and development in rural Bangladesh. In EPW 11,22 (1976) 809-16.

25348 MUKHERJI, K.M. Agriculture, famine, and rehabilitation in South Asia, a regional approach. Santiniketan: Visva-Bharati, 1965. 218p.

25349 SAMAD, M.A. Cyclone of 1970 and agricultural rehabilitation. Dacca: Agri. Info. Service, 1972. 82p.

25350 SOBHAN, REHMAN. Politics of food and famine in Bangladesh. In EPW 14,48 (1979) 1978-80.

c. rice and other food crops; the promotion of wheat

25351 ALIM, ABDUL. Rice improvement in East Pakistan. Dacca: East Pakistan Govt. Press, 1968. 136p.

25352 ALIM, ABDUL & S.M. HASANUZZAMAN. Means of increasing rice production in East Pakistan. Dacca: East Pakistan Govt. Press, 1962. 54p.

25353 ALLISON, A. & MOTIOR RAHMAN & S. ZEIDENSTEIN. Vegetable, fruit & spice gardening in Bangladesh. Dacca?: Zeidenstein and Allison, 1974. 86p.

25354 ANDERSON, R.G. & E.E. SAARI. Bangladesh, a new wheat country. Dacca: Ford Foundation, 1975. 45p.

25355 BANGLADESH RICE RES. INST. Workshop on ten years of modern rice and wheat cultivation in Bangladesh, March 7-10, 1977. Dacca: 1977. 318p.

25356 Deep water rice in Bangladesh. Dacca: Bangladesh Rice Res. Inst., 1974. 156p.

25357 EAST PAKISTAN. SUGAR ENQUIRY CMTEE. Report, 1961-62. Dacca: East Pakistan Govt. Press, 1963. 142p.

25358 KHAN, M. SALAR. Flowers and fruits of Bangladesh. Dacca: Dept. of Pub., MIB, 1974. 55p.

d. jute, tea and other commercial crops

25359 AHMED, RAKIBUDDIN. The progress of the jute industry and trade, 1955-1966. Dacca: Pakistan Central Jute Cmtee., 1966. 526p.

25360 ALIM, ABDUL. A handbook of Bangladesh jute. Dacca: Effat Begum, 1978. 218p.

25361 CARRUTHERS, I.D. & G.D. GYER. Prospects for Pakistan tea industry. In PDR 8 (1968) 431-51.

25362 CHOWDHURY, NAIMUDDIN. Tea industry of Bangladesh: problems and prospects. Dacca: BIDS, 1974. 74p.

25363 EAST PAKISTAN. TEA ENQUIRY CMSN. Report, 1962. Dacca: East Pakistan Govt. Press, 1964. 80p.

25364 HABIBULLAH, M. Some aspects of productivity in the jute industry of Pakistan. Dacca: Bureau of Econ. Res., U. of Dacca, 1968. 180p.

25365 ______. Tea industry in Pakistan. Dacca: U. of Dacca, Bureau of Econ. Res., 1964. 330p.

25366 PAKISTAN, BUREAU OF NATL. RES. & REFERENCE. The growth of jute industry in Pakistan. Rawalpindi: MIB, 1968. 56p.

25367 PAKISTAN. FOOD & AGRI. DIV. PLANNING UNIT. Survey report on jute marketing in East Pakistan. Islamabad: 1971. 69p.

25368 PAKISTAN. JUTE BOARD. Jute: a great decade, 1958-1968. Dacca: 1968. 76p.

25369 PAKISTAN. JUTE ENQUIRY CMSN. Report of the Jute Enquiry Commission, 1960. Karachi: MPGOP, 1961. 319p.

25370 THOMAS, P.S. & IRSHAD AHMED. Some factors affecting tea production in Pakistan. In PDR 4,3 (1964) 404-61.

25371 ZONDAG, C.H. Pakistan jute: its problems and promise; staff study. Karachi?: USAID, 1967. 96p.

e. agricultural planning and development
i. general studies

25372 AHMAD, MOHIUDDIN. Initiating development: BRAC's economic support programme in Sulla: some case studies. Dacca: Bangladesh Rural Advancement Cmtee., 1978. 53p.

25373 AHMED, NOAZESH. Development agriculture of Bangladesh. Dacca: Bangladesh Books Intl., 1976. 184p.

25374 ALI, QAZI AZHER. Rural development in Bangladesh. Comilla: BARD, 1975. 64p.

25375 AMINUL ISLAM, M. The future relationship between rural population and agriculture in East Pakistan. In Pakistan Geog. R. 21,2 (1966) 39-55.

25376 DUMONT, R. Problems and prospects for rural development in Bangladesh: second tentative report. Dacca: Ford Foundation, 1973. 82p.

25377 ______. A self-reliant rural development policy for the poor peasantry of Sonar Bangladesh: a tentative report. Dacca: Ford Foundation, 1973. 79p.

25378 HABIBULLAH, M. & A. FAROUK. Some aspects of rural capital formation in East Pakistan. Dacca: Dacca U., Bureau of Econ. Res., 1963. 122p.

25379 HUQ, MAZHARUL. Impact of development programme on agriculture (a study of the position in East Pakistan). In PEJ 17 (1967) 25-36.

25380 MAY, B. Die Entwicklung der Landwirtschaft in Bangladesh und Pakistan. In IAF 4,2 (1973) 279-305.

25381 SEMINAR ON INTEGRATED RURAL DEV., DACCA, 1975. Proceedings. Dacca: Inst. of Engineers, 1978. 2 v.

25382 STEVENS, R.D. & HAMZA ALAVI & P.J. BERTOCCI, eds. Rural development in Bangladesh and Pakistan: past achievements and present challenges. Honolulu: UPH, 1976. 399p.

ii. agricultural research, technology, and innovation

25383 Agricultural Research Institute, Bangladesh. Dacca: Dir. of Agri. (Res. & Educ.), 1976. 34p.

25384 ASADUZZAMAN, M. & FARIDUL ISLAM. Adoption of HYVs in Bangladesh: some preliminary hypotheses and tests. Dacca: BIDS, 1976. 33p. (Its Res. reports, 23)

25385 BARI, FAZLUL. An innovator in a traditional environment. Comilla: BARD, 1974. 45p.

25386 BIGGS, S.D. Bangladesh, 1975: interaction between technological and institutional development: what is appropriate, where, when, and for whom? Dacca: Ford Foundation, 1975. 29p.

25387 ______. Science and agricultural technology for Bangladesh: a framework for policy analysis. Dacca: Ford Foundation, 1976. 38p.

25388 BYRNE, J. & M. WILLIS & N.M. STRAUGHAN. The Savar experiment: a model for village technology action programmes. Dacca: Lutheran World Federation, Dept. of World Service, Rangpur Dinajpur Rehabilitation Service, 1978. 183p.

25389 CARRUTHERS, I.D. A study of the needs and capacity for agro-economic planning and research in Bangladesh. Dacca: Ford Foundation, 1976. 49p.

25390 Directory of agricultural scientists. Dacca: Bangladesh Agri. Res. Council, 1976. 301p.

25391 FAROUK, A. & S.A. RAHIM. Modernizing subsistence agriculture: an experimental survey. Dacca: U. of Dacca, Bureau of Econ. Res., Dacca U., 1967. 147p. 147p. [Comilla Dist., 1963-64]

25392 MAHBUB-E-ILAH. Farmers' knowledge on modern agriculture and adoption of improved practices. Comilla: BARD, 1974. 21p.

25393 MANNAN, M.A. Adoption of IR-20; a social psychological study in Comilla Kotwali Thana. Comilla: BARD, 1972. 39p.

25394 MCCOLLY, H.F. Special report on introducing farm mechanization in the Comilla Cooperative Project. Comilla: PARD, 1962. 28p.

25395 NATL. SEMINAR ON AGRI. RES. MGMT. IN BANGLADESH, DACCA, 1978. Proceedings. Dacca: Bangladesh Agri. Res. Council, 1978. 211p.

25396 QUASEN, M. ABUL. Fertilizer use in Bangladesh, 1965-66 to 1975-76. Dacca: BIDS, 1978. 37p. (Its Res. reports, ns 25)

25397 RAHIM, SYED A. Diffusion and adoption of agricultural practices. Comilla: Pakistan Academy for Village Dev., 1961. (Its Technical pub., 7)

25398 ______. Use of commercial fertilizers in East Pakistan. In J. of PARD 3 (1963) 182-98.

iii. irrigation and water control

25399 AHMED, BADARUDDIN & W. COWARD, JR. Village, technology & bureaucracy; irrigation development in Bangladesh. In J. of BARD 7,1 (1977) 7-28.

25400 ALAM, MAHMUDUL. Capacity-utilisation of low-lift pump irrigation in Bangladesh. Dacca: BIDE, 1974. 70p.

25401 BANGLADESH. MIN. OF FLOOD CONTROL & WATER RESOURCES. Seminar on flood control and water resource development in Bangladesh. Dacca: 1972. 171p.

25402 BANGLADESH WATER DEV. BOARD. Water resources development in Bangladesh. Dacca: 1979. 109p.

25403 EAST PAKISTAN WATER & POWER DEV. AUTHORITY. EPWAPDA: decade of development, 1958-1968. Dacca: 1968. 108p.

25404 FAROUK, A. Irrigation in a monsoon land; economics of farming in the Ganges-Kobadak. Dacca: Bureau of Econ. Res., U. of Dacca, 1968. 169p.

25405 HAMID, M. ABDUL, ed. Irrigation technologies in Bangladesh: a study in some selected areas. Rajshahi: Dept. of Econ., Rajshahi U., 1978. 308p.

25406 KHAN, A. AZIZ. Tube-well irrigation in Comilla Thana. Comilla: BARD, 1972. 158p. [Rpt. 1965 ed.]

25407 KHAN, HAMIDUR RAHMAN & J. ROMM. Some issues of water resource management in Bangladesh. Dacca: Ford Foundation, 1978. 39p.

25408 KHAN, Z.A., ed. Basic documents on Farakka conspiracy from 1951 to 1976. Dacca: Khoshroz Kitab Mahal, 1976. 197p.

25409 MANNAN, M.A. Knowledge and interest of the farmers in winter irrigation; an investigation among fifty farmers in ten villages of Comilla Kotwali Thana. Comilla: PARD, 1966. 19p.

25410 MOHAMMAD, GHULAM. Development of irrigated agriculture in East Pakistan: some basic considerations. In PDR 6,3 (1966) 315-75.

iv. the Comilla project: Bangladesh Academy of Rural Development (est. 1957)

25411 AHMED, BADARUDDIN. Manual of Comilla co-operatives. Comilla: BARD, 1972. 80p.

25412 ______. Who decides? Role of managing committee in decision making in A.C.F. Comilla: BARD, 1972. 38p. [= Agri. Coop. Federation]

25413 CHOLDIN, H.M. The development project as natural experiment: the Comilla, Pakistan, projects. In EDCC 17,4 (1969) 483-500.

25414 ______. An organizational analysis of rural development projects at Comilla, East Pakistan. In EDCC 20,4 (1972) 671-90.

25415 ______. Urban cooperatives at Comilla, Pakistan; a case study of local-level development. In EDCC 16,2 (1968) 189-218.

25416 DUPREE, L. The Comilla experiment; a scheme for village development in East Pakistan. In American Universities Field Staff, Reports service, South Asia series 8,2 (1964). 20p.

25417 KHAN, A. AZIZ. Comilla co-operative pilot project, 1961-1965. Comilla: PARD, 1965. 16p.

25418 KHAN, A.Z.M. OBAIDULLAH. The Comilla district development project. Comilla: PARD, 1964. 59p.

25419 KHAN, AKHTER HAMEED. Tour of twenty thanas: impressions of drainage-roads, irrigation & co-operative programmes. Comilla: BARD, 1973. 114p. [Rpt. 1971 ed.; Comilla dist.]

25420 KHAN, ALI AKHTAR & M.R. SAHA & M. AMEERUL HUQ. Training at BARD: a review of course catalogue, participants, and training contents, 1959-74. Comilla: BARD, 1975. 51p.

25421 KHAN, AZIZUR RAHMAN. The Comilla model and the integrated rural development programme of Bangladesh; an experiment in "cooperative capitalism." In Dharam Ghai, et al., eds. Agrarian systems and rural development. NY: Holmes & Meier, 1979, 113-58.

25422 OBAIDULLAH, A.K.M. The Comilla dairy cattle programme; a study of an experimental dairy project. Comilla: PARD, 1969. 48p.

25423 PAKISTAN ACADEMY FOR RURAL DEV., COMILLA. The Comilla pilot project in irrigation and rural electrification. Comilla: 1963. 65p.

25424 ______. An evaluation report on the progress of the seven thana projects under the Comilla District Integrated Rural Development Programme (September, 1967). Comilla: 1967. 58p.

25425 ______. The works programme in Comilla; a case study. Comilla: 1966. 174p.

25426 RAHIM, SYED A. The Comilla Program in East Pakistan. In C.R. Wharton, Jr., ed. Subsistence agriculture and economic development. Chicago: Aldine, 1969, 415-24.

25427 RAHMAN, MAHMOODUR. Special co-operatives by night. Comilla: PARD, 1966. 66p.

25428 RAPER, A.F. Rural development in action: the comprehensive experiment at Comilla, East Pakistan. Ithaca: CornellUP, 1970. 320p.

25429 SCHUMAN, H. Economic development and individual change; a social-psychological study of the Comilla experiment in Pakistan. Cambridge: Center for Intl. Affairs, Harvard U., 1967. 59p. (Its Occ. papers, 15)

25430 STEVENS, R.D. Agricultural economics report: rural development programs for adaptation from Comilla, Bangladesh. East Lansing: Dept. of Agri. Econ., Michigan State U., 1972. 75p.

f. rural credit and cooperatives

25431 AHSANULLAH, M. Capital accumulation through co-operatives. Comilla: BARD, 1973. 65p.

25432 CO-OP. FARMING SEMINAR, BANGLADESH ACADEMY FOR RURAL DEV., 1972. Co-operative farming. Comilla: BARD, 1972. 208p.

25433 EAST PAKISTAN. REGISTRAR OF CO-OP. SOCIETIES. Co-operative movement in East Paksitan. Dacca: Co-op. Dir., Govt. of East Pakistan, 1967. 53p.

25434 GUNAWARDANA, L. & D.D. NAIK. Status of cooperative and rural housing programmes in Bangla Desh today. ND: Intl. Coop. Alliance, 1973. 37p.

25435 HUSSAIN, M. ZAKER. Study of Bamail Co-operative Farm. Comilla: BARD, 1973. 125p.

25436 INTL. WORKSHOP ON PROVIDING FINANCIAL SERVICES TO THE RURAL POOR, DACCA, 1978. Problems and issues of agricultural credit and rural finance: deliberations .... Dacca: Bangladesh Bank, 1979. 298p.

25437 KHAN, ALI AKHTAR. Rural credit in Gazipur village. Comilla: PARD, 1968. 68p.

25438 ______. Rural credit programme of Agricultural Co-operative Federation. Comilla: PARD, 1971. 104p.

25439 SHAHJAHAN, MIRZA. Agricultural finance in East Pakistan. Dacca: 1968. 248p.

g. rural labor and unemployment

25440 CLAY, E.J. Institutional change and agricultural wages in Bangladesh. In BDS 4,4 (1974) 423-40.

25441 HABIBULLAH, M. The pattern of agricultural unemployment, a case study of an East Pakistan village. Dacca: Bureau of Econ. Res., Dacca U., 1962. 90p.

25442 Report on the survey of rural credit and rural unemployment in East Pakistan, 1956. Dacca: Socio-Econ. Res. Board, Dacca U., 1958. 205p.

25443 ROBINSON, W.C. "Disguised" unemployment once again: East Pakistan, 1951-61. In American J. of Farm Econ. 51 (1969) 592-603.

h. land tenure and reform

25444 ABDULLAH, ABU. Land reform and agrarian change in Bangladesh. In BDS 4,1 (1976) 67-114.

25445 ABDULLAH, ABU & MOSHARAFF HOSSAIN & R. NATIONS. Agrarian structure and the IRDP; preliminary considerations. In BDS 4,2 (1976) 209-66.

25446 ALIM, ABDUL. Land reforms in Bangladesh: social changes, agricultural development, and eradication of poverty. Dacca: Samina, 1979. 150p.

25447 GHULAM RABBANI, A.K.M. & J.T. PEACH & F.T. JANNUZI. Summary report of the 1977 Land Occupancy Survey of rural Bangladesh. Dacca: Govt. of Bangladesh, Bureau of Stat., 1977. 135p.

25448 HOSSAIN, MAHABUB. Factors affecting tenancy: the case of Bangladesh agriculture. In BDS 6,2 (1978) 139-60.

25449 ______. Farm size, tenancy and land productivity: an analysis of farm level data in Bangladesh agriculture. In BDS 5,3 (1977) 285-348.

25450 ISLAM, SIRAJUL. Rural history of Bangladesh: a source study. Dacca: Tito Islam, 1977. 122p.

25451 JABBAR, M.A. Relative productive efficiency of different tenure classes in selected areas of Bangladesh. In BDS 5,1 (1977) 17-50.

25452 JANNUZI, F.T. The agrarian structure of Bangladesh: an impediment to development. Boulder: Westview, 1980. 150p.

25453 MUKHERJI, I.N. Agrarian reforms in Bangladesh. In AS 16,5 (1976) 452-64.

25454 ZAMAN, M.A. Bangladesh: the case for further land reform. In SAR 8,2 (1975) 97-116.

6. Industry in Bangladesh since 1947
a. general studies

25455 AHMAD, NAFIS & A.K.M. HAFIZUR RAHMAN. Development of industry in Chittagong. In Oriental Geographer 6 (1962) 139-58.

25456 AHMAD, NAFIS & DEEN MUHAMMAD KHAN. Manufacturing industries in the Narayanganj area. In Oriental Geographer 6 (1962) 1-22.

25457 AHMAD, QAZI KHOLIQUZZAMAN. Aspects of the management of nationalised industries in Bangladesh. In BDS 2,3 (1974) 675-703.

25458 BHANWAR SINGH. Industrial structure of Bangladesh and neighbouring states of India: a partial and systems analysis. In SAS 10,1/2 (1975) 33-46.

25459 HABIBULLAH, M. Some aspects of industrial efficiency and profitability in Bangladesh. Dacca: Bureau of Econ. Res., U. of Dacca, 1974. 109p.

25460 INDUSTRIAL DEV. BANK OF PAKISTAN. Investment opportunities in East Pakistan. Dacca: Public Relations Dept., Industrial Dev. Bank of Pakistan, 1965. 49p.

25461 JAHAN, AFROZ. A review of recent industrial development in east Pakistan. In Oriental Geographer 10 (1966) 103-22.

25462 KHAN, AZIZUR RAHMAN. Financing private sector industries in Bangladesh. Dacca: Bureau of Business Res., U. of Dacca, 1980. 78p.

25463 PAPANEK, H. Entrepreneurs in East Pakistan. In Robert Beech & M.J. Beech, eds. Bengal: change and continuity. East Lansing: Asian Studies Center, Michigan State U., 1971, 119-50. (Its occ. papers, S.A. series, 16)

25464 TAIYEB, M. Localisation of industries in East Pakistan. In Commerce & Industry 5,12 (1962) 17-26.

25465 TALUKDER, ALAUDDIN. Bangladesh industry studies: a select bibliography. Dacca: BIDS, 1975. 28p. (Its bibl. series 8.1)

c. small-scale and cottage industries

25466 AUSIN, V. Development of cottage industries in Bangladesh: report. Dacca: Agri. Dev. Agencies in Bangladesh, 1977. 140p.

25467 BHATTACHARJEE, D.D. & A. KHALED. Marketing of small industries products in East Pakistan; a case study of handloom products. Dacca: Bureau of Econ. Res. & East Pakistan Small Industries Corp., 1969. 155p.

25468 HUQ, M.NURUL. Comilla khaddar: a case-study of an artisan co-operative society. Comilla: BARD, 1973. 45p.

7. Labor and Trade Unions in Bangladesh since 1947

25469 AHMAD, K. Labour movement in East Pakistan. Dacca: Progati, 1969. 136p.

25470 CHOWDHURY, NUIMUDDIN. Industrial conflict in Bangladesh, 1947-75: a preliminary analysis. In BDS 5,2 (1977) 211-26.

25471 FAROUK, A. & A.N.M. MUNIRUZZAMAN & T. ISLAM. Science trained manpower; a study of employment problem in Bangladesh. Dacca: Bureau of Econ. Res., U. of Dacca, 1972. 161p.

25472 HABIBULLAH, M. Motivation mix. Dacca: Bureau of Econ. Res., U. of Dacca, 1974. 192p.

25473 HUSAIN, A.F.A. & A. FAROUK. Social integration of industrial workers in Khulna. Dacca: U. of Dacca, Bureau of Econ. Res., 1963. 207p. [1st pub. 1961]

25474 KAMRUDDIN AHMAD. Labour movement in Bangladesh. 2nd ed., rev. Dacca: Inside Library, 1978. 125p.

8. Commerce and Transportation in Bangladesh

25475 AHMED, SHAHID UDDIN. Insurance business in Bangladesh: a study of the pattern, problems & prospects. Dacca: Bureau of Business Res., U. of Dacca, 1977. 168p.

25476 BARY, M.A. Railway development in East Pakistan. In J. of the Inst. of Engineers 2 (1964) 25-55.

25477 FAROUK, A. & M. SAFIULLAH. Retailing of consumer goods in East Pakistan. Dacca: Bureau of Econ. Res., Dacca U., 1965. 153p.

25478 Government of Bangladesh transport survey, final report. London: The Economist Intelligence Unit, 1974. 11pts. in 17v.

25479 MAHMUDUR RAHMAN, KHANDKER. Development of agricultural marketing in Bangladesh. Comilla: BARD, 1973. 135p.

25480 ______. The experience of marketing with regard to small farmers in Bangladesh, with particular reference to Comilla rural development program. Comilla: BARD, 1975. 47p.

25481 MOLLA, M.K.U. The port of Chittagong; a study of its growth and expansion at the beginning of the twentieth-century. In J. of the Inst. of Bangladesh Studies 1,1 (1976) 30-42.

25482 PATEL , A.M. The rural markets of Rajshahi district. In Oriental Geographer 7 (1963) 140-51.

25483 Porte grande: prospect and retrospect. Chittagong: Chittagong Port Authority, 1978. 84p.

25484 REDDAWAY, W.B. & M. MIZANUR RAHMAN. The scale of smuggling out of Bangladesh. Dacca: BIDS, 1975. 22p. Its Res. reports, 21) [1st pub. in EPW 11,23 (1976) 843-49]

25485 Seminar on basic marketing problems of our traders. Dacca: Mgmt. Dev. Centre, 1966. 1 v.

25486 SIDDIQI, AKHTAR HUSAIN. Geographical factors in the development of rail transport in East Pakistan. In Oriental Geographer 12,1 (1968) 24-38.

D. Society and Social Change in Bangladesh since 1947

1. General Studies

25487 ANISUZZAMAN, M. Violence and social change in Bangladesh. In SAS 13,1 (1978) 25-35.

25488 BESSAIGNET, P., ed. Social research in East Pakistan. 2nd rev. ed. Dacca: ASP, 1964. 406p. (Its pub., 5)

25489 KARIM, ABUL KHAIR NAZMUL. The dynamics of Bangladesh society. ND: Vikas, 1980. 242p.

25490 MUKHERJEE, R.K. Social background of Bangladesh. In EPW 7,5-7 (1972) 265-74.

25491 OWEN, J.E., ed. Sociology in East Pakistan. Dacca: ASP, 1962. 275p. (Its occ. studies, 1)

25492 SCHUMAN, H. Social change and the validity of regional stereotypes in East Pakistan. In Sociometry 29 (1966) 428-40.

2. Social Categories, incl. Kinship and Marriage
a. general studies

25493 AZIZ, K.M. ASHRAFUL. Kinship in Bangladesh. Dacca: Intl. Centre for Diarrhoeal Disease Res., 1979. 228p. (Its monograph, 1)

25494 ELLICKSON, J. Symbols in Muslim Bengali family rituals. In P. Bertocci, ed. Prelude to crisis. East Lansing: Asian Studies Center, Michigan State U., 1972, 65-78. (Its occ. papers, S.A. series, 18)

25495 GANKOVSKY, Y.V. The social structure of society in the People's Republic of Bangladesh. In AS 14,3 (1974) 220-30.

25496 KARIM, ABUL KHAIR NAZMUL. Changing patterns of an East Pakistan family. In B.E. Ward, ed. Women in the new Asia. Paris: UNESCO, 1963, 296-322.

b. Muslims of Bangladesh (85.4% in 1974), incl. the Bihari Muslim minority

25497 ELLICKSON, J. Islamic institutions; perception and practice in a village in Bangla Desh. In CIS ns 6 (1972) 53-65.

25498 GLASSE, R.M. La société musulmane dans le Pakistan rural de l'Est; étude préliminaire. In Études rurales 22-24 (1966) 188-205.

25499 MOHSIN ALI, ed. The Bengali Muslim; plight before freedom, progress after freedom, peril to freedom. Karachi: Pakistan Dept. of Films & Pub., 1971. 74p.

25500 THORP, J.P. Masters of earth: conceptions of "power" among Muslims of rural Bangladesh. Ph.D. diss., U. of Chicago, 1978. 222p.

25501 WHITAKER, B.C.G. The Biharis in Bangladesh. London: Minority Rights Group, 1972. 24p. (Its Report, 11)

25502 WISE, J. The Muhammadans of Eastern Bengal. In JASBengal 63,3 (1894-98) 28-64.

c. Hindus (6.9% caste Hindu, 6.6% scheduled castes, in 1974)

25503 BESSAIGNET, P. Family and kinship in a Hindu village of East Pakistan. In M. Afsaruddin, ed. Sociology and social research in Pakistan. Dacca: Pakistan Sociol. Assn., E. Pakistan Unit, 1963, 69-92.

25504 DATTA, J.M. & H.K. SAHA. Inflation of the number of Kayasthas in Chittagong. In MI 42 (1962) 217-22.

25505 SINHA, B.C. The structure of the Varendra Brahmanical order of North and East Bengal. In his Changing times. Calcutta: AnthSI, 1968, 128-36.

d. tribals (Buddhist, Hindu, Muslim, & other): meeting with Burmese culture

25506 BERNOT, L. Les Cak. Contribution a l'étude ethnographique d'une population de langue "loi". Paris: CNRS, 1967. 276p.

25507 ______. Les paysans arakanais du Pakistan oriental; L'histoire, le monde végétal et l'organisation sociale des réfugiés Marma (Mog). The Hague: Mouton, 1967. 2 v.

25508 BESSAIGNET, P. Tribesmen of the Chittagong Hill tracts. Dacca: ASP, 1958. 109p. (Its pub., 1)

25509 CHOWDHURY, RAFIQUL ISLAM. Tribal leadership and political integration: a case study of Chakma and Mong tribes of Chittagong Hill Tracts. Chittagong: Faculty of Social Science, U. of Chittagong, 1979. 248p.

25510 LÖFFLER, L.G. Chakma und Sak; ethnolinguistische Beiträge zur Geschichte eines Kulturvolkes. In Internationales Archiv für Ethnographie 50,1 (1964) 72-115.

25511 RAJPUT, A.B. L'aube sur la foret profonde; Chittagong Hill Tracts (Pakistan oriental). In O&M 6 (1966) 225-36.

25512 ______. Les Murung de la forêt de Bandarban (Pakistan Oriental). In O&M 4,2 (1964) 119-148.

25513 SATTAR, ABDUS. In the sylvan shadows. Dacca: Saquib Bros., 1971. 349p.

25514 ______. Tribal culture in Bangladesh. Dacca: Muktadhara, 1975. 256p.

25515 SOPHER, D.E. Population dislocation in the Chittagong Hills. In Geographical R. 53 (1963) 337-62.

e. women of Bangladesh

25516 ABDULLAH, TAHRUNNESSA AHMED. Village women as I saw them. Comilla: BARD, 1976. 36p.

25517 ALAMGIR, S.F. Profile of Bangladeshi women: selected aspects of women's roles and status in Bangladesh. Dacca: USAID, 1977. 82p.

25518 GERMAIN, A. Women's roles in Bangladesh development: a program assessment. Dacca: Ford Foundation, 1976. 48p.

25519 JAHAN, ROUNAQ. Women in Bangladesh. In R. Rohrlich-Leavitt, ed. Women cross-culturally.... The Hague: Mouton, 1975, 5-30. (WA)

25520 ______. Women in Bangladesh. In W.A. Veenoven, ed. Case studies on human rights and fundamental freedoms. The Hague: Nijhoff, 1975-76, v. 5, 533-61.

25521 LINDENBAUM, S. Woman and the left hand: social status and symbolism in East Pakistan. In Mankind (Sydney) 6 (1968) 537-44.

25522 MAHMUDA ISLAM. Bibliography on Bangladesh women, with annotation. Dacca: Women for Women, Res. & Study Group, 1979. 63p.

25523 MCCARTHY, F.E. & SALEH SABBAH & ROUSHAN AKHTER. Bibliography and selected references regarding rural women in Bangladesh. Dacca: Women's Section, Planning & Dev. Div., Min. of Agri., 1978. 44p.

25524 SATTAR, E. Women in Bangladesh: a village study. Dacca: Ford Foundation, 1974. 60p.

25525 The situation of women in Bangladesh. Ed. by Women for Women, Research and Study Group at the request of Women's Development Programme, UNICEF, Dacca. Dacca: 1979. 454p.

25526 SOBHAN, SALMA. Legal status of women in Bangladesh. Dacca: Bangladesh Inst. of Law & Intl. Affairs, 1978. 53p.

25527 Women for women: Bangladesh 1975. Dacca: University Press, 1975. 248p.

3. Villages and Rural Society

a. village studies

25528 AFSARUDDIN, MOHAMMAD. Rural life in Bangladesh: a study of five selected villages. 2nd ed. Dacca: Nawroze Kitabistan, 1979. 114p. [1st ed. 1964]

25529 AHMED, GIASUDDIN. A sociological study of the rural life of Kadamtali in the district of Comilla. Dacca: Soc. for Pakistan Studies, 1970. 67p.

25530 BAZLUL KARIM, KAZI & GHOLAM MORSHED AKHTER & ABDUN NOOR CHOWDHURY. Village Jamunna: a socio-economic survey. Bogra: RARD, 1975. 43p.

25531 ______. Village Mirjapur: a socio-economic survey. Bogra: RARD, 1975. 42p.

25532 BERTOCCI, P.J. Elusive villages: social structure and community organization in rural East Pakistan. Ph.D. diss., Michigan State U., 1971. 234p. [UM-71,2030]

25533 ______. Patterns of rural social organization in East Bengal. In A. Lipski, ed. Bengal: East and West. East Lansing: Asian Stud. Ctr., Michigan State U., 1970, 107-137. (Its occ. papers, 13)

25534 ______. Rural communities in Bangladesh: Hajipur and Tinpara. In C. Maloney, ed. South Asia: seven community profiles. NY: Holt, Rinehart & Winston, 1974, 81-130.

25535 MUKHERJEE, R.K. Six villages of Bengal. Bombay: Popular Prakashan, 1971. 303p. [1st pub. in JASBengal, 1958]

25536 QADIR, S.A. Village Dhanishwar: three generations of man-land adjustment in an East Pakistan village. Comilla: Pakistan Academy of Village Dev., 1960. 35p.

25537 RAHIM, SYED A. Communications and personal influence in an East Pakistan village. Comilla: PARD, 1965. 43p. (Its Technical Report, 18)

25538 WESTERGAARD, K. Boringram: an economic and social analysis of a village in Bangladesh. Bogra: RARD, 1979. 55p.

25539 ZAIDI, S.M. HAFEEZ. The village culture in transition; a study of East Pakistan rural society. Honolulu: EWCP, 1970. 159p.

b. stratification and exploitation

25540 AMEERUL HUQ, M., ed. Exploitation and the rural poor: a working paper on the rural power structure in Bangladesh. Comilla: BARD, 1976. 282p.

25541 BANGLADESH RURAL ADVANCEMENT CMTEE. Who gets what and why: resource allocation in a Bangladesh village. Dacca: 1979. 269p.

25542 BERTOCCI, P.J. Community structure and social rank in two villages in Bangladesh. In CIS 6 (1972) 28-52.

25543 CHOWDHURY, ANWARULLAH. A Bangladesh village: a study in social stratification. Dacca: Centre for Social Studies, 1978. 177p.

25544 ______. Social stratification in a Bangladesh village. In JASBangla 20,3 (1975) 60-84.

25545 JAHANGIR, BURHANUDDIN KHAN. Differentiation, polarisation, and confrontation in rural Bangladesh. Dacca: Centre for Social Studies, 1979. 324p.

25546 MUFAKHARUL ISLAM, M., et al. Studies in rural history. Dacca: Bangladesh Itihas Samiti, 1979. 140p.

c. community development; the svanirvār ("self-reliance") program

25547 ABDULLAH, M. MOHIAUDDIN. Rural development in Bangladesh: problems and prospects. Dacca: Nurjahan Begum, 1979. 98p.

25548 ALI, QAZI AZHER. Rural development in Bangladesh. Comilla: BARD, 1975. 64p.

25549 ARIF, M. TAUFIQUL & KAZI BAZLUL KARIM & GOLAM MORSHED AKHTER. Visit to selected swanirvar villages of Rangpur District. Bogra: Rural Dev. Academy, 1976. 46p.

25550 BADRUD DUZA, M. & M. MIZANUR RAHMAN & RUHUL AMIN. Modernizing rural Bangladesh: an experiment in selected Chittagong villages. Chittagong: Dept. of Sociology, U. of Chittagong, 1973. 58p.

25551 HAMID, M. ABDUL, et al. Christian Service Society, Dacope. Rajshahi: Dept. of Econ., Rajshahi U., 1976. 66p.

25552 HUQ, M. NURUL. Pioneers of rural development in Bangladesh: their programmes and writings. Bogra: Rural Dev. Academy, 1978. 120p.

25553 ______. Village development in Bangladesh; a study of Monagram Village. Comilla: BARD, 1973. 121p.

25554 Integrated rural development programme: an evaluation of Natore and Gaibandha projects. Rajshahi: Dept. of Econ., U. of Rajshahi, 1975. 116p.

25555 KARIM, KAZI BAZLUL & MANZURUL MAHMOOD SULTAN. Evaluation of Swanirvar Programme in five villages of Mithapukur Thana, Ranjpur. Bogra: Rural Dev. Academy, 1976. 26p.

25556 LATIFEE, H.I. A report on swanirvar programmes in Pashchim Sultanpur, Raozan, Chittagong, Aug. 1976. Chittagong: Dept. of Econ., Chittagong U., 1976. 53p.

25557 Rural development programmes in Chittagong: an observation report on some rural development projects of Chittagong. Comilla: BARD, 1976. 145p.

25558 SATTAR, M. GHULAM. Introductory notes on some locally initiated development projects in Bangladesh. Comilla: BARD, 1975. 27p.

25559 SOBHAN, REHMAN. Basic democracies works programme and rural development in East Pakistan. Dacca: Bureau of Econ. Res., U. of Dacca, 1968. 328p.

25560 The Ulashi villages: a summary report of three village studies. Dacca: Natl. Foundation for Res. on Human Resource Dev., 1978. 61p. (NFRHRD res. report, 1)

4. Cities and Urbanization
a. general studies

25561 ABEDIN, M. JAINUL, ed. Our cities and towns; collected papers presented and circulated in the Conference on Our Cities and Towns. Dacca: NIPA, 1970. 278p.

25562 AHMAD, NAFIS. Urban centers in East Pakistan. In R.L. Park, ed. Urban Bengal. East Lansing: Asian Studies Center, Michigan State U., 1969, 117-23. (Its occ. papers, S.A. series, 12)

25563 KHAN, FAZLE KARIM & MOHAMMAD MASOOD. Urban structure of Comilla Town. In Oriental Geographer 6,2 (1962) 109-38.

25564 SIDDIQI, M.I. An urban profile of Rajshahi. In Geographia 3,2 (1964) 83-98.

25565 TOFAYELL, Z.A. History of Kushtia. Dacca: Ziaunnahar Khanam, 1966. 1 v.

b. Dacca: Mughal provincial capital; capital and cultural center of Bangladesh [1974 pop. 1,679,572]

25566 ATIQULLAH, M. & F. KARIM KHAN. Growth of Dacca city; population and area, 1608-1981. Dacca: Dept. of Statistics, U. of Dacca, 1965. 42p.

25567 BRADLEY-BIRT, F.B. The romance of an eastern capital. Delhi: Metropolitan, 1975. 349p. [Rpt. 1906 ed.]

25568 DANI, A.H. Dacca; a record of its changing fortunes. 2nd rev. & enl. ed. Dacca: Mrs. S.S. Dani, 1962. 276p. [1st pub. 1956]

25569 FAROUK, A. The vagrants of Dacca City: a socio-economic survey, 1975. Dacca: Bureau of Econ. Res., U. of Dacca, 1978. 84p.

25570 HAIDER, AZIMUSSHAN, comp. A city and its civic body; a description of facts and events spotlighting certain aspects of life in and around Dacca during the last hundred years, and an account of the evolution of Dacca municipality. Dacca: Dacca Municipality, 1966. 136p.

25571 MAJID, ROSIE. The CBD (Central Business District) of Dacca: delimitation and internal structure. In Oriental Geographer 14,1 (1970) 44-63.

5. Social Problems and Social Welfare

25572 AFSARUDDIN, MOHAMMAD. Juvenile delinquency in East Pakistan. Dacca: Dept. of Sociology, U. of Dacca, 1965. 103p.

25573 AHMED, SALAHUDDIN. Studies in juvenile delinquency and crime in East Pakistan. Dacca: College of Social Welfare & Res. Centre, 1966. 143p.

25574 ALI AKBAR, M & AHMADULLAH MIA & SYED AHMED KHAN, ed. Studies in social needs and problems. Dacca: Social Welfare & Res. Centre, U. of Dacca, 1970. 89p.

25575 FAROUK, A. & MUHAMMAD ALI. The hardworking poor: a survey on how people use their time in Bangladesh. Dacca: Bureau of Econ. Res., U. of Dacca, 1977. 196p.

25576 HAMID, M. ABDUL, et al. CORR-Caritas, Bangladesh. Rajshahi: Dept. of Econ., Rajshahi U., 1976. 70p. (Rural dev. studies series, 4)

25577 LAURÉ, J. Joi Bangla! the children of Bangladesh. NY: Farrar, Straus & Giroux, 1974. 153p.

25578 MIA, AHMADULLAH, et al. Social stratification and social welfare services in emerging urban communities in Dacca. Dacca: Inst. of Social Welfare & Res., U. of Dacca, 1975. 101p.

25579 MIA, AHMADULLAH & MOHAMMED ALAUDDIN, eds. Problems of children and adolescents in Bangladesh. Dacca: Inst. of Social Welfare & Res., U. of Dacca, 1973. 106p.

25580 OLSEN, V.B. Daktar: diplomat in Bangladesh. Chicago: Moody Press, 1973. 352p.

25581 Private investment in social welfare: a study of registered voluntary social welfare agencies of Dacca and Chittagong Divisions sponsored and funded by the Planning Division, Government of Pakistan. Dacca: College of Social Welfare & Res. Centre, U. of Dacca, 1971. 184p.

25582 ROBINS, A.J. Voluntary social welfare agencies in Dacca: a critical appraisal. Dacca: College of Social Welfare & Res. Centre, 1962. 77p. (Social welfare studies, 1)

25583 Statistical profile of children and mothers in Bangladesh. Dacca: Inst. of Stat. Res. & Training, U. of Dacca, 1977. 80p.

6. Health Services and Family Planning
a. health and medical services

25584 ABDULLAH, MOHAMMAD. Nutrition surveillance of WFP Projects 2226 for vulnerable group feeding in distressed areas of Bangladesh: report on first phase. Dacca: Inst. of Nutrituion & Food Science, U. of Dacca, 1977. 67p.

25585 BRISCOE, J. The role of water supply in improving health in poor countries, with special reference to Bangladesh. Dacca: Cholera Res. Lab., 1977. 34p.

25586 CHEN, L.C., ed. Disaster in Bangladesh: health crisis in a developing nation. NY: OUP, 1973. 290p.

25587 MCCORMACK, W.M., et al. Endemic cholera in rural East Pakistan. In American J. of Epidemiology 89,4 (1969) 393-404.

25588 Nutrition survey of rural Bangladesh, 1975-76. Dacca: Inst. of Nutrition & Food Science, U. of Dacca, 1977. 237p.

25589 Survey of health, MCH, and family planning infrastructure in Bangladesh. Dacca: Min. of Health & Population Control, 1978. 2 v.

b. family planning

25590 AHMED, MOHIUDDIN & FATIMA AHMED. Male attitudes toward family limitation in East Pakistan. In Eugenics Q. 12 (1965) 209-26.

25591 BADRUD DUZA, M., et al. Dynamics of family and fertility: a comparative study of low and high fertility couples in Chittagong. Chittagong: Dept. of Sociology, U. of Chittagong, 1975. 59p.

25592 BANGLADESH. DIR. OF POPULATION CONTROL & FAMILY PLANNING. RESEARCH, EVAL., STAT. & PLANNING UNIT. Annotated bibliography on social, psychological research in family planning. 2nd ed. Dacca: 1978. 62p.

25593 BAYBASTHAPANA SHANGSAD LTD. A desk research report on family planning activities in Bangladesh, 1952-1974. Dacca: The Shangsad, 1974. 133p.

25594 ______. Study report on knowledge, attitude, and practice of family planning. Dacca: The Shangsad, 1975. 142p.

25595 BAZLUL KARIM, KAZI & ABDUN NOOR CHOWDHURY & GOLAM MORSHED AKHTER. Socio-economic study of three villages under zero population growth programme in Bogra District. Bogra: Rural Dev. Academy, 1977. 46p.

25596 COMMUNITY DEV. FOUNDATION. Impact of family planning through village leadership: an experimental project. Dacca: 1976. 78p.

25597 HUBER, S.C. Oral contraceptive users and their children: a health survey in rural Bangladesh. Dacca: Johns Hopkins U. Fertility Res. Project, 1977. 33p.

25598 KHAN, ATIQUR KHAN. Preliminary experience with a clinic-based oral contraceptive programme in rural Bangladesh. Dacca: Johns Hopkins U. Fertility Res. Project, 1976. 36p.

25599 ROBERTS, B.J., et al. Family planning survey in Dacca, East Pakistan. In Demography 2 (1965) 74-96.

25600 SEMINAR ON FAMILY PLANNING, 1st, DACCA, 1972. Proceedings. Dacca: Min. of Health & Family Planning,

1973. 925p.

25601 SIRAGELDIN, ISMAIL, et al. Family planning in Bangladesh: an empirical investigation. In BDS 3,1 (1975) 1-26.

25602 STOECKEL, J.E. Social and demographic correlates of contraceptive adoption in a rural area of East Pakistan. In Demography 5,1 (1968) 45-54.

25603 STOECKEL, J.E. & MOQBUL A. CHOUDHURY. Factors related to knowledge and practice of family planning in East Pakistani villages. In Social Biology 16 (1969) 29-38. [also in Pakistan J. of Family Planning 3,1 (1969) 60-73]

25604 ______. Family planning knowledge, attitudes, and practice in a rural area of East Pakistan. In Intl. R. of Sociology 1,2 (1971) 1-11.

25605 ______. Fertility, infant mortality, and family planning in rural Bangladesh. Dacca: OUP, 1973. 154p.

7. Education in Bangladesh since 1947
a. general studies

25606 AHMED, SALAHUDDIN. Men and matters. Dacca: Bangladesh Books Intl., 1980. 131p.

25607 BANGLADESH. BUREAU OF EDUC. INFO. & STAT. Education in Bangladesh.... Dacca: 1974. 37p.

25608 BANGLADESH. PLANNING CMSN. MANPOWER SECTION. An educational geography of Bangladesh: locational availability against ideal requirement. Dacca: 1974. 142p.

25609 BENGALI ACADEMY. What people read in East Pakistan: a survey.... Karachi: Natl. Book Centre, 1965. 91p. (Reading habits in Pakistan, 4)

25610 ______. What women read in East Pakistan, a survey.... Karachi: Natl. Book Centre, 1964. 60p.

25611 EAST PAKISTAN. EAST BENGAL EDUC. SYSTEM RECONSTRUCTION CMTEE. Report. Dacca: Supt. Govt. Printing, 1952. 445p.

25612 GERARD, R. & MEHERUNNESSA ISLAM & MEHRAJ JAHAN. Training for women in Bangladesh: an inventory and sample survey of training programmes. Dacca: UNICEF, Women's Dev. Programme, 1977. 100p.

25613 ISLAM, SHAMIMA. Women's education in Bangladesh: needs and issues. Dacca: Foundation for Res. on Educ. Planning & Dev., 1977. 145p.

25614 SHARAFUDDIN, ABDULLA AL-MUTI, ed. Education for all; papers and proceedings of the symposia, East Pakistan Education Week, 1966-67. Dacca: Symposium Cmtee., East Pakistan Educ. Week, 1968. 226p.

25615 SYED, MOHAMMAD ABU. Public libraries in East Pakistan: yesterday & today. Dacca: Green, 1968. 116p.

b. higher education; University of Dacca (est. 1921)

25616 BANGLADESH. UNIV. GRANTS CMSN. Role, functions, and procedure. Dacca: 1977. 53p.

25617 BANGLADESH. UNIV. INQUIRY CMSN. Report, 1976-78. Dacca: Min. of Educ., 1979. 1228p. [Chm., Zahirul Huq]

25618 HAKIM, ABDUL. The University of Dacca. In JPHS 16, 1&4 (1968) 46-61, 231-41.

25619 JILANI, GHULAM. From college to university; a study based on the findings of a research project on high percentage of failures in examinations in East Pakistan. 2nd ed. Lahore: U. of the Panjab, 1968. 377p.

25620 ______. Teacher-student relationships at the Dacca University. Dacca: U. of Dacca, 1961. 206p.

25621 Overviews on university education and research in science in Bangladesh. Dacca: Univ. Grants Cmsn., 1977. 114p.

25622 RAHMAN, N. MIZANUR, et al. What university students think?: a profile of Chittagong University students. Chittagong: Dept. of Sociology, U. of Chittagong, 1975. 48p.

25623 ROBINSON, E.A.G. The functions of a social science research council in Bangladesh: some comments. Dacca: Ford Foundation, 1974. 35p.

25624 SATTAR, E. Socio-economic survey of Dacca University students. Dacca: Univ. Grants Cmsn., 1975. 65p.

25625 STOCK, A.G. Memoirs of Dacca University, 1947-51. Dacca: Green Book House, 1973. 202p.

25626 TALUKDER, M.A.H. , ed. Rajshahi University students and the Bangladesh liberation struggle; a survey report. Rajshahi: Rajshahi U., 1973. 99p.

c. elementary and secondary education

25627 DACCA UNIV. INST. OF EDUC. & RES. Teachers in East Pakistan. Karachi: MPGOP, 1972. 237p. (Natl. Cmsn. on Manpower & Educ., Res. study, 13)

25628 ISLAM, TAHERUL. Social justice and the education system of Bangladesh. Dacca: Bureau of Econ. Res., U. of Dacca, 1975. 120p.

25629 NATL. FOUNDATION FOR RES. ON HUMAN RESOURCE DEV. Primary education network in Bangladesh: capacity and utilization. Dacca: 1979. 275p.

25630 UNIV. OF DACCA. INST. OF EDUC. & RES. Survey of primary schools and evaluation of primary school agriculture programme in Bangladesh: a research report. Dacca: 1977. 2 v.

d. rural education and literacy (1974 literacy 22.2%)

25631 ISLAM, SHAMINA. Strengthening non-formal education for women in Bangladesh. In R. Jahan & H. Papanek, eds. Women and development. Dacca: Bangladesh Inst. of Law and Intl. Affairs, 1979, 379-401.

25632 KHATUN, SHARIFA. Women's education in a rural community in Bangladesh. In R. Jahan & H. Papanek, eds. Women and development. Dacca: Bangladesh Inst. of Law and Intl. Affiars, 1979, 253-74.

25633 MOHAMMAD SOLAIMAN. The Comilla rural education experiment. Comilla: BARD, 1975. 36p.

25634 SADEQUE, MOHAMMAD. A study of the educated rural youth. Rajshahi: Dept. of Social Work, Rajshahi U., 1978. 105p.

25635 YUNUS, MUHAMMAD. A report on the programmes of the Mass Education Division, CURDP. Chittagong: Chittagong U. Rural Dev. Project, 1974. 35p. (CURDP report, 5)

E. Religions of Bangladesh: Islam, Hinduism, Buddhism

25636 BARUA, R.B. Rituals and festivals of the Buddhists of East Pakistan. In JASP 8 (1963) 13-25.

25637 ______. The Uposatha ceremony of the Buddhist monks. In DUS 12,A (1964) 73-87.

25638 BECHERT, H. Contemporary Buddhism in Bengal and Tripura. In Educational Miscellany (Tripura) 4 (Dec. 1967-Mar. 1968) 1-25.

25639 HAROON, SHARIF ABDULLAH, ed. Thoughts on Islam: an anthology. Dacca: Islamic Academy, 1970. 130p.

25640 KARIM, A.K. NAZMUL. Some aspects of popular beliefs among Muslims of Bengal. In EA 9,1 (1955) 29-41.

25641 MATIN, ABDUL, ed. Second General Conference, Bangladesh Darshan Samiti (Bangladesh Philosophical Association), Rajshahi, March 9-11, 1975. Dacca: The Assoc., 1977. 219p.

25642 RAHMAN, M. MUSTAFIZUR. Religious education in Bangladesh. In Islam & the Modern Age 8,3 (1977) 77-88.

25643 ELLICKSON, J. A believer among believers: the religious beliefs, practices and meanings in a village in Bangladesh. Ph.D. diss., Michigan State U., 1972. 207p. [UM 72-22,212]

25644 ROY, A. The social factors in the making of Bengali Islam. In SA 3 (1973) 23-35.

F. Literature and Media in Bangladesh

1. Bengali Literature since 1947

25645 AMIN, RAZIA KHAN. Modern poetry in East Pakistan: a survey. In Mahfil 3,4 (1967) 62-84.

25646 ASHRAF, SYED ALI. Bengali poetry since independence; tradition and change. In Pakistan Q. 15 (1967) 289-90, 318.

25647 CHOWDHURY, KABIR, ed. & tr. Fifty poems from Bangladesh. Calcutta: United Writers, 1977. 87p.

25648 CHOWDHURY, MUNIER. Three plays. Dacca: Bengali Academy, 1972. 76p.

25649 NANDY, P., tr. Bangla Desh: a voice of a new nation; fifty poets, seventyfive poems. Calcutta: Dialogue Pub., 1971. 48p.

25650 NOOR, ABUL ASHRAF. Poems of the unsung from Bangladesh. Dacca: BFH Pub. House, 1973. 63p.

25651 RAHMAN, SHAMSUR. A word called freedom: poems tr. by P. Nandy. In IL 14,4 (1971) 4-38.

25652 RASHID, M. HARUNUR, ed. Three poets: Shamsur Rahman, Al Mahmud, Shaheed Quaderi. Dacca: Bangladesh Books Intl., 1976. 73p. (Poems from Bangladesh series)

25653 TAMBIMUTTU, T., comp. Poems from Bangla Desh: the voice of a new nation. Tr. by P. Nandy. London: Lyrebird Press, 1972. 80p.

2. Folk Literature

25654 ABBASI, MUSTAFA ZAMAN, ed. Folkloric Bangladesh. Dacca: Bangladesh Folklore Parishad, 1979. 80p.

25655 BOULTON, J. Eastern Bengali ballads. In Bengali Academy J. 2,1 (1971) 45-75.

25656 CHOWDHURY, KABIR. Folktales of Bangladesh. Dacca: Bangla Academy, 1972-. [to be 2 v.]

25657 DAMANT, G.H. Tales from Bangladesh. Ed. by Ashraf Siddiqui. Dacca: Bangladesh Books Intl., 1976. 135p. [1st pub. in IA, 1872-75]

25658 JASIMUDDIN. Folk tales of Bangladesh. Tr. of his Bangalir hasir galpa, by C. Painter & Hasna Jasimuddin. 2nd ed. Dacca: OUP, 1974. 105p.

25659 SEN, D.C. Eastern Bengal ballads, Mymensingh. Calcutta: U. of Calcutta, 1923. 4 v.

25660 SIDDIQUI, ASHRAF. Folkloric Bangladesh: a collection of essays on folk literature of Bangladesh. Dacca: Bangla Academy, 1976. 94p.

25661 ______. Our folklore, our heritage. Dacca: Barnamichhil, 1977. 136p.

3. Journalism and the Press

25662 KHAN, ATIQUZZAMAN. A study of the newspaper industry in East Pakistan. In DUS 14,A (1966) 1-34.

25663 SHAMSUR RAHMAN, GHAZI. Coypright law in Bangladesh. Dacca: Natl. Book Centre, Bangladesh, 1979. 197p.

25664 TOFAYELL, Z.A. The journalist and Bangladesh. Dacca: Ziaunnahar, 1972. 112p. [History of journalism]

G. Art of Bangladesh

25665 ABEDIN, ZAINUL. Zainul Abedin. Ed. by Muhammad Sirajul Islam. Dacca: Bangladesh Shilpakala Academy, 1977. 64p. (Art of Bangladesh series, 1)

25666 ASAFUDDOWLA, M., ed. Fourth National Art Exhibition. Dacca: Bangladesh Shilpakala Academy, 1978. 32p. (Contemporary art series of Bangladesh, 11)

25667 BASHIR, MURTAZA. Murtaja Baseer. Ed. by Syed Zillur Rahman. Dacca: Bangladesh Shilpakala Academy, 1979. 21p. (Contemporary art series of Bangladesh, 14)

25668 CHOWDHURY, QAYYUM. Qayyum Chowdhury. Ed. by M. Sirajul Islam. Dacca: Bangladesh Shilpakala Academy, 1977. 32p. (Contemporary art series of Bangladesh, 6)

25669 Contemporary art of Bangladesh. Dacca: Bangladesh Shilpakala Academy, 1978. 32p.

25670 HUQ, ANWARUL. Anwarul Huq. Ed. by M. Sirajul Islam. Dacca: Bangladesh Shilpakala Academy, 1976. 22p. (Contemporary art series of Bangladesh, 4)

25671 ISLAM, M. SIRAJUL, ed. Art in Bangladesh, 76-77. Dacca: Bangladesh Shilpakala Academy, 1977. 37p. (Contemporary art series of Bangladesh, 7)

25672 ______, ed. Life in Bangladesh. Dacca: Bangladesh Shilpakala Academy, 1976. 43p. (Contemporary art series of Bangladesh, 2)

25673 ______, ed. Sculpture in Bangladesh. Dacca: Bangladesh Shilpakala Academy, 1976. 22p. (Contemporary art series of Bangladesh, 5)

25674 ______, ed. Young artist, '76. Dacca: Bangladesh Shilpakala Academy, 1976. 22p. (Contemporary art series of Bangladesh, 3)

25675 JAHANGIR, BURHANUDDIN KHAN. Contemporary painters, Bangladesh. Dacca: Bangla Academy, 1974. 71p. + 16pl.

25676 RAHMAN, SYED ZILLUR. Fifth National Art Exhibition. Dacca: Bangladesh Shilpakala Academy, 1980. 8p. + 12pl. (Contemporary art series of Bangladesh, 16)

III. ASSAM: THE PLAINS AND FOOTHILLS OF THE BRAHMAPUTRA VALLEY

A. General and Political History since 1826

1. Assam under the British (annexed 1826)

a. general studies

25677 BAROOAH, N.K. David Scott in North-East India, 1802-1831; a study in British paternalism. ND: Munshiram, 1970. 278p.

25678 BARPUJARI, H.K. Assam in the days of the Company, 1826-1858.... Gauhati: Lawyer's Book Stall, 1963. 312p.

25679 ______, ed. Political history of Assam. Gauhati: Govt. of Assam, 1977. 2 v., 293, 394p. [covers 1826-1939]

25680 BHUYAN, S.K. Anglo-Assamese relations, 1771-1826.... Gauhati: Lawyer's Book Stall, 1974. 641p.

25681 DE, A. The Muslims as a factor in Assam politics, 1826-1947. In BPP 96,2 (1977) 114-20.

25682 GUHA, A. Impact of Bengal Renaissance on Assam 1825-1875. In IESHR 9,3 (1972) 288-304.

25683 HUNTER, W.W. A statistical account of Assam. Delhi: B.R. Pub. Corp., 1975. 2 v., 420, 490p. [Rpt. 1879 ed.]

25684 LAHIRI, R.M. The annexation of Assam, 1824-1854. Calcutta: KLM, 1975. 250p. [1st pub. 1954]

25685 PEMBERTON, R.B. Report on the Eastern frontier of British India. Gauhati: Dept. of Hist. & Antiquarian Studies in Assam, 1966. 269 + 123p. [1st pub. 1835]

25686 SCOTT, DAVID. The correspondence of David Scott. Ed. by C.H. Philips. London: Royal Hist. Soc., 1951. 2 v.

b. accounts by travellers and officials

25687 BUCHANAN, F.H. An account of Assam, first compiled in 1807-1814. Ed. by S.K. Bhuyan. Gauhati: Dept. of Hist. & Antiquarian Studies, Assam, 1963. 104p. [Rpt. 1940 ed.]

25688 BUTLER, J. Travels and adventures in the province of Assam.... Delhi: Vivek, 1978. 272p. [Rpt. 1855 ed.]

25689 M'COSH, J. Topography of Assam. Delhi: Sanskaran Prakashak, 1975. 166p. [Rpt. 1837 ed.]

25690 ROBINSON, W. A descriptive account of Asam: with a sketch of the local geography and a concise history of the tea-plant of Asam.... Delhi: Sanskaran Prakashak, 1975. 433p. [Rpt. 1841 ed.]

c. administrative studies and local government, 1826-1947

25691 BHATTACHARJEE, K.K. Constitution of Chief Commissionership in Assam. In JIH 57,1 (1979) 97-128.

25692 DATTA-RAY, B. Assam Secretariat, 1874-1947: an administrative history of North-East India. Calcutta: K.P. Bagchi, 1978. 287p.

25693 SINGH, B.P. Evolution of the office of the Deputy Commissioner in Assam. In IJPA 23,4 (1977) 890-912.

25694 VENKATA RAO, V. A hundred years of local self-government in Assam. 2nd ed., rev. & enl. Gauhati: Bani Prakash Mandir, 1965. 551p.

d. nationalist movement and provincial politics

25695 BARUA, H. August revolution in Assam. Gauhati: Anu Barua, 1978. 26p. [1942]

25696 DIHINGIA, H. Assam's struggles against British rule, 1826-1863. ND: Asian Pub. Services, 1980. 157p.

25697 DUTT, K.N. Landmarks of the freedom struggle in Assam. Gauhati: Lawyer's Book Stall, 1969. 138p.

25698 GUHA, A. East Bengal immigrants and Maulana Abdul Khan Bhasani in Assam politics, 1928-47. In IESHR 13,4 (1976) 419-53.

25699 ______. Planter raj to swaraj: freedom struggle and electoral politics in Assam, 1826-47. ND: ICHR, 1977. 392p.

2. Government and Politics of Assam since 1947
a. states reorganization: separation of the tribal hill areas from Assam [see also Chap. Sixteen, VII.]

25700 BHATTACHARYA, B.K. A separate Assam hills state, what does it mean? In EPW 2,9 (1967) 491-94.

25701 CHURCH, R.A. Roots of separatism in Assam hill districts. In EPW 4,17 (1969) 727-32.

25702 DOMMEN, A.J. Separatist tendencies in eastern India. In AS 7,10 (1967) 726-39.

25703 GARG, J.P. & B.N. SINGH. Reorganisation of Assam: a study in the politics of regional alienation in India. In United Asia 21,2 (1969) 77-82.

25704 MUKERJEE, D. Assam reorganization. In AS 9 (1969) 297-311.

25705 SHARMA, P.K. Reorganization of Assam. In J. of African and Asian Studies 2,1 (1968) 37-46.

b. general studies of Assam politics

25706 CHAUHAN, S.K. Party preferences: a study of political attitudes in upper Assam. In MI 52,4 (1972) 371-78.

25707 ______. Social structure and political consciousness: a study of political attitudes in upper Assam. In Interdiscipline 8,4 (1971) 35-42.

25708 DEKA, K.M. Profiles of women in Assam [state politics]. In Vina Mazumdar, ed. Symbols of power.... Bombay: Allied, 1979, 191-99.

25709 NAIDU, M.A. Dev Kant Borooah: a political biography. Hyderabad: Naidu, 1976. 76p.

25710 VENKATA RAO, V. Assam state politics from 1947 to 1967. In JUG 21-23,1 (1970-72) 1-54.

25711 ______. Congress politics in Assam. In IJPS 26,4 (1965) 72-82.

c. election studies

25712 ASSAM, INDIA. DIR. OF INFO. & PUBLIC RELATIONS. General elections, Assam Legislative Assembly, 1978: results. Gauhati: 1978. 68p.

25713 PRABHAKER, M.S. More elections. In EPW 9,6/8 (1974) 181-84.

25714 VENKATA RAO, V. Assam. In S.V. Kogekar & R.L. Park, eds. Report on the Indian general elections 1951-52. Bombay: Popular, 1956, 1-16.

25715 ______. General elections in Assam. In PSR 6,3/4 & 7,1/2 (1967-68) 119-38.

d. local government and panchayati raj

25716 ASSAM, INDIA. DIR. OF EVAL. & MONITORING. Study on the working of the mahkuma parishad, Silchar. Dispur: 1977. 118p. (Its eval.report, 48) [panchayat at sub-divisional level]

25717 ASSN. OF VOLUNTARY AGENCIES FOR RURAL DEV. Design of a panchayat plan: Pub Kumarikata, District Kamrup, Assam. ND: AVARD, 1978. 144p.

25718 BARDOLOI, U.N. Local finance in Assam. Gauhati: Dutta Baruah, 1972. 291p.

25719 JAIN, S.P. Panchayati raj in Assam. Hyderabad: NICD, 1976. 132p.

25720 SAIKIA, P.D. Village leadership in north-east India: assessment and conclusion on case-studies in six villages. In MI 43 (1963) 92-99.

25721 VENKATA RAO, V. Municipal administration in Assam. In JNAA 16,2 (1971) 27-34.

B. The Assam Economy since 1826

1. Economic History; Dominance of the Tea Plantations

25722 ANTROBUS, H.A. A history of the Assam Company, 1839-1953. Edinburgh: the author, 1957. 501p.

25723 ______. A history of the Jorehaut Tea Co., Ltd., 1859-1946. London: Tea & Rubber Mail, 1947. 368p.

25724 BARKER, G.M. A tea-planter's life in Assam. Calcutta: Thacker, 1884. 247p.

25725 DEB, K. Impact of plantations on the agrarian structure of the Brahmaputra Valley. Calcutta: Centre for Studies in Social Sciences, Calcutta, 1979. 54p. (Its occ. paper, 24)

25726 FLEX, O. Pflanzerleben in Indien: Kulturgeschichtliche Bilder aus Assam. Berlin: 1873. 254p.

25727 GANGULY, DWARKANATH. Slavery in British dominion. Comp. by K.L. Chattopadhyay. Ed. by S.K. Kunda. Calcutta: Jijnasa, 1972. 102p. [tr. from Bengali]

25728 GUHA, A. A big push without a takeoff: a case study of Assam, 1871-1901. In IESHR 5 (1968) 199-221.

25729 ______. Colonisation of Assam: second phase 1840-1859. In IESHR 4 (1967) 289-318.

25730 ______. Colonisation of Assam: years of transitional crisis (1825-40). In IESHR 5 (1968) 125-40.

25731 RAMSDEN, A.R. Assam planter; tea planting and hunting in the Assam jungle. London: J. Gifford, 1945. 159p.

25732 SARMA, M.C. & R. MEHROTRA. The growth of public expenditures and levels of economic activity in Assam. In Assam Econ. J. 3,1 (1977) 126-34.

25733 SHARMA, S.K. Origin and growth of the tea industry in Assam. In Tapan Raychaudhuri, ed. Contributions to Indian economic history. Calcutta: KLM, 1963, 118-43.

2. Demography (1981 est. pop. 19,903,000)

25734 BORDOLOI, U.N. The 1971 population census of Assam: an analysis. In JUG 21-23, 1 (1970-72) 55-61.

25735 DASS, S.K. Immigration and demographic transformation of Assam, 1891-1981. In EPW 15,19 (1980) 850-59.

25736 GOSWAMI, H. Mortality patterns in the Brahmaputra Valley of Assam, 1881-1931. In Assam Econ. J. 4,1 (1978) 83-88.

3. Surveys of Economic Conditions since 1947; Flood Control

25737 GOSWAMI, A. Prices and cost of living in India: a case study of Assam. Delhi: Jain Book Depot, 1979. 231p.

25738 KOULI, R.M. Assam's grim battle against flood. In Assam Info. 30 (1978) 39-45.

25739 NCAER. Techno-economic survey of Assam. ND: 1962. 277p.

25740 RANGASAMI, A. The paupers of Kolisabhita Hindupara: report on a famine. In EPW 10,5-7 (1975) 267-82.

25741 SAHARIA, B.R., ed. Assam, 1977: an exciting tale of Assam's triumphant journey (1947-77) from backwardness to modernity. Gauhati: Dir. of Info. & Public Relations, 1978. 55p.

4. Economic Development and Planning

25742 Assam after independence; a review of Assam's achievements in the various fields of activities during the nineteen year-span of freedom. Shillong: Dir. of Info. & Public Relations, 1966. 72p.

25743 ASSAM. ECON. & STAT. DEPT. Economic background for formulation of fourth five year plan of Assam. Shillong: 1966. 66p.

25744 ASSAM. PLANNING & DEV. DEPT. Third five-year plan, Assam 1961-66. Shillong: 1962? 2 v.

25745 ______. Draft outline; fifth five-year plan. Shillong: 1973. 3 v. in 1.

25746 GOSWAMI, P.C. The economic development of Assam. Bombay: Asia, 1963. 351p.

25747 SARMA, J.N. Problems of economic development in Assam. In EPW 1,7 (1966) 281-86.

5. agriculture in Assam since 1826
a. general studies of agricultural development

25748 AGRO-ECON. RES. CENTRE FOR NORTH EAST INDIA, JORHAT. Cooperative farming in Assam: problems and prospects. Jorhat: dist. KLM, 1969. 163p.

25749 ASSAM AGRI. CMSN. Report of the Assam Agricultural Commission, June 1975. Gauhati: State Planning Board, 1975. 232p. [Chm., L.S. Negi]

25750 ASSAM. DIR. OF ECON. & STAT. World agricultural census, 1970-71: Assam. Gauhati: 1976. 221p.

25751 ASSAM. DIR. OF EVAL. Report on crash scheme for rural employment. Shillong: 1975. 47p. (Its Eval. study, 28)

25752 ______. Report on minor irrigation in Assam (Flood Control and Irrigation Department). Shillong: 1971. 42p. (Its Eval. report, 5)

25753 ______. Report on the Small and Marginal Farmers and Landless Agriculturists Development Agency. Shillong: 1974-1976. 4 v. in 1.

25754 ASSAM. DIR. OF EVAL. & MONITORING. Study on the functioning of the gaon panchayat level multipurpose cooperative societies. Dispur: 1976. 63p.

25755 AWASTHI, R.C. Economics of tea industry in India: with special reference to Assam. Gauhati: United Pub., 1975. 474p.

25756 DAS, M.M. Population pressure and intensity of cropping in Assam. In GRI 41,2 (1979) 105-14.

25757 INDIA (REP.). CMTEE. ON PLAN PROJECTS. MINOR IRRIGATION TEAM. Report on minor irrigation works in Assam State. ND: 1965. 39p.

25758 RESERVE BANK OF INDIA. Review of agricultural development and co-operative credit in Assam, 1961-1976. Bombay: RBI, 1978. 99p.

25759 SAIKIA, P.D. & A.K. BORA. Impact of modern agricultural technology on small farmers - a case study of Assam. In IJAE 30,3 (1975) 224-29.

25760 SAIKIA, P.D. & U. PHUKAN. A study of loans advanced by land mortgage banks and their utilisation in Assam. Jorhat: Agro-Econ. Res. Centre for NE India, 1969. 89p.

25761 SARMA, M.C. Exploration on the land utilization of Kamrup. In Deccan Geographer 8,1/2 (1970) 15-25.

25762 SHARMA, S.C. A survey of the rural economic conditions in Lakhimpur. Shillong: Dept. of Econ. & Stat., 1954. 96p. (Its Rural econ. survey series, 3)

b. land tenure and reform

25763 DUTTA, N.C. Land problems and land reforms in Assam. Delhi: S. Chand, 1968. 159p.

25764 MUKHERJEE, A. Agrarian conditions in Assam, 1880-90: a case study of five districts in the Brahmaputra Valley. In IESHR 16,2 (1979) 207-32.

6. Industry and Labor

25765 ASSAM. DIR. OF EVAL. Report on the industrial estates in Assam. Shillong: 1969. 87p. (Its Eval. report, 8)

25766 ASSAM. DIR. OF INDUSTRIES. Industrial potentiality of Assam and its development. Shillong: 1962. 163p.

25767 ASSAM. FINANCE DEPT. ASSAM LABOUR ENQUIRY CMTEE., 1921. Report. Shillong: 1922. 144p.

25768 BARUAH, B. Investment, employment and output relations and inter-district variations in industrial growth of Assam, 1962-69. In Assam Econ. J. 3,1 (1977) 135-45.

25769 DIBRUGARH UNIV. DEPT. OF ECON. RESEARCH PROJECT ON UNEMPLOYMENT. Survey of unemployment in selected rural and urban areas of Assam: report of findings. ND: Govt. of India, Expert Cmtee. on Unemployment, Min. of Labour & Rehabilitation, 1975. 121p.

25770 Jogighopa paper mill - a survey. In Assam Info. 27,1-2 (1975) 6-10.

25771 NCAER. Industrial programmes for the Fourth Plan for Assam. ND: 1966. 181p.

25772 Oilfields of Assam; a guide. Digboi: Assam Oil Co., 1958. 253p.

25773 SINHA, R.P. The liquid gold of Assam. In Yojana 17,8 (1973) 329-37.

25774 THAVANI, V.D. & S. SARANGAPANI. Report on urban employment and unemployment survey, Assam, 1955. Gauhati: Gauhati U., 1961. 149p.

C. Society and Social Change in Assam since 1826

1. Social Categories of Assam
a. general studies

25775 CHAUHAN, S.K. Caste, class and power: an analysis of the stratification system in rural upper Assam. In EA 25,2 (1972) 149-60.

25776 ______. Caste hierarchy in three villages of upper Assam. In MI 52,1 (1972) 39-45.

25777 Handbook of census of scheduled castes and scheduled tribes population of Assam, based on the census report of 1971. Shillong: Gen. Admin., 197-. 9 v. in 5.

25778 TEA DISTRICTS LABOUR ASSN. Handbook of castes and tribes employed on tea estates in North-East India. Calcutta: TDLA, 1924. 360p.

b. Bengalis in Assam (19.7% of pop. in 1971): unwelcome immigrants, Hindu and Muslim

25779 The Assam problem. In Gandhi Marg 1,12 (1980) 793-97.

25780 BARUAH, S.K. Cudgel of chauvinism, or tangled nationality question. In EPW 15,11 (1980) 543-45.

25781 GOSWAMI, P.C. Immigration into Assam. In EPW 15,44 (1973) 1827-33.

25782 HAQUE, MOHAMMED NAZRUL. Foreigners in Assam: myth and reality. In Secular Democracy 12 (1979) 27-33.

c. Assamese Hindus and Muslims

25783 IRSHAD ALI, A.N.M. Kinship and marriage among the Assamese Muslims. In Imtiaz Ahmad, ed. Family, kinship, and marriage among the Muslims in India. ND: Manohar, 1976, 1-26.

25784 THOMPSON, R.C.M. Assam Valley: beliefs and customs of the Assamese Hindus. London: Luzac, 1948. 96p.

d. Tribals of Assam [see also Chap. Sixteen, VII.]

25785 BARKATAKI, S., ed. Tribes of Assam. ND: NBT, 1969. 167p.

25786 DANDA, D.G. Among the Dimasa of Assam: an ethnographic study. ND: Sterling, 1978. 192p.

25787 ENDLE, S. The Kacharis. London: Macmillan, 1911. 128p.

25788 GOKULANATHAN, P.P. Achievement-related motivation among tribal adolescent pupils. Bombay: Himalaya Pub. House, 1979. 154p.

25789 KAR, R.K. A migrant tribe in a tea plantation in India: economic profile. In Anthropos 74,5/6 (1979) 770-84.

25790 ______. A tribe in the context of a tea industry in India: some preliminary considerations and observations. In Anthropos 71,5/6 (1976) 868-77.

25791 SAIKIA, P.C. The Dibongiyas: social and religious life of a priestly community. Delhi: B.R., 1976. 109p.

25792 SAIKIA, P.D. Changes in Mikir society; a report on socio-economic resurvey of Kanther in the United Mikir and N. Cachar Hills District, Assam. Jorhat, Assam: Agro-Econ. Res. Center for NE India, 1968. 82p.

25793 SHARMA THAKUR, G.C. The plains tribes of Lakhimpur, Dibrugarh, Sibsagar and Nowgong. Shillong: Tribal Res. Inst., Govt. of Assam, 1972. 102p.

2. Villages and Rural Society

25794 AGRO-ECON. RES. CENTER FOR NORTH EAST INDIA, JORHAT. Rural life in Assam hills; case studies of four villages. Jorhat: dist. KLM, 1969. 293p.

25795 BARUA, I. Changing occupational structure in two villages in Assam. In MI 59,2 (1979) 106-19.

25796 ______. Social relations in an Ahom village. ND: Sterling, 1978. 187p.

25797 BHADRA, R.K. Emerging patterns of agrarian classes in rural Assam. In EA 32,4 (1979) 273-85.

25798 BORA, C.K. & D.K. BURAGOHAIN. Khonajan: a village resurvey report of an immigrant village in Lakhimpur District of Assam, 1963-1968. Jorhat: Agro-Econ. Res. Centre for NE India, 1974. 66p. (Indian village studies: Village resurvey, 6)

25799 GOSWAMI, P.C. A study in rural change in Assam: Dispur; a report on socio-economic resurvey of a village in Kamrup District. Jorhat: Agro-Econ. Res. Centre for NE India, 1967. 165p.

25800 GUHA, A. Assamese peasant society in the late 19th century: structure and trends. Calcutta: Centre for Studies in Social Sciences, 1979. 82p. (Its occ. papers, 25)

25801 JAIN, S.P. & N.Y. NAIDU. Panchayati raj and social change: a study in Assam. Hyderabad: NICD, 1978. 101p.

25802 RATHA, S.N. Caste and occupation in two pre-urban Assamese villages. In EA 21 (1968) 155-65.

4. Social Services, Health, and Education

25803 ASSAM. DEPT. OF PUBLIC INSTRUCTION. Report on the Second Educational Survey in the state of Assam, 1965. Shillong: Dept. of Educ., 1967. 1 v.

25804 ASSAM. DIR. OF EVAL. Report on the drinking water supply programme in the rural areas in Assam. Shillong: 1969. 87p. (Its Eval. report, 6)

25805 ______. Report on the polytechnic institutes in Assam. Shillong: Assam Govt. Press, 1971. 65p. (Its Eval. report, 4)

D. Religions of Assam: Hinduism, Islam, Folk Religions

25806 BARPUJARI, H.K. Management and control of the religious endowments in Assam. In JUG 15,1 (1964) 35-44.

25807 BARUA, H. & J.D. BAVEJA. The fairs and festivals of Assam. Gauhati: B.N. Dutt Barua, 1956. 61p.

25808 DOWNS, F.S. The mighty works of God: a brief history of the Council of Baptist Churches in North East India: the mission period, 1836-1950. Gauhati: Christian Literature Centre, 1971. 252p.

25809 ______. Missionaries and the language controversy in Assam. In IChHR 8,1 (1979) 29-69.

25810 GOSWAMI, M.C. An annual shamanistic dance (Deodha nach) at Kamakhya, Assam. In JUG 11,2 (1960) 37-60.

25811 KAKATI, B.K. The mother goddess Kāmākhyā: or, Studies in the fusion of Aryan and primitive beliefs of Assam. Gauhati: Lawyer's Book Stall, 1967. 83p. [Rpt. 1948 ed.]

25812 RAJKHOWA, B. Assamese popular superstitions and Assamese demonology. Gauhati: Dept. of Folklore Res., Gauhati U., 1973. 163p.

25813 SARMA, D. Religious fairs and festivals of Assam. In J. of the Assam Res. Soc. 18 (1968) 22-45.

E. Modern Assamese Literature

1. General Studies

25814 BARUA, B.K. Modern Assamese literature. Gauhati: Lawyer's Book Stall, 1957. 101p.

25815 BARUA, D.K. Assamese literary magazines. In IWT 3,4 (1969) 7-12.

25816 BARUA, H., ed. Modern Assamese poetry; an anthology. ND: Kavita, 1960. 69p.

25817 BARUA, N. Assamese. In K.R. Srinivasa Iyengar, ed. Indian literature since independence. ND: Sahitya Akademi, 1973, 1-9.

25818 BAHALI, S. Tragic outlook in Assamese drama. Delhi: Shree, 1980. 160p.

25819 BORA, P.P. Cinema in Assam. Gauhati: Performing Arts Centre, 1978. 47p.

25820 BORRA, I.N. Bolinarayan Borrah: his life, work, and musings. Calcutta: 1967. 293p.

25821 GOSWAMI, P.D. Raghunath Chaudhary (1879-1967). In IL 11,1 (1968) 113-24.

25822 KULSHRESHTHA, C.M. Navakanta Barua's poetry: a reappraisal. In IL 22,3 (1979) 108-14.

2. Lakshminath Bezbarua (1868-1938): Nationalist Poet, Dramatist, and Fiction Writer

25823 Assamese language and literature and Sahityarathi Lakshminath Bezbaroa. Delhi: Sahityarathi Lakshminath Bezbaroa Birth Centenary Celebration Cmtee., 1968. 37p.

25824 BARUA, H. Lakshminath Bezbaroa. ND: Sahitya Akademi, 1967. 72p.

25825 BEZBAROA, LAKSHMINATH. Tales of a grandfather from Assam. Tr. by A.D. Mukherjea. Bangalore: Indian Inst. of Culture, 1955. 130p.

25826 A bibliography: Lakshminath Bezbaroa (1868-1938). In IL 11,3 (1968) 43-46.

25827 NEOG, M., ed. Lakshminath Bezbaroa, the sāhityarathī of Assam. Gauhati: Gauhati U., 1972. 272p.

3. Folk Literature

25828 DAS, J. Folklore of Assam. ND: NBT, 1972. 142p.

25829 GOSWAMI, P.D. Ballads and tales of Assam: a study of the folklore of Assam. 2nd ed. Gauhati: U. of Gauhati, 1970. 271p.

25830 ______. Bihu songs of Assam. Gauhati: Lawyer's Book Stall, 1957. 174p.

25831 ______. Folk-literature of Assam; an introductory survey. 2nd ed. Gauhati: Dept. of Hist. & Antiquarian Studies in Assam, 1965. 111p.

25832 PAKRASI, M. Folk tales of Assam. Delhi: Sterling, 1969. 119p. (Folk tales of India series, 3)

16

The Himalayas and Eastern Mountain Rim of India, Nepal and Bhutan: Fringes of Tibetan, Buddhist, and Southeast Asian Cultures, 1816–

I. GENERAL STUDIES OF THE NORTHERN AND EASTERN BORDERLAND SINCE 1800

A. Historical Accounts and Studies

25834 LLOYD, WILLIAM, Sir. Narrative of a journey from Caunpoor to the Boorendo Pass, in the Himalaya Mountains, via Gwalior, Agra, Delhi, and Sirhind. London: J. Madden, 1846. 2 v. [1st pub. 1840]

25835 MEHRA, P.L. Sikkim and Bhutan: an historical conspectus. In JIH 46 (1968) 89-124.

25836 RAWAT, I.S. Indian explorers of the nineteenth century; account of explorations in the Himalayas, Tibet, Mongolia, and central Asia. ND: PDMIB, 1973. 228p.

25837 SHERRING, C.A. Western Tibet and the British borderland; the sacred country of Hindus and Buddhists... London: E. Arnold, 1906. 376p.

25838 TEMPLE, R. Travels in Nepal and Sikkim. Kathmandu: Ratna Pustak Bhandar, 1977. 131p. + 15 pl. (Bibliotheca Himalayica, 20) [1st pub. 1887]

B. Political Studies

25840 CHAUHAN, R.S. Struggle and change in South Asian monarchies. ND: Chetana Pub., 1977. 262p. [Nepal, Sikkim & Bhutan]

25841 GOYAL, N. Prelude to India, a study of India's relations with Himalaya states. ND: Cambridge Book & Stationery Store, 1964. 179p.

25842 HECKER, H. Sikkim und Bhutan: die verfassungsgeschichtliche und politische Entwicklung der indischen Himalaya-Protektorate. Frankfurt: A. Metzner Verlag, 1970. 73p.

25843 RAHUL, RAM. The Himalaya as a frontier. ND: Vikas, 1978. 154p.

25844 ______. The Himalaya borderland. Delhi: Vikas, 1970. 157p.

25845 ______. The system of administration in the Himalaya. In AS 9,9 (1969) 694-702.

25846 ROSE, L.E. The Himalayan border states: "buffers" in transition. In AS 3,2 (1963) 116-21.

25847 ZETLAND, L.J.L. DUNDAS, 2nd Marquis of. Himalayan Bhutan, Sikhim and Tibet. Delhi: Ess Ess, 1977. 267p. [Rpt. 1923 ed., Lands of the thunderbolt....]

C. Economic, Social, and Cultural Studies

25848 BOSE, S.C. Land and people of the Himalaya. Calcutta: Indian Publications, 1968. 284p.

25849 DANG, HARI. Studying the Himalayan region. In JUSI 105,438 (1975) 70-87.

25850 FISHER, J.F., ed. Himalayan anthropology: the Indo-Tibetan interface. The Hague: Mouton, 1978. 567p.

25851 GUPTA, K.M. & DESH BANDHU, eds. Man and forest: a new dimension in the Himalaya: proceedings of the seminars held in Shillong, Dehradun, and New Delhi and organised by Himalaya Seva Sangh, Rajghat, New Delhi. ND: Today & Tomorrow's, 1979. 329p.

25852 Himalaya; écologie-ethnologie. Paris: CNRS, 1977. 591p.

25853 L'homme et la haute montagne: l'Himalaya. In O&M 14,4 (1974) 205-355.

25854 JOHRI, S. Our borderlands. Lucknow: Himalaya Pub., 1964. 376p.

25855 RIEGER, H.C. Zur ökologischen Situation des Himalaya. In IAF 8,1 (1977) 81-109.

II. HIMACHAL PRADESH: THE WESTERN PAHARI-SPEAKING REGION

A. General and Political History since 1800

1. The Himachal Area under the Raj: Rajput Hill States and British Districts of Punjab

25856 BRUCE, C.G. Kulu and Lahoul. London: E. Arnold, 1914. 307p.

25857 BUCK, E.J. Simla, past and present. Delhi: Sumit Pub., 1979. 270p. + 20 pl. [Rpt. 1904 ed.]

25858 GERARD, J.G. Observations on the Spiti Valley and the adjacent countries within the Himalayas. In Asiatic Researches 18 (1833) 238-78.

2. Government and Politics since 1948 (from Union Territory to State, 1971)

25859 BHATNAGAR, S. Panchayati raj in Kangra district. ND: Orient Longmans, 1974. 266p.

25860 HIMACHAL PRADESH. SHRI GURDWARA PAONTA SAHIB POLICE FIRING ENQUIRY CMSN. Report. Simla: Himachal Pradesh, Home Dept., 1965. 92p.

25861 KHOSLA, G.D. Himalayan circuit: the story of a journey in the Inner Himalayas. London: Macmillan, 1956. 233p.

25862 KUMAR, SHANTA. A chief minister's prison diary. ND: Vikas, 1979. 90p.

25863 PARMAR, Y.S. Himachal Pradesh: case for statehood. Simla: Dir. of Public Relations, 1968. 64p.

25864 ______. Himachal Pradesh, its proper shape and status. Simla: Dir. of Public Relations, Himachal Pradesh, 1965. 76p.

25865 SHARMA, R. Party politics in a Himalayan state. ND: National, 1977. 286p.

25866 ______. The politics of statehood: a search for identity. In PSR 14,3/4 (1975) 65-79.

25867 TINKER, I. Himachal Pradesh. In S.V. Kogekar & R.L. Park, eds. Reports on the Indian general elections, 1951-52. Bombay: Popular, 1956, 296-303.

25868 TYAGI, A.R. General elections in Himachal Pradesh: a case of feudal politics. In PSR 6,3/4 & 7,1/2 (1967-68) 221-34.

B. The Economy of Himachal Pradesh

1. Demography (1981 pop. 4,237,569)

25869 INDIA (REP.). CENSUS OF INDIA, 1971. Himachal Pradesh; portrait of population. Delhi: Cont. of Pub., 1978. 129p.

2. Economic Development and Planning

25870 HIMACHAL PRADESH. DIR. OF ECON. & STAT. First five year plan; an appraisal. Simla: 1958. 87p.

25871 ______. Second five year plan; progress report for 1957-58. Simla: 195-. 89p.

25872 ______. State national income of Himachal Pradesh for 1950-51 to 1960-61. Simla: 1963. 115p.

25873 HIMACHAL PRADESH. PLANNING & DEV. DEPT. Impact of plans on Himachal Pradesh. Simla: 1963. 50p.

25874 ______. Third five year plan, 1961-66. Abridged ed. Simla: Himachal Pradesh Administration Press, 1961. 170p.

25875 NCAER. Techno-economic survey of Himachal Pradesh. ND: 1961. 182p.

25876 Symposium on social and economic problems of hilly areas. Simla: Dir. of Econ. & Stat., Himachal Pradesh, 1973. 258p.

3. Agriculture

25877 MISRA, S.D. Agricultural geography of Himachal Pradesh. In Oriental Geographer 7 (1963) 46-58.

25878 PARMAR, H.S. Subsistence economy of rural Himachal Pradesh: a case study of three small villages. In Economic Affairs 24,10-12 (1979) 249-55.

25879 RAJAGOPALAN, C. & JASPAL SINGH. Adoption of agricultural innovations; a sociological study of the Indo-German Project, Mandi. Delhi: National, 1971. 120p.

C. Society and Social Change in Himachal Pradesh

25880 ATAL, Y. A Kulu hill village: prefatory notes. In J. of Social Sciences 3,2 (1963) 41-58.

25881 KAYASTHA, S.L. Ghirths of the Kangra Valley. In NGJI 5,1 (1959) 12-24.

25882 ______. The Himalayan Beas Basin; a study in habitat, economy, and society. Varanasi: BHU, 1964. 346p.

25883 MISRA, S.D. Social groups in Himachal Pradesh. In Bull. de la Soc. de Géog. d'Egypte 35 (1962) 217-62.

25884 NEWELL, W.H. An upper Ravi village; the process of social change in Himachal Pradesh. In K. Ishwaran, ed. Change and continuity in India's villages. NY: ColUP, 1970, 21-36.

25885 PARRY, J.P. Caste and kinship in Kangra. London: Routledge & Kegan Paul, 1979. 353p.

25886 ROSSER, C. A "hermit" village in Kulu. In M.N. Srinivas, ed. India's villages. Calcutta: West Bengal Govt. Press, 1955, 70-81.

25887 SAKSENA, R.N. Marriage and family in the polyandrous Khasa tribe of Jaunsar-Bawar. In G. Kurian, ed. The family in India: a regional view. The Hague: Mouton, 1974, 107-17.

25888 SHASHI, S.S. The Gaddi tribe of Himachal Pradesh: a sociological study. ND: Sterling, 1977. 199p.

25889 ______. The nomads of the Himalayas. Delhi: Sundeep, 1979. 213p.

25890 SINGH, I.P., et al. A socio-biologic study of a scheduled tribe - Bodhs of Lahul, Himachal Pradesh. In IAnth 9,2 (1979) 111-24.

25891 Tibetans in exile, 1959-1969; a report on ten years of rehabilitation in India. Dharamsala: Bureau of H.H. the Dalai Lama, 1969. 366p.

D. Religion and Folklore

25892 CAMPBELL, J.G. Saints and householders: a study of Hindu ritual and myth among the Kangra Rajputs. Kathmandu: Ratna Pustak Bhandar, 1976. 175p.

25893 GILL, M.S. Folk tales of Lahaul. ND: Vikas, 1977. 98p.

25894 HANDA, O.C. Pahari folk art. Bombay: Taraporevala, 1975. 118p.

25895 IBBETSON, D. & E. MACLAGAN. The cult of Mahasu in the Simla hills. In their A glossary of the tribes and castes of the Punjab and Northwest Frontier Province. Lahore: Supt., Govt. Printing, 1919. v. 1, 303-15 et passim.

25896 SEETHALAKSHMI, K.A. Folk tales of Himachal Pradesh. ND: Sterling, 1972. 117p. (Folk tales of India series, 8)

25897 SHARMA, D. Jagra festival. In Folklore(C) 5,9 (1964) 371-74.

25898 SHARMA, U. Public shrines and private interests: the symbolism of the village temple. In SB 23,1 (1974) 71-92.

III. KUMAON AND GARHWAL: THE U.P. HIMALAYAS, SACRED SOURCE OF THE GANGA AND YAMUNA

A. General History and Accounts of the Central Himalayas since 1815

25899 FRASER, J.B. Account of a journey to the sources of the Jamuna and Bhagirathi rivers. In Asiatic Researches 13 (1810) 171-249.

25900 HEIM, A. & A. GANSSER. The throne of the Gods; an account of the first Swiss expedition to the Himalayas. NY: Macmillan, 1939. 233p.

25901 HODGSON, I.A. Journal of a survey to the heads of the rivers Ganges and Jamuna. In Asiatic Researches 14 (1822) 60-152.

25902 KALA, G.R. Memoirs of the Raj: Kumaon (1911-1945). ND: Mukul Prakashan, 1974. 192p.

25903 OAKLEY, E.S. Holy Himalaya: the religion, traditions, and scenery of a Himalayan province (Kumaon and Garhwal). Edinburgh: Oliphant, Anderson & Ferrier, 1905. 319p.

25904 TIWARI, J.G. Communist activities on U.P. Himalayan Border. II: Tehri Garhwal and Uttarkashi. In Indian Communist 1,3 (1968) 1-24.

B. The Economy of the U.P. Himalayas

25905 All-round development of Kumaun. Allahabad: Supt., Printing & Stationery, U.P., 1956. 226p.

25906 KAUSHIC, S.D. Human settlement and occupational economy in Garhwal-Bhot Himalayas. In JASBengal 4th ser. 1,1 (1959) 23-34.

25907 PANT, S.D. The social economy of the Himalayans; based on a survey in the Kumaon Himalayas. London: Allen & Unwin, 1935. 264p.

25908 SAKSENA, R.N. Economic serfdom among the Koltas of Jaunsar-Bawar. Agra: Inst. of Social Sciences, Agra U., 1960. 52p.

25909 SEN, LALIT K. & ABDUL L. THANA. Regional planning for a hill area; a case study of Pauri Tehsil in Pauri Garhwal District. Hyderabad: NICD, 1976. 326p.

25910 TRAILL, G.W. Statistical sketch of Kumaon. In Asiatic Researches 16 (1828) 137-234.

25911 UTTAR PRADESH. BUR. OF AGRI. INFO. Conquest of Tarai; a pictorial survey of the reclamation and colonisation of the Tarai Tract in the District of Naini Tal... Lucknow: The Bureau, 1953. 141p.

C. Society and Social Change in the Central and Eastern Pahari-Speaking Areas

25912 ALLEN, N.J. Byansi kinship terminology: a study in symmetry. In Man ns 10,1 (1975) 80-94.

25913 BERREMAN, G.D. Behind many masks; ethnography and impression management in a Himalayan village. Ithaca: Soc. for Applied Anthro., 1962. 24p. (Its monograph, 4)

25914 ______. Caste and economy in the Himalayas. In EDCC 10 (1962) 386-94.

25915 ______. Cultural variability and drift in the Himalayan hills. In AA 61 (1960) 774-794.

25916 ______. Hindus of the Himalayas; ethnography and change. 2nd ed., rev. enl. Berkeley: UCalP, 1972. 440p.

25917 ______. Pahari polyandry: a comparison. In AA 64,1 (1962) 60-75.

25918 ______. Peoples and cultures of the Himalayas. In

AS 3,6 (1963) 289-304.

25919 ______. Sib and clan among the Pahari of North India. In Ethnoloby 1 (1962) 524-28.

25920 BOSE, S.C. Nomadism in high valleys of Uttarakhand and Kumaon. In GRI 22,3 (1960) 34-39.

25921 DHAPOLA, T.S. The Kumaoni character: a study of an Indian socio-cultural group. Varanasi: Rupa Psychological Centre, 1977. 231p.

25922 FANGER, A.C. Diachronic and synchronic perspectives on Kumaoni society and culture. Ph.D. diss., Syracuse U., 1980. 486p.

25923 GALEY, J.-C. Le créancier, le roi, la mort. Essai sur les relations de dépendance au Tehrī-Gaṛhwāl (Himalaya indien). In Puruṣārtha 4 (1980) 93-164.

25924 GOVILA, J.P. The Tharus of Tarai and Bhubar. In Indian Folklore 2,3 (1959) 228-48.

25925 HASAN, AMIR. The Buxas of the Tarai: a study of their socio-economic disintegration. Delhi: B.R., 1979. 264p.

25926 INDIA (REP.). CENSUS OF INDIA, 1971. Special survey reports on selected towns: Nainital. ND: Dir. of Census Operations, 1978. 718p. (series 21, U.P.; pt. 6B)

25927 JOSHI, L.D. The Khasa family law in the Himalayan districts of the United Provinces. Allahabad: Govt. Press, 1929. 368p.

D. Religions and Folklore of the Garhwal and Kumaon Himalayas [for sacred centers, see Chap. One, IV. B. 2. g.]

25928 ATKINSON, E.T. Notes on the history of religion in the Himalaya of the N.W. Provinces. In JASBengal 53,1 (1884) 39-103; 54,1 (1885) 1-16.

25929 BERREMAN, G.D. Brahmins and shamans in Pahari religion. In E.B. Harper, ed. Aspects of religion in South Asia. Seattle: UWashP, 1964, 53-70. [1st pub. in JAS 23 (1964)]

25930 ______. Himalayan rope sliding and village Hinduism: an analysis. In SWJA 17 (1961) 326-42.

25931 BHANDARI, N.S. Snowballs of Garhwal. In D.N. Majumdar, ed. Folkculture series. Lucknow: Universal Pub., 1946, 21-87. [folksongs]

25932 HASAN, AMIR. The folklore of Buxar. Gurgaon: Academic Press, 1978. 202p.

25933 MAJUMDAR, D.N. Himalayan polyandry: structure, functioning and culture change; a field-study of Jaunsar-Bawar. London: Asia, 1962. 389p.

25934 ______. Lineage structure in a Himalayan society, Himalayan District. In Intl. J. of Comparative Sociology 1 (1960) 17-42.

25935 MATHUR, S. Marriage among Tharus of Chandanchowki. In EA 20,1 (1967) 33-46.

25936 ______. A note on the problems of the Tharu of Chandanchowki. In EA 24,1 (1971) 93-95.

25937 OAKLEY, E.S. & T.D. GAIROLA. Himalayan folklore: Kumaon and west Nepal. Kathmandu: Ratna Pustak Bhandar, 1977. 38 + 315p. (Bibliotheca Himalayica, 2,10) [1st pub. 1935]

25938 SANWAL, R.D. Social stratification in rural Kumaon. Delhi: OUP, 1976. 213p.

25939 SHERRING, C.A. Notes on the Bhotias of Almora and British Garhwal. In MASB 1,8 (1906) 98-119.

25940 SINGH, L.R. The Tarai region of U.P.; a study in human geography. Allahabad: Ram Narain Lal Beni Prasad, 1965. 145p.

25941 SRIVASTAVA, R.P. Tribe-caste mobility in India and the case of Kumaon Bhotias. In C. von Fürer-Haimendorf, ed. Caste and kin in Nepal, India and Ceylon. Bombay: Asia, 1966, 161-212.

25942 SRIVASTAVA, S.K. The Tharus, a study in culture dynamics. Agra: Agra U. Press, 1958. 343p.

25943 TURNER, A.C. Caste in the Kumaun division and Tehri-Garhwal state. In Census of India, 1931, v. 18 (1933) United Provinces, pt. 1, 553-87.

IV. NEPAL: INDEPENDENT HIMALAYAN KINGDOM BETWEEN INDIA AND TIBET

A. General and Political History since 1816

1. General Histories of Modern Nepal

25944 GAIGE, F.H. National integration in Nepal: a study of the Nepal Terai. Ph.D. diss., U. of Pennsylvania, 1970. 714p. [UM 71-19, 226]

25945 HASRAT, B.J. History of Nepal as told by its own and contemporary chroniclers. Hoshiarpur: dist. VVRI Book Agency, 1970. 84 + 356p.

25946 LANDON, P. Nepal. London: Constable, 1928. 2v., 358, 363p.

25947 REGMI, D.R. Modern Nepal. Calcutta: KLM, 1975. 2v.

25948 SHAHA, R. Heroes and builders of Nepal. 5th ed. Calcutta: OUP, 1970. 112p.

25949 SHASTRI, G.C. Historical glimpses of modern Nepal; the other side of the medal. 2nd ed. Kathmandu: Arya Sanskritik Sangha, 1969. 116p.

25950 STILLER, L.F. The silent cry: the people of Nepal, 1816-1839. Kathmandu: Sahayogi Prakashan, 1976. 344p.

2. Accounts by Travellers and Officials

25951 BALLANTINE, J. On India's frontier, or Nepal, the Gurkhas' mysterious land. NY: J.S. Tait, 1895. 192p.

25952 DAVID-NEEL, A. Au coeur des Himalayas, le Népal. Paris: C. Dessart, 1949. 227p.

25953 HODGSON, B.H. Essays on the languages, literature, and religion of Nepal and Tibet. ND: Manjusri Pub. House, 1972. 145 + 124p. (Bibliotheca Himalayica, 2,7) [Rpt. 1874 ed.]

25954 LANDOR, A.H.S. Tibet and Nepal. ND: Light & Life, 1975. 233p + 75pl. [1st pub. 1905]

25955 OLDFIELD, H.A. Sketches from Nepal, historical and descriptive, with an essay on Nepalese Buddhism and illustrations of religious monuments and architecture. Delhi: Cosmo, 1974. 2v. [Rpt. 1881 ed.]

25956 PRANAVANANDA, Swami. The sources of the Brahmaputra, Indus, Sutlej and Karnali. In GJ 102 (1949) 126-35.

3. The Hindu Monarchy of Nepal: A Rajput Dynasty
a. general studies

25957 AGRAWAL, H.N. Monarchical Hindu state in Nepal. In Patna U. J. 21,1 (1966) 94-104.

25958 BHATTARAI, M. Culture and monarchy. Kathmandu: Pustak Bhandar, 1960. 70p.

25959 NEPALI, C.R. The Shah kings of Nepal. 3rd ed. rev. Kathmandu: MIB, 1966. 17p.

25960 ROSE, L.E. Secularization of a Hindu polity: the case of Nepal. In D.E. Smith, ed. Religion and political modernization. New Haven: YUP, 1974, 31-48.

25961 SATISH KUMAR. The Nepalese monarchy from 1769 to 1951. In IS 4,1 (1962) 46-73.

b. hereditary rule by Rana prime-ministers ("mahārājās"), 1846-1951

25962 JAIN, M.S. Emergence of a new aristocracy in Nepal (1937-58). Agra: Sri Ram Mehra, 1972. 220p.

25963 PRASAD, ISHWARI. The life and times of Maharaja Juddha Shamsher Jung Bahadur Rana of Nepal. ND: Ashish Pub. House, 1975. 384p.

25964 RANA, PRAMODE SHAMSHERE JUNG BAHADUR. Rana Nepal: an insider's view. Kathmandu: R. Rana, 1978. 175p.

25965 RANA, PUDMA J.B. Life of Maharaja Sir Jung Bahadur of Nepal. Kathmandu: Ratna Pustak Bhandar, 1974. 314p. (Bibliotheca Himalayica, 2,8)

25966 REGMI, D.R. A century of family autocracy in Nepal. (Being the account of the condition and history of Nepal during the last hundred years of Rana autocracy, 1846-1949). Varanasi: Nepali Natl. Congress, 1958. 268p. [1st pub. 1950]

25967 SATISH KUMAR. Rana polity in Nepal; origin and growth. Bombay: Asia, 1967. 195p.

25968 SHAHA, R. Jung Bahadur, the strongman of Nepal. s.l.: Durga Pokhrel, 1978. 37p.

c. King Tribhuvan Bir Bikram Shaha Deva (1906-1955) and the restoration of royal authority in 1951

25969 JOSHI, B.L. & L.E. ROSE. King Tribhuvan's political experiments. In their Democratic innovations in Nepal.... Berkeley: UCalP, 1966, 103-24.

d. King Mahendra Bir Bikram Shaha Deva (1920-1972): continued autocracy under 1962 "Panchayat" Constitution

i. general studies

25970 BARAL, L.S. The new order in Nepal under King Mahendra, 1960-1962: as assessment. In IS 13,1 (1974) 29-74.

25971 The Citizen King: biography of Mahendra Bir Bikram Shah Deva, the ruler of Nepal. ND: Nepal Trading Corp., 1959.

25972 King Mahendra and the R.S.S. Karnatak: RSS, 1965. 31p.

25973 KRISHNAMURTI, Y.G. His Majesty, King Mahendra, Bir Bikram Shaha Deva; an analytical biography. Bombay: Nityanand Soc., 1965? 399p.

25974 MAHENDRA BIR BIKRAM SHAHA DEVA, Maharajadhiraja of Nepal. Proclamations, speeches and messages. Kathmandu: MIB, 1966-71. 7v.

ii. the 1959 and 1962 Constitutions

25975 APPADORAI, A. & L.S. BARAL. The new constitution of Nepal. In IS 1,3 (1960) 217-47.

25976 GOYAL, N. The King and his constitution. ND: Nepal Trading Corp., 1959. 140p.

25977 JOSHI, B.L. & L.E. ROSE. Democratic innovations in Nepal. A case study of political acculturation. Berkeley: UCalP, 1966. 552p.

25978 KAPHEY, I.P. Fundamental basis of panchayat democratic system. Kathmandu: Nepal Press, 1967. 239p.

25979 NEPAL. CONSTITUTION. The Constitution of the Kingdom of Nepal. Kathmandu: Min. of Law & Parliamentary Affairs, 1959. 67p.

25980 ______. The Constitution of Nepal; English translation. Kathmandu: Min. of Law & Justice, 1963. 64p.

25981 ______. The Constitution of Nepal. Kathmandu: Min. of Law and Justice, Law Books Mgmt. Cmtee, 1976. 68p. [as amended by the 1st & 2nd amendments]

25982 NEUPANE, P. The constitution and constitutions of Nepal. Kathmandu: Ratna Pustak Bhandar, 1969. 206p.

25983 PRADHAN, P.P. A guide to the constitution of Nepal. Kathmandu: Sagar Prasad Mishra, 1965. 170p.

25984 Pronouncements of King Mahendra (on Panchayatcracy). Tr. by D. R. Tuladhar. Kathmandu: HMG Press, 1968. 223p.

25985 ROSE, L.E. Nepal's experiment with "traditional democracy". In PA 36 (1963) 16-31.

25986 SATISH KUMAR. The panchayat constitution of Nepal and its operation. In IS 6,2 (1964) 133-52.

25987 SCHOENFELD, B.N. Nepal's constitution, model 1962. In IJPS 24 (1963) 326-36.

25986 TULADHAR, T.R. The constitution of Nepal. Kathmandu: HMG Press, 1966. 124p.

e. King Birendra Bir Bikrama Shaha Deva (1945-): rejection of parliamentary democracy in favor of partyless Panchayat System

25989 BAJRACHARYA, M.L. Birendra, the king with a difference. Kathmandu: Eastern Trading & Investment Co., 1975. 151p.

25990 HAYES, L.D. The monarchy and modernization in Nepal. In AS 15,7 (1975) 616-28.

25991 MUNI, S.D., ed. Nepal: an assertive monarchy. ND: Chetana, 1977. 251p.

25992 SINGH, R.L. Crown and coronation in Nepal. Kathmandu: Min. of Communication, Dept. of Info., 1975. 19p. + 5pl.

4. Nepali Politics

a. general studies

25993 AGRAWAL, H.N. Nepal, a study in constitutional change. ND: Oxfored & IBH, 1980. 218p.

25994 BARAL, L.R. The dynamics of student politics in Nepal, 1961-75. In IS 14,2 (1974) 303-14.

25995 CHAUHAN, R.S. The political development in Nepal, 1950-70; conflict between tradition and modernity. ND: Associated Pub. House, 1971. 336p.

25996 KAISHER BAHADUR K.C. Nepal after the Revolution of 1950. Kathmandu: Sharada Prakashan Griha, 1976. 2v., 266, 200p.

25997 KUMAR, D.P. Nepal, year of decision. ND: Vikas, 1980. 222p.

25998 MALLA, SHASHI P.B. Political participation in an Asian monarchy: a case study of Nepal. In IAF 6,1 (1975) 66-76.

25999 NATH, TRIBHUVAN. The Nepalese dilemma, 1960-74. ND: Sterling, 1975. 528p.

26000 PARMANAND. The Nepali Congress in exile. Delhi: University Book House, 1978. 152p.

26001 RAJ, P.A. A Nepalese discovers his country. Kathmandu: Sajha Prakashan, 1979. 112p.

26002 RANA, DAMAN SHUMSER JANG BAHADUR. Nepal, rule and misrule. ND: Rajesh, 1978. 240p.

26003 ROSE, L.E. & J.T. SCHOLZ. Nepal: profile of a Himalayan kingdom. Boulder: Westview, 1980. 150p.

26004 ROSE, L.E. & M.W. FISHER. The politics of Nepal: persistence and change in an Asian monarchy. Ithaca: CornellUP, 1970. 197p.

26005 SHAHA, R. Nepali politics: retrospect and prospect. Delhi: OUP, 1975. 208p.

26006 WEINER, M. The political demography of Nepal. In AS 13,6 (1973) 617-630.

b. pre-1951 politics: demand for a constitution and opposition to the Ranas

26007 CHATTERJI, B. A study of recent Nepalese politics. Calcutta: World Press, 1967. 190p.

26008 REGMI, D.R. The Nepali democratic struggle. Its aim and character. Banaras: Nepali Natl. Congress, 1948. 46p.

c. 1951-61: experiment with party politics

26009 CHATTERJI, B. Nepal's experiment with democracy. ND: Ankur Pub. House, 1977. 131p.

26010 DRIVER, J.E.A. Party and government in Nepal. In S. Rose, 3d. Politics in Southern Asia. NY: St. Martins Press, 1963, 75-104.

26011 GUPTA, A. Politics in Nepal, a study of post-Rana political developments and party politics. Bombay: Allied, 1964. 332p.

26012 PANT, R.D. First general elections in Nepal. In EW 11,8 & 14 (1959) 284-90, 483-85.

26013 ROSE, L.E. Communism under high atmospheric conditions: the Party in Nepal. In R.A. Scalapino, ed.

The Communist revolution in Asia. Englewood-Cliffs, NJ: Prentice-Hall, 1965, 343-72.

d. the Panchayat System: a "partyless democracy"?

26014 BARAL, L.R. Party-like institutions in "partyless" polities: the GVNC in Nepal. In AS 16,7 (1976) 672-81.

26015 BARAL, L.S. "Class organizations" in Nepal: social control and interest articulation. In Asia Q. 3 (1974) 173-202.

26016 ______. The First Panchayat Elections in Nepal, 1962-63: the emergency of a new political generation. In IS 12 (1973) 462-477.

26017 ______. Opposition groups in Nepal, 1960-70. In IQ 28,1 (1972) 12-45.

26018 CHAUHAN, R.S. Working of panchayat system in Nepal. In SAS 4 (1969) 174-96.

26019 MOHSIN, M. & PASHUPATI SHUMSHERE. Some aspects of panchayat system in Nepal. Kathmandu: MIB, 1966. 43p.

26020 SHARMA, K.N. The panchayat system in Nepal; an experiment in partyless democracy. Kathmandu: Ratna Pustak Bhandar, 1973. 140p.

26021 SINHA, U.N. Development of panchayats in Nepal. Aligarh: P.C. Dwadash Shreni, 1972. 124p.

5. Administrative Studies

26022 AGRAWAL, H.N. The administrative system of Nepal: from tradition to modernity. ND: Vikas, 1976. 397p.

26023 DHUNGANA, B., et al. An analysis of tax structure of Nepal. Kirtipur: CEDA, 1979. 130p.

26024 EDWARDS, D.W. Patrimonial and bureaucratic administration in Nepal: historical change and Weberian theory. Ph.D. diss., U. of Chicago, 1977. 383p.

26025 FISCHER, W. Personnel administration in Nepal: a report. In Nepalese J. or Public Admin. 3,2 (1972) 33-55.

26026 GOODALL, M.R. Administrative change in Nepal. In R. Braibanti, ed. Asian bureaucratic systems emergent from the British imperial tradition. Durham: DUP, 1966, 605-642.

26027 GONGAL, S.D. Foreign experts in the administration of Nepal; a survey of their reports. Kirtipur: CEDA, 1973. 168p.

26028 JOSHI, N.L. Evolution of public administration in Nepal; experiences and lessons. Kirtipur: CEDA, 1973. 122p.

26029 MALHOTRA, R.C. Public administration in Nepal. In IJPA 4 (1958) 451-64.

26030 PRADHAN, K.P. Government and administration and local government of the Kingdom of Nepal. Kathmandu: S.P. Pradhan & K.P. Pradhan, 1969. 177p.

26031 PRADHAN, P. Public administration in Nepal. Kathmandu: Curriculum Dev. Center, Tribhuvan U., 1976. 192p.

26032 SHRESTHA, M.K. A handbook of public administration in Nepal. Kathmandu: MIB, 1962. 121p.

26033 ______. Public administration in Nepal. Kathmandu: Educ. Enterprise, 1975. 263p.

26034 ______. Trends in public administration in Nepal. Kathmandu: MIB, 1969. 115p.

26035 SHRESTHA, S.B. How Nepal is governed. Kathmandu: Pashupati Press, 1965. 293p.

26035a STAHL, O.G. A strong civil service for Nepal; a charter for merit, incentive, control, and simplicity. Kathmandu: Ford Foundation, 1969. 52p.

6. Law and Judiciary

26036 ADAM, L. Criminal law and procedure in Nepal a century ago: notes left by Brian H. Hodgson. In FEQ 9 (1950) 146-68.

26037 KAISHER BAHADUR K.C. The judicial customs of Nepal. 2nd ed., rev. and enl. Kathmandu: Ratna Pustak Bhandar, 1971-. v.1, 432p.

26038 SATISH KUMAR. Nepal's new legal code. In EW 16,2 (1964) 62-64.

7. Local Government and Politics

26039 CAPLAN, L. Administration and politics in a Nepalese town: the study of a district capital and its environs. London: OUP, 1975. 266p.

26040 RANA, PASHUPATI SHUMSHERE J.B. & MOHAMMAD MOHSIN. A study report on the pattern of emerging leadership in panchayats; with special reference to district and village panchayats of Mechi, Kosi and Sagaramatha zones. Kathmandu: Res. Div., Home Panchayat Min., 1967. 73p.

8. Foreign Relations of Nepal: From Isolationism to Non-Alignment

a. documents

26041 BHASIN, A.S., ed. Documents on Nepal's relations with India and China, 1949-66. Bombay: Academic Books, 1970. 295p.

26042 MAHENDRA BIR BIKRAM SHAHA DEVA. Statement of principles. Major foreign policy speeches. Kathmandu: Dept. of Publicity & Broadcasting, 1962-64. 2v.

26043 RANA, B.B., ed. Documents of Nepalese foreign policy, 1973-July 1979. Kathmandu: Foreign Affairs J., 1979. 68p.

b. general studies

26044 KHANAL, Y.N. Nepal, transition from isolationism. Kathmandu: Sajha Prakashan, 1977. 298p.

26045 KOZICKI, R.J. Nepal and Israel: uniqueness in Asian relations. In AS 9,5 (1969) 331-42.

26046 MOJUMDAR, K. Foreign policy of Nepal: persistence of tradition. In SAS 13,2 (1978) 1-19.

26047 MUNI, S.D. Foreign policy of Nepal. Delhi: Natl., 1973. 320p.

26048 PRADHAN, J.S. Understanding Nepal;s foreign policy. Kathmandu: L. Pradhan, 1969. 90p.

26049 REGMI, J.C. Nepal and her friends: historical approach to Nepal's foreign relations, 1923-1976, and other articles. Kathmandu: Office of the Nepal-Antiquary, 1976. 66p.

26050 ROSE, L.E. Nepal - strategy for survival. Berkeley: UCalP, 1971. 375p.

26051 ROSE, L.E. & R. DIAL. Can a mini-state find true happiness in a world dominated by protagonist powers: the Nepal case. In Annals of the American Academy of Political & Social Science 386 (1969) 89-101.

26052 SHARMA, J.P. Nepal's foreign policy, 1947-1962. Philadelphia: U. of Pennsylvania, 1968. 318p.

c. relations with British India: protectorate and buffer state

26053 HUNTER, W.W. Life of Brian Houghton Hodgson, British Resident at the Court of Nepal.... London: J. Murray, 1896. 390p.

26054 HUSAIN, ASAD. British India's relations with the kingdom of Nepal, 1857-1947: a diplomatic history of Nepal. London: Allen & Unwin, 1970. 408p.

26055 JHA, S.K. British India's policy towards Nepal. In JBRS 60,1/4 (1974) 190-219.

26056 MOJUMDAR, K. Background to Anglo-Nepalese Treaty, 1923. In JIG 48 (1970) 599-655.

26057 ______. British impact on Nepal. In BPP 90,1 (1971) 1-29.

26058 ______. Nepal and the Indian mutiny, 1857-58. In BPP 85,1(159) (1966) 13-39.

26059 ______. Nepal and the Indian nationalist movement. Calcutta: KLM, 1975. 110p.

26060 ______. Nepal's relations with Indian states (1800-50). In JIH 43,2 (1965) 402-65.

26061 ______. Political relations between India and Nepal, 1877-1923. ND: Munshiram, 1971. 331p.

26062 RAMAKANT. Indo-Nepalese relations, 1816 to 1877. Delhi: S. Chand, 1968. 390p.

26063 SANWAL, B.D. Nepal and the East India Company. NY: Asia, 1965. 347p.

d. Nepal and its neighbors
i. relations with India and other South Asian nations

26064 BHATTACHARJEE, G.P. India and politics of modern Nepal. Calcutta: Minerva, 1970. 244p.

26065 DHARAMDASANI, M. Indian diplomacy in Nepal. Jaipur: Aalekh Pub., 1976. 256p.

26066 JHA, S.K. Uneasy partners: India and Nepal in the post-colonial era. ND: Manas, 1975. 344p.

26067 KHANAL, Y.N. Reflections on Nepal-India relations. ND: 1964. 96p.

26068 MOHAMMED AYOOB. India and Nepal: politics of aid and trade. In JIDSA 3 (1970) 127-56.

26069 MOOKERJEA, S.L. Indo-Nepalese relations. In CR 176,1 (1965) 35-50.

26070 MUNI, S.D. Nepal-Pakistan relation: partnership in expediency. In SAS 5,1 (1970) 63-78.

26071 RAMAKANT. Indo-Nepal relations: geopolitical compulsions. In SAS 6,1 (1971) 49-58.

26072 SEN, JAHAR. Slave trade on the Indo-Nepal border in the nineteenth century. In Kailash 1,2 (1973) 159-65.

26073 SHARMA, J.R. Nepal-India relations. Kathmandu: Dept. of Publicity and Broadcasting, 1963. 40p.

26074 SHRIMAN NARAYAN. India and Nepal: an exercise in open diplomacy. Bombay: Popular, 1970. 172p.

ii. relations with Tibet and China

26075 GRÜNDLER, U. The Chinese interests in the Himalayas. The People's Republic of China and Nepal: a case study. In IAF 2,1 (1971) 44-54.

26076 MUNI, S.D. Sino-Nepalese relations: two troubled years - 1959-60. In SAS 3,1 (1968) 33-46.

26077 NIGAM, A.K. Chinese claim of suzerainty over Nepal. In MR 123 (1968) 570-84.

26078 SATISH KUMAR. Nepal and China. In IJPS 24 (1963) 79-93.

iii. Sino-Indian rivalries over Nepal

26079 HUSAIN, ASAD & ASIFA ANWAR. Conflict in Asia: a case study of Nepal. ND: Classical, 1979. 88p.

26080 JAIN, GIRILAL. India meets China in Nepal... Bombay: Asia, 1959. 177p.

26081 RAMAKANT. Nepal-China, and India: Nepal-China relations. ND: Abhinav, 1976. 334p.

26082 REGMI, D.R. Nepal's foreign policy in relation to India and China. In SAS 4 (1969) 127-34. [also in S.P. Varma & K.P. Misra, eds. Foreign policies in South Asia. Bombay: Orient Longmans, 1969, 258-265]

26083 ROSE, L.E. Sino-Indian rivalry and the Himalayan border states. In Orbis 5,2 (1961) 198-215.

26084 SINHA, M. Nepal's role in Sino-Indian relations: 1949-1969. In JIDSA 2 (1970) 456-86.

e. foreign economic relations of Nepal: trade and aid

26085 BEYER, J.C. Economic integration among developing countries; the advantages and disadvantages for Nepal. In Development R. 2,1 (1970) 1-14.

26086 CENTRE FOR ECON. DEV. & ADMIN. Trade and transit: Nepal's problem with her Southern neighbour. Kathmandu: 1970. 35p.

26087 CHAND, D. The foreign trade of Nepal. Dehra Dun: Himachal Times Press, 1977. 103p.

26088 Facts about American aid to Nepal, FY 1952-1969. Kathmandu: USAID, 1969. 32p.

26089 JAYARAMAN, T.K. Some trade problems of landlocked Nepal. In AS 16,12 (1976) 1113-23.

26090 MIHALY, E.B. Foreign aid and politics in Nepal, a case study. London: OUP, 1965. 202p.

26091 Nepal and the Colombo Plan; a review. Kathmandu: Natl. Planning Cmsn. Secretariat, 1971. 34p.

26092 NEPAL. TREATIES. Nepal's trade agreements: as of force in April 2, 1976. 2nd ed. Kathmandu: Trade Promotion Centre, 1977. 127p.

26093 PANT, Y.P. Nepal's economic development on international basis; an analysis of foreign aid utilization. Kathmandu: Educ. Enterprise, 1962. 87p.

26094 ______. Nepal's recent trade policy. In AS 4,7 (1964) 947-57.

26095 RAJBHANDARI, B.L. Foreign assistance in Nepal; a brief review. Lalitpur: Savitri Devi Rajbhandari, 1973. 257p.

26096 SEN, JAHAR. Indo-Nepal trade in the nineteenth century. Calcutta: KLM, 1977. 192p.

26097 STILLER, L.F. A note on Himalayan trade. In J. of Tribhuvan U. 7,1 (1972) 1-34.

26098 Twenty years of Nepalese-American cooperation; a summary of American aid to Nepal, 1951-1971. Kathmandu: 1971. 42p.

26099 UNTAWALE, M.G. The political dynamics of functional collaboration: Indo-Nepalese river projects. In AS 14,8 (1974) 716-32.

B. The Nepal Economy

1. General Economic History of Modern Nepal

26100 REGMI, M.C. Readings in Nepali economic history. Varanasi: Kishor Vidya Niketan, 1979. 88p.

26101 REGMI, M.C. A study in Nepali economic history, 1768-1846. ND: Manjusri, 1971. 235p. (Bibliotheca Himalayica, 1,14)

2. Demography and Population Policy

26102 KROTKI, K.J. & H.N. THAKUR. Estimates of population size and growth from the 1952-54 and 1961 censuses of the Kingdom of Nepal. In Population Studies 25,1 (1971) 89-103.

26103 LINDSEY, Q.W. & M.M. SAINJU. Population and development policy in Nepal: a proposal for implementation. Kathmandu: CEDA, 1972. 41p.

26104 NEPAL. CENTRAL BUREAU OF STAT. The analysis of the population statistics of Nepal. Kathmandu: 1977. 208p.

26105 ______. The demographic sample survey of Nepal: third year survey, 1977-78. Kathmandu: 1978. 33p.

26106 Population and development.... Kathmandu: CEDA, 1971. 201p. (CEDA study series, Seminar paper, 2)

26107 THAPA, Y.S. & M. BANSKOTA. Population study of Nepal. Kathmandu: CEDA & USAID, 1972. 104p.

26108 TULADHAR, J.M. & B.B. GUBHAJU & J.E. STOECKEL. Population and family planning in Nepal. Kathmandu: Ratna Pustak Bhandar, 1978. 118p.

26109 UPADHYAYA, D.C. & J.V. ABUEVA, eds. Population and development in Nepal.... Kathmandu: Tribhuvan U., 1975. 165p. [CEDA seminar]

3. Surveys of Economic Conditions

26110 DONNER, W. Nepal; Raum, Mensch, Wirtschaft. Wiesbaden: Harrassowitz, 1972. 506p. (SIAK, 32)

26111 IIJIMA, S. Ecology, economy, and social system in the Nepal Himalayas. In Developing Economies 2 (1964) 91-105.

26112 MALLA, K.P. Nepal: a conspectus. Kathmandu: Preparatory Cmtee., 26th Colombo Plan Consultative Cmtee.

Meeting, 1977. 152p. + 15 pl.

26113 PRICE, H.B. Economic survey of Nepal. NY: UN, 1961. 71p. (Report TAO/NEP/3)

26114 RANA, RATNA S.J.B. An economic study of the area around the alignment of the Dhanagadi-Dandeldhura Road, Nepal. Kathmandu: CEDA, 1971. 163p.

26115 RANA, SHUMSHERE PASHUPATI J.B. The Nepalese economy: problems and prospects. In AS 14,7 (1974) 651-662.

26116 RANA, SHUMSHERE PASHUPATI J.B. & K.B. MALLA, eds. Nepal in perspective. Kathmandu: CEDA, 1973. 310p.

26117 SHARMA, C.K. Natural resources of Nepal. Kathmandu: Sangeeta Sharma, 1978. 271p. + 30 pl.

26118 ______. Natural resources of Pokhara valley. Kathmandu: S. Sharma, 1977. 106p.

26119 ______. River system of Nepal. Kathmandu: S. Sharma, 1977. 224p.

26120 SHRESTHA, A.M. Problems of Nepalese economy. 2nd ed. Kathmandu: Gayetri Shrestha, 1967. 263p.

26121 SHRESTHA, B.P. An introduction to Nepalese economy. Kathmandu: Nepal Press, 1962. 264p.

4. Economic Development and Planning

26122 BHATTA, B.D. Development administration in Nepal. Kathmandu: Indira Bhatta, 1979. 177p.

26123 BHOOSHAN, B.S. The development experience of Nepal. ND: Concept, 1978. 195p.

26124 CENTRE FOR ECON. DEV. & ADMIN. Organization manual, CEDA as an institution. Kirtipur: CEDA, 1978. 132p.

26125 FRY, M.J. Pitfalls in partial adoption of the McKinnon-Shaw development strategy; the Nepalese experience. In BDS 6,3 (1978) 157-70.

26126 Mountain environment and development: a collection of papers published on the occasion of the twentieth anniversary of the Swiss Association for Technical Assistance in Nepal (SATA). Kathmandu: Tribhuvan U. Press, 1976. 214p.

26127 NEPAL. MIN. OF ECON. PLANNING. The third plan, 1965-70. Kathmandu: 1965. 194p.

26128 ______. The three year plan, 1962-1965. Kathmandu: 1963. 285p.

26129 NEPAL. NATL. PLANNING CMSN. Basic principles of the sixth plan, 1980-85. Kathmandu: 1979. 72p.

26130 ______. Nepal: policy guidelines for the Fifth plan, 1975-1980. Kathmandu: 1974. 132p.

26131 OKADA, F.E. Preliminary report on regional development areas in Nepal. Kathmandu: Natl. Planning Cmsn., 1970. 125p. (Regional planning series, 2)

26132 PANT, Y.P. Planning for prosperity: planning experiences in Nepal. Rev. 4th ed. Kathmandu: Sahayogi Prakashan, 1975. 202p. [1st pub. 1957]

26133 POKHREL, D. Birendra ra bikas: birthday souvenir, development special. Kathmandu: Pokhrel, 1977. 108p.

26134 PRADHAN, P., ed. A new dimension in Nepal's development: the regional approach in Nepalese planning and people-oriented development strategy. Kirtipur: CEDA, 1973. 106p. (Its occ. paper, 3)

26135 SHRESHTHA, B.P. & S.C. JAIN. Regional development in Nepal: an exercise in reality. Delhi: Development Pub., 1978. 160p.

26136 SINGH, B.K. Co-operative development in Nepal. Allahabad: Kitab Mahal, 1965. 128p.

26137 STILLER, L.F. & R.P. YADAV. Planning for people: a study of Nepal's planning experience. Kathmandu: Sahayogi Prakashan, for Research Centre for Nepal & Asian Studies, Tribhuvan U., 1979. 334p.

26138 THWEATT, W.O. The concept of elasticity and the growth equation; with emphasis on the role of capital in Nepal's economic development. London: Asia, 1962. 91p.

26139 WEISS, D. Problems of implementing regional development programs, the case of Nepal. In IAF 3,4 (1972) 560-70.

5. Finance and Banking

26140 Agricultural credit and banking. Kathmandu: Agri. Dev. Bank, 1972. 254p. [1970 seminar]

26141 BEYER, J.C. Budget innovations in developing countries: the experience of Nepal. NY: Praeger, 1973. 187p.

26142 FRY, M.J. Resource mobilisation and financial development in Nepal. Kathmandu: CEDA & Nepal Rashtra Bank, 1974. 94p.

26143 OJHA, J.C. & R.P. RAJBAHAK. Banking and modern currency in Nepal. 2nd ed. Kathmandu: Educational Enterprise, 1965. 173p. [1st ed. 1961]

26144 PANT, Y.P. Banking and development. Kathmandu: Nepal Rastra Bank, 1971. 99p.

26145 ______. Problems of fiscal and monetary policy: a case study of Nepal. Kathmandu: Sahayogi Prakashan, 1970. 205p.

26146 SINGH, S.K. The fiscal system of Nepal. Kathmandu: Ratna Pustak Bhandar, 1977. 268p.

26147 SHRESTHA, B.P. Monetary policy in an emerging state; a case study of Nepal. Kathmandu: Ratna Pustak Bhandar, 1965. 89p.

6. Agriculture
a. general studies of agricultural development

26148 Agricultural Development Bank: operations and achievements. Kathmandu: Agri. Dev. Bank, 1976. 37p.

26149 AMATYA, S.L. Cash crop farming in Nepal. Kirtipur: Inst. of Humanities & Social Sciences, Tribhuvan U., 1976. 114p. + 24 pl.

26150 AUGUSTHY, K.T. Fish farming in Nepal. Rampur: Augusthy, 1979. 147p.

26151 CHAND, D. Critical appraisal of rural economy of Nepal. Kathmandu: Adarsh Chhapakhana, 1976. 168p.

26152 ELDER, J.W. et al. Planned resettlement in Nepal's Terai; a social analysis of the Khajura/Barida Punarvas projects. Madison: U. of Wisconsin, Dept. of Sociology, 1976. 307p.

26153 JHA, K.K. Agricultural finance in Nepal: an analytical study. ND: Heritage, 1978. 241p.

26154 JOSHI, D.D. Animal health, livestock and dairy development statistics of Nepal. Kathmandu: Agri. Projects Service Centre, 1977. 97p.

26155 KIHARA, H., ed. Land and crops of Nepal Himalaya. Scientific results of the Japanese Expeditions to Nepal Himalaya, 1952-53; v. 2. Kyoto: Fauna & Flora Research Society, Kyoto University, 1956. 561p.

26156 MATHEMA, P.R.B. Agricultural development in Nepal. 2nd ed., rev. & enl. Kathmandu: Jaya Shree Mathema, 1969. 200p.

26157 NEPAL. MIN. OF ECON. PLANNING. Mobility of agricultural labor in Nepal. Kathmandu: 1967. 145p.

26158 PANT, Y.P. & S.C. JAIN. Agricultural development in Nepal: a search for new strategy. 2nd rev. & enl. ed. Bombay: Vora, 1979. 162p. [1st ed. 1968]

26159 ______. Long term planning for agriculture in Nepal. Delhi: Vikas, 1972. 182p.

26160 RANA, R.S. & T.R. JOSHI. Nepal's food grain surplus and deficit regions. In NGJI 14 (1968) 165-75.

b. agricultural technology and innovation; irrigation

26161 ASIAN DEVELOPMENT BANK. Feasibility report on the Kankai irrigation project, Nepal. Tokyo: Nippon Koei, 1972. 68, 286, 74p.

26162 BAIDYA, HUTA RAM. Farm irrigation and water management (principles and practices). Kathmandu: Royal Nepal Academy, 1968. 236p.

26163 DHUNGANA, B., ed. Research, productivity, and

mechanization in Nepalese agriculture. Kirtipur: CEDA, Tribhuvan U., 1976. 308p.

26164 Master plan of irrigation development in Nepal. Kathmandu: Min. of Water & Power, 1970. 120p.

26165 THEUVENET, S. Report to the Government of Nepal on irrigation. Rome: FAO, 1953. 44p. (Its Report, 162)

c. agrarian relations, land tenure and reform

26166 CAPLAN, L. The multiplication of social ties: the strategy of credit transactions in East Nepal. In EDCC 20,4 (1972) 691-702.

26167 ______. Some political consequences of state land policy in East Nepal. In Man 2,1 (1967) 107-14.

26168 PRINDLE, P.H. "Exploitation" in peasant societies: a Nepalese example. In MAS 12,1 (1978) 59-76.

26169 REED, H.B. Education and land in Nepal: complementary reforms. In CAS 5 (1974) 78-86.

26170 REGMI, M.C. Land tenure and taxation in Nepal. 2nd ed. Kathmandu: Ratna Pustak Bhandar, 1978. 895p. (Bibliotheca Himalayica, 1,26) [1st pub. 1963-68, 4 v.]

26171 ______. Thatched huts and stucco palaces: peasants and landlords in nineteenth-century Nepal. ND: Vikas, 1978. 173p.

26172 SAGANT, P. Usuriers et chefs du clan. Ethnographie de la dette au Nepal orientale. In Puruṣārtha 4 (1980) 227-78.

26173 ZAMAN, M.A. Evaluation of land reform in Nepal... Kathmandu: Min. of Land Reforms, 1973. 124p.

7. Industry in Nepal

26174 INDUSTRIAL SERVICES CENTRE. Investors' guide to Nepal, 1975. Kathmandu: 1975. 123p.

26175 NEPAL. CORPORATION CO-ORDINATION COUNCIL. Performance of public enterprises in Nepal: macro study - part I & II. Kathmandu: 1977. 240p.

26176 ______. Profiles of public enterprises in Nepal. Kathmandu: 1978. 296p.

26177 NEPAL. MIN. OF INDUSTRY AND COMMERCE. Industrial policy, 1974. Kathmandu: 1974. 30p.

26178 SHRESTHA, B.P. The economy of Nepal; or, A study in problems and processes of industrialization. Bombay: Vora, 1967. 274p.

26179 TOFFIN, G. La presse à huile Néwar de la Vallée de Kathmandu: analyse technologique et socio-économique. In J. d'agriculture tropicale et de botanique appliquée 23,7-12 (1976) 183-204.

8. Labor in Nepal

26180 GOIL, R.M. Wages in manufacturing in Nepal. In IJIR 8,1 (1972) 47-66.

26181 NEPAL. NATL. PLANNING CMSN. SECRETARIAT. Employment of graduates in Nepal. Kathmandu: 1968. 2 v.

26182 NEW EDUCATIONAL REFORM ASSOCIATES. Middle-level manpower follow-up study; a study of attrition among middle-level technical personnel in Nepal. Kathmandu: Natl. Planning Cmsn. Secretariat, 1974. 82p.

26183 PANT, Y.P. Planning for employment in Nepal. In Far Eastern Econ. R. 30,2 (Oct. 13, 1960) 69-71.

9. Commerce and Transportation

26184 CHUDLEY, F.J. The East-West highway. In Royal Nepal Economist 7,5-11 (1965) 70-81.

26185 MAILLART, E.K. Nepal. The China road. In J. of the Royal Central Asian Soc., 53,2 (1966) 143-46.

26186 PRADHAN, I.K. Travel and tourism in perspective. Kathmandu: Nepal Res. Group, 1979. 262p. + 14 pl.

26187 RAJ, P.A. Road to the Chinese border. Kathmandu: Foreign Affairs J. Pub., 1978. 77p.

26188 RIEGER, H.C. & B. BHADRA. Comparative evaluation of road construction techniques in Nepal. Kathmandu: CEDA, Tribhuvan U., 1978. 257p.

26189 SCHMID, R. Zur Wirtschaftsgeographie von Nepal: Transport- und Kommunikationsprobleme Ostnepals im Zusammenhang mit der schweizerischen Entwicklungshilfe in der Region Jiri. Zurich: 1969. 247p.

C. Society and Social Change in Nepal since 1816

1. Social Categories, incl. Kinship and Marriage
a. general studies

26190 ADAM, L. The social organization and customary law of the Nepalese tribes. In AA 38,4 (1936) 533-47.

26191 BISTA, D.B. People of Nepal. 2nd ed. Kathmandu: Ratna Pustak Bhandar, 1972. 210p. [1st pub. 1967]

26192 FÜRER-HAIMENDORF, C. VON. Caste in the multi-ethnic society of Nepal. In CIS 4 (1960) 12-32.

26193 ______., ed. Contributions to the anthropology of Nepal. London: Aris & Phillips, 1974. 260p.

26193a HÖFER, A. The caste hierarchy and the state in Nepal; a study of the Muluki Ain of 1854. Innsbruck: Universitätsverlag Wagner, 1979. 240p. (Khumbu Himal, 13,2)

26194 KIHARA, H. Scientific results of the Japanese expeditions to Nepal Himalaya, 1952-53. Kyoto: Kyoto U., Fauna and Flora Res. Soc., 1955-57. 3 v. [1. Fauna and flora; 2. Land and crops; 3. Peoples]

26195 LOBSIGER-DELLENBACH, M. Recherches ethnologiques au Népal; (Vallée de Katmandou). In Le Globe 92 (1953) 1-62; 93 (1954) 1-79.

26196 MACDONALD, A.W. Essays on the ethnology of Nepal and South Asia. Kathmandu: Ratna Pustak Bhandar, 1975. 317p. (Bibliotheca Himalayica, 3,3)

26197 ______. La hiérarchie des jāt inférieurs dans le Muluki ain. In Échanges et communications, mélanges offerts à Claude Lévi-Strauss. The Hague: Mouton, 1970, v. 1, 139-152. (Studies in general anthro., 5)

26198 MAJUPURIA, I. & T.C. MAJPURIA. Marriage customs in Nepal: ethnic groups, their marriage customs and traditions. Kathmandu: I. Majpuria, dist. Intl. Book House, 1978. 206p. + 8 pl.

26199 [Nepal ethnography issue]. In O&M 6,2 (1966) 83-184.

26200 [Nepal ethnography issue]. In O&M 9,1 (1969) 1-142.

26201 Népal, hommes et dieux. In O&M 9,4 (1969) 383-98.

26202 Nepalese society: an introductory account of the main specialties of different ethnic and occupational groups of Nepalese society. Kathmandu: Natl. Museum, 1975. 51p. + 10 pl.

26203 REGMI, J.C. Dictionary of Nepalese cultural geography. Kathmandu: Office of Nepal-Antiquary, Ratna Pustak Bhandar, 1980. 264p.

26204 VANSITTART, E. The tribes, clans, and castes of Nepal. In JASBengal 63,1 (1894) 213-49.

b. Tibeto-Nepalese peoples of the northern border: Sherpas and other Bhotiyas

26205 ALLEN, N.J. Sherpa kinship terminology in diachronic perspective. In Man ns 11,4 (1976) 569-87.

26206 AZIZ, B.N. Social cohesion and reciprocation in a Tibetan community in Nepal. In J.J. Preston & B. Misra, eds. Community, self, and identity. The Hague: Mouton, 1978, 45-78.

26207 ______. Tibetan frontier families: reflections of three generations from D'ing-ri. ND: Vikas, 1978. 292p

26208 BANERJEE, B. Report on Kuti, a Himalayan village. In Folklore(C) 12,3 (1971) 99-118.

26209 BOURDILLON, J. Visit to the Sherpas. London: Collins, 1956. 256p.

26210 FÜRER-HAIMENDORF, C. VON. Caste concepts and status distinctions in Buddhist communities of western Nepal. In his Caste and kin in Nepal, India and Ceylon Bombay: Asia, 1966, 140-60.

26211 ______. Himalayan traders: life in highland Nepal London: Murray, 1975. 316p. + 16 pl.

26212 ______. The Sherpas of Nepal, Buddhist highlanders. 2nd ed. London: Murray, 1972. 298p. [1st pub. 1964]

26213 JEST, C. Dolpo: communautés de langue tibétaine du Népal. Paris: CNRS, 1975. 481p.

26214 HARDIE, N. In highest Nepal; our life among the Sherpas. London: Allen & Unwin, 1957. 191p.

26215 KLEINERT, C. Bau- und Siedlungsweise ostnepalischer Bhotiyas. In IAF 6,1 (1975) 77-87.

26216 ______. Haus- und Siedlungsformen im Nepal-Himalaya unter Berücksichtigung klimatischer Faktoren. München: Universitätsverlag Wagner, 1973. 127p. (Hochgebirgsforschung, 4)

26217 MAILLART, E.K. The land of the Sherpas. London: Hodder & Stoughton, 1955. 60p.

26218 OPPITZ, M. Geschichte und Sozialordnung der Sherpa. Mit einem Vorwort zum Gesamtwerk von Friedrich W. Funke. Mit Titelbild, 20 Abb., 8 Tab., 3 Taf., 6 Genealogien u. 2 Kt. Innsbruck: München, Universitätsverlag Wagner, 1968. 170p.

26219 ORTNER, S.B. Sherpa purity. In AA 75,1 (1973) 49-63.

26220 ______. Sherpas through their rituals. NY: CamUP, 1978. 195p.

26221 PEISSEL, M. Mustang, the forbidden kingdom; exploring the lost Himalayan land. NY: Dutton, 1967. 318p.

26222 TENZING NORKEY. After Everest: an autobiography. ND: Vikas, 1977. 184p.

c. peoples of the middle hills and valleys

i. the Magar, Gurung, and Rai, sources of the Gurkha regiments [see also Chap. Six, II. B. 7. b.]

26223 ANDORS, E.B. The Rodi: female associations among the Gurung of Nepal. Diss., Columbia U., 1976. 247p. [UM 76-29,575]

26224 BARNOUW, V. Eastern Nepalese marriage customs and kinship organization. In SWJA 11,1 (1955) 15-30.

26225 ______. Some eastern Nepalese customs: the early years. In SWJA 12 (1956) 257-71.

26226 CAPLAN, L. Land and social change in east Nepal; a study of Hindu-tribal relations. Berkeley: UCalP, 1970. 224p.

26227 CHEMJONG, I.S. History and culture of the Kirat people. 3rd ed. Phidim, E. Nepal: Tumeng Hang & Chandraw Hang, 1966. 101p.

26228 HITCHCOCK, J.T. Himalayan ecology and family religious variation. In G. Kurian, ed. The family in India: a regional view. The Hague: Mouton, 1974, 119-38.

26229 ______. The Magars of Banyan Hill. Case studies in cultural anthropology. NY: Holt, Rinehart & Winston, 1966. 115p.

26230 ______. Sub-tribes in the Magar community in Nepal. In AS 5,4 (1965) 207-15.

26231 JEST, C. Les Thakali (Notes sur Népal). In Ethnographie 58/59 (1964-65) 26-49.

26232 JONES, R.L. Courtship in an Eastern Nepal community. In Anthropos 72,1/2 (1977) 288-99.

26233 ______. Sanskritization in Eastern Nepal. In Ethnology 15,1 (1976) 63-75.

26234 JONES, S.K. & R. JONES. Limbu women, divorce, and the domestic cycle. In Kailash 4,2 (1976) 169-84.

26235 MCDOUGAL, C. The Kulunge Rai: a study in kinship and marriage exchange. Kathmandu: Ratna Pustak Bhandar, 1979. 170p. (Bibliotheca Himalayica, 3,14)

26236 MACFARLANE, A. Resources and population; a study of the Gurungs of Nepal. Cambridge: CamUP, 1976. 364p.

26237 MESSERSCHMITT, D.A. The Gurungs of Nepal; conflict and change in a village society. Warminster: Aris & Phillips, 1976. 151p.

26238 ______. Rotating credit in Gurung society; the dhikur associations of Tin Gaun. In Himalayan R. 5,4 (1972) 23-35.

26239 PIGNÈDE, B. Clan organization and hierarchy among the Gurungs. In CIS 6 (1962) 102-19.

26240 ______. Les Gurungs. Une population himalayenne du Népal. The Hague: Mouton, 1967. 414p.

26241 SAGANT, P. Les travaux et les jours dans un village du Népal oriental. In O&M 13,4 (1973) 247-72.

26242 UPRETI, B.P. Analysis of change in Limbu-Brahmin interrelationship in Limbuwan, Nepal. Diss., U. of Wisconsin, 1975. 303p. [UM 75-18,625]

ii. the Newars: dominant group of the Kathmandu Valley

26243 BAJRACHARYA, P.H. Newar marriage customs and festivals. In SWJA 15,4 (1959) 418-28.

26244 CHATTOPADHYAY, K.P. An essay on the history of Newar culture; social organization of the Newars. In JASBengal 19,10 (1923) 465-560.

26245 DUMONT, L. Nepal compared to India: the Newar and others. In CIS 7 (1964) 90-102.

26246 FÜRER-HAIMENDORF, C. VON. Elements of Newar social structure. In JRAI 86,2 (1956) 15-38.

26247 NEPALI, G.S. The Newars; an ethno-sociological study of a Himalayan community. Bombay: United Asia Pub., 1965. 476p.

26248 ROSSER, C. Social mobility in the Newar caste system. In C. von Fürer-Haimendorf, ed. Caste and kin in Nepal, India, and Ceylon. Bombay: Asia, 1966, 68-139.

26249 TOFFIN, G. Pyangaon; une communauté newar de la vallée de Kathmandou; la vie matérielle. Paris: CNRS, 1977. 218p.

iii. other groups of the middle region

26250 BIRMINGHAM, J. Traditional potters of the Kathmandu valley: an ethno-archaeological study. In Man ns 10,3 (1975) 370-86.

26251 BOULLIER, V. Naître renonçant. Une caste de Sannyāsi villageois dans un village du Népal central. Paris: Klincksieck, 1979. 264p.

26252 CAUGHLEY, R.C. & B.M. DAHAL & C. BANDHU. Notes on Chepang culture. In J. of Tribhuvan U. 6,1 (1971) 77-89.

26253 DOBREMEZ, J.F. & C. JEST. Manaslu: hommes et milieux des vallées du Népal central. Paris: CNRS, 1976. 202p.

26254 FÜRER-HAIMENDORF, C. VON. Ethnographic notes on the Tamangs of Nepal. In EA 9,3/4 (1956) 166-77.

26255 GABORIEAU, M. Les curauté du Moyen Népal: place d'un groupe de Musulmans dans une société des castes. In L'homme 6 (1966) 81-91.

26256 JEST, C. Les Chepang, ethnie népalaise de langue tibeto-birmane. In O&M 6 (1966) 169-84.

26257 MACDONALD, A.W. Les Tamang vu par l'un d'eux. In L'homme 6,1 (1966) 27-58.

26258 PRINDLE, P.H. Fictive kinship (mit) in East Nepal. In Anthropos 70,5/6 (1975) 877-82.

26259 REINHARD, J. The Kusunda: ethnographic notes on a hunting tribe of Nepal. In Intl. Cmtee. on Urgent Anthropological & Ethnological Res., Bull. 10 (1968) 95-100.

d. Brahmans and Chetris: Nepali Hindu castes

26260 FÜRER-HAIMENDORF, C. VON. The interrelations of castes and ethnic groups in Nepal. In BSOAS 20 (1957) 243-53.

26261 ______. Status differences in a high Hindu caste of Nepal. In EA 12 (1959) 223-33.

26262 ______. Unity and diversity in the Chetri caste of Nepal. In his Caste and kin in Nepal, India and Ceylon. Bombay: Asia, 1966, 11-67.

26263 PRINDLE, P.H. The closed corporate community in South Asia. In MI 55,2 (1975) 98-117.

e. people of the Tarai, marshy plain and forests of the Indian border

i. the Tharus, immigrants from the Indian Tarai

26264 BISTA, D.B. The forgotten people of Dang valley. In Vasudha 12,10 (1969) 10-14.

26265 JOSHI, T.R. Tharus of Rapti valley. In Vasudha 8, 3 (1970) 39-43.

26266 MACDONALD, A.W. Notes sur deux fêtes chez les Tharu de Dang. In O & M 9 (1969) 69-80.

26267 SINGH, L.R. The Tharus: a study in human ecology. In NGJI 2,3 (1956) 153-66.

26268 SRIVASTAVA, S.K. The Tharus; a study in cultural dynamics. Agra: Agra U. Press, 1958. 343p.

ii. Nepali Muslims (2% of pop.), mostly merchants of the Tarai

26269 GABORIEAU, M. Minorités musulmanes dans le royaume hindou du Népal. Nanterre: Laboratoire d'ethnologie, 1977, 282p.

26270 ______. Muslims in the Hindu kingdom of Nepal. In CIS 6 (1972) 84-105.

26271 ______. Les Musulmans du Népal. In O & M 6 (1966) 121-32.

f. women of Nepal

26272 ACHARYA, M. Statistical profile of Nepalese women: a critical review. Kathmandu: CEDA, Tribhuvan U., 1979. 101p. (Status of women in Nepal, 1, pt. 1)

26273 BENNET, L. Tradition and change in the legal status of Nepalese women. Kathmandu: CEDA, Tribhuvan U., 1979. 107p. (Status of women in Nepal, 1, pt. 2)

26274 BENNETT, L. The wives of the rishis: an analysis of the Tif-Rishi Pancham; women's festival. In Kailash 4,2 (1976) 185-207.

26275 GHIMIRE, D. The role of women in development in Nepal. In R. Jahan & H. Papanek, eds. Women and development. Dacca: Bangladesh Inst. of Law and Intl. Affairs, 1979, 95-114.

26276 ______, ed. Women and development. Kathmandu: CEDA, Tribhuvan U., 1977. 77p.

26277 JOSHI, C., ed. Rural women in today's horizon: a report on the National Workshop for the Promotion and Training of Rural Women in Income-Raising Group Activities, 5-7 Feb. 1979, Mujelia, Janakpur, Nepal. Kathmandu: Social Service Natl. Co-ordination Council, Women Servies Co-ordination Cmtee., Nepal, 1979. 68p.

26278 PRADHAN, B. Institutions concerning women in Nepal. Kathmandu: CEDA, Tribhuvan U., 1979. 140p.

26279 Women of Nepal: approaches to change: a seminar sponsored by the U.S. International Communication Agency and the Centre for Economic Development and Administration, May 17-18, 1978, Kathmandu. Kathmandu: Tribhuvan U., 1978. 95p.

2. Villages and Rural Development

26280 Bajhang small area development program survey.... Kathmandu: Res. Div., Min. of Home Panchayat, 1976. 264p.

26281 CAPLAN, A.P. Priests and cobblers: a study of social change in a Hindu village in Western Nepal. Scranton, PA: Chandler, 1972. 103p.

26282 GABORIEAU, M. Systèmes traditionnels des échanges de service specialisés contre remuneration dans une localité du Népal centrale. In Puruṣārtha 3 (1977) 3-70.

26283 HITCHCOCK, J.T. Some effects of recent change in rural Nepal. In HO 22,1 (1963) 75-82.

26284 Jumla small area development program survey.... Kathmandu: Res. Div., Min. of Home Panchayat, 1976. 239p.

26285 MCDOUGAL, C. Village and household economy in far western Nepal. Kirtipur: Tribhuvan U., 1968. 125p.

3. Urbanization, Migration, and Settlement Patterns

26286 DAHAL, D.R. & N.K. RAI & A.E. MANZARDO. Land and migration in far-western Nepal. Kirtipur: Inst. of Nepal & Asian Studies, Tribhuvan U., 1977. 170p.

26287 HOSKEN, F.P. The Kathmandu Valley towns; a record of life and change in Nepal. NY: Weatherhill, 1974. 327p.

26288 JHA, M. Aspects of a great traditional city in Nepal: an anthropological appraisal. Varanasi: Kishor Vidya Niketan, 1978. 188p + 7pl.

26289 KLEINERT, C. Stadtentwicklung und Stadterneuerung in Nepal; das Bhaktapur Development Project. In IAF 9, 3/4 (1978) 271-93.

26290 NEPAL. DEPT. OF HOUSING & PHYSICAL PLANNING. The Physical development plan for the Kathmandu Valley. Kathmandu: 1969. 195p.

26291 PRUSCHA, C., ed. Kathmandu Valley, the preservation of physical environment and cultural heirtage: a protective inventory. Vienna: Schroll, 1975. 2v., chiefly ill.

26292 SHRESTHA, C.B. Urbanisation trends and emerging pattern in Nepal. In Himalayan R. 7,7 (1975) 1-13.

26293 THAPA, Y.S. & P.N. TIWARI. In-migration on pattern in Kathmandu urban areas. Kirtipur: CEDA, Tribhuvan U., 1977. 119p.

4. Social Welfare and Health Services, incl. Family Planning

26294 ALLEN, N.J. Approaches to illness in the Nepalese Hills. In J.B. Landon, ed. Social anthropology and medicine. London: Academic Press, 1976, 550-52.

26295 DUNN, F.L. Medical-geographical observations in central Nepal. In Milbank Mem. Fund Q. 40 (1962) 125-48.

26296 JHA, P. Family planning in Nepal. In J. of the Nepal Medical Assn. 6,1 (1968) 16-26.

26297 JOSHI, D.D. Veterinary public health hazards in Nepal. Kathmandu: Chandra Kumar Bhattarai, 1973. 87p.

26298 PITT, P. Surgeon in Nepal. London: Murray, 1970. 255p.

26299 Report of a study in the primary health care unit (district) of Tanaha, Nepal. Kathmandu: Tribhuvan U., Inst. of Medicine, Health, Manpower Dev. Res. Project, 1977. 110p. (Rural health needs study, 1)

26300 SHAH, MOIN & M. SHRESHTA & R. PARKER. Report of a study in the primary health care unit (district) of Dhankuta, Nepal. Kathmandu: Tribhuvan U., Inst. of Medicine, Health, Manpower Dev. Res. Project, 1979. 125p.

26301 STABLEIN, W. A medical-cultural system among the Tibetan and Newar Buddhists: ceremonial medicine. In Kailash 1,3 (1973) 193-203.

26302 WORTH, R.M. & N.K. SHAH. Nepal health survey, 1965-1966. Honolulu: UPH, 1969. 158p.

5. Education in Nepal (16% literacy)

26303 AGARWAL, G.R. The challenge of educational finance in Nepal. Kathmandu: CEDA, Tribhuvan U., 1978. 73p.

26304 ARYAL, K.R. Education for the development of Nepal. Kathmandu: Shanti Prakashan, 1970. 166p.

26305 Development of higher education in Nepal. Kathmandu: Planning, Stat & Res. Div., 1970. 33p.

26306 Development of primary education in Nepal. Kathmandu: Min. of Educ., 1967. 22p.

26307 GURUNG, HARKA. Distribution and mobility of graduates in Nepal. In Himalayan R. 5,4 (1972) 36-60.

26308 HAYES, L. Educational reform and student political behaviour in Nepal. In AS 16,8 (1976) 752-69.

26309 KASAJU, P. & S.R. LAMICHCHANE & G.S. PRADHAN, eds. Education for rural development, National Seminar, Dhunche, Rasuwa, 17-25 December 1979. Kathmandu: Tribhuvan U., Res. Centre for Educ. Innovation & Dev., 1980. 117p.

26310 MALLA, K.P. English in Nepalese education. Kathmandu: Ratna Pustak Bhandar, 1977. 40p.

26311 MOHSIN, M & P. KASAJU, eds. Education and development. Kathmandu: Natl. Educ. Cmtee., 1975. 174p.

26312 NEPAL. MIN. OF EDUC. The national educational system: plan for 1971-76. Kathmandu: 1971. 79p.

26313 NEPAL. MIN. OF EDUC. Secondary education in Nepal. Kathmandu: 1970. 54p.

26314 PANDEY, R.R. & KAISHER BAHADUR K.C. & H.B. WOOD, Eds. Education in Nepal. Report of the Nepal National Planning Commission.... Kathmandu: College of Educ., 1956. 259p.

26315 REED, H.B. & M.J. REED. Nepal in transition; educational innovation. Pittsburgh: U. of Pittsburgh Press, 1968. 215p.

26316 SAKYA, T.M. & P.K. KASAJU, eds. Education and development. Kathmandu: Centre for Educ. Res. Innovation & Development, Natl. Education Cmtee., 1977. 104p.

26317 WOOD, H.B. The development of education in Nepal. Washington: U.S. Dept of Health, Educ. & Welfare, 1965. 78p. (U.S. Office of Educ. Bulletin, 5, 1965)

D. Religions of Nepal: Buddhism, Hinduism, Islam and Folk Cults

26318 ALLEN, M. Buddhism without monks: the Vajrayana religion of the Newars of Kathmandu valley. In SA 3 (1973) 1-14.

26319 BISTA, K.B. Le culte du Kuldevata au Népal en particulier chez certains Ksatri de la vallée de Kathmandu. Paris: CNRS, 1972. 169p.

26320 BROUGH, J. Nepalese Buddhist rituals. In BSOAS 12,3/4 (1948) 668-76.

26321 CAPLAN, A.P. Ascetics in western Nepal. In EA 26, 2 (1973) 173-81.

26322 DEEP, D.K. The Nepal festivals: with some articles enquiring into Nepalese arts, religion, and culture. Kathmandu: Ratna Pustak Bhandar, 1978. v. 1, 128p.

26323 FUNKE, F.W. Religiöses Leben der Sherpa. Innsbruck: München, Universitätsverlag Wagner, 1969. 369p. (Khumbu Himal, 9)

26324 FÜRER-HAIMENDORF, C. VON. A nunnery in Nepal. In Kailash 4,2 (1976) 121-54.

26325 ______. The role of the monastery in Sherpa society. In Ethnologica ns 2 (1960) 12-28.

26326 GABORIEAU, M. Le culte des saints chex les Musulmans au Népal et en Inde du nord. In Social Compass 25, 3-4 (1978) 477-94.

26327 ______. Legende et culte du saint musulman Ghazi Miya au Népal occidental et en Inde du Nord. In O & M 15,3 (1975)289-318.

26328 ______. Note préliminaire sur le dieu Masta. In O & M 9,1 (1969) 19-50.

26329 ______. Le transe rituelle dans l'Himalaya central: folie, avatar, meditation. In Purusartha 2 (1975) 147-172.

26330 HITCHCOCK, J.T. A Nepalese shamanism and the classic inner Asian tradition. In HR 7,2 (1967) 149-58.

26331 HITCHCOCK, J.T. & R.L. JONES, Eds. Spirit possession in the Nepal Himalayas. Warminster: Aris & Phillips, 1976. 401p.

26332 HÖFER, A. Notes sur le culte du terroir chez les Tamang du Népal. In J.M.C. Thomas & L. Bernot, eds., Langues et techniques, nature et société. Paris: Klincksieck, 1972, v.2, 147-56.

26333 HÖFER, A. & B.P. SHRESTHA. Ghost exorcism among the Brahmans of central Nepal. In CAJ 17,1 (1973) 51-77.

26334 LIENHARD, S. Religionssynkretismus in Nepal. In H. Bechert, ed. Buddhism in Ceylon and studies on religious syncretism in Buddhist countries. Göttingen: Vandenhoeck & Ruprecht, 1978, 146-77.

26335 MILLER, C.J. Faith-healers in the Himalayas: an investigation of traditional healers and their festivals in Dolakha District of Nepal. Kirtipur: Centre for Nepal & Asian Studies, Tribhuvan U., 1979. 201p.

26336 SCHMID, T. Shamanistic practice in northern Nepal. In Symposium on Shamanism, Abo, 1962. Studies in shamanism.... Ed. by C.-M. Edsman. Stockholm: Almqvist & Wiksell, 1967, 82-89.

26337 SNELLGROVE, D.L. Buddhist Himalaya; travels and studies in quest of the origins and nature of Tibetan religion. Oxford: Cassirer, 1957. 324p.

26338 ______. Himalayan pilgrimage: a study of Tibetan religion by a traveller through Western Nepal. Oxford: Cassirer, 1961. 304p.

26339 ______, ed. & tr. Four Lamas of Dolpo; Tibetan biographies. Cambridge: HUP, 1967. [v.1, Intro. & trans., 302p. + 46pl. v.2, Tibetan texts & commentaries, 345p.]

E. Literatures of Modern Nepal

1. Modern Literature in Nepal

26340 DIWAS, T., ed. Seven poets. Kathmandu: Royal Nepal Academy, 1975. 163p.

26341 MAHENDRA BIR BIKRAM SHAHA DEVA, King of Nepal. A harvest of poems. 2nd ed. T.R. Tuladhar. Kathmandu: HMG Press, 1964. 58p. [1st pub. 1960]

26342 Modern Nepali poems. Kathmandu: Royal Nepal Academy, 1972. 327p.

26343 Poems of today in Nepal bhasa. Kantipur: Nepal Bhasa Parishad, 196-. 127p.

26344 PRADHAN, P.M. Adikavi Bhanubhakta Acharya. Kalimpong: Bhagya Laxmi Prakashan, 1979. 96p. (Makers of Nepali literature series, 3) [Nepali poet, 1812-68]

26345 ______. Mahakavi Laxmi Prasad Devkota. Kalimpong: Bhagya Laxmi Prakashan, 1978. 82p. (Makers of Nepali Literature) [poet, 1980-59]

26346 ______. Modern Nepali literature and India. In IL 20,1 (1977) 19-26.

26347 RUBIN, D., tr. Nepali visions, Nepali dreams; the poetry of Laxmiprasad Devkota. NY: ColUP, 1980. 192p.

26348 SANKRITYAYAN, K. Indian Nepali literature: Himalayan echoes. In IL 21,6 (1978) 154-177.

26349 SUBEDI, A. Nepali literature: background & history. Kathmandu: Sajha Prakashan, 1978. 228p.

26350 VAIDYA, K.K. Nepalese short stories. Kathmandu: Purna Book Stall, 1971. 152p.

2. Newari Literature

26351 LIENHARD, S. Maṇicūḍavadānoddhṛta: a Buddhist rebirth story in the Nevārī language. Stockholm: Almqvist & Wiksell, 1963, 106p. (Stockholm Oriental Studies, 4)

26352 ______. Nevārīgītimañjari; religious and secular poetry of the Nevars of the Kathmandu Valley. Stockholm: Almqvist & Wiksell, 1974. 332p. (Stockholm Oriental Series, 10)

3. Folk Literature

26353 KAUFMANN, W. The folksongs of Nepal. In Ethnomusicology 6 (1962) 93-114.

26354 LALL, K. Lore and legend of Nepal. 2nd ed. Kathmandu: Ratna Pustak Bhandar, 1966. 46p.

26355 SHARMA, M.M. Folklore of Nepal. ND: Vision Books, 1978. 192p.

26356 SHARMA, N. Folk tales of Nepal. ND: Sterling, 1976. 112p.

26357 VAIDYA, K.K. Folk tales of Nepal; First series. 2nd ed. Kathmandu: Ratna Pustak Bhandar, 1971. 121p.

V. SIKKIM STATE AND DARJEELING DISTRICT OF WEST BENGAL (SINCE 1817)

A. General and Political History

1. General Histories of Modern Sikkim

26358 BASNET, L.B. Sikkim; a short political history. ND: S. Chand, 1974. 216p.

26359 RAGHUNADHA RAO, P. Indian and Sikkim, 1814-1970. ND: Sterling, 1972. 227p.

2. The Sikkim Raj as a British Protectorate, 1817-1947

26360 BENGAL. SECRETARIAT. The gazetteer of Sikhim. ND: Manjusri, 1972. 392p.

26361 BUCHANAN, W.J. Notes on towns in Darjeeling and Sikkim. Darjeeling: Improvement Fund, 1916. 40p.

26362 CHATTERJEE, A. Indo-Sikkim relations (1816-1935). In QRHS 16,2 (1976-77) 85-93.

26363 DONALDSON, F. Lepcha land, or six weeks in the Sikkim Himalayas. London: Sampson, Low, Marston, 1900. 213p.

26364 EDGAR, J.W. Report on a visit to Sikhim and the Thibetan frontier in Oct., Nov., & Dec., 1873. ND: Manjusri, 1969. 93p. [1st pub. 1874]

26365 KIERNAN, E.V.G. India, China, and Sikkim, 1886-1890. In IHQ 31 (1955) 32-51.

26366 LEBEDEVA, N.B. British colonial policy in Sikkim. In Central Asian R. 13 (1965) 258-66.

26367 MAJUMDAR, A.K. Hooker and Campbell in Sikkim. In BPP 81 (1962) 132-39.

26368 WADDELL, L.A. Among the Himalayas. 2nd ed. Kathmandu: Ratna Pustak Bhandar, 1977. 452p. (Bibliotheca Himalayica, 1, 18) [Rpt. 1900 ed.]

3. Sikkim as an Indian Protectorate, 1847-75: from Buddhist Theocracy towards Constitutional Democracy

26369 BELFIGLIO, V.J. India's economic and political relations with Sikkim. In AsSt 10,1 (1972) 131-144.

26370 BHOWMICK, D.J. & K.S. BHATTACHARJI. Constitutional and political development in Sikkim. In JCPS 8,3 (1974) 350-66.

26371 CHAUHAN, R.S. Constitutional development in Sikkim. In SAS 10,1/2 (1975) 68-93.

26372 COOKE, H. Time change: an autobiography. NY: Simon & Schuster, 1980. 285p.

26373 GROVER, B.S.K. Sikkim and India: storm and consolidation. ND: Jain Bros., 1974. 248p.

26374 GUPTA, K.P. Protest and change in Sikkim. In China Report 10,3 (1974) 8-13.

26375 RAO, P.R. The political parties of Sikkim. In MR 124 (1969) 819-22.

26376 ROSE, L.E. India and Sikkim; redefining the relationship. In PA 42 (1969) 32-46.

26377 ______. Sikkim and the Sino-Indian dispute. In PSR 8 (1969) 41-58.

26378 SINGH, A.C. Politics of Sikkim: a sociological study. Faridabad: Thomson Press, 1975. 205p.

26379 SINHA, A.C. The feudal polity and political development in Sikkim. In IAnth 3,2 (1973).

4. Integration of Sikkim as an Indian State, 1975- (1981 pop. 315,682)

26380 BHOWMIK, D.J. & K.S. BHATTACHARJI. Political and administrative development in Sikkim. In JCPS 11,3 (1977) 78-98.

26381 GUPTA, R. Sikkim: the merger with India. In AS 15,9 (1975) 786-98.

26382 MISRA, R.C. Sikkim joins the motherland. Bharatpur: Ajay Bandhu Fort, 1977. 114p.

26383 RAGHUNADHA RAO, P. Sikkim, the story of its integration with India. ND: Cosmo, 1978. 139p.

26384 SHUKLA, S.R. Sikkim: the story of integration. ND: S.Chand, 1976. 280p.

5. The Darjeeling area, ceded by Sikkim in 1835

26385 DOZEY, E.C. A concise history of the Darjeeling district since 1835, with a complete itinerary of tours in Sikkim and the district. 2nd ed. Calcutta: N. Mukherjee, 1922. 350p. [1st pub. 1917]

26386 HATHORN, J.G. A handbook of Darjeeling; with brief notes on the culture and manufacture of tea. Calcutta: R.C. Lepage, 1863. 175p.

26387 NAMGYAL, HOPE (COOKE). The Sikkimese theory of land-holding and the Darjeeling grant. In Bull. of Tibetology 3,2 (1966) 47-61.

26388 SEN, JAHAR. The military importance of Darjeeling in the nineteenth-century. In BPP 91,1 (1972) 81-92.

B. The Economy of Sikkim and Darjeeling

26389 CHAKRAVARTY, P.K. The causes of economic underdevelopment in Sikkim. In GRI 39,3 (1967) 141-43.

26390 MITRA, S. The economy of the Gielle basin in the sub-Himalayan region of Darjeeling district. In GRI 37,4 (1975) 315-28.

26391 MUKHERJEE, S. Emergence of Bengalee entrepreneurship in tea plantation in a Bengal district, 1879-1933. In IESHR 8,4 (1976) 487-513.

26392 NCAER. Techno-economic survey of Darjeeling tea industry. ND: 1977. 44p.

26393 NEBESKY-WOJKOWITZ, R. VON. Sikkim. In Zeitschrift für Wirtschaftsgeographie 4 (1960) 182-94.

26394 SYMINGTON, J. In a Bengal jungle: stories of life on the tea gardens of Northern India. Chapel Hill: U. of North Carolina Press, 1935. 245p.

26395 TEA MANUFACTURING AND MARKETING CONSULTANTS. Techno-economic survey of Darjeeling tea industry. Calcutta: 1979. 82p.

C. Society and Religion: Buddhist Lepchas and Bhotes, and Hindu Nepalese (literacy 33.8% in 1981)

26396 AWASTY, I. Between Sikkim and Bhutan: the Lepchas and Bhutias of Pedong. Delhi: B.R., 1978. 128p.

26397 BOSE, S. The Bhot of Northern Sikkim. In MI 46,2 (1966) 164-71.

26398 CHATTOPADHYAY, G. Lepchas of Kalimpong and Sikkim; a comparison. In Vanyajati 10 (1962) 99-109.

26399 DAS, A.K. The Lepchas of Darjeeling district. Calcutta: Tribal Welfare Dept., Govt. of W. Bengal, 1962. 168p.

26400 ______. The Lepchas of West Bengal. Calcutta: Editions Indian, 1978. 276p.

26401 GORER, G. Himalayan village; an account of the Lepchas of Sikkim. 2nd ed. NY: Basic Books, 1967. 488p. [1st ed. 1938]

26402 JEST, C. Religious beliefs of the Lepchas in the Kalimpong district, West Bengal. In JRAS (1960) 124-34.

26403 MACDONALD, A.W. Notes préliminaires sur quelques jhakri du Muglan. In JA 250 (1962) 107-39.

26404 MAZUMDAR, S. Folk-lore of the Lepchas. In Folklore(C) 2 (1961) 294-97.

26405 MITRA, S. The Lepchas of Darjeeling district: a study in acculturation. In GRI 38,2 (1976) 123-39.

26406 MORRIS, J. Living with Lepchas; a book about the Sikkim Himalayas. London: Heinemann, 1938. 312p.

26407 NAKANE, C. A plural society in Sikkim - a study of the interrelations of Lepchas, Bhotias and Nepalis. In C. von Fürer-Haimendorf, ed. Caste and kin in Nepal, India, and Ceylon. Bombay: Asia, 1966, 213-263.

26408 SIIGER, H. Fate in the religion of the Lepchas.... In Symposium on Fatalistic Beliefs, Abo, 1964. Fatalistic beliefs in religion, folklore and literature.... Ed. by H. Ringgren. Stockholm: Almqvist & Wiksell, 1967, 150-157.

26409 ______. The Lepchas: culture and religion of a Himalayan people. Pt. 1, results of anthropological field work in Sikkim, Kalimpong, and Git. Copenhagen: Natl. Museum of Denmark, 1967. 251p. (Its Ethnographical ser., 9,1)

26410 SIIGER, H. & J. RISCHEL. The Lepchas: culture and religion of a Himalayan people. Pt. 2, Lepcha ritual texts and commentary. Copenhagen: Natl. Museum of Denmark, 1967, 153p. (Its Ethnographical ser., 9,2)

26411 STOCKS, C. DE B. Folklore and customs of the Lepchas of Sikkim. In JASBengal ns 21,4 (1925) 327-505.

VI. BHUTAN/DRUKYUL: INDEPENDENT BUDDHIST MONARCHY OF THE EASTERN HIMALAYAS

A. General and Political History since 1772

1. General Histories and Accounts of Modern Bhutan

26412 NAGENDRA SINGH. Bhutan: a kingdom in the Himalayas; a study of the land, its people, and their government. rev. 2nd ed. ND: Thomson, 1978. 262p. [1st pub. 1972]

26413 PEMBERTON, R.B. Report on Bootan, with an appendix and maps, 1838. Calcutta: Bengal Military Orphan Press, 1839. 109p. [Rpt. in ISPP 2 (1961) 665-723; 3 (1961) 31-82]

26414 RAHUL, RAM. Modern Bhutan. Delhi: Vikas, 1971. 173p.

26415 RATHORE, L.S. The changing Bhutan. ND: Jain Bros., 1974. 168p.

2. Government and Politics

26416 BELFIGLIO, V.J. The structure of national law-making authority in Bhutan. In AsSt 12 (1974) 77-87.

26417 BONN, G. Bhutan - das verschlossene Königreich in Himalaya. In Indo Asia 15,1 (1973) 38-52.

26418 DEB, A. Diarchy in Bhutan: the Dharma Raja - Deb Raja system. In BPP 91,2 (1972) 158-165.

26419 LAMITARE, D.B. Murder of democracy in Himalayan kingdom. Tr. from Hindi by Lekh Chander & Rakesh. ND: Amarko Book Agency, dist. Classical, 1978. 172p.

26420 MISHRA, R.C. Recent trends in Bhutanese politics. In SAS 12,1/2 (1977) 132-44.

26421 ROSE, L.E. The politics of Bhutan. Ithaca: CornellUP, 1977. 237p. (South Asian political systems)

26422 RUSTOMJI, N.K. Bhutan, the dragon kingdom in crisis. Delhi: OUP, 1978. 150p.

3. Foreign Relations of Bhutan
a. general studies

26423 LABH, K. The international status of Bhutan before 1947. In IS 13,1 (1974) 75-93.

26424 ROSE, L.E. Bhutan's external relations. In PA 47, 2 (1974) 192-208.

b. relations with British India, 1772-1947

26425 DEB, A. Bhutan and India: a study in frontier political relations, 1772-1865. Calcutta: KLM, 1976. 190p.

26426 ______. Cooch Behar and Bhutan in the context of Tibetan trade. In Kailash 1,1 (1973) 80-88.

26427 ______. George Bogle's treaty with Bhutan (1775). In Bull. of Tibetology 8,1 (1971) 5-14.

26428 GRIFFITH, W. Bhutan, 1837-1838. ND: Skylark Printers, 1974? 197-312p. [1st pub. 1847]

26429 GUPTA, S.S. British relations with Bhutan. Jaipur: Panchsheel Prakashan, 1974. 223p.

26430 RENNIE, D.F. Bhotan and the story of the Doar War. ND: Manjusri, 1970. 408p. (Biblioteca Himalayica, 1,5) [1st pub. 1866]

c. relations with Independent India, 1947-

26431 AGRAWAL, K.N. Indo-Bhutanese relations. In Political Scientist 4,1 (1967-68) 41-46.

26432 BELFIGLIO, V.J. India's economic and political relations with Bhutan. In AS 12,8 (1972) 676-685.

26433 LABH, K. India and Bhutan. ND: Sindhu, 1974. 144p.

26434 MISRA, R.C. Indo-Bhutan relations in context of India's Himalayan policy. In PSR 16,1 (1977) 110-15.

26435 POULOUSE, T.T. Bhutan's external relations and India. In Intl. & Comp. Law Q. 20,2 (1971) 195-212.

B. Society and Religion in Bhutan (1977 pop. 1,100,000)

26436 ARIS, M. "The admonition of the Thunder-bolt cannonball" and its place in the Bhutanese new year festival. In BSOAS 39,3 (1976) 601-35.

26437 BONN, G. Religion and magic in Bhutan. In Indo Asia 16,1 (1974) 156-167.

26438 LAUF, D.I. Vorläufiger Bericht über die Geschichte und Kunst einiger lamaistischer Tempel und Klöster in Bhutan. In Ethnologische Zeitschrift 2 (1972) 79-110.

26439 MISHRA, R.C. Bhutan's social strucutre. In SAS 9, 1/2 (1974) 109-19.

26440 WARD, M. Some geographical and medical observations in North Bhutan. In GJ 132 (1966) 491-506.

VII. THE NORTHEAST INDIAN MOUNTAIN RIM: TRIBAL INTERFACE WITH BURMA AND CHINA

A. General Studies of the Arunachal, Purvanchal and Meghalaya Areas Bordering Assam

1. Historical Accounts and Studies

26441 BANERJEE, ANIL C. Eastern frontier of British India: 1784-1826. 2nd rev. ed. Calcutta: A. Mukherjee, 1946. 584p.

26442 BARPUJARI, H.K. Problem of the hill tribes: North-East Frontier; a critical analysis of the problems and policies of the British Government towards the hill tribes of the Frontier.... Gauhati: Lawyer's Book Stall, 1970-. v. 1, 1822-42, 207p.

26443 CHAKROVORTY, B.C. British relations with the hill tribes of Assam since 1858. Calcutta: KLM, 1964. 222p.

26444 ELWIN, V., ed. India's northeast frontier in the nineteenth century. Bombay: OUP, 1959. 473p.

26445 Historical and constitutional documents of north-eastern India, 1824-1973. Delhi: Concept, 1979. 378p.

26446 JOHNSTONE, J. Manipur and the Naga Hills. Delhi: Vivek, 1971. 286p.

26447 MACKENZIE, A. The north-east frontier of India. Delhi: Mittal Pub., 1979. 586p. [Rpt. 1884 ed.]

26448 MICHELL, ST. JOHN F. The North-East Frontier of India; a topographical, political, and military report. Delhi: Vivek, 1973. 374p. [1st pub. 1883]

26449 REID, R. History of the frontier areas bordering on Assam, from 1883-1941. Shillong: Assam Govt. Press, 1942. 303p.

26450 VENKATA RAO, V. A century of tribal politics in North East India, 1874-1974. ND: S. Chand, 1976. 556p.

2. Political Studies

26451 AGRAWAL, B.N. The North-Eastern Council: a study. In JCPS 12,2 (1978) 218-30.

26452 BHAT, S. The challenge of the northeast. Bombay: Popular, 1975. 146p.

26453 CHAUBE, S.K. Hill politics in north-east India. Bombay: Orient Longman, 1973. 258p.

26454 ______. The sixth Lok Sabha elections in the hill states of North-East India. In PSR 18,2 (1979) 105-20.

26455 FÜRER-HAIMENDORF, C. VON. Recent developments in Nagaland and NEFA. In Asian Affairs 59(ns 3),1 (1972) 3-13.

26456 NATL. SEMINAR ON HILL PEOPLE OF NORTH EASTERN INDIA, CALCUTTA, 1966. A common perspective for north-east India; speeches and papers.... Calcutta: Das Gupta, 1967. 256p.

26457 North Eastern Council. Shillong: NE Council, 1974. 41p.

26458 SARIN, V.I.K. India's north-east in flames. ND: Vikas, 1980. 194p.

26459 VENKATA RAO, V. & N. HAZARIKA. Local self-government in India: with special reference to Assam and north east India. ND: S. Chand, 1980. 348p.

3. Economic, Social, and Cultural Studies

26460 DAS, S.T. The people of the eastern Himalayas. ND: Sagar Pub., 1978. 230p.

26461 DATTA RAY, B. Social and economic profile of north-east India. Delhi: B.R., 1978. 356p.

26462 DUBEY, S.M., ed. North East India: a sociological study. Delhi: Concept, 1978. 426p. [1975 seminar at Dibrugarh]

26463 FÜRER-HAIMENDORF, C. VON. Himalayan Barbary. London: Murray, 1955. 241p.

26464 INDIA (REP.). CENSUS OF INDIA, 1961. Demographic and socio-economic profiles of the hill areas of north-east India, by B.K. Roy Burman. ND: Office of the Registrar General, 1970. 379 + 191p.

26465 SHARMA, T.C. & D.N. MAJUMDAR. Eastern Himalayas: a study on anthropology and tribalism. ND: Cosmo, 1980. 221p.

26466 SIMOONS, F.J. & E.S. SIMOONS. A ceremonial ox of India: the mithan in nature, culture, and history. Madison: UWiscP, 1968. 323p.

4. Religions and Folklore of the NE Tribal Areas

26467 BARKATAKI, S., comp. Tribal folk-tales of Assam (hills). Gauhati: Pub. Board, Assam, 1970. 237p.

26468 BORGOHAIN, B.K. Folk tales of Meghalaya and Arunachal Pradesh. ND: Sterling, 1979. 112p. (Folk tales of India series, 19) [1st pub. 1974]

26469 BORGOHAIN, B.K. & P.C. ROY CHAUDHURY. Folk tales of Nagaland, Manipur, Tripura and Mizoram. ND: Sterling, 1975. 120p. (Folk tales of India series, 20)

26470 BRAHMA, M.M., comp. Folk-songs of the Bodos. Gauhati: Gauhati U., 1960. 192p.

26471 ELWIN, V. Myths of the north-east frontier of India. Shillong: NEFA, 1968. 495p. [1st pub. 1958]

26472 ______. A new book of tribal fiction. Shillong: NEFA, 1970. 376p.

26473 GOHAIN, B.C. Human sacrifice and head-hunting in north-eastern India. Gauhati: Lawyer's Book Stall, 1977. 102p.

26474 MIRI, SUJATA, ed. Religion and society of north-east India. ND: Vikas, 1980. 122p.

B. Arunachal Pradesh: The Former North-East Frontier Agency (NEFA) of the Eastern Himalaya (1981 pop. 628,050)

1. Historical and Political Studies
a. the British period, 1827-1947

26475 BOSE, M.L. British policy in the North-East Frontier Agency. ND: Concept, 1979. 236p.

26476 CHAKRAVARTI, L.N. Glimpses of the early history of Arunachal. Shillong: Res. Dept., Arunachal Pradesh Admin., 1973. 134p.

26477 NYMAN, L.-E. Tawang: a case study of British frontier policy in the Himalayas. In JAH 10 (1976) 151-71.

b. post-1947: from NEFA (1954) to Arunachal Pradesh U.T. (1972)

26478 ELWIN, V. Democracy in NEFA. Shillong: NEFA, 1965. 195p.

26479 NEFA. A brief account of administrative and development activities in North-East Frontier Agency since independence. Calcutta: A. Dhar, 1957. 40p.

26480 ROSE, L.E. & M.W. FISHER. The North-East Frontier Agency of India. Berkeley: Inst. of Intl. Studies, U. of California, 1967. 95p.

26481 SEN, G.E. Sortie over NEFA. In EW 12 (1960) 139-44.

2. Economic and Social Development (Literacy 20.1% in 1981)

26482 GHOSH, S.K. Education and social change: NEFA. In Ethnos 34 (1969) 118-29.

26483 INDIA (REP.). OFFICE OF THE DIRECTOR OF CENSUS OPERATIONS, ARUNACHAL PRADESH. A portrait of population: series 24: Arunachal Pradesh. Delhi: Cont. of Pub., 1975. 128p.

26484 NCAER. Techno-economic survey of NEFA. ND: 1967. 197p.

26485 NEFA on the march. Shillong: Cultural Research Officer for the NEFA, 1964. 44p.

3. Tribal People of Arunachal
a. general studies

26486 BARDOLOI, M.N. Land of the hornbill and myna. Shillong: NEFA, 1971. 98p.

26487 ______., ed. Our festivals. Shillong: Dir. of Info. & Public Relations, NEFA, 1968. 58p.

26488 CHOWDHURY, J.N. Arunachal panorama: a study in profile. Shillong: Jaya Chowdhury, 1973. 289p. + 26 pl.

26489 ______. A comparative study of Adi religion. Shillong: NEFA, 1971. 127p.

26490 DAS, A.K. Tribal art and craft. Delhi: Agam, 1979. 190p.

26491 DUTTA, P.C., ed. Solung, a festival of the Adis of NEFA. Shillong: NEFA, 1969. 61p.

26492 ELWIN, V. A philosophy for NEFA. 2nd rev. ed. Shillong: P.C. Dutta, for the Governor of Assam, 1964. 296p. [1st pub. 1959]

b. tribals of Kameng District

26493 SHARMA, R.R.P. The Sherdukpens. Shillong: P.C. Dutta, for the Research Dept., Adviser's Secretariat, 1961. 101p. (People of NEFA)

26494 SINHA, R. The Akas. Shillong: Res. Dept., Adviser's Secretariat, 1962. 143p. (People of NEFA)

26495 SINHA, R. The conception of an ideal individual in Aka society. In Bull. of the Res. Dept., NEFA 1,1 (1958) 64-89.

c. tribals of Subansiri District

26496 FÜRER-HAIMENDORF, C. VON. The Apa Tanis and their neighbours: a primitive civilization of the Eastern Himalayas. NY: Free Press of Glencoe, 1962. 166p.

26497 ______. A Himalayan tribe: from cattle to cash. ND: 1980. 224p. [Apa Tanis]

26498 MAHAPATRA, L.K. The Daphalā and the Miji society: a preliminary ecological analysis. In Sociologus ns 12,2 (1962) 158-66.

26499 PANDEY, B.B. The Hill Miri. Shillong: Dir. of Info. & Public Relations, Govt. of Arunachal Pradesh, 1974. 176p. + 16 pl.

26500 SAIKIA, P.D. Studies in Dafla social and religious life. Gauhati: Dept. of Tribal Culture & Folklore Res., U. of Gauhati, 1964. 70p.

26501 SHUKLA, B.K. The Daflas of the Subansiri Region. Shillong: NEFA, 1965. 118p. (People of NEFA)

26502 STONOR, C.R. Notes on religion and ritual among the Dafla tribes of the Assam Himalayas. In Anthropos 52 (1957) 1-23.

d. tribals of Siang District

26503 BANERJEE, G.S. Adis of Arunachal: a chapter in the social history of North-East India. Bhatpara, 24 Parganas Dist.: Banerjee, 1975. 272p.

26504 BHATTACHARJEE, T.K. The Tangams. Shillong: Res. Dept., Govt. of Arunachal Pradesh, 1975. 96p.

26505 DHASMANA, M.M. The Ramos of Arunachal: a socio-cultural study. ND: Concept, 1979. 298p.

26506 LAL, P. & B.K. DAS GUPTA. Lower Siang people: a study in ecology and society. Calcutta: AnthSI, 1979. 158p. (Its memoir, 50)

26507 ROY, S. Aspects of Padam-Minyong culture. 2nd rev. ed. Shillong: NEFA, 1966. 311p.

26508 SRIVASTAVA, L.R.N. The Gallongs. Shillong: Res. Dept., Adviser's Secretariat, 1962. 128p. (People of NEFA)

e. tribals of Lohit District

26509 BARUAH, T.K.M. The Idu Mishmis. Shillong: NEFA Res. Dept., 1960. 110p.

26510 ______. The Singphos and their religion. Shillong: Dir. of Info. & Public Relations, Govt. of Arunachal Pradesh, 1977. 177p.

26511 SEN, B. The Khamptis: an outline of their culture. In MI 45 (1965) 237-43.

f. tribals of Tirap District

26512 DUTTA, P.C. Social organisation of the Wanchos of Tirap District, Arunachal Pradesh. In Resarun 4,1 (1978) 14-36.

26513 ______. The Tangsas of the Namchik and Tirap valleys. Shillong: NEFA, 1969. 96p. (People of NEFA) [1st pub. 1957]

26514 SRIVASTAVA, L.R.N. Among the Wanchos of Arunachal Pradesh. Shillong: Res. Dept., Arunachal Pradesh Admin., 1973. 188p.

C. Nagaland: Fiercely Independent Naga Tribes of the Indo-Burmese Border

1. Historical and Political Studies

a. general studies

26515 ALEMCHIBA, M. A brief historical account of Nagaland. Kohima: Naga Inst. of Culture, 1971. 213p.

26516 ELWIN, V., ed. The Nagas in the nineteenth century. Bombay: OUP, 1969. 650p.

26517 LUTHRA, P.N. Nagaland from a district to a state. Shillong: Dir. of Info. & Public Relations, Arunachal Pradesh, 1974. 118p.

26518 YONUO, A. The rising Nagas: a historical and political study. Delhi: Vivek, 1974. 440p.

b. accounts by travellers and officials

26519 BOWER, U.G. The hidden land. London: Murray, 1953. 244p.

26520 ______. Naga path. London: Murray, 1950. 260p.

c. Nagaland State (est. 1963) - government and politics (1981 pop. 773,281)

26521 AGRAWAL, B.N. The political scene of Nagaland: the role of political parties. In JCPS 12,3 (1978) 330-41.

26522 FRANDA, M.F. The Naga National Council: origins of a separatist movement. In EW 13,4-6 (1961) 153-56.

26523 CHAKRAVARTI, K.C. Nehru government's Naga policy. In EW 10,26-28 (1958) 939-40.

26524 GUJRAL, R. General elections of Nagaland - 1969. In IPSR 4 (1970) 255-64.

26525 JOHARI, J.C. Creation of Nagaland: triumph of ebullient infra-nationalism. In IJPS 36,1 (1975) 13-38.

26526 The Naga challenge. In IQ 12,4 (1956) 426-35. [By "Kautilya"]

26527 NAGALAND. Nagaland is born. Kohima: Director of Info. & Publicity, 1963. 123p.

26528 NAGALAND. LEGISLATIVE ASSEMBLY. First Nagaland Legislative Assembly 1964-69; a review. Kohima: 1969. 72p.

26529 PARANJPE, H.G. Practice and procedure in Nagaland Legislative Assembly. Kohima: Assembly Secretariat, 1971. 130p.

26530 RAMASUBBAN, R. The Naga impasse in India. In EA 31,4 (1978) 393-412.

d. continuing independence demands and guerrilla insurgency

26531 ARAM, M. Peace in Nagaland: eight year story, 1964-72. ND: Arnold-Heinemann, 1974. 335p.

26532 GUNDEVIA, Y.D. War and peace in Nagaland. Dehra-Dun: Palit & Palit, 1975. 250p.

26533 HORAM, M. Nagaland: waiting for the peace that never comes. In EPW 9,31 (1974) 1226-39.

26534 MANKEKAR, D.R. On the slippery slope in Nagaland. Bombay: 1967. 202p.

26535 MAXWELL, N.G.A. India and the Nagas. London: Minority Rights Group, 1973. 32p.

26536 MEANS, G.P. & I.N. MEANS. Nagaland - the agony of ending a guerrilla war. In PA 39 (1966-67) 290-313.

26537 MISRA, U. The Naga national question. In EPW 13,14 (1978) 618-24.

26538 NIRMAL NIBEDON. Nagaland, the night of the guerrillas. ND: Lancers Pub., 1978. 404p.

26539 STRACEY, P.D. Nagaland nightmare. Bombay: Allied, 1968. 319p.

2. Economic and Social Development (literacy 41.99% in 1981)

26540 ASSN. OF VOLUNTARY AGENCIES FOR RURAL DEV. Rural development plan of selected blocks in Nagaland. ND: AVARD, 1978. 179p.

26541 Educational administration in Nagaland: a survey report, 1978. ND: Natl. Staff College for Educ. Planners & Admin., 1978. 62p.

26542 HORAM, M. Social change in Nagaland. In MI 55,2 (1975) 149-58.

26543 MUKERJEE, S. Nagaland: a regional study. In DG 15,1 (1977) 209-34.

26544 ______. Potentiality for industrial development in Nagaland. In GRI 36,2 (1974) 171-77.

26545 NAGALAND. TOWN PLANNING ORG. Development plan of Mokokchung Sub-Division, Mokokchung Tuli-Changki belt, and Mokokchung urban area, 1971-1991. Kohima: 1978. 128p. + 16 pl.

26546 ______. Kohima master plan, 1974-1994. Kohima: 1975. 63p. + 21 pl.

26547 ______. The master plan for Dimapur. Kohima: 1975. 141p. + 18 pl.

26548 NAGALAND. CMSN. TO SURVEY THE WORK DONE BY THE TRIBAL, RANGE, AND AREA COUNCILS IN THE DISTRICTS OF KOHIMA & MOKOKCHUNG AND REGIONAL AND AREA COUNCILS IN THE DISTRICT OF TUENSANG. Report. Kohima: Nagaland Govt. Press, 1968. 179p. [Chm., R. Khating]

26549 NAGALAND. DIR. OF EDUC. Statistics on Nagas completing secondary and higher education and their state of employment, as on 31st March 1971. Kohima: 1971. 48p.

26550 NAGALAND. PLANNING & CO-ORDINATION DEPT. Draft Fifth five year plan, 1974-1979. Kohima: 1973. 2 v.

26551 ______. Fourth five year plan; a brief outline. Kohima: 1970. 52p.

26552 NAGALAND. PLANNING AND COORDINATION DEPT. EVAL. UNIT. Evaluation report on the impact of block programmes in Nagaland. Kohima: 1975. 41p.

26553 NCAER. Techno-economic survey of Nagaland. ND: 1968. 132p.

26554 SINHA, D.P., et al., eds. Descriptive cum analytical study of Nagaland education system. Hyderabad: Centre for Educ. Policy & Mgmt., Admin. Staff College of India, 1977. 238p.

26555 SMALL INDUSTRIES SERVICE INST., CALCUTTA. Report on industrial potentiality survey in Nagaland. ND: Dev. Commissioner, Small Scale Industries, 1970. 68p.

3. The Naga Tribes - Ethnographic Studies

26556 ANAND, V.K. Nagaland in transition. ND: Associated Pub. House, 1967. 144p.

26557 BHATTACHARYA, P.K. Position of women in the Naga society. In Highlander 3,1 (1975) 11-18.

26558 FÜRER-HAIMENDORF, C. VON. The Konyak Nagas; an Indian frontier tribe. NY: Holt, Rinehart & Winston, 1969. 111p.

26559 ______. Morality and prestige among the Nagas. In M.C. Pradhan, et al., eds. Anthropology and archaeology. Bombay: OUP, 1969, 154-81.

26560 ______. The naked Nagas. 2nd rev. ed. Calcutta: Thacker Spink, 1962. 239p.

26561 ______. Return to the naked Nagas: an anthropologist's view of Nagaland, 1936-1970. ND: Vikas, 1976. 268p.

26562 HARTWIG, W. Wirtschaft und Gesellschaftsstruktur der Naga: in der zweigen Hälfte des 19. und zu Beginn des 20. Jahrhunderts. Berlin: Akademie-Verlag, 1970. 274p.

26563 HORAM, M. Naga polity. Delhi: B.R., 1975. 161p.

26564 ______. Social and cultural life of Nagas: the Tangkhul Nagas. Delhi: B.R., 1977. 122p.

26565 HUTTON, J.H. The Angami Nagas; with some notes on neighbouring tribes. 2nd ed. Bombay: Indian Branch, OUP, 1969. 499p. [1st pub. 1921]

26566 ______. The mixed culture of the Naga tribes. In JRAI 95 (1965) 16-43.

26567 ______. The Sema Nagas. 2nd ed. London: OUP, for Govt. of Nagaland, 1968. 467p. [1st pub. 1921]

26568 KAPADIA, K.M. The matrilineal social organisation of the Nagas of Assam.... Bombay: Popular, 1950. 34p.

26569 MAJUMDAR, S.N. The Ao Nagas. Calcutta: S. Majumder, 1925. 58p.

26570 MILLS, J.P. The Ao Nagas. 2nd ed. Bombay: OUP, 1973. 510p. [Rpt. 1926 ed.]

26571 ______. The Lhota Nagas. London: Macmillan, 1922. 255p.

26572 ______. The Rengma Nagas. London: Macmillan, 1937. 381p.

26573 SMITH, W.C. The Ao Naga tribe of Assam; a study in ethnology and sociology. London: Macmillan, 1925. 244p.

4. Folklore

26574 Folk tales from Nagaland. Kohima: Naga Inst. of Culture, 1971. 82p.

D. Manipur: Former Princely State, Founded by a Hinduized Naga in 1714 (1981 pop. 1,433,691)

1. Historical and Political Studies (Statehood Granted, 1972)

26575 BANERJEE, S.K. Manipur state constitution act, 1947. In IJPS 19 (1958) 35-38.

26576 BHADRA, G. The Kuki (?) uprising (1917-19): its causes and nature. In MI 55,1 (1975) 10-56.

26577 CHANDRAMANI SINGH, L. The boundaries of Manipur. Imphal: Pan Manipuri Youth League, 1970. 63p.

26578 ROY, J. History of Manipur. Calcutta: KLM, 1958. 190p.

2. Economic and Social Development (1981 literacy 41.99%)

26579 ASSN. OF VOLUNTARY AGENCIES FOR RURAL DEVEL. Meitei villages, Imphal (East Bloc), Manipur: rural development plan. ND: AVARD, 1975. 119p.

26580 INDIA (REP.). CENSUS OF INDIA, 1971. A portrait of population, Manipur. Imphal: Dir. of Census Operations, 1979. 107p.

26581 NCAER. Techno-economic survey of Manipur; economic report. Imphal: Manipur Admin., 1961. 128p.

3. Social Categories in Manipur
a. the Meithei Hindu community: Brahmans, Kshatriyas, and outcastes

26582 HODSON, T.C. The Meitheis. London: D. Nutt, 1908. 227p.

26583 SADASHIVAIAH, K. & RANGA RAO. A study on the demographic and socio-cultural aspects of the tribes of Manipur. In Tribe 10,1/2 (1977) 1-10.

b. Purums and other tribal groups of Manipur

26584 ACKERMAN, C. Structure and process: the Purum case. In AA 67 (1965) 83-91.

26585 ______. Structure and statistics: the Purum case. In AA 66 (1964) 53-65.

26586 COWGILL, G. Statistics and sense: more on the Purum case. In AA 66 (1964) 1358-65.

26587 GEOGHEGAN, W.H. & P. KAY. The Purum case: more structure and statistics: a critique of C. Ackermann's analysis of the Purum. In AA 66 (1964) 1351-58.

26588 GOSWAMI, M.C. & H. KAMKHENTHANG. Mother's brother in Paite society. In MI 52,1 (1972) 21-38.

26589 HODSON, T.C. The Naga tribes of Manipur. Delhi: B.R., 1974. 212p. + 15 pl. [Rpt. 1911 ed.]

26590 An introduction to tribal language and culture of Manipur (seven tribes). Imphal: Manipur State Kala Akademi, 1976. 163p.

26591 KHOKAR, M. Dance and ritual in Manipur. In SN 10 (1968) 35-47.

26592 LIVINGSTONE, F.B. A further analysis of Purum social structure. In AA 61 (1959) 1084-87.

26593 NEEDHAM, R. Chawte social structure. In AA 62 (1969) 236-53.

26594 ______. A synoptic examination of Anāl society. In Ethnos 28,2-4 (1963) 219-36.

26595 WILDER, W. Confusion vs. classification in the study of Purum society. In AA 66 (1964) 1365-71.

4. Chaitanya Vaishnavism of Manipur, State Religion 1714 - 1949

26596 PARRATT, S.N. The religion of Manipur: beliefs, rituals, and historical development. Calcutta: KLM, 1980. 218p.

26597 SINGH, K.B. Manipur Vaishnavism: a sociological interpretation. In SB 12 (1963) 66-72.

26598 THUMRA, J.H. Vaisnavism in Manipur. In R.M. Taylor, ed. Society and religion, essays in honour of M.M. Thomas. Bangalore: CISRS, 1976, 105-22.

5. Manipuri Language and Literature (Tibeto-Burman Language in Bengali Script)

26599 Glimpses of Manipuri language, literature, and culture. Imphal: Manipuri Sahitya Parishad, 1970. 42p.

26600 KHELCHANDRA SINGH, N. Manipuri language: status and importance. Imphal: N. Tombi Raj Singh, 1975. 67p.

26601 Manipuri. In IL 23,1/2 (1980) 299-313. [translations]

26602 Manipuri literature: a year of stagnation. In IL 22,6 (1979) 170-73.

26603 MANIPURI SAHITYA PARISHAD. A catalogue of Manipuri books, 1891-1969. Imphal: 1970. 51p.

6. Manipuri Dancing [See Chap. One, VII. D. 3. e.]

E. Mizoram: Land of the Christianized Mizo Tribes of the Lushai Hills (1981 pop. 481,774)

1. Historical and Political Studies (from Assam District to U.T., 1972)
a. general studies

26604 MCCALL, A.G. Lushei chrysalis. London: Luzac, 1949. 320p.

26605 REID, A.S. Chin-Lushai land, including a description of the various expeditions into the Chin-Lushai Hills and the final annexation of the country. Calcutta: KLM, for Tribal Res. Inst., Aizawl, 1976. 235p.

b. the Mizo National Front under Laldenga (1919 -) and the armed struggle for secession

26606 GOSWAMI, B.B. The Mizo unrest: a study of politicisation of culture. Jaipur: Aalekh, 1979. 220p.

26607 NIRMAL NIBEDON. Mizoram, the Dagger Brigade. ND: Lancers Pub., 1980. 269p.

26608 NUNTHARA, C. MNF holds key to political stability. In EPW 9,50 (1974) 2053-54.

26609 RANGASAMI, A. Mizoram: tragedy of our own making. In EPW 13,15 (1978) 653-62.

2. Economic and Social Development (1981 literacy 59.5%)

26610 HARDEV SINGH. Mizoram: peace comes slowly. In EE 71,26 (1978) 1473-74.

26611 A paper mill in offing. In Commerce (Suppl.) 127,3250 (1973) 65-67.

26612 SUBRAHMANYAM, S.M. Rail line to Mizoram: a difficult survey in progress. In Indian Railways 21,3 (1976) 23-24.

3. Tribals of Mizoram - Ethnography and Religion (86% Christian)

26613 CHAPMAN, E. & M. CLARK. Mizo miracle. Ed. by Marjorie Syies. Madras: CLS, 1968. 192p.

26614 CHATTERJI, N. Status of women in earlier Mizo society. Aizawl: Tribal Res. Inst., 1975. 31p.

26615 GOSWAMI, B.B. A note on the Lushai family. In EA 16 (1963) 201-07.

26616 ______. Structural phenomenon of kinship with regard to the Lushai (Mizo). In K.S. Mathur & B.C. Agrawal, eds. Tribe, caste, and peasantry. Lucknow: Ethnographic & Folk Culture Soc., 1973, 40-47.

26617 ______. Tribe to peasant, not caste: some comments on the Mizo situation. In EA 31,3 (1978) 259-67.

26618 KUMAR, KRISHAN. The changing Lushai society. In Quest 45 (1965) 37-47.

26619 LEACH, E. Alliance and descent among the Lakher: a reconsideration. In Ethnos 28 (1963) 237-49.

26620 PARRY, N.E. The Lakhers. London: Macmillan, 1932. 640p.

26621 ______. Lushai custom. A monograph on Lushai customs and ceremonies. Shillong: Assam Govt. Press, 1928. 130p.

26622 PUDAITE, R. The education of the Hmar people; with historical sketch of the people. Sielmat: Indo-Burma Pioneer Mission, 1963. 134p.

26623 SENGUPTA, A.K. "Lushei-Kuki clans" - re-examined. In EA 22,3 (1969) 349-59.

26624 SHAKESPEAR, J. The Lushei-Kuki clans. Aizawl: Tribal Res. Inst., 1975. 238p. [Rpt. 1912 ed.]

26625 SHAW, W. Notes on the Thadou Kukis. Calcutta: Asiatic Society, 1929. 175p. [Rpt. JASBengal ns 24 (1928)]

26626 THANGA, L.B. The Mizos: a study in racial personality. Gauhati: United Publishers, 1978. 185p.

F. Tripura: Former Princely State, Bengali-Speaking Hindu Salient into Bangladesh (1981 pop. 2,060,189)

1. Historical and Political Studies (Statehood Granted 1972)

26627 GAN-CHAUDHURI, J., ed. Tripura, the land and its people. Delhi: Leeladevi, 1980. 186p.

26628 LONG, J. Rajmala: or, An analysis of the chronicles of the kings of Tripura. Rev. by S. Chaudhuri. Calcutta: KLM, 1978. 59p.

26629 MAJUMDER, B.M. The political movement in native Tripura (1905-49). In Socialist Perspective 6,1-2 (1978) 83-93.

26630 ______. Tribe and politics in Tripura: past and present. In Socialist Perspective 5,1 (1977) 21-35.

26631 ROYCHOWDHURY, N.R. Kuki disturbances in Tripura, 1860-61. In SocSci 4,9 (1976) 59-65.

26632 SAIGAL, O. Tripura, its history and culture. Delhi: Concept, 1978. 164p. + 8pl.

26633 Tripura. In S.V. Kogekar & R.L. Park, eds. Report on the Indian general elections, 1951-52. Bombay: Popular, 1956, 312-15.

26634 TRIPURA (U.T.). DIR. OF EDUC. Who's who of persons in Tripura who participated in the struggle for India's freedom, 1818-1947. Agartala: 1964. 44p.

26635 TRIPURA. DIR. OF PUBLIC RELATIONS & TOURISM. One year of Left Front Government in Tripura. Agartala: 1979. 26p.

2. Economic and Social Development (1981 literacy 41.58%)

26636 GANGULY, J.B. Economic problems of the Jhumias of Tripura; a socio-economic study of the system of shifting cultivation in transition. Calcutta: Bookland, 1969. 129p.

26637 INDIA (REP.). CENSUS OF INDIA, 1971. Tripura; a portrait of population. Delhi: Cont. of Pub., 1975. 200p.

26638 INDIA (REP.). CENTRAL TEA BOARD. Report of techno-economic survey of Tripura tea industry. Calcutta: 1978. 40p.

26639 ______. Survey of the living conditions of tea plantation labour in Tripura. Calcutta: 1962. 43p.

26640 LAHIRI, R.K. Family farming in a developing economy: a study based on farm management survey of Tripura. ND: Concept, 1979. 132p.

26641 NCAER. Techno-economic survey of Tripura. ND: 1961. 161p.

26642 TRIPURA. AGRI. INFO. UNIT. A guide to Tripura agriculture, 1977. Agartala: 1977. 250p.

26643 TRIPURA (U.T.). State development plan for 1958-59. Agartala: 1960. 91p.

3. Social Categories in Tripura
a. Bengali residents and refugees from Bangladesh

26644 TRIPURA (U.T.). Statistical survey of displaced persons from East Pakistan in Tripura (1956). Agartala: Govt. Printing, 1956. 52p.

b. tribals of Tripura (30% of pop.), incl. Bodo-speaking Tripuris, Riangs, Chakmas, and Kukis

26645 CHAKRAVORTY, P. Social structure of the tribals of Tripura as reflected through their dances. In Folklore (C) 20,2 (1979) 31-39.

26646 DEV VARMAN, S.B.K. The tribes of Tripura. Agartala: Director of Tribal Res., Govt. of Tripura, 197-. 32p. + 9pl.

26647 MISRA, B.P. Socioeconomic adjustments of tribals: case-study of Tripura jhumias. ND: PPH, 1976. 137p.

26648 SINGH, R.G. The Kukis of Tripura: a socio-economic survey. Agartala: Dir. of Res., Dept. of Welfare for Sch. Castes & Sch. Tribes, Govt. of Tripura, 1978. 52p.

G. Meghalaya ("Abode of Clouds"): The Garo, Khasi and Jaintia Hills of the Shillong Plateau (1981 pop. 1,327,874)

1. Historical and Political Studies (Autonomous States within Assam, 1970; Statehood, 1972)

26649 BAREH, H. Meghalaya. Shillong: NE India News & Feature Service, 1974. 222p.

26650 BHATTACHARJEE, J.B. The Garos and the English, 1765-1874. ND: Radiant, 1978. 264p.

26651 BHATTACHARJYA, U. Local government in Khasi Hills. Delhi: Vivek, 1980. 263p.

26652 KAR, P.C. British annexation of Garo Hills. Calcutta: Nababharat, 1970. 154p.

26653 KAUTILYA, M. Tribal electoral politics: a case study of the Khasis. In Janata 35,6 (1980) 9-12; 35,7 (1980) 14-16.

26654 INDIA (REP.). CMSN. ON THE HILL AREAS OF ASSAM. Report, 1965-66. Delhi: Min. of Home Affairs, 1966. 198p.

26655 MEGHALAYA. ELECTIONS DEPT. Report on the general elections to the Meghalaya Legislative Assembly and the bye-election from 2-Tura (ST) Parliamentary Constituency (1972). Shillong: 1975. 51p.

2. Economic and Social Development (33.22% literacy in 1981)

26656 ASSAM. ECON. & STAT. DEPT. Report on rural economic survey in United Khasi & Jaintia hills. Shillong: 1963. 155p.

26657 ______. Report on socio-economic survey in Garo hills, 1961. Shillong: 1964. 96p.

26658 ______. Report on socio-economic survey in United Khasi and Jaintia Hills, 1966-67. Shillong: 1972. 66p.

26659 CHOUDHURY, R.C. Meghalaya - its agricultural economy. In IJE 22,5 (1974) 312-16.

26660 LYNGDOH, SNGI. The Bhoi land-tenure system. In MI 46,2 (1966) 95-102.

26661 MALI, D.D. An introduction to the economy of Meghalaya. Shillong: Ratna's Mascot, 1978. 147p.

26662 MEGHALAYA. DIR. OF ECON. & STAT. A report on socio-economic survey of Garo Hills District, 1970. Shillong: 1975. 105p.

26663 MEGHALAYA. LAND REFORMS CMSN. FOR KHASI HILLS. Report of the Land Reforms Commission for Khasi Hills. Shillong: 1975. 276p. [U.R. Tokin-Rymbai, Chm.]

26664 MEGHALAYA. PLANNING DEPT. Fifth five year plan: draft proposals. Shillong: 1973. 2 v. in 1.

26665 ______. Five year plan, 1978-83: draft proposals. Shillong: 1978-. v. 2-.

26666 MONGIA, J.N. Economy of Meghalaya: temporal trends in sectoral growth. Shillong: Dir. of Econ., Stat. & Eval., Govt. of Meghalaya, 1978. 24p. (Its Staff occ. papers, 1,1)

26667 PAKEM, B., et al., ed. Agriculture in the hills: a case study of Meghalaya. Shillong: NE India Council for Social Science Res., 1979. 154p.

26668 VINCENT, K. Socio-economic study of Bhoilymbong, a village in Meghalaya. Madras: CLS, for CISRS, 1978. 378p.

3. Matrilineal Tribes of Meghalaya
a. general studies

26669 NAKANE, C. Garo and Khasi: a comparative study in matrilineal systems. The Hague: Mouton, 1967. 187p.

26670 SENGUPTA, K. Without root: a study of tribal-non tribal relationship in Meghalaya. Shillong: B. Sengupta, 1978-. v. 1-.

b. the Garos, a Bodo (Tibeto-Burman) speaking people

26671 BURLING, R. Garo avuncular authority and matrilateral cross-cousin marriage. In AA 60 (1958) 743-49.

26672 ______. Garo kinship terms and the analysis of meaning. In Ethnology 2 (1963) 70-85.

26673 ______. An incipient caste organization in the Garo Hills. In MI 40 (1960) 283-99.

26674 ______. Linguistics and ethnographic description. In AA 71 (1969) 817-27.

26675 ______. Rengsanggri; family and kinship in a Garo village. Philadelphia: UPaP, 1963. 377p.

26676 CHAUDHURI, B.N. Some cultural and linguistic aspects of the Garos. Gauhati: Lawyer's Book Stall, 1969. 84p. [1st pub. 1958]

26677 COSTA, G. Fr. G. Costa's The Garo code of law. Ed. by P.C. Kar. Tura, Dt. Garo Hills: Catholic Church, 1975. 42p.

26678 GOSWAMI, M.C. & D.N. MAJUMDAR. Clan organisation among the Garo of Assam. In MI 47 (1967) 249-62.

26679 ______. Social institutions of the Garo of Meghalaya. Calcutta: Nababharat, 1972. 142p.

26680 MAJUMDAR, D.N. Culture change in two Garo villages. Calcutta: AnthSI, 1978. 188p. (Its Memoir, 42)

26681 MUKHERJEE, B. Garo family. In EA 11 (1957) 25-30.

26682 PLAYFAIR, A.L. The Garos. Gauhati: United Publishers, 1975. 172p. [Rpt. 1909 ed.]

26683 SINHA, T.C. The psyche of the Garos. Calcutta: AnthSI, 1966. 122p.

c. the Khasis, a Mon-Khmer speaking people

26684 BAREH, H. The history and culture of the Khasi people. Shillong: 1967. 485p.

26685 ______. Khasi democracy. Shillong: 1964. 122p.

26686 CANTLIE, K. Sir Keith Cantlie's Notes on Khasi law. Ed. by A.S. Khnogphai. Shillong: Khongphai, 1974. 192p. [Rpt. 1934 ed.]

26687 CHAUDHURI, J. The Khasi canvas: a cultural and political history. Shillong: Jaya Chowdhury, 1978. 426p. + 26pl.

26688 EHRENFELS, U.R. VON. The double sex character of the Khasi great deity. In L.P. Vidyarthi, ed. Aspects or religion in Indian Society.... Meerut: Kedar Nath Ram Nath, 1961, 268-81.

26689 GURDON, P.R.T. The Khasis. 2nd ed. London: Macmillan, 1914. 232p.

26690 KYNPHAM SINGH. A collection of writings about Khasi hills and Khasis; A collection of poems. Shillong: Kynpham Singh, 1979. 91 + 9p.

26691 MATHUR, P.R.G. The Khasi of Meghalaya: study in tribalism and religion. ND: Cosmo, 1979. 198p.

26692 MUKHERJEE, B. Social groupings among the Khasis of Assam. In MI 38 (1958) 208-12.

26693 MUKHERJEE, B.N. Restrictions on married women's activities and some aspects of husband-wife relations in Khasi culture. In IAnth 4,2 (1974) 104-30.

26694 NAIR, P. THANKAPPAN. Nongkrem - the national festival of Khasis. In Folklore (C) 11 (1970) 224-31.

26695 ROY, HIPSHON, ed. Khasi heritage: a collection of essays on Khasi religion and culture. Rev. and enl. ed. Shillong: Seng Khasi, 1979. 218p.

26696 ROY, P. Christianity and the Khasis. In MI 44 (1964) 105-15.

d. other tribes of Meghalaya

26697 MAJUMDAR, D.N. Acculturation among the Hagong of Meghalaya. In MI 52,1 (1972) 46-63.

26698 SYAMCHAUDHURI, N.K. & M.M. DAS. The Lalung society: a theme for analytical ethnography. Calcutta: AnthSI, 1973. 165p. (Its Memoir, 31) [Jaintia Hills & Assam plains]

4. Religions in Meghalaya: Preference for Christianity over Hinduization (1971 47% Christian, 18% Hindu, 3% Muslim, 31% Tribal)

26699 MINATTUR, J. Khasi religion. In MI 35 (1955) 233-36.

26700 NALINI NATARAJAN. The missionary among the Khasis. ND: Sterling, 1977. 212p.

5. Languages and Literatures of Meghalaya

26701 BAREH, H. Khasi fables and folk-tales. Calcutta: KLM, 1971. 87p.

26702 ______. The language and literature of Meghalaya. Simla: IIAS, 1977. 108p.

26703 ______. A short history of Khasi literature. Rev. ed. Shillong: Don Bosco Press, 1969. 108p.

26704 RABEL, L. Khasi, a language of Assam. Baton Rouge: Louisiana State U. Press, 1961. 248p.

26705 RONGMUTHU, D.S. The epic lore of the Garos. Gauhati: Dept. of Tribal Culture & Folklore Res., U. of Gauhati, 1967. 160p.

26706 SIMON, I.M. Khasi and Jaintia tales and beliefs. Gauhati: Dept. of Tribal Culture & Folklore Res., Gauhati U., 1966. 130p.

VIII. THE ANDAMAN AND NICOBAR ISLANDS: INDIA'S OCEAN FRONTIER IN THE BAY OF BENGAL

A. General and Historical Studies (British Chief Commissioner's Province, a U.T. since 1956)

26707 IQBAL SINGH, N. The Andaman story. ND: Vikas, 1978. 321p. + 10pl.

26708 KLOSS, C.B. Andamans and Nicobars; the narrative of a cruise.... Delhi: Vivek, 1971. 373p. [Rpt. of 1903 ed., In the Andamans and Nicobars]

26709 MAJUMDAR, R.C. Penal settlement in the Andamans. ND: Gazetteers Unit, Dept. of Culture, Min. of Educ. & Social Welfare, 1975. 339p.

26710 MAN, E.H. The Nicobar Islands and their peoples. London: Billing, for Royal Anthro. Inst., 1933. 186p. [posthumous collection of papers]

26711 MATHUR, L.P. History of the Andaman and Nicobar Islands, 1756-1966. Delhi: Sterling, 1968. 335p.

26712 TARLING, N. Pirates and convicts; British interest in the Andaman and Nicobar islands in the mid-nineteenth century. In JIH 38 (1960) 505-26.

26713 WHITEHEAD, G. In the Nicobar Islands.... London: Seeley Service, 1924. 276p. + 19pl.

B. The Economy of the Bay Islanders (1981 pop. 188,254; literacy 51.27%)

26714 Andaman and Nicobar [special issue]. In Yojana 20,13 (1976) 12-102.

26715 LAL, PARMANAND. Evolution of Port Blair: a study in urban geography. In NGJI 8,2 (1962) 93-113.

26716 ______. Utilization of agricultural resources of Andaman Islands. In Indian Geographer 9,1/2 (1964) 25-62.

26717 MANN, R.S. An analysis of Nicobarese economic system under changing conditions. In JSR 18,1 (1975) 66-78.

26718 MYLIUS, K. Wirtschaftsformen auf den Nikobaren-Inseln. In Zeitschrift für Ethnologie 87 (1962) 39-50.

26719 NCAER. Techno-economic survey of Andaman and Nicobar Islands. ND: 1972. 131p.

C. Tribals of the Andamans and Nicobars (1971 pop. 18,102)

26720 BOSE, S. Economy of the Onge of Little Andaman. In MI 44 (1964) 298-310.

26721 CIPRIANI, L. The Andaman Islanders. Ed. & tr. by D. Taylor Cox. NY: Praeger, 1966. 159p.

26722 ______. Hygiene and medical practices among the Onge (Little Andaman). In Anthropos 56 (1961) 481-500.

26723 DUTTA, P.C. The great Andamanese: past and present. Calcutta: AnthSI, 1978. 77p.

26724 GUSINDE, M. Neueste Berichte über die letzten Andamaner. In Anthropos 60 (1965) 838-44.

26725 KOCHAR, V.K. The Great Andamanese today. In MI 49,2 (1969) 247-52.

26726 MAN, E.H. Aboriginal inhabitants of the Andaman Islands. Delhi: Sanskaran Prakashak, 1975. 224p. [Rpt. 1883 ed.]

26727 MANN, R.S. The Bay islander. Bidisa: Inst. of Soc. Research & Applied Anthro., 1979. 156p.

26728 ______. "Change" and "continuity" among the Nicobarese. In EA 28,4 (1975) 327-39.

26729 ______. Depopulation among Andaman aborigines - an analysis. In JSR 19,2 (1975) 37-50.

26730 ______. Innovation perspective in Nicobarese ethnography: some observations. In MI 58,4 (1978) 349-65.

26731 MONDAL, S.R. Some preliminary notes on Nicobarese and their changing life pattern - a micro study. In Folklore (C) 19,6 (1978) 197-84.

26732 MOUAT, F.J. The Andaman Islanders. Delhi: Mittal Pub., 1979. 367p. [Rpt. 1863 ed.]

26733 RADCLIFFE-BROWN, A.R. The Andaman Islanders; a study in social anthropology. NY: Free Press, 1964. 510p. [Rpt. of 1948 ed.; 1st pub. 1922]

26734 SYAMCHAUDHURI, N.K. The social structure of Car Nicobar Islanders: an ethnic study of cognation. Calcutta: AnthSI, 1977. 184p.

26735 TEMPLE, R.C. Remarks on the Andaman islanders and their country. Bombay: British India Press, 1930. 121p.

26736 The tribes of Andaman and Nicobar Islands [special issue]. In JSR 19,2 (1976) 1-132.

17

The Indic Diaspora: South Asian Communities throughout the World

I. SOUTH ASIAN COMMUNITIES OVERSEAS AFTER 1800 - GENERAL STUDIES

A. Histories and Surveys

26737 CUMPSTON, I.M. Indians overseas in British territories, 1834-1854. London: Dawsons, 1969. 198p. [1st pub. 1953]

26738 DEV, D.Y. Our countrymen abroad; a brief survey of the problems of Indians in foreign lands. Allahabad: Swaraj Bhawan, M.B. Kripalani, 1940. 98p.

26739 Factions in Indian and overseas Indian societies. In British J. of Sociology 8 (1957) 291-342.

26740 GANGULEE, N.N. Indians in the Empire overseas: a survey. London: New India Pub. House, 1947. 263p.

26741 GREAT BRITAIN. SECRETARY OF STATE. CMTEE. ON EMIGRATION FROM INDIA TO THE CROWN COLONIES & PROTECTORATES, 1909. [Report with evidence] London: HMSO, 1910. 1v. in 3 pts. (Cd. 5192-4) [Chm., Sanderson]

26742 INDIA. CMTEE. TO ENQUIRE INTO THE CONDITION OF INDIAN IMMIGRANTS INTO THE FOUR BRITISH COLONIES: TRINIDAD, BRITISH GUIANA OR DEMERARA, JAMAICA & FIJI, AND IN THE DUTCH COLONY OF SURINAM, 1912. Report. Delhi: MPGOI, 1912. 150 + 334p. (Cd. 7744-7745) [Chm., J. McNeill]

26743 KONDAPI, C. Indians overseas, 1838-1949. ND: ICWA, 1951. 558p.

26744 LOHIA, R.M. Indians in foreign lands. Allahabad: AICC, 1938. 37p.

26745 Mother India's children abroad. In Vivekananda Kendra Patrika 2,1 (1973) 280p.

26746 The Other India: the overseas Indians and their relationship with India: proceedings of a seminar. Ed. by I.J. Bahadur Singh. ND: Arnold-Heinemann, 1979. 263p.

26747 The overseas Indians [special section]. In Far Eastern Econ. R. 106,47 (1979) 35-42.

26748 RAJKUMAR, N.V. Indians outside India, a general survey.... ND: AICC, 1950. 96p.

26749 SMILLIE, E.E. Historical survey of Indian migration throughout the Empire. In Canadian Hist. R. 4 (1923) 217-57.

26750 TINKER, H. The banyan tree: overseas emigrants from India, Pakistan, and Bangladesh. Oxford: OUP, 1977. 204p.

26751 ______. Separate and unequal: India and the Indians in the British Commonwealth, 1920-1950. London: C. Hurst, 1976. 460p.

26752 VEDALANKAR, N. & M. SOMERA. Arya Samaj and Indians abroad. ND: Sarvadeshik Arya Pratinidhi Sabha, 1975. 204p.

B. Sociological Studies of Overseas Indians

26753 DAVIDS, L. The East Indian family overseas. In Social & Econ. Studies 13 (1964) 384-94.

26754 D'SOUZA, V.S. Indian migrants in Asia and Africa: socio-cultural aspect. In SocAct 20 (1970) 334-41.

26755 JAYAWARDENA, C. Migration and social change: a survey of Indian communities overseas. In GR 58 (1968) 426-49.

26756 MAYER, A.C. Patrons and brokers: rural leadership in four Overseas Indian communities. In M. Freedman, ed. Social organization: essays presented to Raymond Firth. Chicago: Aldine, 1967, 167-188.

26757 SCHWARTZ, B.M., ed. Caste in overseas Indian communities. San Francisco: Chandler Pub. Co., 1967. 350p.

C. Export of Indian Coolies to British Tropical Colonies

26758 INDIA. CMTEE. TO INQUIRE INTO THE ABUSES ALLEGED TO EXIST IN EXPORTING FROM BENGAL HILL COOLIES & INDIAN LABOURERS OF VARIOUS CLASSES TO OTHER COUNTRIES, 1938. Report [with evidence]. London: HMSO, 1941. 195p. (HC 45) [Chm., T. Dickens]

26759 SAHA, P. Emigration of Indian labour, 1834-1900. Delhi: PPH, 1970. 180p.

26760 TINKER, H. New system of slavery: the export of Indian labor overseas, 1830-1920. London: OUP, 1974. 432p.

II. THE SUGAR PLANTATION COLONIES AND THEIR SUCCESSOR INDEPENDENT NATIONS

A. Mauritius: Anglo-French Island in the Indian Ocean (South Asian pop. 66%)

26761 BEEJADHUR, A. Les Indiens à l'Île Maurice. Port Louis: 1935. 124p.

26762 BENEDICT, B. Indians in a plural society: a report on Mauritius. London: HMSO, 1961. 168p.

26763 ______. Mauritius: problems of a plural society. NY: Praeger, 1965. 72p.

26764 BISSOONDOYAL, B. The truth about Mauritius. Bombay: BVB, 1968. 246p.

26765 HAZAREESINGH, K. Histoire des Indiens à l'Île Maurice. Paris: Librairie d'Amérique et d'Orient, 1973. 223p.

26766 ______. A history of Indians in Mauritius. Mauritius: General Printing & Stationery Co., 1950. 231p.

26767 ______. The religion and culture of Indian immigrants in Mauritius and the effect of social change. In CSSH 8 (1966) 241-57.

26728 MUKHERJI, S.B. The indenture system in Mauritius, 1837-1915. Calcutta: KLM, 1962. 66p.

26729 NAPAL, D. Manilall Maganlall Doctor, pioneer of Indo-Mauritian emancipation. Port-Lewis, Mauritius: Neo Press Service, 1963. 213p.

26770 ROY, J.N. Mauritius in transition. Mauritius: 1960. 501p.

26771 SANGEELEE, M. A brief history of the Tamilians of Mauritius. In Intl. Conf. Seminar of Tamil Studies, 1st, 1966, Proceedings. Kuala Lumpur: IATR, 1968, 242-250.

26772 TINKER, H. Odd man out: the loneliness of the Indian colonial politician - the career of Manilal Doctor. In JICH 2,2 (1974) 226-43.

B. The Caribbean and South America: British, French, and Dutch Colonies

1. General Studies

26773 NIEHOFF, A. & J. NIEHOFF. East Indians in the west Indies. Milwaukee: Milwaukee Public Museum, 1960. 192p.

26774 THANI NAYAGAM, X.S. Tamil emigration to the Martinique. In JTS 1,2 (1969) 75-123.

2. The Guianas: Guyana, Surinam, and French Guiana

26775 ARYA, U. Ritual songs and folksongs of the Hindus of Surinam. Leiden: Brill, 1968. 200p. (ORT, 9)

26776 DESPRES, L.A. Cultural pluralism and nationalist politics in British Guiana. Chicago: Rand McNally, 1967. 310p.

26777 GREAT BRITAIN. HOUSE OF COMMONS. Report of the Commissioners appointed to enquire into the treatment of immigrants in British Guiana. London: HMSO, 1871. 2v. (c.393)

26778 INDIA. DELEGATION TO BRITISH GUIANA ON SCHEME FOR INDIAN EMIGRATION. Reports on the scheme for Indian emigration to British Guiana. Simla: Supt. Govt. Monotype Press, 1924. 230p.

26779 JAGAN, C. The West on trial: they fight for Guyana's freedom. Rev. ed. Berlin: Seven Seas Publ., 1975. 435p. [1st pub. 1967]

26780 JAYAWARDENA, C. Conflict and solidarity in a Guianese plantation. London: Athlone press, 1963. 150p.

26781 ______. Religious belief and social change: aspects of the development of Hinduism in British Guiana. In CCSH 8 (1966) 211-40.

26782 JHA, J.C. The first batch of indentured Indian labourers in British Guiana (1838-43). In JBRS 60,1/4 (1974) 69-88.

26783 MOORE, B.L. The retention of caste notions among the Indian immigrants in British Guiana during the nineteenth century. In CSSH 19,1 (1977) 96-107.

26784 NATH, D. A history of Indians in Guyana. 2nd rev. ed. London: D. Nath, 1970. 281p. [1st pub. 1960]

26785 RUHOMON, P. Centenary history of the East Indians in British Guiana, 1838-1938. Georgetown: 1947. 297p.

26786 SINGER, P. & E. ARANETA. Hinduization and creolization in Guyana: the plural society and basic personality. In Social & Economic Studies (Mona, Jamaica) 16 (1967) 221-236.

26787 SMITH, R.T. & C. JAYAWARDENA. Caste and social status among the Indians of Guyana. In B.M. Schwartz, ed. Caste in overseas Indian Communities. San Francisco: Chandler Pub. Co., 1967, 43-92.

26788 ______. Marriage and the family amongst East Indians in British Guiana. In Social & Economic Studies (Mona, Jamaica) 8 (1969) 321-76.

26789 SPECKMAN, J.D. The Indian group in the segmented society of Surinam. In Caribbean studies 3,1 (1963) 3-17.

26790 VATUK, V.P. Protest songs of East Indians in British Guiana. In his Thieves in my house.... Varanasi: Vishwavidyalaya Prakashan, 1969, 35-62.

3. Trinidad and Tobago

26791 CROWLEY, D.J. Plural and differential acculturation in Trinidad. In AA 59 (1957) 817-24.

26792 GREEN, J.B. Socialization values in the Negro and East Indian subcultures of Trinidad. In J. of Social Psychology 64 (1964) 1-20.

26793 JHA, J.C. The background of the legalisation of non-Christian marriages in Trinidad and Tobago. In QRHS 16,2 (1976-77) 63-80.

26794 ______. Indian heritage in Trinidad. In EA 27,3 (1974) 211-34.

26795 KLASS, M. East Indians in Trinidad; a study in cultural persistance. NY: ColUP, 1961. 265p.

26796 LA GUERRE, J.G., ed. Calcutta to Caroni; the East Indian of Trinidad. Trinidad: Longman Caribbean, 1974. 112p.

26797 MALIK, Y.K. Agencies of political socialization and East Indian ethnic identification in Trinidad. In SB 18 (1969) 101-21.

26798 ______. East Indians in Trinidad: a study in minority politics. NY: OUP, for Inst. of Race Relations, 1971. 199p.

26799 ______. Socio-political perceptions and attitudes of East Indian elites in Trinidad. In Western Political Q. 23,3 (1970) 552-63.

26800 NIEHOFF, A. The survival of Hindu institutions in an alien environment. In EA 12 (1959) 171-87.

26801 SCHWARTZ, B.M. Caste and endogamy in Trinidad. In SWJA 20 (1964) 58-66.

26802 WELLER, J.A. The East Indian indenture in Trinidad. Rio Piedras: Inst. of Caribbean Studies, U. of Puerto Rico, 1968. 172p.

C. Fiji: British Islands in the South Pacific, Independent since 1970 (South Asian pop 51%)

26803 AHMED ALI. Aspects of Fiji Indian history, 1879-1949; a society in transition, I & II. In EPW 12,42-43 (1977) 1782-90, 1821-30.

26804 ______. Fiji Indians and the politics of disparity In IQ 32,4 (1976) 413-32.

26805 ANDERSON, A.G. Indo-Fijian small farming: profiles of a peasantry. Auckland: Auckland U. Press, 1975. 199p.

26806 BROWN, C.H. Coolie and freeman: from hierarchy to equality in Fiji. Ph.D. diss., U. of Washington, 1978. 390p. [UM 78-23, 439]

26807 CHAUHAN, I.S. Town, region and nation: study of a small town in Fiji. In JSR 8,2 (1965) 1-24.

26808 COULTER, J.W. Fiji: little India of the Pacific. Chicago: UChiP, 1942. 156p.

26809 GILLION, K.L. The Fiji Indians: Challenge to European dominance, 1920-46. Canberra: ANU Press, 1977. 231p.

26810 ______. Fiji's Indian migrants; a history to the end of indenture in 1920. Melbourne: OUP, 1962. 234p.

26811 BLICK, C.E. Attitudes of Indians toward their position in Fiji. In Intl. Conf. Seminar of Tamil Studies, 1st, 1966. Proceedings. Kuala Lumpur: IATR, 1968, 217-226.

26812 MAYER, A.C. Indians in Fiji. London: OUP, 1963. 142p. (for Inst. of Race Relations)

26813 ______. Peasants in the Pacific: a study of Fiji Indian rural society. Berkeley: UCalP, 1961. 300p.

26814 SUBRAMANI, ed. The Indo-Fijian experience. Brisbane: U. of Queensland Press, 1979. 222p.

26815 WILSON, J. Text and context in Fijian Hinduism: uses of religion; religion as a framework for life. In Religion 5, 1 & 2 (1975) 54-68, 101-16.

III. SOUTH ASIANS IN AFRICA SINCE 1800

A. General Studies

26816 BOUTE, J. La démographie de la branche indo-pakistanaise d'Afrique. Louvain: Soc. d'études morales, sociales, et juridiques, 1965. 412p.

26817 CHATTOPADHYAYA, H.P. Indians in Africa: a socio-economic study. Calcutta: Bookland, 1970. 464p.

26818 RAMCHANDANI, R.R. India and Africa. ND: Radiant, 1980. 314p.

B. South Africa: the Smallest and Most Vulnerable Minority of the Apartheid System (South Asian pop. 3%)

1. Histories and General Studies

26819 BURROWS, H.R. Indian life and labour in Natal. Johannesburg: South African Inst. of Race Relations, 1952. 64p.

26820 CURRIE, J.C. A bibliography of material published during the period 1946-56 on the Indian question in South Africa. Cape Town: U. of Cape Town Libraries, 1969. 27p.

26821 KUPER, H. Indian people in Natal. Pietermaritzburg: Natal U., 1965. 305p. [1st pub. 1960]

26822 MAASDORP, G.G. A Natal Indian community; a socio-economic study in the Tongaar-Verulam area. Durban: Dept. of Econ., U. of Natal, 1968. 142p.

26823 MUKHERJI, S.B. Indian minority in South Africa. ND: PPH, 1959. 211p.

26824 PALMER, M.A. The history of Indians in Natal. Cape Town: OUP, for U. of Natal, 1957. 197p.

2. Early Indian Immigration to the Crown Colony of Natal, 1860-1893

26825 HEY, P. The rise of the Natal Indian elite. Pietermaritzburg: 1962. 78p.

26826 TAYAL, M. Indian indentured labour in Natal, 1890-1911. In IESHR 14,4 (1977) 518-47.

3. Gandhi and the Birth of Satyagraha, 1893-1914 [See also Chap. Six, IV. A.]

26827 DOKE, J.J. M.K. Gandhi; an Indian patriot in South Africa. Delhi: PDMIB, 1967. 116p. [1st pub. 1909 in London Indian Chronicle]

26828 GANDHI, M.K. Satyagraha in South Africa. Tr. from Gujarati by B.G. Desai. 2nd rev. ed. Ahmedabad: Navajivan, 1950. [1st ed. 1928]

26829 HUTTENBACK, R.A. Gandhi in South Africa: British Imperialism and the Indian question, 1860-1914. Ithaca: CornellUP, 1971. 368p.

26830 ______. Indians in South Africa, 1860-1914: the British imperial philosophy on trial. English Hist. R. 81,319 (1966) 273-91.

26831 NARAIN, IQBAL. The politics of racialism; a study of the Indian minority in South Africa down to the Gandhi-Smuts agreement. Agra: S.L. Agarwala, 1962. 304p.

4. Continuing Discrimination against South Asians, 1914-

26832 CALPIN, G.H. A.I. Kajee: his work for the South-African Indian community. Durban: Iqbal Study Group, 195-? 172p. + 13pl.

26833 ______. Indians in South Africa. Pietermaritzburg: Shuter & Shooter, 1949. 310p.

26834 TRELAND, R.R. Apartheid and the education of the Indian community in the Republic of South Africa. In Plural Societies 6,2 (1975) 3-17.

26835 KHAN, S.A. The Indian in South Africa. Allahabad: Kitabistan, 1946. 596p.

26836 JOSHI, P.S. The struggle for equality. Bombay: Hind Kitabs, 1951. 304p.

26837 ______. The tyranny of colour; a study of the Indian problem in South Africa. Durban: the author, 1942. 316p.

26838 MEER, F. Portrait of Indian South Africans. Durban: Avon House, 1969. 236p.

26839 PACHAI, B. The international aspects of the South African Indian question, 1860-1971. Cape Town: C. Struik, 1971. 318p.

26840 SEN, S.D.K. The position of Indians in South Africa. Calcutta: Indian Law R., 1950. 83p.

26841 SOUTH AFRICA. INDIAN PENETRATION CMSN. Report of the Indian penetration commission. Pretoria: Govt. Printer, 1942. 76p.

C. East and Central Africa: British and German Colonies

1. General Studies

26842 BHARATI, A. The Asians in East Africa; Jayhind and Uhuru. Chicago: Nelson Hall, 1973. 362p.

26843 DELF, G. Asians in East Africa. NY: OUP, for Inst. of Race Relations, 1963, 73p.

26844 DOTSON, F. & L.O. DOTSON. The Indian minority of Zambia, Rhodesia, and Malawi. New Haven: YUP, 1968. 444p.

26845 GHAI, D.P. & Y.P. GHAI, eds. Portrait of a minority; Asians in East Africa. Rev. ed. Nairobi: OUP, 1970. 154p. [1st pub. 1965]

26846 HOLLINGSWORTH, L.W. The Asians of East Africa. London: Macmillan, 1960. 174p.

26847 MANGAT, J.S. A history of the Asians in East Africa, c. 1886 to 1945. Oxford: OUP, 1969. 216p.

26848 MORRIS, H.S. The Indians in Uganda: caste and sect in a plural society. London: Weidenfeld & Nicolson, 1968. 230p.

26849 POCOCK, D.F. "Difference" in East Africa; a study of caste and religion in modern Indian society. In SWJA 13 (1957) 189-300.

26850 ______. Generations in East Africa. In EW 12,4-6 (1960) 153-162.

26851 ROTHERMUND, I. Die Inder in Ostafrika. In Indo-Asia 7 (1965) 329-42.

26852 ______. Die politische und wirtschaftliche Rolle der asiatischen Minderheit in Ostafrika (Kenya, Tangyanika/Sansibar, Uganda). Berlin: Springer-Verlag, 1965. 75p.

2. British Colonial Rule: Indians as Laborers, Traders, and Minor Bureaucrats

26853 GREGORY, R.G. India and East Africa: a history of race relations within the British Empire, 1890-1939. London: OUP, 1971. 555p.

26854 LÜTHY, H. India and East Africa: Imperial partnership at the end of the First World War. In J. of Contemporary History 6,2 (1971) 55-86.

26855 POCOCK, D.F. Slavery and Indo-Arab relations in 19th century Zanzibar. In EW 11,4-6 (1959) 165-72.

26856 YOUÉ, C.D. The threat of settler rebellion and the imperial predicament: the denial of Indian rights in Kenya, 1923. In Canadian J. of History 7,3 (1978) 347-360.

3. South Asians under the Independent African States

a. general studies

26857 BHARATI, A. Ritual tolerance and ideological rigour: the paradigm of the expatriate Hindus in East Africa. In CIS ns 10,2 (1976) 317-39.

26858 DOTSON, F. & L. DOTSON. Indians and Coloureds in Rhodesia and Nyasaland. In Race 5,1 (1963) 61-75.

26859 MORRIS, H.S. The divine kingship of the Aga Khan - a study of theocracy in East Africa. In SWJA 14,4 (1958) 454-72.

26860 MUKHERJEE, R.K. The problem of Uganda: a study in acculturation. Berlin: Akademie-Verlag, 1956. 281p.

26861 NELSON, D. Problems of power in a plural society: Asians in Kenya. In SWJA 28,3 (1972) 255-264.

26862 RIZVI, S.A.A. & N.Q. KING. The Khoja Shia Ithna-asheriya community in East Africa. In MW 64 (1974) 194-204.

26863 ROTHCHILD, D. Racial bargaining in Independent Kenya; a study of minorities and decolonization. London: OUP, for Inst. of Race Relations, 1973. 476p.

26864 SHEIKH-DILTHEY, H. Die Punjabi-Muslim in Kenya: Leistungen und Schicksal einer asiatischen Minoritat in Afrika. Munich: Weltforum-Verlag, 1974. 205p.

b. the 1972 expulsion of Asians from Uganda by Idi Amin

26865 BHATIA, P. Indian ordeal in Africa. Delhi: Vikas, 1973. 152p.

26866 HALBACH, AXEL J., ed. Die Ausweisung der Asiaten aus Uganda; sieben Monate Amin'scher Politik in Dokumenten. Munich: IFO-Inst. fur Wirtschaftsforschung, Weltforum Verlag, 1973. 281p. [most documents in English]

26867 MAMDANI, MAHMOOD. From citizen to refugee; Uganda Asians come to Britain. London: F. Pinter, 1973. 127p.

26868 RAMCHANDANI, R.R. Uganda Asians: the end of an enterprise: a study of the role of the people of Indian origin in the economic development of Uganda and their expulsion, 1894-1972. Bombay: United Asia Pub., 1976. 318p.

26869 TILBE, D. The Ugandan Asian Crisis. London: Community and Race Relations Unit, British Council of Churches, 1972. 19p.

26870 TWADDLE, M., ed. Expulsion of a minority; essays on Ugandan Asians. London: Athlone Press, 1975. 240p.

IV. SOUTH ASIANS IN THE MIDDLE EAST

26871 KUSHNER, G. Immigrants from India to Israel, planned change in an administered community. Tucson: U. of Arizona Press, 1973. 151p.

26872 KUSHNER, G. Indians in Israel: guided change in a new immigrant village. In HO 27 (1968) 352-61.

26873 TINKER, H. Indians in Israel; the acceptance model and its limitations. In Race 13,1 (1971) 81-84.

V. SOUTH ASIANS IN SOUTHEAST ASIA AND HONG KONG

A. General

26874 KOLB, A. Die Chinesen, Japaner und Inder auf den Philippinen. Wiesbaden: Harrassowitz, 1974. 142p. (SIAK, 38)

26875 MAHAJANI, U. Role of Indian minorities in Burma and Malaya. Vancouver: U. of British Columbia, 1964. 342p. [1st pub. 1960]

26876 MUHAMMAD KUNHI, M.K. Indian minorities in Ceylon, Burma and Malaysia. In IYIA 1 (1964) 405-72.

B. Burma: Part of the Indian Empire until 1937; Expulsion of Indians from Independent Burma, 1962

26877 ADAS, M. Immigrant Asians and the economic impact of European imperialism: the role of the South Indian Chettiars in British Burma. In JAS 33,3 (1974) 385-402.

26878 CHAKRAVARTI, N.R. The Indian minority in Burma, the rise and decline of an immigrant community. London: OUP, 1971. 214p.

26879 MAHADEVAN, R. Immigrant entrepreneurs in colonial Burma - an explanatory study of the role of Nattukottai Chettiars of Tamil Nadu, 1880-1930. In IESHR 15,3 (1978) 329-58.

26880 NADARAJAN, M. The Nattukkottai Chettiar community and South-East Asia. In Intl. Conf Seminar of Tamil Studies, 1st, 1966. Proceedings. Kuala Lumpur: IATR, 1968, 251-260.

C. Malaysia and Singapore: South Asians as a Third Minority Between Malays and Chinese (South Asian pop. 11%)

26881 ARASARATNAM, S. Indians of Malaysia and Singapore. Rev. ed. NY: OUP, 1980. 260p. [1st pub. 1970]

26882 BURMA. DEPT. OF COMMERCE & INDUSTRY. CMSN. OF INQUIRY TO EXAMINE THE QUESTION OF INDIAN IMMIGRATION INTO BURMA, 1939. Report. Rangoon: 1941. 192p. [Chm., J. Baxter]

26883 GLICK, C.E. Leaders of Indian origin in Kuala Lumpur; a study of minority group leadership and trends toward national cohesion. In Intl. Conf. Seminar of Tamil Studies, 1st, 1966. Proceedings. Kuala Lumpur: IATR, 1968, 227-241.

26884 JAIN, R.K. Leadership and authority in a plantation: a case study of Indians in Malaya (c. 1900-42). In G. Wijeyewardene, ed. Leadership and authority.... Singapore: U. of Malaya Press, 1968, 163-73.

26885 ______. South Indians on the plantation frontier in Malaya. New Haven: YUP, 1970. 459p.

26886 NETTO, G. Indians in Malaya: historical facts and figures. Singapore: Privately printed, 1963. 100p.

26887 SANDHU, K.S. Indians in Malaya: some aspects of their immigration and settlement (1786-1957). London: CamUP, 1969. 246p.

26888 ______. Sikh immigration into Malaya during British rule. In PPP 10,2 (1976_ 425-43. [1st pub. in J. Chen and N. Turling, eds., Studies in the social history of China and South-East Asia. Cambridge: CamUP, 1970]

26889 WIEBE, P.D. & S. MARIAPPEN. Indian Malaysians: the view from the plantation. ND: Manohar, 1978. 196p.

26890 WIKKRAMATILEKE, R. & KARPAL SINGH. Tradition and change in an Indian dairying community in Singapore. In Annals of the Assn. of American Geographers 60,4 (1970) 717-42.

D. The Hong Kong Indian Community

26891 VAID, K.N. The overseas Indian community in Hong Kong. Hong Kong: U. of Hong Kong, Center for Asian studies, 1972. 108p.

V. SOUTH ASIAN COMMUNITIES IN THE UNITED KINGDOM

A. General Studies

26892 ALLEN, S. New minorities, old conflicts: Asian and West Indian migrants in Britain. NY: Random House, 1971. 223p.

26893 BUTTERWORTH, E. A Muslim community in Britain. London: Church Info. Office, 1967. 60p.

26894 ______, ed. Immigrants in West Yorkshire: social conditions and the lives of Pakistanis, Indians and West Indians. London: Inst. of Race Relations, 1967. 68p.

26895 HILL, M.H. & R.M. ISSACHAROFF. Community action and race relations: a study of community relations committees in Britain. NY: OUP, 1971. 317p.

26896 KHAN, V.S. Asian women in Britain; strategies of adjustment of Indian and Pakistani migrants. In SocAct 25,3 (1975) 302-20.

26897 PAREKH, B. Colour, culture and consciousness; immigrant intellectuals in Britain. London: Allen & Unwin, 1974. 249p.

26898 PATTERSON, S. Immigration and race relations in Britain, 1960-1967. London: OUP, 1969. 460p.

26899 PREM, D.R. The parliamentary leper; a history of colour prejudice in Britain. Aligarh: Metric Pub., 1965. 177p.

26900 SASTHI BRATA. Traitor to India: a search for home. London: P. Elek, 1976. 159p.

26901 TAJFEL, H. & J.L. DAWSON, eds. Disappointed guests: essays by African, Asian, and West Indian students. London: OUP, for Inst. of Race Relations, 1965. 158p.

26902 TAYLOR, J.H. The half-way generation: a study of Asian youths in Newcastle on Tyne. Windsor: NFER, 1976. 276p.

B. Indian Immigrants to Britain

1. General Studies

26903 AURORA, G.S. Process of social adjustment of Indian immigrants in Britain. In SB 14 (1965) 39-49.

26904 DESAI, R.H. Indian immigrants in Britain. London: OUP, for Inst. of Race Relations, 1963. 154p.

26905 HIRO, D. The Indian family in Britain. London: Natl. Cmtee. for Commonwealth Immigrants, 1967. 13p.

26906 JOHN, D. Indian workers' associations in Britain. London: OUP, for Inst. of Race Relations, 1969. 194p.

26907 POCOCK, D.F. Preservation of the religious life: Hindu immigrants in England. In CIS 10,2 (1976) 341-65.

26908 RAM, J.K. My efforts for both India and England, 1918-1968. London: New India Pub. Co., 1968. 144p. [1st pub. 1947]

26909 SHARMA, U. Rampal and his family. London: Collins, 1971. 222p.

26910 SINGH, A.K. Indian students in Britain; a survey of their adjustment and attitudes. NY: Asia, 1963. 208p.

2. The Sikhs: a Distinctive and Visible Punjabi-Speaking Minority

26911 AURORA, G.S. The new frontiersmen; a sociological study of Indian immigrants in the United Kingdom. Bombay: Popular, 1967. 176p.

26912 BEETHAM, D. Transport and turbans; a comparative study in local politics. London: OUP, for Inst. of Race Relations, 1970. 86p.

26913 HELWEG, A.W. Sikhs in England; the development of a migrant community. Delhi: OUP, 1980. 204p.

26914 JAMES, A.G. Sikh children in Britain. London: OUP, for Inst. of Race Relations, 1974. 114p.

26915 JANJUA, H.S. Sikh temples in the U.K. and the poeple behind their management. London: Jan Pub., 1976. 106p.

26916 MARSH, P. The anatomy of a strike: unions, employers, and Punjabi workers in a Southall factory. London: Inst. of Race Relations, 1967. 119p.

3. The Ugandan Indian Refugees

26917 HUMPHREY, D. & MICHAEL WARD. Passports and politics. Harmondsworth: Penguin, 1974. 187p.

26918 KIDMAN, B. A handful of tears. London: BBC, 1975. 200p.

C. Pakistani and Bangladeshi Muslims in the U.K.

26919 ANWAR, MUHAMMAD. The myth of return: Pakistanis in Britain. London: Heinemann, 1979. 278p.

26920 DAHYA, BADR. The nature of Pakistani ethnicity in industrial cities in Britain. In A. Cohen, ed. Urban ethnicity. London: Tavistock, 1974, 77-118.

26921 ______. Pakistanis in Britain: transients or settlers? In Race 14,3 (1973) 241-78.

26922 HASHMI, FARRUKH. The Pakistani family in Britain. 2nd ed. London: Natl. Cmtee. for Commonwealth Immigrants, 1967. 13p.

26923 HUNTER, K. History of Pakistanis in Britain. London: K. Hunter, 1962. 115p.

26924 JEFFREY, P. Migrants and refugees: Muslim and Christian Pakistani refugees in Bristol. York: CamUP, 1976. 221p.

D. South Asian Women: Varying Adaptations to British Society

26925 DAHYA, ZAYNAB. Pakistani wives in Britain. In Race 6 (1965) 311-321.

26926 WILSON, AMRIT. A burning fever: the isolation of Asia women in Britain. In Race & Class 20,2 (1978) 129-42.

26927 ______. Finding a voice: Asian women in Britain. ND: Allied, 1980. 179p.

VI. SOUTH ASIANS IN NORTH AMERICA

A. General Studies

26928 DAS, R.K. Hindustani workers on the Pacific Coast. Berlin: W. de Gruyter, 1923. 126p.

26929 GANDA SINGH. The Sikhs in Canada and California. In PPP 4,2 (1970) 380-400.

26930 HARJINDER SINGH. Caste and marriage among Sikhs in India, U.S.A. and Canada. In EA 30,1 (1977) 15-21.

26931 MISROW, J.C. East Indian immigration on the Pacific coast. San Francisco: R & E Res. Associates, 1971. 46p.

B. Canada, A Commonwealth Partner

1. Early Immigration: South Asian Laborers on the West Coast before Exclusion 1913-1947

26932 HOLLAND, R. Indian immigration into Canada: the question of franchise. In Asiatic R. 39,138 (1943) 162-72.

26933 MILLIS, H.A. East Indian immigration to British Columbia and the Pacific States. In American Econ. R. 1,1 (1911) 72-76.

26934 SIHRA, NAND SINGH. Indians in Canada: a pitiable account of their hardships by one who comes from the place and knows them. In MR 14,2 (1913) 140-49.

26935 SINGH, SANT NIHAL. The triumph of the Indians in Canada. In MR 6,2 (1909) 99-108.

2. Post-Independence Immigration; Encouragement of Professional and Technical Immigrants after 1967

26936 KURIAN, G. Indian children in Canada: changing patterns of socialisation. In SocAct 24,4 (1974) 345-54.

26937 MAYER, A.C. A report on the East Indian community in Vancouver; working paper. Vancouver: Inst. of Social & Econ. Res., U. of British Columbia, 1960. 37p.

26938 SIDDIQUE, M. CHAUDRY. On migrating to Canada; the first generation Indian and Pakistan families in the process of change. In SB 26,2 (1977) 203-26.

26939 SRIVASTAVA, R.P. Family organization and change among the overseas Indians with special reference to Indian immigrant families of British Columbia, Canada. In G. Kurian, ed. The family in India: a regional view. The Hague: Mouton, 1974, 369-91.

26940 VIRENDRA KUMAR. Alimony and maintenance in the light of the changing concept of marriage and divorce. Chandigarh: Pub. Bureau, Panjab U., 1978. 368p. [study in Ontario]

C. The United States

1. Early Immigration: Swamis, Sikhs, and Students, 1893 - 1945

26941 HESS, G.R. The "Hindu" in America: immigration and naturalization policies and India, 1917-1946. In Pacific Hist. R. 38 (1969) 59-79.

2. The Post-War Influx of Students and Elite Immigrants, 1945 -

26942 FISHER, M.P. The Indians of New York City: a study of immigrants from India. ND: Heritage, 1980. 165p.

26943 GANDHI, R.S. Locals and cosmopolitans of little India: a sociological study of the Indian student community at Minnesota, U.S.A. Bombay: Popular, 1974. 214p.

26944 HASAN, MOHAMMAD. The social geography of South Asians in Syracuse, New York. Diss., Syracuse U., 1978. 454p. [UM 79-14,219]

26945 IRELAND, R.R. Indian immigration to the United States, 1901-1964: retrospect and prospect. In IJE 46,4 (1966) 465-76.

26946 KAUL, M.L. The adaptive styles of immigrants from India in the American communities of Akron, Canton, Cleveland, and Kent. Diss., Case Western Reserve U., 1977. 282p. [UM 77-25,169]

26947 MOHAPATRA, M.K. Overseas Indians in urban America: a study of their attitudes and experiences involving discrimination in American society. In Nagarlok 11,1 (1979) 120-41.

26948 ______. Perceptions of discrimination among overseas Indians in America: an empirical study. In AsProf 7,2 (1979) 141-58.

26949 VATUK, V.P. Protest songs of east Indians on the west coast, U.S.A. In his Thieves in my house.... Varanasi: Vishwavidyalaya Prakashan, 1969, 63-80.

26950 VENKATARAMAN, B. A Hindu in America. Bangalore: Raman Pub., 1969. 285p.

26951 WENZEL, L.A. Rural Punjabis in California: a religio-ethnic group. In Phylon Q. 29 (1968) 245-56.

Part Five

Reference Resources

18

Introductions and General Research Guides for Travellers and Scholars

I. GENERAL REFERENCE

26952 Encyclopaedia Britannica. 11th ed. NY: Encyclopaedia Britannica, 1910-11. 29 v. [Nineteenth century British imperialist bias; Indological and humanistic emphasis]

26953 Encyclopedia of religion and ethics. Ed. by J. Hastings, et al. NY: Scribner's, 1955. 13 v. [Rpt. 1908-26; articles on art, folklore, language, econ., and other humanistic and social science subjects]

26954 Index Islamicus, 1906-1955. Comp. by J.D. Pearson. Cambridge: Heffer, 1958. 897p. [with Suppl. 1956-75; now issued as Quarterly Index Islamicus, 1977-.]

26955 New Encyclopaedia Britannica. 15th ed. Chicago: Encyclopaedia Britannica, 1974. 30 v.

26956 Times of India directory and yearbook, including Who's who, 1914-. Bombay: Bennett, Coleman, 1914-. [latest ed.: 1979]

II. PHYSICAL AND HUMAN ECOLOGY: A SCHOLAR'S AND TRAVELLER'S INTRODUCTION

A. Overall Works on India and South Asia

1. Reference Works

26957 BALFOUR, E.G. Cyclopaedia of India and of eastern and southern Asia, commercial, industrial and scientific: products of the mineral, vegetable and animal kingdoms, useful arts and manufactures. 3rd ed. London: B. Quaritch, 1885. 3 v. [1st pub. 1857]

26958 BLENCK, J. & D. BRONGER & H. UHLIG. Sudasien. Frankfurt: Taschenbuch-Verlag, 1977. 477p. (Fischer Landerkunde, 2)

26959 CHANDRA, P.T., ed. National cyclopaedia, 1923: a manual of useful information. Karachi: the editor, 1923. 1 v.

26960 India: a reference annual. Delhi: PDMIB. [Annual]

26961 NYROP, RICHARD F., et al. Area handbook for India. 3rd ed. Washington: Govt. Printing Office, 1975. 648p.

26962 WALKER, B. Hindu world. NY: Praeger, 1968. 2 v. [articles are often inaccurate and unscholarly; critical review by V. Raghavan in ALB 33 (1969) 284-302.]

26963 WATT, G. The commercial products of India: being an abridgement of The dictionary of the economic products of India. ND: Today & Tomorrow's, 1969. 1198p. [Rpt. 1908 ed.]

26964 ______. A dictionary of the economic products of India. Delhi: Cosmo, 1972. 10 v. [Rpt. 1889-96 ed.]

26965 The wealth of India; a dictionary of Indian raw materials and industrial products: industrial products. ND: Council of Scientific & Industrial Res., 1948-76. 9v.

26966 The wealth of India; a dictionary of Indian raw materials and industrial products: raw materials. ND: Council of Scientific & Industrial Res., 1948-76. 11 v.

2. Selected Introductions

26967 ANAND, M.R. Is there a contemporary Indian civilization? NY: Asia, 1963. 207p.

26968 BOSSERT, J. India: land, people and culture. Delhi: Gulistan, 1974. 292p.

26969 BROWN, W.N. The United States and India, Pakistan, Bangladesh. 3rd ed. Harvard: HUP, 1972. 462p. [1st ed. 1953]

26970 HEIMSATH, C.H. Teachers' introduction to India. ND: Educ. Resources Center, 1973. 66p.

26971 HILL, J. The Indian sub-continent. London: Barrie & Rockliff, 1963. 312p.

26972 India: portrait of a people. ND: Min. of External Affairs, 1976. 224p.

26973 JOHNSON, D.J. & J.E. JOHNSON, eds. Through Indian eyes: the wheel of life. NY: Praeger, 1974. 136p.

26974 KEAY, J. Into India. London: Murray, 1973. 202p.

26975 KURIYAN, G. India: a general survey. ND: NBT, 1969. 179p. (ILP)

26976 LAMB, B.P. India; a world in transition. 4th ed. NY: Praeger, 1975. 428p.

26977 MEHTA, VED P. Portrait of India. NY: Farrar, Straus, Giroux, 1970. 544p.

26978 MEYER, M.W. India-Pakistan and the border lands. Totowa, NJ: Littlefield, Adams, 1968. 261p.

26979 NAIPAUL, V.S. India: a wounded civilization. NY: Knopf, 1977. 191p.

26980 RAGHAVAN, G.N.S. Introducing India. 2nd rev. ed. ND: ICCR, 1978. 166p. [1st ed., 1976, Understanding India]

26981 ROY, P.B. India: land and culture. Narendrapur: Saturday Mail Pub., 1976. 162p.

26982 SCARFE, W. & A. SCARFE, comps. People of India; a sourcebook for Asian studies. N. Melbourne: Cassell Australia, 1972. 188p.

26983 South Asia: a strategic survey. Washington: Dept. of the Army, 1966. 175p. (Its Pamphlet, 550-3)

3. Geography and Climate; Atlases
a. bibliography and reference

26984 AMERICAN GEOGRAPHICAL SOC. OF NEW YORK. LIBRARY. Research catalogue of the American Geographical Society. Boston: G.K. Hall, 1961. 16 v. [suppl., 1972, 1978]

26985 GOSLING, L.A.P. Maps, atlases and gazetteers for Asian studies: a critical guide. NY: Foreign Area Materials Center, U. of the State of New York, 1965. 27p. (Its Occ. pub., 2)

26986 INDIA (REP.). POSTS & TELEGRAPH DEPT. Post office guide, pt. 3: list of Indian post offices, v. 1: A-K; v. 2: L-Z. Calcutta: 1972. 2 v. 517, 449p. [Revised periodically]

26987 LA TOUCHE, T.H.D. Bibliography of Indian geology. Rev. & enl. ed. Delhi: Geological Survey of India, GOI, 19--. [1st pub. 1917-26]

26988 MARKHAM, C.R. Memoir on the Indian surveys. London: W.H. Allen, 1871. 303p. [Trigonometrical, topographic, geological, archaeological, etc. surveys]

26989 PRASAD, S.N., ed. Catalogue of the historical maps of the Survey of India, 1700-1900. ND: Natl. Archives of India, 1975. 543p.

26990 RAZA, MOONIS, ed. A survey of research in geography, 1969-1972. Bombay: Allied, 1979. 234p. [sponsored by ICSSR]

26991 SANTHANAM, R. Latitudes, longitudes, and local mean times for 5000 places in India. Delhi: Kalyani, 1976. 133p.

26992 SUKHWAL, B.L. South Asia: a systematic geographic bibliography. Metuchen, NJ: Scarecrow Press, 1974. 827p.

26993 Survey of research in geography. Bombay: Popular, 1972. 397p. [sponsored by ICSSR]

b. Atlases

26994 Atlas of India. Edinburgh: W. & A.K. Johnston, 1894. 38 + 19p. + 16 maps.

26995 BARTHOLOMEW, J., ed. The Times atlas of the world, mid-century edition, vol. 2: South-west Asia and Russia.... London: Times Pub. Co., 1959. 51p.

26996 DUTT, A. & S.P. CHATTERJEE & M.M. GEIB. India in maps. Dubuque, IO: Kendall/Hunt, 1976. 124p.

26997 Imperial gazetteer of India, v. 26: Atlas. Rev. ed. Oxford: OUP, 1931. 66 pl. + 41p. [1st ed.: 1909]

26998 INDIA (REP.). NATL. ATLAS ORG. National atlas of India. Calcutta: 1977. 309p.

26999 INDIA (REP.). CENSUS OF INDIA, 1961. Census atlas. ND: Office of the Registrar Genl., 1970. 423p. (v. 1, pt. 9)

27000 INDIA (REP.). CENSUS OF INDIA, 1971. Indian census centenary atlas. ND: Office of the Registrar Genl., 1974. 198p.

27001 INDIA (REP.). NATL. ATLAS ORG. Tourist atlas of India. Calcutta: 1974. 25 maps.

27002 INDIA (REP.). SURVEY OF INDIA. Maps for the nation: stepping stones to planned progress. Dehra Dun: 197-. 43p.

27003 ______. School atlas. Bombay: Allied, 1961. 62p.

27004 KINGSBURY, R.C. South Asia in maps. Chicago: Denoyer-Geppert, 1969. 96p.

27005 Oxford school atlas. 24th ed. Delhi: OUP, 1980. 72p.

27006 UNITED STATES. CENTRAL INTELLIGENCE AGENCY. Indian Ocean atlas. Washington: 1976. 80p.

c. surveys and studies

27007 DAS, P.K. The monsoons. ND: NBT, 1968. 162p. (ILP)

27008 DEY, A.K. Geology of India. ND: NBT, 1968. 178p. (ILP)

27009 GOPAL SINGH. Geography of India. 2nd ed., rev. & enl. Delhi: Atma Ram, 1976. 488p.

27010 JANAKI, V.A. Some aspects of the political geography of India. Baroda: MSUB, 1977. 265p. (Its Geog. series, 8)

27011 JOHNSON, B.L.C. South Asia: selective studies of the essential geography of India, Pakistan and Ceylon. London: Heinemann Educ., 1969. 164p.

27012 LAW, B.C., ed. Mountains and rivers of India. Calcutta: Natl. Cmtee. for Geography, 1968. 437p.

27013 MISRA, R.P. Medical geography of India. ND: NBT, 1970. 205p. (ILP)

27014 MISRA, S.D. Rivers of India. ND: NBT, 1970. 188p. (ILP)

27015 PICHAMUTHU, C.S. Physical geography of India. ND: NBT, 1967. 212p. (ILP)

27016 PLATT, R.R. et al., eds. India: a compendium. NY: American Geog. Soc., 1962. 586p.

27017 RAYCHAUDHURI, S.P. Land and soil. 2nd ed. ND: NBT, 1969. 190p. (ILP)

27018 SINGH, R.L., ed. India: a regional geography. Varanasi: NGSI, 1971. 992p.

27019 SOPHER, D.E., ed. An exploration of India: geographical perspectives on society and culture. Ithaca, NY: CornellUP, 1980. 334p.

27020 SPATE, O.H.K. & A.T.A. LEARMONTH. India and Pakistan: a general and regional geography; with a chapter on Ceylon by B.H. Farmer. 3rd rev. ed. London: Methuen, 1967. 877p. [1st ed. 1954]

27021 ______. India and Pakistan: land, people and economy. 3rd rev. ed. London: Methuen, 1972. 439p. [Rpt. of pt. 1, India and Pakistan: a general and regional geography. 3rd rev. ed. 1967]

27022 ______. India, Pakistan and Ceylon: the regions. 3rd rev. ed. London: Methuen, 1972. 407-862p. [Rpt. of pt. 2, India and Pakistan: a general and regional geography. 3rd rev. ed. 1967]

27023 SPENCER, J.E. & W.L. THOMAS. Asia, east by south: a cultural geography. NY: John Wiley, 1971. 669p.

4. Natural History

27024 ALI, SALIM A. The book of Indian birds. 10th ed., rev. & enl. Bombay: Bombay Natural History Soc., 1977. 175p. + 46 pl.

27025 ALI, SALIM A. & LAEEQ FUTEHALLY. Common birds. ND: NBT, 1967. 118p. (ILP)

27026 ALI, SALIM A. & S.D. RIPLEY. Handbook of the birds of India and Pakistan together with those of Nepal, Sikkim, Bhutan and Ceylon. Bombay: OUP, 1968-. v. 1-.

27027 ARACHI, J.K. Pictorial presentation of Indian flora: special study of the flowering plants of Courtalam. Madras: Higginbothams, 1968. 189p.

27028 BEDDOME, R.H. Handbook to the ferns of British India, Ceylon, and the Malay Peninsula. ND: Today & Tomorrow's, 1969. 500 + 110p. [1st ed. 1863]

27029 COWEN, D.V. Flowering trees and shrubs in India. 4th rev. & enl. ed. Bombay: Thacker, 1965. 159p.

27030 DASTUR, J.F. Useful plants of India and Pakistan: a popular handbook of trees and plants of industrial, economic, and commercial utility. 2nd ed. Bombay: Taraporevala Sons, 1977. 185p.

27031 DEORAS, J.K. Snakes of India. 3rd rev. ed. ND: NBT, 1978. 156p. (ILP)

27032 FLETCHER, T.B. Some south Indian insects and other animals of importance: considered especially from an economic point of view. Dehra Dun: Bishen Singh Mahendra Pal Singh, 1977. 565p. [Rpt. 1914 ed.]

27033 The Gir lion sanctuary project. Gandhinagar: Dir. of Info. & Tourism, Govt. of Gujarat, 1972. 100p.

27034 INDIA (REP.). DEPT. OF TOURISM. Wild life sanctuaries in India. ND: PDMIB, 1961. 96p.

27035 INDIA (REP.). INDIAN BOARD FOR WILD LIFE. EXPERT CMTEE. Wildlife conservation in India: report of the Expert Committee, Indian Board for Wildlife. Dehra Dun: Forest Res. Inst. Press, 1970. 149p.

27036 KALYANAM, N.P. Common insects of India. Bombay: Asia, 1967. 136p.

27037 KHAJWIA, H., ed. India's wild life. Rev. ed. Delhi: PDMIB, 1963. 62p.

27038 PAL, B.P. & S. KRISHNAMURTHI. Flowering shrubs. ND: ICAR, 1967. 155p.

27039 PRATER, S.H. The book of Indian animals. 2nd rev. ed. Bombay: Bombay Natural History Soc., 1965. 323p.

27040 RANDHAWA, M.S. Flowering trees. ND: NBT, 1965. 171p. (ILP)

27041 SANTAPAU, H. Common trees. ND: NBT, 1966. 142p. (ILP)

27042 SCHALLER, G.B. The deer and the tiger; a study of wildlife in India. Chicago: UChiP, 1967. 370p.

27043 SETH, S.K. & M.B. RAIZADA & M.A. WAHEED. Trees for Vana mahotsava. Dehra Dun: Forest Res. Inst. & Colleges, 1962. 130p.

27044 STRACY, P.D. Wild life in India: its conservation and control. ND: Dept. of Agri., 1964. 281p.

27045 SWARUP, V. Garden flowers. ND: NBT, 1967. 261p. (ILP)

27046 WHITAKER, R. Common Indian snakes: a field guide. Delhi: Macmillan, 1978. 154p.

5. Travellers' Accounts

27047 ADAM, K. Journey into India. Sydney: Australian Broadcasting Cmsn., & Hodder & Stoughton, 1978. 160p.

27048 ARMSTRONG, R.G. Sisters under the sari. Ames: Iowa State U. Press, 1964. 498p.

27049 BENY, R. India. London: Thames & Hudson, 1969. 236p.

27050 BOWLES, C. At home in India. NY: Harcourt, Brace, 1956. 180p.

27051 DAY, C.B. The Indian interlude. San Francisco: Chinese Materials Center, 1977. 151p.

27052 FARLEY, M.F. & C.A. KELLY. Indian summer: an account of a visit to India. Washington: Univ. Press of America, 1976. 211p.

27053 FORBES, D. The heart of India. London: R. Hale, 1968. 205p.

27054 GODDEN, J. & R. GODDEN. Shiva's pigeons: an experience of India. NY: Viking, 1972. 372p.

27055 HANKS, J. Tender hearts of India. Delhi: Vikas, 1970. 255p.

27056 HÜRLIMANN, M. India. Tr. from German by D.J.S. Thomson. London: Thames & Hudson, 1967. 331p.

27057 MORAVIA, A. L'Inde comme je l'ai vue. Tr. from Italian by Claude Poncet. Paris: Flammarion, 1963. 167p.

27058 NERLICH, G. ...und weiter fliesst der Ganges; Reisebilder aus Indien. Berlin: Verlag Neues Leben, 1962. 340p.

27059 NOSSITER, B.D. Soft state: a newspaperman's chronicle of India. NY: Harper & Row, 1970. 185p.

27060 POPE, C. Sahib; an American misadventure in India. NY: Liveright, 1972. 176p.

27061 RICE, E. Mother India's children: meeting today's generation in India. NY: Pantheon Books, 1971. 176p.

27062 ROOSEVELT, E. India and the awakening east. NY: Harper, 1953. 237p.

27063 WILES, J. The Grand Trunk Road; Khyber to Calcutta. London: Elek, 1972. 161p.

27064 WOODCOCK, G. Faces of India; a travel narrative. London: Faber & Faber, 1964. 280p.

27065 ZINKIN, T. India. London: OUP, 1967. 126p. (Modern World)

6. Travel, City, and Hotel Guides

27066 All-India hotel and restaurant guide, 19--. Delhi: Federation of Hotel & Restaurant Assns. Irregular. Most recent v.: 1977/78.

27067 BALARAM IYER, T.G.S. North India and Andaman, Nicobar, Laccadive Minicoy, Amindivi Islands: tourist guide. Madurai: Sri Karthikeiya, 1978. 83p.

27068 BOULANGER, R. Inde, Népal, Bhutan, Céylan (Sri-Lanka). Paris: Hachette, 1976. 810p. (Guides bleus)

27069 Fodor's India, 1980. Ed. by E. Fodor & W. Curtis. NY: David McKay & Co., 1979. 608p.

27070 GUPTA, S.P. & K. LAL. Tourism, museums, and monuments in India. Delhi: Oriental, 1974. 216p.

27071 A handbook for travellers in India, Pakistan, Nepal, Bangladesh and Sri Lanka (Ceylon). 22nd ed. Ed. by L.F. Rushbrook Williams. London: Murray, 1975. 762p. ["Murray's guide," 1st pub. 1859-82]

27072 Hardy's encyclopaedia: hotels des India and Nepal; a travellers guide. ND: 1964-. [latest ed. 1977]

27073 Hill resorts of India and Nepal: a travellers guide. ND: Nest & Wings, 1971. 1 v.

27074 KAUL, H.K., ed. Travels in South Asia: a selected and annotated bibliography of guide-books and travel-books on South Asia. ND: Arnold-Heinemann, 1979. 215p.

27075 NAGEL PUBLISHERS. India, Nepal. Ed. by P. Wagret. Geneva: Nagel, 1974. 830p.

27076 Newman's Indian Bradshaw: a complete guide for railway and airway travellers in India, Bangladesh, Pakistan, and Sri Lanka. Calcutta: W. Newman. Publ. monthly. [list of routes, timetables & fares]

27077 NILSSON, S.A. The new capitals of India, Pakistan and Bangladesh. Tr. by E. Andreasson. Lund: Studentlitteratur, 1973. 230p. (Scandinavian Inst. of Asian Studies, monograph 12)

27078 RIDGE, B. & P.E. MADSEN. Traveler's guide to India: a complete, up-to-date guide for student and tourist. NY: Scribner's, 1973. 190p.

27079 ROY, P.B. India: a handbook of travel. 4th rev. & enl. ed. Narendrapur: Saturday Mail Pub., 1975. 500p.

7. Images and Stereotypes of South Asia and South Asians

27080 GOETZ, H. Growth of western ideas about India. In Greater India Soc. J. 4 (1937) 49-63.

27081 GOKHALE, B.G. Images of India. Bombay: Popular, 1971. 196p. (Asian studies, 2)

27082 ISAACS, H.R. Images of Asia: American views of China and India. NY: Harper & Row, 1972. 416p. [1st pub. 1958, Scratches on our minds....]

27083 KOESTLER, A. The lotus and the robot. London: Hutchinson, 1960. 296p.

27084 SINGER, M.B. Passage to more than India: a sketch of changing European and American images. In his When a great tradition modernizes. NY: Praeger, 1972, 11-38.

27085 TAYLOR, E. Richer by Asia. Boston: Houghton Mifflin, 1947. 432p.

27086 VISHAL SINGH et al. Images of contemporary India abroad.... ND: IIC, 1967. 56p.

B. Overall Introductions to Pakistan

1. Reference

27087 MASUD-UL-HASAN. Short encyclopaedia of Pakistan. Lahore: Ferozsons, 1975. 203p.

27088 NYROP, R.F. et al. Area handbook for Pakistan. 4th ed. Washington: Govt. Printing Office, 1975. 455p.

27089 PAKISTAN. POST OFFICE DEPT. List of post offices in Pakistan, corrected up to 31-5-74. Karachi: 1974. 316p. [reissued periodically]

27090 Pakistan year-book, 1969-. Karachi: Natl. Pub. House. [Annual. Continues the monograph: Twenty years of Pakistan, 1947-1967]

2. Introductions

27091 Crescent and green: miscellany of writings on Pakistan. Freeport: Books for Libraries Press, 1970. 170p. [Rpt. 1955 ed.]

27092 FAIRLEY, J. The lion river: the Indus. NY: John Day, 1975. 290p.

27093 FAIZI, S.F. HASAN. Pakistan: a cultural unity. Lahore: Sh. M. Ashraf, 1970. 198p.

27094 IKRAM, S.M. & T.G.P. SPEAR, eds. The cultural heritage of Pakistan. NY: OUP, 1955. 204p.

27095 KINGSBURY, P. & R. KINGSBURY. Pakistan. Garden City, NY: Doubleday, 1963. 64p.

27096 KUREISHI, RAFIUSHAN. The nation of Pakistan. Oxford: Pergamon Press, 1969. 109p.

27097 ______. The new Pakistan. London: Bell, 1977. 146p.

27098 LANG, R.P. The land and people of Pakistan. Philadelphia: Lippincott, 1968. 159p.

27099 MALIK, M. USMAN & A. SCHIMMEL, eds. Pakistan: das Land und seine Menschen: Geschichte, Kultur, Staat und Wirtschaft. Tübingen: H. Erdmann Verlag, 1976. 562p. (Buchreihe Landermonographien, 6)

27100 MARON, S., ed. Pakistan: society and culture. New Haven: HRAF, 1957. 192p.

27101 Pakistan: a land of many splendours. Karachi: Pakistan Pub., 1970. 148p.

27102 Pakistan panorama. Rawalpindi: Pakistan Pub., 1974. 102p.

27103 Pakistan, past and present: a comprehensive study published in commemoration of the centenary of the birth of the founder of Pakistan. London: Stacey Intl., 1977. 288p.

27104 RAJPUT, A.B. Social customs and practices in Pakistan. Islamabad: Pakistan Branch, R.C.D. Cultural Institute, 1977. 293p. (Its pub. 59)

27105 SABIR, MOHAMMAD SHAFI. Pakistan: culture, people and places. Peshawar: University Book Agency, 1970. 418p.

27106 SAMINA QURAESHI. Legacy of the Indus; a discovery of Pakistan. NY: Weatherhill, 1974. 223p.

27107 STEPHENS, I.M. Pakistan. 3rd ed. NY: Praeger, 1967. 304p.

27108 WEEKES, R.V. Pakistan: birth and growth of a Muslim nation. Princeton: Van Nostrand, 1964. 278p.

27109 WILBER, D.N., et al. Pakistan, its people, its society, its culture. New Haven: HRAF Press, 1964. 487p. (Survey of world cultures, 13)

3. Geography and Natural History

27110 AHMAD, KAZI SAID UDDIN. A geography of Pakistan. 2nd ed. Karachi: OUP, 1969. 262p.

27111 AHMAD, KAZI S. & NAFIS AHMAD, eds. Oxford school atlas for Pakistan. Karachi: OUP, 1959. 57p.

27112 JOHNSON, B.L.C. Pakistan. Exeter, NH: Heinemann, 1979. 224p.

27113 KURESHY, K.U. A geography of Pakistan. 4th ed. Karachi: OUP, 1977. 199p.

27114 PLATT, R.R. et al., eds. Pakistan: a compendium. NY: American Geographical Soc., 1961. 383p.

27115 RAHMAN, MUSHTAQUR. Bibliography of Pakistan geography, 1947-1973. Monticello, IL: Council of Planning Librarians, 1974. 117p.

27116 TAYYEB, ALI. Pakistan; a political geography. London: OUP, 1966. 250p.

27117 UNITED STATES BOARD ON GEOGRAPHIC NAMES. Pakistan; official standard names... 2nd ed. Washington: 1978. 523p.

4. Travellers' Accounts

27118 BALNEAVES, E. The waterless moon. Karachi: Indus Pub., 1977. 175p.

27119 JENKINS, L. Pakistan Zindabad. Paris: Berger-Levrault, 1970. 288p.

27120 LINCK, O.F. A passage through Pakistan. Detroit: Wayne State U. Press, 1959. 261p.

27121 MAREK, J. & D. ZBAVITEL. Zweimal Pakistan. Tr. from Czech into German by G. Muller & D. Lokys. Leipzig: Brockhaus, 1966. 266p.

27122 MIREPOIX, C. Now Pakistan. Karachi: Grenich, 1967. 350p.

27123 SCHIMMEL, A. Pakistan: ein schloss mit tausend toren. Zurich: Orell Füssli Verlag, 1965. 278p.

27124 STEPHENS, I.M. Horned moon: an account of a journey through Pakistan, Kashmir, and Afghanistan. 3rd ed. London: Benn, 1966. 288p. [1st ed. 1955]

27125 TETA, J.A. Pakistan and Bangladesh in pictures. NY: Sterling, 1973. 64p.

27126 TOYNBEE, A.J. Between Oxus and Jumna. NY: OUP, 1961. 211p.

5. Travel, City, and Hotel Guides

27127 MASUD-UL-HASAN. Pakistan: places of interest. Lahore: Ferozsons, 1977. 404p.

27128 Pakistan. Paris: Editions Vilo, 1970. 309p. (Les guides modernes Fodor)

27129 Pakistan hotels and tourism, 1975-. Lahore: Bhatti Publications. [annual; supersedes Hotels and restaurants of Pakistan]

C. Sri Lanka

1. Reference

27130 Ferguson's Ceylon directory, 1858-. Colombo: Associated Newspapers of Ceylon. [annual]

27131 NYROP, R.F. et al. Area handbook for Ceylon. Washington: Govt. Printing Office, 1971. 525p.

27132 Sri Lanka year book, 1972-. Colombo: Dept. of Census and Statistics, Govt. of Sri Lanka. [annual; supersedes Ceylon year book, 1948-1971]

2. Introductions

27133 BROHIER, R.L. Seeing Ceylon in vistas of scenery, history, legend, and folklore. Colombo: LHI, 1965. 262p.

27134 DEVENDRA, D.T. Tanks and rice. Colombo: M.D. Gunasena, 1965. 210p.

27135 FERNANDO, T. & R.N. KEARNEY, eds. Modern Sri Lanka: a society in transition. Syracuse: Maxwell School of Citizenship & Public Affairs, Syracuse U., 1979. 297p. [Its Foreign & comp. studies, South Asian series, 4]

27136 PAKEMAN, S.A. Ceylon. NY: Praeger, 1964. 256p.

27137 PHADNIS, U. Sri Lanka. ND: NBT, 1973. 116p.

27138 RAGHAVAN, M.D. Ceylon: a pictorial survey of the peoples and arts. Colombo: Gunasena, 1962. 260p. + 42 pl.

27139 TRESIDDER, A.J. Ceylon: an introduction to the resplendent land. Princeton: Van Nostrand, 1960. 237p.

27140 WIJESEKERA, N.D. The people of Ceylon. Colombo: Gunasena, 1965. 311p.

27141 ZUBER, C. Sri Lanka, island civilisation. Colombo: Lake House Bookshop, 1978. 212p.

3. Geography and Natural History

27142 CEYLON. DEPT. OF CENSUS & STAT. The Ceylon economic atlas. Colombo: 1969. 69p. + 29 maps.

27143 A concise atlas geography of Ceylon. Colombo: Atlas & Maps Industries, 1971. 35p.

27144 COOK, E.K. Ceylon: its geography, its resources and its people. Madras: Macmillan, 1951. 360p.

27145 DE SILVA, S.F. A regional geography of Ceylon. Rev. & enl. ed. Colombo: Colombo Apothecaries, 1954. 301p.

27146 DOMRÖS, M. Sri Lanka: die Tropeninsel Ceylon. Darmstadt: Wissenschaftliche Buchgesellschaft, 1976. 298p.

27147 FERNANDO, S.N.U. The natural vegetation of Ceylon: the forests, the grasslands, and the soils of Ceylon. Colombo: dist. Lake House Bookshop, 1968. 85p.

27148 SIEVERS, A. Ceylon, Gesellschaft und Lebensraum in den orientalischen Tropen; eine sozialgeographische Landeskunde. Wiesbaden: Steiner, 1964. 398p.

27149 UNITED STATES BOARD ON GEOGRAPHIC NAMES. Gazetteer. Official standard names.... Washington: 1955-. [no. 49; Ceylon, 1960]

4. Travellers' Accounts

27150 ADITHIYA, L. Ceylon vagabond. Colombo: K.V.G. De Silva, 1969. 194p.

27151 BENY, R. & J.L. OPIE. Island Ceylon. NY: Viking, 1971. 224p.

27152 DE LANEROLLE, S.D. River in the jungle = Vana nadiya. Tr. into English by K.D. de Lanerolle. Colombo: Kalyani, 1977. 122p.

27153 GOONETILEKE, H.A.I., ed. Images of Sri Lanka through American eyes: travellers in Ceylon in the nineteenth and twentieth centuries: a select anthology. Colombo: Intl. Communication Agency, 1976. 411p.

27154 UCHIYAMA, A. Sri Lanka: travels in Ceylon. Tokyo: Kodansha Intl., 1973. 120p.

5. Travel Guides

27155 Ceylon (Sri Lanka). Geneva: Nagel Pub., 1977. 271p.

27156 Handbook for the Ceylon Traveller. Colombo: Studio Times, 1974. 354p.

27157 HULUGALLE, H.A.J. Guide to Ceylon. Colombo: LHI, 1969. 125p.

D. South India: Tamil Nadu, Kerala, Karnataka, Andhra Pradesh

1. Introductions

27158 ADVERTISING & SALES PROMOTION CO. Karnataka. Bangalore: Dir. of Info. & Tourism, Govt. of Karnataka, 1973? 96p.

27159 BALACHANDRAN NAYAR, K., ed. In quest of Kerala. Trivandrum: Accent, 1974-? 2 v.

27160 CHAITANYA, K. Kerala. ND: NBT, 1972. 202p. (ILP)

27161 CHOUDHARY, R. Andhra Pradesh. ND: NBT, 1979. 112p. (ILP)

27162 DAS, M. Pondicherry. ND: PDMIB, 1976. 59p. (SOU, 29)

27163 JAGADESAN, T.D. Andhra Pradesh. ND: PDMIB, 1969. 81p. (SOU, 2)

27164 Kerala. Delhi: PDMIB, 1974. 43p. (SOU, 1) [Rpt. 1968 ed.]

27165 KRISHNA IYER, L.A. Kerala and her people. Palghat: Educ. Supplies Depot, 1961. 177p.

27166 KRISHNA RAO, M.V. Karnataka. ND: PDMIB, 1975. 112p. (SOU, 19)

27167 RAMACHANDRIAH, N.S. Mysore. ND: NBT, 1972. 196p. (ILP)

27168 RAMUNNY, M. Laccadive, Minicoy, and Amindivi Islands. ND: PDMIB, 1972. 69p. (SOU, 13)

27169 VIRA RAGHAVAN, C. Tamil Nadu. ND: PDMIB, 1973. 81p. (SOU, 16)

27170 WOODCOCK, G. Kerala: a portrait of the Malabar coast. London: Faber & Faber, 1967. 323p.

2. Geography

27171 ANDHRA PRADESH. BUREAU OF ECON. & STAT. Andhra Pradesh in maps. Hyderabad: 1969. 122p.

27172 BALAKRISHNA REDDY, N. & G.S. MURTY. Regional geography of Mysore state. Hubli: Book Centre, 1967. 189p.

27173 INDIA (REP.). METEOROLOGICAL DEPT. Climate of Andhra Pradesh. ND: 1976. 143p. + 10pl. (State climatological summaries, 2)

27174 LEARMONTH, A.T.A. & L.S. BHAT, ed. Mysore State. Bombay: Asia, 1961-63. 2 v., 294, 165p. (Indian stat. series, 196) [v. 1, Atlas of resources; v. 2, Regional synthesis]

27175 MISRA, R.P. Geography of Mysore. ND: NBT, 1973. 165p. (ILP)

3. Travellers' Accounts

27176 MORAES, D.F. The open eyes: a journey through Karnataka. Bangalore: Dir. of Info. & Publicity, Govt. of Karnataka, 1976. 127p.

27177 NAGARAJAN, K. Cauveri, from source to sea. ND: Arnold-Heinemann, 1975. 96p.

27178 NARAYAN, R.K. The emerald route. Bangalore: Dir. of Info. & Publicity, Govt. of Karnataka, 1977. 147p. [sketches by R.K. Laxman]

4. Travel, City, and Hotel Guides

27179 A guide to Hyderabad. Hyderabad: Inst. of Asian Studies, 1976. 77p.

27180 KAUJALGI, H.S. A visit to Bijapur. 4th ed. Hubli: M.H. Kaujalgi, 1950. 79p.

27181 MEHTA, A., ed. Pondicherry Town tourist guide. Madras: the editor, 1977. 56p.

27182 Trivandrum city guide. Trivandrum: Printed at St. Joseph's Press, 19--. 133p.

27183 VALLATT, G. Discovery of Kerala: a tourist guide of Kerala. Trivandrum: S.B. Press and Book Depot, 1977. 225p.

E. Middle India: Maharashtra, Gujarat, Rajasthan, Madhya Pradesh, Orissa

1. Introductions

27184 BHAGWAT, A.K., ed. Maharashtra, a profile: Vishnu Sakharam Khandekar felicitation volume. Kolhapur: V.S. Khandekar Amrit Mahotsava Satkar Samiti, 1977. 593p.

27185 BHATT, N.K. Gujarat. ND: PDMIB, 1972. 73p. (SOU, 12)

27186 CHATURVEDI, S.N. New image of Rajasthan. Jaipur: Dir. of Public Relations, Govt. of Rajasthan, 1966. 200p.

27187 CHIB, S.S. Rajasthan. ND: Light & Life, 1979. 147p.

27188 DAS, M. Goa, Daman and Diu, Dadra and Nagar Haveli. ND: PDMIB, 1976. 62p. (SOU, 21)

27189 DASH, S.C. Orissa. ND: PDMIB, 1970. (SOU, 3)

27190 KARVE, I. Maharashtra: land and its people. Bombay: Dir. of Govt. Printing, 1968. 201p. (Maharashtra State Gazetteer)

27191 Know the colourful Rajasthan. Jaipur: Vidya Bhawan, 1973? 122p.

27192 PAL, DHARM. Rajasthan. ND: NBT, 1968. 190p. (ILP)

27193 POTDAR, D.V. Inside Maharashtra. ND: Maharashtra Info. Centre, 1974. 52p.

2u194 SHARMA, M.L. Rajasthan. ND: PDMIB, 1972. 91p. (SOU, 9)

27195 TIKEKAR, S.R. Maharashtra. ND: PDMIB, 1972. 76p. (SOU, 11)

27196 ______. Maharashtra: the land, its people and their culture. ND: Maharashtra Info. Centre, 1966. 62p.

2. Geography and Natural History

27197 ARUNACHALAM, B. Maharashtra: a study in physical and regional setting and resource development. Bombay: A.R. Sheth, 1967. 308p.

27198 DESHPANDE, C.D. Geography of Maharashtra. ND: NBT, 1971. 218p. (ILP)

27199 DIKSHIT, K.R. Geography of Gujarat. ND: NBT, 1970. 260p. (ILT)

27200 GUPTA, R.K. & ISHWAR PRAKASH. Environmental analysis of the Thar Desert. Dehra Dun: English Book Depot, 1975. 484p.

27201 MISRA, V.C. Geography of Rajasthan. ND: NBT, 1969. 188p. (ILP)

27202 SHAH, G.L. Flora of Gujarat State. Vallabh Vidyanagar: Sardar Patel U., 1978. 2 v., 1074p.

27203 SINHA, B. Geography of Orissa. ND: NBT, 1971. 172p. (ILP)

3. Travel, City and Hotel Guides

27204 AMLADI, D.R. & P.N. NARKHEDE. Aurangabad, queen of

the Deccan. Bombay: Dir. of Archives, Govt. of Maharashtra, 197-. 24p.

27205 DEODHAR, D., ed. Nagpur guide. Nagpur: Yuvak Prakashan, 1977. 220p.

27206 DESAI, S.H. Junagadh and Girnar. Junagadh: Sorath Res. Society, 1972. 100p.

27207 Guide to Rajasthan. ND: India Tourism Development Corp., 1975. 217p.

27208 MEHTA, J.S. Abu to Udaipur: Celestial Simla to City of Sunrise. Delhi: Motilal, 1970. 193p.

27209 ORISSA. DEPT. OF TOURISM & CULTURAL AFFAIRS. Accommodation facilities in Orissa. Bhubaneswar: 1976. 66p.

27210 SHARMA, N.K. Jaisalmer, the golden city. Jaisalmer: Seemant Prakashan, 1978. 47p.

27211 Tourist guide of Goa, Daman and Diu: a travellers' guide. ND: Nest & Wings, 1976. 56p.

F. Indus Valley and Mountain Frontier: Sind, Baluchistan, Punjab, NWFP, Kashmir

1. Introductions

27212 BAMZAI, P.N.K. Jammu and Kashmir. ND: PDMIB, 1973. 62p. (SOU, 15)

27213 BAZAZ, P.N. Inside Kashmir. Srinagar: Kashmir Pub. Co., 1941. 412p.

27214 BEG, M. HAMID ALI, ed. Baluchistan: an introduction. Quetta: Dir. of Info., Govt. of Baluchistan, 1970. 28p.

27215 CHIB, S.S. Jammu and Kashmir. ND: Light & Life, 1977. 158p. (This beautiful India, 6)

27216 ______. Punjab. ND: Light & Life, 1977. 136p. (This beautiful India, 3)

27217 Cultural heritage of Ladakh. ND: Min. of Educ. & Social Welfare, 1978. 100p.

27218 GERVIS, P. This is Kashmir. London: Cassell & Co., 1954. 330p.

27219 GOYAL, D.R. Kashmir. ND: R & K Pub. House, 1965. 141p.

27220 GUPTA, S.S. Punjab. ND: PDMIB, 1971. 41p. (SOU, 7)

27221 HAMID, S. SHAHID. Karakuram Hunza; the land of just enough. Karachi: Maᶜaref, 1979. 175p.

27222 HASSNAIN, F.M. Hindu Kashmir. ND: Light and Life, 1977. 149p.

27223 HUGHES, A.W. The country of Baluchistan: its geography, topography, ethnology, and history. Quetta: Gosha-e-Adab, 1977. 294p. [1st pub. 1878]

27224 LAMBRICK, H.T. Sind: a general introduction. 2nd ed. Hyderabad: Sindhi Adabi Board, 1975. 247p. + 21pl. (History of Sind series, 1)

27225 MOINUDDIN. Sind: land of legends. Karachi: Natl. Book Foundation, 1975. 127p.

27226 RODALE, J.I. The healthy Hunzas. Emmaus, PA: Rodale Press, 1948. 263p.

2. Geography

27227 DICHTER, D. The North-West Frontier of West Pakistan: a study in regional geography. Oxford: OUP, 1967. 231p.

27228 ISHIDA, H., ed. Dynamic regional geographical studies of the Punjab, India. Hiroshima: U. of Hiroshima, 1975. 344p.

27229 KOUL, A. Geography of the Jammu & Kashmir State. ND: Light & Life, 1978. 200p. + 10pl.

27230 PITHAWALLA, M.B. Physical and economic geography of Sind, the lower Indus basin. Karachi: Sindhi Adabi Board, 1959. 389p.

27231 RAHMAN, MUSHTAQUR. A geography of Sind Province, Pakistan. Karachi: Karachi Geographers Assn., 1975. 217p. (Its pub. 12)

27232 RAINA, A.N. Geography of Jammu & Kashmir. ND: NBT, 1971. 183p.

27233 RAZA, M., AIJAZUDDIN AHMAD & ALI MOHAMMAD. The valley of Kashmir: a geographical interpretation.... ND: Vikas, 1978-. v. 1-.

3. Travellers' Accounts

27234 BALSAN, F. La colline mystérieuse, nouvelles recherches au Baloutchistan. Paris: Bibliothèque le livre contemporain, 1957. 209p.

27235 ______. Étrange Baloutchistan... Paris: Soc. continentale d'éditions modernes illustrées, 1969. 371p.

27236 BENYUKH, O. & DARSHAN SINGH. Burglars of hearts. Bombay: Jaico, 1969. 232p. [Punjab and the Ukraine]

27237 CLARK, J. Hunza, lost kingdom of the Himalayas. Karachi: Indus Pub., 1980. 270p. [Rpt. 1956 ed.]

27238 DUARTE, A. The beggar saint of Sehwan and other sketches of Sind. Karachi: printed by Elite Pub., 1974. 98p.

27239 LORIMER, E.O. Language hunting in the Karakorum. London: Allen & Unwin, 1939. 310p.

27240 MARAINI, F. Karakoram; the ascent of Gasherbrum IV. Tr. from Italian by J. Cadell. NY: Viking, 1961. 319p.

27241 MATHESON, S.A. The tigers of Baluchistan. London: A. Barker, 1967. 213p.

27242 MAYNE, P. The narrow smile; a journey back to the North-West Frontier. London: Murray, 1955. 263p.

27243 MONS, B. High road to Hunza. London: Faber & Faber, 1958. 157p.

27244 MURPHY, D. Where the Indus is young: a winter in Baltistan. London: Murray, 1977. 266p.

27245 PRIOR, L.F.L. Punjab prelude. London: Murray, 1952. 218p.

27246 SMITH, N. Golden doorway to Tibet. Indianapolis: Bobbs-Merrill Co., 1949. 288p. [Ladakh]

27247 SUMI, TOKAN, et al. Ladakh; the moonland. ND: Light & Life, 1975. 66p.

4. Travel, City, and Hotel Guides

27248 AGARWALA, A.P., ed. Holiday resorts of Jammu & Kashmir: a travellers' guide. ND: Nest & Wings, 1977. 160p. + 12pl.

27249 DRIEBERG, T. Jammu and Kashmir: a tourist guide. ND: Vikas, 1978. 140 + 32p.

27250 FUJIWARA, S. Kashmir. Tr. by M.F. Breer. Tokyo & New York: Kodansha Intl., 1978. 85p. + 12pl.

27251 HASSNAIN, F.M. Gilgit, the northern gate of India. ND: Sterling, 1978. 194p.

27252 MASUD-UL-HASAN. Guide to Lahore. Lahore: Ferozsons, 1978. 144p.

27253 The moonland Ladakh: a travellers' guide. ND: Nest & Wings, 1978. 134p.

27254 NEVE, A., ed. The tourist's guide to Kashmir, Ladakh, Skardo, &c. 17th ed. Rev. by E.F. Neve. Lahore: Civil & Military Gazette, 1942. 200p.

27255 RAGHU RAI. Amritsar, city of the golden temple. Chandigarh: Dir., Public Relations, Punjab, 1977. 18p. + 34pl.

G. The Ganga Plains of North India: Haryana, Delhi, Uttar Pradesh, Bihar

1. Introductions

27256 BACON, E.E. Uttar Pradesh, an area handbook. New Haven: HRAF, 1956. 453p.

27257 BUDDHA PRAKASH. Glimpses of Haryana. Kurukshetra: U. of Kurukshetra, 1967. 122p.

27258 CHATURVEDI, J.P. Uttar Pradesh. ND: PDMIB, 1970.

59p. (SOU, 4)

27259 CHIB, S.S. Haryana. ND: Light & Life, 1977. 138p. (This beautiful India, 4)

27260 HOULTON, J.W. Bihar,the heart of India. Bombay: Orient Longmans, 1949. 223p.

27261 POLK, E. Delhi, old and new. Chicago: Rand McNally, 1963. 144p.

27262 ROY CHAUDHURY, P.C. Bihar. ND: PDMIB, 1975. 86p.

27263 ______. Inside Bihar. Calcutta: Bookland, 1962. 297p.

27264 SAINA, P. Discovery of Haryana. Jhajjar, Haryana: Hira Parkashan, 1968. 68p.

27265 SINGHAL, S.B. Haryana. ND: PDMIB, 1971. 46p. (SOU, 8)

2. Geography and Natural History

27266 DUTHIE, J.F. Flora of the Upper Gangetic Plain and of the adjacent Siwalik and Sub-Himalayan tracts. Dehra Dun: Bishen Singh Mahendra Pal Singh, 1973. 3 v. in 2. [Rpt. 1903 ed.]

27267 ENAYAT AHMAD. Bihar: a physical, economic and regional geography. Ranchi: Ranchi U., 1965. 420p.

27268 ISHIDA, H. A cultural geography of the Great Plains of India; essays, techniques and interim report-cum-methods. Hiroshima: U. of Hiroshima, Dept. of Geography, 1972. 304p.

27269 PRASAD, A. Chotanagpur: geography of rural settlements. Ranchi: Ranchi U., 1973. 467p.

27270 TIWARI, A.R. Geography of Uttar Pradesh. ND: NBT, 1971. 135p. (ILP)

3. Travellers' Accounts

27271 BUCKHORY, S. The call of the Ganges. ND: Vikas, 1978. 189p.

27272 HILLARY, E. From the ocean to the sky. NY: Viking, 1979. 273p. + 16pl.

27273 NEWBY, E. Slowly down the Ganges. NY: Scribners, 1966. 326p.

27274 PERRIN, M. Le Gange de l'Himalaya à Benares. Paris: Berger-Levrault, 1964. 275p. [trip by kayak]

27275 RAGHUBIR SINGH. Ganga: sacred river of India. Hongkong: Perennial Press, 1974. 158p. (incl. 151p. of col. pls.)

4. Travel, City, and Hotel Guides

27276 CHAKRAVORTY, P.M. Banaras: the most ancient city of the world. Varanasi: Orient, 1969. 114p.

27277 CHOPRA, P., ed. Delhi; history and places of interest. Delhi: 1970. 233p. [comprises 2 chaps. from the Delhi gazetteer]

27278 Delhi city map. ND: Indian Tourism Dev. Corp., 1972. 188p.

27279 Guide to Delhi. ND: Indian Tourism Dev. Corp., 1975. 212p.

27280 Hardy's encyclopaedic guide to Agra, Delhi, Jaipur, and Varanasi. 1970-. ND: Hardy & Ally (India). [annual]

27281 SHARMA, Y.D. Delhi and its neighbourhood. 2nd ed. ND: ASI, 1974. 161p. [1st ed., 1964. 125p.]

27282 Thacker Spink's guide to Patna and its neighbourhood. Calcutta: Thacker Spink, 1963. 107p.

H. The Northeast: The Bengal-Bangladesh and Assam Area of the Ganga Delta and Brahmaputra Valley

1. Bengal and Assam
a. introductions

27283 BARKATAKI, S. Assam. ND: NBT, 1969. 161p.

27284 BARTHAKUR, P.B. Assam. ND: PDMIB, 1971. 67p. (SOU, 6)

27285 BARUA, H. The red river and the blue hill. 3rd rev. and enl. ed. Gauhati: Lawyer's Book Stall, 1962. 205p.

27286 CHATTERJEE, A.B. & A. GUPTA & P.K. MUKHOPADHYAY, eds. West Bengal. Calcutta: KLM, 1970. 213p.

27287 CHOUDHURY, B. Portrait of West Bengal. Calcutta: Print-O-Craft, 1975. 143p.

27288 NEOG, D. Introduction to Assam. Bombay: Vora, 1947. 226p.

b. geography

27289 BAGCHI, KANAGOPAL. The Ganges delta. Calcutta: U. of Calcutta, 1944. 157p.

27290 BOSE, S.C. Geography of West Bengal. ND: NBT, 1968. 185p. (ILP)

27291 CHATTERJEE, S.P. Bengal in maps. Bombay: Orient Longmans, 1949. 105p.

27292 DAS, H.P. Geography of Assam. ND: NBT, 1970. 168p. (ILP)

c. travel, city and hotel guides

27293 ISCOT MARBANIANG. Assam in a nutshell. Shillong: Chapala Book Stall, 1970. 139p.

27294 LATIMER, E. Handbook to Calcutta and environs. 2nd ed. Calcutta: Oxford Book Co., 1966. 160p. [1st pub. 1962]

27295 Newman's comprehensive Calcutta city guide and directory. Calcutta: W. Newman, 1959. 445p.

27296 ROY, A.C. Calcutta atlas and guide; comprehensive handbook of Calcutta and its suburbs with 41 maps, showing streets, places of interest, tram and bus routes, house-numbers at many points, suburban towns, environs of Calcutta. Calcutta: the author, 1965. 384p.

27297 ______. Calcutta & environs; a comprehensive guidebook of the city of Calcutta & its suburbs, with 45 maps. Calcutta: Lake Pub., 1966. 373p.

27298 SUHRAWARDY, HASSAN. Calcutta and environs; an illustrated guide to places of interest and to excursions in and around Calcutta. Calcutta: 1921. 156p.

27299 THAPAR, Y.P., ed. Thapar's Calcutta pocket guide: West Bengal, Bihar, Orissa, Assam, Manipur, Tripura, North East Frontier Agency, Nagaland and Andaman and Nicobar Islands. 2nd ed. Calcutta: Indian Industrial Directory, 1963? 486p.

2. Bangladesh
a. introductions

27300 AHMED, N. Bangladesh. Dacca: Eastern Regal Industries, 1977. 150p.

27301 HAQ, ENAMUL, ed. Meet Bangladesh. Dacca: Dept. of Films & Publications, Govt. of Bangaldesh, 1979. 145p.

27302 JOHNSON, B.L.C. Bangladesh. London: Heinemann Educ. Books, 1975. 104p.

27303 LOCKERBIE, J. On duty in Bangladesh. Grand Rapids: Zondervan, 1973. 191p.

27304 MAHMOOD, ABU ZAFAR SHAHABUDDIN. Introducing East Pakistan: geography, everyday life, places of interest. Dacca: Roushan Akhter Begum, 1969. 118p.

27305 NYROP, R.F., et al. Area handbook for Bangladesh. Washington: U.S. Govt. Print. Off., 1975. 346p.

27306 RAHMAN, C.S. Bangladesh: land and the people. Dacca: MIB, 1973. 86p.

b. geography and natural history

27307 AHMAD, NAFIS. A new economic geography of Bangladesh. ND: Vikas, 1976. 249p.

27308 HAROUN ER-RASHID. East Pakistan; a systematic regional geography and its development planning aspects. 2nd ed. Lahore: Sh. Ghulam Ali, 1976. 409p.

27309 ______. Geography of Bangladesh. Boulder: Westview, 1977. 579p.

27310 U.S. BOARD ON GEOGRAPHICAL NAMES. Bangladesh: official standard names.... Washington: 1976. 526p.

27311 ZAKER HUSAIN, ZAKI. An introduction to the wildlife of Bangladesh. Dacca: F. Ahmed, 1974. 81p.

J. The Himalayas and Eastern Mountain Rim of India, Nepal, and Bhutan

1. India and Bhutan
a. introductions

27312 Arunachal Pradesh. ND: PDMIB, 1979. 34p. + 6pl. (SOU, 24)

27313 BAREH, H. Meghalaya. Shillong: NE India News & Feature Service, 1974. 222p.

27314 CHAK, B.L. Andaman and Nicobar Islands. ND: PDMIB, 1971. 61p. (SOU, 10)

27315 ______. Kumaon and Garhwal hill districts. ND: PMDIB. 1975. 22p.

27316 CHIB, S.S. Himachal Pradesh. ND: Light & Life, 1977. 139p.

27317 ______. Sikkim. ND: Light & Life, 1977. 100p. (This beautiful India, 5)

27318 CHOPRA, P.N. Sikkim. ND: S. Chand, 1979. 113p.

27319 COELHO, V.H. Sikkim and Bhutan. ND: ICCR, 1970. 138p.

27320 DAVE, R.K. Manipur, including who's who. Jodhpur: Surya, 1980. 157p.

27321 DUPUIS, J. L'Himâlaya. Paris: PUF, 1972. 128p.

27322 ELWIN, VERRIER. Nagaland. Shillong: P. Datta, 1961. 108p.

27323 FONIA, K.S. Uttarakhand, Garhwal Himalayas. Rev. by I. Turner. Dehra Dun: Asian Journals, 1977. 271p.

27324 JHALAJIT SINGH, R.K. Manipur. ND: PDMIB, 1976. 78p. (SOU, 18)

27325 MATHUR, K.K. Nicobar Islands. ND: NBT, 1967. 239p. (ILP)

27326 MEHRA, G.N. Bhutan, land of the peaceful dragon. Delhi: Vikas, 1974. 151p.

27327 MELE, P.F. Sikkim. ND: Oxford & IBH, 1971. 18p. + 81pl. [text by D. Doig & J. Perrin]

27328 MITTOO, H.K. Himachal Pradesh. ND: PDMIB, 1978. 118p. (ILP)

27329 NAGENDRA SINGH. Bhutan; a kingdom in the Himalayas: a study of the land, its people and their government. ND: Thomson Press, 1972. 202p.

27330 NEFA, land and the people. Shillong: Dir. of Info. & Public Relations, NEFA, 1970? 16p.

27331 PEISSEL, M. Bhoutan; royaume d'Asie inconnu. Paris: Arthaud, 1971. 225p.

27332 PRAKASH SINGH. Nagaland. 2nd ed., rev. ND: NBT, 1977. 231p. (ILP)

27333 RANDHAWA, M.S. The Kumaon Himalayas. ND: Oxford & IBH, 1970. 185p.

27334 RAY, A.C. Mizoram. ND: PDMIB, 1972. 25p. (SOU, 14)

27335 SARASWAT, H.C. Himachal Pradesh. ND: PDMIB, 1970. 41p. (SOU, 5)

27336 SEN, P.K. Land and people of the Andamans: a geographical and socio-economical study with a short account of the Nicobar Islands. Calcutta: Post-Graduate Book Mart, 1962. 197p.

27337 SHAH, GIRIRAJ. The kingdom of Gods; Uttarakhand. ND: Abhinav, 1975. 104p.

27338 SHASHI, S.S. Himachal: nature's peaceful paradise. ND: Indian School Supply Depot, 1971. 311p.

27339 entry deleted

27340 SINHA, K. Meghalaya: triumph of the tribal genius. Delhi: Indian School Supply Depot, 1970. 328p.

27341 TOMBI SINGH, N. Manipur: a study. Delhi: Rajesh, 1972. 116p.

b. geography and natural history

27342 BOSE, S.C. Geography of the Himalaya. ND: NBT, 1972. 210p. (ILP)

27343 BRÜHL, P. A guide to the orchids of Sikkim: being a guide to the identification of those species of orchids found between the Terai and the northern frontier of independent Sikkim including the Chumbi Valley and British Bhutan. Dehra Dun: Bishen Singh Mahendra Pal Singh, 1978. 208p. [Rpt. 1926 ed.]

27344 KARAN, P.P. Bhutan; a physical and cultural geography. Lexington: U. of Kentucky Press, 1967. 103p.

27345 LAL, P. Andaman Islands: a regional geography. Calcutta: AnthSI, 1976. 228p. (Its Memoirs, 25)

c. travellers' accounts

27346 Arunachal, 1947-72. Shillong: Dir. of Info. & Public Relations, Arunachal Pradesh, 1972. 1 v. [chiefly ill.]

27347 GIBBS, H. The hills of India. London: Jarrolds, 1961. 254p.

27348 KINGDON-WARD, F. Plant hunter in Manipur. London: Cape, 1952. 254p.

27349 OLSCHAK, B.C. Bhutan: land of hidden treasures. NY: Stein & Day, 1971. 63p. [1st German ed. 1969]

27350 ______. Sikkim: Himalajastaat zwischen Gletschern und Dschungeln. Zürich: Schweizer Verlagshaus, 1965. 219p.

27351 PEISSEL, M. Lords and lamas: a solitary expedition across the secret Himalayan kingdom of Bhutan. London: Heinemann, 1970. 180p.

27352 RANDHAWA, M.S. Travels in the Western Himalayas in search of paintings. Delhi: Thomson Press, 1974. 240p.

27353 RUSTOMJI, N.K. Enchanted frontiers: Sikkim, Bhutan, and India's northeastern borderlands. Bombay: OUP, 1971. 333p.

27354 SANYAL, P.K. Himalaja; Erlebnisse mit Menschen, Bergen, Göttern. Tr. from Bengali by G.K. Mookerjee. Herrenalb-Schwarzwald: H. Erdmann, 1963. 231p.

27355 SHIRAKAWA, Y. Himalayas: photos and text. NY: H.N. Abrams, 1976. 128p.

d. travel, city, and hotel guides

27356 AGARWALA, A.P., ed. Holiday resorts and tribals of north-eastern India: including Assam, Arunachal Pradesh, Manipur, Meghalaya, Nagaland, Tripura, and Mizoram. ND: Nest & Wings, 1976. 106p.

27357 ______. Tourist guide to Simla: including Chail, Kasauli, Kufri, Sanjauli, Solan, and Nahan etc.: a travellers' guide. ND: Nest & Wings, 1978. 64p.

27358 SHARMA, N.K. Tourist guide to Himachal Pradesh. Simla: H.P. Tourism Dev. Corp., 1977? 149p.

27359 Tourist guide to Darjeeling, Sikkim and Bhutan: a travellers' guide. ND: Nest & Wings, 1977. 64p.

27360 Tourist guide to Kumaon Region: a travellers' guide. ND: Nest & Wings, 1977. 68p.

2. Nepal
a. introductions

27361 DHAKHWA, D.R. Exclusive encyclopaedia of Nepal. Kathmandu?: Sahayogi Prakashan, 1974. 309p.

27362 HAGEN, T., et al. Mount Everest: formation, population and exploration of the Everest region. Tr. from German by E.N. Bowman. London: OUP, 1963. 195p.

27363 HAGEN, T. & F.T. WAHLEN & W.R. CORTI. Nepal: the kingdom in the Himalayas. Berne: Kümmerly & Frey, 1961. 117p.

27364 HARRIS, G.L., et al. Area handbook for Nepal, Bhutan and Sikkim. Washington: U.S. Govt. Printing Office, 1973. 431p.

27365 KARAN, P.P. & W.M. JENKINS. The Himalayan kingdoms: Bhutan, Sikkim and Nepal. Princeton: Van Nostrand, 1963. 144p.

27366 MAJUPURIA, T.C. & I. MAJUPURIA. Glimpses of Nepal: ancient & modern glories of a charming country. Gwalior: Maha Devi, 1979/80. 328p. + 48pl.

27367 Nepal: a profile. Kathmandu: Nepal Council of Applied Econ. Res., 1970. 253p.

27368 RANA, PASHUPATI SHUMSHERE, J.B. & K.P. MALLA, eds. Nepal in perspective. Kathmandu: CEDA, 1973. 310p.

27369 SARMA, N. This is Nepal: lores, legends, and life styles. Kathmandu: Sajha Prakashan, 1977. 100p.

27370 SEEMANN, H. Nepal 2029, gestern noch verbotenes Land. Stuttgart: Verlag Bandell, 1973. 196p.

27371 SHAHA, R. An introduction to Nepal. Kathmandu: Ratna Pustak Bhandar, 1975. 374p.

27372 SLUSSER, M.S. Nepal mandala: a cultural study of the Kathmandu Valley. Princeton: PUP, 1980.

b. geography and natural history

27373 FLEMING, R.L. The general ecology, flora, and fauna of midland Nepal. Kathmandu: USAID, 1973. 105p. + 39pl.

27374 HAFFNER, W. Nepal, Himalaya: Untersuchung zum vertikalen Landschaftsaufbau Zentral- und Ostnepals. Wiesbaden: Steiner, 1979. 125p.

26375 KARAN, P.P. Nepal, a cultural and physical geography. Lexington: U. of Kentucky Press, 1960. 100p.

27376 NEPAL. DEPT. OF HOUSING & PHYSICAL PLANNING. Kathmandu valley; the preservation of physical environment and cultural heritage: a protective inventory. Vienna: Schroll, 1975. 2 v.

27377 NEPAL. DEPT. OF PUBLICITY. Nepal in maps. Kathmandu: 1966. 18p. + 26 maps.

27378 SHARMA, C.K. River system of Nepal. Kathmandu: S. Sharma, 1977. 224p.

27379 SHRESHTHA, S.H. Modern geography of Nepal. Kathmandu: Visvakarma Press, 1968. 164p.

27380 THAPA, NETRA BAHADUR & D.P. THAPA. Geography of Nepal: physical, economic, cultural and regional. Bombay: Orient Longmans, 1969. 205p.

c. travellers' accounts

27381 AHLUWALIA, H.P.S. Faces of Everest. ND: Vikas, 1978. 238p.

27382 BERNSTEIN, J. The wildest dreams of Kew: a profile of Nepal. NY: Simon & Schuster, 1970. 186p.

27383 BISHOP, R.N.W. Unknown Nepal. London: Luzac, 1952. 124p.

27384 BOON, J. Nepal. München: Verlag Volk & Heimat, 1970. 104p.

27385 ESKELUND, K. The forgotten valley: a journey into Nepal. London: Alvin Redman, 1959. 187p.

27386 GURUNG, H. Annapurna to Dhaulagiri: a decade of mountaineering in Nepal Himalaya, 1950-1960. Kathmandu: Dept. of Info., 1968. 121p.

27387 ______. Vignettes of Nepal. Kathmandu: Sajha Prakashan, 1980. 435p. + 41pl.

27388 HILLARY, E. & D. DOIG. High in the thin, cold air. London: Hodder & Stoughton, 1963. 287p.

27389 JEST, CORNEILLE. Tarap: une vallée dans l'Himalaya. Paris: Éditions du Seuil, 1974. 157p.

27390 KAZAMI, T. The Himalayas: a journey to Nepal. Tokyo: Kodansha Intl., 1968. 154p. + 3pl.

27391 MATTHIESSEN, P. The snow leopard. NY: Viking, 1978. 352p.

27392 MORRIS, H. Winter in Nepal. London: Hart-Davis, 1963. 232p.

27393 PEISSEL, MICHEL. The great Himalayan passage: across the Himalayas by hovercraft. London: Collins, 1974. 254p. + 32pl.

27394 RANA, I.S. & M. DIXIT. Those were the days. Kathmandu: Sharda Prakashan Griha, 1977. 168p.

27395 SAKYA, K. Dolpo: the world behind the Himalayas. Kathmandu: Sharda Prakashan Griha, 1978. 198p. + 14pl.

27396 SHARMA, MAN MOHAN. Through the valley of gods: travels in the central Himalayas. 2nd ed. ND: Vision Books, 1978. 278p.

27397 STONOR, C.R. The Sherpa and the Snowman; an account of a journey through the Himalayas in search of a yeti. London: Hollis & Carter, 1955. 209p.

27398 TUCCI, G. Journey to Mustang, 1952. Tr. from Italian by D. Fussell. Kathmandu: Ratna Pustak Bhandar, 1977. 85p. + 10pl. (Bibliotheca Himalayica 1,23)

d. travel, city, and hotel guides

27399 AMATYA, J.M.S. Picturesque Nepal: a handbook for tourists. 3rd rev. ed. Kathmandu: Ratna Pustak Bhandar, 1970. 128p.

27400 BHATTACHARYA, D. Bhutan: the Himalayan paradise.... Calcutta: M. Mazumder, 1975. 62p.

27401 BISTA, S.D. & Y.R. SATYAL. Nepal travel companion. Kathmandu: 1967. 153p.

27402 FLEMING, R.L. & L.F. FLEMING. Kathmandu Valley. Tokyo: Kodansha Intl., 1978. 129p. + 4pl.

27403 FRANK, D. Traumland Nepal. Munich: Süddentscher Verlag, 1974. 192p.

27404 HOAG, K. Exploring mysterious Kathmandu. Kathmandu: Avalok, 1976. 75p.

27405 NEPAL. DEPT. OF TOURISM. Nepal. Kathmandu: 1974. 96p.

27406 RAJ, P.A. 1975-76 edition of Nepal on $4 a day. 2nd ed. Kathmandu: R.C. Joshi, 1975. 153p.

27407 SIMPSON, C. Katmandu. Sydney: Angus & Robertson, 1967. 104p.

III. TEACHING AND STUDY OF SOUTH ASIA

A. The State of Academic Study of South Asia (Outside the Subcontinent)

1. The United States and Canada

27408 ASSN. FOR ASIAN STUDIES. SOUTH ASIA REGIONAL COUNCIL. Programs in South Asian studies: a directory. Ann Arbor: the Assn., 1972. 123p.

27409 BROWN, W. NORMAN, ed. Resources for South Asian language studies in the United States. Philadelphia: UPaP, 1960. 103p.

27410 ______. South Asian studies: a history. In Annals of the American Academy of Political & Social Science 365 (1964) 54-62.

27411 CORMACK, M.L. Guidelines to South and Southeast Asia studies resources in the U.S. Berkeley: Center for S. & SE Asian Studies, U. of California, 1969. 63p. (Its Occ. paper, 3)

27412 HART, H.C. Campus India: an appraisal of American college programs in India. East Lansing: Michigan State U. Press, 1961. 217p.

27413 Indian studies in the United States [special issue]. In Fulbright Newsletter, New Delhi (Winter 1974) 74p.

27414 LAMBERT, R.D. Language and area studies review. Philadelphia: American Academy of Political & Social Science, 1973. 350p. (Its monograph, 17)

27415 ______, ed. Resources for South Asian area studies in the United States. Philadelphia: UPaP, 1962. 320p. [Report of a conference on strengthening and integration of South Asian language and area studies, New York, 1961]

27416 MOULTON, E.C. South Asian studies in Canada, and the Shastri Indo-Canadian Institute. In PA 51,2 (1978) 245-64.

27417 PATTERSON, M.L.P. The South Asian P.L. 480 library program, 1962-1968. In JAS 28,4 (1969) 743-54.

27418 WARD, R.E. The presidential address: a case for Asian studies. In JAS 32,3 (1973) 391-403.

2. Europe and the United Kingdom

27419 ALAYEV, L.B. & A.K. VAPHA. Fifty years of Soviet Oriental studies. In QUHS 8,1 (1968-69) 7-24.

27420 Europe stakes its claim in South Asian studies. In EPW 5,29/31 (Jul. 1970) 1145-51.

27421 HEIDELBERG. UNIVERSITÄT. SÜDASIEN-INSTITUT. South Asia Institute - the first decade, 1962-72. Ed. by D. Rothermund & A.K. Ray. Heidelberg: 1973. 119p. (Its Bulletin)

27422 O'FLAHERTY, W.D. Disregarded scholars: a survey of Russian Indology. In SAR 5,4 (1972) 289-304.

27423 PHILIPS, C.H. Modern Asian studies in the universities of the United Kingdom. In MAS 1,1 (1967) 1-14.

B. Guides to Study in South Asia: Teaching and Research Centers

27424 BOEWE, C. The green book: American scholar in Pakistan. Islamabad: U.S. Educ. Foundation in Pakistan, 1977. 86p.

27425 CORMACK, M.L. Guidelines for academic opportunities in India: travel, work, training, teaching, study and research information for faculty and students. Berkeley: Center for S. & SE Asian Studies, 1969. 54p. (Its Occasional papers, 2)

27426 DICKINSON, R. & N. DICKINSON. Directory of information for Christian colleges in India. Madras: CLS, 1967. 276p.

27427 Directory of social science research institutions in India. ND: ICSSR, 1971. 200p. [List of 95 institutions not affiliated with universities]

27428 Handbook of the universities of Pakistan. Islamabad: Inter-univ. Board of Pakistan, 1968. 204p.

27429 HOLMES, W.R. Research facilities in Hyderabad. Delhi: Graphic Aids, 1967. 41p.

27430 HOLMES, W.R. & S.R. GOPAL. Research facilities in Bangalore, Mysore, Ahmedabad. Delhi: Graphic Aids, 1969. 71p.

27431 ______. Research facilities in Bombay, Calcutta and Madras. Delhi: Graphic Aids, 1968. 167p.

27432 ______. Research facilities in Delhi. 2nd ed. Delhi: Graphic Aids, 1969. 1 v.

27433 INDIA (REP.). MIN. OF EDUC. STAT AND INFO. DEPT. Directory of institutions for higher education, 1973-74. ND: 1976. 391p.

27434 INDIA (REP.). RASHTRIYA SANSKRIT SANSTHAN. Inventory of Sanskrit institutions in India. ND: Min. of Educ. & Social Welfare, 1972. 120p.

27435 ______. Sanskrit in India. ND: Min. of Educ. & Social Welfare, 1972. 120p.

27436 INDIA (REP.). UNIV. GRANTS CMSN. Centres of advanced study in Indian universities. Rev. ed. ND: 1972. 119p.

27437 INDIAN COUNCIL FOR CULTURAL RELATIONS. Studying in India. ND: 1965. 104p.

27438 JAFAR, S.M., comp. Research facilities in Uttar Pradesh. Gurgaon: Indian Documentation Service, 1971. 221p.

27439 MEHENDIRATTA, P.R. Coming to India and to Delhi: the gateway to modern India for foreign scholars. Ed. by A.K. Butani. ND: Promila, 1972. 204p.

27440 MIAN, TASNIM Q. Principal research institutions in Pakistan. Lahore: Social Science Research Centre, U. of Punjab, 1964. 2 v.

27441 MOHINDER SINGH, ed. Learned societies and institutions in India: activities and publications, including over 4,000 research oriented titles. Rev. & enl. ed. Delhi: Metropolitan, 1975. 459p.

27442 PADMAVATHI, P., comp. The directory of Indian higher educational institutions. Hyderabad: Panchayat Pub., 1970. 486p.

27443 PATIL, H.S., ed. Directory of cultural organisations in India. ND: ICCR, 1975. 251p.

27444 SAHA, J. Special libraries and information services in India and in the U.S.A. Metuchen, NJ: Scarecrow Press, 1969. 216p.

27445 SINHA, S.C., ed. Research programmes on cultural anthropology and allied disciplines. Calcutta: AnthSI, 1970. 444p. [1967 seminar]

27446 U.S. EDUC. FOUNDATION IN PAKISTAN. American scholars in Pakistan. Islamabad: 1975. 30p.

27447 Universities handbook: India. 20th ed. ND: Assn. of Indian Univ., 1979. 1142p. [annual]

C. Teaching and Research Aids

1. Syllabi

27448 BROWN, E.C., comp. Foreign area studies, India: a syllabus. Cedar Falls: U. of Northern Iowa, 1969. 118p.

27449 ELDER, J.W., ed. Chapters in Indian civilization. 2nd ed. Dubuque, IA: Kendall/Hunt, 1970. 2 v., 245, 319p. [1st ed. Madison: U. of Wisconsin, 1967]

27450 ELDER, J.W. & W.L. JOHNSON & C. KING. Lectures in Indian civilization. Dubuque, IA: Kendall, Hunt, 1970. 453p. [1st ed.: Civilization of India syllabus, Madison: Dept. of Indian Studies, U. of Wisconsin, 1965]

27451 GORDON, L.A. & B.S. MILLER. A syllabus of Indian civilization. NY: ColUP, 1971. 182p.

27452 HARRISON, B.J., ed. Learning about India: an annotated guide for non-specialists. Albany: Center for Intl. Programs & Coop. Studies, NY State Educ. Dept., 1977. 349p.

2. Indic Names and their Transliteration

27453 DENHAM, E.B. Nomenclature. In Ceylon at the Census of 1911: being the review of the results of the census of 1911. Colombo: H.C. Cottle, 1912, 177-93.

27454 DOGRA, R.C. Cataloguing Urdu names. In Intl. Library R. 5,3 (1973) 351-77. [Appendices list various surnames & pen-names]

27455 HUQ, A.M. ABDUL. Study of Bengali Muslim personal names to ascertain the feasibility of application of a mechanistic rule for their arrangement. Ph.D. diss., Graduate School of Library & Info. Sciences, U. of Pittsburgh, 1970. 87p. [UM 71-14,487]

27456 Indic names, including proceedings of the seminar on the rendering of Indic names.... Calcutta: Indian Assn. of Special Libraries & Info. Centres, 1961. 162p. (Its Special Pub., 2)

27457 MANGLA, P.B. Punjabi names: an analysis and their rendering. In Herald of Library Science 5,2 (1966) 121-29.

27458 QAZI, M.A. What's in a Muslim name. 3rd ed. Lahore: Kazi Pub., 1978. 54p.

27459 RANGANATHAN, S.R. Classified catalogue code. Bombay: Asia, 1965. 644p. [Indic personal names, 68-85]

27460 SENGUPTA, B. Indic names of person in works in Roman alphabets: problems of their standardization. In Indian Assoc. of Special Libraries & Info. Centers Bull. 4,4 (1959) 1-28.

27461 TEMPLE, R.C. A dissertation on the proper names of Panjābīs. Bombay: Educ. Soc. Press, 1883. 228p.

27462 U.S. LIBRARY OF CONGRESS, PROCESSING DEPT. Cataloging Service Bulletin, Washington, D.C.
- 64. Transliteration, languages of India & Pakistan (Feb 1964) 21p.
- 88. Sinhalese romanization (Jan 1970) 11.
- 90. Tibetan romanization (Sep 1970) 3-4.
- 91. Arabic romanization (Sep 1970) 8p.
- 92. Persian romanization (Oct 1970) 5p.
- 93. Pushto romanization (Oct 1970) 5p.

94. Urdu in Arabic script: romanization. (Nov 1970) 7p.
104. Romanization of Sindhi in Arabic script. (Apr 1972) 19-20.

3. Almanacs and Calendars

27463 INDIA (REP.). CALENDAR REFORM CMTEE. Report. ND: Council of Scientific & Industrial Res., 1955. 280p. [lists festivals, eras, names of months, seasons, etc.]

27464 Rashtriya Panchang. 1958/59. ND: Dir.-Genl. of Meteorology. [annual; official calendar showing Indian festivals & holidays]

4. Who's Whos and Biographical Dictionaries
a. general

27465 ARYAL, D.K. et al. Who is who - Nepal, 1975-1977. 2nd ed., improved, enl., & rev. Kathmandu: Kathmandu School of Journalism, 1977. 378p.

27466 Biographical encyclopedia of Pakistan. Ed. Khan Tahawar Ali Khan. Lahore: Biographical Research Inst., 1956-. [Latest ed. 1972?]

27467 COUR, AJEET & ARPANA COUR. Directory of Indian women today, 1976. ND: India Intl. Pub., 1976. 659p.

27468 Famous India: Nation's who's who. Ed. Ravi Bhushan. Delhi: Famous India Pub., 1975. 384p.

27469 GANDHI, S.C. Directory of scientific, social, and literary awards in India. ND: Sterling, 1979. 306p.

27470 JAIN, N.K. Muslims in India: a biographical dictionary. ND: Manohar, 1979-. [to be 2 v.]

27471 KALIA, D.R. & M.K. JAIN, comps. Eminent Indians: a bibliography of biographies. ND: Marwah, 1977. 200p.

27472 KOTHARI, H., ed. Who's who in India. Calcutta: Kothari, 1973. 464p.

27473 National honours encyclopaedia. Chandigarh: Manu-India Publ. House, 1976-. [to be 4 v.]

27474 Reference guide of India: who's who, 1973-. ND: Premier. [irregular] [Incl. persons in education, library science, and science]

27475 Reference India: biographical notes on men and women of achievements and distinctions in India. 2nd ed. Ed. by K.L. Gupta. Delhi: Tradesman & Men India, 1975-6. 2 v., 416 + 375p.

27476 SEN, S.P. Dictionary of national biography. Calcutta: IHS, 1972-74. 4v. 1925p.

27477 SESYA, C. & D. PAUL. Rare gems of Nepal; short biographical sketches of eminent personages. Kathmandu: Ratna Pustak Bhandar, 1966. 94p.

27478 SHARMA, J.S. The national biographical dictionary of India. ND: Sterling, 1972. 302p.

27479 SINGH, TRILOCHAN. "Personalities": a comprehensive and authentic biographical dictionary of men who matter in India. ND: Arunam & Sheel, 1952. 1 v.

27480 Times of India directory and yearbook, including who's who, 1914-. Bombay: Bennett, Coleman. [annual; latest ed. 1979]

27481 VASHISHTA, B.K., ed. Encyclopaedia of women in India, 1976. ND: Praveen Encyclopaedia Pub., 1976. 548p.

27482 WASTI, SYED RAZI. Biographical dictionary of South Asia. Lahore: Pub. United, 1980. 511p.

27483 Who is who: Nepal, 1975-77. 2nd ed. Ed. by D.K. Aryal, et al. Kathmandu: Kathmandu School of Journalism, 1977. 392p.

27484 Who's who in Pakistan, 1971-72. Ed. by A.M. Barque & Farooq U. Barque. Lahore: Barque & Co., 1971. 280p.

27485 Women in India: who's who? Bombay: Printed at the British India Press for the Natl. Council of Women, India, 1935. 91p.

b. professional

27486 Artists directory, covering painters, sculptors and engravers. ND: Lalit Kala Akademi, 1961. 121p.

27487 BHATTACHARYA, D.K., ed. Anthropologists in India: directory of professional anthropologists. 2nd ed. Delhi: IAS, 1978. [1st pub. 1970]

27488 BISWAS, A.A., ed. A directory of scientists and technologists of Bangladesh. Dacca: Bangladesh Natl. Scientific & Technical Documentation Centre, 1976. 190p. (BANSDOC bibl., 103)

27489 DIL, ANWAR S., comp. A directory of Pakistani linguists and language scholars. Lahore: Linguistic Res. Group of Pakistan, 1962. 60p.

27490 Eminent educationists of India, 1969. ND: Natl. Book Org., 1969. 413p.

27491 India who's who. ND: INFA Pub., 1969-. [Annual. Latest ed. 1977-78.] [leaders listed by profession]

27492 Men of education in India. ND: Premier Pub., 1965-. v.

27493 MENON, REKHA, comp. Cultural profiles. ND: Intl. Cultural Center, 1961-63. 2 v. [lists leaders & org. in the Arts]

27494 ROY, S., comp. Anthropologists in India: short-biography, bibliography and current projects. ND: Indian Anthropological Assn., 1970. 218p.

27495 Who's who in Indian science, 1969. 2nd ed. Ed. by H. Kothari. Calcutta: Kothari Pub., 1969. 200p.

5. Dictionaries of Anglo-Indian Terms

27496 INDIA. DEPT. OF REVENUE & AGRICULTURE. A glossary of vernacular judicial and revenue terms, and other useful words occurring in official documents relating to the administration of the government of British India. Calcutta: Supt. Govt. Printing, 1874. 133p.

27497 NIHALANI, P. & R.K. TONGUE & P. HOSALI. Indian and British English: a handbook of usage and pronunciation. Delhi: OUP, 1979. 260p.

27498 TEMPLE, G. Glossary of Indian terms relating to religion, customs, government, land; and other terms and words in common use: to which is added a glossary of terms used in district work in the N.W. Provinces and Oudh, and also of those applied to labourers. London: Luzac, 1897. 332p.

27499 WHITWORTH, G.C. An Anglo-Indian dictionary: a glossary of Indian terms used in English and of such English or other non-Indian terms as have obtained special meanings in India. Gurgaon: IDS, 1976. 350p. [Rpt. 1885 ed.]

27500 WILSON, H.H. Glossary of judicial and revenue terms, and of useful words occurring in official documents relating to the administration of the government of British India from the Arabic, Persian, Hindustānī, Sanskrit, Hindī, Bengalī, Uṛiya, Marāthī, Guzarāthī, Telugu, Karnātaka, Tamiḻ, Malayālam, and other languages. Compiled and published under the authority...of the East India Company. 2nd ed. Delhi: Munshiram, Manoharlal, 1968. 728p. [1st ed. 1855]

27501 YULE, H. & A.C. BURNELL. Dictionary of Indian English. Ed. by G.B.T. Kurian. Madras: Indian Universities Press, 1966. 353p. [condensation of 27502]

27502 ______. Hobson-Jobson; a glossary of colloquial Anglo-Indian words and phrases, and of kindred terms, etymological, historical, geographical and discursive. Ed. by W. Crooke. 2nd ed. Delhi: Munshiram, 1968. 1021p. [1st pub. 1886]

IV. SOUTH ASIAN RESEARCH MATERIALS: LOCATION AND ACCESS

A. Location and Acquisition of Research Materials

1. Library Collections
a. United States

27503 HARVARD UNIV. PEABODY MUSEUM OF ARCHAEOLOGY & ETHNOLOGY. LIBRARY. Author catalogue. Boston: G.K. Hall, 1963. 26 v. [with Subject catalogue. Boston: G.K. Hall, 1963. 27 v.]

27504 MISSIONARY RES. LIBRARY OF THE UNION THEOLOGICAL SEMINARY. Dictionary catalogue. Boston: G.K. Hall, 1965. 17v.

27505 NEW YORK PUBLIC LIBRARY. Catalog of government publications in the Research Libraries. Boston: G.K. Hall, 1972. 40 v.

27506 NEW YORK PUBLIC LIBRARY. REFERENCE DEPT. Dictionary catalog of the Oriental collection. Boston: G.K. Hall, 1960. 16 v. [with First suppl., 1976. 8 v.]

27507 PATTERSON, M.L.P. South Asian area studies and the library. In Library Q. 35 (1965) 223-38.

27508 ______., ed. South Asian library resources in North America: a survey prepared for the Boston Conference, 1974. Zug, Switzerland: Inter Documentation Co., 1975. 23 + 223p. (Bibliotheca Asiatica, 12)

27509 PATTERSON, M.L.P. & M. YANUCK, eds. South Asian library resources in North America: papers from the Boston Conference, 1974. Zug, Switzerland: Inter Documentation Co., 1975. 42 + 362p. (Bibliotheca Asiatica, 11)

27510 UNIV. OF MINNESOTA. Catalog of the Ames Library of South Asia, University of Minnesota. Boston: G.K. Hall, 1980. 16 v.

b. United Kingdom
i. general

27511 COLLISON, R. Directory of libraries and special collections on Asia and North Africa. Hamden, CT: Archon Books, 1970. 123p. [covers Great Britain and Ireland]

27512 DATTA, R. Union catalogue of the central Government of India publications held by libraries in London, Oxford and Cambridge. London: Mansell, 1971. 242p.

27513 ______., ed. Union catalogue of the Government of Pakistan publications held by libraries in London, Oxford and Cambridge. London: Mansell, 1967. 64p.

27514 HEWITT, A.R. Guide to resources for Commonwealth studies in London, Oxford and Cambridge. London: Athlone Press, 1957. 219p.

27515 MACDONALD, T. Union catalogue of the Government of Ceylon publications held by libraries in London, Oxford and Cambridge. London: Mansell, 1970. 44p.

27516 ______. Union catalogue of the serial publications of the Indian government 1858-1947 held in libraries in Britain. London: Mansell, 1973. 154p.

27517 ROYAL ASIATIC SOC. OF GREAT BRITAIN & IRELAND. LIBRARY. Catalogue of printed books published before 1932 in the library. London: 1940. 541p.

27518 ROYAL EMPIRE SOC. Subject catalogue of the library. London: Dawsons, 1967. 4 v. [v. 4: Mediterranean, Colonies, India & the East; Rpt. 1937 ed.]

27519 Union catalogue of Asian publications, 1965-1970. Ed. by D.E. Hall. London: Mansell, 1971. 4 v. [1971 Suppl.: 1973] [indicates location of 39,000 South Asian titles - 46% of total entries - in sixty-seven U.K. libraries other than SOAS]

ii. British Library (formerly British Museum)

27520 BARRIER, N.G. South Asia vernacular publications: modern Indian-language collections in the British Museum and the India Office Library, London. In JAS 28,4 (1969) 803-10.

27521 BRITISH LIBRARY. REFERENCE DIV. Guide to the Department of Oriental Manuscripts and Printed Books. Comp. by H.J. Goodacre & A.P. Pritchard. London: British Museum Pub., 1977. 72p.

27522 BRITISH MUSEUM. DEPT. OF PRINTED BOOKS. General catalog of printed books, to 1955. London: British Museum, 1959-66. 263 v. [with suppl., 1956-65, 1966-70, 1971-75; latest suppl. issued under new name, British Library]

27523 CAMPBELL, F.B.F. Index catalogue of Indian official publications in the library, British Museum. 1900. 579p.

iii. India Office Library and Records

27524 BAXTER, I.A., ed. A brief guide to biographical sources. London: India Office Library & Records, 1979. 53p.

27525 DATTA, R. The India Office Library: its history, resources, and functions. In Library Q. 36 (1966) 99-148.

27526 FOSTER, W., ed. A guide to the India Office Records, 1600-1858. London: Eyre & Spottiswoode, 1919. 130p.

27527 GREAT BRITAIN. INDIA OFFICE LIBRARY. Catalogue of European printed books. Boston: G.K. Hall, 1964. 10 v.

27528 LANCASTER, J.C. A guide to lists and catalogues of the India Office Records. London: Commonwealth Office, 1966. 26p.

27529 ______. The scope and uses of the India Office Library and Records, with particular reference to the period 1600-1947. In Asian Affairs ns 9,1 (1978) 31-43.

27530 SUTTON, S.C. A guide to the India Office Library, with a note on the India Office Records. London: HMSO, 1971. 122p. [1st pub. 1967]

iv. School of Oriental and African Studies, London University

27531 LONDON UNIVERSITY. SCHOOL OF ORIENTAL & AFRICAN STUDIES. LIBRARY. Library catalogue. Boston: G.K. Hall, 1963. 23 v. [1st suppl. 1968, 11 v.; 2nd suppl. 1973, 13 v.; 3rd suppl. 1979, 19v.]

27352 ______. Library guide. 3rd rev. ed. London: SOAS, 1976. 91p.

c. South Asia

27533 CHATTERJEE, N.K. Directory of research and special libraries in India and Sri Lanka. Calcutta: Info. Res. Academy, 1979-. v. 1-.

27534 DIEHL, K.S. Early Indian imprints. NY: Scarecrow Press, 1964. 533p. ["Based on the William Carey Historical Library of Serampore College."]

27535 ______., comp. Primary sources for 16th - 19th century studies in Bengal, Orissa, and Bihar libraries: seminar papers. Calcutta: AIIS, 1971. 280p.

27536 INDIA (REP.). NATIONAL LIBRARY. Author catalogue of printed books in European languages. Calcutta: GOI Press, 1941-1964. 10 v.

27537 ______. Catalog of periodicals, newspapers and gazettes. Calcutta: Natl. Library, 1956. 285p.

27538 INDIAN ASSN. OF SPECIAL LIBRARIES & INFO CENTRES. Directory of special and research libraries in India. Calcutta: 1962. 282p.

27539 KAUL, H.K., ed. Early writings on India: a union catalogue of books on India in English language published up to 1900 and available in Delhi libraries. ND: Arnold-Heinemann, 1975. 324p.

27540 KESAVAN, B.S. India's national library. Calcutta: Natl. Library, 1961. 300p.

27541 MALLICK, A., ed. Seminar on the Role of the National Library of India, Calcutta, 23 November 1978. Calcutta: Natl. Library Employees' Assn., 1979. 124p.

27542 PAKISTAN BIBLIOGRAPHICAL WORKING GROUP. A guide to Pakistan libraries, learned and scientific societies and educational institutions, including museums and art galleries. Karachi: 1957. 132p. (Its Pub., 3)

27543 Works on Nepal in the Kaiser Library: an annotated bibliography reproduced from the Union catalogue being established at INAS. Ed. by Thakurlal Manandhar, et al. Kirtipur: Inst. of Nepal & Asian Studies, Tribhuvan U., 1974. 119 + 13p.

2. Archival and Manuscript Collections
a. America and Europe

27544 GREAT BRITAIN. INDIA OFFICE LIBRARY. Catalogue of manuscripts in European languages belonging to the library of the India Office. London: OUP, 1916-. 2 v.

27545 ______. Index of post-1937 manuscript accessions. London: G.K. Hall, 1964. 156p.

27546 ______. List of India Office records, 1702-1936. Zug, Switzerland: Inter Documentation Co., 196-. [Microfiche ed., 179 fiches]

27547 JANERT, K.L. An annotated bibliography of catalogs of Indian manuscripts. Wiesbaden: Steiner, 1965. 175p. [covers mss. in Germany]

27548 PEARSON, J.D. Oriental manuscripts in Europe and North America: a survey. Zug, Switzerland: Inter Documentation Co., 1971. 512p. (Bibliotheca Asiatica, 7)

27549 PUGH, R.B. The records of the Colonial and Dominions Offices. London: HMSO, 1964. 119p. (Public Record Office handbooks, 3)

27550 SAMARAWEERA, V. A catalogue of nineteenth century British Parliamentary Papers relating to Ceylon. In CJHSS ns 2,2 (1972) 170-75.

27551 SAMP catalog; 1980 cumulative edition. Chicago: Center for Res. Libraries, 1980. 246p. [2096 entries & indices; SAMP = South Asia Microform Project]

27552 Verzeichnis der orientalischen Handschriften in Deutschland. Wiesbaden: Steiner, 1961-. [To be complete in 25 to 30 vols. incl. several vols. of South Asian mss.]

27553 WAINRIGHT, M.D. & N. MATTHEWS. A guide to Western manuscripts and documents in the British Isles relating to South and South East Asia. London: OUP, 1965. 532p.

b. South Asia

27554 DESAI, S.P. The hand book of the Bombay Archives. Bombay: Dept. of Archives, Govt. of Maharashtra, 1978. 196p.

27555 DE SILVA, H. Blue books of Ceylon, 1821-1938. In Ceylon Today 14 (1965) 20-27.

27556 GHOSE, S. Archives in India; history and assets. Calcutta: KLM, 1963. 358p.

27557 A handbook of the Bihar and Orissa provincial records, 1771 to 1859. Patna: Supt., Govt. Printing, Bihar and Orissa, 1933. 139p.

27558 INDIA. IMPERIAL RECORD DEPT. Handbook to the records of the Government of India in the Imperial Record Dept., 1748-1859. Calcutta: 1925. 158p.

27559 INDIA. IMPERIAL RECORD OFFICE. Index to the land revenue records, 1830-59. Delhi: 1940-42. 2 v.

27560 INDIA (REP.). NATL. ARCHIVES. Archives in India. ND: 1979. 35p.

27561 ______. Guide to the records in the National Archives of India. Rev. ed. ND: The Archives, 1959-. v. 1, 2-.

27562 ______. Index to the Foreign & Political Department records. Delhi: MPGOI, 1957-. v. 1, 2-.

27563 INDIA (REP.). NATL. MUSEUM. Manuscripts from Indian collections: descriptive catalogue. ND: 1964. 113p.

27564 LOW, D.A. & J.C. ILTIS & M.D. WAINWRIGHT. Government archives in South Asia: a guide to national and state archives in Ceylon, India and Pakistan. Cambridge: CamUP, 1969. 355p.

27565 WIMALARATNE, K.D.G. An introduction to the National Archives, Sri Lanka. Colombo: Social Science Res. Centre, Natl. Science Council of Sri Lanka, 1978. 31p.

3. Publishers and Bookdealers in South Asia
a. "Books in Print" for Indian books in English

27566 BEPI; a bibliography of English publications in India, 1976-. Delhi: D.K.F. Trust. [annual]

27567 Indian books. Comp. by L.M.P. Singh, S.P. Mukherji & H.D. Sharma. Varanasi: Indian Bibliographic Centre, 1969-. [annual; last issue available: 1974]

27568 Indian books; an annual bibliography. Comp. by R.G. Prasher, et al. Delhi: Researchco, 1971-. [Last issue available: 1974/75]

27569 Reference catalogue of Indian books in print. ND: Today & Tomorrow's, 1973-77. 3 v. [suppl. 1974]

27570 SINGH, S. & S.N. SADHU, comps. Indian books in print, 1966-67; a select bibliography of English books published in India. Delhi: Indian Bureau of Bibliographies, 1969. 1116p. [subsequent eds for 1972, 1973, 1979, each in 3 v., indexed by author, title, subject]

b. book industry of South Asia: directories and journals

27571 AMJAD ALI. Bookworld of Pakistan. Karachi: Natl. Book Centre of Pakistan, 1967. 48p.

27572 BHATKAL, S.G. Asian book trade directory. 2nd ed. Bombay: Nirmala Sadanand, 1967. 439p.

27573 Bookdealers in India, Pakistan, Sri Lanka &c.; a directory of dealers in secondhand and antiquarian books in the sub-continent of South Western Asia. London: Sheppard Press, 1977. 108p.

27574 Indian book industry, Oct. 1969-. ND: Sterling. [monthly]

27575 Indian publisher and bookseller, 1950-. Bombay: Popular. [monthly]

27576 KHOSLA, R.K., ed. Directory of booksellers, publishers, libraries and librarians in India. ND: Premier, 1973. 300p.

27577 NATIONAL BOOK CENTRE OF PAKISTAN. Lahore booktrade directory. Karachi: 1974. 106p.

27578 NCAER. Survey of Indian book industry. ND: 1976. 2 v.

27579 SHARMA, J.K., ed. Directory of book trade in India. ND: Natl. Guide Books Syndicate, 1973. 647p.

27580 SUBHASH CHANDRA. All India book trade directory, 1979. Delhi: Modern Pub., 1979. 768p.

27581 TRIVEDI, D. New directory of Indian publishers. ND: Federation of Publishers & Booksellers Assns. in India, 1973. 591p.

27582 USMANI, M. ADIL & GHANIUL AKRAM SABZWARI. Pakistan book trade directory. Karachi: Library Promotion Bureau, 1966. 220p.

4. Access to Periodical Literature on and from South Asia
a. lists and bibliographies of periodicals

27583 A general list of newspapers and periodicals published in Pakistan, 19--. Karachi: Press Info. Dept., Govt. of Pakistan. [semi-annual]

27584 GIDWANI, N.N. & K. NAVALANI. Current Indian periodicals in English: an annotated guide. 2nd rev. & enl. ed. Jaipur: Saraswati Pub., 1978. 403p.

27585 GOYAL, SATYA PAUL. Index catalogue of backsets of learned Indian serials. Hissar: General Book Depot, 1972. 86 + 39p. (S.R. Bhatia series in library science, 1)

27586 HEWITT, A.R. Union list of Commonwealth newspapers... London: U. of London, 1960. 101p.

27587 IENS press handbook, 1940-. ND: Indian & Eastern Newspaper Society. [annual]

27588 Indian periodicals in print, 1973. Ed. by H.N.D. Gandhi, et al. Delhi: Vidya Mandal, 1973-4. 2 v. [annual supplements planned]

27589 List of newspapers and periodicals published in Sind, 1970-. Karachi: Dept. of Public Relations, Govt. of Sind. [annual]

27590 MAJUMDAR, GOPAL KUMAR. Newspaper microfilming; a plea for newsprint documentation. Calcutta: KLM, 1974. 132p. [On the history and process of microfilming newspapers; incl. list of South Asian newspapers and periodicals on microfilm.]

27591 NATL. BOOK CENTRE OF PAKISTAN. English language periodicals from Pakistan: a guidelist. Karachi: 1967. 55p.

27592 Press in India. ND: Office of the Registrar of Newspapers, 1957-. [annual in 2 parts; pt. 1, analytical survey of all periodicals submitted for registration; pt. 2, lists by state, periodicity, language, subject; latest ed 1975]

27593 SIDDIQUI, AKHTAR H. Periodicals directory of Pakistan. Karachi: Documentation Info. Bureau, 1966. 42p.

27594 SOCIAL SCIENCE DOCUMENTATION CENTRE. Union catalogue of social science serials: Delhi. ND: the Centre, ISCCR, 1975-. (Union catalogue series, (S), 1-2) [to be 3v.]

27595 U.S. LIBRARY OF CONGRESS. Accessions list: India, list of serials. ND and Karachi: 1962/63-. [separate lists issued periodically for India, Pakistan, Bangladesh, Sri Lanka, Nepal]

27596 WAJID, J.A. & H.K. KAUL. Periodicals in humanities: union catalogue of periodicals in humanities and newspapers in Delhi libraries. ND: Arnold-Heinemann, 1973. 155p.

b. guides to contents of periodicals

27597 ABIDI, SARTAJ A. & S.K. SHARMA, eds. Fifty years of Indian historical writings: index to articles in Journal of Indian history, vols. 1-50 (1921/22-1972). ND: Gitanjali Prakashan, 1974. 248p.

27598 Asian Recorder, v.1, 1 Jan. 1955-. ND: P.S. Sankaran. [Weekly]

27599 ASIATIC SOCIETY, CALCUTTA. Index to the publications of the Asiatic Society, 1788-1953. Compiled by Sibadas Chaudhuri. Calcutta: 1956-59. (JASCalcutta, 22 & 23 (1956-1967) extra numbers)

27600 ______. Index to the publications of the Asiatic Society: first supplement, 1954-1968. Comp. by Sibadas Chaudhuri. Calcutta: Asiatic Soc., 1971-. v.1-.

27601 BELKNAP, B.J. A selected index of articles from the Rising Nepal form 1969-1976. Kathmandu: Documentation Center, Center for Nepal and Asian Studies, 1978. 202p.

27602 CHAUDHURI, S., comp. Index to Indian culture, 1934-1949. Calcutta: KLM, 1975. 108p. (Index Asia Series in Humanities, 4)

27603 ______. Index to Poona Orientalist, 1936-1963. Calcutta: KLM, 1976. 31 + 12p. (Index Asia Series in Humanities, 5)

27604 Classified subject index to Calcutta review, 1844-1920. Comp. by Gita Chattopadhyay, et al. Calcutta: India Book Exchange, 1974. 382p.

27605 Dawn index, 19_?-March 1966. Karachi: Documentation and Info. Bureau. Monthly. [Superseded by Pakistan Press Index, Apr. 1966-]

27606 Guide to Indian periodical literature (social sciences and humanities), 1964-. Gurgaon: IDS. (quarterly; cumulated annually)

27607 HARI RAO, R. Bibliography of articles published in the Quarterly journal of the Mythic society on the history, art, and culture of Karnataka and on Kannada language and literature. In QJMS ns 47,1 (1956) 150-75.

27608 ISCCR journal of abstracts and reviews; sociology and social anthropology. ND: ICSSR, 1971-. [semi-annual]

27609 Index India: a quarterly documentation list of selected articles, editorials, notes, and letters, etc. from periodicals and newspapers published in English language all over the world. Jaipur: Rajasthan U. Library. v.1, Jan./Mar. 1967-.

27610 Index Indo-Asiaticus, 1968-. v.1-. Calcutta. [Quarterly index to periodical literature; ed. by Sibadas Chaudhuri]

27611 Index to Indian economic journals, Jan/June 1966-. Calcutta: Info. Res. Academy. [Quarterly]

27612 Index to the Times of India, Bombay. Jan./Apr. 1973-. Bombay: Microfilm and Index Service, Ref. Dept., Times of India. [3 times a year]

27613 Indian economic diary. Jan 1970-. ND: H.S. Chhabra. [weekly]

27614 Indian press index. v.1-. April 1968-. Delhi: Delhi Library Assn. [Monthly; with Book review suppl. Apr./June 1968-.]

27615 KHAN, M. SHAHABUDDIN. A subject index on articles published in the Pakistan Observer (now Bangladesh Observer). Dacca: Dir. of Archives & Libraries, Govt. of the People's Republic of Bangladesh, 1975-. v.1-.

27616 MANAVALAN, A.A. Tamil research through journals: an annotated bibliography. Madras: Intl. Inst. of Tamil Studies, 1975. 228p.

27617 Prācī-Jyoti: digest of indological studies. v.1-. Dec. 1963-. Kurukshetra: Inst. of Indic Studies, Kurukshetra U. [semiannual; abstracts of articles]

27618 RAM, SADHU. Index to the Indian historical quarterly, 1925-1963. ND: Vijay Mohan, 1970. 187p.

27619 RATH, VIMAL. Index of Indian economic journals, 1016-1965. Poona: Orient Longman, 1971. 302p. (GIPE studies, 57)

27620 SARMA, K.V., comp. Decennial index to Vishveshvaranand Indological Journal, vols. 1-10, 1963-1972. Hoshiarpur: VVRI, 1973. (VIS, 60)

27621 SHAH, N.N. Index to Journal of the Oriental Institute, vols. 1-25, 1951-76. Baroda: Oriental Inst., 1978. 185p. (MSU oriental series, 13)

27622 TIVAREKAR, G.K. Index to the Transactions of the Literary Society of Bombay, vo.s I-III and to the journals of the Bombay Branch, Royal Asiatic Society, vols. I-XVII with a historical sketch of the society. Bombay: Royal Asiatic Soc., 1886. 196p.

5. Access to Books: Reviews of Current Publications

27623 Book Review. v.1-. Jan. 1976-. ND. [bi-monthly]

27624 CHAUDHURI, B., ed. Indian book review digest. Edmonton: U. of Alberta, 1979-. [v.1, 1977, 406p.]

27625 Indian book chronicle: news and reviews. v.1-. Jan 1976-. ND: Vivek Inst. [fortnightly]

27626 New books from India. v.1-. Jan. 1977-. ND: UBS Pub. Distributors.

27627 South Asia in review: Quarterly review of new books on South Asia. v.1-. Oct. 1976-. Colombia, MO. [quarterly]

6. Access to Festschriften

27628 Guide to Festschriften. v.1: The retrospective Festschriften collection of the New York Public Library: materials cataloged through 1971. [by main entry only] v.2: A dictionary catalog of Festschriften in the New York Public Library (1972-1976) and the Library of Congress (1972-1976) [by person honored, editor, title, and subject]. Boston: G.K. Hall, 1977. 2v. 597, 467p.

27629 Index to papers in commemorative volumes. Poona: Bhandarkar Oriental Res. Inst., 1963. 647p.

27630 LEISTNER, O. International bibliographie der Festschriften mit Sachregister. International bibliography of Festschriften) Osnabruck: Biblio Verlag, 1976. 889p.

B. General Bibliographies Containing South Asia Materials

1. Bibliographies of Bibliographies

27631 BESTERMAN, T. A world bibliography of Oriental bibliographies. Rev. and brought up to date by J.D. Pearson. Totowa, NJ: Rowman & Littlefield, 1975. 727 columns. [Orig.: 1939; South Asia, columns 285-434]

27632 CAMPBELL, F.B.F. Index-catalogue of bibliographical works, chiefly in the English language, relating to India. London: Library Supply Co., 1899. 99p.

27633 KALIA, D.R. & M.K. JAIN. A bibliography of bibliographies on India. Delhi: Concept, 1975. 204p.

27634 NUNN, G.R. South and Southeast Asia; a bibliography of bibliographies. Honolulu: East West Center Library, U. of Hawaii, 1966. 59p. (Its occ. papers, 4)

27635 USMANI, M. ADIL. Bibliographical services throughout Pakistan. Karachi: Dr. Mahmud Husain Library, U. of Karachi, 1978. 74p.

27636 ______. Status of bibliography in Pakistan. Karachi: Library Promotion Bureau, 1968. 108p. (Its pub., 4)

2. Bibliographies of Reference Works

27637 BHATIA, K. Reference sources on South Asia. Rev. ed. Philadelphia: South Asia Regional Studies, U. of Pennsylvania, 1978. 77p.

27638 CHATTERJEE, A. & N. GHOSE. Indian reference publications: a bibliography. Calcutta: Mukherji Book House, 1974. 119p. (Indian reference series,2)

27639 GIDWANI, N.N. & K. NAVALANI. A guide to reference materials on India. Jaipur: Saraswati, 1974. 2v., 1536p.

27640 PATTERSON, M.L.P. Bibliographical controls for South Asian studies. In Library Q. 41 (1971) 83-105.

27641 SHARMA, H.D. Indian reference sources: an annotated guide to Indian reference books. Varanasi: Indian Bibliographic Centre, 1972. 313p.

27642 SIDDIQUI, A.H. A guide to reference books published in Pakistan. Karachi: Pakistan Reference Pub., 1966. 41p.

27643 ______. Reference sources on Pakistan; a bibliography. Karachi: Natl. Book Centre of Pakistan, 1968. 32p.

27644 WAGLE, IQBAL, comp. Reference aids to South Asia. Toronto: U. of Toronto Library, 1977. 133p. (Reference Series, 22)

3. General Bibliographies for South Asia
a. South Asia and India

27645 Bibliography of Asian studies. 1956-. Ann Arbor: Assn. for Asian Studies, 1957-. [Until 1969 in JAS: no. 5 of each vol.]

27646 A bibliography of indology. Calcutta: Natl. Library, 1960-. [3v. publ. to date: Indian anthropology; botany; Bengali language & literature - early period. 56v. planned]

27647 CASE, M.H. South Asian history, 1750-1950: a guide to periodicals, dissertations and newspapers. Princeton: PUP, 1968. 561p.

27648 CHAMBARD, J.-L. Bibliographie de civilisation de l'Inde contemporaine. Paris: Pub. Orientalistes de France, 1977. 340p.

27649 DA CUNHA, U. India on film: a catalogue of films on India for teaching and special interest. ND: Educ. Resources Center, U. of State of New York, 1973. 80p.

27650 Early writings on India; a catalogue of books on India in English language published before 1900: an exhibition organised by the India International Centre, New Delhi, December 19-25, 1968. ND: IIC, 1969. 124 + 34p.

27651 INDIAN COUNCIL FOR CULTURAL RELATIONS. Aspects of Indian culture; select bibliographies. H.S. Patil and R.N. Sar, eds. ND: 1966-. [v.1, Arts, 261p.; v.2, History & Culture, 1970, 216p.; v.3 Indian literature, 1972, 262p.; v.4, Econ & Social Life, 1976, 218p.]

27652 Indian national bibliography. 1957-. Calcutta: Central Reference Library. [monthly; all title entries romanized; personal names in Sanskritized, not popular form; latest cumulated annual volume, 1973]

27653 MAHAR, J.M. India: a critical bibliography. Tucson: U. of Arizona Press, 1964. 119p.

27654 MOHINDER SINGH. Government publications of India: a survey of their nature, bibliographical control and distribution systems, including over 1500 titles. Delhi: Metropolitan Book Co., 1967. 270p.

27655 NAKAMURA, H., ed. India. In Comité Japonais des Sciences Historiques. Le Japon au XIe Congres international des sciences historiques à Stockholm. Tokyo: 1960, 365-78. [Bibl. of Japanese studies on India during 1940-1960]

27656 PATTERSON, M.L.P & R.B. INDEN. South Asia; an introductory bibliography. Chicago: Syllabus Div., UChiP, 1962. 412p.

27657 ROERICH, G. Bibliography of Soviet Indology, 1918-1958. In JORM 27,1/4 (1957-8) 48-73.

27658 South Asia: a bibliography for undergraduate libraries. By Louis A. Jacob, et al. Williamsport, PA: Bro-Dart, 1970. 103p. (U. of the State of NY, Foreign Area Materials Center, Occ. pub., 11)

27659 U.S. LIBRARY OF CONGRESS. Accessions list: India. ND: v.1-. Jul 1962-. [Monthly with cumulated author and subject indexes]

b. Pakistan

27660 ABERNETHY, G.L., comp. Pakistan: a selected, annotated bibliography. 3rd ed., rev. & enl. Vancouver: dist. U. of British Columbia, 1968. 56p.

27661 AHMED, U., comp. Bibliographie des Deutschen Pakistanschrifttums bis 1974 / bibliography of German literature on Pakistan up to 1974. Hamburg: Deutsch-Pakistanisches Forum, 1975. 302p.

27662 ALI, SHAUKAT & R.W. GABLE. Pakistan: a selected bibliography. Los Angeles: Intl. Public Admin. Center, U. of S. Calif., 1966. 44p. (Internatl. Public Admin. ser., 7)

27663 ANWAR, MUMTAZ A. & BASHIR ALI TIWANA. Pakistan; a bibliography of books and articles published in the United Kingdom from 1947-64. Lahore: Res. Soc. of Pakistan, U. of the Punjab, 1969. 102p. (Its pub., 18)

27664 Bibliografiia Pakistana, 1947-1967. Comp. by D.A. Birman & M.N. Kafitina; ed. by Iurii V. Gankovskii. Mowcow: Nauka, 1973. 53p.

27665 GHANI, A.R. Pakistan: a select bibliography. Lahore: Pakistan Assn. for the Advancement of Science, Univ. Inst. of Chemistry, 1951. 339p.

27666 KHAN, DILAWAR, comp. Pakistan: a subject guide. Islamabad: Dept. of Pakistan Studies, Quaid-i-Azam U., 1977. 63p.

27667 MORELAND, G.B. & AKHTAR H. SIDDIQUI. Publications of the Government of Pakistan, 1947-1957. Karachi: Inst. of Public & Business Admin., U. of Karachi, 1958. 187p.

27668 NATL. BOOK CENTRE OF PAKISTAN. Books from Pakistan published during the decade of reforms, 1958-1968. 2nd ed. Karachi: 1968. 159p. [subsequent annual vols.]

27669 ______. English language publications from Pakistan; a guidelist. Karachi: 1967. 242p.

27670 ______. Publications of learned bodies and research organizations in Pakistan. Karachi: 1973. [v. 1, Humanities, 140p.; to be 4 v.]

27671 The Pakistan national bibliography, 1947-1961. Karachi: Natl. Book Centre of Pakistan, 1973-. [to be 3 v.]

27672 The Pakistan national bibliography, 1962-. Karachi: Dept. of Libraries, Min. of Educ. & Provincial Co-ordination, Govt. of Pakistan. [annual]

27673 SATYAPRAKASH, comp. & ed. Pakistan: a bibliography, 1962-1974. Gurgaon: IDS, 1975. 338p. [incl. 6,500 articles from 109 Indian journals & Times of India]

27674 SIDDIQUI, AKHTAR H. A guide to Pakistan government publications, 1958-1970. Karachi: Natl. Book Centre of Pakistan, 1973. 276p.

27675 U.S. LIBRARY OF CONGRESS. Accessions list: Pakistan. Karachi: v. 1-, July/Dec. 1962-. [monthly, with cumulative author & subject indexes annually]

4. Special Subject Bibliographies

27676 Annual bibliography of Indian archaeology, v. 1-, 1926-. Leiden: Kern Inst., 1928-. [Irregular. Most recent v. 21 (1964/66) published in 1972.]

27677 DIXIT, H., ed. Medical bibliography of Nepal.

Kathmandu: Inst. of Med., Res., & Rev. Div., Tribhuvan U., 1978. 62p.

27678 GAUTAM, B.P. Researches in political science in India: a detailed bibliography. Kanpur: Oriental Publ. House, 1965. 116p.

27679 GREAT BRITAIN. PARLIAMENT. HOUSE OF COMMONS. EAST INDIA. Annual list and general index of the Parliamentary papers relating to the East Indies published during the years 1801 to 1907 inclusive. London: HMSO, 1909. 194p. (Parl. Papers 89 (1909) 64:757)

27680 GUSTAFSON, W.E., ed. Pakistan and Bangladesh: bibliographic essays in social science. Islamabad: U. of Islamabad Press, 1976. 364p.

27681 HIRIYANNA, M. Reviews. Mysore: Kavyalaya Pub., 1970. 291p.

27682 JAGDISH CHANDRA, comp. Bibliography of Indian art, history and archaeology. Delhi: Delhi Printers Prakashan, 1978-. v. 1, Art, 318p.

27683 NAYAK, S. & MALA SINGH. Children's books on India: an annotated bibliography. 2nd ed. ND: Educational Resources Center, 1973. 78p.

27684 SIDDIQUI, AKHTAR H. Publications of learned bodies and research organizations in Pakistan in the field of social sciences. Karachi: Natl. Book Council of Pakistan, 1978. 88p.

27685 SILVA, M. Bibliography on the Sri Lanka child. Colombo: Sri Lanka IYC Secretariat, 1979. 179p.

27686 TEXAS UNIVERSITY. POPULATION RESEARCH CENTER. International population census bibliography: Asia. Austin: Bureau of business research, U. of Texas, 1966. (census bibl., 5) [Ceylon, India, Nepal, Pakistan; 130p.]

5. Bibliographies of Theses and Dissertations

27687 ANWAR, MUHAMMAD, comp. Doctoral dissertations on Pakistan. Islamabad: Natl. Cmsn. on Hist. & Cultural Res., 1976. 124p. (Its Bibl. series, 2)

27688 Bibliography of doctoral dissertations; social sciences & humanities, 1970-75. ND: Assn. of Indian Universities. [annual; continues InterUniversity Board of India & Ceylon. A bibliography of doctoral dissertations...1957-70.]

27689 BLOOMFIELD, B.C. Theses on Asia accepted by universities in the United Kingdom and Ireland, 1877-1964. London: Cass, 1967. 127p.

27690 GOPAL, K., comp. & DHANPAT RAI, ed. Theses on Indian sub-continent, 1877-1971: an annotated bibliography of dissertations in social sciences and humanities accepted with the universities of Australia, Canada, Great Britain and Ireland, and United States of America. Delhi: Hindustan Pub. Corp., 1977. 462p.

27691 INDIAN COUNCIL OF SOCIAL SCIENCE RESEARCH. Doctorates in social sciences awarded by Indian universities up to 1967. ND: 1971. 401p. (Its Res. info. series 1, v. 1)

27692 INDIAN COUNCIL OF SOCIAL SCIENCES RESEARCH. Doctorates in social sciences awarded by Indian universities, 1968 and 1969. ND: 1970. 2 v., 88, 90p. (Its Res. info. series 1, v. 2)

27693 KAYASTHA, V.P., comp. Master's and doctoral theses on South Asia accepted by Cornell University, 1922-1977. Ithaca, NY: South Asia Program, Cornell U., 1978. 45 + 33p. (South Asia Occ. Papers and Theses)

27694 KOZICKI, R.J. & P. ANANDA, comps. South and Southeast Asia: doctoral dissertations and master's theses completed at the University of California at Berkeley, 1906-1968. Berkeley: Center for S. & SE Asia Studies, U. of Calif., 1969. 49p. (Its Occ. paper, 1)

27695 MAHESHWARY, A.C. Research on Southern Asia at Duke University: an annotated list of doctoral dissertations and master's theses, mainly on India and Pakistan, completed at Duke University through 1972. Durham, NC: DUPCSSA, 1973. 43p. (Its monograph & occ. papers series, 2)

27696 SHULMAN, F.J. Doctoral dissertations on South Asia, 1966-70: an annotated bibliography covering North America, Europe, and Australia. Ann Arbor: Center for S. & SE Asian Studies, 1971. 228p. (MPSSA, 4)

27697 ______. Doctoral dissertations on Asia, v. 1-, 1975-. Ann Arbor: Assn. for Asian Studies. [irregular; latest issue, 3,1 (1980)]

27698 STUCKI, C.W. American doctoral dissertations on Asia, 1933-1962, including appendix of Master's theses at Cornell University. Ithaca, NY: Dept. of Asian Studies, SE Asia Program, Cornell U., 1963. 204p. (Its Data paper, 50)

27699 SUKHWAL, B.L. A bibliography of theses and dissertations in geography on South Asia. Monticello, IL: Council of Planning Librarians, 1973. 70p. (Its Exchange Bibliography, 438)

6. Regional Bibliographies

a. Sri Lanka

27700 ALWIS, N.A.W.A.T., comp. Bibliography of scientific publications relating to Sri Lanka, 1960-1976. Colombo: Social Science Res. Centre, Natl. Science Council of Sri Lanka, 1978. 244p.

27701 ______. Bibliography of scientific literature relating to Sri Lanka: supplement. Colombo: Social Science Res. Centre, Natl. Science Council of Sri Lanka, 1979-. v. 1-.

27702 Ceylon national bibliography, v. 1-, Jan. 1963-. Nugegoda: Natl. Bibl. Branch, Dept. of the Govt. Archivist, Govt. of Ceylon. [monthly. Divided by language: Sinhalese, Tamil, English.]

27703 DE SILVA, C.R. Peradeniya research: a bibliography of research publications by the academic staff of the Faculties of Arts and Oriental Studies, University of Ceylon, Peradeniya, 1952-1974. Peradeniya: Ceylon Studies Seminar, 1974. 99p.

27704 GOONETILEKE, H.A.I. Bibliography of Ceylon: a systematic guide to the literature on the land, people, history, and culture published in Western languages from the sixteenth century to the present day. Zug, Switzerland: Inter Documentation Co., 1970-. (Bibliotheca Asiatica 5,14) [v. 1-2, 1970, 865p. (2nd ed., 1973); v. 3, 1976, 566p.]

27705 U.S. LIBRARY OF CONGRESS. Accessions list: Sri Lanka. ND: v. 1-, March 1967-. [quarterly, with cumulative annual author & subject indexes]

27706 WARE, E.W. Bibliography of Ceylon. Coral Gables: U. of Miami Press, 1962. 181p. [Supplemented by microfilm addition in 1964 by American Documentation Inst., Washington, c/o Photodup. Service, Library of Congress. 49p. (Micro.-ADIM no. 722-3)]

b. South India

27707 HOCKINGS, P.E. A bibliography for the Nilgiri Hills of Southern India, 1603-1978. New Haven: HRAF Press, 1978. 2 v., 303p.

27708 ______. Bibliography of studies on the Nilgiri Hills of Madras. 3rd ed. Poona: S.M. Katre, 1968. 116p. (BDCRI 26,1/2)

27709 PANIKKAR, A.K. & C.V. RAJAN PILLAI. Kerala: a bibliography of books on Kerala in the University Library, Trivandrum. Trivandrum: Kerala U. Library, 1977. 276p.

27710 SATYAPRAKASH. Andhra Pradesh: a select bibliography, 1962-1975. Gurgaon: IDS, 1976. 175p. (Indian states bibl. series, 1)

27711 ______. Karnataka: a select bibliography. Gurgaon: IDS, 1978. 276p. (Indian states bibl. series, 8)

27712 ______. Kerala, a select bibliography. Gurgaon: IDS, 1979. 205p. (Indian states bibl. series, 9)

c. Middle India

27713 CHAVDA, V.K. A select bibliography of Gujarat; its history and culture, 1600-1857. Ahmedabad: New Order Book Co., 1972. 232p.

27714 COSTA, A.M. DA. Literatura goesa; apontamentos bio-bibliográficos para a sua história. Lisbon: Agência-Geral do Ultramar, 1967. 476p.

27715 GONÇALVES, J.J. Síntese bibliográfica de Goa. Lisboa: Agência-geral do Ultramar, 1966-. v. 1, 2-.

27716 KHARBAS, D.S. Maharashtra and the Marathas: their history and culture; a bibliographic guide to western language materials. Boston: G.K. Hall, 1975. 642p.

27717 SATYAPRAKASH. Gujarat: a select bibliography. Gurgaon: IDS, 1976. 168p. (Indian states bibl. series, 4)

d. Indus Valley and Mountain Frontier

27718 AHMED, AKBAR S. A bibliography of the North-West Frontier Province. Islamabad: Pakistan Publications, 1979. 66p.

27719 BILLIMORIA, N.M. Bibliography of publications relating to Sind and Baluchistan. Rev. & enl. ed. Lahore: Sh. Mubarak Ali, 1977. 136p.

27720 JONES, S. Bibliography of Nuristan (Kafiristan) and the Kalash Kafirs of Chitral. Copenhagen: Munksgaard, 1969. 264p.

27721 KHAN, DILAWAR. Baluchistan: a selected bibliography. Islamabad: English Book House, 1977. 23p.

27722 ______. Northern areas: a select bibliography. Islamabad: Dept. of Anthro., Quaid-i-Azam U., 1977. 23p.

27723 NAQVI, S. FAKHRE ALAM. Sind: a select bibliography. Rawalpindi: Friends Own Press, 1977. 37p.

27724 NAWAZ, M.A. Source material on the Punjab. Lahore: Pakistani Adabi Board, 1979. 491p.

27725 NORTH, R. The literature of the North-West Frontier of India; a select bibliography. Peshawar: the author, 1945. 66p.

27726 PANHWAR, M. HUSSAIN. Source material on Sind. Hyderabad: U. of Sind, Jamshoro Inst. of Sindhology, 1977. 581p. (Its pub., 44)

27727 GANDA SINGH. A bibliography of the Panjab. Patiala: Punjab U., 1966. 245p.

27728 WARIKOO, KULBHUSHAN. Jammu, Kashmir, and Ladakh: a classified and comprehensive bibliography. ND: Sterling, 1976. 555p.

e. the Ganga Plains of North India

27729 SATYAPRAKASH, comp. & ed. Bihar: a select bibliography, 1962-1975. Gurgaon: IDS, 1976. 155p. (Indian states bibl. series, 3)

f. the Northeast: Assam and the Bengals

27730 BERTOCCI, P.J. Bangladesh history, society and culture: an introductory bibliography of secondary materials. East Lansing: Asian Studies Center, Michigan State U., 1973. 18p.

27731 KOPF, D. Bibliographic essay on Bengal studies in the United States. In R. Van M. Baumer, ed. Aspects of Bengali history and society. Honolulu: UPH, 1975, 200-42. (Asian Studies at Hawaii, 12)

27732 SATYAPRAKASH. Assam: a select bibliography, 1962-1975. Gurgaon: IDS, 1976. 100p. (Indian states bibl. series, 2)

27733 SHAMSUDDOULAH, A.B.M. Introducing Bangladesh through books: a select bibliography with introductions and annotations, 1855-1976. Dacca: Great Eastern Books, 1976. 45p.

27734 SUKHWAL, B.L. A systematic geographic bibliography on Bangla Desh. Monticello, IL: Council of Planning Librarians, 1973. 63p. (Its Exchange bibl., 455)

27735 U.S. LIBRARY OF CONGRESS. Accessions list: Bangladesh. ND: v. 1-, 1967-. [semi-annual, with cumulative annual author & subject indexes]

g. the Himalayan Rim

27736 BHATTACHARJEE, KAMANA KUMAR & S.C. CHOUDHURY, comps. & eds. Tripurana; a selected and annotated bibliography on Tripura. Agartala: Tripura Library Assn., 1970. 63p.

27737 Bibliografiia Nepala, 1917-1967. Comp. by D.A. Birman & M.N. Kafitina. Moscow: Nauka, 1973. 22p.

27738 Bibliographie du Népal. Comp. by L. Boulnois, et al. Paris: CNRS, 1969-. [v. 1, Sciences humaines, 289p.; v. 1, suppl. 1967-73, 435p.; v. 3,1, Sciences naturelles, cartes du Népal, 117p.; v. 3,2, Sciences naturelles, botaniques, 126p.; v. 2 not yet pub.]

27739 CHAUDHURI, S. Bibliography of the published material on the people of the north-eastern frontier of India. In QJMS 45,3/4 & 46,1/2 (1955) 171-86, 258-69, 32-42, 119-26; 47,1 (1956) 47-51.

27740 GYAWALI, B.M. & G. STANDROD. Information resources on Nepal. Kirtipur: Documentation Centre, CEDA, 1973. 84p. [Incomplete worldwide listing of libraries, centers & bibliographies for Nepal studies.]

27741 HEDRICK, B.C. et al., ed. A bibliography of Nepal. Metuchen, NJ: Scarecrow Press, 1973. 302p.

27742 MALLA, K.M., ed. Bibliography of Nepal. Kathmandu: Royal Nepal Academy, 1975. 529p.

27743 MANANDHAR, T. Works on Nepal in the Kaiser Library: an annotated bibliography, reproduced from the Union catalogue being established at INAS. Kirtipur: Inst. of Nepal and Asian Studies, Tribhuvan U., 1974. 119p.

27744 Nepal documentation. Kathmandu: Documentation Centre, CEDA, 1972. 100p. (Its occ. bibl., 1) [covers journal articles, 1950 to date]

27745 SCHAPPERT, L.G. Sikkim, 1800-1968; an annotated bibliography. Honolulu: East-West Center Library, 1968. 69p. (Its occ. papers, 10)

27746 U.S. LIBRARY OF CONGRESS. Accessions list: Nepal. ND: v. 1-, 1967-. [semiannual, with cumulative author & subject indexes]

27747 WOOD, H.B. Nepal bibliography. Eugene, OR: American-Nepal Educ. Foundation, 1959. 108p.

C. Statistical and Codified Information on South Asia

1. Guides to the Statistics of South Asia

27748 GUPTA, DEVENDRA B. & M.K. PREMI. Sources and nature of the official statistics of the Indian Union. Delhi: Ranjit Printers & Pub., 1970. 335p.

27749 INDIA (REP.). CENTRAL STAT. ORG. Guide to official statistics. ND: 1979. 138p.

27750 ______. Statistical system in India. ND: 1951-. [Rev. periodically. Latest issue verified: 1970, 74p.]

27751 PAKISTAN. CENTRAL STAT. OFFICE. Key to official statistics. Karachi: 1962-. [index to statistical agencies by ministries & depts. and by subjects]

27752 RAJASTHAN. DIR. OF ECON. & STAT. Statistical system in the states in India: growth, organisation, functions, publications. Jaipur: 1970. 130p.

27753 RAZA, MOONIS & SHAFEEQ NAQVI & JAGANATH DHAR. Sources of economic and social statistics of India. ND: Eureka, 1978. 451p.

27754 SALUJA, M.R. Indian official statistical systems. Calcutta: Stat. Pub. Soc., 1972. 276p.

27755 ZAHURUL HUQ, A.T.M. Sources of statistics on Bangladesh: a guide to researchers. Dacca: Bureau of Econ. Res., U. of Dacca, 1978. 86p.

2. Major Statistical Compendia
a. South Asian censuses: guides and descriptions

27756 BOSE, A. The census of India: a historical perspective. In Demography India 2,1 (1973) 18-39.

27757 The census of India, 1872-1951. Zug: Inter Documentation Co., 1965. [4458 microfiches in 100 boxes]

27758 INDIA (REP.). CENSUS OF INDIA, 1971. Bibliography of census publications in India. By C.G. Jadhar & B.K. Roy Burman. ND: Office of the Registrar Genl., 1972. 520p. (Census centenary pub., 5)

27759 ______. Indian census in perspective. By S.C. Srivastava. ND: Office of the Registrar Genl., 1972. 416p. (Census centenary monograph, 1)

27760 ______. Indian census through a hundred years. By Dandapani Natarajan. ND: Office of the Registrar Genl., 1972. 2 v., 550, 706p. (Census centenary monograph, 2)

27761 INDIA (REP.). OFFICE OF THE REGISTRAR GENL. A guide to the 1961 census publication programme. ND: 1965. 230p.

27762 ______. 1971 Indian census publications. ND: 1975. 92p.

27763 INDIA (REP.). VITAL STAT. DIV. Civil registration system in India: a perspective. ND: 1972. 213p. (Census centenary monograph, 4)

27764 MAHALANOBIS, P.C. & D.B. LAHIRI. Analyses of errors in censuses and surveys with special emphasis on the experience of India. In Sankhya 23-A,4 (1961) 325-58.

27765 SRI LANKA. DEPT. OF CENSUS & STAT. Census of population, 1971, Sri Lanka: general report. Moratuwa: Industrial Development Board of Ceylon, 1978. 153 + 66p.

b. national statistical yearbooks and abstracts [volumes also pub. at state & district level]

27766 CHAUDHURI, M.R., ed. India in statistics. Calcutta: Oxford & IBH, 1978. 108p.

27767 India: a statistical outline. Bombay: Indian Oxygen Ltd., 1965-. [biennial. latest, 1976]

27768 INDIA (REP.). CENTRAL STAT. ORG. Statistical abstract, India, ns v.1-, 1949-. [annual. Supersedes India. Dept. of Commercial intelligence and statistics. Statistical abstract for British India.]

27769 INDIA (REP.). OFFICE OF THE REGISTRAR GENL. Pocket book of population statistics. ND: 1972. 148p.

27770 PAKISTAN. CENTRAL STAT. OFFICE. Twenty-five years of Pakistan in statistics, 1947-1972. Karachi: MPGOI, 1972. 557p.

27771 Pakistan statistical yearbook, 19-- - 1971, 1973-. Karachi: Central Stat. Office. [annual; 1972 special ed.: 25 years of Pakistan in statistics, 1947-1972.]

27772 Statistical abstract of Bangladesh. 2nd ed., rev. & enl. Calcutta: Soc. & Commerce Pub., 1975. 127p.

27773 Statistical abstract of Sri Lanka, 1973-. Colombo: Dept. of Census and Statistics, Govt. of Sri Lanka. [annual; supersedes: Statistical abstract of Ceylon, 1949-1972.]

27774 Statistical digest of Bangladesh, 1972-. Dacca: Bureau of Statistics, Govt. of Bangladesh. [annual; supersedes: Statistical digest of East Pakistan]

27775 Statistical pocket-book of Pakistan, 1962-. Karachi: Central Statistical Office, Govt. of Pakistan. [annual]

27776 Statistical pocket-book of the Indian Union, 1956-. ND: Central Stat. Org. [annual]

27777 Statistical pocket book of the Republic of Sri Lanka, 1972-. Colombo: Dept. of Census and Statistics, Govt. of Sri Lanka. [annual; supersedes: Statistical pocket book of Ceylon, 1967-71.]

3. Gazetteers: Historical and Geographical Compendia

27778 CHAUDHURI, SASHI BHUSAN. History of the gazetteers of India. ND: Min. of Educ., GOI, 1964. 230p.

27779 The gazetteer of India; Indian Union. ND: PDMIB, 1965-78. 4 v. [v. 1, Country and people; v. 2, History and culture; v. 3, Economic structure and activities; v. 4, Administration and public welfare]

27780 The gazetteers of India in the British period: Imperial, provincial and district series, published up to 1947. Zug, Switzerland: Inter Documentation Co., 1972. [1210 v. in 131 boxes of microfiches]

27781 Imperial gazetteer of India. ND: Today & Romorrow's Pub., 1972. 26 v. [Rpt. 1908-09 ed.]

27782 INDIA (REP.). MIN. OF EDUC. The Indian gazetteers. ND: 1967. 76p. (Its pub., 765)

27783 SCHOLBERG, H. The district gazetteers of British India: a bibliography. Zug, Switzerland: Inter Documentation Co., 1970. 12 + 131p. (Bibliotheca Asiatica, 3)

V. TOOLS FOR THE STUDY OF THE LITERARY LANGUAGES OF SOUTH ASIA

A. Bibliographies and Reference Works on South Asian Languages

27784 CALCUTTA. NATL. LIBRARY. A bibliography of dictionaries and encyclopaedias in Indian languages. Calcutta: 1964. 165p.

27785 JOHNSON, D.E. et al. Survey of materials for the study of the uncommonly taught languages, v. 4: Languages of South Asia. Arlington, VA: Center for Applied Linguistics, 1976. 41p.

27786 LAMBERT, H.M. Introduction to the Devanagari script: for students of Sanskrit, Hindi, Marathi, Gujarati, and Bengali. London: OUP, 1953. 231p.

27787 NAVALANI, K. & N.N. GIDWANI. Dictionaries in Indian languages: a bibliography. Jaipur: Saraswati, 1972. 370p. [comprehensive, annotated, 3000 entries]

27788 PATTANAYAK, D.P. Indian languages bibliography of grammars, dictionaries and teaching materials. 2nd rev. ed. ND: Educ. Resources Center, 1973. 91p.

27789 SHARMA, D.N. Transliteration into Roman and Devanagari of the languages of the Indian group. Dehra Dun: Survey of India, 1972. 44p.

27790 SIITAA DEVII, A.P. Indian language highway for all: a broad seventeen-language highway through the mother tongues of India and her neighbours; Sindh, Burma, Ceylon. Madras: Adyar Library & Res. Centre, 1967. 427p.

B. Pan-South Asian Languages

1. Sanskrit: Vedic and Classical
a. dictionaries

27791 APTE, V.S. The practical Sanskrit-English dictionary. Poona: Prasad Prakashan, 1977-79. 3 v. [Rpt. 1957-59 ed.]

27792 BÖHTLINGK, O. Sanskrit-Wörterbuch. St. Petersburg: Buchdruckerei des Kaiserlichen Akademie der Wissenschaften, 1855-75. 7 v. [Abridged ed., St. Petersburg: 1879-89. 3 v.]

27793 CAPPELLER, C. A Sanskrit-English dictionary based upon the St. Petersburg lexicons. Varanasi: CSSO, 1972. 672p. [Rpt. of 1891 ed.; orig. pub. in German in 1887]

27794 EDGERTON, F. Buddhist hybrid Sanskrit grammar and dictionary. Delhi: Motilal Banarsidass, 1970-71. 2 v., 238, 627p. [Rpt. 1953 ed.]

27795 MACDONELL, A.A. A practical Sanskrit dictionary with transliteration, accentuation, and etymological analysis throughout. London: OUP, 1974. 382p. [Rpt. of 1924 ed.]

27796 MONIER-WILLIAMS, M. A dictionary, English and Sanskrit. Delhi: Motilal, 1971. 859p. [Rpt. of 1851 ed.]

27797 ______. Sanskrit-English dictionary. Delhi: Motilal, 1970. 1333p. [Rpt. of 1956 ed.; based on 1899 ed.]

b. learning aids: grammars and readers

27798 ABHYANKAR, K.V. & J.M. SHUKLA. A dictionary of Sanskrit grammar. 2nd rev. ed. Baroda: Oriental Inst., 1977. 448p. (GOS, 134)

27799 GONDA, J. A concise elementary grammar of the Sanskrit language, with exercises, reading selections, and a glossary. Tr. from German by G.B. Ford, Jr. University, AL: U. of Alabama Press, 1966, 1966. 152p.

27800 LANMAN, C.R. A Sanskrit reader. Cambridge: HUP, 1963. 405p. [1st pub. 1884-89]

27801 MACDONELL, A.A. Vedic grammar. Varanasi: Indological Book House, 1968. 456p. [1st pub. 1916]

27802 ______. A Vedic reader for students, containing fifty hymns of the Rigveda. Oxford: OUP, 1917. 263p.

27803 PERRY, E.D. A Sanskrit primer. NY: ColUP, 1969. 230p. [1st pub. 1885; based on G. Bühler's Leitfaden für den Elementarcursus des Sanskrit]

27804 RENOU, L. Grammaire sanscrite ... phonétique, composition, dérivation, le nom, le verbe, la phrase. 2nd ed. rev. & enl. Paris: Librairie d'Amerique et d'Orient, Adrien-Maison-neuve, 1968. 589p.

27805 VARENNE, J. Grammaire du sanskrit. Paris: PUF, 1971. 127p.

27806 WHITNEY, W.D. Sanskrit grammar, including both the classical language and the other dialects of Veda and Brahmana. 2nd ed. Cambridge: HUP, 1941. 551p. [2nd ed., 1st pub. 1889]

2. Pali and Prakrits
a. dictionaries

27807 BUDDHADATTA, A.P. English-Pali dictionary. London: Luzac, 1970. 588p. (Pali Text Soc. series) [Rpt. of 1955 ed.]

27808 PATHAK, P.P. Dictionary for students: Ardhamagadhi-English, English-Ardhamagadhi. Poona: 1951. 135p.

27809 RHYS-DAVIDS, T.W. & W. STEDE, eds. Pali-English dictionary. London: Luzac, 1966. 4 v. (Pali Text Soc. series) [Rpt. of 1921 ed.]

27810 TRENCKNER, W. & D. ANDERSON. Critical Pali dictionary. Copenhagen: Royal Danish Academy of Sciences & Letters, 1924-1965. 2 v.

b. learning aids

27811 ANDERSON, D. A Pali reader, with notes and glossary. Kyoto: Rinsen-Shoten Bookstore, 1968. 288p. [1st pub. 1886, Copenhagen]

27812 MÜLLER, E. A simplified grammar of the Pali language. Varanasi: Sharad Publications, 1967. 143p.

27813 SIRCAR, D.C. A grammar of the Prakrit language, based mainly on Vararuchi, Hemachandra, and Purushottama. 2nd enl. ed. Delhi: Motilal, 1970. 176p.

27814 WARDER, A.K. Introduction to Pali. London: Luzac, 1963. 458p. (Pali Text Society)

27815 WOOLNER, A.C. Introduction to Prakrit. Varanasi: R.S. Panna Lal, 1966. 235p.

3. Persian

27816 ELWELL-SUTTON, L.P. Elementary Persian grammar. Cambridge: CamUP, 1963. 223p.

27817 LAMBTON, A.K.S. Persian grammar. Cambridge: CamUP, 1960. 275p.

27818 STEINGASS, F.J. Comprehensive Persian-English dictionary: including the Arabic words and phrases to be met with in Persian literature, being Johnson and Richardson's Persian, Arabic and English dictionary, revised, enlarged and entirely reconstructed. ND: OBRC, 1973. 1539p. [Rpt. 1892 ed.]

4. Hindi, Urdu, Hindustani
a. dictionaries

27819 BULCKE, C. Angrezi-Hindi kosh: an English-Hindi dictionary. 2nd ed. Ranchi: Catholic Press, 1971. 890p.

27820 CHATURVEDI, M. & B.N. TIWARI, eds. Practical Hindi-English dictionary. ND: Natl. Pub. House, 1970. 738p.

27821 FALLON, S.W. Urdu-English dictionary. Lahore: Central Urdu Board, 1976. 1216p. [1st pub. 1879, as New Hindustani-English dictionary]

27822 Ferozsons' English-Urdu dictionary: English words with their equivalents in Urdu. 4th & 5th eds. Lahore: Ferozsons, 1961. 910p.

27823 Ferozsons' Urdu-English dictionary: Urdu words, phrases and idioms with English meanings and synonyms. 4th ed. Lahore: Ferozsons, 1964. 831p.

27824 PATHAK, R.C. Bhargava's standard illustrated dictionary of the English language: Anglo-Hindi edition. 12th ed., rev. & enl. Varanasi: Bhargava Book Depot, 1978. 1432p.

27825 PATHAK, RAM CHANDRA. Bhargava's standard illustrated dictionary of the Hindi language: Hindi-English. Rev. & enl. Varanasi: Bhargava Book Depot, 1967. 1280p.

27826 PLATTS, J.T. Dictionary of Urdu, classical Hindi, and English. London: OUP, 1968. 1259p. [Rpt. 1884 ed.]

b. grammars

27827 KELLOGG, S.H. A grammar of the Hindi language; in which are treated the High Hindí, Braj, and the Eastern Hindí of the Rámáyan of Tulsí Dás, also the colloquial dialects of Rajputáná, Kumáon, Avadh, Ríwá, Bhojpur, Magadha, Maithila, etc., with copious philological notes. ND: OBRC, 1972. 584p. [Rpt. 1875 ed.]

27828 MCGREGOR, R.S. Outline of Hindi grammar, with exercises. 2nd ed. Delhi: OUP, 1977. 261p.

27829 PLATTS, J.T. A grammar of the Hindustānī or Urdū language. Delhi: Munshiram, 1967. 399p. [1st pub. 1874]

27830 SOUTHWORTH, F.C. The student's Hindi-Urdu reference manual. Tucson: U. of Arizona Press, 1971. 238p.

27831 VAN OLPHEN, H. Elementary Hindi grammar and exercises. Austin: Center for Asian Studies, U. of Texas, 1972. 209p.

c. introductory texts

27832 BAILEY, T.G. Teach yourself Urdu. London: English Universities Press, 1970. 39 + 314p. [Rpt. of 1956 ed., rev. from Teach yourself Hindustani, 1950]

27833 BARKER, M. ABD-AL-RAHMAN, et al. A course in Urdu. Ithaca, NY: Spoken Language Services, 1975-. v. [Rpt. of Montreal: Inst. of Islamic Studies, McGill U., 1967. Cover title: Spoken Urdu.]

27834 BARZ, R.K. An introduction to Hindi and Urdu. Canberra: Faculty of Asian Studies, ANU, 1977. 250p.

27835 BENDER, E. Urdu: grammar and reader. Philadelphia: UPaP, 1967. 458p.

27836 FAIRBANKS, G.H. & B.G. MISRA. Spoken and written Hindi. Ithaca: CornellUP, 1966. 468p.

27837 MCGREGOR, R.S. Exercises in spoken Hindi, from tape-recordings in Hindi by A.S. Kalsi. NY: CamUP, 1970. 85p.

27838 NAIM, C.M. Introductory Urdu. Chicago: Cmtee. on Southern Asian Studies, U. of Chicago, 1975. 2 v., 385 + 370p.

27839 POŘIZKA, V. Hindština Hindī language course. Prague: Státní Pedagogické Nakladatelství, 1972. 747p.

27840 SHARMA, D.N. & J.W. STONE. Hindi: an active introduction. Washington: Foreign Services Inst., 1970. 131p. (Foreign Services Inst. Basic course series)

27841 WAZIR CHAND, L. Urdu conversation: a practical handbook for the use of European travellers, also adapted to the requirements of the students. Lahore: Sheikh Mubarak Ali, 1975. 141p. [Prev. ed., Hindustani conversation.]

d. readers

27842 ANSARI, D. Chrestomathie der Hindi-Prosa des 20. Jahrhunderts. Leipzig: Verlag Enzyklopädie VEB, 1967. 221p.

27843 ANSARI, M.A. & D. ANSARI. Chrestomathie der Urdu-prosa des 19. und 20. Jahrhunderts. Leipzig: Verlag Enzyklopädie, 1965. 135p.

27844 BARKER, M. ABD-UL-RAHMAN et al. An Urdu newspaper reader. Ithaca, NY: Spoken Language Services, 1974. 453p.

27845 BENDER, E. Introductory Hindi readings. Philadelphia: UPaP, 1971. 277p.

27846 BRIGHT, W. & SAEED A. KHAN. The Urdu writing system. Ithaca, NY: Spoken Language Services, 1976. 48p.

27847 NAIM, C.M. Readings in Urdu: prose and poetry. Honolulu: EWCP, 1965. 396p.

27848 NARANG, G.C. Urdu: readings in literary Urdu prose. Madison: UWiscP, 1967. 381p.

C. Regional Literary Languages

1. Sinhala: the Indo-Aryan Language of Sri Lanka

27849 CARTER, C. English-Sinhalese dictionary. Colombo: M.D. Gunasena, 1968. 535p. [1st ed. 1889]

27850 DE SILVA, M.W.S. Colloquial Sinhalese reader. York, England: the author, 1971. 211p.

27851 FAIRBANKS, G.H. & J.W. GAIR & M.W.S. DE SILVA. Colloquial Sinhalese. Ithaca, NY: South Asia Program, CornellUP, 1968. 2 v.

27852 GAIR, J.W. & W.S. KARUNATILAKA. Literary Sinhala. Ithaca, NY: Dept. of Modern Languages & Linguistics, Cornell U., 1974. 453p.

27853 ______. Samples of contemporary Sinhala prose with glossary and grammatical notes. Ithaca, NY: South Asia Program, Cornell U., 1976. 52p.

27854 GEIGER, W. Grammar of the Sinhalese language. Colombo: Royal Asiatic Soc., Ceylon Branch, 1938. 200p.

27855 GEIGER, W., ed. & D.B. JAYATILAKA et al., comps. A dictionary of the Sinhalese language. Colombo: Royal Asiatic Soc., Ceylon Branch, and U. of Ceylon, 1935-. [issued in fascicles]

27856 GUNASEKARA, A.M. A comprehensive grammar of the Sinhalese language. Colombo: Sri Lanka Sahitya Mandalaya, 1962. 516p. [Rpt. 1891 ed.]

27857 RANAWAKE, E. Spoken Sinhalese for beginners. Rev. 5th ed. Colombo: M.D. Gunasena, 1968. 80p.

27858 RATNA ENGLISH-SINHALESE POCKET DICTIONARY. Colombo: Ratna Poth Prakasakayo, 1970. 503p.

27859 WIJERATNE, D.G. Sinhalese through English. 3rd ed. Colombo: M.D. Gunasena, 1968. 302p.

2. South Indian Dravidian Languages
a. Tamil
i. dictionaries

27860 CHIDAMBARANATH CHETTIAR, A. English-Tamil dictionary. Madras: U. of Madras, 1963-65. 3 v.

27861 DHAMOTHARAN, A. Tamil dictionaries; a bibliography. Wiesbaden: Steiner, 1978. 185p.

27862 FABRICIUS, J.P. J.P. Fabricius's Tamil and English dictionary, based on Johann Philipp Fabricius's Malabar-English dictionary. 4th ed., rev. & enl. Tranquebar: Evangelical Lutheran Mission Pub. House, 1972. 910p. [1st pub. 1779]

27863 The great Lifco-dictionary: English-English-Tamil. 10th ed. Madras: Little Flower Co., 1967. 694p. [1st ed. 1952]

27864 The Lifco Tamil-Tamil-English dictionary. Madras: Little Flower Co., 1968. 671p. + 84 illus.

27865 Tamil lexicon. Ed. by S. Vaiyapuri Pillai. Madras: U. of Madras, 1926-1956. 6 v. 3944p. + suppl. 1939, 423p.

27866 VISVANATHA PILLAI, V. A Tamil-English dictionary. Rev. and enl. with an appendix of modern scientific terms. 8th ed. Madras: Madras School Book & Literature Soc., 1972. 742p. [1st ed.: A Dictionary: Tamil and English, 1888]

ii. learning aids

27867 ANDRONOV, M.S. A standard grammar of modern and classical Tamil. Tr. by the author from Russian. Madras: New Century Book House, 1969. 342p.

27868 ARDEN, A.H. A progressive grammar of common Tamil. 5th ed. rev. by A.C. Clayton. Madras: CLS, 1969. 342p. [Rpt. 1962 ed.]

27869 ASHER, R.E. & R. RADHAKRISHNAN. A Tamil prose reader: selections from contemporary Tamil prose with notes and glossary. Cambridge: CamUP, 1971. 237p.

27870 JOTHIMUTTHU, P. Guide to Tamil by the direct method. 3rd rev. ed. Madras: CLS, 1970. 264p. [1st ed. 1956]

27871 KOTHANDARAMAN, P. A course in modern standard Tamil: laboratory manual, texts and exercises. Madras: Intl. Inst. of Tamil Studies, 1975. 98 + 107p.

27872 KUMARASWAMI RAJA, N. & K. DORASWAMY. Conversational Tamil. Annamalainagar: Annamalai U., 1966. 360p.

27873 PATTANAYAK, D.P. & M.S. THIRUMALAI & K. RANGAN. Advanced Tamil reader. Mysore: CIIL, 1974. 2 v.

27874 RAJARAM, S. Tamil phonetic reader. Mysore: CIIL, 1972. 82p. (Its Phonetic reader series, 3)

27875 SHANMUGAM PILLAI, M. Spoken Tamil. Annamalainagar: Annamalai U., 1968-71. 2 v.

27876 ______. Tamil reader for beginners. Annamalainagar: S. Muthu Chidambaram, 1966-68. 2 v. in 1.

b. Malayalam of Kerala
i. dictionaries

27877 BAILEY, B. Malayāḷam-Inglīsh nighaṇṭu. Kottayam: Gurunadhan, 1970. 930p. (Its Publication, 12) [1st ed.: A dictionary of high and colloquial Malayalam and English. 1846.]

27878 GEORGE, M.A. Current English-Malayalam dictionary. Trichur: Current Books, 1965. 500p.

27879 GUNDERT, H. Malayalam and English dictionary. Rev. ed. Kottayam: Natl. Book Stall, 1962. 988p. [Rpt. of 1872 ed.]

27880 KARUNAKARA MENON, V. Śrīdevī Malayāḷam-Inglīs nighaṇṭu. 2nd ed. rev. & enl. Cochin: C.I.C.C. Book House, 1969. 1220p.

27881 KUNJAN PILLAI, S., ed. Malayalam lexicon: a comprehensive Malayalam-Malayalam-English dictionary on historical and philological principles. Trivandrum: U. of Kerala, 1965. 2 v.

ii. learning aids

27882 ANDREWSKUTTY, A.P. Malayalam: an intensive course. Trivandrum: Dept. of Linguistics, U. of Kerala, 1971. 141p.

27883 GEORGE, K.M. Malayalam grammar and reader. Trivandrum: the author, 1971. 342p.

27884 MOAG, R. & R. MOAG. Course in colloquial Malayalam. Milwaukee: U. of Wisconsin, 1967. 470p.

27885 ROY, C.J. Introductory Malayalam: a text book based on modern techniques of applied linguistics. Madurai: Dept. of Malayalam, Madurai U., 1976. 134p.

27886 SYAMALA KUMARI, B. Malayalam phonetic reader. Mysore: CIIL, 1972. 68p. (Its Phonetic Reader series, 2)

c. Kannada of Karnataka
i. dictionaries

27887 BÜCHER, J. A Kannada-English school dictionary. Rev. & enl. ed. by C. Watsa. Mangalore: Kanarese Mission Press, 1923. 539p. [1st pub. 1899]

27888 KITTEL, F. Kittel's Kannada-English dictionary. Rev. & enl. by M. Mariappa Bhat. Madras: U. of Madras, 1968-69. 4 v.

27889 Mysore University English-Kannada dictionary. Mysore: U. of Mysore, 1965. 1479p.

ii. learning aids

27890 BRIGHT, W., S. RAU & M. NARVEKAR. Spoken Kannada: lessons 1-12. Berkeley: Center for South Asia Studies, Inst. of Intl. Studies, U. of California, 1960. 184p.

27891 MCCORMACK, W. Kannada: a cultural introduction to the spoken styles of the language. Madison: UWiscP, 1966. 204p.

27892 RAJAPUROHIT, B.B. An intensive course in Kannada: with grammar and note on graphemics. Mysore: Dravidian Linguistic Assn., 1975. 148p. (Its Pub., 14)

27893 SCHIFFMAN, H. A reference grammar of spoken Kannada. Seattle: Dept. of Asian Languages, 1979. 161p.

27894 UPADHYAYA, U.P. Kannada phonetic reader. Mysore: CIIL, 1972. 68p.

27895 UPADHYAYA, U.P. & N.D. KRISHNAMURTY. Conversational Kannada: a microwave approach. Dharwar: Bharatiya Sahitya Mandira, 1972. 380p.

d. Telugu of Andhra Pradesh
i. dictionaries

27896 BROWN, C.P. Brauṇya Telugu nighaṇṭu: Telugu-English dictionary. Hyderabad, India: Andhra Pradesh Sahitya Akademi, 1966. 1330p. [Rpt. 1852 ed.]

27897 ______. A dictionary: English and Telugu, explaining the English idioms and phrases in Telugu with the pronunciation of English words. Freeport, NY: Books for Libraries Press, 1973. 2 v. [Rpt. 1853 ed.]

27898 PERCIVAL, P. Telugu-English dictionary. 2nd ed. Madras: Pub. Instruction Press, 1967. 487p. [Rpt. 1862 ed.]

27899 SANKARANARAYANA, P. Telugu-English dictionary. Rev. & enl. ed. Madras: V. Ramaswamy Sastrulu, 1964. 1372p. [1st ed. 1900]

ii. learning aids

27900 ARDEN, A.H. A progressive grammar of the Telugu language. 4th rev. ed. by F.L. Marler. Madras: CLS, 1955. 475p. [Rpt. 1937 ed.]

27901 KRISHNAMURTI, Bh. & P. SIVANANDA SARMA. Basic course in modern Telugu. Hyderabad: the authors, 1968. 287p.

27902 LISKER, L. Introduction to spoken Telugu. NY: American Council of Learned Societies, 1963. 345p.

27903 MASTER, A. Introduction to Telugu grammar. London: Luzac, 1947. 31p.

27904 SIVARAMA MURTY, N. Intensive course in Telugu. Trivandrum: Dept. of Linguistics, U. of Kerala, 1971. 110p.

27905 SUBRAHMANYAM, P.S. An introduction to modern Telugu. Annamalainagar: Annamalai U., 1974. 344p.

27906 VENKATESWARA SASTRY, J. Telugu phonetic reader. Mysore: CIIL, 1972. 100p. (Its Phonetic reader series, 4)

27907 VENKATESWARA SASTRY, J. & N.D. KRISHNAMURTHY. Conversational Telugu: a microwave approach. Secunderabad: M. Seshachalam, 1975. 378p.

3. Middle India
a. Marathi of Maharashtra
i. dictionaries

27908 BERNTSEN, M. & J. NIMBKAR. A basic Marathi-English dictionary. Philadelphia: South Asia Regional Studies, U. of Pennsylvania, 1975. 176p.

27909 DESHPANDE, M.K., comp. Marathi-English dictionary. 2nd rev. ed. Poona: Suvichar Prakashan Mandal, 1968. 604p.

27910 MOLESWORTH, J.T. Molsvarthakṛta Marāṭhī-Iṅgrajī śabdakośa: Molesworth's Marathi-English dictionary. 2nd ed. Poona: Shubhada-Saraswat, 1975. 920p. [Rpt. of Dictionary of Marathi and English, 1857]

27911 RANADE, N.B. The twentieth century English-Marathi dictionary. Pune: Shubhada-Saraswat, 1977. 2 v. [Rpt. 1903-16 ed., 16v.]

27912 SARMUKADAM, M.S. New standard dictionary: Marathi-English-Marathi. Bombay: Keshav Bhikaji Dhawale, 1970. 2 v., 1300p.

27913 VAZE, S.G. Aryabhushan school dictionary: Marathi-English. 11th ed. Poona: Aryabhushan Press, 1962. 577p. [Rpt. 1911 ed.]

27914 VIRKAR, H.A. The popular modern dictionary: English-English-Marathi. 2nd rev. & enl. ed. Bombay: Educ. Pub. Co., 1965. 912p.

ii. learning aids

27915 BERNTSEN, M. & J. NIMBKAR. Advanced Marathi reader: texts, vocabulary and notes. Philadelphia: South Asia Regional Studies, U. of Pennsylvania, 1975. 2 v., 79, 78p.

27916 ______. Intermediate Marathi reader. Philadelphia: South Asia Regional Studies, U. of Pennsylvania, 1975. 2 v., 45, 66p.

27917 ______. Marathi reference grammar. Philadelphia: South Asia Regional Studies, U. of Pennsylvania, 1975. 206p.

27918 DAS GUPTA, B.B. Marathi self-taught. Calcutta: Das Gupta Prakashan, 1967. 180p.

27919 KAVADI, N.B. & F.C. SOUTHWORTH. Spoken Marathi, book 1: first year intensive course. Philadelphia: UPaP, 1965. 252p.

27920 LAMBERT, H.M. Marathi language course. Bombay: OUP, 1943. 301p.

27921 NAVALKAR, G.R. The student's Marathi grammar. 4th ed. Poona: Scottish Mission Press, 1925. 377p.

b. Konkani of Goa and the West Coast

27922 AIYAGAL, B.D. Konkani self taught. Bombay: Konkan Cultural Assn., 1968. 172p.

27923 DALGADO, SEBASTIÃO RODOLPHO. Diccionario Portuguez-Komkaṇī. Lisboa: Min. da Marinha e Ultramar, 1905. 905p.

27924 MAFFEI, A.F.X. A Konkani-English dictionary. Mangalore: Basel Mission Press, 1883. 12 + 157p.

c. Gujarati
i. dictionaries

27925 BELSARE, M.B. An etymological Gujarati-English dictionary. 2nd ed. rev. & enl. Ahmedabad: H.K. Pathak, 1904. 1207p.

27926 DESAI, D.M. & K.M. MEHTA. The students' modern combined dictionary: English into English and Gujarati and Gujarati into Gujarati and English. 7th enl. ed. Bombay: A.R. Sheth, 1969. 602 + 510p.

27927 DESHPANDE, P.G., ed. English-Gujarati dictionary. Vallabh Vidyanagar: Sardar Patel U., 1970. 809p.

27928 Gala's advanced dictionary: English-English-Gujarati. Ahmedabad: Gala, 1969. 1360p.

27929 OZA, S.S. The universal modern dictionary: English into English and Gujarati. 2nd ed. Bombay: A.R. Sheth, 1967. 1022p.

ii. learning aids

27930 CARDONA, G. Gujarati reference grammar. Philadelphia: UPaP, 1965. 188p.

27931 LAMBERT, H.M. Gujarati language course. Cambridge: CamUP, 1971. 309p.

27932 SHAHANI, A.T. Gujarati self-instructor. 3rd ed. Bombay: School & College Bookstall, 1965. 128p.

27933 TISDALL, W.S. A simplified grammar of the Gujarati language. NY: F. Ungar, 1961. 189p. [Rpt. 1892 ed.]

d. Oriya of Orissa
i. dictionaries

27934 BROOKS, W. Oriya-English dictionary. Rev. ed. Cuttack: Orissa Mission Press, 1908. 314p.

27935 GOSWAMI, P.D. Biswanath dictionary: English-English-Oriya, containing about 40,000 word-meanings. Berhampur: Sankar Prasad Misra, 1964. 1379p.

27936 PADHI, B.B. Bruhat Oḍiā Abhidhāna: a large Oriya dictionary. Cuttack: Friends Pub., 1964. 1305p. [Oriya-Eng.-Oriya]

27937 SUTTON, A. An Oriya dictionary. Cuttack: Orissa Mission Press, 1841-43.[v.1. English and Oriya dictionary; v.2. Oriya dictionary with Oriya synonyms; v. 3. Oriya and English dictionary]

ii. learning aids

27938 ANDERSON, A. A grammar of the Oriya language. Copenhagen: Danish Missionary Soc., 1959. 134p.

27939 MATSON, D.M. Introduction to Oriya: and The Oriya writing system. East Lansing: Asian Studies Center, Michigan State U., 1971. 2v. in 1. (Its S.A. series occ. papers, 15)

27940 MATSON, D.M. & B.P. MAHAPATRA. The Oriya language textbook series. NY: CornellUP, 1970-71. 8 v.

27941 PATTANAYAK, D.P. & G.N. DAS. Conversational Oriya. Mysore: Sulakshana Pattanayak, 1972. 243p.

4. Indus Valley and Mountain Frontier
a. Sindhi
i. dictionaries

27942 DULAMALA, B. A Sindhi-English dictionary. Karachi: Mercantile Steam Press, 1910. 262p.

27943 MEWARAM, P., comp. A new English-Sindhi dictionary. ND: Sahitya Akademi, 1971. 465p. [1st ed. 1933]

27944 SANAULLAH, Shaikh. The Mehran English-Sindhi dictionary, with pronouneations [sic], measurements, abbreviations, French phrases, idioms, singlewords for phrases, and proverbs. Sukkur: Ajaib Stores, 1967. 631p.

27945 SHAHANI, A.T. The English-Sindhi dictionary. New rev. ed. Bombay: School & College Bookstall, 1968. 916p. [Rpt. 1961 ed.]

27947 ______. The Sindhi-English dictionary. 5th rev. & enl. ed. Bombay: School & College Bookstall, 196-? 560p.

ii. learning aids

27947 ANANDRAM. The Sindhi instructor; a useful book to acquire working knowledge of Sindhi language. Rev. ed. by Mohammed Ibrahim M. Joyo. Hyderabad, Pak.: Sindhi Adabi Board, 1971. 130p. [1st ed. 1930]

27948 TRUMPP, E. Grammar of the Sindhi language, compared with the Sanskrit-Prakrit and the cognate Indian vernaculars. Osnabrück: Biblio Verlag, 1970. 540p. [Rpt. 1872 ed.]

b. Baluchi

27949 BARKER, M. ABD-AL-RAHMAN & AGIL KHAN MENGAL. A course in Baluchi. Montreal: Inst. of Islamic Studies, McGill U., 1969. 2 v.

27950 ELFENBEIN, J.H. The Baluchi language: a dialectology with texts. London: Luzac, 1966. 48p.

27951 GILBERTSON, G.W. English-Balochi colloquial dictionary. Hertford: the author, 1925. 2 v., 826p.

27952 MAYER, T.J.L. English-Biluchi dictionary. Lahore: Sh. Mubarak Ali, 1975. 219p. [1st pub. 1909]

c. Panjabi
i. dictionaries

27953 BAILEY, T.G. An English-Panjabi dictionary. Delhi: Ess Ess, 1976. 16 + 159p. [Rpt. 1919 ed.]

27954 Dictionary of the Punjabi language. Patiala: Languages Dept. Punjab U., 1970. 438p. [Rpt. 1854 ed.]

27955 HARES, W.P. An English-Punjabi dictionary. Lahore: Maktaba Mayar, 1965? 478p. [Rpt. 1929 ed.]

27956 SINGH, B.M. The Panjabi dictionary. 3rd ed. Patiala: Punjabi Language Dept., Punjabi U., 1972. 1221p. [Rpt. 1895 ed.]

ii. learning aids

27957 BAHRI, H. Teach yourself Panjabi; based on modernmost linguistic, pedagogical, and psychological methodologies. Patiala: Punjabi U., 1973. 269p.

27958 BAHRI, U.S. Introductory course in spoken Punjabi: a microwave approach to language teaching. Chandigarh: Bahri Pub., 1972. 252p. (SILL series in Indian language & linguistics, 1)

27959 BAHRI, U.S. & P.S. WALIA. Introductory Punjabi. Patiala: Dept. of Linguistics, Punjabi U., 1968. 114p.

27960 GILL, H.S. & H.A. GLEASON. A reference grammar of Punjabi. Rev. ed. Patiala: Dept. of Linguistics, Punjabi U., 1969. 317p.

27961 NEWTON, E.P. Panjabi manual and grammar. 2nd ed. Patiala: Panjabi Language Dept., Punjabi U., 1961. 521p. [1st ed. 1898]

27962 SHACKLE, C. Punjabi. London: Teach Yourself Books, 1972. 223p.

27963 TISDALL, W.S.T. A simplified grammar and reading book of the Panjabi language. NY: F. Ungar, 1961. 136p. [Rpt. 1889 ed.]

27964 VATUK, V.P. Panjabi reader: levels 1 and 2. Fort Collins: Colorado State U., 1964. 2 v.

27965 WILSON, J. Grammar and dictionary of Western Panjabi as spoken in the Shahpur district. Patiala: Language Dept., Punjab U., 1962. 279p. [Rpt. 1899 ed.]

27966 ______. Shahpur Kangri glossary, a grammar, and glossary of the dialects as spoken in Shahpur and Kangra districts. Patiala: Language Dept., Punjab U., 1962. 1 v.

d. Kashmiri: the Dardic language of Kashmir

27967 GRIERSON, G.A. A dictionary of the Kashmiri language. Calcutta: ASB, 1932. 1252p.

27968 ______. Manual of the Kashmiri language comprising grammar, phrase book and vocabularies. Oxford: OUP, 1911. 2 v.

27969 HANDOO, J. Kashmiri phonetic reader. Mysore: CIIL, 1973. 110p.

27970 KACHRU, B.B. An introduction to spoken Kashmiri: a basic course and reference manual for learning and speaking Kashmiri as a second language. Urbana: Dept. of Linguistics, U. of Illinois, 1973. 117p.

27971 ______. A reference grammar of Kashmiri. Urbana: Dept. of Linguistics, U. of Illinois, 1969. 416p.

e. Pashto of the Frontier

27972 BELLEW, H.W. A dictionary of the Pukkhto, or Pukshto, language. London: W.H. Allen, 1867. 12 + 355p.

27973 CHAVARRIA-AGUILAR, O.L. Pashto basic course. Ann Arbor: U. of Michigan, 1962. 159p.

27974 ______. Pashto instructor's handbook. Ann Arbor: U. of Michigan, 1962. 73p.

27975 ______. A short introduction to the writing system of Pushto. Ann Arbor: U. of Michigan, 1962. 22p.

27976 ENEVOLDSEN, J. An introduction to Pakhto. Copenhagen: Dansk Pathan Missions, 1968. 133p.

27977 MORGENSTIERNE, G. An etymological vocabulary of Pashto. Oslo: Norske Videnskaps-Akademie, 1927. 120p.

27978 PENZL, H. A grammar of Pashto. Washington: American Council of Learned Societies, 1955. 169p.

27979 ______. A reader of Pashto. Ann Arbor: U. of Michigan, 1962. 274p.

27980 RAVERTY, H.G. The Pushto manual. London: C. Lockwood, 1880? 257p.

27981 ROOS-KEPPEL, G.O. A manual of Pushtu. London: OUP, 1937. 310p.

27982 SHAFEEV, D.A. A short grammatical outline of Pashto. Trans. and ed. by Herbert H. Paper. Bloomington: Indiana U., 1964. 89p. (Its Res. center in anthropology, Folklore & Linguistics pub., 33)

27983 TRUMPP, E. Grammar of the Pasto or language of the Afghans. Osnabrück: Biblio-verlag, 1969. 412p. [1st ed. 1875]

5. The Ganga Plains of North India [for Hindi, see V. B. 4. above]

6. The Northeast: Bengal-Bangladesh and Assam
a. Bengali of West Bengal and Bangladesh
i. dictionaries

27984 BISWAS, S. Samsad Bengali-English dictionary. Rev. by S.C. Sengupta. Calcutta: Sahitya Samsad, 1968. 1278p.

27985 BONNERJEE, G.L. Dictionary of foreign words in Bengali. Rev. & enl. ed. by Jitendriya Bonnerjee. Calcutta: U. of Calcutta, 1968. 337p.

27986 DABBS, J.A. A short Bengali-English, English-Bengali dictionary. College Station, Texas: Texas A & M U., 1962. 173p.

27987 DEV, A.T.. Dev's concise dictionary: Bengali to English. Rev. & enl. ed. Calcutta: S.C. Mazumdar, 1968. 784p.

27988 ______. Students' favorite dictionary. (English to Bengali & English). 21st ed., rev. Calcutta: S.C. Mazumder, 1965. 1630p.

27989 MALLIK, B.P. Dictionary of the underworld argot: West Bengal and the Bhojpuri and Magahi areas of Bihar. Calcutta: Praci Bhasha Vijnan, Indian J. of Linguistics, 1976-. v. 1-.

27990 PAUL, H.C. A vocabulary of Perso-Arabic words in Bengali with illustrative examples. In Indian Linguistics 22 (1961) 116-44.

27991 SEN, S. An etymological dictionary of Bengali, c. 1000-1800 A.D. Calcutta: Eastern, 1971. 968p.

ii. learning aids

27992 ANDERSON, J.D. Manual of the Bengali language. NY: F. Ungar, 1962. 178p. [Rpt. 1928 ed.]

27993 BHATTACHARJI, S. Introduction to Bengali, part 2: introductory Bengali reader. Honolulu: EWCP, 1966. 417p.

27994 CHOWDHURY, MOFAZZAL HAIDER. Colloquial Bengali: Bengali texts with broad phonetic transcription and meaning in English. Dacca: Bengali Academy, 1966. 47 + 112p.

27995 DIMOCK, E.C. & S. BHATTACHARJI & S. CHATTERJEE. Introduction to Bengali: a basic course in spoken Bengali, with emphasis upon speaking and understanding the language. ND: Manohar Book Service, 1976. 383p. [1st pub. 1965]

27996 ISLAM, RAFIQUL. Introduction to colloquial Bengali. Dacca: Central Board for Dev. of Bengali, 1970. 164p.

27997 MACLEOD, A.G. Colloquial Bengali grammar: an introduction. 3rd ed. Calcutta: Baptist Mission Press, 1967. 97p.

27998 MAJUMDAR, A. Bengali language: historical grammar. Calcutta: KLM, 1972-73. 2 v.

27999 RAY, P.S. & MUHAMMAD ABDUL HAI & LILA RAY. Bengali language handbook. Washington, D.C.: Center for Applied Linguistics, 1966. 137p.

28000 UČIDA, N. Der Bengali-Dialekt von Chittagong: Grammatik, Texte, Wörterbuch. Wiesbaden: Harrassowitz, 1970. 160p.

b. Assamese

28001 Anglo-Assamese dictionary: a most up-to-date and authoritative dictionary comprising full range of words and phrases with their adequate and elaborate meanings in Assamese. 10th ed., rev. & enl. Gauhati: Dutta Baruah, 1965. 859 + 23p.

28002 BARUA, B.K., ed. Ahom lexicons. Gauhati: Dept. of Hist. & Antiquarian Studies in Assam, 1964. 205p.

28003 BARUA, H.C. Etymological Assamese words and idiomatic phrases done into English. Ed. by Anandarama Baruva. Jorhat: Barkataki Co., 1941. 1030p.

28004 ______. Hemakośa, the Assamese-English dictionary. 3rd ed. Sibsagar: Barakataki Co., 1955. 1030p.

28005 BARUA, M.K., ed. Chandrakānt abhidhān. 2nd ed. Gauhati: Gauhati U., 1964. 1045p. [1st ed. 1932; Assamese-Assamese-English dictionary]

28006 GOSWAMI, G.C. Introduction to Assamese phonology. Poona: DCPRI, 1966. 160p. (Its Monograph series)

28007 SHARMA, M.M. Assamese for all, or Assamese self-taught. Jorhat: Asam Sahitya Sabha, 1963. 123p.

7. Nepal
a. Nepali: an Indo-Aryan language

28008 CLARK, T.W. Introduction to Nepali: a first year language course. London: SOAS, 1976. 421p. [1st pub. 1963]

28009 HARI, A.M. Conversational Nepali. Kathmandu: Summer Inst. of Linguistics & Inst. of Nepal Studies, Tribhuvan U., 1971. 599p.

28010 JOSHI, A.B. Nepali thru English. Kathmandu: Himalayan Pioneer Pub., 1963. 169p.

28011 KARKI, T.B. & C.K. SHRESTHA. Basic course in spoken Nepali. Kathmandu: Karki, 1974. 233p.

28012 PRADHAN, P.M. & N.M. PRADHAN. New standard dictionary, English-Nepali. Rev. new ed. Kalimpong: Bhagyalaxmi Prakashan, 1970. 830p. [Prev. ed. The standard dictionary, English-Nepali, 1961]

28013 RANA, G. & B.A. VISHARAD. Nepali-English dictionary. Darjeeling: Shyam Bros., 1968. 302p.

28014 SCHMIDT, R.L. A Nepali conversation manual. Philadelphia: Inst. of South Asia Regional Studies, U. of Pennsylvania, 1968. 113 + 26p.

28015 TURNER, R.L. A comparative and etymological dictionary of the Nepali language.... Comp. by D.R. Turner. London: Routledge & K. Paul, 1965. 923p. [1st pub. 1931]

8. Newari: a Tibeto-Burman language

28016 HALE, M. & A. HALE. Vocabulary of the Newari language. Kirtipur, Nepal: Summer Inst. of Linguistics & Inst. of Nepal Studies, Tribhuvan U., 1971. 80p. (Comparative vocabularies of Nepal)

28017 ISHWARA NANDA, S. & J.N. MASKEY & A. HALE. Conversational Newari. Kathmandu: Summer Inst. of Linguistics & Inst. of Nepal Studies, Tribhuvan U., 1971. 255p.

THE INDEXES

Author Index

Aal, Ingrid, 08968
Aalto, Penti, 03637
Abbas, Khwaja Ahmad, 13413, 13576, 13605
Abbas, M.B.A., 17338
Abbas, Rabeya, 18124
Abbas, S. Zia, 18201
Abbas, Saiyid Asghar, 17713, 17860
Abbasayulu, Y.B., 19784, 19792
Abbasi, Mustafa Zaman, 25654
Abbi, Behari L., 15703
Abbott, A., 10607
Abbott, Freeland, 07674, 17392, 17467, 18097
Abbott, J., 22440
Abbott, John, 02124
Abbott, Justin Edwards, 06744-7, 08425-6, 08431, 08448
ʿAbd al-Ghani, Muhammad, 02519, 07688
ʿAbd al-Laṭīf Bhitāʾī, Shāh (1689-1752), 08671, 08679, 08680
Abd-er-Razzak, 06218
Abdel-Aziz, Mahmoud, 13787
Abduhu, G. Rasool, 10641
Abdul Ali, A.F.M., 08316, 20691, 24180
Abdul Hamid, 09762, 22921
Abdul Haye, Chowdhry, 20634
Abdul Husain, 21847
Abdul Latif (1828-1893), 24332
ʿAbdul Qādir bin-Muluk Shāh. *See* al-Badāonī
Abdul Wadud, Wali of Swat, 23048
ʿAbdulhaʾī ibn Fakhruddīn al-Hasanī, 07404
Abdullah, Abu, 25444, 25445
Abdullah, Mohammad, 25584
Abdullah, Mohammad, Sheikh (1905-), 12081, 23183, 23188
Abdullah, Mohammad Mohiuddin (1953-), 25547
Abdullah, Tahrunnessa Ahmed, 25516
Abdullāh Muḥammad al-Makki al-Aṣafī al-Ulughkhanī Hajjī ad-Dabir, 06718
Abdur Rab, A.S.M., 24341
Abdur Rahim, 07579
Abdur Rahim Khan, Khan Khanan (1556-1627), 07701
Abdur Rashid, 06983, 23073
Abdur Rashid, Sheikh, 07437
Abdurrashid, Mian, 10308
Abedin, Mohammad Jainul, 25561
Abedin, Najmul, 24277, 25229
Abedin, Zainul, 25665
Abegg, Emil, 05792
Abeille, Mireille, 15907
Aberigh-Mackay, George Robert, 20662
Aberle, Eleanor Kathleen Gough. *See* Gough, Eleanor Kathleen
Abernethy, George L., 27660
Abeyagoonasekera, Justin, 18882
Abeyasinghe, Tikiri, 08069
Abeyratna, Oscar M., 19033
Abeysinghe, Ariya, 00905, 18762
Abhedananda, Swami, 01456, 11344
Abhinavagupta, Rājānaka, 05990, 06966, 06974, 06975
Abhishiktananda, Swami. *See* Le Saux, Henri
Abhyankar, Kashinath Vasudev, 27798
Abhyankar, Keshav, 10521
Abhyankar, M.G., 13759
Abhayaratne, O.E.R., 18605, 18606, 18610
Abichandani, C.T., 22025
Abid Husain, Syed, 15848
Abidi, S.A.H., 07689
Abidi, Sartaj A., 00092, 27597
Abraham, C.E., 08954
Abraham, C.M., 19444, 20081, 20086, 20094
Abraham, J.M., 03294
Abraham, M. Francis, 13673
Abraham, P.M., 15525
Abrahamson, Julia, 21884
Abrams, Tevia, 03029
Abrol, Mridula, 09408
Abu Abraham, 13114
Abu Baker, M., 16430
Abu Imam, 00577
Abū Raihān Muhammad ibn Ahmad al-Bīrūnī. *See* al-Bīrūnī
Abu Taleb Khan, Mirza, 11870
Abū-al-Fazl ibn Mubārak, 07468-70
Abuava, Jose V., 26109
Abul Hasanat, 12138, 12139
Abul Hashim, 25150
Abul Khair, Mohammad, 09384
Academy of Comparative Philosophy and Religion, Belgaum, 20552
Academy of Educational Research, Karachi, 18183
Acharji, Nilima, 15652
Acharya, B.T., 06488
Acharya, Hemalata. *See* Acharya, Hemlata
Acharya, Hemalatha. *See* Acharya, Hemlata
Acharya, Hemlata, 01993, 01994, 21419, 21821
Acharya, K.P., 02315
Acharya, K.R., 13526, 19670
Acharya, M.A., 21895
Acharya, Meena, 26272
Acharya, Paramananda, 06694, 06900
Acharya, Prasanna Kumar, 03149, 03150, 03155, 06103-4
Acharya, Ram, 15397, 15448
Acharyya, Nagendra Nath, 07192
Achaya, K.T., 14904
Achyuta Menon, Chelnat, 08228
Achyuthan, Mavelikara, 04508
Ackerley, Joe Randolph, 11930
Ackerman, Charles, 26584, 26585
Acworth, Harry Arbuthnot, 08458a
Adam, Keith, 27047
Adam, Leonard, 26036, 26190
Adam, William, 10568, 10569, 24824
Adamo, Pierre, 01905
Adams, Charles J., 01101, 17468
Adams, John, 00864, 00867-8, 10930, 11056, 12300, 20305, 21991
Adarsh, B.K., 16959
Adas, Michael, 09458, 26877
Adaval, Niti, 05406
Addison, James T., 11518
Adel, Daljit Sen, 14026
Adeney, M., 19102
Adenwalla, Minoo, 10255
Adhikari, Gangadhar M., 10039, 13223
Adhya, Govinda Lal (1924-), 04346
Adiceam, Emmanuel, 19286
Adiceam, Marguerite E., 01739, 01851
Adie, W.A.C., 11986
Adiga, M. Gopala Krishna, 20571
Adigal, Maraimalai. *See* Vedachalam Pillai, Nagapattinam R.S.
Adikaram, E.W., 05041
Adiseshiah, Malcolm S., 16621, 16385, 19469, 19476
Adithiya, Lala, 27150
Administrative Staff College of India, Hyderabad, 19770
Adriel, Jean, 16745
Advani, B.T., 13171
Advani, Gopal, 22486
Advani, K.R., 21889
Advani, Kalyan B., 08672, 08673
Advani, L.K., 13337, 13527, 13606
Adwani, Nirmala H. (1946-), 22128
Adyanthaya, N. Mahalinga, 02867

Afroz, Qamar, 17292
Afsaruddin, Mohammad, 18074, 25528, 25572
Afzal, M. Rafique, 17448
Afzal, Mohammad, 17783, 17923, 22501
Afzal Khan, Mohammad, 23116
Agarawala, Ram Avatar, 00463, 03401
Agarkar, A.J., 03030
Agarwal, Balmukund, 14102
Agarwal, Bhushan Kumar, 22857
Agarwal, D.C., 22216
Agarwal, G.C., 15382
Agarwal, Govind Ram, 26303
Agarwal, Hans Raj, 02463
Agarwal, Hari Om, 12084
Agarwal, K.K., 23276
Agarwal, Lalit P., 16174
Agarwal, Madan Gopal, 15996
Agarwal, Prem Chandra, 20881, 24033
Agarwal, R.D., 15613, 15733
Agarwal, S.L., 15569
Agarwal, Shriman Narayan. *See* Shriman Narayan
Agarwal, Urmila, 01767, 06880
Agarwal, Usha, 07611
Agarwal, Vinod K., 15289
Agarwala, A.P., 27248, 27356-7
Agarwala, Amar Narain, 11111, 16549
Agarwala, Balmukand Rangilal, 12821
Agarwala, G.C., 03759
Agarwala, Manmohan Lal, 10272
Agarwala, N.N., 10522
Agarwala, P.N., 13840
Agarwala, Sri Krishan, 12822
Agarwala, S.N., 01016, 14141-2, 14497, 15908, 23343, 23424
Agarwala, V.S., 01845
Agarwala, Viney K., 02696
Agarwalla, Nursindas, 12435
Agashe, Diwakar (1927-), 21577
Agesthialingom, S., 02353, 02359-60, 02548, 05230, 19371
Aggarwal, Arjun Prakash, 15570, 15658-9
Aggarwal, Jagdish Chand, 10551, 16386, 16400, 16415, 16617
Aggarwal, M.R., 12247
Aggarwal, Narinder K., 02640
Aggarwal, Partap C., 22095-8, 22756
Aggarwal, S.N., 12411
Aggarwala, Dharma Vira, 16377
Aggarwala, Rama Nand, 09554, 12799
Agha Mirza Beg, Nawab Bahadur, 19611
Agnes, M., Sister, 20489
Agnew, Vijay, 00947, 09583
Agnihotri, H.L., 22644
Agnihotri, Vidyadhar, 15614, 23678, 23864
Agniveśa, 04553, 04560
Agochiya, Devendra, 15951
Agrapura, J.G., 04675
Agrarian Research and Training Institute, 18763
Agrawal. *See also* Agarwal, Aggarwala, etc.
Agrawal, A.L., 23813
Agrawal, B.L., 22129
Agrawal, B.N., 26451, 26521
Agrawal, Binod Chand, 01028, 16949-50, 22167, 22273
Agrawal, C.M., 07557
Agrawal, Dharma Pal, 00586, 03487, 03493-4, 03509, 03568
Agrawal, Hem Narayan, 25957, 25993, 26022
Agrawal, K.N., 26431
Agrawal, O.P., 03286
Agrawal, Suraj Bhan (1939-), 14642
Agrawal, Suren (1928-), 16378
Agrawal, Sushila, 10838
Agrawal, Usha, 00600-1
Agrawal, Veena, 12783
Agrawala, Prithvi Kumar, 01807, 01817, 03232, 05449, 05554
Agrawala, Rajkumari, 15930, 15973
Agrawala, S.K. (1929-), 12691
Agrawala, Ratna Chandra, 01725, 01774, 02031-2, 05582, 06855-6
Agrawala, Vasudeva Sharana, 01642, 01664, 01740, 02078, 03078, 03113, 03174, 03208, 04029-30, 04731, 05555, 05562-3, 05572, 05752-3, 05801, 05807, 05812, 06017
Agricultural Development Bank, Planning, Research, and Project Division, 26148.
Agricultural Economics Research Centre, University of Delhi, 16592
Agriculture Development Bank, Kathmandu, 26140
Agriculturists' Association, Hyderabad State, 19633
Agro-Economics Research Centre for North East India, Jorhat, 25748, 25794
Aguilar, H., 03858
Ahir, D.C., 01235-6, 12274, 16761
Ahluwalia, Aneeta, 16207
Ahluwalia, B.K., 10176, 10197-8, 12575, 12580, 13362
Ahluwalia, H.P.S., 27381
Ahluwalia, Isher Judge, 14643-4
Ahluwalia, Jasbir Singh, 22996-7
Ahluwalia, M.L., 22581, 22632
Ahluwalia, M.M., 22955
Ahluwalia, Manjeet Singh, 06683, 06731
Ahluwalia, S.P., 16607
Ahluwalia, Sagar, 19214
Ahluwalia, Shashi, 10189
Ahmad, Aijaz, 11649
Ahmad, Aijazuddin, 00219
Ahmad, Aquiel, 17244
Ahmad, Bashir, 17379
Aḥmad, Bashīr al-Dīn Maḥmūd, Hazrat Mirzā (1889-), 11519-20
Ahmad, Bashiruddin Mahmud, 17836
Ahmad, Enayat, 14471, 23824, 27267
Ahmad, Imtiaz, 00752-3, 00963, 10746, 12414, 23759-60
Ahmad, Jaleel, 15175
Ahmad, Jamil-ud-Din, 10333, 10339
Ahmad, K., 25469
Ahmad, Kabir Uddin, 12158
Ahmad, Kamaluddin, 18067
Ahmad, Karuna, 13101, 15531, 16442
Ahmad, Kazi Said Uddin, 12239, 27110-1
Ahmad, Khurshid, 18102-3
Ahmad, Laiq, 07558
Ahmad, M.B., 07058
Ahmed, M.G. Zubaid, 02520
Ahmad, M.M. Zuhuruddin, 10642
Ahmad, M. Riazuddin, 10511
Ahmad, Makhdum Tasadduq, 15750, 23103
Ahmad, Manazir, 07037
Ahmad, Mansoor, 18030
Ahmad, Masud, 17316
Ahmad, Mohammad, 17508
Ahmad, Mohiuddin, 11443, 25372
Ahmad, Muhammed Basheer, 07572
Ahmad, Muneer, 17326, 17339-40, 17377, 17441
Ahmad, Mushtaq, 13330, 17306, 17421, 17661, 17665
Ahmad, Muzaffar, 10048, 10056
Ahmad, Nazir, 07763
Ahmad, Nafis, 10340, 18002, 25159, 25287-8, 25455-6, 25562, 27111, 27307
Ahmad, Nazir, 17789, 17796, 17970, 18284
Ahmad, Naziruddin, 25165
Ahmad, Qadeeruddin, 17592
Ahmad, Qazi Kholiquzzaman, 25457
Ahmad, Qazi Mohammad, 05646
Ahmad, Qazi Shakil, 16044, 18111-4
Ahmad, Qeyamuddin, 09797, 11444
Ahmad, Rafiq, 08535, 08561, 17846
Ahmad, Rafiuddin. *See* Ahmed, Rafiuddin
Ahmad, S. Hasan, 10320
Ahmad, S. Saqhir, 22871, 22872
Ahmad, Sayed Riaz, 17469
Ahmad, Shaikh Mahmud, 18176
Ahmad, Syed Jamil, 17810
Ahmad, Tasneem, 07494, 07499
Ahmad, Zainul A., 12485
Ahmad, Zarina, 23761
Ahmad, Zeyauddin, 24155, 24156
Ahmad, Ziauddin, 10371, 17488
Ahmad Khan, M., 23081
Ahmad Khan, Muin-ud-din, 11447, 24911-2
Ahmad Khan, Syed, Sir (1817-1898), 07169, 09491, 09763 09789, 11466
Ahmad Saeed, 10372
Ahmad Shah, 07096
Ahmad Yar Khan, 22515
Ahmed, Akbar S., 17442, 18073, 02636, 23060, 23082, 23104-5, 27718
Ahmed, Badaruddin, 25411, 25412
Ahmed, Bashiruddin, 13040, 13072, 13082, 19946, 22160, 23491, 23508
Ahmed, Emajuddin, 17847, 25221
Ahmed, Fatima, 25590

Ahmed, Feroz, 18098, 22523
Ahmed, Giasuddin, 25529
Ahmed, Irshad, 25370
Ahmed, Jalaluddin, 18276
Ahmed, Manazir, 09111
Ahmed, Manzooruddin, 17393, 17516-7
Ahmed, Mohiuddin, 25590
Ahmed, Moudud, 25151
Ahmed, Munir D., 18224
Ahmed, Nasiruddin, 00615
Ahmed, Noazesh, 25373, 27300
Ahmed, Rafiq, 18026
Ahmed, Rafiuddin, 24910
Ahmed, Rakibuddin, 24521, 25359
Ahmed, Raquibuddin, 25256
Ahmed, Salahuddin, 25573, 25606
Ahmed, Shahid Uddin, 25475
Ahmed, Sheikh, 17380
Ahmed, Sufia, 24647
Ahmed, Uta, 27661
Ahmed, Zahir, 19612
Ahmed Ali, 26803, 26804
Ahmed Ali, M., 10686
Ahmednagar College, 21593
Ahrens, Heinz, 00737, 25303, 25329
Ahsan Ullah, 22493
Ahsanullah, Mohammad, 25431
Ahuja, A.M., 07671
Ahuja, B.N., 16831, 16861
Ahuja, Kanta, 15083, 22026
Ahuja, Man Mohan Singh, 16217
Ahuja, N.D., 07671
Ahuja, N.D., 08630
Ahuja, Ram, 20798-9, 23974
Ahuja, Roshan Lal, 16455
Ahuja, S.P., 15398
Aijazuddin, F.S., 08695, 22564
Aijazuddin Ahmad, 27233
Aikara, Jacob, 20160
Airan, Judson William, 16401, 16485
Aitchison, Charles Umpherston, Sir, 09134, 09356
Aitchison, J.E.T., 23208
Aiyagal, Baindoor Deorai, 27922
Aiyangar, A.N.K., 06453
Aiyappan, A., 00664, 02135, 05494, 19372, 20105, 20144, 20153
Aiyar, Jayanthi S., 13651
Aiyar, R.P., 09630
Aiyar, Sadashiv Prabhakar, 12012, 12350, 12516, 13009, 13083, 13550
Aiyar, Shankar Arjun, 03151
Aiyer, A.K. Yegna Narayan, 14845
Aiyer, H.R., 15391
Ajudhia Parshad, Dewan, 22582
Ajwani, Lalsing Hazarising, 02612
Akanda, S.A., 25166
Akbar, Muhammad, 07573, 08536
Akhmedzyanov, A.V., 19870
Akhtar, Abdul Hafeez, 10358, 11482, 17998
Akhtar, J., 22886
Akhtar, Jamila, 18198
Akhtar, Jamna Das, 05802, 17422
Akhtar, M.S., 08827
Akhtar, Rafique, 10373
Akhtar, Sardar Mohammad, 17811, 17823, 22873
Akhtar Aman, 17662
Akhtar Zaman, 17583
Akhter, Gholam Morshed, 25530-1, 25549, 25595
Akhter, Mohammad Saleem, 05943
Akhter, Nilufar, 25332
Akhter, Roushan, 25523
Aklujkar, Ashok, 02496, 05989, 06037
Akram, Chaudhuri Muhammad, 17978
Al-George, Sergiu, 05197
Alagh, Y.K., 14744
Alagh, Yoginder K., 15192, 15194
Alagiyavanna Mukaveti, 08104-8
Alam, Ahmed Fakhrul, 25257
Alam, Bilquis Ara, 25230
Alam, Mahmudul, 25400
Alam, Muzaffar, 08402
Alam, Shah Manzoor, 19834, 19835
Alamgir, Mohiuddin, 12231, 25289-91, 25314
Alamgir, Muhiuddin Khan, 25315
Alamgir, Susan Fuller, 25517
Alauddin, Mohammad, 25579
Alavi, Hamza, 14228, 17731, 17931, 17941, 22703, 22841, 22874-5, 25382
Alavi, Rafi Ahmad, 00441, 07405
Alayev, L.B., 27419
Alberuni. *See* al-Bīrūnī
Albuquerque, Affonso de, 07858
Alder, Garry J., 07973, 09395, 23157
Alekseev, G.V., 03638
Alemchibe, M., 26515
Alemenas-Lipowsky, Angeles J., 15868
Alexander, Alexander, 18300
Alexander, Horace Gundry, 09909, 10404, 10490, 10760
Alexander, Kanjirathara Chandy, 15255, 15631, 19304, 20020-1, 20033-4, 20055, 20114, 20145
Alexander, Michael, 22583
Alexander, Mithrapuram K., 13402, 13414
Alexander, P.C., 15335
Alexander, Paul, 18697, 18764
Alexander, T.M., 14866
Alexandrowicz, Charles Henry, 00916, 12326, 12532, 16557
Ali, Abdul, 25351-2
Ali, Abdullah Yusuf, 07585, 09026
Ali, Ahmad, 02538-9
Ali, Ahmed, 11650
Ali, Ansaf, 17837
Ali, B. Sheik, 08162
Ali, Chaudhri Muhammad, 10288, 17478-9
Ali, Fawzia, 19108
Ali, Hamid, 09260
Ali, Hasan, 24157
Ali, Imran, 22645, 22659
Ali, Kausar, 00174
Ali, Mansoor, 14368
Ali, Mehrunnisa, 12120, 14085, 17674, 17749, 17753
Ali, Mohamed, Maulana (1878-1931), 09798-9
Ali, Muhammad Mohar, 24915
Ali, Qazi Azher, 25231, 25374, 25548
Ali, Rahman, 03522
Ali, S. Amjad, 18250, 18255, 18277
Ali, S. Muzafer, 05751
Ali, Salim A., 27024-6
Ali, Shaukat, 17286, 17650, 17770, 27662
Ali, Syed Anwer, 17476
Ali, Syed Mohammed, 25194
Ali, Syed Murtaza, 07328
Ali, Tariq, 17307
Ali, Ahmed, 17341
Ali Akbar, Mohammad, 25574
Ali Ashraf, 16102
ʿAlī ibn Ḥamīd, al-Kūfī, 04158
Ali Mohammad, 14757, 23590, 23871, 27233
Ali Muhammad Khan, 08340, 08341
Alim, Abdul, 25335, 25360, 25446
Alkazi, E., 17205
All Ceylon Buddhist Congress. National Development Enquiry Committee, 18920
All India Adult Education Conferences, 16670-2
All-India Colloquium on Ethical and Spiritual Values as the Basis of National Integration, Bombay (1966-1967), 12386
All India Conference of Linguists (1970), 02335
All India Conference of Linguists (1972), 02336
All India Conference on the Role of Cooperatives in the Development of Hill Areas and Hill States, New Delhi (1976), 14712
All India Congress Committee, 13164, 13433, 14437
All-India Coordinated Rice Improvement Project, 14864
All-India directory of welfare agencies for the blind, 16175
All India Dogri Writers Conference, 23252
All India Education Board, 10630
All-India Institute of Local Self-Government, Bombay, 12975, 21152
All-India Juvenile Literary Conference, Mysore (1975), 17007
All-India Language Conference, Calcutta (1958), 12487
All India Muslim League, 10273
All-India National Education Conference, Wardha (1937), 10631, 10636
All-India Newspaper Editors' Conference, 16880
All India Panchayat Parishad. Study and Research Unit, 19238
All India Ramayana Conference, Trivandrum (1973), 04709

All India Seminar on Church in India Today, Bangalore (1969), 16815
All India Seminar on Cooperative Industrial Estates, Kolhapur (1964), 15336
All India Seminar on Environmental Pollution, Bombay (1975), 16236
All India Seminar on Family Planning Problems in India, Bombay (1972), 16283
All-India Seminar on Industrial Cooperative Banks, Sholapur (1965), 14720
All India Seminar on Sociology for India: Teaching and Research, Mount Abu (1964), 15702
All-India Seminar on the Development of Backward Regions, Sardar Patel University (1972), 21716
All India Seminar on the Indian Family in the Change and Challenge of the Seventies, New Delhi (1971), 15900
All India Workshop on Health Education in Hospital Services, Chandigarh (1977), 16357
All Pakistan Sociology Seminar, Dacca (1963), 18074
All Parties Conference (1928), 10125
Allahabad University Enquiry Committee (1953), 23905
Allan, J.A., 23618
Allana, Gulam Ali, 10374, 18261
Allchin, Bridget, 03488, 03495, 03559-60, 03567
Allchin, Frank Raymond, 00340, 03495, 03569, 03621, 03670-1, 06537, 08790-1, 08800
Allen, Charles, 11949, 11950
Allen, George Francis, 04974
Allen, Michael, 26318
Allen, N.J., 26205, 25912, 26294
Allen, Richard F., 06375
Allen, Sheila, 26892
Allen, William Sidney, 05175
Alles, Anthony Christopher, 18432, 18524
Allison, Adrienne, 25353
Allison, Howard C., 18189
Almeida, José Conceiçao, 21071, 21084
Alphonso-Karkala, John B., 02417, 05440, 11703, 11710
Alsdorf, Ludwig, 00029, 01144, 01563, 05246
Alse, A.J., 20517
Altbach, Philip Geoffrey, 13093-5, 13198, 16486-7, 16517, 16897, 21185, 21594, 23906
Altekar, Anant Sadashiv, 00951, 01029, 04098, 04253, 04509, 05654, 06205, 06680
Alter, James P., 23910
Aluwihare, Richard, 01934
Alvi, Shahiruddin, 17942
Alvi, Shum Sun Nisa, 21992
Alwis, N.A.W.A.T., 27700-1
Amalorpavadass, D.S., 16787, 16806
Amani, K.Z., 23269
Amarasingham, M., 18661
Amarjit Singh, 15180
Amatya, Jagdish Man Singh, 27399
Amatya, Soorya Lal, 26149
Ambannavar, Jaipal P., 14171, 21205
Ambasht, Nawal Kishore, 24204
Ambashthya, B.P., 07664
Ambedkar, Bhimrao Ramji, 04440, 04875, 09587, 09910, 10341, 10771-5, 11148, 11163, 12275, 12504, 21115, 21413
Ambedkar, V.N., 16091
Ambekar, G.R., 22474
Ambirajan, Srinivasa, 10922-3, 11012, 14571, 19247
Ambrose, Kay, 02946
Ameer Ali, A.C.L., 18718
Ameer Ali, Maulavi Saiyid, 09790-1
Ameerul Huq, M., 25420, 25540
Amerasinghe, Anthony Ranjit Bevis, 18782
Amerasinghe, Chittharanjan Felix, 18363
Amerasinghe, Nihal, 18735-7
American Geographical Society of New York. Library, 26984
Ames, Michael M., 00621, 18932, 18996, 19004, 19013-4, 24187
Amin, K.N., 21891
Amin, R.K., 21746, 21853-4
Amin, Razia Khan, 25645
Amin, Ruhul, 25550
Aminul Islam, A.K.M., 25199, 25232
Aminul Islam, M., 25336, 25375
Aminullah, 25183
Aminur Rahman, A.H.M., 25233
Aminuzzaman, Salahuddin M., 25234
Amir Ali, Hashim, 22099
Amīr Khusrau, Hazrat, 07027
Amirthan, Samuel, 16788
Amjad Ali, 27571
Amjad, Rashid, 18020
Amladi, D.R., 21485, 27204
Amonker, R.G., 16284
Amrik Singh, 16487, 16537
Amrit Kaur, Rajkumari, 15734
Amrita, 11800
Amrita, K., 11385
Amrita Pritam, 23018-9
Amunugama, Sarath, 18611, 18738, 18889, 18921, 19056
Amur, G.S., 17078, 17147, 20565
Anacker, Stefan, 05109
Anand, Balwant Singh, 06984, 08616, 08639, 10491
Anand, Indira, 07811
Anand, J.C., 22689
Anand, J.P., 18565, 19103
Anand, Jagjit Singh, 13962
Anand, Kewal Krishnan, 16372
Anand, Kulwant, 15918
Anand, M., 23412
Anand, M.M., 15399
Anand, Mulk Raj, 00602, 02918, 02932, 02995, 03114, 03419, 03130, 03295, 05509, 05544, 06813, 06881, 07784, 08696, 11581, 11801, 12486, 17105-6, 17185, 23021, 26967
Anand, Satyapal, 16673
Anand, Sushila, 22583
Anand, V.S., 16538
Anand, Vijay Kumar, 26556
Anand Krishna, 07728, 07750, 08516, 17184
Ananda, Peter, 27694
Anandaghana, 08826
Ānandamayī, Mā, 24902-3
Anandappe, J.B. Clinton, 19041
Anandaranga Pillai, 07926
Ānandatīrtha. *See* Madhva
Ānandavardhana, 05984
Anandram, 27947
Anant, Santokh Singh, 23688
Anantapadmanaban, N., 19426
Anantapadmanabhan, Kavasseri Narayana, 05363
Anantaraman, K.N., 19739, 19785
Anantha Krishna Iyer, L. Krishna, 20056, 20067-8, 20115, 20361-2
Anantha Murthy, T.S., 11405
Anantha Murthy, U.R., 20566
Ananthakrishna Sastry, R., 05813
Ananthalwar, M.A., 03156
Ananthanarayanan, N., 11419
Anantharangachar, N.S., 06443
Andarawewa, Asoka B., 18687
Andersen, Walter Korfitz, 13265, 13279, 23330, 23907
Anderson, A., 27938
Anderson, Allan Grant, 26805
Anderson, Bernard, 03589
Anderson, David D., 18262, 18263
Anderson, Dines, 27810-1
Anderson, J.D., 27992
Anderson, Jack, 12159
Anderson, Jon, 23107
Anderson, M.M., 02079
Anderson, Philip, 08379
Anderson, R.L., 02080
Anderson, Robert Glenn, 25354
Anderson, Robert S., 17267, 25195
Anderson, Robert T., 19848
Andhare, Shridhar K., 08492, 08507-8
Andhra Pradesh. Administrative Reforms Committee, 19700
Andhra Pradesh. Backward Classes Commission, 19785
Andhra Pradesh. Bureau of Economics and Statistics, 19738, 19767-8, 27171
Andhra Pradesh. Committee on Nationalised Textbooks, 19857
Andhra Pradesh. Committee on the Working of the Social Welfare Hostels in Andhra Pradesh, 19849
Andhra Pradesh. Committee on Welfare of Scheduled Tribes, 19803-4
Andhra Pradesh Congress Committee, 19728
Andhra Pradesh. Dept. of Town Planning, 19836-7
Andhra Pradesh. Education Dept., 19858
Andhra Pradesh. General Administration (Elections) Dept., 19671-2

Andhra Pradesh. Health, Housing, and Municipal Administration Dept., 19838
Andhra Pradesh. High Power Committee on Panchayati Raj, 19708
Andhra Pradesh. Irrigation Committee, 19739
Andhra Pradesh. Joint Select Committee on the Andhra Pradesh Industrial Relations Commission Bill, 19776
Andhra Pradesh. Joint Select Committee on the Andhra Pradesh Land Reforms, 19758
Andhra Pradesh. Joint Select Committee on the Andhra Pradesh Tenancy Bill (1970), 19756-7
Andhra Pradesh. Laws, statutes, 19709
Andhra Pradesh. Official Language Review Committee, 19653
Andhra Pradesh. Panchayati Raj Dept., 19710
Andhra Pradesh. Planning and Cooperation Dept., 19725-6, 19777
Andhra Pradesh. Planning Dept., 19727
Andhra Pradesh. Rayalaseema Development Board. Sub-Committee on Irrigation, 19740
Andhra Pradesh. State Seminar on Educational Planning and Administration, Hyderabad (1970), 19859
Andhra Pradesh. Village Officers Enquiry Committee, 19711
Andhra University, 01871
Andiappon, P., 15532
Andors, Ellen B., 26223
André de Sainte Marie, Father, 20177
Andrews, Charles Freer, 09631, 09934, 10643, 10761, 11528, 11555, 22980, 23061
Andrews, Edith Wall, 18051
Andrews, F.H., 03079
Andrews, Robert Douglas, 12749
Andrewskutty, A.P., 27882
Andronov, Mikhail Sergeevich, 02354, 02357-8, 02549, 19233, 27867
Andrus, James Russell, 17884
Angadi, S.M., 06547, 06548
Anglo-Indian Survey Committee, Calcutta, 24590
Angrish, A.C., 14589
Angusthy, K.T., 26150
Anikeev, Nikolai Petrovich, 16692
Anis Nagi, 18264
Anisuzzaman, Mohammad, 17342, 17651, 25487
Anjaneyulu, D., 19885-6, 19903
Anjaneyulu, V., 15655
Anjaria, Jashwantrai Jayantilal, 14957
Anna Rao, C., 19871
Annadurai, C.N., 19215-9
Annamalai, E., 05434, 12505, 19552
Annamalai University, 19477
Annand, A. McKenzie, 23035
Anniah Gowda, H.H., 17093, 17118
Annigeri, A.M., 06648
Annotated bibliography on the economic history of India (1500 A.D. to 1947 A.D.), 00236, 10853
Annual bibliography of Indian Archaeology, 03060, 27676
Ansari, A., 22239
Ansari, A.S. Bazmee, 06797, 11445
Ansari, Abdul Wahid, 24158
Ansari, Dagmar, 17040-2, 27842-3
Ansari, Ghaus, 23762
Ansari, Hasan Nishat, 07038
Ansari, J.H., 20157
Ansari, M.A., 27843
Ansari, Mohammed Azher, 07775
Ansari, Muhammad Azhar, 07821
Ansari, Mukhtar Ahmad, 10127
Ansari, Nasim, 14874, 22783
Ansari, Zainuddin Dawood, 03672
Ansari, Zoe, 07122
Anstey, Vera Powell, 10857
Āṇṭāl, 06293
Antes, Peter, 02173
Anthonisz, B.V.A., 18576
Anthonisz, Richard Gerald, 08082
Anthony, Frank, 15861
Anthropological bibliography of South Asia, 00612
Antoine, Robert, 04710, 05364
Anton, Rita, 19523
Antonova, Koka Alexandrovna, 00163
Antrobus, Hinson Allan, 25722-3
Antulay, Abdur Rahman, 12835, 12925
Anuruddha, 06160
Anwar, Asifa, 26079
Anwar, Abdul Aziz, 17932, 18033-4, 18042
Anwar, Muhammad, 10359, 26919, 27687
Anwar, Muhammad Rafi, 17544
Anwar, Mumtaz A., 27663
Anwari, Khawaja Arshad Mubeen, 18104
Anwarul Haq, M., 22142

Anwer Azeem, 13963
Ao, P. Shilu, 15793
Aphale, Champa, 21543
Appa Rao, Ponangi Sri Rama, 05294
Appa Rao, T., 19116, 19701
Appadorai, Angadipuram, 06243, 09530-1, 10217, 10228, 12013, 13010-1, 13172, 13691-2, 25975
Appadurai, Arjun, 00793, 01877, 06263
Appadurai, R.R., 18682, 18686, 18688
Appasamy, Aiyadurai Jesudasen, Bishop, 05828, 26820, 22981
Appasamy, Jaya, 11781, 11802, 17186-9
Appaswamy, Paul, 10693
Appleby, Paul Henson, 12606
Appuswami, P.N., 06585
Aprem, Metropolitan, 20178-9
Apte, Bhalchandra Krishna, 08263, 08278
Apte, D.P., 21558
Apte, M.D., 08413, 21320
Apte, Mahadeo L., 16832, 21633, 21637-8
Apte, P.P., 04252, 04775
Apte, Shivaram Shankar, 08443
Apte, Usha Mukund, 01040
Apte, Vinayak M., 03995, 04463
Apte, Vaman Shivaram, 27791
Apurvananda, Swami, 11294
Aquerone, J.B., 07859
Aquila Kiani, 17652, 18052, 18137
Aquique, Mohammad, 00510
Ara, Matsuo, 07172
Arachi, J.X., 27027
Arai, Toshikazu, 06790
Aram, M., 26531
Aran, Lydia, 03447
Araneta, Enrique, 26786
Aranjaniyil, Augustine G., 01391
Arapura, John Geeverghese, 11432
Arasaratnam, Sinnappah, 00379, 07616, 08055, 08065-6, 08083-8, 08187, 08191-2, 18433, 18473, 19042, 26881
Arasarkadavil, Denis John, 20161
Aravaanan, K.P., 00073
Aravamuthan, T.G., 01808, 03395
Arberry, Arthur John, 02262, 05937-8
Archbold, William Arthur Jobson, 09073
Archer, John Clark, 08567
Archer, Mildred, 03295, 11792-4, 11830, 11974-6
Archer, William George, 01775, 03265-6, 03279, 03350, 03373, 08463, 08476-7, 08493, 08517, 08697-9, 08719, 08733, 08750, 11782, 11793-6, 20913, 20928, 20940, 20983-4
Arden, Albert H., 27868, 27900
Arden, John, 03036
Ardeshir, A.C., 07729, 07764-5
Argal, R., 12962
Argov, Daniel, 09679, 10256
Arguelles, Jose, 05869
Arguelles, Miriam, 05869
Arickal, George, 24034
Arif, Mohammad Taufiqul, 25549
Aris, Michael, 07369, 26436
Ariyadasa, K.D., 18943
Ariyapala, M.B., 06135
Ariyaratne, A.T., 18883
Arjan Singh, 15085, 22775-5a
Arles, J.P., 15806
Armelin, Indumati, 04276
Armstrong, Ruth, 27048
Arnim, Bernd von, 14183
Arnold, David, 19142, 19163-4, 19326
Arnold, Edwin, Sir, 04625, 04659, 06047, 06079, 07244, 09121
Arnold, Thomas W., Sir, 07711
Arnold, Thomas Walker, 05932
Arokiaswami, M., 00406, 04142, 04202, 19294
Aronson, Alex, 25026
Arora, A.C., 22602
Arora, D.R., 16574
Arora, J.S.B., 12160

Arora, Kamla, 16456
Arora, N.D., 13332, 13551
Arora, R.C., 14758-9, 15018
Arora, Radhe Sham, 15230
Arora, Raj Kumar, 22970
Arora, Ramesh Kumar, 12607, 12640, 14400, 15223, 22117
Arora, Satish Kumar, 13060, 13084
Arora, U.P., 15100
Arquivo historico do Estado da Índia, 07852
Arquivo portugues oriental, 07853
Arshad, A.D., 07690
Arshad, A.R., 22873
Arshad, Muhammad, 07406
Arthur, W. Brian, 25273
Artists' Handicrafts Association of Cholamandal Artists' Village, 17195
Artola, George Thomas, 02464
Arulappa, R., 04497
Arumuga Mudaliar, S., 06277, 06285
Arumugam, M., 13186, 14489
Arumugam, Sanmugam, 18699
Arumugham, B., 19564
Arunachal, 27346
Arunachalam, B., 21209, 27197
Arunachalam, Kadalangudi Palaniyappa Pillai, 00074
Arunachalam, M., 02559, 04744-5, 06534
Arunachalam, Ponnambalam, Sir, 18342, 19028
Arya, H.P.S., 15057
Arya, Harish Chandra, 17730
Arya, Satya Prakash, 23911-2, 23933-7
Arya, Usharbudh, 01480, 05261, 26775
Aryal, Deepak Kumar, 27465, 27483
Aryal, Krishna Raj, 26304
Aryan, K.C., 01802, 03351, 03420, 08734
Aryan, Subhashini, 01802, 03339
Asaduzzaman, Mohammad, 25384
Asafuddawla, M., 25666
Asboe, W., 23209
Aschwin, Lippe, 03221
Ascoli, Frank David, 08903, 22478
Asgar Khan, M. Ali, 09986
Ashby, Philip H., 16706, 23913
Ashe, Geoffrey, 09955
Asher, Frederick M., 05608
Asher, Ronald E., 02560, 19127, 19565-7, 20199, 27869
Ashfaq Ali, Syed, 22188, 22254
Ashfaq Naqvi, Syed, 05549
Ashley-Brown, William, 21625
Ashraf, Ali, 12963, 24731
Ashraf, Khalid, 23083-4, 23106
Ashraf, K.M., 09764
Ashraf, Muhammad, 10461, 17381
Ashraf, Mohammad, Kunwar, 07077, 09459
Ashraf, Shaukat, 14109
Ashraf, Syed Ali, 02656, 25646
Ashta, Mahesh Chandra, 11040
Ashton, Leigh, 03066
Ashton, Martha Bush, 03026-7
Ashton, Roger, 02734
Asia Foundation, 17190
Asian-African Conference, Bandung, Java (1955), 13737-8
Asian Development Bank, 26161
Asian Recorder, 11982, 27598
Asian Relations Conference, New Delhi, 13739
Asian social science bibliography, 00613, 11983
Asiatic Society, Calcutta, 27599, 27600
Asiri, Fazl Mahmud, 02531
Askari, Sayed Hasan, 05669, 07039, 07111, 07123, 07523, 07617
Aslam, A.H., 17646
Aslam, M.M., 18021
Aslam, Mohamed, 23210
Asopa, Jai Narayan, 06732
Asopa, Sheel K., 17754
Asopa, V.N., 21735, 21747
Aspinall, Arthur, 08038
Assam Agriculture Commission, 25749
Assam. Dept. of Public Instruction, 25803
Assam. Directorate of Economics and Statistics, 25750
Assam. Directorate of Evaluation, 25751-3, 25765, 25804-5
Assam. Directorate of Evaluation and Monitoring, 25716, 25754
Assam. Directorate of Industries, 25766
Assam. Directorate of Information and Public Relations, 25712, 25742
Assam. Economics and Statistics Dept., 25743, 26656-8
Assam. Finance Dept. Assam Labour Enquiry Committee (1921), 25767
Assam. General Administration Dept., 25777
Assam. Planning and Development Dept., 25744-5
Association for Asian Studies. South Asia Regional Council, 27408
Association of Indian Universities, 16436, 16515
Association of Voluntary Agencies for Rural Development, 12989, 22189, 25717, 26540, 26579
Asthana, Pratima, 10741
Asthana, Shashi, 04561
Aśvaghoṣa, 04889-91
Atal, Yogesh, 00770, 00869, 15685, 15761, 23523, 25880
Ate, Lynn Marie, 06288
Athalye, D.V., 11318
Athalye, V.V., 16436
Athar Ali, M., 07524, 07533, 07544-5, 07548-9
Athavale, Pandurang Vaijnath, 04711
Athavale, Parvatibai, 21356
Athavale, V.R., 02843
Athavale, Vasant Balaji, 16333
Atherton, Pauline, 16909
Athilakshmi, 06303
Atiqullah, Mohammad, 25566
Atiqur Rahman, 25314
Atkins, A.G., 08792
Atkins, S.D., 03831
Atkinson, E.T., 25928
Atkinson, George Franklin, 11951
Atreya, B.L., 11433
Ātreya Punarvasu, 04553
Attar, Abdulgani Dadamiya, 16184
Attar Chand, 13960
Attar Singh, 02282, 16906, 22998
Attiqur Rahman, Mohammed, 17364
Atwal, Avtar Singh, 15058
Auber, Peter, 07974
Auboyer, Jeannine, 01588, 01643, 03080-1, 04277, 04395, 05522, 05538
Auchinleck, Claude, Field-Marshal Sir, 10468
Aufderlandwehr, Werner, 19839
Aufrecht, Theodor, 00001
Auld, J.W., 20586
Aurangzīb, 07495
Aurobindo, Sri. *See* Ghose, Aurobindo
Aurora, Gurdip Singh, 16249, 16347, 20843, 22229, 26903, 26911
Austin, Granville, 12085, 12327
Austin, H., 19969
Austin, Vincent, 25466
Auti, V.B., 21283, 21327
Autran, Charles, 04635
Avadhani, V.A., 14490
Avalon, Arthur. *See* Woodroffe, John George
Avasthi, A., 14400
Avasthi, Abha, 15904
Avasthi, Amreshwar, 12964, 22168
Avasthy, A., 22161
Avasthy, Rama Shanker, 07457
Avatar Singh, 22774
Avinashilingam, T.S., 16421
Avtar Singh, 08580, 15038, 22855
Awan, Akhtar Hussain, 18131
Awan, Asghari K., 18132
Awasthi, A.B.L., 04038, 05788, 06788
Awasthi, Dhyaneshwar, 23456-8
Awasthi, R.C., 25755
Awasthi, R.K., 10073
Awasthy, G.C., 16935
Awasthy, Indira, 26396
Awchat, Anil, 21309
Anwal, Mohammad Abdul, 24953
Ayoob, Mohammed, 12014, 12059, 12121, 12161, 12191, 17365, 17568, 17732, 17743, 26068
Ayrookuzhiel, A.M. Abraham, 20167
Ayub Khan, Mohammad, Field-Marshal, 17453, 17509-11, 18159
Ayubi, Fahima, 04178
Ayyangar, M. Ananthasayanam, 20955
Ayyappapanicker, K., 02586, 20196
Ayyar, N.P., 22177
Azad, Abul Kalam, Maulana, 10289

al-Azad, Alauddin, 24952
Azad, Jagdish Lal, 16508
Azam, Kousar J., 15849
Azam, Kouzar J., 19673
Azeez, A.M.A., 18850
Azevedo, Carlos de, 03402
Azhar, Ansari Mohammed, 07629
Azhar, Malik Mueen Nawaz, 11483
Azhar, Mohammad, 18138
Azim, M., 17915
Azim, S. Viqar, 18265
Aziz, A., 23380
Aziz, Abdul, 07565, 07605, 07646, 07798, 20351
Aziz, Barbara Nimri, 26206, 26207
Aziz, K.M. Ashraful, 25493
Aziz, Khursheed Kamal, 08987, 09027, 09765, 09800, 09987, 10342, 10309-10, 17394, 17750
Aziz, Muhammed Abdul, 12060
Aziz, Sartaj, 17697, 18003
Aziz, Syed Abdul, 23956
Aziz Ahmad, 00979, 02268-9, 06985, 07653, 07665, 07677, 08457, 09766, 10321, 11448-9, 11468, 12203-4, 17395, 18206, 18218
Aziz Ahmad, Muhammad, 07023

Baagha, Ajit Singh, 08647
Baagø, Kaj, 02234, 11529-30
Babar, Iftikharullah, 18115
Babar, Sarojini Krishnarao, 21652
Bābar, Zahiruddīn Muhammad, Pādshāh Ghāzī, 07448-9
Babb, Lawrence Alan, 22274-6
Babbitt, Irving, 04989
Baber, Sattar, 17733
Babineau, Edmour J., 08801
Bachal, V.M., 12413
Bachhofer, Ludwig, 05450
Bacon, Elizabeth E., 27256
Bada, C.R., 20251
Badal, R.K., 11711, 17119
al-Badāonī, 07407
Badari, V.S., 16053
Baden-Powell, Baden Henry, 10943-4, 10966-7, 21464, 22084
Baden-Powell, Robert Stephenson Smyth, Lt.-Genl. Sir, 09314
Badrud Duza, M., 25273a, 25550, 25591
Bafna, C.L., 16989
Bag, A.K., 00290, 04006, 04540
Bagal, Jogesh Chandra, 17272, 24286, 24815, 24855, 24868-9
Bagchee, Moni, 24976
Bagchi, Amalendu, 01457
Bagchi, Amiya Kumar, 10884, 11077-8, 11183-4, 15176
Bagchi, Asoke K., 00295
Bagchi, Deepika, 20844
Bagchi, K., 24747
Bagchi, Kanangopal, 27289
Bagchi, Prabodh Chandra, 00361, 00368, 04961, 05894-5, 05923, 07219, 24708
Bagga, V., 16002
Bahadur, F., 20846
Bahadur, K.P., 22085
Bahadur, Kalim, 17470
Bahadur, Satya Prakash, 08793-4
Bahadur, Krishna Prakash, 04805, 04873-8, 08802, 14143, 23938
Bahadurji, G.J., 09219
Bahiṇā Bāī, 08425
Bahirat, Bhalchandra Pandharinath, 06757-8
Bahl, Kali Charan, 02621, 08832
Bahri, H.P., 23423
Bahri, Hardev, 27957
Bahri, Ujjal Singh, 27958, 27959
Bahuleyan, K.S., 21494
Bahulikar, Saudamani, 05198
Baidya, Huta Ram, 26162
Baig, Mirza Rashid Ali, 15850, 24289
Baig, Nafees, 15266, 15290
Baig, Tara Ali, 00952, 11770, 15936
Bailey, Benjamin, 27877
Bailey, Frederick George, 00771, 01091, 22287-8, 22309-10, 22366-7
Bailey, Thomas Grahame, 02532, 11593, 27832, 27953
Baillie, Alexander F., 22494
Bainbridge, R.B., 20994
Baines, Jervoise Athelstane, 00690
Bains, J.S., 09727, 14121
Baird, J.G.A., 09122
Baird, Robert D., 12414
Bajaj, R.K., 22066
Bajpai, K.D., 00150, 00551
Bajpai, Shiva Chandra, 09409
Bajracharya, Manik Lal, 25989
Bajracharya, Purna Harsha, 02779, 26243
Bajwa, Fauja Singh. *See* Fauja Singh
Bajwa, Ijaz, 22776
Bake, Arnold A., 02698, 03876-7, 05839, 25049
Baker, Christopher John, 19143-4, 19165, 19188, 19295
Baker, David E.U., 10021, 20769-71
Baker, Samuel White, 18319
Bakhshi, Ghulam Mohammad, 23164
Bakhtiar, Yahya, 17460
Baks, Chris, 21865
Bakshi, A.R., 21813
Bakshi, Chandrakant, 21932
Bakshi, N.S., 23337
Bakshi, Santosh, 12290, 15000
Bakshi, Shiri Ram, 07975, 08046, 10250-2
Bakshish Singh, 12823
Bal, Sarjit Singh, 08598, 08609, 08651, 22590, 22584
Bal Krishan, 00546
Bala Ratnam, L.K., 00656, 00664, 02081
Balabushevich, Vladimir Vasil'evich, 09970, 13964
Balachandran Nayar, K., 27159
Balakrishna, Kulamarva, 21537
Balakrishna, Ramachandra, 14472
Balakrishna Menon, K.C., 02947
Balakrishna Reddy, Nalagatla, 27172
Balakrishnan, N., 18622, 18648
Balakrishnan, V., 20087
Balakrishnan Nair, A., 12800
Balakrishnan Nayar, T., 03715, 03716
Balambal, V., 06176
Balaram, Nhalileveettil Edavalath, 13199
Balaram Iyer, T.G.S., 01947, 27067
Balarama Gupta, Grandhyam Subbarama, 17107
Balasingham, C., 16737, 18519
Balasingham, S.V., 18320
Balasubrahmanyam, Sirkali Ramaswamy, 06632-6, 06882
Balasubramaniam, K.M., 04489, 19189, 19492
Balasubramaniam, Krishnamurthy, 14946
Balasubramanian, R., 06289
Balasubramanian, S.C., 16252
Balbir Singh, 01360
Balchin, Marianne, 02775
Baldaeus, Philippus, 07893
Balding, J.W., 19046
Baldwin, George Benedict, 19122
Baldwin, Stephen C., 25274
Balendu Sekaram, Kandavalli, 00418
Balfour, Edward Green, 26957
Balfour, Elizabeth, 09143
Balfour, Margaret Ida, 10673
Bali, Saraswati, 03832
Baliga, B.S., 19145
Baljit Singh, 13665, 13714, 14429, 14971, 23571, 23610, 23649-50, 23674, 23842, 23856
Baljon, Johannes Marinus Simon, 07680, 11450, 11467
Balkrishna, 04377, 07998
Balkrishna, S., 19850
Balkrishnan, 03233
Ball, V., 07504
Ballantine, Henry, 25951
Ballantyne, James R., 05998
Ballhatchet, K., 21342
Ballin, L., 04626
Ballinger, Thomas O., 02779
Balneaves, Elizabeth, 27118
Baloch, Aziz, 02735
Baloch, Mir Khudabuk Bijarani Marri, 00487
Baloch, N.A. *See* Baloch, Nabi Bakhsh
Baloch, Nabi Bakhsh, 02780, 02816, 18160, 22487
Balsan, François, 27234-5
Balsara, Pestanji Phirozshah, 02301
Balse, Mayah, 02209
Baluch, Muhammad Sardar Khan, 00489, 06925, 08690
Balys, Jones, 02429
Bamboat, Zenobia, 07909
Bamford, P.C., 09988
Bamzai, Anand Kaul, Pandit, 23225

Bamzai, Prithvi Nath Kaul, 00500, 23131, 27212
Bāṇabhaṭṭa, 06011-6
Banaji, Dady Rustomji, 20627
Bandara, H.H., 19057
Bandaranaike, Malini Yasmine Dias, 19072
Bandaranaike, Solomon West Ridgeway Dias, 18343, 18350, 18411-2, 18553, 18797
Bandaranayake, S., 06164
Bandaranayake, Senake, 05617
Bandhu, Chudamani, 26252
Bandyopadhyay, Nandita, 07316
Bandyopadhyay, Pranab, 17012
Bandyopadhyay, Pratap, 06054
Bandyopadhyay, Sarit Kumar, 24947
Bandyopadhyay, Suraj, 24585
Bandyopadhyaya, Jayantanuja, 09605, 09911, 15766
Bandyopadhyaya, Kalyani, 14760, 24510
Bandyopadhyaya, Shripada, 02753, 02817
Banerjea, Akshaya Kumar, 07303
Banerjea, Jitendra Nath, 01589, 04732, 04754
Banerjea, Pradeep, 25086
Banerjea, Pramathanath, 10858, 11149-51
Banerjea, Surendranath, Sir, 09651
Banerjee.... *See also* Banerji
Banerjee, A.K., 23425
Banerjee, Anukul Chandra, 04966
Banerjee, Anil Chandra, 00464, 07672, 08296, 08350, 08594, 08610, 09074-5, 10290, 10462, 12276, 26441
Banerjee, Arun Kumar, 11057
Banerjee, B.N., 16911
Banerjee, Bani, 09652
Banerjee, Bhavani, 20400
Banerjee, Bibhuti Bhusan, 25087-8
Banerjee, Bireswar, 24460, 24511
Banerjee, Biswanath, 26208
Banerjee, Brajendra Nath, 16784, 24954
Banerjee, D.N., 12898, 24377
Banerjee, Debendra Nath, 08894, 10446, 10451
Banerjee, Gauranga Nath, 04569
Banerjee, Gobinda Lall, 14670
Banerjee, Gooroodas, Sir, 10737
Banerjee, Gopa, 24633
Banerjee, Gouri Sankar, 26503
Banerjee, Hemendra Nath, 24447
Banerjee, Hiranmay. *See* Banerji, Hiranmay
Banerjee, Indubhusan, 08537
Banerjee, Jamini Mohan, 07040
Banerjee, Jyotirmoy, 13978
Banerjee, Manabendu, 04056
Banerjee, Maya, 24205
Banerjee, Mrityunjoy, 13173
Banerjee, Narayanachandra, 04347
Banerjee, Nikunja Vihari, 04422
Banerjee, Nil Ratan, 03448, 03467, 03469, 03686, 05573, 06637
Banerjee, Nirmala, 24349
Banerjee, P.K., 15103, 15147
Banerjee, Prajananda, 24752
Banerjee, Priyatosh, 01611, 01776, 04587, 04739
Banerjee, R.M., 24522
Banerjee, S.K., 26575
Banerjee, S.P., 16700
Banerjee, Sarmila, 24261a
Banerjee, Satya Ranjan, 05247, 05248
Banerjee, Shailendra Nath, 24030
Banerjee, Shyamananda, 24905, 25127
Banerjee, Somendu K., 09606
Banerjee, Sukumar, 21023
Banerjee, Sumanta, 13246, 16300
Banerjee, Swapan Kumar, 24516
Banerjee, Tarasankar (1898-1971), 24671
Banerjee, Tarasankar (1934-   ), 00121, 11034-5, 24545
Banerjee, Usha, 23426
Banerji.... *See also* Banerjee
Banerji, A.C., 03933
Banerji, Adris, 01655, 03691, 05461, 06857, 08464, 08494, 08518, 08969
Banerji, Albion Rajkumar, 24551
Banerji, Anjan Kumar, 12100
Banerji, Aparna, 06569
Banerji, Arun Kumar, 14056-7
Banerji, Benoyendra Nath, 15735
Banerji, Brajendranath, 08755, 24870
Banerji, Debabar, 16285, 16358
Banerji, Debendra Nath, 25160
Banerji, Gauri Rani, 16141
Banerji, Hiranmay, 24683, 24968, 25012, 25027
Banerji, Jayantanuja, 13693
Banerji, Mrityunjoy, 01188
Banerji, Nripendra Chandra, 10621, 24305
Banerji, Projesh, 02996
Banerji, R.N., 08193
Banerji, Rakhal Das, 00475, 02378, 04144, 05574, 06649, 06896, 07174, 07335, 07350
Banerji, Srikumar, 25050
Banerji, Sujit, 16027
Banerji, Sunil Kumar, 24977
Banerji, Sures Chandra, 02465-6, 02486-7, 03787, 04031, 04414, 05237, 05240, 05323, 06048, 07204
Banerji, Tarasankar (1934-   ). *See* Banerjee, Tarasankar (1934-   )
Banga, Indu, 08562
Bangaruswami, R., 19568
Bangladesh Academy for Rural Development, 25557
Bangladesh. Agricultural Research Council, 25390
Bangladesh. Agro-Economic Research Section, 25337
Bangladesh. Bureau of Educational Information and Statistics, 25607
Bangladesh. Bureau of Statistics, 25338
Bangladesh. Census (1974), 25275-6
Bangladesh. Constitution, 25184
Bangladesh. Directorate of Agriculture (Research and Education), 25383
Bangladesh. Directorate of Population Control and Family Planning, 25286, 25592
Bangladesh Institute of Development Studies, 25344
Bangladesh. Laws, statutes, 25196
Bangladesh. Ministry of Flood Control and Water Resources, 25401
Bangladesh. Ministry of Health and Population Control, 25589
Bangladesh. National Foundation for Research on Human Resource Development, 25629
Bangladesh. National Pay Commission, 25222
Bangladesh. Planning Commission, 25316, 25317
Bangladesh. Planning Commission. Manpower Section, 25608
Bangladesh. Population Control and Family Planning Division, 25283, 25284
Bangladesh Rice Research Institute, 25355, 25356
Bangladesh Rural Advancement Committee, 25541
Bangladesh Shilpakala Academy, 25669
Bangladesh. University Grants Commission, 25616, 25621
Bangladesh. University Inquiry Commission, 25617
Bangladesh Water Development Board, 25402
Banhatti, G.S., 11319
Bank of India. Economic and Statistical Dept., 21268
Bankey Behari, 02210, 05829, 05957, 06783, 07245
Banks, Michael, 18851
Bansal, Prem Lata, 12627
Bansal, Usha Rani, 16116
Bansil, Puran Chand, 14734, 14743, 18683
Banskota, M.,
Bantock, Geoffrey Herman, 11923
Banvir Singh, 15721
Bapat, Meera, 21544
Bapat, Nilkanth Gangadhar, 21196
Bapat, Purushottam V., 01249, 04961
Bapat, Vasant, 25068
Baptista, Elsie Wilhelmina, 21450
Baqai, Mohammad Sabihuddin, 18075
Baqai, Moinuddin, 17908
Baqar, S. Ali, 18015
Bar Association of India. Commission of Enquiry on Alleged Police Excesses in Punjab (1966), 22674
Barakrishna, R., 20341
Baral, J.K., 22301
Baral, Lok Raj, 25994, 26014
Baral, Lok S., 25970, 25975, 26015-7
Barannikov, A., 11594
Baranson, Jack, 13879
Baranwal, Rajesh, 15201
Barat, Amiya, 09298
Barbarua, Srinath Duara, 08848
Barber, Noel, 08017
Barber, William J., 10924-5, 11164
Barbarka, Geoffrey A., 11353
Barbarosa, Duarte, 05660-1
Bardhan, Amita, 14173
Bardhan, Ardhendu Bhushan, 15785

Bardhan, Kalpana, 14286
Bardoloi, Muktinath, 26486-7
Bardoloi, U.N., 25718, 25734
Bareau, André, 01392, 01679-80, 04892-4, 04823, 04942, 05019, 05079, 05495, 06149, 18989
Bareh, Hamlet, 26649, 26684-5, 26701-3, 27313
Barfivala, Chunelal Damodardas, 20714
Barger, Evert, 03421
Bari, Fazlul, 25385
Barik, Radhakanta, 13478
Barik, Sourindra, 22404
Barjor Dayal, 23165
Barkat Ali, Malik, 22646
Barkataki, S., 25785, 26467, 27283
Barker, Alfred F., 23211
Barker, George M., 25724
Barker, Muhammad Abd-al-Rahman, 27833, 27844, 27949
Barlingay, Surendra Sheodas, 01426
Barman, J., 22306
Barman, Kiran, 14509
Barmeda, J.N., 21762
Barnabas, A.P., 00827, 12692, 14184, 14783, 15762, 23334, 23799
Barnabas, T., 16401
Barnds, William J., 12015, 14004
Barnett, Elise B., 02686-7
Barnett, Lionel David, 00203, 01696, 06977
Barnett, Marguerite Ross, 13652, 19206, 19417
Barnett, Richard B., 08762
Barnett, Stephen Alan, 01055, 19340-1, 19417, 19445
Barnouw, Erik, 16964
Barnouw, Victor, 21606, 26224-5
Barnow, Finn, 00888
Barns, Margarita, 10291, 10796
Baroda. Economic Development Committee, 21706
Barooah, Debo Prasad, 14058
Barooah, Nirode Kumar, 09385, 25677
Barpujari, H.K., 25678-9, 25806, 26442
Barque, A.M., 27484
Barque, Farooq U., 27484
Barr, Pat, 11952, 11966
Barratt, Barnaby B., 14986
Barrett, Douglas E., 03267, 05483, 05499-500, 06638-9, 06923, 08465-7
Barrier, Norman Gerald, 00494, 10839, 22554, 22633, 22660, 22737-8, 22944, 23030, 27520
Barros, João de, 07866
Barth, Fredrik, 23096-7, 23108-10
Barthakur, Pulin Behari, 27284
Barthélemy-Saint-Hilaire, Jules, 01237, 05647
Bartholemew, Richard L., 17206
Bartholomew, John, 26995
Barthwal, Pitambar Datt, 07084
Barton, William Pell, Sir, 09343, 10452, 10762, 23049
Barua, Benimadhab, 01250, 02057, 03812, 04132, 04924, 05052, 05479
Barua, Bimala Kanta, 28002
Barua, Birinchi Kumar, 00525-6, 02066, 02669-70, 07292, 25814
Barua, Dipak Kumar, 02058, 04984, 25815
Barua, Hem, 02440, 02449, 02671, 25695, 25807, 25816, 25824, 27285
Barua, Hemachandra, 28003-4
Barua, Indira, 25795-6
Barua, Kanak Lal, 00527-8
Barua, M.K., 28005
Barua, Navakanta, 25817
Barua, P.R., 01846
Barua, R.P., 25185
Barua, Rabindra Bijay, 01889, 25636-7
Barua, Tushar Kanti, 25197
Baruah, B., 25768
Baruah, Sanjib Kumar, 25780
Baruah, Tapan Kumar M., 26509-10
Barui, Balai Chandra, 24397
Bary, M.A., 25476
Barz, Richard Keith, 06500, 08813, 27834
Basak, B., 24306
Basak, Radhagovinda, 04293, 04299, 07175
Basal, S.C., 14700
Basava, 06546, 06548, 06550, 06553, 06556
Basavarajappa, K.G., 15909
Basham, Arthur Llewellyn, 00204-6, 00303, 01437, 04179, 04242, 04265, 04278, 04599, 04925, 05009
Basheer Hussain, M., 12926
Bashir, Muhammad, 17979
Bashir, Murtaza, 25667
Bashir Ahmad, Mirza, 18225
Baskara Rao, N., 20504
Basnet, Lal Bahadur, 26358
Basrao, Sharda, 22003
Bastedo, T.G., 24206
Bastiampillai, Bertram, 18321-2, 18489, 18712
Basu, A., 01030
Basu, Anath Nath, 10570, 10582, 10590, 10601
Basu, Aparna, 09584, 09598, 10600-8
Basu, Arabinda, 03694, 05770
Basu, B.N., 04482
Basu, Baman Das, 09028, 10571, 11079, 20603
Basu, C.R., 14623
Basu, D.N., 14241
Basu, D.N., 24695
Basu, Dilip, 24626-7
Basu, Durga Das, 12320, 12328-9, 12844
Basu, Jitendra Nath, 16862
Basu, Jogiraj, 03745
Basu, Jyotirmayee, 04441
Basu, K.K., 05696, 07041
Basu, Latika, 11743
Basu, Mrinal Kumar, 23954
Basu, Nirmal Kumar, (1915-), 00529
Basu, Patricia Lyons, 05162
Basu, Praphullachandra, 03781
Basu, Purnendu, 08763
Basu, R.N., 16260
Basu, Rabindra Nath, 05003
Basu, Ramala, 24816
Basu, S.K., 21748
Basu, Sachindranath, 10661
Basu, Sajal, 13538
Basu, Sankari Prasad, 11313
Basu, Saroj Kumar, 14656, 15277, 15492, 24050, 24495, 24512
Basu, Satyabrata, 24796
Basu, Subhas K., 15118
Basu, Sunil Kumar, 24635, 24689
Basu, Syama Prasad, 07024, 07042
Basu, Tara Krishna, 24672
Basu, Tarapada, 25069
Bateman, C.H., 25251
Bateson, William McKallip, 23629
Batley, Claude, 03157
Batra, H.C., 20651
Batra, Jagdish Chander, 17610
Batra, Madan Mohan, 14831
Batra, Satkartar, 11041, 21797-8
Batra, Shakti, 16831
Batra, Ved Parkash, 15493
Bauer, Pèter Tamàs, 14036
Baumann, George, 06791
Baumer, Rachel R. van Meter, 24250, 24561, 24991
Baumgartel, Howard, 15256
Bausani, Alessandro, 02387a, 02617, 02637, 07691, 11650, 11652
Baveja, G.C., 15440
Baveja, J.D., 25807
Baviskar, B.S., 13007, 15667
Bawa, Arjan Singh, 11276
Bawa, V.K., 00442
Baxi, Upendra, 12824
Baxter, Craig, 13267, 13316, 13674, 17411, 17555, 22647, 22715-6
Baxter, Ian A., 27524
Baxter, James, 26882
Baybasthapana Shangsad Ltd., 25593-4
Bayley, David H., 12700-2, 13085-6
Bayley, Edward Clive, 06712
Bayly, Christopher Alan, 08784, 08997, 10687, 23467, 23533, 23825
Bayne, Stephen Fielding, Bishop, 16821
Bazaz, Prem Nath, 04676, 12086, 23166-8, 23190-1, 23203, 27213
Bazlul Karim, Kazi, 25530-1, 25595
Beach, Milo Cleveland, 07727, 07730, 08495-6, 08509, 08700
Beaglehole, J.H., 15858
Beaglehole, T.H., 09179
Beal, Samuel, 04052, 05648
Beale, Thomas William, 00157
Beals, Alan R., 20265, 20425-7, 20505, 20533

Beames, John, 02347, 24262
Bean, Lee L., 17784, 17792-4, 18043, 18091, 18139-40
Beane, Wendell Charles, 05848
Bearce, George D., 07647, 11791, 11836
Beatson, W.B., 10674
Beaumont, Roger, 09283
Beautrix, Pierre, 01123, 05068
Bechert, Heinz, 01124, 01238-9, 01818, 01860, 04229, 04935, 04951, 04955, 18466-7, 18974, 19005, 25638
Bechtoldt, Heinrich, 14272
Beck, Brenda E.F., 00682, 05441, 06255, 19333, 19342-4, 19493
Becker, Raymond de, 16707
Beddome, Richard Henry, 27028
Bedekar, Dinkar Keshav, 09912
Bedi, Baba Pyare Lal, 06055
Bedi, Kishan Singh, 22757
Bedi, Mohinder S., 14110, 22130
Bedi, Sohinder Singh, 23022
Beech, Mary Jane, 24598
Beejadhur, Aunauth, 26761
Beers, Howard W., 15050-1
Beetham, D., 26912
Beg, Aziz, 12066, 17629
Beg, M. Hamid Ali, 27214
Beg, Mohammad Afzel, 23184
Beg, Mohammad Ibrahim, 23124
Begde, Prabhakar V., 04519
Begg, Wahiduddin, 05944
Begley, Wayne Edison, 01759, 05591
Behanan, Kovoor Thomas, 02181
Behari, Chandra, 12851
Behari, Bepin, 15151
Behere, N.K., 08253
Behm, Allan J., 03981
Behura, Nab Kishore, 03259, 22357
Beidelman, Thomas O., 00893
Beidler, William, 01458
Bejwa, Harcharan Singh, 22559
Belfiglio, Valentine J., 26369, 26416, 26432
Belknap, Bruce J., 27601
Bell, Evans, 20223-4, 22585
Bell, Harold Wilberforce. *See* Wilberforce-Bell, Harold
Bell, Harry Charles Purvis, 19104-5
Bell, Thomas Evans, Major, 19134
Bellew, Francis John, 09200
Bellew, Henry Walter, 27972
Belliappa, Meena, 11712, 17140, 17152, 17166
Belsare, Keshav Vishnu, 08432
Belsare, Malhar Bhikaji, 27925
Belvalgidad, M.I., 15909
Belvalkar, S.K., 01296
Belvalkar, Shripad Krishna, 06023
Benares Hindu University. Library, 10138, 23893
Benary, Barbara Lynn, 02852, 02873
Bence-Jones, Mark, 08005, 11831
Bender, Ernest, 00015, 08460, 27835, 27845
Bendre, Dattatreya Ramachandra, 20572
Bendre, Vinod Pandharinath, 15400
Bendrey, Vasudeo Sitaram, 05675
Benedict, Burton, 26762, 26763
Benegal, Som, 02933
Benesh, Jaon, 02775
Benesh, Rudolph, 02775
Bengal Chamber of Commerce and Industry, 24427-8
Bengal. Dacca University Committee (1912), 24847
Bengal. Indigo Commission, 24443
Bengal. Land Revenue Commission (1938), 24479
Bengal. Moslem Education Advisory Committee, 24860
Bengal. Retrenchment Committee, 24263
Bengal. Secretariat, 26360
Bengali Academy, 25609-10
Benisti, Mireille, 01628, 01679-80, 05508
Benjamin, N., 00237, 08391, 10854, 10983
Benjamin, V., 16311
Benjamin ben Jonah of Tudela, 05662
Bennett, John W., 01564
Bennett, Lynn, 26273-4
Bennett, Richard George, 21904
Benson, Charles Scott, 18161
Benson, Janet, 00894
Bentley, John, 00274
Beny, Roloff, 27049, 27151
Benyukh, Oles, 27236
Berard, Father, 01297
Berber, F.J., 12241
Berg, Alan, 16250
Bergaigne, Abel Henri Joseph, 03891
Bergan, Asbjörn, 17805-6
Bergmann, Jean Noel, 04483
Bergmann, Theodor, 14273, 14761, 14871, 14987, 15341
Berindranath, Dewan, 17423, 17551
Beringer, Christoph, 17964, 23085
Berkes, Ross N., 14110
Berlage, Lodewijk J.J.B., 25290-1
Berna, James J., 19316
Bernard, Theos, 04793
Bernet Kempers, A.J., 07351
Bernier, Francois, 07496, 07910
Bernier, Ronald M., 03470-1
Bernot, Lucien, 25506-7
Bernstein, Henry T., 11042
Bernstein, Jeromy, 27382
Bernstorff, Dagmar, 19654-5, 19674-5
Berntsen, Rita Maxine, 02598, 27908, 27915-7
Berreman, Gerald Duane, 00719-22, 00731, 00794, 25913-9, 25929-30
Berridge, P.S.A., 23086
Berry, Brian Joe Lobley, 19840, 24759
Berry, Margaret, 17108, 17120
Berry, Willard, 23071
Bertocci, Peter J., 17941, 25208, 25292, 25382, 25532-4, 25542, 27730
Bertolacci, Anthony, 18584
Bertrand, Josef, S.J., 08216-7
Besant, Annie Wood, 04660, 09546, 09632, 11360-2
Bessaignet, Pierre, 25488, 25503, 25508
Besterman, Theodore, 27631
Betai, Ramesh, 06031
Béteille, André, 00622, 00700, 00723, 00738, 00772, 00784, 00851, 00870, 15751, 15807, 15830, 19345, 19418, 19514
Betham, Robert Mitchell, 21393
Bettelheim, Charles, 14229, 14369, 14436
Betty, L. Stafford, 01352
Beven, F. Lorenz, 19047
Beveridge, Annette Susannah Akroyd, 07448, 07458, 07475
Beveridge, Henry, 07397, 07470, 07483, 08026, 24181
Beyer, John C., 26085, 26141
Beyer, Stephen, 01265
Bezbaroa, Lakshminath, 25825-6
Bezboruah, Monoranjan, 11987
Bhabha, Homi Jehangir, 13788, 15407, 17245
Bhade, Gangadhar S., 21189
Bhadra, Binayak, 26188
Bhadra, Gautam, 08920, 26576
Bhadra, Ranajit K., 20862
Bhadra, Ranajit K., 25797
Bhaduri, Manindra B., 20838
Bhaduri, Taroon Coomar, 22263
Bhagabat Kumar, Sastri, 04733, 04738
Bhagat, A.K., 09703
Bhagat, Dhanraj, 17207
Bhagat, G., 09386
Bhagat, K.P., 10292, 19958
Bhagat, Mahadeo Gopal, 02186, 15061, 15104, 21403
Bhagat, P.S., 13760
Bhagat Singh (1921-), 22565
Bhagavati, B., 15496
Bhagbati, Ananda, 24634
Bhagi, M.L., 04086
Bhagvat, Durga, 20845, 20863, 21653-4
Bhagvat Sinh Jee, Maharaja of Gondal, 00304
Bhagwan Singh, 23175
Bhagwat, Achyut Keshav, 00450, 27184
Bhagwat, Ramchandra Keshav, 06759
Bhagwati, Jagdish N., 13653, 13819, 14128, 14370, 15202
Bhakti Prajnan Yati Maharaj, 16708
Bhaktivedanta Swami, A.C., 04661, 05761, 07270, 07278, 07284-5
Bhaktivinode, Thakur, 05772
Bhalerao, C.N., 14401
Bhalerao, S.S., 12774
Bhalla, G.S., 14744, 15245
Bhalla, M.M., 02934
Bhalla, R.P., 13333, 23333
Bhalla, Sheila, 23292
Bhāmaha, 05972

Bhambri, Chandra Prakash, 10087, 12608, 12628-9, 12670, 12744, 12801, 13334, 13455, 17327, 17352, 17518, 21973, 21993, 22004-5
Bhan, B.K., 15517
Bhan, Radha Krishna, 23212
Bhanawat, Narendra, 01289
Bhandare, L.S. (b. 1881), 05336
Bhandare, L.S., 09630
Bhandare, R.D., 21414
Bhandari, Arvind, 13607
Bhandari, J.S., 15786, 23743
Bhandari, Labdhi, 16301
Bhandari, N.S., 25931
Bhandari, S.S., 13268
Bhandarkar, Devadatta Ramkrishna, 04125, 04755-6
Bhandarkar, Ramkrishna Gopal, 00444, 01167
Bhandarkar, S.S., 16488
Bhaneja, Balwant, 12016
Bhansali, Kamalini, 16691
Bhanwar Singh, 25458
Bharadvaja, Brahma, 13335
Bharadwaj, A.N., 15808
Bharadwaj, Krishna, 14745, 22340
Bharadwaj, Krishna Datta, 06426
Bharadwaj, Ramdat, 08803
Bharadwaj, Ranganath, 13820
Bharadwaja, E., 19872
Bharali, Sailena, 25818
Bharara, L.P., 22010
Bharat Krishak Samaj, 14846
Bharat Sevak Samaj. Delhi Pradesh, 23398
Bharati, Agehananda, 00639, 00980, 01647, 01861, 01906-7, 02220, 05857, 11219, 14347, 16722, 16965, 18434, 26842, 26857
Bharati, Shuddhananda, 04490, 06290, 06320, 08207, 19896
Bharati, Swadesh, 17013
Bharati Tamil Sangam, 19584
Bharatiya, Rajendra Kumar, 04279
Bharatiya Jan Sangh, 13266
Bhartiya, Mahesh Chandra, 04839
Bhardwaj, H.C., 00341
Bhardwaj, K.K., 18382
Bhardwaj, K.S., 23433
Bhardwaj, R.K., 12703, 12965, 13012, 16082
Bhardwaj, Surinder Mohan, 01908, 22795
Bhargav, Abhay, 17712
Bhargava, B.S., 12938, 12982, 13675, 20327, 21979, 21996
Bhargava, Dayanand, 01509
Bhargava, Ganti Suryanarayana, 10088, 11128, 12162-3, 12184, 12671-2, 12745, 13565, 13621, 13942, 14005, 14086, 17545
Bhargava, K.D., 10576, 10609
Bhargava, Kusum, 21963
Bhargava, Madhuri, 14521
Bhargava, Manohar Lal, 03730
Bhargava, Moti Lal, 09472, 23468
Bhargava, Prahlad Kumar, 14498, 14590, 23584
Bhargava, Purushottam Lal, 03746, 03771, 04121
Bhargava, Rajendra Nath, 14510, 14531
Bhargava, Visheshwar Sarup, 08365
Bhargawa, Rochana, 16941
Bharill, Chandra, 10776
Bharti, R.K., 15337
Bhartṛhari, 01438, 06039-46
Bharucha, Ervad Sheriarji Dadabhai, 02288
Bharuci, 04423
Bhasin, A.S., 26041
Bhasin, Prem, 13174, 13466
Bhaskar Rao, U., 10492
Bhaskara Rao, B., 16065
Bhaskara Rao, N., 12101, 19656
Bhaskara Rao, Vasireddy, 15615
Bhāskarācārya, 05732
Bhaskaran, R., 13037
Bhaskaran, T.R., 24794
Bhaskaran Nair, M., 17327, 17352, 25141
Bhat, A. Vishnu, 06064
Bhat, Govind Keshav, 02497, 03813, 05277-8, 05284, 05289, 05312, 06024, 06032
Bhat, K.S., 21153
Bhat, Laxminarayana Sanna, 14194, 14473, 20273, 23277, 27174
Bhat, Sudhakar, 26452
Bhate, Govind Chimnaji, 21634
Bhate, Vaijayanti, 16315, 21466, 21564-5
Bhatia, Arjun Kumar, 15401
Bhatia, B., 14691
Bhatia, B.M., 10992, 11013, 11058, 14806, 17848, 19334
Bhatia, Gurbachan Singh, 22960
Bhatia, Harbans Lal, 14522
Bhatia, Harbans Singh, 00221, 04336, 11953, 12301, 17611
Bhatia, J.C., 16312
Bhatia, Kanta, 27637
Bhatia, Krishan, 13013, 13415
Bhatia, Mohan, 17231
Bhatia, O.P. Singh, 04145
Bhatia, Pratipal, 06708
Bhatia, Prem, 16882, 26865
Bhatia, Shyam, 13772
Bhatia, Shyam Sunder, 23381, 23598-9
Bhatia, Sohan Lal, 00305-6
Bhatiya, S.L., 20506
Bhatkal, Ramdas G., 13141
Bhatkal, Sadanand G., 27572
Bhatkhande, Vishnu Narayan, 02736, 02818
Bhatnagar, Akshay Kumar, 12775
Bhatnagar, G.D., 23441
Bhatnagar, Gurnam Saran, 22245, 22931
Bhatnagar, I., 06976
Bhatnagar, K.P., 15415
Bhatnagar, Ram Ratan, 10797
Bhatnagar, Shyam Krishna, 11475
Bhatnagar, Sudha, 14532
Bhatnagar, Suresh, 16416
Bhatnagar, V.S., 08371
Bhatt, Anil Harilal, 00812, 13061, 13073, 13082, 15752, 21690, 21885, 22140
Bhatt, B.D., 10551
Bhatt, B.N., 06379
Bhatt, Bhagavatprasad Natvarlal, 06056
Bhatt, Bharat L., 00683, 01920
Bhatt, G.S., 23744
Bhatt, Govindlal Hargovind, 04695-6, 06501
Bhatt, Lalshankar Jasubhai, 21889
Bhatt, Mahesh, 21715, 21875-6
Bhatt, N.R., 04746
Bhatt, Narhari K., 27185
Bhatt, Ram Krishen Kaul, 23181
Bhatt, Ramanbhai G., 10610
Bhatt, S.C., 05266
Bhatt, Siddheshwar Rameshwar, 04776-7, 06427
Bhatt, Usha, 16176
Bhatt, Vinayak Vijayshanker, 10859, 14217, 14230
Bhatta, Bhim Dev, 26122
Bhatta, Shrikrishna Datta, 22264
Bhaṭṭa Nārāyaṇa, 06981
Bhattacharjea, Ajit, 12140, 13479
Bhattacharjee, A.K., 24817
Bhattacharjee, Amal Kanti, 24810
Bhattacharjee, Arun, 04087, 07352, 16863
Bhattacharjee, Durgadas, 25467
Bhattacharjee, Gauri Pada, 10074, 25167, 26064
Bhattacharjee, J.P., 24056
Bhattacharjee, Jayanta Bhusan, 26650
Bhattacharjee, Jyoti Prasad, 24673
Bhattacharjee, K.K., 25691
Bhattacharjee, K.S., 13126
Bhattacharjee, Kamana Kumar, 16910, 27736
Bhattacharjee, P.J., 14161
Bhattacharjee, Siva Sadhan, 01312
Bhattacharjee, Tarun Kumar, 26504
Bhattacharji, K.S., 26370, 26380
Bhattacharji, Somdev, 27993-5
Bhattacharji, Sukumari, 01697
Bhattacharjya, Umasaday, 26651
Bhattacharya, A.K., 01612, 01687, 07136, 07342
Bhattacharya, A.R., 01393
Bhattacharya, Ahibhushan, 05814
Bhattacharya, Ajit R., 06380
Bhattacharya, Amarendra Nath, 22090
Bhattacharya, Amitabha, 00521
Bhattacharya, Arun, 02722
Bhattacharya, Ashoka Nath, 06005
Bhattacharya, Asok K., 03287
Bhattacharya, Asutosh, 01576, 03037-8, 03051, 06588, 07299, 08962-3, 24897, 25109, 25121
Bhattacharya, Bhabani, 09861, 24552
Bhattacharya, Bholanath, 07343, 24874
Bhattacharya, Bimalendu, 00889
Bhattacharya, Birendra Kumar, 25700

Bhattacharya, Bishnupada, 05178
Bhattacharya, Brajamadhaba, 01754
Bhattacharya, Brindavan Chandra, 01688
Bhattacharya, D., 10885
Bhattacharya, D.K., 21377, 27487
Bhattacharya, Deben, 07228, 07258-9, 08946
Bhattacharya, Devaprasad, 04806
Bhattacharya, Dhires, 24429
Bhattacharya, Dilip, 27400
Bhattacharya, Dinesh Chandra, 06389
Bhattacharya, Durgaprasad, 14950
Bhattacharya, Haridas, 04822
Bhattacharya, Harisatya, 01273, 01368, 01510
Bhattacharya, Jogendranath, 00757
Bhattacharya, K.R., 17263
Bhattacharya, Kalidas, 01052, 11425
Bhattacharya, Kamaleswar, 01459, 05090
Bhattacharya, Karuna, 06381
Bhattacharya, Krishna Chandra, 01394
Bhattacharya, Lokenath, 17018
Bhattacharya, Mahashveta Devi, 25089
Bhattacharya, Mohit, 12947, 12966-70, 14402, 24732-3
Bhattacharya, N., 15474
Bhattacharya, N.D., 24696
Bhattacharya, Narendra Nath, 01328, 01711, 02125, 05849
Bhattacharya, P.K., 26557
Bhattacharya, R., 24461
Bhattacharya, Rakhal, 24825
Bhattacharya, Ranjit, 24468, 24620, 24687
Bhattacharya, Ranjit K., 24648
Bhattacharya, S.A., 05830
Bhattacharya, Sabyasachi, 08904, 10860, 10926
Bhattacharya, Sachchidananda, 00138
Bhattacharya, Sauripada, 13726
Bhattacharya, Shashthi Prasad, 05988
Bhattacharya, Shiva Chandra Vidyarnava, 05886
Bhattacharya, Shyam S., 18086
Bhattacharya, Sibesh Chandra, 04396
Bhattacharya, Siddheswar, 05771
Bhattacharya, Sivaprasad, 05965-6
Bhattacharya, Sudhibhushan, 02897
Bhattacharya, Sudhindra Nath, 08849, 10432
Bhattacharya, Sukanta, 25090
Bhattacharya, Sukumar, 08889, 24495
Bhattacharya, Sunil Kumar, 01777
Bhattacharya, Tarapada, 01804, 06853
Bhattacharya, Tarasankar, 07317
Bhattacharya, Tarundev, 02097
Bhattacharya, Vidhushekhara, Mahamahopadhyaya, 04911, 06336
Bhaṭṭāchārya, Viśvanātha Nyāyapañcānana. *See* Viśvanātha Nyāyapañcānana Bhaṭṭācārya
Bhattacharya, Vivek Ranjan, 16135, 23382
Bhattacharyya, Anima, 14162
Bhattacharyya, Asit Kumar, 14474, 24430, 24474
Bhattacharyya, Asutosh. *See* Bhattacharya, Asutosh
Bhattacharyya, Benoytosh, 05896, 05917-8, 07220
Bhattacharyya, Buddhadeva, 24307-8, 09738, 09935
Bhattacharyya, Dipak Chandra, 01656, 01829
Bhattacharyya, Gopikamohan, 07318
Bhattacharyya, Janaki Vallabha, 04840
Bhattacharyya, Jnanabrata, 24500
Bhattacharyya, Kalidas. *See* Bhattacharya, Kalidas
Bhattacharyya, Mrinal Kanti, 24772
Bhattacharyya, N.C., 11803
Bhattacharyya, Narendra Nath, 00267, 01031, 02388, 04895
Bhattacharyya, Nirmal Chandra, 24665
Bhattacharyya, Pares Chandra, 14624
Bhattacharyya, Pranab Kumar, 00472
Bhattacharyya, S.K., 14737, 16180-1
Bhattacharyya, Sabyasachi, 11152, 11153
Bhattacharyya, Sailendra Nath, 10822
Bhattacharyya, Sibajiba, 07319
Bhattacharyya, Sivaprasad, 02882, 05840
Bhattacharyya, Sudhindra Nath, 15019
Bhattacharyya, Sukumar, 08351
Bhattacharyya, Suresh Mohan, 05967
Bhattacharyya, Tarapada, 05468
Bhattarai, Muralidhar, 25958
Bhattasali, Nalini Kanta, 01590, 07182, 08843
Bhatti, Allah Ditta, 17781, 17784, 18139
Bhatti, Faiz Muhammad, 18044
Bhatti, K.M., 17916
Bhatty, I.Z., 15084
Bhatty, Zarina, 23763
Bhaumik, D.J. *See* Bhowmik, D.J.
Bhavabhūti, 06023-30
Bhave, Vinayak Narahar. *See* Bhave, Vinoba
Bhave, Vinoba, 04677, 08601, 12469, 14312-5, 14988-9, 16457
Bhavnani, Enakshi, 02920, 03308
Bhawe, Shrikrishna Sakharam, 03922, 05326
Bheem Rao, K., 19803-4
Bhende, Asha A., 14132, 14144, 16275
Bhesania, N.C., 09989
Bhide, V.G., 17232
Bhim Deva, 04005
Bhimbhetka, 03532
Bhimsen, 07497
Bhishagratna, K.L., 04552
Bhogle, Shantaram K., 12940
Bhole, L.M., 14491
Bhooshan, B.S., 16036, 26123
Bhoosnurmath, S.S., 06538
Bhoothalingam, Mathuram, 19583
Bhoothalingam, S., 14563
Bhore, Joseph William, 10682
Bhowmik, D.J., 26370, 26380
Bhowmick, K.N., 02834
Bhowmick, Kanai Lal, 01077, 24417
Bhowmick, Prabodh Kumar, 24578-80, 24599, 24634, 24674, 24875, 24882-3
Bhoymeeah, Tyabjee, 21331
Bhujanga Rao, M., 02581
Bhuleshkar, Ashok V., 14231, 14287, 14323
Bhupal Singh, 11888
Bhupendra Chandra Sinha, Maharaja of Susanga, 24251
Bhupinder Singh, 15786
Bhūriyā, Mahipāla, 20802
Bhushan, Ravi, 27468
Bhushan, V.N., 11744
Bhutani, Kamla, 15926
Bhutani, V.C., 10945
Bhutto, Benazir, 17663
Bhutto, Zulfikar Ali, 12185-6, 17612-4, 17462-3, 17579-82, 17657-8, 17664, 17685, 17755, 17766
Bhuyan, Arun Chandra, 10413
Bhuyan, Ayubur Rahman, 12248
Bhuyan, Suryya Kumar, 00530, 02672, 07193, 07336, 08848-9, 08851, 25680
Biardeau, Madeleine, 01189, 01460, 01792, 05163, 05221, 05754, 06390
Bibliografiia Nepala (1917-1967), 27737
Bibliografiia Pakistana (1947-67), 27764
Bibliographie du Népal, 27738
Bibliographie védique, 00014
Bibliography of Asian Studies, 27645
Bibliography of English publications in India, 27566
Bibliography of Indology, 27646
Bibliothèque Nationale, Paris, 24992
Biddulph, Charles Hubert, 06196
Bidwell, Shelford, 07822
Bidya Nand, 09439
Bidyabinod, B.B., 01760
Bierwirth, Gerhard, 14070
Biggs, Stephen D., 25386, 25387
Bigler, Luc, 25279
Bihar. Agricultural Census, 24057
Bihar. Commission to Inquire into the Affairs of the Patna Improvement Trust..., 24182
Bihar. Education Re-Organisation Committee (1938), 24207
Bihar. Finance Dept., 24035
Bihar. Home (Election) Dept., 23999
Bihar Institute of Economic Development, 24106
Bihar. Labour Dept., 24123, 24188
Bihar. Mudholkar Commission of Inquiry, 23975
Bihar. Public Relations Dept., 23976
Bihar. Secondary Education Committee, 24208
Bihar State Seminar on Educational and Administration, Patna (1970), 24209
Bihar. T.L. Venkatarama Aiyar Commission of Inquiry, 23977
Bihar. Town Planning Organisation, 24171
Bihārī Lāl, 08835
Bijalwan, C.D., 02136, 04841
Bijlani, H.U., 16083
Bilgrami, Asghar Husain, 09421
Bilgrami, Jafar Raza, 14111
Bilgrami, S. Athar Raza, 14046
Bilgrami, Saiyid Husain, 19613

Bilhaṇa, 06047-53
Bilimoria, Jamshid H., 07495
Billard, Roger, 00275
Billimoria, H.M., 15968
Billimoria, N.M., 27719
Billimoria, R.N., 21190
Billings, Martin H., 15085, 22775-5a
Bilung, Alphonse, 20892
Bimal Prasad, 12028, 13694, 13965
Bimla Prasad, 09607, 13964, 14288
Binder, Leonard, 17396-7
Binford, Mira R., 02009
Bingley, Alfred Harsford, Sir, 22086, 22822, 23226
Binney, Edwin, 3rd, 07712, 07731, 08477
Binyon, Robert Laurence, 07473, 07732
Biographical Encyclopedia of Pakistan, 27466
Bipan Chandra, 00133, 09558, 10105, 10900, 10962
Birch, Walter de Gray, 07858
Bird, Kai, 25214
Birdwood, Christopher Bromhead Birdwood, Baron, 10474, 12087
Birdwood, George Christopher Molesworth, Sir, 03296, 03310, 07963
Birdwood, William Riddell Birdwood, Field-Marshal Baron, 09315
Birendra Prasad, 09608
Birindranath, Dewan. *See* Berindranath Dewan
Birkhead, Guthrie S., 17328, 17828
Birla, Basant Kumar, 11797
Birla, Ghanshyam Dass, 09890-1
Birla, L.N., 22150
Birmingham, Judy, 26250
al-Bīrūnī, 05636, 05641, 05643
Al-Bīrūnī International Congress of Pakistan (1973), 05644
Birwé, Robert, 05793
Bisaliah, S., 20328
Bishnoi, O.P., 23914
Bishnoi, R.N., 13545, 16293
Bishnoi, Usha, 14572
Bishop, C. James, 00177
Bishop, Donald H., 01175, 11199, 11345
Bishop, Raymond Norman Wear, 27383
Bishui, Kalpana, 10840
Bissoondoyal, Basdeo, 09913, 11875, 26764
Bista, Dor Bahadur, 26191, 26264
Bista, Khem Bahadur, 02098, 26319
Bista, Soma Dhot, 27401
Biswas, Ahsan A., 27488
Biswas, Arabinda, 16378, 16386, 16402, 24760
Biswas, Atreyi, 04193
Biswas, Basudeb, 13841
Biswas, Dilip Kumar, 11233
Biswas, Dipti Kumar, 24927
Biswas, P.C., 20914
Biswas, Sailendra, 27984
Biswas, Sukumar, 13464
Biswas, T.K., 01629
Bjorkman, James Warner, 15020
Black, R.D. Collison, 10927
Blackburn, Stuart H., 19373, 19597
Blackton, Charles S., 18334, 18338, 18392
Blair, Charles, 11014
Blair, Harry Wallace, 24000-1, 24014, 25176, 25209
Blaise, Clark, 24709
Blakiston, J.F., 07159
Blanckenburg, Peter von, 14847
Blang, Mark, 15512
Blank, Judith, 03039
Blaschke, Dieter, 24210
Blavatsky, Helene Petrovna, 11354
Blechynden, Kathleen, 24710
Blenck, Jürgen, 26958
Blinkenberg, Lars, 12067
Bloch, Jules, 02348-9, 02361, 02599, 04133
Blochmann, H., 07468
Blofeld, John, 05897
Blondeel, Emmerich, 22982
Bloomfield, Barry Cambray, 27689
Bloomfield, Maurice, 03798, 03814, 03926, 03929, 03960, 05130
Blunt, Edward Arthur Henry, Sir, 09180, 10694, 23586, 23689, 23800
Blunt, Wilfred Scawen, 09144, 10788
Bly, Robert, 07097
Blyn, George, 08895, 10931
Boag, George Townsend, 19146
Boal, Barbara M., 22403
Boatwright, Howard, 02776
Bobrinskoy, George V., 00026
Bodding, Paul Olaf, 20911, 20915, 20929, 20941
Bodewitz, H.W., 03934, 03945
Böhtlingk, Otto, 05973, 27792
Boel, J., 00828
Boetzelaer, J.M. van, 06391
Boewe, Charles, 27424
Bogaert, Michael van den, 15632, 15640, 15668, 24107, 24201
Bois, Pierre, 12164
Bokil, Vinayak Pandurang, 08444
Bolitho, Hector, 10375
Bolle, Kees W., 04662, 11376
Bollee, Willem Boudewijn, 03946
Bolton, Glorney, 10210
Bolz, Klaus, 13858
Boman-Behram, B.K., 10572, 21877
Bombay Chamber of Commerce and Industry, 20002, 21516
Bombay Metropolitan Regional Planning Board, 21517
Bombay (Presidency), 21284-5
Bombay (Presidency). Committee on the Riots in Poona and Ahmednagar, 21273
Bombay (Presidency). Labour Office, 21324
Bombay (Presidency). Provincial Banking Enquiry Committee, 21227
Bombay (Province). Provincial Industries Committee. Cottage and Small-Scale Industries Sub-Committee, 21306
Bombay (State). Committee for a History of the Freedom Movement in India, 20719
Bombay (State). Education Dept., 21569
Bombay (State). Legislature, 21110
Bombay. University, 21600
Bombwall, K.R., 12517-8, 12912, 13014
Bon, Bhakti Hṛdaya, 01461, 03878, 07271, 07286
Bonarjee, N.B., 12657
Bonarjee, Pitt D., 09284
Bonazzoli, Giorgio, 02099, 05783, 23915
Bondurant, Joan Valérie, 09956, 12506, 13038, 13175, 13338, 13927
Boner, Alice, 01748, 03228, 06910-1, 06916
Bongard-Levin, Grigorii Maksimovich, 00163, 04134
Bongert, Yvonne, 04386
Bongirwar, L.N., 21159
Bonn, Gisela, 26417, 26437
Bonnerjee, Gobin Lal, 27985
Bonerjee, Jitindriya, 24748
Bonerjee, Sadhona, 09653
Boon, Jan, 27384
Bopegamage, A., 09285, 19346, 21378, 23386-7
Bora, Ajit Kumar, 25759
Bora, C.K., 25798
Bora, Prafulla Prasad, 25819
Borah, M.I., 08847
Borale, P.T., 15778
Borgohain, B.K., 26468-9
Borkar, Vishnu Vinayak, 14573, 21247
Borooah, Renee, 16952
Borpujari, Jitendra G., 11029, 11154
Borra, Indra Narayun, 25820
Borthwick, Meredith, 11251
Bosch, Frederik David Kan, 01577-8
Bose, A.B., 21997, 22027, 22037, 22074, 22091-2, 22105-6
Bose, A.N., 24753
Bose, Abinash Chandra, 03881
Bose, Ajoy, 13566, 23326
Bose, Amalendu, 11745
Bose, Anima, 10591-2
Bose, Arun, 24309
Bose, Arun Coomer, 09609
Bose, Ashish, 12971, 14133-4, 14145, 14163, 16021-2, 16028-30, 23400, 27756
Bose, Asoke Nath, 10153
Bose, Atindranath, 04348
Bose, Buddhadeva, 24919-20, 25054
Bose, D.M., 00252
Bose, Dakshina Ranjan, 10462
Bose, Devabrata, 00732
Bose, Dhirendra Nath, 05858
Bose, Jyoti, 15059
Bose, K., 16546
Bose, Mandakranta, 02904

Bose, Manilal, 26445, 26475
Bose, Manindra Mohan, 08940
Bose, Narendra Kumar, 02829
Bose, Nemai Sadhan, 06702, 09556, 10823, 24562, 24713
Bose, Nirmal Kumar, 00623, 00640, 00665-7, 00684, 00724, 00733, 00871, 01078, 01092, 02100, 06912, 09892, 09928, 09936, 10517, 12387, 13304, 15704, 15809, 19805, 21019, 22358, 22400, 24581-2, 24761-2
Bose, P.K., 10660, 17270, 24854
Bose, Phanindra Nath, 06105
Bose, Pramatha Nath, 09053, 10908, 25128
Bose, Prem Sundar, 06345
Bose, Ramendra Mohan, 05349
Bose, Roma, 06495
Bose, S.C., 24050a, 25920
Bose, S.K., 10008
Bose, Samar, 22329
Bose, Santipriya, 24462
Bose, Saradindu, 26397, 26720
Bose, Sarat Chandra, 24310-11
Bose, Saroj Ranjan, 24031, 24036, 24058-9
Bose, Shib Chunder, 24583
Bose, Sisir Kumar, 10160
Bose, Subhas Chandra, 09971-2, 10154-9
Bose, Subodh Chandra, 14195, 25848, 27290, 27342
Bose, Sudhansu Mohan, 10274
Bose, Sukla, 01073
Bose, Sunil, 02838
Bose, Sunil Kumar, 09654, 24969, 24978
Bose, Suresh Chandra, 10433
Bose, Swadesh R., 17703, 17849, 17885, 17950, 25304-5, 25339, 25345
Bose, Tara, 21947
Boserup, Ester, 15533
Bossert, Jeanette, 26968
Bosu, Jyotirmoy, 15452
Bosworth, Clifford Edmund, 06929
Botelho de Sousa, Alfredo, 07854
Bothra, Pushpa, 01411
Botlivala, Soli S., 10437
Botto, Oscar, 06071
Bottomore, T.B., 15831
Bouchon, Geneviève, 08130
Bouda, Karl, 03717
Boudens, R., 08098
Bouglé, Celestin Charles Alfred, 00758
Boulanger, Robert, 27068
Boulding, Kenneth E., 10909
Boulger, Demetrius Charles, 09112
Boullier, Véronique, 26251
Boulnois, L., 27738
Boulton, J.V., 22405
Boulton, John, 25655
Bouquet, Alan Coates, 01190
Bourdillon, Jennifer, 26209
Bourke-White, Margaret, 10518
Boute, Joseph, 26816
Bowen, John Charles Edward, 07692
Bower, Ursula Graham, 26519-20
Bowers, Faubion, 02910, 02921
Bowery, Thomas, 07941
Bowes, Pratima, 01313, 16709
Bowles, Chester, 14017-9
Bowles, Cynthia, 27050
Bowman, Arthur Herbert, 11556
Bowring, Lewin Bentham, 08163, 20232
Boxer, Charles Ralph, 07841-3, 07874-5, 07899, 08334
Boyee, Mary, 02289
Boyd, James W., 01548
Boyd, Robin H.S., 02237, 16789
Bradfield, E.W.C., 10675
Bradley-Birt, Francis Bradley, 20893, 24133, 25567
Brahaspati, K.C.D., 02810, 02853
Brahm Dutt, 13608
Brahma, Mohini Mohan, 26470
Brahmagupta, 05733
Brahmananda, P.R., 14203, 14255, 14466
Brahmananda Reddy, K., 19756
Brahme, Sulabha, 21545
Braibanti, Ralph J.D., 12205, 14348, 14403, 17305, 17329, 17343-5
Brailsford, Henry Noel, 10142
Braisted, Paul Judson, 10593
Brander, Laurence, 18266
Brandon, James R., 02911
Brass, Paul R., 12206, 12388, 13317, 16359, 22675, 23486, 23492-3, 23509, 23944
Braun, D., 12045
Bray, Denys de Saumarez, Sir, 22532-3
Brayne, C.V., 18728
Brayne, Frank Lugard, 10977, 15165, 22849, 23303-4
Brecher, Irving, 17713
Brecher, Michael, 12088, 12750, 13062, 13363-4, 13375-6, 13727, 14027, 14063
Breckenridge, Carol Appadurai, 01877, 19515-6
Breloer, Bernhard, 04300-1
Breman, Jan, 21763, 21787
Brembeck, Cole Spencer, 16379, 18146
Brennan, L., 23448, 23469, 23642
Brennig, Joseph J., 08194
Brent, Peter, 02211
Breton, Roland J.L., 02316-7, 12507
Breuer, Helmut, 14371
Bridge, Carl, 10211
Briggs, George Weston, 07304, 23745, 23773
Briggs, Henry George, 19614
Briggs, John, 07410
Bright, Jagat Singh, 10089, 13495, 13577
Bright, William, 27846, 27890
Brij Bhushan, Jamila, 03234, 03311-2
Brines, Russell, 12102
Brinkhaus, Horst, 04442
Briscoe, John, 25585
British Library. Reference Division, 27521
British Museum. Dept. of Printed Books, 27522
Brittain, Vera-Mary, 12751
Broadfoot, William, 22611
Broadley, A.M., 05609
Brock, Irving, 07496, 07910
Brockington, J.L., 04712
Brockway, K. Nora, 19478
Brodkin, E.I., 09492, 23449
Broehl, Wayne C., Jr., 14848
Broekmeijer, M.W.J.M., 12207
Brohi, Allahbukhsh Karimbukhsh, 17601, 18207
Brohi, Nasser, 00490
Brohier, Richard Leslie, 06136, 08089, 18689, 18700, 18705, 27133
Broker, Gulabdas, 21933
Bronger, Dirk, 00895, 19729, 19817, 26958
Brook-Shepherd, Gordon, 11954
Brooke, Robert Taliaferro, 16738
Brooks, Robert R.R., 03533-4
Brooks, Williams, 27934
Broome, Francis Napier, 26841
Broomfield, J.H., 10747
Broomfield, John H., 24290, 24312, 24326-8, 24333, 24628
Brosse, Thérèse, 02182
Brou, Alexandre, 08218
Brough, John, 03833, 26320
Broughton, Gladys M., 11112
Broughton, Thomas Duer, 08317
Brow, James, 18829-30
Brown, C.J., 00552
Brown, Carolyn Henning, 26806
Brown, Charles Philip, 06599, 19887, 27896-7
Brown, Cheever Mackenzie, 05784
Brown, Donald Mackenzie, 00222, 04424, 09352, 09697
Brown, Dorris D., 14797
Brown, Emily C., 09739, 27448
Brown, Hilton, 11955, 19317
Brown, John Coggin, 12238, 15351
Brown, Judith M., 09929, 10143, 10212
Brown, Leslie Wilfrid, 02249
Brown, Melvyn, 17273
Brown, Michael H., 20671
Brown, Percy, 03158, 03188, 03268, 07733, 07776
Brown, Robert Edward, 02699-700, 02800
Brown, William Norman, 00030, 00852, 01361-2, 01535, 01565, 01579, 05164, 05400, 05841-2, 06831-8, 07137-8, 26969, 27409-10
Browne, James, 07964
Brubaker, Richard Lee, 01712
Bruce, Charles Gagranville, 25856
Bruce, George Ludgate, 09231
Bruce, J.F., 22919
Brucker, Egon, 04302
Bruce, Reginald Isaac, 09422
Brühl, Paul, 27343
Bruhn, Klaus, 06897

Brunel, Francis, 03313
Brunet, Jacques, 02688
Brunner, Elizabeth, 17208
Brunner, Elizabeth Farkas, 17209
Brunner, Hélène, 04747-8, 06509-10, 06557
Brunner-Lachaux, Hélène. *See* Brunner, Hélène
Brunswig, Robert H., Jr., 03590, 03634
Brunton, Paul, 11406
Brush, John E., 07951, 16045
Brush, S.E., 18226-7
Bruteau, Beatrice, 11377
Bruton, Henry J., 17703
Bryant, Kenneth E., 08814
Bryce, Lucy Winifred Robinson, 22151
Brynn, Edward, 18301
Buch, M.B., 16380-1
Buch, Maganlal Amritlal, 09533
Buchan, John, 09823
Buchanan, Daniel Houston, 10861
Buchanan, Francis Hamilton, 08974, 19135, 24251a, 25687
Buchanan, Walter James, Sir, 10676, 26361
Buck, Cecil Henry, 02082
Buck, Edward John, Sir, 25857
Buck, Harry M., 00075
Buck, William, 04627, 04702
Buckhory, Somduth, 27271
Buckingham, James Silk, 10824
Buckland, Charles Edward, 09012, 24264
Buckley, Robert Burton, 11025
Buddha Prakash. *See* Prakash, Buddha
Buddhadatta, Ambalangoda Polvatte, 27807
Buddhist Committee of Inquiry, 18468
Buddhist Council of Ceylon, 18997
Budhasvāmin of Nepal, 06075
Budhraj, Vijay Sen, 12046, 12122, 17744
Budruddin, S.G.M., 17556
Bücher, J., 27887
Bühler, Georg, 00569, 02379, 04415, 04419
Bürkle, Horst, 16790
Bukhari, Shankat Ali, 22805
Bukhari, Syed Abdul Wahab, 07131, 07703, 11678
Bukhari, Y.K., 07160
Bulcke, Camille, 04713, 04842, 27819
Bullock, H., 07161
Bulsara, Jal Feerose, 16031, 21497, 21507
Bumb, Balu, 21991
Buradkar, M.P., 20864
Buragohain, D.K., 25798
Burch, George Bosworth, 01401, 16693, 16768
Burger, Angela Sutherland, 23494
Burgess, James, 00139, 01689, 01972, 03175, 03178, 03403, 05501-2, 05523, 05592, 06816, 06825, 06876-7
Burgess, Tyrrell, 16438
Burgi-Kyriazi, Maria, 11407
Burke, Mary Louise, 11314
Burke, R.C., 20584
Burke, S.M., 12017, 12187-8, 17665-6
Burkhart, Geoffrey, 19494
Burki, Shahid Javed, 17346, 17546-7, 17569, 17877, 17943, 17951, 18117, 22705, 22716
Burkill, Isaac Henry, 10649
Burleigh, Peter, 08973
Burling, Robbins, 26671-5
Burlingame, Eugene Watson, 04975, 04990
Burma. Dept. of Commerce and Industry. Commission of Inquiry to examine the question of Indian immigration into Burma (1939), 26882
Burman, Debajyoti, 15314-5, 24265
Burne, Owen Tudor, 09486
Burnell, Arthur Coke, 00570, 04420, 05183, 07844, 09011, 20534, 27501-2
Burnes, Alexander, 22426
Burnes, James, 22441
Burnet-Hurst, Alexander, 21310
Burnier, Radha, 02685
Burnouf, Eugene, 05762
Burrell, R.M., 11989-90
Burrow, Thomas, 02362-3, 02369, 02469
Burrows, Harry Raymond, 26819
Burt, Richard, 11988
Burton, Ian, 16243
Burton, Reginald George, 08318
Burton, Richard Francis, Sir, 04484, 22442-4
Burton-Page, J., 02273, 06096
Burtt, Edwin Arthur, 01266, 01342
Burway, Mukund Wamanrao, 20672
Busch, Briton Cooper, 09396
Businessmen's Conference, Karachi (1973), 18022
Bussabarger, Robert F., 03297
Bussagli, Mario, 03082, 03280, 05524
Busteed, Henry Elmsley, 08924
Butenschön, Andrea, 07491
Butler, Iris, 11931
Butler, John, 25688
Butterworth, Alan, 19136
Butterworth, Eric, 26893-4
Byres, T.J., 14771
Byrne, Jim, 25388
Byrski, Maria Christopher, 05267

Cabinetmaker, Perin H., 10510
Cadell, Patrick Robert, 09299
Caillat, Colette, 01145, 01274, 02187, 02204, 05141, 05930
Cairns, Grace E., 00122-3
Caland, Willem, 03859, 03947-8, 03998-9, 04457-8
Calcott, Maria. *See* Graham, Maria
Calcutta Review. Subject index (1844-1920), 27604
Calcutta. University, 24839
Calcutta. University. Dept. of Commerce, 24533
Calcutta. University. Dept. of Economics, 24534, 24840
Calder, Grace J., 17489
Caldwell, Robert, 02364, 08149
Calkins, Philip B., 07574, 08861, 08896, 08921
Callahan, Raymond, 07976
Callard, Keith, 17308-9
Callewaert, Winand M., 08450-3
Calpin, George Harold, 26832-3
Calvert, H., 22731
Cambridge University Asian Expedition, 22876
Camoens, Luiz de, 07867-8
Campataraya, 11286
Campbell, Andra, 20942
Campbell, Colin, 09473
Campbell, Ernest Y., 22983
Campbell, Francis Bunbury Fitzgerald, 27523, 27632
Campbell, George, Sir, 09159, 09170, 09201
Campbell, George Douglas, 09100
Campbell, J. Gabriel, 25892
Campbell-Johnson, Alan, 10475
Campos, Arnulf, 07685
Campos, J.J.A., 08853
Caṇḍidāsa, 07258
Cannon, Garland Hampton, 11847-50
Cantlie, Audrey, 02194
Cantlie, Keith, Sir, 26686
Cape, Charles Phillipps, 02043
Caplan, A. Patricia, 26281, 26321
Caplan, Lionel, 19405, 26039, 26166-7, 26226
Cappeller, Carl, 05380, 27793
Capper, John, 09160
Capwell, Charles H., 08947
Caraka, 04553, 04560
Cardew, Alexander Gordon, 07977
Cardew, Francis Gordon, 09300
Cardona, George, 05190-1, 05199-201, 27930
Cardwell, Pamela, 09513
Carey, W.H., 11932
Carman, John Braisted, 06428, 19876
Carmichael, Amy Wilson, 19524-6
Caroe, Olaf Kirkpatrick, 00498, 13923, 23033
Carpenter, Joseph Estlin, 05831
Carpenter, Mary, 11234
Carr, W.K., 19102
Carras, Mary C., 13416, 21161-2
Carré, Henri, 07918
Carrère D'Encausse, Hélène, 23074
Carrington, Charles Edward, 11898
Carroll, David, 07792
Carroll, James J., 16023
Carroll, Lucy, 10695, 10798, 16009, 23725-8
Carruthers, Ian D., 17958, 25361, 25389
Carstairs, G. Morris, 20363, 20800-1, 22075, 22131-3, 22143
Carstairs, Robert, 24278-9
Carter, Anthony T., 21154-5, 21394
Carter, Charles, 27849
Carter, John Ross, 01536
Carthill, Al, 09244
Cartman, James, 19029
Casal, Geneviève, 04570

Casal, Jean-Marie, 03578, 03595, 04570
Case, Margaret H., 08988, 09792, 11692, 27647
Casey, David F., 05095
Cashman, Richard Ian, 20739-40
Caspersz, Paul, Father, 19034
Cassels, Nancy Gardner, 10696
Cassen, Robert H., 14146
Casserly, Gordon, 09316
Castanheda, Fernão Lopes de. *See* Castanheda, Hernan Lopes de
Castanheda, Hernan Lopes de, 07869-70
Castro Lopo, Lisbet de, 24032
Catalina, Francis V., 01462
Catalogus Catalogorum, 00009
Catanach, Ian J., 21269, 21274
Catholic Association, Bombay, 16810a
Catholic Bishops' Conference of India, 16628
Catholic Directory of India, 16811
Caton, A.R., 10722
Catto, W.E., 09305
Caughley, R.C., 26252
Cavaliero, Roderick, 07936
Cave, Sydney, 01498
Cave-Browne, John, 10716
Center for the Study of Developing Societies, 13127
Central Institute of English and Foreign Languages, Hyderabad, 17088
Central Institute of Research and Training in Public Cooperation, 16151, 16287, 24080
Central Marine Fisheries Research Institute, 14935
Central Provinces and Berar, 20609
Central Provinces and Berar. Berar Co-operative Enquiry Committee, 22213
Central Road Research Institute, 15431-3, 20466
Centre for Economic Development and Administration, Tribhuvan University, 26124
Centre for Training and Research in Municipal Administration, New Delhi, 12972, 12979
Cerulli, Enrico, 17382, 18208
Cevet, David, 17014
Ceylon... *See also* Sri Lanka
Ceylon. Buddhist Sāsana Commission, 18469
Ceylon. Centre for Society and Religion, Colombo, 18483, 18802
Ceylon. Commission Appointed to Inquire into the Incidents at the Peredeniya Campus of the University of Sri Lanka on 11th and 12th November 1976, 18956
Ceylon. Commission of Inquiry into the Film Industry in Ceylon (1964), 19058
Ceylon. Commission of Inquiry on Technical Education in Ceylon, 18968
Ceylon. Commission of Inquiry on the Ceylon Broadcasting Corporation, 19059
Ceylon. Commission on Broadcasting and Information, 19060
Ceylon. Commission on Elementary Education in Ceylon, 18969
Ceylon. Commission on Higher Education in the National Languages, 18953
Ceylon. Commission on Industrial Disputes, 18803
Ceylon. Commission on Profit Sharing, 18798
Ceylon. Committee Appointed to Investigate and Report on the Establishment in Ceylon of an Institute of Theoretical Studies, 19100
Ceylon. Committee of Inquiry into the Teaching of English in Ceylon Schools, 18970
Ceylon. Committee of Inquiry on Local Government, 18541
Ceylon. Committee of Inquiry on the University of Colombo, 18954
Ceylon. Committee of Investigation into the Working of Teacher Training Colleges, 18955
Ceylon Communist Party, 18393
Ceylon. Constitution, 18356, 18369
Ceylon. Dept. of Census and Statistics, 18581, 18614-5, 18684, 18765, 27142
Ceylon. Dept. of Cooperative Development, 18677
Ceylon. Dept. of Inland Revenue, 18654
Ceylon. Dept. of Labour, 18799
Ceylon. Gal Oya Project Evaluation Committee, 18706
Ceylon Government Railway, 18787
Ceylon Indian Congress, 18490
Ceylon. Industrial Development Board, 18776, 18780
Ceylon Institute of Scientific and Industrial Research, 19099
Ceylon. Land Commission, 18751, 18766
Ceylon. Local Government Commission, 18542
Ceylon. Mahaweli Development Board, 18707
Ceylon. Ministry of Agriculture and Food, 18690-1
Ceylon. Ministry of Cultural Affairs. Register of ancient monuments, 03361
Ceylon. Ministry of Educational and Cultural Affairs, 18930
Ceylon. Ministry of Finance, 18627, 18783
Ceylon. Ministry of Planning and Economic Affairs, 18577, 18623, 18652
Ceylon National Bibliography, 27702
Ceylon National Congress, 18351
Ceylon. National Education Commission (1961), 18944
Ceylon. National Planning Council, 18624, 18649-50
Ceylon. Police Commission, 18510
Ceylon. Press Commission, 19061
Ceylon. Royal Commission on the Cooperative Movement in Ceylon, 18676
Ceylon. Special Committee on Education, 18945
Ceylon. State Council, 18543
Ceylon. Treasury, 18578
Ceylon. Universities Commission, 18957-9, 18965
Ceylon. University, 00382, 18872
Ceylon. Viharagam, Dewalagam, and Nindagam Land Tenure Commission, 18752
Chablani, Hashmatrai Lekhraj, 07586
Chablani, S.P., 08563
Chadha, K.R., 22961
Chaghatai, Muhammad Abdulla, 07139-40, 07751-2, 08753
Chagla, Mahomedali Currim, 12077, 14020
Chailleux, Jean-Yves, 19818
Chailley-Bert, Joseph, 08161
Chaitanya, Krishna, 02398, 02468, 02499, 02587, 03269, 27160
Chak, B.L., 27314-5
Chakladar, Haran Chandra, 03510, 03772, 04486, 05337
Chakrabarti, Atulananda, 13015
Chakrabarti, Dilip K., 00342, 03493, 03527, 03596, 03628, 03689-90, 03734
Chakrabarti, Hiren, 24292, 24313
Chakrabarti, S.K., 25152
Chakrabarti, Samiran Chandra, 03815
Chakrabarti, Saroj, 24363-4
Chakrabarti, Satyabrata, 24612
Chakrabarti, Tarapada, 02498
Chakrabarty, Dipesh, 24540, 24563
Chakrabarty, Ramakanta, 24884
Chakrabarty, Chandra, 00691
Chakraborti, A.M., 15251
Chakraborti, B., 24675
Chakraborti, Haripada, 02015, 04146, 04378, 04757
Chakraborti, Manindra Kumar, 03324
Chakraborti, Smarajit, 25129
Chakrabortty, Krishna, 24763
Chakraborty, Chhanda, 03788
Chakraborty, Ratan Lal, 08872
Chakraborty, S.C., 24754
Chakraborty, S.K., 14692, 15257
Chakraborty, Sunil Ranjan, 24350
Chakraborty, Trailokya Nath, 24314
Chakraborty, Usha, 24660
Chakravarthy, G.N., 03892
Chakravarthy, P., 19178
Chakravarti, A.K., 14858, 24791-2
Chakravarti, Anand, 21964-5, 21998
Chakravarti, Appaswami, 01146
Chakravarti, Atul Chandra, 01778
Chakravarti, B., 00537
Chakravarti, Basudha, 25079
Chakravarti, Chintaharan, 05859, 08935
Chakravarti, Haripada, 04057
Chakravarti, Jadab Chandra, 09344
Chakravarti, Janardana, 07264
Chakravarti, K.C., 26523
Chakravarti, Kisor Kumar, 04843, 04844
Chakravarti, Kshitish Chandra, 06382
Chakravarti, L.N., 26476
Chakravarti, Nalini Ranjan, 10862, 26875
Chakravarti, Nihar Chandra, 15152
Chakravarti, Nirmal, 24621
Chakravarti, Nirod Baran, 01427
Chakravarti, P.C., 04341, 09410
Chakravarti, Parimal, 14449
Chakravarti, Prabhatchandra, 05165
Chakravarti, Prithvindra, 08948

Chakravarti, Prithwis Chandra, 13924
Chakravarti, Pulinbihari, 04807
Chakravarti, S.R., 12226
Chakravarti, Santi K., 14645
Chakravarti, Satis Chandra, 10758
Chakravarti, Sudhindra Chandra, 07229
Chakravarti, Sukumara, 07279
Chakravarti, Sures Chandra, 03982
Chakravarti, Taponath, 07205
Chakravarti, Tarini Sankar, 10414
Chakravartty, Nikhil, 23515
Chakravarty, Apurba Kumar, 00277, 04530
Chakravarty, B., 24773
Chakravarty, Basudha, 11338
Chakravarty, Indira, 00837
Chakravarty, Lalita, 11113
Chakravarty, Mohan, 24365
Chakravarty, Pranab Kumar, 26389
Chakravarty, R., 23289
Chakravarty, S.C., 24600
Chakravarty, S.R., 25252, 25293
Chakravarty, Sudeshna, 24938
Chakravarty, Sukhamoy, 14128, 15460
Chakravarty, T.K., 15057
Chakravorti, Bankabehari, 03639
Chakravorti, Robi, 24734
Chakravorty, Byomkesh Chandra, 25052
Chakravorty, P.M., 27276
Chakravorty, Padmini, 26645
Chakravorty, Upendra Narayan, 08319
Chakravorty, Birendra Chandra, 26443
Chalapathi Rao, I.V., 17035
Chalapathi Rau, M., 10147, 10799, 13353, 13417, 16864, 16883-4
Chaliha, Bhaba Prasad, 07293
Chambard, Jean-Luc, 08403, 22230-1, 27648
Chamber of Commerce and Industry, Karachi, 18001, 18019
Chamberlain, Jacob, 19873
Chamberlain, Muriel Evelyn, 09029
Chamling, Dhiraj R., 14112
Champion, Harry George, Sir, 17974
Champness, Ernest, 10612
Chan, Wing Tsit, 01325
Chana, Mahboob Ali, 22508
Chanana, Charanjit, 12249, 15119, 15166, 25294
Chanana, Dev Raj, 04387
Chanchreek, Kanhaiyalal, 13640-1
Chand, Diwaker, 26087, 26151
Chand, Hari, 12380
Chand, Mahesh, 23836
Chand, Sansar, 23260
Chand, Tara, 00164, 02283, 07424, 09557
Chand, Tej Pratap, 23459
Chand Bardāī, 06724
Chanda, Ashok K., 16835, 16937
Chanda, Asok Kumar, 12609, 22913, 13016
Chanda, Ramaprasad, 00692, 05451, 06097
Chandar, Krishan, 11697-8
Chandavarkar, G.A., 01511, 22920
Chandavarkar, Ganesh Lakshman, 10742, 21357-8, 21370
Chander, Jag Parvesh, 23325
Chander, Prabha, 22758
Chander, R., 15513
Chandernagor. Conseil, 07905
Chandhok, H.L., 14646
Chandhoke, S.K., 20995
Chandidas, Raj, 13318, 22162, 22690, 23335
Chandiram, Jai, 16947
Chandna, R.C., 23274a
Chandola, Anoop C., 02759, 02764
Chandola, L.M., 22368
Chandra, Asit Math, 03760
Chandra, Bipan. *See* Bipan Chandra
Chandra, Jag Parvesh, 16891
Chandra, K. Rishabh, 05249, 05279
Chandra, Lokesh, 00355
Chandra, N.K., 24369
Chandra, N.R., 13868
Chandra, P.T., 26959
Chandra, Prabhat, 22243
Chandra, Pramod, 01726, 03176-7, 03210, 03235, 05472, 05575, 05610, 06089, 06826, 06883, 07713, 07719, 07756, 07772-3, 08497, 08501
Chandra, Pratap, 01314, 01463
Chandra, Rai Govind, 05516
Chandra, Ramprasad, 01761
Chandra, S.C., 06884
Chandra, Savitri, 08804
Chandra, Sudhir, 09582, 20720
Chandra, Sushil, 16185
Chandra Prabha, 06057
Chandra Shekhar, 13087
Chandrachud, Y.V., 13272
Chandrakant, L.S., 16441, 16550, 16618-9
Chandramani, G.Y., 19787
Chandramani Singh, Leishangthem, 26577
Chandran, C.S., 19446
Chandran, Praphulla Satish, 20576
Chandrasekara Naidu, V., 19259
Chandrasekaran, C., 16276, 21562
Chandrasekhar, A., 02588
Chandrasekhar, Sripati, 16677, 14037, 14147, 14185, 16313, 19431
Chandrasekhara Aiyer, N., 04703
Chandrasekharan, K., 25028
Chandrasekharan, Kannankulangarai Ranganathasastry, 17155, 17173
Chandrasekharan, S., 14904
Chandrasoma, M., 18877
Chandu Menon, Oyyarattu, 20200-1
Chandy, M., 14924
Changkakati, Keshav, 02760
Channa, V.C., 23362
Chapekar, Laxman Narayan, 20819, 21459
Chapekar, Nalinee M., 04571
Chaplin, William, 20693
Chapman, Edith, 26613
Chapman, John Alexander, 08932
Charak, Sukh Dev Singh, 00538, 08557, 23133
Charan Singh, 14292, 23916
Charanjit Chanana. *See* Chanana, Charanjit
Chari, A.S.R., 10057, 12865
Chari, P.R., 17690-1
Chari, V.K., 05980
Charlesworth, Neil, 21275
Charpentier, C.J., 00838
Charpentier, Jarl, 02126
Chassaigne, Marc, 07927
Chatalian, G., 05096
Chatfield, Charles, 09914
Chatham, Doris Clark, 06817
Chatterjea, A.B., 15411
Chatterjee... *See also* Chatterji
Chatterjee, A.C., 00178
Chatterjee, Amitabha, 27638
Chatterjee, Amiya Bhusan, 24422, 24513, 24711, 24749-50, 27286
Chatterjee, Anathnath, 20977
Chatterjee, Anil K., 15576
Chatterjee, Anjan, 26362
Chatterjee, Anjali Basu, 08844
Chatterjee, Arun Kumar, 21520
Chatterjee, Arun Prokas, 12787
Chatterjee, Asim Kumar, 00042, 10819, 05142
Chatterjee, Asoke, 05815, 07300
Chatterjee, B.R., 16261
Chatterjee, Basant Kumar, 13622
Chatterjee, Basudeb, 24387
Chatterjee, Bimalananda, 16286
Chatterjee, Bimanesh, 12565
Chatterjee, Bina, 05733
Chatterjee, Bishwa Bandhu, 15035, 15744, 22359, 23865, 23887
Chatterjee, Chanchal Kumar, 01042, 04467
Chatterjee, Debiprasad, 24937
Chatterjee, Dilip Kumar, 10022
Chatterjee, Dipankar, 01379
Chatterjee, Enakshi, 24928
Chatterjee, Heramba, 04468
Chatterjee, Krishna Nath, 01041
Chatterjee, Lalita, 03324
Chatterjee, Margaret, 16103, 16694
Chatterjee, Mary, 21508, 23746
Chatterjee, N.N., 22038
Chatterjee, Niharkanti, 27533
Chatterjee, Nirmal Chandra, 12373
Chatterjee, Pareshnath, 14450
Chatterjee, Rama Krishna, 16833
Chatterjee, S.P., 17233, 26996
Chatterjee, Sabitri Prasanna, 09740

Chatterjee, Santa, 25122
Chatterjee, Santosh, 10732
Chatterjee, Satischandra, 04845, 01315, 11295
Chatterjee, Shiba Prasad, 27291
Chatterjee, Sila, 25122
Chatterjee, Sisir, 12123, 25153
Chatterjee, Suhas, 27995
Chatterjee, U.N., 15036
Chatterji... *See also* Chatterjee
Chatterji, A., 24854
Chatterji, Amiya, 14523
Chatterji, Bankim Chandra, 24979-85
Chatterji, Basant Kumar, 13449
Chatterji, Basant Kumar, 13966
Chatterji, Bhaskar, 04180
Chatterji, Bhola, 13480, 24826, 26007, 26009
Chatterji, Heramba Nath, 05968
Chatterji, Jagadish Chandra, 04846, 06956
Chatterji, Kalyan Kumar, 16653
Chatterji, M., 24735
Chatterji, N., 26614
Chatterji, Nandalal, 08006, 08862, 08873-4, 09645
Chatterji, Prashanto K., 09093
Chatterji, Saratchandra, 25070-4
Chatterji, Sanjiv Chandra, 24480
Chatterji, Santimay, 10662
Chatterji, Saral Kumar, 12351, 13456, 13578, 16314, 13654, 16575
Chatterji, Shiba Prasad, 24423
Chatterji, Sris Chandra, 03432
Chatterji, Suniti Kumar, 00016, 00065, 00476, 00531, 00701-2, 02657, 04714, 05945, 07132, 07250, 08949, 11567, 17063, 24712, 25053
Chatterjia, P.K., 24793
Chattopadhyay... *See also* Chattopadhyaya
Chattopadhyay, Gouranga, 20978, 24584, 24676, 26398
Chattopadhyay, Kshitis Prasad, 00981, 24853, 26244
Chattopadhyay, Kumar Ananda, 24221, 24585
Chattopadhyay, P., 15207
Chattopadhyay, Raghabendra, 11080
Chattopadhyaya, Alaka, 04933
Chattopadhyaya, Amal Kumar, 00238, 24398
Chattopadhyaya, Aparna, 04464
Chattopadhyaya, B.D., 06734
Chattopadhyaya, Brajadulal, 06244
Chattopadhyaya, Debiprasad, 00017, 00039, 00253, 01298, 01380, 04594, 04832, 04933, 16695
Chattopadhyaya, Gautam, 13200, 24241, 24315, 24564
Chattopadhyaya, Haraprasad, 09493, 18852, 26817
Chattopadhyaya, K., 03347
Chattopadhyaya, K.P., 03747
Chattopadhyaya, Kamaladevi, 01079, 03298, 03340, 03348
Chattopadhyaya, Ksetreschandra, 00024, 02040
Chattopadhyaya, Shyamal, 25054
Chattopadhyaya, Siddheswar, 05999
Chattopadhyaya, Sudhakar, 04108-9, 04175, 04195, 04428, 04562, 04734, 05860
Chaturvedi, B.N., 12927, 19730
Chaturvedi, Benarsidas, 11541
Chaturvedi, H.R., 16332, 22107, 23510
Chaturvedi, Jagdish Prasad, 27258
Chaturvedi, M.G., 16639
Chaturvedi, M.S., 12717
Chaturvedi, Mahendra, 27820
Chaturvedi, Ram Gopal, 12546, 12816
Chaturvedi, S.C., 12538
Chaturvedi, Shrinath, 27186
Chaturvedi, Sitaram, 10130
Chaturvedi, T.N., 16152
Chaube, J., 06713, 07529
Chaube, Ram Kumar, 05626
Chaube, Sarayu P., 16608
Chaube, Shibanikinkar, 26453-5
Chaubey, B.B., 04320
Chaubey, Ganesh, 24222
Chaubey, Hira Lal, 13627
Chaubey, N.P., 15100, 23611
Chaudhari, Haider Ali, 22776
Chaudhari, Radha Krishna, 00511
Chaudhary, Muhammad Ikram, 17473
Chaudhary, N.D., 20818
Chaudhary, Radhakrishna, 06256
Chaudhary, Vijay Chandra Prasad, 00128, 09646
Chaudhory, Fazlul Quader, 17454
Chaudhri, D.P., 14849
Chaudhri, Mohammed Ahsen, 17667, 17686
Chaudhry, K.C., 09680
Chaudhry, Mahinder D., 14221, 23346
Chaudhry, Mohammad Ghaffar, 17889, 17981
Chaudhry, Nazir Ahmad, 09494, 22556, 22991, 17682
Chaudhry, Ranbir Singh, 22676, 23263
Chaudhry, Shahid Amjad, 17714
Chaudhuri... *See also* Chaudury, Choudhuri, Chowdhury
Chaudhuri, Amiya K., 12836
Chaudhuri, Asim, 15267, 15283
Chaudhuri, Bhupendranath, 26676
Chaudhuri, Binay Bhushan, 10946, 24101, 24436-7, 24444, 24474, 24501
Chaudhuri, Brahma, 27624
Chaudhuri, Dipak Basu Ray, 15352
Chaudhuri, Dulal, 03040
Chaudhuri, Harendra Narayan, 24481
Chaudhuri, Haridas, 01395, 02156, 11378
Chaudhuri, J.N., 08246
Chaudhuri, Joyanto Nath, 12735, 12736
Chaudhuri, Jyotirindra Nath, 26687
Chaudhuri, K.N., 00239, 07623, 07803-4, 07952, 07999, 10863, 11059
Chaudhuri, Keshab, 09681
Chaudhuri, Kshitish Chandra, 08975, 22482
Chaudhuri, M.A., 09181
Chaudhuri, M.K., 10886
Chaudhuri, M.R., 27766
Chaudhuri, Manoranjan, 14196, 14905, 15353, 15383, 24514-5
Chaudhuri, Muzaffer Ahmed, 17347
Chaudhuri, Nani Gopal, 08875, 19615
Chaudhuri, Narayan, 11252, 24929
Chaudhuri, Nibaran Chandra, 24446
Chaudhuri, Nirad Chandra, 00703, 01191, 03314, 08007, 11852, 11971, 15834, 17174
Chaudhuri, P.D., 03439
Chaudhuri, P.K., 21980
Chaudhuri, Pabitra Kumar, 04250
Chaudhuri, Pradip, 24713
Chaudhuri, Pramit, 14242, 14256
Chaudhuri, Pratap Chandra, 00532
Chaudhuri, Radha Krishna, 04405
Chaudhuri, Ranjit, 24390-1
Chaudhuri, Roma, 06496
Chaudhuri, Roop Lal, 01017
Chaudhuri, Sachin, 14389
Chaudhuri, Sankho, 17210
Chaudhuri, Sashi Bhusan, 04039, 09454, 09460-1, 09495, 27778
Chaudhuri, Sibadas, 00002-4, 00296, 00559, 09462, 27600-3, 27739
Chaudhuri, Sukomal, 05110
Chaudhuri, Susil, 08910-3, 08925
Chaudhury, Binayendra Nath, 04078
Chaudhury, Jogindra Nath, 08239
Chaudhury, Kabir, 12124
Chauhan, Arvind Balubhai, 21773
Chauhan, Brij Raj, 00773, 00865, 14998, 16443, 22108, 22118
Chauhan, D.S., 23623, 23837
Chauhan, Eklavya, 16237
Chauhan, I.E.N., 02898
Chauhan, I.S., 26807
Chauhan, Jagmal Singh, 14679
Chauhan, K.K.S., 21240
Chauhan, Randhir Singh, 25840, 25995, 26018, 26371
Chauhan, S.K., 25706-7, 25775-6
Chaurasia, G., 16539
Chavan, Anita, 14204
Chavan, B.W., 14204
Chavan, Yashwantrao Balwantrao, 13131, 13642, 13742
Chavarria-Aguilar, Oscar Luis, 27973-5
Chavda, V.K., 08342, 09411, 20624, 27713
Chawda, V.K., 21715, 21875-6
Chawla, D.R., 16273
Chawla, Om Prakash, 14574
Chawla, V.N., 12352, 12941, 12978
Chawla, Vijay, 17745
Cheema, Aftab Ahmad, 18004
Chekki, Danesh A., 01002, 15037, 15686, 15887, 15974, 20380-2, 20401-2
Chelliah, J.V., 18960
Chelliah, Raja Jesudoss, 14499, 14533, 14575, 22123
Chemjong, Iman Singh, 26227

Chen, Kuan-I, 14274
Chen, Lincoln C., 25346, 25586
Chenchiah, Pandipeddi, 02581
Chenery, Hollis B., 17715
Chengal Reddy, A., 19849
Chengalvaraya Pillai, V.S., 19569
Chennakesavan, Sarasvati, 01192, 01464
Cherian, A., 06573
Cheriyan, C.V., 04600
Cherukupalle, Nirmala Devi, 16056
Chesney, George Tomkyns, 09162
Chethimattam, John Britto, 01369, 16791
Chettur, Sankara Krishna, 12658
Chetwode, Penelope, 03472
Chhabra, B. Chandra, 01613
Chhabra, Bahadur Chand, 04584
Chhabra, G.S., 08538, 09054, 22561
Chhabra, Hari Sharan, 19616
Chhaju Singh, 11277
Chhavi: golden jubilee volume, 03109
Chhibbar, Yash Pal, 15754
Chhibber, H.L., 22198
Chiao, Chien, 01706
Chib, Som Nath, 10594
Chib, Sukhdev Singh, 16674, 27187, 27215-6, 27259, 27316-7
Chicherov, Alexander I., 07587, 13979
Chickermane, D.V., 16648
Chidambaram, S., 19918
Chidambaram, V.C., 21562
Chidambaram Aiyar, N., 04533
Chidambaram Pillai, P., 19517
Chidambaranath Chettiar, A., 27860
Chidananda Murthy, M., 06539
Child, Frank C., 17698, 22806
Childe, Vere Gordon, 03773
Childs, John Norris, 20012
Chimpa, Lama, 04933
Chinai, Babubhai Maneklal, 14340
Chinchunsure, B.S., 21405
Chinmayananda, Swami, 06346
Chinmulgund, P.J., 00043
Chintamani, Chirravoori Yajneswara, Sir, 09084, 10275, 10697
Chinzen, Akanuma, 05124
Chirayath, John Thomas, 20013, 20042
Chirol, Valentine, Sir, 09682, 10229
Chishti, Anees, 12581
Chishti, Sumitra, 14080
Chitale, Kamalabai, 21546
Chitale, Vasant Parsharam, 13842, 13859, 15357
Chitkara, H.L., 16360
Chitnis, K.N., 05704, 06558, 08164
Chitnis, Suma, 16382, 16444-5, 21406, 21601
Chitra, M.N., 20518
Chitre, Dilip, 21646
Chittagong Port Authority, 25483
Chittagong. University. Dept. of Sociology, 25591
Choksey, Rustom Dinshaw, 08320, 20267, 20585, 20604-5, 20685-6, 20701, 21198-201, 21707
Chokshi, C.C., 14567
Chokshi, Hiralal Punjalal, 21699
Choksy, N.K., 18542-4
Choldin, Harvey M., 25413-25415
Choondal, Chummar, 20219
Chopra, Barkat Rai, 22586
Chopra, Devi Saran, 12630
Chopra, Gulshan Lal, 22566, 22570
Chopra, I.C., 16201
Chopra, Kusum, 14906, 22777
Chopra, Prabha, 23320
Chopra, Prabha, 27277
Chopra, Pran, 12141, 12165, 12208, 13017, 13236, 13988
Chopra, Pran Nath, 00190, 00395, 07630, 09599, 23470, 27318
Chopra, R.N., 16337
Chopra, Surendra, 12089, 23075
Chopra, V.P., 13843
Choubey, Hutendra Kumar, 22221
Choudhary, Abhay Kant, 05722
Choudhary, B.C., 22301
Choudhary, K.M., 21753
Choudhary, L.K., 12018
Choudhary, Radhakrishna, 02641, 04009, 04303, 04321, 04388, 05711, 07078, 07183, 07211, 07370
Choudhary, Ramesh, 27161
Choudhary, Sukhbir, 09559, 09990, 10033, 12166, 13987, 20121
Choudhry, Kapil, 23290-1
Choudhry, L.P., 13014
Choudhry, Mohammad Iqbal, 18077-8
Choudhry, P.S., 20635
Choudhuri, Keshab, 24736
Choudhury, A.H., 18182
Chowdhury, Abdul Momin, 07176, 07178
Choudhury, B., 14907
Choudhury, Biswanath, 27287
Choudhury, Deba Prosad, 09440-1
Choudhury, Golam Wahed, 12019, 12068, 17317-8, 17424, 17500, 17560, 25161-2
Choudhury, Lutful Hoq, 12265, 25223
Choudhury, Mamata, 04322
Choudhury, Moqbul A., 25603-5
Choudhury, N.C., 00624, 20949
Choudhury, Pratap Chandra, 07194
Choudhury, R.C., 26659
Choudhury, Ranabir Ray, 24714
Choudhury, S.C., 27736
Choudhury, Sadananda, 22315
Choudhury, Serajul Islam, 25080
Chowdary, P.U.C., 19888
Chowdhary, S.N., 05583
Chowdhry, D. Paul, 16126
Chowdhry, Kamla, 12641, 14737, 15258, 15957, 21774
Chowdhry, Prem, 22739
Chowdhury, A.K.M. Alauddin, 25346
Chowdhury, Abdun Noor, 25530-1, 25595
Chowdhury, Anwarullah, 25543-4
Chowdhury, Bhawani Sankar, 09245
Chowdhury, Jyotirindra Nath, 26488-9
Chowdhury, Kabir, 25647, 25656
Chowdhury, Khurshid Alam, 17324
Chowdhury, Mofazzal Haider, 27994
Chowdhury, Munier, 25648
Chowdhury, Naimuddin, 25362
Chowdhury, Neerja, 16892
Chowdhury, Nuimuddin, 25470
Chowdhury, P.N., 17264
Chowdhury, Qayyum, 25668
Chowdhury, Rafiqul Islam, 25509
Christa Seva Ashram, 19039
Christian Institute for the Study of Religion and Society, Bangalore, 16782, 16795
Christie, Anthony, 04585
Christie, Bruce, 03027
Chudgar, Popatlal L., 09357
Chudley, F.J., 26184
Chughtai, M.I.D., 18285
Chughtai, Muhammad Abdullah Rahman, 11825
Chunder, Pratapchandra, 04304, 24553
Chung, Tan, 11060
Chunkath, A., 12415
Church, Roderick, 23534, 25701
Church of South India, 16822-3, 19527
Churchill, Awnsham, 07826
Churchill, Edward D., Jr., 22975
Churchill, John, 07826
Churchill, Winston Leonard Spencer, Sir, 23036
Cipriani, Lidio, 26721-2
Cirlot, Juan Eduardo, 03056
Citizens for Democracy. Nathwani Commission, 21848
Civil Rights (Tarkunde) Committee, 19695
Cizikova, Ksenija, 02654
Clark, Colin, 14875-6
Clark, Edwin Hill, 17950, 22784
Clark, Ian Duncan Lindsay, 11542
Clark, John, 27237
Clark, M., 26613
Clark, Thomas Welbourne, 02677, 07301, 11568, 24715, 24955, 28008
Clark, Walter Eugene, 00291, 04525, 04534
Clarke, C. Stanley, 07766
Clarke, W. Hyde, 11967
Clarkson, Stephen, 14243, 14264
Clason, A.T., 03570
Claus, Peter James, 20364, 20383, 20535-7
Clavel, Leotiny S., 11679
Clay, Edward J., 24073, 25333, 25440
Clay, Mavis N., 25333
Clements, Ernest, 02743

Clinard, Marshall Barron, 15687, 16076
Closets d'Errey, Henri de, 07907-8, 07915
Clothey, Frederick W., 01948, 02101
Clunes, John, 09358
Coale, Ansley J., 14148
Coates, William Ames, 19073
Coatman, John, 10213, 10244, 10276, 10763
Coats, Thomas, 21465
Cobden-Ramsay, Louis E.B., 20680
Codd, Clara M., 11355
Codrington, Humphrey William, 00380, 04362, 06121
Codrington, Kenneth de Burgh, 05452, 06098
Coedès, George, 06273
Coelho, Vincent H., 00381, 12199, 27319
Coffin, Merrill M., 22280
Cohen, Benjamin I., 13844
Cohen, Stephen Philip, 09816, 10434, 12020, 12051, 12718, 12730-2, 13695, 17366, 19657
Cohen, Sulman Samuel, 06347, 11408
Cohn, Bernard Samuel, 00641, 00652, 00846, 07618, 07978, 08764-5, 08989, 08998, 09194, 09272, 10546, 10947-8, 11200-1, 23460-1, 23690, 23747
Cohn, William, 03197
Cole, W. Owen, 08568
Colebrooke, Henry Thomas, 04798, 05699, 05732, 08914, 20702
Collet, Joseph, 07965
Collet, Sophia Dobson, 11235
Collins, Charles Henry, 18357
Collins, Charles Henry, 18504-5
Collins, Larry, 10476
Collis, Maurice, 04704
Collison, Robert, 27511
Colombo Plan Consultative Committee, 12250-1
Columbia University. School of Law, 13869
Columbia University. Southern Asian Institute, 14103
Colvin, Ian Duncan, 09843
Combaz, Gisbert, 01681, 03067
Comfort, Alex, 05723
Commissariat, Manekshah Sorabshah, 06714, 08343-5
Commonwealth Education Conference, Canberra (1971), 18150
Communist Party of India, 10040, 12454, 12463, 13202, 13235, 14457, 13580, 13943, 14925
Communist Party of India (Marxist), 13224-7, 13560
Community Development Foundation, 25596
Compagnie Nouvelle des Indes, 07906
Compton, J.M., 09195
Conference on Bengal Studies, 1st-7th, 24252
Conference on Problems of Resource Mobilisation in the States (1969), 14555
Conference on the Impact of Cooperative Agricultural Credit on Weaker Sections, New Delhi (1976), 15129
Conference on the Teaching of English in Schools, Delhi (1963), 16654
Conference on the Teaching of Preventive and Social Medicine in Relation to the Health Needs of the Country, Delhi (1965), 16361
Conference on Traditional Cultures, Ceylon University (1956), 18835
Conference on University Adult Education, Bhopal (1965), 16675
Conio, Caterina, 06336
Conklin, George H., 15888, 15845, 20365, 20384
Conlon, Frank Fowler, 20393-4
Conn, Harvie M., 17398
Connell, John, 13925
Connor, Lieut., 20244
Conrad, Dieter, 17519
Constable, Archibald, 07496
Contractor, Meher, 03006
Contractor, Minocher K., 02380
Converse, Hyla Stuntz, 03860
Conze, Edward, 01141, 01224, 01252, 01267-8, 01537, 02174, 04952, 05029, 05062-7, 05069-71, 07344
Cook, Elsie Kathleen, 27144
Cook, Nilla Cram, 02631
Cooke, Charles Northcote, 11165
Cooke, Gerald B., 16710
Cooke, Henry Reade, 21803
Cooke, Hope. *See* Namgyal, Hope
Coomaraswamy, Ananda Kentish, 00910, 01335, 01439, 01583, 01591, 01630, 01657, 01665-7, 01693, 01727, 01747, 01847, 03068, 03083-5, 03115-6, 03152, 03159, 03198, 03243-4, 03262, 03277, 03288, 03352, 03362, 03473, 03834, 04926, 05300, 05453, 05469, 05480, 06839, 07260, 07734, 08109-10, 08232, 08478-80, 11983, 19090
Cooper, Judith Elias, 24655
Cooper, Leonard, 09317
Co-operative Farming Seminar, Bangladesh Academy for Rural Development (1972), 25432
Cooray, Joseph A.L., 18364, 18445, 18525
Cooray, L.J. Mark, 18365-7, 18446, 18526
Copland, Ian F.S., 20591, 20625
Copleston, Reginald Stephen, 01240
Copley, Antony R.H., 10199, 13096
Coppola, Carlo, 16993, 17054-6
Corea, Gamini, 18579, 18625, 18692
Corea, J.C.A., 18933
Corfield, Conrad, Sir, 09359
Cormack, Margaret Lawson, 16576, 27411, 27425
Cornelius, A.R., 17360
Cornelius, John Jesudasan. *See* Kumarappa, Jagadisan Mohandas
Cornell, Louis L., 11899
Corpus Inscriptionum Indicarum, 00564
Corr, Gerald H., 10435
Correa, Gaspar, 07860
Correia-Afonso, John, 00059, 07876, 07883
Corti, W.R., 27363
Corwin, Lauren Anita, 15919
Cosens, Francis Richard, 09514
Costa, Aleixo Manuel da, 27714
Costa, Giulio, 26677
Coster, Geraldine, 02183
Cotton, Arthur Thomas, 11026
Cotton, Harry Evan Auguste, Sir, 10223, 10678, 24523
Cotton, Henry John Stedman, Sir, 09202
Cotton, James Sutherland, 20703
Cottrell, Alvin J., 11989-90
Coulborn, Rushton, 05712
Coulson, N.J., 18105-6
Coulter, John Wesley, 26808
Council for Old World Archaeology Bibliography, 00575
Council for Social Development, New Delhi, 14193
Council of Scientific and Industrial Research, New Delhi, 17271, 26965-6
Council on World Tensions, 21602
Coupland, Reginald, Sir, 10214-5, 10405, 10512
Cour, Ajeet, 27467
Cour, Arpana, 27467
Courbe, Nicole, 17520
Courtney, W., 20586
Cousens, Henry, 03403-4, 03422, 06858, 08233
Cousin, Françoise, 03341
Cousins, William J., 19841
Cousins, William T., 24690
Couto, Diogo do, 07866
Cove, John J., 00795-6
Coward, Harold G., 01412, 05224, 06038
Coward, Walter, Jr., 25399
Cowasjee, Saros, 17110
Cowell, Edward Byles, 03973, 04794, 05007, 05060, 05302, 05353, 06011
Cowell, Herbert, 09246
Cowen, D.V., 27029
Cowgill, George, 26586
Cownie, John, 17952
Cox, Edmund Charles, Sir, 09222, 20694
Crabb, Cecil van Meter, Jr., 13748
Craddock, Reginald Henry, Sir, 09973
Crafts Museum, New Delhi, 03299
Craig, J. Edwin, Jr., 18585
Crane, Robert I., 00685, 09006, 10552, 10611, 12266, 13039
Craven, Roy C., 03086, 03211, 17192
Crawford, Arthur Travers, 20695
Crawford, Dirom Grey, 10679
Crawford, H.L., 18990
Crawford, S. Cromwell, 01512
Crawley, W.F., 23656
Creagh Coen, Terence, Sir, 09360
Creel, Austin B., 01538, 12416
Creswell, Keppel Archibald Cameron, 03153-4, 03263
Crocker, Walter, 13365
Crone, G.R., 07805
Cronin, Richard Paul, 24291
Cronin, Vincent, 08219
Crook, Nigel, 21544
Crooke, William, 00512, 00693, 01566, 01713, 02102, 02137, 02450, 07504, 23691, 23917

Crouch, Harold A., 15669
Crouzet, Francois, 00212
Crowe, Philip K., 19107
Crowe, Sylvia, 07777
Crowley, Daniel J., 26791
Cullen, Gordon, 23413
Culshaw, Wesley J., 20916, 20921, 20928, 20943
Cultural Heritage of India, 00207
Cultural Heritage of Ladakh, 27217
Cumming, John Ghest, Sir, 09085
Cummings, Ralph W., Jr., 14793
Cumpston, Ina Mary, 09655, 26737
Cunha, Tristão de Bragança, 21036
Cunningham, Alexander, Sir, 00140, 03160, 04063, 04079, 04135, 05473, 05481, 05676, 23142
Cunningham, Henry Stewart, 09129
Cunningham, Joseph Davey, 08539
Cunningham, W.B., 23226
Curle, Adam, 18162-3
Curran, Jean Alonzo, 13280
Currell, Melville, 14302
Currie, Julia Clare, 26820
Curry, John Court, 09223
Curtis, Lionel, 10230
Curtis, William, 27069
Curzon of Kedleston, George Nathaniel Curzon, 1st Marquess, 09101, 09412, 09817, 10586
Cutt, James, 14576
Cytrynbaum, Solomon, 18825
Czekus, Sandor, 09610

Dabadghao, P.M., 14897
Dabbs, Jack A., 27986
Dabral, M.P., 23833
Dabu, Khurshed S., 02290
Dacca. University. College of Social Welfare and Research Centre, 25581
Dacca. University. Institute of Education and Research, 25627, 25630
Dacca. University. Institute of Nutrition and Food Science, 25588
Dacca. University. Institute of Statistical Research and Training, 25583
Da Cruz, Antonio, 21037
Da Cunha, J. Gerson, 08385
Da Cunha, Uma, 27649
Da Cunha Rivara, J.H., 02593
Dadachanji, Serozh, 02925
Dādūdayāla, 08454
Daftary, G.D., 21799
Dagens, Bruno, 06607-8
Dagli, Vadilal Jechand, 13994, 14033, 14071, 14197, 14232, 14492, 14746-7, 15153, 15177, 15208, 15217
Dahal, Ballabh Mani, 26252
Dahal, Dilli Ram, 26286
Dahama, Om Prakash, 15060
Dahejia, Vidya, 06901
Dahiya, B.S., 22823
Dahiya, M.S., 12883
Dahlquist, Allan, 04588
Dahmen-Dallapiccola, A.L., 06106, 03281-2
Dahya, Badr, 26920-1
Dahya, Zaynab, 26925
Dalal, Chandulal Bhagubhai, 09854
Dalal, Minakshi L., 05280
Dalaya, Chandra, 13794, 14511
Dale, Stephen F., 08131, 08212, 20122-3
Dales, George F., 03483, 03489, 03579, 03612, 03622, 03651-4
Dalgliesh, Wilbert Harold, 07928
Dalip Singh, 08569
Daljeet Singh, 08581
Daljit Singh, Raja Sir, 08640
Dallas, Dumi, 17211
Dalton, Dennis G., 09937, 10075, 10764
Dalton, Edward Tuite, 24636
Dalton, Eira, 20180
Dalvi, J.P., 13944
Dalwai, Hamid Umar, 12446
Damant, Gaborn Henry, 25657
Dames, Mansel Longworth, 22534, 22551
Damle, Yashwant Bhaskar, 00847, 15688, 21476, 21607
Damodara Gupta, 05674, 06055
Damodaran, G.R., 16622
Damodaran, Gurusamy, 06291
Damodaran, K., 01155, 01299
Damodaran, Nettur P., 20072
Damodaran Nambiar, K., 05794
D'Ancona, M.L., 05503
Danda, Ajit Kumar, 20996, 24469, 24691
Danda, Dipali Ghosh, 24469, 24691, 25786
Dandekar, Gopal Krishna, 21257
Dandekar, Kumudini, 16315, 21206-8, 21466, 21563-5
Dandekar, Ramchandra Narayan, 00005, 00044-8, 00060, 00268-9, 01193, 01525, 01698, 02488, 03748, 03799-801, 03835-6, 04254, 04735, 04764, 05250, 05758
Dandekar, Shankar Vaman, 06760
Dandekar, Vishnu Mahadeo, 01567, 04129, 14277, 14826, 14832-3, 14926, 14947, 15526, 21206, 21258
Daṇḍin, 05973, 06062, 06068
Dandiya, C.K., 22076
Daner, Francine Jeanne, 16756
Dang, Hari, 25849
Dange, Sadashiv Ambadas, 02032, 03749, 03861, 03893, 05268
Dange, Shripad Amrit, 11127, 13201, 14335, 21111
Dange, Sindhu S., 05268
Dani, Ahmad Hasan, 00571, 03511, 03580, 03735-6, 04181, 05525, 05636, 07185-6, 07353, 23125, 25568
Dani, R.S., 14594
Daniel, David, 02250
Daniel, Harry F.J., 20354
Daniell, Thomas, 11977
Daniell, William, 11977
Daniélou, Alain, 00175, 01699, 02157, 02689, 02811, 02830, 02883, 02969, 03131, 04443, 05437
Dantwala, Mohanlal Lalloobhai, 14834, 14972, 15140, 15495, 21259
Danvers, Frederick Charles, 07845, 07877, 09766
Danzig, Richard, 10231-2
Dapper, Olfert, 07894
Dar, Abdul Ghani, 22667
Dar, Bashir Ahmad, 11469, 11495
Dar, Saifur Rahman, 00604-5
Dar, Shiv Nath, 03315
Dar, Shivanandan Lal, 23894-5
Darbara Singh, 10415, 13581
Darda, Ranjeet Singh, 20636, 21994
Darian, Steven G., 01837-8, 04349, 05898, 07212
Darling, Malcolm Lyall, Sir, 09818, 10477, 14702, 22661, 22740, 22850-1
Darmesteter, James, 02297
Darshan Singh, 07093, 27236
Darshankar, Arjunrao Y., 21156
Daruwalla, Keki N., 17015, 17094
Das, Abinas Chandra, 03750
Das, Aioswarjya Kumar, 03353, 26490
Das, Amal Kumar, 20985, 24447, 24516, 24637-40, 24677, 26399-400
Das, Amritananda, 14293
Das, Arvind N., 14951
Das, Asok Kumar, 07767, 07768
Das, Asutosh, 24463
Das, Babagopal, 14603
Das, Bhagwan, 01768
Das, Bhaskar Chandra, 12302, 12552-3, 13018, 13305, 22289, 22299
Das, Binod Sankar, 08392
Das, Biswanath, 22383
Das, Biswarup, 06695
Das, Dipakranjan, 04350
Das, Durga, 09547
Das, Frieda Mathilda Hauswirth, 10734
Das, G.K., 11909
Das, G.N., 27941
Das, Gopabandhu, 20790
Das, Hari Prasanna, 27292
Das, Harihar, 07498, 11762
Das, Harish Chandra, 22311, 22369
Das, Jibanananda, 25091
Das, Jogesh, 25828
Das, K.K., 24470
Das, Kirem, 24316
Das, Kumudranjan, 07559
Das, Kunjabehari, 22420
Das, M.M., 25756, 26698
Das, M.N., 10841
Das, Maheshwar, 06005
Das, Man Singh, 15527, 15727-8

Das, Manmath Nath, 00190, 09633, 09824, 09829, 10717, 13366
Das, Manindra Nath, 09123, 21007
Das, Manoj, 11771, 27162, 27188
Das, Nabagopal, 15218, 15548, 15633
Das, Narendra Nath, 24283
Das, Nirmala, 00539
Das, P.K., 22340
Das, Padmalaya, 02016
Das, Parimal Kumar, 14093
Das, Prosad Kumar, 27007
Das, R.B., 12942, 12973
Das, R.K., 02017, 03386
Das, R.N., 07112
Das, Rajani Kanta, 11129, 11141, 26928
Das, Rajendra Prasad, 06916
Das, Rashvihari, 06348
Das, S.R., 22683
Das, Sambidananda, 07272
Das, Santwana Kumar, 14233
Das, Satyajit, 24242
Das, Shiva Tosh, 26460
Das, Sisir Kumar, 11557, 24848, 24916, 24956
Das, Sudhendu Kumar, 01714
Das, Sudhir Ranjan, 24885
Das, Sukla, 04351
Das, Tapan, 17425
Das, Tarak Chandra, 01098, 20977
Das, Taraknath, 09361
Das, Veena, 00741, 02128, 04444, 12814, 18099, 22842
Das Gupta... *See also* Dasgupta
Das Gupta, Ashin, 08203, 08297, 08414
Das Gupta, Bidhu Bhusan, 27918
Das Gupta, Biman Kumar, 26506
Das Gupta, Binayendra Nath, 10076
Das Gupta, Chidananda, 25092, 25138
Das Gupta, Harendra Mohan, 24957
Das Gupta, Hemendra Nath, 09634, 10023
Das Gupta, Jogendra Nath, 08845
Das Gupta, Jyoti Bhusan, 12068a, 12090
Das Gupta, Narendra Kumar, 20930
Das Gupta, Nilima, 24993
Das Gupta, Pranab Kumar, 24108
Das Gupta, Rajatananda, 03440, 03474, 07345
Das Gupta, S., 13481
Das Gupta, S.B., 20997
Das Gupta, Sadhana Prasad, 02997
Das Gupta, Subrata Kumar, 07354
Dasaradha Rama Rao, G., 19748
Dasgado, Sebastião Rodolpho, 27923
Dasgupta... *See also* Das Gupta
Dasgupta, A., 15259, 15268
Dasgupta, A.K., 12470
Dasgupta, A.K., 14372
Dasgupta, Ajit Kumar, 14762
Dasgupta, Alokeranjan, 07230, 24921, 25093
Dasgupta, Amar Prasad, 07979-80, 24841
Dasgupta, B.C., 16238
Dasgupta, Biplab, 00872, 13237-8, 13336, 13831, 14186, 15086, 15365, 22163
Dasgupta, Charu Chandra, 03245-8, 05564
Dasgupta, Jayanti Kumar, 24986
Dasgupta, Jyotirindra, 12471
Dasgupta, K.C., 15272
Dasgupta, Kalpana, 00948, 15869, 16953
Dasgupta, Kalyan Kumar, 04064, 04323
Dasgupta, Mary Ann, 11746, 11763
Dasgupta, S., 24589
Dasgupta, S.C., 07337
Dasgupta, Sajadal, 24471
Dasgupta, Samir, 25094
Dasgupta, Satadal, 15038, 23780, 24692
Dasgupta, Shashibhushan, 05899, 07206
Dasgupta, Subhachari, 15061, 15104
Dasgupta, Subhayu, 14349
Dasgupta, Subhoranjan, 17175, 24938
Dasgupta, Sugata, 10978, 14990, 15005, 15700, 16142, 24693, 24854
Dasgupta, Sukharanjan, 25177, 25210
Dasgupta, Surama, 01513, 11426
Dasgupta, Surendranath, 01168, 01381, 02142, 04823-5
Dasgupta, Tamonashchandra, 07207, 08890
Dasgupta, Uma, 09224, 10800, 10842-3
Dash, Bhagwan, 00307-8, 04560
Dash, Bijay Kumar, 16898
Dash, G.N., 07251, 20791
Dash, Mahesh P., 01728, 06802
Dash, P.C., 22322
Dash, Shreeram Chandra, 12330, 20779, 20792, 22290, 27189
Da Silva, O.M., 08056
Dass, Sudhir Ranjan, 22670
Dass, Susanta Krishna, 25735
Dassanayake, M.B., 01935
Dastur, Aloo J., 13388, 21112, 21191
Dastur, Jehangir Fardunji, 27030
Daswani, Chander J., 02613
Datar, Asha L., 13901
Date, Govind Tryambak, 04342
Date, Sankara Ramacandra, 19617
Date, Vinayak Hari, 02158, 04678, 06349, 08445
Datey, C.D., 15105
Datir, R.N., 21559
Datt, Pitambar. *See* Pitambar Datt
Datta, Abhijit, 12974, 16084, 24737-8, 24775
Datta, Amlan, 14324
Datta, Ansu K., 24392
Datta, B.K., 21567
Datta, Bhabatosh, 00240, 10901, 14390, 16868
Datta, Bhupendranath, 00925, 03117
Datta, Bibhutibhusan, 00292, 04541, 05734
Datta, Bimal Kumar, 03441, 04510
Datta, C.L., 12554
Datta, Chaman Lal, 23134
Datta, Churamani, 06368
Datta, Dipankar, 12447
Datta, Guru Saday, 10743
Datta, Jatindra Mohan, 24622, 24697, 25504
Datta, Kali Kumar, 02489
Datta, Kalikinkar, 00193, 07513, 07631, 08854, 08863-4, 08891, 08990, 09455, 09496, 12566, 10698, 20931, 23945-7, 23955, 23964, 24236
Datta, Rabindra Chandra, 24958
Datta, Rajeshwari, 27512-3, 27525
Datta, Samir Kumar, 05303
Datta, Shib Chandra, 10902-3
Datta, Sudhindranath, 25095
Datta, Vishwa Nath, 09741, 09844-5, 22910
Datta Gupta, Sobhanlal, 12852
Datta-Majumdar, Nabendu, 20932
Datta-Ray, Basudeb, 25692, 26461
Datta-Ray, Sunanda K., 13482
Dattaray, Rajatbaran, 06072
Datza, Sanjib, 25168
Daumal, René, 05290
Da Vanzo, Julie, 25281
Davar, Firoze Cowasji, 00369
Davar, Rustom S., 15624
Davar, Sohrab Rustanji, 21431
Dave, Dayashankar Trikamji, 16339
Dave, H.T., 21921
Dave, Jagdish P., 16631
Dave, Jayantkrishna Harikrishna, 00018, 01921
Dave, Mahendra, 15260
Dave, Radhekant, 17049
Dave, Rajendra Kumar, 27320
Dave, Ramesh M., 21922-3
Dave, Ravindra, 16526
Dave, Suresh Kanaiyalal, 01805, 06777
Dave, T.N., 03983
Davey, Cyril J., 23037
Davey, Hampton Thompson, Jr., 13128, 13269
David, H.S., 00076
David, Kenneth, 00797, 18853
David, M.D., 08386
David-Neel, Alexandra, 25952
Davids, Leo, 26753
Davidson, J. Leroy, 03069, 05539
Davierwalla, A.M., 17212
Davies, Alfred Mervy, 08008, 08027
Davies, Cuthbert Colin, 00152, 08766, 23050
Davis, Kingsley, 10493, 14149
Davis, Marvin, 00966, 24586, 24601-2
Davis, Walter Bruce, 08955
Davtar, Vasant, 21635
Davy, John, 18311
Daw, Prasanta, 11804
Dawn index, 27605
Dawson, John L., 26901
Dawson, William Albert, 15571
Day, Charles Russell, 02854

Day, Clarence Burton, 01194, 27051
Day, Francis, 19919
Day, Lal Behari, 24613, 25123
Day, Richard H., 14774
Day, Upendra Nath, 06709, 06735, 07025, 07059, 07534
Daya, E., 21786
Daya Krishna, 14772, 16696
Dayal, Deen, Raja, 19618
Dayal, Edison, 13821
Dayal, Har, 05084
Dayal, Ishwar, 12547, 12947
Dayal, John, 13566, 23326
Dayal, Raghubir, 13089
Dayal, Rajeshwar, 12991, 14807, 15044
Dayanand, Y.J., 17148-50
Dayananda Saraswati, Swami, 01023, 03816, 11269-73
Dayanandan, P., 06617
Dayanandan Francis, T., 19580
Daykin, David S., 15937, 15941
D' Costa, Ronald, 18804
De, A.K., 16563
De, Amalendu, 24334, 24342, 25681
De, Barun, 09182, 09558
De, Bimaleswar, 15689
De, Brajendranath, 07420
De, Gokuldas, 04936, 05010
De, Krishna Prasad, 12417
De, Nitish Ranjan, 15832, 19769, 24536
De, S.C., 03761
De, Samir, 24939
De, Satyendra Lal, 24810, 24817
De, Sushil Chandra, 06913, 20774
De, Sushil Kumar, 02469, 02490, 02500-2, 07221, 07231-2, 24871, 24959
De Alwis, C.M., 06130
Deb, Arabinda, 26418, 26425-7
Deb, Binaya Krishna, 24716
Deb, Harit Krishna, 01648
Deb, Kalipada, 13845
Deb, Keya, 25725
Deb, Prafulla Chandra, 14850, 22769, 22856-7, 22914
De Bary, William Theodore, 00191, 01269
Débidour, A., 11858
Debnath, P.K., 01629
De Cardi, Beatrice, 03571
Deep, Dhruba Krishna, 02103, 26322
Defourny, Michel, 01700
Deglurkar, G.B., 03405
Dehejia, Vidya, 03087, 05484-5, 05504
Dehlavi, S.A., 18278
Dehon, P.S., Rev., 20986
De Jong, J.W., 01142, 01396, 04572, 04607
Deka, K.M., 25708
De Kalbermatten, G., 16723
De Lanerolle, S.D., 04243, 27152
Del Bontà, Robert John, 06670
Deleury, Guy A., 00642, 01995-6, 08433, 08438
Delf, George, 26843
Delfendahl, Bernard, 21467
Delhi. Development Authority, 23414
Delhi. Municipal Corporation. Dept. of Urban Community Development, 23415
Delhi Orthodox Syrian Church Society, 02251
Delhi (Union Territory). Bureau of Economics and Statistics, 23347
Delhi (Union Territory). Directorate of Public Relations, 23348-9
Delhi. University, 23434
De Lippe, Aschwin, 06100
Della Casa, Carlo, 01275
Deloche, Jean, 00343
DeLubac, Henri, 01143
Dembo, Morris, 09502
Demiéville, Paul, 04943, 05004
Deming, Wilbur Stone, 08427, 08446
Denham, E.B., 27453
Deo, Shantaram Bhalchandra, 00593, 01891, 03672, 03692-4, 06808
Deodhar, Dilip, 27205
Deodhar, Y.N., 08321
Deogirikar, T.R., 09668
Deol, Gurdev Singh, 09742, 10106
Deopujari, Murlidhar Balkrishna, 08264
Deoras, Jaikrishna, 27031
Dep, A.C., 18513
Deraniyagala, P.E.P., 18831, 19074
Deraniyagala, S., 03512, 03523, 03673, 05618
Derozio, Henry, 11764
Derrett, John Duncan Martin, 00918-9, 00924, 00926-7, 00934, 00990, 01546, 04406, 04423, 04429, 04573, 05700, 06215, 07578, 08057, 08208, 09261-3, 12418-9, 12853, 15896, 15980-3, 15986-7, 16002
Derrett, Margaret E., 11726
Desai, Akshayakumar Ramanlal, 09600, 10996, 11006, 13019, 15001, 15736, 16077, 21531
Desai, Ashok V., 07588, 13832, 13860, 14033a, 16834, 21202
Desai, B.G., 21890
Desai, B.L., 21913
Desai, B.M., 14908, 21736, 21751
Desai, Balvant A., 15369
Desai, Batuk, 16507
Desai, Bhadra, 13418
Desai, Bhulabhai J., 10456
Desai, Chaitanya, 02839
Desai, Chitra, 16686
Desai, Devangana, 03132
Desai, Dhanwant M., 16588, 21896, 21905, 27926
Desai, Dhirajlal Keshavlal, 14798, 20306, 21724, 21754, 24060
Desai, Govindbhai H., 20626
Desai, Gunvantrai Maganlal, 14867
Desai, Ishwarlal Pragji, 16444-5, 21585, 21822, 21841, 21856
Desai, K.G., 15625
Desai, K.S., 21700
Desai, Kalpana S., 01762
Desai, Kirtidev D., 21665, 21686
Desai, Kishor Gopal, 21538
Desai, Kumud Ghurye, 16003
Desai, M.D., 21891
Desai, M.V., 16847
Desai, Madhukar N., 20428
Desai, Maganbhai Prabhudas, 16640
Desai, Maganlal Bhagwanji, 21560, 21714, 21725-6, 21737-8, 21764-5, 21864, 21736-9
Desai, Mahadev Haribhai, 09893, 10192, 19920, 20745
Desai, Mahendra Dahyabhai, 22028
Desai, Makarand, 13539
Desai, Meghnad, 11106
Desai, Morarji Ranchodji, 13623-4, 16334
Desai, N.B., 20715, 21727
Desai, N.C., 21823
Desai, Narayan, 21067
Desai, Neera, 15870, 16691, 21804-5
Desai, Nileshvari Y., 05808
Desai, P.B., 05143, 14134-5, 14373, 16277, 23394, 23838
Desai, Padma, 13833, 14370, 15178, 15202, 24109
Desai, Pandurang Bhimrao, 00430, 06540
Desai, Pravina, 12461
Desai, Rajanikanta C., 10887
Desai, Rashmi H., 26904
Desai, S.K., 17078, 17176, 20557
Desai, S.S.M., 15120
Desai, Sanjiv P., 27554
Desai, Santosh N., 04715
Desai, Sapur Faredun, 21432-3
Desai, Shambhuprasad Harprasad, 02002-3, 27206
Desai, Shripad Raghunath, 21099
Desai, Sudha R., 03031
Desai, Tripta, 10293, 14038, 14047
Desai, Urmiben, 21831
Desai, V.V., 14755
Desai, Vasant. *See* Mutalik Desai, V.R.
Desai, Walter Sadgun, 08298, 08387
Desai, Z.A., 06715-6, 07580
Desai, Ziyand-Din A., 03189-90, 16774
Desauvage, Alain, 18626
Desh Bandhu, 16237, 25851
Deshmukh, Chintaman Dwarkanath, Sir, 12659
Deshmukh, D.G., 11859
Deshmukh, Durgabai, 12660, 16689, 19788
Deshmukh, M.B., 23388
Deshmukh, Nana, 13281
Deshpande, Bani, 06324
Deshpande, Chandrasekhar Dundiraj, 20429, 27198
Deshpande, Gauri, 11747, 17095
Deshpande, Indu C., 03962
Deshpande, Kusumavati, 02600
Deshpande, L.K., 15592

Deshpande, M.N., 05486
Deshpande, Madhav, 02399, 05184, 05202
Deshpande, Madhav Kashinath, 27909
Deshpande, Madhav M., 00704
Deshpande, Manohar Sriniwas, 04679, 08428, 20538, 21617
Deshpande, Pandurang Ganesa, 09855, 27927
Deshpande, S.H., 13197, 21219
Deshpande, Shantaram Ramkrishna, 24448
Deshpande, U.G., 21468
Deshpande, V.V., 04040, 15985
Deshpande, Vamanrao H., 02790, 02819-20
Deshpande, Vasant Dattatraya, 21260, 21408
Deshpande, Vinayak A., 14170
Desika Chariar, N.V., 06463
Desikachar, S.V., 09152
Desikacharya, N., 01892
De Silva, C.C., 18922
De Silva, C.M. Austin, 08108
De Silva, C.R., 18451, 18961
De Silva, Chandra Richard, 08048, 08070-2, 27703
De Silva, Colvin Reginald, 18312, 18805
De Silva, D., 08048
De Silva, E.P., 18413
De Silva, G.A.C., 18733
De Silva, G.P.S. Harischandra, 18403, 18908
De Silva, H., 27555
De Silva, K.D., 19061
De Silva, K.M., 18289, 18295, 18313, 18323-5, 18352-4, 18460, 18472, 18491, 18753-5, 19035
De Silva, L., 18693
De Silva, Lynn A., 01481
De Silva, M.A., 19062
De Silva, M.W. Padmasiri, 01353
De Silva, M.W. Sugathapala, 02541-2, 27850-1
De Silva, Mervyn, 18371
De Silva, P.H., 00603
De Silva, P.H.D.H., 03363
De Silva, R.H., 03289, 05622
De Silva, S.F., 18970, 27145
De Silva, Sugathapala M.W., 06144
De Silva, W.A., 01241
De Silva, W.P.N., 18806
Desjardins, Arnand, 01890
De Smet, Richard V., 01053, 01482, 01526
Desmond, Ray, 11966
De Souza, Alfred, 13063-4, 15871, 15938, 16057, 16085, 16458, 16625
De Souza, Armand, 18335
De Souza, J.P., 00105
De Souza, Robert, 21092
De Souza, Teotonio Robert, 08393
De Soysa, A.B. Colin, 18527
Despres, Emile, 17903
Despres, Leo A., 26776
Dessigane, R., 01741-2, 01820
Deterra, H., 03546
Detmold, Geoffrey, 01592
Dettman, Paul R., 19528
Deussen, Paul, 03984, 06325
Deutch, Eliot S., 01465, 04663, 06326-7, 11379
Deutsch, Karl W., 11900
Dev, Ashu Tosh, 27987-8
Dev, Dharam Yash, 26738
Dev, Haramohan, 09713
Dev Varman, S.B.K., 26646
Deva, Bigamudre Chaitanya, 02701-2, 02744, 02754, 02781-2
Deva, Indra, 00663, 02424
Deva, Narendra, Acharya, 10090-1, 03177
Deva Sangeetham, Daniel, 19570
Devadas, Rajammal P., 16506, 16676, 19458
Devadas Pillai, S., 00657, 13552, 16077, 16156, 20612, 21311, 21531, 21865
Devadason, E.D., 00920
Devadhar, C.R., 05350
Devadoss, T.S., 14294, 15889
Devahuti, 00129
Devahuti, D., 07002
Devalle, Susana B.C., 20959, 20969
Devanandan, Paul David, 01402, 15897, 19190
Devanesen, Chandra David Srinivasagam, 09873
Devapriam, Emma, 07735
Devaraja, Nand Kishore, 01343, 06369, 16697-8, 16711
Devaraja Mudaliar, A., 11409
Devasenapathi, V.A., 04498, 06292, 06519, 06527
Devassey, M.K., 02970
Devasthali, Govind Vinayak, 03957, 05203, 05308, 05376
Devdas, Nalini, 11296, 11320
Deve Gowda, A.C., 16540
Devendra, Don Titus, 00578, 01668, 05613, 27134
Devi, Akshaya K., 05744
Devi, V. Yasoda, 01793
Devi Chand, 03909, 03917
Devillers, Philippe, 18492
Devra, Ghanshyam Lal, 00465
Devrajani, Bherulal T., 22475
Dewaraja, Lorna Srimathie, 08058-9
Dewey, Clive J., 00239, 09196, 10864, 10968, 11084
Dexter, Wilfrid E., 21655
Dey, Abani Kumar, 12238, 15351, 27008
Dey, Bishnu, 11805-6, 25096-7
Dey, Lilian, 16307
Dey, Nundo Lal, 00151
Dey, Surendra Kumar, 13020, 14703, 15021, 23305
Deydier, Henri, 05526
De Zoete, Beryl, 02948, 03014
Dhabhar, Ervad Bamanji Nusserwanji, 02298
Dhadda, Siddharaj, 24081
Dhakhwa, Dev Ratna, 27361
Dhaky, Madhusudan A., 02004, 03147, 03345, 06099, 06641, 06849, 06859-66, 06871-2, 06878
Dhal, Upendra Nath, 01729
Dhalla, Maneckji Nusservanji, 02291-2, 18235
Dhama, B.L., 06884
Dhami, M.S., 13295
Dhamija, J., 03347
Dhamija, Jasleen, 03295, 03354
Dhammaratana, U., 05036
Dhamotharan, A., 27861
Dhan, R.O., 20987, 20998
Dhanagre, D.N., 10997-8, 19634, 20124, 23657
Dhanañjaya, 02680, 06001
Dhanapala, D.B., 03364-6
Dhandayudham, R., 19571
Dhangare, D.N., 13088
Dhanpat Rai, Lala, 09728
Dhapola, T.S., 23535, 25921
Dhar, D.P., 15737
Dhar, Jaganath, 27753
Dhar, K.N., 06937
Dhar, Kanahaya Lal, 23197
Dhar, M.K., 13625
Dhar, Nil Ratan, 10663
Dhar, Niranjan, 08876, 10077
Dhar, P.N., 14374, 15193, 23356
Dhar, Pannalal, 21051
Dhar, Sailendra Nath, 11321, 20663
Dhar, Somnath, 06938, 23259
Dhar, Triloki Nath, 08667, 15514, 15519, 16439-40
Dharaiya, Ramanlal Kakalbhai, 09497
Dharam Pal, 09729, 12719
Dharamdasani, Murlidhar, 26065
Dharampal, 07812, 09456
Dharap, B.V., 16960
Dharia, Mohan, 13497
Dharm Narain, 13876
Dharma Deva, Vidya Martanda, 03882, 03910
Dharma Kumar. *See* Kumar, Dharma
Dharma Vir, 09856
Dharma Vira, 12661
Dharmadasa, K.N.O., 18983, 19075
Dharmapala, Anagarika, 18984
Dharmavira, 09743-4
Dharmendra, 23336
Dhasmana, M.M., 26505
Dhavalikar, Madhukar Keshav, 01809, 03249, 03258, 05593, 05913
Dhavamony, Mariasusai, 06408, 06528
Dhavan, Rajeev, 12331, 12374, 12825-7, 12837, 13522
Dhawan, B.D., 14888
Dhawan, Banarsi Dass, 16944
Dhawan, Gopi Nath, 09938
Dhekney, B.R., 20486
Dhekney, Malhar Ramchandra, 15310, 15449
Dhekney, Vishwas Malhar, 16931
Dhillon, G.S., 16611
Dhillon, Gurdarshan Singh, 22677
Dhillon, Gurbax Singh, 10460
Dhillon, Naginder Singh, 14113
Dhiman, R., 22792
Dhingra, H.L., 15464

Dhingra, M.M., 15450
Dholakia, Bakul H., 15534
Dholakia, Jitendra L., 21788
Dholakia, Ravindra H., 15534
Dhoomi Mal's Gallery, 03326
Dhooria, Ram Lall, 13282
Dhuleep Singh, 22587
Dhungama, Bhawani, 26023, 26163
Dhyani, S.N., 15549
Dial, Roger, 26051
Di Bona, Joseph, 16422, 22932, 23908
Dibrugarh University. Dept. of Economics, 25769
Dichter, David, 27227
Dickens, T., 26758
Dickie, James, 11680
Dickinson, Eric, 08510
Dickinson, John, 20664
Dickinson, Nancy, 27426
Dickinson, Richard, 27426
Dickinson, Richard D.N., 16489
Dictionary of Oriental Literatures, 02318
Diederich, Georg, 18698
Diehl, Anita, 19191
Diehl, Carl Gustav, 02127, 19486
Diehl, Katherine Smith, 07393, 07888, 08090, 24243, 27534-5
Dietrich, Gabriele, 19487
Digambaraji, Swami, 02153
Digby, Simon, 07060, 07113-4, 07141, 07162
Digby, William, 10801-2, 10910-1, 11015, 18327
Dighe, Anita, 22029
Dighe, Vishvanath Govind, 08299, 09819, 20721, 21504
Dignan, Don K., 09745
Dihingia, Hemeswar, 25696
Dikshit, K.N., Rai Bahadur, 07361
Dikshit, Kamal Ramprit, 27199
Dikshit, Kashinath Narayan, 03598
Dikshit, Moreshwar Gangadhar, 00344, 05487, 06846
Dikshit, Ratnamayidevi, 05281
Dikshit, Sadanand Kashinath, 01715
Dikshit, Sankara Balkrishna, 00278, 03793
Dil, Afia, 01062, 18194
Dil, Anwar S., 02337-9, 17824, 18194, 27489
Dil, S., 12125
Dilgeer, Harjinder Singh, 22945
Dilks, David, 09820
Dimand, Maurice Sven, 03283
Dimmitt, Cornelia, 01710
Dimock, Edward Cameron, Jr., 02389, 02658, 07233-5, 07265, 07287, 07309-10, 08865, 08941, 08950, 24886, 24960, 25055, 25098, 27995
Dinesh, Deendayal, 12167
Dinesh, Kamini, 22152
Dinesh Singh, 14007
Dionne, Russell Jude, 10932, 16566
Disalkar, D.B., 04251
Diskalkar, P.D., 21469
Disney, A.R., 07878, 08203a
Dissanayake, Gamini, 18417
Dissanayake, T.B., 18527
Dissanayake, T.D.S.A., 18414
Dittmer, Kerrin, 17449, 23487
Divakaran, Odile, 06660
Divatia, Harisdhbhai Vajubahi, Sir, 04680
Divekar, V.D., 00236, 14375
Diver, Katherine Helen Maud Marshall, 09183, 09345
Diwakar, Ranganath Ramachandra, 00431, 00513, 04876, 09957, 11380, 16867
Diwaker, S.C., 16769
Diwan, Paras, 12321, 13523, 16010
Diwas, Tulsi, 26340
Dixit, Hemang, 27677
Dixit, Krishna Kumar, 01370, 01428, 05144-5
Dixit, Mani, 27394
Dixit, Narayan Gopal, 20772
Dixit, Prabha, 10115
Dixit, Veena, 16162
Djurfeldt, Göran, 19419
D'Mello, Rudolf Gyan, 21059-60
Dnyāndev. *See* Jñānesvara
Dobbin, Christine E., 09067, 09273, 21178-9, 21434
Dobell, W.M., 17512, 17538, 17737
Dobremez, Jean François, 26253
Dockhorn, Kurt, 11381, 16792
Doctor, Adi Hormusji, 13306, 13696
Documentation on Asia, 11984
Documentos remittidos da Índia, 07884
Dodge, Patrick, 25347
Dodwell, Henry Herbert, 00192, 07965, 08009, 08179-80
Dogra, R.C., 27454
Dogri Sanstha, Jammu, 23253
Dohanian, Diran Kavork, 03367, 06165, 06171
Doidge, Charles, 18905
Doig, Desmond, 24717, 27388
Doig, Ronald P., 18328
Doke, Joseph J., 26827
Dolapihilla, Punchibandara, 18302
Domin, Dolores, 09397, 22741
Dommen, Arthur J., 25702
Domrös, Manfred, 27146
Don Peter, W.L.A., 08073
Donaldson, Florence, 26363
Donaldson, Robert H., 13980-1
Donaldson, Thomas, 05611, 06902
Dongerkery, Kamala Sunderrao Kulkarni, 03316-7, 03342
Dongerkery, Sunderrao Ramrao, 16490, 16509, 21595-6, 21906
Dongre, Rajas Krishnarao, 21359
Donner, Wolf, 26110
Donoughmore, the Earl of, 18359
Dool Singh, 22043, 22067
Doraswamy, K., 27872
Doré, Francis, 12303
Dorfman, Robert, 17959
Doshi, Harish C., 21878-9
Doshi, J.K., 20803
Doshi, R.T., 15405
Doshi, Shambhu Lal, 16581, 20804-5, 22101
Doshi, Saryu, 07142
Doss, Veda, 14524
Dotson, Arch, 23416
Dotson, Floyd, 26844, 26858
Dotson, Lillian O., 26844, 26858
Douglas, James, 20579, 20687
Douglas, Janet, 12306
Douglas, Mary, 00785
Douglas, Nik, 05861
Douglas, William Orville, 12332
Douie, James McCrane, Sir, 22427
Dover, Cedrick, 11765
Dow, Alexander, 07409
Dow, H., 22450
Downs, Frederick Sheldon, 25808, 25809
Downton, James V., 16724
Dowsett, Norman C., 16459
Dowson, John, 01116, 07408, 07482
Doxiadēs, Kōnstantinos Apostolou, 16086
D'Oyly, Charles, Sir, 09203
D'Oyly, John, Sir, 08060
Dozey, E.C., 26385
Drach, George, 19874
Draguhn, Werner, 14350
Dravid, Raja Ram, 01371
Dravid, V.V., 22222
Drekmeier, Charles, 04280
Drevet, Camille, 09939
Drew, Frederic, 23143
Drewery, Mary, 08956
Drewitt, Frederick George Dawtrey, 21180
Dreyfus, Paul, 25154
Driḍhabala, 04553
Drieberg, Trevor, 13419, 13498, 27249
Driver, Edwin D., 22178,
Driver, John E.S., 26010
Driver, Peshotan Nasserwanji, 14952
Drummond, H.J.H., 03554
Drury, Michael, 14073
D'Silva, Louis, 12339
D'Souza, Anthony A., 16164
D'Souza, Bento Graciano, 21093
D'Souza, Austin Anthony, 16626, 24856
D'Souza, S., 15859
D'Souza, Stan, 25277-8
D'Souza, Victor Salvadore, 00774-5, 00798, 15898, 15970, 16024, 20057, 20125-7, 20366, 20385, 20457, 22824, 22900-1, 26754
D'Souza, Vitus L., 20268
Dua, B.D., 12375
Dua, M.R., 16945
Dua, R.P., 09611, 10699

Dua, Veena, 22691-2
Duarte, Adrian, 07919, 27238
Dube, B.K., 20846
Dube, Bechan, 04080
Dube, Kamala Kant, 02044, 23839
Dube, Leela, 00829, 00960-1, 20135-6
Dube, R.S., 22177
Dube, Shyama Charan, 00813, 01080, 12610, 15705, 15713-4, 19819, 20847, 23801
Dube, S.L., 22217
Duberly, Frances Isabella Locke, 09474
Dubey, Bhagwant Rao, 22077
Dubey, Dinesh Chandra, 14173, 16278, 16302, 23427
Dubey, K.C., 21024
Dubey, Rishi Mani, 23564
Dubey, S.M., 23545, 26462
Dubey, Sumati Narain, 12992, 14953, 16127
Dubey, Swaroop Rani, 18435, 19063, 25198
Dubhashi, P.R., 12662, 12948, 14404, 14784
Dubois, Jean Antoine, Abbé, 11837
Ducat, Walter M., 21880
Duchesne-Guillemin, Jacques, 02299
Duff, Bart, 17952
Duff, James Grant, 07438
Dufferin and Ava, Hariot Georgina Hamilton-Temple-Blackwood, Marchioness of, 09147, 11933
Dufty, Norman F., 15616
Duggal, Kartar Singh, 16899, 16936, 17022
Duggal, S.L., 22759
Duggirala, G.K., 05300
Du Jarric, Pierre, 07686
Dulaharaj, Muni, 05133
Dulai, Surjit Singh, 17161, 22999-23000
Dulamala, Bulacanda, 27942
Dumarçay, Jacques, 06613
Dumasia, Naoroji M., 20613
Dumézil, George, 04636-7
Dumont, Georges H., 08855
Dumont, Louis, 00625, 00643, 00668, 00725, 00759, 00783, 00818, 00873, 00968, 00982-3, 01006-8, 01043, 01054, 01093, 01852, 01862, 02104, 02195, 04281, 09767, 10969, 19374, 20095, 21011, 26245
Dumont, Paul Émile, 03958, 05816
Dumont, René, 25376, 25377
Dunbar, William, 13021
Duncan, George T., 13908
Dundas, Henry. *See* Melville, Henry Dundas
Dunn, Fred L., 16328, 26295
Dunn, Theodore Douglas, 11748, 11876
Dupleix, Joseph François, 07929
Dupree, Louis, 25416
Dupree, Nancy H., 05544
Dupuis, Jacques, 19248, 27321
Duraiswamy Pillai, Avvai S., 04499
Durand, Algernon, 23144
Durand, Henry Marion, Sir, 09423
Durand, Henry Mortimer, 20764
Durand-Dastes, François, 21328
Durbin, Mridula A., 01276
Durdin-Robertson, Lawrence, 01716
Durga, S.A.K., 02855, 02949
Durga Parshad, Ignatius, 11061
During Caspers, Elisabeth C.L., 03629-30
Durlab Singh, 10172, 25040
Dushkin, Lelah, 13074, 13301, 15767, 20225
Dustoor, P.E., 17087
Duthie, John Firminger, 27266
Dutt, Ashok Kumar, 16092, 24189, 24754, 26996
Dutt, Balai Chandra, 10457
Dutt, Binode Behari, 04520
Dutt, K. Guru, 20395
Dutt, Kalpana, 24317
Dutt, Kalyan, 24496
Dutt, Kanai Lal, 24887
Dutt, Keshab Narayan, 25697
Dutt, Manmatha Nath, 04317, 04430, 04620, 04656, 04698, 05763, 05779, 05795-6
Dutt, Nalinaksha, 04937, 04944, 04953, 05045, 05900
Dutt, Nripendra Kumar, 00760, 03774, 24587
Dutt, Paramananda, 25130
Dutt, Rajani Palme, 09030, 10469
Dutt, Romesh Chunder, 04628, 09031, 10912, 11016, 24666
Dutt, Subimal, 13728
Dutt, Sukumar, 01893, 04927, 04938, 22044
Dutt, Sunitee, 16402
Dutt, Toru, 02418, 11766
Dutt, V.P., 13499
Dutt Gupta, Bela, 24554
Dutt Mulick, V., 16278
Dutta, Alok K., 24764
Dutta, Amita, 18569, 18586
Dutta, Bimal Chandra, 03623
Dutta, Kund, 24694
Dutta, Maya, 24190
Dutta, Narendra Chandra, 25763
Dutta, Parul Chandra, 26491, 26512-3
Dutta, Pratap C., 03694, 26723
Dutta, Prithwis, 13749, 18554
Dutta, S.C., 16678
Dutta, S.J., 24794
Dutta, Vijay Ranjan, 23530, 23531
Dvivedi, H.P., 05192
Dvivedī, Sudhāraka, 04539
Dwarkadas, Kanji, 09974, 10294, 11130
Dwarkadas, R., 12631
Dwivedi, Amar Nath, 11767, 11860
Dwivedi, D.N., 23600
Dwivedi, Gyan Chandra, 13517
Dwivedi, Hari Prasad, 10700
Dwivedi, R.C., 01290, 01555, 02503, 05994
Dwivedi, R.K., 03731
Dwivedi, R.L., 23840
Dwivedi, Radhey Dhar, 07546
Dwivedi, Ram Awadh, 02642
Dwivedi, Ramchandra, 03873
Dwivedi, Vinod Prakash, 00607, 03250, 06996-7, 08833
Dwivedy, Surendranath, 12672
Dyakov, A.M., 09970
Dye, Joseph M., 05527
Dyer, Helen S., 21360
Dyson, Ketaki Kushari, 11934
Dyson, Robert H., 03587

Eakin, Terry Clay, 13097, 21126
Eames, Edwin, 14164, 23781
Eapen, K.E., 16865-6
East Pakistan. Bureau of Educational Information and Statistics, 24827
East Pakistan. Bureau of Statistics, 25258, 25267
East Pakistan. East Bengal Educational System Reconstruction Committee, 25611
East Pakistan. Registrar of Co-operative Societies, 2543
East Pakistan. Sugar Enquiry Committee, 25357
East Pakistan. Tea Enquiry Commission, 25363
East Pakistan. Water and Power Development Authority, 25403
Eastwick, Edward Backhouse, 22445
Easwaran Nampoothiry, E., 02491
Ebeling, Klaus, 08481
Eaton, Richard M., 05946, 08213, 22976
Eberhard, Wolfram, 17284, 17771, 18209
Ebersole, R., 06917
Ebon, Martin, 16725
Eck, Diana L., 02045
Eckaus, Richard S., 14265
Economic and Scientific Research Association, Calcutta, 13861, 24432
Economic and Scientific Research Foundation, Delhi, 13834
Economic Conference on Second Five Year Plan, Rawalpindi (1961), 17863
Economic Cooperation Study Group (1968), 13996
The Economist Intelligence Unit Ltd., London, 18582
Eddy, John Percy, 10277
Edgar, John Ware, 26364
Edgerton, Eleanor, 05358
Edgerton, Franklin, 03874, 03985, 04664, 04864, 05358, 05394-5, 27794
Edwardes, Allen, 08010
Edwardes, Michael, 07514, 08018, 08028, 09045, 09135, 09413, 09515-6, 10295, 13367, 23442
Edwardes, Stephen Meredyth, 02451, 07425, 07450, 08404, 09232, 21181, 21435, 21498-9
Edwards, Daniel Walker, 26024
Edwards, Thomas, 25131
Edwards, James Fairbrother, 06761, 08434
Edwards, William, 09475, 24266
Edwin, P.G., 20181
Eek, Sven, 11356
Eekelen, William Frederik van, 13926
Eger, Gudrun, 18141

Egerton, Wilbraham Egerton, Earl, 03318
Eggeling, Julius, 03959
Egger, Rowland A., 17330
Eggermont, P.H.L., 04126, 04165, 04379
Eglar, Zekiye Suleyman, 22877
Ehrenfels, Umar Rolf Leopold Werner von, 00991-2, 15833, 15899, 19363, 20146, 26688
Eidlitz, Walther, 07280
Eisemon, Thomas, 16564
Eister, Allan W., 17838, 18202
Ekanātha, 08429
Ekbote, Gopalrao, 16558
Elahi, Maqbool, 06986
Elavia, B.H., 21755
Elayaperumal, L., 15768
Elayath, K.N.N., 01499
Elder, George R., 05901
Elder, Joseph Walter, 15687, 23718, 26152, 27449-50
Elder, Robert Ellsworth, 23872
Eldersveld, Samuel James, 13040, 13430, 23334
Eldridge, Philip John, 13870
Elenkath, K.R., 19921
Elfenbein, J.H., 27950
Elgin, James Bruce, 8th Earl of, 09131
Eliade, Mircea, 01440, 02159-62, 04826, 05862, 07305
Elias, Flower, 24655
Elias, Jiri, 12252
Eliot, Charles Norton Edgecombe, 01169, 08943
Elisofon, Eliot, 06918
Eliya, E., 02311
Elizarenkova, Tatiana Yakovleuna, 05241
Elkins, David J., 12294, 19117
Ellawala, H., 04397
Ellenborough, Edward Law, 1st Earl of, 09117-8
Ellickson, Jean, 25494, 25497, 25643
Ellinwood, Dewitt Clinton, 09398
Elliot, Henry Miers, Sir, 07043, 07408, 07482, 07484, 07490
Elliot, J.G., Major-General, 10398
Elliot, Walter, 00553
Elliott, Carolyn Margaret, 19635, 19658-9, 19860
Elliott, James Gordon, 23051
Ellis, C.G., 03347
Ellman, Anthony Oliver, 18739-42
Elmhirst, Leonard K., 10628
Elmore, Wilbur Theodore, 01853
Elphinstone, Mountstuart, 09055, 09424, 20688, 20696
Elsmie, George Robert, 09322, 22612
Elson, Vickie C., 03406
Elwell-Sutton, Laurence Paul, 27816
Elwin, Verrier, 00626, 03407, 03449, 15787, 20848, 20865-70, 20882-3, 21008, 21012-3, 21019, 21025, 24110, 26444, 26471-2, 26478, 26492, 26516, 27322
Embree, Ainslie Thomas, 01218, 05643, 09463, 09560, 10538, 11965, 12389-90, 22439
Emeneau, Murray Barnson, 01063, 02319, 02329-31, 02340, 02363, 02365-9, 05351, 06086, 19385-92, 19398, 20408-9
Emerson, Gertrude, 10789
Emerson, H.W., 22628
Emmerick, Ronald Eric, 04545, 05080
Enayat Ahmad. *See* Ahmad, Enayat
Enayetullah, Anwar, 18279
Encyclopaedia of Islam, 02257
Encyclopaedia of Religion and Ethics, 01108
Encyclopaedia of social work in India, 16113
Encyclopedia of world art, 03057
Endle, Sidney, 25787
Enevoldsen, Jens, 02638, 27976
Engels, F., 09504
Engineer, Asghar Ali, 21443, 22078
English records on Shivaji (1659-82), 08271
Enriquez, Colin Metcalfe Dallas, 23038
Ensminger, Douglas, 15002, 15022
Enthoven, Reginald Edward, 21379, 21656
Epigraphia Indica, 00565
Epigraphia Indica. Arabic and Persian supplement, 05677
Epstein, Trude Scarlett, 20307, 20430-1, 20539
Erdman, Howard Lloyd, 13298, 13716, 21775-6
Erdman, Joan L., 02844
Erickson, Eugene C., 22776
Erikson, Erik Homburger, 09874
Erikson, Joan, 21914
Erskine, William, 07449
Eschmann, Anncharlott, 02018, 11202, 22394
Eskelund, Karl, 27385
Esnoul, Anne Marie, 04736, 04778, 04799, 06429
Esposito, Bruce J., 17980
Esser, A. Albert M., 04554
Estborn, Sigfrid, 19406
Esteller, A., 03894-5
Esteves, Sarto, 21061-2, 21132
Eswara Reddy, V., 15952
Etheridge, A.T., 21286
Étienne, Gilbert, 12253, 12519, 14748, 14763, 17785, 17960
Ettinghausen, Richard, 07143, 07714
Eustis, F.A., 24297
Evans, Humphrey, 12737
Evenson, Norma, 22902
Everitt, Elizabeth, 24037
Evers, Hans-Dieter, 18461, 18777, 18991-3, 19006
Ewing, James Caruthers Rhea, 22984
Eyde, Lorraine D., 16577
Eyre, Vincent, Sir (1811-1881), 09425
Ezekiel, Hannan, 14266
Ezekiel, Isaac A., 07102

Fa-hsien, 04052
Faaland, Just, 25318
Fabian, Paul, 14059
Fabri, Charles Louis, 03161, 03199, 03319, 03408, 06881, 06998, 11822
Fabricius, Johann Philipp, 27862
Faccenna, Domenico, 03737
Faddegon, Barend, 03912, 04847, 05204
Fadia, Babulal, 13041
Fahim-ud-din, Muhammad, 24061
Fairbanks, Gordon H., 27836, 27851
Fairley, Jean, 27092
Fairservis, Walter Ashlin, 03496, 03581-2, 03599, 03738
Faiz, Faiz Ahmad, 11693, 18267-8
Faizi, S.F. Hasan, 27093
Fakhar Zaman, 17583
Fakirbhai, Dhanjibhai, 16793, 16800
Falcon, Walter P., 17825, 17835, 17924, 17933, 17944, 17992
Falk, Harry, 05401
Fallon, Pierre, 11558
Fallon, S.W., 27821
Fane, Hannah, 01717
Faneuff, Charles T., 20519
Fanger, Allen C., 01113, 25922
Fanī, Muḥammad Muḥsin, 07655
Farber, Carole, 03052
Faria y Sousa, Manuel de, 07871
Farid, G.S., 07362
Farley, M. Foster, 27052
Farmer, Bertram Hughes, 14895, 18475-6, 18651, 18729, 18743-4, 19287, 27022
Farooki, Nasir Ahmad, 18269
Farooq, Daniel M., 18043, 18140
Farooq, Ghazi Mumtaz, 12232, 18045, 22495
Farooqi, Anis, 07753-4
Farooqi, Ishrat H., 15219
Farooqi, M., 10049, 25306
Farooqi, Mian Bashir Ahmed, 22603
Farooque, Abul Khair Muhammad, 07612
Farooquee, Qamar Husain, 16552
Farouk, A., 25319, 25378, 25391, 25404, 25471, 25473-7, 25569, 25575
Farquhar, John Nicol, 01170, 01195, 01894, 02200, 04601-2, 11203, 11357, 11559
Farrington, J., 18719
Farrukhi, Aslam, 18270
Fartyal, H.S., 12762
Faruki, Kemal A., 18107
Faruki, Zahiruddin, 07505
Faruqi, Burhan Ahmad, 07678
Faruqi, Hafiz Abbadullah, 07778
Al-Faruqi, Isma'il Ragi, 01107
Faruqi, Ziya-ul-Hasan, 11516
Faruqui, Jalees A., 18251
Fatima, Nasim, 11485
Fatima, Qamar, 18140
Fauche, Hippolyte, 04621, 05347
Fauja Singh, 00106, 00491-2, 06930, 08531, 08570, 08599, 08648, 22567, 22588, 22634, 22887, 22911-2, 22956
Faulwetter, Helmut, 14244
Fautz, Bruno, 23112
Fawcett, Charles, 07967, 09247
Fayyaz, Muhammad, 18079, 18143

Fazal, Cyril P.K., 22722-3
Fazal, M. Abdul, 12846, 17353
Fazal-e-Rab, Syed, 13483
Fazelbhoy, Rehmut S., 16177
Fazili, Manzoor A., 18035, 23169
Fazl-i Husain, Mian, Sir, 10260, 22652
Fazlul Hasan, M., 20467
Fazlul Huq, Abul Kasem, 24343-6
Fazlur Rahman, A.K. Mohammad, 07666
Federici, Cesare, 07834
Feer, Henri Leon, 05011
Feiling, Keith Grahame, 08029
Fein, Helen, 09846
Feldbaek, Ole, 07813, 07835, 24524
Feldhaus, Anne, 06772
Feldman, Herbert, 12436, 17490, 17501, 17539, 17552, 22496
Feldsieper, Manfred, 15154, 15319, 24930
Fellenberg, Theodor von, 18878, 18884
Felton, Monica, 10200, 19454
Fenner, Peter, 23888
Ferguson, Alastair Mackenzie, 18756
Ferguson, Charles A., 02341, 02654
Ferguson, Frances N., 01895
Ferguson, James P., 00501
Ferguson's Ceylon Directory, 27130
Fergusson, James, 03162, 03178
Fermar, Lewis, 10650
Fernandes, B.G., 15438, 23417
Fernandes, George, 13179
Fernandes, Praxy, 08165
Fernando, A., 18975
Fernando, B.J. Philip, 18404
Fernando, Edgar, 18545
Fernando, J.L., 18415
Fernando, M.E., 08104
Fernando, Neil, 18546
Fernando, P.E.E., 06172, 08099
Fernando, P.T.M., 18336, 18338, 18512, 18836
Fernando, S. Nihal U., 18620, 27147
Fernando, Tissa, 18344-5, 18372, 18462, 18815, 18867, 27135
Fernando, W.B. Marcus, 05619, 06173
Fernando, W.L., 19064
Feroz Chand, 09730
Ferozsons English-Urdu Dictionary, 27822
Ferozsons Urdu-English Dictionary, 27823
Ferreira, John Vincent, 00969, 16032, 21509
Ferrell, D.W., 23321
Ferrier, Joseph Pierre, 22516
Ferro-Luzzi, Gabriella Eichinger, 00839, 19495-6
Ferroli, D., Rev., 08220
Feuerstein, Georg A., 02163-4, 04681, 04827
Feys, Jan, 11382
Fic, Victor M., 13218, 19970
Fick, Richard, 04392
Fickett, Lewis P., Jr., 12508, 13180, 13432
Field, Harry H., 10790
Field, John Osgood, 24370
Filliozat, Jean, 00032, 00077-8, 00208, 00254-5, 00279, 00309, 01300, 01741-3, 01848, 04214, 04526-7, 04574, 04749, 04956, 06293, 06511
Filliozat, Pierre-Sylvain, 05995, 06392
Filliozat, Vasundhara, 06219
Finance Commission Act, 14534
Findly, Ellison Banks, 21415
Firishtah, Muḥammad Qāsim, 07409-10
Firminger, Walter Kelly, 07981
Firn, John, 14061
Firth, Cyril Bruce, 02238
Fischel, Walter J., 02312, 20140
Fischer, Christa-M. Friedrika, 03191
Fischer, Eberhard, 01691, 03140, 03409, 20829
Fischer, George, 10296, 13373, 18358
Fischer, H.J., 16059
Fischer, Klaus, 03088, 03163, 03191, 03251
Fischer, Louis, 09875
Fischer, W., 26025
Fišer, Ivo, 04487
Fisher, Douglas, 15320
Fisher, Frederick B., 09915
Fisher, James F., 25850
Fisher, Margaret W., 13038, 13175, 13338, 13927, 13945, 21052, 26004, 26480
Fisher, Marlene, 17177
Fisher, Maxine P., 26942
Fisher, Michael Herbert, 08767
Fishman, Alvin Texas, 19793
Fiske, Adele M., 11727, 16762, 17070, 21416-7
Fitze, Kenneth, Sir, 09362
Fitzler, M.A. Hedwig, 08077
Fitzroy, Yvonne Alice Gertrude, 11935
Fleet, John Faithfull, 04058, 06512
Fleming, Linda F., 27402
Fleming, Peter, 09442
Fleming, Robert Leland, 27374, 27402
Flemming, Leslie A., 02528
Fletcher, Thomas Bainbrigge, 27032
Flex, Oscar, 25726
Fliegel, Frederick C., 14851, 19741
Fløystad, Gunnar, 18177
Floris, George A., 09233
Flory, Marcel, 06885
Floud, Francis, Sir, 24479
Floyer, Ernest Ayscoghe, 22517
Flynn, Vincent John Adams, 07790
Fodermayr, Franz, 20861
Fodor's Guides, 27069, 27128
Folke, Steen, 19249, 20308
Folkert, Kendall W., 01147-8
Fonia, K.S., 27323
Fonseca, Aloysius Joseph, 15577, 15586-7
Fonseca, José Nicolay da, 08335
Fonseca, Mabel B., 15931-2
Fonseka, H.N.C., 18745
Fontera, Richard M., 10765
Food Corporation of India, 14819
Foote, Robert Bruce, 03497
Forbes, Alexander Kinloch, 00452
Forbes, Andrew, 19108, 19990, 20137
Forbes, Duncan, 27053
Forbes, Geraldine Hancock, 24555, 24661
Forbes, Rosita Torr, 09346
Ford Foundation, 24774
Foreign Trade Seminar, Bombay (1978), 13822
Forest Research Institute and Colleges, 14918-9
Forgue, Stella Sandahl, 07252
Forman, Werner, 03200
Fornaro, Robert John, 11420
Forrest, Denys Mostyn, 08166, 18720
Forrest, George William, 07968, 08011, 08030, 09068, 09469, 09487, 10688, 20580
Forrester, Duncan B., 12892, 19199, 19223, 19224, 19234, 19682, 20410
Forster, Edward Morgan, 11910-1, 20665
Forsyth, James, 20849
Forum of Education. Committee on Education and Total Employment, 15517
Foster, William, Sir, 07488, 07942, 07953, 07966, 07969, 07982, 08000, 27526
Foucaux, Philippe E., 04896
Foucher, Alfred Charles Auguste, 01658, 01669-70, 03459, 04877, 04878, 05012-3, 05462, 05517, 05528
Fouchet, Max Pol, 03133
Fox, Douglas A., 05046
Fox, Richard Gabriel, 00223, 00627, 00742, 00890, 01082, 23462, 23692, 23735-6, 23855
Fox-Strangways, Arthur Henry, 02723
Foxe, Barbara, 11339
Fraad, Irmah, 07143
Francis, T.S., 14843
Franck, Dorothea Seelye, 23076
Francke, R.O., 04945
Francklin, William, 07515
Franda, Marcus F., 12143, 12206, 12520, 13161, 13247, 24351-3, 24366, 24370-1, 25163, 25285, 26522
Frank, Dietmar, 27403
Franke, Rudolf Otto, 00031
Frankel, Francine R., 14234, 14773, 24472
Franks, Horace George, 20592
Franz, Heinrich Gerhard, 03089, 03141
Fraser, Andrew Henderson Leith, Sir, 09204
Fraser, J.B., 25899
Fraser, James Nelson, 08434, 21597
Fraser, Lovat, 09821
Fraser, Thomas M., 22370
Frauwallner, Erich, 01301, 04979, 05115, 07320
Fredericks, Pierce G., 09426
Freed, Ruth S., 01568, 01649, 01730, 02084, 23344, 23351, 23370-1, 23428-9

Freed, Stanley A., 00799, 01568, 01649, 01730, 02084, 23344, 23351, 23363, 23369-71, 23428-9
Freeman, James M., 22360-1
Freitas, William John, 07872
French, Harold W., 11346
French, Joseph Charles, 07340, 08720
Frenz, Albrecht, 01336
Frere, Henry Bartle Edward, Sir, 09171, 10720, 20705
Fretty, Ralph E., 18405
Frey, Hans, 12069
Freydig, Constance A., 23652, 23659
Friedman, Edward, 13946
Friedmann, Yohanan, 05958, 07679, 10392
Friend, Corinne, 10107
Fripp, Peter, 23918
Frith, Nigel, 01779
Fritz, Daniel Allen, 20259, 20449-50
Fruzzetti-Ostor, Lina, 00984, 01055, 24649
Fry, Maxwell J., 22903, 26125, 26142
Fryer, John, 07943
Frykenberg, Robert Eric, 10478, 10949-50, 19300, 19702, 19820-2
Fuchas, Mother, 02659, 24876-7, 25110-1
Fuchs, Stephen, 01083, 03718, 11001-3, 20392, 20850, 20871, 20884, 22233, 23774
Führer, Alois Anton, 03433, 07163
Fürer-Haimendorf, Christoph von, 01878, 03719-20, 05670, 13075, 15788-9, 19806-8, 20885, 26192-3, 26210-2, 26246, 26254, 26260-2, 26324-5, 26455, 26463, 26496-7, 26558-61
Fürer-Haimendorf, Elizabeth von, 00612
Fujita, Kotatsu, 05076
Fujiwara, Shin'ya, 27250
Fukazawa, Hiroshi, 08112, 08394, 08405-6
Fukutake, Tadashi, 00884
Fuller, A.R., 07026
Fuller, Christopher J., 20088-9, 20116
Fuller, Joseph Bampfylde, 20765
Fuller, Mary, 01064
Funke, Friedrich W., 26323
Furber, Holden, 07806, 07983-4, 08019, 08040, 08188, 08380, 08415, 08926
Furedy, Christine, 24546, 24739
Furneaux, Rupert, 09847
Furtado, Christopher L., 19048
Furtado, Raul de Loyola, 11788
Fussman, Gerard, 02320, 04127
Futchally, Laeeq, 27025
Futteh Sing, Bahadur, Raja of Khetri, 20637
Fuzli Rubbee, Kondkar, 07329
Fyle, Clifford, 16902
Fyzee, Asaf Ali Asghar, 00940-1, 16011-2
Fyzee Rahamin, Atiya Begum, 02703, 11682

Gable, Richard W., 27662
Gaborieau, Marc, 00669, 26255, 26269-71, 26282, 26326-9
Gabriel, Gwen, 17017
Gabriel, M.C., 17017
Gadbois, George H., Jr., 12817, 12828
Gadgil, Dhananjaya Ramchandra, 10865, 11143, 12277, 12521, 14257, 14376, 14423, 14431, 14494, 14704, 15139, 21248, 21486, 21547
Gadhok, D.N., 12802-3
Gaeffke, Hans Peter Theodore, 11584, 11615, 17038
Gagzow, Burkhard, 18570
Gahlot, Purnima, 00141
Gahlot, Sukhvir Singh, 00142
Gaige, Frederick H., 25944
Gaikwad, B.K., 13302
Gaikwad, V.R., 14737, 15032, 15862, 19771, 21157, 22244-5, 23613
Gail, Adalbert J., 01794-5, 05773
Gair, James W., 27851-3
Gairola, C. Krishna, 01650
Gairola, Tara Dutt, 25937
Gait, Edward Albert, 00533
Gaitonde, Pundlik, 21043
Gajarajan, C.S., 20280
Gajendragadkar, Aswathama Balacharya, 05996
Gajendragadkar, K.V., 06748
Gajendragadkar, Pralhad Balacharya, 12333, 12353, 12391-2, 12420, 12866, 15553, 15988, 16510, 16649, 23176, 23215, 23897
Gajendragadkar, S.N., 00743, 04870
Gajjar, Irene N., 03535
Galanter, Marc, 00921, 09274, 12421-2, 12854-5, 12872, 15779-81, 15810, 15821
Galbraith, John Kenneth, 14021, 03275
Galey, Jean-Claude, 25923
Gallagher, John, 09062, 24329
Gallais, Jean, 19823
Galle Municipal Council, 18907
Galloway, Archibald, Sir, 10951
Gama, Vasco da, 08761
Gambhirananda, Swami, 11297, 11347-8
Gamburd, Geraldine, 18628
Gan-Chaudhuri, Jagadis, 26627
Gananakennan, I., 14411
Gananathan, V.S., 14198
Ganapathy, B.D., 20411
Ganda Singh, 08532, 08565, 08585, 08600, 08617, 08649, 09731, 10495, 22589-91, 22941, 22950, 22957, 22985, 23011, 26929, 27727
Gandhi, D.V., 13500
Gandhi, H.N.D., 27588
Gandhi, H.S., 16219
Gandhi, Indira Nehru, 12114-5, 13410-2, 13518
Gandhi, Kishor, 16491
Gandhi, Manubehn (Jaysukhlal), 09894-6, 10519
Gandhi, Mohandas Karamchand, 04682, 09669, 09862-72, 09940-1, 09991, 10116-7, 10144, 10416-7, 10632-4, 10744, 10766-8, 11560, 12472, 14295-6, 16202, 16316, 16460, 22635, 26825
Gandhi, N.K., 16087, 21521
Gandhi, Raj S., 02205, 26943
Gandhi, Rajmohan, 10201
Gandhi, Shanta, 02998
Gandhi, Subhash Chander, 27469
Gandhi, Surjit Singh, 08595
Gandhi, Ved Parkash, 14577, 14591
Gandhi, Virchand Raghavji, 01302
Gandhi Peace Foundation, New Delhi, 15101
Gandhi Smarak Nidhi, 16128
Gandhigram Institute of Rural Health and Family Planning, 16220
Ganesan, Jayalakshmi, 19277
Ganesan, S., 00020
Ganeshi Lal, 23145
Gangadhara Rao, M., 15617
Gangadharan, A., 20022
Gangadharan, K., 13567
Gangadharan, K.K., 09561, 13253, 21139
Gangadharan Pillai, V., 20043
Gangal, Suresh Chandra, 12021, 12593, 13744, 14064
Gangoly, Ordhendra Coomar, 01671, 03164, 03252, 03396, 06614, 06809, 06903, 06919, 07715, 08482
Gangopadhyay, Anantlal, 06000
Gangopadhyay, Bela, 24603
Gangopadhyay, Mrinalkanti, 04832, 04848, 07321
Gangrade, Kesharichand Dasarathasa, 15052, 15745, 15756, 15953-4, 16143, 22706, 23341, 23324, 24081
Gangulee, N., 10680
Gangulee, Nagendranath, 10278, 10933, 10963
Gangulee, Narendranath, 26740
Ganguli, Birendranath, 00874, 09601, 09942, 10701, 10866, 10904, 10913, 11062, 13804, 14150, 14223, 16046, 16117, 23601, 23826
Ganguli, H.C., 16578
Ganguli, Kalyan Kumar, 03418, 03837, 06830
Ganguli, Radharaman, 04363
Ganguli, Sobhanlal, 24996
Ganguly, Anil Baran, 05454, 09746
Ganguly, Bangendu, 24354, 24379-80
Ganguly, Debi Sankar, 24431
Ganguly, Dhirendra Chandra, 06206, 06710
Ganguly, Dilip Kumar, 00477, 04255
Ganguly, Dwarkanath, 25727
Ganguly, J.B., 26636
Ganguly, Mano Mohan, 03423
Ganguly, Mira, 15231, 24380
Ganguly, S.M., 10065
Ganguly, S.N., 14351
Ganguly, Shivaji, 12052
Gangwar, A.C., 23289
Gangwar, R.M., 23609
Ganhar, J.N., 02068
Gani, H.A., 12448
Ganju, M., 23213
Gankovsky, Yuri Vladimirovich, 00705, 17293, 25495
Gansser, August, 25900

Garbe, Richard von, 04808
Garcin de Tassy, Joseph Héliodore, 02643, 11585
Gard, Richard Abbott, 01125, 01225
Garde, D.K., 04252, 12907
Garde, Raghunath Krishna, 16335
Gardezi, Hassan Nawaz, 18080, 18144
Gardner, Brian, 07954
Gardner, Peter M., 00628, 00776, 00814, 15790
Gardner, Philip, 11912
Garg, J.P., 25703
Garg, J.S., 23624
Garg, Pulin K., 15955
Garg, R.P., 22265
Garg, Rajender Kumar, 16712
Garg, Vipin Krishna, 14808
Gargi, B.D., 16970
Gargi, Balwant, 02105, 02912, 02935, 02999, 22962
Garman, Michael, 17136
Garratt, Geoffrey Theodore, 00209, 09044
Garrett, Herbert Leonard Offley, 07425, 22570, 22921
Garrett, John, 01117
Garrett, Richard, 08012
Garuḍa-purāṇa, 05797
Gauba, Khalid Latif, 09248, 10524, 11872, 12867, 15851
Gaudani, H.R., 06865-6
Gaudart, Edmond, 07902
Gaudino, Robert L., 16492
Gauntia, R., 24172
Gaur, Damodar Sharma, 00324
Gaur, Dharmendra, 10108
Gaur, K.D., 14604
Gaur, Madan, 15392, 16971
Gaur, R.C., 03662
Gaur, V.P., 09958
Gauri Shankar, V., 13893
Gautam, Brijendra Pratap, 27678
Gautam, Ghanshyam, 16493
Gautam, Mohan K., 20933
Gautam, Vinayshil, 10867, 15261, 15291
Gaya Improvement Trust, 24173
Gayathri, P.K., 06294
Gazetteer of India, 27779-81
Geddes, Arthur, 10879, 24667
Geddes, J.C., 11017
Geddes, Patrick, 10664, 10689, 22255
Gehlot, N.S., 12885
Gehrts, Heine, 04638
Geib, M. Margaret, 26996
Geib, Ruprecht, 02019, 05402
Geiger, Rudolf, 12091
Geiger, Wilhelm, 02543, 04230-2, 05242, 06137, 27854-5
Geldner, Karl Friedrich, 03883
Gena, C.B., 13435
Gense, James H., 20627
Gentil, Jean Baptiste Joseph, 07911
Geoghegan, William H., 26587
Geological Survey of India, 17281
George, C.M., 24537
George, K.A., 20000
George, K.C., 19922
George, Karimpumannil Mathai, 02589, 06593, 20192-4, 20210, 20213, 27883
George, M.A., 27878
George, Nedumpalakunnel, 11383
George, P.V., 15221
George, Poykayil Simon, 14908, 15122, 21482, 23613
George, Puthukudy Thomas, 19296, 19759-61, 20333
George, Robert Esmonde Gordon, 11877
George, Thayil Jacob Sony, 12752, 24008
George, V.C., 04603
Gera, Vimla, 06033
Gerard, J.G., 25858
Gerard, Renée, 25612
Gerber, William, 01184
Germain, Adrienne, 25518
Germain, Ernest, 18394
Gerow, Edwin Mahaffey, 02504, 05355, 05989, 17121
Gerson-Kiwi, Edith, 02812
Gervis, Pearce, 27218
Getman, Julius G., 16559
Getty, Alice, 01659, 01810
Geyl, P., 07486
Ghai, Dharam P., 26845
Ghai, Yash P., 26845
Ghalib, Mirza Asadullah Khan, 09476, 11634-48
Ghanananda, Swami, 11322
Ghani, A.R., 27665
Ghatage, A.M., 05250
Ghatak, Subrata, 15106
Ghatate, Narayan Madhav, 13989
Ghate, Vinayaka Sakharama, 06328
Ghauri, Iftikhar Ahmad, 07506, 08113
Ghaznawi, Khalid, 12070
Ghimire, Durga, 26275-6
Ghirshmann, Roman, 05540
Gholām Hoseyn Khān Ṭabāṭabāʾī, 07561 , 08866
Ghori, S.A.K., 00345
Ghosal, A.K., 24381
Ghosal, Hari Ranjan, 24399
Ghosal, Sourendra Nath, 14662, 15123
Ghose... *See also* Ghosh
Ghose, Abhijit, 24939
Ghose, Abulya, 13450
Ghose, Akshaya Kumar, 09163
Ghose, Aurobindo, 01483, 03968, 04683, 09718-20, 09959, 10615, 11220, 11367, 11374-5, 11749, 11772, 24987
Ghose, Benoy, 11253, 24244, 24614-5, 24668, 24970
Ghose, Bijon, 24931, 24940
Ghose, D.K., 09057
Ghose, Dilip Kumar, 23158
Ghose, Hemendra Prasad, 10803, 10844
Ghose, Kamal Kumar, 10993, 15087
Ghose, Lotika, 24961-63
Ghose, Manmathanath, 10826
Ghose, Manmohan, 24962-3
Ghose, Nagendra Nath, 03775, 03806
Ghose, Nemai, 27638
Ghose, Nirmal, 24941
Ghose, O.K., 05407
Ghose, Sachindra Lal, 10827
Ghose, Sailen, 27556
Ghose, Sankar, 09534-5, 09562, 09635, 09683, 13142-3, 13151, 14289, 24424
Ghose, Santidev, 10622
Ghose, Shishir Kumar, 07273, 24502
Ghose, Sisirkumar, 11773, 24922, 25056
Ghose, Sookamal, 25043
Ghose, Sudhansu Kumar, 13561, 13609
Ghose, Sudhir, 24382
Ghose, Sukumar, 24932, 24942
Ghosh... *See also* Ghose
Ghosh, A., 00579, 03494
Ghosh, Alak, 14416, 14625, 24512
Ghosh, Amalananda, 03142, 04521, 05594, 07213
Ghosh, Ambika, 24456
Ghosh, Amiya Bhushan, 11107, 14647
Ghosh, Arabinda, 14809, 15252, 15269
Ghosh, Arun K., 09524, 10934, 11166, 12286
Ghosh, Asok K., 03498, 03506, 03547-8
Ghosh, Asoklal, 09457
Ghosh, B.R., 23389
Ghosh, Bijit, 16088, 22119, 23418
Ghosh, Bimal, 15715
Ghosh, Biswanath, 08322
Ghosh, Damayanti, 11861
Ghosh, D.P., 07346
Ghosh, Deva Prasad, 00608
Ghosh, Dhruba Narayan, 14610
Ghosh, G.B., 16911
Ghosh, Grish, 24400
Ghosh, Jamini Mohan, 02201, 08846, 08933
Ghosh, Jajneswar, 02165, 24836
Ghosh, Juthika, 02470
Ghosh, Jyotish Chandra, 02660
Ghosh, Kali Charan, 24450
Ghosh, Kalyan Kumar, 10436
Ghosh, Kedar, 16885
Ghosh, Lotika, 24872
Ghosh, M.G., 14776
Ghosh, Manomohan, 05269, 05291, 05295, 05301, 05381
Ghosh, Moni, 24541
Ghosh, Murari, 24764
Ghosh, Nikhil, 02745
Ghosh, Oroon, 02419
Ghosh, P., 15626
Ghosh, Pabitra Kumar, 24388
Ghosh, Pansy Chaya, 09636
Ghosh, Parimal Chandra, 13967
Ghosh, Prafulla Chandra, 09897
Ghosh, Pramita, 10050

Ghosh, Prodyot, 11798
Ghosh, Rabindra Nath, 22760
Ghosh, Ranjit, 09524, 12286
Ghosh, Ratan, 24497-8
Ghosh, S.C., 10216
Ghosh, Sachindralal, 25132
Ghosh, Samir K., 26482
Ghosh, Sankar, 24355-6, 24372
Ghosh, Shyamali, 24347
Ghosh, Srikanta, 12704-5, 15811, 16186, 22307
Ghosh, Subarna, 09457
Ghosh, Subratesh, 15593
Ghosh, Suchita, 09443
Ghosh, Sudhir, 09898
Ghosh, Sunanda, 24389
Ghosh, Sunilkumar, 24942
Ghosh, Sunit, 22291
Ghosh, Suresh Chandra, 08927, 09124, 10539, 10581, 10595, 20934
Ghosh, Tapan, 10525
Ghosh, Tarak Chandra, 25099
Ghosh, Tushar Kanti, 24451
Ghosh, Yatinkumar, 16461, 24293-6, 24318
Ghoshal, S.N., 04000
Ghoshal, Sarat Chandra, 05159
Ghoshal, Satyendranath, 08964
Ghoshal, Shivanarayana, 02401
Ghoshal, Upendra Nath, 00108, 00198, 00906, 03782, 04010-1, 04256, 04266, 04293, 04328, 04364, 04445-6
Ghouse, Agha Mohamed, 17826, 17846-50, 18028
Ghouse, Mohammad, 12423, 23902
Ghuge, V.B., 14512, 14597, 21276
Ghulam Ahmad, Mirza, 11521-2
Ghulam Ali, 17716
Ghulām Farīduddīn, Khvājah, 23001
Ghulām Husain Khān, Ṭabāṭabā'ī. *See* Gholam Huseyn Khan
Ghulam Husain Zaidpuri, 08840
Ghulam Mohammad, 17961-4
Ghulam Rabbani, A.K.M., 25447
Ghurye, Govind Sadashiv, 00629, 00670-1, 00761, 00891, 00970, 01003, 01081, 01863, 02188, 02212, 03320, 03751, 04215, 04716, 12437, 13582, 15843, 20820, 21470, 21548
Ghurye, Kumud G., 00853
Giasuddin Ahmed, Syed, 25224, 25235
Gibb, Hamilton Alexander Roskeen, 02358, 02263, 05637, 11451
Gibbs, Henry, 27347
Gibbs, Mildred E., 02239, 11531
Gibson, G.E., 00280
Gideon, Helen, 22843
Gidvani, M.M., 08674
Gidwani, N.N., 19959, 27584, 27639, 27787
Gidwani, P.M., 12415
Gierth, Roland, 20555
Gilani, Arifshah C., Sayyid, 11653
Gilani, Asad, 18219
Gilbert, Irene A., 10553-4, 10577
Gilbert, Martin, 09825
Gilbertson, George Waters, 27951
Giles, Herbert A., 04053
Gill, Azam, 17367
Gill, Harjeet Singh, 27960
Gill, Manohar Singh, 22761, 25893
Gill, Pritam Singh, 08540, 08571, 08637, 08641
Gillion, Kenneth Lowell Oliver, 20746, 21881, 26809-10
Gimaret, Daniel, 05959
Giri, Kalipada, 02505
Giri, Raghunath, 05850
Giri, V. Shanker, 12587
Giri, Varahagiri Venkata, 11131, 12588-90, 15594, 19947-8
Gispert-Sauch, G., 01344
Gist, Noel Pitts, 15863-4, 15920, 20468-9
Glachant, Roger, 07916
Glamann, Kristof, 07900, 08019
Glasenapp, Helmuth von, 01196, 01277, 01484, 01500, 01922, 04962, 05902-3, 06475, 06502, 11862-3
Glass, Ruth, 12144
Glassburner, Bruce, 17697-9
Glasse, Robert M., 25498
Gleason, Henry Allan, 27960
Gledhill, Alan, 09275, 12334, 12354, 17319, 17491
Glendevon, John Hope, Baron, 10394
Glick, Clarence E., 26811, 26883
Glück, Heinrich, 07755
Glynn, Catherine, 01839, 03274
Gnanambal, K., 01896, 02085, 06464
Gnanamurthy, T.E., 06586
Gnanapragasam, V.M., 08221
Gnoli, Raniero, 04750, 05971, 05990, 06966
Goa, Daman and Diu, 21073
Goa, Daman and Diu. Bureau of Economics, Statistics, and Evaluation, 21074-5, 21085
Goa, Daman and Diu. Committee of the Problems of Mundkars..., 21089
Goa, Daman and Diu. Directorate of Education, 21094
Goa, Daman and Diu. Directorate of Fisheries, 21086
Goa, Daman and Diu. General Statistics Dept., 21076-7
Goa, Daman and Diu. Land Reform Commission, 21090-1
Goa, Daman and Diu. University Committee, 21095
Gochwal, Balbir Singh, 01354
Godakumbura, Charles Edmund, 02106, 02544, 03368, 05614, 06174
Godard, André, 05545
Godard, Y., 05545
Godbole, M.D., 21291
Godbole, N.N., 03732
Godbole, N.R., 06746-7
Godbole, Narayan Haribhau, 20497
Godden, Jon, 11925, 27054
Godden, Rumer, 11924-5, 27054
Gode, P.K., 02041
Godinho, Vitorino de Magalhães, 07855
Godse, Nathuram Vinayak, 10526
Godwin, Clement J., 11543, 16812, 21451
Goekoop, C., 07322
Goel, Bhim Sain, 10583, 16650
Goel, D.R., 23314
Goel, M.L., 13144
Goel, R.C., 23291
Goetz, Hermann, 00033, 00165, 00176, 03070, 03091, 03165, 03284, 03410, 03424, 05455, 05556-7, 05595, 06784, 06818, 06840, 06867, 06886, 06931, 06944, 06999, 07380, 07716, 07769, 07779, 08502, 08555, 08735, 27080
Gogoi, Padmeswar, 07195
Gohain, Bikash Chandra, 26473
Goheen, John, 14352
Goil, R.M., 26180
Goitein, S.D., 07814
Gokak, Vinayak Krishna, 02402, 11570, 11750-1, 16657, 16739, 17071, 17096, 20573
Gokhale, Balkrishna Govind, 00107, 01242, 01363, 01539, 04088, 04128, 04147, 04267, 04282, 04957, 05017, 05456, 08395-7, 08416-8, 09656, 09809, 11878, 18985, 21418, 27081
Gokhale, Gangadhar Nilkanth, 10616
Gokhale, Gopal Krishna, 09670
Gokhale, Jayashree B., 20741
Gokhale, Kamal Shrikrishna, 08292
Gokhale, R.G., 21312
Gokhale, S.D., 16128a
Gokhale, S.M., 10463
Gokhale, Sharad D., 16153
Gokhale, Sharacchandra Damodar, 16262
Gokhale, V.V., 04961
Gokhale Institute of Politics and Economics, Poona, 00236, 10853
Gokulanathan, K.S., 15939
Gokulanathan, P.P., 25788
Golant, William, 09047
Golay, Wasant Hari, 21598
Gold, Norman Leon, 15370
Goldberg, Helen, 20083
Goldberg, N.M., 09705
Goldman, Robert P., 03762, 04639, 05803
Goldstein, Rhoda L., 20367
Goldstuecker, Theodor, 05205
Gole, Prakash, 21545
Gole, R.M., 21639
Gollenesse, Julius Stein van, 08091
Goloubew, Victor, 01936, 05596
Golwalkar, Alka R., 21461-2
Golwalkar, Madhav Sadashiv, 10527, 13283-4
Goman, Thomas G., 03986
Gombrich, Richard, 01660, 06049, 06150, 19015-6
Gomes, Francisco Luiz, 21100
Gomes Soliz, Duarte, 07873
Gomez, Luis O., 05053
Gonçalves, Diogo, 08132
Gonçalves, Jose Julio, 27715

Gonda, Jan, 00210, 01033, 01156, 01171, 01701, 02129, 02390, 03807-8, 03838-9, 03862, 03896-7, 03935, 04283, 04459, 04589, 04737, 04751, 04765-6, 04779, 04789-90, 05166, 05832, 05843, 27799
Gondi, M.G., 20309
Gongal, Sushila Devi, 26027
Goodall, Merrill R., 26026
Goode, Richard, 18655
Goode, Samuel Walter, 24740
Goodfriend, Arthur, 14022
Goodman, J.M., 23483
Goodnow, Henry Frank, 17331
Goodwin, Buster, 23113
Goonatilleka, M.H., 03015-6
Gooneratne, Tilak E., 18679
Gooneratne, W., 18746
Gooneratne, Yasmine, 00109, 19076
Goonetileke, Henry Alfred Ian, 00547, 00560, 18430-1, 18832, 19077, 19082, 19092-3, 27153, 27704
Goonetilleke, D.C.R.A., 11879
Goonetilleke, Lionel Perera, 18701a
Goonewardena, Karunadasa Wijesiri, 08092, 09006
Goonewardene, Leslie, 18395-6
Gopal, B., 16248
Gopal, Krishan, 27690
Gopal, Krishna, 23919
Gopal, Krishna Kanti, 05678, 05713
Gopal, Lallanji, 00021, 00540, 04122, 04318, 04365-6, 04372, 04380, 04447, 05714-6, 07070
Gopal, Madan, 11598-601, 11625, 22648
Gopal, Mysore Hatti, 08206, 14578, 15203, 17246, 20226
Gopal, Ram. *See* Ram Gopal
Gopal, Sarvepalli, 00111, 08905, 09086, 09145, 10257, 13354
Gopal, Surendra, 08398, 08419-20, 23948
Gopal Iyer, K., 24134
Gopal Krishan, 16664, 22319, 22747, 22904
Gopal Krishna, 09995-6, 12438, 12449, 23328
Gopal Sharma, P., 12488
Gopal Singh, 08572-3, 08611, 08638, 08650, 08661, 27009
Gopala Sarana, 00660
Gopala Reddy, Y., 06661
Gopalachari, K., 04222
Gopalacharya, Majuli Ramacharya, 03884
Gopalakrishna Murthy, S., 06662
Gopalakrishna, M.D., 19742
Gopalakrishnan, T.P., 15975
Gopalan, Avilliath Kutteri, 19971-2
Gopalan, Coluthur, 16251-3
Gopalan, Gopalan V., 21934
Gopalan, R., 06185
Gopalan, Subramania, 01329, 16699
Gopalan Nair, C., 20128
Gopalaswami, K., 20747
Gopalkrishna, D., 12539
Gopalkrishna Naidu, G.T., 05833
Gopalkrishnan, Panikkanparambil Kesavan, 10905
Gopalratnam, V.C., 19147
Gopi, K.N., 19842
Gopinath, C., 02991
Gopinath, Meenakshi, 17570
Gopinatha Rao, T.A., 01593-4
Gopinathan Nair, P.R., 20154
Goradia, Prafull, 14909
Gorakh Nātha, 07307
Gorakṣa Nātha. *See* Gorakh Nātha
Gorakshkar, Sadashiv, 01614
Gordon, A.D.D., 21203
Gordon, Corrie, 10602
Gordon, Douglas Hamilton, 03499
Gordon, John Everett, 22750, 22918
Gordon, John James Hood, Sir, 08541
Gordon, Leonard A., 09721, 10078, 24284, 24319, 27451
Gordon, Richard, 09992, 10131
Gordon, Stewart Nelson, 08305-8
Gordon-Polonskaya, Ludmilla R., 10322, 17293
Gore, Madhav S., 00971, 01000, 14683, 15940, 16182, 16444-5, 21510, 23390-1, 23399
Gore, N.A., 04697
Gore, N.Y., 19996
Gorekar, N.S., 02521, 07581
Gorer, Geoffrey, 26401
Gorman, M., 11036
Gorrie, Robert Maclagan, 22732
Gorvine, Albert, 17348
Gosal, Gurdev Singh, 16025, 16660, 22762, 22888, 22942
Gosling, L.A. Peter, 26985
Goswami, A., 03179, 25737
Goswami, B.B., 01923, 20540, 23775, 26606, 26615, 26617
Goswami, Birendra Nath, 17738
Goswami, Golock Chandra, 28006
Goswami, H., 25736
Goswami, K.P., 09857
Goswami, M.C., 25810, 26588, 26678-9
Goswami, Niranjan, 01744
Goswami, O., 01750, 02704
Goswami, Prabhas Chandra, 25746, 25781, 25799
Goswami, Praphulladatta, 25821, 25829-31
Goswami, Purushottam Das, 27935
Goswami, Tulsi Chandra, 24330
Goswami Bhagabat Kumar, Mahamahopadhyaya. *See* Bhagabat Kumar, Sastri
Goswamy, B.N., 00097, 01909, 06106, 08468, 08668-9, 08701-7, 08712, 08721-2, 08736-9, 08751, 17194
Goswamy, Jaya, 04159
Goswamy, Karuna, 02069, 08670
Gotsch, Carl Hugo, 17934, 17944, 17953, 17992
Goud, M. Basavana, 20322
Goudriaan, Teun, 01403, 04791-2, 05887-8
Gough, Archibald Edward, 04794, 04835
Gough, Charles John Stanley, Sir, 22568
Gough, Eleanor Kathleen, 00800, 01034, 10999, 12209, 19347, 19420-1, 19353, 19960, 19986-7, 20035, 20069-70, 20090, 20096-100, 20162
Gould, Harold A., 00830, 13636, 15004, 15763-4, 19348, 23471, 23524, 23537, 23693, 23782-3, 23707-9, 23873, 23889
Gouldsbury, Charles Elphinstone, 09225
Gour, Raj Bahadur, 19636
Gover, Charles E., 02107, 02452, 19598
Government of India act (1935), 10280
Govil, Rishi Kumar, 23585
Govila, J.P., 25924
Govind Narain, 11062
Govinda, Anagarika, 01682-3, 04996
Govinda Rajulu Chetty, Tranquebar Venkatram, 19497
Govinda Rao, M., 14535
Govinda Reddy, C., 00297
Govindan, M., 20211
Govindankutty, A., 03630
Govindarajan, S.A., 10828
Govindasamy, M.S., 06186
Gowdra, Gurumurthy K., 20541
Gowen, Herbert Henry, 02471
Goyal, D.R., 13285, 27219
Goyal, Narendra, 12753, 25841, 25976
Goyal, O.P., 09684, 12304, 13458, 13655
Goyal, Om Prakash, 14493
Goyal, R.C., 15641
Goyal, Ravinder Kumar, 22256
Goyal, S.K., 12648-9
Goyal, Satya Paul, 16912, 27585
Goyal, Shravan Kumar, 15477
Goyal, Shriram, 04148
Goyal, Surinder Kumar, 22763
Goyder, Catherine, 19841
Graaf, Nikolaas van, 07895
Gracias, Valerian, Cardinal, 16813-4
Grag, Hugh, 19824
Graham, Bruce D., 13270-1, 13321, 23483, 23511
Graham, Carol, 19529
Graham, D.C., 20593
Graham, Gail Minault. *See* Minault, Gail
Graham, George Farquhar Irving, 11470
Graham, Gerald Sandford, 11043
Graham, Maria, 11936
Granoff, Phyllis E., 06393
Granovsky, A., 13995
Grant, Charles, 10540
Grant, Colesworthey, 11937
Graveley, Frederic Henry, 03212-3, 03397
Graves, Daniel R., 13129
Gray, A., 07912
Gray, Basil, 03267, 08483
Gray, Hugh, 19676-8, 19683-4
Gray, John E.B., 02453
Graziosi, Paolo, 03513
Great Britain. Cabinet mission to India, 10464-5
Great Britain. Colonial Office, 18359

Great Britain. Commission on Constitutional Reform in Ceylon, 18362
Great Britain. India Office, 09214, 10233-4, 11018-9
Great Britain. India Office Library, 27527, 27544-6
Great Britain. Indian Franchise Committee (1932), 10263
Great Britain. Indian Railway Committee, 11044
Great Britain. Indian States Committee, 09376-7
Great Britain. Indian Statutory Commission, 10253, 10584
Great Britain. Ministry of Defence, 09301
Great Britain. Parliament. House of Commons, 09470, 26777, 27679
Great Britain. Parliament. Joint Committee on Indian Constitutional Reform, 10279
Great Britain. Royal Commission on Agriculture in India, 10935
Great Britain. Royal Commission on Decentralization in India, 09830
Great Britain. Royal Commission on Indian currency and finance (193), 11167
Great Britain. Royal Commission on labour (1891), 11114-5
Great Britain. Royal Commission on the public services in India, 09184
Great Britain. Royal Commission on the superior civil services in India, 09185
Great Britain. Secretary of State, 26741
Greaves, Monica Alice, 10549
Greaves, Rose, 09414
Green, Helen Bagenstose, 26792
Green, Lawrence W., 18145, 22488
Green, Leslie, 24775
Greenberg, Michael, 11063, 18664
Greenberger, Allen J., 11880
Greenlees, Duncan, 07246
Greenough, Paul, 24452
Greenwall, Harry James, 21444
Gregory, Robert G., 26853
Grenard, Fernand, 07451
Grenell, Peter, 22375
Grewal, B.S., 14525
Grewal, Jagtan Singh, 00493, 05627-8, 07411, 08542, 08618, 08642, 08651, 08668-9
Grewal, S.S., 22764
Grey, Basil. *See* Gray, Basil
Grey, Henry George Grey, 3rd Earl, 18326, 18329
Gribble, James Dunning Baker, 08240
Grierson, George Abraham, Sir, 02321, 02622, 06977, 11571, 23258, 24159, 27967-8
Griffin, Keith B., 17717, 17827, 17851, 25326
Griffin, Lepel Henry, Sir, 22571, 22604, 22613
Griffin, Willis H., 16403
Griffith, M., 09336
Griffith, Ralph Thomas Hotchkin, 03885, 03911, 03918, 03927, 04699, 05368
Griffith, William, 26428
Griffiths, Percival Joseph, Sir, 09032, 09046, 09226, 11030
Griffiths, Walter G., 20979
Grigson, Wilfred Vernon, 20851, 20872
Grimshaw, Allen D., 15865
Griswold, Hervey de Witt, 03898
Grohma, Otto, 04849
Gros, Francois, 05415, 06587
Gross, Rita M., 01718
Grousset, René, 01303, 05649, 07341
Grover, B.L., 09033, 09831
Grover, B.R., 07597-8
Grover, B.S.K., 26373
Grover, D.C., 10079
Grover, Krishan Lal, 12382, 13492
Grover, Satish, 03166
Grover, Ved Prakash, 21981
Grover, Verinder, 22668
Growse, Frederic Salmon, 02036-7, 08795, 23450
Gründler, Ulrich, 26075
Grünwedel, Albert, 03143, 19017
Gubbannavar, S.Y., 15227
Gubbannavar, Shivanand, 20247
Gubernatis, Angelo de, 01569
Gubhaju, B.B., 26108
Guénon, René, 01210, 01316
Guenther, Herbert V., 01319, 04997, 05125, 05904-7
Guérinot, Armand Albert, 01149, 01278
Guha, Amalendu, 07196-7, 21234, 21332-3, 25682, 25698-9, 25728-30, 25800
Guha, Aravinda, 11807
Guha, Arun Chandra, 09685, 09722, 15323
Guha, Biraja Sankar, 00694, 24812
Guha, C.R., 13814
Guha, Charuchandra ("Krishnadas"), 09993
Guha, Dinesh Chandra, 07323
Guha, K., 23920
Guha, Meera, 24698, 24755, 24765, 24784
Guha, Meghna, 25253
Guha, Nikhiles, 25100
Guha, Ranajit, 08906
Guha, S.K., 15375
Guha, Sunil, 14764
Guha, Uma, 23694, 24650
Guha-Thakurta, Prabhucharan, 24948
Guide to Festschriften, 27628
Guide to Indian periodical literature, 27606
Guillaume, Alfred, 02264
Guisinger, Stephen, 18046
Gujarat. Agriculture Dept., 21728-9
Gujarat. Bureau of Economics and Statistics, 20830, 21740, 21777, 21789-90, 21800
Gujarat. Chief Electoral Officer, 21681-2
Gujarat. Commission of Inquiry on Communal Disturbances at Ahmedabad..., 21811
Gujarat. Commission on Modernization of University Acts, 21906
Gujarat. Committee to Review the State of Higher Education in Gujarat, 21907
Gujarat. Directorate of Evaluation, 21766
Gujarat. Directorate of Industries, 21778
Gujarat. Directorate of Information and Tourism, 27033
Gujarat. General Administration Dept., 21717
Gujarat. High Level Team on District Administration, 21696
Gujarat. Labour, Social Welfare, and Tribal Development Dept., 21812
Gujarat. Panchayat and Health Dept., 21701
Gujarat. Socially and Educationally Backward Class Commission, 21813
Gujarat. Zanzmer Inquiry Commission, 21842
Gujarati, Damodar, 15578
Gujral, M.L., 14235
Gujral, Rajinder, 26524
Gujrati, Balwant Singh, 16913
Gulati, C.L., 22960
Gulati, I.S., 14605-6, 14820
Gulati, J.S., 15494
Gulati, Kailash Chander, 13296, 22649
Gulati, Kuldip S., 14606
Gulati, Leela, 15535-8
Gulati, Raj Kumar, 02105, 21395
Gulati, Y.B., 09302
Gulawani, V.N., 16961
Gulbadan, Begam, 07458
Guleria, J.S., 23012
Gulhati, Niranjan Das, 12242, 12931, 14878
Guliani, T.D., 14735
Gulik, Robert Hans van, 00049
Gulraj, Jethamal Parsram, 08675
Gumperz, Ellen McDonald, 20726, 20743, 21343-4, 21487, 21659
Gumperz, John Joseph, 02341-2, 23819-21
Gunadasa, J.M., 18730
Gunaji, Nagesh Vasudev, 21619
Gunaratne, M.H., 18788
Gunaratne, Shelton A., 18885, 19065-6
Gunasegaram, S.J., 05446
Gunasekara, Abraham Mendis, 27856
Gunasekera, H.A. de Silva, 18665-7
Gunasekhara, Alex, 08061
Gunasinghe, Newton, 18767
Gunasinghe, P.A.T., 04389
Gunasinghe, Siri, 03290, 06107, 08111
Gunatilleke, Godfrey, 18893
Gunatunga, C., 18583
Gunawardana, Amaradasa, 18882
Gunawardana, Lionel, 25434
Gunawardana, R.A.L.H., 06138, 06151-3
Gunawardena, D.C.R., 18957
Gunawardena, Kusuma, 18906
Gunawardene, C.A., 18653
Gundert, Hermann, 27879
Gundevia, Y.D., 23188, 26532
Gune, Vithal Trimbak, 03411, 08265

Gunewardena, Elaine, 18587
Gunjal, S.R., 12555
Gunther, Frances, 10418
Gunthorpe, Edward James, 20708
Gupta, A.B., 15363
Gupta, A.K., 09016, 23062
Gupta, Alka, 14114
Gupta, Amal Kumar, 06048
Gupta, Amit Kumar, 20697
Gupta, Anand P., 14580, 15550
Gupta, Anand Swarup, 05745, 05755, 05817, 09227-8
Gupta, Anirudha, 10804, 13553, 26011
Gupta, Anupam, 14579
Gupta, Arvind, 14821
Gupta, Atulchandra, 24565
Gupta, Avijit, 24422, 27286
Gupta, B.L., 02821
Gupta, B.N., 14513, 15928
Gupta, Babu Lal, 10635, 18493
Gupta, Badlu Ram, 15302
Gupta, Badri Prasad, 22006
Gupta, Baldev Raj, 02623
Gupta, Beni, 08352
Gupta, Bhabani Sen, 04933
Gupta, Bhagwan Das, 08377
Gupta, Bharat Bhushan, 12611, 12943
Gupta, Bhim Sen, 08643
Gupta, Bhupesh, 13234, 13505, 13519, 24373

Gupta, Brahmananda, 04850, 24818
Gupta, Brijen Kishore, 08020, 08867, 09647, 11881
Gupta, Chandra Bhan, 02936
Gupta, Chandra Bhanu, 23495
Gupta, Chitra, 13258
Gupta, D.L., 22123
Gupta, Devendra B., 14133, 14223, 15478, 23400, 27748
Gupta, Dharmendra Kumar, 05671, 05974-5, 06058
Gupta, Dharam Chand, 09563, 12305
Gupta, Dipankar, 21140
Gupta, Ghanshyam Singh, 22156, 22678
Gupta, Giri Raj, 15890, 15921
Gupta, Giriraj Prasad, 14125, 14626
Gupta, H.C., 16536
Gupta, Hirendra Nath, 04558
Gupta, Hari Ram, 08300, 08543-44, 22592
Gupta, J.P., 13510
Gupta, Jagdeo, 23522
Gupta, K.L., 16462, 27475
Gupta, K.P., 11323, 26374
Gupta, Karunakar, 13729
Gupta, Khadija Ansari, 23538
Gupta, Kishore Mohan, 06257
Gupta, Krishna Murti, 25851
Gupta, Krishna Prakash, 01864
Gupta, Krishna Swaroop, 08358
Gupta, Kulwant Rai, 15179, 15232, 15465
Gupta, Kunj Bihari Lal, 20659
Gupta, Lakshmi Chandra, 15262
Gupta, Lakshmi Narain, 15233
Gupta, Mahendra Nath, Rai Bahadur, 24483
Gupta, Manmathnath, 10109-11
Gupta, N.L., 22030
Gupta, Narain Saran, 15180
Gupta, Narayani, 23383
Gupta, Nolini Kanta, 11384-5
Gupta, Om Prakash, 02010, 11168
Gupta, P.H., 04717
Gupta, Pabitra, 03694
Gupta, Parmanand, 00153, 04081-2
Gupta, Parmeshwari Lal, 00548-9, 00554, 03214, 03295, 04149, 05457

Gupta, Prabhat Das, 24373
Gupta, Prakash Chandra, 11603
Gupta, Pratul Chandra, 08323, 08865, 09498
Gupta, R.L., 13459, 14060
Gupta, R.N., 05506
Gupta, Raghuraj, 12439, 23546, 23764
Gupta, Raj Narain, 12335
Gupta, Rajkumar, 27200
Gupta, Ram Chandra, 13403, 16579
Gupta, Ram Kishore, 04268, 15222, 16589
Gupta, Ram Pratap, 22199
Gupta, Ramesh Chand, 12053
Gupta, Ramesh Shankar, 06650
Gupta, Rameshwar, 11774
Gupta, Ranjan, 11992, 20935, 26381
Gupta, Ranjan Kumar, 24438, 24484
Gupta, Ranjit, 12145, 14452, 15466
Gupta, Ranjit Kumar, 14278, 24433, 24461, 24678
Gupta, S.C., 12682
Gupta, S.C., 23784
Gupta, S.K., 24812
Gupta, S.L., 01631-2, 10132, 23282, 23294
Gupta, S.P., 14267
Gupta, Samir Kumar, 20666
Gupta, Sanjukta, 01796, 04780, 05888, 06394, 08942
Gupta, Saryoo Prasad, 10657, 17234
Gupta, Satya, 16154
Gupta, Satya Pal, 00310
Gupta, Satya Prakash, 20999
Gupta, Shaibal, 07589
Gupta, Shakti M., 01633, 01702, 01769, 01826
Gupta, Shakti Madan, 10665
Gupta, Sham Sunder, 15822
Gupta, Shanti Nath, 01514
Gupta, Shanti Swarup, 14297, 23612, 26429
Gupta, Sher Singh, 22765, 27220
Gupta, Shiva Kumar, 15866
Gupta, Shyamala, 03118
Gupta, Sisir, 12092, 13717, 13902
Gupta, Sisir K., 12450, 17683
Gupta, Sisir Kumar, 08944
Gupta, Sulekh Chandra, 10952, 14048, 23591, 23644
Gupta, Sunil Kumar, 09588
Gupta, Suraj B., 14627
Gupta, Surendra K., 14165
Gupta, Suresh Chandra, 10112
Gupta, Swarajya Prakash, 02381, 03543, 03663-4, 03695, 03763, 27070
Gupta, Tarun, 25103
Gupta, V.K. (1941-), 20673
Gupta, V.K. (1930-), 23613
Gupta, Vinod, 12168
Gupte, Balkrishna Atmaram, 01035, 02086, 20628, 21396-7
Gupte, Ramesh Shankar, 06810, 06819, 06827
Gupte, Shankar Vinayak, 09264
Gur Rattan Pal Singh, 22946
Gurbachan Singh, 16377, 22766
Gurdial Singh, 22069
Gurdip Singh, 13823
Gurdon, Phillip Richard Thornbagh, 26689
Gurmit Singh, 08631, 22958
Gurnam Singh, 22679
Gursaran Singh, 08602
Gurtoo, Dukh Haran Nath, 11064, 13795
Gurukkal, P.M. Rajan, 20141
Gurumurthy, S., 00860
Gurung, Harka, 26307, 27386-7
Gururaja Bhatt, P., 00432
Gururaja Rao, Bairathnahalli Krishnamurthy, 03696
Gururajachar, S., 06245
Guseva, Natal'ia Romanovna, 01279
Gusfield, Joseph R., 13043
Gusinde, Martin, 20147, 26724
Gussin, Carl Mark, 21456
Gussner, Robert E., 06350-1
Gustafson, Donald Rudolph, 20227
Gustafson, Elizabeth, 17793
Gustafson, W. Eric, 17285, 17878-9, 22557, 25142, 27680
Guthrie, Katherine Blanche, 20581
Gutschow, Niels, 03167
Gutteridge, William, 09286
Guyot, James F., 12230
Gwyer, Maurice Linford, Sir, 10217
Gyan Chand, 14151, 14325
Gyani, Shiva Datta, 05798
Gyawali, Bharat M., 27740
Gyer, G.D., 25361

Haas, George C.O., 02680, 06001
Habenstein, R.W., 01044
Habib, Hassan, 17325, 17828
Habib, Irfan, 00111, 07386, 07525, 07590, 07599, 07606-8, 08564, 08785, 10868
Habib, Kemal, 11681
Habib, Mohammad, 06932, 07014-5, 07027, 07061, 07115, 07124
Habibullah, A.B.M., 07028
Habibullah, M., 25364-5, 25378, 25441, 25459, 25472

Hacker, Paul, 01404, 01466, 01540-1, 01770, 06361, 06395, 11204
Hackin, J.R., 05542
Hackin, Joseph, 05545-6, 03071, 03215, 05541-2
Hadi, Abdul, 23085
Hadi, Husain, Muhammad, 11472
Haeckel, Ernst, 18330
Haekel, Josef, 20852, 21915
Hänsch, Harald von, 24074
Hafeez, Sabeeha, 18059-61
Hafeez, Saeed, 17928, 17935-6
Haffner, Willibald, 27374
Hafiz Mohammad Tahir Ali, 08828
Hafizuddin, 15384
Hafizullah, M., 23204
Hafizur Rahman, A.K.M., 25455
Hagen, Toni, 27362-3
Haggerty, William J., 16494
Hahn, Emily, 02302
Hahn, Harlan, 13655
Haider, Agha Sajjad, 22878
Haider, Azimusshan, 22497, 25570
Haider, Husain, 17620
Haider, Syed Mohammad, 17332, 17349, 17354-5, 17375, 17653, 18047
Haig, M.R., 00484
Haithcox, John Patrick, 10080-1
Hájek, Lubor, 03285, 07736, 07774
Hajela, P.D., 14628
Hajjar, Sami G., 12295
Hajra, Durgadas, 20886
Hajra, Sridhar, 14648, 14910, 15195, 16065a
Hakari, Devendra Kumar, 06553
Hakeda, Yoshita S., 05111
Hakim, Abdul, 25618
Hakluyt, Richard, 07827
Hakluyt Society, 07828
Haksar, Urmila, 13528
Halappa, G.S., 12928, 20248, 20252, 21065
Halayya, M., 14911
Halbach, Axel J., 26866
Halbar, B.G., 20520, 20523
Halbfass, Wilhelm, 01114, 04851-2
Haldane, John Burdon Sanderson, 17256
Halder, Gopal, 24971, 25081, 25112
Haldar, Jnanranjan, 01661-2, 04546
Halder, Animesh, 13846
Halder, D.K., 24795-6
Haldipur, R.N., 12993, 14999
Hale, Austin, 28016-7
Hale, H.W., 10042
Hale, Margrit, 28016
Hale, Sylvia M., 00801, 23802
Ḥālī, Ḵhvājah Alṭāf Ḥusain, 11471
Halifax, Edward Frederick Lindley Wood, Earl of, 10258
Halim, A., 05834
Halim, Abdul, 07044-5, 07089, 07116, 07133-4
Halim, S.A., 08834
Hall, David E., 27519
Hall, Fernau, 02737, 02971
Hall, Kenneth R., 06201, 06246
Hall, Margaret, 03329, 03344
Hallade, Madeleine, 03144, 03201, 05529
Hallak, Jacques, 18946
Halliday, James, 09205
Hallikeri, R.K., 14468
Hallissey, Robert C., 08353
Halse, Michael, 15138
Halverson, John, 18976
Hambly, G.R.G., 20722, 22742
Hambly, Gavin, 07785
Hambye, Edward René, 02235, 02244, 04604, 16781
Hameed, Abdul, 17782
Hameed-ud-din, 05629, 06736
Hamid, Muhammad, 14087
Hamid, Muhammad Abdul, 25405, 25551, 25576
Hamid, S.M., 17350
Hamid, S. Shahid, 27221
Hamid-ud-Din, Chaudhuri, 22718
Hamied, Khwaja Abdul, 11094, 18165, 21297
Hamilton, Alexander, 07944
Hamilton, Charles Joseph, 08001, 11065
Hamilton, Clarence, 01270
Hamilton, Richard E., 24051
Hamilton, W.G., 08976
Hamiuddin Khan, Mohammad, 00861
Hammond, Norman, 00594
Hamoodur Rahman, 17389
Hamsananda, Swami, 16336
Hanafi, Zawar Ahmad, 09768
Hanaki, Taiken, 05150
Hanayama, Shinsho, 01126
Hanayama, Shoyu, 05072
Hanchett, Suzanne Lorraine, 02432, 20432, 20542
Handa, Om Chand, 25894
Handa, Rajendra Lal, 02644, 09378, 12567
Handbook of the Universities of Pakistan, 27428
Handbuch der Orientalistik, 00210
Handiqui, Krishna Kanta, 05251, 05672, 06059
Handoo, Chandra Kumari, 08805
Handoo, Jawaharlal, 02425, 02433, 27969
Hanefeld, Erhardt, 02987
Hangen, Welles, 13377
Hanif, M.W., 13511
Hanifi, Manzoor Ahmad, 07412
Hanks, Jane, 27055
Hanna, Henry Bathurst, 09427
Hans Raj, 12788
Hansen, G. Eric, 13947
Hansen, Jan, 02793
Hansen, Lillian E., 11544
Hanson, Albert Henry, 12306, 14417, 14475
Hanumanta Rao, S., 06476
Hanumantha Rao, B.S.L., 06278
Hanumantha Rao, C.H., 14842, 14929, 19762, 22767
Hanumantha Rao, G., 03119
Hanumanthaiya, K., 12876, 15455
Haq, Enamul, 27301
Haq, M.M., 07331
Haq, Mahbubul, 17852
Haq, Muhammad Enamul, 02661, 05947, 07330
Haq, Mushir Ul, 09769, 16013, 16775
Haq, Syed Moinul, 07016, 07046, 07117, 07657-8
Haqqi, Anwarrul Haque, 12914, 23539, 23765, 23903
Haqqi, S.A.H. *See* Haqqi, Anwarrul Haque
Haque, Enamul, 24861
Haque, Mahmudul, 25253
Haque, Mohammed Nazrul, 25782
Haque, Zulekha, 07355
Hara, Minoru, 01009, 04284, 04758
Harbans Singh, 00494, 02624, 08574, 08619, 08652, 14930-2, 22922, 23002, 23013
Harbir Singh, 22680
Harcharan Singh, 22693
Hardee, J. Gilbert, 18138
Hardev Singh, 14105-6, 26610
Hardgrave, Robert L., Jr., 12307, 13451, 19118, 19179, 19207, 19225-6, 19235, 19358-60, 19550-1, 19961, 19973-4, 20106, 20129-30
Hardie, Martin, 11978
Hardie, Norman, 26214
Hardiman, David, 11000, 21767
Harding, D.W., 11926
Hardinge, Charles Stewart, 2nd Viscount, 09120
Hardwari Lal, 13529, 13568
Hardy, Friedhelm, 01879, 06295, 07236
Hardy, Peter, 05630-1, 05933, 07029, 07528, 09770, 10393, 11452, 22977
Hardy, S.M., 18314
Hardy's Encyclopaedia, 27072
Hardy's encyclopaedic guide to Agra, Delhi, Jaipur, and Varanasi, 27280
Hare, E.M., 04985
Hares, Walter Pullin, 27955
Hari, Anna Marie, 28009
Hari Hara Sarma, T.R., 02801
Hari Mohan, 21000-2
Hari Om, 23192
Hari Rao, R., 27607
Hari Rao, V.N., 01973-4, 06615
Hari Singh, 14934
Harichand, 12540
Hariharan, K.V., 20490
Hariharan, M., 02708-9, 02913, 06492, 07253
Harijan Sevak Sangha. Cawnpore Branch, 23750
Harilal Savailal, 20615
Harit, H.L., 23307
Harjinder Singh, 00754, 12738, 22707, 22858-9, 26930
Harle, James C., 05552, 05558
Harmandar Singh, 12613

Harnam Singh, 09617, 18494
Harnek Singh, 15296
Harnetty, Peter, 10928, 11031, 11066-8, 19782, 22218, 22200
Haroon, Sharif Abdullah, 25639
Haroun er-Rashid, 27308-9
Harper, Edward Burnette, 00777, 00819, 00896, 01865, 20543-5, 20433-4
Harper, Judith W., 20368
Harper, Katherine, 01719
Harper, Marvin Henry, 16726
Harrex, S.C., 11728, 17072, 17122, 17156
Harris, Frank Reginald, 11095
Harris, George Lawrence, 27364
Harris, John, 09517
Harris, Leslie, 09428
Harris, M.A., 10377
Harris, Marvin, 01570
Harris, Mary Belli, 05338
Harris, Nigel, 21522
Harris, R.L., 18507a
Harrison, Barbara J., 27452
Harrison, Godfrey, 11096
Harrison, H.L., 24857
Harrison, John B., 07846, 08999
Harrison, Selig S., 12393, 14006, 19660
Harriss, Barbara, 14822, 14860, 19270
Harṣavardhana, 06008-9, 06078
Harshé, R.G., 06034
Hart, George Luzerne, III, 02411-2, 04474, 05416, 05418, 05430, 06279
Hart, Henry Cowles, 12929, 13583, 13672, 27412
Hart, S.G., 24280
Hartenberger, John Russell, 02802
Hartley, Lois, 11927, 17167
Hartmann, Horst, 13130, 19962
Hartog, Philip Joseph, Sir, 10555, 10584
Hartwig, Werner, 26562
Harvard University. International Program in Taxation, 14581
Harvard University. Peabody Museum of Archaeology and Ethnology. Library, 27503
Harvey, M.E., 22795
Haryana. Dept. of Industries, 23295
Haryana. Directorate of Health Services, 23275
Haryana. Directorate of Industries, 23296
Haryana. Directorate of Public Relations, 23264-5
Haryana. Economic and Statistical Organisation, 23278, 23283-5, 23297, 23309
Haryana. Marketing and Economic Research Bureau, 23288
Haryana. Planning Dept., 23279
Hasalkar, J.B., 20459
Hasan, Amir, 20980, 25925, 25932
Hasan, Aziza, 07609
Hasan, K.A., 23874
Hasan, K. Sarwar, 10297, 12031, 12078, 17724, 17751, 17767
Hasan, Khaja Shoeb, 14611
Hasan, Masood, 13824
Hasan, Masudul, 17630, 17649
Hasan, Masuma, 12243, 17668
Hasan, Mohammad, 07704, 11654, 23863, 26944
Hasan, Mohibbul, 05632, 06945
Hasan, Mushirul, 10118, 11453
Hasan, Parvez, 17700, 17909
Hasan, S.M., 18176
Hasan, S. Nurul, 07480, 07600
Hasan, Syed Mahmudul, 07363
Hasan, Zubeida, 17746
Hasan Ibn Yazīd, Abū Zaīd (Al Sirāf), 05638
Hasanuzzaman, S.M., 25352
Hashim, M., 18280
Hashmat Ara Begum, 25271
Hashmi, Alamgir, 18271
Hashmi, Farrukh, 26922
Hashmi, Riaz, 22719
Hashmi, Shafik H., 18116, 22498
Hashmi, Sultan S., 18081, 22499-500
Hasrat, Bikrama Jit, 07507, 22593-4, 25945
Hassan, M.C.A., 01937, 18859
Hassan, Mohammad, 17057
Hassan, Riffat, 11683
Hassan, S. Masihul, 02326
al-Hassan, Siraj, 19786
Hassan, Syed Riazul, 00942, 09265
Hassnain, F.M., 23159, 27222, 27251
Hassnain, S.E., 12451
Hasson, Joseph A., 15371
Hastings, Francis Rawdon-Hastings, 1st Marquis of, 09107
Hastings, James, 26953
Hastings, Warren, 08031, 08768-70
Haswell, Margaret Rosary, 19271
Hatalkar, V.G., 07930, 08247
Hatch, William John, 20148
Hathorn, James George, 26386
Hattiangdi, Gopal S., 01897
Hauer, J.W., 03817
Haug, Martin, 02293, 03941
Hause, E. Malcolm, 14065
Hauser, Walter, 24085, 24102
Hausherr, Klaus, 01938
Hauvette-Besnault, M., 05762
Havanur, L.G., 15812, 20369, 20372
Havell, Ernest Binfield, 01651, 02046, 03092-3, 03120, 03168-9, 07793
Hawley, John Stratton, 08815, 23921
Hay, Stephen, 11228, 25029
Hayashida, Tatsuo, 10161
Hayavadana Rao, Conjeevaram, 08167
Hayes, Louis D., 25990, 26308
Hayley, Frederick Austin, 18528
Haynes, Edward S., 20638
Hayward, Victor Evelyn William, 15860
Haywood, Sheila, 07777
Hazareesingh, Kissoonsingh, 26765-7
Hazari, Bharat R., 15479
Hazari, Rabindra Kishen, 13872, 13880, 15270, 15279, 15284
Hazarika, Niru, 12643, 26459
Hazlehurst, Leighton W., 16047, 22815, 23298
Hazra, Rajendra Chandra, 01542, 04416, 05756, 05758, 05823
Healey, John Michael, 14684
Healy, Derek T., 17829
Hearn, Gordon Risley, 23384
Heathcote, T.A., 09287
Hebbar, Kattingeri Krishna, 17213
Heber, Reginald, 11938, 12061, 19106-9, 25842
Hedayetullah, Muhammad, 07103, 11446
Hedrick, Basil C., 27741
Heeger, Gerald A., 22650, 22669
Heeramaneck, Alice N., 03216
Heesterman, Johannes Cornelius, 00022, 03783-4, 04285, 04305, 07807
Hegde, Kawdoor Sadananda, 12368
Heginbotham, Stanley J., 12192, 12650, 19196
Heidelberg. Universität. Südasien-Institut, 27421
Heidenreich, Herbert, 23978, 24009
Heim, Arnold, 25900
Heimann, Betty, 01176, 01345
Heimsath, Charles Herman, 10702, 10725, 11205, 13697, 13750, 14008, 26970
Hein, Norvin J., 01118, 02109, 03053, 07281
Heinz, Wilhelm, 02522
Heitler, Richard, 23472
Held, Gerrit Jan, 04640
Helfer, Mireille, 02110
Helweg, Arthur Wesley, 26913
Hemacandra, 06792-6
Hemenway, Stephen Ignatius, 11729, 17073
Hena, Abu, 24862
Henderson, Michael, 13584
Henderson, Patrick David, 15358
Hendley, Thomas H., 08527
Hendre, Sudhir Laxman, 13544
Henige, David P., 05679
Henley, Nancy S., 23310
Hennessy, Maurice N., 08756
Henry, Edward O., 02899
Henry, Victor, 03859
Hensman, C.R., 18506, 18641
Hensman, Howard, 09429
Henty, George Alfred, 22595
Heras, Henry, 03600, 06187-8, 06220-1
Herath, J.W., 18621
Herdt, Robert W., 14793
Heredero, J.M., 21897
Heredia, Susana, 10177
Herir, Patrick, Sir, 10681
Herman, Arthur L., 01159, 01549, 06396
Hermanns, Matthias, 01097, 20853, 22281

Herrenschmidt, Olivier, 20873
Herring, Ronald J., 14954, 17571, 17981, 18768
Herringham, Lady, 05597
Hershman, P., 22825
Hertel, Bradley R., 01866, 15937-41
Hertel, Johannes, 02454, 05396, 05403-4
Hertz, Willard J., 14054
Hess, Gary R., 09387, 26941
Hess, Peter, 12169-70
Hester, Donald D., 14663
Heston, Alan W., 01571, 14224

Hettiarachchy, Tilak, 04286
Hettne, Bjørn, 14298, 20228
Hewavitharana, Buddhadasa, 18642, 18656
Hewitt, Arthur R., 27514, 27586
Hey, Peter, 26825
Hiatt, Lester R., 19007
Hibbert, Christopher, 09518
Hicks, J.R., 18657
Hicks, Ursula K., 18657
Hidayatullah, M., 12838, 12847
Hiebert, Paul G., 00802, 19825
Higgins, Jon Borthwick, 02874, 02957
Hikata, Ryusho, 05073
Hill, Archibald Vivian, 10652
Hill, John, 26971
Hill, John Lowell, 23473
Hill, Michael J., 26895
Hill, Polly, 20334
Hill, Samuel Charles, 08150, 08868
Hill, Thomas, 16553
Hill, W. Douglas P., 08796
Hill, Walker, 16526
Hillary, Edmund, Sir, 27272, 27388
Hillebrandt, Alfred, 03840
Hiltebeitel, Alf, 04641-3
Himachal Pradesh. Directorate of Economics and Statistics, 25870-2, 25876
Himachal Pradesh. Planning and Development Dept., 25873-4
Himachal Pradesh. Shri Gurdwara Paonta Sahib Police Firing Enquiry Commission, 25860
Himachal Times, 15368
Hinchcliffe, Doreen, 01019
Hindery, Roderick, 01516
Hindustan Motors, Ltd. Dept. of Economic and Market Research, 15434
Hingne Stree-Shikshan Samstha, 21361
Hingorani, Ratan Pribhdas, 00576, 03058, 03264
Hingston, Walter George, 10401
Hingwe, K.S., 16474
Hinnells, John R., 01211
Hira Lall, 12961
Hirakawa, Akira, 05054
Hiramani, A.B., 21471
Hiran, S.L., 22030
Hiremath, K.C., 20328
Hiremath, N.R., 16595
Hiremath, R.C., 02370, 06549
Hiriyanna, Mysore, 01177, 01304, 01515, 02506, 03969, 27684
Hiriyanniah, K.N., 16624
Hiro, Dilip, 13105, 26905
Hirsch, Leon V., 23664
Hirsch, Paul, 04897
Hirsh, Herbert, 12829
Hirt, Howard F., 01880
Hirudayam, Ignatius, 19488
Hirway, Indira, 21741
History of Ceylon, 00382
A History of Indian literature, 02390
Hita Harivaṁśa Gosvāmī, 08825
Hitchcock, John Thayer, 23547, 23732-3, 26228-30, 26283, 26330-1
Hitopadeśa, 06079-85
Hitrec, Joseph George, 22087
Hivale, Shamrao, 20870, 20887
Hjejle, Benedicte, 19250
Hoag, Katharine, 27404
Hobogirin. Dictionnaire encyclopédique du Bouddhisme, 01135
Hobsbawm, Eric J., 00875
Hocart, Arthur Maurice, 00762, 01939
Hoch, Erna M., 20922, 23875
Hockings, Paul Edward, 00848, 11838, 19375-7, 27707-8
Hockley, T.W., 19110
Hoda, Mansur, 15500
Hodgson, Brian Houghton, 25953
Hodgson, I.A., 25901
Hodgson, Marshall Goodwin Simms, 02265
Hodivala, Shahpurji K., 07413
Hodivala, Shahpurshah Hormasji, 07014, 07394
Hodson, Henry Vincent, 10298
Hodson, T.C., 00695, 26582, 26589
Hoebel, E. Adamson, 17383
Höfer, András, 26193a, 26332-3
Hoefer, Herbert, 16807
Hoens, Dirk Jan, 05888
Höpker, Wolfgang, 11993
Horhager, Herbert, 23098
Hoernle, August Friedrich Rudolf, 00311, 04555-6, 06724
Hoey, William, 23558
Hoffman, Helmut, 05924
Hoffman, Johann, 20948, 20964, 20967
Hoffman, Karl, 03949
Hofinger, Marcel, 04946, 04963
Hogan, W.P., 12233
Hogben, W. Murray, 09415
Hogg, V.W., 18789
Hohenberger, A., 05818-9, 05804, 06415, 06430
Holck, H. Frederick, 02196
Holcomb, Helen Harriet Howe, 11545
Holden, Edward Singleton, 07426
Holdich, Thomas Hungerford, Sir, 22428, 22518
Holland, Barron Gregory, 01119, 08835
Holland, Robert, Sir, 26932
Holland, T.H., 20370
Holland-Pryor, Pomeroy, 20131
Hollingsworth, Lawrence William, 26846
Hollis, Michael, 19530
Hollister, John Norman, 02270
Holman, Dennis, 09318
Holmes, Thomas Rice Edward, 09319, 09488
Holmes, Walter Robert, 27429-32
Holmstrom, Lakshmi, 17123
Holroyde, Peggy, 02705
Holtzmann, Adolf, 04644
Hone, Angus, 13852, 14454, 25259
Honigmann, John Joseph, 22879-80
Hooda, Radha Krishan, 13628
Hoogt, J.M. van der, 03913
Hooja, Rakesh, 22015, 22117
Hooja, Swarna Lata, 01020, 23364
Hook, Peter Edwin, 00704
Hoole, Elijah, 19531
Hooper, John Stirling Morley, 06296
Hoover, Edgar M., 14148, 17786
Hope, A. Guy, 09612, 10864
Hopkins, Edward Washburn, 00911, 01160, 01517, 03950, 04420, 04448, 04608, 04629, 04645
Hopkins, Thomas J., 01197, 05774
Hopkinson, Henry Thomas, 16746
Horam, Mashangthei, 26533, 26542, 26563-4
Horne, Eric Arthur, 10235
Harnell, James, 01854
Horner, Isaline Blew, 01253, 01527, 04475, 04980, 05020
Horniman, B.G., 09848
Horsburgh, H.J.N., 09877, 09960
Horsch, Paul, 04912
Hosali, Paroo, 27497
Hoselitz, Berthold Frank, 12234, 15107, 15155, 15320, 16033, 23346
Hosken, Fran P., 26287
Hossain, Mahabub, 25448-9
Hossain, Mosharaff, 25445
Hotchand, Tirithdas, 08676
Hough, Eleanor Margaret, 10984, 14705
Houlton, John Wardle, 27260
Houpert, Joseph C., 02240
Hourani, George Fadlo, 04563
Houtart, François, 16375, 18456, 19043, 20058, 20182
Howard, Louise, 10666
Howe, Susanne, 11882
Howell, Evelyn Berkeley, Sir, 23052
Howland, Marie, 23419
Hoyland, John Somervell, 07471, 07837, 09671
Hrdayakumari, B., 20206
Hridaya, Chitta Dhar, 02891
Hsu, Francis L.K., 00726

Hu, Chi-hsi, 13909
Hua, Jan Yun, 05097
Huart, A., 02087
Hubbeck, J.A., 20780
Huber, Sallie Craig, 25597
Hudson, D. Dennis, 19489
Hügel, Carl Alexander Anselm, 22429
Hürlimann, Martin, 27056
Hufbauer, Gary C., 22807
Hughes, Albert Williams, 22519, 27223
Hughes, Arthur, 00473
Hughes, Russell M., 02992
Hughes, Thomas Patrick, 02259
Hughes, Thomas Robert, 20606

Hugoniot, Richard D., 02322
Hukam Singh, 22681
Hulin, Michel, 01467, 04809
Hullur, S.I., 20355
Hultzsch, Eugen, 04136
Hulugalle, H.A.J., 08050, 18296, 18416, 18898, 19067-8, 27157
Human Resources Foundation, 15627
Hume, Robert Ernest, 03970
Hummel, Reinhardt, 16727
Humphrey, Derek, 26917
Humphreys, Christmas, 01136, 04967, 16763
Hunashal, S.M., 06559
Hunck, Josef Maria, 14074-5
Hunt, James D., 09878
Hunter, Guy, 14785
Hunter, Kathleen, 26923
Hunter, Robert, 11532
Hunter, Thelma, 19975
Hunter, William Wilson, Sir, 09125, 09139, 09771, 10578, 11956, 20698, 22316, 24245, 24268, 24453, 25683, 26053
Huntington, Susan Lubin, 07356
Huq, A.M. Abdul, 27455
Huq, Abu Nasar Husain, 25236
Huq, Abul Fazl, 25186
Huq, Anwarul, 25670
Huq, M. Mahfuzul, 17474
Huq, M. Nurul, 25340, 25468, 25552-3
Huq, Mahfuzul, 17492
Huq, Mazharul, 08897, 25379
Huq, Muhammad Shamsul, 18195
Huq, Obaidul, 25178
Huq, Sayeedul, 18006
Huq, Zahirul, 25617
Hurd, John, II, 11045
Hurvitz, Leon, 05077
Husain, A.B. Musharaf, 03192, 07365
Husain, A.F.A., 17910, 18082, 25473
Husain, Abid, 10119
Husain, Agha Mahdi, 06687-8, 07047-8
Husain, Ahmed, 17426
Husain, Asad, 26054, 26079
Husain, Azim, 22651
Husain, Fazli, Mian Sir. *See* Fazl-i-Husain, Mian Sir
Husain, I.Z., 16317
Husain, Imtiaz, 23645
Husain, Imtiazuddin, 22501
Husain, Ishrat Zafar, 14136, 23561
Husain, Khalifa Amjad, 17976
Husain, Mahdi, 05639
Husain, Majid, 14199
Husain, Maqbul Fida, 17214-5
Husain, Mazhar, 16165
Husain, Muhammad Afzal, 18166
Husain, Sheikh Abrar, 23766
Husain, Wahed, 07575
Husain, Yusuf, 23729
Husain, Zakir, 12583, 16388
Husain ᶜAlī, Kirmānī, 08168
Husaini, Abdul Qadir, 00407
Husaini, Abdul Qualir, 06689
Huss, Carol Ann, 16376
Hussain, Altaf, 08521
Hussain, Arif, 17684
Hussain, Asaf, 17443-4
Hussain, M., 23087
Hussain, M. Zaker, 25435
Hussain, Mushtaq, 17925
Hussain, Riaz, 10323
Hussain, S.M., 24863
Hussain, S. Manzoor, 18120
Hussain, S. Mushtaq, 17905
Hussain, Sajjad, 25237
Hussain, Serajuddin, 25169
Hussain, Shahanara, 07198, 07357
Hussain, Syed Sajjid, 11901, 17427
Hussain, T. Karki, 12032
Hussain Khan, C.G., 20412
Hussam-ul-Mulk, Shahzada, 23117
Hutchins, Francis G., 09034, 10419
Hutchinson, David, 09477
Hutchinson, George, 09489
Hutchinson, Lester, 07823, 09048, 10058
Hutchison, J., 22605
Hutchison, John, 08556
Hutheesing, Krishna Nehru, 09589, 13420
Hutten, Kurt, 16728
Huttenback, Robert Arthur, 09430, 13945, 22446-9, 23135-6, 23160-1, 26829-30
Hutton, John Henry, 00763, 26565-7
Hutton, William Holden, 08042
Hyde, Harford Montgomery, 10245
Hyder, Ghulam, 13290
Hyder, Khursid, 12022
Hyder, Qurratulain, 11655, 17020
Hyderabad. Central Records Office, 19620
Hyderabad, Pakistan (Division). Directorate of Basic Democracies, 22463

ICAR. *See* Indian Council of Agricultural Research
ICSSR. *See* Indian Council of Social Science Research
ICSSR journal of abstracts and reviews, 27608
IIPA. *See* Indian Institute of Public Administration
IIPO. *See* Indian Institute of Public Opinion
I.M.C. Economic Research and Training Foundation, 14209
ISAE. *See* Indian Society of Agricultural Economics
Ibbetson, Denzil Charles Jeff, Sir, 22826, 25895
Ibn Batuta, 05637-9
Ibn Hasan, 07535
Ibrahim Kunju, A.P., 06177, 06240, 06574, 08133-5, 08169
Ibrahim, R., 20044
Ibrahim Beg, Mohammad, 23088
Ibrahim Khan, Mohammed, Sardar, 23205
Iengar, Haravu Venkatanarasingha Verada Raj, 14391-2, 14629
Iftikhar Ahmad, 17557
Iijima, Shigeru, 26111
Ikeda, Daisaku, 04882
Ikegami, Yoshihiko, 02993
Ikram, Muhammad, 17553
Ikram, S.M., 27094
Ikram, Sheikh Mohammad, 07414, 09772
Ikram Azam, R.M., 17294, 17428, 17669
Ilakkuvankar, Singaravel, 05231
Ilbert, Courtenay Peregrine, Sir, 09087, 10236
Ilchman, Alice Stone, 15062, 16439
Ilchman, Warren F., 13698, 13875, 15518-9, 16439-40
Iltis, J.C., 27564
Imadi, Saidul Haq, 19861
Imam, Mohammed, 12541, 12830, 12900, 15823, 15844
Imam, Syed Mehdi, 04684
Imam, Zafar, 02275, 09613, 13968, 13982, 15852
Imdad Ali Khan, 17945
Imfeld, Al, 18571
Imlah, Albert Henry, 09119
Immanuel, Rajappan D., 16794
Immerwahr, George, 18598
Imran, Muhammad, 17839
Imtiaz Ahmad, 23512. *See also* Ahmad, Imtiaz
Imtiazi, I.A., 22808
Inada, Kenneth K., 01320, 01468, 05091
Inam Mohammad, 06987
Inamdar, N.R., 21167, 21578, 21660
Inamdar, P.L., 10528
Inayatullah, 17333, 17356, 17647-8, 17954, 18144, 22881-3
Inden, Ronald Bertrand, 00224, 00782, 07200, 24604, 27656
Inderjit Singh, 14774
Index India, 27609
Index Indo-Asiaticus, 27610
Index to Indian economic journals, 27611
Index to Papers in Commemorative Volumes, 27629
India: A Statistical Outline, 27767
India. Age of Consent Committee, 10726
India. Army, 09431

India. Banking Enquiry Committee (Bengal) (1929-30), 24400a
India. Calcutta University Commission (1917-19), 24842
India. Central advisory board of education, 10585
India. Central Banking Enquiry Committee (1929), 11169
India. Chamber of Princes, 09379
India. Commission of Enquiry against Maharaja Gulab Singh, 23137
India. Committee to enquire into the condition of Indian immigrants into the four British colonies ... and in Surinam, 26742
India. Committee to inquire into the abuses alleged to exist in exporting from Bengal hill coolies..., 26758
India. Corruption Enquiry Committee, Bihar, 23956
India. Delegation to British Guiana on Scheme for Indian Emigration, 26778
India. Dept. of Revenue and Agriculture, 27496
India. Disorders Inquiry Committee (1919-1920), 09849
India. Education Commission, 10578
India. Famine Commission, 11020-2
India. Famine Inquiry Commission, 24455
India. Finance Dept. Taxation Enquiry Committee (1924), 11155
India. Fiscal Commission (1921), 11156
India. Health Survey and Development Committee, 10682
India. Hindu Law Committee, 09266, 10738
India. Home Dept., 10420, 10727
India. Imperial Record Dept., 02088, 27558-9
India. Indian Central Committee, 10254
India. Indian Cinematograph Committee, 16972
India. Indian Universities Commission, 10596
India. Industrial Commission, 11085
India. Intelligence branch (Army), 09432
India. Irrigation Commission, 11027
India. Law Commission, 10721
India. Laws, statutes, 10280, 10728, 10845-6
India. Memoranda on Native States in India (1915), 09337
India. National Income Committee, 14205
India News and Features Alliance, 16830
India. Office of the Adjutant General, 09303
India. Orissa Administration Committee, 20780
India. Orissa Committee, 20781
India. Police Commission, 09229
India Population Project, Karnataka, 16327
India. Public Service Commission (1886-87), 09186
India. Reconstruction Committee of Council, 11192
India. Reforms Enquiry Committee (1924), 10246
India. Sedition Committee, 09841
India. Sind Administrative Committee, 22450
India Society, London, 05597
India. The Indian Councils Acts (1861, 1892), 09153
India Tourism Development Corporation, 26972
India. U.P. Provincial Banking Enquiry Committee Report (1929-30), 23586
India Who's Who, 27491
India (Dominion), 12079, 19621
India (Dominion). Committee on Indigenous Systems of Medicine, 16337
India (Dominion). Constituent Assembly, 12278
India (Dominion). Fiscal Commission (1949-50), 14515
India (Dominion). University Education Commission, 16480
India (Dominion). White paper on Indian States, 10534
India (Rep.). Administrative Reforms Commission, 12684-5, 12874-7, 12904, 12915-6, 12949, 14405-7, 14514, 14786-7, 15212, 15321, 15423, 15455
India (Rep.). Advisory Committee on After-Care Programmes (1954), 16187
India (Rep.). Advisory Committee on Social and Moral Hygiene (1954), 16166
India (Rep.). Advisory Committee on the Revision of the Lists of Scheduled Castes and Scheduled Tribes, 15813
India (Rep.). Agricultural Meteorology Division, 14724
India (Rep.). Agricultural Prices Commission, 14835
India (Rep.). Air Transport Enquiry Committee (1950), 15451
India (Rep.). All-India Agricultural Labour Enquiry, 15075
India (Rep.). All India Radio, 16946
India (Rep.). Archaeological Survey, 00609
India (Rep.). Assessment Committee on Basic Education, 16596
India (Rep.). Ayurvedic Pharmacopoeia Committee, 16209
India (Rep.). Backward Classes Commission, 15814
India (Rep.). Banaras Hindu University Enquiry Committee, 23896-7
India (Rep.). Banking Commission, 14612
India (Rep.). Bureau of Public Enterprises, 15210
India (Rep.). Calendar Reform Committee, 27463
India (Rep.). Census of India (1961), 01975, 02089, 02323, 03300, 03387, 10880, 14166, 14476, 14963, 15679, 16034, 16288, 19335, 19378, 19393, 19447, 19997, 24418, 24766, 26464, 26999
India (Rep.). Census of India (1971), 14137, 14152, 14167, 15910, 16661, 19257, 19364, 19998, 20269, 21078, 21709, 22320, 23214, 23345, 25869, 25926, 26483, 26580, 26637, 27000, 27758-60
India (Rep.). Central Board for the Prevention and Control of Water Pollution, 21087
India (Rep.). Central Board of Irrigation and Power, 14879, 14889
India (Rep.). Central Bureau of Correctional Services, 16188, 16189
India (Rep.). Central Bureau of Health Intelligence, 16210, 16373-4
India (Rep.). Central Council for Research in Indian Medicine and Homoeopathy, 16208
India (Rep.). Central Council of Local Self-government, 14558
India (Rep.). Central Hindi Directorate, 02382
India (Rep.). Central Social Welfare Board. Research, Evaluation, and Statistics Division, 20498, 24804
India (Rep.). Central Statistical Organisation, 14122, 27749-50, 27768
India (Rep.). Central Tea Board, 26638-9
India (Rep.). Central Water and Power Commission, 14880, 14890, 15354
India (Rep.). Commission of Enquiry on Certain Allegations against S. Pratap Singh Kairon, Chief Minister of Punjab, 22670
India (Rep.). Commission of Inquiry into Conspiracy to Murder Mahatma Gandhi, 10529
India (Rep.). Commission of Inquiry into the Affairs of the Bharat Sevak Samaj (1969), 16129
India (Rep.). Commission of Inquiry into the Disappearance of Netaji Subhas Chandra Bose, 10169
India (Rep.). Commission of Inquiry into the Sadar Bazar Disturbances, 23365
India (Rep.). Commission of Inquiry on Communal Disturbances, 13089
India (Rep.). Commission of Inquiry on Communal Disturbances, Ranchi-Hatia (1967), 24010
India (Rep.). Commission of Inquiry on Maruti Affairs, 13546
India (Rep.). Commission of Inquiry to Enquire into ... the Death of Shri Deen Dayal Upadhyaya, 13272
India (Rep.). Commission on Maharashtra-Mysore-Kerala Boundary Disputes, 12930
India (Rep.). Commission on the Hill Areas of Assam, 26654
India (Rep.). Commissioner for Scheduled Castes and Scheduled Tribes, 15815
India (Rep.). Committee of Direction on Cooperative Farming, 15139
India (Rep.). Committee of Experts on Unemployment Estimates, 15495
India (Rep.). Committee of Members of Parliament on Education, 16417
India (Rep.). Committee on Broadcasting and Information Media (1966), 16835, 16937
India (Rep.). Committee on Colleges, 16481
India (Rep.). Committee on Cooperation Marketing (1964), 15140
India (Rep.). Committee on Defections, 13131
India (Rep.). Committee on Distribution of Income and Levels of Living (1960), 14212
India (Rep.). Committee on Emotional Integration, 12394
India (Rep.). Committee on Evaluation of Therapeutical Claims of Yogic Practices, 02184
India (Rep.). Committee on Fertilisers, 14868
India (Rep.). Committee on Finance for the Private Sector (1953), 14693
India (Rep.). Committee on Governance of Universities and Colleges (1969), 16510
India (Rep.). Committee on Higher Education for Rural Areas, 16567
India (Rep.). Committee on Integration of Health Services, 16221
India (Rep.). Committee on Labour Welfare, 15595
India (Rep.). Committee on Land Reforms, 14964
India (Rep.). Committee on News Agencies, 16893

India (Rep.). Committee on Panchayati Raj Institutions, 12982-3
India (Rep.). Committee on Plan Projects. Minor Irrigation Team, 22330, 24075, 25757
India (Rep.). Committee on Plan Projects. Study Team for Selected Education Schemes, 16679
India (Rep.). Committee on Plan Projects. Study Team on Metropolitan Transport, 15439
India (Rep.). Committee on Plan Projects. Study Team on Selected Educational Schemes, 16568
India (Rep.). Committee on Prevention of Corruption, 12673
India (Rep.). Committee on Recruitment Policy and Selection Methods, 12642
India (Rep.). Committee on Rural Higher Education, 16569
India (Rep.). Committee on Social Science Research, 15690
India (Rep.). Committee on Takavi Loans and Cooperative Credit (1961), 15130
India (Rep.). Committee on Taxation of Agricultural Wealth and Income, 14592
India (Rep.). Committee on Tea Marketing, 14912
India (Rep.). Committee on Transport Policy and Coordination, 15416
India (Rep.). Committee on Unemployment, 15496
India (Rep.). Committee on Unemployment. Working Group on Industries, 15497
India (Rep.). Committee on Untouchability, Economic and Educational Development of the Scheduled Castes, 15768
India (Rep.). Committee on Urban Land Policy, 16048
India (Rep.). Committee on Utilisation of External Assistance (1963), 13862
India (Rep.). Committee to Assess and Evaluate the Present Status of Ayurvedic System of Medicine, 16338
India (Rep.). Committee to Look Into the Causes for Lack of Public Support ... for Girls' Education, 16687
India (Rep.). Committee to Review the Progress of the Tanning and Leather Industries, 15406
India (Rep.). Committee to Review the State Trading Corporation of India, 15467
India (Rep.). Committee to Review the Structure and Organisation of the Indian Foreign Service, 12747
India (Rep.). Committee to Study the Question of Formulating Uniform Standards in Respect of Education and Regulation of Practice of Vaidyas, Hakims, and Homeopaths (1956), 16339
India (Rep.). Committee to Study the Question of Legalisation of Abortion (1964), 16318
India (Rep.). Constitution, 12319
India (Rep.). Council of Scientific and Industrial Research, 14740, 17247
India (Rep.). Damodar Valley Corporation Enquiry Committee, 24052
India (Rep.). Dept. of Atomic Energy, 15371a
India (Rep.). Dept. of Commercial Intelligence and Statistics, 13815
India (Rep.). Dept. of Community Development, 12984
India (Rep.). Dept. of Economic Affairs, 14039
India (Rep.). Dept. of Industry, 15182
India (Rep.). Dept. of Justice, 12819
India (Rep.). Dept. of Labour and Employment, 15484, 15551
India (Rep.). Dept. of Personnel and Administrative Reforms, 15824
India (Rep.). Dept. of Rural Development, 12980
India (Rep.). Dept. of Social Welfare, 15791
India (Rep.). Dept. of Steel, 15385
India (Rep.). Dept. of Tourism, 27034
India (Rep.). Development Commissioner, Small Scale Industries, 15331
India (Rep.). Direct Tax Laws Committee, 14567
India (Rep.). Direct Taxes Administration Enquiry Committee, 14565
India (Rep.). Direct Taxes Enquiry Committee, 14566
India (Rep.). Directorate General of Employment and Training, 15520
India (Rep.). Directorate of Adult Education, 15956, 16662, 16680
India (Rep.). Directorate of Economics and Statistics, 14725-6, 14765, 22799
India (Rep.). Directorate of Research and Statistics, 13816
India (Rep.). Education Commission, 16418-9, 16688
India (Rep.). Election Commission, 13324-7, 13380, 13385, 13390, 13436, 13460, 13629, 19679, 19963
India (Rep.). Electronics Committee, 15407
India (Rep.). Energy Survey of India Committee, 15355
India (Rep.). English Review Committee, 16656
India (Rep.). Enquiry Committee on Film Censorship, 16988
India (Rep.). Enquiry Committee on Small Newspapers, 16867
India (Rep.). Environmental Hygiene Committee (1948), 16238
India (Rep.). Expert Committee on ... Intensive Agricultural District Programme, 14799-802, 15141
India (Rep.). Expert Committee on the Environmental Impact of Mathura Refinery, 23665
India (Rep.). Expert Committee on Unemployment. Working Group on Education, 16441
India (Rep.). Fact-Finding Committee on Newspaper Economics (1972), 16868
India (Rep.). Fact Finding Committee: Slum Clearance, Demolitions, etc. ..., 23401
India (Rep.). Film Enquiry Committee (1949), 16973
India (Rep.). Finance Commissions, 14536-42, 14547
India (Rep.). Foodgrains Policy Committee, 14811
India (Rep.). Foodgrains Prices Committee, 14836
India (Rep.). Geological Survey, 10656-8, 14200
India (Rep.). Health Survey and Planning Committee, 16222
India (Rep.). High-powered Expert Committee on Companies and MRTP Pacts, 15271
India (Rep.). Hindu Religious Endowments Commission, 01881
India (Rep.). Import and Export Policy Committee, 13835
India (Rep.). Indian Board for Wild Life, 14933, 27035
India (Rep.). Industrial Licensing Policy Inquiry Committee, 15285
India (Rep.). Information Services, 17204
India (Rep.). Irrigation Commission, 14891
India (Rep.). Joint Technical Group for Transport Planning, 15417
India (Rep.). Khadi and Village Industries Commission, 15156-7, 24160
India (Rep.). Khadi Evaluation Committee, 15158
India (Rep.). Krishna Godavari Commission, 12931, 21249
India (Rep.). Labour Bureau, 15076, 15485, 15552, 15579
India (Rep.). Land Reforms Implementation Committee, 14965
India (Rep.). Law Commission, 12818, 12899-902, 13006
India (Rep.). Laws, Statutes, 15915-6, 15990, 15997-6000, 16004-7, 16989
India (Rep.). Local Finance Enquiry Committee, 14559
India (Rep.). Managing Agency Enquiry Committee, 15280
India (Rep.). Manual of election law, 13323
India (Rep.). Medical Education Committee, 16363
India (Rep.). Meteorological Dept., 10659, 27173
India (Rep.). Metropolitan Transport Team, 21527, 24797
India (Rep.). Ministry of Commerce, 13836
India (Rep.). Ministry of Community Development and Cooperation, 14560, 15131
India (Rep.). Ministry of Education, 16404, 16463, 16609, 16620, 16681, 27782
India (Rep.). Ministry of Education and Social Welfare, 16383, 16389, 16405, 16682, 17062, 22509, 27433
India (Rep.). Ministry of External Affairs, 12113
India (Rep.). Ministry of Food and Agriculture, 14872
India (Rep.). Ministry of Health, 16211-2
India (Rep.). Ministry of Health and Family Planning, 16263
India (Rep.). Ministry of Home Affairs, 19650
India (Rep.). Ministry of Home Affairs. Tribal Development Division, 15792
India (Rep.). Ministry of Information and Broadcasting, 17191, 17268, 26960
India (Rep.). Ministry of Labour and Employment, 15077, 15634
India (Rep.). Ministry of Rehabilitation, 10496
India (Rep.). Ministry of States, 10535, 12534
India (Rep.). Monopolies Inquiry Commission, 15272
India (Rep.). Narmada Water Resources Development Committee, 14892
India (Rep.). National Archives, 08878-9, 27560-2
India (Rep.). National Atlas Organisation, 26998, 27001
India (Rep.). National Commission on Agriculture, 14749-50, 14899
India (Rep.). National Commission on Labour, 15553, 15596-7
India (Rep.). National Committee on Science and Technology. Panel on Housing, Urbanisation, and Construction Technology, 16067

India (Rep.). National Committee on Women's Education, 16689
India (Rep.). National Employment Service, 19327
India (Rep.). National Library, 27536-7, 27784
India (Rep.). National Museum, 27563
India (Rep.). National Review Committee on Higher Secondary Education, 16621
India (Rep.). National Water Supply and Sanitation Committee, 16239
India (Rep.). Office of the Development Commissioner, Small Scale Industries, 15322, 20045
India (Rep.). Office of the Registrar General, 27761-2, 27769. *See also* India (Rep.). Census of India...
India (Rep.). Official Language Commission, 12489-90
India (Rep.). P. Jaganmohan Reddy Commission of Inquiry, 13569
India (Rep.). Panel on Literacy among Industrial Workers, 16663
India (Rep.). Parliament Advisory Committee on the Press Council, 16869
India (Rep.). Parliament. House of the People, 12287
India (Rep.). Parliament. House of the People. Committee on Public Undertakings, 15213, 15408, 15452
India (Rep.). Parliament. House of the People. Secretariat, 12377
India (Rep.). Parliament. Joint Committee on Air (Prevention and Control of Pollution) Bill (1978), 16240
India (Rep.). Parliament. Joint Committee on Amendments to Election Law, 13328
India (Rep.). Parliament. Joint Committee on the Banaras Hindu University (Amendment) Bill, 23898
India (Rep.). Parliament. Joint Committee on the Delhi Secondary Education Bill, 23435
India (Rep.). Parliament. Joint Committee on the Lokpal and Lokayuktas Bill (1968), 12696
India (Rep.). Parliament. Joint Committee on the Mental Health Bill (1978), 16269
India (Rep.). Parliament. Joint Committee on the Untouchability (Offences) Amendment and Miscellaneous Provision Bill (1972), 15782
India (Rep.). Parliamentary Committee on the Demand for Punjabi Suba, 22681
India (Rep.). Part B States (Special Assistance) Enquiry Committee, 12535
India (Rep.). Petro-Chemical Committee, 15409
India (Rep.). Planning Commission, 14424-7, 14432-3, 14438-42, 14455-7, 14461-3, 14469, 14966-8, 15198-200, 15746, 16118-9, 23572
India (Rep.). Planning Commission. Programme Evaluation Organisation, 14225, 14408, 14861, 14869, 15078, 16590
India (Rep.). Planning Commission. Prohibition Enquiry Committee, 16203-4
India (Rep.). Planning Commission. Research Programmes Committee, 21830, 22039
India (Rep.). Planning Commission. Working Group on Libraries, 16914
India (Rep.). Posts and Telegraph Dept., 26986
India (Rep.). Press Commission, 16870
India (Rep.). Punjab Boundary Commission, 22682
India (Rep.). Punjab Commission (1961), 22683
India (Rep.). Rail Tariff Enquiry Committee, 15424
India (Rep.). Railway Board, 15427
India (Rep.). Railway Corruption Enquiry Committee (1953), 15425
India (Rep.). Rashtriya Sanskrit Sansthan, 27434-5
India (Rep.). Regional Transport Survey Unit, Eastern Region, Calcutta, 24547
India (Rep.). Review Committee on Upgraded and Post-graduate Departments in Medical College, 16364
India (Rep.). Reviewing Committee for the three Akademies (Sahitya, Lalit Kala and Sangeet Natak) and the ICCR, 16991
India (Rep.). Rural Banking Enquiry Committee, 15124
India (Rep.). Rural Urban Relationship Committee, 16104
India (Rep.). Sanskrit Commission (1956), 17063
India (Rep.). Sarkaria Commission of Inquiry, 19227
India (Rep.). Secondary Education Commission, 16610
India (Rep.). Shah Commission of Inquiry, 13570, 13573
India (Rep.). Shuddha Ayurvedic Education Committee, 16340
India (Rep.). Small Family Norm Committee, 14187
India (Rep.). Special Committee on ... Polytechnic Education in India, 16622
India (Rep.). Special Committee to Review the ... National Malaria Eradication Programme, 16264
India (Rep.). Special Working Group on Cooperation for Backward Classes, 15816
India (Rep.). Special Working Group on Financing of Industrial Cooperatives by Cooperative Banks, 14717
India (Rep.). States Reorganisation Commission, 12536
India (Rep.). Study Group for Plantations (Tea), 14913
India (Rep.). Study Group for Tribal Labour, 15794
India (Rep.). Study Group for Wage Policy, 15588
India (Rep.). Study Group on Credit Cooperatives in the Non-agricultural Sector, 14718
India (Rep.). Study Group on Employment and Training, 15498
India (Rep.). Study Group on Indigenous Bankers, 14681
India (Rep.). Study Group on Labour Problems in the Public Sector, 15554
India (Rep.). Study Group on Non-Banking Financial Intermediaries, 14613
India (Rep.). Study Group on Sociological Aspects of Labour-Management Relations, 15618
India (Rep.). Study Group on Supervision and Inspection, 16431
India (Rep.). Study Group on the Teaching of English at the School Stage, 16657-8
India (Rep.). Study Group on Wages, Incomes, and Prices, 15589
India (Rep.). Study Group on Wayside Amenities, 15435
India (Rep.). Study Group on Wild Life and Wild Life Products (1964), 14934
India (Rep.). Study Team of Community Development Agency and Panchayati Raj Institutions in the Implementation of Basic Land Reform Measures (1967), 14969
India (Rep.). Study Team on Administration of Union Territories and NEFA, 12905
India (Rep.). Study Team on Machinery of the Government of India and its Procedures of Work, 12612
India (Rep.). Study Team on Nyaya Panchayats, 13005
India (Rep.). Study Team on Personnel Planning, Staffing of Public Sector Undertakings, and Personnel Management, 15214
India (Rep.). Study Team on Promotion Policies, Conduct Rules, Discipline, and Morale, 12632
India (Rep.). Study Team on Public Sector Undertakings, 15215
India (Rep.). Study Team on Railways, 15426
India (Rep.). Study Team on Recruitment, Selection, U.P.S.C./State P.S.C.'s and Training, 12644
India (Rep.). Study Team on Reforms in Accounts and Role of Audit, 15216
India (Rep.). Study Team on Social Welfare and Welfare of Backward Classes (1958), 15817
India (Rep.). Study Team on Tribal Development Programmes, 15793
India (Rep.). Śuddha Unani Education Committee, 16365
India (Rep.). Superintendent of Census Operations, Rajasthan, 22079
India (Rep.). Survey of India, 27002-3
India (Rep.). Tariff Commission, 14914
India (Rep.). Task Force to Examine ... Small and Medium Towns and Cities, 16088
India (Rep.). Taxation Enquiry Commission, 14568
India (Rep.). Team for the Study of Community Projects and National Extension Service (1956), 15023
India (Rep.). Textile Enquiry Committee, 21298
India (Rep.). University Grants Commission, 16475, 16482-4, 16518-20, 16527, 16529-31, 16915, 27436
India (Rep.). Village and Small Scale Industries Committee, 15129
India (Rep.). Vimadalal Commission of Inquiry, 19661
India (Rep.). Vital Statistics Division, 14168, 22763
India (Rep.). Women's Welfare Division, 15872
India (Rep.). Working Group on Autonomy for Akashvani and Doordarshan, 16938
India (Rep.). Working Group on Developmental, Control and Regulatory Organizations, 12548
India (Rep.). Working Group on Educational Technology, 16406
India (Rep.). Working Group on Industrial Co-operatives, 15342
India (Rep.). Working Group on Labour Administration, 15555-8
India (Rep.). Working Group on Metropolitan Transport Services, 15440

India (Rep.). Working Group on Posts and Telegraphs, 15456
India (Rep.). Working Group on Small Scale Industries, Handicrafts and Sericulture. Sub-Group on Small Scale Industries, 15160
India (Rep.). Working Group on Small Scale Sector, 15323
India (Rep.). Working Group on the Reserve Bank of India, 14630
India (Rep.). Working Group on Vocationalisation of Education and Work Experience, 16623
India (Rep.). Working Group to Consider ... the Change of the Medium of Instruction from English to an Indian Language, 16651
Indian and Eastern Newspaper Society Press Handbook, 27587
Indian Anthropological Society, 15800
Indian Archaeological Society, 03601
Indian Association of Special Libraries and Information Centres, 27538
Indian Banks' Association, 14664
Indian Behavioural Sciences Abstracts, 15680
Indian Book Chronicle: News and Reviews, 27625
Indian Books, 27567
Indian Books; An Annual Bibliography, 27568
Indian Chamber of Commerce, Calcutta, 13847, 14076, 14094, 19976, 24780, 24782
Indian Committee for Cultural Freedom, 21120
Indian Conference of Social Work, 16078
Indian Conference on Research in National Income, 14206
Indian Council for Child Welfare, 23357
Indian Council for Cultural Relations, 16692, 27437, 27651
Indian Council of Agricultural Research, 03789, 14723, 14738-9, 14741, 14810, 14898, 15003
Indian Council of Social Science Research, 09858, 12291, 13443, 14733, 14782, 15172-3, 15677-8, 15683-4, 15873, 26993, 27691-2
Indian Council of World Affairs, 11984, 11991, 14115
Indian Economic Conference, Bombay (1963), 14635
Indian Economic Diary, 27613
Indian Federation of Labour, 11193
Indian Institute of Foreign Trade, 13813, 13825-6, 13848, 15393, 21340
Indian Institute of Foreign Trade Alumni Association, 14081
Indian Institute of Management, Ahmedabad. Centre for Management in Agriculture, 21742
Indian Institute of Mass Communication, 14862, 16894
Indian Institute of Personnel Management, 15628
Indian Institute of Public Administration, 12602-3, 15209
Indian Institute of Public Administration, Maharashtra, 08279, 21148
Indian Institute of Public Opinion, 13796, 13801, 14222, 14453, 15475-6, 19549
Indian Investment Centre, 13881, 15204
The Indian Law Institute, 16855
Indian Merchants' Chamber, 21211
Indian National Bibliography, 27652
Indian National Committee for International Commission on Large Dams (1979), 14883
Indian National Congress, 09525, 09637, 09850, 13512, 13562
Indian National Congress. Linguistic Provinces Committee, 12509
Indian National Congress. Maharashtra Provincial Congress Committee, 21277
Indian National Congress. National Planning Committee (1938), 11194
Indian National Congress. Village Panchayat Committee, 12985
Indian National Science Academy, New Delhi, 17262
Indian National Trade Union Congress, 15559-60
Indian Parliamentary and Scientific Committee, 16632
Indian Periodicals in Print, 27588
Indian Political Science Association, 12613
Indian Press Index, 27614
Indian Public Schools Conference, 16627
Indian Publisher and Bookseller, 27575
Indian Round Table Conference, 10264-6, 10268
Indian Science Congress, Nagpur (1920), 21488
Indian Society of Agricultural Economics, 14859, 14927, 15088, 21855
Indian Society of International Law, 12103, 13922, 13928
Indian Society of Labour Economics, 15486
Indian Society of Oriental Art, 11808
Indian States' People's Conference. Patiala Enquiry Committee, 22606
Indian Statistical Institute, 14443, 15079, 15499
Indian Statistical Institute. Bombay Branch, 21523
Indira Devi, 02119
Indra Prakash, 10135-6, 13259
Indrajit, 08838
Indrajit Singh, 20874
Indrapala, Karthigesu, 00389, 06122, 06139
Indraratne, A.D.V. de Silva, 18588
Induchudan, V.T., 01976-7, 03863
Indule, C.B., 14719
Industrial Development Bank of India, 15181, 21072
Industrial Development Bank of Pakistan, 18036, 25460
Industrial Services Centre, 26174
Ingalls, Daniel Henry Holmes, 00854, 01364, 02507, 04407, 04759, 05339, 06060-1, 06370, 06383, 07324
Ingham, Kenneth, 11564
Ingholt, Harold, 05531
Ingram, Edward, 08943, 09416
Innaiah, N., 19890
Innes, Arthur Donald, 22568
Inscriptions of Ceylon, 00566
Institute of Applied Manpower Research, 15487, 19778
The Institute of Asian Studies, 01871
Institute of Chartered Accountants of Ceylon, 18658, 18668
Institute of Constitutional and Parliamentary Studies, 16587
Institute of Development Studies, University of Sussex, 00866, 17288
Institute of Economic Growth, 11983
Institute of Economic Research, Demographic Research Centre, 20487, 20507
Institute of Indo-Middle East Cultural Studies, Hyderabad, 12402
Institute of International Affairs, Karachi, 17808
Institute of Public Enterprise, Hyderabad, 15234
Institute of Secretariat Training and Management, 12614
Institute of Town Planning. Bombay Regional Chapter, 21495
International Atomic Energy Agency. Mission to Study Prospects of Nuclear Power in Pakistan (1962), 18031
International Bank for Reconstruction and Development, 18572, 18629-30, 25295
International Bibliography of the History of Religions, 01103
International Commission of Jurists, 18244
International Conference Seminar of Tamil Studies, 1st, 2nd, 3rd, 00079-82
International Co-operative Alliance. Regional Office and Education Centre for South-East Asia, 14701
International Economic Conference on Problems of Unemployment in India, London (1971), 15500
International Labour Office, 11116, 18792, 18794
International Planning Team on Small Industry in India, 15324
International Workshop on Providing Financial Services to the Rural Poor, Dacca (1978), 25436
Ions, Veronica, 01580
Iqbal, Afzal, 09801
Iqbal, Javid, 17399
Iqbal, Mehrunnisa H., 17670, 17718
Iqbal, Muhammad, Sir (1877-1938), 10324, 11487-94, 11523, 11634, 11672-7
Iqbal, Muhammad (1913-), 11684
Iqbal, S.M., 00502
Iqbal Singh, 11236, 11497
Iqbal Singh, N., 26707
Irani, C.R., 24374
Irani, Meherwanja Sheheriyarji. *See* Meher Baba
Ireland, Ralph R., 26834, 26945
Irfan, Mohammed, 18046
Iriyagolle, Gamini, 18708
Irschick, Eugene F., 19166, 19180
Irshad, Mohammed, 17911
Irshad Ali, A.N.M., 25783
Irshad Khan, Shaheen, 17725
Iria, Alberto, 07856
Irvine, William, 07517, 07566
Irwin, Henry Crossley, 23451
Irwin, John, 03072, 03327-31, 03343-4, 03347, 05463-4, 08528-9, 11806
Irwin, P.G., 21756
Isaac, Light, 02746

Isaacs, Harold Robert, 15769, 27082
Iscot Marbaniang, 27293
Isenberg, Shirley Berry, 23227
Ishak Lebbe, M.U., 18873
Ishaq, Muhammad, 02271
Ishaq, Shahid, 02986
Ishar Singh, 08620
Ishar Singh, 08632
Isherwood, Christopher, 02221, 04668, 04820, 06359, 11298
Ishida, Hiroshi, 27228, 27268
Ishvani, 21445
Ishwara Nanda, Sresthacharya, 28017
Ishwaran, Karigoudar, 00922, 00993, 15006, 20403, 20435-7
Ishwarcharandas, Shastri, 21924
Ishwardas Nagar, 07499
Islam, Faridul, 25384
Islam, Khurshidul, 07709, 11694
Islam, M. Mufakharul, 24439
Islam, M. Rafiqul, 25170
Islam, Mazharul, 02434
Islam, Meherunnessa, 25612
Islam, Muhammad Sirajul, 25671-4
Islam, Nurul, 17704-5, 18010, 18068, 18133, 25321
Islam, Rafiqul, 27996
Islam, Shamima, 25613, 25631
Islam, Sirajul, 08907, 25450
Islam, T., 25471
Islam, Taherul, 25628
Islam, Zaferul, 09773
Ismail, M.M., 02287
Ismail, Mirza Mahomed, Sir, 20233-34

Ispahani, Mirza Abol Hassan, 10378, 17687
Israel, Benjamin J., 21457
Israel, Samuel, 16900
Israr-ud-din, 23118
Issacharoff, Ruth M., 26895
Issarani, H.R., 15242
Iswara Dutt, Kunduri, 09638, 12576
Ittaman, K.P., 20138
Ittiavira, Verghese, 20202
Ivanow, W., 08458
Iver, George Grosvenor Bruce, 22629
Ivern, Francis, 24198
Iyengar, A.S.K., 14706
Iyengar, Sreerangapatna Kesava, 10964, 13806, 14377, 19731, 19843
Iyengar, Shanta, 19662
Iyer, K. Bharatha, 01615, 02972, 03112
Iyer, Raghavan, 09943, 10541
Iyer, Shakuntala (Ayatonde), 03914
Iyer, Vishwanath, 10806
Izmirlian, Harry, 22708, 22860
Izzat Majeed, 18436

Jabbar, M.A., 25451
Jabeen, Qamar, 22884
Jack, James Charles, 24401
Jackson, A.V. Williams, 06007
Jackson, Arthur Mason Tippetts, 00764, 21657
Jackson, Barbara Ward, 14444
Jackson, Charles Robert Mitchell, Sir, 09126
Jackson, Robert Victor, 12172
Jackson, William Collins, 08181
Jacob, Alice, 12331, 12336, 12837, 12932
Jacob, Georg, 03007
Jacob, George, 12994
Jacob, George Adolphus, 03967
Jacob, George L., General Sir, 09478
Jacob, H.K. 's, 08136
Jacob, K., 20220
Jacob, K.K., 16144
Jacob, Lucy M., 18448, 18566, 20071
Jacob-Pandian, Ebenezer Titus, 19181, 19498-9
Jacobi, Hermann Georg, 05134, 05151, 05981
Jacobs, Hans, 02185
Jacobs, Joseph, 02455
Jacobson, Doranne, 00972, 22234-5
Jacobson, Leo, 16035
Jacobson, Nolan Pliny, 01226
Jacquemont, Victor, 11939
Jacques, Claude, 01910, 02059, 02138
Jadhav, Dilip, 15964
Jaeckel, Horst, 09433
Jafar, Malik Mohammad, 17384
Jafar, Saiyid Mohammad, 27438
Jaʿfar Sharif, 02276
Jaffar, S.M., 07415, 07427, 07648
Jaffrey, Ali A., 22536
Jafri, A.B.S., 17531
Jafri, Ali Sardar, 11655
Jafri, Rais Ahmad, 09802
Jafri, S.N.A., 23630
Jafri, Zamir, 22896
Jag Mohan, 11854, 12146, 14082
Jag Mohan, Sarla, 21935
Jagadananda, Swami, 06352-3
Jagadeesan, N., 01949, 06454
Jagadesan, T.D., 27163
Jagadisa Ayyar, P.V., 02090, 19128
Jagadisan, T.N., 10009
Jagalpure, L.B., 21472
Jagan, Cheddi, 26779
Jaganathan, Maithily, 02950
Jagannadha Rao, N., 03764
Jagannadham, Vedula, 12674, 12694, 15738, 16120, 23334-7
Jagannarayanan, S., 13368
Jagannathan, N.S., 16871
Jagat Singh, 13547
Jagdish Chandra, 03059, 27682
Jagdish Singh, 24129-30
Jaggi, Om Prakash, 00256-7, 16366
Jagirdar, Prabhakar Janardan, 21347
Jagjit Singh, 08545, 17275
Jagmohan, 16079, 23402, 23420
Jahan, Afroz, 25461
Jahan, Rounaq, 12267, 17513, 17561, 25187, 25200, 25211, 25519-20
Jahānārā Begam, 07491
Jahangir, 07481-4
Jahangir, Burhanuddin Khan, 25545, 25675
Jahanian, Chaudhuri Mohammad Husain, 17982
Jahn, Karl, 05640
Jahn, Wilhelm, 05824
Jai Gopal, 24375
Jai Ratan, 17043
Jai Singh, 12071
Jaideva Singh, 01358, 06957-8, 06967
Jain, Ajit Prasad, 13991, 14891, 23474
Jain, Akshaya Kumar, 05135
Jain, Anil Kumar, 14582
Jain, B.C., 15376
Jain, B.K., 18477
Jain, B.S., 07576, 13022
Jain, C.M., 12296, 15053, 16581, 21951-2
Jain, Champat Rai, 01330
Jain, Chhote Lal, 01150
Jain, Dharma Chandra, 12464, 12791, 13524
Jain, D.P., 16213
Jain, Girilal, 13939, 26080
Jain, H.C., 12815
Jain, H.R., 22751
Jain, Hari Mohan, 12549
Jain, Hiralal, 05136
Jain, Jagdish Chandra, 04032, 05252, 05389, 10530-1
Jain, Jagdish Prasad, 12033, 12043, 13774, 13789, 15372
Jain, Jasbir, 17178
Jain, Jawaharlal, 22120
Jain, Jyoti Prasad, 01280, 04033
Jain, Jyotindra, 01691, 03140
Jain, K.S.S., 22905
Jain, Kailash Chand, 00474, 01281, 02011, 03500, 05137, 06737
Jain, Kanta Prasad, 05146
Jain, Kapila, 23270
Jain, Kesharlal Ajmera, 22120
Jain, Kul Bhushan, 24086
Jain, Lakshmi Chandra, 11170-1
Jain, Lila Ram, 15482
Jain, M.K., 14155, 14735, 27471, 27633
Jain, M.S., 11476, 25962
Jain, Mahabir Prashad, 09250, 12337, 12695
Jain, Naresh Kumar, 27470
Jain, P.C., 23286
Jain, P.K., 09187, 13554, 15911
Jain, Pratibha, 08880
Jain, Prem Suman, 01289
Jain, Purushottam Chandra, 05705
Jain, R.B., 12615, 12686, 12763, 12893
Jain, R.K., 12033, 12044, 22236

Jain, Rajendra Kumar, 14552, 14598
Jain, Ram Chandra, 04646
Jain, Ranbir Singh, 09102
Jain, Ratan Kumar, 16554
Jain, Ravindra K., 22220, 26884-5
Jain, Rikhab Dass, 16976
Jain, S.A., 05152
Jain, S.C., 01469
Jain, S.K., 14915, 23814
Jain, S.N., 12917, 12932, 16155
Jain, S.P., 14134, 14139, 15024, 15654, 23695, 23767, 25719, 25801
Jain, Sagar C., 15292, 23310
Jain, Satish Kumar, 16770
Jain, Sharad Chandra, 14766, 14837, 26135, 26158-9
Jain, Subash C., 12932
Jain, Sugan Chand, 15045
Jain, Sushil Kumar, 11705
Jain, Takhatmal, 12949
Jain, Tara Chand, 14727
Jain, Uttam Kamal, 01282
Jaina, Nirmal Kumar, 08582
Jaini, Jagmandar Lal, 01283
Jaini, Padmanabh S., 01151, 01284, 04590, 05116, 05131
Jaipur, H.H. Maharaja of, 09288
Jairazbhoy, Nazir A., 02706, 02747, 02765, 02791, 02831
Jairazbhoy, Rafique Ali, 00356
Jaishanker, S., 15373
Jaiswal, H.K., 20854
Jaiswal, P.L., 14881
Jaiswal, Suvira, 04767
Jakhade, V.M., 15127
Jalan, Bimal, 14393
Jalbani, G.N. *See* Jalbani, Ghulam Husain
Jalbani, Ghulam Husain, 07681, 07683-4
Jambhekar, G.G., 21371
James, A.G., 26914
James, Harold Douglas, 09304
James, Henry Rosher, 10556, 10597
James, Josef, 11826, 19260
James, P.A., 19703
James, V., 20821
Jamiat Rai, Diwan, 22537
Jamil Ahmad, 17830
Jamiluddin, K., 11902
Jamkhedkar, A.P., 05673
Jammu, Parkash Singh, 22861
Jammu and Kashmir, 23193, 23228
Jammu and Kashmir. Backward Classes Committee, 23229
Jammu and Kashmir. Commission of Enquiry: Jammu Firing, 23194
Jammu and Kashmir. Commission of Inquiry to Inquire into ... Shri Bakhshi Ghulam Mohammad, 23195
Jammu and Kashmir. Committee of Enquiry on Amarnath Yatra (1970), 23242
Jammu and Kashmir. Committee on Development of Education..., 23230
Jammu and Kashmir. Constitution, 23177-8
Jammu and Kashmir. Directorate of Education, 23231
Jammu and Kashmir. Education Dept., 23232
Jammu and Kashmir. Jammu and Kashmir Commission of Inquiry, 23215
Jammu and Kashmir. Planning and Development Dept., 23216
Jamspal, L., 03475
Jana, M.M., 24699
Janacek, A., 04828
Janaki, Vengalil A., 00216, 06717, 21801, 21857, 21869-71, 27010
Jānakīrām, Ācaṇṭa, 06600
Janakiraman, T., 17018
Janarthanam, A.P., 19220-1
Janata Party, 13563, 13610-1, 13626
Janbaz Khan, 23128
Janert, Klaus Ludwig, 00006, 27547
Jangam, R.T., 12928, 20257, 21172, 21195
Jani, A.N., 17064
Janik, Brigitte, 25143, 25279
Janjua, Harbhajan Singh, 26915
Janki Dass, 16975
Jannuzi, F. Tomasson, 24062, 25447, 25452
Janvier, Ernest Paxton, 05313
Japheth, Maurice David, 02313
Jariwala, C.M., 15473
Jasbir Singh, 14728, 23287
Jasdanwalla, Zaibun Y., 14812
Jash, Pranabananda, 01755
Jasimuddin, 02462, 25101, 25658
Jaspal Singh, 22846, 25879
Jatar, D.P., 22266
Jatava, Daya Ram, 10778-81, 16764
Jatoi, Hyder Baksh, 22464
Jauhari, Manorama, 03388, 04269
Jauhri, Ramesh Chandra, 07049, 09614
Javed, Ghufranullah, 23089
Jawaharlal Nehru University, 23439
Jawaid, Sohail, 13249, 24376
Jawed, Nasim Ahmad, 11454, 17400
Jawhar, 07460
Jay, Edward J., 20875
Jaya Chamaraja Wadiyar Bahadur, Maharaja of Mysore, 20235
Jayadeva, 07244-9
Jayakanthan, Dandapani, 19197
Jayakar, Mukundrao Ramrao, 20748
Jayakar, Pupul, 03331
Jayakar, R.B.K., 16167
Jayal, Shakambari, 04476
Jayalakshmi, Salem S., 02856
Jayamaha, Gratien, 18659
Jayanta Bhatta, 04840
Jayaraj, D., 19964
Jayaram, B.D., 16647
Jayaram, N., 16367, 20521
Jayaraman, K., 19239
Jayaraman, N., 06588
Jayaraman, R., 18495, 18816
Jayaraman, T.K., 12254, 21718, 25260, 26089
Jayaratne, B.C.F., 18520
Jayasekera, U.D., 00862, 04244
Jayasenapati, 02681
Jayashankar, D.C., 16108
Jayasundera, M.G., 18923
Jayasuriya, D.C., 18924
Jayasuriya, D.L., 18962
Jayasuriya, J.E., 18934, 18944, 18947
Jayasuriya, V.C., 18541
Jayasuriya, W.F., 18909
Jayaswal, Kashi Prasad, 00225, 04110, 04431, 07371
Jayaswal, Sita Ram, 16459
Jayaswal, Vidula, 03549-51
Jayatilaka, D.B., 27855
Jayatilleke, Kulatissa Nanda, 01227, 01413, 05021
Jayawardena, Chandra, 26755, 26780-1, 26787-8
Jayawardena, Lal, 18643
Jayawardena, Visakha Kumari, 18338, 18397, 18807
Jayawardene, C.H.S., 18605-6, 18610, 18910
Jayawardene, H.W., 18803
Jayaweera, N.D., 19069
Jayaweera, Swarna, 18869, 18935-6, 18948
Jayawickrama, Nicholas Abeydeera, 00023, 05037, 06145
Jayawickrama, Nihal, 18529
Jayewardene, E.D.W., 19094
Jayewardene, Junius Richard, 18418-9, 18470, 18555
Jeanneret-Gris, Charles Édouard, 22906
Jeejeebhoy, Jeejeebhoy Rustomji Byramji, 21182
Jefferey, Roger, 16228
Jeffery, Roger, 10683, 23430
Jeffrey, Mary Pauline, 19459
Jeffrey, Patricia, 26924
Jeffrey, Robin, 09347, 10497, 19923-4, 19938
Jeffries, Charles, Sir, 18373, 18420
Jena, B.B., 12804, 22292, 22300-1
Jena, Krishnachandra, 22317, 22341
Jenkins, Liliane, 27119
Jenkins, Richard, 20610
Jenkins, William M., 27365
Jennings, James George, 04879
Jennings, William Ivor, Sir, 12338, 17493, 18370, 18478, 18530, 18631
Jensen, Hans, 03007
Jensen, Irene Khin Khin, 12754
Jensen, Raymond L., 09773
Jerstad, Luther Gerald, 03054
Jest, Corneille, 02111, 26213, 26231, 26253, 26256, 26402, 27389
Jesudasan, C., 02561, 05419
Jesudasan, Hephzibah, 02561
Jethabai, Ganeshji, 02456
Jetley, Surinder, 23803
Jetly, Nancy, 13910
Jettmar, Gabriele, 03476

Jevoor, S.V., 20522
Jeyasingham, Shakuntala Jean, 18437
Jha, A.P., 20936
Jha, Akhileshwar, 15836
Jha, Amar Nath, 11635
Jha, Badri Vishal, 14838
Jha, Baidyanath, 24063
Jha, Chakradhar, 12848
Jha, Chetakar, 23979, 24002
Jha, Dayadhar, 04287, 12894
Jha, Dayanath, 23352, 23354
Jha, Dinesh Chandra, 12072
Jha, Divakar, 24076
Jha, Durga Nand, 23602, 24064
Jha, Dwijendra Narayan, 04089, 04352, 04373
Jha, Ganganatha, Mahamahopadhyaya, 00928, 04800, 04833, 04853, 04862, 04865-7, 05997, 11428
Jha, Hetukar, 24087
Jha, Hit Narayan, 04324
Jha, J.C., 26782, 26793-4
Jha, Jagdish Chandra, 20957, 20970, 24088, 24215
Jha, Jata Shankar, 08324, 09797, 23949, 23957-8, 24211-3, 24237
Jha, Kalanath, 02508
Jha, Kumar Kant, 26153
Jha, Lakshmana, 23980
Jha, Lakshmikant, 13330, 14836
Jha, Makhan, 01911, 01918, 02020, 02056, 02074, 22376, 24139-40, 24228, 26288
Jha, Manoranjan, 09615, 10218, 10791
Jha, Mitra Nandan, 09536
Jha, Munishwar, 05253
Jha, Nagesh, 23981
Jha, P.N., 14865
Jha, Parameshwar, 09832, 13132
Jha, Pitamber, 26296
Jha, Ram Chandra, 01372
Jha, Ramanatha, 07261
Jha, Shaktidhar, 01690
Jha, Shashishekhar, 16032, 23982-3
Jha, Shiva Chandra, 11132, 14948
Jha, Shree Krishna, 26055, 26066
Jha, Shree Nagesh, 12594, 23532, 23979
Jha, Subhadra, 02645
Jha, Ugra Nath, 24141-2
Jha, Y.N., 00744, 04449
Jha Committee, 14569, 14836
Jhabvala, Ruth Prawer, 17168
Jhala, Jaipal Singh, 17952
Jhalajit Singh, R.K., 27324
Jhambhaladatta, 06086
Jhangiani, Motilal A., 13145
Jhaveri, Krishnalal Mohanlal, 02603-4, 21936
Jhaveri, Mansukhlal Maganlal, 02605
Jhaveri, N.J., 14543
Jhaveri, Vithalbhai K., 10437
Jhavery, Mohanlal Bhagvandas, 05908
Jhingran, V.G., 14936
Jhirad, J.F.M., 21278
Jiggins, Janice, 18406, 18439, 18837
Jilani, Ghulam, 25619-20
Jilani, S.G., 25164
Jillani, M.S., 10498, 18152
Jinarājadāsa, Curuppumullage, 11358
Jindal, K.B., 02646
Jindel, Rajendra, 02012
Jinnah, Mahomed Ali, 10334-5, 10363-70, 10395
Jñānadeva. *See* Jñāneśvara
Jnanatmananda, Swami, 11349
Jñāneśvara, 06757-68
Joad, Cyril Edwin Mitchison, 11434
Joag, Vishvanath Keshav, 21599
Joarder, Safiuddin, 24567
Jodh Singh, 07104
Jodha, N.S., 22031, 22105
Jörgensen, Hans, 03951
Jörgensen, I., 20308
Jog, Narayan Gopal, 09698, 10162, 21334
Jogendra Singh, Sir, 08586-7, 21372
Johannson, Rune Edvin Anders, 01470
Johansen, Robert C., 14040
Johar, Surinder Singh, 08575, 08588, 08652-4, 22913
Johari, Jagdish Chandra, 13250, 21141, 26525
Johl, S.S., 22780
John, Dewitt, 26906
John, K.C., 19949
John, N.C., 19966
John, P. John, 20117
John, Patrick, 14937
John, Perukattu Verkey, 14751
John, V.V., 13044, 16464, 16495, 16511, 16641, 21907
John-Peter, S., 19409
John Samuel, G., 02562, 19581
Johnson, B.B., 03291
Johnson, B.F., 17952
Johnson, Basil Leonard Clyde, 27011, 27112, 27302
Johnson, Clive, 01219
Johnson, David L., 11386
Johnson, Donald J., 26973
Johnson, Dora E., 27785
Johnson, Edward William, II, 13254
Johnson, Francis, 06080
Johnson, Gordon, 09062, 20723, 20752, 24298
Johnson, J., 15428
Johnson, Jean E., 26973
Johnson, Willard L., 27450
Johnson, William Arthur, 15386
Johnston, Edward Hamilton, 04810, 04898, 05304-5
Johnston, Hugh J.M., 09747
Johnston, J., 11046
Johnston, James, 10579
Johnstone, James, Sir, 26446
Johnstone, P.D.L., 05365
Johri, C.K., 15561, 15642, 23358
Johri, Sitaram, 13948-9, 25854
Joint Committee for Diagnostic Survey of the Damodar Valley Region, 24054
Joint Indo-American Study Team on ... Agricultural Universities in India, 16570
Jolly, Julius, 00312, 00929, 04432-4
Jonathan, Kanchan F., 08806
Jones, Allan Keith, 22461
Jones, Betty True, 02973, 02975
Jones, Clifford Reis, 02958, 02974-5
Jones, Dawn E., 21666-7
Jones, Edward T., 05055
Jones, G.G., 11108
Jones, Garth N., 17286, 17770, 17993, 18118
Jones, Gavin W., 18599, 18894
Jones, George E., 10499
Jones, J.J., 04899
Jones, Kenneth W., 11287-8, 22557, 22662, 22827, 22968-9
Jones, Rex L., 02139, 26232-4, 26331
Jones, Rodney W., 21666-7, 22170
Jones, Schuyler, 27720
Jones, Shirley Kurz, 26234
Jones, William, Sir, 02754, 05352, 11850
Jorapur, T.B., 20271
Jordanus Catalani, 05663
Jordens, J.T.F., 11279-80
Jorge, Evagrio, 21039
Jose, A.V., 20036
Jose, P.K., 10024
Joseph, C.A., 20195
Joseph, Marietta, 03477
Joseph, P., 03721
Josh, Bhagwan, 22636
Josh, Sohan Singh, 09748-9, 10052
Joshi, Achut B., 28010
Joshi, Ambelal Naranji, 21437
Joshi, Arun, 15303-4
Joshi, Baburao, 02707
Joshi, Bhuwan Lal, 25969, 25977
Joshi, Chandni, 26277
Joshi, Dhirendra Kumar, 23196
Joshi, Durga Dutt, 26154, 26297
Joshi, Gajanan Narayan, 01454, 02822
Joshi, Hari Ram, 24906
Joshi, Hariprasad Shivprasad, 01806
Joshi, Heather, 21313
Joshi, J.P., 03621
Joshi, Janardan Raghunath, 03841-3
Joshi, K.C., 12464
Joshi, K.L., 16512
Joshi, Kalidas Sadashiv, 01056, 02166
Joshi, L.A., 15273
Joshi, L.M., 05909
Joshi, Laksmi Dat, 25927
Joshi, Lal Mani, 04913, 05650, 05925-6
Joshi, M.S., 14614

Joshi, Madan Mohan, 20876
Joshi, Moropant Vishvanath, Sir, 10726
Joshi, Murli Dhar, 14553
Joshi, N.D., 15263
Joshi, Nanda Lall, 26028
Joshi, Nandini, 14279, 17269
Joshi, Narendra Prakash, 04150
Joshi, Navin Chandra, 14258
Joshi, Nilakanth Purushottam, 01780, 04111, 05565
Joshi, Nilkanth Maheshwar, 21307
Joshi, Nirmala, 09616
Joshi, Om Prakash, 03412
Joshi, P.C., 23675, 23890-1
Joshi, Puran Chandra (1907-), 09499, 13219, 16977
Joshi, Puran Chandra (1928-), 14949, 14973, 15691
Joshi, P.M., 00354, 06773
Joshi, Pranshankar, 26836-7
Joshi, R.B., 01405
Joshi, R.L., 15468
Joshi, R.V., 21549
Joshi, Ram, 12339, 21066, 21142, 21166
Joshi, Ramanlal, 21937
Joshi, Ramchandra Bhikaji, 21640
Joshi, Ramchandra Vinayak, 03514
Joshi, Rasik Vihari, 01036, 01781
Joshi, Rekha, 07017, 07030
Joshi, S.D., 05219
Joshi, S.L., 22080
Joshi, Shanti, 06371
Joshi, Shreedhar Mahadev, 13192
Joshi, Subhadra, 13286
Joshi, Suresh, 21938-9
Joshi, Tryambak Mahadeo, 14593, 21228
Joshi, Tukaram Dattaram, 08447
Joshi, Tulsi Ram, 26160, 26265
Joshi, V.C., 11237, 11387
Joshi, V.N., 20589
Joshi, V.V., 07439
Joshi, Vasant, 16994
Joshi, Venkatachar, 14631
Joshi, Vijay, 21313
Joshi, Vishnu Shridar, 20724
Joshi, Vishnushankar Hargovind, 21473, 21866
Joshi, Vishvanath Ranchodji, 21743
Joshua, Alexander, 19470
Jothimutthu, P., 27870
Jotwani, Motilal Wadhumal, 02614, 08677-8, 16995
Jourdain, John, 07945
Journal of the Music Academy, Index, 02690
Jouveau-Dubreuil, Gabriel, 01595, 03379-80, 03697, 06616
Joy, J.L., 24037
Jozefowicz, Adam, 18049
Judah, J. Stillson, 16757
Juergensmeyer, Mark, 09750-1
Jukes, Geoffrey, 11995
Jullien, François, 19977
Junaid, Mien Muhammad, 17429
Junankar, Nagorao Sitaram, 04854
Jungalwalla, N., 16221
Jungblut, Leonard J., 20806
Junghare, Indira Y., 01065
Junius, Manfred, 02738
Jupp, James, 18367-8, 18374
Jurriaanse, M.W., 08093
Jussawalla, Adil J., 17019
Jussawalla, J.M., 16341
Jussawalla, M.F., 19743
Justice Party, 19182, 19187
Juyal, B.N., 23751

Kabadi, Waman P., 09013
Kabeer, Rokeya Rahman, 24269
Kabīr, 07096-101
Kabir, Alamgir, 18256-7
Kabir, Humayun, 02383, 09774, 10193, 12395, 16465, 16521, 24923, 24943, 25057, 25075
Kabir, Lutful, 24485
Kabir, Mafizullah, 12147
Kabir, Muhammad Ghulam, 25201
Kabra, Kamal Nayan, 15528, 16089-90
Kachru, Braj B., 02343, 02632, 12510, 17089, 27970-1
Kacker, Madhav P., 13882
Kadankavil, Kurian T., 03988, 11427
Kadetotad, N.K., 20415-6
Kaduskar, M.R., 20877
Kaelber, Walter O., 03818
Kaeppelin, Paul, 07920
Kagzi, Mangal Chandra Jain, 12322
Kahagalle, S., 18669
Kahin, George McTurnan, 13740
Kahlon, A.S., 22768-9, 22778, 22800
Kahnert, F., 17926
Kahol, Om Prakash, 22684
Kail, Owen C., 03180
Kailasapathy, K., 05435, 19553
Kaisher Bahadur K.C., 25996, 26037, 26314
Kaji, Biralal Lallubhai, 10985, 21270, 21299
Kajiyama, Yuichi, 05117
Kak, B.L., 12073, 17615, 23233
Kak, Ram Chandra, 03425
Kakade, Raghunath Govind, 20371, 21398
Kakar, D.N., 16214, 16349, 23879
Kakar, Sudhir, 01057, 15942-3, 15957
Kakati, Banikanta, 01763, 02673, 07208, 25811
Kakkar, N.K., 11117, 16683
Kala, Govind Ram, 25902
Kala, Satish Chandra, 03217
Kalamdani, N.B., 06489
Kalani, K.L., 06778
Kalansuriya, A.D.P., 18636
Kaldor, Nicholas, 14570
Kale, Baburao Balaji, 13644
Kale, Balkrishna Damodar, 15912, 20270-1, 20342, 20458, 20508-10
Kale, D.N., 21399
Kale, K.D., 21472
Kale, Moreshvar Ramchandra, 05354, 05356, 05369, 05374, 06012, 06025-6, 06039, 06062, 06081
Kale, Pramod, 05296
Kale, Pramodh, 21410
Kale, Pratima, 21586-7
Kalelkar, Dattatrey Balakrishna, "Kaka", 09899, 15814
Kalghatgi, T.G., 00435, 01291, 01331, 01485, 05135
Kalhan, Promilla, 13585, 13645
Kalhaṇa, 06940-1
Kalia, Barkat Ram, 22622
Kalia, Dev Raj, 14735, 27471, 27633
Kalia, Narendra Nath, 16633
Kālidāsa, 05347-75
Kalidos, Raju, 00408
Kalim, M. Siddiq, 18153
Kalimuddin Ahmed, 25341
Kalimullah, A.F., 18258
Kaliyanam, G., 01978
Kalmar, George, 14083
Kalota, Narain Singh, 04018
Kalupahana, David J., 01321, 06154
Kalyanam, N.P., 27036
Kamal, Abu Hena Mustafa, 25133
Kamal, K.L., 13023, 20652, 21953-4
Kamal, Kazi Ahmed, 17457, 24335, 25179
Kamal, Rahimuddin, 11498
Kamal Azfar, 22466
Kamalamanchar Rao, P., 19809
Kamalanathan, K., 13751
Kamalavijayan, D., 16476
Kamaliah, K.C., 04500
Kamaluddin Ahmed, 25342
Kāmandaki, 04317
Kamaraj, Kumaraswami, 14326
Kamat, A.R., 21579, 21603
Kamat, Gopal Sadashiv, 14707
Kamat, Jyotsna K., 06247
Kamatchinathan, Arunachalam, 02550
Kamath, M.G., 15063
Kamban, 06576-7
Kambi, V.S., 06542, 06560-1
Kamble, B.R., 03819
Kamble, Jeewan R., 15818
Kamble, N.D., 20451, 21474
Kame, G.P., 15409
Kameshwara Rao, N.V., 19826
Kameswara Rao, V., 06672, 06678
Kamil, Dost Muhammad Khan, 08691
Kamil Al-Qadri, S.M., 02618-9, 22552
Kaminsky, Arnold P., 09103
Kamkhenthang, H., 26588
Kamoji, D.C., 21626
Kampar. *See* Kamban
Kamruddin Ahmad, 25155, 25474

Kanakasabhai, K.V., 04203
Kanal, Parasram Verhomal, 11263-6
Kanal, Satewan Parsram, 11267
Kanchan, Mani Ram, 23568
Kandaswamy, S.N., 05447
Kandiah, T., 03017
Kane, Pandurang Vaman, 00451, 00935, 01066, 01925, 02509, 04408, 04435, 04609, 09276, 23730
Kaneda, Hiromitsu, 17946, 17955, 17965, 22806
Kanesalingam, V., 18547
Kanesathasan, S., 18580
Kanetkar, B.D., 11028
Kang, Kanwarjit, 03426
Kangle, R.P., 04306
Kanhere, Sadashiv Govind, 08461
Kanitkar, Helen, 00612
Kanitkar, J.M., 00614
Kanitkar, N.V., 21479
Kanitkar, Tara, 14132, 14144, 15949
Kanjilal, S., 16901
Kannaiyan, V., 02384
Kannan, C.T., 15929, 21380
Kannan, K.P., 20003
Kannangara, A.P., 11092
Kannangara, C.W.W., 18945
Kannangara, D.M., 18670
Kannangara, P.D., 18514
Kannappan, Subbiah, 15488, 15604, 15620, 15650
Kansal, S.M., 14213, 15580
Kansara, N.M., 06018
Kant, Rama, 13940
Kantawala, S.G., 02042, 04041-2
Kantirava Narasimharaja Wadiyar, Yuvaraja of Mysore, 20236
Kantowsky, Detlef, 23548, 23555, 23804
Kanungo, Kissen, 15142
Kanungo, Nityananda, 21298
Kanwar, H.I.S., 07786, 07794
Kanwar Lal, 13586
Kanwar Sain, 17276
Kapadia, Hiralal Rasikdas, 05153
Kapadia, Kanailal Motilal, 00658, 00974, 16156, 21779, 21824, 21867, 21872, 26568
Kaphey, Indra Prasad, 25978
Kapileshwari, Bal Krishnabuwa, 02766
Kapoor, Ashok, 13883
Kapoor, Badri Prasad, 23587
Kapoor, J.M., 16665
Kapoor, Krishna Das, 15605
Kapoor, L.D., 01636
Kapoor, O.B.L., 07266
Kapoor, P.N., 14179, 16267-8
Kapoor, S.K., 16462
Kapoor, Saroj, 23366
Kapoor, T.N., 15183, 15629
Kapp, Karl W., 14353
Kapur, Ashok, 13775, 13911, 13990
Kapur, Banwari Lal, 08797
Kapur, D.K., 22623
Kapur, Geeta, 17196-8
Kapur, Harish, 13903, 13983
Kapur, J.L., 16129
Kapur, Jagdish C., 14268
Kapur, Jagga, 13571
Kapur, Karam Narain, 10134
Kapur, Kishori, 22709
Kapur, Manohar Lal, 06946-8, 23162-3
Kapur, Promilla, 15539, 15874, 15905, 15922, 16168
Kapur, Raghu Pati, 19200
Kapur, Ravi L., 20363
Kapur, Shiv S., 17206
Kar, Chintamoni, 03236, 17216
Kar, Jasobanta, 10163
Kar, N.R., 24756-8
Kar, Parimal Chandra, 26652
Kar, Ramendra Kumar, 25789-90
Karachi Development Authority. Master Plan Dept., 22502
Karachi encyclopaedia, 22503
Karachi. Joint Research Project for Slum Improvement and Urban Development, 22507
Karaka, Dosabhoy Framjee, 02303
Karaka, Dosoo Framjee, 08280, 16886, 19622
Karalasingham, V., 18389, 18398, 18496
Karam Singh, 26146
Karambelkar, Vinayak Waman, 03752, 03930, 07306
Karan, Pradyumna Prasad, 24038, 24174, 27344, 27365, 27375
Karan Singh, 16240
Karandikar, Maheshwar, 06769, 16776, 21641
Karandikar, Shivaram Laxman, 08254, 09699
Karandikar, Shivaram Vithal, 01004
Karanjia, Rustom Khurshedji, 13484
Karanth, Kota Shivarama, 03028, 13587
Karashima, Noboru, 05680, 06258
Karat, Prakash, 20037-8
Karat Prakash, 12473
Karavelane, 06304
Karennavar, M.F., 20343
Karim, Abdul, 05681, 07187-8, 07199, 08869, 08922
Karim, Abul Khair Nazmul, 24556, 24913, 25489, 25496, 25640
Karim, Arshad Syed, 17603
Karim, Kazi Bazlul, 25549, 25555
Karim, Khondkar Mahbubul, 08892
Karkal, Gopal, 14615, 14682
Karkal, Malini, 15913
Karkaria, Bachi J., 16753
Karkaria, R.P., 21373
Karki, Tika B., 28011
Karmarkar, Anantrao Parashurampant, 04610, 06489
Karmarkar, Raghunath Damodar, 05327, 06019, 06027, 06035, 06372
Karnani, Chetan, 02823, 17137
Karnatak Historical Research Society, 00433
Karnataka. Backward Classes Commission, 20372
Karnataka. Commission for Reorganisation of Districts and Taluks..., 20260
Karnataka. Directorate of Evaluation and Manpower, 20295, 20310-1, 20319
Karnataka. Directorate of Evaluation, Manpower, and Project Formulation, 20281, 20312-3
Karnataka. Municipal Finance Enquiry Committee, 20261
Karnataka. Pay Commission (1976), 20253
Karnataka. Planning Dept., 20282, 20314, 20511
Karnataka. Public Works Dept., 20356
Karnataka. Rural Development and Cooperation Dept., 20452
Karni Singh, 20657
Karnik, Dwarkanath Bhagwant, 12789, 13646, 21127
Karnik, Vasant Bhagwant, 10082, 11133, 13950, 15643-4, 15661, 15670
Karokaran, Anto, 16808
Karpal Singh, 26890
Karpov, Alexander V., 17966
Kartar Singh, 08613, 08655
Karthikeya Sarma, I., 03674
Karunakara Menon, Vadakkekkra, 27880
Karunakaran, Kotta Patikal, 09537-9, 11206, 13024, 17401
Karunakaran Nair, K., 19925, 19939
Karunanithi, M., 05438, 19208
Karunaratne, N.D., 18778
Karunaratne, T.B., 01644-5
Karunatilaka, W.S., 27852-3
Karunatilake, H.N.S., 18337, 18573, 18616, 18632, 18637, 18671-2, 18911
Karve, Dattatraya Gopal, 14352, 21348
Karve, Dhondo Keshav, 10723, 10745, 21362-3
Karve, Dinkar Dhondo, 16424, 21391, 21570
Karve, Irawati Karmarkar, 00644, 00727, 00734, 00975, 01067, 01997, 20386, 20807, 21250, 21381-2, 21392, 21419, 21475-6, 21489, 21825, 27190
Karwanski, Ryszard A., 18178
Kasaju, Prem K., 26309, 26311, 26316
Kashappagouder, N.B., 16319
Kashikar, C.G., 03864, 04001
Kashkari, Chaman, 15356
Kashyap, J., 04998
Kashyap, Ram Anant, 06477
Kashyap, S.P., 15192, 15332
Kashyap, Subhash Chandra, 12126, 12764, 12917-8, 13133, 13146, 13339, 13656
Kasinathan, Natana, 19500
Kasipati, Kapila, 19663
Kasliwal, Kastoor Chand, 01152
Kasliwal, R.R., 12542
Kasturi, G., 10807
Katare, Sant Lal, 06207
Katare, Shyam Sunder, 22267
Katiyar, T.S., 22081
Katrak, Sorab K.H., 02304
Katre, Sumitra Mangesh, 02510, 02594, 05193, 05254

Katti, A.P., 20459, 20488, 20512
Kattikaran, K., 15958
Katz, Alan N., 13098
Katz, Nathan, 05098
Katz, S. Stanley, 13873
Katzenstein, Mary Fainsod, 21143-4
Kaufman, Harold Frederick, 15038
Kaufmann, Walter, 02777-8, 02832, 02868, 26353
Kaujalgi, H.S., 27180
Kaul, Brij Mohan, 12104, 13951
Kaul, Gwasha Lal, 00503
Kaul, Hari Krishen, 00350, 11369, 27074, 27539
Kaul, J.L., 23247-8
Kaul, Jagan Nath, 16496-7
Kaul, Jaya Lal, 02633-4, 06978
Kaul, Jolly Mohan, 16932
Kaul, K.K., 12054
Kaul, M.N., 12765, 12784, 23242
Kaul, Mohan Lal, 26946
Kaul, N.N., 23694
Kaul, P.N., 03347
Kaul, Ravi, 13762, 13776
Kaul, S.N., 23217
Kaul, Santosh, 23181-2
Kaul, Triloki Nath, 12755, 13904, 14023
Kaula, Prithvi Nath, 16916-7, 23197
Kaur, Manmohan, 09585
Kaura, Uma, 10311-2
Kaushal, G., 10870
Kaushal, Mohinder Paul, 22862
Kaushal, R.K., 00541
Kaushic, S.D., 25906
Kaushik, Brij Mohan, 13777, 13790-1, 17692
Kaushik, Devendra, 11996, 12034, 12047
Kaushik, Harish P., 09639
Kaushik, Meena, 01045
Kaushik, Pitambar Datt, 09975, 22155
Kaushik, Ram Pal, 14028
Kaushik, Surendra Nath, 17584, 17604
Kauṭalya, 04298
Kautilya, Mitra, 26653
Kautsky, John Hans, 13203
Kavadi, Naresh B., 27919
Kaveeshwar, Gajanan Wasudeo, 04685
Kavic, Lorne J., 13763
Kaviraj, Gopi Nath, 04855
Kaviraj, Narahari, 08898
Kaviratna, Abinash Chandra, 04557
Kavlekar, K.K., 20594
Kaw, R.K., 06959, 06968
Kawata, Kazuyoshi, 16241
Kay, Paul, 26587
Kayani, Malik Rustam, 17357, 17385, 17502
Kayastha, S.L., 23666, 25881-2
Kayastha, Ved P., 12116, 27693
Kaye, Cecil, Sir, 10045
Kaye, George Rusby, 00281, 00293, 01827, 05735
Kaye, John William, 02241, 07985, 09014, 09172-4, 09490
Kazami, Takehide, 27390
Kazi, Elsa, 08671
Kazi, Fazul Haque, 17386
Kazmi, Aqdas Ali, 17701
Keane, John, Sir, 18702
Kearney, Robert Norman, 12210, 18338, 18375-7, 18399-400, 18438-9, 18479-80, 18507-7a, 18808-10, 27135
Keatinge, Gerald Francis, 21235-6
Keay, Frank Ernest, 00863, 02252, 02647, 04511, 07105
Keay, John, 23146, 26974
Kedar Singh, 23549
Keenan, John L., 24111
Keene, Henry George, 07416, 07428, 07518, 08309
Keer, Dhananjay, 09700, 09879, 10782, 13260, 20595, 20753
Keith, Arthur Berriedale, 01322, 02472-3, 03802, 03820, 03919, 03942, 03963-5, 04811, 04856, 04868, 05270, 09069, 09076
Kelegama, J.B., 18731
Kelekar, Ravindra, 02595
Kelkar, D.G., 03302
Kelkar, Govind S., 23658
Kelkar, Narsinha Chintaman, 09701, 09759, 09994
Keller, Carl A., 06309, 06529
Keller, Dale, 19095
Keller, P., 19095
Keller, Stephen L., 22816
Kellock, James, 21349
Kellogg, Samuel Henry, 27827
Kelly, Colleen A., 27052
Kelman, Janet Harvey, 11118
Keluskar, Krishnarau Arjuna, 08281
Kemp, Tom, 09602
Kemp-Ashraf, P.M., 09618
Kemper, Steven E.G., 01010
Kennedy, Bennett Christian Huntington Calcraft. *See* Carthill, Al
Kennedy, Brian E., 08856
Kennedy, D.E., 12023
Kennedy, Edward M., 12148
Kennedy, Kenneth A.R., 03552, 03675, 03898
Kennedy, Melville T., 07267
Kennedy, Pringle, 07429
Kennedy, Richard S., 00226, 24934
Kennedy, Van Dusen, 15645
Keppel, Arnold, 23039
Ker, James Campbell, 09686
Kerala. Administrative Reorganisation and Economy Committee (1965-67), 19950
Kerala. Agricultural Census Division, 20014
Kerala. Backward Classes Reservation Commission, 20072
Kerala. Bureau of Economics and Statistics, 20004-5, 20015, 20073-4, 20051
Kerala. Commission for Enquiry into the Scales of Pay..., 19951
Kerala. Commission for Reservation of Seats in Educational Institutions, 20163
Kerala. Dept. of Public Relations, 12460, 20189
Kerala. Expert Committee on Ayurveda, 16342
Kerala. High Level Committee for Unification of Laws Relating to Hindu Religious Institutions and Endowments, 20168
Kerala. Laws, Statutes, 20164
Kerala. Public Works Dept., 20016
Kerala. Regional Records Survey Committee, 19937
Kerala. State Planning Board, 20017, 20046-7
Kerala. Town Planning Dept., 20158
Keravala, Perin C., 16190
Kern, Fritz, 04958
Kern, Hendrik, 01137, 04535, 05078
Kern Institute, Leiden, 00093, 03060, 27676
Kerr, Robert, 07829
Kesava Iyengar, S. *See* Iyengar, Sreerangapatna Kesava
Kesava Menon, K.P., 12491
Keśavadāsa, 08836
Kesavan, B.S., 16918, 27540
Kesavan, Veluthat, 06264
Kesavanarayana, B., 19604
Keshava Iyenger, B.R., 03899
Keshavadas, Swami, 01998
Keshwani, N.H., 05739
Keskar, Balkrishna Vishwanath, 02813
Kessinger, Tom G., 00876, 22863
Keswani, Nandkumar H., 00313-4
Ketkar, Venkatesh Balpuji, 00143
Keynes, John Maynard, 11172
Keyt, George, 07247, 19083
Khāfī Khān, Muḥammad Hāshim, 07500
Khair, Gajanan Shripat, 04686
Khajwia, H., 27037
Khaled, A., 25467
Khalid, Detlev, 09803
Khalid, Karim Bakhsh, 08679
Khalid, Mohammad, 18125
Khalifa, Abdul Mannan, 23206
Khalilzad, Zalmay, 17693
Khaliq, Sheikh Abdul, 17295
Khaliquzzaman, Choudhry, 10343
Khallaque, A., 07026
Khalsa College, 22923
Khambata, K.J., 10897
Khan, A. Aziz, 25406, 25417
Khan, A.Z.M. Obaidullah, 25418
Khan, Abdul Ghaffar, Khan, 23063
Khan, Abdul Halim Jaffer, 07125
Khan, Abdul Karim, 02766
Khan, Abdul Majid, 10178
Khan, Abdul Waheed, 10299
Khan, Ahmad Nabi, 03613
Khan, Ahsan Raza, 07550
Khan, Akhter Hameed, 17947, 17983, 17994, 25419
Khan, Ali Akhtar, 25420, 25437-8
Khan, Ansar Zahid, 06988, 08530

Khan, Anwar Tahmasp, 17356
Khan, Ataur R., 12193
Khan, Atiqur Khan, 25598
Khan, Atiquzzaman, 25662
Khan, Azizur Rahman, 17717, 17827, 17853, 17864, 18048, 25296, 25322-3, 25421, 25462
Khan, Badiuddin A., 18062-3
Khan, Deen Muhammad 25456
Khan, Dilawar, 27666, 27721-2
Khan, F.A., 03094, 03583, 03631
Khan, Fazal Muqueem, 17368, 17430, 18094
Khan, Fazle Karim, 25563, 25566
Khan, Fazlur Rashid, 18083
Khan, Gangadhar, 14672
Khan, Ghani Mohammad, 17707
Khan, Ghulam Hassan, 23234
Khan, Ghulam Jilani, 23099
Khan, Gulzar Mohammad, 03584
Khan, Hamidur Rahman, 25407
Khan, Iltija, 12995
Khan, Inayat, 18281
Khan, Iqtidar Alam, 07118, 07459, 07560, 07667
Khan, Izzat Ullah, 22493
Khan, Khan Tahawar Ali, 27466
Khan, Khushi Mohammed, 25307
Khan, M. Akram, 18027
Khan, M.E., 16303, 23877
Khan, M. Fathulla, 19623
Khan, M.R., 18043
Khan, M.S., 05641
Khan, M. Sarwar, 18149
Khan, M. Siddiq, 08965
Khan, M.Z., 22266
Khan, Mahmood Hasan, 17937-8
Khan, Masihur Rahman, 17792, 17794, 22500, 25280
Khan, Mazhar-ul-Haq, 18092
Khan, Mohamed Shabbir, 13863
Khan, Mohammad Abdul Waheed, 03218
Khan, Mohammad Irshad, 17925
Khan, Mohammad Ishaq, 23235
Khan, Mohammad Mohabbat, 12687
Khan, Mohammad Salar, 25358
Khan, Mohammad Shahabuddin, 27615
Khan, Mohammad Shamsul Islam, 25272
Khan, Mohammed Ashiqullah, 20766
Khan, Mohammed Irshad, 17984
Khan, Mohammed Yunus, 14694
Khan, Mohibbul Hasan, 08170-1
Khan, Muhammad Ahmad, 17932
Khan, Muhammad Shamsul Islam, 25332
Khan, Muhammad Zafrullah, 17671
Khan, Mukhtar Ahmad, 22733
Khan, Mumtaz Ali, 15148, 20417-8, 20499
Khan, Mushtaq Ahmad, 18078
Khan, N.A.G., 18087
Khan, R.R., 15325
Khan, Rahat Nahi, 12452
Khan, Rahmatullah, 11997
Khan, Rasheeduddin, 13969, 15853, 19664-5
Khan, S. Mohammad Reza Ali, 24700
Khan, Saeed A., 27846
Khan, Saleh Mohammad, 22720
Khān, Shafā‘at Ahmad, Sir, 07387, 07970, 08002, 26835
Khan, Shafique Ali, 10379, 18203
Khan, Shamsul Islam, 17927, 25147, 25272
Khan, Shoaib Sultan, 17995
Khan, Syed Ahmed, 18179, 25574
Khan, Taufiq M., 17807
Khan, Verity Saifullah, 26896
Khan, Yusuf Husain, 05948, 05960, 07018, 07062, 07632, 07705, 08126
Khan, Z.A., 12244, 25408
Khan, Ziauddin, 15223
Khan, Zillur R., 00755, 12024, 25171, 25212, 25188
Khanal, Yadu Nath, 26044, 26067
Khanapurkar, D.P., 03032
Khandaker, A.M., 12127
Khandalavala, Karl J., 03073, 03270, 03237, 03478, 05488, 06841, 07144-50, 07156, 07718-9, 07738, 08498-9, 08511, 08708, 08723-4, 08740, 11823
Khandekar, Mandakini, 16068, 21539
Khandewale, S.V., 21251, 21265
Khandwala, Vidyut, 10550
Khanna, B.S., 14409, 22694
Khanna, Girija, 15875
Khanna, Hans Raj, 12355, 12868
Khanna, Krishen, 17199
Khanna, Rattan Lal, 12976, 12996, 22710-1
Khanna, S.S., 23667
Khanolkar, Gangadhar Devrao, 21335, 25030
Khanolkar, Savitribai, 06749
Khanolkar, Vaman Pandurang, 21588
Khanolkar, Vasant Ramji, 17235
Kharbas, Datta Shankarrao, 27716
Khare, Brij B., 13045
Khare, M.P., 21241
Khare, Prem Shanker, 10808
Khare, Ravindra S., 00778, 00820, 00840-1, 01441, 12856, 16242, 23550, 23710, 23719-23, 23785
Kharge, M. Mallikarjun, 20261
Khatana, R.P., 23236
Khating, R., 26548
Khatkhate, Deena R., 15837, 15838
Khatri, A.A., 15891, 21826-7
Khatri, A.P., 03536
Khattak, G.M., 17974
Khatun, Sharifa, 25632
Khazan Singh, 22653-4, 22952
Khelchandra Singh, Ningthoukhongjam, 26600
Kher, Inder Nath, 17138
Kher, Narendra Nath, 04374
Kher, Sitaram Pandit, 20296
Khera, P.N., 09289, 21053, 22451
Khera, Sucha Singh, 12550, 12950, 13764, 15224, 15366, 22223
Khetarpal, S.P., 15991
Khilnani, N.M., 12595, 22614-5
Khobragade, B.D., 13302
Khobrekar, Vithal Gopal, 07497, 08272-3, 20742
Khodwe, Achyut, 19637
Khokar, Mohan, 02951, 02959-60, 02987-8, 26591
Khosla, A.N., 14892
Khosla, C.L., 16466
Khosla, D.N., 16544
Khosla, Gopal Das, 10438, 10479, 10532, 12869-70, 16848, 16988, 25861
Khosla, Raj K., 27576
Khosla, Ram Prasad, 07551
Khosla, Sarla, 01243
Khoso, Abdul Wahab, 22476
Khubchandani, Lachman M., 02615, 16642
Khudanpur, G.J., 21258
Khuhro, Hamida, 17310, 22452
Khundmiri, Alam, 19890
Khurshid, Abdus Salam, 10344, 10809, 18247
Khurshid, Anis, 10360
Khurshid, Muhammad Idris, 17985
Khurshid, Zahiruddin, 18252
Khushdeva Singh, 10500
Khushwant Singh, 00111, 08566, 08576-7, 08656, 09752, 13106, 13630, 15304, 17020, 17163, 22562, 22596, 22947, 23004
Khusro, Ali Mohammed, 14245, 14823, 14974, 15501, 19763, 23436
Khusro, Amir, 17731
Khwushhāl Khān, 08692
Kibbee, Robert J., 18184
Kibria, A.B.M.G., 25225
Kidder, David E., 24535, 24828
Kidder, Robert L., 12857, 20470-1
Kidman, Brenda, 26918
Kidron, Michael, 12261, 13884, 17762
Kielhorn, Franz, 05176, 05185
Kieniewics, J., 08204
Kiernan, E.V.G., 26365
Kihara, Hitoshi, 26155, 26194
Kihlberg, Mats, 12997
Kikani, L.T., 09277
Kilam, Jia Lal, 23237
Killion, Howard Ray, 07937
Kimura, Ryukan, 05056
Kincaid, Charles Augustus, 02457, 06750, 07440, 20616
Kincaid, Dennis, 08282, 11957
Kinch, Arne, 18612
King, Anthony D., 10690, 11968, 16580
King, Christopher R., 11595, 27450
King, Denise E., 03484
King, James Stewart, 06690
King, Noel Q., 26862
King, William Ross, 19379

King, Winston Lee, 01518, 05030
Kingdon-Ward, Frank, 27348
Kingsbury, Francis, 06305
Kingsbury, Patricia, 27095
Kingsbury, Robert C., 27004, 27095
Kingscote, Georgianna Wolff, 19599
Kini, N.G.S., 21133-4
Kinnier-Wilson, J.V., 03640
Kinsley, D.A. *See* Edwardes, Allen
Kinsley, David R., 01703, 01731, 01782-3, 08816
Kipling, Rudyard, 11893, 24718
Kirfel, Willibald, 00034, 00270, 01581-2
Kiribamune, S., 06123
Kirk, James A., 01607
Kirkland, Edwin Capers, 02426
Kirkpatrick, Joanna, 22915-6
Kirkpatrick, William, 08977
Kirloskar Consultants Ltd., 22054
Kirpā Rām, 23138
Kirpal, Prem, 15959, 16390-1
Kirpal Singh (1894-1974), 23922
Kirpal Singh (1924-), 08599, 08603, 10501, 22632
Kishan, Ram, 15456
Kishore, Brij, 08293
Kishore, Mohammed Ali, 13718
Kistaiah, M., 19685
Kittel, Ferdinand, 27888
Kitts, Eustace John, 00696
Kiyota, Minoru, 02175
Kizilbash, H.H., 17621, 17672, 17726
Kjaer, Jakob, 20308
Klaes, Norbert, 04647
Klass, Morton, 00728, 24605, 26795
Klatt, W., 25297
Klausen, Arne Martin, 20018
Klein, Ira, 10881, 11069, 11157, 14299, 21237, 24819
Kleinert, Christian, 26215-6, 26289
Klimburg-Salter, Deborah Elizabeth, 05547
Klimkeit, Hans-Joachim, 03000, 11281, 19183-4
Kling, Blair B., 11097, 24503, 24517, 24548
Kloss, Cecil Boden, 26708
Klostermaier, Klaus, 01198, 02038, 06002, 16713, 16796, 21608
Knight, Edward Frederick, 23147
Knight, L.A., 09363
Knight, Lionel, 20237
Knighton, William, 23443
Knipe, David Maclay, 01046, 03844-5
Knizkova, H., 07757
Knox, Robert, 08051-2
Kochanek, Stanley A., 12790, 13152, 13165. 14116, 15311, 15316
Kochar, Vijay K., 20923-4, 26725
Kodanda Rao, Pandurangi, 10010, 12279
Koder, S.S., 00420
Kodesia, J., 15108
Kodesia, Krishna, 12511
Kodikara, S.U., 12200, 18481, 18556-7
Koelman, Gaspar M., 04829
Kölver, Bernhard, 06939
Koestler, Arthur, 27083
Koffsky, Peter L., 07613
Kogekar, Sadanand Vasudeo, 13381, 22695, 23513, 26633
Kohli, Devendra, 17179
Kohli, K.L., 14174
Kohli, Mohinder Pal, 23003
Kohli, S.N., 11998
Kohli, Sita Ram, 08546, 22597
Kohli, Suresh, 12675, 16996, 17021
Kohli, Surinder Singh, 08578, 08583, 08621-2, 08657-62
Kolb, Albert, 26874
Kolenda, Pauline Mahar, 00779, 00803, 00897, 00994-5, 01486, 15901, 23754-5
Kolhapur. Development Dept., 21220
Kollaparambil, Jacob, 08222
Koller, John M., 01543, 04595, 14354
Komarov, E.N., 08991
Komma, 22948
Kondapi, C., 26743
Koninckx, Christian, 07836
Konow, Sten, 04182, 04307, 05271, 05567
Konrad, Paul, 20808
Kooij, K.R. van, 01596, 01720
Kopf, David, 00177, 11238, 24246, 24566-7, 27731
Koppar, D.H., 20831
Koppel, Bruce, 19123
Koppers, Wilhelm, 20809-10
Koptevsky, V., 13995
Korbel, Josef, 12093, 23198
Karson, J. Henry, 17572-3, 18095, 18100-1, 18167, 22489-91
Kortzfleisch, Siegfried von, 16728
Kosambi, Damodar Dharmanand, 00007, 00166, 00446, 00672, 01721, 03515, 03790, 04090, 04687, 05315, 05706, 06040
Koschwitz, Hansjurgen, 16872
Koshy, Manaloor Joseph, 07847, 19926-7, 19940, 20188
Koskenniemi, Kimmo, 03641
Koskenniemi, Seppo, 03642
Koss, Stephen E., 09833
Kotelawala, John Lionel, Sir, 18421-2
Koteshwar, Raghavendra Krishna, 20272, 20488
Kothandaraman, Ponnusamy, 27871
Kothari, D.S., 16418, 16425
Kothari, Ganpatlal M., 15572
Kothari, Hemraj, 27472
Kothari, Kamal S., 02783-4, 22145
Kothari, M.L., 15274
Kothari, M.M., 13807
Kothari, Manu, 17277
Kothari, Rajni, 12308, 12396, 13025, 13076, 13134, 13395, 13438, 15739, 21668-9, 21683
Kothari, Shantilal, 12951
Kothari, Sunil, 03042-4
Kothari, V.N., 21843
Kothari, Valchand P., 01556
Kothekar, S.V., 08310
Koti, V. Bhanu, Shri, 13815
Kotnala, M.C., 11239
Kotoky, P.C., 11752
Kotovsky, Grigory Grigorevich, 00163, 14975
Kotturan, George, 01557
Koul, Anand, 06979, 27229
Koul, Omkar N., 02635
Koul, Samsar Chand, 23238
Kouli, Ramesh Mohan, 25738
Kowdi, A.V., 21068
Kozicki, Richard J., 14090, 26045, 27694
Kramer, Fred A., 19288
Kramer, Samuel Noah, 03632
Kramers, J.H., 02258
Kramrisch, Stella, 00912, 01722, 03095, 03181, 03202, 03219, 03253, 03271, 03356, 03381, 03460-1, 03479, 03846, 03900-1, 05559, 06108, 06881, 07358, 08470, 11809, 20944
Krasa, Miloslav, 02112, 09619-20
Kraus, Georg, 18886
Kripalani, Jiwatram Bhagwandas, 09640, 09880, 10092-3, 13588
Kripalani, Krishna, 11572, 25031-2
Kripalani, Sucheta, 23496
Krishan, Gopal. *See* Gopal Krishan
Krishan, Y., 01616, 01634, 01672-3, 05126, 05489
Krishen, Prakash, 12663
Krishna, Gopal. *See* Gopal Krishna
Krishna, Kalyan, 03337
Krishna Ayyar, K.V., 00421
Krishna Deva, 03182, 06868-9, 06887-8
Krishna Iyer, E., 02961-3
Krishna Iyer, L.A., 00422, 03699, 27165
Krishna Iyer, Vaidyanathapuram Rama, 12858, 14410, 15747
Krishna Kumar, Tummala, 12688
Krishna Lal, 04465
Krishna Mani, P.N., 13340
Krishna Menon, Vengalil Krishnan, 13952
Krishna Murari, 06208
Krishna Murthy, K., 04223, 05510
Krishna Murthy, K.G., 16281, 19965
Krishna Murthy, Panuganty, 12309
Krishna Murthy, R., 02213
Krishna Murthy, Sonti, 19862
Krishna Rao, Angara Venkata, 11730
Krishna Rao, B., 19311
Krishna Rao, H., 20513
Krishna Rao, M.V., 04308, 06178, 06490-1, 20248, 27166
Krishna Reddy, N., 17217
Krishna Shetty, K.P., 18497, 18558
Krishna Warrier, A.G., 05851, 06373
Krishnadasa, Rai, 07151
Krishnamachari, Vangal Thiruvenkatachari, Rao Bahadur Sir, 12952, 14378, 15039
Krishnamachariar, Madabhushi, 02474

Krishnamacharya, Ekkirala, 04818
Krishnamoorthy, Keralapura, 02404-5, 02511, 05328, 05982-4, 06020
Krishnamoorthy Vaidehi, A., 06248
Krishnamurthi, M.G., 06596
Krishnamurthi, S.R., 06197
Krishnamurthi, Sundaram, 27038
Krishnamurti, Bhadriraju, 02344, 02371, 27901
Krishnamurti, Y.G., 08604, 25973
Krishnamurti Sharma, B.N., 06469, 06478-9
Krishnamurty, J., 10888, 10994, 11081
Krishnamurty, R., 07668
Krishnan, M.V., 03229
Krishnan, N., 12173
Krishnan, T.N., 14820, 19999
Krishnan, V., 19124
Krishnan Nair, T., 16145
Krishnanath, 13874
Krishnaraja Wadiyar Bahadur, Maharaja of Mysore, 20238
Krishnarao, Bhavaraju Venkata, 04224
Krishnasvami Aiyangar, Sakkotai, 00396-7, 01956, 04091, 04781, 05448, 06179, 06222, 06241
Krishnaswami, Arcot, 06223, 10281, 12522
Krishnaswami, S., 02785, 02803
Krishnaswami, V.D., 03572, 03700
Krishnaswami Aiyangar, S. *See* Krishnasvami Aiyangar, Sakkotai
Krishnaswami Aiyar, R., 02222
Krishnaswami Aiyar, V., 05408
Krishnaswami Iyengar, K.S., 19455
Krishnaswami Nayudu, W.S., 12871
Krishnaswamy, K.S., 00659, 14434
Krishnaswamy, O.R., 15132, 20315
Krishnaswamy, S., 12933, 15346, 16964
Krishnaswamy, Sucheendrum Yegnanarayana, 04367, 19272, 19899, 20546
Krishnaswamy Iyer, Kaveripatnam Anikollu, 06329
Krisṇamurthy, N.D., 27895
Kṛṣṇadāsa Kavirāja, Gosvāmī, 07270, 07274, 07276-7, 08945
Kṛṣṇalīlāśukamuni, 05845-6
Krom, N.J., 04900
Kropp, Erhard Werner, 23786, 24112
Krotki, Karol J., 17787-8, 17795-6, 17800, 22488, 22500, 26102
Krüger, Horst, 00025
Kṣemarāja, Rājānaka, 06967, 06971, 06973
Kṣemendra, 06069
Kshire, Vasant K., 21374
Kshirsagar, K.S., 21134
Kshirsagar, S.S., 12619, 14413
Kshirsagar, Shiwaram Krishnarao, 10179
Kshirsagar, Sumati, 14169
Kuber, W.N., 10783-4
Kuckertz, Josef, 02869
Kuder, Calvin F., 19874
Kuder, Katherine, 21562
Kudva, Venkataraya Narayan, 20396
Kühnel, Ernst, 07720, 07739, 07769
Külz, Helmut R., 12245
Kuhnen, Frithjof, 17939, 25324
Kuiper, F.B.J., 03821
Kukar, Jagdish C., 12640
Kulandran, Sabapathy, 19049
Kulasrestha, Mahendra, 25045
Kulasuriya, Ananda S., 06131
Kulatillake, C. de S., 02892-3
Kuldip Singh, 24193
Kulendran, S., 05835
Kulkarnee, Narayan H., 08283
Kulkarni, A.G., 15497
Kulkarni, Anant Ramachandra, 08284, 08407, 21113
Kulkarni, Digambar Gopinath, 21252-3
Kulkarni, G.M., 00105
Kulkarni, G.T., 08408
Kulkarni, Krishnarao Ramrao, 14708
Kulkarni, M.V., 21232
Kulkarni, Madhav Gururao, 20387, 20822, 21490
Kulkarni, Malhar Raghavendra, 15184
Kulkarni, Maya, 13970
Kulkarni, P.D., 15740, 16130, 21329
Kulkarni, R.G., 14500
Kulkarni, R.R., 15421
Kulkarni, Shreedhar Rangnath, 08430
Kulkarni, Sumati, 21491
Kulkarni, Venkatesh Balkrishna, 00158, 08285, 09104, 09590, 12397, 15394, 20749
Kulke, Eckehard, 02305, 19686, 21438
Kulke, Hermann, 01962, 02018, 22386
Kulli, J.S., 02370
Kulshreshta, D.K., 23686
Kulshreshtha, C.M., 25822
Kulshreshtha, Jinesh Chandra, 15573, 16157
Kulshreshtha, S.S., 07591
Kulshreshtha, Visheshwar Dayal, 16560
Kulshresth, S.K., 16049
Kulshrestha, Chirantan, 13044, 17111, 17162
Kulta Jati Mahasabha, 22362
Kumar, Anil, 24044
Kumar, Ashok, 00319, 16065a, 16279-80, 16320
Kumar, Baldev, 04183
Kumar, D.P., 25997
Kumar, Devendra, 15211
Kumar, Dharma, 10855, 14072, 19251, 19297
Kumar, Jitendra, 11207
Kumar, Joginder, 00996
Kumar, Krishan, 26618
Kumar, Krishna, 06847
Kumar, Lal Chand, 13961
Kumar, Nagendra, 24011, 24183
Kumar, P., 14882, 22331
Kumar, Praduman, 23352
Kumar, Pramod, 00037
Kumar, Ravinder, 09399, 09842, 20725, 29750, 21261, 21279, 21330, 21345, 22637
Kumar, Satish. *See* Satish Kumar
Kumar, Shanta, 25862
Kumar, Sushil, 21966
Kumar, Sushil Venkataraman, 19240
Kumar, Tej B., 23359
Kumar, V., 15933
Kumar, Virendra, 09838, 12292, 26940
Kumara Pillai, G., 20163
Kumara Swamiji, 06543, 06562
Kumaramangalam, S. Mohan, 12383, 12492, 12839
Kumaran Asan, 20212
Kumarappa, Bharatan, 06431, 11573
Kumarappa, Jagadisan Mohandas, 10623
Kumarappa, Joseph Cornelius, 10979, 21730
Kumaraswami, T.J., 19365
Kumaraswami Raja, N., 02359, 05230, 27872
Kumaraswami Raja, P.S., 19651
Kumareson, J., 16826
Kumbha, Maharana of Udaipur, 02682
Kumedan, B.S., 15854
Kunbae, Bak, 05314
Kundu, C.L., 23316
Kundu, Nundo Lall, 05889
Kunhan Raja, Chittenjoor, 02475, 04801, 05297, 05329, 06013
Kunhappa, Murkot, 02458
Kunhi Krishnan, T.V., 13647, 14009
Kunjan Pillai, Elamkulam P.N., 00423
Kunjan Pillai, Suranad, 27881
Kunjunni Raja, K., 01429, 02492, 02590, 02685, 02977
Kunst, Arnold, 01253
Kunte, B.G., 20689
Kunte, Mahadev Moreshwar, 04257
Kunwar, Mayura Jang, 08978
Kunzru, Hriday Nath, 15426
Kuper, Hilda, 26821
Kuppūswāmī, A., 06362
Kuppuswamy, Bangalore, 01544, 14153, 15716, 15934, 20373, 23668
Kuppuswamy, G.R., 06249
Kuppuswamy, Gowry, 02708-9, 02913, 06492, 07253
Kuraishi, Muhammad Hamid, 02060
Kural, Shreeprakash, 06785
Kureishi, Rafiushan, 27096-7
Kureishy, M.A., 17358
Kureshy, K.U., 27113
Kurian, George, 00976, 15892, 20059-60, 20118, 26936
Kurian, K. Mathew, 13046, 13864, 15692
Kurien, C.T., 14246, 14280-1, 19260
Kuriyan, George, 26975
Kurk, Neal M., 13865
Kurtakoty, K.D., 20567
Kurti, Kitty, 10164
Kurukulasuriya, G., 18680
Kurup, K.K.N., 02978, 19912, 19941, 19991, 20221

Kurup, P.N.V., 16343
Kurup, R.S., 14175, 20000
Kurz, Otto, 07740
Kushawaha, R., 23556
Kushner, Gilbert, 00898, 26871-2
Kust, Matthew J., 13885
Kusuman, K.K., 08205, 08223, 19942, 19993
Kusumgar, Sheela, 03487
Kutty, Abdul Rahman, 20139
Kutumbiah, P., 00315, 04547
Kuznets, Simon, 14207, 14276
Kvaerne, Per, 07222
Kwatra, R.D., 13513
Kydd, J.C., 11144
Kynpham Singh, 26690

Labernadie, Marguerite V., 07938
Labh, Kapileshwar, 26423, 26433
Labh Singh, 22963
Lach, Donald F., 07815
Lachman Singh, Major General, 12174
Lacombe, Olivier, 01397, 06416
Lacôte, Felix, 05390-1, 06073
Lad, Ashok Kumar, 01501
Ladakh National Congress, 23218
Ladejinsky, Wolf Isaac, 14775, 14955, 21288, 22770, 24065
Ladendorf, Janice M., 09465
Laet, Joannes de, 07837
Lafir, A.L.M., 02279, 18860
Lago, Mary M., 25058-9, 25102-3
La Guerre, John Gaffar, 26796
Lahiri, A., 14201, 14259
Lahiri, Amar, 10165
Lahiri, Amarendra Nath, 04065
Lahiri, Ashish, 13252
Lahiri, B.N., 12707
Lahiri, Bela, 04142
Lahiri, Bibher Kumar, 08807
Lahiri, D.B., 27764
Lahiri, K.C., 11753
Lahiri, Nirmal Kumar, 24518
Lahiri, P.C., 05969
Lahiri, Ranjan Kumar, 26640
Lahiri, Rebati Mohan, 25684
Lahiri, T.B., 14477
Lahiry, Ashutosh, 09930
Lahore Municipal Corporation, 22893
Lahovary, N., 03722
Laird, Michael Andrew, 08957, 11940
Lajpat Rai, Lala, 04688, 09548, 09732-5, 10617, 10792, 10914, 11289
Lakdawala, Dansukhlal Tulsidas, 14526, 14544, 14583, 15194, 21308, 21524, 21714, 21898
Lakhanpal, P.L., 10094, 11656, 12080
Lakhi, M.V., 17321, 17402, 17412, 17532, 17673
Lakshman, P.P., 11134
Lakshman, T.K., 20344
Lakshman Singh, Bhagat, 22655
Lakshmana, C., 15693
Lakshmana Rao, G., 13047, 16105, 19965, 19978
Lakshmana Rao, Y.V., 19744, 19827
Lakshmanam Chettiar, S.L., 19545
Lakshmanna, Chintamani, 19789, 19794
Lakshmi Devi, 00534
Lakshminarasiah, P., 24247
Lakshminarayana, H.D., 19481, 20262, 20374, 20388, 22314
Lal, A.B., 12766
Lal, A.K., 13678, 14283
Lal, Basant Kumar, 11429
Lal, Brij Basi, 00580, 03665, 03701, 03739, 05544
Lal, Brij Behari, 03561
Lal, Chaman, 00351, 00363, 00375, 09035
Lal, Chhotey, 16479
Lal, Deepak, 21254
Lal, Hira, 22241
Lal, J.N., 12556
Lal, K. Sajun, 10810
Lal, Kanhaiya, 13857
Lal, Kanwar, 01784, 01926, 02013, 03134, 06889-90, 06914, 06920, 07795, 13501
Lal, Kishori Saran, 02277, 07031, 07050
Lal, Krishna, 27070
Lal, Magan, 07702
Lal, Mohan. *See* Mohan Lal
Lal, Muni, 07452, 07461, 23266, 23280
Lal, Narendra Nath, 03754
Lal, P., 02403, 02608, 02676, 04614, 04622, 04991, 05382, 06063, 11754, 17097, 17142
Lal, Parmanand, 26506, 26715-6, 27345
Lal, Prem Chand, 10980, 24669
Lal, Purushottam. *See* Lal, P.
Lal, Ram N., 14575
Lal, Rama Shanker, 24131
Lal, S.N., 14501
Lal, Sheo Kumar, 22121
Lal Baha, 23053
Lal Bahadur, 09810
Laleshwari. *See* Lalla Ded
Lalishri. *See* Lalla Ded
Lalit Kumar, 12201
Lalitha, N.V., 16131
Lall, G.S., 14502
Lall, H.K., 14938
Lall, Inder Jit, 11657
Lall, Kesar, 26354
Lall, R.B., 20988
Lalla Ded, 06977, 06980
Lalou, M., 01130
Lalwani, Kastur Chand, 05138, 05154-5
Lalye, Pramod Ganesh, 05825
Lamb, Alastair, 09444-5, 12094, 13929-30
Lamb, Beatrice Pitney, 09591, 26976
Lamb, Frederick, 19875
Lamb, Harold Albert, 07453
Lamb, Helen B., 00913
Lambat, Ismail A., 21849-50
Lamberg-Karlovsky, C.C., 03573, 03585, 03633
Lambert, Hester Marjorie, 27786, 27920, 27931
Lambert, Richard David, 12234, 13255, 21314, 24357, 25172, 27414-5
Lambert, William W., 15944
Lambrick, Hugh Trevor, 00485, 03614, 03655, 22454-4, 27224
Lambton, Ann Katharine Swynford, 27817
Lameis, W.M., 01044
La Méri. *See* Hughes, Russell M.
Lamichhane, S.R., 26309
Lamitare, Devi Bhakat, 26419
Lamotte, Étienne, 01255, 04575-6, 04880, 04914, 04928, 04959, 05057, 05085, 05092, 05112
Lamsweerde, F. van, 02814
Lancaster, Joan Cadogan, 27528-9
Lancereau, Édouard, 05397, 06082
Landon, Perceval, 25946
Landor, Arnold Henry Savage, 25954
Lane-Poole, Stanley, 07395, 07417, 07454, 07508
Lang, Robert Peregrine, 27098
Langlois, Simon Alexandre, 04657
Langton, Maurice, 06589
Lanka Sundaram, 12424
Lanman, Charles Rockwell, 05255, 27800
Lannoy, Richard, 00645
Lapierre, Dominique, 10476
Laporte, Robert, 17337, 17431, 17548, 17562
Lapp, John Allen, 11533
L'Armand, Adrian, 02857
L'Armand, Kathleen, 02857
La Roche, Emmanuel, 03170
Larson, Gerald James, 01545, 04689, 04812, 06969
Larwood, H.J.C., 10653
Laska, John A., 16407
Lasswell, Harold C., 13060
Laszlo, Franz, 05820
Lath, Mukund, 02683
Latif, Syed Abdul, 10380, 11631, 11658
Latifee, H.I., 25556
Latifi, Alma, 22724
Latifi, Danial, 16008, 16014
Latimer, Eardly, 27294
La Touche, Thomas Henry Digges, 26987
Latthe, Anna Babaji, 01285, 20596
Laubach, Frank Charles, 10613
Lauf, Detlef Inge, 05871, 26438
Laufer, Berthold, 06109
Laumas, K.R., 16321
Laura, Ronald S., 03986
Lauré, Jason, 25577
Laurie, William F.B., 22387
Laushey, David M., 24320

La Vallée-Poussin, Louis de, 01323-4, 01502, 03753, 03822, 04092-3, 04947, 05127
Lavan, Spencer, 11524, 16827
Lavania, Gauri Shanker, 23603, 23625
Law, Bimala Churn, 00217, 01256, 01519, 04034, 04083-5, 04115, 04137, 04233-4, 04245, 04325-7, 04477, 04901, 05015, 05038, 05139, 05156, 05243, 05306, 05341, 06155, 27012
Law, Narendra Nath, 04258, 04337, 07649
Law de Lauristan, Jean, 07519
Lawford, James Philip, 07986, 08013, 09305
Lawrence, Bruce B., 02272, 05949, 05961
Lawrence, George, 07741, 08709
Lawrence, Lee, 21054
Lawrence, Rosamond, 09320
Lawrence, Walter Roper, Sir, 09175, 23148
Lawson, Charles, Sir, 08199
Lawson, Charles Allen, 19137
Lawton, F.H., 10277
Laxman, R.K., 13115
Laxman Singh, 20639
Laxminarayan, H., 15142
Layard, Richard, 15512, 16438
Lazarus, Frederick Kumar, 06444
Leach, Edmund Ronald, 00729-30, 00740, 06140, 18769, 18838-9, 18879, 18998, 19008, 26619
Leaf, Murray J., 22779, 22864
League of Nations, Health Organisation, 10684
Lear, Edward, 11941
Learmonth, Andrew Thomas Amos, 14194, 20273, 27020-2, 27174
Lebedeva, N.B., 26366
Lebra, Joyce C., 10439
Le Corbusier. *See* Jeanneret-Gris, Charles Édouard
Lederle, M., 21615
Lee, Orlan, 04915
Lee, Sherman E., 03462, 07756
Lee, Terence, 16243
Lee-Warner, William, Sir, 09127, 09348
Leela, S.V., 02767, 02794
Leeladevi, R., 02591, 20203
Leeson, Francis, 03135
Lefeber, Louis, 12255, 14478
Lefebvre D'Argencé, René-Yvon, 03220
Lefroy, George Alfred, 11546
Legge, James, 04054
Legrand, Michel, 16375
Lehman, Frederic K., 00646
Lehman, Fritz, 07706
Lehmann, David, 14976
Lehmann, E. Arno, 19532
Lehmann, Edgar, 00154
Lehot, Maurice, 06006
Leidecker, Kurt Friedrich, 06971
Leifer, Walter, 00352, 21500
Leighton, David, 08200
Leistner, Otto, 27630
Leitan, G.R. Tressie, 18548
Leitner, Gottlieb William, 22924, 23149
Le Joly, Edward, 16132, 16809
Lekhi, P.N., 13572
Lele, Purushottam Ramchandra, 10282
Lele, Uma J., 14824, 21336
Lelyveld, David, 11477-9
Lemaître, Solange, 11350
Lemercinier, Geneviève, 16375, 19043, 20058, 20182
Lengyel, Emil, 12756
Lentz, Donald A., 02768
Leonard, G.S., 11249
Leonard, John G., 19605, 19704
Leonard, Karen Isaksen, 19624-7, 19795
Leonard, T.J., 12523
Lerski, George Jan, 17727, 18355
Le Saux, Henri, 02223, 16797, 16816, 19501
Leshnik, Lawrence S., 00587, 00673, 03544, 03562, 03624, 03676, 03702-3, 22201, 22246
Leslie, Charles, 16329, 16350
Lester, Robert C., 06445-6, 06460-1
Lethbridge, Roper, Sir, 09338, 10811, 10848, 24525
Leuva, K.K., 21003
Levertov, D., 07235
Lévi, Sylvain, 00542, 03450, 03936, 05086, 05118, 05272, 05651
Levin, Sergey, 22467
Levine, Deborah, 07758, 06814
Levine, Faye, 16758
Levkovsky, Aleksei I., 10871
Levy, Arieh, 18937
Levy, Harold Lewis, 15992
Levy, John, 01528
Lévy, Paul, 00786
Lewandowski, Susan J., 08195, 19427, 19432-3, 19448
Lewin, Thomas Herbert, 09321
Lewis, C.A., 04043
Lewis, Dearing, 17029
Lewis, John Prior, 14247-8
Lewis, Martin Deming, 09917
Lewis, Oscar, 23372-3
Lewis, Primila, 13530
Lewis, Reba, 21501
Lewis, Robin Jared, 11913
Lewis, Stephen R., 17887, 17890, 17904-5, 17911, 18005, 18007-8
Leyden, J., 07449
Leyden, R.V., 05490
L'Hernault, Françoise, 01821, 06613
Li, Yung-Hsi, 04055
Liaquat Ali Khan, 17485-6
Liebert, Gosta, 01597
Liebich, Bruno, 05167
Liedholm, Carl, 15387
Lieftinck, Pieter, 17973
Lienhard, Siegfried, 04992, 05431, 26334, 26351-2
Liesch, James R., 22936
Lieten, Georges Kristoffel, 19952
Lifco Tamil-Tamil-English dictionary, 27864
Lifschultz, Lawrence, 25202, 25213-4
Lightfoot, Louise, 02989
Lim, Youngil, 18574, 18721
Limaye, Madhu, 13719, 13953
Limaye, P.N., 21364
Limaye, Parashuram Mahadev, 20587, 21571
Limaye, V.P., 05220
Limby, E.W.R., 24457
Linck, Orville F., 27120
Lincoln Institute of Social Research and Public Opinion, Dharwar, 12934
Lindauer, John, 22744, 22789
Lindberg, Staffan, 19419
Linde, Gerd, 12128
Lindenbaum, Shirley, 25521
Lindholm, Charles, 17445
Lindsay, Jack, 17112
Lindsey, Q.W., 26103
Ling, Catherine F., 19533
Ling, Trevor Oswald, 01138, 01244-5, 01550, 07214, 12425, 25189
Liṅga-purāṇa, 05789
Lingat, Robert, 00930, 01442
Linlithgow, Victor A.J. Hope, Marquess of, 10396
Linschoten, John Hughen van, 07896
Linton, Erica, 14992
Linus, Joseph, 13931
Lipkin, John Phillip, 16541
Lippe, Aschwin, 06652-3
Lipski, Alexander, 09714, 11208, 24888-9, 24907-8
Lipstein, Kurt, 09278
Lipton, Michael, 14061, 14422, 14767, 14788, 18791
Lisker, Leigh, 27902
Little, I.M.D., 14445
Little, J.H., 24402
Livingston, Flora V., 11895
Livingstone, F.B., 26592
Liyanagamage, Amaradasa, 06124, 06132
Liyanaratne, Jinadasa, 06166
Llewellyn, Alexander, 09519
Llewelyn, Bernard, 17480
Lloyd, William, Sir, 25834
Lobligeois, Mireille, 19318
Lobo, Antsher, 02769
Lobo, Crescencio, 21079
Lobsiger-Dellenbach, Marguerite, 26195
Locke, John Courtenay, 07946
Lockerbie, Jeannie, 27303
Lockhart, Laurence, 07520
Lockwood, Brian, 14863
Lockwood, David E., 23185, 23199
Lockwood, Michael, 06064, 06617
Lodha, Raj Mal, 22122
Lodrick, Deryck O., 12465

Loebner, Hugh Gene, 22179
Löffler, Lorenz G., 25238, 25510
Loehlin, C.H., 08633
Logan, William, 19913
Login, Lena Campbell, Lady, 22598
Lohia, Rammanohar, 10480, 13187-8, 13720, 13954, 15765, 26744
Lohuizen, Jan van, 08172
Lohuizen-de Leeuw, J.E. van, 00595-6, 03223, 03619, 05518-9, 05620, 07366
Lok Sabha who's who, 12792
Lokāchārya Swāmī. *See* Pillai Lokācārya
Lokanathan, Palamadai Samu, 11086, 14214, 15293, 15359
Lokhande, G.S., 10785
Lokhandwalla, S.T., 16015-6, 16777, 21851
Lokhanwala, M.F., 06718
Lokre, Shrinivas L., 14077
Lokus, B.N., 15813
Lommel, Andreas, 03074
London. University. School of Oriental and African Studies. Library, 27531-2
Long, James, 24719, 26628
Long, Joe Bruce, 02114, 04615
Longer, V., 09290
Longhurst, Albert Henry, 05511, 06618-20, 06679
Loomba, Joanne F., 14041
Loomis, Charles Price, 13204, 14355, 16351
Loomis, Zona K., 14355
Lord, James Henry, 02314
Lorenzen, Daivd N., 02202, 06513, 08934
Lorimer, E.O., 27239
Losch, Hans, 03007, 04288, 04436
Lothian, Philip Henry Kerr, 11th Marquis of, 10263
Loti, Pierre, 11942
Lott, Eric J., 06447
Lougheed, A.L., 13877
Louis-Fréderic, 03183
Love, D.E., 23475
Love, Henry Davidson, 08182
Loveday, Alexander, 11023
Lovett, Harrington Verney, Sir, 09549
Low, Donald Anthony, 09000, 09036, 09063, 09976, 09997, 10145, 10259, 10267, 27564
Lowe, W.H., 07407
Luard, Charles Eckford, 20667, 20811
Lubell, H., 24776
Lucas, Edmund DeLong, 22852
Lucas, Heinz, 19018
Ludden, David Ellsworth, 00409, 05429, 06254, 19289
Ludowyk, Evelyn Frederick Charles, 00383, 03369, 08053, 18290
Lüthy, Herbert, 26854
Lütt, Jurgen, 23476
Luiz, A.A.D., 20149, 20423
Luiz, Tomy, 16873
Luke, P.Y., 19876
Lumby, Esmond Walter Rawson, 10406, 10422, 10448-9, 10481
Lumsden, Peter Stark, Sir, 09322
Luniya, Bhanwarlal Nathuram, 05633, 05724
Lupi, Nita, 21101
Lupsa, Michèle, 08936
Luschinsky, Mildred Stroop, 23787
Lutfullah, Syed, 09500
Luthera, Ved Prakash, 12426, 21045
Luthra, Pran Nath, 26517
Lutze, Lothar, 20558
Luyster, Robert W., 01471
Luz, Francisco Pavlo Mendes da, 07879
Lyall, Alfred Comyns, Sir, 09056
Lynch, Owen M., 00787, 13077, 16106, 21409, 21532, 23752-3
Lyngdoh, Sngi, Rev. Fr., 26660
Lynton, Harriet Ronken, 19628
Lyon, Peter, 25254
Lyons, Islay, 05531

Maan Singh, 06065
Maasdorp, Gavin G., 26822
Mabbett, Ian W., 04270
McAlpin, David W., 03723-4
McAlpin, Michelle Burge, 11047
Macan Markar, A.H., 18860
Macartney, George Macartney, 1st Earl, 08183
Macaulay, Thomas Babington, 10542
Macauliffe, Max Arthur, 06989, 08663
McAuliffe, Robert Paten, 19629
McCall, Anthony Gilchrist, 26604
McCarthy, Florence E., 25523
McColly, Howard F., 25394
McCormack, W.M., 25587
McCormack, William Charles, 06563, 09279, 14029, 20389, 20404, 20547, 27891
M'Cosh, John, 25689
McCrindle, John Watson, 04020-3, 04577
McCrory, James T., 23676
McCully, Bruce Tiebout, 09526, 09603
McCune, Evelyn B., 01882
McCurdy, David Whitwell, 20812
McCutchion, David J., 02406, 03443-5, 08970, 11713, 11832
McDermott, A.C.S., 02130
McDermott, James P., 01487-8
McDermott, Robert A., 11390, 11435, 16729
MacDonald, Alexander W., 26196-7, 26257, 26266, 26403
MacDonald, Archibald, 08325
McDonald, Ellen E. *See* Gumperz, Ellen McDonald
MacDonald, James Ramsay, 09088, 10264-5
MacDonald, Kenneth Somerled, 03937
MacDonald, Teresa, 17515-6
MacDonell, Arthur Anthony, 00211, 02476, 03802, 03847-8, 03902, 27795, 27801-2
McDonough, Peter, 13341
McDonough, Sheila, 09775, 10313, 10381, 11455, 17408, 18210
McDougal, Charles, 21020, 26235, 26285
MacDougall, Donald, Sir, 13797
MacDougall, John, 20894
MacDowall, D.W., 04171
McDowell, Bart, 00376
McDowell, Frederick P.W., 11914
MacEwan, Arthur, 17715, 17831, 17854, 25308
MacFarlane, Alan, 26236
MacFarlane, Iris, 02459, 08021
Macfie, John Mandeville, 04630, 05780
McGavran, Donald Anderson, 10557, 16810
MacGeorge, George Walter, 00346
McGovern, William Montgomery, 00271
McGregor, Ronald Stuart, 08809, 08838, 11587, 11596-7, 17044, 27828, 27837
Machek, Václav, 01764
Machwe, Prabhakar Balvant, 06770, 07106, 11574, 11626, 16999-17001, 17039, 17047, 21648
Mackay, Ernest John Henry, 03602, 03615, 03625
Mackay, G.P.G., 18789
Mackenzie, Alexander, Sir, 26447
Mackenzie, E., 07469
McKeon, Richard, 04138
McKinley, Jim, 12129
Maclagan, Edward Douglas, 07687, 25875
MacLagan, Michael, 09130
McLane, John R., 09564, 09648, 10915, 10986, 24299, 24331
MacLeod, A.G., 27997
MacLeod, Roderick Donald, 09206
MacLeod, Roy M., 10654
McLeod, W.H., 08548, 08623, 08634, 22829, 22959
Macmillan, Margaret, 12720
Macmunn, George Fletcher, Sir, 09234, 09291-2, 09323, 09349, 09417
Macmurdo, James, 08346
McNeill, James, 26742
McNeill, William H., 04100
Macnicol, Nicol, 01161-2, 01220, 06751, 21365
McNicoll, Geoffrey, 25273
Maconochie, Evan, Sir, 09207
Macphail, J.R., 16522
McPherson, Kenneth, 00998, 19167, 19410, 24336, 24651
MacPherson, W.J., 11048
Macrory, Patrick, 09434
Macy, Joanna Rogers, 01608, 16765
Madalgi, S.S., 14813
Madan, A.K., 15347
Madan, Gurmukh Ram, 10906, 11839, 15717-8, 23780
Madan, Indar Nath, 11586, 11604, 25076
Madan, Tara, 23551
Madan, Triloki Nath, 00622, 00630-1, 00660, 00788, 00962, 01005, 02278, 18925, 20520, 20523, 23239, 23243, 23431, 23878
Madan Gopal, 08808, 13700
Madanjeet Singh, 03451
Madappa, P.P., 21751
Maddern, Marian, 24944, 24946

Maddick, Henry, 12998
Maddison, Angus, 10872
Maddox, S.L., 22342
Madge, Elliot Walter, 11768
Mādhava, son of Māyaṇa, 06397, 06398
Madhava Rao, P. Setu, 07126, 08533
Mādhava Vidyāraṇya, 06363
Madhavadasa Raghunathadasa, 21366
Madhavananda, Swami, 00159, 04861, 05764, 06354
Madho Rao Sindhia, Maharaja of Gwalior, 20674
Madhok, Balraj, 13273-5, 13531, 13721
Madhok, R.N., 16264
Madhukara, Mani, 17050
Madhuri, S., 15653
Madhusūdana Sarasvatī, 08944
Madhva, 06471-4
Madhya Pradesh. Christian Missions' Activities Enquiry Committee, 22282
Madhya Pradesh. Directorate of Economics and Statistics, 22180-4, 22224
Madhya Pradesh. Directorate of Industries, 22225-6
Madhya Pradesh. Directorate of Land Records, 22202-4
Madhya Pradesh. Planning, Economics, and Statistics Dept., 22190-1
Madhya Pradesh. Prohibition Enquiry Committee, 22268
Madhya Pradesh. Town and Country Planning Dept., 22257-9
Madlani, S.S., 21791
Madras. Conseil provincial, 07907
Madras Institute of Development Studies, 19245
Madras Metropolitan Development Authority. Urban Node Division, 19449-51
Madras. Partition Committee, 19651
Madras Tercentenary Celebration Committee, 19435
Madras. University, 16506, 19471, 19479-80
Madras (Presidency), 19148-9, 19243, 19273, 19482
Madras (Presidency). Depts. of State and Public Institutions, Army, 08137
Madras (Presidency). Dutch records, 07897
Madras (Presidency). Record Office, 08184-5
Madras (State). Committee on Agricultural Production, 19274
Madras (State). Dept. of Statistics, 19244, 19328
Madras (State). Finance Dept., 19261-2
Madras (State). Jail Reforms Committee, 19455
Madras (State). Land Revenue Reform Committee, 19298
Madras (State). Rural Development and Local Administration Dept., 19241
Madras (State). State Employment Market Information Unit, 19329
Madsen, Peter Eric, 27078
Maffei, Angelus Francis Xavier, 27924
Magsi, Muhammad Aslam Khan, 22630
Mahadev, P.D., 16108, 20482
Mahadeva Sastry, Alladi, 04665
Mahadevan, Iravatham, 03643
Mahadevan, K., 19258
Mahadevan, Raman, 26879
Mahadevan, Telliyavaram Mahadevan Ponnambalam, 00123, 01178, 01199, 01305, 02214-5, 02224, 03971, 06330, 06339, 06364, 06355-6, 11325
Mahadevan, Thopil Krishnan, 09921, 09931, 13485
Mahādevī, Mate, 06544, 20548
Mahajan, Amarjit, 22844
Mahajan, B.D., 06810
Mahajan, B.K., 16223-4
Mahajan, D.K., 22702
Mahajan, Jagmohan, 22599
Mahajan, Mehr Chand, 12840, 12930
Mahajan, Savitri, 07019
Mahajan, Skumar, 12095
Mahajan, V.S., 13166
Mahajan, Vidya Dhar, 07019, 07418, 09077, 09565, 12323, 12841-3
Mahajan, Yadav S., 20345
Mahajani, Usha, 26875
Mahakoshal Provincial Congress Committee, 22156
Mahalanobis, B., 15474
Mahalanobis, Prasanta Chandra, 10882, 14205, 14269, 14294, 24456, 25033, 27764
Mahalé, M.K.J., 09961
Mahaley, K.L., 08399
Mahalingam, T.V., 00398-9, 00572, 01883, 03389, 04059, 04227, 04760, 06189-91, 06224, 06250, 06514, 06642
Mahanambrata, Brahmachari, 07288
Mahanta, D., 16408
Mahanty, Surendra, 20793, 24949
Mahapatra, Kedarnath, 02021, 06904
Mahapatra, Lakshman Kumar, 20500, 21009, 21026-7, 22388, 26498
Mahapatra, Manamohan, 22363
Mahapatra, Piyush Kanti, 24878, 24898
Mahapatra, Sitakant, 17030, 20895, 20937, 20945, 20965, 22406-8, 22421-3
Mahar, J. Michael, 15770, 27653
Mahar, Pauline Moller. *See* Kolenda, Pauline Mahar
Maharajan, Subramania, 04501, 06575
Maharashtra. Administrative Reorganisation Committee, 21149-50
Maharashtra. Badli Labour Inquiry Committee. Cotton Textile Industry, 21325
Maharashtra. Committee ... for Evaluation of Land Reforms, 21262
Maharashtra. Committee on Democratic Decentralisation, 21158
Maharashtra. Dept. of Agriculture, 21477
Maharashtra. Directorate of Education. Research Unit, 21581
Maharashtra. Directorate of Publicity, 21117
Maharashtra Economic Development Council, 21212-6, 21222-3, 21243, 21292-3, 21525
Maharashtra. Education and Social Welfare Dept., 21580
Maharashtra. Evaluation Committee on Panchayati Raj, 21159
Maharashtra. Finance Dept. Planning Division, 21242
Maharashtra. High Court of Judicature, 20709
Maharashtra. Night High School Committee, 21589
Maharashtra. Norms Committee, 21326
Maharashtra. Planning Dept., 21221
Maharashtra State Co-operative Union, 21271
Maharashtra. Town Planning and Valuation Dept., 21492, 21528
Maharashtra. Urban Development, Public Health and Housing Dept., 21493
Mahashveta Devi. *See* Bhattacharya, Mahasveta
Mahavir, 05206
Mahāvīrācārya, 05737
Mahbub-e-Ilah, 25392
Mahdi, S. Ali, 11636
Maheep Singh, 17009
Mahendra, K.L., 13287
Mahendra Bir Bikram Shaha Deva, Maharajadhiraja of Nepal, 25974, 25984, 26042, 26341
Mahendra Vikrama Varma Pallava, 06063-4
Mahendru, K.C., 12543
Mahesh Yogi, Maharishi, 16730
Maheshwar Dayal, 08757
Maheshwari, B., 14042, 22007
Maheshwari, B.L., 12919
Maheshwari, Hiralal, 22971
Maheshwari, Shriram, 12376, 12524, 12616, 12633, 12683, 12689, 12805, 12878, 12944, 12986, 13391, 16555, 17359, 25226
Maheshwari, Vinod Kumar, 14679
Maheshwary, Avinash C., 27695
Mahfooz Ali, 17734
Mahindru, K.C., 12356
Mahipati, 08431, 08435, 08448
Mahler, Walter R., 14584
Mahmood, A.B.M., 08899
Mahmood, Abu Zafar Shahabuddin, 27304
Mahmood, Afzal, 17631
Mahmood, Ayyaz, 17334
Mahmood, Hameeduddin, 16978
Mahmood, Khalid, 17645
Mahmood, M., 16643
Mahmood, M., 17593
Mahmood, Mansoor, 22720
Mahmood, Naushin, 18199
Mahmood, Safdar, 17311, 17320
Mahmood, Shaukat, 17475, 17521, 17594
Mahmood, Syed Tahir, 15976, 16017-9
Mahmud, Hassan, 17494
Mahmud, Sayyid Fayyaz, 02266, 11659
Mahmud Ali, 10382, 17840
Mahmūd Shām, 17586
Mahmuda Islam, 25522
Mahmudur Rahman, Khandker, 25479-80
Mahroof, M.M.M., 18938, 19055
Mahtab, Harekrushna, 00478, 20681
Mahtab, Nazmunnessa, 25239

Mahtab, Pronoy Chand, 24616-7
Mahto, S., 20896, 24223
Maillant, Ella Katherine, 26185, 26217
Mailvaganam, A.W., 19100
Main, Thomas Forster, 22477
Maine, Henry James Sumner, Sir, 10970
Maini, Darshan Singh, 23005
Mainkar, Trimbak Govind, 04690, 04802, 05285-6, 05330
Maisey, Frederick Charles, 05474
Maitin, Tarkeshwar P., 14695
Maitra, M.S., 24786
Maitra, Sankar, 12748
Maitra, Susil Kumar, 01520, 11388-9
Maitraye Devi, 12149
Maître, Luce-Claude, 11500
Maity, A., 04450
Maity, A.B., 11145
Maity, Pradyot Kumar, 07311, 24899
Maity, Sachindra Kumar, 04066, 04151-2, 04353, 06673, 24285
Majeed Khan, Abdul, 08881
Majendie, Vivian Dering, Sir, 09479
Majid, Abdul, 23591
Majid, Rosie, 25571
Majithia, Surendra Singh, Sir, 08604
Majmudar, Harshadrai Ambashanker, 06848
Majmudar, Manjulal Ranchhodlal, 00453-4, 03413, 07152-3, 08512
Majmundar, Paresh, 21792
Major, Richard Henry, 05664
Majumdar, A.G., 14226, 15410
Majumdar, Abhay Kumar, 04813
Majumdar, Amiya Kumar, 11326
Majumdar, Asoke Kumar, 03765, 04094, 06432, 06719, 07268, 07282, 09057, 10120, 12493, 26367
Majumdar, Atindra, 27998
Majumdar, Bhagaban Prasad, 10573
Majumdar, Bhakat Prasad, 07071
Majumdar, Bhavatośa, 05566
Majumdar, Bimal Kanti, 04343
Majumdar, Bimanbehari, 01785, 09154, 09540, 09566, 09641, 09687, 10126, 14632, 24015, 25060
Majumdar, Dhirendra Nath, 00698, 20966, 20981, 21814, 23696, 23776, 23822, 23841, 24419, 25933-4, 26465, 26678-80, 26697
Majumdar, Ganesh Gangadhar, 03677
Majumdar, Geeta, 25124
Majumdar, Girija Prasanna, 00258
Majumdar, Gopal Kumar, 27590
Majumdar, Ila, 23403
Majumdar, Kshitindranath, 11810
Majumdar, N., 08882
Majumdar, Nani Gopal, 03224
Majumdar, Niloy, 13798
Majumdar, Prasanta S., 23403
Majumdar, Purna Chandra, 24253
Majumdar, Ramesh Chandra, 00110-1, 00159, 00193-4, 00227, 00522-3, 02033, 04019, 04095-8, 04329, 04528, 04961, 05687-8, 06274, 06926, 07006-7, 07020, 07201, 07430, 09001, 09057, 09501, 09567, 11240, 11327-8, 24254-5, 24322, 24557, 24917, 26709
Majumdar, S., 13409
Majumdar, S.K., 09592, 10383
Majumdar, Surendra Nath, 20782, 26569
Majumdar, Tapan K., 23404
Majumder, Benimadhab, 26629, 26630
Majumder, Niranjan, 10812
Majupuria, I., 01635, 03136, 26198, 27366
Majupuria, Trilok Chandra, 01617, 01635, 03136, 26198, 27366
Makhija, Hem Raj, 15064
Makuloluwa, W.B., 03018
Mal, Bahadur, 11278
Mala Singh, 27683
Malabari, Behramji M., 00455, 10729, 21503
Malalasekara, Gunapala Piyasena (originally George Pieris Malalasekara), 01139, 04235, 04968, 05244
Malalgoda, K., 18977, 18999, 19036
Malamoud, Charles, 03938
Malathvi, Muzaffar Hussain, 17813
Malaviya, Harsh Dev, 12025, 12987, 13167, 14010, 14970, 19979
Malaviya, Madan Mohan, 10137
Malcolm, John, Sir, 07987-8, 20582
Malenbaum, Wilfred, 13827, 14236, 14446
Malgavkar, P.D., 15205
Malgonkar, Manohar, 08294, 08311, 10533, 20597, 20668
Malhotra, Kailash Chandra, 03675, 03680
Malhotra, Madan Lal, 17151-3
Malhotra, P.C., 14685
Malhotra, P.L., 09151
Malhotra, Prem Chand, 22260
Malhotra, Ram Chand, 26029
Malhotra, S.L., 11209, 15033, 22638, 22663
Malhotra, S.P., 22027, 22082, 22091-2, 22106
Mali, Dharani Dhar, 26661
Malik, Arjan Dass, 08547
Malik, Hafeez, 07419, 09502, 09793-4, 11501, 11685, 17002, 17413, 17841
Malik, Ikram Ali, 22558, 22563, 23031
Malik, M.B.K., 11049
Malik, M. Usman, 27099
Malik, Marcus Abraham ("Hazari"), 23756
Malik, Mohammad Riaz, 10386
Malik, Ram, 11660
Malik, Rashid A., 18069
Malik, Salahuddin, 09464, 09503
Malik, Shiva N., 22644
Malik, Subhash Chandra, 00130, 00167, 00241, 00588-90, 00632, 03490, 03501, 03563, 04012, 16513
Malik, Suneila, 15771
Malik, Surendra, 12357
Malik, Yogendra K., 12936, 15839, 17025, 17045, 22933, 26797-9
Malik, Zahiruddin, 07521, 07561, 08127, 08558, 08900
Malini, S., 20240
Malkani, H.C., 21886
Malkani, K.R., 13532
Malkani, M.U., 22510
Malkani, Naraindas Rattanmal, 16244
Malla, Kamal Prakash, 26112, 26116, 26310, 27368
Malla, Khadga Man, 27742
Malla, Shashi P.B., 25998
Malleson, George Bruce, 07474, 07921, 07931, 07939, 09136, 09350, 09490
Mallet, Bernard, Sir, 09141
Mallick, Achintya, 27541
Mallick, Azizur Rahman, 24864
Mallik, Basanta Kumar, 01058
Mallik, Bhaktiprasad, 24805, 27989
Mallik, Deva Narayan, 13752
Mallik, Girindra Narayan, 07237
Mallik, Kameshwar, 14418
Mallison, Françoise, 06781, 21925
Mallman, Marie Thérèse de, 03463, 05087-8, 05872-5, 06110
Mallya, N.N., 12767, 15235
Malone, Carl Curtis, 14843, 19290
Maloney, Clarence, 00581, 00706, 00885, 04219, 19111-2
Malurkar, S.L., 02091
Malvania, Dalsukh Bhai, 05157
Malviya, R.K., 15595
Malya, Paramjit, 20324
Mamdani, Mahmood, 22865, 26867
Mammaṭa, 05994, 05996-7
Mamoria, Chaturbhuj, 14752, 15133, 15468, 16121, 15046
Man, Edward Horace, 26710, 26726
Man Mohan, 22607
Manaktala, T.R., 14633
Manandhar, Thakurlal, 27543, 27743
Manavalan, A.A., 00067, 27616
Manchanda, Jaishree, 03332
Manchanda, Mohinder K., 09388
Manchanda, Omi, 03603
Manchanna, 06601
Manchester, Frederick, 03977
Mandal, Bipan Bihari, 24199
Mandal, Bishweshwar, 24113
Mandal, G.C., 14776, 24679
Mandal, Kumar Kishore, 01443
Mandal, Ram Bahadur, 15167, 16197
Mandelbaum, David Goodman, 00647, 00877, 00977, 01867, 09881, 14176-7, 16330, 19380, 19399-400, 20142, 20675
Mandlik, Visvanath Narayan, 08409
Mangat, J.S., 26847
Mangat Rai, Edward Nirmal, 12617, 12664, 22699
Mangla, Pramod B., 27457
Mani, A.D., 21043
Mani, Vathsala, 11070
Mani, Vettam, 01120, 05746
Maniar, Umadbhai M., 21940-1

Manickam, Sundararaj, 19490
Manickam, T.M., 04425
Manickam, Valiappa Subramaniam, 00083, 05432
Manickavasagom Pillai, M.E., 04220
Manikka-vacagar, 06313
Manipur State Kala Akademi, Imphal, 26590
Manipuri Sahitya Parishad, Imphal, 26599, 26603
Maniruzzaman, Talukder, 17446, 17549, 17855, 18204, 25173, 25203, 25215
Manjappa, Hardekar, 06545
Manjur-ul-Alam, Mohammad, 25240-2, 25248
Mankar, Ganapatirava Amritarava, 21350
Mankekar, D.R., 08359, 12175, 13404-5, 13540, 13589, 13955, 16849, 16895, 19980, 21055, 21439, 26534
Mankekar, Kamla, 13589, 15876, 16290
Mankowski, Leo von, 06074
Manmohan Reddy, Vedre, 11370-3
Manmohan Singh, 08664, 13849
Mann, Harbans Singh, 15025
Mann, Harold Hart, 08410, 10965, 21289, 21478-9
Mann, K.S., 22780
Mann, Rann Singh, 15719, 15805, 20818, 23374, 23432, 26717, 26727
Mann, Trilochan Kaur, 22700
Mannan, Muhammad Abdul, 25393, 25409
Mannan, Qazi Abdul, 08966
Manne, Alan Sussmann, 15185
Manocha, Lalita, 16565
Manohar Rao, G., 19863
Manor, James, 20229-30, 20249-50, 20254-5, 20405
Mansergh, Nicholas, 10300, 10406, 10422, 10448-9, 10453-4, 10466-7, 24457
Manshardt, Clifford, 10121
Mansingh, Surjit, 13697
Mansinghka, Shyamsunder, 14594
Mansinha, Mayadhar, 02609, 05342, 22409-10
Mansukhani, Gobind Singh, 08636, 08657, 13099, 16498, 16611
Mansukhani, H.L., 12676, 13837
Manucci, Niccolao, 07501-2
Manuel, Vimala, 19572
Manwaring, Alfred, 02601
Manzardo, Andrew E., 26286
Mappilaparambil, Annie, 15877
Maprayil, Cyriac, 14066
Maquet, Jacques, 01898
Maṟaimalai Aṭikaḷ. *See* Vedachalam Pillai, Nagapattinam R.S.
Maraini, Fosco, 27240
Marāṭhī Nāṭya Parishad, 21650
Marby, Heidrun, 18722
March, Arthur C., 01129
Marco. *See* Mountbatten, Louis
Marek, Jan, 02523, 07396, 27121
Marek, Jiri, 07757
Marenco, Ethne K., 22828
Marfatia, Mrudula I., 06503
Marga Institute, Colombo, 18678, 18890, 18912-3, 18917, 18919, 18949, 19070
Margul, Tadeusz, 01572, 01899
Mariappen, S., 26889
Marikar, A.I.L., 02279, 18860
Markandan, K.C., 12369, 12384, 19150
Markar, A.H. Macan, 02279
Markensten, Klas, 13886
Markey, Jagan Nath, 28017
Markham, Clements R., 00582, 26988
Markose, Anithottam Thomas, 12849
Maron, Stanley, 27100
Marquardt, Hertha, 11903
Marquette, Jesse F., 22933
Marr, J.R., 05420, 06643
Marr, John T., 06321
Marriott, McKim, 00780-2, 00789-90, 00804-6, 00846, 00849, 00878, 00887, 02155, 22866, 23788, 23805-6, 23815, 23879
Marsh, Peter, 26916
Marshall, Dara Nusserwanji, 07388, 07392
Marshall, George N., 04881
Marshall, Henry, 18303
Marshall, John Hubert, Sir, 03616, 05475-6, 05520, 05530, 05550-1, 05567, 05598, 04160
Marshall, Peter James, 07816, 07955-6, 08786, 08915-7, 11864, 23444
Marshman, John Clark, 08958, 09324
Martel, Gabrielle, 20917
Martin, Briton, 09148, 09649
Martin, François, 07922
Martin, James Luther, 19502-3, 19518
Martin, Larry Joe, 23614
Martin, Montgomery, 08045
Martin, Robert Montgomery, 00524
Martin-Dubost, Paul, 06399, 08234
Martineau, Alfred Albert, 07932-3
Martineau, John, 09176
Maru, Rushikesh, 21669, 21684
Maruf, Mohammed, 11501a-2
Marwah, I.S., 22100
Marwah, Onkar, 12176
Marx, Karl, 09504
Maryam Jameela, 18211
Masaldan, P.N., 23477, 23573-4
Masani, Mehra, 16939
Masani, Minocheher Rustom ("Minoo"), 10053, 10275, 12793, 13205, 13299, 13486
Masani, Rustom Pestonji, 00914, 01068, 02294, 09037, 09657-8, 20716
Masani, Zareer, 13421
Mascarenhas, Anthony, 08100, 12150
Mascarenhas, Marie Mignon, 16304
Mascarenhas, Telo de, 21040, 21102
Mascaró, Juan, 03972, 04666
Masica, Colin P., 00707, 02332, 02334
Masih, Inayat, 17404
Masih Uddin Khan, Mohammad, 23445
Masodkar, B.A., 13329
Mason, Edward Sagendorph, 12256
Mason, Gene L., 12829
Mason, Philip ("Philip Woodruff"), 00678, 07962, 09025, 09208, 09259, 09293, 11904, 12398
Masood, Mohammad, 25563
Massa, François, 12130
Masselos, James Cosmas, 09568, 20727-8, 21446, 21183, 21187
Massey, Jamila, 02710
Massey, Reginald, 02710, 02929
Masson, Charles, 22430
Masson, J.L., 01609, 01786, 05292, 05315, 05985, 05991-2
Masson, Jeffrey Moussaieff, 02143, 02197, 02512, 06066
Masson, Joseph, 04969
Masson-Oursel, Paul, 04099, 05128
Mast, Mahesh Kumar, 15646
Master, Alfred, 27903
Master, Mansukhlal Atmaram, 15444
Master, Meher K., 12340
Master, Streynsham, 08186
Masud-ul-Hasan, 02460, 10326, 11686, 27087, 27127, 27252
Maswani, A.M.K., 25174
Matani, Pushpa R., 16158
Mate, Madhukar Shripad, 01999, 03502, 03617, 06621, 08522-3
Mateer, Samuel, Rev., 20061
Maten, E.P., 06075
Mathai, Isaac, 12494
Mathai, M.O., 13355-6
Mathai, Samuel, 16514
Mathema, Pushpa Ram Bhakta, 26156
Matheson, Sylvia A., 27241
Mathew, Anjilvel V., 20754
Mathew, C.P., 02253
Mathew, Elangikal Thomas, 14595, 20154
Mathew, George, 13555
Mathew, K.S., 06251
Mathew, Kuttyil Kurien, 12873
Mathew, M.O., 15418
Mathew, T., 14503
Mathews, D.J., 02540
Mathieu, G.K., 25216
Mathpal, Yashodhar, 03537-8
Mathur, A.S., 11146
Mathur, Agam Prasad, 23923
Mathur, B.L., 24200
Mathur, B.P., 15246, 22907
Mathur, B.S., 14709, 15125, 15143
Mathur, D.B., 09672, 21968
Mathur, D.C., 22068
Mathur, D.P., 21752
Mathur, G.C., 15169
Mathur, G.L., 06090

Mathur, Girish, 13912
Mathur, Hari Mohan, 22045, 22055
Mathur, J.C., 03295
Mathur, J.S., 12677, 14300, 15647, 15720
Mathur, Jagannath Swaroop, 09944
Mathur, Jagdish Chandra, 03001, 15065
Mathur, Jai Krishna, 23562
Mathur, K.M., 22129
Mathur, K.S., 15721, 22056, 22277, 23777
Mathur, Kamala, 15562
Mathur, Kaushal Kumar, 27325
Mathur, Kripa Shankar, 22247-8
Mathur, Kuldeep, 12947, 15054
Mathur, Laxman Prasad, 09146, 09753, 26711
Mathur, M.L., 14945
Mathur, Mukut Vehari, 12999, 21982, 22123
Mathur, N.L., 03203
Mathur, O.P., 14665
Mathur, Om Prakash, 15338
Mathur, P.C., 12474, 12514, 13078, 14545, 21956, 21967, 22005
Mathur, P.N., 09188
Mathur, P.R.G., 20062, 20082, 20107, 20132, 20150-1, 26691
Mathur, Prakash Lal, 21999
Mathur, R.M., 08354
Mathur, R.S., 14901
Mathur, Ray Bahadur, 23350
Mathur, Ramesh, 08837
Mathur, Ramesh Narain, 12335
Mathur, Saroj, 25935-6
Mathur, Shabd Prasad, 23677
Mathur, Shashi, 22117
Mathur, Umrao Bahadur, 22153
Mathur, Yaduvansh Bahadur, 09776-7, 10314, 10389, 10423, 10558, 16778, 22624-6, 22725, 22925
Matics, Marion L., 05093
Matilal, Bimal Krisna, 01414, 01430, 02144-5, 07325
Matin, Abdul, 25641
Matson, Dan M., 27939-40
Matsui, Toru, 05680
Matsya-purāṇam, 05802, 05805
Mattam, Joseph, 11561
Matthai, John, 09215, 10971
Matthews, Bruce, 18378, 18482
Matthews, Christine M.E., 19460
Matthews, Desmond S., 24224
Matthews, Gordon, 06520
Matthews, N., 27553
Matthews, William, 08992
Matthiessen, Peter, 27391
Maudoodi, Syed Abūl ᶜAlā, Maulānā, 00954, 17405, 17387, 17471, 17842, 18220-3, 18228
Maurice, David, 04976
Mauroof, Mohamed, 18861
Maurya, B.P., 13302
Mavalankar, Purushottama Gaṇeśa, 13502
Mavinkurve, Brahmanand S., 20397
Maxwell, Neville George Anthony, 13956, 26535
May, Bernhard, 22809, 25380
May, Jacques, 01382
May, Lini S., 11456, 11503
Mayeda, Sengaku, 06357, 06374
Mayer, Adrian C., 00807, 13392, 20023, 22171-3, 22237, 22249-51, 22978, 26756, 26812-3, 26937
Mayer, Albert, 22908, 23815
Mayer, Thomas John Lee, 27952
Mayhew, Arthur Innes, 10559, 11534
Mayne, John Dawson, 09267
Mayne, Peter, 27242
Mayo, Katherine, 00955, 10730, 10793
Mayur, Rashmi, 21540
Mayūra, 06014
Mazumdar, Amiya Kumar, 11340
Mazumdar, Ammu Menon, 16122
Mazumdar, B.P., 07238
Mazumdar, Bhakat Prasad, 09641
Mazumdar, Bijay Chandra, 20783, 21028
Mazumdar, Keshab Chandra, 07787
Mazumdar, Nirode, 17193
Mazumdar, Pradip Kumar, 05168
Mazumdar, Satyen, 26404
Mazumdar, Satyendra Narayan, 12475
Mazumdar, Shudha, 07242, 24662
Mazumdar, Vina, 10560, 15007, 15878, 24829
Mazumder, Amiya Kumar, 01179
Meadows, Philip. *See* Taylor, Meadows
Means, Gordon P., 26536
Means, Ingunn N., 26536
Mecking, Ludwig, 02047
Medhora, Pheroze Bahramshaw, 15186
Medlycott, Adolphus E., 04605
Meegama, S.A., 18613
Meena, V., 01950
Meenai, Saeed Ahmed, 17894-5
Meenakshisundaram, Kaliappa, 00084
Meenakshisundaram, T.P., 02551-2, 02563-4, 06400, 19554
Meer, Fatima, 26838
Meer Hasan Ali, Mrs. B., 11457, 23768
Meersman, Achilles, 07885, 07889, 08102
Meerwarth-Levina, Ludmila, 19009
Mees, Gualtherus Hendrik, 00745
Meester, Marie E. de, 11865
Megginson, Leon C., 18028
Meghalaya. Directorate of Economics and Statistics, 26662
Meghalaya. Elections Dept., 26655
Meghalaya. Land Reforms Commission for Khasi Hills, 26663
Meghalaya. Planning Dept., 26664-5
Meghe, Dinkar R., 15984
Mehan, Kewal Krishna, 15326
Mehar Singh, 08589
Mehdi, Syed Sikander, 17763
Mehendale, Madhukar Anant, 05179, 05238
Mehendiratta, P.R., 27439
Meher Baba, 16747-50
Mehra, C., 16542-3
Mehra, G.N., 27326
Mehra, L.S., 15960
Mehra, P.L., 25835
Mehra, Parshotam, 09446-8, 23054
Mehraj Jahan, 25612
Mehrish, Brijesh Narain, 12151, 13701
Mehrotra, Gopal Naresh, 14686, 15598, 15619
Mehrotra, H.C., 23686
Mehrotra, K.K., 23909
Mehrotra, Nanak Chand, 13189
Mehrotra, O.N., 17692, 17739
Mehrotra, R., 25732
Mehrotra, R.K., 16829
Mehrotra, S.N., 22261
Mehrotra, Sriram, 09400-1, 09569, 09621, 09642, 09650, 10237, 20729
Mehta, Aban B., 21315
Mehta, Ashok. *See* Mehta, Asoka
Mehta, Asoka. 10122, 12982-3, 12988, 13193-6, 13382, 14327-8, 14484, 15157
Mehta, Avinash, 27181
Mehta, B., 12879
Mehta, B.H., 20832
Mehta, Balwant Sinha, 08360
Mehta, Balwantrai Gopalji, 15023
Mehta, Bhoopal Chandra, 22011, 22124
Mehta, Chandravadan Chimanlal, 02905
Mehta, Dalpat Singh, 16837
Mehta, Dharma Deva, 03794
Mehta, Gaganvihari Lallubhai, 14341
Mehta, Gita, 16731
Mehta, Harbans Rai, 22926
Mehta, Hemangiri, 13461
Mehta, I.M., 13297
Mehta, J.D., 21780-1
Mehta, J.L., 22934
Mehta, Jamshed N.R., 22504
Mehta, Jarava L., 01337, 01355
Mehta, Jaswant Lal, 05689
Mehta, Jodh Singh, 02014, 08360, 27208
Mehta, Kantilal M., 27926
Mehta, Kumud A., 11755
Mehta, M.M., 15187
Mehta, Mahesh M., 04648
Mehta, Makrand J., 21609, 21806-7, 21899-900
Mehta, Manu Nandshankar, 09339
Mehta, Markand Nandshankar, 09339
Mehta, Mohan Lal, 01286, 01332, 01489
Mehta, Mohan Sinha, 09364, 20617
Mehta, Nanalal Chamanlal, 03272
Mehta, Pherozeshah Merwanji, Sir, 09660-1
Mehta, Pranjivan M., 00331
Mehta, Prayag, 13342, 15961, 23327
Mehta, Purushottam Pragji, 11731, 17074

Mehta, R.C., 14696
Mehta, R.N., 00456, 03334, 08513
Mehta, R.S., 21737, 21864
Mehta, Rama, 15879, 15935
Mehta, Ramanlal Nagarji, 05583
Mehta, Ramanlal V., 10739
Mehta, Ravi Ravinder S., 13679, 14666
Mehta, Rustam Jehangir, 03184, 03193, 03204, 03238, 03303, 03333, 06921
Mehta, S.C., 14710, 15343
Mehta, S.D., 11109, 13872, 15395
Mehta, S.R., 16312
Mehta, S.S., 06786
Mehta, Shirin M., 21807
Mehta, Subhash C., 15762
Mehta, Sukh Sampat, 15581
Mehta, Surinder K., 21550-1
Mehta, Sushila, 15041, 16446
Mehta, T.S., 16426
Mehta, Usha, 16136, 21112, 21192
Mehta, Vadilal Lallubhai, 14301
Mehta, Vaikunth L., 15131, 15161
Mehta, Ved Parkash, 09918, 13307, 13590, 22817, 26977
Mehta, Veena, 23259
Mehta, Vinod (1941-), 13548
Mehta, Vinod (1945-), 13997
Mehta, Y.S., 20640
Meile, Pierre, 04578
Meisezahl, R.O., 05876-7
Meister, Michael W., 06111, 06870, 06891
Mele, Pietro Francesco, 27327
Meller, H.E., 10691
Mellor, Andrew, 14249
Mellor, John W., 13702, 14789
Melville, Henry Dundas, 08040
Melwani, Murli Das, 11714-5
Memon, Muhammed Umar, 11499, 18272
Memons International, 22468
Menachery, George, 02236
Menant, Delphine, 02306
Mencher, Joan P., 00735, 15089, 19129, 19275, 19291,19366, 20024, 20075, 20083-5, 20091, 20101
Mendelsohn, Oliver, 13591
Mendes Pinto, Fernão, 07862
Mendis, G.C., 04246
Mendis, Garrett Champness, 00098, 04236, 18297, 18315
Mendis, M.W.J.G., 18549, 18710
Mendis, V.L.B., 18304
Menefee, Audrey G., 20438
Menefee, Selden Cowles, 20398, 20438
Menen, Aubrey, 02216, 04705
Menezes, Antonio de, 00447
Menezes, Luis Mathias Armando, 06546-9
Menezes Bragança, Luis de, 21041
Mengal, Agil Khan, 27949
Menge, P.E., 12604
Menges, K.H., 03725
Menon, K.B., 10849
Menon, K.N., 04536
Menon, K.P.S., 13992
Menon, K.S.V., 14479, 15590
Menon, Kumara Padmanabha Sivasankara, 12757-8, 13971
Menon, Mambillikalathil Govind Kumar, 17257
Menon, Panampilli Govinda, 12794
Menon, Raghava R., 02711, 02845, 16979
Menon, Rekha, 27493
Menon, Saraswathi, 19198
Menon, Vapal Pangunni, 10238, 10301, 10536, 23174
Menon, Y. Keshava, 06375
Menuhin, Yehudi, 02739
Merchant, Bharat B., 15286
La Mère. *See* The Mother
Merillat, Herbert Christian Laing, 14956
Merivale, Herman, 08034
Merkrebs, Allen Hillel, 03823
Merriam, Marshal F., 15529
Mersey, Clive Bingham, Viscount, 09105
Merwin, W.S., 06066
Mesquita, Roque, 06409-10
Messegee, Gordon H., 15445
Messerschmitt, Donald A., 26237-8
Metcalf, Barbara, 11517
Metcalf, Thomas R., 09064, 09521, 10953-4, 10987, 23631, 23637-8
Metcalfe, Charles Theophilus, 09480
Meti, T.K., 20283-5
Métraux, Guy S., 00212
Meuwese, Catherine, 05652
Mewaram, Parmanand, 27943
Meyer, Elizabeth, 18819
Meyer, Éric, 18589-90, 18819
Meyer, Johann Jacob, 04296, 04478
Meyer, Milton W., 26978
Meyer, Ralph C., 13023
Meyer-Dohm, Peter, 14260
Meykand Deva, 06521
Mhetras, V.G., 15635
Mia, Ahmadullah, 25574, 25578-9
Mian, Inam-ul-Haq, 17986
Mian, Nurul-Islam, 17702, 18037, 23072, 23090-1
Mian, Tasnim Q., 27440
Michael, Aloysius, 11436
Michel, Aloys Arthur, 10513, 12246, 17967
Michell, George Alexander, 03185, 06654
Michell, St. John F., 26448
Michie, Aruna N., 14977
Michie, Barry H., 15305
Micklin, Michael, 15902
Middlebrook, John Bailey, 08959
Mies, Maria, 15880
Migot, André, 04907
Mihaly, Eugene Bramer, 26090
Mileham, S.M.K., 18583
Miles, Arthur, 01756
Milhaud, G., 04542
Mill, James, 09058-9
Mill, John Stuart, 10537
Millar, Thomas Bruce, 11999
Miller, Barbara Stoler, 02477, 06041-2, 06050-1, 07248, 07254, 27451
Miller, Beatrice Diamond, 21420
Miller, Casper J., 26335
Miller, Charles, 23055
Miller, D.B., 02116, 23306
Miller, David M., 01900
Miller, Donald F., 12953, 13680
Miller, J.D.B., 13905
Miller, J. Melvin, 17432
Miller, J.O., 20767
Miller, Jeanine, 02164
Miller, Robert J., 21410, 21421-2
Miller, Roland E., 20187
Millis, H.A., 26933
Millot, Jacques, 00842
Mills, James Philip, 26570-2
Mills, Lennox Algernon, 18298
Miltner, Vladimir, 08839
Minakshi, C., 06192, 06622
Minattur, Joseph, 12211, 12854, 16850, 17504, 26699
Minault, Gail, 07656, 09999-10001, 11479
Mines, Mattison, 19319, 19411-4
Minh-Chau, Thich, 05653
Minhas, Bagicha Singh, 14458, 14978, 22785
Minhas, Ilyasib, 17896
Minkes, A.L., 18784
Minnesota. University. 27510
Minocha, A.C., 14685-7, 22174, 22192-3
Minor, Robert Neil, 11391
Minto, Gilbert Elliot, 1st Earl of, 08047
Minto, Mary Caroline Elliott-Murray-Kynynmound, Countess of, 09826
Minturn, Leigh, 15944, 23733
Minz, Nirmal, 11562
Mira Behn. *See* Slade, Madeleine
Mīrābāī, 06785, 06789
Mirando, Mario, 13116
Mirashi, Vasudev Vishnu, 00043, 03766, 04196, 05331, 06036, 06703
Mirchandani, G.G., 13107, 13520, 13556, 13631, 13778
Mirepoix, Camille, 27122
Miri, Sujata, 26474
Mirza, A.H., 07799
Mirza, Agha Iqbal, 11695
Mirza, Anis, 03304
Mirza, Kayoji, 02307
Mirza, Manzoor, 17832
Mirza, Mohammad Wahid, 07127
Mirza, Mukarram, 18108
Mirza, Sarfaraz Hussain, 22927
Mirzā Nathan, 08847

Mishra, Adya Prasad, 06384
Mishra, Bambahadur, 05799
Mishra, Bhagawati Sharan, 14599
Mishra, Chandranarayan, 01415
Mishra, Debakanta, 17279
Mishra, Dina Nath, 13288
Mishra, Dip Narain, 23984
Mishra, G.P., 13305
Mishra, Girish, 13514, 23965-6, 24089-90
Mishra, Jagannath, 24039, 24091
Mishra, Jagdish Prasad, 11588
Mishra, Jayakanta, 02648-9, 24226-7
Mishra, Kanhu Charan, 02022
Mishra, Laxman Prasad, 11627
Mishra, M.L., 14237
Mishra, Madaneshwar, 24066
Mishra, Narayan, 24149, 24153-5, 24161
Mishra, P.K., 20794
Mishra, Phanikanta, 04204
Mishra, Pramod Kumar, 12062, 13746
Mishra, R.C., 26420, 26439
Mishra, R.R., 21768
Mishra, Ram Sagar, 13153
Mishra, Ramkumar, 15247
Mishra, Rammurti S., 04819
Mishra, Ramnandan, 24103
Mishra, Ratneshwar, 08778
Mishra, S.N. (1935-), 14939
Mishra, S.N. (1942-), 13667, 24016-7
Mishra, Shree Govind, 08779, 09977
Mishra, Shridhar, 24229
Mishra, Shyam Manohar, 05707, 07008
Mishra, Sudama, 04330
Mishra, Sudhakanta, 13808, 13856
Mishra, Umesha, 06497
Mishra, Vibhuti Bhusan, 07009, 07085
Mishra, Vijayakanta, 00514, 03434
Mishra, Vikas, 14356
Mishra, Vishwa Mohan, 23405
Mishra, Y.K., 04112
Misra, Atmanand, 16432
Misra, B.N., 05514, 06052
Misra, Babagrahi, 01732
Misra, Babu Ram, 14993, 23632, 24191
Misra, Baidyanath, 14504, 22333
Misra, Bal Govind, 27836
Misra, Bani Prasanna, 26647
Misra, Bankey Bihari, 07989, 09166, 09189, 09978, 10748, 23967
Misra, Benudhar, 22332
Misra, Bhabagrahi, 02435
Misra, Bidyadhar, 22332, 22379
Misra, Binayak, 06696
Misra, Brahm Sankar, Maharaj Saheb, 23924
Misra, D.K., 16581
Misra, G.K., 19831
Misra, G.S., 07990
Misra, Girija Shankar Prasad, 04981
Misra, Girish Kumar, 23406
Misra, H.M., 23679
Misra, Jagannath Prasad, 09149
Misra, Janardan, 08817
Misra, Jogesh, 16919
Misra, Kashi Prasad, 12000, 12065, 12131, 12152, 13703-5, 13745, 17321, 17532
Misra, Krishna Kant, 12096
Misra, Krishna Kumar, 23680
Misra, Lakshmi, 10587
Misra, Om Prakash, 14329
Misra, P.K., 16447, 22102
Misra, Panchanand, 12280
Misra, Promode Kumar, 20839
Misra, R.N., 03096
Misra, R.N., 12551, 12557
Misra, Raghavendra Nath, 14994
Misra, Rajalakshmi, 19381
Misra, Ram Asrey, 23517
Misra, Ramesh Chandra, 26382, 26434
Misra, Rameshwar Prasad, 14480, 14790, 15026, 15446, 16036, 16060, 16108, 16265, 20335, 27013, 27175
Misra, Rekha, 07644
Misra, S.P., 23627
Misra, Sadasiv, 22323
Misra, Satish Chandra, 06720-1
Misra, Shivadhar, 03077
Misra, Shivenandan, 04331
Misra, Shri Dev, 27014
Misra, Shridhar, 23610, 23615, 23650-1, 23697, 25877, 25883
Misra, Udayon, 26537
Misra, V.D., 03666, 05597
Misra, Vidya Niwas, 05207, 11616
Misra, Vinod Chandra, 27201
Misra, Virendra Nath, 03485, 03491, 03502, 03516, 21745
Misrow, Jogesh Chander, 26931
Missionary Research Library, Union Theological Seminary, 27504
Mistry, Dhan K., 15945
Mital, Nemi Sharan, 13135
Mital, S.S., 11329
Mitchell, Donald W., 05074
Mitchell, John Murray, 21627
Mitchell, Kate L., 10407
Mitchell, Nora, 11969
Mitchiner, John E., 01444, 03644
Mitchiner, Michael, 04067
Mitra, Achyut Kumar, 05465
Mitra, Ajit Kumar, 22332
Mitra, Ashok (1928-), 13592, 24383-4, 24787
Mitra, Ashok K., 15090
Mitra, Asok (1917-), 11811-2, 14154, 14188, 15881, 16051, 17200, 23392, 24588, 24720, 24777
Mitra, Bejan, 10424
Mitra, Bhupendra Nath, Sir, 11169
Mitra, Debala, 01828, 03145, 03239, 06905-6, 06922, 07000
Mitra, Debendra Bijoy, 08918
Mitra, Dinabandhu, 24964
Mitra, Haridas, 03061
Mitra, Jyotir, 04548
Mitra, Kalipada, 10708
Mitra, N.N., 09007
Mitra, P.C., 24798
Mitra, Pramada Dasa, 05998
Mitra, Priti, 03755
Mitra, R., 01636
Mitra, R.C., 05927
Mitra, Rajendralal, 02493, 03414, 03973, 04902, 05470, 05576, 24858
Mitra, Saroj Mohan, 25104
Mitra, Satis Chandra, 08361
Mitra, Sevati, 26390, 26405
Mitra, Sisir Kumar, 06704, 09723, 11392-3
Mitra, Subal Chandra, 24972
Mitra, Subrata Kumar, 13657
Mitra, Veda, 04417
Mitrokhin, Leonid V., 10399
Mittal, Amar Chand, 00479
Mittal, J.K., 09251
Mittal, Jagdish, 08235, 08471, 08710, 08741-4
Mittal, Kewal Krishan, 01383
Mittal, S.K., 09778, 23968
Mittelsten Scheid, Jörg, 10482
Mitter, Partha, 11840-1
Mitter, S.C., 24403
Mitterwallner, Gritli von, 03415
Mittoo, Hari Krishan, 27328
Mittra, Kissory Chand, 11229
Mittra, Sid, 14634
Miyamoto, Shoson, 01503
Mizami, Majid, 18248
Mizanur Rahman Shelly, 17450
Mizuno, Kōgen, 04929
Mizuno, Seiichi, 05548
Moag, Rachel, 27884
Moag, Rodney, 27884
Modak, D.S., 21263
Modak, K.K., 24823
Modak, M.S., 03989
Modak, Manorama Ramkrishna, 21628
Modak, Narayan Vinayak, 16091
Modder, Frank H., 18531
Moddie, A.D., 14357
Mode, Heinz, 03097, 03370, 03604, 25125

Modi, I.P., 21968
Modi, Jivanji Jamshedji, 02308, 21440
Mody, Hormasji Peroshaw, Sir, ("Homi"), 09662-3, 23240
Mody, Jehangir R.P., 11098
Moeenud-Din, Syed, 23129
Möller, Birger, 18644

Moffatt, Michael, 19367-8
Moffitt, John, 01901, 16715, 16798
Mohale, B.V., 16639
Mohammad, Ghulam, 25410
Mohammad, Noor, 14900
Mohammad Solaiman, 25633
Mohammad, Tila, 23092
Mohammed, Azizali F., 17884
Mohan, Anand, 13422
Mohan, Brij, 16271
Mohan, C. Raja, 15373
Mohan, Jag, 19096
Mohan, K.T.J., 13026
Mohan, Mehta Vasishtha Deva, 04161, 04332
Mohan, Pearay, 09851
Mohan, Radhey, 12584
Mohan, Ramesh, 11716
Mohan, Ramesh, 17075
Mohan, Vishwa Mitra, 04176
Mohan Lal, 11873
Mohan Lal, 13344, 21955, 21984-5
Mohan Ram, 12498, 13209, 13251, 13913, 19192, 19236, 19666
Mohan Singh, 02537, 02626, 07307, 10440, 20654
Mohanti, Prafulla, 22371, 22424
Mohanty, Ajit K., 22384
Mohanty, Amiya Kumar, 22379
Mohanty, Gopi Nath, 22411
Mohanty, J.N., 16700
Mohanty, Manoranjan, 13239
Mohanty, Shanti, 22425
Mohanty, Shiv Prasad, 16275, 16305, 21145
Mohanty, Surendra, 22412
Mohapatra, B.P., 27940
Mohapatra, Gopal Chandra, 03517
Mohapatra, Gopinath, 02023
Mohapatra, Kulamoni, 21010
Mohapatra, Manindra Kumar, 26947-8, 22293-4
Mohapatra, Prasant Kumar, 21029
Moharir, V.V., 12690
Mohatta, Ramgopal G., 06331
Mohinder Singh, 14674, 14729, 15000, 16159, 22953, 27441, 27654
Mohnot, Sohan Raj, 14395, 15275, 15287
Mohota, R.D., 15396
Mohsin, Khan Mohammad, 24404
Mohsin, Mohammad, 15253, 16070, 23604, 24701, 26019, 26040, 26311
Mohsin Ali, 25499
Moinuddin, 27225
Moinul Haq, S., 05950
Moitra, Mohit, 10813, 25134
Moitra, Suresh Chandra, 24248
Mojumdar, Atindra, 07223
Mojumdar, Kanchanmoy, 09306, 26046, 26056-61
Mojumder, Mohammad Abu Taher, 11866
Mokashi-Punekar, Shankar, 11717, 17076, 20559, 20568
Molesworth, J.T., 27910
Molla, M.K.U., 25481
Momen, Humaira, 24348
Momen, Nurul, 25144
Monahan, Francis John, 04117
Monckton-Jones, Mary Evelyn, 08032
Mondal, Sekh Rahim, 24652, 26731
Mondal, Sushila, 07189
Money, N., 19534
Mongia, J.N., 26666
Monier-Williams, Monier, Sir, 01200, 01338, 09197, 27796-7
Morley, John Morley, Viscount, 09834
Monod, Odette, 03075, 03464
Monod-Bruhl, O., 07381
Mons, Barbara, 27243
Monserrate, Antonio, 07471
Montagno, George L., 17756
Montagu, Edwin Samuel, 10226
Monteiro, John B., 12678
Montgomery, Edward, 19461-2
Montgomery, George, 08484
Montgomery, Stephen E., 02355
Moodgal, Hari Mohan K., 13409
Moody, J.F., 16759
Mookenthottham, Antony, 16799
Mookerjea, Sobhanlal, 26069
Mookerjee, Ajitcoomar, 03098, 03309, 03357, 05878, 05890, 11784
Mookerjee, Amalendu Prasad, 09715
Mookerjee, Girija Kanta, 09631, 10166, 10168
Mookerjee, Monotosh, 07382-3
Mookerjee, Nanda, 10441, 11300
Mookerjee, Satkari, 01398, 01445, 06792
Mookerjee, Subodh Kumar, 16920
Mookerjee, Syama Prasad, 24950
Mookerji, Radha Kumud, 00242, 00679, 00907, 04123, 04129, 04153, 04259, 04512, 07003
Mookherjea, Sailoz, 17218
Mookherjee, Debnath, 16037
Mookherjee, Harsha Nath, 24589
Moon, Penderel, 08033, 09550, 09919, 10302, 10453-4, 10466-7
Moorcroft, William, 22431
Moore, Brian L., 26783
Moore, C.V., 22780
Moore, Charles, 24270
Moore, Charles Alexander, 01180, 01187, 01325, 01346
Moore, Frank J., 23652, 23659
Moore, M.P., 14940
Moore, M.P., 18723, 18757, 18873
Moore, Raymond A., Jr., 17369, 17540
Moore, Robin James, 00228, 09094-5, 09198, 09979, 10303, 10408, 10929
Moore, Sarah Jane, 23516
Moorhouse, Geoffrey, 24767
Moorthy Rao, Akkihebbal Narasimha, 20574
Mooss, N.S., 19928
Moosvi, Shireen, 07552
Mootham, H.P., 23905
Morab, S.G., 01923, 20424, 21400
Moraes, Dom F., 12153, 17143-4, 27176
Moraes, Francis Robert, 09980, 11099, 13027, 13108-9, 13357-8, 16887-8
Moraes, Frank. *See* Moraes, Francis Robert
Moraes, George Mark, 02242, 06180
Morah, S.G., 20540
Morarka, R.R., 12905
Moravia, Alberto, 27057
More, Paul Elder, 06044
Morehouse, Ward, 13343, 17236, 17248, 17258-9, 18286
Moreland, George B., 27667
Moreland, William Harrison, 00178, 07486, 07553, 07592-3, 07601, 08114, 23592, 23633
Moreno, H.W.B., 25128
Morgan, Kenneth William, 01212
Morgenstierne, Georg, 27977
Morison, John Lyle, 09132-3
Morley, Grace, 08725
Morley, William Hook, 09252
Morrill, Richard L., 16037
Morris, Brian, 19382
Morris, C.J., 09308
Morris, H.S., 26848, 26859
Morris, Henry, 10543, 19535
Morris, John, 26406, 27392
Morris, Morris David, 00243, 10856, 10873, 10936, 11119-20, 14827-8, 15502, 15606, 21300, 21316, 24124
Morris-Jones, Wyndraeth Humphreys, 09945, 12310, 12512, 12768, 13028, 13048, 13154, 13336, 13383, 13462, 22163
Morrison, Barrie M., 04013, 07177, 08274, 12257, 18873
Morrison, Charles, 12872-3, 22845, 23300
Morrison, Diana, 01109
Morrison, William A., 21460, 21566
Moses, S.T., 19415
Mosley, Leonard Oswald, 10304
Mossé, Claude, 12177
The Mother (1878-1973), 11400
Moti, Shardi, 21968
Moti Chandra, 01652, 01723, 01849, 03073, 03225, 03254-6, 03273, 03335, 04381, 04479, 05457, 05488, 05584, 06841-2, 07147-50, 07154-6, 07164, 07718-9, 07742, 08472, 08503-5, 08519, 08986
Motooka, Takeshi, 14777
Motwani, Kewal, 15694
Mouat, Frederic John, 26732
Moulik, T.K., 15329, 15377, 21748, 23375-7
Moulton, Anthony Drummond, 15134
Moulton, Edward C., 09142, 20629, 27416
Moulton, Joseph Langdon, 21452
Mouni Sadhu, 11410
Mountbatten, Louis Mountbatten, Earl, 10470-2

Movius, Hallam L., 03553
Mowry, M. Lucetta, 06310
Moynihan, Daniel Patrick, 14024
Mozoomdar, Protap Chunder, 11254
Mubarak Ahmad, Mirza, 18229
Mudaliar, Arcot Lakshmanaswami, Sir, 16222, 16610, 19151, 23896
Mudaliar, Chandra Y., 19519-20, 20598-9
Mudaliar, N. Murugesa, 19394
Mudaliar, V.S., 05442
Muddhachari, B., 08173-4
Mudford, Peter, 09049
Mudgal, S.G., 01551, 06385
Mudholkar, Gauri-Vrinda Govind, 21301
Mudholkar, J.R., 16851, 23975
Mudiraj, G.N.R., 19790
Mudiyanse, Nandasena, 03371, 06167-8
Muelder, Wallace R., 18950
Mueller, Conrad, 04543
Müller, Eduard, 27812
Müller, Friedrich Max, 01186, 03886, 03974, 04795, 04993, 06083, 11255, 11301, 11359
Müller, Reinhold F.G., 00318
Müller-Stellrecht, Irmstrand, 23244
Mufakharul Islam, M., 25546
Mugali, Ranganath Shrinivas, 02577
Mughal, M. Rafique, 03591, 03618
Mughal, Nazir A., 12194
Muhammad, G., 02070
Muhammad Abdul Hai, 27999
Muhammad Ali, 25575
Muhammad Kunhi, M.K., 26876
Muhammad Latif, Saiyid, 22894
Muhammed Bihamad Khani, 07055
Muhar, P.S., 12679
Muhith, A.M.A., 17632, 25156, 25243
Muir, Ramsay, 09070
al-Mujahid, Sharif, 12453, 17529-30
Mujawar, Isak, 21662
Mujeeb, Mohammad, 02284, 02280, 11661, 12585
Mujibur Rahman, Sheikh, 17458, 25180
Mujtabai, Fathullah, 02285
Mukandi, Lal, 08745-6
Mukerjee, Dilip, 17587, 25704
Mukerjee, Hirendranath, 09882, 10167
Mukerjee, Radhakamal, 00195, 00213, 07594, 10750, 10937, 10955, 11121, 11135, 14396, 15563, 15706, 23593, 23842, 23856
Mukerjee, Sudarshan, 26543-4
Mukerjee, Tapan, 10909
Mukerji, Anath Bandhu, 23738, 23757, 23769, 23827
Mukerji, Abhay Charan, 02092
Mukerji, B., 10660
Mukerji, Basudeva, 23194
Mukerji, Bishnu, 17237
Mukerji, Dhan Gopal, 10751
Mukerji, Hirendranath. *See* Mukherjee, Hirendranath
Mukerji, Krishna Prasanna, 12533
Mukerji, Kshitimohan, 11186, 21321-2, 24843
Mukerji, Mohan, 12665
Mukerji, S., 14158
Mukerji, Shridhar Nath, 16612
Mukharji, Nalinimohan, Sastri, 06376
Mukharji, Prasanta Bihari, 12341, 12358
Mukharji, T.N., 03305
Mukherjea, A.K., 07326
Mukherjea, Ajita Ranjan, 12785
Mukherjee, Ajit Kumar, 00008, 01618
Mukherjee, Ajitcoomar. *See* Mookerjee, Ajitcoomar
Mukherjee, Aditya, 25764
Mukherjee, Amitabha, 24568
Mukherjee, B., 24194
Mukherjee, Bhabananda, 00997, 26681, 26692
Mukherjee, Bharati, 24709
Mukherjee, Bishwa Nath, 26693
Mukherjee, Biswadeb, 04908
Mukherjee, Bratindra Nath, 04014, 04068, 04172, 04184-6, 04354
Mukherjee, Chittapriya, 24702-4, 24778
Mukherjee, Dhurjati, 13308
Mukherjee, Dilip Kumar, 07269
Mukherjee, Haridas, 09688-9, 09716, 09724-5, 10618-9
Mukherjee, Himangshu Bhushan, 10624
Mukherjee, Hirendranath, 08485, 12769, 12795, 13359
Mukherjee, Ila, 07645
Mukherjee, K.K., 24694
Mukherjee, K.L., 24890
Mukherjee, Meenakshi, 11718, 17113
Mukherjee, Meera, 03240, 22238
Mukherjee, Moni, 14208
Mukherjee, Narayan Chandra, 24830
Mukherjee, Nilmani, 19299-300, 24618, 24721
Mukherjee, P.K., 14863
Mukherjee, Prabhat. *See* Mukhopadhyay, Prabhat
Mukherjee, Rajni, 24542
Mukherjee, Ramkrishna, 00633, 07957, 15695-7, 15707, 16291, 24456, 24606, 24680-1, 25190, 25490, 25535, 26860
Mukherjee, Robin N., 24779
Mukherjee, Rudrangshu, 08787
Mukherjee, S., 26391
Mukherjee, S.B., 24050, 24420
Mukherjee, Sadhan, 18291
Mukherjee, Sailas Kumar, 24385
Mukherjee, Soumyendra Nath, 09570, 11851, 24558, 24722, 24741
Mukherjee, Subhas, 25105
Mukherjee, Subimal Kumar, 12178
Mukherjee, Subrata Kumar, 24393, 24394
Mukherjee, Sujit, 02391, 25034
Mukherjee, Tara Bhusan, 04338
Mukherjee, Uma, 09688-9, 09716, 09724-5, 09754, 10619
Mukherji... *See also* Mookerjee, Mookherjee, Mukerji, Mukherjee, etc.
Mukherji, Amulya Dhan, 02513, 07255
Mukherji, B., 17270
Mukherji, Bharati, 04339
Mukherji, Brahmadeva, 15027
Mukherji, Charu Lal, 20918
Mukherji, Girija Kanta. *See* Mookerjee, Girija Kanta
Mukherji, Harendra Chandra, 09946
Mukherji, Hirendranath. *See* Mukherjee, Hirendranath
Mukherji, I.N., 25261, 25298, 25453
Mukherji, Jagomohon, 02655, 24924
Mukherji, Kalinath, 00282
Mukherji, Kamal Krishan, 23023
Mukherji, Karunamoy, 24486-8, 25348
Mukherji, Krishna Prasanna, 18424
Mukherji, Mahamaya, 24175
Mukherji, Meenakshi, 11732
Mukherji, Nirod, 12399
Mukherji, Panchanandas, 09078, 10988
Mukherji, Prabhati, 00956
Mukherji, R., 13998
Mukherji, Ramaranjan, 02407
Mukherji, Rasacharya Kaviraj Bhudeb, 00336
Mukherji, S.B., 25061, 26768, 26823
Mukherji, Samarendra Nath, 24465
Mukherji, Sarit Kumar, 14516
Mukherji, Satyanshu Kumar, 16191
Mukherji, Shobha, 04333
Mukherji, Shridhar Nath, 16433
Mukherji, Shyam Chand, 07239
Mukherji, Tarapada, 07338
Mukhia, Harbans, 00133, 07472, 08455
Mukhopadhyay, Amal Kumar, 13049, 24569
Mukhopadhyay, Amitabha, 10709
Mukhopadhyay, Asok Kumar, 24395
Mukhopadhyay, Chittapriya. *See* Mukherjee, Chittapriya
Mukhopadhyay, Durgadas, 03002
Mukhopadhyay, Mohini Mohan, 24965
Mukhopadhyay, Prabhat, 06697, 06803-4
Mukhopadhyay, Prabhat Kumar, 25035
Mukhopadhyay, Pradip K., 24422, 27286
Mukhopadhyay, S., 24806
Mukhopadhyay, Sankarananda, 01085
Mukhopadhyay, Subhas Chandra, 08870
Mukhopadhyay, T., 24629
Mukhopadhyaya, Girindranath, 00316-7
Mukhtar, Ahmad, 11133, 11136
Mukhtyar, Gatoolal Chhaganlal, 21858
Muktananda, Swami (c. 1757-1829), 21926
Mukund, S., 02870
Mukundan, Thyan Kariyadan, 19992
Mul Raj, Rai Bahadur, 22639
Muley, D.S., 21168
Mulji, Karsondas, 21916
Mulla, Dinshah Fardunji, 00943, 20710
Mullatti, L.C., 07327
Muller, Mette, 02786
Mullick, K.S., 16940

Mullik, B.N., 12097, 12708, 13932
Mullins, Edwin B., 17219
Mumtaz, Khawar, 17672, 17726
Mumtaz Ahmad, 17622
Mumtaz Moin, 11480
Munasinghe, T.P. de S., 18968
Munasinghe, V.G.B., 18971
Munawwar Khan, 13933
Munda, Ram Dayal, 20963, 25120
Mundadan, A. Mathias, 08224-5
Mundle, Sudipto, 24092
Mundy, Peter, 07947
Muneer, Nur-ud-din, 18230
Muni, S.D., 12064, 25991, 26047, 26070, 26076
Munim, F.K.M.A., 25191
Munir, Muhammad, 17296, 17595, 22505
Muniruzzaman, A.N.M., 25471
Munshi, Kanaiyalal Maneklal, 00457, 01787, 01797, 02005, 02606, 09079, 12558, 19630, 21118, 21663
Munshi, Mantubhai Champaklal, 20346
Munshi, R.N., 07165
Munshi, Sunil K., 24768
Munson, Arley, 19851
Munson, Fred C., 15648, 23360
Muppathyil, Cyriac, 11351
Murad, Mehr Afroz, 11458
Muranjan, S.K., 11182
Muranjan, S.W., 21082
Murdia, B.S., 22035
Murdia, Ratna, 12992, 14953
Murphet, Howard, 16740-1
Murphey, Rhoads, 04247, 08928, 09038, 10692
Murphy, Dennis, 02804
Murphy, Dervla, 27244
Murphy, Gardner, 01472, 12440
Murphy, Lois B., 01472
Murphy, Ray Livingstone, 10473
Murray, Hugh, 07817
Murray, John, 22432
Murthi, R.K., 09593, 10180, 10202, 13423
Murthi, V.K., 13029, 13632
Murthy, A.S., 19745
Murthy, Guruprasad, 15260
Murthy, Nadig Krishna, 10814
Murti, Mulakaluri Srimannarayana, 02514
Murti, T.R.V., 05099
Murton, Brian J., 06260, 19156, 19301
Murty, G.S., 27172
Murty, K. Radhakrishna, 19799
Murugesa Mudaliar, Nallur, 12618, 14358
Murugesan, K., 10059
Mus, Paul, 01684-5, 04903
Museum für Indische Kunst, Berlin, 03076
Musgrave, P.J., 23634
Mushtaq, M., 22895
Music Academy, Madras, 02692
Musleah, Ezekiel N., Rabbi, 24656
Muslehuddin, Mohammad, 00944, 17843, 17897
Mustafa, Khursheed, 07614
Mustafa, Sami, 17719, 17735, 17814
Mustafa, Zubeida, 12189, 17757
Musto, A.A., 22478
Mutalik, Keshav, 11943
Mutalik Desai, V.R., 14616, 14814, 20316
Mutatkar, R.K., 16266, 22239
Muthanna, I.M., 00436, 12739-40, 20245, 20413
Muthayya, B.C., 14411, 14852-3, 16254, 19712, 19852
Muthiah, C., 22214
Muthiah, S., 15403
Muthian, Thiru A.R., 19573
Muthoo, M.K., 23219
Muthulakshmi Reddy, S., 19168
Muthuraman, Munisamy, 04502
Muttalib, M.A., 12645, 14791
Muttam, John, 12055
Muttucumaraswamy, V., 18854
Muztar, Allah Ditta, 07682
Muztar, Bal Krishna, 00515
Muzumdar, Haridas Thakardas, 09622, 10146
Myer, Prudence, 05471
Myers, Charles Andrew, 15620
Myers, Margaret Anne, 09307
Mylius, Klaus, 03865, 20169, 26718
Myrdal, Gunnar, 12258-9
Mysore. Backward Classes Committee, 20375
Mysore. Bangalore Metropolitan Planning Board, 20472
Mysore. Bureau of Economics and Statistics, 20286, 20317
Mysore Chamber of Commerce and Industry, 20347
Mysore. Committee for Educational Reform, 20525
Mysore. Committee for the Revision of the Land Revenue System, 20336
Mysore. Committee on Panchayati Raj, 20263
Mysore. Dept. of Co-operation, 20297-8
Mysore. Dept. of Planning, Housing and Social Welfare, 20419
Mysore. Dept. of Publicity and Information, 20357, 20492
Mysore. Development, Housing, Panchayatraj, and Co-operation Dept., 20318
Mysore. Directorate of Evaluation and Manpower, 20275
Mysore. Education Dept., 20524
Mysore Pay Commission (1966-68), 20256
Mysore University English-Kannada Dictionary, 27889

NCAER. *See* National Council of Applied Economic Research
NEFA. *See* North East Frontier Agency
Naayar, S. Guptan, 20204
Nabi, Mohammad Noor, 05943
Nadaraja, Tambyah, 18532
Nadarajah, Devapoopathy, 04480
Nadarajan, M., 26880
Nadda, N.L., 14698
Nadesan, P., 18425
Nadesan, S., 18447
Nadkarni, Dnyaneshwar Ganpat, 03033, 21636, 21651
Nadkarni, Jnaneshvar Ganpat. *See* Nadkarni, Dnyaneshwar Ganpat
Nadkarni, K.M., 00332
Nadkarni, M.V., 14600, 14839, 20330
Nadkarni, Rajaram Vyankatesh, 08255
Nadvī, Abulḥasan ʿAlī, 11459, 11504, 11525
Nadvi, Syed Sulaiman, 02286
Nadwi, S. Abul Hasan Ali, 15855
Nafziger, E. Wayne, 15294, 19772
Nag, Daya Shankar, 20888, 22194
Nag, Jamuna, 11242
Nag, Kalidas, 24872
Nag, Moni, 24807
Nag, Salil Kumar, 09155
Naga Institute of Culture, Kohima, 26574
Nagabhushanam, Kandula, 19828
Nagaiya, D., 15339, 21224
Nagaiah, Samudrala, 05332, 19864
Nagaland. Commission to Survey the Work done by Tribal, Range, and Area Councils..., 26548
Nagaland. Director of Information and Publicity, 26527
Nagaland. Directorate of Education, 26549
Nagaland. Legislative Assembly, 26528
Nagaland. Planning and Co-ordination Dept., 26550-2
Nagaland. Town Planning Organisation, 26545-7
Nagan Gowda, R., 20375
Naganatha Sastry, P.V., 05972
Nagao, Gadjin, 05129
Nagar, Malti, 03485
Nagar, Purushottam, 09736
Nagaraj, K., 24498
Nagaraj, M.N., 09016
Nagaraj, Nalini, 06674
Nagaraja Rao, Mirle Srivastava, 03678-80, 06209
Nagaraja Rao, P., 06332, 06480, 11221, 11430
Nagaraja Sarma, R., 06470
Nagarajan, K.S., 00410
Nagarajan, Kolar Sesha Iyer, 02494
Nagarajan, Krishnaswami, 19484, 27177
Nagarajan, N., 19305
Nagarajan, R., 14201
Nagarajan, R., 14259
Nagarajan, S., 17005, 17145
Nāgārjuna, 05090-2
Nagarkar, V.V., 10345
Nagaswamy, R., 00085, 00400, 03382, 04205, 06265, 06611, 06644
Nagda, Sohanlal, 16306, 19853
Nagel Publishers, 27075, 27155
Nagendra, 02392, 02408-9, 08818-9, 11575
Nagendra Kumar (1917-), 24238
Nagendra Kumar (1944-), 23959
Nagendra Singh, 00233, 26412, 27329
Nagnajit, 06106
Nagpaul, Hans, 16114, 16123
Nagraj, Muni, 04916

Nahar, Puran Chand, 05147
Nahar, Shamsun, 24504
Nahata, Amrit, 15408
Naib, V.P., 20320
Naidis, Mark, 11928, 22743
Naidu, Bijayeti Venkata Narayanaswami, 05293
Naidu, D.S., 04197
Naidu, Inderjeti Janakiram, 14736
Naidu, M.A., 12591, 25709
Naidu, N.Y., 25801
Naidu, Pasupuleti Srinivasulu, 05293
Naik, Chhotubhai Ranchhodji, 07693, 21832
Naik, D.D., 25434
Naik, J.A., 12132, 13515, 13612, 13637, 13984
Naik, J.P., 10561, 10580-1, 15825, 16225, 16392, 16409, 16420, 16591, 16684
Naik, K.N., 21272
Naik, Kullal Chickappu, 16571-2
Naik, M.K., 11733, 11756-7, 17077-8, 17098, 17114, 17131-2
Naik, Ramesh Devidas, 00998, 21538
Naik, T.B., 15708, 20813-4, 20855-6, 20878, 21815, 21833, 21917
Naik, V.N., 10011
Naim, C.M., 02385, 02529, 10346, 11637, 11662, 11687, 12455, 17058, 27838, 27847
Naimuddin, Sayyid, 11688
Naipaul, Vidiadhar Surajprasad, 26979
Nair, A.A., 19130
Nair, Balakrishna Narayan, 00370, 12154, 19354, 20170
Nair, K.S., 21552-3
Nair, Krishnapillai Krishnan. *See* Chaitanya, Krishna
Nair, Kusum, 14854-5, 15028
Nair, P.A., 21323
Nair, P.K.B., 20063
Nair, P.S.G., 20001
Nair, P. Thankappan, 01619, 02117-8, 26694
Nair, Pyarelal, 09900-1, 23064-5
Nair, V.G., 16771
Najibullah Khan, Mohammad, 17388
Najm Husain Sayyid, 02627
Najmir Nur Begum, 25145
Nakamura, Hajime, 00363, 01104, 01127-8, 01153, 01446, 05047, 05058, 05225, 06340-1, 27655
Nakamura, Hisashi, 19422
Nakane, Chie, 00884, 26407, 26669
Nakkiran, S., 14721
Nalini Natarajan, 26700
Nallaswami Pillai, J.M., 06521-2, 06530
Nāmadeva, 06771
Namasivayam, Sagarajasingham, 18379, 18521
Nambi Arooran, K., 06322
Nambiar, K.V., 14583
Nambiar, Odayamadath Kunjappa, 00371, 08138
Namboodiri, P.K.S., 17694-5
Namboodiripad, E.M.S., 13155, 13229-30, 13309, 13574, 10060, 12400, 14336-7, 19943, 19945
Nambyar, M.K., 12901
Namdar Khan, 18196
Namgyal, Hope Cooke, 26372, 26387
Namjoshi, A.N., 16209
Namjoshi, Madhukar Vinayak, 15276, 15312, 21244
Nānak, Guru, 08605-8, 08612
Nānamoḷi, Bhikkhu, 02225, 04883, 05039
Nanavati, J.M., 03345, 06849, 06871-2
Nanavati, Manilal Balabhai, Sir, 12441, 14957, 21697, 21757
Nanavaty, Jal Jehangir, 04513
Nanavutty, Piloo, 02309, 21441
Nanayakkara, Vesak, 08062, 18292
Nand, Nitya, 22012
Nand Lal, 14117
Nanda, A.K., 14156
Nanda, Bal Ram, 09594-5, 09673, 09884, 10025, 10034, 10095, 13176, 13730, 15882, 17238
Nanda, Sukadev, 22295
Nanda Lāla, 07694
Nandakumar, Prema, 06590, 11401, 19585-7
Nandargikar, Bopal Raghunath, 05383
Nanddās, 08820
Nandedkar, V.G., 21163
Nandi, Dwijendra, 10043
Nandi, Proshanta Kumar, 16351, 23698
Nandi, Ramendra Nath, 06280, 06564
Nandi, Santibhusan, 20152
Nandi, Sudhirkumar, 03121, 11785
Nandi, Tapasvi S., 05977
Nandimath, S.C., 04740, 04752, 06549, 06565
Nandurkar, G.M., 10181, 10183
Nandy, Ashis, 10668-9, 10710, 13050-1, 13779, 24630, 24808
Nandy, Pritish, 11758, 17023, 17099-100, 25649
Nandy, R.K., 17264
Nandy, Santosh Kumar, 14359
Nanekar, K.R., 21264-5, 22227
Nanekar, S.R., 21169
Nangia, Sudesh, 23393
Nanjundappa, Dogganahal Mahadevappa, 14255, 14282, 14600, 15419, 15437, 20287, 20321-2
Nanjundayya, Hebbalalu Velpanuru, 20362
Nannithamby, Loganayagy, 19555
Naoroji, Dadabhai, 09659, 09664, 10916
Napal, D., 26769
Napier, Charles James, Sir, 09089, 09165
Napier, William Francis Patrick, Sir, 09325, 22455
Naqvi, G.A., 02906
Naqvi, Hameeda Khatoon, 07624-7
Naqvi, Rafiq Ahmad, 11706
Naqvi, S. Fakhre Alam, 27723
Naqvi, Shafeeq, 27753
Naqvi, Syed Nawab Haider, 18070
Nārada, 04434
Nārada, Mahāthera, 01490, 04999, 06156
Narain, A.K., 01257-8
Narain, Awadh K., 04166
Narain, Brij, 07898, 10035
Narain, Dharm, 10938, 22735
Narain, Dhirendra, 01059, 13197, 15893, 15946
Narain, Govind, 14187, 16363
Narain, Harsh, 05100
Narain, Iqbal, 12226, 12401, 12525, 12886, 12999-13000, 13030, 13322, 13344, 13444, 13658-61, 13706, 17633, 21955-6, 21969, 21974, 21983-5, 22000, 22109, 22135, 26831
Narain, Jai Prakash. *See* Narayan, Jayaprakash
Narain, K., 06481-2
Narain, Lakshmi, 10891, 23260
Narain, Lala Aditya, 05466
Narain, Laxmi, 12806, 15225
Narain, Prem, 09795, 10815
Narain, Raj, 16532
Narain, Virendra, 17321, 17532, 17567, 25252
Narain, Vishnu Anugrah, 11210
Narang, Gokul Chand, Sir, 01213, 02528, 08549, 11638, 11699, 27848
Narang, Satya Pal, 05324, 06793
Narasaiah, Panjala, 12895
Narasimha Ayyangar, M.B., 06417
Narasimha Das, C.V., 22413
Narasiṁha Mahetā/Mehta, 06782
Narasimha Murthy, A.V., 06684
Narasimha Murthy, N.K., 20239
Narasimha Rao, P.V., 12896
Narasimha Swami, B.V., 11411, 21620-1
Narasimhachar, R., 03390, 06675
Narasimhachari, M., 06411
Narasimhacharya, Vinjamuri Varaha, 02922
Narasimhaiah, B., 03704
Narasimhaiah, Closepet Dasappa, 11576, 11719, 17004-5, 17026, 17079, 17133-4, 25062
Narasimhan, C., 19708
Narasimhan, Chakravarthi V., 04631
Narasimhan, J.K. 10830
Narasimhan, Raji, 11734, 17080
Narasimhan, V.K., 16852, 16874, 19202, 19546
Narasimhan, V.M., 06623-4
Naravane, Vishwanath S., 05409, 09541, 11211, 11222, 11855, 25036, 25077
Narawane, Kavita, 13593
Narayan, B.K., 14255, 19125, 19773
Narayan, Badri, 17201
Narayan, Basudev, 03518
Narayan, Jayaprakash, 10096-8, 13470-7, 14989
Narayan, R.K., 01704, 04706, 27178
Narayan, Rajan, 13116
Narayan, T.G., 24458
Narayan Pillai, G., 20063
Narayan Reddy, Ravi, 19638
Narayana, D.L., 15503, 19746
Narayana, G., 16443

Narayana, Shyamala A., 17180
Narayana Ayyar, C.V. *See* Sadananda, Swami
Nārāyaṇa Bhaṭṭa, 01912
Narayana Guru, 20172
Narayana Menon, Vallathol, 20207
Narayana Menon, Vatakke Kurupath, 16838
Narayana Pai, A., 20253
Narayana Rao, K. 21046
Narayana Rao, K.S., 17157-8
Narayana Rao, K.V., 19606, 19687
Narayana Rao, Velcheru, 19891
Narayana Sastri, Tandalam Sankara, 06365
Nārāyaṇabhaṭṭapāda, 01979
Narayanampoullé, 08151
Narayanan, A.V.S., 21754
Narayanan, M.G.S., 00401, 00424, 04118, 04216
Narayanan Kutty, V.A., 20019
Narayanaswamy, S.R., 19437
Narde, A.D., 16136
Narendra Kumar, 14673, 16942, 16947
Nargolkar, Vasant Sadashiv, 13487-8, 13533, 14317, 22269
Nariman, G.K., 06007
Narkhede, P.N., 21485, 27204
Narla, V.R. *See* Venkateswar Rao, Narla
Narsimhachar, K.T., 10203
Narula, R.K., 16192
Narula, Shamsher Singh, 02650
Narvekar, Meera, 27890
Naseem, S.M., 17846, 18126
Nasenko, Yuri Petrovich, 13731
Nash, Manning, 01868
Nasir Ahmad, Mirza, 18231
Nasir Ahmed, 08473
Nasiruddin and Associates, Ltd., 18040
Nasri, S. Navaid, 17968
Nataraja Ayyar, A.S., 04409
Nataraja Guru, 20172-3
Nataraja Sarma, T., 05232
Natarajan, B., 01963, 06523, 19256
Natarajan, D., 06266
Natarajan, Dandapani, 16661
Natarajan, J., 10816, 16870
Natarajan, L., 11004, 14011
Natarajan, Swaminath, 10567, 10703, 10817, 16399, 16853
Natarajan, T., 05233
Natarajan, T.S., 19463
Natarajan, V., 16533
Natesa Sastri, Sangendi Mahalinga, 02461
Natesan, L.A., 24665
Nath, Birendra, 04260
Nath, Dharmendra, 23338
Nath, Dwarka, 26784
Nath, Kamla, 15540-2
Nath, Narendra Chandra, 05208
Nath, R. (1933-   ), 02684, 06892, 06898, 07166-9, 07530, 07780-2, 07788-9, 07796, 07800
Nath, Rabindra (1929-   ), 15582
Nath, Raj Mohan, 00535
Nath, S., 03667
Nath, Shaileshwar, 23960
Nath, Tribhuvan, 25999
Nath, V., 00879, 14481-2, 22867
Nath, Viswa, 21808
Nath, Y.V.S., 20815
Nathamal, Muni, 16772
Nathan, Leonard, 05359
Nathwani, N.P., 21848
National Bank of Pakistan, 17898
National Book Centre of Pakistan, 27577, 27591, 27668-70
National Commission on Manpower and Education, 18161
National Conference on Control of Communicable Diseases, Lahore (1968), 18134
National Conference on Municipal Health, Lahore (1968), 18135
National Conference on Population Control, New Delhi, 14190, 16292
National Conference on Women Doctors in India, New Delhi (1975), 16352
National Cooperative Union of India, 14711
National Council of Applied Economic Research, New Delhi, 13850, 14130, 14215, 14227, 14447, 14517, 14675, 14697, 14753-4, 14870, 15135, 15188, 15196, 15281, 15327, 15436, 15480, 16052, 19126, 19246, 19263-4, 19320, 19436, 19732-3, 20006, 20049, 20288, 20299, 20329, 20348-9, 20358-9, 20460, 20494, 20857, 21080-1, 21213, 21225, 21711, 21720, 22016-7, 22032, 22185, 22324-5, 22327, 22752, 22771, 22781, 22793, 23220, 23281, 23569, 23575-6, 24040, 24114-5, 24425, 24473, 24549, 25739, 25771, 25875, 26392, 26484, 26553, 26581, 26641, 26719, 27578
National Council of Educational Research and Training, 16547, 16613, 16634-6
National Federation of Indian Women, 15883
National Foundation for Research on Human Resource Development, 25560
National Gallery of Modern Art, New Delhi, 17202
National honours encyclopaedia, 27473
National Institute of Basic Education, Delhi, 16597-9
National Institute of Community Development, 15017
National Institute of Education, Delhi, 16624
National Institute of Educational Planning and Administration, 16437
National Institute of Health and Family Welfare, 16226, 16348
National Institute of Nutrition, India, 16255
National Institute of Rural Development, 15010
National Institute of Sciences of India, 17280
National Institute of Social and Economic Research, Pakistan, 17815, 17969, 18009, 18089, 25309-10
National Museum, Kathmandu, 26202
National Science Council, 17772
National Science Council of Sri Lanka, 19101
National Seminar on Adult Education of Women in the Changing Pattern of Society, Delhi (1968), 16690
National Seminar on Agricultural Research Management in Bangladesh, Dacca (1978), 25395
National Seminar on Hill People of North Eastern India, Calcutta (1966), 26456
National Seminar on Industrial Relations in a Developing Economy, Varanasi (1968), 15561
National Seminar on Pakistani Nationhood, Dacca (1961), 17414
National Seminar on Social Security and National Development, New Delhi (1977), 16140
National Seminar on Special Nutrition Programme, Srinagar (1978), 16256
National Seminar on the Role of Voluntary Agencies in the Implementation of Public Health..., Madras (1965), 19464
National Seminar on Tribal Education in India, Udaipur (1965), 16448
National Staff College for Educational Planners and Administrators, New Delhi, 20526, 21582, 22382, 24831, 26541
National Symposium on Alternative Approaches to Health Care, National Institute of Nutrition (1976), 16218
National Symposium on the Traditional Rural Culture of Sri Lanka, Colombo National Museum (1977), 18887
National Workshop on Famine Relief and Reconstruction, New Delhi (1971), 14829
Nations, Richard, 25445
Natraj, V.K., 20335
Nattier, Janice J., 04954
Natu, Bal, 16751
Natwar Singh, K., 11582, 11915
Naudou, Jean, 01653, 06949, 06955
Nautiyal, Govind Prasad, 02071
Nautiyal, K.C., 15826
Navalani, K., 27584, 27639, 27787
Navalkar, Ganpatrao R., 27921
Navaratna, Ratna, 01822
Navaratnam, C.S., 19030
Navaratnam, Kandiah, 00086, 01214
Navaratnam, Ratna Chelliah, 01811, 06311-2, 19031
Navaratne, Gamini, 18567
Navlekar, Narayan Raghunath, 05331
Navrekha Singh, 16286
Nawab, A.W., 15236, 15453
Nawab, Sarabhai Manilal, 01694, 06844-5
Nawab, Vidya Sarabhai, 02914
Nawang Tsering, 08689
Nawaz, M.K., 12179
Nawaz, Malik Ahmad, 27724
Nawaz, Mohammed, 18053
Nayak, B.J., 20717
Nayak, G.C., 01552
Nayak, G.H., 20560
Nayak, Harogadde Manappa, 02578, 20561
Nayak, Pandav, 17433, 17816
Nayak, R.K., 10026
Nayak, Sharada, 27683

Nayak, V.T., 16323
Nayar, Baldev Raj, 12056, 12495, 14012, 14342, 14379, 16193, 22685
Nayar, D.P., 16368
Nayar, Kuldip, 12063, 13110-1, 13534, 13594, 16889, 16893
Nayar, Mehander Pratap, 15211
Nayar, P.K.B., 14412, 20007, 20039
Nayar, S.K., 20171
Nayar, Sushila, 16205, 16269
Nayar, T.N.K., 16732
Nayar, Usha, 18870
Nayeem, M.A., 08115, 08266
Naylor, George W., 18785
Nayudamma, Y., 15406
Nayyar, Deepak, 13851
Nayyar, Sushila. *See* Nayar, Sushila
Naz, 02533
Nazim, Muhammad, 06933
Nazrul Islam, Kazi, 25082-4
Neale, Walter C., 00899, 12300, 15029, 22801, 22635
Nebesky-Wojkowitz, René von, 26393
Nederlandsche Oostindische Compagnie, 08094
Needham, J., 18959
Needham, Rodney, 26593-4
Neelakantan Nair, K., 19988
Neelkant, Kalyanarama, 13972
Neelsen, John Peter, 16449, 16582
Neevel, Walter G., Jr., 06412, 11302
Neff, Muriel, 06828
Negandhi, Anant R., 13887, 15264
Negi, L.S., 25749
Negotiating Committee for Church Union in Ceylon, 19050
Nehru, Jawaharlal, 00168, 09902, 10148-51, 13349-52, 13732, 13916, 13919-20, 14330, 15047, 21047
Nehru, Motilal, 10027-8
Nehru, Rameshwari, 16169
Nehru, Shri Shridhar, 08821, 23626
Neidhart, Anthony C., 19551
Neil, J.W., 21280
Neild, Susan M., 19438
Neill, Stephen, 02243
Nelson, Amirtharaj, 19536
Nelson, Donald, 02576, 05392
Nelson, Donna, 26861
Nema, Shree Ram, 06698
Nemade, Bhalchandra, 21647
Neog, Dimbeswar, 02674, 27288
Neog, Maheswar, 02760, 07294-6, 25827
Neogi, Panchanan, 00347
Neogy, Ajit K., 09365
Nepal. Central Bureau of Statistics, 26104-5
Nepal. Centre for Economic Development and Administration, 26023, 26086
Nepal. Constitution, 25979-81
Nepal. Corporation Co-Ordination Council, 26175-6
Nepal. Dept. of Housing and Physical Planning, 26290, 27376
Nepal. Dept. of Publicity, 27377
Nepal. Dept. of Tourism, 27405
Nepal documentation, 27744
Nepal. Ministry of Economic Planning, 26127-8, 26157
Nepal. Ministry of Education, 26312-3, 26306
Nepal. Ministry of Home Panchayat, 26280-4
Nepal. Ministry of Industry and Commerce, 26177
Nepal. Ministry of Water and Power, 26164
Nepal. National Planning Commission, 26091, 26129-30, 26181
Nepali, Chitta Ranjan, 25959
Nepali, Gopal Singh, 26247
Nerlich, Gunter, 27058
Ness, Gayle D., 07808
Nethercot, Arthur Hobart, 11363-4
Netto, George, 26886
Neugebauer, O., 00283, 04537
Neumann, Daniel M., 02824, 02846
Neupane, P., 25982
Neurath, Paul M., 16943
Neve, Arthur, 23150-1, 27254
Neve, Ernest Frederic, 23152-3
Nevill, Hugh Lewis, 23040
Nevinson, Henry Woodd, 09551
New Educational Reform Associates, 26182
New India Industries Ltd. Market Research Division, 21719
New York Public Library, 27505-6
Newbigin, James Edward Lesslie, Bishop, 19537
Newby, Eric, 27273
Newcombe, Alfred Cornelius, 11944
Newell, Richard S., 23653
Newell, William H., 25884
Newman, Karl John, 17481, 17495, 17505
Newman, Peter, 18575
Newman, Robert S., 00756
Newman, Ruth Einsidler, 23114
Newman's Indian Bradshaw, 27076
Newton, E.P., 27961
Niaz, A.Q., 18273
Niaz, Aslam, 17334
Niaz, Shafi, 17956
Nicholas, Cyril Wace, 00384, 04368
Nicholas, Marta R., 12133, 25146
Nicholas, Ralph Wallace, 24358, 24396, 24604, 24607, 24682-3, 24879
Nicholas, Samuel Ernest N., 18591
Nichols, Beverley, 10794
Nicholson, Arthur Pole, 09366
Nicholson, Kai, 17081
Nicholson, Norman Kibby, 12597, 13065, 14050, 14792, 14815-6
Nicholson, Reynold Alleyne, 05939
Nicholson, Sydney, 19796
Nichter, Mark, 20515, 20549
Nidhiry, Abraham Mani, 20183
Niehoff, Arthur, 23711, 26773, 26800
Niehoff, Juanita, 26773
Niemeijer, A.C., 10002
Nigam, Ashok Kumar, 26077
Nigam, Brij Mohan Lall, 14657
Nigam, K.K., 12920
Nigam, M.N., 23843-4, 23857
Nigam, Mohan Lal, 03398
Nigam, O.P., 15471
Nigam, Raj Kumar, 15237, 15263, 15282
Nigam, Ramesh Chandra, 02325
Nigam, Saliq Ram, 12709
Nigam, Shiva Bindeshwari Prasad, 07032
Nigam, Shyamsunder, 04355
Niggemeyer, Hermann, 21030
Nighat Ayub, 18093
Nightingale, Florence, 10685, 24489
Nightingale, Pamela, 07958, 08381
Nihal Singh, 09351, 20619
Nihal Singh, Gurmukh, 08624
Nihal Singh, Surendra, 13595
Nihalani, Paroo, 27497
Nijenhuis, Emmie Te, 02712-3, 02725, 02755
Nijhawan, B.R., 15411
Nijjar, Bakhshish Singh, 06934, 08550-1, 22600, 22616
Nikam, N.A., 04138
Nikhilananda, Swami, 03975-6, 04667, 06358, 11303-4
Nikitin, A.N., 05664-5
Nilakant, V., 14951
Nilakanta of Rajamangalam, 01620
Nilakanta Sastri, Kallidaikurichi Aiyah Aiyar, 00099-101, 00111, 00179, 00196, 00357, 00364, 00402-3, 00411-2, 02964, 04101, 04217-8, 04586, 05048, 05421, 06125, 06198-9, 06225, 06281, 06297, 06681, 07934
Niles, D.T., 18986
Nilsson, Sten Ake, 11833, 12235, 27077
Nilsson, Usha Saksena, 06787
Nimbkar, Jai, 21250, 27908
Nimbkar, Krishnabai, 13031, 19228
Nirala. *See* Tripathi, Surya Kant
Nirash, K.L., 00502
Nirmal, C.J., 19547
Nirmal Nibedon, 26538, 26607
Nisar Ali, 23221
Nissanka, H.S.S., 18559
Nitti-Dolci, Luigia, 05256
Nivedita, Sister. *See* Noble, Margaret Elizabeth
Niven, Alastair, 17115
Niyogi, Jitendra Prasad, 11158
Niyogi, M.B., Justice, 22282
Niyogi, Puspa, 07072, 07202
Niyogi, Roma, 07010
Nizam, Taufiq Ahmad, 13206
Nizām al-Dīn Aḥmad, Khvājah, 07420
Nizam Ali Khan, Mir, 08128
Nizami, Khaliq Ahmad, 05690, 05951, 06798, 07014-5, 07086, 07695, 11473
Nizami, Taufiq Ahmad, 09779, 13722

Nizami, Z.A., 09016
Njammasch, Marlene, 04939
Noble, A., 20019
Noble, Allen G., 16092
Noble, Margaret Elizabeth, 11330, 11341-2, 01583, 01733
Noble, William A., 03705, 19395
Noboru, Tabe, 15295
Nölle, Wilfried, 00068, 01115
Noer, Friedrich Christian Karl August, Graf von, 07475
Noman, Mohammad, 09811
Non-Party Political Conference, 10447
Noor, Abul Ashraf, 25650
Noor Nabi, Mohammad, 06990
Noorani, Abdul Ghafoor Abdul Majeed, 09253, 12098, 12311, 12586, 12921, 13707, 14095, 16854, 20730, 23186
Norbye, Ole David Koht, 17833
Norman, K.R., 01253
Noronha, R.P., 22157
Norr, Kathleen Fordham, 19276, 19423
Norris, J.A., 09435
North, R., Lt. Col., 27725
North East Frontier Agency, 26479, 26485
Northey, William Brook, 09308
Norton, George, 19472
Norton, John Bruce, 19138
Nossiter, Bernard D., 27059
Nossiter, Thomas Johnson, 19981
Ntsoha, Dama, 00372
Nulty, Leslie, 17957
Numismatic Society of India, 00555-6
Nunes, Judilia, 08524
Nuniz, Fernao, 06226
Nunn, G. Raymond, 27634
Nunthara, C., 26608
Nurkse, Ragner, 14435
Nuruddin, Abu Sayeed, 11505
Nurul Islam, Mustafa, 25136
Nurullah, Syed, 10561
Nuruzzaman, Syed, 25244
Nyanaponika, Mahathera, 05022, 05031
Nyanatiloka, Mahathera, 01140, 04986, 05000
Nyholm, Klaus, 20323
Nyman, Lars-Erik, 26477
Nyrop, Richard F., 26961, 27088, 27131, 27305

Oad, L.K., 16393
Oakley, David, 15168
Oakley, E. Sherman, 25903, 25937
Oaten, Edward Farley, 07824, 11883
Obaidullah, A.K.M., 25422, 25557
Oberhammer, Gerhard, 01416, 02146, 02177, 06413
Obeyesekere, Gananath, 01260, 01940, 06116, 18440, 18457, 18770, 18914, 18926-7, 18978, 19000, 19010-2, 19019-21
Obeyesekere, Ranjini, 19078
Obhrai, Diwan Chand, 23056
O'Connell, Joseph T., 07289, 25218
Oddie, G.A., 11565-6, 19877-8, 24918
O'Donnell, Charles James, 09690, 24068
Oertel, Hanns, 03952-3, 03966
O'Flaherty, Wendy Doniger, 00050, 01491, 01546, 01553, 01610, 01705, 01745-6, 03856, 04616, 27422
Ogale, S.L., 16227
Ogden, Charles J., 06007
Ogibenin, Boris Leonidovich, 03903
Ohdedar, Aditya Kumar, 07650
Ohri, Vishwa Chander, 03452, 03519
Ojha, B.S., 22762
Ojha, Divakar, 00319
Ojha, Gopesh Kumar, 16561
Ojha, Gyaneshwar, 24093
Ojha, Jagdish Chandra, 26143
Ojha, P.D., 14216-7
Ojha, P.N., 05725, 07633
Okada, Ferdinand E., 26131
Olcott, Mason, 10603
Oldenberg, Hermann, 03824, 03886, 04237, 04460, 04917, 04983
Oldenburg, Philip Kantorowicz, 12133, 23339, 25146
Oldenburg, Veena Talwar, 23845
Oldfield, Henry Ambrose, 25955
Olivelle, Patrick, 02189, 02206, 04451
Oliver, Edward Emmerson, 22433
Oliver, Henry Madison, Jr., 18645
Oliver, Revilo Pendleton, 05309
Olivier, Georges, 19336
Olschak, Blanche Christine, 27349-50
Olsen, Viggo B., 25580
Olson, Carl, 01037
Om Prakash. *See* Prakash, Om
O'Malley, Lewis Sydney Steward, 00765, 02140, 09039, 09190, 10704, 24256
Oman, John Campbell, 02141, 02217
Omer, Salma, 17634
Omodeo Salé, Marino, 04909
Omvedt, Gail, 12212, 20755-9, 21383
O'Neil, L. Thomas, 11394
Onkar Singh, 23563, 23828-9
Oommen, M.A., 20008, 20025, 20050
Oommen, T.K., 00815, 10972, 13100, 14778, 14995, 16109, 16133, 16353, 20040, 22046, 22110-1, 23437
Opie, John Lindsay, 27151
Opler, Morris Edward, 00634, 23525, 23699, 23789-90, 23925-6
Oppitz, Michael, 26218
Orans, Martin, 00808, 00900, 20919
Oren, Stephen, 22656
Orenstein, Henry, 00821-2, 00901, 01047, 15902, 21401, 21480
Organ, Troy Wilson, 01201-2, 01473
Orissa. Board of Revenue, 22343
Orissa. Bureau of Statistics and Economics, 22326, 22334-5
Orissa. Committee of Enquiry: Orissa Students' Disquietude, 22383
Orissa Cultural Forum, 00480
Orissa. Dept. of Tourism and Cultural Affairs, 27209
Orissa. Forest Dept., 22336
Orissa. Home (Boundary) Dept., 22296
Orissa. Home (Elections) Dept., 22302-4
Orissa. Industries Dept., 22348
Orissa. State Evaluation Organisation, 22349
Orissa. State Family Planning Bureau, 22380
Orissa State's People's Conference. Orissa States Enquiry Committee, 20682
Orlich, Leopold von, 11945
Orme, Robert, 07948, 07991
Ornati, Oscar A., 15599
Orr, Inge C., 11605
Orr, J. Edwin, 11536
Orr, P., and Sons, 19321
Orr, William Gladstone, 02203, 08456
Orta, Garcia da, 00333
Ortner, Sherry B., 26219-20
Osborne, Arthur, 11412, 21622
Osborne, William Godolphin, Lord, 22572-3
Osman, Mohammad Taib, 02436
Ostergaard, Geoffrey N., 14302
Ostor, Akos, 00984, 01055, 02131, 24891
Oswell, George Devereux, 09017
Otto, Rudolf, 02147
Ouchi, Tsutomo, 00884
Ouden, Jan Hendrik Barend den, 19349, 19361, 19369
Outram, James, Sir, 22456
Overstreet, Gene D., 10054, 13207, 13973, 15993-4
Ovington, John, 08382
Owen, Hugh F., 09758, 09812
Owen, John E., 25491
Owen, Sidney J., 07441, 07526
Owen, Wilfred, 15420
Owens, John E., 17913
Owens, Raymond Lee, 24608, 24630, 24808
Oza, Shantilal S., 27929
Oza, Uchhrangrai Keshavra, 21769

Pachai, B., 26839
Paddaya, K., 03564, 03681
Padhi, Baba Baidyanath, 27936
Padhy, Kishore Chandra, 15126
Padhye, M.D., 21247
Padki, M.B., 21082, 21511
Padmanabhacharya, C.M., 06483
Padmanabhan, C.B., 16434
Padmanabhan, R.A., 19169
Padmanabhan, Sivan Pillai, 01951, 01980
Padmanabhan Tampy, K.P., 08714
Padmanji, Baba, 21629
Padmarajjah, Yelekyatharahali Jinadathiah, 01373
Padmasha, 10315
Padmavalli, R., 19306
Padmavathi, Padala, 27442

Padoux, André, 02132, 05169
Paes, Domingos, 06226
Pagdi, Setumadhava Rao, 19810
Page, James Alfred, 07170-1
Pahadiya, S.M., 06742
Pai, D.N., 21859
Pai, G.K., 04044
Pai, Mangalore Ramakrishna, 14343-5, 19705
Pai Panandikar, D.H., 14649
Pai Panandikar, V.A., 12619, 12651, 12954, 13545, 14413, 15205, 16293
Painter, C., 02462
Pakem, B., 26667
Pakeman, Sidney Arnold, 00385, 27136
Pakistan Academy for Rural Development, 17942, 25423-5
Pakistan. Advisory Panels for the Fourth Five-Year Plan, 17880
Pakistan Association of Scientists and Scientific Professions, 18287
Pakistan. Atomic Energy Commission, 18032
Pakistan Bibliographical Working Group, 27542, 27671
Pakistan. Bureau of National Reconstruction, 17635
Pakistan. Bureau of National Research and Reference, 25366
Pakistan. Central Statistical Office, 22897, 27751, 27770
Pakistan. Census Commissioner, 17918
Pakistan. Commission for Eradication of Social Evils, 18127
Pakistan. Commission on Marriage and Family Laws of 1956, 18109
Pakistan. Commission on National Education, 18169
Pakistan. Commission on Student Problems and Welfare, 18205
Pakistan. Constituent Assembly, 17496-7
Pakistan. Constitution, 17498, 17522-3, 17596-8
Pakistan. Constitution Commission, 17524
Pakistan. Curriculum Wing, 18154, 18185-6
Pakistan. Dept. of Films and Publications, 17654, 25325
Pakistan. Dept. of Investment Promotion and Supplies, 17999
Pakistan. Economic Advisor's Wing, 17773, 17818
Pakistan. Education Division, 18170
Pakistan. Education Division. Quaid-i-Azam Papers Cell, 10361
Pakistan. Election Commission, 17525, 17533-5, 17558
Pakistan. Environment and Urban Affairs Division, 17975
Pakistan. Experts' Committee of Economists on Prices, 17907
Pakistan. Finance Division, 17891
Pakistan. Food and Agriculture Division. Planning Unit, 25367
Pakistan Group for the Study of Local Government, Karachi, 17886
Pakistan Historical Society, 09571
Pakistan. Information and Broadcasting Division, 17575
Pakistan Institute of Development Economics, 17775, 17906
Pakistan International Family Planning Conference, Dacca (1969), 17801
Pakistan. Jute Board, 25368
Pakistan. Jute Enquiry Commission, 25369
Pakistan. Land Reforms Commission for West Pakistan, 17987
Pakistan. Law Reform Commission, 17389
Pakistan. Laws, statutes, 17606, 17636
Pakistan Manpower Institute, 17920
Pakistan. Ministry of Agriculture and Works. Planning Unit, 17917
Pakistan. Ministry of Economic Affairs, 17858-9
Pakistan. Ministry of Education, 18171
Pakistan. Ministry of Finance, 17888
Pakistan. Ministry of Foreign Affairs, 12082, 17659
Pakistan. Ministry of Health, Labour and Social Welfare, 17802
Pakistan. Ministry of Information and National Affairs, 12116a
Pakistan. Ministry of Law, 17477
Pakistan. Ministry of Law and Parliamentary Affairs. Law Division, 17526
Pakistan. Ministry of Refugees and Rehabilitation, 10503
Pakistan. Ministry of Religious Affairs, 18212
Pakistan. National Assembly, 17599
Pakistan National Bibliography, 27672
Pakistan. National Income Commission, 17809
Pakistan. Pay and Services Commission, 17360
Pakistan. Planning Commission, 17819, 17861-2, 17865-74, 17881-3, 17919, 18121
Pakistan. Post Office Dept., 27089
Pakistan. Press Commission, 18242
Pakistan. Radio Pakistan, 18259
Pakistan Sociological Association, 18085
Pakistan. Special Committee on Cottage Industries for the Rehabilitation of Refugees of Karachi, 22469
Pakistan Statistical Yearbook, 27771
Pakistan. Study Group on Examinations in Universities, 18187
Pakistan. Supreme Court, 17616-7
Pakistan. Taxation Commission, 17892
Pakistan. Taxation Enquiry Commission, 17893
Pakistan. Textile Enquiry Commission, 18038
Pakistan. Textile Industry Capacity Committee, 18039
Pakistan. Treaties, 17660
Pakistan. Waterlogging and Salinity Study Cell, 17970
Pakistan Year-Book, 27090
Pakrasi, Kanti B., 21809, 24609, 24813-4
Pakrasi, Mira, 24230, 25832
Pal, Benjamin Peary, 27038
Pal, Binay Krishna, 24466
Pal, Bipin Chandra, 09717, 24844, 24892
Pal, Dharm, 09137, 27192
Pal, Keshav Ram, 00037
Pal, Mrinal Kanti, 00915
Pal, Pratapaditya, 01765, 01829, 03099, 03226, 03274, 03427, 03453, 03465-6, 05560, 05585, 07347-8, 07384, 08486
Palakshappa, T.C., 20376-7
Palaniappan, K., 01966
Palanisami, M., 19324
Palchoudhuri, Ila, 03321
Palekar, Shreekant A., 10892, 15591
Pali Text Society, London, 04972
Palit, Chittabrata, 24405, 24490
Palit, D.K., 12180, 17695
Paliwal, D.L., 20645
Palmer, J.A.B., 09505
Palmer, Mabel Atkinson, 26824
Palmer, Norman Dunbar, 12026-7, 12057, 12213, 12312, 13345, 13439, 13662, 21193-4
Palsapure, P.Z., 21294
Palsokar, R.D., 13780
Palwal, A. Raziq, 23119
Panandikar, Satyashraya Gopal, 14617, 24406
Panandikar, Sulabha, 16691
Pancamukhi, R.S., 05497
Panchal, Goverdhan, 02979
Panchamukhi, Vadiraj Raghawendracharya, 13799, 13828, 14096
Panchanadikar, J., 21868
Panchanadikar, K.C., 21868
Panchapakesa Ayyar, Aiylam Subramanier, 02420
Panchbhai, Sudhir, 20907
Panda, Basudev, 12680
Panda, Daityari, 22396
Panda, Debabrata, 13252
Panda, Kamala Kant, 13746
Pande, B.M., 00586, 03509, 03592
Pande, D.K., 21610
Pande, Dinesh C., 12710, 15288
Pande, Govind Chandra, 04591, 04931
Pande, K.C., 12514, 21970, 21984-5, 22109
Pande, M.P., 21262
Pande, Ram, 08993, 20660, 22047, 23739
Pande, Trilochan, 02441
Pande, Vinayak Krishnarao, 21173
Pande, Vindhyeshwari Prasad, 00880, 15030
Pandey, Awadh Bihari, 05691-2, 07051, 07431
Pandey, B.B., 26499
Pandey, Bishwa Nath, 08883, 09572, 10347, 12214, 13066, 13360, 16543, 24271
Pandey, Deena Bandhu, 01674
Pandey, Deepak, 10316
Pandey, Dhanpati, 11290, 22640
Pandey, Gyanendra, 23478-9, 23497
Pandey, Indu Prakash, 02651
Pandey, Jawaharlal, 23985-6
Pandey, Kanhaiya Lal, 22240
Pandey, Kanti Chandra, 02515, 03122, 05993, 06972
Pandey, Lalta Prasad, 01830, 04369
Pandey, M.K., 21758
Pandey, Mahendra Prasad, 24077

Pandey, Mithila Sarma, 00516
Pandey, Prabha Shanker, 23807
Pandey, R.E., 16272
Pandey, R.N., 15543
Pandey, Raj Bali, 01024-5, 02048, 04198
Pandey, Rajendra, 02049, 15962
Pandey, Rajeshwar, 14303
Pandey, Ram Kewal, 01771
Pandey, Ram Kishore, 07562
Pandey, Ram Shakal, 15947
Pandey, Rewati Raman, 06333
Pandey, Rudra Raj, Sardar, 26314
Pandey, Sangam Lal, 07094
Pandey, Shiva Mohan, 11005, 15091, 16038, 23358
23376, 23619, 23681-2
Pandey, Shyam Manohar, 06788, 07119, 08822
Pandey, Triloki N., 01706
Pandey, Uma Kant, 03923
Pandey, V.K., 23620
Pandeya, Avinash C. (Gayanacharya), 02980
Pandeya, P., 24176
Pandeya, R.C., 05101
Pandhe, M.K., 16160
Pandhe, Pramila, 24966
Pandit, Baljit Nath, 06960
Pandit, C.S., 13596
Pandit, Dhairyabala Prabodh, 21793
Pandit, H.N., 12559, 15521
Pandit, Prabodh Bechardas, 00680, 02333, 02607, 12476
Pandit, Raghunath Vishnu, 21103-4
Pandit, Ranjit Sitaram, 06940
Pandit, Saraswati Shantipriya, 10588, 21905
Pandit, Sneh, 03123
Pandit, Vijay Lakshmi Nehru, 12759
Pandit, Yeshwant Sakharam, 11071, 21204
Panditaradhya, H.K., 20493
Panditha, Vincent, 06157
Panditratna, Bernard L., 18779, 18895-7, 18899-904
Panduranga Rao, Ilapavuluri, 04718
Panduranga Rao, V., 17124
Pandurangi, Krishnacharya Tamanacharya, 00010
Pandya, Indubala H., 16933
Pandya, Jayendra F., 14585
Pandya, N.M., 21873
Pandya, T.R., 21901
Panemanglor, Krishnarao N., 20630
Pangborn, Cyrus R., 11305
Panhwar, Muhammed Hussain, 27726
Pani, Jiwan, 03008
Pani, P.K., 14270
Panigrahi, Krishna Chandra, 04761, 06907, 06915
Panigrahi, Lalita, 10718
Panikar, Puthenveetil Govinda Kerala, 15109, 16228, 20009
Panikkar, A.K., 27709
Panikkar, C.V.K., 19982
Panikkar, K.K., 20155
Panikkar, K.N., 13208, 20026, 20076, 23322
Panikkar, Kavalam Madhava, 00111, 00124, 00169, 00218,
00229, 00365, 00373, 00648, 07809, 08139-40, 09367-8,
09380, 10239, 12281, 20092, 20658, 23139
Panikkar, Raymond, 01185, 01492, 16716-7
Pāṇini, 05195-6
Panini, M.N., 23299
Panjabi, Kewalram Lalchand, 09209, 10184, 12568
Panjatan, S. Ghulam, 17899
Pannu, Nisar Ahmad, 10384
Panse, M.G., 06743, 20731
Pant, Apa, 12760-1
Pant, Alok, 23907
Pant, Chandra, 07485
Pant, D., 07619
Pant, G.N., 03322
Pant, Govind Ballabh, 22048
Pant, H.G., 13743
Pant, Ika Paul, 16161
Pant, Mahes Raj, 00855
Pant, Niranjan, 13681, 24018
Pant, Pitambar, 16438
Pant, Rama Devi, 26012
Pant, S.C., 15600
Pant, Shiva D., 25907
Pant, Sumitra Nandan, 11617
Pant, Yadav Prasad, 23669, 26093-4, 26132, 26144-5,
26158-9, 26183
Panter-Brick, Simone, 09963
Panter-Downes, Mollie, 11971
Pantham, Thomas, 21670, 21685, 21691
Pantulu, Ongole Venkata Rangayya, 05293
Papachristou, Garald C., 21986
Papanek, Gustav F., 17720, 17825, 17834, 18011-2, 18023
Papanek, Hanna, 10735, 12267, 18024, 22470, 25463
Papola, T.S., 15583, 21794
Pappacena, Enrice, 02937
Paradkar, M.D., 04691
Parakatil, Francis, 14118
Paramahamsa, V.R.K., 12993, 15042, 20289
Paramesvara Pillai, Govinda, 19152
Parameswar Iyer, Ulloor S., 20214
Parameswara, P., 01455
Parameswara Rao, P., 12373
Parameswaran, E.G., 19884
Parameswaran, P., 09596, 20174
Parameswaran, Uma, 11735, 17159
Parameswaran Nair, P.K., 02592
Paranavitana, Senerat, 00366, 00384, 01598, 01686,
03372-3, 04167, 04514, 05042, 05049, 05615-6, 05623-4,
06117, 06146, 06158-9, 06175, 08074
Paranjape, H.D., 15238
Paranjape, H.K., 14414-5, 14485, 15424
Paranjape, N.V., 12370
Paranjoti, Violet, 06531, 10562, 11547
Paranjpe, Anand Chintaman, 21384
Paranjpe, H.G., 12897, 26529
Parasnis, Dattatraya Balwant, 07440, 20607
Parasnis, N.R., 21572
Parate, Dadappa Chintappa, 21583
Parchani, S., 02613
Pardaman Singh, 09827, 24300-1
Pardesi, Ghanshyam, 13974
Pareek, H.S., 22062
Pareek, Radhey Shyam, 11291
Pareek, Ratan Nath, 19811
Pareek, Suraj Narain, 22049
Pareek, Udai Narain, 14139, 15681-2, 15948, 16403, 16574,
23377, 23526
Parekh, Bhikhu, 26897
Parekh, Hasmukhlal Thakordas, 12260, 14681, 21229
Parekh, M.T., 21686
Parekh, Manilal Chhotalal, 06504, 16800, 21927
Parel, Anthony, 12466
Parganika, B.L., 22278
Pargiter, Frederick Eden, 04045, 05809, 24491
Parida, Gurupada, 21014
Parihar, G.R., 08366
Parihar, R.R., 23200
Parikh, Balchandra, 21942
Parikh, Govardhan Dhanraj, 16499, 21095
Parikh, H.B., 21799
Parikh, Indira J., 15955
Parikh, Jivanlal Trikamlal, 05282
Parikh, Kirit S., 14265, 22785
Parikh, Narahari Dwarkadas, 10185
Parikh, P.C., 16467
Parikh, R.D., 21950
Parikh, R.T., 01736
Parikh, S.S., 15364
Parimoo, B.N., 06980
Parimoo, Ratan, 11786-7, 11814
Park, Richard Leonard, 12313, 13032, 13067, 13381, 13384,
13503, 13695, 23328, 23513, 23815, 24705, 26633
Parkash Singh, 23014
Parker, Henry, 04248, 19084
Parker, Rebecca Jane, 11548, 22986
Parker, Robert, 26300
Parkes, Joseph, 08034
Parkinson, J.R., 25318
Parmanand, 26000
Parmanand, T., 24542
Parmar, H.S., 25878
Parmar, Shyam, 02900, 02902, 16839-40, 22285-6, 23939
Parmar, Y.S., 25863-4
Parmu, R.K., 06950, 08559, 21332
Parnerkar, Y.M., 14932
Parpola, Asko, 00051, 03593, 03634, 03641-2, 03645-7,
03706, 04002
Parpola, Simo, 03634, 03642
Parrain, Philippe, 16980
Parratt, Saroj Nalini, 26596
Parrinder, Edward Geoffrey, 01474, 01772, 11322
Parry, Benita, 11884

Parry, John Horace, 07818
Parry, Jonathan P., 00791, 25885
Parry, Nevill Edward, 26620-1
Parsons, Constance E., 08175, 20483
Partap Singh, 23272
Parthasarathi, R., 19170
Parthasarathy, Gogula, 19307, 19688, 19747-8, 19764, 19829
Parthasarathy, Rangaswami, 06433, 10818, 17101, 17146
Parthasarathy, V.S., 15730
Parui, Sasanka Sekhar, 04046
Parulekar, Godavari, 20823, 21281
Parulekar, Ramchandra Vithal, 10614, 10620, 21573-5
Parvate, T.V., 21230
Parvate, Trimbak Vishnu, 09674, 09702, 21351, 21661
Parvathamma, C., 20264, 20337, 20406-7, 20439-40, 20453, 20550
Parveen, Khalida, 17788
Parveen Feroze Hassan, 10327
Parviz, Naim, 18054
Parwez, Ghulam Ahmad, 18213
Pasricha, Prem, 16394
Pastner, Carroll M., 22525, 22538, 22541
Pastner, Stephen L., 22525, 22539-41
Patankar, Mamatha, 14380
Patankar, P.G., 21529
Patankar, Pandit, 16307
Pataudi, Sher Ali Khan, Nawabzada, 17373
Patel, Ahmed M., 24421, 25343, 25482
Patel, Ambalal, 03358
Patel, Arun S., 21721, 21749
Patel, Ashvin J., 16229
Patel, B.P., 15130
Patel, Baburao, 06752, 13369
Patel, D.A., 21724
Patel, Dadubhai N., 21928
Patel, G.D., 21770
Patel, Gordhanbhai I., 10029
Patel, Govindlal Dalsukhbhai, 14958, 21266, 21692
Patel, Gunavant A., 21731
Patel, Haribhai G., 21894
Patel, Himmat, 14554
Patel, I.G., 15280
Patel, Jhaverbhai P., 16110
Patel, Kamla, 16629
Patel, Keshavlal Virdas, 19749, 21750
Patel, Kunj, 21317
Patel, M.S., 10637, 21748
Patel, Madhubhai, 21948-9
Patel, Mahendra Lal, 20889, 22186
Patel, S.D., 21816
Patel, Shantibhai Mangaldas, 21750-1, 21758
Patel, Shirish B., 21526
Patel, Surendra J., 10995, 14271
Patel, Tara, 21892
Patel, Vallabhbhai Jhaverbhai, Sardar, 10182, 10186-7, 12271
Patel, Viharidas Gopaldas, 14419
Paterson, Thomas Thomson, 03546, 03554
Pathak, D.S., 14618
Pathak, Devavrat N., 21686, 21693
Pathak, Gopal Swarup, 12860
Pathak, H.N., 14420, 21782, 22794
Pathak, Haldhar, 04154
Pathak, Lalit P., 15881
Pathak, M.C., 15388
Pathak, Madhusudan Madhavlal, 04719
Pathak, Mahesh T., 21721
Pathak, P.P., 27808
Pathak, Raghunath Prasad, 11274
Pathak, Ram Chandra, 27824-5
Pathak, S.H., 16230
Pathak, Shankar, 16124, 16294
Pathak, Sushil Madhava, 11563
Pathak, Vishuddhanand, 04116
Pathak, Vishwambhar Sharan, 00112
Pathan, Mumtaz Husain, 06927
Pathare, Rajani, 16295
Pathik, Bijai Singh, 09353
Pathik, Jyoteeshwar, 00504
Pathmanathan, S., 06133, 06141, 08067
Pathy, Jaganath, 01074
Patil, B.R., 16125
Patil, Bal, 01274
Patil, Devendrakumar Rajaram, 03435, 04047, 05577
Patil, H.S., 02326, 03062, 27443, 27651
Patil, N.P., 20338
Patil, Pandurang Chimnaji, 21214
Patil, R.K., 21255, 21783
Patil, R.L., 20274
Patil, S.K., 16973
Patil, V.T., 10152
Patkar, M.M., 04418, 04437
Patna Improvement Trust, 24184
Patnaik, Dhirendranath, 03045-6
Patnaik, Gorachand, 22318
Patnaik, K.C., 16267-8
Patnaik, Lal Mohan, 20785
Patnaik, Nityananda, 02024, 21021, 22312-4, 22337, 22364-5, 23372, 22389-91, 22400
Patnaik, Srish Chandra, 22328
Patni, R.L., 15195
Patra, A.N., 08022
Patra, Kishor Mohan, 22392, 22397
Patra, Kishori Mohan (1938-   ), 20775-96
Patra, M.K., 15100
Patra, S.C., 20786
Patra, Saral, 12001
Patro, A.P., 19185
Pattabhi Raman, N., 15671
Pattabhi Sitaramayya, Bhogaraju, 09643
Pattabhiram, M., 12946, 13440
Pattabiramin, P.Z., 01741-2, 01820
Pattanaik, Kavichandra Kalicharan, 03047
Pattanaik, Prafulla Kumar, 08378
Pattanayak, Debi Prasanna, 02345, 16644-5, 17007, 27788, 27873, 27941
Pattanshetti, C.C., 20331
Patterson, George Neilson, 13957
Patterson, Josephine E., 21359
Patterson, Maureen L.P., 20760, 21114, 21385, 21389-90, 27417, 27507-9, 27640, 27656
Patterson, Sheila, 26898
Patvardhan, Vinayak Sadashiv, 14051, 21290
Patwant Singh, 13710, 23421
Patwardhan, Achyut, 10122, 15741
Patwardhan, Chintamani Nilkant, 21590
Patwardhan, Daya, 11891
Patwardhan, Dileep, 21048
Patwardhan, Moreshwar Vishwanath, 04426, 05292, 05992
Patwardhan, P.H., 09928
Patwardhan, R.P., 08248, 09675
Patwardhan, Sunanda, 21411, 21423
Patyal, Hukam Chand, 03961
Paul, Ashit, 17220
Paul, D., 27477
Paul, Harendra Chandra, 08951, 27990
Paul, Joginder, 17059
Paul, Manomatha Nath, 06462
Paul, Rajaiah David, 16824-6, 19538
Paul, Samuel, 13803, 13896
Paul, Sharda, 13557, 13633
Paulus, Caleb R., 14178
Paustian, Paul William, 22726
Pavaskar, Madhoo G., 15421-2
Pavate, Dadappa Chintappa, 22701
Pavlov, Vladimir Ivanovich, 10917, 14043
Pawar, A.G., 20600
Pawar, S.N., 21283
Pawate, Ishtalingappa Siddharamappa, 05701
Payne, Charles Herbert, 08552
Payne, Ernest Alexander, 05852
Payne, Geoffrey K., 23407
Payne, Robert, 09883
Pe Maung Tin, 05032, 05040
Peace, M.L., 22954
Peach, J.T., 25447
Peach, William Nelson, 17774
Pearl, David, 15977, 25219
Pearse, Hugh Wodehouse, 11958
Pearson, Hugh Nicholas, 08226
Pearson, James Douglas, 26954, 27548
Pearson, Michael Naylor, 07528, 07536, 07880, 08286, 08411, 08347
Pearson, Roger, 24657
Pearson, William Winstanley, 10625
Pederson, Mathew A., 20920
Peebles, Patrick, 18592
Peeradina, Saleem, 17102
Peethambara Rao, B.T., 20300

Peggs, James, 10547
Pehrson, Robert Niez, 22542
Peiris, Edmund, 00386, 04579, 08101-2, 18820
Peiris, G.H., 18771-3
Peiris, Gerald, 18694
Peiris, H. Shelton A.T., 18963
Peiris, K.R.S., 18905
Peiris, L.L.T., 18533
Peiris, William, 18703
Peissel, Michel, 26221, 27331, 27351, 27393
Pelsaert, Francisco, 07486
Pelz, Donald Campbell, 14783
Pemberton, Robert Boileau, 25685, 26413
Pemble, John, 08326, 08979, 23446
Pendharkar, V.G., 15127
Pendse, R.G., 21558
Pendse, Shripad Narayan, 21530
Pennell, Alice Maud Sarabji, 23041
Pennell, Theodore Leighton, 23042
Penner, Hans H., 05781
Penny, Fanny Emily Farr, 08201
Penzl, Herbert, 27978-9
Percival, Peter, 02565, 27898
Percival, Robert, 08054, 18305
Pereira, A.B.M., 20495
Pereira, Jose, 01317, 02596, 06820, 21105
Pereira, Rui Gomes, 00448
Pereira, Theodore, 01048
Perera, A.D.T.E., 05621
Perera, B.J., 06118
Perera, Edward Walter, 18339
Perera, G.F., 18790
Perera, Jayantha, 18886
Perera, L.H. Horace, 00387, 18293
Perera, Lakshman S., 04238, 04370
Perera, Nanayakkarapathirage Martin, 18452
Perera, S.G., 08103-4
Periakaruppan, Ramasamy, 05422
Peries, O.S., 18696
Peringalloor, Joseph, 16801
Perlin, Frank, 08412
Perlman, Mark, 17786
Perniola, Vito, 18980
Perowne, Thomas Thomason, 19539
Perrill, Jeffrey Price, 22928
Perrin, Michel, 27274
Perry, Edward Delavan, 27803
Pershad, Madho, 23340
Perti, Rajesh Kumar, 09150
Pertold, Otaker, 03019, 19022-3
Perumal, Nilkan, 10204
Perumalil, A.C., 04606
Perumalil, H.C., 02244
Pescatello, Ann M., 07881
Peshawar. University. Board of Economic Enquiry, 23093, 23126
Peshawar. University. Dept. of Economics, 23094
Petech, Luciano, 00505, 07372, 08980
Peter, H.R.H. Prince of Greece and Denmark, 01011, 20102
Peters, Thomas, 09018
Pethe, Vasant P., 14826, 16053, 21207, 21554, 21591
Petrie, David, Sir, 10044
Petros, Prince of Greece. *See* Peter, H.R.H. ...
Petterson, Richard E., 19123
Pettigrew, Joyce, 22671, 22686
Pfaffenberger, Bryan, 01941
Pfeffer, Karl Heinz, 18188, 18236
Pfeiffer, Martin, 01869
Phadke, H.A., 00062
Phadke, Raghunath Krishna, 20669
Phadke, Yasavanta Dinakara, 21119
Phadnis, Urmila, 09381, 12064, 12202, 18390, 18441, 18448, 18471, 18498, 18560-1, 18862, 27137
Phear, John Budd, Sir, 10973
Philips, Cyril Henry, 00113, 00144, 07959, 07992, 09002, 09071, 09113, 10305, 13052, 25686, 27423
Phillips, G.E., 06305
Phillips, W.W.A., 19113
Phogat, Silak Ram, 02034
Phukan, Umananda, 25760
Phul, Raj Kumar, 07567
Phul Chand, 14527
Piantelli, Mario, 06386
Pichamuthu, Charles S., 27015
Pichholiya, K.R., 21732
Pickering, A.K., 22529
Pickett, Jarrell Waskom, 11535
Pickford, John, 06028
Pieper, J., 03167
Pieris, Paulus Edward, 08068, 08075-7, 08095-6, 18306
Pieris, Ralph, 00674, 08063, 18638, 18711, 18811, 18817, 18888, 18964
Piet, David, 11707
Piet, John H., 06524
Piggott, Stuart, 03503, 03668, 05458
Pignède, Bernard, 26239-40
Pilat, Jan, 13370
Pilcher, G., 10248
Pillai, A.P., 10981
Pillai, Govinda Krishna, 00767, 06112
Pillai, K.K., 01981, 04452, 19157
Pillai, K.S., 13117
Pillai, Kesavakurup Raman, 13711
Pillai, P. Mohanan, 13900
Pillai, Padmanabh Vijal, 04271
Pillai, S. Devadas. *See* Devadas Pillai, S.
Pillai, Velu Pillai Raman, 20009
Piḷḷai Lokācārya, 06461-2
Pillay, Kolappa Pillai Kanakasabhapathi ("K.K."), 00388, 00413, 01884, 19350
Pingle, Bhavanrav A., 02726
Pingree, David Edwin, 00247, 00284-5, 04531, 04537
Pinkerton, John, 07830
Pinto, C.D., 16817
Pinto, Marina, 12339
Pinto, Moragodage Newton, 02545
Piplai, Tapen, 24538
Pippet, G.K., 18513
Pirenne, Jacquéline, 04024
Pirzada, Syed Sharifuddin, 09813, 10336, 17298, 17322
Pischel, Richard, 05257
Pissurlencar, Panduronga S.S., 07848, 08256, 08421
Pitambar Datt, 04005
Pithawalla, Manekji Bejanji, 22457, 22471, 22530, 27230
Pitman, Emma Raymond, 10736
Pitt, Peter, 26298
Piyadassi, 01259
Piyadassi, Widurupola, Thera, 05023
Placid, Father, C.M.I., 20119
Plaeschke, Herbert, 06101
Plaeschke, Ingeborg, 06101
Planalp, Jack M., 23880, 23927
Platt, Raye Roberts, 27016, 27114
Plattner, F., 16819
Platts, John Thompson, 27826, 27829
Playfair, Archibald Lewis, 26682
Playne, Somerset S., 19139, 20246
Plott, John C., 06448
Plunkett, Frances Taft, 22088
Plunkett, Hugh Sheridan, 21995, 22008
Pochhammer, Wilhelm von, 09573
Pocock, David F., 00625, 00759, 00818, 00873, 00902, 00968, 01447, 01862, 16111, 21011, 21671, 21817, 21835-6, 21918, 26849-50, 26855, 26907
Poddar, Arabinda, 02393, 24570-1
Podder, Vishnu Prasad, 15412-3
Podipara, Placid J., 02254
Poduval, R. Vasudeva, 02858
Poffenberger, Shirley B., 21860
Poffenberger, Thomas, 21860, 21893-4
Pogson, Wredenhall Robert, 06705
Pohlman, Edward, 16308
Pokhrel, Durga, 26133
Poleman, Horace Irvin, 00011
Polk, Emily, 27261
Pollack, Oliver B., 09405
Pollock, John, 21128
Polo, Marco, 05666-8
Pomerantz, G.S., 05928
Pondicherry. Conseil supérieur, 07908
Ponette, P., 20950
Ponniah, J.S., 19407
Ponniah, S.M., 06576
Ponniah, V., 01417
Pool, John J., 00160
Poona Sarvajanik Sabha, 20692, 20704, 21282
Poonawala, Rashida, 17764
Poonen, T.I., 08141-2
Pope, Carl, 27060
Pope, George Uglow, 02553, 04491, 06313, 06591

Poplai, Sunder Lal, 12272, 13386, 13393, 14015
Popley, Herbert Arthur, 02714, 04492
Porcher, Marie-Claude, 08211, 08229
Pore, S.H., 21082
Pořizka, Vincent, 27839
Porter, George, S.J., 11549
Porter, Richard C., 17900
Portugal. Agência Geral do Ultramar, 07849
Portugal. National Secretariat for Information, 21056
Portugal. Treaties, etc., 07857
Porwal, L.S., 22023
Porwal, S.K., 22067
Possehl, Gregory L., 03525, 03594, 03605, 03656
Postans, Thomas, 22458
Potdar, K.R., 03866
Potdar, Datto Vaman, Mahamahopadhyaya, 27193
Pothacamury, Thomas, Archbishop, 16818
Pothan, S.G., 20120
Pott, Janet, 20473
Pott, Pieter Hendrik, 01599
Potter, David C., 09191, 12620, 12634, 12807, 12955, 22018
Potter, Karl H., 01105, 01356, 01365, 01384, 04857, 06342
Pottinger, Henry, Sir, 22434
Potts, Eli Daniel, 08960, 09066
Pouchepadass, Jacques, 09050, 23969-70, 24094
Poullada, Leon B., 23077
Poulose, K. Thomas, 16093
Poulose, T.T., 12002, 13781, 26435
Powell, A.A., 11460
Powell, Geoffrey, 18307
Power, Paul F., 09920, 09947, 13733, 13753, 15360
Powers, Harold Stone, 02693, 02756, 02833, 02871
Prabartak Samgha, 24809
Prabha, Krishna, 22890
Prabhakar, M.S., 25713
Prabhakar, Manohar, 00466, 08462
Prabhakar Singh, 16426
Prabhakara Sastri, J., 05978
Prabhavalkar, B.H., 21494
Prabhavananda, Swami, 03825, 03977, 04668, 04820, 05765, 06359
Prabhu, K. Sanjiva, 03013
Prabhu, Pandhari Nath, 00736
Prachand, S.L.M., 13090
Pradhan, Bina, 26278
Pradhan, G.P., 09703, 21375
Pradhan, G.S., 26309
Pradhan, I.K., 26186
Pradhan, Janardan S., 26048
Pradhan, Krishna Prasad, 26030
Pradhan, Mahesh Chandra, 00661, 23740
Pradhan, Nagendra Mani, 28012
Pradhan, Paras Mani, 26344-6, 28012
Pradhan, Prachanda Prasad, 25983, 26031, 26134
Pradhan, R.G., 10850
Pradhan, S., 14902
Pradhan, S.N., 17237
Pradhan, S.V., 11916
Pradhan, Sita Nath, 03785
Pradhan, Vithal Ganesh, 06762
Pragwat, R.B., 05140
Praja Socialist Party, 13181-2
Prajnanananda, Swami, 01179, 01406, 02715, 02727-30, 02741, 11352
Prakasa, Sri, 11365
Prakasa Rao, V.L.S., 19840, 20461, 20474, 23605
Prakash, Buddha, 00199, 00358, 00517, 03606, 03756, 03791, 04162, 04174, 06935, 07073, 27257
Prakash, Hari, 24060
Prakash, Ishwar, 07628, 27200
Prakash, Om, 00843, 04289, 05757, 08857-8, 08919, 15226, 16902
Prakash, Prem, 23519
Prakash, Satya (1905-), 00259, 04069, 05736
Prakash, Satya, 16297
Prakash Rao, V.L.S. *See* Prakasa Rao, V.L.S.
Prakash Singh, 27332, 27339
Pramanik, P., 01038
Prananatha, Vidyalankara, 04356
Pranavananda, Swami, 25956
Prasad, Akhowri Braj Ballav, 07011
Prasad, Amba, 10425, 15429
Prasad, Awadhesh, 15055, 24022, 24162
Prasad, Ayodhya, 24116, 24163, 27269
Prasad, B.K., 16953
Prasad, Beni, 04272, 07487, 10123
Prasad, Bhagwan, 23700
Prasad, Bindeshwari, 00518
Prasad, Bisheshwar, 08758, 09065, 09389-91, 10400
Prasad, Bishwanath, 12635
Prasad, Brahmanand, 14688
Prasad, Brajkishore, 13597
Prasad, Chandi, 16183
Prasad, Chandra Shekhar, 05024
Prasad, D.N., 13866
Prasad, Dharmendra, 06282
Prasad, Dhirendra Mohan, 18562-3
Prasad, Dineshwar, 20967
Prasad, G.K., 12652
Prasad, Gangeshwar, 23521
Prasad, Hanuman, 23882
Prasad, Hari Kishore, 04113
Prasad, Harishchandra, 24230a
Prasad, Ishwari, 05693, 07052, 07421, 07432, 07442, 07462, 09780, 25963
Prasad, Jai Shankar, 11618-9
Prasad, Jwala, 01418
Prasad, K.M., 13244
Prasad, Kedarnath, 15162, 24041, 24117
Prasad, Mahadeva, 09948
Prasad, Mantrini, 05180
Prasad, Narmadeshwar, 00746, 15031, 20897, 24143
Prasad, Nawal Kishore, 12477
Prasad, Onkar, 02742
Prasad, Parmanand, 24055
Prasad, Prakash Charan, 04564
Prasad, R., 23365, 24003
Prasad, R.K., 24203
Prasad, Rajendra. *See* Rajendra Prasad
Prasad, Rajeshwar, 08908, 22917
Prasad, Rajiva Nain, 08372
Prasad, Ram Chandra, 07949, 13002, 16754, 24004, 24019
Prasad, Ramayan, 22175
Prasad, S. Benjamin, 15264
Prasad, S.N., 05393
Prasad, Saileshwar, 20898
Prasad, Sri Nandan, 00114, 09370, 12722, 26989
Prasad, Umesh, 23564
Prasad, Vishnu, 24020
Prasad Rao, C.R., 19741
Prasada Rao, B., 19764
Prasada Rao, N., 14980
Prasada Rao, P.D.P., 11137
Prasanna Kumar, A., 19641
Prasannan, R., 19953
Prashad, Baini, 07397
Prashad, Ganesh, 13372
Prashant Bhushan, 13493
Prasher, Ram Gopal, 16921
Pratap, D. Rabinandan, 19812
Prater, Stanley Henry, 27039
Pratt, James Bissett, 01228
Praval, K.C., 12721
Pravir Chandra Bhanjdeo Katatiya, Maharaja of Bastar, 22176
Prebish, Charles S., 01261, 04940, 04948, 04954, 04982
Prem, Dhani R., 26899
Prem Vedant, Swami. *See* Hansen, Jan
Premakumar, 02994
Prematilleke, Leelananda, 00389, 06169
Premchand (1880-1936), 11609-14
Premchand, A., 12808, 14505
Premi, Mahendra Kumar, 16410, 27748
Presidency College, Calcutta, 24849
Presler, Franklin Anderson, 19521-2
Presler, Henry H., 01100, 01870, 01913, 21424
Press in India, 27592
Press Institute of India, 16855, 16875
Preston, James John, 22401-2
Price, David, 07481
Price, H.B., 26113
Price, James Cattarall, 24257
Price, John Frederick, Sir, 07926, 11972
Price, Ralph B., 14331
Prichard, Iltudus Thomas, 09481, 11946
Prindle, Peter H., 26168, 26258-63
Prinsep, Henry Thoby, 09108, 22574
Prinsep, James, 00035
Priolkar, Anant Kakba, 07651, 08336

Prior, L.F. Loveday, 27245
Pritam, A., 17018
Pritam Singh, 02219, 16538, 22753, 23006
Pritchett, Frances W., 02530, 07707
Prithipal, D., 06334
Proctor, Raja, 19079
Proctor, Robert Chelvathurai, 06609
Progress of education in India; quinquennial review, 10563
Progressive Painters' Association, 17195
Pruscha, Carl, 26291
Przyluski, Jean, 01130, 01646, 04914, 04949, 04960
Pudaite, Rochunga, 26622
Pugh, R.B., 27549
Puligandla, R., 01306
Pulla Reddi, O., 12666
Pullapilly, Cyriac K., 20108
Pulparampil, John K., 17250, 21694
Pumphrey, Caroline W., 22283
Punalekar, S.P., 16097
Punekar, S.D., 11138, 15621, 15653, 21461-2, 21541, 21561
Punekar, Vijaya Bhaskar, 20475, 20824
Punit, A.E., 15008
Punjab. Board of Economic Enquiry, 22853
Punjab. Education Dept. Punjab University Enquiry Committee, 22929
Punjab, India. Agricultural Census Wing, 22772
Punjab, India. Board of Economic Inquiry, 22786, 22891
Punjab, India. Community Development Organisation, 22868
Punjab, India. Economic and Statistical Organisation, 22754-5, 22802, 22869
Punjab, India. Elections Dept., 22696-7
Punjab, India. Evaluation Committee on Welfare, 22830
Punjab, India. Pay Commission, 22702
Punjab, India. Planning Dept., 22796
Punjab, Pakistan. Bureau of Education, 22937
Punjab, Pakistan. Court of Enquiry ... Punjab Disturbances of 1953, 18232
Punjab University, Pakistan. Institute of Education and Research, 18147-51
Puran Singh, 02421, 08596, 22972
Purani, Ambalal Balkrishna, 11775
Puranik, S.N., 12442
Purchas, Samuel, 07831
Purdom, C.B., 16752
Puri, Baij Nath, 00180, 00190, 00536, 04025, 04035, 04187-8, 04273, 04371, 04522, 04950, 07012
Puri, Balraj, 13504, 13598, 15856, 23179, 23186, 23353
Puri, Geeta, 23329
Puri, Rajinder, 13112
Puri, Shashi Lata, 21957
Purkayastha, Kshetra M., 24887
Purnaiya, R., 06477
Purnalingam Pillai, M.S., 04503
Purohit, Swami, 02226, 03978
Purohit, B.R., 09691, 22164-5
Purohit, M.C., 22019
Purushothaman, E.N., 19898
Purwar, Vijaya Lakshmi, 23527
Pusalker, Achyut Dattatraya, 04611, 05316, 05747, 21504
Pushpendra Kumar, 05853
Pushpindar Singh, 12723
Puthenkalam, J., 20077-8
Puthnangady, Paul, 01049
Puttappa, K. Venkatappa Gowda, 20575
Puttaswamaiah, K., 14893, 15504, 15564, 20290-1
Putte Gowda, K., 20502
Pyarelal. *See* Nair, Pyarelal
Pyatt, Graham, 18633
Pylee, Moolamattom Varkey, 12314, 12342, 15636, 19966
Pyrard de Laval, François, 07912
Pyyappan, 01855

Qadeer, Mohammad A., 17996
Qadir, Abdul, Sir, 11632
Qadir, M.A.A., 07367
Qadir, S.A., 25536
al-Qadir, S.M. Kamil, 22550
Qadri, Sayyid Ahmad-ullah, 08241
Qaisar, A. Jan, 07615, 07620-1
Qaiser Ali Khan, 18128
Qaiyum, Abdul, 23066
Qamar Rais, 11578
Qamaruddin, 07128
Qamarul Ahsan, Syed, 17434
Qanungo, Kalika Ranjan, 00467, 07463-4, 07509, 08759
Qanungo, Sudhindra Nath, 07797, 08312
Qazi, M.A., 27458
Qeyamuddin, Ahmad, 08780
Quackenbos, George Payn, 06014, 06067
Quaderi, Fazlul Quader, 12155
Quadir, C.A., 18238
Quasem, Mohammad Abul, 25396
Quddus, Mohammed, 14677
Quddus, Syed Abdul, 18172
Quentric, Martine, 23120
Queyroz, Fernao de, 08078
Quraishi, M.A., 21902
Quraishi, Mansooruddin (1914-), 08400
Quraishi, Mansooruddin A. (1922-), 06799
Quraishi, Waheed, 02628
Quraishi, Zaheer Masood, 12561-2, 13291-2, 13446, 23201
Quraishi, Salma Mustafa, 23130
Qureshi, Aijaz Ahmad, 08680, 22479
Qureshi, Anwar Iqbal, 17790, 17820, 17875, 19722
Qureshi, Ishtiaq Hussain, 00181, 02273, 02281, 07063, 07476, 07537, 07659, 09506, 10348, 11461, 17407-8, 18084, 18155
Qureshi, Jamil A., 22884
Qureshi, Khalida, 17563, 17674, 17758-9
Qureshi, M.A., 14290
Qureshi, M. Anwar A., 23095
Qureshi, M. Aslam, 17675, 17752
Qureshi, M.H.K., 17056
Qureshi, M. Naeem, 10004
Qureshi, M. Toaha, 22480
Qureshi, Mahmud Shah, 24337
Qureshi, Regula, 02885-7, 11639
Qureshi, S.A., 17618
Qureshi, Saleem M.M., 17415, 17452, 17482, 23078
Qureshi, Sarfaraz Khan, 17890

Rabel, Lili, 26704
Rabitoy, Neil, 08383, 08422, 20699-700
Rabra, R.C., 22887
Radcliffe-Brown, Alfred Reginald, 26733
Radhakrishna, K.S., 12145
Radhakrishna, P., 00299
Radhakrishna Rao, Calyampudi, 24419
Radhakrishna Sarma, Challa, 02582-3, 06601
Radhakrishna Sarma, Mukkamala, 06663-6
Radhakrishnamurti, Baddepudi, 16856
Radhakrishnan, N., 12526, 15827
Radhakrishnan, R., 27869
Radhakrishnan, Sarvepalli, Sir, 01157, 01172, 01187, 01318, 01347-8, 01529, 03979, 03990, 04669, 04871, 04994, 06401, 09019, 11437-9, 12577-8, 16480, 25014
Radhu, G.M., 17721
Radwan, Ann Bos, 07901, 08348
Raeside, Ian Matthew Paton, 06774-5, 21642-3
Rafiqi, Abdul Qaiyum, 06991
Rafique Afzal, M., 10349
Rafiqur Rahman, A.T., 25245
Rafiuddin, 11506
Ragam, V.R., 02072
Raghava Aiyangar, M., 02566
Raghava Rao, D.V., 20454
Raghava Rao, G., 12237, 12264, 21238
Raghavachar, S.S., 06418-20, 06434, 06449, 06484
Raghavachariar, Navalpakkam R., 00936
Raghavacharyulu, Dhupaty V.K., 11720
Raghavaiah, Y., 14486
Raghavan, G.N.S., 26980
Raghavan, K., 16565
Raghavan, Manayatt Dharmadam, 00390, 02981, 03020-1, 03374, 18499, 18840, 18855, 27138
Raghavan, Thevur Subramanya, 19556
Raghavan, Venkataram, 00012-3, 00019, 00048, 00052-5, 00348, 00649, 00681, 01221, 01831, 02409, 02413, 02478, 02516, 02681, 02795, 03879, 03915, 04720-3, 04782, 04796, 05264, 05287, 05836, 05970, 06003, 17065-6
Raghavan, V.K.S.N., 06455
Raghavan Pillai, K., 05226
Raghavender Rao, J.V., 19854
Raghavendra, Swami, 08209
Raghavendra Rao, K., 11754, 21065
Raghavendracharya, H.N., 06471
Raghaviah, V., 01086-7, 15795, 19813
Raghavulu, C.V., 19657
Raghu Rai, 27255

Raghu Ram, N.V., 13118
Raghu Singh, 17948
Raghu Vira, 02346
Raghubir Singh (1908-), 10283
Raghubir Singh, 27275
Raghubir Sinh (1908-), 08367
Raghunadha Rao, L., 19750
Raghunadha Rao, P., 19607, 26359, 26383
Raghunath Ram, 17747
Raghunatha Rao, P., 19608
Raghunathan, N., 01419, 05766
Raghuvanshi, V.P.S., 07634, 07641, 09542
Raghuvira, 00353, 12496
Ragini Devi, 02923-4
Raha, Kironmoy, 24951
Raha, Manis Kumar, 20985, 24639-40
Rahamathulla, Bellary, 14013
Rahbar, Hans Raj, 11606
Raheja, Bhagwan Dass, 16094, 23422
Rahi, Krishin, 08681
Rahim, A., 07332-3
Rahim, A.M.A., 17856, 25299-30
Rahim, Muhammad Abdur, 06239, 06572, 07203, 07582, 08368, 08952, 09128, 24338
Rahim, Syed A., 25391, 25397-8, 25426, 25537
Rahim, Syed Bazlur, 25192
Rahimtoola, Ibrahim, 11156
Rahman, A., 00345
Rahman, A.T.R., 25188, 25227
Rahman, Abdur, 17240, 17251, 17260-1, 17265
Rahman, Choudhury Shamsur, 27306
Rahman, Fazlur, 18173
Rahman, Fazlur (1919-), 02267, 10328, 11507, 18110, 17409, 17600, 18174, 18214-5
Rahman, Habibur, 17637
Rahman, I.A., 18260
Rahman, M.A., 17361
Rahman, M. Akhlaqur, 18016, 18050, 18071
Rahman, M. Anisur, 17722
Rahman, M. Fazlur, 24865
Rahman, M.L., 07696
Rahman, M. Mizanur, 25550, 25622
Rahman, M. Mustafizur, 25642
Rahman, Mahfoozur, 23222
Rahman, Mahmoodur, 25427
Rahman, Matiur, 09814
Rahman, Muhammad Habibur, 00615
Rahman, Mofakhkhar, 25217
Rahman, Mohammad Ataur, 17728
Rahman, Mohammed Mahafoozur, 13452, 13754
Rahman, Mohammad Mizanur, 25484
Rahman, Motior, 25353
Rahman, Muhammad Anisur, 25311
Rahman, Munibur, 18274
Rahman, Mushtaqur, 22810, 27115, 27231
Rahman, Pares Islam Syed Mustafizur, 07801
Rahman, Qamrun, 09216
Rahman, R., 11462
Rahman, S., 25278
Rahman, Saulat, 16954
Rahman, Shamsur, 25651
Rahman, Sultan Hafeez, 25262
Rahman, Syed Sabahuddin Abdur, 07697
Rahman, Syed Zillur, 25676
Rahmat ʿAlī, Choudhary, 10329-31
Rahul, Ram, 25843, 26414
Rahula, Telwatte, 04904
Rahula, Walpola, 01229, 01246, 05043, 05089, 05113, 19001
Rai, Binay Kumar, 01099, 24069
Rai, Dhanpat, 27690
Rai, G.K., 04390
Rai, Hameed Ali Khan, 12215, 17312, 17768
Rai, Haridwar, 09217, 12621, 12956-9, 13244, 23985-6, 24021-3
Rai, Jamal, 04523
Rai, Navin Kumar, 26286
Rai, Satya M., 22664
Rai Chowdhuri, Satyabrata, 10036
Raikar, Yashavant Anant, 00170, 06779
Raikes, Charles, 09482, 23452
Raikes, Robert L., 03526, 03586-7, 03654, 03657-60
Raina, A.N., 23249, 27232
Raina, B.L., 16282, 23883
Raina, S.M.N., 12861
Raina, Trailokinath, 23250
Rais, Jon P., 13231
Rais, Rasul Bux, 17740
Raitsin, L., 13995
Raizada, Harish, 17125
Raizada, M.B., 27043
Raizada, R.K., 16326
Raj, Arumai Besant Creeper, 15239
Raj, J.S., 14620
Raj, Jagdish, 09522, 23639-40
Raj, Kakkadan Nandanath, 01573, 14381, 14459, 14464, 14487, 14650, 14959, 15081, 15505, 16500, 22787
Raj, Prakash A., 26001, 26187, 27406
Raj Gopal, S., 27429-32
Raj Krishna, 14825, 14964, 14979, 22734, 22788
Raj Singh, 23315
Raja, C.K.N., 12359
Raja, Irfan-ur-Rehman, 17335
Raja Ram, 09852
Rajadhyaksha, G.S., 15451, 16870
Rajadhyaksha, N.D, 21174
Rajagopal, M.V., 16431, 19865
Rajagopala Ayyangar, M.R., 06465-6
Rajagopala Chariar, T., 06298
Rajagopala Iyengar, T.S., 12770, 12831
Rajagopala Rao, Narayanamurthy, 20301-2
Rajagopalachari, Chakravarti, 04493, 04632, 04707, 06577, 10205-6, 12497
Rajagopalan, C., 21512-3, 22846, 25879
Rajagopalan, Subrahmanya, 08337
Rajagopalan, T.R., 01947
Rajagopalan, V., 06299
Rajaguru, Satyanarayan, 06699
Rajaguru, Sharad Narahar, 03677
Rajalakshmi, C.R., 20152
Rajamanickam, Savarimuthu, 08227
Rajamanickkam Pillai, Manickkam Pillai, 06515
Rajamanikkam, M., 04398, 04741
Rajamannar, P.V., 19231
Rajan, M.A.S., 20339
Rajan, Mannaraswamighala Sreeranga, 10012, 12074, 12105, 12196, 13734, 13755, 14067-8
Rajan, Mohini, 19628
Rajan, R., 22195
Rajan, T.N., 02694
Rajan, V.N., 16137
Rajan Pillai, C.V., 27709
Rajanayagam, M.J.L., 18534
Rajaneesh, Acharya, 16755
Rajannan, Busnagi, 02356
Rajapurohit, A.R., 20455
Rajapurohit, B.B., 27892
Rajaram, S., 27874
Rajaraththinam, A., 18856
Rajaratnam, S., 18713, 18724
Rajasekhariah, Avaragere Math, 10786, 15227, 21065
Rajasthan. Administrative Reforms Committee, 21975
Rajasthan. Bureau of Statistics, 21971
Rajasthan Chamber of Commerce and Industry, 22059
Rajasthan. Demographic and Evaluation Cell, 20840
Rajasthan. Directorate of Economics and Statistics, 22020, 22063, 27752
Rajasthan. Directorate of Education, 22136
Rajasthan. Directorate of Industries and Civil Supplies, 22057, 22064
Rajasthan. Directorate of Public Relations, 22050
Rajasthan. Education Dept., 22137
Rajasthan. Evaluation Organisation, 22112
Rajasthan. Khudkasht Enquiry Committee, 22051
Rajasthan. Panchayati Raj Study Team, 21987
Rajasthan. State Archives, 08373
Rajasthan State Industrial and Mineral Development Corporation, 22060
Rajasthan. State Land Commission, 22052
Rajasthan. State Primary Education Committee, 22138
Rajasthan. Town Planning Dept., 22125
Rajasthan. University. Dept. of Adult Education, 22139
Rajasthan. Zamindari Abolition Committee, 22053
Rajayyan, K., 00414, 08143, 08152-5, 08189
Rajbahak, Ram Prasad, 26143
Rajbhandari, Bharat Lall, 26095
Raje, Sudhakar, 13276-7
Rajeke, Barakat Ahmad, 11526
Rajendra, M., 18747
Rajendra Prasad, 09903, 10350, 12569-73, 23971
Rajendra Prasad, B., 03383

Rajendra Ram, 07379
Rajendra Singh, 04069, 09297, 12724, 23660
Rajendra Singh, K., 12003-4
Rajendran, G., 20109
Rajendran, N., 08144
Rajeśvararāv, A.V., 11583
Rajeswara Rao, C., 13505, 19689
Rajinder Singh, 23015
Rajkhowa, Banudhar, 25812
Rajkumar, Nagoji Vasudev, 13162, 13724, 26748
Rajpurohit, Jaithirth, 19119
Rajput, A.B., 09815, 23121, 25511-2, 27104
Rajput, P., 22672
Rajput, Pam, 12321
Rajsekhar Reddy, N., 13220
Rajshahi. University. Dept. of Economics, 25554
Raju, D.M., 19709
Raju, K.N.M., 20278, 20516
Raju, Poolla Tirupati, 01307, 01339, 01357, 01385, 01530, 02584
Raju, S.V., 13550
Raju, Vadrevu Bhadir, 12324
Rakhral, K.R., 22040
Rakshit, Gangadhar, 14465
Rakshit, Hirendra K., 00710-1
Raleigh, T., 10896
Ram, Eric R., 21567
Ram, J.K., 26908
Ram, Mohan. *See* Mohan Ram
Ram, Jagjivan, 13643
Ram, N., 19186, 19209
Ram, N.V. Raghu, 14189
Ram, Pars, 23858
Ram, Sadhu, 00094, 27618
Ram, Vani, 02716
Ram Avtar, 02796, 02805, 02847
Ram Chander, 23293
Ram Chandra, Guru, 23929
Ram Gopal, 02925, 02946, 02952, 08877, 09041, 09090, 09574, 09704, 09781, 12478, 13938
Ram Krishna, Lajwanti, 08686
Ram Kumar, 17221
Ram Reddy, Gaddam, 12712, 13003, 19667, 19690, 19705, 19714, 19718
Rama, G. Dasaradha, 19688
Rama, K.G., 19456, 19879
Rama, Swami (1903-1972), 02227
Rama, Swami (1925-), 02228
Rama Rao, Bhagavatam, 00300
Rama Rao, Damerla, 11827
Rama Rao, G., 14132
Rama Rao, K., 10831
Rama Rao, M., 01952, 04225, 06227, 06655
Rama Rao, Maremanda, 06181
Rama Rao, S., 12938, 20476
Rama Rao, T.P., 22140
Rama Rao, T.S., 12937, 15748
Rama Rau, Dhanwanthi, 16166
Rama Sastri, B.V., 16252
Rama Sharma, M.H., 06228
Ramābāī Sarasvatī, Paṇḍitā, 21367-8
Rāmacandra Kaulācāra, 06911
Ramachandra Dikshitar, V.R., 03520, 03726, 04119, 04155, 04344, 04494, 05439, 05748, 05806, 05821, 06286, 06306
Ramachandra Raj, G., 20052, 20079, 20093
Ramachandra Rao, Basavarasu, 11173-4, 21231
Ramachandra Rao, Bommatapalli, 17154
Ramachandra Rao, C.V., 06700
Ramachandra Rao, P.R., 05512, 11789, 17203
Ramachandra Rao, Saligrama Krishna, 01885, 05863, 05929
Ramachandra Rao, V., 00320
Ramachandran, C.E., 05433
Ramachandran, G., 09921, 16569
Ramachandran, K., 02872
Ramachandran, Kattalai Subrahmanyayyar, 02381, 03592, 03707-8, 03763
Ramachandran, K.V., 14170
Ramachandran, L., 23311
Ramachandran, N., 18660, 18714
Ramachandran, P., 16146, 21318, 21534-6, 21542, 21561
Ramachandran, R., 19292
Ramachandran, S.P., 01957
Ramachandran, T.N., 05513, 06625, 06645
Ramachandran, T.P., 01407, 06485
Ramachandran, Velandai Gopalayyar, 12622
Ramachandran Nair, K., 20053
Ramachandrasekhara Rao, R.V., 12403
Ramachandriah, N.S., 01914, 27167
Ramadas, R., 19439
Rāmadāsa, 08449
Ramakant, 26062, 26071, 26081
Ramakrishna, 11306-7
Ramakrishna Aiyer, Viravavallur Gopalier, 01964
Ramakrishna Rao, Adapa, 19894
Ramakrishna Rao, K.B., 04814, 04918
Ramakrishna Reddy, T., 14119
Ramakrishnan, K.C., 19285
Ramakrishnan, R., 00438, 20240
Ramakrishnan, V., 01340
Ramakrishnan Nair, R., 19954-5, 19967
Ramakrishnananda, Swami, 06435
Ramalinga, Swami, 19504
Ramalinga Reddy, D., 06229
Ramalingaswami, Prabha, 15698
Ramalingeswara Rao, T., 01982-3
Ramamurthy, M., 19457
Ramamurthy, S.R., 19857
Ramamurty, 06210
Ramamurty, Dharmala, 02806
Raman, A., 15127
Raman, K.V., 05148
Raman, Sunder, 13525
Raman Nayar, R., 16468
Raman Rao, Ajjarapu Venkata, 13004, 15649, 15662, 19723
Raman Unni, K., 15168, 20103, 20156
Ramana, Maharshi, 11413-4, 11417
Ramana, Duvvuri V., 11175, 14210
Ramana, H.S., 00099
Ramana, K.V., 19688
Ramana Rao, M.V., 13163
Ramana Rao, S.V., 02991
Ramanadham, Venkata Vemuri, 15240, 15248-9, 19734
Ramanamma, Angara, 21555
Ramananda Bharati, Swami. *See* Sastry, Kadayam Ramachandra Ramabhadra
Ramananda Tirtha, Swami, 19646
Ramanathan, Gopalakrishna, 10638, 12653
Ramanathan, Ponnambalam, 18340
Ramanathan, S., 19383-4
Ramanathan, Subrahmanya, 05443
Ramanathan, V., 14969
Ramani, Hashoo Kewal, 22511
Ramani, R., 03003
Ramanna, R., 15374
Rāmānuja, 06415-25
Ramanuja Rao, Devulapalli, 19906
Ramanujachari, K., 10752
Ramanujachariar, C., 19899
Ramanujam, B.V., 04768
Ramanujam, G., 11139
Ramanujam, Kummattithidal Santhanam, 19210, 19229
Ramanujam, P.S., 04858
Ramanujan, A.K., 02334, 05423, 05428, 06550, 06596, 07309, 19337
Rāmaprasāda Sena, 08936-8
Ramaraju, B., 19910-1
Ramareddi, Padala, 19713
Ramasubban, Radhika, 26530
Ramasubramanian, V., 01493, 02907
Ramaswami, N.S., 06626
Ramaswami, S., 16331
Ramaswami Aiyar, Chetpat Pattabhirama, Sir, 10598, 11366, 19931
Ramaswami Aiyar, M.S., 02695
Ramaswami Naicker, E.V., 04724
Ramaswami Sastri, K.S., 00415, 02748, 02953, 11421
Ramaswamy, E.A., 00637, 14180, 15622, 15672-4, 19330-1
Ramaswamy, Suhasini, 12533
Ramaswamy, Thanu, 15228
Ramaswamy, Tumkur Narasimhiah, 04297
Ramaswamy, Uma, 19797-8
Ramaswamy Naidu, Yenuga, 19715
Rambousek, Walter Heinrich, 20441
Ramchandani, Ram R., 26818, 26868
Ramdev, Joginder Singh, 08658
Ramesan, N., 00028, 01953, 06667
Ramesh, K.V., 00437, 02372
Rameshwar Rao, Shanta, 07312
Rami Reddy, V., 03682, 03709
Ramkrishna Rao, T., 19742

Ramkrishnan, E.M., 02859
Rammohun Roy, Raja, 03809, 11228, 11230-1
Ramnath Aiyer, S., 19929
Rampal Singh, Sir, 23932
Ramsaran, John A., 07090
Ramsbotham, Richard Bury, 08901
Ramsden, A.R., 25731
Ramu, G.N., 00963, 15722, 20420-2, 20464
Ramunny, Murkot, 27168
Ramusack, Barbara N., 09382-3, 22608-9
Rana, A.P., 13735
Rana, Bhola Bikrum, 26043
Rana, Daman Shumser Jang Bahadur, 26002
Rana, Gabriel, 28013
Rana, Ina Shumshere, 27394
Rana, M.B., 15213
Rana, Mahendra Singh, 09080, 12288
Rana, Narendra Singh, 23318
Rana, Netra Rajya Laxmi, 08981
Rana, Pashupati Shumshere Jung Bahadur, 26040, 26115-6, 27368
Rana, Pramode Shamshere Jung Bahadur, 25964
Rana, Pudma Jung Bahadur, 25965
Rana, Ratna S.J.B., 26114, 26160
Rana, Satya Paul, 13934
Rana, Swadesh, 14120
Ranade, Ganesh Hari, 02825-6
Ranade, Mahadev Govind, 08249, 08257, 10874, 11223, 21352
Ranade, N.B., 27911
Ranade, Pandharinatha Vishnupanta, 06821
Ranade, Ramabai, 21353
Ranade, Ramchandra Dattatraya, 01296, 03991, 04692, 06335, 06493, 06753, 07091, 21616
Ranade, S.N., 15545, 16115
Ranade, Vinayak Govind, 20588-9, 21463
Ranadive, Bhalchandra Trimbak, 14427, 20761
Ranadive, J.S., 21489
Ranadive, K.R., 14218
Ranadive, Vimal, 15544
Ranasinge, Douglas D., 18346
Ranasingha, Arthur, Sir, 18426
Ranasinghe, H., 18910
Ranasinghe, W., 18583
Ranawake, Edwin, 27857
Ranbhise, N.P., 21215
Ranbir Singh, 23267
Ranbir Singh, Sardar, 10284
Ranchi Improvement Trust, 24195
Randhawa, Mohindar Singh, 01637, 03275, 08500, 08711, 08715-7, 08726-30, 08747-8, 10505, 14742, 14803, 22773, 22870, 27040, 27333, 27352
Randle, Herbert Niel, 04859
Ranga, N.G., 11007, 13300, 19642
Ranga Ayengar, K., 06464
Ranga Rao, K., 19799
Ranga Rao, M., 19854
Rangacarya, M., 05737
Rangachar, S., 05317
Rangachari, K., 07926, 19355
Rangacharya, Adya, 02938, 05273, 05298, 17036
Rangacharya, Matur, 06421
Rangacharya, V., 06456
Rangan, K., 27873
Ranganath, H.K., 02939
Ranganathan, Edwina, 02966
Ranganathan, Padma, 05366
Ranganathan, Shiyali Ramamrita, 10670, 16922-4, 27459
Ranganathananda, Swami, 16718
Rangarajan, V., 19322, 24988
Rangaramanuja Ayyangar Raghunathswami, 02860, 02875
Rangasami, Amrita. *See* Rangasami, Amritha
Rangasami, Amritha, 26609, 25740
Rangaswami, A., 07917
Rangaswami Aiyangar, K.V., 04360
Range, Willard, 13736
Rangnath, 23552
Rangnekar, D.K., 14078
Rangnekar, S.B., 22803
Rangoonwalla, Firoze, 16962-3, 16981-2
Ranjit Singh, 14916
Rankin, George C., 09254
Ranking, George S.A., 07407, 24850
Ranney, David C., 24738
Rao, Amiya, 05318, 13119, 13371, 13542
Rao, B.G., 05318, 13119, 13371, 13542
Rao, B.S.R., 14619
Rao, Bachcha Prasad, 19783, 19844
Rao, C.R., 14131
Rao, C.R.M., 15727
Rao, C.S.S., 15069
Rao, D.V.R., 23408, 23423
Rao, G.N., 19751
Rao, G.R., 19265
Rao, G.R.S., 19691
Rao, Jagannath, 13328, 16344
Rao, K.L., 14885
Rao, K.V., 22297
Rao, K.V.N., 19692
Rao, Kamala, 21541
Rao, Kanatur Bhaskara, 11905
Rao, Karanam Ramachandra, 17135
Rao, M.B., 09623, 10061
Rao, M.C.R., 03920
Rao, M.J., 13549
Rao, M.L., 16477
Rao, M.R., 23890-1
Rao, M.S.A., 12733, 14360, 15723-5, 16061, 20064, 20110, 23378
Rao, M.S.V., 23409, 24799
Rao, M. Shama, 20231
Rao, M.U., 21189
Rao, N.V., 15362
Rao, P.R., 26375
Rao, Pattadakal Venkanna Raghavendra, 12667, 13765
Rao, R.P., 08338, 13453
Rao, R.V., 10639, 16600
Rao, Rampalli Visweswar, 15163-6, 15328, 19735
Rao, Ranga, 26583
Rao, S.B., 15469, 21337
Rao, S.K., 14884
Rao, S.R., 05586, 06656
Rao, Shikaripur Ranganatha, 03626, 03635
Rao, Sudha V., 14091
Rao, T.S., 24201
Rao, T.V., 15329, 16477
Rao, T.V.S., 19765, 20027
Rao, V.D., 07443
Rao, V.G., 14586, 20324
Rao, V.M., 21560
Rao, Vasant D., 10240, 21146
Rao, Vijendra Kasturi Ranga Varadaraja, 10894, 11176, 11331, 12479, 13310, 13378, 13876, 14211, 14361, 14428, 14651, 15080, 15092, 20292, 23394, 25301
Raper, Arthur F., 25428
Raphael, R., 03124, 11856
Raphy, Sabeena, 02982
Rapson, Edward James, 04102
Rasa, Mian Sayed Rasul, 17589
Rasaputram, Warnasena, 18593, 18617
Rashid, A., 05726, 07079
Rashid, Abdul, 17362
Rashid, Khwaja Abdul, 11508, 18216
Rashid, Mohammad Harunur, 07178, 24945, 25652
Rashid-al-Din Tabib, 05640
Rashiduzzaman, M., 10219, 17313, 17459-61, 17536, 17564, 17638-9, 17655, 25204
Rashtriya Panchang, 27464
Rashtriya Swayamsevak Sangh, 25972
Rastogi, J.L., 23683
Rastogi, Krishna Gopal, 16637
Rastogi, Navjivan, 06961-2
Rastogi, P.N., 00831, 23553, 23791
Rastogi, Satish Kumar, 13156
Rastogi, T.N., 11123, 15470
Rasul, Mohammad Abdullah, 11008
Ratan, Ram, 23367
Ratanjankar, S.N., 02761, 02790, 02848
Rath, Nilakantha, 14051, 14277, 22339
Rath, R., 22384
Rath, Radhanath, 20683, 20797
Rath, S.N., 22305, 22381
Rath, Sharda, 16134
Rath, Vimal, 14126, 27619
Ratha, S.N., 25802
Ratha, Satyanarayana, 01094
Rathore, Laxman Singh, 26415
Ratnam, R., 19252
Ratnam, S., 15216
Ratnapala, Nandasena, 18915
Ratnasabapathy, M., 00387

Ratnaswami, Subramaniam, 04206
Ratnatunga, Manel, 19085
Ratnawat, B.P., 22205
Ratnaweera, D. de S., 18740-1, 18748
Rattan, Ram, 09949
Rau, Benegal Narsinga, Sir, 12282
Rau, Heimo, 01600, 03100, 03125
Rau, P.S., 24052
Rau, Shantha, 27890
Rau, Wilhelm, 03887, 05227
Rauf, Abdur, 17997, 18175, 18197, 18217
Raulet, Harry M., 22870a
Raut Ray, Satchidananda, 22415
Raval, Ravishankar M., 03416
Raven-Hill, Leonard, 11947
Raverty, Henry George, 02639, 27980
Ravindra, 11402
Ravindra Prasad, D., 19706, 19752
Ravindran, T.K., 00200, 00395, 00425, 19914-6, 19930, 19944, 20111
Ravindranath, P.K., 10188
Rawal, Anantray J., 05785-6
Rawat, Indra Singh, 25836
Rawlinson, Alfred Edward John, Bishop of Derby, 16828
Rawlinson, Henry Creswicke, Sir, 09418
Rawlinson, Hugh George, 00214, 04168, 04580, 08248, 08287, 08384, 09040
Rawson, Philip Stanley, 03101, 03137, 03205, 03230, 03276, 03323, 05864, 05879, 07313
Ray.... *See also* Roy
Ray, A., 05509
Ray, A.C., 15144
Ray, Ajit K., 22400
Ray, Ajit Kumar, 11232, 11243
Ray, Alok, 24723-4
Ray, Amal, 12527, 12908, 22298, 24386
Ray, Amalendu, 10306
Ray, Amita, 03454, 03527, 04524, 06815
Ray, Anil Baran, 23890, 24302
Ray, Animesh Chandra, 27334
Ray, Annadasankar, 02662, 09904, 25106
Ray, Asish Kumar, 13240
Ray, Benoy Gopal, 24880, 25015
Ray, Bhabani Charan, 20776, 20787
Ray, Bharati, 12528
Ray, Bishwanath, 24526, 24764
Ray, Hem Chandra, 05694, 07373
Ray, Hemen, 09922, 13210
Ray, Indrani, 08859
Ray, Jayanta Kumar, 12075, 13766. 17336. 25255
Ray, Kamalesh, 15522
Ray, Kshitis, 25037
Ray, L., 02662
Ray, Lila, 24935, 27999
Ray, N.R., 11979, 24725
Ray, Naresh Chandra, 12513
Ray, Niharranjan, 03126, 05459, 07743, 07892, 08597, 09575, 09738, 22601, 25063
Ray, P.C., 24591
Ray, Parimal, 11072
Ray, Prafulla Chandra, 00339, 10671
Ray, Pramode Chandra, 20925, 24642
Ray, Prithwis Chandra, 10030
Ray, Priyadaranjan, 00337-8, 04558, 17241
Ray, Punya Sloka, 27999
Ray, R., 24492
Ray, R.M., 16983
Ray, Rajat K., 09003, 11087, 24323, 24440-1, 24492, 24726, 24742
Ray, Ram Kumar, 02154
Ray, Ratna, 08909
Ray, Ratnalekha, 24441, 24670
Ray, Renuka, 15995
Ray, S.B., 03607
Ray, Sally, 13211
Ray, Samirendra Nath, 12850
Ray, Santosh Kumar, 12579
Ray, Saradaranjan, 05377
Ray, Sarojendra Nath, 10758
Ray, Satyajit, 16984
Ray, Shyamal Kumar, 00616-7
Ray, Sibnarayan, 09923, 10083, 24946
Ray, Subrata, 24512
Ray, Sudhansu Kumar, 03359, 24893-4
Ray, Sukumar, 02894, 07465
Ray, Sunil Chandra, 06951
Ray, Susanta Kanta, 14793
Ray, Syamal Kumar, 12636
Ray Chaudhuri, Tarak Chandra, 24623
Rayapati, J.P. Rao, 11867
Raychaudhuri, G.C., 06211, 06212
Raychaudhuri, Gaurisankar, 10895, 14133
Raychaudhuri, H.C., 00193
Raychaudhuri, Hemchandra, 04103, 04769
Raychaudhuri, Manas, 02849
Raychaudhuri, Pranab Chandra, 09885, 23951
Raychaudhuri, Satya Prasad, 14903, 27017
Raychaudhuri, Tapan Kumar, 07595, 07602, 08196, 08893, 10875, 16534, 24493
Raychoudhury, Prafulla, 24426
Raychowdhury, Tarak Chandra, 20971
Raye, Narendra Nath, 08781, 23950
Raza, M. Ali, 18064
Raza, Moonis, 00219, 26990, 27233, 27753
Raza, Muhammad Rafique, 22885
Raza Khan, Mohamed, 10307
Razdan, Prithve Nath, 23256
Razvi, Mujtaba, 17676
Razzack, M.A., 05742, 16216
Rea, Alexander, 03156, 05498, 06627, 06657, 08236
Read, Hadley, 16573
Read, Hollis, 21453
Read, Margaret, 11124
Reading, Gerald Rufus Isaacs, 2nd Marquess of, 19619
Reat, Noble Ross, 01494
Reck, David, 03048
Reddaway, W.B., 14251, 25484
Reddy, C.G.K., 13535, 16896
Reddy, D.V.S., 19465-6
Reddy, Duvur Jaganatha, 16501
Reddy, G. Asvatthanarayana, 17082
Reddy, K.N., 09294, 10896
Reddy, N.B.K., 19845-6
Reddy, N.S., 23712, 23758
Reddy, P.H., 20278, 20516
Reddy, Philomena Royappa, 19855
Reddy, V. Kodanda, 19853
Reddy, V. Krishnamurthy, 15024
Reddy, V.M., 19608
Reddy, V.M.M., 19706
Reddy, V. Narayan Karan, 15906
Redfield, Robert, 00892
Reed, Horace B., 26169, 26315
Reed, Mary J., 26315
Reed, Stanley, Sir, 10832
Reed, Wallace, 24550
Rees, J.D., 09840
Rees, Philip H., 24759
Reeves, Peter D., 23453, 23480-3
Reeves, Ruth, 03231, 03360
Refaqat Ali Khan, Kunwar, 08374
Régamey, Constantin, 00708, 01131, 01531
Regani, Sarojini, 08129, 19643-4
Rege, P.W., 13516
Reginer, R., 01163
Regional Centre for Research and Training in Municipal Administration, Lucknow, 23536
Regional Development Plan for Peshawar Valley, 23127
Regional Seminar on Planning and Development, Bohawalpur (1963), 22811
Regmi, Dilli Raman, 04114, 07374-6, 25947, 25966, 26008, 26082
Regmi, Jagadish Chandra, 26049, 26203
Regmi, Mahesh Chandra, 26100, 26170-1
Rego, Antonio da Silva, 07886
Rehm, Klaus E., 04549
Rehmaney, Fazle Ahmed Aziz, 12592
Reid, Adam Scott, 26605
Reid, Donald N., 24104
Reid, Robert, 24258, 26449
Reinaud, Joseph Toussaint, 05642
Reindorp, Julian, 20352
Reinhard, Johan, 26259
Reinhart, William W., 22617
Reiniche, Marie-Louise, 00903, 19505-6
Reisner, I.M., 09705
Reitz, Jeffrey, 14191
Rele, J.R., 14155
Rele, Subhash J., 15378
Remaiah, C., 01374

Renault-Roulier, Gilbert, 08339
Rennie, David Fields, 26430
Renou, Louis, 00014, 01164, 01203, 01222, 02394, 02479-80, 03757, 03803, 03849, 03867, 03916, 03996, 04104, 04872, 05170, 05195, 05209-10, 05262, 05367, 05986, 06087, 27804
Repetto, Robert C., 14382
Republican Party of India, 13303
Reserve Bank of India, 10990, 13800, 13867, 14494, 14636, 14620, 14667, 15110-6, 15121, 15136, 15265, 19312, 21759, 22215, 25758
Retzlaff, Ralph Herbert, 13212, 22001
Reu, Bisheshwar Nath, 06682
Revankar, Ratna G., 15819
Revelle, Roger, 17959, 17972
Revri, Chamanlal, 11140
Reyes-Hocking, Amelia, 15923
Reymond, Lizelle, 11343
Reyna, Ruth, 01308, 01408
Reynolds, C.H.B., 02546, 18981, 19114
Reynolds, Frank E., 01132-3, 01260, 04932, 05025, 05044, 18973
Reynolds, Reginald, 09042, 09886
Reza, Sadrel, 25263
Rhodes, Dennis E., 10819
Rhys, Ernest, 25039
Rhys-Davids, Caroline Augusta Foley, 01477, 04919, 04995, 05005-6, 05033, 06160
Rhys Davids, Thomas William, 04070, 04105, 04983, 04987, 27809
Riazul Islam, 07583
Ribbentrop, Berthold, 11032
Ribeiro, João, 08079
Riccardi, Theodore, 06088
Rice, Edward, 27061
Rice, Edward Peter, 02579, 04617
Rice, Stanley Pitcairn, 05398, 20631
Richards, F.J., 00686
Richards, John F., 00063, 00230, 05935, 07528, 07531, 08116-9
Richards, Norah, 10672
Richards, P.J., 18685, 18793
Richards, Philip Ernest, 22618
Richardson, H.B., 10612
Richardson, Jane. *See* Hanks, Jane Richardson
Richey, J.A., 10565
Richmond, Farley P., 02908, 02940-1, 03034
Richmond, Herbert William, 07993
Richter, Julius A., 11537
Richter, William L., 09383
Rickmers, Christian Mable Duff, 00145
Ridding, Caroline Mary, 06015
Ridge, Betsy, 27078
Rieger, Hans Christoph, 25855, 26188
Riemenschneider, Dieter, 11736
Riepe, Dale Maurice, 01386, 11868, 16701
Ries, Raymond E., 02861
Rinpoche, Samdhong, 05102
Ripley, Sidney Dillon, II, 17282, 27026
Rischel, Jorgen, 26410
Risabh Chandra, K., 05258
Rishi, Padmashri Weer Rajendra, 00377
Risley, Herbert Hope, 00698-9, 24592
Ritchie, Anne Isabella, 09110
Ritschl, Eva, 04309
Rittenberg, Stephen, 23057
Ritti, Shrinivas, 06685
Rivers, William Halse, 01012-3, 19396
Rivière, Juan Roger, 01812, 05749
Rizvi, Dolly, 02815
Rizvi, Gowher, 10397
Rizvi, Hasan Askari, 12048, 13782, 17370, 17464
Rizvi, Jamil Hussain, 10483
Rizvi, S.A. Sarwar, 18065
Rizvi, S. Ehtisham Husain, 11663
Rizvi, S.M. Akram, 23368
Rizvi, S.M.Z., 17641
Rizvi, S. Shahid Ali, 17640
Rizvi, Saiyid Athar Abbas, 02273, 05952, 05962, 07554, 07675-6, 07790, 09782, 09472, 11463
Rizvi, Seyyid Saeed Akhtar, 26862
Rizvi, Shahid Ali, 17623-6
Rizvi, Syed Amjad Ali Bahadur, 22501
Rizvi, Syed Jamil Ahmad, 11484
Roach, David, 02835
Roach, James Robert, 13387
Roadarmel, Gordon Charles, 11589, 11628-9
Roarke, Jesse, 11395
Robb, Peter, 09760, 10241, 23961, 24095
Robbin, Jeanette, 10787
Roberge, Gaston, 16841, 16985
Robert, Bruce L., Jr., 19313
Roberts, Beryl J., 25599
Roberts, Frederick Sleigh Roberts, 1st Earl, 09326
Roberts, John M., 01706
Roberts, Joseph, 00766
Roberts, Michael Webb, 18331, 18347-8, 18351, 18484-5, 18500, 18704, 18715, 18758-60, 18800, 18812, 18818, 18821, 18841
Roberts, Paul Ernest, 08044, 09060
Roberts, Warren E., 02446
Robertson, Alexander, 21412
Robertson, Donald, 02836
Robertson, George Scott, 23043, 23122
Robins, Arthur J., 25582
Robins, Betty Dashew, 03297
Robins, Robert Sidwar, 12598, 23554, 23557
Robinson, Duane, 16742
Robinson, Edward Austin Gossage, 12261, 15361, 25326, 25623
Robinson, F.C.R., 23463
Robinson, Francis, 10317, 23488-9
Robinson, Frederick Bruce, Jr., 20711
Robinson, Frederick Percival, 08003
Robinson, Marguerite S., 18550, 18842, 19086
Robinson, Richard H., 01230, 01475, 05103
Robinson, Sandra Pocahontas, 24900
Robinson, Warren C., 17791, 17803-4, 25443
Robinson, William, 25690
Roche, Paul, 19408
Rocher, Ludo, 00747, 00917, 00931, 03904, 04290, 09268, 19120, 19362
Rocher, Rosane, 00056, 00064, 05211
Rochin, Refugio I., 14856, 22481
Rockhill, William Woodville, 04884
Rodale, Jerome Irving, 27226
Rodgers, Charles J., 05682, 07398
Rodgers, G.B., 24042
Rodhe, Sten Olof, 03826
Rodrigues, Lucio, 21107-8
Roe, Alan, 18633
Roe, Thomas, Sir, 07488
Röh, Klaus, 22350-1
Roerich, George, 05654, 27657
Rösel, Jakob, 02025-6, 22393
Rogers, Alexander, 07483, 21267
Rogers, Everett M., 15066
Rogers, Leonard, 24820
Rogers, Millard Buxton, 03171
Roghair, Gene Henry, 06602-3
Rokadiya, B.C., 15963
Roland, Joan G., 16780
Rolland, Pierre, 03921, 04461, 11308
Rolland, Romain, 11332
Rolnick, Phyllis L., 13147
Romm, Jeff, 25407
Ronaldshay, Lord. *See* Zetland, Lawrence John Lumley Dundas, 2nd Marquis of
Rongmuthu, Dewansingh Shangma, 26705
Rooke, G.H., 05360
Rooksby, R.L., 19397
Rooman, M. Anwar, 02620, 22543, 22553
Roonwal, M.L., 22021
Roop Singh, 20841
Roos-Keppel, George Olof, Sir, 27981
Roosevelt, Eleanor, 27062
Root, Helen I., 19051
Roschmann, Hans, 17371
Rose, Horace Arthur, 22831, 23100
Rose, Leo E., 13945, 25846, 25960, 25969, 25977, 25985, 26003-4, 26013, 26050-1, 26083, 26376-7, 26421, 26424, 26480
Rose, Saul, 12216-7
Roseberry, James Royal, 22631, 22665
Roselli, John, 23646
Rosen, George, 10918, 11088, 14250, 14658, 15009
Rosenfield, John M., 05521, 05569
Rosenstein-Rodan, P.N., 14506, 14689
Rosenthal, Donald B., 13668-71, 20601, 21129, 21164-5, 21175-6, 21584, 23540

Rosenthal, Ethel, 02731
Rosner, Victor, 22279
Ross, Aileen Dansken, 16583, 20390
Ross, David, 22435
Ross, Floyd Hiatt, 01532
Ross-of-Bladensburg, John Foster George, Sir, 09109
Rosselli, John, 09114-5
Rosser, Colin, 16039, 24781, 25886, 26248
Rossi, A.V., 22992
Roşu, Arion, 01476, 01654, 11842
Rotary Club of Bombay, 21197
Roth, Gustav, 05158
Rothchild, Donald, 26863
Rothenstein, William, Sir, 25016
Rothermund, Dietmar, 02260, 09576, 09604, 09676, 09932, 09981-2, 10099, 10956-9, 11177, 13975, 23032, 24118, 24494, 25038
Rothermund, Indira Nalin, 09950, 09964, 13213, 20751, 24125, 26851-2
Roussel, Alfred, 05762, 05767
Rousselet, Louis, 09354, 20583
Rout, Savitri, 22416
Rout, Siba Prasad, 21022
Routh, S.K., 00937
Rowe, William L., 15969, 16062, 23701, 23713
Rowland, Benjamin, Jr., 01675, 03102, 03277, 05532-5, 05544, 05599, 11843
Rowland, John, 13914
Roy.... *See also* Ray
Roy, A.K., 23515, 24641
Roy, Ajit, 13467, 13634, 14044, 14338-9, 22373
Roy, Anandya Chandra, 27296
Roy, Ashim Kumar, 22126
Roy, Asim, 17844, 25644
Roy, Asishkumar, 14621
Roy, Asoke Chandra, 27297
Roy, Aswini K., 12035
Roy, Atul Chandra, 07568, 08841, 08884
Roy, B.B., 22025
Roy, Basanta Koomar, 25064
Roy, Benoy Krishna, 08885
Roy, Bhabesh Chandra, 15348
Roy, Bidhan Chandra, 24367
Roy, Brajdeo Prasad, 04274
Roy, Buddhadev, 25113
Roy, C.J., 27885
Roy, Debika, 24511
Roy, Dilip Kumar, 02119, 10170
Roy, Ellen, 10066a
Roy, Evelyn, 10005
Roy, Girish Chandra, 15726
Roy, Gouri Kant, Rai Bahadur, 10852
Roy, Hipshon, 26695
Roy, Hirendra Nath, 14637
Roy, Jay Narain, 26770
Roy, Jyotirmoy, 26578
Roy, K.C., 13877
Roy, Kuldip K., 19588
Roy, M., 15357
Roy, Mahendra Prakash, 08327
Roy, Manabendra Nath, 09924, 10005, 10067-72, 10919, 11193-5
Roy, Manisha, 24663
Roy, Nagendra Kumar, 07274
Roy, Naresh Chandra, 12637, 15318, 24272, 24281
Roy, Phani Bhushan, 26981, 27079
Roy, Pratap Chandra, 04623
Roy, Prodipto, 01574, 14857, 15066, 16665, 26696
Roy, Putul, 24675
Roy, Ramashray, 12951, 13157, 13468, 13663, 23514, 23987-90
Roy, Ramesh Chandra, 21005
Roy, Ranajit, 24359
Roy, S.K., 15442
Roy, Sachin, 00610, 00618, 26507, 27494
Roy, Samaren, 10084
Roy, Santimoy, 09783
Roy, Sarat Chandra, 20951, 20989-90, 21004-5, 21031
Roy, Satindra Narayan, 21015
Roy, Satis Chandra, 04693, 10989
Roy, Shashanka Bhushan, 03492, 03767
Roy, Shibani, 00957, 23770
Roy, Siddheshwari Narain, 05759
Roy, Sita Ram, 03740
Roy, Somendra Lal, 04340
Roy, Somir Kumar, 15189
Roy, Somnath, 09081, 09577, 23991
Roy, Sourindranath, 00583, 11844
Roy, Sripati Charan, 09280
Roy, Subodh, 10045-6
Roy Burman, B.K., 14138, 15699, 15820, 16296
Roy Chaudhury, Indu, 20946, 23319
Roy Choudhury, Bani, 22154, 23261
Roy Choudhury, Makhan Lal, 07660, 07669
Roy Choudhury, Pranab Chandra, 02061, 02067, 02075, 10031, 11550, 23972, 24231-2, 26469, 27262-3
Roy Chowdhury, Bidyut Kumar, 24639-40
Roy Chowdhury, Bulu, 09586, 20732
Roy Chowdhury, Devi Prosad, 17222
Roy Chowdhury, Subrata, 12134
Roy Chowdhury, Uma Dutta, 15481
Royal Asiatic Society of Great Britain and Ireland. Library, 27517
Royal Empire Society, 27518
Royal Institute of International Affairs, 17688
Roychowdhury, Krishna Chandra, 05361
Roychowdhury, Nalini Ranjan, 26631
Rubel, Mary, 01592, 01601
Ruben, Walter, 00057, 00182, 00244, 03992, 04106, 04334, 04391, 04453, 04612, 04834, 05333, 05378, 05405
Ruberu, T. Ranjit, 18939
Rubin, David, 11620, 26347
Rubinoff, Arthur G., 13756, 21057
Rudduck, Grenfell, 18119
Rudolph, Lloyd Irving, 09281, 09933, 12734, 13079-80, 13101, 13441, 13638, 13672, 15772, 16535, 19203, 20641, 20654-5, 21908, 22089
Rudolph, Susanne Hoeber, 09281, 09933, 12734, 13053, 13080, 13101, 13441, 13469, 13638, 15772, 16535, 20641-2, 20654-5, 21908, 22089
Rudra, Abani Bhushan, 09106
Rudra, Ashok, 10876, 14219, 14460, 24475
Rudrabasavaraj, M.N., 15630
Rudramoorthy, B., 15067
Rudrappa, J., 06963
Rudrayya Chowdari, Garigipati, 19645
Ruegg, David Seyfort, 01341, 05119, 05171
Rüping, Klaus, 06402
Ruhela, Satya Pal, 16395, 16450-3, 16469, 16638, 16742, 20842, 22103
Ruhomon, Peter, 26785
Rukmani, T.S., 05775
Rule, Pauline, 00125
Rumbold, Algernon, Sir, 10220
Rungta, Radhe Shyam, 11089
Rūpa Gosvāmī, 07285-6
Rupp, George, 01505
Rural Health Research Centre, 16289
Rusch, Thomas Alvin, 10100, 13442, 13792
Rushbrook Williams, L.F. *See* Williams, L.F. Rushbrook
Russell, George E., 19609
Russell, Martin, 19097
Russell, R.V., 22241
Russell, Ralph, 07708-9, 09784, 11640-1, 11664-5, 11694, 11700
Russell, Thomas Brian, 09218
Russell, Wilfred, 11101
Russell, William Howard, 09483
Rustomji, Kaikhosru Jehangir, 12713, 22832
Rustomji, Nari K., 26422, 27353
Ruswa, Mirza Mohammad Hadi, 11696
Ruthnaswamy, Mariadas, 09167, 09951
Ruths, Gernot W., 23992
Rutnagar, S.M., 21302
Rutnam, James T., 18341
Ruud, Kaare, 18180
Ryan, Bryce F., 18607, 18822, 18843-4, 18880, 18928, 18940
Ryder, Arthur William, 05310, 05348, 05399, 06043, 06068
Ryland, Shane, 10242
Ryley, John Horton, 07950
Rytina, Joan, 13204

Sa, Fidelis de, 20899
Saadullah Khan, 12181
Saari, E.E., 25354
Sabade, B.R., 15312
Sabanayagam, P., 16406
Sabavala, Jehangir, 17223
Sabbah, Saleh, 25523

Saberwal, Satish, 00687, 15703, 16040, 22833, 23515
Sabharwal, Nirmal, 16543-4
Sabikhi, Ranjit, 23418
Sabir, Mohammad Shafi, 27105
Sable, Alan, 22385
Sabnis, R.V., Rai Bahadur, Sir, 20602
Sabnis, S.A., 05334
Sabzwari, Ghaniul Akram, 27582
Sachar, Rajinder, 15271
Sachau, Edward C., 05636, 05643
Sachchidananda, 03295, 14283, 15773, 20900-2, 20952, 20958, 20991, 24005, 24070, 24134, 24150-1, 24164, 24214
Sachidanand, 20041
Sachithanandan, V., 19589-90
Sachs, Curt, 02787
Sackett, F. Colyer, 19880
Sacred books of the Buddhists, 01271, 04973
Sacred books of the Hindus, 01223
Sacred books of the Jainas, 01295, 05159
Sadananda, Swami, 04742
Sadananda Giri, Swami, 01902
Sadarangani, H.I., 02524, 22512-3
Sadashivaiah, K., 26583
Sadasivaiah, H.M., 20551
Sadasivan, D., 19171
Sadasivan, S.N., 13136
Sadequain, 18283
Saddhatissa, H., 01521, 05026
Sadeque, Mohammad, 25634
Sadhu, S.N., 16162, 27570
Sadhu, Shyam Lal, 23262
Sadhu Om, 11415
Sadik, Nafis, 17801
Sadiq, Muhammad, 02534, 11633
Sadler, Albert W., 01903
Saeed, Ahmad, 23024
Saeed, Khawaja Amjad, 17821
Saeed, Mian Muhammad, 07021
Saeed, S.A., 17514
Saeed Ahmad, 12106
Safi Ahmad, 23447
Safiullah, M., 17912, 25477
Sagant, Philippe, 26172, 26241
Sager, Peter, 13985
Saggi, P.D., 09692, 12404
Sagreiya, K.P., 14920
Saha, Gobindalal, 24461
Saha, H., 24821
Saha, Hare Krishna, 25504
Saha, Jibananda, 16925, 27444
Saha, Kshanika, 04964
Saha, Leena, 24800
Saha, Maya Rani, 25420
Saha, N.K., 20926
Saha, Panchanan, 10063, 24543, 26759
Saha, Ramendra Nath, 24635, 24689
Saha, Subhas Chandra, 11759-60
Sahai, Bhagvant. *See* Sahai, Bhagwant
Sahai, Bhagwant, 01602, 03850
Sahai, Govind, 10426, 13289
Sahai, Indu, 23737
Sahai, Jawala, Nazim of Deegi, 20661
Sahai, Jugendra, 24706
Sahai, Mahajot, 02153
Sahai, Sachchidanand, 05612
Sahai, Shrinath, 16926
Sahajānanda, Swami, 21929
Sahajānanda Saraswatī. *See* Saraswatī, Sahajānanda, Swāmī
Saharaj, H.K., 09082
Saharia, B.R., 25741
Sahasrabuddhe, V.G., 21217
Sahasrabudhe, A.W., 22344
Sahasrabudhe, M.T., 06343
Sahay, B.N., 15069, 15712, 24024
Sahay, Bhagwan, 23230
Sahay, Binode Kumar, 07652
Sahay, K.N., 01638
Sahay, K.N., 24029, 24165, 24225
Sahay, Keshari N., 20962, 20992
Sahgal, N.P., 13536
Sahgal, Nayantara Pandit, 13424, 13536
Sahgal, Prem K., 10460
Sahi, A.F., 22886
Sahi, Joginder Singh, 08580
Sahir Ludhianvi, Abdul Haye, 17060
Sahitya Akademi, 17008, 17024
Sahney, Vimala, 03710
Sahni, Balbir Singh, 14690
Sahni, Daya Ram, 05570
Sahni, Jogendra Nath, 10834, 11050, 13113, 16890
Sahni, Naresh Chander, 13664, 17435
Sahota, G.S., 14107
Sahota, Sohan Singh, 13425
Sahu, Biswanath, 22338
Sahu, Kishori Prasad, 05727
Sahu, Lakshminarayan, 21032
Sahu, Nabin Kumar, 00481-2
Said, Hakim Mohammed, 05644, 18239
Saidookhail, Ayub Khan, 22892
Saif-ud-din, M., 08560
Saigal, Jaswant Rai, 13958
Saigal, Omesh, 26632
Saikia, Paban Chandra, 25791
Saikia, Padma Dhar, 25720, 25759-60, 25792, 26500
Saina, Pritam, 27264
Saini, B.S., 16523, 22727
Saini, Krishan G., 10893, 10920
Saini, Mahender Kumar, 23330
Saini, Shiv Kumar, 16427, 16650
Sainju, M.M., 26103
Sainsbury, E.B., 07971
Sainy, H.C., 13829
Saiyed, A.R., 21447
Saiyid, Matlubul Hasan, 10385
Saiyidain, Khwaja Ghulam, 10564, 10645, 11666, 16470, 16535, 16614
Sakala, Carol, 00950
Sakhare, M.R., 06566
Sakharov, I.V., 24593
Saksena, B.R., 00027
Saksena, Baburam, 02652
Saksena, Banarsi Prasad, 07492
Saksena, D.N., 23565, 24202
Saksena, Jogendra, 03417
Saksena, Kashi Prasad, 00945
Saksena, R.N., 10506, 21069, 25887, 25908
Saksena, Ram Babu, 02535
Saksena, Ram Mohan, 14659
Saksena, Shri Krishna, 01181, 01478
Sakthivel, S., 02353, 02427, 19371
Sakya, Karna, 27395
Sakya, Thakur M., 26316
Salahuddin Ahmed, A.F., 24572
Salamatullah, 16453
Salazar, Antonio de Oliviera, 21049
Saldanda, Jerome Antony, 21096
Saletore, Bhasker Anand, 00359, 00458, 04026, 04261, 06182, 06230, 06570, 08267
Saletore, Rajaram Narayan, 04357, 04399
Salim Khan, Afsar Umar, 07061
Salima Hashmi, 18200
Salmin, Muhammad Ali al-Haj, 06800
Salomon, Richard G., 01912, 01915, 04177
Saluja, M.R., 27754
Salunke, S.P., 12190
Salvi, Purushottam Gangaram, 14034
Sama, G.V.I., 19534
Sama Rao, P., 06676
Samad, M.A., 25349
Samaddar, Sivaprasad, 24743
Samal, J.K., 20777
Samant, Dattatraya Ramkrishna, 14652
Samant, S.V., 21170
Samanta, D.K., 21402
Samarasinge, S.W.R. de A., 18732
Samarasinghe, S.G., 19024
Samaraweera, Vijaya, 18308, 18316-8, 18535, 18725, 18863-5, 27550
Samarth, Anil, 20744
Samartha, Michael Prakash, 06551
Samartha, S.J., 11440, 16802
Sambamoorthy, Pichu, 02788, 02792, 02797, 02807, 02862-4, 02876, 19900
Sambhi, Piara Singh, 08568
Samboo, Gopalgee, 00321
Sambrani, Shreekant, 21732
Sami, Abdus, 24185
Samina Quraeshi, 27106
Samiuddin, 23606

Samiuddin, Abida, 23528
Sammani, Saiyid Ghulam, 07129
Sampath, Rajan Kasturi, 19277
Sampatkumaran, M.R., 06422
Sampooran Singh, 13783
Sampurnanand, 01707, 13178, 14332, 23498
Samuel, C.M., 13687
Samuel, Getsie R., 19478
Samuel, V.T., 20175
Samyukta Maharashtra Parishad, 21121
Sanātana, Gosvāmī, 07291
Sanaullah, Shaikh, 27944
Sanceau, Elaine, 07863-4
Sandal, Mohan Lal, 04863, 04869
Sanderatne, A.E.H., 18515
Sanderatne, Nimal, 17988, 19601, 18774-5, 18891, 11834
Sandes, Edward Warren Caulfield, 09327
Sandesara, J.C., 15330, 15592, 21308
Sandhu, Harjit S., 15840
Sandhu, Kernial Singh, 26887, 26888
Sandhu, Nirmal, 03426
Sandhu, S.K., 23433
Sandhu, Swaran S., 01558
Sandweiss, Samuel H., 16743
Sangal, P.S., 13897
Sangar, S.P., 07802
Sangat Singh, 17677, 23323
Sangave, Vilas Adinath, 20825, 21386, 16773
Sangharakshita, Bhikshu, 01231-2, 02229, 18987
Sanghvi, Prafulla, 15093
Sanghvi, R.L., 15340
Sangeelee, M., 26771
Sangoram, K.D., 21617
Sanial, S.C., 10820, 10833, 24866
Sanjana, Jehangir Edalji, 10753
Sanjeeva Rao, T.S.A., 11051
Sanjeeva Reddy, G., 19776
Sanjeevi, N., 04504
Sanjivi, K.S., 16231
Sankalia, Hasmukhlal Dhirajlal, 00459, 00584-5, 00591-2, 00598, 02006-7, 03258, 03504-5, 03521, 03529-31, 03539, 03555-6, 03565, 03574-5, 03683, 04725, 07215
Sankara Kurup, G., 20217-8
Sankara Menon, T.C., 20205
Sankara Rama Sastri, C., 05319, 06008
Śankarācārya, 06345-60
Sankaram, A., 16572
Sankaran, A., 05979
Sankaran, Kamala, 04505, 06578
Sankaran, P.S., 04559
Sankaran Nair, Chettu, Sir, 10705
Sankaranarayana, Paluri, 27899
Sankaranarayanan, N., 16904
Sankaranarayanan, S., 04226
Sankhdher, Lalit Mohan, 23778
Sankhder, M.M., 23079, 23331
Sanklecha, S.N., 15447
Sankrityayan, Kamala, 26348
Sankrityayana, Rahula, 01262, 05059, 05910
Sanmuganathan, M., 18673
Sanon, C.G., 22706
Sanoo, M.K., 20176
Santapau, H., 27041
Santhanam, Kasturiranga Iyengar, 02422, 09581, 12315, 12360, 12673, 12922, 13337, 14560, 19314
Santhanam, R., 26991
Śāntideva, 05093
Santos, S.R., 19540
Santucci, James A., 03804
Sanwal, Bhairava Dat, 26063
Sanwal, R.D., 25938
Sanyal, Amiya Nath, 08487
Sanyal, Bhabesh Chandra, 17224
Sanyal, Hitesranjan, 08923, 08971, 24519, 24527, 24631-2
Sanyal, J.M., 05768
Sanyal, Nalinaksha, 11052
Sanyal, Nirmal Chandra, 05826
Sanyal, Nisikanta, 07275
Sanyal, Prabodh Kumar, 27354
Sanyal, Rajat, 24573
Sanyal, Ranjit Kumar, 14156
Sanyal, S.N., 16309
Sanyal, Shanta, 23241
Sanyal, Shubhendu, 15820
Sanyal, Suprakash, 08771
Sanyal, Tapan Kumar, 24643
Saparamadu, Sumana D., 06126, 06147
Sapra, C.L., 16593
Sapre, S.G., 21256
Sapru, Tej Bahadur, Sir, 10014, 10447
Sapru Committee (1945), 10447
Saqi, M.F., 18013
Sar, R.N., 03062, 27651
Sarabhai, Mrinalini, 02926-7, 02954, 02967
Sarabhai, Vikram A., 17252
Sarachchandra, E.R. *See* Sarathchandra, E.R.
Sarada Raju, A., 19253
Saradamoni, K., 20028-9
Saradananda, Swami, 11309
Saradhi, K.P., 17103
Saraf, Muhammad Yusuf, 23171
Saraf, Mulk Raj, 10835, 23202
Saraf, R.K., 16245
Saraf, R.N., 06763
Saraf, Samarendra, 00823, 02133, 05865
Saraiya, R.G., 14612
Saram, P.A.S., 18639
Saran, Anirudha Behari, 20903
Saran, Parmatma, 06725, 07547, 24025
Saran, Saraswati, 02387, 11667
Sarangapani, S., 25774
Sarasvati, Sarasi Kumar, 03206, 03336, 03446, 05460, 05880, 06908, 07349, 07359, 07368, 07744, 07783
Sarasvati, Satya Prakash, Swami, 04830
Saraswat, Har Charan, 27335
Saraswat, Rawat, 22146-7
Saraswathy Rao, Y., 15430
Saraswati, Baidyanath, 00856-7, 01026, 01928, 02039, 02050, 02054, 02056, 03259, 21097, 24144-5
Saraswati, P.N., 09009
Saraswati, S., 19338
Saraswati, S.K. *See* Sarasvati, Sarasi Kumar
Saraswati, Sahajanand, Swami, 24096
Sarathchandra, Ediriweera Ranjita, 01409, 03022-3, 18640
Sarda, Har Bilas, 00468, 11275, 11282, 22127
Sardar, Gangadhar Balkrishna, 06754
Sardesai, Damodar Ramaji, 14097
Sardesai, Govind Sakharam, 07444-5, 08250, 08252
Sardesai, S.G., 08288, 13102, 13221, 13809
Sareen, Tilak Raj, 09624-5
Sargant, Norman Carr, 19541
Sargeant, Winthrop, 04670
Sargent, John, Sir, 10585, 16396
Sargunam, M. Ezra, 19542
Sargunam, M.J., 19473
Sarhadi, Ajit Singh, 13767, 22688
Sarikwal, R.C., 23859
Sarin, Dharam Paul, 11590
Sarin, L.N., 23499
Sarin, V.I.K., 26458
Sarjit Singh, 22744, 22789
Sarkar, Amal, 02327, 07302
Sarkar, Anil Kumar, 01349
Sarkar, Benoy Kumar, 00231, 00260, 02442, 04319, 05708, 12273
Sarkar, Bhupendra Nath, 10626
Sarkar, Chanchal, 16842, 16857, 16876-8, 21447
Sarkar, D.C., 01734
Sarkar, H., 03391
Sarkar, H.C., 11256
Sarkar, Hemchandra, 24287
Sarkar, Haribishnu, 05505, 05514
Sarkar, Himansu Bhushan, 04382
Sarkar, Indira, 24967
Sarkar, Jadunath, 00126, 00522, 01904, 07276-7, 07389, 07503, 07510-2, 07522, 07527, 07538, 07569, 08023, 08251-2, 08258, 08275, 08289, 08842, 08860
Sarkar, Jagadish Narayan, 05634-5, 07080, 07334, 07399-400, 07446, 07563, 07570-1, 07596, 07622, 07673, 07698, 08295, 08788, 08953, 24215
Sarkar, Javanata, 20378
Sarkar, K.R., 04375
Sarkar, Kobita, 16986
Sarkar, Krishnakant, 24505
Sarkar, N.K., 12268
Sarkar, P.L., 13898
Sarkar, Pabitra, 03055, 18245
Sarkar, Ranajit, 05370
Sarkar, Sasanka Sekhar, 01088, 03684
Sarkar, Sourindranath, 16584

Sarkar, Subhas, 16397
Sarkar, Subhash Chandra, 24239
Sarkar, Subimal Chandra, 04515
Sarkar, Subrata, 12923
Sarkar, Sudhir Chandra, 13464
Sarkar, Sumit, 11212, 24303, 24339
Sarkar, Sunil Chandra, 25046
Sarkar, Susobhan Chandra, 24574-5
Sarkar, Tanika, 24324
Sarkar, U.C., 00932, 00938
Sarkaria, R.S., 19227
Sarma, Atul, 15194
Sarma, Binod, 04613
Sarma, Dimbeswar, 25813
Sarma, Dittakavi Subrahmanya, 01204, 11213, 11224
Sarma, Gobinda Prasad, 11737
Sarma, Harishcandra, 22024
Sarma, I.R.K., 14220
Sarma, J.N., 25747
Sarma, Jyotirmoyee, 24610, 24624-5, 24684, 24895
Sarma, K.S.R.N., 23406
Sarma, Kotacheri Madhava Krishna, 05186
Sarma, Krishna Venkateswara, 00286, 03795, 27620
Sarma, Madhab Chandra, 25732, 25761
Sarma, N.A., 14421
Sarma, Nagendra, 27369
Sarma, P.V., 19736
Sarma, P. Sivananda, 27901
Sarma, S., 20208
Sarma, Sadasiva Rath, 06911, 06916
Sarma, Satyendranath, 02675, 07297
Sarma, V., 17278
Sarma, V. Anjaneya, 06403
Sarmah, Jogeswar, 03792
Sarmukadam, M.S., 27912
Sarna, S.R., 15398
Sarngadeva, 02685
Sarojini Reddy, Palnaty, 12361
Sarton, George, 00261
Sarup, Lakshman, 05181, 05322
Sarvesvara Iyer, P., 06161
Sarveswara Rao, Bhavaraju, 19766, 19828, 19830
Sasaki, Shigetsu, 04910
Sassani, Abul Hassan K., 18156
Sassetti, Filippo, 07838
Sasthi Brata, 26900
Sastri, Gaurinath, 05228
Sastri, Haraprasad, 07209
Sastri, Hirananda, 05914, 06829, 07216
Sastri, Khandrika Venkata Subrahmanya, 14546
Sastri, Pothukuchi Subrahmanya, 01387, 05104, 11857
Sastri, Satyavrat, 00036, 01448
Sastri, Sibnath, 11250
Sastry, D.V., 15193
Sastry, Kadayam Ramachandra Ramabhadra, 00933, 04506, 09371, 19172
Sastry, S.A.R., 19791
Sastry, S.M.Y., 19892, 21188
Satapathy, Binapani, 22345
Satchidananda Murty, K., 00201
Sathasivam, A., 02554
Sathasivampillai, K., 18733
Sathe, Madhusudan D., 21244
Sathe, Satyaranjan Purushottam, 12362, 12832
Sathianathaier, R., 06193, 08156
Sathianathan, M.A., 15380
Sathyamurthy, T.V., 13447, 19211
Sathyanarayana, R., 02772, 02968
Sathyanatha Aiyar, R. *See* Sathianathaier, R.
Satin, Nora, 11885
Satindra Singh, 09752
Satish Chandra, 05728, 07539, 07610, 07635, 07661, 12514, 13406
Satish Kumar, 13688, 14318, 17574, 17585, 25961, 25967, 25986, 26038, 26078
Satpathy, Nandini, 22417
Satprakashananda, Swami, 01420, 02179, 11333
Satprem, 11403
Sattanathan, A.N., 19352
Sattar, Abdus, 25513-4
Sattar, Ellen, 25524, 25624
Sattar, Mohammad Ghulam, 25558
Satthianadhan, Samuel, 19474
Satyal, Yajna Raj, 27401
Satyamurti, T., 01965
Satyanand Agnihotri, 11268
Satyananda Saraswati, Swami, 04831
Satyanarayana, J., 15241
Satyanarayana, Kambhampati, 00419
Satyanarayana, M., 12499
Satyanarayanamurti, Varanasi, 12500
Satyaprakash, 01134, 04007-8, 09859, 14730, 17289, 25148, 27673, 27710-2, 27717, 27729-32
Satyapriya, V.S., 20353
Satyavrat, Usha, 17067
Sauliere, A., 08158
Saunders, E. Dale, 01663
Saunders, Kenneth James, 04885
Saundranayagam, Terrence, 18618
Savale, R.S., 21468
Savara, Sudershan K., 12107, 13407, 13506
Savarkar, Vinayak Damodar, 00171, 08259, 09507, 13261-4
Savdasia, V.B., 21718
Save, Khanderao Jagannath, 20826
Savita, 15742
Savla, Chandan, 21710
Savur, Manorama G., 15621
Sawant, Shashikant B., 21338, 21556
Sawhney, P.K., 15585
Saxena, A.P., 12647
Saxena, Brijendra Swarup, 15471
Saxena, D.P., 03733, 23860
Saxena, Hari Mohan, 22071
Saxena, Hori Lal, 12099
Saxena, J.C., 22113
Saxena, J.N., 12182
Saxena, J.P., 15523
Saxena, K.C., 12076
Saxena, K.M.L., 09295
Saxena, K.S., 20643
Saxena, Kiran, 09543
Saxena, Kishore Kumar, 03661
Saxena, Krishna Swarup, 00506, 06952
Saxena, P.C., 15949
Saxena, R.C., 23621
Saxena, Rajendra Kumar, 08355, 10711
Saxena, Ranvir Prakash, 20858
Saxena, S.P., 15471
Saxena, Sateshwari, 16411
Saxena, Sudha, 23830
Saxena, Sushil Kumar, 02827, 02837
Saxena, T.P., 00161
Saxena, Vinod Kumar, 09693, 13852
Sayaji Rao Gaekwar III, Maharaja of Baroda, 20633
Sayana, V.V., 19278
Sayed, G.M., 22462
Sayed, Z.A., 21869
Sayeed, Khalid Bin, 10351, 17314, 17351, 17372, 17410, 17465, 17472, 17483, 17503, 17537, 17541, 17678, 23080
Saymi, Dhooswan, 00543
Scarfe, Allan, 13489, 24082, 24166, 26982
Scarfe, Wendy, 13489, 24082, 24166, 26982
Schaefer, E.S., 18789
Schaller, George B., 27042
Schams, M. Radul, 12236
Schappert, Linda G., 27745
Scharfe, Hartmut, 04310, 05187, 05212
Scharpé, A., 00561, 05325
Schastok, Sara W., 05587
Schayer, Stanislaw, 01449
Schechtman, Joseph B., 10507
Schendel, Willem van, 25149
Schermerhorn, Richard Alonzo, 00709, 15796, 15845
Schetelich, Maria, 04309
Scheuer, Jacques, 04649
Schiffman, Harold, 27893
Schimmel, Annemarie, 02525, 02536, 02616, 05940, 05953, 08682-4, 08829-30, 11509-10, 11668-9, 22514, 27099, 27123
Schleicher, Charles P., 14121
Schlesinger, Lee I., 21171
Schlingloff, Dieter, 04311
Schlipp, Paul Arthur, 11441
Schlumberger, Daniel, 05536
Schmeits, Eric, 19977
Schmid, Robert, 26189
Schmid, Toni, 26336
Schmidt, Hanns Peter, 01559, 03851
Schmidt, Richard, 06091-4
Schmidt, Ruth Laila, 28014

Schmitt, Erika, 05537, 20938
Schmitthener, Samuel, 12872
Schneider, Ulrich, 03868, 04139
Schneiderman, Leo, 11310
Schoenfeld, Benjamin N., 12378, 13183, 25987
Schoff, Wilfred H., 04027
Schokker, G.H., 00022
Scholberg, Henry, 07903, 27783
Scholz, Fred, 22544-6
Scholz, John T., 26003
Schomberg, R.C.F., 23044
Schomerus, Hilko Wiardo, 06314, 06323, 06532
Schorowsky, Michael, 07960
Schrader, Friedrich Otto, 04592, 04783
Schramm, Harold, 02798, 02915
Schregel, Johannes, 18066
Schreiner, Peter, 16702
Schrenk-Notzing, Caspar, 09091
Schubring, Walther, 01287, 01292, 01333, 21930
Schuler, Edgar Albert, 17527, 17948
Schuler, Kathryn R., 17527
Schulman, Arnold, 16744
Schultz, Friedrich A., 04762
Schultz, T. Paul, 25281
Schuman, Howard, 17565, 25429, 25492
Schurhammer, Georg, 07850, 08080
Schuster, Nancy, 04860
Schuyler, Montgomery, 05265, 06009
Schwab, Raymond, 11845
Schwartz, Barton M., 26757, 26801
Schwartz, P.R., 03330
Schwartzberg, Joseph E., 00156, 00232, 15506, 23703
Schwarz, Walter, 18501
Schweinfurth, Ulrich, 18823
Schweitzer, Albert, 01158
Schwerin, Detlef, 20904, 24097
Schwerin, Kerrin Gräfin, 00737, 06992
Scott, Dixon, 06045
Scott, George Batley, 23101
Scott, Roland Waldeck, 11214, 16719
Scrafton, Luke, 08871
Sdasyuk, Galina, 14476
Seal, Anil, 09062, 09578
Seal, Brajendranath, 00263
Seal, Srish Chandra, 16232, 24822-3
Seaver, George, 09449
Sebastian, M., 13999
Sederberg, Peter C., 25181
Sedlar, Jean W., 04100
Seely, Clinton Booth, 25107
Seely, John Benjamin, 06822
Seemann, Heinrich, 27370
Seervai, H.M., 12820
Seetal, Sohan Singh, 08659, 22575-6
Seetalakshmi, R., 19978
Seetaraman, M.V., 11776
Seethalakshmi, K.A., 19600, 25896
Seetharam, K.S., 14172
Seevanayagam, 12786
Sehgal, Amar Nath, 17225
Selbourne, David, 13599
Seligmann, Brenda Z., 18833
Seligmann, Charles Gabriel, 18833
Seltmann, F., 03009
Selvadurai, A.J., 18824, 19025
Selvajayam, S., 18661
Selvaraj, C., 19351
Selvaratnam, S., 18599, 18602, 18613, 18894
Semeka-Pankratov, Elena, 01621
Seminar on a Policy for Skilled Manpower, Dacca (1967), 18055
Seminar on Agricultural Marketing, West Pakistan (1965), 17929
Seminar on Basic Marketing Problems of our Traders, Dacca (1966), 25485
Seminar on Bombay's Development and Master Plan, Bombay (1968), 21519
Seminar on Book Publishing, New Delhi (1969), 16905
Seminar on Calcutta and its Problems, Calcutta (1970), 24785
Seminar on Casteism and Removal of Untouchability, Delhi (1955), 15775
Seminar on Cultural Action for Social Change, Delhi (1974), 15102
Seminar on Defence, Delhi (1966), 13761
Seminar on Editorial Content, Delhi (1965), 16879
Seminar on Educational Research, Delhi (1969), 16387
Seminar on Environmental Pollution and Urban Administration, New Delhi (1973), 16058
Seminar on Environmental Pollution in the Context of Present Industrial Developments in India, Trivandrum (1974), 16246
Seminar on Family Planning, Dacca (1972), 25600
Seminar on Fertiliser Production and Technology, Delhi (1969), 14866
Seminar on Fiction and the Reading Public in India, University of Mysore (1965), 17026
Seminar on Government Regulation of Private Enterprise, Delhi (1969), 15288
Seminar on Health Information System, New Delhi (1973), 16233
Seminar on Higher Education and Development, Delhi (1975), 16423
Seminar on Indian Aesthetics and Art Activity, Simla (1966), 03127
Seminar on Indian English, Hyderabad (1972), 17075
Seminar on Industrial Co-operation, Delhi (1961), 15344
Seminar on Industrial Relations in a Developing Economy, 15567, 15675
Seminar on Integrated Rural Development, Dacca (1975), 25381
Seminar on Law and Urbanization in India, Allahabad (1967), 16095
Seminar on Market Towns and Spatial Development, New Delhi (1971), 16054
Seminar on Mass Communication Media and Adult Literacy, New Delhi (1966), 16843
Seminar on Medical and Socio-Economic Aspects of Abortion, Calcutta (1972), 16325
Seminar on Medieval Inscriptions, Aligarh Muslim University, 05683
Seminar on Methodology of Social Science Research, Gandhian Institute of Studies (1964), 15700
Seminar on Metropolitan Area Problems in Pakistan, Karachi (1963), 18122
Seminar on National Integration, Delhi (1958), 12405
Seminar on Non-violence and Social Change, University of Allahabad (1971), 15720
Seminar on OCP and NBP, 03669
Seminar on Panchayati Raj, Planning and Democracy, Jaipur (1964), 12981
Seminar on Pollution and Human Environment, Bombay (1970), 16247
Seminar on Population and Development, Kathmandu (1970), 26106
Seminar on Problems and Prospects of Local Government, Islamabad (1972), 17627
Seminar on Problems of Development of Tribal Areas, Warora (1979), 15797
Seminar on Problems of Farm Mechanization, Sardar Patel University (1971), 14873
Seminar on Public Administration and Police in Pakistan, Peshawar (1962), 17375
Seminar on Removal of Untouchability in Gujarat, Gujarat University (1973), 21844
Seminar on Renascent Bengal, 1817-1857, Calcutta (1971), 24576
Seminar on Rural Housing and Village-Planning, Vallabh Vidyanagar (1960), 15169
Seminar on Sanskrit Learning through the Ages, 00858
Seminar on Science in India's Basic Problems, 17253
Seminar on "Secularism: Its Implications for Law and Life in India," Delhi (1965), 12429
Seminar on Social Problems of Urbanization in Pakistan, Karachi (1962), 18123
Seminar on Socialism in India (1919-1939), 10037
Seminar on States' Taxation in Indian Federation, Shivaji University (1977), 14597
Seminar on the Current Economic Problems of Pakistan, Karachi (1967), 17822
Seminar on the Eradication of Social Evils, Lahore (1961), 18129
Seminar on the Hindu Marriage, 1956 and the Special Marriage Act, 1954, New Delhi (1975), 16001
Seminar on the Indian Ocean, Hyderabad (1972), 11994
Seminar on the Police and the Citizen, Lahore (1961), 17376
Seminar on the Problem of Goa's Integration with India, Margao (1964), 21070

Seminar on the Role of Documentary Films in National Development, Delhi (1967), 16967
Seminar on the Social Responsibilities of Trade Unions, Delhi (1966), 15657
Seminar on Urban Planning and Development Authorities, New Delhi (1974), 16100
Sen, A., 15454
Sen, A.C., 02121
Sen, Amal Kumar, 22013, 22033
Sen, Amarendralal, 14950
Sen, Amartya Kumar, 11187-8
Sen, Amiya Kumar, 07819, 11244
Sen, Arun, 07260
Sen, Asis, 01622
Sen, Asit Kumar, 07033
Sen, Asok, 24973
Sen, Asoke Kumar, 12888
Sen, Benoychandra, 05014
Sen, Bhowani, 10960, 13233, 14960
Sen, Biswajit, 26511
Sen, Chanakya. *See* Sen Gupta, Bhabani
Sen, Chitrabanu, 03869
Sen, D.C., 07243
Sen, D.K., 00712
Sen, Dharam, 02073
Sen, Dharanidhar, 03486, 03506, 03557-8
Sen, Dinesh Chandra, 02663, 07210, 07240, 07290, 25126, 25659
Sen, Gertrude Emerson, 26481
Sen, Girish Chandra, 06764
Sen, Jahar, 26072, 26096, 26388
Sen, Jitendra Mohan, 10604-5
Sen, Jyoti, 20907, 23993, 24167
Sen, Keshab Chandra, 11257-60
Sen, Kshitimohan, 01205, 05963, 07092
Sen, Lalit Kumar, 15032, 15043, 15068, 15072, 19737, 19831, 20289, 25909
Sen, Madhu, 05160
Sen, Makhan Lal, 04700
Sen, Mohan Lal A., 22082
Sen, Mohit, 10055, 10061, 13168, 13234, 13241, 13505
Sen, N.B., 16927-8, 22642
Sen, Nabaneeta, 04726
Sen, Nani Lal, 01421
Sen, Narayan Chandra, 05655
Sen, Nilratan, 07224-5
Sen, Paritosh, 17226
Sen, Prabir, 24931
Sen, Prabodh Chandra, 25085
Sen, Pranab Kumar, 01069
Sen, Priyaranjan, 06805, 07262, 22418, 24832, 24925
Sen, Probhat Kumar, 27336
Sen, Pulinbihari, 24994-6
Sen, Rajaniranjan, 02051
Sen, Rajendra Nath, 05787
Sen, Ranen, 24373
Sen, S.N., 09466, 10655
Sen, Sachin, 10352, 16858, 17484, 25017
Sen, Sailendra Nath, 08328
Sen, Samar, 12118, 13252
Sen, Samar Ranjan, 14794, 15108
Sen, Samarendra Nath, 00248-9, 00264
Sen, Sanat Kumar, 01450
Sen, Satyendranath, 24476, 24538, 24769
Sen, Shila, 24340
Sen, Siba Pada, 00095, 00115-6, 00172, 02395, 07904, 07923, 07940, 09004, 09020, 09282, 09527, 10706, 10821, 27476
Sen, Sirdar D.K., 26840
Sen, Sudhir, 14817
Sen, Sukumar, 02664, 05213, 05239, 05307, 07226, 07241, 07263, 07308, 08967, 24901, 27991
Sen, Sunil Kumar, 10921, 10961, 11102, 24506
Sen, Sunil Madhav, 11815
Sen, Surendranath, 05656, 07851, 07913, 08268-9, 08276-7, 08313, 09508
Sen, Sushanta, 01375
Sen Gupta, Anima, 03993, 04797, 04815, 06436
Sen Gupta, Bhabani, 12029, 12049, 13214, 13232
Sen Gupta, Jyoti, 13757, 25157
Sen Gupta, Kalyan Kumar, 09467
Sen Gupta, Kanti Prasanna, 08961
Sen Gupta, Nares Chandra, 04410-1
Sen Gupta, P., 14476
Sen Gupta, Sankar, 00958, 01639, 02428, 02437, 02443-4, 02901-2, 11799, 25114-7
Sen Gupta, Santosh Chandra, 25048
Sen Gupta, Santosh Kumar, 14179, 16273
Sen Gupta, Subodh Chandra, 25078
Senapati, Nilamani, 22398
Senaratne, K.M.L.B., 01942
Sénart, Émile Charles Marie, 00768, 04886, 04905
Senaveratne, John M., 03375
Sencourt, Robert, 11886
Seneviratna, Anuradha, 03024
Seneviratne, H.L., 08064
Seneviratne, Heraliwala L., 01943-5
Seneviratne, Maureen, 04240, 18427
Senewiratne, S.T., 18686
Sengupta, Anil Kumar, 24544, 26623
Sengupta, B.K., 24788
Sengupta, Barun, 10443, 13613
Sengupta, Benoyendra, 27460
Sengupta, Kalyan Kumar, 24507-9
Sengupta, Kollel, 26670
Sengupta, N.K., 15268
Sengupta, Nanda Gopal, 02665
Sengupta, Nilakshi, 04469
Sengupta, Nirmal, 24152
Sengupta, P.R., 15011
Sengupta, Padmini (Sathianadhan), 11769, 11777, 24325, 24838
Sengupta, Prabodh Chandra, 00287, 04532
Sengupta, R., 05544
Sengupta, S.C., 24989
Sengupta, Subroto, 16934
Sengupta, Sunil C., 24611, 24670a, 24679
Sengupta, Syamalkanti, 24594, 24644, 24685-6
Sensarma, P., 07466
Serajuddin, Alamgir Muhammad, 08902
Serajul Haque, 25147, 25272-2a, 25331
Serampore College, 24851
Serebryakov, Igor Dmitrievitch, 02481, 02629
Sesha Aiyer, K.G., 04221
Seshachar, B.R., 19868
Seshadri, K., 12316, 12712, 13682, 15056, 19693, 19714, 19716-7, 19753
Seshadri, Pundi, 10599, 10724
Seshadri, Sadagopan, 12809
Seshadri Aiyangar, Pundi. *See* Seshadri, Pundi
Seshadri Iyer, Kumarapuram, Sir, 20241
Seshagiri, Narasimhiah, 13784
Seshagiri Rao, K., 16308
Seshagiri Rao, K.L., 01366
Seshagiri Rao, K.R., 19883
Seshagiri Rao, L.S., 20562-9
Seshaiah, S., 15730
Seshanna, A.V., 12684
Sestini, Valerio, 03480
Sesya, C., 27477
Setalvad, Motilal Chimanlal, 12343, 12427, 12601, 12818, 12862-3, 12924
Seth, Bhoj Raj, 17242
Seth, Hira Lal, 10101, 10171, 10390
Seth, K.N., 06711
Seth, Krishnan Lal, 18072, 25264-5, 25302
Seth, M.J., 24658
Seth, S.P., 12005, 12050, 14014
Seth, Shiam Kishore, 17974, 27043
Seth, Veena, 23025
Sethi, Amarjit Singh, 15663
Sethi, Jai Chand Dev ("J.D."), 09925, 12317, 13311, 13337, 13993, 14304, 14451
Sethi, Kamla, 23332
Sethi, M.L., 22022
Sethi, Narendra Kumar, 15171
Sethi, R.R., Sir, 09033, 22577, 22934, 23172
Sethna, Kaikhushru Dhunjibhoy, 03776-7, 04048, 11778-9
Sethna, Minocher Jehangirji, 00923, 16194
Sethu, C., 19306
Sethuraman, N., 06183, 06200
Sethuraman, T.V., 14495
Seton, Malcolm Catter Cariston, 09096
Seton, Marie, 13361, 16987, 25139
Seton-Karr, Walter Scott, 08039, 08929, 24443
Settar, S., 06677
Sewell, Robert, 00146, 00567, 06231
Seybold, Theodore C., 11538
Seyid Muhammad, Valiyaveetil Abdulazeez, 13521

Seymour, Susan, 22377
Shackle, C., 02540, 06993, 22979, 22993-5, 27962
Shafāᶜat Ahmad Khān, Sir, 08388, 08994, 10285
Shafeev, D.A., 27982
Shaffer, Jimmie Gray, 03588
Shafi, M., 18056-7
Shafi, Q.M., 22883
Shafiqur Rahman, A.B. Muhammad, 25246-7
Shafqat, C.M., 17499
Shah, A.C., 21232
Shah, A.R., 21861
Shah, Ambalal Premchand, 05157
Shah, Amita, 21672
Shah, Amritlal B., 12428, 12467, 13712, 15727, 15853, 16401, 16454, 16502, 16524, 16646, 16859, 17254
Shah, Arvindbhai Manilal, 00637, 00964-5, 08349, 10975, 21828, 21837, 21861
Shah, B.V., 13103, 21909-11
Shah, C.H., 14731, 14768, 14972, 21259, 21726, 21734, 21760
Shah, Chandulal M., 13648
Shah, G.L., 27202
Shah, Ghanshyam, 20833, 21673-5, 21687, 21733, 21845, 23510
Shah, Giriraj, 27337
Shah, Haku, 03409, 20829
Shah, Ikbal Ali, 02423
Shah, J.M., 20516
Shah, Jayantilal Chottalal, 12344
Shah, Jethalal Govardhandas, 06505-7
Shah, Jyotsna H., 16163
Shah, K.K., 16869
Shah, K.R., 21898
Shah, Khushal Talaksi, 04361, 09219, 10286-7, 10353, 10897, 11037, 11159-60, 11194, 22728
Shah, Manubhai, 14630, 14638, 21698, 21761, 21784
Shah, Moin, 26300
Shah, Mowahid H., 17619
Shah, N.K., 26302
Shah, Naginchand Jagjiwandas, 11073
Shah, Navinchandra N., 27621
Shah, Nazeer Ali, 22610
Shah, Popatlal Govindlal, 20834-6, 21818
Shah, Priyabala, 06113
Shah, Ramesh Chandra, 11621, 17051
Shah, Ranchhodlal M., 12977
Shah, S.M., 14804
Shah, Sarla, 21862
Shah, Shantilal H., 16318
Shah, Umakant Premanand, 01832, 03146-7, 03260, 03418, 05588-90, 06830, 06843, 06850-1, 08475
Shah, V.B., 21829
Shah, Vimal, 21734, 21862
Shah, Vimal P., 15894
Shah Husain, 08687
Shah Nawaz, Jahan Ara, Begum, 22657
Shah Nawaz Khan, Major-General, 10442-4, 10459-60
Shaha, Rishikesh, 25948, 25968, 26005, 27371
Shahamat ᶜAli, 22578
Shahane, Vasant Anant, 11906, 11917-21, 17164-5, 17169, 21649
Shahani, Anandram T., 27932, 27945-6
Shahani, Dayaram Gidumal, 21376
Shahani, Savitri, 21481, 21838
Shahbuddin, Muhammad, 17390
Shahidullah, M., 07227
Shahjahan, Mirza, 25439
Shahu Chhatrapati, Maharaja of Kolhapur, 20596
Shaikh, A.U., 14713
Shakdher, Shyam Lal, 12771-2, 12778-80, 12784, 12810-1, 13564
Shakespear, John, 26624
Shakespear, Leslie Waterfield, 08329, 21557
Shakir, Moin, 09544, 09983, 10194, 12456-7, 13054, 13293, 13635, 16779
Sham Lal, 13465
Sham Rao, D.P., 21623
Shamasastry, Rudrapatna, Mahamahopadhyaya, 01451, 04298
Shami, Parwaiz, 18157
Shamlal, 17227
Shams-ud-din, Abu Zafar, 25205
Shamsuddoulah, A.B.M., 27733
Shamsul Hoque, Abunasar, 17363
Shamsul Islam, 11887, 11907, 25327
Shamsur Rahman, Ghazi, 25663
Shan, Harnam Singh, 08605
Shan Muhammad, 09796, 09805-6, 10391, 11481
Shanbhag, D.N., 02597
Shand, Alexander Innes, 22459
Shand, R.T., 14863
Shankar, 13120
Shankar, Girija, 10102
Shankar, Kripa, 23577-8, 23607
Shankar, Lakshminarayana, 02799
Shankar, Ravi, 02850
Shankar, Shyam, 10139
Shankar, V., 10189
Shankar Raju Naidu, S., 06579, 08810
Shankar Rao, U. Bhavani, 00155
Shankaranarayanan, S., 05810, 05881
Shankarnarayan, K., 14897
Shanker, Uday, 23316
Shanmugam, S.V., 02360, 02548
Shanmugam Pillai, M., 05429, 27875-6

Shanmugasundaram, V., 14805
Shanmugasundaram, Yasodha, 19266, 19339
Shanta, 01070
Shantha, K., 20222
Sharab, Zahur al-Hasan, 06801
Sharad, Onkar, 13190, 13490
Sharafuddin, Abdulla al-Muti, 18189, 25614
Sharan, Girja, 21752
Sharan, Mahesh Kumar, 04071, 04438, 04694
Sharan, Parmatma, 09156, 12623, 17315
Sharar, Abdul Halim, 23847
Sharda, Ram Dev, 00809
Sharda, Sadhu Ram, 08688
Sharib, Zahurul Hassan, 12945, 21988, 23808
Sharif, C.M., 17940
Sharif, M. Raihan, 25328
Sharif, Mian Mohammad, 17416
Sharif al Mujahid, 18249
Sharifa Begum, 25282
Sharma, A.C., 22769, 22782, 22797
Sharma, Akhileshwar, 12833
Sharma, Ambika Prasad, 09392, 10221
Sharma, Arvind (1940-), 01182, 03943, 06437, 06567, 10712, 14362, 16760
Sharma, Arvind K., 12525, 15242
Sharma, B.A.V., 19667, 19690, 21172, 21195
Sharma, B.D., 15798, 23223
Sharma, B.L., 02895, 17748
Sharma, B.M., 23355
Sharma, B.R., 01814
Sharma, B.S., 15250
Sharma, Baldev R., 15607-8
Sharma, Basudeo, 09665
Sharma, Benishankar, 11335
Sharma, Bodh Raj, 22698, 23180
Sharma, Brij Bhushan, 11835
Sharma, Brij Lal, 12036, 17741, 23187
Sharma, Brij Mohan, 12318
Sharma, Brij Narain, 07074
Sharma, Brijendra Nath, 01708, 01747, 01798, 01813, 02093, 07075
Sharma, Brijnath, 07004
Sharma, Chandra K., 26117-9, 27378
Sharma, Chandradhar, 01309, 01431
Sharma, D.P., 14755
Sharma, Dasharatha, 00469, 06738-9
Sharma, Daya Nand, 27789
Sharma, Deoki N., 27840
Sharma, Dev, 12108
Sharma, Devendra Prasad, 13649
Sharma, Devichand, 25897
Sharma, Dhirendra, 01432, 13614
Sharma, E.P., 14668
Sharma, G.D., 08369-70, 16503, 22009, 22061
Sharma, G.R., 03566, 04189
Sharma, G.S., 12371, 12429, 16412
Sharma, Gian Chand, 08356
Sharma, Girdhar Behari, 15783-4
Sharma, Giriraj Kishore, 15650
Sharma, Gollapalli Nagabhushana, 09544
Sharma, Gopi Nath, 00470, 06780, 07390, 08362, 08401, 08506, 08514
Sharma, Hari, 09372
Sharma, Hari Dev, 27641
Sharma, Hari P., 12209

Sharma, Hari Shanker, 22206
Sharma, Harish Chandra, 14678
Sharma, Hira Lal, 08301
Sharma, I.K., 22148
Sharma, Indrajeet, 02035
Sharma, Ishwar Chandra, 01522
Sharma, J.N., 21771
Sharma, J.V.M., 20503
Sharma, Jagadish Prasad, 26052
Sharma, Jagdish, 04335
Sharma, Jagdish Narayan, 14528
Sharma, Jagdish P., 06794
Sharma, Jagdish Saran, 00147, 09008, 09528, 09860, 13125, 13348, 14319, 14996, 15846, 27478
Sharma, Jai Kishore, 27579
Sharma, Jitendra Raj, 26073
Sharma, K.D., 14290
Sharma, Kailash Nath, 00748, 00844, 23809
Sharma, Kamla Kant, 22072
Sharma, Kaushal Kishore, 11721, 17116, 17181
Sharma, Kanhaiyalal, 22114-5, 23994
Sharma, Khagendra Nath, 26020
Sharma, Krishan, 21033
Sharma, Krishan Dev, 23438
Sharma, Krishan Kumar, 09737
Sharma, Krishan Lal, 15296
Sharma, Krishna Kumar, 14639
Sharma, Krishna Murti, 16138
Sharma, Kuldeepak, 16297
Sharma, L.C., 14921
Sharma, Lakshmi Nidhi, 06964
Sharma, Lal Narain, 12599
Sharma, M., 23529
Sharma, M.D., 14662
Sharma, M.L., 14850, 23315
Sharma, Mahadeo Prasad, 09220, 23541
Sharma, Man Mohan, 12725, 26355, 27396
Sharma, Mathura Lal, 20656, 27194
Sharma, Mohan L., 01575, 13661, 21969, 22109, 23500
Sharma, Mukunda Madhava, 05987, 28007
Sharma, Murari Lal, 24119
Sharma, N.K., 27358
Sharma, N.N., 04462
Sharma, Nagendra, 26356
Sharma, Nand Kishore, 27210
Sharma, Narinder Kumar, 17068
Sharma, Neel Kamal, 22144
Sharma, Neeta, 06021
Sharma, Nilamber Dev, 23254
Sharma, Nilima, 11225, 11431
Sharma, O.P., 13545, 16293, 23007
Sharma, P.C., 09944
Sharma, P. Dash, 20905
Sharma, P.K., 25705
Sharma, P.N., 23207
Sharma, P.R., 03455
Sharma, Padmaja, 20647
Sharma, Phool Kumar, 12037, 12529, 12537
Sharma, Prabhu Datta, 12714, 21989-90
Sharma, Prakash C., 17921
Sharma, Prem Sarup, 14756
Sharma, Premlata, 02682
Sharma, Priya Vrat, 00334, 04550
Sharma, R.A., 15297
Sharma, R.K., 13409, 13878, 14000-1
Sharma, Raj Kumar, 03522, 06899
Sharma, Rajendra, 12372
Sharma, Rajendra Narayan, 12290, 14729, 14732, 15000, 16159
Sharma, Rajiv, 19698
Sharma, Rakesh R.P., 26493
Sharma, Ram Chandra, 16310, 22014
Sharma, Ram Karan, 04560, 04650
Sharma, Ram Nath, 11396, 15012
Sharma, Ram Sharan, 00908, 04262, 04358, 04400, 04454, 05709, 05717-8
Sharma, Ram Swarup, 04007-8
Sharma, Ramashraya, 04727
Sharma, Ramesh Chandra, 07636, 16384, 16593
Sharma, Ranbir, 25865-6
Sharma, Ravindra, 22002
Sharma, S.C., 25762
Sharma, S.L., 08290
Sharma, S.P., 23741
Sharma, Satgur Lal, 16504
Sharma, Savitri, 15885
Sharma, Shambhu Nath, 03810
Sharma, Shiv, 00322
Sharma, Shri Ram, 12135, 12183, 13689
Sharma, Shripad Rama (1879-), 06765, 07422, 07433, 08260-1, 08436-7, 21618, 22973
Sharma, Sita Ram (1932-), 16398
Sharma, Sri Ram (1900-76), 06936, 07391, 07540, 08364, 07662, 08363, 12345, 12530, 12834, 22643, 22909, 22930
Sharma, Sudesh Kumar, 12297, 12624, 12906, 12978, 22712
Sharma, Sunil K., 25733
Sharma, Suraj Bhan, 20653
Sharma, Suresh Kumar, 00092, 15033, 27597
Sharma, Surya Prakash, 12109, 13713, 13906
Sharma, T.C., 26465
Sharma, T.R., 13215, 24192
Sharma, Tej Ram, 04060
Sharma, Tirth Raj, 15229
Sharma, Udayan, 13615
Sharma, Ursula M., 01788, 11292, 25898, 26909
Sharma, Vishnu Datt, 22149
Sharma, Y.D., 03436, 15826, 27281
Sharma Thakur, G.C., 25793
Sharman, Gopal, 02717
Sharp, Gene, 09965-7
Sharp, Henry, Sir, 10565, 23385
Sharpe, Bryan, 21592
Sharpe, Elizabeth, 20620
Sharpe, Eric J., 01211, 11551
Sharrock, John Alfred, 19543
Shashi, Shyam Singh, 12726, 14941, 25888-9, 27338
Shashi Bhushan, 13426, 13758
Shashi Kant, 04061
Shasmal, Kartick Chandra, 24645
Shastri, Ajay Mitra, 04036, 04072-3, 04538, 05645, 05674
Shastri, Ashokanath, 02122
Shastri, C.P., 24078
Shastri, Dakshinaranjan, 01050, 04596-8
Shastri, Dharmendra Nath, 00037, 01388
Shastri, G.C., 25949
Shastri, G.N., 14161
Shastri, Gaurinath Bhattacharya, 02482
Shastri, Hari Prasad, 02004, 02148, 04701
Shastri, Joyadeva Ganguly, 24146
Shastri, K. Vasudeva, 02928
Shastri, Kali Charan, 05188
Shastri, Lal Bahadur, 13399-401
Shastri, P.N., 02608, 02676
Shastri, Prabhu Dutt, 01410
Shastri, Raghuvara Mitthulal, 23731
Shastri, Surendra Nath, 05288
Shastri, Vaidyanath, 03796, 11293
Shastry, B.S., 06232
Shastry, Badrinarayan Damodar, 14843
Shaw, David C., 17797
Shaw, William, 26625
Shay, Theodore L., 09706
Shea, David, 07655
Shea, Thomas William, 20030
Sheean, Vincent, 09887
Sheik Ali, B., 06184, 06216
Sheikh, Atique Zafar, 10386
Sheikh-Dilthey, Helmtraud, 26864
Sheil-Small, Denis, 09304
Shejwalkar, P.C., 21339
Shejwalkar, Tryambak Shankar, 08302
Shekhar, Indu, 05274
Shekhar, Raj, 16647
Shelat, Jayendra Manilal, 07477, 12430
Shelat, Nanoobhai Gaurishanker, 12864, 12875
Shellim, Maurice, 11790, 11980
Shende, K.K., 21303
Shende, N.J., 03931-2, 03944
Shendge, Malati J., 03608
Shenoi, P.V., 14795
Shenoy, Bellikoth Rahunath, 14052, 14383, 18674
Shenoy, J.P.L., 01967
Shenoy, Sudha R., 14384-5
Sheorey, Indumati, 21658
Sheppard, Eric William, 08024
Sher-Gil, Amrita, 11824
Sher Singh, 22834-5
Sher Singh, Gyani, 08584, 08660
Sherer, John Walter, 09484
Sherring, Charles Atmore, 25837, 25939

Sherring, Matthew Atmore, 02052, 23704
Sherwani, Haroon Khan, 00444, 06691-2, 07434, 08120-4, 08237, 19631, 19866
Sherwani, Latif Ahmed, 10354, 12038
Sheshadri, P., 13526
Sheth, Bhanu, 19968
Sheth, Chimanlal Bhailal, 06795
Sheth, D.L., 13081, 13137
Sheth, Hansa, 16195
Sheth, Jayana, 21944
Sheth, Narayan Ranchhodlal, 15489, 15562, 15637, 15609-10, 15654, 16112, 21795
Sheth, Pravin N., 20733, 21676-7, 21688-9, 21819
Sheth, Surabhi, 05822
Sheth, Tarun, 15623, 21683
Shetty, S.L., 14238
Shetty, V.V., 20340
Shibly, Atful Hye, 09296
Shils, Edward Albert, 13068, 15841, 16525
Shinde, Anandrao Baliram, 21604
Shinde, B.G., 21644
Shinde, Suresh D., 21245
Shingi, Prakash M., 15377, 15964
Shinohara, Miyohei, 15320
Shirakawa, Yoshikazu, 27355
Shirali, Vishnudass, 02718
Shirer, William L., 09926
Shirgaonkar, S.B., 17229
Shiri, G., 20556
Shirsat, K.R., 09761, 21630
Shirwadkar, Meena, 11738, 17083
Shiv Dās Lakhnavī, 07523
Shiv Lal, 10318, 12443, 12563, 13148-9, 13319, 13331, 13346-7, 13494, 13600, 13616, 14239
Shiva Rao, Benegal, 11125, 12283-4, 13337
Shivakumar, Chitra, 20527
Shivakumar, K., 19324
Shivamaggi, H.V., 15099
Shivamurthy, M., 20276-7
Shivanath, 02630, 23255
Shivarudrappa, A.D.G., 06568
Shive Kumar, 11009
Shiveshwarkar, Leela, 07157
Shiviah, 10085, 12909
Shiviah, M., 12531
Shodan, Manisha, 00888
Shore, Frederick John, 09328
Shourie, Arun, 01206, 12262, 13601, 13617
Shourie, H.D., 14035
Shraddhananda, Swami, 10133, 10140-1
Shrader, Lawrence L., 21166, 21961
Shrawan Kumar, 17047
Shreedharan, G., 20190, 20197
Shreshtha, B.P., 26178
Shreshtha, Mathura, 26300
Shreshtha, S.H., 27379
Shrestha, Amrit Man, 26120
Shrestha, Badri Prasad, 26121, 26135, 21647
Shrestha, Bishnu P., 26333
Shrestha, Chandra Bahadur, 26292
Shrestha, Chij K., 28011
Shrestha, Mangal Krishna, 26032-4
Shrestha, Surendra B., 26035
Shri Prakash, 16435, 22195
Shridevi, S., 19893
Shridharani, Krishnalal Jethalal, 09968, 11038
Shrimali, K.L., 13033
Shrimali, Kalulal, 16601
Shriman Narayan, 09905, 11196, 13169-70, 13312, 14305-7, 14320, 14333-4, 21678, 26074
Shrimany, Adhir K., 15881
Shringy, R.K., 02773
Shrinivas Iyengar, P.T., 06973
Shrinivas Rao, K., 16585
Shrishrimal, Walchand Chunilal, 14714
Shrivastava, B.K., 09393, 10412, 10428, 17736
Shrivastava, Gopinath, 12480
Shrivastava, Narendra Nath, 14640
Shrivastava, Rama Shanker. *See* Srivastava, Rama Shanker
Shroff, A.D., 14693
Shroff, Bomi K.F., 11973
Shroff, Phiroze Jamshedji, 14346
Shroff, R.G., 21837, 21861
Shujauddin, Mohammad, 07489
Shujauddin, Razia, 07489
Shukla, B.D., 23627
Shukla, B.R.K., 15721
Shukla, Bisheshwar Dayal, 10015
Shukla, Brahma Kumar, 26501
Shukla, Dinesh Chandra, 04163
Shukla, Dinesh M., 21820
Shukla, H.C., 00323
Shukla, H.N., 23684, 24126
Shukla, Harkant, 03035
Shukla, Harshadrai Sankleshwar, 21882
Shukla, Hira Lal, 17069
Shukla, Jadavrai Bhavanishankar, 21863
Shukla, Janardan Datt, 12880, 12960
Shukla, Jayadev Mohan, 27798
Shukla, K.B., 12988
Shukla, K.S., 03954
Shukla, Kamla Shanker, 22270
Shukla, Kripa Shankar, 05738
Shukla, Lalit Kumar, 03063
Shukla, Madan Mohan, 14622, 14679
Shukla, Mani Shanker, 03306
Shukla, Manorama, 14092
Shukla, N.K., 24168
Shukla, Narayan S., 08945
Shukla, P.D., 16413
Shukla, Pratap Chandra, 01479
Shukla, R.S., 16545
Shukla, Ram Lakhan, 09402
Shukla, Ravi Shankar, 12501
Shukla, Santosh Kumar, 22228
Shukla, Satyendra R., 26384
Shukla, Shaligram, 23699
Shukla, Vishnoo Prasad, 22207
Shulman, David Dean, 01735, 01823, 01954, 06580
Shulman, Frank Joseph, 27696-7
Shumshere, Pashupati, 26019
Shungoonny Menon, P., 00426
Shyam, Madhav, 16664
Shyam, Radhey, 07455, 08242-3
Shyamlal, 22094
Siauve, Suzanne, 06472-3, 06486
Siddayya, S.M., 15782
Siddeswarananda, Swami, 02180
Siddhānta Saraswatī, 07283
Siddhantashastree, Rabindra Kumar, 01757
Siddharthan, N.S., 15206
Siddiq, Malik Muhammad, 17650
Siddiqi, Abdul Haleem, 12406
Siddiqi, Asiya, 23647-8
Siddiqi, Iqtidar Husain, 02261, 05646, 07034, 07053-4, 07064-6, 07081, 07467, 08553
Siddiqi, M.I., 25564
Siddiqi, M. Idris, 23123
Siddiqi, Majid Hayat, 23661-2
Siddiqi, Mazheruddin, 11464
Siddiqi, Mohammad Mazharuddin, 11511
Siddiqi, Mohammed Murtuza, 10195
Siddiqi, Noman Ahmad, 07604
Siddique, A.F.M., 00096
Siddique, M. Chandry, 26938
Siddiqui.... *See also* Siddiqi
Siddiqui, Akhtar Hussain, 17290-2, 17708, 17776-9, 17782, 17922, 18000, 18253, 25486, 27593, 27642-3, 27667, 27674, 27684
Siddiqui, Anwar H., 18017
Siddiqui, Ashraf, 25118, 25660-1
Siddiqui, Aslam, 17689
Siddiqui, Kalim, 17679
Siddiqui, M. Atique, 11591
Siddiqui, M.K.A., 24789
Siddiqui, M. Sulaiman, 05955
Siddiqui, Mahmud Husain, 05954
Siddiqui, Misbah-ul-Haq, 11689
Siddiqui, Muhammad Khalid ʿAbbas, 24653
Siddiqui, Muhammad Nejatullah, 17901, 17845
Siddiqui, Nafis Ahmad, 15857
Siddiqui, Nurul Hasan, 23654
Siddiqui, S.A., 25220
Siddiqui, S.I., 17989
Siddiqui, Sharif Ahmed, 22482
Siddons, Joachim Heywood. *See* Stocqueler, J.H.
Sidhanta, Nirmal Kumar, 03768
Sidhu, Baldev Singh, 14981
Sidhu, Dalip Singh, 14840, 22764
Sidky, Mohammad Habib, 12039

Siegel, Bernard J., 20265, 20427
Siegel, Lee, 07256
Sievers, Angelika, 27148
Sihra, Nand Singh, 26943
Siiger, Halfdan, 26408-10
Siitaa Devii, Adeltha P., 27790
Sikka, Ajit Singh, 08635
Sil, Jogendra Nath, 20768
Silananda, Brahmachari, 05001
Silburn, Lilian, 01376, 06974-5, 06981
Silva, Manil, 18662, 27685
Silva, Maria Madalena de Cagigal E., 08525
Silva, Nimalasiri, 18502
Silva, Percy, 18906
Silva, R., 06169
Silva, Severine, 20392
Silver, Arthur W., 11033
Silver, Brian Q., 02851, 11642
Silverberg, James, 00810, 00825
Simcox, Arthur Henry Addenbrooke, 09309
Simeonov, L.A., 18929
Simha, H., 11178
Simha, Seshadriiyengar Lakshmi Nara, 11179, 14641, 14699, 20303
Simhadri, Y.C., 09235, 19814-5
Simmons, Colin P., 11110, 11147
Simmons, George Bradford, 14192
Simon, I.M., 26706
Simon, Robert Leopold, 02889
Simon, Sheldon R., 23792
Simoons, Elizabeth S., 26466
Simoons, Frederick J., 26466
Simpson, Colin, 27407
Simpson, Hassell A., 11929
Sinari, Ramakant, 06377
Sind, Pakistan. Hari Enquiry Committee, 22483
Sinder, Leon, 07642
Sinderby, Donald, 20133
Singammal, M.A., 25206
Singaravelu, S., 04383, 04401, 06581
Singer, Marshall R., 18380
Singer, Milton Borah, 00650-2, 00675, 00850, 00892, 01789, 02890, 11846, 13672, 14352, 14363-5, 15298, 19323, 19440-1, 19507, 27084
Singer, Philip, 02198, 26789
Singh, A.K., 14045
Singh, A.N., 02053, 23848
Singh, Abha Lakshmi, 14896, 23616
Singh, Amal Dhari, 05335
Singh, Amar Kumar, 26910
Singh, Anand Bahadur, 23887
Singh, Andrea Menefee, 16080, 23395-6, 23410
Singh, Avadhesh Narayan, 00292
Singh, Awadhesh Coomar, 26378
Singh, B.K., 11283, 26136
Singh, B.N., 24132, 25703
Singh, B.P., 25693
Singh, Baljit. *See* Baljit Singh.
Singh, Basant Kumari, 23008
Singh, Bawa Satinder, 23140-1
Singh, Bhai Maya, 27956
Singh, Bhawani, 12776
Singh, Bhim Sen, 10409
Singh, Birendra Pratap, 23779
Singh, Birkeshwar Prasad, 15048
Singh, Bishwanath, 19237
Singh, Biveshwar P., 07217
Singh, Brij Pal, 22935
Singh, C.P., 20982, 23618
Singh, Candradeva, 16556
Singh, Chintamani, 16234
Singh, D.P., 12942
Singh, Devendra, 08811
Singh, Devendra Kumar, 14471
Singh, Digvijaya, 09090
Singh, Diwakar Prasad, 09626
Singh, Durganand, 23851
Singh, Durgashankar Prasad, 24233-4
Singh, Ghanshyam Narain, 14519, 23628
Singh, Govind Saran, 21122
Singh, H., 14850
Singh, H.K., 17255
Singh, Harendra Pal, 23579
Singh, Hari Har, 23849
Singh, Hari Kishore, 10103, 13184
Singh, Herbert Jai, 13379, 23910
Singh, Hira Lal, 09092, 11180
Singh, I.J., 23289-91
Singh, I.J. Bahadur, 26746
Singh, Indera Paul, 00713, 22870b, 22949, 23307, 25890
Singh, Indra Jeet, 16196
Singh, J.P., 20332
Singh, Jai Prakash, 04156, 05149
Singh, Jitendra, 12881, 19983
Singh, Jiwitesh Kumar, 24043
Singh, K.N., 14865, 15069, 22252
Singh, K.P., 22158
Singh, K. Suresh, 14830, 15799, 20960, 24083
Singh, Kailash Kumar, 23705
Singh, Kalpa Nath, 22208
Singh, Kamal Prasad, 04003
Singh, Kamaldeo Narain, 24177
Singh, Kashi Nath, 07082-3
Singh, Keisham Romani Kumar, 14098
Singh, Kulwant Pritam, 22748
Singh, Kumar Sangram, 08488, 08515
Singh, Kunj Bihari, 26597
Singh, L.P., 13034, 14030
Singh, L.R., 26267
Singh, Lalan Prasad, 05866
Singh, Lalita Prasad, 13741
Singh, Lekh Raj, 23570, 25940
Singh, M.B., 23666
Singh, M.L., 14252
Singh, M.M., 12346
Singh, M.M., 24744
Singh, M.R., 05760
Singh, Madan Mohan, 04393, 04941
Singh, Madanjeet, 05600-1
Singh, Mahendra Prasad, 23995
Singh, Meera, 05695
Singh, Mohinder, 10754
Singh, N.P., 15964
Singh, Nau Nihal, 13650
Singh, O.P., 08423
Singh, Om Prakash, 04074, 23831-2
Singh, P., 15299
Singh, P.N., 20993
Singh, Prabhu Narain, 14660
Singh, Purushottam, 03545, 12889
Singh, R.B., 06740-1
Singh, R.C., 15457
Singh, R.D., 23793
Singh, R.K., 15414
Singh, R.L., 15170, 16026, 20477, 22196, 23861-2, 27018
Singh, R.P., 23833, 24044
Singh, R.Y., 20816
Singh, Raghuraj, 15584
Singh, Rajendra Pal, 10646, 11442, 16472, 16630
Singh, Ram Bali, 23734
Singh, Ram Bhushan, 04049
Singh, Ram Bhushan Prasad, 06571
Singh, Ram Briksh, 23687
Singh, Ram Charitra Prasad, 07056
Singh, Ram Gopal, 22271, 26648
Singh, Ram Lal, 01359, 07083
Singh, Ram Nath, 13785
Singh, Ram Pratap, 15095
Singh, Ram Sagar, 15345
Singh, Ram Sewak, 11739, 17126
Singh, Rama Yagya, 22253
Singh, Ramashray Prasad, 17628, 22116
Singh, Rana P.B., 15170, 24135-7
Singh, Reginald Lal, 23850
Singh, Renu Lall, 25992
Singh, Rudra Dutt, 23789-90
Singh, S.B., 24407-8
Singh, S.D., 24012
Singh, S.K., 16326
Singh, S.N., 09097, 19745, 22208, 22252
Singh, S.P., 23794
Singh, Sakendra Prasad, 12621, 24023
Singh, Samar Bahadur, 07699
Singh, Sankatha Prasad, 16703
Singh, Sant Nihal, 26935
Singh, Sarva Daman, 03786, 04470
Singh, Satish Chandra, 23834
Singh, Satyavrata, 06467
Singh, Shailendra Dhari, 09468
Singh, Sheo Bahadur, 01603

Singh, Sheo Swarath, 15744, 23865
Singh, Sher, 27570
Singh, Shri Gopal, 12822
Singh, Shri Narain, 14661
Singh, Shrinath, 23617
Singh, Sita Ram, 10707
Singh, Sundra Rani, 16096
Singh, Surendra Kumar, 23580
Singh, T. Gopal, 20577
Singh, T.P., 22346
Singh, T.R., 00824
Singh, Tapeshwar, 14886
Singh, Thakur Jaideva, 02828
Singh, Thakur Rajendra, 23795
Singh, Trilochan. *See* Trilochan Singh
Singh, Trilok, 01799
Singh, Tulja Ram, 16443, 19800
Singh, Udai Vir, 03601
Singh, Uma Shankar, 14099, 23354
Singh, Upendra Narayan, 24045
Singh, V.B., 10877-8, 10907, 15486, 15601-2, 22160, 23501, 23685
Singh, V.R., 23594
Singh, Vijai P., 15757
Singh, Vir Bahadur, 13899, 15472
Singh, Yogendra Pal, 16574
Singh Deo, Juga Bhanu, 03049
Singh Roy, P.N., 24288
Singha, Rina, 02929
Singhal, Chanan Ram, 00550, 05684
Singhal, Damodar P., 00360, 09006, 09406, 09436, 17299
Singhal, G.P., 00324
Singhal, H.S., 16537
Singhal, Harish K., 13888
Singhal, R.P., 16402
Singhal, Shashi Bhushan, 27265
Singhal, Sushila, 13104, 16586
Singhi, Narendra Kumar, 21976
Singhvi, G.C., 12715, 21977
Singhvi, Laxmi Mall, 12363, 12385, 12812, 13810, 15965
Sinha, A.C., 26379
Sinha, Ajit Kumar, 16720
Sinha, Alakh Kumar, 09230, 24013
Sinha, Archana, 14308
Sinha, Arun, 23771
Sinha, Avanindra Kumar, 11780
Sinha, B., 22378
Sinha, B.B., 23271
Sinha, B.K., 14715, 15145
Sinha, B.N., 20355, 20462, 22321, 22347
Sinha, Bagishwar Prasad, 23962
Sinha, Bakshi D., 16072
Sinha, Balbir Sahai, 09255
Sinha, Bejoy Kumar, 10113
Sinha, Bhupendra Chandra, 25505
Sinha, Bichitrananda, 15197, 22352-3, 27203
Sinha, Bindeshwari Prasad, 03103, 03528, 04312, 05466, 07179
Sinha, Binod Chandra, 01623, 01640, 04143
Sinha, Bipin Bihari, 20906, 24046
Sinha, Birendra Kumar, 08330
Sinha, Braj Kishore, 10520
Sinha, Braj Mohan, 01452
Sinha, Brajdhar Prasad, 16957
Sinha, Chandreshwar Prasad Narayan, 07181
Sinha, Chittaranjan, 09256, 24273
Sinha, D.K., 01676
Sinha, D.P., 23706, 24047, 24169, 24833
Sinha, Devi P., 09116
Sinha, Dharnidhar Prasad, 24138, 26554
Sinha, Durganand, 15689, 23810-1, 23866
Sinha, G.P., 15545
Sinha, Ganesh Prasad, 05719
Sinha, Har Narain, 00234, 04291, 08303
Sinha, J.K.P., 23996
Sinha, J.N., 15507, 15585
Sinha, Jadunath, 01310, 01389, 01422, 04772, 05854-5, 06404, 06498
Sinha, Jagdamba Prasad, 04651
Sinha, Janki, 12058
Sinha, Jogis Chandra, 24409
Sinha, K.N., 08331
Sinha, Kamaleshwar, 17590, 27340
Sinha, Kanchan, 01824
Sinha, Krishna Kishore, 14601
Sinha, Krishna Nandan, 17084, 17117
Sinha, Kumar Ganganand, 23952
Sinha, Lalal Prasad, 10038
Sinha, M.R., 12407
Sinha, Mahesvari, 07135
Sinha, Manas Ranjan, 15565
Sinha, Mihir, 24926
Sinha, Mira, 26084
Sinha, Murli Manohar Prasad, 24186
Sinha, N.K., 24990
Sinha, N.K.P., 12298
Sinha, Nandalal, 04816, 04836
Sinha, Narendra Krishna, 08554, 22579, 24259, 24410-2, 24845
Sinha, Naval Kishore, 24217
Sinha, Nirmal C., 09627, 11245, 13941, 24249
Sinha, Niroj, 24216
Sinha, P.B., 17760
Sinha, Pabitra Bhaskar, 24120
Sinha, Pandey Rawati Raman, 15057
Sinha, Parmeshwar Prasad, 07564
Sinha, Phulgenda, 13185
Sinha, Pradip, 24559, 24727-9
Sinha, Pramod Kumar, 16139
Sinha, Prem Bahadur, 09628, 25228
Sinha, Purnima, 02749-50, 02840, 02903
Sinha, R., 26495
Sinha, R.C.P., 11722
Sinha, R.K., 23863
Sinha, R.M., 08314
Sinha, R.P., 25773
Sinha, Raghavir, 26494
Sinha, Raghuvir, 17048
Sinha, Raj Kishore, 14548, 15073
Sinha, Rajeshwar Prasad Narain, 11761
Sinha, Ram Mohan, 20611
Sinha, Ram Narain, 24098
Sinha, Rama, 13121
Sinha, S.C., 20907
Sinha, S.K., 06693, 12668, 14779, 24196
Sinha, S.P., 04345, 20837
Sinha, Sachchidananda, 09021, 10836, 11690, 13150, 23963, 24048, 24240, 25137
Sinha, Sasadhar, 24846, 25018
Sinha, Satyadev Narain, 15435
Sinha, Satyanarayan, 13959
Sinha, Shyam Narain, 09520
Sinha, Surajit Chandra, 00265, 00635-6, 00662, 00715-6, 01095, 01872, 02054, 15709, 15798, 20859-60, 20972-6, 24595, 24620, 24678, 24770-1, 24896, 27445
Sinha, Surendra Nath, 08772-4, 08789
Sinha, Surendra Prasad, 10589, 16659, 20959, 24071
Sinha, Tarunchandra, 26683
Sinha, Upendra Narain, 26021
Sinha, V.C., 14157
Sinha, V.K., 12431
Sinha, Vishwa Nath Prasad, 24172, 24178
Sinha, Vraj Mohan, 21958
Sinnatamby, J.R., 04028
Sirageldin, Ismail, 25601
Sircar, Dineschandra, 00038, 00220, 00272, 00557, 00562-3, 00573-4, 01183, 01929, 02062, 03727, 03769, 04062, 04075-6, 04140-1, 04190, 04199-200, 04228, 04263, 04359, 04402-3, 04565, 04770, 05657, 05685, 05720, 05856, 05915, 27813
Sirdar Ali Khan, Sayyid, 09694, 09836, 10249
al-Sirhindi, Yahya ibn Ahmad, 05696
Sirisena, U.D.I., 18951
Sirisena, W.M., 06127, 06276
Siriwardena, B.S., 18871
Siriwardene, C.D.S., 18982
Siriwardene, Reggie, 19062
Siriweera, W.I., 06142-3, 18486
Sirohi, A.S., 23355
Siromoney, Gift, 06617
Sirsikar, V.M., 21130, 21135-7, 21160, 21605
Sirvya, Bhagvan Das, 10740
Sisson, Richard, 21959-60, 22093
Sita, S., 02877
Sitapati, Gidugu Venkata. *See* Venkata Sitapati, Gidugu
Sitapati, Pidatala, 01958
Sitarama, Subahdar, 09329
Sitaramiah, G., 03997
Sitaramiah, Venkataramiah, 06494, 06597, 20293, 20563, 20570

Siva Dharma Sastry, B., 12781
Śiva-purāṇa, 05790
Sivaganacharya, Swami, 02230
Sivagnanam, M.P., 19173
Sivakumaran, 19080
Sivananda, Swami, 01825, 01840, 04671, 04873, 11422-4
Sivanatha Sastri, 24577
Sivaraja Pillai, K. Narayan, 04207
Sivaram, Mysore, 06405, 10445
Sivarama Menon, C.P., 00273
Sivarama Murty, Nunnagoppula, 27904
Sivaramakrishnan, K.C., 16041, 24790
Sivaramamurti, Calambur, 00215, 00611, 01604, 01751, 01841, 02483, 03082, 03207, 03212-3, 03227, 03241, 03278, 03292, 03399-400, 05343, 05507, 05543, 06022, 06114-5, 06366, 06612, 06628, 06658, 06668
Sivaraman, Krishna, 01412
Sivaramayya, Bhamidipati, 01021, 15978
Sivaramkrishnan, K.C., 24520
Sivaratnam, C., 04249
Sivasubramonian, S., 11090
Sivaswami Aiyar, Pazhamaneri Sundaram, Sir, 10016
Sivaswamy, Kodaganallur Ganapattri, 19302, 19994
Sivaswamy, Tirumangalakudy Chinnasamy, 19222
Sivathamby, Kartigesu, 19037, 19557
Sivayya, K.V., 19779-81
Sivertsen, Dagfinn, 19424
Siveson, Randolph M., 13908
Siwach, J.R., 12564, 12890
Sjoberg, Andrée F., 00087, 01071, 03728
Skelton, Robert, 07723, 07770, 08474, 08489, 08972
Sköld, Hannes, 05182
Skorpen, Erling, 02190
Skorupski, Tadeusz, 00507, 03428
Skurzak, Ludwik, 02191
Slade, Madeleine, 09906
Slater, Gilbert, 00088, 19153, 19279
Sleeman, James Lewis, 09236
Sleeman, William Henry, Major-General Sir, 09237-8, 09330, 23454
Slocum, W.L., 22886
Slusser, Mary Shepherd, 05882, 07385, 27372
Small, Walter Joseph Tombleson, 19052
Small Industries Service Institute, Calcutta, 26555
Small Industries Service Institute, Jaipur, 22065
Smarananda, Swami, 11311
Smart, Ninian, 01350, 01433, 01506
Smet, Richard V. de, 18240
Smillie, E.E., 26749
Smith, Bardwell L., 01216, 01260, 01533, 01873-4, 04241, 06128, 06162, 12218, 19002
Smith, Donald Eugene, 12219-20, 12432, 13373, 18455, 18458
Smith, Edmund W., 07791
Smith, George, 09022
Smith, Graham, 00924, 07578
Smith, Harry Daniel, 01605, 01766, 04784-7
Smith, John D., 06726-7
Smith, Margaret, 05941
Smith, Marian W., 19401, 22818, 22870c
Smith, Mary Carroll, 04652
Smith, Nicol, 27246
Smith, R. Morton, 03827, 03924, 04050
Smith, Ray T., 10017-8, 26787-8
Smith, Reginald Bosworth, 09138, 22627
Smith, Robert Aura, 10484
Smith, Ronald Bishop, 07865
Smith, T. Lynn, 15728
Smith, Vincent Arthur, 00197, 03104, 04130, 05553, 05659, 07401, 07478, 10243
Smith, W.H. Saumarez, 09210
Smith, Wilfred Cantwell, 07643, 07663, 09785, 19639
Smith, William Carlson, 26573
Smith, William L., 07314
Smith, William Roy, 09579, 11215
Smithsonian Institution, 07724
Smyth, Douglas C., 13256
Smyth, George Carmichael, 22569
Snelgrove, Alfred Kitchener, 17971
Snellgrove, David Llewellyn, 00507, 01677, 03428, 03481, 04906, 05919, 26337-9
Snodgrass, Donald R., 18634
Soares, Aloysius, 22284
Sobhan, Rehman, 25312, 25350, 25559
Sobhan, Salma, 25526
Sobhanan, B., 08145, 19932-3
Social Science Documentation Centre, 27594
Society for Developing Gramdans, 14991
Society for the Promotion and Improvement of Libraries, 18254
Socio-Economic Research Board, Dacca, 25442
Socio-Economic Research Institute, Calcutta, 11091
Sodhi, J.S., 23376
Sodhi, Tarlochan Singh, 16428
Sörensen, Soren, 04618
Sogani, Kamal Chand, 01523, 02149
Sohan Singh, 08570, 22918
Sohoni, Neera K., 16153
Sohoni, S.V., 23953
Soifer, Deborah, 01773
Solaiman, M., 25248
Solheim, Wilhelm Gerhard, 03523
Soligo, Ronald, 17709
Solomon, Esther Abraham, 04817
Solomon, Ted J., 04771
Solomon, William Ewart Gladstone, 03105
Solovʼyev, O.F., 09419
Somadeva Bhaṭṭa, 06077
Somalay, 01984
Somaratne, Gintota Parana Vidanage, 06134
Somasekhara, N., 20294, 20350
Somasekhara Rao, V.B.R.S., 19761
Somasundara Bharathiar, Navalar S., 05412
Somasundara Rao, B., 19442
Somasundaram Pillai, J.M., 01752, 02568, 05413
Somayaji, D.A., 00288
Somayajulu, V.V.N., 15190
Somera, Manohar, 26752
Somigli, Enzo, 03480
Somjee, Abdulkarim Husseinbhoy, 21679, 21695, 21702-5, 21888
Sompura, Kantilal F., 06873
Sompura, Prabhashankar Oghadbhai, 01709, 03172, 06854
Sonachalam, K.S., 19267, 19293, 19308
Sonarikar, Sunanda S., 15574
Sondhi, M.L., 13715
Soni, R.C., 14922
Soni, Ravinder Nath, 22790
Soni, Veena, 21568
Sontheimer, Günther Dietz, 00673, 00999, 09269, 15903, 20827, 21611
Sood, D.R., 22580, 22974
Sood, P., 13055, 13618
Soodan, Kirpal Singh, 15971, 23881
Sootha, C.D., 15381
Sopher, David E., 00688, 01107, 16666, 21919, 25515, 27019
Sorabjee, Soli J., 13543, 16860
Sorabji, Cornelia, 10769
Sorensen, Niels Roed, 03010
Sorley, Herbert Tower, 08685
Sorrell, Neil, 02719
Sottas, Jules, 07924
Soulbury, Herwald Ramsbotham, Baron, 18362
Soundara Rajan, K.V., 01051, 01736, 03186, 03384, 03392, 03576, 03687, 03741, 04208, 05561, 05578, 06610, 06852, 06874
Sourirajan, Pon, 08210
South Africa. Indian Penetration Commission, 26841
South Asia Microform Project Catalog, 27551
South Indian inscriptions, 00568
Southard, Barbara, 09726
Southern States Official Language Seminar, Mysore (1976), 19119
Southwick, E.M., 02080
Southworth, Franklin C., 02602, 03778, 19558, 27830, 27919
Souza, Francis Newton, 17228
Sovani, Nilkanth Vitthal, 11074, 16042, 21208, 21218, 21496, 21558, 22339
Sovani, Y.K., 21123
Spagnoli, Maria Mariottini, 05482
Spain, James William, 00499, 23034, 23058, 23115
Spangenberg, Bradford, 09192, 09199
Sparks, S., 12262
Spate, Oskar Hermann Khristian, 10508, 10514, 27020-2
Spear, Thomas George Percival, 00183-4, 07961, 08014, 08760, 09051, 09061, 10544, 10574, 23324, 27094
Speckman, J.D., 26789
Speight, Ernest Edwin, 11740
Spellman, John W., 04292, 09755

Spencer, Arthur Marshman, 08939
Spencer, Daniel L., 15254
Spencer, Dorothy Mary, 11708, 20968
Spencer, George W., 06119, 06201, 06267-9, 06307
Spencer, J., 17090
Spencer, Joseph E., 27023
Spengler, Joseph John, 00245, 14291, 14348, 14403
Sperling, Jan Bodo, 22354-5
Speyer, J.S., 05008
Spiegelberg, Frederic, 11378
Spielmann, Karl F., Jr., 19984
Spink, Walter M., 01737, 01790, 05477, 05491, 05579, 05602-5, 06811, 06823, 07758
Spittel, Richard Lionel, 18834
Spodek, Howard, 09005, 09969, 20621, 21680, 21785, 21874
Spooner, Brian, 22547
Spratt, Philip, 01060, 10064, 19230
Spreen, Hildegard L., 03003
Sprockhoff, Joachim Frederick, 02192
Sprung, Mervyn, 01423
Spry, Graham, 10410
Sree Rama Sarma, P., 06233
Sreedhar, 13915
Sreedhara Menon, A., 00428
Sreekantaradhya, B.S., 14520, 20304
Sreedhara Variar, K., 20080
Sreekanthaiya, T.N., 20564
Sreekumaran Nair, M.P., 09580, 09707
Sreenivas, M.A., 14653
Sreenivasa Iyengar, N., 15482
Sreenivasa Murthy, H.V., 00404, 00438, 02066, 07298
Sreenivasan, Kasthuri, 04495
Sreenivasan, Kasthuriswami, 14261, 19425
Sreenivasulu, K., 17230
Sreevenkateswara mahatmyam, 01959
Sri Chandra, 17266
Śrī Krishna Prem, 02231
Sri Lanka.... *See also* Ceylon
Sri Lanka. Constitution, 18449-54
Sri Lanka. Dept. of Census and Statistics, 18603, 27765
Sri Lanka. Dept. of Labour, 18813
Sri Lanka. Dept. of Rural Development, 18695
Sri Lanka Foundation Institute, 18801
Sri Lanka. Ministry of Labour, 18814
Sri Lanka. Ministry of Lands and Land Development and Mahaweli Development, 18709
Sri Lanka. National Institute of Management, 18786
Sri Lanka Year Book, 27132
Sri Prakasa, 12891
Sri Ram, V., 13842
Sri Venkatesvara University, Tirupati, 19868
Sridhar, S.N., 02343
Śrīharṣa (12th century), 06059
Srikanta Murthy, K.R., 00301
Srikantha Sastri, S., 00439
Srinath, C.N., 11709
Srinivas, Mysore Narasimhachar, 00637, 00717, 00749, 00816-7, 00826, 00832-3, 00851, 00881-3, 00886, 01856, 10974-5, 12409, 14180, 14352, 15701, 15729-30, 15776, 15807, 19601, 20391, 20414, 20443-8
Srinivas Kini, K., 00155
Srinivasa Aiyangar, Muttusvami, 00089
Śrīnivāsa Aiyangār, Piḷḷaipūndagudi Tiruvengaḍatt'aiyangār, 04209
Srinivasa Chari, S.M., 06468
Srinivasa Iyengar, C.R., 02930
Srinivasa Iyengar, K.R., 08625, 11397, 11404, 11723, 17010, 17027, 17037
Srinivasa Iyengar, S., 10032
Srinivasa Raghavaiyangar, Seshayangar, 19254
Srinivasa Raghavan, A., 06300
Srinivasa Rao, C.B., 04633, 04708
Srinivasa Rao, R., 16844
Srinivasa Rao, V.N., 01960
Srinivasa Sastri, Valangiman Sankaranarayana, 09666, 09677-8, 10019-20
Srinivasachari, Chidambaram S., 07935, 08190, 08197, 09373, 19443
Srinivasachari, G., 00179, 00196
Srinivasachari, P.N., 06406, 06438, 06499
Srinivasan, C.K., 08159, 08304
Srinivasan, C.R., 00416, 01970
Srinivasan, Comaraswamy, 19508
Srinivasan, Doris M., 03852-3, 03905
Srinivasan, Gummaraju, 01351
Srinivasan, K., 14158, 15949, 20278
Srinivasan, Kuthur Ramakrisna, 03393, 06629-31
Srinivasan, K.S., 21533
Srinivasan, N., 12299, 12910, 12917, 14796
Srinivasan, P.R., 01753, 05494, 06646
Srinivasan, R., 11261, 13009, 19212, 21131, 21138
Srinivasan, T.N., 13819, 22785
Srinivasiengar, C.N., 00294
Srirama Sastry, P., 02942
Śrīśa Chandra Vidyārṇava, 04439
Srisaila Chakravarti, V.R., 06439
Srivastav, K.M., 03711
Srivastava, A.K., 16647
Srivastava, Akhileshwar Lal, 16354
Srivastava, Anand Prakash, 16929
Srivastava, Ashirbadi Lal, 05697, 05936, 07022, 07087, 07435, 07479, 07637, 08375, 08775-6
Srivastava, Ashok Kumar, 07035
Srivastava, B.L., 13857
Srivastava, Balram, 01738, 04384, 05883, 06202
Srivastava, Bireshwar Nath, 07005
Srivastava, Dayanand, 02678
Srivastava, Dhanapat Rai. *See* Premchand
Srivastava, Dharma Bhanu, 23464
Srivastava, G.P., 00335
Srivastava, G.P.L., 24200
Srivastava, Girish K., 14587
Srivastava, Gur Prasad, 12638
Srivastava, Gursharanlal, 15664
Srivastava, Hari Shanker, 11024, 16538
Srivastava, Harish Chandra, 13069, 15842, 23900
Srivastava, K.P., 07402
Srivastava, Lala Rai Niranjan, 21016, 24218, 26508, 26514
Srivastava, M.P., 07541, 07638, 09509
Srivastava, Mahesh Chandra Prasad, 01724
Srivastava, Nagendra Mohan Prasad, 09629, 09756
Srivastava, Om Prie, 23542
Srivastava, Prabhat, 25175
Srivastava, Prem Kumar, 13889
Srivastava, Ram P., 25941, 26939
Srivastava, Rama Shanker, 11226, 15458, 16704, 23622
Srivastava, Ramesh Chandra (1922-), 09257
Srivastava, Ramesh Chandra (1929-), 16546
Srivastava, Ratish, 00676, 20908
Srivastava, Ripusudan Prasad, 11227
Srivastava, S.K., 00834, 25942
Srivastava, S.L., 23796
Srivastava, Sahab Lal, 02445
Srivastava, Saraswati, 23502, 23543
Srivastava, Shankar Sahai, 23867
Srivastava, Sita, 12777
Srivastava, Surendra Kumar, 26268
Srivastava, Suresh, 15490, 24536
Srivastava, Suresh Narain, 15777
Srivastava, Uma Kant, 14908, 15122, 15377, 21482, 22209
Srivastava, V.C., 01815, 01833-4, 04763
Srivastava, V.K., 24049
Srivastava, V.N., 03077
Srivastava, Veena, 23319
Srivastava, Vinita, 15546
Srivastava, Virendra Lal, 24127
Staal, J. Frits, 00835, 02150, 03880, 05172-3, 05189, 05214
Stablein, Marilyn, 02063
Stablein, W., 26301
Stache-Rosen, Valentina, 03011
Stacul, Giorgio, 03742-3
Stahl, Kathleen M., 18594
Stahl, Oscar Glenn, 26035a
Stahl, William, 07808
Stahnke, Arthur A., 12040, 13935
Staley, John, 23117, 23224
Stallybrass, Oliver, 11922
Standing Committee in Defence of Democracy, West Bengal, 24360
Standing Conference of Public Enterprises, 15243
Standrod, Garland L., 27740
Stanford, John Keith, 11959
Stanford Research Institute, 15191
Stang, Friedrich, 15389
Stanislaus, M. Sebastian, 14002
Stanley, John M., 21612
Staples, A.C., 11053
Stark, Claude Alan, 11312
Stark, Craig M., 20743

Stark, Herbert A., 24834
State Bank of Pakistan, 17902, 17990-1
The Statesman, 10805
Statistical abstract of Bangladesh, 27772
Statistical abstract of Sri Lanka, 27773
Statistical digest of Bangladesh, 27774
Statistical pocket-book of Pakistan, 27775
Statistical pocket-book of the Indian Union, 27776
Statistical pocket book of ... Sri Lanka, 27777
Staude, Wilhelm, 07759-60
Stcherbatskoi, Fedor Ippolitovich, 00039, 01377, 01434, 01507, 05081, 05114
Stcherbatsky, Theodore. *See* Stcherbatskoi, Fedor Ippolitovich
Stchoukine, Ivan Vasilevitch, 07745-6
Stchoupak, Nadine, 06029
Stede, William, 27809
Steed, Gitel P., 21839
Steel, Flora Annie, 02462, 11892, 23026
Steele, Arthur H., 20712
Steele, Thomas, 08106
Steensgaard, Niels, 07810
Stein, Arthur Benjamin, 13976-7
Stein, Burton, 00090, 00131, 00243, 00909, 01955, 06194, 06203, 06252-3, 06261-2, 06270-2, 06457, 18635
Stein, Dorothy, 10713
Stein, Mark Aurel, Sir, 03429, 06941, 22436
Steinberg, Blema S., 14031
Steingass, Francis Joseph, 27818
Steinvorth, Klaus, 17085
Stephen, Carr, 03437
Stephens, Donald Ryder. *See* Sinderby, Donald
Stephens, Ian Melville, 27107, 27124
Stephenson, Glenn V., 22898
Stern, Elizabeth G. Levin, 09907
Stern, Henri, 14366, 22083
Stern, Joseph J., 17709-10, 17835
Stern, Philippe, 04099, 05508
Stern, Robert W., 13138, 13222, 20652, 21124
Sternbach, Ludwik, 01547, 04294, 04313, 04412, 05387-8, 06069, 06084
Stevens, George Richard, 10401
Stevens, George Roy, 09310
Stevens, Robert D., 17941, 25382, 25430
Stevenson, Henry Noel Cochran, 00811
Stevenson, John, 05161
Stevenson, Margaret Sinclair, 01027, 01288, 21846
Stewart, Anthony Terence Quincey, 09407
Stewart, Charles, 07190, 07460
Stewart, James M., 11897
Stewart, Rebecca Marie, 02762, 02808
Stewart, William, 16803
Stiebler, Klaus, 13242
Stier, Peter, 14244
Stietencron, Heinrich von, 01835, 02207, 17566
Stiglmayr, Engelbert, 20861
Still, John, 04239
Stiller, Ludwig Francis, 08982-3, 08985, 25950, 26097, 26137
Stirling, Andrew, 20778
Stirrat, R.L., 00985, 18868
Stock, Amy Geraldine, 25625
Stock, Frederick, 22987
Stock, Margaret, 22987
Stocks, C. de Beauvoir, 26411
Stocqueller, Joachim Heyward, 11960-2
Stoddard, Robert H., 01916, 01930
Stoddard, Theodore L., 19115
Stoddart, Brian, 19158, 19647
Stoeckel, John E., 25602-5, 26108
Stönner, Heinrich, 03955
Stokes, Eric T., 09510, 10545, 10939, 11010-1, 11216, 23663
Stone, James W., 27840
Stonor, Charles Robert, 26502, 27397
Storey, Charles Ambrose, 02526
Story, Francis, 01263
Stoudt, Howard W., 00714
Stoutjesdijk, E., 18685
Stracey, P.D., 26539
Strachey, John, Sir, 08761, 09168, 11161
Strachey, Oliver, 08389
Strachey, Ray, 08389
Strachey, Richard, Lieutenant General, 11161
Stracy, P.D., 27044
Straughan, Nancy M., 25388
Straus, Jaqueline, 18916
Straus, Murray Arnold, 18825, 18916, 21387-8
Streefland, Pieter H., 22836
Streeten, Paul, 14422
Streeter, Carroll P., 14055
Strehly, Georges, 04421, 06030
Streik, Lucien, 01272
Streng, Frederick John, 01399, 05094, 05105
Strettell, Dashwood, Sir, 12727
Strizower, Schifra, 21458
Stroup, Herbert Hewitt, 01207
Stuart, Charles, 08176
Stucki, Curt W., 27698
Study Conference on the Indian Ocean in International Politics, 12006
Stutley, James, 01121
Stutley, Margaret, 01121
Styler, William Edward, 16685
Subba Rao.... *See also* Subbarao
Subba Rao, G., 17091
Subba Rao, G.V., 19610
Subba Rao, Koka, 12347, 12364, 12408, 15749
Subba Rao, T.V., 02720
Subba Rau, Khasa, 19548
Subba Rau, S., 06474
Subba Reddy, D.V., 00325, 04551, 05740
Subbannachar, N.V., 06487
Subbaramaiah, S., 19881
Subbaraman, P.S., 19205
Subbarao, Bendapudi, 00460, 00689, 02758, 03507, 03712
Subbarao, K., 19754
Subbarayalu, Y., 05680, 06204
Subbarayan, G.R., 14961
Subbayya, K.K., 03713
Subbiah, B.V., 14159
Subbu Reddiar, N., 06458
Subedar, Manu, 06766
Subedar, S.K., 09780
Subedi, Abhi, 26349
Subhan, Abdus, 24914
Subhan, John A., 05956
Subhani, S.M. Mohiuddin, 13725
Subhash Chandra, 16097, 27580
Subrahmanian, Kalarickal Kumaran, 13890, 13900, 15192, 15332, 21794
Subrahmanian, Nainar, 00117, 00132, 00173, 00395, 00417, 04210-2, 06217
Subrahmanya Aiyer, K.V., 00405
Subrahmanya Ayyar, C., 02865
Subrahmanya Bharati, C., 19591-4
Subrahmanya Sastri, P.S., 02414
Subrahmanya Sastry, V.V., 00302
Subrahmanyam, B.R., 03688
Subrahmanyam, Krishnaswami, 12161, 13768-9, 13786, 14100
Subrahmanyam, N., 19428
Subrahmanyam, P.S., 02372-4, 27905
Subrahmanyam, Padma, 05299
Subrahmanyam, R., 05515
Subrahmanyam, S.M., 26612
Subrahmanyam, Y. Subhashini, 19832
Subrahmanyan, M., 10411
Subrahmanyan, S., 05234
Subramani, 26814
Subramania, N., 06516
Subramania Aiyar, A.V., 06535, 06592
Subramania Aiyar, N., 04728
Subramania Iyer, K.A., 05222-3, 05229
Subramaniam, Chidambaram, 14284, 14780
Subramaniam, K.R., 04743
Subramaniam, Kamala, 04634
Subramaniam, Kuppu, 19356
Subramaniam, P.S., 20553
Subramaniam, S., 09169
Subramaniam, V., 12299, 14032, 14108, 19357
Subramaniam, V.I., 00022
Subramaniam, Venkateswarier, 12654, 15300
Subramanian, K., 19305
Subramanian, K.R., 08160
Subramanian, P., 19255
Subramanian, R.R., 17696
Subramanian, Ramayyar, 19324
Subramanian, Vadakaymadam Krishnier, 05844, 14496
Subramanya Aiyar, Varaganeri Venkatesa, 06582-3
Subramanya Sastri, S., 06397

Subramanyam, C.S., 10059
Subramanyam, Ka. Naa., 02245, 02415, 19559, 19574
Subramanyam, R., 00028
Subramanyan, K.G., 03128
Subramonia Iyer, R., 10196
Subuddhi, Umakanta, 06701
Subudhi, Nabin Sundar, 22419
Sud, Kidar Nath, 11670
Sudan, M.L., 19280
Sudarshan Kumari, 15966, 23887
Sudersen, V., 03524
Sufi, Ghulam Muhyi'd Din, 00508, 23245
Sugatananda, Anagarika. *See* Story, Francis
Sugathan, N., 20054
Sugimoto, T., 05478
Sugiyama, Koichi, 20953
Suhrawardy, Hassan, Sir, 24867, 27298
Suhrawardy, Shaista Akhtar Banu, 11701
Sujan, M.A., 14607
Sukh Deo, 14608
Sukhatme, P.V., 16257-8
Sukhatme, Pandurang Vasudeo, 14818
Sukhee, G.V., 24542
Sukhthanker, Vinayak Sadashiw, 21109
Sukhwal, B.L., 12410, 26992, 27699, 27734
Sukhwant Singh, 12741-2
Sukla, Ananta Charana, 02410
Sukthankar, Vishnu Sitaram, 04619, 04653-4, 05320
Sukul, Kuber Nath, 02055
Sukumar Azhicode, 20215
Sukumara Barakatha, 01624
Sukumaran Nair, K., 19989
Sukumaran Nayar, V.K., 19956
Sulaiman, S.M., 02287
Suleri, Ziauddin Ahmad, 10387, 17436-7
Sulivan, Raymond J.F., 21505
Sullivan, Edward Eugene, 21903
Sullivan, Herbert P., 03609
Sullivan, Michael J., III, 13793
Sultan, Manzurul Mahmood, 25555
Sultan Jahan Begam, Nawab of Bhopal, 20676-8
Sultan Muhammad Shah, Aga Khan, Sir, 09807
Suman, H.N.P.S., 14588
Suman, R.D., 10777
Sumathipala, K.H.M., 18941
Sumi, Tōkan, 27247
Sumitra, L.G., 20578
Summers, T., 22484
Sunasinghe, Siri, 01678
Sunda, K., 15096
Sundar-Isanon, A.N., 09340
Sundar Singh, Sadhu, 22988-9
Sundara, A., 03714
Sundara Rajan, Mohan, 17243
Sundara Ramaiah, G., 01400
Sundara Reddi, G., 12481
Sundaraj Iyengar, S., 19303
Sundarajan, P.G., 19575
Sundaram, K., 01985, 06254
Sundaram, K.N., 15524
Sundaram, Kavasseri Vanchi, 14790, 15026, 22197
Sundaram, P.S., 17127
Sundaram, V.A., 23901
Sundaram, Vivan, 11821
Sundarananda, Swami, 10755
Sundararajan, K.R., 01217
Sundararajan, Parthasarathy, 13122
Sundarayya, Puchalapalli, 14982, 19640, 19652, 19680, 19833
Sunder Rao, Mark, 13379, 16804
Sunderlal, 09043
Sundkler, Bengt Gustaf Malcolm, 19544
Suneet Vir Singh, 08656
Suntharalingam, R., 19159, 19174-6
Sur, Atul Krishna, 01014, 24596
Sur, Mary, 15665
Sūradāsa. *See* Sūrdās
Sūrdās, 08823
Surendra, Lawrence, 19699
Surendra Singh, 16171
Surendranathan, P.K., 15117
Suresh Kumar, 12488
Suresh Ram, 14997
Suresh Singh, K. *See* Singh, K. Suresh
Suresvara, 06391
Suri, Kul Bhushan, 16275, 20478
Suri, Mushter Shahnaz, 16505
Suri, Promila, 09157
Suri, Pushpa, 07639
Suri, Sohan Lal, 08534
Suri, Surindar, 13056, 13394
Suri, Vidya Sagar, 00495
Surjit Kaur, 16298, 23312
Surya Sena, Devar, 02896
Suryakanta, 05371
Suryanarayana, A.V., 10627
Suryanarayana, M., 19801
Suryanarayana, Peri, 19908-9
Suryanarayana Murti, Chaganty, 19856
Suryanarayana Murty, A., 06924
Suryanarayana Sastri, Satalur Sundra, 04803
Suryanarayanarao, M.K., 06598
Suryavanshi, Bhagwansingh, 04201
Sussman, Gerald Edward, 23816
Sutantar Singh, 01560
Sutherland, Lucy Stewart, 07994-5
Sutradharamandana, 01692
Sutton, Amos, Rev., 27937
Sutton, Stanley C., 27530
Sutton, Thomas, 11981
Suzuki, Beatrice Lane, 05050
Suzuki, Daisetz Teitaro, 01424, 05051, 05075, 05082
Swaan, Wim, 05625
Swain, A.C., 01800
Swaminathan, K., 11416, 19576
Swaminathan, K.D., 08177
Swaminathan, Monkombu Sambasivan, 14769
Swaminathan, R., 05384
Swaminathan, S., 19213
Swaminathan, V., 19560
Swammikannu, S., 12798
Swamy, B.G.L., 00250, 03854, 06517
Swamy, G.L., 20484
Swamy, Gurushri, 14906
Swamy, Subramanian, 14983
Swan, Robert O., 11607
Swaran Singh, 12117-8
Swaroop, Bhagwat, 22034
Swarup, Bishan, 02751
Swarup, Har, 23544
Swarup, Jagadish, 12365
Swarup, Ram, 14309
Swarup, Shanti, 03106
Swarup, Vishnu, 27045
Swearer, Donald Keeney, 04988, 05018, 05034, 19003
Swenson, Geoffrey C., 19281
Swidler, Nina Bailey, 22520, 22526, 22548
Swidler, Warren W., 22531, 22549
Swinson, Arthur, 09853, 23059
Swiss Association for Technical Assistance in Nepal, 26126
Swynnerton, Charles, 23027
Syamala Kumari, B., 27886
Syamchaudhuri, Nirupam Kumar, 26698, 26734
Sydenham, George Sydenham Clarke, Baron, 20707
Syed, Anees Jahan, 07500
Syed, Anwar, 12110
Syed, Anwar Hussain, 17466, 17742
Syed, Hasan Ali, 17711, 22812
Syed, Mohammad Abu, 25615
Syed, Mujtaba Ali, 21448
Syed, Reza H., 18018
Syed, Sabiha Hassan, 17798
Syed Mahmud (1889-1971), 07423
Syed Mohamed, 07710
Sykes, Marjorie, 11541
Sykes, Percy Molesworth, Sir, 09437
Symington, David. *See* Halliday, James
Symington, John, 26394
Symonds, Richard, 10355, 18516
Symposium: Decline of the Mughal Empire, 07528
Symposium on al-Bīrūnī and Indian Science, 05731
Symposium on Base Metals, Calcutta (1966), 15349
Symposium on Fish Processing Industry in India, Mysore (1975), 14928
Symposium on Telecommunications in India - Growth and Gaps, Calcutta (1971), 15459
Symposium on the History of Sciences in India, 00266
Symposium on the Mineral Resources of Kerala and their Utilisation, Trivandrum (1975), 20048
Symposium: The Contributions of Louis Dumont, 00792

Synod Theological Commission of the Church of South India, 16822

Tachibana, Shundo, 01524
Tada, Hirokazu, 15013
Taddei, Maurizio, 00599, 07001
Tadpatrikar, S.N., 06053
Tagare, Ganesh Vasudeo, 05769
Tagore, Abanindranath, 11816
Tagore, Devendranath, 11262
Tagore, Gaganendranath, 11817-9
Tagore, Rabindranath, Sir, 03129, 07098, 09908, 10628, 11820, 24998-25013, 25019-25, 25041-2
Tagore, Saumyendranath, 10427, 11246-7
Tagore, Sourindro Mohun, 00750, 02774, 02732-3
Tahilramani, Parsram V., 10509
Tahir, Naeem, 18275
Tahir-Kheli, Shirin, 17680, 17761
Tahmankar, Dattatraya Vishwanath, 09708, 10190
Tahtinen, Unto, 01561
Takakusu, Junjiro, 01325
Taimni, I.K., 01606, 06965
Taimni, K.K., 15461
Taiyeb, Mohammad, 25464
Tajfel, Henry, 26901
Tajima, Ryūjun, 05920
Takakusu, J., 04804
Takasaki, J.N., 04961
Takata, Osamu, 03107
Takulia, Harbans S., 16355
Talbot, Phillips, 14015
Taleyarkhan, Feroza, 02232
Talib, Gurbachan Singh, 01293, 06994-5, 08570, 08614, 08644
Talim, Meena, 04481
Talukdar, J.N., 03779
Talukdar, Muhammad H.R., 06928
Talukdar, Suhas Chandra, 21083
Talukder, Alauddin, 17780, 25266, 25268-72, 25334, 25465
Talukder, M.A.H., 25626
Talwar, Bhagat Ram, 10173
Talwar, G.P., 14139
Talwar, Kay, 03337
Talwar, Sada Nand, 10086
Tamaskar, B.G., 08244-5
Tambad, S.B., 20306
Tambiah, Henry Wijayakone, 18530, 18536-40, 18994
Tambiah, Stanley Jeyaraj, 00751, 01022, 05174, 12221, 12482, 14367, 18675, 18681, 18845-7
Tambimuttu, Francis, Rev., 19045
Tambimuttu, Thurairajah, 25653
Tamil Nadu. Backward Classes Commission, 19352
Tamil Nadu. Centre-State Relations Inquiry Committee, 19231
Tamil Nadu. Committee on Co-operation, 19314
Tamil Nadu. Dept. of Agriculture, 19292-3
Tamil Nadu. Expert Committee on Handloom Industry, 19325
Tamil Nadu. Finance Dept., 19268
Tamil Nadu. Laws, statutes, 19309
Tamil Nadu. Legislature. Joint Select Committee on the Tamil Nadu Agriculturists Relief (Amendment) Bill (1972), 19284
Tamil Nadu Slum Clearance Board, 19452
Tamilnadu Muslim Education Standing Committee, 19416
Tamm, Gordon, 14298
Tanasarma, 02679
Tandan, R.C., 06789
Tandon, Bharat Chandra, 15244, 15301
Tandon, Brij Kishore, 14397-8, 22035
Tandon, J.K., 14079
Tandon, P.D., 09023, 14321
Tandon, P.L., 15307
Tandon, Prakash, 15306, 15467, 22819-20
Tandon, Purushottam Das, 10104
Tandon, Rajesh, 15832
Tandon, Vishwanath, 13313, 14310
Taneja, Kusum Lata, 16055
Taneja, S.K., 13802
Tangri, Shanti S., 11217, 16073
Tanic, Zivan, 15638
Tanvir Ahmad, 18015
Tanzer, Michael, 13838
Tanzil-ur-Rahman, 17391
Tapasyananda, Swami, 19509
Tapper, Bruce Elliott, 19882
Tara Chand. *See* Chand, Tara
Tarafdar, Momtazur Rahman, 03194, 07158, 07191
Taran Singh, 08626-7
Taranath, Rajeev, 17139-40
Tāranātha, 01247, 04933
Taraporevala, Vicaji Dinshah B., 07392
Taraporewala, Irach Jehangir Sorabji, 02300
Tarkalankar, G.C., 09009
Tarlekar, Ganesh Hari, 02789
Tarlekar, N., 02789
Tarling, Nicholas, 26712
Tarlok Singh, 10982, 15743
Tarn, William Woodthorpe, 04169
Tarr, Gary, 06659
Taseer, Muhammad Din, 11691
Taseer, Salmaan, 17591
Taskar, A.D., 16259
Tasneem, Niranjan S., 23009
Tata Economic Consultancy Services, 21226
Tata Institute of Fundamental Research, 17274
Tate, George Passman, 22521
Tatia, Nathmal, 01334
Tattvabhushan, Sitanath, 24560
Taub, Doris L., 22356
Taub, Richard P., 12656, 22308, 22356
Taunk, Bengali Mal, 10006
Tavernier, Jean Baptise, 07504, 07914
Tawale, S.N., 21369
Tawde, M.D., 21341
Tawney, C.H., 05357, 06076-7
Tayal, Maureen, 26826
Taylor, Carl Cleveland, 15014
Taylor, Carl Ernest, 16356, 16369
Taylor, David, 12222
Taylor, Edmond, 27085
Taylor, James, 24260
Taylor, John J., 26902
Taylor, Keith, 06129
Taylor, Meadows, 09239
Taylor, Richard Warren, 02246
Taylor, W.S., 16274
Tayyeb, A., 17417
Tayyeb, Ali, 27116
Tea Districts Labour Association, 25778
Tea Manufacturing and Marketing Consultants, 26395
Tegh Bahadur, Guru, 08645
Teignmouth, Charles John Shore, Lord, 08040-1
Teja Singh, 08579, 08592
Tejvir Singh, 23670
Telang, Kashinath Trimbak, 20734-5
Telang, R.T., 08257
Telkar, Shridhar, 21085
Temple, G., 27498
Temple, Richard, Sir (1826-1902), 09177, 09211, 23465, 25838
Temple, Richard Carnac, Sir (1850-1931), 01072, 06982, 08262, 23028, 26735, 27461
Temple Entry Enquiry Committee, Trivandrum, 20112
Templin, Ralph T., 09952
Tendulkar, Dinanath Gopal, 09888, 23067, 23973
Teng, Krishan Mohan, 23181-2
Tennant, William, Rev., 10548
Tennent, James Emerson, Sir (1804-1869), 18332, 19038
Tennyson, Hallam, 14322
Tenzing Norkey, 26222
Tepper, Elliot L., 17300, 17577, 17642
Terry, John, 03195
Terway, Vinodini, 09420
Tessitori, L.P., 06728
Teta, Jon A., 27125
Tewari, Abnash Chander, 22713
Tewari, D.D., 23892
Tewari, I.P., 16845
Tewari, Laxmi Ganesh, 23940
Tewari, Rajendra Nath, 14770, 22041, 23608
Tewari, S.C., 14016
Tewari, S.M., 09953
Tewari, V.K., 20474
Tewari, Vishwa Nath, 13427
Tewary, Indra Narayan, 12119, 23503
Texas. University. Population Research Center, 14140, 27686
Thacker Spink's Guide to Patna, 27282
Thadani, Jaya, 23004
Thairani, Kala, 22460

Thakar, Jai Narain, 24121
Thakaran, K.M., 20198
Thaker, J.D., 21911
Thakker, G.K., 21319
Thakore, J.M., 20718
Thakur, B., 24179
Thakur, B.C., 19884
Thakur, C.P., 23360
Thakur, D.S., 21758
Thakur, Gopal, 10114
Thakur, Hari Kishore, 13491
Thakur, Harsha N., 26102
Thakur, Janardan, 13602-3, 13619
Thakur, R.N., 09193
Thakur, Ramesh C., 13507
Thakur, Shrinivas Y., 14253
Thakur, U.T., 22492
Thakur, Umakant, 01931-3, 05791
Thakur, Upendra, 00519, 00558, 01061, 04107, 04194, 04262, 04385, 04413, 07377, 08782
Thakur, Vijay Kumar, 04015
Thakurdas, Purshotamdas, Sir, 11197-8, 15124
Thalgodapitiya, W., 18428
Thaliath, Joseph, 22242
Thana, Abdul L., 25909
Thanawala, Kishor H., 13818
Thanga, Lal Biak, 26626
Thangamani, K., 15404
Thangappa, M.L., 05417
Thangasamy, D.A., 16785
Thani Nayagam, Xavier Stanislaus, 00069, 00070-1, 00091, 04212, 04516-7, 05414, 05425-5, 18487, 18857, 19563, 19577, 26774
Thankappan Nair, Parameswaran, 01015, 01625, 08930, 20143
Thapa, D.P., 27380
Thapa, Netra Bahadur, 27380
Thapa, Ramesh J., 03467
Thapa, Yadab S., 26107, 26293
Thapar, Bal Krishen, 03627, 03685
Thapar, Daya Ram, 03242, 12743
Thapar, P.N., 22837
Thapar, Raj, 11948
Thapar, Romila, 00103, 00111, 00118, 00133-4, 00185, 00496, 02199, 03636, 03758, 04016-7, 04051, 04131, 04376, 04404, 04455, 04566-7, 04593, 04729
Thapar, S.D., 14923, 24467
Thapar, Yash Pal, 27299
Thapar's Indian Industrial Directory, 15174
Thapliyal, Uma Prasad, 04568
Tharyan, P., 13035
Thatcher, Mary, 08995
Thavani, V.D., 25774
Thavaraj, M.K., 11189-90
Thawfeeq, M.M., 18866
Theodore, A. Sunderaraj, 06553
Theroux, Paul, 17182
Theuvenet, S., 26165
Thiagarajah, A., 18781
Thiagarajan, K., 01968, 08238
Thibaut, George, 04539, 04544, 04874
Thieme, Paul, 05215-6
Thien, Ton That, 14101
Thierry, Solange, 00845, 07315
Thimmaiah, Gujjarappa, 14529, 14549, 15015, 20503
Thingalaya, N.K., 20325-6
Thipperudra Swamy, Honnali, 06554-5
Thirtha, N.V., 16652
Thirumalai, M.S., 27873
Thirumalai Muthuswamy, A., 04488
Thirunaranan, B.M., 19429
Thistlethwaite, Frank, 18966
Thite, Ganesh Umakant, 03870, 03925, 03939
Thittila, U., 05027
Tholal, Bishambhar Nath, 23641
Thomas, Abraham Vazhayil, 16786
Thomas, Annie Mrithulakumari, 00072
Thomas, Catherine, 11608
Thomas, Edward (1813-1886), 04077, 04157
Thomas, Edward Joseph, 01326, 03888, 04887, 04977, 05061
Thomas, F.W., 06011
Thomas, Harold, 17959
Thomas, K.P., 24368
Thomas, Madathilparampil Mammen, 02253, 13604, 15897, 20184, 20354, 21425
Thomas, Parakunnel Joseph, 11162, 19256, 19285
Thomas, Paul, 01584, 02094, 02447-8, 03138
Thomas, Peedikayil Thomas, 01857
Thomas, Philip S., 25370
Thomas, Raju G.C., 12728, 13770-1
Thomas, Roger, Sir, 22483, 22485
Thomas, Sunny, 20185
Thomas, T.K., 11552
Thomas, T.M., 16414, 16473
Thomas, W.L., 27023
Thompson, Edward John, 08939, 09044, 09178, 09355, 09511, 09552, 10714-5, 25065-6
Thompson, Harry Craufuird, 23045
Thompson (J. Walter) Co., 13853
Thompson, R.C. Muirhead, 25784
Thompson, Stith, 02429, 02446
Thompson, Virginia McLean, 07929
Thompson, William Percy, 22736
Thomson, Dale C., 14069
Thomson, George G., 12007
Thomson, Thomas, 22437
Thoothi, Noshirwan Ardeshir, 21920
Thorat, Sudhakar S., 21246
Thorburn, Septimus Smet, 22619, 22745, 22838, 23046
Thoreau, Henry David, 04658
Thorner, Alice, 00669, 10898, 10941, 11082, 15508-9, 20010
Thorner, Daniel, 10899, 10941, 11054-5, 11082, 11126, 14984, 15082, 15146, 23817
Thornton, Edward, 09240
Thornton, Thomas Henry, 22522
Thorp, John Putnam, 25500
Thorpe, C. Lloyd, 09786
Thotappa, K.B.Y., 20257
Thrasher, Allen Wright, 01425
Three-Day Seminar on Mental Health in Pakistan, Karachi (1960), 18136
Thulaseedharan, K., 20065-6
Thumra, Jonathan H., 26598
Thundy, Zacharias P., 20196
Thurman, Robert A.F., 05083
Thursby, G.R., 10124
Thurston, Edgar, 19132-3, 19140
Thusu, Kidar Nath, 20890-1, 21034
Thweatt, William Oliver, 26138
Thyagarajan, R., 00327
Tiagi, B., 16248
Tidmarsh, Kyril, 09927
Tiemann, Günter, 23301, 23742
Tika Ram, 22658
Tikekar, Shripad Ramachandra, 00127, 27195-6
Tikku, Girdhari Lal, 02527, 06953, 07700
Tikku, Somnath, 23173
Tiku, M.K., 23251
Tilak, Bal Gangadhar, 03780, 03811, 04672, 09709-11
Tilak, Jandhyala B.G., 16667
Tilak, Lakshmibai (Gokhale), 21454, 21631-2
Tilak Maharaj, Swami, 01495
Tilakaratna, W.M., 18892
Tilakasiri, J., 03012
Tilbe, Douglas, 26869
Tiliander, Bror, 19491
Timberg, Thomas Arnold, 11093, 11103, 15308, 24413-4, 24659
Times of India Directory and Yearbook, 27480
Times of India, Index, 27612
Tims, Wouter, 17876
Tinker, Hugh Russell, 00186, 09221, 09523, 09984, 10402, 10455, 10485-6, 11553, 12223-5, 13314, 26750-1, 26760, 26772, 26873
Tinker, Irene, 21972, 25867
Tipnis, Shantaram Narayan, 21613
Tipu Sultan, K.M., 25207, 25249
Tirimagni-Hurtig, Christiane, 12111, 12197
Tirmizi, F.A.M., 17949
Tirmizi, Sayyid Akbarali Ibrahimali, 06722, 08376
Tirtha, Ranjit, 16668
Tirumūlar, 06523
Tirupati Naidu, V., 15137
Tiruvaḷḷuvar, 04489-90, 04496
Tischler, Johann, 00058
Tisdall, William St. Clair Towers, 27933, 27963
Titus, Murray Thurston, 02274
Tivarekar, Ganpatrao Krishna, 27622
Tiwana, Bashir Ali, 27663
Tiwari, Angelo Rajkumar, 23852, 27270
Tiwari, Arya Ramchandra G., 10191

Tiwari, Bhola Nath, 27820
Tiwari, J.G., 13243, 25904
Tiwari, Kapil Nath, 02193
Tiwari, Maruti Nandan Prasad, 01695
Tiwari, Padma N., 26293
Tiwari, Prem Shanker, 22262, 23595
Tiwari, Ramchandra G., 06824, 20646
Tiwari, Shri Gopal, 23559
Tiwari, Udai Narain, 07339
Tiwary, Uma Kant, 12285
Tobias, George, 15097, 15510, 15566
Tod, James, 00471
Todhunter, Charles, Sir, 11155
Tofayell, Z.A., 25182, 25565, 25664
Toffin, Gerard, 26179, 26249
Tokin-Rymbai, U.R., 26663
Tomar, D.S., 22804
Tombi Singh, N., 27341
Tomlinson, B.R., 09403, 09985, 11181, 11191
Tomlinson, J.D., 11075
Tomlinson, James W.C., 12263, 13891
Tongue, Ray K., 27497
Tōṇṭada Siddhaliṅgeśvara, 06547
Toomey, Paul M., 01039
Toosy, M.S., 10388
Topa, Ishwara Nath, 07067, 07107
Tope, Trimbak Krishna, 00066, 12325
Toporov, Vladimir Nikolaevich, 05241
Torri, Michelguglielmo, 14680, 14781
Torrington, George Byng, 7th Viscount, 18326
Toth, E., 03468
Toussaint, Auguste, 00374
Townend, Harry Douglas, Sir, 11104
Toy, Sidney, 06102
Toye, Hugh, 10174
Toynbee, Arnold Joseph, 27126
Toynbee, George, 24282
Trabold, Jeanne L., 05492
Trade Promotion Centre, Kathmandu, 26092
Trager, Frank N., 17729
Traill, G.W., 25910
Tranchell, Carlton L., 18564
Trautmann, Thomas R., 00104, 00978, 04314, 04471-2
Travancore Education Reorganization Committee, 20165
Travancore University Committee, 20166
Trebeck, George, 22431
Trehan, Girdhari Lal, 04518
Trench, Victor, 10269
Trenckner, Wilhelm, 27810
Tresidder, Argus John, 27139
Trevaskis, Hugh Kennedy, 00497, 22729-30
Trevelyan, Charles Edward, 10575
Trevelyan, Ernest John, Sir, 09258
Trevelyan, George Otto, 09212
Trevelyan, Humphrey, 09213
Tribhuvan University. Institute of Medicine, Health, Manpower Development, 26299
Tribhuwan, Jyotsna, 16172
Trier, Jasper, 00349
Trilochan Singh, 08570, 08615, 08646, 08665, 12797, 27479
Trimingham, J. Spencer, 05942
Trinidade, Paulo da, Fr., 08081
Tripathi, Akhilesh Dutt, 14156
Tripathi, Amales, 09558, 09695, 24415, 24974
Tripathi, B.D., 23930
Tripathi, B.L., 21735, 21747, 22244-5
Tripathi, Ganga Prasad, 09438
Tripathi, Gaya Charan, 01801, 02018, 02028-9, 05750
Tripathi, Kishore Sharan, 05776
Tripathi, Kunjabihari, 02610-1
Tripathi, L.K., 06893
Tripathi, Pradyumna Kumar, 12366, 12433
Tripathi, Prakash Chandra, 22073
Tripathi, R.N., 25193
Tripathi, Ram Prasad, 07068, 07436, 07542
Tripathi, Rama Shankar, 07013
Tripathi, S.D., 15676, 23588
Tripathi, Surya Kant ("Nirala"), 11622
Tripathi, Vibha, 03744
Tripathy, P., 02030
Tripathy, Ram Niranjan, 14507, 14561, 19771
Tripura. Agriculture Information Unit, 26642
Tripura. Directorate of Public Relations and Tourism, 26635
Tripura (Union Territory), 26643-4
Tripura (Union Territory). Directorate of Education, 26634
Trivadi, V.D., 14607
Trivedi, A.K., 21912
Trivedi, Anantray B., 21708, 21713
Trivedi, Dinkar, 27581
Trivedi, H.N., 12582, 15651
Trivedi, H.V., 06806
Trivedi, Harshad R., 16063-4, 21840, 23397
Trivedi, M.L., 14654
Trivedi, Pratibha, 16733
Trivedi, R.D., 05344
Trivedi, Ram Naresh, 12041, 24026
Trivedi, Ramchandra, 11398
Trivedi, Vasantrai Jatashanker, 21945
Troger, Ralph, 25119
Troisi, Joseph, 20912, 20927, 20939, 20947
Troll, Christian W., 11474
Trotter, Lionel James, 08035, 09331-2
Troyer, Anthony, 07655
Trumpp, Ernst, 08666, 27948, 27983
Tse, Therese, 03220
Tsuji, N., 03956, 04466
Tsumikowa, Tokifusa, 07172
Tubini, Bernadette, 05372
Tucci, Giuseppe, 00040, 01173, 01390, 03139, 03430, 05120, 05884, 05921, 08984, 27398
Tucker, Richard Philip, 20736-7, 21239, 21346, 21354-5
Tufail, Mian Muhammad, 10647
Tukārāma, 08437-42
Tuker, Francis Ivan Simms, Sir, 09241, 09311, 10487
Tukol, T.K., 02208
Tuladhar, Jayanti M., 26108
Tuladhar, Tirtha R., 25988
Tulasīdās. *See* Tulsīdās
Tulpule, Bagaram, 24528
Tulsī Sāhib, 23931
Tulsīdās, 08792-9
Tunio, M.M., 22465
Tupper, Charles Lewis, 09374-5
Turlach, Manfred, 19957, 20031
Turnbull, Patrick, 08015, 08036
Turner, Alfred Charles, 25943
Turner, Dorothy Rivers, 02352
Turner, James, 00986
Turner, Ralph E., 10837
Turner, Ralph Lilley, 02350-2, 28015
Turner, Roy, 16043
Turner, Victor Witter, 01917, 21017
Twaddle, Michael, 26870
Tyabji, Husain B., 20738
Tyabji, Raiz Hassan Badrudin, 16020
Tyagaraja, Swami, 19901
Tyagi, A.R., 12639, 18382, 25868
Tyagi, B.N., 23609
Tyagi, D.S., 14841, 21745
Tyagi, R.B., 14716
Tyberg, Judith M., 01110
Tyler, Mary, 16197
Tyler, Stephen A., 00653
Tyndale-Biscoe, Cecil Earle, 23154
Tysen, Frank J., 24733, 24745
Tyson, Geoffrey William, 13374, 24416

UN-UNESCO Panel Meeting on SITE Experiences, Ahmedabad (1977), 16958
UNESCO Conference on History, Archaeology, and Culture of Central Asia in the Kushan Period, 04191
Uberoi, J.P. Singh, 08570
Uchiyama, Akira, 27154
Uči̇da, Norihiko, 28000
Udayalinga Rao, S., 01986
Udeshi, J.J., 21483
Udgaonkar, Padma B., 07057
Udhrain, S.D., 07701
Udupa, K.N., 16338, 16345
Uebach, H., 02076
Ueda, Yoshifumu, 05121
Ueno, Teruo, 03107
Uhde, Bernard, 02173
Uhlig, Harald, 26958
Uhrenbacher, Werner Josef, 17723
Ujagir Singh, 21506, 23853-4
Ullah, Salamat, 16603
Ullman, Manfred, 05741

Ullrich, Helen E., 12269, 20379
Umamaheshwara Rao, T., 14609
Umapathi Sivacharya, 06522
Umapathy Setty, K., 16930
Umar, Badruddin, 25158
Umar, Muhammad, 07555-6, 08831, 10128
al-ʿUmarī, Shihāb al-Dīn, 05646
Umarji, Varadaraj R., 02580
Umashankar, Pejavar, 06556
Ummul Fazal, 05742, 16216
Underhill, Evelyn, 07098
Underhill, Muriel Marion, 02095
Union Catalogue of Asian Publications, 27519
United Nations. Centre for Regional Development, 22472
United Nations. Dept. of Economic and Social Affairs, 20011
United Nations Economic and Social Commission for Asia and the Pacific, 18600
United Nations Economic Commission for Asia and the Far East, 23812
United Nations Educational, Scientific and Cultural Organization. Research Centre on Social and Economic Development in Southern Asia, 15334
United Nations Educational, Scientific and Cultural Organization. South Asia Science Cooperation Office, 18288
United Nations. Food and Agriculture Organization, 18701
United Nations. Industrial Development Organisation, 13854
United Nations. Information Centre for Pakistan, 17769
United Nations. Research Institute for Social Development, 18734
United Nations. Secretariat, 20279
United Nations. Security Council Representative for India and Pakistan, 12083
United Nations. Technical Assistance Program, 16299
United Provinces Chamber of Commerce, 23560
United Provinces of Agra and Oudh. Hindu Religious and Charitable Endowments Committee, 23932
United Provinces. Zamindari Abolition Committee, 23655
United States. AID Mission to Nepal, 26088
United States. AID Mission to Pakistan, 17930
United States. Board on Geographic Names, 27117, 27149, 27310
United States. Central Intelligence Agency, 27006
United States Congress. House. Committee on Foreign Affairs, 12008
United States Congress. Senate. Subcommittee to Investigate Problems Connected with Refugees and Escapees, 12156
United States. Dept. of the Army, 26983
United States Educational Foundation in Pakistan, 27446
United States. General Accounting Office, 14053
United States. Library of Congress, 27462, 27595, 27659, 27675, 27705, 27735, 27746
United States. White House - Department of Interior Panel on Waterlogging and Salinity in West Pakistan, 17972
Universities handbook, India, 16478, 27447
University of Agricultural Sciences, Bangalore, 20528
Unni, K.P.K., 13123
Unni, K. Raman. *See* Raman Unni, K.
Unni, Narayanan Parameswaran, 05321, 06070
Unnithan, Thottamon Kantan Kesavan Narayanan, 00663, 13315, 15702, 20104
Untawale, Mukund G., 26099
Upadhyay, Geeta, 00235
Upadhyay, Govind Prasad, 04456
Upadhyay, M.D., 23596
Upadhyay, Madhusoodhan Narasimhacharya, 03307, 19774
Upadhyay, V.S., 02008, 24203
Upadhyay, Vasudev, 07088
Upadhyaya, Baldev, 02000, 06755
Upadhyaya, Bhagwat Saran, 03906, 04037
Upadhyaya, D.C., 26109
Upadhyaya, Deendayal, 13278
Upadhyaya, Ganga Prasad, 11284
Upadhyaya, Hari S., 00959, 02438, 24234a
Upadhyaya, K.D., 02444
Upadhyaya, K.S., 03013
Upadhyaya, Kashi Nath, 04920
Upadhyaya, Krishna Kumar, 23671
Upadhyaya, Nirmala M., 20648
Upadhyaya, S.C., 04485, 05729
Upadhyaya, Uliyar Padmanabha, 27894-5
Upadhye, Adinath Neminath, 01274, 01294, 05136, 05259
Upadhye, P.M., 06756
Upasak, C.S., 07218
Uppal, Joginder S., 14274, 14488, 22791, 22798, 22870a
Uppal, Swinder Singh, 23010
Upreti, Bodh Prakash, 26242
Upreti, H.C., 15924
Upreti, Nandini, 12773, 21962
Uprety, Prem, 22666
Urff, Winfried von, 14285, 25313, 25329
Urquhart, Margaret M., 24664
Ursekar, H.S., 05283
Usmani, Abid Hasan, 22938-9
Usmani, Abul Fazl, 07532
Usmani, Muhammad Adil, 10362, 11485, 27582, 27635-6
Usmani, Muhammad Taqi, 18233
Uswatte-Aratchi, G., 18967
Utkal University history of Orissa, 00483
Utpaladeva, 06968
Uttar Pradesh. Banda Police Firing Inquiry Commission, 23517
Uttar Pradesh. Bhasha Vibhag, 23505
Uttar Pradesh. Bureau of Agricultural Information, 25911
Uttar Pradesh. Commission of Inquiry for Renukoot, 23518
Uttar Pradesh. Dept. of Fisheries, 23597
Uttar Pradesh. High Court of Judicature, 23520
Uttar Pradesh. Industries Dept., 23673
Uttar Pradesh. Jal Nigam, 23885
Uttar Pradesh. Language Committee, 23506
Uttar Pradesh. Modinagar Firing Inquiry Commission, 23519
Uttar Pradesh. Planning Dept., 23581-3
Uttar Pradesh. Planning Research and Action Institute, 23818, 23881
Uttar Pradesh. Police Commission, 23521
Uttar Pradesh. Sarvajanik Udyog Bureau, 23672
Uwise, M. Mohamed, 02569
Uzair, Mohammad, 18029

Vācaspati Miśra, 05702-3
Vacek, Jaroslav, 02558, 03649
Vachha, Phirozeshah Bejanji, 20713
Vācissaratthera, 06145
Vadivelu, A., 09341
Vagale, L.R., 22042
Vagiswari, Alladi, 19370
Vahid, Syed Abdul, 11512-3
Vahiduddin, Syed, 11514
Vaid, Kanwal Narain, 15567-8, 15603, 15611-2, 15666, 22069-70, 23361, 24539, 26891
Vaidya, Chintaman Vinayak, 05698, 08291
Vaidya, Karuna Kar, 26350, 26357
Vaidya, Kisori Lal, 00544, 03456
Vaidya, Murarji Jadhavji, 14399
Vaidya, Raghunath Vinayak, 03797
Vaidya, S.G., 08332
Vaidyanatha Ayyar, R.S., 04427
Vaidyanathan, K.E., 14181, 16669
Vaidyanathan, Kunissery Ramakrishnaier, 01987-8
Vaidyanathan, P.S., 19485
Vaish, Devi Charan Lal, 07447
Vaish, M.C., 14669
Vaiyapuri Pillai, S., 02570, 27865
Vajirañana, Paravahera, Mahathera, 05035
Vajpayee, Atal Bihari, 13747
Vajpeyi, Ambikaprasad, 02653
Vajpeyi, D.A., 13070
Vajpeyi, Dhirendra K., 13665, 23823, 23868
Vajpeyi, J.N., 09696
Vajpeyi, Kailash, 17052
Vajracharya, Gautam Vajra, 08985
Vakil, A.K., 21151
Vakil, Chandulal Nagindas, 10510, 10515-6, 11182, 12237, 12264, 13812, 14262, 14311, 14655, 21714
Vakil, Krishnalal Suranjram, 10567, 16399
Vakil, Mitra R., 12907
Vakil, Rustom Jal, 00328
Vali, Ferenc Albert, 12009
Valiuddin, Mir, 11515
Vallatt, George, 27183
Valle, Pietro Della, 07839
Valsan, E.H., 15049
Valunjkar, T.N., 16332, 21484
Vāmana, 05976
Vamathevan, S., 18608
Vamśāvalī. History of Nepal, 00545, 07378

Vanamamalai, N., 05436, 05444, 19602
Vanamamalai Pillai, N., 01989
Van Buitenen, Johannes Adrianus Bernardus, 01367, 01710, 03871-2, 03980, 04624, 04673, 04788, 05311, 05379, 05410, 05777, 06327, 06414, 06423-4
Vandendriesen, Ian H., 18503, 18595-6, 18716, 18726, 18761
Van den Dungen, Piet H.M., 22746, 22821
van der Kroef, Justus M., 13248, 18401, 18442
Vanderbok, William, 13057
Van der Veen, K.W., 21834
van de Wiele, Micheline, 18626
van Emelen, A., 20948
Van Gelder, J.M., 04004
Vangeyzel, L.C., 19098
Vanjari, Srikrishna, 14550, 21088
Van Meter, Rachel Rebecca. *See* Baumer, Rachel R. Van Meter
Vanmikanathan, G., 04496, 06315-7, 12669
van Nooten, Barend Adrian Anske Johannes, 04655
Van Olphen, Herman, 27831
Vansittart, Eden, 26204
Vansittart, Henry, 08886
Van Troy, Joseph, 06533
Van Wart, Reginald Bramley, 20649
van Wijk, W.E., 00148
Van Zile, Judy, 02909
Vapya, A.K., 27419
Varada Tatacharya, R., 01971
Varadachari, K.C., 06301, 06440
Varadachari, V.K., 01887, 06302
Varadachariar, S., 00939
Varadaraja Aiyangar, M.B., 06421
Varadarajan, M., 05427, 05445, 19578, 19603
Varadarajan, S., 23665
Varadpande, M.L., 02945
Vararuchi, 05260
Varat, T.M., 21338
Varde, P.S., 21098
Varenne, Jean, 01836, 01850, 02167-8, 03875, 03940, 05811, 05885, 27805
Varghese, K.V., 16075
Varghese, Mariamma A., 15875
Varghese, T.C., 20032
Varghese, V.E., 16783
Variar, K.M.P., 20209
Vāris Shāh. *See* Wāris Shāh
Varkey, Chunkat J., 10640
Varkey, Ouseph, 13936
Varkhedkar, Vasant, 13537
Varma, Eileen, 16604
Varma, K.M., 02916
Varma, Madan Mohan, 16734
Varma, Monika, 01791, 07249
Varma, P.N., 17170
Varma, Paripurnanand, 16198-9
Varma, Poornima, 20909
Varma, Raghubir Saran, 12625
Varma, Rajani Kant, 13191
Varma, Ram Kumar, 07108
Varma, Ramesh Chandra, 07584
Varma, Ravi, 11828
Varma, Ravindra, 12010
Varma, S.C., 22134, 23869
Varma, S.K., 21738
Varma, S.P., 12681, 17567, 18246, 24182
Varma, Sat Dev, 22749
Varma, Satyakama, 13620
Varma, Shanti Prasad, 08333, 12065, 13444, 13937, 21973-4
Varma, Sharad Chandra, 08628
Varma, Siddheshwar, 02328, 05177
Varma, Sushil Chandra, 20817
Varma, Vishwanath Prasad, 04275, 04921, 04934, 09545, 09712, 16705, 20961, 24006
Varshney, Manga Ram, 13257
Varthema, Lodovico de, 07840
Vartikar, V.S., 15462
Varughese, K.V., 19985
Vas, Luis S.R., 21106
Vasantha Devi, M.N., 19430
Vashisht, R.S., 16426
Vashishta, B.K., 15886, 27481
Vashishta, H.B., 08270
Vashishth, Satish, 23189
Vashishtha, Vijay Kumar, 20644
Vasishtha, Krishna Kant, 16548
Vasu, Nagendranath, 22399
Vasu, Srisa Chandra, 05196
Vasudev, Aruna, 16990
Vasudev, Uma, 02917, 02983, 13428-9
Vasudeva Rao, M., 20260
Vasudevan, A., 14386
Vasumati, E., 08230
Vaswani, A.S., 08731
Vats, Madho Sarup, 03620, 05580
Vatsyayan, Kapila M., 02969, 02955-6, 03004, 03050, 07257
Vatsyayan, Sachchidananda H. ("Agyeya"), 11579, 11623-4, 17011
Vātsyāyana, 04482, 04484-5
Vatuk, Sylvia J., 00677, 00987, 15972, 23029, 23589, 23714-7, 23835, 23943
Vatuk, Ved Prakash, 02447, 07130, 23029, 23589, 23941-3, 26790, 26949, 27964
Vaudeville, Charlotte, 02001, 02416, 04773, 06729, 06767-8, 07099-101, 07109, 08798-9, 08812
Vaz, J. Clement, 02172
Vaze, Sridhara Ganesa, 27913
Ved Kumari, 06942
Ved Prakash, 16035, 16101
Vedachalam Pillai, Nagapattinam R.S., 02571, 19510
Vedalankar, Nardev, 26752
Vedalankar, Shardadevi, 11592
Vedānta Deśika, 06465-6
Vedic Bibliography, 00005, 03800
Vedavalli, Rangaswamy, 13892
Veeghinathan, N., 01496
Veeraraghavachar, S.M., 14530
Veereraghavan, P.V., 19346, 21378
Veeraswamy, Enugula, 23455
Veerathappa, K., 10222
Veit, Lawrence A., 14254
Velankar, Hari Damodar, 03889-90
Velayudhan, V.K., 19951
Velayudhan Pillai, P.V., 06594
Vellaivaranan, K., 05235
Vellian, J., 02255
Velupillai, C.D., Rev., 19053
Veluppillai, A., 02555
Veluthat, Kesavan, 00429
Vemana, 06599
Venguswamy, N.S., 10207
Venkata Ramanan, K., 05106
Venkata Ramanayya, N., 06213
Venkata Rao, V., 12483, 19160, 25694, 25710-1, 25714-5, 25721, 26450, 26459
Venkata Ratnam, A.V., 06237
Venkata Reddy, K., 19755
Venkata Sitapati, Gidugu, 19907, 02585
Venkata Subbarao, G.C., 12348, 15979
Venkata Subbiah, A., 06518
Venkatachalam, Govindaraj, 02931
Venkatachalam, S.K., 24801
Venkatachari, K., 17128
Venkatachari, Koli Kandadai Appan, 06459
Venkatachelam, Keta, 00149
Venkaṭādhvarin, 08211
Venkataiah, N., 19867
Venkatakrishna Rao, Bhavaraju, 06214
Venkatakrishna Rao, U., 02484
Venkaṭanātha. *See* Vedānta Deśika
Venkatappa, K., 11829
Venkatappiah, B., 15074, 15116
Venkataram Raju, Shinganelur, 12350
Venkatarama Aiyar, T.L., 12349
Venkatarama Aiyer, C.P., 06584
Venkatarama Iyer, M.K., 06378
Venkatarama Iyer, Tinniam, 02809
Venkatarama Iyer, V.T., 02763
Venkataramaiah, S., 07493
Venkataraman, Balasubrahmanyam, 06647
Venkataraman, Bangalore, 26950
Venkataraman, K., 19242
Venkataraman, K.R., 01990-2, 02964
Venkataraman, Krishnaswamy, 14556, 14562
Venkataraman, T.S., 12434
Venkataramani, G., 19310
Venkataramani, M.S., 09393, 10412, 10428, 17730, 24459
Venkataramayya, M., 05345
Venkataramanayya, N., 06225, 06234-6, 06242

Venkatarangaiya, Mamidipudi, 12531, 12946, 19648, 19718, 19161
Venkatarao, Nidathavolu, 08231
Venkatarathnam, R., 02763
Venkataratnam, L., 22210
Venkataratnam, Rajagopalan, 16235
Venkataratnam Naidu, R., 10733
Venkataraya Sastry, Vedam, 19895
Venkatarayappa, K.N., 20456, 20479, 20485
Venkatasubba Ayyar, V., 06195
Venkatasubba Sastri, Kasi Nageswara, 20243
Venkatasubbiah, Agaram, 03908
Venkatasubbiah, Ambale, 03907
Venkatasubbiah, Hiranyappa, 11076, 14240, 14387, 15313
Venkatasubramanian, K., 19475
Venkataswamy, P.R., 10757
Venkatavadhani, Divakarla, 06604
Venkatesa Iyengar, Masti, 10208
Venkateswar Rao, Narla, 06605-6
Venkateswara Rao, Talam, 14139, 16371, 22140
Venkateswara Sastry, Jonnalagadda, 27906-7
Venkateswaran, A.L., 12729
Venkateswaran, C.S., 05758, 06004
Venkateswaran, R.J., 12600
Venkateswaran, Shyamala, 17160
Venkateswaran, T.K., 19511
Venkatraman, S.R., 10756
Venkatswamy, P.R., 19802
Venkitasubramonia Iyer, Subramonia, 02495, 02878-9
Venkoba Rao, R., 09342
Venn, T.W., 20496
Venu, A.S., 12502
Venu, S., 14378
Venugopal, C.V., 11741, 17129
Venugopal Reddy, Y., 14388
Venugopala Rao, S., 16200
Vepa, Ram Krishna, 12626, 15333, 19707, 19719, 19775
Vequaud, Yves, 03438
Verba, Sidney, 13082
Verbenko, V.A., 16507
Verelst, Harry, 07996, 08887
Verghese, B.G., 12198, 17578, 24084
Verghese, C. Paul, 11724, 11742, 17086, 17141, 17183
Verghese, Habel G., 11554, 20186
Verghese, I., 19402-4, 20152
Verghese, Jamila, 15917
Verghese, K.E., 11039
Verghese, K.P., 15939
Verghese, Paul, 02256
Verghese, S.K., 13830
Verma, Babu Ram, 00946
Verma, Bhagwati Charan, 07076
Verma, Dina Nath, 09394
Verma, Dinesh Chandra, 08125
Verma, G.P., 15828
Verma, Ganeshilal, 23484-5
Verma, Ganpat Lal, 15032
Verma, Harish Chandra, 05710
Verma, I.B., 16605
Verma, Jag Mohan Singh, 23567
Verma, K.K., 02752, 02757
Verma, K.M., 03261
Verma, Kripa Nath, 23566
Verma, Mahabir Singh, 23507
Verma, Manju, 22673
Verma, Mukut Behari, 10770
Verma, Nawal Kishore Prasad, 24027-8
Verma, Onkar Prasad, 06686, 06776, 06812
Verma, Pramod, 21796, 21883
Verma, Prem Mohan, 12379, 12468
Verma, R.L., 05739, 05743
Verma, Rajendra, 16429
Verma, S.L., 12698, 21978
Verma, S.N., 02123
Verma, Som Prakash, 07761
Verma, Surendra, 09954
Verma, Thakur Prasad, 00540
Verma, Yogendra Prasad, 13839
Vermeer, Hans Josep, 17092
Verneuil de Marval, 01816
Verstraeten, A., 16629
Verzeichnis der Orientalischen Handschriften in Deutschland, 27552
Vetscher, Trande, 22104
Vetter, Tilmann, 06344
Vettickathadam, C., 15958
Viaud, Louis Marie Julien. *See* Loti, Pierre
Vibhakar, Jagdish, 12011
Victor, M.A., 19315
Victoria and Albert Museum, 07820
Victoria Memorial (Museum), 24730
Vicziany, Marika, 11083
Vidya Prakash, 06706, 06894
Vidya Sagar, 13690
Vidya Shankar, 02880
Vidyabhusana, Amulyacharan, 06796
Vidyabhusana, Satish Chandra, 01435
Vidyākara, 06060
Vidyāpati Ṭhakura, 07259-60
Vidyāraṇya. *See* Mādhava Vidyāraṇya
Vidyarthi, Lalita Prasad, 00620, 00638, 00654, 00718, 00836, 01075-6, 01090, 01099, 01875, 01918, 02056, 02064-5, 02430-1, 02439, 13071, 15710-2, 15731, 15801-4, 20910, 20962, 21006, 23997, 24029, 24072, 24105, 24122, 24147-8, 24153-4, 24197, 24203, 24219-20, 24235
Vidyarthi, Pandeya Brahmeshwar, 06441-2, 06450-1
Vidyarthi, R.D., 15575
Vidyarthi, Ram Sharan, 10429
Vidyasagar, Ishwarchandra, 10731, 24975
Viennot, Odette, 01641, 01843, 05581, 06807, 06875
Vig, O.P., 14160
Vijai Govind, 16479
Vijaya Bharati, Sundaram, 19595-6
Vijaya Raghavan, K., 16253
Vijayakumar, S., 14853
Vijayanagar, R.L.N., 21304
Vijnanananda, Swami, 05827
Vijayatunga, Jinadasa, 19087
Vijayavardhana, D.C., 18472
Vijayawardhana, G. Hemapala, 02517
Vijia Kumar, N., 12903
Vimadalal, Jal Rustamji, 02310
Vimalananda, T., 18463-4
Vimalananda, Tennakoon, 18309-10, 18459
Vimochanananda, Swami, 19512
Vimuktananda, Swami, 06360
Vincent, Kaushal, 26668
Vinod Kumar, 16908
Vinod Kumar, R.M., 20159
Vipulananda, Swami, 06283
Vir Singh, Bhai, 23016-7
Vira Raghavan, Conjeevaram, 27169
Viraraghavacharya, T.K.T., 01961
Viraswami Pathar, S., 01888
Viresalingam, Kandukuri, 19905
Virji, Krishnakumari J., 06723
Virkar, H.A., 27914
Virottam, Balmukund, 08783
Visaria, Leela, 14182
Visaria, Pravin, 15491, 15551
Vishal Singh, 27086
Visharad, B.A., 28013
Vishnoo Bhagwan, 09083, 09555, 23273
Vishnu Dutt, 13639
Vishnu-Mittre, 03577
Vishva Bandhu, 04005
Vishvanathan, S., 06016
Vishwa Prakash, 11285
Visswanathan, E. Sa., 19232
Visva-Bharati University, 10629, 24477, 24499
Viśvanātha Nyāyapañcānana Bhaṭṭācārya, 04861
Visvanatha Pillai, V., 27866
Viswanadham, Garimella, 19847
Vishwanath, M.S., 20463
Viswanath, Maya, 21752
Viswanathaiah, K.V., 20258, 20266, 20360
Viswanatham, Kalive, 11889
Viswanathamurthi, J., 19332
Viswanathan, E.S., 19194
Vitsaxis, Basile, 01585, 03994
Vithiananthan, S., 03025
Vittachi, Tarzie, 18488
Vittal, S.P., 12684
Vittal Rao, Y., 19724, 19869
Vivekananda, Swami, 11315-7, 11874
Viyogi Hari. *See* Dwivedi, Hari Prasad
Voelcker, John Augustus, 10940
Vogel, Claus, 02518
Vogel, Jean Phillippe, 01626-7, 01844, 03148, 03457, 05571, 08556, 08754, 22605

Vohra, Bikram, 12716
Voigt, Johannes H., 00119, 04315, 10403, 11853
Vollmer, Franz-Josef, 00246, 12545
Volwahsen, Andreas, 03173, 03196
von Grünebaum, G.E., 11449
von Mehren, Arthur Taylor, 16562
Vora, M.P., 03345
Voretzsch, Ernst Arthur, 08080
Vorys, Karl von, 17438
Vreede-de Stuers, Cora, 00988, 15925, 22141
Vriddhagirīsan, V., 08161
Vyas, Kantilal C., 11218, 16452
Vyas, Mohanlal P., 16340
Vyas, N.N., 15805, 20818
Vyas, R.P., 20650
Vyas, Ramnarayan, 04774, 05778, 06367
Vyas, Ravindra Nath, 22090
Vyas, Shantikumar Nanooram, 03770
Vyas, V.S., 15098-9, 15150, 21744-5, 21772, 22031
Vythilingam, M., 18349

Wace, H., 18969
Wacha, Dinshaw Edulji, 11105, 15309, 21184, 21233
Waddell, Laurence Austine, 04120, 05467, 26368
Wade, Bonnie C., 02721, 02841-2
Wade, Henry William Rawson, 12699
Wade, John Peter, 08852
Wade, Robert, 14887, 14894
Wadhva, Charan D., 13803
Wadhwa, D.C., 10942, 14962, 24118
Wadhwa, Kamlesh Kumar, 12367
Wadhwa, O.P., 12911
Wadia, Ardeshir Ruttonji, 12503, 16147
Wadia, Meher D.N., 15350
Wadia, Pestonji Ardesir, 14430, 21442
Wadia, Ruttonjee Ardeshir, 21305
Wadley, Susan Snow, 02448
Wadlington, Truman Caylor, 19513
Waerden, Hans van der, 00289, 08777
Waghorne, Joanne Punzo, 10209
Wagle, Dileep M., 15362
Wagle, Iqbal, 27644
Wagle, Narendra Kashinath, 04394, 04473, 04730, 20399
Wagret, Paul, 27075
Wahab, Abdul, 12157
Waheed, K.A., 11486
Waheed, M.A., 27043
Waheed, Zuhra, 22721
Waheed-uz-Zaman, 10356
Wahlen, F.T., 27363
Wainwright, Mary Doreen, 10305, 27553, 27564
Waisanen, Frederick B., 15066
Wajid, J.A., 27596
Wakankar, Vishnu S., 03534, 03541-2
Wake, William H., 22211
Wakefield, William, 00509
Wakil, Parvez A., 22847
Walatara, D., 18952, 19088
Walch, James, 19121
Waldschmidt, Ernst, 03458, 08490-1, 08749
Waldschmidt, R.L., 03458
Wales, Horace Geoffrey Quaritch, 00367
Waley, Sigismund David, 10227
Walhouse, M.J., 20554
Wali, B.M., 15463
Walia, Paramjit Singh, 227959
Waliullah, Shah, 07683-4
Waliullah Khan, Mohammad, 03431, 08593
Walker, Benjamin, 26962
Walker, George Benjamin, 01111
Wall, David, 18795
Wallace, Charles Lindsay, 09514
Wallace, D.R., 24529
Wallace, Paul, 23030
Wallbank, Thomas Walter, 10488
Walleser, Max, 05107
Walli, Koshelya, 01497, 01562
Walsh, Cecil Henry, Sir, 09242
Walsh, John Henry Tull, 24261
Walter, Howard Arnold, 11527, 23246
Walter, Otto, 05373
Wanchoo, K.N., 14566
Wanigaratne, R.D., 18749, 18874-5
Wanigatunga, S., 06148
Ward, Michael, 26440, 26917
Ward, Robert E., 27418
Ward, William E., 06170
Warder, Anthony Kennedy, 00120, 00135, 01248, 01311, 01436, 02485, 04922, 04970, 05245, 05263, 27814
Ware, Edith W., 27706
Warikoo, Kulbhushan, 27728
Waris Kirmani, Mohammed, 11671
Wāris Shāh, 08693-4
Warmington, Eric Herbert, 04581
Warnasuriya, W.M.A., 18972
Warren, Henry Clarke, 04888, 04978
Wasan, R.P., 17656
Waseem, Muhammad Tariq, 22813
Wasey, Akhtarul, 10648
Washbrook, David A., 19144, 19154-5, 19162
Wasi, S.M., 12574
Wasiullah Khan, Mohammad, 22940
Wasson, R. Gordon, 03855-6
Wasti, S. Razi, 10007
Wasti, Syed Razi, 09828, 27482
Waterfield, William, 06730
Waterston, Albert, 17857
Watney, John Basil, 08016
Watson, Francis, 00187
Watson, Ian, 03828
Watson, James B., 01096
Watson, Vincent C., 12444
Watt, George, Sir, 26963-4
Wattal, H.K., 03347
Wattal, Pyare Kishan, 12813, 14559
Watters, Thomas, 05659
Wauchope, R.S., 05493
Wavell, Archibald Percival Wavell, 1st Earl, 10450
Waverley, John Anderson, Viscount, 24274
Wayman, Alex, 01233, 01327, 01586, 02134, 05016, 05108, 05122, 05912, 05916, 05922
Wayman, Hideko, 05016
Wazir, J.N., 23229
Wazir Chand, L., 27841
Wazir Singh, 08629
The wealth of India, 14202
Weatherford, W.D., 18058
Weaver, Thomas F., 22212
Weber, Albrecht Friedrich, 02396
Weber, Henry, 07925
Weber, Max, 01876
Webster, John C.B., 00136, 22943, 22965
Webster, Warren, 18237
Wedderburn, William, Sir, 09667
Weekes, Richard V., 27108
Weeramantry, Lucian G., 18429
Weerasooria, N.E., 00391
Weerasooria, Wickrema S., 18646, 18858
Weerawardana, I.D.S., 18360, 18407-8, 18826
Weidner, Edward W., 16379, 18146
Weijland, Hermien, 18647
Weiner, Myron, 12227, 13058-9, 13091, 13139-40, 13158, 13395-6, 13559, 13666, 13672, 15847, 19720, 21050, 24746, 26006
Weiner, Sheila L., 05606, 07360
Weiss, Dieter, 26139
Weisse, Hildegard, 00154
Weitzman, Sophie, 08037
Welbon, Guy Richard, 01508, 02096
Welch, Stuart Cary, Jr., 07725-7, 07747-8, 07762, 11791
Weling, A.N., 20828
Weller, Jac, 07997
Weller, Judith Ann, 26802
Wellesley, Richard Colley Wellesley, Marquess, 08043, 08045
Wellesz, Emmy, 07670
Wells, Henry Willis, 05275, 05385-6
Wenzel, L.A., 26951
Werner, Karel, 02169, 03805, 03829, 03857
Werner International Management Consultants, 18041
Werth, Alexander, 10175
Wertz, Dorothy C., 01900
West, Algernon Edward, Sir, 09098
West, Edward William, 20590
West Bengal. Agriculture and Community Development Dept., 24442
West Bengal. Asansol Planning Organisation, 24707
West Bengal. Calcutta Metropolitan Planning Organisation, 24434, 24751, 24783, 24802

West Bengal. Education Dept., 24835
West Bengal. Forest Directorate, 24449
West Bengal Pradesh Congress Committee, 24362
West Bengal. State Planning Board, 24435
West Bengal. State Statistical Bureau, 24530-2
West Bengal. Tribal Welfare Dept., 24646
West Pakistan. Bureau of Education, 18148, 18191
West Pakistan. Bureau of National Reconstruction, 10337
West Pakistan. Cooperative Inquiry Committee, 17914
West Pakistan. Director General of Social Welfare, 18130
West Pakistan. Directorate of Fisheries, 17977
West Pakistan. Industrial Development Corporation, 18014, 22473
Westbrook, Jessie Duncan, 07702
Westbrook, Perry D., 17130
Westcott, George Herbert, 07110
Westcott, Jay B., 12262
Westergaard, Kirsten, 25538
Western India Shippers' Association, 21802
Western India States Agency, 20622
Westheim, Paul, 03064
Westphal, Heinz, 18090, 22839
Westphal-Hellbusch, Sigrid, 18090, 22839, 23102
Wezler, Albrecht, 05217-8
Wheeler, James Talboys, 07825, 07832, 07972, 08202, 09072
Wheeler, Richard S., 17323, 17418, 17528, 25250
Wheeler, Robert Eric Mortimer, Sir, 00188, 03508, 04164
Wheeler-Bennett, John Wheeler, 24275
Wherry, Elwood Morris, 11539
Whish, C.W., 23466
Whitaker, Benjamin Charles George, 25501
Whitaker, Romulus, 27046
Whitcombe, Elizabeth, 23636
White, Carl Milton, 23440
White, Charles Sydney John, 07120, 08824, 16735, 21614, 21625
White, David, 01534
White, Emmons E., 02572, 02866
White, John Claude, 25839
White, Lawrence J., 18025
Whitehead, George, 26713
Whitehead, Henry, 01858, 22990
Whitehead, R.B., 07403
Whiteway, Richard Stephen, 07882
Whitney, William Dwight, 03928, 27806
Whitworth, George Clifford, 27499
Whyte, Robert Orr, 14942-5
Wickenden, T., 10430
Wicki, Josef, 07887, 07890
Wickramaratne, L.A., 18727
Wickramasinghe, Gamini, 18757
Wickramasinghe, Jotiyasena, 19058
Wickramasinghe, Martin, 00392-3, 02547, 06163, 19081
Wickremeratne, Lakdasa Ananda, 18299, 18465, 18942, 18988
Wickremesinghe, Percy, 19054
Wiebe, Paul D., 19409, 19453, 19721, 20421-2, 20464, 25347, 26889
Wielenga, Bastiaan, 00137
Wiener, Norbert, 11900
Wiener, Sita, 16736
Wiersma - te Nijenhuis, Emmie. *See* Nijenhuis, Emmie te
Wiesinger, Rita, 01001
Wiesner, Ulrich, 03482
Wightman, Archibald John, 09243
Wijayatilake, S.R., 01919
Wijeratne, David G., 27859
Wijesekera, Nandadeva, 03376-7, 18361, 18887, 27140
Wijesekera, O.H. de A., 01264
Wijesinghe, Mallory E., 18597
Wijetunga, W.M. Karunaratna, 06120, 18294
Wijetunge, Edmund P., 08105, 08107
Wijewardana, Dayapala, 18604
Wijeyewardena, E.A.L., 18953
Wikeley, J.M., 22840
Wikkramatileke, Rudolph, 18750, 26890
Wilber, Donald Newton, 27109
Wilberforce, Reginald Garton, 09485
Wilberforce-Bell, Harold, 00461, 08461
Wilbur, Marguerite Knowlton Eyer, 09404
Wilcox, Wayne Ayers, 12042, 12228-9, 17374, 17419, 17439, 17506, 17542, 17550, 22159
Wild, Roland, 20623
Wilder, William, 26595
Wiles, John, 27063
Wilhelm, Friedrich, 04316
Wilkins, Charles, 06085
Wilkinson, J.V.S., 07749, 07771
Wilkinson, T.S., 20879, 21425
Wilkinson, Theon, 11963
Wilks, Mark, 19141
Willard, N. Augustus, 02724
Willetts, William, 06909
Willey, Arthur, 03378
Williams, Donovan, 09066, 09099
Williams, George Mason, 11337
Williams, Haydn Moore, 11725, 17171-2
Williams, John, Captain, 09312
Williams, K., 18619
Williams, Lawrence Frederic Rushbrook, 00162, 00462, 07465, 17302, 17642, 12136, 27071
Williams, Paul M., 05028
Williams, Robert Hamilton Blair, 05931
Williamson, Horace, Sir, 10047
Williamson, Thomas, 11964
Willingdon, Freeman Freeman-Thomas, Lord, 10270-1
Willis, Malcolm, 25388
Willman-Grabowska, Helena de, 04099
Wills, C.U., 06707, 08315
Willson, Amos Leslie, 11869
Wilson, Alfred J., 18383-6, 18402, 18409, 18443, 18508-9
Wilson, Amrit, 26926-7
Wilson, Angus, 11908
Wilson, Charles Robert, 08888, 08931
Wilson, D. Kanagasabai, 19040
Wilson, Dorothy Clark, 19467-8
Wilson, Frances A., 05845-6
Wilson, Horace Hayman, 01208, 04798, 05276, 05362, 05375, 05782, 09010, 27500
Wilson, J.G., 06452
Wilson, James, Sir, 27965-6
Wilson, Jim, 26815
Wilson, John, 00769, 10719, 21810
Wilson, Patrick, 00251, 08996, 10066, 12293
Wilson, Pitiyage, 18796
Wilson, Roland Knyvet, Sir, 09270
Wilson-Carmichael, Amy. *See* Carmichael, Amy Wilson
Wimadalal, J.R., 19661
Wimaladharma, Kapila Pathirana, 18717, 18742
Wimalaratne, D., 18956
Wimalaratne, K.D.G., 27565
Windey, M.A., 15016
Windmiller, Marshall Louis, 10054, 12515, 13207, 21125
Winius, George Davison, 08097
Winkelmann, Dorethea, 21388
Winks, Robin W., 09006
Winslow, John Copley, 02151, 21455
Wint, Guy, 17507
Winter, H.J.J., 04529
Winternitz, Moriz, 02397
Winther, Paul Christian, 22272
Wirsing, Robert G., 21177
Wirth, Peter, 25279
Wirz, Paul, 01946, 19026
Wise, James, 24597, 25502
Wiser, Charlotte Melina Viall, 23797-8, 23886
Wiser, William Henricks, 00904, 23798
Wiswa Warnapala, W.A., 18387, 18444, 18450, 18454, 18517-8, 18522-3, 18551-2, 19071
Withana, R.M., 18784
Wodeyar, Sadashiva S., 08178
Wolcott, Leonard T., 01803
Wolff, Henry William, 10991
Wolpert, Stanley A., 00189, 09597, 09837
Wolseley, Roland E., 16881
Wolseley, T., 07407
Woltemade, Uwe J., 00864, 00868
Women for Women, Research and Study Group, Dacca, 25525-7
Women of Nepal: a seminar, Kathmandu (1978), 26279
Wood, Arthur Lewis, 18876, 18918
Wood, Conrad, 08146, 20134
Wood, Ernest, 01122, 02155, 02170-1, 05800
Wood, Ernest Egerton, 10795
Wood, Geoffrey, 24170
Wood, Glynn, 16516, 20529-32
Wood, Hugh Bernard, 26314, 26317, 27747
Wood, John B., 13216
Wood, John R., 13092, 21664
Wood, Robin, 25140
Wood, S.H., 10607
Woodcock, George, 04170, 09450, 09899, 11890, 27064, 27170

Woodford, Peggy, 09052
Woodhall, Maureen, 15512
Woodman, Dorothy, 09451, 13907
Woodroffe, John George, Sir, 05847, 05867, 05891-3
Woodruff, Gertrude Marvin, 20480
Woodruff, Philip. *See* Mason, Philip
Woods, James Houghton, 04821
Woodward, Calvin A., 18391, 18410
Woodward, F.L., 04971
Woolf, Leonard Sidney, 18333, 18881
Woolner, Alfred Cooper, 05322, 27815
Workman, Fanny (Bullock), 22438
Workman, William Hunter, 22438
Workshop on Bipartism, New Delhi (1976), 15639
World Fertility Survey, 17799
World Health Organization, 24803
World Telugu Conference, Hyderabad (1975), 19888
Worswick, Clark, 11965
Worth, Robert M., 26302
Wortham, Biscoe Hale, 06010, 06046, 06078, 06095
Wretts-Smith, Mildred, 08004
Wriggins, William Howard, 12230, 17303, 17305, 18388
Wright, Arnold, 08390, 08424
Wright, H. Nelson, 05686
Wright, H.R.C., 08198
Wright, Nicholas H., 18609
Wright, Philip, 03421
Wright, Roy Dean, 15864-7
Wright, Susan W., 15867
Wright, Theodore P., Jr., 12458-9, 13294, 17447, 19669, 21449, 21852, 23772, 23904
Wunderlich, Gene L., 14985
Wylie, Turrell, 02077
Wylly, Harold Carmichael, 08025, 22620
Wyon, John B., 22750, 22848, 22918

Yadav, Babu Ram, 05346
Yadav, C.S., 23411
Yadav, Dharam Raj, 15744, 23865
Yadav, Jai Narain Singh, 12782, 13408, 23268
Yadav, Jai Pal Singh, 22036
Yadav, K.C., 23317
Yadav, K.S., 20880
Yadav, Kripal Chandra, 00520, 09512, 22621
Yadav, R.K., 12484
Yadav, R.S., 16179
Yadav, Ram Prakash, 26137
Yadav, S.S., 15914
Yadava, B.N.S., 05730, 05837
Yadava, J.S., 22714, 23274, 23302
Yaduvansh, Uma, 09271, 20679
Yāḥiya bin Aḥmad bin ʿAbdullah Sirhindī, 07041
Yajnik, Indulal Kanaiyalal, 09757
Yajnik, Jayendrakumar Anandji, 21931
Yajnik, Ramanlal Kanaiyalal, 11580
Yalman, Nur O., 00989, 18827-8, 18848-9, 18995, 19027
Yamada, Isshi, 05123
Yamada, Ryuji, 20954
Yamamoto, Tatsuro, 07172
Yāmunācārya, 06414
Yamunacharya, M., 06425
Yang, Anand Alan, 24099-100
Yanuck, Martin, 11465, 23490, 27509
Yapp, Malcolm, 12222
Yar, Muhammad Khan, 07543
Yasas, Frances Maria, 16148
Yashpal, 11630
Yasin, Madhvi, 06943, 09158
Yasin, Mohammad, 07640
Yasmin Azra Jan, 18145
Yati, Bhakti Prajñān, 07291
Yazdani, Ghulam, 00445, 03385, 05607, 06669, 06879
Yazdani, Zubaida, 19632
Yeats, William Butler, 03978
Yeats-Browne, Francis Charles Claypon, 09333
Yelaja, Shankar A., 16149
Yesudas, R.N., 19934-6, 20113
Yocum, Glenn E., 00075, 02096, 06284, 06287, 06318-9
Yogananda, Paramahansa, 02233
Yogaswami, 19032
Yogendra, Jayadeva, 02172
Yogendra Singh, 00663, 14263, 15732, 15758-60, 23870
Yonuo, Asoso, 26518
Yorke, Michael, 19816
Youé, Christopher P., 26856
Young, Miriam, 22854
Young, Ruth, 10673
Younger, Paul, 01165-6
Younghusband, Francis Edward, Sir, 09452, 23047, 23155
Younghusband, George John, Sir, 09313, 09334, 20347
Yule, Henry, Sir, 09011, 27501-2
Yungblut, Leonard J., 20810
Yunus, Mohammad (1916-   ), 13036, 23069
Yunus, Muhammad (1940-   ), 25330, 25635
Yusafji, Habib, 16721
Yusuf, Hamid, 17304
Yusuf, K.M., 07069
Yusuf, S.M., 05964
Yusuf Jamal, Begam, 02666
Yusufi, Allah Bakhsh, 09808

Zachariae, Theodor, 00041
Zachariah, Kunniparampil C., 10883, 14171-2, 21514-5
Zachariah, Kuruvila, 24852
Zachariah, Mathew, 16606, 16615-6
Zachariah, Michael, 15829
Zaehner, Robert Charles, 01112, 01209, 02152, 02296, 04674, 11399
Zafar, S.M., 17592
Zafar Hasan, Maulvi, 07173
Zagoria, Donald S., 13217, 13245
Zaheer, Ehsan Elahi, 18234
Zahir, Mohammad (1935-   ), 14508
Zaheer, Muhammad (1916-   ), 23522
Zahra, Irene, 17053
Zahrul Huq, A.T.M., 27755
Zaidi, A. Moin, 09644, 09787, 10129, 10319, 10338, 10431, 10489, 13454
Zaidi, S.M. Hafeez, 18096, 25539
Zaidi, Shaheda, 09644
Zaidi, Z.H., 24297, 24304
Zain al-Din, al-Maʾbari, 08147
Zakaria, Nasim, 17378
Zakaria, Rafiq, 07036, 09788
Zaker Husain, Kazi, 27311
Zaki, Muhammad, 07055
Zaki, Wali Muhammad, 18149, 18181, 18192-3
Zaman, Hasan, 12137
Zaman, M.A., 25454, 26173
Zaman, Mukhtar, 10357, 11702
Zamora, Mario D., 10976
Zannas, Eliky, 06895
Zarrilli, Phillip Barry, 02984
Zaveri, J.S., 01378
Zbavitel, Dušan, 02667-8, 25067, 27121
Zeb-un-Nissa, Begum, 07702
Zeidenstein, Sondra, 25353
Zeimal, E.V., 04192
Zelliot, Eleanor Mae, 05838, 10787a, 16765-7, 20762-3, 21426-30
Zetland, Lawrence John Lumley Dundas, 2nd Marquess of, 09553, 09822, 24276, 25847
Zeuner, Frederick, 03567
Zeuner, Tim H., 22814
Zeylanicus, 00394
Zia-ud-Din Barani, 07026, 07043, 07061
Zia-ul-Haq, Mohammad, 17607-9
Zide, Arlene R.K., 03650
Zide, Norman H., 08822, 20963, 25120
Ziegenbalg, Bartholomeus, 01859
Ziegler, Norman P., 08357
Zieseniss, Alexander, 01758
Zimmer, Heinrich Robert, 00329, 01174, 01587, 03108, 05868, 11418
Zimmerman, Francis, 00330
Zingel, Wolfgang-Peter, 18157
Zinkin, Maurice, 13398, 14062
Zinkin, Taya, 14062, 27065
Ziring, Lawrence, 12030, 17305, 17337, 17420, 17440, 17543, 17554, 17644, 17681
Zondag, Cornelius Henry, 25371
Zuber, Christian, 27141
Zürcher, Erik, 01234, 04965
Zulfi, Sahba, 17515
Zutshi, G.L., 23070
Zutshi, N.K., 06954
Zvelebil, Kamil Veith, 02375-7, 02556-8, 02573-6, 03650, 03729, 05236, 06536, 06595, 19579, 19582

Subject Index

NOTE

The small roman numerals refer to the Introduction (pages xiii-xxiii).
One- or two-digit arabic numbers refer to the Outline of Headings (pages 1-83).
Five-digit arabic numbers refer to the Bibliographic Entries (00001-28017).

ᶜAbd al-Quddūs Gangōhī (1456-1537), 07113, 17118
ᶜAbd-al-Razzāk, Samsām al-Daulah Shāh-navāz Khān (1700-58), 07397
ᶜAbd al-Samad, 07752
Abdul Ghaffar Khan. *See* Khan, Abdul Ghaffar Khan
Abdul Karīm, Shāh (1536-1624), 28, 08671-85
Abdul Latif (1828-1893), 24332, 24861
Abdul Latīf, Shāh (Sindhi poet, 1689-1752), 28, 08671-85
Abdullah, Sheikh Mohammed (1905-), 69, 23170, 23173, 23183-9, 23193
ᶜAbdur-Rahīm Khān (1556-1627), 07693, 07699
Abhedananda, Swami (1866-1939), 01179, 11344, 11352
Abhidammattha-sangaha, 06160
Abhidhamma-piṭaka (Buddhist texts), 14, 04996-5002
Abhidharmakośa, 05110, 05114
Abhidharmasamuccaya, 05113
Abhijñāna-Śakuntalā. *See* Śakuntalā
Abhinava Vidyateertha (1917-), 20546, 20553
Abhinavagupta (c. 1000), 18, 22, 05989-93, 06966-75
Abhinayadarpaṇa (dance text), 15, 05300-1
Abhīras, early pastoral group in Deccan, 04201
aboriginals. *See* adivasis
Abors (tribe), 26489, 26504, 26507
"aborted growth" theory (economics), 36, 10908-21, 11077-83
Abraham, K.E. (1899-), 20186
Abraham Malpan (1796-1845), 20184
absolute, in Indic thought, 4, 01391-400
Abu, Mount, 02010, 02013-4
Abul Fazl (1551-1602), 07468-72, 07532, 07676
accounts, of travellers, officials, etc. *See* travellers' accounts
Acintya-Bhedābheda Vedānta, 23, 07264-98
acculturation of tribes, 01091-6
Adhikari, Gangadhar M., 10061
Adi-Dravida, 58, 19363-70
Ādi-Granth, 28, 08661-6
Adi Karnatakas, 61, 20415-22
Ādi-Siddha. *See* Gorakh Nāth
Adigal, Ilango. *See* Iḷaṅkōvaṭikaḷ
Ādil Shāhī Sultanate, 26, 08112-25
adivasi art, 03407, 03350-60
adivasi folklore and religion. *See* sections on specific tribes
adivasi uprisings, 11002-3, 20928-39, 20955-63
ādivāsis (tribal peoples), xxii, 3, 48, 01073-1100, 15785-805. *See also* names of specific tribes; for regions not listed below, *see* social conditions
- Andaman & Nicobar Islands, 79, 26720-36
- Andhra Pradesh, 59, 19803-16
- Arunachal Pradesh, 78-9, 26486-514
- Assam, 76, 25785-93
- Bangladesh, 75, 25506-15
- bibliography, 01073-6, 19371, 19376, 27739
- Bihar, 72, 20892-1006, 24014-29
- Chota Nagpur, 62-63, 20892-1006
- Gujarat, 62, 20829-37
- Karnataka, 61, 20423-4
- Kerala, 60, 20144-52
- Maharashtra, 62, 20819-28
- Manipur, 79, 26584-95
adivasis -- *continued*
- Middle India, 62-3, 20798-1034
- Mizoram, 79, 26613-26
- Nagaland, 79, 26556-73
- Rajasthan, 62, 66, 20838-42, 22101-4
- Sri Lanka, 57, 18829-34
- Tamil Nadu, 58, 19371-404
- Tripura, 79, 26646-8
- Uttar Pradesh, 71, 23773-9
- West Bengal, 73, 24516, 24633-46
administration, xvi-xvii
- Andhra Pradesh, 59, 19700-7
- Assam, 76, 25691-4
- Bangladesh, 75, 25221-8
- Bengal Presidency, 73, 24261a-76
- Bihar, 72, 24011-3
- Bombay Presidency, 62, 20691-707
- British India, 30-31, 71, 09159-243
- Delhi U.T., 70, 23333-4
- East India Company, 26, 07973-97, 08187-90
- Gujarat, 65, 21695-8
- India (Rep.), 40-1, 12602-761
- Maharashtra, 63, 21148-51
- Marathas, 27, 08263-70
- Mughal Empire, 24, 07533-43
- Nepal, 77, 26022-35a
- Orissa, 67, 22306-8
- Pakistan, 52, 17326-63
- Punjab, 68, 22622, 22699-702
- Rajasthan, 66, 21975-78
- Rajputs, 08356
- Sri Lanka, 56, 18504-18
- Tamil Nadu, 58, 19196
- Uttar Pradesh, 71, 23456, 23520-2
- West Bengal, 73, 24387-9
administrative documents, xvi-xviii
Administrative Reforms Commission (1966-69), 41, 12684-90
adolescents. *See* youth
Advaita Vedānta, 19, 06324-407
advertising in India, 51, 16931-4
adult education. *See* education
aesthetics
- literary, 6, 18, 02398-416, 02496-518
- music, 7, 02743-74, 02826-37, 02867-72
- visual arts, 8, 03113-29
Afghanistan and the Afghans, xiv
- ancient art, 16, 05516-53
- British India, relations, 31, 09421-38, 22430
- Islam and, 18, 05932-56
- Mughal period, relations, 24, 27-9, 07457-67, 08296-304, 08535-54, 08034-8
- Pakistan, relations, 69, 17753, 17756, 17760, 23074-80
- prehistory, 03573, 03578-88
Africa
- historical contacts, 00073, 00370-2, 07881
- India (Rep.), relations, 44, 14105
- South Asians in, 80, 26816-70
āgamas (Pāñcarātra texts), 13, 04775-88
āgamas (Śaiva texts), 13, 19-20, 04744-53, 06607
Agaria (tribe), 20882
Agarkar, Gopal Ganesh (1856-95), 21375

Agarwals, 15302, 23390-1
Agastya, 11, 04214-8
age of consent controversy, 35, 49, 10725-31
aged, 49, 15968, 20501, 21538, 23884
Aggarwals. *See* Agarwals
Agni (deity), 03837, 03850
agnihotra, 03934
Agnihotri, Satyanand. *See* Satyanand Agnihotri
Agnipurāṇa, 17, 05793, 05795, 05798-9, 05967
agnistoma (Vedic sacrifice), 03859
Āgniveśyagṛhyasūtra, 04466
Agra, 25, 71, 07784-91, 23837, 23852
agrarian relations. *See* land tenure
agrarian unrest. *See* peasant movements
Agrawala, Vasudev Saran, 03111
agricultural credit. *See also* cooperatives
- Assam, 25758, 25760
- Bangladesh, 75, 25431-9
- British India, 10983-91
- India (Rep.), 47, 15103-50
- Maharashtra, 64, 24474-7
- Nepal, 26140, 26153, 26172
- Pakistan, 54, 17984, 17990
- Sri Lanka, 57, 18889-92
- Tamil Nadu, 19311-5
- Uttar Pradesh, 71, 23623-8
- West Bengal, 73, 24474-7
agricultural education, 50, 16566-74
Agricultural Labour Enquiry, 47, 15075-82
agricultural pests, 14898, 14901
agricultural research
- Bangladesh, 25583
- India (Rep.), 46, 14737-42
agricultural taxation, 45, 14589-96. *See also* finance, public
agriculture. For regions not listed below, *see also* economic conditions
- ancient, 11, 03789, 04362-71
- Andhra Pradesh, 59, 19738-66
- Assam, 76, 25748-64
- Bangladesh, 75, 25331-454
- Bihar, 72, 24056-105
- British India, 36, 10930
- Delhi U.T., 70, 23351-5
- Goa, 63, 21084-91
- Gujarat, 65, 21722-72
- Haryana, 70, 23282-93
- Himachal Pradesh, 77, 25877-79
- India (Rep.), 46, 14723-997
- Jammu & Kashmir, 23209, 23221
- Karnataka, 61, 14847, 20305-40
- Kerala, 60, 20012-41
- Madhya Pradesh, 66, 22198-220
- Maharashtra, 64, 21234-41
- Meghalaya, 26656-68
- Nepal, 77, 26148-60
- Orissa, 67, 22329-47
- Pakistan, 54, 17915-97
- Punjab, 68, 14847, 22731-46, 22757-91, 22805-14
- Rajasthan, 66, 22025-53
- Sind, 67, 22474-85
- Sri Lanka, 56, 18682-775
- Tamil Nadu, 58, 19270-315
- Tripura, 26642
- Uttar Pradesh, 71, 23590-687
- West Bengal, 73, 24436-509
Agris (caste), 21399
Agyeya (Hindi writer, 1911-), 11623-4
ahaṁkāra (individuality, "ego"), 01456-79
Ahilyābāī (d. 1795), 08301
ahiṁsā (non-violence), 4, 33, 01555-62
Ahmad, Yar Khan of Kalat (1904-), 22515
Ahmad Khan, Sir Syed (1817-98), 09789-96, 11466-74
Ahmad Maghribi, Shaikh, 06798
Ahmadabad, 65, 08395, 21693, 21781, 21785-6, 21796, 21875-83
Ahmadiyyas, 37, 55, 11518-26, 18224-34
Ahmadnagar Sultanate, 27, 08239-45
Ahmed, Fakhruddin Ali (1905-77), 40, 12591-2
Ahmed Lahori, Ustad, 07786
Ahmedabad. *See* Ahmadabad
Ahmednagar. *See* Ahmadnagar
Ahmednagar College, 21593
Ahoms (Assamese people), 23, 29, 00529, 00534, 07192-6, 25796
aid, economic. *See* foreign aid
Aihole, 06650-1
Ain-i-Akbari, 07468-72
air transport, India, 47, 15448-54
Aiyannār (deity), 5, 01851-9
Aiyappan. *See* Ayyappan
Ajaṇṭā cave temple, 16, 05591-607, 06810-1
Ajitāgama (Śaiva text), 06607
Ājīvikas (ancient sect), 12, 04599
Ajmer, Rajasthan, 27, 00468, 08376, 22125, 22127
Ajudhianath, Pandit (1840-92), 23468
Akal Takht, 22945
Akali Dal (political party), 42, 13295-7
Akali Movement (Sikhism), 69, 22950-4
Akali Party, British Punjab, 22649, 22653
akam (love) poetry, 16, 05428-33
Akanāṉūṟu, 05433
Akas (tribe), 26494-5
Ākāshvāṇī (All-India Radio), 51, 16941-3
Akbar (1542-1605), 24, 07468-79, 07548, 07550, 07552, 07562, 07564
- religious policy, 25, 07653-73, 07686
Akbar Ilāhābādī (1846-1921), 11692, 11694
Akbar-nāma, 07468-72
Akhil Bhārat Hindu Mahāsabhā. *See* Hindu Mahasabha
ākhyāyika. *See* story literature
alaṁkāraśāstra, 18, 05965-76
Alampur, 06666-7
Alanahally, Srikrishna, 20558
ᶜAlā ud-dīn Khaljī (fl. 1296-1316), 07026-7
Albuquerque, Affonso de, 07858, 07863
alchemy. *See* chemistry
alcohol use and abuse, 49, 16201-6, 21560-1, 22268, 22914
Alekhā sect. *See* Mahimā Dharma
Alexander the Great, 11, 04165, 04569-83
Ali, Ahmed, 18262, 18266
Ali, Mohamed, Maulana (1878-1931), 09798-9, 09801-2, 09804-6, 09808
Ali, Salim A. (1896-), 17282
Ali, Shaukat (1872-1936), 09805-6
Ali Khan, Nizam of Hyderabad (1732/3-1803), 19614
Aligarh Movement, 37, 11475-81
Aligarh Muslim University, 24, 27, 72, 11475-81, 23902-4
"Aligarh school" of history, 24, 07524-8
Aligarh, Uttar Pradesh (city), 23858
Alivardi Khan (fl. 1740-56), 08863
All-India Muslim Conference, 10309-10
All-India Radio (AIR), 51, 16941-3
All-India services. *See* civil service, India
All-India Trade Union Congress, 48, 11127, 15640-76
Allahabad, 71, 08772, 08774, 08789, 23533, 23836, 23840, 23846
- as sacred center, 5, 02040-2, 02099
Allahabad University, 72, 23905-9
almanacs, 82, 27463-4
aluminum industry, 15410
Āḻvārs (Tamil Vaiṣṇava saint-poets), 19, 06285-302
Alwar, princely state, Rajputana, 20638
Amar Singh, 23945
Amarāvatī, stūpa, Andhra, 16, 05499-508
Ambedkar, Bhimrao Ramji (1892-1956), 35, 42, 64, 10771-87a, 12274, 21413-30
Amber, Rajasthan, 27, 08371-5
Ameer Ali, 09800
amendments, Indian constitution, 40, 43, 12380-5, 13517-37
American Ceylon Mission, 19053
Americas, Hindu influence in, 00351
Amherst, William Pitt Amherst, Earl (1773-1857), 30, 09110
Amin, Idi, 80, 26865-70
Amīr Chākar Rind (1454-1551), 06925
Amīr Khusrau (1253-1325), 22, 07027, 07121-30
Amjad Ali Shah, King of Avadh (1801-47), 23447
Amrita Pritam (1919-), 23018-20
Amritsar, Punjab, 68, 22910-3
Amritsar massacre (1919). *See* Jallianwala Bagh
Anāl (tribe), 26594
Anand, Mulk Raj (1905-), 51, 17105-17
Anandaghana (fl. 1719-39). *See* Ghanānanda
Ānandamayī Mā, 74, 24902-9
Anandaranga Pillai, 26, 07926-35
Ānandavardhana (writer on poetics), 18, 05980-7
Ananta Krishna Iyer, L.K., 00656
Anasuya Devi, 19872
anātman (no-soul concept), 01456-79
Anāvil Brahmans, 21833-4, 21917

ancestors, rites for, 3, 01043-51, 20090, 21915
ancient India, 10-17, 04009-5625 (Chapter Three)
Andal. *See* Āṇṭāl
Andaman & Nicobar Islands, xxii, 79, 26707-736, 27345
Andamans prison colony, 10113
Andhra Pradesh, xxi
- ancient, 11, 04222-6
- art, 8, 03383, 03398, 05495-515, 06923-4
- bibliography, 27710
- general history, 2, 00418-9
- geography, 81, 27173
- introductions, 81, 27161, 27163, 27179
- medieval, 06181
- modern (1818-), 59-60, 19604-911
- Mughal period, 26, 08148-61, 08191-98
- sacred centers, 01956-61, 01986
Āndhra-Sātavāhana dynasty, 11, 04195-201
- art, 16, 05494-8
Andrews, Charles Freer (1871-1940), 11540-2, 11550, 11553
Anglican Church. *See* Christianity
Anglo-Indian literature. *See* English literature
Anglo-Indian terms, 82, 27496-502
Anglo-Indians, 48, 15861-67, 21377, 24590, 24856
Anglo-Sikh wars, 68, 22581-601
Āngre dynasty of Kolaba, 27, 08311, 08313
animal husbandry, 46, 14924-45, 18688, 23095, 23301, 23351, 26154
animal symbolism, 4, 01611-27
animals, early domestication of, 9, 03569-70, 03670, 03702
Annadurai, C.N. (1908-69), 58, 19214-22
Annamalai University, 59, 19477, 19484
Āṇṭāḷ (Tamil Vaiṣṇava saint-poet), 05833
anthropology in India, 48, 15677-712, 27487, 27494
anthropology of religion, 5, 01860-76
anthropology of South Asia, 2, 00612-01100
anthropology, physical, xvi, 2, 00710-4
anti-Brahmanism. *See* Non-Brahman movements
Anurādhapura, Ceylon, 19, 04242-9, 06116-20
- art, 16, 05617-21
Anuruddha, 06160
Anushilan Samiti, 32, 09738, 24308
Apa Tanis (tribe), 26496-7
Apabhraṁśas (medieval vernaculars), 15, 05246-60
apartheid (South Africa), 80, 26819-41
Āpastambagṛhyasūtra, 04464
Āpastambaśulvaśāstra, 04542
Appa Sahib, Raja of Nagpur, 20609
Apparao, Guruzada Venkata (1861-1915), 60, 19906-9
Appaya Dīkṣita (16th cent.), 06000, 06392
Apte, Hari Narayan (1864-1919), 31640-1
Arab accounts of South Asia, 17, 05636-46
Arab invasion of Sind (711 AD), 18, 21, 04157, 06926-8, 07022
Arabic literature, 6, 02520, 02525
Arabs, ancient contacts, 04563
Arabs in Sri Lanka. *See* Muslims, Sri Lanka
Arakanese, 25507
Arakkal, House of, 19912
Āraṇyakas, 10, 03962-6
Aravidu dynasty of Vijayanagar, 06220
Archaeological Survey of India, xvi
archaeology, xvi, 2, 9, 00575-611, 03483-797
architecture. *See* art and architecture
archives and documents, 82, 27544-65
- British India, 07963-72, 08180-90, 08252, 08271, 08878-9, 09067-83, 09469-72, 10565, 10576, 10609, 21575, 23946, 23951
- Dutch, 07897, 08093-4
- French, 07902-8, 08247
- Jaipur, 08373
- Maratha, 08249-50, 08272-3, 08413
- Mughal, 07402, 07493, 07523, 08251
- Nepal, 26041-3
- Pakistan, 17657
- Portuguese, 07841-57
- Sri Lanka, 18375
Arcot districts. *See* Tamil Nadu
Ardhamāgadhī language and literature, 14-15, 05150-61, 05253
Arikamedu (ancient site), 04570, 04582
aristocracy. *See* nobility
armed forces and military history, 00114
- ancient, 11, 03786, 04341-5
- Bangladesh, 25228
armed forces and military history -- *continued*
- British India, 31, 34, 09283-334, 10398-403, 10456-60, 10468
- East India Company, 26, 07973-97, 08137
- French in India, 25-26, 07915-25
- India (Rep.), 41, 63, 12717-43, 21051-8
- Marathas, 02263-70
- medieval, 21, 22, 07056-69
- Mughal Empire, 24, 07565-71
- Pakistan, 39, 52-3, 12138-57, 17364-74, 17540, 17736
- Sikhs, 28, 08535-54, 08636-60
- Sri Lanka, 18511
Armenians in Bengal, 73, 24658
arms and armor, 8, 03310-23, 07798
arms control, 44, 13787-93
arranged marriages. *See* kinship
Arrian (Greek writer), 04023
art and architecture, xvi, 8, 03056-482. *See also* names of specific schools, sites, and artists
- ancient, 16-7, 03096, 05449-625
- Bangladesh, 76, 25665-76
- British in India, 39, 11974-81
- British India, 38, 11781-829
- India (Rep.), 51, 17184-230
- Islamic, 8, 23, 25, 03188-97, 06877-9, 07159-73, 07711-802
- medieval, 18, 19, 20, 21, 22, 23, 06096-102, 06164-75, 06607-79, 06806-924, 06877-9, 06996-7001, 07136-73, 07340-68, 07380-5
- Mughal period, 25, 27, 28, 29, 30, 07711-802, 08109-11, 08232-8, 08463-529, 08695-754, 08968-72, 08985-6
- Nepal, 8, 23, 30, 03447-69, 07380-5, 08985-6
- Pakistan, 55, 18276-83
- prehistoric, 9, 03532-42
- South India, 8, 16, 20, 27, 03379-95, 05494-515, 06607-78, 08232-8
- Sri Lanka, 8, 19, 26, 57-8, 03361-78, 05613-25, 06164-75, 08109-11, 19089-98
- tantric, 17, 05869-85
- texts, 18, 21, 03287, 06103-15, 06168, 06853-4, 06910-12, 06916, 08232
artha, bibliography, 01547
Arthaśāstra, 11, 04293-319
artists, 03096, 03127
- Bangladesh, 76, 25665
- British India, 38, 11800-29
- British, in India, 39, 11974-81
- India (Rep.), 51, 17184-230
- Sri Lanka, 58, 19089
Arumuga Navalar (1822-79), 18859, 18854
Arunachal Pradesh, 78-9, 26475-514, 27312, 27330, 27346
Arunachalam, Ponnambalam, 18352
Ārya Samāj, 32, 36-7, 69, 10588, 11269-93, 22633, 22640, 22662, 22966-9, 26752
Āryabhaṭa I (b. 476 AD), 12, 04533-9
Aryan and Non-Aryan interactions, 11, 00704, 00708, 04214-8, 07201
Aryan invasion, xx, 9, 03706, 03734, 03771-80
Āryavarta (land of the Aryans). *See* North India Area
Asaf Jah I, Nizam of Hyderabad (1671-1748), 26, 08126-9
Asan, Kumaran. *See* Kumaran Asan
Asaṅga (Buddhist philosopher, 4th-5th cent.), 14, 05112-3, 05120
Asansol, West Bengal, 24520, 24707
asceticism, 5, 12-3, 02186-2208, 06533, 26321. *See also* sannyāsa
Ashraf, Kunwar Mohammed (1903-62), 20634
ashrams. *See* āśramas
Asiatic Society of Bengal, 35, 38, 10656-60, 11847-51
Asian Relations Conference (1947), 43, 13739
Aśoka Maurya (3rd cent. BC), 11, 04124-41
- as patron of Buddhism, 13, 04955-60
- edicts, 11, 04061, 04132-41
aśoka (plant), 01629
āśramas (four life stages), 5, 04440-56
āśramas (religious communities), 5, 01889-904. *See also* specific gurus and sects
Assam, xxii
- bibliography, 27732
- general history, 2, 00526-36
- geography, 82, 27292
- introductions, 82, 27283-5, 27288, 27293
- medieval, 23, 07192-6
- modern, 73-76, 78-79, 24258, 25677-832, 26441-706
- Mughal period, 29, 08840-72

Assam -- *continued*
- music, 02894
- temples, 02066

Assam Company, 25722
Assam hill areas (formerly part of Assam State), 78-9, 25700-5, 26441-706, 27312-56
Assamese dictionaries and learning aids, 83, 28001-7
Assamese language and literature, 7, 76, 02669-76, 07208, 07336, 25814-27
assassinations
- Bandaranaike, S.W.R., 18429
- Gandhi, M.K., 34, 10521-33
- Liaquat Ali Khan, 52, 17485-8
- Mujibur Rahman, Sheikh, 75, 25208-17

Aṣṭachāp (group of Hindi poets), 29, 08813-24
Aṣṭādhyāyi of Pāṇini, 15, 05190-218
aṣṭāṅga yoga, 13, 04818-31
āstika (orthodox) systems of Hindu philosophy, 13, 04793-874
astral deities, 5, 01826-36
astrology. *See* astronomy
astronomy and astrology, 1, 12, 17, 00274-89, 03793-7, 04530-44
Asurs (tribe), 20997, 20999, 21003
Aśvaghoṣa (1st cent. AD), 15, 05111, 05302-7
Aśvalāyanagṛhyasūtra, 04462
aśvamedha (horse sacrifice), 03922
Atharvaveda saṁhitā. *See* Vedas
atlases and maps
- general, 81-83, 01107, 14723-32, 26994-7006
- historical, 1, 00150-6, 07386
- linguistic, 02316, 02320, 02625
- state and provincial, 20689, 22033, 22202, 24423

Ātmabodha (Vedānta text), 06347, 06356, 06358
Ātmajñānopadeśavidhi (Vedānta text), 06353
ātman ("self" in Indic thought), 4, 01456-79
atomic energy, atomic weapons. *See* nuclear
atoms (philosophy), 01378, 04832-61
Atreya, Bikhan Lal, 16704
Attlee, Clement Richard (1883-1967), British Prime Minister (1945-51), 34
Attorney-General for India, 40, 12601
Auckland, George Eden, Earl of (1784-1849), 30, 09116
Aurangabad cave temples, 16, 21, 06810, 06813-5
Aurangabad city, 21485, 21490
Aurangzīb (1619-1707), 24, 25, 27-28, 07494-512, 07549, 07557-8, 07563, 07544
- religious policy, 25, 07653-73

Aurobindo, Sri. *See* Ghose, Aurobindo
authority, ideas of. *See* kingship; political thought
Avadh (region now in Uttar Pradesh), 29, 71, 08762-77, 08786-7, 23441-7, 23637-41, 23827
Avadhī language and literature, 29, 02652, 08790-812
Avalokiteśvara (Bodhisattva), 05088
avatāra (divine "descent," incarnation), 5, 13, 01767-1801, 06071, 11202
Avesta (Zoroastrian texts), 6, 02297-300
avidyā (nescience), 01415, 01425
Avimāraka (play), 05314-5
Avtar Singh (1899-1969), 22960
Awadh, Awadhi. *See* Avadh
Awami League, 52, 75, 17456-9
Ayub Khan, Mohammad (1907-), 52, 17508-15, 17538-50, 17673
āyurveda. *See* medicine
Ayyappan (deity), 5, 01851-9, 19512, 20171
Azad, Abul Kalam, Maulana (1888-1958), 33, 10194-6, 10289, 10299, 10306, 10641
"Azad Hind," 34, 10432-45
"Azad Kashmir," 69, 23203-7
Azariah, Vedanayagam Samuel (1874-1945), 19529

Bābar (1483-1530), Mughal Emperor, 24, 07448-56
Backward Classes, 48, 15806-42. *See also* Scheduled Castes; adivasis
Bactria, 04158-94
Badagas (tribe), 19375
Bādāmi (Vātāpi, capital of Western Cālukya dynasty), 19, 96205-14
- art, 20, 06648-59

Bādarāyana's Brahmasūtra, 13, 04870-4
Baden-Powell, Robert Stephenson Smyth, Sir, 09314
Badrinath, Uttar Pradesh, 02071, 02073
Badu (caste), 22363
Bāgh (archaeological site), 05591-607
Bāghelkhand, medieval, 21, 06702-7
Bahāristān-ī-Ghaybī, 08847
Bahāwalpur, princely state, Punjab, 22610
Bahiṇā Bāī (1629?-1700), 08425
Bāhman Shāh (Hasan Gangawī), 20, 06689
Bāhmanī Sultanate, 20, 06687
Baiga (tribe), 20853, 20883-4, 20888
Bairam Khan (d. 1561), 07562
Baji Rao I, Peshwa, 08299, 08304
Baji Rao II, Peshwa, 08323, 08332
Baker, Samuel, 22283
Balahis (tribe), 20850
balance of payments. *See* foreign trade
Balarāma (Kṛṣṇa's brother), 01774, 01780
Baluchi dictionaries and learning aids, 83, 27949-52
Baluchi language and literature, 7, 28, 68, 02617-20, 08690, 22553
Baluchistan
- bibliography, 27719, 27721
- general history, 2, 00487-90
- introductions, 81, 27214, 27223, 27234-5, 27241
- medieval, 21, 06925
- modern (1800-), 67-68, 22430, 22433-4, 22439, 22515, 22553
- Mughal period, 28
- prehistory, 9, 03526, 03571, 03578-88, 03738

Baluchs, 68, 22532-49
Bāmiyān (ancient site in Afghanistan), 16, 05544-8
Bāṇa / Bāṇabhaṭṭa (Sanskrit writer, c. 625), 18, 06011-22
Bāna dynasty, 06189
Banaras. *See* Vārāṇasī
Banaras Hindu University, 72, 23893-901
Bandaranaike, Sirimavo (1916-), 18424, 18427, 18562-3
Bandaranaike, Solomon West Ridgeway Dias (1899-1959), 18411-2, 18429, 18467, 18559, 18562-3
Bande Mataram (journal), 32, 09689, 09718, 10841
Bande Mataram (song), 24976, 24988
Bandung Asian-African Conference (1955), 43, 13737-40
Bandyopadhyay, Manik (1908-56), 25104
Bandyopadhyay, Tarashankar (1898-1971), 25089
Banerjea, Surendranath (1848-1925), 32, 09651-2, 09654, 09679
Banerjee, Gooroo Dass, Sir (1844-1918), 24826
Banerji, Sevabrata Sasipada, 24551
Bangabasi (journal), 25127
Bangalore, Karnataka capital, 61, 20465-80
Bangladesh, xiv, xxi-xxii, 73-6, 25141-676
- bibliography, 27730, 27733-4
- census, xviii
- introductions, 82, 27300-11
- origins of, 39, 43, 12113-190
- statistics, guides, 27755

Bangladesh Academy of Rural Development, 75, 25411-30
Bangladesh War of Independence (1971), 39, 12113-90, 25165
Bangladesh refugees, 39, 76, 79, 12138-57, 25779-82, 26644
Bania/Baniya (merchant castes), 15305, 24626-7
banking. For areas not listed below, *see* economic conditions
- Bihar, 24039
- British India, 36, 11163-82, 24411
- cooperative, 14717-22
- India (Rep.), 45, 47, 14610-99, 15118-28
- indigenous, 00914, 11170, 19124-5
- Karnataka, 61, 20295-304, 20306, 20324
- Madhya Pradesh, 22193
- Maharashtra, 64, 21227-33
- Nepal, 77, 26140-7
- Pakistan, 53, 17894-902, 17991
- Rajasthan, 66, 22024
- Sri Lanka, 56, 18663-75
- Uttar Pradesh, 23586

Baptista, Joseph, "Kaka" (1864-1930), 09761
Barani, Zia-ud-din, 07026, 07043, 07046, 07061
bardic poetry
- Kashmiri, 22, 06937-43
- Rajasthani, medieval, 21, 06724-30
- Tamil, 16, 05434-6

Bardoli, Gujarat, 21787
Bardoli satyagraha, 20745
Barisal District Conference (1908), 24298
Baroda, Gujarat (city), 65, 00460, 21683, 21685, 21695, 21699, 21775, 21782, 21884-8, 21890, 21901
Baroda, princely state, Gujarat, 27, 62, 20624-33
Bāroṭs (Gujarati bardic caste), 21837
Barrier, N. Gerald, xvii, xviii

Barros, João de (1496-1570), 07843, 07856, 07866
Bartholomew, Saint, 04606
Barua, Devakanta (1914-), 25709
Barua, Navakanta, 25822
Basava (Vīraśaiva saint, 12th cent.), 20, 06538-56
Basāwan (Mughal painter) 07762
Bashir, Murtaza, 25667
Basic Democracies (Pakistan 1959-65), 17538-43, 17629-44
basic education, India, 35, 10630-40, 16595-606
Basohli painting, 29, 08712-8
Bastar, Madhya Pradesh, 22197, 24033
- adivasis, 20862-91
- Maharaja of, 20666
Bastar, princely state, Central India, 20666
bastis/bustees. *See* slums
batik, 03324, 03326
Bāuls (Bengali mendicant singers), 30, 08946
Bauris (caste), 24152, 24645
Bazaar painting, 38, 11794-9
Bedi, Rajinder Singh, 17055
beggars (as social problem) 49, 16180-3, 18915, 22134, 22379, 23399, 24201, 24808
Begrām (ancient site), 16, 05538-43
behavioral sciences in India, 48, 15677-712
Belgians in India, 29, 07811, 08855
Belūr temples, Karnataka, 06673-4
Bendre, Dattatreya Ramachandra (1896-), 20572-3
Bene Israel (Jews of Bombay), 24, 21456-8
Bengal (areas now in Bangladesh and West Bengal State of India)
- ancient, 04382
- bibliography, 27751
- general history, 2, 00521-4
- medieval, 23, 07174-368
- modern (1813-), 73-76, 24241-5676
- Mughal period, 29, 08840-72
- prehistory, 03510-1, 03561
- Sanskrit literature, 02489-90
- temples, 02067
Bengal-Assam Area. *See* Northeast Area
Bengal, Darjeeling district. *See* Darjeeling
Bengal Presidency, xxii, 72-3, 24241-348
Bengal Provincial Conference (1905), 24294-5, 24318
Bengal Renaissance, 37, 73, 24561-77, 24991, 25682
Bengal school of painting, 38, 11800-20
Bengali dictionaries and learning aids, 83, 27984-8000
Bengali language and literature, 7, 23, 30, 74, 76, 02654-68, 07207-9, 07228-98, 07335-9, 08962-7, 24919-5108, 25645-53
Bengali script, 02378
Bengalis in Assam, 76, 25698, 25779-82
Bengalis in Punjab, 22827
Bengalis in Tripura, 79, 26644
Bentinck, William Henry Cavendish, Lord (1774-1839), 30, 09111-5, 10574
Berar. *See* Vidarbha
Berar Sultanate, 27
Besant, Annie (1847-1933), 32, 37, 09760, 11360-6, 18988
Beschi, Constanzo Guiseppe (1680-1746), 08221
betel-nut, 00837-45
Bezbarua, Lakshminath (1868-1938), 76, 25823-7
Bhabha, Homi Jehangir (1909-66), 17278-9
Bhadrabāhu (Jaina astronomer and religious leader d. 298 BC), 04538
bhadralok (Bengali, "respectable people"), 73, 24612-20
Bhagat Singh (1907-31), 10105-14
Bhagavadajjuka-prahasana (Sanskrit farce), 06064
Bhagavadgītā, 13, 01206, 01220, 01354, 01366, 01482, 01534, 04502, 04659-94, 06368
- commentaries, 06419-23, 06757-68, 07289, 08944
Bhagavat Simhaji, Maharaja of Gondal (1865-1944), 20614, 20619
Bhāgavata Dharma (Vaisnava sect), 13, 04773-4, 06367
Bhāgavata Meḷa (South Indian dance form), 02958-9, 02961
Bhāgavata-purāṇa, 17, 05761-78
Bhairon (Śaiva deity), 23920
bhajnopdeshak (folk performer), 23941
Bhakra dam, Himachal Pradesh, 22785-7
Bhaktalīlāmṛta of Mahīpati, 06746, 08425-49
Bhaktavijaya of Mahīpati, 06744-71
bhakti (devotional Hinduism), xx, 13, 17, 04772-4, 05773, 05828-56
- Bengal, 23, 30, 07228-98, 08935-52
- Gujarat-Rajasthan, 21, 28, 06777-89
- Kashmir, 22, 06976-82
bhakti -- *continued*
- Maharashtra, 21, 27-8, 06744-71, 08425-56
- origins, 13, 04731-92
- North India (Hindi area), 22, 29, 07089-110, 08790-826
- South India, 19-20, 06285-323, 06379-568
Bhāmaha (writer on poetics, c. 600 AD), 18, 05260, 05971-2
Bhandara district, Maharashtra, 21168
Bhandaris (Maharashtrian caste), 21400
Bhandarkar, Ramakrishna Gopal (1837-1925), 00060, 00062
Bhangis (sweeper caste), 66, 71, 22094, 23367, 23746
Bhanubhakta Acharya (1812-68), 26344
Bhānudās (Marathi poet-saint), 06744
Bharata Nāṭyam (South Indian dance style), 7, 02957-68
Bharatamuni. *See* Nāṭyaśāstra
Bhāratendu. *See* Hariśchandra
Bharati, C. Subrahmanya (1882-1921), 59, 19583-603
Bharatiya Jan Sangh. *See* Jana Sangh
Bharatpur, princely state, Rajasthan, 62, 20659-60
Bhāravi (Sanskrit writer, 7th cent. AD), 05380
Bharhut (archaeological site), 16, 05479-82
Bhartṛhari (Sanskrit grammarian), 15, 18, 01438, 05521-9
Bhartṛhari (Sanskrit poet, 7th cent.?), 18, 06037-46
Bharuci (legal commentator, c. 6th cent. AD), 04423
Bhāsa (c. 4th cent. AD), 15, 05312-22
Bhasani, Abdul Hamid Khan, Maulana (1880-1976), 52, 17460-1, 24335, 25698
Bhāskara (Vedānta philosopher, 9th cent.), 20, 06495-9
Bhāskara I (astronomer, c. 600 AD), 17, 05734, 05738
Bhāskara II (astronomer, b. 1114), 17, 05732, 05734
Bhaṭ (Gujarati bardic caste), 20699
Bhāṭkhaṇḍe, Vishnu Narayan (1860-1936), 02848
Bhatnagar, Shanti Swarup (1894-1955), 10672
Bhaṭṭa Nārāyaṇa (Śaiva Bhakta, Kashmir), 22, 06981
Bhattacharya, Bhabani, 17173, 17177, 17181
Bhattacharya, Kalidas, 16700
Bhattacharyya, Krishna Chandra (1875-1949), 11425, 11427
Bhaumakāra dynasty, 21, 06694-701
Bhavabhūti (dramatist, c. 700), 18, 06024-36
Bhavāī folk drama, 8, 03031-5
Bhāvaviveka, 05117
Bhave, Vinayak Narahar. *See* Bhave, Vinoba
Bhave, Vinoba (1895-), 45-6, 14314, 14986-97
Bhaviṣya-purāṇa, 17, 05818, 05820
Bhavnagar, princely state, Kathiawar, 20615
Bhedābheda (school of Vedānta), 20, 06495-9
Bhilalas (tribe), 20852-3, 20861
Bhils (tribal people), 62, 20798-818, 20853
Bhilwara city, Rajasthan, 22122
Bhimbhetka rock paintings, Madhya Pradesh, 03532, 03537
Bhoja (Sanskrit writer, 11th cent.), 06003
Bhojpuri language and literature, 07339, 24229, 24233-5
Bhonsle/Bhonsla dynasty of Nagpur, 27, 08314-5, 20609-11
Bhoodan/Bhūdān (land-gift movement) and gramdam (village-gift), 46, 14986-97, 20041, 21265, 22046, 22344, 22346
Bhopal city, Madhya Pradesh, 22188, 22254, 22257, 22260
Bhopal, princely state, 62, 20676-9
Bhor, princely state, Maharashtra, 20588-9
Bhotias/Bhotiyas (Tibetan peoples of the Himalayas), 78, 25889, 25939, 25941, 26396-7, 26407. *See also* Tibetans
Bhoymeeah, Tyabjee, 21331
Bhṛgus (warrior-priests), 04639, 04653
Bhubaneshwar, capital of Orissa, 21, 06913-5, 22363, 22375, 22377
Bhuiyas (tribe), 20871, 21027-8
Bhumihar Brahmans, Bihar, 72
Bhumij (tribe), 63, 20969-76
Bhunjias (tribe), 21024
bhūta ("devils" of folk religion), 20534, 20549, 20554
Bhutan, xiv, xx, xxii
- general history, 2, 00537-45
- geography, 27344
- introductions, 82, 27319, 27326, 27329, 27331
- medieval, 07369
- modern (1800-), 25834-55, 26412-40
- Mughal period, 08980
- travel accounts, 25835, 25839, 27349, 27351, 27353
Bhutto, Zulfiqar Ali (1928-79), 52-3, 17462-6, 17555-9, 17579-91, 17619-20, 17681
Bhuvanesvara. *See* Bhubaneshwar
bibliography, general, ix, 82-83, 27631-741. *See also* bibliography sections under specific subject headings
Bihar, xxii
- adivasis, 62-3, 20892-1006
- ancient, 04113
- art, Gupta period, 16, 05608-12

Bihar -- *continued*
- bibliography, 27729
- general history, 2, 00510-20
- geography, 27267-8
- introductions, 82, 27260, 27262-3
- medieval, 23, 07076, 07078, 07080, 07179-81, 07183, 07370, 07377
- modern (1801-), 72, 23944-4240
- Mughal period, 29, 08778-83, 08788, 08892
- prehistory, 03518, 03548
- sacred centers, 5, 02057-65

Bihārī Lāl, Hindi poet (1595-1664), 08835
Biharis in Bangladesh, 25501
Bijapur architecture, 08233
Bijapur sufis, 08215
Bijapur Sultanate, 26, 08112-25
Bijaykrishna Goswāmī. *See* Gosvāmī, Vijay Kṛṣṇa
Bikaner, princely state, Rajasthan, 62, 20640, 20657-8
Bilgrami, Saiyid Husain (1844-), 19861
Bilhaṇa, Sanskrit poet (11th cent.), 18, 06047-53
Bilvamaṅgalastava, Sanskrit devotional poem, 05845
Bimbisāra, King of Magadha (6th cent. BC), 04108
biography and biographical dictionaries, 1, 30, 82, 00059-66, 00121-7, 00157-62, 09012-25, 27465-95
Birbhum district, West Bengal, 24484, 24486
- land tenure, 24488
- iron industry, 24519

Bird & Co., Calcutta, 11096
birds. *See* wildlife
Birdwood, William Riddell Birdwood, Baron, 09315
Birendra Bir Bikram Shaha Deva (1945-), King of Nepal, 77, 25989-92
Birhors (tribe), 21004, 24047
Birjhia Asurs (tribe), 20997
Birla, business family, 15314-5
Birsa Munda (1874-1901), 63, 20956, 20959-60, 20963
birth control. *See* family planning
al-Bīrūnī (Arab traveller, 978?-1048), 17, 05636-46, 05731
Bishandās (Mughal painter), 07767
Biswas, Prophilla Chander (1904-), 00655
Black and Red Ware culture, 03691, 03711
"black money", 14602-9
Blavatsky, Helene Petrovna (1831-91), 11353-4
blindness and the blind, 16174-9
Bobrinskoy, George V., 00026
Bodhgayā. *See* Gayā
Bodhicaryavatāra (Buddhist text), 05093
bodhisattvas, 14, 18, 05084-9
Bodhs (Himalayan people), 25890
Bodas (tribe), 79, 26470. *See also* Garo
Bohras (Muslim sect), 21443, 21847-52
Bokaro, Bihar, 24109
Bokaro steel plant, 14042
Bombay city
- modern (1818-), 63-4, 21497-542
- Mughal period, 27, 08298, 08385-90, 03413-23
- politics, 63, 21178-95

Bombay Plan, 11198
Bombay Presidency, 62, 08379-90, 20685-763
Bombay State, 21110-4 *See also* Maharashtra; Gujarat
Bombay, University of, 64, 21594-5, 21600
Bondo (tribe), 21025
Bongaism, Santal tribal cult, 20940-7, 20966
Bonnerjee, W.C., 32, 09653
bookdealers, 82, 27566-82
Border Security Force, India, 12706, 12716
Borrah, Bolinarayan (1852-1927), 25820
Bose, Ananda Mohan (1847-1906), 11256, 24287
Bose, Buddhadeva (1908-74), 25093
Bose, Jagadis Chandra, Sir (1858-1937), 10661, 10664, 10668-9
Bose, Nandalal (1882-1966), 11813
Bose, Nirmal Kumar, 00635, 00662
Bose, Pramath Nath, 17272
Bose, Rash Behari (1880-1945), 09740, 09743, 09754
Bose, Satyendranath (1894-1974), 10662, 17273, 17279
Bose, Subhas Chandra (1877-1945), 33, 34, 10153-75, 10432-45
botany
- flora of South Asia, 27027-30, 27038, 27040-1, 27043, 27045, 27147, 27202, 27266, 27343, 27373
- history, 00250, 00258, 10649, 10665

boundary disputes. *See also* partition
- India, internal, 41, 12925-37
- India-Pakistan, 39, 12066-202

boundary disputes -- *continued*
- Sino-Indian, 44, 13916-59

Bourdonnais, Bertrand François Mahé, Comte de (1699-1753), 07907
Bower Manuscript (medieval medical text), 04555
Bowne, Borden Parker (1847-1910), 06444
Brahmā (deity), 5, 08904-6
Brahmagupta (b. 598 AD), 17, 05733, 05736
brahman, the Hindu absolute, 4, 01391-400, 01459
brāhmaṇas (Vedic texts), 10, 01366, 03745, 03933-61
Brahmāṇḍa-purāṇa, 17, 05813
Brahmanism. *See* Hinduism
Brahmans (first of the four varṇas), xiii. *See also* names of specific Brahman castes
- Andhra Pradesh, 19799
- Bangladesh, 25505
- Bengal, 73, 24621-5
- Bihar, 72, 24139-48
- Gujarat, 65, 21831-4
- Jammu & Kashmir, 23225, 23237, 23239-40
- Karnataka, 61, 20393-9
- Kerala, 60, 20081-5
- kinship, 01003-5
- Kumaon, 25929
- Maharashtra, 64, 21389-92
- Manipur, 79
- Nepal, 78, 26242, 26260-3
- origins, 04445, 04456
- Orissa, 22373
- ritual, 01026-7, 01038
- Tamil Nadu, 58, 19353-7
- Uttar Pradesh, 71, 23718-23

Brahma-purāṇa, 17, 05822
Brahmaputra Valley. *See* Assam
Brahmasūtra, 13, 01206, 04870-4, 06325
- commentaries, 06348-9, 06415, 06421, 06474

Brahmavaivarta-purāṇa, 17, 05783-7
Brāhmi script, 02379, 02381, 04057
Brāhmo Samāj, 36, 10758, 11248-62
Brahui language, 68, 02365, 02619, 22552
Brahuis, 00590, 22526, 22533, 22546, 22548-9
"brain drain", 48, 15525-30
Braj/Vraj (region now in Uttar Pradesh), 5, 29, 02036-9
Brajabūli literature, 07241, 08967
Brajbhāṣā literature (Hindi dialect), 29, 08813-25
brass industry, 23667, 24530
bratas. *See* vrata rituals
Brazil-India relations, 14107
Bṛhad-devatā, index of Vedic gods, 03847
Bṛhad-jātaka (astronomy text), 04533, 04535
Bṛhaspati (deity), 03832, 03851
Bṛhaspati (writer on law). *See* Dharmaśāstras
Bṛhatkathā (story collection), 15, 18, 05389-92, 06071-8
Bṛhatkathāmañjarī (story collection), 06074
Bṛhatkathāślokasaṁgraha (story collection), 06073, 06075
bridges, ancient, 00343
Brindaban. *See* Vrindavan
British colonies, South Asians in, 80, 26758-891
British in India, xx
- art, 39, 11974-81
- early settlement, 26, 27, 29, 07437-43, 07841-8047, 08199-202, 08379-90, 08853-88, 08924-31
- social life, 39, 08199-202, 08924-31, 11930-81

British India, xxi, 30-39, 08987-11981 (Chapter Six); *also* Chapter Five and Chapters Eleven-Seventeen, *passim*
British India, relations with Nepal and Bhutan, 77, 78, 26053-63, 26425-30
British Indian Association, 24288
British Library, ix, 82, 27520-3
British Museum. *See* British Library
British rule in South Asia. *See* government and politics
Broadfoot, George, Major, 22611
Bronze Age in South Asia, 9, 03568-685
bronze sculpture, 8, 23, 03232-42, 07361-8. *See also* art and architecture
Brown, William Norman, ix, 00015
Buckingham, James Silk, 10824, 10837
Buddha. *See* Gautama Buddha
Buddha Gayā. *See* Gayā
Buddhacarita, 15, 05302-7
Buddhaghoṣa (Buddhist writer, 5th cent. AD), 14, 05036-40
Buddhism, xxii, 3-5, 01101-859
- Abhidharma, 01452
- art, 8, 16, 21, 03140-8, 03361-78, 05449-625
- Bangladesh, 76, 25636-8

Buddhism -- *continued*
- Bengal, 07211-27
- bibliography and reference, 01123-43
- Bihar, 07211-27
- comparative studies, 19, 01335-59, 01423, 01430-1, 01481, 06379-86
- cosmology, 00267, 00271
- decline in India, 05923-9, 06569
- early history, 13-4, 01459, 01463, 01470, 04875-5129
- ethics, 01509-75
- Hīnayāna, 05017-44
- iconography, 01655-86
- Kashmir, 70, 06955
- Kuṣāṇa Empire, 11, 04178-93
- Ladakh, 08689
- logic, 01426-36
- Mādhyamika, 05053, 05095-109
- Mahāyāna, 01128, 02175, 05945-129, 06158
- Mauryan Empire, 11, 13, 14124-41, 04955-60
- medieval, 17-8, 06742, 06955, 07211-27, 07379
- meditation, 02174, 05029-35
- metaphysics, 01368-1410
- modern Indian ("Neo-Buddhism"), 50, 64, 16761-7, 21413-30
- monasticism, 01893, 04935-65, 06149-63, 18989-95, 25637, 26488, 26324-5
- Mughal period, 28, 08689
- Muslim views, 05959
- Nepal, 78, 07379, 26318-39
- philosophy, 01319-27
- political thought, 04267, 04282
- sacred centers, 17, 01934-46, 02057-65, 02077, 04078
- Sikkim, 78, 26402, 26408
- Sri Lanka, 14, 19, 26, 55-56, 57, 01237-41, 01244-6, 05041-4, 06149-63, 08099, 18342-9, 18455-72, 18973-9027
- surveys, 01224-64
- tantric. *See* Buddhism, Vajrayāna
- texts, 4, 12, 14, 01266-72, 04966-5016, 05060-83
- Theravāda, 01127, 01132, 01260, 01868, 01889, 04951-4, 05017-47
- Tibetan, 77, 01341, 02063, 02077, 26318-39
- Vajrayāna (tantric), 18, 05047, 05857-922, 26318-39
- women in early, 04474-81

Buddhism and modernization, 56, 18636-40
Budhasvāmin, 06071-8
Bundelas, ruling group in Central India, 06705, 22236
Bundelkhaṇḍ (region now in Madhya Pradesh)
- Mughal period, 21, 28, 08377

Bundī painting, 28, 08492-500
bureaucracy. *See* administration; civil service
Burghers (Euro-Ceylonese), 57, 18867-8
Burhanpur, Madhya Pradesh
- Mughal period, 08396

burial, prehistoric, 9, 03543-5
Burma, xiv, xxii
- British India, relations, 31, 34, 08872, 09405-7
- India (Rep.), relations, 14099
- South Asians in, 78-80, 26875-6, 26877-80, 26812

business communities
- British India, 36, 11092-110
- India (Rep.), 47, 15289-318
- Pakistan, 54, 18020-5

Bussy, Charles Joseph Patissier, Marquis de, 07932
bustees. *See* slums
Butler, Spencer Harcourt, Sir, 23456, 23458
Buxas (tribe), 25925

cabinet, India, 40, 12593-600
Cabinet Mission (1946), 34, 10461-6
cabinet, Sri Lanka, 55, 18383-4, 18387
Caitanya (1486-1533), Bengali Vaiṣṇava saint, 23, 07264-98
Caitanya sect, 50, 79, 06803, 16708, 16756-60, 26596-8
Cāk (tribe), 25506
Cakma (tribe). *See* Chakma
cakra (wheel symbol), 4, 01642-6, 01759
Cakradhar, Śrī, 21, 06772-7, 06779
Calcutta Journal, 24242
Calcutta Metropolitan Planning Organization, 74, 24772-83
Calcutta, University of, 74, 24839-46, 24859
Calcutta, West Bengal, 32, 74, 24654, 24708-803, 24938
- "Black Hole" (1756), 08017-25
- early history, 08924-31

calendar, sacred. *See* festivals
calendars, 82, 27463-4. *See also* chronology
calendrical science, 1, 12, 00274-89, 04530-2
Calicut/Kozhikode, Kerala, 26, 08138
calligraphy, Muslim, 07800-1
Cāḷukya dynasty, Eastern (of Vengi), 19, 06205-14, 06660-9
- art, 20, 06660-9

Cāḷukya dynasty, Western (of Badami), 19, 06205-14, 06719
- art, 20, 06648-59

Cama, Bhikaji, Madam (1861-1963), 09586, 20732
Cama, Kharshedji Rustamji (1831-1909), 21435, 21440
Camār. *See* Chamar
Camoens, Luiz de (1524?-80), 07867-8, 07872
Campbell, George, Sir (1825-92), 09170, 09201
Campbellpur, Attock Dist., Punjab (Pak.), 22892
campu, mixed prose and verse literary form, 18
Canada
- India, relations, 14069
- South Asian Studies, 27416
- South Asians in, 81, 26928-40

Cāṇakya. *See* Kauṭilya
Canarese language. *See* Kannada
Candella dynasty, 21, 06702
Caṇḍī (deity), 07301, 22402, 24890
Caṇḍīdāsa (Bengali bhakti poet, 1417-77), 23, 07258-63
Caṇḍīśataka, 06014
Cankam. *See* Sangam
Cannanore, Kerala, 19912
Canning, Charles John Canning, Earl (1812-62), 30, 09100, 09129-30
capital formation. *See also* savings
- India, 46, 14683-99
- Pakistan, 54, 17908-12

Caraka-saṁhitā (medical text), 12, 04552-60
Carey, William (1761-1834), 30, 08954-61
Cariappa, K.M., Gen., 12739
Caribbean, South Asians in, 80, 26773-802
Carnatic (South Indian) music. *See* Karnatak music
carpets, 8, 03347-9
Cartier, John (1733-1802), 08875
cartoons, political, Indian, 42, 13114-23
Cārvāka (ancient philosophy), 12, 04594-8
caryāgīti (medieval Bengali songs), 23, 07219-27
cashew cultivation, Kerala, 20013
caste and caste system, xviii, 2-3, 00678-845. *See also* names of specific castes; for caste in rural society, *see also* villages
- ancient, 12, 04440-56
- Andhra Pradesh, 59, 19784-802
- Assam, 25775-78
- Bangladesh, 75, 25493-505
- Bengal, 73, 24578-646
- Bihar, 72, 24134-154
- British India, 10746-87a, 11292
- Delhi U.T., 23362-8
- Gujarat, 65, 21668-9, 21673, 21811-46, 21909
- Himachal Pradesh, 25885
- India (Rep.), 48, 13072-82, 15761-84, 15926-9
- Jammu and Kashmir, 23228
- Karnataka, 20361-79, 20520, 20523
- Kerala, 60, 20067-113
- law and, 31, 48, 09272-82, 15778-85, 15806-20. *See also* Scheduled Castes
- Madhya Pradesh, 66, 22229-42
- Maharashtra, 21377-430
- Meghalaya, 26673
- Mughal period, 24, 07641-3, 08394
- Muslims, 2, 00752-6, 20135, 24155, 24157, 24650, 24653
- Nepal, 78, 26190-204
- Orissa, 67, 22357-65
- overseas South Asians, 26757
- Pakistan, 54
- Punjab, 68, 22822-40
- Rajasthan, 66, 22074-94
- Sri Lanka, 57, 18815-18
- Tamil Nadu, 58, 19340-70
- Uttar Pradesh, 71, 23688-758
- Vedic period, 03943
- West Bengal, 73, 24578-646

caste and marriage, 49, 15926-9
caste and politics, 52, 13072-82
caste discrimination, 35, 48, 10746-87, 15766-84, 15806-20
caste ranking, 2, 00793-836
Castro, João de, 07859, 07864
Catholic Church. *See* Christianity
Cāttaṉār (Tamil poet, fl. 550 AD), 16, 05446-8
cattle. *See* animal husbandry; cow

Caturbhānī (Sanskrit drama), 05381
Caurapañcāśikā (Sanskrit erotic poem), 06047-53, 07157
Caurāsī pad (Braj Bhāṣā poem), 29, 08825
causation (philosophy), 01376, 01480-97, 04806, 04839
cave temples, 16, 21, 05483-93, 06813-29. *See also* specific sites
Cēkkiḻār (Tamil poet, 12th cent.), 12, 06320-3
cement industry, India, 15412
censorship
- British India, 35, 00119, 10838-52
- India (Rep.), 43, 51, 14538-43, 16847-60, 16988-90
- Pakistan, 55, 18241-6
- Sri Lanka, 19063, 19065-6
censuses, xiv, xvi-xviii, 27686, 27746-65. *See also* demography
Central Bank of Ceylon, 18663-75
Central India Agency, 20667
Central India Area. *See* Middle India Area.
Central Intelligence Agency (U.S.), 14026
Central Provinces and Berar, 62, 20764-73
Central Social Welfare Board, 49, 16150
centre-state relations, India, 41, 45, 12912-24, 14521-50, 21951
Cēra kingdom, 11, 16, 04219-21
ceremonies. *See* ritual
Cerenga Kulha (tribe), 21026
Ceylon. *See* Sri Lanka
Ceylon Communist Party, 18393
Ceylon National Congress, 55, 18350-4
Chaitanya. *See* Caitanya
Chakmas (tribe), 79, 25510
Chalcolithic (Copper-Stone Age), 9, 03568-685
Chamar (leather worker caste), 22, 71, 23744-5, 23747-9, 23757
Chambā painting, 29, 08732-49
Chambā, princely state, Himachal Pradesh, 06931, 08555
Chambal Valley, Madhya Pradesh, 66, 22189, 22206, 22263-72
Chamber of Princes, 31, 09376-83
Chambers of Commerce, 15310-3, 21516, 24416
Champaran, Bihar, 72, 24089-90
Champaran Satyagraha (1917), 72, 23964-73
Chand Bardāī (Hindi poet, 12th cent.), 06724
Chānd Bībī (d. 1600), 27, 08239-45
Chandavarkar, Narayan Ganesh, Sir (1855-1923), 21370
Chandella dynasty, 21, 06702
Chandernagore, French enclave in Bengal, 07902-40
Chandigarh city, 68, 22899-909
Chandragupta Maurya (321-296 B.C.), Emperor, 11, 04121-3
Chandrakīrti, Buddhist philosopher, 05095
Chandrasekharendra Sarasvatī, Sankarācārya of Kāñchī, 02224
Chandu Menon, Oyyarattu (1846-99), 20200-1, 20205
Channabasava (Vīraśaiva saint, 12th cent.), 06541
Charan Singh (1899-), 13627-35
Charnock, Job, 08930
Chārsada, NW Frontier archaeological site, 04164
Chatterjee, Kali Charan (1839-1916), 22984
Chatterjee, Ramananda (1865-1943), 10823
Chatterji, Bankim Chandra (1833-94), 74, 11220, 24976-91
Chatterji, Saratchandra (1876-1938), 74, 25068
Chatterji, Suniti Kumar (1890-1977), 00065
Chattopadhyaya, Ksetresh Chandra (1896-1974), 00024
Chaudhary, Raghunath (1879-1967), 25821
Chaudhuri, Joyanto Nath (1908-), 12735-6
Chaudhuri, Nirad Chandra (1897-), 17174, 17183
Chaudhuri, Sachin, journalist, 00659
Chauhān dynasties, 07631-41
chauth, 08127, 08266-7
Chavan, Yashwantrao Balwantrao (1913-), 13642-8
Chawte (tribe), 28593
chāyāvād (Hindi literary "romanticism"), 38, 11615-24
Chelmsford, Frederic John Napier Thesiger, Viscount (1858-1944), 33, 10223-8
chemistry, history of, 1, 00336-9
Chennamma, Rani of Kittur (1778-1829), 08178
Chepangs (Nepalese people), 26252, 26256
Cheros (tribe), 08783, 21000
Chetris (Nepal caste), 78, 26260-3
Chettiyars. *See* Komutti Chettiyars; Vellalar Chettiyars
Chhau dance (Orissa), 03036-50
chhotolok, Bengali "ordinary" people, 24612, 24620. *See also* bhadralok
Chhotu Ram, Chaudhri (1882-1945), 22644, 22648, 22658
Chidambaram (sacred center in Tamil Nadu), 5, 01962-5
Chidambaram Pillai, V.U. (1872-1936), 19169, 19173
child marriage. *See* marriage, age of
childhood, India, 49, 15936-50
children and child welfare
- Bangladesh, 25577, 25579, 25583
- India, 49, 16150-63, 19852, 22130, 23875
- Sri Lanka, 18913
children's literature, India, 17007, 27683
China
- British India, relations, 08978, 11060, 11062-3, 24397, 24407
- historical contacts, 1, 00361-7, 04052-5, 04586, 05647-59
- India (Rep.), relations, 44, 13901-59, 26079-84
- Nepal, relations, 77, 26075-8
- Pakistan, relations, 53, 17737-42
- South Asia, relations, 39, 12012-42
- Sri Lanka, relations, 19, 18565, 18567
Chinese accounts of South Asia, 8, 17, 04052-5, 05647-59
Chintamani, Chiravoori Yajneswara (1880-1949), 33, 09084, 10275, 10697
Chiplunkar, Vishnushastri Krishna (1850-1882), 21633
Chishtī Sufi order, 22, 05955, 06800-1, 07112-20
Chitpāvan Brahmans, Maharashtra, 27, 64, 20723, 21389-92
Chitral, NW Frontier, 69, 23043, 23045, 23047, 23116-23
Chittagong, Bangladesh, 25455, 25481, 25483
Chittagong Hill Tracts, 25506-15
Chittagong, University of, 25622
Chittaranjan, West Bengal, 24520, 24701
Chodhris (tribe), 20829, 20823-3
Cholas. *See* Cola dynasty.
cholera, 16267, 24816, 25587
Chota Nagpur plateau
- adivasis, 62-3, 20892-1006
- economic conditions, 72, 24038, 24046, 24069, 24088, 24116
- education, 72, 24218-20
- geography, 81, 27269
- religion, 24223-5
- social conditions, 72, 24167, 24198
- urbanization, 72, 24172, 24176-7
Christian law in India, 00920
Christianity (South Asia)
- ancient, 12, 04600-6
- Andhra Pradesh, 60, 19870-82
- Assam, 25808-9
- Bengal, 74, 24915-18
- Bihar, 24223-4
- British India, 37, 11528-66
- Chota Nagpur, 20899, 21034
- comparative studies, 6, 01342-59
- general history, 6, 02234-56
- India (Rep.), 50-1, 16781-828
- Karnataka, 61, 20555-6
- Kerala, 12, 27, 60, 20177-86
- Madhya Pradesh, 60, 22280-4
- Maharashtra, 64, 21625-32
- Meghalaya, 79, 26700
- Mizoram, 79
- Mughal period, 25-27, 06785-7, 08216-27, 08954-61
- Orissa, 22403
- Pakistan, 18235-6
- Punjab, 69, 22980-90
- Sri Lanka, 26, 57, 08056, 08080-1, 08098-103, 19033-54
- Tamil Nadu, 59, 19486-91, 19523
- Uttar Pradesh, 23910
Christians (as a social group)
- India (Rep.), 48, 15858-60
- Karnataka, 20385, 20392, 20422, 20555-6
- Kerala, 60, 20114-21
- Maharashtra, 20821, 21450-55
- Pakistan, 55
- Punjab, 22836
- Sri Lanka, 18867-8
- Tamil Nadu, 59, 19405-9
chronology
- ancient, 04009-17, 04014, 04207
- British India, 09008-9
- general, 00104, 00138-49, 01437-53
- prehistory, 03487-92
Chughtai, Ismat, Urdu writer (1915-), 17054
Chughtai, Muhammad Abdullah Rahman (1899?-), painter, 11825
Church of India, Pakistan, Burma, and Ceylon, 16823
Church of South India, 16820, 16825-6, 16828, 19528, 19537, 19544, 20117. *See also* Christianity
Churchill, Winston Leonard Spencer, Sir (1875-1965), 10303

Cilappatikāram (Tamil epic), 16, 05437-45
cinchona cultivation, Sri Lanka, 18718
cinema
- Assam, 25819
- Bengal, 74, 25138-40
- India (Rep.), 51, 16959-90
- Maharashtra, 65, 21662
- Pakistan, 55, 18255-60
- Sri Lanka, 57, 19056, 19058
- Tamil Nadu, 59, 19549-51
cinnamon cultivation, Sri Lanka, 18723, 18725
cities. *See* urbanization; sacred centers
Citralakṣaṇa (art text), 06106, 06109, 08232
Citsukha (fl. 1200), commentator on Vedanta, 06403
Cīvakacintāmaṇi (Tamil epic), 06586
Civañaṇacittiyār (Śaiva Siddhānta Tamil text), 06519-24
Civañāṇapotam (Śaiva Siddhānta Tamil text), 06519-24
Civil Disobedience (1930-2), 33, 10142-6, 19166, 24324
civil rights
- Bangladesh, 25191
- India (Rep.), 12350-67, 13517-37
- Sri Lanka, 18364, 18529
civil service. *See also* administration
- Bangladesh, 25221-8
- British India, 09179-213
- India (Rep.)., 41, 12602-716
- Nepal, 26022-35a
- Pakistan, 52, 17324, 17326-63
- Sri Lanka, 56, 18510-8
Claessen, George (Ceylonese artist), 19093
classes, social, 48-9, 54, 57. *See also* social conditions
climate, 81-2, 27007, 27173
Clive, Robert (1725-74), 26, 08005-25
Cloud Messenger (Sanskrit poem). *See* Meghadūta
coal industry, 47, 11107, 15363
Cochin, princely state, Kerala, xxi, 60, 19917-36, 19945
coconut cultivation, Sri Lanka, 56, 18763
coffee cultivation, Sri Lanka, 18712, 18715, 18726
coiffures, 8
Coimbatore, Tamil Nadu, 19292, 19331, 19333, 19344, 19368
coins. *See* numismatics
Cōḷa dynasty, 11, 19, 04219, 06196-204
- art, 20, 06632-47
- conquest of Ceylon, 19, 06116-20
- epigraphy, 05680
- literature, 16
Colebrooke-Cameron Reforms (Ceylon, 1833), 55, 18311-8
collective bargaining. *See* labor
Colombo city, Sri Lanka, 57, 18898-906
Colombo Plan, 12250-1, 26091
colonization, agricultural. *See* land reclamation
Comilla, Bangaldesh, 25563
Comilla rural development project, 75, 25411-30, 25633
commerce. For regions not listed below, *see* economic conditions
- ancient, 11, 04377-84
- Andhra Pradesh, 59, 19782-83
- Bangladesh, 75, 25475-86
- Bengal, 73, 24545-50
- Bihar, 24132
- British India, 36, 11034-76
- early European, 07803-10
- East India Company, 07998-8004, 08187
- Gujarat, 65, 21797-802
- India (Rep.), 48, 15460-82
- Maharashtra, 64, 21331-41
- medieval, 17, 05104-10, 06139, 06252
- Mughal period, 24, 27, 29, 07611-22, 08191-206, 08413-24, 08787, 08910-9
- Nepal, 77, 26184-9
- Pakistan, 54, 18067-72
- Punjab, 68, 22799-804
- Uttar Pradesh, 71, 23686-8
Commonwealth, British, 31, 40, 44, 53, 09400-1, 12012, 12021, 14063-9, 17749-52
communalism
- Bengal, 24302
- Bihar, 24008-10
- British India, 32-4, 10115-41, 10308-393
- general, 00128, 00133-4
- Gujarat, 21674
- India (Rep.), 40, 42, 12435-44, 13253-97
- Punjab, 68-9, 22659-66
- Sri Lanka, 55-6, 18334-41, 18402, 18473-503
- Uttar Pradesh, 71, 23486-90
communication. *See* transportation and communication; media
communications in rural development, 47, 51, 15058-70, 16949-58, 19744, 23819-23
Communism and Communist Parties
- Andhra Pradesh, 19633-40, 19666, 19694-9
- Bengal, 73, 24309, 25315, 24320, 24369-76, 24542
- British India, 33, 09605-29, 10039-64
- Himachal Pradesh, 25904
- India (Rep.), 42, 13143, 13198-252
- Kerala, 60, 19985, 20031
- Nepal, 26013
- Punjab (British), 22636
- South Asia, general, 12206-7
- Sri Lanka, 18392-401
community development, rural. *See* villages
community development, urban, 16076-81. *See also* planning, urban
Compagnie Royale des Indes Orientales. *See* French in India
Company painting, 38, 11792-3
Comrade (journal), 09802
concepts of Indic thought, 01360-1575
Congress Party. *See* Indian National Congress
Congress Socialist Party, 33, 10087-104
conservatism, Indian, 42, 45
Conservative Party (Great Britain), 10216, 10222
Constituent Assembly, India, 34, 40, 12274-85
Constitution
- Bangladesh, 75, 25183-93
- British India, 30, 32, 33, 34, 09073-83, 10210-22, 10272-87
- India (Rep.), 34, 40, 43, 12274, 12288, 12319-85, 13517-37
- Jammu & Kashmir, 69, 23175-82
- Maldives, 19106
- Nepal, 25975-88
- Pakistan, 52-3, 17316-23, 17489-99, 17516-28, 17592-600
- Sri Lanka, 55, 18356-9, 18363-70, 18445-54
consumers, India, 48, 15474-82
Cooch Behar, princely state, Bengal, 24481, 26426
coolie traffic, 80, 26758
Coomaraswamy, Ananda Kentish (1877-1947), 38, 03112, 11854-7
cooperative banks. *See* banking
cooperatives
- Andhra Pradesh, 19750, 19752
- Assam, 25728, 25748
- Bangladesh, 75, 25411-39
- Bihar, 24039
- British India, 36, 10983-91
- Gujarat, 65, 21753-61, 21784
- India (Rep.), 46-7, 14700-22, 15103-50
- industrial, 15345-319
- Jammu & Kashmir, 23222-3
- Madhya Pradesh, 66, 22213-5
- Maharashtra, 64, 21268-72
- Nepal, 26136
- Pakistan, 54
- Punjab, 22812
- Sri Lanka, 56, 18676-81, 18890
- Tamil Nadu, 19313, 19439
- Uttar Pradesh, 71, 23623-8
- West Bengal, 73, 24476-7
Coorg district, Karnataka, 61, 20244-6
Coorgs/Koḍagu (people), 61, 20361, 20370, 20408-14
Coote, Eyre, Sir (1726-83), 08024-25
Copper Age (prehistory), 9, 23568-685
Copper Hoards Culture, 9, 03662-9
copper industry, 00347
Cornwallis, Charles Cornwallis, 1st Marquess (1738-1805), 26, 29, 08038-9
Coromandel/Cōḻamaṇḍalam Coast, Mughal period, 26, 08148-61
Cosmas Indicopleustes (6th cent. AD), 04022
cosmology and cosmography, 1, 00267-73, 01312, 03892, 03949, 06374
costume, 8, 03310-23
cottage industries. *See* industry
cotton cultivation and industry. *See also* textile industry
- Bengal, 24407
- Bombay, 11120, 21302, 21305, 21312, 21316, 21319
- British India, 11029-33, 11066-8, 11106, 11109
- Haryana, 23291

cotton cultivation and industry -- *continued*
- India (Rep.)., 15391-6
- Maharashtra, 21234, 21251
- Mughal period, 08918
- Pakistan, 18036, 18038-9, 18041
- Punjab, 22805
- Sind, 22484
- Sri Lanka, 18719
- Uttar Pradesh, 23682, 23685

Council of Ministers
- India, 40, 12546, 12593-600
- Pakistan, 52

Council of States, India. *See* Rajya Sabha
Councils, Buddhist, 04942-50
courtesans, 35, 04479, 06055, 10732-3
courts. *See* law and judiciary
Couto, Diogo de, 07843, 07846, 07866
cow in Ṛgveda, 03905
cow, sanctity of, 4, 01563-75
cow slaughter bans, 40, 12460-8
cows. *See also* animal husbandry
craftsmen, 3, 00910-5
credit, rural. *See* agricultural credit
crime. *See also* law and judiciary; social welfare
- Bangladesh, 25773
- Bombay city, 21537
- Bombay Presidency, 20708-13
- British period, 31, 09222-43, 20708-13
- India (Rep.), 49, 16184-200
- Madhya Pradesh, 22189, 22263-72
- Rajasthan, 22128, 22131
- Sri Lanka, 18909-19
- West Bengal, 24805

criminal tribes, 09235, 19814-5
Cripps Mission (1942), 34, 10404-12
Cripps, Richard Stafford, Sir (1889-1952), 10303, 10404-12
crops. *See* agriculture
Cubbon, Mark, Sir, 20243
Cūlavaṁsa (Pāli chronicle of Ceylon), 11, 04229-41
cultural transmission, 3, 00846-63
cultural unity of South Asia, xiv, 2, 00678-714, 02329-35
Cumaratunga, Munidasa, Sinhala nationalist, 19075
currency. *See* finance, public; banking
curriculum. *See* education
Curzon of Kedleston, George Nathaniel Curzon, Marquess (1859-1925), 32, 09816-21, 10945
Cuttack, Orissa, 22356, 22401-2
cyclones, 25349

Dacca, Bangladesh, 75, 08922, 12235, 24260, 25230, 25566-71
Dacca, University of, 24847, 25618, 25620, 25624-5
dacoity, 31, 66, 09231-43, 22189, 22263-72. *See also* crime
Dadra and Nagar Haveli U.T., 63, 21043-070
Dādū (1544-1603), Hindi poet-saint, 28, 08450-6
Daflas (tribe), 26498, 26500-2
Da Gama, Vasco, 25, 07860-1
dāī (midwife), 16349, 18144
dairies, 14937, 20312, 20323, 21754, 21756, 21758, 21761, 23289
Dakhni language, 25, 07710
Dalhousie, James Andrew Broun Ramsay, 1st Marquess of (1812-60), 30, 09100, 09121-8, 09370, 10539, 11036, 20934
Dalit Panthers (low caste movement in Maharashtra), 21404, 21407
Damale, Krsnaji Kesava (1866-1905), 21648
Damaṇ. *See* Goa, Daman & Diu
Dambadeniya (early Ceylon kingdom), 19, 06132, 06134
Damodar Valley Corporation, 72, 24050-15
dance and dance-drama, 7-8, 51, 02680-5, 02904-3055
dancing girls, 35
Daṇḍakāraṇya, tribal plateau in eastern Middle India, 24812
Daṇḍin (writer on poetics, 7th cent.), 18, 05671, 06058, 06062, 06065
Dangis (farming caste, Rajasthan), 22090
Dāngs (tribal subregion of Gujarat), 20831
Daniell, Thomas (1749-1840), artist, 11974-81
Daniell, William (1769-1837), artist, 11974-81
Danish in India, 29-30, 07813, 07835
Dara Shukoh (1615-1659), 24, 07505-12
Darbhanga Raj (now in Bihar), 23949, 23952-3
Dardic languages, 7, 83
Dardistan, 23149
Darjeeling district, West Bengal, xxii, 78, 26385-8
Das, Chittaranjan (1870-1925), 33, 10022-3, 10030-1
Das, Gopalbandhu (1877-1928), 20790, 20792, 20795, 20797
Das, Jatindra Nath (1904-29), 24316
Das, Jibanananda (1899-1954), 25091-2, 25093, 25103, 25107
Das, Kamala, 17179
Das, Madhusudan (1858-1934), 20793, 24949
Das, Tarak Chandra, 00636
Daśakumāracarita (Sanskrit prose-romance), 06062, 06065, 06068
Daśanāmi (sannyāsis of Vedānta), 01894, 01902, 01904
Daśarūpa (10th cent. drama text), 02680, 06001
Daśavatāracarita (Vaiṣṇava work by Kṣemendra), 06071
Dasgupta, Surendranath (1885-1952), 11426
Datta, Dhirendranath (1886-1971), 25168
Datta, Saroj Nalini (1887-1925), 10743
Dattātreya (deity), 5, 01806
Dattilam (music text), 02683, 02712
Dāūd, Maulānā, 07119
Daudi Bohras. *See* Bohras
Daulat Singh (1868-), 20620
Dave, Narmadashankar Lalshankar (1833-86), 21933
Dayābhāga (school of Hindu law), 17, 05699
Dayal, Har (1884-1939), 09739, 09744
Dayanand Anglo-Vedic College, 22920
Dayānanda Saraswatī, Swāmī (1824-83), 36-7, 01023, 11220, 11269-85
death and death rites, 3-4, 01043-51, 21915, 24139
Deccan/Dakṣinapatha
- ancient economy, 04350
- general history, 2, 00441-5
- Mughal period, 07543
- prehistory, 03515

Deccan College, Poona, 21597
Deccan Education Society, Poona, 21570-1
Deccan Riots (1875), 64, 21273-82
Deccani painting, 28, 08463-74
decorative arts, 8, 28, 03294-349, 08526
defense. *See also* armed forces
- British India, 07973
- India (Rep.), 44, 13759-93
- Pakistan, 17685-769

Delhi city, 25, 29, 32, 70, 23335-40
- architecture, 07159-73, 07784-91
- Mughal period, 08757, 08760

Delhi Durbar (1911), 32, 09839-40
Delhi Sultanate, 20, 22, 06731, 06737, 07014-55, 07058-69, 07077-83
Delhi U.T., xxii, 70, 23320-440
Delhi, University of, 23424, 23436-7, 23440
democracy, ancient, 11, 04328-35
demography, xvii
- Arunachal Pradesh, 26483
- Assam, 76, 25734
- Bangladesh, 75, 25272-86
- Bihar, 72, 24030-2
- British India, 36, 10879-83
- Delhi U.T., 70, 23343-5
- Goa, 21078
- Gujarat, 65, 21709-10
- Haryana, 70, 23274a-5
- Himachal Pradesh, 77, 25869
- India (Rep.), 44-5, 14132-93
- Jammu & Kashmir, 23214
- Karnataka, 61, 20269-79
- Kerala, 60, 19995-20001
- Madhya Pradesh, 22177-9
- Maharashtra, 63, 21205-8
- Manipur, 26580
- Nepal, 77, 26102-9
- Orissa, 67, 22319-21
- Pakistan, 53, 17781-804
- Punjab, 68, 22747-50
- Rajasthan, 22010
- South Asia, general, 12230
- Sri Lanka, 56, 18598-613
- Tamil Nadu, 58, 19257-8
- Uttar Pradesh, 71, 23561-7
- West Bengal, 73, 24417

demons, 5, 01845-50, 25812
Deoband madrasah, Uttar Pradesh, 37, 11516-7
Deokota, Laxmi Prasad (1908-59), 26345, 26347
Deogarh temples, 16, 05572-81
depressed classes. *See* Scheduled Castes

Derozio, Henry Louis Vivian (1808-31), 11763-5, 11768
Desai, Anita (1937-), 51, 17152-4
Desai, Morarji Ranchodji (1896-), 43, 13621-5
Deshmukh, Chintaman Dwarkanath (1896-), 12660
Deshmukh, Gopal Hari (1823-92), 21374, 21633
Deshmukh, Punjabrao, 14846
Desh (region of Maharashtra), 64
Deshastha Brahmans, Maharashtra, 64
design motifs, 8, 03308-9
detenus (Emergency 1975-77), 43, 13527-37
Dev Samāj, 36, 11263-8
Devadasan, Neelakantan, 19538
devadāsīs, 35, 10732-3
Devanāgarī script, 02382
development, agricultural. *See* agriculture
development banks, 14656-61
development, economic. *See* planning, economic
development, industrial. *See* industry
development, rural. *See* villages
development, urban. *See* planning, urban
Devī (deity), 4, 01711-18
Devī Bhāgavata-purāṇa, 05825-7
Devīmahātmya, 17, 05807-11
Dewas Senior, princely state, Madhya Pradesh, 20665, 20668-9
devotional music, 7, 02881-90
Dey, Bishnu (1909-), 25094, 25096-7
Dey, Ramdoolal, 24400
Dhalla, Maneckji Nusservanji (1875-1956), 18235
dhamma. *See* dharma
Dhanaṁjaya (Sanskrit writer on drama), 02680, 06001
Dhammapada (Buddhist text), 14, 04989-95
Dhanapāla (Sanskrit writer, 10th cent.), 06018
Dhanbad district, Bihar, 24112
Dhangars (tribe in Maharashtra), 20827
Dhanjibhai Fakirbhai (1895-1967), 16800
Dhanka (tribe), 20836
Dhār, princely state, Madhya Pradesh, 21, 06708-11, 20664
Dharampur, princely state, Gujarat, 20612
dharma/dhamma ("duty, law"), 4, 12, 13, 00745, 01364, 01367, 01442, 01536-47, 04392-524, 24561
  - bibliography, 01547
dharma (metaphysics), 01377
Dharma Thakur (deity), 24897-901
Dharmapāla (Buddhist philosopher), 05117
Dharmapāla, Anagārika (1864-1933), 57, 18983-8
Dharmasāstras, 3, 12, 00926-7, 04419-39
Dharmasūtras, 12, 04414-8
Dharmasvāmin, 05654
Dharwar, city and district, Karnataka, 61, 20487-8
Dheds (caste in Gujarat), 21846
Dhingra, Madan Lal (1887-1909), 09741
Dhurwa (tribe), 20890-1
dhvani theory (aesthetics), 18, 05977-6004
Dhvanyāloka (aesthetics text), 18, 05980-7
dhyāna. *See* meditation
diaspora, Indic, xxii-xxiii
Dibongiyas (tribe), 25761
dictionaries
  - Anglo-Indian terms, 82, 27496-502
  - biographical, 1, 30, 82, 00157-62, 09012-25, 27465-502
  - South Asian languages, 82-3, 27784-8017
Digambara (Jain sect), 14, 05141-9
dīkṣā, initiation ritual, 3, 01028-39
Dimasa (tribe), 25786
Dīn-i-Ilāhī (Akbar's syncretic faith), 25, 07664-71
Dinkar Rao (1819-96), 20672
Dinshaw, Framroze (1885-), 21437
Dīpavaṁśa (Pāli chronicle of Ceylon), 11, 04229-41
diplomacy. *See* international relations
diplomats, memoirs, 41, 44, 12749-61, 14017-24
directive principles of state policy, Constitution of India, 40, 12368-72
diseases. *See* medicine
dissertations, bibliography, 82, 27687-99
district government and politics. *See* local government
Divālī (festival), 02102
Divarus (caste), 20368
Diu. *See* Goa, Daman & Diu
Divine Life Society, 37, 11419-24
Divine Light Mission, 16724
divorce, 49, 15930-5. *See also* kinship and marriage
Dnyāndev. *See* Jñāneśvara
Doctor, Manilall Maganlall, 26769, 26772
documents. *See* archives
Dogras (people of Jammu), 69, 00504
Dogrī literature, 7, 70, 02630, 23252-5
dohā (verse form), 23, 07219-27
Dolpo district, Nepal, 26213
domestic ritual, 12, 04457-66
Dominion of India, 34, 40, 12270-85
Dominion of Pakistan, 34, 52
dominant castes, 2, 00812-7, 19818, 20374, 20445, 22237, 24584
Doms (tribe), 23773
Donoughmore Commission (1928), 55, 18356-9
Doordarshan (Indian TV network), 51, 16944-8
Dorla (tribe), 20886
dowry, 3, 49, 01016-22, 15915-7, 18100, 22490, 23364
"drain theory" (economics), 36, 10908-21, 11077-83
drama
  - traditional, 7-8, 02932-3055
  - modern, 17034-7, 21650-1, 24948, 24950-1, 24954, 24964-6
  - Sanskrit, 15, 18, 02497, 05264-386, 06005-70
Dravida Kazhagam (DK), 58, 19178-94
Dravida Munnetra Kazhagam (DMK), 58, 19206-32
Dravidian languages
  - general, 6, 02548-92
  - comparative studies, 02353-77
Dravidian regionalism, 58, 19178-94, 19206-32
Dravidian South. *See* South India Area
Dravidians, 1, 00067-91
  - ancient, 11, 04214-8
  - kinship, 00982, 00985, 00989, 01006-7
  - origins (prehistoric), 9, 03715-29
Dravidology, 1, 00067-91
drug abuse, 49, 16201-6, 18924, 21601, 22132
Dublas (tribe), 20834
Dubois, Jean Antoine, Abbé (1765-1848), 11838
dualism (philosophy), 13, 20, 04798-817, 06469-94
dualistic Vedānta. *See* Dvaita
Dufferin and Ava, Frederick Temple Blackwood, 1st Marquess of (1826-1902), 30, 09147, 09407, 10840, 11943
Duleep Singh (1838-98), 22583, 22585, 22587
Dumézil, Georges, 00063
Dumont, Louis (1911-), 2, 00783-92
Dundas, Henry. *See* Melville, H. Dundas, 1st Viscount
Dupleix, Joseph François (1697-1763), 26, 07907, 07926-35, 08009
Durand, Henry Mortimer, Sir (1850-1924), 09437
Durgadas Rathor (fl. 1679), 08367
Durgā-pūjā (festival), 02122
Durgapur, West Bengal, 24514, 24520, 24528, 24706
Durlabhram Mahindra, Raja (1710-70), 08870
Dusadh (caste), 24149
Dutch architecture, 08236
Dutch in Ceylon, 26, 08082-97
Dutch in India, 25-7, 29, 55, 07891-901, 08136, 08140-2, 08172, 08196, 08348, 08854-60
Dutt, Aswini Kumar (1856-1923), 24296
Dutt, Romesh Chunder (1848-1909), 00125, 24958
Dutt, Toru (1856-77), 11762, 11766-7, 11769
duty. *See* dharma
Dvaita Vedānta, 20, 06469-94
Dvārasamudra, medieval town, Karnataka, 19, 06215-38
Dwārkā (sacred center in Gujarat), 5, 02002-8
Dwivedi, Mahavir Prasad, modern Hindi writer (1864-1938), 11625
Dyer, Reginald Henry Harry, Gen. (1864-1927), 09843-53

East Africa, South Asians in, 80, 26842-70
East Bengal, 39, 25141-676. *See also* Bangladesh
East India Company, xvii, 26, 30, 07951-8047; *also* Chapters Five, Six, and Eleven through Sixteen, passim.
  - Avadh, 29, 08755-77
  - Bengal, 29, 08872-88
  - Ceylon, 18298, 18301
  - Marathas, relations, 27, 08316-33
  - relations with native states, 08128-9, 08162, 08315, 08351, 19615
East Pakistan (now Bangladesh), xxii, 39, 25303-13, 25141-676. *See also* Bangladesh
economic conditions, xvi
  - ancient, 11, 04346-91
  - Andaman & Nicobar Islands, 79, 26714-9
  - Andhra Pradesh, 59, 19722-83
  - Arunachal Pradesh, 78, 26482-3
  - Assam, 76, 25722-74
  - Baluchistan, 68, 22527-31

economic conditions -- *continued*
- Bangladesh, 75, 25267-486
- Bengal Presidency, 73, 24397-416
- Bihar, 72, 24030-132
- British India, 36, 10853-1198
- Darjeeling, 78, 26389-95
- Delhi U.T., 70, 23343-61
- general history, 00236-46
- Goa, 63, 21071-91
- Gujarat, 65, 21709-802
- Haryana, 70, 23274a-23299
- Himachal Pradesh, 77, 25869-79
- India (Rep.), 44-5, 10511-6, 13794-900
- Jammu & Kashmir, 69, 23208-24
- Karnataka, 61, 20267-360
- Kerala, 60, 19993-20054
- Kumaon and Garhwal, 77, 25905-11
- Madhya Pradesh, 66, 22177-226
- Madras Presidency, 58, 19247-56
- Maharashtra, 63-4, 21196-463
- Manipur, 79, 26581
- medieval, 17, 22, 23, 05704-21, 06135-43, 06243-72, 07070-83, 07197-203
- Meghalaya, 79, 26656-68
- Mizoram, 79, 26610-2
- Mughal period, 24, 27-9, 07585-628, 08191-206, 08391-423, 08561-5, 08784-9, 08889-931
- Nagaland, 78, 26540-55
- Nepal, 77, 26100-89
- North West Frontier Province, 69, 23081-95
- Orissa, 67, 22315-56
- Pakistan, 53, 17770-8072
- Punjab, 68, 22722-814
- Rajasthan, 66, 22010-73
- Sikkim, 78, 26389-95
- Sind, 67, 22466-85
- South Asia, general, 39-40, 12231-64
- Sri Lanka, 56-7, 18581-814, 18685-711
- Tamil Nadu, 58, 19243-69
- Tripura, 79, 26636-43
- Uttar Pradesh, 71, 23558-687
- Uttar Pradesh Himalayas, 77, 25905-11
- West Bengal, 73, 24397-416

economic effects of Partition (1947), 34, 10511-6
economic research, India, 44, 14122-31
economic thought, 00240, 00245, 04360-1, 10900-29, 14286-367
economy. *See* economic conditions
economy, traditional, 3, 00893-915
education
- agricultural, 14849, 15058-70, 16566-74, 16943, 16949-58
- ancient, 12, 03792, 04508-18
- Andhra Pradesh, 60, 19857-69
- Arunachal Pradesh, 26482
- Assam, 76, 25803, 25805
- Baluchistan, 22543
- Bangladesh, 76, 25606-35
- Bengal, 73-4, 24824-72
- Bihar, 72, 24204-20
- British India, 35, 09598, 09603-4, 10549-648
- Delhi U.T., 70, 23434-40
- general history, 00859-63
- Goa, 21094, 21098
- Gujarat, 65, 21895-912
- Haryana, 70, 23313-7
- Hindu, 02286
- India (Rep.), 50, 15512-30, 16377-691, 27490, 27494
- Jammu & Kashmir, 23230-2
- Karnataka, 61, 20517
- Kerala, 60, 19952, 20160-6
- Maharashtra, 64, 21343-4, 21569-605
- medical and health, 49, 16357-71
- medieval, 06568, 06799
- Mughal period, 24, 07646-52, 08400, 08957
- Muslim, 37, 06799, 16774, 18174-5, 18938, 19416, 19861, 22927, 23438, 24860-7
- Nagaland, 26541, 26554
- Nepal, 78, 26303-17
- North-West Frontier Province, 69, 23128-30
- Orissa, 67, 22382-5
- Pakistan, 54, 18133, 18146-205
- Punjab, 68, 22919-40
- Rajasthan, 66, 22135-54
- Sikh, 22922-3

education -- *continued*
- Sind, 22487
- Sri Lanka, 57, 08073, 18930-72
- Tamil Nadu, 59, 19416, 19469-85
- Uttar Pradesh, 71-2, 23887-909
- West Bengal, 74, 24824-72

Education Commission (India, 1964-66), 50, 16415-20
Egypt-India relations, 09620, 14092
Ekanātha (c. 1548 - c. 1609), Marathi poet-saint, 27, 08427-31
elections
- Andhra Pradesh, 59, 19670-80
- Assam, 76, 25712-5
- Bangladesh, 75, 25198, 25206, 25209, 25248
- Bengal, 73, 24328, 24348
- Bihar, 72, 23999-4007
- British India, 33, 10008-32, 10272-87
- Delhi U.T., 23327-8, 23331-3, 23335
- Goa, 21059-66
- Gujarat, 65, 21681-9
- Haryana, 70, 23269-71
- Himachal Pradesh, 25867-8
- India (Rep.), 41-3, 13316-47, 13380-98, 13430-48, 13626-39
- Jammu & Kashmir, 23200-1
- Karnataka, 20251, 20257, 20264
- Kerala, 60, 19958-68
- Madhya Pradesh, 66, 22160-5
- Madras Presidency, 19165
- Maharashtra, 63, 21132-8
- Nagaland, 26524
- Nepal, 26012, 26016
- Orissa, 67, 22299-305
- Pakistan, 52, 17473-7, 17529-37, 17555-9, 17604, 17655, 18086-90
- Punjab (India), 68, 22689-98
- Rajasthan, 66, 21963-74
- South Asia, general, 12213
- Sri Lanka, 55, 18403-10
- Tamil Nadu, 19201, 19210
- Tripura, 26633
- Uttar Pradesh, 71, 23480, 23483, 23504, 23508-14, 23535
- West Bengal, 73, 24351, 24377-86

elections, President of India, 12562-3, 13446-8, 13455-65, 13550-64
electrification, rural, 47, 15071-4, 21750, 23580, 23612
electronics industry, 15407
elephant symbolism, 4, 01611-27
Elephanta cave temples, 21, 06825-9
Elgin, James Bruce, 8th Earl of (1811-63), 30, 09131-3
Elgin, Victor Alexander Bruce, 9th Earl of (1849-1917), 31, 09151
élites
- British India, 11200
- India (Rep.), 48, 13060-71, 15830-42
- Sri Lanka, 18817

Ellenborough, Edward Law, 1st Earl of (1790-1871), 30, 09117-9, 22-49
Ellora cave temples, 21, 06810-1, 06816-24
Elphinstone, Mountstuart (1779-1859), 20701-3
Elwin, Verrier, 00626, 00661, 02435
embroidery, 8, 03339-46
Emergency (India, 1975-77), 43, 13495-604, 23326
emergency powers, Indian Constitution, 40, 12373-9
emigration overseas, 80-81, 26737-951 (Chapter Seventeen)
employment. *See* labor
endowments, religious. *See* temples
energy industries
- India, 47, 15351-81, 19126
- Pakistan, 54, 18030-2

engineering education, 50, 16563-65
English, Indian, 6, 40, 50, 09010-1, 17087-92
English language education, 50, 16653-9, 26310
English literature of South Asia, 6, 38, 55, 57, 11703-80, 17070-183, 18262, 19076
English literature, South Asia in, 39, 11875-929
entrepreneurs. *See* business communities
Epic age, 9, 03759-70
epics, Sanskrit, xx, 9, 12-3, 04607-730
epics, Tamil, 16, 05437-48
epigraphy, xvi
- ancient, 10, 04056-62, 04081-2
- general, 2, 00559-74
- Gupta, 04056, 04058, 04060, 04146

epigraphy -- *continued*
- Kuṣāṇa, 04182
- Mauryan, 04061, 04132-41
- medieval, 17, 05675-86
- Pallavas, 06195
- Tamil, 02548, 02555, 02557
- Vijayanagara, 06219
epistemology, 4, 01412-25, 06398, 06480
erotic art, 8, 03130-9, 06916-22
erotic literature, 12, 02388, 04483-7
Erukulas (tribe). *See* Yerukulas
Etawah Pilot Project, Uttar Pradesh, 71, 23813-8
ethics, 4, 12, 01509-75
- Sikh, 28, 01560, 08580, 08583
ethnic groups, 2, 57, 00690-714, 24419, 24760, 26195-6
ethnomusicology, 7, 02897-2903
Eṭṭuttokai (eight anthologies of Tamil verse), 05415-36
etymology, Indic, 15, 05178-82
Europe
- early modern contacts, 25-6, 29, 73, 05660-8, 07803-8047, 08049-54
- medieval contacts, 17, 05660-8
- South Asian studies in, 00054, 00084, 01142, 01147, 11836-53, 27419-23
Europe, Eastern
- India, relations, 44, 13901, 14080-4
- Pakistan, relations, 17762
Europe, Western
- India, relations, 44, 14070-9
European Economic Community, 44, 14070-9
Europeans in British India, 39, 11930-81, 24657
evil in Indic thought, 4, 01548-54
examinations, educational, India, 50, 16526-38
executive offices
- British India, 30-1, 09073-158
- India (Rep.), 40, 12546-601
- Pakistan, 52, 17324-5
- Sri Lanka, 55
exports. *See* foreign trade
extremists (Nationalist movement), 32, 09679-761, 19942
Ezekiel, Nissim (1924-), 51, 17136-41
Ezhavas (caste in Kerala), 60, 61, 20105-13
Eẓuttucchan. *See* Tuñcatt' Eẓuttacchan

Fa-hsien (5th cent.), 04052-5
Faiz, Faiz Ahmad (Urdu poet, 1911-), 11693, 18267-8
Faizabad, town and district in Uttar Pradesh, 23471, 23863
Faizī, Abū'l-Faiz, Shaikh (1547-95), 07690
family. *See* kinship
family planning. For regions not listed below, *see* social conditions
- Andhra Pradesh, 19850, 19853
- Bangladesh, 76, 25589-605
- Bihar, 24200, 24202
- Delhi U.T., 70, 23424-33
- Gujarat, 21892-4
- Haryana, 70, 23308-12
- India (Rep.), 49, 13544-5, 16275-327
- Karnataka, 61, 20504-16
- Maharashtra, 64, 21562-8
- Nepal, 78, 26296
- Orissa, 22380
- Pakistan, 55, 18137-45
- Rajasthan, 22129
- Sind, 22488
- Sri Lanka, 18610-3, 18922, 18928
- Uttar Pradesh, 71, 23871-85
- West Bengal, 74, 24821
famines. For regions not listed below, *see* agriculture
- ancient, 04369
- Assam, 25740
- Bangladesh, 75, 25344-50
- Bengal, 73, 24450-9
- Bihar, 72, 24079-84
- British India, 36, 10992, 11012-23, 19273
- India (Rep.), 46, 14826-30
- Kerala, 19994
- Maharashtra, 64, 21283-90
- Orissa, 22318
- South Asia, general, 12231
Farā'idī Movement, 37, 24911-2, 24504, 24914
Farakka dam, Murshidabad district, West Bengal, 25255
Farīd-uddīn, Shaikh (1175?-1265), 06984-95
Faridabad, city, Haryana, 23294, 23299
Faridkot city, Punjab, 22887
farmāns (official order), Mughal, 07402
farmers, farming. *See* agriculture
Farquhar, John Nicol (1861-1929), 11551
Farrukh Beg (Mughal painter), 07763, 07770
Farrukh Chela (Mughal painter), 07750
Farrukhsiyar (1687-1719), Mughal Emperor, 07523, 08788
Fateh Singh, Akali Sikh leader, 22680
Fatehpur Sikri, architecture of, 25, 07784-91, 07793
fauna. *See* wildlife; animal husbandry
Fazl-i-Husain, Mian Sir (1877-1936), Punjabi Muslim leader, 22651-2
Fazlul Huq, Abdul Kasem (1873-1962), Bengali leader, 73, 24335, 24341-8
federalism
- British India, 33, 10272-85
- India (Rep.), 40, 12516-45, 12907-37, 17411-20
- Pakistan, 52, 17411-20
female infanticide, 35, 10716-9
Ferazi Movement. *See* Farā'idī
Fergusson, James, Sir (1808-86), 20697, 20704
fertility. *See* demography; family planning
fertilizer industry, 15405, 21776
fertilizers, use of. *See* technology, agricultural
festivals, 5, 02078-123. For areas not listed below, *see also* religio-philosophical traditions
- Arunachal Pradesh, 26487, 26491
- Assam, 25807, 25813
- Bhutan, 26436
- Karnataka, 20533, 20542
- Himachal Pradesh, 25897
- Jammu & Kashmir, 23244
- Nepal, 26266, 26274, 23222, 26355
- Uttar Pradesh, 23912, 23914-5
- West Bengal, 24877, 24883, 24891
Festschriften, 1, 2, 8, 00015-28, 00655-63, 03109-12
- bibliography, 27628
feudalism, 17, 19, 05704-21, 06141, 06255-62
fiction. *See* names of specific languages, e.g. Kannada language and literature
Fiji, South Asians in, 80, 26803
films. *See* cinema
Finance Commissions, India, 45, 14531-50
finance, public (incl. taxation); for land taxes, *see also* land tenure; for local finance, *see also* local government
- ancient, 11, 04302, 04372-6
- Bangladesh, 25230
- British India, 36, 11148-62
- Gujarat, 65, 21720
- Haryana, 23286
- India (Rep.), 45-6, 12799-813, 14489-609
- Karnataka, 61, 20295-304, 20476
- Maharashtra, 64, 21227-33
- Mughal empire, 24, 07597-610
- Nepal, 77, 26140-7
- Orissa, 22328
- Pakistan, 54, 17884-93
- Rajasthan, 66, 21978, 22023
- Sri Lanka, 56, 18654-62
- Uttar Pradesh, 23584-9, 23600
fire (symbolism), 03844-5
Firūz Shāh Tughluq (1351-88), King of Delhi, 07037-55, 07184
fishing and fishing communities, 46, 14924-45, 17976-7, 19276, 19351, 19801, 20012, 20018-9, 20313, 20455, 21086, 23597, 26150
five-year plans. *See* planning, economic
floods and flood control, 36, 76, 21545, 25340-50, 25738
flora. *See* botany
folk art, 8, 03350-60
folk music, general, 02897-2903
folk religion. *See* religio-philosophical traditions
folklore, folk literature, and folk music, xx, 6-7, 02424-62, 02897-903
- Andhra Pradesh, 60, 19910-1
- Arunachal Pradesh, 26488
- Assam, 25828-32
- Bangladesh, 76, 25654-61
- Bengal, 74, 25109-26
- Bihar, 72, 24228-35
- Goa, 63, 21108-9
- Gujarat, 65, 21947-9
- Haryana, 70, 23318-9
- Himachal Pradesh, 77, 25893-8

folklore -- *continued*
- Jammu & Kashmir, 70, 23257
- Karnataka, 61, 20576-8
- Kerala, 61, 20219-22
- Kumaon & Garhwal, 77, 25931-2, 25937
- Madhya Pradesh, 66, 22285-6
- Maharashtra, 65, 21652-8
- Meghalaya, 26488, 26701-6
- Nagaland, 79, 26574
- Nepal, 78, 26353-7
- Northeast hill tribes, 78, 26469-74
- Orissa, 67, 22420-25
- Punjab, 69, 23021-9
- Rajasthan, 66, 22150-4
- Sikkim, 26404, 26411
- Sri Lanka, 57, 19082-8
- Tamil Nadu, 59, 19385, 19389, 19398, 19401, 19597-603
- tribal. *See* names of specific tribes
- Uttar Pradesh, 27, 23933-43
- West Bengal, 74, 25109-26

Food Corporation of India, 46, 14819-25
food habits, 3, 00837-45, 23886. *See also* nutrition
food production, early, 9, 03568-686
food supply, India, 46, 14806-30
Ford Foundation, 14054
foreign aid
- Bangladesh, 75, 25256-66
- India (Rep.), 44, 13994-4002, 14036-55
- Nepal, 77, 26085-99
- Pakistan, 53, 17712-23, 17732-6
- Sri Lanka, 56, 18576-80

foreign contacts, historical, 00350-74, 04561-86, 07803-20
foreign investment. *See* foreign trade
foreign opinion of South Asia, 27080-6
foreign policy. *See* international relations
Foreign Service, India, 12744-61
foreign trade
- Bangladesh, 25256-66
- British India, 36, 11056-76
- India (Rep.), 44, 13794-900
- Nepal, 26085-99
- Pakistan, 53, 17697-711
- Sri Lanka, 56, 18569-75

forests and forestry, 36, 41, 46, 11032, 14917-23, 17974-5, 21239, 22336, 24449, 25851
Forster, Edward Morgan (1879-1970), 39, 11879, 11909-22
Fort St. George, Madras, 26, 08179-90, 08199-202
Fort William, Calcutta, 29, 08924-31, 24270
Fort William, College of, 38, 24848, 24850
42nd Amendment, Indian Constitution, 43, 13522-6
Forward Bloc, 24309
Francis, Philip, Sir (East India Company councillor), 08034, 08037
Franciscans (Roman Catholic order), 07885-90, 08056
Fraser, Andrew Henderson Leith (1848-1919), 24267
Freedom Movement. *See* Nationalist Movement
freedom of the press. *See* censorship
Freemasons, 21440, 24553
French Guiana, South Asians in, 80, 26775-90
French in India, 2506, 29, 07902-40, 08170, 08856-60, 19195, 22448
French literature, India in, 11875
Frere, Henry Bartle Edward, Sir (1815-84), 09171, 09176, 20705
Freud, Sigmund, 01353
Friends, Society of (Quakers), 22280, 22283
fruits
- Bangladesh, 25353, 25358
- India, 14916

fundamental rights. *See* civil rights
Futūhat-i-ʿĀlamgīrī (account of Aurangzīb's reign), 07499

Gaddis (tribe), 25888-9
Gadgil, Dhananjaya Ramchandra (1901-71), 14335
Gaduliya Lohars (tribe), 20839, 20842, 22102-3
Gaekwad... *See* Gaikwad
Gāhadavāla dynasty, 07010
Gaikwad dynasty of Baroda, 27, 62, 08310, 20624-33
Gajabāhu, King of Ceylon, 06116
Gajabāhu II, King of Ceylon, 06123
Gajapati dynasty, 21, 06694-701
Gajendragadkar, Pralhad Balacharya, 12841
Gal Oya Valley Project, Sri Lanka, 18705-6, 18711
Galle, Sri Lanka, 18907
Gallongs (tribe), 26508
Gamits (tribe), 20829
Gampola, Ceylon, 19, 06130-4, 06167
Gaṇapati. *See* Gaṇeśa
Gaṇapati festival/Gaṇeśotsava, 62, 20740, 21606
Gandhara, 04159
- art, xx, 16, 05482, 05516-53

Gandhi, Feroze (1912-60), 13426
Gandhi, Indira Nehru (1917-), 42-3, 13409-682, 13742-3
Gandhi, Mohandas Karamchand, Mahatma (1969-1948), 32-33, 34, 72, 09587-96, 09854-969, 09989, 09993, 10119, 10142-6, 10256, 10313, 10383, 10517-33, 11562, 22663, 22635, 22638, 23964-73
- as journalist, 10822
- assassination, 10521-33
- communalism, 10119, 10383, 10517-21
- educational ideas, 35, 10630-40
- in South Africa, 80, 26827-31
- untouchability, 35, 10760-70

Gandhi, Sanjay (1946-80), 43, 13546-9
Gandhism (Gandhian economic and social movements), 33, 42, 45, 48, 50, 09928-69, 10979, 11196, 13304-15, 14292-35, 24166
Gaṇeśa (deity), 5, 01807-16
Ganga Delta and Brahmaputra Valley Area. *See* Northeast Area
Gaṅga dynasty, Eastern, 06694-701
Gaṅga dynasty, Western, 06178, 06184
Ganga Narain, Bhirmij tribal leader, 20969-70
Gaṅgā/Ganges River, 27058, 27271-5
- as deity, 5, 01837-44
- as sacred place, 5, 01905

Ganga Singh, Sir, Maharaja of Bikaner (1880-), 20658
Ganges. *See* Gaṅgā
Ganges water dispute, 12240, 12243-4
Gaṅgeśa (13th cent.), philosopher, 07316-27
Ganīmat Kunğāhi, 07691
Gaṇitasārasaṅgraha, 9th cent. mathematics text, 05737
Garhwal. *See* Kumaon and Garhwal
Garhwal painting, 29, 08745-6, 08748
Garo Hills, 79, 26649-706
Garos (tribal people), 79, 26650, 26669, 26671-83
Garuḍa (deity, vāhana/"carrier", of Viṣṇu), 01788
Garuḍa-purāṇa, 17, 05792, 05796-7, 05800
Gauḍa Saraswat Brahmans, 61, 20393-9
Gauḍapāda (c. 700), 06336-44
Gauḍiya Vaiṣṇavism, 23, 07264-98
Gaurāṅga. *See* Caitanya
Gautama Akṣapāda (founder of Nyāya), 04832-4
Gautama Buddha, xx, 13, 04875-910, 05302, 05304
- image in art, 10, 01664-78

Gayā, 5, 02057-65, 05468-71, 23951, 24173
Gayāwal Brahmans, 72, 24143, 24147-8
gazetteers, xvi-xvii, 83, 27778-83
Geddes, Patrick, Sir (1854-1932), 10623
Gemelli-Careri, Giovanni Francesco, 07913
generation gap, India, 49, 15941-67
geography, xvi
- economic, 45, 14104-202, 18581, 25287-8
- general, 81, 26984-7023
- historical, 1, 10, 00150-6, 00216-20, 03730-3, 04078-85, 05751, 05760, 07386
- regional, 81-2, 27110-7, 27142-9, 27171-5, 27200-3, 27233, 27266-9, 27289-92, 27308-11, 27342-5, 27373-80

Geological Survey of India, 10656, 10658, 17281
geology, 27008
geometry (śulvaśāstra), 12, 04006-8, 04540-44
George, S.K. (1900-60), 11552
Germany (incl. East and West)
- British India, relations, 32, 09385
- historical relations, 00352
- India (Rep.), relations, 14070-9, 14082, 14084, 21500
- South Asian Studies, 00057, 01114, 27421

Ghadar Party, 32, 09738-57
Ghālib, Urdu poet (1797-1869), 38, 11634, 11642-71
Ghanānand (fl. 1719-39), 29, 08829
Ghārapuri (Elephanta) cave temples, 21, 06816-24
Gharuas (caste), 22238
Ghate, S.V., 10063
ghazal. *See* Urdu literature; Persian literature
Ghaziabad, Uttar Pradesh, 23859
Ghaznavid dynasty, 976-1186 AD, 06929-36
gherao. *See* labor; students
Ghirths (tribe), 25881
Ghose, Aurobindo (1872-1950)
- political role, 32, 09718-26

Ghose, Aurobindo -- *continued*
- religious ideas, 37, 11227, 11367-99
- poetry of, 38, 11770-80

Ghose, Girish Chunder, 10826
Ghose, Manmohan (1869-1924), 24961-3
Ghose, Motilal (1847-1922), 10827, 25130, 25132
Ghose, Sudhindra Nath, 17180
Ghosh, Atulya, 24366
Ghosh, Shishir Kumar, 10829
Ghulam Ahmad, Mirza (1839?-1908), 37, 11518-26
Ghulām Farīd, Khwāja (1845-1901), 22979, 23001
Ghurye, Govind Sadashiv (1892-), 00629, 00657-8
Gilgit, district and town in Kashmir region, 02070, 23144, 23146-7
Giri, Varahagiri Venkata (1894-1980), 40, 43, 11128, 11131, 11135, 12587-90, 19947-8
Gītā. *See* Bhagavad-gītā
Gīta-Govinda, Sanskrit poem, 23, 07244-57
Glasenapp, Helmuth von (1891-), 01115
glass, history of, 00344
Gnānānanda, 02223, 19501
Goa, Daman, & Diu U.T., xxii
- art, 03402, 08524-5
- bibliography, 27714
- general history, 2, 00446-8
- modern (1818-), 63, 21035-109
- Mughal period, 27, 08334-9, 08393, 08411

Gobind Singh, Sikh guru (1666-1708), 28, 08647-60
God, gods, in Indic religions, 4, 01161, 01696-859. *See also* theology; mythology
Godden, Rumer (1907-), 11927, 11929
Gode, Parashuram Krishna (1861-1961), 00127
Godse, Nathuram Vinayak (1912-49), 10521-33
Gokak, Vinayak Krishna, 20559
Gokhale, Gopal Krishna (1866-1915), 32, 09594, 09597, 09668-78
gold mining, 00340
Golkonda Sultanate, 26, 08112-25
Gondal, princely state, Kathiawar, 20614
Gonds (tribal people), 62, 19808, 19810, 19816, 20853, 20862-80, 20884
Gonsalvez, Jacome, 08103
Goonetilleke, Oliver Ernest, Sir (1896-), 18420
goose in Indic art, 01626
Gopālakṛṣṇa. *See* Kṛṣṇa
Gorakh Natha (9th cent.), 23, 07303-8
Gorakhpur, Uttar Pradesh, 23855-6, 23860-1
Gorakṣa. *See* Gorakh Nātha
Gorkhas. *See* Gurkhas
Gosvāmī, Vijay Kṛṣṇa (1841-1900), 24889, 24892
Goswāmī, Tulsi Chandra (1898-1957), 24330
Goswāmīs (disciples of Chaitanya), 23, 07284-91
gotra, 3, 01002-5
government and politics
- ancient, 11, 04250-64
- Andhra Pradesh, 59, 19604-721
- Arunachal Pradesh, 78, 26475-81
- Assam, 76, 25677-721
- Baluchistan, 67, 22515-26
- Bangladesh, 75, 25150-266
- Bengal Presidency, 73, 24241-348
- Bhutan, 78, 25840-7, 26412-22
- Bihar, 72, 23944-4029
- British India, 31, 62, 09073-10536, 19142-55, 20579-797, 24241-348
- Delhi U.T., 70, 23320-42
- East India Company, 26, 07973-97, 08187-90
- East Pakistan, 75, 25159-82
- general history, 1, 00221-35
- Goa, 63, 21035-70
- Gujarat, 65, 21663-705
- Haryana, 70, 23263-74
- Himachal Pradesh, 77, 25859-68
- India (Rep.), 40-3, 12270-14121, 15314-8, 15667-76
- Karnataka, 61, 20223-66
- Kerala, 60, 19912-92
- Madhya Pradesh, 66, 22155-76
- Madras Presidency, 58, 19142-55
- Maharashtra, 63, 21110-195
- Manipur, 79, 26575-7
- Marathas, 27, 08247-333
- medieval, 06116-34, 06179-242, 06680-741, 06925-55, 07002-69, 07174-96
- Mughal Empire, 24, 07448-584
- Mughal period, 08048-97, 08112-90, 08239-390, 08530-60,

government and politics -- *continued*
- Mughal period -- *continued* 08755-83, 08840-88, 08973-84
- Nagaland, 79, 26521-39
- Nepal, 77, 25040-7, 25957-6099
- North-East hill states, India, 78, 26451-9
- North-West Frontier Province, 69, 23035-79
- Orissa, 67, 22787-314
- Pakistan, 52-3, 17306-769
- Punjab, 68, 22554-721
- Rajasthan, 65, 21951-2009
- Sikkim, 78, 25840-7, 26369-84
- Sind, 67, 22410-65
- South Asia, general, 39, 12205
- Sri Lanka, 55-6, 18295-580
- Tamil Nadu, 58, 19196-242
- Tripura, 79, 26627-35
- Uttar Pradesh, 71, 23441-557
- West Bengal, 73, 24349-96

Government College, Lahore, 22951
Government of India Act (1919), 33, 10228-43
Government of India Act (1935), 33, 10272-87
government publications, guides to, 27505, 27512-5, 27526. *See also* archives
governors of Indian states
- general, 41, 12883-91
- West Bengal, 24338

Governors-general, Ceylon, 55, 18295-333, 18386
Governors-general, India, 26, 29, 30-1, 08026-47, 09100-09151, 09816-28, 09838, 10223-7, 10244-9, 10255-9, 10269-71, 10394-7, 10448-50, 10468-73
Governors-general, Pakistan, 52, 17324-5
Govinda Siṁha. *See* Gobind Singh
gram panchayats (village councils). *See* panchayati raj
grāmdān. *See* Bhoodan
grammar and grammarians, indigenous
- Prakrit, 15, 05246-60
- Sanskrit, 15, 05183-289
- Tamil, 15, 05230-6

Granth (Sikh scripture). *See* Ādi-Granth
Grant, Charles, 10538, 10540, 10543
Great Britain. *See also* British India
- India, relations, 44, 14056-62
- Pakistan, relations, 53, 17749-52
- South Asian libraries, 82, 27511-43
- South Asian studies, 82, 27423
- South Asians in, 80, 26892-918
- Sri Lanka, relations, 18565

Great Tradition, xix, 1-8, 38, 00001-3482 (Chapter One), 11836-57
Greek accounts of ancient South Asia, 10, 04018-28
Greek dynasties in ancient South Asia, 12, 04165-70
Greeks, ancient contacts, 04165-70, 04569-83, 05522-37
green revolution. *See* agriculture
Gregory, William, Sir, 18321-2
Grey, Henry George Grey, 3rd Earl (1802-94), 18326, 18754
Gṛhyasūtras (domestic ritual texts), 12, 03869, 04457-66
Gūhyasamāja-tantra, 05917, 05921-2
guilds, 00910-5
Gujarat, xxii
- adivasis (tribals), 62, 20829-37
- art, 16, 21, 28, 03403-18, 06830-79, 05582-91, 08475
- bibliography, 08342, 27713, 27717
- folk drama, 8, 03031, 03034
- general history, 2, 00452-62
- geography, 27199
- introductions, 81, 27185
- medieval, 21, 06712-23, 06777-801, 06830-79
- modern (1818-), 62, 65, 20612-33, 20685-763, 21663-950
- Mughal period, 27, 08340-9
- prehistory, 03509, 03562-3, 03628
- Princely States, 62, 20612-33
- sacred centers, 5, 02002-8

Gujarati dictionaries and learning aids, 83, 27925-33
Gujarati language and literature, 7, 65, 02603-8, 06791, 21932-46
Gujarat painting, 28, 08475
Gūjars (caste), 22822, 23236, 25889
Gulab Singh, Maharaja of Jammu (1792-1857), 69, 23133-41
Guler painting, 29, 08742
Guṇāḍhya (4th cent. AD), author of Bṛhat-Kathā, 15, 05389-93
Gunatitanand Swami (1873/74-), 21924
Guntupalle, Andhra Buddhist site, 05495

Guntur district, Andhra Pradesh, 19702
Gupta, Chandra Bhanu (1902-), 23499
Gupta dynasty, 10-11, 0209708, 04144-57, 04373
- art, xx, 16, 05554-612
- inscriptions, 04056-62
Gupta, Iswarchandra (1812-59), 24952
Gurbachan Singh (1930-80), 22961-2
Gurdwara (Sikh shrines), 28, 69. *See* Sikhism
Gurjara-Pratīhāra dynasty, 07006-13
Gurkhas (Nepalese people), 78, 08973-84, 09298-313
Guru Dutt (1925-65), 16981
Guru Granth Sahib. *See* Ādi-Granth
Guru Nānak. *See* Nānak, Guru
Gurung (Himalayan people), 78, 26223, 26236-40
Gurus, Sikh, 28, 08598-660
Guruvayur, Kerala, 01979, 01988
Guyana, South Asians in, 80, 26775-90
Gwalior, princely state, Madhya Pradesh, 27, 62, 00473, 08309, 20672-5
Gyananneshun (Bengali-English journal), 24248
Gypsies, 1, 00375-8

Haidar Ali (c. 1722-1782), 26, 08162-78
Hailey, William Malcolm Hailey, Baron (1872-1969), 22654
Haileybury College, 31, 09194-9
Hajong (tribe), 26697
hakīms (unānī physicians). *See* medicine
Halebid, Karnataka, 06673
Halifax, Charles Wood, 1st Viscount (1800-85), 09095, 09098
Halifax, Edward Frederick Lindley Wood, 1st Earl of (Lord Irwin, 1881-1959), 33, 10255-9
Hamied, K.A., 11094
Hamilton, Alexander (1762-1824), xvii, 00064
handicapped persons, 49, 16174-9, 22130, 24199
handicrafts, 8, 36, 03294-349, 19095, 19774
Hansrāj, Lālā, Punjab leader (1864-1938), 22930
Hanumān (deity), 5, 01802-3, 08797
Hanumanthaiah, Kengal, 20254
Har Gobind, Guru (1595-1644), 28, 08637-8
Harappan civilization, xx, 9, 03589-661
Hardinge, Charles Stewart, 2nd Viscount (1785-1856), 30, 09120
Hardinge of Penshurst, Charles Hardinge, Lord (1858-1944), 32, 09838
Hare, David, educator in Bengal (1775-1842), 24825
"Hare Krishna" Movement, 50, 16756-60
Hari Singh, Maharaja of Jammu & Kashmir, 69, 23174
Haridāsas (medieval Karnataka saint-poets), 20, 06488-94
Harijans. *See* Scheduled Castes
Harikathā (devotional drama in Maharashtra), 21607
Hariścandra, "Bharatendu", Hindi author, (1850-85), 38, 11598-9
Harivaṁśa, supplement to Mahabharata, 13, 04656-8
Harṣacarita, 7th cent. prose composition by Bana, 06011-6
Harṣavardhana (fl. 606-647), 18, 22, 05385, 06005-16, 07002-5
hartals (strikes, boycotts), 32, 09841
Haryana, xxii, 70, 23263-319
- formation of state, 68, 22674-88, 23263
- general history, 2, 00510-20
- introductions, 82, 27257, 27259, 27264-5
- sacred centers, 5, 02031-5
Hasan, Yakub, 19167
Hastings, Francis Rawdon-Hastings, 1st Marquess (1754-1826), 30, 09107-9, 09364
Hastings, Warren (1732-1818), 26, 08026-37, 08761-77
haṭhayoga, 23, 07303-8
Havelock, Henry, Sir, 09317
health services. *See* medicine
Heber, Reginald, Bishop (1783-1826), 11938, 11940
Heidelberg University, South Asia Institute, 27421
Hemacandra, Jain writer on philosophy and poetics (1089-1172), 06792-6
Henriques, P. (1520-1600), 07890
Henty, George Alfred, British author (1832-1902), 11928
Heras, Henry, historian in Bombay (1888-1955), 00059
heroic poetry, Tamil. *See* puṟam
Hevajra-tantra, 05919
Heyer, Christian Frederick (1793-1873), 19874
high-yielding varieties (HYV), 46, 14858-65. *See also* technology, agricultural
hill stations, 39, 11966-73
Himachal Pradesh, xxii, 77, 25856-98
- general history, 2, 00537-45
Himachal Pradesh -- *continued*
- prehistory, 0, 03519
Himalayan Rim Area, xx-xxii. *See also* Himachal Pradesh, Kumaon & Garhwal, Nepal, Sikkim, Darjeeling, Bhutan, Arunachal Pradesh, Nagaland, Manipur, Mizoram, Tripura, Meghalaya, Andaman & Nicobar Islands
- art, 8, 23, 30, 03447-82, 07380-5, 08985-6
- bibliography, 83, 27736-47
- general history, 2, 00537-45
- introductions, 82, 27312-407
- languages, 83, 28008-17
- medieval, 23, 07369-85
- modern (1800-), 76-80, 25834-6736 (Chapter Sixteen)
- Mughal period, 30, 08973-86
- performing arts, 7-8, 02988-9, 03054
- sacred centers, 5, 02068-73
Himalayas in art and myth, 01651
Hīnayāna Buddhism, 14, 05017-44
- origins, 04951-54
Hindi as official language, controversy, 40, 12279, 19233-7, 23488
Hindi dictionaries and learning aids, 83, 27819-48
Hindi language and literature, xxii, 6, 7, 22, 29, 37-8, 51, 02640-53, 07131-5, 08790-839, 11584-630, 17038-53, 23256
Hindi-Urdu controversy, Uttar Pradesh, 23487, 23505, 23506
The Hindu, Madras newspaper, 10807, 10818, 19174
Hindu Code Bill (1955), 49, 15985-95
Hindu law, 3, 12, 17, 49, 00925-39, 09260-70, 10737-40, 15980-6008
Hindu Mahasabha, 33, 42, 10130-41, 14358-64, 19617
Hindu-Muslim relations
- Bengal, 24339, 24591
- British period, 33, 34, 10308-393
- Delhi Sultanate, 07087, 07103
- India (Rep.), 12435-44, 23243
- Mughal period, 07653-73
Hindu Renaissance, 36, 73, 11219-362, 24561-77
Hinduism, xix-xx, 3-6, 01101-2233. For areas not listed below, *see also* religio-philosphical traditions; *see also* names of specific sects, leaders, sites
- ancient, 12-3, 04731-874
- Andhra Pradesh, 5, 60, 01956-61, 19870-82
- Assam, 23, 76, 07292-8, 25806
- Bengal, 23, 29-30, 74, 75, 07204-327, 08932-53, 24873-909
- bibliography, 01116-22
- Bihar, 24222, 24225
- British period, 36-7, 11199-442
- Christianity and, 4, 37, 50, 01342-69, 11555-63, 16787-805
- ethics, 4, 01509-75
- Gujarat, 5, 21, 65, 02003-8, 06777-89, 21913-20
- India (Rep.), 50, 16706-60
- Islam and, 18, 22, 30, 15957-64
- Karnataka, 20, 61, 06469-94, 20533-54
- Kashmir, 22, 70, 06956-92, 08667, 23242-6
- Kerala, 19-20, 20167-76
- logic, 4, 01426-36
- Madhya Pradesh, 66, 22273-9
- Maharashtra, 5, 20, 27-8, 64, 01993-2002, 06742-76, 08424-56, 21606-14
- Manipur, 79, 26596-8
- medieval, 17, 19-20, 21, 22, 23, 05744-885, 06277-568, 06742-805, 06955-92, 07084-110, 07204-315
- metaphysics, 4, 01368-1410
- Mughal period, 24, 25, 27, 28, 07653-70, 08207-11, 08424-56, 08667-70, 08790-826, 08932-52
- Nepal, 5, 78
- Orissa, 5, 67, 02015-30, 22386-402
- overseas, 26800, 26907, 26950
- Pakistan, 55
- philosophy, 4, 01313-8
- Punjab, 69, 08669-70, 22966-79
- Sri Lanka, 26, 57, 06161, 19028-32
- surveys, 01188-1217
- Tamil Nadu, 5, 19, 27, 59, 01947-92, 16277-568, 08207-11, 19492-22
- texts, 01218-23
Hindus in Baluchistan, 22537
Hindus in Bangladesh, 75, 25503-5
Hindustan Ghadar Party. *See* Ghadar Party
Hindustan Socialist Republican Army, 33, 10105-14
Hindustani dictionaries and learning aids, 83, 27819-48
Hindustani music, 7, 02816-51

Hirachand, Walchand (industrialist), 21335
Hirakud Dam, Orissa, 22334, 22339
historical geography. *See* geography, historical
historiography
- ancient, 04009-17
- Bihar, 23991
- British period, 08997-9006, 09458-68, 19625
- Europeans in India, 07824, 07843, 07846-7, 07904
- general, 1, 00105-62
- medieval, 17, 05626-35
- Mughal period, 07393-403, 07472
- Sikhs, 08531
- Sri Lanka, 04229-49
history. *See also* specific places and topics
- ancient, 19-11, 04009-4586
- British period, 09027-72
- general, 00092-00545
- medieval, 20-1, 05626-743, 06116-43, 06176-272, 06680-741, 06925-54, 07002-83, 07174-203, 07369-78
- Mughal period, 07404-7652, 07803-8097, 08112-206, 08239-432, 08530-64, 08755-89, 08840-931, 08973-84
- Pakistan, 17293-305
- sources, 01909, 04018-77, 05636-86
Hit Harivaṁśa Gosvāmī (1502-52), 29, 08825
Hitopadeśa (Sanskrit story collection), 18, 06079-85
Hmar (tribe), 26622
Hobson-Jobson, 09011, 27502
Hodgson, Brian Houghton, 26053
Holi (festival), 02115-6
Holkar dynasty of Indore, 27, 08312
Holland. *See* Dutch in India,...Ceylon
Home Rule Leagues, 32, 09758-61
homeopathy, 16346
Hong Kong, South Asians in, 80, 26891
Hooghly College, 24852
horse sacrifice. *See* aśvamedha
Hos (tribe), 63, 20977-82
hospitals, 49, 16372-6, 22915, 22917
hotel industry, 15399
House of the People. *See* Lok Sabha
household rites. *See* Gṛhyasūtras
housing. For areas not listed below, *see also* urbanization; villages
- Bangladesh, 25434
- Bombay, 64, 21310, 21531-6
- Calcutta, 74, 24786-90
- Delhi, 23398-411
- Gujarat, 21875-6
- India (Rep.), 47, 15165-9, 16065-75
- North-West Frontier Province, 23124
- Pakistan, 18120-1
- Poona, 21544
- rural, India, 47, 15165-70
- Sri Lanka, 18912
- Uttar Pradesh, 23864
Howard, Albert, Sir, 10666
Howrah city, West Bengal, 74, 24513, 24630, 24747-51
Hoysala dynasty, Karnataka, 19, 06215-7
- art, 20, 06670-7
Hsüan-tsang (c. 596-664 AD), traveller, 05647-59
Hubli city, Karnataka, 61, 20486
Hujwīrī (Dātā Jang Bakhsh, d.c. 1072), 06983
Humāyūn, Mughal emperor (1508-1556), 24, 25, 07457-67
Hume, Allan Octavian, Sir (1828-1912), 32, 09667
Hume, David, 01352
Hūṇas (Central Asian tribe), 11, 04193-4
Hungary
- India, relations, 14083
Hunter Commission (1882), 35, 10578
Hunter, William Wilson, Sir (1840-1900), xvii, 09763
Hunza, district in Kashmir region, 09430, 27221, 27226, 27237, 27243
Hur Rebellion in Sind, 2nd (1942-47), 22424
Husain, Fazli. *See* Fazl-i-Husain
Husain, Maqbul Fida, 11788, 17205-6, 17214-5
Husain, Mir Musharraf (1869-99), 24953
Husain Shāh, 07191
Husain, Zakir (1897-69), President of India, 40, 10646, 12580-6
Hyderabad city, Andhra Pradesh, 59, 19834-47
- architecture, 08237
- Mughal period, 26, 08116-29
Hyderabad, princely state, South India, xxi, 26, 59, 19611-40, 21048
Hyderabad State (1949-1956), 19611-40
hygiene. *See* medicine

Ibn Battūta (1304-77), 17, 05636-46
Ichalkaranji, princely state, Maharashtra, 20592
iconography, xx, 4, 01567-1859
- Mahāyāna, 14, 05069
- Tantric, 17, 05869-85
idealism in Indic thought, 4, 01379-90
Ikṣvāku dynasty, 11, 04222-6
- art, 16, 05494-508
Ilango Adigal. *See* Iḷankovāṭikal
Iḷankovāṭikal (5th-6th cent. AD), 16, 05437-45
Iḻavas. *See* Ezhavas
Ilbert Bill (1883), 09182, 09273
illiteracy. *See* literacy; education
Iltutmish, Shams-ud-din, King of Delhi (fl. 1211-36), 07030
Ilyās, Muhammad, Maulānā (1885-1944), 22142
ʿImād-Shāhī dynasty, Berar, 27, 08246
images of South Asia, 39, 81, 11875-929, 27080-6
Imperial Legislative Council, 30
Imperial Library, Calcutta, ix. *See also* National Library
Impey, Elijah, Sir (1732-1809), 08883, 24271
imports. *See* foreign trade
incarnation, divine. *See* avatāra
income distribution, India, 45, 14212-20
income, national. *See* national income
Independenc, India and Pakistan (1947), 34, 10474-89
Independence Movement. *See* Nationalist Movement
India-Bangladesh relations, 12191-8
India-Bhutan relations, 78, 26425-35
India, British, 08987-12269 (Chapter Six); *see also* Chapter Five, *passim*; for regional and local studies, *see* Chapters Eleven through Sixteen
India-China relations, 26079-84
India-Nepal relations, 26053-74
India Office, history, 09096
India Office Library and Records, ix, 82, 27524-30
India-Pakistan relations, 39, 12066-198
India, Republic of (1947-), xiv, 40-52, 12270-7282 (Chapter Eight); for regional and local studies, *see* Chapters Eleven-Sixteen
- bibliography, 83, 27645-59
- introductions, 81, 26957-7086
India-Sri Lanka relations, 12199-202
Indian Administrative Service (IAS), 12627-69
Indian Agricultural Service, 09187
Indian Army. *See* armed forces
Indian Association (1876-1951), 24286
Indian Civil Service (ICS), 31, 09179-213, 12627-69. *See also* Indian Administrative Service.
Indian Council of Historical Research, xiv
Indian Council of Social Science Research, xiv
Indian Councils Act of 1909, 32, 09829-37
Indian English
- dictionaries, 27496-502
- linguistic studies, 17087-92
- literature. *See* English literature
Indian Foreign Service, 41, 12744-61
Indian League, 20720
Indian Medical Service, 10674, 10678-9
Indian music, 7, 02686-904
Indian National Army, 34, 10432-45, 10456-60
Indian National Congress (est. 1885)
- Assam, 25711
- Bengal, 24329
- Bihar, 23988-90, 23995, 24085
- British India (1885-1947), 32, 33, 09525, 09528-9, 09530, 09678, 11134
- Central Provinces & Berar, 20769
- Delhi U.T., 23330
- India (Rep.), 1947-, 41-2, 45, 13151-70
- Kerala, 19938
- Madras Presidency, 58, 19163-77
- Maharashtra, 62, 21112, 21131
- Mysore State, 20250
- Punjab, 68, 22650, 22656
- Rajasthan, 21960
- Tamil Nadu, 58, 19199-205
- Uttar Pradesh, 23473, 23478-9, 23492, 23497, 23508
- West Bengal, 24362
Indian National Trade Union Congress, 48, 15640-76
Indian Ocean, xxi, 1, 30, 00370-4, 11985-2011, 14014
Indian Political Service, 31, 09356-75
Indian Science Congress Association, 10660

Indian Statutory Commission (1927). *See* Simon Commission
Indian Union Muslim League. *See* Muslim League
Indians in Sri Lanka. *See* Tamils in Sri Lanka
indigo cultivation, 73, 23964-73, 24090, 24503, 24918, 24964
individual in Indic society, 3, 01052-61
Indo-Anglian literature. *See* English literature
Indo-Aryan philology, 6, 02347-52
Indo-Aryan, Middle. *See* Middle Indo-Aryan
Indo-Greeks, 11, 04165-70
- art, 16, 05522-51
- numismatics, 11, 04065, 04067
Indo-Islamic architecture, 8, 03188-96. *See also* art and architecture, Islamic
Indo-Pakistan War, 1965, xxi, 39, 12100-12
Indo-Pakistan War, 1971, xxi, 39, 75, 12113-90
Indo-Soviet Treaty (1971), 44, 13987-93
Indology, ix, 1, 00001-66
Indonesia-India seminar, 1975, 14100
Indore city, Madhya Pradesh, 22255-6
Indore, princely state, Madhya Pradesh, 27, 08312, 20663
Indra (deity), 03851
Indus River, 27092
Indus Valley and Mountain Frontier Area. *See* Northwest Area
Indus Valley civilization. *See* Harappan civilization
Indus script, 9, 03637-50
Indus water disputes, 39, 12239-46
industrial arts, 8, 28, 03294-349, 08526-9
industrial estates, 15335-40, 22349, 25765
industrial finance, 45, 14656-62. *See also* banking; industry
industrial relations. *See* labor
industry. For regions not listed below, *see also* economic conditions
- ancient, 11, 04377-84
- Andhra Pradesh, 15, 19767-75
- Assam, 76, 25765-74
- Bangladesh, 75, 25455-68
- Bengal, 29, 73, 75, 08910-9, 24510-32, 25455-68
- Bihar, 72, 24106-22
- British India, 36, 11077-147
- Delhi U.T., 70, 23356-61, 23390
- Gujarat, 65, 21773-85, 21866-7
- Haryana, 70, 23294-9
- India (Rep.), 47-8, 15151-64, 15172-414, 19122-3
- Karnataka, 61, 20341-50
- Kerala, 60, 20042-50
- Madhya Pradesh, 66, 22221-8
- Maharashtra, 64, 21291-308
- medieval, 07079
- Mughal period, 24, 29, 07623-8, 08910-9
- Nepal, 77, 26174-9
- Orissa, 67, 22348-56
- Pakistan, 54, 17998-8041
- Punjab, 68, 22728, 22792-4
- Rajasthan, 66, 22054-65
- Sri Lanka, 56, 18776-86
- Tamil Nadu, 58, 19316-25
- Uttar Pradesh, 71, 23664-85
- West Bengal, 73, 24510-32
industry, rural, India, 47, 15151-74. *See also* village industry
infanticide, female, 35, 10716-9, 21803-10
inflation. *See* prices
inheritance, law of, 35, 49, 00925, 10737-40, 15996-6000, 18102-10
initiation rites, 3, 01028-39
inscriptions. *See* epigraphy
insurance, health, 16136, 23425
insurance, life, 25475
insurance, social, 49, 16135-40
insurrection of April, 1971, Sri Lanka, 55, 18430-44
integration, national. *See* national integration
intellectuals, Indian, 48, 11217, 15834-42
Intensive Agricultural District Program, India, 46, 14797-805, 20017
inter-governmental relations, India, 41, 12907-37
inter-state relations, India, 41, 12925-37
Interim Government (1946-47), 34, 10467
international relations
- ancient, 11, 04336-40
- Bangladesh, 75, 25251-66
- Bhutan, 78, 26423-35
- British India, 31, 09384-453, 09605-29

international relations -- *continued*
- India (Rep.), 43-4, 13683-4121
- Mughal Empire, 24, 07579-84
- Nepal, 77, 26041-99
- Pakistan, 53, 17656
- South Asia, general, 39, 12012-202
- Sri Lanka, 56, 18553-80
investment, foreign
- India (Rep.), 44, 13855-900
- Pakistan, 53, 17712-23
- Sri Lanka, 56, 18576-80
Iqbāl, Muḥammad, Sir (1877-1938)
- educational thought, 10644-5, 10647
- poetry, 38, 11634, 11672-91
- political thought, 34, 10313, 10320-31, 10346
- religious thought, 37, 11482-515
Iran
- British India, relations, 09414
- historical relations, 1, 00368-9, 03575, 03631, 04562
- India (Rep.), relations, 14085
- Mughal Empire, relations, 07579-84
- Pakistan, relations, 17755, 17761
Iranians in ancient India, 11, 04171-4
Iron Age, 9, 03686-797
iron industry. *See* steel industry
iron industry, early, 03689-90
irrigation. For regions not listed below, *see also* technology, agricultural
- ancient Ceylon, 11, 06136-42
- ancient India, 11, 04362-71
- Andhra Pradesh, 19739-40
- Assam, 25748, 25757
- Bangladesh, 75, 25399-410
- Bihar, 72, 24050-5, 24073-8
- British India, 36, 11025-8
- Gujarat, 21746-52
- India (Rep.), 46, 14874-96
- Karnataka, 61, 20327-32
- Kerala, 20016
- Maharashtra, 64, 21247-56
- medieval South India, 06259
- Nepal, 77, 26161-5
- Orissa, 22330-1, 22334, 22339
- Pakistan, 54, 17958-73
- Punjab, 68, 22726
- Rajasthan, 67, 22037-42
- Sind, 22477-9
- Sri Lanka, 11, 56, 06136-42, 18699-704
- Tamil Nadu, 19280-93
- Uttar Pradesh, 71, 23610-7
Irwin, Lord. *See* Halifax
Ishwardas Nagar, Mughal historian (b. 1654?), 07494, 07499
Islam, 6, 02257-87. *See also* Muslims, *for* social, economic, and political studies; *see also* religio-philosophical traditions, for areas not listed below
- Andhra Pradesh, 60, 19799, 19870-82
- Bangladesh, 76, 25636-44
- Bengal, 74, 76, 24879, 24910-4, 25636-44
- British India, 37, 11443-517
- entry and early history in South Asia, 05712, 05932-64, 06239-42
- India (Rep.), 50, 16774-9
- Jammu & Kashmir, 70, 23243, 23245-6
- Kerala, 60, 20187
- medieval, 17, 18, 22, 23, 06239-42, 06572-4, 06797-801, 06983-95, 07111-30, 07328-34
- Mughal period, 24-5, 26, 27, 28, 29, 07674-84, 08212-5, 08457-8, 08671-88, 08827-31, 08953
- Nepal, 78, 26326-7
- Pakistan, 52-5, 18206-23
- Punjab, 69, 22975-9
- Rajasthan, 22142
- Sri Lanka, 26, 57, 19055
Islam, Kazi Nazrul. *See* Nazrul Islam
Islam and modernization, 53, 17836-45
Islam and politics, 39, 12203-4
Islamabad (capital of Pakistan), 68, 12235, 22896-8
Islamic architecture, 8, 23, 29, 03154, 03188-96, 07159-73, 07775-97, 08753-4. *See also* names of specific sites
Islamic ideology of Pakistan, 53, 17392-410, 17682-4, 17836-45
Islamic law. *See* law, Islamic
"Islamic Socialism," 52, 17568-600

Ismail, Mirza Mahomed, Sir (1883-1959), Dewan of Mysore, Jaipur, 20242
Isma'īlīs, 06988. *See also* Muslims; Bohras
Israel-India relations, 14087-91
Israel, Indians in, 26871-3
Īśvarakṛṣṇa's Sāṁkhya-kārikā (3rd cent. AD), 13, 04798-804
Italians in early modern India, 25, 07834, 07838-40
ivory sculptures, 8, 16, 03243-61, 05538-43, 06996-7

"J.P." *See* Narayan, Jaya Prakash
Jabalpur, Madhya Pradesh, 22258
Jacob, John, Gen., 22459
Jaffna city, Sri Lanka, 18850-9
Jaffna kingdom, 26, 06133, 08065-8
Jagannāth (deity) and his cult at Puri, 5, 67, 02015-30, 02121, 20791, 22386-93
Jagatseth (firm), 24402
Jagdish Kashyap, Bhikku, 01258
Jaggayapeta stūpa, Andhra, 16, 05499-508
Jahānārā (daughter of Shāh Jahān), 07491
Jahāngīr (1569-1627), Mughal Emperor, 24, 25, 07480-89
Jahāngīrnāma, Persian history of Jahangīr, 07484
Jaimini (author of Mīmāṁsā-sūtra, 4th cent. BC?), 04862-3
Jaiminigṛhyasūtra, 04458
Jains and Jainism, xx, 3-6, 01101-2233. For regions and topics not listed below, *see also* religio-philosophical traditions
- ancient, 14, 05130-61
- art, 8, 21, 03140-8, 05553, 06831-45, 07148, 08475
- bibliography, 0144-53
- ethics, 01509-75
- logic, 01426-36
- medieval, 20, 21, 05930-1, 06570-1, 06790-6
- metaphysics, 01368-1410
- modern (Rep. of India), 50, 16768-73
- monasticism, 01891, 02187, 05141
- philosophy, 01328-34
- Rajasthan, 22144
- ritual, 01028
- surveys, 01273-94
- texts, 01328-34, 05150-61
Jaintia Hills (now in Meghalaya), 79, 26649-706
Jaipal Singh (Munda leader), 63
Jaipur city, Rajasthan, 62, 22005, 22007, 22117, 22120, 22123, 22126
Jaipur, princely state, Rajasthan, 27, 08371-5, 20640, 20651-6
- art, 08520
- music, 02844
Jaisalmer, princely state, Rajasthan, 00463, 03401, 22119
jajmānī system (non-monetary village economy), 3, 00893-904, 19348, 19817, 22105, 23783
Jalal, Shah, 07332
Jalal al-Din Tabrizi, Sheikh, 07332
Jallianwala Bagh massacre, Amritsar (1919), 32, 09843-53
Jām Durrak, 22550
Jama'āt-e-Islāmī-e-Hind, 52, 13290, 13293
Jama'āt-i-Islāmī, 17467-72
Jāmbhekar, Bāl-shāstri Gangādhar, Marathi journalist (1810-1846), 21371
Jam'iāt al-'ulamā -i-Hind, 34, 10392-3
Jammu & Kashmir, 2, 69, 23131-262. *See also* Kashmir, for historical and cultural studies
Jammu Kingdom, 28, 08557-60
Jammu, literature of. *See* Dogri
Jammu painting, 29, 08740
Jammū, sacred centers, 02068
Jamshedpur city, Bihar, 72, 24124, 24128, 24174, 24187-92
Jamnagar, princely state, Kathiawar, 20613
Jamuna. *See* Yamunā
Jana Sangh, political party, 42, 13145, 13257, 13265-78, 13527, 13718, 22669, 23329, 23494, 23501
Jānakīharaṇam, epic by Kumāradāsa (6th cent. AD?), 05383-4
Janakpur, Nepal, 02074, 26288
Janata Party, 43, 13605-25, 13744-7, 23265
Janatha Vimukthi Peramuna, Sri Lanka political party, 55, 18430-44
Jang Bahadur, Maharaja of Nepal (1817-77), 25965, 25968
Japan
- historical contacts, 1, 00363-3
- India, relations, 44, 14102-4
- Pakistan, relations, 17764
- South Asian studies, 00049, 01147
- World War II, 34, 10432-45
Jasimuddin (1903-76), Bengali poet, 25101
Jātaka tales, Buddhist, 14, 05007-14
- art, 05478-9, 07342
- as historical source, 04473
Jātaka tales, Jaina, 06796
Jatapus (tribe), 19811
jāti. *See* caste
Jats (North Indian cultivating caste), 62, 66, 72, 08545, 08759, 18090, 22092-3, 22532, 22671, 22822-3, 22839, 23301, 23738-42
Jatti, Basappa Danappa (1912-), 12555
Jaunpur Sultanate, 22, 07021
- architecture, 07163
Jaunsar-Bawar tract (now in Chakrata tehsil of Dehra Dun district of Uttar Pradesh), 25887, 25908
Jawaharlal Nehru University, 23439
Jayadeva (12th cent.), Sanskrit poet, 23, 07244-57
Jayakar, Mukund Ramrao (1875-1959), 20748-9
Jayatilaka, Don Baron, Sir (1868-1944), 18361
Jayewardene, Junius Richard (1906-), 18417-9
Jehan Begum, Nawab of Bhopal, 20676-8
Jehangeermian Saheb, Shaikh (1860-?), 20617
Jeejeebhoy, Jamsetjee, Sir (1783-1859), 11098
Jesuits in Ceylon, 08080, 08100
Jesuits in India, 07883-90, 08216-27
jewellery, 8, 03310-23, 05516, 07798, 07802
Jews of India, 6, 60, 64, 73, 00420, 00756, 02311-4, 16780, 20140-3, 24055-6, 24659, 21456-8
Jhabbar, Kartar Singh (1874-1962), 22954
Jhabwala, Ruth Prawer (1927-), 51, 17166-72
Jharkhand Party, Bihar, 23993-4, 23997
Jimutavāhana, legal writer (12th cent.?), 05699
Jinnah, Mahomed Ali (1876-1948), 34, 52, 09587, 09592, 10334-5, 10346, 10358-88, 10395
jīva ("soul"), 01456-79
Jīva Gosvāmī (16th cent.), 07288
Jīvaka-pustaka (medical text), 04545
Jñānānveshana/Gyananneshun (Bengali-English journal), 24248
Jñāneśvara, Marathi poet-saint (1275-1296), 21, 27, 06757-68
Jñāneśvarī, 21, 06757-68
Joag, C.V., 21219
Jodhpur city, Rajasthan, 62, 22121
Jodhpur, princely state. *See* Mārwāṛ
Jogeśvarī (deity), 01737
Johnson, Louis, U.S. emissary to India (1942), 34
joint family. *See* kinship, drug use
joint sector industries, India, 47, 15251-4
Jones, Eli Stanley, Methodist missionary (1884-1973), 11547
Jones, William, Sir (1746-94), 38, 11847-51, 11866
Jorehaut Tea Company, Assam, 25723
Joshi, Narayan Malhar (1879-1955), 11133
Joshi, Umashankar (1911-), 21946
journal literature, guides to, 82, 27583-622
journalism. *See* press
Juang (tribe), 63, 21019
Judaism. *See* Jews
judicial system. *See* law and judiciary
judicial review, India, 41, 12845-50
Junnar cave temples, Maharashtra, 05484
Justice Party, South India, 58, 19178-94
jute cultivation and industry, 73, 75, 14910, 24446, 24521, 24525, 24529, 24538, 24540, 25359-71
juvenile delinquency, 49, 16184-200, 23867, 23869, 24806, 25572-3
jyotiṣa. *See* astronomy

Kabīr (1440-1518), 22, 28, 07096-110
Kabir, Humayun (1906-1969), 12447
Kaccha. *See* Kutch
Kacchwāh clan, Jaipur, 27, 08371-5
Kacharis (tribe), 25787
Kadamba dynasty, 04204, 06180
Kādambarī (Sanskrit novel) by Bāṇa (7th cent.), 06012-5
Kadar (tribe), 20146-7
Kafiristan, North-West frontier, 69, 23116-23
Kafirs, 69, 23044, 23116-23
Kahnapāda. *See* Kanha
Kairon, Pratap Singh (1901-1965), 22667, 22670
Kaji, Abdulla Ismail (d. 1947), 26832
Kākatīya dynasty, art, 06660-9
kāla. *See* time
Kālacakra (Buddhist sect), 05924
Kalacuri dynasty, 11

Kalady, Kerala, birthplace of Śaṅkara, 01982, 01990
kalamkari (textile art), 03325
Kālamukhas (Saiva sect), 06513
Kalat, khanate of (Baluchistan), 67, 22515-22
Kalhaṇa (fl. 1148 AD), chronicler of Kashmir, 22, 06937-43
Kālī (deity), 01703, 01731, 01733
Kalibangan (Harappan site), northwest Rajasthan, 03627, 03658
Kālidāsa (c. 400 AD), 15, 05323-75
- as historical source, 04037
Kalighat paintings, 11794-9
Kālikā-purāṇa, 01720
Kaliṅga dynasty, Ceylon, 06127
Kaliṅga region. *See* Orissa
Kallars (tribe), 19373-4
Kalpa-sūtra (Jain text), 05154, 05161
Kalpa-sūtras (Vedāngas), 10, 03998-4008
Kama, Bhikaji. *See* Cama, Bhikaji
Kāmakhyā (goddess), 25811
Kāmandakīya-nītisāra, work on polity (c. 700-750 AD), 04317
Kamar (tribe), 20847
Kamaraj, Kumaraswami (1903-), Tamil Nadu political leader, 58, 19199-205
Kāmarūpa. *See* Assam
Kāmasūtra, work on erotics (c. 300 AD), 12, 04482-7
Kambar. *See* Kampan
Kampan/Kampar (Tamil poet, c. 1180-1250), 04505, 06575-85, 08810
Kamsavaho (Prakrit poem), 05259
Kaṇāda (author of Vaisesika-sūtra), 13, 04835-6
Kanara districts. *See* Karnataka
Kanauj/Kānyakubja, 18, 22, 05687, 07002-13
Kāñchīpuram, Tamil Nadu, 5, 11, 19, 00416, 01741, 01969-71, 04227-8, 06185-95
- art, 06622
Kandla, Gujarat, 21797-8, 21801
Kandy, Sri Lanka, 18292, 18298-9
- as sacred center, 5, 01934-46
Kandy kingdom, Ceylon, 26, 55, 08055-64
- conquest by British, 18300-10
Kandyan dance, 8, 03014-25
Kandyan law, 18527-8, 18531
Kandyans. *See* Sinhalese
Kāṇe, Pāṇḍurang Vāman (1880-1972), 00066
Kangra district. *See* Himachal Pradesh
Kāngrā painting, 29, 08719-31
Kanha, Bengali Sahajiya poet (10th cent. AD), 07227
Kānhojī Āngre, Maratha admiral (d. 1729), 08311, 08313
Kaniṣka (Kuṣāṇa king, c. 2nd cent. AD), 04179
Kannada dictionaries and learning aids, 83, 27887-95
Kannada language and literature, 6, 20, 61, 02577, 06488-94, 06538-56, 06593-4, 20557-78
Kānphaṭa yogis (sect), 07303-8
Kanpur/Cawnpore, Uttar Pradesh, 71, 23490, 23678, 23685, 23698, 23838, 23841, 23850
Kant, Immanuel (1724-1804), 01354, 01359, 11863
Kāṇva dynasty, 11
- art, 16
Kānyakubja. *See* Kanauj
Kanyakubja Brahmans, 23719-23
Kapālikas (Saivite sect), 06513, 06883
Kapila (founder of Sāṁkhya philosophy), 13
Kapilar (Tamil poet), 06588, 06592
Kapiśi (modern Begrām), Afghanistan, 16, 04159
Kappa Sutta. *See* Kalpa Sūtra
Karachi, Sind, 67, 22493-507
Karakoram Mountains, 27239-40
Karāva (Sinhalese caste), 18840
"Karīmpur," village in Mainpuri dist., Uttar Pradesh, 71
Kārla cave temples, Maharashtra, 05483, 05488
karma, 4, 01480-97, 01552, 17070
Karma-Mīmāṁsā. *See* Mīmāṁsā
Karmasiddhiprakaraṇa (Buddhist text), 05109
Karṇāṭa dynasty of Mithila, 07181, 07370, 07377
Karnatak (South Indian) music, 7, 02852-90, 19896-902
Karṇāṭaka, xxii
- ancient, 04204
- bibliography, 27711
- drama, 8, 02939
- general history, 2, 00359, 00430-40
- geography, 27172
- introductions, 81, 27158, 27166-7, 27176, 27178
- medieval, 06176-84
- modern (1799-), 61, 20223-578
Karnataka -- *continued*
- Mughal period, 26, 08162-78, 08206
- prehistory, 03679, 03713-4
Karpūra-mañjarī (Prakrit text), 05255
Kārttikeya (deity). *See* Skanda
Karunanidhi, M. *See* Karunanithi, M.
Karunanithi, M. (1924-), Tamil Nadu political leader, 19213
Karve, Dhondo Keshav (1858-62), 10723, 10742, 21357-8, 21361-3
Kashmir, xxii
- bibliography, 27728
- general history, 2, 00500-9
- geography, 27229, 27232-3
- introductions, 81, 27212-3, 27215, 27218-9, 27222
- medieval, 22, 06937-54
- modern (1799-), 69, 70, 22427, 22429, 22431-2, 23131-262
- Mughal period, 28, 08557-60
- prehistory, 03555
- Sanskrit literature, 02486, 02494
Kashmir question, 39, 12077-99
Kashmir Śaivism, xiii, 22, 06956-75
Kashmir shawls, 8, 03327, 03335
Kashmiri dictionaries and learning aids, 83, 27967-71
Kashmiri language and literature, 7, 70, 02631-5, 23247-51
Kāśī. *See* Vārāṇasī
Kataragama, sacred center, Sri Lanka, 5, 01934-46, 18978
kathā (story literature), 15, 18, 05387-411, 06071-95
Kathak dance, 7, 02985
Kathākalī (Kerala dance-drama), 7, 02969-84, 02994
Kathākośa (story collection), 06076
Kathāsaritsāgara (story collection), 06077-8
Kathiawar (region in Gujarat), 00461, 21714, 21874
Kāṭhmaṇḍu, capital of Nepal, 78, 26287, 26290-1, 26293
Katkaris (tribe), 20828
Kātyāyanasmṛti. *See* Dharmaśāstras
Kaul, Zinda (1884-1966), 23249
Kauravas, descendants of Kuru. *See* Kurukṣetra, Battle of
Kauśika sūtra, 04457, 04459
Kauṭilya/Kauṭalya (author of Arthaśāstra), 11, 01542, 04293-319
KAVAL cities, Uttar Pradesh, 71, 23836-54
kāvya (courtly poetry or poetic prose), 15, 02485, 05261-411, 06005-95
Kāvyadarśa (poetics text), 18, 05973-6
Kāvyālaṁkāra (poetics text), 18, 05971-2
Kāvyālaṅkāra-sūtra (poetics texts), 05976
Kāvyaprakāśa (poetics text), 05994-7
Kawar (tribe), 20996
kāya (bodies of the Buddha), 05124-9
Kāyasthas (caste), 71, 19795, 21396-7, 23725-31, 25504
Kayyūr riot (1941), Malabar dist., 19941
Keḷadi kingdom, 08164
Kelkar, Narasinha Chintaman (1872-1947), 21639
Kenya, South Asians in, 26856, 26861, 26863-4
Kerala, xxi
- bibliography, 27709, 27712
- drama, 7, 02969-84, 02994
- general history, 2, 00420-9
- introductions, 81, 27159-60, 27164-5, 27170, 27177
- medieval, 06177
- modern (1800-), 60-1, 19912-20222
- Mughal period, 08169, 08130-47, 08203-5
- music, 02858
- sacred centers, 01972-92
- Sanskrit literature, 02491-2, 02495
Kesarī (Marathi newspaper), 32
Keśavadāsa, Hindi poet (1555?-1617?), 08836
Keshavsūt. *See* Dāmale, Kṛṣṇajī Keśava
Keyt, George (1901-), Ceylonese painter, 11788, 19091-2, 19097-8
khādī, also khaddar (homespun cloth made by Indian nationalists), 47, 15151-64
Khajuraho, Madhya Pradesh, 21, 06704, 06706
- art, 28, 06880-95
Khāksār Movement (1926-46), 34, 10389-91
Khaljī dynasty of Delhi (1290-1320 AD), 22, 06683, 07023-36
Khālsā (Sikh brotherhood), 28
Khalsa College, Amritsar, 22923
Khamtis (tribe), 26511
Khan, Abdul Ghaffar, Khan (1891-), 69, 23063-70
Khan, Liaquat Ali (1895-1951), first Prime Minister of Pakistan, 52, 17485-8

Khan, Muhammad Reza (1717?-91), 08881
Khandagiri cave temple, Orissa, 05489
Khaṇḍakhādyaka (mathematical text) by Brahmagupta (c. 598 AD), 05733
Khandesh district, Maharashtra
- medieval, 06687-8
Khani, Muhammad Bihamad, chronicler of Firoz Shah (14th cent.), 07055
Khan-i-Dauran, 07561
Khaṇḍobā (deity), 21611-2
Kharak Singh, Maharaja of the Punjab (1801?-1840), 22588
Khāravela, king of Kalinga, 04061
Khāriā (tribe), 20892, 21005, 21002
Kharwar Movement (1871), Chota Nagpur, 63, 20928-39
Khasa (tribe), Jaunsar-Bawar, Uttar Pradesh, 25887, 25927
Khāsī Hills (now in Meghalaya), 26649-706
Khāsīs (tribal people), 79, 26653, 26669, 26699-706
Khazan Singh, 22654
Khetri, princely state, Rajasthan, 20637
Khilafat Movement, 33, 09986-10007
Khiljī dynasty. *See* Khaljī
Khojas (Muslim sect), 21445-6, 21448
Khuddaka-nikāya (Buddhist texts), 14, 04989-95
Khushwant Singh (1915), author, 51, 17161-5
Khwushhāl Khān (Pashtu poet, 17th cent.), 08691
Kidwai, Rafi Ahmed, Uttar Pradesh Congress leader (1894-1954), 23470, 23474
kingship, xiii, 00221-35
- ancient, 11, 13, 04236, 04279-92, 06143
- medieval, 06194, 06790, 06949, 07056
- Mughal period, 24, 07529-32, 07551, 08061
- Vedic, 9, 03781-6
kinship, marriage, and the family. For regions not listed below, *see also* social conditions; *see also* names of specific social categories. 3, 00960-01072
- ancient, 12, 04467-73, 04730
- Bangladesh, 75, 25493-6
- Bengal, 73, 00967, 07200, 24598-611, 25493-6
- Bihar, 72, 24133-70
- Delhi U.T., 70, 23362-8, 23391, 23410
- Gujarat, 65, 21815, 21821-30
- Haryana, 70, 23300, 23302
- Himachal Pradesh, 25885, 25887
- India (Rep.), 49, 15887-6020
- Karnataka, 61, 20380-92
- Kerala, 60, 20067-80
- Madhya Pradesh, 22229-42
- Maharashtra, 64, 21377-88
- Nepal, 78, 26190-204
- overseas South Asians, 26753
- Pakistan, 54, 18094-110
- Punjab, 68, 22841-8
- Rajasthan, 66, 22074-83
- Sind, 22490
- Sri Lanka, 57, 18824
- Tamil Nadu, 58, 19333-9, 19390
- Uttar Pradesh, 71, 23707-17
- West Bengal, 73, 24598-611
kinship terminology, 00979-89, 21381, 23716, 25912
Kipling, Rudyard (1865-1936), 39, 11879, 11893-908
Kirātārjūniya, mahākāvya by Bhāravi (7th cent.?), 05380
Kisān Sabhās. *See also* peasant movements, 23656, 24102
Kitchener, Horatio Herbert Kitchener, 1st Earl (1850-1916), 09816
Knight, Robert, 10833
knowledge, theory of, 4, 01368-433
Knox, Robert (1640?-1720), 08051-3
Koch Bihar. *See* Cooch Behar
Koḍagus. *See* Coorgs
Koka Shastra, erotic text, 05723, 05729
Kokkoka (c. 8th cent. AD), 05723, 05729
Kolhapur city, Maharashtra, 21175, 21496
Kolhapur, princely state and district, 27, 62, 08294, 20591-602, 20825, 21165, 21220
Kolis (tribe), 20820-1, 20824
Kols (tribe), 63, 20957, 20977-82, 23779
Koltas (caste), 25908
Komutti Chettiyar (caste), 19361
Konārak Sun Temple, Orissa, 21, 06916-22
Konds (tribal people), 21030, 21033, 22403, 22421, 22423
Kongu. *See* Koṅkunāḍu
Konkani dictionaries and learning aids, 83, 27922-4
Konkani language and literature, 7, 63, 02593-7, 21099-106
Koṅkunāḍu/Kongu (region in Tamil Nadu), 00406, 19342
Koras (tribe), 24637
Korās (tribe), 24637
Korava (tribe). *See* Yerukulas
Korea, Indian Custodian Force in, 12722
Korean War, 12722, 14028, 14031
Korku (tribe), 20853
Korwas (tribe), 23743, 23776
Kośala kingdom, 11, 04116
Kosambi, Damodar Dharmanand (1907-66), historian, 00021
Kosi region, Bihar, 24037, 24042
Koṭā painting, Rajasthan, 28, 08492-500
Kotas (tribe), Nilgiris district, 58, 19398-404
Kotelawala, John Lionel, Sir (1897-), 18422, 18425
Kotte, Sri Lanka, 19, 06130
Koya (tribe), 21029
krama (Kashmir Śaivism), 06955-75
Kripalani, Jiwatram Bhagwandas, Acharya (1888-), Congress leader, 10088-9, 10104
Kripalani, Sucheta (1908-74), 23496
Krishak Praja Party, Bengal, 73, 24348
Krishna-Godavari Commission, 21249
Krishna-Godavari delta (Vengi), art, 16
Krishna Menon, Vengalil Krishnan (1896-1974), 12750-6, 13727
Krishna Pillai, H.A. (1827-1900), 10489, 19580
Krishnadeva Raya (d. 1530), King of Vijayanagara, 06227
Krishnavarma, Shyamaji (1857-1930), 09759
Kṛṣṇa (avatāra of Viṣṇu) and his cult. *See also* Vaiṣṇavism, 5, 13, 17, 21, 01703, 10768, 01774-91, 01979, 10988, 02036-9, 04772-88, 06288-302, 06408-507, 06744-89, 07228-91, 08211, 08940-5, 16756-60
Kṛṣṇadāsa Kavirāj Gosvāmi (b. 1518/19), 07270-7, 08945
Kṛṣṇakarṇāmṛta, bhakti poem by Līlāśuka, 05846
Kṛttibās (Bengali poet, 15th cent.), 23, 07242-3
Kṣatrapas (dynasty), 04177
Kṣemarāja (11th cent.), Kashmiri Śaiva philosopher, 22, 06959, 06967, 06971, 06973
Kṣemendra (11th cent.), Kashmiri Sanskrit poet, 18, 06069, 06071-8
Kshatriya movements, 20972, 21669, 21673, 24641
Kuchipudi dance, 02959
Kuiper, Franciscus Bernardus Jacobus (1907-), 00022
Kukas (Sikh sect), 69, 22955-9
Kuki uprising (1917-19), 26576, 26631
Kukis (tribe), 79, 26624-5, 26631, 26648
Kulaśekhara Varman (fl. 1100 AD), royal dramatist of Kerala, 06070
kulinism, Bengal, 24600
Kulta (caste), 22362
Kula school of Pahari painting, 29, 08743-4
Kumaon and Garhwal, Uttar Pradesh region, xxii, 77, 25899-943
- introductions, 27315, 27323, 27337
Kumāra, Śrī (16th cent.), 08232
Kumāradāsa (6th cent. AD Sanskrit poet), 05383-4
Kumaran Asan (1873-1924), Malayalam writer, 61, 19944, 20111, 20210-2
Kumārasambhava (mahākāvya) by Kālidāsa, 15, 05368-73
Kumārila Bhaṭṭa (writer on mīmāṁsā), 04865
Kumbars (caste), 20378
Kumbha Melā (festival), 02099, 02112-3, 02119, 23914-5
Kunjalis of Calicut, 08138
Kunwar Singh, 23945
Kunzru, Hriday Nath (1887-1978), Liberal leader, 33, 10012
Kuraver (tribe). *See* Yerukulas
Kurma-purāna, 17, 05814, 05816
Kurmis (caste), 22242
Kurukhs (tribal people). *See* Oraons
Kurukṣetra, Battle of, in Mahabharata, 03759-70
Kurukshetra, sacred center in Haryana, 5, 00515, 02031-5
kuṟuntokai (Tamil anthology), 05429
Kuṣāṇa dynasty, 11, 04068, 04178-92, 04354
- art, 16, 05521
Kushtia, Bangladesh, 25565
Kusunda (tribe), 26259
Kutch/Cutch/Kaccha, princely state, region in Gujarat, 00462
- art
Kutiyattam (dance), 02977
Kuṭṭanāḍ, Kerala, 20003, 20020, 20033-4
Kuṭṭanimata (Sanskrit kāvya), 05674, 06055
Kuvalayamālā (story collection), 05673, 05707
Kuvi-kandha (tribe), 21023

labor (incl. industrial relations, trade unions). For regions not listed below, *see* economic conditions
- Andhra Pradesh, 59, 19776
- Assam, 76, 25765-74
- Bangladesh, 75, 25469-74
- Bihar, 72, 24123-8
- British India, 36, 11147, 12232
- Delhi U.T., 70, 23356-61
- Gujarat, 65, 21786-96
- Haryana, 70, 23297
- India (Rep.), 48, 15483-76
- Karnataka, 61, 20351
- Kerala, 60, 20051-4
- Madhya Pradesh, 66
- Maharashtra, 64, 21309-30
- Nepal, 77, 26180-3
- Pakistan, 54, 18042-66
- Punjab, 68, 22795-8, 22807
- Rajasthan, 66, 22066-70
- Sri Lanka, 57, 18791-814
- Tamil Nadu, 58, 19326-32
- Uttar Pradesh, 71, 23678-85
- West Bengal, 73, 24533-44

labor, bonded, 15100-2, 23679
labor legislation, 11141-7
Labour Party (Great Britain), 34, 10296, 18358
labor, rural. For regions not listed below, *see also* agriculture, villages
- Andhra Pradesh, 19748
- Assam, 25751
- Bangladesh, 25440-3
- British India, 10992-5, 19251
- India (Rep.), 47, 15075-102
- Karnataka, 20325, 20353
- Nepal, 21657
- Rajasthan, 22026, 22029
- Sind, 22482
- Tamil Nadu, 19332
- Uttar Pradesh, 71, 23618-22
- West Bengal, 24448

Laccadives. *See* Lakshadweep
Ladakh (region in Jammu & Kashmir), 2, 22, 28, 44, 22431, 22437-8, 23131-262, 27246-7
Lahiri, Ramtanu (1813-98), 24577
Lahore, Punjab, 68, 22893-5, 23497
- art, 29, 18753-4

Lahore conspiracy case, 32
Lajpat Rai, Lala (1865-1928), 32, 09679, 09727-37
Lakhers (tribe), 26619-20
Lakshadweep, U.T. (islands west of Kerala), 60, 19990-2, 27168
Lakshmi Bai, Rani of Jhansi (1835?-58), 09520
Lakshmishwar Singh, Maharaja of Dharbanga, 23957
Lakṣmaṇa/Lakshman (Rama's brother), 04723
Lakṣmī/Lakshmi (deity, consort of Viṣṇu), 01726, 01726, 01734
Lakulīśa (founder of Paśupati sect), 04754-63
Lal, Bansi (1927-), Haryana politician, 13569, 23266
Lal Singh, Raja, 23172
Laldenga (1919-), Mizo nationalist leader, 79, 26606-9
Lalit Kalā Akademi, 16991
Lalla Ded (Śaiva poetess, 14th cent. Kashmir), 22, 06976-82
Lally, Thomas Arthur, baron de Tolendal, comte de (1702-66), 07927
Lalung (tribe), 26698
Lamaism. *See* Buddhism, Tibetan
Land Army, Karnataka rural development group, 20320
land reclamation and colonization
- India (Rep.), 46, 14895-6
- Nepal, 26152
- Pakistan, 17982
- Sri Lanka, 18735-50
- Uttar Pradesh, 23616

land reform. *See* land tenure
land revenue. *See* land tenure
land revenue records, Index, 27559
land settlement reports, xvi
land tenure, revenue, and reform
- ancient, 04362-71
- Andhra Pradesh, 59, 19756-66
- Assam, 76, 25763-4
- Bangladesh, 75, 25444
- Bengal, 73, 24478-99
- Bihar, 72, 23964-73, 24085-100

land tenure -- *continued*
- British India, xvii, 36, 08383, 09522, 10943-61
- Delhi U.T., 23353
- general history, 3, 00905-9
- Goa, Daman, & Diu, 63, 21089-91
- Gujarat, 65, 21762-72
- Haryana, 70, 23292-3
- India (Rep.), 46, 14589-96, 14946-97
- Jammu & Kashmir, 23210
- Karnataka, 61, 20333-40, 20368, 20439
- Kerala, 60, 20020-32
- Madhya Pradesh, 66, 22216-20
- Madras Presidency, 10294-304
- Maharashtra, 64, 21257-67
- medieval, 05711-8, 06142-3, 06255-62, 07073, 07081
- Meghalaya, 26660, 26663
- Mughal period, 24, 27, 29, 07552, 08270, 08402-12, 08561-4, 08785, 08894-909
- Nepal, 77, 26166-73
- North-West Frontier Province, 23085
- Orissa, 67, 22340-7
- Pakistan, 54, 17978-91
- Punjab, 68, 22737-46, 22788-91
- Rajasthan, 66, 22043-53
- Sind, 22483
- Sri Lanka, 56, 06142-3, 18318, 18323, 18751-75, 18992-3
- Tamil Nadu, 58, 19305-10
- Uttar Pradesh, 71, 23481, 23629-55
- West Bengal, 73, 24478-99

land, urban, 16089-90
Lansdowne, Henry Charles Keith Petty-Fitzmaurice, 5th Marquess of (1845-1927), 09149-50
Langhnaj (prehistoric site), Gujarat, 03562, 03565
language and politics
- Andhra Pradesh, 19653
- India (Rep.), 50, 12504-15
- South Asia, general, 12221
- Sri Lanka, 56, 18473-503
- Tamil Nadu, 58, 19233-7

language in education (medium of instruction), India, 50, 16639-59
language, official, India, 50, 12279, 12485-503
languages and literatures of South Asia, xvi, 6-7, 02315-679. *See also* names of specific languages
- ancient, 14-16, 05162-449
- British period, 37-8, 11567-780
- dictionaries and learning aids, 83, 27784-8017
- India (Rep.), 16993-7183
- medieval, 18, 19, 20, 21, 22, 23, 05965-6095, 06144-8, 06285-323, 06488-94, 06534-68, 06575-98, 06742-805, 06976-92, 07084-135, 07219-0339
- Mughal period, 25, 26, 27, 28, 29, 30, 07688-710, 08104-8, 08228-31, 08601-8, 08671-89, 08690-4, 08790-39, 08932-67
- Pakistan, 18261-75
- Sri Lanka, 06114-8, 18104-8, 19072-88

Lanka Sama Samaja Party, 18355, 18395-6, 18398, 18413
Laṅkavatārasūtra (Mahāyāna Buddhist text), 05082
Latin America-India relations, 44, 14106-7
law and caste, 31, 48, 09272-83, 15778-84
law and judiciary, 3, 00916-46. For regions not listed below, *see* government and politics
- ancient, 12, 04405-59
- Bengal Presidency, 73, 24271, 24273
- Bihar, 24011
- Bombay Presidency, 62, 20708-13
- British India, 31, 09244-82, 19147
- India (Rep.), 41, 12814-75, 13005-6
- Jammu & Kashmir, 23192
- Marathas, 08265
- Mughal Empire, 07572-8
- Mughal period, 24, 25, 08882-3
- Nagpur state, 08314
- Nepal, 77, 26036-8, 26190, 26193a
- Orissa, 67, 22306
- Pakistan, 52, 17379-91
- Punjab, 22628, 22633, 22635, 22700
- Sri Lanka, 56, 18317, 18524-40
- Uttar Pradesh, 71, 23461, 23520, 23555-7

law and social change, India, 48, 15745-49, 23865
law, Buddhist, 18994
law, Christian, 00920
law, constitutional. *See* constitutions
law, election. *See* elections

law, family, 3, 12, 49, 54, 15973-6020, 18102-10
law, Hindu, 3, 12, 17, 49, 00916-39, 09260-70, 10737-40, 15980-6008
law, Islamic, 3, 00940-6, 09260-70, 16011-20, 17379-91, 18102-10
law, Kandyan, 08057, 18527-8, 18531
law, labor
- British India, 36, 11141-7
- India (Rep.), 48, 15569-75
- Pakistan, 54, 18051-8
- Sri Lanka, 57, 18797-801
law, Parsi, 00923
Lawrence, John Laird Mair Lawrence, 1st Baron (1811-79), 30, 09134-8, 22615, 22627, 22743
lawyers, 41, 00931, 09281, 12865-75
leadership. *See* elites
League of Nations, 09394
leather industry, 15406, 24531
legal education, India, 50, 16557-62, 24206
legislatures. For regions not listed below *see also* government and politics
- Bihar, 23984
- British India, 31, 09152-8, 10218-9, 19150-1
- India (Rep.), 41, 12762-813, 12892-97
- Jammu & Kashmir, 23165
- Maharashtra, 21151
- Meghalaya, 26655
- Nagaland, 26528-9
- Nepal, 26014-21
- Orissa, 20796, 22287, 22294
- Pakistan, 17377-8
- Punjab, 22617, 22668
- Rajasthan, 21952, 21957, 21961
- Sri Lanka, 56, 18519-23
- Tamil Nadu, 19224
- West Bengal, 24389
legitimation of power, 5, 01871, 01873-4
Lenin, V.I., 09623
Lepchas (Himalayan people), 78, 26363, 26396, 20398-402, 26404-11
leprosy, 16261-2, 16266
Liberal Party (Great Britain), 09094
Liberal Party, India (National Liberal Federation), 10008-20
Liberation Movement, Goa, 63, 21036-42
libraries holding South Asian materials, 82, 27503-43
libraries of South Asia, 51, 55, 04510, 04518, 07646, 07650, 06909-30, 18252-4, 23440, 25615
Library of Congress, U.S., ix-x, 27417, 27508
Liccavis of Vaiśālī (ancient tribal state), 04324
licensing of business, India, 15283-8
Life Insurance Corporation of India, 14619, 16070
Līlāvatī (mathematical text), 05732
Limbdi, princely state, Kathiawar, 20620
Limbu (tribe), 26226, 26234, 26241-2
Liṅga-purāṇa, 17, 05789
Liṅgarāj temple, Bhubaneswar, 22363, 22400
Lingayats. *See* Virasaivas
linguistic philosophy, 01411-36, 15162-74
linguistic regionalism, India, xviii, 40, 12504-15
linguistic studies of South Asia, 6, 02315-679
linguistics, Indic, 14, 05162-36
Linlithgow, Victor Alexander John Hope, 2nd Marquess of (1887-1952), 34, 10394-7
literacy, 50, 54, 16660-9, 18198-9. *See also* education
literary criticism, 6, 15, 18, 02398-416, 02496-518, 05284-99, 05965-6004, 17039
literatures. *See* languages and literatures
local government. For regions not listed below, *see* government and politics
- Andhra Pradesh, 59, 19700-21
- Assam, 76, 25694, 25716-21, 25801
- Bangladesh, 75, 25229-50
- Bengal Presidency, 73, 24277-82
- Bihar, 72, 24014-29
- Bombay Presidency, 62, 20714
- British India, 31, 09214-21
- Calcutta, 74, 24731-46
- Delhi Sultanate, 07066
- Delhi U.T., 70, 23335-42
- Gujarat, 65, 21690-705, 21877
- Haryana, 70, 23272-4
- Himachal Pradesh, 25859
- India (Rep.), 41, 43, 45, 12938-3006, 13667-82, 14557-62, 15044-57, 19116
local goverment -- *continued*
- Karnataka, 61, 20259-66, 20450
- Kerala, 60, 19986-89
- Madhya Pradesh, 66, 22167-76
- Madras Presidency, 58, 19156-62
- Maharashtra, 63, 21152-95
- Meghalaya, 26657
- Mughal Empire, 24, 07544-7
- Nepal, 77, 26039-40
- Orissa, 67, 22309-14
- Pakistan, 53, 17620-55
- Punjab, 68, 22628-31, 22703-14
- Rajasthan, 66, 21979-2009
- Sri Lanka, 56, 18541-52
- Tamil Nadu, 58, 19238-42
- Uttar Pradesh, 71, 23488, 23523-57
- West Bengal, 73, 24390-6
Lodhas (tribe), 24634, 24642
Lodī dynasty, Kings of Delhi (1451-1526), 22, 07037-55
logic, 4, 13, 23, 01426-36, 04832-61, 07316-27
Login, John Spencer (1809-68), 22598
Lohars (caste), 22102-3, 23758
Lohia, Rammanohar (1910-67), Socialist leader, 09596, 13186-97
Lok Sabha (Indian parliament's lower house), 41, 12778-82
Lokahitawadi. *See* Deshmukh, Gopal Hari
lokāyata (philosophy), 12, 04594-8
lokayukta. *See* ombudsman
lokpal. *See* ombudsman
Lollaṭa (writer on poetics, 9th cent.), 05978
Lonad cave temples, Maharashtra, 05490
London, University of. *See* School of Oriental and African Studies
Lothal (Harappan site), Gujarat, 03624, 03626
lotus in Indic art, 01628, 01636, 01654
Lotus Sūtra (Mahāyāna Buddhist text), 14, 05076-8
Lucknow Pact (1916), 32, 09809-15
Lucknow, Uttar Pradesh, 71, 23693, 23842-5, 23847
Lumsden, Harry Burnett (1821-96), 09322
Lushai (tribal people), 26604-26
Lushei. *See* Lushai
Lusiad (Portuguese epic by Camoens, 1626), 07867-8, 07872
Lyall, Alfred Comyn, Sir, 20764
Lytton, Edward Robert Bulwer-Lytton, Earl of (1831-91), 30, 09143

Maathir-ul-umarā, 07397
Macartney, George Macartney, 1st Earl (1737-1806), 07795, 08183
Macaulay, Thomas Babington Macaulay, 1st Baron (1800-59), 10542
Mādhava Rāo Sindhia (1727-1794), 08309
Mādhavendra Purī, 07236
Madhu Rao I, Peshwa (1744?-72), 08296
Madhusūdana Sarasvatī (1540-1648), 30, 06394, 08942, 08944
Madhva (Ācārya of Dvaita Vedānta, 1197-1296 AD?), 20, 06469-94
Madhva (d. 1386), 06387, 06397-8
Madhya Pradesh, xxii
- adivasis, 62, 20798-818, 20843-1006
- British period, 62, 20662-79, 20764-73
- general history, 2, 00472-4
- medieval, 06702-7
- medieval art, 06880-99
- modern (1818-), 66, 22155-286
- prehistory, 03514, 03522
Mādhyamika (Mahāyāna Buddhist school), 14, 01391-100, 05090-108
Madiga (caste), 19800
Madras city, capital of Tamil Nadu, 59, 19431-53
- early history, 08195, 08199-202
- urban politics, 19158
Madras Native Association, 19175
Madras Presidency, xxi, 26, 58-9, 08179-90, 19134-95
Madras State. *See* Tamil Nadu
Madras, University of, 59, 19476, 19479, 19485
Madurai, Tamil Nadu
- as sacred center, 5, 01752, 01966-8
- modern (1801-), 19311, 19324, 19427
- Mughal period, 26, 08148-61, 08195
Madurai University, 59
Magadha kingdom, 11, 04115, 0717-81
Māgadhī (a Prakrit language), 05253
Magars (tribe), 78, 26229-30
Maghs (Arakan raiders), 08846

Magha (Kaliṅga king), 19, 06121-9
magic, 01403, 02135-41, 03925, 04457
Mahābalipuram, 19, 06185-95
- art, 20, 06613-31
Mahābhārata (Sanskrit epic), xiii, 12-3, 02413, 03759-70, 04269, 04274, 046-7=13, 04614-94
Mahābhāṣya of Patañjali, 15, 05219-20
Mahābhāṣyadīpikā (grammatical commentary), 15
Mahābodhi Temple, 05468-71
Mahadev Kolis (tribe), 20820
Mahadevan, Telliyavaram Mahadevan Ponnambalam (1911-), 00122-3
Mahādjī Shinde. *See* Mādhava Rāo Sindhia
Mahajan, Mehr Chand, jurist (1889-1967), 12840, 12843
Mahalis (tribe), 24644
Mahanadi Valley, Orissa, 22334, 22339
Mahānirvāṇa-tantra, 05892, 09263
Mahānubhāva sect, 21, 06772-6
Mahāparinirvāṇasūtra (Mahāyāna Buddhist text), 05079
Mahāprajñāpāramitāśāstra (Mahāyāna Buddhist text), 05092, 05106
Maharaj Ji, Guru, 16724
Maharaja Sayajirao University of Baroda (MSUB), 21905
Mahārājās. *See* Vallabha sect
Mahārāṣhṭa purāṇa, 08865
Maharashtra, xxii
- art, 8, 03405, 05483-93, 05572-607, 06808-29
- bibliography, 27716
- British period, 62, 20584-611, 20685-773
- drama and dance, 8, 03029-30, 03032
- general history, 2, 00449-51
- geography, 81, 17197-8
- introductions, 81, 27184, 27190, 27193, 27195-6
- medieval, 20-1, 06680-93, 06744-76
- modern (1818-), 62, 20584-611, 20685-763, 21110-1662
- Mughal period, 27, 08239-333
- music, 7, 02820, 02822, 02825
- prehistory, 03521
- sacred centers, 5, 01993-2001
- tribes, 62, 20819-28
Mahārs (caste), 35, 62, 64, 20752-63, 21403-30
Mahāsaṅghikas (Buddhist sect), 13, 04951-4
Mahāsu (deity), 25895
Mahāvairocanasūtra (tantric Buddhist text), 05920
Mahāvaṁśa (Pali chronicle of Ceylon), 11, 04229-41
Mahāvīra (540?-477 BC), founder of Jainism, 4, 01289, 01294, 01693-5, 05133-40, 05154-5
Mahāvīrācārya (c. 850 AD), mathematician, 17, 05737
Mahaweli Ganga Development Project, Sri Lanka, 18707-10
Mahāyāna Buddhism, 14, 05045-129
- origins, 13, 04951-4
Mahāyānasaṁgraha (Buddhist text), 05112
Mahé, Bertrand François. *See* Bourdonnais
Mahendra Bir Bikram Shaha Deva, King of Nepal (1920-72), 77, 25974-88
Mahesh Yogi, Maharishi, 16725, 16730
Mahimā Dharma sect, Orissa, 67, 22394-9
Mahimnastava (Śaiva text), 05841
Mahīpati (1715-90), Marathi poet, 06744-71, 08425-49
Mahisya (caste), 24630
al-Mahmud (1936-), 24945
Mahmūd Gāwān, Bāhmanī minister, 06692
Mahmūd of Ghaznī (971-1030), 06932-3
Mahratta (English newspaper from Poona), 32
Mahsud tribe, NWFP, 23052
Maithil Brahmans, 72, 24139-42, 24144-6
Maithilī language and literature, 23, 72, 02641, 02645, 02648-9, 23944, 23980, 24226-7
Maitreya (Bodhisattva), 05086
Maitreyanātha (Buddhist philosopher), 05120
Majlis-e-Mushawarat, 13291-2
Majlis Ittihad-ul-Muslimin, 19669
Majumdar, Dhirendra Nath (1903-1960), 00660
Majumdar, Kshitindranath (b. 1819), 11810
Mala Ulladan (tribe), 20152
Malabar district (now in Kerala), 26, 27, 60, 08130-47, 19912-6. *See also* Kerala
Malabari, Behramji Merwanji (1853-1912), 21372-3, 21376
Malalasekara, G.P. (1899-1973), 10264
malaria, 16264, 24810
Malas (tribe), 19796
Mālatīmādhava (Sanskrit play), 18, 06025, 06030
Mālavikāgnimitra (Sanskrit play), 15, 05355-7
Malaviya, Madan Mohan, Pandit (1861-1946), 33, 10130, 10132, 10137-8
Malaya. *See* Malaysia
Malayalam dictionaries and learning aids, 83, 27877-86
Malayalam language and literature, 7, 29, 60-1, 02586, 06593-6, 08228, 19565, 20191-222
Malaysia
- Ceylon, relations, 00366
- South Asians in, 80, 26875-6, 26881-90
Malcolm, John, Sir (1769-1833), 08319, 09173, 20706
Maldives, Republic of the, xiv, xx, 58, 19102-15
Maler (tribe), 21006
Malgonkar, Manohar (1913-), 51, 17147-51
Malik Ambar (1549-1626), 27, 08239-45
Malla dynasty, Nepal, 08984
Malpaharias (tribe), 24640
Malpan, Abraham. *See* Abraham Malpan
Malwa (plateau region of west central India), 11, 21, 28, 62, 00474, 04199, 06708-11, 08306-8
- art, 21, 28, 08463-74, 08516-9
Mamale, Māpiḷḷa merchant ruler of Cannanore, Kerala (d. 1527?), 08130
Mamallāpuram. *See* Mahābalipuram
Māmluk dynasty of Delhi, 22, 07023-36
Mammanmappila, K.C. (1873-1953), 20188
Mammaṭa (writer on poetics, fl. 1074), 18, 05994-7
man, in Indic thought, 01525-34
Man Singh, Maharaja of Marwar (1783-1843), 20647
Man Singh, Raja of Amber (1550-1614), 08372
management education, 50, 16549-56
management, industrial
- India, 48, 15230-44
- Pakistan, 54, 18026-9
management, personnel, India, 48, 15624-30
managing agency system, 36, 47, 11094-105, 15227-82
Manasā (goddess of snakes), 23, 07301, 07309-15, 24881
Mānasāra (architecture text), 06103
Manav Sewa Sangh, 16734
Mānbhāo sect. *See* Mahanubhava
Manchanna (Telugu poet, 13th cent.), 06601
maṇḍala (tantric symbolic diagram), 05869-85
Maṇḍana Miśra (Vedānta philosopher, 8th or 9th cent.), 01425, 06370
Mandi painting, 29
Mandi, princely state, Punjab Hills, 22607
Mandla, Madya Pradesh, 20889
Māndū (city in Malwa), 06879
Mangalore, Karnataka, 61, 20489-96
Mangesha Rao, Panje, 20563
Mangrol, princely state, Kathiawar, 20617
Māṇikkavācakar (Tamil poet-saint, 9th cent.), 19, 06308-23
Maṇimēkalai (Tamil epic), 16, 05446-8
Manipur, 79, 26446, 26575-603
- introductions, 81, 27320, 27324, 27341, 27348
Manipuri dance, 7, 02988-9
Manipuri language and literature, 79, 26599-603
Manjappa, Hardekar (1866-1947), 20247-50
Mañjuśrī (Bodhisattva), 05085, 05087
Maṅkha (fl. 1135-50), poet in Kashmir, 06056
Manning, William, Sir, 18353
manpower planning. *See* labor
mansabdārī system, mansabdārs, 24, 07548-71
al-Mansurah kingdom, 06927
mantra (ritual formula), 5, 14, 14790, 02124-34, 05162-74
Manu, Laws of (Manusmṛti), 04419-27, 05820
- as source, 04029
- Tirukkuraḷ and, 04506
manuscript collections, 82, 27544-65
manuscript painting. *See* miniatures
manuscripts, Sanskrit, 1, 00001-14
Manusmṛti. *See* Manu, Laws of
Maoism in India. *See* Naxalites
Mappilla uprisings, 60, 20121-34
Māppiḷḷas/Māpiḷḷas/Moplahs (Muslim group of Kerala), 27, 60, 08131, 08146, 08212-5, 20121-34, 20187
maps. *See* atlases
Mar Dionysius, 08222
Mar Gregorios, Saint (1848-1902), 20185
Māra (death, as a god), 01548
Maratha Confederacy (dominant power in pre-British India), xx, 24, 27, 07437-47, 08173-4, 08247-333, 08387
Maratha dominance, period of, xx, 24, 07437-47
Maratha-Rajput relations, 08350-78
Maratha War with British (1816-18), 08318, 08326
Marāṭhās (caste group of Maharashtra), 64, 21393, 21401
Marāṭhī dictionaries and learning aids, 83, 27908-21

Marathi language and literature, 7, 21, 27, 65, 02598-601, 06092, 06744-71, 08425-49, 08458a-61, 21633-50, 25068
Marāthwāḍā (region in Maharashtra), 64, 21173, 21464-84, 21405, 21596
Marathwada University, Aurangabad, 21405, 21596
Mardhekar, Bal Sitaram (1909-1956), Marathi poet, 21649
Maria Gonds (tribe), 20868, 20872, 20878
Markandaya, Kamala (1924-), 51, 17155-60
Mārkaṇḍeya-purāṇa, 17, 05807-11
marketing, cooperative, 15140. *See also* cooperatives
marketing, India, 46, 48, 14819-25, 15464-72
marriage. *See* kinship
marriage, age of, 35, 49, 10722-4, 15907-14
Mārtaṇḍa Varma, Maharaja of Travancore, 08134
martial law
- Bangladesh, 75, 25208-17
- Pakistan, 52-3, 17500-7, 17551-4
- South Asia, general, 1211
Martin, François (1634-1706), 26, 07918-25
Martin, Robert Montgomery, xvi
Martinique, South Asians in, 26774
Maru-Gurjara architecture, 06855-75
Mārwāṛ (Jodhpur), princely state, Rajasthan, 27, 62, 08365-70, 20640, 20647-50
Marwaris (commercial group), 11093, 11103, 15308, 24413-4
Marxism, 33, 45, 55, 10039-64, 12206-7, 12212, 13198-52, 18392-401. *See also* Communism
Marxism in literature, 16993, 17002
Marxist economic ideas, India, 14243, 14335-9
Marxist historiography of South Asia, 00137, 00163, 00166
Marxists, India, 10039-64, 12206-7, 13198-52
Marxists, Sri Lanka, 18392-401
Maryam Jameela (1934-), 18220
Mashriqī, Ināyat Allāh Khān (1888-1963), 34, 10389-91
mass media. *See* media
mass transportation, urban, India, 47, 64, 15438-43, 21527-30. For specific cities, *see* transportation
Mastā (deity), 26327
Master, Streynsham, Sir (1640-1724), 18186
materialism in Indic thought, 4, 12, 01379-90, 04594-8
maṭhas. *See* monasticism
mathematics, history of, 1, 12, 17, 00290-4, 04530-44, 05732-8, 17274
Mathurā, Uttar Pradesh
- art, 03077, 05516-53, 05562-71
- as sacred center, 5, 27, 02036-9, 03053, 08813-26
- modern, 23450, 23665, 23697
matriliny, 60, 79, 00992, 20094-104, 20137, 26669-700. *See also* kinship
mātṛkās (divine "mothers", tutelary deities), 4, 01711-38
Matsya (fish avatāra of Viṣṇu), 01799
Matsya-purāṇa, 17, 05801-6
Matsyendranātha (d.c. 1210), 07306-7
Mattavilāsaprahasana (play), 06063
Maudoodi, Syed Abul ʿAla Maulana (1903-79), 54, 17467-72, 18218-23
Maududi. *See* Maudoodi
Mauritius, South Asians in, 80, 26761-72
Maurya dynasty, 11, 04097, 05101, 04117-41
- art, 16, 05461-7
- economic history, 04374-6
- Greeks, relations, 04167
Mawdudi. *See* Maudoodi
māyā, 4, 01401-10
Mayamata (architectural text), 06608
Mayaśāstra (architectural text), 06105
Mayo, Katherine (1868?-1940), 10788-95
Mayo, Richard Southwell Bourke, 6th Earl of (1822-72), 30, 09139-40
Mayūra (Sanskrit poet, 7th cent.), 06014, 06067
Mazharul Haque (1866-1930), 09797
McMahon Line, 09445-6
mechanization of agriculture. *See* technology, agricultural
media (press, cinema, radio, TV, etc.)
- Andhra Pradesh, 60, 19883-4
- Bangladesh, 76, 25662-4
- Bihar, 72, 24236-40
- British India, 32, 10796-852
- Gujarat, 65, 21950
- India (Rep.), 51, 13538-43, 16829-16990, 19130
- Kerala, 60, 20188-90
- Maharashtra, 64, 21659-62
- Pakistan, 55, 18241-60
- Punjab, 69, 24236-40
media -- *continued*
- Sri Lanka, 57, 19056-71
- Tamil Nadu, 59, 19545-51
- Uttar Pradesh, 23484
- West Bengal, 74, 25127-40
medicine and health services. For regions not listed below, *see* social conditions
- ancient, 12, 04545-60
- Andhra Pradesh, 60, 19848-56
- āyurveda, 12, 37, 49, 00303-30, 04545-60, 16333-45, 18926-7
- Bangladesh, 76, 25584-9
- Bihar, 72, 24198-203
- British India, 35, 10673-85
- Delhi U.T., 70, 23424-33
- education, 49, 16357-76
- geography, 16210, 16251, 16253, 16265, 27013
- Gujarat, 65, 21891
- Haryana, 70, 23308-12
- India (Rep.), 41, 49, 16207-376
- Karnataka, 61, 20504-16
- Maharashtra, 64, 21546, 21562-8
- medieval, 17, 05739-43
- Nepal, 78, 26294-302, 26335, 27677
- Orissa, 67
- Pakistan, 54, 18131-45
- Punjab, 68, 22914-5, 22918
- Rajasthan, 66, 22133
- siddha, 00298, 00315, 00327
- Sri Lanka, 57, 18920-9
- Tamil Nadu, 59, 19458-68
- traditional, 00295-335, 04545-60, 95739-43, 16333-45, 16349-50, 18926-7, 26301
- unānī (Greco-Arab), 17, 05739-43
- Uttar Pradesh, 71, 23871-85
- West Bengal, 74, 24815-23
meditation in Indic religions, 5, 14, 02173-80, 05029-35
Meenakshi. *See* Mīnākṣī
Meenakshisundaran, T.P. (1901-), 02552
medium of instruction, India, 50, 16639-59
Meerut conspiracy trial (1929), 10050, 10052, 10058
megaliths, 03691-714
Megasthenes (Greek writer, 3rd cent. BC), 00403, 04018-28, 04134, 14583
Meghadūta (Sanskrit poem) by Kālidāsa, 15, 05358-62
Meghalaya, 78-9, 26649-706
- introductions, 27313, 27340
Meghani, Zaverchand Kalidas (1897-1947), 21945
Meher Bābā (1894-1969), 50, 16745-52
Mehta, Asoka, 12982-3, 13193-6
Mehta, Pherozeshah Merwanji (1845-1915), 32, 09660-3, 09666
Mehtar (caste), 22233
Meiteis (Manipur tribe), 79, 26579, 26582-3
Melville, Henry Dundas, 1st Viscount (1742-1811), 07983, 08043
Memons, 22467-8, 22470
melodic structures, Indian music (rāga), 7, 02753-8, 02829-33
Menander, Indo-Bactrian king (c. 150 BC), 14, 05003-6. *See also* Milindapañha
Menezes Bragança, Luis de (1878-1938), 21041-2
Menon, Vallathol Narayana. *See* Narayana Menon
mental health. *See also* medicine
- India, 49, 16269-74, 20363, 20922, 23875
- Pakistan, 18136
- Sri Lanka, 18923, 18926
Meos (caste), 66, 22095-100
mercenaries, European, 07822-3
La Mère. *See* The Mother
Mers (caste), 21810
merchants. *See* commerce
Mesolithic (middle stone-age), 9, 03559-67
metalanguage, 05172, 05212
metaphysics, Indic, 4, 01178, 01368-01453, 05070. *See also* religio-philosophical traditions
Metcalfe, Charles Theophilus (1837-92), 09172, 09174, 09178
meteorology in India, 10659
Mewar painting, 28, 08501-6
Mewāṛ, princely state, Rajasthan, 27, 62, 06735, 08358-64, 20645-6
Mewat, tract in Rajasthan, 66, 20634
Mesopotamia-Harappan contacts, 03628-36
mica industry, 22056

microliths, 9, 03559-67
Middle East, relations with
- British India, 31, 09395-404
- India, 44, 14085-92
- Pakistan, 53, 17753-61
- South Asians in, 80, 26871-3
Middle India Area, xxi-xxii. *See also* Goa, Maharashtra, Gujarat, Rajasthan, Madhya Pradesh, Orissa
- ancient, 11, 04195-201
- art, 8, 16, 21, 28, 03401-18, 05483-94, 05582-612, 06806-924, 08463-525
- bibliography, 82, 27713-7
- general history, 2, 00441-83
- introductions, 81, 27184-211
- languages, 83, 27908-41
- medieval, 20-1, 06680-924
- modern (1818-), 62-7, 20579-2425 (Chapter Twelve)
- Mughal period, 27-8, 08239-529
- performing arts, 8, 03029-50
- sacred centers, 5, 01993-2030
Middle Indo-Aryan language and literature,15, 05237-60
Midnapore. *See* Midnapur
Midnapur, West Bengal, 24257, 24283, 24285, 24321, 24699, 24857
migration. *See* demography; urbanization
Miji (tribe), 26498
Mikir (tribe), 25792
Milindapañha (Buddhist text), 14, 05003-6
- as source, 04573
military assistance to Pakistan, United States, 53, 17731-6
military history. *See* armed forces
milk industry. *See* dairies
Mill, James, (1773-1836)
Mīmāṁsā (school of philosophy), 13, 04862-9, 05168
Mīmāṁsā law, 04409
Mīnākṣī temple, Madurai, 5, 01966-8, 08238
Minas (tribe), 22104
miniatures (painting), 8, 25, 28, 29, 03279-85, 06830-45, 07136-58, 07342-9, 07396, 07711-27, 08463-519, 08695-752
mining, India, 47, 15346-50
minorities in India, 34, 48, 15843-67
Minto, Gilbert Elliot Murray-Kynynmound, 1st Earl of (1751-1814), 26, 08046-7
Minto, Gilbert John Elliot-Murray-Kynynmound, 4th Earl of (1845-1914), 32, 09823-37, 24301
mints, 00558
Minyong (Himalayan people), 26507
Mīr Dard (18th cent.), Sufi poet of Sind, 08682, 08829-30
Mīr Ḥasan (1727-87), Urdu poet, 07709
Mīr Jāfar (fl. 1757-65), Bengal general, 08880, 08884
Mīr Jumla (1591-1663), Aurangzib's general, 07563
Mīr, Mīr Taqī (d. 1810), Urdu poet, 07707, 07709
Mīrābāī (1515-1546), princess and poet-saint, 21, 05833, 06783-89
Mirat-i-Ahmadī, 08340-1
Mirat-i-Sikandarī, 06715
Miri (tribe), 26490
Mirzā Kamrān (d. 1557), Humāyun's brother, 07459
Mirzapur, Uttar Pradesh, 23855, 23862
misal (village group in Punjab), 22818
Mishmis (tribe), 26509
Mishra, Lalit Narayan (1923-65), 23998
Mishra, Umesha, 00027
missionaries. *See* Christianity
Mītākṣara (school of Hindu law), 17, 04439, 05703
Mithilā (region in Bihar), 29, 00510, 00514, 00519, 08782, 23980
Mitra (Vedic deity), 03839
"Mitra" dynasty, art, 16
Mitra, Rajendralala, Raja (1824-91), 24858
Mitra, Sarat Chandra, 25118
Mizo (tribe), 79, 26613-26
Mizo National Front, 79, 26606-9
Mizoram, 79, 26604-26
- introduction, 27334
mobility, social, 3, 00825-45
Modak, Ramkrishna Shahu, 21628
modern art, 38, 51, 55, 58, 76, 11800-29, 17184-204, 18276-83, 19089-98, 25665-77
modernization, economic. *See* planning, economic
modernization, social, 48, 00647, 00651, 15713-49, 18073, 18082, 21342-76, 23515-6, 24551-77. *See also* social conditions
Mody, Hormasji Peroshaw (1881-1969), 21439
Mog (tribe), 25507
Moghuls/Moguls. *See* Mughal Empire
Mohammed. *See* Muhammad
Mohenjo Daro, 9, 03612-20. *See also* Harappan civilization
Mohīniyāṭṭam (dance), 02973
Moira, Earl of. *See* Hastings, 1st Marquess of, 30, 09107-9
mokṣa ("liberation" in Indic religions), 4, 5, 01364, 01367, 10498-508
monasticism, 5, 13, 14, 01878, 01889-904, 02209-33
- Buddhist, 57, 04935-65, 06149-63, 18989-95, 25637, 26324-5, 26488
- Hindu, 02209-33, 06558, 06568, 16715
- Jain, 01891, 02187, 05141
monetary system and policy
- India, 36, 11163-82
- India (Rep.), 45, 14610-90
- Nepal, 77, 26140-7
- Pakistan, 53, 17884-912
- Sri Lanka, 56, 18654-81
moneylenders, 36, 10983-91. *See also* agricultural credit; villages
Mongoloid peoples of India, 00702
Mon-Khmer speaking peoples, 79
monsoons, 27007
Montagu, Edwin Samuel (1879-1924), 33, 10223-7, 10242
Montagu-Chelmsford Reforms. *See* Government of India Act, 1919
Mookerjee. *See also* Mukerji; Mukherjee; Mukherji; Mukhopadhyay; etc.
Mookerjee, Syama Prasad (1901-53), 13271
Mookerji, Harendra Coomar, Bengal educator, 24838
moon in Indic mythology, 5, 01836
Moplahs. *See* Mapillas
Moraes, Dom (1938-), poet, 51, 17142-4
Moraes, G.M., 00105
Morarjee, Narottam, 21334
Morgan, Richard F., Sir, 18327
Morley, Grace, 00607
Morley, John Morley, Viscount (1838-1923), 32, 09829-37
Morley-Minto Reforms. *See* Indian Councils Act of 1909
Mornington, Earl of. *See* Wellesley, R.C., Marquess
mortality. *See* demography
mosques. *See* Islamic architecture
Mossel, Jacob, 19362
The Mother (1878-1973), 47, 11400-4
Mother Goddess, 4, 01711-18
"Mother India" (critique of Indic society), 35, 10788-95
Moti Chandra, art historian (1909-74), 13110
motion pictures. *See* cinema
Mountbatten, Louis Mountbatten, Earl (1900-79), 34, 10468-73
Mṛcchakaṭikā (Sanskrit play), 15, 05308-11, 05385
mṛdaṅgam (kind of drum), 7
Mudrārākṣasa (Sanskrit play), 15, 05376-9
mudrās (gestures or poses in religion and dance), 7, 01588, 02990-4, 05300-1
Mughal Empire, xx, 24-25, 07404-802
- art, 25, 01711-802, 17184
- decline of, 24, 07524-28, 08286
Mughal period, xx, 24-30, 07386-8986 (Chapter Five)
Mughal-Rajput relations, 08350-78
Muhammad Ali Shah, King of Avadh (1777-1842), 23447
Muhammad bin Tughluq (d. 1351), King of Delhi, 07038, 07047
Muhammad Jaunpuri, 06797
Muhammad Shah (1702-48), Mughal king, 07523, 07561
Muḥammad Ṭāhir Ghani (17th cent.), 07700
Muhammadan Anglo-Oriental College. *See* Aligarh Muslim University
Muʿinuʾdīn Chishtī, Khwāja (d. 1274), 06800-1
Mujibur Rahman, Sheikh (1922-75), 52, 75, 17456-9, 17555-9, 25176-82, 25194, 25210-1, 25213-7
Mukerji, Dhurjati Prasad (1894-1961), 00663
Mukhalingam (archaeological site), 21, 06923-4
Mukherjee, Binode Behari (1904-), 11802
Mukherjee, Jyotindra Nath (1880-1915), 09754
Mukherji, Asutosh, Sir (1864-1924), 74, 24841, 24844-6
Muktananda Paramahansa, Swami, 16733, 21614
Mul Raj, A.B., 22639
Mūlamādhyamakakārikā (Buddhist text), 05091, 05094
Mulkis, Hyderabadi "insiders", 19624-7
Muller, Archibald Herman (1878-1960), 17229
Müller, Friedrich Max (1823-1900), Indologist, 38, 11852-3

Multan, Punjab, 06988, 22631, 22889
multinational corporations, 44, 13893-900
Muluki Ain, first Nepali law code, 26193a, 26197
Mumtāz (Shāh Jahān's Empress), 25
Mundari literature, 20967, 25120
Mundari-speaking tribes, 63, 20892-982
Mundas (tribal people), 63, 20892, 20948-68
municipal government and politics. *See* local government
Munᶜim Khān (1497-1575), 07560
Munje, Balkrishna Shivram (1872-1942), 20772
Munro, John (British Resident of Travancore, 1810-19), 19935-6
Munshi, Kanaiyalal Maneklal (1887-1971), 00018, 21944
Muntakhab al-lubab, 07500
Muntakhab-ut-tawarikh, 07407
murder (crime as a social problem), 18910, 18914, 18916, 20868, 20903. For political murders, *see* assassinations
Murdoch, John, evangelist in South India, 19535
Murias (tribe), 20866, 20868-9, 20879
Mushid Quli Khan, Nawab of Bengal (1695?-1727), 08869
Mushidabad, Bengal, 24253, 24261, 24696, 24700
- art, 08972
- Mughal period, 98920-1, 24404
Murugan/Murukaṉ (deity), 5, 57, 01817-25, 01948, 06511, 19029-30
Murungs (tribe), 25512
museums, 2, 00600-11, 03058
- catalogs and guides, 03065-77, 03208-27, 03456-68
music of South Asia, 7-8, 02680-903
- in literature, 05283, 05443
- Pakistan, 55, 18278-9, 18281
- Sikh, 08591
musical instruments, 02779-809
musical texts, 7, 02680-5
musicians, 7, 02810-6, 02843-5, 02873-80, 19896-902
Muslim education. *See* education, Muslim
Muslim law. *See* law, Islamic
Muslim League
- British India, 09809-15, 22461, 22645
- India, 42
- Pakistan, 52, 17453-5
Muslim literature, 02569, 02519-25, 02661. *See also* Urdu; Persian; Arabic
Muslim music and musicians, 02884-7, 02853
Muslim rule in South Asia, general histories, 07404-23
Muslims as a social group
- Assam, 76, 25681, 25783
- Bangladesh, 75, 25497-502
- Bengal, 73-4, 07199, 25332-48, 24647-54, 24739, 25136, 25497-502
- Bihar, 72, 24155-7
- British India, 37, 09599, 09762-815, 10308-93, 10641-8, 11443-527
- caste among, 2, 00752-5
- Delhi U.T., 23438
- general studies, 02257-87
- Gujarat, 65, 06712, 21847-52
- India (Rep.), 40, 48, 12445-59, 15848-57
- Karnataka, 20365-6, 20513
- Kashmir, 23234
- Kerala, 60, 20121-34, 20187
- kinship, 00979, 00988
- Lakshadweep, 20135-39
- Madhya Pradesh, 22234, 22239
- Maharashtra, 64, 21393, 21443-9
- Nepal, 78, 20269-71, 26255, 26326-7
- Punjab, 68, 22644-66
- Rajasthan, 66, 22078
- Sri Lanka, 12, 55, 56, 02279, 18860-6
- Tamil Nadu, 19, 59, 19319, 19410-5
- Uttar Pradesh, 71, 23486-90, 23759-72, 23877
- West Bengal, 73-4, 24332-48, 24647-54, 24674
Muslims, South Asian, in Africa, 26859, 26862
Muslims, South Asian, in Great Britain, 80, 26893
Mutiny, Indian, of 1857. *See* Rebellion of 1857
mutt/maṭh/maṭha. *See* monasticism
Muttollāyiram (6th? to 10th? cent. Tamil text), 06585
Myers, Leopold Hamilton (1882-1944), historical novelist, 11923, 11926
Mysore, princely state and Indian Union state, xxii, 61, 20223-43
- Mughal period, 26-27, 08162-78
Mysore city, Karnataka, 61, 20481-5
mysticism, 5, 18, 01178, 02142-52, 05937-56, 16722
mythology, xx, 4, 01576-1859
- Purāṇic, 17, 05744-5828
- Vedic, 10, 03830-57

NEFA. *See* North-East Frontier Agency
NWFP. *See* North-West Frontier Province
Nabha, princely state, Punjab, 22608
Nadars (caste), 19358-60
Nādir Shāh, King of Persia (c. 1688-1747), 07520, 07522
Nagaland State, 79, 26446, 26515-74, 27322, 27332, 27339
Nāgānanda (Sanskrit play), 05385, 06008, 06010
Nagar Haveli. *See* Dadra and Nagar Haveli
Nāgara Brahmans, Gujarat, 21831-2
Nāgārjuna (Buddhist philosopher, 2nd cent. AD?), 14, 05090-108
Nāgārjunakoṇḍa, Andhra Pradesh, 04223
- art, 16, 05509-15
Nagas (tribal people), 78, 26515-74, 26556-73, 26589
nāgas. *See* serpents
Nāgasena (Buddhist monk, c. 150 BC), 14, 05003-6
Nagbanshis (tribe), 08783
Nagpur city, Maharashtra, 64, 21133, 21177, 21488
Nagpur, princely state, 27, 62, 08314-5, 20609-11
Naidu, Sarojini (1879-1949), poet and Congress leader, 11770-80
Naikas-Naikdas (tribes), 20835
Nainital, Uttar Pradesh, 25926
Naipaul, Vidiadhar Surajprasad, Trinidad-born author, 17182
Naisadacarita (Sanskrit mahakavya), 06054, 06059, 06115
Nakkirar (Tamil poet, 8th cent.), 06511
Nalanda (medieval Buddhist center in Bihar), 07212-3, 07215-6, 07218
Nalavira Divyaprabandham (Tamil text), 19, 06288-302
Nalini, Saroj. *See* Datta, Saroj Nalini
Nallaswami Pillai, J.M. (1864-1920), Śaiva Siddhāntin, 19492
Nāmadeva (1270-1350), Marathi poet-saint, 21, 06769-71
Namboodiripad, E.M.S. (1909-), Communist leader, 10060, 13223-34
Nāmbūdiri Brahmans, Kerala, 60, 20081-5
Nāmdev. *See* Nāmadeva
Nāmdhāris (Sikh sect), 69, 22955-9
names, personal, 3, 01062-72, 19386, 20409, 17453-62
names, transliteration, 82, 27453-62
Nānā Phaḍnīs (1741-1800), Peshwa Minister, 27, 08316-33
Nānak, Guru (1469-1538), 28, 08598-635
Nanalal Dalpatram (1877-1946), 21941-3
Nanda dynasty, 11, 04101
Nando Lāla (1633-1705), writer of Persian, 07694
Nandakumāra, Maharaja (1705-1775), Dewan of Bengal, 08885
Nanddās (16th cent. Braj Bhasa poet), 08820
Nandikeśvara (Sanskrit writer on drama), 15, 05300-1
Nandy, Pritish, poet, 17175
Nanoo Pillay (1826-86), 19921
Naoroji, Dadabhai (1825-1917), nationalist leader, 32, 09657-9, 09664, 10913
Napier, Charles James, Sir (1782-1853), 09319-20, 09325, 22449, 22453
Naqshbandī Sufi order, 25, 05950
Nārada, Mahāthera, 01259
Nārada-purāna, 17, 05794
Nāradīya-dharmaśāstra. *See* Dharmaśāstras
Narain, Jai Prakash. *See* Narayan, Jayaprakash
Narasiṁha (avatāra of Viṣṇu), 01792, 01800
Narasiṁha Mehetā (1414-1481), Gujarati poet, 21, 06781-2
Narayan, Jayaprakash (1902-79), nationalist leader, 43, 10096-8, 13470-91, 14288, 24166
Narayan, R.K. (1906-), writer, 51, 17118-30
Narayana Guru (1840-1928), Kerala social reformer, 60, 20172-6
Narayana Menon, Vallathol (1878-1958), Malayalam poet, 61, 20207-9
Narayana Pillai, P.K. (1910-), Malayalam litterateur, 02590
Narmadā/Narbada River, 14892
Naropa (Tantric Buddhist philosopher), 07217
Narsiṅha Mehtā. *See* Narasiṁha Mehetā
Nāśik, city and sacred center, Maharashtra, 5, 01993-4, 21163
Natal. *See* South Africa
Nāṭakalakṣana-ratnakośa, of Sāgaranandin (11th to 13th cent.), 05999
Naṭarāja, Śiva as "Lord of the Dance," 5, 01748-53, 01962-5

Natarajan, D., xviii
Natesa Sastri, S.M. (1859-1906), 19566
Nātha sect. *See also* Gorakh Nāth, 23, 05962, 07303-8
Nāthadwāra (sacred center in Rajasthan), 02012
National Awami Party, Pakistan, 52, 17460-1
National Education Movement, 35, 10615-20
national income
- Bangladesh, 25290-1
- British India, 10884-99
- India (Rep.), 14203-11
- Pakistan, 17805-9
- Sri Lanka, 18614-9
national integration
- India (Rep.), 50, 12386-545
- Pakistan, 17411-20, 17560-7
- Sri Lanka, 18473-503
National Liberal Federation, 33, 10008-21
National Library, Calcutta, 16917-8, 27540-1
National Population Policy, India (1976), 43, 13544-5
National Social Conference, 64
Nationalist Movement, India, xiv, 31-32, 09454-10536. For regions not listed below, *see also* government and politics
- Andhra Pradesh, 59, 19641-8
- Assam, 76, 25695
- Bengal, 73, 24249, 24283-348
- Bihar, 72, 23947, 23955-73
- Bombay Presidency, 62, 20719-63
- Delhi U.T., 23323
- Jammu & Kashmir, 29, 23164-72
- Karnataka, 61, 20247-50
- Kerala, 60, 19937-44
- Madhya Pradesh, 20773
- Madras Presidency, 58, 19163-77
- Maharashtra, 20719-63
- Orissa, 20683, 20788-97
- Punjab, 68, 22632-66
- Rajasthan, 20634, 20683
- Uttar Pradesh, 71, 23467-85
Nationalist Movement, Ceylon, 55, 18342-61
nationalization of banks, India, 46, 14670-80
Native States. *See* Princely States
Nattukottai Chettiars (caste)
- Southeast Asia, 26879-80
- Sri Lanka, 18852, 18858
natural history, 8, 27024-46
natural resources
- India, 45, 14194-202
- Nepal, 26117-8
- Sri Lanka, 56, 18620-1
naturopathy, 16333-45
Nātyaśāstra (Sanskrit dramaturgy text), 15, 05289-99
"nautch" (dancing) girls, 35, 10732-4
Nav Nirman political movement, Gujarat (1974), 21666-7, 21672, 21676
Nava-Bauddhas. *See* Neo-Buddhists
Navayats (Muslim group in South Kanara), 20366
Navya-Nyāya, medieval school of Hindu logic, 07316-27
Nawanagar, princely state, Kathiawar, 20616, 20618, 20623
Naxalbari peasant revolt, 42, 13235-45
Naxalites, Maoist rebels, 42, 59, 73, 13235-52, 19694-9, 24372-6
Nayadis (tribe), 20144
Nayak dynasty of Ikkeri in Tulunadu (1500-1763), 26, 08177
Nayak dynasty of Madurai and Tanjore (16th - 17th cent.), 26, 08148-61
Nāyanārs (Tamil Śaiva poet-saints), 19, 06285-323
Nayars (caste), Kerala, 60, 19923, 20086-104
Nazīr Akbarābādī (d. 1830?), 07704
Nazrul Islam, Kazi (1899-1976), Bengali poet, 74, 25080-5
Nehru, Jawaharlal (1889-1964), 33-34, 42, 09588-95, 10087, 10095, 10099, 10147-52, 10256, 10335, 10455, 13348-98, 13726-40, 13976, 14066
Nehru, Motilal (1861-1931), 33, 09589-95, 10025, 10027-8
Nehru Report (1928), 33
Neo-Buddhists, India, 50, 64, 16761-7, 21413-30
Neolithic in South Asia, 9, 03568-685
Nepal, xiv, xx, xxii
- ancient, 04108-14
- arts, 8, 23, 30, 03447-82, 07380-5, 08985-6
- bibliography, 27738-47
- folk drama, 8, 03054
- general history, 2, 00540, 00542-3, 00545
- geography, 27373-8
- introductions, 82, 27361-407
Nepal -- *continued*
- medieval, 28, 07370-85
- modern (1816-), 76, 77-78, 25834-55, 25944-6357
- Mughal period, 30, 08973-86
- music, 7, 02779, 02891
- sacred centers, 5, 02074-7
- Sanskrit literature, 02493
- religions, 01596, 01601, 01829
- travel accounts, 25838, 27381-98
Nepal-India relations, 26053-74
Nepali Congress, 26000
Nepali dictionaries and learning aids, 83, 28008-15
Nepali language and literature, 7, 78, 02677-9, 06088, 26340-50
Netherlands. *See* Dutch in India, . . . Ceylon
networks, cultural, 3, 00846-51
neutralism (foreign policy)
- Bangladesh, 25253
- India (Rep.), 43, 13726, 13748-58
- Sri Lanka, 56, 18554
New Delhi, 70, 12235, 23418
New India (journal), 32
Newari dictionaries and learning aids, 83, 28016-7
Newari literature, 78, 26351-2
Newars (Nepalese people), 78, 26243-9, 26318
news agencies, India, 51, 16891-6
Niazi, Amir Abdullah Khan, Pakistani general, 12127
Nicholson, John (1892-1857), British general, 09332
Nicobar Islands, xxii, 79, 26710, 26713, 26717-8, 26730-1, 26734. *See also* Andaman and Nicobar Islands
Nidhiri, Emmannuel (1842-1904), 20183
Nighaṇṭu, Vedic glossary, 05181
Nihal Singh, Sant (d. 1856), Punjabi political leader, 22581
nikāyas (Buddhist texts), 14, 04984-95
Nilakanta Sastri, Kallidaikurichi Aiyah Aiyar (1892-75), historian, 00020
Nīlamata-purāṇa, Kashmiri Sanskrit text, 06942
Niles, Daniel Thambyrajah, Ceylon Christian leader, 19048
Nilgiri Hills, Tamil Nadu
- bibliography, 27708
- adivasis, 58, 19348, 19371-404
Nimbargi Maharaj (1789-1884), 20052
Nimbārka (11th cent.), philosopher of bhedabheda, 20, 06495-9
Nimbārka Sampradāya, Vaiṣṇava sect, 29, 08829
Nirālā, pseudonym of Sūrya Kānt Tripāṭhi (1896-1961), Hindi writer, 11620, 11622
Nirankāri (Sikh sect), 69, 22960-65
Nirmalā Devī (1923-), yogini, 16723
Nirukta (etymology text), 15, 05178-82
nirvāṇa, Buddhist liberation from rebirth, 4, 01498-508
Nisr ᶜAlī, Mīr. *See* Titu Mīr
Nītisāra (Sanskrit text on polity), 11, 04317
Niveditā, Sister (Margaret Elizabeth Noble, 1867-1911), 37, 11338-43
Niyogi Committee (1956), 50, 16806-10, 22282, 22284
Nizam-ud-din Ahmad (1871-1955), official of Hyderabad princely state, 19612
Nizām-ud-Dīn Awliya, Shaikh (d. 1325), Sufi saint, 22, 07112-20
Nizam's Dominions (Hyderabad-Deccan), xxi, 26, 59-60, 19611-40, 19786, 21048. *See also* Hyderabad, princely state
Nobili, Roberto de (1577-1656), Jesuit missionary, 08219
nobility
- Bengal, 24616-7
- Delhi Sultanate, 07032-4, 07065
- Marwar, 20650
- Mughal, 24, 07548-70, 07667
Noble, Margaret Elizabeth. *See* Nivedita, Sister
nomads and nomadism, 00673, 01086, 03702, 22532-49, 23102, 23774, 25889, 25920
non-alignment. *See* neutralism
Non-Brahman movements, 58, 62, 64, 19178-94, 20225, 20591-602, 20752-63
Non-Cooperation Movement (1920-22), 33, 62, 09986-10007, 24312, 24323
non-dualism. *See* advaita
Non-Mulkis, "outsiders" in Hyderabad administration, 19624-7
Non-Party Political Conference (1943-45), 10446-7
Non-Proliferation Treaty, 44, 13787-93
nonviolence, 4, 33, 01555-62, 09934-69
North America, South Asians in, 81, 26928-52

North-East Frontier Agency (NEFA), 44, 78, 26475-514. *See also* its present name, Arunachal Pradesh
North-East Area. *See* Northeast
North India Area, xx-xxii. *See also* Haryana, Delhi U.T., Uttar Pradesh, Bihar
- ancient, 11, 04108-57
- art, 8, 16, 23, 25, 03432-8, 05468-93, 05552-71, 07136-73, 07711-802
- bibliography, 83, 27729
- general history, 2, 00510-20
- introductions, 82, 27256-82
- languages, 83, 27819-48
- medieval, 22-3, 07002-173
- modern (1801-), 70-2, 23263-4240 (Chapter Fourteen)
- Mughal period, 29, 08755-839
- performing arts, 7-8, 02985-8, 03053
- prehistory, 9, 03662-9, 03730-97
- sacred centers, 5, 02031-65
North-West Area. *See* Northwest
North-West Frontier Province
- bibliography, 27725, 27727
- geography, 81, 27227
- modern (1799-), 22427, 22439, 23033-130
- travel accounts, 69, 81, 22427, 22433, 23035-47, 27242
North-Western Provinces and Oudh (now in Uttar Pradesh), 71, 00512, 23450-90
Northbrook, Thomas George Baring, 1st Earl of (1826-1904), 30, 09141-2
Northeast Area, xxi-xxii. *See also* Bengal, Assam
- art, 8, 23, 30, 03439-46, 07340-68, 08968-72
- bibliography, 83, 27730-5
- general history, 2, 00521-36
- introductions, 82, 27283-311
- languages, 83, 27984-8007
- medieval, 23, 07174-368
- modern (1813-), 73-6, 24241-5833 (Chapter Fifteen)
- Mughal period, 29-30, 08840-973
- performing arts, 8, 03051-2, 03055
- sacred centers, 5, 02066-7
Northwest Area, xxi. *See also* Sind, Baluchistan, Punjab, North-West Frontier Province, Jammu & Kashmir
- ancient, 11, 04158-94
- art, 8, 16, 22, 29, 03419-31, 05522-51, 06996-7001, 08695-754
- bibliography, 83, 27718-28
- general history, 2, 00484-509
- introductions, 81, 27212-55
- languages, 83, 27942-83
- medieval, 21-2, 06925-7001
- modern (1799-), 67-70, 22426-3262 (Chapter Thirteen)
- Mughal period, 28-9, 08530-839
- prehistory, 9, 03578-661
Nowrosjee Wadia College, Poona, 21599
Nṛttaratnāvalī (Sanskrit text on dance, c. 1253), 02681
nuclear power
- India (Rep.), 47, 15369-74
- Pakistan, 18030-2
nuclear weapons policy
- India (Rep.), 44, 13772-86, 14030
- Pakistan, 53, 17690-6
numismatics, xvi, 2, 00546-58
- ancient, 10, 04063-77
- medieval, 17, 05675-86, 06196
- Mughal period, 24, 07394-403
Nūr Jahān (1577?-1646?), Mughal Empress, 24, 07480-9
nutrition, 16249-59, 23871, 23886, 24203, 24643, 25584, 25588. *See also* medicine and health services
Nuwara Eliya, Sri Lanka hill station, 18908
nyāya (Hindu system of logic), 13, 23, 01430, 04832-61, 07316-27
nyaya panchayats (village courts), 71, 23555-7. *See also* law and judiciary
Nyāyasūtra, of Gautama (2nd cent. BC?), 13, 04832-61

Ochre Colored Pottery, 9, 03662-9
Odissi, style of dance in Orissa, 03036-50
official language
- India, 40, 12485-503
- Sri Lanka, 56, 18489-509
O'Flaherty, Wendy Doniger, xv
oil industry. *See* petroleum
oil, vegetable, 14904, 14908, 26179
Oman, prehistoric contacts with, 03695, 03708
ombudsman, proposals for, India, 41, 12691-9, 21977
omens, 5, 02136
Onam (festival), Kerala, 02117
Onges (tribe), 26720
Ootacamund, Nilgiri district, 11971-2
opium trade, 73, 24397
oral tradition. *See* folklore
Oraons (tribal group), 63, 20892, 20983-93
orientalism, 39, 11836-53, 24566
Orissa, xxii
- art, 16, 21, 03408, 03414, 06900-24
- general history, 2, 00475-83
- geography, 27203
- introductions, 81, 27189
- medieval, 21, 00694-701, 06802-5
- modern (1818-), 62, 67, 72, 20680-4, 20774-97, 22287-425
- Mughal period, 27, 08378, 08392
- prehistory, 03517
- sacred centers, 5, 02015-30
- tribals, 21007-34
Oriya dictionaries and learning aids, 83, 27934-41
Oriya language and literature, 7, 67, 02609-11, 22404-19
Osmania University, Hyderabad, 19866
Ostend Company, 07811, 08855
Oudh. *See* Avadh
overseas South Asians, 26737-951

PL 480. *See* Public Law 480
Pabna, Bengal, peasant unrest, 24508-9
Padams (tribe). *See* Abors
Padamsee, modern artist, 17227
Padmanabhan, Mannath (1878-1970), Nayar social worker, 20087
Padma-purāṇa, 17, 05815
Padmāvat, story of Queen Padminī of Chitor, 07689
Padra, town, Gujarat, 21869
Padshah-buranji, Assamese chronicle, 07193
Pahāṛī language, 02677
Pahari painting, 08695-752
Paharis (mountain people), 77, 25856-943
Paharpur (ancient Somapura), Bengal, 07361-8
Pai, Nath (1924-71), socialist leader, 21127
Pai, Tonse Madhava Anantha, Dr. (1898-1970), educator in Karnataka, 20517
painting. *See* art and architecture; miniatures
Paite (tribe), 26588
Pakhtunistan movement (of Pashto speakers), 69, 23074-80
Pakhtuns. *See* Pathans
Pakistan, xiv, xxi, 52-55, 17283-8288 (Chapter Nine)
- bibliography, 27660-75
- general history, 2, 00181
- geography, 27110-7
- introductions, 81, 27087-129
- origins, 34, 10288, 10320-393
Pakistan People's Party, founded by Bhutto, 52, 17462-6, 17568-600, 22715-6
Pal, Bipin Chandra (1858-1932), Bengali nationalist, 32, 09713-7, 24888
Pāla dynasty (730-1197), 23, 07174-81, 07198
- art, 23, 07340-68
palaeography. *See* epigraphy
palaeolithic in South Asia, 9, 03546-58
Pali Canon. *See* Buddhism, texts
Pali chronicles of Ceylon, 11, 04429-41
Pali dictionaries and learning aids, 83, 27807-15
Pāli language and literature, 11, 14-15, 19, 04229-41, 05240-5, 05968, 06144-8
Pallava dynasty (250-900 AD), 11, 19, 04227-8, 04584, 06185-95
- art, 20, 06613-31
Palnāṭi-vīracaritra, Telugu epic, 06602-3
Paluskar, Vishnu Digambar (1872-1931), musician, 02843, 02847
Pampa (Kannada poet, 10th cent.), 06597
Pāñcarātra (Vaisnava sect), 13, 20, 04775-88, 06408-4, 19901
Pañcasiddhāntikā (astronomy text), 04537, 04539
Pañcatantra (Sanskrit story collection), 15-6, 05394-405, 06074
Panchasheel ("Five Principles"), 43, 13737-40
panchayat system, Nepal, 77, 25975-88, 26014-21
panchayati raj. *See* local government
Pāṇḍavas, opponents of Kauravas in Mahabharata, 12-13
Paṇḍharpur (sacred center in Maharashtra), 5, 21, 01993-2001

Pandit, Vijaya Lakshmi (Nehru) (1900-), nationalist leader and diplomat, 12749-61
Pandits, Brahmans of Kashmir, 23168, 23225, 23237, 23239-40
Pāṇḍuranga (deity). *See* Viṭhobā
Pāṇḍya dynasty, early Tamil kingdom, 11, 00407, 00412, 04202-21, 02555, 06183
- art, 20, 06611-12
Panikkar, Kavalam Madhava (1896-1960), administrator and diplomat, 00121, 00124
Pāṇini (4th cent. B.C. Sanskrit grammarian), 15, 05168, 05190-218
- as historical source, 04030
Panipat, battle of (1761), 27, 08300, 08302
Panjab. *See* Punjab
Panjab University, Chandigarh, 22934
panji system (genealogies of Maithil Brahmans), 24141-2, 24144-6
paper industry, 00345, 00349, 05413, 25770, 26611
Parajas (tribe), 22423
Paramāra dynasty of Malwa, 21, 06708-11
Paramārthasāra (Kashmir Saiva text), 06975
Parameśvara Iyer, Ulloor S. (1877-1949), Malayalam poet, 61, 20213-15
paramilitary forces
- Bangladesh, 25196
- India (Rep.), 41, 12706, 12713, 12715, 12716
Paramountcy, British, in relation to princely states, 31, 09335-83
Paranavitana, Senarat (1896-1972), 00023, 00389
Paranjpe, Vasudeva Gopal (1887-), Indologist, 00016
Paraśurāma (avatāra of Viṣṇu), 01794, 01797
pardā/purdah, "curtain" (seclusion of women), 35, 00954, 10734-6, 22234, 22538, 24664
Pardhāns (tribe), 20885, 20887
Parekh, Manilal Chhotalal (1885-1967), historian of religions, 16800
Parhaiyas (tribe), 21001
Parikh, Govardhan Dhanaraj (1915-76), Radical Humanist and author, 13197
Paripāṭal (Sangam period Tamil anthology), 05415, 06587
Parliamentary Papers, Great Britain, guides, xvii, 27679
parliamentary privileges, India, 09155, 12787-98
parliaments. *See also* legislatures
- India (Rep.), 41, 12551, 12762-813
- Pakistan, 52, 17377-8
- Sri Lanka, 18379, 18382, 18519-23
Parsis (Indian Zoroastrians), 6, 50, 64, 00923, 02288-310, 07664, 09155, 18235, 21202, 21332-3, 21431-42
Pārśvanātha (Jaina saint), 14, 05130, 05132
Parthians in India, 11, 04171-5
parties, political
- India (Rep.), 41-3, 13124-13315, 13716-25, 19121
- Pakistan, 17448-72
- Sri Lanka, 18389-402
partition of Bengal (1905), 73, 24289-304
partition of India (1947), 34, 10288-536
Parulekar, Ramachandra Vithal (1886-), educationist, 21576
Pārvatī (goddess), 5, 15
Pashto/Pakhto dictionaries and learning aids, 83, 27972-83
Pashto language and literature, 7, 28, 02636-9, 08691-2
Pāśupatas (early Śaiva sect), 13, 04754-63
Pātaliputra (ancient Patna), Bihar, 04120, 05466-7
Patañjali (author of Yogasūtra), 13, 04818-31
Patañjali (grammarian), 15, 05194, 05219-20
- as historical source, 04035
Patel, Vallabhbhai Jhaverbhai (1875-1950), Congress leader, 33, 09590, 10176-91
Patel, Vithalbhai Jhaverbhai (1873-1933), legislator, 33, 10029
"Path of Purity", Theravāda Buddhist text. *See* Visuddhimagga
Pathan language and literature. *See* Pashto
Paṭhāns (Pashto-speaking tribes), 2, 69, 00498-9, 22433, 23033-4, 23042, 23103-15
Patiala, princely state, Punjab, 22606
Patiala and East Punjab States Union (PEPSU), 22695
Patidars (caste), in Gujarat, 65, 21767, 21835-6
Patil, Bhaurao (1887-1959), rural educator, Maharashtra, 20754
Patna, Bihar, 72, 24174, 24180-6
Patna College, 24215
pats/patas, Bengali drawings, 11798-9
Pattabhi Sitaramayya, Bhogaraju, 19641
Pattini (deity), Sri Lanka, 19007, 19009, 19011
patwaris (village registrars), 17653
Paumacariyam (Prakrit text), 05259
Pawar dynasty. *See* Puar
peacock, in art and symbolism, 01612, 01618-9, 01625
peasant life. *See* villages
peasant movements and revolts
- Bengal, 73, 08898, 24101, 24500-9
- Bihar, 72, 23964-73, 24101-5
- British period, 36, 10996, 20759
- India (Rep.), 13235-45
- Kerala, 60, 20033-41
- Maharashtra, 64, 20823, 21273-82
- Punjab, 68, 22737-46
- Tamil Nadu, 19304
- Uttar Pradesh, 71, 23656-63
Pengo Porajas (tribe), 21034
Pennell, Theodore Leighton (1867-1912), 23041
percussion instruments, 7, 02800-09
Perera, Edward Walter, Ceylon nationalist leader, 18346
Perera, Nananayakkarapathirage Martin (1905-), Ceylon political leader, 18413
performing arts, xx, 7-8, 02680-3055
- ancient drama, 15, 05264-387
periodical literature, guides to, 82, 27583-622
Periplus of the Erythraean Sea, 04024, 04027
Periya-purāṇam (biographies of Tamil Śaiva saints), 19, 06320-3, 06643
Permanent Settlement (1793), 29, 08903-9
Persian dictionaries and learning aids, 83, 27816-8
Persian Gulf States, South Asians in, xxiii
Persian literature of South Asia, 6, 22, 02519-27, 07688-702, 11642-71
Persian historical sources, 07392
person and group in Indic society, 3, 12, 01052-61
Peshawar, NWFP, 69, 23124-7
Peshwa Daftar (Marathi records), 08249-50, 08413
Peshwas (Brahman prime ministers in 18th cent. Maharashtra) 27, 08296-333
petroleum industry, India, 47, 11108, 15365-8, 15409, 25772-3
Phadke, Vasudeo Balvant (1845-83), rebel leader, 20724
Phanse-Paradhis (tribe), 20825
pharmaceuticals industry, Pakistan, 18035
pharmacology, Indic, 00331-5
Philippines, South Asians in, 26874
philology, 6, 38, 02329-86, 11836-53
philosophy, contemporary, 37, 50, 55, 11425-42, 11692-705, 18238-40
philosophy, Indic. *See* religio-philosophical traditions
phonetics, classical Indic, 15, 05175-7
Phule, Jotirao Govindrao (1827-90), Maharashtrian social reformer, 20753, 20756
Phulkian princely states, Punjab, 22602
physicians. *See* medicine
Pieris, Hannadige Jeronis Pieris (elite member of Karava caste, Ceylon), 18331, 18841
pilgrimage, xii-xiii, 5, 01905-2977, 21919, 24222, 23243. *See also* sacred centers; temples
Piḷḷai Lokācārya (1264-1327), Śrī-Vaiṣṇava leader, 20, 06456-68
Pindaris, early 19th cent. marauding bands, 08316-33
Pithalkhora rock temples, 05486
plague, 24823
planning, agricultural. *See* agriculture; planning, economic
Planning Commission, India, 45, 14400-15
planning, economic. For areas not listed below, *see also* economic conditions
- Andhra Pradesh, 59, 19725-37
- Assam, 76, 25742-7
- Bangladesh, 75, 25314-30, 25372-430
- Bihar, 72, 24033-49
- British India, 36, 11192-8
- Delhi U.T., 70, 23346-50
- Goa, 63, 21071-83
- Gujarat, 65, 21716-19, 21735-45
- Haryana, 70, 23276-81
- Himachal Pradesh, 77, 25873-4
- India (Rep.), 44-46, 13510-6
- Karnataka, 61, 20280-94
- Kerala, 60, 20002-11
- Madhya Pradesh, 66, 22188-97
- Maharashtra, 63, 21219-26
- Nepal, 77, 26122-39

planning, economic -- *continued*
- Orissa, 67, 22327-8
- Pakistan, 53, 17846-83
- Punjab, 56, 22751-5
- Rajasthan, 66, 22015-22
- Sri Lanka, 56, 18622-53
- Tamil Nadu, 58, 19259-69
- Uttar Pradesh, 71, 23571-83, 23598
- West Bengal, 73, 24429-35
planning, education
- India, 50, 16400-41
- Pakistan, 54, 18159-80
planning, social, India, 48, 15733-43
planning, urban. For cities not listed below, *see also* urbanization
- ancient period, 04519-24
- Bombay, 64, 21516-26
- Calcutta, 74, 24772-82
- Delhi, 70, 23412-23
- India (Rep.), 49, 16082-101
- Madras, 59, 19444-53
plant diseases, 14898, 14901
plant symbolism, 4, 01628-41
plantations and plantation labor
- Assam, 76, 11030, 25722-33, 25789-90
- Bengal, 73, 24443-49
- Darjeeling, 26391-2, 26394-5
- overseas, 80, 26761-815
- South India, 19249
- Sri Lanka, 56, 18727
- Tripura, 26639
plants of South Asia. *See* botany
Plassey, battle of (1757), 26, 08017-25
Plato, 03994
poetics, 02496-2518, 05965-6004
Point Four (1950), 44, 14036-45
Pokharan (Rajasthan), nuclear test, 1974, 44, 13782, 13784, 13786
Poleman, Horace I., ix
police. For regions not listed below, *See also* administration
- Bangladesh, 25196, 25225
- Bihar, 24013
- Bombay city, 21184
- British India, 31, 09222-43, 19142
- Himachal Pradesh, 25860
- India (Rep.), 41, 12700-16
- Orissa, 22307
- Pakistan, 52, 17375-6
- Punjab, 22622, 22626, 22629
- Sri Lanka, 18510, 18513
- Uttar Pradesh, 71, 23521
- West Bengal, 24360, 24387
political cartoons, 42, 13114-23
political history. *See* government and politics
political parties. *See* parties, political
political science, bibliography, 12286-93, 27678
political science in India, 40, 12294-9
political thought, 00221-35. *See also* kingship
- ancient, 04265-319
- British period, 09530-45
- medieval, 05757
- Mughal period, 07529-32
- Vedic, 03781-6, 03923
pollution, environmental, India, 49, 16236-48
pollution, ritual. *See* purity and pollution
Polonnāruva, Ceylon, 19, 06118, 06121-9
- art, 19, 06171-5
polyandry, 01011, 04470, 18838, 19402-3, 20102-3, 25887, 25917, 25933. *See also* kinship
Pondicherry/Pondichéry (former French colony, now a Union Territory in South India), 26, 58, 07902-40, 19195, 19264, 19318, 19320, 27162
Pongal (festival), 02107-8
Poona/Pune, Maharashtra, 27, 74, 08296-333, 21175-6, 21337-8, 21378, 21539-58
Poona Sarvajanik Sabha, social reform group, 20729
Poona, University of, 21598
population. *See* demography; family planning
pornography, 16848. *See also* censorship
Port Blair, Andaman Islands, 26715
Portuguese in Ceylon, 26, 08056, 08069-81
Portuguese in India, 25, 27, 29, 63, 07841, 08130, 08132, 08147-8, 08203a-4, 08255, 08334-9, 08347, 08388, 08853, 21035-109
Portuguese literature of Goa, 63, 21099-106
Posnett, Charles Walker (1870-1950), Methodist missionary in Andhra, 19880
postal service, 47, 15455-9, 19928
Potana, Bammēra (Telugu poet, 15th cent.?), 06604
potato cultivation, 23290
pottery
- Harappan, 03603
- prehistoric, 03528-9, 03740
poverty. *See also* economic conditions
- India, 45, 14277-85
- Pakistan, 18126
power, legitimation of. *See* legitimation
Prabartak Samgha, Bengal social reform group founded by Motilal Roy, 24809
Prabhavananda, Swami, Vedanta leader in Hollywood, 02221
Prabhus (caste), 21396-7
Praja Socialist Party, 13184-5, 23494
Prajāpati (deity), 03842
Prājñāpāramitā literature (Mahāyāna Buddhism), 14, 05062-75
Prakasam, Tangutur (1872-1957), Madras and Andhra Congress leader, 19645
Prakrit dictionaries and learning aids, 83, 27807-15
Prakrit languages and literatures (vernaculars of ancient India), 13, 15, 05246-60, 05279
prāṇāyāma (yogi breath control), 02166
prapatti (divine grace), 06445, 06448
Prasad, Jai Shankar (1889-1937), Hindi writer, 11618-9, 11621
Prasad, Rajendra. *See* Rajendra Prasad
Pratap Singh (d. 1597), Rana of Mewāṛ, 08360-1, 08363
Pratap Singh, Sir (1845-1922), Maharaja of Idar, Gujarat, 20649
Pratapsingh (d. 1847), Raja of Satara, 20604
Pratyabhijñāhṛdayam (Kashmir Śaiva text), 06959, 06967, 06971
Pratyabhijñā-kārikā (Kashmir Śaiva text), 06968
Pravarasena II Vakataka (c. 410-440 AD), 05251
pravargya (Vedic ritual), 03871-2
Pravir Chandra Bhanjdeo Katatiya, Maharaja of Bastar (1929-66), 20666, 22176
Prayāg, sacred center, 5, 02040-2, 02099. *See also* Allahabad
prehistory of South Asia, xx, 9-10, 03483-797 (Chapter Two)
Premchand (1880-1936), Hindi and Urdu author, 38, 11600-30
Presidency College, Calcutta, 24849
President, office of
- India, 40, 12546, 12551, 12565-92
- Pakistan, 52, 17324-5
President's rule, India, 40, 12373-9
- Gujarat, 21678
- Orissa, 22292
press and journalism
- Andhra Pradesh, 60, 19883-4
- Bangladesh, 76, 25662
- Bengal, 74, 25127-37
- Bihar, 72, 24236
- British India, 35, 10796-852
- Gujarat, 65, 21950
- India (Rep.), 43, 51, 13538-43, 16831-96, 19130
- Kerala, 60, 20188-90
- Maharashtra, 21660-1
- Pakistan, 55, 18241-9
- Punjab, 69, 23030-2
- Sri Lanka, 57, 19056-71
- Tamil Nadu, 59, 19545-8
- Uttar Pradesh, 23484
- West Bengal, 74, 25127-37
prices
- British India, 10891, 10938
- India (Rep.), 45, 14642-55, 14831-41
- Pakistan, 54, 17903-7
prices, agricultural, India, 46, 14831-41
Prime Minsiter
- India, 40, 42-3, 12593-600
- Pakistan, 52, 17324-25
Princely States, xvii, xxi, xxiii, 27, 31, 09288, 09335-83, 10463, 20584-684
- Himalayan rim area, 77, 79, 25856-8, 26627-35
- integration of, 34, 40, 10534-6, 12538-45
- Middle India, 62, 20584-685
- Northwest area, 67, 68, 69, 22515-22, 22602-10, 23133-73

Princely States -- *continued*
  South India, 59, 60, 61, 19611-33, 19917-44, 20223-43
printing, 07651, 10819, 24237
prisons, 16184-200, 19455, 21559, 22128, 26709, 26712
Pritam, Amrita. *See* Amrita Pritam
Prithvirāja rāsau (Hindi bardic romance), 06724
private sector industries. *See also* industry
  - India, 42, 45, 47, 15255-45
  - Pakistan, 54, 18020-5
privy purses (of former Princes), 40, 12538-45
Priyadarsīka (Sanskrit play), 06007
products, agricultural, 46, 14897-945
prohibition of alcohol. *See* alcohol use; temperance movements
property rights of women, 3, 35, 01016-22, 19737-40. *See also* law
prostitution, 35, 49, 10732-3, 16164-73, 19854, 21541
Protestantism. *See also* Christianity
protohistory, 9-10, 03483-4008 (Chapter Two)
proverbs
  - Marathi, 02601
  - Panjabi, 22757
  - Pashto, 02636
  - Tamil, 02565
provincial and state government. *See also* names of specific states and provinces
  - British India, 31, 09214-21
  - India (Rep.), 41, 12876-938
  - Mughal Empire, 24, 07544-7
  - Pakistan, 53
psychology
  - comparative, 4, 01353
  - Indic, 4, 01456-79
psychology in India, 48, 15677-712
Ptolemaeus, Claudius (Ptolemy), Greek account, 04021, 04028
Puar dynasty of Dewas Senior princely state, 20665, 20668-9
public administration. *See* administration
public administration education, 50, 16549-56
public assistance, 49, 16141-9
public finance. *See* finance, public
public health. *See* medicine
public investment, foreign. *See* foreign aid
Public Law 480 (U.S.), x, 44, 14046-53
public relations in India, 51, 16931-4
public schools, 50, 16625-30
public sector industry. *See also* industry
  - India (Rep.), 47, 15207-50, 10768-9, 22061, 23672
  - Nepal, 26175-6
  - Pakistan, 54, 18015-9
  - Sri Lanka, 56, 18782-86
Public Service Commission, Ceylon, 18509
Public Service Commissions, India, 41, 12640-47
publishing industry
  - Bangladesh, 25609-10, 25663
  - India (Rep.), 51, 64, 16897-908, 21659
  - Pakistan, 55, 18250
  - reference guides, 82, 27566-82
pūjā (ritual of worship), 5, 02124-34
Pūjyapāda (Jaina philosopher), 05152
Pukalēnti (Tamil poet, 13th cent.), 06589
Pulayas (tribe), Kerala, 20145
Pulleyar (deity), Sri Lanka, 19008
Pune. *See* Poona
Punjab (incl. both the Indian state and the Pakistan province), xxii
  - ancient, 11, 03756, 04162
  - bibliography, 27724
  - general history, 2, 00491-7
  - geography, 27228
  - introductions, 81, 27216, 27210, 27245
  - medieval, 22, 06929-36
  - modern (1799-), 68, 69, 22427, 22429, 22432, 22435, 22554-3032
  - Mughal period, 28, 08531-56, 08565-666
  - partition (1947), 10486, 10490-510
  - prehistory, 03513, 03623
Punjab Hill States (princely states), xxii, 08555-6, 22602-10
Punjab National Unionist Party, 22645, 22656
Punjab University, Lahore, 22919, 22928-9
Punjabi dictionaries and learning aids, 83, 27953-66
Punjabi language and literature, 7, 28, 83, 69, 02621-9, 08686-8, 08693-4, 22996-3020
Punjabi Suba (linguistic state) movement, 22674-88
puppet plays, 8, 03005-13
puṟam (heroic) poetry in Tamil, 16, 05434-6
Puran Singh (1881-1931), Punjabi author, 23008
Purāṇa-mayamataya (Sinhalese text on architecture), 06166
purāṇas (Hindu mythological texts in Sanskrit), xxi, 10, 17, 01120, 01705, 01710, 04052-6, 05744-827
  - as sources, 04038-51
  - Kannada versions, 06598
  - minor (Upa-purāṇas), 05823-7, 06777
Purandaradāsa (fl. 1550), Kannada poet-saint, 06488-94
purdah (seclusion of women). *See* pardā
Purī, Orissa, city and sacred center, 02015-30, 22376, 22386-93
purity and pollution, 00818-24
Purnea district, Bihar, 08778
Purniah/Purnaiya (1732-1812), dewan of Mysore State, 20239-40
Purums (tribe), 79, 26584-7, 26592, 26595
puruṣa, "consciousness" in Sāṅkhya, 13
Pūrva-mīmāṁsā, school of philosophy, 13, 04862-9
Pūrva-mīmāṁsā-sūtra of Jaimini, 13, 04862-9
Pūrvānchal, eastern frontier region of Nagaland, Manipur, Tripura, and Mizoram, 78-9
Pūṣan (Vedic deity), 03831, 03846
Pushtu. *See* Pashto
Pushtuns. *See* Pathans
Puṣṭimārga (Hindu sect), 20, 06500-7
Puttappa, K. Venkatappa Gowda (1904-), pseud. Kuvempu Kannada poet, 20575

Qadian (town in Punjab) and Qadianism. *See* Ahmadiyya
Qādirī Sufi order, 05950
Qaᶜid-i-Aᶜẓam. *See* Jinnah, Mahomed Ali
Qalandar Lal Shahbaz (1177-1274), Sind sufi, 06987
Quaderi, Shaheed, 24945
Quaid-e-Azam. *See* Jinnah, Mahomed Ali
Quakers. *See* Friends, Society of
"Qualified Non-Dualism" (Viśiṣṭādvaita), 20, 06408-68
"Quit India" Movement (1942), 34, 10413-31, 25695
Qutb Minar (monument at Delhi), 07159-73
Qutb Shāhī Sultanate of Golkoṇḍa, 26, 08112-25
Qutb-ud-dīn Aibak (d. 1210), Sultān of Delhi, 07035

RSS. *See* Rashtriya Swayamsevak Sangh
races of South Asia, 2, 00690-709
Rādhā-Kṛṣṇa Vaiṣṇavism, 20, 23, 29, 06408-507, 07228-92, 08113-27, 08940-5, 16756-60. *See also* Vaiṣṇavism
Radha Soami sect, 23913, 23916, 23918, 23923-4, 23928
Radhakrishnan, Sarvepalli, Sir (1888-1975), philosopher and President of India, 37, 40, 11227, 11432-42, 12575-9
Rādhāvallabha Sampradāya (Vaiṣṇava sect), 29, 08825
Rāḍhiya Brahmans of Bengal, 24621
Radical Humanism, philosophy of M.N. Roy, 33, 10065-86
radio, 51, 55, 57, 16935-43, 18259, 21746
rāga in Indic music, 7, 02753-8
Raghavan, Venkatarama (1908-1979), 00019
Raghavendra, Swami (1601-61), Dvaita Vedānta exponent, 08209
Raghunātha Śiromaṇi (15th cent.?), Navya Nyāya logician, 07316-27
Raghuvaṁśa (Sanskrit mahākāvya), 15, 05363-7
Ragland, Thomas Gajetan (d. 1858), missionary, 19539
Rahman, Mujibur, Sheikh. *See* Mujibur Rahman, Sheikh
Rahman, Shamsur, Bengali poet, 24945
Rahman, Ziaur, Gen. *See* Ziaur Rahman
Rahmat ᶜAlī, Choudhary (1897-1951), author of "Pakistan" idea, 34, 10329-31
Rahula, Śrī (Sinhala poet, 15th cent.), 06148
Rai, Lajpat. *See* Lajpat Rai, Lala
Rai (Nepalese ethnic group), 78, 26235
Raidās (North Indian Rām bhakta, 15th cent.), 22, 07093-4
railways. *See* transportation
Raj. *See* British India; *see also* present states/provinces for history during British rule
Raj Singh (fl. 1651-80), Rāṇā of Mewāṛ, 08364
Raja Birbal (d. 1586), Mughal courtier, 07564
Raja Rao (1909-), Indo-Anglian novelist, 51, 17131-5
Rāja Yoga of Patañjali, 13, 04818-31
Rajagopalachari, Chakravarti (1879-1972), Indian statesman, 33, 10197-209
Rājagṛha. *See* Rājgīr
Rajaji. *See* Rajagopalachari, Chakravarti
Rajan, Ponambala Tyagarajan (1892-), Tamil political leader, 19187

Rajaraja Varma, A.R. (1863-1918), Malayalam and Sanskrit scholar, 20192
Rājārām I (second son of Shivājī), King of Marathas (1689-1700), 27
Rājaśekhara (Prakrit writer, c. 860-c. 930), 05255
Rajasthan, xxii
- ancient, 16, 04163
- art, 16, 21, 28, 03401, 03410, 03412, 03417-8, 06830-79, 08476-519
- general history, 2, 00463-71
- geography, 81, 27200-1
- introductions, 27186-7, 27192, 27194, 27207, 27210
- Jainism, 01152, 01281
- medieval, 21, 06724-41, 06777-801
- modern (1818-), 62, 67, 20634-61, 21951-2154, 22432
- Mughal period, 27, 08350-76, 08401
- music, 8, 02784, 02844, 02895
- prehistory, 03509, 03516
- Princely states, 62, 20634-61
- sacred centers, 5, 02009-14
- tribes, 62, 20828-42
Rajasthan Canal, 66, 22038
Rajasthani literature, 66, 08462, 22145-9
Rajasthani painting, 28, 08479-519
rājasūya (Vedic royal consecration), 04285
Rājataraṅgiṇī (Kashmir chronicle, c. 1148 AD), 22, 06937-43
Rājendra (fl. 1012-44), Cōḷa king, 06202
Rajendra Prasad (1884-63), first President of India, 33, 40, 12565-74
Rajgir (sacred center in Bihar), 5, 02060
Rajneesh, Acharya (1931-), 50, 16753-55
Rajputana. *See* Rajasthan
Rajputana Agency, 20644
Rajput clans
- general history, 2, 00463-71
- medieval, 21, 06707-11, 06724-41
- Mughal period, 21, 27, 08350-76
- modern, 62, 67, 77, 21402, 22084-9, 23732-4, 25892, 25957-92
Rajshahi city, Bangladesh, 25564
Rajshahi University, 25626
Rajya Sabha (Indian upper house of Parliament), 41, 12774-7
Ram, Jagjivan (1908-), "untouchable" Congress leader, 13640-50
Rām Dās, Sikh Guru (1534-81), 28, 08636
Ram Mohun Roy. *See* Roy, Ram Mohan
Ram Tirth, Swami (1873-1906), Punjabi spiritual leader, 69, 22970-4
Rāma (avatār of Viṣṇu), 5, 13, 15, 18, 04695-730, 05363-8. *See also* Rāmāyaṇa; Vaiṣṇavism
- cult of, 22, 29, 07089-110, 08790-24
Ramā Devī (1911-78), yoginī, 16732
Rāma Pāṇivāda (late Mahārāṣṭri Prakrit writer, c. 1707-75), 05259
Rama Rao, Damerla (1897-1925), painter of Andhra school, 11827
Rama Rao, Santha (1923-), Indo-Anglian writer, 17176
Rama Varma, Maharaja of Travancore (1758-98), 08145
Rama Varma Kulaśekhara Perumal (1813-46), Maharaja of Travancore, 02879
Ramābāī Sarasvatī, Panditā (1858-1922), social reformer, 21359-60, 21365, 21367-8
Ramachandran, M.G., Tamil Nadu politician, 19225-6, 19550
Rāmadāsa (Maharashtrian poet-saint, 1608-81), 28, 08443-9
Ramakrishna Mission, religious and social reform organization, 37, 11344-52, 16735
Rāmakrishna Paramahaṁsa (1834-86), Bengali mystic, 37, 11294-312
Ramakrishnananda, Swami (1863-1911), 19509
Ramalinga Reddy, Cattamanchi. *See* Reddy, Cattamanchi Ramalinga
Ramalinga Swami (1823-74), Tamil devotee of Murugan, 19497, 19504, 19508
Raman, Chandrasekhara Venkata (1888-1970), Indian physicist, 17279
Ramana Maharṣi (1879-1950), 37, 02232, 11405-18
Rāmānanda (1400-1470), North India Rama-bhakta, 22, 07093-5
Ramanathan, Ponnambalam (1851-1930), Ceylon nationalist leader, 18342, 18349
Rāmānuja (1017?-1137?), Vedānta philosopher, 20, 01400, 06396-468
Ramanujam, C.P. (1938-74), Indian mathematician, 17274
Ramanujan, A.K. (1929-), poet and scholar, 51, 17145-6
Ramanujan Aiyangar, Srinivasa (1887-1920), Indian mathematician, 10670
Ramaswami Aiyar, Chetpat Pattabhirama, Sir (1879-1966), Dewan of Travancore and statesman, 18817-8
Ramaswami Naicker, E.V. (1878-1973), Dravidian political leader, 19188-94
Rāmavilliam Kalākam (folk performance), 20221
Rāmāyaṇa (epic of King Rāma), 02413
- Bengali, 23, 07242-3
- Hindi, 29, 08790-812
- Sanskrit, 12-3, 03759-70, 04607-13, 04695-730
- Tamil, 06575-85
Rāmcaritmānas (Rāmāyaṇa of Tulsīdās in Avadhī), 29, 08790-812
Rameśvarama temple, Tamil Nadu, 01972, 01989
Rāmlīlā (festival), 02105, 02109
Ramos (tribe), 26506
Rāmprasād Sen (1718-75), Bengali sakta poet, 30, 08935-9
Ramsurat Kumar, Yogi (1918-), 19518
Rana "Maharajas" of Nepal, 25962-8
Ranade, Mahadev Govind (1842-1901), Indian jurist and social reformer, 32, 64, 09587, 12347-55, 20737
Ranade, Ramachandra Dattatraya (1886-1957), Maharashtrian philospher, 64, 21615-8
Ranchi city and district, Bihar, 72, 24107, 24193-7
Ranganathan, Shiyali Ramamrita (1892-1972), librarian, 16929
Ranjit Dev, Maharaja of Jammū (fl. 1725-82), 08557
Ranjit Singh (1780-1839), Maharaja of the Punjab, xxi, 28, 68-9, 22570-80, 23131-2
Ranjitsinghji Vibhaji, Maharaja of Nawanazar, "Ranji" (1877-1933), cricketer, 20623
rasa, "flavor," "mood," in Indian literature, 6, 18, 05292, 05977-6004
Rashtrapati (President of India). *See* president, office of
Rashtriya Swayamsevak Sangh (RSS), 42, 13257, 13279-89
Rastogis (caste), 23737
Rāṣṭrakūṭa dynasty, 19, 06205-14, 06680-2
- art, 20, 06809
Rāthoḍ/Rathor, dynasty of Mārwāṛ, 27, 08365-70
Ratirahasya (erotic text, 12th cent.?), 05723, 05729
Ratnāgiri district, Maharashtra, 20686
Ratnagotravibhāga (4th cent. AD text), 05119
Ratnāvalī (Sanskrit drama, 7th cent.), 06005-6
Rauravāgama (Śaiva text), 06607
Ravidās. *See* Raidās
Rawalpindi, Punjab, Pakistan, 68, 22896-8
Ray, Niharranjan (1903-), scholar and educator, 00017
Ray, Prafulla Chandra, Sir (1861-1944), Indian chemist, 10663, 10671
Ray, Radhanath (1848-1908), Oriya poet, 22411
Ray, Satyajit (1922-), Bengali cinema director, 25138-40
Razik Farid (1893-), Ceylon Muslim leader, 18859
Raẓiyya, daughter of Iltutmish and Sultan of Delhi (1236-40), 07036
Reading, Rufus Daniel Isaacs, Marquess of (1860-1935), 23, 10244-9, 20630
Rebellion of 1857 (*also called* Sepoy Mutiny, Indian Mutiny, The Mutiny, Great Rebellion, Sepoy Rebellion, and "War of Independence," etc.), 31, 09458-523
rebirth, in Indic religions, 4, 01032, 01454-1508, 01552
Reddi Naidu, Kurma Venkatta (1875-1942), Justice Party leader, 19610
Reddy, Cattamanchi Ramalinga (1880-1951), Telugu litterateur and politician, 19885
Reddy, N. Sanjeeva. *See* Sanjeeva Reddy, Neelam
Redfield, Robert (1897-1958), American anthropologist, ix
refugees and rehabilitation, 34, 74, 12138-57, 22469, 22816, 24810-14, 24817, 25891, 26644
regional development, 45, 14471-82. *See also* planning, economic; economic conditions
regionalism, India, 40, 12469-515
- Maharashtra, 63, 21115-25
- Punjab, 69, 22674-88
- Tamil, 58, 19178-94, 19206-36
- Telangana (Andhra Pradesh), 59, 19681-93
regions of South Asia (cultural, linguistic, economic), 00103, 00223, 00682-9, 02329-34, 12504, 14471-88
Regulating Act of 1773, 26
regulation of business, India, 47, 15283-8
reincarnation. *See* rebirth
religio-philosophical traditions, 3-6, 01101-2314. *See also* names of specific religions, sects, and leaders
- ancient, 12-6, 04587-5161

religio-philosophical traditions -- *continued*
- Andhra Pradesh, 60, 01986, 06278, 06282, 06463-8, 19870-82, 19896-902
- Assam, 23, 30, 76, 02066, 07292-8, 25806-13
- Baluchistan, 22541
- Bangladesh. *See* Bengal
- Bengal (incl. present Bangladesh and West Bengal), 23, 29-30, 74, 76, 07204-334, 08932-61, 24873-918, 25636-44
- Bhutan, 78, 26436-38
- Bihar, 23, 29, 72, 01240, 02057-65, 07211-8, 07258-63, 07316-27, 24221-5
- British India, 36-7, 11199-566
- Goa, 63, 21097
- Gujarat, 21, 27, 65, 02002-8, 06777-801, 08457-8, 21913-31
- Harappan, 9, 03609
- Haryana, 02031-5
- Himachal Pradesh, 77, 25892-8
- India (Rep.), 50-51, 16692-828
- Jammu & Kashmir. *See* Kashmir
- Karnataka, 19-20, 27, 61, 01972-92, 06469-94, 06537-68, 06571, 20533-56
- Kashmir, 22, 28, 70, 01243, 06956-82, 06991, 08667, 23242-6
- Kerala, 19-20, 60, 01972-92, 04600-6, 06572-4, 08212, 08216-27, 20167-87
- Kumaon and Garhwal, 77, 25928-43
- Ladakh, 00507, 08689
- Madhya Pradesh, 66, 22273-84
- Maharashtra, 21, 27, 64-5, 01993-2001, 06744-71, 08425-49, 21606-32
- Manipur, 26596-8
- medieval, 17-8, 19-20, 21, 22, 23, 05744-964, 06149-63, 06277-574, 06742-805, 06955-99, 07084-130, 07204-334, 07379
- Meghalaya, 79, 26699-700
- Mizoram, 79
- Mughal period, 24-5, 26, 27, 28, 29, 29-30, 07653-87, 08093-103, 08207-27, 08424-58, 08565-689, 08790-839, 08932-61
- Nepal, 23, 78, 01592, 01596, 01601, 02074-7, 07379, 26318-39
- Orissa, 21, 67, 02015-30, 06802-5, 22386-403
- Pakistan, 54-5, 18206-37
- Punjab, 22, 28, 69, 06983-95, 08565-688, 22941-90
- Rajasthan, 21, 27, 66, 02009-14, 06780-801, 08450-6, 22142-4
- Sikkim, 26396-411
- Sind, 22, 28, 06987-8, 08671-85
- South India, 19-20, 59, 60, 61, 01947-92, 05143, 06277-574, 08207-27, 19486-544, 19870-82, 20167-87, 20533-56
- Sri Lanka, 19, 26, 55, 57, 01237-46, 01934-46, 05041-4, 06149-63, 18973-9055
- Tamil Nadu, 19-20, 27, 59, 01947-92, 05158, 06277-574, 08207-27, 19486-544
- tribal, 01097-1100. *See also* names of specific tribes
- Uttar Pradesh, 22, 29, 72, 02036-56, 07084-130, 08790-831, 23910-32
- Vedic, 10, 03812-29
- West Bengal. *See* Bengal

religious music, 7, 02881-90
religious orders, 5, 01877-88
Renaissance, Bengal. *See* Bengal Renaissance
Renaissance, Hindu, 11219-352, 20721, 24561-77
Renou, Louis (1896-1966), French indologist, 2, 00061
renunciation (Indic religions). *See* sannyāsa
Republic of India (1950-), 40-52, 12270-7282 (Chapter Eight); for regional and local studies, *see* Chapters Eleven through Sixteen
Republican Party of India, 42, 13301-3
"republics" of ancient India, 04328-35
research centers and facilities in South Asia, 27424-47
research guides, 81-3
Reserve Bank of India, 36, 45, 11163-82, 14523-41
resources. *See* natural resources
Revanta (deity, protector of huntsmen), 01708
revelation, in Indic religions, 01412, 01416
revenue surveys, xvii
revenue systems. *See* finance, public; land tenure
Revolt of 1857-59. *See* Rebellion of 1857
revolutionaries. *See* Nationalist Movement
Ṛgveda, 10, 01220, 03881-908, 03941-4, 05170
Ṛgveda on Harappan culture, 03606, 03608
rhythm, in Indian music, 7, 02759-63, 02800-9, 02834-7
Riangs (tribal people), 79
rice cultivation and trade
- Bangladesh, 75, 25351-8
- India, 19270, 19754, 20917, 22329, 23591, 24462
- Sri Lanka, 18730-50

right and left hand castes, 00793
right and left, in ritual, 03862, 19343
rights. *See* civil rights
Riot of 1915, Ceylon, 18334-41
riots and mob violence
- Bihar, 72, 24008-10
- India (Rep.), 42, 13083-104
- Uttar Pradesh, 23515-9

Ripon, George Frederick Samuel Robinson, 1st Marquess of (1827-1902), 30, 09144-6
rites and ritual, 5, 13, 01023-51, 01720, 01781, 02124-34, 08064, 19493, 19495-6, 22276, 22279, 24221, 24885, 24893-4
- Jaina, 05141, 05930
- Sikh, 08585-93
- Vaikhānasa, 04789-92
- Vedic, 10, 03853-72, 20169

rivers. *See also* names of rivers
- India, 5, 27012, 27014
- Nepal, 26119

Riyāzu-s-salatīn (late 18th cent. Persian history of Bengal), 08840
road transport. *See* transportation
Roberts, Frederick Sleigh Roberts, 1st Earl (1832-1914), Indian Army Commander-in-Chief, 09326
rock paintings, 03532-42
Rockefeller Foundation, in India, 14055
Roe, Thomas, Sir (1581?-1644), English Ambassador to Mughal Court, 07488
Rohilkhand (region in Uttar Pradesh), 29, 71, 23448-9, 23469, 23544
Rohilla War (1773), 08761
Rohillas, Afghan settlers in Rohilkhand, 08758, 08761
Rohtak, town and district, Haryana, 23272
Roman Catholic Church. *See* Christianity
romanization of South Asia languages and names, 02386, 27453-62
Rome, ancient contacts with India, 12, 04569-83
Round Table Conferences, London, 1st-3rd (1930-32), 33, 10260-8
Rourkela, steel plant, Sundergarh district, Orissa, 22350-1, 22354-5
Rowlatt Acts (1919), satyagraha against, 32, 09841-2, 20771, 22637
Roy, Bidhan Chandra, Dr. (1882-1962), West Bengal Chief Minister, 24363-5, 24367-8
Roy, Ellen (1904-60), wife of M.N. Roy, 33, 10066a
Roy, Jaimini (1887-1972), Bengali artist, 11800-20
Roy, Manabendra Nath (1893-1954), Communist and Radical Humanist, 33, 10065-86
Roy, Motilal (1882-1959), founder of Prabartak Sangh, 24809
Roy, Ram Mohan, Raja (1772?-1835), Bengali Hindu reformer, 36, 10851, 11228-47
Roy, Sarat Chandra (1871-1942), Indian anthropologist, 02439, 25116
Royal Indian Navy Mutiny (1946), 34, 10457-8
Ṛsabha (Jaina saint), 14, 05131, 06796
Ṛtusaṁhāra (Sanskrit poem, attrib. to Kālidāsa), 15, 05374-5
rubber plantations, Ceylon, 56, 18713-4
Ruben, Walter (1899-), German indologist, 00025
Rūpā (Kashmir saint-poetess, d. 1721), 08667
Rūpa Gosvāmī (16th cent.), Vaiṣṇava disciple of Caitanya, 07284-6
rupee, Indian, 44, 13794-812
Ruqᶜāt-i-ᶜĀlamgīrī (Letters of Aurangzīb), 07495
rural credit. *See* agricultural credit
rural development. *See* villages
Russia, relations with, British India, 31, 09408-53. *See also* Soviet Union
Russell, Henry (1783-1852), British Resident at Hyderabad, 19632
ryotwari system (land tenure), 58, 19294-304

SOAS. *See* School of Oriental and African Studies
Sabarimalai (Kerala shrine to Ayyappan), 01857, 01987
Sacchal Sarmast (1739-1826), Sindhi poet, 08672
sacred centers, 5, 00097, 01877-2077, 22144, 22386-93

sacred thread, 01028-39
sacrifice, Vedic, 10, 03853-72, 03936, 03939
Ṣaḍdarśana ("six views", orthodox systems of Hindu philosophy), 13, 04793-870
Saddhamma-sangaha (medieval Ceylon Buddhist text), 06155
Saddharmapuṇḍarīkasūtra ("Lotus Sutra", Mahayana Buddhist text), 14, 05076-8
Sādhanamālā (Tantric text), 05870, 05918
sādhus (ascetics), 5, 02209-33. *See also* asceticism; sannyāsa
Sāgaranandin (medieval writer on drama), 05999
Saha, Meghnad (1893-1956), Indian scientist, 17279
Sahajānanda, Swami (1781-1830), founder of Svaminarayana sect, 65, 21921-31
Sahajiya cult, Bengal, 23, 30, 08940-1
Sahgal, Nayantara (1927-), Indo-Anglian novelist, 17178
Sahir Ludhianvi, Abdul Haye (192-), Urdu poet, 17056
Sahitya Akademi, India's "Academy of Literature," xiv, 16991
Sāhitya-darpaṇa (medieval poetics text), 05998
Sahni, Balraj (1913-73), Hindi film star, Punjabi writer, Communist worker, 13219
Sahni, Birbal (1891-1949), Indian botanist, 10665
Sai Baba (d. 1918), Muslim-Hindu saint, 64, 21619-24
Sai Baba, Sathya (1926-), miracle-worker and spiritual leader, 50, 16737-44
Saigal, Kundan Lal (1904-46), Indian singer and film actor, 02845, 16979
St. Thomas Christians of Kerala, 6, 27, 60, 02249-56, 08222-5. *See also* Christianity; Christians
Śaiva Siddhānta (Hindu sect, primarily Tamil), 20, 01340, 01417, 06519-33, 19510
Śaivāgamas (Śaiva texts), 22, 04744-53
Śaivism. *See* Śiva
Śaka era, Indian national calendar (began in 78 AD), 11, 04014
Śakas (Scythian dynasty), 11, 04175-7
- art, 16, 05519
- coins, 04067
Saklatvala, Shapurji (1874-1936), Indian Communist leader, 10063
Śākta, cult and worshipper of Śakti. *See* Śakti and Śākta
Śākta pīthas (centers of Śakti worship), 01929
Śakti ("power" of a god, usually Śiva, personified as his wife) and Śākta/Shaktism, 17, 20, 27, 30, 74, 01711-38, 05848-56, 06514, 06516, 06802, 08935-8, 09681
Śaktism/Shaktism. *See* Śakti and Śākta
Śakuntalā (play by Kālidāsa), 15, 05349-52, 05385
Śākyamuni. *See* Gautama Buddha
Śākyas (ancient tribe), 13
Sālār Masʿūd Gāzī (11th cent.), Indian Muslim saint, 06992
Salem district, Tamil Nadu, 19159, 19311
Sālivāhana, Ustād (Mughal artist), 07773
salt industry, 21303
Salt Satyāgraha (1930), 33, 10144
Saluva dynasty of Vijayanagara, 06233
salvation, in Indic religions, 01498-508
Sāma Veda. *See* Vedas
Samaldas Parmananddas (1828-84), Dewan of Bhavnagar princely state, 20615
Saman (deity, in Sri Lanka), 01598. *See also* Yama
Sāmantas ("vassals"), 05713, 05716
Samaraiccakaha (Prakrit text by Haribhadra, fl. 12th cent.), as historical source, 05707
Sāmaveda. *See* Vedas
Sambhājī I (1657-89), Chhatrapati ("King") of Maratha state after Shivājī, 27, 08292
saṁsāra (cycle of birth and death), 4, 01454-1508
saṁskāras (life and death rituals), 3, 12, 01023-51. *See also* rites and ritual
Samudra Gupta (fl. 335-76 AD), Emperor, 04147
Samyukta Maharashtra Movement, 63, 21115-25
Sanātana Goswāmī (1484-1558), Vaiṣṇava disciple of Caitanya, 07291
Sāñchī (archaeological site), Madhya Pradesh, 16, 05472-8
Sandeman, Robert Groves, Sir (1835-92), administrator in Baluchistan, 22522
Sāng (folk opera), 23943
Sangam age, South India, 5, 11, 04202-28, 04399, 04401, 04452
- literature, 16, 05412-48
Sangeet Nāṭak Akademi, "Academy of Music and Drama", 16991
saṅgha (Buddhist monastic community), early history, 13, 04935-65
Saṅgitarājā (music text), 02682
Saṅgitaratnākara (dance text), 02685
Saṅgītis (Buddhist councils), 13, 04942-50
Sangli, princely state, Maharashtra, 20584, 20587
sanitation, public, 49, 16236-48, 21880, 23885, 24794
Sanjeeva Reddy, Neelam (1913-), President of India, 1977-, 40, 43
Sankara Kurup, G. (1901-), Malayalam poet, 61, 20191, 20216-8
Śaṅkarācārya (9th cent.), Vedānta philosopher, 19, 01359, 01372, 01400, 06324-407
Śaṅkaradeva (1496?-1568), Assam Vaiṣṇava saint, 23, 07292-8
Sāṁkhya (school of philosophy), 13, 01450, 01452, 01462, 04798-817
Sankrityayan, Rahul (1893-1963), Buddhist scholar and Hindi writer, 11626
sannyasa (renunciation), 5, 02186-2208, 08208
Sansis (tribe), 22834
saṅskāras. *See* saṁskāras
Sanskrit dictionaries and learning aids, 83, 27791-806
Sanskrit language and literature, xx, 6, 15, 01124, 02411, 02414, 02463-518
- classical, 6, 15, 18, 27, 05261-411, 06005-95, 06144-8
- modern, 51, 17062-9
- Vedic, 10, 03798-994
Sanskrit manuscripts, 1, 00001-14
Sanskritization (emulation of high caste custom), 3, 00827-36, 01091-6
Santal Rebellion (1855), 63, 20928-39
Santals (tribal people), 63, 20894, 20911-47, 24070a
Śāntarakṣita (Buddhist philosopher), 01409
śāntarasa, "mood of repose" in poetics, 18, 05988-93
Santas (poet-saints)
- Maharashtra, 21, 27, 06744-71, 08425-49
- North India (Hindi area), 23, 28, 07089-110, 08790-826
Śāntideva (Buddhist poet, 7th cent.), 05093
Śāntiniketan, Tagore's educational center in West Bengal, 35, 10621-9
Sanyal, Sachindra Nath (1895-1945), Indian revolutionary, 09756
Saoras (tribe), 63, 21011-7
Saorias (tribe), 20994
Sapru Committee (1943-45), on constitutional proposals, 34, 10446-7
Sapru, Tej Bahadur, Sir (1875-1949), jurist and Liberal leader, 33, 10008, 10014, 10446-7
Saptamātṛkās (female deities), 01719, 01728, 01736
Sarabhai, Vikram Ambalal (1919-71), Indian scientist, 17279
Saraha (medieval Bengal Buddhist poet), 07227
Saran district, Bihar, 24099, 24135-37
Śaraṇas (Vīraśaiva saints), 20, 06538-68
Sarosothimalai (South Indian architecture text), 06609
Sarasvatī (goddess), 01734, 05872
Sarasvatī (river in ancient India), 01837
Sāraswat Brahmans, 61, 20393-9
Sarda Canal, Uttar Pradesh, 23610
Sarda, Har Bilas (1867-1955), social reformer, 10724
Sardesai, Govind Sakharam (1865-1959), historian of Maharashtra, 00127
sargabandha (narrative verse), 15
Sarkar, Jadunath (1870-1958), Indian historian, 00126-7, 07497
Śarma, Īshwar Chandra. *See* Vidyāsāgar
Sarma, Mallampalli Somasekhara (1891-1963), 00028
Sārnāth (archaeological site near Vārāṇasī), 16, 01646, 05562-71
Sarojavajra. *See* Saraha
Sarton, George, historian of science, xiii
Sarva-darśana-saṁgraha (philosophy text), 04794
Sarva-siddhānta-saṁgraha (Vedanta text), 06345
Sarvodaya, "uplift of all" (Gandhian economic program), 45, 13304-15, 14292-322, 18883, 24166
Śāstā (South Indian deity), 5, 01851-9
Sātārā, princely state, Maharashtra; Maratha royal capital, 27, 62, 20603-8
Sātavāhana dynasty, 11, 04195-201
- coins, 04072
Satchidananda, Swami (1914-), 16736
Satellite Instructional Television Experiment (SITE), India, 51, 16949-58
Sathya Sai Baba. *See* Sai Baba, Sathya

satī/suttee, "a woman who is pure", the practice of widow-burning, 35, 10708-15
Satī-gīta (18th cent. text on feminine ideal), 21926
satire, political, 42, 13114-23
Satnāmi, movement and sect, 22278
satyāgraha (Gandhian strategy of "truth force"), 33, 09955-69
Satyamurti, S. (1887-1943), Tamil Nadu educator and Congress leader, 19170
Satyanand Agnihotri (1850-1929), founder of Dev Samaj, 36, 11263-8
Satyashodhak Samaj, Maharashtrain social reform group founded by Phule, 20759
Saudā, Mirzā Rafiᶜ (1907-81), Urdu poet, 07708, 07709
Saudi Arabia, xxiii
Saundarānanda (mahākāvya by Aśvaghoṣa), 15, 05302-7
Saundaryalaharī (tantric text), 05842, 05844
Saurashtra. *See* Kathiawar
Savaras (tribe). *See* Saoras
Savarkar, Vinayak Damodar, "Veer" (1883-1966), Maharashtrain Hindu leader, 42, 13258-64
savings
- Bangladesh, 25314
- India (Rep.), 46, 14683-99, 23589
- Pakistan, 54, 17903-12
- Sri Lanka, 18675
Sawan Singh (1858-1948), North Indian religious leader, 23922
Sawantwadi, princely state, Maharashtra, 20585-6
Sayajirao III, Maharaja of Baroda (1863-1939), 20631, 20633
Sayyid Ahmad of Rae Bareli (1786-1831), leader of Farāᶜidī movement, 37, 11443-6
Sayyid dynasty (1414-1451), Kings of Delhi, 23, 07037-55
scale in Indian music, 7, 02764-74
Scandinavia, Indology in, 00051
scepticism, in Indic thought, 4, 01379-90
Scheduled Castes (former "Untouchables"). *See also* social conditions, for regions not listed below.
- Bihar, 24149-54
- British India, 35, 10749-87a
- Gujarat, 21675, 21812-3, 21841-6, 21911
- India (Rep.), 48, 15766-84, 15806-29
- Karnataka, 61, 20415-22
- Maharashtra, 21403-30
- Rajasthan, 66, 22094
- Tamil Nadu, 19335, 19363-70
- Uttar Pradesh, 71, 23743-58
- West Bengal, 73, 24633-46
Scheduled Tribes. *See* adivasis
Scholberg, Henry, xvii
School of Oriental and African Studies, University of London, 82, 27531-2
Schwartz, Christian Friedrich, Rev. (1726-98), missionary, 08226
science and technology
- ancient, 12, 04525-60
- Bangladesh, 27488
- British period, 35, 10649-72
- general history, 00247-349
- India (Rep.), 51-2, 17231-82, 27494
- medieval, 17, 04731-43
- Mughal period, 07812
- Pakistan, 55, 18284-8
- Sri Lanka, 58, 19099-101
- Vedic period, 9, 03793-7
Scindia. *See* Sindhia
Scindia Steam Navigation Company, 21334
Scott, David (1786-1831), British official in Assam, 25677, 25686
scripts, Indic, 6, 02378-86, 03637-50, 07335
Scudder, Ida S. (1870-1960), medical missionary, 19459, 19467
sculpture. *See* art and architecture
Scythian (Śaka) dynasty, 11, 04175-7
seasons, in literature, 02416, 02518, 02668, 05374-5
seclusion of women. *See* pardā
secondary education. *See* education
secularism
- Bangladesh, 75, 25218-20
- India (Rep.), 40, 00128, 12411-68, 19183-4
- Nepal, 25960
Secunderabad city, Andhra Pradesh, 19834-47. *See also* Hyderabad city
security and defense
- India, 44, 13759-93
- Pakistan, 53, 17685-96
seed varieties. *See* technology, agricultural
Seir mutaqherin. *See* Siyar-al-muta akhkhirīn
self in Indic thought, 4, 01456-79
Sen, Keshub Chunder/Keshab Chandra (1838-84), Brāhmo Samāj leader, 11251-62
Sen, Nabin Chandra (1847-1909), Bengali poet, 24967
Sen, Sunil Madhav (1910-), Indian artist, 11815
Sen, Surya (1892-1934), Indian revolutionary, 24322
Sena dynasty (12th cent.), 23, 07174-81
- art, 23, 07340-68
Senanayake, Don Stephen, Ceylon's first Prime Minister (1948-52), 18416, 18555, 18689
Senanayake, Dudley (1911-73), Ceylon Prime Minister 1952-53, 1960, 1965-70, 18414
Senapati, Fakir Mohan (1843-1918), Oriya novelist, 22405, 22409, 22413
Sengupta, Jatindra Mohan (1885-1933), Bengal Congress leader, 24325
separatism, Muslim. *See* communalism
Sepoy Rebellion (1857-58). *See* Rebellion of 1857
Serampore College, Srirampur, West Bengal, 24851
Serampore mission (Baptist), est. in Bengal in 1793, 30, 08954-61
serpent symbolism, 4, 01611-27, 25109. *See also* Manasā, goddess of snakes
settlement reports, xvi
settlements. *See* village; urbanization
Setubandha (Prakrit epic), 05251
Sevunas/Seunas. *See* Yādava dynasty
sexual life, 12, 04482-7, 05723, 05729
sexual symbolism, 4, 01607-10, 01754, 03861, 03893
shadow plays, 8, 03005-13
Shāh Ālam II (1738-1806), Mughal Emperor, 07513-5
Shah Commission, inquiry into 1975-77 Emergency abuses, 43, 13565-75
Shah Din, Muhammad (1868-1918), Indian jurist, 17379
Shāh dynasty of Nepal, 25957-92
Shāh Husain (Punjabi Sufi poet, 1539-99), 08687
Shāh Jahān (1592-1666), Mughal Emperor, 24-25, 07490-3, 07545
Shah, Jayantilal Chottalal (1906-), Indian jurist, 13566-75
Shāhjī, Rājā of Sātārā (1839-48), 20605
Shahrastānī (Muslim scholar), 05961
Shāhu Chhatrapati, Maharaja of Kolhapur (1874-1922), 20594-6, 20600
Shakti, Shaktism. *See* Śakti
shamanism, 3, 5, 01097-1100, 02139, 02159, 06284, 19499, 20545, 20968, 21017, 25810, 25929, 26330, 26336
shariᶜat. *See* law, Islamic
Sharqi Sultanate of Jaunpur, 1394-1477, 07021
- art, 07163
Shastri, Lal Bahadur (1904-66), India's second Prime Minister, 42-3, 12100, 13399-408, 13741
Shaṭṭari Sūfi order, 07331
Shaw Wallace & Co., British managing agency in Calcutta, 11104
Sher-Gil, Amrita (1913-41), painter, 38, 11788, 11821-4
Sher Shāh (fl. 1538-45), Afghan conqueror of North India, 24, 29, 07457-67
Sherdukpens (tribe), 26493
Sherpas (Himalayan people), 78, 01878, 03054, 26205-22, 26323, 26325
Shīᶜā (Muslim sect), 25, 02270, 08458
Shīᶜā-Sunni conflict, 23771-2
Shilappadikaram. *See* Cilappatikāram
Shinde. *See* Sindhia
shipping. *See* transportation
Shiromani Akali Dal, Sikh political party, 13295-7
Shiv Kumar (1937-73), Punjabi poet, 23007
Shiv Sena, Maharashtrian nativist party, 63, 21139-47
Shivājī Chhatrapati (1627-80), Maratha king, 27, 28, 08262, 08271-95, 08399, 08408
Shivaji memorial movement, 22, 20742, 20744
Sholapur city, Maharashtra, 21486
Shore, John. *See* Teignmouth
Shraddhānanda, Swāmī (1856?-1926), leader of suddhi movement for reconversion to Hinduism, 33, 10141
Shri Ram (1884-1943), Indian industrialist, 15303-4
siddha. *See* medicine
Siddhānta (Jain canon), 05150-61. *See also* Jainism
Siddhārtha. *See* Gautama Buddha

Siddhas, Tamil tantric adepts, 20, 06534-6
Siddhis (peasant caste in Karnataka), 20376
Sīgiriya/Sīgiri (Ceylon archaeological site), 16, 06146, 05623-5
Sikandar Begum (d. 1888), Nawab of Bhopal, 20679
Sikh rule in Kashmir (1819-46), 23131-2
Sikh Wars, 22581-601
Sikhs and Sikhism, xx, 28, 08565-666
- ethics, 28, 01560, 08580, 08583
- historiography, 00106
- Kashmir, 69, 23131-2
- modern Punjab, 68, 22564-601, 22621, 22674-88, 22828-9, 22944-65
- Mughal period, 24, 25, 28, 07673, 08531-51, 08565-666
- music, 02888
- painting, 08751-2
Sikhs in Great Britain, 80, 26911-6
Sikkim, principality, and Indian State, 1975-, xxii, 78, 26358-26411
- bibliography, 27748
- introductions, 27317-9, 27327, 27350
- travel accounts, 25835, 25838-9, 27350, 27353
Sikligars (tribe), 22835
Śikṣā (phonetics), 15, 05175-7
silk industry, 04377, 08911, 14914, 24121, 24532
Śilpa-prakāśa (art text), 06911
Śilparatna (medieval art text), 08232
Śilpasāriṇi (medieval Orissan art text), 06910
Śilpaśastras. *See* art and architecture, texts
Simhāla. *See* Sri Lanka
Simla, hill station in Himachal Pradesh, 11966, 25857
Simla Agreement (1972), between India and Pakistan, 39, 12184-90
Simla Conference (1945) on India's independence, 34, 10451-5
Simon Commission (1928) on Indian constitutional reform, 33, 10250-4, 19158
Sind, xxii
- ancient, 16, 04158
- Arab invasion (711 AD), 04157-8, 06926-8, 07022
- bibliography, 27719, 27723, 27726
- general history, 2, 00484-6
- geography, 81, 27230-1
- introductions, 81, 27224-5
- medieval, 18, 21, 06925-8
- modern (1799-), 67, 22410-514
- Mughal period, 28, 08530, 08563
- music, 02735, 02780, 02816
- prehistory, 03738
- travel accounts, 22432, 22434-5, 22440-60
Sindhi dictionaries and learning aids, 83, 27942-8
Sindhi language and literature, 7, 28, 67, 02612-6, 08671-85, 22508-14
Sindhia/Scindia dynasty of Gwalior, 27, 62, 08309, 20672-5
Singapore, South Asians in, 80, 26876, 26881-90
Singaravelu, M. (1860-1946), South Indian Communist leader, 10059
Singer, Milton Borah, American anthropologist, ix, 00621
Singh, Charan. *See* Charan Singh
Singh, Khushwant. *See* Khushwant Singh
Singphos (tribe), 26510
Sinha, Sachchidananda (1871-1950), Bihar journalist and Kayastha leader, 10836, 23962, 24236, 24240
Sinhala dictionaries and learning aids, 83, 27849-59
Sinhala language and literature, 6, 19, 26, 47, 00393, 02541-7, 06144-8, 08101-8, 19072-81
Sinhalese (Sinhala-speaking population of Sri Lanka), 18835-49
Sinhalese language. *See* Sinhala
Sino-Indian relations, 39, 44, 13901-59
Siraiki language (Punjab), 69, 22995
Siraj-ud-Daulah (d. 1757), Nawab of Bengal, 08864, 08867
Sirājuddīn Uthmān, Sheikh (Akhi Sirāj), Bengal Muslim saint, 07333
Sirhind tract, Indo-Gangetic divide in Punjab, 00492
Sirhindī, Aḥmad, Shaikh (1564-1625), Muslim reformer, 25, 07677-84
Sisodia dynasty of Mewāṛ, 27, 08358-64
Śītalā (goddess of smallpox), 01732
Sitaramayya, B. Pattabhi. *See* Pattabhi Sitaramayya, B.
Sittannavasal cave temple, Tamil Nadu, 06625
Śiva and Śaivism, 405, 10067, 01739-58. *See also* Hinduism and names of specific sects: Kashmir Śaivism, Pāśupatas, Śaiva Siddhānta, Vīraśaivism
- ancient, 13, 87, 04649, 04739-63
Śiva and Śaivism -- *continued*
- medieval, 20, 23, 05889, 06303-23, 06508-68, 06780, 06956-75, 07299-315
Śivājī. *See* Shivājī
Śiva-jnāna-bodha (Śaiva Siddhānta text), 06519-24
Śivajñana-siddhiyār (Śaiva Siddhānta text), 06519-24
Śivānanda Saraswatī, Swami (1887-1963), 37, 11419-24
Śiva-purāṇa, 17, 05790
Śiva-sūtras (Kashmir Śaiva texts), 22, 06957, 06965, 06973
Sivaswami Aiyar, Pazhamarneri Sundaram (1864-1946), South Indian Liberal leader, 10016
six systems of orthodox Hindu philosophy (ṣaḍdarśana), 13, 04793-874
Siyar al-muta akhkhirīn/Siyar-ul-Mutakherīn, Persian history of 18th cent. India, 07516, 08866
Skanda (deity), 5, 01817-25, 04215
Skandagupta Kramāditya (fl. 455-67 AD), 04156
Skanda-purāṇa, 17, 01931-3, 02076, 05788, 05791
Skanda-ṣaṣṭi (South Indian festival), 02101
Skinner, James (1778-1841), Colonel, 09318
Skinner, William, x
"Slave" dynasty of Delhi (Māmluks), 22, 07023-36
slavery, 00238
- ancient, 11, 04386-91
- British India, 35, 26072, 10720-1, 19250, 10003, 20028, 24398, 25727
Sleeman, William Henry (1789-1856), British official in North India, 23453-4
slums, 16076-81. *See also* urbanization for cities not listed below
- Bombay, 21531-6
- Calcutta, 74, 24786-90
- Delhi, 23398-411
- Karachi, 22498, 22507
- Madras, 19444-53
- Mysore, 20485
- Poona, 21544
smallpox, 16260, 16263, 16268
small-scale industry. *See* industry
smuggling, 25484
Soān, prehistoric culture, 03554, 03556
social conditions and social change. *See also* demography
- ancient, 12, 04392-519
- Andhra Pradesh, 59-60, 19784-869
- Arunachal Pradesh, 78, 26482-92
- Assam, 76, 25775-93
- Baluchistan, 68, 22532-49
- Bangladesh, 75-6, 25487-92
- Bengal, 73-5, 24551-872
- Bhutan, 78, 26436-40
- Bihar, 72, 24133-220
- British period, 34-5, 10538-852, 11199-218
- Delhi, 70, 23362-440
- Goa, 63, 21092-8
- Gujarat, 65, 21803-912
- Haryana, 70, 23300-17
- Himachal Pradesh, 77, 25880-91
- India (Rep.), 46-7, 48, 13037-123, 15677-6691
- Jammu & Kashmir, 70, 23225-41
- Karnataka, 61, 20361-532
- Kerala, 60, 20055-166
- Kumaon and Garhwal, 77, 25912-27
- Madhya Pradesh, 66, 22229-72
- Maharashtra, 64, 21342-605
- Manipur, 79, 26582-95
- medieval, 17, 22-23, 05722-30, 06135-43, 06243-72, 07074-83, 07197-203
- Meghalaya, 79, 26669-98
- Mizoram, 79, 26610-2
- Mughal period, 24, 27, 28, 29, 07629-52, 08048-97, 08191-205, 08391-423, 08561-4, 08784-9, 08889-931
- Nagaland, 79, 26540-73
- Nepal, 78, 26190-317
- North-East hill states, India, 78-9, 26460-6. *See also* names of states
- North-West Frontier Province, 69, 23096-130
- Orissa, 67, 22357-85
- Pakistan, 54, 18073-205
- Punjab, 68, 22815-940
- Rajasthan, 66, 22074-141
- Sikkim and Darjeeling, 78, 26396-411
- Sind, 67, 22486-72
- South Asia, general, 40, 12265-9

social conditions and social change -- *continued*
- South India, general, 19127-33, 06243-72, 08191-205, 19127-33
- Sri Lanka, 57, 06135-43, 08048-97, 18815-972
- Tamil Nadu, 58-9, 19333-485
- Tripura, 79, 26636-48
- Uttar Pradesh, 71, 23688-909
- West Bengal, 73, 24551-872

social conditions, rural. *See* villages
social policy, India, 15713-43
social reform movements, 35-6, 64, 65, 11564-66, 21803-10, 24551-60
social sciences in India, 15677-712
social services and welfare. For regions not listed below, *see* social conditions
- Andhra Pradesh, 60, 19848-56
- Assam, 76, 25803-5
- Bangladesh, 75, 25572-83
- Bihar, 72, 24198-203
- Bombay city, 64, 21537-42
- British India, 35, 10694
- Calcutta, 74, 24784-803
- Gujarat, 65, 21889-94
- India (Rep.), 49, 16113-206
- Karnataka, 61, 20497-503
- Madras city, 19444-53
- Maharashtra, 64, 21559-61
- Nepal, 78, 26294-302
- Orissa, 67, 22379-81
- Pakistan, 54, 18124-30
- Punjab, 68, 22914-8
- Rajasthan, 66, 22128-34
- Sri Lanka, 57, 18909-19
- Tamil Nadu, 59, 19454-7
- Uttar Pradesh, 71, 23864-70
- West Bengal, 74, 24784, 24804-9

social systems, Indic, 2-3, 00612-01100
social welfare, social work. *See* social services
socialism
- British India, 33, 10033-114, 23169
- India (Rep.), 42, 13125, 13145, 13164-70, 13171-97, 14323-46
- South Asia, general, 12206, 12216
- Sri Lanka, 55, 18392-401

Socialist Parties, India, 13179-97, 23494
socialization, 3, 49, 01052-61, 15936-72
sociology in India, 48, 15685-712
sociology of religion, 5, 01860-76
Soma (Vedic intoxicating drink, personified as a god), 03833, 03854-6, 03859, 03865, 03868
Somadeva (Sanskrit poet, 11th cent.), 18, 06071-8
Somadeva Sūri (Jain Sanskrit writer, 10th cent. AD), 05672
Somanātha. *See* Somnath
Somapura. *See* Pahārpur
Somaśambhupaddhati (Śaiva ritual text), 06510
Somasundaram, S.S. (1877-1967), Ceylon Christian educationist, 19049
Somnath (sacred center in Gujarat), 5, 02202-8, 06858
Somnāthpur temples, Karnataka, 06673, 06675
Son River Basin, Bihar, 24049
Son Kolis (tribe), 20821, 20824
sorcery. *See* magic
soul, in Indic thought, 4, 01456-79
Soulbury Constitutional Commission (Ceylon, 1944-45), 55, 18362
South Africa, South Asians in, 80, 26819-41
South America
- India (Rep.), relations, 44, 14106-7
- South Asians in, 80, 26775-90

South-east Asia, xxii
- historical contacts, 1, 12, 19, 04584-6, 06273-6
- India (Rep.), relations, 44, 14093-101
- South Asians in, 80, 26874-90
- Sri Lanka, relations, 18568

South India Area (*See also* Tamil Nadu, Andhra Pradesh, Kerala, Karnataka)
- ancient, 11, 04204-28
- art, 8, 16, 27, 03379-400, 05494-508, 06607-77, 08232-8
- bibliography, 83, 27707-12
- dance and drama, 7-8, 02957-68, 03026-8
- deities, 5, 01817-25, 01851-9
- general history, 1, 00067-91, 00395-440
- historiography, 00100-1

South India Area -- *continued*
- introductions, 81, 27158-83
- languages, 6, 83, 02548-92, 27860-907
- medieval, 19, 06176-679
- modern (1800-), 58-61, 19116-20578 (Chapter Eleven)
- Mughal period, 26-7, 08112-238
- music, 7, 02852-80
- performing arts, 708, 02957-84, 03026-8
- prehistory, 9, 03520, 03524, 03670-85, 03691-729
- relations with north India, 00172, 04214-8
- sacred centers, 5, 01877-88, 01947-92

South Kanara district. *See* Karnataka
Souza, Francis Newton, Indian artist, 17219, 17228
Soviet Union
- British India, relations, 09605-29
- India (Rep.), relations, 44, 13901, 13960-4002, 24109
- Pakistan, relations, 17743-8
- South Asia, relations, 11986-2058, 12122
- South Asian studies, 00050, 04607, 13986, 14243, 27419, 27422

Spaniards in early modern India, 25, 07834
speech (vāc), philosophy of, 14, 05162-74
śraddhā (faith), 01366
śrāddha. *See* ancestors, rites for
śramanas (adherents of Buddhism, Jainism, and other "heterodoxies"), 12, 04590-1
Śrautasūtras, rules for Vedic sacrifice, 10, 03869, 03998-4005
Sri Lanka (Ceylon), xiv, xx, xxiii
- ancient, 11, 16, 04229-49, 04370, 04387, 05613-25
- art, 8, 16, 26, 58, 03289, 03361-78, 05613-25, 06114-34, 08109-11, 19089-98
- bibliography, 27703-6
- dance, 8, 03014-25
- general history, 2, 00379-94
- historiography, 00098
- introductions, 81, 27130-57
- languages, 6, 83, 02541-76, 27849-76
- medieval, 19, 06116-75
- modern (1796-), 55-8, 18289-9115 (Chapter Ten)
- Mughal period, 26, 08048-111
- music, 7, 02892-4, 02896
- prehistory, 9, 03512, 03523, 03559, 03673
- sacred centers, 5, 01920-33
- South Asian states, relations, 39, 12199-202

Sri Aurobindo. *See* Ghose, Aurobindo
Sri Narayana Paripalana Movement, Kerala social reform, 20110
Sri Ramakrishna. *See* Ramakrishna Paramahansa
Śrī Vaiṣṇavas. *See* Śrīvaiṣṇavas
Śrī Veṅkaṭeśvara temple, 5, 20, 01956-61
Śrīharṣa (Sanskrit poet, 12th cent.), 06393
Srikakulam Naxalite uprisings (Andhra Pradesh, 59, 19694-9
Srikantayya, B.M. (Kannada writer, 1884-1946), 20574
Śrīkaṇṭhacaritam (Sanskrit mahākāvya), 06056
Śrīmad Bhāgavatam. *See* Bhāgavata-purāṇa
Śrīnagar city, Kashmir, 23227, 23235, 23238
Śrīnātha (Telugu poet, fl. 1400-1440), 06602-3
Śringeri (sacred center in Karnataka), 01983, 01991-2
Śrīniketan, educational center, West Bengal, 35, 10621-9
Srinivasa Iyengar, Seshadri (1874-1941), Madras Congress leader, 19172
Srinivasa Sastri, Valangiman Sankaranarayana (1869-1946), Indian Liberal leader, 33, 10009-20
Srinivasan Iyengar, Kasturi (1887-1959), Madras journalist, 10830
Śrīrāmpur. *See* Serampore
Śrīraṅgam temple, Tamil Nadu, 5, 20, 01973-4
Śrīsailam temple, Andhra, 01986
Śrīvaiṣṇavas (Hindu sect), 20, 01879, 01949, 06415-68, 19355
Srivastava, Dhanpat Rai. *See* Premchand
Śṛṅgāra-prakāśa (aesthetics text), 06003
śruti ("revealed", Vedic literature), 10, 03798-994
śruti, "scale" in Indian music, 7, 02764-74
standard of living
- India, 45, 14203-7
- Pakistan, 53, 17805-9
- Sri Lanka, 56, 18614

stars (mythology), 01826-36
State Bank of Pakistan, 53
state economic plans, India, 14483-8
state finance. *See* finance, public
state government and politics, India, 41, 12876-937, 13651-66, 14551-6. *See also* government and politics,

state government and politics -- *continued*
for individual states
state planning, 45, 14483-8. For specific states, *see* planning, economic
State Trading Corporation, India, 48
states reorganization, Assam, 76, 25700-5
states reorganization, India, 50, 12532-37, 21125, 22156, 22296, 23976, 24361-2, 25700-5
The Statesman (Calcutta newspaper), 10805, 10812
statistics, guides to, 83, 27748-83
stava (Sanskrit hymns), 17, 05839-47
Stavacintāmaṇi (Śaiva text), 06981
Steel, Flora Annie (1847-1929), British writer, 39, 11891-2
steel industry, 47, 11110, 15282-89, 24110-1, 24549
stereotypes of South Asians, 39, 81, 11875-923, 27080-7
sterilization, 43, 13544-6. *See also* family planning
Sthaviras. *See* Buddhism, Theravāda
Sthaviravāda. *See* Buddhism, Theravāda
Sthiramati (Buddhist philosopher), 05117
Stone Ages in South Asia, 9, 03546-67
story literature, 15, 18, 05387-411, 06071-95
stotra (Sanskrit hymns), 17, 05839-47
Stotramālā (Marathi Hindu devotional text), 06745
stratification, social, 24, 35, 48, 54, 57, 00715-845, 15750-842, 18086-90, 18815-8, 25540-6, 25578, 25797, 25938. *See also* caste; social conditions; villages
strikes, 32, 48, 11137, 15658-66, 21330, 24124, 24128. *See also* labor
stringed instruments in Indian music, 7, 02793-9
students -- life, attitudes, and movements. For regions not listed below, *see also* education
- India (Rep.), 42, 50, 13093-104, 16575-87
- Maharashtra, 64, 21126, 21601-4
- Nepal, 25994
- Pakistan, 54, 18201-5
- Uttar Pradesh, 71, 23893-901
- West Bengal, 74, 24853-4
study in South Asia, guides, 81, 27424-47
stūpa (Buddhist reliquary), 4, 01679-86, 05054, 06145
stuti (Sanskrit hymns), 17, 05839-47
Subandhu (Sanskrit writer, 7th cent.), 06065
Subba Rao, Koka (1902-), Indian jurist, 12842, 15980
Subhāṣitaratnakośa (anthology of didactic verses), 06060-1
Subhāṣita-saṁgraha (anthology of didactic verses), 04313
Subrahmanya Aiyar, G. (1855-1916), South Indian journalist, 10828
Subramanya (deity), 5, 01817-25
Śuddhādvaita Vedānta, 20, 06500-7
Śūdraka (Sanskrit dramatist, 3rd cent. AD?), 15, 05308-11
śūdras (lowest of the four classical varnas), 03943, 04440-56
Suffren St. Tropez, Pierre Andre de (1726-88), French admiral, 07936-7
Sufism (Islamic mysticism), 18, 21, 22, 25, 27, 28, 02152, 02272,05937-56, 05669, 07111-30, 07328-34, 07658, 07674-84, 08212-5, 08671-88, 22142. *See also* Islam
sugar cultivation and industry, 15345, 18034, 23591, 23664, 23680, 25357
Suhrawardy, Hussein Shaheed (1893-1963), Bengal political leader, 24335
suicide, 01061, 16272, 18916, 20868, 20903
- religious, 5, 02040, 02204-8
Śukasaptati (story collection), 18, 06089-95
Śukranīti (text of polity), 11, 04318-9
Śulvasūtras (geometry texts), 10, 12, 04006-8, 04540-4
sun. *See* Sūrya
Sundar Singh, Sadhu (1889-1933), Punjab Christian leader, 22980-90
Sundarbans district, West Bengal, 24478, 24491
Śunga dynasty (c. 183-71 BC), 11, 04143
- art, 16
Sung-Yun (Chinese pilgrim, 6th cent. AD), 04052
Śūnyasampādane (Vīraśaiva text), 06538, 06542, 06549, 06561
śūnyatā/śūnya ("void" or "emptiness" in Indic philosophy), 4, 14, 01391-400
Supreme Court
- India (Rep.), 41, 12821-34
- Pakistan, 17381
- Sri Lanka, 18525
Surat (port in Gujarat), 27, 08297, 08385-90, 08413-23, 20733, 21870, 21783
Sūrdās (Braj poet-saint, 1483-1563), 29, 02120, 08813-24
Sureśvara (Vedāntin philosopher), 06391
surgery, traditional, 00317, 00325. *See also* medicine
Surinam (Dutch Guiana), South Asians in, 80, 26775-90
Sūrya (Sun god), 5, 01576, 01826-36, 07354
Sūryamalla (Rajasthani poet, 1815-68), 22149
Sūrya Temple, Konārak, Orissa, 21, 06916-22
Suśruta Saṁhitā (medical text), 12, 04552-60
sūtras (Jaina), 05150-61
sūtras (Mahāyāna Buddhist), 05060-83
Sutta-piṭaka (Buddhist sūtras), 14, 04984-95
suttee. *See* satī
Suvarṇabhaṣottamasūtra (Mahāyāna Buddhist text), 05080
Svāminārāyaṇa sect, 65, 21921-31
svanirvār ("self-reliance") program of community development, Bangladesh, 75, 25547-60
Svapnavāsavadatta (play by Kālidāsa), 15, 05312-22
svara, "note", in Indian music, 7, 02764-74
Śvetāmbara (Jain sect), 14, 05141-9
Swadeshi ("of one's own country") Movement, for promotion of indigenous industry, 32, 09688, 10618, 24289-304
Swaraj/Swarājya Party, founded in 1922 by Motilal Nehru and others,33, 10021-32
Swartz, Christian Frederick. *See* Schwartz, Christian Friedrich
Swarūpānanda, Swāmī (1903-74), Nātha yogi, in Ratnagiri district, Maharashtra, 21610
swastika/svastika, symbol "of good fortune", 01648-9
Swāt, princely state and district in Pakistan, 23048
- prehistory, 03742-3
Swatantra Party, founded in 1959 by C. Rajagopalachi and others, 42, 13145, 13298-300, 21665
Swati Tirunal. *See* Rama Varma Kulasekhara Perumal
Sweden, early modern contacts, 07836
Śyāmasāstri (1762-1827), Indian musician, 02880
syllabi on South Asia, 82, 27448-52
symbolism and iconography, 4, 17, 01576-1859, 03056, 03830, 05869-85
"synthetic bibliography", xiii
Syrian Orthodox Church in Kerala, 6, 27, 60, 02249-56, 08222-5, 20114-20. *See also* Christianity

Ṭabaqāt-i-Akbarī, Persian chronicle, 07420
tablā (type of drum), 7, 02800-9
Tagore, Abanindranath (1871-1951), Bengali artist, 11806-8, 11812, 11814, 11816
Tagore, Devendranath (1817-1905), Bengali religious leader, 11252, 11262
Tagore, Dwarkanath (1794-1846), banker and philanthropist, 24546
Tagore, Gaganendranath (1867-1938), Bengali artist, 11811-2, 11814, 11817-9
Tagore, Rabindranath (1861-1941), Bengali poet, 74, 24992-5067
- educational thought, 35, 10621-9
- painting, 11800-20
- rural development work, 10978
Tai kingdoms in Assam, 07195
Tāj Mahal, tomb of Mughal Empress Mumtāz, 25, 07792-7
Takṣaśīla. *See* Taxila
tāla, "rhythm", in Indian music, 7, 02759-63
Tāluqdārī system (land tenure), 71, 23637-41
Tamangs (Himalayan people). 26254, 26257
tamāshā, folk drama of Maharashtra, 03029, 03032
Tamber, A.E. (1904-71), Ceylon educationist, 18931
Tamil dictionaries and learning aids, 83, 27860-76
Tamil grammar, classical, 15, 05230-6
Tamil language and literature, xx, 6, 16-7, 27, 57, 59, 01146, 02411-2, 02414, 02548-58, 02559-76, 05412-58, 06519-24, 06575-92, 08228-9, 19080, 19552-96
Tamil law, Sri Lanka, 18536-8
Tamil Nadu, xxi
- ancient, 11, 04204-28, 04383, 04474, 04480
- dance and drama, 7, 02957-68
- general history, 2, 00406-17
- introductions, 81, 27169, 27177
- modern (1900-), 58, 19196-603
- Mughal period, 26, 08148-61, 08191-202
- music, 02856-7
- prehistory, 03567, 03704-5
- sacred centers, 5, 01962-92
Tamil studies, 1, 00067-73
Tamils in Sri Lanka, 56, 57, 00086, 04249, 06139, 12201, 08489-503, 18850-9
Tana Bhagats (tribe), 20995, 20998

Tangams. *See* Abors
Tangsas (tribe), 26513
Tanjore. *See* Thanjavur
Tantrākhyāyikā (story collection), 05396, 05404
Tantra-tattva (tantric text), 05886
tantrism, 17-8, 20, 22, 23, 30, 05169, 05856-922, 06163, 07204, 08935-8. *See also* Saktism; Buddhism, Vajrayana
Tārābāī Bhosale (1675-1761), wife of Maratha king, 27, 08293
Tarai (marshy plain along India-Nepal border), 78, 23570, 25911, 25940, 25944, 26152, 26264-71
Tārās (saviour-goddesses of tantric Buddhism), 18, 05913-6
tariffs. *See* foreign trade
Tārīkh-i-Firishtah, Persian chronicle, 07409
Tārīkh-i-Firūz Shāhī, Persian chronicle, 07026, 07043, 07046
Tārīkh-i-Mubārakshāhī, Persian chronicle, 05696, 07041
Tārīkh-i-Muḥammadī, Persian chronicle, 07055
Tarkabhāṣā (Nyāya text on logic), 04853
Tashkent Conference (1966), end of Indo-Pakistan war, 39, 12100-12
Tata Industries, Ltd., 11102
Tata Iron and Steel Company (est. 1907), 72, 24110
Tata, Jamsetji Nusserwanji (1839-1904), Parsi industrialist, 11095, 11105, 15309
Tattvacintāmaṇi (Navya-Nyāya text), 07322
tax evasion, India, 45, 14602-9, 18662
taxation. *See* finance, public
Taxila (ancient city in Northwest), 16, 04160, 05520, 05549-51
Tāyumāṉavar (1705-42), Tamil saint, 08207, 08210
tea cultivation, xxii
- Assam, 76, 25722-33, 25755, 25789-90
- Bangladesh, 75, 25359-71
- British India, 11030
- Darjeeling, 24447, 26391-2, 26394-5
- India (Rep.), 14905-13
- Sri Lanka, 56, 18712-27, 18816
- Tripura, 26639
teachers and teacher education. *See* education
tebhāga peasant movement to gain "two-thirds share" of land produce, 24505-6
Technical Cooperation Mission, U.S. (1952), 44
technology, agricultural. For regions not listed below, *see also* agriculture
- Assam, 76, 25759
- Bangladesh, 75, 25383-98
- Bengal, 73, 24468-73
- Bihar, 72, 24073-8
- Gujarat, 65, 21746-7
- Himachal Pradesh, 25879
- India (Rep.), 46, 14842-96
- Karnataka, 20327-32
- Maharashtra, 64, 21247-56
- Nepal, 77, 26161-5
- North-West Frontier Province, 23088
- Pakistan, 54, 17950-73
- Punjab, 68, 22774-82, 22809
- Rajasthan, 22037-42
- Sind, 22474, 22480-1
- Sri Lanka, 56, 18697-8
- Tamil Nadu, 58, 19286-93
- Uttar Pradesh, 71, 23610-7
technology, history of. *See* science and technology
technology, prehistoric, 9, 03525-31
technology transfer, 13898
Tegh Bahādur, Guru of the Sikhs (1621-75), 28, 08639-46
Teignmouth, John Shore, Lord (1751-1834), 26, 08040-41
Telangana regionalism (in Andhra Pradesh), 59, 19681-93
Telangana uprising (1946-51), 59, 19633-40
telecommunications, 47, 15455-59. *See also* communications; media
telegraph, 11036, 11038
television
- India, 51, 16935-58
- Pakistan, 55, 18258
Telugu dictionaries and learning aids, 83, 27896-907
Telugu language and literature, 7, 29, 60, 02581-5, 06599-606, 08230-1, 19885-911
temperance movement, Ceylon, 18344-5
temperance movement, India, 10695
Temple, Richard, 1st Bart. (1826-1902), British official, 09177, 22743
temple architecture, 8, 03174-87. *See also* art and architecture
- ancient, 16-7, 05449-612
- medieval, 06103-15, 06164, 06169, 06607-79, 06806-924, 07000, 07361-8
temple entry movements, on behalf of "untouchables", 10756, 10769
temple prostitutes. *See* devadāsīs
temples and religious endowments, 5, 19, 59, 01877-2077, 06263-72. *See also* religio-philosophical traditions; temple architecture
- Andhra Pradesh, 5, 01956-61, 19871, 19879, 18881
- Goa, 21097
- Jammu & Kashmir, 23242
- Karnataka, 20540, 20550-1
- Kerala, 20168
- Orissa, 22386-88a, 22400-2
- Tamil Nadu, 5, 19, 59, 01947-92, 06263-72, 08208, 09514-22
- United Provinces, 23932
Tengalai (South Indian Vaiṣṇava sect), 20, 19503
Terai. *See* Tarai
Terehpanth (Jaina sect), 16771
terra-cotta sculpture, 8, 23, 03243-61, 03597, 05564, 06998
terrorism (in Indian nationalist movement), 32, 33, 10105-14, 24313, 24320
Tetrus, Khojah (Bengal Armenian leader), 24658
textbooks in education, India, 50, 16631-8
textile arts, 8, 03324-49, 08526-9, 21914
textile industry, 47, 04380, 15391, 18036-41, 21774, 23211, 23213, 24524
Thacker Spink & Company, Calcutta, 24523
Thackersey, Vithaldas Damodar, Sir (1873-1922), Gujarati industrialist, 21299
Thackwell, Joseph, Lt. Gen., Sir, 22620
ṭhags. *See* thugs
Thakalis (Nepalese people). 26231
Thakkar, Amritlal Vithaldas (1869-1951), Indian social reformer, 10700
Thakurdas, Purshotamdas, Sir, Bombay industrialist (1879-1961), 11099
Thakurs (cultivating caste in North India), 23741
Thakurs (tribe in Maharashtra), 20819
Thana district. *See* Maharashtra
Thanjavur/Tanjore district, Tamil Nadu, 19, 58-9, 19198, 29280-1, 19290, 19304, 19420
- Mughal period, 26, 08148-61
Tharus (Tarai ethnic group), 78, 25924, 25935-6, 25942, 26264-8
theatre. *See* drama
theology
- Hindu, 01317, 04814, 05828-56, 06373, 06426-42, 06525-33
- Indian Christian, 02234, 16787-805
- Sikh, 08581
Theosophical Society (est. 1875), 37, 57, 11353-66, 18988
Therāgāthā (Buddhist text), 14, 04992, 04995
Theravāda Buddhism, 14, 57, 05017-44. *See also* Buddhism, Sri Lanka
Therīgāthā (Buddhist text), 14, 04992
Thesawalamai. *See* Tamil law, Sri Lanka
theses on South Asia, guides to, 82, 27687-700
Thevenot, Jean de (1633-67), French traveller, 07913
Thimayya, Kodendera Subayya (1906-), Indian general, 12737, 12740
Thomas, St., Apostle, 12, 04600-6
Thomason, James, Sir (1804-53), British official in North India, 23457, 23465
Thompson, Stith (folklore scholar), 02438
Thoreau, Henry David (1812-62), 11859
throne (symbolism), 04277
thugs/ṭhags and thuggee/ṭhagī, practice of ritual murder, 31, 09231-43
Thūpavaṁsa (Ceylon chronicle), 06145
Tibet, xiv, xxii
- British India, relations, 31, 09439-53
- Nepal, relations, 77, 26075-78
- Sino-Indian relations, 44, 13938-41
Tibetans. *See also* Bhotiyas
- India, 20377, 25891
- Nepal, 78, 26206-7, 26213, 26215
Tieffenthaler, Joseph (b. 1710), French traveller and writer, 08773

Tilak, Bal Gangadhar (1856-1920), Maharashtrian nationalist leader, 32, 62, 09597, 09697-712, 09758-9, 11220, 20739-44
Tilak, Lakshmibai Gokhale (1873-1936), Maharashtrian Christian convert, 21631-2
Tilak, Narayan Waman, Rev. (1862?-1919), Maharashtrian Christian leader and poet, 21454-5, 21630
Tili (caste in Bengal), 24632
time, kāla, in Indic thought, 4, 01437-53
Tīmūr/Tamerlane, Mongol ruler, 24
Tinnevelly. *See* Tirunelveli
Tipū Sultān (1753-99), ruler of Mysore (1782-99), 26, 08162-78
Tirhut (region in Bihar), 29
Tīrthaṅkaras (Jaina saints), 4, 14, 01695, 05130-40
Tirukkuṟaḷ (Tamil ethics text), 12, 04488-507, 06578
Tirumurai (Tamil devotional anthrology), 19, 06303-23
Tirumurukāṟṟuppatai (Tamil anthology), 06511
Tirunelveli/Tinnevelly, city and district, Tamil Nadu, 02550, 08149
Tirupati (sacred center in Andhra), 5, 20, 01956-61
Tiruttakkatēvar (Tamil poet, 10th cent.), 06586
Tiruvācakam (Tamil Śaiva text), 19, 06308-23
Tiruvaḷḷuvar (c. 5th cent.), Tamil writer, 12, 04488-507
Titū Mīr (Mīr Niser ᶜAlī), 19th cent. Bengali Muslim leader, 24503
tobacco industry, Pakistan, 18037
Ṭoḍaramalla (Mughal official, d. 1589), 07559
Todas (tribal people), 58, 19385-97, 19533
Tolkāppiyam (classic Tamil grammar), 15, 05230-6
Toṇḍaimaṇḍalam, ancient region within Tamil Nadu, 11, 04227-8
Tōṇtada Siddhēśvara (Vīraśaiva poet-saint, fl. 1467-78), 06547
Torrington, George Byng, 7th Viscount (1812-84), Governor of Ceylon, 18326, 18328
totemism, 3, 00969, 01097-1100
tourism, India (as industry), 47, 15397-404, 23670
tourist guides. *See* travel guides
town planning. *See* planning, urban
trade. *See* commerce; foreign trade
trade unions. *See* labor
Tranquebar, Danish mission in Tamil Nadu, 19532
transfer of power (1947), 10468-89
transliteration of Indic names, 82, 27453-62
transmigration. *See* rebirth
transnational corporations. *See* multinational
transportation and communication. For regions not listed below, *see* economic conditions
- ancient, 11, 04377-85
- Andhra Pradesh, 59, 19782-3
- Bangalore city, 20466
- Bangladesh, 5, 25475-86
- Bengal, 73, 24545-50
- Bihar, 24129-31
- Bombay city, 21527-30
- British India, 36, 11034-76
- Calcutta city, 74, 24791-803
- Delhi city, 23409
- Gujarat, 65, 21797-802
- India (Rep.), 47, 15415-59
- Karnataka, 61, 20355-60, 20466
- Kerala, 60, 20042-50
- Madhya Pradesh, 66, 22211, 22221
- Maharashtra, 64, 21331
- medieval, 05704-10
- Mizoram, 26612
- Mughal period, 24, 07611-22
- Nepal, 77, 26184-9
- North-West Frontier Province, 23086
- Pakistan, 54, 18067-72
- Punjab, 68, 22799-804
- Rajasthan, 66, 22071-3
- Sri Lanka, 56, 18787
- Tamil Nadu, 58, 19316-25
- Uttar Pradesh, 71, 23686
- West Bengal, 73, 24545-50
Travancore, princely state, Kerala, xxi, 26, 60, 00426, 19917-36, 19945
travel accounts, contemporary, 81-82, 27047-407. *See also* travellers' accounts, historical
travel guides (incl. city guides, listed by province/state/U.T.)
- Andhra Pradesh, 81, 27179
- Assam, 82, 27293, 27356
travel guides -- *continued*
- Bihar, 82, 27282
- Delhi U.T., 82, 27277-81
- Goa, Daman, & Diu, 81, 27211
- Gujarat, 81, 27206
- Himachal Pradesh, 82, 27357-8
- Himalayan Rim Area, 82, 27356-60, 27399-407
- India, 81, 27066-79
- Jammu & Kashmir, 81, 27248-50, 27253-5
- Karnataka, 81, 27180
- Kashmir. *See* Jammu & Kashmir
- Kerala, 81, 27182-83
- Maharashtra, 81, 27204-5
- Nepal, 82, 27399-407
- Orissa, 81, 27209
- Pakistan, 81, 27127-9
- Pondicherry, 27181
- Punjab, 81, 27252, 27255
- Rajasthan, 81, 27207-8, 27210
- South Asia, general, 81, 27066-79
- Sri Lanka, 81, 27155-7
- Uttar Pradesh, 82, 27276, 27281, 27360
- West Bengal, 82, 27294-9
travellers' accounts, historical, incl. accounts by officials, soldiers, etc.
- ancient, 11, 04018-55
- Assam, 76, 25687-90
- British India, 31, 39, 09200-13, 09314-34, 11930-48
- Ceylon, 08049-54, 18300, 18305, 18311, 18319, 18327, 18330, 18332-3
- Himalayan Rim Area, 76, 77-9, 25834-9, 25856-8, 25899-904, 25951-6, 26361-8, 26413, 26441-50, 26519-20, 26604-5
- medieval, 17, 05636-68
- Mughal period, 24, 07471, 07496, 07498, 07501-2, 07504, 07821-40, 07858-65, 07893-8, 07909-14, 07941-50
- North India Area, 71, 23450-5
- Northwest Area, 67, 69, 22426-38, 22441-5, 22458, 22516, 22521, 22612, 22618, 22620, 23035-47, 23142-56
- South India, modern, 58, 19134-41, 20232
tree symbolism, 4, 01628-41, 04675
tribal agencies (North-West Frontier Province), 69, 23035-70
tribal states, ancient, 11, 04320-7
- coins, 04064, 04071
tribals. *See* adivasis
tribes (North-West Frontier), 69, 23033-128. *See also* Baluchs; Pathans
Tribhuvan Bir Bikram Shaha Deva, King of Nepal (1906-55), 77, 25969
Trika Śaivism of Kashmir, 22, 06956-75
trikāya (three "bodies" of Buddha), 14, 05124-29
Trinidad and Tobago, South Asians in, 80, 26791-802
Tripathi, Govardhanram Madhavram (Gujarati writer, 1855-1907), 21937
Tripathi, Surya Kant. *See* Nirālā
Tripiṭaka (Buddhist scriptures), 14, 04966-5002
Tripura, 79, 26627-48
- bibliography, 27736
- temples, 08969
Trivandrum city, Kerala, 20063
Tṛtsus (ancient tribe), 04320
Tughluq dynasty, kings of Delhi (1320-1411), 22, 07037-55
Tukārāma (1608-40), Marathi Vaiṣṇava poet-saint, 27, 08432-42
Tulsī, Ācārya (1914-), Jain religious leader, 16772
Tulsī Sāhib (1763-1843), North Indian poet-saint, 23931
Tulsīdās (1532-1623), author of Avadhī version of Rāmāyaṇa and other poems on Rāma, 29, 08790-812
Tuḷu, Dravidian language in South Kanara, 02372, 02374
Tuḷuva, subregion of Karnataka, 00432, 06182
Tuñcatt' Eẓuttachan, Rāmānujan (Malayalam poet, 16th cent.), 08228
Tutī-nāma (story collection, "Tales of a Parrot"), 06089, 07756. *See also* Śukasaptati
Tūzuk-i-Jahāngīrī (Memoirs of Jahāngīr), 07483
Twain, Mark (Samuel Langhorne Clemens, 1835-1910), American writer, 11943
20-Point Economic Programme (1975-77), 43, 13510-6
Tyabji, Badruddin (1844-1906), Indian Muslim nationalist, 20730, 20738
Tyāgarāja, Swāmī (1767-1847), Telugu poet-musician, 60, 19896-902

U.P. *See* Uttar Pradesh (formerly United Provinces)
Udaigiri cave temples, Orissa, 05489, 05577
Udaipur painting, 28, 08501-6
Udaipur princely state. *See* Mewāṛ
Udipi town and matha, Karnataka, 20
Uganda, South Asians in, 80, 26848, 26860, 26865-70
Ugandan South Asian refugees, 80, 26917-8
Ujjain city, Madhya Pradesh, 22259
ʿulamā (Islamic scholars), 37, 07654, 07659, 09999
Umadīkara, Bhausāheba, Mahārāja (1843-1914), Karnataka yogi, 20538
Umar (caste), 23736
unānī-tibb (Greco-Arabic medicine), 17, 05739-43
underground literature during Emergency (1975-77), 43, 13538-43
union territories, India, 12876-937. *See also* names of specific union territories
Unionist Party (Punjab), 68, 22645, 22656
Unitarians in India, 16827
United Kingdom. *See* Great Britain
United Nations
- India, relations, 44, 14109-21
- Kashmir, role in, 39, 12089
- Pakistan, relations, 53, 17765-9
United Provinces of Agra and Oudh (now Uttar Pradesh), 23450-90
United States
- British India, relations, 09384-94, 09605-29, 10293
- India (Rep.), relations, 44, 14003-55
- Indian Ocean, role in, 11986-2058
- Nepal, economic relations, 26088, 26098
- Pakistan, relations, 53, 17724-36
- South Asia, general, relations, 39, 12158-83
- South Asia libraries, 87, 27503-10
- South Asian studies, 00053, 01142, 14025, 14029, 14032, 27408-18
- South Asians in, 81, 26928-31, 26941-51
unity of Indic civilization, 2, 00678-81, 02329-34
universals, in Indic thought, 01368-78
universities. *See* education; *see also* names of universities and colleges
University Grants Commission, Bangladesh, 25616-7
University Grants Commission, India, 50, 16514
University of Chicago, ix, x, xv
University of Delhi. *See* Delhi, University of
Untouchables. *See* Scheduled Castes
Upadeśasāhasrī (Vedānta text), 06352, 06357
Upadhyaya, Deendayal (1916-68), Jana Sangh leader, 09596, 13265-78
upanayana (Hindu initiation rite), 01028-39
Upaniṣads, minor or sectarian, 02167, 02192, 05851
Upaniṣads, Vedic, 13, 01206, 01220, 01350, 01366, 01391, 01471, 03792, 03967-94
- commentaries, 06337-8, 06345-60, 06415-25
Upapurāṇas, "lesser puranas," 17, 05823-7
Upasakajanālankara (Ceylon historical text), 06124
Upāsani Bābā (1870-1941), Maharashtra yogi, 21613
urban development. *See* planning, urban
urban government and politics. *See* local government
urbanization and cities. *See also* names of cities; for regions not listed below, *see* social conditions
- ancient, 12, 04519-24
- Andhra Pradesh, 59, 19834-47
- Bangladesh, 75, 25561-71
- Bengal, 74, 08920-31, 24696-707
- Bihar, 72, 24171-203
- British India, 35, 10686-92
- Delhi U.T., 70, 23378-423
- general history, 3, 00882-92
- Gujarat, 65, 21869-88
- Harappan, 10, 03612-27
- India (Rep.), 49, 16021-112
- Karnataka, 61, 20457-96
- Kerala, 60, 20157-9
- Madhya Pradesh, 66, 22254-62
- Maharashtra, 64, 21485-558
- medieval, 07082-3
- Mughal period, 24, 29, 08784, 08920-31
- Nepal, 78, 26286-93
- North-West Frontier Province, 23124-7
- Orissa, 67, 22375-8
- Pakistan, 54, 18111-23
- Punjab, 68, 22887-913
- Rajasthan, 66, 22117-27
- Sri Lanka, 57, 18893-908
urbanization and cities -- *continued*
- Tamil Nadu, 59, 08199-202, 19416, 19426-53
- Uttar Pradesh, 71, 07082-3, 08784, 23824-63
- West Bengal, 74, 08920-31, 24696-707
Urdu dictionaries and learning aids, 83, 27819-48
Urdu in Uttar Pradesh, 23487, 23505, 23506
Urdu language and literature, xxii, 6, 25, 37-8, 51, 55, 02528-40, 07603-10, 10001, 11631-702, 17054-61, 18261-75, 19890, 22991
Urdu press, 10810
Utkal. *See* Orissa
Utilitarianism in British India, 10537-45, 18535
Utpaladeva (Kashmir Śaiva author, 10th cent.), 22, 06969
Uttar Pradesh, xxii
- ancient, 11, 04106-57, 05552
- general history, 2, 00510-20
- geography, 82, 27270
- Himalayan region. *See* Kumaon and Garhwal
- introductions, 82, 27256, 27258
- medieval, 07002-73
- modern (1801-), 71-2, 23441-943
- Mughal period, 08755-839
- prehistory, 03662-9
- sacred centers, 5, 02036-56, 02071, 02073
- travel accounts, 82, 23450-5, 27271-5
Uttara-Mīmāṁsā. *See* Vedānta
Uttara-Rāma-carita, Sanskrit drama by Bhavabhūti (8th cent. AD), 06023-31

vac, vāc, "speech," and speech personified as a goddess, 14, 05162-74
vacanas (Vīrasaiva poems), 20, 06538-56
Vadagalai Tamil Hindu sect, 20, 06463-8
Vaḍodara. *See* Baroda
vaidyas (āyurvedic physicians). *See* medicine
Vaikhanasas (South Indian Vaisnava sect), 13, 04789-92
Vaikkam/Vaikom Satyāgraha (village in Travancore), 19930
Vaināyakī (female form of Gaṇeśa), 01813
Vaiśeṣika (school of philosophy), 13, 04835-61
Vaiśeṣikasūtra, philosophic text by Kaṇāda, 13, 04835-6
Vaiṣṇavism (worship of Viṣṇu in various forms), 4, 01667, 01759-1801, 16756-60. *See also* names of specific sects and leaders
- ancient period, 13, 04764-92
- Assam, 23, 07292-8
- Bengal, 23, 30, 07228-98, 08940-5, 24879, 24881-96
- Bihar, 07238-9, 07258-63
- Gujarat, 21, 65, 06777-89, 21920-31
- Maharashtra, 21, 27, 06744-76, 08424-49
- Manipur, 79, 26596-8
- North India (Hindi region), 22, 29, 07084-110, 08790-826
- Orissa, 67, 06802-5, 22386-93
- Rajasthan, 21, 28, 06777-89, 08450-7
- South India, 19-20, 06285-302, 06408-507
Vajrayāna, "Vehicle of the Thunderbolt" (Tantric Buddhism), 18, 23, 05047, 05857-922, 026318-39
Vākāṭaka dynasty, 11, 04098, 04196
- art, 16
Vākyapadīya (medieval text on grammar), 15, 05221-9
Vallabha sect of Vaisnavas, 20, 29, 08813-24, 21609, 21916
Vallabhācārya (1479-1531?), Telugu Brahman bhakta, 20, 06500-7
Vallathol. *See* Narayana Menon, Vallathol
Vālmīki. *See* Rāmāyaṇa
Vāmana (writer on poetics, c. 700), 05976
Vāmana Trivikrama ("dwarf" avatāra of Visnu), 01793, 01798, 01801
Vāmana-purāṇa, 05812, 05817, 05819
Vaṁśāvalī (history of Nepal), 00545
Vande Mātaram. *See* Bande Mataram
Varadārāja temple, in Kanchipuram, 5, 01969-71
Varadarajan, M. (1912-74), Tamil writer, 19564, 19570
Varāha ("boar" avatāra of Visnu), 01765
Varāhagṛhyasūtra (text on household rites), 04461
Varāhamihira (astronomer, c. 505 BC), 12, 04533-9
- as source, 04036
Vārakarī sect. *See* Vārkarī panth
Vārāṇasī/Banāras/Benares, Uttar Pradesh
- as sacred center, called Kāsī/Kāshī, 5, 02043-56
- modern (1801-), 71, 23460, 23472, 23497, 23848-9
- Mughal period, 08764-5, 08768-70, 08777
- music in, 02835-6
Vararuci (Prakrit grammarian), 05260

Vardhamāna. *See* Mahāvīra
Varendra Brahmans of Bengal, 24623, 25505
Vārkarī panth (Maharashtrian Vaisnava sect), 21, 01993-2001, 06744-71
Vāris Shāh. *See* Warīs Shāh
Varmā, Ravi, modern Indian artist, 11828
varṇa (four classes or ranks of classic Hindu society), 00778
varṇāśramadharma, "duties according to ranks and stages of life," 2, 12, 00741-51
Vasanta-vilāsa (poem in Old Gujarati), 06838
Vasava (tribe in Gujarat), 20829
Vāsavadattā (Sanskrit prose kāvya by Subandhu), 06065
Vāstuvidyā (Sanskrit architectural text), 06853-4
Vasubandhu (Buddhist philosopher, c. 300 AD), 14, 01409, 05109, 05129
Vāsudevahiṇḍī (Prakrit story collection), 05252, 05389
Vasugupta. *See* Śivasūtra
Vātāpi. *See* Bādāmi
Vatsyayan, Sachchidanand Hiranand. *See* Agyeya
Vātsyāyana, called Mallanāga (c. 3rd cent. AD?), author of Kāmasūtra, 12, 04483-7
Vāyu-purāna, 05821
Vaz, Joseph (1651-1711, Ceylonese poet), 08100
Vedāṅgas ("limbs," appendices to the Vedas), 10, 14, 03995-4008, 04525-44
Vedānta (school of Hindu philosophy), 13, 19-20, 01122, 01219, 01337, 01339, 01410
- Acintya-bhedābheda, 23, 07264-98
- Advaita, 19, 01357, 01420, 01465, 06324-407
- Bhedābheda, 20, 06495-9
- Dvaita, 20, 06469-94
- early, 13, 04870-4
- modern, "Neo-Vedānta," 37, 11209, 11294-352, 16693
- Śuddhādvaita, 20, 06500-7
- Viśiṣṭādvaita, 20, 06415-68
Vedānta Deśika (1268-1369), Srivaisnava philosopher, 20, 06453-68
Vedāntasūtra. *See* Brahmasūtra
Vedas (basic scriptures of Hinduism), xx, 10, 00269, 01185, 03798-994
Veddas (Ceylon aboriginals), 57, 18829-34
Vedic Age, xx, 9, 03730-97
Vedic chant, 02778, 03913
Vedic recitation, 03876-80
Vedic ritual, 10, 20158-72
Vedic studies, xiii, 1, 00044
Vellalar Chettiyars (caste in Tamil Nadu), 19362
Velu Thampi (1765-1809), Dewan of Travancore, 19932
Vemana (Telugu poet, 15th cent.), 06599, 06605-6
Veṅgī region (Krishnā-Godāvarī delta), 19
- art, 16, 20, 05494-515
Veṅkaṭādhvarin (Sanskrit writer, 17th cent.), 08229
Veṅkaṭanatha. *See* Vedānta Deśika
Venkatappa, K. (1887-), modern Indian painter, 11829
Venkataraya Sastri, Vedam (Telugu writer, 1853-1929), 19895
Venkaṭeśvara temple. *See* Śrī Veṅkaṭeśvara temple
Vereenigde Oostindesche Compagnie (Dutch United East India Company), 25, 07891-901
Verelst, Harry (d. 1785), East India Company official in Bengal, 08874, 08887
Verghese, Mary Puthusseril, Dr. (1925-), physical rehabilitation specialist, 19468
Vernacular Press Act (1878), 10842
Vetālapañcaviṁśati (story collection), 18, 06086-8
Viceroys of India. *See* Governors-General
Vidarbha (region in Maharashtra), 20609-11, 21464-83, 21560-1
Vidarbha Sultanate, 27, 08246
Vidyākara (Sanskrit anthologist, 12th cent.), 06060-1
Vidyāpati (Maithilī poet, 15th cent.), 23, 07258-63
Vidyāraṇya. *See* Mādhava (d. 1386)
Vidyāsāgar, Ishwarchandra (1820-91), Bengali educator, 75, 24870, 24968-75
vidūṣaka (jester in classical Sanskrit drama), 05278, 05282
Vietnam
- India, relations, 14095
Vietnam War, 14093
Vijaya, Prince (legendary Aryan conqueror of Ceylon), 11, 04242-9
Vijayabāhu I of Ceylon, 06125
Vijayanagara Empire, 19, 06218-38
- art, 20, 06678-9
Vijayawada/Bezwada, city in Andhra Pradesh, 19837
Vijñānabhairava (Kashmir Saiva text), 06958
Vijñānavāda (school of Mahayana Buddhism), 14, 05109-29
Vijñaptimātra (Buddhist school), 05118, 05123
Vikrama Bahu, king of Kandy, 08056
Vikramabāhu I, king of Ceylon, 06123
Vikramāditya, king of Ujjayini (1st cent. AD), 04198-9
Vikramāṅkadevacarita, historical poem by Bilhana, 06048, 06052
Vikramaśīla, medieval Buddhist center in Bihar, 07211
Vikramorvaśīya (Sanskrit play), 15, 05353-4
village community, 00446, 10966-76
village government and politics. *See* local government
village industry. *See* industry
village studies, xiii, 3, 00864-887
villages, rural society, and rural development. For regions not listed below, *see* social conditions; for economic aspects of rural development, *see also* agriculture
- Andhra Pradesh, 59, 19817-33
- Assam, 76, 25794-802
- Bangladesh, 75, 25528-60
- Bengal, 73-4, 24665-94
- Bihar, 72, 20904, 24158-70
- British India, 36, 10962-11011
- Delhi U.T., 70, 23369-78
- Gujarat, 65, 21853-68
- Haryana, 70, 23303-7
- India (Rep.), 46, 14998-5169
- Karnataka, 61, 20425-56
- Kerala, 60, 20153-6
- Madhya Pradesh, 66, 22243-53
- Maharashtra, 64, 21259-84
- medieval, 05722, 06258
- Meghalaya, 26668, 26680
- Mughal period, 29, 08402-12
- Nepal, 78, 26280-5
- North-West Frontier Province, 23087
- Orissa, 67, 22366-74
- Pakistan, 54, 17992-7
- Punjab, 68, 22849-86
- Rajasthan, 66, 22105-16
- Sind, 22486
- Sri Lanka, 57, 18872-92
- Tamil Nadu, 59, 19270-85, 19417-25
- Uttar Pradesh, 71, 23780-818
- West Bengal, 73-4, 24665-94
Vimalakīrtinirdeśa (Mahāyāna Buddhist text), 05083
Vinaya-piṭaka (Buddhist texts), 14, 04979-83
Vināyaka. *See* Gaṇeśa
Vīr Singh, Bhai (1872-1957), Punjabi writer, 69, 23011-7
Vīraśaiva sect (Liṅgāyats) in Karnataka, 20, 61, 06537-68, 20400-7, 20547-8, 20551
Viresalingam, Kandukuri (Telugu writer, 1848-1919), 60, 19903-5
Viśākhadatta (Sanskrit dramatist, 5th cent. AD), 15, 05376-86
Visakhapatnam/Vizagapatam, port in Andhra Pradesh, 19701, 19779-81, 19783, 19844
Vīsaḷadevarāsa (medieval Hindi bardic romance), 06727
Viśiṣṭādvaita Vedānta, 20, 06415-68
Viṣṇu (deity), 5, 01759-1801. *See also* Vaiṣṇavism
Viṣṇudharmottara (upapurāṇa, of special interest for art history), 06108-10, 06113-4
Viṣṇu-purāṇa, 17, 05779-82, 06108, 06110, 06113-4
Viṣṇukuṇḍin dynasty of Veṅgi (7th cent. AD), 04226
Viṣṇuśarma, traditional author of Pañcatantra, 15, 05389-405
Viśuddhimagga (Buddhist text), 14, 05036-40
Viśva-Bhāratī, university founded by Rabindranath Tagore, 35, 10621-9
Viśvakarma (author of Sanskrit architectural text), 06853-4
Viśvanātha (writer on poetics, fl. 1350), 05998
Visvesvaraya, Mokshagundam (1861-1962), Mysore statesman and engineer, 20293
Viṭhobā (Vaiṣṇava deity), 5, 21, 01993-2001
Vivādachintāmaṇi (law text), 05702
Vivekacūḍamaṇi (Vedānta text), 06346, 06350, 06354, 06359
Vivekānanda, Swāmī (1863-1902), apostle of Vedanta to the West, 37, 11227, 11313-37
vocal music, 7, 02838-42, 02855, 02881, 02887, 02894, 02896
vocational education, 50, 16617-24. *See also* education
Vohras. *See* Bohras

Voice of America, 14027
Vokkaligas/Okkaligas (caste in Karnataka), 61, 20400-7
Voltaire, François Marie Arouet de (1694-1778), 11858
vrata rituals, "vows" of fasting etc., 24885, 24893-4
Vrātyas (ancient non-Vedic tribe), 04321
Vrindāvan, sacred center of Braj, 5, 29, 02036-9, 23921
vyākaraṇa. *See* grammar
Vyāsa (traditional "author" of Mahabharata and other texts), 12-13
Vyavahāracintāmaṇi (law text), 05703

Wadiyar dynasty of Mysore, 26, 61, 08162-78, 20223-43
wages. *See also* labor
- British India, 10885, 10892
- India (Rep.), 48, 15576-92
- Pakistan, 54, 18044-50
Wahhabis (Muslim puritan revivalist movement), 37, 11443-6, 24911-2, 24914
Wajid Ali Shah (1821-96), king of Avadh, 23441
Walīullāh, Shāh (1703-63), Muslim reformer, 25, 07680-4
Wanchos (tribe), 26512, 26514
Wang Hsüan-ts'e (Buddhist pilgrim, 7th cent. AD), 05651
war, art of. *See* armed forces
"War of Independence" (1857-58). *See* Rebellion of 1857
Warangal, Andhra (capital of Kakatiya dynasty), 20
Ward, Henry, Sir (1797-1860), Governor of Ceylon, 18320
Wardha Scheme of Basic Education, 35, 10630-40, 16595-606
warfare. *See* armed forces
Wārīs Shāh (Punjabi poet, fl. 1766), 08693-4
Warlis (tribe), 20823, 20826, 21281
water disputes
- India, interstate, 41, 12925-37
- international, 39, 12239-46
water resources. *See* irrigation
water supply, urban, 21880, 24791-803, 23885, 25585, 25804
water transport. *See* transportation
Wavell, Archibald Percival Wavell, 1st Earl (1883-1950), Viceroy, 34, 10448-50, 10451-2
Waverley, John Anderson, 1st Viscount (1882-1958), Governor of Bengal, 24274-5
Weber, Max (1864-1920), 01876
Weber thesis, 45, 53, 56, 14347-67, 17836-45, 18636-40
Wellesley, Richard Colley Wellesley, Marquess (1760-1842), 26, 08042-5, 18301
Wellington, Arthur Wellesley, 1st Duke of (1769-1852), 07997
West, relations with South Asia, 25, 38, 07803-40, 11836-980
West Bengal (1813-), xxii, 73, 78, 24349-5140. *See also* Bengal
West Bengal, Darjeeling District. *See* Darjeeling
Western India Association, 20720
Western India States Agency, 20622
"Western Indian Art," 16, 21, 06830-79
wheat cultivation, 75, 23609, 25354-5
wheel (cakra) symbolism, 4, 01642-6
Who's Whos, 82, 27465-95. *See also* biography
widow-burning. *See* satī
widows in Indic society, 3, 35, 01016-22, 10725-31, 19454, 21356, 21366
Wijewardene, D.R., Ceylon journalist, 19068
wildlife, 46, 81, 14933-4, 27024-46
Williamson, Thomas, British writer of guidebooks, xvii
Willingdon, Freeman Freeman-Thomas, Marquess of (1866-1941), 33, 10269-71
Wilmot-Horton, Robert John, Bart. (1784-1841), Governor of Ceylon, 18314, 18316
Wilson, Horace Hayman (1786-1860), indologist, 11233
Wilson, Patrick, American bibliographer, ix
Wimalasurendra, D.J. (1874-1953), Ceylon engineer, 18701a, 18703
wind instruments, 7, 02790-2
women in literature and art, 03097, 04718, 05281, 17041, 17083, 17177, 19555, 22416, 24934
women in religion and mythology, 01610, 01711-38, 03906, 05913-6, 19882
women in the Nationalist Movement, India, 31, 09583-6
women in the labor force, 48, 15531-47, 18091, 21555, 25612
women -- status and role, 3, 00947-59, 01016-22. For regions not listed below, *see* social conditions
- ancient period, 04474-81
- Andhra Pradesh, 19787-8
- Assam, 25708
- Bangladesh, 75, 25496, 25516-27, 25612, 25632
women -- status and role -- *continued*
- Bihar, 24125
- British India, 35, 09583-6, 10722-745
- Delhi U.T., 23410
- European, in India, 11949-65
- Great Britain, South Asian women in, 80, 26896
- Gujarat, 21804, 21819-20, 21926
- India (Rep.), 48, 15868-86
- Karnataka, 20367, 20379
- Kerala, 20071, 20074
- Madhya Pradesh, 22234-5
- Maharashtra, 64, 21356-69, 21555
- Mizoram, 26614
- Mughal period, 24, 07644-5
- Nagaland, 26557
- Nepal, 26223, 26234, 26272-9
- Pakistan, 54, 18091-3
- Punjab, 22672, 22748
- Rajasthan, 22077
- social service, 10673
- South Asia, general, 12267
- Sri Lanka, 57, 18869-71
- Tamil Nadu, 19456
- Uttar Pradesh, 23503, 23770
- West Bengal, 73, 24349, 24354, 24660, 24763
women's education, 50, 54, 74, 10558, 10587, 16689-91, 18200, 20527, 22141, 23130, 24868, 25613, 25632
Wood, Charles. *See* Halifax
workers. *See* labor
World War I, 32
World War II, 34, 10288-10450

Xavier, Francis, St. (1506-52), Spanish Jesuit missionary to "the East," 08080, 08218
Xavier, Jerome, Jesuit at Mughal court, 07685

Yādava dynasty of Devagiri, in Maharashtra (1150-1313), 20-1, 06683-6
Yahya Khan, Agha Muhammad, Gen. (1917-), President of Pakistan (1969-71), 52, 17551-4
yajña (sacrifice, especially Vedic), 10, 13, 03853-72
Yājñavalkyasmṛti. *See* Dharmaśāstras
Yajurveda. *See* Vedas
Yakṣagāna dance drama, of South Kanara, 8, 03013, 03027-30
yakṣas (godlings), 5, 01845-50, 05472
Yama (god of death), 03836
Yamunā (river, as deity), 5, 01842-4
Yāmunācārya (10th cent.), philosopher, 20, 06408-14
Yanadis (tribe), 19813
yantra (symbolic diagram), 01599. *See also* mandala
Yaśastilaka (Jain text), as source, 05672
Yashpāl (1903-76), Hindi writer, 11630
Yāska's Nirukta (etymology text), 15, 05178-82
Yaśovarman (8th cent.), king of Kanauj, 07008
yātrā/jātrā, Bengali folk drama, 03051-5
Yayāti myth, 01700
Yemens, South Asians in the, xxiii
Yerukula (tribe), 19814, 20148
Yeruvas (caste), 20370
Yoga (school of Hindu philosophy), 13, 01450, 04818-31, 06446
yoga (spiritual discipline), 5, 01056, 01599, 02153-80, 03817, 03829
- haṭha, 23, 07303-8
- tantric, 17, 05857-60
Yogācāra (school of Mahāyāna Buddhism), 14, 05081, 05109-29
Yogasūtra of Patañjali, 13, 04818-31
Yogaswami, Ceylon yogi, 19031-2
yogis, biographies and studies, 5-6, 02209-33
Younghusband, Francis Edward, Sir (1863-1942), British traveller and official, 09448-53
youth
- India (Rep.), 49, 15951-67, 21672, 21889-90, 23870
- Pakistan, 18094
- Sri Lanka, 18913, 18919, 18937
Youth Congress, promoted by Sanjay Gandhi, 43, 13546-50
Yue-tchi/Yüeh-chih (Central Asian nomadic people), 04093

Zakā'ullāh, Muḥammad (1832-1910), Muslim educator in Delhi, 10643
Zakāt (annual levy on "persons of substance," under Islamic law), 08413
zamīndārs, "holder of land." *See* land tenure; villages
Zamorin of Calicut, 26

Zeb-un-Nissa, Begum (17th cent.), Persian poetess, 07702
zenāna/zanānah (women's quarters). *See* pardā
Zend Avesta (Zoroastrian scriptures), 6, 02297-300
Zia-ul-Haq, Mohammad, Gen. (1924-), President of Pakistan (1977-), 53, 17601-9
Zia-ur-Rahman (1936-81), President of Bangladesh (1977-81), 75, 25208-17
zilla parishads, "district committees." *See* local government
zonal councils, India, 12524, 12526
Zoroastrianism, 02288-2310. *See also* Parsis